ROTHMANS

FOOTBALL

YEARBOOK

1999-2000

ROTHMANS

EDITORS: GLENDA ROLLIN AND **JACK ROLLIN**

HEADLINE

First published in 1999
by HEADLINE BOOK PUBLISHING

10 9 8 7 6 5 4 3 2 1

Front cover photographs: (left) Marcel Desailly (Chelsea) – *Actionimages*; (centre and background) Steve Bould (Arsenal) and Michael Owen (Liverpool) – *Colorsport*; (right) Dwight Yorke (Manchester U) – *Colorsport*.

Back cover photographs: (top) Henrik Larsson (Celtic) and Giovanni van Bronckhorst (Rangers) – *Actionimages*; (bottom) Paul Merson (Aston Villa) and George Boateng (Coventry C) – *Colorsport.*

British Library Cataloguing in Publication Data
Rothmans Football Yearbook.—1999–2000
1. Association Football—Serials
796.334'05

ISBN 0 7472 2166 9 (hardback)
ISBN 0 7472 7627 7 (trade paperback)

Typeset by Wearset, Boldon, Tyne and Wear

Printed and bound in Great Britain by
Mackays of Chatham PLC,
Chatham, Kent

HEADLINE BOOK PUBLISHING
A division of the Hodder Headline Group
338 Euston Road
London NW1 3BH

www.headline.co.uk
www.hodderheadline.com

CONTENTS

INTRODUCTION

The 30th edition of Rothmans Football Yearbook features an increased amount of historical and record information for the 92 English clubs. This includes each club's full record in the previous ten seasons and the latest sequences recorded for wins, draws and defeats, etc. There is also an article by our guest writer, the FA Premier League and FIFA referee David Elleray. Full coverage is given for the Euro 2000 European Championship qualifying competition, with results, scorers, teams and attendances.

Detailed and varied coverage involves the FA Premier League, Football League, Scottish, Welsh and Irish football, amateur, schools, university, reserve team, extensive non-League information, awards, records and international directory, the Football Trust, Football and the Law, coaching, women's football, referees and the work of chaplains.

Transfer fees are given where known. When two clubs have differed as to the amount of a record move, the lower figure has been quoted in both instances. For certain entries, the figure given in the list of transfers may be the original figure quoted without extra finance built in for appearances etc., which would appear subsequently as a record fee on the relevant club page. Also the date when a player is signed often varies from the one given as his registration. A frequent question asked is why Football League records have not been changed since the advent of the Premier League. The answer is quite simple, the Football League still consider their First Division to be a championship which has existed for 100 years. In fact, they celebrated the event with a match between the record holders Liverpool and the most recent champions, Sunderland.

The Editors would like to thank Alan Elliott for the Scottish section, Bob Hennessy for the Milestones Diary and Ian Vosper for the obituaries. Thanks are also due to John English and Christine Forrest who provided their invaluable and conscientious reading of the proofs. The editors would like to pay tribute to the various organisations who have helped to make this edition complete, especially Debbie Birch from the Football League, Mike Foster of the FA Premier League and the secretaries of all the FA Premier League, Football League and Scottish League clubs for their kind cooperation. The ready availability of Football League secretary David Dent and his staff to answer queries, was as usual, most appreciated, as was Chris Hull's help from the Press Office. Thanks are also due in equal measure to the Scottish Football Association, Scottish Premier League, Scottish Football League as well as Adrian Cook and Jonathan Hargreaves of the FA Premier League.

ACKNOWLEDGEMENTS

The Editors would also like to express appreciation of the following individuals and organisations for their cooperation: Glynis Firth, Sandra Whiteside, Lorna Parnell, Louise Standing, Andrea Stock (all from the Football League), David C. Thomson of the Scottish League, Alan Dick, Heather Elliott, Malcolm Brodie, Peter Hughes (English Schools FA), Wally Goss (AFA), Paul Reaney for Nationwide Conference information, Rev. Nigel Sands, Edward Grayson, Ken Goldman, Grahame Lloyd, Marshall Gillespie, Sean Creedon, Manuel Márquez, Ben Jerram, Jane Parsons and Juliana Lessa (Headline Books).

Special thanks are due to Lorraine Jerram, Headline's House Editor for her expertise, constant support, unflagging patience, sincerity, understanding, perspicacity and appreciation, not to mention her unfailing humour, quick-wittedness and understated authority.

Finally, sincere thanks to John Anderson, Simon Dunnington, Geoff Turner, Carl Gillingham and the staff at Wearset for their efforts in the production of this book, which was much appreciated throughout the year.

VIEWPOINT

by David Elleray

'To err is human'

In the course of this season the outcome of thousands of matches will be decided by a variety of decisions. Some of these will be made in a flicker of an eye; others will have taken much longer. Football is a wonderful game played at a frantic pace with the outcome resting not on a single decision but on a multitude of judgements made by human beings of different ages, emotions and experience. Who will be making the vital decisions this season?

In a year's time *Rothmans Football Yearbook* and the millions of newspaper column inches devoted to football matches may well give the impression that the destiny of the FA Cup, the Premier League Championship and Euro 2000 were all determined by referees. However, referees are not the only people in football who make decisions – and they are certainly not alone in making *wrong* ones. Throughout every game at every level players are making decisions all the time: where to run, who to mark, whether to pass or shoot, whether to foul or not. Like referees, players' decisions are usually made in a split second based on what they believe they can see and what they think other people are doing, or trying to do. More crucial decisions, however, have been made even before the game has started. Managers spend hours agonising over team selection and playing tactics, while administrators debate who should referee each match and what Law changes should be implemented. Yet it is rare that these decisions, taken under little time pressure, are held responsible for the outcome of games or championships – everyone tends to lay responsibility on the referees and players and discuss at length whether their instant judgements were correct or not. However, part of the attraction of the game we all love is this very lack of perfection, for discussing decisions, be they team selections or disallowed goals, involves the spectator, fanatical or casual, in the game.

As this season begins the Premier League referees are physically and technically better prepared than ever before to face the pressures and demands of the modern game. Before the first whistle is blown we will all have passed a stringent FIFA fitness test, submitted details of our daily diets for analysis, and undergone scientific fitness, strength and flexibility tests similar to those applied to most top professional footballers. Seminars will have been held to discuss the Law changes and styles of refereeing, and further attempts will have been made to achieve greater consistency within the group of top referees. During the season there will be regular weekend courses to review performances, receive media training and study the development of the game with inputs coming from the League Managers' Association and Professional Footballers' Association. After each match we will complete a detailed self-assessment form to send to our personal referee coach and several days later we will receive the independent Premier League Match Observer's considered views on the quality of our match-day performance. As the season progresses each of us will be told how well we are performing and whether we risk demotion from the panel at the end of the season or, if young enough, whether we are performing well enough to be nominated as one of England's FIFA International Referees. Many hours will be spent each week training, watching videos of matches and reviewing performances in an attempt to improve the quality of our refereeing. But, like the players, the managers and all those actively involved in the game, each of us will still make mistakes and we shall find our failure to be 100 per cent correct deeply frustrating and disappointing.

What help will the new millennium bring? Many believe that technology holds the key but the introduction of widespread use of video replays is highly unlikely as most important decisions are not black and white and therefore not easily decided by TV. Anyway, who really wants to interrupt at regular intervals the almost non-stop, free-flowing excitement and entertainment that raises soccer above rugby, cricket and most other sports? However, if we can develop technology so that the referee can be told in an instant whether the ball has crossed the line (especially within the goal) then technology will have done a great service but to go beyond that will undermine so much of what is attractive about the game.

Progress may come in the form of the sin bin replacing the yellow card so that justice is done *during* a game not afterwards. Perhaps then we can, once and for all, remove the ridiculous situation of a player receiving a card in one game and missing a match several weeks later. Surely, if a player commits offences when playing against, say, West Ham, then any suspension should be during that game so that West Ham, who probably suffered by the player's misconduct, benefit and not another team later in the season? Why should one team benefit from the opponents having a player suspended for offences against other, possibly rival, teams? It is illogical and unfair. The use of sin bins might also prevent ill-discipline and any measure that prevents rather than merely punishes has to be good for the game.

In this context, therefore, perhaps one way forward will come from the Central Midlands Football League who this season are experimenting with the '10 yards rule' from rugby. Whenever after conceding a player fails to retire 10 yards, shows dissent, delays the free-kick or kicks the ball away, the referee will show the player the yellow card and the position of the kick will be advanced 10 yards. This experiment had spectacular success in Jersey last year and may be a major step towards tackling the dissent and delaying tactics which annoy spectators even more than players. It also had the great benefit of preventing problems and led to a reduction in yellow cards rather than an increase. I am sure we would all welcome any move in that direction.

Whether you love them or hate them, referees are here to stay. Some competitions are trying two referees rather than one, on the Premier League we will be wired up to our assistants and, one day, referees might become full time. But if anyone believes that this will produce perfect decision-making then they have lost touch with reality. Do we expect Alan Shearer to score every time he shoots simply because he is a consummate professional paid a huge salary? And if his salary was doubled would he then be expected to win every tackle, pass perfectly every time and score with every shot? Of course not! Well, such unrealistic expectations should not be made of referees. We will always make mistakes but at least they are honest mistakes. I was once heard on television saying to Tony Adams, who had criticised a decision, 'We may be useless but we don't cheat.' Whatever else you think of the British referee he, or she, is straight as a die and long may that continue.

We must not make 'perfect decision-making' a quest which destroys football. The beautiful game has become very big business and will continue to evolve but, fundamentally, it will always remain a game played, refereed, managed, administered and watched by humans, and humans are fallible and different (thank goodness). So, on behalf of all those actively involved in football, but especially the referees, please remember:

'To forgive is divine'

EDITORIAL

The introduction of professional referees will not guarantee improvement in the control of matches. Since the intention is to pay the same officials more money, the whole exercise seems illogical. Moreover, the argument that they will be more accountable to the game as full-time referees is little more than a slur on the integrity of people who are already carrying out the game's most difficult job to the best of their ability.

What is needed is a revolutionary approach to the subject, to cope with the increasing demands of the modern game.

There has never been more criticism of top referees than at present, as their on-the-spot decisions are coming under the intense scrutiny of progressively intrusive television techniques. FIFA are unhappy about how the game is refereed. Experiments with two referees, first tried out in the 1930's, are being reintroduced. Gerhard Aigner, General Secretary of UEFA, wants all footballers to be trained as referees and pass a test before signing their first professional contract. He also proposes that players should then have to referee one match a month at local youth level. This is an excellent idea, but it should not be left there. There should be provision for former professional footballers to take up refereeing when their playing days are over, either through old age or injury. They would have the edge when it comes to spotting gamesmanship.

But there must be a faster system of promotion to the top and not only for ex-players, but referees who have to come up through the various grades from grassroots level.

Assistant referees must be given more responsibility and the fourth official provided with more serious duties. For a start, he could take time-keeping out of the referee's hands or wrist, if you prefer. This is not a new idea, Willy Meisl that European visionary, suggested it to the then FA Secretary Stanley Rous nearly forty years ago. At the same time, if good use of electronic devices is sought, the fourth official can keep the watch and an electronically controlled scoreboard will show legitimate stoppages monitored during play and not added on in time at the end of 90 minutes.

We know John Motson leads the cause of those who want to get home for tea at a reasonable hour, but paying customers are entitled to more actual playing time. It would put an end to the farce of more goals being scored in the 90th minute than at any other time in the game, since these 60 seconds can last on up to seven or eight minutes in the extreme.

You only have to look at the problems created when Manchester United's Ole Gunnar Solskjaer scored four goals in 13 minutes 46 seconds, though the best they could manage was about ten minutes.

Goals remain the life blood of the game and providing you score more than the opposition, you can have as many faith-healers you like, providing you keep controversially personal thoughts to yourself. As it stands, the full England International team needs plenty of faith, even more hope and possibly charity from the opposition to win the next two matches in order to qualify for even Euro 2000 play-offs.

But there have been mixed fortunes in tournaments at other levels. The Under-21's did exceptionally well, but the manager left to run a Second Division team. The Under-18's failed to score sufficient goals, the Under-20's didn't manage one at all.

The Government is so obsessed with having the 2006 World Cup held here in England that they persuaded Manchester United to participate in the Club World Championship in Brazil in the winter and opt out of defending their FA Cup title. This competition is so named to prevent it being confused with the World Club Championship...

Manchester United's FA Cup commitments could easily be accommodated with the tournament by changes of dates. This has to be done when television requires it or when Mother Nature takes a hand and causes a backlog of fixtures. United showed the strength they possessed in depth by winning three major trophies. They have the playing resources and after all, if one wishes to be pedantic, they should have been fined for failing to start the European Cup Final with their best team. It was left to two of their substitutes to score the winning goals.

United could always field their Worthington Cup team in some of the Club World Championship matches – those against the champions of Africa, Asia and Oceania for a start – and there are many ways of circumventing the problem without dropping out of the FA Cup. If they had to, would they be forced to start the 2000–2001 competition at the Preliminary Round stage? That would concentrate thinking along the right lines.

Lack of international success has been blamed on the influx of foreign players. Manchester United have more than their fair share but understandably not a voice was raised against their memorable achievements. The top four clubs finishing in the FA Premier League had foreign (non-English) managers, the bottom four were led by English ones. A wise person remarked on the subject saying that it meant the bigger clubs could afford expensive foreign managers, just as they can costly foreign players.

ROTHMANS FOOTBALL YEARBOOK
HONOURS

For the fourth consecutive year, members of the Football Writers' Association selected their team of the season for Rothmans Football Yearbook. As in previous years, players eligible had to have appeared in FA Carling Premiership matches during the season.

Although fewer players received votes, 53 compared with 61 last year, a record number of FWA members recorded their preferences. As last year the majority plumped for a 4-4-2 formation.

Despite Manchester United's triple triumph, Arsenal players were well represented in the closeness of the voting, mirroring the tight finish to the Premier League. In fact these two teams split all but one place in the final selection, that going to David Ginola of Tottenham Hotspur, the FWA's choice as Footballer of the Year. But in fact Ginola was closely pressed by Harry Kewell of Leeds United.

Once again the only player to have appeared in the team for the four years of the honours was Gary Neville of Manchester United. He was joined by colleagues Peter Schmeichel, Jaap Stam, Roy Keane, David Beckham and Dwight Yorke. Keane and Beckham received the most votes.

The most fiercely contested place was at centre-back as two Arsenal players Martin Keown and Tony Adams fought for the right to partner Stam in the heart of the rearguard. In the end Keown just edged it. Two other Arsenal players, Emmanuel Petit and Patrick Vieira tenaciously vied for a midfield place before Petit succeeded.

Another close contest was at left-back where Nigel Winterburn was hard pressed by Manchester United's Denis Irwin.

Other players who figured prominently in the final analysis included Albert Ferrer (Chelsea), Sol Campbell (Tottenham Hotspur), Ryan Giggs (Manchester United), Marcel Desailly (Chelsea), Michael Owen (Liverpool) and Nicolas Anelka (Arsenal).

Sir Alex Ferguson had overwhelming support as manager of the season, following his team's unique success on three fronts.

Rothmans Football Yearbook Team of the Season

Peter Schmeichel
(*Manchester U*)

Gary Neville	Martin Keown	Jaap Stam	Nigel Winterburn
(*Manchester U*)	(*Arsenal*)	(*Manchester U*)	(*Arsenal*)

David Beckham	Roy Keane	Emmanuel Petit	David Ginola
(*Manchester U*)	(*Manchester U*)	(*Arsenal*)	(*Tottenham H*)

Dennis Bergkamp   Dwight Yorke
(*Arsenal*)   (*Manchester U*)

Manager:
Sir Alex Ferguson (*Manchester U*)

Substitutes:
Tony Adams (*Arsenal*)
Patrick Vieira (*Arsenal*)
Harry Kewell (*Leeds U*)

MILESTONES DIARY 1998–99

June 1998

England start WC with Tunisia win ... Scotland out early ... Pen shoot-out heartache ... Platini and Blatter request strict refs ... Sir Alf Ramsey has stroke ... England v Argentina huge TV audience ... WC 66 booking surfaces for Bobby Charlton

13 Fancied Holland, playing in blue, held 0-0 by near neighbours Belgium. Patrick Kluivert dismissed in 80th min. South Korea's hopes of first WC win evaporate (lost 3-1 to Mexico) when Seok-Ju Ha sent off a minute after scoring. Olympic champs Nigeria shock Spain with 3-2 success.

14 English football hooligans fight running battle with Marseilles police and rival supporters on eve of England's opener v Tunisia. Argentina unconvincing but make winning 1-0 start over Japan. Croatia comfortable 3-1 winners over Caribbean reggae boys Jamaica. Robbie Earle scores as the colour of the occasion provides the real excitement. On their quest to qualify, Iran and Yugoslavia scored a combined 98 goals, but a 72nd free kick from Mihajlovic secures this result for the Yugoslavs.

15 Skipper Alan Shearer (his 19th in 39 appearances) shows the way with Paul Scholes completing England's solid start against Tunisia. Romania beat disappointing Colombia 1-0. Germany, not at their best, see off gallant USA 2-0. Double-winning Arsenal to kick off new season, Monday Aug 17, home to promoted Forest.

16 Scotland keep hopes alive thanks to Craig Burley's 1-1 equaliser against Norway. Champs Brazil cruise to 3-0 success over Morocco with Ronaldo at times dormant then brilliant. Michel Platini and Sepp Blatter complain that some referees are not following FIFA guidelines. Former Blackburn, Everton and England defender Keith Newton dies a week before 57th birthday.

17 Italian artistry overcomes Cameroon foul play and 10 men, for 3-0 win. Austria's last gasp 1-1 equaliser deprives Chile of a win whose Marcelo Salas hits 3rd of tournament. Faustino Asprilla walks out of Colombia camp. Scotland's Colin Calderwood flies to London for treatment to a broken hand.

18 S Africa's 1-1 with Denmark brings petty squabbles. Colombian ref John Jairo Toro Rendon cautions 7 and dismisses 3 reducing the Danes to 9 men. The 3 red-carded – all subs – lasted a combined total of 35 mins. Before 75,000 France advance to 2nd stage with 4-0 win over S Arabia – but Zinedine Zidane sent off for stamping.

19 Nigeria's 1-0 win over Bulgaria puts them through. Stalemate against 80-1 Paraguay leaves under-achievers Spain on verge of early exit. Newcastle sell Jon Dahl Tomasson to Feyenoord for £2.5m and complete £3.5m signing of Stephane Guivarc'h from Auxerre.

20 Three goals in 11 min spell sees Holland put 5 past S Korea. Dennis Bergkamp starts his first game since injury against Derby on April 29. Mexico felt 105°F temperature to their liking in Bordeaux pegging back Belgium's 2-0 lead. Around 100 fans treated for sunstroke. Scots ref Hugh Dallas sends off Pavel Pardo. Japan predictably eliminated by Croatia's 1-0 win. Going into Day 12: 11 sent off and 87 players with 1 caution.

21 With typical resolve, lethargic Germany wake up to pull back the 2-0 lead of the technically gifted Yugoslavs. Coach Berti Vogts compliments his opponents' 'brilliant' play. Lothar Matthaus comes on for 125th cap and appearance in 5th WC finals. In politically charged confrontation Iran beat USA 2-1. Argentina crush Jamaica 5-0. Plymouth sack manager Mick Jones.

22 England's progress falters – they now need a draw at least against Colombia – after Toulouse defeat v Romania. Petrescu pounces on Chelsea colleague Le Saux's 90th min slip to snatch 2-1 win. Sub Michael Owen had earlier replied to Moldovan's opener. Colombia beat ordinary-looking Tunisia 1-0. Charlton break transfer record paying £825,000 for Derby's Chris Powell. Allan Evans appointed to coaching staff at Stoke, Sheff Utd requiring new boss, given permission to talk with Brum's Steve Bruce.

23 Scotland, in their 8th appearance at WC finals, knocked out of tournament beaten 3-0 by Morocco in St Etienne. Burley sent off in 54th min. Behind, 12 mins from time, Norway with 6 Premiership players in line-up stun WC holders Brazil to win 2-1. The S Americans had not lost a group game since 1974. Both now advance to knock-out phase. Earlier, Chile draw 1-1 with Cameroon and over tedious 90 mins Italy beat Austria 2-1.

24 Spain the first major casualty of WC. They tumble out despite a 6-1 demolition of demoralised Bulgaria. Arsenal's Emmanuel Petit and Patrick Vieira play key roles as France beat Denmark 2-1. Paraguay secure surprise place beating much-weakened Nigeria 3-1 to set up meeting with hosts. S Africa's 2-2 with S Arabia features 3 pens. Munich air tragedy testimonial between Man U and Eric Cantona XI re-scheduled for Aug 18. Plymouth appoint former player Kevin Hodges, 38, as manager.

25 Sloppy Holland, 2-0 up with 15 mins to go, let Mexico retrieve 2 goals, but both progress. S Korea gain a little glory in their 1-1 with Belgium – but head home. Yugoslavia top their group beating USA 1-0 who lost all 3 of 1st round games. German coach Vogts makes changes and his selection sees off Iran 3-0. Spain veteran goalie Andoni Zubizarreta, 36, announces retirement. Belgian coach Georges Leekens set to quit post.

26 England rekindle the fire and move into 2nd round with exciting 2-0 win over a Colombian side neat and tidy but lacking a cutting edge. Darren Anderton and Beckham do the damage. Coach Hoddle yields to clamour of critics and promotes Owen to start in preference to Teddy Sheringham. Moldovan's 73rd min strike rescues Romania to earn 1-1 with Tunisia and showdown with Argentina. In show of solidarity, the entire Romanian side dye their hair yellow! Germany, only team of 32 to keep a clean sheet in each group match, beat Croatia 1-0. With only pride at stake, Jamaica get first WC victory, 2-1 over Japan who notch their first goal. Afterwards coach Okada says he will quit the post. Belgian playmaker Enzo Scifo, 32, to quit the international scene. FIFA deny Nigeria–Paraguay group match-rigging claim.

27 In 2nd round Brazil, beaten earlier by Norway, respond to knockout competition with a sparkling 4-1 dismissal of Chile. Unsung hero Cesar Sampaio – who opened the scoring at France 98 – with a brace, and Ronaldo two, 1 a spot-kick. Salas reduced Italy book a last 8 place thanks to Vieri's 18th min goal against Norway, his 5th so far.

28 France totter into quarter-finals courtesy of extra time Golden Goal from central defender Laurent Blanc. Paraguay's stout defending held out for 113 mins. Denmark, the tournament's big surprise, have a quarter-final encounter with Brazil. Moller, Brian Laudrup, Sand and Helveg seal a comfortable 4-1 win over enthusiastic Nigeria. Sir Alf Ramsey, 78, manager of England's 1966 WC winners, resting in Ipswich hospital after a mild stroke.

29   An opportunistic injury time drive from Juventus midfielder Davids gains Holland a 2-1 win over Yugoslavia and sets up clash with either England or Argentina. Komljenovic headed in after 49 mins to equalise Bergkamp's opener 11 mins beforehand. Mijatovic misses a pen. Methodical Germany, behind to Hernandez's 47th mins score, chisel out a triumph over Mexico. Jurgen Klinsmann levels and with 4 mins remaining Bierhoff's powerful header beats pint-sized Campos. Germany meet winners of Romania-Croatia tie. Steve Sampson (USA) becomes 5th WC boss to quit. Going into Day 20: 138 goals; 197 cautions and 16 red cards (52 matches). Jack Rowley, former Man U and England forward, dies, aged 79.

30   England's WC adventure ends in heroic failure at St Etienne beaten on pens by Argentina. Reduced to 10 men for 73 mins after Beckham's dismissal, England hold the opposition to a 2-2 draw after extra time. With the score in the penalty shoot-out 4-3 to the S Americans, David Batty, on as sub, sees his spot-kick saved by Carlos Roa. Earlier and within 5 mins of start, Gabriel Batistuta scored from a pen. But when Owen was decked, Shearer levelled. The Liverpool lad then brought the house down with a spectacular solo run and finish only for Zanetti to reply on stroke of half-time. A record TV home audience of 28 million watched Hoddle's team fail after a match laced with high drama. Swansea part company with Alan Cork. A FIFA scan of the archives shows WC winner Bobby Charlton received his first international booking – 32 years after it was administered during England's storming quarter-final clash with Argentina at Wembley.

July
Bass pour in £23m for Worthington League Cup ... Wilson gets Sheff Wed post ... Bruce is boss at Blades ... Pele unimpressed by WC refs ... Ronaldo mystery as France lift World Cup ... Wright swaps Gunners for Hammers ... Kanchelskis links with Rangers

1   Beckham will miss Euro 2000 start after FIFA issue 2 match ban and £2,000 fine. Walter Smith on a 3 year contract becomes Everton's 4th manager in 4 years. Brentford chairman Ron Noades announces he will also manage the team. Former Chelsea boss John Hollins takes charge at Swansea.

2   Steve Bruce, 37, installed as Sheff Utd manager. Wes Saunders appointed Torquay boss. Steve Staunton, 29, returns to Liverpool on free transfer under Bosman rule 7 years after leaving to join Villa. FL announce Worthington League Cup details in 5 year, £23m sponsorship with brewers Bass.

3   In quarter-final clash before 77,000 France should have ended the Italian dream long before the 4-3 penalty shoot-out success which followed the stalemate extra time. The all-round brilliance of Rivaldo weighs in with 2 goals to ensure Brazil storm into last 4, 3-2 winners over a Denmark side true to its honest and open-style football.

4   Croatia with 2 in last 10 mins gatecrash the party in earnest (3-0) to push aside the ageing might of Germany hampered by the red-carded Christian Worns. A wonderfully controlled 89th min goal by Bergkamp enables Holland to rectify a 20 year hurt since losing unluckily to the Argentines in the 1978 WC final. Earlier Lopez had equalised Kluivert's 12th min finish. Each had a man dismissed, Numan and Ortega.

5   At least half the 32 coaches at France 98 will be out of a job after the tournament.

6   Danny Wilson, 41, installed as Sheff Wed boss. John Hendrie succeeds him at Barnsley. Boro who signed Dean Gordon for £900,000 from Palace expect to land Man U's Gary Pallister for £2m. Shaka Hislop completes Newcastle to W Ham on free move. Stuart Ripley leaves Blackburn in £1.5m switch to Southampton. Man U's Euro travels start against either LKS Lodz or little known Kopaz from Azerbaijan. Welsh minnows Barry again draw Dynamo Kiev and Hearts head to Estonia. Celtic paired with St Patrick's, Rangers also draw a Dublin club, Shelbourne.

7   After gripping 1-1 aet encounter Brazil beat Holland 4-2 on penalties in Marseilles and reach their 6th WC Final. Ronaldo's early 2nd half score triggers celebrations. Van der Sar keeps the Dutch in it and with 4 in attack, Kluivert rises to score. Cocu and Ronald de Boer have their spot-kicks saved by Taffarel. Former England captain David Platt, 32, retires with a year still to run on Arsenal contract. W Ham sign £3m, 3 year sponsorship deal with Dr Martens.

8   Joy for France but despair for Laurent Blanc sent off in clash with Slaven Bilic and misses the final. 76,000 pack the stadium in St Denis as hosts France with 2 goals from Thuram overcome Croatia who had stolen a 46th minute lead through Suker.

9   Despite French appeals to FIFA, defender Blanc will miss WC final against Brazil and the opening Euro qualifier. Said Belqola, 41, of Morocco to referee WC final and Nationwide ref Mark Warrel, 38, a former traffic policeman selected on the line.

10   Pele describes refereeing standards as 'low point of tournament'. Chelsea's Mark Hughes, 34, completes £500,000 move to Southampton.

11   Croatia's Suker (the leading scorer in the tournament with 6) notches the 2-1 winner over Holland to take the 3rd place play-off spot at Parc des Princes. Zenden (21 mins) had equalised Prosinecki's 13th min opener. Every touch defender Bilic made was booed. In Croatia's semi-final his reaction had caused the dismissal of France's centre-half Blanc.

12   France put their name on the trophy for the first time beating Brazil 3-0 before 75,000 at Stade de France. The win sparks unprecedented celebrations on the streets of Paris. Favourites Brazil are disappointing, hampered by a mystery injury/illness to star Ronaldo who played despite being distinctly off-colour. In hospital, he only joined the squad 45 mins before kick-off. Ronaldo's late, late appearance meant that a second team sheet was submitted in time to FIFA officials. Zidane got 2 from corners with Arsenal's Petit adding the 3rd in injury time. France saw out the last 20 mins without red-carded Marcel Desailly.

13   A total of 257 cautions and 22 red cards dished out during WC. Mexican offical Arturo Carter in charge for 3 games flashed 16 yellows and 4 red cards. Ian Wright, 34, who broke Cliff Bastin's club record of 178 League and Cup goals, moves from Arsenal to W Ham for a fee around £750,000. Liverpool to sign Norway's WC defender Vegard Heggem from Rosenborg for £3m.

14   Man U's Beckham gets police protection on his return to training.

15   France's WC winning coach Aime Jacquet, honoured by President Chirac, is to step down as planned. England and France named joint winners in FIFA's WC Fair Play awards. England also won it in 1990. Beaten finalists Brazil receive low-key return welcome from an estimated 3,000 crowd.

16   Former Man U and Everton winger Andrei Kanchelskis joins Rangers from Fiorentina in Scottish record £5.5m transfer. Rangers UEFA Cup tie in Dublin against Shelbourne called off for security reasons, neutral venue likely. Long-serving Ronnie Moran is to retire after 50 years Liverpool service. Walter Smith completes first signing for

Everton paying £2.8m for Marco Materazzi. Ronaldo's convulsive fit before WC final could have been triggered by side effects of pain-killing injections on his knee.

17   Liverpool announce Gerard Houllier, 50, a former French national team coach to share joint managerial duties with Roy Evans. Coventry receive a club record £3.5m for Viorel Moldovan. FIFA say all 256 players who underwent drug tests during WC provided negative results. Celtic end 10 week search with surprise announcement that Jozef Venglos, 62, who briefly took charge at Villa, to succeed Wim Jansen.

18   German's confirm Berti Vogts to stay as national coach.

19   Palace lose 2-0 at home to Samsunspor in UEFA Intertoto Cup prelim round. England U-18 win opening UEFA finals match 2-1 in Cyprus against hosts.

20   UEFA give the OK for Arsenal's Champions League matches to be staged at Wembley. Doncaster Rovers to entice Ian Snodin as boss following relegation from the FL.

21   Arsenal give 6 year contract to Matthew Upson, 19.

22   Dino Zoff who skippered Italy's 1982 WC winning side succeeds Cesare Maldini as national coach. S Korea, co-hosts of WC 2002, ask FIFA to switch dates and avoid rainy season. Switched to Prenton Park, Shelbourne race to an astonishing 3-0 UEFA Cup lead against money-bags club Rangers – but run out of steam late on and lose 5-3. In European Cup qualifier mighty Celtic held 0-0 by St Patrick's before 56,864. Dynamo Kiev inflict 8-0 defeat on Barry Town.

23   England U-18 crash out of championship finals in Cyprus, on goal difference losing 3-0 to Croatia. ROI win the group and face Germany in Sunday's final. FA Cup, linked with £25m deal, is to be known as the AXA-sponsored FA Cup.

24   Disgraced Newcastle directors Freddy Shepherd and Douglas Hall return to the board with apologies and promise of money for new signings. Villa complete £3m signing of W Ham's David Unsworth who failed to settle in London.

25   Celtic beat Spurs 2-0 in pre-season friendly.

26   Everton agree fee for French-based players, John Collins (Monaco) £2.5m, and Strasbourg's Oliver Dacourt, £4m. ROI are EC U-18 champs beating fancied Germany in penalty shoot-out in Cyprus.

27   Roger Lemerre, 57, assistant to Aime Jacquet, is new national coach to France. Forest striker Kevin Campbell heads to Trabzonspor in £3m deal.

28   Brazil dismiss Mario Zagallo and the entire WC coaching staff. Zagallo managed for 148 games, over 2 periods, with 107 victories, 29 draws and 12 defeats. Scotland will miss out Glasgow and use Edinburgh and Aberdeen venues for EC 2000 qualifiers. Blackburn put £5.15m valuation on under contract Colin Hendry who wants to join Rangers.

29   Newcastle sign Bayern Munich's Dietmar Hamann for £5.5m and pay Boca Jnrs £2.5m for Nolberto Solano. In Euro action Celtic beat St Patrick's 2-0 and Rangers win by same margin against fellow Dublin part-timers Shelbourne. Linfield, 5-1 behind to Omonia from 1st leg and 3-1 down in 2nd leg, come back to win 5-3 – but go out 8-6 on agg.

30   In an amazing U-turn Villa's Unsworth wants to quit a week after a £3m transfer from W Ham to link up with Everton. Sky announce £45m, 4 year package for Scottish football. The deal to show 30 live games on Sunday evenings this season.

31   Villa call off Dwight Yorke's proposed move to Man U when told Andy Cole was not part of a £16m package. Man U with £10.5m record signing Jaap Stam making debut, hit Brondby for six in Copenhagen friendly. In UEFA Cup Rangers paired with PAOK Salonika; Kilmarnock meet Czech side Sigma Olomouc.

August

Kluivert not for Man U ... Hendry heads to Ibrox ... Big Two eye Super League ... Arsenal lift Charity Shield ... FA drop Clough 'bung' charges ... Beckham long term at Old Trafford ... Yorke off to Man U ... David Unsworth double U-turn ... Madejski stadium opening ... Super Cup for Chelsea

1   Scotland's 10-club Premier Division kicks off. Teams permitted five subs – two must be U-21 – and only three can be used.

2   Kenny Dalglish furious at Boro statement that they had captured Keith Gillespie for £3.5m on a five year agreement. 'Something I never knew', said the Newcastle boss before the two clubs clashed in JD Sports Cup. Rangers, Britain's biggest spenders on £23m and under Dick Advocaat, crash 2-1 at Hearts in their League opener, live on TV. FA chairman Keith Wiseman dismisses proposed European Super League as 'Harlem Globetrotters stuff'.

3   Patrick Kluivert snubs £9m Man U offer to remain at AC Milan.

4   In-dispute Pierre van Hooijdonk, remains in his native Holland, and fails to report for training at Nottm Forest, as scheduled. Rangers pay £4m for Blackburn's Colin Hendry. The Football League announces 100 League Legends, named by 15 journalists. WC 66 winners Jack Charlton, George Cohen, Ray Wilson and Roger Hunt not included.

5   Ian Rush signs one year p/c deal at Wrexham. Wimbledon's much-travelled Mick Harford, 39, forced to quit. Man U and Arsenal own up to conducting secret talks on formation of the ultimate money-spinning 32-club European Super League. Both issue almost identical statements within minutes of each other. Speaking at Worthington Cup launch Alex Ferguson says that the idea is hypothetical and 10 years away. Leeds, who had five players red-carded and 79 cautioned last season, fined £50,000 by FA.

6   Man U and Arsenal would be offered £100m a year to take part if European Super League took off. Media Partners is the company behind the £2 billion project backed by American bank JP Morgan. Still on finance, accountants Deloitte and Touche disclose over £250m spent by clubs bringing in overseas players during last five years. Arsenal pay £1.6m to sign Argentine defender Nelson Vivas, 28, from Lugano. Arsenal's double-winning squad dominate the *Rothmans Yearbook* Team of the Season. Only Gary Neville and Michael Owen interrupted a clean sweep of the first XI selected by the Football Writers' Association: Seaman; Neville, Keown, Adams, Winterburn; Parlour, Vieira, Petit, Overmars; Bergkamp, Owen. Subs: Beckham, Giggs, Sutton. Manager: Arsène Wenger.

7   FIFA President Sepp Blatter and UEFA Gen Sec Gerald Aigner urge Europe's elite to abandon breakaway plans and instead discuss the situation with UEFA. Coventry agree £2.6m signing of Croatian Robert Jarni, 29, of Real Betis.

8   Centenary season of FL kicks off with time allowed boards displayed by reserve officials in all 3 divisions. Opening weekend attendances total 347,740, highest for over 20 years. Sunderland's Stadium of Light attracts 41,008 for defeat of QPR.

9   Overmars, Wreh and Anelka score in Arsenal's 3-0 Wembley Charity Shield win over Man U before 67,342 crowd. Credibility doubts expressed about Ron Atkinson's book *A Different Ball Game* which claims drug abuse rife in the game. But FA confirm random drug tests have doubled to over 500 although the number of positive fines fell to three last year.

10   Former chairman Sir John Hall says Newcastle could not afford to be excluded from European Super League plans. £3,000 match fee to be offered to referees in new Super League. Glenn Hoddle makes a series of stinging criticisms in his serialised book *World Cup Story* including a detailed description of Paul Gascoigne's reaction to being told he was not in the England squad for France.

11   Bryan Robson labels Glenn Hoddle's book revelations 'pathetic'. Dennis Wise gets three match ban for his stamping dismissal on Atletico Madrid's Carlos Aguilera.

12   Sub Darren Jackson's second half strike before 51,500 gives Celtic a slender 1st leg lead over Croatia Zagreb. A goal apiece from Man U's Ryan Giggs and Andy Cole seals a 2-0 win over LKS Lodz before 50,906. PFA chief exec Gordon Taylor says England players will be wary of Glenn Hoddle after serialisation of his controversial book. Swedish hero Tomas Brolin who had an unhappy spell at Leeds and Palace announces retirement at 28. Leicester sign Chelsea's Frank Sinclair for £2m. FA lift life ban on former WBA defender Shane Nicholson after clinical reports show progress at a drug rehab centre.

13   The FA pursuing their three year 'Bung Inquiry' drop charges against former Nottm Forest manager Brian Clough, on health grounds.

14   Ron Noades, Brentford's new chairman and manager says win bonuses only paid if the side is in top half of Div 3 table. David Beckham signs five year Man U deal worth £5m. Arsenal get Marc Overmars' signature on a two year contract extension. Steffen Effenberg recalled to German squad after four years' exile for obscene gestures to fans during USA 94. Lincoln put up for sale. Chelsea and Arsenal could lose French WC players required for FIFA-backed Confederation Cup tournament in Mexico Jan 6–20.

15   Four 0-0 draws on Premiership opening day which included new boys Charlton, down to ten men for 70 minutes, at Newcastle. Jurgen Klinsmann says he has no interest in returning to the Bundesliga. UEFA issue ultimatum and threaten to expel Man U, Arsenal, Liverpool and 13 others from European competitions unless they abandon breakaway plans by August 27, the draw date of the various European competitions. Halifax return to League Football with a 1-0 win over Brentford while Doncaster experiencing life in the Football Conference lose at Dover. Dermot Gallagher first referee this season to send off a Premiership player – Charlton's Richard Rufus at St James' Park.

16   Scores from Karlheinz Reidle and Michael Owen secure Liverpool's opening season 2-1 win at Southampton.

17   Neville Southall, 40 next month, agrees match to match arrangement with Doncaster. In a massive U-turn, Croatia World Cup star Robert Jarni abandons the agreed £2.6m move to Coventry and signs three year contract at Real Madrid. N Ireland cancel friendly against Malta as a mark of respect after Omagh bombing.

18   Steve Bull takes his tally to 304 goals for Wolves with a hat-trick in the 5-0 rout of Barnet. Espanyol's Marcelo Bielsa succeeds Daniel Passarella as coach to Argentina. Eric Cantona returns to Old Trafford to help raise £1m for survivors and families of those who died in Munich air disaster in 1958. His record at the Reds reads: played 185, won 117, drawn 45, lost 23.

19   Bruce Grobbelaar joins Ryman League side Chesham. Man City hit Notts Co 7-1 in Worthington Cup. And in night of shocks holders Celtic and Premier leaders Aberdeen crash out of Scottish League Cup. Coventry made £750,000 selling Robert Jarni to Real Madrid although he never kicked a ball for them. David Platt appointed assistant coach to England U-18 and U-19 teams.

20   Dwight Yorke joins Man U for £12.6m, a club record purchase. Aged 26, on a five year contract, Yorke had been at Aston Villa nine years, enticed from Tobago by Graham Taylor. Wolves agree one year loan with Feyenoord for Irish striker David Connolly. Blackburn beat European deadline with £5.3m capture of Derby's Christian Dailly. Villa sell unsettled defender David Unsworth to Everton for £3m. Nottm Forest complete £2.5m Colin Cooper move to Boro and are set to pay £2.5m for QPR's Nigel Quashie.

21   England to meet newly formed Yugoslavia, seventh in FIFA's rankings, in Wembley friendly on Nov 18. Patrick Vieira puts pen to paper on new four year Arsenal contract. Gordon Strachan tells Nottm Forest boss Dave Bassett to let striking contract rebel Pierre van Hooijdonk rot in exile. A late safety certificate allows Reading's opening match v Luton in new £37m 22,000 all-seater Madejski Stadium, to go ahead. It is now up to the player as Tottenham agree a £5.5m fee with Man U for Ole Gunnar Solskjaer.

22   First time that The Valley had seen top flight football since 1947, Charlton oblige by trouncing Southampton 5-0 to stand top of Premiership table. Christian Gross, tipped to be Premiership first casualty, orders Sunday training after Spurs crash 3-0 home to Sheff Wed. Hearts top in Scotland. Liverpool's Michael Owen, 18, signs lucrative five year contract reportedly worth £5m and doubling his wages to £20,000 weekly. FA launch inquiry after injury time 21-man brawl in the 0-0 Gillingham–Bristol Rovers Div II game. Marseille score five second half goals to beat Montpellier 5-4 and go top.

23   Barcelona barracked by 40,000 Nou Camp fans after losing 1-0 and 3-1 on aggregate to Mallorca in the Spanish Super Cup.

24   Ole Gunnar Solskjaer £5.5m departure to Spurs scrapped. UEFA decline Media Partners' offer to be Regulators of the proposed European Super League.

25   The 140 year old oak tree on the terraces which cost St Albans City a place in the Football Conference is to be felled. FIFA say the eight nations in the Confederation Cup in Mexico in January need not select their strongest squad.

26   Man U draw 0-0 against LKS Lodz, win 2-0 on aggregate to secure European Champions place. Robert Prosinecki's double in Croatia Zagreb's 3-0 success ends Celtic's ambitions. Roy Keane back in Ireland squad for EC tie with Croatia after 12 months' injury absence. Officials have suggested the 2002 World Cup be rescheduled to start in May to avoid rainy season in South Korea and Japan. BBC TV pundit Jimmy Hill quits after 25 years and joins Sky Sports. Tottenham appoint former captain Martin Peters, 54, to the board.

27   In dramatic and whirlwind fashion Newcastle axe manager Kenny Dalglish after 19 months in charge. The former Liverpool and Blackburn boss had two years remaining. His No. 2 Terry McDermott is also out. Ruud Gullit immediately installed on a two year contract worth £1m a year. Man U drawn in Champions League Group D

alongside Barcelona, Bayern Munich and Brondby. Arsenal (Group E) have Lens, Dynamo Kiev and Panathinaikos. Les Ferdinand sole member of England World Cup 22 failing to make first squad of new season, the EC tie with Sweden. Steve Archibald has joined Benfica as Executive Director.

28 Chelsea lift the European Super Cup beating Real Madrid 1-0 in Monaco. Gustavo Poyet's 81st minute winner gave Blues player/coach Gianluca Vialli his third trophy in six months. Ruud Gullit will ask his former Chelsea colleague Steve Clarke, 35, to be his No. 2 at Newcastle. In Cup-Winners' Cup draw Chelsea paired with Helsingborg, Newcastle against Partizan, Hearts tackle Mallorca. In the UEFA Cup 1st leg it is Leeds v Maritimo, Kosice v Liverpool, A Villa v Stromsgodset, Blackburn v Lyon, Vitoria Guimaraes v Celtic, Beitar Jerusalem v Rangers. Christian Vieri returns to Italy joining Lazio from Atletico Madrid in a £19m deal. Patrick Kluivert joins Barcelona in £9m transfer from AC Milan. Kenny Dalglish insists he did not resign but was sacked.

29 Blackburn drop £7.5m Kevin Davies, replaced by Kevin Gallacher, who gets 1-0 winner over Leicester. Villa establish themselves as early season pacesetters after 1-0 win at Sheff Wed.

30 Michael Owen hits a 16 minute hat-trick in Liverpool's 4-1 win at Newcastle. The Magpies line up selected by coach Alan Irvine with Ruud Gullit taking a back seat – until half time. Requiring dental treatment Nicky Butt pulls out of England squad for qualifier in Sweden. But Ally McCoist, not included in Scotland's World Cup panel, recalled for Lithuania tie after his hat-trick for Kilmarnock v Hearts.

31 On Bank Holiday Monday Wolves share Div I top spot with Sunderland after 2-2 with Stockport in front of 22,217.

September
Jackie Blanchflower dies ... Ince sees red in EC tie ... BSkyB big bid for Man U ... Chinese TV view Worthington Cup ... McMahon quits Swindon ... No replay for FA Cup Final ... Ref Paul Alcock in knock-down controversy

1 Refs at start of Jersey European Combination season will move the ball forward a further 10 yards for dissent. Ron Noades becomes first chairman to win Nationwide Manager of Month award. He is also club owner. A back injury has forced Liverpool's Mark Wright to quit at 35.

2 Assistant manager Peter Shreeves leaves Sheff Wed. Premiership refs to take fitness tests and have diets assessed every 3 months. Newcastle pay Chelsea £250,000 compensation for Clarke who becomes Ruud Gullit's No. 2. Jackie Blanchflower, a survivor of Munich air crash dies of cancer, aged 65.

3 To head off breakaway, UEFA hint that 3 English clubs could play in Champions League next season, and a further 7 in a competition combining existing UEFA and Cup-Winners' Cup. Motherwell appoint Pat Nevin, 35, as chief executive. Arsenal slash prices for Champions League 'home' ties at Wembley. 20,000 tickets available at £10.

4 Jamie Carragher and Frank Lampard see England U-21 make a winning start in EC qualifier against Sweden. Wales lose 2-1 to Italy in Wrexham; Scotland draw 0-0 in Lithuania; N Ireland go under 2-0 in Turkey and ROI draw 2-2 with Croatia.

5 England's Paul Ince sent off as they crash 2-1 to Sweden in opening EC qualifier, losing shape and discipline after Shearer netted in 75 secs. Scotland draw 0-0 in Lithuania; Wales, at Anfield, lose 2-0 to Italy and N Ireland go under 3-0 in Turkey. ROI pull off shock 2-0 home win over Croatia. No-hopers Cyprus humiliate Spain 3-2, only their 3rd victory in 30 years. Under pressure Christian Gross' inevitable parting from Tottenham ends torrid 10 months' reign.

6 *Sunday Telegraph* disclose Rupert Murdoch's satellite television group BSkyB bid to buy Man U in £575m deal. Martin Edwards, chief executive and chairman, to sell his 14 per cent stake for over £80m. Just 10 years ago he failed to sell the club for £20m. Man U was floated on the stock market in 1991 for £47m. Controversially, the deal would give BSkyB a key position in negotiations for a European Super League, and with the launch of the digital service an opportunity to broadcast the club's own new television channel and screen all live games. Anderlecht, Belgium's most successful club with 24 titles, left propping up Div I after 6-0 defeat at Westerlo.

7 FA call for talks with government over BSkyB proposed purchase of Man U, the country's most profitable club. Amid speculation of a rival bidder the club's stock market value soared by over £123m. Berti Vogts, 51, resigns German post. From 102 games in charge he had 67 wins; 23 draws and 12 defeats.

8 Man U's plc board accept an increased offer of £625m from BSkyB. Ex-boss Tommy Docherty says the sale would 'rip the heart' out of the club. Paul Merson completes £6.75m move to Villa and claims gambling and drinking at Boro was too much a temptation. His comments provoke anger at Riverside with Bryan Robson refuting the allegations. Leeds who last led the way in 1995 head the Premiership after 3-0 win over Southampton.

9 Two debut scores for big signing Dwight Yorke as Man U sweep aside Charlton 4-1 and deflect terrace 'sell out' chants. First glimpse of £4.4m Jesper Blomqvist from Parma. Caretaker David Pleat engineers Tottenham 2-1 win over Blackburn, while the Dons stage the comeback of the evening pulling back a 3-0 deficit at W Ham to win 4-3. Liverpool beat Coventry 2-0 to go top. Six cautions and Lee Dixon dismissed as Chelsea and Arsenal draw 0-0 in capital clash. No more international club matches in Stockholm because of high policing costs supervising Chelsea's European Cup-Winners' Cup final which cost £400,000 with 1,000 police on duty.

10 In the wake of BSkyB deal with Man U reports say that Carlton Communications are in talks with Arsenal about a possible take-over, and Tyne Tees Television believed to be interested in Newcastle. Former Magpies skipper Kevin Keegan claims his successor Kenny Dalglish 'lost the plot' at Newcastle, and backs Gullit's more stylish approach. Chinese internationals Fan Zhiyi and Sun Jihai (combined cost £500,000) finally granted visas to turn out for Palace. Javier Clemente resigns as Spanish boss in the wake of defeat v Cyprus. Scottish League Cup semi-final draw: Rangers v Airdrie; St Johnstone v Hearts

11 Arsenal agree £3m fee to Halmstad for Fredrik Ljungberg, 21. Wayne Allison's double in 3-2 win at Tranmere puts Huddersfield top of Div I.

12 Villa with debut goal from Merson sit top after 2-0 win over the Dons, Leeds 0-0 at Everton remain unbeaten in 5 matches. Newcastle's Shearer nets two in 4-0 win over pointless Saints.

13 Spurs fall flat at home and lose 3-0 to Boro. As takeover talks rumble on American investment bank Salomon Smith Barney show interest to gazump Murdoch's Man U deal with reported £700m bid.

14 Liverpool launch their 26th Euro campaign against Kosice. Chinese TV with potential audience of 1,208,000,000 will give in-depth report of tomorrow's Worthington Cup tie at Bury when Palace are set to include first Chinese imports to be involved in English football.

15   Dramatic late UEFA drama at Villa Park against Stromsgodset. Down 2-0 and 10 mins remaining Villa send on Darius Vassell, 18, who follows up Gary Charles' score by netting two injury-time goals. Liverpool chalk up 3-0 away win in Kosice, a late Lyon goal deflates Blackburn. Leeds overcome Maritimo 1-0. Rangers draw 1-1 away in Beitar Jerusalem, but Celtic lose 2-1 at Vitoria Guimaraes. Woking, bottom of Conference, sack manager John McGovern. Bruce Grobbelaar appointed caretaker Zimbabwe coach for tie with Zambia on Sep 27.

16   Arsenal squander a precious away win when Lens squeeze home late 1-1 equaliser with secs to go. Disappointing night for Man U who draw 3-3 with Barcelona after leading 2-0 at the interval. They concede 2 pens and play last 20 mins without red-carded sub Nicky Butt. Ray Harford offers to stand down as QPR lose Worthington tie 2-0 at home to Charlton. Steve Burtenshaw, former Arsenal chief scout, admits to receiving an illegal payment. He apologises to FA for accepting £35,000 fee from Rune Hauge 2 months after John Jensen joined Highbury in Sep 1992.

17   Chelsea make heavy weather of defeating Helsingborg 1-0 at home through Frank Leboeuf's 43rd min goal. Nikos Dabizas gives Newcastle 2-1 win over Partizan Belgrade; Hearts lose 1-0 at home to Real Mallorca. Ron Atkinson declines chance to take charge of S Africa.

18   John Gregory signs 4 year manager deal at Villa reported to be worth £2m.

19   Dave Watson becomes only 3rd Everton player to make 500 appearances. Brentford's Jamie Bates chalks up 500 games at Scarborough. Villa remain in top spot despite 0-0 at Leeds; Liverpool and Charlton share 6 at Anfield, and Newcastle have 5-1 win at Coventry.

20   Nicky Butt sent off 2nd time in 5 days in 3-0 defeat by Arsenal who produce championship performance. First Old Firm clash ends scoreless at Ibrox before 50,026.

21   Glenn Hoddle voted to UEFA's technical committee. Graeme Le Saux off as Chelsea win 4-3 at Blackburn in stormy affair.

22   FL to pioneer screening of some fixtures to pay-per-view subscribers in late December and early January. Man U 1st club charged with misconduct after Wes Brown fails to report for England U-18 squad duty.

23   Abuse to his family triggered Steve McMahon's decision to quit at Swindon after 4 years. Michael Owen only England player in Euro all-Star XI chosen by 51 international coaches. First time in 127 year history no replay of FA Cup final. FA say extra time and penalties to decide Wembley May 22 clash.

24   In Premiership showdown Man U defeat Liverpool 2-0. FA impose £7,500 fine on Steve Burtenshaw, 62, for breaking rules.

25   Swindon with estimated £5m debts place entire playing staff on list.

26   Ref Paul Alcock knocked to ground by Sheff Wed red-carded fiery Italian Paolo Di Canio. Arsenal's Martin Keown also off. A total of 21 sendings-off in England and Scotland, one of the worst for indiscipline. John Gregory, 70, former QPR owner who hired and fired 14 managers in 22 years, dies after long illness.

27   Ray Harford who won only 5 of 44 games, quits his QPR post.

28   Sheff Wed's Paolo Di Canio charged with misconduct by FA. Australia thrash Cook Islands 16-0 in Brisbane in Oceania Nations Cup, one goal less than world record victory Iran recorded over Maldive Islands in WC qualifier.

29   Liverpool wallop Kosice 5-0 and agg 8-0 scoreline. Blackburn exit after 2-2 (agg 3-2) in Lyon, Jason Wilcox dismissed. Villa's Stan Collymore hits hat-trick to seal Villa win in Stromsgodset. Henrik Larsson's late 2-1 home winner eases Celtic passage into next round (agg 4-2) over Vitoria Guimaraes. Leeds with George Graham probably in charge for last time lose 1-0 away to Maritimo (agg 1-1) but go through 4-1 on pens.

30   Bayern Munich snatch 90th min score (2-2) at home to Man U in Champions League; Arsenal beat Panathinaikos 2-1 and hail the switch to Wembley (73,500) a success despite crowd congestion which delayed ko 25 mins.

October
George Graham in charge at Spurs ... Champions League to expand says UEFA ... Hartson horror kick ... Villa Park gets Euro final ... Francis returns to QPR helm ... O'Neill loyal to Leicester ... Laudrup's Stamford Bridge shock ... Full time officials next season ... Van Hooijdonk the rebel back to Forest

1   George Graham installed as Tottenham boss, signs 4 year contract reportedly worth around £6m. European Cup-Winners' Cup holders Chelsea, with a slender 1-0 lead, draw 0-0 in Helsingborg. Ruud Gullit's Euro dream with Newcastle ends in 1-0 Belgrade defeat to Partizan (agg 2-2). Hearts draw 1-1 away but Mallorca progress (agg 2-1). Scots lodge protest over cross-bar measurements pointed out beforehand. Rangers move into UEFA 2nd round with 4-2 home win over Beitar Jerusalem. Former Arsenal and Spurs defender Laurie Brown dies, age 60.

2   Jimmy Quinn is new boss at Swindon. Villa's John Gregory wins Carling Manager of Month award. Cup-Winners' Cup 2nd round draw pairs: Chelsea v FC Copenhagen. In UEFA Cup: Liverpool v Valencia; Celta Vigo v Villa; Celtic v FC Zurich; Roma v Leeds.

3   Villa get 6th consecutive Premiership win, 2-1 at Coventry and stay top. Boro hit Sheff Wed 4-0. Huddersfield 2-0 v Oxford lead Div 1.

4   Chelsea, winners only once in 39 visits to Liverpool, draw 1-1 in niggling clash, 7 booked. Dennis Bergkamp whose last score was for Holland in WC against Argentina in July, notches a double and misses pen in Arsenal's 3-0 win over Newcastle. Tranmere's John Aldridge who threatened to quit is to stay. Rangers edge 2 points clear after slender home win over Dundee. Manager Advocaat orders rest after punishing 8 games in 23 day period.

5   Because of political situation, UEFA postpone ROI Euro 2000 qualifier in Belgrade. Both countries advised to keep Nov 18 free.

6   UEFA announce sweeping changes to Euro cups. Confirm expanded 32 team Champions League from next season with winners expected to receive £40m. Lennart Johansson states the merging of Cup-Winners' Cup, inaugurated in 1960-61 season, with UEFA Cup. The changes prompted by talks of breakaway Super League. Nigel Clough gets £180,000 pay off by Man City. His 38 first team outings cost £40,000 apiece. Leicester boss Martin O'Neill insists on his right to talk to Leeds about vacant manager's post.

7   *Daily Mirror* splash picture of W Ham John Hartson's horrific training ground kick at the head of colleague Eyal Berkovic sparking nationwide outrage. UEFA choose Villa Park to stage what could be the last ever European Cup-Winners' Cup Final on May 19. Barcelona host the Champions League (May 26) and UEFA Cup Final in Luzhniki Stadium, Moscow (May 12).

8   Bobby Gould to recall Robbie Savage against Denmark a month after the Wales boss described the midfielder as 'disrespectful' prior to clash with Italy. Bristol City unveil plans for £30m out of town stadium.

9   Paul Ince's 3 match UEFA ban (dismissed in Sweden) rules him out for England fixtures until June. W Ham's Frank Lampard on his home ground skippers and scores (pen) in the 1-0, U-21 EC win over Bulgaria. Scotland beat Estonia 2-0; Wales draw 2-2 in Denmark; and NI 1-1 with Finland.

10   Dreary fare at Wembley as England with one serious attempt on goal stumble 0-0 with Bulgaria before 72,974. Scotland avoid humiliating defeat v Estonia at Tynecastle with a Billy Dodds winner, his 2nd, 5 mins from time in a 3-2 success. Dream victory in Denmark for Wales with Craig Bellamy's 86th min winner. Boro make £3m swoop for Benfica's striker Brian Deane subject to medical. Wycombe only team in the FL without a victory.

11   Following dismal draw with Bulgaria, Glenn Hoddle refuses to accept the flak directed was aimed at him. 'You might think it was for me but it was for the team going off together.' Paul Philipp, coach to Luxembourg who face England on Wednesday said just 2 players in his squad are professional. Boro admit Paul Gascoigne has checked into a specialist clinic suffering from stress and alcohol problems.

12   As the squad prepare for Euro clash with Faeroe Islands, Scots keeper Jim Leighton, 40, capped a record 90 times, suddenly announces his international retirement – with no reason given. New Swindon boss Jimmy Quinn has banned players from supermarket shopping 3 days before games!

13   In EC U-21, England hit Luxembourg 5-0; Wales draw 0-0 with Belarus; ROI snatch a late 2-1 win over Malta.

14   England labour to a 3-0 win over Luxembourg part-timers. Owen, Shearer (pen) and Southgate score but home side miss a spot-kick after 5 mins. Scotland see off a spirited Faeroe Islands 2-1. Another boost for Wales who come back from the dead with 2nd victory in 5 days and beat Belarus 3-2. Teenager Robbie Keane, just turned 18, into record books as ROI youngest scorer hitting two in 3 mins in 5-0 win over Malta. World Cup winners France beat Andorra 2-0 with keeper Bernard Lama only touching the ball twice.

15   John Richards, Wolves managing director and former player, voted to FL board of directors as a Div 1 rep. Motherwell appoint Billy Davies to succeed Harri Kampman. Steve Chettle, longest serving player on Forest ground staff, signs 1 year contract extension. Steve Watson, 24, at Newcastle since 10, leaves for Villa in £4m move. French WC winner colleague at St James' Park Stephane Guivarc'h stalls on £2.5m move to Rangers.

16   Gerry Francis, 46, rejoins QPR saying he has turned down 12 job offers since he quit his Tottenham post. Gary Stevens, 35, former England, Everton and Rangers defender has been forced to retire after clocking up over 500 appearances. UEFA dismiss Hearts appeal against non-regulation dimensions of Real Mallorca goal-posts. Berkovic and Hartson put on show of unity at W Ham following highly publicised training ground confrontation.

17   Merseyside's 159th Derby at Goodison ends in stalemate. Man U brush aside Wimbledon 5-1. Villa despite score-less draw at W Ham remain top. Huddersfield maintain Div 1 lead with 2-0 success over QPR, now bottom. Table-toppers Rangers take revenge for opening day defeat to overwhelm Hearts 3-0. Ref Eddie Wolstenholme issues 10 yellow cards – 8 to Millwall players who had a player red-carded – in the 1-0 home defeat by Fulham.

18   Former Boro colleagues Juninho and Emerson, booked and 14 players cautioned as Atletico Madrid beat Tenerife 2-0. Chelsea's Frank Leboeuf, speaking at Oxford University Union, brands Man U's David Beckham 'arrogant' and accuses Liverpool's Karlheinz Riedle of 'cheating'.

19   Chester City face a winding up order with £350,000 owing to the Inland Revenue. Fluorescent yellow balls to be used in all Nationwide league matches from Nov 20 until at least Feb 27. Bryan Robson signs 5 year contract at Boro. Kevin Keegan has emergency surgery on a nerve in his neck. After emotional demonstrations at Filbert St and Leicester's 2-0 win over Spurs, Martin O'Neill says he will decide within 24 hrs whether to break his contract and take Leeds managerial post. In Danish newspapers Brian Laudrup hits out again at Chelsea's 'rotation' system.

20   Despite dismissal of Bruno Ribeiro, Leeds, under caretaker David O'Leary, battle hard to hold Roma to a 1-0 UEFA Cup lead. David James the Anfield hero as Liverpool held scoreless against Valencia. Liverpool forsook their red shirts for what is believed 1st time in more than 30 yrs. Julian Joachim scores a priceless away goal in Villa's win on Celta Vigo. Celtic, a goal up at home, have skipper Boyd sent off and are well held 1-1 by FC Zurich. John Toshack threatens resignation at Besiktas after interference by directors.

21   Dynamo Kiev's last min goal costs Arsenal dear in Champions League at Wembley. Although outclassed for long periods, Bergkamp's 74th min header looked to have secured a win. Man U, aided by a brace from dazzling Giggs, eased past Brondby 6-2 at Parken Stadium and shoot to top of Group D. On domestic front over 20,000 pack McAlpine Stadium to see high-flying Huddersfield and Sunderland draw 1-1. Martin O'Neill calls press conference and ends speculation: he stays as manager of Leicester. Paul Ince charged with misconduct by FA following his V-sign after he was sent off on England duty in Sweden last month. He has already received a 3-match UEFA ban. Man U sign 3 year promotion with Pepsi, worth £1,500,000.

22   Marcel Desailly's 90th min score preserves Chelsea's unbeaten home record in Europe after Goldbaek's shock goal for FC Copenhagen. Rangers pull off a storming 2-1 away win at Bayer Leverkusen with the Germans pulling 1 back on full-time whistle. Sheff Wed take ex-Newcastle keeper Pavel Srnicek. Philip Don, Premier League's referees' official, announces plans to pay 6 full-time refs from start of next season.

23   Disgraced Sheff Wed star Paolo Di Canio given 11 match ban and a £10,000 fine for his assault on ref Paul Alcock on Sep 26 against Arsenal. The name Clough back in management. Nigel, 30, son of Brian, takes charge at Burton Albion.

24   George Graham gets 1st win as Spurs boss, 2-0 over Newcastle. Speed merchant Owen, with a virtuoso performance, hits 4 in Liverpool, 5-1 thrashing of beleaguered Forest. Hard-working Leicester complete a good week with a 1-1 draw at Villa leaders over Man U who drew 1-1 at Derby. Rod Wallace's double helps Rangers coast to a 5-0 defeat of Airdrie, at Celtic Park, and into League Cup Final. The Ibrox club now on a 17 match undefeated run. Northampton and Preston face disciplinary action following a 12-man brawl.

25   Leeds v Chelsea 0-0 brings red card for Leboeuf and 13 cautions. Later David O'Leary, 41, ends a month of speculation by agreeing two and a half year contract as new boss at Elland Rd. Eddie Gray will be No. 2. A late 'X'-rated tackle by Sutton on Vieira the talking point at Ewood Park as out of sorts Blackburn floored by Anelka and Petit with Johnson replying. FL give Everton chairman Peter Johnson a New Year's Day deadline to cease his involvement with Tranmere. Two S African club players hospitalised after a bolt of lightning struck the pitch during Moroka Swallows v Jomo Cosmos. Captured on TV, 7 players and the ref were knocked to the ground.

26   England hopes of staging WC 2006 suffer double blow: FIFA's President Blatter tells Tony Blair during visit to London that Africa was the 'logical' choice. Germans insist that should an African country fail to meet the criteria they – not England – would have the influential support of UEFA.

27 Bristol City manager John Ward ends 18 months in charge and walks out. Benny Lennartsson, technical director to Sweden's 1994 WC squad, will take over. St Johnstone are in their 1st domestic final for 29 years. They beat Hearts 3-0 and face Rangers on Nov 29. Feyenoord's De Kuip Stadium the venue for EC Final 2000.

28 Chelsea's Vialli nets hat-trick in 4-1 over Villa. Arsenal's weakened side win 2-1 at Derby. Boro go under 3-2 to Everton and Man U stumble through League Cup tie, in extra time, against Bury.

29 Happy Wanderer Brian Laudrup, rumoured to be highest paid player in the country on £50,000 a week, is to leave Chelsea and return home to Denmark and FC Copenhagen. Insists he and his family are just homesick, have not settled in London, and that it probably was 'a mistake' to sign a 3 year contract. Wimbledon snap up Vale's Gareth Ainsworth for £2m. Man City's major shareholder Stephen Boler dies of heart attack at Johannesburg airport.

30 Pierre van Hooijdonk ends his 3 month exile dispute in Holland and returns to Forest. The club looking to claw back some of the £4m they paid Celtic, by off-loading the striker. Nathan Blake leaves Bolton to join Blackburn in £4.25m deal.

31 10,000 kids in free swell gate to 30,078 for Sheff Wed v Southampton. Everton lose 4-1 to Man City. An Ian Wright double as W Ham pull off 3-0 win at Newcastle. Jason McAteer dismissed 5 mins from time in Liverpool 1-0 defeat at Leicester. The death of a Coventry steward after a collision with the Arsenal team coach outside Highfield Road mars the fixture won 1-0 by the Gunners. Just under 20,000 witness Birmingham, with more games played, go top although held 1-1 at home by 2nd place Huddersfield. Blues Peter Ndlovu controversially sent off for taking an alleged 'double' dive. Mark Hughes chalks up 8th booking in 12 games for Southampton. Kilmarnock keep pressure on Rangers with 2-0 win over stuttering Celtic. Rangers beat Dundee Utd 2-1. A near 7,000 crowd brave atrocious conditions to see Aldershot and Woking finish 0-0 in FA Cup 4th qualifying round. Glenn Hoddle agrees lucrative revised terms for 2nd half of his 4 year contract believed to be a £100,000 increase on his previous £250,000 a year terms.

November
Butcher sells medals ... Dublin opts for Villa ... McGhee out at Molineux ... Dalglish bid for Celtic ... Schmeichel to leave Man U ... Anfield goodbye for Roy Evans ... FAW admit cash help ... Welcome to yellow balls ... Celtic heap misery on Rangers ... Shock exit of Roy at Rovers ... Newcastle splash cash for striker Ferguson ... Man U and Barcelona serve up thriller

1 New £3m arrival Brian Deane shows the way for 4th placed Boro against Forest, but Marlon Harewood snatches 88th min precious equaliser .

2 Terry Butcher puts his career mementoes up for auction in Stirling. His 1989 Sports Personality of the year souvenir sells for around £400. Hull City owner David Lloyd sells the struggling Div 3 club to a Sheffield-based consortium.

3 Sir Geoff Hurst, ambassador for England's 2006 WC bid, kick-starts his new role in Zurich. Villa's UEFA Cup hopes end as Celta Vigo dish out a lesson and win 3-1 (agg 3-2). Celtic go under 4-2 at FC Zurich and exit (agg 5-3). Liverpool draw 2-2 in Valencia but progress on away goals. Ince and McManaman off in heated ending. Leeds youngsters fail to break 10 man Roma to finish 0-0 and lose out (agg 1-0). Cash-strapped Oxford fail to pay staff for third month.

4 Red machine rolls on in Champions League, as Man U thump in 5 without reply against Brondby. Dynamo Kiev turn on the power (3-1) and put Arsenal's qualification in the melting pot. Sub Stephen Hughes scores an 84th min consolation as Gunners feel the absence of Bergkamp, Adams, Overmars and Anelka. Boro give keeper Mark Schwarzer a new 6 and half year contract.

5 Brian Laudrup's stooped header secures 1-0 (agg 2-1) win which sends Chelsea into quarter-final for 3rd time in 4 years. It wrecks the Cup-Winners' Cup hopes of FC Copenhagen – the club the Danish international joins in 4 days' time. Rangers fly the flag for Scotland with a 1-1 (agg 3-2) success over Bayer Leverkusen at Ibrox. Coventry's much sought-after Dion Dublin turns down Blackburn and Leeds to sign for Villa in a £5.75m deal and a 5 and half year contract. Kevin Keegan discloses that the money men at Newcastle forced him to quit. Mark McGhee parts company with Wolves 7 months before his £200,000 a year contract was due to expire.

6 FA fine Paul Ince £1,500 for his V-sign when sent off against Sweden. Rangers complete £3.5m signing of Newcastle's Stephane Guivarc'h. Pele in his Brazilian Minister for Sport role says the only country in Africa with potential to hold WC 2006 is South Africa. Sunderland's Alex Rae checks into clinic suffering from stress and alcohol-related problems.

7 Dublin scores twice on Villa debut and 3-2 win over Spurs. Boro's Robbie Mustoe and Phil Stamp shown red cards in 3-3 draw at Southampton. Kop fans jeer Liverpool's 2-1 defeat to weakened Derby. Van Hooijdonk returns for Forest, but another defeat, this time to Wimbledon. Irish striker David Connolly, on loan from Feyenoord, hits 4 in Wolves 6-1 win at Bristol City. General manager Jock Brown quits Celtic.

8 Anelka's goal against Everton keeps Arsenal 2 pts behind Villa but having played one more game. Chelsea keep up challenge 1-1 at W Ham. Man U on a crumbling below-par surface fail to get to grips with Gullit's Newcastle who grafted for a point in scoreless draw. Teenage defender Jonathan Woodgate notches 1st league goal in 2-1 win over Sheff Wed as Leeds soar into top 6. Rampant Rangers wallop St Johnstone 7-0 in Perth. Fiorentina thrown out of UEFA Cup following an explosive device which injured an official and caused suspension of the tie against Grasshoppers. Swiss side now advance to meet Bordeaux.

9 Roy Evans, hurt by criticism of his role, hits out at comments by former Liverpool stars. Chelsea's Pierluigi Casiraghi could be out for a year if surgeon confirms ruptured cruciate knee ligaments. Wembley's most famous voice Kenneth Wolstenholme joins chorus of outrage at the possible bulldozing of the Twin Towers.

10 Kenny Dalglish and pop star Jim Kerr prepare to launch multi-million takeover bid of Celtic. Hull sack manager Mark Hateley. FA appoint South Yorks Force policeman Graham Bean, 37, as its new 'Sleazebuster'.

11 ROI reject FIFA suggestion to release players to face Yugoslavia and allow them turn out for their clubs this weekend. Lincoln chairman John Reames will take charge of team after sacking of Shane Westley. In Worthington Cup 4th round, Vialli bags 2 and gives lively display as Chelsea hit Arsenal's 'reserve' team 5-0. Blackburn come from behind to beat Newcastle on spot-kicks. Sunderland win shoot-out at Everton. Man U win 2-1 over Forest and Garry Parker's late pen puts Leicester through against Leeds.

12   Leeds list Lee Sharpe, a record £4.5m signing from Man U 2 years ago. Watford boss Graham Taylor rushed to hospital after contracting serious throat infection. UEFA postpone U-18 qualifying tourney in Israel over safety concern in the Gulf. Former Ipswich hero Kevin Beattie reveals he made £36,000 selling FA Cup final tickets for 1978 clash with Arsenal. Peter Schmeichel, nearing 35, announces his decision to quit Man U at end of season, citing the increasing demands of the English game. At emotional press conference Liverpool joint manager Roy Evans bows out leaving partner Gerard Houllier to assume full control. Evans spent 34 years at Anfield. Ex Reds skipper Phil Thompson, 44, is new No. 2.

13   Paul Ince's miserable season continues with 3 match UEFA Cup ban following dismissal in Valencia. Chester face being wound up unless new owner can be found.

14   Chelsea's Tore Andre Flo starts for 1st time this season in 3-0 win over Wimbledon. Dublin gets hat-trick in Villa's 4-1 success at Southampton. Arsenal and Spurs cancel each other out in scoreless North London clash. Man U 3 up, take foot off pedal and allow Blackburn, with Tim Sherwood sent off, to pull back 2 goals. Sunderland's 2-0 away win at Vale keeps them 5pts clear in Div 1. Celtic stumble to 2-1 defeat against St Johnstone.

15   Alan Shearer to have hamstring scan and expects to be ruled out of England friendly with Czech Republic. BBC to pay £650,000 to Celta Vigo and show UEFA Cup clash with Liverpool next week.

16   Man U engage in feeder 'link-up' with Belgian club Antwerp. Europe's top clubs meet in Madrid to discuss how monies from next season's revamped Champions League should be divided. Sheff Utd part company with asst/man Steve Thompson, victim of backroom re-shuffle by boss Steve Bruce. Macclesfield boss Sammy McIlroy fines himself for his part in a touch-line punch-up after 2-2 FA Cup draw with Slough. Confirmation that FA of Wales agreed to accept £3.2 m over 8 years as reward for supporting Keith Wiseman in his bid for FIFA vice-presidency provokes questions at Lancaster Gate. The arrangement was £400,000 per year until 2006 to help fund development of youth football.

17   Kevin Keegan takes his Fulham spending to over £11m by signing Bristol Rovers hit man Barry Hayles for £2m. Palace ask FA to investigate alleged £400,000 shortfall in deal with 2 Chinese clubs for the £1.35m transfer of 2 recruits, Fan Zhiyi and Sun Jihai. Australian company which laid Old Trafford pitch blames Manchester's poor weather – 5 days sunshine since June – on its crumbling state. Sol Campbell named England skipper for tomorrow's friendly with Czech Republic. Frank Lampard misses 87th min pen as Czech Republic win U-21 friendly 1-0 at Portman Road. Villa's Gareth Barry, still 17, makes debut. In EC U-21 N Ireland draw 1-1 with Moldova.

18   Darren Anderton and Paul Merson seal a welcome England victory over Czech Republic before 38,535 at Wembley. Ian Wright turns back clock with lively performance. In EC qualifiers N Ireland draw 2-2 in Belfast with Moldova, Iain Dowie and Neil Lennon score. ROI give fine away display but go under 1-0 to Yugoslavia. At U-21 level Kevin Kilbane's 90th min pen equaliser (1-1) gets ROI, down to 9 with the dismissals of Robbie Ryan (32) and Steve Baker (52), out of jail. Scotland fight back from 2 down to share points with Belgium in Wales lose U-21 friendly 3-0 in Portugal.

19   Martin Edwards faced calls for resignation during noisy AGM at Old Trafford attended by 700 shareholders. Celtic pay £1.5m for Swedish midfielder Johan Mjallby, 27, from AIK Stockholm. Tomorrow's Div 2 Stoke–York fixture brings manager brothers Brian and Alan Little in opposition. Steve McManaman's adviser says 13 clubs have enquired about his availability.

20   New Mitre Ultimax Fluoflare yellow ball introduced in Div 3 Mansfield–Barnet fixture. Derby give 18 month contract to Tony Dorigo, 32, after his spell at Torino.

21   Villa 2 Liverpool 4 and action from start to finish. Stan Collymore sent off in clash with Steve Harkness. Robbie Fowler grabs a treble, but Villa remain top. Chelsea extend undefeated run to 17 games with win at Leicester. Before biggest attendance Sheff Wed overcome Man U 3-1. Arsène Wenger says 1-0 winners Wimbledon were more determined than his Arsenal who lost where Vieira and Bergkamp, both injured. Following Blackburn's 2-0 home defeat by fellow strugglers Southampton which put the Ewood Park club bottom, manager Roy Hodgson, 51, was dramatically relieved of the reins he assumed just 16 months ago. In Scotland, Celtic's 5-1 drubbing of Rangers was biggest Old Firm win in 32 years. Near 60,000 attendance, Rangers down to 10 with the dismissal of Scott Wilson after 22 mins. For the 1st time in 29 years and part of the N Ireland Peace Process, Cliftonville and Linfield draw 1-1 at the Solitude ground.

22   W Ham move to 6th after 2-0 away win at Derby. But Harry Redknapp rages at board's request to omit Andy Impey pending a £1.5m departure to Leicester.

23   Everton celebrate 1st Premiership win with Michael Ball's 18th min pen against lack-lustre Newcastle. UEFA postpone until Dec 2 the Juventus-Galatasaray Champions League match set for Wednesday because of the escalating tension between the 2 countries. Blackburn turn to long-serving Tony Parkes, 4th time in 12 seasons, to take temporary charge after Roy Hodgson's departure.

24   In UEFA Cup a stoppage time defensive error spoils Liverpool's gallant effort and leaves Celta Vigo with 3-1 lead and difficult for the Reds to retrieve. Outplayed for an hour, Rangers dig deep to earn spirited 1-1 (Wallace) draw at Ibrox against favourites Parma. Ruud Gullit will parade new £7m Everton signing Duncan Ferguson at press conference tomorrow. Ipswich keeper Richard Wright skippers Nationwide U-21 rep side in Terni against Italian Serie B. Everton boss Walter Smith seething about the Ferguson transfer when disclosed it was thrashed out by chairman Peter Johnson while Smith was master-minding from the dugout Monday's win over the Geordies.

25   Man U's twin-pronged attack of Andy Cole (2) and Dwight Yorke (1) provide real handful for Barcelona in a thrilling, cut and thrust Champions League tie which ends 3-3 before 67,650. United probably have to beat Bayern Munich at Old Trafford to guarantee quarter-final spot. Lens extinguish Arsenal's Euro ambitions. In a frenzied closing moment Ray Parlour is sent off after wild challenge and Lee Dixon accused of getting Vairelles red-carded. Luton's Sean Evers scores as Nationwide U-21 draw 1-1 with Italian Serie B. Barnsley sell Jan Aage Fjortoft to Eintracht Frankfurt. Controversial ref Graham Poll books 13 and sends 2 off in UEFA tie between Atletico Madrid and Real Sociedad. Gerard Houllier's first Liverpool signing is Jean-Michel Ferri, 29, from Istanbulspor for £1.2m.

26   Sepp Blatter says it was 'logical' for an African bid to host WC 2006 Finals – when he meets Nelson Mandela in Johannesburg. In aftermath of Arsenal's Champions League exit, conceding crucial late goals, Marc Overmars says they should have won their group 'in a gallop'.

27   Duncan Ferguson paid in the region of £900,000 by Everton, the severance payment covering the 4 yrs to run on his contract and the reward for not asking for a transfer.

28   Villa remain top despite 2-2 at lowly Forest. W Ham move into 3rd defeating Spurs 2-1. Sunderland's 4-0 win at
      Sheff Utd keeps them top of Div 1. Wolves confirm Colin Lee as manager at least until end of season.
29   Man U have 3-2 win over Leeds. Liverpool add to Blackburn anxiety winning 2-0 at Anfield. Nicholas Anelka gets
      last minute equaliser at Highbury to deprive Boro of success. All eyes on Ferguson and he obliges with a brace in
      Newcastle's 3-1 win over Wimbledon. Dick Advocaat, having spent £31m, gains his 1st trophy at Rangers with a
      League Cup win over St Johnstone, at Parkhead. Portsmouth chairman, Martin Gregory forced to borrow
      £150,000 from PFA to pay his players. Former Liverpool favourite Craig Johnston appointed head of Reebok's
      worldwide football and rugby business.
30   Everton chairman Peter Johnson forced to stand down after 4 years. Predecessor Sir Philip Carter, 71, back tem-
      porarily at the helm persuades Walter Smith to remain as boss. Palace's Terry Venables cleared of any involve-
      ment in alleged financial irregularities concerning transfer of Australian players to his old club Portsmouth.
      Blackburn make official approach to lure Brian Kidd as boss. Norway, Sweden, Denmark and Finland agreed to
      launch unique 4-way bid to host EC Finals 2008.

December
Kinnear denies betting claims ... Kidd is boss at Ewood ... Ardiles returns from Japan action ... Wise off again ...
Wanderer Saunders to sample Portugal ... Batty back at Leeds ... Arsenal's Wenger signs up ... Beardsley leaves
Cottagers ... UEFA announce new look competitions ... Owen wins BBC award ... Graham Kelly shock exit at FA ...
Chelsea top at last ... Zidane is Europe's Player of Year ... Graham Taylor glad to be alive

1   Chelsea's 3 month undefeated run ends with 2-1 Worthington Cup loss to Wimbledon. Newcastle's David Batty,
      subject of transfer speculation, says he only wants to rejoin Leeds. To stem likely political demonstrations 20,000
      police on duty for Galatasaray–Juventus Champions League clash in Istanbul. Real Madrid crowned World Club
      Champions for first time since 1960 after beating Vasco da Gama (Brazil) in Toyko. Gerry Francis Div 1 manager
      of month.
2   David Ginola lights up Tottenham with a brilliant goal to seal Spurs 3-1 over Man U. UEFA suspension means
      Arsenal pair Parlour and Dixon miss final Champions League tie against Panathinaikos. Celtic complete £3m
      signing of Australian Marco Viduka from Croatia Zagreb. Neil Lennon's 67th min goal against Blackburn earns
      Leicester a Worthington Cup semi-final spot, 2nd in 3 years. Millwall escape FA punishment but warned about
      future crowd trouble.
3   Premiership agree that clubs playing Euro ties on Thursday nights can switch their following game to Sunday. FA
      to write to Wimbledon and Joe Kinnear over allegations that their players bet on matches. Kinnear insists that he
      was joking about 66-1 odds taken to lift Worthington Cup. Michael Zen-Ruffingen, 39, a former international ref,
      replaces Sepp Blatter as Gen Sec of FIFA. Brian Kidd, 49, Man U No. 2, breaks long time links to accept
      Blackburn post and will be installed before fixture v Charlton.
4   Dublin with 7 goals in his first 4 games for Villa named Carling Player of the Month. Jimmy Ryan steps up for
      time being to assist Alex Ferguson. Former Spurs boss Ossie Ardiles ends 3 year stint in Japan as Manager of the
      Season for transforming lowly Shimizu S-Pulse.
5   Renowned FA Cup battlers Yeovil take their 18th League club scalp defeating Northampton 2-0. Southport, bot-
      tom half of Conference, knock out Mansfield. Top of table clash Villa–Man U ends in stalemate. Improving Leeds
      with 6 players under 21, go 3rd with emphatic 4-0 win over W Ham. Blackburn welcome Kidd with a 1-0 home win
      over Charlton. For 3rd time this season Chelsea's Dennis Wise sent off in 0-0 draw at Everton. Sunderland's 1-0
      over Stockport sets the pace at the top of Div 1 before a 36,000 crowd. Motherwell fixture against Dundee post-
      poned after death previous night of striker Andy Thomson, 19.
6   FA Cup 3rd round draw sees Boro's boss Bryan Robson return to Man U who have won the trophy a record
      9 times. Holders Arsenal have a tricky away tie at Preston. Kevin Keegan in charge of Fulham will return to for-
      mer club Southampton. Liverpool travel to Port Vale while Palace head to Newcastle and Spurs entertain
      Watford. The winners of non-league Doncaster v Rushden & Diamonds have a dream tie against Leeds. Yeovil
      face Cardiff. Australia's attempts to qualify for WC 2002 potentially more difficult by FIFA's announcement that
      the Oceania zone winners – likely to be Australia or New Zealand – will face a S American team for a place in
      finals.
7   Sheff Utd agree to sell Welsh international striker Dean Saunders, 34, to Benfica in £500,000 deal. Three-match
      ban for Chelsea's Wise. Tottenham's Steffen Iversen breaks his jaw; out 6 weeks. Coach Derek Fazackerley leaves
      Blackburn. Two Benito Carbone goals help Sheff Wed to 3-2 win over struggling Forest.
8   David Batty's £4.4m transfer from Newcastle to Leeds goes through. The 30 year old midfielder who left for
      Blackburn in 1993 has a four and a half year contract. Roy Hodgson reveals he didn't see the axe falling at
      Blackburn despite low position. Aberdeen have parted with manager Alex Miller by mutual consent. Liverpool's
      UEFA Cup ambitions end at subdued Anfield losing 1-0 (agg 4-1) to Celta Vigo who did not need to repeat their
      sparkling display in Spain. Rangers rattle Parma with a good 1st half performance and a 1-0 lead – but they are
      undone by Sergio Porrini's dismissal in 1st half injury time and eventually overwhelmed 3-1 (agg 4-2). Arsène
      Wenger finally puts pen to paper on new Arsenal 4 year contract and despite enticing offers elsewhere insists he
      did not even consider them. Sacked Bristol City manager John Ward to become assistant manager at Wolves.
9   Arsenal's makeshift team – 14 players not considered – produce a stunning Champions League finale and shock
      3-1 away win in freezing Athens against Panathinaikos. Scores from Mendez, Anelka and Boa Morte. This rare
      Euro success, only their 2nd of the season, left them to rue precious points squandered late on against Lens and
      Kiev. Roy Keane's effort in 1-1 draw with Bayern Munich deservedly put Man U through to last 8 of European
      Cup – but only confirmation mins after the whistle that Juventus had disposed of Rosenborg relieved the anxiety.
      With 10 mins to go boss Ferguson had communicated to his players that a draw was sufficient. Uwe Rosler, ex-
      Man City, notched a hat-trick in Champions League for Kaiserslautern. Domestically, Chelsea come more and
      more into the reckoning. In pulsating game they snatch a 4th min stoppage time 2-1 win over Villa through Tore
      Andre Flo's goal. He was making his 35th appearance as a sub. Peter Beardsley, 37, looking for 9th club after
      release from Fulham.
10   Champions League increases to 32 teams, instead of 24, and the UEFA and European Cup-Winners' Cup merge
      into one tournament from next season. This was formally announced at UEFA meeting in Lausanne. Premiership
      winners and runners-up assured of places with the 3rd placed team to join at the 3rd qualifying round. The new
      look UEFA Cup to include England's 4th placed side plus the winners of the FA Cup and Worthington Cup. If

England's 3rd placed club fails to survive the 3rd qualifying round of Champions League they will also enter the UEFA Cup. With 32 teams in new Champions League and 121 starting the new UEFA Cup competition there will be a total of 526 European club matches next season. First ties set for July 14. Arsenal to end 18 year link with sponsors JVC. The revolt of Premiership chairmen against chief executive Peter Leaver collapses with confirmation he is to keep his job.

11 Brighton hope to play 1st match at their new temporary home at Withdean Athletic ground against Barnet on Mar 27. Norwich fans to decide at next Saturday's game against Bristol City whether the team sticks with an all-yellow kit or reverts to yellow and green. UEFA say TV and marketing rights for new-look European club competition will generate £375m.

12 Man U surrender 2-0 lead at Tottenham (2-2) with Sol Campbell heading in twice, the equaliser right on time. Gary Neville sent off and 5 Utd players cautioned. Charlton with 4 consecutive defeats go under 3-0 at Sheff Wed. Everton's 1-0 win keeps Southampton rooted to bottom. Blackburn's fickle fans desert before the end after team let Newcastle away with a point (0-0). Dean Sturridge's stoppage time strike gives Derby 2-2 draw with Chelsea, still unbeaten since opening day. Sunderland's 2-0 win over Port Vale maintains top position while Birmingham (7-1) subject cash-strapped Oxford to their heaviest Manor Ground defeat. Rangers top, win against Kilmarnock (2nd) while Celtic (3rd) draw at Dundee Utd.

13 Alan Ball helps break up a pitch demo by around 500 fans after troubled Portsmouth lose at home to Grimsby. Two down at half time to Bergkamp's goals Villa stage a recovery against Arsenal for full points thanks to Julian Joachim and a double from Dublin. Second half delayed when member of RAF Hawks Parachute team landed on the main stand roof then fell 60 ft onto the touchline. Wimbledon beat Liverpool 1-0 with Owen missing a late pen. But the Kop Kid, 19 tomorrow, was handed a perfect pick-me-up hours later when named 1998 BBC Sports Personality of the Year.

14 New signing Batty booked for wild challenge 5 mins into his home debut for Leeds against Coventry. Disciplinary committee clear Arsenal's Vieira of assaulting police officer but hand out a £20,000 fine – a record for FA – for a V-sign gesture. Swindon incur £20,000 penalty suspended and Sheff Utd £5,000 for mass brawl on Aug 8. Blackpool put up for sale with midlands based leisure company negotiating for £18m purchase. Rangers take Neil McCann from Hearts for £1.6m.

15 England's football administration in turmoil with the shock resignation after 6 hour meeting of FA executive committee of chief executive Graham Kelly, 52. Also unanimous vote of no confidence in chairman Keith Wiseman. This follows internal investigation into alleged £3.2m misuse of FA funds, a grant over 8 years to the Welsh FA in exchange for votes to support Mr Wiseman's bid to secure a place on FIFA Executive Committee. Both men were undermined in Sept when an invoice for £400,000 – representing the first of eight annual payments – was received from the FAW. The pair had brokered the deal on Cup Final morning last May with David Collins. Three months later the Wales FA backed Wiseman in a fallen bid to unseat Scotland's David Will as Britain's FIFA vice-president. David Davies, director of public affairs, takes temporary executive director's role in charge of daily running at Lancaster Gate. FAW president John Hughes stated there was 'nothing sinister' and that the finance was earmarked to help develop youth and women's football. Brian Kidd makes his 1st Blackburn signing enticing Newcastle's Keith Gillespie for £2.35m while Motherwell give Brian McClair, who spent 11 years at Man U, permission to leave and join Ewood Park as No. 2. Sunderland, with Niall Quinn signing contract until 2002, open up 10 point lead with 2-0 over Palace. In FA Cup replays Leyton Orient put out Kingstonian but non-league Rushden & Diamonds fly the flag with 4-2 defeat of Doncaster. David Platt, 32, with no managerial experience heads to Sampdoria, but will need to overcome red-tape to take the coaching appointment.

16 Man U and Chelsea battle it out with 7 bookings and countless contentious decisions in 1-1 draw. Zola's equaliser cancels Andy Cole's 10th of the season. FAW say the £3.2m from FA funds was a 'gift' and did not need repaying. FIFA say the FA internal problems should not damage England's bid to host WC 2006. Prime Minister Tony Blair throws weight behind WC bid. Approaching 21st Century opinion polls point to radical overhaul at Lancaster Gate where the FA has £60m turnover, a full-time staff of 150, and a Council comprising 91 members. Bobby Robson is replaced by Eric Gerets who signs 3 year contract at PSV.

17 Former FA chairman Sir Bert Millichip demands total overhaul at Lancaster Gate following 'cash for votes' scandal. Revealed that Thailand national coach Peter Withe's £100,000 contract funded by English FA. Sunderland attract a staggering 20,583 attendance in reserve fixture v Man U. Graham Allner, Conference's longest serving boss relinquishes his Kidderminster Harriers post after 15 years.

18 Sheff Wed's Paolo Di Canio goes AWOL for 2nd time. Portsmouth's Martin Gregory, 46, who instigated a cut-price sale of entire playing staff to tackle £5m debts, stands down as chairman.

19 Chelsea overtake Villa and land top spot for 1st time this decade after 2-0 win over Tottenham who had Chris Armstrong sent off. The Blues' good day complete when title rivals Man U crash 3-2 at home to Boro. Nathan Blake's added-time 2nd score gives Blackburn a point just as home side Forest look to have secured their 1st Premiership victory in 15 outings. Liverpool had a rare clean sheet winning 2-0 over Sheff Wed. Leicester experience 9th defeat in 10 visits to Newcastle going under 1-0. Struggling Southampton with 2 from Egil Ostenstad surprise Wimbledon 3-1. Watford's 10 game unbroken run ends 2-1 at Grimsby. Mansfield's much-travelled Tony Ford's 821st appearance at Cardiff. Fulham, 1-0 winners at PNE, go top. Celtic put 5 past Dunfermline. Don Goodman returns from J-League side Hiroshima to join Barnsley on loan.

20 Arsenal defeat Leeds 3-1 but sub Gilles Grimandi dismissed for head-butt on teenager Alan Smith. Highbury's 5th red card and 17th sent off since Arsène Wenger took charge Oct 1996. David Platt gets emotional ovation after Sampdoria fight back to earn 2-2 with AC Milan in Genoa.

21 Villa gain full points and top 3 pts over Chelsea at Charlton. Rangers all set to land German goalie Stefan Klos, 27, from Borussia Dortmund for £700,000. Zinedine Zidane, 26, who notched twice in WC final v Brazil named European Footballer of Year, the 4th Frenchman to win the award.

22 UEFA, reacting to France 98 arrangements, agree fairer distribution on EC 2000 tickets: 16% to opposing countries upped to 20% in case of joint-hosts Holland and Belgium. Southampton's Mark Hughes, 1st to reach 11 cautions, given 2 match ban and £1,000 fine. Damaged cruciate knee ligaments rule out Leeds defender Robert Molenaar for season. At Watford press conference Graham Taylor reveals his recent throat illness left him 2 hours from death. Chairman Elton John slams the huge money paid to many top players with little community time given in return. Jean-Marc Bosman given £280,000 by Belgian FA to end legal conflict caused by his case. Aldershot of the Ryman League the 8th most popular club (Liverpool tops) according to Clubcall sports service who have 75 clubs on line. Shots have taken 500,000 calls since relaunch April 1992.

23   Ruud Gullit reaffirms loyalty to Newcastle after suggestions he spends too much time in Holland. England 9th in FIFA world rankings for December – a rise of 2 places; Scotland slip 2 spots to 38th. ROI move up 1 to 56th, N Ireland jump 7 to 86th and Wales leap 5 to 97th. Brazil top, France 2nd, Germany 3rd.

24   Blackburn agree £4.25m with Barnsley for striker Ashley Ward. Newcastle pull out of proposed £5.2m deal for AC Milan's Ibrahim Ba after the winger fails medical.

26   Chelsea class shows as they win 2-0 at Southampton and stay top. Villa have goalie Michael Oakes sent off and lose ground 2-1 at Blackburn, 4 games unbeaten under new boss Brian Kidd. Man U with 2 from Ronny Johnsen overcome lowly Forest 3-0. Leeds shock Newcastle at St James' with 3-0 success. Boro seeking to break a 61 year club record going nearly 15 months without losing at home, go under 3-1 to Liverpool. Overmars seals a 1-0 home win for Arsenal over W Ham. Stenhousemuir's Graeme Armstrong, 42, marks a 23 year career when he plays his 864th league game (2-2) v East Stirling, the most by a Scot. John McGrath, former Southampton and Newcastle stalwart, dies after heart attack, aged 60.

27   Celtic coast to a 3-0 win over lowly Dundee. Eight Liverpool players to be quizzed by the club about sordid antics at their Christmas party.

28   Villa reclaim Premiership lead from Chelsea with 2-1 win over Sheff Wed. Arsenal, down to 10 with Vieira's elbow-raised sending off, increase gloom for Charlton with 53rd pen win from winger Overmars. A Chris Armstrong hat-trick helps Tottenham to 4-1 over Everton. Liverpool come from 2 down to storm Newcastle and win a thriller 4-2. Magpies' Dietmar Hamann red-carded after 29 mins. After W Ham 2-0 win Coventry fans turn on team for 1st time after 7 games without a win. Sunderland, 8 points ahead, attract 41,333 for hard-earned 2-0 over Crewe. In Div 2, Man City beat Stoke 2-1 before 30,478.

29   Eagerly awaited Chelsea–Man U clash ends scoreless, Zola and Flo guilty of missing a string of chances. Yellow-carded Frank Leboeuf admits he should have gone for tripping Beckham. Wimbledon put a halt to the Leeds run at Elland Road grabbing an 83rd min (2-2) equaliser before near 40,000 crowd. Ref Dermot Gallagher after viewing video evidence admits a 'genuine error' in red-carding Villa goalie Oakes on Boxing Day. First British pay-per-view League game will be Oxford v Sunderland on Feb 27. Millwall survive 2 dismissals and still get 1-1 at Gillingham who remain unbeaten in 16 League games.

30   Rod Wallace hits 17th of season to gain Rangers a late 2-1 win at Dundee Utd. Greek League cancel matches over late payments of pools revenue. Newcastle pay £4m to Paris St Germain for defender Didier Domi. Burnley break club record paying Luton £750,000 for return of Steve Davis. In the Queen's New Year Honours Stuart Pearce, 36, currently at Newcastle gets an MBE. Trevor Brooking, 49, capped 47 times and now a television pundit, is awarded CBE.

31   Peter Beardsley, soon 38, joins Div 3 Hartlepool. Nicola Berti leaves Tottenham for Spanish side Alaves.

January 1999
Rushden & Diamonds hold Leeds ... Blatter wants WC every 2 years ... Forest and Bassett part ... Ford equals Paine's record ... Big Ron in at Forest ... Hammer Hartson becomes £7m Don ... Venables leaving Palace ... Kidd splashes cash ... Rudge out at Vale ... Mabbutt retires ... Red again for Petit ... Beardsley's Magpie benefit ... Hoddle's comments spark uproar ... Chelsea's 1st defeat since August

1   In unprecedented move ref Paul Danson is taken off tomorrow's FA Cup 3rd round tie between Lincoln and Sunderland after requests from both clubs. FA refuse request from FL to install six cameras in the woodwork of the goalposts; the experiment was earmarked for recent Spurs v Man U Worthington Cup tie. Last night's FIFA deadline to host WC finals 2006 closed with official candidates Germany, England, Brazil, S Africa, Morocco, Egypt and Ghana.

2   In FA Cup Forest lose at home to Portsmouth, Coventry hit 7 past Macclesfield and Swansea concede late goal in 1-1 at W Ham. Villa put out Hull, Blackburn overcome Charlton, Everton win at Bristol City, Newcastle see off Palace and Leicester advance past Brum. But Rushden & Diamonds provide the biggest shock holding Leeds 0-0 at their £20m Nene Park Stadium. Jermaine Pennant, 15, makes sub appearance for Notts Co at Sheff U.

3   Two late scores seal a 3-1 Man U FA Cup win over Boro. Liverpool notch up comfortable 3-0 win at Vale. Sheff Wed punish Norwich errors in easy 4-1 win. Man U v Liverpool is the plum tie in the FA Cup 4th rd draw, the 10th time the teams have been drawn against each other. If they win at Preston tomorrow, holders Arsenal will travel to Wolves. Dons and Spurs draw means 4 clashes in a month – Premiership fixture, FA Cup, then two Worthington Cup semi-final meetings. Cash-strapped Portsmouth given home tie against Leeds/Rushden & Diamonds and Oxford host Chelsea. Last New Year Old Firm clash of this century ends 2-2 at Ibrox. The largest shake-up in the history of international football has been launched by Sepp Blatter who announces proposals to hold the WC finals every 2 years. The FIFA President claims the current 4-year rotation is outdated.

4   Keith Wiseman, 52, elected in summer of 1996, quits as FA chairman saying it was because of two 'grave errors' of judgement. Hit by injuries and down 2-0 to Preston FA Cup holders Arsenal fight back with 2 from Petit, for 4-2 win at Deepdale before 21,500. Leeds winger Lee Sharpe becomes David Platt's first signing as Sampdoria coach, on loan for remainder of the season.

5   Dave Bassett and Nottm Forest part company, the 7th Premiership boss to lose his job since the end of last season. Duncan Ferguson, Newcastle's £7m new signing, undergoes surgery and is out for 6 weeks. Bert Paton resigns at Dunfermline, bottom of Premier League.

6   Premiership refs and their assistants to link using radio mikes in experiment next season, says officer Philip Don. Inland Revenue issue High Court winding-up order against Portsmouth claiming unpaid tax of £435,000.

7   Lennart Johansson slams Sepp Blatter for not informing UEFA of his proposals to stage the WC every 2 years. David Ginola is Carling Player of the Month for December. WC finals in France made pre-tax profit of £39m. Ex WC ref Clive Thomas pledges £50,000 to set up new association to train officials. Pompey boss Alan Ball suffers humiliation of having his company car repossessed. Jack Taylor is the only ref inducted into FIFA's new Hall of Champions.

8   Blackburn's Brian Kidd named December Carling Manager of the Month. Confirmation that Oldham, Bury and Rochdale have held merger talks. Arsenal win race for wonderkid Jermaine Pennant, 15, in a deal which could eventually net Notts Co £2m. Chairman Gordon Taylor quits Football Task Force after PFA not invited to the launch of a major 'Investing in the Community' report.

9   Blackburn skipper Tim Sherwood sent-off in 1-0 win over Leeds. Chelsea who had not won at Newcastle for 14 years get 3 pts through Petrescu's score. Liverpool display defensive resilience to hold Arsenal scoreless at

Highbury. Demoralised Forest 18 successive matches without a win, lose 4-0 at Coventry with Darren Huckerby netting a hat-trick. Chelsea and Villa share top. Sunderland on 57 pts in Div 1 lead Brum (48), Fulham lead Div 2 and Cardiff Div 3. Tony Ford, 39, makes 824th league appearance for Mansfield against Brentford. Ford's league debut came in 1975, and he now equals Terry Paine's record for an outfield player; only Peter Shilton has had more League outings – a staggering 1,005.

10 A power failure delays start for 45 min as Man U maul West Ham 4-1 with much-hyped Joe Cole, 17, making his Premiership Hammers debut.

11 Villa chase up interest in Juninho, unsettled at At Madrid. Paul Gascoigne reveals that he is taking anti-depressant drugs. Nottm Forest confirm Ron Atkinson to be new boss until end of the season with Peter Shreeves his assistant. Wycombe sack Neil Smillie and put Terry Evans in temporary charge.

12 FA finally secure acquisition of Wembley and its surrounding land for £103m with plans already underway to redevelop the site. A budget of £320m which includes a contribution of £120m from the Sports Council through National Lottery funding has been set aside to create a new National Stadium which will be the focal point of the proposed WC bid. Oldham chairman Ian Stott resigns.

13 Martin Thomas is hero as Swansea deserve their 1-0 FA Cup 3rd replay win over W Ham. But Leeds are comfortable 3-1 winners over Rushden & Diamonds who score first. Fulham march on 1-0 over Southampton. Villa agree £1.5m deal with Benfica for Gary Charles. Returning from Lisbon to W Ham in £1m transaction is former Chelsea defender Scott Minto who spent 18 months at Benfica. Man U's fringe player Jordi Cruyff is to link up with Celta Vigo on loan. Coventry pay £2m to AS Monaco for Mohamed Konjic, 28, captain of Bosnia.

14 Wimbledon break their transfer record paying £7m for W Ham striker John Hartson, 23, who signs a 6 year contract. Hammers to receive an immediate £3m payment and the remainder in instalments. Colchester and Torquay each receive £50,000 FA compensation for lost revenue from last season's Div 3 play-off final being switched to a Friday to make way for an England international. The game attracted just 19,486.

15 Terry Venables is to leave Palace after 6 months in charge. He and chairman Mark Goldberg meet in Kensington hotel but settlement details rumoured to be around £1m is not agreed. Arsenal complete signing of Nigerian striker Nwankwo Kanu, 22, from Inter with the fee believed to be £4.5m. The player returns immediately to Italy to await work permit clearance.

16 A full-scale scuffle between the two benches as Chelsea beat Coventry 2-1. Home team's kit-man booked and Gordon Strachan sent to the stands. Ron Atkinson flies in from Barbados to meet his new players at the team hotel before clash with Arsenal, but Martin Keown seals win for the champs. A Dwight Yorke hat-trick inspires Man U in 6-2 success at Leicester. More misery at W Ham as they crash 4-0 to Sheff Wed. Robbie Fowler nabs 2nd hat-trick of the season as Liverpool thrash Southampton 7-1.

17 Charlton spare supporters a new Premiership record of 9 successive defeats with a comeback and two goals (2-2) with Newcastle who have Nikos Dabizas sent off. Sunderland strengthen hold on pole position to beat Ipswich 2-0, screened live on Danish television.

18 Brian Kidd takes his Blackburn spending to nearly £12m in 5 weeks by paying Palace £4.1m for striker Matt Jansen. After a run of 14 games, 12 defeats and a solitary win, Vale terminate contract of John Rudge, 54, who was in charge 15 years. Julian Joachim's double in Villa's 3-0 win over Everton puts them joint-top with Chelsea.

19 Forest agree to pay former manager Dave Bassett £200,000 following his sacking. New boss Ron Atkinson makes first signing Carlton Palmer, 33, from Southampton for £1.1m. Former Spurs defender Gary Mabbutt, 37, forced to retire after 21-year career, 5 spent at Bristol Rovers. He won 16 England caps, made 618 appearances for Tottenham and received an MBE. Mabbutt gained admiration for his sportsmanship and ability to cope with diabetes.

20 Sir Jack Hayward, chairman and owner of Wolves, issues writ against his son, Jonathan, 41, over alleged financial irregularities at the club between 1992 and 1997. Palace's Attilio Lombardo heads back to Italy for talks with a move to Lazio reported as having been agreed. N Ireland named joint-winners of FIFA's Fair Play prize for their efforts to unite Protestant and Catholic communities. They share with US and Iran who exchanged gifts before their highly publicised WC finals clash last summer. The FAI announce plans for £65m stadium seating 45,000 in Dublin to be known as The Arena. It will have a removable pitch and retractable roof. Four Home Countries agree that present representative David Will (Scotland) should continue to represent Britain as a vice-president on FIFA's Executive Committee.

21 Steve Wignall resigns as manager of Colchester after 4 years. In Sky TV experiment designed to give viewers an insight into stress levels of football management, Mansfield boss Steve Parkin and Rotherham's Ronnie Moore agree to be wired-up to heart monitors in tonight's Div 3 fixture. Nationwide Building Society sign £15m sponsorship with FA. The 4-year investment is to the international squad, youth development, the Football Conference and women's football.

22 Brighton's Brian Horton appointed as new boss at Vale where he spent 5 years as a player. Liverpool complete £2.6m formalities for Cameroon international Rigobert Song, 22, from Salernitana. Coventry chairman promises supporters 'the best arena stadium in Europe' in time for start of the 2001 season. The £120m project will have sliding roof and retractable pitch and has already been included among 16 category A grounds for England's 2006 WC bid.

23 In FA Cup 4th round tie Kevin Keegan's Fulham pull off shock 2-0 win at Villa. Leeds overcome Pompey 5-1 at Fratton and Everton knock out Ipswich. Leicester lose at home 3-0 to Coventry who score twice in the 90th min. Newcastle eliminate Bradford 3-0 and the Swansea venture ends with 1-0 home defeat to Derby. The Dons v Spurs tie predictably ends 1-1. As Premier sides fall to lower opposition in Scottish Cup 3rd rd biggest upset sees Aberdeen crash 1-0 at home to Div 2 leaders Livingston. In pulsating tie, holders Hearts go out 3-1 at Motherwell.

24 In bristling FA Cup clash favourites Man U knock out Liverpool 2-1 with dramatic 88th and 90th min scores from Yorke and Solskjaer. Emmanuel Petit's dismissal, his 3rd red card since he joined, takes gloss off Arsenal's 2-1 success at Wolves. In 5th rd draw Arsenal entertain Sheff Utd or Cardiff, and George Graham could meet his former club Leeds if Tottenham overcome Wimbledon in replay. Sheff Wed will meet either Oxford or Chelsea, Wrexham or Huddersfield v Derby and Barnsley face Bristol Rovers. It is Everton v Coventry, Newcastle v Blackburn with Man U home to Fulham.

25 Villa's £7m record signing Stan Collymore seeks stress counselling to help 'current difficulties'. A controversial 90th min Frank Leboeuf pen rescues Chelsea (1-1) after being outplayed by an Oxford side given 52nd min lead by Dean Windass.

26 Striker Mike Sheron leaves QPR for Barnsley. Liverpool confirm Robbie Fowler, 23, has signed a lucrative four and a half year contract rumoured to be worth £35,000 a week. In Worthington Cup semi-final 1st leg Tony Cottee, 35, poaches 2 goals in Leicester's 2-1 win at Sunderland.

27 Tottenham and Wimbledon stumble scoreless through another clash, this time the Worthington Cup semi-final 1st leg. Sheff Utd, FA Cup semi-finalists last year, defeat Cardiff 4-1 to claim the rich pickings of a 5th rd visit to Highbury. Keegan and Dalglish back for the occasion as a sell-out St James' gathering of 36,733 turn up for Peter Beardsley's Newcastle–Celtic testimonial. W Ham splash £4.2m on Cameroon international Marc-Vivien Foe from Lens, and £1.7m to capture Paolo Di Canio from Sheff Wed. Sunderland give free admission and attract an incredible 33,517 for Pontins League fixture against Liverpool reserves.

28 Scarborough's Mick Wadsworth is new manager at Colchester. Premier League meeting sanction an extension of the domestic season for 1999–2000 with the starting date brought forward 7 days to Aug 7 with May 14 finish. Blackburn complete Jason McAteer's £4m move from Liverpool. Villa fail in attempt to land Juninho from At Madrid.

29 Sacked John Rudge declines Director of Football post at Vale. Wolves announce £25m loss over last 5 years. Arsenal tie-up £2.5m signing of French striker Kaba Diawara, 23, from Bordeaux. Liverpool's Steve McManaman discloses he has already signed a transfer agreement with Real Madrid which will earn him around £14m over the next 5 years.

30 In article in *The Times* Glenn Hoddle's controversial comments regarding reincarnation, and that people born disabled were paying for sins committed in a previous life, provoke furious condemnation from sports bodies, church and government. Later, on BBC *Football Focus*, Hoddle says his remarks were 'misconstrued', 'misinterpreted' and 'misunderstood'. Newcastle's Shearer ends 126 days Premiership drought scoring after 4 min in 2-1 defeat of Villa. Mark Hughes picks up 14th booking of the season as Saints beat Leeds 3-0. Forest end 19-game losing run at Everton. Jason Wilcox becomes 3rd Blackburn player dismissed in successive home games in 1-1 with Tottenham. Sheff Wed keeper Pavel Srnicek red-carded in home defeat by Derby. In Div 1 Sunderland still way out on top despite 2-1 reverse at Watford. Rangers, down to 10 men, clinch late 4-2 win at Aberdeen.

31 Chelsea suffer Premiership defeat for 1st time since opening day, at Arsenal. Bergkamp nets winner as Gunners extend record of not conceding a League goal to 7hrs 54 min. Man U go top thanks to Yorke's 89th min away winner which breaks Charlton hearts. The future of England boss Glenn Hoddle seriously under threat as government ministers call for his resignation after his 'What you sow, you have to reap' comments. Nationwide's £8m deal with FA is in jeopardy while the Association's acting chairman seeks explanation as to how a football interview ended up in a discussion about reincarnation with hurtful implications towards the disabled.

February 1999
FA terminate Hoddle's contract ... Man U is world's richest club ... Wilkinson is caretaker England coach ... Wise off for 4th time ... McClaren is new No 2 at Old Trafford ... Fluent French give England a lesson ... Arrests follow Valley light failure ... Historic Gunners–Blades rematch ... Twin Towers for Spurs ... Keegan says yes for 4 games ... Toshack for Real

1 Glenn Hoddle's views on the disabled dominate the front pages of virtually every national newspaper and lead radio and television news bulletins. Tony Blair lines up behind growing numbers demanding the England boss resigns. John Hartson is fined record-equalling £20,000 and gets 3 game ban by FA for kicking former W Ham colleague Eyal Berkovic in the face at training. Zinedine Zidane is crowned FIFA World Player of the Year at Barcelona function. In a poll of national coaches he earns 518 points, Ronaldo (164), Davor Suker (108), and Michael Owen (43). Team of the Year: Brazil. Top Goalie: Fabien Barthez (France). Most Entertaining Team: France.

2 FA's David Davies announces termination of England coach Glenn Hoddle's contract after 30 months in the post. On a reported £350,000 yearly salary, Hoddle, 41, reads a terse statement acknowledging he had made 'a serious error of judgement.' His international record reads: P28 W17 D4 L7. FA's Technical Director Howard Wilkinson is immediately installed on a temporary basis. Tottenham's 3-0 win over Wimbledon gives new boss George Graham an FA Cup 5th rd trip to his last club Leeds. David Platt resigns from his role as team supervisor with Serie A strugglers Sampdoria. Survey by chartered accountants Deloitte & Touche acclaims Man U as world's richest club. Their turnover in season ended 1997 was £87.94m, nearly £30m more than 2nd placed Barcelona. Rangers (14th) higher than Ajax, Lazio and Arsenal.

3 Howard Wilkinson who managed clubs from Boston to Sheff Wed and Leeds for 24 years until 1996 steps into limelight with 1st press conference as England caretaker boss, but Fulham's Kevin Keegan remains the people's choice. Arthur Mann, 51, who played for Man City in 1970 League Cup final, dies in works accident. Chelsea's Dennis Wise sent off for 4th time this season in 4-2 FA Cup replay win over Oxford. Huddersfield triumph 2-1 over Wrexham and will now entertain Derby. In the Premiership Man U stretch lead after 1-0 win over Derby.

4 Newcastle sign Croatia Zagreb midfielder Silvio Maric. Tim Sherwood completes £3m Blackburn to Tottenham move.

5 Icelandic international Arnar Gunnlaugsson, 25, leaves Bolton for Leicester for £2m. Man U confirm Derby's Steve McClaren as new No 2 to Alex Ferguson. Ray Harford will be Jim Smith's assistant at Derby for remainder of the season. Brighton give Jeff Wood the managerial post until end of season. Wycombe appoint Lawrie Sanchez as new boss. Tim Flowers asks Blackburn for a transfer after losing his spot to John Filan. Dwight Yorke and his boss Alex Ferguson take the Carling Player and Manager of the Month awards for January.

6 Sub Ole Gunnar Solskjaer bags 4 quickfire goals at the City ground for rampant Man U who dish out 8-1 drubbing to lowly Forest. Chelsea keep in contention beating Southampton 1-0, Arsenal sweep aside W Ham 4-0. Sunderland continue to steam ahead in Div 1 after 2-0 over Swindon, revitalised Fulham remain top of Div 2 and Cardiff lead the way in Div 3. Germany lose 3-0 to US in Jacksonville, Florida with all three scorers earning their living at German clubs.

7 Rangers secure 12-point lead with 3-0 defeat of Dunfermline. Derby into 6th place following 2-1 win over Everton.

8 Newcastle's out of favour John Barnes joins Charlton on a free and watches 2-0 win over Wimbledon, their 1st victory since Oct 24. Surprised Lee Dixon, 35 next month, gets drafted in to face France at Wembley. His last England appearance was in Nov 1993 v San Marino.

9   Peter Reid signs 2 year extension to his Sunderland contract. Record crowd of 32,865 pack Derby's Pride Park to watch England U-21's beat France.

10   Toothless England made to look ordinary by World Cup holders France who win 2-0 at Wembley inspired by Zidane and the clinical finishing of Nicolas Anelka. In Dublin friendly ROI dominate in 2-0 success over Paraguay.

11   Southampton's Mark Hughes who has the worst disciplinary record in the Premiership with 14 yellow cards receives £2,000 fine, an additional 2 match suspension, and a warning. Growing speculation that Kevin Keegan, Chief Operations Officer at Fulham, is FA's favoured choice to take charge of England. Los Angeles attendance of over 91,000, the biggest in the US since WC 94, watches Mexico lose 1-0 to Argentina. Three Malaysians and a member of Charlton's security team arrested after break-in at The Valley's power room where electrical cable was tampered with. Police believe they may have thwarted a major betting sting linked to blowing the floodlights, stopping Premiership matches, and involving big-money gambling syndicates in the Far East. Lights have suddenly blown at Derby v Wimbledon (Aug 14 1997), W Ham v Palace (Nov 3 1997), Wimbledon v Arsenal (Dec 22 1997) and Man U v W Ham (Jan 10 1999).

12   FIFA clear English and Welsh FAs of any misconduct in the affair that led to the resignation of Chief Executive Graham Kelly and Chairman Keith Wiseman. Concern by Chelsea players has led to re-laying of their substandard Stamford Bridge pitch. Work commences immediately after Wednesday's fixture against Blackburn.

13   In FA Cup 5th rd tie holders Arsenal beat Sheff Utd 2-1 but within minutes of the end and prompted by Arsène Wenger's public gesture, the FA in the interest of 'fair play' agree to an historic rematch. Earlier, Utd had angrily protested over the 76th winner by Marc Overmars and play was held up 8 min amidst much jostling and finger-pointing. Utd's keeper Alan Kelly had kicked the ball out to enable an injured colleague to receive treatment, but at the restart Ray Parlour's throw-in 'return' was naively seized upon by Gunners' sub Nwankwo Kanu, making his debut, and he ran on to cross for the Dutch international to slide home as the Blades defence hastily scrambled back. Afterwards, embarassed Kanu says that he was confused about procedure after the long hold-up. However, many feel the rule book does not allow for this 'sporting' gesture and the result should have stood. It is the 1st time in 127 years of the FA Cup such a rematch has been ordered.

14   In FA Cup Andy Cole's strike enables Man U put out gutsy Fulham 1-0. Newcastle and Blackburn must meet again after a scoreless draw. Meanwhile, the quarter-final draw throws up Man U v Chelsea, Blackburn/Newcastle v Everton, Barnsley/Spurs v Leeds, Arsenal/Sheff U v Derby/Huddersfield. In Scottish Cup 4th rd Hamilton concede 6 to rampant Rangers. Philip Don, Premier League referees' spokesman, says FA sanctioning an Arsenal–Sheff U rematch is a dangerous precedent and that under the laws ref Peter Jones' decision, to allow the controversial goal to stand, is correct.

15   Sheff U board drop plans to bid for Bramall Lane FA Cup rematch and will meet Arsenal once again at Highbury. Indications suggest Kevin Keegan is expected to say 'yes' to the England coaching job – on a part-time basis.

16   In their 6th meeting this season Spurs overcome the Dons 1-0 to reach Worthington Cup final with Steffen Iversen clinching the Wembley visit.

17   Massive blow to FA. Keegan, 48, accepts new managerial post for 4 games on a reported £200,000 arrangement, but states that he does not want to be considered beyond that. Keegan, Chief Operations Officer at Fulham, will supervise England against Poland, Hungary, Sweden, and bow out after the Bulgaria clash, June 9. For 2nd time in 3 years Martin O'Neill guides Leicester to the League Cup final. They draw 1-1 (agg 3-2) at home to Sunderland. In action-packed Premiership clash Man U and Arsenal draw 1-1. Two red and 7 yellow cards sees Chelsea's Vialli and Blackburn's Marlon Broomes dismissed in stormy 1-1 draw. Everton chalk up 5-0 result against Boro.

18   Kevin Keegan, who captained his country in WC 82, faces 1st press conference vowing supporters will see a passionate approach to singing the national anthem and performance on the pitch. But he is adamant he will not abandon Fulham duties when his caretaker stint ends. In staff reshuffle only Ray Clemence and U-21 coach Peter Taylor survive. Out goes John Gorman replaced by ex-Newcastle coach Derek Fazackerley. Fulham's chief scout Arthur Cox comes on board. Howard Wilkinson says Keegan will be involved in preparation and tactics. Reading's Robert Fleck, 33, retires because of back problems.

19   John Toshack, 49, quits as coach to Turkish club Besiktas. Luton chairman David Kohler quits after a petrol bomb and matches were pushed through home letterbox. Leeds, with 8 youngsters on stand-by, harbour concerns over safety at WC Youth finals in Nigeria and are refusing release.

20   Nicolas Anelka fires 1st Arsenal hat-trick as champions sweep aside Leicester 5-0. Coventry lose 1-0 to Man U and slip into bottom 3. Forest problems deepen with 3-1 home defeat to Chelsea. Liverpool and W Ham share 4 at Anfield. Sheff Wed win 4-1 at Blackburn. Lowly Saints gain precious 2-1 win over Newcastle who have not won at The Dell since 1972. Charlton ease their position with 2-0 win at Derby.

21   The Dons and out of sorts Villa end scoreless. Henrik Larsson with 4 goals leads Celtic 7-1 rout of 10-man Motherwell. FIFA considering tomorrow the FA-sanctioned Arsenal v Sheff U rematch. They are undecided whether regulations allow the replaying of a game in which no law was broken.

22   Against background of confusion FIFA finally sanction tomorrow's FA Cup 5th rd rematch between Arsenal and Sheff U. In bizarre fashion they also insist both clubs sign a declaration, for legal reasons, that the winner of the rematch or any replay will advance to the next rd even though the result of the prior game, a 2-1 win for Arsenal, will stand in the record books. Wales ordered to play their EC 2000 qualifier v Denmark at Anfield rather than the proposed switch to Ninian Park. Much-travelled Colin Addison, 58, appointed boss at Scarborough.

23   First half goals from Bergkamp and Overmars smooth Arsenal's 2-1 passage in FA Cup 5th rd rematch with Sheff U. All 75,000 tickets to see England's EC 2000 qualifier v Poland on March 27 – Kevin Keegan's 1st at the helm – sold within 36 hours. Phone poll shows 58% of fans in the city thought a Dundee–Dundee Utd merger was the correct way forward. Tom Finney officially opens FL's new HQ in Preston.

24   Stylish Spurs close in on Wembley again after stunning FA Cup goals from Anderton and Ginola prove too much for Leeds. In other replay Derby see off Huddersfield 3-1 and Newcastle overcome Blackburn 1-0 at Ewood Park. FIFA world rankings list England in 11th place, Scotland (26), N Ireland (67), Wales (74). All remain static but ROI jump 4 places to joint 40th. After UEFA–FIFA meeting in Geneva, Sepp Blatter, President of FIFA who floated the proposal of a WC every 2 years, agrees to put his controversial plan on the back burner. Hartlepool appoint Wolves youth coach Chris Turner, 40, to succeed manager Mick Tait.

25   Real Madrid who sacked Guus Hiddink after 23 league games install John Toshack as their 4th coach in a year. The Spanish giants will pay up the Welshman's £370,000 contract at Besiktas. FA invite former Sampdoria coach David Platt back into the fold to assist England U-18 squad in Spanish tourney next month.

26   Steve Stone says he will exercise a contract clause and quit Forest if they are relegated. Clayton Blackmore, 34, leaves Boro for Barnsley on a free. Glenn Hoddle gets blame for Nationwide League fixture chaos on March 27, the day of the England v Poland EC clash. Refusal to move kick-off time from 3pm means 26 scheduled fixtures are now strung out over 3 days with 7 different start times. Newcastle to unveil Croatia midfielder Silvio Maric, 23, a £3.6m capture from Zagreb.

27   On newly laid pitch, Chelsea continue snapping at Man U's heels after 2-1 win over Liverpool. In running battle Le Saux's alleged elbow assault on Fowler is missed by ref Paul Durkin but captured on television and could bring disciplinary action. Man U rest key players in all departments but 2 goals in 4 min earn the pts in 2-1 win over Saints. Villa, losing all confidence, go under 4-1 at home to Coventry. Forest recall Mark Crossley after 22 months and he saves a pen in 0-0 at Charlton. Spurs, with a 1st goal from new £3m signing Tim Sherwood, extend 15 game unbeaten sequence in 1-1 with Derby. Oxford v Sunderland is first in a series of 6 'screen tests' to be shown nationally on a pay-per-view basis, at a Sky TV charge of £7.95. The 6pm kick-off attracts a 9,044 attendance and ends 0-0.

28   George Graham installs Ipswich coach Stewart Houston as his No 2 reuniting their successful Highbury partnership. Arsenal lose championship ground held 1-1 at St James' by improving Newcastle.

March 1999
Simeone comes clean on Beckham tap ... Kinnear's heart attack ... Man U's Viollet dies ... Vinnie calls it a day ... Gregory spends £30m ... New faces in under Keegan ... Euro return greets Spurs Worthington win ... NATO strikes bring EC disruption ... Prison for Chelsea's Rix ... Caretaker Kev starts with win ... UEFA give Magpies surprise Euro spot

1   Tony Cottee poaches his 199th league goal, but Leicester go under 2-1 to Leeds. Scottish FA suspend chief executive Jim Farry over negligence in processing Jorge Cadete's move from Sporting Lisbon in 1996. SFA offer apologies to Celtic and agree to pay compensation and legal fees. John Gorman, 49, who lost his job as asst England manager, returns as Ipswich coach.

2   Following incidents last Saturday, Chelsea's Graeme Le Saux and Liverpool's Robbie Fowler both charged with misconduct by FA. On eve of Man U v Inter clash Argentinian midfielder Diego Simeone admits to feigning injury to get England's David Beckham sent off in the WC. Thomas Ravelli, 39, the goalie who won a world record 143 caps for Sweden retires after 22 years a pro.

3   In European Cup quarter-final a brace of headers from Dwight Yorke without reply from an Inter side missing Ronaldo secures Man U valuable lead for 2nd leg. Reds ride their luck in last 20 min, grateful to Schmeichel and Berg for vital interventions. Palace's Mark Goldberg wrestling with £9m debts and the club losing £3m a year, calls in administrators. Joe Kinnear spends the night in a Sheffield hospital after suffering chest pains an hour before Wimbledon's uplifting 2-1 victory at Sheff Wed.

4   Doctors advise long rest for Kinnear, out for the season after his heart attack scare. Goals from Babayaro, Zola and Wise give Chelsea a comfortable cushion for European Cup-Winners' Cup return leg in Oslo against Valerenga.

5   Steve McManaman passes medical at Real Madrid but refuses to pose in a club shirt. Richard Gough, 36, joins bottom club Forest on loan until end of season after action with San Jose Clash.

6   Nwankwo Kanu, much criticised for cheating in the previous FA Cup rd v Sheff Utd, is blameless this time and nets a last-gasp winner to put holders Arsenal through against Derby. Snow postpones Barnsley–Spurs tie. Dogfight continues at the bottom as Coventry, Southampton and Leicester all notch crucial victories. Dennis Viollet, former Man U striker who survived Munich air crash in 1958, dies in US from a brain tumour. He was 65. Viollet set a club record for most League goals in a season netting 32 times in 1959–60.

7   In FA quarter-final clash Chelsea stand defiant (0-0) at Man U to gain replay. Di Matteo sent off on 45 min and Scholes red-carded after 85 min. Temur Ketsbaia scores twice as Newcastle overpower Everton 4-1 to move into the semi-final. After appearing twice for QPR this season, Vinnie Jones retires to concentrate on new career as an actor. Capped 9 times for Wales, Jones, 35, made 486 first team appearances and was sent off 13 times.

8   Jim Farry is sacked for 'gross misconduct' from his post as SFA Chief Executive. FL refs will revert to traditional black kit next season.

9   Arsenal, undefeated at Highbury in the last 24 matches, move into 2nd place above Chelsea after 3-0 win over Sheff Wed. Benfica boss Graeme Souness completes £750,000 signing of Liverpool's Steve Harkness who joins Mark Pembridge, Dean Saunders, Gary Charles and Michael Thomas at the Lisbon club. Sunderland's Niall Quinn scores 72nd min 1-0 winner at Bradford then takes the goalie's jersey after Thomas Sorensen's injury.

10   Yorke's clinical finishing and Schmeichel's masterly display provides the difference as Man U triumph 2-0 in FA Cup quarter-final replay at Chelsea, and will now meet Arsenal. In Premiership, improved Spurs lose at Leeds and Derby increase Villa worries with 2-1 win. Forest go under 2-1 to Newcastle while Bakayoko's brace eases concern in Everton's 2-1 success at Blackburn. Figures from City analysts Capel-Cure Sharp reveal the total wage bill in the Premiership and FL for 1996–97 was a massive £361m – a rise of 25 per cent on previous season. Over the same period 70 Premiership players earned £1m compared to just two the previous year.

11   Villa's John Gregory takes his spending to £30.5m in 12 months paying £5.5m for Forest's Steve Stone, 27, who won 9 caps under Terry Venables, and had been at the City ground 12 years. Premier League chief executive Peter Leaver and chairman Sir John Quinton forced to resign after awarding television consultancy contracts worth millions – without asking clubs for approval – to former BSkyB executives Sam Chisholm and David Chance. Club reps voted overwhelmingly 19 to one.

12   Domestic season before the 2002 World Cup finals in Japan and S Korea may have to start in mid-July following news the finals will kick-off on June 1 to avoid rainy season. The date is to be ratified at FIFA's Los Angeles congress in July. Everton and Leeds incur wrath of FIFA over refusal to allow release of youngsters for WC Youth finals in Nigeria, citing health and security fears.

13   Ex-Magpie Andy Cole nets double as Man U, unbeaten in 17 matches, gain impressive 2-1 away win at Newcastle. Don Hutchison and Emmanuel Petit dismissed as Arsenal have easy win over Everton. In Div 2 Man City attract

30,321 for Lancs clash with Oldham but lose 2-1. Rangers defeat Motherwell and top the table on 62 pts with Celtic, a game in hand, on 49.

14   Police give escort to Graeme Souness after Benfica's 3-0 home defeat to Boavista. France's richest club Paris St-Germain sacks manager Artur Jorge. Mark Viduka, the £3.5m striker, scores his 2nd double in two starts, as Celtic thrash Aberdeen 5-1.

15   Scottish FA fine Rangers boss Dick Advocaat £1,000 with severe censure, for touchline behaviour v Dunfermline last month. Allan MacDonald, 47, confirmed as Celtic's next chief executive to succeed Fergus McCann.

16   Tottenham knock out Barnsley and earn FA Cup semi-final spot with a weaving run and splendid goal from David Ginola. Millwall draw 1-1 (agg 2-1) at Walsall and book place in Auto Windscreens Shield final at Wembley. Fulham extend Div 2nd lead by 12 pts after 1-0 win at Stoke.

17   With Henning Berg outstanding, Man U survive intense hostility of San Siro, to earn a 1-1 draw against Inter (agg 3-1) and reach last 4 of Champions League. Super sub Paul Scholes nets 88th min equaliser after Nicola Ventola, replacing the ineffective Ronaldo, scores in 63 min. Ref Gilles Veissiere (France) ignores play-acting antics of the Italians. Mark Goldberg admits Palace debts of £22m. Chris Ramsey, 36, becomes the 1st black England manager, put in charge of the U-20 squad for the WC Youth finals in Nigeria. Five sent off in mass pitch brawl as Arsenal beat Palace 1-0 in FA Youth Cup 5th rd tie.

18   Chelsea dictate and comfortably win 3-2 (agg 6-2) in Oslo against Valerenga for a semi-final spot in Cup-Winners' Cup with Vialli, Lambourde and Flo scoring. Ronnie Whelan's Greek side Panionios lose 3-0 (agg 7-0) to Lazio. For EC qualifier v Poland Kevin Keegan springs surprises and makes 6 changes from the last England squad picked by Glenn Hoddle. In 24-man panel with 9 defenders and 6 forwards, Chris Sutton is the big shock as is Tim Sherwood. Fit-again Gary McAllister returns to Scottish squad for EC tie with Bosnia. He last figured in November 1997 v France.

19   American Cable TV company NTL to pay Rangers and Celtic £13m in a unique 4-year shirt sponsorship deal. Champions League draw pairs Man U v Juventus, Dynamo Kiev v Bayern Munich. In Cup-Winners' Cup Chelsea entertain Real Mallorca and Loko Moscow meet Lazio.

20   Arsenal reduce Man U advantage to a single point beating Coventry 2-0. Lee Dixon makes his 500th club appearance. The youthful Leeds team shoot into 3rd place with 4-1 win over Derby. Table-toppers Sunderland, in front of 41,506, dominate Bolton and win 3-1. Rangers get a shock at Ibrox losing 1-0 to Dundee Utd. Cheltenham move to top of Nationwide Conference displacing Kettering with 3-0 win – and still have 3 games in hand.

21   Tottenham return to European action after 8 year break. Before 77,892 they snatch Worthington Cup Final win over Leicester at Wembley thanks to a stoppage-time header from Allan Nielsen, and despite having Justin Edinburgh sent off in 63 min. Martin O'Neill sends Frank Sinclair home and puts him on the transfer-list after the player arrives an hour late for the hotel team meeting. Man U, after 6 crucial games in 18 days and after beating Everton 3-1, sense an unprecedented treble of Champions League, Premiership and FA Cup. Chelsea with 2 from Flo keep up chase winning 3-0 at dispirited Villa.

22   Kevin Keegan brokers a 20 min handshake and make-up agreement between feuding players, Le Saux and Fowler, at England's team hotel. Lee Carsley completes £3.375m move from Derby to relegation-threatened Blackburn.

23   In refreshing change to his predecessor new England boss Keegan appears open and honest discussing injuries in build-up to vital EC tie with Poland. In lively session Keegan gives individual tuition. Luton Town goes into receivership with estimated debts of £3m. Sheff U transfer David Holdsworth to Brum for £1.2m and Graham Stuart to Charlton for £1.1m. Everton take Kevin Campbell on loan from Trabzonspor until end of season.

24   UEFA call off ROI's EC 2000 qualifier against Macedonia in Skopje. Also cancelled because of the possibility of NATO air strikes is Yugoslavia's Group 8 games in Belgrade against Croatia and Macedonia. Bradford entice Lee Sharpe on loan from Leeds after his 3 month spell with Sampdoria. Villa's Stan Collymore is to undergo full-time treatment to overcome clinical depression. Tottenham's Chris Armstrong gets surprise call-up to England's squad.

25   UEFA fine Alex Ferguson £2,200 for 'unnecessary provocation' following anti-Italian jibes towards Inter. Scotland's qualifier at Ibrox on Saturday is postponed because Bosnia face travel disruption from the Balkan region caused by NATO air strikes on Serbia. No huge transfers on deadline-day but Sheff Wed snap up York striker Richard Cresswell for £950,000 and Southampton get Marian Pakhar (Pahars) for £800,000 from Skonto Riga. Idiosyncrasies of UEFA reorganisation on qualification means that on the back of Tottenham's Worthington Cup victory Newcastle have unexpectedly gained Euro action for next term.

26   Alvin Martin resigns as Southend manager. Chelsea will keep Graham Rix's coaching job open following his 12 months' jail sentence and appoint Ray Wilkins 1st team coach until Rix returns. England U-21 beat Poland 5-0 at The Dell to virtually assure qualification for next stage of EC. In Group 3 N Ireland beats Germany 1-0.

27   With 3-1 on the scoreboard thanks to a hat-trick from Paul Scholes and chants of 'Keegan–Keegan' England supporters revel in celebration with this EC qualifying win over Poland who had not won at Wembley in 6 attempts over the past 26 years. An uplifting and inspirational start represents considerable improvement on performances against Sweden and Bulgaria, under Glenn Hoddle. In Group 3 N Ireland boasting just 4 Premiership players could not contain Germany who win comfortably 3-0. David Will who represents Britain at FIFA reveals he was sent gifts by Asian countries seeking to influence his vote on the staging of 2002 WC finals.

28   Music to the ears of the FA. After 3-1 over Poland Keegan admits 'there might be a solution somewhere' enabling him to take England's job full-time or combine his international post with Fulham duties. Before fixture with Bradford, Sasa Curcic, Palace's Serbian midfielder, does a one-man pitch protest with placard requesting 'NATO Stop Bombing.'

29   Blackburn's Jason Wilcox signs 5-year contract. Watt Nicoll, 63, a colourful Scots-born folk-singing ex-dustman now a sports motivator who addressed England players, gets a 'thank you' phone call from Keegan. Organisers of EC finals in Holland and Belgium put one third of tournament's 1.2m tickets on sale.

30   U-21 coach Peter Taylor reveals he is leaving in June despite having 15 months to run on his contract. He claims he was told he did not fit into Howard Wilkinson's long-term plans. Bryan Gunn, former Norwich and Scotland goalie, announces retirement following injury. In EC U-21 ties Wales lose 1-0 in Switzerland, N Ireland draw 0-0 in Moldova and Scotland, at Fir Park, lose 1-0 to Czech Rep. Alex Ferguson who brought Aberdeen European Cup-Winners success in 1983 receives the Freedom of the Scottish city. UEFA tell Newcastle they are in Europe as FA Cup winners – before their semi-final clash with Tottenham on Sunday week!

31   In Euro 2000 tie at Celtic Park, Scotland fall to Czech Rep's 2-1 smash-and-grab raid. N Ireland's shortage of fire-power exposed when held scoreless in Moldova. Qualification for Wales looks difficult after losing 2-0 in

Switzerland. In England's group, Bulgaria win 2-0 in Luxembourg and Sweden surge 3 pts clear with 1-0 success in Poland.

April 1999

Fowler's cocaine prank earns fine and ban ... O'Leary matches Revie's record ... Giggs goal checks Juventus ... McAllister closes Scottish chapter ... Magpies home in on Wembley again ... Owen's season looks over ... Sunderland secure Premiership spot ... Div II for King Kev's Fulham ... Giggs solo winner wins Wembley day out ... Liverpool remember Hillsborough ... Larsson tops say fellow pros ... Man U clinch Euro Final place but Chelsea miss out ... Cheltenham win FL status ... Ginola is PFA choice ... Keegan wants England job

1   Millionaire hotelier Firoz Kassam buys debt-ridden Oxford Utd. Irish FA President Jim Boyce quells sudden speculation over Lawrie McMenemy's future as international boss.

2   Arsenal's Ray Parlour wins Carling award for March a week after his England debut. David O'Leary takes his 1st managerial award after Leeds chalk up 6 consecutive Premiership victories. Former York boss Alan Little, who played for Southend as a striker in the mid 70s, is new Roots Hall manager.

3   After scoring a penalty in Liverpool's 3-2 win over Everton at Anfield, Robbie Fowler appears to simulate snorting cocaine by rubbing his nose along the 6-yard line – in front of furious Evertonians. Alex Ferguson's horse, Candleriggs, wins at nearby Kempton Pk but his Man U team is denied by Neil Sullivan in 1-1 with Wimbledon. End to end Pride Pk action as Derby go under 4-3 to Newcastle. Leeds notch up 7 Premierhip wins on the bounce beating Forest 3-1 and equalling a post-war record set by Don Revie's team 26 yrs ago. Ipswich score 6 without reply at Swindon.

4   Liverpool's Fowler, facing police action and FA misconduct charge, quickly issues apology for sick cocaine joke in Merseyside derby. St Johnstone keep Premier title race open beating Rangers 3-1, while Hibs are crowned Div 1 champions after 2-0 win over Hamilton Accies.

5   Fabian De Freitas misses Albion's afternoon match v Crewe thinking the Bank Holiday fixture has a 7:45 pm start. Baggies thrashed 5-1. In 5th relegation fight in 6 seasons Everton gift 2 goals to Sheff Wed's Carbone. John Barnes makes 1st League start since last May for struggling Charlton in 1-0 win over W Ham. England slip to surprise 1-0 defeat against US at WC Youth finals in Nigeria.

6   In rugged Arsenal–Blackburn encounter with 5 bookings Keown and Gillespie are sent off. Bergkamp keeps title chase open with a sweetly struck winner. Villa surrender 2-goal lead and draw at Leicester. Liverpool formally warn Fowler over his cocaine-snorting stunt and fine him a substantial amount, believed to be in the region of £60,000.

7   In European Cup semi-final 1st leg v Juventus, Man U salvage some hope for return with a late Giggs equaliser (1-1). Davids and Zidane control the tie but manager Ferguson is adamant his team will score in Turin. Charlton investigating the possibility of building 45,000 all-seater stadium at the Millennium Dome site in Greenwich. Halifax sack p/m Kieran O'Regan.

8   In Cup-Winners' Cup semi-final a 50th min Flo volley equaliser v Real Mallorca (1-1) maintains Chelsea's record of not having lost a home Euro tie in 27 matches stretching back 41 years. Skipper Wise is caught out by cameras in a 'biting' attempt to the arm of defender Marcelino. Scots captain Gary McAllister, 34, capped 57 times, retires from international action because of continuous terrace barracking. More misery for England at WC Youth finals in Nigeria as they lose 1-0 to Cameroon.

9   FA fine Robbie Fowler a record £32,000 and ban him for 4 games for mimicking cocaine-snorting during recent Merseyside derby. On his 24th birthday, he also receives a further 2-match suspension for his distasteful gesture to Graeme Le Saux at Chelsea. Le Saux escapes with a one-match ban and £5,000 fine for the use of an elbow on Fowler. Brighton fire Jeff Wood and obtain permission to approach Micky Adams, the reserve coach at Forest.

10 Chelsea keep up challenge winning 2-1 at Wimbledon. Villa end 11-match run without a win and keep Saints in bottom three with 3-0 success. Derby get 1-0 win over Forest who have Van Hooijdonk dismissed. Boro's 2-0 victory deepens Charlton gloom. Celtic beat Dundee Utd 2-0 in Scottish Cup semi-final.

11 The Arsenal–Man U FA Cup semi-final tie at Villa Pk ends in stalemate. In extra-time Nelson Vivas becomes 10th Gunner dismissed this season and the 22nd red-carded since Arsène Wenger took control. In extra-time Shearer scores twice against Spurs to take Newcastle back to Wembley. It will be Ruud Gullit's 2nd FA Cup final appearance in 3 seasons after leading Chelsea to the trophy in 1997. Gustavo Poyet, returning after a Dec 26 injury, scores in Chelsea's 2-1 win at Wimbledon. Rangers through to Scottish Cup final after 4-0 defeat of St Johnstone at half-empty Celtic Pk.

12 Leeds and Liverpool scoreless as Michael Owen limps off in 25 min with hamstring trouble. W Ham's £2m injured signing Javier Margas says he is staying in Chile. Brighton appoint Micky Adams, the former Brentford, Swansea and Fulham boss, as their new manager.

13 Wearsiders celebrate. Kevin Phillips nets 4 in 5-2 win at Bury to make Premiership football certain for Sunderland. Kevin Keegan steers Fulham into Div II defeating Gillingham with Cottagers celebrating a 2nd promotion in 3 years. Henrik Larsson the leading scorer in Scotland with 37, signs 4-year contract at Celtic.

14 A Ryan Giggs extra-time winner of breathtaking brilliance sends Man U into their 15th FA Cup final. The 2-1 defeat of Arsenal in the Villa Pk replay is achieved despite playing for 42 min with 10 men after Keane's dismissal. Yet in injury-time scorer Dennis Bergkamp has the chance to clinch it but his penalty is dramatically saved by Peter Schmeichel. Chelsea miss opportunity to climb into Premiership driving seat ending scoreless at Boro. Hamstring and tendon injuries may keep Liverpool's Michael Owen sidelined for 3 months. New England coaching staff member, Derek Fazackerley, 47, joins backroom boys at Bolton until end of the season.

15 Following highly successful trials in Jersey, the FL will experiment with rugby's 10-yard rule for offences in next year's Auto Windscreens Shield. In a moving symbol marking the 10th anniversary of Hillsborough, when 96 died, a ref's whistle blows at 3:06, and 14,000 people on Liverpool's Anfield Kop stand to observe a 1 min silence.

16 Newcastle's new strip to be worn at the Cup final goes on sale with Ruud Gullit winning his battle with sponsors Adidas and insisting on white socks. Devotees can purchase parts of Wembley stadium when it is knocked down next year. Prize possession is likely to be the seat in the Royal Box where the Queen sat during WC 66. David Beckham is the only Englishman among 6 players in contention for PFA Players' Player of the Year award. His Man U colleagues Keane and Yorke are completed with Arsenal's Bergkamp and Petit and Tottenham's Ginola.

17 W Ham hit 5 against Derby. Sheff Wed offer little resistance and lose 3-0 at Man U while Charlton get a point at home to Leeds, but miss a penalty. Mark Hughes ends the long drought and nets his 1st for Saints in the 3-3 home

draw with Blackburn. Liverpool get the bird after limp display and 1-0 defeat to Villa who were winning for just the 3rd time in 28 trips to Anfield.

18   Chelsea title hopes fade as they let slip a 2-goal lead and draw 2-2 with visiting Leicester. Wigan's Paul Rogers gets stoppage-time match-winner against Millwall in Auto Windscreens Shield final at Wembley before 55,349. Lions take massive 45,000 following. Dundee secure unexpected but well-earned 1-1 draw with Rangers. Celtic's Larsson is named Player of the Year in Scottish Premier by fellow pros.

19   Arsenal move within a point of Man U and give vintage display scoring 4 in a 10 min spell to cruise 5-1 past the Dons. Berwick Rangers captain Martin Neil, 29, admits he has been playing football with a drug problem for over a decade. Two former Premiership managers get the sack, John Hendrie goes at Barnsley and Graeme Souness is to leave Benfica. Dennis Wise escapes UEFA punishment over alleged 'bite' on Real Mallorca's Marcelino.

20   Honest Gianluca Vialli admits his tactical gaffes against Leicester could now cost Chelsea the Premiership crown. Spurs win 4-1 and give sinking feeling to Charlton. Fulham crowned Div II Champs without playing when 2nd placed Walsall lose at Preston.

21   Man U buy their dream ticket to the European Cup final against Bayern Munich in Barcelona's Nou Camp stadium. The 31-year wait is over following an amazing comeback in Turin to win 3-2 (agg 4-3). Dazzling Inzaghi scores twice in opening 10 min to put Juventus in the driving seat (agg 3-1). But skipper Keane glances one in, and Yorke's diving header levels matters before, 6 min from time, Cole coolly slots in the sensational winner. Afterwards, Alex Ferguson says the opening 45 min was the best performance United has played in his time at Old Trafford. Fitting that May 26 should be the 90th anniversary of the birth of Sir Matt Busby whose team lifted the trophy. The only sour note was cautions for Keane and Scholes which rule them out of the final.

22   Despite numerous chances to force extra-time, Chelsea lose Cup-Winners' Cup semi-final 2nd leg 1-0 (agg 2-1) against Real Mallorca, with players agreeing the tie was effectively lost at Stamford Bridge, not in Palma. Sidelined Joe Kinnear spends time at Wimbledon's training ground after his heart attack 7 weeks ago. Arsenal will wear the name of computer company Sega Europe on shirts next season, ending an 18-year link with JVC. Spurs announce 3-year kit deal with Adidas, worth £3m. A Cheltenham Town stoppage-time winner over Yeovil seals the Nationwide Conference title and gains entry to the FL.

23   Peter Storrie, Director of Football at W Ham, controversially departs from the club. Man U given an extra 5,000 tickets to bring their allocation to 30,000 for European Cup final in Barcelona.

24   Spain win WC Youth final in Lagos beating Japan 4-0, with Mali finishing 3rd. Defending champs Arsenal thrash Boro 6-1, their best away win for 40 years. Everton celebrate Premiership survival with 4-1 win over Charlton. Blackburn's suicidal defending at home proves costly losing 3-1 to Liverpool with revved-up Brian Kidd and Phil Thompson engaging in touchline confrontation. Saints grab a precious point in scoreless clash at Derby. John Hartson, the Dons' £7m purchase, ends his 3-month goal drought scoring against Newcastle, earning himself a special £10,000 goal bonus! Celtic lose 1-0 at St Johnstone and end their 17-match unbeaten run. Much-travelled Ron Atkinson, 60, announces his intention to retire while on the Forest team bus.

25   David Ginola is PFA Player of the Year, Dwight Yorke is runner-up, Emmanuel Petit 3rd. Nicolas Anelka wins Young Player of the Year, ahead of Michael Owen and Harry Kewell. Six withdrawals on the eve of England's trip to Hungary force Kevin Keegan to call up Everton teenager Francis Jeffers. Rod Wallace hits his 26th of the season as Rangers overcome Aberdeen 3-1. Mick Harford is appointed Wimbledon manager until Joe Kinnear is fit to return to work. Feyenoord win their 14th League title despite being held 2-2 at home by bottom club NAC Breda.

26   Sheff Wed's David Richards takes over as chairman of Premier League. Forest confirm ex-Liverpool boss Roy Evans a candidate for the managerial vacancy.

27   In Belfast, Paul McVeigh, a Tottenham reserve, rescues NI with an injury-time equaliser (1-1) against Canada, 92nd in FIFA rankings, though an og is given. In U-21 fixture England recover from 2-down to draw with Hungary. Scotland lose 2-1 in Germany and ROI go under 3-0 to Sweden. Axed Blackburn boss Roy Hodgson answers Inter SOS and returns as stand-in technical director.

28   Keegan bloods youngsters such as Phillips, Brown, Carragher, Gray and Heskey as England draw 1-1 in Hungary at Nep stadium. Shearer's penalty makes it his 23rd goal in 49 appearances. David Seaman reaches his 50th cap. Afterwards, caretaker Keegan surprises everyone by confirming his desire for the full-time role. "It's time to stop playing games – I want the job." Don Hutchison scores on his full debut to give Scotland a famous victory in Germany who had Lothar Matthaus chalking up his 135th appearance. ROI fight eager understudies and gains 2-0 win over Sweden. Arsenal's Anelka, reportedly at a nearby nightclub at the time, apologises for failing to collect his Young Player of the Year award.

29   Accountants Deloitte and Touche warn about spiralling salaries, and they report three-quarters of Premiership clubs paid out more than half their income in wages last season. Chelsea emerge as the highest spenders with a £27m wages bill, Man U (£26.9m) and Liverpool (£24m) with Wimbledon (£9m) and Southampton (£7m). Worthington Cup finalists Leicester told by FL they must reveal which players or staff passed Wembley tickets to the black market. Saturday's Bass Irish Cup final between Cliftonville and Portadown is cancelled after Cliftonville fielded an ineligible player in a semi-final replay. Portadown awarded the trophy and qualify for UEFA Cup.

30   FA liaise with Foreign office over England's EC 2000 tie with Bulgaria in Sofia on June 9 after stray NATO missiles land near to the city. Play-off hopefuls Bolton and Wolves draw 1-1. Alex Ferguson is named Carling Manager of the Month for 2nd time this season. He has lifted the award a record 8 times.

May 1999
Football mourns Sir Alf's loss ... Rangers are champs ... Ginola is Footballer of the Year ... Goalie Glass keeps Carlisle up ... King Kev leaves the Cottage ... Brian's Blackburn go down ... Keegan takes England job full-time ... Man U pip Arsenal for title ... Bruce severs with Blades ... United end Newcastle's Wembley dream ... Glory, Glory Man U win European Cup ... Bassett back with Barnsley ... Clough recognition at Forest ... Rangers make it triple scotch ... Watford in top flight

1   Football is in mourning after the death of Sir Alf Ramsey is announced. The WC 66 winning manager, 79, died peacefully during the week at a Suffolk nursing home following a long illness. His wife Vickie was at his side when he passed away last Wednesday. Sir Bobby Charlton said, 'Alf Ramsey gave all of us the proudest moment we have ever had in football.' Sir Alf suffered a stroke on June 9th last year before the start of England's WC cam-

paign in France. At Liverpool v Spurs fixture ref Stephen Lodge is wired up to his 2 linesmen and 4th official in Premiership experiment. Wright, Hislop and Lomas all dismissed in Hammers 5-1 defeat by Leeds. Beckham's 30-yard free-kick helps lack-lustre Man U to 2-1 win over Villa. Down in drop zone Saints smile with 2-1 success over Leicester as relegation rivals Charlton and Blackburn slug out scoreless draw. Walsall clinch promotion to Div 1 and Brentford move up to Div 2. Div 1 champs Hibs beat basement boys Stranraer and create an incredible 72-point gap between top and bottom club.

2   Rangers roar to their 48th Scottish title, at Parkhead, beating Celtic 3-0 and chalk up their 100th victory in Old Firm clashes. But ref Hugh Dallas is felled by a missile. Sloppy Arsenal, a goal up in 14 min, come close to messing it up but hang on against Derby.

3   Antonio Lopez Nieto creates Spanish history by showing 16 yellow cards, plus 2 reds, during At Madrid's 2-1 win over Ath Bilbao. Jan Molby is set to take charge at non-league Kidderminster. Arsenal beat Saints 2-0 to land the AXA-sponsored Women's FA Cup at the Valley before 6,450. Rochdale sack manager Graham Barrow.

4   Ray Wilkins is to sue Fulham over his sacking last year. Charlton's Mark Bright whose career spans 15 yrs and 6 clubs announces he is to retire. Alex Ferguson becomes Britain's highest-paid manager after signing a new contract worth £5m. Watford's Graham Taylor is Nationwide Div 1 Manager of the Month, with Walsall's Ray Graydon and Brentford's Ron Noades picking up the Divs 2 and 3 awards.

5   Two up with 22 min remaining Man U looks set fair for victory at Anfield. Redknapp then nets a penalty and Irwin is sent-off, and with 2 min left Ince snatches a dramatic equaliser. Boss Ferguson blows a fuse – and blames ref David Elleray! Chelsea secure a definite qualifying rd Euro spot after win over Leeds. Prompted by the outstanding Bergkamp, Arsenal win the North London derby 3-1 at Tottenham. If new proposals come into force Premiership refs will be driven to and from matches in 'safe' cars. George Reynolds, 84th in recent list of Britain's richest people, completes £4m takeover of Darlington.

6   Chelsea's Zola hints at retiring at the end of next season. David Ginola, winner of the PFA award, completes the double when named Footballer of the Year, the 5th year running the FWA nomination has been an overseas player. FL confirm attendances will approach 14 million in this the 100th championship season.

7   FAI disclose fascist group has made phone and letter threats against Irish players playing in England. Saints get go-ahead to build new £30m 32,000 all-seater stadium in the St Mary's area of the city centre. Mohammed Al Fayed confirms Kevin Keegan is no longer Chief Operations Officer at Fulham and will seek compensation from the FA. Meanwhile, Paul Bracewell takes temporary charge.

8   Saints march towards safety with 2-0 win at Wimbledon, while Forest's defeat of Blackburn leaves the Ewood Pk club staring relegation in the face and brings a stinging rebuke from manager Brian Kidd to his players. A last min free-kick winner from Danny Mills keeps Charlton hopes alive in see-saw 4-3 struggle at Villa. Kevin Campbell nets hat-trick in Everton's 6-0 rout of W Ham. In most dramatic finish imaginable, and in injury-time, on-loan goalie Jimmy Glass races upfield for a corner to crash in Carlisle's 2-1 winner over Plymouth which saves their 71-year League record and prevents the drop into Nationwide Conference. Glass' strike ends Scarborough's 12-year league status. Brentford are Div 3 champs defeating 2nd place Cambridge 1-0. At Craven Cottage Keegan gets a mixed reception as he bows out. Northampton relegated despite being unbeaten in last 9 games.

9   As title race heads to an exciting climax Man U leap back to top, at Boro, thanks to Yorke's header. They look jaded, this being their 59th game of a campaign that has also taken them to 5 countries. Bradford hold their nerve

Kevin Keegan exchanged a bench mark at Fulham who won automatic promotion, for one with an England who will be only too grateful for the opportunity of a play-off. (Actionimages).

to clinch a Premiership place beating Wolves 3-2, the result meaning Ipswich must face the agonies of the play-offs for 3rd time in 3 years.

10   Ginola scores a cracker and helps inspire Spurs in 2-2 draw with Chelsea. Hugh Dallas, the Motherwell ref struck by a missile, will control Wednesday's UEFA Cup final between Marseille and Parma in Moscow. New Brighton boss Micky Adams gives frees to 11 players. Huddersfield dismiss Peter Jackson who took over in October 1997. Nigeria pull out of the race to stage WC 2006.

11   Brian Horton's reward for keeping Vale in Div 1 is a 3-year contract. Hasselbaink's late Leeds strike ends Arsenal's 19-match unbeaten run and effectively does the same to hopes of retaining the Premiership crown.

12   On a tension-packed night Blackburn hold Man U scoreless but a point is not enough. Premiership champs in 1995, Rovers now join Forest in Div 1 next season. Stoke to be put up for sale. Parma lift UEFA Cup beating Marseille 3-0 before 61,000 in Moscow's Luzhniki stadium.

13   Ginola ends speculation at Spurs by signing new 3-year contract putting his earnings in the £1m a year bracket. Pompey to be sold to Miami-based tycoon Milan Mandarac in £4m takeover, with ex-Arsenal defender Bob McNab becoming chief executive.

14   Kevin Keegan unveiled as England's full-time coach on a £3m, 3-year deal. Paul Bracewell is Keegan's successor at Fulham. W Ham win FA Youth Cup for 3rd time defeating Coventry 6-0 (agg 9-0) before 26,463 at Upton Pk.

15   In Div 2 play-off semi-final Wigan and Man C end 1-1. Rangers hit 5 at Motherwell. Stars of England's WC 66 squad among over 500 mourners at Sir Alf Ramsey's memorial service in Ipswich.

16   Jubilant scenes as Man U beat Spurs 2-1 to reclaim the Premiership with 79pts from Arsenal who finish a point behind. However, had Spurs equalised, the Gunners would have claimed the title because of their 1-0 win at home over Villa. Utd's victory makes it 5 League titles for manager Ferguson who affectionately hugs Peter Schmeichel, soon to leave after 8 glory-filled yrs. Chelsea finish 3rd, their highest spot for 29 yrs. Hammers finish 5th and are back in Europe after 18 yrs. With Forest and Blackburn already down Charlton have to win at home to Sheff Wed and trust Saints slip up at The Dell to Everton, but neither prayer is answered. In play-off semis Bolton steal a late 1-0 advantage over Ipswich and Watford, down to 10 men, hang on to slender lead over Brum. Gillingham get a 1-1 draw at Preston, Swansea establish 1-0 lead over Scunthorpe and Rotherham come away scoreless at Leyton Orient.

17   Steve Bruce leaves cash-strapped Sheff Utd after 10 turbulent months as manager. Everton snap up Richard Gough on a free from Forest. Paul Bracewell makes his first Fulham capture taking ex-Sunderland colleague Andy Melville on a free. Trabzonspor sack Gordon Milne midway through a 2-year contract. Alex Ferguson is Carling Manager of the Year. Nigel Pearson is sacked a fortnight after securing Carlisle's Div 3 future. Liverpool pay £3.25m to Dutch club Willem II for Sami Hyypia, 25, a Finnish international central defender.

18   Roy Keane will skipper Man U in FA Cup final, and will not be punished, after being arrested and having spent Monday night in a police cell following an alleged bar altercation. Liverpool beat Sunderland 3-2 to win the FL 100th Championship Challenge at the Stadium of Light. Derby complete £3m club record signing of Crewe's U-21 midfielder Seth Johnson.

19   In play-off semi clash Bolton come from behind 3 times, and advance on away goals, in a thriller at Ipswich, to set up a Wembley final date. Leyton Orient clinch their place, at Rotherham, in a dramatic (4-2) pen shoot-out after both teams fail to muster a goal in either leg. Shaun Goater's score v Wigan has Man C heading to the Twin Towers. Andy Hessenthaler's Golden Goal over Preston (agg 2-1) gives Gillingham a 1st Wembley appearance in their 106-yr history. Two extra-time goals see Scunthorpe beat Swansea 3-1 (agg 3-2). Big-spending Lazio snatch late 2-1 win over Real Mallorca to land the European Cup-Winners' Cup at Villa Pk.

20   In Div 1 play-off 2nd leg Watford, inspired by goalie Alec Chamberlain, win a dramatic shoot-out 7-6 at St Andrews after drawing 1-1 on aggregate with Brum. Blues battle with 10 men after David Holdsworth's 54th min dismissal. Pat Jennings is replaced by Hans Segers as goalie coach at Tottenham. Joe Cole, 17, yet to complete 90 min with W Ham, gets invite to train with England preparing for qualifier against Sweden.

21   Wigan sack Ray Mathias 2-days after losing to Man C in the Div 2 play-offs. Man U establish links with S African club FC Fortune, Cape Town, allowing selected youths to attend trials in England.

22   Man U just one step from a unique treble after lifting the FA Cup with a comfortable 2-0 victory over a disappointing Newcastle at Wembley. Always in command the Reds never look like losing despite the loss of injured skipper Keane inside the opening 10 min. Sub Sheringham and Scholes show the way as Utd, capturing their 10th FA Cup, become the 1st team to do the double 3 times. The 44-year-long wait for domestic success drags on and on for long-suffering Geordie fans. Former W Ham and Southend forward Jeroen Boere, 31, loses the sight of his left eye after a knife attack leaving a Tokyo bar.

23   In exciting finale to Dutch season Bobby Robson takes PSV Eindhoven into Champions League, coming from 2-0 down at half-time to beat FC Utrecht 3-2 in injury-time. A 1-0 win over Dundee puts St Johnstone into Europe for the 1st time in 28 yrs, but Dunfermline who lose to Motherwell, bid farewell to Premier League.

24   Steve Bruce agrees to become Huddersfield new boss on a 3-year contract. Grimsby win the Bobby Moore Fair Play Trophy awarded by the PFA. Man C fans queue for 15 hrs to snap up 40,000 tickets allocated for Sunday's play-off Wembley clash with Gillingham. European Cup finalists Man U fly to Barcelona on Concorde to discover the Nou Camp pitch has been narrowed by 4 metres.

25   Wolves boss Colin Lee and asst John Ward agree new 2-year deals. About 20,000 ticketless Man U fans descend on Barcelona fuelling the black market with £41 seats being offered by touts for upwards of £280.

26   Fittingly, on what would have been Sir Matt Busby's 90th birthday, tears of joy in the Nou Camp as Man U pull off an astonishing last-gasp 2-1 victory over shell-shocked Bayern Munich in the Champions League final. And so Utd complete their historic treble with injury-time goals from subs Sheringham and Solskjaer. Before Champions League record crowd of 90,000 the Germans take the lead through Basler's 6th min free-kick, and also rattled the woodwork, twice, near the close. Bayern's bench were on the point of celebrating with the huge clocks clicking 45:00. Goalie Schmeichel, skipper on his last game, runs the length of the pitch for a corner, and in the confusion Sheringham swivels to side-foot home. Incredibly, from another Beckham corner, in-form Sheringham heads on for Solskjaer to stab home from close range, and provide the most thrilling night ever for English football.

27   Four months after losing his job at Forest, ex-Blades boss Dave Bassett bounces back to management at Barnsley with a 3-yr contract. FA give 3-match ban and £17,500 fine to Ian Wright for damaging personal property in the ref's room following his dismissal v Leeds. Everton's Thomas Myhre breaks a leg in training with Norway. Liverpool release former England defender Rob Jones.

28   Brian Clough learns that Forest will name a grandstand after him, and also erect a bronze bust in the reception area. David Taylor, 45, director of Scottish Trade International, replaces Jim Farry as new SFA chief executive and secretary. Arsenal spend £3m on Oleg Luzhny, 30, the Dynamo Kiev right-back.

29   Rangers land the domestic treble beating Celtic 1-0 in the Scottish Cup with a Rod Wallace effort, his 29th of the season. A Danny Griffin goal gives N Ireland a 1-0 success over ROI in Dublin friendly for the Omagh Fund. In Div 3 play-off final before 36,985, Scunthorpe beat Leyton Orient with a goal from Spaniard Alex Calvo-Garcia.

30   Man C return to Div 1 equalising against Gillingham with 2 goals in the dying seconds, then winning the Wembley play-off final in a pen shoot-out (3-1). Blackburn's French midfielder Sebastian Perez joins Marseille at £2.5m.

31   Ebbe Skovdahl, currently in charge at Brondby, is to become Aberdeen boss. Graham Taylor, with a team assembled for £700,000, leads Watford back to the top flight after 11 yrs. His unfancied side beat Bolton 2-0 in Div 1 play-off with scores from Nick Wright and sub Allan Smart. On the League run-in the Hornets collect 22 points from a possible 24. Brian Laudrup quits FC Copenhagen months after leaving Chelsea.

June 1999

Kinnear out, Olsen in at Dons ... Government block Irish v Yugoslavia tie ... Bosnich replaces Schmeichel ... Reid gets Taylor's U-21 job ... England poor, Scholes off against Sweden ... Faeroe Islands hold Scots, Gould quits Wales ... Sofia draw bring qualification gloom ... Dalglish and Barnes at Celtic helm ... O'Neill stays at Foxes, Little leaves Stoke ... Alec Ferguson is knighted ... FL vote for goal difference

1   Joe Kinnear's 7-year managerial reign is to end after the Dons confirm he wishes to be involved at a bigger club. Kinnear, 52, was appointed in January 1991 as the 4th-longest-serving boss in the country. A representative of the Norwegian company, Windmore, which owns 80% of the Dons, says ex-national coach Egil Olsen is expected to take charge after compensation is reached with the Valerenga club.

2   ROI's EC tie with Yugoslavia is called off by the Irish government who withdraw 170 visas to the visiting party. Villa's Mark Bosnich completes his free transfer move to Man U as replacement for Peter Schmeichel. The Australian international, 27, stands to make around £7m over the next 4 years at Old Trafford where he began his English career before returning to play with Sydney Croatia.

3   Croatia Zagreb confirm the appointment of Ossie Ardiles as manager. Irish government promise total backing to FAI if UEFA hand out heavy punishment for postponing EC tie with Yugoslavia.

4   England U-21's beat Sweden 3-0 at McAlpine stadium, the last home fixture departing manager Peter Taylor supervises. Martin Edwards says that with a heavy programme next season the FA Cup will not be a priority for Man U. The Reds will meet Lazio in the Super Cup in Monaco, Aug 27, and agree to play in the World Cup Championship in Tokyo, Nov 30.

5   The honeymoon is over for Keegan, after just 3 games, as disappointing England, poorly balanced, especially in midfield, fail miserably to make an impact v Sweden at Wembley. A reckless tackle sees Paul Scholes – fortunate not to go for a woeful 1st min lunge – sent-off. The scoreless draw leaves qualifying for Euro 2000 finals on a knife-edge. Angry Bobby Gould resigns immediately after Wales are completely outsmarted 4-0 by Italy in Bologna. Scotland have a shocker in the Faeroe Islands. Matt Elliott is sent-off for 'slapping' before half-time, the 11th dismissed in an international. Scots concede an injury-time equaliser (1-1) to give the minnows only their 2nd point in the group. Chelsea's Gianluca Vialli says his playing days are now over. Sunderland's Peter Reid is chosen to replace Peter Taylor as U-21 coach, and is to work part-time alongside Howard Wilkinson.

6   W Ham's Eyal Berkovic scores twice in Israel's 5-0 EC defeat of Austria in Tel Aviv. Speaking on BBC TV's *Frost* Kevin Keegan admits media criticism he has received is 'fair.'

7   A knee injury forces Liam Daish, 30, Coventry's Irish defender, to quit. The LMA support Arsenal's call for UEFA to investigate the 'illegal' approaches made by Real Madrid to striker Nicolas Anelka. Sunderland stress that Peter Reid will not be allowed to spend more than 30 days a season with England's U-21 set-up.

8   Coach Peter Taylor bows out as England's U-21's win 1-0 in Bulgaria and qualify for EC finals with a 100% record. Scotland lose 3-2 in Czech Rep, Wales go under 2-1 to Denmark and ROI end scoreless hosting Macedonia. Inter pay world record £28m for Lazio's Australian-raised striker Christian Vieri. Doug Livermore replaces Bryan Hamilton as asst to Norwich manager Bruce Rioch. Ray Harford quits his coaching post at Derby.

9   England take little comfort from their 1-1 draw in Bulgaria leaving them needing to defeat Luxembourg and Poland to ensure they reach just the EC play-offs. Pegged back shortly after Shearer's 14th min lead, England fail to capitalise on playing 10 men for most of the game, looking short on ideas and inspiration. A series of outstanding saves from Paul Jones prevents an embarrassing scoreline as Wales, under Neville Southall, rarely threaten and lose 2-0 to Denmark at half-empty Anfield. In positive mood Scotland go into a 2-goal lead in Czech Rep but succumb to a home rally and suffer the killer-blow 3 min from time. ROI share top spot in Grp 8 after enjoying the lion's share of play against defiant Macedonia to win 1-0.

10   John Rudge wins court battle with Vale for compensation following his controversial dismissal in January. Kenny Dalglish returns to Celtic and assumes newly created post of Director of Football Operations with John Barnes as head coach. In FIFA-inspired experiment 2 refs will be used for Italian Cup matches next season. England has 11 players carrying yellow cards into September qualifying ties against Luxembourg and Poland.

11   Malcolm Crosby replaces Ray Harford as Derby coach. Martin O'Neill finally signs a new 3-year contract worth £600,000 per annum, at Leicester. Brian Little quits Stoke after a year, citing personal problems.

12   Alex Ferguson receives his knighthood in the Queen's Birthday Honours list in recognition of a remarkable season which sees the Premiership title, FA Cup and the European Cup, all end up at Old Trafford. Arsenal's Tony Adams gains an MBE, Scots boss Craig Brown becomes a CBE, and there is an MBE for Wimbledon's Jamaican international Robbie Earle. At their AGM near Chester the FL vote to revert to goal difference rather than goals scored to separate teams next season. Players' names and squad numbers will also be displayed on shirts in the Nationwide League. From next season teams can use 3 out of 5 players on the bench.

13   Chelsea complete signing of Ajax defender Marion Malchiot, 22, on a Bosman free.

ENGLISH LEAGUE TABLES 1998–99

FA CARLING PREMIERSHIP

		P	W	D	L	F	A	W	D	L	F	A	GD	Pts
			Home			*Goals*		*Away*			*Goals*			
1	Manchester U	38	14	4	1	45	18	8	9	2	35	19	+43	79
2	Arsenal	38	14	5	0	34	5	8	7	4	25	12	+42	78
3	Chelsea	38	12	6	1	29	13	8	9	2	28	17	+27	75
4	Leeds U	38	12	5	2	32	9	6	8	5	30	25	+28	67
5	West Ham U	38	11	3	5	32	26	5	6	8	14	27	−7	57
6	Aston Villa	38	10	3	6	33	28	5	7	7	18	18	+5	55
7	Liverpool	38	10	5	4	44	24	5	4	10	24	25	+19	54
8	Derby Co	38	8	7	4	22	19	5	6	8	18	26	−5	52
9	Middlesbrough	38	7	9	3	25	18	5	6	8	23	36	−6	51
10	Leicester C	38	7	6	6	25	25	5	7	7	15	21	−6	49
11	Tottenham H	38	7	7	5	28	26	4	7	8	19	24	−3	47
12	Sheffield W	38	7	5	7	20	15	6	2	11	21	27	−1	46
13	Newcastle U	38	7	6	6	26	25	4	7	8	22	29	−6	46
14	Everton	38	6	8	5	22	12	5	2	12	20	35	−5	43
15	Coventry C	38	8	6	5	26	21	3	3	13	13	30	−12	42
16	Wimbledon	38	7	7	5	22	21	3	5	11	18	42	−23	42
17	Southampton	38	9	4	6	29	26	2	4	13	8	38	−27	41
18	Charlton Ath	38	4	7	8	20	20	4	5	10	21	36	−15	36
19	Blackburn R	38	6	5	8	21	24	1	9	9	17	28	−14	35
20	Nottingham F	38	3	7	9	18	31	4	2	13	17	38	−34	30

NATIONWIDE FOOTBALL LEAGUE DIVISION 1

		P	W	D	L	F	A	W	D	L	F	A	GS	Pts
			Home			*Goals*		*Away*			*Goals*			
1	Sunderland	46	19	3	1	50	10	12	9	2	41	18	91	105
2	Bradford C	46	15	4	4	48	20	11	5	7	34	27	82	87
3	Ipswich T	46	16	1	6	37	15	10	7	6	32	17	69	86
4	Birmingham C	46	12	7	4	32	15	11	5	7	34	22	66	81
5	Watford	46	12	8	3	30	19	9	6	8	35	37	65	77
6	Bolton W	46	13	6	4	44	25	7	10	6	34	34	78	76
7	Wolverhampton W	46	11	10	2	37	19	8	6	9	27	24	64	73
8	Sheffield U	46	12	6	5	42	29	6	7	10	29	37	71	67
9	Norwich C	46	7	12	4	34	28	8	5	10	28	33	62	62
10	Huddersfield T	46	11	9	3	38	23	4	7	12	24	48	62	61
11	Grimsby T	46	11	6	6	25	18	6	4	13	15	34	40	61
12	WBA	46	12	4	7	43	33	4	7	12	26	43	69	59
13	Barnsley	46	7	9	7	35	30	7	8	8	24	26	59	59
14	Crystal Palace	46	11	10	2	43	26	3	6	14	15	45	58	58
15	Tranmere R	46	8	7	8	37	30	4	13	6	26	31	63	56
16	Stockport Co	46	7	9	7	24	21	5	8	10	25	39	49	53
17	Swindon T	46	7	8	8	40	44	6	3	14	19	37	59	50
18	Crewe Alex	46	7	6	10	27	35	5	6	12	27	43	54	48
19	Portsmouth	46	10	5	8	34	26	1	9	13	23	47	57	47
20	QPR	46	9	7	7	34	22	3	4	16	18	39	52	47
21	Port Vale	46	10	3	10	22	28	3	5	15	23	47	45	47
22	Bury	46	9	7	7	24	27	1	10	12	11	33	35	47
23	Oxford U	46	7	8	8	31	30	3	6	14	17	41	48	44
24	Bristol C	46	7	8	8	35	36	2	7	14	22	44	57	42

NATIONWIDE FOOTBALL LEAGUE DIVISION 2

		P	W	Home D	L	Goals F	A	W	Away D	L	Goals F	A	GS	Pts
1	Fulham	46	19	3	1	50	12	12	5	6	29	20	79	101
2	Walsall	46	13	7	3	37	23	13	2	8	26	24	63	87
3	Manchester C	46	13	6	4	38	14	9	10	4	31	19	69	82
4	Gillingham	46	15	5	3	45	17	7	9	7	30	27	75	80
5	Preston NE	46	12	6	5	46	23	10	7	6	32	27	78	79
6	Wigan Ath	46	14	5	4	44	17	8	5	10	31	31	75	76
7	Bournemouth	46	14	7	2	37	11	7	6	10	26	30	63	76
8	Stoke C	46	10	4	9	32	32	11	2	10	27	31	59	69
9	Chesterfield	46	14	5	4	34	16	3	8	12	12	28	46	64
10	Millwall	46	9	8	6	33	24	8	3	12	19	35	52	62
11	Reading	46	10	6	7	29	26	6	7	10	25	37	54	61
12	Luton T	46	10	4	9	25	26	6	6	11	26	34	51	58
13	Bristol R	46	8	9	6	35	28	5	8	10	30	28	65	56
14	Blackpool	46	7	8	8	24	24	7	6	10	20	30	44	56
15	Burnley	46	8	7	8	23	33	5	9	9	31	40	54	55
16	Notts Co	46	8	6	9	29	27	6	6	11	23	34	52	54
17	Wrexham	46	8	6	9	21	28	5	8	10	22	34	43	53
18	Colchester U	46	9	7	7	25	30	3	9	11	27	40	52	52
19	Wycombe W	46	8	5	10	31	26	5	7	11	21	32	52	51
20	Oldham Ath	46	8	4	11	26	31	6	5	12	22	35	48	51
21	York C	46	6	8	9	28	33	7	3	13	28	47	56	50
22	Northampton T	46	4	12	7	26	31	6	6	11	17	26	43	48
23	Lincoln C	46	9	4	10	27	27	4	3	16	15	47	42	46
24	Macclesfield T	46	7	4	12	24	30	4	6	13	19	33	43	43

NATIONWIDE FOOTBALL LEAGUE DIVISION 3

		P	W	Home D	L	Goals F	A	W	Away D	L	Goals F	A	GS	Pts
1	Brentford	46	16	5	2	45	18	10	2	11	34	38	79	85
2	Cambridge U	46	13	6	4	41	21	10	6	7	37	27	78	81
3	Cardiff C	46	13	7	3	35	17	9	7	7	25	22	60	80
4	Scunthorpe U	46	14	3	6	42	28	8	5	10	27	30	69	74
5	Rotherham U	46	11	8	4	41	26	9	5	9	38	35	79	73
6	Leyton Orient	46	12	6	5	40	30	7	9	7	28	29	68	72
7	Swansea C	46	11	9	3	33	19	8	5	10	23	29	56	71
8	Mansfield T	46	15	2	6	38	18	4	8	11	22	40	60	67
9	Peterborough U	46	11	4	8	41	29	7	8	8	31	27	72	66
10	Halifax T	46	10	8	5	33	25	7	7	9	25	31	58	66
11	Darlington	46	10	6	7	41	24	8	5	10	28	34	69	65
12	Exeter C	46	13	5	5	32	18	4	7	12	15	32	47	63
13	Plymouth Arg	46	11	6	6	32	19	6	4	13	26	35	58	61
14	Chester C	46	6	12	5	28	30	7	6	10	29	36	57	57
15	Shrewsbury T	46	11	6	6	36	29	3	8	12	16	34	52	56
16	Barnet	46	10	5	8	30	31	4	8	11	24	40	54	55
17	Brighton & HA	46	8	3	12	25	35	8	4	11	24	31	49	55
18	Southend U	46	8	6	9	24	21	6	6	11	28	37	52	54
19	Rochdale	46	9	8	6	22	21	4	7	12	20	34	42	54
20	Torquay U	46	9	9	5	29	20	3	8	12	18	38	47	53
21	Hull C	46	8	5	10	25	28	6	6	11	19	34	44	53
22	Hartlepool U	46	8	7	8	33	27	5	5	13	19	38	52	51
23	Carlisle U	46	8	8	7	25	21	3	8	12	18	32	43	49
24	Scarborough	46	8	3	12	30	39	6	3	14	20	38	50	48

Goals scored determine Nationwide Football League position where clubs are level on points. If teams still cannot be separated, the team that has conceded fewer goals is placed higher.

FOOTBALL LEAGUE PLAY-OFFS 1998–99

DIV 2 SEMI-FINALS FIRST LEG

15 MAY

Wigan Ath (1) 1 *(Barlow 1)*
Manchester C (0) 1 *(Dickov 76)*   6762

Wigan Ath: Carroll; Bradshaw (Green), Sharp, McGibbon, Balmer, Porter, Liddell (Lee), Greenall, Haworth (Jones), O'Neill, Barlow.
Manchester C: Weaver; Crooks, Edghill, Vaughan, Horlock, Wiekens, Brown, Jeff Whitley, Dickov, Goater (Taylor), Cooke (Allsop).

16 MAY

Preston NE (0) 1 *(Eyres 54)*
Gillingham (0) 1 *(Taylor 79)*   18,584

Preston NE: Lucas; Alexander, Ludden, Murdock, Jackson, Gregan, Cartwright, Rankine, Nogan (Appleton), Macken (Harris), Eyres.
Gillingham: Bartram; Southall, Carr, Smith, Butters, Pennock, Patterson (Hodge), Hessenthaler, Asaba (Saunders), Galloway (Brown), Taylor.

DIV 1 SEMI-FINALS FIRST LEG

16 MAY

Bolton W (0) 1 *(Johansen 84)*
Ipswich T (0) 0   18,295

Bolton W: Banks; Cox, Elliott, Frandsen, Todd, Fish (Bergsson), Johansen, Jensen, Gudjohnsen (Hansen), Taylor, Gardner (Warhurst).
Ipswich T: Wright; Wilnis, Clapham, Thetis, Mowbray, Venus, Dyer, Holland, Johnson (Naylor), Scowcroft, Magilton.

Watford (1) 1 *(Ngonge 5)*
Birmingham C (0) 0   18,535

Watford: Chamberlain; Bazeley, Kennedy, Page, Palmer, Robinson, Ngonge (Hazan), Hyde, Mooney, Johnson, Wright (Smart).
Birmingham C: Poole; Rowett, Grainger, Robinson (Ndlovu), Holdsworth, Johnson M, McCarthy, O'Connor, Furlong, Bradbury (Adebola), Holland.

DIV 3 SEMI-FINALS FIRST LEG

16 MAY

Leyton Orient (0) 0
Rotherham U (0) 0   9419

Leyton Orient: Barrett; Joseph M (Stimson), Lockwood, Smith, Joseph R, Clark, Ling, Richards, Watts (Maskell), Simba, Beall.
Rotherham U: Pollitt; Varty, Hurst, Thompson, Knill (Williams), Dillon, Scott R, Hudson, Fortune-West, Warne, Roscoe.

Swansea C (1) 1 *(Bound 44)*
Scunthorpe U (0) 0   7828

Swansea C: Freestone; Jones S, Howard, Cusack, Smith, Bound, Roberts (Appleby), Thomas, Alsop, Watkin (Bird), Coates.
Scunthorpe U: Clarke; Housham, Dawson, Fickling, Wilcox, Hope, Walker, Forrester, Eyre, Gayle, Calvo-Garcia.

DIV 1 SEMI-FINALS SECOND LEG

19 MAY

Ipswich T (1) 4 *(Holland 14, 116, Dyer 52, 90)*
Bolton W (0) 3 *(Taylor 51, 96, Frandsen 84)*   21,755

Ipswich T: Wright; Wilnis (Stockwell), Clapham, Magilton, Mowbray (Thetis), Venus, Dyer, Holland, Johnson (Naylor), Scowcroft, Petta.
Bolton W: Banks; Cox, Elliott (Warhurst), Frandsen, Todd, Fish, Johansen, Jensen, Gudjohnsen (Hansen), Taylor, Gardner (Bergsson).
aet; Bolton W won on away goals.

20 MAY

Birmingham C (1) 1 *(Adebola 2)*
Watford (0) 0   29,100

Birmingham C: Poole; Rowett, Grainger, McCarthy (Purse), Holdsworth, Johnson M, Furlong, O'Connor (Bradbury), Adebola (Holland), Hughes, Ndlovu.
Watford: Chamberlain; Bazeley, Gibbs, Palmer, Page, Kennedy, Ngonge (Hazan), Hyde, Mooney, Johnson, Wright (Smart).
aet; Watford won 7-6 on penalties.

Manchester City goalkeeper Nick Weaver celebrates his play-off penalty save at Wembley which enabled his team to win promotion to the First Division. (Colorsport)

Scunthorpe United players, officials and supporters celebrate after their 1-0 play-off win at Wembley. (Colorsport)

DIV 2 SEMI-FINALS SECOND LEG

19 MAY

Gillingham (1) 1 *(Hessenthaler 2)*

Preston NE (0) 0   10,505

Gillingham: Bartram; Southall, Ashby, Smith, Butters, Pennock, Patterson, Hessenthaler, Asaba (Hodge), Galloway (Saunders), Taylor.
Preston NE: Lucas; Alexander, Ludden (Harris), Murdock (Darby), Jackson, Gregan, Cartwright, Appleton, Macken, Rankine (Nogan), Eyres.

Manchester C (1) 1 *(Goater 27)*

Wigan Ath (0) 0   31,305

Manchester C: Weaver; Crooks, Edghill, Vaughan, Wiekens, Horlock, Brown, Jeff Whitley, Dickov, Goater (Taylor), Cooke (Pollock).
Wigan Ath: Carroll; Bradshaw, Sharp, McGibbon, Balmer, Porter (Lee), Liddell, Greenall, Green (Kilford), Lowe (Jones), Barlow.

DIV 3 SEMI-FINALS SECOND LEG

19 MAY

Rotherham U (0) 0

Leyton Orient (0) 0   9529

Rotherham U: Pollitt; Varty, Hurst, Thompson, Knill (Williams), Dillon, Scott R (Sedgwick), Hudson, Fortune-West, Warne, Roscoe.
Leyton Orient: Barrett; Stimson (Hicks), Lockwood, Smith, Joseph R, Clark, Ling, Richards (Morrison), Watts (Inglethorpe), Simba, Beall.
aet; Leyton Orient won 4-2 on penalties.

Scunthorpe U (1) 3 *(Dawson 2, Sheldon 92, 102)*

Swansea C (0) 1 *(Bird 98)*   7089

Scunthorpe U: Clarke; Wilcox, Dawson, Logan, Hope, Walker, Forrester (Sheldon), Eyre, Gayle, Calvo-Garcia.
Swansea C: Freestone; Jones S (O'Leary), Howard, Cusack, Smith, Bound, Roberts (Price), Thomas, Bird, Alsop, Coates (Appleby).
aet.

DIV 3 FINAL (at Wembley)

29 MAY

Leyton Orient (0) 0

Scunthorpe U (1) 1 *(Calvo-Garcia 6)*   36,985

Leyton Orient: Barrett; Joseph R, Lockwood, Smith, Hicks (Maskell), Clark, Ling, Richards (Inglethorpe), Watts, Simba, Beall.
Scunthorpe U: Evans; Wilcox, Dawson, Logan, Harsley, Hope, Walker, Forrester (Bull), Gayle (Stamp), Sheldon, Calvo-Garcia (Housham).

DIV 2 FINAL (at Wembley)

30 MAY

Gillingham (0) 2 *(Asaba 81, Taylor 86)*

Manchester C (0) 2 *(Horlock 89, Dickov 90)*   76,935

Gillingham: Bartram; Southall, Ashby, Smith, Butters, Pennock, Patterson (Hodge), Hessenthaler, Asaba (Carr), Galloway (Saunders), Taylor.
Manchester C: Weaver; Crooks (Taylor), Edghill, Wiekens, Morrison (Vaughan), Horlock, Brown (Bishop), Jeff Whitley, Dickov, Goater, Cooke.
aet; Manchester C won 3-1 on penalties.

DIV 1 FINAL (at Wembley)

31 MAY

Bolton W (0) 0

Watford (1) 2 *(Wright 38, Smart 89)*   70,343

Bolton W: Banks; Cox, Elliott, Frandsen, Todd, Fish, Johansen (Sellars), Jensen, Gudjohnsen, Taylor, Gardner (Hansen).
Watford: Chamberlain; Bazeley, Kennedy, Palmer, Page, Robinson, Ngonge (Smart), Hyde, Mooney, Johnson, Wright (Hazan).

LEADING GOALSCORERS 1998–99

FA CARLING PREMIERSHIP	League	FA Cup	Worthington Cup	Other	Total
Dwight Yorke *(Manchester U)*	18	3	0	8	29
Michael Owen *(Liverpool)*	18	2	1	2	23
Jimmy Floyd Hasselbaink *(Leeds U)*	18	1	0	1	20
Andy Cole *(Manchester U)*	17	2	0	5	24
Nicolas Anelka *(Arsenal)*	17	0	0	2	19
Hamilton Ricard *(Middlesbrough)*	15	0	3	0	18
Alan Shearer *(Newcastle U)*	14	5	1	1	21
Robbie Fowler *(Liverpool)*	14	1	1	2	18
Julian Joachim *(Aston Villa)*	14	1	0	1	16
Dion Dublin *(Aston Villa)*	14	0	1	0	15
(Including 3 League and 1 Worthington Cup goal for Coventry C)					
Ole Gunnar Solskjaer *(Manchester U)*	13	1	3	2	19
Gianfranco Zola *(Chelsea)*	13	1	0	1	15
Dennis Bergkamp *(Arsenal)*	12	3	0	1	16
Gustavo Poyet *(Chelsea)*	11	0	2	1	14
Noel Whelan *(Coventry C)*	10	2	1	0	13
Tony Cottee *(Leicester C)*	10	1	5	0	16
Tore Andre Flo *(Chelsea)*	10	0	1	2	13
Jason Euell *(Wimbledon)*	10	0	0	0	10
Marcus Gayle *(Wimbledon)*	10	0	1	0	11

NATIONWIDE DIVISION 1

	League	FA Cup	Worthington Cup	Other	Total
Lee Hughes *(WBA)*	31	0	1	0	32
Kevin Phillips *(Sunderland)*	23	0	2	0	25
Lee Mills *(Bradford C)*	23	1	0	0	24
Marcus Stewart *(Huddersfield T)*	22	2	2	0	26
Iffy Onuora *(Swindon T)*	20	0	0	0	20
Iwan Roberts *(Norwich C)*	19	1	3	0	23
Ade Akinbiyi *(Bristol C)*	19	0	4	0	23
Niall Quinn *(Sunderland)*	18	0	3	0	21
Brett Angell *(Stockport Co)*	17	1	0	0	18
Craig Bellamy *(Norwich C)*	17	0	2	0	19
Marcelo *(Sheffield U)*	16	3	0	0	19
Robbie Blake *(Bradford C)*	16	0	1	0	17
Dean Windass *(Oxford U)*	15	3	0	0	18
Kenny Irons *(Tranmere R)*	15	0	3	0	18
Bob Taylor *(Bolton W)*	15	0	1	0	16
Paul Groves *(Grimsby T)*	14	0	1	0	15

DIVISION 2

	League	FA Cup	Worthington Cup	Other	Total
Jamie Cureton *(Bristol R)*	25	2	1	1	29
Carl Asaba *(Gillingham)*	20	0	1	1	22
(Includes 1 Worthington Cup goal for Reading)					
Andy Payton *(Burnley)*	19	2	1	0	22
Stuart Barlow *(Wigan Ath)*	19	1	1	4	25
Kurt Nogan *(Preston NE)*	18	3	0	0	21
Andy Rammell *(Walsall)*	18	0	1	1	20
Shaun Goater *(Manchester C)*	17	1	2	0	20
Barry Hayles *(Fulham)*	17	1	1	0	19
(Includes 9 League and 1 Worthington Cup goal for Bristol R)					
Jason Roberts *(Bristol R)*	16	7	0	0	23
Richard Cresswell *(York C)*	16	3	0	0	19
(Also scored 1 League goal for Sheffield W)					
Robert Taylor *(Gillingham)*	16	0	0	3	19
Carlo Corazzin *(Northampton T)*	16	0	0	1	17
Geoff Horsfield *(Fulham)*	15	2	0	0	17
(Also scored 7 League and 1 Worthington Cup goal for Halifax T)					
Mark Stein *(Bournemouth)*	15	1	5	4	25
Neil Harris *(Millwall)*	15	0	0	3	18
Steve Robinson *(Bournemouth)*	13	1	1	1	16
Darren Wrack *(Walsall)*	13	0	0	1	14

DIVISION 3

	League	FA Cup	Worthington Cup	Other	Total
Marco Gabbiadini *(Darlington)*	23	0	0	1	24
Lloyd Owusu *(Brentford)*	22	1	2	0	25
Jamie Forrester *(Scunthorpe U)*	20	2	1	0	23
Scott Partridge *(Brentford)*	19	1	0	1	21
(Including 12 League, 1 Worthington and 1 other goal for Torquay U)					
Martin Butler *(Cambridge U)*	17	1	2	1	21
John Taylor *(Cambridge U)*	17	0	1	1	19
Lee Peacock *(Mansfield T)*	17	0	0	2	19
Steve Watkin *(Swansea C)*	17	0	0	0	17
Ken Charlery *(Barnet)*	16	0	0	0	16
Kevin Nugent *(Cardiff C)*	15	3	0	0	18
John Eyre *(Scunthorpe U)*	15	2	0	0	17
Guiliano Grazioli *(Peterborough U)*	15	0	0	0	15
Lee Steele *(Shrewsbury T)*	13	0	0	0	13

REVIEW OF THE SEASON

Manchester United's unique treble of FA Premier League, FA Cup and European Cup had seemed an unlikely prospect on 19 December when they were beaten 3-2 at Old Trafford by Middlesbrough, but it proved to be the beginning of a remarkable unbeaten run of 33 matches, achieved by a combination of quality in depth, confidence just short of arrogance and a strengthening determination to achieve all three prizes.

Not one of the 23 players used in the championship alone was an ever present. Roy Keane influentially combative in midfield, appeared in 35 matches, two of them as a substitute. The occasionally unpredictable goalkeeper Peter Schmeichel, right-back Gary Neville and midfield player David Beckham, missed four games each.

Two crucial captures proved to be Dutch central defender Jaap Stam and striker Dwight Yorke, who formed an effective spearhead in attack with Andy Cole. The midfield area was also well served and Paul Scholes often proved the player for the big occasion. The Neville brothers Gary and Phil were reliably adaptable and both Ole Gunnar Solskjaer and Teddy Sheringham made the most of a handful of opportunities up front. Manipulating the entire assembly was Alex Ferguson, whose successful efforts on behalf of the Old Trafford club deservedly gained him a knighthood. Outside of the domestic achievements, the European Cup win against Juventus in Italy and the dramatic last gasp victory over Bayern Munich in Spain were unforgettable moments.

In one of the closest endings to the title race, Arsenal finished just a point behind United and in fact themselves only suffered their first defeat for five months after 19 unbeaten games on 11 May, when they lost 1-0 at Leeds where Manchester United had drawn 1-1 the previous month. While this was not the entire story, too many drawn matches – half of them in the first 16 matches – and no goals at all in seven games were other contributory factors to Arsenal losing their crown. Defensively, the Gunners were formidable as ever with 23 clean sheets and just one goal conceded in others, except when losing 3-2 at Aston Villa. They also managed to beat United 3-0 (a score repeated from the Charity Shield game) and also drew 1-1 at Old Trafford.

Chelsea managed to achieve a European honour quite early in the season, when they defeated Real Madrid 1-0 in the Super Cup. Unfortunately, injuries played havoc with the team, which was top on 16 January. Unbeaten in the last ten games, they needed not to have drawn four of them, otherwise the four point gap between themselves and the leaders might have proved even more interesting in the final outcome.

But for a draw-ridden start with eight such results out of the first 11, Leeds United might have challenged for the title themselves. They had a change of manager during the season when George Graham left for Tottenham Hotspur and was replaced by his No. 2 David O'Leary. Seven successive wins into April launched them into fourth place and confirmed the new manager's status.

It was a season of contrasts for West Ham United, who managed fifth place even though they failed to score in 16 games and during the season conceded a 6, a 5 and six 4's.

Aston Villa were still top at the end of the year, but subsequently lost ground in dramatic fashion, gaining only three points from a possible 30 and for Liverpool, seventh place was poor by their standards. Yet their 4-2 win at Villa Park had been arguably the finest match of the Premier season. They lost Michael Owen through injury late in the season and Robbie Fowler also missed many games. Only once did they achieve three wins in a row.

A dip in fortunes during mid-season proved costly for Derby County and they failed to make the most of a solid start, but Middlesbrough's 3-2 win at Old Trafford were their first success there in 69 years. Fourth at that time, they then failed to win any of the next nine and none of the last four.

Ryan Giggs sets off on his marathon through the Arsenal defence in the FA Cup replay. The run ended with what has been generally described as the goal of the season. (Actionimages)

Switching European Cup games to Wembley proved to be a crowd-puller for Arsenal. Here Martin Keown heads a goal against Panathinaikos. (Colorsport)

Leicester's highest position was seventh on 31 October. They were occasionally let down by their defence, letting in six goals to Manchester United, five against Arsenal and four at home to Chelsea. Tottenham Hotspur took some silverware when they won the Worthington Cup against Leicester, but in the League, four of their 11 wins came against teams relegated and only three others against teams who finished above them.

Sheffield Wednesday's second half of the season was marginally better than the first half, but they failed to score in 17 games and the team selection problems at Newcastle were underlined by the fact that they used 34 players. They had no wins in the last seven matches, scored only six goals and three of these from penalties, but they did finish runners-up in the FA Cup.

Everton went 480 minutes before scoring a goal at home and slipped into the bottom three in April and needed three straight wins to escape the probability of relegation. Coventry again freed themselves early from the possibilities of going down and had five wins from their last 12 games.

For Wimbledon, there was an alarming slump after manager Joe Kinnear was taken ill on 3 March at Sheffield Wednesday. The Dons were in the top half of the table at the time. They failed to win any of their remaining 11 fixtures.

Southampton's first win did not arrive until 24 October and unbeaten at home in 1999, they only emerged from the bottom three in the last three weeks, which yielded three precious wins. The crash which affected relegated Charlton was spectacular since they were top on 22 August. Despite some brave performances in the last few months, eight straight defeats had put them in a precarious position. For Blackburn Rovers, they made history by being the first Premier League champions to suffer relegation. They fell on 12 May after holding Manchester United to a goalless draw. They scraped just one win in their last 14 outings.

Nineteen matches without a win signalled severe problems for Nottingham Forest, who were never off the bottom from mid-December. Already relegated but apparently relaxed, they won their last three matches.

In the Nationwide First Division, Sunderland proved runaway champions, sustaining only three defeats – two of them in a spell of five games at the turn of the year. They failed to score in only five matches, impressively piling up 91 goals and 105 points and recording a club record 19 matches without defeat.

Bradford City were never out of the top three from mid-January and snatched the other automatic promotion spot with a 3-2 win at Wolves on the last day of the season. City's success was at the expense of Ipswich, who had to be content with a place in the play-offs again. After failing to score a goal in their first four games they ended the season by losing three of their last five, which led to their subsequent failure.

Even though Birmingham managed three separate spells of eight games without defeat and won 7-1 at Oxford on 12 December, they showed a failure to be consistent. However, it was Watford who came through the play-offs successfully. Second in November, they faded until a recovery which saw them drop only two points from their last eight matches.

Six successive wins at the turn of the year promised much for Bolton and put them second, only to see this solid foundation crumble and they had to be satisfied with a play-off place. Wolves also failed at the wrong time, producing just one win and five drawn games from their last seven.

Sheffield United were fourth on 21 November, but they, too, hit erratic form and though Norwich won their first three games to go top, they were never above fourth place afterwards and endured just one win in 16 matches into April. Huddersfield led the table in mid-October before sliding out of contention and goalscoring problems for Grimsby were illustrated from Boxing Day when they were unable to score more than one goal a game and only ten in the last 22.

A 2-0 win against Oxford on 6 March seemed likely to precipitate West Bromwich Albion into the play-offs, only then to experience five successive defeats. Barnsley were stuck in mid-table halfway through the season and a 7-1 win against Huddersfield proved an isolated flurry of scoring.

Ten matches without defeat into March gave false hopes of the play-offs for Crystal Palace, who called upon the services of 43 different players during the season. Tranmere were the draw champions of the competition, with 20 such results to keep them in mid-table. While for Stockport, four goals in one game, three in another but not more than two in any other match highlighted their problem area. A 6-0 home defeat by Ipswich on 3 April threatened to send Swindon into the relegation zone, until three wins in their last seven saved them.

A run of 18 matches without a win lasting four months into December, left Crewe firmly at the foot of the table, until three wins in their last four lifted them to safety. Portsmouth hovered above the relegation zone from mid-October and they managed only one win from their last ten. For Queens Park Rangers, an incredible 6-0 win over Crystal Palace on the last day gave them sufficient goals to escape, even though they managed only one goal in their previous five games. Port Vale were also saved by scoring ten more goals than Bury. Their problems were underlined with only one win in 15 to the end of January. A disastrous spell of 18 matches without a win from 11 December, including a club record of six successive draws, laid the foundations for Bury's relegation, even though they were on the same points as Portsmouth, QPR and Port Vale.

The highest position for Oxford during the season was 18th at the end of November after three wins, but only four came in the second half of the season and they were relegated with Bristol City, who never recovered from a wretched opening, which did not produce a win until the 10th game and they were in the bottom three from the end of January.

Fulham achieved 101 points on winning the championship of the Second Division. They were never headed from 19 December and eight successive wins from March equalled a club record. They were accompanied in automatic promotion by Walsall, whose solid work from November ensured they were never out of second or third place for the rest of the campaign. Manchester City effected gradual improvement during the season. They lost only twice after the turn of the year and only Fulham conceded fewer goals. They were also successful in the play-offs.

Gillingham's sluggish start was forgotten when they went 17 games without defeat, lifting them to play-off proportions. Top as late as 13 February, Preston fell away and had to be satisfied with a play-off place after just one win from their last nine. Wigan were forced to play six League games in 12 days, but scraped into the play-offs. They also found time to win the Auto Windscreens Shield just before this marathon. An end to the season decline which produced just one win in the last seven, cost Bournemouth and though Stoke had never been headed by 12 December, their collapse was extraordinary as they merely managed only seven more wins.

Goals dried up from early March for Chesterfield, with only nine from their last 14 games, while from 19 December Millwall were unable to move above eighth or 10th place, though they did finish runners-up for the Auto Windscreens Shield.

The play-offs seemed probable for Reading after 20 March when they were seventh, but only one win came from the next ten. Luton were fourth in October. Then came eight matches and no wins, followed by a lack of scoring in the second half of the season. Jamie Cureton and Jason Roberts scored 41 goals between them for Bristol Rovers but there were too many leaks in defence and though Blackpool achieved five wins in a row to the end of September to take them to third place, there was a gentle slide to mid-table afterwards.

Four consecutive defeats in which no goals were scored and 14 conceded, left Burnley in the relegation zone before a marked recovery. And by 20 February, Notts County had dropped to last but one place. They, too, embarked on serious improvement.

Stan Collymore of Aston Villa steps over Liverpool's Paul Ince during one of the best Premier League matches of the 1998–99 season, when Liverpool won 4-2 at Villa Park. (ASP)

Wrexham were unable to recover from a spell of only one win in 13 into January and Colchester's bright beginning was eroded with ten matches without a win to the end of January. Wycombe did not achieve their first win until the 13th game and they were still bottom on 20 March, before winning seven of their last 11, while only four wins in the last six edged Oldham to safety.

The relegated quartet were York, Northampton, Lincoln and Macclesfield. York fell into the relegation trap on the last day, losing 4-0 at Manchester City. Eleven games without a win to mid-March had started the problem and just one win in the first 11 laid the base for Northampton's demise, despite being unbeaten in the last nine.

Infrequent victories and several heavy defeats were such that not even three wins in the last six could save Lincoln and failing to score at all in the first five games for newly-promoted Macclesfield was followed by never being out of the bottom two in the second half of the season and a club record ten games without a win.

Once Brentford had improved their indifferent away form from mid-February, they ended the season in confident fashion, unbeaten in a club record-equalling 16 matches, to secure first place on the last day by winning 1-0 at Cambridge. For their part, Cambridge had to be content with runners-up, having earned first place by early March. They surrendered this in the last seven games, which yielded just one victory. Cardiff joined them in automatic promotion, their only disappointment being to drop from first to third place in successive matches at the end of the season.

Scunthorpe finished fourth and were able to gain promotion through the play-offs. Top on 24 October, they had settled into the top seven in succeeding months. Despite matching Brentford for goalscoring, Rotherham still failed to score at all in 13 games, but were top on 7 November.

A better second half of the season ensured play-off place for Leyton Orient, after a run of ten games without defeat had put them second by the send of November. Swansea just made the last play-off spot with three wins out of the last four, having been as low as 20th at the start of November.

Mansfield were second on Boxing Day, but too many sequences of successive defeats proved costly and though Peterborough were capable of free scoring as witnessed by a 9, a 5 and two 4's, they showed erratic form.

On 21 November newly-promoted Halifax were top. Then came seven games without a win. While Darlington were also at the head of the Third Division on 10 October before settling into mid-table, a position which Exeter held in the second half of the term.

Plymouth's useful opening and still in 8th place on 3 April, was ruined with only one success in the next eight. Chester were 10th on 3rd October, but did not manage to win any of the next eight games and Shrewsbury were bottom in September, after nine games with no wins and only three goals to their credit.

Barnet suffered their heaviest League defeat, losing 9-1 at home to Peterborough on 5 September and three successive wins into December was the highlight of their season. On 30 January, Brighton had seen a climb to seventh place. Alas, the next win came after 11 matches. By mid-April, Southend had dropped to 21st, only six points above bottom place and Rochdale were the poorest scorers in the division, only twice achieving as many as three goals.

Matters improved for Torquay after a run of 13 games without a win had sent them next to bottom by 28 November. Favourites to go down for many months, Hull won 2-0 at Brentford on 6 February and hauled themselves away from trouble. But problems began for Hartlepool on 28 November. Only two wins came from the next 19 games and a battle to avoid the drop.

Carlisle escaped from the clutches of the Conference, thanks to an injury-time winning goal from on-loan goalkeeper Jimmy Glass against Plymouth on the last day of the season. It shot Scarborough out of the League. Caught first by Hull and then Carlisle, they really owed their relegation to five successive defeats in a busy April. Up from the Conference came Cheltenham Town.

Goalkeeper Jimmy Glass on loan to Carlisle United from Swindon Town, scores a dramatic last-minute winner against Plymouth Argyle to keep his temporary team in the Football League. (Actionimages)

INTRODUCTION TO THE CLUB SECTION

For this year's Rothmans Football Yearbook, the players again appear under the club with whom they finished the season and in an A–Z form for easy reference (see pages 414–540). The names of Trainees, Scholarships and Associated Schoolboys are also included under each club's name.

The club section again comprises four pages but this year, the first two feature increased historical and record details for each club, including new entries in the 'Did you know?' series. Record transfer fees are usually left to the discretion of the club concerned.

The third and fourth pages of this section present a complete record of the League season, including date, venue, opponents, results, half-time score, League position, goalscorers, attendances and complete line-ups including substitutes where used, for every League game in the 1998–99 season. Again goal times have been added, though not official they give an indication of when goals were scored. These appear as superior figures [10, 20, 30].

Squad numbers in the Premier League have been ignored; those used are the familiar ones, 1–11 while the introduction of a third outfield substitute has been recognised as follows:- the first substitute No. 12, the second No. 13 and the third No. 14. However, if there is a substitute goalkeeper he is represented by No. 15 but *only* if he replaces the first choice goalkeeper. Otherwise he adopts one of the other three substitute numbers, as there have been several instances where a goalkeeper has been used as an outfield player because of injuries during the game. Players replaced are respectively noted with superior figures [1], [2], [3] and [g] for goalkeeper. These third and fourth pages also include consolidated lists of goalscorers for the club in League, Worthington Cup and FA Cup matches plus a summary of results in these two main domestic competitions.

The continued increase in the number of matches played on Sundays has resulted in the League positions shown after every League result being taken on that day. Full holiday programmes are also recorded, but the position after mid-week fixtures will not normally have been updated. Attendance figures quoted for the Nationwide Football League are those which appeared in the Press at the time. But those in the FA Carling Premiership are official. The attendance statistics published on pages 568–570 are those officially issued by the FA Premier League and the Football League at the end of the season.

In the totals at the top of each column on page 4, substitute appearances are listed separately by the '+', but have been amalgamated in the totals which feature in the players historical section in the directory mentioned above. Thus these appearances include those as substitute. In fact the directory again features those names appearing on the FA Premier League and Football League's Retained list, which is published at the end of May. Each player's height and weight where known, plus birth place, birth date and source together with total League goals and appearances for each club he has represented, can be found as in previous editions. The player's details remain under the club which retained him at the end of the season. An asterisk '*' by a player's name indicates that he was given a free transfer at the end of the 1998–99 season, a dagger '†' against a name means that he is a non-contract player, a double dagger '‡' indicates that the player's registration was cancelled during the season and a section mark '§' shows the player to be a trainee or associated schoolboy who has made League appearances. The symbol # indicates players aged 24 and over who are out of contract but who were offered re-engagement by their clubs. Appearances by players in the play-offs are not included in their career totals.

FA Premiership

ARSENAL

FOUNDATION

Formed by workers at the Royal Arsenal, Woolwich in 1886, they
began as Dial Square (name of one of the workshops), and
included two former Nottingham Forest players, Fred Beardsley
and Morris Bates. Beardsley wrote to his old club seeking help and
they provided the new club with a full set of red jerseys and a ball.
The club became known as the 'Woolwich Reds' although their
official title soon after formation was Woolwich Arsenal.

Arsenal Stadium, Highbury, London N5 1BU.
Telephone: (0171) 704 4000.
Fax: (0171) 704 4001.
Box Office: (0171) 413 3366.
Commercial & Marketing: (0171) 704 4100.
Recorded Information: (0171) 704 4242.
Clubline: 0891 202021.
Ground Capacity: 38,500 all seated.
Record Attendance: 73,295 v Sunderland, Div 1, 9 March 1935.
At Wembley: 73,455 v Panathinaikos, European Cup Group E, 30 September 1998.
Record Receipts: £392,726.50 v Sampdoria, European
Cup-Winners' Cup, semi-final first leg, 6 April 1995.
Pitch Measurements: 110yd x 73yd.
Life President: Sir Robert Bellinger GBE, D.SC.
Chairman: P.D. Hill-Wood.
Vice-Chairman: D. Dein.
Directors: R.G. Gibbs, C.E.B.L. Carr, R.C.L. Carr,
D.D. Fiszman.
Managing Director: K.J. Friar.
Manager: Arsène Wenger.
Assistant Manager/Coach: Pat Rice.
Head Youth Coach: Don Howe.
Head of Youth Development: Liam Brady.
Physio: Gary Lewin.
Reserve Coach: George Armstrong.
Youth Coach: Don Givens.
Company Secretary: David Miles.
Commercial Manager: John Hazell.
Stadium Manager: John Beattie.

HONOURS

FA Premier League: Champions
1997–98. Runners-up 1998–99.

Football League: Division 1 –
Champions 1930–31, 1932–33,
1933–34, 1934–35, 1937–38, 1947–48,
1952–53, 1970–71, 1988–89, 1990–91;
Runners-up 1925–26, 1931–32,
1972–73; Division 2 – Runners-up
1903–04.

FA Cup: Winners 1930, 1936, 1950,
1971, 1979, 1993, 1998; Runners-up
1927, 1932, 1952, 1972, 1978, 1980.

Double performed: 1970–71, 1997–98.

Football League Cup: Winners 1987,
1993; Runners-up 1968, 1969, 1988.

European Competitions: Fairs Cup:
1963–64, 1969–70 (winners), 1970–71.
European Cup: 1971–72, 1991–92,
1998–99. *UEFA Cup:* 1978–79,
1981–82, 1982–83, 1996–97, 1997–98.
European Cup-Winners' Cup:
1979–80 (runners-up), 1993–94
(winners), 1994–95 (runners-up).

LATEST SEQUENCES
Longest Sequence of League Wins: 10, 11.3.98 – 3.5.98.
Longest Sequence of League Defeats: 7, 12.2.77 – 12.3.77.
Longest Sequence of League Draws: 6, 4.3.61 – 1.4.61.
Longest Sequence of Unbeaten League Matches: 26,
28.4.90 – 19.1.91.
Longest Sequence Without a League Win: 23, 28.9.12 –
1.3.13.

Colours
Red shirts with white sleeves, white shorts, red and white hooped stockings.

Change Colours
Yellow and navy blue shirts, navy blue shorts, navy blue stockings.

Year Formed: 1886.

Turned Professional: 1891.

Ltd Co: 1893.

Previous Names: 1886, Dial Square; 1886, Royal Arsenal; 1891, Woolwich Arsenal; 1914 Arsenal.

Club Nickname: 'Gunners'.

Previous Grounds: 1886, Plumstead Common; 1887, Sportsman Ground; 1888, Manor Ground; 1890, Invicta Ground; 1893, Manor Ground; 1913, Highbury.

First Football League Game: 2 September 1893, Division 2, v Newcastle U (h) D 2–2 – Williams; Powell, Jeffrey; Devine, Buist, Howat; Gemmell, Henderson, Shaw (1), Elliott (1), Booth.

Record League Victory: 12–0 v Loughborough T, Division 2, 12 March 1900 – Orr; McNichol, Jackson; Moir, Dick (2), Anderson (1); Hunt, Cottrell (2), Main (2), Gaudie (3), Tennant (2).

Record Cup Victory: 11–1 v Darwen, FA Cup 3rd rd, 9 January 1932 – Moss; Parker, Hapgood; Jones, Roberts, John; Hulme (2), Jack (3), Lambert (2), James, Bastin (4).

MANAGERS
Sam Hollis 1894–97
Tom Mitchell 1897–98
George Elcoat 1898–99
Harry Bradshaw 1899–1904
Phil Kelso 1904–08
George Morrell 1908–15
Leslie Knighton 1919–25
Herbert Chapman 1925–34
George Allison 1934–47
Tom Whittaker 1947–56
Jack Crayston 1956–58
George Swindin 1958–62
Billy Wright 1962–66
Bertie Mee 1966–76
Terry Neill 1976–83
Don Howe 1984–86
George Graham 1986–95
Bruce Rioch 1995–96
Arsène Wenger September 1996–

Record Defeat: 0–8 v Loughborough T, Division 2, 12 December 1896.

Most League Points (2 for a win): 66, Division 1, 1930–31.

Most League Points (3 for a win): 83, Division 1, 1990–91.

Most League Goals: 127, Division 1, 1930–31.

Highest League Scorer in Season: Ted Drake, 42, 1934–35.

Most League Goals in Total Aggregate: Cliff Bastin, 150, 1930–47.

Most League Goals in One Match: 7, Ted Drake v Aston Villa, Division 1, 14 December 1935.

Most Capped Player: Kenny Sansom, 77 (86), England, 1981–1988.

Most League Appearances: David O'Leary, 558, 1975–93.

Youngest League Player: Gerry Ward, 16 years 321 days v Huddersfield T, 22 August 1953.

Record Transfer Fee Received: £5,000,000 from Middlesbrough for Paul Merson, July 1997.

Record Transfer Fee Paid: £7,500,000 to Internazionale for Dennis Bergkamp, June 1995.

Football League Record: 1893 Elected to Division 2; 1904–13 Division 1; 1913–19 Division 2; 1919–92 Division 1; 1992– FA Premier League.

TEN YEAR LEAGUE RECORD

		P	W	D	L	F	A	Pts	Pos
1988-89	Div 1	38	22	10	6	73	36	76	1
1989-90	Div 1	38	18	8	12	54	38	62	4
1990-91	Div 1	38	24	13	1	74	18	83	1
1991-92	Div 1	42	19	15	8	81	46	72	4
1992-93	PR Lge	42	15	11	16	40	38	56	10
1993-94	PR Lge	42	18	17	7	53	28	71	4
1994-95	PR Lge	42	13	12	17	52	49	51	12
1995-96	PR Lge	38	17	12	9	49	32	63	5
1996-97	PR Lge	38	19	11	8	62	32	68	3
1997-98	PR Lge	38	23	9	6	68	33	78	1

DID YOU KNOW ?

Arsenal supplied a record seven players for England's team against Italy in 1934 and seven for the England v France match at Wembley on 10 February 1999 – four on the English team and three Frenchmen.

ARSENAL 1998–99 LEAGUE RECORD

Match No.	Date	Venue	Opponents	Result	H/T Score	Lg. Pos.	Goalscorers	Attendance
1	Aug 17	H	Nottingham F	W 2-1	0-0	—	Petit [58], Overmars [79]	38,064
2	22	A	Liverpool	D 0-0	0-0	5		44,429
3	29	H	Charlton Ath	D 0-0	0-0	6		38,014
4	Sept 9	A	Chelsea	D 0-0	0-0	—		34,647
5	12	A	Leicester C	D 1-1	0-1	9	Hughes [90]	21,628
6	20	H	Manchester U	W 3-0	2-0	5	Adams [13], Anelka [44], Ljungberg [84]	38,142
7	26	A	Sheffield W	L 0-1	0-0	9		27,949
8	Oct 4	H	Newcastle U	W 3-0	2-0	3	Bergkamp 2 (1 pen) [21, 66 (p)], Anelka [29]	38,102
9	17	H	Southampton	D 1-1	1-0	5	Anelka [34]	38,027
10	25	A	Blackburn R	W 2-1	2-0	3	Anelka [25], Petit [39]	27,012
11	31	A	Coventry C	W 1-0	0-0	3	Anelka [63]	23,039
12	Nov 8	H	Everton	W 1-0	1-0	2	Anelka [6]	38,088
13	14	H	Tottenham H	D 0-0	0-0	3		38,278
14	21	A	Wimbledon	L 0-1	0-0	3		26,003
15	29	H	Middlesbrough	D 1-1	0-1	4	Anelka [89]	38,075
16	Dec 5	A	Derby Co	D 0-0	0-0	4		29,018
17	13	A	Aston Villa	L 2-3	2-0	6	Bergkamp 2 [14, 45]	39,217
18	20	H	Leeds U	W 3-1	1-0	6	Bergkamp [28], Vieira [53], Petit [82]	38,025
19	26	H	West Ham U	W 1-0	1-0	5	Overmars [7]	38,098
20	28	A	Charlton Ath	W 1-0	0-0	3	Overmars (pen) [53]	20,043
21	Jan 9	H	Liverpool	D 0-0	0-0	4		38,107
22	16	A	Nottingham F	W 1-0	1-0	4	Keown [34]	26,021
23	31	H	Chelsea	W 1-0	1-0	4	Bergkamp [32]	38,121
24	Feb 6	A	West Ham U	W 4-0	2-0	3	Bergkamp [35], Overmars [45], Anelka [83], Parlour [87]	26,042
25	17	A	Manchester U	D 1-1	1-0	—	Anelka [47]	55,171
26	20	H	Leicester C	W 5-0	4-0	3	Anelka 3 [23, 27, 44], Parlour 2 [42, 48]	38,069
27	28	A	Newcastle U	D 1-1	1-0	3	Anelka [36]	36,708
28	Mar 9	H	Sheffield W	W 3-0	0-0	—	Bergkamp 2 [83, 88], Kanu [86]	37,792
29	13	A	Everton	W 2-0	1-0	2	Parlour [16], Bergkamp (pen) [69]	38,049
30	20	H	Coventry C	W 2-0	1-0	2	Parlour [16], Overmars [80]	38,074
31	Apr 3	A	Southampton	D 0-0	0-0	2		15,255
32	6	H	Blackburn R	W 1-0	1-0	—	Bergkamp [42]	37,762
33	19	H	Wimbledon	W 5-1	1-0	—	Parlour [34], Vieira [49], Thatcher (og) [56], Bergkamp [57], Kanu [59]	37,982
34	24	A	Middlesbrough	W 6-1	3-0	1	Overmars (pen) [4], Anelka 2 [38, 78], Kanu 2 [45, 60], Vieira [58]	34,630
35	May 2	H	Derby Co	W 1-0	1-0	1	Anelka [14]	37,323
36	5	A	Tottenham H	W 3-1	2-1	—	Petit [17], Anelka [33], Kanu [85]	36,019
37	11	A	Leeds U	L 0-1	0-0	—		40,124
38	16	H	Aston Villa	W 1-0	0-0	2	Kanu [66]	38,308

Final League Position: 2

GOALSCORERS

League (59): Anelka 17, Bergkamp 12 (2 pens), Kanu 6, Overmars 6 (2 pens), Parlour 6, Petit 4, Vieira 3, Adams 1, Hughes 1, Keown 1, Ljungberg 1, own goal 1.
Worthington Cup (2): Vivas 1, own goal 1.
FA Cup (10): Bergkamp 3, Overmars 3, Petit 2, Boa Morte 1, Kanu 1.

Seaman D 32	Dixon L 36	Winterburn N 30	Vieira P 34	Keown M 34	Adams T 26	Parlour R 35	Anelka N 34 + 1	Petit E 26 + 1	Bergkamp D 28 + 1	Overmars M 37	Bould S 14 + 5	Vivas N 10 + 13	Hughes S 4 + 10	Wreh C 3 + 9	Garde R 6 + 4	Ljungberg F 10 + 6	Manninger A 6	Mendez A — + 1	Boa Morte L 2 + 6	Grimandi G 3 + 5	Caballero F — + 1	Grondin D 1	Upson M — + 5	Diawara K 2 + 10	Kanu N 5 + 7	Match No.
1	2	3	4	5	6	7	8	9	10	11																1
1	2	3	4	5		7	8[1]	9	10	11	6	12														2
1	2[1]	3	4[2]	5	6	7	8[3]	9	10	11	12	13	14													3
1	2	3	4	5	6	7	8[1]	9	10[2]	11[3]	12	13	14													4
1	2[3]	3	4[2]	5		7	12		10	11	6	14	9	8[1]	13											5
1	2	3	4	5	6	7	8[1]		10	11	9		12													6
		3	4	5	6	7[3]	8	9[2]	10	11[1]	12	2	13			14	1									7
1	2	3	4	5[1]	6		8	9[2]	10	11	12	13			7[3]	14										8
1	2	3	4	5	6	7[1]	8		10	11	9	12														9
1	2	3	4	5			8	9	10	11	6		7													10
1	2	3	4	5		7	8	9		11[1]	6	12	10[2]			13										11
1	2	3	4	5		7	8	9		11			10			6										12
1	2	3	4	5	6	7	8[2]	9		11		12	10[1]			13										13
1	2	3	4[1]	5	6	7	8	9	10[2]	11[3]	12	13	14													14
1	2	3[2]		5		7	8			11	6	13	9[1]	4	10[3]	12	14									15
1	2			5		7	8		11		6	3	9[1]	4[2]	13	10			12							16
1	2		4	5		7[1]	9		10	11	6	3		8[2]		12			13							17
	2			4	5			8	9	10	11[1]	6	3		7[2]	1			13							18
	2			4	5		8[1]	9	10	11	12[2]					1			13							19
	2	3[1]	4	5		7			9	10[2]	11	6	12	13			1		8[3]	14						20
	2		4	5		7	8[1]	9		11[2]	6[3]		12	13		1			10			3	14			21
	2	3		5	6	7	8[2]	9	10	11[1]		12			4	1				13						22
1	2	3		5	6	7	8[1]	9	10[2]	11[3]		12			4					13	14					23
1	2	3	4	5	6	7	8	9	10	11																24
1	2	3[1]	4		6	7	8			11[3]	5	12	9		13								14	10[2]		25
1	2		4[1]		6	7	8[2]		10	11[3]	3	12	9						5				13	14		26
1	2	3	4	5	6	7	8		10	11[2]		12			9[1]								13			27
1	2		4	5	6	7[1]	8[3]	12	10	11		3				9[2]							13	14		28
1	2	3	4	5	6	7	8[1]	9	10	11[2]		12										13				29
1	2[1]	3	4	5	6	7	8[3]	9	10	11[2]						12							13	14		30
1	2	3	4	5[1]	6	7	8			12	13					10[3]			14					9[2]	11	31
1	2	3	4	5	6	7			10	11[1]	12	8											9[2]	13		32
1		3	4	5[1]	6	7			9	10[2]	11	12	2										13	8		33
1	2	3	4		6	7	8	9[1]		11[3]	5	13	12										14	10[2]		34
1	2	3	4		6	7	8[3]	9	12	11[1]	5		13										14	10[1]		35
1	2	3	4	5	6	7[1]	8	9	10[2]	11[3]	12											14		13		36
1	2	3[1]	4	5	6	7[2]	8	9	10	11[3]	12												13	14		37
1	2		4	5	6	7	8[3]	9	10	11[2]				3[1]						12			13	14		38

Worthington Cup

Third Round	Derby Co	(a)	2-1
Fourth Round	Chelsea	(h)	0-5

FA Cup

Third Round	Preston NE	(a)	4-2
Fourth Round	Wolverhampton W	(a)	2-1
Fifth Round	Sheffield U	(h)	2-1
Sixth Round	Derby Co	(h)	1-0
Semi-Final	Manchester U (at Villa Park)		0-0
Replay	(at Villa Park)		1-2

FA Premiership

ASTON VILLA

FOUNDATION

Cricketing enthusiasts of Villa Cross Wesleyan Chapel, Aston, Birmingham decided to form a football club during the winter of 1874–75. Football clubs were few and far between in the Birmingham area and in their first game against Aston Brook St Mary's Rugby team they played one half rugby and the other soccer. In 1876 they were joined by a Scottish soccer enthusiast George Ramsay who was immediately appointed captain and went on to lead Aston Villa from obscurity to one of the country's top clubs in a period of less than 10 years.

Villa Park, Trinity Rd, Birmingham B6 6HE.
Telephone: (0121) 327 2299. *Fax:* (0121) 322 2107. *Commercial Dept:* (0121) 327 5399.
Commercial Fax: (0121) 328 2099. *Clubcall:* 09068 121148. *Ticketline:* 09068 121848.
Ticket Information: (0121) 327 5353. *Club Shop:* (0121) 327 2800.
Ground Capacity: 39,217.
Record Attendance: 76,588 v Derby Co, FA Cup 6th rd, 2 March 1946.
Record Receipts: £1,196,712 Portugal v Czech Republic, Euro '96, 23 June 1996.
Pitch Measurements: 115yd × 72yd.
President: J. A. Alderson.
Chairman: H. D. Ellis.
Directors: S. M. Stride, M. J. Ansell, D. M. Owen, A. Hales.
Manager: John Gregory.
First Team Coach: Steve Harrison.
Coaches: Kevin MacDonald, Gordon Cowans.
Physio: Jim Walker.
Reserve Team Manager: Malcolm Beard.
Chief Scout: Ross MacLaren.
Fitness Consultant: Paul Barron.
Youth Development Officer: Alan Miller.
Secretary: Steven Stride.
Commercial Manager: Abdul Rashid.
Stadium Manager: Tony Diffley.
Football Academy Director: Bryan Jones.
Assistant Academy Director: Steve Burns.

LATEST SEQUENCES
Longest Sequence of League Wins: 9, 15.10.10 – 10.12.10.
Longest Sequence of League Defeats: 11, 23.3.63 – 4.5.63.
Longest Sequence of League Draws: 6, 12.9.81 – 10.10.81.
Longest Sequence of Unbeaten League Matches: 15, 12.3.49 – 27.8.49.
Longest Sequence Without a League Win: 12, 27.12.86 – 25.3.87.

HONOURS

FA Premier League: Runners-up 1992–93.

Football League: Division 1 – Champions 1893–94, 1895–96, 1896–97, 1898–99, 1899–1900, 1909–10, 1980–81; Runners-up 1888–89, 1902–03, 1907–08, 1910–11, 1912–13, 1913–14, 1930–31, 1932–33, 1989–90; Division 2 – Champions 1937–38, 1959–60; Runners-up 1974–75, 1987–88; Division 3 – Champions 1971–72.

FA Cup: Winners 1887, 1895, 1897, 1905, 1913, 1920, 1957; Runners-up 1892, 1924.

Double Performed: 1896–97.

Football League Cup: Winners 1961, 1975, 1977, 1994, 1996; Runners-up 1963, 1971.

European Competitions: European Cup: 1981–82 (winners), 1982–83. UEFA Cup: 1975–76, 1977–78, 1983–84, 1990–91, 1993–94, 1994–95, 1996–97, 1997–98, 1998–99. World Club Championship: 1982. European Super Cup: 1982–83 (winners).

Colours
Claret and blue broad striped shirts, claret shorts, claret stockings with blue trim.

Change Colours
White shirt, claret and blue collar and claret and blue diagonal stripe, white shorts with claret and blue trim, white stockings with claret and blue trim.

Year Formed: 1874.

Turned Professional: 1885.

Ltd Co.: 1896.

Club Nickname: 'The Villans'.

Previous Grounds: 1874 Wilson Road and Aston Park (also used Aston Lower Grounds for some matches); 1876 Wellington Road, Perry Barr; 1897 Villa Park.

First Football League Game: 8 September 1888, Football League, v Wolverhampton W (a) D 1–1 – Warner; Cox, Coulton; Yates, H. Devey, Dawson; A. Brown, Green (1), Allen, Garvey, Hodgetts.

Record League Victory: 12–2 v Accrington S, Division 1, 12 March 1892 – Warner; Evans, Cox; Harry Devey, Jimmy Cowan, Baird; Athersmith (1), Dickson (2), John Devey (4), L. Campbell (4), Hodgetts (1).

Record Cup Victory: 13–0 v Wednesbury Old Ath, FA Cup 1st rd, 30 October 1886 – Warner; Coulton, Simmonds; Yates, Robertson, Burton (2); R. Davis (1), A. Brown (3), Hunter (3), Loach (2), Hodgetts (2).

Record Defeat: 1–8 v Blackburn R, FA Cup 3rd rd, 16 February 1889.

Most League Points (2 for a win): 70, Division 3, 1971–72.

Most League Points (3 for a win): 78, Division 2, 1987–88.

Most League Goals: 128, Division 1, 1930–31.

Highest League Scorer in Season: 'Pongo' Waring, 49, Division 1, 1930–31.

Most League Goals in Total Aggregate: Harry Hampton, 215, 1904–15.

Most League Goals in One Match: 5, Harry Hampton v Sheffield W, Division 1, 5 October 1912; 5, Harold Halse v Derby Co, Division 1, 19 October 1912; 5, Len Capewell v Burnley, Division 1, 29 August 1925; 5, George Brown v Leicester C, Division 1, 2 January 1932; 5, Gerry Hitchens v Charlton Ath, Division 2, 18 November 1959.

Most Capped Player: Paul McGrath, 51 (83), Republic of Ireland.

Most League Appearances: Charlie Aitken, 561, 1961–76.

Youngest League Player: Jimmy Brown, 15 years 349 days v Bolton W, 17 September 1969.

Record Transfer Fee Received: £12,600,000 from Manchester U for Dwight Yorke, August 1998.

Record Transfer Fee Paid: £7,000,000 to Liverpool for Stan Collymore, May 1997.

Football League Record: 1888 Founder Member of the League; 1936–38 Division 2; 1938–59 Division 1; 1959–60 Division 2; 1960–67 Division 1; 1967–70 Division 2; 1970–72 Division 3; 1972–75 Division 2; 1975–87 Division 1; 1987–88 Division 2; 1988–92 Division 1; 1992– FA Premier League.

MANAGERS

George Ramsay 1884–1926
(Secretary-Manager)
W. J. Smith 1926–34
(Secretary-Manager)
Jimmy McMullan 1934–35
Jimmy Hogan 1936–44
Alex Massie 1945–50
George Martin 1950–53
Eric Houghton 1953–58
Joe Mercer 1958–64
Dick Taylor 1964–67
Tommy Cummings 1967–68
Tommy Docherty 1968–70
Vic Crowe 1970–74
Ron Saunders 1974–82
Tony Barton 1982–84
Graham Turner 1984–86
Billy McNeill 1986–87
Graham Taylor 1987–90
Dr Jozef Venglos 1990–91
Ron Atkinson 1991–94
Brian Little 1994–1998
John Gregory February 1998–

TEN YEAR LEAGUE RECORD

		P	W	D	L	F	A	Pts	Pos
1988-89	Div 1	38	9	13	16	45	56	40	17
1989-90	Div 1	38	21	7	10	57	38	70	2
1990-91	Div 1	38	9	14	15	46	58	41	17
1991-92	Div 1	42	17	9	16	48	44	60	7
1992-93	PR Lge	42	21	11	10	57	40	74	2
1993-94	PR Lge	42	15	12	15	46	50	57	10
1994-95	PR Lge	42	11	15	16	51	56	48	18
1995-96	PR Lge	38	18	9	11	52	35	63	4
1996-97	PR Lge	38	17	10	11	47	34	61	5
1997-98	PR Lge	38	17	6	15	49	48	57	7

DID YOU KNOW ?

On 20 October 1998 Aston Villa fielded a team in the UEFA Cup second round first leg at Celta Vigo which consisted entirely of players born in England. They won 1–0 with a goal from Julian Joachim.

ASTON VILLA 1998–99 LEAGUE RECORD

Match No.	Date	Venue	Opponents	Result	H/T Score	Lg. Pos.	Goalscorers	Attendance
1	Aug 15	A	Everton	D	0-0	0-0	—		40,112
2	23	H	Middlesbrough	W	3-1	1-0	3	Joachim [6], Charles [52], Thompson [78]	29,559
3	29	A	Sheffield W	W	1-0	1-0	2	Joachim [37]	25,989
4	Sept 9	H	Newcastle U	W	1-0	0-0	—	Hendrie (pen) [63]	39,241
5	12	H	Wimbledon	W	2-0	1-0	1	Merson [45], Taylor [57]	32,959
6	19	A	Leeds U	D	0-0	0-0	1		33,162
7	26	H	Derby Co	W	1-0	1-0	1	Merson [15]	38,007
8	Oct 3	A	Coventry C	W	2-1	2-0	1	Taylor 2 [29, 39]	22,650
9	17	A	West Ham U	D	0-0	0-0	1		26,002
10	24	H	Leicester C	D	1-1	0-1	1	Ehiogu [68]	39,241
11	Nov 7	H	Tottenham H	W	3-2	2-0	1	Dublin 2 [31, 35], Collymore [48]	39,241
12	14	A	Southampton	W	4-1	1-0	1	Dublin 3 [3, 56, 85], Merson [77]	15,242
13	21	H	Liverpool	L	2-4	0-2	1	Dublin 2 [47, 63]	39,241
14	28	A	Nottingham F	D	2-2	0-2	1	Joachim 2 [58, 63]	25,753
15	Dec 5	H	Manchester U	D	1-1	0-0	1	Joachim [55]	39,241
16	9	A	Chelsea	L	1-2	1-1	—	Hendrie [32]	34,765
17	13	H	Arsenal	W	3-2	0-2	1	Joachim [62], Dublin 2 [65, 83]	39,217
18	21	A	Charlton Ath	W	1-0	1-0	—	Rufus (og) [3]	20,043
19	26	A	Blackburn R	L	1-2	0-1	2	Scimeca [81]	27,536
20	28	H	Sheffield W	W	2-1	1-1	1	Southgate [7], Ehiogu [85]	39,217
21	Jan 9	A	Middlesbrough	D	0-0	0-0	2		34,643
22	18	H	Everton	W	3-0	1-0	—	Joachim 2 [40, 51], Merson [78]	32,488
23	30	A	Newcastle U	L	1-2	0-2	3	Merson [61]	36,766
24	Feb 6	H	Blackburn R	L	1-3	0-1	4	Joachim [69]	37,404
25	17	A	Leeds U	L	1-2	0-2	—	Scimeca [76]	37,510
26	21	A	Wimbledon	D	0-0	0-0	4		15,582
27	27	H	Coventry C	L	1-4	0-1	4	Dublin (pen) [55]	38,799
28	Mar 10	A	Derby Co	L	1-2	1-2	—	Thompson [44]	26,836
29	13	A	Tottenham H	L	0-1	0-0	5		35,963
30	21	H	Chelsea	L	0-3	0-0	6		39,217
31	Apr 2	H	West Ham U	D	0-0	0-0	—		36,813
32	6	A	Leicester C	D	2-2	1-0	—	Hendrie [2], Joachim [49]	20,652
33	10	H	Southampton	W	3-0	1-0	5	Draper [13], Joachim [66], Dublin [89]	32,203
34	17	A	Liverpool	W	1-0	1-0	5	Taylor [33]	44,306
35	24	H	Nottingham F	W	2-0	1-0	5	Draper [45], Barry [57]	34,492
36	May 1	A	Manchester U	L	1-2	1-1	5	Joachim [33]	55,189
37	8	H	Charlton Ath	L	3-4	1-1	5	Barry [7], Joachim 2 [66, 79]	37,705
38	16	A	Arsenal	L	0-1	0-0	6		38,308

Final League Position: 6

GOALSCORERS

League (51): Joachim 14, Dublin 11 (1 pen), Merson 5, Taylor 4, Hendrie 3 (1 pen), Barry 2, Draper 2, Ehiogu 2, Scimeca 2, Thompson 2, Charles 1, Collymore 1, Southgate 1, own goal 1.
Worthington Cup (1): Draper 1.
FA Cup (3): Collymore 2, Joachim 1.

Bosnich M 15	Charles G 10 + 1	Wright A 38	Southgate G 38	Scimeca R 16 + 2	Barry G 27 + 5	Taylor I 31 + 2	Hendrie L 31 + 1	Joachim J 29 + 7	Yorke D 1	Thompson A 20 + 5	Draper M 13 + 10	Ehiogu U 23 + 2	Grayson S 4 + 11	Vassell D — + 6	Collymore S 11 + 9	Merson P 21 + 5	Oakes M 23	Watson S 26 + 1	Dubin D 24	Rachel A — + 1	Stone S 9 + 1	Calderwood C 8	Delaney M — + 2	Match No.
1	2	3	4	5	6	7	8	9	10	11[1]	12													1
1	2	3	4	10[2]	6	7	8[1]	9[3]		11	12	5	13	14										2
1	2	3	4	6		8		9		11	7[1]	5	12		10									3
1	2	3	4	10[1]	6	12	8	9		11[2]	7[1]	5	13	14										4
1	2	3	4	12	6	7[2]	8	9		11[3]	13	5		14		10[1]								5
1	2	3	4		6	7	8	9		11[1]	12	5	13		10									6
1	2[2]	3	4		6	7	8	9		11[1]	12	5	13	14	10									7
1	2[2]	3	4		6	7	8	12		11		5	13		9	10[1]								8
1	2[2]	3	4		6	7	8	12		11		5			9	10[1]								9
	2	3	4		6	7	8			11		5			9	10	1							10
		3	4		6	7	8	12		11		5				10	1	2	9[1]					11
		3	4		6	7	8	12		11		5				10	1	2	9					12
		3	4		6	7	8	12		11[2]	13	5				10[1]	1	2	9					13
12		3[2]	4		6	7[3]	8			11		5	13	14		10	1	2[1]	9					14
		3	4		6	7	8			11	12	5				10[1]	1	2	9					15
		3	4		6	7	8			11		5			10		1	2	9					16
		3	4		6	7	8			11	12	5				10[1]	1	2	9					17
		3	4		6[2]	7	8			11	12	5	13			10[1]	1	2	9					18
		3	4	12	6	7[2]	8			11		5				10[1]	1	2	9					19
		3	4	11[2]	6	7[1]	8					5	13			10	1	2	9					20
		3	4	10[1]	6	7	8			11	12	5					1	2	9					21
		3	4	11	6	7[3]	8[1]				12	5	13	14		10	1	2	9[2]					22
		3	4	11	6	7	8	9			12	5[1]	13			10	1	2[2]						23
		3	4	5	6[1]	7	8			11	12					10	1	2	9					24
		3	4	5	6[1]	7	8			11	12	13				10	1	2	9[2]					25
		3	4	5	6	7	8			11[1]	12					10	1	2	9					26
		3	4	5	6	7[2]	8			11	12		13[3]	14		10	1	2[1]	9					27
		3	4	2[1]	6	7	8			11					9	10	1					5		28
1		3	4	5	6	7	8			11	12					10[1]		2	9			5		29
1		3	4	5	6	8[1]	12			13		10[2]	14					2	9[3]	7		5		30
1		3	4		7		10	11[1]		8	12							2[1]	9		6	5		31
1		3	4	12	7	11	10			8								2[1]	9		6	5		32
1		3	4	12	7	13	10	8[3]					14					2	9[1]		6	5		33
1		3	4	12	7	11[2]	10[1]	8			13							2	9		6	5		34
		3	4	12	7		11	8		13						10	1	2[2]	9[1]		6[3]	5	14	35
		3	4	12	7		11	8[1]		13						10	1	2	9[2]		6	5		36
		3	4	11	7		9	8[2]		12	13					10	1	2			6	5[1]		37
		3	4	11			9	7		5	8[1]	12				10	1	2[3]			13	6[2]	14	38

Worthington Cup
Third Round　　Chelsea　　(a)　1-4

FA Cup
Third Round　　Hull C　　(h)　3-0
Fourth Round　　Fulham　　(h)　0-2

Division 3

BARNET

Underhill Stadium, Barnet Lane, Barnet, Herts EN5 2BE.

Telephone: (0181) 441 6932.

Fax: (0181) 447 0655.

Ticket Office: (0181) 449 6325.

Clubcall: 0891 121544.

Ground Capacity: 4057.

Record Attendance: 11,026 v Wycombe Wanderers. FA Amateur Cup 4th Round 1951–52.

Record Receipts: £31,202 v Portsmouth, FA Cup 3rd Round, 5 January 1991.

Pitch Measurements: 113yd × 72yd.

Chairman: A. Kleanthous.

Vice-Chairman: D. J. Buchler FCA.

Manager: John Still.

Coach: Lil Fuccillo.

Secretary: David Stanley.

LATEST SEQUENCES

Longest Sequence of League Wins: 5, 29.1.93 – 2.3.93.

Longest Sequence of League Defeats: 11, 8.5.93 – 2.10.93.

Longest Sequence of League Draws: 4, 22.1.94 – 12.2.94.

Longest Sequence of Unbeaten League Matches: 12, 5.12.92 – 2.3.93.

Longest Sequence Without a League Win: 14, 11.12.93 – 8.3.94.

HONOURS

Football League: Division 2 best season: 24th, 1993–94.

FA Amateur Cup: Winners 1946.

FA Trophy: Finalists 1972.

GM Vauxhall Conference: Winners 1990–91.

FA Cup: never past 3rd rd.

League Cup: never past 2nd rd.

Colours
Amber shirts with black trim, black shorts, black stockings.

Change Colours
All white with orange trim.

Year Formed: 1888.

Turned Professional: 1965.

Previous Names: 1906, Barnet Alston FC; 1919 Barnet.

Club Nickname: The Bees.

Previous Grounds: 1888, Queens Road; 1901, Totteridge Lane, 1907 Barnet Lane.

First Football League Game: 17 August 1991, Division 4, v Crewe Alex (h) L 4–7 – Phillips; Blackford, Cooper (Murphy), Horton, Bodley (Stein), Johnson, Showler, Carter (2), Bull (2), Lowe, Evans.

Record League Victory: 6–0 v Lincoln C (a), Division 4, 4 September 1991 – Pape; Poole, Naylor, Bodley, Howell, Evans (1), Willis (1), Murphy (1), Bull (2), Lowe, Showler, (1 og).

Record Cup Victory: 6–1 v Newport Co, FA Cup 1st rd, 21 November 1970 – McClelland; Lye, Jenkins, Ward, Embery, King, Powell (1), Ferry, Adams (1), Gray, George (3), (1 og).

Record Defeat: 1–9 v Peterborough U, Division 3, 5 September 1998.

Most League Points (3 for a win): 79, Division 3, 1992–93.

Most League Goals: 81, Division 4, 1991–92.

Highest League Scorer in Season: Dougie Freedman, 24, Division 3, 1994–95.

Most League Goals in Total Aggregate: Sean Devine, 47, 1995–99.

Most League Goals in One Match: 4, Dougie Freedman v Rochdale, Division 3, 13 September 1994; 4, Lee Hodges v Rochdale, Division 3, 8 April 1996.

Most Capped Player: None

Most League Appearances: Paul Wilson, 244, 1991–99.

Youngest League Player: Kieran Adams, 17 years 71 days v Mansfield T, 31 December 1994.

Record Transfer Fee Received: £800,000 from Crystal Palace for Dougie Freedman, September 1995.

Record Transfer Fee Paid: £130,000 to Peterborough U for Greg Heald, August 1997.

Football League Record: Promoted to Division 4 from GMVC 1991; 1991–92 Division 4; 1992–93 Division 3; 1993–94 Division 2; 1994– Division 3.

MANAGERS

Lester Finch
George Wheeler
Dexter Adams
Tommy Coleman
Gerry Ward
Gordon Ferry
Brian Kelly
Bill Meadows
Barry Fry
Roger Thompson
Don McAllister
Barry Fry
Edwin Stein
Gary Phillips *(Player-Manager)* 1993–94
Ray Clemence 1994–96
Alan Mullery *(Director of Football)* 1996–97
Terry Bullivant 1997
John Still June 1997–

TEN YEAR LEAGUE RECORD

		P	W	D	L	F	A	Pts	Pos
1988-89	Conf	40	18	7	15	64	69	61	8
1989-90	Conf	42	26	7	9	81	41	85	2
1990-91	Conf	42	26	9	7	103	52	87	1
1991-92	Div 4	42	21	6	15	81	61	69	7
1992-93	Div 3	42	23	10	9	66	48	79	3
1993-94	Div 2	46	5	13	28	41	86	28	24
1994-95	Div 3	42	15	11	16	56	63	56	11
1995-96	Div 3	46	18	16	12	65	45	70	9
1996-97	Div 3	46	14	16	16	46	51	58	15
1997-98	Div 3	46	19	13	14	61	51	70	7

DID YOU KNOW ?

Outside-left Lester Finch made 476 appearances for Barnet and scored 226 between 1928 and 1953. He won 24 England amateur international caps and appeared in one full wartime game in 1941.

BARNET 1998–99 LEAGUE RECORD

Match No.	Date	Venue	Opponents	Result	H/T Score	Lg. Pos.	Goalscorers	Attendance
1	Aug 8	A	Darlington	W 2-0	0-0	—	Currie [70], McGleish [81]	4200
2	15	H	Hartlepool U	L 0-2	0-1	13		2049
3	22	A	Plymouth Arg	L 0-2	0-1	17		5080
4	29	H	Brentford	L 0-3	0-1	24		2710
5	31	A	Shrewsbury T	W 2-0	0-0	13	Manuel [69], Charlery [88]	2369
6	Sept 5	H	Peterborough U	L 1-9	1-4	20	Bodley (og) [28]	2330
7	8	A	Cardiff C	L 0-1	0-0	—		3742
8	12	H	Hull C	W 4-1	2-1	18	Currie [13], Charlery [45], McGleish 2 [78, 88]	2025
9	19	A	Exeter C	L 0-1	0-0	20		2523
10	26	H	Rotherham U	W 4-2	3-0	17	McGleish [19], Charlery [40], Doolan [45], Devine [86]	1989
11	Oct 3	A	Carlisle U	L 1-2	1-0	19	Charlery [37]	2834
12	11	H	Chester C	D 0-0	0-0	20		2236
13	16	A	Halifax T	D 1-1	0-1	—	Charlery [90]	2223
14	21	A	Scarborough	D 0-0	0-0	—		1056
15	24	H	Brighton & HA	L 0-1	0-0	22		2299
16	31	H	Rochdale	L 0-1	0-0	23		1413
17	Nov 7	A	Cambridge U	L 2-3	1-2	23	Charlery 2 [42, 89]	3832
18	10	H	Scunthorpe U	W 1-0	0-0	—	Goodhind [82]	1314
19	20	A	Mansfield T	L 0-5	0-3	—		2965
20	28	H	Torquay U	W 3-1	1-0	20	Alsford [44], McGleish [59], Ford [83]	1665
21	Dec 12	A	Southend U	W 3-2	2-1	19	Charlery 2 [18, 45], King [89]	4311
22	19	H	Leyton Orient	W 3-2	1-0	17	Wilson (pen) [31], Basham [86], Charlery [89]	3129
23	26	A	Plymouth Arg	D 1-1	0-1	17	Currie [58]	2519
24	28	A	Swansea C	L 1-2	0-2	17	Arber [74]	6514
25	Jan 2	A	Brentford	L 1-3	0-2	19	Charlery [88]	6011
26	9	H	Darlington	W 3-0	1-0	18	Searle [7], Charlery [46], Wilson (pen) [60]	1723
27	16	A	Hartlepool U	D 2-2	0-1	18	Arber [75], King [85]	2233
28	23	A	Shrewsbury T	D 2-2	1-1	18	King [16], Currie [68]	2029
29	30	H	Swansea C	L 0-1	0-0	18		2259
30	Feb 6	A	Peterborough U	L 2-5	2-1	21	Charlery [4], King [34]	4668
31	13	H	Cardiff C	W 1-0	0-0	18	Searle [70]	2234
32	20	A	Hull C	D 1-1	1-1	19	Heald [4]	6823
33	27	H	Exeter C	L 0-1	0-0	19		2072
34	Mar 9	H	Carlisle U	W 1-0	1-0	—	Charlery [34]	1428
35	13	H	Cambridge U	W 3-0	1-0	17	King [9], McGleish [78], Onwere [89]	2748
36	20	A	Rochdale	D 0-0	0-0	17		1502
37	27	A	Brighton & HA	W 1-0	0-0	16	McGleish [74]	2384
38	Apr 3	H	Halifax T	D 2-2	1-1	15	Charlery [35], Onwere [54]	2055
39	5	A	Chester C	L 0-3	0-2	15		2122
40	10	H	Scarborough	W 1-0	0-0	14	King [48]	1679
41	13	A	Torquay U	D 1-1	0-0	—	McGleish [73]	2132
42	17	H	Mansfield T	D 0-0	0-0	14		1861
43	24	A	Scunthorpe U	L 1-3	0-2	16	Charlery [72]	3930
44	27	A	Rotherham U	D 1-1	1-0	—	Heald [31]	3526
45	May 1	A	Southend U	L 0-2	0-0	15		2704
46	8	A	Leyton Orient	D 2-2	1-1	16	Doolan [22], Searle [47]	5808

Final League Position: 16

GOALSCORERS
League (54): Charlery 16, McGleish 8, King 6, Currie 4, Searle 3, Arber 2, Doolan 2, Heald 2, Onwere 2, Wilson 2 (2 pens), Alsford 1, Basham 1, Devine 1, Ford 1, Goodhind 1, Manuel 1, own goal 1.
Worthington Cup (2): Currie 1, McGleish 1.
FA Cup (1): Currie 1.

Harrison L 43	Stockley S 40 + 1	Sawyers R 21 + 1	Goodhind W 15	Ford J 15	Simpson P 11 + 2	Wilson P 31	Charlery K 40 + 2	Currie D 33 + 5	McGleish S 25 + 11	Onwere U 14 + 5	Manuel B 3 + 9	Doolan J 40 + 2	Devine S 10 + 10	Basham M 32	Harle M 11	Rust N 2	Searle S 33 + 2	Alsford J 9	Arber M 35	Barnes S 3 + 9	King M 17 + 5	Heald G 19	Dearden K 1	Hackett W 3 + 4	Gledhill L — + 1	Match No.
1	2	3	4	5	6	7¹	8	9	10	11	12															1
1	2	3¹	4	5	6	7²	8³	9	10	11	12	13	14													2
1	2		4	5		7		9	10	11				6	8	3										3
1	2		4			7¹	11	9	10			12		6	8	5	3									4
1	2²		4	5		8	11	12	14	10		13	7²	9¹	6	3										5
			4	5	7	11	9		12		2²	8	10¹	6	3	1	13									6
	2		4²	5	7	11¹	9	14	12		13	8³	10	6	3	1										7
1	2		4	5		9	11	12	13	14	8	10¹	6²	3			7³									8
1	2		4	5		9	11	10	4		8			3			7	5	6							9
1	2²	13	4			9	11	10¹			8	12		3			7	5	6							10
1		2¹	4			9	11	10²	12		8	13		6	3		7	5								11
1		4				9¹	11	10	13	3	8	12	5	2			7²		6							12
1	2	3¹		11		9		10			8	12	5				7	4	6							13
1		3	2	6		9	11				8	10	5				7	4								14
1	12	3¹	2	6		9	11				8	10	5				7²		4	13						15
1	2		3	12		9	11				13	8	10³	5			4²		6	7¹	14					16
1	2		3	7³		9	11	12			13	8	10¹	5²			4		6	14						17
1	2		4			7	9	11	10			8			3		5	6								18
1	2			7¹		9	11²	10		12	8			3			4	5	6	13						19
1	2		5			9	11	10			8						7	4	6	3						20
1	2		5	11	9		10¹	3			8						7	4	6	12						21
1	2		5	11¹	9	3	10				8		4				7		6	12						22
1	2		5	11¹	9	3	10				8		4				7		6	12						23
1	2	3	5	13	11¹	9	12	10³			8		4				7²		6	14						24
1	2	3¹	5	11	9		12				8		4				7		6	10						25
1	2		5	11	9	3¹	12				8		4				7		6	13	10¹					26
1	2		5	11	9	3	12				8¹		4				7		6	10						27
1	2			11	9¹	3	12	8					4				7		6	10	5					28
1	2	3		9	11	12	6¹	8	13		4						7			10²	5					29
	2	3		4¹	9	11		12	8	13							7		6	10²	5	1				30
1	2			11	9	3		8	12	4							7		6	10¹	5					31
1	2	3		11	9			8	12	4							7		6	10	5					32
1	2¹			11²	9	3		8	12	4							7		6	13	10	5				33
1	2	3		9			11	8	12	4							7²		6	13	10¹	5				34
1	2			11	9	7	12	13			8		4						6	3²	10¹	5				35
1	2	3		11	9		12	7			8		4						6		10¹	5				36
1	2¹	3²		11	9	12	10	7			8		4						6			5		13		37
1		3		11¹	9	7	10	2			8		4						6			5		12		38
1	2	3		9	11	10	7	8¹			4²						12		6			5		13		39
1	2			11			8	10	4								7		6	9		5		3		40
1	2	3²		11¹	12	13	10	8			14						7³		6	9	9	5		4		41
1	2	3		11¹		8	10				4						7		6	12	9	5				42
1	2			11	9	4¹	10				8						7		6	12		5		3		43
1	2	3		11	9		10				8		4				7		6			5				44
1	2¹	3		11	9	4					8						7		6	13	10²	5			12	45
1	2			11	9	3					8		4¹				7		6		10	5		12		46

Worthington Cup
First Round   Wolverhampton W   (h) 2-1
                                   (a) 0-5

FA Cup
First Round   Hednesford T   (a) 1-3

Division 1

BARNSLEY

Oakwell Stadium, Grove St, Barnsley, South Yorkshire S71 1ET.

Telephone: (01226) 211211.

Fax: (01226) 211444.

Website: barnsleyfc.co.uk.

Email: thereds@barnsleyfc.co.uk.

Clubcall: 09068 121152.

Ground Capacity: 23,000.

Record Attendance: 40,255 v Stoke C, FA Cup 5th rd, 15 February 1936.

Record Receipts: undisclosed.

Pitch Measurements: 110yd × 75yd.

Chairman: J. A. Dennis.

Directors: C. B. Taylor (Vice-Chairman), M. Hanson, C. H. Harrison, M. R. Hayselden, J. N. Kelly, I. D. Potter.

Manager: Dave Bassett.

Assistant Manager: Peter Shirtliff.

First Team Coach: Eric Winstanley.

Physios: Michael Tarmey, Nigel Cox.

General Manager/Secretary: Michael Spinks.

Lotteries Manager: Gerry Whewall.

Sales and Marketing Manager: Graham Barlow.

HONOURS

Football League: Division 1 – Runners-up 1996–97; Division 3 (N) – Champions 1933–34, 1938–39, 1954–55; Runners-up 1953–54; Division 3 – Runners-up 1980–81; Division 4 – Runners-up 1967–68; Promoted 1978–79.

FA Cup: Winners 1912; Runners-up 1910.

Football League Cup: best season: 5th rd, 1982.

LATEST SEQUENCES

Longest Sequence of League Wins: 10, 5.3.55 – 23.4.55.

Longest Sequence of League Defeats: 9, 14.3.53 – 25.4.53.

Longest Sequence of League Draws: 7, 28.3.11 – 22.4.11.

Longest Sequence of Unbeaten League Matches: 21, 1.1.34 – 5.5.34.

Longest Sequence Without a League Win: 26, 13.12.52 – 26.8.53.

Colours
Red shirts, white shorts, red stockings.

Change Colours
Royal blue and black striped shirts, black shorts, black stockings.

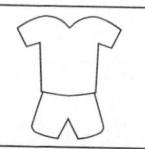

Year Formed: 1887.

Turned Professional: 1888.

Ltd Co.: 1899.

Previous Name: 1887, Barnsley St Peter's; 1897, Barnsley.

Club Nickname: 'The Tykes', 'Reds' or 'Colliers'.

First Football League Game: 1 September 1898, Division 2, v Lincoln C (a) L 0–1 – Fawcett; McArtney, Nixon; King, Burleigh, Porteous; Davis, Lees, Murray, McCullough, McGee.

Record League Victory: 9–0 v Loughborough T, Division 2, 28 January 1899 – Greaves; McArtney, Nixon; Porteous, Burleigh, Howard; Davis (4), Hepworth (1), Lees (1), McCullough (1), Jones (2). 9–0 v Accrington S, Division 3 (N), 3 February 1934 – Ellis; Cookson, Shotton; Harper, Henderson, Whitworth; Spence (2), Smith (1), Blight (4), Andrews (1), Ashton (1).

Record Cup Victory: 6–0 v Blackpool, FA Cup 1st rd replay, 20 January 1910 – Mearns; Downs, Ness; Glendinning, Boyle (1), Utley; Bartrop, Gadsby (1), Lillycrop (2), Tufnell (2), Forman. 6–0 v Peterborough U, League Cup 1st rd 2nd leg, 15 September 1981 – Horn; Joyce, Chambers, Glavin (2), Banks, McCarthy, Evans, Parker (2), Aylott (1), McHale, Barrowclough (1).

Record Defeat: 0–9 v Notts Co, Division 2, 19 November 1927.

Most League Points (2 for a win): 67, Division 3 (N), 1938–39.

Most League Points (3 for a win): 80, Division 1, 1996–97.

Most League Goals: 118, Division 3 (N), 1933–34.

Highest League Scorer in Season: Cecil McCormack, 33, Division 2, 1950–51.

Most League Goals in Total Aggregate: Ernest Hine, 123, 1921–26 and 1934–38.

Most League Goals in One Match: 5, Frank Eaton v South Shields, Division 3N, 9 April 1927; 5, Peter Cunningham v Darlington, Division 3N, 4 February 1933; 5, Beau Asquith v Darlington, Division 3N, 12 November 1938; 5, Cecil McCormack v Luton T, Division 2, 9 September 1950.

Most Capped Player: Gerry Taggart, 35 (45), Northern Ireland.

Most League Appearances: Barry Murphy, 514, 1962–78.

Youngest League Player: Glyn Riley, 16 years 171 days v Torquay U, 11 January 1975.

Record Transfer Fee Received: £4,250,000 from Blackburn R for Ashley Ward, December 1998.

Record Transfer Fee Paid: £1,500,000 to Partizan Belgrade for Georgi Hristov, June 1997.

Football League Record: 1898 Elected to Division 2; 1932–34 Division 3 (N); 1934–38 Division 2; 1938–39 Division 3 (N); 1946–53 Division 2; 1953–55 Division 3 (N); 1955–59 Division 2; 1959–65 Division 3; 1965–68 Division 4; 1968–72 Division 3; 1972–79 Division 4; 1979–81 Division 3; 1981–92 Division 2; 1992–97 Division 1; 1997–98 FA Premier League; 1998– Division 1.

MANAGERS

Arthur Fairclough 1898–1901
  (Secretary-Manager)
John McCartney 1901–04
  (Secretary-Manager)
Arthur Fairclough 1904–12
John Hastie 1912–14
Percy Lewis 1914–19
Peter Sant 1919–26
John Commins 1926–29
Arthur Fairclough 1929–30
Brough Fletcher 1930–37
Angus Seed 1937–53
Tim Ward 1953–60
Johnny Steele 1960–71
  (continued as General Manager)
John McSeveney 1971–72
Johnny Steele *(General Manager)*
  1972–73
Jim Iley 1973–78
Allan Clarke 1978–80
Norman Hunter 1980–84
Bobby Collins 1984–85
Allan Clarke 1985–89
Mel Machin 1989–93
Viv Anderson 1993–94
Danny Wilson 1994–98
John Hendrie 1998–99
Dave Bassett June 1999–

TEN YEAR LEAGUE RECORD

		P	W	D	L	F	A	Pts	Pos
1988-89	Div 2	46	20	14	12	66	58	74	7
1989-90	Div 2	46	13	15	18	49	71	54	19
1990-91	Div 2	46	19	12	15	63	48	69	8
1991-92	Div 2	46	16	11	19	46	57	59	16
1992-93	Div 1	46	17	9	20	56	60	60	13
1993-94	Div 1	46	16	7	23	55	67	55	18
1994-95	Div 1	46	20	12	14	63	52	72	6
1995-96	Div 1	46	14	18	14	60	66	60	10
1996-97	Div 1	46	22	14	10	76	55	80	2
1997-98	PR Lge	38	10	5	23	37	82	35	19

DID YOU KNOW ?

A weekly wage bill in 1909 for 23 Barnsley players, two trainers and three secretaries was £63. Dicky Downs on £4 was the highest paid player, who later won England international honours while with Everton.

BARNSLEY 1998–99 LEAGUE RECORD

Match No.	Date	Venue	Opponents	Result	H/T Score	Lg. Pos.	Goalscorers	Attendance
1	Aug 8	H	WBA	D 2-2	1-2	—	De Zeeuw 2 [22, 87]	18,114
2	15	A	Crewe Alex	L 1-3	0-1	15	McClare [54]	5289
3	21	H	Stockport Co	D 1-1	1-0	—	Fjortoft [24]	16,377
4	29	A	Birmingham C	D 0-0	0-0	17		19,825
5	31	H	Oxford U	W 1-0	1-0	15	Hendrie [43]	15,328
6	Sept 8	H	Norwich C	L 1-3	1-0	—	Ward [6]	15,695
7	12	A	Grimsby T	W 2-1	1-0	14	Ward 2 [16, 62]	8149
8	19	H	Crystal Palace	W 4-0	2-0	13	Ward 2 [7, 17], McClare [61], Fjortoft [71]	15,597
9	26	A	Bradford C	L 1-2	0-0	13	Ward [56]	15,887
10	29	A	Bristol C	D 1-1	0-0	—	Sheridan [73]	12,005
11	Oct 3	H	Bolton W	D 2-2	1-2	15	Ward [9], Van der Laan [85]	17,362
12	11	H	Port Vale	L 0-2	0-0	16		16,195
13	17	A	Sheffield U	D 1-1	1-0	18	Fjortoft [31]	23,180
14	20	A	Tranmere R	L 0-3	0-2	—		5194
15	24	H	Portsmouth	W 2-1	1-0	16	Ward [25], Barnard [59]	15,152
16	31	A	Wolverhampton W	D 1-1	0-1	16	Ward (pen) [52]	20,714
17	Nov 4	A	QPR	L 1-2	0-2	—	Bullock M [47]	8218
18	7	H	Bury	D 1-1	1-0	18	Ward [16]	15,115
19	14	H	Ipswich T	L 0-1	0-1	19		15,966
20	21	A	Sunderland	W 3-2	1-0	16	Ward [33], Dyer [46], Barnard (pen) [82]	40,231
21	27	H	Huddersfield T	W 7-1	6-0	—	Dyer 2 [10, 70], Hignett 2 [19, 26], Tinkler [28], Ward [37], Barnard [41]	16,648
22	Dec 5	A	Watford	D 0-0	0-0	13		10,165
23	12	A	Ipswich T	W 2-0	0-0	13	McClare [69], Turner [90]	16,021
24	19	A	Swindon T	L 1-3	0-3	13	Barnard (pen) [85]	15,342
25	26	A	Stockport Co	W 1-0	1-0	13	De Zeeuw [26]	10,263
26	28	H	QPR	W 1-0	0-0	13	Hignett [81]	17,083
27	Jan 9	A	WBA	L 0-2	0-0	13		15,029
28	16	A	Birmingham C	D 0-0	0-0	13		17,114
29	30	A	Oxford U	L 0-1	0-0	13		6174
30	Feb 6	H	Crewe Alex	D 2-2	0-1	13	Tinkler [72], De Zeeuw [75]	15,377
31	16	A	Norwich C	D 0-0	0-0	—		13,232
32	20	H	Grimsby T	D 0-0	0-0	13		16,343
33	28	A	Crystal Palace	L 0-1	0-1	15		17,021
34	Mar 3	H	Bradford C	L 0-1	0-0	—		16,866
35	9	A	Bolton W	D 3-3	2-2	—	Hignett 2 [34, 48], Jones [43]	16,537
36	13	A	Bury	D 0-0	0-0	17		4696
37	20	H	Wolverhampton W	L 2-3	2-1	17	Richards (og) [31], Jones [33]	16,587
38	23	H	Bristol C	W 2-0	1-0	—	Dyer [32], Hignett [88]	14,733
39	28	A	Portsmouth	W 3-1	0-1	15	Hignett [66], Whitbread (og) [70], Dyer [76]	13,337
40	Apr 3	H	Sheffield U	W 2-1	1-0	13	Hignett 2 [14, 90]	17,566
41	5	H	Port Vale	L 0-1	0-1	14		5968
42	10	H	Tranmere R	D 1-1	0-1	14	Dyer [54]	15,133
43	16	H	Sunderland	L 1-3	0-1	—	Sheron [86]	17,390
44	24	A	Huddersfield T	W 1-0	1-0	14	Sheron [20]	15,353
45	May 1	H	Watford	D 2-2	0-1	14	Eaden [64], Tinkler [89]	17,098
46	9	A	Swindon T	W 3-1	2-1	13	Jones [9], Bullock M [28], Dyer [75]	8182

Final League Position: 13

GOALSCORERS

League (59): Ward 12 (1 pen), Hignett 9, Dyer 7, Barnard 4 (2 pens), De Zeeuw 4, Fjortoft 3, Jones 3, McClare 3, Tinkler 3, Bullock M 2, Sheron 2, Eaden 1, Hendrie 1, Sheridan 1, Turner 1, Van der Laan 1, own goals 2.
Worthington Cup (10): Fjortoft 4, Ward 3 (1 pen), Barnard 1, Eaden 1, Van der Laan 1.
FA Cup (10): Hignett 5, Bullock M 2, Dyer 1, McClare 1, Sheridan 1.

Watson D 6	Eaden N 38 + 2	Jones S 28 + 1	Richardson K 24 + 2	Moses A 33 + 1	De Zeeuw A 38	Hendrie J 6 + 3	Van der Laan R 13 + 4	Hristov G 2 + 1	Liddell A 3 + 5	Barnard D 26	Bullock M 20 + 12	Fjortoft J 9 + 10	Morgan C 18 + 1	Ward A 17	McClare S 23 + 7	Sheridan D 15 + 10	Appleby M 33 + 1	Leese L 8	Marcelle C 2 + 7	Bullock T 32	Tinkler E 21 + 4	Dyer B 28	Moore A 4 + 1	Hignett C 24	Rose K 2 + 2	Bagshaw P — + 1	Burton D 3	Turner M 2 + 11	Goodman D 5 + 3	Markstedt P 2	Sheron M 14 + 1	Blackmore C 4 + 3	Krizan A 1	Pirri 2	Parkin J — + 2	Match No.
1	2	3	4	5	6	7^1	8	9^2	10	11	12	13																								1
1	2		4	5	6		8^1		7	10	11		12	3	9	13																				2
1	2		4	5	6	12	8^1		10	11	13			3	9^1	7^2	14																			3
1	2		4	5	6	12	8			11^2		10^1		3	9	13	7																			4
1	2		4	5		10^1	8^3			11		7^2	12	3	9	13	14	6																		5
1	2		4^1	5		7	8			11	12		10^2	3	9	13	6																			6
	2		4	5	3		8^2		10	11		7^1	12		9	13	6			1																7
	12		4	5	3		8^1		10	11		7^2			9		6		2	1	13															8
	12		4	5	3		8^2			11	13	7	10^1		9		6		2	1																9
	2	4^3			3		8		10		13	7^2	12	5	9		14	6^1		1																10
	2	6			3		8		10^2		13	12		5	9	8^1	4			1														7^2		11
	2	4			3		8		10^1	11	13	12		5	9	14	6^3			1														7^2		12
	2	4			3		8		10^1	5		11		7	9		6			1	12															13
		4	2		3		8		10^2	5^1		11		7	9	12	6			1	13															14
		4	2		3		8					11		7	12	9	6			1			5	10^1												15
		4	2		3		8					11		7	12	9	6			1			5	10^1	11											16
			2		3		8					11		7^1	12	9	6			1			5	10	4											17
		12			3	4	8		7		13			2	9	8^3	14		6^1	1			5	10^2	11											18
	4	12			3	13	8			11		7^1	9^2	2		5^3	8	6		1				10	14											19
	4				3		8			11				2	9	7				1			5	10^1	8^3											20
	4				6	3				11	12			2	9	7^2	13			1	14		5	10^1		8^3										21
	4				3					11				2		7				1	5			10		8	9^1	12	10							22
	2	4			3					11						7				1	5			10		8		9^1	12							23
	2	4	12		3					11						7^2			13	1	5^1	10				8		9^3	14							24
	2	11			3							4				7				1	5	10^1				8		12	9							25
	2				3							4				7				1	5	10^1				8		12	9							26
	2	12			3	4				11	13					7^2				1	5^1					8	10^3	14	9							27
	2	6	4		3	5				11^2	12					7^1	13			1						8	14	10^3	9							28
	2		4	3	5					10						7^1	11	6^2		13	1	12				8		14	9^3							29
	2					5									9	3				1	4	10^1				8	12	13			6^2					30
	2	8	4		3												6^2	7		1	5	11		9				10								31
	2	7	4^1		3			12				13				11^2	6			1	5	10		8			14				9^3					32
	2	6	4	5^1	3							13				7^3	12^2			1		10		8				14			9	11				33
	2	11			3			7				12		6						1	5	10		8				13	4^1		9^2					34
	2	11		4	3								6		7^1					1	5	10		8					12		9^2	13				35
	2	11		4	3	12							6		7^1					1	5	10^2		8							13	9				36
	2	11		4	3	7							6							1	5	10		8				12			9^1					37
	2	11		4	5	3				7^2	12						6			1		10^1		8							9	13				38
	2	11		4^2	5	3				7^1							6			1		10		8							9	13				39
	2	5	4								11					12	6			1	10			8				13			9^2	7		3^1		40
	2	11		4^1	5	3				7							6			1	12	10		8				13			9^2					41
	2	11		4	5	3				12						13	6^2			1		10		8				9						7^1		42
	2	6		4^1	5	3	12									11^3				1	14	10		8				9						7^2		43
		11		4	5	3				7		12	13				6			1	8^2	10^3						9	2^1				14			44
	2	3	4	5						7						11	6			1	12	10		8^1				9^2					13			45
	2	3	4		5					11	7					12	6			1		8^1	10					9								46

Worthington Cup

First Round	Scarborough	(a)	1-0
		(h)	3-0
Second Round	Reading	(h)	3-0
		(a)	1-1
Third Round	Bournemouth	(h)	2-1
Fourth Round	Luton T	(a)	0-1

FA Cup

Third Round	Swindon T	(a)	0-0
		(h)	3-1
Fourth Round	Bournemouth	(h)	3-1
Fifth Round	Bristol R	(h)	4-1
Sixth Round	Tottenham H	(h)	0-1

Division 1

BIRMINGHAM CITY

FOUNDATION

In 1875 cricketing enthusiasts who were largely members of Trinity Church, Bordesley, determined to continue their sporting relationships throughout the year by forming a football club which they called Small Heath Alliance. For their earliest games played on waste land in Arthur Street, the team included three Edden brothers and two James brothers.

St Andrews, Birmingham B9 4NH.

Telephone: 0709 111 25837.

Fax: (0121) 766 7866.

Website: www.bcfc.com.

Clubcall: 0891 121188.

Club Soccer Shop: 0709 111 25837 (ext. 8).

Ground Capacity: 30,009.

Record Attendance: 66,844 v Everton, FA Cup 5th rd, 11 February 1939.

Record Receipts: £230,000 v Aston Villa, Coca-Cola Cup 2nd rd 1st leg, 21 September 1993.

Pitch Measurements: 110yd × 74yd.

Chairman: D. Gold.

Vice-Chairman: J. F. Wiseman.

Directors: D. Sullivan, R. Gold, B. Gold, H. Brandman, A. G. Jones, M. Wiseman.

Managing Director: K. R. Brady.

Manager: Trevor Francis.

Coach: Mick Mills.

Physio: N. McDiarmid.

Commercial Manager: Simon Bradley.

Stadium Manager: Brian Tew.

Secretary: A. G. Jones BA, MBA.

LATEST SEQUENCES

Longest Sequence of League Wins: 13, 17.12.1892 – 16.9.1893.

Longest Sequence of League Defeats: 8, 28.9.85 – 23.11.85.

Longest Sequence of League Draws: 8, 18.9.90 – 23.10.90.

Longest Sequence of Unbeaten League Matches: 20, 3.9.94 – 2.1.95.

Longest Sequence Without a League Win: 17, 28.9.85 – 18.1.86.

HONOURS

Football League: Division 1 best season: 4th, 1998–99; Division 2 – Champions 1892–93, 1920–21, 1947–48, 1954–55, 1994–95; Runners-up 1893–94, 1900–01, 1902–03, 1971–72, 1984–85; Division 3 Runners-up 1991–92.

FA Cup: Runners-up 1931, 1956.

Football League Cup: Winners 1963.

Leyland Daf Cup: Winners 1991.

Auto Windscreens Shield: Winners 1995.

European Competitions: *European Fairs Cup:* 1955–58, 1958–60 (runners-up), 1960–61 (runners-up), 1961–62.

Colours

Blue shirts, blue shorts, blue and white stockings.

Change Colours

White shirts, shorts and stockings all with red trim.

Year Formed: 1875.

Turned Professional: 1885.

Ltd Co.: 1888.

Previous Names: 1875, Small Heath Alliance; 1888, dropped 'Alliance'; 1905, Birmingham; 1945, Birmingham City.

Club Nickname: 'Blues'.

Previous Grounds: 1875, waste ground near Arthur St; 1877, Muntz St, Small Heath; 1906, St Andrews.

First Football League game: 3 September 1892, Division 2, v Burslem Port Vale (h) W 5–1 – Charsley; Bayley, Speller; Ollis, Jenkyns, Devey; Hallam (1), Edwards (1), Short (1), Wheldon (2), Hands.

Record League Victory: 12–0 v Walsall T Swifts, Division 2, 17 December 1892 – Charsley; Bayley, Jones; Ollis, Jenkyns, Devey; Hallam (2), Walton (3), Mobley (3), Wheldon (2), Hands (2). 12–0 v Doncaster R, Division 2, 11 April 1903 – Dorrington; Goldie, Wassell; Beer, Dougherty (1), Howard; Athersmith (1), Leonard (3), McRoberts (1), Wilcox (4), Field (1). Aston, (1 og).

Record Cup Victory: 9–2 v Burton W, FA Cup 1st rd, 31 October 1885 – Hedges; Jones, Evetts (1); F. James, Felton, A. James (1); Davenport (2), Stanley (4), Simms, Figures, Morris (1).

Record Defeat: 1–9 v Sheffield W, Division 1, 13 December 1930. 1–9 v Blackburn R, Division 1, 5 January 1895.

Most League Points (2 for a win): 59, Division 2, 1947–48.

Most League Points (3 for a win): 89, Division 2, 1994–95.

Most League Goals: 103, Division 2, 1893–94 (only 28 games).

Highest League Scorer in Season: Joe Bradford, 29, Division 1, 1927–28.

Most League Goals in Total Aggregate: Joe Bradford, 249, 1920–35.

Most League Goals in One Match: 5, Walter Abbott v Darwen, Division 2, 26 November, 1898; 5, John McMillan v Blackpool, Division 2, 2 March 1901; 5, James Windridge v Glossop, Division 2, 23 January 1915.

Most Capped Player: Malcolm Page, 28, Wales.

Most League Appearances: Frank Womack, 491, 1908–28.

Youngest League Player: Trevor Francis, 16 years 7 months v Cardiff C, 5 September 1970.

Record Transfer Fee Received: £2,500,000 from Coventry C for Gary Breen, January 1997.

Record Transfer Fee Paid: £1,850,000 to Port Vale for Jon McCarthy, September 1997.

Football League Record: 1892 elected to Division 2; 1894–96 Division 1; 1896–1901 Division 2; 1901–02 Division 1; 1902–03 Division 2; 1903–08 Division 1; 1908–21 Division 2; 1921–39 Division 1; 1946–48 Division 2; 1948–50 Division 1; 1950–1955 Division 2; 1955–65 Division 1; 1965–72 Division 2; 1972–79 Division 1; 1979–80 Division 2; 1980–84 Division 1; 1984–85 Division 2; 1985–86 Division 1; 1986–89 Division 2; 1989–92 Division 3; 1992–94 Division 2; 1994–95 Division 2; 1995– Division 1.

MANAGERS

Alfred Jones 1892–1908
(Secretary-Manager)
Alec Watson 1908–10
Bob McRoberts 1910–15
Frank Richards 1915–23
Billy Beer 1923–27
Leslie Knighton 1928–33
George Liddell 1933–39
Harry Storer 1945–48
Bob Brocklebank 1949–54
Arthur Turner 1954–58
Pat Beasley 1959–60
Gil Merrick 1960–64
Joe Mallett 1965
Stan Cullis 1965–70
Fred Goodwin 1970–75
Willie Bell 1975–77
Jim Smith 1978–82
Ron Saunders 1982–86
John Bond 1986–87
Garry Pendrey 1987–89
Dave Mackay 1989–1991
Lou Macari 1991
Terry Cooper 1991–93
Barry Fry 1993–96
Trevor Francis May 1996–

TEN YEAR LEAGUE RECORD

		P	W	D	L	F	A	Pts	Pos
1988-89	Div 2	46	8	11	27	31	76	35	23
1989-90	Div 3	46	18	12	16	60	59	66	7
1990-91	Div 3	46	16	17	13	45	49	65	12
1991-92	Div 3	46	23	12	11	69	52	81	2
1992-93	Div 1	46	13	12	21	50	72	51	19
1993-94	Div 1	46	13	12	21	52	69	51	22
1994-95	Div 2	46	25	14	7	84	37	89	1
1995-96	Div 1	46	15	13	18	61	64	58	15
1996-97	Div 1	46	17	15	14	52	48	66	10
1997-98	Div 1	46	19	17	10	60	35	74	7

DID YOU KNOW ?

Jack Hall scored three hat-tricks for Birmingham in the Second Division during the 1911–12 season against Leeds City (when he actually hit four goals), Wolverhampton Wanderers and Clapton Orient.

BIRMINGHAM CITY 1998–99 LEAGUE RECORD

Match No.	Date	Venue	Opponents	Result	H/T Score	Lg. Pos.	Goalscorers	Attendance
1	Aug 8	A	Port Vale	W 2-0	1-0	—	Furlong [21], Adebola [68]	10,465
2	16	H	Crystal Palace	W 3-1	2-0	10	Adebola [12], O'Connor (pen) [29], Forster [90]	16,699
3	22	A	Sheffield U	W 2-0	0-0	2	Adebola [55], Forster [81]	17,528
4	29	H	Barnsley	D 0-0	0-0	4		19,825
5	31	A	Bradford C	L 1-2	0-0	5	Ndlovu [56]	13,910
6	Sept 5	H	Bury	W 1-0	0-0	3	Adebola [20]	15,935
7	8	H	Stockport Co	W 2-0	1-0	—	Marsden [15], Hughes [67]	16,429
8	12	A	Bolton W	L 1-3	1-2	2	Rowett [40]	19,637
9	19	H	Grimsby T	L 0-1	0-0	3		17,563
10	26	A	Norwich C	L 0-2	0-0	7		16,584
11	29	A	Portsmouth	W 1-0	0-0	—	O'Connor (pen) [59]	11,843
12	Oct 3	H	Tranmere R	D 2-2	1-1	4	Johnson M 2 [40, 72]	17,189
13	10	A	Watford	D 1-1	1-0	3	Adebola [22]	10,096
14	17	H	Crewe Alex	W 3-1	2-1	3	Ndlovu [8], O'Connor (pen) [43], Furlong [53]	20,087
15	20	A	Swindon T	D 1-1	0-0	—	Marsden [58]	19,485
16	25	A	QPR	W 1-0	1-0	2	Adebola [6]	10,272
17	31	H	Huddersfield T	D 1-1	0-0	2	Ndlovu [53]	19,170
18	Nov 7	A	WBA	W 3-1	3-0	3	Ndlovu 2 [5, 34], Adebola [12]	19,472
19	14	H	Oxford U	L 0-1	0-1	4		18,216
20	22	A	Wolverhampton W	L 1-3	1-0	8	Furlong [21]	23,037
21	28	H	Bristol C	W 4-2	3-2	4	Johnson M [5], Ndlovu [11], Forster 2 [42, 72]	17,577
22	Dec 5	A	Ipswich T	L 0-1	0-1	7		15,901
23	12	A	Oxford U	W 7-1	4-0	4	Rowett 2 [16, 31], Furlong 2 [17, 43], Grainger [55], Ndlovu [72], Hughes [89]	7189
24	19	H	Sunderland	D 0-0	0-0	7		22,095
25	26	H	Sheffield U	W 1-0	1-0	4	Furlong (pen) [20]	22,005
26	28	A	Bury	W 4-2	2-1	3	Furlong 2 [32, 56], O'Connor [35], Adebola [74]	7024
27	Jan 9	H	Port Vale	W 1-0	1-0	2	Furlong [25]	18,632
28	16	A	Barnsley	D 0-0	0-0	4		17,114
29	31	H	Bradford C	W 2-1	1-1	4	Furlong 2 (1 pen) [45, 90 (p)]	19,291
30	Feb 6	A	Crystal Palace	D 1-1	0-0	5	Furlong (pen) [50]	15,996
31	13	A	Stockport Co	L 0-1	0-1	5		9056
32	21	H	Bolton W	D 0-0	0-0	5		26,051
33	27	A	Grimsby T	W 3-0	1-0	5	Ndlovu [36], Adebola [85], Rowett [90]	7807
34	Mar 2	H	Norwich C	D 0-0	0-0	—		20,749
35	6	H	Portsmouth	W 4-1	1-1	4	Adebola 2 [26, 60], Forster [50], Hughes [84]	20,617
36	9	A	Tranmere R	W 1-0	0-0	—	Johnson M [46]	7184
37	13	H	WBA	W 4-0	1-0	4	Adebola 2 [24, 62], Ndlovu [50], Grainger [88]	29,060
38	20	A	Huddersfield T	D 1-1	0-0	4	Johnson M [47]	14,667
39	Apr 2	A	Crewe Alex	D 0-0	0-0	—		5582
40	5	H	Watford	L 1-2	0-1	4	Holdsworth [87]	24,877
41	10	A	Swindon T	W 1-0	0-0	4	Rowett [83]	8896
42	17	H	Wolverhampton W	L 0-1	0-1	4		28,143
43	20	H	QPR	W 1-0	0-0	—	Forinton [85]	20,888
44	24	A	Bristol C	W 2-1	0-0	4	Grainger (pen) [48], Ndlovu [70]	15,845
45	May 2	H	Ipswich T	W 1-0	0-0	4	Furlong [60]	27,685
46	9	A	Sunderland	L 1-2	1-0	4	Grainger [38]	41,634

Final League Position: 4

GOALSCORERS

League (66): Adebola 13, Furlong 13 (3 pens), Ndlovu 10, Forster 5, Johnson M 5, Rowett 5, Grainger 4 (1 pen), O'Connor 4 (3 pens), Hughes 3, Marsden 2, Forinton 1, Holdsworth 1.
Worthington Cup (13): Marsden 3, Adebola 2, Johnson M 2, Ndlovu 2, Rowett 2, Forster 1, own goal 1.
FA Cup (2): Adebola 1, Robinson 1.

Bennett I 10	Gill J 3	Charlton S 27 + 1	Marsden C 20	Ablett G 23 + 3	Johnson M 43 + 2	McCarthy J 35 + 8	O'Connor M 35 + 2	Furlong P 24 + 5	Adebola D 33 + 6	Ndlovu P 37 + 6	Grainger M 30 + 10	Forster N 8 + 25	Hughes B 20 + 8	Purse D 11 + 9	Rowett G 42	Holland C 7 + 7	Robinson S 20 + 11	Johnson A — + 4	Poole K 36	Bass J 9 + 2	Marsh S 6 + 1	Wassall D — + 3	Hyde G 13	Holdsworth D 8	Bradbury L 6 + 1	Forinton H — + 3	Match No.
1	2	3	4	5	6	7	8		9¹	10	11²	12	13														1
1	2	3	4	5	6	7¹	8		9	11²	12	13	10¹	14													2
1		3²	4	5	6	7	8		9	11²	10¹	12	13		2	14											3
1		3	4	5	6	7	8		9	12	10	11¹			2												4
1				4	5	6²	7¹	8	9	11	3	10²		13	2	12	14										5
1				4²	5	6		8	9³	11	3	10¹		12	2	13	14	7									6
1				4	5	6²	12	8	9	11¹	3	10³		13	2	14		7									7
1				4	5²	6	11	8³	9		3	12	10¹	14	2	13		7									8
1		3	4	5²	6	7²	8		9	11	10¹	12	13		2	14											9
1		3	4	5	6	7	8²		9	11	10¹	12			2	13											10
		3	4	5	6	7	8		9	11¹	10	12			2				1								11
		3	4	5²	6	7²	8		9	11	10¹	12		13	2	14			1								12
	11¹	5²		6		8	9⁶	10	12	3	13			4	2			7	1	14							13
	3¹	6	5	12	13	8	9	10²	11					4	2			7	1								14
	3	5	12	6	7	10	9	8¹	11					4	2²	13			1								15
	3	5	12	6	7	10²	9	8³	11¹		13			4	2	14			1								16
	3	6³	5²	13	7		9¹	12	11	10				4	2	8	14		1								17
		5¹	12	6	7		9³	8²	11	3	13			4	2	10	14		1								18
	12	5		6	7		9	8²	11	3¹	14	13		4³	2	10			1								19
	3²	5		6	7		9		11	12	13	10¹		4	2	8			1								20
	3¹			6	7		11	5	9²	12	4			2	8	10	13		1								21
			5	6	7²	8³	12		11	3	9	13		2	10¹	4			1	14							22
			5	6	7³	10	9	8¹	11	3²	13	12		2	4				1		14						23
			5	6	7	10	9	8	11					2	4				1	3¹	12						24
			5	6	7	10	9¹	8²	11	12	13			2	4				1	3							25
			5	6	7¹	10	9	8	11	13		12		2	4				1	3²							26
			5	6	7	10	9	8²	11	12	13			2	4				1	3							27
			5	6²	7	10	9	8	11	12				2	13	4			1	3¹							28
2¹			5	6	7		9	8	11	13		12			10	4			1	3²							29
	3		5¹	6	7	10	9	8²	11²	12	14	13		2	4				1								30
	3			6	7	10²	9	8	11		13	12		5	2	4¹			1								31
	3				8	9¹	12	11³	6	13	10		4	5	14		2		1			7²					32
	3¹			6	12	8	9³	13	11²	7	14	10		5			1		2		4						33
	3			6	7¹	8	9²	12	11			10		5	13		1		2		4						34
	3			6	12	8	9³	7	11²	13	14	10		5			1		2		4¹						35
	3			6	12	8	13	9²	14	7	11³	10		5			1		2		4¹						36
	3			6	12	8¹	13	9³	11²	7	14	10		5			1		2		4						37
	3			6	7	8	12	9¹	11³	4	14	10²		5	13		1		2								38
	3			6	7²	8¹		11	4	13	10			2	12		1		5						9³	14	39
	3²			6	12	8		11	7	13	10			1	2¹		4		5						9³	14	40
				6²	7	13		9¹	12	3	8	10		2	11		1						4	5			41
				6¹	7	8		9	11²	3	10			2	12		1			14			4³	5	13		42
				6	7³			11²	3	10	2	12	8		1				13				4¹	5	9	14	43
				6	12		13	11	3	10	2		8¹		1	7							4	5	9²		44
				6	7		9¹	12	13	3	10	14		2	8				1				4³	5	11²		45
	3²			6	7	12	9	14	13	8		10		2					1				4¹	5	11³		46

Worthington Cup

First Round	Millwall	(h)	2-0
		(a)	1-1
Second Round	Macclesfield T	(a)	3-0
		(h)	6-0
Third Round	Wimbledon	(h)	1-2

FA Cup

Third Round	Leicester C	(a)	2-4

Division 1

BLACKBURN ROVERS

FOUNDATION

It was in 1875 that some Public School old boys called a meeting at which the Blackburn Rovers club was formed and the colours blue and white adopted. The leading light was John Lewis, later to become a founder of the Lancashire FA, a famous referee who was in charge of two FA Cup Finals, and a vice-president of both the FA and the Football League.

Ewood Park, Blackburn BB2 4JF.
Telephone: (01254) 698888.
Fax: (01254) 671042.
Website: www.rovers.co.uk.
Email: enquiries@rovers.co.uk.
Ticket Hotline: 08080 10 10 10.
Clubcall: 0891 121179.
Mail Order: 08080 20 20 20.
Club Shop: 01254 672333.
Ground Capacity: 31,367.
Record Attendance: 62,522 v Bolton W, FA Cup 6th rd, 2 March 1929.
Record Receipts: £333,067 v Liverpool, Coca-Cola Cup 4th rd, 30 November 1994.
Pitch Measurements: 115yd × 72yd.
Chairman: R. D. Coar BSc.
Vice-Chairman: R. L. Matthewman.
Directors: J. O. Williams BSc. (Chief Executive), K. C. Lee, I. R. Stanners, G. R. Root FCMA. T. M. Finn.
Manager: Brian Kidd.
Physio: Mark Taylor.
Assistant Manager: Tony Parkes.
Coach: Brian McClair.
Commercial Manager: Ken Beamish.
Secretary: Tom Finn.
Stadium Manager: M. Highmore.

LATEST SEQUENCES
Longest Sequence of League Wins: 8, 1.3.80 – 7.4.80.
Longest Sequence of League Defeats: 7, 12.3.66 – 16.4.66.
Longest Sequence of League Draws: 5, 11.10.75 – 1.11.75.
Longest Sequence of Unbeaten League Matches: 23, 30.9.87 – 27.3.88.
Longest Sequence Without a League Win: 16, 11.11.78 – 24.3.79.

HONOURS

FA Premier League: Champions 1994–95; Runners-up 1993–94.
Football League: Division 1 – Champions 1911–12, 1913–14; Division 2 – Champions 1938–39; Runners-up 1957–58; Division 3 – Champions 1974–75; Runners-up 1979–80.
FA Cup: Winners 1884, 1885, 1886, 1890, 1891, 1928; Runners-up 1882, 1960.
Football League Cup: Semi-final 1962, 1993.
Full Members' Cup: Winners 1987.
European Competitions: European Cup: 1995–96. UEFA Cup: 1994–95, 1998–99.

Colours
Blue and white halved shirts, white shorts with blue trim, white stockings with blue trim.

Change Colours
Yellow and royal blue or navy blue and red.

Year Formed: 1875.

Turned Professional: 1880.

Ltd Co.: 1897.

Club Nickname: Rovers.

Previous Grounds: 1875, all matches played away; 1876, Oozehead Ground; 1877, Pleasington Cricket Ground; 1878, Alexandra Meadows; 1881, Leamington Road; 1890, Ewood Park.

First Football League Game: 15 September 1888, Football League, v Accrington (h) D 5–5 – Arthur; Beverley, James Southworth; Douglas, Almond, Forrest; Beresford (1), Walton, John Southworth (1), Fecitt (1), Townley (2).

Record League Victory: 9–0 v Middlesbrough, Division 2, 6 November 1954 – Elvy; Suart, Eckersley; Clayton, Kelly, Bell; Mooney (3), Crossan (2), Briggs, Quigley (3), Langton (1).

Record Cup Victory: 11–0 v Rossendale, FA Cup 1st rd, 13 October 1884 – Arthur; Hopwood, McIntyre; Forrest, Blenkhorn, Lofthouse; Sowerbutts (2), J. Brown (1), Fecitt (4), Barton (3), Birtwistle (1).

Record Defeat: 0–8 v Arsenal, Division 1, 25 February 1933.

Most League Points (2 for a win): 60, Division 3, 1974–75.

Most League Points (3 for a win): 89, FA Premier League, 1994–95.

Most League Goals: 114, Division 2, 1954–55.

Highest League Scorer in Season: Ted Harper, 43, Division 1, 1925–26.

Most League Goals in Total Aggregate: Simon Garner, 168, 1978–92.

Most League Goals in One Match: 7, Tommy Briggs v Bristol R, Division 2, 5 February 1953.

Most Capped Player: Bob Crompton, 41, England.

Most League Appearances: Derek Fazackerley, 596, 1970–86.

Youngest League Player: Harry Dennison, 16 years 155 days v Bristol C, 8 April 1911.

Record Transfer Fee Received: £15,000,000 from Newcastle U for Alan Shearer, July 1996.

Record Transfer Fee Paid: £7,250,000 to Southampton for Kevin Davies, June 1998.

Football League Record: 1888 Founder Member of the League; 1936–39 Division 2; 1946–48 Division 1; 1948–58 Division 2; 1958–66 Division 1; 1966–71 Division 2; 1971–75 Division 3; 1975–79 Division 2; 1979–80 Division 3; 1980–92 Division 2; 1992–99 FA Premier League; 1999– Division 1.

MANAGERS

Thomas Mitchell 1884–96
(Secretary-Manager)
J. Walmsley 1896–1903
(Secretary-Manager)
R. B. Middleton 1903–25
Jack Carr 1922–26
(Team Manager under Middleton to 1925)
Bob Crompton 1926–30
(Hon. Team Manager)
Arthur Barritt 1931–36
(had been Secretary from 1927)
Reg Taylor 1936–38
Bob Crompton 1938–41
Eddie Hapgood 1944–47
Will Scott 1947
Jack Bruton 1947–49
Jackie Bestall 1949–53
Johnny Carey 1953–58
Dally Duncan 1958–60
Jack Marshall 1960–67
Eddie Quigley 1967–70
Johnny Carey 1970–71
Ken Furphy 1971–73
Gordon Lee 1974–75
Jim Smith 1975–78
Jim Iley 1978
John Pickering 1978–79
Howard Kendall 1979–81
Bobby Saxton 1981–86
Don Mackay 1987–91
Kenny Dalglish 1991–95
Ray Harford 1995–97
Roy Hodgson 1997–98
Brian Kidd December 1998–

TEN YEAR LEAGUE RECORD

		P	W	D	L	F	A	Pts	Pos
1988-89	Div 2	46	22	11	13	74	59	77	5
1989-90	Div 2	46	19	17	10	74	59	74	5
1990-91	Div 2	46	14	10	22	51	66	52	19
1991-92	Div 2	46	21	11	14	70	53	74	6
1992-93	PR Lge	42	20	11	11	68	46	71	4
1993-94	PR Lge	42	25	9	8	63	36	84	2
1994-95	PR Lge	42	27	8	7	80	39	89	1
1995-96	PR Lge	38	18	7	13	61	47	61	7
1996-97	PR Lge	38	9	15	14	42	43	42	13
1997-98	PR Lge	38	16	10	12	57	52	58	6

DID YOU KNOW ?

Centre-forward Jimmy Brown, who scored 28 FA Cup goals for Blackburn Rovers between 1879–80 and 1885–86, was only 5ft 5in tall and weighed less than 10st. He captained the team to three final successes.

BLACKBURN ROVERS 1998–99 LEAGUE RECORD

Match No.	Date	Venue	Opponents	Result	H/T Score	Lg. Pos.	Goalscorers	Attendance
1	Aug 15	H	Derby Co	D 0-0	0-0	—		24,235
2	24	A	Leeds U	L 0-1	0-1	—		30,541
3	29	H	Leicester C	W 1-0		11	Gallacher 12	22,544
4	Sept 9	A	Tottenham H	L 1-2	1-1	—	Gallacher 11	28,338
5	12	A	Sheffield W	L 0-3	0-2	18		20,846
6	21	H	Chelsea	L 3-4	1-1	—	Sutton 2 (1 pen) 22, 79 (p), Perez 57	23,113
7	26	A	Everton	D 0-0	0-0	18		36,404
8	Oct 3	H	West Ham U	W 3-0	1-0	17	Flitcroft 2 10, 47, Davidson 68	25,213
9	17	A	Middlesbrough	L 1-2	0-0	17	Sherwood 56	34,413
10	25	H	Arsenal	L 1-2	0-2	17	Johnson 64	27,012
11	31	A	Wimbledon	D 1-1	0-0	17	Sutton (pen) 47	12,526
12	Nov 7	H	Coventry C	L 1-2	0-0	18	Sherwood 73	23,779
13	14	A	Manchester U	L 2-3	0-2	18	Marcolin 65, Blake 74	55,198
14	21	H	Southampton	L 0-2	0-1	20		22,812
15	29	A	Liverpool	L 0-2	0-2	20		41,753
16	Dec 5	H	Charlton Ath	W 1-0	0-0	18	Davies 75	22,568
17	12	H	Newcastle U	D 0-0	0-0	18		27,569
18	19	A	Nottingham F	D 2-2	0-2	18	Blake 2 49, 90	22,013
19	26	H	Aston Villa	W 2-1	1-0	16	Gallacher 44, Sherwood 88	27,536
20	28	A	Leicester C	D 1-1	1-1	16	Gallacher 38	21,083
21	Jan 9	H	Leeds U	W 1-0	1-0	16	Gillespie 22	27,620
22	16	A	Derby Co	L 0-1	0-0	16		27,386
23	30	H	Tottenham H	D 1-1	1-0	17	Jansen 43	29,643
24	Feb 6	A	Aston Villa	W 3-1	1-0	15	Southgate (og) 32, Ward 62, Dunn 64	37,404
25	17	A	Chelsea	D 1-1	0-1	—	Ward 84	34,382
26	20	H	Sheffield W	L 1-4	0-3	17	McAteer 68	24,643
27	27	A	West Ham U	L 0-2	0-2	18		25,529
28	Mar 10	A	Everton	L 1-2	1-1	—	Ward 2	27,219
29	13	A	Coventry C	D 1-1	0-1	18	Wilcox 67	19,694
30	20	H	Wimbledon	W 3-1	3-0	17	Ward 7, Jansen 2 18, 26	21,754
31	Apr 3	H	Middlesbrough	D 0-0	0-0	16		27,482
32	6	A	Arsenal	L 0-1	0-1	—		37,762
33	17	A	Southampton	D 3-3	2-1	18	Ward 14, Peacock 25, Wilcox 47	15,209
34	24	H	Liverpool	L 1-3	0-3	17	Duff 63	29,944
35	May 1	A	Charlton Ath	D 0-0	0-0	18		20,043
36	8	H	Nottingham F	L 1-2	1-1	19	Gallacher 25	24,565
37	12	H	Manchester U	D 0-0	0-0	—		30,436
38	May 16	A	Newcastle U	D 1-1	1-0	19	Wilcox 37	36,623

Final League Position: 19

GOALSCORERS

League (38): Gallacher 5, Ward 5, Blake 3, Jansen 3, Sherwood 3, Sutton 3 (2 pens), Wilcox 3, Flitcroft 2, Davidson 1, Davies 1, Duff 1, Dunn 1, Gillespie 1, Johnson 1, Marcolin 1, McAteer 1, Peacock 1, Perez 1, own goal 1.
Worthington Cup (2): Sherwood 1, Sutton 1.
FA Cup (3): Davies 1, Gillespie 1, Wilcox 1.

Filan J 26	Kenna J 22+1	Davidson C 34	Sherwood T 19	Peacock D 27+3	Henchoz S 34	Flitcroft G 8	Perez S 4+1	Sutton C 17	Davies K 9+12	Wilcox J 28+2	Gallacher K 13+3	Dahlin M 2+3	Duff D 18+10	Flowers T 10+1	Dailly C 14+3	McKinlay B 14+2	Croft G 10+2	Dunn D 10+5	Johnson D 14+7	Blake N 9+2	Marcolin D 5+5	Fettis A 2	Broomes M 8+5	Gillespie K 13+3	Ward A 17	McAteer J 13	Jansen M 10+1	Taylor M 1+2	Carsley L 7+1	Match No.
1	2	3	4	5	6	7	8^1	9	10^2	11^3	12	13	14																	1
1	2	3	4	5	6	7	8	9	10^2	11^1	12	13																		2
	2	3	4	5	6	7	10^9	9	12	13	8^1		11^2	1	14															3
2^1	3		5	6	10	12	9		11^2	8		13	1	4	7															4
	2	8	5	6			9	10	12			11^1	1	4	7	3														5
	3	4	5	6	7	8	9		11^1		10		1	2	12															6
2	3	8	5	6	10			11		9	7^1	1	4	13		12^2														7
12	3	4	5	6^1	10			11	8^2	13	9^3	1	2	7			14													8
	2	3	4	5	6	7		10^1	11		9	1		12	8															9
	2	3	4	5	6		9	12	11^1		10	1		8																10
	2	3	4	5	6		9	10^2		11	1	12	7^1		8	13														11
	2	3	4	5^1	6		9^1	12		11	1	7		8	10	13														12
1	2	3^1	4	5	6			10^1	12	11^3	7		13	8	9	14														13
1	2		4	5^1	6		12		8	11	7		3^2	10	9	13														14
1	2	3		6			12		8	11	5		10	7^1	9	4														15
	3		6				12		8^1	11	5	7	2	10^5	4	9	1	13												16
	2	3	4	6			10	11		5	7		8	9	1															17
1	2	3	4	6			9		11^1	12	5	7		13	10		8^2													18
1	2	3	4	6^3			9^1	12	11	8^2	13	5	7			14	10													19
1	2	3	4	5			10	11	9	6^1	7		12	8																20
1	2	3	4		6			11		10^1	7	12					5	8	9											21
1	2	3	4		6			11		7		10					5	8	9											22
1	2	3	12	6			13	11	10^3		8^1	14	5					9	4	7^2										23
	3		5			9	11	13^3	12	6	7		4	10	2	8^1														24
1	2		14	6	9			13^3		3	11	4^1	5	12	10	7	8^2													25
1	2	3	12	6^1			11		7	13		5	8	9	4	10^2														26
1		3	5	6			12	11^2	13		14^3	10	6	8	9	2	7^1													27
1		3	5	6			10^2	11	7	2^1		8	12		9	4	13													28
1		3		6			9	11	12	7^2	13	4		10	2	8^1	5													29
1		3	5	6			9	11^1	13	7^3	4		12	10	2	8^2	14													30
1		3	5	6			9	12	11	7^2	4^3		13	10	2	8^1		14												31
1		3	5	6			9	11	4^1		12		13	8	10	2	7^2													32
1		3	5	6^2			12	11	9^1	14	4^3		13	8	10	2	7													33
1			5	6			11	9	8	3	12	4^1	10	2	7															34
1		3	5	6			11	9^1	12	2	8	10	4	7																35
1		3	5	6			12	11	9	4^3	2^2	14	13	8	10^1	7														36
1		3	5	6			11	2	4	12	8^1	9	10	7																37
1^6		3		5			11	9^2	15	2	4^1	12	6	8	10	13	7													38

Worthington Cup

Third Round	Crewe Alex	(a)	1-0
Fourth Round	Newcastle U	(a)	1-1
Fifth Round	Leicester C	(a)	0-1

FA Cup

Third Round	Charlton Ath	(h)	2-0
Fourth Round	Sunderland	(h)	1-0
Fifth Round	Newcastle U	(a)	0-0
		(h)	0-1

Division 2

BLACKPOOL

FOUNDATION

Old boys of St John's School who had formed themselves into a football club decided to establish a club bearing the name of their town and Blackpool FC came into being at a meeting at the Stanley Arms Hotel in the summer of 1887. In their first season playing at Raikes Hall Gardens, the club won both the Lancashire Junior Cup and the Fylde Cup.

Bloomfield Rd Ground, Blackpool FY1 6JJ.

Telephone: (01253) 404331 (Ticket/Credit Bookings), (01253) 405331 (Shop/General Enquiries).

Fax: (01253) 405011.

Website: http://www.cyberscape.co.uk/users/bfc/default.htm

Email: bfc@cyberscape.net

Ground Capacity: 11,295.

Record Attendance: 38,098 v Wolverhampton W, Division 1, 17 September 1955.

Record Receipts: £79,420 v Preston NE, Division 2, 21 November 1998.

Pitch Measurements: 112yd × 74yd.

Chairman: Mr K. Oyston.

Deputy Chairman: K. Chadwick.

Directors: C. Muir OBE, O. J. Oyston, G. Warburton, M. Joyce.

Manager: Nigel Worthington.

Secretary: Carol Banks.

Commercial Director: Geoff Warburton.

Physio: Paul Kelly.

Stadium Manager: John Turner.

LATEST SEQUENCES

Longest Sequence of League Wins: 9, 21.11.36 – 1.1.37.

Longest Sequence of League Defeats: 8, 26.11.1898 – 7.1.1899.

Longest Sequence of League Draws: 5, 4.12.76 – 1.1.77.

Longest Sequence of Unbeaten League Matches: 17, 6.4.68 – 21.9.68.

Longest Sequence Without a League Win: 19, 19.12.70 – 24.4.71.

HONOURS

Football League: Division 1 – Runners-up 1955–56; Division 2 – Champions 1929–30; Runners-up 1936–37, 1969–70; Division 4 – Runners-up 1984–85.

FA Cup: Winners 1953; Runners-up 1948, 1951.

Football League Cup: Semi-final 1962.

Anglo-Italian Cup: Winners 1971; Runners-up 1972.

Colours
All tangerine.

Change Colours
Tangerine and white.

Year Formed: 1887.

Turned Professional: 1887.

Ltd Co.: 1896.

Previous Name: 'South Shore' combined with Blackpool in 1899, twelve years after the latter had been formed on the breaking up of the old 'Blackpool St John's' club.

Club Nickname: 'The Seasiders'.

Previous Grounds: 1887, Raikes Hall Gardens; 1897, Athletic Grounds; 1899, Raikes Hall Gardens; 1899, Bloomfield Road.

First Football League game: 5 September 1896, Division 2, v Lincoln C (a) L 1–3 – Douglas; Parr, Bowman; Stuart, Stirzaker, Norris; Clarkin, Donnelly, R. Parkinson, Mount (1), J. Parkinson.

Record League Victory: 7–0 v Reading, Division 2, 10 November 1928 – Mercer; Gibson, Hamilton, Watson, Wilson, Grant, Ritchie, Oxberry (2), Hampson (5), Tufnell, Neal. 7–0 v Preston NE (away), Division 1, 1 May 1948 – Robinson; Shimwell, Crosland; Buchan, Hayward, Kelly; Hobson, Munro (1), McIntosh (5), McCall, Rickett (1). 7–0 v Sunderland, Division 1, 5 October 1957 – Farm; Armfield, Garrett, Kelly (J), Gratrix, Kelly (H), Matthews, Taylor (2), Charnley (2), Durie (2), Perry (1).

Record Cup Victory: 7–1 v Charlton Ath, League Cup 2nd rd, 25 September 1963 – Harvey; Armfield, Martin; Crawford, Gratrix, Cranston; Lea, Ball (1), Charnley (4), Durie (1), Oates (1).

Record Defeat: 1–10 v Small Heath, Division 2, 2 March 1901 and v Huddersfield T, Division 1, 13 December 1930.

Most League Points (2 for a win): 58, Division 2, 1929–30 and Division 2, 1967–68.

Most League Points (3 for a win): 86, Division 4, 1984–85.

Most League Goals: 98, Division 2, 1929–30.

Highest League Scorer in Season: Jimmy Hampson, 45, Division 2, 1929–30.

Most League Goals in Total Aggregate: Jimmy Hampson, 246, 1927–38.

Most League Goals in One Match: 5, Jimmy Hampson v Reading, Division 2, 10 November 1928; 5, Jimmy McIntosh v Preston NE, Division 1, 1 May 1948.

Most Capped Player: Jimmy Armfield, 43, England.

Most League Appearances: Jimmy Armfield, 568, 1952–71.

Youngest League Player: Trevor Sinclair, 16 years 170 days v Wigan Ath, 19 August 1989.

Record Transfer Fee Received: £750,000 from QPR for Trevor Sinclair, August 1993.

Record Transfer Fee Paid: £275,000 to Millwall for Chris Malkin, October 1996.

Football League Record: 1896 Elected to Division 2; 1899 Failed re-election; 1900 Re-elected; 1900–30 Division 2; 1930–33 Division 1; 1933–37 Division 2; 1937–67 Division 1; 1967–70 Division 2; 1970–71 Division 1; 1971–78 Division 2; 1978–81 Division 3; 1981–85 Division 4; 1985–90 Division 3; 1990–92 Division 4; 1992– Division 2.

MANAGERS

Tom Barcroft 1903–33
 (Secretary-Manager)
John Cox 1909–11
Bill Norman 1919–23
Maj. Frank Buckley 1923–27
Sid Beaumont 1927–28
Harry Evans 1928–33
 (Hon. Team Manager)
Alex 'Sandy' Macfarlane 1933–35
Joe Smith 1935–58
Ronnie Suart 1958–67
Stan Mortensen 1967–69
Les Shannon 1969–70
Bob Stokoe 1970–72
Harry Potts 1972–76
Allan Brown 1976–78
Bob Stokoe 1978–79
Stan Ternent 1979–80
Alan Ball 1980–81
Allan Brown 1981–82
Sam Ellis 1982–89
Jimmy Mullen 1989–90
Graham Carr 1990
Bill Ayre 1990–94
Sam Allardyce 1994–96
Gary Megson 1996–97
Nigel Worthington July 1997–

TEN YEAR LEAGUE RECORD

		P	W	D	L	F	A	Pts	Pos
1988-89	Div 3	46	14	13	19	56	59	54	19
1989-90	Div 3	46	10	16	20	49	73	46	23
1990-91	Div 4	46	23	10	13	78	47	79	5
1991-92	Div 4	42	22	10	10	71	45	76	4
1992-93	Div 2	46	12	15	19	63	75	51	18
1993-94	Div 2	46	16	5	25	63	75	53	20
1994-95	Div 2	46	18	10	18	64	70	64	12
1995-96	Div 2	46	23	13	10	67	40	82	3
1996-97	Div 2	46	18	15	13	60	47	69	7
1997-98	Div 2	46	17	11	18	59	67	62	12

DID YOU KNOW ?

Blackpool had won the first three First Division matches of the 1939–40 season when the competition was abandoned. When the same fixtures were used to start 1946–47, they were again successful in all three.

BLACKPOOL 1998–99 LEAGUE RECORD

Match No.	Date		Venue	Opponents	Result		H/T Score	Lg. Pos.	Goalscorers	Atten- dance
1	Aug	8	A	Manchester C	L	0-3	0-1	—		32,134
2		15	H	Oldham Ath	W	3-0	1-0	12	Bent [40], Malkin [61], Bushell [73]	5258
3		22	A	Wigan Ath	L	0-3	0-2	17		4853
4		29	H	Gillingham	D	2-2	0-0	15	Thompson [69], Clarkson [90]	3994
5	Sept	1	A	Bournemouth	D	1-1	0-0	—	Clarkson [72]	6785
6		5	H	Northampton T	W	2-1	0-1	11	Clarkson [71], Thompson [82]	4017
7		8	H	Notts Co	W	1-0	0-0	—	Shuttleworth [76]	3849
8		12	A	Lincoln C	W	2-1	1-1	4	Clarkson [14], Aldridge [66]	2949
9		19	H	Luton T	W	1-0	0-0	4	Nowland [87]	5695
10		26	A	Stoke C	W	3-1	2-0	3	Carlisle [6], Aldridge 2 [35, 86]	15,002
11	Oct	3	H	York C	L	1-2	0-1	5	Bushell [58]	5633
12		10	H	Millwall	L	2-3	1-2	7	Aldridge 2 [39, 58]	5295
13		17	A	Walsall	L	0-1	0-1	8		4728
14		21	A	Reading	D	1-1	0-0	—	Bryan [90]	8450
15		31	H	Fulham	L	2-3	1-3	12	Hills [30], Aldridge [62]	5904
16	Nov	7	A	Wrexham	D	1-1	0-0	12	Lawson [48]	3511
17		10	A	Bristol R	W	2-0	0-0	—	Ormerod [69], Lawson [70]	5361
18		21	H	Preston NE	D	0-0	0-0	11		10,868
19		28	A	Burnley	L	0-1	0-0	12		11,925
20	Dec	5	H	Chesterfield	D	1-1	0-0	13	Lawson [70]	3278
21		12	H	Wycombe W	D	0-0	0-0	13		2990
22		18	A	Colchester U	D	2-2	1-1	—	Ormerod [11], Hughes [88]	3228
23		26	H	Wigan Ath	D	1-1	0-0	12	Garvey [56]	5147
24		28	A	Macclesfield T	W	1-0	0-0	10	Howarth (og) [52]	3919
25	Jan	2	H	Gillingham	L	0-1	0-0	12		7022
26		9	H	Manchester C	D	0-0	0-0	14		9752
27		16	A	Oldham Ath	L	0-3	0-0	14		5353
28		30	H	Macclesfield T	W	2-1	0-1	12	Ormerod [61], Clarkson [73]	4569
29	Feb	6	A	Northampton T	D	0-0	0-0	13		5592
30		13	A	Notts Co	W	1-0	1-0	10	Bushell [5]	4778
31		20	H	Lincoln C	L	0-1	0-0	12		4215
32		27	A	Luton T	L	0-1	0-0	13		4646
33	Mar	6	H	Stoke C	L	0-1	0-1	14		5504
34		13	H	Wrexham	D	1-1	0-0	13	Ormerod (pen) [72]	3905
35		16	H	Bournemouth	D	0-0	0-0	—		3186
36		20	A	Fulham	L	0-4	0-1	13		12,869
37		27	A	Chesterfield	W	2-1	1-0	12	Sturridge [15], Clarkson [56]	4027
38	Apr	3	H	Walsall	L	0-2	0-1	14		5432
39		5	A	Millwall	L	0-1	0-1	14		6672
40		10	H	Reading	W	2-0	1-0	13	Aldridge (pen) [31], Clarkson [47]	3617
41		13	H	Burnley	L	0-2	0-1	—		5658
42		17	A	Preston NE	W	2-1	1-0	12	Nowland [45], Ormerod [89]	15,337
43		24	H	Bristol R	L	1-2	0-0	14	Ormerod [47]	5033
44		27	A	York C	L	0-1	0-1	—		2971
45	May	1	H	Wycombe W	D	2-2	1-2	16	Ormerod [15], Clarkson [61]	5286
46		8	H	Colchester U	W	2-1	1-1	14	Ormerod [1], Clarkson [88]	4866

Final League Position: 14

GOALSCORERS

League (44): Clarkson 9, Ormerod 8 (1 pen), Aldridge 7 (1 pen), Bushell 3, Lawson 3, Nowland 2, Thompson 2, Bent 1, Bryan 1, Carlisle 1, Garvey 1, Hills 1, Hughes 1, Malkin 1, Shuttleworth 1, Sturridge 1, own goal 1.
Worthington Cup (5): Aldridge 2, Bent 1, Conroy 1, Malkin 1.
FA Cup (3): Aldridge 1, Blunt 1, Ormerod 1.

Banks S 35	Bryan M 37+4	Bardsley D 29	Butler T 20	Hughes I 31+2	Bushell S 31	Clarkson P 44	Blunt J 1+1	Hills J 27+1	Aldridge M 19+3	Bent J 21+18	Conroy M 7+1	Malkin C 24+5	Brabin G 5+2	Carlisle C 34+5	Ormerod B 30+10	Thompson P 18+4	Rogan A 9+5	Shuttleworth B 12+2	Robinson P 2+3	Nowland A 13+24	Garvey S 6+9	Lawson I 9	Patterson M 7	Barnes P 1	Jarrett J 2	Couzens A 6	Sturridge S 5	Caig T 10	Watts J 9	Coid D —+1	Barnes K 2+2	Match No.
1	2	3	4	5	6	7	8[1]	9	10	11[2]	12	13																				1
1		2	4	5[1]	10	8		3		7	9	11[1]	6	12	13																	2
1		2			10	8		3		7	9	11	6	5		4																3
1	2	4			10	8		3[2]	12		9[1]	11	6	5	14	7	13[3]															4
1	2	4			10	8			11[2]		9			5	6	7		3[1]	12	13												5
1	2	4			10[2]	8			6[3]		9[1]	11		5	12	7		3	13	14												6
1	2	4			10	8			9[1]			11		5	6	7		3	12													7
1	2	4	12		10	8			9[1]			11		5	6[2]	7		3	13													8
1	2	5	12		10	8			9[2]	13		11[1]		6	7[3]	4		3	14													9
1	2	4[1]	7		10	8			9[3]	13		11[2]	12	5	6			3	14													10
1	2		7		10	8			9[1]	12		11	4	5	6[2]			3	13													11
1	2	4[2]	10[1]			8			9	12		11	13	5	6[3]	7		3	14													12
1	2				10	8		3	9	7[1]		11		5			4		6[2]	12	13											13
1	2		4		10	8		3		7[1]		11		5	12	6			9[2]	13												14
1	2		4		10	8		3	7	12		11[2]		5	6				9[1]	13												15
1	2		4		10	8		3	7[1]	12		11[2]		5	13	6[1]				9												16
1	2		4		10	8		3	7[2]	12		11		5	13	6[1]	14			9[1]												17
1	2		4	6	10	8		3	7[1]			11		5	12					9												18
1	2		4	6	10	8		3		12	7[2]	5	11[1]					13		9												19
1	2		4	6	10	8				12		11[1]		5	7[2]		3		13	9												20
1	2	4		6	10	8		3		13		11		5	7[1]			12[2]	9													21
		4	6	2	10[1]	8		3		12	11[2]	5	9				13						7	1								22
1	2	6	4	5		8		3				11		9	7					10												23
1	2	6	4	5		8		3[3]		12		14	11[1]	9	7[2]					10												24
1	2	6	4	5[1]		8			12			11		9[2]	14	3	13		10		7[1]											25
1	2	6	4		10	8			7[2]			11[1]		5	12		13		9		3											26
1	2	6[1]			10	8			7			11[2]		5	13	3[3]	12		14	9	4											27
1		6	4	5	10	8			12			13		11	2	3[1]	7[2]		14	9[3]												28
1	2	6	4	5	10	8			12	13		14		11		3[2]	7[3]			9[1]												29
1	2	6	4	5	10	8			12			11		9[2]	3	13				7[1]												30
1	2	6	4	5	10	8			3	9		11[1]						13		7	12											31
1	2	6[1]			5	10	8		3	9[2]	14	7		4	11	12[2]				13												32
1	2		4	10		8		3	13	12		5		11						9					6[2]				7[1]			33
1	12		4	6	10	8		3[1]		13		5		11						9[3]					2	7[2]			14			34
1	12		4	6	10[1]	8		3		7		5		11						13					2	9[2]						35
1	2			6		8		3		7		5		11						12					4	9		10[1]				36
	12			6		8		3		7		5		13						10	11[3]				2[1]	9[2]	1	4	14			37
	2			6				3		7		12		5	13			14		10[3]	11		8[2]			9[1]	1	4				38
	2			6		8		3[1]	9	7		5		10		12				13	11[2]						1	4				39
	2			6		8			10	9[1]		7[2]		12		5		11		3	13						1	4				40
	2			6		8			10[1]	7		9		5		11		3		12							1	4				41
	2	6				8				7		5		11	4[1]	3	12		9[2]	13			10			1						42
	4		2			8		10[3]	7[2]			5		11		12	3		13	9[1]	14						1	6				43
	2	4		10		8		12		7		13		11	5[2]	3[1]			9[2]	14							1	6				44
	2[3]	4		10		8				7		9		11[2]	12	3[1]		5		13	14						1	6				45
	12	2	4			8				7		9[2]		11		5		3[3]		13	10[1]						1	6	14			46

Worthington Cup

First Round	Scunthorpe U	(h)	1-0
		(a)	1-1
Second Round	Tranmere R	(h)	2-1
		(a)	1-3

FA Cup

First Round	Wigan Ath	(a)	3-4

Division 1   **BOLTON WANDERERS**

FOUNDATION

In 1874 boys of Christ Church Sunday School, Blackburn Street, led by their master Thomas Ogden, established a football club which went under the name of the school and whose president was Vicar of Christ Church. Membership was 6d (two and a half pence). When their president began to lay down too many rules about the use of church premises, the club broke away and formed Bolton Wanderers in 1877, holding their earliest meetings at the Gladstone Hotel.

Reebok Stadium, Burnden Way, Lostock, Bolton BL6 6JW.

Telephone: (01204) 673673.

Fax: (01204) 673773.

Ticket Office: (01204) 673601.

Ground Capacity: 25,000.

Record Attendance: 69,912 v Manchester C, FA Cup 5th rd, 18 February 1933.

Record Receipts: £289,784 v West Ham U, FA Premier League, 21 February 1998.

Pitch Measurements: 114yd × 74yd.

President: Nat Lofthouse.

Chairman: G. Hargreaves.

Directors: P. A. Gartside, G. Ball, G. Seymour, G. Warburton, W. B. Warburton, B. Scowcroft.

Team Manager: Colin Todd.

Physio: E. Simpson.

Chief Executive & Secretary: Des McBain.

Commercial Manager: T. Holland.

LATEST SEQUENCES

Longest Sequence of League Wins: 11, 5.11.04 – 2.1.05.

Longest Sequence of League Defeats: 11, 7.4.02 – 18.10.02.

Longest Sequence of League Draws: 6, 25.1.13 – 8.3.13.

Longest Sequence of Unbeaten League Matches: 23, 13.10.90 – 9.3.91.

Longest Sequence Without a League Win: 26, 7.4.02 – 10.1.03.

HONOURS

Football League: Division 1 – Champions 1996–97; Division 2 – Champions 1908–09, 1977–78; Runners-up 1899–1900, 1904–05, 1910–11, 1934–35, 1992–93; Division 3 – Champions 1972–73.

FA Cup: Winners 1923, 1926, 1929, 1958; Runners-up 1894, 1904, 1953.

Football League Cup: Runners-up 1995.

Freight Rover Trophy: Runners-up 1986.

Sherpa Van Trophy: Winners 1989.

Colours
White shirts, navy blue shorts, blue stockings.
Change Colours
Blue shirts with white sash, white shorts, blue stockings.

Year Formed: 1874.

Turned Professional: 1880.

Ltd Co.: 1895.

Previous Name: 1874, Christ Church FC; 1877, Bolton Wanderers.

Club Nickname: 'The Trotters'.

Previous Grounds: Park Recreation Ground and Cockle's Field before moving to Pike's Lane ground 1881; 1895, Burnden Park; 1997, Reebok Stadium.

First Football League Game: 8 September 1888, Football League, v Derby Co (h) L 3–6 – Harrison; Robinson, Mitchell; Roberts, Weir, Bullough, Davenport (2), Milne, Coupar, Barbour, Brogan (1).

Record League Victory: 8–0 v Barnsley, Division 2, 6 October 1934 – Jones; Smith, Finney; Goslin, Atkinson, George Taylor; George T. Taylor (2), Eastham, Milsom (1), Westwood (4), Cook, (1 og).

Record Cup Victory: 13–0 v Sheffield U, FA Cup 2nd rd, 1 February 1890 – Parkinson; Robinson (1), Jones; Bullough, Davenport, Roberts; Rushton, Brogan (3), Cassidy (5), McNee, Weir (4).

Record Defeat: 1–9 v Preston NE, FA Cup 2nd rd, 10 December 1887.

Most League Points (2 for a win): 61, Division 3, 1972–73.

Most League Points (3 for a win): 98, Division 1, 1996–97.

Most League Goals: 100, Division 1, 1996–97.

Highest League Scorer in Season: Joe Smith, 38, Division 1, 1920–21.

Most League Goals in Total Aggregate: Nat Lofthouse, 255, 1946–61.

Most League Goals in One Match: 5, Tony Caldwell v Walsall, Division 3, 10 September 1983.

Most Capped Player: Nat Lofthouse, 33, England.

Most League Appearances: Eddie Hopkinson, 519, 1956–70.

Youngest League Player: Ray Parry, 15 years 267 days v Wolverhampton W, 13 October 1951.

Record Transfer Fee Received: £4,500,000 from Liverpool for Jason McAteer, September 1995.

Record Transfer Fee Paid: £3,500,000 for Dean Holdsworth from Wimbledon, October 1997.

Football League Record: 1888 Founder Member of the League; 1899–1900 Division 2; 1900–03 Division 1; 1903–05 Division 2; 1905–08 Division 1; 1908–09 Division 2; 1909–10 Division 1; 1910–11 Division 2; 1911–33 Division 1; 1933–35 Division 2; 1935–64 Division 1; 1964–71 Division 2; 1971–73 Division 3; 1973–78 Division 2; 1978–80 Division 1; 1980–83 Division 2; 1983–87 Division 3; 1987–88 Division 4; 1988–92 Division 3; 1992–93 Division 2; 1993–95 Division 1; 1995–96 FA Premier League; 1996–97 Division 1; 1997–98 FA Premier League; 1998– Division 1.

MANAGERS

Tom Rawthorne 1874–85
(Secretary-Manager)
J. J. Bentley 1885–86
(Secretary-Manager)
W. G. Struthers 1886–87
(Secretary-Manager)
Fitzroy Norris 1887
(Secretary-Manager)
J. J. Bentley 1887–95
(Secretary-Manager)
Harry Downs 1895–96
(Secretary-Manager)
Frank Brettell 1896–98
(Secretary-Manager)
John Somerville 1898–1910
Will Settle 1910–15
Tom Mather 1915–19
Charles Foweraker 1919–44
Walter Rowley 1944–50
Bill Ridding 1951–68
Nat Lofthouse 1968–70
Jimmy McIlroy 1970
Jimmy Meadows 1971
Nat Lofthouse 1971
(then Admin. Manager to 1972)
Jimmy Armfield 1971–74
Ian Greaves 1974–80
Stan Anderson 1980–81
George Mulhall 1981–82
John McGovern 1982–85
Charlie Wright 1985
Phil Neal 1985–92
Bruce Rioch 1992–95
Roy McFarland 1995–96
Colin Todd January 1996–

TEN YEAR LEAGUE RECORD

		P	W	D	L	F	A	Pts	Pos
1988-89	Div 3	46	16	16	14	58	54	64	10
1989-90	Div 3	46	18	15	13	59	48	69	6
1990-91	Div 3	46	24	11	11	64	50	83	4
1991-92	Div 3	46	14	17	15	57	56	59	13
1992-93	Div 2	46	27	9	10	80	41	90	2
1993-94	Div 1	46	15	14	17	63	64	59	14
1994-95	Div 1	46	21	14	11	67	45	77	3
1995-96	PR Lge	38	8	5	25	39	71	29	20
1996-97	Div 1	46	28	14	4	100	53	98	1
1997-98	PR Lge	38	9	13	16	41	61	40	18

DID YOU KNOW ?

Jack Milsom is the only Bolton Wanderers player to be the club's leading scorer in six consecutive seasons; a feat he achieved from 1931–32 to 1936–37. He had cost £1,750 from Rochdale in December 1929.

BOLTON WANDERERS 1998–99 LEAGUE RECORD

Match No.	Date	Venue	Opponents	Result	H/T Score	Lg. Pos.	Goalscorers	Attendance
1	Aug 8	A	Crystal Palace	D 2-2	1-0	—	Holdsworth 33, Gunnlaugsson 90	19,029
2	15	H	Grimsby T	W 2-0	0-0	5	Blake 56, Holdsworth (pen) 70	16,584
3	23	A	Bradford C	D 2-2	1-1	8	Gunnlaugsson 19, Blake 60	13,163
4	29	H	Sheffield U	D 2-2	2-0	8	Strong 5, Blake 36	18,263
5	Sept 8	A	WBA	W 3-2	2-1	—	Gunnlaugsson 19, Blake 26, Gardner 88	15,789
6	12	H	Birmingham C	W 3-1	2-1	8	Taylor B 2 1,49, Frandsen 5	19,637
7	19	A	Crewe Alex	D 4-4	3-2	8	Gunnlaugsson 2 23,44, Taylor B 37, Frandsen 50	5744
8	26	H	Huddersfield T	W 3-0	3-0	5	Frandsen 15, Blake 26, Gunnlaugsson 43	20,971
9	29	H	Swindon T	W 2-1	0-0	—	Blake 46, Gunnlaugsson 86	16,497
10	Oct 3	A	Barnsley	D 2-2	2-1	3	Gunnlaugsson 21, Johansen 42	17,362
11	17	H	Oxford U	D 1-1	1-1	5	Frandsen 37	17,064
12	20	H	Watford	L 1-2	1-1	—	Gunnlaugsson 25	15,921
13	23	A	Bristol C	L 1-2	1-2	—	Gunnlaugsson 6	12,026
14	Nov 1	H	Sunderland	L 0-3	0-2	12		21,676
15	4	A	Port Vale	W 2-0	2-0	—	Taylor B 5, Frandsen 20, Gunnlaugsson 69	13,324
16	7	A	QPR	L 0-2	0-1	12		11,814
17	14	H	Tranmere R	D 2-2	0-1	13	Johansen 53, Holdsworth (pen) 56	16,564
18	21	A	Ipswich T	W 1-0	0-0	10	Taylor B 90	17,225
19	24	A	Stockport Co	W 1-0	0-0	—	Taylor B 81	8520
20	28	H	Bury	W 4-0	1-0	5	Johansen 2 21,57, Gunnlaugsson 2 64,67	21,028
21	Dec 5	A	Wolverhampton W	D 1-1	0-0	5	Taylor B 58	22,537
22	12	A	Tranmere R	D 1-1	1-0	7	Taylor B 11	6959
23	19	H	Portsmouth	W 3-1	0-1	6	Taylor B 70, Frandsen 78, Holdsworth 84	15,981
24	26	H	Bradford C	D 0-0	0-0	7		24,625
25	28	A	Port Vale	W 2-0	0-0	5	Sellars 48, Holdsworth (pen) 75	8201
26	Jan 10	H	Crystal Palace	W 3-0	3-0	5	Taylor B 3, Johansen 26, Jensen 33	15,410
27	16	A	Sheffield U	W 2-1	1-1	3	Holdsworth 2 45,72	15,787
28	30	H	Norwich C	W 2-0	1-0	3	Holdsworth 38, Cox 65	17,269
29	Feb 6	A	Grimsby T	W 1-0	0-0	3	Holdsworth 54	8674
30	13	H	WBA	W 2-1	1-1	2	Taylor B 43, Cox 51	20,657
31	21	A	Birmingham C	D 0-0	0-0	2		26,051
32	27	H	Crewe Alex	L 1-3	0-2	4	Holdsworth (pen) 55	19,437
33	Mar 2	A	Huddersfield T	L 2-3	1-2	—	Holdsworth 19, Johansen 50	13,867
34	6	A	Swindon T	D 3-3	0-1	5	Fish 60, Jensen 70, Gudjohnsen 77	8392
35	9	H	Barnsley	D 3-3	2-2	—	Sellars 15, Holdsworth (pen) 25, Gudjohnsen 80	16,537
36	13	H	QPR	W 2-1	1-0	5	Taylor B 2 30,58	17,919
37	20	A	Sunderland	L 1-3	0-2	—	Frandsen 49	41,505
38	Apr 3	A	Oxford U	D 0-0	0-0	5		7547
39	5	H	Stockport Co	L 1-2	0-1	6	Taylor B 49	18,587
40	10	A	Watford	L 0-2	0-1	6		13,001
41	13	H	Bristol C	W 1-0	1-0	—	Gudjohnsen 7	14,459
42	17	H	Ipswich T	W 2-0	1-0	5	Taylor B 37, Gudjohnsen 69	19,894
43	20	A	Norwich C	D 2-2	0-2	—	Cox 48, Frandsen 74	11,137
44	23	A	Bury	L 1-2	0-2	—	Cox 90	7680
45	30	H	Wolverhampton W	D 1-1	1-0	6	Gardner 36	20,208
46	May 9	A	Portsmouth	W 2-0	1-0	6	Johansen 20, Gudjohnsen 67	16,015

Final League Position: 6

GOALSCORERS

League (78): Taylor B 15, Gunnlaugsson 13, Holdsworth 12 (5 pens), Frandsen 8, Johansen 7, Blake 6, Gudjohnsen 5, Cox 4, Gardner 2, Jensen 2, Sellars 2, Fish 1, Strong 1.
Worthington Cup (12): Blake 3, Jensen 2, Elliott 1, Frandsen 1, Gardner 1, Gunnlaugsson 1, Johansen 1, Phillips 1, Taylor B 1.
FA Cup (1): Sellars 1.

Jaaskelainen J 34	Cox N 42+2	Phillips J 14+1	Todd A 18+2	Bergsson G 15+2	Fish M 36	Jensen C 44	Frandsen P 44	Blake N 11+1	Holdsworth D 22+10	Sellars S 22+3	Johansen M 40+3	Gunnlaugsson A 22+5	Whitlow M 27+1	Strong G 4+1	Taylor B 32+6	Gardner R 19+11	Gudjohnsen E 8+6	Branagan K 3	Elliott R 14+8	Aljofree H 1+3	Newsome J 6	Warhurst P 17+3	Hansen B 1+7	Banks S 9	Fullarton J 1	Match No.
1	2	3	4	5	6	7^1	8	9	10	11^2	12	13														1
1	2	3	4	5	6	7^1	8	9	10	12	11															2
1	2	3	4	5	6	7	8	9	10		11															3
1	2		4^1	12	6	7^2	8	9	10		11		3	5	13											4
1	2		4	5	6	7^3	8	9^1	10^2	14	11		3		12	13										5
1	2			5	6	4^2	8	12			7		11		3	9	10^1		13							6
1	2			5^1	6	4^2	8	13			7		11		3	12	9		10							7
1	2			5	6	4	8	9			7		11		3	10										8
1	2			5	6	4	8	9			7		11		3	10										9
1	2	3		5	6	4	8	9			7		11			10										10
1	2			5	6	4	8	9	12		7		11		3	13	10^2									11
	2			5	6	4	8	9			7		11		3	12	10^1	1								12
	2			5	6	4	8^2	9	12		7		11		3	13	10^1	1								13
	3	4	5	6^1	10	8	12				7^2		11		9			1	2	13						14
1	12	3	4	5	10^2	8		14	13		7		11^3		6	9^1			2							15
1	12	3	4	5^1		8		13	14		7^2		11		6	9			2^3			10				16
1	2				6	4^3	8		10^1		11	7	9		3^2	5	12		13	14						17
1	2			5		8	4		9^1		11	7	12		3	10					6					18
1	2			5		8	12			11		7^1	9		3	10			4^2	13	6					19
1	2					8	4		12	11		7	9		3^2	10^1	13				6	5				20
1	2					8	4			11		7	9^1		10	12			3		6	5				21
1	2					8^3	4		12	11		7	9^1		13	10	14		3^2		6	5				22
1	2					8	4		12	11^2		7	9^3		3	10	13				6	5				23
1	2				6	8	4^1		9		11	12	3		10	7			5							24
1	2				6	8	4		9		11	7	12		3	10^1			5							25
1	2				6	8	4		12	11^2		7	9		3	10^1	13			14		5				26
1	2				6	8^1	4		9		11	7	3		10	12						5				27
1	2				6	8	4^3		9^1		11	7	12		3	10	14			13		5^2				28
1	2				6	8^2	4		9		11	7	3		10	13	12					5^1				29
1	2				6	8^1	4		9		11	7	3		10	12						5				30
1	2				6	8^1	4		9^2		11	7	3		10	12						5	13			31
1	2	12			6^2	8			9		11	7	3		10^3	4^1			5			13	14			32
1	2				6	8	4		9		11	7	3		10^1				5			12				33
1	2				6	8	4		9		11	7	3		10^1				12			5				34
1	2				6	8	4		9		11	7	3			12			5			10^1				35
1	2	12			6	8	4		9^2		11	7	3^1		10		13					5				36
1	2	12			6	8	4		9	11^2		7^1			10^3	13	14		3			5				37
	2	3			6	8	4		9						7	12	10^2		5			13		1	11^1	38
	2				6	8	4		9^1						7	10	11		12	3		5		1		39
	2				6	8	4								7	10	11		9	3		5		1		40
	2	3		5	6	8	4								7	10	11					9		1		41
	2	3		5	6^1	8	4								7	10	11		9^2			12	13	1		42
	2	3			6	8	4								7	10	11		9			5		1		43
	2	3		5	6	8	4								7	10	11		9					1		44
	2	3^1		5	6	8	4								7	10	11		9^3	12		13	14	1		45
	2^1		5	12	6	8	4^2								7	10^3	11		9	3		13	14	1		46

Worthington Cup

First Round	Hartlepool U	(h)	1-0
		(a)	3-0
Second Round	Hull C	(h)	3-1
		(a)	3-2
Third Round	Norwich C	(a)	1-1
Fourth Round	Wimbledon	(h)	1-2

FA Cup

Third Round	Wolverhampton W	(h)	1-2

Division 2

AFC BOURNEMOUTH

FOUNDATION

There was a Bournemouth FC as early as 1875, but the present club arose out of the remnants of the Boscombe St John's club (formed 1890). The meeting at which Boscombe FC came into being was held at a house in Gladstone Road in 1899. They began by playing in the Boscombe and District Junior League.

Dean Court Ground, Bournemouth, Dorset BH7 7AF.

Telephone: (01202) 395381.

Fax: (01202) 309797.

Website: http://www.afcb.co.uk.

Clubcall: 0891 121 163.

Ticket Office: (01202) 397939.

Ground Capacity: 10,770.

Record Attendance: 28,799 v Manchester U, FA Cup 6th rd, 2 March 1957.

Record Receipts: £80,267 v Walsall, Auto Windscreens Shield Southern Area Final, 17 March 1998.

Pitch Measurements: 112yd × 74yd.

Chairman: T. S. Watkins.

Directors: A. H. Kaye (Vice-Chairman), K. R. Dando, P. W. Aldersey (Managing Director), A. Dawson (Deputy Managing Director), A. Swaisland.

Secretary: K. R. J. MacAlister.

Manager: Mel Machin.

Assistant Manager: John Williams.

First Team Coach: Sean O'Driscoll.

Physio: Steve Hardwick.

Corporate Manager: Miss D. Edwards.

Groundsman: D. Edwards.

LATEST SEQUENCES

Longest Sequence of League Wins: 7, 22.8.70 – 23.9.70.

Longest Sequence of League Defeats: 7, 13.8.94 – 13.9.94.

Longest Sequence of League Draws: 5, 10.11.79 – 21.12.79.

Longest Sequence of Unbeaten League Matches: 18, 6.3.82 – 28.8.82.

Longest Sequence Without a League Win: 14, 6.3.74 – 27.4.74.

HONOURS

Football League: Division 3 – Champions 1986–87; Division 3 (S) – Runners-up 1947–48; Division 4 – Runners-up 1970–71; Promotion from Division 4 1981–82 (4th).

FA Cup: best season: 6th rd, 1957.

Football League Cup: best season: 4th rd, 1962, 1964.

Associate Members' Cup: Winners 1984.

Auto Windscreens Shield: Runners-up 1998.

Colours

Red shirts with 3¾-inch black stripe and black collar with red and white trim, black shorts, black stockings.

Change Colours

Green shirts with 3¾-inch black stripe and black collar with green and white trim, green shorts, green stockings.

Year Formed: 1899.

Turned Professional: 1912.

Ltd Co.: 1914.

Previous Names: 1890, Boscombe St Johns; 1899, Boscombe FC; 1923, Bournemouth & Boscombe Ath FC; 1971, AFC Bournemouth.

Club Nickname: 'Cherries'.

Previous Grounds: 1899, Castlemain Road, Pokesdown; 1910, Dean Court.

First Football League Game: 25 August 1923, Division 3 (S), v Swindon T (a), L 1–3 – Heron; Wingham, Lamb; Butt, C. Smith, Voisey; Miller, Lister (1), Davey, Simpson, Robinson.

Record League Victory: 7–0 v Swindon T, Division 3 (S), 22 September 1956 – Godwin; Cunningham, Keetley; Clayton, Crosland, Rushworth; Siddall (1), Norris (2), Arnott (1), Newsham (2), Cutler (1). 10–0 win v Northampton T at start of 1939–40 expunged from the records on outbreak of war.

Record Cup Victory: 11–0 v Margate, FA Cup 1st rd, 20 November 1971 – Davies; Machin (1), Kitchener, Benson, Jones, Powell, Cave (1), Boyer, MacDougall (9 incl. 1p), Miller, Scott (De Garis).

Record Defeat: 0–9 v Lincoln C, Division 3, 18 December 1982.

Most League Points (2 for a win): 62, Division 3, 1971–72.

Most League Points (3 for a win): 97, Division 3, 1986–87.

Most League Goals: 88, Division 3 (S), 1956–57.

Highest League Scorer in Season: Ted MacDougall, 42, 1970–71.

Most League Goals in Total Aggregate: Ron Eyre, 202, 1924–33.

Most League Goals in One Match: 4, Jack Russell v Clapton Orient, Division 3S, 7 January 1933; 4, Jack Russell v Bristol C, Division 3S, 28 January 1933; 4, Harry Mardon v Southend U, Division 3S, 1 January 1938; 4, Jack McDonald v Torquay U, Division 3S, 8 November 1947.

Most Capped Player: Gerry Peyton, 7 (33), Republic of Ireland.

Most League Appearances: Sean O'Driscoll, 423, 1984–95.

Youngest League Player: Jimmy White, 15 years 321 days v Brentford, 30 April 1958.

Record Transfer Fee Received: £800,000 from Everton for Joe Parkinson, March 1994.

Record Transfer Fee Paid: £210,000 to Gillingham for Gavin Peacock, August 1989.

Football League Record: 1923 Elected to Division 3 (S) and remained a Third Division club for record number of years until 1970; 1970–71 Division 4; 1971–75 Division 3; 1975–82 Division 4; 1982–87 Division 3; 1987–90 Division 2; 1990–92 Division 3; 1992– Division 2.

MANAGERS

Vincent Kitcher 1914–23
(Secretary-Manager)
Harry Kinghorn 1923–25
Leslie Knighton 1925–28
Frank Richards 1928–30
Billy Birrell 1930–35
Bob Crompton 1935–36
Charlie Bell 1936–39
Harry Kinghorn 1939–47
Harry Lowe 1947–50
Jack Bruton 1950–56
Fred Cox 1956–58
Don Welsh 1958–61
Bill McGarry 1961–63
Reg Flewin 1963–65
Fred Cox 1965–70
John Bond 1970–73
Trevor Hartley 1974–75
John Benson 1975–78
Alec Stock 1979–80
David Webb 1980–82
Don Megson 1983
Harry Redknapp 1983–92
Tony Pulis 1992–94
Mel Machin August 1994–

TEN YEAR LEAGUE RECORD

		P	W	D	L	F	A	Pts	Pos
1988-89	Div 2	46	18	8	20	53	62	62	12
1989-90	Div 2	46	12	12	22	57	76	48	22
1990-91	Div 3	46	19	13	14	58	58	70	9
1991-92	Div 3	46	20	11	15	52	48	71	8
1992-93	Div 2	46	12	17	17	45	52	53	17
1993-94	Div 2	46	14	15	17	51	59	57	17
1994-95	Div 2	46	13	11	22	49	69	50	19
1995-96	Div 2	46	16	10	20	51	70	58	14
1996-97	Div 2	46	15	15	16	43	45	60	16
1997-98	Div 2	46	18	12	16	57	52	66	9

DID YOU KNOW ?

The first player to gain international honours while with Bournemouth was Sammy Beswick, selected to appear at inside-left for England in the amateur international against Wales at Aberystwyth on 15 February 1930. England won 2–1.

AFC BOURNEMOUTH 1998–99 LEAGUE RECORD

Match No.	Date	Venue	Opponents	Result	H/T Score	Lg. Pos.	Goalscorers	Attendance
1	Aug 8	H	Lincoln C	W 2-0	2-0	—	Cox [11], Stein [29]	5573
2	15	A	Notts Co	W 2-1	0-1	4	Berthe [51], Robinson [63]	5269
3	22	A	Millwall	W 3-0	0-0	2	Cox [56], Tindall (pen) [89], O'Neill [90]	6956
4	29	A	Fulham	D 0-0	0-0	2		12,107
5	Sept 1	H	Blackpool	D 1-1	0-0	—	Stein [50]	6785
6	5	A	Stoke C	L 0-2	0-0	4		13,443
7	8	A	Manchester C	L 1-2	0-1	—	Fletcher [48]	26,696
8	12	H	Wigan Ath	W 1-0	0-0	5	Berthe [83]	5151
9	19	A	Wycombe W	W 2-0	2-0	3	Fletcher [25], O'Neill [31]	4267
10	26	H	Oldham Ath	W 2-0	1-0	4	Robinson [6], Stein [49]	5877
11	Oct 3	A	Bristol R	L 0-1	0-0	6		7526
12	10	A	Macclesfield T	D 2-2	1-1	5	Robinson (pen) [45], Stein [89]	2974
13	17	H	Northampton T	D 1-1	1-0	6	Stein [26]	6362
14	20	H	Gillingham	D 3-3	1-1	—	Young [44], Hughes [57], Stein [88]	5183
15	Nov 7	A	Reading	D 3-3	1-2	9	Warren [40], Stein 2 (1 pen) [51] [pl], [89]	13,004
16	10	A	Chesterfield	L 1-3	1-2	—	Curtis (og) [32]	3797
17	21	H	Burnley	W 5-0	0-0	9	Warren [55], Robinson 2 (1 pen) [60] [pl], [69], Stein 2 [74], [89]	5907
18	28	A	Walsall	L 0-1	0-0	11		3895
19	Dec 12	H	York C	W 2-1	0-1	7	Robinson [63], Fletcher [74]	4863
20	19	A	Wrexham	W 1-0	1-0	6	Fletcher [21]	2716
21	26	A	Millwall	W 2-1	1-0	6	Warren [28], Stein [81]	7807
22	28	H	Luton T	W 1-0	0-0	5	Cox [53]	8863
23	Jan 9	A	Lincoln C	L 1-2	1-1	6	Fletcher [33]	3141
24	16	A	Notts Co	W 2-0	1-0	6	Stein [22], Cox [56]	5968
25	26	H	Preston NE	W 3-1	1-0	—	O'Neill [26], Howe [54], Stein [64]	6170
26	30	A	Luton T	D 2-2	0-1	5	Robinson [62], Vincent [69]	5426
27	Feb 6	H	Stoke C	W 4-0	2-0	4	Fletcher 2 [21], [39], Robinson [71], Hayter [76]	7637
28	13	A	Manchester C	D 0-0	0-0	5		10,964
29	20	A	Wigan Ath	L 1-2	0-0	6	Robinson [90]	4144
30	27	H	Wycombe W	W 2-0	2-0	5	Robinson 2 [24], [34]	6693
31	Mar 2	H	Fulham	D 1-1	0-0	—	Vincent [72]	9928
32	6	A	Oldham Ath	W 3-2	2-0	5	Cox [2], Stein [44], Warren [63]	4453
33	9	H	Bristol R	W 1-0	0-0	—	Howe [66]	7181
34	13	H	Reading	L 0-1	0-0	4		9445
35	16	A	Blackpool	D 0-0	0-0	—		3186
36	20	A	Preston NE	W 1-0	1-0	4	Fletcher [13]	12,882
37	27	H	Colchester U	W 2-1	2-1	4	Warren [35], Hughes [40]	6447
38	Apr 2	A	Northampton T	L 1-2	1-2	—	Robinson [17]	6858
39	6	H	Macclesfield T	W 1-0	0-0	—	Stein [84]	8033
40	9	A	Gillingham	L 1-2	1-0	—	Robinson [18]	7813
41	13	H	Walsall	L 0-1	0-1	—		8390
42	17	A	Burnley	D 0-0	0-0	6		9802
43	24	H	Chesterfield	D 0-0	0-0	6		6890
44	27	H	Colchester U	L 1-2	1-1	—	Greene (og) [34]	4168
45	May 1	A	York C	W 1-0	0-0	6	Hayter [47]	3503
46	8	H	Wrexham	D 0-0	0-0	7		8439

Final League Position: 7

GOALSCORERS

League (63): Stein 15 (1 pen), Robinson 13 (2 pens), Fletcher S 8, Cox 5, Warren 5, O'Neill 3, Berthe 2, Hayter 2, Howe 2, Hughes 2, Vincent 2, Tindall 1 (pen), Young 1, own goals 2.
Worthington Cup (8): Stein 5, Fletcher S 1, Howe 1, Robinson 1.
FA Cup (5): Howe 2, O'Neill 1, Robinson 1, Stein 1.

Overdale M 46	Young N 44	Vincent J 31 + 1	Howe E 45	Berthe M 12 + 3	Bailey J 30 + 2	Cox I 46	Robinson S 42	Stein M 43	Fletcher S 38 + 1	Hughes R 43 + 1	Tindall J 6 + 11	O'Neill J 18 + 6	Dean M 1 + 8	Town D 1 + 9	Warren C 26 + 6	Rodrigues D — + 5	Boli R 5 + 1	Griffin A 1 + 5	Rawlinson M 5 + 2	Jenkins J — + 1	Hayter J 16 + 4	Huck W 6 + 2	Day J — + 2	Lovell S 1 + 6	Fletcher C — + 1	Match No.
1	2	3	4	5	6^1	7	8	9	10	11	12															1
1	2	3	4	5^1	6	7	8	9	10	11	12															2
1	2	3	4	5	6^1	7		9	10	11	8	12														3
1	2	3	4	5^1		7	8	9	10	11	6		12													4
1	2	3	4	5^1	6^2	7	8	9	10	11^3	14	12	13													5
1	2	3	4	5^2	6^1	7	8	9	10	11	14		12	13^3												6
1	2^2	3	4		6^1	7	8	9	10	11	5^3		12	13	14											7
1	2	3	4	5	6	7	8	9	10	11																8
1	2	3	4		6	7	8^1	9	10	11	12				5											9
1	2		4		6	7	8^1	9	10	11	3	5^2			12	13										10
1	2^2	12	4		6^1	7	8	9	10	11	3^3	5			13	14										11
1	2		4	5	6	7	8	9		11	3^2	10^1			12	13										12
1	2	3	4	5		7	8	9		11					10	6										13
1	2	3^1	4	5	6	7	8	9		11					12	10										14
1	2		4	5^1	6	7		9		11	12	8^2			3	13	10									15
1	2	12	4	5	6	7		9		11^3	13	8^2		14	3		10^1									16
1	2	3	4		6	7	8^2	9		11^1					5	10		12	13							17
1	2	3^1	4	12	6	7	8	9	13	11					5^1	10										18
1		3	4	12	6	7	8	9^2	10	11^3					5	13	14		2^1							19
1	2	3	4			7	8	9	10						5	12	11				6^1					20
1	2	3	4		6	7	8	9	10					12	5			11^1								21
1	2	3	4		6	7	8	9	10	11					5											22
1	2	3	4		6^1	7	8	9	10	11					5	12										23
1	2	3	4		6	7	8	9	10	11			12		5^1											24
1	2	3	4		6	7	8	9	10	11					5											25
1	2	3	4		6	7	8	9	10	11					5											26
1	2	3^3	4		6	7	8		10	11					5	12^2		9^1			14	13				27
1	2	3	4		6	7^1	8		10	11					5^2	12	13				9					28
1	2	3	4		6^2	7^1	8	9	10	11		12			5^3	13					14					29
1	2	3	4		6^2	7	8	9	10	11			12		5^1						13					30
1	2	3	4		6^1	7	8	9	10	11					5						12					31
1	2	3	4			7	8	9^2	10	11		12	13		5						6^1					32
1	2	3	4			7	8	9	10	11					5						6					33
1	2	3	4	12		7	8	9	10	11					5^1						6					34
1	2	3	4			7	8	9	10	11					5^1				12		6					35
1	2	3				7	8	9^1	10	11					5^3	4^2	12		14	13	6					36
1			4		6	7		9		11					5	12	3		2		10	8^1				37
1	2^2		4			7	8	9	10	11		12			3^1						5	6	13			38
1	2		4			7	8^2	9	10	11		12			3						5	6^1	14	13^3		39
1	2		4			7	8	9	10	11^2		12			3						6^1			13		40
1	2		4^1			7	8	9	10	11				6^3	3^2				13	12	5			14		41
1	2		4			7	8	9^2	10	11					3^1					6	5	12		13		42
1	2		4			7	8		10	11			12		3		6				5		3^1	9^2	13	43
1	2		4			7	8	9	10	11					3				12		5^2	6^1		13		44
1	2		4	12		7	8	9	10	11					3						5	6^1				45
1	2		4		6^1	7	8	9	10	11		12			3^3						5^2	14		13		46

Worthington Cup

First Round	Colchester U	(h)	2-0
		(a)	2-3
Second Round	Wolverhampton W	(h)	1-1
		(a)	2-1
Third Round	Barnsley	(a)	1-2

FA Cup

First Round	Basingstoke T	(a)	2-1
Second Round	Torquay U	(a)	1-0
Third Round	WBA	(h)	1-0
Fourth Round	Barnsley	(a)	1-3

FA Premiership

BRADFORD CITY

FOUNDATION

Bradford was a rugby stronghold around the turn of the century but after Manningham RFC held an archery contest to help them out of financial difficulties in 1903, they were persuaded to give up the handling code and turn to soccer. So they formed Bradford City and continued at Valley Parade. Recognising this as an opportunity of spreading the dribbling code in this part of Yorkshire, the Football League immediately accepted the new club's first application for membership of the Second Division.

Valley Parade, Bradford BD8 7DY.

Telephone: (01274) 773355 (Office).

Fax: (01274) 773356.

Ticket Office: (01274) 770022.

Website: www.bradfordcity.co.uk.

Email: bradfordcityfc@compuserve.com.

Ground Capacity: 18,018.

Record Attendance: 39,146 v Burnley, FA Cup 4th rd, 11 March 1911.

Record Receipts: £164,567 v Sheffield Wednesday, FA Cup 5th rd, 16 February 1997.

Pitch Measurements: 110yd × 73yd.

Chairman: Geoffrey Richmond. *Vice-Chairman:* David Thompson FCA.

Directors: David Richmond, Elizabeth Richmond, Terry Goddard, Michael Richmond, Julian Rhodes, Prof. David Rhodes.

Managing Director: Shaun Harvey.

Manager: Paul Jewell.

Assistant Manager: Chris Hutchings.

Youth Coach: Steve Smith.

Physio: Steve Redmond.

Secretary: Jon Pollard.

Stadium Manager: Allan Gilliver.

HONOURS

Football League: Division 1 – Runners-up 1998–99; Division 2 – Champions 1907–08; Promoted from Division 2 1995–96 (play-offs); Division 3 – Champions 1984–85; Division 3 (N) – Champions 1928–29; Division 4 – Runners-up 1981–82.

FA Cup: Winners 1911.

Football League Cup: best season: 5th rd, 1965, 1989.

LATEST SEQUENCES

Longest Sequence of League Wins: 10, 26.11.83 – 3.2.84.

Longest Sequence of League Defeats: 8, 21.1.33 – 11.3.33.

Longest Sequence of League Draws: 6, 30.1.76 – 13.3.76.

Longest Sequence of Unbeaten League Matches: 21, 11.1.69 – 2.5.69.

Longest Sequence Without a League Win: 16, 28.8.48 – 20.11.48.

Colours
Claret and amber shirts, claret shorts, amber stockings.

Change Colours
Blue shirts and shorts, blue stockings.

Year Formed: 1903.

Turned Professional: 1903.

Ltd Co.: 1908.

Club Nickname: 'The Bantams'.

First Football League Game: 1 September 1903, Division 2, v Grimsby T (a) L 0–2 – Seymour; Wilson, Halliday; Robinson, Millar, Farnall; Guy, Beckram, Forrest, McMillan, Graham.

Record League Victory: 11–1 v Rotherham U, Division 3 (N), 25 August 1928 – Sherlaw; Russell, Watson; Burkinshaw (1), Summers, Bauld; Harvey (2), Edmunds (3), White (3), Cairns, Scriven (2).

Record Cup Victory: 11–3 v Walker Celtic, FA Cup 1st rd (replay), 1 December 1937 – Parker; Rookes, McDermott; Murphy, Mackie, Moore; Bagley (1), Whittingham (1), Deakin (4 incl. 1p), Cooke (1), Bartholomew (4).

Record Defeat: 1–9 v Colchester U, Division 4, 30 December 1961.

Most League Points (2 for a win): 63, Division 3 (N), 1928–29.

Most League Points (3 for a win): 94, Division 3, 1984–85.

Most League Goals: 128, Division 3 (N), 1928–29.

Highest League Scorer in Season: David Layne, 34, Division 4, 1961–62.

Most League Goals in Total Aggregate: Bobby Campbell, 121, 1981–84, 1984–86.

Most League Goals in One Match: 7, Albert Whitehurst v Tranmere R, Division 3N, 6 March 1929.

Most Capped Player: Harry Hampton, 9, Northern Ireland.

Most League Appearances: Cec Podd, 502, 1970–84.

Youngest League Player: Robert Cullingford, 16 years 141 days v Mansfield T, 22 April 1970.

Record Transfer Fee Received: £2,000,000 from Newcastle U for Des Hamilton, March 1997.

Record Transfer Fee Paid: £1,300,000 to Arsenal for Isaiah Rankin, August 1998.

Football League Record: 1903 Elected to Division 2; 1908–22 Division 1; 1922–27 Division 2; 1927–29 Division 3 (N); 1929–37 Division 2; 1937–61 Division 3; 1961–69 Division 4; 1969–72 Division 3; 1972–77 Division 4; 1977–78 Division 3; 1978–82 Division 4; 1982–85 Division 3; 1985–90 Division 2; 1990–92 Division 3; 1992–96 Division 2; 1996–99 Division 1; 1999– FA Premier League.

MANAGERS

Robert Campbell 1903–05
Peter O'Rourke 1905–21
David Menzies 1921–26
Colin Veitch 1926–28
Peter O'Rourke 1928–30
Jack Peart 1930–35
Dick Ray 1935–37
Fred Westgarth 1938–43
Bob Sharp 1943–46
Jack Barker 1946–47
John Milburn 1947–48
David Steele 1948–52
Albert Harris 1952
Ivor Powell 1952–55
Peter Jackson 1955–61
Bob Brocklebank 1961–64
Bill Harris 1965–66
Willie Watson 1966–69
Grenville Hair 1967–68
Jimmy Wheeler 1968–71
Bryan Edwards 1971–75
Bobby Kennedy 1975–78
John Napier 1978
George Mulhall 1978–81
Roy McFarland 1981–82
Trevor Cherry 1982–87
Terry Dolan 1987–89
Terry Yorath 1989–90
John Docherty 1990–91
Frank Stapleton 1991–94
Lennie Lawrence 1994–95
Chris Kamara 1995–98
Paul Jewell May 1998–

TEN YEAR LEAGUE RECORD

		P	W	D	L	F	A	Pts	Pos
1988-89	Div 2	46	13	17	16	52	59	56	14
1989-90	Div 2	46	9	14	23	44	68	41	23
1990-91	Div 3	46	20	10	16	62	54	70	8
1991-92	Div 3	46	13	19	14	62	61	58	16
1992-93	Div 2	46	18	14	14	69	67	68	10
1993-94	Div 2	46	19	13	14	61	53	70	7
1994-95	Div 2	46	16	12	18	57	64	60	14
1995-96	Div 2	46	22	7	17	71	69	73	6
1996-97	Div 1	46	12	12	22	47	72	48	21
1997-98	Div 1	46	14	15	17	46	59	57	13

DID YOU KNOW ?

Against Southport on 11 October 1961, Bradford City fielded their youngest pair of full-backs: Brian Kelly and Roy Ellam. Their aggregate age was only 37 years 48 days. City won 1–0 with a goal from David 'Bronco' Layne.

BRADFORD CITY 1998–99 LEAGUE RECORD

Match No.	Date	Venue	Opponents	Result	H/T Score	Lg. Pos.	Goalscorers	Atten- dance
1	Aug 8	H	Stockport Co	L 1-2	0-1	—	Beagrie (pen) 76	14,360
2	15	A	Watford	L 0-1	0-0	23		10,731
3	23	H	Bolton W	D 2-2	1-1	19	Rankin 42, Mills 88	13,163
4	28	A	Crewe Alex	L 1-2	1-2	—	McCall 38	5759
5	31	H	Birmingham C	W 2-1	0-0	18	Mills 59, Moore 73	13,910
6	Sept 8	A	Ipswich T	L 0-3	0-1	—		11,596
7	12	H	Sheffield U	D 2-2	2-1	21	Mills 18, Blake 28	13,169
8	20	A	WBA	W 2-0	2-0	18	Mills 2 4, 16	12,426
9	26	H	Barnsley	W 2-1	0-0	15	Watson 2 87, 89	15,887
10	29	H	Port Vale	W 4-0	1-0	—	Blake 31, Moore 57, Mills 60, Beesley (og) 89	13,245
11	Oct 3	A	Sunderland	D 0-0	0-0	13		37,828
12	9	H	Bury	W 3-0	1-0	—	Blake 15, McCall 55, Beagrie 67	15,697
13	17	A	Grimsby T	L 0-2	0-1	9		7473
14	20	A	Portsmouth	W 4-2	3-0	—	Whalley 22, Rankin 32, Mills 33, Beagrie 80	10,062
15	31	H	Bristol C	W 5-0	2-0	8	Carey (og) 14, Mills 17, Rankin 51, Beagrie 57, Blake 90	14,468
16	Nov 7	A	Norwich C	D 2-2	1-0	7	Rankin 19, Mills 88	14,722
17	10	A	Tranmere R	W 1-0	1-0	—	Beagrie (pen) 44	6002
18	14	H	Swindon T	W 3-0	0-0	5	Beagrie (pen) 48, Pepper 79, Jacobs 90	14,897
19	21	A	Huddersfield T	L 1-2	1-0	9	Blake 18	18,173
20	28	H	QPR	L 0-3	0-0	10		15,037
21	Dec 5	A	Oxford U	W 1-0	1-0	8	Mills 22	5969
22	12	A	Swindon T	W 4-1	1-1	5	Blake 2 20, 83, Mills 2 48, 61	7447
23	19	H	Wolverhampton W	W 2-1	1-0	3	Blake 20, Mills 50	13,846
24	26	A	Bolton W	D 0-0	0-0	5		24,625
25	28	H	Tranmere R	W 2-0	1-0	4	Blake 27, Mills 61	14,076
26	Jan 9	A	Stockport Co	W 2-1	1-0	4	Blake 9, Beagrie 72	8975
27	16	H	Crewe Alex	W 4-1	2-0	2	Mills 3 25, 41, 55, Blake 66	12,595
28	19	H	Crystal Palace	W 2-1	0-0	—	Westwood 75, Beagrie (pen) 87	14,368
29	31	A	Birmingham C	L 1-2	1-1	2	Lawrence 27	19,291
30	Feb 6	H	Watford	W 2-0	1-0	2	McCall 9, Mills 62	14,142
31	13	H	Ipswich T	D 0-0	0-0	3		15,024
32	19	A	Sheffield U	D 2-2	1-1	—	Blake 2 32, 82	14,675
33	27	H	WBA	W 1-0	1-0	2	Jacobs 3	14,278
34	Mar 3	A	Barnsley	W 1-0	0-0	—	Watson 74	16,866
35	9	H	Sunderland	L 0-1	0-0	—		15,124
36	13	H	Norwich C	W 4-1	4-0	3	Moore 13, Beagrie (pen) 25, Mills 34, Lawrence 45	13,331
37	20	A	Bristol C	W 3-2	2-0	3	Mills 30, Jacobs 40, Whalley 83	10,870
38	28	A	Crystal Palace	L 0-1	0-1	3		15,626
39	Apr 3	H	Grimsby T	W 3-0	1-0	3	Blake 11, Sharpe 76, Beagrie 90	14,522
40	5	A	Bury	W 2-0	2-0	3	Windass 2 28, 43	8000
41	10	H	Portsmouth	W 2-1	2-0	3	Mills 25, Sharpe 36	13,552
42	13	A	Port Vale	D 1-1	1-1	—	Mills 33	6998
43	17	H	Huddersfield T	L 2-3	1-3	2	Blake 8, Windass 72	15,124
44	24	A	QPR	W 3-1	1-0	2	Beagrie 32, Westwood 62, Watson 90	11,641
45	May 1	H	Oxford U	D 0-0	0-0	2		15,064
46	9	A	Wolverhampton W	W 3-2	2-1	2	Beagrie 25, Mills 40, Blake 64	27,589

Final League Position: 2

GOALSCORERS

League (82): Mills 23, Blake 16, Beagrie 12 (5 pens), Rankin 4, Watson 4, Jacobs 3, McCall 3, Moore 3, Windass 3, Lawrence 2, Sharpe 2, Westwood 2, Whalley 2, Pepper 1, own goals 2.
Worthington Cup (7): Beagrie 3 (1 pen), Blake 1, Moore 1, Pepper 1, Rankin 1.
FA Cup (2): Lawrence 1, Mills 1.

Walsh G 46	Wright S 21+1	Todd L 14+1	McCall S 43	Moore D 44	O'Brien A 19+12	Lawrence J 33+2	Edinho 1+2	Mills L 44	Whalley G 45	Beagrie P 43	Grant G 1+4	Dreyer J 19+2	Bolland P 2	Rankin I 15+12	Jacobs W 42+2	Westwood A 17+2	Pepper N 5+4	Ramage C —+3	Blake R 35+4	Watson G 5+13	Windass D 6+6	Sharpe L 6+3	Match No.
1	2	3	4	5	6	7	8^1	9	10	11	12												1
1	2			5	6	7	12	9^2	10	11	13	3	4		8^1								2
1				5	6	7		9	10	11		4^2	3	2^1	8	12	13						3
1			4	5	6	7		9	10	11		3			8	12	2^1						4
1			4	5	6	7^2		9	10	11	12	3			8^1	2			13				5
1	12		4	5	6^1			9^2	10	11	13	3			8	2^3		7	14				6
1	2		4	5				9	10	11		6		3	7				8				7
1	2		4	5	6			9	10	11				7^1	3		13		8	12^2			8
1	2^1		4	5	6^3			9	10	11		12		13	3	7^2			8	14			9
1		2	4^1	5	13			9	10	11^2				6	12	3		14	8	7^3			10
1		2	4	5				9	10	11				6	12	3			8	7^1			11
1		2	4	5	12		13	9		11^2				6	14	3^1		10	8	7^2			12
1		2	4	5				9	10^1	11				6	13	3		12	8	7^2			13
1		2	4	5	12			9	10	11				6	7^2	3			8^1	13			14
1		2	4^1	5	12	13		9^2	10	11^2				6	7	3			8	14			15
1			4	5	6	2		9	10	11					7	3			8				16
1			4	5		2		9^1	10	11					7	3	6		8	12			17
1				5	12	2		9^2	10	11					7	3	6^1	4	8	13			18
1			4	5	6	2		9	10^1	11					7^2	3		12	8	13			19
1		12	4	5	6^1	2		9	10	11					7	3			8^2	13			20
1	2		4	5	6	7		9	10	11					12	3			8^1				21
1	2		4	5	6	7		9	10	11					3				8				22
1	2^2		4	5	6	7		9^1	10	11					3	13			8	12			23
1	2		4	5	6	7			10	11					12	3			8	9^1			24
1	2		4	5	6	7		9	10	11					3				8				25
1	2		4	5	6	7		9	10	11					3				8				26
1	2		4^2	5		7		9	10	11					12	3	6		8^1	13			27
1	2^1		4	5		7		9	10	11					12	3	6		8				28
1	2		4	5		7		9	10	11						3	6		8				29
1	2		4			5	7	9	10	11						3	6		8				30
1	2		4	5		7		9	10	11					12	3	6		8^1				31
1	2^2		4	5	12	7			10	11					9^1	3	6		8	13			32
1		2	4	5	11	7^2		9	10					12	13	3	6^1		8				33
1		2	4	5	12	7		9	10					6	11^2	3			8^1	13			34
1		2	4	5		7		9	10					6		3			8	11			35
1		2^1	4	5	12	7		9	10	11				6		3			8^2	13			36
1		2	4	5		7		9	10	11				6	12	3			8^1				37
1		2^2	4	5		7		9	10	11					3	6		12	8^1	13			38
1		2^3	4	5	12	7		9^2	10	11					3	6			8^1	13	14		39
1			4	5	12	7		9	10	11					3	6		13	8^2			2^1	40
1			4	5	12	7		9	10	11^1					3	6		13	8^2			2	41
1			4	5		7		9	10	11					3	6			8^1		12	2	42
1	7^1		4	5				9	10^2	11					3	6			8	12	13	2	43
1	7		4		12			9^2	10	11		5			3^1	6			8^3	13	14	2	44
1	7		4	5			12	9^2	10	11		6			3					13	8	2^1	45
1	2		4	5		7		9	10	11^2			6		3				8^1		12	13	46

Worthington Cup

First Round	Lincoln C	(h)	1-1
		(a)	1-0
Second Round	Halifax T	(a)	2-1
		(h)	3-1
Third Round	Leeds U	(a)	0-1

FA Cup

Third Round	Grimsby T	(h)	2-1
Fourth Round	Newcastle U	(a)	0-3

Division 2

BRENTFORD

FOUNDATION

Formed as a small amateur concern in 1889 they were very successful in local circles. They won the championship of the West London Alliance in 1893 and a year later the West Middlesex Junior Cup before carrying off the Senior Cup in 1895. After winning both the London Senior Amateur Cup and the Middlesex Senior Cup in 1898 they were admitted to the Second Division of the Southern League.

Griffin Park, Braemar Rd, Brentford, Middlesex TW8 0NT.
Telephone: (0208) 847 2511.
Fax: (0208) 568 9940.
Commercial Dept: (0208) 847 2511
Press Office: (0208) 847 2511.
Clubcall: 09068 121108.
Ground Capacity: 12,763.
Record Attendance: 38,678 v Leicester C, FA Cup 6th rd, 26 February 1949.
Record Receipts: £162,314 v Tottenham H, Worthington Cup 2nd rd, 15 September 1998.
Pitch Measurements: 111yd × 74yd.
Chairman: Ron Noades.
President: E. J. Radley-Smith.
Managing Director: G. Hargraves.
Directors: S. Ebbs, J. Herting, D. Miller, D. Tana.
Manager: Ron Noades.
First Team Coach: Ray Lewington.
Director of Youth Football: Geoff Taylor.
Coaches: Terry Bullivant, Brian Sparrow.
Community Officer: Lee Doyle.
Secretary: Polly Kates.
Physio: Gerry Delahunt.
Safety Officer: Jill Dawson.
Communications Manager: Peter Gilham.
Commercial Manager: Samantha Marmara.

LATEST SEQUENCES
Longest Sequence of League Wins: 9, 30.4.32 – 24.9.32.
Longest Sequence of League Defeats: 9, 20.10.28 – 25.12.28.
Longest Sequence of League Draws: 5, 16.3.57 – 6.4.57.
Longest Sequence of Unbeaten League Matches: 16, 20.2.99 – 8.5.99.
Longest Sequence Without a League Win: 16, 19.2.94 – 7.5.94.

HONOURS

Football League: Division 1 best season: 5th, 1935–36; Division 2 – Champions 1934–35; Division 3 – Champions 1991–92, 1998–99; Division 3 (S) – Champions 1932–33, Runners-up 1929–30, 1957–58; Division 4 – Champions 1962–63.

FA Cup: best season: 6th rd, 1938, 1946, 1949, 1989.

Football League Cup: best season: 4th rd, 1983.

Freight Rover Trophy: Runners-up 1985.

Colours
Red and white vertical striped shirts, black shorts, black stockings.

Change Colours
Blue and yellow shirts, blue shorts, yellow stockings.

Year Formed: 1889.

Turned Professional: 1899.

Ltd Co.: 1901.

Club Nickname: 'The Bees'.

Previous Grounds: 1889, Clifden Road; 1891, Benns Fields, Little Ealing; 1895, Shotters Field; 1898, Cross Road, S. Ealing; 1900, Boston Park; 1904, Griffin Park.

First Football League Game: 28 August 1920, Division 3, v Exeter C (a) L 0–3 – Young; Hodson, Rosier, Elliott J, Levitt, Amos, Smith, Thompson, Spreadbury, Morley, Henery.

Record League Victory: 9–0 v Wrexham, Division 3, 15 October 1963 – Cakebread; Coote, Jones; Slater, Scott, Higginson; Summers (1), Brooks (2), McAdams (2), Ward (2), Hales (1), (1 og).

Record Cup Victory: 7–0 v Windsor & Eton (away), FA Cup 1st rd, 20 November 1982 – Roche; Rowe, Harris (Booker), McNichol (1), Whitehead, Hurlock (2), Kamara, Joseph (1), Mahoney (3), Bowles, Roberts.

Record Defeat: 0–7 v Swansea T, Division 3 (S), 8 November 1924 and v Walsall, Division 3 (S), 19 January 1957.

Most League Points (2 for a win): 62, Division 3 (S), 1932–33 and Division 4, 1962–63.

Most League Points (3 for a win): 85, Division 2, 1994–95 and Division 3, 1998–99.

Most League Goals: 98, Division 4, 1962–63.

Highest League Scorer in Season: Jack Holliday, 38, Division 3 (S), 1932–33.

Most League Goals in Total Aggregate: Jim Towers, 153, 1954–61.

Most League Goals in One Match: 5, Jack Holliday v Luton T, Division 3S, 28 January 1933; Billy Scott v Barnsley, Division 2, 15 December 1934; Peter McKennan v Bury, Division 2, 18 February 1949.

Most Capped Player: John Buttigieg, (63), Malta.

Most League Appearances: Ken Coote, 514, 1949–64.

Youngest League Player: Danis Salman, 15 years 243 days v Watford, 15 November 1975.

Record Transfer Fee Received: £720,000 from Wimbledon for Dean Holdsworth, August 1992.

Record Transfer Fee Paid: £850,000 to Crystal Palace for Hermann Hreidarsson, September 1998.

Football League Record: 1920 Original Member of Division 3; 1921–33 Division 3 (S); 1933–35 Division 2; 1935–47 Division 1; 1947–54 Division 2; 1954–62 Division 3 (S); 1962–63 Division 4; 1963–66 Division 3; 1966–72 Division 4; 1972–73 Division 3; 1973–78 Division 4; 1978–92 Division 3; 1992–93 Division 1; 1993–98 Division 2; 1998 –99 Division 3; 1999– Division 2.

TEN YEAR LEAGUE RECORD

		P	W	D	L	F	A	Pts	Pos
1988-89	Div 3	46	18	14	14	66	61	68	7
1989-90	Div 3	46	18	7	21	66	66	61	13
1990-91	Div 3	46	21	13	12	59	47	76	6
1991-92	Div 3	46	25	7	14	81	55	82	1
1992-93	Div 1	46	13	10	23	52	71	49	22
1993-94	Div 2	46	13	19	14	57	55	58	16
1994-95	Div 2	46	25	10	11	81	39	85	2
1995-96	Div 2	46	15	13	18	43	49	58	15
1996-97	Div 2	46	20	14	12	56	43	74	4
1997-98	Div 2	46	11	17	18	50	71	50	21

DID YOU KNOW ?

The team group photograph taken after Brentford had won promotion to the First Division in successive seasons in the 1930s had this 'sponsorship' note: 'each member is an enthusiastic user of a Waterman's Pen!'

BRENTFORD 1998–99 LEAGUE RECORD

Match No.	Date	Venue	Opponents	Result	H/T Score	Lg. Pos.	Goalscorers	Attendance
1	Aug 8	H	Mansfield T	W 3-0	1-0	—	Rapley 2 [32, 71], Freeman [83]	4846
2	15	A	Halifax T	L 0-1	0-1	7		3876
3	22	H	Brighton & HA	W 2-0	2-0	5	Thomas (og) [7], Scott [18]	6355
4	29	A	Barnet	W 3-0	1-0	3	Quinn [8], Rowlands [60], Owusu [80]	2710
5	31	H	Rochdale	W 2-1	1-1	2	Powell [2], Rapley [71]	4873
6	Sept 5	A	Hull C	W 3-2	1-1	1	Owusu [26], Aspinall [58], Scott [79]	4058
7	8	A	Torquay U	L 1-3	1-0	—	Bates [44]	2340
8	12	H	Rotherham U	L 0-3	0-1	4		4803
9	19	A	Scarborough	L 1-3	0-2	7	Owusu [64]	2028
10	26	H	Darlington	W 3-0	2-0	5	Powell [20], Rowlands [32], Owusu [69]	4486
11	Oct 3	A	Peterborough U	W 4-2	1-1	2	Freeman [45], Scott 2 [76, 82], Folan [79]	6056
12	17	H	Hartlepool U	W 3-1	2-0	1	Freeman [14], Aspinall (pen) [27], Rowlands [50]	4883
13	20	H	Scunthorpe U	W 2-1	0-1	—	Scott [67], Owusu [77]	4700
14	Nov 3	A	Plymouth Arg	L 0-3	0-1	—		4650
15	7	A	Shrewsbury T	L 0-2	0-2	6		2799
16	10	H	Southend U	W 4-1	2-0	—	Owusu 3 [22, 36, 83], Freeman [59]	4285
17	21	A	Leyton Orient	L 1-2	1-0	7	Folan [21]	6340
18	28	H	Chester C	W 2-1	1-0	6	Owusu [20], Rowlands [73]	5173
19	Dec 12	A	Exeter C	W 1-0	1-0	3	Owusu [40]	2793
20	18	H	Cambridge U	W 1-0	1-0	—	Folan [5]	5069
21	26	A	Brighton & HA	L 1-3	0-2	3	Freeman [61]	4838
22	28	H	Cardiff C	W 1-0	0-0	2	Hreidarsson [53]	9535
23	Jan 2	H	Barnet	W 3-1	2-0	2	Freeman [18], Bryan [36], Mahon [65]	6011
24	9	A	Mansfield T	L 1-3	1-2	2	Owusu [45]	4095
25	23	A	Rochdale	L 0-2	0-0	4		2113
26	30	A	Cardiff C	L 1-4	0-2	6	Boxall [57]	11,509
27	Feb 2	H	Carlisle U	D 1-1	0-0	—	Barr (og) [46]	3674
28	6	H	Hull C	L 0-2	0-1	6		5086
29	13	H	Torquay U	W 3-2	1-1	4	Owusu [20], Bryan [62], Hreidarsson [90]	4299
30	16	A	Swansea C	L 1-2	1-1	—	Hreidarsson [42]	5109
31	20	A	Rotherham U	W 4-2	3-1	3	Mahon [10], Owusu 3 [26, 40, 80]	3899
32	27	H	Scarborough	D 1-1	0-1	3	Bryan [79]	4783
33	Mar 9	A	Peterborough U	W 3-0	1-0	—	Partridge [11], Mahon [73], Owusu [76]	4195
34	13	H	Shrewsbury T	D 0-0	0-0	3		5082
35	16	H	Halifax T	D 1-1	1-1	—	Partridge [28]	3713
36	20	A	Carlisle U	W 1-0	0-0	3	Partridge [54]	2564
37	Apr 3	H	Hartlepool U	W 1-0	1-0	3	Owusu [42]	2719
38	5	H	Plymouth Arg	W 3-1	2-0	3	Evans [42], Mahon [45], Folan [89]	6979
39	10	A	Scunthorpe U	D 0-0	0-0	3		5604
40	13	A	Chester C	W 3-1	2-0	—	Anderson [2], Evans [4], Bryan [89]	1766
41	17	H	Leyton Orient	D 0-0	0-0	3		8245
42	24	A	Southend U	W 4-1	1-0	3	Owusu 3 [13, 50, 83], Partridge [66]	5248
43	27	A	Darlington	D 2-2	1-1	—	Scott [44], Partridge [70]	2514
44	May 1	H	Exeter C	W 3-0	1-0	3	Quinn [12], Scott [47], Partridge [71]	6977
45	4	H	Swansea C	W 4-1	1-0	—	Owusu [27], Evans [46], Hreidarsson [75], Partridge [87]	7156
46	8	A	Cambridge U	W 1-0	0-0	1	Owusu [61]	8936

Final League Position: 1

GOALSCORERS

League (79): Owusu 22, Partridge 7, Scott 7, Freeman 6, Bryan 4, Folan 4, Hreidarsson 4, Mahon 4, Rowlands 4, Evans 3, Rapley 3, Aspinall 2 (1 pen), Powell 2, Quinn 2, Anderson 1, Bates 1, Boxall 1, own goals 2.
Worthington Cup (8): Owusu 2, Scott 2, Bates 1, Freeman 1, Oatway 1, Rapley 1.
FA Cup (8): Folan 2, Freeman 2 (1 pen), Bates 1, Hreidarsson 1, Owusu 1, Quinn 1.

Pearcey J 17	Boxall D 37 + 1	Watson P 12	Cullip D 2	Powell D 33	Bates J 27	Rowlands M 32 + 4	Aspinall W 17 + 2	Owusu L 42 + 4	Rapley K 3 + 9	Scott A 31 + 3	Oatway C 7 + 17	Freeman D 16 + 6	Dearden K 7	Quinn R 34 + 9	Coyne C 7	Anderson I 35 + 3	Hebel D 6 + 9	Hreidarsson H 33	Folan T 19 + 10	Broughton D 1	Bryan D 9 + 11	Mahon G 29	Fortune-West L 2 + 9	Woodman A 22	Partridge S 12 + 2	Evans P 14	Jenkins S — + 1	Match No.
1	2	3	4	5	6	7	8	9^1	10	11^2	12	13																1
	2	3	4^1	5	6	7	8^2	12	10	11		13	1	9														2
1	2	3		5^2	6	10	8	12	13	11^2				7^1														3
1	2	3^2		5	6	10	8	7	12	11^1	13			9^2	4	14												4
1		3^1		5	6	10	8^3	7	12	11	13			9^2	4	2	14											5
1		3		5	6	10^3	8	7	12	11	13			9^2	4	2^1	14											6
1	2	3		5	6		12	7	13	11	8			9^2	4		10^1											7
1	2	3		5	6	10	8^3	7	12	11		13		9^2	4^1		14											8
1	2			5	6	10	12	13	14	11		7		9^1	4^2	3	8^3											9
1	2		5^2	6	10	8	9	12	11^1		7^3		13		3		4	14										10
1	2			5	6	10	8^2	9		11				7^1		12		3^3	13	4	14							11
1	2			5^1	6	10	8	9		11				7^2		12		3^3	13	4	14							12
1	2			5	6	10	8	9^2		11				7		12		3^1		4	13							13
1	2			5	6	10	8^3	9	12	11^1				13				3^2	14	4	7							14
1	2			5^1	6	10	8	9	4^2					12				13	3	7	11^3	14						15
1	2	3			6	10	8^1	9						7^2		5		12	4	11		13						16
1		3					8^1	9			7^2			5		2	12	4	11		13	6	10					17
1		3		6	10			9			7			5		2	8		11		4							18
	2			6	10			9			12	7^2	1	5			4^1	3	11		13	8						19
				6	10			9^2			12	7	1	5		3	8^1	4	11			2	13					20
				6^2	10			9			12	7	1	5		3	8^3	4	2^1		13	11	14					21
	2			6	10			9^2				7^1	1	5		3		4	8		12	11	13					22
	2				10			9			12	13	7^3	1	5	3		4	8^1		6^2	11	14					23
			2		10	8	9			11	12		1	5		3		4			6^2	7	13					24
	2			6^1	10			9^3			11	13	12	5		3		4	7			8^2	14	1				25
	2			6	10^2	8	12			11^1	13	7		5		3		4	14			9^3		1				26
	2			6	10			9			3	12	7^1	5		13		4^2	11			8		1				27
	2		5	6				9			12		7^2	13		3		4	11			8	10^1	1				28
	2		5	6^1	10			9						12		3		4	11		7^2	8	13	1				29
	2		5		10^1			9^2				12		6		3		4	11		7	8	13	1				30
	2	3	5		10			9^2			12			6				4	11^1		7^3	8	13	1	14			31
	2^1		5		10^2			9			12			6		3		4	11		7	8		1	13			32
	2		5	10				9			4					3					11	6		1	8	7		33
	2		5	12				9		10^1						3		4	7^2		13	6		1	8	11		34
	2		5	10^3				9		12	13			14		3^1		4^2	7			6		1	8	11		35
	2		5					9		10^1	7			4		3					12	6		1	8	11		36
			5	10^1				9		7^2	6			2		3		4	12					1	8	11	13	37
12			5					9		7^2	6^1			2		3		4	14		13	10^2		1	8	11		38
	2		5					9		7				6		3		4	12			10		1	8^1	11		39
	2		5					9		7^1				6		3		4	12		8	10		1		11		40
	2		5					9		7^1				6		3		4	12		10	6		1		11		41
	2			12				9^2		7	5^1	13		8		3		4				6		1	10	11		42
	2		4	12				9		7	5^1			8		3						6		1	10	11		43
	2		5	12				9^1		7	13			8		3		4^2			14	6^1		1	10	11		44
	2		5					9		7^1				8		3		4			12	6		1	10	11		45
	2		5					9		7	12			8		3		4				6		1	10	11^1		46

Worthington Cup

First Round	WBA	(a)	1-2
		(h)	3-0
Second Round	Tottenham H	(h)	2-3
		(a)	2-3

FA Cup

First Round	Camberley T	(h)	5-0
Second Round	Oldham Ath	(a)	1-1
		(h)	2-2

Division 3   **BRIGHTON & HOVE ALBION**

FOUNDATION

A professional club Brighton United was formed in November 1897 at the Imperial Hotel, Queen's Road, but folded in March 1900 after less than two seasons in the Southern League at the County Ground. An amateur team, Brighton & Hove Rangers was then formed by some prominent United supporters and after one season at Withdean, decided to turn semi-professional and play at the County Ground. Rangers were accepted into the Southern League but then also folded June 1901. John Jackson the former United manager organised a meeting at the Seven Stars public house, Ship Street on 24 June 1901 at which a new third club Brighton & Hove United was formed. They took over Rangers' place in the Southern League and pitch at County Ground. The name was changed to Brighton & Hove Albion before a match was played because of objections by Hove FC.

Offices: Fifth floor, Hanover House, 118 Queens Road, Brighton BN1 3XG.
Telephone: (01273) 778855.
Fax: (01273) 321095.
Ground Address: Withdean Stadium, Tongdean Lane, Brighton.
Albion Clubline: 09068 800609.
Ground Capacity: 10,952.
Record Attendance: 36,747 v Fulham, Division 2, 27 December 1958.
Record Receipts: £109,615.65 v Crawley T, FA Cup 3rd rd, 4 January 1992.
Pitch Measurements: 114yd × 77yd (at Gillingham).
Directors: H. R. Knight (Chairman), Ray Bloom, Derek Chapman, M. J. Perry, R. L. Pinnock FCA.
Non-Executive Directors: R. O. Faulkner, Sir John Smith QPM.
Manager: Micky Adams.
Assistant Manager: Alan Cork.
General Manager: Nick Rowe.
Secretary: Derek Allan.
Physio: Malcolm Stuart.
Youth Development Officer: Martin Hinshelwood.
Youth Team Coach: Dean Wilkins.

LATEST SEQUENCES
Longest Sequence of League Wins: 9, 2.10.26 – 20.11.26.
Longest Sequence of League Defeats: 12, 11.11.72 – 27.1.73.
Longest Sequence of League Draws: 6, 16.2.80 – 15.3.80.
Longest Sequence of Unbeaten League Matches: 16, 8.10.30 – 28.1.31.
Longest Sequence Without a League Win: 15, 21.10.72 – 27.1.73

HONOURS

Football League: Division 1 best season: 13th, 1981–82; Division 2 – Runners-up 1978–79; Division 3 (S) – Champions 1957–58; Runners-up 1953–54, 1955–56; Division 3 – Runners-up 1971–72, 1976–77, 1987–88; Division 4 – Champions 1964–65.

FA Cup: Runners-up 1983.

Football League Cup: best season: 5th rd, 1979.

Colours
Blue and white striped shirts, white shorts, blue stockings.

Change Colours
Red and black striped shirts, black shorts, black stockings.

Year Formed: 1901.

Turned Professional: 1901.

Ltd Co.: 1904.

Previous Grounds: 1901, County Ground;
1902, Goldstone Ground.

Club Nickname: 'The Seagulls'.

First Football League Game: 28 August 1920, Division 3,
v Southend U (a) L 0–2 – Hayes; Woodhouse, Little; Hall,
Comber, Bentley; Longstaff, Ritchie, Doran, Rodgerson,
March.

Record League Victory: 9–1 v Newport Co, Division 3 (S),
18 April 1951 – Ball; Tennant (1p), Mansell (1p); Willard,
McCoy, Wilson; Reed, McNichol (4), Garbutt, Bennett (2),
Keene (1). 9–1 v Southend U, Division 3, 27 November 1965
– Powney; Magill, Baxter; Leck, Gall, Turner; Gould (1),
Collins (1), Livesey (2), Smith (3), Goodchild (2).

Record Cup Victory: 10–1 v Wisbech, FA Cup 1st rd,
13 November 1965 – Powney; Magill, Baxter; Collins (1),
Gall, Turner; Gould, Smith (2), Livesey (3), Cassidy (2),
Goodchild (1), (1 og).

Record Defeat: 0–9 v Middlesbrough, Division 2, 23 August
1958.

Most League Points (2 for a win): 65, Division 3 (S),
1955–56 and Division 3, 1971–72.

Most League Points (3 for a win): 84, Division 3, 1987–88.

Most League Goals: 112, Division 3 (S), 1955–56.

Highest League Scorer in Season: Peter Ward, 32, Division 3, 1976–77.

Most League Goals in Total Aggregate: Tommy Cook, 114, 1922–29.

Most League Goals in One Match: 5, Jack Doran v Northampton T, Division 3S, 5 November 1921;
5, Adrian Thorne v Watford, Division 3S, 30 April 1958.

Most Capped Player: Steve Penney, 17, Northern Ireland.

Most League Appearances: 'Tug' Wilson, 509, 1922–36.

Youngest League Player: Ian Chapman, 16 years 259 days v Birmingham C, 14 February 1987.

Record Transfer Fee Received: £900,000 from Liverpool for Mark Lawrenson, August 1981.

Record Transfer Fee Paid: £500,000 to Manchester U for Andy Ritchie, October 1980.

Football League Record: 1920 Original Member of Division 3; 1921–58 Division 3 (S); 1958–62
Division 2; 1962–63 Division 3; 1963–65 Division 4; 1965–72 Division 3; 1972–73 Division 2; 1973–77
Division 3; 1977–79 Division 2; 1979–83 Division 1; 1983–87 Division 2; 1987–88 Division 3; 1988–96
Division 2; 1996– Division 3.

MANAGERS

John Jackson 1901–05
Frank Scott-Walford 1905–08
John Robson 1908–14
Charles Webb 1919–47
Tommy Cook 1947
Don Welsh 1947–51
Billy Lane 1951–61
George Curtis 1961–63
Archie Macaulay 1963–68
Fred Goodwin 1968–70
Pat Saward 1970–73
Brian Clough 1973–74
Peter Taylor 1974–76
Alan Mullery 1976–81
Mike Bailey 1981–82
Jimmy Melia 1982–83
Chris Cattlin 1983–86
Alan Mullery 1986–87
Barry Lloyd 1987–93
Liam Brady 1993–95
Jimmy Case 1995–96
Steve Gritt 1996–98
Brian Horton 1998–99
Jeff Wood 1999
Micky Adams February 1999–

TEN YEAR LEAGUE RECORD

		P	W	D	L	F	A	Pts	Pos
1988-89	Div 2	46	14	9	23	57	66	51	19
1989-90	Div 2	46	15	9	22	56	72	54	18
1990-91	Div 2	46	21	7	18	63	69	70	6
1991-92	Div 2	46	12	11	23	56	77	47	23
1992-93	Div 2	46	20	9	17	63	59	69	9
1993-94	Div 2	46	15	14	17	60	67	59	14
1994-95	Div 2	46	14	17	15	54	53	59	16
1995-96	Div 2	46	10	10	26	46	69	40	23
1996-97	Div 3	46	13	10	23	53	70	47	23
1997-98	Div 3	46	6	17	23	38	66	35	23

DID YOU KNOW ?

On 10 November 1998 at
Hull City, Brighton & Hove
Albion recorded their fourth
away win to beat a 62-year-
old club record. This 2–0
success was achieved despite
having two players sent off in
the 55th and 56th minutes.

BRIGHTON & HOVE ALBION 1998–99 LEAGUE RECORD

Match No.	Date	Venue	Opponents	Result		H/T Score	Lg. Pos.	Goalscorers	Attendance
1	Aug 8	A	Carlisle U	L	0-1	0-1	—		5184
2	15	H	Chester C	D	2-2	0-1	19	Barker [69], Woods (og) [73]	2703
3	22	A	Brentford	L	0-2	0-2	23		6355
4	29	H	Torquay U	W	2-0	0-0	17	Minton (pen) [62], Hart [87]	2703
5	31	A	Scarborough	W	2-1	1-0	10	Minton [25], Hart [65]	2528
6	Sept 5	H	Swansea C	W	1-0	1-0	10	Hart [36]	2931
7	8	A	Exeter C	L	0-1	0-0	—		2519
8	12	H	Southend U	L	0-2	0-1	15		3840
9	19	A	Leyton Orient	L	0-1	0-0	19		5620
10	26	H	Scunthorpe U	L	1-3	0-1	21	Hart [55]	2625
11	Oct 3	A	Cardiff C	L	0-2	0-0	22		6143
12	9	A	Cambridge U	W	3-2	1-1	—	Thomas R [22], Allan [55], Minton (pen) [81]	4602
13	17	H	Mansfield T	L	1-3	1-1	22	Moralee [31]	2808
14	20	H	Plymouth Arg	L	1-3	0-1	—	Barker [84]	1793
15	24	A	Barnet	W	1-0	0-0	19	Ifejiagwa [53]	2299
16	31	H	Hartlepool U	W	3-2	1-1	16	Minton 2 (1 pen) [33 (p), 81], Thomas R [62]	2765
17	Nov 7	A	Darlington	W	2-1	0-1	13	Hart [70], Minton (pen) [72]	3069
18	10	A	Hull C	W	2-0	2-0	—	Barker [6], Hart [30]	4433
19	21	H	Halifax T	L	0-1	0-1	13		3305
20	28	A	Shrewsbury T	W	3-1	2-0	11	Hart [33], Minton [45], Barker [82]	3168
21	Dec 12	H	Rotherham U	W	4-1	0-0	10	Barker 2 [52, 54], Hart [86], Minton [88]	2870
22	19	A	Rochdale	L	1-2	0-0	11	Mayo [65]	2153
23	26	H	Brentford	W	3-1	2-0	9	Thomas R [26], Minton [33], Arnott [79]	4838
24	28	A	Peterborough U	W	2-1	1-0	7	Barker 2 [39, 60]	7912
25	Jan 2	A	Torquay U	D	1-1	0-1	7	Arnott [70]	3663
26	9	H	Carlisle U	L	1-3	1-0	7	Hart [43]	4163
27	15	A	Chester C	D	1-1	0-1	—	Armstrong (pen) [90]	3869
28	23	H	Scarborough	W	1-0	0-0	8	Armstrong [83]	3499
29	30	H	Peterborough U	W	1-0	0-0	7	Barker [47]	4444
30	Feb 5	A	Swansea C	D	2-2	0-1	—	Johnson 2 [55, 86]	6563
31	13	H	Exeter C	L	0-1	0-0	8		4005
32	20	A	Southend U	L	0-3	0-2	9		6066
33	27	H	Leyton Orient	L	1-2	0-0	13	Nicholls [70]	4825
34	Mar 6	A	Scunthorpe U	L	1-3	0-2	13	Ryan [67]	4148
35	9	H	Cardiff C	L	0-2	0-2	—		2312
36	13	H	Darlington	L	0-4	0-1	13		3053
37	20	A	Hartlepool U	D	0-0	0-0	14		2353
38	27	H	Barnet	L	0-1	0-0	17		2384
39	Apr 3	A	Mansfield T	L	0-2	0-2	17		3015
40	6	H	Cambridge U	L	1-3	0-1	—	Hart [87]	2621
41	10	A	Plymouth Arg	W	2-1	1-1	15	Hart [6], Moralee [75]	4911
42	13	H	Shrewsbury T	W	1-0	1-0	—	Hart [19]	2207
43	17	A	Halifax T	L	0-1	0-1	15		2773
44	24	H	Hull C	D	0-0	0-0	14		3481
45	May 1	A	Rotherham U	L	1-2	0-0	16	Moralee [47]	4458
46	8	H	Rochdale	D	1-1	1-0	17	Barker [32]	4646

Final League Position: 17

GOALSCORERS

League (49): Hart 12, Barker 10, Minton 9 (4 pens), Moralee 3, Thomas R 3, Armstrong 2 (1 pen), Arnott 2, Johnson 2, Allan 1, Ifejiagwa 1, Mayo 1, Nicholls 1, Ryan 1, own goal 1.
Worthington Cup (2): Barker 1, Storer 1.
FA Cup (2): Barker 1, Mayo 1.

Walton M 19	Bennett M 37 + 1	Tuck S 2	Minton J 35	Johnson R 30 + 4	Hobson G 12 + 1	Allan D 21 + 1	Mayo K 21 + 4	Barker R 33 + 10	Browne S 2 + 1	Smith P 8 + 6	Storer S 14 + 9	Andrews B — + 1	Hart G 42 + 2	Moralee J 22 + 9	Thomas G 2 + 1	Westcott J — + 4	Atkinson G 7	Culverhouse I 35	Armstrong P 21 + 7	Hinshelwood D 3 + 1	Ansah A 3 + 8	Sturgess P 28 + 2	Mills D 1 + 1	Thomas R 11 + 1	Ormerod M 27	Browne T 13	Ifejiagwa E 2	Arnott A 27	Davies L 2 + 6	Nicholls K 4	Ryan D 3 + 2	Davis D — + 1	King P 3	Doherty L 3	McPherson K 10	McArthur D 3	Match No.
1	2	3	4	5	6	7¹	8	9²	10³	11	12	13	14																								1
1	11	3	4	5²	6		8³	12			2	7	10¹	9	13	14																					2
1	11		4	12	5		8³	10			2²	13	14	9	6¹				3	7																	3
1	11		4	5	6			10					8	9					3	7	2																4
1	11		4	5	6			10					8	9					3	7	2																5
1	11		4	5	6			10¹			12		8	9					3	7	2																6
1	11		4	5		6¹				10³			8	9			12		3	7	2²	13	14														7
1	11		4	5¹	12	6		10		13			8						3	7³	9²	2	14														8
1			4	5	6	11		10					8	9²					7	12	2¹	3		13													9
1			4	5¹	6			10			12		8	9					7	13	2²	3		11													10
1		5	4		6			10¹			12	2	8	9					11²	7		13	3														11
1	9		4	5		6					12	2	8¹	10				11							3	7											12
1	9		4	12		6				13	2²		8	10		5¹		11³			14				3	7											13
1	9		4	5		6					12	13	8²	10				11			2³				3¹	7											14
			4	6				10			12		9¹					11							3	7	1	2	5	8							15
	12		4	6				10²					9	13				11							3	7	1	2	5	8¹							16
	7		4	6				5¹	12	10			9					11							3¹		1	2		8							17
	7		4	6				10				5	9¹	12				11							3		1	2		8							18
	5		4	6				12	10²		14		9	13				11³							3		1	2		8							19
	5		4			6		10					9					11	8			3			7	1	2									20
	5		4			3		10					9					11	8			3			7	1	2	6									21
	5¹		4	12		3		10				13	9					11	8			7²			1	2	6										22
			4	5				10					9¹	12				11	8			3			7	1	2	6									23
			4	5				10					9					11	8			3			7	1	2	6									24
	2		4	5				7¹			12		9	10				11	8²	13	3				1		6										25
	8		4	5²				10					9	7¹	12			11	13			3			1	2	6										26
	8		4¹	5				12	10				9		13			11	7			3²			1	2	6										27
1	8			5				2	10¹		4		9²	12			13	11	7			3					6										28
1	8			5		6		2	10		4		9					11	7			3															29
1	8			5		6		2¹	10				9	12				11	7			3					4										30
1	8			5		6		2	10²				9	12				11	7			3¹					4	13									31
1	8			5		6¹		10			2		9					11	7			3					4	12									32
	8		5	6			3²	10					12						7							1	2¹	4	9	11	13						33
	8		5²	6				10					9	12				2¹	13			3					1	4	7³	11	14						34
	8			6				10²				7¹	9					2	12			3					1	4	13	11	5						35
				6¹	12			10			5	7	9					2	4³			3					1		13	11	8²	14					36
	8		4					10					9¹					2	7								1		12				3	5	6	11	37
	8³		4	12				10			13		9					2									1		7	14			3²	5	6	11¹	38
	8		4	11				12			10		9³					2	13	14	3						1		7					5¹	6²		39
	8		4	5				7	12	11			9	10				2¹									1						3		6	11	40
	2		4		5			3			12	7¹	9	10													1		8						6	11	41
	2		4		5			3	12		14	7³	9¹	10								13					1		8		11²				6		42
	2³		4		5			3	12		14	7¹	9	10							13	11²					1		8						6		43
	2				5			3	12			7	9	10							4	11¹					1		8						6		44
			4		5¹	2		3	11		12	7	9	10													1		8						6		45
			4¹		5	2		3	11		13	7²	9³	10								12	14	1				8							6		46

Worthington Cup
First Round Northampton T (a) 1-2
(h) 1-1

FA Cup
First Round Leyton Orient (a) 2-4

Division 2

BRISTOL CITY

FOUNDATION

The name Bristol City came into being in 1897 when the Bristol South End club, formed three years earlier, decided to adopt professionalism and apply for admission to the Southern League after competing in the Western League. The historic meeting was held at The Albert Hall, Bedminster. Bristol City employed Sam Hollis from Woolwich Arsenal as manager and gave him £40 to buy players. In 1901 they merged with Bedminster, another leading Bristol club.

Ashton Gate, Bristol BS3 2EJ.
Telephone: (0117) 9630630 (5 lines).
Fax: (0117) 9630700.
Website: www.bcfc.co.uk.
Commercial: (0117) 9630600.
Shop: (0117) 9630637.
Clubcall: 09068 121176.
Supporters Club: (0117) 9665554.
Community Dept: (0117) 9630636.
Ground Capacity: 21,479.
Record Attendance: 43,335 v Preston NE, FA Cup 5th rd, 16 February 1935.
Record Receipts: £251,612 v Everton, FA Cup 4th rd, 23 January 1999.
Pitch Measurements: 115yd × 75yd.
Executive Chairman: S. Davidson.
Directors: J. Laycock, J. Clapp, R. Neale, S. Lansdown, K. Dawe, A. Gooch.
Sales Manager: Elaine White.
General Manager: Ian Wilson.
Football Administrator: Michelle McDonald.
Manager: Tony Pulis.
Coach: Terry Connor.
Physio: Gill O'Shea.
Stadium Manager: Dave Lewis.
Safety Officer: Keith Draisey.

LATEST SEQUENCES

Longest Sequence of League Wins: 14, 9.9.05 – 2.12.05.
Longest Sequence of League Defeats: 7, 3.10.70 – 7.11.70.
Longest Sequence of League Draws: 4, 9.1.99 – 5.2.99.
Longest Sequence of Unbeaten League Matches: 24, 9.9.05 – 10.2.06.
Longest Sequence Without a League Win: 15, 29.4.33 – 4.11.33.

HONOURS

Football League: Division 1 – Runners-up 1906–07; Division 2 – Champions 1905–06; Runners-up 1975–76, 1997–98; Division 3 (S) – Champions 1922–23, 1926–27, 1954–55; Runners-up 1937–38; Division 3 – Runners-up 1964–65, 1989–90.
FA Cup: Runners-up 1909.
Football League Cup: Semi-final 1971, 1989.
Welsh Cup: Winners 1934.
Anglo-Scottish Cup: Winners 1978.
Freight Rover Trophy: Winners 1986; Runners-up 1987.

Colours
Red shirts, red shorts, white stockings.

Change Colours
White shirts, white shorts, white stockings.

Year Formed: 1894.

Turned Professional: 1897.

Ltd Co.: 1897. Bristol City Football Club Ltd.

Previous Name: 1894, Bristol South End; 1897, Bristol City.

Club Nickname: 'Robins'.

Previous Grounds: 1894, St John's Lane; 1904, Ashton Gate.

First Football League Game: 7 September 1901, Division 2, v Blackpool (a) W 2–0 – Moles; Tuft, Davies; Jones, McLean, Chambers; Bradbury, Connor, Boucher, O'Brien (2), Flynn.

Record League Victory: 9–0 v Aldershot, Division 3 (S), 28 December 1946 – Eddols; Morgan, Fox; Peacock, Roberts, Jones (1); Chilcott, Thomas, Clark (4 incl. 1p), Cyril Williams (1), Hargreaves (3).

Record Cup Victory: 11–0 v Chichester C, FA Cup 1st rd, 5 November 1960 – Cook; Collinson, Thresher; Connor, Alan Williams, Etheridge; Tait (1), Bobby Williams (1), Atyeo (5), Adrian Williams (3), Derrick, (1 og).

Record Defeat: 0–9 v Coventry C, Division 3 (S), 28 April 1934.

Most League Points (2 for a win): 70, Division 3 (S), 1954–55.

Most League Points (3 for a win): 91, Division 3, 1989–90.

Most League Goals: 104, Division 3 (S), 1926–27.

Highest League Scorer in Season: Don Clark, 36, Division 3 (S), 1946–47.

Most League Goals in Total Aggregate: John Atyeo, 314, 1951–66.

Most League Goals in One Match: 6, Tommy 'Tot' Walsh v Gillingham, Division 3S, 15 January 1927.

Most Capped Player: Billy Wedlock, 26, England.

Most League Appearances: John Atyeo, 597, 1951–66.

Youngest League Player: Nyrere Kelly, 16 years 213 days v Hartlepool U, 16 October 1982.

Record Transfer Fee Received: £1,750,000 from Newcastle U for Andy Cole, March 1993.

Record Transfer Fee Paid: £1,200,000 to Gillingham for Ade Akinbiyi, May 1998.

Football League Record: 1901 Elected to Division 2; 1906–11 Division 1; 1911–22 Division 2; 1922–23 Division 3 (S); 1923–24 Division 2; 1924–27 Division 3 (S); 1927–32 Division 2; 1932–55 Division 3 (S); 1955–60 Division 2; 1960–65 Division 3; 1965–76 Division 2; 1976–80 Division 1; 1980–81 Division 2; 1981–82 Division 3; 1982–84 Division 4; 1984–90 Division 3; 1990–92 Division 2; 1992–95 Division 1; 1995–98 Division 2; 1998–99 Division 1; 1999– Division 2.

TEN YEAR LEAGUE RECORD

		P	W	D	L	F	A	Pts	Pos
1988-89	Div 3	46	18	9	19	53	55	63	11
1989-90	Div 3	46	27	10	9	76	40	91	2
1990-91	Div 2	46	20	7	19	68	71	67	9
1991-92	Div 2	46	13	15	18	55	71	54	17
1992-93	Div 1	46	14	14	18	49	67	56	15
1993-94	Div 1	46	16	16	14	47	50	64	13
1994-95	Div 1	46	11	12	23	42	63	45	23
1995-96	Div 2	46	15	15	16	55	60	60	13
1996-97	Div 2	46	21	10	15	69	51	73	5
1997-98	Div 2	46	25	10	11	69	39	85	2

DID YOU KNOW ?

When England met Wales at Ashton Gate on 17 March 1913, Bristol City's centre-half Billy Wedlock, who had 25 caps at the time, was chosen to play but had to withdraw because of injury. England won 4–3.

BRISTOL CITY 1998–99 LEAGUE RECORD

Match No.	Date	Venue	Opponents	Result	H/T Score	Lg. Pos.	Goalscorers	Atten- dance
1	Aug 8	H	Oxford U	D 2-2	2-1	—	Andersen S 2 [26, 44]	13,729
2	15	A	QPR	D 1-1	1-0	13	Hewlett [28]	13,337
3	22	H	Watford	L 1-4	0-1	17	Andersen S [59]	13,063
4	29	H	Tranmere R	D 1-1	1-1	16	Akinbiyi [32]	5960
5	31	H	Huddersfield T	L 1-2	1-0	19	Goodridge [12]	11,801
6	Sept 5	A	Swindon T	L 2-3	0-3	20	Akinbiyi [62], Bell (pen) [75]	8537
7	8	A	Sunderland	D 1-1	0-1	—	Andersen S [88]	34,111
8	13	H	WBA	L 1-3	0-2	22	Watts [69]	13,761
9	19	A	Ipswich T	L 1-3	0-2	23	Akinbiyi [88]	13,657
10	26	H	Crewe Alex	W 5-2	3-0	22	Doherty [13], Goodridge [29], Murray [37], Akinbiyi [78], Hutchings [89]	9810
11	29	H	Barnsley	D 1-1	0-0	—	Bell [68]	12,005
12	Oct 3	A	Bury	W 1-0	0-0	19	Bell (pen) [67]	4794
13	10	H	Portsmouth	D 2-2	1-1	19	Murray [11], Andersen S [85]	13,056
14	17	A	Port Vale	L 2-3	0-1	20	Murray [55], Akinbiyi [59]	6691
15	20	A	Grimsby T	L 1-2	1-0	—	Andersen S [33]	5082
16	23	H	Bolton W	W 2-1	2-1	—	Akinbiyi [28], Bell (pen) [45]	12,026
17	31	A	Bradford C	L 0-5	0-2	21		14,468
18	Nov 7	H	Wolverhampton W	L 1-6	1-2	21	Hutchings [12]	15,432
19	14	A	Crystal Palace	L 1-2	1-1	23	Andersen S [35]	17,821
20	21	H	Stockport Co	D 1-1	1-0	23	Thorpe [43]	11,032
21	28	A	Birmingham C	L 2-4	2-3	23	Thorpe [4], Andersen S [45]	17,577
22	Dec 5	H	Sheffield U	W 2-0	1-0	23	Bell (pen) [33], Akinbiyi [64]	11,134
23	12	H	Crystal Palace	D 1-1	1-1	23	Akinbiyi [25]	13,014
24	19	A	Norwich C	L 1-2	1-2	23	Akinbiyi [20]	17,022
25	26	A	Watford	L 0-1	0-0	23		15,081
26	28	H	Swindon T	W 3-1	1-0	23	Torpey 2 [8, 50], Akinbiyi [75]	16,257
27	Jan 9	A	Oxford U	D 0-0	0-0	23		9434
28	16	H	Tranmere R	D 1-1	1-1	21	Locke [25]	13,217
29	30	A	Huddersfield T	D 2-2	1-1	22	Akinbiyi [16], Locke [62]	14,034
30	Feb 5	A	QPR	D 0-0	0-0	—		13,841
31	13	H	Sunderland	L 0-1	0-0	23		15,736
32	20	A	WBA	D 2-2	0-1	23	Akinbiyi 2 [60, 85]	16,490
33	27	H	Ipswich T	L 0-1	0-0	23		14,065
34	Mar 9	A	Bury	D 1-1	0-1	—	Andersen S [80]	11,606
35	13	A	Wolverhampton W	L 0-3	0-1	23		25,237
36	20	H	Bradford C	L 2-3	0-2	24	Akinbiyi [51], Andersen S [81]	10,870
37	23	A	Barnsley	L 0-2	0-1	—		14,733
38	Apr 3	H	Port Vale	W 2-0	2-0	24	Akinbiyi [31], Howells [36]	11,039
39	5	A	Portsmouth	W 1-0	0-0	24	Locke [86]	13,026
40	10	H	Grimsby T	W 4-1	2-1	23	Torpey [21], Akinbiyi 2 [43, 62], Tinnion [55]	11,616
41	13	A	Bolton W	L 0-1	0-1	—		14,459
42	17	A	Stockport Co	D 2-2	0-0	23	Brennan [60], Torpey [76]	7602
43	24	H	Birmingham C	L 1-2	0-0	24	Akinbiyi [46]	15,845
44	27	A	Crewe Alex	L 0-1	0-1	—		5579
45	May 1	A	Sheffield U	L 1-3	0-1	24	Akinbiyi [61]	17,310
46	9	H	Norwich C	W 1-0	1-0	24	Pinamonte [40]	11,362

Final League Position: 24

GOALSCORERS

League (57): Akinbiyi 19, Andersen S 10, Bell 5 (4 pens), Torpey 4, Locke 3, Murray 3, Goodridge 2, Hutchings 2, Thorpe 2, Brennan 1, Doherty 1, Hewlett 1, Howells 1, Pinamonte 1, Tinnion 1, Watts 1.
Worthington Cup (8): Akinbiyi 4, Andersen S 1, Doherty 1, Hutchings 1, Thorpe 1.
FA Cup (0).

Welch K 21	Locke A 26 + 2	Bell M 33	Hewlett M 8 + 2	Watts J 16 + 1	Dyche S 4 + 2	Goodridge G 15 + 15	Hutchings C 16 + 5	Akinbiyi A 44	Andersen S 26 + 13	Tinnion B 32 + 3	Carey L 40 + 1	Doherty T 15 + 8	Thorpe T 9 + 7	Edwards R 19 + 4	Murray S 27 + 5	Cramb C 4 + 9	Zwijnenberg C 1 + 2	Brennan J 29	Shail M 21 + 3	Hill M — + 3	Torpey S 19 + 2	Phillips S 15	Brown A 14	Edwards C 3	Testimiteanu I 8	Sebok V 10 + 2	Langan K 1	Heaney N 2 + 1	Andersen B 10	Taylor S 8	Howells D 8	Jordan A 1	Meechan A — + 1	Pinamonte L 1	Match No.
1	2	3	4	5	6¹	7²	8	9	10³	11	12	13	14																						1
1	2	3	4	5	13	7²		9	10¹	11	6	8	12																						2
1	2	3	4²	5¹	12	7	8	9	10	11	6		13																						3
1	2	3	4	5	12		8	9	10¹	11	6				7																				4
1	2	3	4	5		7		9	10¹	11	6	13	12	8²																					5
1	2	3	12	5	6			9		11		4	10¹	8²	7	13																			6
1	2	3	8	5¹	6	13		9	12	11²	10	4			7																				7
1	2	3	8¹	13	6²	12		9	10	11	5	4			7³	14																			8
1	2³	3		5			8⁷	9	10	11	6				12	13	14	4	7¹																9
1		3		5		7	12	9	13	11	6	4		8¹				2			10²														10
1		3		5		7²	8	9	12	11	6	4						2		13	10¹														11
1		3		5		7¹	8	9		11	6	4			12			2			10														12
1		3		5		7	8	9	12	11	6	4²						2		13	10¹														13
1		3		5		7¹	12	9	10	11²	6	4		8				2		13															14
1		3		5		7²	12	9	10	11	6	4¹	13	8				2																	15
1		3		5		7	8	9²	10¹	11	6	4			12			2		13															16
1		3		5		7	4	9	10	11	6			8				2¹			12														17
1		3¹				7	4	9	10³	11	6			8¹	12			2	5	14	13														18
1		3					4	9	10	11	6			8	7			2	5																19
1		3				12	4	9	10	11²	6	13		8¹	7			2	5																20
1		3				12	4	9	10¹	11²	6	13		8	7			2	5																21
		3					4	9	10³	11	6	13	7²	8	12			2	5			1													22
		3					12	9¹	10	11¹²	6	13		8	7			2	5			1		4											23
		3				12	4	9	10	11²	6			8	7¹			2	5	13		1													24
		3				12	4¹	9		11	6	13	14	8²	7³			2	5			1	10												25
		3				12		9		11	6	4		8	7			2¹	5			1	10												26
	12	3				7¹		9		11	6	4		8				2	5			1	10												27
	4¹	3				12		9		11²	6	13		8	7			2	5			1	10												28
	4	3				12		9¹		11	6	13		8²	7			2	5			1	10												29
	4	3				12		9		11	6			8	7¹			2	5			1	10												30
	4	3²				12		9		11	6			8	7			2	5	13		1	10¹												31
	4	3²				12		9		11	6			8¹	7			2	5	13		1	10												32
	4	3				12		9		11	6			8¹	7			2	5			1	10												33
	4	3				12		9		11	6	13		8	7¹			2⁴	5³	14		1	10												34
	4¹	3				12		9		11²	6			8	7			2	5	13		1	10												35
	12	3						9	10	11	6	4		8¹	7²			2	5	13		1													36
	4	3				12		9	10	11	6	13		8¹	7²			2	5										1						37
	4					12		9		11	6							2					10		8	3			1	5	7¹				38
	4					12		9		11	6							2					10¹		8	3			1	5	7				39
	4					12		9		11	6	13						2		14			10²		8	3			1	5³	7¹				40
	4					12		9²		11	6	13						2					10		8¹	3			1	5	7				41
	4					12		9²		11	6							2		13			10		8¹	3			1	5	7				42
	4					12		9		11¹	6³	13						2		14			10		8²	3			1	5	7				43
	4³							9		11	6	14			12			2		13			10		8²	3			1	5	7¹				44
	4					12		9		11	6	14						2		13			10		8	3¹			1	5²	7³				45
	3¹					7²		9	12	11	6			8				2	5			1										4	13	10	46

Worthington Cup

First Round	Shrewsbury T	(h)	4-0
		(a)	3-4
Second Round	Crewe Alex	(h)	1-1
		(a)	0-2

FA Cup

Third Round	Everton	(h)	0-2

Division 2

BRISTOL ROVERS

FOUNDATION

Bristol Rovers were formed at a meeting in Stapleton Road, Eastville, in 1883. However, they first went under the name of the Black Arabs (wearing black shirts). Changing their name to Eastville Rovers in their second season, they won the Gloucestershire Senior Cup in 1888–89. Original members of the Bristol & District League in 1892, this eventually became the Western League and Eastville Rovers adopted professionalism in 1897.

Registered Offices: The Memorial Stadium, Filton Avenue, Horfield, Bristol BS7 0AQ. (0117) 9096648.

Ground: The Memorial Stadium.

Training Ground: (0117) 977 2000.

Matchday Ticket Office: (0117) 909 8848.

Pirates Hotline: 0891 121131.

Fax: (0117) 924 4454.

Community Office: (0117) 977 3111.

Ticket Office: (0117) 924 3200.

Ground Capacity: 10861.

Record Attendance: 9274 v Leyton Orient, FA Cup 4th rd, 23 January 1999 (Memorial Ground). 9464 v Liverpool, FA Cup 4th rd, 8 February 1992 (Twerton Park). 38,472 v Preston NE, FA Cup 4th rd, 30 January 1960 (Eastville).

Record Receipts: £75,935 v Leyton Orient, FA Cup 4th rd, 23 January 1999.

Pitch Measurements: 101m × 68m.

Vice-Presidents: Dr W. T. Cussen, A. I. Seager, R. Redmond.

Chairman: D. H. A. Dunford.

Vice-Chairman: G. M. H. Dunford.

Directors: R. Craig, B. Andrews, V. Stokes, B. Bradshaw.

Player/Manager: Ian Holloway.

Player-coach: Gary Penrice.

Physio: Phil Kite.

Director of Youth: Phil Bater.

Community Scheme Organiser: Alan Walsh.

Chief Administrator/Club Secretary: Roger Brinsford.

Office Manager: Mrs Angela Mann.

LATEST SEQUENCES

Longest Sequence of League Wins: 12, 18.10.52 – 17.1.53.

Longest Sequence of League Defeats: 8, 29.4.61 – 9.9.61.

Longest Sequence of League Draws: 5, 1.11.75 – 22.11.75.

Longest Sequence of Unbeaten League Matches: 32, 7.4.73 – 27.1.74.

Longest Sequence Without a League Win: 20, 5.4.80 – 1.11.80.

HONOURS

Football League: Division 2 best season: 4th, 1994–95; Division 3 (S) – Champions 1952–53; Division 3 – Champions 1989–90; Runners-up 1973–74.

FA Cup: best season: 6th rd, 1951, 1958.

Football League Cup: best season: 5th rd, 1971, 1972.

Colours
Blue and white quartered shirts, white shorts, blue stockings.

Change Colours
White shirts, black shorts, white stockings.

Year Formed: 1883.

Turned Professional: 1897.

Ltd Co.: 1896.

Previous Names: 1883, Black Arabs; 1884, Eastville Rovers; 1897, Bristol Eastville Rovers; 1898, Bristol Rovers.

Club Nickname: 'Pirates'.

Previous Grounds: 1883, Purdown; Three Acres, Ashley Hill; Rudgeway, Fishponds; 1897, Eastville; 1986, Twerton Park; 1996, The Memorial Stadium.

First Football League Game: 28 August 1920, Division 3, v Millwall (a) L 0–2 – Stansfield; Bethune, Panes; Boxley, Kenny, Steele; Chance, Bird, Sims, Bell, Palmer.

Record League Victory: 7–0 v Brighton & HA, Division 3 (S), 29 November 1952 – Hoyle; Bamford, Fox; Pitt, Warren, Sampson; McIlvenny, Roost (2), Lambden (1), Bradford (1), Petherbridge (2), (1 og). 7–0 v Swansea T, Division 2, 2 October 1954 – Radford; Bamford, Watkins; Pitt, Muir, Anderson; Petherbridge, Bradford (2), Meyer, Roost (1), Hooper (2), (2 og). 7–0 v Shrewsbury T, Division 3, 21 March 1964 – Hall; Hillard, Gwyn Jones; Oldfield, Stone (1), Mabbutt; Jarman (2), Brown (1), Biggs (1p), Hamilton, Bobby Jones (2).

Record Cup Victory: 6–0 v Merthyr Tydfil, FA Cup 1st rd, 14 November 1987 – Martyn; Alexander (Dryden), Tanner, Hibbitt, Twentyman, Jones, Holloway, Meacham (1), White (2), Penrice (3) (Reece), Purnell.

Record Defeat: 0–12 v Luton T, Division 3 (S), 13 April 1936.

Most League Points (2 for a win): 64, Division 3 (S), 1952–53.

Most League Points (3 for a win): 93, Division 3, 1989–90.

Most League Goals: 92, Division 3 (S), 1952–53.

Highest League Scorer in Season: Geoff Bradford, 33, Division 3 (S), 1952–53.

Most League Goals in Total Aggregate: Geoff Bradford, 242, 1949–64.

Most League Goals in One Match: 4, Sidney Leigh v Exeter C, Division 3S, 2 May 1921; 4, Jonah Wilcox v Bournemouth, Division 3S, 12 December 1925; 4, Bill Culley v QPR, Division 3S, 5 March 1927; Frank Curran v Swindon T, Division 3S, 25 March 1939; Vic Lambden v Aldershot, Division 3S, 29 March 1947; George Petherbridge v Torquay U, Division 3S, 1 December 1951; Vic Lambden v Colchester U, Division 3S, 14 May 1952; Geoff Bradford v Rotherham U, Division 2, 14 March 1959; Robin Stubbs v Gillingham, Division 2, 10 October 1970; Alan Warboys v Brighton & HA, Division 3, 1 December 1973; Jamie Cureton v Reading, Division 2, 16 January 1999.

Most Capped Player: Neil Slatter, 10 (22), Wales.

Most League Appearances: Stuart Taylor, 546, 1966–80.

Youngest League Player: Ronnie Dix, 15 years 180 days v Norwich C, 3 March 1928.

Record Transfer Fee Received: £2,000,000 from Fulham for Barry Hayles, November 1998.

Record Transfer Fee Paid: £370,000 to QPR for Andy Tillson, November 1992.

Football League Record: 1920 Original Member of Division 3; 1921–53 Division 3 (S); 1953–62 Division 2; 1962–74 Division 3; 1974–81 Division 2; 1981–90 Division 3; 1990–92 Division 2. 1992–93 Division 1; 1993– Division 2.

MANAGERS

Alfred Homer 1899–1920
 (*continued as Secretary to 1928*)
Ben Hall 1920–21
Andy Wilson 1921–26
Joe Palmer 1926–29
Dave McLean 1929–30
Albert Prince-Cox 1930–36
Percy Smith 1936–37
Brough Fletcher 1938–49
Bert Tann 1950–68
 (*continued as General Manager to 1972*)
Fred Ford 1968–69
Bill Dodgin Snr 1969–72
Don Megson 1972–77
Bobby Campbell 1978–79
Harold Jarman 1979–80
Terry Cooper 1980–81
Bobby Gould 1981–83
David Williams 1983–85
Bobby Gould 1985–87
Gerry Francis 1987–91
Martin Dobson 1991
Dennis Rofe 1992
Malcolm Allison 1992–93
John Ward 1993–96
Ian Holloway May 1996–

TEN YEAR LEAGUE RECORD

		P	W	D	L	F	A	Pts	Pos
1988-89	Div 3	46	19	17	10	67	51	74	5
1989-90	Div 3	46	26	15	5	71	35	93	1
1990-91	Div 2	46	15	13	18	56	59	58	13
1991-92	Div 2	46	16	14	16	60	63	62	13
1992-93	Div 1	46	10	11	25	55	87	41	24
1993-94	Div 2	46	20	10	16	60	59	70	8
1994-95	Div 2	46	22	16	8	70	40	82	4
1995-96	Div 2	46	20	10	16	57	60	70	10
1996-97	Div 2	46	15	11	20	47	50	56	17
1997-98	Div 2	46	20	10	16	70	64	70	6

DID YOU KNOW ?

Three Bristol Rovers players scored hat-tricks on their League debut for the club: Joe Riley 1931 v Bournemouth, Jimmy McCambridge 1933 v Bristol City and Bobby Gould against Blackburn Rovers in 1977.

BRISTOL ROVERS 1998–99 LEAGUE RECORD

Match No.	Date		Venue	Opponents	Result	H/T Score	Lg. Pos.	Goalscorers	Attendance
1	Aug	8	A	Burnley	L 1-2	1-2	—	Cureton [8]	11,781
2		15	H	Reading	W 4-1	3-1	9	Hayles [32], Meaker [36], Cureton (pen) [40], Roberts [84]	7529
3		22	A	Gillingham	D 0-0	0-0	8		4896
4		29	H	Wigan Ath	W 3-2	1-0	6	Hayles 2 [44, 65], Ipoua [86]	6140
5		31	A	Wycombe W	D 1-1	0-0	7	Hayles [84]	4318
6	Sept	5	H	Preston NE	D 2-2	2-0	8	Hayles [5], Tillson [24]	6702
7		8	H	Chesterfield	D 0-0	0-0	—		5416
8		12	A	Luton T	L 0-2	0-2	13		5558
9		19	H	Lincoln C	W 3-0	0-0	9	Cureton [48], Hayles 2 [65, 73]	6091
10		26	A	York C	L 0-1	0-0	13		3305
11	Oct	3	H	Bournemouth	W 1-0	1-0	10	Shore [29]	7526
12		10	H	Northampton T	L 1-3	1-2	13	Meaker [21]	6023
13		17	H	Wrexham	D 0-0	0-0	13		6072
14		20	H	Stoke C	W 1-0	1-0	—	Cureton [8]	6752
15		24	A	Notts Co	D 1-1	0-0	10	Shore [59]	4822
16		31	H	Walsall	L 3-4	2-2	11	Cureton [3], Hayles 2 [4, 50]	5753
17	Nov	7	A	Fulham	L 0-1	0-1	13		11,575
18		10	H	Blackpool	L 0-2	0-0	—		5361
19		21	A	Millwall	D 1-1	0-1	15	Roberts [66]	5755
20		28	H	Oldham Ath	D 2-2	0-1	16	Cureton [71], Roberts [89]	5614
21	Dec	12	H	Manchester C	D 0-0	0-0	17		24,976
22		18	H	Macclesfield T	D 0-0	0-0	—		5039
23		28	A	Colchester U	W 3-0	2-0	15	Cureton [2], Roberts [43], Ipoua [84]	4609
24	Jan	9	H	Burnley	L 3-4	3-3	16	Cureton [25], Roberts [35], Lee [45]	7129
25		16	A	Reading	W 6-0	0-0	15	Cureton 4 (1 pen) [49, 57 (pl), 63, 70], Roberts 2 [88, 90]	13,258
26		30	H	Colchester U	D 1-1	1-0	16	Roberts [28]	6249
27	Feb	6	A	Preston NE	D 2-2	2-1	15	Cureton [28], Roberts [45]	12,170
28		20	H	Luton T	W 1-0	1-0	14	Tillson [26]	6361
29		23	H	Gillingham	L 0-1	0-1	—		5735
30		27	A	Lincoln C	L 0-1	0-0	16		4235
31	Mar	6	H	York C	W 2-0	1-0	15	Roberts [17], Ellington [76]	5749
32		9	A	Bournemouth	L 0-1	0-0	—		7181
33		12	H	Fulham	L 2-3	1-2	—	Thomson [45], Roberts [47]	8011
34		20	A	Walsall	D 3-3	0-2	15	Cureton 3 (1 pen) [53 (pl), 63, 89]	4967
35		23	H	Wycombe W	L 0-2	0-1	—		4833
36		27	H	Notts Co	D 1-1	1-1	15	Ipoua [34]	5899
37		30	A	Wigan Ath	L 0-1	0-1	—		3568
38	Apr	3	A	Wrexham	L 0-1	0-1	17		3087
39		5	H	Northampton T	D 1-1	0-1	16	Penrice [64]	6580
40		10	A	Stoke C	W 4-1	0-1	16	Roberts [53], Foster [81], Cureton 2 [84, 88]	17,823
41		13	A	Oldham Ath	L 1-2	1-0	—	Roberts [23]	3913
42		20	A	Chesterfield	D 0-0	0-0	—		2621
43		24	A	Blackpool	W 2-1	0-0	15	Cureton 2 (1 pen) [61, 71 (pl)]	5033
44		27	H	Millwall	W 3-0	1-0	—	Cureton [29], Roberts 2 [66, 70]	5755
45	May	1	H	Manchester C	D 2-2	0-2	13	Roberts [83], Cureton (pen) [88]	8033
46		8	A	Macclesfield T	W 4-3	1-2	13	Cureton 3 (1 pen) [41, 57 (pl), 85], Bennett [55]	3186

Final League Position: 13

GOALSCORERS

League (65): Cureton 25 (6 pens), Roberts 16, Hayles 9, Ipoua 3, Meaker 2, Shore 2, Tillson 2, Bennett 1, Ellington 1, Foster 1, Lee 1, Penrice 1, Thomson 1.
Worthington Cup (2): Cureton 1, Hayles 1.
FA Cup (15): Roberts 7, Cureton 2, Shore 2, Lee 1, Leoni 1, Penrice 1, Zabek 1.

Jones L 32	Trees R 33+3	Challis T 38	Zabek L 9+2	Foster S 41+2	Andreasson M 4+1	Holloway J 33+4	Meaker M 17+3	Roberts J 32+5	Cureton J 46	Hayles B 17	Ipoua G 15+9	Basford L 6+3	Leoni S 25+5	Smith M 11+3	Penrice G 10+16	Tillson A 18+1	Low J 5+3	Collett A 3	Shore J 18+6	Trought M 6+3	McKeever M 5+2	Lee D 10+1	Thomson A 21	Pritchard D 11+1	Pethick R 9	Ellington N 1+9	Phillips M 2	Hillier D 13	Kuipers M 1	Andrews B 3	Williams A 9	Bennett F 1+3	Johnston R 1	Match No.
1	2	3	4	5	6	7	8	9	10^1	11	12																							1
1	2	3	4^1	5	6	7	8	9	10	11		12																						2
1	2	3		5		7^2	8^3	9	10	11	12		4	6	13	14																		3
1	4	3		5		7	8	9	10	11	12		2		6																		4
1	4		5		7		9^2	10	11	12	3	2		13	6	8^1																		5
	4		5		7	8	12	10	11		9^1	3	2^2	13		6		1																6
	4		5			8^3	12	10	11		9^1	3	2^2	13	7	6		1	14															7
	4		5		7^1	8	9	10	11		3	2		6		1	12																	8
1	4	3		5			9	10	11		2		6	7	8																			9
1	4^1	3		5		12	13	9^3	10	11	14	2		6	7^2	8																		10
1	4	3	12	5		14	8^2	9	10^1	11	13	2^3	6		7																			11
1	4	3	12	5		13	8	9	10^3	11	14	2^1	6		7^2																			12
1		3	4^1	5		7	8		10^2	11	9		2	6	12	13																		13
1	12	3	4	5		7	8		10	11	9^2		2^1	6	13																			14
1	2		4	5		7			10		9^2	12	3	6	11	8^1	13																	15
1	3		4	5		7	8^2	12	10	11	9^1	13	2^3	6		14																		16
1	8^1		5		7	12	13	10	11	9^2		2^3	6	4																				17
1	2	3^1	4^2	5		8	12	10^1	11	9		14	6	13		7																		18
1	2	3		5	4	8^2	11	10		9^1	13	6	12		7																			19
1	2	3		5	4	8	11	10	12		6	9		7^1																				20
1	8	3	4	5		11	10	9^3	2	13	12		7	6^1	14																			21
1	8^2	3	4	5		11	10	9^1	2	12		7	6	13																				22
1		3			4	8	11	10	12	2		7	6	9	5																			23
1		3	5		4	8	11	10	2	12		7^1	9	6																				24
1	4	3	5		7	11	10	2				9	8	6																				25
1	4	3	5		7	11	10	12				13	8^1	9	6	2^2																		26
1	4^3	3	5		7	11	10	12		13	14		9	8^2	6	2^1																		27
1	4	3		9		11	10			12	6	8^1	7			5	2																	28
1		3	12	4		11	10^3	9^2		13	5		7					8^1	6	2	14													29
1	4^1	3		11		10					5		7			6		2	12	9	8													30
1		3	6	7		11	10		4		5		2			12	9^1	8																31
		6	7	11	10		3	4^1	9^2		12			5^1	2	13	8	1																32
1	4^2	3	6	9		11	10		7	12		5^1	2	13	8																			33
1	12	3	6	4		11	10		7^1	13		5	2^2		8	9																		34
1	4^1	3	5	7		11	10		2			6			12	8	9																	35
	4	3	12			10	11^3	2	13	6				7	5	14					8^2	9^1	1											36
1	4^2	3	2	9^1		10	11			12	13		6	7	5						8													37
	4	3	9	6	12	10	11^3		13			8^1	7	5	14	2^2					1													38
	3	6	11	7		10			9					8	5	2	4^1	12			1													39
	3	4	7			11	10					9	6			5	2				8	1												40
	3	4	7			11	10		12			9^2	6			13	5	2			8^1	1												41
	3	4	9			11	10					6	7			5	2				8	1												42
	7	4				10			3	12	9^3	6	13			5	2	11^2	8^1		1	14												43
12	3	4	9			11	10					6	7^2			5	2				8^1	1	13											44
8^1	3	4	7			11	10					9	6			5	2				1	12												45
11	3	4	13			12	10		7^1			6				5	8	2^2	13		9^2	1												46

Worthington Cup
First Round   Leyton Orient   (a) 1-1
                              (h) 1-2

FA Cup
First Round   Welling U   (h) 3-0
Second Round   Exeter C   (a) 2-2
                              (h) 5-0
Third Round   Rotherham U   (a) 1-0
Fourth Round   Leyton Orient (h) 3-0
Fifth Round   Barnsley   (a) 1-4

Division 2

BURNLEY

FOUNDATION

The majority of those responsible for the formation of the Burnley club in 1881 were from the defunct rugby club Burnley Rovers. Indeed, they continued to play rugby for a year before changing to soccer and dropping 'Rovers' from their name. The changes were decided at a meeting held in May 1882 at the Bull Hotel.

Turf Moor, Burnley BB10 4BX.

Telephone: (01282) 700000.

Fax: (01282) 700014.

Clubcall: 0891 121153.

Ticket Office: (01282) 70010.

Community Programme: (01282) 70011.

Commercial Department: (01282) 70007.

Ground Capacity: 22,546.

Record Attendance: 54,775 v Huddersfield T, FA Cup 3rd rd, 23 February 1924.

Record Receipts: £150,000 v Liverpool, FA Cup 4th rd, 28 January 1995.

Pitch Measurements: 114yd × 72yd.

Chairman: B. Kilby.

President: Dr R. D. Iven MRCS (Eng), LRCP (Lond), MRCGP.

Directors: F. J. Teasdale, C. Holt, R. Blakeborough, R. Ingleby.

Manager: Stan Ternent.

General Manager: A. Watson.

Company Secretary: Cathy Pickup.

Coaches: Terry Pashley, Michael Docherty, James Robson.

Commercial Manager: Peter Davis.

LATEST SEQUENCES

Longest Sequence of League Wins: 10, 16.11.12 – 18.1.13.

Longest Sequence of League Defeats: 8, 2.1.95 – 25.2.95.

Longest Sequence of League Draws: 6, 21.2.31 – 28.3.31.

Longest Sequence of Unbeaten League Matches: 30, 6.9.20 – 25.3.21.

Longest Sequence Without a League Win: 24, 16.4.79 – 17.11.79.

HONOURS

Football League: Division 1 – Champions 1920–21, 1959–60; Runners-up 1919–20, 1961–62; Division 2 – Champions 1897–98, 1972–73; Runners-up 1912–13, 1946–47; Promoted from Division 2, 1993–94 (play-offs); Division 3 – Champions 1981–82; Division 4 – Champions 1991–92. Record 30 consecutive Division 1 games without defeat 1920–21.

FA Cup: Winners 1914; Runners-up 1947, 1962.

Football League Cup: Semi-final 1961, 1969, 1983.

Anglo–Scottish Cup: Winners 1979.

Sherpa Van Trophy: Runners-up 1988.

European Competitions: European Cup: 1960–61. European Fairs Cup: 1966–67.

Colours
Claret body with blue sleeves and white collar, blue shorts, blue stockings.

Change Colours
White shirts with blue collar, blue shorts, blue stockings.

Year Formed: 1882.

Turned Professional: 1883.

Ltd Co.: 1897.

Previous Name: 1881, Burnley Rovers; 1882, Burnley.

Club Nickname: 'The Clarets'.

Previous Grounds: 1881, Calder Vale; 1882, Turf Moor.

First Football League Game: 8 September 1888, Football League, v Preston NE (a) L 2–5 – Smith; Lang, Bury, Abrams, Friel, Keenan, Brady, Tait, Poland (1), Gallocher (1), Yates.

Record League Victory: 9–0 v Darwen, Division 1, 9 January 1892 – Hillman; Walker, McFettridge, Lang, Matthews, Keenan, Nicol (3), Bowes, Espie (1), McLardie (3), Hill (2).

Record Cup Victory: 9–0 v Crystal Palace, FA Cup 2nd rd (replay), 10 February 1909 – Dawson; Barron, McLean; Cretney (2), Leake, Moffat; Morley, Ogden, Smith (3), Abbott (2), Smethams (1). 9–0 v New Brighton, FA Cup 4th rd, 26 January 1957 – Blacklaw; Angus, Winton; Seith, Adamson, Miller; Newlands (1), McIlroy (3), Lawson (3), Cheesebrough (1), Pilkington (1). 9–0 v Penrith, FA Cup 1st rd, 17 November 1984 – Hansbury; Miller, Hampton, Phelan, Overson (Kennedy), Hird (3 incl. 1p), Grewcock (1), Powell (2), Taylor (3), Biggins, Hutchison.

Record Defeat: 0–10 v Aston Villa, Division 1, 29 August 1925 and v Sheffield U, Division 1, 19 January 1929.

Most League Points (2 for a win): 62, Division 2, 1972–73.

Most League Points (3 for a win): 83, Division 4, 1991–92.

Most League Goals: 102, Division 1, 1960–61.

Highest League Scorer in Season: George Beel, 35, Division 1, 1927–28.

Most League Goals in Total Aggregate: George Beel, 178, 1923–32.

Most League Goals in One Match: 6, Louis Page v Birmingham C, Division 1, 10 April 1926.

Most Capped Player: Jimmy McIlroy, 51 (55), Northern Ireland.

Most League Appearances: Jerry Dawson, 522, 1907–28.

Youngest League Player: Tommy Lawton, 16 years 174 days v Doncaster R, 28 March 1936.

Record Transfer Fee Received: £750,000 from Luton T for Steve Davis, August 1995.

Record Transfer Fee Paid: £800,000 to Luton T for Steve Davis, December 1998.

Football League Record: 1888 Original Member of the Football League; 1897–98 Division 2; 1898–1900 Division 1; 1900–13 Division 2; 1913–30 Division 1; 1930–47 Division 2; 1947–71 Division 1; 1971–73 Division 2; 1973–76 Division 1; 1976–80 Division 2; 1980–82 Division 3; 1982–83 Division 2; 1983–85 Division 3; 1985–92 Division 4; 1992–94 Division 2; 1994–95 Division 1; 1995– Division 2.

MANAGERS

Arthur F. Sutcliffe 1893–96
(Secretary-Manager)
Harry Bradshaw 1896–99
(Secretary-Manager)
Ernest Magnall 1899–1903
(Secretary-Manager)
Spen Whittaker 1903–10
R. H. Wadge 1910–11
(Secretary-Manager)
John Haworth 1911–25
Albert Pickles 1925–32
Tom Bromilow 1932–35
Alf Boland 1935–39
(Secretary-Manager)
Cliff Britton 1945–48
Frank Hill 1948–54
Alan Brown 1954–57
Billy Dougall 1957–58
Harry Potts 1958–70
(General Manager to 1972)
Jimmy Adamson 1970–76
Joe Brown 1976–77
Harry Potts 1977–79
Brian Miller 1979–83
John Bond 1983–84
John Benson 1984–85
Martin Buchan 1985
Tommy Cavanagh 1985–86
Brian Miller 1986–89
Frank Casper 1989–91
Jimmy Mullen 1991–96
Adrian Heath 1996–97
Chris Waddle 1997–98
Stan Ternent June 1998–

TEN YEAR LEAGUE RECORD

		P	W	D	L	F	A	Pts	Pos
1988-89	Div 4	46	14	13	19	52	61	55	16
1989-90	Div 4	46	14	14	18	45	55	56	16
1990-91	Div 4	46	23	10	13	70	51	79	6
1991-92	Div 4	42	25	8	9	79	43	83	1
1992-93	Div 2	46	15	16	15	57	59	61	13
1993-94	Div 2	46	21	10	15	79	58	73	6
1994-95	Div 1	46	11	13	22	49	74	46	22
1995-96	Div 2	46	14	13	19	56	68	55	17
1996-97	Div 2	46	19	11	16	71	55	68	9
1997-98	Div 2	46	13	13	20	55	65	52	20

DID YOU KNOW ?

Burnley purchased Turf Moor and the surrounding area of eight acres for £4,500 in 1922. At the time the capacity of the ground was 60,000. Two years later the club recorded its record attendance.

BURNLEY 1998–99 LEAGUE RECORD

Match No.	Date	Venue	Opponents	Result	H/T Score	Lg. Pos.	Goalscorers	Attendance
1	Aug 8	H	Bristol R	W 2-1	2-1	—	Payton 2 [2, 31]	11,781
2	15	A	Chesterfield	L 0-1	0-0	14		5426
3	22	A	York C	L 0-1	0-1	19		9715
4	29	A	Walsall	L 1-3	0-1	20	Armstrong [69]	4599
5	Sept 1	H	Millwall	W 2-1	2-0	—	Cooke 2 [21, 30]	8526
6	5	A	Luton T	L 0-1	0-0	19		5554
7	9	A	Reading	D 1-1	0-1	—	Payton [76]	10,080
8	12	H	Wycombe W	D 1-1	1-1	17	Payton [6]	9120
9	19	A	Gillingham	L 1-2	1-1	19	Payton [31]	5702
10	26	H	Wigan Ath	D 1-1	0-0	18	Reid [68]	10,183
11	Oct 3	A	Manchester C	D 2-2	1-1	20	Payton [34], Cooke [54]	30,722
12	9	A	Colchester U	W 4-0	2-0	—	Payton 2 [2, 11], Vindheim [50], Cooke [72]	5532
13	17	H	Notts Co	D 1-1	0-1	18	Vindheim [90]	10,559
14	20	H	Oldham Ath	W 1-0	0-0	—	Cooke [64]	9539
15	24	A	Macclesfield T	L 1-2	0-1	15	Little [71]	3995
16	31	H	Wrexham	W 2-1	1-0	14	Payton 2 [29, 55]	10,109
17	Nov 7	A	Preston NE	L 1-4	1-1	18	Eastwood [15]	15,888
18	10	H	Stoke C	L 0-2	0-0	—		10,575
19	21	A	Bournemouth	L 0-5	0-0	19		5907
20	28	H	Blackpool	W 1-0	0-0	17	Payton (pen) [67]	11,925
21	Dec 12	A	Fulham	L 0-4	0-2	18		9983
22	19	H	Northampton T	L 0-2	0-0	19		8783
23	26	A	York C	D 3-3	1-0	19	Payton [23], Robertson [58], Armstrong [87]	5630
24	28	H	Lincoln C	D 1-1	0-0	17	Henderson [81]	9635
25	Jan 2	A	Walsall	D 0-0	0-0	17		10,892
26	9	A	Bristol R	W 4-3	3-3	15	Davis [15], Branch [30], Payton [44], Cooke [54]	7129
27	16	H	Chesterfield	L 1-2	0-1	16	Cooke [86]	10,985
28	23	A	Millwall	W 2-1	1-0	15	Cooke [11], Davis [80]	7407
29	30	A	Lincoln C	D 1-1	0-1	15	Reid [66]	6361
30	Feb 6	H	Luton T	L 1-2	1-1	16	Mellon [29]	10,285
31	13	H	Reading	D 1-1	0-0	16	Reid [90]	9366
32	20	A	Wycombe W	L 0-2	0-0	18		5195
33	27	A	Gillingham	L 0-5	0-4	18		8981
34	Mar 9	H	Manchester C	L 0-6	0-2	—		17,251
35	14	H	Preston NE	L 0-1	0-0	21		11,561
36	20	A	Wrexham	D 1-1	0-1	21	Mellon [75]	4151
37	28	H	Macclesfield T	W 4-3	1-2	19	Little [17], Davis 2 [57, 90], Payton [79]	10,500
38	Apr 3	A	Notts Co	D 0-0	0-0	19		6625
39	5	H	Colchester U	W 3-1	0-1	17	Johnrose [57], Payton 2 [82, 89]	10,747
40	10	A	Oldham Ath	D 1-1	0-1	18	Payton [52]	8542
41	13	A	Blackpool	W 2-0	1-0	—	Payton [26], Little [57]	5658
42	17	H	Bournemouth	D 0-0	0-0	17		9802
43	24	A	Stoke C	W 4-1	2-1	15	Pickering [5], Payton [11], Little 2 [68, 90]	10,965
44	May 1	H	Fulham	W 1-0	0-0	14	Jepson [82]	13,086
45	3	A	Wigan Ath	D 0-0	0-0	—		5528
46	8	A	Northampton T	D 2-2	0-1	15	Cook (pen) [69], Cooke [88]	7435

Final League Position: 15

GOALSCORERS

League (54): Payton 19 (1 pen), Cooke 9, Little 5, Davis 5, Reid 3, Armstrong 2, Mellon 2, Vindheim 2, Branch 1, Cook 1 (pen), Eastwood 1, Henderson 1, Jepson 1, Johnrose 1, Pickering 1, Robertson 1.
Worthington Cup (2): Cooke 1, Payton 1.
FA Cup (2): Payton 2 (1 pen).

Crichton P 29	Brass C 33 + 1	Morgan S 17	Ford M 11 + 1	Blatherwick S 3	Howey L 3	Little G 32 + 2	Williams M 2	Cooke A 36	Payton A 39 + 1	Smith P 11 + 1	Smith C 5 + 5	Moore N 10 + 2	Jepson R 3 + 12	Ward G 17	Robertson M 19 + 5	Winstanley M 1	Carr-Lawton C 2 + 2	Heywood M 11 + 2	Scott C 9 + 5	Eastwood P 6 + 7	Armstrong G 40	Weller P 1	Swan P 11 + 6	Reid B 30 + 1	Henderson K — + 7	Vindheim R 8	Maylett B — + 17	O'Kane J 8	Hewlett M 2	Pickering A 21	Davis S 19	Branch G 14 + 6	Mellon M 20	Johnrose L 9 + 3	Cowan T 12	Cook P 12	Williamson J — + 1	Match No.
1	2	3	4¹	5	6²	7	8	9	10³	11	12	13	14																									1
	2	3		5	6	7		9²	10	11	8¹	4	12	1	13																							2
		2		5¹	6²	7³			10	11	8	4		1			3	9	12	13	14																	3
					6	7		9	10	11				1	2			8	12		3		4¹	5														4
					6	7		9	10	11	4	2¹		1				8	12		3			5														5
					6	7		9	10	11	8			1	2						3			5	4													6
			4			7		9	10	11²	8¹			1	2			13	12		3			5	6													7
			4			7		9	10		12			1	2		11¹	8			3			5	6													8
			4			7		9	10		8			1	2			11			3			5	6													9
			4			7		9	10	11¹				1				8	5	2	3		12	6														10
						7		9	10	11				1				8	5	2	3		6		4¹													11
						7		9	10²	11		12		1				8	5	2	3		6		4¹	13												12
						7		9	10	11¹				1				8	5	2	3		6		4	12												13
						7		9	10	11¹				1				8	5	2	3		6	13	4²	12												14
						7		9	10				12²	1				8	5		3		6	13	4					11								15
	8	3				7		9	10					1	2				5		4¹		6	13						11	12²							16
	8	3		12		7		9³	10					1	2				5		4¹		6²	13						11		14						17
	8	3		10		7		9²						1	2				5		4¹		6	13		12				11								18
1	5	8	4			7		9	10						2						11¹		6								12	3						19
1	5		4			7		9	10						2²			11	13	12			6									3¹	8					20
1	11		4					9¹	10						2			5			7		6		12						13	3	8²					21
1	8		4					9	10						7¹			5	13		11		6		12						2	3²						22
1	5	3	4					9	10¹						7			8	13		11²		6		12						2							23
1	5	3	4					9							7²			8			11¹		10	6	12						13							24
1		3	4					9	10						7						8		12	6							2	5	11¹					25
1		3						9¹	10						4						8		12	6							2	5	11	7				26
1	12	3				7		9	10			13									8¹		6				14				2³	5	11²	4				27
1		3	11			7		9²	10²			2									8		12	6			14					5	13³	4				28
1		3				7¹		9	10²			2					12				8		6			13						5	11	4				29
1		3				7²		9	10¹			2					12				8		6			13	14					5	11³	4				30
1		3				7¹		9			12		13					8					6				14				2	5	11³	4	10			31
1	12	3¹	4					9					8		13						7		12²	6			14				2	5	11		10			32
1	7²							9	8		12				5¹	13					3			6							2		11	4	10			33
1		3	4			7		9					2¹										10		6		12					5	11	4				34
1	6					7			10												8¹									12	2	5	11	4	3	9		35
1	6					7			10												8										2	5	11	4	3	9		36
1	6					7			10			12									8¹									12	2³	5	11²	4	13	3	9	14	37
1	6					7²			10			12									8									13	2	5	11	4	11	3	9¹		38
1	6³					7			10			12									8									13	2¹	5	11	4	14	3	9²		39
1	6							9¹	10³												8		7²								2	5	13	4	11	3	9		40
1	6		13					9¹	10³			12									7										2	5	14	4	11	3²	8		41
1	6							9					12								13		7								2	5	11²	4	10	3	8¹		42
1	6					7		9	10²			12									11										2	5	13³	4	14	3	8¹		43
1	6					7²		9				12									11										2³	5	10¹	4	13	3	8		44
1	6					7		9²				12									11			5			13				2		4	10	3	8¹		45
1	6					7		9		12		10¹									11			5			13				2²		4	3	8			46

Division 2

BURY

FOUNDATION

A meeting at the Waggon & Horses Hotel, attended largely by members of Bury Wesleyans and Bury Unitarians football clubs, decided to form a new Bury club. This was officially formed at a subsequent gathering at the Old White Horse Hotel, Fleet Street, Bury on 24 April 1885.

Gigg Lane, Bury BL9 9HR.
Telephone: (0161) 764 4881.
Fax: (0161) 764 5521.
Commercial Dept: (0161) 705 2144.
Fax: (0161) 763 3103.
Clubcall: 0891 121197.
Community Programme: (0161) 797 5423.
Social Club: (0161) 764 6771.
Ground Capacity: 11,841.
Record Attendance: 35,000 v Bolton W, FA Cup 3rd rd, 9 January 1960.
Record Receipts: £86,000 v Manchester C, Division 1, 12 September 1997.
Pitch Measurements: 112yd × 72yd.
Chairman: T. Robinson.
Directors: J. Smith, F. Mason, N. Neville.
Manager: Neil Warnock.
Assistant Manager: Kevin Blackwell.
Coach: Brian Taylor.
Physio: Alan Raw.
Youth Development: Dave Cowling.
Stadium Manager: Wilf Linton.
Secretary: J. Neville.
Commercial Manager: Neville Neville.

LATEST SEQUENCES

Longest Sequence of League Wins: 9, 26.9.60 – 19.11.60.
Longest Sequence of League Defeats: 6, 14.1.67 – 4.3.67.
Longest Sequence of League Draws: 6, 6.3.99 – 3.4.99.
Longest Sequence of Unbeaten League Matches: 18, 4.2.61 – 29.4.61.
Longest Sequence Without a League Win: 19, 1.4.11 – 2.12.11.

HONOURS

Football League: Division 1 best season: 4th, 1925–26; Division 2 – Champions 1894–95, 1996–97; Runners-up 1923–24; Division 3 – Champions 1960–61; Runners-up 1967–68; Promoted from Division 3 (3rd) 1995–96.
FA Cup: Winners 1900, 1903.
Football League Cup: Semi-final 1963.

Colours
White shirts, royal blue shorts, royal blue stockings.

Change Colours
Red shirts, navy blue shorts, navy blue stockings.

Year Formed: 1885.

Turned professional: 1885.

Ltd Co.: 1897.

Club Nickname: 'Shakers'.

Club Sponsors: Birthdays.

First Football League Game: 1 September 1894, Division 2, v Manchester C (h) W 4–2 – Lowe; Gillespie, Davies; White, Clegg, Ross; Wylie, Barbour (2), Millar (1), Ostler (1), Plant.

Record League Victory: 8–0 v Tranmere R, Division 3, 10 January 1970 – Forrest; Tinney, Saile; Anderson, Turner, McDermott; Hince (1), Arrowsmith (1), Jones (4), Kerr (1), Grundy, (1 og).

Record Cup Victory: 12–1 v Stockton, FA Cup 1st rd (replay), 2 February 1897 – Montgomery; Darroch, Barbour; Hendry (1), Clegg, Ross (1); Wylie (3), Pangbourn, Millar (4), Henderson (2), Plant, (1 og).

Record Defeat: 0–10 v West Ham U, Milk Cup 2nd rd 2nd leg, 25 October 1983.

Most League Points (2 for a win): 68, Division 3, 1960–61.

Most League Points (3 for a win): 84, Division 4, 1984–85 and Division 2, 1996–97.

Most League Goals: 108, Division 3, 1960–61.

Highest League Scorer in Season: Craig Madden, 35, Division 4, 1981–82.

Most League Goals in Total Aggregate: Craig Madden, 129, 1978–86.

Most League Goals in One Match: 5, Eddie Quigley v Millwall, Division 2, 15 February 1947; 5, Ray Pointer v Rotherham U, Division 2, 2 October 1965.

Most Capped Player: Bill Gorman, 11 (13), Republic of Ireland and (4), Northern Ireland.

Most League Appearances: Norman Bullock, 506, 1920–35.

Youngest League Player: Brian Williams, 16 years 133 days v Stockport Co, 18 March 1972.

Record Transfer Fee Received: £1,100,000 from Ipswich T for David Johnson, November 1997.

Record Transfer Fee Paid: £200,000 to Ipswich T for Chris Swailes, November 1997 and to Swindon T for Darren Bullock, February 1999.

Football League Record: 1894 Elected to Division 2; 1895–1912 Division 1; 1912–24 Division 2; 1924–29 Division 1; 1929–57 Division 2; 1957–61 Division 3; 1961–67 Division 2; 1967–68 Division 3; 1968–69 Division 2; 1969–71 Division 3; 1971–74 Division 4; 1974–80 Division 3; 1980–85 Division 4; 1985–96 Division 3; 1996–97 Division 2; 1997–99 Division 1; 1999– Division 2.

MANAGERS

T. Hargreaves 1887
(Secretary-Manager)
H. S. Hamer 1887–1907
(Secretary-Manager)
Archie Montgomery 1907–15
William Cameron 1919–23
James Hunter Thompson 1923–27
Percy Smith 1927–30
Arthur Paine 1930–34
Norman Bullock 1934–38
Jim Porter 1944–45
Norman Bullock 1945–49
John McNeil 1950–53
Dave Russell 1953–61
Bob Stokoe 1961–65
Bert Head 1965–66
Les Shannon 1966–69
Jack Marshall 1969
Les Hart 1970
Tommy McAnearney 1970–72
Alan Brown 1972–73
Bobby Smith 1973–77
Bob Stokoe 1977–78
David Hatton 1978–79
Dave Connor 1979–80
Jim Iley 1980–84
Martin Dobson 1984–89
Sam Ellis 1989–90
Mike Walsh 1990–95
Stan Ternent 1995–98
Neil Warnock June 1998–

TEN YEAR LEAGUE RECORD

		P	W	D	L	F	A	Pts	Pos
1988-89	Div 3	46	16	13	17	55	67	61	13
1989-90	Div 3	46	21	11	14	70	49	74	5
1990-91	Div 3	46	20	13	13	67	56	73	7
1991-92	Div 3	46	13	12	21	55	74	51	21
1992-93	Div 3	42	18	9	15	63	55	63	7
1993-94	Div 3	42	14	11	17	55	56	53	13
1994-95	Div 3	42	23	11	8	73	36	80	4
1995-96	Div 3	46	22	13	11	66	48	79	3
1996-97	Div 2	46	24	12	10	62	38	84	1
1997-98	Div 1	46	11	19	16	42	58	52	17

DID YOU KNOW ?

Tommy Cornthwaite, who kept goal for Bury on 89 League occasions between 1919 and 1923, was a part-time player and policeman. He missed several games in 1920 during a miners' strike when police leave was cancelled.

BURY 1998-99 LEAGUE RECORD

Match No.	Date	Venue	Opponents	Result		H/T Score	Lg. Pos.	Goalscorers	Attendance
1	Aug 8	H	Huddersfield T	W	1-0	1-0	—	Ellis [20]	7659
2	15	A	Ipswich T	D	0-0	0-0	7		13,267
3	22	H	Crewe Alex	W	1-0	1-0	7	D'Jaffo [36]	5073
4	29	A	QPR	D	0-0	0-0	7		8612
5	31	H	Swindon T	W	3-0	0-0	3	Barrick [62], Matthews [66], Preece [76]	4513
6	Sept 5	A	Birmingham C	L	0-1	0-1	4		15,935
7	8	H	Portsmouth	W	2-1	2-1	—	Preece [23], D'Jaffo [44]	4310
8	13	A	Norwich C	D	0-0	0-0	4		16,919
9	19	H	Tranmere R	D	0-0	0-0	4		5030
10	26	A	Wolverhampton W	L	0-1	0-0	8		20,155
11	30	A	Crystal Palace	L	2-4	2-1	—	Daws [9], Preece [45]	13,219
12	Oct 3	H	Bristol C	L	0-1	0-0	12		4794
13	9	A	Bradford C	L	0-3	0-1	—		15,697
14	17	H	Stockport Co	D	1-1	0-0	16	Matthews [72]	5732
15	20	H	Oxford U	W	1-0	0-0	—	Swailes [69]	3436
16	24	A	Sunderland	L	0-1	0-0	15		38,049
17	31	H	Watford	L	1-3	1-2	15	Ellis [7]	4342
18	Nov 7	A	Barnsley	D	1-1	0-1	16	D'Jaffo [52]	15,115
19	14	A	Sheffield U	L	1-3	1-0	17	James [39]	14,164
20	21	H	Grimsby T	W	1-0	0-0	14	Lucketti [47]	4198
21	28	A	Bolton W	L	0-4	0-1	16		21,028
22	Dec 5	H	WBA	W	2-0	2-0	15	Johnrose [9], D'Jaffo (pen) [28]	5007
23	11	H	Sheffield U	D	3-3	1-1	—	D'Jaffo [36], Williams [52], Swailes [54]	5002
24	19	A	Port Vale	L	0-1	0-0	16		6425
25	26	A	Crewe Alex	L	1-3	0-0	19	Woodward [79]	5333
26	28	H	Birmingham C	L	2-4	1-2	19	D'Jaffo 2 (1 pen) [17, 85 (p)]	7024
27	Jan 9	A	Huddersfield T	L	0-2	0-1	19		10,788
28	16	H	QPR	D	1-1	1-0	19	James [24]	4609
29	30	A	Swindon T	D	1-1	0-0	18	Littlejohn [68]	7797
30	Feb 6	H	Ipswich T	L	0-3	0-0	20		4750
31	13	A	Portsmouth	L	1-2	0-1	21	Avdiu [89]	9062
32	20	H	Norwich C	L	0-2	0-1	22		4285
33	27	A	Tranmere R	L	0-4	0-1	22		6002
34	Mar 6	H	Crystal Palace	D	0-0	0-0	21		4334
35	9	A	Bristol C	D	1-1	1-0	—	D'Jaffo [17]	11,606
36	13	H	Barnsley	D	0-0	0-0	22		4696
37	16	H	Wolverhampton W	D	0-0	0-0	—		5204
38	20	A	Watford	D	0-0	0-0	20		9336
39	Apr 3	A	Stockport Co	D	0-0	0-0	21		7483
40	5	H	Bradford C	L	0-2	0-2	23		8000
41	10	A	Oxford U	W	1-0	1-0	21	Lilley [29]	6358
42	13	H	Sunderland	L	2-5	1-4	—	Bullock [23], Daws [65]	8669
43	17	A	Grimsby T	D	0-0	0-0	21		5132
44	23	H	Bolton W	W	2-1	2-0	—	West [27], Swailes [45]	7680
45	May 1	A	WBA	L	0-1	0-0	22		12,918
46	9	H	Port Vale	W	1-0	0-0	22	West [67]	7567

Final League Position: 22

GOALSCORERS

League (33): D'Jaffo 8 (2 pens), Preece 3, Swailes C 3, Daws 2, Ellis 2, James 2, Matthews 2, West 2, Avdiu 1, Barrick 1, Bullock 1, Johnrose 1, Lilley 1, Littlejohn 1, Lucketti 1, Williams 1, Woodward 1.
Worthington Cup (9): Matthews 3, Johnrose 2, Armstrong 1, Daws 1, D'Jaffo 1, own goal 1.
FA Cup (0).

Kiely D 45	Woodward A 36+1	Barrick D 16+4	Daws N 46	Luckett C 43	Redmond S 26	Swailes C 43	Ellis T 3+13	Matthews R 12+4	Johnrose L 26+1	Preece A 19+20	Armstrong G —+2	D'Jaffo L 35+2	Rigby T 1+1	Patterson M 9+4	Foster J 6+1	Jemson N 6+8	Grobbelaar B 1	Baldry S —+5	Billy C 35+2	Avdiu K —+6	James L 10+7	Williams P 14+1	West D 18+5	Littlejohn A 11+9	Forrest M —+1	Souter R —+1	Serrant C 15	Bullock D 12	Hall P 7	Barnes P 6+2	Lilley D 5	Match No.
1	2	3¹	4	5	6	7	8²	9³	10	11	12	13	14																			1
1	2	3	4	5	6	7	12		10	11¹		9		8																		2
1	2	3²	4	5	6	7	12	8³	10	11	13	9¹	14																			3
1	2	3	4	5	6	7	12		10	11		9¹			8																	4
1	2	3	4	5	6	7	12	8	10	11		9¹				13																5
	2	3	4	5	6	7	12	13³	10	11		9¹		14	8²		1															6
1	2	3	4	5	6	7	12	8²	10	11		9¹						13														7
1	2	3	4	5	6	7	12	8¹	10	11		9																				8
1		3	4¹	5	6	7	12	8³	10	11		9²		13				14	2													9
1		3	4	5	6	7	12	8³	10	11¹		9						13	2													10
1	2	3	4	5	6	7		8²	10³		12	9¹						13	11	14												11
1	2	3	4	5	6	7¹		8¹		11						10		13	12²	9	14											12
1	2	3	4	5	6	7¹	12	13	10	11		9²				8																13
1	2	12	4	5	6		13	8	10	11		9²		3¹				7														14
1	2	12	4	5	6²	7	14	8¹	13	11³		9		10				3														15
1	2	3	4	5		7	11	12	10¹	13		9²		8				6														16
1	2	12	4	5	6¹	7²	11³	8	10	13		9						3	14													17
1	2		4	5		7		12	10			9		8¹				6			11²	3	13									18
1	2		4	5		7		10				9¹		13		12		6²	11		3	14	8¹									19
1	2		4	5		7		10	12			9		11¹				6			3		8									20
1	2		4	5		7		10	12			9¹		13				6	14	11³	3²		8									21
1	2		4	5		7		10	12			9¹		11				6²	13	3			8									22
1	2		4	5		7		10	12			9¹		11				6		3			8									23
1	2	7	4	5				10	11			9²			8¹			6	12	13	3											24
1	2	12	4	5					11²					13				10	14	9	3	6	8²									25
1	2	11¹	4	5		7						9						10		12	3	6	8									26
1	2		4	5		7	12	10	13						8			11²		9¹	3	6										27
1	2		4	5		7		10	12						8¹			11		9²	3	6	13									28
1	2		4	5²		7		10	12						8¹			11		9	3	6	13									29
1	2		4			7		10	12		11²				8¹			5		9	3	6		13								30
1	2³		4		6	5			12					8		10²		11¹	13	9	3	7			14							31
1	2	4³	5			7			12	9¹		8		10²						14	13						3	6	11			32
1	2		4	5	6					9¹		8²		12		13		14		7³							3	10	11			33
1	12		4	5	6	7			11³	9²				13		10				2¹	14						3		8			34
1			4	5	6	7			12	9³				13		10				2	11¹						3		8			35
1			4	5	6	7			12	9²				13		10				2	11¹						3		8			36
1			4	5	6	7			12	9¹						2					13			3	11²	8	10					37
1			4	5	6	7										2		10¹			12			3	11	8	9					38
1			4	5	6	7			12							11				2	13			3	10			9²	8¹		39
1			4	5	6	7				12						11				2²	13			3	10			9	8¹		40
1			4	5	6¹	7³			12	9						2				14	13			3	10			11²	8		41
1	6		4	5		7				9						11				2				3	10				8		42
1	6		4	5					12	9¹						11				2	13			3	10				8²		43
1	6		4	5		7			11	9²						8¹			12	2				3	10	13					44
1	6		4			7			11²	9						3		12		2¹	8			5	10	13					45
1	6		4	5		7			12	9¹						13		14		2³	11			3	10²			8			46

Worthington Cup
First Round   Burnley   (h) 1-1
                                      (a) 4-1
Second Round   Crystal Palace   (h) 3-0
                                      (a) 1-2
Third Round   Manchester U   (a) 0-2

FA Cup
Third Round   Stockport Co   (h) 0-3

Division 2

CAMBRIDGE UNITED

FOUNDATION

The football revival in Cambridge began soon after World War II when the Abbey United club (formed 1912) decided to turn professional and in 1949 changed their name to Cambridge United. They were competing in the United Counties League before graduating to the Eastern Counties League in 1951 and the Southern League in 1958.

Abbey Stadium, Newmarket Rd, Cambridge, CB5 8LN.

Telephone: (01223) 566500.

Fax: (01223) 566502.

Abbey Update: 0891 555885.

Website: www.cambridgeunited.com.

Ground Capacity: 9247.

Record Attendance: 14,000 v Chelsea, Friendly, 1 May 1970.

Record Receipts: £86,308 v Manchester U, Rumbelows Cup 2nd rd 2nd leg, 9 October 1991.

Pitch Measurements: 110yd × 74yd.

Chairman: R. H. Smart.

Vice-Chairman: R. F. Hunt.

Directors: G. Harwood, J. Howard, R. Hunt, G. Lowe, R. Summerfield.

Manager: Roy McFarland.

Player/coach: David Preece.

Youth Manager: Dale Brooks.

Physio: Ken Steggles.

Secretary: Andrew Pincher.

Commercial Manager: Carla Frediani.

Stadium Manager: Ian Darler.

LATEST SEQUENCES

Longest Sequence of League Wins: 7, 19.2.77 – 1.4.77.

Longest Sequence of League Defeats: 7, 8.4.85 – 30.4.85.

Longest Sequence of League Draws: 6, 6.9.86 – 30.9.86.

Longest Sequence of Unbeaten League Matches: 14, 9.9.72 – 10.11.72.

Longest Sequence Without a League Win: 31, 8.10.83 – 23.4.84.

HONOURS

Football League: Division 2 best season: 5th, 1991–92; Division 3 – Champions 1990–91; Runners-up 1977–78, 1998–99; Division 4 – Champions 1976–77; Promoted from Division 4 1989–90 (play-offs).

FA Cup: best season: 6th rd, 1990 (shared record for Fourth Division club), 1991.

Football League Cup: best season: 5th rd, 1993.

Colours
Amber shirts with black trim, black shorts, black stockings.

Change Colours
Light and dark blue halved shirts, dark blue shorts, dark blue stockings.

Year Formed: 1912.

Turned Professional: 1946.

Ltd Co.: 1948.

Previous Name: 1919, Abbey United; 1949, Cambridge United.

Club Nickname: The 'U's'.

First Football League Game: 15 August 1970, Division 4, v Lincoln C (h) D 1–1 – Roberts; Thompson, Meldrum (1), Slack, Eades, Hardy, Leggett, Cassidy, Lindsey, McKinven, Harris.

Record League Victory: 6–0 v Darlington, Division 4, 18 September 1971 – Roberts; Thompson, Akers, Guild, Eades, Foote, Collins (1p), Horrey, Hollett, Greenhalgh (4), Phillips, (1 og). 6–0 v Hartlepool U, Division 4, 11 February 1989 – Vaughan; Beck, Kimble, Turner, Chapple (1), Daish, Clayton, Holmes, Taylor (3 incl. 1p), Bull (1), Leadbitter (1).

Record Cup Victory: 5–1 v Bristol C, FA Cup 5th rd second replay, 27 February 1990 – Vaughan; Fensome, Kimble, Bailie (O'Shea), Chapple, Daish, Cheetham (Robinson), Leadbitter (1), Dublin (2), Taylor (1), Philpott (1).

Record Defeat: 0–6 v Aldershot, Division 3, 13 April 1974; v Darlington, Division 4, 28 September 1974. 0–6 v Chelsea, Division 2, 15 January 1983 and v Brentford, Division 2, 28 January 1995.

Most League Points (2 for a win): 65, Division 4, 1976–77.

Most League Points (3 for a win): 86, Division 3, 1990–91.

Most League Goals: 87, Division 4, 1976–77.

Highest League Scorer in Season: David Crown, 24, Division 4, 1985–86.

Most League Goals in Total Aggregate: John Taylor, 77, 1988–92; 1996–99.

Most League Goals in One Match: 5, Steve Butler v Exeter C, Division 2, 4 April 1994.

Most Capped Player: Tom Finney, 7 (15), Northern Ireland.

Most League Appearances: Steve Spriggs, 416, 1975–87.

Youngest League Player: Andy Sinton, 16 years 228 days v Wolverhampton W, 2 November 1982.

Record Transfer Fee Received: £1,000,000 from Manchester U for Dion Dublin, August 1992.

Record Transfer Fee Paid: £190,000 to Luton T for Steve Claridge, November 1992.

Football League Record: 1970 Elected to Division 4; 1973–74 Division 3; 1974–77 Division 4; 1977–78 Division 3; 1978–84 Division 2; 1984–85 Division 3; 1985–90 Division 4; 1990–91 Division 3; 1991–92 Division 2; 1992–93 Division 1; 1993–95 Division 2; 1995–99 Division 3; 1999– Division 2.

MANAGERS

Bill Whittaker 1949–55
Gerald Williams 1955
Bert Johnson 1955–59
Bill Craig 1959–60
Alan Moore 1960–63
Roy Kirk 1964–66
Bill Leivers 1967–74
Ron Atkinson 1974–78
John Docherty 1978–83
John Ryan 1984–85
Ken Shellito 1985
Chris Turner 1985–90
John Beck 1990–1992
Ian Atkins 1992–93
Gary Johnson 1993–95
Tommy Taylor 1995–96
Roy McFarland November 1996–

TEN YEAR LEAGUE RECORD

		P	W	D	L	F	A	Pts	Pos
1988-89	Div 4	46	18	14	14	71	62	68	8
1989-90	Div 4	46	21	10	15	76	66	73	6
1990-91	Div 3	46	25	11	10	75	45	86	1
1991-92	Div 2	46	19	17	10	65	47	74	5
1992-93	Div 1	46	11	16	19	48	69	49	23
1993-94	Div 2	46	19	9	18	79	73	66	10
1994-95	Div 2	46	11	15	20	52	69	48	20
1995-96	Div 3	46	14	12	20	61	71	54	16
1996-97	Div 3	46	18	11	17	53	59	65	10
1997-98	Div 3	46	14	18	14	63	57	60	16

DID YOU KNOW ?

Cambridge United's first meeting with a Football League club was in the FA Cup when they were drawn against Newport County at home on 2 November 1953. After a 2–2 draw, United surprisingly won the replay 2–1.

CAMBRIDGE UNITED 1998–99 LEAGUE RECORD

Match No.	Date	Venue	Opponents	Result	H/T Score	Lg. Pos.	Goalscorers	Attendance
1	Aug 8	A	Torquay U	W 1-0	0-0	—	Butler (pen) [80]	2428
2	15	H	Swansea C	W 2-1	1-1	4	Butler 2 [32, 82]	3074
3	22	A	Rotherham U	L 0-2	0-0	9		3773
4	29	H	Hartlepool U	L 1-2	0-0	9	Campbell [88]	2825
5	Sept 1	A	Chester C	W 3-0	1-0	—	Russell [28], Wanless 2 (1 pen) [57, 90 (p)]	2199
6	5	H	Scarborough	L 2-3	2-1	12	Butler 2 [8, 10]	2385
7	8	A	Scunthorpe U	L 2-3	1-1	—	Butler [21], Preece [80]	2431
8	12	H	Leyton Orient	W 1-0	0-0	11	Campbell [52]	3684
9	19	A	Southend U	W 1-0	0-0	8	Benjamin [72]	5009
10	26	H	Exeter C	D 1-1	1-0	9	Taylor [27]	3061
11	Oct 3	A	Hull C	W 3-0	2-0	8	Duncan [33], Wanless [40], Benjamin [81]	3882
12	9	H	Brighton & HA	L 2-3	1-1	—	Taylor 2 [31, 85]	4602
13	17	A	Cardiff C	W 1-0	0-0	6	Taylor [90]	6886
14	20	A	Halifax T	D 3-3	2-2	—	Butler [6], Russell [40], Ashbee [66]	1906
15	24	H	Shrewsbury T	D 0-0	0-0	5		3127
16	31	A	Mansfield T	W 3-1	2-0	4	Russell [31], Benjamin [35], Butler [51]	2674
17	Nov 7	H	Barnet	W 3-2	2-1	3	Taylor [15], Benjamin [26], Russell [67]	3832
18	10	A	Peterborough U	L 1-2	1-2	—	Benjamin [18]	10,168
19	21	H	Darlington	W 2-1	0-1	3	Taylor [57], Reed (og) [80]	3395
20	Dec 12	H	Plymouth Arg	W 1-0	1-0	4	Taylor [44]	3933
21	18	A	Brentford	L 0-1	0-1	—		5069
22	26	H	Rotherham U	W 3-2	2-0	4	Taylor [2], Benjamin [25], Mustoe [90]	5325
23	28	A	Carlisle U	D 1-1	1-1	4	Russell [3]	4419
24	Jan 2	A	Hartlepool U	D 2-2	0-1	3	Clark (og) [48], Russell [62]	3788
25	9	H	Torquay U	W 2-0	0-0	3	Taylor [63], Mustoe [71]	3936
26	23	H	Chester C	W 2-1	1-1	2	Wanless [38], Campbell [54]	3635
27	30	H	Carlisle U	W 1-0	1-0	2	Butler [38]	4128
28	Feb 6	A	Scarborough	W 5-1	2-1	2	Taylor [6], Butler 2 [44, 83], Ashbee 2 [48, 54]	1650
29	13	A	Scunthorpe U	D 0-0	0-0	2		5596
30	20	A	Leyton Orient	L 0-2	0-1	2		6222
31	27	H	Southend U	W 3-0	1-0	2	Taylor 2 [45, 79], Butler [74]	5013
32	Mar 6	A	Exeter C	W 3-0	2-0	1	Preece [3], Taylor [24], Butler [83]	3478
33	9	H	Hull C	W 2-0	0-0	—	Benjamin [80], Ashbee [90]	4948
34	13	A	Barnet	L 0-3	0-1	1		2748
35	20	H	Mansfield T	W 7-2	3-1	1	Taylor [13], Butler 3 (1 pen) [33, 48 (p), 78], Benjamin [45], Mustoe [82], Walker [90]	4343
36	26	A	Shrewsbury T	D 1-1	0-0	—	Wanless [61]	3247
37	Apr 3	A	Cardiff C	D 0-0	0-0	2		7787
38	6	A	Brighton & HA	W 3-1	1-0	—	Wanless [22], Campbell [56], Mackenzie [73]	2621
39	10	H	Halifax T	W 4-0	0-0	1	Walker [51], Wanless [67], Butler [83], Taylor [87]	4838
40	13	H	Rochdale	D 1-1	0-1	—	Walker [86]	4690
41	17	A	Darlington	D 0-0	0-0	1		2668
42	24	H	Peterborough U	D 1-1	1-1	2	Wanless [26]	8307
43	27	A	Rochdale	W 2-0	0-0	—	Taylor 2 (1 pen) [83 (p), 88]	1408
44	May 1	A	Plymouth Arg	D 2-2	1-1	1	Benjamin 2 [38, 70]	5006
45	6	A	Swansea C	L 0-2	0-1	—		6086
46	8	H	Brentford	L 0-1	0-0	2		8936

Final League Position: 2

GOALSCORERS

League (78): Butler 17 (2 pens), Taylor 17 (1 pen), Benjamin 10, Wanless 8 (1 pen), Russell 6, Ashbee 4, Campbell 4, Mustoe 3, Walker 3, Preece 2, Duncan 1, Mackenzie 1, own goals 2.
Worthington Cup (7): Benjamin 4, Butler 2 (1 pen), Taylor 1 (pen).
FA Cup (3): Benjamin 1, Butler 1, Campbell 1.

Appearances and goalscorers (goals shown as [n]).

Van Heusden A 27	Chenery B 44	Ashbee I 25+6	Duncan A 45	Joseph M 28+1	Campbell J 45	Wanless P 45	Russell A 36+1	Butler M 46	Benjamin T 37+5	Mustoe N 28+6	Taylor J 29+11	Kyd M 5+7	Preece D 5+9	Youngs T 6+4	Wilde A 1	McCammon M 1+1	McAvoy L 1	Andrews W 1+1	Marshall S 19	McNeil M 4+2	Walker R 7+14	Eustace S 15+1	McMahon S 1+2	Mackenzie N 3+1	Bruce P 2+2	Match No.
1	2	3	4	5	6	7	8[1]	9	10	11	12															1
1	2	3	4	5	6	7	11	9	8	12	10[1]															2
1	2	3[2]	4	5	6	7	11[3]	9	8[1]	13	12	10	14													3
1	2	3[4]	4	5	6	7	11	9[2]	8	13	12	10[1]	14													4
1	2	3	4	5	6	7	11	9[1]	12		10			8												5
1	2	3[1]	4	5	6	7	11	9	13	14	12			10[2]	8[3]											6
1	2		4	5	6	7	11	9	12	13	14			10[2]	8[1]	3[3]										7
1	2		4	5	6	7	11	9	10[1]	3	8			12												8
1	2		4	5	6	7[1]	11	9	10	3	13			12				8[2]								9
1	2		4	5	6	7	11	9	10	3	8															10
1			4	5	6	7	11	9	10	3	12			13			2[1]	8[2]								11
1[1]	2		4	5	6	7	11	9[1]	10	3	8			12[2]	14				13							12
	2		4	5	6	7	11	9		3	8	12	10[1]						1							13
	2	12	4	5	6	7	11	9		3	8[1]	10							1							14
	2[1]	8	4	5[2]	6	7	11	9		3	10			12					1	13						15
	2	3	4		6	7	11	9	10		8								1	5						16
	2	3	4		6	7	11	9	10		8								1	5						17
	2	3[1]	4		6	7	11	9	10[2]		8	13	12						1	5						18
	2	3	4		6	7	11	9	10		8								1	5						19
	2		4	5	6	7	11	9	10	3	8								1							20
	2	3	4	5	6	7	11	9	10		8[1]								1		12					21
1	2	3	4	5	6	7	11	9	10	12	8[1]															22
1	2		4	5	6	7	11	9	10[1]	3	8										12					23
1	2	12	4	5	6	7[1]	11[2]	9	13	3	8										10					24
1	2		4	5	6	7	11	9	10	3	8															25
1	2		4	5	6	7	11	9	10	3	12											8[1]				26
1	2		4	5	6	7	11	9	10	3[1]	8										12					27
1	2	11	4	5	6	7[1]		9	10	3	8[2]			12							13					28
1	2	12	4	5	6	7	11[1]	9	10[2]	3	8										13					29
1	2	11[2]	4	5	6	7		9	12	3	8[3]			10[1]							13	14				30
1	2	11	4	5	6	7		9	10[2]	3	8[1]			12							13					31
1	2	3		5[2]		7	11[3]	9	10[1]	8	6										13	12	4	14		32
1	2	3	4		6	7	11[1]	9	10		8										12	5				33
1	2	3	4		6	7		9	10	8[2]				12							13	5	11[1]			34
1	2	12	4		6	7		9[2]	10	3	8[2]		11[1]	14							13	5				35
1	2	12	4		6	7[1]		9	10	3	8[2]											5	13		11	36
	2	11	4		6	7		9		3	8[1]								1		12	5	10			37
	2		4		6	7		9	10	3									1		11	5	8			38
	2		4	12	6	7		9	10	3[2]	13								1		11[3]	5	8[1]	14		39
	2		4		6	7	12	9	10[2]	3	13								1		8	5			11	40
	2	12	4		6	7	11[1]	9	10	3	13								1		8	5				41
	2		4		6	7	11	9	10	3[1]	8[2]		12						1		13	5				42
	2	3	4		6	7	11	9	10		12								1		8[1]	5				43
	2	3	4		6	7	11	9	10		12								1		8[1]	5				44
	2	3	4		6	7	11[1]	9	10[2]	8[3]	12								1			5	13	14		45
	2	3[1]	4		6[3]	7	11[2]	9	10	12	8	13							1		14	5				46

Worthington Cup

First Round	Watford	(h)	1-0	
		(a)	1-1	
Second Round	Sheffield W	(a)	1-0	
		(h)	1-1	
Third Round	Nottingham F	(a)	3-3	

FA Cup

First Round	Telford U	(a)	2-0
Second Round	Macclesfield T	(a)	1-4

Division 2

CARDIFF CITY

FOUNDATION

Credit for the establishment of a first class professional football club in such a rugby stronghold as Cardiff, is due to members of the Riverside club formed in 1899 out of a cricket club of that name. Cardiff became a city in 1905 and in 1908 the local FA granted Riverside permission to call themselves Cardiff City.

Ninian Park, Cardiff CF1 8SX.

Telephone: (01222) 221001.

Fax: (01222) 341148.

Ticket Office: (01222) 222857/222858.

Clubcall: 09068 121171.

Website: www.cardiffcityfc.co.uk.

Email: ccafc@baynet.co.uk.

Ground Capacity: 15,585.

Record Attendance: 61,566, Wales v England, 14 October 1961.

Club record: 57,893 v Arsenal, Division 1, 22 April 1953.

Record Receipts: £141,756 v Manchester C, FA Cup 4th rd, 29 January 1994.

Pitch Measurements: 100yd × 70yd.

Directors: S. Kumar, J. Hill, P. Guy, R. Phillips, S. Borley, D. Temme, K. Walker, P. Jardine, M. Price.

Director of Football Development: Kenny Hibbitt.

Chief Executive Director: Joan Hill.

Secretary: Ceri Whitehead.

Manager: Frank Burrows.

Physio: Mike Davenport.

LATEST SEQUENCES

Longest Sequence of League Wins: 9, 26.10.46 – 28.12.46.

Longest Sequence of League Defeats: 7, 4.11.33 – 25.12.33.

Longest Sequence of League Draws: 6, 29.11.80 – 17.1.81.

Longest Sequence of Unbeaten League Matches: 21, 21.9.46 – 1.3.47.

Longest Sequence Without a League Win: 15, 21.11.36 – 6.3.37.

HONOURS

Football League: Division 1 – Runners-up 1923–24; Division 2 – Runners-up 1920–21, 1951–52, 1959–60; Division 3 (S) – Champions 1946–47; Division 3 – Champions 1992–93. Runners-up 1975–76, 1982–83; Division 4 – Runners-up 1987–88.

FA Cup: Winners 1927 (only occasion the Cup has been won by a club outside England); Runners-up 1925.

Football League Cup: Semi-final 1966.

Welsh Cup: Winners 21 times.

Charity Shield: Winners 1927.

European Competitions: *European Cup-Winners' Cup:* 1964–65, 1965–66, 1967–68, 1968–69, 1969–70, 1970–71, 1971–72, 1973–74, 1974–75, 1976–77, 1977–78, 1988–89, 1991–92, 1992–93, 1993–94.

Colours
Blue shirts, white shorts, white stockings.

Change Colours
Yellow shirts, blue shorts, yellow stockings.

Year Formed: 1899.

Turned Professional: 1910.

Ltd Co.: 1910.

Previous Names: 1899, Riverside; 1902, Riverside Albion; 1908, Cardiff City.

Club Nickname: 'Bluebirds'.

Previous Grounds: Riverside, Sophia Gardens, Old Park and Fir Gardens. Moved to Ninian Park, 1910.

First Football League Game: 28 August 1920, Division 2, v Stockport Co (a) W 5–2 – Kneeshaw; Brittain, Leyton; Keenor (1), Smith, Hardy; Grimshaw (1), Gill (2), Cashmore, West, Evans (1).

Record League Victory: 9–2 v Thames, Division 3 (S), 6 February 1932 – Farquharson; E. L. Morris, Roberts; Galbraith, Harris, Ronan; Emmerson (1), Keating (1), Jones (1), McCambridge (1), Robbins (5).

Record Cup Victory: 8–0 v Enfield, FA Cup 1st rd, 28 November 1931 – Farquharson; Smith, Roberts; Harris (1), Galbraith, Ronan; Emmerson (2), Keating (3); O'Neill (2), Robbins, McCambridge.

Record Defeat: 2–11 v Sheffield U, Division 1, 1 January 1926.

Most League Points (2 for a win): 66, Division 3 (S), 1946–47.

Most League Points (3 for a win): 86, Division 3, 1982–83.

Most League Goals: 93, Division 3 (S), 1946–47.

Highest League Scorer in Season: Stan Richards, 30, Division 3 (S), 1946–47.

Most League Goals in Total Aggregate: Len Davies, 128, 1920–31.

Most League Goals in One Match: 5, Hugh Ferguson v Burnley, Division 2, 5 September 1928; 5, Walter Robbins v Thames, Division 3S, 6 February 1932; 5, William Henderson v Northampton T, Division 3S, 22 April 1933.

Most Capped Player: Alf Sherwood, 39 (41), Wales.

Most League Appearances: Phil Dwyer, 471, 1972–85.

Youngest League Player: John Toshack, 16 years 236 days v Leyton Orient, 13 November 1965.

Record Transfer Fee Received: £500,000 from Coventry C for Simon Haworth, June 1997.

Record Transfer Fee Paid: £180,000 to San Jose Earthquakes for Godfrey Ingram, September 1982.

Football League Record: 1920 Elected to Division 2; 1921–29 Division 1; 1929–31 Division 2; 1931–47 Division 3 (S); 1947–52 Division 2; 1952–57 Division 1; 1957–60 Division 2; 1960–62 Division 1; 1962–75 Division 2; 1975–76 Division 3; 1976–82 Division 2; 1982–83 Division 3; 1983–85 Division 2; 1985–86 Division 3; 1986–88 Division 4; 1988–90 Division 3; 1990–92 Division 4; 1992–93 Division 3; 1993–95 Division 2; 1995–99 Division 3; 1999– Division 2.

MANAGERS

Davy McDougall 1910–11
Fred Stewart 1911–33
Bartley Wilson 1933–34
B. Watts-Jones 1934–37
Bill Jennings 1937–39
Cyril Spiers 1939–46
Billy McCandless 1946–48
Cyril Spiers 1948–54
Trevor Morris 1954–58
Bill Jones 1958–62
George Swindin 1962–64
Jimmy Scoular 1964–73
Frank O'Farrell 1973–74
Jimmy Andrews 1974–78
Richie Morgan 1978–82
Len Ashurst 1982–84
Jimmy Goodfellow 1984
Alan Durban 1984–86
Frank Burrows 1986–89
Len Ashurst 1989–91
Eddie May 1991–94
Terry Yorath 1994–95
Eddie May 1995
Kenny Hibbitt *(Chief Coach)* 1995
Phil Neal 1996
Russell Osman 1996–97
Kenny Hibbitt 1996–98
Frank Burrows February 1998–

TEN YEAR LEAGUE RECORD

		P	W	D	L	F	A	Pts	Pos
1988-89	Div 3	46	14	15	17	44	56	57	16
1989-90	Div 3	46	12	14	20	51	70	50	21
1990-91	Div 4	46	15	15	16	43	54	60	13
1991-92	Div 4	42	17	15	10	66	53	66	9
1992-93	Div 3	42	25	8	9	77	47	83	1
1993-94	Div 2	46	13	15	18	66	79	54	19
1994-95	Div 2	46	9	11	26	46	74	38	22
1995-96	Div 3	46	11	12	23	41	64	45	22
1996-97	Div 3	46	20	9	17	56	54	69	7
1997-98	Div 3	46	9	23	14	48	52	50	21

DID YOU KNOW ?

Of the 43 professionals on the books of Cardiff City in 1946, only one had been signed from another Football League club: Bryn Allen who had been transferred from Swansea Town the previous season.

CARDIFF CITY 1998–99 LEAGUE RECORD

Match No.	Date	Venue	Opponents	Result	H/T Score	Lg. Pos.	Goalscorers	Attendance
1	Aug 8	A	Hartlepool U	D	1-1	0-1	—	Earnshaw [52]	2591
2	15	H	Peterborough U	L	1-3	1-0	20	Saville [17]	5629
3	21	A	Shrewsbury T	W	3-0	2-0	—	Eckhardt [8], Thomas [29], Nugent [76]	3003
4	29	H	Rotherham U	L	0-1	0-0	14		5356
5	31	A	Darlington	L	0-3	0-1	18		2085
6	Sept 5	H	Plymouth Arg	W	1-0	0-0	15	Wotton (og) [88]	3939
7	8	H	Barnet	W	1-0	0-0	—	O'Sullivan [61]	3742
8	11	A	Halifax T	W	2-1	0-0	—	Fowler [80], Thomas [94]	2814
9	19	H	Rochdale	W	2-1	0-1	6	Brazier [54], Bonner [58]	4643
10	26	A	Chester C	D	2-2	0-0	8	Jarman [62], Brazier [79]	2842
11	Oct 3	H	Brighton & HA	W	2-0	1-0	5	Nugent [8], Williams [74]	6143
12	9	A	Hull C	W	2-1	1-1	—	Thomas 2 [10, 52]	8594
13	17	H	Cambridge U	L	0-1	0-0	5		6886
14	20	H	Leyton Orient	D	0-0	0-0	—		5001
15	31	H	Exeter C	W	1-0	0-0	5	Middleton [76]	5411
16	Nov 7	A	Torquay U	D	0-0	0-0	5		3342
17	10	H	Scarborough	W	1-0	0-0	—	Williams [50]	4422
18	22	A	Swansea C	L	1-2	1-0	6	Williams [4]	7757
19	28	H	Southend U	W	2-0	2-0	3	Middleton [2], Nugent [32]	4638
20	Dec 1	A	Carlisle U	W	1-0	0-0	—	Nugent (pen) [49]	2700
21	12	H	Scunthorpe U	W	2-0	1-0	1	Williams 2 [45, 54]	3200
22	19	H	Mansfield T	W	4-2	1-0	1	Williams 2 [12, 46], Nugent 2 [61, 81]	9013
23	26	A	Shrewsbury T	W	3-0	1-0	1	Williams [40], Nugent [49], Hill [53]	12,452
24	28	A	Brentford	L	0-1	0-0	1		9535
25	Jan 9	H	Hartlepool U	W	4-1	2-0	1	O'Sullivan [4], Nugent [12], Eckhardt [67], Middleton [68]	7766
26	16	A	Peterborough U	L	1-2	1-0	1	Nugent [25]	5890
27	23	A	Darlington	W	3-2	1-1	1	Carpenter [23], Williams [53], Middleton [81]	5803
28	30	H	Brentford	W	4-1	2-0	1	Williams [20], Eckhardt [28], Fowler [52], Nugent [76]	11,509
29	Feb 6	A	Plymouth Arg	D	1-1	0-1	1	Legg [63]	6062
30	13	A	Barnet	L	0-1	0-0	1		2234
31	19	H	Halifax T	D	1-1	1-0	—	Eckhardt [44]	8570
32	27	A	Rochdale	D	1-1	0-1	1	Legg [76]	2431
33	Mar 5	H	Chester C	D	0-0	0-0	—		7526
34	9	A	Brighton & HA	W	2-0	2-0	—	Nugent [16], Young [31]	2312
35	13	H	Torquay U	D	2-2	1-1	2	Hill [36], Fowler [58]	6956
36	16	A	Rotherham U	L	0-1	0-0	—		3669
37	20	A	Exeter C	W	2-0	1-0	2	Nugent 2 [39, 60]	3653
38	27	H	Carlisle U	W	2-1	1-1	1	Nugent [27], Bowen [54]	7094
39	Apr 3	A	Cambridge U	D	0-0	0-0	1		7787
40	5	H	Hull C	D	1-1	0-1	1	Nugent (pen) [74]	8252
41	10	A	Leyton Orient	D	1-1	1-0	2	Williams [40]	5238
42	13	A	Southend U	W	1-0	0-0	—	Williams [70]	4076
43	18	H	Swansea C	D	0-0	0-0	2		10,809
44	24	A	Scarborough	W	2-1	1-1	1	Eckhardt [24], Bowen [69]	1834
45	May 1	H	Scunthorpe U	D	0-0	0-0	2		12,455
46	8	A	Mansfield T	L	0-3	0-0	3		4032

Final League Position: 3

GOALSCORERS

League (60): Nugent 15 (2 pens), Williams 12, Eckhardt 5, Middleton 4, Thomas 4, Fowler 3, Bowen 2, Brazier 2, Hill 2, Legg 2, O'Sullivan 2, Bonner 1, Carpenter 1, Earnshaw 1, Jarman 1, Saville 1, Young 1, own goal 1.
Worthington Cup (2): Eckhardt 1, Williams 1.
FA Cup (13): Fowler 3, Nugent 3, Williams 3, Middleton 2, Delaney 1, Eckhardt 1.

Hallworth J 41	Delaney M 28	Ford M 25	Mitchell G 46	Young S 33	Carpenter R 41 + 1	Bonner M 21 + 4	Williams J 25 + 18	Saville A 2	Earnshaw R 1 + 4	Fowler J 32 + 5	Nugent K 40 + 1	Phillips L 2	O'Sullivan W 38 + 4	Eckhardt J 31 + 4	Thomas D 16 + 8	Penney D 1	Middleton C 20 + 15	Jarman L 2 + 4	Brazier M 11	Allen C 3 + 1	Roberts C - + 4	Hill D 14 + 12	Legg A 18 + 6	Bowen J 10 + 7	Kelly S 5	Match No.
1	2	3	4	5	6	7	8	9	10^1	11	12															1
1	2		4	5	6^2	7	8^1	9	12	11	10		3	13												2
1	2		4	5	6	7	12				10^1		11	3	9		8^2	13								3
1	2		4^3	5	6^2	7	10^1	12					11	3	9		13	14	8							4
1	2		4^1	5	6	7	10	12					11	3	9		8									5
1	2		4	5	6^1	7^2	14	12			10		11	3	9^3		13		8							6
1	2		4	5^2	6^1	7	14	12			10		11	3	9		13		8							7
1	2		4	5	6	7	12	13			10^1		11^2	3	9		8									8
1	2^1		4	5	6	7	13	12			10		11	3	9^2		8									9
1	2		4	5	6	7^2	14				10		11	3^1	9^3		13	12	8							10
1	2		4	5	6^1	7^2	14	12			10		11		9^3		13	3	8							11
1		3	4	5	6	7	12				2		10	11			9^1		8							12
1		3	4	5	6	7^1	13				2		10	11			9^2	12	8							13
1		3	4	5	6	7	12				2		10	11			9^1		8							14
1	2		4	5	6		12				7^2		10	11^1	3		9^3	13			8	14				15
1	2	3^2	4	5	6		12				10		11^1	13	9^3		7				8	14				16
1	2	3	4^1	5	6		9				7		10		12		11				8					17
1	2	3	4	5	6		9^1			7	10		8				11^2			12		13				18
1	2	3	4	5	6		9^1			7	10		8				11^2				12	13				19
1	2	3	4	5	6		9^1			7	10		8	12			11^2					13				20
1	2	3	4	5	6		9			7^2	10		8^1	12			11					13				21
1	2	3	4	5	6		9				10^1		8	12			11					7^2	13			22
1	2	3	4	5	6		9			11	10^1		8^3	12			13					7^2	14			23
1	2	3	4	5^1	6		9			11	10		8	12			7^2					13				24
1	2	3	4		6		9				10		8	5			11					7^1	12			25
1	2	3	4		6					7	10		8	5	9^1		11^2					13	12			26
1	2	3	4		6		9^1			7	10		8	5	12		11									27
1	2	3^2	4		6		9			7^1	10		8	5			11					12	13			28
1			4	2	6		9^2			7	10		8	5			11^1					12	3	13		29
1			4	2	6^1		9	13	7			8^3	5	10^2			12					11	3^1	14		30
1	8		4	2	6		9^3			7	10	12	5				11^2	13					3^1	14		31
1	8		4	2	6		9^1			7	10		5	12			11^2	3								32
1	2		4	8	6^2		9^3			7	10	12	5				11^1	13					3	14		33
1			4	8	6		13	12		7	10		2	5			11^2					3	9^1			34
1			4	8	6		12			7	10		2	5			11^1					3	9			35
1			4^1	8	6^2		13	14		7	10		2	5			12					11^3	3	9		36
1			4	8	6		7	12			10		2^2	5	14		13					11^3	3	9^1		37
1			4	8	6		12			7	10		2^2	5			13					11^1	3	9		38
1	8		4		6		12			7	10		2	5			13					11^2	3	9^1		39
1	8^3		4		6		11^1	12		7	10		2^2	5			13	14					3	9		40
1	8		4		6		12	10		7^1			2	5	13		14					11^3	3	9^2		41
1	8		4		6		10			7			2	5			11						3	9	1	42
	8		4		6		9^2			7	10		2^1	5			11					12	3	13	1	43
	8		4	12	6		9				10		2	5			11^1					7^2	3	13	1	44
	8		4		6		9^2			7	10		2	5			11^1	12					3	13	1	45
	8^3		4		6					7^2	10		12	5	13		11				14	2^1	3	9	1	46

Worthington Cup
First Round   Fulham   (a)   1-2
                                               (h)   1-2

FA Cup
First Round   Chester C   (h)   6-0
Second Round   Hednesford T   (h)   3-1
Third Round   Yeovil T   (h)   1-1
                                        (a)   2-1
Fourth Round   Sheffield U   (a)   1-4

Division 3

CARLISLE UNITED

FOUNDATION

Carlisle United came into being in 1903 through the amalgamation of Shaddongate United and Carlisle Red Rose. The new club was admitted to the Second Division of the Lancashire Combination in 1905–06, winning promotion the following season. Devonshire Park was officially opened on 2 September 1905, when St Helens Town were the visitors. Despite defeat in a disappointing 3-2 start, a respectable mid-table position was achieved.

Brunton Park, Carlisle CA1 1LL.

Telephone: (01228) 526237.

Fax: (01228) 530138.

Commercial Dept: (01228) 524014.

Information Line: 0891 230011.

Ground Capacity: 16,651.

Record Attendance: 27,500 v Birmingham C, FA Cup 3rd rd, 5 January 1957 and v Middlesbrough, FA Cup 5th rd, 7 February 1970.

Record Receipts: £146,000 v Tottenham H, Coca-Cola Cup 2nd rd, 30 September 1997.

Pitch Measurements: 117yd × 72yd.

Directors: M Knighton (Chairman), J. T. T. Fuller (Managing), B. Chaytow, R. McKnight, A. Doweck, H. A. Jenkins.

General Manager: Martin Wilkinson.

First Team Coach: Keith Mincher.

Physio: Neil Dalton.

Commercial Manager: Daphne Tweddle.

Secretary: J. T. T. Fuller.

LATEST SEQUENCES

Longest Sequence of League Wins: 6, 27.8.94 – 17.9.94.

Longest Sequence of League Defeats: 8, 8.11.86 – 3.1.87.

Longest Sequence of League Draws: 6, 11.2.78 – 11.3.78.

Longest Sequence of Unbeaten League Matches: 19, 1.10.94 – 11.2.95.

Longest Sequence Without a League Win: 14, 19.1.35 – 19.4.35.

HONOURS

Football League: Division 1 best season: 22nd, 1974–75; Promoted from Division 2 (3rd) 1973–74; Division 3 – Champions 1964–65, 1994–95; Runners-up 1981–82; Promoted from Division 3 1996–97; Division 4 – Runners-up 1963–64.

FA Cup: best season: 6th rd 1975.

Football League Cup: Semi-final 1970.

Auto Windscreens Shield: Winners 1997; Runners-up 1995.

Colours
Blue shirts, white shorts, white stockings.

Change Colours
All gold with red, white and green trim.

Year Formed: 1903.

Ltd Co.: 1921.

Previous Name: 1903, Shaddongate United; 1904, Carlisle United.

Club Nickname: 'Cumbrians' or 'The Blues'.

Previous Grounds: 1903, Milholme Bank; 1905, Devonshire Park; 1909, Brunton Park.

First Football League Game: 25 August 1928, Division 3 (N), v Accrington S (a) W 3–2 – Prout; Coulthard, Cook; Harrison, Ross, Pigg; Agar (1), Hutchison, McConnell (1), Ward (1), Watson.

Record League Victory: 8–0 v Hartlepool U, Division 3 (N), 1 September 1928 – Prout; Smiles, Cook; Robinson (1) Ross, Pigg; Agar (1), Hutchison (1), McConnell (4), Ward (1), Watson. 8–0 v Scunthorpe U, Division 3 (N), 25 December 1952 – MacLaren; Hill, Scott; Stokoe, Twentyman, Waters; Harrison (1), Whitehouse (5), Ashman (2), Duffett, Bond.

Record Cup Victory: 6–0 v Shepshed Dynamo, FA Cup 1st rd, 16 November 1996 – Caig; Hopper, Archdeacon (pen), Walling, Robinson, Pounewatchy, Peacock (1), Conway (1) (Jansen), Smart (McAlindon (1)), Hayward, Aspinall (Thorpe), (2 og).

Record Defeat: 1–11 v Hull C, Division 3 (N), 14 January 1939.

Most League Points (2 for a win): 62, Division 3 (N), 1950–51.

Most League Points (3 for a win): 91, Division 3, 1994–95.

Most League Goals: 113, Division 4, 1963–64.

Highest League Scorer in Season: Jimmy McConnell, 42, Division 3 (N), 1928–29.

Most League Goals in Total Aggregate: Jimmy McConnell, 126, 1928–32.

Most League Goals in One Match: 5, Hugh Mills v Halifax T, Division 3N, 11 September 1937; 5, Jim Whitehouse v Scunthorpe U, Division 3N, 25 December 1952.

Most Capped Player: Eric Welsh, 4, Northern Ireland.

Most League Appearances: Allan Ross, 466, 1963–79.

Youngest League Player: Rory Delap, 16 years 306 days v Scarborough, 8 May 1993.

Record Transfer Fee Received: £1,500,000 from Crystal Palace for Matt Jansen, February 1998.

Record Transfer Fee Paid: £121,000 to Notts Co for David Reeves, December 1993.

Football League Record: 1928 Elected to Division 3 (N); 1958–62 Division 4; 1962–63 Division 3; 1963–64 Division 4; 1964–65 Division 3; 1965–74 Division 2; 1974–75 Division 3; 1975–77 Division 2; 1977–82 Division 3; 1982–86 Division 2; 1986–87 Division 3; 1987–92 Division 4; 1992–95 Division 3; 1995–96 Division 2; 1996–97 Division 3; 1997–98 Division 2; 1998– Division 3.

MANAGERS

Harry Kirkbride 1904–05
(Secretary-Manager)
McCumiskey 1905–06
(Secretary-Manager)
Jack Houston 1906–08
(Secretary-Manager)
Bert Stansfield 1908–10
Jack Houston 1910–12
Davie Graham 1912–13
George Bristow 1913–30
Billy Hampson 1930–33
Bill Clarke 1933–35
Robert Kelly 1935–36
Fred Westgarth 1936–38
David Taylor 1938–40
Howard Harkness 1940–45
Bill Clark 1945–46 *(Secretary-Manager)*
Ivor Broadis 1946–49
Bill Shankly 1949–51
Fred Emery 1951–58
Andy Beattie 1958–60
Ivor Powell 1960–63
Alan Ashman 1963–67
Tim Ward 1967–68
Bob Stokoe 1968–70
Ian MacFarlane 1970–72
Alan Ashman 1972–75
Dick Young 1975–76
Bobby Moncur 1976–80
Martin Harvey 1980
Bob Stokoe 1980–85
Bryan 'Pop' Robson 1985
Bob Stokoe 1985–86
Harry Gregg 1986–87
Cliff Middlemass 1987–91
Aidan McCaffery 1991–92
David McCreery 1992–93
Mick Wadsworth *(Director of Coaching)* 1993–96
Mervyn Day 1996–97
David Wilkes and John Halpin *(Directors of Coaching)*
Michael Knighton 1997–99
Martin Wilkinson June 1999–

TEN YEAR LEAGUE RECORD

		P	W	D	L	F	A	Pts	Pos
1988-89	Div 4	46	15	15	16	53	52	60	12
1989-90	Div 4	46	21	8	17	61	60	71	8
1990-91	Div 4	46	13	9	24	47	89	48	20
1991-92	Div 4	42	7	13	22	41	67	34	22
1992-93	Div 3	42	11	11	20	51	65	44	18
1993-94	Div 3	42	18	10	14	57	42	64	7
1994-95	Div 3	42	27	10	5	67	31	91	1
1995-96	Div 2	46	12	13	21	57	72	49	21
1996-97	Div 3	46	24	12	10	67	44	84	3
1997-98	Div 2	46	12	8	26	57	73	44	23

DID YOU KNOW ?

On 26 September 1972, Carlisle United met Blackpool under new floodlights. So bright were the twelve 3.5 kilowatt Mercury Halide lamps that motorists on the M6 two miles away were dazzled and required adjustment.

CARLISLE UNITED 1998–99 LEAGUE RECORD

Match No.	Date	Venue	Opponents	Result	H/T Score	Lg. Pos.	Goalscorers	Attendance
1	Aug 8	H	Brighton & HA	W 1-0	1-0	—	Stevens [17]	5184
2	15	A	Scunthorpe U	L 1-3	0-2	14	Stevens [90]	2810
3	22	H	Rochdale	L 0-1	0-0	18		3627
4	29	A	Exeter C	L 0-2	0-2	23		2661
5	Sept 1	H	Southend U	W 3-0	0-0	—	Dublin (og) [61], Stevens [74], Scott [86]	2638
6	5	A	Leyton Orient	L 1-2	1-0	19	Stevens [22]	3730
7	8	H	Swansea C	L 1-2	1-2	—	Scott [5]	2816
8	12	A	Mansfield T	D 1-1	1-0	23	Brightwell [16]	2292
9	19	H	Chester C	D 1-1	0-0	21	Scott [84]	2971
10	26	A	Shrewsbury T	D 1-1	0-0	22	Stevens [87]	2180
11	Oct 3	H	Barnet	W 2-1	0-1	20	Stevens [81], McGregor [84]	2834
12	9	H	Scarborough	W 1-0	0-0	—	McGregor [53]	3502
13	17	A	Torquay U	D 2-2	2-2	16	Finney [30], Brightwell [35]	2211
14	20	A	Peterborough U	W 1-0	0-0	—	Stevens [67]	3785
15	Nov 7	H	Halifax T	L 0-1	0-0	19		3636
16	21	H	Rotherham U	D 0-0	0-0	20		3281
17	28	A	Hull C	L 0-1	0-0	21		4452
18	Dec 1	H	Cardiff C	L 0-1	0-0	—		2700
19	12	H	Hartlepool U	W 2-1	2-0	21	Searle [22], Mendes [26]	3025
20	19	A	Plymouth Arg	L 0-2	0-1	22		4236
21	26	A	Rochdale	D 1-1	0-1	21	Monington (og) [83]	2900
22	28	H	Cambridge U	D 1-1	1-1	22	McGregor [27]	4419
23	Jan 2	H	Exeter C	L 1-3	1-2	22	Dobie [24]	3340
24	9	A	Brighton & HA	W 3-1	0-1	20	Dobie [57], Finney [75], Paterson [80]	4163
25	16	H	Scunthorpe U	L 0-1	0-0	21		3044
26	23	A	Southend U	W 1-0	1-0	21	Finney [19]	4120
27	30	A	Cambridge U	L 0-1	0-1	21		4128
28	Feb 2	A	Brentford	D 1-1	0-0	—	Finney [47]	3674
29	6	A	Leyton Orient	D 1-1	1-0	22	Finney (pen) [30]	2794
30	13	A	Swansea C	D 1-1	0-0	21	Boertien [75]	4753
31	20	H	Mansfield T	D 0-0	0-0	21		2273
32	27	A	Chester C	L 1-2	0-0	21	Stevens [50]	2450
33	Mar 6	H	Shrewsbury T	W 2-1	1-1	20	Dobie 2 [36, 85]	2501
34	9	A	Barnet	L 0-1	0-1	—		1428
35	13	A	Halifax T	L 0-1	0-0	21		2432
36	20	H	Brentford	L 0-1	0-0	22		2564
37	23	A	Darlington	D 1-1	1-0	—	Finney [40]	3028
38	27	A	Cardiff C	L 1-2	1-1	22	Tracey [22]	7094
39	Apr 3	H	Torquay U	W 3-0	2-0	22	Searle [9], Bowman [21], Tracey [90]	3765
40	5	A	Scarborough	L 0-3	0-1	22		3604
41	10	H	Peterborough U	D 1-1	1-0	23	Brightwell [39]	3064
42	13	A	Hull C	D 0-0	0-0	—		3743
43	17	A	Rotherham U	L 1-3	1-0	23	Dobie [45]	4267
44	24	H	Darlington	D 3-3	2-1	23	Dobie (pen) [39], Tracey [42], Stevens [68]	3808
45	May 1	A	Hartlepool U	D 0-0	0-0	23		4468
46	8	H	Plymouth Arg	W 2-1	0-0	23	Brightwell [62], Glass [90]	7599

Final League Position: 23

GOALSCORERS

League (43): Stevens 9, Dobie 6 (1 pen), Finney 6 (1 pen), Brightwell 4, McGregor 3, Scott 3, Tracey 3, Searle 2, Boertien 1, Bowman 1, Glass 1, Mendes 1, Paterson 1, own goals 2.
Worthington Cup (0).
FA Cup (1): Stevens 1.

Caig T 37	Kubicki D 7	Searle D 43+2	Whitehead S 36+1	Paterson S 18+1	Brightwell D 41	Barr B 21+2	Couzens A 10+5	Stevens I 31+10	McAlindon G 3+13	Dobie S 26+7	Prokas R 33+1	Thorpe J 6+7	Finney S 22+11	Anthony G 21+5	Scott R 7	Varty W 5+1	Hopper T 17+6	McGregor P 9+1	Bowman R 24	Clark P 35+1	Mendes J 5+1	Douglas A —+1	Ormerod A 5	Boertien P 8	Bridge-Wilkinson M 4+3	Tracey R 10+1	Knight R 6	Bagshaw P 5+4	Bass D 8+1	Glass J 3	Match No.
1	2	3	4	5	6	7	8¹	9²	10³	11	12	13	14																		1
1	3¹	7	4	5	6	2	12	9	11²	8			10	13																	2
1		3	2	5	6	4¹	12	9²	13	8	11	7	10																		3
1	2¹	3		5	6	13	12	9	11³	8			14	7²	10	4															4
1	2	3	5²		6	4		9		8	12		11¹	7			10	13													5
1	2	3			6	4		9		8	12		11¹	7			10	5													6
1	2¹	3			6	4		9	13	8	12		11	7			10	5²													7
1	2²	3	5		6	4		9		8			11¹	12			7	10	13												8
1		3	4	5	6	2	8²	9	13		12		11¹	7			10														9
1		3	4	5	6	2		9		8	12		11	7²				13	10¹												10
1		3	4	5	6			9			12		11	7¹			10		2	8											11
1		3	4	5	6			9			12		11	7¹			10		2	8											12
1		3	4	5	6			9			12		11	7			10¹		2	8											13
1		3	4	5	6			9			12		11	7¹			10		2	8											14
1		3	4	5	6			9			12		11	7			10		2	8¹											15
1		3	4	5	6			9	10¹		12		11²	7					2	8	13										16
1		3	4	5	6			9			12		11	7			10		2	8¹											17
1		3	4¹	5	6			9	13		12		11	7²			10		2	8											18
1		3	4	5	6	2	8¹	9	13		12	7	11				10²														19
1	13	3	4	5	6²	2		9¹		11	12	7³	14				10			8											20
1		3	4	5	6			9¹	13		12	7²	11				10		2	8											21
1		3	4	5	6	2		9²	13	11	12	7¹	14				10³			8											22
1		3²	4	5	6			9¹	13		12	7	11				10		2	8											23
1		3	4	5	6		8	9		11		7					10		2												24
1		3¹	4	5	6		8	9		11	12	7					10		2												25
1		3	4	5	6		8	9¹		11	12	7							2	3			10								26
1		3	4			2	8	9¹	13	11	12	7							6	5			10²								27
1		3	4			2	8	9¹	13	11	12	7²							6	5			10								28
1		3	4		6	2	8	9	13	11³	12	7¹	14							5			10²								29
1		3	4			2	8	9	13	11¹	12	7	14						6³	5			10²								30
1		3	4			2	8	9¹	13	11	12	7							6²	5			10								31
1		3	4			2	8	9¹	13	11	12	7							6²	5			10								32
1		3	4	5		2		9¹	13	11	12	7							6²						8	10					33
1		3	4	5		2		9		11	12	7¹							6						8	10					34
1		3	4	5		2		9¹		11	12	7²							6						8	10		13			35
1		3	4	5		2		9²	13	11	12	7							6						8	10¹					36
1		3	4	5		2		9		11		7¹							6						8	10			12		37
		3	4²	5		2		9¹			12	7¹							6	8					13	11	1	14	10		38
		3	4	5		2						7							6	8¹					12	11	1	9	10		39
		3	4	5		2					12	7							6¹	8²					13	11	1	9	10		40
		3	4	5		2					12	7							6	8						11¹	1	9	10		41
		3	4	5		2					12	7							6	8					13	11¹	1	9²	10		42
		3	4	5		2					12	7							6	8						11¹	1	9	10		43
		3	4	5		2			13		12	7²	14						6¹	8						11		9²	10	1	44
		3	4	5		2¹			13		12	7							6	8						11		9²	10	1	45
		3¹	4	5		2			13		12	7	14						6	8²						11		9³	10	1	46

Worthington Cup
First Round   Tranmere R   (a) 0-3
                              (h) 0-1

FA Cup
First Round   Hartlepool U   (a) 1-2

Division 1   **CHARLTON ATHLETIC**

FOUNDATION

The club was formed on 9 June 1905, by a group of 14 and 15-year-old youths living in streets by the Thames in the area which now borders the Thames Barrier. The club's progress through local leagues was so rapid that after the First World War they joined the Kent League where they spent a season before turning professional and joining the Southern League in 1920. A year later they were elected to the Football League's Division 3 (South).

The Valley, Floyd Road, Charlton, London SE7 8BL.
Telephone: (0208) 333 4000.
Fax: (0208) 333 4001.
Website: www.cafc.co.uk.
Email: info@cafc.co.uk.
Box Office: (0208) 333 4010.
Clubcall: 09068 121146.
Ground Capacity: 20,043.
Record Attendance: 75,031 v Aston Villa, FA Cup 5th rd, 12 February 1938 (at The Valley).
Record Receipts: £163,864 v Newcastle United, FA Cup 3rd rd, 5 January 1997.
Pitch Measurements: 111yd × 73yd.
Chairman: M. A. Simons.
Vice-Chairman: R. A. Murray.
Managing Director: P. D. Varney.
Directors: R. N. Alwen, G. P. Bone, N. E. Capelin, R. D. Collins, D. J. Hughes, R. D. King, M. C. Stevens, D. C. Sumners, D. G. Ufton, R. C. Whitehand.
Manager: Alan Curbishley.
Assistant Manager: Keith Peacock.
First Team Coach: Mervyn Day.
Reserve Team Coach: Gary Stevens.
Academy Director: Mick Browne.
Physio: Andy Jones.
Football Secretary: Chris Parkes.
Safety Officer: John Little.
Media and PR: Rick Everitt.

LATEST SEQUENCES

Longest Sequence of League Wins: 8, 21.3.98 – 25.4.98.
Longest Sequence of League Defeats: 10, 11.4.90 – 15.9.90.
Longest Sequence of League Draws: 6, 13.12.92 – 16.1.93.
Longest Sequence of Unbeaten League Matches: 15, 4.10.80 – 20.12.80.
Longest Sequence Without a League Win: 16, 26.2.55 – 22.8.55.

HONOURS

Football League: Division 1 – Runners-up 1936–37; Promoted from Division 1, 1997–98 (play-offs); Division 2 – Runners-up 1935–36, 1985–86; Division 3 (S) – Champions 1928–29, 1934–35; Promoted from Division 3 (3rd) 1974–75, 1980–81.

FA Cup: Winners 1947; Runners-up 1946.

Football League Cup: best season: 4th rd, 1963, 1966, 1979.

Full Members' Cup: Runners-up 1987.

Colours
Red shirts, white shorts, red stockings.

Change Colours
All yellow.

Year Formed: 1905.

Turned Professional: 1920.

Ltd Co.: 1919.

Club Nickname: 'Addicks'.

Previous Grounds: 1906, Siemen's Meadow; 1907, Woolwich Common; 1909, Pound Park; 1913, Horn Lane; 1920, The Valley; 1923, Catford (The Mount); 1924, The Valley; 1985, Selhurst Park; 1991, Upton Park; 1992, The Valley.

First Football League Game: 27 August 1921, Division 3 (S), v Exeter C (h) W 1–0 – Hughes; Mitchell, Goodman; Dowling (1), Hampson, Dunn; Castle, Bailey, Halse, Green, Wilson.

Record League Victory: 8–1 v Middlesbrough, Division 1, 12 September 1953 – Bartram; Campbell, Ellis; Fenton, Ufton, Hammond; Hurst (2), O'Linn (2), Leary (1), Firmani (3), Kiernan.

Record Cup Victory: 7–0 v Burton A, FA Cup 3rd rd, 7 January 1956 – Bartram; Campbell, Townsend; Hewie, Ufton, Hammond; Hurst (1), Gauld (1), Leary (3), White, Kiernan (2).

MANAGERS
Bill Rayner 1920–25
Alex McFarlane 1925–27
Albert Lindon 1928
Alex McFarlane 1928–32
Jimmy Seed 1933–56
Jimmy Trotter 1956–61
Frank Hill 1961–65
Bob Stokoe 1965–67
Eddie Firmani 1967–70
Theo Foley 1970–74
Andy Nelson 1974–79
Mike Bailey 1979–81
Alan Mullery 1981–82
Ken Craggs 1982
Lennie Lawrence 1982–91
Steve Gritt/Alan Curbishley 1991–95
Alan Curbishley June 1995–

Record Defeat: 1–11 v Aston Villa, Division 2, 14 November 1959.

Most League Points (2 for a win): 61, Division 3 (S), 1934–35.

Most League Points (3 for a win): 88, Division 1, 1997–98.

Most League Goals: 107, Division 2, 1957–58.

Highest League Scorer in Season: Ralph Allen, 32, Division 3 (S), 1934–35.

Most League Goals in Total Aggregate: Stuart Leary, 153, 1953–62.

Most League Goals in One Match: 5, Wilson Lennox v Exeter C, Division 3S, 2 February 1929; 5, Eddie Firmani v Aston Villa, Division 1, 5 February 1955; 5, John Summers v Huddersfield T, Division 2, 21 December 1957; 5, John Summers v Portsmouth, Division 2, 1 October 1960.

Most Capped Player: John Hewie, 19, Scotland.

Most League Appearances: Sam Bartram, 583, 1934–56.

Youngest League Player: Paul Konchesky, 16 years 93 days v Oxford U, 16 August 1997.

Record Transfer Fee Received: £2,800,000 from Leeds United for Lee Bowyer, July 1996.

Record Transfer Fee Paid: £1,017,000 to Barnsley for Neil Redfearn, July 1998.

Football League Record: 1921 Elected to Division 3 (S); 1929–33 Division 2; 1933–35 Division 3 (S); 1935–36 Division 2; 1936–57 Division 1; 1957–72 Division 2; 1972–75 Division 3; 1975–80 Division 2; 1980–81 Division 3; 1981–86 Division 2; 1986–90 Division 1; 1990–92 Division 2; 1992–98 Division 1; 1998–99 FA Premier League; 1999– Division 1.

TEN YEAR LEAGUE RECORD								
		P	W	D	L	F	A	Pts	Pos
1988-89	Div 1	38	10	12	16	44	58	42	14
1989-90	Div 1	38	7	9	22	31	57	30	19
1990-91	Div 2	46	13	17	16	57	61	56	16
1991-92	Div 2	46	20	11	15	54	48	71	7
1992-93	Div 1	46	16	13	17	49	46	61	12
1993-94	Div 1	46	19	8	19	61	58	65	11
1994-95	Div 1	46	16	11	19	58	66	59	15
1995-96	Div 1	46	17	20	9	57	45	71	6
1996-97	Div 1	46	16	11	19	52	66	59	15
1997-98	Div 1	46	26	10	10	80	49	88	4

DID YOU KNOW ?

Don Welsh, Charlton Athletic's 1947 FA Cup winning captain, owned a car pre-war and teammates helped to keep it on the road by paying 2d for a lift up Charlton Church Lane and 1d for the return journey.

CHARLTON ATHLETIC 1998–99 LEAGUE RECORD

Match No.	Date	Venue	Opponents	Result	H/T Score	Lg. Pos.	Goalscorers	Attendance
1	Aug 15	A	Newcastle U	D 0-0	0-0	—		36,719
2	22	H	Southampton	W 5-0	1-0	1	Robinson 3, Redfearn 46, Mendonca 3 (1 pen) 65 (p), 81, 90	16,488
3	29	A	Arsenal	D 0-0	0-0	4		38,014
4	Sept 9	A	Manchester U	L 1-4	1-2	—	Kinsella 32	55,147
5	12	H	Derby Co	L 1-2	0-1	13	Mendonca (pen) 89	19,516
6	19	A	Liverpool	D 3-3	1-1	14	Rufus 24, Mendonca 61, Jones S 83	44,526
7	26	H	Coventry C	D 1-1	0-0	14	Hunt 74	20,048
8	Oct 3	A	Nottingham F	W 1-0	1-0	13	Youds 5	22,661
9	17	A	Chelsea	L 1-2	0-1	14	Youds 58	34,642
10	24	H	West Ham U	W 4-2	1-2	9	Tiler 30, Mills 73, Hunt 88, Redfearn (pen) 90	20,043
11	Nov 2	A	Tottenham H	D 2-2	1-0	—	Hunt 2 32, 75	32,202
12	7	H	Leicester C	D 0-0	0-0	12		20,021
13	14	H	Middlesbrough	D 1-1	1-0	11	Mendonca (pen) 37	19,906
14	21	A	Leeds U	L 1-4	0-1	13	Mortimer 65	32,487
15	28	H	Everton	L 1-2	0-1	15	Kinsella 72	20,043
16	Dec 5	A	Blackburn R	L 0-1	0-0	16		22,568
17	12	A	Sheffield W	L 0-3	0-1	16		26,010
18	21	H	Aston Villa	L 0-1	0-1	—		20,043
19	26	A	Wimbledon	L 1-2	1-1	18	Redfearn 29	19,106
20	28	H	Arsenal	L 0-1	0-0	18		20,043
21	Jan 9	A	Southampton	L 1-3	1-1	19	Hunt 13	15,222
22	17	H	Newcastle U	D 2-2	0-1	18	Bright 64, Pringle 90	20,043
23	31	H	Manchester U	L 0-1	0-0	19		20,043
24	Feb 8	H	Wimbledon	W 2-0	1-0	—	Pringle 37, Blackwell (og) 68	20,002
25	13	H	Liverpool	W 1-0	0-0	18	Jones K 70	20,043
26	20	A	Derby Co	W 2-0	0-0	16	Hunt 64, Pringle 86	27,853
27	27	H	Nottingham F	D 0-0	0-0	16		20,007
28	Mar 6	A	Coventry C	L 1-2	0-0	17	Hunt 55	20,255
29	13	A	Leicester C	D 1-1	0-0	17	Mendonca 90	20,220
30	Apr 3	H	Chelsea	L 0-1	0-1	19		20,046
31	5	A	West Ham U	W 1-0	0-0	16	Stuart 75	26,041
32	10	A	Middlesbrough	L 0-2	0-1	17		34,529
33	17	H	Leeds U	D 1-1	1-1	17	Stuart 20	20,043
34	20	H	Tottenham H	L 1-4	1-0	—	Stuart 5	20,043
35	24	A	Everton	L 1-4	0-2	18	Stuart (pen) 81	40,089
36	May 1	H	Blackburn R	D 0-0	0-0	19		20,043
37	8	A	Aston Villa	W 4-3	1-1	18	Barry (og) 3, Mendonca 56, Robinson 68, Mills 89	37,705
38	16	H	Sheffield W	L 0-1	0-0	18		20,043

Final League Position: 18

GOALSCORERS
League (41): Mendonca 8 (3 pens), Hunt 7, Stuart 4 (1 pen), Pringle 3, Redfearn 3 (1 pen), Kinsella 2, Mills 2, Robinson 2, Youds 2, Bright 1, Jones K 1, Jones S 1, Mortimer 1, Rufus 1, Tiler 1, own goals 2.
Worthington Cup (4): Mortimer 1, Newton 1, Redfearn 1, Youds 1.
FA Cup (0).

Ilic S 23	Mills D 36	Powell C 38	Redfearn N 29 + 1	Rufus R 27	Youds E 21 + 1	Newton S 13 + 3	Kinsella M 38	Hunt A 32 + 2	Mendonca C 19 + 6	Robinson J 27 + 3	Brown S 13 + 5	Jones S 7 + 18	Mortimer P 10 + 7	Jones K 13 + 9	Tiler C 27	Petterson A 7 + 3	Barness A — + 3	Parker S — + 4	Lisbie K — + 1	Pringle M 15 + 3	Royce S 8	Konchesky P 1 + 1	Bright M 1 + 5	Barnes J 2 + 10	Stuart G 9	Bowen M 2 + 4	Match No.
1	2	3	4	5	6	7	8	9^1	10^2	11^3	12	13	14														1
1	2	3	4	5	6	7^2	8^1	9	10	11			13	12													2
1	2	3	4		6	7	8	9	10	11^2	5	12	13														3
1	2	3	4		6	7^2	8^3	9	10^1	11	5	12	13	14													4
1	2	3	4		6	7^1	8^2	9	10	11	5	12	13														5
1	2	3	4	5	6	7	8^2	9^1	10	11			12		13												6
1	2	3	4	5	6	7^2	8	9	10^1				12	11	13												7
1	2	3	4^3	5	6		8	9^1	10		14	12	11^2	13	7												8
1°	2	3	8	5	6	7^2		9	10		12		11^1		4	15							13				9
	2	3	8	5	6	7		9	10^1	13			12	11	4^2	1											10
1	2	3	8^2	5^3	6	7		9	10	14	13	12	11^1		4												11
1	2	3		6			8	9	10		7	12	11^1		4	5											12
1	2^1	3	12	5	6		8	9	10^2	11			13		7	4											13
1	2^3	3	8	5	6	7^2		9^1	10	11			12	14	13	4											14
1	2	3	8	5	6	12	7	9	10				13	11^1	4^2												15
1	2	3	4	5	6	12	8	9	10^2	11			13		7^1												16
1	2	3	4^2	5	6	7^3	8	9^1	12	11			10		13		14										17
1	2	3	4	5		7^1	8	9	12	11			10		6												18
1	2^2	3	4	5	12	7^1	8		11	10			9		6			13									19
1	2	3	10^1	5	6	7	8		11				9		4^2			12	13								20
1	2	3	4	5	6	7	8	9		11			10^1							12							21
	2	3		6		7^2	8	9^2		11					4^1	5				12	10	1	13	14			22
		3	8	5		7		9^2			2	4	11		6					12	10	1	13				23
	2	3	4			12	7	9		11^1	5				6					10		1	8				24
	2	3	8^2			7		9		11	5				4	6				10^1		1		12	13		25
	2	3	8			7^2		9	12	11	5				4^3	6	14			10		1		13			26
	2	3	8			7		9^1	12	11	5				4	6				10		1					27
	2	3	8^3			7		9^1		11^2	5		12		4	6		13		10		1		14			28
1	2	3	8^3	5		7		9^2	12		6	13	11		4					10^1				14			29
1	2^3	3^3		5				8	12	10^1	11	6	13		4			9						14	7		30
1°	2	3		5		7		9^1		4^2			12		6	15				8				10	11	13	31
	2	3		5		7^3		9^2	12	13			14		6	1				8				10	11	4^1	32
	2	3		5			8	9					7^2		4	6	1			10^1			12		11	13	33
		3		5			8	9	12				7^2		4	6	1			10^1			13		11	2	34
	2	3^3	5^2	6		7	12								8	4	1			10		9^1	13	11	14	35
	2	3	4	5			8	9^1		11^2			12		6	15				10		1°	13		7		36
	2	3	4^3	5			8		10^2	11^1	12	9			6	1				13				14	7		37
	2	3	4^2				8		10	11^1	5^3	9			6	1				12				13	7	14	38

Worthington Cup
Second Round	QPR	(a)	2-0
		(h)	1-0
Third Round	Leicester C	(h)	1-2

FA Cup
| Third Round | Blackburn R | (a) | 0-2 |

FA Premiership

CHELSEA

FOUNDATION

Chelsea may never have existed but for the fact that Fulham rejected an offer to rent the Stamford Bridge ground from Mr H. A. Mears who had owned it since 1904. Fortunately he was determined to develop it as a football stadium rather than sell it to the Great Western Railway and got together with Frederick Parker, who persuaded Mears of the financial advantages of developing a major sporting venue. Chelsea FC was formed in 1905, and when admission to the Southern League was denied, they immediately gained admission to the Second Division of the Football League.

Stamford Bridge, London SW6 1HS.
Telephone: (0171) 385 5545.
Fax: (0171) 381 4831.
Clubcall: 0891 121159.
Ticket News and Promotions: 0891 121011.
Ticket Credit Card Service: (0171) 386 7799.
Ground Capacity: 35,421 (during ground development); 41,000 (eventually).
Record Attendance: 82,905 v Arsenal, Division 1, 12 October 1935.
Record Receipts: £488,960 v Liverpool, FA Premier League, 30 December 1995.
Pitch Measurements: 113yd × 74yd.
Chairman: K. W. Bates.
Directors: C. Hutchinson (Managing), Ms Y. S. Todd.
Player/Manager: Gianluca Vialli.
Assistant Manager: Gwyn Williams.
Coach: Graham Rix.
Physio: Michael Banks.
Reserve Team Manager: Mick McGiven.
Company Secretary: Alan Shaw.
Match Secretary: Keith Lacy.
Commercial Manager: Carole Phair.
Safety Officer: David Lowery.

HONOURS

Football League: Division 1 – Champions 1954–55; Division 2 – Champions 1983–84, 1988–89; Runners-up 1906–07, 1911–12, 1929–30, 1962–63, 1976–77.
FA Cup: Winners 1970, 1997; Runners-up 1915, 1967, 1994.
Football League Cup: Winners 1965, 1998; Runners-up 1972.
Full Members' Cup: Winners 1986.
Zenith Data Systems Cup: Winners 1990.
European Competitions: European Fairs Cup: 1958–60, 1965–66, 1968–69. *European Cup-Winners' Cup:* 1970–71 (winners), 1971–72, 1994–95, 1997–98 (winners), 1998–99 (semi-finals). *Super Cup:* 1998–99 (winners).

LATEST SEQUENCES

Longest Sequence of League Wins: 8, 15.3.89 – 8.4.89.
Longest Sequence of League Defeats: 7, 1.11.52 – 20.12.52.
Longest Sequence of League Draws: 6, 20.8.69 – 13.9.69.
Longest Sequence of Unbeaten League Matches: 27, 29.10.88 – 8.4.89.
Longest Sequence Without a League Win: 21, 3.11.87 – 2.4.88.

Colours

Royal blue with white and amber trim shirts and shorts, white stockings with royal blue and amber trim.

Change Colours

White shirts and shorts with royal blue/yellow trim, white stockings with royal blue/yellow trim on turnover.

Year Formed: 1905.

Turned Professional: 1905.

Ltd Co.: 1905.

Club Nickname: 'The Blues'.

First Football League Game: 2 September 1905, Division 2, v Stockport Co (a) L 0–1 – Foulke; Mackie, McEwan; Key, Harris, Miller; Moran, J. T. Robertson, Copeland, Windridge, Kirwan.

Record League Victory: 9–2 v Glossop N E, Division 2, 1 September 1906 – Byrne; Walton, Miller; Key (1), McRoberts, Henderson; Moran, McDermott (1), Hilsdon (5), Copeland (1), Kirwan (1).

Record Cup Victory: 13–0 v Jeunesse Hautcharage, ECWC, 1st rd 2nd leg, 29 September 1971 – Bonetti; Boyle, Harris (1), Hollins (1p), Webb (1), Hinton, Cooke, Baldwin (3), Osgood (5), Hudson (1), Houseman (1).

Record Defeat: 1–8 v Wolverhampton W, Division 1, 26 September 1953.

Most League Points (2 for a win): 57, Division 2, 1906–07.

Most League Points (3 for a win): 99, Division 2, 1988–89.

Most League Goals: 98, Division 1, 1960–61.

Highest League Scorer in Season: Jimmy Greaves, 41, 1960–61.

Most League Goals in Total Aggregate: Bobby Tambling, 164, 1958–70.

Most League Goals in One Match: 5, George Hilsdon v Glossop, Division 2, 1 September 1906; 5, Jimmy Greaves v Wolverhampton W, Division 1, 30 August 1958; 5, Jimmy Greaves v Preston NE, Division 1, 19 December 1959; 5, Jimmy Greaves v WBA, Division 1, 3 December 1960; 5, Bobby Tambling v Aston Villa, Division 1, 17 September 1966.

Most Capped Player: Ray Wilkins, 24 (84), England.

Most League Appearances: Ron Harris, 655, 1962–80.

Youngest League Player: Ian Hamilton, 16 years 138 days v Tottenham H, 18 March 1967.

Record Transfer Fee Received: £2,500,000 from QPR for John Spencer, November 1996; £2,500,000 from Celtic for Craig Burley, July 1997.

Record Transfer Fee Paid: £10,000,000 to Blackburn R for Chris Sutton, July 1999.

Football League Record: 1905 Elected to Division 2; 1907–10 Division 1; 1910–12 Division 2; 1912–24 Division 1; 1924–30 Division 2; 1930–62 Division 1; 1962–63 Division 2; 1963–75 Division 1; 1975–77 Division 2; 1977–79 Division 1; 1979–84 Division 2; 1984–88 Division 1; 1988–89 Division 2; 1989–92 Division 1; 1992– FA Premier League.

MANAGERS

John Tait Robertson 1905–07
David Calderhead 1907–33
Leslie Knighton 1933–39
Billy Birrell 1939–52
Ted Drake 1952–61
Tommy Docherty 1962–67
Dave Sexton 1967–74
Ron Suart 1974–75
Eddie McCreadie 1975–77
Ken Shellito 1977–78
Danny Blanchflower 1978–79
Geoff Hurst 1979–81
John Neal 1981–85 *(Director to 1986)*
John Hollins 1985–88
Bobby Campbell 1988–91
Ian Porterfield 1991–93
David Webb 1993
Glenn Hoddle 1993–96
Ruud Gullit 1996–98
Gianluca Vialli February 1998–

TEN YEAR LEAGUE RECORD

1988-89	Div 2	46	29	12	5	96	50	99	1
1989-90	Div 1	38	16	12	10	58	50	60	5
1990-91	Div 1	38	13	10	15	58	69	49	11
1991-92	Div 1	42	13	14	15	50	60	53	14
1992-93	PR Lge	42	14	14	14	51	54	56	11
1993-94	PR Lge	42	13	12	17	49	53	51	14
1994-95	PR Lge	42	13	15	14	50	55	54	11
1995-96	PR Lge	38	12	14	12	46	44	50	11
1996-97	PR Lge	38	16	11	11	58	55	59	6
1997-98	PR Lge	38	20	3	15	71	43	63	4

DID YOU KNOW ?

In 1971 Chelsea's European Cup-Winners' Cup success was achieved by all British-born players. In 1998 they used only four Englishmen in winning it. In 1998–99 they frequently fielded a team born outside the mainland of England.

CHELSEA 1998–99 LEAGUE RECORD

Match No.	Date	Venue	Opponents	Result	H/T Score	Lg. Pos.	Goalscorers	Atten- dance
1	Aug 15	A	Coventry C	L	1-2	1-2	—	Poyet [37]	23,042
2	22	H	Newcastle U	D	1-1	1-1	16	Babayaro [23]	34,795
3	Sept 9	H	Arsenal	D	0-0	0-0	—		34,647
4	12	H	Nottingham F	W	2-1	2-0	16	Zola [1], Poyet [35]	34,809
5	21	A	Blackburn R	W	4-3	1-1	—	Zola [15], Leboeuf (pen) [51], Flo 2 [82, 86]	23,113
6	26	H	Middlesbrough	W	2-0	0-0	8	Pallister (og) [46], Zola [81]	34,814
7	Oct 4	A	Liverpool	D	1-1	1-1	6	Casiraghi [10]	44,404
8	17	A	Charlton Ath	W	2-1	1-0	4	Leboeuf (pen) [18], Poyet [88]	34,642
9	25	A	Leeds U	D	0-0	0-0	6		35,833
10	Nov 8	A	West Ham U	D	1-1	0-1	5	Babayaro [76]	26,023
11	14	H	Wimbledon	W	3-0	1-0	4	Zola [32], Poyet [55], Petrescu [70]	34,800
12	21	A	Leicester C	W	4-2	2-1	4	Zola 2 [28, 90], Poyet [39], Flo [56]	21,401
13	28	H	Sheffield W	D	1-1	1-0	5	Zola [27]	34,451
14	Dec 5	A	Everton	D	0-0	0-0	6		36,430
15	9	H	Aston Villa	W	2-1	—	—	Zola [30], Flo [90]	34,765
16	12	A	Derby Co	D	2-2	0-1	3	Flo [55], Poyet [59]	29,056
17	16	A	Manchester U	D	1-1	0-1	—	Zola [83]	55,159
18	19	H	Tottenham H	W	2-0	0-0	1	Poyet [90], Flo [90]	34,881
19	26	A	Southampton	W	2-0	1-0	1	Flo [20], Poyet [48]	15,253
20	29	H	Manchester U	D	0-0	0-0	—		34,741
21	Jan 9	A	Newcastle U	W	1-0	1-0	1	Petrescu [39]	36,711
22	16	H	Coventry C	W	2-1	1-1	1	Leboeuf [45], Di Matteo [90]	34,869
23	31	A	Arsenal	L	0-1	0-1	2		38,121
24	Feb 6	A	Southampton	W	1-0	1-0	2	Zola [11]	34,920
25	17	H	Blackburn R	D	1-1	1-0	—	Morris [44]	34,382
26	20	A	Nottingham F	W	3-1	2-1	2	Forssell [6], Goldbaek 2 [25, 83]	26,351
27	27	H	Liverpool	W	2-1	2-0	2	Leboeuf (pen) [7], Goldbaek [38]	34,822
28	Mar 13	A	West Ham U	L	0-1	0-0	3		34,765
29	21	H	Aston Villa	W	3-0	0-0	3	Flo 2 [59, 90], Goldbaek [86]	39,217
30	Apr 3	A	Charlton Ath	W	1-0	1-0	3	Di Matteo [11]	20,046
31	11	H	Wimbledon	W	2-1	1-0	3	Flo [24], Poyet [53]	21,577
32	14	A	Middlesbrough	D	0-0	0-0	—		34,406
33	18	H	Leicester C	D	2-2	1-0	2	Zola [30], Petrescu [69]	34,535
34	25	A	Sheffield W	D	0-0	0-0	3		21,652
35	May 1	H	Everton	W	3-1	1-0	3	Zola 2 [25, 81], Petrescu [60]	34,000
36	5	H	Leeds U	W	1-0	0-0	—	Poyet [68]	34,762
37	10	A	Tottenham H	D	2-2	1-1	—	Poyet [4], Goldbaek [72]	35,878
38	16	H	Derby Co	W	2-1	1-0	3	Babayaro [40], Vialli [68]	35,017

Final League Position: 3

GOALSCORERS

League (57): Zola 13, Poyet 11, Flo 10, Goldbaek 5, Leboeuf 4 (3 pens), Petrescu 4, Babayaro 3, Di Matteo 2, Casiraghi 1, Forssell 1, Morris 1, Vialli 1, own goal 1.
Worthington Cup (10): Vialli 6, Poyet 2, Flo 1, Leboeuf 1 (pen).
FA Cup (8): Forssell 2, Vialli 2, Di Matteo 1, Leboeuf 1 (pen), Wise 1, Zola 1.

De Goey E 35	Ferrer A 30	Le Saux G 30 + 1	Babayaro C 26 + 2	Leboeuf F 33	Desailly M 30 + 1	Poyet G 21 + 7	Di Matteo R 26 + 4	Vialli G 9	Casiraghi P 10	Wise D 21 + 1	Zola G 35 + 2	Flo T 18 + 12	Duberry M 18 + 7	Petrescu D 23 + 9	Lambourde B 12 + 5	Laudrup B 5 + 2	Newton E 1 + 6	Morris J 14 + 4	Nicholls M — + 9	Goldbaek B 13 + 10	Terry J — + 2	Forssell M 4 + 6	Myers A 1	Hitchcock K 2 + 1	Kharine D 1	Match No.
1	2	3	4	5	6	7	8^1	9^2	10	11	12	13														1
1	2	3^2	11	5	6	7^1	8		10		9	12	4	13												2
1		3	11	5	6	12	8		10		9^2	13	4	14	2^3	7^1										3
1		3	11	5	6	7^1			10^2		9		4	2	12	13	8									4
1	2	3	7	5	6	8	12		10^2	11^1	9^3	13	4					14								5
1	2	3	4	5^3	6	7	8		10^1		9	12	14	13				11^2								6
1	2	3		5	6	12	8		10^2		9^1	13	4	7			14	11^3								7
1	2	3		5	6^1	7	8		10^2	12	9^2	13	4	14				11								8
1	2	3		5	6	12	8		10^2	11	9^1	13	4				7									9
1	2	3	4		6	7	8^2		10^1	11	9^3	12	13	5				14								10
1		3	4	5	6	7^1	8^3				9^2	10	12	2	11			14	13							11
1	2	3	11	5	6	7	8			9	10	12	4^1													12
1	2	3	11	5	6	7	8^2			9	10	12			13			4^1								13
1	2	3		5	6	7	8			11	9^2	10	12	4				13								14
1	2	3	11^1	5	6	12	8	9			10^2	13	4	7												15
1		3	12	5		7				11	9^3	10	6	13	2			8^1	14	4^2						16
1	2	3^1	4			12	8			11	9	10	6	7	5											17
1	2	3	5			7		9			10^1	12	6	11	4^2		8		13							18
1	2	3	5			11^1				9	10^1	6	7				8	12	4	13						19
1	2	3^2	4	5	12		8			11	9	6	7				10^1		13							20
1	2	3		5	6		8	9		11	10^1	4	7					12								21
1	2^1	3	4	5			8	9		11	10		7	6				12								22
1		3	7	5	6		8	9		11	10^2	4^1	2					12	13							23
1		3	7^1	5	6		8			11	10		2					4	13	12	9^2					24
1		3^1	11	5	6		8	9			10		7^2	2	12		4^3	13	14							25
1	2		11	5	6					10^1	12	7^2	3	13		8	14	4		9^3						26
1	2	3^1		5^2	6		8			10	9^3		7	13		12	11	4		14						27
1	2	3^2	7		6^1		8			11	10	9	12	13				4		14	5^3					28
1	2	3		5	6					11	10	9^2		7^1	12		8	13		4						29
1^6	2	3		5	6	12	8^2			11	10	9	13				7^1	4				15				30
1		3		5			11	8^1			10^3	9	6	7^2	2	13	12	14	4							31
1	2	3			6		8^2	12		11	10	9	5	7^1				13	4							32
1	2^3	12		5	6	13	8			11	10	9	14	7				4^2	3^1							33
	2		3	5	6	8^2		9		11	12			7				4		10^1		1				34
1	2	3	12	5^2	6	8				11	10		7^3	13				4^1	14	9						35
1	2	3		5	6	8	12			11	10^3	9^1	7					4^2	13	14						36
	2	3		5	6	8	12			11	10^2	9		7^2				4^1	13	14		1				37
	2^2	3	4^1			7	8	9		11		10	6^3	12	5		13			14		1				38

Worthington Cup

Third Round	Aston Villa	(h)	4-1
Fourth Round	Arsenal	(a)	5-0
Fifth Round	Wimbledon	(a)	1-2

FA Cup

Third Round	Oldham Ath	(a)	2-0
Fourth Round	Oxford U	(a)	1-1
		(h)	4-2
Fifth Round	Sheffield W	(a)	1-0
Sixth Round	Manchester U	(a)	0-0
		(h)	0-2

Division 3   **CHELTENHAM TOWN**

FOUNDATION

Although a scratch team representing Cheltenham played a match against Gloucester in 1884, the earliest recorded match for Cheltenham Town FC was a friendly against Dean Close School on 12 March 1892. The School won 4–3 and the match was played at Prestbury (half a mile from Whaddon Road). Cheltenham Town played Wednesday afternoon friendlies at a local cricket ground until entering the Mid Gloucester League. In those days the club played in deep red coloured shirts and were nicknamed 'the Rubies'. The club moved to Whaddon Lane for season 1901–02 and changed to red and white colours two years later.

Whaddon Road, Cheltenham, Gloucester GL52 5NA.

Telephone: (01242) 573558.

Fax: (01242) 224675.

Clubcall: 09066 555833.

Ground Capacity: 6114.

Record Attendance: at Whaddon Road: 8326 v Reading, FA Cup 1st rd, 17 November 1956; at Cheltenham Athletic Ground: 10,389 v Blackpool, FA Cup 3rd rd, 13 January 1934.

Record Receipts: £40,000 v Yeovil T, Nationwide Conference, 22 April 1999.

Pitch Measurements: 111yd × 72yd.

Chairman: Paul Baker.

Directors: Wayne Allen, Dave Bathers, Rod Burge, Colin Farmer, Paul Roberts, Brian Sandland, John Wood.

Chief Executive: Arthur Hayward.

Manager: Steve Cotterill.

First Team Coach: Mike Davis.

Secretary: Reg Woodward.

Youth Team Manager: David May.

Commercial Manager: Gordon Cook.

Physio: John Atkinson.

HONOURS

Football Conference: Champions 1998–99, runners-up 1997–98.

FA Trophy: Winners 1997–98.

Southern League: Champions 1984–85; *Southern League Cup:* Winners 1957–58, runners-up 1968–69, 1984–85; *Southern League Merit Cup:* Winners 1984–85; *Southern League Championship Shield:* Winners 1985.

Gloucestershire Senior Cup: Winners 1998–99; *Gloucestershire Northern Senior Professional Cup:* Winners 30 times; *Midland Floodlit Cup:* Winners 1985–86, 1986–87, 1987–88; *Mid Gloucester League:* Champions 1896–97; *Gloucester and District League:* Champions 1902–03, 1905–06; *Cheltenham League:* Champions 1910–11, 1913–14; *North Gloucestershire League:* Champions 1913–14; *Gloucestershire Northern Senior League:* Champions 1928–29, 1932–33; *Gloucestershire Northern Senior Amateur Cup:* Winners 1929–30, 1930–31, 1932–33, 1933–34, 1934–35; *Leamington Hospital Cup:* Winners 1934–35.

Colours
Red and white striped shirts, white shorts, red stockings.

Change Colours
All white with blue and yellow trim.

Year Formed: 1892.

Turned Professional: 1932.

Ltd Co.: 1937.

Club Nickname: 'The Robins'.

Previous Grounds: Grafton Cricket Ground, Whaddon Lane, Carter's Field (pre 1932).

Record League Victory: 11–0 v Bourneville Ath, Birmingham Combination, 29 April 1933 – Davis; Jones, Williams; Lang (1), Blackburn, Draper; Evans, Hazard (4), Haycox (4), Goodger (1), Hill (1).

Record Cup Victory: 12–0 v Chippenham R, FA Cup 3rd qual. rd, 2 November 1935 – Bowles; Whitehouse, Williams; Lang, Devonport (1), Partridge (2); Perkins, Hackett, Jones (4), Black (4), Griffiths (1).

Record Defeat: 1–10 v Merthyr T, Southern League, 8 March 1952.

Most League Points (2 for a win): 60, Southern League Division 1, 1963–64.

Most League Points (3 for a win): 86, Southern League Premier Division, 1994–95.

Most League Goals: 115, Southern League, 1957–58.

Highest League Scorer in Season: Dave Lewis, 33 (53 in all competitions), Southern League Division 1, 1974–75.

Most League Goals in Total Aggregate: Dave Lewis, 205 (290 in all competitions), 1970–83.

Most League Appearances: Roger Thorndale, 524 (701 in all competitions), 1958–76.

Record Transfer Fee Received: £60,000 from Southampton for Christer Warren, 1995.

Record Transfer Fee Paid: £25,000 to Kidderminster H for Kim Casey, 1991.

MANAGERS

George Carr 1936–39
Jimmy Brain 1945–48
Cyril Dean 1948–50
George Summerbee 1950–52
William Raeside 1952–53
Arch Anderson 1953–58
Ron Lewin 1958–60
Peter Donnelly 1960–61
Tommy Cavanagh 1961
Arch Anderson 1961–65
Harold Fletcher 1965–66
Bob Etheridge 1966–73
Willie Penman 1973–74
Dennis Allen 1974–79
Terry Paine 1979
Alan Grundy 1979–82
Alan Wood 1982–83
John Murphy 1983–88
Jim Barron 1988–90
John Murphy 1990
Dave Lewis 1990–91
Ally Robertson 1991–92
Lindsay Parsons 1992–95
Chris Robinson 1995–97
Steve Cotterill 1997–

TEN YEAR LEAGUE RECORD

		P	W	D	L	F	A	Pts	Pos
1988–89	Conf	40	12	12	16	55	58	48	15
1989–90	Conf	42	16	11	15	58	60	59	11
1990–91	Conf	42	12	12	18	54	72	48	16
1991–92	Conf	42	10	13	19	56	82	43	21
1992–93	Sth L	40	21	10	9	76	40	73	2
1993–94	Sth L	42	21	12	9	67	38	75	2
1994–95	Sth L	42	25	11	6	87	39	86	2
1995–96	Sth L	42	21	11	10	76	57	74	3
1996–97	Sth L	42	21	11	10	76	44	74	2
1997–98	Conf	42	23	9	10	63	43	78	2

DID YOU KNOW ?

Amongst the famous players to have appeared for Cheltenham Town are Ronny Radford, scorer of the Hereford United goal that knocked Newcastle out of the F. A. Cup in the early 1970s; TV personality Andy Gray; and England 1966 World Cup player Terry Paine.

CHELTENHAM TOWN 1998–99 LEAGUE RECORD

Match No.	Date	Venue	Opponents	Result	H/T Score	Lg. Pos.	Goalscorers	Atten- dance
1	Aug 15	A	Welling U	L	1-2	1-1	—	Banks [7]	820
2	18	H	Hednesford T	D	0-0	0-0	—		2186
3	22	H	Hayes	D	3-3	0-2	—	Eaton [53], Howells [75], Smith [89] (pen)	1879
4	26	A	Forest Green Rovers	W	2-1	0-0	12	Eaton [59], Norton [82]	1909
5	29	A	Leek T	W	2-0	1-0	8	Grayson [12], Victory [73]	704
6	31	H	Barrow	W	4-1	2-1	4	Walker C 2 [16, 34], Brough [52], Eaton [88]	2005
7	Sept 5	A	Morecambe	W	4-1	2-1	3	Grayson 2 [2, 65], Howells 2 [32, 69],	1959
8	8	A	Kettering T	W	2-0	1-0	2	Eaton [4], Grayson [70]	1615
9	12	A	Kingstonian	W	2-1	1-0	2	Freeman [37], Eaton [56]	1801
10	19	H	Southport	W	3-0	3-0	2	Norton [13], Eaton [16], Walker C [41]	2594
11	22	H	Woking	D	1-1	0-1	1	Grayson [79]	2406
12	26	A	Farnborough T	W	4-2	2-1	1	Freeman 2 [2, 47], Knight [28], Grayson [90]	1067
13	Oct 3	H	Dover Ath	D	1-1	0-0	1	Grayson [67]	2575
14	10	A	Yeovil T	D	2-2	2-1	1	Norton [19], Grayson [32]	2955
15	24	A	Doncaster R	W	2-1	2-1	1	Brough [6], Duff [30]	2428
16	Nov 7	A	Woking	L	0-1	0-0	1		2738
17	28	H	Rushden & D	W	1-0	1-0	1	Knight [32]	4051
18	Dec 5	A	Dover Ath	D	0-0	0-0	2		972
19	12	H	Leek T	D	0-0	0-0	2		1912
20	19	H	Stevenage B	W	3-0	2-0	2	Eaton 2 [21, 33], Watkins [55] (pen)	2772
21	26	A	Telford U	W	3-0	0-0	2	Watkins [67], Eaton [75], Jones [84] (og)	1304
22	28	A	Kidderminster H	W	1-0	1-0	2	Watkins [34]	3295
23	Jan 2	H	Telford U	W	2-0	1-0	2	Walker C [37], Howells [67]	3027
24	9	A	Doncaster R	D	2-2	2-0	2	Watkins 2 [28] (pen) [34]	3082
25	23	H	Northwich V	L	0-1	0-1	2		2460
26	30	A	Southport	W	2-0	1-0	2	Howells [29], Grayson [60]	1224
27	Feb 13	A	Morecombe	W	2-0	1-0	2	Watkins [35], Grayson [71]	1354
28	20	A	Hereford U	W	2-0	1-0	2	Freeman [16], Victory [84]	3480
29	Mar 6	A	Barrow	D	1-1	0-1	2	Knight [73]	1773
30	9	H	Hereford U	D	2-2	1-1	2	Victory [39], Brough [61]	3341
31	13	A	Stevenage B	D	2-2	1-1	2	Brough [3], Howells [74]	2576
32	16	H	Farnborough T	D	0-0	0-0	2		2265
33	20	H	Kettering T	W	3-0	2-0	1	Matthews [35] (og), Grayson [38], Hone [73] (og)	5202
34	22	A	Hednesford T	L	2-3	1-2	1	Grayson [37], Bailey [90]	1651
35	Apr 3	A	Rushden & D	W	2-1	0-1	2	Freeman [89], Grayson [90]	6312
36	5	H	Kidderminster H	W	1-0	0-0	1	Grayson [55]	4518
37	13	H	Kingstonian	H	1-0	1-0	1	Grayson [25] (pen)	3184
38	20	H	Forest Green Rovers	D	1-1	1-0	1	Bailey [30]	3058
39	22	H	Yeovil T	W	3-2	2-1	1	Victory [4], Grayson [22], Duff [90]	6150
40	24	A	Hayes	L	2-3	1-1	1	Grayson [45], Duff [56]	2105
41	27	A	Northwich V	L	0-1	0-0	1		1155
42	May 1	H	Welling U	D	0-0	0-0	1		5400

Final League Position: 1

GOALSCORERS

League (71): Grayson 17, Eaton 9, Howells 6, Watkins 6, Freeman 5, Brough 4, Victory 4, Walker C 4, Duff 3, Knight 3, Norton 3, Bailey 2, Banks 1, Smith 1, own goals 3.
FA Cup (4). Eaton 3, Howells 1.
Other Cups (25): Grayson 7, Watkins 3, Brough 2, Hopkins 2, Victory 2, Bloomer 1, Duff 1, Eaton 1, Freeman 1, Howarth 1, Knight 1, Smith 1, Walker C 1, Yates 1.

Book 42	Duff 41	Victory 42	Banks 34 + 1	Brough 34 + 6	Milton 6 + 11	Howells 37 + 1	Norton 35 + 1	Eaton 27 + 7	Grayson 39 + 2	Bloomer 15 + 13	Knight 8 + 15	Walker C 17 + 7	Smith 2 + 5	Freeman 36 + 1	Howarth 5 + 3	Walker R 14 + 2	Yates 12	Watkins 9 + 10	Bailey 7 + 1	Jackson 0 + 1	Match No.
1	2	3	4	5	6^2	7	8^1	9	10	11	12	13									1
1	2	3	4	5	11	7	6^1	9	10		12	8									2
1	2	3	4	5	10	7	6^3	9^2	8^1		12	11	13			14					3
1	2	3	4	6	12	7	11	9	10			8^1		5							4
1	2	3	4	6	12	7	11	9	10			8^1		5							5
1	2	3	4	6	13	7	11	9^1	10^3		12	8^2	14	5							6
1	2	3	4	6	13	7	11^1	9	10		12	8^2		5							7
1	2	3	4	6^1	8	7	11	9^1	10		12			5				13			8
1	2	3	4	6	12	7	11	9^2	10			8^1		5				13			9
1	2	3	4^1	6	13	7	11	9^3	10		12	8^2		5				14			10
1	2	3		6		7	11	9^1	10	13	4	8^2		5				12			11
1	2	3	14	6	13	7	11^2	9	10	12	4^1	8^3		5							12
1	2	3	4	6		7	11^2	9^1	10	13	12	8		5							13
1	2	3	4	6		7	11	9	10	12		8^1		5							14
1	2	3	4	6^1		7	11	9	10	8				5			12				15
1	2	3	4	6		7		9	10	8			11^1	5			12				16
1	2	3	4	6		7	11		10	8^1				5	9		12				17
1	2	3	4	6^1		7	11		10^1			8		5	9		12				18
1	2	3	4	6^1	8^3	7	11	12	10^2			14	9	5		13					19
1	2	3	4	12	14	7	11^1	9				8^2		5	6^3		13	10			20
1		3	4	2		7	11	9	13		12	8^1	14	5	6^2			10^3			21
1	2	3	4	14		7	11	9^2	13		12	8^1		5	6^2			10			22
1	2	3	4	14		7	11	9	6^1		12	8^3	13	5				10^2			23
1	2	3	4	5		7	11	9^1	8		12		13		6			10^2			24
1	2	3	4	13		7	11	9^3	8		12		14	5	6^2			10^1			25
1	2	3	4	14		7	11	9^1	10^3	13				5	6^2	8		12			26
1	2	3	4				11	9	8					5	6			10	7		27
1	2	3	4				11	9	8		12			5	6			10^1	7		28
1	2	3	4				11^1	9	8		12			5	6			10	7		29
1	2	3	4^2				10^3	9	8	11^1	12			5	14	6		13	7		30
1	2	3	4			13	10^1	9	8	11^2				5	12	6			7		31
1	2	3	4	10		7	12	9	13	11				5^1	14	6^2		8^3			32
1	2	3	4			7	12	9	11					5	6	8^1		10			33
1	2	3	4^3			7^1	8	12	9	11^2	13		14	5	6			10			34
1	2	3	4	5	13	7	11	9	8^2	14	12				6^1			10^3			35
1	2	3	4	10^1	8^2	7	11^3	9	13	14	12			5	6						36
1	2	3	4	6	12	7	11^1	13	9	8				5				10^2			37
1	2	3	4	6		7	11	12	9					5		8		10^1			38
1	2	3	4	6		7	11	9	8	12				5				10^1			39
1	2	3	4	12		7	10^3	9^1	13	11^2				5	6	8		14			40
1	2	3	4	6^2		7	13	12	9	11				5		8		10^1			41
1	2	3	4	12		7	11^3	10^2	9	8	14			5		6^1		13			42

FA Cup

Third Qual Round	Barnstable T	(a)	1-0
Fourth Qual Round	Taunton T	(h)	3-2
First Round	Lincoln C	(h)	0-1

Division 3   CHESTER CITY

FOUNDATION

All students of soccer history have read about the medieval games of football in Chester, but the present club was not formed until 1884 through the amalgamation of King's School Old Boys with Chester Rovers. For many years Chester were overshadowed in Cheshire by Northwich Victoria and Crewe Alexandra who had both won the Senior Cup several times before Chester's first success in 1894–95. The final against Macclesfield saw Chester face the team that had not only beaten them in the previous year's final, but also knocked them out of the FA Cup two seasons in succession. The final was held at the Drill Field, Northwich and Chester had the support of more than 1000 fans. Chester won 2-1.

The Deva Stadium, Bumpers Lane, Chester CH1 4LT.

Telephone: (01244) 371376, 371809.

Fax: (01244) 390265.

Commercial: (01244) 390243.

Ground Capacity: 6000.

Record Attendance: 20,500 v Chelsea, FA Cup 3rd rd (replay), 16 January 1952 (at Sealand Road).

Record Receipts: £30,609 v Sheffield W, FA Cup 4th rd, 31 January 1987.

Pitch Measurements: 115yd × 75yd.

Honorary President: C. Thompson.

Chief Executive: W. Wingrove.

Manager: Kevin Ratcliffe.

Honorary Vice-Presidents: J. F. Kane, L. Lloyd, Dr. M. D. Swallow.

Assistant Secretary: Gill Dugan.

Physio: Joe Hinnigan.

LATEST SEQUENCES

Longest Sequence of League Wins: 8, 12.4.78 – 26.8.78.

Longest Sequence of League Defeats: 9, 30.4.94 – 13.9.94.

Longest Sequence of League Draws: 6, 11.10.86 – 1.11.86.

Longest Sequence of Unbeaten League Matches: 18, 27.10.34 – 16.2.35.

Longest Sequence Without a League Win: 25, 19.9.61 – 3.3.62.

HONOURS

Football League: Division 3 – Runners-up 1993–94; Division 3 (N) – Runners-up 1935–36; Division 4 – Runners-up 1985–86.

FA Cup: best season: 5th rd, 1977, 1980.

Football League Cup: Semi-final 1975.

Welsh Cup: Winners 1908, 1933, 1947.

Debenhams Cup: Winners 1977.

Colours
Blue and white striped shirts, white shorts, blue and white stockings.

Change Colours
Claret and white.

Year Formed: 1885.

Turned Professional: 1902.

Ltd Co.: 1909.

Previous Name: Chester until 1983.

Club Nickname: 'Blues' and 'City'.

Previous Grounds: 1885, Faulkner Street; 1898, The Old Showground; 1901, Whipcord Lane; 1906, Sealand Road; 1990, Moss Rose Ground, Macclesfield; 1992, Deva Stadium, Bumpers Lane.

First Football League Game: 2 September 1931, Division 3 (N), v Wrexham (a) D 1–1 – Johnson; Herod, Jones; Keeley, Skitt, Reilly; Thompson, Ranson, Jennings (1), Cresswell, Hedley.

Record League Victory: 12–0 v York C, Division 3 (N), 1 February 1936 – Middleton; Common, Hall; Wharton, Wilson, Howarth; Horsman (2), Hughes, Wrightson (4), Cresswell (2), Sargeant (4).

Record Cup Victory: 6–1 v Darlington, FA Cup 1st rd, 25 November 1933 – Burke; Bennett, Little; Pitcairn, Skitt, Duckworth; Armes (3), Whittam, Mantle (2), Cresswell (1), McLachlan.

Record Defeat: 2–11 v Oldham Ath, Division 3 (N), 19 January 1952.

Most League Points (2 for a win): 56, Division 3 (N), 1946–47 and Division 4, 1964–65.

Most League Points (3 for a win): 84, Division 4, 1985–86.

Most League Goals: 119, Division 4, 1964–65.

Highest League Scorer in Season: Dick Yates, 36, Division 3 (N), 1946–47.

Most League Goals in Total Aggregate: Stuart Rimmer, 135, 1985–88, 1991–98.

Most League Goals in One Match: 5, Tom Jennings v Walsall, Division 3N, 30 January 1932; 5, Barry Jepson v York C, Division 4, 8 February 1958.

Most Capped Player: Bill Lewis, 13 (27), Wales.

Most League Appearances: Ray Gill, 406, 1951–62.

Youngest League Player: Aidan Newhouse, 15 years 350 days v Bury, 7 May 1988.

Record Transfer Fee Received: £300,000 from Liverpool for Ian Rush, May 1980.

Record Transfer Fee Paid: £94,000 to Barnsley for Stuart Rimmer, August 1991.

Football League Record: 1931 Elected Division 3 (N); 1958–75 Division 4; 1975–82 Division 3; 1982–86 Division 4; 1986–92 Division 3; 1992–93 Division 2; 1993–94 Division 3; 1994–95 Division 2; 1995– Division 3.

MANAGERS

Charlie Hewitt 1930–36
Alex Raisbeck 1936–38
Frank Brown 1938–53
Louis Page 1953–56
John Harris 1956–59
Stan Pearson 1959–61
Bill Lambton 1962–63
Peter Hauser 1963–68
Ken Roberts 1968–76
Alan Oakes 1976–82
Cliff Sear 1982
John Sainty 1982–83
John McGrath 1984
Harry McNally 1985–92
Graham Barrow 1992–94
Mike Pejic 1994–95
Derek Mann 1995
Kevin Ratcliffe April 1995–

TEN YEAR LEAGUE RECORD

		P	W	D	L	F	A	Pts	Pos
1988-89	Div 3	46	19	11	16	64	61	68	8
1989-90	Div 3	46	13	15	18	43	55	54	16
1990-91	Div 3	46	14	9	23	46	58	51	19
1991-92	Div 3	46	14	14	18	56	59	56	18
1992-93	Div 2	46	8	5	33	49	102	29	24
1993-94	Div 3	42	21	11	10	69	46	74	2
1994-95	Div 2	46	6	11	29	37	84	29	23
1995-96	Div 3	46	18	16	12	72	53	70	8
1996-97	Div 3	46	18	16	12	55	43	70	6
1997-98	Div 3	46	17	10	19	60	61	61	14

DID YOU KNOW ?

Full-back Baden Herod was Chester's first ever-present player in Division Three (North) in 1931–32. This included taking over in goal for part of the game with Gateshead on 26 September when the team finished with only nine men through injury in a 1–1 draw.

CHESTER CITY 1998–99 LEAGUE RECORD

Match No.	Date		Venue	Opponents	Result		H/T Score	Lg. Pos.	Goalscorers	Attendance
1	Aug	8	H	Leyton Orient	L	0-2	0-1	—		2541
2		15	A	Brighton & HA	D	2-2	1-0	21	Smith [1], Flitcroft (pen) [61]	2703
3		23	H	Hull C	D	2-2	1-1	21	Flitcroft (pen) [33], Crosby [59]	2577
4		29	A	Southend U	W	1-0	0-0	12	Bennett [75]	4241
5	Sept	1	H	Cambridge U	L	0-3	0-1	—		2199
6		5	A	Exeter C	W	1-0	0-0	14	Richardson [54]	2551
7		8	A	Peterborough U	L	0-3	0-3	—		4548
8		12	H	Torquay U	W	2-0	1-0	13	Richardson [37], Murphy [90]	1729
9		19	A	Carlisle U	D	1-1	0-0	16	Flitcroft [53]	2971
10		26	H	Cardiff C	D	2-2	0-0	15	Priest [64], Thomas [67]	2842
11	Oct	3	A	Scarborough	W	4-2	2-0	10	Priest [24], Thomas 2 [33, 56], Flitcroft [59]	1832
12		11	A	Barnet	D	0-0	0-0	11		2236
13		17	H	Swansea C	D	1-1	1-1	11	Murphy [24]	3926
14		20	H	Hartlepool U	D	1-1	1-0	—	Woods [39]	2182
15		31	H	Shrewsbury T	D	1-1	0-0	13	Murphy [54]	3699
16	Nov	7	A	Scunthorpe U	L	1-2	0-2	17	Murphy [90]	3160
17		10	A	Halifax T	L	2-3	0-1	—	Beckett [53], Murphy [68]	2427
18		21	H	Rochdale	D	1-1	1-0	19	Wright [24]	2495
19		28	A	Brentford	L	1-2	0-1	19	Davidson [88]	5173
20	Dec	12	H	Darlington	W	1-0	0-0	17	Shelton [53]	2011
21		18	A	Rotherham U	W	4-2	1-0	—	Priest [17], Conroy 2 [51, 74], Murphy [83]	2696
22		26	A	Hull C	W	2-1	2-0	14	Flitcroft [9], Whitney (og) [11]	6695
23		28	H	Mansfield T	D	1-1	0-1	15	Reid [75]	3320
24	Jan	2	H	Southend U	D	1-1	0-0	14	Murphy [77]	2574
25		9	A	Leyton Orient	D	2-2	1-1	15	Murphy [34], Smith (pen) [60]	4132
26		15	H	Brighton & HA	D	1-1	1-0	—	Conroy [45]	3869
27		23	A	Cambridge U	L	1-2	1-1	16	Crosby (pen) [45]	3635
28		30	A	Mansfield T	L	0-3	0-0	17		2654
29	Feb	6	A	Exeter C	D	0-0	0-0	19		2243
30		13	H	Peterborough U	W	1-0	1-0	17	Murphy [26]	2087
31		20	A	Torquay U	W	3-0	1-0	16	Beckett [12], Alsford [69], Cross [89]	2384
32		23	A	Plymouth Arg	L	0-2	0-2	—		4208
33		27	A	Carlisle U	W	2-1	0-0	14	Richardson [62], Murphy [72]	2450
34	Mar	5	A	Cardiff C	D	0-0	0-0	—		7526
35		9	H	Scarborough	L	1-3	0-1	—	Beckett [60]	1954
36		13	H	Scunthorpe U	L	0-2	0-1	15		2115
37		20	A	Shrewsbury T	L	0-2	0-1	16		2903
38		27	H	Plymouth Arg	W	3-2	0-1	14	Beckett 2 [46, 67], Murphy [75]	1982
39	Apr	3	A	Swansea C	D	1-1	0-1	13	Beckett [58]	5994
40		5	H	Barnet	W	3-0	2-0	13	Murphy [11], Crosby (pen) [25], Beckett [48]	2122
41		10	A	Hartlepool U	L	0-2	0-1	13		2413
42		13	H	Brentford	L	1-3	0-2	—	Crosby (pen) [56]	1766
43		17	A	Rochdale	L	1-3	1-0	17	Beckett [25]	1712
44		24	H	Halifax T	D	2-2	1-1	15	Priest [20], Beckett [65]	2461
45	May	1	A	Darlington	W	2-1	1-1	14	Flitcroft [36], Beckett [59]	2564
46		8	H	Rotherham U	D	1-1	1-0	14	Beckett [44]	3792

Final League Position: 14

GOALSCORERS

League (57): Murphy 12, Beckett 11, Flitcroft 6 (2 pens), Crosby 4 (3 pens), Priest 4, Conroy 3, Richardson 3, Thomas 3, Smith 2 (1 pen), Alsford 1, Bennett 1, Cross 1, Davidson 1, Reid 1, Shelton 1, Woods 1, Wright 1, own goal 1.
Worthington Cup (4): Beckett 2, Smith 1, own goal 1.
FA Cup (0).

Brown W 23	Davidson R 40	Cross J 33+2	Richardson N 41+2	Crosby A 41	Woods M 41+2	Flitcroft D 42	Priest C 35	Murphy J 41+1	Beckett L 24+4	Smith A 32	Bennett G 5+2	Thomas R 3+3	Shelton A 5+17	Wright D 6+12	Reid S 16+6	Jones J 2+6	Cutler N 23	Carson D 1+1	Lancaster M 8+3	Moss D 5+2	Alston S 11	Conroy M 11+4	Alsford J 9+1	Smeets J 1+2	Fisher N 7+1	Match No.
1	2	3	4	5	6	7[1]	8	9	10	11	12															1
1	2	3	4	5	6	10	8	9		11	7[1]	12														2
1	2	3	4	5	6	10	8	9		11	7[1]	12														3
1	2	3	4	5	6	10[1]	8	9		11	7		12													4
1	2	3	4	5	6	10	8	9		11	7[1]				12											5
1	2	3	4	5	6	7	8[2]			11			12	10	13	9[1]										6
1		3	2	5	6	7	8			11	12		10	4	9[1]											7
1	2	3	4	5	6	7	8	12		11		9[2]	13	10[1]												8
1	2	3		5	6	7	8	9		11		10		4												9
1	2	3	12	5	6	7	8			11		10		9	4[1]											10
1	2	3	4	5	6	7	8	9[1]	12	11					10											11
1	2	3	4	5	6	7	8	9	10[1]	11					12											12
1	2	3	4	5	6	7[1]		9	10	11				12	8											13
1	2	3	4	5	6	7		9	10	11					8											14
1	2	3	4	5	6	7		9	10	11					8											15
1		3	2	5	6	7	8	9	10	11[1]				12	4											16
	2[2]	3	4	5	6	7[1]	8	9	10[3]	11		13	14	12			1									17
	2	3	4[2]	5	6	7	8	9		11[1]			12	10[3]	13	14	1									18
	2	3		5				9		11			8	12	4[3]	13	1		14	6	7[2]	10[1]				19
	2		4	5	6	7		9		3			8[2]	13	12		1					11	10[1]			20
	2		4	5	6	7	8	9		3				12			1					11[1]	10			21
5	2			6	7	8	9		3				12	13	4		1					11[1]	10[2]			22
5	2[2]			6		8	9		3				7[1]	12	4		1		13			11	10			23
	2			6		8	9		3				7		4		1		5	12		11	10[1]			24
2[1]		12		6	7	8	9		3						4		1		5			11	10			25
	4	5	2	7	8	9			3				12				1		6			11[1]	10			26
	2	4	5	3	7	8	9	12					11[1]				1		6				10			27
	2[2]		4		6	7	8	9	12	3			13		11		1		5				10[1]			28
	2		4	5	3[2]	7		9	12	11			13		8		1						10[1]		6	29
	2		7	5		8	9	10[1]	3				12		4	13	1					11[2]			6	30
	2	12	4	5	13	7	8[2]	9	10[1]	3			14				1					11[3]			6	31
	2	12	4	5	13	7	8[2]	9	10[1]	3			14				1					11[3]			6	32
	2	3	4	5[3]	8	7		9	10[1]	11[2]				12			1		14	13			6			33
	2	3	4	5	8	7		9	10[1]					12	11		1						6			34
		3	4	5	8	7		9	10				12		11					2[1]			6			35
	2	3	4	5	8	7		9	10	11[1]	12						1		13				6[2]			36
1	2	3	4	5		7		9	10	11	12		8[1]										6			37
1	2	3	4	5	6	7	8[1]	9	10														12	11[2]	13	38
1	2	3	4	5	6	7	8	9	10[1]														12		11	39
1	2	3	4	5	6	7	8	9[1]	10														12	13	11[2]	40
1	2	3	4	5	6	7[1]	8		10					12									9	13	11[2]	41
1	2	3	4	5	6	7	8	9	10														12		11[1]	42
1	2	3	4	5	6	7	8	9	10												11[1]		12			43
	2[1]	3	4	5	6	7	8	9	10				13		12		1								11[2]	44
		3	4	5	6	7[1]	8	9	10				13		12		1			2					11[2]	45
		3	4	5	6	7	8[2]	9	10				13	14	12		1			2[1]					11[3]	46

Worthington Cup

First Round	Port Vale	(a)	2-1	
		(h)	2-2	
Second Round	Sunderland	(a)	0-3	
		(h)	0-1	

FA Cup

First Round	Cardiff C	(a)	0-6

Division 2   **CHESTERFIELD**

FOUNDATION

Chesterfield are fourth only to Stoke, Notts County and Nottingham Forest in age for they can trace their existence as far back as 1866, although it is fair to say that they were somewhat casual in the first few years of their history playing only a few friendlies a year. However, their rules of 1871 are still in existence showing an annual membership of 2s (10p), but it was not until 1891 that they won a trophy (the Barnes Cup) and followed this a year later by winning the Sheffield Cup, Barnes Cup and the Derbyshire Junior Cup.

Recreation Ground, Chesterfield S40 4SX.

Telephone: (01246) 209765.

Fax: (01246) 556799.

Commercial Dept: (01246) 231535.

Spireites Hotline: 0891 555818.

Ground Capacity: 8880.

Record Attendance: 30,968 v Newcastle U, Division 2, 7 April 1939.

Record Receipts: £45,000 v Mansfield T, Division 3 play-off semi-final, 17 May 1995.

Pitch Measurements: 113yd × 71yd.

President: His Grace the Duke of Devonshire MC, DL, JP.

Chairman: J. Norton Lea.

Vice-Chairman: B. W. Hubbard.

Directors: R. F. Pepper, M. L. Warner.

Manager: John Duncan.

Assistant Manager: Kevin Randall.

Physio: Dave Rushbury.

Secretary: Stephanie Otter.

Commercial Manager: Jim Brown.

Stadium Manager: W. W. Kenworthy.

LATEST SEQUENCES

Longest Sequence of League Wins: 10, 6.9.33 – 4.11.33.

Longest Sequence of League Defeats: 9, 22.10.60 – 27.12.60.

Longest Sequence of League Draws: 5, 19.9.90 – 6.10.90.

Longest Sequence of Unbeaten League Matches: 21, 26.12.94 – 29.4.95.

Longest Sequence Without a League Win: 16, 26.2.83 – 14.5.83.

HONOURS

Football League: Division 2 best season: 4th, 1946–47; Division 3 (N) – Champions 1930–31, 1935–36; Runners-up 1933–34; Division 4 – Champions 1969–70, 1984–85.

FA Cup: Semi-final 1997.

Football League Cup: best season: 4th rd, 1965.

Anglo-Scottish Cup: Winners 1981.

Colours
Blue shirts, white shorts, blue stockings.

Change Colours
White shirts, blue shorts, white stockings.

Year Formed: 1866.

Turned Professional: 1891.

Ltd Co: 1871.

Previous Name: Chesterfield Town.

Club Nickname: 'Blues' or 'Spireites'.

First Football League Game: 2 September 1899, Division 2, v Sheffield W (a) L 1–5 – Hancock; Pilgrim, Fletcher; Ballantyne, Bell, Downie; Morley, Thacker, Gooing, Munday (1), Geary.

Record League Victory: 10–0 v Glossop NE, Division 2, 17 January 1903 – Clutterbuck; Thorpe, Lerper; Haig, Banner, Thacker; Tomlinson (2), Newton (1), Milward (3), Munday (2), Steel (2).

Record Cup Victory: 5–0 v Wath Ath (a), FA Cup 1st rd, 28 November 1925 – Birch; Saxby, Dennis; Wass, Abbott, Thompson; Fisher (1), Roseboom (1), Cookson (2), Whitfield (1), Hopkinson.

Record Defeat: 0–10 v Gillingham, Division 3, 5 September 1987.

Most League Points (2 for a win): 64, Division 4, 1969–70.

Most League Points (3 for a win): 91, Division 4, 1984–85.

Most League Goals: 102, Division 3 (N), 1930–31.

Highest League Scorer in Season: Jimmy Cookson, 44, Division 3 (N), 1925–26.

Most League Goals in Total Aggregate: Ernie Moss, 161, 1969–76, 1979–81 and 1984–86.

Most League Goals in One Match: 4, Jimmy Cookson v Accrington S, Division 3N, 16 January 1926; 4, Jimmy Cookson v Ashington, Division 3N, 1 May 1926; 4, Jimmy Cookson v Wigan Borough, Division 3N, 4 September 1926; 4, Tommy Lyon v Southampton, Division 2, 3 December 1938.

Most Capped Player: Walter McMillen, 4 (7), Northern Ireland; Mark Williams, 4, Northern Ireland.

Most League Appearances: Dave Blakey, 613, 1948–67.

Youngest League Player: Dennis Thompson, 16 years 160 days v Notts Co, 26 December 1950.

Record Transfer Fee Received: £750,000 from Southampton for Kevin Davies, May 1997.

Record Transfer Fee Paid: £250,000 to Watford for Jason Lee, August 1998.

Football League Record: 1899 Elected to Division 2; 1909 failed re-election; 1921–31 Division 3 (N); 1931–33 Division 2; 1933–36 Division 3 (N); 1936–51 Division 2; 1951–58 Division 3 (N); 1958–61 Division 3; 1961–70 Division 4; 1970–83 Division 3; 1983–85 Division 4; 1985–89 Division 3; 1989–92 Division 4; 1992–95 Division 3; 1995– Division 2.

MANAGERS

E. Russell Timmeus 1891–95 *(Secretary-Manager)*
Gilbert Gillies 1895–1901
E. F. Hind 1901–02
Jack Hoskin 1902–06
W. Furness 1906–07
George Swift 1907–10
G. H. Jones 1911–13
R. L. Weston 1913–17
T. Callaghan 1919
J. J. Caffrey 1920–22
Harry Hadley 1922
Harry Parkes 1922–27
Alec Campbell 1927
Ted Davison 1927–32
Bill Harvey 1932–38
Norman Bullock 1938–45
Bob Brocklebank 1945–48
Bobby Marshall 1948–52
Ted Davison 1952–58
Duggie Livingstone 1958–62
Tony McShane 1962–67
Jimmy McGuigan 1967–73
Joe Shaw 1973–76
Arthur Cox 1976–80
Frank Barlow 1980–83
John Duncan 1983–87
Kevin Randall 1987–88
Paul Hart 1988–91
Chris McMenemy 1991–93
John Duncan February 1993–

TEN YEAR LEAGUE RECORD

		P	W	D	L	F	A	Pts	Pos
1988-89	Div 3	46	14	7	25	51	86	49	22
1989-90	Div 4	46	19	14	13	63	50	71	7
1990-91	Div 4	46	13	14	19	47	62	53	18
1991-92	Div 4	42	14	11	17	49	61	53	13
1992-93	Div 3	42	15	11	16	59	63	56	12
1993-94	Div 3	42	16	14	12	55	48	62	8
1994-95	Div 3	42	23	12	7	62	37	81	3
1995-96	Div 2	46	20	12	14	56	51	72	7
1996-97	Div 2	46	18	14	14	42	39	68	10
1997-98	Div 2	46	16	17	13	46	44	65	10

DID YOU KNOW ?

On 10 November 1998, Tom Curtis made a 40-yard run before scoring his second goal of the game in the 3–1 win over Bournemouth. It was an historic strike since it was the 5000th in Chesterfield's Football League history.

CHESTERFIELD 1998–99 LEAGUE RECORD

Match No.	Date	Venue	Opponents	Result	Score	H/T Lg. Pos.	Goalscorers	Attendance
1	Aug 8	A	Colchester U	L	0-1	0-0	—		4042
2	15	H	Burnley	W	1-0	0-0	15	Reeves (pen) [89]	5426
3	22	A	Oldham Ath	L	0-2	0-1	20		4548
4	29	H	Reading	W	1-0	1-0	12	Howard [35]	4145
5	31	A	Preston NE	L	0-2	0-0	13		9249
6	Sept 5	H	Gillingham	W	1-0	0-0	10	Holland [53]	3766
7	8	A	Bristol R	D	0-0	0-0	—		5416
8	12	H	Walsall	L	0-1	0-0	15		4169
9	19	A	Manchester C	D	1-1	1-1	15	Reeves [28]	27,500
10	26	H	Wrexham	W	2-1	2-0	12	Howard 2 [8, 17]	3681
11	Oct 3	A	Millwall	D	0-0	0-0	15		5178
12	12	A	Stoke C	D	0-0	0-0	—		10,557
13	17	H	York C	W	2-1	1-1	11	Williams [45], Reeves (pen) [67]	4113
14	20	A	Notts Co	W	3-0	2-0	—	Holland 2 [19, 62], Williams [44]	4506
15	Nov 7	H	Lincoln C	W	3-0	1-0	8	Reeves (pen) [29], Perkins [50], Howard [90]	4694
16	10	H	Bournemouth	W	3-1	2-1	—	Curtis 2 [25, 77], Ebdon [39]	3797
17	21	A	Fulham	L	1-2	0-1	8	Howard [62]	10,005
18	28	H	Macclesfield T	W	2-0	1-0	6	Reeves [31], Hewitt [82]	4788
19	Dec 5	A	Blackpool	D	1-1	0-0	6	Howard [77]	3278
20	12	A	Northampton T	L	0-1	0-0	6		5282
21	19	H	Wigan Ath	D	1-1	1-1	7	Wilkinson [22]	3896
22	26	H	Oldham Ath	L	1-3	1-1	8	Wilkinson [1]	5448
23	28	A	Wycombe W	L	0-1	0-0	11		5391
24	Jan 2	A	Reading	W	2-1	2-0	8	Curtis [33], Breckin [44]	10,409
25	9	H	Colchester U	W	3-1	0-0	7	Wilkinson [62], Howard [69], Reeves [82]	3761
26	16	H	Burnley	W	2-1	1-0	7	Pickering (og) [30], Beaumont [65]	10,985
27	23	H	Preston NE	L	0-1	0-0	7		6138
28	30	H	Wycombe W	W	2-0	1-0	7	Howard [20], Wilkinson [65]	4248
29	Feb 6	A	Gillingham	L	1-3	0-1	8	Howard [71]	6582
30	20	A	Walsall	D	1-1	1-1	10	Williams [11]	5268
31	27	H	Manchester C	D	1-1	1-0	10	Reeves [32]	8245
32	Mar 2	H	Millwall	W	2-1	0-0	—	Reeves 2 [46, 47]	3372
33	6	A	Wrexham	D	0-0	0-0	8		3224
34	13	A	Lincoln C	L	0-2	0-1	10		5262
35	20	H	Luton T	W	3-1	0-0	10	Wilkinson 2 [52, 56], Reeves [66]	3921
36	27	H	Blackpool	L	1-2	0-1	11	Lee [81]	4027
37	Apr 3	A	York C	W	2-1	1-0	10	Lenagh [44], Beaumont [60]	3356
38	5	H	Stoke C	D	1-1	1-1	10	Blatherwick [26]	5290
39	10	A	Notts Co	L	0-2	0-1	10		5121
40	13	A	Macclesfield T	L	0-2	0-1	—		2216
41	17	H	Fulham	W	1-0	0-0	10	Hewitt [77]	5800
42	20	A	Bristol R	D	0-0	0-0	—		2621
43	24	A	Bournemouth	D	0-0	0-0	9		6890
44	27	A	Luton T	L	0-1	0-0	—		4287
45	May 3	H	Northampton T	D	0-0	0-0	—		5110
46	8	A	Wigan Ath	L	1-3	1-1	9	Breckin [28]	5858

Final League Position: 9

GOALSCORERS

League (46): Reeves 10 (3 pens), Howard 9, Wilkinson 6, Curtis 3, Holland 3, Williams 3, Beaumont 2, Breckin 2, Hewitt 2, Blatherwick 1, Ebdon 1, Lee 1, Lenagh 1, Perkins 1, own goal 1.
Worthington Cup (4): Holland 2, Howard 1, Reeves 1.
FA Cup (0).

Mercer B 44	Hewitt J 40	Perkins C 32 + 2	Curtis T 24	Williams M 40	Breckin I 44	Willis R 7 + 10	Holland P 32 + 1	Reeves D 37 + 3	Wilkinson S 18 + 5	Howard J 34 + 3	Beaumont C 35 + 4	Jules M 19 + 4	Ebdon M 39 + 1	Lee J 14 + 8	Lomas J 5 + 2	Leaning A 2	Blatherwick S 9 + 5	Nicholson S 23 + 1	Pearce G — + 1	Morris A — + 1	Lenagh S 6 + 4	Carss T 2 + 2	Simpkins M — + 1	Match No.
1	2	3	4	5	6	7	8	9	10	11¹	12													1
1	2	3	4	5	6	7	8	9	10¹	11	12													2
1	2	3		5	6	7	8	9	10¹	11		4	12											3
1	2	3		5	6	7¹	8	9	10	11			4	12										4
1	2	3		5	6	12	8		9	13	11²	4		10¹	7									5
1	2	3		5	6		8	9	4¹	11	12		10		7									6
1	2	3		5	6		8	9	12	11¹	13		10		7	4²								7
1	2	3		5	6	12	8	9	4¹	11			10		7									8
	2	3			6	7¹	8	9	4²	12	5	11	10	13		1								9
	2	11			6		8²	9		7¹	4	3	10	12	13	1	5							10
1					6		8	9		7	2	3	10	12	4¹		5	11¹²	13					11
1	2	11		5	6		8	9		7		4	10					3						12
1	2	11	4	5	6		8	9		7			10					3						13
1	2	11	4	5	6		8	9		7			10					3						14
1	2	11	4	5	6		8	9		7			10					3						15
1	2	11	4	5	6		8	9		7			10					3						16
1	2	11²	4	5	6		8	9	12	7	10¹	3										13		17
1	2	11	4	5	6			9		7	8	3	10											18
1	2	11¹	4	5	6			9	12	7	8	3	10											19
1	2	11²	4	5	6			9		7	8	3¹	10				12					13		20
1	2		4	5	6			9	11¹	7	8	3	10				12							21
1	2		4	5	6	7¹		11		8	12	10					9	3²				13		22
1	2		4	5	6	12		11¹		8	7	10					3	9						23
1	2		4	5	6	12		11¹		8	7	10					3	9						24
1	2	12	4	5	6		13	11	7¹	8		10					3	9²						25
1		2¹	4³	5	6		9	11²	7	8	13	10	12		14		3							26
1	2			5	6	12		9	11	7	8	4¹	10					3						27
1	2			5	6			9	11	7	8	4	10					3						28
1	2³		4	5	6		12	9²	11	7	8¹		10	13			14	3						29
1		2	4	5	6		8	9		7	11		12					3						30
1		2	4²	5	6		8	9		7¹	11		10	12			13	3						31
1		2	4	5	6		8	9		7	11		10					3						32
1		2	4	5	6		8	9¹		7	11		10	12				3						33
1	2	3³	4			12		8	9	13	7	6	10²	11¹			5	14						34
1	2		4	5				8	9	11	7¹	10		12			6	3						35
1	2		4		6	12	8²	9	11		7¹	14	13	10			5	3³						36
1	2	11		5	6		8	12			4		10	9¹				3			7			37
1	2		5	6	12		9		8	11	10	7	4	3¹										38
1	2	4²	5	6	7¹		12		8	11	10	9					3³				13	14		39
1	2¹	11		5	6	12	8	9			4	3	10	7										40
1	2	11		5	6		8	9			4	3	10	7										41
1	2			5	6		8	9		12	4	3¹	10	7	11									42
1	2	3		5	6		8	9		7¹	4		10		11²						12	13		43
1	2	12			6	13	8			7	4		3¹	10			5				9²	11		44
1	2	3		5	6		8			7	4			9			10					11		45
1	2	3		5	6		8			12	4		10²	9	11						7¹	13		46

Worthington Cup

First Round	Rotherham U	(a)	1-0
		(h)	2-0
Second Round	Leicester C	(a)	0-3
		(h)	1-3

FA Cup

First Round	Wycombe W	(a)	0-1

Division 2   **COLCHESTER UNITED**

FOUNDATION

Colchester United was formed in 1937 when a number of enthusiasts of the much older Colchester Town club decided to establish a professional concern as a limited liability company. The new club continued at Layer Road which had been the amateur club's home since 1909.

Layer Rd Ground, Colchester, Essex CO2 7JJ.
Telephone: (01206) 508800.
Fax: (01206) 508803.
Club Shop: (01206) 561180.
Soccer Centre: (01206) 571581.
Lottery: (01206) 508820.
Ground Capacity: 7556.
Record Attendance: 19,072 v Reading, FA Cup 1st rd, 27 November 1948.
Record Receipts: £26,330 v Barrow, GM Vauxhall Conference, 2 May 1992.
Pitch Measurements: 110yd × 71yd.
Patron: The Mayor of Colchester.
Chairman: Peter Heard.
Directors: Gordon Parker, John Worsp, Peter Powell.
Managing Director: Stephen Gage.
Manager: Mick Wadsworth.
Assistant Manager/Coach: Steve Whitton.
Youth Coach: Micky Cook.
Physio: Brian Owen.
Consultant Physio: Ray Cole.
Secretary: Mrs Marie Partner.
Marketing Manager: John Schultz.
Commercial Manager: Brian Wheeler.
Lottery Manager: John Cross.
Stadium Manager: David Blacknall.

LATEST SEQUENCES
Longest Sequence of League Wins: 7, 29.11.68 – 1.2.69.
Longest Sequence of League Defeats: 8, 9.10.54 – 4.12.54.
Longest Sequence of League Draws: 6, 21.3.77 – 11.4.77.
Longest Sequence of Unbeaten League Matches: 20, 22.12.56 – 19.4.57.
Longest Sequence Without a League Win: 20, 2.3.68 – 31.8.68.

HONOURS

Football League: Promoted from Division 3 – 1997–98 (play-offs); Division 4 – Runners-up 1961–62.

FA Cup: best season: 6th rd, 1971.

Football League Cup: best season: 5th rd, 1975.

Auto Windscreens Shield: Runners-up 1997.

GM Vauxhall Conference: Winners 1991–92.

FA Trophy: Winners 1992.

Colours
Blue and white striped shirts, navy shorts, white stockings.

Change Colours
All white with blue trim.

Year Formed: 1937.

Turned Professional: 1937.

Ltd Co.: 1937.

Club Nickname: 'The U's'.

First Football League Game: 19 August 1950, Division 3 (S), v Gillingham (a) D 0–0 – Wright; Kettle, Allen; Bearryman, Stewart, Elder; Jones, Curry, Turner, McKim, Church.

Record League Victory: 9–1 v Bradford C, Division 4, 30 December 1961 – Ames; Millar, Fowler; Harris, Abrey, Ron Hunt; Foster, Bobby Hunt (4), King (4), Hill (1), Wright.

Record Cup Victory: 7–1 v Yeovil T (away), FA Cup 2nd rd (replay), 11 December 1958 – Ames; Fisher, Fowler; Parker, Milligan, Hammond; Williams (1), McLeod (2), Langman (4), Evans, Wright. 7–1 v Yeading, FA Cup 1st rd (replay), 22 November 1994 – Cheesewright; Betts, English, Cawley, Caesar, Locke (Dennis), Fry, Brown (2), Whitton (2) (Thompson), Kinsella (1), Abrahams (2).

Record Defeat: 0–8 v Leyton Orient, Division 4, 15 October 1989.

Most League Points (2 for a win): 60, Division 4, 1973–74.

Most League Points (3 for a win): 81, Division 4, 1982–83.

Most League Goals: 104, Division 4, 1961–62.

Highest League Scorer in Season: Bobby Hunt, 38, Division 4, 1961–62.

Most League Goals in Total Aggregate: Martyn King, 130, 1956–64.

Most League Goals in One Match: 4, Bobby Hunt v Bradford C, Division 4, 30 December 1961; 4, Martyn King v Bradford C, Division 4, 30 December 1961; 4, Bobby Hunt v Doncaster R, Division 4, 30 April 1962.

Most Capped Player: None.

Most League Appearances: Micky Cook, 613, 1969–84.

Youngest League Player: Lindsay Smith, 16 years 218 days v Grimsby T, 24 April 1971.

Record Transfer Fee Received: £150,000 from Charlton Ath for Mark Kinsella, September 1996.

Record Transfer Fee Paid: £50,000 to Ipswich T for Neil Gregory, March 1998.

Football League Record: 1950 Elected to Division 3 (S); 1958–61 Division 3; 1961–62 Division 4; 1962–65 Division 3; 1965–66 Division 4; 1966–68 Division 3; 1968–74 Division 4; 1974–76 Division 3; 1976–77 Division 4; 1977–81 Division 3; 1981–90 Division 4; 1990–92 GM Vauxhall Conference; 1992–98 Division 3; 1998– Division 2.

MANAGERS

Ted Fenton 1946–48
Jimmy Allen 1948–53
Jack Butler 1953–55
Benny Fenton 1955–63
Neil Franklin 1963–68
Dick Graham 1968–72
Jim Smith 1972–75
Bobby Roberts 1975–82
Allan Hunter 1982–83
Cyril Lea 1983–86
Mike Walker 1986–87
Roger Brown 1987–88
Jock Wallace 1989
Mick Mills 1990
Ian Atkins 1990–91
Roy McDonough 1991–94
George Burley 1994
Steve Wignall 1995–99
Mick Wadsworth February 1999–

TEN YEAR LEAGUE RECORD

		P	W	D	L	F	A	Pts	Pos
1988-89	Div 4	46	12	14	20	60	78	50	22
1989-90	Div 4	46	11	10	25	48	75	43	24
1990-91	Conf	42	25	10	7	68	35	85	2
1991-92	Conf	42	28	10	4	98	40	94	1
1992-93	Div 3	42	18	5	19	67	76	59	10
1993-94	Div 3	42	13	10	19	56	71	49	17
1994-95	Div 3	42	16	10	16	56	64	58	10
1995-96	Div 3	46	18	18	10	61	51	72	7
1996-97	Div 3	46	17	17	12	62	51	68	8
1997-98	Div 3	46	21	11	14	72	60	74	4

DID YOU KNOW ?

On 23 August 1947 at the start of their English tour, the Dutch club PEC Zwolle were beaten 3–2 by Colchester United for whom Bob Allen, Bob Curry and Arthur Turner (penalty) were on the goalscoring mark.

COLCHESTER UNITED 1998–99 LEAGUE RECORD

Match No.	Date	Venue	Opponents	Result	H/T Score	Lg. Pos.	Goalscorers	Attendance
1	Aug 8	H	Chesterfield	W 1-0	0-0	—	Sale [90]	4042
2	15	A	Wrexham	W 4-2	2-0	2	Abrahams [16], Haydon [43], Gregory N [48], Gregory D (pen) [64]	4157
3	22	H	Fulham	L 0-1	0-0	5		6377
4	29	A	Luton T	L 0-2	0-0	11		5005
5	31	H	Stoke C	L 0-1	0-0	12		4728
6	Sept 5	A	York C	W 2-1	1-0	9	Gregory N [2], Forbes [87]	2699
7	8	A	Wigan Ath	D 1-1	0-0	—	Sale [52]	2784
8	12	H	Gillingham	D 1-1	1-1	11	Gregory N [28]	4612
9	19	A	Reading	D 1-1	0-1	12	Duguid [87]	9058
10	26	H	Wycombe W	W 2-1	0-0	10	Forbes [65], Gregory D (pen) [89]	4205
11	Oct 3	A	Oldham Ath	L 0-1	0-1	13		4231
12	9	H	Burnley	L 0-4	0-2	—		5532
13	17	A	Preston NE	L 0-2	0-2	17		10,483
14	20	A	Walsall	D 1-1	0-0	—	Lock [81]	3319
15	31	A	Manchester C	L 1-2	0-0	20	Dozzell [58]	24,820
16	Nov 6	H	Macclesfield T	D 1-1	0-1	—	Greene [75]	3927
17	10	H	Northampton T	W 1-0	0-0	—	Greene [88]	3597
18	21	A	Notts Co	W 3-1	2-0	14	Greene 2 [10, 22], Gregory D [47]	4598
19	28	H	Millwall	D 0-0	0-0	15		4476
20	Dec 12	A	Lincoln C	D 0-0	0-0	15		4513
21	18	H	Blackpool	D 2-2	1-1	—	Greene [7], Gregory D [78]	3228
22	26	A	Fulham	L 0-2	0-1	15		11,939
23	28	H	Bristol R	L 0-3	0-2	16		4609
24	Jan 2	H	Luton T	D 2-2	1-1	16	Gregory D (pen) [21], Abrahams [84]	4694
25	9	A	Chesterfield	L 1-3	0-0	17	Lua-Lua [75]	3761
26	15	A	Wrexham	L 1-3	1-3	—	Wilkins [16]	3491
27	23	A	Stoke C	D 3-3	2-3	17	Betts [9], Gregory D [45], Dozzell [79]	12,507
28	30	A	Bristol R	D 1-1	0-1	18	Gregory D (pen) [88]	6249
29	Feb 5	H	York C	W 2-1	2-0	—	Betts [1], Greene [4]	3982
30	12	A	Wigan Ath	W 2-1	2-0	—	Wilkins [22], Gregory D [28]	3934
31	20	A	Gillingham	D 1-1	0-1	16	Duguid [64]	7276
32	27	H	Reading	D 1-1	1-0	15	Gregory N [8]	4686
33	Mar 6	A	Wycombe W	D 2-2	1-0	16	Dozzell [18], Gregory D (pen) [90]	4670
34	9	A	Oldham Ath	D 2-2	1-0	—	Allen [40], Gregory D (pen) [67]	3616
35	13	A	Macclesfield T	L 0-2	0-0	16		2796
36	20	H	Manchester C	L 0-1	0-0	17		6554
37	27	A	Bournemouth	L 1-2	1-2	19	Greene [20]	6447
38	Apr 2	H	Preston NE	W 1-0	0-0	—	Aspinall [78]	5644
39	5	A	Burnley	L 1-3	1-0	18	Gregory D [26]	10,747
40	10	H	Walsall	W 1-0	1-0	17	Greene [45]	4082
41	14	A	Millwall	L 0-2	0-2	—		4686
42	16	H	Notts Co	W 2-1	1-0	—	Buckle [37], Aspinall (pen) [86]	4215
43	24	A	Northampton T	D 3-3	1-2	18	Buckle [3], Aspinall (pen) [47], Duguid [71]	6146
44	27	H	Bournemouth	W 2-1	1-1	—	Hayter (og) [11], Dozzell [67]	4168
45	May 1	H	Lincoln C	L 1-3	0-2	17	Duguid [49]	4613
46	8	A	Blackpool	L 1-2	1-1	18	Pounewatchy [27]	4866

Final League Position: 18

GOALSCORERS
League (52): Gregory D 11 (6 pens), Greene 8, Dozzell 4, Duguid 4, Gregory N 4, Aspinall 3 (2 pens), Abrahams 2, Betts 2, Buckle 2, Forbes 2, Sale 2, Wilkins 2, Allen 1, Haydon 1, Lock 1, Lua-Lua 1, Pounewatchy 1, own goal 1.
Worthington Cup (3): Gregory D 2 (2 pens), Abrahams 1.
FA Cup (1): Adcock 1.

Emberson C 37	Betts S 22 + 6	Stamps S 19 + 2	Williams G 38 + 1	Greene D 42	Buckle P 39 + 4	Wilkins R 25 + 1	Gregory D 43 + 1	Sale M 21 + 10	Lock T 14 + 9	Abrahams P 13 + 14	Duguid K 23 + 10	Dunne J 32 + 4	Gregory N 29 + 9	Haydon N 7 + 6	Adcock T — + 6	Wiles I — + 1	Forbes S 8 + 7	Rainford D — + 1	Skelton A 7 + 2	Branston G — + 1	Dozzell J 23 + 6	Dublin K 2	Fernandes T 8	Lua-Lua L 6 + 7	Pounewatchy S 15	Aspinall W 15	Allen B 4	Fumaca J 1	Richard F 10	Launders B 1	Germain S 1 + 5	Walker A 1	Okafor S — + 1	Opara C — + 1	Match No.
1	2	3	4	5	6	7[1]	8[2]	9	10[3]	11	12	13	14																						1
1	2	3	4	5	6		8	9		11[3]	12	10[2]	7[1]	13	14																				2
1		3	4	5	6	7	8	9[1]		11[3]		2[3]	10	13	12		14																		3
1		3[2]	4	5	6	7	8	9		11	12	2[3]	10[1]	13			14																		4
1		3	4	5	6[2]	7	8	9		12	11[1]	10	2		13																				5
1	12	3	4	5	6	7[1]	8	9		11[2]		10[3]	2			13	14																		6
1	12	3	4	5	6		8	9		11[2]		13	10	2[1]			7																		7
1		3[1]	4	5	6		8	9		11		13	2	10	12		7[2]																		8
1	12	3	4	5	6		8	9		11[3]		14	2	10[2]		13	7[1]																		9
1		3	4	5	6		8	9		11[2]		13	2	10[1]	12		7																		10
1		3	4[2]	5	6[3]		8	9		11[1]	12	2	10				7		13	14															11
1		3[1]	4	5	6		8	9[3]	12	11	13	2	10				7[2]		14																12
1	12	3	4[1]	5	6		8	9		11[2]	13	2	10				7[3]				14														13
1		3	4	5	6		8	9[1]	12	11		2	10		13						7[2]														14
1		3	4	5	6		8	12	9	13	11[2]	2	10[1]								7														15
1			4[1]	5	6		8	12	9		11[2]	2	10[3]	3		14	13				7														16
1		3	4	5	6		8	9	10[2]			2	12	13		11[1]					7														17
1		3	4	5	6		8	9[2]	10[1]	11		2	12		13						7														18
1		3	4	5	6		8	9[2]	10[2]	11[1]		2	12		13	14					7														19
1		3[1]	11	4	5	6	7	8		13	12	10[2]	2								9														20
1		3	11	4	5	7	8		12	13	6[1]	2	10[2]								9														21
1		3	11[2]	4	5	6	7	8	12	14	10[1]	2		13							9[1]														22
1		3	4[1]	5	6	7	8	12	11	13		2[3]	10[2]	14							9														23
		3	4[3]	5	6	7	8	9[2]	12	10	11[1]	2	13	14									1												24
		3	4	5	6	7	8[1]	9	12	10[2]	11		2										1	13											25
			4	5		7	8	9	6[1]	10	11	2		3								3	1	12											26
1		3	4	5	6	7	8		12	11[1]		2	10[2]				9				13														27
1		3	4	5	6	7[2]	8		12	11[1]		2	10[3]				9				13				14										28
1		3	4	5		7	8			11		2	10[1]				6				9					12									29
1		3	4	5	12	7	8			11[2]		2	10[2]				6				9					13									30
				5	10	7[2]	8[3]	12	13	11		2		14			6				9[1]				3	4									31
1		3	4[1]	5			8			12	13	2	10[2]						14		6			9					7		11[3]				32
1		5		4		12		8	13	14		2	10						6[1]		11[3]					7	3		9[2]						33
1		3	4[2]		6		8	12	13			2	10[3]	11[1]			14		5							7			9[2]						34
1			12	6	7	8[1]	11		2	3	13	10			14				5							4[3]			9[2]						35
1	13		5	6		8	12[2]		3	2	10		9								4					7			11[1]						36
1	12		4	5	6[3]	8		13		2[1]	10[2]			14			11				7				3	9									37
1			4	5	12	8		11		3	13		9[3]				10[2]	6	7[1]		2				14										38
1	12		4[3]	5	13	3[1]	8	11		9	10			6	7[2]				2					14											39
1			4	5	7	12	8	13		11[2]	3[1]		9	10			6		2																40
			4[2]	5	6	7	8[1]	14	13[3]	12			9	1		10	3	11		2															41
			4	5	6	7		12		10[1]			9	1		11	3	8		2															42
			4	5	6	7	12			11[2]	13		10[1]	9[3]			1		3		8							2			14				43
			4[1]	12		5	6[2]	7	8		13		11[3]	9			1		3		10							2			14				44
				4		5	6	7[1]	8		12		11	9[2]			1		3		10							2			13				45
					5	6	7	8[1]		4			11		3		10		2		9[2]		1								12	13			46

Worthington Cup
First Round　　Bournemouth　　(a)　0-2
　　　　　　　　　　　　　　　　(h)　3-2

FA Cup
First Round　　Bedlington T　　(a)　1-4

FA Premiership

COVENTRY CITY

Highfield Road Stadium, King Richard Street, Coventry CV2 4FW.
Telephone: (02476) 234000.
Fax: (02476) 234099.
Ticket Office: (02476) 234020.
Ticket Office Fax: (02476) 234023.
Sales & Marketing: (02476) 234010.
Clubcall: 0891 121166.
Website: http://www.ccfc.co.uk.
Email: chris.m@ccfc.co.uk.
Ground Capacity: 23,611.
Record Attendance: 51,455 v Wolverhampton W, Division 2, 29 April 1967.
Record Receipts: £375,510 v Sheffield U, FA Cup 6th Rd, 7 March 1998.
Pitch Measurements: 110yd × 75yd.
President: E. W. Grove.
Chairman: B. A. Richardson.
Deputy Chairman: M. C. McGinnity.
Directors: A. M. Jepson, J. F. W Reason, D. A. Higgs, Miss B. Price.
Secretary: Graham Hover.
Manager: Gordon Strachan.
Coaches: Garry Pendrey and Trevor Peake.
Physio: Stuart Collie.
Marketing: Ric Allison.
Stadium Manager: Don Blair.
Club Statistician: Jim Brown.

LATEST SEQUENCES
Longest Sequence of League Wins: 6, 25.4.64 – 5.9.64.
Longest Sequence of League Defeats: 9, 30.8.19 – 11.10.19.
Longest Sequence of League Draws: 6, 28.9.96 – 16.11.96.
Longest Sequence of Unbeaten League Matches: 25, 26.11.66 – 13.5.67.
Longest Sequence Without a League Win: 19, 30.8.19 – 20.12.19.

HONOURS

Football League: Division 1 best season: 6th, 1969–70; Division 2 – Champions 1966–67; Division 3 – Champions 1963–64; Division 3 (S) – Champions 1935–36; Runners-up 1933–34; Division 4 – Runners-up 1958–59.

FA Cup: Winners 1987.

Football League Cup: Semi-final 1981, 1990.

European Competitions: European Fairs Cup: 1970–71.

Colours
Sky blue shirts with navy panels and white trim, sky blue shorts with navy panels, sky blue stockings with navy trim.

Change Colours
White shirts with black panels and red trim, black shorts, white stockings with black trim.

Year Formed: 1883.

Turned Professional: 1893.

Ltd Co.: 1907.

Previous Names: 1883, Singers FC; 1898, Coventry City FC.

Club Nickname: 'Sky Blues'.

Previous Grounds: 1883, Binley Road; 1887, Stoke Road; 1899, Highfield Road.

First Football League Game: 30 August 1919, Division 2, v Tottenham H (h) L 0–5 – Lindon; Roberts, Chaplin, Allan, Hawley, Clarke, Sheldon, Mercer, Sambrooke, Lowes, Gibson.

Record League Victory: 9–0 v Bristol C, Division 3 (S), 28 April 1934 – Pearson; Brown, Bisby; Perry, Davidson, Frith; White (2), Lauderdale, Bourton (5), Jones (2), Lake.

Record Cup Victory: 7–0 v Scunthorpe U, FA Cup 1st rd, 24 November 1934 – Pearson; Brown, Bisby; Mason, Davidson, Boileau; Birtley (2), Lauderdale (2), Bourton (1), Jones (1), Liddle (1).

Record Defeat: 2–10 v Norwich C, Division 3 (S), 15 March 1930.

Most League Points (2 for a win): 60, Division 4, 1958–59 and Division 3, 1963–64.

Most League Points (3 for a win): 63, Division 1, 1986–87.

Most League Goals: 108, Division 3 (S), 1931–32.

Highest League Scorer in Season: Clarrie Bourton, 49, Division 3 (S), 1931–32.

Most League Goals in Total Aggregate: Clarrie Bourton, 171, 1931–37.

Most League Goals in One Match: 5, Clarrie Bourton v Bournemouth, Division 3S, 17 October 1931; 5, Arthur Bacon v Gillingham, Division 3S, 30 December 1933.

Most Capped Player: Peter Ndlovu 26 (37) Zimbabwe.

Most League Appearances: Steve Ogrizovic, 504, 1984–99.

Youngest League Player: Gary McSheffrey, 16 years 198 days v Aston Villa, 27 February 1999.

Record Transfer Fee Received: £5,750,000 from Aston Villa for Dion Dublin, November 1998.

Record Transfer Fee Paid: £4,000,000 to Deportivo La Coruna for Mustapha Hadji, July 1999.

Football League Record: 1919 Elected to Division 2; 1925–26 Division 3 (N); 1926–36 Division 3 (S); 1936–52 Division 2; 1952–58 Division 3 (S); 1958–59 Division 4; 1959–64 Division 3; 1964–67 Division 2; 1967–92 Division 1; 1992– FA Premier League.

MANAGERS

H. R. Buckle 1909–10
Robert Wallace 1910–13
(Secretary-Manager)
Frank Scott-Walford 1913–15
William Clayton 1917–19
H. Pollitt 1919–20
Albert Evans 1920–24
Jimmy Kerr 1924–28
James McIntyre 1928–31
Harry Storer 1931–45
Dick Bayliss 1945–47
Billy Frith 1947–48
Harry Storer 1948–53
Jack Fairbrother 1953–54
Charlie Elliott 1954–55
Jesse Carver 1955–56
Harry Warren 1956–57
Billy Frith 1957–61
Jimmy Hill 1961–67
Noel Cantwell 1967–72
Bob Dennison 1972
Joe Mercer 1972–75
Gordon Milne 1972–81
Dave Sexton 1981–83
Bobby Gould 1983–84
Don Mackay 1985–86
George Curtis 1986–87
(became Managing Director)
John Sillett 1987–90
Terry Butcher 1990–92
Don Howe 1992
Bobby Gould 1992–93
Phil Neal 1993–95
Ron Atkinson 1995–96
(became Director of Football)
Gordon Strachan *(Player-Manager)* November 1996–

TEN YEAR LEAGUE RECORD

		P	W	D	L	F	A	Pts	Pos
1988-89	Div 1	38	14	13	11	47	42	55	7
1989-90	Div 1	38	14	7	17	39	59	49	12
1990-91	Div 1	38	11	11	16	42	49	44	16
1991-92	Div 1	42	11	11	20	35	44	44	19
1992-93	PR Lge	42	13	13	16	52	57	52	15
1993-94	PR Lge	42	14	14	14	43	45	56	11
1994-95	PR Lge	42	12	14	16	44	62	50	16
1995-96	PR Lge	38	8	14	16	42	60	38	16
1996-97	PR Lge	38	9	14	15	38	54	41	17
1997-98	PR Lge	38	12	16	10	46	44	52	11

DID YOU KNOW ?

On 27 February 1999, Coventry City's 4–1 win at Aston Villa was their first in the League at Villa Park in 25 attempts starting in 1936 and a year after their first ever on the ground in an FA Cup tie.

COVENTRY CITY 1998–99 LEAGUE RECORD

Match No.	Date	Venue	Opponents	Result	H/T Score	Lg. Pos.	Goalscorers	Atten- dance
1	Aug 15	H	Chelsea	W	2-1	2-1	—	Huckerby [10], Dublin [16]	23,042
2	22	A	Nottingham F	L	0-1	0-0	9		22,546
3	29	H	West Ham U	D	0-0	0-0	10		20,818
4	Sept 9	A	Liverpool	L	0-2	0-1	—		41,771
5	12	A	Manchester U	L	0-2	0-1	19		55,193
6	19	H	Newcastle U	L	1-5	1-3	19	Whelan [4]	22,639
7	26	A	Charlton Ath	D	1-1	0-0	19	Whelan [69]	20,048
8	Oct 3	H	Aston Villa	L	1-2	0-2	19	Soltvedt [71]	22,650
9	18	H	Sheffield W	W	1-0	0-0	19	Dublin [74]	16,003
10	24	A	Southampton	L	1-2	0-2	18	Dublin [60]	15,152
11	31	H	Arsenal	L	0-1	0-0	19		23,039
12	Nov 7	A	Blackburn R	W	2-1	0-0	17	Huckerby [54], Whelan [74]	23,779
13	15	H	Everton	W	3-0	1-0	15	Froggatt [15], Huckerby [48], Whelan [89]	19,279
14	21	A	Middlesbrough	L	0-2	0-0	16		34,287
15	28	H	Leicester C	D	1-1	0-0	17	Huckerby [78]	19,887
16	Dec 5	A	Wimbledon	L	1-2	0-0	17	McAllister (pen) [54]	11,717
17	14	A	Leeds U	L	0-2	0-1	—		31,799
18	19	H	Derby Co	D	1-1	1-0	17	Whelan [16]	16,602
19	26	H	Tottenham H	D	1-1	0-1	17	Aloisi [81]	23,091
20	28	A	West Ham U	L	0-2	0-1	17		25,662
21	Jan 9	H	Nottingham F	W	4-0	1-0	17	Huckerby 3 [45, 46, 75], Telfer [54]	17,158
22	16	A	Chelsea	L	1-2	1-1	17	Huckerby [9]	34,869
23	30	H	Liverpool	W	2-1	0-0	16	Boateng [60], Whelan [71]	23,057
24	Feb 6	A	Tottenham H	D	0-0	0-0	16		34,376
25	17	A	Newcastle U	L	1-4	1-1	—	Whelan [18]	36,352
26	20	H	Manchester U	L	0-1	0-0	18		22,594
27	27	A	Aston Villa	W	4-1	1-0	17	Aloisi 2 [25, 73], Boateng 2 [51, 84]	38,799
28	Mar 6	H	Charlton Ath	W	2-1	0-0	15	Whelan [67], Soltvedt [85]	20,255
29	13	H	Blackburn R	D	1-1	1-0	15	Aloisi [22]	19,694
30	20	A	Arsenal	L	0-2	0-1	15		38,074
31	Apr 3	A	Sheffield W	W	2-1	1-0	15	McAllister (pen) [19], Whelan [84]	28,136
32	5	H	Southampton	W	1-0	0-0	15	Boateng [64]	21,404
33	11	A	Everton	L	0-2	0-1	15		32,341
34	17	H	Middlesbrough	L	1-2	0-0	16	McAllister [72]	19,228
35	24	A	Leicester C	L	0-1	0-1	16		20,224
36	May 1	H	Wimbledon	W	2-1	2-0	16	Huckerby [16], Whelan [29]	21,198
37	8	A	Derby Co	D	0-0	0-0	16		32,450
38	16	H	Leeds U	D	2-2	0-1	15	Aloisi [63], Telfer [72]	23,049

Final League Position: 15

GOALSCORERS

League (39): Whelan 10, Huckerby 9, Aloisi 5, Boateng 4, Dublin 3, McAllister 3 (2 pens), Soltvedt 2, Telfer 2, Froggatt 1.
Worthington Cup (5): Boateng 1, Dublin 1, Hall P 1, Soltvedt 1, Whelan 1.
FA Cup (11): Huckerby 3, Froggatt 2, Whelan 2, Boateng 1, McAllister 1, Telfer 1, own goal 1.

Hedman M 36	Nilsson R 28	Burrows D 23	Williams P 20+2	Shaw R 36+1	Boateng G 29+4	Telfer P 30+2	Soltvedt T 21+6	Dublin D 10	Whelan N 31	Huckerby D 31+3	Hall P 2+7	Hall M 2+3	Breen G 21+4	Wallemme J 4+2	Edworthy M 16+6	Shilton S 1+4	Quinn B 6+1	Haworth S 1	Froggatt S 23	McAllister G 29	Clement P 6+6	Jackson D —+3	Aloisi J 7+9	Ogrizovic S 2	Konjic M 3+1	McSheffrey G —+1	Gioacchini S —+3	Match No.
1	2	3	4	5	6¹		8	9	10²	11	12	13																1
1	2²	3		5	6	7	8¹	9	10	11	12		4	13														2
1		3		5	6	7	8¹	9	10	11	12		4	2²	13													3
1	2¹	3	12		6	7	8²	9		11	10³		4	5	13	14												4
1		3	2		6	7		9		11¹	12		4	5	8		10											5
1		3			6			9	10			7¹	4	5	2	12	8	11										6
1	2	3²		5	6	7		9	10		12		4		13	11¹	8											7
1	2			5	6	7	12	9	10				4²	13	3		8¹		11									8
1	2			5	6	7¹		9	8	12			4		3				11	10								9
1	2¹	3³		5	6²	12	13	9	8	7			4		14				11	10								10
1	2			5	6³	7	12		8	9²	13		4		3				11	10¹	14							11
1	2	12		5	13	7			8	9			4¹		3				11	10²	6							12
1	2	4	5			7		8	9						3				11	10	6							13
1	2	4	5	12		7		8	9²						3				11	10¹	6	13						14
1	2	4	5	12		7	8		9						3				11	10	6¹							15
1	2	4	5	6		7	8	9					12		3				11	10								16
1	2	4	5	6¹			8		9		12		3						11	10	7²	13						17
1	2	4	5	12		7¹	6	8	9				13		3²				11	10³			14					18
	2	4¹	5	6		7		8	9²				12		3³	13			11	10			14	1				19
	2	5	6	12		7		8	13				4		3¹				11	10			9²	1				20
1	2	3¹	4	5		7	6		8	11				12	13					10²			14	9¹				21
1	2	3	4	5	6	7	8		9										11	10¹	12							22
1	2¹	3	4	5	6	7		8	9				12						11	10								23
1	2	4³	5		7	6¹	8	9				3²							11	10	12		13		14			24
1	2	3		5	6	7¹		8	9²										11	10	12		13		4			25
1	2	3¹	4	5	6	7	12	8²	9										11	10			13					26
1	2	3	4	5	6	7			9¹										11	10			8			12		27
1	2	3	4	5		7	12	6	9¹										11	10			8					28
1	2	3	4	5	6	7	8		12										11	10¹	13		9			4²		29
1	2¹	3		5	6²	7		9	12				8						11	10						4	13	30
1		4	5	6	7		8	9					2	3					11	10¹	12							31
1	3	4	5	6	7	8	11	9¹					2							10						12		32
1	3	4	5	6	7¹	11	8	9					2							10			12					33
1	3	4	5	6		11	8	9					2¹							10	12		7					34
1	3	4	5	6	7²	12		9	13	2					8							11¹	10³		14			35
1	3¹		5	6	7	11	8	9	12	4	2									10								36
1			5	6	7	11	8	9¹	3	4	2									10			12					37
1	2	3²	12	5	6	7	11	8	9³				4¹	13						10			14					38

Worthington Cup

Second Round	Southend U	(h)	1-0	
		(a)	4-0	
Third Round	Luton T	(a)	0-2	

FA Cup

Third Round	Macclesfield T	(h)	7-0
Fourth Round	Leicester C	(a)	3-0
Fifth Round	Everton	(a)	1-2

Division 1

CREWE ALEXANDRA

FOUNDATION

The first match played at Crewe was on 1 December 1877 against Basford, the leading North Staffordshire team of that time. During the club's history they have also played in a number of other leagues including the Football Alliance, Football Combination, Lancashire League, Manchester League, Central League and Lancashire Combination. Two former players, Aaron Scragg in 1899 and Jackie Pearson in 1911, had the distinction of refereeing FA Cup finals. Pearson was also capped for England against Ireland in 1892.

Football Ground, Gresty Rd, Crewe CW2 6EB.

Telephone: (01270) 213014.

Ground Capacity: 10,046.

Record Attendance: 20,000 v Tottenham H, FA Cup 4th rd, 30 January 1960.

Record Receipts: £41,093 v Liverpool, FA Cup 3rd rd, 6 January 1992.

Pitch Measurements: 112yd × 74yd.

President: N. Rowlinson.

Chairman: J. Bowler.

Vice-Chairman: N. Hassall.

Directors: D. Rowlinson, R. Clayton, J. McMillan, D. Gradi.

Manager: Dario Gradi MBE.

Secretary: Mrs Gill Palin.

Marketing Manager: Alison Bowler.

LATEST SEQUENCES

Longest Sequence of League Wins: 7, 30.4.94 – 3.9.94.

Longest Sequence of League Defeats: 10, 16.4.79 – 22.8.79.

Longest Sequence of League Draws: 5, 31.8.87 – 18.9.87.

Longest Sequence of Unbeaten League Matches: 17, 25.3.95 – 16.9.95.

Longest Sequence Without a League Win: 30, 22.9.56 – 6.4.57.

HONOURS

Football League: Promoted from Division 2 1996–97 (play-offs).

FA Cup: Semi-final 1888.

Football League Cup: best season: 3rd rd, 1975, 1976, 1979, 1993, 1999.

Welsh Cup: Winners 1936, 1937.

Colours
Red shirts, white shorts, red stockings.

Change Colours
Blue shirts, white shorts, blue stockings.

Year Formed: 1877.

Turned Professional: 1893.

Ltd Co.: 1892.

Club Nickname: 'Railwaymen'.

First Football League Game: 3 September 1892, Division 2, v Burton Swifts (a) L 1–7 – Hickton; Moore, Cope; Linnell, Johnson, Osborne; Bennett, Pearson (1), Bailey, Barnett, Roberts.

Record League Victory: 8–0 v Rotherham U, Division 3 (N), 1 October 1932 – Foster; Pringle, Dawson; Ward, Keenor (1), Turner (1); Gillespie, Swindells (1), McConnell (2), Deacon (2), Weale (1).

Record Cup Victory: 8–0 v Hartlepool U, Auto Windscreens Shield 1st rd, 17 October 1995 – Gayle; Collins (1), Booty, Westwood (Unsworth), Macauley (1), Whalley (1), Garvey (1), Murphy (1), Savage (1) (Rivers (1p)), Lennon, Edwards, (1 og).

Record Defeat: 2–13 v Tottenham H, FA Cup 4th rd replay, 3 February 1960.

Most League Points (2 for a win): 59, Division 4, 1962–63.

Most League Points (3 for a win): 83, Division 2, 1994–95.

Most League Goals: 95, Division 3 (N), 1931–32.

Highest League Scorer in Season: Terry Harkin, 35, Division 4, 1964–65.

Most League Goals in Total Aggregate: Bert Swindells, 126, 1928–37.

Most League Goals in One Match: 5, Tony Naylor v Colchester U, Division 3, 24 April 1993.

Most Capped Player: Bill Lewis, 9 (27), Wales.

Most League Appearances: Tommy Lowry, 436, 1966–78.

Youngest League Player: Steve Walters, 16 years 119 days v Peterborough U, 6 May 1988.

Record Transfer Fee Received: £1,500,000 from Liverpool for Danny Murphy, July 1997.

Record Transfer Fee Paid: £650,000 to Torquay U for Rodney Jack, June 1998.

Football League Record: 1892 Original Member of Division 2; 1896 Failed re-election; 1921 Re-entered Division 3 (N); 1958–63 Division 4; 1963–64 Division 3; 1964–68 Division 4; 1968–69 Division 3; 1969–89 Division 4; 1989–91 Division 3; 1991–92 Division 4; 1992–94 Division 3; 1994–97 Division 2; 1997– Division 1.

MANAGERS

W. C. McNeill 1892–94
  (Secretary-Manager)
J. G. Hall 1895–96
  (Secretary-Manager)
R. Roberts *(1st team Secretary-Manager)* 1897
J. B. Blomerley 1898–1911
  (Secretary-Manager, continued as Hon. Secretary to 1925)
Tom Bailey *(Secretary only)* 1925–38
George Lillycrop *(Trainer)* 1938–44
Frank Hill 1944–48
Arthur Turner 1948–51
Harry Catterick 1951–53
Ralph Ward 1953–55
Maurice Lindley 1956–57
Willie Cook 1957–58
Harry Ware 1958–60
Jimmy McGuigan 1960–64
Ernie Tagg 1964–71
  (continued as Secretary to 1972)
Dennis Viollet 1971
Jimmy Melia 1972–74
Ernie Tagg 1974
Harry Gregg 1975–78
Warwick Rimmer 1978–79
Tony Waddington 1979–81
Arfon Griffiths 1981–82
Peter Morris 1982–83
Dario Gradi June 1983–

TEN YEAR LEAGUE RECORD

		P	W	D	L	F	A	Pts	Pos
1988-89	Div 4	46	21	15	10	67	48	78	3
1989-90	Div 3	46	15	17	14	56	53	62	12
1990-91	Div 3	46	11	11	24	62	80	44	22
1991-92	Div 4	42	20	10	12	66	51	70	6
1992-93	Div 3	42	21	7	14	75	56	70	6
1993-94	Div 3	42	21	10	11	80	61	73	3
1994-95	Div 2	46	25	8	13	80	68	83	3
1995-96	Div 2	46	22	7	17	77	60	73	5
1996-97	Div 2	46	22	7	17	56	47	73	6
1997-98	Div 1	46	18	5	23	58	65	59	11

DID YOU KNOW ?

In 1888 when the Football League was being formed, Crewe Alexandra joined the short-lived Combination for its only season before becoming members of the Football Alliance for 1889–90, the competition which became the Second Division in 1892.

CREWE ALEXANDRA 1998–99 LEAGUE RECORD

Match No.	Date	Venue	Opponents	Result		H/T Score	Lg. Pos.	Goalscorers	Attendance
1	Aug 8	A	Norwich C	L	1-2	1-2	—	Rivers [36]	15,016
2	15	H	Barnsley	W	3-1	1-0	8	Smith S (pen) [5], Lightfoot 2 [69, 77]	5289
3	22	A	Bury	L	0-1	0-1	12		5073
4	28	A	Bradford C	W	2-1	2-1	—	Lunt [12], Collins [19]	5759
5	31	A	Sheffield U	L	1-3	1-1	13	Jack [6]	15,922
6	Sept 8	H	Crystal Palace	L	0-1	0-0	—		4977
7	12	A	Stockport Co	D	1-1	1-0	18	Wright J [34]	7302
8	19	H	Bolton W	D	4-4	2-3	17	Little [13], Charnock [32], Rivers [72], Smith S (pen) [80]	5744
9	26	A	Bristol C	L	2-5	0-3	20	Anthrobus 2 [72, 85]	9810
10	29	A	Grimsby T	D	1-1	1-1	—	Rivers [16]	5024
11	Oct 3	H	Wolverhampton W	D	0-0	0-0	21		5759
12	17	A	Birmingham C	L	1-3	1-2	23	Johnson [29]	20,087
13	20	A	Port Vale	L	0-1	0-0	—		8205
14	24	H	Tranmere R	L	1-4	0-4	23	Little [82]	5080
15	31	A	Oxford U	D	1-1	0-0	23	Little [87]	5607
16	Nov 3	A	Sunderland	L	1-4	0-3	—	Little [78]	5361
17	7	H	Swindon T	L	0-2	0-1	24		4489
18	14	H	QPR	L	0-2	0-1	24		5001
19	21	A	Watford	L	2-4	0-3	24	Jack [66], Little [82]	9405
20	28	A	Ipswich T	L	0-3	0-1	24		5165
21	Dec 5	A	Portsmouth	L	0-2	0-0	24		9800
22	8	H	WBA	D	1-1	0-1	—	Anthrobus [64]	5007
23	12	A	QPR	W	1-0	1-0	24	Wright J [26]	11,296
24	19	H	Huddersfield T	L	1-2	0-1	24	Jack [76]	5102
25	26	H	Bury	W	3-1	0-0	24	Little [47], Rivers [63], Wright J [90]	5333
26	28	A	Sunderland	L	0-2	0-1	24		41,433
27	Jan 9	H	Norwich C	W	3-2	0-2	24	Street 2 [82, 90], Rivers [87]	4782
28	16	A	Bradford C	L	1-4	0-2	24	Little [73]	12,595
29	30	A	Sheffield U	L	1-2	1-0	24	Jack [5]	5243
30	Feb 6	H	Barnsley	D	2-2	1-0	24	Jack 2 [27, 70]	15,377
31	13	A	Crystal Palace	D	1-1	0-1	24	Walton [63]	14,823
32	20	H	Stockport Co	L	0-2	0-1	24		5473
33	27	A	Bolton W	W	3-1	2-0	24	Johnson [18], Jack 2 [33, 46]	19,437
34	Mar 13	A	Swindon T	W	2-1	2-0	24	Jack [16], Charnock [32]	7434
35	16	H	Grimsby T	D	0-0	0-0	—		4855
36	20	H	Oxford U	W	3-1	0-0	23	Murphy [57], Little [85], Smith S (pen) [88]	4791
37	26	A	Tranmere R	L	0-3	0-2	—		9359
38	30	A	Wolverhampton W	L	0-3	0-2	—		24,197
39	Apr 2	H	Birmingham C	D	0-0	0-0	—		5582
40	5	A	WBA	W	5-1	2-0	22	Wright D [13], Wright J 2 [24, 54], Johnson [51], Rivers [83]	12,308
41	10	A	Port Vale	D	0-0	0-0	24		5606
42	17	A	Watford	L	0-1	0-1	24		5461
43	24	A	Ipswich T	W	2-1	0-0	22	Rivers [64], Macauley [84]	20,845
44	27	H	Bristol C	W	1-0	1-0	—	Johnson [23]	5579
45	May 1	H	Portsmouth	W	3-1	3-0	19	Little 2 [21, 30], Smith S [45]	5759
46	9	A	Huddersfield T	D	0-0	0-0	18		15,105

Final League Position: 18

GOALSCORERS

League (54): Little 10, Jack 9, Rivers 7, Wright J 5, Johnson 4, Smith S 4 (3 pens), Anthrobus 3, Charnock 2, Lightfoot 2, Street 2, Collins 1, Lunt 1, Macauley 1, Murphy 1, Walton 1, Wright D 1.
Worthington Cup (7): Rivers 3, Jack 2, Little 2.
FA Cup (1): Johnson 1.

Kearton J 46	Bignot M 26	Smith S 46	Lightfoot C 19+3	Walton D 38	Wright J 44	Lunt K 6+12	Johnson S 42	Rivers M 38+15	Little C 27+10	Street K 4+19	Unsworth L 15+9	Charnock P 40+4	Smith P —+4	Collins J 5+1	Jack R 37+2	Anthrobus S 16+5	Foster S —+1	Wicks M 4+2	Wright D 20	Macauley S 12+8	Foran M 4+2	Murphy D 16	Newell M 1+3	Match No.
1	2	3	4^1	5	6	7	8^2	9	10	11^3	12	13	14											1
1	2	3	12	5	7	13	8	9	10			4^1	14		6^2	11								2
1	2	3	4^3	5	7	12	8	9	10^2			13	14		6^1	11								3
1	2	3		5	7	12	8	9^1	10			13	14		6^1	11^2		4						4
1	2	3		5^3	7	12	8	9	10			13	14		6^2	11^1		4						5
1	2	3		5	7	12	8	9	10						6^1	11		4						6
1	2	3		5	7	12	8^2	9	10			13	14		6^1	11^3		4						7
1	2	3		5	7		8	11	10			4			6	9^1		12						8
1	2	3		5	7	12	8	9	10		13	4			6^2	11								9
1	2	3		5	7	12	8	10	11^1		13	4			6	9^2								10
1	2	3		5	7	12	8	10	11			4			6	9^1								11
1	2	3		5	7	12	8	9	10		13	4			6^1	11								12
1	2	3		5	7	12	8	9	10			4			6^1	11								13
1	2^2	3		5	7	12	8	9	10		13	4^1			6	11								14
1	2	3	4^1	5	7	12	8	9	10						6	11								15
1	2	3	4	5^1	7	12	8	9^1	10			13			6	11								16
1	2^1	3	4^3	5	7	12	8	9	10		12	13	14		6^2	11								17
1	2	3	4^3	5	7		8	9	10		12	13	14		6^1	11^2								18
1	2	3		5	7		8	9	10			4			6	11								19
1	2	3			7	12	8	9	10^1		13	4			6^2	11				5				20
1	2	3			7	12	8	9	10^1			4			6	11				5				21
1	2	3		5	7	12	8	9^4	10		13	4			6	11^1								22
1	2	3		5	7	12	8	9^2	10^1		13	4			6	11								23
1	2^2	3			7	12	8	9	10^1			13		5	6	11		4						24
1	2	3	12		7		8	9	10^1		13			5	6	11				4^2				25
1	2	3	12		7^1	13	8	9	10^3			4	14		6^2	11				5				26
1	2	3		5	7^2	12	8	9	10^3			13	14		6	11^1		4						27
1	2^2	3		5	7^3	12	8	9	10^1		13		14		6	11		4						28
1		3		5	7		8	9	10^1			13			6	11^2		12	2	4				29
1		3	4	5	7		8	9	10		12				6	11^1			2					30
1		3	4	5	7		8^1	9			12				6	11^2			2	13		10		31
1		3	4	5	7		8	9	10		12				6	11^1			2^2	13		8		32
1		3	4^2	5	7		8	9^1			12				6	11			2	13		10		33
1		3	4^3	5	7	12	8	9^1				13			6	11			2	14		10^2		34
1		3	4	5	7^2	12	8	9				13^3			6	11^1			2	14		10		35
1		3	4	5	7^2	12	8	9							6	11^1			2	13		10		36
1		3	4	5	7	12	8	9							6	11^1			2			10		37
1		3	4	5^1	7	13	8	9			12				6^3				2	14		10	11^2	38
1		3	4	5	7		8	9							6	11			2			10		39
1		3	4	5	7	12	8	9							6^1	11			2			10		40
1		3	4	5	7^1		8	9							6	11^2		12	2			10	13	41
1		3		5	7^1		8	9							6	11			2		4	10	12	42
1		3		5	7	12	8	9^1							6^2	11			2		4	10	13	43
1		3		5	7	12	8	9^1							6	11			2		4	10		44
1		3		5	7	12	8	9^1							6	11			2		4	10		45
1		3		5	7^2	12	8	9^1							6	11			2		4	10	13	46

Worthington Cup

First Round	Oldham Ath	(a)	2-3	
		(h)	2-0	
Second Round	Bristol C	(a)	1-1	
		(h)	2-0	
Third Round	Blackburn R	(h)	0-1	

FA Cup

Third Round	Oxford U	(h)	1-3

Division 1

CRYSTAL PALACE

FOUNDATION

There was a Crystal Palace club as early as 1861 but the present organisation was born in 1905 after the formation of a club by the company that controlled the Crystal Palace (building), had been rejected by the FA who did not like the idea of the Cup Final hosts running their own club. A separate company had to be formed and they had their home on the old Cup Final ground until 1915.

Selhurst Park, London SE25 6PU.

Telephone: (0181) 768 6000. *Fax:* (0181) 771 5311.

Lottery Office: (0181) 768 6094.

Club Shop: (0181) 768 6100.

Dial-A-Seat Ticketline: (0181) 771 8841.

Palace Publications: (0181) 768 6021. *Fax:* (0181) 653 6312.

Palace Clubline: 0891 400 333.

Palace Ticket Line: 0891 400 334 (normal 0891 charges apply for these services).

Press Office: (0181) 768 6020. *Fax:* (0181) 768 6114.

Ground Capacity: 26,400.

Record Attendance: 51,482 v Burnley, Division 2, 11 May 1979.

Record Receipts: £327,124 v Manchester U, FA Premier League, 21 April 1993 (League); £336,583 v Chelsea, Coca-Cola Cup 5th rd, 6 January 1993.

Pitch Measurements: 110yd × 74yd.

Chairman: M. Goldberg.

Directors: R. E. Anderson, C. Carlsen, J. Cole, S. Coppell, L. W. Grimes, S. Hume-Kendall, P. L. Morley CBE JP, V. E. Murphy.

Manager: Steve Coppell.

Physio: Gary Sadler.

Stadium Manager: Vic Worrall.

Company Secretary: Peter Morley CBE, JP.

Club Secretary: Mike Hurst.

PR and Communications Manager: Terry Byfield.

LATEST SEQUENCES

Longest Sequence of League Wins: 8, 9.2.21 – 26.3.21.

Longest Sequence of League Defeats: 8, 10.1.98 – 14.3.98.

Longest Sequence of League Draws: 5, 30.12.78 – 24.2.79.

Longest Sequence of Unbeaten League Matches: 18, 22.2.69 – 13.8.69.

Longest Sequence Without a League Win: 20, 3.3.62 – 8.9.62.

HONOURS

Football League: Division 1 – Champions 1993–94; Promoted from Division 1, 1996–97 (play-offs); Division 2 – Champions 1978–79; Runners-up 1968–69; Division 3 – Runners-up 1963–64; Division 3 (S) – Champions 1920–21; Runners-up 1928–29, 1930–31, 1938–39; Division 4 – Runners-up 1960–61.

FA Cup: Runners-up 1990.

Football League Cup: Semi-final 1993, 1995.

Zenith Data Systems Cup: Winners 1991.

Colours
Red and blue vertical striped shirts, red shorts, red stockings with blue tops.

Change Colours
White shirts, royal blue shorts, royal blue stockings with red tops.

Year Formed: 1905.

Turned Professional: 1905.

Ltd Co.: 1905.

Club Nickname: 'The Eagles'.

Previous Grounds: 1905, Crystal Palace; 1915, Herne Hill; 1918, The Nest; 1924, Selhurst Park.

First Football League Game: 28 August 1920, Division 3, v Merthyr T (a) L 1–2 – Alderson; Little, Rhodes; McCracken, Jones, Feebury; Bateman, Conner, Smith, Milligan (1), Whibley.

Record League Victory: 9–0 v Barrow, Division 4, 10 October 1959 – Rouse; Long, Noakes; Truett, Evans, McNichol; Gavin (1), Summersby (4 incl. 1p), Sexton, Byrne (2), Colfar (2).

Record Cup Victory: 8–0 v Southend U, Rumbelows League Cup 2nd rd (1st leg), 25 September 1989 – Martyn; Humphrey (Thompson (1)), Shaw, Pardew, Young, Thorn, McGoldrick, Thomas, Bright (3), Wright (3), Barber (Hodges (1)).

Record Defeat: 0–9 v Burnley, FA Cup 2nd rd replay, 10 February 1909. 0–9 v Liverpool, Division 1, 12 September 1990.

Most League Points (2 for a win): 64, Division 4, 1960–61.

Most League Points (3 for a win): 90, Division 1, 1993–94.

Most League Goals: 110, Division 4, 1960–61.

Highest League Scorer in Season: Peter Simpson, 46, Division 3 (S), 1930–31.

Most League Goals in Total Aggregate: Peter Simpson, 153, 1930–36.

Most League Goals in One Match: 6, Peter Simpson v Exeter C, Division 3S, 4 October 1930.

Most Capped Player: Eric Young, 19 (21), Wales.

Most League Appearances: Jim Cannon, 571, 1973–88.

Youngest League Player: Phil Hoadley, 16 years 112 days v Bolton W, 27 April 1968.

Record Transfer Fee Received: £4,500,000 from Tottenham H for Chris Armstrong, June 1995.

Record Transfer Fee Paid: £2,750,000 to RC Strasbourg for Valerien Ismael, January 1998.

Football League Record: 1920 Original Members of Division 3; 1921–25 Division 2; 1925–58 Division 3 (S); 1958–61 Division 4; 1961–64 Division 3; 1964–69 Division 2; 1969–73 Division 1; 1973–74 Division 2; 1974–77 Division 3; 1977–79 Division 2; 1979–81 Division 1; 1981–89 Division 2; 1989–92 Division 1; 1992–93 FA Premier League; 1993–94 Division 1; 1994–95 FA Premier League; 1995–97 Division 1; 1997–98 FA Premier League; 1998– Division 1.

MANAGERS

John T. Robson 1905–07
Edmund Goodman 1907–25
(had been Secretary since 1905 and afterwards continued in this position to 1933)
Alec Maley 1925–27
Fred Mavin 1927–30
Jack Tresadern 1930–35
Tom Bromilow 1935–36
R. S. Moyes 1936
Tom Bromilow 1936–39
George Irwin 1939–47
Jack Butler 1947–49
Ronnie Rooke 1949–50
Charlie Slade and Fred Dawes
(Joint Managers) 1950–51
Laurie Scott 1951–54
Cyril Spiers 1954–58
George Smith 1958–60
Arthur Rowe 1960–62
Dick Graham 1962–66
Bert Head 1966–72
(continued as General Manager to 1973)
Malcolm Allison 1973–76
Terry Venables 1976–80
Ernie Walley 1980
Malcolm Allison 1980–81
Dario Gradi 1981
Steve Kember 1981–82
Alan Mullery 1982–84
Steve Coppell 1984–93
Alan Smith 1993–95
Steve Coppell *(Technical Director)* 1995–96
Dave Bassett 1996–97
Steve Coppell 1997–98
Attilio Lombardo 1998
Terry Venables *(Head Coach)* 1998–99
Steve Coppell January 1999–

TEN YEAR LEAGUE RECORD

		P	W	D	L	F	A	Pts	Pos
1988-89	Div 2	46	23	12	11	71	49	81	3
1989-90	Div 1	38	13	9	16	42	66	48	15
1990-91	Div 1	38	20	9	9	50	41	69	3
1991-92	Div 1	42	14	15	13	53	61	57	10
1992-93	PR Lge	42	11	16	15	48	61	49	20
1993-94	Div 1	46	27	9	10	73	46	90	1
1994-95	PR Lge	42	11	12	19	34	49	45	19
1995-96	Div 1	46	20	15	11	67	48	75	3
1996-97	Div 1	46	19	14	13	78	48	71	6
1997-98	PR Lge	38	8	9	21	37	71	33	20

DID YOU KNOW ?

Bill Davies was the first player to appear in a full international while with Crystal Palace, when he was selected to turn out for Wales v Scotland at Dundee on 7 March 1908. It was the first of four caps.

CRYSTAL PALACE 1998–99 LEAGUE RECORD

Match No.	Date	Venue	Opponents	Result		H/T Score	Lg. Pos.	Goalscorers	Attendance
1	Aug 8	H	Bolton W	D	2-2	0-1	—	Jansen [50], Curcic [61]	19,029
2	16	A	Birmingham C	L	1-3	0-2	16	Mullins [73]	16,699
3	22	H	Oxford U	W	2-0	2-0	9	Dyer [5], Lombardo [12]	14,827
4	29	A	Stockport Co	D	1-1	1-0	10	Shipperley [27]	7739
5	Sept 8	A	Crewe Alex	W	1-0	0-0	—	Jansen [65]	4977
6	12	H	Port Vale	L	0-1	0-0	17		15,983
7	19	A	Barnsley	L	0-4	0-2	19		15,597
8	27	H	Sheffield U	W	1-0	0-0	17	Curcic [74]	20,370
9	30	H	Bury	W	4-2	1-2	—	Warhurst [13], Dyer [48], Morrison [64], Lombardo (pen) [66]	13,219
10	Oct 3	A	Ipswich T	L	0-3	0-1	16		16,837
11	17	H	Norwich C	W	5-1	2-1	14	Rizzo [38], Jansen 2 [42, 50], Svensson [48], Lombardo [79]	18,100
12	20	H	Wolverhampton W	W	3-2	1-0	—	Moore [40], Burton [52], Curcic [84]	16,417
13	31	A	Grimsby T	L	0-2	0-1	14		6948
14	Nov 3	A	WBA	L	2-3	1-1	—	Jansen [30], Moore [87]	11,606
15	7	H	Portsmouth	W	4-1	1-1	13	Moore [6], Thomson (og) [57], Mullins [64], Foster [81]	20,188
16	14	H	Bristol C	W	2-1	1-1	11	Bradbury [5], Jansen [89]	17,821
17	21	A	Swindon T	L	0-2	0-1	12		11,718
18	28	H	Watford	D	2-2	1-2	13	Tuttle [33], Curcic (pen) [75]	19,521
19	Dec 5	A	Huddersfield T	L	0-4	0-2	14		10,453
20	8	H	Tranmere R	D	1-1	0-0	—	Jansen [68]	12,919
21	12	A	Bristol C	D	1-1	1-1	14	Bell (og) [24]	13,014
22	15	A	Sunderland	L	0-2	0-1	—		33,870
23	19	H	QPR	D	1-1	0-0	14	Rodger [61]	17,684
24	26	A	Oxford U	W	3-1	0-0	14	Foster [59], Morrison [78], Bradbury (pen) [80]	8375
25	28	H	WBA	D	1-1	1-0	14	Morrison [10]	19,137
26	Jan 10	A	Bolton W	L	0-3	0-3	14		15,410
27	16	H	Stockport Co	D	2-2	1-2	14	Morrison [44], Zhiyi [47]	15,517
28	19	A	Bradford C	L	1-2	0-0	—	Tuttle [56]	14,368
29	30	A	Tranmere R	D	1-3	1-2	14	Bradbury [39]	6017
30	Feb 6	H	Birmingham C	D	1-1	0-0	14	Rowett (og) [90]	15,996
31	13	H	Crewe Alex	D	1-1	1-0	15	Morrison [6]	14,823
32	20	A	Port Vale	L	0-1	0-1	16		6051
33	28	H	Barnsley	W	1-0	1-0	14	Mullins [24]	17,021
34	Mar 2	A	Sheffield U	D	1-1	1-0	—	Petric [9]	12,896
35	6	A	Bury	D	0-0	0-0	14		4334
36	9	H	Ipswich T	W	3-2	1-1	—	Mullins [45], Morrison 2 [46, 70]	16,360
37	13	A	Portsmouth	D	1-1	1-0	13	Bradbury [3]	15,520
38	20	H	Grimsby T	W	3-1	2-1	12	Morrison 2 [44, 45], Mullins [46]	15,228
39	28	H	Bradford C	W	1-0	1-0	12	Zhiyi [45]	15,626
40	Apr 3	A	Norwich C	W	1-0	1-0	10	Austin [13]	16,754
41	5	H	Sunderland	D	1-1	1-1	10	Morrison [34]	22,096
42	10	A	Wolverhampton W	D	0-0	0-0	9		23,643
43	17	H	Swindon T	L	0-1	0-0	10		18,660
44	24	A	Watford	L	1-2	0-1	11	McKenzie [87]	15,590
45	May 1	H	Huddersfield T	D	2-2	1-2	13	Morrison 2 [10, 58]	17,282
46	9	A	QPR	L	0-6	0-2	14		18,498

Final League Position: 14

GOALSCORERS

League (58): Morrison 12, Jansen 7, Mullins 5, Bradbury 4 (1 pen), Curcic 4 (1 pen), Lombardo 3 (1 pen), Moore 3, Dyer 2, Foster 2, Tuttle 2, Zhiyi 2, Austin 1, Burton 1, McKenzie 1, Petric 1, Rizzo 1, Rodger 1, Shipperley 1, Svensson 1, Warhurst 1, own goals 3.
Worthington Cup (5): Lombardo 2, Hreidarsson 1, Morrison 1, Zhiyi 1.
FA Cup (1): Bradbury 1.

Miller K 28	Austin D 17+3	Smith J 25+1	Curcic S 4+11	Tuttle D 17+5	Hreidarsson H 6+1	Lombardo A 19	Warhurst P 5	Hibburt J —+2	Dyer B 5+1	Woozley D 7	Jansen M 18	Mullins H 38+2	Edworthy M 1+2	Linighan A 19+1	Bent M 3+9	Martin A 2+1	Digby F 18	Rodger S 18	Padovano M —+2	Graham G —+1	Amsalem D 6+4	Morrison C 27+10	Shipperley N 3	Rizzo N 13+6	Zhiyi F 28+1	Harris R —+1	Del Rio W 1+1	Burton S 18+5	Thomson S 11+5	Svensson M 6+2	Foster C 30+2	Jihai S 22+1	Moore C 23	Bradbury L 19+3	Petric G 18	Crowe J 8	Turner A —+2	Fullarton J 7	McKenzie L 10+6	Evans S —+4	Carlisle W 2+4	Frampton A 4+2	Match No.
1	2	3¹	4	5	6	7	8		9		10	11	12																														1
1	12	3	4¹			5		7	8	9²	10	11		2	6	13																											2
	2	3	4²	12				7	8¹	9	10³	11	13	6		1	5	14																									3
	2	3					8	7			10	11			6	12	1	5²			4	13	9¹																				4
	2	3					8	7			10²	11			6	12	1	5			4	13	9¹																				5
	2	3					8	7			10	11			6	12	1	5¹			4²		9	13																			6
	12	3¹					8	7			10	11			6	9²	1	5³			13	3¹	9	4³	8	14	2	4															7
		12	5					7	10²			11			6		1			13	3¹	9	4³	8	14	2	4																8
		12	5			7	8	10			11			6		1					9²	4	11		2	3¹	13																9
		4¹	5			7	8	12			11			1						10	3		2	13	9	6²																	10
	3	12						7			10¹	11			1						8	4	13	14	9²	6³	2	5															11
	3¹	12						7			10	11			1					13	8¹	4	14		9²	6	2	5															12
2								7³			10	11		12	1					9²	8¹	4	13		6	3	5	14														13
2								7			10¹	11		9²	1		12				4	6		8	3	5	13															14
2								7			10²	11		12	1					13		4	14		6³	3	5	9¹														15
2¹		13	12					7			10	11			1					14	8²	5		6	3	9	4															16
		12	13					7¹				11		14	1					10	8³	2²	6	5	9	4	3															17
	2	12	11					7			13	1			10²	8¹		6	5	9	4	3																					18
	2	12	11					10	6			1				13	14	8¹		7³	5	9	4	3²																			19
	2		11					10	5			1	7¹	12	13	4	9²	6	8	3																							20
1			11					10	8			7	2	5	12	9¹	6	13	4²	3																							21
1	2							11				5	7	8¹	10	4	6	9		3	12																						22
1	11	12						10	8			5	7	13	3¹	4	6	9²	2																								23
1	3					7		10¹				5	11	12²	13	8	7	6	2	4	9																						24
1	3		7					12	5	9²	11³	10	13	8	6¹	2	4			14																							25
1		7						5			12	11²	14	10¹	13	8	4	6	2	9	3³																						26
1	12	13	3	7²				11				10	2¹	8	6	5	9³		4	14																							27
1		6						11				10	8¹	2	7	3	5	9	4	12																							28
1	13	6²						12	11³			10	8	2	7¹	3	5	9	4	14																							29
1	2				8	6		10			12	7¹	5	9	3	4	10²	13	11																							30
1	2				8	6	11	10	12	13	5	9	3	4²	7¹																												31
1	2	12				11¹	6	10	8³	7	13	5	3	4	9²	14																											32
1	2				11	6	10	8¹	9⁴	7	4	5	3	12	13																												33
1	2	6		9	11	10	8¹	13	7²	4	5	3	12																														34
1	2	6	12	11²	10	13	7	4¹	5	9	3	8																															35
1	2	12	11	6	10²	8	7	4¹	5	9	3	13																															36
1	2	4	11	6	10	8	7	5	9	3¹	12																																37
1	2	12	3	11	6	10	8¹	13	7²	5	9	4																															38
1	4	6	11	10	8	2	7	3	5	9																																	39
1	4	13	5	11	9	10¹	8	6	7	3	12	2²																															40
1	4	5	11	10	8	6	7	2	3	9																																	41
1	4	5	11	10	8	6	7	2¹	3	9	12																																42
1	4	11	10	5¹	6	12²	7	2	3	9	13	8																															43
1	4	5	11	14	10	8	6³	7	2¹	3²	9	12	13																														44
1	4	12	5	11	13	10	14	8	6	7¹	9²	3³	2																														45
1	4	12	3	11	9³	10	14	8	13	6	7²	5¹	2																														46

Worthington Cup

First Round	Torquay U	(a)	1-1
		(h)	2-1
Second Round	Bury	(a)	0-3
		(h)	2-1

FA Cup

Third Round	Newcastle U	(a)	1-2

Division 3

DARLINGTON

FOUNDATION

A football club was formed in Darlington as early as 1861 but the present club began in 1883 and reached the final of the Durham Senior Cup in their first season, losing to Sunderland in a replay after complaining that they had suffered from intimidation in the first. On 5 April 1884, Sunderland had defeated Darlington 4-3. Darlington's objection was upheld by the referee and the replay took place on 3 May. The new referee for the match was Major Marindin, appointed by the Football Association to ensure fair play. Sunderland won 2-0. The following season Darlington won this trophy and for many years were one of the leading amateur clubs in their area.

Feethams Ground, Darlington DL1 5JB.

Telephone: (01325) 240240.

Fax: (01325) 381377.

Ground Capacity: 8500.

Record Attendance: 21,023 v Bolton W, League Cup 3rd rd, 14 November 1960.

Record Receipts: £32,300 v Rochdale, Division 4, 11 May 1991.

Pitch Measurements: 110yd × 74yd.

President: A. Noble.

Chairman: B. Lowery.

Vice-Chairman: G. Hodgson.

Manager: David Hodgson.

Assistant Manager: Ian Butterworth.

Coach: Gary Bennett.

Chief Executive: M. J. Peden.

Secretary: K. J. Lavery.

LATEST SEQUENCES

Longest Sequence of League Wins: 5, 31.8.98 – 19.9.88.

Longest Sequence of League Defeats: 8, 31.8.85 – 19.10.85.

Longest Sequence of League Draws: 5, 31.12.88 – 28.1.89.

Longest Sequence of Unbeaten League Matches: 17, 27.4.68 – 19.10.68.

Longest Sequence Without a League Win: 19, 27.4.88 – 8.11.88.

HONOURS

Football League: Division 2 best season: 15th, 1925–26; Division 3 (N) – Champions 1924–25; Runners-up 1921–22; Division 4 – Champions 1990–91; Runners-up 1965–66.

FA Cup: best season: 5th rd, 1958.

Football League Cup: best season: 5th rd, 1968.

GM Vauxhall Conference: Champions 1989–90.

Colours
Black and white.

Change Colours
All red.

Year Formed: 1883.

Turned Professional: 1908.

Ltd Co.: 1891.

Club Nickname: 'The Quakers'.

First Football League Game: 27 August 1921, Division 3 (N), v Halifax T (h) W 2–0 – Ward; Greaves, Barbour; Dickson (1), Sutcliffe, Malcolm; Dolphin, Hooper (1), Edmunds, Wolstenholme, Winship.

Record League Victory: 9–2 v Lincoln C, Division 3 (N), 7 January 1928 – Archibald; Brooks, Mellen; Kelly, Waugh, McKinnell; Cochrane (1), Gregg (1), Ruddy (3), Lees (3), McGiffen (1).

Record Cup Victory: 7–2 v Evenwood T, FA Cup 1st rd, 17 November 1956 – Ward; Devlin, Henderson; Bell (1p), Greener, Furphy; Forster (1), Morton (3), Tulip (2), Davis, Moran.

Record Defeat: 0–10 v Doncaster R, Division 4, 25 January 1964.

Most League Points (2 for a win): 59, Division 4, 1965–66.

Most League Points (3 for a win): 85, Division 4, 1984–85.

Most League Goals: 108, Division 3 (N), 1929–30.

Highest League Scorer in Season: David Brown, 39, Division 3 (N), 1924–25.

Most League Goals in Total Aggregate: Alan Walsh, 90, 1978–84.

Most League Goals in One Match: 5, Tom Ruddy v South Shields, Division 2, 23 April 1927; 5, Maurice Wellock v Rotherham U, Division 3N, 15 February 1930.

Most Capped Player: Jason Devos, 3, Canada.

Most League Appearances: Ron Greener, 442, 1955–68.

Youngest League Player: Dale Anderson, 16 years 254 days v Chesterfield, 4 May 1987.

Record Transfer Fee Received: £400,000 from Dundee U for Jason Devos, October 1998.

Record Transfer Fee Paid: £95,000 to Motherwell for Nick Cusack, January 1992.

Football League Record: 1921 Original Member Division 3 (N); 1925–27 Division 2; 1927–58 Division 3 (N); 1958–66 Division 4; 1966–67 Division 3; 1967–85 Division 4; 1985–87 Division 3; 1987–89 Division 4; 1989–90 GM Vauxhall Conference; 1990–91 Division 4; 1991– Division 3.

MANAGERS

Tom McIntosh 1902–11
W. L. Lane 1911–12
    (Secretary-Manager)
Dick Jackson 1912–19
Jack English 1919–28
Jack Fairless 1928–33
George Collins 1933–36
George Brown 1936–38
Jackie Carr 1938–42
Jack Surtees 1942
Jack English 1945–46
Bill Forrest 1946–50
George Irwin 1950–52
Bob Gurney 1952–57
Dick Duckworth 1957–60
Eddie Carr 1960–64
Lol Morgan 1964–66
Jimmy Greenhalgh 1966–68
Ray Yeoman 1968–70
Len Richley 1970–71
Frank Brennan 1971
Ken Hale 1971–72
Allan Jones 1972
Ralph Brand 1972–73
Dick Conner 1973–74
Billy Horner 1974–76
Peter Madden 1976–78
Len Walker 1978–79
Billy Elliott 1979–83
Cyril Knowles 1983–87
Dave Booth 1987–89
Brian Little 1989–91
Frank Gray 1991–92
Ray Hankin 1992
Billy McEwan 1992–93
Alan Murray 1993–95
Paul Futcher 1995
David Hodgson/Jim Platt
    (Director of Coaching) 1995
Jim Platt 1995–96
David Hodgson November 1996–

TEN YEAR LEAGUE RECORD

		P	W	D	L	F	A	Pts	Pos
1988-89	Div 4	46	8	18	20	53	76	42	24
1989-90	Conf	42	26	9	7	76	25	87	1
1990-91	Div 4	46	22	17	7	68	38	83	1
1991-92	Div 3	46	10	7	29	56	90	37	24
1992-93	Div 3	42	12	14	16	48	53	50	15
1993-94	Div 3	42	10	11	21	42	64	41	21
1994-95	Div 3	42	11	8	23	43	57	41	20
1995-96	Div 3	46	20	18	8	60	42	78	5
1996-97	Div 3	46	14	10	22	64	78	52	18
1997-98	Div 3	46	14	12	20	56	72	54	19

DID YOU KNOW ?

Before becoming founder members of the Third Division (North), Darlington had a highly successful first season in the North-Eastern League, finishing as champions in 1920–21 with 60 points.

DARLINGTON 1998–99 LEAGUE RECORD

Match No.	Date	Venue	Opponents	Result	H/T Score	Lg. Pos.	Goalscorers	Attendance
1	Aug 8	H	Barnet	L	0-2	0-0	—	4200
2	15	A	Hull C	W	2-1	1-0	15	Gaughan [6], Atkinson [53]	5217
3	22	H	Halifax T	D	2-2	1-0	14	Naylor [1], Gabbiadini [59]	4200
4	29	A	Rochdale	D	0-0	0-0	13		1953
5	31	H	Cardiff C	W	3-0	1-0	8	Roberts 2 [42, 70], Devos [75]	2085
6	Sept 5	A	Mansfield T	W	1-0	1-0	6	Gabbiadini [33]	2428
7	8	H	Hartlepool U	W	2-0	0-0	—	Roberts [61], Gabbiadini [78]	5899
8	12	A	Plymouth Arg	W	2-1	1-1	1	Gabbiadini [35], Devos [69]	5709
9	19	H	Shrewsbury T	W	1-0	1-0	1	Oliver [41]	4484
10	26	A	Brentford	L	0-3	0-2	2		4486
11	Oct 3	H	Swansea C	D	2-2	0-1	4	Reed [72], Shutt [90]	3046
12	10	H	Peterborough U	W	3-0	2-0	1	Naylor 2 [7, 18], Reed [90]	3178
13	17	A	Rotherham U	L	1-3	1-2	3	Shutt [7]	4004
14	20	A	Torquay U	D	2-2	0-1	—	Gabbiadini [52], Atkinson [71]	1775
15	31	A	Southend U	L	1-2	1-1	7	Roberts [30]	3527
16	Nov 7	H	Brighton & HA	L	1-2	1-0	9	Naylor [17]	3069
17	21	A	Cambridge U	L	1-2	1-0	12	Naylor [35]	3395
18	28	H	Scarborough	W	3-0	1-0	10	Carter [31], Gabbiadini [52], Barnard [65]	2660
19	Dec 12	A	Chester C	L	0-1	0-0	11		2011
20	19	H	Scunthorpe U	W	3-1	1-0	10	Naylor [5], Leah [58], Bennett [89]	2465
21	26	A	Halifax T	D	0-0	0-0	11		3557
22	28	H	Leyton Orient	D	1-1	0-0	13	Gabbiadini [67]	3424
23	Jan 2	H	Rochdale	W	3-0	1-0	10	Roberts [45], Dorner [68], Naylor [89]	2807
24	9	A	Barnet	L	0-3	0-1	11		1723
25	23	A	Cardiff C	L	2-3	1-1	12	Naylor [1], Gabbiadini [87]	5803
26	30	A	Leyton Orient	L	2-3	1-2	14	Gabbiadini [20], Liddle [49]	3972
27	Feb 6	H	Mansfield T	W	5-1	0-1	12	Liddle [52], Duffield [56], Gabbiadini 2 [58, 63], Costa [90]	2708
28	13	A	Hartlepool U	W	3-2	2-0	12	Bennett [2], Gabbiadini [18], Duffield [60]	3980
29	16	H	Hull C	L	0-1	0-1	—		3107
30	20	H	Plymouth Arg	L	1-2	0-1	14	Dorner [75]	2643
31	27	A	Shrewsbury T	L	0-3	0-1	17		2624
32	Mar 9	A	Swansea C	L	0-2	0-2	—		4078
33	13	A	Brighton & HA	W	4-0	1-0	14	Gabbiadini 3 [24, 48, 86], Smith (og) [72]	3053
34	20	A	Southend U	W	2-1	1-0	12	Bennett [26], Dorner [90]	2516
35	23	H	Carlisle U	D	1-1	0-1	—	Gaughan [54]	3028
36	26	A	Exeter C	D	0-0	0-0	—		3179
37	Apr 3	H	Rotherham U	L	1-2	0-1	12	Gabbiadini [73]	3468
38	5	A	Peterborough U	W	1-0	1-0	12	Gabbiadini [33]	5107
39	10	H	Torquay U	L	0-2	0-2	12		2248
40	14	A	Scarborough	W	2-0	1-0	—	Carruthers [18], Gabbiadini [71]	2125
41	17	H	Cambridge U	D	0-0	0-0	11		2668
42	24	A	Carlisle U	D	3-3	1-2	12	Liddle [7], Carruthers [54], Campbell [64]	3808
43	27	H	Brentford	D	2-2	1-1	—	Himsworth [10], Gabbiadini [83]	2514
44	May 1	H	Chester C	L	1-2	1-1	13	Naylor [26]	2564
45	4	H	Exeter C	W	4-0	0-0	—	Bennett [60], Gabbiadini 3 [66, 77, 82]	2450
46	8	A	Scunthorpe U	W	1-0	0-0	11	Gabbiadini [84]	4238

Final League Position: 11

GOALSCORERS

League (69): Gabbiadini 23, Naylor 9, Roberts 5, Bennett 4, Dorner 3, Liddle 3, Atkinson 2, Carruthers 2, Devos 2, Duffield 2, Gaughan 2, Reed 2, Shutt 2, Barnard 1, Campbell 1, Carter 1, Costa 1, Himsworth 1, Leah 1, Oliver 1, own goal 1.
Worthington Cup (3): Devos 1, Roberts 1, own goal 1.
FA Cup (4): Atkinson 1, Barnard 1, Bennett 1, Dorner 1.

Preece D 46	Pepper C 5+1	Barnard M 29+4	Liddle C 44	Tutill S 33+3	Devos J 12	Gaughan S 12+11	Naylor G 32+10	Dorner M 9+13	Gabbiadini M 40	Atkinson B 42+1	Shutt C 8+6	Roberts D 10+14	Hope R 8	Reed A 25+4	Brumwell P 24+13	Oliver M 33+3	Ellison L 3+17	Kubicki D 2+1	Bennett G 26+3	Carter M 1	Campbell P 6+3	Leah J 7	Duffield P 10+4	Costa R —+3	Scott K 4	Himsworth G 14	Heckingbottom P 10	Carruthers M 11	Kilty M —+2	Match No.
1	2[1]	3	4	5	6	7	8	9[2]	10	11	12	13																		1
1	2	3	4		6	7	8	9	10[1]	11		12		5																2
1	2		4	5[1]	6	7[1]	8	9[2]	10	11	13	12	3	14																3
1	2[3]		4		5	7[1]	8	9[2]	10	11	12	13		6	14	3														4
1			4	5	12		8		10	11	7	9[4]		6	2	3[1]	13													5
1			4	5	12			13	10[2]	11	7[1]	9	3	2	6	8														6
1			4	5	12				10[1]	11	7	9	3	2	6	8														7
1			4	12	5			13	10[3]	11	7[2]	9	3	2	6[1]	8	14													8
1			4	12	5	7			10	11		9[2]	3[1]	2	6	8	13													9
1	13		4	12	5	7[2]			10	11		9[3]	3	2	6[1]	8	14													10
1		3	4	6	5		9		10	11	7	12		2		8[1]														11
1		3	4	5	12			9[2]	10[3]	11	7[1]	13		2	6	8	14													12
1		3		5	12			9	10	11[3]	7[1]	13		4	6	8[2]		2[1]	14											13
1		3	4	5	12			9	10	11	7[1]	13		2	6	8[2]														14
1		3	4	5		7[1]	8		10	11		9		2	6[2]				12		13									15
1		3		6	7		8		10	11		9[2]		4	12	13		2[1]	5											16
1	8		4	5		7[3]	9	12	10[2]	11		13		3	2	14			6[1]											17
1		3	4	5		7	8		10	11[3]		12[2]		2	13				6		9[1]		14							18
1		3	4	5		11[1]	8[3]	9	10					2	12	13	14				6		7[2]							19
1		3	4	5			9[1]	12	10[2]	11				2	13	8			6				7							20
1		3	4	5			9[1]		10	11	12			2		8			6				7							21
1		3	4	5			9[2]	12	10	11		14		2[1]	13	8			6				7[3]							22
1		3	4	5	12		9[2]	13	10	11[1]		14		2		8			6				7[3]							23
1		3		5	12	6			10[1]	11[3]		13	9	14	2	8			4				7[2]							24
1		3	4	5	12				10	11[3]		13		2	6	8			7[1]				9[2]							25
1	2	3	4		12				10	11		13	14		6[1]	8			7[2]		9[3]				5					26
1		3	4	5		7			10[3]	11[1]		12		2	13	8			6		9[2]		14							27
1		3	4	5	12				10	11				2[2]	13	8	14				9[1]		7	6[3]						28
1		3	4	5	12				10	11				2		8					9[1]	13	7	6[2]						29
1		3	4	5	12	7[1]			10	11				2	13	8	14		6[2]				9[3]							30
1	12	3	4			7[1]		13	10	11[2]				5	2	8	14		6[3]				9							31
1		3	6	5	12		9[3]		10	11[1]				4	2[2]	8					13		14			7				32
1		3	2	5	12	6[3]			10	11				14	13	8			4				9[1]			7[2]				33
1		3	2	5	12	6			10	11				13		8			4				9[1]			7[2]				34
1		3	2	5	11	6			12	10						8			4				9[1]			7				35
1	12		2	5		6[2]	9[1]		11					13		8			4				14			7	3	10[3]		36
1	12		2	5		6[1]			13	10	11					8[9]			4							7	3	9[2]	14	37
1			2	5		6[1]			10	11	12					8			4				13			7	3	9[2]		38
1	8		4		12	6[3]			10	11		2[2]		13	5											7[1]	3	9	14	39
1			2	5	12				10	11[2]		6		13					4					8		7[1]	3	9		40
1	12		2	5		13	14		11			6		10					4					8[9]		7[1]	3	9[2]		41
1		3	2	5	12		13		10	11				6[2]		8	14		4				7[3]					9[1]		42
1			2	5	12				10	11[2]		13				8[1]			7				4			14	3	9		43
1			2	5					10	12	11[2]					13			8[3]		7[1]		4			14	3	9		44
1			4	5	12				10	11[1]		2		13		14			6						7	8[3]	3	9[3]		45
1			4	5[1]					10	11		2		12		13			6						7[2]	8[3]	3	9	14	46

Worthington Cup
First Round — Sheffield U — (a) 1-3 / (h) 2-2

FA Cup
First Round — Burnley (at Middlesbrough) — (h) 3-2
Second Round — Manchester C — (h) 1-1 / (a) 0-1

FA Premiership

DERBY COUNTY

Pride Park Stadium, Derby DE24 8XL.

Telephone: (01332) 202202.

Fax: (01332) 667519.

Clubcall: 0891 121187.

Ground Capacity: 33,258.

Record Attendance: 41,826 v Tottenham H, Division 1, 20 September 1969.

Record Receipts: £425,804 v Huddersfield T, FA Cup 5th rd replay, 24 February 1999.

Pitch Measurements: 115yd × 75yd.

Chairman: L. V. Pickering.

Vice-Chairman: P. J. Gadsby.

Directors: J. N. Kirkland OBE, A. S. Webb, R. Clarke.

Manager: Jim Smith.

Assistant Manager: Billy McEwan.

Chief Scout: Bobby Roberts.

First Team Coach: Malcolm Crosby.

Physio: Peter Melville.

Stadium Manager: David Goodwin.

Chief Executive: Keith Loring.

Secretary: Keith Pearson ACIS.

Sales and Marketing Manager: Gary Hodder.

LATEST SEQUENCES

Longest Sequence of League Wins: 9, 15.3.69 – 19.4.69.

Longest Sequence of League Defeats: 8, 12.12.87 – 10.2.88.

Longest Sequence of League Draws: 6, 26.3.27 – 18.4.27.

Longest Sequence of Unbeaten League Matches: 22, 8.3.69 – 20.9.69.

Longest Sequence Without a League Win: 20, 15.12.90 – 23.4.91.

HONOURS

Football League: Division 1 – Champions 1971–72, 1974–75; Runners-up 1895–96, 1929–30, 1935–36, 1995–96; Division 2 – Champions 1911–12, 1914–15, 1968–69, 1986–87; Runners-up 1925–26; Division 3 (N) Champions 1956–57; Runners-up 1955–56.

FA Cup: Winners 1946; Runners-up 1898, 1899, 1903.

Football League Cup: Semi-final 1968.

Texaco Cup: Winners 1972.

European Competitions: *European Cup:* 1972–73, 1975–76. *UEFA Cup:* 1974–75, 1976–77. *Anglo-Italian Cup:* Runners-up 1993.

Colours
White shirts with black trim, black shorts with white stripes, white stockings.

Change Colours
Yellow shirts with royal blue sleeves, blue shorts with yellow stripes, blue stockings with yellow turnover.

Year Formed: 1884.

Turned Professional: 1884.

Ltd Co.: 1896.

Club Nickname: 'The Rams'.

Previous Grounds: 1884, Racecourse Ground; 1895, Baseball Ground; 1997, Pride Park.

First Football League Game: 8 September 1888, Football League, v Bolton W (a) W 6–3 – Marshall; Latham, Ferguson, Williamson; Monks, W. Roulstone; Bakewell (2), Cooper (2), Higgins, H. Plackett, L. Plackett (2).

Record League Victory: 9–0 v Wolverhampton W, Division 1, 10 January 1891 – Bunyan; Archie Goodall, Roberts; Walker, Chalmers, Roulston (1); Bakewell, McLachlan, Johnny Goodall (1), Holmes (2), McMillan (5). 9–0 v Sheffield W, Division 1, 21 January 1899 – Fryer; Methven, Staley; Cox, Archie Goodall, May; Oakden (1), Bloomer (6), Boag, McDonald (1), Allen, (1 og).

Record Cup Victory: 12–0 v Finn Harps, UEFA Cup 1st rd 1st leg, 15 September 1976 – Moseley; Thomas, Nish, Rioch (1), McFarland, Todd (King), Macken, Gemmill, Hector (5), George (3), James (3).

Record Defeat: 2–11 v Everton, FA Cup 1st rd, 1889–90.

Most League Points (2 for a win): 63, Division 2, 1968–69 and Division 3 (N), 1955–56 and 1956–57.

Most League Points (3 for a win): 84, Division 3, 1985–86 and Division 3, 1986–87.

Most League Goals: 111, Division 3 (N), 1956–57.

Highest League Scorer in Season: Jack Bowers, 37, Division 1, 1930–31; Ray Straw, 37 Division 3 (N), 1956–57.

Most League Goals in Total Aggregate: Steve Bloomer, 292, 1892–1906 and 1910–14.

Most League Goals in One Match: 6, Steve Bloomer v Sheffield W, Division 1, 2 January 1899.

Most Capped Player: Peter Shilton, 34 (125), England.

Most League Appearances: Kevin Hector, 486, 1966–78 and 1980–82.

Youngest League Player: Steve Powell, 16 years 33 days v Arsenal, 23 October 1971.

Record Transfer Fee Received: £5,300,000 from Blackburn R for Christian Dailly, August 1998.

Record Transfer Fee Paid: £3,000,000 to Crewe A for Seth Johnson, May 1999.

Football League Record: 1888 Founder Member of the Football League; 1907–12 Division 2; 1912–14 Division 1; 1914–15 Division 2; 1915–21 Division 1; 1921–26 Division 2; 1926–53 Division 1; 1953–55 Division 2; 1955–57 Division 3 (N); 1957–69 Division 2; 1969–80 Division 1; 1980–84 Division 2; 1984–86 Division 3; 1986–87 Division 2; 1987–91 Division 1; 1991–92 Division 2; 1992–96 Division 1; 1996– FA Premier League.

MANAGERS

Harry Newbould 1896–1906
Jimmy Methven 1906–22
Cecil Potter 1922–25
George Jobey 1925–41
Ted Magner 1944–46
Stuart McMillan 1946–53
Jack Barker 1953–55
Harry Storer 1955–62
Tim Ward 1962–67
Brian Clough 1967–73
Dave Mackay 1973–76
Colin Murphy 1977
Tommy Docherty 1977–79
Colin Addison 1979–82
Johnny Newman 1982
Peter Taylor 1982–84
Roy McFarland 1984
Arthur Cox 1984–93
Roy McFarland 1993–95
Jim Smith June 1995–

TEN YEAR LEAGUE RECORD

		P	W	D	L	F	A	Pts	Pos
1988-89	Div 1	38	17	7	14	40	38	58	5
1989-90	Div 1	38	13	7	28	43	40	46	16
1990-91	Div 1	38	5	9	24	37	75	24	20
1991-92	Div 2	46	23	9	14	69	51	78	3
1992-93	Div 1	46	19	9	18	68	57	66	8
1993-94	Div 1	46	20	11	15	73	68	71	6
1994-95	Div 1	46	18	12	16	66	51	66	9
1995-96	Div 1	46	21	16	9	71	51	79	2
1996-97	PR Lge	38	11	13	14	45	58	46	12
1997-98	PR Lge	38	16	7	15	52	49	55	9

DID YOU KNOW ?

Though in previous seasons they had occasionally used the Baseball Ground, it was not officially opened until 14 September 1895 when a crowd of 10,000 saw two goals from Steve Bloomer account for Sunderland.

DERBY COUNTY 1998–99 LEAGUE RECORD

Match No.	Date	Venue	Opponents	Result	H/T Score	Lg. Pos.	Goalscorers	Attendance
1	Aug 15	A	Blackburn R	D 0-0	0-0	—		24,235
2	22	H	Wimbledon	D 0-0	0-0	13		25,710
3	29	A	Middlesbrough	D 1-1	1-0	13	Wanchope 31	34,087
4	Sept 9	H	Sheffield W	W 1-0	1-0	—	Sturridge 23	26,209
5	12	A	Charlton Ath	W 2-1	1-0	4	Wanchope 5, Baiano 60	19,516
6	19	H	Leicester C	W 2-0	1-0	2	Schnoor 34, Wanchope 51	26,738
7	26	A	Aston Villa	L 0-1	0-1	2		38,007
8	Oct 3	H	Tottenham H	L 0-1	0-0	7		30,083
9	17	A	Newcastle U	L 1-2	0-2	10	Burton 73	36,750
10	24	H	Manchester U	D 1-1	0-0	11	Burton 74	30,867
11	31	H	Leeds U	D 2-2	1-2	10	Schnoor (pen) 3, Sturridge 56	27,034
12	Nov 7	A	Liverpool	W 2-1	2-0	7	Harper 6, Wanchope 27	44,020
13	16	A	Nottingham F	D 2-2	0-0	—	Dorigo (pen) 56, Carbonari 72	24,014
14	22	H	West Ham U	L 0-2	0-1	11		31,366
15	28	A	Southampton	W 1-0	1-0	9	Carbonari 33	14,762
16	Dec 5	H	Arsenal	D 0-0	0-0	10		29,018
17	12	H	Chelsea	D 2-2	1-0	10	Carbonari 26, Sturridge 90	29,056
18	19	A	Coventry C	D 1-1	0-1	12	Carsley 50	16,602
19	26	A	Everton	D 0-0	0-0	11		39,206
20	28	H	Middlesbrough	W 2-1	1-0	11	Sturridge 29, Hunt 85	32,726
21	Jan 9	A	Wimbledon	L 1-2	0-1	11	Wanchope 76	12,732
22	16	A	Blackburn R	W 1-0	0-0	10	Burton 84	27,386
23	30	A	Sheffield W	W 1-0	0-0	8	Prior 54	24,440
24	Feb 3	A	Manchester U	L 0-1	0-0	—		55,174
25	7	H	Everton	W 2-1	0-1	6	Burton 2 51, 85	27,603
26	20	H	Charlton Ath	L 0-2	0-0	7		27,853
27	27	A	Tottenham H	D 1-1	0-0	8	Burton 46	35,392
28	Mar 10	A	Aston Villa	W 2-1	2-1	—	Baiano 17, Burton 21	26,836
29	13	H	Liverpool	W 3-2	2-1	6	Burton 12, Wanchope 2 44, 49	32,913
30	20	A	Leeds U	L 1-4	1-3	7	Baiano (pen) 4	38,992
31	Apr 3	H	Newcastle U	L 3-4	2-3	7	Burton 8, Baiano (pen) 22, Wanchope 90	32,039
32	10	H	Nottingham F	W 1-0	0-0	7	Carbonari 85	32,217
33	17	A	West Ham U	L 1-5	0-2	8	Wanchope 79	25,485
34	24	H	Southampton	D 0-0	0-0	8		26,557
35	May 2	A	Arsenal	L 0-1	0-1	9		37,323
36	5	A	Leicester C	W 2-1	1-1	—	Sturridge 17, Beck 60	20,535
37	8	H	Coventry C	D 0-0	0-0	7		32,450
38	16	A	Chelsea	L 1-2	0-1	8	Carbonari 88	35,017

Final League Position: 8

GOALSCORERS

League (40): Burton 9, Wanchope 9, Carbonari 5, Sturridge 5, Baiano 4 (2 pens), Schnoor 2 (1 pen), Beck 1, Carsley 1, Dorigo 1 (pen), Harper 1, Hunt 1, Prior 1.
Worthington Cup (3): Delap 1, Sturridge 1, Wanchope 1.
FA Cup (9): Burton 3, Baiano 2, Dorigo 2 (1 pen), Eranio 1 (pen), Harper 1.

Hoult R 23	Delap R 21 + 2	Schnoor S 20 + 3	Laursen J 37	Carbonari H 28 + 1	Dailly C 1	Powell D 30 + 3	Sturridge D 23 + 6	Baiano F 17 + 5	Wanchope P 33 + 2	Carsley L 20 + 2	Elliott S 7 + 4	Bohinen L 29 + 3	Burton D 14 + 7	Stimac I 14	Prior S 33 + 1	Eranio S 18 + 7	Kozluk R 3 + 4	Harper K 6 + 21	Dorigo T 17 + 1	Bridge-Wilkinson M — + 1	Poom M 15 + 2	Hunt J — + 6	Christie M — + 2	Borbokis V 3 + 1	Launders B — + 1	Beck M 6 + 1	Murray A — + 4	Robinson M — + 1	Boertien P — + 1	Match No.
1	2	3	4¹	5	6	7	8	9²	10³	11	12	13	14																	1
1	2	3	4			7	8	12	10	11		9¹			5	6²	13													2
1	12	3¹	4			7	8²	13	10	11	6	9			5	2														3
1	2³	3	4			12	8	9¹	10	11		7²			5	6	13	14												4
1	2	3¹	4			12	8	9²	10	11		7			5	6	13													5
1	2	3	4			7	8²		10	11	12	9			5¹	6		13												6
1	3		4	5²		7	8	12	10	11		9			6	13	2¹													7
1	2	3²	4	5¹		7	12	9	10	11		8¹	14		6	13														8
1	3	12	4	5		7	8	9²	10	11			13		6	2¹														9
1	2	3	4¹			7	8		10	11		9		5	6				12											10
	3		4			7	8²	12	10		6¹	9	13	5		2³	14	11												11
1	2¹		4	5		7			10		6	9	11			12	8²	3	13											12
1⁶			4	5		7	12		10		2	11	9		6		8¹	3			15									13
	2		4	5⁴		7²	8	9¹	10	12		11			6	13	14		3		1									14
	2		4	5		7	8¹		10	11		9²	12		6	13	14		3		1									15
	2		4	5		7	8		10			9			6	11¹	12		3		1									16
	2	12	4	5²		7	13	9¹	10			8¹			6	11	14		3		1									17
	2		4	5		7	8²		10	12	13	9			6			11¹	3³		1	14								18
9²		3¹	5			8			10	11	4				6	7	2	13			1	12								19
	3		5			7	8²		10	11	4	9¹			6	2³	14	13			1	12								20
	2		5			9²	8		10	11	4³	12	13		6	7¹	14		3		1									21
		4	5				8	9²	11			7¹	10		6	2	13	12	3		1									22
1	12	2	5				8³	9²	11			10¹			4	6	13	7	3				14							23
1		2	5			7²			10	11		9	12	4	6			8¹	3				13							24
1		2²	5			12		9¹	10³	11		8	4		6		7	13	3				14							25
1	2²		4³					9	8¹	12	11	13	10		5	6	7	14	3											26
1	6		4	5				9²	10	11		7	8		12	2¹		13	3²²				14							27
1		3	4	5					9	10¹		7	8	5	6			12												28
1		3¹	4	12					9³	10		7	8	5	6	2²		13							14					29
		2	5					11	9²		12	7³	8	4¹	6			10		1		13	3	14						30
1	10²		4	5¹				13	9	12		7	8		6			3					2	11						31
1	3		4	5				11	12	9²	10	7	8⁶		6			13				15	2¹							32
1	2		4	5				11	8	10		7			6			12	3¹							9²	13			33
1	12	3²	4	5				11	13		10	7	8³		6	2		14			1					9¹				34
	3		4	5				11		10		7²	8¹		6	2		12³			1					9	13	14		35
	2	3	4	5				8		10		11¹			6	7					1					9	12			36
	2²	3	4	5				11	8	12		10			6	7³		13			1					9¹	14			37
	2	3¹	4	5				11	8³	9²		10			6	7		12			1					13		14		38

Worthington Cup

Second Round	Manchester C	(h)	1-1
		(a)	1-0
Third Round	Arsenal	(h)	1-2

FA Cup

Third Round	Plymouth Arg	(a)	3-0
Fourth Round	Swansea C	(a)	1-0
Fifth Round	Huddersfield T	(a)	2-2
		(h)	3-1
Sixth Round	Arsenal	(a)	0-1

FA Premiership

EVERTON

Goodison Park, Liverpool L4 4EL.
Telephone: (0151) 330 2200.
Fax: (0151) 286 9112.
Ticket Infoline: 0891 121599.
Clubcall: 0891 121199.
Dial-A-Seat Service: (0151) 471 8000.
Ground Capacity: 40,200.
Record Attendance: 78,299 v Liverpool, Division 1, 18 September 1948.
Record Receipts: £450,000 v Liverpool, FA Premier League, 16 April 1996.
Pitch Measurements: 112yd × 78yd.
Chairman: Sir Philip Carter.
Vice-Chairman: Bill Kenwright.
Directors: Keith Tamlin, Arthur Abercromby, Lord Grantchester.
Manager: Walter Smith OBE.
Assistant Manager: Archie Knox.
First Team Coach: Dave Watson.
Physio: A. Jones.
Secretary: Michael J. Dunford.
Sales Promotion Manager: Graham Cass.
Stadium Manager: A. Bowen.
Communications Manager: Alan Myers.

LATEST SEQUENCES

Longest Sequence of League Wins: 12, 24.3.1894 – 13.10.1894.
Longest Sequence of League Defeats: 6, 26.12.96 – 29.1.97.
Longest Sequence of League Draws: 5, 4.5.77 – 16.5.77.
Longest Sequence of Unbeaten League Matches: 20, 29.4.78 – 16.12.78.
Longest Sequence Without a League Win: 14, 6.3.37 – 4.9.37.

HONOURS

Football League: Division 1 – Champions 1890–91, 1914–15, 1927–28, 1931–32, 1938–39, 1962–63, 1969–70, 1984–85, 1986–87; Runners-up 1889–90, 1894–95, 1901–02, 1904–05, 1908–09, 1911–12, 1985–86; Division 2 – Champions 1930–31; Runners-up 1953–54.

FA Cup: Winners 1906, 1933, 1966, 1984, 1995; Runners-up 1893, 1897, 1907, 1968, 1985, 1986, 1989.

Football League Cup: Runners-up 1977, 1984.

League Super Cup: Runners-up 1986.

Simod Cup: Runners-up 1989.

Zenith Data Systems Cup: Runners-up 1991.

European Competitions: *European Cup:* 1963–64, 1970–71. *European Cup-Winners' Cup:* 1966–67, 1984–85 (winners), 1995–96. *European Fairs Cup:* 1962–63, 1964–65, 1965–66. *UEFA Cup:* 1975–76, 1978–79, 1979–80.

Colours
Royal blue shirts with white trim, white shorts, blue stockings.

Change Colours
White shirts, blue shorts with white trim, blue stockings.

Year Formed: 1878.

Turned Professional: 1885.

Ltd Co.: 1892.

Previous Name: 1878, St Domingo FC; 1879, Everton.

Club Nickname: 'The Toffees'.

Previous Grounds: 1878, Stanley Park; 1882, Priory Road; 1884, Anfield Road; 1892, Goodison Park.

First Football League Game: 8 September 1888, Football League, v Accrington (h) W 2–1 – Smalley; Dick, Ross; Holt, Jones, Dobson; Fleming (2), Waugh, Lewis, E. Chadwick, Farmer.

Record League Victory: 9–1 v Manchester C, Division 1, 3 September 1906 – Scott; Balmer, Crelley; Booth, Taylor (1), Abbott (1); Sharp, Bolton (1), Young (4), Settle (2), George Wilson. 9–1 v Plymouth Arg, Division 2, 27 December 1930 – Coggins; Williams, Cresswell; McPherson, Griffiths, Thomson; Critchley, Dunn, Dean (4), Johnson (1), Stein (4).

Record Cup Victory: 11–2 v Derby Co, FA Cup 1st rd, 18 January 1890 – Smalley; Hannah, Doyle (1); Kirkwood, Holt (1), Parry; Latta, Brady (3), Geary (3), Chadwick, Millward (3).

Record Defeat: 4–10 v Tottenham H, Division 1, 11 October 1958.

Most League Points (2 for a win): 66, Division 1, 1969–70.

Most League Points (3 for a win): 90, Division 1, 1984–85.

Most League Goals: 121, Division 2, 1930–31.

Highest League Scorer in Season: William Ralph 'Dixie' Dean, 60, Division 1, 1927–28 (All-time League record).

Most League Goals in Total Aggregate: William Ralph 'Dixie' Dean, 349, 1925–37.

Most League Goals in One Match: 6, Jack Southworth v WBA, Division 1, 30 December 1893.

Most Capped Player: Neville Southall, 92, Wales.

Most League Appearances: Neville Southall, 578, 1981–98.

Youngest League Player: Joe Royle, 16 years 282 days v Blackpool, 15 January 1966.

Record Transfer Fee Received: £8,000,000 from Fiorentina for Andrei Kanchelskis, February 1997.

Record Transfer Fee Paid: £5,750,000 to Middlesbrough for Nick Barmby, October 1996.

Football League Record: 1888 Founder Member of the Football League; 1930–31 Division 2; 1931–51 Division 1; 1951–54 Division 2; 1954–92 Division 1; 1992– FA Premier League.

MANAGERS

W. E. Barclay 1888–89
(Secretary-Manager)
Dick Molyneux 1889–1901
(Secretary-Manager)
William C. Cuff 1901–18
(Secretary-Manager)
W. J. Sawyer 1918–19
(Secretary-Manager)
Thomas H. McIntosh 1919–35
(Secretary-Manager)
Theo Kelly 1936–48
Cliff Britton 1948–56
Ian Buchan 1956–58
Johnny Carey 1958–61
Harry Catterick 1961–73
Billy Bingham 1973–77
Gordon Lee 1977–81
Howard Kendall 1981–87
Colin Harvey 1987–90
Howard Kendall 1990–93
Mike Walker 1994
Joe Royle 1994–97
Howard Kendall 1997–98
Walter Smith July 1998–

TEN YEAR LEAGUE RECORD

		P	W	D	L	F	A	Pts	Pos
1988-89	Div 1	38	14	12	12	50	45	54	8
1989-90	Div 1	38	17	8	13	57	46	59	6
1990-91	Div 1	38	13	12	13	50	46	51	9
1991-92	Div 1	42	13	14	15	52	51	53	12
1992-93	PR Lge	42	15	8	19	53	55	53	13
1993-94	PR Lge	42	12	8	22	42	63	44	17
1994-95	PR Lge	42	11	17	14	44	51	50	15
1995-96	PR Lge	38	17	10	11	64	44	61	6
1996-97	PR Lge	38	10	12	16	44	57	42	15
1997-98	PR Lge	38	9	13	16	41	56	40	17

DID YOU KNOW ?

Everton established a club record 28 consecutive matches without defeat in the 1984–85 season. The run comprised 18 League, six FA Cup ties and four in the European Cup-Winners' Cup. They won the League, Cup-Winners' Cup and were FA Cup runners-up.

EVERTON 1998–99 LEAGUE RECORD

Match No.	Date	Venue	Opponents	Result	H/T Score	Lg. Pos.	Goalscorers	Attendance
1	Aug 15	H	Aston Villa	D	0-0	0-0	—	40,112
2	22	A	Leicester C	L	0-2	0-2	18	21,037
3	29	H	Tottenham H	L	0-1	0-1	19	39,378
4	Sept 8	A	Nottingham F	W	2-0	0-0	—	Ferguson 2 [73, 83]	25,610
5	12	H	Leeds U	D	0-0	0-0	17	36,687
6	19	A	Middlesbrough	D	2-2	0-2	15	Ball (pen) [47], Collins [48]	34,563
7	26	H	Blackburn R	D	0-0	0-0	15	36,404
8	Oct 3	A	Wimbledon	W	2-1	1-1	14	Cadamarteri [32], Ferguson [59]	16,054
9	17	H	Liverpool	D	0-0	0-0	12	40,185
10	24	A	Sheffield W	D	0-0	0-0	15	26,592
11	31	H	Manchester U	L	1-4	1-2	15	Ferguson [30]	40,087
12	Nov 8	A	Arsenal	L	0-1	0-1	15	38,088
13	15	A	Coventry C	L	0-3	0-1	17	19,279
14	23	H	Newcastle U	W	1-0	1-0	—	Ball (pen) [18]	30,357
15	28	A	Charlton Ath	W	2-1	1-0	14	Cadamarteri 2 [45, 73]	20,043
16	Dec 5	H	Chelsea	D	0-0	0-0	14	36,430
17	12	H	Southampton	W	1-0	1-0	14	Bakayoko [31]	32,073
18	19	A	West Ham U	L	1-2	0-1	15	Cadamarteri [71]	25,998
19	26	H	Derby Co	D	0-0	0-0	14	39,206
20	28	A	Tottenham H	L	1-4	1-1	14	Bakayoko [31]	36,053
21	Jan 9	H	Leicester C	D	0-0	0-0	14	32,792
22	18	A	Aston Villa	L	0-3	0-1	—	32,488
23	30	H	Nottingham F	L	0-1	0-0	15	34,175
24	Feb 7	A	Derby Co	L	1-2	1-0	17	Barmby [38]	27,603
25	17	H	Middlesbrough	W	5-0	2-0	—	Barmby 2 [1, 16], Dacourt [62], Materazzi [67], Unsworth [74]	31,606
26	20	A	Leeds U	L	0-1	0-0	15	36,344
27	27	H	Wimbledon	D	1-1	0-1	15	Jeffers [57]	32,574
28	Mar 10	A	Blackburn R	W	2-1	1-1	—	Bakayoko 2 [15, 65]	27,219
29	13	H	Arsenal	L	0-2	0-1	16	38,049
30	21	A	Manchester U	L	1-3	0-0	16	Hutchison [80]	55,182
31	Apr 3	A	Liverpool	L	2-3	1-2	17	Dacourt [1], Jeffers [84]	44,852
32	5	H	Sheffield W	L	1-2	1-0	18	Jeffers [12]	35,270
33	11	H	Coventry C	W	2-0	1-0	16	Campbell 2 [29, 88]	32,341
34	17	A	Newcastle U	W	3-1	2-0	15	Campbell 2 [1, 44], Gemmill [88]	36,775
35	24	H	Charlton Ath	W	4-1	2-0	15	Hutchison [24], Campbell 2 [31, 60], Jeffers [75]	40,089
36	May 1	A	Chelsea	L	1-3	0-0	15	Jeffers [69]	34,000
37	8	H	West Ham U	W	6-0	3-0	14	Campbell 3 [14, 52, 77], Ball (pen) [25], Hutchison [38], Jeffers [87]	40,029
38	16	A	Southampton	L	0-2	0-1	14	15,254

Final League Position: 14

GOALSCORERS

League (42): Campbell 9, Jeffers 6, Bakayoko 4, Cadamarteri 4, Ferguson 4, Ball 3 (3 pens), Barmby 3, Hutchison 3, Dacourt 2, Collins 1, Gemmill 1, Materazzi 1, Unsworth 1.
Worthington Cup (7): Bakayoko 1, Collins 1, Dacourt 1, Ferguson 1, Hutchison 1, Materazzi 1, Watson 1.
FA Cup (6): Bakayoko 2, Barmby 1, Jeffers 1, Oster 1, Unsworth 1.

Myhre T 38	Cleland A 16+2	Ball M 36+1	Short C 22	Materazzi M 26+1	Tiler C 2	Collins J 19+1	Barmby N 20+4	Ferguson D 13	Dacourt O 28+2	Spencer J 2+1	Hutchison D 29+4	Cadamarteri D 11+19	Unsworth D 33+1	Watson D 22	Thomas T —+1	Farrelly G —+1	Oster J 6+3	Grant T 13+3	Bakayoko I 17+6	Ward M 4+2	Dunne R 15+1	Milligan J —+3	Jeffers F 11+4	Bilic S 4	Madar M 2	Branch M 1+6	Farley A —+1	Weir D 11+3	Jevons P —+1	O'Kane J 2	Degn P —+4	Gemmill S 7	Campbell K 8	Match No.
1	2	3	4	5	6	7	8	9	10^1	11^2	12	13																						1
1	2	3	4	5^2	6	7	8^2	9	10	11^1	13	12	14																					2
1	2^1	3	4	5		7	8^2	9	10		13	12	11	6																				3
1	2	3		6		7	8^1	9^1	10		11	12	4	5	13																			4
1	2	3		6		7	8^1	9	10		11^2	12	4	5	13																			5
1	2	3		6		7	8	9	10		11^1	12	4	5																				6
1	2^2	3	10	6		7	8^1	9			11	12	4	5		13																		7
1		3	2	6				9	10		11	8	4	5	13																			8
1	2	3	4			7		9			11	12	6	5				8^1	10^2	13														9
1	2	3		6		7		9	10	8		12	4	5					11^1															10
1		3	2^1	6		7		9	10			8	4	5					11	12														11
1	2^1	3		6^2		7		9	10		12	13	8	5^2					11		4	14												12
1	2^2	3	4	5		7		9			10	12	6					8	11^1			13												13
1		3	4			7					10	9^2	6	5				8	11^1		2	12	13											14
1	12	3	4	13		7					10	9	6	5^2			14	8^3	11^1		2													15
1	2	3	4	5		7					10	9						8	11		6													16
1	2	3				7	12		13		10		6					8^1	11		4			5	9^2									17
1		3		5		12	13				10		11		7	6	2^1	8^2			4				9^3	14								18
1	2	3		6		7^2	12				10		11					8^1			4		9	5		13								19
1	12	3	2	4^1		7^3					10		6					8	11			14	13	5		9^2								20
1	2	3		5		7^1	12				10		6					8	11		4		9											21
1	2	3		6		7^2	12				10			5				8	11		4^1	13	9^3			14								22
1		3		5		7	12				10		6					8	11	2^3		13	9^2	4		14								23
1		3		5		7	12				10		6					8	11	2	4^1		9											24
1		3		5		7	12				10		6					8	11	2	4^2	13	9^1											25
1		3		5		7^2	12				10		6					8	11	2	4^3	13	9^1			14								26
1	11	3		5		7	12				10		6					8		2	4^1		9											27
1		3	4	5			12				10		6					8^3					9^1	2		13		7	14	11^2				28
1		3		5			12				10							8^1	11		4		13	2^2		9^3		7	14					29
1		3	4	5			12				10		6					8^1	11				9^1	2		13		7^2	14					30
1		3	2				12				10		6^3					8^2	11^1		4		13	5		14						7	9	31
1	12	3	4	5^1							10		6^3					8^2	11				13	2		14						7	9	32
1		3	4	5			12				10		6					8	11^1					2								7	9	33
1		3	4	5			12				10		6					8^1	11				13	2								7	9^2	34
1		3	4	5							10		6					8	11					2								7	9	35
1		3	4				12				10		6					8	11					2				7^1	5^2		13		9	36
1		3	4	5							10		6					8	11					2								7	9	37
1		3	4^1	5							10		6					8^2	11				13	2		14						7^3	9	38

Worthington Cup

Second Round	Huddersfield T	(a)	1-1
		(h)	2-1
Third Round	Middlesbrough	(a)	3-2
Fourth Round	Sunderland	(h)	1-1

FA Cup

Third Round	Bristol C	(a)	2-0
Fourth Round	Ipswich T	(h)	1-0
Fifth Round	Coventry C	(h)	2-1
Sixth Round	Newcastle U	(a)	1-4

Division 3

EXETER CITY

FOUNDATION

Exeter City was formed in 1904 by the amalgamation of St. Sidwell's United and Exeter United. The club first played in the East Devon League and then the Plymouth & District League. After an exhibition match between West Bromwich Albion and Woolwich Arsenal was held to test interest as Exeter was then a rugby stronghold, Exeter City decided at a meeting at the Red Lion Hotel to turn professional in 1908.

St James Park, Exeter EX4 6PX.

Telephone: (01392) 254073.

Fax: (01392) 425885.

Training Ground: (01395) 232784.

Ground Capacity: 10,570.

Record Attendance: 20,984 v Sunderland, FA Cup 6th rd (replay), 4 March 1931.

Record Receipts: £59,862.98 v Aston Villa, FA Cup 3rd rd, 8 January 1994.

Pitch Measurements: 114yd × 73yd.

Honorary President: W. C. Hill.

Chairman: A. I. Doble.

Directors: P. Carter, I. M. Couch, S. W. Dawe, L. G. Vallance, M. Shelbourne, P. Dobson.

Manager: Peter Fox.

Assistant Manager/Coach: Noel Blake.

Physio: Simon Shakeshaft.

Chief Executive: Bernard Frowd OBE.

Secretary: Stuart Brailey.

Company Secretary: P. Carter.

Marketing Manager: Julie Richards.

LATEST SEQUENCES

Longest Sequence of League Wins: 7, 23.4.77 – 20.8.77.

Longest Sequence of League Defeats: 7, 14.1.84 – 25.2.84.

Longest Sequence of League Draws: 6, 13.9.86 – 4.10.86.

Longest Sequence of Unbeaten League Matches: 13, 23.8.86 – 25.10.86.

Longest Sequence Without a League Win: 18, 21.2.95 – 19.8.95.

HONOURS

Football League: Division 3 best season: 8th, 1979–80; Division 3 (S) – Runners-up 1932–33; Division 4 – Champions 1989–90; Runners-up 1976–77.

FA Cup: best season: 6th rd replay, 1931, 6th rd 1981.

Football League Cup: never beyond 4th rd.

Division 3 (S) Cup: Winners 1934.

Colours

Red and white striped shirts, black shorts, black stockings.

Change Colours

All purple.

Year Formed: 1904.

Turned Professional: 1908.

Ltd Co.: 1908.

Club Nickname: 'The Grecians'.

First Football League Game: 28 August 1920, Division 3, v Brentford (h) W 3–0 – Pym; Coleburne, Feebury (1p); Crawshaw, Carrick, Mitton; Appleton, Makin, Wright (1), Vowles (1), Dockray.

Record League Victory: 8–1 v Coventry C, Division 3 (S), 4 December 1926 – Bailey; Pollard, Charlton; Pullen, Pool, Garrett; Purcell (2), McDevitt, Blackmore (2), Dent (2), Compton (2). 8–1 v Aldershot, Division 3 (S), 4 May 1935 – Chesters; Gray, Miller; Risdon, Webb, Angus; Jack Scott (1), Wrightson (1), Poulter (3), McArthur (1), Dryden (1), (1 og).

Record Cup Victory: 9–1 v Aberdare, FA Cup 1st rd, 26 November 1927 – Holland; Pollard, Charlton; Phoenix, Pool, Gee; Purcell (2), McDevitt, Dent (4), Vaughan (2), Compton (1).

Record Defeat: 0–9 v Notts Co, Division 3 (S), 16 October 1948. 0–9 v Northampton T, Division 3 (S), 12 April 1958.

Most League Points (2 for a win): 62, Division 4, 1976–77.

Most League Points (3 for a win): 89, Division 4, 1989–90.

Most League Goals: 88, Division 3 (S), 1932–33.

Highest League Scorer in Season: Fred Whitlow, 33, Division 3 (S), 1932–33.

Most League Goals in Total Aggregate: Tony Kellow, 129, 1976–78, 1980–83, 1985–88.

Most League Goals in One Match: 4, Harold 'Jazzo' Kirk v Portsmouth, Division 3S, 3 March 1923; 4, Fred Dent v Bristol R, Division 3S, 5 November 1927; 4, Fred Whitlow v Watford, Division 3S, 29 October 1932.

Most Capped Player: Dermot Curtis, 1 (17), Eire.

Most League Appearances: Arnold Mitchell, 495, 1952–66.

Youngest League Player: Cliff Bastin, 16 years 31 days v Coventry C, 14 April 1928.

Record Transfer Fee Received: £500,000 from Manchester C for Martin Phillips, November 1995.

Record Transfer Fee Paid: £65,000 to Blackpool for Tony Kellow, March 1980.

Football League Record: 1920 Elected Division 3; 1921–58 Division 3 (S); 1958–64 Division 4; 1964–66 Division 3; 1966–77 Division 4; 1977–84 Division 3; 1984–90 Division 4; 1990–92 Division 3; 1992–94 Division 2; 1994– Division 3.

MANAGERS

Arthur Chadwick 1910–22
Fred Mavin 1923–27
Dave Wilson 1928–29
Billy McDevitt 1929–35
Jack English 1935–39
George Roughton 1945–52
Norman Kirkman 1952–53
Norman Dodgin 1953–57
Bill Thompson 1957–58
Frank Broome 1958–60
Glen Wilson 1960–62
Cyril Spiers 1962–63
Jack Edwards 1963–65
Ellis Stuttard 1965–66
Jock Basford 1966–67
Frank Broome 1967–69
Johnny Newman 1969–76
Bobby Saxton 1977–79
Brian Godfrey 1979–83
Gerry Francis 1983–84
Jim Iley 1984–85
Colin Appleton 1985–87
Terry Cooper 1988–91
Alan Ball 1991–94
Terry Cooper 1994–95
Peter Fox June 1995–

TEN YEAR LEAGUE RECORD

		P	W	D	L	F	A	Pts	Pos
1988-89	Div 4	46	18	6	22	65	68	60	13
1989-90	Div 4	46	28	5	13	83	48	89	1
1990-91	Div 3	46	16	9	21	58	52	57	16
1991-92	Div 3	46	14	11	21	57	80	53	20
1992-93	Div 2	46	11	17	18	54	69	50	19
1993-94	Div 2	46	11	12	23	52	83	45	22
1994-95	Div 3	42	8	10	24	36	70	34	22
1995-96	Div 3	46	13	18	15	46	53	57	14
1996-97	Div 3	46	12	12	22	48	73	48	22
1997-98	Div 3	46	15	15	16	68	63	60	15

DID YOU KNOW ?

Exeter City became the first English club to undertake an extensive tour of South America in the summer of 1914, playing eight matches in Argentina and Brazil. They lost only the first fixture.

EXETER CITY 1998–99 LEAGUE RECORD

Match No.	Date	Venue	Opponents	Result	H/T Score	Lg. Pos.	Goalscorers	Attendance
1	Aug 8	A	Swansea C	L 0-2	0-1			5809
2	15	H	Scarborough	W 1-0	1-0	18	Gittens [21]	2703
3	22	A	Torquay U	L 0-1	0-0	20		3739
4	29	H	Carlisle U	W 2-0	2-0	10	Breslan [26], Flack [40]	2661
5	31	A	Peterborough U	L 1-4	1-3	14	Rowbotham [19]	4256
6	Sept 5	H	Chester C	L 0-1	0-0	21		2551
7	8	H	Brighton & HA	W 1-0	0-0	—	Breslan [70]	2519
8	12	A	Hartlepool U	L 3-4	2-2	19	Rowbotham [28], McConnell [35], Breslan [68]	2106
9	19	H	Barnet	W 1-0	0-0	14	Rowbotham [90]	2523
10	26	A	Cambridge U	D 1-1	0-1	16	Richardson [90]	3061
11	Oct 3	H	Mansfield T	W 2-1	1-1	11	Flack [21], Rowbotham [63]	3024
12	9	A	Leyton Orient	L 0-2	0-1	—		3349
13	17	H	Scunthorpe U	D 2-2	0-2	15	Wilkinson [75], Flack [90]	2885
14	20	H	Hull C	W 3-0	0-0	14	McConnell [69], Richardson [70], Rowbotham [83]	2101
15	31	A	Cardiff C	L 0-1	0-0	14		5411
16	Nov 7	H	Southend U	W 2-1	0-1	11	McConnell [86], Flack [90]	3085
17	10	A	Rochdale	D 1-1	0-1	—	Gittens [85]	1639
18	21	H	Shrewsbury T	L 0-1	0-0	16		3510
19	28	A	Rotherham U	D 0-0	0-0	15		3489
20	Dec 12	H	Brentford	L 0-1	0-1	15		2793
21	19	A	Halifax T	D 1-1	1-0	18	Stoneman (og) [33]	2342
22	26	H	Torquay U	D 1-1	0-0	18	Flack [88]	5575
23	28	A	Plymouth Arg	L 0-1	0-0	19		11,936
24	Jan 2	A	Carlisle U	W 3-1	2-1	17	Rees [11], Holloway [25], Flack [86]	3340
25	9	H	Swansea C	W 4-0	2-0	16	Curran [7], Flack 2 [26, 82], Quailey [66]	3213
26	16	A	Scarborough	L 0-1	0-0	16		2002
27	23	H	Peterborough U	W 2-0	0-0	13	Flack 2 [58, 68]	2933
28	30	H	Plymouth Arg	D 1-1	1-1	13	Fry [9]	6746
29	Feb 6	A	Chester C	D 0-0	0-0	14		2243
30	13	A	Brighton & HA	W 1-0	0-0	13	Rowbotham [64]	4005
31	20	H	Hartlepool U	W 2-1	0-1	12	Quailey [89], Flack [90]	2987
32	27	A	Barnet	W 1-0	0-0	12	Tosh [50]	2072
33	Mar 6	H	Cambridge U	L 0-3	0-2	12		3478
34	13	A	Southend U	D 0-0	0-0	12		3695
35	20	H	Cardiff C	L 0-2	0-1	13		3653
36	26	H	Darlington	D 0-0	0-0	—		3179
37	Apr 3	A	Scunthorpe U	L 0-2	0-0	14		3419
38	5	H	Leyton Orient	D 1-1	1-0	14	Wilkinson [24]	2764
39	10	H	Hull C	L 1-2	0-1	16	McConnell [53]	5836
40	13	H	Rotherham U	W 3-0	1-0	12	Curran [20], Whelan (og) [56], McConnell (pen) [90]	1929
41	17	A	Shrewsbury T	D 1-1	0-0	13	Tosh [88]	2419
42	24	H	Rochdale	W 2-1	1-0	13	Curran [45], Fry [75]	2543
43	27	A	Mansfield T	W 1-0	0-0	—	Breslan [47]	2830
44	May 1	A	Brentford	L 0-3	0-1	12		6977
45	4	A	Darlington	L 0-4	0-0	—		2450
46	8	H	Halifax T	W 2-1	1-1	12	Thackeray (og) [44], Curran [90]	3180

Final League Position: 12

GOALSCORERS

League (47): Flack 11, Rowbotham 6, McConnell 5 (1 pen), Breslan 4, Curran 4, Fry 2, Gittens 2, Quailey 2, Richardson 2, Tosh 2, Wilkinson 2, Holloway 1, Rees 1, own goals 3.
Worthington Cup (2): Richardson 2.
FA Cup (8): Flack 2, Rowbotham 2, Gardner 1, Gittens 1, Richardson 1, own goal 1.

Player appearances (starts + substitute):

Bayes A 41 · Gale S 21 + 6 · Power G 40 · Curran C 30 + 4 · Blake N 4 + 3 · Gittens J 44 · Rowbotham D 28 + 4 · Rees J 44 · Flack S 38 + 6 · Clark B 8 + 2 · Breslan G 24 + 10 · Richardson J 39 + 1 · Crowe G 3 + 6 · Gardner J 23 + 4 · Fry C 27 + 5 · Holloway C 27 + 7 · McConnell B 15 + 7 · Wilkinson J 6 + 12 · Baddeley L 23 · Quailey B 8 + 4 · Waugh W — + 7 · Tosh P 8 + 2 · Speakman R — + 1 · Potter D 5 · Smith P — + 1

Bayes A	Gale S	Power G	Curran C	Blake N	Gittens J	Rowbotham D	Rees J	Flack S	Clark B	Breslan G	Richardson J	Crowe G	Gardner J	Fry C	Holloway C	McConnell B	Wilkinson J	Baddeley L	Quailey B	Waugh W	Tosh P	Speakman R	Potter D	Smith P	Match No.
1	2[1]	3	4	5	6	7	8	9	10	11[2]	12	13													1
1	2	3[1]	4		6	7[2]	8	9	10	11[3]	5			12	13	14									2
1	2		4		6	7[1]	8[2]	9[3]	10	11	5	14	3	12	13										3
1	2	3			6	7	8	12		11[2]	5		9	10[1]	4	13									4
1	2	3[3]		14	6	7	8	12		11	5		9[2]	4[1]	13	10									5
1	2	3		12	6	7[2]	8	9[1]		11	5	13		4		10[3]	14								6
1	2	3			6	7	8	12		11	5	9[1]		4	10										7
1	2	3		4[1]	6	7	8	13		11	5	12			10	9[2]									8
1	2	3			6	7	8	12		11	5	13		4	10[2]	9[1]									9
1		3	2		6	7		9		11	5	13	12	4[2]	10[1]			8							10
1		3	12		6	7	8	9		11	5				10		2[1]	4							11
1	10[1]	3	2		6	7	8	9		11[2]	5			12		13		4							12
1		3	12		6	7	8[1]	9		11	5				2[3]	10[2]	13	14	4						13
1		3	10		6	7	8[1]	9		11[2]	5				2[3]	12	13	14	4						14
1		3	10[2]		6		8	9		11	5			2[1]	12	13	7		4						15
1		3	10		6	7	8	9		11	5			2[2]		12	13		4						16
1		3	10[1]		6	7	8	9			5			12	11[2]	2	13		4						17
1		3			6	7	8	9		11[2]	5			2	10[1]		12	13	4						18
1		3	10	4	6	7	8	9	2		5							11							19
1	12	3[1]	10	4	6	7	8			2[3]	14	5		11	13		9[2]								20
1	5	3	10		6	7		9						11	2	8			4						21
1	5	3	10		6	7[3]	8	9			12			11[2]	2	13			4[1]	14					22
1	5	3	10		6	12	8				13			11[1]	2	4					7[2]				23
1		3	10		6	12	8	9	13		5			11	2[2]	4					7[1]				24
1		3	10	12			8	9[3]	6	13	5			11[1]	2[2]	4					7	14			25
1		3	10		6		8	9	12	13	5			11	2[2]	4[1]					7[3]	14			26
1	12	3			6		8	9	4		5			11	2	10[1]					7[2]	13			27
1		3			6		8	9	4	12	5			11[1]	2	10					7[2]	13			28
1	3		12		6	13	8[1]	9			5			11	2[3]	10	14	4			7[2]				29
1		3	12		6	7	8	9			5			11	2	10[1]		4							30
1		3			6	7	8	9			5			11[2]	2[1]	10	12	4	13						31
1	3				6	7	8	9			5			11	10			4			2				32
1	12	3	10		6	7	8	9			5[1]			11				4[2]	13		2				33
1	5[1]	3	10		6	7[2]	8	9		12				11				4	13		2				34
1	2	3	5				8	12		6[1]				11		10		13	4		7[2]	9			35
1	2	3[3]	5		6	7	8	9[1]		12				11		10		13		14	10[2]				36
1	3				6		8	9		2[1]	5				10		12	4			7				37
1	3	4			6		8	9		2[1]	5				10	12	11				7[2]	13			38
1	3		2		6		8				5		12		10	9	11[1]	4			7				39
1	12	3	2		6		8	9			5			7[2]		10	11[1]	4	13						40
	3		2		6		8	9		12	5			7[2]		10	11	4[1]	13				1		41
	3		2		6		8	9		11	5			7[1]	4	10							1		42
	12	3	2		6		8	9		11	5			7[1]	4	10							1		43
	3		2		6		8	9		11[2]	5			7	4	10[1]	12		13				1		44
1	12	3	2		6		8	9		11[2]	5			7	4[1]	10			13						45
	3	2			6	7[2]	8	9		12	5			10	4[3]		11[1]		13				1	14	46

Worthington Cup
First Round   Ipswich T   (h) 1-1   (a) 1-5

FA Cup
First Round   Tamworth   (a) 2-2   (h) 4-1
Second Round   Bristol R   (h) 2-2   (a) 0-5

Division 1 **FULHAM**

Established 1879

FOUNDATION

Churchgoers were responsible for the foundation of Fulham, which first saw the light of day as Fulham St Andrew's Church Sunday School FC in 1879. They won the West London Amateur Cup in 1887 and the championship of the West London League in its initial season of 1892–93. The name Fulham had been adopted in 1888.

Craven Cottage, Stevenage Rd, Fulham, London SW6 6HH.
Telephone: (0171) 893 8383.
Fax: (0171) 384 4715.
Website: http://www.fulhamfc.co.uk.
Clubcall: 0891 440044.
Ground Capacity: 19,250.
Record Attendance: 49,335 v Millwall, Division 2, 8 October 1938.
Record Receipts: £139,235 v Watford, Division 2, 2 May 1998.
Pitch Measurements: 110yd × 75yd.
Chairman: M. Al Fayed.
Directors: W. F. Muddyman (Vice-Chairman), Stuart Benson, Mark Griffiths, Andy Muddyman, Tim Delaney.
Manager: Paul Bracewell.
Assistant Manager: Frank Sibley.
Coach: John Marshall.
Chief Scout: Arthur Cox.
Director of Youth: Alan Smith.
Youth Team Coach: Glenn Cockerill.
Community Officer: Gary Mulcahey (0171) 384 4759.
Stadium Manager: Francis Broughton.
Club Secretary: Etain Wist.
Sales and Marketing Director: Juliet Slot.
Communications Manager: Mark Maunders.

LATEST SEQUENCES

Longest Sequence of League Wins: 8, 6.3.99 – 13.4.99.
Longest Sequence of League Defeats: 11, 2.12.61 – 24.2.62.
Longest Sequence of League Draws: 6, 14.10.95 – 18.11.95.
Longest Sequence of Unbeaten League Matches: 15, 26.1.99 – 13.4.99.
Longest Sequence Without a League Win: 15, 25.2.50 – 23.8.50.

HONOURS

Football League: Division 1 best season: 10th, 1959–60; Division 2 – Champions 1948–49, 1998–99; Runners-up 1958–59; Division 3 (S) – Champions 1931–32; Division 3 – Runners-up 1970–71, 1996–97.
FA Cup: Runners-up 1975.
Football League Cup: best season: 5th rd, 1968, 1971.

Colours

White shirts, red and black trim, black shorts, white stockings red and black trim.

Change Colours

Lime green shirts with navy trim, navy shorts, navy stockings.

Year Formed: 1879.
Turned Professional: 1898.
Ltd Co.: 1903.
Reformed: 1987.
Previous Name: 1879, Fulham St Andrew's; 1888, Fulham.
Club Nickname: 'Cottagers'.
Previous Grounds: 1879 Star Road, Fulham; c.1883 Eel Brook Common, 1884 Lillie Road; 1885 Putney Lower Common; 1886 Ranelagh House, Fulham; 1888 Barn Elms, Castelnau; 1889 Purser's Cross (Roskell's Field), Parsons Green Lane; 1891 Eel Brook Common; 1891 Half Moon, Putney; 1895 Captain James Field, West Brompton; 1896 Craven Cottage.
First Football League Game: 3 September 1907, Division 2, v Hull C (h) L 0–1 – Skene; Ross, Lindsay; Collins, Morrison, Goldie; Dalrymple, Freeman, Bevan, Hubbard, Threlfall.
Record League Victory: 10–1 v Ipswich T, Division 1, 26 December 1963 – Macedo; Cohen, Langley; Mullery (1), Keetch, Robson (1); Key, Cook (1), Leggat (4), Haynes, Howfield (3).
Record Cup Victory: 7–0 v Swansea C, FA Cup 1st rd, 11 November 1995 – Lange; Jupp (1), Herrera, Barkus (Brooker (1)), Moore, Angus, Thomas (1), Morgan, Brazil (Hamill), Conroy (3) (Bolt), Cusack (1).
Record Defeat: 0–10 v Liverpool, League Cup 2nd rd 1st leg, 23 September 1986.
Most League Points (2 for a win): 60, Division 2, 1958–59 and Division 3, 1970–71.
Most League Points (3 for a win): 101, Division 2, 1998–99.
Most League Goals: 111, Division 3 (S), 1931–32.
Highest League Scorer in Season: Frank Newton, 43, Division 3 (S), 1931–32.
Most League Goals in Total Aggregate: Gordon Davies, 159, 1978–84, 1986–91.
Most League Goals in One Match: 5, Fred Harrison v Stockport Co, Division 2, 5 September 1908; 5, Bedford Jezzard v Hull C, Division 2, 8 October 1955; 5, Jimmy Hill v Doncaster R, Division 2, 15 March 1958; 5, Steve Earle v Halifax T, Division 3, 16 September 1969.
Most Capped Player: Johnny Haynes, 56, England.
Most League Appearances: Johnny Haynes, 594, 1952–70.
Youngest League Player: Tony Mahoney, 17 years 38 days v Cardiff C, 6 November 1976.
Record Transfer Fee Received: £800,000 from Bristol C for Tony Thorpe, February 1998.
Record Transfer Fee Paid: £2,100,000 to Blackburn R for Chris Coleman, December 1997.
Football League Record: 1907 Elected to Division 2; 1928–32 Division 3 (S); 1932–49 Division 2; 1949–52 Division 1; 1952–59 Division 2; 1959–68 Division 1; 1968–69 Division 2; 1969–71 Division 3; 1971–80 Division 2; 1980–82 Division 3; 1982–86 Division 2; 1986–92 Division 3; 1992–94 Division 2; 1994–97 Division 3; 1997–99 Division 2; 1999– Division 1.

MANAGERS

Harry Bradshaw 1904–09
Phil Kelso 1909–24
Andy Ducat 1924–26
Joe Bradshaw 1926–29
Ned Liddell 1929–31
Jim MacIntyre 1931–34
Jimmy Hogan 1934–35
Jack Peart 1935–48
Frank Osborne 1948–64
  (was Secretary-Manager or General Manager for most of this period)
Bill Dodgin Snr 1949–53
Duggie Livingstone 1956–58
Bedford Jezzard 1958–64
  (General Manager for last two months)
Vic Buckingham 1965–68
Bobby Robson 1968
Bill Dodgin Jnr 1969–72
Alec Stock 1972–76
Bobby Campbell 1976–80
Malcolm Macdonald 1980–84
Ray Harford 1984–96
Ray Lewington 1986–90
Alan Dicks 1990–91
Don Mackay 1991–94
Ian Branfoot 1994–96
  (continued as General Manager)
Micky Adams 1996–97
Ray Wilkins 1997–98
Kevin Keegan 1998–99
  (Chief Operating Officer)
Paul Bracewell May 1999–

TEN YEAR LEAGUE RECORD

		P	W	D	L	F	A	Pts	Pos
1988-89	Div 3	46	22	9	15	69	67	75	4
1989-90	Div 3	46	12	15	19	55	66	51	20
1990-91	Div 3	46	10	16	20	41	56	46	21
1991-92	Div 3	46	19	13	14	57	53	70	9
1992-93	Div 2	46	16	17	13	57	55	65	12
1993-94	Div 2	46	14	10	22	50	63	52	21
1994-95	Div 3	42	16	14	12	60	54	62	8
1995-96	Div 3	46	12	17	17	57	63	53	17
1996-97	Div 3	46	25	12	9	72	38	87	2
1997-98	Div 2	46	20	10	16	60	43	70	6

DID YOU KNOW ?

Before turning professional in 1952 at 17, Johnny Haynes played for Feltham in the Middlesex League, Wimbledon (Isthmian League) and Woodford Town (Delphian League). Fulham had no youth team at that time.

FULHAM 1998–99 LEAGUE RECORD

Match No.	Date	Venue	Opponents	Result	H/T Score	Lg. Pos.	Goalscorers	Attendance
1	Aug 8	A	Macclesfield T	W 1-0	1-0	—	Salako [19]	3933
2	14	H	Manchester C	W 3-0	3-0	—	Beardsley [21], Lehmann 2 [33, 39]	14,284
3	22	A	Colchester U	W 1-0	0-0	3	Collins [82]	6377
4	29	H	Bournemouth	D 0-0	0-0	4		12,107
5	31	A	Oldham Ath	D 1-1	0-0	2	Moody [50]	4744
6	Sept 8	H	Stoke C	W 1-0	0-0	—	Brevett [60]	12,055
7	12	A	Notts Co	L 0-1	0-1	7		5805
8	19	H	York C	D 3-3	2-1	8	Cornwall [19], Coleman [32], Symons [56]	9071
9	26	A	Lincoln C	W 2-1	0-0	6	Beardsley 2 [47, 64]	4731
10	29	H	Wycombe W	W 2-0	1-0	—	Coleman [13], Bracewell [65]	7447
11	Oct 3	A	Luton T	L 1-3	0-1	4	Neilson [87]	11,886
12	17	A	Millwall	W 1-0	0-0	5	Symons [89]	11,876
13	24	H	Walsall	W 4-1	1-0	3	Peschisolido [30], Symons [63], Hayward [75], Horsfield [83]	8452
14	31	A	Blackpool	W 3-2	3-1	2	Morgan [24], Hayward (pen) [26], Horsfield [35]	5904
15	Nov 7	A	Bristol R	W 1-0	1-0	2	Collins [38]	11,575
16	10	A	Wrexham	W 2-0	2-0	—	Uhlenbeek [14], Peschisolido [30]	3485
17	21	H	Chesterfield	W 2-1	1-0	2	Peschisolido 2 (1 pen) [16, 54 (p)]	10,005
18	28	A	Gillingham	L 0-1	0-0	3		7614
19	Dec 1	A	Wigan Ath	L 0-2	0-0	—		3951
20	12	H	Burnley	W 4-0	2-0	2	Morgan 2 [27, 38], Hayles [57], Peschisolido [73]	9983
21	19	H	Preston NE	W 1-0	0-0	1	Coleman [86]	12,321
22	26	H	Colchester U	W 2-0	1-0	1	Smith N [26], Hayles (pen) [73]	11,939
23	28	A	Northampton T	D 1-1	0-0	1	Horsfield [49]	7315
24	Jan 9	H	Macclesfield T	W 1-0	0-0	1	Horsfield [55]	10,153
25	16	H	Manchester C	L 0-3	0-2	1		30,251
26	26	H	Oldham Ath	W 1-0	1-0	—	Morgan [22]	8160
27	30	H	Northampton T	W 2-0	1-0	1	Hayles [18], Albert [70]	11,641
28	Feb 6	A	Wycombe W	D 1-1	1-1	1	Symons [33]	7538
29	20	H	Notts Co	W 2-1	1-0	1	Horsfield 2 [36, 67]	11,909
30	23	H	Reading	W 3-1	0-1	—	Horsfield 2 [49, 51], Symons [67]	11,247
31	27	A	York C	W 3-0	2-0	1	Horsfield [40], Hayles [45], Peschisolido [52]	6169
32	Mar 2	A	Bournemouth	D 1-1	0-0	—	Symons [61]	9928
33	6	H	Lincoln C	W 1-0	1-0	1	Horsfield [44]	11,702
34	9	A	Luton T	W 4-0	1-0	—	Horsfield 2 [34, 73], Trollope [64], Hayles [85]	7424
35	12	A	Bristol R	W 3-2	2-1	—	Symons [9], Horsfield [38], Trollope [56]	8011
36	16	H	Stoke C	W 1-0	1-0	—	Symons [10]	12,298
37	20	H	Blackpool	W 4-0	1-0	1	Hayles [20], Horsfield [63], Finnan [74], Symons [87]	12,869
38	Apr 5	A	Reading	W 1-0	0-0	1	Morgan [77]	18,741
39	10	H	Wigan Ath	W 2-0	0-0	1	Albert [56], Symons [64]	12,140
40	13	H	Gillingham	W 3-0	1-0	—	Hayles [22], Coleman [81], Horsfield [88]	13,119
41	17	A	Chesterfield	L 0-1	0-0	1		5800
42	21	A	Millwall	W 4-1	2-0	—	Betsy [19], Hayles [44], Symons [48], Finnan [89]	11,266
43	24	H	Wrexham	D 1-1	1-1	1	Peschisolido [43]	11,754
44	May 1	A	Burnley	L 0-1	0-0	1		13,086
45	4	A	Walsall	D 2-2	1-1	—	Smith J [45], Hayward [88]	8326
46	8	H	Preston NE	W 3-0	0-0	1	Moody 3 (1 pen) [64, 74 (p), 77]	17,176

Final League Position: 1

GOALSCORERS

League (79): Horsfield 15, Symons 11, Hayles 8 (1 pen), Peschisolido 7 (1 pen), Morgan 5, Coleman 4, Moody 4 (1 pen), Beardsley 3, Hayward 3 (1 pen), Albert 2, Collins 2, Finnan 2, Lehmann 2, Trollope 2, Betsy 1, Bracewell 1, Brevett 1, Cornwall 1, Neilson 1, Salako 1, Smith J 1, Smith N 1, Uhlenbeek 1.
Worthington Cup (7): Lehmann 2, Beardsley 1, Coleman 1, Morgan 1, Peschisolido 1, Salako 1.
FA Cup (11): Hayward 2, Horsfield 2, Morgan 2, Peschisolido 2 (1 pen), Hayles 1, Lehmann 1, own goal 1.

Taylor M 46	Lawrence M 1	Brevett R 45	Symons K 45	Coleman C 45	Morgan S 32+2	Trollope P 17+3	Bracewell P 25+1	Lehmann D 16+10	Collins W 18+3	Salako J 7+3	Hayward S 42	Beardsley P 11+2	Moody P 2+5	Uhlenbeek G 11+12	Peschisolido P 19+14	Davis S 1+5	Cornwall L 1+3	Brooker P —+1	Scott R 2+1	Neilson A 3+1	Smith N 20+9	Horsfield G 26+2	Finnan S 21+1	Hayles B 26+4	Keller F —+1	Brazier M 1+1	Albert P 12+1	Betsy K 1+6	McAnespie S 1+2	Smith J 9	Match No.
1	2	3	4	5	6	7	8	9	10	11																					1
1		3	6	5	2		8	9^1	10	11^2	4	7	12	13																	2
1		3	6	5	4		8	9^1	13	11^2	10	7^3	12	2	14																3
1		3	6	5	4		8	9^1	2	11^2	10	7	12		13																4
1		3	6	5	4		8		2	11^1	10	7	9		12																5
1		3	6	5	4		8	12	2^2	11^3	10	7	9^1	13		14															6
1		3	6	5	4		8^1	9	11		10	7^2	2		12	13															7
1		3	6	5	4		8	9	2		10	7^1	12				11^2		13												8
1		3	6	5	4		8	9^1	10	11		7	2								12										9
1		3	6	5	4^3		8		2	11		7	12			10^1	13				9^2	14									10
1		3	6	5			8^2	10^3	2	11		7	12			13	14				9^1	4									11
1		3	6	5	2		8	9	4^1	11		7	12								10										12
1		3	6	5	4		8^1	9			7	11	2			10^2					12	13									13
1		3	6	5	4		8	12			7	11	2		10							9^1									14
1		3	6	5	4		8^3	9^2	7	13	11	12	2		10^1						14										15
1		3	6	5	4		8^1	9			7	11	2		10						12										16
1		3	6	5	4		8^2				11		12		10						13	9	2	7^1							17
1		3	6	5	4		11								10						8	9	2	7							18
1		3	6	5	4		12	8^2			11	13	14		10^3						9	2^1		7							19
1		3	6	5	4						12	7	2		10						8^2	9^1	11	13							20
1		3	6	5	4		8^1					7	2		10^2						11	9	12	13							21
1		3	6	5	4	12	8^1			13		7	2		10^2						11	9^3	14								22
1		3	6	5	4		8					7	2		10^1						11	9	12								23
1		3	6	5			8	12	13		4		10						2		9^1	7	11^2								24
1		3	6	5			8^3	9^1			4		12						2		13	14	7	11	10^2						25
1		3	6	5	4^1				12			13			10^2						7	9	2	11		8					26
1		3		5	10		8	12			4	13									7	9^2	2	11^2		6					27
1		3	6	5	11		8	12				7			10^2						9	2	13	4^1							28
1		3	6	7	12		8^2								10						4	9	2	11^1		5	13				29
1		3	6	5					13			7	12		10^2						4	9^1	2	11^3			8	14			30
1		3	6	5					10			7	12								4	9^1	2	11^3			13	8^2	14		31
1		3	6	5	4			9	10			7	12								8	2	11^1								32
1		3	6	5	4				10^1			7	13		12						8	2	11^2								33
1		3	6	5	4				10			7	12								8^3	9^2	2	11^1				13	14		34
1		3	6	5	4				10			7	12								8	9	2	11^1							35
1		3	6	5	4				10			7									8	9	2	11							36
1		3	6	5	4^3				10			7	12	13							8^1	9	2	11				14			37
1			6	5	4				10^1			7	12								13	8	9	11^2			3			2	38
1		3	6^1	5	12				10			7^3	13								14	9	8	11			4			2^2	39
1		3	6	5	12				10^2			7	13								14	9	8	11^2			4^1			2	40
1		3	6	5								7	12								10^1	9	8	11			4			2	41
1		3	6	5								7			10	12						8	11				4	9^1		2	42
1		3	6	5								7			10	12					8	9^2	11				4^1	13		2	43
1		3	6	5	4^2		8		12			7			10^3						13	9^1	11					14		2	44
1		3	6	5					10^1	12	9^3	8^2	7	14							13		11						4	2	45
1		3	6	5	4				9^3	10		7	14	12							8^2		11						13	2^1	46

Worthington Cup

First Round	Cardiff C	(h)	2-1
		(a)	2-1
Second Round	Southampton	(h)	1-1
		(a)	1-0
Third Round	Liverpool	(a)	1-3

FA Cup

First Round	Leigh RMI	(h)	1-1
		(a)	2-0
Second Round	Hartlepool U	(h)	4-2
Third Round	Southampton	(a)	1-1
		(h)	1-0
Fourth Round	Aston Villa	(a)	2-0
Fifth Round	Manchester U	(a)	0-1

Division 2

GILLINGHAM

FOUNDATION

The success of the pioneering Royal Engineers of Chatham
excited the interest of the residents of the Medway Towns and led
to the formation of many clubs including Excelsior. After winning
the Kent Junior Cup and the Chatham District League in 1893,
Excelsior decided to go for bigger things and it was at a meeting in
the Napier Arms, Brompton, in 1893 that New Brompton FC
came into being, buying and developing the ground which is now
Priestfield Stadium.

Priestfield Stadium, Gillingham, ME7 4DD.

Telephone: (01634) 851854/576828.

Fax: (01634) 850986.

Ground Capacity: 10,600.

Record Attendance: 23,002 v QPR, FA Cup 3rd rd, 10 January 1948.

Record Receipts: £80,184 v Sheffield W, FA Cup 3rd rd, 7 January 1995.

Pitch Measurements: 114yd × 75yd.

Chairman/Chief Executive: P. D. P. Scally.

Director: P. A. Spokes.

Associate Director: Yvonne Paulley.

Manager: Peter Taylor.

Assistant Manager: Andy Hessenthaler.

Coach: Steve Butler.

Physio: Wayne Jones.

Secretary: Mrs G. E. Poynter.

Sales and Marketing Manager: J. Swaby.

LATEST SEQUENCES

Longest Sequence of League Wins: 7, 18.12.54 – 29.1.55.

Longest Sequence of League Defeats: 10, 20.9.88 – 5.11.88.

Longest Sequence of League Draws: 5, 28.8.93 – 18.9.93.

Longest Sequence of Unbeaten League Matches: 20,
13.10.73 – 10.2.74.

Longest Sequence Without a League Win: 15, 1.4.72 –
2.9.72.

HONOURS

Football League: Division 3 –
Runners-up 1995-96; Division 4 –
Champions 1963–64; Runners-up
1973–74.
FA Cup: best season: 5th rd, 1970.
Football League Cup: best season:
4th rd, 1964, 1997.

Colours
Blue and black.

Change Colours
Red and black.

Year Formed: 1893.

Turned Professional: 1894.

Ltd Co.: 1893.

Previous Name: 1893, New Brompton; 1913, Gillingham.

Club Nickname: 'The Gills'.

First Football League Game: 28 August 1920, Division 3, v Southampton (h) D 1–1 – Branfield; Robertson, Sissons; Battiste, Baxter, Wigmore; Holt, Hall, Gilbey (1), Roe, Gore.

Record League Victory: 10–0 v Chesterfield, Division 3, 5 September 1987 – Kite; Haylock, Pearce, Shipley (2) (Lillis), West, Greenall (1), Pritchard (2), Shearer (2), Lovell, Elsey (2), David Smith (1).

Record Cup Victory: 10–1 v Gorleston, FA Cup 1st rd, 16 November 1957 – Brodie; Parry, Hannaway; Riggs, Boswell, Laing; Payne, Fletcher (2), Saunders (5), Morgan (1), Clark (2).

Record Defeat: 2–9 v Nottingham F, Division 3 (S), 18 November 1950.

Most League Points (2 for a win): 62, Division 4, 1973–74.

Most League Points (3 for a win): 83, Division 3, 1984–85 and Division 3, 1995–96.

Most League Goals: 90, Division 4, 1973–74.

Highest League Scorer in Season: Ernie Morgan, 31, Division 3 (S), 1954–55; Brian Yeo, 31, Division 4, 1973–74.

Most League Goals in Total Aggregate: Brian Yeo, 135, 1963–75.

Most League Goals in One Match: 6, Fred Cheesmur v Merthyr T, Division 3S, 26 April 1930.

Most Capped Player: Tony Cascarino, 3 (38), Republic of Ireland.

Most League Appearances: John Simpson, 571, 1957–72.

Youngest League Player: Billy Hughes, 15 years 275 days v Southend U, 13 April 1976.

Record Transfer Fee Received: £1,200,000 from Bristol C for Ade Akinbiyi, May 1998.

Record Transfer Fee Paid: £600,000 to Reading for Carl Asaba, August 1998.

Football League Record: 1920 Original Member of Division 3; 1921 Division 3 (S); 1938 Failed re-election; Southern League 1938–44; Kent League 1944–46; Southern League 1946–50; 1950 Re-elected to Division 3 (S); 1958–64 Division 4; 1964–71 Division 3; 1971–74 Division 4; 1974–89 Division 3; 1989–92 Division 4; 1992–96; Division 3; 1996– Division 2.

MANAGERS

W. Ironside Groombridge
   1896–1906 *(Secretary-Manager)*
   (previously Financial Secretary)
Steve Smith 1906–08
W. I. Groombridge 1908–19
   (Secretary-Manager)
George Collins 1919–20
John McMillan 1920–23
Harry Curtis 1923–26
Albert Hoskins 1926–29
Dick Hendrie 1929–31
Fred Mavin 1932–37
Alan Ure 1937–38
Bill Harvey 1938–39
Archie Clark 1939–58
Harry Barratt 1958–62
Freddie Cox 1962–65
Basil Hayward 1966–71
Andy Nelson 1971–74
Len Ashurst 1974–75
Gerry Summers 1975–81
Keith Peacock 1981–87
Paul Taylor 1988
Keith Burkinshaw 1988–89
Damien Richardson 1989–93
Mike Flanagan 1993–95
Neil Smillie 1995
Tony Pulis 1995–99
Peter Taylor July 1999–

TEN YEAR LEAGUE RECORD

		P	W	D	L	F	A	Pts	Pos
1988-89	Div 3	46	12	4	30	47	81	40	23
1989-90	Div 4	46	17	11	18	46	48	62	14
1990-91	Div 4	46	12	18	16	57	60	54	15
1991-92	Div 4	42	15	12	15	63	53	57	11
1992-93	Div 3	42	9	13	20	48	64	40	21
1993-94	Div 3	42	12	15	15	44	51	51	16
1994-95	Div 3	42	10	11	21	46	64	41	19
1995-96	Div 3	46	22	17	7	49	20	83	2
1996-97	Div 2	46	19	10	17	60	59	67	11
1997-98	Div 2	46	19	13	14	52	47	70	8

DID YOU KNOW ?

Robert Taylor's five goals for Gillingham at Burnley on 27 February 1999 included a hat-trick in seven minutes. But Jimmy Scarth once hit three in two minutes on 1 November 1952 against Leyton Orient.

GILLINGHAM 1998–99 LEAGUE RECORD

Match No.	Date	Venue	Opponents	Result	H/T Score	Lg. Pos.	Goalscorers	Attendance
1	Aug 8	H	Walsall	L	0-1	0-1	—	5712
2	15	A	York C	D	1-1	1-1	17	Williams [41]	2634
3	22	H	Bristol R	D	0-0	0-0	22		4896
4	29	A	Blackpool	D	2-2	0-0	19	Saunders [61], Carr [65]	3994
5	Sept 1	H	Wrexham	W	4-0	2-0	—	Smith [8], Hessenthaler 2 [45, 49], Asaba [90]	5349
6	5	A	Chesterfield	L	0-1	0-0	17		3766
7	8	H	Northampton T	L	2-3	1-1	—	Smith 2 (1 pen) [2 (p), 56]	4897
8	12	A	Colchester U	D	1-1	1-1	18	Asaba [27]	4612
9	19	H	Burnley	W	2-1	1-1	16	Galloway [11], Taylor [86]	5702
10	26	A	Preston NE	D	1-1	0-0	16	Asaba [71]	10,506
11	Oct 3	H	Macclesfield T	D	2-2	0-1	17	Carr [70], Hodge [90]	6093
12	10	H	Wycombe W	W	3-0	2-0	14	Saunders [38], Taylor 2 [45, 70]	4575
13	17	A	Reading	D	0-0	0-0	15		11,467
14	20	A	Bournemouth	D	3-3	1-1	—	Asaba 2 [12, 81], Southall [76]	5183
15	24	H	Luton T	W	1-0	0-0	12	Asaba [61]	5602
16	31	A	Lincoln C	W	2-1	0-1	7	Asaba 2 [80, 90]	4366
17	Nov 7	H	Wigan Ath	W	2-0	1-0	7	Asaba [6], Balmer (og) [66]	5869
18	10	H	Oldham Ath	W	2-1	0-0	—	Asaba [76], Patterson [77]	5188
19	21	A	Manchester C	D	0-0	0-0	5		26,529
20	28	H	Fulham	W	1-0	0-0	5	Taylor [90]	7614
21	Dec 12	A	Stoke C	D	0-0	0-0	5		17,233
22	19	H	Notts Co	W	4-0	1-0	5	Asaba 3 [33, 81, 89], Taylor [71]	6072
23	29	H	Millwall	D	1-1	1-0	—	Galloway [13]	9221
24	Jan 2	H	Blackpool	W	1-0	0-0	5	Southall [87]	7022
25	9	A	Walsall	L	1-2	0-1	5	Patterson [69]	5495
26	16	H	York C	W	3-1	1-0	5	Asaba [17], Taylor [53], Butters [83]	6242
27	30	A	Millwall	D	3-3	1-0	6	Southall [23], Taylor [73], Saunders [81]	10,442
28	Feb 6	H	Chesterfield	W	3-1	1-0	5	Asaba [45], Hessenthaler [60], Southall [67]	6582
29	13	A	Northampton T	W	1-0	0-0	4	Smith [49]	5981
30	20	H	Colchester U	D	1-1	1-0	4	Asaba [22]	7276
31	23	A	Bristol R	W	1-0	1-0	—	Hessenthaler [29]	5735
32	27	A	Burnley	W	5-0	4-0	4	Taylor 5 (1 pen) [14, 27, 41, 43 (p), 48]	8981
33	Mar 6	H	Preston NE	D	1-1	0-1	4	Taylor [90]	9581
34	9	A	Macclesfield T	L	0-1	0-1	—		1868
35	13	A	Wigan Ath	L	1-4	1-2	5	Lisbie [8]	4248
36	20	H	Lincoln C	W	4-0	1-0	5	Hessenthaler 2 [13, 57], Lisbie 2 [79, 90]	7023
37	27	H	Luton T	L	0-1	0-1	6		6705
38	Apr 1	H	Reading	W	2-1	1-0	—	Saunders [4], Asaba [64]	8195
39	5	A	Wycombe W	W	2-0	0-0	5	Ashby [68], Asaba [74]	6688
40	9	H	Bournemouth	W	2-1	0-0	—	Hessenthaler [69], Lisbie [90]	7813
41	13	A	Fulham	L	0-3	0-1	—		13,119
42	17	H	Manchester C	L	0-2	0-1	5		10,400
43	20	A	Wrexham	L	1-2	0-1	—	Butters [48]	1871
44	24	A	Oldham Ath	W	4-1	3-1	5	Asaba [4], Smith [10], Galloway [27], Taylor [78]	5331
45	May 1	H	Stoke C	W	4-0	3-0	5	Taylor 2 [30, 45], Butters [33], Smith [69]	8289
46	8	A	Notts Co	W	1-0	0-0	4	Asaba [75]	7815

Final League Position: 4

GOALSCORERS

League (75): Asaba 20, Taylor 16 (1 pen), Hessenthaler 7, Smith 6 (1 pen), Lisbie 4, Saunders 4, Southall 4, Butters 3, Galloway 3, Carr 2, Patterson 2, Ashby 1, Hodge 1, Williams 1, own goal 1.
Worthington Cup (0).
FA Cup (0).

Bartram V 44	Patterson M 42	Pennock A 39 + 1	Smith P 45	Ashby B 38	Carr D 22 + 8	Hessenthaler A 36 + 3	Hodge J 7 + 27	Butler S 4 + 3	Taylor R 43	Williams P 9 + 1	Bryant M 16 + 7	Galloway M 19 + 6	Southall N 34 + 8	Saunders M 28 + 6	Pinnock J — + 4	Asaba C 40 + 1	Dobson T 2	Rolling F 1	Edge R 1 + 7	Elliott S 4 + 1	Stannard J 2	Browning M 1 + 3	Nosworthy N — + 3	Butters G 23	Lisbie K 4 + 3	Brown K 2 + 2	Match No.
1	2^1	3	4	5	6	7	8	9^2	10	11^3	12	13	14														1
1	2	3^1	4	5	6	7	8			11	10	12		13		9^2											2
1	2^1	3	4	5	6	7	8^2	9		11^3	10	12	14	13													3
1	2	3	4	5	6		8	12		11^1	10	13	14	7^2		9^2											4
1	2	3	4	5	6		8		10^1	11^3	12	13	14	7^2		9											5
1			4		8		11	5	7^2	2	10	12				9	3	6^1	13								6
1	2		4		6	8		7	11^1	5	12	10^2		13		9	3										7
1	2		4		6	8	12	11^1	5^2	3	10	7				9			13								8
1	7	3	4	2	6	8^1	12	11	5^1		10	13				9											9
1	7	3^1	4	2	6		12		11^1	5	10^2	13	8			9			14								10
1	7	3	4	2	6		12	13	11	5^1	10			8^2		9											11
1	2		4	5	6	7^2	12		11	3	13	10	14	8^3		9^1											12
1	8	2	4	3	5		12	9^1	11		10	6^2	7	13													13
1	2	3	4	5	6^3		12		11	7^2	13	10		8^1		9			14								14
1	3	2	4	5		7^1			11	6		10		12		9						8					15
1	7	2^1	4	5	3		12		11	6				10^2		9			13	8							16
1	7		4	5	3		12		11	6			2	10		9				8^1							17
	7		4	5	3		12	13	11	6			2	10^1		9				8^3	1						18
	7^1	12	4	5	3		10		11	6^2		13	2			9			14		1	8^3					19
1		6	4	5	3				11	13	10		2			9			7^1	8		12^2					20
1	7	6	4	3		8	12		11^1				2	10		9								5			21
1	7	6	4	3		8^1	12		11				2	10		9								5			22
1	7	6	4	3		8^2	12		11			13	2	10^2		9								5			23
1	7	6	4	3		8^2	12		11			13	2	10^1		9								5			24
1	7	6	4	3		8^1	12		11			13	2	10^2		9								5			25
1	7	6	4	3		8^3	12		11			13	2	10^1	14	9^2								5			26
1	7	6	4	3		8	12		11				2	10		9								5			27
1	7	6	4	3		8			11				2	10		9								5			28
1	7	6	4	3		8			11				2	10		9								5			29
1	7	6	4	3		8	12		11				2	10^1		9								5			30
1	7	6	4	3		8			11		12		2	10^1		9								5			31
1	7	6	4^1	3		8^2	12		11^3			13	2	10	14	9								5			32
1	7	6	4	3		8	12		11				2^1	10^2		9								5	13		33
1	7	6	4	3		8	12		11			13	2	10^1		9						7^2		5	11		34
1	7	6	4	3		8	12		11				2	10^1		9								5			35
1	7	6	4	3		8	12		11				2	10		9								5^1			36
1	7	6	4	3^2		8	12		11			13	2	10^1		9^3						14		5			37
1	7	6	4	3		8	12		11				2	10^2		9^1							13	5			38
1	7	6	4	3		8	12		11				2	10^2		9^1							13^3	5	14		39
1	7	6	4	3		8	12		11^1			13	2	10^2		9^3								5	14		40
1	7	6	4	3^1		8	12		11			13	2	10^2	14	9^3								5			41
1	7	6	4	3		8	12		11			13		10		9								5^1		2^2	42
1	7	6	4	3		8	12		11				2	10		9^1								5			43
1		6	4	3		8	12		11				2	10^2		9^1						13		5		7	44
1	7^3	6	4	3		8	12		11				2	10^1	13	9^1								5		14	45
1	7^2	6	4^1	3		8^3	12		11				2	10	13	9								5		14	46

Worthington Cup
First Round   Southend U   (a) 0-1
                                      (h) 0-1

FA Cup
First Round   Oldham Ath   (a) 0-2

Division 1

GRIMSBY TOWN

FOUNDATION

Grimsby Pelham FC as they were first known, came into being at a meeting held at the Wellington Arms in September 1878. Pelham is the family name of big landowners in the area, the Earls of Yarborough. The receipts for their first game amounted to 6s. 9d. (approx. 39p). After a year, the club name was changed to Grimsby Town.

Blundell Park, Cleethorpes, North East Lincolnshire DN35 7PY.

Telephone: (01472) 605050.

Fax: (01472) 693665.

Clubcall: 09068 555855.

Ground Capacity: 10,033.

Record Attendance: 31,657 v Wolverhampton W, FA Cup 5th rd, 20 February 1937.

Record Receipts: £119,799 v Aston Villa, FA Cup 4th rd, 29 January 1994.

Pitch Measurements: 111yd × 75yd.

Life Presidents: T. Aspinall, T. J. Lindley.

Chairman: W. H. Carr.

Vice-Chairman: J. Teanby.

Directors: C. Aspinall, S. Bygott FCA, J. Fenty, M. Rouse.

Manager: Alan Buckley.

Assistant Manager: John Cockerill.

Chief Executive/Company Secretary: Ian Fleming.

Commercial Manager: Tony Richardson.

Assistant Commercial Manager: Tim Harvey.

Physio: Paul Mitchell.

LATEST SEQUENCES

Longest Sequence of League Wins: 11, 19.1.52 – 29.3.52.

Longest Sequence of League Defeats: 9, 30.11.07 – 18.1.08.

Longest Sequence of League Draws: 5, 6.2.65 – 6.3.65.

Longest Sequence of Unbeaten League Matches: 19, 16.2.80 – 30.8.80.

Longest Sequence Without a League Win: 18, 10.10.81 – 16.3.82.

HONOURS

Football League: Division 1 best season: 5th, 1934–35; Division 2 – Champions 1900–01, 1933–34; Runners-up 1928–29; Promoted from Division 2 1997–98 (play-offs); Division 3 (N) – Champions 1925–26, 1955–56; Runners-up 1951–52; Division 3 – Champions 1979–80; Runners-up 1961–62; Division 4 – Champions 1971–72; Runners-up 1978–79; 1989–90.

FA Cup: Semi-finals, 1936, 1939.

Football League Cup: best season: 5th rd, 1980, 1985.

League Group Cup: Winners 1982.

Auto Windscreen Shield: Winners 1998.

Colours

Black and white striped shirts, black shorts with red and white trim, black stockings with red and white turnover.

Change Colours

Sky blue and navy hooped shirts, sky blue shorts with navy trim, sky blue stockings.

Year Formed. 1878.

Turned Professional: 1890.

Ltd Co.: 1890.

Previous Name: 1878, Grimsby Pelham; 1879, Grimsby Town.

Club Nickname: 'The Mariners'.

Previous Grounds: 1880, Clee Park; 1889, Abbey Park; 1899, Blundell Park.

First Football League Game: 3 September 1892, Division 2, v Northwich Victoria (h) W 2–1 – Whitehouse; Lundie, T. Frith; C. Frith, Walker, Murrell; Higgins, Henderson, Brayshaw, Riddoch (2), Ackroyd.

Record League Victory: 9–2 v Darwen, Division 2, 15 April 1899 – Bagshaw; Lockie, Nidd; Griffiths, Bell (1), Nelmes; Jenkinson (3), Richards (1), Cockshutt (3), Robinson, Chadburn (1).

Record Cup Victory: 8–0 v Darlington, FA Cup 2nd rd, 21 November 1885 – G. Atkinson; J. H. Taylor, H. Taylor; Hall, Kimpson, Hopewell; H. Atkinson (1), Garnham, Seal (3), Sharman, Monument (4).

Record Defeat: 1–9 v Arsenal, Division 1, 28 January 1931.

Most League Points (2 for a win): 68, Division 3 (N), 1955–56.

Most League Points (3 for a win): 83, Division 3, 1990–91.

Most League Goals: 103, Division 2, 1933–34.

Highest League Scorer in Season: Pat Glover, 42, Division 2, 1933–34.

Most League Goals in Total Aggregate: Pat Glover, 180, 1930–39.

MANAGERS
H. N. Hickson 1902–20
(Secretary-Manager)
Haydn Price 1920
George Fraser 1921–24
Wilf Gillow 1924–32
Frank Womack 1932–36
Charles Spencer 1937–51
Bill Shankly 1951–53
Billy Walsh 1954–55
Allenby Chilton 1955–59
Tim Ward 1960–62
Tom Johnston 1962–64
Jimmy McGuigan 1964–67
Don McEvoy 1967–68
Bill Harvey 1968–69
Bobby Kennedy 1969–71
Lawrie McMenemy 1971–73
Ron Ashman 1973–75
Tom Casey 1975–76
Johnny Newman 1976–79
George Kerr 1979–82
David Booth 1982–85
Mike Lyons 1985–87
Bobby Roberts 1987–88
Alan Buckley 1988–94
Brian Laws 1994–96
Kenny Swain 1997
Alan Buckley May 1997–

Most League Goals in One Match: 6, Tommy McCairns v Leicester Fosse, Division 2, 11 April 1896.

Most Capped Player: Pat Glover, 7, Wales.

Most League Appearances: Keith Jobling, 448, 1953–69.

Youngest League Player: Tony Ford, 16 years 143 days v Walsall, 4 October 1975.

Record Transfer Fee Received: £1,500,000 from Everton for John Oster, July 1997.

Record Transfer Fee Paid: £400,000 to Preston NE for Lee Ashcroft, August 1998.

Football League Record: 1892 Original Member Division 2; 1901–03 Division 1; 1903 Division 2; 1910 Failed re-election; 1911 re-elected Division 2; 1920–21 Division 3; 1921–26 Division 3 (N); 1926–29 Division 2; 1929–32 Division 1; 1932–34 Division 2; 1934–48 Division 1; 1948–51 Division 2; 1951–56 Division 3 (N); 1956–59 Division 2; 1959–62 Division 3; 1962–64 Division 2; 1964–68 Division 3; 1968–72 Division 4; 1972–77 Division 3; 1977–79 Division 4; 1979–80 Division 3; 1980–87 Division 2; 1987–88 Division 3; 1988–90 Division 4; 1990–91 Division 3; 1991–92 Division 2; 1992–97 Division 1; 1997–98 Division 2; 1998– Division 1.

TEN YEAR LEAGUE RECORD

		P	W	D	L	F	A	Pts	Pos
1988-89	Div 4	46	17	15	14	65	59	66	9
1989-90	Div 4	46	22	13	11	70	47	79	2
1990-91	Div 3	46	24	11	11	66	34	83	3
1991-92	Div 2	46	14	11	21	47	62	53	19
1992-93	Div 1	46	19	7	20	58	57	64	9
1993-94	Div 1	46	13	20	13	52	47	59	16
1994-95	Div 1	46	17	14	15	62	56	65	10
1995-96	Div 1	46	14	14	18	55	69	56	17
1996-97	Div 1	46	11	13	22	60	81	46	22
1997-98	Div 2	46	19	15	12	55	37	72	3

DID YOU KNOW ?

Best individual FA Cup scoring performance by a Grimsby Town player was the five goals scored by Bob Blanthorne against Carlisle United on 1 February 1908 in a 6–2 win. He subsequently transferred to Newcastle United.

GRIMSBY TOWN 1998–99 LEAGUE RECORD

Match No.	Date	Venue	Opponents	Result	H/T Score	Lg. Pos.	Goalscorers	Attendance
1	Aug 9	H	Ipswich T	D 0-0	0-0	—		7211
2	15	A	Bolton W	L 0-2	0-0	22		16,584
3	22	H	Huddersfield T	W 1-0	0-0	11	Groves (pen) [61]	6974
4	29	A	Oxford U	D 0-0	0-0	12		5587
5	31	H	WBA	W 5-1	4-0	8	Handyside [6], Burnett [17], Smith D [27], Groves (pen) [45], Black [88]	7931
6	Sept 5	A	Stockport Co	L 0-2	0-0	10		6199
7	8	A	Sheffield U	L 2-3	1-0	—	Lester [28], Burnett [71]	12,293
8	12	H	Barnsley	L 1-2	0-1	16	Ashcroft [51]	8149
9	19	A	Birmingham C	W 1-0	0-0	14	Smith D [50]	17,563
10	26	H	Port Vale	D 2-2	0-2	14	Clare 2 [65, 90]	5747
11	29	H	Crewe Alex	D 1-1	1-1	—	Nogan [23]	5024
12	Oct 3	A	QPR	W 2-1	1-1	11	Smith D [40], Black [50]	10,240
13	17	H	Bradford C	W 2-0	1-0	8	Nogan [24], Groves [73]	7473
14	20	H	Bristol C	W 2-1	0-1	—	Groves 2 (1 pen) [50, 60 (p)]	5082
15	24	A	Wolverhampton W	L 0-2	0-2	8		18,480
16	31	A	Crystal Palace	W 2-0	1-0	7	Widdrington [13], Lester [53]	6948
17	Nov 7	A	Sunderland	L 1-3	0-0	10	Groves [70]	40,077
18	14	H	Portsmouth	D 1-1	1-1	12	Groves [26]	6236
19	21	A	Bury	L 0-1	0-0	13		4198
20	28	H	Swindon T	W 1-0	1-0	12	Lester [10]	5657
21	Dec 2	A	Norwich C	L 1-3	0-1	—	Smith D [83]	12,024
22	5	A	Tranmere R	W 2-1	1-1	11	Groves (pen) [23], Ashcroft [46]	4937
23	13	A	Portsmouth	W 1-0	0-0	9	Groves [67]	8180
24	19	H	Watford	W 2-1	0-0	9	Smith D [48], Groves [86]	6679
25	26	A	Huddersfield T	L 0-2	0-0	9		16,186
26	28	H	Stockport Co	W 1-0	0-0	8	Groves [68]	8058
27	Jan 9	A	Ipswich T	W 1-0	1-0	7	Handyside [14]	15,575
28	16	H	Oxford U	W 1-0	1-0	6	Groves [32]	6626
29	30	A	WBA	D 1-1	1-0	7	Black [28]	17,843
30	Feb 6	H	Bolton W	L 0-1	0-0	7		8674
31	20	A	Barnsley	D 0-0	0-0	7		16,343
32	27	H	Birmingham C	L 0-3	0-1	8		7807
33	Mar 13	A	Sunderland	L 0-2	0-0	11		9528
34	16	A	Crewe Alex	D 0-0	0-0	—		4855
35	20	A	Crystal Palace	L 1-3	1-2	11	Groves [11]	15,228
36	23	H	Port Vale	W 1-0	0-0	—	Groves [71]	4980
37	Apr 3	A	Bradford C	L 0-3	0-1	12		14,522
38	5	H	Norwich C	L 0-1	0-1	13		6302
39	10	A	Bristol C	L 1-4	1-2	13	Ashcroft [13]	11,616
40	13	H	QPR	W 1-0	0-0	—	Lester [72]	4789
41	17	H	Bury	D 0-0	0-0	11		5132
42	20	H	Sheffield U	L 1-2	0-0	—	Black [51]	5109
43	24	A	Swindon T	L 0-2	0-1	12		7197
44	May 1	H	Tranmere R	W 1-0	1-0	11	Clare [34]	5916
45	4	H	Wolverhampton W	D 0-0	0-0	—		7009
46	9	A	Watford	L 0-1	0-1	11		20,303

Final League Position: 11

GOALSCORERS

League (40): Groves 14 (4 pens), Smith D 5, Black 4, Lester 4, Ashcroft 3, Clare 3, Burnett 2, Handyside 2, Nogan 2, Widdrington 1.
Worthington Cup (4): Ashcroft 1, Clare 1, Groves 1, Nogan 1.
FA Cup (1): McDermott 1.

Davison A 35	McDermott J 37	Gallimore T 43	Handyside P 30 + 1	Smith R 29 + 1	Widdrington T 16 + 10	Coldicott S 35 + 2	Black K 29 + 13	Nogan L 30 + 8	Lester J 26 + 7	Groves P 46	Smith D 30 + 1	Burnett W 15 + 5	Ashcroft L 21 + 6	Livingstone S 15 + 8	Clare D 7 + 15	Lever M 15 + 9	Dobbin J — + 4	Donovan K 27 + 1	Butterfield D 9 + 3	Bloomer M — + 4	Love A 9	Buckley A — + 2	Croudson S 2	Chapman B — + 1	Match No.
1	2	3	4	5	6	7	8¹	9	10	11	12														1
1	2	3³	4	5		7	12	10²	13	11	8	6¹	9	14											2
1	2	3	4	5	12	7		9²	10	11	8	6¹				13									3
1	2	3	4	5	12	7			10	11	8¹	6	9												4
1	2	3¹	4	5		7	12	13	10²	11	8	6	9												5
1	2	3¹	4³	5		7²	12	13	10	11	8	6	9		14										6
1	2	3	4²			7¹	12		10	11	8	6	9	13		5									7
1	2	3		4	7		12	13	10	11	8¹	6²	9	14		5³									8
1	2	3		5		7	12	10²	13	11	8	6¹	9	4											9
1	2³	3		5			8		10	11	6²	9¹	4	12	13	14	7								10
1	2	3³		4	6²		8	9¹	12	11				10	5	13	7	14							11
1	2	3		4	12	6¹	10	9		11	8				5		7								12
1	2	3		4	6		10	9		11	8				5	12	7¹								13
1	2	3		4	6		10	9	12	11	8¹			13		5	7²								14
1	2	3	12	4	6³		7²	9	10	11	8			13		5¹	14								15
1		3	4		6	7	12	9¹	10	11	8			5					2²	13					16
1	2	3	4		6¹	7	12	9²	10	11	8²		14	5		13									17
1	2	3	4		6	7²	12	9¹	10	11	8³		14	5		13						1			18
1		3³	4		6	7¹		9²	10	11	8		13	5	14	12			2						19
1	2	3	4		6	12	13	14	10	11	8²		9²	5		7¹									20
1	2	3	4		6	12	5¹	13	10	11	8		9²			7³		14							21
1	2	3¹	4			6	12	9	10²	11	8	13	5					7							22
1	2	3	4	12		6	13	9²		11	8	10	5¹					7							23
1	2	3	4	5	12	6¹	10²	9		11	8	7		13											24
1	2		4	5	12	6	3³	9²	13	11	8	10	14					7¹							25
1	2		4	5	6		8		10	11	3		9					7							26
1	2	3	4	5	12	6	10²	9¹		11	8			13				7							27
1	2¹	3	4	5	12	6	10²	9	13	11	8							7							28
1	2	3	4	5		6	10¹	9		11	8		12					7							29
1	2	3³	4	5	12	6	10	9		11	8¹		14	13				7²							30
1	2		4		8	6	10	9		11	3¹					5		7	12						31
1	2	3		4	12	6¹	8	9²		11		13	10		14	5³		7							32
1	2	3	4	5	6		12			11	8¹		9			10		7							33
1	2	3	4	5	12	6	8²			11			9			10¹	13	7							34
1	2	3	4²	5	10	6	8³			11		12	9¹		13	14		7							35
1	2	3	4	5		6	10	9		11	8¹			12				7							36
	2	3	4	5¹		6	10²	9	8³	11		13	14	12				7			1				37
	2	3			6	12	9³	10¹	11		13	8	4	14	5²		7				1				38
	2³	3			7	8	12	10¹	11		6²	9	4	13	5			14			1				39
	3				7¹	8	9	12	11		6	10	4		5			2		1					40
	3	5				8¹	12	10²	11		6	9³	4	13	14		7	2		1					41
	3³				5	8¹	9²	10	11		6	12	4	13			7	2	14	1					42
	3²				4	8³	9	10¹	11		6		12	5		7	2	13	14	1					43
	3	4			6	8	9²	10	11		12		13	5¹		7	2		1						44
	3	4			6	8		10	11		5			9		7	2					1			45
	3³	4			6	8¹		10	11					9²	5	7	2	12		13		1	14		46

Worthington Cup

First Round	Preston NE	(h)	0-0
		(a)	0-0
Second Round	Sheffield U	(a)	1-2
		(h)	2-0
Third Round	Sunderland	(a)	1-2

FA Cup

Third Round	Bradford C	(a)	1-2

Division 3

HALIFAX TOWN

FOUNDATION

The real pioneer behind the setting up of the club was Mr A. E. Jones, who, using the *nom de plume* 'Old Sport', wrote to the *Halifax Evening Courier*. His letter suggesting a club be set up and inviting public opinion was published on 20 April 1911. A public meeting was held at the Saddle Hotel on 23 May 1911, whereafter Dr A. H. Muir became the club's first president and Joe McClelland its first secretary. Mr Jones proposed the following: "That this meeting of townsmen of Halifax heartily approves of the establishment of a town's Association football club on the basis of scheme 1 (the formation of a limited company) and pledges itself to adopt every legitimate means to that end". Mr Charles Deantry seconded the motion and the resolution was carried unanimously. The chairman asked for a show of hands of those willing to become guarantors of £1. There was an immediate response from 46 of the assembly.

The Shay Stadium, Shaw Hill, Halifax HX1 2YS.

Telephone: (01422) 345543.

Fax: (01422) 349487.

Souvenir Shop: (01422) 353423.

Info Line: 0891 227328.

Ground Capacity: 9900.

Record Attendance: 36,885 v Tottenham H, FA Cup 5th rd, 15 February 1953.

Record Receipts: £36,267 v Bradford C, Worthington Cup, 2nd rd, 1st leg, 15 September 1998.

Pitch Measurements: 110yd × 70yd.

President: Robert Holmes.

Vice-President: Jack Haymer.

Chairman: S. J. Brown.

Directors: D. C. Greenwood, A. Hall, D. Cairns, M. Hitchen, Dr M. Choucri.

Manager: Mark Lillis.

Coach: Peter Butler.

Physio: A. Russell-Cox.

Youth Team Coach: Steve Thornber.

Club Secretary: Hilary Molyneux Horrocks.

LATEST SEQUENCES

Longest Sequence of League Wins: 7, 22.2.64 – 21.3.64.

Longest Sequence of League Defeats: 8, 7.12.46 – 13.1.47.

Longest Sequence of League Draws: 7, 22.1.82 – 20.2.82.

Longest Sequence of Unbeaten League Matches: 17, 14.1.69 – 21.4.69.

Longest Sequence Without a League Win: 22, 26.8.78 – 10.2.79.

HONOURS

Football League: Division 3 best season: 3rd, 1970–71; Division 3 (N) – Runners-up 1934–35; Division 4: Runners-up 1968–69.

FA Cup: best season: 5th rd, 1933, 1953.

Football League Cup: best season: 4th rd, 1964.

Vauxhall Conference: Champions 1997–98.

Colours

Blue and white striped shirts, blue shorts, white stockings.

Change Colours

Green shirts with yellow trim, green shorts, green stockings.

Year Formed: 1911.

Turned Professional: 1911.

Ltd Co.: 1911.

Club Nickname: 'The Shaymen'.

Previous Grounds: 1911, Sandhall; 1919, Exley; 1921, The Shay.

Club Sponsors: Nationwide.

First Football League Game: 27 August 1921, Division 3 (N), v Darlington (a) L 0-2 – Haldane; Hawley, Mackrill; Hall, Wellock, Challinor; Pinkey, Hetherington, Woods, Dent, Phipps.

Record League Victory: 6–0 v Bradford PA, Division 3 (N), 3 December 1955 – Johnson; Griffiths, Ferguson; Watson, Harris, Bell; Hampson (2), Baker (3), Watkinson (1), Capel, Lonsdale. 6–0 v Doncaster R, Division 4, 2 November 1976 – Gennoe; Trainer, Loska (Bradley), McGill, Dunleavy (1), Phelan, Hoy (2), Carroll (1), Bullock (1), Lawson (1), Johnston.

Record Cup Victory: 7–0 v Bishop Auckland, FA Cup 2nd rd (replay), 10 January 1967 – White; Russell, Bodell; Smith, Holt, Jeff Lee; Taylor (2), Hutchison (2), Parks (2), Atkins (1), McCarthy.

Record Defeat: 0–13 v Stockport Co, Division 3 (N), 6 January 1934.

Most League Points (2 for a win): 57, Division 4, 1968–69.

Most League Points (3 for a win): 66, Division 3, 1998–99.

Most League Goals: 83, Division 3 (N), 1957–58.

Highest League Scorer in Season: Albert Valentine, 34, Division 3 (N), 1934–35.

Most League Goals in Total Aggregate: Ernest Dixon, 129, 1922–30.

Most League Goals in One Match: 6, William Chambers v Hartlepools U, Division 3N, 7 April 1934.

Most Capped Player: None.

Most League Appearances: John Pickering, 367, 1965–74.

Youngest League Player: Phil Whitehead, 16 years 284 days v Burnley, 27 September 1986.

Record Transfer Fee Received: £350,000 from Fulham for Geoff Horsfield, October 1998.

Record Transfer Fee Paid: £50,000 to Hereford U for Ian Juryeff, September 1990.

Football League Record: 1921 Original Member of Division 3 (N); 1958–63 Division 3; 1963–69 Division 4; 1969–76 Division 3; 1976–92 Division 4; 1992–93 Division 3; 1993–98 Vauxhall Conference; 1998– Division 3.

MANAGERS

A. M. Ricketts 1911–12
(Secretary-Manager)
Joe McClelland 1912–30
Alec Raisbeck 1930–36
Jimmy Thomson 1936–47
Jack Breedon 1947–50
William Wootton 1951–52
Gerald Henry 1952–54
Willie Watson 1954–56
Billy Burnikell 1956
Harry Hooper 1957–62
Willie Watson 1964–66
Vic Metcalfe 1966–67
Alan Ball Snr 1967–70
George Kirby 1970–71
Ray Henderson 1971–72
George Mulhall 1972–74
Johnny Quinn 1974–76
Alan Ball Snr 1976–77
Jimmy Lawson 1977–78
George Kirby 1978–81
Mick Bullock 1981–84
Mick Jones 1984–86
Bill Ayre 1986–90
Jim McCalliog 1990–91
John McGrath 1991–92
Peter Wragg 1992–93
John Bird 1993–95
John Carroll 1996
George Mulhall 1996–98
Kieran O'Regan 1998–99
Mark Lillis June 1999–

TEN YEAR LEAGUE RECORD

		P	W	D	L	F	A	Pts	Pos
1988-89	Div 4	46	13	11	22	69	75	50	21
1989-90	Div 4	46	12	13	21	57	65	49	23
1990-91	Div 4	46	12	10	24	59	79	46	22
1991-92	Div 4	42	10	8	24	34	75	38	20
1992-93	Div 3	42	9	9	24	45	68	36	22
1993-94	Conf	42	13	16	13	55	49	55	13
1994-95	Conf	42	17	12	13	68	54	63	8
1995-96	Conf	42	13	13	16	49	63	52	15
1996-97	Conf	42	12	12	18	55	74	48	19
1997-98	Conf	42	25	12	5	74	43	87	1

DID YOU KNOW ?

On 7 November 1998 Halifax Town were away to Carlisle United. When goalkeeper Tim Carter was injured in the first half, Kevin Hulme took over, kept a clean sheet and became man of the match in a 1–0 win.

HALIFAX TOWN 1998–99 LEAGUE RECORD

Match No.	Date		Venue	Opponents	Result	H/T Score	Lg. Pos.	Goalscorers	Attendance
1	Aug	8	A	Peterborough U	W 2-0	0-0	—	Hanson [48], Horsfield [78]	5746
2		15	H	Brentford	W 1-0	1-0	3	Horsfield [32]	3876
3		22	A	Darlington	D 2-2	0-1	2	Horsfield 2 [73, 76]	4200
4		28	H	Shrewsbury T	W 2-0	1-0	—	Hulme [41], Horsfield [63]	3424
5		31	A	Plymouth Arg	L 0-1	0-1	4		6544
6	Sept	4	H	Hartlepool U	W 2-1	2-0	—	Hulme [21], Horsfield [23]	3820
7		8	A	Southend U	D 0-0	0-0	—		3620
8		11	H	Cardiff C	L 1-2	0-0	—	O'Regan [60]	2814
9		19	A	Hull C	W 2-1	0-0	5	Horsfield [62], Hanson [79]	4719
10		26	H	Torquay U	D 1-1	0-0	6	Paterson [77]	2753
11	Oct	3	A	Scunthorpe U	W 4-0	0-0	3	Paterson 2 [50, 76], Williams 2 [58, 82]	4989
12		11	A	Rochdale	L 0-1	0-1	5		3628
13		16	H	Barnet	D 1-1	1-0	—	Guinan [31]	2223
14		20	H	Cambridge U	D 3-3	2-2	—	Stoneman [20], Thackeray [25], Paterson [59]	1906
15		24	A	Leyton Orient	L 0-1	0-1	8		3655
16		31	H	Swansea C	W 2-0	1-0	6	Hulme [35], Paterson [88]	2383
17	Nov	7	A	Carlisle U	W 1-0	0-0	4	Stoneman [89]	3636
18		10	H	Chester C	W 3-2	1-0	—	Paterson [21], Thackeray 2 [70, 74]	2427
19		21	A	Brighton & HA	W 1-0	1-0	1	Paterson [8]	3305
20		27	H	Mansfield T	D 2-2	0-2	—	Thackeray [63], Paterson (pen) [90]	3227
21	Dec	12	A	Scarborough	L 0-1	0-1	5		2251
22		19	H	Exeter C	D 1-1	0-1	4	Williams [85]	2342
23		26	H	Darlington	D 0-0	0-0	5		3557
24		28	A	Rotherham U	L 1-3	1-2	6	Guinan [2]	4728
25	Jan	2	A	Shrewsbury T	D 2-2	1-1	6	Power [42], O'Regan [87]	2806
26		9	H	Peterborough U	D 2-2	0-1	6	Stoneman (pen) [52], Williams [73]	2784
27		23	H	Plymouth Arg	W 2-0	0-0	6	Williams 2 [63, 76]	2762
28		30	H	Rotherham U	L 2-4	1-1	8	Stoneman [29], Power [69]	4251
29	Feb	6	A	Hartlepool U	L 0-2	0-2	9		2374
30		13	H	Southend U	W 3-1	0-0	7	Hulme [49], Power 2 [50, 90]	2302
31		19	A	Cardiff C	D 1-1	0-1	—	Bradshaw [66]	8570
32		27	H	Hull C	L 0-1	0-0	10		4455
33	Mar	6	A	Torquay U	L 0-4	0-1	10		1715
34		13	H	Carlisle U	W 1-0	0-0	10	Bradshaw [81]	2432
35		16	A	Brentford	D 1-1	1-1	—	Stansfield [45]	3713
36		20	A	Swansea C	W 2-1	0-1	8	Murphy J [77], Paterson [90]	4974
37		26	H	Leyton Orient	L 1-2	0-2	—	Butler [68]	2978
38	Apr	3	A	Barnet	D 2-2	1-1	11	Paterson [22], Bradshaw [82]	2055
39		5	H	Rochdale	D 0-0	0-0	11		2759
40		10	A	Cambridge U	L 0-4	0-0	11		4838
41		13	A	Mansfield T	W 1-0	1-0	—	Thackeray [31]	2471
42		17	H	Brighton & HA	W 1-0	1-0	7	Jackson [28]	2773
43		24	A	Chester C	D 2-2	1-1	8	Newton [44], Bradshaw [86]	2461
44		27	H	Scunthorpe U	W 1-0	0-0	—	Jackson [67]	3486
45	May	1	H	Scarborough	L 1-2	1-2	7	Jackson [24]	3308
46		8	A	Exeter C	L 1-2	1-1	10	Jackson [43]	3180

Final League Position: 10

GOALSCORERS
League (58): Paterson 10 (1 pen), Horsfield 7, Williams 6, Thackeray 5, Bradshaw 4, Hulme 4, Jackson 4, Power 4, Stoneman 4 (1 pen), Guinan 2, Hanson 2, O'Regan 2, Butler 1, Murphy J 1, Newton 1, Stansfield 1.
Worthington Cup (4): Hanson 2, Horsfield 1, Paterson 1.
FA Cup (0).

Martin L 37	Thackeray A 37 + 1	Bradshaw M 41	Lucas R 29 + 7	Stoneman P 40	Murphy S 10 + 2	Duerden I 1 + 1	Hulme K 30	Hanson D 19 + 12	Horsfield G 10	Brown J 32 + 8	Sertori M 39 + 1	Butler P 33	O'Regan K 15 + 4	Murphy J 21 + 2	Williams M 18 + 6	Paterson J 19 + 5	Carter T 9 + 1	Guinan S 12	Newton C 8 + 6	Power L 14 + 4	Stansfield J 12	Etherington C 4	Grant G — + 3	Jackson J 16	Match No.
1	2	3	4	5	6	7		8	9	10	11														1
1	2	3	7	6	5	12		8	9	10[1]	11		4												2
1	2	3	5	6				8	9	10	11[1]		4	7	12										3
1	2	3	4	6				8	9	10	11		5	7											4
1	2	3	5	6				8	9	10	11		4	7											5
1	2	3	5	6				8[1]	9	10	11		4		7	12									6
1	2	3	5	6				8	9[1]	10	11		4	7	13	12[2]									7
1	2	3	5	6				8	9	10	11		4	7[1]	12										8
1	2	3	5[1]	6				8	9	10	11		4	7		12									9
1	2[2]	3	12	6				8	9[1]	10			4	5	11	13	7								10
1[0]		3	11	6			8			12	4	10	2[1]	5	9	7	15								11
1	2	3	11	6			8[1]			12	4	10		5	9	7									12
1	2	3	11	6						12	4	10		5	9[1]	7	8								13
1	2	3		6							4	10	11	5	9	7	8								14
1	2	3		6							4	10	11	5	9	7	8								15
1	2	3		6			8[1]			12	4		11	5	9	7	10								16
	2	3	12	6			8			11	4			5	9	7	1[1]	10							17
1	2	3	12	6			8			11	4			5	9[1]	7	10								18
1	2	3	4	6	12					11	8			5	9[1]	7	10								19
1	2	3	4	6[1]						11	8			5	9	7	10	12							20
1	2	3	4	6						11[2]	8			5	9	7	10[1]	12	13						21
1	2	3[1]	5	6					13	11	4	8			9	7	10[2]	12							22
1	2	3[1]	8	6						10	11	4			5	9	7	12							23
	2	3	12	6					9[2]	11	4	8[1]		5	13	1	10	7							24
	2	3		6					9	11	4		7	5[1]	12	1	10	8							25
	2	3		6			8	10[1]			4	5	7	9		12	11								26
	2	3		6			8			12	4	11	7[1]	9		1		10	5						27
	2	3		6			8	12		7	4	11	5[1]	9		1		10							28
	2	3		6	8[1]			12		4	11			9		1		10	5	7					29
1	2	3		6			8			12	4[2]			9			11	5	7[1]	13	10				30
1	2	11	3	6			8[2]	12		13	4		14				9[1]	5	7		10[3]				31
1	2	11[1]	3				8	10		6	4		12					5	7	13	9[2]				32
1	2	3		6			8[1]	10		12	4	11	7[2]					5	13		9				33
1		3	12	6			8[1]			13	4			7	2				11[2]	10	5		9		34
1		3		6							8	4	11	7	2				10	5			9		35
1		3	12					8	9	6	4	11	7[1]	2	13				10	5[2]			9		36
1		3					8	12		2	4	11	6[1]	5		7			10				9		37
		3	8[2]		13			12		2	4	11		5		7	1		10[1]	6			9		38
		3					8			2[2]	4	11	12	5		7	1[1]		13	10	6		9		39
1		3	4	6	8					10	2[1]		11			12			7	5			9		40
1	2	3	4	6	10[2]		8[3]	12		5	13	11							7	14			9[1]		41
1	2	3	10	6			8[3]	12		5	4	11		13		14			7[1]				9[2]		42
1	2	3	10	6			8	12		5	4	11[1]		13		7							9[2]		43
1	2		3	6	5		8[1]	12			4	11		7					10				9		44
1	12	3	13	6	5			10		2[1]	4	11		7[3]					8[2]	14			9		45
1	2	3		6	5		8[1]	12		10[2]	4	11		7					13				9		46

Worthington Cup
First Round	Wrexham	(a)	2-0
		(h)	0-2
Second Round	Bradford C	(h)	1-2
		(a)	1-3

FA Cup
First Round	Manchester C	(a)	0-3

Division 3 — **HARTLEPOOL UNITED**

FOUNDATION

The inspiration for the launching of Hartlepool United was the West Hartlepool club which won the FA Amateur Cup in 1904–05. They had been in existence since 1881 and their Cup success led in 1908 to the formation of the new professional concern which first joined the North-Eastern League. In those days they were Hartlepools United and won the Durham Senior Cup in their first two seasons.

Victoria Park, Clarence Road, Hartlepool TS24 8BZ.
Telephone: (01429) 272584.
Commercial Dept: (01429) 272584.
Fax: (01429) 863007.
Football in the Community: (01429) 862595.
Ground Capacity: 7229.
Record Attendance: 17,426 v Manchester U, FA Cup 3rd rd, 5 January 1957.
Record Receipts: £42,300 v Tottenham H, Rumbelows Cup 2nd rd, 2nd leg, 9 October 1990.
Pitch Measurements: 110yd × 75yd.
Chairman: K. Hodcroft.
Directors: H. Hornsey, I. Prescott, M. Downey.
Manager: Chris Turner.
Coach: Brian Honour.
Youth Coach: Mick Smith.
Physio: Gary Hinchley.
Commercial Manager: John Breward.
Secretary: Maureen Smith.
Football in the Community Officer: Keith Nobbs.
Safety Officer: Maurice Russell.

LATEST SEQUENCES

Longest Sequence of League Wins: 7, 1.4.68 – 26.4.68.
Longest Sequence of League Defeats: 8, 27.1.93 – 27.2.93.
Longest Sequence of League Draws: 4, 27.2.99 – 20.3.99.
Longest Sequence of Unbeaten League Matches: 17, 24.2.68 – 10.8.68.
Longest Sequence Without a League Win: 18, 9.1.93 – 3.4.93.

HONOURS

Football League: Division 3 (N) – Runners-up 1956–57.
FA Cup: best season: 4th rd, 1955, 1978, 1989, 1993.
Football League Cup, best season: 4th rd, 1975.

Colours
Royal blue and white striped shirts.

Change Colours
White with blue trim.

Year Formed: 1908.

Turned Professional: 1908.

Ltd Co.: 1908.

Previous Names: 1908, Hartlepools United; 1968, Hartlepool; 1977, Hartlepool United.

Club Nickname: 'The Pool'.

First Football League Game: 27 August 1921, Division 3 (N), v Wrexham (a) W 2–0 – Gill; Thomas, Crilly; Dougherty, Hopkins, Short; Kessler, Mulholland (1), Lister (1), Robertson, Donald.

Record League Victory: 10–1 v Barrow, Division 4, 4 April 1959 – Oakley; Cameron, Waugh; Johnson, Moore, Anderson; Scott (1), Langland (1), Smith (3), Clark (2), Luke (2), (1 og).

Record Cup Victory: 6–0 v North Shields, FA Cup 1st rd, 30 November 1946 – Heywood; Brown, Gregory; Spelman, Lambert, Jones; Price, Scott (2), Sloan (4), Moses, McMahon.

Record Defeat: 1–10 v Wrexham, Division 4, 3 March 1962.

Most League Points (2 for a win): 60, Division 4, 1967–68.

Most League Points (3 for a win): 82, Division 4, 1990–91.

Most League Goals: 90, Division 3 (N), 1956–57.

Highest League Scorer in Season: William Robinson, 28, Division 3 (N), 1927–28; Joe Allon, 28, Division 4, 1990–91.

Most League Goals in Total Aggregate: Ken Johnson, 98, 1949–64.

Most League Goals in One Match: 5, Harry Simmons v Wigan Borough, Division 3N, 1 January 1931; 5, Bobby Folland v Oldham Ath, Division 3N, 15 April 1961.

Most Capped Player: Ambrose Fogarty, 1 (11), Republic of Ireland.

Most League Appearances: Wattie Moore, 447, 1948–64.

Youngest League Player: John McGovern, 16 years 205 days v Bradford C, 21 May 1966.

Record Transfer Fee Received: £300,000 from Chelsea for Joe Allon, August 1991.

Record Transfer Fee Paid: £60,000 to Barnsley for Andy Saville, March 1992.

Football League Record: 1921 Original Member of Division 3 (N); 1958–68 Division 4; 1968–69 Division 3; 1969–91 Division 4; 1991–92 Division 3; 1992–94 Division 2; 1994– Division 3.

MANAGERS

Alfred Priest 1908–12
Percy Humphreys 1912–13
Jack Manners 1913–20
Cecil Potter 1920–22
David Gordon 1922–24
Jack Manners 1924–27
Bill Norman 1927–31
Jack Carr 1932–35
(had been Player-Coach since 1931)
Jimmy Hamilton 1935–43
Fred Westgarth 1943–57
Ray Middleton 1957–59
Bill Robinson 1959–62
Allenby Chilton 1962–63
Bob Gurney 1963–64
Alvan Williams 1964–65
Geoff Twentyman 1965
Brian Clough 1965–67
Angus McLean 1967–70
John Simpson 1970–71
Len Ashurst 1971–74
Ken Hale 1974–76
Billy Horner 1976–83
Johnny Duncan 1983
Mike Docherty 1983
Billy Horner 1984–86
John Bird 1986–88
Bobby Moncur 1988–89
Cyril Knowles 1989–91
Alan Murray 1991–93
Viv Busby 1993
John MacPhail 1993–94
David McCreery 1994–95
Keith Houchen 1995–96
Mick Tait 1996–99
Chris Turner March 1999–

TEN YEAR LEAGUE RECORD

		P	W	D	L	F	A	Pts	Pos
1988-89	Div 4	46	14	10	22	50	78	52	19
1989-90	Div 4	46	15	10	21	66	88	55	19
1990-91	Div 4	46	24	10	12	67	48	82	3
1991-92	Div 3	46	18	11	17	57	57	65	11
1992-93	Div 2	46	14	12	20	42	60	54	16
1993-94	Div 2	46	9	9	28	41	87	36	23
1994-95	Div 3	42	11	10	21	43	69	43	18
1995-96	Div 3	46	12	13	21	47	67	49	20
1996-97	Div 3	46	14	9	23	53	66	51	20
1997-98	Div 3	46	12	23	11	61	53	59	17

DID YOU KNOW ?

In 1936 Jack Howe was transferred from Hartlepools United to Derby County, after signing forms on the platform at Lincoln railway station. He later played for England and won an FA Cup medal in 1946.

HARTLEPOOL UNITED 1998–99 LEAGUE RECORD

Match No.	Date	Venue	Opponents	Result	H/T Score	Lg. Pos.	Goalscorers	Attendance
1	Aug 8	H	Cardiff C	D 1-1	1-0	—	Beech [9]	2591
2	15	A	Barnet	W 2-0	1-0	5	Midgley [29], Beech [81]	2049
3	22	H	Scunthorpe U	L 1-2	0-1	11	Ingram (pen) [56]	2697
4	29	A	Cambridge U	W 2-1	0-0	6	Howard [81], Lee [90]	2825
5	31	H	Hull C	W 1-0	0-0	5	Di Lella [57]	3277
6	Sept 4	A	Halifax T	L 1-2	0-2	—	Beech [49]	3820
7	8	A	Darlington	L 0-2	0-0	—		5899
8	12	H	Exeter C	W 4-3	2-2	9	Beech 2 [13, 88], Blake (og) [45], Lee [56]	2106
9	19	A	Rotherham U	L 0-3	0-0	11		3769
10	26	H	Peterborough U	L 1-2	1-1	14	Heckingbottom [41]	2385
11	Oct 3	A	Leyton Orient	D 1-1	0-0	15	Midgley (pen) [76]	3745
12	10	H	Shrewsbury T	D 1-1	0-0	16	Beech [47]	1897
13	17	A	Brentford	L 1-3	0-2	17	Miller [83]	4883
14	20	A	Chester C	D 1-1	0-1	—	Beech [53]	2182
15	24	H	Torquay U	W 4-1	1-0	13	Stephenson [33], Howard [47], Lee [61], Beech [67]	1593
16	31	A	Brighton & HA	L 2-3	1-1	15	Beech [45], Midgley [54]	2765
17	Nov 7	H	Plymouth Arg	W 2-0	2-0	12	Wotton (og) [3], Midgley [9]	2121
18	10	H	Mansfield T	L 1-2	0-2	—	Ingram (pen) [58]	1779
19	21	A	Scarborough	W 2-1	2-0	11	Midgley [14], Brightwell [26]	1715
20	28	H	Swansea C	L 1-2	1-0	14	Midgley [26]	2051
21	Dec 12	A	Carlisle U	L 1-2	0-2	14	Ingram (pen) [90]	3025
22	19	H	Southend U	L 2-4	1-3	19	Di Lella [5], Howard [90]	1889
23	26	H	Scunthorpe U	L 0-1	0-0	19		3621
24	28	H	Rochdale	L 0-1	0-0	21		2218
25	Jan 2	H	Cambridge U	D 2-2	1-0	21	Beardsley [18], Barron [68]	3788
26	9	A	Cardiff C	L 1-4	0-2	22	Clark [70]	7766
27	16	H	Barnet	D 2-2	1-0	22	Midgley [25], Miller [86]	2233
28	23	A	Hull C	L 0-4	0-4	22		5808
29	30	A	Rochdale	W 1-0	1-0	22	Clark [18]	1943
30	Feb 6	H	Halifax T	W 2-0	2-0	20	Howard 2 [3, 15]	2374
31	13	A	Darlington	L 2-3	0-2	22	Irvine [71], Miller [80]	3980
32	20	A	Exeter C	L 1-2	1-0	22	Ingram (pen) [23]	2987
33	27	H	Rotherham U	D 0-0	0-0	22		2680
34	Mar 6	A	Peterborough U	D 1-1	1-0	22	Miller [32]	4854
35	13	A	Plymouth Arg	D 0-0	0-0	23		4441
36	20	H	Brighton & HA	D 0-0	0-0	23		2353
37	27	A	Torquay U	L 0-3	0-1	23		1927
38	Apr 3	H	Brentford	L 0-1	0-1	24		2719
39	6	A	Shrewsbury T	W 1-0	0-0	—	Baker [87]	3187
40	10	H	Chester C	W 2-0	1-0	22	Freestone [32], Jones [50]	2413
41	13	A	Swansea C	L 0-1	0-0	—		4429
42	17	H	Scarborough	W 3-0	2-0	22	Freestone 2 (1 pen) [26, 41 (p)], Baker [90]	5098
43	24	A	Mansfield T	L 0-2	0-2	22		3337
44	27	H	Leyton Orient	W 1-0	1-0	—	Beardsley [13]	3152
45	May 1	H	Carlisle U	D 0-0	0-0	22		4468
46	8	A	Southend U	D 1-1	0-1	22	Stephenson [79]	4865

Final League Position: 22

GOALSCORERS

League (52): Beech 9, Midgley 7 (1 pen), Howard 5, Ingram 4 (4 pens), Miller 4, Freestone 3 (1 pen), Lee 3, Baker 2, Beardsley 2, Clark 2, Di Lella 2, Stephenson 2, Barron 1, Brightwell 1, Heckingbottom 1, Irvine 1, Jones 1, own goals 2.
Worthington Cup (0).
FA Cup (4): Howard 2, Midgley 1, Miller 1.

Hollund M 41	Knowles D 46	Ingram D 37+1	Barron M 38	Lee G 23+1	Beech C 16	Stephenson P 24+3	Di Lella G 18+5	Irvine S 10+8	Midgley C 26+3	Clark I 36+3	Brightwell S 8+9	Howard S 25+3	Miller T 29+5	Pemberton M —+4	McDonald C 5	Evans N —+1	Rush D 5+5	Smith J 2+1	Davies L 2+1	Stokoe G 15+5	Heckingbottom P 5	Hutt S 2+2	Baker P 3+10	McGuckin I 8	Miotto S 5	Beardsley P 22	Elliott S 5	McKinnon R 7	Strodder G 13	Jones G 12	Hughes D 6+2	Westwood C 3+1	Freestone C 9+1	Dunwell M —+1	Match No.
1	2	3	4	5	6	7^1	8	9	10^2	11	12	13																							1
1	2	3	4	5	6	10^1		9	8	11		12	7																						2
1	2	3	4	5	6			9^1	8	11		10	7	12																					3
1	2	3^2	4	5	6	13	12	8^3		11		10^1	7	14	9																				4
1	2		4	5	6		3^1	12	8	11^2		10	7	13	9																				5
1	2	3	4	5	6			12	8^2	11^1		10	7	13	9^9	14																			6
1	2	3	4	5	6				8	11		10	7		9^1		12																		7
1	2	3	4	5	6	11^3			8^1	9^2		10	7							12	13	14													8
1	2	3	4		6	11^1	13		8	12		14	7		5					9^9	10^2														9
1	2	3	4		6	11^1	12		8	13			7							9^2	10	5													10
1	2		4	5	6				11			12			9		8			7^1	10			3											11
1	2	4		5	6			12	11						9		8^1			7	10			3											12
1	2	5	4		6			11	7^1	9	3	12					8				10														13
1	2	7	4	5	6	11		12							9		8				10^1			3											14
1	2	7	4	5	6	11^1		10	13	12	9^3	8								14				3^2											15
1	2		4		5	6		11	10^1	3	7	9	8		12																				16
1	2		4		5	11^2	6^1	12	10	3	7	9^9	8							13								14							17
1	2		4		5	11	6	10	3	7	9	8																							18
1	2		4		5	11	6	10	3	7	9									8															19
1	2		4		5	11	6	10	3	7	9	12								8^1															20
1	2	6	4	5		11	8	10	3^2	12					9^1					7			13												21
1	2	3	4	5		11	8	12	10^2		7^1	9								13						6									22
	2		4	5				10					9	7						3			8	11	1	6									23
	2		4	5		11	7	10^1		12	9									3			8		1	6									24
	2	6	4	5^2		11	10		3	12	9	13								8^1					1	7									25
	2^1	6	4			11	10^2	12	3	9	8									13					1	5	7								26
	2		4			11^1	6	10	3	12	9	13								8^2					1	5	7								27
1	2	11		5		12	13	9^2	10^3	3	14		8^1										4			6	7								28
1	2^1	3	4			7		13	10^2	11	9	12														5	8	6							29
1	2	3	4			7		12	10^1	11	9															5	8	6							30
1	2	5	4			7^1		10		11		9	12													8	6	3							31
1	2	5	4			12		10		11^1		9	7													8	6	3							32
1	2		4					9^1		11	7		10^2				12				13					8	6	3	5						33
1	2	6	4					10^1		11	7		12								9					8	3	5							34
1	2	6^2	4	12				11		7											9					8	3	5	10^1	13					35
1	2		4		6	10^1		11		7^2			12													8	3	5	9	13					36
1	2			6				11^1	12		7		9^2													8	3	5	10	4	13				37
1	2^1	12	4			7		3		11^3	13		14							8^2						5	10	6		9					38
1	2	3	4			7^2		11	13	12			8													5	10^1	6		9					39
1	2	3	4			11		7		8			10													6	5	9							40
1	2	3	4			11		7		12			8													5	10	6^1		9					41
1	2	3	4			12		11^1		7	13		8													5	10^2	6		9					42
1	2	3	4			11		7		12			8^1													5	10	6		9					43
1	2	3	4	6		11		7		12			8													5	10^1			9					44
1	2	3	4	6		11		7^1		8																5	10		12	9					45
1	2	3	4	12	6	11		13		8													13			5	10^3		7^1	9^2				14	46

Worthington Cup
First Round — Bolton W — (a) 0-1
(h) 0-3

FA Cup
First Round — Carlisle U — (h) 2-1
Second Round — Fulham — (a) 2-4

Division 1 **HUDDERSFIELD TOWN**

FOUNDATION

A meeting, attended largely by members of the Huddersfield &
District FA, was held at the Imperial Hotel in 1906 to discuss the
feasibility of establishing a football club in this rugby stronghold.
However, it was not until a man with both the enthusiasm and the
money to back the scheme came on the scene, that real progress
was made. This benefactor was Mr Hilton Crowther and it was at a
meeting at the Albert Hotel in 1908, that the club formally came
into existence with a capital of £2,000 and joined the
North-Eastern League.

The Alfred McAlpine Stadium, Leeds Rd, Huddersfield HD1 6PX.
Telephone: (01484) 484100.
Fax: (01484) 484101.
Ticket Office: (01484) 484123.
Club Shop: (01484) 484144.
Clubcall: 09068 121635.
Ground Capacity: 24,500.
Record Attendance: 67,037 v Arsenal, FA Cup 6th rd, 27 February 1932 (at Leeds Road);
20,741 v Sunderland, Division 1, 21 October 1998 (at Alfred McAlpine Stadium).
Record Receipts: £155,149 v Wimbledon, FA Cup 5th rd, 17 February 1996.
Pitch Measurements: 115yd × 76yd.
President: Lawrence Batley OBE.
Chairman: Ian Ayre.
Directors: B. Rubery, G. Rubery, P. Slaman, T. Cherry.
Manager: Steve Bruce.
First Team Coach: John Deehan
Coach: Terry Dolan.
Secretary: Ann Hough.
Commercial Manager: Brian Hewitt.
Physio: John Dickens.
Stadium Manager: Phil Armitage.

LATEST SEQUENCES
Longest Sequence of League Wins: 11, 5.4.20 – 4.9.20.
Longest Sequence of League Defeats: 7, 8.10.55 – 19.11.55.
Longest Sequence of League Draws: 6, 3.3.87 – 3.4.87.
Longest Sequence of Unbeaten League Matches: 27,
24.1.25 – 17.10.25.
Longest Sequence Without a League Win: 22, 4.12.71 –
29.4.72.

HONOURS

Football League: Division 1 –
Champions 1923–24, 1924–25,
1925–26; Runners-up 1926–27,
1927–28, 1933–34; Division 2 –
Champions 1969–70; Runners-up
1919–20, 1952–53; Promoted from
Division 2 1994–95 (play-offs);
Division 4 – Champions 1979–80.
FA Cup: Winners 1922; Runners-up
1920, 1928, 1930, 1938.
Football League Cup: Semi-final 1968.
Autoglass Trophy: Runners-up 1994.

Colours
Blue and white striped shirts, white shorts, white stockings with single
navy hoop.

Change Colours
Red and black striped shirts, black shorts with red stripe down side, black
stockings with red cuff.

Year Formed: 1908.

Turned Professional: 1908.

Ltd Co.: 1908.

Club Nickname: 'The Terriers'.

Previous Ground: 1908, Leeds Road; 1994, The Alfred McAlpine Stadium.

First Football League Game: 3 September 1910, Division 2, v Bradford PA (a) W 1–0 – Mutch; Taylor, Morris; Beaton, Hall, Bartlett; Blackburn, Wood, Hamilton (1), McCubbin, Jee.

Record League Victory: 10–1 v Blackpool, Division 1, 13 December 1930 – Turner; Goodall, Spencer; Redfern, Wilson, Campbell; Bob Kelly (1), McLean (4), Robson (3), Davies (1), Smailes (1).

Record Cup Victory: 7–0 v Lincoln U, FA Cup 1st rd, 16 November 1991 – Clarke; Trevitt, Charlton, Donovan (2), Mitchell, Doherty, O'Regan (1), Stapleton (1) (Wright), Roberts (2), Onuora (1), Barnett (Ireland).

Record Defeat: 1–10 v Manchester C, Division 2, 7 November 1987.

Most League Points (2 for a win): 66, Division 4, 1979–80.

Most League Points (3 for a win): 82, Division 3, 1982–83.

Most League Goals: 101, Division 4, 1979–80.

Highest League Scorer in Season: Sam Taylor, 35, Division 2, 1919–20; George Brown, 35, Division 1, 1925–26.

Most League Goals in Total Aggregate: George Brown, 142, 1921–29; Jimmy Glazzard, 142, 1946–56.

Most League Goals in One Match: 5, Dave Mangnall v Derby Co, Division 1, 21 November 1931; 5, Alf Lythgoe v Blackburn R, Division 1, 13 April 1935.

Most Capped Player: Jimmy Nicholson, 31 (41), Northern Ireland.

Most League Appearances: Billy Smith, 520, 1914–34.

Youngest League Player: Denis Law, 16 years 303 days v Notts Co, 24 December 1956.

Record Transfer Fee Received: £2,700,000 from Sheffield W for Andy Booth, July 1996.

Record Transfer Fee Paid: £1,200,000 to Bristol R for Marcus Stewart, July 1996.

Football League Record: 1910 Elected to Division 2; 1920–52 Division 1; 1952–53 Division 2; 1953–56 Division 1; 1956–70 Division 2; 1970–72 Division 1; 1972–73 Division 2; 1973–75 Division 3; 1975–80 Division 4; 1980–83 Division 3; 1983–88 Division 2; 1988–92 Division 3; 1992–95 Division 2; 1995– Division 1.

MANAGERS

Fred Walker 1908–10
Richard Pudan 1910–12
Arthur Fairclough 1912–19
Ambrose Langley 1919–21
Herbert Chapman 1921–25
Cecil Potter 1925–26
Jack Chaplin 1926–29
Clem Stephenson 1929–42
David Steele 1943–47
George Stephenson 1947–52
Andy Beattie 1952–56
Bill Shankly 1956–59
Eddie Boot 1960–64
Tom Johnston 1964–68
Ian Greaves 1968–74
Bobby Collins 1974
Tom Johnston 1975–78
   (had been General Manager since 1975)
Mike Buxton 1978–86
Steve Smith 1986–87
Malcolm Macdonald 1987–88
Eoin Hand 1988–92
Ian Ross 1992–93
Neil Warnock 1993–95
Brian Horton 1995–97
Peter Jackson 1997–99
Steve Bruce June 1999–

TEN YEAR LEAGUE RECORD

		P	W	D	L	F	A	Pts	Pos
1988-89	Div 3	46	17	9	20	63	73	60	14
1989-90	Div 3	46	17	14	15	61	62	65	8
1990-91	Div 3	46	18	13	15	57	51	67	11
1991-92	Div 3	46	22	12	12	59	38	78	3
1992-93	Div 2	46	17	9	20	54	61	60	15
1993-94	Div 2	46	17	14	15	58	61	65	11
1994-95	Div 2	46	22	15	9	79	49	81	5
1995-96	Div 1	46	17	12	17	61	58	63	8
1996-97	Div 1	46	13	15	18	48	61	54	20
1997-98	Div 1	46	14	11	21	50	72	53	16

DID YOU KNOW ?

In 1919–20, Huddersfield Town set up several club records: most home wins (16); most away (12); most overall (28); most 'double' wins over opponents (9) and least 'doubles' against (none). They finished as runners-up.

HUDDERSFIELD TOWN 1998–99 LEAGUE RECORD

Match No.	Date	Venue	Opponents	Result	H/T Score	Lg. Pos.	Goalscorers	Attendance
1	Aug 8	A	Bury	L	0-1	0-1	—	7659
2	15	H	Port Vale	W	2-1	1-0	11	Dalton 40, Stewart 60	10,030
3	22	A	Grimsby T	L	0-1	0-0	14		6974
4	29	H	Portsmouth	D	3-3	1-1	13	Stewart 2 45, 84, Allison 89	10,085
5	31	A	Bristol C	W	2-1	0-1	10	Horne 48, Stewart 52	11,801
6	Sept 5	H	Sheffield U	W	1-0	0-0	6	Allison 88	12,192
7	8	H	Watford	W	2-0	2-0	—	Stewart 21, Allison 41	9811
8	11	A	Tranmere R	W	3-2	2-0	—	Stewart 21, Allison 2 45, 69	5770
9	19	H	Wolverhampton W	W	2-1	1-0	1	Dalton 19, Thornley 90	13,854
10	26	A	Bolton W	L	0-3	0-3	2		20,971
11	29	A	Stockport Co	D	1-1	1-1	—	Allison 40	8023
12	Oct 3	H	Oxford U	W	2-0	2-0	1	Dalton 24, Stewart 33	10,968
13	9	A	Swindon T	L	0-3	0-3	—		8316
14	17	H	QPR	W	2-0	1-0	1	Edwards 12, Thornley 48	11,276
15	21	H	Sunderland	D	1-1	1-1	—	Stewart 28	20,741
16	24	A	Norwich C	L	1-4	0-3	3	Beresford 59	15,403
17	31	A	Birmingham C	D	1-1	0-0	3	Stewart 61	19,170
18	Nov 7	H	Ipswich T	D	2-2	0-1	5	Edwards 65, Allison 74	14,240
19	14	A	WBA	L	1-3	1-1	9	Beresford 6	13,626
20	21	H	Bradford C	W	2-1	0-1	7	Barnes 70, Johnson 72	18,173
21	27	A	Barnsley	L	1-7	0-6	—	Facey 74	16,648
22	Dec 5	H	Crystal Palace	W	4-0	2-0	6	Stewart 3 15, 24, 82, Facey 90	10,453
23	12	H	WBA	L	0-3	0-0	8		11,947
24	19	A	Crewe Alex	W	2-1	1-0	8	Stewart 2 13, 48	5102
25	26	H	Grimsby T	W	2-0	0-0	6	Stewart 53, Beech 66	16,186
26	28	A	Sheffield U	L	1-2	0-0	7	Stewart (pen) 67	17,359
27	Jan 9	A	Bury	W	2-0	1-0	8	Allison 32, Johnson 83	10,788
28	16	A	Portsmouth	L	0-1	0-1	10		10,334
29	30	H	Bristol C	D	2-2	1-1	10	Phillips 3, Johnson 59	14,034
30	Feb 6	A	Port Vale	L	0-2	0-2	11		6499
31	16	H	Watford	D	1-1	0-0	—	Beech 71	10,303
32	20	H	Tranmere R	D	0-0	0-0	12		11,411
33	27	A	Wolverhampton W	D	2-2	0-1	12	Gray 59, Hamilton 90	21,778
34	Mar 2	H	Bolton W	W	3-2	2-1	—	Stewart 36, Johnson 41, Armstrong 46	13,867
35	6	H	Stockport Co	W	3-0	0-0	8	Stewart 2 (1 pen) 64 (p), 68, Jenkins 72	11,914
36	9	A	Oxford U	D	2-2	1-1	—	Thornley 29, Stewart (pen) 86	6034
37	13	A	Ipswich T	L	0-3	0-2	10		17,170
38	20	H	Birmingham C	D	1-1	0-0	9	Facey 55	14,667
39	24	H	Norwich C	D	1-1	0-1	—	Hughes (og) 83	9717
40	Apr 3	A	QPR	D	1-1	0-0	9	Lawson 79	11,113
41	5	H	Swindon T	L	1-2	0-1	9	Lawson 80	11,719
42	10	A	Sunderland	L	0-2	0-2	10		41,074
43	17	A	Bradford C	W	3-2	3-1	9	Stewart 22, Allison 24, Thornley 36	15,124
44	24	H	Barnsley	L	0-1	0-1	10		15,353
45	May 1	A	Crystal Palace	D	2-2	2-1	10	Dyson 33, Stewart (pen) 40	17,282
46	9	H	Crewe Alex	D	0-0	0-0	10		15,105

Final League Position: 10

GOALSCORERS

League (62): Stewart 22 (4 pens), Allison 9, Johnson 4, Thornley 4, Dalton 3, Facey 3, Beech 2, Beresford 2, Edwards 2, Lawson 2, Armstrong 1, Barnes 1, Dyson 1, Gray 1, Hamilton 1, Horne 1, Jenkins 1, Phillips 1, own goal 1.
Worthington Cup (6): Allison 2, Stewart 2, Dalton 1 (pen), Johnson 1.
FA Cup (7): Allison 2, Beech 2, Stewart 2, Thornley 1.

Vaassen N 43	Jenkins S 36	Edwards R 45	Browning M 2+4	Morrison A 12	Collins S 22+1	Johnson G 36	Horne B 20	Stewart M 43	Allison W 44	Thornley B 32+3	Phillips D 15+8	Facey D 5+15	Dalton P 7+2	Gray K 28+6	Francis S 3	Barnes P 2+13	Hessey S 7+3	Richardson L 13+2	Dyson J 10+4	Beresford D 13+6	Jackson M 5	Beech C 13+4	Cowan T 5	Lawson L 2+4	Edmondson D 1+2	Baldry S 8+5	Hamilton D 10	Armstrong C 13	Vincent J 7	Heary T 3	Mattis D —+2	Schofield D 1	Match No.
1	2	3	4	5	6	7¹	8	9²	10	11	12	13																					1
1	2	3	12	5	6	4	8	9²	10	11			7¹	13																			2
	2	3		5¹	6	4	8	9	10	11			7²	12	1	13																	3
1		3	12	5	6	4¹	8	9	10	11			7	13				2²															4
1	2	3	4¹	5	6	7	8	9	10	11								12															5
1	2	3	5²		6	4	8	9	10	11				12		13	7¹																6
1	2	3			6	4	8	9	10¹	11				5		12		7															7
1	2	3			6	4	8	9	10	11²				12		5		7¹	13														8
1	2	3			6	4	8	9	10	11						7	5																9
1	2	3			6	4	8		10	11					5	9		7¹		12													10
1	2	3	7		6	4¹	8	9	10	11						5		12															11
1	2¹	3	5		6	4	8	9²	10	11				7		12	13																12
1		3	12	5	6²	4	8	9	10	11³	2		7¹			14		13															13
1	2	3	5			4	8	9²	10	11	12					13		6	7¹														14
1	2	3	5			4	8	9	10	11¹	12					13		6	7²														15
1	2	3	12	5			8	9	10²	11¹	13				6⁴	14		4	7														16
1	2	3¹				4	8	9	10	11²	12					6	13		7		5												17
1	2	3				4	8	9	10		12	13	7¹			6		11²		5													18
1	2	3				4	8	9	10			7	12			6	13	11²		5													19
1	2	3			6	4	8¹	9	10			12	7			13		11²		5													20
1	2	3			6	4		9²	10			8	13	12		11³	7¹			5	14												21
	2	3			4²			9	10¹			8	7	6	1			5	12	13	11												22
	2	3						9				8	7	6	1	12		5	13	4²	11	10¹											23
1	2	3			4			9	10					6			5	7		11		8											24
1	2	3			4			9	10					6			5	7		11		8											25
1	2	3			4			9	10		12			6			5	7¹		11²		8			13								26
1	2	3²			4			9	10			8	12	6			13	5		7¹		11											27
1	2	3	7²		4			9	10			8¹	12	6			13	5				11											28
1	2	3	5		4¹			9	10	11	8			6²			13		12	7													29
1	2¹	3						9	10	11²	8			6			13	5		7	4					12							30
1		3			4			9		11¹	2	12		6				5		10							7	8					31
1		3	6		4			9²	10	12	2	13				14	5			11¹							7³	8					32
1		3						9	10	11	2	12		6						4						7¹	8	5					33
1			4¹					9	10	11	2	12		6						7	3²	13					8	5					34
1	2²	3	4¹					9	10	11	13	12		6						7							8	5					35
1	2	3	4					9	10	11		12		6						7							8¹	5					36
1	2	3	4					9	10²	11¹	8	12		6						7						13		5					37
1	2	3	4					9	10	11			7²	6						12						13	8¹	5					38
1		3	4					9	10	11				6						7²					12	2¹	13	8	5				39
1	2	7	4						10	11²		9¹		6						5					12	13	8	3					40
1	2	7	12					9	10	11²		6¹		4						13	14				8³	5	3						41
1	2	8	6					9	10	12		13	4²	11¹	7					5	3												42
1	2	8	6					9	10	11¹			4	12						7					5	3							43
1		8¹	6					9	10	11		12		4						7					5	3	2						44
1		8	6					9¹	10	11²		12		4	6³	13				7					5	3	2	14					45
1		8	6¹						10	11²			4³	12			13			7					5	3	2	14	9				46

Worthington Cup

First Round	Mansfield T	(h)	3-2
		(a)	1-1
Second Round	Everton	(h)	1-1
		(a)	1-2

FA Cup

Third Round	QPR	(a)	1-0
Fourth Round	Wrexham	(a)	1-1
		(h)	2-1
Fifth Round	Derby Co	(h)	2-2
		(a)	1-3

Division 3

HULL CITY

Boothferry Park, Hull HU4 6EU.
Telephone: (01482) 575263.
Fax: (01482) 565752.
Sales/Marketing Manager: Andy Daykin (01482) 327200.
Football in the Community Office: John Davies (01482) 568088.
Club Shop: (01482) 575263.
Ground Capacity: 12,439.
Record Attendance: 55,019 v Manchester U, FA Cup 6th rd, 26 February 1949.
Record Receipts: £79,604 v Liverpool, FA Cup 5th rd, 18 February 1989.
Pitch Measurements: 115yd × 75yd.
Vice-President: S. Hinchliffe.
Chairman: Nick Buchanan.
Directors: Phillip Webster, Richard Ibbotson, Tom Belton, Andy Daykin.
Manager: Warren Joyce
Assistant Manager: John McGovern.
Assistant Secretary: Jackie Bell.
Physio: Keith Warner.
Ticket Office Manager: Carol Taylor.
Hon. Medical Officers: Mr F. R. Howell MA, FRCS, Dr B. Kell MBBS.

LATEST SEQUENCES

Longest Sequence of League Wins: 10, 23.2.66 – 20.4.66.
Longest Sequence of League Defeats: 8, 7.4.34 – 8.9.34.
Longest Sequence of League Draws: 5, 30.3.29 – 15.4.29.
Longest Sequence of Unbeaten League Matches: 15, 23.4.83 – 18.10.83.
Longest Sequence Without a League Win: 27, 27.3.89 – 4.11.89.

HONOURS

Football League: Division 2 best season: 3rd, 1909–10; Division 3 (N) – Champions 1932–33, 1948–49; Division 3 – Champions 1965–66; Runners-up 1958–59; Division 4 – Runners-up 1982–83.
FA Cup: Semi-final 1930.
Football League Cup: best season: 4th, 1974, 1976, 1978.
Associate Members' Cup: Runners-up 1984.

Colours

Black and amber striped shirts, black shorts with amber stripe, black and amber stockings with white tops.

Change Colours

All white.

Year Formed: 1904.

Turned Professional: 1905.

Ltd Co.: 1905.

Club Nickname: 'The Tigers'.

Previous Grounds: 1904, Boulevard Ground (Hull RFC); 1905, Anlaby Road (Hull CC); 1944, Boulevard Ground; 1946, Boothferry Park.

First Football League Game: 2 September 1905, Division 2, v Barnsley (h) W 4–1 – Spendiff; Langley, Jones; Martin, Robinson, Gordon (2); Rushton, Spence (1), Wilson (1), Howe, Raisbeck.

Record League Victory: 11–1 v Carlisle U, Division 3 (N), 14 January 1939 – Ellis; Woodhead, Dowen; Robinson (1), Blyth, Hardy; Hubbard (2), Richardson (2), Dickinson (2), Davies (2), Cunliffe (2).

Record Cup Victory: 8–2 v Stalybridge Celtic (a), FA Cup 1st rd, 26 November 1932 – Maddison; Goldsmith, Woodhead; Gardner, Hill (1), Denby; Forward (1), Duncan, McNaughton (1), Wainscoat (4), Sargeant (1).

Record Defeat: 0–8 v Wolverhampton W, Division 2, 4 November 1911.

Most League Points (2 for a win): 69, Division 3, 1965–66.

Most League Points (3 for a win): 90, Division 4, 1982–83.

Most League Goals: 109, Division 3, 1965–66.

Highest League Scorer in Season: Bill McNaughton, 39, Division 3 (N), 1932–33.

Most League Goals in Total Aggregate: Chris Chilton, 195, 1960–71.

Most League Goals in One Match: 5, Ken McDonald v Bristol C, Division 2, 17 November 1928; 5, Simon 'Slim' Raleigh v Halifax T, Division 3N, 26 December 1930.

Most Capped Player: Terry Neill, 15 (59), Northern Ireland.

Most League Appearances: Andy Davidson, 520, 1952–67.

Youngest League Player: Matthew Edeson, 16 years 63 days v Fulham, 10 October 1992.

Record Transfer Fee Received: £750,000 from Middlesbrough for Andy Payton, November 1991.

Record Transfer Fee Paid: £200,000 to Leeds U for Peter Swan, March 1989.

Football League Record: 1905 Elected to Division 2; 1930–33 Division 3 (N); 1933–36 Division 2; 1936–49 Division 3 (N); 1949–56 Division 2; 1956–58 Division 3 (N); 1958–59 Division 3; 1959–60 Division 2; 1960–66 Division 3; 1966–78 Division 2; 1978–81 Division 3; 1981–83 Division 4; 1983–85 Division 3; 1985–91 Division 2; 1991–92 Division 3; 1992–96 Division 2; 1996– Division 3.

MANAGERS

James Ramster 1904–05
(Secretary-Manager)
Ambrose Langley 1905–13
Harry Chapman 1913–14
Fred Stringer 1914–16
David Menzies 1916–21
Percy Lewis 1921–23
Bill McCracken 1923–31
Haydn Green 1931–34
John Hill 1934–36
David Menzies 1936
Ernest Blackburn 1936–46
Major Frank Buckley 1946–48
Raich Carter 1948–51
Bob Jackson 1952–55
Bob Brocklebank 1955–61
Cliff Britton 1961–70
(continued as General Manager to 1971)
Terry Neill 1970–74
John Kaye 1974–77
Bobby Collins 1977–78
Ken Houghton 1978–79
Mike Smith 1979–82
Bobby Brown 1982
Colin Appleton 1982–84
Brian Horton 1984–88
Eddie Gray 1988–89
Colin Appleton 1989
Stan Ternent 1989–91
Terry Dolan 1991–97
Mark Hateley 1997–98
Warren Joyce November 1998–

TEN YEAR LEAGUE RECORD

		P	W	D	L	F	A	Pts	Pos
1988-89	Div 2	46	11	14	21	52	68	47	21
1989-90	Div 2	46	14	16	16	58	65	58	14
1990-91	Div 2	46	10	15	21	57	85	45	24
1991-92	Div 3	46	16	11	19	54	54	59	14
1992-93	Div 2	46	13	11	22	46	69	50	20
1993-94	Div 2	46	18	14	14	62	54	68	9
1994-95	Div 2	46	21	11	14	70	57	74	8
1995-96	Div 2	46	5	16	25	36	78	31	24
1996-97	Div 3	46	13	18	15	44	50	57	17
1997-98	Div 3	46	11	8	27	56	83	41	22

DID YOU KNOW ?

On their re-formation after the Second World War, Hull City drew a crowd of 25,586 for the visit of Lincoln City in a Division Three (North) match. In that 1946–47 season Hull's average attendance was 19,673.

HULL CITY 1998–99 LEAGUE RECORD

Match No.	Date	Venue	Opponents	Result	H/T Score	Lg. Pos.	Goalscorers	Attendance
1	Aug 8	A	Rotherham U	L	1-3	1-2	—	D'Auria [6]	5447
2	15	H	Darlington	L	1-2	0-1	22	Whitworth [52]	5217
3	23	A	Chester C	D	2-2	1-1	22	Brown [40], Hateley (pen) [89]	2577
4	29	A	Peterborough U	W	1-0	1-0	15	Hateley (pen) [39]	4636
5	31	A	Hartlepool U	L	0-1	0-0	19		3277
6	Sept 5	H	Brentford	L	2-3	1-1	22	Hocking [12], Whitworth [63]	4058
7	8	H	Rochdale	W	2-1	1-0	—	Peacock [23], Brown [63]	3433
8	12	A	Barnet	L	1-4	1-2	22	Peacock [8]	2025
9	19	A	Halifax T	L	1-2	0-0	23	McGinty [81]	4719
10	26	A	Mansfield T	L	0-2	0-0	23		2603
11	Oct 3	H	Cambridge U	L	0-3	0-2	24		3882
12	9	H	Cardiff C	L	1-2	1-1	—	Brown [42]	8594
13	17	A	Scarborough	W	2-1	2-1	24	Mann [14], Hateley [39]	2760
14	20	A	Exeter C	L	0-3	0-0	—		2101
15	24	H	Southend U	D	1-1	0-0	24	McGinty [84]	3551
16	31	A	Plymouth Arg	D	0-0	0-0	24		4285
17	Nov 7	A	Leyton Orient	L	0-1	0-0	24		5288
18	10	H	Brighton & HA	L	0-2	0-2	—		4433
19	21	A	Scunthorpe U	L	2-3	1-2	24	Dudley [38], Brown [46]	5633
20	28	H	Carlisle U	W	1-0	0-0	24	Dudley [89]	4452
21	Dec 12	A	Torquay U	L	0-2	0-2	24		2033
22	19	H	Swansea C	L	0-2	0-2	24		4280
23	26	H	Chester C	L	1-2	0-2	24	D'Auria [63]	6695
24	28	A	Shrewsbury T	L	2-3	1-2	24	D'Auria (pen) [14], Joyce [67]	2879
25	Jan 9	H	Rotherham U	W	1-0	1-0	24	Bonner [35]	5575
26	23	H	Hartlepool U	W	4-0	4-0	24	Brown 2 [10, 14], McGinty 2 [28, 41]	5808
27	26	A	Peterborough U	D	1-1	0-0	—	Whitney [86]	4405
28	30	H	Shrewsbury T	D	1-1	0-0	24	Gayle (og) [86]	7331
29	Feb 6	A	Brentford	W	2-0	1-0	23	Alcide [16], Brown [80]	5086
30	12	A	Rochdale	L	0-3	0-1	—		5374
31	16	A	Darlington	W	1-0	1-0	—	Brabin [38]	3107
32	20	H	Barnet	D	1-1	1-1	23	Whittle [12]	6823
33	27	A	Halifax T	W	1-0	0-0	23	Brown [54]	4455
34	Mar 6	H	Mansfield T	D	0-0	0-0	23		6692
35	9	A	Cambridge U	L	0-2	0-0	—		4948
36	13	A	Leyton Orient	W	2-1	1-0	22	Brabin [3], Brown [83]	5481
37	20	H	Plymouth Arg	W	1-0	0-0	21	Brabin [51]	6294
38	26	A	Southend U	W	1-0	0-0	—	D'Auria [81]	4149
39	Apr 3	H	Scarborough	D	1-1	0-0	21	Brabin [49]	13,949
40	5	A	Cardiff C	D	1-1	1-0	21	Alcide [25]	8252
41	10	H	Exeter C	W	2-1	1-0	20	Williams [43], Alcide [90]	5836
42	13	A	Carlisle U	D	0-0	0-0	—		3743
43	17	H	Scunthorpe U	L	2-3	0-2	21	Joyce [82], Brown [89]	9835
44	24	A	Brighton & HA	D	0-0	0-0	21		3481
45	May 1	H	Torquay U	W	1-0	1-0	20	Brown [31]	7789
46	8	A	Swansea C	L	0-2	0-1	21		9226

Final League Position: 21

GOALSCORERS

League (44): Brown 11, Brabin 4, D'Auria 4 (1 pen), McGinty 4, Alcide 3, Hateley 3 (2 pens), Dudley 2, Joyce 2, Peacock 2, Whitworth 2, Bonner 1, Hocking 1, Mann 1, Whitney 1, Whittle 1, Williams 1, own goal 1.
Worthington Cup (5): Brown 3, McGinty 1, Rioch 1 (pen).
FA Cup (4): Dewhurst 1, McGinty 1, Morley 1, Rioch 1.

Wilson S 23	Gage K 2+1	Edwards M 28+2	Hocking M 24+2	Whitworth N 18	Joyce W 28+1	French J 9+6	D'Auria D 42	Brown D 38+4	Ellington L 3+3	Hawes S 18+1	Mann N 16+4	McGinty B 22+10	Peacock R 13+1	Morley B 1+11	Greaves M 18+7	Hateley M 8+4	Rioch G 10+3	Dewhurst R 4+4	Saville A 3	Gibson P 4	Dudley C 4+3	Whittle J 24	Williams G 24+1	Swales S 20+2	Oakes A 19	Perry J 7+1	Whitney J 21	Faulconbridge C 4+6	Bonner M 1	Brabin G 21	Bolder A —+1	Alcide C 17	Harrison G 8	Darby D 4+4	Match No
1	2	3[1]	4	5	6[2]	7[3]	8	9	10	11	12	13	14																						1
1	3			2			8	9	10	4	11[1]	6	7	12																					2
1		3	4	5		10[1]	9[2]	12		6	11[3]	8	7	13	2	14																			3
1		2	4	5		11	9[1]	6	12	8	7	13	10	3[2]																					4
1		2	4	5		11	9	6[2]	12	8	7	3	10[1]	13																					5
1		2[2]	4	5		12	10	9	6	11	8	7	3[1]	13																					6
1		3	4	5		2	10	9[2]	6	11[1]	8	7	12	13																					7
1	12	4[1]	5		13	8[2]	9	6[3]	3	11	7	2	14	10																					8
1		4	5	2[2]	9[1]	8	6	3	11	7	12	13	10																						9
1		4	5	8	9	12	2	3	11	7	6[1]	10																							10
1		4	5	6	2[1]	3	7	12	11	10																									11
1	12	4	5	6[1]	8[2]	9	2	3	7	13	10	11																							12
1		4	5	2	8	9	3	6	7	10	11																								13
1		4	5	2	12	8	9	3	6	7[1]	10	11																							14
1		4	5	2	7[1]	8	9	12	3	6	10	11																							15
1		4	5	2	7	8	9[1]	13	3	6[2]	12	10	11																						16
		4	5	2	7[1]	8		9	6	3	12	10	11	1																					17
		4	5	2	12	8[1]	6	3	7		11		1	10																					18
		5	2		6		8	9		7	3[1]	11		4		12	1	10																	19
		3	2		6		8	9		7				5			1	10	4	11															20
1		3[3]	2[2]			7		9		6		8		10	12			5[1]		13	4	11	14												21
		2		7			9		8[1]	12	13						11	4		3	1	5	6	10[2]											22
1		2[1]			8					7[2]	11	12					13	4	9	3		5	6	10											23
		12	2[3]		6	9[1]	8					13						14	3	10	5[2]	1	4	7	11										24
		5			6		8	9[1]					2						11		1	4	3	12	7	10									25
		5[2]			7		8	9[1]		10	12	2						4	11	3	1		6			13									26
					7		8	9[1]		10		5						4	11	3	1		6	12	2										27
1		4	12[1]		7		8[3]			9		13	2[1]					5	11	3			6	14	10										28
		4	13		7	14	2	9[3]		12			6[2]					5	11	3	1			8	10[1]										29
		4			12	2[2]	9			7[1]				13	5			11	3	1		6		8	10										30
		4		7	8	9[1]		12										5	11	2	1	3		6	10										31
		4		7	8	9[1]			12									5	11	2	1	3		6	10										32
1		4		7	8	9				3								5	11	2			6	10											33
1		4		7	8[1]	9		12		6	13							5		2		3[2]	10	11											34
1		4		7	8[1]	9[2]		12		2								5	11			3	13	6	10[1]										35
1		4		7	8	9[2]				12								5	11	2		3	13	6	10[1]										36
		4		7		9[2]				12								5	11	3	1		6	13	8[1]	10									37
		4		12		8	13											5	11	2	1	3		6	10[1]	7	9[1]								38
		4			8	12				13			5						11	2	1		6	10	7[2]	9[1]									39
		4		7		8[2]	12					13			14			5	11	2[1]	1	3		6	10		9[1]								40
		4		7		8[1]	13			14			3					5	11	12	1		6[2]	10	2	9[3]									41
				7			9[1]						2					5	11			1	4	3	6	10	8	12							42
				7		8[1]	9			4								5	12		1	6	3	11	10[2]	2	13								43
		4			8	9[1]												5	11	2	1	3		6	10	7	12								44
		4			8[1]	9[3]				12								5	11	2	1	13	3	6	10	7[2]	14								45
		4			8	9		12		13								5	11[1]	2[2]	1	3		6	10	7									46

Division 1

IPSWICH TOWN

FOUNDATION

Considering that Ipswich Town only reached the Football League in 1938, many people outside of East Anglia may be surprised to learn that this club was formed at a meeting held in the Town Hall as far back as 1878 when Mr T. C. Cobbold, MP, was voted president. Originally it was the Ipswich Association FC to distinguish it from the older Ipswich Football Club which played rugby. These two amalgamated in 1888 and the handling game was dropped in 1893.

Portman Road, Ipswich, Suffolk IP1 2DA.
Telephone: (01473) 400500 (4 lines).
Fax: (01473) 400040.
Ticket Office: (01473) 400555.
Sales & Marketing Dept: (01473) 400523.
Ground Capacity: 22,600.
Record Attendance: 38,010 v Leeds U, FA Cup 6th rd, 8 March 1975.
Record Receipts: £105,950 v AZ 67 Alkmaar, UEFA Cup Final 1st leg, 6 May 1981.
Pitch Measurements: 112yd × 72yd.
Chairman: David Sheepshanks.
Vice-Presidents: Kenneth H. Brightwell, Harold R. Smith.
Directors: P. Hope-Cobbold, R. Moore, John Kerr MBE, R. J. Finbow, Lord Ryder OBE.
Manager: George Burley.
Assistant Manager: Dale Roberts.
First Team Coach: Tony Mowbraw.
Reserve Team Coach: Dale Roberts.
Youth Team Coach: Paul Goddard.
Chief Scout: Colin Suggett.
Director of Football: Bryan Klug.
Physio: Dave Williams.
Secretary: David C. Rose.
Sales & Promotions Manager: Mike Noye.
Director of Sales & Marketing: Paul Clouting.

HONOURS

Football League: Division 1 – Champions 1961–62; Runners-up 1980–81, 1981–82; Division 2 – Champions 1960–61, 1967–68, 1991–92; Division 3 (S) – Champions 1953–54, 1956–57.
FA Cup: Winners 1978.
Football League Cup: Semi-final 1982, 1985.
Texaco Cup: Winners 1973.
European Competitions: *European Cup:* 1962–63. *European Cup-Winners' Cup:* 1978–79. *UEFA Cup:* 1973–74, 1974–75, 1975–76, 1977–78, 1979–80, 1980–81 (winners), 1981–82, 1982–83.

LATEST SEQUENCES

Longest Sequence of League Wins: 8, 23.9.53 – 31.10.53.
Longest Sequence of League Defeats: 10, 4.9.54 – 16.10.54.
Longest Sequence of League Draws: 7, 10.11.90 – 21.12.90.
Longest Sequence of Unbeaten League Matches: 23, 8.12.79 – 26.4.80.
Longest Sequence Without a League Win: 21, 28.8.63 – 14.12.63.

Colours
Blue shirts, white shorts, blue stockings.

Change Colours
Orange shirts, navy shorts, orange stockings.

Year Formed: 1878.

Turned Professional: 1936.

Ltd Co.: 1936.

Club Nickname: 'Blues' or 'Town'.

First Football League Game: 27 August 1938, Division 3 (S), v Southend U (h) W 4–2 – Burns; Dale, Parry; Perrett, Fillingham, McLuckie; Williams, Davies (1), Jones (2), Alsop (1), Little.

Record League Victory: 7–0 v Portsmouth, Division 2, 7 November 1964 – Thorburn; Smith, McNeil; Baxter, Bolton, Thompson; Broadfoot (1), Hegan (2), Baker (1), Leadbetter, Brogan (3). 7–0 v Southampton, Division 1, 2 February 1974 – Sivell; Burley, Mills (1), Morris, Hunter, Beattie (1), Hamilton (2), Viljoen, Johnson, Whymark (2), Lambert (1) (Woods). 7–0 v WBA, Division 1, 6 November 1976 – Sivell; Burley, Mills, Talbot, Hunter, Beattie (1), Osborne, Wark (1), Mariner (1) (Bertschin), Whymark (4), Woods.

Record Cup Victory: 10–0 v Floriana, European Cup prel. rd, 25 September 1962 – Bailey; Malcolm, Compton; Baxter, Laurel, Elsworthy (1); Stephenson, Moran (2), Crawford (5), Phillips (2), Blackwood.

Record Defeat: 1–10 v Fulham, Division 1, 26 December 1963.

Most League Points (2 for a win): 64, Division 3 (S), 1953–54 and 1955–56.

Most League Points (3 for a win): 86, Division 1, 1998–99.

Most League Goals: 106, Division 3 (S), 1955–56.

Highest League Scorer in Season: Ted Phillips, 41, Division 3 (S), 1956–57.

Most League Goals in Total Aggregate: Ray Crawford, 203, 1958–63 and 1966–69.

Most League Goals in One Match: 5, Alan Brazil v Southampton, Division 1, 16 February 1981.

Most Capped Player: Allan Hunter, 47 (53), Northern Ireland.

Most League Appearances: Mick Mills, 591, 1966–82.

Youngest League Player: Jason Dozzell, 16 years 56 days v Coventry C, 4 February 1984.

Record Transfer Fee Received: £1,900,000 from Tottenham H for Jason Dozzell, August 1993.

Record Transfer Fee Paid: £1,100,000 to Bury for David Johnson, November 1997.

Football League Record: 1938 Elected to Division 3 (S); 1954–55 Division 2; 1955–57 Division 3 (S); 1957–61 Division 2; 1961–64 Division 1; 1964–68 Division 2; 1968–86 Division 1; 1986–92 Division 2; 1992–95 FA Premier League; 1995– Division 1.

MANAGERS

Mick O'Brien 1936–37
Scott Duncan 1937–55
(continued as Secretary)
Alf Ramsey 1955–63
Jackie Milburn 1963–64
Bill McGarry 1964–68
Bobby Robson 1969–82
Bobby Ferguson 1982–87
Johnny Duncan 1987–90
John Lyall 1990–94
George Burley December 1994–

TEN YEAR LEAGUE RECORD

		P	W	D	L	F	A	Pts	Pos
1988-89	Div 2	46	22	7	17	71	61	73	8
1989-90	Div 2	46	19	12	15	67	66	69	9
1990-91	Div 2	46	13	18	15	60	68	57	14
1991-92	Div 2	46	24	12	10	70	50	84	1
1992-93	PR Lge	42	12	16	14	50	55	52	16
1993-94	PR Lge	42	9	16	17	35	58	43	19
1994-95	PR Lge	42	7	6	29	36	93	27	22
1995-96	Div 1	46	19	12	15	79	69	69	7
1996-97	Div 1	46	20	14	12	68	50	74	4
1997-98	Div 1	46	23	14	9	77	43	83	5

DID YOU KNOW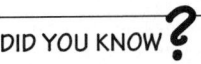

On 20 March 1999, Ipswich Town won 1–0 at West Bromwich Albion. It was their 22nd clean-sheet in the League in the season, a club record. At the time they had conceded only 25 goals in 38 First Division matches.

IPSWICH TOWN 1998–99 LEAGUE RECORD

Match No.	Date	Venue	Opponents	Result	H/T Score	Lg. Pos.	Goalscorers	Attendance
1	Aug 9	A	Grimsby T	D 0-0	0-0	—		7211
2	15	H	Bury	D 0-0	0-0	14		13,267
3	22	A	Portsmouth	D 0-0	0-0	15		12,002
4	29	H	Sunderland	L 0-2	0-2	18		15,813
5	31	A	Port Vale	W 3-0	1-0	16	Scowcroft [22], Johnson [57], Holland [90]	5485
6	Sept 8	H	Bradford C	W 3-0	1-0	—	Scowcroft 2 [22, 83], Venus [65]	11,596
7	12	A	Oxford U	D 3-3	1-1	11	Scowcroft [39], Johnson [64], Dyer [86]	6632
8	19	A	Bristol C	W 3-1	2-0	10	Johnson 2 [13, 90], Scowcroft [33]	13,657
9	26	A	Watford	L 0-1	0-1	12		13,109
10	29	A	Tranmere R	W 2-0	1-0	—	Stockwell [43], Scowcroft [78]	5072
11	Oct 3	H	Crystal Palace	W 3-0	1-0	5	Venus (pen) [45], Taricco [82], Mathie [90]	16,837
12	17	H	Swindon T	W 1-0	1-0	4	Johnson [31]	13,212
13	20	H	Norwich C	L 0-1	0-0	—		22,079
14	24	A	Stockport Co	W 1-0	0-0	4	Dyer [60]	7432
15	31	H	WBA	W 2-0	0-0	4	Johnson 2 [66, 74]	15,568
16	Nov 3	H	Wolverhampton W	W 2-0	1-0	—	Scowcroft [17], Stockwell [90]	14,680
17	7	A	Huddersfield T	D 2-2	1-0	2	Venus [25], Johnson [89]	14,240
18	14	A	Barnsley	W 1-0	1-0	2	Johnson [5]	15,966
19	21	H	Bolton W	L 0-1	0-0	3		17,225
20	28	A	Crewe Alex	W 3-0	1-0	2	Scowcroft 3 (1 pen) [37, 57, 74 (p)]	5165
21	Dec 2	H	QPR	D 1-1	0-0	—	Holland [90]	12,449
22	5	H	Birmingham C	W 1-0	1-0	2	Petta [16]	15,901
23	12	H	Barnsley	L 0-2	0-0	2		16,021
24	20	A	Sheffield U	W 2-1	0-0	2	Abou [49], Naylor [90]	12,944
25	26	H	Portsmouth	W 3-0	3-0	2	Naylor 2 [23, 25], Dyer [31]	21,805
26	28	A	Wolverhampton W	L 0-1	0-0	2		24,636
27	Jan 9	H	Grimsby T	L 0-1	0-1	3		15,575
28	17	A	Sunderland	L 1-2	1-2	5	Holland [38]	39,835
29	30	H	Port Vale	W 1-0	1-0	5	Clapham [40]	16,328
30	Feb 6	A	Bury	W 3-0	0-0	4	Venus (pen) [50], Mowbray [70], Harewood [76]	4750
31	13	H	Bradford C	D 0-0	0-0	4		15,024
32	20	H	Oxford U	W 2-1	2-1	4	Holland [6], Venus (pen) [8]	16,920
33	27	A	Bristol C	W 1-0	0-0	3	Naylor [56]	14,065
34	Mar 2	H	Watford	W 3-2	2-0	2	Dyer [17], Venus [27], Johnson [74]	18,818
35	6	H	Tranmere R	W 1-0	0-0	2	Thetis [78]	15,929
36	9	A	Crystal Palace	L 2-3	1-1	—	Johnson [10], Clapham [62]	16,360
37	13	H	Huddersfield T	W 3-0	2-0	2	Magilton [13], Johnson [45], Petta [83]	17,170
38	20	A	WBA	W 1-0	1-0	2	Thetis [15]	15,552
39	Apr 3	A	Swindon T	W 6-0	4-0	2	Venus 2 (2 pens) [6, 61], Scowcroft [18], Mowbray [22], Clapham [43], Wilnis [74]	10,337
40	5	H	QPR	W 3-1	1-1	2	Johnson [12], Scowcroft [65], Holland [75]	22,162
41	11	A	Norwich C	D 0-0	0-0	2		19,511
42	17	A	Bolton W	L 0-2	0-1	3		19,894
43	20	H	Stockport Co	W 1-0	1-0	3	Magilton [39]	17,056
44	24	A	Crewe Alex	L 1-2	0-0	3	Venus (pen) [70]	20,845
45	May 2	A	Birmingham C	L 0-1	0-0	3		27,685
46	9	H	Sheffield U	W 4-1	3-0	3	Magilton [18], Scowcroft [32], Dyer [45], Naylor [79]	21,689

Final League Position: 3

GOALSCORERS

League (69): Johnson 13, Scowcroft 13 (1 pen), Venus 9 (6 pens), Dyer 5, Holland 5, Naylor 5, Clapham 3, Magilton 3, Mowbray 2, Petta 2, Stockwell 2, Thetis 2, Abou 1, Harewood 1, Mathie 1, Taricco 1, Wilnis 1.
Worthington Cup (10): Holland 2, Johnson 1, Mason 1, Mathie 1, Scowcroft 1, Stockwell 1, Taricco 1, Thetis 1, own goal 1.
FA Cup (1): own goal 1.

Wright R 46	Stockwell M 23 + 7	Taricco M 16	Clapham J 45 + 1	Mowbray T 40	Venus M 44	Dyer K 36 + 1	Holland M 46	Johnson D 41 + 1	Holster M 1 + 9	Petta B 26 + 6	Mathie A 2 + 6	Sonner D — + 4	Naylor R 10 + 20	Scowcroft J 29 + 3	Tanner A 13 + 6	Thetis M 29 + 2	Vernazza P 2	Hunt J 2 + 4	Kennedy J 6 + 1	Hodges L — + 4	Abou S 5	Bramble T 2 + 2	Brown W — + 1	Logan R — + 2	Wilnis F 17 + 1	Magilton J 19	Harewood M 5 + 1	Cundy J 1 + 3	Match No.
1	2	3	4	5	6	7	8	9	10¹	11²	12	13																	1
1	2	3	4	5	6	7	8	9		11	12		10¹																2
1	2	3	4	5	6	7	8	9		11	10¹		12																3
1	2¹	3	4	5	6	7	8	9	12	11	10²			13															4
1		3	4	5	6	7	8	9	13	11²	12		10¹	2															5
1		3	4	5²	6	7¹	8	9		11	12	13	10	2															6
1	12	3	4²		6	7	8	9		11		13	10	2¹	5														7
1	2	3	4			7	8	9	12	11²		13	10	6	5¹														8
1	2²	3	12		6	7	8	9		11	13		10	4¹	5														9
1	2¹	3	4		6	7	8	9	12	11²			10	13	5														10
1	2	3	4		6	7	8	9		11²	12		10¹	13	5														11
1	2	3	4	5	6		8	9	12	11¹			13	10²	14		7³												12
1	2	3	4	5	6		8	9		11				10			7¹	12											13
1	2¹	3	4	5	6	7	8	9					12	10		11													14
1	2¹	3	4	5	6	7	8	9	12				13	10²	14	11³													15
1	2	3²	4	5	6	7	8	9					12	10¹	11	13													16
1	2²		4	5	6	7	8	9		11			10	12	3¹	13													17
1			4	5	6	7	8	9²		11¹			12	10		3	13	2											18
1			4	5	6	7	8	9		11¹				10		3		2	12										19
1			4	5	6	7	8	9		11³			12	10¹	13	3		2²	14										20
1			4	5²	6	7	8			11				10		3	13	12											21
1			4	5	6	7	8			11¹			12	10		2	3					9							22
1			4	5	6	7	8			11			12	10¹		2	3					9							23
1			4	5			7	8		11			10		3²			2	12	9¹	6	13							24
1			4	5	6	7³	8	12	13	11²			10			3		2	9¹	14									25
1			4	5	6	7¹	8	9	12				10			3		2²	11				13						26
1			4	5	6	7	8	9		11			10¹			3					13	12	2²						27
1			4			6	7	8	9				10			3			5		2	11	10						28
1			4	5	6	7	8	9¹					12			3					2	11	10						29
1	12		4	5	6	7	8	9²					13		3					2¹	11	10							30
1			4	5	6	7	8	9					12			3					2	11	10¹						31
1			4	5	6	7	8	9					12			3					2	11	10¹						32
1	12		4	5	6	7	8		13				9			3					2¹	11	10²						33
1	12		4	5	6	7²	8	9	13				10³			3¹					2	11	14						34
1	12		4	5	6		8	9	7¹				10²	13		3					2	11							35
1	7		4	5	6		8	9	12				10¹	13		3					2²	11							36
1	7¹		4	5	6		8	9	12				13	10²	14	3³					2	11							37
1	7		4	5	6		8	9						10		3					2	11							38
1	7²		4	5	6		8	9	12				13	10¹	3³						2	11		14					39
1	7		4	5	6		8	9¹	12				13	10²		3					2	11	3						40
1	7		4	5	6		8	9						10	3¹						2	11	12						41
1	2²		4	5	6	12	8	9		7¹			13	10	3							11							42
1	2¹		4	5	6	7³	8	9²	12				13	10	3							11	14						43
1	2¹		4	5	6	7	8	9					12	10	3²						13	11							44
1	12		4	5	6	7	8	9						10	3¹						2	11							45
1	12		3	5	6	7	8	9²		11³			13	10	14						2	4¹							46

Worthington Cup

First Round	Exeter C	(a)	1-1
		(h)	5-1
Second Round	Luton T	(h)	2-1
		(a)	2-4

FA Cup

Third Round	Tranmere R	(a)	1-0
Fourth Round	Everton	(a)	0-1

FA Premiership

LEEDS UNITED

FOUNDATION

Immediately the Leeds City club (founded in 1904) was wound up by the FA in October 1919, following allegations of illegal payments to players, a meeting was called by a Leeds solicitor, Mr Alf Masser, at which Leeds United was formed. They joined the Midland League playing their first game in that competition in November 1919. It was in this same month that the new club had discussions with the directors of a virtually bankrupt Huddersfield Town who wanted to move to Leeds in an amalgamation. But Huddersfield survived even that crisis.

Elland Road, Leeds LS11 0ES.
Telephone: (0113) 2266000.
Fax: (0113) 2266050.
Ticket Information: 0891 121680.
Clubcall: 0891 121180.
Ground Capacity: 40,204.
Record Attendance: 57,892 v Sunderland, FA Cup 5th rd (replay), 15 March 1967.
Record Receipts: £780,697 v Tottenham Hotspur, FA Cup 5th rd, 13 February 1999.
Pitch Measurements: 105m × 65m.
President: The Right Hon. The Earl of Harewood KBE, LLD.
Chairman: Peter Ridsdale.
Managing Director: Jeremy Fenn.
Directors: A. Hudson, A. Pearson, D. Spencer.
Manager: David O'Leary.
Assistant Manager: Eddie Gray MBE.
Club Secretary: Ian Silvester.
Physio: David Swift.
Commercial Manager: Phil Brining.
Stadium Manager: Harry Stokey.

LATEST SEQUENCES

Longest Sequence of League Wins: 9, 26.9.31 – 21.11.31.
Longest Sequence of League Defeats: 6, 6.4.96 – 2.5.96.
Longest Sequence of League Draws: 5, 19.4.97 – 9.8.97.
Longest Sequence of Unbeaten League Matches: 34, 26.10.68 – 26.8.69.
Longest Sequence Without a League Win: 17, 1.2.47 – 26.5.47.

HONOURS

Football League: Division 1 – Champions 1968–69, 1973–74, 1991–92; Runners-up 1964–65, 1965–66, 1969–70, 1970–71, 1971–72; Division 2 – Champions 1923–24, 1963–64, 1989–90; Runners-up 1927–28, 1931–32, 1955–56.

FA Cup: Winners 1972; Runners-up 1965, 1970, 1973.

Football League Cup: Winners 1968; Runners-up 1996.

European Competitions: *European Cup:* 1969–70, 1974–75 (runners-up), 1992–93. *European Cup-Winners' Cup:* 1972–73 (runners-up). *European Fairs Cup:* 1965–66, 1966–67 (runners-up), 1967–68 (winners), 1968–69, 1970–71 (winners). *UEFA Cup:* 1971–72, 1973–74, 1979–80, 1995–96, 1998–99.

Colours

All white with yellow and blue trim.

Change Colours

Sky blue shirts with navy blue band across chest and navy blue and white trim, navy blue shorts with sky blue and white trim, sky blue stockings with navy blue and white trim.

Year Formed: 1919, as Leeds United after disbandment (by FA order) of Leeds City (formed in 1904).

Turned Professional: 1920.

Ltd Co.: 1920.

Club Nickname: 'United'.

First Football League Game: 28 August 1920, Division 2, v Port Vale (a) L 0–2 – Down; Duffield, Tillotson; Musgrove, Baker, Walton; Mason, Goldthorpe, Thompson, Lyon, Best.

Record League Victory: 8–0 v Leicester C, Division 1, 7 April 1934 – Moore; George Milburn, Jack Milburn; Edwards, Hart, Copping; Mahon (2), Firth (2), Duggan (2), Furness (2), Cochrane.

Record Cup Victory: 10–0 v Lyn (Oslo), European Cup 1st rd 1st leg, 17 September 1969 – Sprake; Reaney, Cooper, Bremner (2), Charlton, Hunter, Madeley, Clarke (2), Jones (3), Giles (2) (Bates), O'Grady (1).

Record Defeat: 1–8 v Stoke C, Division 1, 27 August 1934.

Most League Points (2 for a win): 67, Division 1, 1968–69.

Most League Points (3 for a win): 85, Division 2, 1989–90.

Most League Goals: 98, Division 2, 1927–28.

Highest League Scorer in Season: John Charles, 42, Division 2, 1953–54.

Most League Goals in Total Aggregate: Peter Lorimer, 168, 1965–79 and 1983–86.

Most League Goals in One Match: 5, Gordon Hodgson v Leicester C, Division 1, 1 October 1938.

Most Capped Player: Billy Bremner, 54, Scotland.

Most League Appearances: Jack Charlton, 629, 1953–73.

Youngest League Player: Peter Lorimer, 15 years 289 days v Southampton, 29 September 1962.

Record Transfer Fee Received: £3,500,000 from Everton for Gary Speed, June 1996.

Record Transfer Fee Paid: £4,500,000 to Parma for Tomas Brolin, November 1995; £4,500,000 to Manchester U for Lee Sharpe, August 1996.

Football League Record: 1920 Elected to Division 2; 1924–27 Division 1; 1927–28 Division 2; 1928–31 Division 1; 1931–32 Division 2; 1932–47 Division 1; 1947–56 Division 2; 1956–60 Division 1; 1960–64 Division 2; 1964–82 Division 1; 1982–90 Division 2; 1990–92 Division 1; 1992– FA Premier League.

MANAGERS

Dick Ray 1919–20
Arthur Fairclough 1920–27
Dick Ray 1927–35
Bill Hampson 1935–47
Willis Edwards 1947–48
Major Frank Buckley 1948–53
Raich Carter 1953–58
Bill Lambton 1958–59
Jack Taylor 1959–61
Don Revie OBE 1961–74
Brian Clough 1974
Jimmy Armfield 1974–78
Jock Stein CBE 1978
Jimmy Adamson 1978–80
Allan Clarke 1980–82
Eddie Gray MBE 1982–85
Billy Bremner 1985–88
Howard Wilkinson 1988–96
George Graham 1996–98
David O'Leary October 1998–

TEN YEAR LEAGUE RECORD

		P	W	D	L	F	A	Pts	Pos
1988-89	Div 2	46	17	16	13	59	50	67	10
1989-90	Div 2	46	24	13	9	79	52	85	1
1990-91	Div 1	38	19	7	12	65	47	64	4
1991-92	Div 1	42	22	16	4	74	37	82	1
1992-93	PR Lge	42	12	15	15	57	62	51	17
1993-94	PR Lge	42	18	16	8	65	39	70	5
1994-95	PR Lge	42	20	13	9	59	38	73	5
1995-96	PR Lge	38	12	7	19	40	57	43	13
1996-97	PR Lge	38	11	13	14	28	38	46	11
1997-98	PR Lge	38	17	8	13	57	46	59	5

DID YOU KNOW ?

Leeds United needed to beat Tottenham Hotspur in the last match of 1925–26 to preserve their First Division status. They did so handsomely, winning 4–1 having scored only three times in the previous seven games.

LEEDS UNITED 1998–99 LEAGUE RECORD

Match No.	Date	Venue	Opponents	Result	H/T Score	Lg. Pos.	Goalscorers	Attendance
1	Aug 15	A	Middlesbrough	D 0-0	0-0	—		34,160
2	24	H	Blackburn R	W 1-0	1-0	—	Hasselbaink [18]	30,541
3	29	A	Wimbledon	D 1-1	0-0	7	Bowyer [61]	16,473
4	Sept 8	H	Southampton	W 3-0	1-0	—	Marshall (og) [38], Harte [52], Wijnhard [86]	30,637
5	12	H	Everton	D 0-0	0-0	3		36,687
6	19	H	Aston Villa	D 0-0	0-0	6		33,162
7	26	A	Tottenham H	D 3-3	2-1	6	Halle [4], Hasselbaink [26], Wijnhard [61]	35,535
8	Oct 3	H	Leicester C	L 0-1	0-0	11		32,120
9	17	A	Nottingham F	D 1-1	0-0	9	Halle [53]	23,911
10	25	H	Chelsea	D 0-0	0-0	10		35,833
11	31	A	Derby Co	D 2-2	2-1	9	Molenaar [16], Kewell [43]	27,034
12	Nov 8	H	Sheffield W	W 2-1	1-1	6	Hasselbaink [40], Woodgate [61]	30,012
13	14	A	Liverpool	W 3-1	0-0	5	Smith [79], Hasselbaink 2 [81, 86]	44,305
14	21	H	Charlton Ath	W 4-1	1-0	5	Hasselbaink [34], Bowyer [51], Smith [67], Kewell [87]	32,487
15	29	A	Manchester U	L 2-3	1-1	6	Hasselbaink [29], Kewell [52]	55,172
16	Dec 5	H	West Ham U	W 4-0	1-0	3	Bowyer 2 [8, 61], Molenaar [68], Hasselbaink [79]	36,315
17	14	H	Coventry C	W 2-0	1-0	—	Hopkin [40], Bowyer [90]	31,799
18	20	A	Arsenal	L 1-3	0-1	5	Hasselbaink [66]	38,025
19	26	H	Newcastle U	W 3-0	1-0	4	Kewell [38], Bowyer [62], Hasselbaink [90]	36,759
20	29	H	Wimbledon	D 2-2	1-1	—	Ribeiro [26], Hopkin [57]	39,901
21	Jan 9	A	Blackburn R	L 0-1	0-1	5		27,620
22	16	H	Middlesbrough	W 2-0	2-0	5	Smith [21], Bowyer [27]	37,394
23	30	A	Southampton	L 0-3	0-1	5		15,236
24	Feb 6	H	Newcastle U	L 0-1	0-0	7		40,202
25	17	A	Aston Villa	W 2-1	2-0	—	Hasselbaink 2 [8, 32]	37,510
26	20	H	Everton	W 1-0	0-0	5	Korsten [55]	36,344
27	Mar 1	A	Leicester C	W 2-1	1-0	—	Kewell [24], Smith [60]	18,101
28	10	H	Tottenham H	W 2-0	1-0	—	Smith [42], Kewell [68]	34,561
29	13	A	Sheffield W	W 2-0	1-0	4	Hasselbaink [4], Hopkin [73]	28,142
30	20	H	Derby Co	W 4-1	3-1	4	Bowyer [18], Hasselbaink [32], Korsten [45], Harte [85]	38,992
31	Apr 3	H	Nottingham F	W 3-1	1-0	4	Hasselbaink [43], Harte [60], Smith [84]	39,645
32	12	H	Liverpool	D 0-0	0-0	—		39,372
33	17	A	Charlton Ath	D 1-1	1-1	4	Woodgate [24]	20,043
34	25	H	Manchester U	D 1-1	1-0	4	Hasselbaink [32]	40,255
35	May 1	A	West Ham U	W 5-1	2-0	4	Hasselbaink [1], Smith [45], Harte (pen) [62], Bowyer [78], Haaland [79]	25,997
36	5	A	Chelsea	L 0-1	0-0	—		34,762
37	11	H	Arsenal	W 1-0	0-0	—	Hasselbaink [86]	40,124
38	16	A	Coventry C	D 2-2	1-0	4	Wijnhard [43], Hopkin [90]	23,049

Final League Position: 4

GOALSCORERS

League (62): Hasselbaink 18, Bowyer 9, Smith 7, Kewell 6, Harte 4 (1 pen), Hopkin 4, Wijnhard 3, Halle 2, Korsten 2, Molenaar 2, Woodgate 2, Haaland 1, Ribeiro 1, own goal 1.
Worthington Cup (2): Kewell 2.
FA Cup (9): Harte 2, Smith 2, Hasselbaink 1, Kewell 1, Ribeiro 1, Wetherall 1, Wijnhard 1.

Martyn N 34	Hiden M 14	Harte I 34+1	Haaland A 24+5	Radebe L 29	Molenaar R 17	Hopkin D 32+2	Wijnhard C 11+7	Kewell H 36+2	Sharpe L 2+2	Bowyer L 35	Lilley D —+2	Hasselbaink J 36	Wetherall D 14+7	Ribeiro B 7+6	Halle G 14+3	Granville D 7+2	McPhail S 11+6	Woodgate J 25	Robinson P 4+1	Smith A 15+7	Batty D 10	Karsten W 4+3	Jones M 3+5	Match No.
1	2	3	4	5	6	7	8	9	10^1	11	12													1
1	2	3	4	5	6	7	8^1	10	12	11		9												2
1	2	3	4	5	6	7	8	10		11		9												3
1	2	3	4	5	6^1	7	8^2	10		11		9	12	13										4
1	2	3	4	5	6	7	8^1	10^2		11	12	9	13											5
1	2	3	12	5	6	7		10^1	13	11		9		8^2	4									6
1	2	3		5	6	7	8^1	10		11		9	12		4									7
1	2	3^3	10		6		8^1	12	7	11^2		9	5		4	14	13							8
1	2			5	6	7	12	10^1		11		9^2	13		14	3	8^3	4						9
	2		12	5	6	7^1	13	10		11		9^2				3	8	4	1					10
		3		5^1	6	7	12	10		11		9^1	13		2		8	4	1					11
1	2	3	12		6	7	13	10		11		9	5^2		4		8^1							12
1	5	3			6	7	8^1	10		11		9			2			4		12				13
1	5	3			6	7	8^1	10		11		9			2			4		12				14
1	5^1	3	6			7		10				9	12	11^2	2		8	4		15			13	15
		3	2	5	6	7	12	10^1		11		9	13					4	1	8^2				16
1		3		5^1	6	7		10		11		9	12	13		4	2			8^2				17
1		3	6	5^1		7		10		11		9	12		2		8^2	4		13				18
1		3	6			7		10^2		11		9	5	8^1	2		12	4		13				19
1		3	6			7		10		11		9	5	8^1	2		12	4						20
1			6			7		10		11		9	5	8^1	2	3	12	4^2		13				21
1	2	12	5			7		10		11		9	6			3	4^1			8^2		13		22
1		3	2	5		7		10		11		9	6					4		8				23
1		2	6	5		7	8^2			11		9	12			3^1	4			10		13		24
1		3	4	5		7		10		11		9	6		2		12			8			11^1	25
1		3	4	5		7		10^1		11^2		9	6		2			12		8		13		26
1		3	2	5		7		10		11		9^1	6	12						8	4			27
1		3	2	5				10		11		9	6					4		7	8			28
1		3	2	5^1		7		10^2		11		9	12					4		8	6	13		29
1		3	2	5		7		10		11		9				6	4			8^1	12			30
1		3		5		7		10^1		11		9	6			4	2			8			12	31
1		3		5		7		10^1		11		9	12		2^2			6		8	4	13		32
1		3	12	5		7^1		10		11		9	6				2			8	4	13		33
1		3		5				12	10		11		9^1	13		7	4^2		8	6			2	34
1		3	2	5				12	10		11		9^1	13		7	4		8^2	6				35
1		3	2	5				12		10		11	9				7^1	4		8	6			36
1		3	2	5						10		11	9					4		8	6			37
		12	2^2	5				13	8	14		9	6	10^3		3^1	7		1		4		11	38

Worthington Cup

Third Round	Bradford C	(h)	1-0
Fourth Round	Leicester C	(a)	1-2

FA Cup

Third Round	Rushden & D	(a)	0-0
		(h)	3-1
Fourth Round	Portsmouth	(a)	5-1
Fifth Round	Tottenham H	(h)	1-1
		(a)	0-2

FA Premiership

LEICESTER CITY

FOUNDATION

In 1884 a number of young footballers who were mostly old boys of Wyggeston School, held a meeting at a house on the Roman Fosse Way and formed Leicester Fosse FC. They collected 9d (less than 4p) towards the cost of a ball, plus the same amount for membership. Their first professional, Harry Webb from Stafford Rangers, was signed in 1888 for 2s 6d (12p) per week, plus travelling expenses.

City Stadium, Filbert St, Leicester LE2 7FL.
Telephone: (0116) 2915000.
Fax: (0116) 2470585.
Ticket Office: (0116) 2915232.
Clubcall: 0891 121185.
Ground Capacity: 22,000.
Record Attendance: 47,298 v Tottenham H, FA Cup 5th rd, 18 February 1928.
Record Receipts: £302,714 v Northampton T, FA Cup 3rd rd, 3 January 1998.
Pitch Measurements: 110yd × 76yd.
President: T. W. Shipman.
Chairman: J. M. Elsom FCA.
Group Chief Executive: Barrie Pierpoint.
Directors: G. K. Kinch, S. A. Kind, B. J. Pierpoint, P. H. Smith.
Manager: Martin O'Neill.
Assistant Manager: John Robertson.
First Team Coach: Steve Walford.
Youth Academy Director: David Nish.
Physios: Alan Smith and Mick Yeoman.
Finance Director and Company Secretary: Steve Kind FCCA.
Football Press Officer: Paul Mace.
Leicester City PLC Communications: Paul Barker.
Football Secretary: Andrew Neville.
Stadium Manager: John Petherick.

LATEST SEQUENCES

Longest Sequence of League Wins: 7, 28.2.93 – 27.3.93.
Longest Sequence of League Defeats: 7, 28.8.90 – 29.9.90.
Longest Sequence of League Draws: 6, 21.8.76 – 18.9.76.
Longest Sequence of Unbeaten League Matches: 19, 6.2.71 – 18.8.71.
Longest Sequence Without a League Win: 18, 12.4.75 – 1.11.75.

HONOURS

Football League: Division 1 – Runners-up 1928–29; Promoted from Division 1 1993–94 (play-offs) and 1995–96 (play-offs); Division 2 – Champions 1924–25, 1936–37, 1953–54, 1956–57, 1970–71, 1979–80; Runners-up 1907–08.

FA Cup: Runners-up 1949, 1961, 1963, 1969.

Football League Cup: Winners 1964, 1997; Runners-up 1965, 1999.

European Competitions: European Cup-Winners' Cup: 1961–62. UEFA Cup: 1997–98.

Colours
Royal blue shirts, white shorts, blue stockings.

Change Colours
White shirts, royal blue shorts, white stockings.

Year Formed: 1884.

Turned Professional: 1888.

Ltd Co: 1897.

Previous Name: 1884, Leicester Fosse; 1919, Leicester City.

Club Nickname: 'Foxes'.

Previous Grounds: 1884, Victoria Park; 1887, Belgrave Road; 1888, Victoria Park; 1891, Filbert Street.

First Football League Game: 1 September 1894, Division 2, v Grimsby T (a) L 3–4 – Thraves; Smith, Bailey; Seymour, Brown, Henrys; Hill, Hughes, McArthur (1), Skea (2), Priestman.

Record League Victory: 10–0 v Portsmouth, Division 1, 20 October 1928 – McLaren; Black, Brown; Findlay, Carr, Watson; Adcock, Hine (3), Chandler (6), Lochhead, Barry (1).

Record Cup Victory: 8–1 v Coventry C (a), League Cup 5th rd, 1 December 1964 – Banks; Sjoberg, Norman (2); Roberts, King, McDerment; Hodgson (2), Cross, Goodfellow, Gibson (1), Stringfellow (2), (1 og).

Record Defeat: 0–12 (as Leicester Fosse) v Nottingham F, Division 1, 21 April 1909.

Most League Points (2 for a win): 61, Division 2, 1956–57.

Most League Points (3 for a win): 77, Division 2, 1991–92.

Most League Goals: 109, Division 2, 1956–57.

Highest League Scorer in Season: Arthur Rowley, 44, Division 2, 1956–57.

Most League Goals in Total Aggregate: Arthur Chandler, 259, 1923–35.

Most League Goals in One Match: 6, John Duncan v Port Vale, Division 2, 25 December 1924; 6, Arthur Chandler v Portsmouth, Division 1, 20 October 1928.

Most Capped Player: John O'Neill, 39, Northern Ireland.

Most League Appearances: Adam Black, 528, 1920–35.

Youngest League Player: Dave Buchanan, 16 years 192 days v Oldham Ath, 1 January 1979.

Record Transfer Fee Received: £3,250,000 from Aston Villa for Mark Draper, July 1995.

Record Transfer Fee Paid: £2,050,000 to Chelsea for Frank Sinclair, August 1998.

Football League Record: 1894 Elected to Division 2; 1908–09 Division 1; 1909–25 Division 2; 1925–35 Division 1; 1935–37 Division 2; 1937–39 Division 1; 1946–54 Division 2; 1954–55 Division 1; 1955–57 Division 2; 1957–69 Division 1; 1969–71 Division 2; 1971–78 Division 1; 1978–80 Division 2; 1980–81 Division 1; 1981–83 Division 2; 1983–87 Division 1; 1987–92 Division 2; 1992–94 Division 1; 1994–95 FA Premier League; 1995–96 Division 1; 1996– FA Premier League.

MANAGERS

Frank Gardner 1884–92
Ernest Marson 1892–94
J. Lee 1894–95
Henry Jackson 1895–97
William Clark 1897–98
George Johnson 1898–1912
Jack Bartlett 1912–14
Louis Ford 1914–15
Harry Linney 1915–19
Peter Hodge 1919–26
Willie Orr 1926–32
Peter Hodge 1932–34
Arthur Lochhead 1934–36
Frank Womack 1936–39
Tom Bromilow 1939–45
Tom Mather 1945–46
John Duncan 1946–49
Norman Bullock 1949–55
David Halliday 1955–58
Matt Gillies 1958–68
Frank O'Farrell 1968–71
Jimmy Bloomfield 1971–77
Frank McLintock 1977–78
Jock Wallace 1978–82
Gordon Milne 1982–86
Bryan Hamilton 1986–87
David Pleat 1987–91
Gordon Lee 1991
Brian Little 1991–94
Mark McGhee 1994–95
Martin O'Neill December 1995–

TEN YEAR LEAGUE RECORD

		P	W	D	L	F	A	Pts	Pos
1988-89	Div 2	46	13	16	17	56	63	55	15
1989-90	Div 2	46	15	14	17	67	79	59	13
1990-91	Div 2	46	14	8	24	60	83	50	22
1991-92	Div 2	46	23	8	15	62	55	77	4
1992-93	Div 1	46	22	10	14	71	64	76	6
1993-94	Div 1	46	19	16	11	72	59	73	4
1994-95	PR Lge	42	6	11	25	45	80	29	21
1995-96	Div 1	46	19	14	13	66	60	71	5
1996-97	PR Lge	38	12	11	15	46	54	47	9
1997-98	PR Lge	38	13	14	11	51	41	53	10

DID YOU KNOW ?

Frank Gardner, 18, was elected secretary and treasurer at the inaugural Leicester Fosse meeting in 1884 and also figured at left-half in the club's initial fixture against Syston Fosse on 1 November.

LEICESTER CITY 1998–99 LEAGUE RECORD

Match No.	Date	Venue	Opponents		Result	H/T Score	Lg. Pos.	Goalscorers	Atten- dance
1	Aug 15	A	Manchester U	D	2-2	1-0	—	Heskey [7], Cottee [76]	55,052
2	22	H	Everton	W	2-0	2-0	2	Cottee [11], Izzet [38]	21,037
3	29	A	Blackburn R	L	0-1	0-1	9		22,544
4	Sept 9	H	Middlesbrough	L	0-1	0-1	—		20,635
5	12	H	Arsenal	D	1-1	1-0	15	Heskey [28]	21,628
6	19	A	Derby Co	L	0-2	0-1	17		26,738
7	27	H	Wimbledon	D	1-1	0-0	17	Elliott [86]	17,725
8	Oct 3	A	Leeds U	W	1-0	0-0	16	Cottee [76]	32,120
9	19	H	Tottenham H	W	2-1	1-1	—	Heskey [37], Izzet [85]	20,787
10	24	A	Aston Villa	D	1-1	1-0	12	Cottee [37]	39,241
11	31	H	Liverpool	W	1-0	0-0	7	Cottee [79]	21,837
12	Nov 7	A	Charlton Ath	D	0-0	0-0	8		20,021
13	14	A	West Ham U	L	2-3	1-1	9	Izzet [28], Lampard (og) [87]	25,642
14	21	H	Chelsea	L	2-4	1-2	12	Izzet [40], Guppy [60]	21,401
15	28	A	Coventry C	D	1-1	0-0	13	Heskey [89]	19,887
16	Dec 5	H	Southampton	W	2-0	0-0	12	Heskey [61], Walsh [63]	18,423
17	12	H	Nottingham F	W	3-1	1-1	9	Heskey [43], Elliott (pen) [55], Guppy [75]	20,891
18	19	A	Newcastle U	L	0-1	0-0	11		36,718
19	26	H	Sheffield W	W	1-0	1-0	10	Cottee [34]	33,513
20	28	H	Blackburn R	D	1-1	1-1	10	Walsh [44]	21,083
21	Jan 9	A	Everton	D	0-0	0-0	10		32,792
22	16	H	Manchester U	L	2-6	1-1	12	Zagorakis [35], Walsh [73]	22,091
23	30	A	Middlesbrough	D	0-0	0-0	12		34,631
24	Feb 6	H	Sheffield W	L	0-2	0-0	13		20,113
25	20	A	Arsenal	L	0-5	0-4	14		38,069
26	Mar 1	H	Leeds U	L	1-2	0-1	—	Cottee [76]	18,101
27	6	A	Wimbledon	W	1-0	1-0	14	Guppy [6]	11,801
28	13	H	Charlton Ath	D	1-1	0-0	14	Lennon [60]	20,220
29	Apr 3	A	Tottenham H	W	2-0	1-0	13	Elliott [43], Cottee [67]	35,415
30	6	H	Aston Villa	D	2-2	0-1	—	Savage [63], Cottee [71]	20,652
31	10	H	West Ham U	D	0-0	0-0	13		20,402
32	18	A	Chelsea	D	2-2	0-1	13	Duberry (og) [82], Guppy [88]	34,535
33	21	A	Liverpool	W	1-0	0-0	—	Marshall [90]	36,019
34	24	H	Coventry C	W	1-0	1-0	11	Marshall [45]	20,224
35	May 1	A	Southampton	L	1-2	1-1	11	Marshall [17]	15,228
36	5	H	Derby Co	L	1-2	1-1	—	Sinclair [28]	20,535
37	8	H	Newcastle U	W	2-0	2-0	10	Izzet [20], Cottee [41]	21,125
38	16	A	Nottingham F	L	0-1	0-0	10		25,353

Final League Position: 10

GOALSCORERS

League (40): Cottee 10, Heskey 6, Izzet 5, Guppy 4, Elliott 3 (1 pen), Marshall 3, Walsh 3, Lennon 1, Savage 1, Sinclair 1, Zagorakis 1, own goals 2.
Worthington Cup (14): Cottee 5, Heskey 3, Fenton 1, Izzet 1, Lennon 1, Parker 1 (pen), Taggart 1, Wilson 1.
FA Cup (4): Cottee 1, Guppy 1, Sinclair 1, Ullathorne 1.

Keller K 36	Savage R 29 + 5	Guppy S 38	Elliott M 37	Walsh S 17 + 5	Sinclair F 30 + 1	Lennon N 37	Izzet M 31	Cottee T 29 + 2	Zagorakis T 16 + 3	Heskey E 29 + 1	Arphexad P 2 + 2	Taggart G 9 + 6	Wilson S 1 + 8	Campbell S 1 + 11	Parker G 2 + 5	Kamark P 15 + 4	Ullathorne R 25	Fenton G 3 + 6	Oakes S 2 + 1	Impey A 17 + 1	Marshall I 6 + 4	Gunnlaugsson A 5 + 4	Miller C 1 + 3	Match No.
1^6	2	3	4^1	5	6	7	8	9^5	10	11		15	12	13										1
1	2	3	4	5	6	7	8	9	10	11	12	13	14											2
1	2	3	4^1	5	6	7^2	8	9	10^3	11	12	13	14											3
1	2^2	3	4		6	7	8	9^1	10^3	11		12	13	14		5								4
1	2	3	4		6	7	8	9	10^1	11		12				5								5
1	2^2	3	4		6	7	8	9^3		11		12	14	10^1	13	5								6
1	2	3	4		6	7	8	9^2		11		5	13			12	10^1							7
1	2	3	4			7	8	9	10^1	11		5				12		6						8
1	2	3	4		6	7	8	9		11				5^1	12	12^2	13	10						9
1	2	3	4		6	7	8	9	10^1	11				12		5								10
1	2^2	3	4	12	6	7	8	9	10^1	11				13		5								11
1	2	3	4	9	6	7	8		10^1	11				12		5								12
1	2	3	4	5	6	7	8^1					12	13	14		11^3	10	9^2						13
1	2^1	3	11	5	6	7	8		10					12		4	9^2	13						14
1	12	3	4	5	6	7	8	9^1	10	11						2								15
1	12	3	9	5^2	6	7	8		10^1	11				13		4	2							16
1	12	3	9	5^2		7	8		10^1	11^3				14		4	6	13	2					17
1	12	3	4	6^3		7	8^1	9^2		11				5		14	10	13	2					18
1	12	3	4	5	6	7	8^2	9		11				13		10	2^1							19
1	2^1	3	4	5	6	7	8	9	12^2	11						10	13							20
1		3	4	5	6	7	8	9		11						10	2							21
1		3		5		7	8	9	10					6	11^{12}	14	13	2^3	4	12				22
1		3	11	5^1			9		10						6	13	8^2		4	7	12	2		23
1		3	4	5^1	12	7	8	9	13	11				6^3		10	2^2	14						24
1	2	11	4	12	6	7	8		10^3					5^1	3	13				14	9^2			25
1	10	3	4			7	8	9		11^1					5	6			2^2	12	13			26
1^6	2	3	4	5		7	8	9						15		6	11	10						27
1	2	3	4	5		7	8							11^1		6	9	12						28
1	10	3	4		6	7	8^1	9		11						12	5		2					29
1	10	3	4		6	7		9		11						5			2		8^1	12		30
1	10	3	4		6	7		9		11						5			2^1	13	8^2	12		31
1	10	3	4		6	7		9		11						12	5^1		2	13	8^2			32
1	10	3	4		6	7		9						12		5			2	11	8^1			33
1	10	3	4		6	7^3		9^2		11				13		5	12		2		8^1	14		34
1	10	3	4	12	6	7		9^2		11						5^1			2		8	13		35
1	10^2	3	4	12	6	7	8							13		5			2		9^1			36
	2	3	4		6	7	8	9			1			12		5	10					11^1		37
	2	3	4	12	6^1	7	8	9	10		1			13		5						11^2		38

Worthington Cup

Second Round	Chesterfield	(h)	3-0
		(a)	3-1
Third Round	Charlton Ath	(a)	2-1
Fourth Round	Leeds U	(h)	2-1
Fifth Round	Blackburn R	(h)	1-0
Semi-Final	Sunderland	(a)	2-1
		(h)	1-1
Final	Tottenham H (at Wembley)		0-1

FA Cup

Third Round	Birmingham C	(h)	4-2
Fourth Round	Coventry C	(h)	0-3

Division 3

LEYTON ORIENT

FOUNDATION

There is some doubt about the foundation of Leyton Orient, and, indeed, some confusion with clubs like Leyton and Clapton over their early history. As regards the foundation, the most favoured version is that Leyton Orient was formed originally by members of Homerton Theological College who established Glyn Cricket Club in 1881 and then carried on through the following winter playing football. Eventually many employees of the Orient Shipping Line became involved and so the name Orient was chosen in 1888.

Leyton Stadium, Brisbane Road, Leyton, London E10 5NE.

Telephone: (0181) 926 1111.

Fax: (0181) 926 1110.

Clubcall: 0891 121150.

Ground Capacity: 13,842.

Record Attendance: 34,345 v West Ham U, FA Cup 4th rd, 25 January 1964.

Record Receipts: £87,867.92 v West Ham U, FA Cup 3rd rd, 10 January 1987.

Pitch Measurements: 110yd × 80yd.

Chairman: Barry Hearn.

Chief Executive: Steve Dawson.

Directors: Tony Wood OBE, John Goldsmith FRIBA, David Dodd, Steve Davis, Nick Levene.

Team Manager: Tommy Taylor.

First Team Coach: Paul Clark.

Physio: Tony Flynn.

Secretary: Frank Woolf.

Commercial Manager: Lyn Newman.

Stadium Manager: Janet Hasler.

LATEST SEQUENCES

Longest Sequence of League Wins: 10, 21.1.56 – 30.3.56.

Longest Sequence of League Defeats: 9, 1.4.95 – 6.5.95.

Longest Sequence of League Draws: 6, 30.11.74 – 28.12.74.

Longest Sequence of Unbeaten League Matches: 13, 30.10.54 – 19.2.55.

Longest Sequence Without a League Win: 23, 6.10.62 – 13.4.63.

HONOURS

Football League: Division 1 best season: 22nd, 1962–63; Division 2 – Runners-up 1961–62; Division 3 – Champions 1969–70; Division 3 (S) – Champions 1955–56; Runners-up 1954–55; Promoted from Division 4 1988–89 (play-offs).

FA Cup: Semi-final 1978.

Football League Cup: best season: 5th rd, 1963.

Colours
White shirts with red V, black shorts, red stockings.

Change Colours
Blue and yellow.

Year Formed: 1881.

Turned Professional: 1903.

Ltd Co.: 1906.

Previous Names: 1881, Glyn Cricket and Football Club; 1886, Eagle Football Club; 1888, Orient Football Club; 1898, Clapton Orient; 1946, Leyton Orient; 1966, Orient; 1987, Leyton Orient.

Club Nickname: 'The O's'.

Previous Grounds: 1884, Glyn Road; 1896, Whittles Athletic Ground; 1900, Millfields Road; 1930, Lea Bridge Road; 1937, Brisbane Road.

First Football League Game: 2 September 1905, Division 2, v Leicester Fosse (a) L 1–2 – Butler; Holmes, Codling; Lamberton, Boden, Boyle; Kingaby (1), Wootten, Leigh, Evenson, Bourne.

Record League Victory: 8–0 v Crystal Palace, Division 3 (S), 12 November 1955 – Welton; Lee, Earl; Blizzard, Aldous, McKnight; White (1), Facey (3), Burgess (2), Heckman, Hartburn (2). 8–0 v Rochdale, Division 4, 20 October 1987 – Wells; Howard, Dickenson (1), Smalley (1), Day, Hull, Hales (2), Castle (Sussex), Shinners (2), Godfrey (Harvey), Comfort (2). 8–0 v Colchester U, Division 4, 15 October 1988 – Wells; Howard, Dickenson, Hales (1p), Day (1), Sitton (1), Baker (1), Ward, Hull (3), Juryeff, Comfort (1). 8–0 v Doncaster R, Division 3, 28 December 1997 – Hyde; Channing, Naylor, Smith (1p), Hicks, Clark, Ling, Joseph R, Griffiths (3) (Harris), Richards (2) (Baker (1)), Inglethorpe (1) (Simpson).

Record Cup Victory: 9–2 v Chester, League Cup 3rd rd, 15 October 1962 – Robertson; Charlton, Taylor; Gibbs, Bishop, Lea; Deeley (1), Waites (3), Dunmore (2), Graham (3), Wedge.

Record Defeat: 0–8 v Aston Villa, FA Cup 4th rd, 30 January 1929.

Most League Points (2 for a win): 66, Division 3 (S), 1955–56.

Most League Points (3 for a win): 75, Division 4, 1988–89.

Most League Goals: 106, Division 3 (S), 1955–56.

Highest League Scorer in Season: Tom Johnston, 35, Division 2, 1957–58.

Most League Goals in Total Aggregate: Tom Johnston, 121, 1956–58, 1959–61.

Most League Goals in One Match: 4, Wally Leigh v Bradford C, Division 2, 13 April 1906; 4, Albert Pape v Oldham Ath, Division 2, 1 September 1924; 4, Peter Kitchen v Millwall, Division 3, 21 April 1984.

Most Capped Players: Tunji Banjo, 7 (7), Nigeria; John Chiedozie, 7 (9), Nigeria; Tony Grealish, 7 (45), Eire.

Most League Appearances: Peter Allen, 432, 1965–78.

Youngest League Player: Paul Went, 15 years 327 days v Preston NE, 4 September 1965.

Record Transfer Fee Received: £600,000 from Notts Co, for John Chiedozie, August 1981.

Record Transfer Fee Paid: £175,000 to Wigan Ath for Paul Beesley, October 1989.

Football League Record: 1905 Elected to Division 2; 1929–56 Division 3 (S); 1956–62 Division 2; 1962–63 Division 1; 1963–66 Division 2; 1966–70 Division 3; 1970–82 Division 2; 1982–85 Division 3; 1985–89 Division 4; 1989–92 Division 3; 1992–95 Division 2; 1995– Division 3.

MANAGERS

Sam Omerod 1905–06
Ike Ivenson 1906
Billy Holmes 1907–22
Peter Proudfoot 1922–29
Arthur Grimsdell 1929–30
Peter Proudfoot 1930–31
Jimmy Seed 1931–33
David Pratt 1933–34
Peter Proudfoot 1935–39
Tom Halsey 1939
Bill Wright 1939–45
Willie Hall 1945
Bill Wright 1945–46
Charlie Hewitt 1946–48
Neil McBain 1948–49
Alec Stock 1949–59
Les Gore 1959–61
Johnny Carey 1961–63
Benny Fenton 1963–64
Dave Sexton 1965
Dick Graham 1966–68
Jimmy Bloomfield 1968–71
George Petchey 1971–77
Jimmy Bloomfield 1977–81
Paul Went 1981
Ken Knighton 1981
Frank Clark 1982–91 *(Managing Director)*
Peter Eustace 1991–94
Chris Turner/John Sitton 1994–95
Pat Holland 1995–96
Tommy Taylor November 1996–

TEN YEAR LEAGUE RECORD

		P	W	D	L	F	A	Pts	Pos
1988-89	Div 4	46	21	12	13	86	50	75	6
1989-90	Div 3	46	16	10	20	52	56	58	14
1990-91	Div 3	46	18	10	18	55	58	64	13
1991-92	Div 3	46	18	11	17	62	52	65	10
1992-93	Div 2	46	21	9	16	69	53	72	7
1993-94	Div 2	46	14	14	18	57	71	56	18
1994-95	Div 2	46	6	8	32	30	75	26	24
1995-96	Div 3	46	12	11	23	44	63	47	21
1996-97	Div 3	46	15	12	19	50	58	57	16
1997-98	Div 3	46	19	12	15	62	47	66	11

DID YOU KNOW ?

Amara Simba, who was playing his first season for Leyton Orient in 1998–99, had been capped three times by France including a match against England at Wembley on 19 February 1992, when England won 2–0.

LEYTON ORIENT 1998–99 LEAGUE RECORD

Match No.	Date		Venue	Opponents	Result		H/T Score	Lg. Pos.	Goalscorers	Atten- dance
1	Aug	8	A	Chester C	W	2-0	1-0	—	Richards 44, Harris 69	2541
2		15	H	Rotherham U	L	1-4	0-2	11	Smith 64	4457
3		22	A	Swansea C	D	1-1	0-0	15	Morrison 70	4629
4		29	H	Scarborough	L	0-3	0-2	19		3845
5	Sept	1	A	Torquay U	D	1-1	1-0	—	Griffiths 40	2384
6		5	H	Carlisle U	W	2-1	0-1	13	Griffiths (pen) 64, Morrison 90	3730
7		8	H	Mansfield T	D	1-1	1-0	—	Clark 28	3186
8		12	A	Cambridge U	L	0-1	0-0	20		3684
9		19	H	Brighton & HA	W	1-0	0-0	15	Smith 69	5620
10		26	A	Rochdale	L	1-2	1-2	18	Smith 45	1742
11	Oct	3	A	Hartlepool U	D	1-1	0-0	17	Clark 52	3745
12		9	H	Exeter C	W	2-0	1-0	—	Inglethorpe 19, Simba 47	3349
13		17	A	Southend U	D	2-2	1-0	14	Inglethorpe 12, Lockwood 81	6700
14		20	A	Cardiff C	D	0-0	0-0	—		5001
15		24	H	Halifax T	W	1-0	1-0	10	Inglethorpe 8	3655
16		31	H	Scunthorpe U	W	1-0	0-0	10	Griffiths 88	3919
17	Nov	7	A	Hull C	W	1-0	0-0	8	Beall 63	5288
18		10	A	Shrewsbury T	D	1-1	0-1	—	Smith 49	2485
19		21	H	Brentford	W	2-1	0-1	5	Smith (pen) 49, Watts 77	6340
20		28	A	Plymouth Arg	W	4-2	1-1	2	Watts 40, Ling 72, Richards 80, Griffiths (pen) 85	4240
21	Dec	12	A	Peterborough U	L	1-2	1-1	6	Smith (pen) 18	4718
22		19	A	Barnet	L	2-3	0-1	7	Simba 58, Beall 68	3129
23		26	H	Swansea C	D	1-1	0-0	8	Smith (pen) 58	5343
24		28	A	Darlington	D	1-1	0-0	10	Ling 79	3424
25	Jan	9	H	Chester C	D	2-2	1-1	9	Simba 2 2, 65	4132
26		16	A	Rotherham U	L	1-3	1-0	11	Watts 26	3139
27		30	H	Darlington	W	3-2	2-1	10	Richards 15, Smith 28, Walschaerts 60	3972
28	Feb	6	A	Carlisle U	D	1-1	0-1	10	Watts 65	2794
29		13	A	Mansfield T	W	2-1	1-1	10	Ling 37, Richards 68	2817
30		20	A	Cambridge U	W	2-0	1-0	7	Griffiths 23, Ling 51	6222
31		27	A	Brighton & HA	W	2-1	0-0	5	Griffiths (pen) 64, Lockwood 71	4825
32	Mar	2	H	Torquay U	W	2-0	0-0	—	Lockwood 52, Watts 82	4099
33		6	H	Rochdale	W	3-0	1-0	3	Ampadu 44, Griffiths 2 62, 70	4927
34		13	H	Hull C	L	1-2	0-1	4	Richards 75	5481
35		20	A	Scunthorpe U	L	0-2	0-0	5		4163
36		26	A	Halifax T	W	2-1	2-0	—	Omoyimni 3, Clark 25	2978
37	Apr	3	A	Southend U	L	0-3	0-2	5		6537
38		5	H	Exeter C	D	1-1	0-1	6	Walschaerts 64	2764
39		10	H	Cardiff C	D	1-1	0-1	6	Eckhardt (og) 49	5238
40		13	H	Plymouth Arg	W	4-3	2-2	—	Watts 7, Morrison 9, Inglethorpe 46, Richards 73	4095
41		17	A	Brentford	D	0-0	0-0	6		8245
42		21	A	Scarborough	W	3-1	1-1	—	Richards 35, Simba 2 61, 70	1410
43		24	A	Shrewsbury T	W	6-1	4-0	5	Simba 2 8, 41, Smith 25, Gayle (og) 39, Walschaerts 47, Clark 52	4957
44		27	A	Hartlepool U	L	0-1	0-1	—		3152
45	May	1	A	Peterborough U	L	0-3	0-0	6		6189
46		8	H	Barnet	D	2-2	1-1	6	Simba 2 40, 68	5808

Final League Position: 6

GOALSCORERS

League (68): Simba 10, Smith 9 (3 pens), Griffiths 8 (3 pens), Richards 7, Watts 6, Clark 4, Inglethorpe 4, Ling 4, Lockwood 3, Morrison 3, Walschaerts 3, Beall 2, Ampadu 1, Harris 1, Omoyimni 1, own goals 2.
Worthington Cup (4): Inglethorpe 1, Reinelt 1, Richards 1, Warren 1.
FA Cup (8): Richards 3, Walschaerts 2, Griffiths 1, Simba 1, Smith 1 (pen).

MacKenzie C 26	Walschaerts W 44	Lockwood M 36+1	Smith D 37	Hicks S 29	Clark S 40	Ling M 44	Ampadu K 26+3	Richards T 28+1	Maskell C 8+7	Martin J 1	Harris J 1+1	Reinelt R 2+5	Warren M 10	Griffiths C 21+3	Baker J —+4	Inglethorpe A 15+8	Raynor P 1+4	Canham S 2+6	Morrison D 7+16	Joseph M 34	Joseph R 13+11	McCormick S 1+3	McDougald J 3+5	Simba A 19+5	Watts S 10+18	Beall B 21+2	Curran D —+1	Barrett S 20	Omoyinmi E 3+1	Stimson M 2	Finney S 2+3	Downer S —+1	Match No.
1	2	3	4	5	6	7	8	9^1	10	11^2	12	13																					1
1	2	3	4	5^1	6	7	8		10		9^2	11	12	13																			2
1	2	3		5^1	6	7	8		10				4	9^1	11	12	13	14															3
1	2		4	5^2	6	7	8		10^1			12	3	9^3	11	13		14															4
1	2			5	6	7	8		10			12	3	9^1		4	13	11^2															5
1	2	11		5	6	7	8		10^1			12	3	9						13	4^1												6
1	2	11		5^2	6	7	8		10^1				3	9					14	4	13^3	12											7
1	2^1	11		5^2	6^2	7	8					12	3	9						13	4	14	10										8
1	2		4	5		7	8					10^3	3	9			12		11^2	6^1	13	14											9
1	2		4			7	8					10^3		3	9	11^2	13	12		6	5^1	14											10
1	2	10	4		6	7^1	8	9^2	13					3	12	11			5														11
1	2	3	4		6	7		9^2						12	11			5		8		13		10^1									12
1	2^1	3	4		6	7	12	9							11			5		8		13		10^3	14								13
1	2	3	4	5	6	7		9						12	11			8		13				10^1									14
1	2	3	4	5	6	7	12	9^2							13	11^1		8						10^3	14								15
1	2^1	3	4	5	6	7	8	12						9							13		10^2		11								16
1	2	3	4	5	6	7	8^2	10^1	12					9						13					11								17
1	2^2	3^1	4	5	6	7	8	11						10						12			13	9									18
1	2	3	4	5	6	7		10^2	12					9					8				13		11								19
1	2^3	3	4^2	5^1	6	7	12	10	13					9					8				14		11								20
1	2^1	3	4^2	5	6	7						13		9			12		8				10^2	14	11								21
1	2	3	4	5	6	7		9						12					8				10^1		11								22
1	2	3	4		6	7		9^2						10^1		5			8				12	13	11								23
1	2	3^4	4		6	7	9							5^1		12			8				10^3	13	11	14							24
1		3	4		6	7	5	8											2				9	10^1	12	11							25
1	5^2	3	4		6	7								12					13	2			9	10^1	8	11							26
	2		4	5		7		9^1						8^2	3		13^3		6				12	10	14	11	1					27
	2		4	5^1	6	7	8	9						12	3^3				13				10	14	11^2		1					28
	2		4	5^2	6	7	8	9						11^3				14	3	13			12	10^1			1					29
	2		4	5	3	7	8	9						10^1					11	6			12				1					30
	2	12	4	5^2	3	7	8	9						10					11^1	6			13				1					31
	2	11^1	4	5^1	3	7	8	9						10					12	6			13				1					32
	2	3	4		7	8	9^2							10^1		12			13	6	5		11^3	14			1					33
	2	3			7	8^1	9							10		4^2			13	6	5		11^3	14	12		1					34
	2	3		5	6	7^2								10	9					8	12			14	13		1	11^1	4^3			35
	2	3		5	6		4	10	12									13	8^3	14				9^2	7		1	11^1				36
		3	4	5^2	6	7	8	11										2					10^1	12		1	13		9		37
	2	3	4		6	7	5^1	10						12	8				13							1	11		9^2		38
	2^3	3	4		6	7	11	10^1		12			14	5^2	8	13		9							1					39
	2^1	3	4		6	7		10						12			5		8				13	9^2	11	1					40
	2		5	6	7		10									12	4^1	8	3				9		11	1					41
	2	3	4	5	6	7		10^1											8				12	9^2	11	1				13	42
	2	3	4		6	7								12				13	8	5		10^3	9^1	11^2	1				14	43
	2	3	4		6	7								12					8	5		10^2	9	11^1	1				13	44
	2	3	4		6^1	7	9							12					8	5		13	10^2	11	1					45
	2	3	4			12		13											8	5		7^2	10	9^3	11	1	6^1		14	46

Worthington Cup

First Round	Bristol R	(h)	1-1
		(a)	2-1
Second Round	Nottingham F	(h)	1-5
		(a)	0-0

FA Cup

First Round	Brighton & HA	(h)	4-2
Second Round	Kingstonian	(a)	0-0
		(h)	2-1
Third Round	Southport	(a)	2-0
Fourth Round	Bristol R	(a)	0-3

Division 3 LINCOLN CITY

FOUNDATION

Although there was a Lincoln club as far back as 1861, the present organisation was formed in 1884 winning the Lincolnshire Senior Cup in only their fourth season. They were founder members of the Midland League in 1889 and that competition's first champions.

Sincil Bank, Lincoln LN5 8LD.

Telephone: (01522) 880011.

Fax: (01522) 880020.

Website: www.redimps.com.

Ground Capacity: 11,729.

Record Attendance: 23,196 v Derby Co, League Cup 4th rd, 15 November 1967.

Record Receipts: £44,184.46 v Everton, Coca-Cola Cup 2nd rd 1st leg, 21 September 1993.

Pitch Measurements: 110yd × 71yd.

President: J. Jennison.

Chairman: K. J. Reames.

Vice-Chairman: J. Hicks.

Directors: N. Woolsey, P. Jackson, S. Tindall.

Chief Executive: J. Lonsdale.

Hon. Consultant Surgeon: Mr Brian Smith.

Hon. Club Doctor: Chris Batty.

Company Secretary: J. Hicks.

Manager: K. J. Reames.

Assistant Manager: Phil Stant.

Physio: Keith Oakes.

Commercial Executive: K. France.

Secretary: L. Jubb.

Stadium Manager: Nigel Dennis.

LATEST SEQUENCES

Longest Sequence of League Wins: 10, 1.9.30 – 18.10.30.

Longest Sequence of League Defeats: 12, 21.9.1896 – 9.1.1897.

Longest Sequence of League Draws: 5, 21.2.81 – 7.3.81.

Longest Sequence of Unbeaten League Matches: 18, 11.3.80 – 13.9.80.

Longest Sequence Without a League Win: 19, 22.8.78 – 23.12.78.

HONOURS

Football League: Division 2 best season: 5th, 1901–02; Promotion from Division 3, 1997–98; Division 3 (N) – Champions 1931–32, 1947–48, 1951–52; Runners-up 1927–28, 1930–31, 1936–37; Division 4 – Champions 1975–76; Runners-up 1980–81.

FA Cup: best season: 1st rd of Second Series (5th rd equivalent), 1887, 2nd rd (5th rd equivalent), 1890, 1902.

Football League Cup: best season: 4th rd, 1968.

GM Vauxhall Conference: Champions 1987–88.

Colours

Red and white striped shirts, black shorts, black stockings.

Change Colours

All purple.

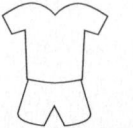

Year Formed: 1884.

Turned Professional: 1892.

Ltd Co.: 1895.

Club Nickname: 'The Red Imps'.

Previous Grounds: 1883, John O'Gaunt's; 1894, Sincil Bank.

First Football League Game: 3 September 1892, Division 2, v Sheffield U (a) L 2–4 – W. Gresham; Coulton, Neill; Shaw, Mettam, Moore; Smallman, Irving (1), Cameron (1), Kelly, J. Gresham.

Record League Victory: 11–1 v Crewe Alex, Division 3 (N), 29 September 1951 – Jones; Green (1p), Varney; Wright, Emery, Grummett (1); Troops (1), Garvey, Graver (6), Whittle (1), Johnson (1).

Record Cup Victory: 8–1 v Bromley, FA Cup 2nd rd, 10 December 1938 – McPhail; Hartshorne, Corbett; Bean, Leach, Whyte (1); Hancock, Wilson (1), Ponting (3), Deacon (1), Clare (2).

Record Defeat: 3–11 v Manchester C, Division 2, 23 March 1895.

Most League Points (2 for a win): 74, Division 4, 1975–76.

Most League Points (3 for a win): 77, Division 3, 1981–82.

Most League Goals: 121, Division 3 (N), 1951–52.

Highest League Scorer in Season: Allan Hall, 42, Division 3 (N), 1931–32.

Most League Goals in Total Aggregate: Andy Graver, 144, 1950–55 and 1958–61.

Most League Goals in One Match: 6, Frank Keetley v Halifax T, Division 3N, 16 January 1932; 6, Andy Graver v Crewe Alex, Division 3N, 29 September 1951.

Most Capped Player: David Pugh, 3 (7), Wales; George Moulson, 3, Republic of Ireland.

Most League Appearances: Tony Emery, 402, 1946–59.

Youngest League Player: Shane Nicholson, 16 years 172 days v Burnley, 22 November 1986.

Record Transfer Fee Received: £500,000 from Port Vale for Gareth Ainsworth, September 1997.

Record Transfer Fee Paid: £75,000 to Carlisle U for Dean Walling, September 1997; £75,000 to Bury for Tony Battersby, August 1998.

Football League Record: 1892 Founder member of Division 2. Remained in Division 2 until 1920 when they failed re-election but also missed seasons 1908–09 and 1911–12 when not re-elected. 1921–32 Division 3 (N); 1932–34 Division 2; 1934–48 Division 3 (N); 1948–49 Division 2; 1949–52 Division 3 (N); 1952–61 Division 2; 1961–62 Division 3; 1962–76 Division 4; 1976–79 Division 3; 1979–81 Division 4; 1981–86 Division 3; 1986–87 Division 4; 1987–88 GM Vauxhall Conference; 1988–92 Division 4; 1992–98 Division 3; 1998–99 Division 2; 1999– Division 3.

MANAGERS

David Calderhead 1900–07
John Henry Strawson 1907–14
(had been Secretary)
George Fraser 1919–21
David Calderhead Jnr. 1921–24
Horace Henshall 1924–27
Harry Parkes 1927–36
Joe McClelland 1936–46
Bill Anderson 1946–65
(General Manager to 1966)
Roy Chapman 1965–66
Ron Gray 1966–70
Bert Loxley 1970–71
David Herd 1971–72
Graham Taylor 1972–77
George Kerr 1977–78
Willie Bell 1977–78
Colin Murphy 1978–85
John Pickering 1985
George Kerr 1985–87
Peter Daniel 1987
Colin Murphy 1987–90
Allan Clarke 1990
Steve Thompson 1990–93
Keith Alexander 1993–94
Sam Ellis 1994–95
Steve Wicks *(Head Coach)* 1995
John Beck 1995–98
Shane Westley 1998
K. J. Reames November 1998–

TEN YEAR LEAGUE RECORD

		P	W	D	L	F	A	Pts	Pos
1988-89	Div 4	46	18	10	18	64	60	64	10
1989-90	Div 4	46	18	14	14	48	48	68	10
1990-91	Div 4	46	14	17	15	50	61	59	14
1991-92	Div 4	42	17	11	14	50	44	62	10
1992-93	Div 3	42	18	9	15	57	53	63	8
1993-94	Div 3	42	12	11	19	52	63	47	18
1994-95	Div 3	42	15	11	16	54	55	56	12
1995-96	Div 3	46	13	14	19	57	73	53	18
1996-97	Div 3	46	18	12	16	70	69	66	9
1997-98	Div 3	46	20	15	11	60	51	72	3

DID YOU KNOW ?

Wing-half George Whyte made 183 consecutive Football League appearances for Lincoln City from April 1934 to September 1938 from a total of 299 League matches for them between 1931 and 1939.

LINCOLN CITY 1998–99 LEAGUE RECORD

Match No.	Date	Venue	Opponents		Result	H/T Score	Lg. Pos.	Goalscorers	Attendance
1	Aug 8	A	Bournemouth	L	0-2	0-2	—		5573
2	15	H	Wigan Ath	W	1-0	0-0	16	Battersby [63]	3355
3	22	A	Macclesfield T	D	0-0	0-0	14		2794
4	29	H	Preston NE	L	3-4	1-1	16	Brown [24], Fortune-West [63], Battersby (pen) [71]	4130
5	31	A	Northampton T	D	0-0	0-0	15		5964
6	Sept 5	H	Oldham Ath	L	1-3	0-2	20	Smith [69]	3224
7	9	A	Millwall	L	0-2	0-0	—		4424
8	12	H	Blackpool	L	1-2	1-1	21	Whitney [13]	2949
9	19	A	Bristol R	L	0-3	0-0	22		6091
10	26	H	Fulham	L	1-2	0-0	23	Whitney [74]	4731
11	Oct 3	A	Wrexham	L	1-2	1-1	23	Hartfield [21]	3048
12	10	A	Notts Co	W	3-2	2-0	23	Thorpe 2 [28, 50], Alcide [32]	6458
13	17	H	Stoke C	L	1-2	1-0	23	Battersby [8]	6159
14	20	H	Manchester C	W	2-1	2-0	—	Battersby [4], Austin [33]	7338
15	31	H	Gillingham	L	1-2	1-0	23	Gordon [36]	4366
16	Nov 7	A	Chesterfield	L	0-3	0-1	24		4694
17	10	A	Walsall	L	1-2	1-0	—	Battersby [8]	3698
18	21	H	Luton T	D	2-2	1-1	24	Smith [40], McGowan (og) [61]	4893
19	28	A	Reading	L	1-2	1-0	24	Holmes (pen) [2]	8694
20	Dec 8	A	York C	L	1-2	1-1	—	Holmes [22]	2075
21	12	H	Colchester U	D	0-0	0-0	24		4513
22	19	A	Wycombe W	L	1-4	0-2	24	Gordon [60]	4731
23	26	H	Macclesfield T	W	1-0	0-0	24	Holmes [50]	3732
24	28	A	Burnley	D	1-1	0-0	24	Finnigan [72]	9635
25	Jan 9	H	Bournemouth	W	2-1	1-1	24	Bimson [19], Battersby [81]	3141
26	23	H	Northampton T	W	1-0	1-0	22	Holmes [35]	4608
27	30	H	Burnley	D	1-1	1-0	22	Gordon [32]	6361
28	Feb 6	A	Oldham Ath	L	0-2	0-0	22		5220
29	13	H	Millwall	W	2-0	1-0	20	Battersby [15], Holmes [69]	4613
30	20	A	Blackpool	W	1-0	0-0	20	Miller [81]	4215
31	23	A	Preston NE	L	0-5	0-2	—		9849
32	27	H	Bristol R	W	1-0	0-0	20	Holmes [71]	4235
33	Mar 6	A	Fulham	L	0-1	0-1	21		11,702
34	13	H	Chesterfield	W	2-0	1-0	20	Bimson [14], Gordon [56]	5262
35	20	A	Gillingham	L	0-4	0-1	20		7023
36	28	H	York C	L	1-2	1-0	21	Miller [4]	5504
37	Apr 3	A	Stoke C	L	0-2	0-1	22		12,845
38	5	H	Notts Co	L	0-1	0-0	23		5745
39	10	A	Manchester C	L	0-4	0-2	23		26,298
40	13	H	Reading	D	2-2	0-1	—	Barnett [53], Thorpe [78]	2518
41	17	A	Luton T	W	1-0	0-0	23	Thorpe [61]	5122
42	24	H	Walsall	L	0-1	0-0	23		4588
43	27	A	Wigan Ath	L	1-3	0-0	—	Thorpe [57]	3728
44	May 1	A	Colchester U	W	3-1	2-0	23	Gordon [43], Thorpe 2 [44, 75]	4613
45	4	H	Wrexham	W	1-0	0-0	—	Thorpe [88]	2926
46	8	H	Wycombe W	L	0-1	0-0	23		8145

Final League Position: 23

GOALSCORERS

League (42): Thorpe 8, Battersby 7 (1 pen), Holmes 6 (1 pen), Gordon 5, Bimson 2, Miller 2, Smith 2, Whitney 2, Alcide 1, Austin 1, Barnett 1, Brown 1, Finnigan 1, Fortune-West 1, Hartfield 1, own goal 1.
Worthington Cup (1): Battersby 1.
FA Cup (5): Alcide 1, Battersby 1, Finnigan 1, Holmes 1, Thorpe 1.

Vaughan J 31	Perry J 10 + 2	Whitney J 13	Brown G 21 + 1	Holmes S 37	Austin K 38 + 1	Smith P 22 + 6	Finnigan J 36 + 1	Fortune-West L 7 + 2	Alcide C 20 + 3	Fleming T 40 + 3	Battersby T 35 + 4	Miller P 26 + 6	Thorpe L 35 + 3	Philpott L 15 + 9	Richardson B 13	Hartfield C 3	Gordon G 21 + 6	Barnett J 29	Bimson S 30 + 1	Oatway C 3	Grobbelaar B 2	Brabin G 3 + 1	Watts J 2	Stant P — + 3	Peacock R 3 + 7	Gain P — + 4	Fenn N — + 4	Stones C — + 1	Phillips D 9	Wilder C 2 + 1	Walling D — + 3	Match No.
1	2	3	4	5^1	6	7	8	9	10	11	12																					1
1	2	3	5		6	7^1	8	9	11	4	10	12																				2
1	2	3	5		6	7^1	8	9	11	4	10		12																			3
1	2	3	5		6		8	9^1	11	4	10		7	12																		4
1	2	3	5		6		8	9	11	4	10^1		7	12																		5
1	2	3	5		6	12	8	9^1	11^2	4	10		7	13																		6
1	2^2	3^3	5		6	7^1	8	9	11	4	10	13	12	14																		7
		3^1	5		6	12	8	13	9	4	10	2^2	7	11	1																	8
		3	5		6		8	9		4	10		7	11^1	1	2	12															9
		3	5		6	12	8		9	4	10^1		7	13	1	11	2^2															10
		3	5		6		8		9	4	10		7	12	1	11	2^1															11
	12	3	5		6	7^2	8		10	4	11^1	9		13	1		2															12
		3^1	5		6	7	8		9	4	10			12	1		2			11												13
	12		5		6	7	8		9	4	11			10	1		2^1		3													14
	2			5	6	7				4	9			10	1	11			3			8										15
	2			5	6	7^1	8			4	9			10	1	12			3													16
	2^1		5		6	7	8		11		9^2	12	10		1	13	3	4														17
			5	2	6	7	8		12	4	9^2	13	10		1		11^1		3													18
			5	2^2	6	7^1	8		9	4	13	11	10	12	1				3													19
			5^1	2	6	7	8		11	4	9	12	10		1				3													20
			5	6	7	8	11^2		9^1	4	10	12								2	3	1	13									21
			8^1	6	7	12	13		4	9	14	10^2								2	3^3	1	11	5								22
1				5	6		8		4	9^1	11	10						2	3			7	12									23
1				5			8	12	4	9^2	11	10^1						2	3			7	6	13								24
1				5	6	7^1	8		4	12	11	10					9	2	3													25
1				5	6	7^2	8		4	9^1	11		12				10	2	3					13								26
1				5	6		8		4	9^1	11	7					10^2	2	3					12	13							27
1				5	6		8		4	9^2	11	7					10	2	3					12		13						28
1				5	6		8		4	9	11	7					10	2	3													29
1				5	6		8		4	9^1	11	10	7					2	3					12								30
1				5	6	7^2			4	9^1	11		8				10	2	3					12	13							31
1				5	6	7			4	9	11		8^1				10	2	3					12								32
1			4	5	6^1	12		9		11	10^2	8					2	3					7		13							33
1			6	5	7			4	11	11^1	10	8	9				2	3					12									34
1			6	5	7^2			4		11	10	8	9					3	2				2^1	12	13							35
1			6	5	12			4	13	11	10^2	8^1	9					3	7					2					7	2		36
1			6	5	12			4	9	11		8					10^1	2						13	3				7	2^2		37
1			6	5	12			4	9^2	11	10	8						2				13	3^1	14					7^3			38
1			6	5	12	7^2	8^3	4	9	13	10	11						2	3^1											14		39
1				5	6		8		4	9	11	7					10	2	3													40
1			12	5	6		8^2		4	9^1	11	7	13				10	2										3				41
1				5	6		8^2		4	9^2	11	12					10	2	3					13				7^1				42
1				5	6		8		4		9	7					10^1	2	3									11		12		43
1				5	6		8		12	9		7	11				10^1	2	3									4				44
1				5	6		8		12	9^2		7	11				10	2	3									4^1		13		45
1				5	6		8		12	9^2		7	11				10	2	3									4^1		13		46

Worthington Cup
First Round   Bradford C   (a) 1-1
  (h) 0-1

FA Cup
First Round   Cheltenham T   (a) 1-0
Second Round   Stevenage B   (h) 4-1
Third Round   Sunderland   (h) 0-1

FA Premiership

LIVERPOOL

FOUNDATION

But for a dispute between Everton FC and their landlord at Anfield in 1892, there may never have been a Liverpool club. This dispute persuaded the majority of Evertonians to quit Anfield for Goodison Park, leaving the landlord, Mr. John Houlding, to form a new club. He originally tried to retain the name 'Everton' but when this failed, he founded Liverpool Association FC on 15 March 1892.

Anfield Road, Liverpool L4 0TH.
Telephone: (0151) 263 2361. *Fax:* (0151) 260 8813.
Clubcall: 09068 121184.
Ticket and Match Information: (0151) 260 9999 (24-hour service) or (0151) 260 8680 (office hours).
Credit Card Bookings: (0151) 263 5727.
International Supporters Club: (0151) 261 1444.
Museum and Stadium Tours: (0151) 260 6677.
LFC Direct Mail Order: (0990) 532532.
Ground Capacity: 45,362.
Record Attendance: 61,905 v Wolverhampton W, FA Cup 4th rd, 2 February 1952.
Record Receipts: £496,000 v Newcastle U, Coca-Cola Cup 4th rd, 29 November 1995.
Pitch Measurements: 111yd × 74yd.
Chairman: D. R. Moores.
Executive Vice-Chairman: Peter B. Robinson.
Chief Executive: Rick Parry BSC, FCA.
Finance Director: David Chestnutt FCA.
Directors: J. T. Cross, N. White FSCA, T. D. Smith, T. W. Saunders, K. E. B. Clayton FCA.
Vice-President: H. E. Roberts.
Manager: Gerard Houllier.
Assistant Manager: Phil Thompson.
Physio: Mark Leather.
Secretary: Bryce Morrison.

LATEST SEQUENCES

Longest Sequence of League Wins: 12, 21.4.90 – 6.10.90.
Longest Sequence of League Defeats: 9, 29.4.1899 – 14.10.1899.
Longest Sequence of League Draws: 6, 19.2.75 – 19.3.75.
Longest Sequence of Unbeaten League Matches: 31, 4.5.87 – 16.3.88.
Longest Sequence Without a League Win: 14, 12.12.53 – 20.3.54.

HONOURS

Football League: Division 1 – Champions 1900–01, 1905–06, 1921–22, 1922–23, 1946–47, 1963–64, 1965–66, 1972–73, 1975–76, 1976–77, 1978–79, 1979–80, 1981–82, 1982–83, 1983–84, 1985–86, 1987–88, 1989–90 (Liverpool have a record number of 18 League Championship wins); Runners-up 1898–99, 1909–10, 1968–69, 1973–74, 1974–75, 1977–78, 1984–85, 1986–87, 1988–89, 1990–91; Division 2 – Champions 1893–94, 1895–96, 1904–05, 1961–62.

FA Cup: Winners 1965, 1974, 1986, 1989, 1992; Runners-up 1914, 1950, 1971, 1977, 1988, 1996;

Football League Cup: Winners 1981, 1982, 1983, 1984, 1995; Runners-up 1978, 1987.

League Super Cup: Winners 1986.

European Competitions: European Cup: 1964–65, 1966–67, 1973–74, 1976–77 (winners), 1977–78 (winners), 1978–79, 1979–80, 1980–81 (winners), 1981–82, 1982–83, 1983–84 (winners), 1984–85 (runners-up). *European Cup-Winners' Cup:* 1965–66 (runners-up), 1971–72, 1974–75, 1992–93, 1996–97 (s-f.). *European Fairs Cup:* 1967–68, 1968–69, 1969–70, 1970–71. *UEFA Cup:* 1972–73 (winners), 1975–76 (winners), 1991–92, 1995–96, 1997–98, 1998–99. *Super Cup:* 1977 (winners), 1978, 1984. *World Club Championship:* 1981 (runners-up).

Colours
All red.

Change Colours
Turf green shirts with white and navy trim, navy shorts, turf green stockings with white and navy trim

Year Formed: 1892.

Turned Professional: 1892.

Ltd Co.: 1892.

Club Nickname: 'Reds' or 'Pool'.

First Football League Game: 2 September 1893, Division 2, v Middlesbrough Ironopolis (a) W 2–0 – McOwen; Hannah, McLean; Henderson, McQue (1), McBride; Gordon, McVean (1), M. McQueen, Stott, H. McQueen.

Record League Victory: 10–1 v Rotherham T, Division 2, 18 February 1896 – Storer; Goldie, Wilkie; McCarthy, McQueen, Holmes; McVean (3), Ross (2), Allan (4), Becton (1), Bradshaw.

Record Cup Victory: 11–0 v Stromsgodset Drammen, ECWC 1st rd 1st leg, 17 September 1974 – Clemence; Smith (1), Lindsay (1p), Thompson (2), Cormack (1), Hughes (1), Boersma (2), Hall, Heighway (1), Kennedy (1), Callaghan (1).

MANAGERS
W. E. Barclay 1892–96
Tom Watson 1896–1915
David Ashworth 1920–23
Matt McQueen 1923–28
George Patterson 1928–36
(continued as Secretary)
George Kay 1936–51
Don Welsh 1951–56
Phil Taylor 1956–59
Bill Shankly 1959–74
Bob Paisley 1974–83
Joe Fagan 1983–85
Kenny Dalglish 1985–91
Graeme Souness 1991–94
Roy Evans January 1994–98
(then Joint Manager)
Gerard Houllier July 1998–

Record Defeat: 1–9 v Birmingham C, Division 2, 11 December 1954.

Most League Points (2 for a win): 68, Division 1, 1978–79.

Most League Points (3 for a win): 90, Division 1, 1987–88.

Most League Goals: 106, Division 2, 1895–96.

Highest League Scorer in Season: Roger Hunt, 41, Division 2, 1961–62.

Most League Goals in Total Aggregate: Roger Hunt, 245, 1959–69.

Most League Goals in One Match: 5, Andy McGuigan v Stoke C, Division 1, 4 January 1902; 5, John Evans v Bristol R, Division 2, 15 September 1954; 5, Ian Rush v Luton T, Division 1, 29 October 1983.

Most Capped Player: Ian Rush, 67 (73), Wales.

Most League Appearances: Ian Callaghan, 640, 1960–78.

Youngest League Player: Michael Owen, 17 years 144 days v Wimbledon, 6 May 1997.

Record Transfer Fee Received: £7,000,000 from Aston Villa for Stan Collymore, May 1997.

Record Transfer Fee Paid: £8,500,000 to Nottingham F for Stan Collymore, June 1995.

Football League Record: 1893 Elected to Division 2; 1894–95 Division 1; 1895–96 Division 2; 1896–1904 Division 1; 1904–05 Division 2; 1905–54 Division 1; 1954–62 Division 2; 1962–92 Division 1; 1992– FA Premier League.

TEN YEAR LEAGUE RECORD								
		P	W	D	L	F	A	Pts	Pos
1988-89	Div 1	38	22	10	6	65	28	76	2
1989-90	Div 1	38	23	10	5	78	37	79	1
1990-91	Div 1	38	23	7	8	77	40	76	2
1991-92	Div 1	42	16	16	10	47	40	64	6
1992-93	PR Lge	42	16	11	15	62	55	59	6
1993-94	PR Lge	42	17	9	16	59	55	60	8
1994-95	PR Lge	42	21	11	10	65	37	74	4
1995-96	PR Lge	38	20	11	7	70	34	71	3
1996-97	PR Lge	38	19	11	8	62	37	68	4
1997-98	PR Lge	38	18	11	9	68	42	65	3

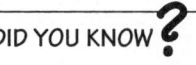

DID YOU KNOW

Willie 'Demon' Devlin made only 19 League appearances for Liverpool but scored 15 goals including four on two separate occasions before being transferred to Hearts in December 1927. He later returned to Cowdenbeath.

LIVERPOOL 1998–99 LEAGUE RECORD

Match No.	Date	Venue	Opponents	Result	H/T Score	Lg. Pos.	Goalscorers	Atten- dance
1	Aug 16	A	Southampton	W 2-1	1-1	—	Riedle [38], Owen [73]	15,202
2	22	H	Arsenal	D 0-0	0-0	6		44,429
3	30	A	Newcastle U	W 4-1	4-1	1	Owen 3 [17, 18, 32], Berger [45]	36,740
4	Sept 9	H	Coventry C	W 2-0	1-0	—	Berger [26], Redknapp [48]	41,771
5	12	A	West Ham U	L 1-2	0-1	2	Riedle [88]	26,010
6	19	H	Charlton Ath	D 3-3	1-1	3	Fowler 2 (1 pen) [33 (p), 82], Berger [67]	44,526
7	24	A	Manchester U	L 0-2	0-1	—		55,181
8	Oct 4	H	Chelsea	D 1-1	0-1	5	Redknapp [83]	44,404
9	17	A	Everton	D 0-0	0-0	7		40,185
10	24	H	Nottingham F	W 5-1	3-1	4	Owen 4 (1 pen) [10, 38, 71 (p), 77], McManaman [23]	44,595
11	31	A	Leicester C	L 0-1	0-0	5		21,837
12	Nov 7	A	Derby Co	L 1-2	0-2	11	Redknapp [84]	44,020
13	14	H	Leeds U	L 1-3	0-0	12	Fowler (pen) [68]	44,305
14	21	A	Aston Villa	W 4-2	2-0	9	Ince [2], Fowler 3 [7, 58, 66]	39,241
15	29	A	Blackburn R	W 2-0	2-0	8	Ince [30], Owen [33]	41,753
16	Dec 5	A	Tottenham H	L 1-2	0-1	9	Berger [55]	36,125
17	13	A	Wimbledon	L 0-1	0-0	12		26,080
18	19	H	Sheffield W	W 2-0	2-0	9	Berger [19], Owen [34]	40,003
19	26	A	Middlesbrough	W 3-1	2-1	9	Owen [17], Redknapp [35], Heggem [88]	34,626
20	28	H	Newcastle U	W 4-2	0-1	7	Owen 2 [67, 80], Riedle 2 [71, 84]	44,605
21	Jan 9	A	Arsenal	D 0-0	0-0	7		38,107
22	16	H	Southampton	W 7-1	3-0	6	Fowler 3 [22, 37, 47], Matteo [35], Carragher [55], Owen [63], Thompson [73]	44,011
23	30	A	Coventry C	L 1-2	0-0	6	McManaman [86]	23,057
24	Feb 6	H	Middlesbrough	W 3-1	3-0	5	Owen [9], Heggem [44], Ince [45]	44,384
25	13	A	Charlton Ath	L 0-1	0-0	5		20,043
26	20	H	West Ham U	D 2-2	2-1	6	Fowler [22], Owen [45]	44,511
27	27	A	Chelsea	L 1-2	0-2	7	Owen [77]	34,822
28	Mar 13	A	Derby Co	L 2-3	1-2	9	Fowler 2 (1 pen) [36 (p), 57]	32,913
29	Apr 3	A	Everton	W 3-2	2-1	8	Fowler 2 (1 pen) [15 (p), 21], Berger [82]	44,852
30	5	A	Nottingham F	D 2-2	1-0	8	Redknapp [15], Owen [72]	28,374
31	12	A	Leeds U	D 0-0	0-0	—		39,372
32	17	H	Aston Villa	L 0-1	0-1	9		44,306
33	21	H	Leicester C	L 0-1	0-0	—		36,019
34	24	A	Blackburn R	W 3-1	3-0	9	McManaman [23], Redknapp [31], Leonhardsen [32]	29,944
35	May 1	H	Tottenham H	W 3-2	0-2	8	Redknapp (pen) [49], Ince [77], McManaman [79]	44,007
36	5	H	Manchester U	D 2-2	0-1	—	Redknapp (pen) [69], Ince [89]	44,702
37	8	A	Sheffield W	L 0-1	0-0	8		27,383
38	16	H	Wimbledon	W 3-0	1-0	7	Berger [12], Riedle [50], Ince [65]	41,902

Final League Position: 7

GOALSCORERS

League (68): Owen 18 (1 pen), Fowler 14 (4 pens), Redknapp 8 (2 pens), Berger 7, Ince 6, Riedle 5, McManaman 4, Heggem 2, Carragher 1, Leonhardsen 1, Matteo 1, Thompson 1.
Worthington Cup (4): Fowler 1 (pen), Ince 1, Owen 1, own goal 1.
FA Cup (4): Owen 2 (1 pen), Fowler 1, Ince 1.

Friedel B 12	Heggem V 27+2	Staunton S 31	McAteer J 6+7	Carragher J 34	Babb P 24+1	McManaman S 25+3	Ince P 34	Riedle K 16+18	Owen M 30	Berger P 30+2	Harkness S 4+2	Redknapp J 33+1	Thompson D 4+10	Matteo D 16+4	Fowler R 23+2	Bjornebye S 20+3	James D 26	Leonhardsen O 7+2	Kvarme B 2+5	Murphy D —+1	Gerrard S 4+8	Song R 10+3	Ferri J —+2	Dundee S —+3	Match No.
1	2	3	4	5	6	7	8	9	10	11^1	12														1
1	2	3	4	5	6	7	8	9	10	11^1		12													2
1	2	3	12	5	6	7^1	8	9	10	11	4^1	13													3
1	2	3		5	6	7	8	9	10	11	4														4
1	2^2	3^3	13	5	6	7	8	12	10	9	11^1	4	14												5
1	2^3	3^1	12	5	6	7			10	8	4^1	11	14	13	9										6
1		2		5	6	7	8	9^1	10	11	4				12	3									7
	12	2^1		5	6^9		8	13	10	11	4		14		9	3	1	7^2							8
	2	6	12	5^3		7	8	13	10	11^2	4^1				9	3	1		14						9
	2	6	4	5		7^1	8	9	10	11					12	3	1								10
	2	6	4	5		7	8	9	10	11^1					12	3	1								11
	2^2	6	12	5		7	8		10	11^1	4	13			9	3	1								12
	2	6		5			8		10^1	11	4	7			9	3	1	12							13
	2	6	12	5	4		8	13	10^2	11^1		3^3	7		9				14						14
	2^2	6^1		5	4		8		10	11			7		9	3	1	12	13						15
	2	6		5	4		8		10	11		12			9	3^2	1			13	7^1				16
	2	6		5	4		8	12	10	11			7		9^1	3	1								17
	2^2	6		5	4		8	12	10^1	11			7		9	3	1	13							18
	2	6		5	4	12	8	13	10^1	11		14		7^3	9^2	3	1								19
	2	6	12	5	4^1	7^2	9	10	11	8			14			3	1				13^3				20
	2	6^1		5	4		8	12	10^1	11		3		7	9		1	13	9						21
	2		5^2	6			8^2	12	10	11		7	13		4	9	3	1	14						22
	2	6^3	12				8	13	10	11^2		7			4	9	3	1		14	5^1				23
	2	6		5		7	8	12	10^2	11					11	4	9^3	1			13				24
	2^2	6		5		7	8	10^1	11					11	4	9	3^2	1			13	14			25
	2	6	8	4	7^2		12	10	13	11					9	3^1	1					5			26
	2^1		6	12	8^9	13		10	11^2			7		5	9	3^1	1	4					14		27
	2	6^2		4			12	10^1	11		7		3	9	13		1		8	5			14		28
	2^2	6				7	8	12	10	11		4		3	9^1		1		13	5					29
		6		5		7^1	8	12	10	11		4		3	9^2		1		13	2					30
			5	6	7		8	12	10^1	11		4		3	9		1			2					31
			5	4	7		8	10		11		6	9	3^1	1		12			2^2		13			32
			5	4	7		8	9		11	10^1			1	6					2		12			33
1		6	5		7	8	9^2		11	10	3			4	12				2^1		13				34
1		6	5		7	8	9		11	10^1	3		12	4^3	2^2		13	14							35
1		6^2	5	4	7	8	9	12		11	13	3		10			2^1								36
1		6	5		7	8	9		11^1		4^3	12	3		10			2^2	13	14					37
1	12	6^2		5	13	7^3	8	9		11	4	14	3		10			2^1							38

Worthington Cup

Third Round	Fulham	(h)	3-1
Fourth Round	Tottenham H	(h)	1-3

FA Cup

Third Round	Port Vale	(a)	3-0
Fourth Round	Manchester U	(a)	1-2

Division 2

LUTON TOWN

FOUNDATION

Formed by an amalgamation of two leading local clubs, Wanderers and Excelsior a works team, at a meeting in Luton Town Hall in April 1885. The Wanderers had three months earlier changed their name to Luton Town Wanderers and did not take too kindly to the formation of another Town club but were talked around at this meeting. Wanderers had already appeared in the FA Cup and the new club entered in its inaugural season.

Kenilworth Road Stadium, 1 Maple Rd, Luton, Beds LU4 8AW.

Telephone: (01582) 411622.

Ticket Office: (01582) 416976.

Credit Hotline: (01582) 30748 (24 hrs).

Clubcall: 09068 121123.

Ground Capacity: 9975.

Record Attendance: 30,069 v Blackpool, FA Cup 6th rd replay, 4 March 1959.

Record Receipts: £115,541.20 v West Ham U, FA Cup 6th rd, 23 March 1994.

Pitch Measurements: 110yd × 72yd.

Chairman: D. A. Kohler BSC (HONS), ARICS.

Directors: C. S. Bassett, C. T. F. Green, N. S. Terry.

Secretary: Cherry Newbery.

Sales and Marketing Manager: John Bailey Jnr.

Stadium Manager: Geoff Lovell.

Manager: Lennie Lawrence.

Coach: John Moore.

Physio: Clive Goodyear.

LATEST SEQUENCES

Longest Sequence of League Wins: 9, 22.1.77 – 8.3.77.

Longest Sequence of League Defeats: 8, 11.11.1899 – 6.1.1900.

Longest Sequence of League Draws: 5, 28.8.71 – 18.9.71.

Longest Sequence of Unbeaten League Matches: 19, 8.4.69 – 7.10.69.

Longest Sequence Without a League Win: 16, 9.9.64 – 6.11.64.

HONOURS

Football League: Division 1 best season: 7th, 1986–87; Division 2 – Champions 1981–82; Runners-up 1954–55, 1973–74; Division 3 – Runners-up 1969–70; Division 4 – Champions 1967–68; Division 3 (S) – Champions 1936–37; Runners-up 1935–36.

FA Cup: Runners-up 1959.

Football League Cup: Winners 1988; Runners-up 1989.

Simod Cup: Runners-up 1988.

Colours

Orange shirts with blue side panels and blue and white knitted collar, blue shorts with orange and white stripe, blue stockings with orange stripes.

Change Colours

White shirts with black side panels and black and orange knitted collar, black shorts with orange and white stripe, black stockings with white stripes.

Year Formed: 1885.

Turned Professional: 1890.

Ltd Co.: 1897.

Club Nickname: 'The Hatters'.

Previous Grounds: 1885, Excelsior, Dallow Lane; 1897, Dunstable Road; 1905, Kenilworth Road.

First Football League Game: 4 September 1897, Division 2, v Leicester Fosse (a) D 1–1 – Williams; McCartney, McEwen; Davies, Stewart, Docherty; Gallacher, Coupar, Birch, McInnes, Ekins (1).

Record League Victory: 12–0 v Bristol R, Division 3 (S), 13 April 1936 – Dolman; Mackey, Smith; Finlayson, Nelson, Godfrey; Rich, Martin (1), Payne (10), Roberts (1), Stephenson.

Record Cup Victory: 9–0 v Clapton, FA Cup 1st rd (replay after abandoned game), 30 November 1927 – Abbott; Kingham, Graham; Black, Rennie, Fraser; Pointon, Yardley (4), Reid (2), Woods (1), Dennis (2).

Record Defeat: 0–9 v Small Heath, Division 2, 12 November 1898.

Most League Points (2 for a win): 66, Division 4, 1967–68.

Most League Points (3 for a win): 88, Division 2, 1981–82.

Most League Goals: 103, Division 3 (S), 1936–37.

Highest League Scorer in Season: Joe Payne, 55, Division 3 (S), 1936–37.

Most League Goals in Total Aggregate: Gordon Turner, 243, 1949–64.

Most League Goals in One Match: 10, Joe Payne v Bristol R, Division 3S, 13 April 1936.

Most Capped Player: Mal Donaghy, 58 (91), Northern Ireland.

Most League Appearances: Bob Morton, 494, 1948–64.

Youngest League Player: Mike O'Hara, 16 years 32 days v Stoke C, 1 October 1960.

Record Transfer Fee Received: £2,500,000 from Arsenal for John Hartson, January 1995.

Record Transfer Fee Paid: £850,000 to Odense for Lars Elstrup, August 1989.

Football League Record: 1897 Elected to Division 2; 1900 Failed re-election; 1920 Division 3; 1921–37 Division 3 (S); 1937–55 Division 2; 1955–60 Division 1; 1960–63 Division 2; 1963–65 Division 3; 1965–68 Division 4; 1968–70 Division 3; 1970–74 Division 1; 1974–75 Division 1; 1975–82 Division 2; 1982–96 Division 1; 1996– Division 2.

MANAGERS

Charlie Green 1901–28
(Secretary-Manager)
George Thomson 1925
John McCartney 1927–29
George Kay 1929–31
Harold Wightman 1931–35
Ted Liddell 1936–38
Neil McBain 1938–39
George Martin 1939–47
Dally Duncan 1947–58
Syd Owen 1959–60
Sam Bartram 1960–62
Bill Harvey 1962–64
George Martin 1965–66
Allan Brown 1966–68
Alec Stock 1968–72
Harry Haslam 1972–78
David Pleat 1978–86
John Moore 1986–87
Ray Harford 1987–89
Jim Ryan 1900–91
David Pleat 1991–95
Terry Westley 1995
Lennie Lawrence December 1995–

TEN YEAR LEAGUE RECORD

		P	W	D	L	F	A	Pts	Pos
1988-89	Div 1	38	10	11	17	42	52	41	16
1989-90	Div 1	38	10	13	15	43	57	43	17
1990-91	Div 1	38	10	7	21	42	61	37	18
1991-92	Div 1	42	10	12	20	38	71	42	20
1992-93	Div 1	46	10	21	15	48	62	51	20
1993-94	Div 1	46	14	11	21	56	60	53	20
1994-95	Div 1	46	15	13	18	61	64	58	16
1995-96	Div 1	46	11	12	23	40	64	45	24
1996-97	Div 2	46	21	15	10	71	45	78	3
1997-98	Div 2	46	14	15	17	60	64	57	17

DID YOU KNOW ?

Ten-goal Joe Payne's name did not appear on the programme for the historical match with Bristol Rovers on 13 April 1936. He was a late replacement for Scottish international Billy Boyd, the only change on either team.

LUTON TOWN 1998–99 LEAGUE RECORD

Match No.	Date	Venue	Opponents	Result		H/T Score	Lg. Pos.	Goalscorers	Attendance
1	Aug 8	A	Wycombe W	W	1-0	1-0	—	Davis S [35]	5252
2	15	H	Preston NE	D	1-1	0-1	7	Marshall [54]	5392
3	22	A	Reading	L	0-3	0-1	12		18,108
4	29	H	Colchester U	W	2-0	0-0	9	Douglas [62], Davis S [82]	5005
5	31	A	Wigan Ath	W	3-1	1-0	5	Davis S [42], Evers [78], Gray [80]	3778
6	Sept 5	H	Burnley	W	1-0	0-0	2	Douglas [47]	5554
7	8	A	Wrexham	D	1-1	1-1	—	McKinnon [35]	2951
8	12	H	Bristol R	W	2-0	2-0	3	Davis S [7], Alexander [9]	5558
9	19	A	Blackpool	L	0-1	0-0	5		5695
10	26	H	Walsall	L	0-1	0-0	7		5530
11	Oct 3	A	Fulham	W	3-1	1-0	4	Gray [5], Douglas [48], Davis S [65]	11,856
12	10	H	York C	D	3-3	2-2	4	Douglas [22], Evers [43], Gray [55]	3780
13	17	H	Oldham Ath	W	2-0	0-0	4	Gray [82], Scarlett [90]	5447
14	20	H	Northampton T	W	1-0	1-0	—	Alexander [20]	6087
15	24	A	Gillingham	L	0-1	0-0	4		5602
16	Nov 7	A	Stoke C	L	1-3	0-2	6	Douglas [81]	12,964
17	21	A	Lincoln C	D	2-2	1-1	6	Gray [43], Doherty [76]	4893
18	28	H	Manchester C	D	1-1	0-1	7	Doherty [76]	9070
19	Dec 12	A	Macclesfield T	D	2-2	1-1	8	Douglas [3], Gray [90]	2905
20	19	H	Millwall	L	1-2	0-1	11	Davis S [69]	5939
21	28	A	Bournemouth	L	0-1	0-0	14		8863
22	Jan 2	A	Colchester U	D	2-2	1-1	14	Alexander (pen) [7], White [72]	4694
23	9	H	Wycombe W	W	3-1	1-0	13	Spring [16], Evers [68], Douglas [75]	5063
24	16	A	Preston NE	L	1-2	1-0	12	Fotiadis [15]	11,034
25	23	H	Wigan Ath	L	0-4	0-2	13		4934
26	30	H	Bournemouth	D	2-2	1-0	14	McKinnon [6], Doherty [53]	5426
27	Feb 6	A	Burnley	W	2-1	1-1	12	Fotiadis [34], Doherty [87]	10,285
28	13	H	Wrexham	L	1-2	0-0	13	Doherty [47]	4759
29	20	A	Bristol R	L	0-1	0-1	13		6361
30	23	H	Notts Co	L	0-1	0-0	—		4021
31	27	H	Blackpool	W	1-0	0-0	12	Douglas [54]	4646
32	Mar 6	A	Walsall	L	0-1	0-0	13		4508
33	9	H	Fulham	L	0-4	0-1	—		7424
34	13	H	Stoke C	L	1-2	0-2	14	Alexander (pen) [47]	5221
35	20	A	Chesterfield	L	1-3	0-0	14	Gray [82]	3921
36	23	H	Reading	D	1-1	1-0	—	Spring [13]	5527
37	27	H	Gillingham	W	1-0	1-0	13	Dyche [42]	6705
38	Apr 2	A	Oldham Ath	D	1-1	1-0	—	Gray [5]	4948
39	6	H	York C	W	2-1	0-1	—	Spring [51], Douglas [90]	4667
40	10	A	Northampton T	L	0-1	0-1	12		6856
41	14	A	Manchester C	L	0-2	0-2	—		26,130
42	17	H	Lincoln C	L	0-1	0-0	14		5122
43	24	A	Notts Co	W	2-1	1-0	12	Thorpe 2 [32, 65]	5583
44	27	H	Chesterfield	W	1-0	0-0	—	Thorpe [63]	4287
45	May 1	H	Macclesfield T	L	1-2	0-2	12	Doherty [88]	5738
46	8	A	Millwall	W	1-0	1-0	12	Thorpe [13]	8494

Final League Position: 12

GOALSCORERS

League (51): Douglas 9, Gray 8, Davis S 6, Doherty 6, Alexander 4 (2 pens), Thorpe 4, Evers 3, Spring 3, Fotiadis 2, McKinnon 2, Dyche 1, Marshall 1, Scarlett 1, White 1.
Worthington Cup (13): Gray 3, Alexander 2 (2 pens), Davis S 2, Douglas 2, Evers 1, Fotiadis 1, Johnson 1, McLaren 1.
FA Cup (4): Davis S 2, Gray 2.

Davis K 44	Alexander G 28+1	Thomas M 26+6	Spring M 45	Davis S 20	Johnson M 42	McKinnon R 29+1	Evers S 27	Bacque H 2+5	Gray P 32+3	Marshall D 3+1	George L 6+6	McGowan G 27+4	White A 18+15	McLaren P 14+9	Douglas S 42	Fotiadis A 8+13	McIndoe M 17+5	Cox J 3+5	Scarlett A 2+4	Doherty G 5+15	Davies S 2	Showler P 2+1	Fraser S 5+3	Harrison G 14	Dyche S 14	Zahana-Oni L 4+4	Abbey N 2	Kandol T 2+2	Willmott C 13+1	Thorpe T 7+1	Boyce E 1	Match No.
1	2	3	4	5	6	7	8	9^1	10	11^2	12	13																				1
1	2		4	5	6	7^3	8	9^1	10	11	12	3^2	13	14																		2
1	2	12	4	5		13	8		10	11^2		3	6	7^3	9^1																	3
1	2	12	4	5	6	7	8	13	10^1	11^2		3		14	9^3																	4
1	2		4	5	6	7	8	12	10	11^2		3			9^1	13																5
1	2	12	4	5	6	7	8		10			3		11^1	9^2	13																6
1	2		4	5	6	7	8	12	10^1			3		11	9																	7
1	2	12	4	5		7^1	8		10			3	6	11	9^2	13																8
1	2	12	4	5	6		8	13	10^2		14	3			9^3	11^1	7															9
1	2		4^1	5	6	7	8		13		12	3		11^3	9^2	10	14															10
1	2	3	4	5	6	7	8		10	11^2					9^1	12	13															11
1	2	3	4	5	6	7^1	8		10				12		9^2	11	13															12
1	2	3	4	5	6	7^2	8		10			13		11^3	9^1		14															13
1	2	3	4^1	5	6	7	8		10			12		11	9^2	13																14
1	2	3	4	5	6	7^1	8		10	11^2	12				9	13																15
1	2	3^1	4^2	5	6	7	8		10	11			12		9	13																16
1		3	4^1		6	7	8		10			2	5	12	9					13		11^2										17
1	2		4	5	6	7	8		10			3^1	12	13	9^3					14		11^2										18
1	2	3	4^1	5	6		8		10			12	7	9^2		11^3				13		14										19
1			4	5	6				10^1			2	12	8	9	13		7				11^2	3									20
1		3	4	5	6			7	12		10		2		9		13			11^2		8^1										21
1	2	3	4		6			11	10			5	7	9^1				12				8										22
1			4		6		7		10			3	8	9^2			13	12		2	5	11^1										23
1			4		6		7				11^2	3	8	9^1	10			13		2	5	11^2										24
1			4		6		7					8	3	9	10^1	13		12		2	5	11^2										25
1			4		6	11	7					3	12	8	9^2			10		2^1	5	13										26
12			4		6	11^1	7					3^2	13	8	9^3	10			14	2^1	5		1									27
1	3		4		6	11^3	7		12			13	8		10^1	14			9	2^2	5											28
1	2			6	11						3	8	9	4^2		7^1	10			5	12		13									29
1	2		6^2	11			12				3	13	8	9^1			7^3	14	10		5											30
1	2	3	4^1			8			10		11^3	12	6	13	9				14				7^2			5					31
1	2	3	4		6	8			10		11^1	12	5	13	9								7^2								32
1	2	3^1	4		6	8			10		11^3	12	5	13	9			14					7								33
1	2	3	4		6	8			10		11^2		5^3	12	9			13					7^1		14							34
1	2	3	4		6	8^1			10		14	11		12	9^3			13					7^2			5						35
1	2	12	4		6				10			3		8	9^3	13		11^1					7^2		14	5						36
1		3	4		6				7		11	12	8	9				5						2	10^1							37
1		3	4		6				7		11	12	8^3	9^1	13	14		5						2	10^2							38
1		3	4		6				7		11			9	8	10		5	12					2								39
1		3	4								11	6		9	8	10		5	12				7^1	2								40
1		3	4								11			9		10		12		13	5	8^1	7^2	2							13	41
1		3	4		6									9		10	12		13	5	8^1		2	7	11^{12}							42
1		3	4		6	8						5		9^1	12	10	13			11			2	7^2								43
1		3	4		6	8						5		9^1	12	10				11			2	7								44
1		3	4		6	8^2						14		9^1	12	10	13		11^3				2	7								45
	3	4		6				8^2				14		9^3	12	10	13		11		1	2	7^1									46

Worthington Cup

First Round	Oxford U	(h)	2-3
		(a)	3-1
Second Round	Ipswich T	(a)	1-2
		(h)	4-2
Third Round	Coventry C	(h)	2-0
Fourth Round	Barnsley	(h)	1-0
Fifth Round	Sunderland	(a)	0-3

FA Cup

First Round	Boreham Wood	(a)	3-2
Second Round	Hull C	(h)	1-2

Division 3   **MACCLESFIELD TOWN**

FOUNDATION

From the mid-19th Century until 1874, Macclesfield Town FC played under rugby rules. In 1891 they moved to the Moss Rose and finished champions of the Manchester & District League in 1906 and 1908. By 1911, they had carried off the Cheshire Senior Cup five times. Macclesfield were founder members of the Cheshire County League in 1919.

The Moss Rose Ground, London Road, Macclesfield, Cheshire SK11 7SP.

Telephone: (01625) 264686.

Fax: (01625) 264692.

Website: www.mtfc.co.uk.

Email: office@mtfc.co.uk.

Commercial Office: (01625) 264693.

Social Club: (01625) 424324.

Press Box: (01625) 264690/1.

Club Call Line: 0930 555835.

Ground Capacity: 6028 (seated 1053, standing 4975).

Record Attendance: 9008 v Winsford U, Cheshire Senior Cup 2nd rd, 4 February 1948.

Pitch Measurements: 100m × 66m.

Chairman: Alan Cash.

Directors: Harry Armstrong, John Brooks, Alan Cash, Reg Flowers, Colin Garlick, Roy Higginbotham, John Chesworth, Jeremy Turner, Andy White, Eddie Furlong, Mike Rance.

Manager: Sammy McIlroy.

Secretary: Colin Garlick.

Administration Manager: Dianne Hehir.

Commercial Manager: Jackie Birks.

Club Doctor: Dr Mike Whiteside.

LATEST SEQUENCES

Longest Sequence of League Wins: 4, 13.4.98 – 2.5.98.

Longest Sequence of League Defeats: 6, 26.12.98 –6.2.99.

Longest Sequence of League Draws: 3, 27.9.97 – 11.10.97.

Longest Sequence of Unbeaten League Matches: 8, 17.1.98 – 21.2.98.

Longest Sequence Without a League Win: 10, 21.11.98 – 6.2.99.

HONOURS

Football League: Division 3 – Runners-up 1997–98.

Vauxhall Conference: Champions 1994–95, 1996–97.

FA Trophy: Winners 1969–70, 1995–96; Runners-up 1988–89.

Bob Lord Trophy: Winners 1993–94; Runners-up 1995–96, 1996–97.

Vauxhall Conference Championship Shield: Winners 1996, 1997, 1998.

Northern Premier League: Winners 1968–69, 1969–70, 1986–87; Runners-up 1984–85.

Northern Premier League Challenge Cup: Winners 1986–87; Runners-up 1969–70, 1970–71, 1982–83.

Northern Premier League Presidents Cup: Winners 1986–87; Runners-up 1984–85.

Cheshire Senior Cup: Winners 19 times; Runners-up 11.

Colours
Royal blue shirts, white shorts, blue stockings.

Change Colours
Old gold shirts, navy shorts, navy stockings.

Year formed: 1874.

Club Nickname: 'The Silkmen'.

Previous Ground: 1874, Rostron Field; 1891, Moss Rose.

First Football League Game: 9 August 1997, Division 3, v Torquay U (h) W 2–1 – Price; Tinson, Rose, Payne (Edey), Howarth, Sodje (1), Askey, Wood, Landon (1) (Power), Mason, Sorvel.

Record League Victory: 3–0 v Doncaster R, Division 3, 23 August 1997 – Price; Tinson, Rose, Payne, Howarth, Sodje, Askey (1) (Mitchell), Wood, Landon (1), Mason (Power), Sorvel, (1 og). 3–0 v Swansea C, Division 3, 13 September 1997 – Price; Tinson, Rose, Payne (Hitchen), Howarth, Sodje, Mitchell (Askey (1)), Gardiner (1), Peel (1), Power (Landon), Sorvel. 3–0 v Doncaster R (away), Division 3, 24 January 1998 – Price; Tinson, Howarth (Edey), Payne, McDonald, Sodje, Askey (Power), Wood (2), Chambers, Sorvel (1), Whittaker.

Record Win: 15–0 v Chester St Marys, Cheshire Senior Cup, 2nd rd, 16 February 1886.

Record Defeat: 1–13 v Tranmere R reserves, 3 May 1929.

Most League Points (3 for a win): 82, Division 3, 1997–98.

Most League Goals: 63, Division 3, 1997–98.

Highest League Scorer in Season: Steve Wood, 13, Division 3, 1997–98.

Most League Appearances: Ryan Price, 88, 1997–99.

Youngest League Player: Peter Griffiths, 18 years 44 days v Reading, 26 September 1998.

Record Transfer Fee Received: £40,000 from Sheffield U for Mike Lake, 1988.

Record Transfer Fee Paid: £30,000 to Stevenage Borough for Efetobore Sodje, August 1997.

Football League Record: Promoted to Division 3 1997; 1998–99 Division 2; 1999– Division 3.

MANAGERS

Since 1967
Keith Goalen 1967–68
Frank Beaumont 1968–72
Billy Haydock 1972–74
Eddie Brown 1974
John Collins 1974
Willie Stevenson 1974
John Collins 1975–76
Tony Coleman 1976
John Barnes 1976
Brian Taylor 1976
Dave Connor 1976–78
Derek Partridge 1978
Phil Staley 1978–80
Jimmy Williams 1980–81
Brian Booth 1981–85
Neil Griffiths 1985–86
Roy Campbell 1986
Peter Wragg 1986–93
Sammy McIlroy 1993–

TEN YEAR LEAGUE RECORD

		P	W	D	L	F	A	Pts	Pos
1988-89	Conf	40	17	10	13	63	57	61	7
1989-90	Conf	42	17	15	10	66	41	66	4
1990-91	Conf	42	17	12	13	63	52	63	7
1991-92	Conf	42	13	13	16	50	50	52	13
1992-93	Conf	42	12	13	17	40	50	49	18
1993-94	Conf	42	16	11	15	48	49	59	7
1994-95	Conf	42	24	8	10	70	40	80	1
1995-96	Conf	42	22	9	11	66	49	75	4
1996-97	Conf	42	27	9	6	80	30	90	1
1997-98	Div 3	46	23	13	10	63	44	82	2

DID YOU KNOW ?

When Macclesfield Town beat Stoke City 3–1 in a Worthington Cup first round first leg game on 11 August 1998, they had 25 goal attempts, 15 on target. Their first League goal came in the sixth game.

MACCLESFIELD TOWN 1998–99 LEAGUE RECORD

Match No.	Date	Venue	Opponents	Result	H/T Score	Lg. Pos.	Goalscorers	Attendance
1	Aug 8	H	Fulham	L 0-1	0-1	—		3933
2	15	A	Stoke C	L 0-2	0-2	24		13,981
3	22	H	Lincoln C	D 0-0	0-0	23		2794
4	29	A	Millwall	D 0-0	0-0	23		5997
5	31	H	Notts Co	L 0-1	0-0	23		3148
6	Sept 5	A	Wrexham	L 1-2	0-1	23	Wood [55]	3384
7	8	A	Oldham Ath	W 2-1	0-1	—	Barclay [55], Wood [66]	5401
8	12	H	Manchester C	L 0-1	0-0	22		6381
9	19	A	Wigan Ath	L 0-2	0-1	23		3839
10	26	H	Reading	W 2-1	1-0	21	Holt [25], Askey [77]	2920
11	Oct 3	A	Gillingham	D 2-2	1-0	21	McDonald 2 [23, 83]	6093
12	10	A	Bournemouth	D 2-2	1-1	22	Smith [19], Whittaker [70]	2974
13	17	A	Wycombe W	L 0-3	0-2	22		4012
14	20	A	Preston NE	D 2-2	2-0	—	Sodje [10], Smith [13]	10,316
15	24	H	Burnley	W 2-1	1-0	20	Sedgemore [18], Smith [84]	3995
16	31	H	Northampton T	L 0-1	0-1	21		3201
17	Nov 6	A	Colchester U	D 1-1	1-0	—	Griffiths [27]	3927
18	10	A	York C	W 2-0	2-0	—	Sedgemore [27], Sorvel [38]	2713
19	21	H	Walsall	D 1-1	0-1	20	Tomlinson [76]	3183
20	28	A	Chesterfield	L 0-2	0-1	20		4788
21	Dec 12	H	Luton T	D 2-2	1-1	21	Sorvel [36], Tomlinson [46]	2905
22	18	A	Bristol R	D 0-0	0-0	—		5039
23	26	A	Lincoln C	L 0-1	0-0	22		3732
24	28	H	Blackpool	L 0-1	0-0	23		3919
25	Jan 9	A	Fulham	L 0-1	0-0	23		10,153
26	26	H	Millwall	L 0-2	0-0	—		1998
27	30	A	Blackpool	L 1-2	1-0	24	Sodje [37]	4569
28	Feb 6	H	Wrexham	L 0-2	0-1	24		2578
29	13	H	Oldham Ath	W 1-0	0-0	24	Sodje [84]	4038
30	20	A	Manchester C	L 0-2	0-1	24		31,086
31	27	H	Wigan Ath	L 0-1	0-1	24		3706
32	Mar 6	A	Reading	L 0-1	0-0	24		8085
33	9	A	Gillingham	W 1-0	1-0	—	Landon [33]	1868
34	13	H	Colchester U	W 2-0	0-0	23	Landon [65], Bailey [90]	2796
35	20	A	Northampton T	W 2-0	0-0	23	Wood [62], Sorvel [84]	5790
36	28	A	Burnley	L 3-4	2-1	24	Durkan 2 [9, 63], Askey [14]	10,500
37	Apr 3	H	Wycombe W	L 1-3	1-2	24	Emblen (og) [11]	3183
38	6	A	Bournemouth	L 0-1	0-0	—		8033
39	10	H	Preston NE	W 3-2	0-1	24	Askey [50], Durkan [63], Wood [65]	4325
40	13	H	Chesterfield	W 2-0	1-0	—	Payne 2 [45, 70]	2216
41	17	A	Walsall	L 0-2	0-0	24		6256
42	24	H	York C	L 1-2	0-2	24	Tomlinson [77]	3077
43	27	H	Stoke C	L 1-2	1-1	04	Matias [44]	3825
44	May 1	A	Luton T	W 2-1	2-0	24	Sorvel [26], Davies [36]	5738
45	4	A	Notts Co	D 1-1	1-0	—	Matias [26]	3747
46	8	H	Bristol R	L 3-4	2-1	24	Askey [3], Tomlinson (pen) [20], Davies [48]	3186

Final League Position: 24

GOALSCORERS

League (43): Askey 4, Sorvel 4, Tomlinson 4 (1 pen), Wood 4, Durkan 3, Smith 3, Sodje 3, Davies 2, Landon 2, Matias 2, McDonald 2, Payne 2, Sedgemore 2, Bailey 1, Barclay 1, Griffiths 1, Holt 1, Whittaker 1, own goal 1.
Worthington Cup (3): Askey 2, Wood 1.
FA Cup (7): Tomlinson 4, Askey 1, Sedgemore 1, Sodje 1.

Price R 42	Tinson D 37	Ingram R 23 + 6	Payne S 32 + 6	McDonald M 23	Sodje E 42	Askey J 31 + 7	Wood S 29 + 13	Landon R 10 + 4	Sedgemore B 25 + 10	Whittaker S 18 + 9	Howarth N 11 + 8	Barclay D 3 + 6	Tomlinson G 15 + 13	Sorvel N 38 + 3	Durkan K 23 + 3	Brown S 1 + 1	Hitchen S 35	Griffiths P 4	Smith P 12	Holt M 3 + 1	Davies S 9 + 3	Matias P 21 + 1	Williams A 4	Bailey A 5 + 5	Soley S 5 + 5	Davenport P — + 1	Lomax M — + 1	Brown G 5	Match No.
1	2	3	4	5	6^1	7	8		9^2	10	11	12	13																1
1	2	3	4	5	6	7	8			11		12		9^1	10														2
1	2	3	4	5	6	7	8			11		12		9^1	10^2	13													3
1	2	3	4	5	6	7^1	8			12		13	9		11	10^2													4
1	2	3	4	5	6	7	8^1			11		13		9^2	12	10^3	14												5
1	2	3	4^2	5	6	7	8			12		13	14	9^3	10^1	11													6
1	2	3	4	5	6	7	8						9		10	11													7
1	2	3^1	4	5	6	7	8		13	14		12	9		10^2	11^3													8
1	2	3^3	4		6	12	8		7^2	11	5^1	9		13	14		10												9
1	2		5	6	12	8^2			11	13	4						3	7	9^1	10									10
1	2		5	6		8			11	12	4						3	7^1	9	10									11
1	2	12	5	6	7	8			11	13	4						3^1		9	10^2									12
1	2	12	5	6	7	8^2			10^3	11	4^1		13				3		9	14									13
1	2		4	5	6	12			10	11				8	7		3		9^1										14
1	2		4	5	6	12	13		10	11				8^1	7^2		3		9										15
1	2		5	6		12			10^1	11	4	13		8	7^2		3		9										16
1	2		4	5^3	6	12			10	11^1	13	14		8			3^2	7	9										17
1	2	14	4	5	6	12			10	11^3		13		8			3	7^1	9^2										18
1		3	4		6^1	7	5		10^2	11	12	13		8			2	9											19
1	6	3	4		7	5^1			10	11	12			8			2	9											20
1		3		5	6	7	10		12	11^1	4		9	8			2												21
1		3		5	6	12	13		14	4			9	10^2			2		8^1		7	11^3							22
1		3^1	12		6	13	5		14	11	4			9^3	8		2				7	10^2							23
1		3	12		6	7	5		11	4				9^2	8	13	2				10^1								24
		3	4	5	6	7^1	9		13	12			10	8			2					11^2	1						25
5		3^2	4		6	12			9	11			2				13		8		7^1	10	1						26
4		3	12	5	6^1	7	11		13	14				8^3			2				9		1	10^2					27
4		3	12	5^2	6	7	13			11^3			14	8^3			2				9		1	10^1					28
1		3^2	4	5	6	7	12		13	14			8				2		11		9^1	10							29
1		3	4		6	7	12		13	14			8^1				2		10		9	11^2							30
1		3	4		6	7	12		13	14			8^3				2		10^1		9	11^2							31
1	2		4		6				11	9	5^2		12	8	7		3				13	10^1							32
1	2^1	12	4		6		7^3		13	9	5		14	8	11^2		3		10										33
1	2		4		6		7^2		12	9	5			8	11		3		10^1					13					34
1	2	12	4		6	7	10^1		9^2		5			8	11		3							13					35
1	2^1	12	4		6	7	10^3		9^2		5			8	11		3					13		14					36
1	2		4		6	7	12				5^2			8	11		3		10^1					9	13				37
1	2		4		6		5		9^1	13				8^2	11		3		10					12	7				38
1	2	12	4		6	7	5		13					8	11		3^1		10						9				39
1	2	14	4^3		6	7^2	5		12					8	11		3		10					13	9				40
1	2	6				7^2	5^1	14	12				13	8	11		3		10						9^3			4	41
1	2	6^3				12	5^2	7	13				14	8	11^3		3		10						9^1			4	42
1	2				6	7	5^1		12				9	8	11^3		13		10					14				4^2	43
1	2		4		6	7^1	12	5					9^3	8	11		3^2				13	10		14					44
1	2		4		6		9	5^1					7^2	8	11				10					12	13			3	45
1			4		6	7	12	5					9^1	8	11^3							2	10		13		14	3^2	46

Worthington Cup

First Round	Stoke C	(h)	3-1
		(a)	0-1
Second Round	Birmingham C	(h)	0-3
		(a)	0-6

FA Cup

First Round	Slough T	(h)	2-2
		(a)	1-1
Second Round	Cambridge U	(h)	4-1
Third Round	Coventry C	(a)	0-7

Division 1 **MANCHESTER CITY**

Maine Road, Moss Side, Manchester M14 7WN.

Telephone: (0161) 232 3000.

Fax: (0161) 232 8999.

Ticket Office: (0161) 226 2224.

Dial-A-Seat: (0161) 227 9229.

Development Office: (0161) 226 3143.

Clubcall: 0891 121191.

Ticketcall: 0891 121591.

Ground Capacity: 31,458.

Record Attendance: 84,569 v Stoke C, FA Cup 6th rd, 3 March 1934 (British record for any game outside London or Glasgow).

Record Receipts: £512,235 Manchester U v Oldham Ath, FA Cup semi-final replay, 13 April 1994.

Pitch Measurements: 117yd × 78yd.

Chairman: D. A. Bernstein.

Directors: J. Wardle, D. Tueart, A. Lewis, A. Thomas.

General Secretary: J. B. Halford.

Commercial Manager: Geoff Durbin.

Manager: Joe Royle.

Head Coach: Willie Donachie.

Reserve Team Coach: Asa Hartford.

Physio: Roy Bailey.

Youth Team Coach: Alex Gibson.

Youth Academy Director: Jim Cassell.

HONOURS

Football League: Division 1 – Champions 1936–37, 1967–68; Runners-up 1903–04, 1920–21, 1976–77; Division 2 – Champions 1898–99, 1902–03, 1909–10, 1927–28, 1946–47, 1965–66; Runners-up 1895–96, 1950–51, 1987–88; Promoted from Division 2 (play-offs) 1998–99.

FA Cup: Winners 1904, 1934, 1956, 1969; Runners-up 1926, 1933, 1955, 1981.

Football League Cup: Winners 1970, 1976; Runners-up 1974.

European Competitions: *European Cup:* 1968–69. *European Cup-Winners' Cup:* 1969–70 (winners), 1970–71. *UEFA Cup:* 1972–73, 1976–77, 1977–78, 1978–79.

LATEST SEQUENCES

Longest Sequence of League Wins: 9, 8.4.12 – 28.9.12.

Longest Sequence of League Defeats: 8, 23.8.95 – 14.10.95.

Longest Sequence of League Draws: 6, 5.4.13 – 6.9.13.

Longest Sequence of Unbeaten League Matches: 22, 16.11.46 – 19.4.47.

Longest Sequence Without a League Win: 17, 26.12.79 – 7.4.80.

Colours
Lazer blue shirts, white shorts, navy stockings.

Change Colours
White shirts, navy shorts, white stockings.

Year Formed: 1887 as Ardwick FC; 1894 as Manchester City.

Turned Professional: 1887 as Ardwick FC.

Ltd Co.: 1894.

Previous Names: 1887, Ardwick FC (formed through the amalgamation of West Gorton and Gorton Athletic, the latter having been formed in 1880); 1894, Manchester City.

Club Nickname: 'Blues' or 'The Citizens'.

Previous Grounds: 1880, Clowes Street; 1881, Kirkmanshulme Cricket Ground; 1882, Queens Road; 1884, Pink Bank Lane; 1887, Hyde Road (1894–1923 as City); 1923, Maine Road.

First Football League Game: 3 September 1892, Division 2, v Bootle (h) W 7–0 – Douglas; McVickers, Robson; Middleton, Russell, Hopkins; Davies (3), Morris (2), Angus (1), Weir (1), Milarvie.

Record League Victory: 10–1 v Huddersfield T, Division 2, 7 November 1987 – Nixon; Gidman, Hinchcliffe, Clements, Lake, Redmond, White (3), Stewart (3), Adcock (3), McNab (1), Simpson.

Record Cup Victory: 10–1 v Swindon T, FA Cup 4th rd, 29 January 1930 – Barber; Felton, McCloy; Barrass, Cowan, Heinemann; Toseland, Marshall (5), Tait (3), Johnson (1), Brook (1).

Record Defeat: 1–9 v Everton, Division 1, 3 September 1906.

Most League Points (2 for a win): 62, Division 2, 1946–47.

Most League Points (3 for a win): 82, Division 2, 1988–89 and 82, Division 2, 1998–99.

Most League Goals: 108, Division 2, 1926–27.

Highest League Scorer in Season: Tommy Johnson, 38, Division 1, 1928–29.

Most League Goals in Total Aggregate: Tommy Johnson, 158, 1919–30.

Most League Goals in One Match: 5, Fred Williams v Darwen, Division 2, 18 February 1899; 5, Tom Browell v Burnley, Division 2, 24 October 1925; 5, Tom Johnson v Everton, Division 1, 15 September 1928; 5, George Smith v Newport Co, Division 2, 14 June 1947.

Most Capped Player: Colin Bell, 48, England.

Most League Appearances: Alan Oakes, 565, 1959–76.

Youngest League Player: Glyn Pardoe, 15 years 314 days v Birmingham C, 11 April 1961.

Record Transfer Fee Received: £4,925,000 from Ajax for Georgi Kinkladze, May 1998.

Record Transfer Fee Paid: £3,000,000 to Portsmouth for Lee Bradbury, July 1997.

Football League Record: 1892 Ardwick elected founder member of Division 2; 1894 Newly-formed Manchester C elected to Division 2; Division 1 1899–1902, 1903–09, 1910–26, 1928–38, 1947–50, 1951–63, 1966–83, 1985–87, 1989–92; Division 2 1902–03, 1909–10, 1926–28, 1938–47, 1950–51, 1963–66, 1983–85, 1987–89; 1992–96 FA Premier League; 1996–98 Division 1; 1998–99 Division 2; 1999– Division 1.

MANAGERS

Joshua Parlby 1893–95
  (Secretary-Manager)
Sam Omerod 1895–1902
Tom Maley 1902–06
Harry Newbould 1906–12
Ernest Magnall 1912–24
David Ashworth 1924–25
Peter Hodge 1926–32
Wilf Wild 1932–46
  (continued as Secretary to 1950)
Sam Cowan 1946–47
John 'Jock' Thomson 1947–50
Leslie McDowall 1950–63
George Poyser 1963–65
Joe Mercer 1965–71
  (continued as General Manager to 1972)
Malcolm Allison 1972–73
Johnny Hart 1973
Ron Saunders 1973–74
Tony Book 1974–79
Malcolm Allison 1979–80
John Bond 1980–83
John Benson 1983
Billy McNeill 1983–86
Jimmy Frizzell 1986–87
  (continued as General Manager)
Mel Machin 1987–89
Howard Kendall 1990
Peter Reid 1990–93
Brian Horton 1993–95
Alan Ball 1995–96
Steve Coppell 1996
Frank Clark 1996–98
Joe Royle February 1998–

TEN YEAR LEAGUE RECORD

		P	W	D	L	F	A	Pts	Pos
1988-89	Div 2	46	23	13	10	77	53	82	2
1989-90	Div 1	38	12	12	14	43	52	48	14
1990-91	Div 1	38	17	11	10	64	53	62	5
1991-92	Div 1	42	20	10	12	61	48	70	5
1992-93	PR Lge	42	15	12	15	56	51	57	9
1993-94	PR Lge	42	9	18	15	38	49	45	16
1994-95	PR Lge	42	12	13	17	53	64	49	17
1995-96	PR Lge	38	9	11	18	33	58	38	18
1996-97	Div 1	46	17	10	19	59	60	61	14
1997-98	Div 1	46	12	12	22	56	57	48	22

DID YOU KNOW ?

Alan Oakes had a testimonial match against Manchester United in 1972. To mark his 500th appearance, he was presented with a silver salver before the game against Stoke City on 9 November 1974.

MANCHESTER CITY 1998–99 LEAGUE RECORD

Match No.	Date	Venue	Opponents	Result	H/T Score	Lg. Pos.	Goalscorers	Atten-dance
1	Aug 8	H	Blackpool	W 3-0	1-0	—	Goater [26], Bradbury [62], Tskhadadze [79]	32,134
2	14	A	Fulham	L 0-3	0-3	—		14,284
3	22	H	Wrexham	D 0-0	0-0	11		27,677
4	29	A	Notts Co	D 1-1	0-0	14	Goater [90]	10,316
5	Sept 2	H	Walsall	W 3-1	1-0	—	Goater 2 [30, 71], Dickov [74]	24,291
6	8	H	Bournemouth	W 2-1	1-0	—	Allsop [25], Dickov [64]	26,696
7	12	A	Macclesfield T	W 1-0	0-0	6	Goater [86]	6381
8	19	H	Chesterfield	D 1-1	1-1	7	Bradbury [36]	27,500
9	26	A	Northampton T	D 2-2	0-1	8	Dickov [54], Goater [88]	7557
10	29	A	Millwall	D 1-1	0-0	—	Bradbury [90]	12,726
11	Oct 3	H	Burnley	D 2-2	1-1	8	Goater [8], Allsop [85]	30,722
12	12	H	Preston NE	L 0-1	0-0	—		28,779
13	17	A	Wigan Ath	W 1-0	0-0	7	Goater [56]	6700
14	20	A	Lincoln C	L 1-2	0-2	—	Holmes (og) [83]	7338
15	24	H	Reading	L 0-1	0-0	11		24,365
16	31	H	Colchester U	W 2-1	0-0	6	Horlock (pen) [49], Morrison [53]	24,820
17	Nov 7	A	Oldham Ath	W 3-0	2-0	5	Horlock 2 [17, 31], Morrison [69]	12,976
18	10	A	Wycombe W	L 0-1	0-1	—		8129
19	21	H	Gillingham	D 0-0	0-0	7		26,529
20	28	A	Luton T	D 1-1	1-0	8	Morrison [29]	9070
21	Dec 12	H	Bristol R	D 0-0	0-0	9		24,976
22	19	A	York C	L 1-2	1-1	12	Russell [33]	7527
23	26	A	Wrexham	W 1-0	0-0	7	Wiekens [56]	9048
24	28	H	Stoke C	W 2-1	0-1	7	Dickov [47], Taylor [85]	30,478
25	Jan 9	A	Blackpool	D 0-0	0-0	9		9752
26	16	H	Fulham	W 3-0	2-0	8	Goater [24], Taylor [32], Horlock [54]	30,251
27	23	A	Walsall	D 1-1	0-0	8	Pollock [74]	9517
28	29	H	Stoke C	W 1-0	1-0	—	Wiekens [20]	13,679
29	Feb 6	H	Millwall	W 3-0	0-0	7	Dickov [61], Cooke [71], Horlock [75]	29,862
30	13	A	Bournemouth	D 0-0	0-0	7		10,964
31	20	H	Macclesfield T	W 2-0	1-0	5	Goater [14], Taylor [67]	31,086
32	27	A	Chesterfield	D 1-1	0-1	6	Crooks [51]	8245
33	Mar 6	H	Northampton T	D 0-0	0-0	6		27,999
34	9	A	Burnley	W 6-0	2-0	—	Horlock [17], Morrison [41], Goater 3 [50, 59, 65], Allsop [82]	17,251
35	13	H	Oldham Ath	L 1-2	0-1	6	Taylor [79]	30,321
36	16	H	Notts Co	W 2-1	2-0	—	Brown [16], Cooke [40]	26,502
37	20	A	Colchester U	W 1-0	0-0	6	Goater [55]	6554
38	27	A	Reading	W 3-1	1-0	5	Cooke 2 [31, 62], Goater [54]	20,055
39	Apr 3	H	Wigan Ath	W 1-0	0-0	4	Cooke [52]	31,058
40	5	A	Preston NE	D 1-1	1-1	4	Brown [22]	20,857
41	10	H	Lincoln C	W 4-0	2-0	4	Dickov 3 [34, 45, 48], Horlock [63]	26,298
42	14	H	Luton T	W 2-0	2-0	—	Dickov [4], Vaughan [10]	26,130
43	17	A	Gillingham	W 2-0	1-0	3	Cooke [31], Horlock [64]	10,400
44	24	H	Wycombe W	L 1-2	1-2	4	Goater [45]	29,337
45	May 1	A	Bristol R	D 2-2	2-0	4	Goater [27], Cooke [42]	8033
46	8	H	York C	W 4-0	1-0	3	Dickov [23], Horlock [76], Jeff Whitley [84], Allsop [88]	32,471

Final League Position: 3

GOALSCORERS

League (69): Goater 17, Dickov 10, Horlock 9 (1 pen), Cooke 7, Allsopp 4, Morrison 4, Taylor 4, Bradbury 3, Brown 2, Wiekens 2, Crooks 1, Pollock 1, Russell 1, Tskhadadze 1, Vaughan 1, own goal 1.
Worthington Cup (10): Dickov 2, Goater 2, Allsop 1, Bradbury 1, Mason 1, Tiatto 1, Tskhadadze 1, Jim Whitley 1.
FA Cup (5): Russell 2, Brown 1, Dickov 1, Goater 1.

Weaver N 45	Edghill R 38	Tskhadadze K 2	Wiekens G 42	Vaughan T 35+3	Mason G 18+1	Pollock J 24+2	Horlock K 36+1	Dickov P 22+13	Goater S 41+2	Bradbury L 11+2	Allsop D 3+21	Whitley Jim 10+8	Whitley Jeff 1+7	Fenton N 15	Tiatto D 8+9	Brown M 26+5	Wright T 1	Crooks L 32+2	Greenacre C 1	Shelia M 3	Russell C 5+2	Morrison A 21+1	Bishop I 21+4	Branch M 4	Taylor G 20+6	Cooke T 21	Robins M —+2	Match No.
1	2	3	4	5	6	7	8	9[1]	10	11[4]	12	13																1
1	2	4[2]	5	6	7[1]	8	3	10	9			13	11	12														2
1	3		5	6	7	8	10		9	11[1]	12	2		4														3
1	3		5	6	7	8	11	10	9		12	2[1]		4														4
1	2		5	6	7	8		10[2]	9	11[1]	12			4	3	13												5
1	2		5	6	7	8	3	10[2]	9		12	11[2]		4	13													6
1	2		5	6	7[1]	8		10[2]	9	11	13	12		4	3													7
	2		5	6	7	8		10[1]	9	11	12			4[2]	3		1	13										8
1	2		5	6		8	3	12[2]	9	11	10[1]		7	4[3]	14			13										9
1	2		5	6		8	3		9	11	12		7[2]	4	13					10[1]								10
1	2		5	6	8			10	9	11	12		7	4	3[1]													11
1	2		5	6			3[2]	10[5]	9	11	12		7	4	13	8												12
1			5		7[1]			10	9	11		8	12	4	3			2	6									13
1			5					10	12	9	11	13	8[4]	7[1]	4	3		2	6									14
1			5		7			10	11[3]	9		12	2[2]	13	4	3		8	6[1]	14								15
1	2		5	3	8			11	12	9		7[2]				6						4	13		10[1]			16
1	2		5	3	8			11	9							12		6				4	7[1]		10			17
1	2		5	3	8[1]			11	13	9		12				14		6				4	7[3]		10[2]			18
1			5	3	6	7[2]		12	9							13		2			11	4	8		10[4]			19
1	2		5	3	7			9				12	13			6					11	4[1]	8[2]		10			20
1	2		5		6[1]	8			7[2]	9[2]		13	12			3					11	4			10			21
1	3		5		8[1]	2			13	12		14				7		6				11[2]			10	9		22
1	3		4	5	8	6		12	13			14				7		2				11[1]	10[3]		9[2]			23
1	3		4	5	8	6		11	12							7		2					10[1]		9			24
1			4	3	8	6		11[1]	10							7		2			12	5			9			25
1	3		4	5	8	6[1]			10			12				7		2							9	11		26
1	3		4	5	8	6			10			12				7		2							9	11[1]		27
1	3		4	5	8[2]	6		12	10			13				7		2[3]					14		9	11[1]		28
1	3[2]		4	5	8	6		12	10[1]							7		2				13			9	11		29
1	3		4	12	8	6		13	10[1]							7		2				5			9	11[2]		30
1	3		4		8[2]	6		12	10							7		2				5	13		9[1]	11		31
1	3		4		8[3]			12	10			13		5	14	7		2				6			9[2]	11[1]		32
1	3		4		6			12	10[1]							7		2				5	8		9	11		33
1	3		4[1]		12	6			10[2]							7		2				5	8		9	11		34
1	2		4	3[3]	12	6		13	10[2]			14				7						5	8[1]		9	11		35
1	3		4		12	6		10				13				7		2				5	8		9[2]	11[1]		36
1	3		4	6				10				12				7		2				5	8		9	11[1]		37
1			4	3	6			9[1]	10[2]			12				7		2				5	8		13	11		38
1	3		4	5		6	12	9[2]	10			13				7		2					8			11[1]		39
1	3		4		6[1]		8		10							7		2				5	12		9[2]	11	13	40
1			4			6		9[2]	10[2]			12		3		7		2				5	8[1]		13	11	14	41
1	3[1]		4	12		6		9	10[2]							7		2				5	8		13	11		42
1			4	3		6		9[2]	10			12				7[1]		2				5	8		13	11		43
1	2		4	3[1]		6		9	10		12[2]					7						5	8		13	11		44
1	3		4[1]	12		6		9	10[2]							7		2				5	8		13	11		45
1	2		4	5		6		9[3]			12	13	14		7	3							8[2]		10[1]	11		46

Worthington Cup

First Round	Notts Co	(a)	2-0
		(h)	7-1
Second Round	Derby Co	(a)	1-1
		(h)	0-1

FA Cup

First Round	Halifax T	(h)	3-0
Second Round	Darlington	(a)	1-1
		(h)	1-0
Third Round	Wimbledon	(a)	0-1

FA Premiership   **MANCHESTER UNITED**

FOUNDATION

Manchester United was formed as comparatively recently as 1902 after their predecessors, Newton Heath, went bankrupt. However, it is usual to give the date of the club's foundation as 1878 when the dining room committee of the carriage and waggon works of the Lancashire and Yorkshire Railway Company formed Newton Heath L and YR Cricket and Football Club. They won the Manchester Cup in 1886 and as Newton Heath FC were admitted to the Second Division in 1892.

Sir Matt Busby Way, Old Trafford, Manchester M16 0RA.

Telephone: (0161) 872 1661, (0161) 930 1968.

Fax: (0161) 876 5502.

Ticket and Match Information: (0161) 872 0199.

Membership Enquiries and Supporters Club: (0161) 872 5208.

Clubcall: 0891 121161.

Ground Capacity: 56,387.

Record Attendance: 76,962 Wolverhampton W v Grimsby T, FA Cup semi-final, 25 March 1939.

Club record: 70,504 v Aston Villa, Division 1, 27 December 1920.

Record Receipts: £723,650.22 (net of VAT), £850,289 (including VAT) v Liverpool, FA Cup 4th rd, 24 January 1999.

Pitch Measurements: 116yd × 76yd.

Chairman/Chief Executive: C. M. Edwards.

Directors: J. M. Edelson, Sir Bobby Charlton CBE, E. M. Watkins LL.M., R. L. Olive, P. F. Kenyon, D. A. Gill.

Manager: Sir Alex Ferguson CBE.

Assistant Manager: Steve McClaren.

Secretary: Kenneth Merrett.

Commercial Manager: Danny McGregor.

Stadium Manager: Alan Bird.

LATEST SEQUENCES

Longest Sequence of League Wins: 14, 15.10.04 – 3.1.05.

Longest Sequence of League Defeats: 14, 26.4.30 – 25.10.30.

Longest Sequence of League Draws: 6, 30.10.88 – 27.11.88.

Longest Sequence of Unbeaten League Matches: 26, 4.2.56 – 13.10.56.

Longest Sequence Without a League Win: 16, 19.4.30 – 25.10.30.

HONOURS

FA Premier League – Champions 1992–93, 1993–94, 1995–96, 1996–97, 1998–99; Runners-up 1994–95, 1997–98.

Football League: Division 1 – Champions 1907–08, 1910–11, 1951–52, 1955–56, 1956–57, 1964–65, 1966–67; Runners-up 1946–47, 1947–48, 1948–49, 1950–51, 1958–59, 1963–64, 1967–68, 1979–80, 1987–88, 1991–92. Division 2 – Champions 1935–36, 1974–75; Runners-up 1896–97, 1905–06, 1924–25, 1937–38.

FA Cup: Winners 1909, 1948, 1963, 1977, 1983, 1985, 1990, 1994, 1996, 1999; Runners-up 1957, 1958, 1976, 1979, 1995.

Football League Cup: Winners 1992; Runners-up 1983, 1991, 1994.

European Competitions: *European Cup:* 1956–57 (s-f), 1957–58 (s-f), 1965–66 (s-f), 1967–68 (winners), 1968–69 (s-f), 1993–94, 1994–95, 1996–97 (s-f), 1997–98, 1998–99 (winners). *European Cup-Winners' Cup:* 1963–64, 1977–78, 1983–84, 1990–91 (winners). 1991–92. *European Fairs Cup:* 1964–65. *UEFA Cup:* 1976–77, 1980–81, 1982–83, 1984–85, 1992–93, 1995–96. *World Club Championship:* 1968. *Super Cup:* 1991 (winners).

Colours
Red shirts, white shorts, black stockings.

Change Colours
All white.

Year Formed: 1878 as Newton Heath LYR; 1902, Manchester United.

Turned Professional: 1885. *Ltd Co.:* 1907.

Previous Name: 1880, Newton Heath; 1902, Manchester United.

Club Nickname: 'Red Devils'.

Previous Grounds: 1880, North Road, Monsall Road; 1893, Bank Street; 1910, Old Trafford (played at Maine Road 1941–49).

First Football League Game: 3 September 1892, Division 1, v Blackburn R (a) L 3–4 – Warner; Clements, Brown; Perrins, Stewart, Erentz; Farman (1), Coupar (1), Donaldson (1), Carson, Mathieson.

Record League Victory (as Newton Heath): 10–1 v Wolverhampton W, Division 1, 15 October 1892 – Warner; Mitchell, Clements; Perrins, Stewart (3), Erentz; Farman (1), Hood (1), Donaldson (3), Carson (1), Hendry (1).

Record League Victory (as Manchester U): 9–0 v Ipswich T, FA Premier League, 4 March 1995 – Schmeichel; Keane (1) (Sharpe), Irwin, Bruce (Butt), Kanchelskis, Pallister, Cole (5), Ince (1), McClair, Hughes (2), Giggs.

Record Cup Victory: 10–0 v RSC Anderlecht, European Cup prel. rd 2nd leg, 26 September 1956 – Wood; Foulkes, Byrne; Colman, Jones, Edwards; Berry (1), Whelan (2), Taylor (3), Viollet (4), Pegg.

MANAGERS
J. Ernest Mangnall 1903–12
John Bentley 1912–14
John Robson 1914–21
(Secretary-Manager from 1916)
John Chapman 1921–26
Clarence Hilditch 1926–27
Herbert Bamlett 1927–31
Walter Crickmer 1931–32
Scott Duncan 1932–37
Walter Crickmer 1937–45
(Secretary-Manager)
Matt Busby 1945–69
(continued as General Manager then Director)
Wilf McGuinness 1969–70
Sir Matt Busby 1970–71
Frank O'Farrell 1971–72
Tommy Docherty 1972–77
Dave Sexton 1977–81
Ron Atkinson 1981–86
Alex Ferguson November 1986–

Record Defeat: 0–7 v Blackburn R, Division 1, 10 April 1926. 0–7 v Aston Villa, Division 1, 27 December 1930. 0–7 v Wolverhampton W, Division 2, 26 December 1931.

Most League Points (2 for a win): 64, Division 1, 1956–57.

Most League Points (3 for a win): 92, FA Premier League, 1993–94.

Most League Goals: 103, Division 1, 1956–57 and 1958–59.

Highest League Scorer in Season: Dennis Viollet, 32, 1959–60.

Most League Goals in Total Aggregate: Bobby Charlton, 199, 1956–73.

Most Capped Player: Bobby Charlton, 106, England.

Most League Appearances: Bobby Charlton, 606, 1956–73.

Youngest League Player: Jeff Whitefoot, 16 years 105 days v Portsmouth, 15 April 1950.

Record Transfer Fee Received: £7,000,000 from Internazionale for Paul Ince, June 1995.

Record Transfer Fee Paid: £12,600,000 to Aston Villa for Dwight Yorke, August 1998.

Football League Record: 1892 Newton Heath elected to Division 1; 1894–1906 Division 2; 1906–22 Division 1; 1922–25 Division 2; 1925–31 Division 1; 1931–36 Division 2; 1936–37 Division 1; 1937–38 Division 2; 1938–74 Division 1; 1974–75 Division 2; 1975–92 Division 1; 1992– FA Premier League.

TEN YEAR LEAGUE RECORD

		P	W	D	L	F	A	Pts	Pos
1988-89	Div 1	38	13	12	13	45	35	51	11
1989-90	Div 1	38	13	9	16	46	47	48	13
1990-91	Div 1	38	16	12	10	58	45	59	6
1991-92	Div 1	42	21	15	6	63	33	78	2
1992-93	PR Lge	42	24	12	6	67	31	84	1
1993-94	PR Lge	42	27	11	4	80	38	92	1
1994-95	PR Lge	42	26	10	6	77	28	88	2
1995-96	PR Lge	38	25	7	6	73	35	82	1
1996-97	PR Lge	38	21	12	5	76	44	75	1
1997-98	PR Lge	38	23	8	7	73	26	77	2

DID YOU KNOW ?

Sir Matt Busby was offered the manager's job at Tottenham Hotspur in 1949 and invited the same year to coach the Italian national team. In 1948 he had coached Great Britain to fourth place in the Olympic Games.

MANCHESTER UNITED 1998–99 LEAGUE RECORD

Match No.	Date	Venue	Opponents	Result	H/T Score	Lg. Pos.	Goalscorers	Attendance
1	Aug 15	H	Leicester C	D	2-2	0-1	—	Sheringham [79], Beckham [90]	55,052
2	22	A	West Ham U	D	0-0	0-0	11		25,912
3	Sept 9	H	Charlton Ath	W	4-1	2-1	—	Solskjaer 2 [38, 63], Yorke 2 [45, 48]	55,147
4	12	H	Coventry C	W	2-0	1-0	5	Yorke [21], Johnsen [48]	55,193
5	20	A	Arsenal	L	0-3	0-2	10		38,142
6	24	H	Liverpool	W	2-0	1-0	—	Irwin (pen) [19], Scholes [79]	55,181
7	Oct 3	A	Southampton	W	3-0	1-0	2	Yorke [11], Cole [59], Cruyff [74]	15,251
8	17	H	Wimbledon	W	5-1	2-1	2	Cole 2 [19, 88], Giggs [45], Beckham [48], Yorke [54]	55,265
9	24	A	Derby Co	D	1-1	0-0	2	Cruyff [85]	30,867
10	31	A	Everton	W	4-1	2-1	2	Yorke [14], Short (og) [23], Cole [59], Blomqvist [64]	40,087
11	Nov 8	H	Newcastle U	D	0-0	0-0	3		55,174
12	14	H	Blackburn R	W	3-2	2-0	2	Scholes 2 [32, 58], Yorke [44]	55,198
13	21	A	Sheffield W	L	1-3	1-1	2	Cole [29]	39,475
14	29	A	Leeds U	W	3-2	1-1	2	Solskjaer [45], Keane [46], Butt [77]	55,172
15	Dec 5	A	Aston Villa	D	1-1	0-0	2	Scholes [47]	39,241
16	12	A	Tottenham H	D	2-2	2-0	2	Solskjaer 2 [11, 18]	36,058
17	16	H	Chelsea	D	1-1	1-0	—	Cole [45]	55,159
18	19	H	Middlesbrough	L	2-3	0-2	3	Butt [62], Scholes [70]	55,152
19	26	H	Nottingham F	W	3-0	1-0	3	Johnsen 2 [28, 59], Giggs [62]	55,216
20	29	A	Chelsea	D	0-0	0-0	—		34,741
21	Jan 10	H	West Ham U	W	4-1	2-0	4	Yorke [10], Cole 2 [40, 67], Solskjaer [80]	55,180
22	16	A	Leicester C	W	6-2	1-1	2	Yorke 3 [10, 63, 84], Cole 2 [49, 61], Stam [90]	22,091
23	31	A	Charlton Ath	W	1-0	0-0	1	Yorke [89]	20,043
24	Feb 3	H	Derby Co	W	1-0	0-0	1	Yorke [65]	55,174
25	6	A	Nottingham F	W	8-1	2-1	1	Yorke 2 [2, 66], Cole 2 [7, 49], Solskjaer 4 [80, 87, 89, 90]	30,025
26	17	H	Arsenal	D	1-1	0-0	1	Cole [60]	55,171
27	20	A	Coventry C	W	1-0	0-0	1	Giggs [78]	22,594
28	27	H	Southampton	W	2-1	0-0	1	Keane [79], Yorke [83]	55,316
29	Mar 13	A	Newcastle U	W	2-1	1-1	1	Cole 2 [25, 51]	36,776
30	21	H	Everton	W	3-1	0-0	1	Solskjaer [54], Neville G [63], Beckham [67]	55,182
31	Apr 3	A	Wimbledon	D	1-1	1-1	1	Beckham [44]	26,121
32	17	H	Sheffield W	W	3-0	2-0	1	Solskjaer [35], Sheringham [44], Scholes [62]	55,270
33	25	A	Leeds U	D	1-1	0-1	2	Cole [56]	40,255
34	May 1	H	Aston Villa	W	2-1	1-1	2	Watson (og) [20], Beckham [46]	55,189
35	5	A	Liverpool	D	2-2	1-0	—	Yorke [23], Irwin (pen) [56]	44,702
36	May 9	A	Middlesbrough	W	1-0	1-0	1	Yorke [45]	34,655
37	12	A	Blackburn R	D	0-0	0-0	—		30,436
38	16	H	Tottenham H	W	2-1	1-1	1	Beckham [42], Cole [47]	55,189

Final League Position: 1

GOALSCORERS

League (80): Yorke 18, Cole 17, Solskjaer 12, Beckham 6, Scholes 6, Giggs 3, Johnsen 3, Butt 2, Cruyff 2, Irwin 2 (2 pens), Keane 2, Sheringham 2, Blomqvist, Neville G 1, Stam 1, own goals 2.
Worthington Cup (5): Solskjaer 3, Nevland 1, Sheringham 1.
FA Cup (12): Yorke 3, Cole 2, Giggs 2, Beckham 1, Irwin 1 (pen), Scholes 1, Sheringham 1, Solskjaer 1.

Schmeichel P 34	Neville G 34	Irwin D 26 + 3	Keane R 33 + 2	Johnsen R 19 + 3	Stam J 30	Beckham D 33 + 1	Butt N 22 + 9	Cole A 26 + 6	Scholes P 24 + 7	Giggs R 20 + 4	Sheringham T 7 + 10	Berg H 10 + 6	Yorke D 32	Neville P 19 + 9	Solskjaer O 9 + 10	Blomqvist J 20 + 5	Van der Gouw R 4 + 1	Brown W 11 + 3	Cruyff J — + 5	Curtis J 1 + 3	Greening J — + 3	May D 4 + 2	Match No.
1	2¹	3	4	5	6²	7	8	9	10	11	12	13											1
1	2²	3	5	6		7	8	9¹		11	12	4	10	13									2
1		2¹	5	4	6	7		13	11		14	12	10³	3	9²	8							3
1	2		5	4²	6	7¹	12		10	11³		13	9	3	8	14							4
1	2	3	5		6	7	8			11		4	9		10								5
1	4	3	5		6	7	12	13	10¹	11			9	2	8²								6
	4	3²	5		6	7	8	9		12		11¹		2	10³		1	13		14			7
	4		5		6	7²		9	12	11¹			10	3³	8		1		2	13	14		8
1	4¹		5		6	7	8³	9	12	11²			10	3	14			2	13				9
1	4	12	5		6	7		9	11			10	3¹	8	2								10
1	4	3	5	12²	6	7	13	9	11			10		14	8³	2¹							11
1	4	14			6	7	8	9	11²			10		2	12	5¹				13³	3		12
1	4	3³	5²		6	7	12	9	11			10	2	13	8¹		14						13
1	4		5		6³		8	9¹	11²	12	13	14	10	3	7		2						14
1	4	3	5		6	7	12	9¹	11	13		10			8²		2						15
1	2		5	4	6	7	8	12	11³			10¹		13	3	9²		14					16
1	4	3	5		6	12	8	9	11³	13	14		10¹			7²		2					17
1	4	3	5	6		7¹	8	9	12	11		10		2²		13							18
1		3	5³	6		7	8		9²	11¹	10		4		2	13	12				14		19
1	2	3	5	4	6	7	8	9	10¹	11	12												20
		3	5²	12	6		8³	9		11			4	10	14	7	1	2¹		13			21
1		3	5	6		7		9		11		4	10	12	8			2¹					22
1	2	3	5		6	7²	8¹	9	12	11		4	10		13								23
1	2	3	5	4	6		8	7		11¹			10		9	12							24
1	2	5²	4		6	7	12	9	11				10³	3	13	8¹		14					25
1	2	5¹	4		6	7	8	9	13	12			10	3		11²							26
1	2	3	5	4	6¹	7		9³	8	11		12	10²	13	14								27
1	2	12	13		6	7		8²	14	5		11	4	10	3¹	9³							28
1⁶	2	3	5	12	6	7		9	8²	11¹			4	10	13		15						29
1	2		5	6		7³	8	9¹		12			4	10	3	11²				13	14		30
1	2	3	5	6		7		9	8				4	10	12	11¹							31
	2	12	5²		6³		8		11	10			3		9	7¹	1	4		13	14		32
1	2	3¹	5			7²	8	9	13		14		10		12	11³		6			4		33
1	2	3			6	7	8	5		10			9	12	11¹	13					4²		34
1	2	3	5	4	6	7	12	9¹	8			10		13		11²							35
1	2	3	5¹		6	7	12	13	8³			10	9		14	11²					4		36
1	2	3	4		6³	7	8	9²	12	11	13		10	5¹							14		37
1	2	3	5	6		7	12	13	8¹	11³	10²		9	14							4		38

Worthington Cup

Third Round	Bury	(h)	2-0
Fourth Round	Nottingham F	(h)	2-1
Fifth Round	Tottenham H	(a)	1-3

FA Cup

Third Round	Middlesbrough	(h)	3-1
Fourth Round	Liverpool	(h)	2-1
Fifth Round	Fulham	(h)	1-0
Sixth Round	Chelsea	(h)	0-0
		(a)	2-0
Semi-Final	Arsenal (at Villa Park)		0-0
Replay	(at Villa Park)		2-1
Final	Newcastle U (at Wembley)		2-0

Division 3   MANSFIELD TOWN

FOUNDATION

The club was formed as Mansfield Wesleyans in 1897, and changed their name to Mansfield Wesley in 1906 and Mansfield Town in 1910. This was after the Mansfield Wesleyan Chapel trustees had requested that the club change its name as 'it has no longer had any connection with either the chapel or school'. The new club participated in the Notts and Derby District League, but in the following season 1911–12 joined the Central Alliance.

Field Mill Ground, Quarry Lane, Mansfield NG18 5DA.

Telephone: (01623) 623567/658070.

Fax: (01623) 625014.

Marketing: (01623) 658070.

Football in the Community: (01623) 625197.

Ground Capacity: 5289.

Record Attendance: 24,467 v Nottingham F, FA Cup 3rd rd, 10 January 1953.

Record Receipts: £46,915 v Sheffield W, FA Cup 3rd rd, 5 January 1991.

Pitch Measurements: 115yd × 70yd.

Chairman/Chief Executive: Keith Haslam.

Associate Directors: T. Hewson, K. Woodcock, S. Whetton, M. Murphy.

Manager: Bill Dearden.

Physio: Barry Statham.

Community Scheme Organiser: D. Bentley.

Secretary: Christine Reynolds.

Marketing Manager: Nicola Wilcockson.

LATEST SEQUENCES

Longest Sequence of League Wins: 7, 13.9.91 – 26.10.91.

Longest Sequence of League Defeats: 7, 18.1.47 – 15.3.47.

Longest Sequence of League Draws: 5, 18.10.86 – 22.11.86.

Longest Sequence of Unbeaten League Matches: 20, 14.2.76 – 21.8.76.

Longest Sequence Without a League Win: 12, 10.11.79 – 16.2.80.

HONOURS

Football League: Division 2 best season: 21st, 1977–78; Division 3 – Champions 1976–77; Division 4 – Champions 1974–75; Division 3 (N) – Runners-up 1950–51.

FA Cup: best season: 6th rd, 1969.

Football League Cup: best season: 5th rd, 1976.

Freight Rover Trophy: Winners 1987.

Colours

Amber shirts with royal blue trim, royal blue shorts with amber flash, royal blue stockings with amber trim.

Change Colours

White shirts, white shorts with thin blue stripe, white stockings with blue stripe.

Year Formed: 1897.

Turned Professional: 1906.

Ltd Co.: 1922.

Previous Name: 1897, Mansfield Wesleyans; 1906, Mansfield Wesley; 1910, Mansfield Town.

Club Nickname: 'The Stags'.

First Football League Game: 29 August 1931, Division 3 (S), v Swindon T (h) W 3–2 – Wilson; Clifford, England; Wake, Davis, Blackburn; Gilhespy, Readman (1), Johnson, Broom (2), Baxter.

Record League Victory: 9–2 v Rotherham U, Division 3 (N), 27 December 1932 – Wilson; Anthony, England; Davies, S. Robinson, Slack; Prior, Broom, Readman (3), Hoyland (3), Bowater (3).

Record Cup Victory: 8–0 v Scarborough (a), FA Cup 1st rd, 22 November 1952 – Bramley; Chessell, Bradley; Field, Plummer, Lewis; Scott, Fox (3), Marron (2), Sid Watson (1), Adam (2).

Record Defeat: 1–8 v Walsall, Division 3 (N), 19 January 1933.

Most League Points (2 for a win): 68, Division 4, 1974–75.

Most League Points (3 for a win): 81, Division 4, 1985–86.

Most League Goals: 108, Division 4, 1962–63.

Highest League Scorer in Season: Ted Harston, 55, Division 3 (N), 1936–37.

Most League Goals in Total Aggregate: Harry Johnson, 104, 1931–36.

Most League Goals in One Match: 7, Ted Harston v Hartlepools U, Division 3N, 23 January 1937.

Most Capped Player: John McClelland, 6 (53), Northern Ireland.

Most League Appearances: Rod Arnold, 440, 1970–83.

Youngest League Player: Cyril Poole, 15 years 351 days v New Brighton, 27 February 1937.

Record Transfer Fee Received: £655,000 from Tottenham H for Colin Calderwood, July 1993.

Record Transfer Fee Paid: £150,000 to Carlisle U for Lee Peacock, October 1997.

Football League Record: 1931 Elected to Division 3 (S); 1932–37 Division 3 (N); 1937–47 Division 3 (S); 1947–58 Division 3 (N); 1958–60 Division 3; 1960–63 Division 4; 1963–72 Division 3; 1972–75 Division 4; 1975–77 Division 3; 1977–78 Division 2; 1978–80 Division 3; 1980–86 Division 4; 1986–91 Division 3; 1991–92 Division 4; 1992–93 Division 2; 1993– Division 3.

MANAGERS

John Baynes 1922–25
Ted Davison 1926–28
Jack Hickling 1928–33
Henry Martin 1933–35
Charlie Bell 1935
Harold Wightman 1936
Harold Parkes 1936–38
Jack Poole 1938–44
Lloyd Barke 1944–45
Roy Goodall 1945–49
Freddie Steele 1949–51
George Jobey 1952–53
Stan Mercer 1953–55
Charlie Mitten 1956–58
Sam Weaver 1958–60
Raich Carter 1960–63
Tommy Cummings 1963–67
Tommy Eggleston 1967–70
Jock Basford 1970–71
Danny Williams 1971–74
Dave Smith 1974–76
Peter Morris 1976–78
Billy Bingham 1978–79
Mick Jones 1979–81
Stuart Boam 1981–83
Ian Greaves 1983–89
George Foster 1989–93
Andy King 1993–96
Steve Parkin 1996–99
Bill Dearden July 1999–

TEN YEAR LEAGUE RECORD

		P	W	D	L	F	A	Pts	Pos
1988-89	Div 3	46	14	17	15	48	52	59	15
1989-90	Div 3	46	16	7	23	50	65	55	15
1990-91	Div 3	46	8	14	24	42	63	38	24
1991-92	Div 4	42	23	8	11	75	53	77	3
1992-93	Div 2	46	11	11	24	52	80	44	22
1993-94	Div 3	42	15	10	17	53	62	55	12
1994-95	Div 3	42	18	11	13	84	59	65	6
1995-96	Div 3	46	11	20	15	54	64	53	19
1996-97	Div 3	46	16	16	14	47	45	64	11
1997-98	Div 3	46	16	17	13	64	55	65	12

DID YOU KNOW ?

On 26 February 1969 in a five-times postponed fifth round FA Cup tie, Mansfield Town beat a West Ham United team including England's 1966 World Cup trio: Bobby Moore, Martin Peters and Geoff Hurst 3–0.

MANSFIELD TOWN 1998–99 LEAGUE RECORD

Match No.	Date	Venue	Opponents	Result	H/T Score	Lg. Pos.	Goalscorers	Attendance
1	Aug 8	A	Brentford	L	0-3	0-1	—	4846
2	15	H	Plymouth Arg	W	2-0	2-0	16	Peacock [8], Gibbs (og) [23]	2451
3	22	A	Scarborough	W	3-2	1-1	6	Peters [22], Christie [63], Kerr [68]	1972
4	29	H	Swansea C	W	1-0	1-0	5	Christie [36]	2421
5	31	A	Rotherham U	D	0-0	0-0	6		5943
6	Sept 5	H	Darlington	L	0-1	0-1	11		2428
7	8	A	Leyton Orient	D	1-1	0-1	—	Clarke [50]	3186
8	12	H	Carlisle U	D	1-1	0-1	12	Clarke [57]	2292
9	19	A	Scunthorpe U	L	2-3	2-2	13	Peacock [12], Harper [36]	3554
10	26	H	Hull C	W	2-0	0-0	10	Christie 2 [56, 90]	2603
11	Oct 3	A	Exeter C	L	1-2	1-1	13	Lormor [28]	3024
12	9	H	Torquay U	W	2-1	1-0	—	Peacock [8], Lormor [68]	3573
13	17	A	Brighton & HA	W	3-1	1-1	8	Peacock [42], Clarke [77], Christie [87]	2808
14	20	A	Southend U	W	2-1	1-1	—	Tallon [43], Harper [49]	3250
15	31	H	Cambridge U	L	1-3	0-2	8	Peacock (pen) [82]	2674
16	Nov 7	A	Rochdale	L	0-1	0-0	10		2142
17	10	A	Hartlepool U	W	2-1	2-0	—	Lormor 2 [20, 44]	1779
18	20	H	Barnet	W	5-0	3-0	—	Ford [24], Peacock 3 [30, 38, 48], Christie [83]	2965
19	27	A	Halifax T	D	2-2	2-0	—	Ford [4], Peacock (pen) [19]	3227
20	Dec 1	H	Peterborough U	W	1-0	0-0	—	Peacock [76]	3169
21	11	H	Shrewsbury T	W	1-0	1-0	—	Peacock (pen) [15]	2865
22	19	A	Cardiff C	L	2-4	0-1	3	Harper [53], Christie [58]	9013
23	26	H	Scarborough	W	3-2	2-0	2	Williams [10], Ryder [38], Harper [55]	3495
24	28	A	Chester C	D	1-1	1-0	3	Lormor [2]	3320
25	Jan 9	H	Brentford	W	3-1	2-1	4	Lormor [12], Harper [15], Christie [86]	4095
26	16	A	Plymouth Arg	L	0-3	0-2	5		4399
27	22	H	Rotherham U	L	0-3	0-0	—		3586
28	30	H	Chester C	W	3-0	0-0	4	Walker [50], Lormor 2 [57, 90]	2654
29	Feb 6	A	Darlington	L	1-5	1-0	4	Harper [34]	2708
30	13	H	Leyton Orient	L	1-2	1-1	5	Peacock [21]	2817
31	20	A	Carlisle U	D	0-0	0-0	5		2273
32	23	A	Swansea C	L	0-1	0-0	—		4361
33	27	H	Scunthorpe U	W	2-1	1-1	4	Peacock 2 [26, 87]	3208
34	Mar 6	A	Hull C	D	0-0	0-0	6		6692
35	13	H	Rochdale	W	3-1	1-0	6	L'Helgoualch [2], Ryder [56], Clarke [68]	2555
36	20	A	Cambridge U	L	2-7	1-3	6	Lormor [30], Peacock (pen) [64]	4343
37	28	A	Peterborough U	L	0-1	0-0	8		5507
38	Apr 3	H	Brighton & HA	W	2-0	2-0	7	Peacock [35], Kerr [45]	3015
39	5	A	Torquay U	D	0-0	0-0	7		2897
40	10	H	Southend U	D	0-0	0-0	7		2624
41	13	H	Halifax T	L	0-1	0-1	—		2471
42	17	A	Barnet	D	0-0	0-0	10		1861
43	24	A	Hartlepool U	W	2-0	2-0	7	Lormor [3], Williams [38]	3337
44	27	H	Exeter C	L	0-1	0-0	—		2830
45	May 1	A	Shrewsbury T	L	0-1	0-0	10		2553
46	8	H	Cardiff C	W	3-0	0-0	8	Lormor [71], Peacock (pen) [76], Clarke [81]	4032

Final League Position: 8

GOALSCORERS
League (60): Peacock 17 (5 pens), Lormor 11, Christie 8, Harper 6, Clarke 5, Ford 2, Kerr 2, Ryder 2, Williams 2, L'Helgoualch 1, Peters 1, Tallon 1, Walker 1, own goal 1.
Worthington Cup (3): Christie 1, Clarke 1, Peters 1.
FA Cup (3): Lormor 2, Clarke 1.

Cherry S 1	Williams L 31+13	Harper S 45	Peters M 37	Kerr D 30+5	Hackett W 24+2	Schofield J 37+5	Clarke D 24+9	Lormor T 35+6	Christie I 18+24	Ford T 39+3	Tallon G 31+5	Peacock L 42+3	Bowling I 37	Ryder S 18+4	Walker J 18+19	Hassell B 1+2	Sedlan J 1+4	Naylor S 6	L'Helgoualch C 3+1	Sisson M —+1	Carruthers M —+5	Willis A 10	Allardyce C 6	Linighan D 10	Rose K —+1	Adamson C 2	Match No.
1	2	3	4	5¹	6	7	8	9²	10	11	12	13															1
	2	3	4²		6	7	8	12	10	5	11	9¹	1	13													2
	2¹	3	4	12	6	7	8		10	5¹	11	9	1	13													3
		3	4	2²	6	7	8	12	10¹	5	11	9	1		13												4
		3	4	2	6	7	8	12	10	5¹	11²	9	1		13												5
	12	3	4		6²	7	8	11	10	5¹		9	1	13	2³	14											6
	2	3	4			7	8		10	5		9	1	6	11												7
	2	3	4			7	8	12	10¹	5	13	9	1	6	11²												8
	2	3	4			7	8²	12	10	5³	11	9	1	6¹	13		14										9
	12	3	4			7		10	13	2¹	11	9	1	6	8	5¹											10
	2³	3	4¹	12		7		10	9		11	5	1	6	8²	13	14										11
	3		4	8	6	7		9	12	5	11	10¹	1		2												12
	2	3	4	8	6		7	12	9²	13	5	11¹	10	1													13
	2	3	4	8¹	6		7	12	9	13	5	11²	10	1													14
	2¹	3	4	8²	6		7	11	9	12	5³		10	1		13	14										15
	2	3	4	8¹	6²		7	11	9	12	5	14	10¹	1		13											16
	12	3	4	13	6		7	5²	9	14	2	11³	10	1		8¹											17
	12	3	4	13	6		7	5²	9¹	14	2¹	11	10	1		8											18
	12	3	4	13	6		7²	5	9²	14	2	11	10	1		8¹											19
	12	3	4		6		5	9²	13	2¹	11	10	1	7	8												20
	12	3		5¹		7	8		9	2¹	11	10		6	13		14	1	4³								21
	12	3		5²	6	7	8		9	2	11¹	10		4	13			1									22
	5¹	3			6	7		9	10	2	11		1	4	8						12						23
	12	3¹	4		6	7		5	9	2	11	10	1		8			1									24
	12	3	4	5	6	7		9²	13	2¹	11	10	1		8			1									25
	12	3	4	5¹	6	7		9	13	2	11	10³	1	14	8¹												26
	8	3	4	5¹	6	7	12	9	13	2¹	11²	10			14			1									27
	11	3	4	6²		7	8	9	10¹	2		12		5	13			1									28
	11¹	3	4	12	13	7²	8	9	10	2		14		5	6³			1									29
	12	3	4		6²	7	8	9	13	2¹	11	10		5				1									30
	12	3	4	8²	6	7		9		2	11¹	10²	1	5	13							14					31
	11	3	4	8²	6	7		9		2¹	12	10	1	5³	13							14					32
	6	3	4	8		7		9²		2¹	11	10	1	5	12							13					33
	6	3	4	8		7		9¹	12	2	11²	10³	1	5								13	14				34
	2	3	4	8¹		7	12	9²	13		11	10	1	5	14			6³									35
	2	3¹		11		7	12	9³	13	8³	14	10	1		5			6²	14								36
	2	3		7				9	12	11	10²	1			8¹									4	5	6	13	37
	2	3		7			12	9²	13	14	11¹	10¹	1											4	5	6	38
	2	3		7		12	13	9	14		11²	10³	1		8¹									4	5	6	39
	2	3		7			12	9²	13		11	10	1		8¹									4	5	6	40
	2	3		7¹		12	11	9²	13	8³		10	1		14									4	5	6	41
	2	3¹		11			7	12	9²	13	8³	14	10	1										4	5	6	42
	11	3	4	7¹		12	8	9	13	2²		10²	1		14										5	6		43
	11	3	4	7³		12	8	9	13	2²		10	1¹		14										5	6		44
	11	3	4	7³		12	8¹	9	13	2²		10			14										5	6	1	45
	11	3	4	8¹			7³	12	13	9		2²			10										5	6	1	46

FA Premiership

MIDDLESBROUGH

FOUNDATION

A previous belief that Middlesbrough Football Club was founded at a tripe supper at the Corporation Hotel has proved to be erroneous. In fact, members of Middlesbrough Cricket Club were responsible for forming it at a meeting in the gymnasium of the Albert Park Hotel in 1875.

Cellnet Riverside Stadium, Middlesbrough, Cleveland TS3 6RS.
Telephone: (01642) 877700.
Fax: (01642) 877840.
Website: www.mfc.co.uk.
Clubcall: 0891 121181.
Ticket Office: (01642) 877745.
Stadium Shop: (01642) 877720.
Town Centre Shop: (01642) 877849.
Tour Booking Line: (01642) 877730.
Ground Capacity: 35,000.
Record Attendance: Ayresome Park: 53,596 v Newcastle U, Division 1, 27 December 1949.
Cellnet Riverside Stadium: 34,687 v Tottenham H, FA Premier League, 20 February 1999.
Record Receipts: £486,229 v Newcastle U, FA Premier League, 6 December 1998.
Pitch measurements: 115yd × 74yd.
Chairman: Steve Gibson.
Director: George Cooke.
Chief Executive: Keith Lamb.
Secretary: Karen Nelson.
Manager: Bryan Robson.
Assistant Manager: Viv Anderson.
Physio: Bob Ward.
First Team Coach: Gordon McQueen.
Reserve Team Coach: David Geddis.
Youth Academy Director: David Parnaby
Chief Scout: Ray Train.
General Manager Business Operations: Reg Corbidge.
Commercial Manager: Graham Fordy.
Public Relations Manager: Dave Allan.
Stadium Manager: Terry Tasker.

LATEST SEQUENCES
Longest Sequence of League Wins: 9, 16.2.74 – 6.4.74.
Longest Sequence of League Defeats: 8, 26.12.95 – 17.2.96.
Longest Sequence of League Draws: 8, 3.4.71 – 1.5.71.
Longest Sequence of Unbeaten League Matches: 24, 8.9.73 – 19.1.74.
Longest Sequence Without a League Win: 19, 3.10.81 – 6.3.82.

HONOURS

Football League: Division 1 – Champions 1994–95; Runners-up 1997–98; Division 2 – Champions 1926–27, 1928–29, 1973–74; Runners-up 1901–02, 1991–92; Division 3 – Runners-up 1966–67, 1986–87.

FA Cup: Runners-up 1997.

Football League Cup: Runners-up 1997, 1998.

Amateur Cup: Winners 1895, 1898.

Anglo-Scottish Cup: Winners 1976.

Zenith Data Systems Cup: Runners-up 1990.

Colours
Red and white.

Change Colours
White and purple.

Year Formed: 1876; re-formed 1986.

Turned Professional: 1889; became amateur 1892, and professional again, 1899.

Ltd Co: 1892.

Club Nickname: 'Boro'.

Previous Grounds: 1877, Old Archery Ground, Albert Park; 1879, Breckon Hill; 1882, Linthorpe Road Ground; 1903, Ayresome Park; 1995, Cellnet Riverside Stadium.

First Football League Game: 2 September 1899, Division 2, v Lincoln C (a) L 0–3 – Smith; Shaw, Ramsey; Allport, McNally, McCracken; Wanless, Longstaffe, Gettins, Page, Pugh.

Record League Victory: 9–0 v Brighton & HA, Division 2, 23 August 1958 – Taylor; Bilcliff, Robinson; Harris (2p), Phillips, Walley; Day, McLean, Clough (5), Peacock (2), Holliday.

Record Cup Victory: 7–0 v Hereford U, Coca-Cola Cup 2nd rd, 1st leg, 18 September 1996 – Miller; Fleming (1), Branco (1), Whyte, Vickers, Whelan, Emerson (1), Mustoe, Stamp, Juninho, Ravanelli (4).

Record Defeat: 0–9 v Blackburn R, Division 2, 6 November 1954.

Most League Points (2 for a win): 65, Division 2, 1973–74.

Most League Points (3 for a win): 94, Division 3, 1986–87.

Most League Goals: 122, Division 2, 1926–27.

Highest League Scorer in Season: George Camsell, 59, Division 2, 1926–27 (Second Division record).

Most League Goals in Total Aggregate: George Camsell, 326, 1925–39.

Most League Goals in One Match: 5, Andy Wilson v Nottingham F, Division 1, 6 October 1923; 5, George Camsell v Manchester C, Division 2, 25 December 1926; 5, George Camsell v Aston Villa, Division 1, 9 September 1935; 5, Brian Clough v Brighton & HA, Division 2, 22 August 1958.

Most Capped Player: Wilf Mannion, 26, England.

Most League Appearances: Tim Williamson, 563, 1902–23.

Youngest League Player: Stephen Bell, 16 years 323 days v Southampton, 30 January 1982; Sam Lawrie, 16 years 323 days v Arsenal, 3 November 1951.

Record Transfer Fee Received: £12,000,000 from Atletico Madrid for Juninho, July 1997.

Record Transfer Fee Paid: £7,000,000 to Juventus for Fabrizio Ravanelli, August 1996.

Football League Record: 1899 Elected to Division 2; 1902–24 Division 1; 1924–27 Division 2; 1927–28 Division 1; 1928–29 Division 2; 1929–54 Division 1; 1954–66 Division 2; 1966–67 Division 3; 1967–74 Division 2; 1974–82 Division 1; 1982–86 Division 2; 1986–87 Division 3; 1987–88 Division 2; 1988–89 Division 1; 1989–92 Division 2; 1992–93 FA Premier League; 1993–95 Division 1; 1995–97 FA Premier League; 1997–98 Division 1; 1998– FA Premier League.

MANAGERS

John Robson 1899–1905
Alex Mackie 1905–06
Andy Aitken 1906–09
J. Gunter 1908–10
(Secretary-Manager)
Andy Walker 1910–11
Tom McIntosh 1911–19
Jimmy Howie 1920–23
Herbert Bamlett 1923–26
Peter McWilliam 1927–34
Wilf Gillow 1934–44
David Jack 1944–52
Walter Rowley 1952–54
Bob Dennison 1954–63
Raich Carter 1963–66
Stan Anderson 1966–73
Jack Charlton 1973–77
John Neal 1977–81
Bobby Murdoch 1981–82
Malcolm Allison 1982–84
Willie Maddren 1984–86
Bruce Rioch 1986–90
Colin Todd 1990–91
Lennie Lawrence 1991–94
Bryan Robson May 1994–

TEN YEAR LEAGUE RECORD

		P	W	D	L	F	A	Pts	Pos
1988-89	Div 1	38	9	12	17	44	61	39	18
1989-90	Div 2	46	13	11	22	52	63	50	21
1990-91	Div 2	46	20	9	17	66	47	69	7
1991-92	Div 2	46	23	11	12	58	41	80	2
1992-93	PR Lge	42	11	11	20	54	75	44	21
1993-94	Div 1	46	18	13	15	66	54	67	9
1994-95	Div 1	46	23	13	10	67	40	82	1
1995-96	PR Lge	38	11	10	17	35	50	43	12
1996-97	PR Lge	38	10	12	16	51	60	39	19
1997-98	Div 1	46	27	10	9	77	41	91	2

DID YOU KNOW ?

Middlesbrough's first floodlit friendly was on 16 October 1957 against First Division Sunderland. Second Division Middlesbrough won 2–0 with goals from Arthur Fitzsimons and Brian Clough watched by a crowd of 27,273.

MIDDLESBROUGH 1998–99 LEAGUE RECORD

Match No.	Date	Venue	Opponents	Result		H/T Score	Lg. Pos.	Goalscorers	Attendance
1	Aug 15	H	Leeds U	D	0-0	0-0	—		34,160
2	23	A	Aston Villa	L	1-3	0-1	17	Beck [62]	29,559
3	29	H	Derby Co	D	1-1	0-1	17	Ricard [48]	34,087
4	Sept 9	A	Leicester C	W	1-0	1-0	—	Gascoigne [45]	20,635
5	13	A	Tottenham H	W	3-0	2-0	6	Ricard 2 [25, 32], Kinder [87]	30,437
6	19	H	Everton	D	2-2	2-0	7	Ricard 2 [27, 35]	34,563
7	26	A	Chelsea	L	0-2	0-0	12		34,814
8	Oct 3	H	Sheffield W	W	4-0	2-0	4	Beck 2 [27, 45], Ricard [49], Gascoigne [90]	34,163
9	17	H	Blackburn R	W	2-1	0-0	3	Ricard (pen) [83], Fleming [90]	34,413
10	24	A	Wimbledon	D	2-2	2-1	5	Mustoe [23], Ricard [37]	14,114
11	Nov 1	H	Nottingham F	D	1-1	1-0	4	Deane [22]	34,223
12	7	A	Southampton	D	3-3	0-0	4	Gascoigne [47], Lundekvam (og) [66], Festa [90]	15,202
13	14	A	Charlton Ath	D	1-1	0-1	7	Stamp [74]	19,906
14	21	H	Coventry C	W	2-0	0-0	7	Gordon [66], Ricard [83]	34,287
15	29	A	Arsenal	D	1-1	1-0	7	Deane [6]	38,075
16	Dec 6	A	Newcastle U	D	2-2	1-1	7	Townsend [13], Cooper [59]	34,629
17	12	H	West Ham U	W	1-0	1-0	4	Deane [40]	34,623
18	19	A	Manchester U	W	3-2	2-0	4	Ricard [23], Gordon [31], Deane [59]	55,152
19	26	H	Liverpool	L	1-3	1-2	6	Deane [32]	34,626
20	28	A	Derby Co	L	1-2	0-1	8	Beck [77]	32,726
21	Jan 9	H	Aston Villa	D	0-0	0-0	9		34,643
22	16	A	Leeds U	L	0-2	0-2	9		37,394
23	30	H	Leicester C	D	0-0	0-0	10		34,631
24	Feb 6	A	Liverpool	L	1-3	0-3	10	Stamp [86]	44,384
25	17	A	Everton	L	0-5	0-2	—		31,606
26	20	H	Tottenham H	D	0-0	0-0	11		34,687
27	27	A	Sheffield W	L	1-3	0-1	13	Mustoe [78]	24,534
28	Mar 14	H	Southampton	W	3-0	2-0	12	Beck [44], Ricard [45], Vickers [62]	33,387
29	20	A	Nottingham F	W	2-1	1-1	11	Ricard [30], Deane [87]	21,468
30	Apr 3	A	Blackburn R	D	0-0	0-0	11		27,482
31	5	H	Wimbledon	W	3-1	3-0	9	Ricard 2 [1, 29], Festa [8]	33,999
32	10	H	Charlton Ath	W	2-0	1-0	8	Ricard [35], Mustoe [60]	34,529
33	14	H	Chelsea	D	0-0	0-0	—		34,406
34	17	A	Coventry C	W	2-1	0-0	7	Kinder [64], Gordon [82]	19,228
35	24	H	Arsenal	L	1-6	0-3	7	Armstrong [87]	34,630
36	May 1	A	Newcastle U	D	1-1	0-0	7	Mustoe [60]	36,784
37	9	H	Manchester U	L	0-1	0-1	9		34,655
38	16	A	West Ham U	L	0-4	0-2	9		25,902

Final League Position: 9

GOALSCORERS

League (48): Ricard 15 (1 pen), Deane 6, Beck 5, Mustoe 4, Gascoigne 3, Gordon 3, Festa 2, Kinder 2, Stamp 2, Armstrong 1, Cooper 1, Fleming 1, Townsend 1, Vickers 1, own goal 1.
Worthington Cup (5): Ricard 3, Festa 1, Summerbell 1.
FA Cup (1): Townsend 1.

Schwarzer M 34	Stockdale R 17+2	Harrison C 3+1	Fleming C 12+2	Gordon D 38	Townsend A 35	Mustoe R 32+1	Gascoigne P 25+1	Stamp P 5+11	Merson P 3	Moore A 3+1	Maddison N 10+11	Beck M 13+14	Festa G 25	Ricard H 32+4	Cooper C 31+1	Kinder V —+5	Vickers S 30+1	Pallister G 26	Campbell A 1+7	Branca M —+1	Beresford M 4	Summerbell M 7+4	Deane B 24+2	Armstrong A —+6	O'Neill K 4+2	Baker S 1+1	Gavin J 2	Cummins M 1	Match No.
1	2	3	4	5	6	7[1]	8	9	10	11[2]	12	13																	1
1		3	4	5	6	7	8[1]	9	10	11[2]		12	2	13															2
1	2		3	6[2]	7	8	9[1]	10			11	5	12	4	13														3
1	12		3			7	8[2]			10	11	2	9[1]	5[1]	13	4	6	14											4
1			3	10	7	8[1]				11[2]	2	9[1]	5	12	4	6	13	14										5
1			3	10	7	8				11	2	9	5		4	6												6
1			3	10	7	8	12			11[1]	2	9	5		4	6												7
1			3	10	7	8				11	2	9[1]	5		4	6	12											8
1		2	3	10	7		12			11[1]	5	9	6		4				1	8[1]	13							9
		2	3	11[1]	7		12			13	5	9[1]	6		4				1	8	10							10
	12		2[1]	3	11	7	8[2]	13			5	9	6		4				1		10							11
		2	3	11	7	8	12				5	9[1]	6		4				1		10							12
1		2	3	11	7	8[1]	12			13	5	9	6		4						10[2]							13
1	2		3	8						12	11	5[1]	9	6	4					7	10							14
1		2	3	11	7	8[2]				13	12	9[1]	5		4	6				14	10[3]							15
1		2	3	11	7[2]	8	13				12	9	5		4	6					10[1]							16
1	2[2]		3	11	7	8	13				12	9[1]	5		4	6					10							17
1			3	11	7[2]		13	8[1]	13	2	9	5		4	6[1]						10							18
1		12	3	11[2]			8	14		7[3]	13	2	9	5		4	6					10							19
1	2[3]	12	3	11			8[1]	7[2]		14	13	6	9	5		4						10							20
1		2	3	11			8			7	12	5	9[1]		4	6						10							21
1		2	3			7	8[2]			11[1]	12	5	9	13	4	6						10							22
1		2	3	11	7[2]	8	13				12	5	9	4			6					10[1]							23
1			3	11[2]	7	8	12			13	9	2[1]		5	4	6						10							24
1	2		3	11	7	8[1]				13	9		12	5	4[3]	6	10[2]				14							25
1	2		3	10	7	8			11[1]		9[2]		12	5	4	6	13											26
1	2[1]	12	3	10	7	8[2]				13	11		9	5	4	6												27
1	2		3		7		8[1]			10	11	5	9[2]	6	4		13					12						28
1	2		3	11	7					8	12[2]	5	9[1]	6	4							10	13					29
1	2	11	3	4[2]		12				8[1]			9	5		6					7	10		13				30
1	2[1]		3	11[3]	7	8				13		5	9	4	12	6					14		10[2]					31
1	2		3	11	7	8[1]				12		5	9[2]	4		6						10[3]	13	14				32
1	2		3	11	7					12		5	9	4		6						10	8[1]					33
1			3	11	13					8		9[1]	5	12[2]	4	6[1]						10	14	7	2			34
1	2[1]		3	11	7					8[3]		9	5[2]	13	4	6					12	10	14					35
1	2		3	11	7							9[1]		4	6						8	10	12			5		36
1	2[2]		3	11	7							9		4	6	12					8	10			13	5[1]		37
1			3	5	7					14		9[2]		4	6	12					8	10[1]	13	11[3]			2	38

Worthington Cup

Second Round	Wycombe W	(h)	2-0	
		(a)	1-1	
Third Round	Everton	(h)	2-3	

FA Cup

Third Round	Manchester U	(a)	1-3

Division 2 **MILLWALL**

FOUNDATION

Formed in 1885 as Millwall Rovers by employees of Morton & Co, a jam and marmalade factory in West Ferry Road. The founders were predominantly Scotsmen. Their first headquarters was The Islanders pub in Tooke Street, Millwall. Their first trophy was the East End Cup in 1887.

Millwall Football & Athletic Company (1985) plc, The Den, Zampa Road, Bermondsey SE16 3LN.
Telephone: (0171) 232 1222.
Ticket Office: (0171) 231 9999.
Club Shop: (0171) 231 9845.
Fax: (0171) 231 3663.
Ground Capacity: 20,146 (all-seater).
Record Attendance: 20,093 v Arsenal, FA Cup 3rd rd, 10 January 1994.
Record Receipts: undisclosed.
Pitch Measurements: 100m × 68m.
Life President: Reg Burr.
Chairman: Theo Paphitis.
Directors: Reg Burr, Peter Mead, Steven Ring, Doug Woodward, David Sullivan.
Secretary: Yvonne Haines.
Joint Managers: Keith Stevens, Alan McLeary.
Reserve Team Coach: Steve Gritt.
Chief Scout: Ronnie Boyce.
Youth Development Officer and Senior Scout: Bob Pearson.
Assistant Youth Development Officer: Mick Beard.
Physio: Gerry Docherty.
Hon. Medical Officer: Dr. Charlotte Cowie.
Stadium Manager: Colin Sayer.
Sales and Promotions Manager: Mark Cole.

LATEST SEQUENCES

Longest Sequence of League Wins: 10, 10.3.28 – 25.4.28.
Longest Sequence of League Defeats: 11, 10.4.29 – 16.9.29.
Longest Sequence of League Draws: 5, 22.12.73 – 12.1.74.
Longest Sequence of Unbeaten League Matches: 19, 22.8.59 – 31.10.59.
Longest Sequence Without a League Win: 20, 26.12.89 – 5.5.90.

HONOURS

Football League: Division 1 best season: 3rd, 1993–94; Division 2 – Champions 1987–88; Division 3 (S) – Champions 1927–28, 1937–38; Runners-up 1952–53; Division 3 – Runners-up 1965–66, 1984–85; Division 4 – Champions 1961–62; Runners-up 1964–65.

FA Cup: Semi-final 1900, 1903, 1937 (first Division 3 side to reach semi-final).

Football League Cup: best season: 5th rd, 1974, 1977, 1995.

Football League Trophy: Winners 1983.

Auto Windscreens Shield: Runners-up 1999.

Colours
White with black trim.

Change Colours
Gold with navy blue trim.

Year Formed: 1885.

Turned Professional: 1893.

Ltd Co.: 1894.

Previous Names: 1885, Millwall Rovers; 1889, Millwall Athletic; 1985, Millwall Football & Athletic Company.

Club Nickname: 'The Lions'.

Previous Grounds: 1885, Glengall Road, Millwall; 1886, Back of 'Lord Nelson'; 1890, East Ferry Road; 1901, North Greenwich; 1910, The Den, Cold Blow Lane; 1993, The Den, Bermondsey.

First Football League Game: 28 August 1920, Division 3, v Bristol R (h) W 2–0 – Lansdale; Fort, Hodge; Voisey (1), Riddell, McAlpine; Waterall, Travers, Broad (1), Sutherland, Dempsey.

Record League Victory: 9–1 v Torquay U, Division 3 (S), 29 August 1927 – Lansdale; Tilling, Hill; Amos, Bryant (3), Graham; Chance, Hawkins (3), Landells (1), Phillips (2), Black. 9–1 v Coventry C, Division 3 (S), 19 November 1927 – Lansdale; Fort, Hill; Amos, Collins (1), Graham; Chance, Landells (4), Cock (2), Phillips (2), Black.

Record Cup Victory: 7–0 v Gateshead, FA Cup 2nd rd, 12 December 1936 – Yuill; Ted Smith, Inns; Brolly, Hancock, Forsyth; Thomas (1), Mangnall (1), Ken Burditt (2), McCartney (2), Thorogood (1).

Record Defeat: 1–9 v Aston Villa, FA Cup 4th rd, 28 January 1946.

Most League Points (2 for a win): 65, Division 3 (S), 1927–28 and Division 3, 1965–66.

Most League Points (3 for a win): 90, Division 3, 1984–85.

Most League Goals: 127, Division 3 (S), 1927–28.

Highest League Scorer in Season: Richard Parker, 37, Division 3 (S), 1926–27.

Most League Goals in Total Aggregate: Teddy Sheringham, 93, 1984–91.

Most League Goals in One Match: 5, Richard Parker v Norwich C, Division 3S, 28 August 1926.

Most Capped Player: Eamonn Dunphy, 22 (23), Republic of Ireland.

Most League Appearances: Barry Kitchener, 523, 1967–82.

Youngest League Player: David Mehmet, 16 years 163 days v Burnley, 14 May 1977.

Record Transfer Fee Received: £2,300,000 from Liverpool for Mark Kennedy, March 1995.

Record Transfer Fee Paid: £800,000 to Derby Co for Paul Goddard, December 1989.

Football League Record: 1920 Original Members of Division 3; 1921 Division 3 (S); 1928–34 Division 2; 1934–38 Division 3 (S); 1938–48 Division 2; 1948–58 Division 3 (S); 1958–62 Division 4; 1962–64 Division 3; 1964–65 Division 4; 1965–66 Division 3; 1966–75 Division 2; 1975–76 Division 3; 1976–79 Division 2; 1979–85 Division 3; 1985–88 Division 2; 1988–90 Division 1; 1990–92 Division 2; 1992–96 Division 1; 1996– Division 2.

MANAGERS

F. B. Kidd 1894–99 *(Hon. Treasurer/Manager)*
E. R. Stopher 1899–1900 *(Hon. Treasurer/Manager)*
George Saunders 1900–11 *(Hon. Treasurer/Manager)*
Herbert Lipsham 1911–19
Robert Hunter 1919–33
Bill McCracken 1933–36
Charlie Hewitt 1936–40
Bill Voisey 1940–44
Jack Cock 1944–48
Charlie Hewitt 1948–56
Ron Gray 1956–57
Jimmy Seed 1958–59
Reg Smith 1959–61
Ron Gray 1961–63
Billy Gray 1963–66
Benny Fenton 1966–74
Gordon Jago 1974–77
George Petchey 1978–80
Peter Anderson 1980–82
George Graham 1982–86
John Docherty 1986–90
Bob Pearson 1990
Bruce Rioch 1990–92
Mick McCarthy 1992–96
Jimmy Nicholl 1996–97
John Docherty 1997
Billy Bonds 1997–98
Keith Stevens May 1998–
   (then Joint Manager)
(plus Alan McLeary May 1999–)

TEN YEAR LEAGUE RECORD

		P	W	D	L	F	A	Pts	Pos
1988-89	Div 1	38	14	11	13	47	52	53	10
1989-90	Div 1	38	5	11	22	39	65	26	20
1990-91	Div 2	46	20	13	13	70	51	73	5
1991-92	Div 2	46	17	10	19	64	71	61	15
1992-93	Div 1	46	18	16	12	65	53	70	7
1993-94	Div 1	46	19	17	10	58	49	74	3
1994-95	Div 1	46	16	14	16	60	60	62	12
1995-96	Div 1	46	13	13	20	43	63	52	22
1996-97	Div 2	46	16	13	17	50	55	61	14
1997-98	Div 2	46	14	13	19	43	54	55	18

DID YOU KNOW ?

When Millwall won 6–1 at Manchester City on 17 September 1938, they were one down in eight minutes. In the second half they scored two goals in a minute, three in seven and five in 27 minutes.

MILLWALL 1998–99 LEAGUE RECORD

Match No.	Date	Venue	Opponents	Result	H/T Score	Lg. Pos.	Goalscorers	Attendance
1	Aug 8	A	Wigan Ath	W 1-0	1-0	—	Shaw [16]	4285
2	15	H	Wycombe W	W 2-1	0-0	5	Sadlier [46], Fitzgerald [90]	7492
3	22	A	Bournemouth	L 0-3	0-0	6		6956
4	29	H	Macclesfield T	D 0-0	0-0	10		5997
5	Sept 1	A	Burnley	L 1-2	0-2	—	Shaw [88]	8526
6	9	H	Lincoln C	W 2-0	0-0	—	Shaw [50], Neill [64]	4424
7	12	A	Stoke C	L 0-1	0-0	14		12,307
8	19	H	Northampton T	W 2-1	0-1	10	Harris [49], Cahill [61]	5997
9	26	A	Notts Co	L 1-3	1-2	14	Neill [2]	5016
10	29	H	Manchester C	D 1-1	0-0	—	Harris [46]	12,726
11	Oct 3	H	Chesterfield	D 0-0	0-0	14		5178
12	10	A	Blackpool	W 3-2	2-1	11	Hughes (og) [10], Shaw 2 [25, 49]	5295
13	17	H	Fulham	L 0-1	0-0	12		11,876
14	21	H	York C	W 3-1	1-0	—	Sadlier [13], Harris [61], Neill [69]	4249
15	24	A	Wrexham	D 0-0	0-0	7		2766
16	31	H	Oldham Ath	D 1-1	0-1	9	Shaw [58]	5609
17	Nov 7	A	Walsall	L 0-3	0-2	11		4237
18	10	A	Preston NE	W 1-0	1-0	—	Shaw [17]	10,228
19	21	H	Bristol R	D 1-1	1-0	10	Harris [11]	5755
20	28	A	Colchester U	D 0-0	0-0	10		4476
21	Dec 12	H	Reading	D 1-1	1-0	12	Neill [33]	6058
22	19	A	Luton T	W 2-1	1-0	8	Harris [45], Neill [82]	5939
23	26	A	Bournemouth	L 1-2	0-1	9	Harris [51]	7807
24	29	H	Gillingham	D 1-1	0-1	—	Neill [82]	9221
25	Jan 9	H	Wigan Ath	W 3-1	1-0	10	Nethercott [45], Sadlier [76], Shaw [83]	5625
26	16	A	Wycombe W	W 1-0	0-0	9	Cahill [79]	5510
27	23	H	Burnley	L 0-1	0-1	9	Sadlier [86]	7407
28	26	A	Macclesfield T	W 2-0	0-0	—	Harris 2 [62, 90]	1998
29	30	H	Gillingham	D 3-3	0-1	9	Cahill [59], Harris 2 (1 pen) [67, 75 (p)]	10,442
30	Feb 6	A	Manchester C	L 0-3	0-0	9		29,862
31	13	A	Lincoln C	L 0-2	0-1	9		4613
32	20	H	Stoke C	W 2-0	1-0	9	Harris [39], Cahill [65]	7855
33	27	A	Northampton T	W 2-1	0-0	8	Nethercott [59], Sadlier [87]	5490
34	Mar 2	A	Chesterfield	L 1-2	0-0	—	Dolan [57]	3372
35	6	H	Notts Co	L 1-3	0-1	10	Hockton [82]	6042
36	13	H	Walsall	L 1-2	1-2	11	Harris [45]	6248
37	20	A	Oldham Ath	W 1-0	1-0	11	Cahill [25]	4565
38	27	H	Wrexham	W 3-0	1-0	10	Grant [10], Harris 2 [79, 89]	7390
39	Apr 5	H	Blackpool	W 1-0	1-0	9	Harris [8]	6672
40	10	A	York C	L 1-2	0-0	9	Shaw [71]	2572
41	14	H	Colchester U	W 2-0	2-0	—	Grant 2 (1 pen) [1, 16 (p)]	4686
42	21	A	Fulham	L 1-4	0-2	—	Shaw [75]	11,266
43	24	H	Preston NE	D 2-2	0-0	10	Cahill [84], Ifill [90]	6016
44	27	A	Bristol R	L 0-3	0-1	—		5755
45	May 1	A	Reading	L 0-2	0-2	10		7943
46	8	H	Luton T	L 0-1	0-1	10		8494

Final League Position: 10

GOALSCORERS

League (52): Harris 15 (1 pen), Shaw 10, Cahill 6, Neill 6, Sadlier 5, Grant 3 (1 pen), Nethercott 2, Dolan 1, Fitzgerald 1, Hockton 1, Ifill 1, own goal 1.
Worthington Cup (1): Shaw 1.
FA Cup (0).

Spink N 22	Lavin G 38	Stuart J 33+2	Bowry B 22+3	Law B 5	Fitzgerald S 32	Neill L 33+2	Newman R 22+2	Sadlier R 18+13	Shaw P 31+3	Carter J 16	McDougald J —+1	Bircham M 20+8	Savage D —+2	Reid S 25	Cahill T 34+2	Harris N 37+2	Roberts T 8	Ryan R 22+4	Roche S 3	Nethercott S 35+2	Grant K 4+12	Hockton D 1+7	Stevens K 1+2	McLeary A 2	Smith P 5	Ifill P 12+3	Roberts B 11	Dolan J 9	Cook A 1+1	Bull R 1	Bubb B 1+2	Hicks M —+1	Odunsi L 2+1	Match No.
1	2	3	4	5	6	7[1]	8	9	10	11	12																							1
1	2	3	4	5	6	7[2]	8	9	10	11[1]		13	12																					2
1	2	3	4	5	6		8[2]	9[3]	10	11				12	7[1]	13	14																	3
		3	4	5	6			9	10	11[1]				2	12	8		1	7															4
		3	4	5[2]	6	12			10	11				2	8	9		1	7[1]	13														5
1	2		4[1]		6		11		10	7[2]				12	8	9			3	5		13												6
1	2		4		6	7			10	11				12	8[1]	9			3	5														7
1	2				6		11	4	12	10					7	8		9[1]	3	5														8
1	2	12			6		11[1]	4	10[2]	7					8	9			3	5	13													9
1	2				6		11	4	10	7					8	9[1]			3	5	12													10
1					6		11	4	10	7				2	8	9[1]			3	5	12													11
	2	3			6		11	4	10	7				12	8[1]	9	1			5														12
	2	3			6		11		10	7[1]		4			8[2]	9	1	12		5	13													13
	2	3			6		11		10[2]	7[3]		4			8	9	1	12		5[1]	13	14												14
	2	3			6		11[1]		10	7		4			8	9[2]	1	12		5	13													15
	2				6		11		10		12	4			7	8	9	1	3[1]	5														16
	2	3[1]	12		6			4[3]	10	11	13				8	9[2]	14	1		5	7													17
1	2	3	4[1]		6		11	9	10						8	7				5			12											18
1	2	3	4[1]		6	12			10	7					8	9	11[2]			5	13													19
1	2	3			6	12			10	8					7	4	9	11[1]		5														20
1	2[1]				6		11	8	10						7	4	9		3		12		5											21
1	2	5			6		11	8[2]	10						7[1]	4	9		3		12	13												22
1		5	8		6		11	12	10						2[1]	7[2]	4	9		3	13													23
	2	5	8		6		11	12	10						7[1]	4	9[2]		3	13		1												24
1	2	3	8		6		11	9	10		12				7[2]	4[1]	13			5														25
1	2	6	8				11	9[1]	10						7	4	12		3	5														26
1	2[1]	6	8				11	12	10						7	4	9		3	5														27
1	2	6	8				11	12	10[1]						7	4	9		3	5														28
1	2	6	8				11	12	10[2]	13					7	4	9[1]		3	5														29
1	2		8		6		11	12	10						7[1]	4	9		3	5														30
	2	12	8		6[1]		11	13	10					4			9	3[2]		5						7	1							31
	2	3	8				11		10		12				7[1]	4	9[2]			5						1	13	6						32
	2		8				11		10						7	4	9[1]	3		5						1	12	6						33
	2	3	8				11		10						7[1]	4	9			5						1	12	6						34
	2	6					11	12		8					7[2]	4	9	3[1]		5	13					1	10							35
	3						11[2]	8	10			2			4	9				5	13	12				7[1]	1	6						36
	2	3	12				11	8	10						4					5	9					7[1]	1	6						37
	2	3					8							11	4	9				5	10[1]					7	1	6	12					38
	2						11[1]	8		12		3			10	4	9			5						7	1	6						39
	2	3						8		10[1]				11	4	9				5	12					7	1	6						40
1		4	5							2							9	6		10	9	6				11	3	7[1]	12	8				41
	2[3]	3						10[1]	12	8				11	4	9				5	13					7	1	6[2]				14		42
		3	12[2]		6		8[1]	13	10			2			11	4	9			5						7	1							43
	2	3			6			12	13	10				11	4	9[2]				5	14					7[3]	1					8[1]		44
	2	3			6		8	12	10[1]			4		11		9				5						7[2]	1				13			45
		3			6	2	8	10				4		11[1]		9				5	12					7[2]	1				13			46

Worthington Cup
First Round   Birmingham C   (a)   0-2
                                                             (h)   1-1

FA Cup
First Round   Swansea C   (a)   0-3

FA Premiership   **NEWCASTLE UNITED**

FOUNDATION

It stemmed from a newly formed club called Stanley in 1881.
In October 1882 they changed their name to Newcastle East End
to avoid confusion with two other local clubs, Stanley Nops and
Stanley Albion. Shortly afterwards another club Rosewood
merged with them. Newcastle West End had been formed in
August 1882 and they played on a pitch which was part of the
Town Moor. Moved to Brandling Park 1885 and St James' Park
1886 (home of Newcastle Rangers). West End went out of
existence after a bad run and the remaining committee men
invited East End to move to St James' Park. They accepted and,
at a meeting in Bath Lane Hall in 1892, changed their name to
Newcastle United.

St James' Park, Newcastle-upon-Tyne NE1 4ST.
Telephone: (0191) 201 8400. *Fax:* (0191) 201 8600.
Lottery Office: (0191) 201 8502. *Commercial Department:* (0191) 201 8422.
Ticket Office Hotline: (0191) 261 1571. *Mail Order:* (0990) 501892.
Football in the Community Scheme: (0191) 261 9715. *Clubcall:* 0891 121590.
Clubcall Main Line: 0891 121190. *Ticket Line:* 0891 121590. *Club Shop:* (0191) 201 8426.
Travel Club: (0191) 201 8550. *Junior Magpies:* (0191) 201 8472. *Corporate Hospitality:* (0191) 201 8424.
Photographic Dept: (0191) 235 3906.
Ground Capacity: 36,834.
Record Attendance: 68,386 v Chelsea, Division 1,
3 September 1930.
Record Receipts: £744,544 v Monaco, UEFA Cup
quarter-final, 4 March 1997.
Pitch Measurements: 114m × 74m.
President: Sir John Hall.
Chairman: W. F. Shepherd.
Chief Executive: A. O. Fletcher.
Deputy Chairman: D. S. Hall.
Directors: R. Jones, A. O. Fletcher, L. Wheatley.
Manager: Ruud Gullit.
Assistant Manager: Steve Clarke.
Coaches: John Carver, Tommy Craig, Terry Gennoe.
Physios: Derek Wright, Paul Ferris.
Director of Football Administration: Russell Cushing.
Director of Marketing: Alec King.
Operations Manager: P. W. Stevens.
Assistant Secretary: Tony Toward.
Academy Director: Alan Irvine.

HONOURS

FA Premier League: Runners-up
1995–96, 1996–97; *Football League:*
Division 1 – Champions 1904–05,
1906–07, 1908–09, 1926–27, 1992–93;
Division 2 – Champions 1964–65;
Runners-up 1897–98, 1947–48.
FA Cup: Winners 1910, 1924, 1932,
1951, 1952, 1955; Runners-up 1905,
1906, 1908, 1911, 1974, 1998, 1999.
Football League Cup: Runners-up
1976.
Texaco Cup: Winners 1974, 1975.
European Competitions: European
Cup: 1997–98. *European Fairs Cup:*
1968–69 (winners), 1969–70, 1970–71.
UEFA Cup: 1977–78, 1994–95,
1996–97. *European Cup Winners' Cup:*
1998–99. *Anglo-Italian Cup:* Winners
1972–73.

LATEST SEQUENCES

Longest Sequence of League Wins: 13, 25.4.92 – 18.10.92.
Longest Sequence of League Defeats: 10, 23.8.77 – 15.10.77.
Longest Sequence of League Draws: 4, 20.1.90 – 24.2.90.
Longest Sequence of Unbeaten League Matches: 14,
22.4.50 – 30.9.50.
Longest Sequence Without a League Win: 21, 14.1.78 – 23.8.78.

Colours
Black and white striped shirts, black shorts, white stockings.

Change Colours
White shirts with teal half sleeve, white shorts, white stockings.

Year Formed: 1881.

Turned Professional: 1889.

Ltd Co.: 1890.

Previous Names: 1881, Stanley; 1882, Newcastle East End; 1892, Newcastle United.

Club Nickname: 'Magpies'.

Previous Grounds: 1881, South Byker; 1886, Chillingham Road, Heaton, 1892, St James' Park.

First Football League Game: 2 September 1893, Division 2, v Royal Arsenal (a) D 2–2 – Ramsay; Jeffery, Miller; Crielly, Graham, McKane; Bowman, Crate (1), Thompson, Sorley (1), Wallace. Graham and not Crate scored according to some reports.

Record League Victory: 13–0 v Newport Co, Division 2, 5 October 1946 – Garbutt; Cowell, Graham; Harvey, Brennan, Wright; Milburn (2), Bentley (1), Wayman (4), Shackleton (6), Pearson.

Record Cup Victory: 9–0 v Southport (at Hillsborough), FA Cup 4th rd, 1 February 1932 – McInroy; Nelson, Fairhurst; McKenzie, Davidson, Weaver (1); Boyd (1), Jimmy Richardson (3), Cape (2), McMenemy (1), Lang (1).

Record Defeat: 0–9 v Burton Wanderers, Division 2, 15 April 1895.

Most League Points (2 for a win): 57, Division 2, 1964–65.

Most League Points (3 for a win): 96, Division 1, 1992–93.

Most League Goals: 98, Division 1, 1951–52.

Highest League Scorer in Season: Hughie Gallacher, 36, Division 1, 1926–27.

Most League Goals in Total Aggregate: Jackie Milburn, 177, 1946–57.

Most League Goals in One Match: 6, Len Shackleton v Newport Co, Division 2, 5 October 1946.

Most Capped Player: Alf McMichael, 40, Northern Ireland.

Most League Appearances: Jim Lawrence, 432, 1904–22.

Youngest League Player: Steve Watson, 16 years 223 days v Wolverhampton W, 10 November 1990.

Record Transfer Fee Received: £8,000,000 from Liverpool for Dieter Hamann, July 1999.

Record Transfer Fee Paid: £15,000,000 to Blackburn R for Alan Shearer, July 1996.

Football League Record: 1893 Elected to Division 2; 1898–1934 Division 1; 1934–48 Division 2; 1948–61 Division 1; 1961–65 Division 2; 1965–78 Division 1; 1978–84 Division 2; 1984–89 Division 1; 1989–92 Division 2; 1992–93 Division 1; 1993– FA Premier League.

MANAGERS

Frank Watt 1895–32
  (Secretary-Manager)
Andy Cunningham 1930–35
Tom Mather 1935–39
Stan Seymour 1939–47
  (Hon. Manager)
George Martin 1947–50
Stan Seymour 1950–54
  (Hon. Manager)
Duggie Livingstone 1954–56
Stan Seymour 1956–58
  (Hon. Manager)
Charlie Mitten 1958–61
Norman Smith 1961–62
Joe Harvey 1962–75
Gordon Lee 1975–77
Richard Dinnis 1977
Bill McGarry 1977–80
Arthur Cox 1980–84
Jack Charlton 1984
Willie McFaul 1985–88
Jim Smith 1988–91
Ossie Ardiles 1991–92
Kevin Keegan 1992–97
Kenny Dalglish 1997–98
Ruud Gullit August 1998–

TEN YEAR LEAGUE RECORD

		P	W	D	L	F	A	Pts	Pos
1988-89	Div 1	38	7	10	21	32	63	31	20
1989-90	Div 2	46	22	14	10	80	55	80	3
1990-91	Div 2	46	14	17	15	49	56	59	11
1991-92	Div 2	46	13	13	20	66	84	52	20
1992-93	Div 1	46	29	9	8	92	38	96	1
1993-94	PR Lge	42	23	8	11	82	41	77	3
1994-95	PR Lge	42	20	12	10	67	47	72	6
1995-96	PR Lge	38	24	6	8	66	37	78	2
1996-97	PR Lge	38	19	11	8	73	40	68	2
1997-98	PR Lge	38	11	11	16	35	44	44	13

DID YOU KNOW ?

Newcastle United scored seven goals in 25 minutes in an FA Cup fourth round second replay against Southport at Hillsborough on 1 February 1932 to win 9–0, amazingly after two 1–1 draws. They went on to win the cup.

NEWCASTLE UNITED 1998–99 LEAGUE RECORD

Match No.	Date	Venue	Opponents	Result	H/T Score	Lg. Pos.	Goalscorers	Attendance
1	Aug 15	H	Charlton Ath	D 0-0	0-0	—		36,719
2	22	A	Chelsea	D 1-1	1-1	12	Andersson [43]	34,795
3	30	H	Liverpool	L 1-4	1-4	16	Guivarc'h [28]	36,740
4	Sept 9	A	Aston Villa	L 0-1	0-0	—		39,241
5	12	H	Southampton	W 4-0	2-0	14	Shearer 2 (1 pen) [8, 38 (p)], Marshall (og) [88], Ketsbaia [90]	36,454
6	19	A	Coventry C	W 5-1	3-1	9	Dabizas [14], Shearer 2 [42, 90], Speed [43], Glass [58]	22,639
7	26	H	Nottingham F	W 2-0	1-0	4	Shearer 2 (1 pen) [11, 89 (p)]	36,760
8	Oct 4	A	Arsenal	L 0-3	0-2	10		38,102
9	17	H	Derby Co	W 2-1	2-0	6	Dabizas [13], Glass [17]	36,750
10	24	A	Tottenham H	L 0-2	0-1	7		36,047
11	31	H	West Ham U	L 0-3	0-0	11		36,744
12	Nov 8	A	Manchester U	D 0-0	0-0	13		55,174
13	14	H	Sheffield W	D 1-1	1-0	13	Dalglish [4]	36,698
14	23	A	Everton	L 0-1	0-1	—		30,357
15	28	H	Wimbledon	W 3-1	1-1	11	Solano [38], Ferguson 2 [59, 90]	36,623
16	Dec 6	A	Middlesbrough	D 2-2	1-1	13	Charvet [38], Dabizas [83]	34,629
17	12	A	Blackburn R	D 0-0	0-0	15		27,569
18	19	H	Leicester C	W 1-0	0-0	10	Glass [66]	36,718
19	26	H	Leeds U	L 0-3	0-1	12		36,759
20	28	A	Liverpool	L 2-4	1-3	13	Solano [29], Andersson [56]	44,605
21	Jan 9	H	Chelsea	L 0-1	0-1	13		36,711
22	17	A	Charlton Ath	D 2-2	1-0	14	Ketsbaia [13], Solano [55]	20,043
23	30	H	Aston Villa	W 2-1	2-0	13	Shearer [4], Ketsbaia [27]	36,766
24	Feb 6	A	Leeds U	W 1-0	0-0	12	Solano [63]	40,202
25	17	H	Coventry C	W 4-1	1-1	—	Shearer 2 [19, 75], Speed [55], Saha [58]	36,352
26	20	A	Southampton	L 1-2	0-2	10	Hamann [86]	15,244
27	28	H	Arsenal	D 1-1	0-1	11	Hamann [77]	36,708
28	Mar 10	A	Nottingham F	W 2-1	1-1	—	Shearer (pen) [45], Hamann [73]	22,852
29	13	H	Manchester U	L 1-2	1-1	11	Solano [16]	36,776
30	20	A	West Ham U	L 0-2	0-1	12		25,997
31	Apr 3	A	Derby Co	W 4-3	3-2	9	Speed 2 [11, 24], Ketsbaia [39], Solano [60]	32,039
32	5	H	Tottenham H	D 1-1	0-0	10	Ketsbaia [78]	36,655
33	17	H	Everton	L 1-3	0-2	11	Shearer (pen) [82]	36,775
34	21	A	Sheffield W	D 1-1	1-0	—	Shearer (pen) [45]	21,545
35	24	A	Wimbledon	D 1-1	1-1	12	Shearer [18]	21,325
36	May 1	H	Middlesbrough	D 1-1	0-0	12	Shearer (pen) [64]	36,784
37	8	A	Leicester C	L 0-2	0-2	12		21,125
38	May 16	H	Blackburn R	D 1-1	0-1	13	Hamann [51]	36,623

Final League Position: 13

GOALSCORERS

League (48): Shearer 14 (6 pens), Solano 6, Ketsbaia 5, Hamann 4, Speed 4, Dabizas 3, Glass 3, Andersson 2, Ferguson 2, Charvet 1, Dalglish 1, Guivarc'h 1, Saha 1, own goal 1.
Worthington Cup (2): Dalglish 1, Shearer 1.
FA Cup (12): Shearer 5, Ketsbaia 3, Georgiadis 1, Hamann 1, Saha 1, Speed 1.

Given S 31	Watson S 7	Pistone A 2+1	Dabizas N 25+5	Charvet L 30+1	Pearce S 12	Lee R 20+6	Hamann D 22+1	Shearer A 29+1	Andersson A 11+4	Speed G 34+4	Barnes J —+1	Barton W 17+7	Ketsbaia T 14+12	Albert P 3+3	Solano N 24+5	Guivarc'h S 2+2	Serrant C 3+1	Glass S 18+4	Gillespie K 5+2	Dalglish P 6+5	Batty D 6+2	Griffin A 14	Hughes A 12+2	Georgiadis G 7+3	Brady G 3+6	Harper S 7+1	Howey S 14	Ferguson D 7	Domi D 14	Saha L 5+6	Maric S 9+1	McClen J 1	Beharall D 4	Match No.
1	2	3	4^1	5	6	7	8	9	10^3	11	12^2	13	14																					1
1	2	3^1	4	5	6	7	8	9	10^2	11					12	13																		2
1	2^1	12		5	6	7	8^3	9		11		13		4	10	3^2	14																	3
1	2		5	3		7		9	10^1	11		12			6	4^2	13	8																4
1	2		5	3		7		9	10^2	11^1		12	8	6	4	13		8																5
1	2		4	5	3	7		9		12		13			8^1	10^3		6	11^2	14														6
1	2^1		4	5	3	7		9		11		12	10^2	8^3				6	11^2	14	13	14												7
1			4	5	3			9		11			10^2	12	8			6^1		13	7	2												8
1			4	5	3	7		9		12			13		6			11^2	8	2														9
1				5	6	7		9		12				8	13	3	11^1		10^2	4	2													10
1	12		4	5	3			9		11			13		10^2			6^1	14	7^3	8	2												11
1			4	5			6^1	9		12					11				10	8	3	2	7											12
1			5			7	4^1	9^2	13	11		2					14		8	10	12	3^5	6											13
1			4	5		7	12		9	11		2^1	13		3^2			8	10^3	6				14										14
1^9			5			8		9	11	2				12	6^1	7			3			15	4	10										15
	12	5		7			10^3	11	2^1				6^2		13	8	14		3				1	4	9									16
	12	5		8			10^2	11	2	13			6		7^3			3^1	14				1	4	9									17
1		4	3	7			12	9	11			2	10^1		6					8			5											18
1		4	3	7			9		11			2^2	12		6				13	8^1			5	10										19
1		12	2	3			8	9	13	11					6^1			7^3		4	14		5	10^2										20
1		2				12	8	9	10^2	11					6^1			7		4			5		3	13								21
		4	12					9		11			2	10^2	6^3			13		14	8	7^1	5	3										22
1		4					8	9	12	11			2	10^1	6^2			7			13		5	3										23
1		4					8		12	11			2	10	6			7^2		3		13	5		9^1									24
1		4	2				8	9		11^2		13	12		6			7^3			14		5	3	10^1									25
1		4	2				12	8	9	11			10		6^1						7		5	3										26
1		4	2				12	8	9	11			13		6^2						7^1		5	3	10									27
1		12	4				13	8	9	11^1		2	14								6		5^1		3	10^3	7							28
1		4	5				12	8	9	11		2^1	10^2		6						7^1			3	13	14								29
1		4	5				12		9	11			13		6			2	8^1				3	10	7^2									30
1		4	5			7			8				10		6^2			3	2	13			11	12	9^1									31
1		4	5					8		12	10		6					3^1	2	13			11	14	9^3	7^2								32
1				7	4	9		11		3	10^1		12					2	5					13	8^2		6							33
	4			7^2	6	9^1		11		3	10		12					2	5	13	1				8									34
1	4				8	9	10	11			6							2					3		7		5							35
	4			7	6	9		11		2	13		12						1				10^3	3	8^1		5							36
	4			7	8	9		11		2	12		6^2		13				1				10^1	3			5							37
	4			7^1	8			11		3	10^2		6		12							2	5		1			13	9					38

Worthington Cup

Third Round	Tranmere R	(a)	1-0	
Fourth Round	Blackburn R	(h)	1-1	

FA Cup

Third Round	Crystal Palace	(h)	2-1
Fourth Round	Bradford C	(h)	3-0
Fifth Round	Blackburn R	(h)	0-0
		(a)	1-0
Sixth Round	Everton	(h)	4-1
Semi-Final	Tottenham H		2-0
	(at Old Trafford)		
Final	Manchester U		0-2
	(at Wembley)		

Division 3   **NORTHAMPTON TOWN**

FOUNDATION

Formed in 1897 by school teachers connected with the
Northampton and District Elementary Schools' Association, they
survived a financial crisis at the end of their first year when they
were £675 in the red and became members of the Midland League
– a fast move indeed for a new club. They achieved Southern
League membership in 1901.

Sixfields Stadium, Upton Way, Northampton NN5 5QA.

Telephone: (01604) 757773.

Fax: (01604) 751613/754960.

Website: http://www.ntfc.co.uk.

Email: secretary@ntfc.co.uk.

Ticket Office: (01604) 588338.

Soccer Line: 0930 555970.

Ground Capacity: 7653 (all seated).

Record Attendance: (at County Ground): 24,523 v Fulham, Division 1, 23 April 1966.
(at Sixfields Stadium): 7557 v Manchester C, Division 2, 26 September 1998.

Record Receipts (at Sixfields): £102,979 v Tottenham H, Worthington Cup 3rd rd, 27 October 1998.

Pitch Measurements: 116yd × 72yd.

Chairman: B. J. Stonhill.

Directors: B. Hancock, D. Kerr, C. Smith, Cllr. T. Clarke MP, P. Randall.

Secretary: Norman Howells.

Company Secretary: B. J. Stonhill.

Manager: Ian Atkins.

Coach: Kevin Wilson.

Physio: Dennis Casey.

Commercial Manager: Jenny Ball.

Stadium Manager: Geoff Harvey.

LATEST SEQUENCES

Longest Sequence of League Wins: 8, 27.8.60 – 19.9.60.

Longest Sequence of League Defeats: 8, 26.10.35 –
21.12.35.

Longest Sequence of League Draws: 6, 18.9.83 – 15.10.83.

Longest Sequence of Unbeaten League Matches: 21,
27.9.86 – 6.2.87.

Longest Sequence Without a League Win: 18, 26.3.69 –
20.9.69.

HONOURS

Football League: Division 1 best
season: 21st, 1965–66; Division 2 –
Runners-up 1964–65; Division 3 –
Champions 1962–63; Promoted from
Division 3 1996–97 (play-offs);
Division 3 (S) – Runners-up 1927–28,
1949–50; Division 4 – Champions
1986–87; Runners-up 1975–76.

FA Cup: best season: 5th rd, 1934,
1950, 1970.

Football League Cup: best season:
5th rd, 1965, 1967.

Colours
Claret with white shirts, white shorts, white stockings.

Change Colours
Orange and black shirts, black shorts, black stockings.

Year Formed: 1897.

Turned Professional: 1901.

Ltd Co.: 1901.

Previous Ground: 1897, County Ground; 1994, Sixfields Stadium.

Club Nickname: 'The Cobblers'.

First Football League Game: 28 August 1920, Division 3, v Grimsby T (a) L 0–2 – Thorpe; Sproston, Hewison; Jobey, Tomkins, Pease; Whitworth, Lockett, Thomas, Freeman, MacKechnie.

Record League Victory: 10–0 v Walsall, Division 3 (S), 5 November 1927 – Hammond; Watson, Jeffs; Allen, Brett, Odell; Daley, Smith (3), Loasby (3), Hoten (1), Wells (3).

Record Cup Victory: 10–0 v Sutton T, FA Cup prel rd, 7 December 1907 – Cooch; Drennan, Lloyd Davies, Tirrell (1), McCartney, Hickleton, Badenock (3), Platt (3), Lowe (1), Chapman (2), McDiarmid.

Record Defeat: 0–11 v Southampton, Southern League, 28 December 1901.

Most League Points (2 for a win): 68, Division 4, 1975–76.

Most League Points (3 for a win): 99, Division 4, 1986–87.

Most League Goals: 109, Division 3, 1962–63 and Division 3 (S), 1952–53.

Highest League Scorer in Season: Cliff Holton, 36, Division 3, 1961–62.

Most League Goals in Total Aggregate: Jack English, 135, 1947–60.

Most League Goals in One Match: 5, Ralph Hoten v Crystal Palace, Division 3S, 27 October 1928.

Most Capped Player: E. Lloyd Davies, 12 (16), Wales.

Most League Appearances: Tommy Fowler, 521, 1946–61.

Youngest League Player: Adrian Mann, 16 years 297 days v Bury, 5 May 1984.

Record Transfer Fee Received: £265,000 from Watford for Richard Hill, July 1987.

Record Transfer Fee Paid: £120,000 to Hartlepool U for Steve Howard, February 1999.

Football League Record: 1920 Original Member of Division 3; 1921 Division 3 (S); 1958–61 Division 4; 1961–63 Division 3; 1963–65 Division 2; 1965–66 Division 1; 1966–67 Division 2; 1967–69 Division 3; 1969–76 Division 4; 1976–77 Division 3; 1977–87 Division 4; 1987–90 Division 3; 1990–92 Division 4; 1992–97 Division 3; 1997–99 Division 2; 1999– Division 3.

MANAGERS

Arthur Jones 1897–1907
(Secretary-Manager)
Herbert Chapman 1907–12
Walter Bull 1912–13
Fred Lessons 1913–19
Bob Hewison 1920–25
Jack Tresadern 1925–30
Jack English 1931–35
Syd Puddefoot 1935–37
Warney Cresswell 1937–39
Tom Smith 1939–49
Bob Dennison 1949–54
Dave Smith 1954–59
David Bowen 1959–67
Tony Marchi 1967–68
Ron Flowers 1968–69
Dave Bowen 1969–72
(continued as General Manager and Secretary to 1985 when joined the board)
Billy Baxter 1972–73
Bill Dodgin Jnr 1973–76
Pat Crerand 1976–77
Bill Dodgin Jnr 1977
John Petts 1977–78
Mike Keen 1978–79
Clive Walker 1979–80
Bill Dodgin Jnr 1980–82
Clive Walker 1982–84
Tony Barton 1984–85
Graham Carr 1985–90
Theo Foley 1990–92
Phil Chard 1992–93
John Barnwell 1993–95
Ian Atkins January 1995–

TEN YEAR LEAGUE RECORD

		P	W	D	L	F	A	Pts	Pos
1988-89	Div 3	46	16	6	24	66	76	54	20
1989-90	Div 3	46	11	14	21	51	68	47	22
1990-91	Div 4	46	18	13	15	57	58	67	10
1991-92	Div 4	42	11	13	18	46	57	46	16
1992-93	Div 3	42	11	8	23	48	74	41	20
1993-94	Div 3	42	9	11	22	44	66	38	22
1994-95	Div 3	42	10	14	18	45	67	44	17
1995-96	Div 3	46	18	13	15	51	44	67	11
1996-97	Div 3	46	20	12	14	67	44	72	4
1997-98	Div 2	46	18	17	11	52	37	71	4

DID YOU KNOW ?

In 1936 Northampton Town signed Jack Rawlings a winger from West Bromwich Albion. His father Archie, a wing-half, had played for the Cobblers in their Southern League days originally from the tender age of 16.

NORTHAMPTON TOWN 1998–99 LEAGUE RECORD

Match No.	Date	Venue	Opponents	Result	H/T Score	Lg. Pos.	Goalscorers	Attendance
1	Aug 8	H	Stoke C	L	1-3	1-1	—	Corazzin [17]	6661
2	15	A	Walsall	D	0-0	0-0	18		4360
3	22	H	Notts Co	D	1-1	0-0	21	Warburton [90]	6141
4	29	A	Wrexham	L	0-1	0-0	22		3534
5	31	H	Lincoln C	D	0-0	0-0	22		5964
6	Sept 5	A	Blackpool	L	1-2	1-0	22	Corazzin (pen) [16]	4017
7	8	A	Gillingham	W	3-2	1-1	—	Hunter [17], Corazzin [54], Spedding [81]	4897
8	12	H	Oldham Ath	D	1-1	0-1	20	Freestone [56]	5210
9	19	A	Millwall	L	1-2	1-0	20	Sampson [31]	5997
10	26	H	Manchester C	D	2-2	1-0	19	Peer [30], Corazzin [64]	7557
11	Oct 3	A	Wigan Ath	L	0-1	0-0	22		4396
12	10	H	Bristol R	W	3-1	2-1	19	Heggs [30], Corazzin (pen) [44], Hunt [52]	6023
13	17	A	Bournemouth	D	1-1	0-1	19	Hodgson [49]	6362
14	20	A	Luton T	L	0-1	0-1	—		6087
15	24	H	Preston NE	D	1-1	0-1	21	Hunt [90]	6085
16	31	A	Macclesfield T	W	1-0	1-0	19	Corazzin [18]	3201
17	Nov 7	H	Wycombe W	D	1-1	1-1	19	Corazzin (pen) [2]	6248
18	10	A	Colchester U	L	0-1	0-0	—		3597
19	21	H	Reading	L	0-1	0-0	21		5970
20	28	A	York C	D	1-1	0-0	21	Corazzin (pen) [61]	2656
21	Dec 12	H	Chesterfield	W	1-0	0-0	20	Howey [71]	5282
22	19	A	Burnley	W	2-0	0-0	18	Wilkinson [71], Corazzin [81]	8783
23	26	A	Notts Co	L	1-3	0-3	20	Howey [72]	6131
24	28	H	Fulham	D	1-1	0-0	18	Freestone [68]	7315
25	Jan 9	A	Stoke C	L	1-3	0-0	18	Howey [90]	11,180
26	23	A	Lincoln C	L	0-1	0-1	20		4608
27	30	A	Fulham	L	0-2	0-1	21		11,641
28	Feb 6	H	Blackpool	D	0-0	0-0	20		5592
29	13	H	Gillingham	L	0-1	0-0	21		5981
30	20	A	Oldham Ath	W	1-0	1-0	21	Corazzin (pen) [10]	4752
31	23	H	Walsall	L	0-1	0-0	—		5631
32	27	H	Millwall	L	1-2	0-0	22	Corazzin [80]	5490
33	Mar 2	H	Wrexham	L	0-2	0-0	—		4710
34	6	A	Manchester C	D	0-0	0-0	22		27,999
35	13	A	Wycombe W	W	2-1	1-0	22	Parrish [15], Corazzin [84]	4861
36	20	H	Macclesfield T	L	0-2	0-0	22		5790
37	27	A	Preston NE	L	0-3	0-1	23		10,686
38	Apr 2	H	Bournemouth	W	2-1	2-1	—	Lee [33], Corazzin [37]	6858
39	5	A	Bristol R	D	1-1	1-0	22	Corazzin [6]	6580
40	10	H	Luton T	W	1-0	1-0	21	Corazzin [34]	6856
41	13	H	York C	D	2-2	1-1	—	Howey [39], Wilson [51]	5220
42	17	A	Reading	W	1-0	0-0	22	Savage [89]	10,132
43	24	H	Colchester U	D	3-3	2-1	21	Savage [18], Corazzin (pen) [41], Howey [63]	6146
44	29	May 3	A	Wigan Ath	D	3-3	1-1	—	Savage 2 [7, 71], O'Neill (og) [58]	5404
45	May 3	A	Chesterfield	D	0-0	0-0	—		5110
46	8	H	Burnley	D	2-2	1-0	22	Savage [7], Howey [90]	7435

Final League Position: 22

GOALSCORERS

League (43): Corazzin 16 (6 pens), Howey 6, Savage 5, Freestone 2, Hunt 2, Heggs 1, Hodgson 1, Hunter 1, Lee 1, Parrish 1, Peer 1, Sampson 1, Spedding 1, Warburton 1, Wilkinson 1, Wilson 1, own goal 1.
Worthington Cup (6): Freestone 3, Heggs 2, Parrish 1.
FA Cup (2): Sampson 1, own goal 1.

Woodman A 18	Matthew D 1	Frain J 40 + 1	Bishop C 4	Warburton R 12	Spedding D 15 + 9	Gibb A 30 + 11	Peer D 21 + 5	Heggs C 6 + 5	Corazzin C 36 + 3	Hill C 22 + 5	Clarkson 13 + 2	Freestone C 17 + 15	Hunt J 24 + 11	Warner M 5 + 4	Witter T 1 + 3	Parrish S 33	Lee C 9 + 10	Sampson I 42	Hunter R 15 + 3	Dobson T 8 + 3	Wilkinson P 12 + 3	Savage D 18 + 9	Hodgson D 7 + 1	Seal D 5 + 1	Wilder C 1	Howey L 25	Turley B 25	Hope R 17 + 2	Clarke A 2 + 2	Howard S 12	Hendon I 7	Wilson K 8	Francis S 3	Match No.
1	2¹	3	4	5	6	7	8²	9³	10	11	12	13	14																					1
1		3	4	5	6¹	7²	8	9	10³	11	2	14	12	13																				2
1		3	4	5	12	13		9	10	2¹	11³	7				6	8²	14																3
1		3		5	12	2	6	9²	10	11	14	13	7				8¹	4³																4
1		3		5	6¹	13	7	8	10²	11	2³	9	12	14				4																5
1		3³	6¹	5		2	7	12	10			9	13	14		8		4	11²															6
1				5	6	2³	7	12	10¹	11		9		13		3	8	4																7
1				5	8¹	2	6²	12	10	11		9				3		4	7	13														8
1	12			5	8¹	2	6		10	11		9				3³		4	7²	14	13													9
1		3		5³		2	6	12	9²	11		13	7			10	8¹	4	14															10
1		3		5¹		2	7²	11	9			12	13			10		4	6	8														11
1		3		5		2		10¹	9³			12	7			11		4	6	8²	13	14												12
1		3				2		10¹	9¹			12	7			11		5	6	8	13	4												13
1		3				2		12	9	11		13	7			6		4		8	10¹	5²												14
1		3				2		9	6			10¹	7			11	12	4			8²	5	13											15
1		3				2		9	6			10²	7	13		11	12	4			8¹	5												16
1		3				2		9	6			10¹	7			11²		4			12	13	5	8										17
1		3							9	11	12	10	7			6²	13	4				14	5			2¹	8³							18
		3				2			9		12		11	13	14	6²		4	7²			8				5	1	10¹						19
		3			7			9¹	12				12		11	13		4			10²		8			5	1							20
		3						9²	11	2					12		6	4		13	10	8				5	1							21
		3							9	5	11	2				7		4			10	8					1	6						22
		3							9	11	2	12				13	7¹	4	14		10³	8				5	1	6²						23
		3							9	11	2	12				13		6¹	4	7	10	8				5	1							24
		3							9²	11	2	12				10		6¹	4	7		8³				5	1	14						25
		3³					2	8		11		9²		12		13		4	7¹		14					5	1	6	10					26
		3			5		2	7		10						11		4			6					8¹	1	12	9					27
		3¹					7²	2	10				13			12		4	11³		8					5	1	6	14					28
		3²					7	10³	5				12			2		11¹	4	13	8					5	1	6	14					29
		3					7		10				12			2		11	9		4	8¹				5	1	6						30
		3		12			7²		10				8³			2		11	4		13	14				5¹	1	6		9				31
		3²				12		10	5¹				8			13		2	11	4	7						1	6		9				32
		3				12		13	10³	5¹			8			2		11²	4	7		14					1	6		9				33
		3					2²		12				8¹	13		11		4	7		10					5	1	6		9³				34
		3		12			2	13	10				14			11²	8¹	4	7							5	1	6		9³				35
		3¹		12			2		10	13			8	14		11		9²	4	7³						5	1	6						36
				11		12			10				8			3¹	13	4	7						9²	5	1	6			2			37
		3		12	13			9					11			10¹		4								5	1	6			2	8²		38
		3		12	13	7		9¹				14	11			10²		4								5	1	6			2	8³		39
		3				7		9					11			12		4			13					5	1	6	10¹		2	8²		40
		3		12		7²		9					10			4		13								5	1	6	11		2	8¹		41
		3							4			11				8	9		6	7						5		10	2				1	42
		3		12	13			9					11			2²		4	6	7						5		10		8¹			1	43
		3				2			12				11			8¹	13	4	6	7						5		9		10²			1	44
		3		12		2	10					13	11			11¹		4	6	7						5	1	9		8²				45
		3		12								13	11			10³	14	4	6¹	7						5	1	9	2	8²				46

Worthington Cup

First Round	Brighton & HA	(h)	2-1
		(a)	1-1
Second Round	West Ham U	(h)	2-0
		(a)	0-1
Third Round	Tottenham H	(h)	1-3

FA Cup

| First Round | Lancaster C | (h) | 2-1 |
| Second Round | Yeovil T | (a) | 0-2 |

Division 1

NORWICH CITY

FOUNDATION

Formed in 1902, largely through the initiative of two local schoolmasters who called a meeting at the Criterion Cafe, they were shocked by an FA Commission which in 1904 declared the club professional and ejected them from the FA Amateur Cup. However, this only served to strengthen their determination. New officials were appointed and a professional club established at a meeting in the Agricultural Hall in March 1905.

NORWICH CITY FC

Carrow Road, Norwich NR1 1JE.

Telephone: (01603) 760760.

Fax: (01603) 613886.

Box Office: (01603) 761661.

Clubcall: 0891 121144.

Ground Capacity: 21,414.

Record Attendance: 43,984 v Leicester C, FA Cup 6th rd, 30 March 1963.

Record Receipts: £261,918 v Internazionale, UEFA Cup 3rd rd 1st leg, 24 November 1993.

Pitch Measurements: 114yd × 74yd.

President: G. C. Watling.

Chairman: Bob Cooper.

Joint Vice-Chairmen: R. J. Munby, B. W. Lockwood.

Company Secretary: N. A. Doncaster.

Directors: M. M. Foulger, B. J. Skipper, M. Wynn Jones, D. Smith.

Chief Executive: G. J. Bennett.

First Team Manager: Bruce Rioch.

Director of Football: Bryan Hamilton.

Youth Team Coach: Keith Webb.

Physio: Tim Sheppard MCSP, SRP.

Football Secretary: Kevan Platt.

LATEST SEQUENCES

Longest Sequence of League Wins: 10, 23.11.85 – 25.1.86.

Longest Sequence of League Defeats: 7, 1.4.95 – 6.5.95.

Longest Sequence of League Draws: 7, 15.1.94 – 26.2.94.

Longest Sequence of Unbeaten League Matches: 20, 31.8.50 – 30.12.50.

Longest Sequence Without a League Win: 25, 22.9.56 – 23.2.57.

HONOURS

FA Premier League: best season: 3rd 1992–93.

Football League: Division 2 – Champions 1971–72, 1985–86; Division 3 (S) – Champions 1933–34; Division 3 – Runners-up 1959–60.

FA Cup: Semi-finals 1959, 1989, 1992.

Football League Cup: Winners 1962, 1985; Runners-up 1973, 1975.

European Competitions: UEFA Cup: 1993–94.

Colours
Yellow shirts, green shorts, yellow stockings.

Change Colours
All navy blue.

Year Formed: 1902.

Turned Professional: 1905.

Ltd Co.: 1905.

Club Nickname: 'The Canaries'.

Previous Grounds: 1902, Newmarket Road; 1908, The Nest, Rosary Road; 1935, Carrow Road.

First Football League Game: 28 August 1920, Division 3, v Plymouth Arg (a) D 1–1 – Skermer; Gray, Gadsden; Wilkinson, Addy, Martin; Laxton, Kidger, Parker, Whitham (1), Dobson.

Record League Victory: 10–2 v Coventry C, Division 3 (S), 15 March 1930 – Jarvie; Hannah, Graham; Brown, O'Brien, Lochhead (1); Porter (1), Anderson, Hunt (5), Scott (2), Slicer (1).

Record Cup Victory: 8–0 v Sutton U, FA Cup 4th rd, 28 January 1989 – Gunn; Culverhouse, Bowen, Butterworth, Linighan, Townsend (Crook), Gordon, Fleck (3), Allen (4), Phelan, Putney (1).

Record Defeat: 2–10 v Swindon T, Southern League, 5 September 1908.

Most League Points (2 for a win): 64, Division 3 (S), 1950–51.

Most League Points (3 for a win): 84, Division 2, 1985–86.

Most League Goals: 99, Division 3 (S), 1952–53.

Highest League Scorer in Season: Ralph Hunt, 31, Division 3 (S), 1955–56.

Most League Goals in Total Aggregate: Johnny Gavin, 122, 1945–54, 1955–58.

Most League Goals in One Match: 5, Tommy Hunt v Coventry C, Division 3S, 15 March 1930; 5, Roy Hollis v Walsall, Division 3S, 29 December 1951.

Most Capped Player: Mark Bowen, 35 (41), Wales.

Most League Appearances: Ron Ashman, 592, 1947–64.

Youngest League Player: Ian Davies, 17 years 29 days v Birmingham C, 27 April 1974.

Record Transfer Fee Received: £5,000,000 from Blackburn R for Chris Sutton, July 1994.

Record Transfer Fee Paid: £1,000,000 to Leeds U for Jon Newsome, June 1994.

Football League Record: 1920 Original Member of Division 3; 1921 Division 3 (S): 1934–39 Division 2; 1946–58 Division 3 (S); 1958–60 Division 3; 1960–72 Division 2; 1972–74 Division 1; 1974–75 Division 2; 1975–81 Division 1; 1981–82 Division 2; 1982–85 Division 1; 1985–86 Division 2; 1986–92 Division 1; 1992–95 FA Premier League; 1995– Division 1.

MANAGERS

John Bowman 1905–07
James McEwen 1907–08
Arthur Turner 1909–10
Bert Stansfield 1910–15
Major Frank Buckley 1919–20
Charles O'Hagan 1920–21
Albert Gosnell 1921–26
Bert Stansfield 1926
Cecil Potter 1926–29
James Kerr 1929–33
Tom Parker 1933–37
Bob Young 1937–39
Jimmy Jewell 1939
Bob Young 1939–45
Cyril Spiers 1946–47
Duggie Lochhead 1947–50
Norman Low 1950–55
Tom Parker 1955–57
Archie Macaulay 1957–61
Willie Reid 1961–62
George Swindin 1962
Ron Ashman 1962–66
Lol Morgan 1966–69
Ron Saunders 1969–73
John Bond 1973–80
Ken Brown 1980–87
Dave Stringer 1987–92
Mike Walker 1992–94
John Deehan 1994–95
Martin O'Neill 1995
Gary Megson 1995–96
Mike Walker 1996–98
Bruce Rioch *(Football Team Manager)* July 1998–

TEN YEAR LEAGUE RECORD

		P	W	D	L	F	A	Pts	Pos
1988-89	Div 1	38	17	11	10	48	45	62	4
1989-90	Div 1	38	13	14	11	44	40	53	10
1990-91	Div 1	38	13	6	19	41	64	45	15
1991-92	Div 1	42	11	12	19	47	63	45	18
1992-93	PR Lge	42	21	9	12	61	65	72	3
1993-94	PR Lge	42	12	17	13	65	61	53	12
1994-95	PR Lge	42	10	13	19	37	54	43	20
1995-96	Div 1	46	14	15	17	59	55	57	16
1996-97	Div 1	46	17	12	17	63	68	63	13
1997-98	Div 1	46	14	13	19	52	69	55	15

DID YOU KNOW ?

On 6 February 1909 Norwich City, then in the Southern League, defeated First Division Liverpool 3–2 in an FA Cup second round tie at Anfield. John Smith scored the winning goal in the last minute of the match before a crowd of 25,000.

NORWICH CITY FC

NORWICH CITY 1998–99 LEAGUE RECORD

Match No.	Date	Venue	Opponents	Result	H/T Score	Lg. Pos.	Goalscorers	Attendance
1	Aug 8	H	Crewe Alex	W 2-1	2-1	—	Bellamy 31, Kenton 35	15,016
2	15	A	Stockport Co	W 2-0	1-0	2	Bellamy 31, Woodthorpe (og) 74	6538
3	22	H	QPR	W 4-2	3-2	1	Bellamy 3 (2 pens) 2, 6 (p), 57 (p), Jackson 8	16,317
4	29	A	WBA	L 0-2	0-0	5		17,401
5	Sept 8	A	Barnsley	W 3-1	0-1	—	Marshall L 58, Roberts 86, Bellamy 90	15,695
6	13	H	Bury	D 0-0	0-0	7		16,919
7	19	A	Sheffield U	L 1-2	0-1	11	Brannan 63	16,155
8	26	H	Birmingham C	W 2-0	0-0	6	Bellamy 79, Roberts 88	16,584
9	29	H	Sunderland	D 2-2	2-1	—	Eadie 19, MacKay 23	17,504
10	Oct 3	A	Port Vale	L 0-1	0-0	10		5580
11	17	A	Crystal Palace	L 1-5	1-2	13	Roberts 36	18,100
12	20	H	Ipswich T	W 1-0	0-0	—	Bellamy 53	22,079
13	24	H	Huddersfield T	W 4-1	3-0	6	Bellamy 2 2, 30, Roberts 2 41, 49	15,403
14	Nov 3	A	Watford	D 1-1	1-1	—	Eadie 34	10,011
15	7	H	Bradford C	D 2-2	0-1	9	O'Brien (og) 77, Adams (pen) 90	14,722
16	10	A	Portsmouth	W 2-1	0-1	—	Roberts 52, Eadie 73	9335
17	14	A	Wolverhampton W	D 0-0	0-0	8		17,275
18	21	A	Tranmere R	W 3-1	2-0	6	O'Neill 10, Bellamy 39, Roberts 83	6319
19	29	H	Oxford U	L 1-3	1-2	7	Bellamy 3	17,851
20	Dec 2	H	Grimsby T	W 3-1	1-0	—	Adams 11, Roberts 80, Bellamy 84	12,024
21	5	A	Swindon T	D 1-1	1-1	4	Roberts 17	9262
22	12	A	Wolverhampton W	D 2-2	1-0	6	Adams (pen) 31, Roberts 60	21,014
23	19	H	Bristol C	W 2-1	2-1	5	Roberts 2 18, 36	17,022
24	26	A	QPR	L 0-2	0-2	8		15,251
25	29	H	Watford	D 1-1	0-0	—	Roberts 54	19,259
26	Jan 9	A	Crewe Alex	L 2-3	2-0	10	Llewellyn 10, Marshall L 33	4782
27	16	H	WBA	D 1-1	0-0	9	Marshall L 78	15,411
28	30	A	Bolton W	L 0-2	0-1	11		17,269
29	Feb 6	H	Stockport Co	L 0-2	0-2	12		14,675
30	16	H	Barnsley	D 0-0	0-0	—		13,232
31	20	A	Bury	W 2-0	1-0	10	Bellamy 29, Fleming 72	4285
32	27	H	Sheffield U	D 1-1	1-0	10	Llewellyn 20	14,224
33	Mar 2	A	Birmingham C	D 0-0	0-0	—		20,749
34	6	A	Sunderland	L 0-1	0-1	12		39,004
35	9	H	Port Vale	L 3-4	1-2	—	Fleming 30, Roberts 68, Bellamy 83	12,960
36	13	A	Bradford C	L 1-4	0-4	12	Roberts 48	13,331
37	20	H	Portsmouth	D 0-0	0-0	13		16,662
38	24	A	Huddersfield T	D 1-1	1-0	—	Russell 3	9717
39	Apr 3	H	Crystal Palace	L 0-1	0-1	14		16,754
40	5	A	Grimsby T	W 1-0	1-0	12	Mulryne 35	6302
41	11	H	Ipswich T	D 0-0	0-0	11		19,511
42	17	A	Tranmere R	D 2-2	1-1	13	Bellamy 15, Mulryne 62	14,735
43	20	H	Bolton W	D 2-2	2-0	—	Roberts 2 3, 5	11,137
44	24	A	Oxford U	W 4-2	1-1	9	Anselin 34, Roberts 65, Fleming 70, Bellamy 88	7345
45	May 1	H	Swindon T	W 2-1	0-0	9	Roberts 62, Hughes 90	17,306
46	9	A	Bristol C	L 0-1	0-1	9		11,362

Final League Position: 9

GOALSCORERS

League (62): Roberts 19, Bellamy 17 (2 pens), Adams 3 (2 pens), Eadie 3, Fleming 3, Marshall L 3, Llewellyn 2, Mulryne 2, Anselin 1, Brannan 1, Hughes 1, Jackson 1, Kenton 1, MacKay 1, O'Neill 1, Russell 1, own goals 2.
Worthington Cup (7): Roberts 3, Bellamy 2, O'Neill 1, own goal 1.
FA Cup (1): Roberts 1.

Marshall A 37	Sutch D 34+2	Kenton D 22	Grant P 31+2	Fleming C 35+2	Jackson M 36+1	Adams N 15+3	Bellamy C 38+2	Carey S 7+3	Eadie D 21+1	O'Neill K 14+4	Marshall L 38+6	Milligan M 1+1	Llewellyn C 21+10	Roberts I 40+5	Brannan G 10+1	Watt M 7+1	Segura V 2+2	Forbes A 7+8	Fuglestad E 22+2	MacKay M 24+3	Wilson C 14+3	Russell D 8+5	Coote A 2+4	Hughes S 7	Mulryne P 2+2	Dalglish P 3+2	Anselin C 7	Green R 2	Match No.
1	2	3	4	5	6	7	8	9	10	11																			1
1	2	3	4	5	6		8	9¹	10	11³	7	12²	13	14															2
1	2	3	4	5	6		8		10¹	11	7		9²	12	13														3
1	2	3	4	5	6		8		10¹	11	7		12	9															4
1²	2	3¹	4	5	6		8		10		7		12	9	11	13													5
1	2		4	5	6¹		8		10		7		9		11²	3			12	13									6
1	2²		4	5			8		10		7		12	9¹	11	6³	13	3	14										7
1	2	3	4	5			8		10		7			9	11¹	12	6												8
1	2	3²	4	5			8		10¹		7			9	11	12	13	6											9
1	2	3²	4	5			8		10		7			9	11¹		13	6			12								10
1	2	3	4¹	5		12	8²		10		7	13	9	11			6												11
1	12	3		5	13		8		10		7			9	11		6²	4¹	2										12
1	4¹	2		5	6	12	8²		10	13	7			9	11			3											13
1	11		4	5	6		8		10		7			9				3	2										14
1	2		4¹	5	6	11	8		10	12	7			9				3											15
1	2²		12	5	6	4	8¹		10	11	7	13	9					3											16
1			4	5	6	11	8¹		10	12	7	2	9					3											17
1			2	4	5	6	11	8		10	7			9				3											18
1			2	4¹	5	6	11	8		10	7¹			9				12	3		13								19
			2	4	5	6	11	8		10	7		1	9					3										20
			2	4	6		8		7	11	9		1		3	5	10												21
			2	4	6	7	8¹	12		13	11³	9	1	14		3	5²	10											22
	12		2	4	6	7¹		8		13	11	9	1			3	5	10²											23
			2²	4	12	6	7			8¹	11	9	1	13		3	5	14	10³									24
	2			4	6	7		10	8	11	9		1			3	5												25
	2			4	6	7		10	8	11¹	9		1			3	5		12										26
1	2			5	6	7		10	8	11	9			3	4														27
1	4	3	12	5	6	7	13			11	8¹	10²	9			2													28
1	10	3¹	4²	5	6	7¹	8			11	12	13	9		14	2													29
1	2		4	5	6		8			7	10	9			11	3													30
1	2		4¹	5	6		8			7	10	9			11³	3²	12	13	14										31
1	2		4	5	6		8	12		7	10¹	9			11	3													32
1	2		4	5	6		8		10	7	12	9			11²	3¹	13												33
1	2		4²	5	6		8¹		10	11	7	12	9			3	10	13											34
1	2		4	5	6		8			11	7	12	9			3¹	10												35
1	2		4¹	5			8			11²	7	10	12	9		13	6	3											36
1	2			5	6		8		10		11	9¹	7				3	4	12										37
1	2			5	6		8	12		10	11¹	9	7²				3	4	13										38
1	2				6		8		7¹	11³	9		12			5	3	4	10²	13	14								39
1	2				6		8	11			12					3	5	4		10	9¹	7							40
	2			5	6¹		8	9		12		13				3	4		10	11²	7		1						41
	2				8	12	5	9								3	4	11	6¹	10	13	7²	1						42
1	2		12	6¹	13		8			4	11³	9				3	5	14		10²	7								43
1	2³		6		8	4	12			11	9²					3	5	14	13	10	7¹								44
1			6	12	4²	13	11	9		3¹	5	2³		8	14	10	7												45
1	2			5	8	12	4	11	9			3	6			10	7¹												46

Worthington Cup

First Round	Swansea C	(a)	1-1
		(h)	1-0
Second Round	Wigan Ath	(h)	1-0
		(a)	3-2
Third Round	Bolton W	(h)	1-1

FA Cup

| Third Round | Sheffield W | (a) | 1-4 |

Division 1   **NOTTINGHAM FOREST**

FOUNDATION

One of the oldest football clubs in the world, Nottingham Forest was formed at a meeting in the Clinton Arms in 1865. Known originally as the Forest Football Club, the game which first drew the founders together was 'shinney', a form of hockey. When they determined to change to football in 1865, one of their first moves was to buy a set of red caps to wear on the field.

City Ground, Nottingham NG2 5FJ.
Telephone: (0115) 982 4444.
Fax: (0115) 982 4455.
Information Desk: (0115) 982 4446.
Commercial Office: (0115) 982 4450.
Commercial Office Fax: (0115) 982 4410.
Ticket Office: (0115) 982 4445.
Souvenir Shop: (0115) 982 4447.
Junior Reds: (0115) 982 4454.
Clubcall: 0891 121174.
Ground Capacity: 30,602.
Record Attendance: 49,946 v Manchester U, Division 1, 28 October 1967.
Record Receipts: £499,099 v Bayern Munich, UEFA Cup quarter-final 2nd leg, 19 March 1996.
Pitch Measurements: 116yd × 76yd.
Deputy Chairman/Chief Executive: P. W. Soar.
Directors: R. W. Dove, R. A. Fairhall, P. R. Markham, T. H. Farr, K. J. Eggleston, I. I. Korn.
Manager: David Platt.
Secretary: Paul White.
Commercial Director: D. Clayton.
Coach: Liam O'Kane.
Physio: John Haselden.

LATEST SEQUENCES

Longest Sequence of League Wins: 7, 9.5.79 – 1.9.79.
Longest Sequence of League Defeats: 14, 21.3.13 – 27.9.13.
Longest Sequence of League Draws: 7, 29.4.78 – 2.9.78.
Longest Sequence of Unbeaten League Matches: 42, 26.11.77 – 25.11.78.
Longest Sequence Without a League Win: 19, 8.9.98 – 16.1.99.

HONOURS

Football League: Division 1 – Champions 1977–78, 1997–98; Runners-up 1966–67, 1978–79; Division 2 – Champions 1906–07, 1921–22; Runners-up 1956–57; Division 3 (S) – Champions 1950–51.
FA Cup: Winners 1898, 1959; Runners-up 1991.
Football League Cup: Winners 1978, 1979, 1989, 1990; Runners-up 1980, 1992.
Anglo-Scottish Cup: Winners 1977;
Simod Cup: Winners 1989.
Zenith Data Systems Cup: Winners: 1992.
European Competitions: European Fairs Cup: 1961–62, 1967–68. European Cup: 1978–79 (winners), 1979–80 (winners), 1980–81. Super Cup: 1979–80 (winners), 1980–81 (runners-up). World Club Championship: 1980. UEFA Cup: 1983–84, 1984–85, 1995–96.

Colours
Red shirts with black shoulders, white shorts, red stockings.
Change Colours
Yellow and navy.

Year Formed: 1865.

Turned Professional: 1889.

Ltd Co.: 1982.

Club Nickname: 'Reds'.

Previous Grounds: 1865, Forest Racecourse; 1879, The Meadows; 1880, Trent Bridge Cricket Ground; 1882, Parkside, Lenton; 1885, Gregory, Lenton; 1890, Town Ground; 1898, City Ground.

First Football League Game: 3 September 1892, Division 1, v Everton (a) D 2–2 – Brown; Earp, Scott; Hamilton, A. Smith, McCracken; McCallum, W. Smith, Higgins (2), Pike, McInnes.

Record League Victory: 12–0 v Leicester Fosse, Division 1, 12 April 1909 – Iremonger; Dudley, Maltby; Hughes (1), Needham, Armstrong; Hooper (3), Marrison, West (3), Morris (2), Spouncer (3 incl. 1p).

Record Cup Victory: 14–0 v Clapton (away), FA Cup 1st rd, 17 January 1891 – Brown; Earp, Scott; A. Smith, Russell, Jeacock; McCallum (2), 'Tich' Smith (1), Higgins (5), Lindley (4), Shaw (2).

Record Defeat: 1–9 v Blackburn R, Division 2, 10 April 1937.

Most League Points (2 for a win): 70, Division 3 (S), 1950–51.

Most League Points (3 for a win): 94, Division 1, 1997–98.

Most League Goals: 110, Division 3 (S), 1950–51.

Highest League Scorer in Season: Wally Ardron, 36, Division 3 (S), 1950–51.

MANAGERS
Harry Radford 1889–97 *(Secretary-Manager)*
Harry Haslam 1897–1909 *(Secretary-Manager)*
Fred Earp 1909–12
Bob Masters 1912–25
John Baynes 1925–29
Stan Hardy 1930–31
Noel Watson 1931–36
Harold Wightman 1936–39
Billy Walker 1939–60
Andy Beattie 1960–63
Johnny Carey 1963–68
Matt Gillies 1969–72
Dave Mackay 1972
Allan Brown 1973–75
Brian Clough 1975–93
Frank Clark 1993–96
Stuart Pearce 1996–97
Dave Bassett 1997–98 *(previously General Manager from February)*
Ron Atkinson 1998–99
David Platt July 1999–

Most League Goals in Total Aggregate: Grenville Morris, 199, 1898–1913.

Most League Goals in One Match: 4, Enoch West v Sunderland, Division 1, 9 November 1907; 4, Tommy Gibson v Burnley, Division 2, 25 January 1913; 4, Tom Peacock v Port Vale, Division 2, 23 December 1933; 4, Tom Peacock v Barnsley, Division 2, 9 November 1935; 4, Tom Peacock v Port Vale, Division 2, 23 November 1935; 4, Tom Peacock v Doncaster R, Division 2, 26 December 1935; 4, Tommy Capel v Gillingham, Division 3S, 18 November 1950; 4, Wally Ardron v Hull C, Division 2, 26 December 1952; 4, Tommy Wilson v Barnsley, Division 2, 9 February 1957; 4, Peter Withe v Ipswich T, Division 1, 4 October 1977.

Most Capped Player: Stuart Pearce, 76, England.

Most League Appearances: Bob McKinlay, 614, 1951–70.

Youngest League Player: Gary Mills, 16 years 302 days v Arsenal, 9 September 1978.

Record Transfer Fee Received: £8,500,000 from Liverpool for Stan Collymore, June 1995.

Record Transfer Fee Paid: £3,500,000 to Celtic for Pierre van Hooijdonk, March 1997.

Football League Record: 1892 Elected to Division 1; 1906–07 Division 2; 1907–11 Division 1; 1911–22 Division 2; 1922–25 Division 1; 1925–49 Division 2; 1949–51 Division 3 (S); 1951–57 Division 2; 1957–72 Division 1; 1972–77 Division 2; 1977–92 Division 1; 1992–93 FA Premier League; 1993–94 Division 1; 1994–97 FA Premier League; 1997–98 Division 1; 1998–99 FA Premier League; 1999– Division 1.

TEN YEAR LEAGUE RECORD

		P	W	D	L	F	A	Pts	Pos
1988-89	Div 1	38	17	13	8	64	43	64	3
1989-90	Div 1	38	15	9	14	55	47	54	9
1990-91	Div 1	38	14	12	12	65	50	54	8
1991-92	Div 1	42	16	11	15	60	58	59	8
1992-93	PR Lge	42	10	10	22	41	62	40	22
1993-94	Div 1	46	23	14	9	74	49	83	2
1994-95	PR Lge	42	22	11	9	72	43	77	3
1995-96	PR Lge	38	15	13	10	50	54	58	9
1996-97	PR Lge	38	6	16	16	31	59	34	20
1997-98	Div 1	46	28	10	8	82	42	94	1

DID YOU KNOW ?

On 27 February 1999, goalkeeper Mark Crossley played in his first League game for Nottingham Forest since 5 April 1997 and kept a clean sheet against Charlton Athletic, including a 69th minute penalty save.

NOTTINGHAM FOREST 1998–99 LEAGUE RECORD

Match No.	Date	Venue	Opponents	Result	H/T Score	Lg. Pos.	Goalscorers	Attendance
1	Aug 17	A	Arsenal	L	1-2	0-0	—	Thomas [76]	38,064
2	22	H	Coventry C	W	1-0	0-0	10	Stone [51]	22,546
3	29	A	Southampton	W	2-1	0-0	3	Darcheville [52], Stone [68]	14,942
4	Sept 8	H	Everton	L	0-2	0-0	—		25,610
5	12	A	Chelsea	L	1-2	0-2	11	Darcheville [69]	34,809
6	19	H	West Ham U	D	0-0	0-0	11		26,463
7	26	A	Newcastle U	L	0-2	0-1	16		36,760
8	Oct 3	H	Charlton Ath	L	0-1	0-1	18		22,661
9	17	H	Leeds U	D	1-1	0-0	18	Stone [85]	23,911
10	24	A	Liverpool	L	1-5	1-3	19	Freedman [17]	44,595
11	Nov 1	A	Middlesbrough	D	1-1	0-1	18	Harewood [88]	34,223
12	7	H	Wimbledon	L	0-1	0-1	19		21,362
13	16	H	Derby Co	D	2-2	0-0	—	Freedman [57], Van Hooijdonk [62]	24,014
14	21	A	Tottenham H	L	0-2	0-0	18		35,832
15	28	H	Aston Villa	D	2-2	2-0	18	Bart-Williams [32], Freedman [44]	25,753
16	Dec 7	A	Sheffield W	L	2-3	0-1	—	Bonalair [55], Van Hooijdonk [70]	19,321
17	12	A	Leicester C	L	1-3	1-1	19	Van Hooijdonk [14]	20,891
18	19	H	Blackburn R	D	2-2	2-0	20	Chettle (pen) [22], Freedman [30]	22,013
19	26	A	Manchester U	L	0-3	0-1	20		55,216
20	28	H	Southampton	D	1-1	0-0	20	Chettle (pen) [54]	23,456
21	Jan 9	A	Coventry C	L	0-4	0-1	20		17,158
22	16	H	Arsenal	L	0-1	0-1	20		26,021
23	30	A	Everton	W	1-0	0-0	20	Van Hooijdonk [51]	34,175
24	Feb 6	H	Manchester U	L	1-8	1-2	20	Rogers [6]	30,025
25	13	A	West Ham U	L	1-2	0-2	20	Hjelde [84]	25,458
26	20	H	Chelsea	L	1-3	1-2	20	Van Hooijdonk [39]	26,351
27	27	A	Charlton Ath	D	0-0	0-0	20		20,007
28	Mar 10	H	Newcastle U	L	1-2	1-1	—	Freedman [45]	22,852
29	13	A	Wimbledon	W	3-1	1-0	20	Rogers [21], Freedman [59], Shipperley [84]	12,149
30	20	H	Middlesbrough	L	1-2	1-1	20	Freedman [37]	21,468
31	Apr 3	A	Leeds U	L	1-3	0-1	20	Rogers [53]	39,645
32	5	H	Liverpool	D	2-2	0-1	20	Freedman [60], Van Hooijdonk [90]	28,374
33	10	A	Derby Co	L	0-1	0-0	20		32,217
34	17	H	Tottenham H	L	0-1	0-0	20		25,181
35	24	A	Aston Villa	L	0-2	0-1	20		34,492
36	May 1	H	Sheffield W	W	2-0	2-0	20	Porfirio [14], Rogers [16]	20,480
37	8	A	Blackburn R	W	2-1	1-1	20	Freedman [12], Bart-Williams [56]	24,565
38	16	H	Leicester C	W	1-0	0-0	20	Bart-Williams [76]	25,353

Final League Position: 20

GOALSCORERS

League (35): Freedman 9, Van Hooijdonk 6, Rogers 4, Bart-Williams 3, Stone 3, Chettle 2 (2 pens), Darcheville 2, Bonalair 1, Harewood 1, Hjelde 1, Porfirio 1, Shipperley 1, Thomas 1.
Worthington Cup (9): Freedman 3, Harewood 2, Stone 2, Armstrong 1, Johnson 1.
FA Cup (0).

Beasant D 26	Bonalair T 24 + 4	Rogers A 34	Stone S 26	Chettle S 32 + 2	Hjelde J 16 + 1	Johnson A 25 + 3	Armstrong C 20 + 2	Darcheville J 14 + 2	Thomas G 5	Hodges G 3 + 2	Lyttle D 5 + 5	Harewood M 11 + 12	Freedman D 20 + 11	Gemmill S 18 + 2	Quashie N 12 + 4	Gray A 3 + 5	Louis-Jean M 15 + 1	Shipperley N 12 + 8	Bart-Williams C 20 + 4	Van Hooijdonk P 19 + 2	Edwards C 7 + 5	Mattsson J 5 + 1	Doig C 1 + 1	Woan I — + 2	Harkes J 3	Stensaas S 8 + 1	Palmer C 13	Porfirio H 3 + 6	Crossley M 12	Gough R 7	Aliou B — + 2	Melton S 1	Match No.
1	2	3	4	5	6^1	7^2	8	9^3	10	11	12	13	14																				1
1	2	3	4	5		12	6	9^2	10^1	11^3	14	13	8	7																			2
1	2	3	4	5		7	6	9^1	10	11			12	8																			3
1	2	3^1	4	5		7	6	9	10			12	13	14					8^2	11^3													4
1	2	3	4	5		7	6	9	10^1			13	12						8	11^2													5
1	11	3	4	5		7	6	9^2	2^3	10^1	12								8	13	14												6
1		3	4	5		7	6	9^2				13	12	8^1	14		2		10	11^3													7
1		3	4	5	12	7	6					13		9			2		8^1	11^2	10												8
1	2	3^1	4	5	6	12	7	9^3				13	8^2	14					10	11													9
1	2	3	4	5	6		7					9	8						10	11													10
1	2^3		4	5	6		3					12	10	13	8	7^1	14		9^2	11													11
1	12	3	4	5		6						2^1	10^2	13	8	7			11	9													12
1	2	3	4	5		6						12	10^1	8	7				11	9													13
1	12	3	4	5	2		6^2						10^1	8	7				11	9	13												14
1	2		4	5	3	12	6	13					10^2	8^1	7				11	9													15
1	2	3		5	6	8	4^1	10^2				13		12	7^3	14			11	9													16
1		3	4	5	2^1	7		10^2	12	8			13	11	9				6														17
1		3^1	4	5	2	7	12					13	9	8					10^2	11							6						18
1	12	3	4^2	5^3		8	6					13		9			7	2	10	11^1							14						19
1	2	3	4	5	6	7						12	9^1	8					10	11													20
1			4	5	6^3	7	10^1					2		12	8^2	13			11	9							3	14					21
1	4^1	3		5	7	6	10^2	2					8	13					12	11	9												22
1	11^3	7		4	6	12	10^2					8		13	9				2	3^1	5						14						23
1	11	7		4	6	3^3	10^1					12	8^2		9				13	2	5						14						24
1	11	7	12	4	6		8^3	13				10		9					2^2	3^1	5						14						25
1	6	3	7	5		8^1	10^2					12	11^3	2	13	9			4	14													26
	4		7	5			10^2					8^1	12	2	13	9	6			3	11						1						27
	6	11	7	5		8						12	10^1	2	13	9	14		3^2								1	4^3					28
	3		5		11^1							8		2	10	12	9	6	4		7						1						29
	12	3	4^2	5^3								13	8^2	2	10	11^1	9	6	4^3		7	14					1						30
	2	11		5	7							10	9^1	12			6		3^2	8	13	1		4									31
	3	11		5	7							10	8^2	2^1	12		9	6	4		1	5	13										32
	3	11	12		7							10^1	8	2	13		9^2	6	4		1	5											33
	3^3	11	5		7	12						8		2	10^1		9	6^2	14		13	1	4										34
		11	5	4	8^2		7	10	9^1			2	12	13	14		6		3^3		1												35
	4	3	5^2			12						10^1	8	2	11	14	13		7	9^3	1	6											36
	3	11	5									8^1	9	2	10	12		6	7^2	1	4	13											37
	3	11	5									8	9	2	10	12		6	7^1	1	4												38

Worthington Cup

Second Round	Leyton Orient	(a)	5-1
		(h)	0-0
Third Round	Cambridge U	(h)	3-3
Fourth Round	Manchester U	(a)	1-2

FA Cup

Third Round	Portsmouth	(h)	0-1

Division 2

NOTTS COUNTY

FOUNDATION

According to the official history of Notts County 'the true date of Notts' foundation has to be the meeting at the George Hotel on 7 December 1864'. However, in the same opening chapter is the following: The Nottingham Guardian on 28 November 1862 carried the following report:- 'The opening of the Nottingham Football Club commenced on Tuesday last at Cremorne Gardens. A side was chosen by W. Arkwright and Chas Deakin. A very spirited game resulted in the latter scoring two goals and two rouges against one and one'.

County Ground, Meadow Lane, Nottingham NG2 3HJ.
Telephone: (0115) 952 9000. *Fax:* (0115) 955 3994.
Ticket Office: (0115) 955 7210. *Clubline:* 0891 888684.
Football in the Community: (0115) 955 7215.
Supporters Club: (0115) 955 7255.
Ground Capacity: 20,300.
Record Attendance: 47,310 v York C, FA Cup 6th rd, 12 March 1955.
Record Receipts: £124,539.10 v Manchester C, FA Cup 6th rd, 16 February 1991.
Pitch Measurements: 114yd × 74yd.
Chairman: D. C. Pavis.
Vice-Chairman: J. Mounteney.
Directors: W. Barrowcliffe, Mrs V. Pavis, M. Youdell MBE, G. Davey (Managing).
Manager: Sam Allardyce.
Assistant Manager: Gary Brazil.
Youth Coach: John Gaunt.
Secretary: Ian Moat.
Commercial Manager: Clair Finnigan.
Conference & Banqueting Manager: Matthew Foote.
Physio: Roger Cleary.
Stadium Manager: Bob Davy.
Year Formed: 1862* (*see Foundation*).
Turned Professional: 1885.
Ltd Co.: 1888.
Club Nickname: 'Magpies'.
Previous Grounds: 1862, The Park; 1864, The Meadows; 1877, Beeston Cricket Ground; 1880, Castle Ground; 1883, Trent Bridge; 1910, Meadow Lane.

HONOURS

Football League: Division 1 best season: 3rd, 1890–91, 1900–01; Division 2 – Champions 1896–97, 1913–14, 1922–23; Runners-up 1894–95, 1980–81; Promoted from Division 2 1990–91 (play-offs); Division 3 (S) – Champions 1930–31, 1949–50; Runners-up 1936–37; Division 3 – Champions 1997–98; Runners-up 1972–73; Promoted from Division 3 1989–90 (play-offs); Division 4 – Champions 1970–71; Runners-up 1959–60.

FA Cup: Winners 1894; Runners-up 1891.

Football League Cup: best season: 5th rd, 1964, 1973, 1976.

Anglo-Italian Cup: Winners 1995; Runners-up 1994.

LATEST SEQUENCES
Longest Sequence of League Wins: 10, 3.12.97 – 31.1.98.
Longest Sequence of League Defeats: 7, 3.9.83 – 16.10.83.
Longest Sequence of League Draws: 5, 2.12.78 – 26.12.78.
Longest Sequence of Unbeaten League Matches: 19, 26.4.30 – 6.12.30.
Longest Sequence Without a League Win: 20, 3.12.96 – 31.3.97.

Colours
Black and white striped shirts, black shorts, black stockings.

Change Colours
All royal blue.

First Football League Game: 15 September 1888, Football League, v Everton (a) L 1–2 – Holland; Guttridge, McLean; Brown, Warburton, Shelton; Hodder, Harker, Jardine, Moore (1), Wardle.

Record League Victory: 11–1 v Newport Co, Division 3 (S), 15 January 1949 – Smith; Southwell, Purvis; Gannon, Baxter, Adamson; Houghton (1), Sewell (4), Lawton (4), Pimbley, Johnston (2).

Record Cup Victory: 15–0 v Rotherham T (at Trent Bridge), FA Cup 1st rd, 24 October 1885 – Sherwin; Snook, H. T. Moore; Dobson (1), Emmett (1), Chapman; Gunn (1), Albert Moore (2), Jackson (3), Daft (2), Cursham (4), (1 og).

Record Defeat: 1–9 v Blackburn R, Division 1, 16 November 1889. 1–9 v Aston Villa, Division 1, 29 September 1888. 1–9 v Portsmouth, Division 2, 9 April 1927.

Most League Points (2 for a win): 69, Division 4, 1970–71.

Most League Points (3 for a win): 99, Division 3, 1997–98.

Most League Goals: 107, Division 4, 1959–60.

Highest League Scorer in Season: Tom Keetley, 39, Division 3 (S), 1930–31.

Most League Goals in Total Aggregate: Les Bradd, 124, 1967–78.

Most League Goals in One Match: 5, Robert Jardine v Burnley, Division 1, 27 October 1888; 5, Daniel Bruce v Port Vale, Division 2, 26 February 1895; 5, Bertie Mills v Barnsley, Division 2, 19 November 1927.

Most Capped Player: Kevin Wilson, 15 (42), Northern Ireland.

Most League Appearances: Albert Iremonger, 564, 1904–26.

Youngest League Player: Tony Bircumshaw, 16 years 54 days v Brentford, 3 April 1961.

Record Transfer Fee Received: £2,500,000 from Derby Co for Craig Short, September 1992.

Record Transfer Fee Paid: £685,000 to Sheffield U for Tony Agana, November 1991.

Football League Record: 1888 Founder Member of the Football League; 1893–97 Division 2; 1897–1913 Division 1; 1913–14 Division 2; 1914–20 Division 1; 1920–23 Division 2; 1923–26 Division 1; 1926–30 Division 2; 1930–31 Division 3 (S); 1931–35 Division 2; 1935–50 Division 3 (S); 1950–58 Division 2; 1958–59 Division 3; 1959–60 Division 4; 1960–64 Division 3; 1964–71 Division 4; 1971–73 Division 3; 1973–81 Division 2; 1981–84 Division 1; 1984–85 Division 2; 1985–90 Division 3; 1990–91 Division 2; 1991–95 Division 1; 1995–97 Division 2; 1997–98 Division 3; 1998– Division 2.

MANAGERS

Edwin Browne 1883–93
  (Secretary-Manager)
Tom Featherstone 1893
  (Secretary-Manager)
Tom Harris 1893–1913 *(Secretary-Manager)*
Albert Fisher 1913–27
Horace Henshall 1927–34
Charlie Jones 1934–35
David Pratt 1935
Percy Smith 1935–36
Jimmy McMullan 1936–37
Harry Parkes 1938–39
Tony Towers 1939–42
Frank Womack 1942–43
Major Frank Buckley 1944–46
Arthur Stollery 1946–49
Eric Houghton 1949–53
George Poyser 1953–57
Tommy Lawton 1957–58
Frank Hill 1958–61
Tim Coleman 1961–63
Eddie Lowe 1963–65
Tim Coleman 1965–66
Jack Burkitt 1966–67
Andy Beattie *(General Manager)* 1967
Billy Gray 1967–68
Jimmy Sirrel 1969–75
Ron Fenton 1975–77
Jimmy Sirrel 1978–82
  (continued as General Manager to 1984)
Howard Wilkinson 1982–83
Larry Lloyd 1983–84
Richie Barker 1984–85
Jimmy Sirrel 1985–87
John Barnwell 1987–88
Neil Warnock 1989–93
Mick Walker 1993–94
Russell Slade 1994–95
Howard Kendall 1995
Colin Murphy June 1995
  (continued as General Manager to 1996)
Steve Thompson 1996
Sam Allardyce January 1997–

TEN YEAR LEAGUE RECORD

		P	W	D	L	F	A	Pts	Pos
1988-89	Div 3	46	18	13	15	64	54	67	9
1989-90	Div 3	46	25	12	9	73	53	87	3
1990-91	Div 2	46	23	11	12	76	55	80	4
1991-92	Div 1	42	10	10	22	40	62	40	21
1992-93	Div 1	46	12	16	18	55	70	52	17
1993-94	Div 1	46	20	8	18	65	69	68	7
1994-95	Div 1	46	9	13	24	45	66	40	24
1995-96	Div 2	46	21	15	10	63	39	78	4
1996-97	Div 2	46	7	14	25	33	59	35	24
1997-98	Div 3	46	29	12	5	82	43	99	1

DID YOU KNOW ?

In 1888–89 the inaugural Football League programme consisted of only 22 matches, but Notts County called upon the services of 33 players, the most used by the club before the introduction of substitutes.

1 8 6 2

NOTTS COUNTY 1998–99 LEAGUE RECORD

Match No.	Date	Venue	Opponents	Result	H/T Score	Lg. Pos.	Goalscorers	Attendance
1	Aug 8	A	Oldham Ath	W 3-1	3-0	—	Richardson [8], Farrell 2 [21, 26]	5709
2	15	H	Bournemouth	L 1-2	1-0	11	Hendon (pen) [40]	5269
3	22	A	Northampton T	D 1-1	0-0	9	Torpey [70]	6141
4	29	H	Manchester C	D 1-1	0-0	13	Hendon (pen) [71]	10,316
5	31	A	Macclesfield T	W 1-0	0-0	8	Hendon [56]	3148
6	Sept 5	H	Wigan Ath	L 0-1	0-1	13		4445
7	8	A	Blackpool	L 0-1	0-0	—		3849
8	12	H	Fulham	W 1-0	1-0	12	Murray [45]	5805
9	18	A	Walsall	L 2-3	0-1	—	Jones [52], Hughes [55]	3991
10	26	H	Millwall	W 3-1	2-1	11	Murray [5], Hendon (pen) [9], Jones [76]	5016
11	Oct 3	A	Wycombe W	D 1-1	0-1	11	Strodder [90]	4164
12	10	H	Lincoln C	L 2-3	0-2	15	Hendon (pen) [56], Hughes [69]	6458
13	17	A	Burnley	D 1-1	1-0	16	Pearce [8]	10,559
14	20	A	Chesterfield	L 0-3	0-2	—		4506
15	24	H	Bristol R	D 1-1	0-0	16	Garcia [60]	4822
16	31	H	Stoke C	W 1-0	1-0	15	Farrell [35]	8546
17	Nov 7	A	York C	D 1-1	1-0	14	Fairclough [50]	3391
18	21	H	Colchester U	L 1-3	0-2	16	Murray [52]	4598
19	28	A	Wrexham	L 0-1	0-1	19		2811
20	Dec 12	H	Preston NE	L 2-3	0-0	19	Kidd (og) [55], Richardson [64]	5096
21	19	A	Gillingham	L 0-4	0-1	20		6072
22	26	H	Northampton T	W 3-1	3-0	18	Grant [1], Tierney [6], Richardson [44]	6131
23	28	A	Reading	L 0-1	0-1	20		13,026
24	Jan 9	H	Oldham Ath	L 0-1	0-1	20		4669
25	16	A	Bournemouth	L 0-2	0-1	21		5968
26	30	H	Reading	D 1-1	0-1	20	Owers [77]	5192
27	Feb 13	H	Blackpool	L 0-1	0-1	22		4778
28	16	A	Wigan Ath	L 0-3	0-0	—		2971
29	20	A	Fulham	L 1-2	0-1	23	Owers [83]	11,909
30	23	A	Luton T	W 1-0	0-0	—	Rapley [72]	4021
31	27	H	Walsall	W 2-1	0-1	21	Creaney [75], Hendon (pen) [81]	6172
32	Mar 6	A	Millwall	W 3-1	1-0	19	Richardson 2 [13, 64], Beadle [59]	6042
33	13	H	York C	W 4-2	3-1	17	Richardson 2 [22, 28], Tierney [29], Beadle [75]	5400
34	16	A	Manchester C	L 1-2	0-2	—	Stallard [72]	26,502
35	20	A	Stoke C	W 3-2	0-0	16	Beadle [54], Liburd [76], Stallard [85]	9565
36	27	A	Bristol R	D 1-1	1-1	16	Creaney [14]	5899
37	Apr 3	H	Burnley	D 0-0	0-0	15		6625
38	5	A	Lincoln C	W 1-0	0-0	15	Tierney [67]	5745
39	10	H	Chesterfield	W 2-0	1-0	14	Owers [45], Stallard [90]	5121
40	13	H	Wrexham	D 1-1	0-0	—	Garcia [76]	3294
41	16	A	Colchester U	L 1-2	0-1	—	Stallard [78]	4215
42	24	H	Luton T	L 1-2	0-1	17	Redmile [55]	5583
43	27	H	Wycombe W	W 1-0	0-0	—	Creaney (pen) [50]	4721
44	May 1	A	Preston NE	D 1-1	0-1	15	Rapley [90]	11,862
45	4	H	Macclesfield T	D 1-1	0-1	—	Hughes [67]	3747
46	8	H	Gillingham	L 0-1	0-0	16		7815

Final League Position: 16

GOALSCORERS

League (52): Richardson 7, Hendon 6 (5 pens), Stallard 4, Beadle 3, Creaney 3 (1 pen), Farrell 3, Hughes 3, Murray 3, Owers 3, Tierney 3, Garcia 2, Jones 2, Rapley 2, Fairclough 1, Grant 1, Liburd 1, Pearce 1, Redmile 1, Strodder 1, Torpey 1, own goal 1.
Worthington Cup (1): Torpey 1.
FA Cup (8): Jones 6, Murray 1, Owers 1.

Ward D 43	Hendon I 32	Pearce D 31+2	Redmile M 39+2	Fairclough C 16	Richardson I 23	Owers G 36+3	Hughes A 21+9	Farrell S 7+4	Jones G 23+5	Murray S 32+3	Liburd R 27+8	Torpey S 4+2	Billy C 3+3	Dyer A 19+10	Robson M —+2	Dudley C —+4	Finnan S 12+1	Goram A 1	Quayle M 2+3	Jackson J 3+7	Strodder G 8+3	Matthews L 4+1	Garcia T 10+9	Parkin B 1	Devlin P 5	Tierney F 13+7	Foley D 2	Grant K 6	Bolland P 12+1	Warren M 18	Creaney G 13+3	Beadle P 13+1	Rapley K 10+6	Holmes R 3+5	Stallard M 13+1	Gibson P 1	Match No.
1	2	3	4	5¹	6	7	8	9²	10	11³	12	13	14																								1
1	2		4	5		6	8	9	10²	11	12	13		7¹	3³	14																					2
1	2		4	5	6	7	8		10¹	11²	3	9		13		12																					3
1	2		4	5	6	7	8	12	9	11²	3	10¹					13																				4
1	2		4	5		7	8	12	10	11²	3	9¹	13			6																					5
	2		4	5		7	8		10	11¹	3	9²	12			6	1	13																			6
1			4	5		7	8¹	9²	10	11	3			6	2		12	13																			7
1	2		5			7	12		10¹	11	3	8			6		9²	13	4																		8
1	2	12	5			7	8¹		10	11³	3	14			6		9²	13	4																		9
1	2		5			7	8		10	11	3¹	12			6		4	9²	13																		10
1	2		5			7³	8²		10	11	12	3¹	13		6		4	9	14																		11
	2¹		5			12	8	13	10	11	3			6		4	9²	7	1																		12
1	2	11	5			8			10	3		12		6		4	9¹	7																			13
1	2	11	5			12	8	9	10	13	3¹			6		4³	14	7²																			14
1	2	11	4	5		7	12	9²	13		3¹			6			8		10																		15
1	2	3	4	5		7		9¹	12	11				6			8		10																		16
1	2	3	4			7	12	9²	13	11				6			8¹		10																		17
1	2	3	4	5	6	7¹	8²		10	11³	12			14					13	9																	18
1	2	3	4		6	7			10	11				5					8	9																	19
1	2	3	4		6	7			10	11				5²					13	12	8³		14	9¹													20
1	2		4		6	7		11	8¹		3						13	10	5	12				9²													21
1	2	3	4		6	7	8		10	11¹	12						13		5				9²														22
1	2	3²	4		6	7	8		10	11	12						13	14	5¹				9														23
1	2	3²	4		6	7	8		10		12			14			11²			13			5¹	9													24
1	2	3	4		6	7	12		10	11²	5			14					13				9³	8¹													25
1	2	12	4			7			10	11	5			3³	13				9¹		14			8²	6												26
1	2		4						10	11	5			3¹	12				8²				13	9	7	6											27
1	2	12	4			6	7		14	11	5			9¹					13				8³	10	3³												28
1	2	3	4			6	7	13		12				5					11²				8	9¹	10												29
1	2	3				6	7				4								11				8	5		10	9										30
1	2	3	12			6	7		4²					10			13		11³				8¹	5	14		9										31
1	2¹	3	8			6	7		4					12					11				5	13	10	9²											32
1		3	8¹	6					4					2					11				5	7¹	10		9²	12	13								33
1		3	8¹	6					4					2²			13		11³				5	7	10	14	12	9									34
1	2	3	8	6					4					5					11					7	10¹	12	9										35
1		3	5				12					13	4¹	8²					11³				6	7	10	14	2	9									36
1		3	5			7	14	12						13					11²				8³	6	10¹		4	2	9								37
1		3	5	8										12			13		4²				11¹		2	6	7	10						9		38
1		3	5			7								11¹			13		12				2	6³	8	10²	4	14	9								39
1		3²	5	6	7									11²			12		13				2³	8	10	4¹	14	9								40
1		3²	5	8	2	4								11¹			12		7²				6	10	13	14	9									41
1		3²	5	8	2	4¹								11³	12		13						6	7	10	14	9									42
1		3	5		2	12								11	4		8¹						6	7	10	9										43
1		3	5		2	12								11	4		8¹		14				6	7³	10²	13	9									44
1		3	5			4								11			8¹		12				6	7	10	2	9									45
		3	5		2	4								11			8¹		12				7	6³	14	13	10²	9	1							46

Worthington Cup
First Round   Manchester C   (h) 0-2
   (a) 1-7

FA Cup
First Round   Hendon   (a) 0-0
   (h) 3-0
Second Round   Wigan Ath   (h) 1-1
   (a) 0-0
Third Round   Sheffield U   (a) 1-1
   (h) 3-4

Division 2

OLDHAM ATHLETIC

FOUNDATION

It was in 1895 that John Garland, the landlord of the Featherstall and Junction Hotel, decided to form a football club. As Pine Villa they played in the Oldham Junior League. In 1899 the local professional club Oldham County, went out of existence and one of the liquidators persuaded Pine Villa to take over their ground at Sheepfoot Lane and change their name to Oldham Athletic.

Boundary Park, Oldham OL1 2PA.
Telephone: (0161) 624 4972.
Fax: (0161) 627 5915.
Website: www.oldhamathletic.co.uk.
Commercial Office: (0161) 627 1802.
Fax: (0161) 652 6501.
Clubcall: 09068 121142.
Ground Capacity: 13,559.
Record Attendance: 47,671 v Sheffield W, FA Cup 4th rd, 25 January 1930.
Record Receipts: £138,680 v Manchester U, FA Premier League, 29 December 1993.
Pitch Measurements: 110yd × 74yd.
Chairman: D. A. Brierley.
Vice-Chairman: I. H. Stott.
Directors: G. T. Butterworth, D. R. Taylor, P. Chadwick, J. Slevin, N. Holden.
Manager: Andy Ritchie.
Chief Executive/Secretary: Alan Hardy.
Commercial Manager: Bob Gorrill.
Public Relations Office: Gordon A. Lawton.
Stadium Manager: Stuart Oddie.
Safety Officer: Frank Carlisle.
Senior Coach: Bill Urmson.
Physio: Alex Moreno MCSP SRP.
Youth Coaches: David Cross, Tony Philliskirk.

LATEST SEQUENCES

Longest Sequence of League Wins: 10, 12.1.74 – 12.3.74.
Longest Sequence of League Defeats: 8, 15.12.34 – 2.2.35.
Longest Sequence of League Draws: 5, 26.12.82 – 15.1.83.
Longest Sequence of Unbeaten League Matches: 20, 1.5.90 – 10.11.90.
Longest Sequence Without a League Win: 17, 4.9.20 – 18.12.20.

HONOURS

Football League: Division 1 – Runners-up 1914–15; Division 2 – Champions 1990–91; Runners-up 1909–10; Division 3 (N) – Champions 1952–53; Division 3 – Champions 1973–74; Division 4 – Runners-up 1962–63.

FA Cup: Semi-final 1913, 1990, 1994.

Football League Cup: Runners-up 1990.

Colours
All blue.

Change Colours
White shirts, claret shorts, claret stockings.

Year Formed: 1895.

Turned Professional: 1899.

Ltd Co.: 1906.

Previous Name: 1895, Pine Villa; 1899, Oldham Athletic.

Club Nickname: 'The Latics'.

Previous Grounds: 1895, Sheepfoot Lane; 1900, Hudson Field; 1906, Sheepfoot Lane; 1907, Boundary Park.

First Football League Game: 9 September 1907, Division 2, v Stoke (a) W 3–1 – Hewitson; Hodson, Hamilton; Fay, Walders, Wilson; Ward, W. Dodds (1), Newton (1), Hancock, Swarbrick (1).

Record League Victory: 11–0 v Southport, Division 4, 26 December 1962 – Hollands; Branagan, Marshall; McCall, Williams, Scott; Ledger (1), Johnstone, Lister (6), Colquhoun (1), Whitaker (3).

Record Cup Victory: 10–1 v Lytham, FA Cup 1st rd, 28 November 1925 – Gray; Wynne, Grundy; Adlam, Heaton, Naylor (1), Douglas, Pynegar (2), Ormston (2), Barnes (3), Watson (2).

Record Defeat: 4–13 v Tranmere R, Division 3 (N), 26 December 1935.

Most League Points (2 for a win): 62, Division 3, 1973–74.

Most League Points (3 for a win): 88, Division 2, 1990–91.

Most League Goals: 95, Division 4, 1962–63.

Highest League Scorer in Season: Tom Davis, 33, Division 3 (N), 1936–37.

Most League Goals in Total Aggregate: Roger Palmer, 141, 1980–94.

Most League Goals in One Match: 7, Eric Gemmell v Chester, Division 3N, 19 January 1952.

Most Capped Player: Gunnar Halle, 24 (62), Norway.

Most League Appearances: Ian Wood, 525, 1966–80.

Youngest League Player: Wayne Harrison, 15 years 11 months v Notts Co, 27 October 1984.

Record Transfer Fee Received: £1,700,000 from Aston Villa for Earl Barrett, February 1992.

Record Transfer Fee Paid: £750,000 to Aston Villa for Ian Olney, June 1992.

Football League Record: 1907 Elected to Division 2; 1910–23 Division 1; 1923–35 Division 2; 1935–53 Division 3 (N); 1953–54 Division 2; 1954–58 Division 3 (N); 1958–63 Division 4; 1963–69 Division 3; 1969–71 Division 4; 1971–74 Division 3; 1974–91 Division 2; 1991–92 Division 1; 1992–94 FA Premier League; 1994–97 Division 1; 1997– Division 2.

MANAGERS

David Ashworth 1906–14
Herbert Bamlett 1914–21
Charlie Roberts 1921–22
David Ashworth 1923–24
Bob Mellor 1924–27
Andy Wilson 1927–32
Jimmy McMullan 1933–34
Bob Mellor 1934–45
    (continued as Secretary to 1953)
Frank Womack 1945–47
Billy Wootton 1947–50
George Hardwick 1950–56
Ted Goodier 1956–58
Norman Dodgin 1958–60
Jack Rowley 1960–63
Les McDowall 1963–65
Gordon Hurst 1965–66
Jimmy McIlroy 1966–68
Jack Rowley 1968–69
Jimmy Frizzell 1970–82
Joe Royle 1982–94
Graeme Sharp 1994–97
Neil Warnock 1997–98
Andy Ritchie May 1998–

TEN YEAR LEAGUE RECORD

		P	W	D	L	F	A	Pts	Pos
1988-89	Div 2	46	11	21	14	75	72	54	16
1989-90	Div 2	46	19	14	13	70	57	71	8
1990-91	Div 2	46	25	13	8	83	53	88	1
1991-92	Div 1	42	14	9	19	63	67	51	17
1992-93	PR Lge	42	13	10	19	63	74	49	19
1993-94	PR Lge	42	9	13	20	42	68	40	21
1994-95	Div 1	46	16	13	17	60	60	61	14
1995-96	Div 1	46	14	14	18	54	50	56	18
1996-97	Div 1	46	10	13	23	51	66	43	23
1997-98	Div 2	46	15	16	15	62	54	61	13

DID YOU KNOW ?

In July 1896 the Mayor of Oldham cut the first turf at Boundary Park. He was presented with a specially engraved silver spade, which was subsequently lost until 1948 when it was presented to the club.

OLDHAM ATHLETIC 1998–99 LEAGUE RECORD

Match No.	Date	Venue	Opponents	Result	H/T Score	Lg. Pos.	Goalscorers	Atten-dance
1	Aug 8	H	Notts Co	L	1-3	0-3	—	Holt [90]	5709
2	15	A	Blackpool	L	0-3	0-1	21		5258
3	22	H	Chesterfield	W	2-0	1-0	18	Williams (og) [1], Graham [82]	4548
4	29	A	Stoke C	L	0-2	0-1	21		12,306
5	31	H	Fulham	D	1-1	0-0	17	Allott [61]	4744
6	Sept 5	A	Lincoln C	W	3-1	2-0	14	Graham [28], Littlejohn [34], Allott [71]	3224
7	8	H	Macclesfield T	L	1-2	1-0	—	Littlejohn [11]	5401
8	12	A	Northampton T	D	1-1	1-0	16	Duxbury [45]	5210
9	19	H	Preston NE	L	0-1	0-1	18		8205
10	26	A	Bournemouth	L	0-2	0-1	20		5877
11	Oct 3	H	Colchester U	W	1-0	1-0	19	Rickers [20]	4231
12	9	H	Wigan Ath	L	2-3	0-1	—	Graham [48], Allott [90]	5499
13	17	A	Luton T	L	0-2	0-0	21		5447
14	20	A	Burnley	L	0-1	0-0	—		9539
15	24	H	Wycombe W	D	0-0	0-0	22		4337
16	31	A	Millwall	D	1-1	0-0	22	McGinlay [13]	5609
17	Nov 7	H	Manchester C	L	0-3	0-2	22		12,976
18	10	A	Gillingham	L	1-2	0-0	—	Whitehall [69]	5188
19	21	H	Wrexham	W	3-2	1-1	22	Whitehall [26], McNiven S [81], Tipton [88]	4446
20	28	A	Bristol R	D	2-2	1-0	22	Rickers [61], Sheridan [81]	5614
21	Dec 12	A	Walsall	L	0-2	0-2	22		4195
22	19	H	Reading	D	1-1	0-1	23	Allott [56]	9390
23	26	A	Chesterfield	W	3-1	1-1	21	Allott 2 [22, 65], Holt [56]	5448
24	28	H	York C	L	0-2	0-1	22		5343
25	Jan 9	A	Notts Co	W	1-0	1-0	21	Mardon [6]	4669
26	16	H	Blackpool	W	3-0	0-0	18	Holt [48], Allott [55], Duxbury [57]	5353
27	26	A	Fulham	L	0-1	0-1	—		8160
28	30	A	York C	W	1-0	1-0	17	Holt [38]	3760
29	Feb 6	H	Lincoln C	W	2-0	0-0	17	Thom [71], Mardon [81]	5220
30	13	A	Macclesfield T	L	0-1	0-0	19		4038
31	20	H	Northampton T	L	0-1	0-1	19		4752
32	27	A	Preston NE	L	1-2	1-1	19	Mardon [45]	12,965
33	Mar 6	H	Bournemouth	L	2-3	0-2	20	Whitehall [47], Duxbury [75]	4453
34	9	A	Colchester U	D	2-2	0-1	—	Whitehall [56], Duxbury [75]	3616
35	13	A	Manchester C	W	2-1	1-0	18	Reid (pen) [27], Duxbury [56]	30,321
36	20	H	Millwall	L	0-1	0-1	18		4565
37	27	A	Wycombe W	L	0-3	0-3	20		4083
38	Apr 2	H	Luton T	D	1-1	0-0	—	Garnett [62]	4948
39	5	A	Wigan Ath	L	0-2	0-1	20		4754
40	10	H	Burnley	D	1-1	1-0	22	Tipton [37]	8542
41	13	H	Bristol R	W	2-1	0-1	—	Sheridan [58], Rickers [65]	3913
42	17	A	Wrexham	W	2-1	1-1	19	Garnett [40], Holt [84]	3267
43	24	H	Gillingham	L	1-4	1-3	20	Beavers [33]	5331
44	May 1	A	Walsall	L	1-3	0-2	22	Duxbury [56]	9184
45	4	H	Stoke C	W	1-0	0-0	—	Beavers [50]	5015
46	8	H	Reading	W	2-0	2-0	20	Innes [5], Rickers [27]	7724

Final League Position: 20

GOALSCORERS

League (48): Allott 7, Duxbury 6, Holt 5, Rickers 4, Whitehall 4, Graham 3, Mardon 3, Beavers 2, Garnett 2, Littlejohn 2, Sheridan 2, Tipton 2, Innes 1, McGinlay 1, McNiven S 1, Reid 1 (pen), Thom 1, own goal 1.
Worthington Cup (3): Allott 1, Littlejohn 1, Reid 1 (pen).
FA Cup (5): McGinlay 2 (1 pen), Duxbury 1, McNiven S 1, Salt 1.

Kelly G 45	McNiven S 33 + 4	Innes M 8 + 5	Duxbury L 41	Graham R 11	Sinnott L 14 + 4	Rickers P 44 + 1	Orlygsson T 19 + 3	McNiven D 1 + 5	Allott M 32 + 9	Reid P 40	Holt A 39 + 4	Littlejohn A 11 + 5	Whitehall S 28 + 8	Garnett S 36 + 1	Salt P 3 + 6	Tipton M 15 + 13	Ritchie A — + 1	Hodgson D — + 1	Clitheroe L 1 + 1	Thom S 19 + 6	McLean I 5	McGinlay J 4 + 3	Sheridan J 30	Spooner N 2	Miskelly D 1	Mardon P 12	Swan I 1	Gray A 4	Walsh D — + 1	Beavers P 7	Hotte M — + 1	Sugden R — + 2	Match No.
1	2	3¹	4	5	6	7²	8	9	10	11	12	13																					1
1	2		6	5	4	7¹	8	9		11	3	10	12																				2
1	2		6	5		7	8²	9		11	3	10¹	12	4	13																		3
1	2		6	5		7	8		9	11	3	10		4																			4
1	2		6	5		7	8	9		11	3	10		4																			5
1	2		6	5		7	8		10	11	3	9		4																			6
1	2		6	5		7	8	12	10	11	3¹	9		4																			7
1	2		6	12		7	8		10	11	3	9	5¹	4																			8
1	2		6	5		7	8	12	9	11	3	10¹³		4²																			9
1	2		6	5	4	7		12	8¹	11	3	9² 10		13																			10
1	2		6	5	4	7				8² 11	3	12 10¹							9³ 13 14														11
1	2	6¹	4	5	7	12			13 11	3³ 10		14	9²		8																		12
1	2		4	7	8	12	10	9 13	11¹	3											5	6²										13
1	2		6	7	8	10¹ 11	9	4	12												5	3										14
1	2		6	7	8	10³	13 12	4²	14												5	3	9¹ 11									15
1			6	9	8			12 13	10	4											5	3¹	7² 11	2								16
1		6		9		12 13		8	14 10¹	4											5	3³	7 11	2¹								17
1		6		2		12	11	3	10¹	4 13	9										5²		7 8									18
1	2		6			5		12 11	3	10²	4	7¹	9										13 8									19
1	2		6			12 5			7 11	3¹	10	4	9										8									20
1	2²		6			5			7¹ 11	3	10³	4	9		13 12						14	8									21
	2 12		6		4	5			13 11	3	10¹		9²							7			8	1								22
1	2 12		6		3	5 9			7	11		10¹	4									13	8									23
1	2 12		6		3	5 9¹			7	11		10²	4									13	8									24
1	2		6		12 5		9	11	3	10²		13							7			8¹			4							25
1	2		6			5		9	11	3	10								7			8			4							26
1	2		6			5		9		3	10¹	4	12						7			8			11							27
1	2		6		12	5		9¹ 11	3	10²	4	13							7			8										28
1			6			5		9	11	3	10¹	4	12						7			8	2									29
1	4		6		3	5		9	11		12								7			8	2									30
1			6			5 12		9	11¹	3	10²	4	13						7			8	2									31
1	5²		6			7		9	11¹	3	10	4	12						13			8	2									32
1	2¹		6			5 12		10² 11³	3	13	4	9						14			8	7									33
1	12		6			5 2			11	3	10	4	9¹						13			8	7²									34
1	12		6			7 5¹			13 11	3	10	4	9²						2			8										35
1	12		6			7² 5³			13 11	3	10	4 14	9						2¹			8										36
1	12	6		3	7	5¹			13 11		10	4² 14										8					2³ 9					37
1	12	6				5			10 11	3		13	4	9²								8				2	7¹					38
1		6				5			10 11	3		12	4	9								8				2	7¹					39
1	5	8³ 6				12			11	3		13	4	9								8				2	7¹ 14	10²			40
1	2	7² 6				5			11	3		12	4	9¹								8							10 13		41
1	2	7 6				5		12 11	3		10¹	4 8		13														9²			42
1	2	7 6				5¹			11	3		10²	4	13								12	8						9			43
1	2¹	6				10		7	11	3			4	12								5	8						9²	13	44
1		7 6				2			10 11	3			4 13	12²								5	8						9¹		45
1	12	7 6²				2		9	11¹	3			4 13									5	8						10³	14	46

Division 2 **OXFORD UNITED**

FOUNDATION

There had been an Oxford United club around the time of World War I but only in the Oxfordshire Thursday League and there is no connection with the modern club which began as Headington in 1893, adding 'United' a year later. Playing first on Quarry Fields and subsequently Wootten's Fields, they owe much to a Dr. Hitchings for their early development.

Manor Ground, Headington, Oxford OX3 7RS.

Telephone: (01865) 761503.

Fax: (01865) 741820.

Website: www.oufc.co.uk.

Email: oxford-united@community.co.uk.

Supporters Club: (01865) 763063.

Clubline: 0891 440055.

Ground Capacity: 9572.

Record Attendance: 22,750 v Preston NE, FA Cup 6th rd, 29 February 1964.

Record Receipts: £136,423 v Chelsea, FA Cup 4th rd, 25 January 1999.

Pitch Measurements: 110yd × 75yd.

President: The Duke of Marlborough.

Directors: G. E. Coppock, N. J. W. Harris, M. G. Evans.

Manager: Malcolm Shotton.

Coach: Mark Harrison.

Physio: John Clinkard.

Secretary: Mick Brown.

Commercial Manager: Trevor Baxter.

Stadium Manager: Mick Moore.

LATEST SEQUENCES

Longest Sequence of League Wins: 6, 6.4.85 – 24.4.85.

Longest Sequence of League Defeats: 7, 4.5.91 – 7.9.91.

Longest Sequence of League Draws: 5, 7.10.78 – 28.10.78.

Longest Sequence of Unbeaten League Matches: 20, 17.3.84 – 29.9.84.

Longest Sequence Without a League Win: 27, 14.11.87 – 27.8.88.

HONOURS

Football League: Division 1 best season: 12th, 1997–98; Division 2 – Champions 1984–85; Runners-up 1995–96; Division 3 – Champions 1967–68, 1983–84; Division 4 – Promoted 1964–65 (4th).

FA Cup: best season: 6th rd, 1964 (shared record for 4th Division club).

Football League Cup: Winners 1986.

Colours
Yellow shirts with navy trim, navy shorts, navy stockings.

Change Colours
All white.

Year Formed: 1893.

Turned Professional: 1949.

Ltd Co.: 1949.

Club Nickname: 'The U's'.

Previous Names: 1893, Headington; 1894, Headington United; 1960, Oxford United.

Previous Grounds: 1893, Headington Quarry; 1894, Wootten's Field; 1898, Sandy Lane Ground; 1902, Britannia Field; 1909, Sandy Lane; 1910, Quarry Recreation Ground; 1914, Sandy Lane; 1922, The Paddock Manor Road; 1925, Manor Ground.

First Football League Game: 18 August 1962, Division 4, v Barrow (a) L 2–3 – Medlock; Beavon, Quartermain; R. Atkinson, Kyle, Jones; Knight, G. Atkinson (1), Houghton (1), Cornwell, Colfar.

Record League Victory: 7–0 v Barrow, Division 4, 19 December 1964 – Fearnley; Beavon, Quartermain; R. Atkinson (1), Kyle, Jones; Morris, Booth (3), Willey (1), G. Atkinson (1), Harrington (1).

MANAGERS

Harry Thompson 1949–58
(Player-Manager) 1949-51
Arthur Turner 1959–69
(continued as General Manager to 1972)
Ron Saunders 1969
George Summers 1969–75
Mike Brown 1975–79
Bill Asprey 1979–80
Ian Greaves 1980–82
Jim Smith 1982–85
Maurice Evans 1985–88
Mark Lawrenson 1988
Brian Horton 1988–93
Denis Smith 1993–97
Malcolm Crosby 1997
Malcolm Shotton January 1998–

Record Cup Victory: 9–1 v Dorchester T, FA Cup 1st rd, 11 November 1995 – Whitehead; Wood (2), Ford M (1), Smith, Elliott, Gilchrist, Rush (1), Massey (Murphy), Moody (3), Ford R (1), Angel (Beauchamp (1)).

Record Defeat: 0–7 v Sunderland, Division 1, 19 September 1998.

Most League Points (2 for a win): 61, Division 4, 1964–65.

Most League Points (3 for a win): 95, Division 3, 1983–84.

Most League Goals: 91, Division 3, 1983–84.

Highest League Scorer in Season: John Aldridge, 30, Division 2, 1984–85.

Most League Goals in Total Aggregate: Graham Atkinson, 77, 1962–73.

Most League Goals in One Match: 4, Tony Jones v Newport Co, Division 4, 22 September 1962; 4, Arthur Longbottom v Darlington, Division 4, 26 October 1963; 4, Richard Hill v Walsall, Division 2, 26 December 1988; 4, John Durnin v Luton T, 14 November 1992.

Most Capped Player: Jim Magilton, 18 (39), Northern Ireland.

Most League Appearances: John Shuker, 478, 1962–77.

Youngest League Player: Jason Seacole, 16 years 149 days v Mansfield T, 7 September 1976.

Record Transfer Fee Received: £1,600,000 from Leicester C for Matt Elliott, January 1997.

Record Transfer Fee Paid: £475,000 to Aberdeen for Dean Windass, August 1998.

Football League Record: 1962 Elected to Division 4; 1965–68 Division 3; 1968–76 Division 2; 1976–84 Division 3; 1984–85 Division 2; 1985–88 Division 1; 1988–92 Division 2; 1992–94 Division 1; 1994–96 Division 2; 1996–99 Division 1; 1999– Division 2.

TEN YEAR LEAGUE RECORD

		P	W	D	L	F	A	Pts	Pos
1988-89	Div 2	46	14	12	20	62	70	54	17
1989-90	Div 2	46	15	9	22	57	66	54	17
1990-91	Div 2	46	14	19	13	69	66	61	10
1991-92	Div 2	46	13	11	22	66	73	50	21
1992-93	Div 1	46	14	14	18	53	56	56	14
1993-94	Div 1	46	13	10	23	54	75	49	23
1994-95	Div 2	46	21	12	13	66	52	75	7
1995-96	Div 2	46	24	11	11	76	39	83	2
1996-97	Div 1	46	16	9	21	64	68	57	17
1997-98	Div 1	46	16	10	20	60	64	58	12

DID YOU KNOW ?

The Rev. Michael Chantry became the Oxford United club chaplain in 1962, two years after the club changed its name. He is the longest serving in this capacity at a football club in the entire country.

OXFORD UNITED 1998–99 LEAGUE RECORD

Match No.	Date	Venue	Opponents	Result	H/T Score	Lg. Pos.	Goalscorers	Attendance
1	Aug 8	A	Bristol C	D 2-2	1-2	—	Murphy 18, Windass 48	13,729
2	15	H	Wolverhampton W	L 0-2	0-1	19		7521
3	22	A	Crystal Palace	L 0-2	0-2	22		14,827
4	29	H	Grimsby T	D 0-0	0-0	21		5587
5	31	A	Barnsley	L 0-1	0-1	22		15,328
6	Sept 6	H	Portsmouth	W 3-0	2-0	22	Marsh 28, Windass 2 (1 pen) 34 (p), 74	6626
7	9	A	Swindon T	L 1-4	1-1	—	Banger 25	8305
8	12	H	Ipswich T	D 3-3	1-1	20	Banger 21, Windass 50, Thomson 90	6632
9	19	A	Sunderland	L 0-7	0-3	21		34,567
10	26	H	QPR	W 4-1	1-0	19	Beauchamp 15, Murphy 64, Thomson 72, Windass 75	7489
11	29	H	WBA	W 3-0	2-0	—	Beauchamp 5, Powell 32, Marsh 73	7437
12	Oct 3	A	Huddersfield T	L 0-2	0-2	18		10,968
13	10	H	Tranmere R	L 1-2	1-1	21	Windass 8	5862
14	17	A	Bolton W	D 1-1	1-1	19	Thomson 40	17,064
15	20	A	Bury	L 0-1	0-0	—		3436
16	24	H	Sheffield U	L 0-2	0-1	22		6586
17	31	H	Crewe Alex	D 1-1	0-0	22	Windass 71	5607
18	Nov 7	A	Watford	L 0-2	0-1	23		10,137
19	14	A	Birmingham C	W 1-0	1-0	22	Murphy 27	18,216
20	21	H	Port Vale	W 2-1	2-1	21	Windass (pen) 6, Powell 13	5964
21	29	A	Norwich C	W 3-1	2-1	18	Wilsterman 34, Windass 45, Thomson 48	17,851
22	Dec 5	A	Bradford C	L 0-1	0-1	20		5969
23	12	H	Birmingham C	L 1-7	0-4	21	Windass 90	7189
24	19	A	Stockport Co	L 0-2	0-1	22		6500
25	26	H	Crystal Palace	L 1-3	0-0	22	Windass 68	8375
26	28	A	Portsmouth	D 2-2	1-0	22	Banger 2 44, 71	12,604
27	Jan 9	H	Bristol C	D 0-0	0-0	21		9434
28	16	A	Grimsby T	L 0-1	0-1	22		6626
29	30	H	Barnsley	W 1-0	0-0	21	Windass 60	6174
30	Feb 6	A	Wolverhampton W	D 1-1	1-1	21	Windass 39	20,811
31	13	H	Swindon T	W 2-0	1-0	20	Windass 2 (1 pen) 17 (p), 81	8179
32	20	A	Ipswich T	L 1-2	1-2	20	Remy 43	16,920
33	27	H	Sunderland	D 0-0	0-0	20		9044
34	Mar 3	A	QPR	L 0-1	0-0	—		9040
35	6	A	WBA	L 0-2	0-1	20		13,875
36	9	H	Huddersfield T	D 2-2	1-1	—	Cook 7, Beauchamp 82	6034
37	13	H	Watford	D 0-0	0-0	21		8137
38	20	A	Crewe Alex	L 1-3	0-0	22	Thomson 60	4791
39	26	A	Sheffield U	W 2-1	1-1	—	Thomson 32, Banger 90	14,115
40	Apr 3	H	Bolton W	D 0-0	0-0	20		7547
41	5	A	Tranmere R	D 2-2	0-2	20	Weatherstone 74, Gilchrist 87	7837
42	10	H	Bury	L 0-1	0-1	20		6358
43	17	A	Port Vale	L 0-1	0-0	22		7393
44	24	H	Norwich C	L 2-4	1-1	23	Wilsterman 29, Francis 77	7345
45	May 1	A	Bradford C	D 0-0	0-0	23		15,064
46	9	H	Stockport Co	W 5-0	3-0	23	Gilchrist 33, Powell 43, Beauchamp 44, Murphy 63, Thomson 90	6830

Final League Position: 23

GOALSCORERS

League (48): Windass 15 (3 pens), Thomson 7, Banger 5, Beauchamp 4, Murphy 4, Powell 3, Gilchrist 2, Marsh 2, Wilsterman 2, Cook 1, Francis 1, Remy 1, Weatherstone 1.
Worthington Cup (4): Murphy 2, Weatherstone 1, Whelan 1.
FA Cup (6): Windass 3 (1 pen), Murphy 2, Gilchrist 1.

Whitehead P 21	Robinson L 44	Marsh S 20+1	Gray M 40	Davis S 3	Gilchrist P 39	Banger N 22+10	Windass D 33	Murphy M 33+10	Thomson A 25+13	Beauchamp J 31+6	Powell P 40+4	Smith D 19+3	Weatherstone S 4+8	Hill D 1+8	Remy C 10+2	Whelan P 14+1	Cook J 9+10	Wilsterman B 12+5	Wright T 4+2	Rose A 1+3	Jackson E 1	Salmon M 1	Gerrard P 16	Watson M 23	Warren M 4	Tait P 17	Francis K 12+6	Williams M —+2	Lundin P 7	Match No.
1	2	3	4	5^1	6	7^2	8	9	10^3	11	12	13	14																	1
1	2	3	4^2	5	6	7	8	10^1		11	12	9^3	13	14																2
1	2	12	4	5	6	13	8	10					3	9^2	11^3	7	14													3
1	2	3	4		6	9^3	8^1	10	14	11	7^2	12			5		13													4
1	2	3	4		6	12	8	10^3	14	11	7^2	13			5		9^1													5
1	2	3	4^1		6^2		8	10	13	11	7	12			5	9														6
1	2	3	4^1		7^2		8	10	13	11	6	12			5	9														7
1	2	3	4			7^2	8	9^1	10	11	12	13			5	6														8
1	2	3	4		6		8	9	10	11	7				5															9
1	2	3	4		6	7^2	8	9	10^3	11	12	13			5^1		14													10
1	2	3	4		6	7^2	8	9^1	10	11	12				5		13													11
1	2	3^3	4		6	7	8	9^1	10	11	12				5^2	13	14													12
1	2	3	4		6	7^2	8	9^1	10	11	12		13		5															13
1	2	3	4		6		8	9	10	11	12			7^1	5															14
1	2	3	4		6		8	9	10	11^1	12		13	7^2	5															15
1	2	3	4		6	7	8^2	9^1	10	11	12				5			13												16
1	2	3	4		6		8	9^1	10	11	12				5	7														17
1	2		4				8	9	10^1		12	3			5	7	13	14	11^2	6^3										18
1	2	3	4		6		8	9	10	11	12			7^1	5															19
1	2	3	4		6		8	9^1	10	11^2	12				5	7	13													20
1	2	3	4		6		8	9^1	10	11	12				5	7														21
	2	3	4		6		8	9	10	11	12			7^1	5						1									22
	2		4		6		8	9^1	10	11	12	3	13		5	7^2						1								23
	2				6^3		8	9	10^1	11^2	12	3	13						4				1	5	14	7				24
	2						8	9	10	11	12	3				7^1		13	14	4^3			1	5	6^2					25
	2						8	9^1	10	11	12	3				7^3		13	14	4^2			1	5	6					26
	2				6		8	9	10	11		3				7			4				1	5						27
	2		4		6			9	10	11^1	12					7^2		13					1	5		3	8			28
	2		4		6			9^1	10	11		3											1	5		7	8	12		29
	2		4		6		8		10	11		3						13					1	5^1		7^2	9	12		30
	2		4		6				10	11	12	3						13					1	5		7^1	8	9^2		31
	2		4		6		8^1		10	11	12	3				7^2		13					1	5			9			32
	2		4		6				10	11	12					7^1		13					1	5			8^2	9		33
	2		4		6				10	11	12	3^1				7		13					1	5			8	9^2		34
	2		4		6				10	11	12	3^3	14			7^1		13					1	5			8	9^2		35
	2		4		6			9	10	11		3				7^1							1	5			8	12		36
	2		4		6			9	10	11	12	3				7^2							1	5			8	13		37
	2		4		6			9	10		12	3			11^2	7^1							1	5			8	13		38
	2		4		6	7			10^1	11^2	12	3											1	5		8	9	13		39
	2		4		6	7			10	11^1		3												5		8	9	12	1	40
	2		4		6	7			10^2	11^1	12	3												5		8	9	13	1	41
	2		4		6	7^1			10^2	11	12	3												5		8	9	13	1	42
	2		4		6	7^2			10	11	12	3												5		8	9	13	1	43
	2		4		6^2	7			10^3	11	12	3			9^1									5		8	14	13	1	44
	2		4		6	7			10^1	11	12	3			9^2									5		8		13	1	45
	2		4		6	7^2			10^3	11	12	3			14									5		8	9^1	13	1	46

Worthington Cup
First Round   Luton T   (a) 3-2 / (h) 1-3

FA Cup
Third Round   Crewe Alex   (a) 3-1
Fourth Round   Chelsea   (h) 1-1 / (a) 2-4

Division 3   **PETERBOROUGH UNITED**

FOUNDATION

The old Peterborough & Fletton club, founded in 1923, was suspended by the FA during season 1932–33 and disbanded. Local enthusiasts determined to carry on and in 1934 a new professional club Peterborough United was formed and entered the Midland League the following year. Peterborough's first success came in 1939–40, but from 1955–56 to 1959–60 they won five successive titles. During the 1958–59 season they were undefeated in the Midland League. They reached the third round of the FA Cup, won the Northamptonshire Senior Cup, the Maunsell Cup and were runners-up in the East Anglian Cup.

London Road Ground, Peterborough PE2 8AL.

Telephone: (01733) 563947.

Fax: (01733) 557210.

Ground Capacity: 15,314.

Record Attendance: 30,096 v Swansea T, FA Cup 5th rd, 20 February 1965.

Record Receipts: £51,315 v Brighton & HA, FA Cup 5th rd, 15 February 1986.

Pitch Measurements: 112yd × 75yd.

Chairman: Peter Boizot MBE, DL.

Vice-Chairman: Roger Terrell.

Directors: A. Hand, N. Hards, P. Sagar.

Company Secretary: Timothy Warren.

Club Secretary: Caroline Hand.

General Manager: David Gledhill.

First Team Manager: Barry Fry.

First Team Coach: Paul Ashworth.

Youth Academy Director: Kit Carson.

Physio: Phil McLoughlin.

LATEST SEQUENCES

Longest Sequence of League Wins: 9, 1.2.92 – 14.3.92.

Longest Sequence of League Defeats: 5, 8.10.96 – 26.10.96.

Longest Sequence of League Draws: 8, 18.12.71 – 12.2.72.

Longest Sequence of Unbeaten League Matches: 17, 17.12.60 – 8.4.61.

Longest Sequence Without a League Win: 17, 23.9.78 – 30.12.78.

HONOURS

Football League: Division 1 best season: 10th, 1992–93; Division 4 – Champions 1960–61, 1973–74.

FA Cup: best season: 6th rd, 1965.

Football League Cup: Semi-final 1966.

Colours

Royal blue shirts, white shorts, blue stockings with white tops.

Change Colours

All red.

Year Formed: 1934.

Turned Professional: 1934.

Ltd Co.: 1934.

Club Nickname: 'The Posh'.

First Football League Game: 20 August 1960, Division 4, v Wrexham (h) W 3–0 – Walls; Stafford, Walker; Rayner, Rigby, Norris; Hails, Emery (1), Bly (1), Smith, McNamee (1).

Record League Victory: 9–1 v Barnet (a) Division 3, 5 September 1998 – Griemink; Hooper (1), Drury (Farell), Gill, Bodley, Edwards, Davies, Payne, Grazioli (5), Quinn (2) (Rowe), Houghton (Etherington) (1).

Record Cup Victory: 7–0 v Harlow T, FA Cup 1st rd, 16 November 1991 – Barber; Luke, Johnson, Halsall (1), Robinson D, Welsh, Sterling (1) (Butterworth), Cooper G (2 incl. 1p), Riley (1) (Culpin (1)), Charlery (1), Kimble.

Record Defeat: 1–8 v Northampton T, FA Cup 2nd rd (2nd replay), 18 December 1946.

Most League Points (2 for a win): 66, Division 4, 1960–61.

Most League Points (3 for a win): 82, Division 4, 1981–82.

Most League Goals: 134, Division 4, 1960–61.

Highest League Scorer in Season: Terry Bly, 52, Division 4, 1960–61.

Most League Goals in Total Aggregate: Jim Hall, 122, 1967–75.

Most League Goals in One Match: 5, Guiliano Grazioli v Barnet, Division 3, 5 September 1998.

Most Capped Player: Tony Millington, 8 (21), Wales.

Most League Appearances: Tommy Robson, 482, 1968–81.

Youngest League Player: Matthew Etherington, 15 years 262 days v Brentford, 3 May 1997.

Record Transfer Fee Received: £450,000 from Birmingham C for Martin O'Connor, November 1996.

Record Transfer Fee Paid: £350,000 to Walsall for Martin O'Connor, July 1996.

Football League Record: 1960 Elected to Division 4; 1961–68 Division 3, when they were demoted for financial irregularities; 1968–74 Division 4; 1974–79 Division 3; 1979–91 Division 4; 1991–92 Division 3; 1992–94 Division 1; 1994–97 Division 2; 1997– Division 3.

MANAGERS

Jock Porter 1934–36
Fred Taylor 1936–37
Vic Poulter 1937–38
Sam Madden 1938–48
Jack Blood 1948–50
Bob Gurney 1950–52
Jack Fairbrother 1952–54
George Swindin 1954–58
Jimmy Hagan 1958–62
Jack Fairbrother 1962–64
Gordon Clark 1964–67
Norman Rigby 1967–69
Jim Iley 1969–72
Noel Cantwell 1972–77
John Barnwell 1977–78
Billy Hails 1978–79
Peter Morris 1979–82
Martin Wilkinson 1982–83
John Wile 1983–86
Noel Cantwell 1986–88
*(continued as
General Manager)*
Mick Jones 1988–89
Mark Lawrenson 1989–90
Chris Turner 1991–92
Lil Fuccillo 1992–93
John Still 1994–95
Mick Halsall 1995–96
Barry Fry May 1996–

TEN YEAR LEAGUE RECORD

		P	W	D	L	F	A	Pts	Pos
1988-89	Div 4	46	14	12	20	52	74	54	17
1989-90	Div 4	46	17	17	12	59	46	68	9
1990-91	Div 4	46	21	17	8	67	45	80	4
1991-92	Div 3	46	20	14	12	65	58	74	6
1992-93	Div 1	46	16	14	16	55	63	62	10
1993-94	Div 1	46	8	13	25	48	76	37	24
1994-95	Div 2	46	14	18	14	54	69	60	15
1995-96	Div 2	46	13	13	20	59	66	52	19
1996-97	Div 2	46	11	14	21	55	73	47	21
1997-98	Div 3	46	18	13	15	63	51	67	10

DID YOU KNOW ?

In 1959–60 as a prelude to gaining Football League status, Peterborough United won the Midland League for the fifth successive time, scoring in every League game and all but one FA Cup tie.

PETERBOROUGH UNITED 1998–99 LEAGUE RECORD

Match No.	Date	Venue	Opponents	Result	H/T Score	Lg. Pos.	Goalscorers	Attendance
1	Aug 8	H	Halifax T	L	0-2	0-0	—	5746
2	15	A	Cardiff C	W	3-1	0-1	9	McKenzie 2 [51, 88], Carruthers [55]	5629
3	22	A	Southend U	D	1-1	0-0	13	Quinn [52]	5323
4	29	A	Hull C	L	0-1	0-1	18		4636
5	31	H	Exeter C	W	4-1	3-1	9	Quinn 2 [22, 24], McKenzie [42], Edwards [61]	4256
6	Sept 5	A	Barnet	W	9-1	4-1	7	Quinn 2 [16, 41], Grazioli 5 [26, 28, 51, 55, 89], Hooper [79], Etherington [90]	2330
7	8	H	Chester C	W	3-0	3-0	—	Grazioli [14], Houghton [16], Davies [37]	4548
8	12	A	Shrewsbury T	D	1-1	0-0	6	Davies [77]	2225
9	19	H	Plymouth Arg	L	0-2	0-1	9		5870
10	26	A	Hartlepool U	W	2-1	1-1	7	Carruthers [26], Scott [66]	2385
11	Oct 3	H	Brentford	L	2-4	1-1	9	Grazioli [21], Etherington [50]	6056
12	10	A	Darlington	L	0-3	0-2	10		3178
13	17	H	Rochdale	W	2-0	2-0	9	Farrell [11], Grazioli [38]	4536
14	20	H	Carlisle U	L	0-1	0-0	—		3785
15	31	H	Rotherham U	L	2-4	2-0	12	Inman [23], McKenzie [42]	4796
16	Nov 7	A	Swansea C	D	0-0	0-0	15		3771
17	10	H	Cambridge U	W	2-1	2-1	—	Castle [20], McKenzie [24]	10,168
18	21	A	Torquay U	W	1-0	0-0	9	Butler [83]	2093
19	28	H	Scunthorpe U	W	2-1	1-1	9	McKenzie [36], Broughton (pen) [72]	5160
20	Dec 1	A	Mansfield T	L	0-1	0-0	—		3169
21	12	A	Leyton Orient	W	2-1	1-1	8	McKenzie [17], Broughton [80]	4718
22	19	H	Scarborough	W	3-1	2-0	5	Farrell [18], Edwards [25], McKenzie [82]	4444
23	26	A	Southend U	L	0-2	0-1	6		6159
24	28	H	Brighton & HA	L	1-2	0-1	9	Broughton [84]	7912
25	Jan 9	A	Halifax T	D	2-2	1-0	8	Castle [13], Butler (pen) [46]	2784
26	16	H	Cardiff C	W	2-1	0-1	6	Castle [46], Grazioli [90]	5890
27	23	A	Exeter C	L	0-2	0-0	9		2933
28	26	H	Hull C	D	1-1	0-0	—	Hanlon [90]	4405
29	30	A	Brighton & HA	L	0-1	0-0	9		4444
30	Feb 6	H	Barnet	W	5-2	1-2	8	Sawyers (og) [33], Andrews 4 [53, 54, 63, 80]	4668
31	13	A	Chester C	L	0-1	0-1	9		2087
32	20	H	Shrewsbury T	D	2-2	1-1	11	Castle [3], Broughton [71]	4608
33	27	A	Plymouth Arg	W	2-0	2-0	8	Andrews [3], Broughton [31]	5959
34	Mar 6	H	Hartlepool U	D	1-1	0-1	7	Broughton (pen) [58]	4854
35	9	A	Brentford	L	0-3	0-1	—		4195
36	13	H	Swansea C	L	0-1	0-1	11		4182
37	20	A	Rotherham U	D	2-2	2-0	11	Grazioli [17], Davies [18]	3979
38	28	H	Mansfield T	W	1-0	0-0	10	Farrell [76]	5507
39	Apr 3	A	Rochdale	W	3-0	1-0	10	Davies [36], Grazioli 2 [46, 74]	1696
40	5	H	Darlington	L	0-1	0-1	10		5107
41	10	A	Carlisle U	D	1-1	0-1	9	Scott [88]	3064
42	13	A	Scunthorpe U	D	1-1	0-1	—	Scott [66]	3296
43	17	H	Torquay U	W	4-0	1-0	9	Grazioli [27], Etherington [58], Hooper [72], Green [90]	4162
44	24	A	Cambridge U	D	1-1	1-1	9	Grazioli [7]	8307
45	May 1	H	Leyton Orient	W	3-0	0-0	8	Farrell (pen) [62], Grazioli [76], Broughton [90]	6189
46	8	A	Scarborough	D	1-1	1-1	9	Scott [7]	4769

Final League Position: 9

GOALSCORERS

League (72): Grazioli 15, McKenzie 8, Broughton 7 (2 pens), Andrews 5, Quinn 5, Castle 4, Davies 4, Farrell 4 (1 pen), Scott 4, Etherington 3, Butler 2 (1 pen), Carruthers 2, Edwards 2, Hooper 2, Green 1, Hanlon 1, Houghton 1, Inman 1, own goal 1.
Worthington Cup (1): Carruthers 1.
FA Cup (0).

Tyler M 27	Scott R 19+8	McMenamin C 4+1	Castle S 26	Bodley M 24	Edwards A 41	Farrell D 28+9	Payne D 8+1	Shields T 6+3	Carruthers M 13+1	Quinn J 7	Koogi A —+1	Houghton S 7+1	Gill M 22+4	Hooper D 36+2	Grazioli G 21+13	Griemink B 17	Drury A 39+1	Davies S 43	McKenzie L 14	Etherington M 21+8	Rowe Z —+7	De Souza M 3	Allardyce C 4	Martin J —+4	Legg A 5	Cleaver C —+2	Inman N 1+2	Linton D 8	Butler S 13+1	Broughton D 14+11	Chapple P 1	Hanlon R —+4	Hann M —+4	Rennie D 9	Connor D 2	Andrews W 8+2	Forbes S 1+2	Wicks M 11	Green F 3+4	Match No.
1	2	3	4	5	6	7^1	8^2	9^3	10	11			12	13	14																									1
	8			5	6			9	10					4	2	1	3	7		11																				2
	8			5	6			9	10					4	2	1	3	7		11																				3
12				5	6		8	9^2	10					4^3	2	1	3	7^1	13	11	14																			4
				5	6		8	9^1	10	11			12	4	2	1	3	7																						5
				5	6	12	8	9	10^3	11^2				4	2	1	3^1	7	13		14																			6
		3		5	6	12	8^1	9^3	10	11^2				4	2	1		7	13		14																			7
		3		5	6	12	8	9^2	10	11				4^1	2	1		7^3	13		14																			8
		3		5	6	12	8^1	9^3	10	11^2				4	2	1		7	13		14																			9
1	8			5				9^1	10					4	2		3	7		11^2	12		6		13															10
1	8			5	6			9	10					4	2		3	7		11^1				12																11
	8	12		5	6	13	7^1	9	10^3					4	2	1	3			11^2	14																			12
				5		7		9	11^1					4	2	1	8			12		10^2	6		3	13														13
						7^3		5^2						4^1	2	1	12	8		11		10	6		3	13	14													14
12		8^3		5	14			13		9^2	1			7	11^1			6		3		4	2	10																15
1	4			8^1	5	6			13	12				3	7	11^3		10	14	2^2	9																			16
1	4^1			8	5	6	13	12						3	7	11		10^2		2^2	9																			17
1	4			5	6	7		12						3	8	11		2^1	10	9																				18
1	4			5	6	7		2						3	8	11	12	10^1	9																					19
1	4^1			5^3	6	7	12	2	13					3	8	11	14	10	9^2																					20
1	12			8		6	7	2						3	4	10	11^1	9	5																					21
1	2			8	5	6	7	12						3	4	10	11^2	9^1	13																					22
1				8	5	7		2	12					3	4	10	11^1	6	9																					23
1	12			8^3	5	6	7^2	13						2^1	3	4	10	11	9	14																				24
1	2^3			8		6	11	10^1						4	12	3	7	13	9^2										14	5										25
1	7			8		6		9^3						2	12	3	4	11^1											10^2	13				14	5					26
1	7			8		6		9^3						2	12	3	4	11^1											10^2	13				14	5					27
1^3				8	5	6	7							2	10^2	3	4	11		12									9^1	13	14									28
				8	5	6	7							2	9^2	3	4	11^3		12									10^1	13	14					1				29
				8	5	6	12	7^1						2	13	3	4	11											10^3	14						1	9^2			30
				8		6	12	7						2	13	1	3	4		11^1									10^2							5	9			31
				8		6	7									1	3	4		11				2					10							5	9			32
	12			8		6	7									1	3	4		11^1				2					10							5	9			33
				8		6	7							11^2	12	1	3	4						2					10^1							5	9	13		34
				8		6	11									1	3	4	12					2					10^1							5	9	7		35
1				8		6	11							4^2	2		3	7	9^1																		12	13	5	10	36
1				8		6	11							4	2	10	3	7	9																			5		37
1	7					6	11	8						4	2	10	3																				9^1	5	12	38
1	13			8		6	11	14						4	2	10^1	3	7^2											12				13				5	9^3	39
1	12			8^1		6	11	14						4^3	2	10	3	7											12								5	9^2	40
1	13			8^3		6	11	14						4^2	2	10	3	7											12							9^1	5		41
1	8					6	11	4						2	10		3	7	9^1																	12	5		42
1	8					6	11	4					12	2^1	10^2		3	7	9^3										13								5	14	43
1	8					6	11	4						2	10		3	7	9^1										12								5		44
1	8					6	11	4^3				14		2	10^1		3	7	9^2										12								5	13	45
1	8						11	4^1						2	10		3	7	9^2										12					6			5	13	46

Worthington Cup
First Round   Reading   (h)   1-1
                                  (a)   0-2

FA Cup
First Round   Wrexham   (a)   0-1

Division 3 **PLYMOUTH ARGYLE**

FOUNDATION

The club was formed in September 1886 as the Argyle Football Club by former public and private school pupils who wanted to continue playing the game. The meeting was held in a room above the Borough Arms (a Coffee House), Bedford Street, Plymouth. It was common then to choose a local street/terrace as a club name and Argyle or Argyll was a fashionable name throughout the land due to Queen Victoria's great interest in Scotland.

Home Park, Plymouth, Devon PL2 3DQ.

Telephone: (01752) 562561.

Fax: (01752) 606167.

Pilgrim Shop: (01752) 558292.

Ground Capacity: 19,630.

Record Attendance: 43,596 v Aston Villa, Division 2, 10 October 1936.

Record Receipts: £128,000 v Burnley, Division 2 play-off, 18 May 1994.

Pitch Measurements: 110yd × 72yd.

President: S. J. Rendell.

Chairman: D. McCauley.

Vice-Chairman: P. Bloom.

Directors: Paul Stapleton, John McNulty, Ken Jones, Roy Griggs.

Manager: Kevin Hodges.

Assistant Manager: Steve McCall.

Physio: Norman Medhurst.

Secretary/Chief Executive: Roger Matthews.

LATEST SEQUENCES

Longest Sequence of League Wins: 9, 8.3.86 – 12.4.86.

Longest Sequence of League Defeats: 9, 12.10.63 – 7.12.63.

Longest Sequence of League Draws: 5, 3.5.97 – 30.8.97.

Longest Sequence of Unbeaten League Matches: 22, 20.4.29 – 21.12.29.

Longest Sequence Without a League Win: 13, 27.4.63 – 2.10.63.

HONOURS

Football League: Division 2 best season: 4th, 1931–32, 1952–53; Division 3 (S) – Champions 1929–30, 1951–52; Runners-up 1921–22, 1922–23, 1923–24, 1924–25, 1925–26, 1926–27 (record of six consecutive years); Division 3 – Champions 1958–59; Runners-up 1974–75, 1985–86, Promoted 1995–96 (play-offs).
FA Cup: Semi-final 1984.
Football League Cup: Semi-final 1965, 1974.

Colours
Green and white shirts, white shorts, green, black and white stockings.

Change Colours
All white.

Year Formed: 1886.

Turned Professional: 1903.

Ltd Co.: 1903.

Previous Name: 1886, Argyle Athletic Club; 1903, Plymouth Argyle.

Club Nickname: 'The Pilgrims'.

First Football League game: 28 August 1920, Division 3, v Norwich C (h) D 1–1 – Craig; Russell, Atterbury; Logan, Dickinson, Forbes; Kirkpatrick, Jack, Bowler, Heeps (1), Dixon.

Record League Victory: 8–1 v Millwall, Division 2, 16 January 1932 – Harper; Roberts, Titmuss; Mackay, Pullan, Reed; Grozier, Bowden (2), Vidler (3), Leslie (1), Black (1), (1 og). 8–1 v Hartlepool U (a), Division 2, 7 May 1994 – Nicholls; Patterson (Naylor), Hill, Burrows, Comyn, McCall (1), Barlow, Castle (1), Landon (3), Marshall (1), Dalton (2).

Record Cup Victory: 6–0 v Corby T, FA Cup 3rd rd, 22 January 1966 – Leiper; Book, Baird; Williams, Nelson, Newman; Jones (1), Jackson (1), Bickle (3), Piper (1), Jennings.

Record Defeat: 0–9 v Stoke C, Division 2, 17 December 1960.

Most League Points (2 for a win): 68, Division 3 (S), 1929–30.

Most League Points (3 for a win): 87, Division 3, 1985–86.

Most League Goals: 107, Division 3 (S), 1925–26 and 1951–52.

Highest League Scorer in Season: Jack Cock, 32, Division 3 (S), 1925–26.

Most League Goals in Total Aggregate: Sammy Black, 180, 1924–38.

Most League Goals in One Match: 5, Wilf Carter v Charlton Ath, Division 2, 27 December 1960.

Most Capped Player: Moses Russell, 20 (23), Wales.

Most League Appearances: Kevin Hodges, 530, 1978–92.

Youngest League Player: Lee Phillips, 16 years 43 days v Gillingham, 29 October 1996.

Record Transfer Fee Received: £750,000 from Southampton for Mickey Evans, March 1997.

Record Transfer Fee Paid: £250,000 to Hartlepool U for Paul Dalton, June 1992.

Football League Record: 1920 Original Member of Division 3; 1921–30 Division 3 (S); 1930–50 Division 2; 1950–52 Division 3 (S); 1952–56 Division 2; 1956–58 Division 3 (S); 1958–59 Division 3; 1959–68 Division 2; 1968–75 Division 3; 1975–77 Division 2; 1977–86 Division 3; 1986–95 Division 2; 1995–96 Division 3; 1996–98 Division 2; 1998– Division 3.

MANAGERS

Frank Brettell 1903–05
Bob Jack 1905–06
Bill Fullerton 1906–07
Bob Jack 1910–38
Jack Tresadern 1938–47
Jimmy Rae 1948–55
Jack Rowley 1955–60
Neil Dougall 1961
Ellis Stuttard 1961–63
Andy Beattie 1963–64
Malcolm Allison 1964–65
Derek Ufton 1965–68
Billy Bingham 1968–70
Ellis Stuttard 1970–72
Tony Waiters 1972–77
Mike Kelly 1977–78
Malcolm Allison 1978–79
Bobby Saxton 1979–81
Bobby Moncur 1981–83
Johnny Hore 1983–84
Dave Smith 1984–88
Ken Brown 1988–90
David Kemp 1990–92
Peter Shilton 1992–95
Steve McCall 1995
Neil Warnock 1995–97
Mick Jones 1997–98
Kevin Hodges June 1998–

TEN YEAR LEAGUE RECORD

		P	W	D	L	F	A	Pts	Pos
1988-89	Div 2	46	14	12	20	55	66	54	18
1989-90	Div 2	46	14	13	19	58	63	55	16
1990-91	Div 2	46	12	17	17	54	68	53	18
1991-92	Div 2	46	13	9	24	42	64	48	22
1992-93	Div 2	46	16	12	18	59	64	60	14
1993-94	Div 2	46	25	10	11	88	56	85	3
1994-95	Div 2	46	12	10	24	45	83	46	21
1995-96	Div 3	46	22	12	12	68	49	79	4
1996-97	Div 2	46	12	18	16	47	58	54	19
1997-98	Div 2	46	12	13	21	55	70	49	22

DID YOU KNOW ?

The only Plymouth Argyle goalkeeper in the club's history to be credited with at least one goal was Fred Craig who scored five times from the penalty spot in 362 League appearances in the 1920s. He had joined the club pre-First World War.

PLYMOUTH ARGYLE 1998–99 LEAGUE RECORD

Match No.	Date	Venue	Opponents	Result	H/T Score	Lg. Pos.	Goalscorers	Attendance
1	Aug 8	H	Rochdale	W 2-1	0-1	—	Mauge 52, Jean 78	5547
2	15	A	Mansfield T	L 0-2	0-2	17		2451
3	22	H	Barnet	W 2-0	1-0	7	Heathcote 5, McCarthy 73	5080
4	29	A	Scunthorpe U	W 2-0	1-0	4	Heathcote 8, Jean 55	2868
5	31	H	Halifax T	W 1-0	1-0	3	Gibbs 42	6544
6	Sept 5	A	Cardiff C	L 0-1	0-0	5		3939
7	8	A	Rotherham U	W 2-0	1-0	—	Gibbs (pen) 32, McCarthy 51	3442
8	12	H	Darlington	L 1-2	1-1	5	Mauge 19	5709
9	19	A	Peterborough U	W 2-0	1-0	4	Heathcote 44, Barlow 54	5870
10	26	H	Scarborough	D 0-0	0-0	4		5216
11	Oct 3	A	Torquay U	D 1-1	0-0	6	Gibbs (pen) 81	5719
12	17	A	Shrewsbury T	L 1-2	0-1	10	Seabury (og) 64	2778
13	20	H	Brighton & HA	W 3-1	1-0	—	Collins 26, Barlow 2 (1 pen) 53, 90 (p)	1793
14	31	H	Hull C	D 0-0	0-0	9		4285
15	Nov 3	H	Brentford	W 3-0	1-0	—	Barlow 28, Taylor 76, Bastow 85	4650
16	7	A	Hartlepool U	L 0-2	0-2	7		2121
17	10	H	Swansea C	L 1-2	0-1	—	Marshall 78	4517
18	21	A	Southend U	L 0-1	0-0	10		3814
19	28	H	Leyton Orient	L 2-4	1-1	12	Joseph M (og) 9, Collins 74	4240
20	Dec 12	A	Cambridge U	L 0-1	0-1	13		3933
21	19	H	Carlisle U	W 2-0	1-0	13	Bastow 22, McCarthy 83	4236
22	26	A	Barnet	D 1-1	1-0	13	Forinton 21	2519
23	28	H	Exeter C	W 1-0	0-0	12	Forinton 73	11,936
24	Jan 9	A	Rochdale	D 1-1	1-0	13	Branston 14	1922
25	16	H	Mansfield T	W 3-0	2-0	10	Marshall 2 13, 43, Hargreaves 46	4399
26	23	A	Halifax T	L 0-2	0-0	10		2762
27	30	A	Exeter C	D 1-1	1-1	11	Forinton 27	6746
28	Feb 6	H	Cardiff C	D 1-1	1-0	11	Marshall 19	6062
29	13	H	Rotherham U	W 1-0	0-0	11	Marshall 59	4336
30	20	A	Darlington	W 2-1	1-0	10	Jean 32, Marshall 72	2643
31	23	H	Chester C	W 2-0	2-0	—	Sweeney 13, Marshall 42	4208
32	27	H	Peterborough U	L 0-2	0-2	7		5959
33	Mar 9	H	Torquay U	D 0-0	0-0	—		7856
34	13	H	Hartlepool U	D 0-0	0-0	8		4441
35	20	A	Hull C	L 0-1	0-0	10		6294
36	27	A	Chester C	L 2-3	1-0	11	Marshall 37, Hargreaves 72	1982
37	30	H	Scunthorpe U	W 5-0	2-0	—	Guinan 3 25, 30, 71, Marshall 58, Sale 75	3589
38	Apr 3	H	Shrewsbury T	W 2-0	1-0	8	Marshall 40, Barlow 61	5749
39	5	A	Brentford	L 1-3	0-2	8	Marshall 80	6979
40	10	H	Brighton & HA	L 1-2	1-1	10	Guinan 42	4911
41	13	A	Leyton Orient	L 3-4	2-2	—	Guinan 36, Marshall 45, Mauge 52	4095
42	17	H	Southend U	L 0-3	0-2	12		3949
43	24	A	Swansea C	W 3-2	0-2	11	Guinan 2 72, 85, Wotton (pen) 77	5660
44	May 1	H	Cambridge U	D 2-2	1-1	11	Eustace (og) 8, Crowe 61	5006
45	5	A	Scarborough	L 0-3	0-1	—		2398
46	8	A	Carlisle U	L 1-2	0-0	13	Phillips 49	7599

Final League Position: 13

GOALSCORERS

League (58): Marshall 12, Guinan 7, Barlow 5 (1 pen), Forinton 3, Gibbs 3 (2 pens), Heathcote 3, Jean 3, Mauge 3, McCarthy 3, Bastow 2, Collins 2, Hargreaves 2, Branston 1, Crowe 1, Phillips 1, Sale 1, Sweeney 1, Taylor 1, Wotton 1 (pen), own goals 3.
Worthington Cup (3): McCarthy 2, Jean 1.
FA Cup (4): Heathcote 1, Sweeney 1, Wotton 1 (pen), own goal 1.

Sheffield J 39	Collins S 40	Gibbs P 27	McCall S 14 + 3	Heathcote M 43	Wotton P 32 + 4	Barlow M 45	Mauge R 31 + 1	Jean E 21 + 8	Power L 7 + 9	Hargreaves C 30 + 2	Gritton M — + 2	McCarthy S 14 + 2	Flash R 4 + 1	Beswetherick J 18 + 4	Ashton J 22 + 4	Wills K — + 2	Edmondson D 4	Marshall D 25 + 3	Taylor C 6	Ford L — + 1	Crittenden N 1 + 1	Bastow D 21 + 8	Phillips L 8 + 7	Branston G 7	Sweeney T 6 + 7	Forinton H 8 + 1	Crowe G 3 + 8	Marker N 4	Sale M 8	Guinan S 11	Dungey J 7	Barrett A — + 1	McGovern B — + 2	Match No.
1	2	3	4	5	6	7	8	9	10^{2}	11	12	13																						1
1	2^{2}	3	4	5	6	7^{1}	10	9	12	11				8	13																			2
1	10	3		5	6	7	4	9^{1}	12	11				8^{2}	2		13																	3
1	10	3		5	6	7	4	9^{1}	12	11				8	2																			4
1	10	3	12	5	6	7	4^{1}	9^{2}	13	11				8	2																			5
1	10	3		5	6	7	4	9^{1}	12	11				8	2^{2}		13																	6
1	10	3		5	6	7	4	9^{1}	12	11				8^{2}			2	13																7
1	10	3		5	6^{2}	7	4	9	12	11^{1}				8				13	2															8
1	10	3		5	6	7	4	12	9^{1}	11				8				2																9
1	10	3	12	5	6	7	4^{1}	13	9^{2}	11				8				2																10
1	10	3	11	5	6	7	4	12	9^{1}					8				2^{2}	13															11
1	2	4^{2}		5	6	7	8	9			12			3^{1}				11				10	13											12
1	2	11		5	6	7	8	9						3								10	4											13
1		11		5	6	7	8	9			12	13		3^{2}							2^{1}	10	4											14
1	2	11^{3}		5	6	7	8	9^{1}			12			3								10^{2}	4				13						14	15
1	2	11		5	6	7	8	9^{1}			12			3								10	4											16
1	2	11^{1}		5	6	7	8		12					3^{2}				9				10	4				13							17
1	2			5	6	7	8							3				9				10	4			11								18
1	2			5	6^{1}	7	8^{3}		12					3				9				10^{2}	4			11	13						14	19
1				5	6	7	8							3^{2}	2			9				10	12	4		11^{1}	13							20
1	6	3		5	7		8		10^{1}						2			9					4	12		11^{2}	13							21
1				5	6	7	8		12					3	2			9				10^{1}		4		11								22
1				5	6	7	8		12					3	2			9				10^{2}	4^{1}			11	13							23
1	6^{1}			5		7	8		12					3	2			9^{2}				10		4		11	13							24
1	6	10^{1}		5	7		8							3	2			9					4	12		11								25
1	6	10^{3}	4^{2}		7		8		12					3	2			9^{1}						5		11	13						14	26
1	6	3		5	7	4	8								2			9				10				11								27
1	6	3		5	7		8		12						2			9^{2}				10^{1}	4			11	13							28
1	6	3		5	7		8		12						2			9^{2}				10	4^{1}			11	13							29
1	6	3		5	7		8								2			9^{1}				10	12	4		11								30
1	6	3		5	7		8^{1}		12						2			9^{2}				10		4		11	13							31
1	6	3		5	7		8^{3}								2			9				10	12	4^{2}		11^{1}	13						14	32
1	6	3		5	7	4	8								2			9				10	12			11^{1}								33
1	6	3^{2}		5	7		8								2			9				10	12	4		11^{1}	13							34
1	6	3		5	7		8		12						2			9^{2}				10		4^{1}		11	13							35
1^{2}	6	3		5	7	4	8		12						2			9^{3}									13		10	11^{1}			14	36
	6^{3}	3^{1}		5	7	4	8		12						2			9									13		10	11^{2}		1	14	37
	6			5	7	4	8		12						2			9^{1}				10					13		10	11		1		38
1	6	3		5	7	4^{2}	8^{1}		12						2			9				10					13			11				39
1	6	3		5	7	4^{1}	8		12						2			9				10^{2}					13			11				40
1	6	3		5	7	4	8								2			9				10								11				41
	6	3^{2}		5	7	4	8		12						2			9^{1}				10					13			11	1			42
	6			5	7	4	8							3	2							10							9	11	1			43
	6			5	7	4	8^{1}		12					3	2							10							9	11	1			44
	6			5	7	4^{2}	8^{1}		12					3	2							10					13		9	11	1			45
	6			5	7	4^{3}	8^{1}		12					3	2							10^{2}					13		9	11	1		14	46

Worthington Cup

First Round	Portsmouth	(h)	1-3
		(a)	2-3

FA Cup

First Round	Kidderminster H	(h)	0-0
		(a)	0-0
Second Round	Wycombe W	(a)	1-1
		(h)	3-2
Third Round	Derby Co	(h)	0-3

Division 1 **PORTSMOUTH**

Fratton Park, Frogmore Rd, Portsmouth PO4 8RA.
Telephone: (01705) 731204.
Fax: (01705) 734129.
Commercial Dept: (01705) 731204.
Ticket Office: (01705) 618777/861963.
Fax: (01705) 750825.
Membership Office: (01705) 825016.
Clubcall: 0891 121182.
Ground Capacity: 19,179.
Record Attendance: 51,385 v Derby Co, FA Cup 6th rd, 26 February 1949.
Record Receipts: £233,000 v Chelsea, FA Cup 6th rd, 9 March 1997.
Pitch Measurements: 110yd × 72yd.
Chairman: Milan Mandaric.
Director: F. Dinenage.
Managing Director: David Deacon.
Manager: Alan Ball.
First Team Coach: Kevin Bond.
Secretary: Paul Weld.
Marketing Manager: David Morton.
Reserve Team Coach: Ted MacDougall.
Youth Team Coach: Neil McNab.
Physio: Jonathon Trigg.

LATEST SEQUENCES

Longest Sequence of League Wins: 7, 22.1.83 – 26.2.83.
Longest Sequence of League Defeats: 9, 21.10.75 – 6.12.75.
Longest Sequence of League Draws: 5, 28.9.77 – 15.10.77.
Longest Sequence of Unbeaten League Matches: 15, 18.4.24 – 18.10.24.
Longest Sequence Without a League Win: 25, 29.11.58 – 22.8.59.

HONOURS

Football League: Division 1 – Champions 1948–49, 1949–50; Division 2 – Runners-up 1926–27, 1986–87; Division 3 (S) – Champions 1923–24; Division 3 – Champions 1961–62, 1982–83.
FA Cup: Winners 1939; Runners-up 1929, 1934.
Football League Cup: best season: 5th rd, 1961, 1986.

Colours
Blue shirts, white shorts, red stockings.

Change Colours
Gold shirts, blue shorts, white stockings.

Year Formed: 1898.

Turned Professional: 1898.

Ltd Co.: 1898.

Club Nickname: 'Pompey'.

First Football League Game: 28 August 1920, Division 3, v Swansea T (h) W 3–0 – Robson; Probert, Potts; Abbott, Harwood, Turner; Thompson, Stringfellow (1), Reid (1), James (1), Beedie.

Record League Victory: 9–1 v Notts Co, Division 2, 9 April 1927 – McPhail; Clifford, Ted Smith; Reg Davies (1), Foxall, Moffat; Forward (1), Mackie (2), Haines (3), Watson, Cook (2).

Record Cup Victory: 7–0 v Stockport Co, FA Cup 3rd rd, 8 January 1949 – Butler; Rookes, Ferrier; Scoular, Flewin, Dickinson; Harris (3), Barlow, Clarke (2), Phillips (2), Froggatt.

Record Defeat: 0–10 v Leicester C, Division 1, 20 October 1928.

Most League Points (2 for a win): 65, Division 3, 1961–62.

Most League Points (3 for a win): 91, Division 3, 1982–83.

Most League Goals: 91, Division 4, 1979–80.

Highest League Scorer in Season: Guy Whittingham, 42, Division 1, 1992–93.

Most League Goals in Total Aggregate: Peter Harris, 194, 1946–60.

Most League Goals in One Match: 5, Alf Strange v Gillingham, Division 3, 27 January 1923; 5, Peter Harris v Aston Villa, Division 1, 3 September 1958.

Most Capped Player: Jimmy Dickinson, 48, England.

Most League Appearances: Jimmy Dickinson, 764, 1946–65.

Youngest League Player: Clive Green, 16 years 259 days v Wrexham, 21 August 1976.

Record Transfer Fee Received: £3,500,000 from Manchester C for Lee Bradbury, August 1997.

Record Transfer Fee Paid: £650,000 to Celtic for Gerry Creaney, January 1994.

Football League Record: 1920 Original Member of Division 3; 1921 Division 3 (S); 1924–27 Division 2; 1927–59 Division 1; 1959–61 Division 2; 1961–62 Division 3; 1962–76 Division 2; 1976–78 Division 3; 1978–80 Division 4; 1980–83 Division 3; 1983–87 Division 2; 1987–88 Division 1; 1988–92 Division 2; 1992– Division 1.

MANAGERS

Frank Brettell 1898–1901
Bob Blyth 1901–04
Richard Bonney 1905–08
Bob Brown 1911–20
John McCartney 1920–27
Jack Tinn 1927–47
Bob Jackson 1947–52
Eddie Lever 1952–58
Freddie Cox 1958–61
George Smith 1961–70
Ron Tindall 1970–73
    (General Manager to 1974)
John Mortimore 1973–74
Ian St. John 1974–77
Jimmy Dickinson 1977–79
Frank Burrows 1979–82
Bobby Campbell 1982–84
Alan Ball 1984–89
John Gregory 1989–90
Frank Burrows 1990–1991
Jim Smith 1991–95
Terry Fenwick 1995–98
Alan Ball January 1998–

TEN YEAR LEAGUE RECORD

		P	W	D	L	F	A	Pts	Pos
1988-89	Div 2	46	13	12	21	53	62	51	20
1989-90	Div 2	46	15	16	15	62	65	61	12
1990-91	Div 2	46	14	11	21	58	70	53	17
1991-92	Div 2	46	19	12	15	65	51	69	9
1992-93	Div 1	46	26	10	10	80	46	88	3
1993-94	Div 1	46	15	13	18	52	58	58	17
1994-95	Div 1	46	15	13	18	53	63	58	18
1995-96	Div 1	46	13	13	20	61	69	52	21
1996-97	Div 1	46	20	8	18	59	53	68	7
1997-98	Div 1	46	13	10	23	51	63	49	20

DID YOU KNOW ?

Portsmouth's first goal in the Southern League was scored by Harold 'Nobby' Clarke on 2 September 1899 at Chatham. Incredibly a substitute was allowed, who went under the name of Edward 'Old Hookey' Turner!

PORTSMOUTH 1998–99 LEAGUE RECORD

Match No.	Date	Venue	Opponents	Result		H/T Score	Lg. Pos.	Goalscorers	Attendance
1	Aug 8	H	Watford	L	1-2	1-0	—	Aloisi [30]	15,275
2	15	A	Tranmere R	D	1-1	1-1	17	Aloisi [3]	6714
3	22	H	Ipswich T	D	0-0	0-0	18		12,002
4	29	A	Huddersfield T	D	3-3	1-1	15	Johnson (og) [5], Aloisi [48], McLoughlin (pen) [90]	10,085
5	31	H	QPR	W	3-0	1-0	12	Aloisi [34], McLoughlin [87], Phillips [89]	12,106
6	Sept 6	A	Oxford U	L	0-3	0-2	13		6626
7	8	A	Bury	L	1-2	1-2	—	McLoughlin (pen) [41]	4310
8	12	H	Swindon T	W	5-2	2-0	13	Aloisi 2 [14, 88], Igoe 2 [28, 62], Claridge [64]	10,105
9	19	A	Port Vale	W	2-0	0-0	12	Aloisi [52], Durnin [89]	5992
10	26	H	Sunderland	D	1-1	1-0	11	Igoe [21]	17,022
11	29	H	Birmingham C	L	0-1	0-0	—		11,843
12	Oct 3	A	Sheffield U	L	1-2	0-1	17	Aloisi [48]	15,386
13	10	A	Bristol C	D	2-2	1-1	15	Igoe [18], Claridge [70]	13,056
14	17	H	Wolverhampton W	W	1-0	0-0	12	McLoughlin (pen) [66]	13,681
15	20	H	Bradford C	L	2-4	0-3	—	Aloisi 2 [59, 68]	10,062
16	24	A	Barnsley	L	1-2	0-1	18	Durnin [75]	15,152
17	Nov 7	A	Crystal Palace	L	1-4	1-1	20	Aloisi [42]	20,188
18	10	H	Norwich C	L	1-2	1-0	—	Aloisi [29]	9335
19	14	A	Grimsby T	D	1-1	1-1	20	Aloisi [23]	6236
20	21	H	WBA	W	2-1	1-1	18	Nightingale 2 [38, 55]	11,144
21	28	A	Stockport Co	L	0-2	0-0	21		7504
22	Dec 5	H	Crewe Alex	W	2-0	0-0	18	McLoughlin [72], Claridge [89]	9800
23	13	A	Grimsby T	L	0-1	0-0	18		8180
24	19	A	Bolton W	L	1-3	1-0	21	Igoe [1]	15,981
25	26	A	Ipswich T	L	0-3	0-3	21		21,805
26	28	H	Oxford U	D	2-2	0-1	20	Claridge 2 (1 pen) [47, 68 (p)]	12,604
27	Jan 9	A	Watford	D	0-0	0-0	20		12,057
28	16	H	Huddersfield T	W	1-0	1-0	20	Claridge [4]	10,334
29	30	A	QPR	D	1-1	0-0	19	Nightingale [63]	12,270
30	Feb 6	H	Tranmere R	D	1-1	1-1	19	Whittingham [17]	10,597
31	13	H	Bury	W	2-1	1-0	18	Robinson [37], Whittingham [64]	9062
32	20	A	Swindon T	D	3-3	1-3	18	Claridge 2 [44, 74], Peron [76]	10,230
33	27	H	Port Vale	W	4-0	3-0	18	McLoughlin (pen) [29], Whittingham 3 [36, 39, 89]	12,838
34	Mar 2	A	Sunderland	L	0-2	0-1	—		37,656
35	6	A	Birmingham C	L	1-4	1-1	18	Whittingham [4]	20,617
36	9	H	Sheffield U	W	1-0	0-0	—	Awford [64]	10,287
37	13	H	Crystal Palace	D	1-1	0-1	16	Whittingham [89]	15,520
38	20	A	Norwich C	D	0-0	0-0	16		16,662
39	28	H	Barnsley	L	1-3	1-0	17	Durnin [12]	13,337
40	Apr 3	A	Wolverhampton W	L	0-2	0-0	17		23,262
41	5	H	Bristol C	L	0-1	0-0	18		13,026
42	10	H	Bradford C	L	1-2	0-2	19	Durnin [67]	13,552
43	17	A	WBA	D	2-2	2-0	18	Durnin 2 [31, 34]	12,750
44	24	H	Stockport Co	W	3-1	2-0	18	Claridge [10], Simpson [17], Durnin [46]	11,212
45	May 1	A	Crewe Alex	L	1-3	0-3	18	McLoughlin [49]	5759
46	9	H	Bolton W	L	0-2	0-1	19		16,015

Final League Position: 19

GOALSCORERS

League (57): Aloisi 13, Claridge 9 (1 pen), Durnin 7, McLoughlin 7 (4 pens), Whittingham 7, Igoe 5, Nightingale 3, Awford 1, Peron 1, Phillips 1, Robinson 1, Simpson 1, own goal 1.
Worthington Cup (9): Aloisi 3, McLoughlin 3 (2 pens), Hillier 1, Vlachos 1, Whitbread 1.
FA Cup (2): Claridge 1, Nightingale 1.

Flahavan A 13	Hillier D 11 + 5	Simpson F 38 + 3	McLoughlin A 41	Thogersen T 29 + 5	Awford A 35	Vlachos M 29 + 1	Kyzeridis N 2 + 2	Aloisi J 22	Durnin J 16 + 10	Thomson A 14	Robinson M 27 + 2	Soley S 1 + 7	Pethick R 4 + 6	Knight A 20	Whitbread A 33	Claridge S 39	Igoe S 39 + 1	Philips M 2 + 15	Peron J 37 + 1	Perrett R 12 + 3	Waterman D 10	Petterson A 13	Nightingale L 6 + 13	Andreasson S — + 2	Whittingham G 9	Miglioranzi S 4 + 3	Match No.
1	2	3[1]	4[2]	5	6	7	8[3]	9	10	11	12	13	14														1
	12	3	4		6	7[1]	11[2]	9	10	2		13		1	5	8											2
1		3	4		6[2]	7	12	9	10	2		13			5	8[1]	11										3
1	8	3	4		6[1]	7		9	12				2		5	10	11[1]	12									4
1	8	3	4		6	7		9					2		5	10	11	12									5
1	8[1]	3	4	7	6		12	9	10[3]				2		5		11[2]	13	14								6
1		3[1]	4	2[2]	6	7		9	12		14	13			5	10	11[3]		8								7
1		3	4	2	6	7[1]		9	12						5	10	11[2]	13	8								8
1		3	4	2	6			9[1]			12	13			5	10	11		8[1]	7							9
1	12	3	4	2	6			9							5	10[1]	11		8	7							10
1	12	3	4	2	6[1]			9				13			5	10	11[3]	14	8[2]	7							11
1	12	3	4	2	6			9[1]							5	10	11		8	7							12
1		3	4	2	6			9[1]	12						5	10	11		8	7							13
		3	4	2				9			12		6	1	5	10	11		7	8[1]							14
		3	4[1]	2			12	9				13	6	1	5	10	11		8[2]	7							15
		3	4	2	6	7		9[2]				13		1	5[1]	10	11	12	8								16
		3	4	2	6	7		9[2]				13		1	5	10	11	12	8[1]								17
		3	4	2	6			9						1	5[1]	10	11	12	8	7							18
		3	4	2	6			9						1	5	10	11		8	7							19
		3	4	2	6			9[1]						1	5	10	11	12	8	7							20
		3	4	2	6	7		9[1]						1	5	10	11	12	8								21
		3	4	2	6	7		9						1	5[1]	10	11	12	8								22
	12	3	4	2	6			9							5	10[2]	11		8[1]	7		1	13				23
	12	3	4[1]	2	6	7[3]		9							5	10[2]	11		8			1	13	14			24
	5		4	2[1]	6	7		9[2]	10[3]		12						11		8			1	13	14			25
	5[1]		4	2[2]	6	7		9			12					10	11		8			1	13				26
	12	3	4[1]	2	6	7		9						1	5	10	11		8				6				27
		3	4	2				9			12			1	5	10	11		8		6		7[1]				28
		3	4	2				9						1	5		11		8		6		7		10		29
	11[1]	3	4	2	6						12[2]	13		1	5				8				7		10		30
	12	3	4	2	6			9				13		1	5	10	11[1]		8[2]				7				31
1		3[1]	4	2	6			9	13						5	10	11[2]		8	12			14		7		32
		3	4	2	6			9[1]						1	5	10[2]	11		8				13		7		33
		3	4	2	6			9[1]						1	5	10	11[2]	12	8				13		7		34
		3	4	2	6			9[2]	12					1	5	10[3]	11[1]		8				13	14	7		35
		3	4	2	6			9						1	5	10	11		8						7		36
		3[1]	4	2	6			9						1	5	10[2]	11		8	12					7	13	37
		3	4	2					10						5		11	7	8		6	1			9		38
		3	4	2	6			9	12						5	10[1]	11		8			1	7				39
		3	4	2	6			9	12			13			5	10	11[2]		8			1			7[1]		40
		3	4	2	6			9	12						5	10	11[2]	13	8			1	7[1]				41
		3	4	2	6			9	12						5	10	11			7	8[1]	1					42
		3	4	2	6	8		9							5	10[1]	11[2]			7		1	12			13	43
		3	4	2	6			9							5	10	11		8	7[1]		1	12				44
		3	4	2	6[3]			9				13			5	10	11	12	8[1]	7[2]		1				14	45
		3	4	2	6			9[2]				13			5	10	11	12	8[1]	7[3]		1		14			46

Worthington Cup

First Round	Plymouth Arg	(a)	3-1
		(h)	3-2
Second Round	Wimbledon	(h)	2-1
		(a)	1-4

FA Cup

Third Round	Nottingham F	(a)	1-0
Fourth Round	Leeds U	(h)	1-5

Division 1

PORT VALE

FOUNDATION

Formed in 1876 as Port Vale, adopting the prefix 'Burslem' in 1884 upon moving to that part of the city. It was dropped in 1909.

Vale Park, Burslem, Stoke-on-Trent ST6 1AW.

Telephone: (01782) 814134.

Fax: (01782) 834981.

Marketing Dept: (01782) 835524.

Clubcall: 0891 121636.

Marketing Fax: (01782) 836875.

Club Shop: (01782) 833545.

Community: (01782) 575594.

Ground Capacity: 22,356.

Record Attendance: 49,768 v Aston Villa, FA Cup 5th rd, 20 February 1960.

Record Receipts: £170,349 v Everton, FA Cup 4th rd, 14 February 1996.

Pitch Measurements: 114yd × 77yd.

President: J. Burgess.

Chairman: W. T. Bell LAE, TECH. ENG, MIMI.

Directors: A. Belfield, I. McPherson, P. Wright, N. Hughes (Marketing Director).

Manager: Brian Horton.

Secretary: F. W. Lodey.

Coach: Bill Dearden.

Physio: Alan Rankin.

Medical Officer: Dr D. Phillips.

Safety Officer: W. Stevenson.

Groundsman: S. Speed.

Community Scheme Officer: Jim Cooper (01782 575594).

LATEST SEQUENCES

Longest Sequence of League Wins: 8, 8.4.1893 – 30.9.1893.

Longest Sequence of League Defeats: 9, 9.3.57 – 20.4.57.

Longest Sequence of League Draws: 6, 26.4.81 – 12.9.81.

Longest Sequence of Unbeaten League Matches: 19, 5.5.69 – 8.11.69.

Longest Sequence Without a League Win: 17, 7.12.91 – 21.3.92.

HONOURS

Football League: Division 2 – Runners-up 1993–94; Division 3 (N) – Champions 1929–30, 1953–54; Runners-up 1952–53; Division 4 – Champions 1958–59; Promoted 1969–70 (4th).

FA Cup: Semi-final 1954, when in Division 3.

Football League Cup: best season: 3rd rd 1992, 1997.

Autoglass Trophy: Winners 1993.

Anglo-Italian Cup: Runners-up 1996.

Colours

White shirts, black shorts, black and white stockings.

Change Colours

All yellow.

Year Formed: 1876.

Turned Professional: 1885.

Ltd Co.: 1911.

Previous Name: 1876, Burslem Port Vale; 1909, Port Vale.

Club Nickname: 'Valiants'.

Previous Grounds: 1876, Limekin Lane, Longport; 1881, Westport; 1884, Moorland Road, Burslem; 1886, Athletic Ground, Cobridge; 1913, Recreation Ground, Hanley; 1950, Vale Park.

First Football League Game: 3 September 1892, Division 2, v Small Heath (a) L 1–5 – Frail; Clutton, Elson; Farrington, McCrindle, Delves; Walker, Scarratt, Bliss (1), Jones. (Only 10 men).

Record League Victory: 9–1 v Chesterfield, Division 2, 24 September 1932 – Leckie; Shenton, Poyser; Sherlock, Round, Jones; McGrath, Mills, Littlewood (6), Kirkham (2), Morton (1).

Record Cup Victory: 7–1 v Irthlingborough, FA Cup 1st rd, 12 January 1907 – Matthews; Dunn, Hamilton; Eardley, Baddeley, Holyhead; Carter, Dodds (2), Beats, Mountford (2), Coxon (3).

Record Defeat: 0–10 v Sheffield U, Division 2, 10 December 1892. 0–10 v Notts Co, Division 2, 26 February 1895.

Most League Points (2 for a win): 69, Division 3 (N), 1953–54.

Most League Points (3 for a win): 89, Division 2, 1992–93.

Most League Goals: 110, Division 4, 1958–59.

Highest League Scorer in Season: Wilf Kirkham 38, Division 2, 1926–27.

Most League Goals in Total Aggregate: Wilf Kirkham, 154, 1923–29, 1931–33.

Most League Goals in One Match: 6, Stewart Littlewood v Chesterfield, Division 2, 24 September 1922.

Most Capped Player: Sammy Morgan, 7 (18), Northern Ireland.

Most League Appearances: Roy Sproson, 761, 1950–72.

Youngest League Player: Malcolm McKenzie, 15 years 347 days v Newport Co, 12 April 1966.

Record Transfer Fee Received: £2,000,000 from Wimbledon for Gareth Ainsworth, October 1998.

Record Transfer Fee Paid: £500,000 to Lincoln C for Gareth Ainsworth, September 1997.

Football League Record: 1892 Original Member of Division 2. Failed re-election in 1896; Re-elected 1898; Resigned 1907; Returned in Oct, 1919, when they took over the fixtures of Leeds City; 1929–30 Division 3 (N); 1930–36 Division 2; 1936–38 Division 3 (N); 1938–52 Division 3 (S); 1952–54 Division 3 (N); 1954–57 Division 2; 1957–58 Division 3 (S); 1958–59 Division 4; 1959–65 Division 3; 1965–70 Division 4; 1970–78 Division 3; 1978–83 Division 4; 1983–84 Division 3; 1984–86 Division 4; 1986–89 Division 3; 1989–94 Division 2; 1994– Division 1.

MANAGERS

Sam Gleaves 1896–1905
  (Secretary-Manager)
Tom Clare 1905–11
A. S. Walker 1911–12
H. Myatt 1912–14
Tom Holford 1919–24 *(continued as Trainer)*
Joe Schofield 1924–30
Tom Morgan 1930–32
Tom Holford 1932–35
Warney Cresswell 1936–37
Tom Morgan 1937–38
Billy Frith 1945–46
Gordon Hodgson 1946–51
Ivor Powell 1951
Freddie Steele 1951–57
Norman Low 1957–62
Freddie Steele 1962–65
Jackie Mudie 1965–67
Sir Stanley Matthews *(General Manager)* 1965–68
Gordon Lee 1968–74
Roy Sproson 1974–77
Colin Harper 1977
Bobby Smith 1977–78
Dennis Butler 1978–79
Alan Bloor 1979
John McGrath 1980–83
John Rudge 1984–99
Brian Horton February 1999–

TEN YEAR LEAGUE RECORD

		P	W	D	L	F	A	Pts	Pos
1988-89	Div 3	46	24	12	10	78	48	84	3
1989-90	Div 2	46	15	16	15	62	57	61	11
1990-91	Div 2	46	15	12	19	56	64	57	15
1991-92	Div 2	46	10	15	21	42	59	45	24
1992-93	Div 2	46	26	11	9	79	44	89	3
1993-94	Div 2	46	26	10	9	79	46	88	2
1994-95	Div 1	46	15	13	18	58	64	58	17
1995-96	Div 1	46	15	15	16	59	66	60	12
1996-97	Div 1	46	17	16	13	58	55	67	8
1997-98	Div 1	46	13	10	23	56	66	49	19

DID YOU KNOW ?

When Port Vale reached the FA Cup semi-final in 1954, 100 coaches and 14 excursion trains helped ferry supporters to Villa Park while a 70 year old fan from Trenton, New Jersey, USA also made the trip.

PORT VALE 1998–99 LEAGUE RECORD

Match No.	Date	Venue	Opponents	Result	H/T Score	Lg. Pos.	Goalscorers	Attendance
1	Aug 8	H	Birmingham C	L	0-2	0-1	—		10,465
2	15	A	Huddersfield T	L	1-2	0-1	24	Ainsworth [71]	10,030
3	22	H	WBA	L	0-3	0-0	24		8146
4	29	A	Swindon T	D	1-1	1-0	24	Ainsworth [22]	7800
5	31	H	Ipswich T	L	0-3	0-1	24		5485
6	Sept 8	H	Wolverhampton W	W	2-1	1-0	—	Beadle [14], Naylor [58]	8087
7	12	A	Crystal Palace	W	1-0	0-0	19	Beadle [83]	15,983
8	19	H	Portsmouth	L	0-2	0-0	20		5992
9	26	A	Grimsby T	D	2-2	2-0	21	Naylor 2, Beesley [45]	5747
10	29	A	Bradford C	L	0-4	0-1	—		13,245
11	Oct 3	H	Norwich C	W	1-0	0-0	20	Ainsworth [61]	5580
12	11	A	Barnsley	W	2-0	0-0	18	Foyle [47], Beadle [56]	16,195
13	17	H	Bristol C	W	3-2	1-0	15	Beesley [1], Ainsworth 2 [47, 86]	6691
14	20	H	Crewe Alex	W	1-0	0-0	—	Beesley [68]	8205
15	24	A	Watford	D	2-2	1-1	13	Foyle [12], Tankard [82]	8750
16	31	A	Sheffield U	L	2-3	0-1	13	Foyle [56], Beadle [71]	6737
17	Nov 4	A	Bolton W	L	1-3	0-2	—	Beadle [79]	13,324
18	8	A	Stockport Co	L	2-4	1-2	15	Beadle [43], Flynn (og) [56]	7612
19	14	H	Sunderland	L	0-2	0-1	16		8839
20	21	A	Oxford U	L	1-2	1-2	20	McGlinchey [29]	5964
21	28	H	Tranmere R	D	2-2	1-0	20	Foyle 2 [30, 63]	5216
22	Dec 5	A	QPR	L	2-3	1-0	22	Foyle [31], Barker [78]	10,498
23	12	A	Sunderland	L	0-2	0-2	22		37,583
24	19	H	Bury	W	1-0	0-0	20	Barker (pen) [72]	6425
25	26	A	WBA	L	2-3	0-1	20	Naylor 2 [50, 56]	14,929
26	28	H	Bolton W	L	0-2	0-0	21		8201
27	Jan 9	A	Birmingham C	L	0-1	0-1	22		18,632
28	16	H	Swindon T	L	0-1	0-1	23		5405
29	30	A	Ipswich T	L	0-1	0-1	23		16,328
30	Feb 6	H	Huddersfield T	W	2-0	2-0	22	Foyle 2 [22, 33]	6499
31	13	A	Wolverhampton W	L	1-3	1-2	22	Bogie [4]	20,952
32	20	H	Crystal Palace	W	1-0	1-0	21	Tankard [40]	6051
33	27	H	Portsmouth	L	0-4	0-3	21		12,838
34	Mar 9	A	Norwich C	W	4-3	2-1	—	Tankard [14], Russell [35], Walsh [50], Bogie [87]	12,960
35	13	H	Stockport Co	D	1-1	0-1	20	Allen [65]	6456
36	20	A	Sheffield U	L	0-3	0-0	21		15,515
37	23	H	Grimsby T	L	0-1	0-0	—		4980
38	Apr 3	A	Bristol C	L	0-2	0-2	22		11,039
39	5	H	Barnsley	W	1-0	1-0	21	Foyle [8]	5968
40	10	A	Crewe Alex	D	0-0	0-0	22		5606
41	13	H	Bradford C	D	1-1	1-1	—	Lee [20]	6998
42	17	H	Oxford U	W	1-0	0-0	20	Tankard [55]	7393
43	24	A	Tranmere R	D	1-1	0-1	20	Lee [61]	7770
44	27	H	Watford	L	1-2	1-1	—	Widdrington (pen) [28]	7126
45	May 1	H	QPR	W	2-0	1-0	20	Gardner [22], Griffiths [66]	9851
46	9	A	Bury	L	0-1	0-0	21		7567

Final League Position: 21

GOALSCORERS

League (45): Foyle 9, Beadle 6, Ainsworth 5, Naylor 4, Tankard 4, Beesley 3, Barker 2 (1 pen), Bogie 2, Lee 2, Allen 1, Gardner 1, Griffiths 1, McGlinchey 1, Russell 1, Walsh 1, Widdrington 1 (pen), own goal 1.
Worthington Cup (3): Naylor 2, Ainsworth 1.
FA Cup (0).

Boxed (shared) columns: **Brammer D 9**, **Butler T 4**, **Griffiths C 3**, **Widdrington T 9**, **Smith A 7+1**

Musselwhite P 38	Carragher M 8+2	Tankard A 37	Bogie I 31+4	Aspin N 28+2	Snijders M 6+4	Ainsworth G 15	Talbot S 29+4	Beadle P 18+5	Foyle M 32+3	Jansson J 5+2	McGlinchey B 10+5	McQuade J —+3	Koordes R 13+2	Walsh M 18+1	Naylor T 14+8	Mean S 1	Burns L 2+2	Corden W 4+12	Pounewatchy S 2	Barnett D 26+1	Beesley P 33+2	Clarke A 2+4	O'Callaghan G 4	Barker S 23+4	McGill D —+3	Gardner A 14+1	Pilkington K 8	Berntsen R 1	Horlaville C 1+1	Eyre R 8+3	Lyttle D 7	Rougier T 8+5	Brisco N 1	Bent M 10+5	Russell C 8	Allen C 2+3	Lee A 7+4	Match No.
1	2	3^{1}	4	5	6	7	8	9^{2}	10	11^{3}	12	13	14																									1
1	12	3	13	5^{1}	6	7	8^{2}	9	10^{3}	11				4	2	14																						2
1	2	3	4		6	7		9		11^{3}	12		14	5^{1}	10		8^{1}	13																				3
1	2	3	4				8^{2}	12	13	14					10						5		9^{3}	11	11^{1}	6												4
1	2	3	4			7	8	12	9^{1}			13			10						5^{2}				11	6												5
1		3	4			7	8^{2}	9		12	13				2	10^{3}					5	14	11^{1}			6												6
1		3	4			7	8	9		11					2	10					5					6												7
1		3^{1}	4			7	8	9							2	10	12				5				13	6	11^{2}											8
1		3	4		12	7	8			11					2	10^{2}					5^{1}			9	13	6												9
1		3	4^{2}			7	8	12							2	10	11^{1}				5			9	13	6												10
1		3	13		12	7	8^{2}	9		11				4	2	10^{1}					5					6												11
1		3			12	7	8^{1}	9	10	11				4	2						5					6												12
1	2	3	4		12	7		9	10^{1}	11											5			8		6												13
1	2	3	4			7			10	11^{1}	12										5		9	8		6												14
1	12	3	4			7			9^{3}					2	10						5^{1}	14		8	13	6												15
1	2	3	4	5		7^{1}		9	10	12														8		6												16
1	2^{2}	3	4		12	7		9	10	11^{3}											5	14		8^{1}	13	6												17
1		3^{2}	4			7^{1}		9	10	11	12				2						5			8	13	6												18
		3	4					9	10	11					2						5			8		6	1			7^{1}	12							19
		3	4				8^{1}		10	11					2						5				13	6	1			7^{2}	12			9				20
	12	3	4^{1}		6	7	8	9	10	11											5						1		1		2							21
		3	4	5	6	7^{1}	8	9	10	11	12																1				2							22
		3	4	6		7^{2}	8	9^{1}	10	11	12				2^{3}						5	14			13		1											23
		3	4	6		7	8	9	10	11					2						5						1											24
		3	4	6		7	8^{2}	12	10		9	14			2						5^{1}		11^{3}		13		1											25
		3	4	6		7	8^{2}	12	10		9^{1}	14			2						5		11^{3}		13		1											26
1		3	4	6			8	12	10		9^{2}	14			2^{3}						5		11^{1}							7								27
1		3					8		10	11	9				2^{1}			12			5			4		6				7								28
1		3	4	5			8		10		12	14			2^{3}										13	6				7^{2}				9	11^{1}			29
1		3	4	5			8^{1}		10	11	12				2											6				7				9				30
1		3	4	5			8^{3}		10	11	12	13			2^{1}											6				7^{2}	14			9^{3}				31
1		3	4	5			8^{2}		10	11	12	13			2^{1}											6				7				9^{3}				32
1		3	4	5			8		10^{2}	11	12	13			2											6				7^{1}				9				33
1		3^{1}	4	5		7			10	11	12	13			2									8		6								9^{2}				34
1		3				7^{1}			10	11	12				2						5			8	4	6								9				35
1		3	4			7^{1}			10	11	12	13			2						5			8^{2}		6								9				36
1		3	4^{3}			7			10^{2}	11	12	13			2						5					6^{1}					14			9				37
1		3	4			7	8^{2}		10	11^{3}	12	13			2						5	14				6^{1}								9				38
1	2	3^{1}	4			7^{2}	8		10	11	12										5					6					13	14					9^{3}	39
1	2	3	4			7	8		10^{1}	11	12										5					6											9	40
1	2	3	4			7^{3}	8		10^{3}	11^{1}	12										5					6						13					9	41
1	2	3	4			7	8^{1}		10^{2}	11											5					6											9	42
1	2	3	4			7	8^{1}		10^{2}	11	12										5				2	6						13					9	43
1	2	3	4			7^{1}	8		10^{2}	11	12										5					6^{2}						13				14	9	44
1	2	3	4			7	8	9^{2}	10^{1}	11											5					6											13	45
1	2	3^{1}	4			7	8		10	11	12										5					6						13					9^{2}	46

Worthington Cup
First Round   Chester C   (h)   1-2
                                        (a)   2-2

FA Cup
Third Round   Liverpool   (h)   0-3

Division 2   **PRESTON NORTH END**

FOUNDATION

North End Cricket and Rugby Club which was formed in 1863, indulged in most sports before taking up soccer in about 1879. In 1881 they decided to stick to football to the exclusion of other sports and even a 16–0 drubbing by Blackburn Rovers in an invitation game at Deepdale, a few weeks after taking this decision, did not deter them for they immediately became affiliated to the Lancashire FA.

Deepdale, Preston PR1 6RU.
Telephone: (01772) 902020.
Fax: (01772) 653266.
Website: www.prestonnorthend.co.uk.
Email: enquiries@prestonnorthend.co.uk.
Ticket Enquiries: (01772) 902000.
Ticket Office Credit Card Bookings: (01772) 902222.
Corporate Hospitality: (01772) 902048.
Publishing: (01772) 902046.
Community: (01772) 902030.
Kit 1 Shop at Deepdale: (01772) 902040.
Kit 2 Shop, Preston Town Centre: (01772) 887088.
Kit 3 Shop, Leyland: (01772) 624600.
Ground Capacity: 21,412.
Record Attendance: 42,684 v Arsenal, Division 1, 23 April 1938.
Record Receipts: £68,650 v Sheffield W, FA Cup 3rd rd, 4 January 1992.
Pitch Measurements: 110yd × 77yd.
President: Sir Tom Finney OBE, JP.
Chairman: Bryan M. Gray.
Directors: K. W. Leeming and M. J. Woodhouse (snr) (Vice-Chairmen), D. Shaw (Non-Executive), T. Scholes (Finance Director/Company Secretary).
Manager: David Moyes.
Coach/Goalkeeping Coach: Kelham O'Hanlon.
Secretary: M. Wearmouth.

LATEST SEQUENCES

Longest Sequence of League Wins: 14, 25.12.50 – 27.3.51.
Longest Sequence of League Defeats: 8, 22.9.84 – 27.10.84.
Longest Sequence of League Draws: 6, 24.2.79 – 20.3.79.
Longest Sequence of Unbeaten League Matches: 23, 8.9.1888 – 14.9.1889.
Longest Sequence Without a League Win: 15, 14.4.23 – 20.10.23.

HONOURS

Football League: Division 1 – Champions 1888–89 (first champions) 1889–90; Runners-up 1890–91, 1891–92, 1892–93, 1905–06, 1952–53, 1957–58; Division 2 – Champions 1903–04, 1912–13, 1950–51; Runners-up 1914–15, 1933–34; Division 3 – Champions 1970–71, 1995–96; Division 4 – Runners-up 1986–87.

FA Cup: Winners 1889, 1938; Runners-up 1888, 1922, 1937, 1954, 1964.

Double Performed: 1888–89.

Football League Cup: best season: 4th rd, 1963, 1966, 1972, 1981.

Colours
White shirts, navy shorts, white stockings.

Change Colours
All Royal blue.

Year Formed: 1881.

Turned Professional: 1885.

Ltd Co.: 1893.

Club Nicknames: 'The Lilywhites' or 'North End'.

First Football League Game: 8 September 1888, Football League, v Burnley (h) W 5–2 – Trainer; Howarth, Holmes; Robertson, W. Graham, J. Graham; Gordon (1), Ross (2), Goodall, Dewhurst (2), Drummond.

Record League Victory: 10–0 v Stoke, Division 1, 14 September 1889 – Trainer; Howarth, Holmes; Kelso, Russell (1), Graham; Gordon, Jimmy Ross (2), Nick Ross (3), Thomson (2), Drummond (2).

Record Cup Victory: 26–0 v Hyde, FA Cup 1st rd, 15 October 1887 – Addison; Howarth, Nick Ross; Russell (1), Thomson (5), Graham (1); Gordon (5), Jimmy Ross (8), John Goodall (1), Dewhurst (3), Drummond (2).

Record Defeat: 0–7 v Blackpool, Division 1, 1 May 1948.

Most League Points (2 for a win): 61, Division 3, 1970–71.

Most League Points (3 for a win): 90, Division 4, 1986–87.

Most League Goals: 100, Division 2, 1927–28 and Division 1, 1957–58.

Highest League Scorer in Season: Ted Harper, 37, Division 2, 1932–33.

Most League Goals in Total Aggregate: Tom Finney, 187, 1946–60.

Most League Goals in One Match: 7, Jimmy Ross v Stoke, Division 1, 6 October 1888.

Most Capped Player: Tom Finney, 76, England.

Most League Appearances: Alan Kelly, 447, 1961–75.

Youngest League Player: Steve Doyle, 16 years 166 days v Tranmere R, 15 November 1974.

Record Transfer Fee Received: £1,250,000 from WBA for Kevin Kilbane, June 1997.

Record Transfer Fee Paid: £500,000 to Manchester U for Michael Appleton, August 1997.

Football League Record: 1888 Founder Member of League; 1901–04 Division 2; 1904–12 Division 1; 1912–13 Division 2; 1913–14 Division 1; 1914–15 Division 2; 1919–25 Division 1; 1925–34 Division 2; 1934–49 Division 1; 1949–51 Division 2; 1951–61 Division 1; 1961–70 Division 2; 1970–71 Division 3; 1971–74 Division 2; 1974–78 Division 3; 1978–81 Division 2; 1981–85 Division 3; 1985–87 Division 4; 1987–92 Division 3; 1992–93 Division 2; 1993–96 Division 3; 1996– Division 2.

MANAGERS

Charlie Parker 1906–15
Vincent Hayes 1919–23
Jim Lawrence 1923–25
Frank Richards 1925–27
Alex Gibson 1927–31
Lincoln Hayes 1931–1932
Run by committee 1932–36
Tommy Muirhead 1936–37
Run by committee 1937–49
Will Scott 1949–53
Scot Symon 1953–54
Frank Hill 1954–56
Cliff Britton 1956–61
Jimmy Milne 1961–68
Bobby Seith 1968–70
Alan Ball Sr 1970–73
Bobby Charlton 1973–75
Harry Catterick 1975–77
Nobby Stiles 1977–81
Tommy Docherty 1981
Gordon Lee 1981–83
Alan Kelly 1983–85
Tommy Booth 1985–86
Brian Kidd 1986
John McGrath 1986–90
Les Chapman 1990–92
John Beck 1992–94
Gary Peters 1994–98
David Moyes January 1998–

TEN YEAR LEAGUE RECORD

		P	W	D	L	F	A	Pts	Pos
1988-89	Div 3	46	19	15	12	79	60	72	6
1989-90	Div 3	46	14	10	22	65	79	52	19
1990-91	Div 3	46	15	11	20	54	67	56	17
1991-92	Div 3	46	15	12	19	61	72	57	17
1992-93	Div 2	46	13	8	25	65	94	47	21
1993-94	Div 3	42	18	13	11	79	60	67	5
1994-95	Div 3	42	19	10	13	58	41	67	5
1995-96	Div 3	46	23	17	6	78	38	86	1
1996-97	Div 2	46	18	7	21	49	55	61	15
1997-98	Div 2	46	15	14	17	56	56	59	15

DID YOU KNOW ?

For their first two FA Cup finals, Preston North End fielded amateur goalkeepers: Dr Mills Roberts in 1889 and James Frederick Mitchell in 1922; a record since the Football League was formed.

PRESTON NORTH END 1998–99 LEAGUE RECORD

Match No.	Date	Venue	Opponents	Result	H/T Score	Lg. Pos.	Goalscorers	Attendance
1	Aug 8	H	York C	W 3-0	2-0	—	Appleton [2], Rankine [23], Nogan [60]	8656
2	15	A	Luton T	D 1-1	1-0	6	Macken [41]	5392
3	22	H	Stoke C	L 3-4	2-0	7	Nogan 2 [6, 63], Eyres [38]	11,587
4	29	A	Lincoln C	W 4-3	1-1	5	Eyres [33], Macken 2 [74, 90], Nogan [86]	4130
5	31	H	Chesterfield	W 2-0	0-0	3	Harris [66], Kidd [84]	9249
6	Sept 5	A	Bristol R	D 2-2	0-2	3	Harris [49], Jackson [83]	6702
7	8	A	Wycombe W	W 1-0	0-0	—	Nogan [75]	3800
8	12	H	Reading	W 4-0	3-0	2	Jackson 2 [19, 34], Eyres 2 [36, 74]	9836
9	19	A	Oldham Ath	W 1-0	1-0	2	Appleton [8]	8205
10	26	H	Gillingham	D 1-1	0-0	2	Harris [74]	10,506
11	Oct 3	A	Walsall	L 0-1	0-1	3		5802
12	12	A	Manchester C	W 1-0	0-0	—	Parkinson (pen) [71]	28,779
13	17	H	Colchester U	W 2-0	2-0	2	Eyres [12], Nogan [39]	10,483
14	20	H	Macclesfield T	D 2-2	0-2	2	Harris [65], Jackson [88]	10,316
15	24	A	Northampton T	D 1-1	1-0	2	Hill (og) [7]	6085
16	Nov 7	H	Burnley	W 4-1	1-1	3	Rankine [23], Nogan [46], Eyres [49], Byfield [57]	15,888
17	10	H	Millwall	L 0-1	0-1	—		10,228
18	21	A	Blackpool	D 0-0	0-0	4		10,868
19	28	H	Wigan Ath	D 2-2	0-1	4	Macken [71], Rankine [85]	11,562
20	Dec 12	A	Notts Co	W 3-2	0-0	4	Gregan [49], Cartwright [52], Harris [90]	5096
21	19	H	Fulham	L 0-1	0-0	4		12,321
22	26	A	Stoke C	W 1-0	1-0	4	Jackson [7]	23,272
23	28	H	Wrexham	W 3-1	2-0	4	Nogan [22], Cartwright 2 [32, 70]	12,106
24	Jan 9	A	York C	W 1-0	0-0	4	Nogan [71]	5744
25	16	H	Luton T	W 2-1	0-1	3	Nogan [56], Harris [90]	11,034
26	23	A	Chesterfield	W 1-0	0-0	1	Kidd [85]	6138
27	26	A	Bournemouth	L 1-3	0-1	—	Nogan [89]	6170
28	30	A	Wrexham	W 5-0	3-0	2	Jackson [7], Nogan [14], Macken [29], Eyres [67], Kidd [89]	6394
29	Feb 6	H	Bristol R	D 2-2	1-2	2	Cartwright [6], Nogan [71]	12,170
30	13	H	Wycombe W	W 2-1	1-1	1	Basham 2 [9, 81]	10,686
31	20	A	Reading	L 1-2	0-0	2	Basham [80]	10,937
32	23	H	Lincoln C	W 5-0	2-0	—	Basham 2 [15, 65], Nogan 2 [45, 48], Macken [89]	9849
33	27	H	Oldham Ath	W 2-1	1-1	2	Nogan [24], Jackson [65]	12,965
34	Mar 6	A	Gillingham	D 1-1	1-0	2	Gregan [10]	9581
35	14	A	Burnley	W 1-0	0-0	2	Nogan [61]	11,561
36	20	H	Bournemouth	L 0-1	0-1	2		12,882
37	27	H	Northampton T	W 3-0	1-0	2	Basham 2 [36, 63], Macken [70]	10,686
38	Apr 2	A	Colchester U	L 0-1	0-0	—		5644
39	5	H	Manchester C	D 1-1	1-1	2	Basham [1]	20,857
40	10	A	Macclesfield T	L 2-3	1-0	3	Basham 2 [35, 66]	4325
41	13	A	Wigan Ath	D 2-2	2-2	—	Murdock [3], Eyres [40]	5396
42	17	H	Blackpool	L 1-2	0-1	4	Nogan [60]	15,337
43	20	H	Walsall	W 1-0	0-0	—	Gregan [60]	13,337
44	24	A	Millwall	D 2-2	0-0	3	Darby [46], Jackson [61]	6016
45	May 1	H	Notts Co	D 1-1	0-0	3	Macken [48]	11,862
46	8	A	Fulham	L 0-3	0-0	5		17,176

Final League Position: 5

GOALSCORERS

League (78): Nogan 18, Basham 10, Eyres 8, Jackson 8, Macken 8, Harris 6, Cartwright 4, Gregan 3, Kidd 3, Rankine 3, Appleton 2, Byfield 1, Darby 1, Murdock 1, Parkinson 1 (pen), own goal 1.
Worthington Cup (0).
FA Cup (7): Nogan 3, Darby 1, Harris 1, McKenna 1, Rankine 1.

Moilanen T 15	Parkinson G 27	Kidd R 27 + 1	Murdock C 28 + 5	Jackson M 44	Gregan S 40 + 1	Appleton M 13 + 12	Rankine M 42	Nogan K 39 + 3	Macken J 30 + 12	Eyres D 33 + 1	Holt M — + 3	McKenna P 31 + 5	Ludden D 26 + 6	Cartwright L 14 + 13	Harris J 9 + 25	Darby J 12 + 8	Lucas D 31	Byfield D 3 + 2	Harrison C 6	Basham S 15 + 2	Gray A 5	Wright M 1	Alexander G 10	McGregor P 1 + 3	Clement N 4	Match No.
1	2	3	4	5	6^1	7^2	8	9	10	11^3	12	13	14													1
1	2		4	5	6	7	8	9	10^2	11	12	3	13													2
1	2	3		5	6	7	8	9	10^1	11	12	4														3
1	2^3	3	4	5	6		8	9	10	11^1		7^2	12	13	14											4
1	2	3	4	5	6		8^2	9^3	10^1	11		7	12	13	14											5
1	2	3		5	6		8	9^2	10	11^2		7^1	4	12	13	14										6
1	2	4		5	6		8	9	10^2	11		7	3	12	13											7
1	2	4		5^1	6	12	8^2	9	10^3	11		7	3	13	14											8
1	2	4^1	12	5		6	8	9^2	10^3	11		7	3	13	14											9
1	2		4	5	6		8	9	10^2	11		7^1	3	12	13											10
1	2		4	5	6	12	8^1	9	10	11^3		7^2	3	13	14											11
1	2		4	5	6	12	8	9	13	11		7^1	3	14	10^2											12
1	2	5	4		6		8	9	10	11		7	3													13
1	2^1	12	4	5	6^2		8	9	10^3	11		7	3	13	14											14
1	2	4		5	6	12	8	9^1		11		7	3		10											15
	2	4		5		6	8^2	9	12	11		7	3	13			1	10^1								16
	2	4		5	12	6^1	8	9		11^3		7^2	3	13	14		1	10								17
	2	4		5	6		8	9	10^1			11	3	7	12		1									18
	2^1	4		5	6		8	9	12			11	3	7	10		1									19
	2	4	12	5	6		8	9^2	13			3	7^1	10	11^3		1	14								20
	2	4		5	6	12	8	9^2	13			3^1	7	10	11^2		1	14								21
	2	3	4	5	6		8	12	9^2	11			7	13			1	10^1								22
	2	3	4	5	6	12	8	9	10^2	11^1		14	7	13^3			1									23
	2	3^1	4	5		6	8	9	10	11		7		12			1									24
	2		4	5	6	12	8	9^3	10^2	11^1		7		13	14		1			3						25
	2^3	4	12	5	6		8	9^1	10^2			11		7	13	14	1			3						26
		4		5	6		8	9	10^2			11^1	12	7	13		1			3	2					27
		4		5	6^1		8	9^2	10^3	11		7	12		13		1			3	2					28
		4		5	6		8	9	10^2	11^1		7	12		13		1			3	2					29
	5	4			6		8	9^1		11^2		7	12		13		1			3	10^1					30
	2^3	4	12	5	6		8	9				11^2	3^1	7	13	14	1						10			31
	4^1	12	5	6			8	9	13			3	7^2	14			1						10^3	11		32
	4	5	6			8	9	12		3			13				1						10^2	7	11^1	33
	4	5	6			8	9	12	11			3					1						10^1	7		34
	4	5	6^1	12		8	9	13	11^2			3					1						10^3	7		35
	4	5	6^2			8	9	12	11			3	13				1						10	7^1		36
	4	5	6			8^1	9	7	3	11			12				1						10^2	2	13	37
	4	5	6	11^2	8	9	7	11^1	12	13							1						10	2	3	38
	4	5	6	12	8^1	9^2	13	11	7								1						10	2	3	39
	4	5	6	12		9	13	11	8	14							1						10	2	7^2 3^1	40
	4	5	6	12	8^1	13	9^2	11	7								1						10	2	3	41
	4	5	6	12	8^1	13	9^2	11	7^3	3	14						1						10	2		42
	4	5	6	8			9	11	7^3	3	10^1	12					1						10	2		43
	4	5	6				9	11	7	3	11^1	8					1						10	2	12	44
	4	5	6	8			9	7	3	11^1							1						10	2	12	45
	3	4	5	6	11	8^1	9	7	10^2	12							1		13					2		46

Worthington Cup
First Round   Grimsby T   (a)   0-0
                                    (h)   0-0

FA Cup
First Round   Ford U   (h)   3-0
Second Round   Walsall   (h)   2-0
Third Round   Arsenal   (h)   2-4

Division 1   **QUEENS PARK RANGERS**

FOUNDATION

There is an element of doubt about the date of the foundation of this club, but it is believed that in either 1885 or 1886 it was formed through the amalgamation of Christchurch Rangers and St Jude's Institute FC. The leading light was George Wodehouse, whose family maintained a connection with the club until comparatively recent times. Most of the players came from the Queen's Park district so this name was adopted after a year as St Jude's Institute.

South Africa Road, London W12 7PA.
Telephone: (0181) 743 0262.
Fax: (0181) 749 0994.
Box office: (0181) 740 0503.
Supporters Club: (0181) 740 2534.
Club Shop: (0181) 749 6862.
Marketing: (0181) 740 2514.
Ticket Master: (0171) 344 9494.
Ground Capacity: 19,148.
Record Attendance: 35,353 v Leeds U, Division 1, 27 April 1974.
Record Receipts: £218,475 v Manchester U, FA Premier League, 5 February 1994.
Pitch Measurements: 112yd × 72yd.
Chairman: Chris Wright.
Executive Directors: Nick Blackburn, Paul Hart, Simon Crane.
Non-Executive Directors: Lord Terence Burns GCB, Peter Ellis, Charles Levison.
Associate Directors: Andrew Ellis, Tony Ingham, Chris O'Donnell, Keith Westcott, Ross Jones.
Manager: Gerry Francis.
Secretary: Sheila Marson.
Sales and Marketing Executive: Brian Rowe.
Physio: Brian Morris.
Year Formed: 1885* (*see Foundation*).
Turned Professional: 1898.
Ltd Co.: 1899.
Previous Name: 1885, St Jude's; 1887, Queens Park Rangers.
Club Nicknames: 'Rangers' or 'Rs'.

LATEST SEQUENCES

Longest Sequence of League Wins: 8, 7.11.31 – 28.12.31.
Longest Sequence of League Defeats: 9, 25.2.69 – 5.4.69.
Longest Sequence of League Draws: 6, 28.3.98 – 25.4.98.
Longest Sequence of Unbeaten League Matches: 20, 11.3.72 – 23.9.72.
Longest Sequence Without a League Win: 20, 7.12.68 – 7.4.69.

HONOURS

Football League: Division 1 – Runners-up 1975–76; Division 2 – Champions 1982–83; Runners-up 1967–68, 1972–73; Division 3 (S) – Champions 1947–48; Runners-up 1946–47; Division 3 – Champions 1966–67.

FA Cup: Runners-up 1982.

Football League Cup: Winners 1967; Runners-up 1986. (In 1966–67 won Division 3 and Football League Cup.)

European Competitions: UEFA Cup: 1976–77, 1984–85.

Colours
Blue and white hooped shirts, blue shorts, blue stockings.

Change Colours
White shirts, black shorts, black stockings.

Previous Grounds: 1885* (*see Foundation*), Welford's Fields; 1888–99; London Scottish Ground, Brondesbury, Home Farm, Kensal Rise Green, Gun Club Wormwood Scrubs, Kilburn Cricket Ground; 1899, Kensal Rise Athletic Ground; 1901, Latimer Road, Notting Hill; 1904, Agricultural Society, Park Royal; 1907, Park Royal Ground; 1917, Loftus Road; 1931, White City; 1933, Loftus Road; 1962, White City; 1963, Loftus Road.

First Football League Game: 28 August 1920, Division 3, v Watford (h) L 1–2 – Price; Blackman, Wingrove; McGovern, Grant, O'Brien; Faulkner, Birch (1), Smith, Gregory, Middlemiss.

Record League Victory: 9–2 v Tranmere R, Division 3, 3 December 1960 – Drinkwater; Woods, Ingham; Keen, Rutter, Angell; Lazarus (2), Bedford (2), Evans (2), Andrews (1), Clark (2).

Record Cup Victory: 8–1 v Bristol R (away), FA Cup 1st rd, 27 November 1937 – Gilfillan; Smith, Jefferson; Lowe, James, March; Cape, Mallett, Cheetham (3), Fitzgerald (3) Bott (2). 8–1 v Crewe Alex, Milk Cup 1st rd, 3 October 1983 – Hucker; Neill, Dawes, Waddock (1), McDonald (1), Fenwick, Micklewhite (1), Stewart (1), Allen (1), Stainrod (3), Gregory.

Record Defeat: 1–8 v Mansfield T, Division 3, 15 March 1965. 1–8 v Manchester U, Division 1, 19 March 1969.

Most League Points (2 for a win): 67, Division 3, 1966–67.

Most League Points (3 for a win): 85, Division 2, 1982–83.

Most League Goals: 111, Division 3, 1961–62.

Highest League Scorer in Season: George Goddard, 37, Division 3 (S), 1929–30.

Most League Goals in Total Aggregate: George Goddard, 172, 1926–34.

Most League Goals in One Match: 4, George Goddard v Merthyr T, Division 3S, 9 March 1929; 4, George Goddard v Swindon T, Division 3S, 12 April 1930; 4, George Goddard v Exeter C, Division 3S, 20 December 1930; 4, George Goddard v Watford, Division 3S, 19 September 1931; 4, Tom Cheetham v Aldershot, Division 3S, 14 September 1935; 4, Tom Cheetham v Aldershot, Division 3S, 12 November 1938.

Most Capped Player: Alan McDonald, 52, Northern Ireland.

Most League Appearances: Tony Ingham, 519, 1950–63.

Youngest League Player: Frank Sibley, 16 years 97 days v Bristol C, 10 March 1964.

Record Transfer Fee Received: £6,000,000 from Newcastle U for Les Ferdinand, June 1995.

Record Transfer Fee Paid: £2,750,000 to Stoke C for Mike Sheron, July 1997.

Football League Record: 1920 Original Members of Division 3; 1921–48 Division 3 (S); 1948–52 Division 2; 1952–58 Division 3 (S); 1958–67 Division 3; 1967–68 Division 2; 1968–69 Division 1; 1969–73 Division 2; 1973–79 Division 1; 1979–83 Division 2; 1983–92 Division 1; 1992–96 FA Premier League; 1996– Division 1.

MANAGERS

James Cowan 1906–13
Jimmy Howie 1913–20
Ted Liddell 1920–24
Will Wood 1924–25
  (had been Secretary since 1903)
Bob Hewison 1925–30
John Bowman 1930–31
Archie Mitchell 1931–33
Mick O'Brien 1933–35
Billy Birrell 1935–39
Ted Vizard 1939–44
Dave Mangnall 1944–52
Jack Taylor 1952–59
Alec Stock 1959–65
  (General Manager to 1968)
Bill Dodgin Jnr 1968
Tommy Docherty 1968
Les Allen 1968–71
Gordon Jago 1971–74
Dave Sexton 1974–77
Frank Sibley 1977–78
Steve Burtenshaw 1978–79
Tommy Docherty 1979–80
Terry Venables 1980–84
Gordon Jago 1984
Alan Mullery 1984
Frank Sibley 1984–85
Jim Smith 1985–88
Trevor Francis 1988–90
Don Howe 1990–91
Gerry Francis 1991–94
Ray Wilkins 1994–96
Stewart Houston 1996–97
Ray Harford 1997–98
Gerry Francis October 1998–

TEN YEAR LEAGUE RECORD

		P	W	D	L	F	A	Pts	Pos
1988-89	Div 1	38	14	11	13	43	37	53	9
1989-90	Div 1	38	13	11	14	45	44	50	11
1990-91	Div 1	38	12	10	16	44	53	46	12
1991-92	Div 1	42	12	18	12	48	47	54	11
1992-93	PR Lge	42	17	12	13	63	55	63	5
1993-94	PR Lge	42	16	12	14	62	61	60	9
1994-95	PR Lge	42	17	9	16	61	59	60	8
1995-96	PR Lge	38	9	6	23	38	57	33	19
1996-97	Div 1	46	18	12	16	64	60	66	9
1997-98	Div 1	46	10	19	17	51	63	49	21

DID YOU KNOW ?

In the summer of 1925 Jack Gregory left Queens Park Rangers after 11 years to become player-manager of Yeovil & Petters United. In 1946 Alec Stock had the same experience with the then Yeovil Town.

QUEENS PARK RANGERS 1998–99 LEAGUE RECORD

Match No.	Date	Venue	Opponents	Result	H/T Score	Lg. Pos.	Goalscorers	Attendance
1	Aug 8	A	Sunderland	L	0-1	0-0	—	41,008
2	15	H	Bristol C	D	1-1	0-1	20	Ready [90]	13,337
3	22	A	Norwich C	L	2-4	2-3	20	Peacock (pen) [4], Sheron [37]	16,317
4	29	H	Bury	D	0-0	0-0	20		8612
5	31	A	Portsmouth	L	0-3	0-1	21		12,106
6	Sept 8	H	Tranmere R	D	0-0	0-0	—		8070
7	12	A	Watford	L	1-2	0-1	23	Slade [73]	14,251
8	19	H	Stockport Co	W	2-0	0-0	22	Gallen 2 [70, 77]	8205
9	26	A	Oxford U	L	1-4	0-1	23	Scully [89]	7489
10	29	A	Wolverhampton W	W	2-1	2-0	—	Sheron 2 [2, 9]	20,201
11	Oct 3	H	Grimsby T	L	1-2	1-1	23	Maddix [28]	10,240
12	17	A	Huddersfield T	L	0-2	0-1	24		11,276
13	21	A	WBA	L	0-2	0-0	—		11,842
14	25	H	Birmingham C	L	0-1	0-1	24		10,272
15	31	A	Swindon T	L	1-3	1-1	24	Sheron [10]	8500
16	Nov 4	H	Barnsley	W	2-1	2-0	—	Langley [11], Gallen [40]	8218
17	7	H	Bolton W	W	2-0	1-0	22	Gallen [4], Sheron [60]	11,814
18	14	A	Crewe Alex	W	2-0	1-0	21	Peacock [34], Sheron [62]	5001
19	21	H	Sheffield U	L	1-2	0-2	22	Peacock (pen) [49]	12,558
20	28	A	Bradford C	W	3-0	0-0	22	Peacock [49], Gallen [53], Sheron [72]	15,037
21	Dec 2	H	Ipswich T	D	1-1	0-0	—	Gallen [57]	12,449
22	5	H	Port Vale	W	3-2	0-1	17	Maddix [47], Talbot (og) [57], Sheron [88]	10,498
23	12	A	Crewe Alex	L	0-1	0-1	17		11,296
24	19	A	Crystal Palace	D	1-1	0-0	19	Steiner [76]	17,684
25	26	H	Norwich C	W	2-0	2-0	18	Murray [11], Peacock [18]	15,251
26	28	A	Barnsley	L	0-1	0-0	18		17,083
27	Jan 9	H	Sunderland	D	2-2	1-1	17	Maddix [43], Gallen [51]	17,444
28	16	A	Bury	D	1-1	0-1	17	Dowie [66]	4609
29	30	H	Portsmouth	D	1-1	0-0	17	Peacock [50]	12,270
30	Feb 5	A	Bristol C	D	0-0	0-0	—		13,841
31	13	A	Tranmere R	L	2-3	1-1	19	Maddix [18], Rowland [47]	5896
32	20	H	Watford	L	1-2	1-1	19	Peacock [45]	14,918
33	27	A	Stockport Co	D	0-0	0-0	19		7694
34	Mar 3	H	Oxford U	W	1-0	0-0	—	Steiner [46]	9040
35	6	H	Wolverhampton W	L	0-1	0-0	19		13,150
36	13	A	Bolton W	L	1-2	0-1	19	Rowland (pen) [69]	17,919
37	20	H	Swindon T	W	4-0	0-0	19	Steiner [47], Kiwomya 2 [50, 59], Rowland [80]	11,184
38	Apr 3	H	Huddersfield T	D	1-1	0-0	18	Baraclough [52]	11,113
39	5	A	Ipswich T	L	1-3	1-1	19	Kiwomya [4]	22,162
40	10	H	WBA	W	2-1	1-1	17	Ready [45], Peacock [87]	11,158
41	13	A	Grimsby T	L	0-1	0-0	—		4789
42	17	A	Sheffield U	L	0-2	0-1	19		14,341
43	20	A	Birmingham C	L	0-1	0-0	—		20,888
44	24	H	Bradford C	L	1-3	0-1	19	Gallen [79]	11,641
45	May 1	A	Port Vale	L	0-2	0-1	21		9851
46	9	H	Crystal Palace	W	6-0	2-0	20	Kulcsar [8], Kiwomya 3 [43, 56, 85], Scully [76], Breacker [82]	18,498

Final League Position: 20

GOALSCORERS

League (52): Gallen 8, Peacock 8 (2 pens), Sheron 8, Kiwomya 6, Maddix 4, Rowland 3 (1 pen), Steiner 3, Ready 2, Scully 2, Baraclough 1, Breacker 1, Dowie 1, Kulcsar 1, Langley 1, Murray 1, Slade 1, own goal 1.
Worthington Cup (3): Maddix 1, Sheron 1, Slade 1.
FA Cup (0).

Harper L 15	Heinola A 23	Baraclough I 41 + 2	Yates S 6	Ready K 40 + 1	Maddix D 37	Murray P 32 + 7	Peacock G 41 + 1	Rowland K 16 + 14	Gallen K 41 + 3	Scully T 10 + 13	Slade S 10 + 10	Sheron M 21 + 2	Rose M 27 + 2	Kiwomya C 12 + 4	Jones V 1 + 1	Dowie I 7 + 12	Kulcsar G 17	Graham R — + 2	Morrow S 24	Miklosko L 31	Breacker T 18	Langley R 7 + 1	Perry M 1	Steiner R 5 + 7	Plummer C 8 + 2	Jeanne L 7 + 3	Linighan A 4 + 3	Darlington J 4	Match No.
1	2	3	4¹	5	6	7	8	9	10	11	12																		1
1	2	3	4¹	5	6	7	8	13	10²	11	12	9																	2
1	2²		4¹	5	6	7	8	3	10	11	12	9	13																3
1		3		5	6	4	8		10¹	11		7	9	2	12														4
1		3		5¹	6	4	8	12	10	11		7	9²	2	13														5
1	2	3		5	6	4	8		10	11²		7	9¹			13	12												6
1	2	3		5	6	7	8		10	11	12	9¹			4														7
1	2	3	4	5	6	11	8		10	12		7					9¹												8
1	2²	3	4	5	6	11³	8		10	13		7	12	14			9¹												9
1		3	4¹	5	6	2²	8		10		12	9	11			13	7												10
		3¹		5	6	2²	8		10	12		9	11			13	7			1	4								11
		3		5	6	2³	8	12	10	14	13	9	11²				7			1	4¹								12
1		3		5	6		8	11¹	10		7	12	9	2							4								13
		3		5	6²	11	8	13³	10		7	12	9	2					4	1									14
1	2	3		5		8		11	10¹	12		9	4						6			13	7²						15
	2	3		5		8³	12	11	10	13		9	4²			14			6	1		7¹							16
	2	3		5		8		11	10¹			9				4			6	1		7		12					17
	2	3		5		8		11	10			9	5			4			6	1		7		7					18
	2¹	3		5		8		11²	10	12		9	4						6	1		7		13					19
	2	3		5	6	8		12	10			9	11						4	1		7¹							20
	2	3		5	6	11	8¹	12	10	13		9³							4	1		7²		14					21
	2	3		5	6	8			11	10		9	7						4¹	1				12					22
	2			5	6	8			11	10	12	9	7²				3¹		4	1				13					23
	2	3		5	6¹	11²	8	12	10			9	7						4	1				13					24
	2	3		5	6	11	8		10			9¹	7						4	1				12					25
	2	3		5	6	11¹	8		10	12		7		13		9²			4	1									26
	2	3		5	6		8		10			7	11			9			4	1									27
	2¹	3			6	12	8		10			7	11			9			4	1				5					28
		3		5	6¹	7	8	12	10	13		11²				9			4	1				2					29
	2¹	3		5	6	12	8		10	13			11²			9			4	1				7					30
		3¹		5	6	11³	8	12	10	14	13		9						4	1	2²			7					31
				5	6	11	8	3²	10			7				9			4¹	1	2			12	13				32
		3		5		8			10			4				9	7			1	2			6	11				33
		3		5	6²	12	8		10			4				7				1	2			9	13	11¹			34
		3		5		12	8		10³			4	14	13	7¹					1	2			9²	6	11			35
		3		5		8		12	10			4	13	14						1	2	7		9³	6¹	11²			36
		3			6	7¹	8	10	12			5	11	13		4				1	2			9²					37
		3		12	6	7		9¹	10²			5¹	11	13		4				1	2					14			38
		3		5²	6	7	8					11		12	9	4¹				1	2				10	13			39
	12			5	6	7²	8	13	10³		14	11				9				1	2					3	4¹		40
	12			5	6	7	8	13	10		14	11				9¹				1	2					3³	4²		41
1		3		5	6	7²	8	12	10¹			11				13	9				2				14	4³			42
1		3		5	6	12	8	7			10	11				13					2				9²				43
1	4¹	3		5	6	12	8	7²	10		11					13	4¹				2				9²	14			44
		3			9²		8	12	13		10	11				7¹				1	2³			5	14	6	4		45
		3			6	12	8	9²	13	7	10	11¹				4				1	2				5				46

Worthington Cup
First Round   Walsall   (a)   0-0
                                              (h)   3-1
Second Round   Charlton Ath   (h)   0-2
                                               (a)   0-1

FA Cup
Third Round   Huddersfield T   (h)   0-1

Division 2

READING

Madejski Stadium, Junction 11, M4, Reading, Berks RG2 0FL.

Telephone: (0118) 968 1100.

Fax: (0118) 968 1101.

Website: www.readingfc.co.uk.

Email: comments@readingfc.co.uk.

Ticket Office: (0118) 968 1000.

Ticket Office Fax: (0118) 968 1001.

Ground Capacity: 24,200.

Record Attendance: 33,042 v Brentford, FA Cup 5th rd, 19 February 1927.

Record Receipts: £171,203 v Manchester C, Division 2, 27 March 1999.

Pitch Measurements: 112yd × 77yd.

President: F. Orton.

Chairman: John Madejski.

Director: I. Wood-Smith.

Manager: Tommy Burns.

Chief Executive: Nigel Howe.

Physio: Paul Turner.

Commercial Manager: Kevin Girdler.

Secretary: Ms Andrea Barker.

LATEST SEQUENCES

Longest Sequence of League Wins: 13, 17.8.85 – 19.10.85.

Longest Sequence of League Defeats: 7, 10.4.98 – 15.8.98.

Longest Sequence of League Draws: 5, 11.10.97 – 1.11.97.

Longest Sequence of Unbeaten League Matches: 19, 21.4.73 – 27.10.73.

Longest Sequence Without a League Win: 14, 30.4.27 – 29.10.27.

HONOURS

Football League: Division 1 – Runners-up 1994–95; Division 2 – Champions 1993–94; Division 3 – Champions 1985–86; Division 3 (S) – Champions 1925–26; Runners-up 1931–32, 1934–35, 1948–49, 1951–52; Division 4 – Champions 1978–79.

FA Cup: Semi-final 1927.

Football League Cup: best season: 5th rd, 1996.

Simod Cup: Winners 1988.

Colours

Royal blue and white hooped shirts, blue shorts, white and blue hooped stockings.

Change Colours

Red shirts with yellow trim, red shorts with yellow trim, red stockings.

Year Formed: 1871.

Turned Professional: 1895.

Ltd Co.: 1895.

Club Nickname: 'The Royals'.

Previous Grounds: 1871, Reading Recreation; Reading Cricket Ground; 1882, Coley Park; 1889, Caversham Cricket Ground; 1896, Elm Park; 1998, Madejski Stadium.

First Football League Game: 28 August 1920, Division 3, v Newport Co (a) W 1–0 – Crawford; Smith, Horler; Christie, Mavin, Getgood; Spence, Weston, Yarnell, Bailey (1), Andrews.

Record League Victory: 10–2 v Crystal Palace, Division 3 (S), 4 September 1946 – Groves; Glidden, Gulliver; McKenna, Ratcliffe, Young; Chitty, Maurice Edelston (3), McPhee (4), Barney (1), Deverell (2).

Record Cup Victory: 6–0 v Leyton, FA Cup 2nd rd, 12 December 1925 – Duckworth; Eggo, McConnell; Wilson, Messer, Evans; Smith (2), Braithwaite (1), Davey (1), Tinsley, Robson (2).

Record Defeat: 0–18 v Preston NE, FA Cup 1st rd, 1893–94.

Most League Points (2 for a win): 65, Division 4, 1978–79.

Most League Points (3 for a win): 94, Division 3, 1985–86.

Most League Goals: 112, Division 3 (S), 1951–52.

Highest League Scorer in Season: Ronnie Blackman, 39, Division 3 (S), 1951–52.

Most League Goals in Total Aggregate: Ronnie Blackman, 158, 1947–54.

Most League Goals in One Match: 6, Arthur Bacon v Stoke C, Division 2, 3 April 1931.

Most Capped Player: Jimmy Quinn, 17 (46), Northern Ireland.

Most League Appearances: Martin Hicks, 500, 1978–91.

Youngest League Player: Steve Hetzke, 16 years 184 days v Darlington, 4 December 1971.

Record Transfer Fee Received: £1,575,000 from Newcastle U for Shaka Hislop, August 1995.

Record Transfer Fee Paid: £800,000 to Brentford for Carl Asaba, August 1997.

Football League Record: 1920 Original Member of Division 3; 1921–26 Division 3 (S); 1926–31 Division 2; 1931–58 Division 3 (S); 1958–71 Division 3; 1971–76 Division 4; 1976–77 Division 3; 1977–79 Division 4; 1979–83 Division 3; 1983–84 Division 4; 1984–86 Division 3; 1986–88 Division 2; 1988–92 Division 3; 1992–94 Division 2; 1994–98 Division 1; 1998– Division 2.

MANAGERS

Thomas Sefton 1897–1901
(Secretary-Manager)
James Sharp 1901–02
Harry Matthews 1902–20
Harry Marshall 1920–22
Arthur Chadwick 1923–25
H. S. Bray 1925–26
(Secretary only since 1922 and 1926–35)
Andrew Wylie 1926–31
Joe Smith 1931–35
Billy Butler 1935–39
John Cochrane 1939
Joe Edelston 1939–47
Ted Drake 1947–52
Jack Smith 1952–55
Harry Johnston 1955–63
Roy Bentley 1963–69
Jack Mansell 1969–71
Charlie Hurley 1972–77
Maurice Evans 1977–84
Ian Branfoot 1984–89
Ian Porterfield 1989–91
Mark McGhee 1991–94
Jimmy Quinn/Mick Gooding 1994–97
Terry Bullivant 1997–98
Tommy Burns March 1998–

TEN YEAR LEAGUE RECORD

		P	W	D	L	F	A	Pts	Pos
1988-89	Div 3	46	15	11	20	68	72	56	18
1989-90	Div 3	46	15	19	12	57	53	64	10
1990-91	Div 3	46	17	8	21	53	66	59	15
1991-92	Div 3	46	16	13	17	59	62	61	12
1992-93	Div 2	46	18	15	13	66	51	69	8
1993-94	Div 2	46	26	11	9	81	44	89	1
1994-95	Div 1	46	23	10	13	58	44	79	2
1995-96	Div 1	46	13	17	16	54	63	56	19
1996-97	Div 1	46	15	12	19	58	67	57	18
1997-98	Div 1	46	11	9	26	39	78	42	24

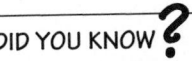

DID YOU KNOW

Joe 'Bubbles' Bailey, scorer of Reading's first League goal was an England amateur international, Berkshire cricketer and Oxfordshire hockey player. He also won the DSO, MC and bar in the First World War.

READING 1998–99 LEAGUE RECORD

Match No.	Date	Venue	Opponents	Result	H/T Score	Lg. Pos.	Goalscorers	Attendance
1	Aug 8	A	Wrexham	L 0-3	0-1	—		6671
2	15	A	Bristol R	L 1-4	1-3	22	Williams [7]	7529
3	22	H	Luton T	W 3-0	1-0	15	Brebner [10], McIntyre [51], Fleck [84]	18,108
4	29	H	Chesterfield	L 0-1	0-1	18		4145
5	Sept 9	H	Burnley	D 1-1	1-0	—	Williams [28]	10,080
6	12	A	Preston NE	L 0-4	0-3	23		9836
7	19	H	Colchester U	D 1-1	1-0	21	Williams [17]	9058
8	26	A	Macclesfield T	L 1-2	0-1	22	Williams (pen) [60]	2920
9	30	A	Walsall	W 2-0	1-0	—	Williams [8], Brebner [66]	3729
10	Oct 3	H	Stoke C	W 2-1	1-0	18	Brebner [44], McIntyre [73]	13,089
11	17	H	Gillingham	D 0-0	0-0	20		11,467
12	21	H	Blackpool	D 1-1	0-0	—	Williams [86]	8450
13	24	A	Manchester C	W 1-0	0-0	18	Williams [56]	24,365
14	31	A	Wycombe W	W 3-2	2-1	18	Brebner 2 [3, 9], Williams [71]	6373
15	Nov 4	H	York C	W 1-0	1-0	—	Brebner [31]	7914
16	7	H	Bournemouth	D 3-3	2-1	10	Caskey [7], Williams [44], Parkinson [80]	13,004
17	11	H	Wigan Ath	L 0-1	0-1	—		9317
18	21	A	Northampton T	W 1-0	0-0	12	Brebner [61]	5970
19	28	H	Lincoln C	W 2-1	0-1	9	Clement [46], Sarr [67]	8694
20	Dec 12	A	Millwall	D 1-1	0-0	10	Sarr [67]	6058
21	19	H	Oldham Ath	D 1-1	1-0	9	McIntyre [29]	9390
22	28	H	Notts Co	W 1-0	1-0	9	Richardson (og) [24]	13,026
23	Jan 2	H	Chesterfield	L 1-2	0-2	11	Sarr [88]	10,409
24	9	H	Wrexham	W 4-0	2-0	8	Williams 2 (2 pens) [7, 53], Brebner [44], Parkinson [82]	8087
25	16	H	Bristol R	L 0-6	0-0	10		13,258
26	23	A	York C	D 1-1	0-0	10	Parkinson [80]	3274
27	30	A	Notts Co	D 1-1	1-0	11	Glasgow [17]	5192
28	Feb 6	H	Walsall	L 0-1	0-1	11		9481
29	13	A	Burnley	D 1-1	0-0	12	Caskey [54]	9366
30	20	H	Preston NE	W 2-1	0-0	11	Caskey [55], Thorpe (pen) [90]	10,937
31	23	A	Fulham	L 1-3	1-0	—	Brebner [3]	11,247
32	27	A	Colchester U	D 1-1	0-1	11	Parkinson [81]	4686
33	Mar 6	H	Macclesfield T	W 1-0	0-0	11	Caskey [62]	8085
34	10	A	Stoke C	W 4-0	0-0	—	McKeever [59], McIntyre 2 [76, 82], Gray [87]	8218
35	13	A	Bournemouth	W 1-0	0-0	8	McKeever [76]	9445
36	20	H	Wycombe W	W 2-1	1-0	7	McIntyre [28], Caskey [73]	10,298
37	23	A	Luton T	D 1-1	0-1	—	Barras [84]	5527
38	27	H	Manchester C	L 1-3	0-1	7	Scott [90]	20,055
39	Apr 1	A	Gillingham	L 1-2	0-1	—	Scott [77]	8195
40	5	H	Fulham	L 0-1	0-0	11		18,741
41	10	A	Blackpool	L 0-2	0-1	11		3617
42	13	A	Lincoln C	D 2-2	1-0	—	Caskey 2 [40, 84]	2518
43	17	H	Northampton T	L 0-1	0-0	11		10,132
44	24	A	Wigan Ath	L 1-4	0-3	11	McLaren [67]	3885
45	May 1	H	Millwall	W 2-0	2-0	11	Parkinson [23], Gray [31]	7943
46	8	A	Oldham Ath	L 0-2	0-2	11		7724

Final League Position: 11

GOALSCORERS

League (54): Williams 11 (3 pens), Brebner 9, Caskey 7, McIntyre 6, Parkinson 5, Sarr 3, Gray 2, McKeever 2, Scott 2, Barras 1, Clement 1, Fleck 1, Glasgow 1, McLaren 1, Thorpe 1 (pen), own goal 1.
Worthington Cup (4): Caskey 2 (2 pens), Asaba 1, Brebner 1.
FA Cup (0).

Van der Kwaak P 3	McLaren A 7	Booty M 7 + 1	Legg A 2	Brebner G 36 + 3	Scott K 5 + 4	Davies G 1	Kromheer E 11	Hunter B 2 + 1	Crawford J 9 + 2	Caskey D 42	McIntyre J 22 + 10	Gray S 25 + 2	Evers S — + 1	Lambert J 1	Stamp N — + 1	Sarr M 18 + 10	Williams M 20 + 6	Bowen J 1	Parkinson P 42	Asaba C — + 1	Houghton R 13 + 5	Bernal A 18 + 4	Primus L 31	Reilly M 4 + 2	Fleck R 2 + 2	Howie S 42	Brayson P 13 + 15	Hammond N 1	McPherson K 13 + 2	Casper C 32	Glasgow B 28 + 4	Roach N 3 + 2	Clement N 11	Polston J 4	Wright A — + 2	Gurney A 5 + 3	Hodges L — + 1	Thorpe T 6	Murty G 8 + 1	McKeever M 6 + 1	Barras T 4 + 2	Maybury A 8	Match No.
1	2	3	4	5	6	7¹	8	9	10	11²	12	13																															1
1	2	3¹	7		6		8	9	10							11			4²	5	12	13																					2
1	12			4	6		8	9³	3							11²	13				7	2¹	5	10	14																		3
	2			4			8		3	11	12					5	7		6		10¹	9²				1	13																4
	2			4			8		3	11	10					5	7¹		6		12	9²				1	13																5
	2			4		7¹			3	10	9					8			6				5	11	12	1																	6
	2			4¹			12	8²	10	11²	9												5	14	13	1				3	6	7											7
	2			7													9		4		8		5	10		1				3	6	11											8
				11				2		8	12						9		4				5			1	7¹			3	6	10											9
				11				2		8	12						9		4				5			1	7¹			3	6	10											10
				11²				2		8	10¹					12	9		4				5			1	13			3	6	7											11
				11¹				2		8	10					12	9		4				5			1				3	6	7											12
				11						8						10¹	9		4			2	5			1	12			3	6	7											13
				11						8						12	9		4			2	5			1	10¹			3	6	7											14
				11			6			8						10¹	9		4			2	5			1				3		7	12										15
				11						8						10	9¹		4			2	5			1	12			3	6	7											16
				11						8						10¹	9		4			2²	5			1	12			3	6	7	13										17
				11³						8	12					10²	9¹		4				5			1	13	14	6	2	7	3											18
										8	12					10¹	9²		4				5			1	13			6	2	7	11	3									19
							6	12		8	9					10			4							1			3	5	7²	2¹	11		13								20
				11			6	2		8	9					10¹			4							1	12			5	7²			3	13								21
				11			5	2		8	9¹					12	13		4							1	10²			6	7			3									22
				11			5	2		8	9²					12	13		4			3				1	10			6	7¹												23
				11						8	12					2²	9		4	13						1	10¹			6	7			3									24
										8	12					13	9		4	11²	14					1	10¹		6	2³	3					7							25
				11						8	12²	13					9		4			2	3			1	10¹			6	7³						14						26
				11						8						10¹	12		4			2	5			1	9			6²	7	3				13							27
				11											4		12	9¹		8²			5			1	13			6	2	3				7		10					28
				11						8	12						13		4				5			1	9¹			6	2	3				7²		10	13				29
				11						8	12	6					13		4				5			1	9¹				2		3					10²	7				30
				11						8	12	6							4²		13		5³			1	9¹				2		3					10	7				31
				11						8	9	14							4			12	5			1	13				6¹	2³		3²				10	7			2	32
				11²						8	9	3							4		12	6	5			1	7¹											13	2			33
										8	9	3					10	6	5							1	12	13		14						7¹			2	9			34
										8	9	3				12			4		10	6	5			1				7¹										2	11		35
	12									8²	9	3				7³			4		10		5			1				6	13									2	11¹	14	36
	12									8	9	3							4		10		2			1				6									7¹	11	5	37
		7		13						8	9	3							4		10¹	12				1				6									11²	5	2	38
		7	12	13						8	9	3							4				5			1				6	10¹								11²	2		39
	9¹	6	10							8		5				11			7				3			1				4									12			40
	7¹	11	10					14			9	3							4	8²			5³			1	12			6	13					2						41
	7	11	12							8	9	3			10¹				4							1				6										5	2	42
	7	11²	13							8	9	3			10¹				4			6				1					12									5	2	43
	7	11²	9							8		3							4		13	5				1	12				6³	10¹								14	2	44
		11¹	10							2	8	9	3						4		12	5				1					6²					13					7	45
			10							5	8	9	11¹	13		12			4		7	3				1					6										2²	46

Worthington Cup
First Round   Peterborough U   (a) 1-1
                               (h) 2-0
Second Round   Barnsley   (a) 0-3
                          (h) 1-1

FA Cup
First Round   Stoke C   (h) 0-1

Division 3   **ROCHDALE**

FOUNDATION

Considering the love of rugby in their area, it is not surprising that Rochdale had difficulty in establishing an Association Football club. The earlier Rochdale Town club formed in 1900 went out of existence in 1907 when the present club was immediately established and joined the Manchester League, before graduating to the Lancashire Combination in 1908.

Spotland, Sandy Lane, Rochdale OL11 5DS.

Telephone: (01706) 644648.

Fax: (01706) 648466.

Commercial: (01706) 647521.

Ground Capacity: 9223.

Record Attendance: 24,231 v Notts Co, FA Cup 2nd rd, 10 December 1949.

Record Receipts: £46,000 v Burnley, Division 4, 5 May 1992.

Pitch Measurements: 114yd × 76yd.

President: Mrs L. Stoney.

Chairman: D. F. Kilpatrick.

Directors: G. R. Brierley, C. Dunphy, J. Marsh, G. Morris, R. Bott.

Manager: Steve Parkin.

Secretary: Mrs Karen Jagger.

Youth Development Manager: David Hamilton.

Lottery and Merchandising Managers: F. Collins, R. Wild.

Advertising & Sponsorship Manager: L. Duckworth.

Stadium Manager: Ronnie Cowgill.

Physio: Andy Thorpe.

LATEST SEQUENCES

Longest Sequence of League Wins: 8, 29.9.69 – 3.11.69.

Longest Sequence of League Defeats: 17, 14.11.31 – 12.3.32.

Longest Sequence of League Draws: 6, 17.8.68 – 14.9.68.

Longest Sequence of Unbeaten League Matches: 20, 15.9.23 – 19.1.24.

Longest Sequence Without a League Win: 28, 14.11.31 – 29.8.32.

HONOURS

Football League: Division 3 best season: 9th, 1969–70; Division 3 (N) – Runners-up 1923–24, 1926–27.
FA Cup: best season: 5th rd, 1990.
Football League Cup: Runners-up 1962 (record for 4th Division club).

Colours
Blue shirts with white trim, blue shorts, blue stockings with white hoop on turnover.

Change Colours
Yellow shirts, black shorts, black stockings.

Year Formed: 1907.

Turned Professional: 1907.

Ltd Co.: 1910.

Club Nickname: 'The Dale'.

First Football League Game: 27 August 1921, Division 3 (N), v Accrington Stanley (h) W 6–3 – Crabtree; Nuttall, Sheehan; Hill, Farrer, Yarwood; Hoad, Sandiford, Dennison (2), Owens (3), Carney (1).

Record League Victory: 8–1 v Chesterfield, Division 3 (N), 18 December 1926 – Hill; Brown, Ward; Hillhouse, Parkes, Braidwood; Hughes, Bertram, Whitehurst (5), Schofield (2), Martin (1).

Record Cup Victory: 8–2 v Crook T, FA Cup 1st rd, 26 November 1927 – Moody; Hopkins, Ward; Braidwood, Parkes, Barker; Tompkinson, Clennell (3) Whitehurst (4), Hall, Martin (1).

Record Defeat: 1–9 v Tranmere R, Division 3 (N), 25 December 1931.

Most League Points (2 for a win): 62, Division 3 (N), 1923–24.

Most League Points (3 for a win): 67, Division 4, 1991–92.

Most League Goals: 105, Division 3 (N), 1926–27.

Highest League Scorer in Season: Albert Whitehurst, 44, Division 3 (N), 1926–27.

Most League Goals in Total Aggregate: Reg Jenkins, 119, 1964–73.

Most League Goals in One Match: 6, Tommy Tippett v Hartlepools U, Division 3N, 21 April 1930.

Most Capped Player: None.

Most League Appearances: Graham Smith, 317, 1966–74.

Youngest League Player: Zac Hughes, 16 years 105 days v Exeter C, 19 September 1987.

Record Transfer Fee Received: £400,000 from West Ham U for Stephen Bywater, August 1998.

Record Transfer Fee Paid: £80,000 to Scunthorpe U for Andy Flounders, August 1991.

Football League Record: 1921 Elected to Division 3 (N); 1958–59 Division 3; 1959–69 Division 4; 1969–74 Division 3; 1974–92 Division 4; 1992– Division 3.

MANAGERS

Billy Bradshaw 1920
Run by committee 1920–22
Tom Wilson 1922–23
Jack Peart 1923–30
Will Cameron 1930–31
Herbert Hopkinson 1932–34
Billy Smith 1934–35
Ernest Nixon 1935–37
Sam Jennings 1937–38
Ted Goodier 1938–52
Jack Warner 1952–53
Harry Catterick 1953–58
Jack Marshall 1958–60
Tony Collins 1960–68
Bob Stokoe 1967–68
Len Richley 1968–70
Dick Conner 1970–73
Walter Joyce 1973–76
Brian Green 1976–77
Mike Ferguson 1977–78
Doug Collins 1979
Bob Stokoe 1979–80
Peter Madden 1980–83
Jimmy Greenhoff 1983–84
Vic Halom 1984–86
Eddie Gray 1986–88
Danny Bergara 1988–89
Terry Dolan 1989–91
Dave Sutton 1991–94
Mick Docherty 1995–96
Graham Barrow 1996–99
Steve Parkin June 1999–

TEN YEAR LEAGUE RECORD

		P	W	D	L	F	A	Pts	Pos
1988-89	Div 4	46	13	14	19	56	82	53	18
1989-90	Div 4	46	20	6	20	52	55	66	12
1990-91	Div 4	46	15	17	14	50	53	62	12
1991-92	Div 4	42	18	13	11	57	53	67	8
1992-93	Div 3	42	16	10	16	70	70	58	11
1993-94	Div 3	42	16	12	14	63	51	60	9
1994-95	Div 3	42	12	14	16	44	67	50	15
1995-96	Div 3	46	14	13	19	57	61	55	15
1996-97	Div 3	46	14	16	16	58	58	58	14
1997-98	Div 3	46	17	7	22	56	55	58	18

DID YOU KNOW ?

Rochdale did not concede a goal at home in the 1923–24 season until 15 December and that a penalty against Barrow. They were never out of the top two placed clubs from then until the end of the season.

ROCHDALE 1998–99 LEAGUE RECORD

Match No.	Date	Venue	Opponents	Result	H/T Score	Lg. Pos.	Goalscorers	Attendance
1	Aug 8	A	Plymouth Arg	L	1-2	1-0	—	Lancashire (pen) [19]	5547
2	15	H	Torquay U	L	0-2	0-1	24		1713
3	22	A	Carlisle U	W	1-0	0-0	19	Diaz [82]	3627
4	29	H	Darlington	D	0-0	0-0	20		1953
5	31	A	Brentford	L	1-2	1-1	21	Diaz [17]	4873
6	Sept 5	H	Shrewsbury T	W	1-0	1-0	16	Bailey [22]	1660
7	8	A	Hull C	L	1-2	0-1	—	Hill [50]	3433
8	12	H	Scunthorpe U	D	2-2	0-1	21	Painter (pen) [51], Monington [67]	1929
9	19	A	Cardiff C	L	1-2	1-0	22	Painter [25]	4643
10	26	H	Leyton Orient	W	2-1	2-1	20	Lancashire [6], Painter [21]	1742
11	Oct 3	A	Southend U	D	1-1	1-0	21	Lancashire [36]	3686
12	11	H	Halifax T	W	1-0	1-0	18	Williams [45]	3628
13	17	A	Peterborough U	L	0-2	0-2	18		4536
14	20	A	Rotherham U	D	2-2	1-1	—	Sparrow [36], Monington [77]	3105
15	31	A	Barnet	W	1-0	0-0	18	Painter [65]	1413
16	Nov 7	H	Mansfield T	W	1-0	0-0	14	Peake [47]	2142
17	10	H	Exeter C	D	1-1	1-0	—	Sparrow [36]	1639
18	17	H	Scarborough	L	0-1	0-0	—		1536
19	21	A	Chester C	D	1-1	0-1	17	Holt [73]	2495
20	Dec 12	A	Swansea C	D	1-1	1-0	16	Peake [34]	4010
21	19	H	Brighton & HA	W	2-1	0-0	14	Painter [69], Monington [88]	2153
22	26	H	Carlisle U	D	1-1	1-0	16	Peake [21]	2900
23	28	A	Hartlepool U	W	1-0	0-0	14	Holt [79]	2218
24	Jan 2	A	Darlington	L	0-3	0-1	15		2807
25	9	H	Plymouth Arg	D	1-1	0-1	17	Holt [62]	1922
26	16	A	Torquay U	L	1-2	0-1	17	Morris [90]	2205
27	23	H	Brentford	W	2-0	0-0	14	Holt [48], Painter [51]	2113
28	30	H	Hartlepool U	L	0-1	0-1	15		1943
29	Feb 6	A	Shrewsbury T	L	2-3	1-2	18	Peake [10], Morris [75]	2561
30	12	H	Hull C	W	3-0	1-0	—	Holt 2 [43, 59], Morris [90]	5374
31	20	A	Scunthorpe U	W	1-0	0-0	15	Bayliss [84]	3749
32	27	H	Cardiff C	D	1-1	1-0	16	Peake [44]	2431
33	Mar 6	A	Leyton Orient	L	0-3	0-1	16		4927
34	13	A	Mansfield T	L	1-3	0-1	19	Lydiate [50]	2555
35	20	H	Barnet	D	0-0	0-0	18		1502
36	26	A	Scarborough	L	0-1	0-1	—		2206
37	30	H	Southend U	W	1-0	1-0	—	Morris [31]	1344
38	Apr 3	H	Peterborough U	L	0-3	0-1	18		1696
39	5	A	Halifax T	D	0-0	0-0	17		2759
40	10	H	Rotherham U	D	0-0	0-0	19		2516
41	13	A	Cambridge U	D	1-1	1-0	—	Stoker [29]	4690
42	17	H	Chester C	W	3-1	0-1	16	Morris 3 [60, 78, 88]	1712
43	24	A	Exeter C	L	1-2	0-1	18	Holt [65]	2543
44	27	H	Cambridge U	L	0-2	0-0	—		1408
45	May 1	H	Swansea C	L	0-3	0-1	21		1654
46	8	A	Brighton & HA	D	1-1	0-1	19	Barlow A [89]	4646

Final League Position: 19

GOALSCORERS

League (42): Holt 7, Morris 7, Painter 6 (1 pen), Peake 5, Lancashire 3 (1 pen), Monington 3, Diaz 2, Sparrow 2, Bailey 1, Barlow A 1, Bayliss 1, Hill 1, Lydiate 1, Stoker 1, Williams 1.
Worthington Cup (0).
FA Cup (3): Bryson 2, Monington 1.

Edwards N 45	Sparrow P 21+4	Stokes D 10+1	Hill K 33	Bayliss D 22+3	Johnson A 13+3	Farrell A 36+2	Lancashire G 7+4	Leonard M 2+6	Peake J 36+2	Stuart M 9+10	Gray D —+3	Bailey M 12+7	Jones G 11+9	Diaz I 12+2	Painter R 35+5	Bryson I 31+8	Monington M 37	Williams M 11+3	Barlow A 25+4	De Souza M 5	Holt M 17+7	Carden P 24+1	Morris A 25	Priestley P 1	Lydiate J 14	Stoker G 11+1	Hicks G 1	Match No.
1	2¹	3	4	5	6	7	8²	9	10³	11	12	13	14															1
1	2³	3¹	4	5		6	8	9	10	12		11²		7	14	13												2
1	2³	3	4	5	6²		10	12	13	11		9		7	8¹	14												3
1		3	4	2		6			11			9		7	8	10	5											4
1	12	3	4	2³		6			11	14		9¹	13	7	8	10²	5											5
1		3	4	2		6			11			7¹	12	9	10	8	5											6
1	12	3	4	2¹		6			11			13	9	7	8	10²	5											7
1	2	3	4			6			11			9		7	8	10	5											8
1	2¹	3	4³			6		9²	13	12		11		7	8	10	5											9
1			4	14	12			9²	13	11		6¹	7³		8	10	5		2	3								10
1			4		12			9²	13	11¹		6	7		8	10	5		2	3								11
1			4			6		9¹	11	12				7	8	10	5		2	3								12
1			4		12			9	11			13	6	7	8	10	5		2²	3¹								13
1		3	4			6		9²	13	11		12		7¹	8	10	5		2									14
1		3	4			6			11			12		7¹	8	10	5		2		9							15
1		3	4		12	6¹			11			13		7²	8	10	5		2		9							16
1		3	4			6			11			12			8	10	5		2¹		9							17
1		3	4			6			11	7		12	13		8	10³	5		2¹		9²	14						18
1		3	4			6			11			12			8	10	5		2¹		9¹	13				7		19
1			4			6			11			12	13		8²	10	5	3	2		9¹	7						20
1	2		4			6			11						8	10	5	3			9	7						21
1	2		4			6	7		11						8	10	5	3			9							22
1	2		4			6			11						8¹	10	5	3			12	7	9					23
1	2		4			6			11			12			8	10¹	5	3²	13³		14	7	9					24
	2		4		12	6³			11			13			8	10²	5	3¹			14	7	9	1				25
1	2³		4		12	6			11			13			8	10²	5	3¹			14	7	9					26
1		3	4	5	12	6			11²			13	14		8	10¹			2³			7	9					27
1	3²		4		6¹				10	12					8		5		2³		14	11	7			9		28
1		4²	13		6				10	12					8		5		2¹		11	7	9					29
1					6	7			10						8		5	3			11	2	9		4			30
1	12				5	7			10			13			8¹			3²			11	2	9		6	4		31
1	2¹		4			6	12		10²			13	14				5	3			11³	7	9		8			32
1			4			6	12		10	13					8¹		5	3²			2	9			7	11		33
1				6²	12				10			2	13				5	3			11¹	7	9		4	8		34
1				7	6				10			2²	12				5	3¹			11	13	9		4	8		35
1			4		6				10	12		13			8		5	3			11²	2¹	9			7		36
1			4		6				10						8	12	5	3			2	9	11			7¹		37
1	12		4		6				10	11³					8	13	5	3			14	2	9²			7¹		38
1			4		6				10						8	12	5	3¹			2	9	11			7		39
1			4		6				10						8	12	5	3			13	2	9²			11	7¹	40
1		4	3		6				10¹	11							5	12				2	9		8	7		41
1		4	3²		6				10	12						11	5	13				8	7		9	6¹		42
1		4	3¹	2					10	11						5	12	13				7	9		6	8²		43
1		4		2					10	8		11				5	3					7	9		6			44
1		4		2					10	12		8¹				5	3				11	7	9		6			45
1	12	3	4						10			6¹			7²		5	11			8		9			13	2	46

Worthington Cup
First Round — Wigan Ath — (a) 0-1 — (h) 0-1

FA Cup
First Round — Scarborough — (a) 1-1 — (h) 2-0
Second Round — Rotherham U — (h) 0-0 — (a) 0-4

Division 3

ROTHERHAM UNITED

FOUNDATION

Rotherham were formed in 1870 before becoming Town in the late 1880s. Thornhill United were founded in 1877 and changed their name to Rotherham County in 1905. The Town amalgamated with Rotherham County to form Rotherham United in 1925.

Millmoor Ground, Rotherham S60 1HR.

Telephone: (01709) 512434.

Fax: (01709) 512762.

Commercial Dept: (01709) 512760.

Fax: (01709) 512763.

Football in the Community: (01709) 512761.

Ground Capacity: 11,514.

Record Attendance: 25,170 v Sheffield U, Division 2, 13 December 1952 and v Sheffield W, Division 2, 26 January 1952.

Record Receipts: £79,155 v Newcastle U, FA Cup 4th rd, 23 January 1993.

Pitch Measurements. 115yd × 75yd.

Chairman: K. F. Booth.

Directors: R. Hull (Vice-Chairman), C. A. Luckock, J. A. Webb, N. Freeman.

Chief Executive: Phil Henson.

Manager: Ronnie Moore.

Assistant Manager: John Breckin.

Youth Development Officer: Fraser Foster.

Physios: Paul Smith, Ian Bailey.

Coach: Billy Russell.

Stadium Manager/Safety Officer: David Sumner.

Commercial Manager: D. Nicholls.

Year Formed: 1870.

Turned Professional: 1905.

Ltd Co.: 1920.

Club Nickname: 'The Merry Millers'.

LATEST SEQUENCES

Longest Sequence of League Wins: 9, 2.2.82 – 6.3.82.

Longest Sequence of League Defeats: 8, 7.4.56 – 18.8.56.

Longest Sequence of League Draws: 6, 13.10.69 – 22.11.69.

Longest Sequence of Unbeaten League Matches: 18, 13.10.69 – 7.2.70.

Longest Sequence Without a League Win: 14, 8.10.77 – 2.1.78.

HONOURS

Football League: Division 2 best season: 3rd, 1954–55 (equal points with champions and runners-up); Division 3 – Champions 1980–81; Division 3 (N) – Champions 1950–51; Runners-up 1946–47, 1947–48, 1948–49; Division 4 – Champions 1988–89; Runners-up 1991–92.

FA Cup: best season: 5th rd, 1953, 1968.

Football League Cup: Runners-up 1961.

Auto Windscreens Shield: Winners 1996.

Colours
Red and white.

Change Colours
White shirts, black shorts, black stockings.

Previous Names: 1877, Thornhill United; 1905, Rotherham County; 1925, amalgamated with Rotherham Town under Rotherham United.

Previous Ground: 1870, Red House Ground; 1907, Millmoor.

First Football League Game: 2 September 1893, Division 2, Rotherham T v Lincoln C (a) D 1–1 – McKay; Thickett, Watson; Barr, Brown, Broadhead; Longden, Cutts, Leatherbarrow, McCormick, Pickering, (1 og). 30 August 1919, Division 2, Rotherham Co v Nottingham F (h) W 2–0 – Branston; Alton, Baines; Bailey, Coe, Stanton; Lee (1), Cawley (1), Glennon, Lees, Lamb.

Record League Victory: 8–0 v Oldham Ath, Division 3 (N), 26 May 1947 – Warnes; Selkirk, Ibbotson; Edwards, Horace Williams, Danny Williams; Wilson (2), Shaw (1), Ardron (3), Guest (1), Hainsworth (1).

Record Cup Victory: 6–0 v Spennymoor U, FA Cup 2nd rd, 17 December 1977 – McAlister; Forrest, Breckin, Womble, Stancliffe, Green, Finney, Phillips (3), Gwyther (2) (Smith), Goodfellow, Crawford (1). 6–0 v Wolverhampton W, FA Cup 1st rd, 16 November 1985 – O'Hanlon; Forrest, Dungworth, Gooding (1), Smith (1), Pickering, Birch (2), Emerson, Tynan (1), Simmons (1), Pugh. 6–0 v Kings Lynn, FA Cup 2nd rd, 6 December 1997 – Mimms; Clark, Hurst (Goodwin), Garner (1) (Hudson) (1), Warner (Bass), Richardson (1), Berry (1), Thompson, Druce (1), Glover (1), Roscoe.

Record Defeat: 1–11 v Bradford C, Division 3 (N), 25 August 1928.

Most League Points (2 for a win): 71, Division 3 (N), 1950–51.

Most League Points (3 for a win): 82, Division 4, 1988–89.

Most League Goals: 114, Division 3 (N), 1946–47.

Highest League Scorer in Season: Wally Ardron, 38, Division 3 (N), 1946–47.

Most League Goals in Total Aggregate: Gladstone Guest, 130, 1946–56.

Most League Goals in One Match: 4, Roland Bastow v York C, Division 3N, 9 November 1935; 4, Roland Bastow v Rochdale, Division 3N, 7 March 1936; 4, Wally Ardron v Crewe Alex, Division 3N, 5 October 1946; 4, Wally Ardron v Carlisle U, Division 3N, 13 September 1947; 4, Wally Ardron v Hartlepools U, Division 3N, 13 October 1948.

Most Capped Player: Shaun Goater, 18, Bermuda.

Most League Appearances: Danny Williams, 459, 1946–62.

Youngest League Player: Kevin Eley, 16 years 72 days v Scunthorpe U, 15 May 1984.

Record Transfer Fee Received: £325,000 from Sheffield W for Matt Clarke, July 1996.

Record Transfer Fee Paid: £150,000 to Millwall for Tony Towner, August 1980; £150,000 to Port Vale for Lee Glover, August 1996.

Football League Record: 1893 Rotherham Town elected to Division 2; 1896 Failed re-election; 1919 Rotherham County elected to Division 2; 1923–51 Division 3 (N); 1951–68 Division 2; 1968–73 Division 3; 1973–75 Division 4; 1975–81 Division 3; 1981–83 Division 2; 1983–88 Division 3; 1988–89 Division 4; 1989–91 Division 3; 1991–92 Division 4; 1992–97 Division 2; 1997– Division 3.

MANAGERS

Billy Heald 1925–29 *(Secretary only for long spell)*
Stanley Davies 1929–30
Billy Heald 1930–33
Reg Freeman 1934–52
Andy Smailes 1952–58
Tom Johnston 1958–62
Danny Williams 1962–65
Jack Mansell 1965–67
Tommy Docherty 1967–68
Jimmy McAnearney 1968–73
Jimmy McGuigan 1973–79
Ian Porterfield 1979–81
Emlyn Hughes 1981–83
George Kerr 1983–85
Norman Hunter 1985–87
Dave Cusack 1987–88
Billy McEwan 1988–91
Phil Henson 1991–94
Archie Gemmill/John McGovern 1994–96
Danny Bergara 1996–97
Ronnie Moore May 1997–

TEN YEAR LEAGUE RECORD

		P	W	D	L	F	A	Pts	Pos
1988-89	Div 4	46	22	16	8	76	35	82	1
1989-90	Div 3	46	17	13	16	71	62	64	9
1990-91	Div 3	46	10	12	24	50	87	42	23
1991-92	Div 4	42	22	11	9	70	37	77	2
1992-93	Div 2	46	17	14	15	60	60	65	11
1993-94	Div 2	46	15	13	18	63	60	58	15
1994-95	Div 2	46	14	14	18	57	61	56	17
1995-96	Div 2	46	14	14	18	54	62	56	16
1996-97	Div 2	46	7	14	25	39	70	35	23
1997-98	Div 3	46	16	19	11	67	61	67	9

DID YOU KNOW ?

Andy Monkhouse's last minute goal for Rotherham United in the 3–0 win over Hartlepool United on 19 September 1998 came after just three minutes of his League debut as a substitute. Rotherham were lying third at the time.

ROTHERHAM UNITED 1998–99 LEAGUE RECORD

Match No.	Date	Venue	Opponents	Result	H/T Score	Lg. Pos.	Goalscorers	Attendance
1	Aug 8	H	Hull C	W 3-1	2-1	—	Warner [10], White [31], Glover [72]	5447
2	15	A	Leyton Orient	W 4-1	2-0	1	Garner [33], Glover [34], Ingledow [67], Roscoe [69]	4457
3	22	H	Cambridge U	W 2-0	0-0	1	White [72], Glover [79]	3773
4	29	A	Cardiff C	W 1-0	0-0	1	Glover [63]	5356
5	31	H	Mansfield T	D 0-0	0-0	1		5943
6	Sept 5	A	Southend U	L 0-3	0-1	2		3479
7	8	H	Plymouth Arg	L 0-2	0-1	—		3442
8	12	A	Brentford	W 3-0	1-0	3	Martindale [44], Hudson [60], Garner [87]	4803
9	19	A	Hartlepool U	W 3-0	0-0	3	Glover [47], Hudson [74], Monkhouse [90]	3769
10	26	A	Barnet	L 2-4	0-3	3	Martindale [58], Sedgwick [82]	1989
11	Oct 3	H	Shrewsbury T	L 0-1	0-1	7		3639
12	9	A	Swansea C	D 1-1	1-0	—	Fortune-West [8]	5180
13	17	H	Darlington	W 3-1	2-1	4	Dillon [22], Glover 2 (2 pens) [42, 87]	4004
14	20	H	Rochdale	D 2-2	1-1	—	Fortune-West [25], Glover [65]	3105
15	24	A	Scunthorpe U	L 3-4	0-2	4	Garner 2 [72, 90], Hurst [87]	4783
16	31	A	Peterborough U	W 4-2	0-2	1	Hudson 2 [50, 69], Sedgwick [57], Berry [77]	4796
17	Nov 7	H	Scarborough	W 4-0	0-0	1	Fortune-West 2 [34, 38], Berry [37], Roscoe [84]	3954
18	10	A	Torquay U	D 2-2	0-1	—	Sedgwick (pen) [86], Raven [88]	3708
19	21	A	Carlisle U	D 0-0	0-0	4		3281
20	28	H	Exeter C	D 0-0	0-0	4		3489
21	Dec 12	A	Brighton & HA	L 1-4	0-0	7	Glover [77]	2870
22	18	H	Chester C	L 2-4	0-1	—	Glover [78], White [89]	2696
23	26	A	Cambridge U	L 2-3	0-2	10	Knill 2 [55, 69]	5325
24	28	H	Halifax T	W 3-1	2-1	8	Roscoe [22], Knill [32], Raven [85]	4728
25	Jan 9	H	Hull C	L 0-1	0-1	10		5575
26	16	H	Leyton Orient	W 3-1	0-1	8	Warne 2 [54, 70], Thompson [64]	3139
27	22	A	Mansfield T	W 3-0	0-0	—	Thompson (pen) [52], Roscoe [67], White [81]	3586
28	30	A	Halifax T	W 4-2	1-1	5	Thompson (pen) [8], Warne 2 [55, 63], Jackson [90]	4251
29	Feb 6	A	Southend U	D 2-2	2-0	5	Ingledow [30], Warne [45]	3895
30	13	A	Plymouth Arg	L 0-1	0-0	6		4336
31	20	H	Brentford	L 2-4	1-3	8	Warne [32], Thompson [75]	3899
32	27	A	Hartlepool U	D 0-0	0-0	9		2680
33	Mar 13	A	Scarborough	W 4-0	2-0	9	Whelan [17], Hurst [37], Warne [55], Fortune-West [72]	3326
34	16	H	Cardiff C	W 1-0	0-0	—	Sedgwick [66]	3669
35	20	A	Peterborough U	D 2-2	0-2	7	Whelan [76], Thompson (pen) [86]	3979
36	27	H	Scunthorpe U	D 0-0	0-0	7		4939
37	Apr 3	A	Darlington	W 2-1	1-0	6	Fortune-West [6], Roscoe [78]	3468
38	5	H	Swansea C	W 1-0	0-0	5	Fortune-West [51]	4257
39	10	A	Rochdale	D 0-0	0-0	5		2516
40	13	A	Exeter C	L 0-3	0-1	—		1929
41	17	H	Carlisle U	W 3-1	0-1	5	Fortune-West 3 [73, 78, 79]	4267
42	20	A	Shrewsbury T	W 3-2	1-1	—	Fortune-West [8], Warne [67], Whelan [86]	1620
43	24	A	Torquay U	L 0-2	0-0	6		2296
44	27	H	Barnet	D 1-1	0-1	—	Fortune-West [78]	3526
45	May 1	H	Brighton & HA	W 2-1	0-0	5	White [50], Whelan [88]	4458
46	8	A	Chester C	D 1-1	0-1	5	Scott R [88]	3792

Final League Position: 5

GOALSCORERS

League (79): Fortune-West 12, Glover 10 (2 pens), Warne 8, Roscoe 5, Thompson 5 (3 pens), White 5, Garner 4, Hudson 4, Sedgwick 4 (1 pen), Whelan 4, Knill 3, Berry 2, Hurst 2, Ingledow 2, Martindale 2, Raven 2, Dillon 1, Jackson 1, Monkhouse 1, Scott R 1, Warner 1.
Worthington Cup (0).
FA Cup (8): Garner 2, Glover 2, Berry 1, Hudson 1, Hurst 1, Scott R 1.

Pollitt M 46	Ingledow J 15 + 6	Beech C 24	Warner V 23	Knill A 35 + 1	Dillon P 25 + 1	Garner D 40	Thompson S 28 + 5	White J 18 + 8	Glover L 18 + 1	Roscoe A 27 + 11	Hudson D 19 + 7	Martindale G 6 + 4	Scott G 13	Hurst P 31 + 1	Richardson N 4 + 1	Sedgwick C 24 + 9	Monkhouse A — + 5	Fortune-West L 20	Berry T 11 + 7	Raven P 11	Bos G 1 + 1	Tracey R — + 3	Scott R 5 + 1	Warne P 19	Strodder G 3	Jackson J 2	Clark M 1	Williams M 10 + 1	Varty W 14	Whelan P 13	Match No.
1	2	3	4	5	6	7	8^1	9	10^2	11	12	13																			1
1	2	3	4	5	6	7	8	9	10	11																					2
1	2	3	4		6	7	8	9	10	11^1			5	12																	3
1	2	3	4	5	6	11	8	9	10					7																	4
1	2^2	3	4	5	6	7	8^1	9	10		13	12	11																		5
1		3	4	5	6	7	8^5	9^2	10	12	14	13		2	11^1																6
1		3	4^3	5	6	7^1	8		10	11	12	9		2^2		13	14														7
1		3		5	11	4		9	10	7	8			2		6															8
1		3		5	6	4		10	11	8	9			2		7	12														9
1		3		5	6	4		10	11	8	9			2^1		7	12														10
1	3^2	2		5	6	4^1	12	10		11	8	9				7	13														11
1	3^1			5	6	4	12		10	11	8			2		7		9													12
1				5	6	4		10	11^1	8			2	3		7		9	12												13
1				5	6	4	12	10^2	11	8			2^1	3		7		9	13												14
1	8			5	6	4		9		11			2	3		7^1	12	10													15
1				5		4		9^1		11	8		2	3	12			10	7	6											16
1	12			5		4				11	8		2	3		7^1		9	10^2	6	13										17
1	12			5	13	4				11^3	8		2^2	3		7			10	6	9^1	14									18
1	2			5		4	12			11	8			3		7^1			10	6	9										19
1	2^2		12	3	4			10	11	8						7	5	13	9^1	6											20
1				5	6	4	12	10	11^2	8^1				3		13			7	2	9										21
1	8		3^3	5		4	12	13	10	11			2^1			7^2			14	6	9										22
1	8		2	5	3	4		7	10	12		11								6	9^1										23
1	2		7	5		4	8	9	10	11				3						6											24
1	7		2	5		8	9		11^1	4^2				3			13		10	6			12								25
1		2	5	3	4	8	9			11						7				6				10							26
1		2	5	6	4	8	9			11				3		7								10							27
1		2	5	11	4	8								3		7								10	6	9					28
1	7	2^2	5	11	4	8^1				12				3			13							10	6	9					29
1	7^2	11	2	5	3^1	4				12						8	13						14	10	6						30
1	12	3^1		5	6	4^2	8	9^3		11	13	14		11		7								10				2			31
1	11^1	6	2	5		4	8			12				3		7		9						10							32
1	3		4				8	13		12				11		7^1		9						10				2	5	6	33
1	3		4				8							11		7		9						10				2	5	6	34
1	3^1		4				8			12				11		7		9						10				2	5	6	35
1	3		4^1				8			12				11		7		9						10				2	5	6	36
1	3	2	4				8^1			12	13			11		7^2		9						10					5	6	37
1	3	5	4^3				8			12	13					7^2		9				14		10^1				2	11	6	38
1	3	5	4				8			10^1				11		7		9						12				2	11	6	39
1	3	5	4				8^1			12	13					7^2		9	14					10				2	11	6	40
1		5	4^2			12	13			11	8			3		7^1		9						10^3				14	2	6	41
1	12	5	4							11	8^1			3			13	9						10				2^2	7	6	42
1	12	5	4^1			13				11	8^2			3			14	9						10				2^2	7	6	43
1		5	4			12				11	8			3		7^1		9						10				2		6	44
1		5	4			8^1				11^2	7			3				9	13				12	10				2		6	45
1	12	3		5	6		8			11					13			9^2	14				7	10^3				2^1	4		46

Worthington Cup

First Round	Chesterfield	(h)	0-1
		(a)	0-2

FA Cup

First Round	Emley	(a)	1-1
		(h)	3-1
Second Round	Rochdale	(a)	0-0
		(h)	4-0
Third Round	Bristol R	(h)	0-1

Football Conference   **SCARBOROUGH**

FOUNDATION

Scarborough came into being as early as 1879 when they were formed by members of the town's cricket club and went under the name of Scarborough Cricketers' FC with home games played on the North Marine Road Cricket Ground.

The McCain Stadium, Seamer Road, Scarborough YO12 4HF.

Telephone: (01723) 375094.

Fax: (01723) 378733.

Ground Capacity: 6899.

Record Attendance: 11,130 v Luton T, FA Cup 3rd rd, 8 January 1938. Football League: 7314 v Wolverhampton W, Division 4, 15 August 1987.

Record Receipts: £37,609.50 v Arsenal, Coca-Cola Cup 4th rd, 6 January 1993.

Pitch Measurements: 114yd × 74yd.

President: John Birley.

Chairman: J. Russell.

Directors: T. Milton, R. Robinson, R. Kemp, R. Green, Mrs G. Russell, A. Walker.

Manager: Colin Addison.

Assistant Manager: Ray McHale.

Secretary: Mrs Gillian Russell.

Physio: L. Taylor.

Year Formed: 1879.

Turned Professional: 1926.

Ltd Co.: 1933.

Club Nickname: 'The Boro'.

LATEST SEQUENCES

Longest Sequence of League Wins: 3, 6.12.97 – 19.12.97.

Longest Sequence of League Defeats: 7, 19.3.96 – 13.4.96.

Longest Sequence of League Draws: 4, 13.4.98 – 2.5.98.

Longest Sequence of Unbeaten League Matches: 9, 28.9.96 – 2.11.96.

Longest Sequence Without a League Win: 16, 17.9.94 – 14.1.95.

HONOURS

Football League: Division 3 best season: 6th, 1997–98.

FA Cup: best season: 3rd rd, 1931, 1938, 1976, 1978, 1995.

Football League Cup: best season: 4th rd, 1993.

FA Trophy: Winners 1973, 1976, 1977.

GM Vauxhall Conference: Winners 1986–87.

Colours
White shirts and shorts with red and green trim, red and white hooped stockings.

Change Colours
Fluorescent lime shirts with black trim, lime shorts, black and lime stockings.

Previous Grounds: 1879, Scarborough Cricket Ground; 1887, Recreation Ground; 1898 Athletic Ground (re-named The McCain Stadium 1992).

First Football League Game: 15 August 1987, Division 4, v Wolverhampton W (h) D 2–2 – Blackwell; McJannet, Thompson, Bennyworth, Richards, Kendall, Hamill, Moss, McHale (1), Mell (1), Graham.

Record League Victory: 4–0 v Bolton W, Division 4, 29 August 1987 – Blackwell; McJannet, Thompson, Bennyworth (Walker), Richards (1) (Cook), Kendall, Hamill (1), Moss, McHale, Mell (1), Graham, (1 og). 4–0 v Newport Co (a), Division 4, 12 April 1988 – Ironside; McJannet, Thompson, Kamara, Richards (1), Short (1), Adams (Cook 1), Brook, Outhart (1), Russell, Graham. 4–0 v Doncaster R, Division 3, 1 November 1997 – Martin; Jackson, Heckingbottom, Snodin, Atkin, Bennett G (1), Williams (2), McElhatton (1), Robinson, Brodie, Bennett T.

Record Cup Victory: 6–0 v Rhyl Ath, FA Cup 1st rd, 29 November 1930 – Turner; Severn, Belton; Maskell, Robinson, Wallis; Small (1), Rand (2), Palfreman (2), A. D. Hill (1), Mickman.

Record Defeat: 1–7 v Wigan Ath, Division 3, 11 March 1997.

Most League Points (3 for a win): 77, Division 4, 1988–89.

Most League Goals: 69, Division 4, 1990–91.

Highest League Scorer in Season: Darren Foreman, 27, Division 4, 1992–93.

Most League Goals in Total Aggregate: Darren Foreman, 35, 1991–95.

Most League Goals in One Match: 3, Darren Foreman v Northampton T, Division 3, 10 October 1992; 3, Darren Foreman v York C, Division 3, 19 December 1992.

Most Capped Player: None.

Most League Appearances: Ian Ironside, 183, 1988–91, 1992, 1994–97.

Youngest League Player: Lee Harper, 17 years 192 days v Scunthorpe U, 2 October 1993.

Record Transfer Fee Received: £240,000 from Notts Co for Chris Short, September 1990.

Record Transfer Fee Paid: £102,000 to Leicester C for Martin Russell, March 1989.

Football League Record: Promoted to Division 4 1987; 1992–99 Division 3; 1999– Football Conference.

MANAGERS

B. Chapman 1945–47 *(Secretary-Manager)*
George Hall 1946–47
Harold Taylor 1947–48
Frank Taylor 1948–50
A. C. Bell *(Director & Hon. Team Manager)* 1950–53
Reg Halton 1953–54
Charles Robson *(Hon. Team Manager)* 1954–57
George Higgins 1957–58
Andy Smailes 1959–61
Eddie Brown 1961–64
Albert Franks 1964–65
Stuart Myers 1965–66
Graham Shaw 1968–69
Colin Appleton 1969–73
Ken Houghton 1974–75
Colin Appleton 1975–81
Jimmy McAnearney 1981–82
John Cottam 1982–84
Harry Dunn 1984–86
Neil Warnock 1986–88
Colin Morris 1989
Ray McHale 1989–93
Phil Chambers 1993
Steve Wicks 1993–94
Billy Ayre 1994
Ray McHale 1994–96
Mitch Cook *(Director of Coaching)* 1996
Mick Wadsworth 1996–99
Colin Addison March 1999–

TEN YEAR LEAGUE RECORD

		P	W	D	L	F	A	Pts	Pos
1988-89	Div 4	46	21	14	11	67	52	77	5
1989-90	Div 4	46	15	10	21	60	73	55	18
1990-91	Div 4	46	19	12	15	59	56	69	9
1991-92	Div 4	42	15	12	15	64	68	57	12
1992-93	Div 3	42	15	9	18	66	71	54	13
1993-94	Div 3	42	15	8	19	55	61	53	14
1994-95	Div 3	42	8	10	24	49	70	34	21
1995-96	Div 3	46	8	16	22	39	69	40	23
1996-97	Div 3	46	16	15	15	65	68	63	12
1997-98	Div 3	46	19	15	12	67	58	72	6

DID YOU KNOW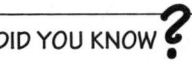

As a non-league club, Scarborough beat the following Football League clubs in the FA Cup: Bradford City, Crewe (twice), Darlington, Lincoln, Oldham, Preston, Rochdale, Stockport and York.

SCARBOROUGH 1998–99 LEAGUE RECORD

Match No.	Date	Venue	Opponents	Result		H/T Score	Lg. Pos.	Goalscorers	Attendance
1	Aug 8	H	Southend U	L	1-2	1-0	—	Brodie [37]	2298
2	15	A	Exeter C	L	0-1	0-1	23		2703
3	22	H	Mansfield T	L	2-3	1-1	24	Brodie [41], Williams [56]	1972
4	29	A	Leyton Orient	W	3-0	2-0	21	Robinson [1], Brodie [19], Russell [88]	3845
5	31	A	Brighton & HA	L	1-2	0-1	22	Bullimore [89]	2528
6	Sept 5	A	Cambridge U	W	3-2	1-2	18	Lydiate [39], Mirankov [51], Williams [79]	2385
7	9	H	Shrewsbury T	W	2-0	2-0	—	Robinson [12], Brodie [13]	1910
8	12	A	Swansea C	L	0-2	0-1	17		3360
9	19	H	Brentford	W	3-1	2-0	12	Brodie 2 [34, 36], Mirankov (pen) [67]	2028
10	26	A	Plymouth Arg	D	0-0	0-0	13		5216
11	Oct 3	H	Chester C	L	2-4	0-2	16	Mirankov [58], Tate [89]	1832
12	9	A	Carlisle U	L	0-1	0-0	—		3502
13	17	H	Hull C	L	1-2	1-2	21	Hoyland [35]	2760
14	21	H	Barnet	D	0-0	0-0	—		1056
15	31	H	Torquay U	D	1-1	0-0	22	Robinson [88]	1365
16	Nov 7	A	Rotherham U	L	0-4	0-3	22		3954
17	10	A	Cardiff C	L	0-1	0-0	—		4422
18	17	A	Rochdale	W	1-0	0-0	—	Russell [73]	1536
19	21	H	Hartlepool U	L	1-2	0-2	21	Hoyland [49]	1715
20	28	A	Darlington	L	0-3	0-1	22		2660
21	Dec 12	H	Halifax T	W	1-0	1-0	23	Brodie [31]	2251
22	19	A	Peterborough U	L	1-3	0-2	23	Dabelsteen [65]	4444
23	26	A	Mansfield T	L	2-3	0-2	23	Greenacre [76], McNaughton [80]	3495
24	28	H	Scunthorpe U	L	1-4	0-2	23	Rennison [82]	2300
25	Jan 9	A	Southend U	L	0-1	0-0	23		3453
26	16	H	Exeter C	W	1-0	0-0	23	Mirankov (pen) [65]	2002
27	23	A	Brighton & HA	L	0-1	0-0	23		3499
28	30	A	Scunthorpe U	L	1-5	0-2	23	Greenacre [62]	3779
29	Feb 6	H	Cambridge U	L	1-5	1-2	24	Tate [17]	1650
30	13	A	Shrewsbury T	L	1-3	0-1	24	Brodie [58]	2378
31	20	H	Swansea C	W	2-1	2-1	24	Tate [26], Roberts [32]	1512
32	27	A	Brentford	D	1-1	1-0	24	Tate [19]	4783
33	Mar 9	A	Chester C	W	3-1	1-0	—	Tate 2 [5, 87], Russell [85]	1954
34	13	H	Rotherham U	L	0-4	0-2	24		3326
35	20	A	Torquay U	W	1-0	0-0	24	Brodie [78]	1891
36	26	H	Rochdale	W	1-0	1-0	—	Brodie [11]	2206
37	Apr 3	A	Hull C	D	1-1	0-0	23	Hoyland [78]	13,949
38	5	H	Carlisle U	W	3-0	1-0	23	Tate 3 [31, 61, 62]	3604
39	10	A	Barnet	L	0-1	0-0	24		1679
40	14	H	Darlington	L	0-2	0-1	—		2125
41	17	A	Hartlepool U	L	0-3	0-2	24		5098
42	21	A	Leyton Orient	L	1-3	1-1	—	Tate [27]	1410
43	24	H	Cardiff C	L	1-2	1-1	24	Roberts [43]	1834
44	May 1	A	Halifax T	W	2-1	2-1	24	Atkinson G [7], Brodie [9]	3308
45	5	H	Plymouth Arg	W	3-0	1-0	—	Brodie [3], Tate 2 [74, 76]	2398
46	8	H	Peterborough U	D	1-1	1-1	24	Roberts [42]	4769

Final League Position: 24

GOALSCORERS

League (50): Brodie 12, Tate 12, Mirankov 4 (2 pens), Hoyland 3, Roberts 3, Robinson 3, Russell 3, Greenacre 2, Williams 2, Atkinson G 1, Bullimore 1, Dabelsteen 1, Lydiate 1, McNaughton 1, Rennison 1.
Worthington Cup (0).
FA Cup (1): Williams 1.

Elliott T 20	Jackson R 19 + 1	Atkinson P 23 + 4	Worrall B 25 + 6	Lydiate J 26 + 1	Mirankov A 22	Bullimore W 33 + 2	Hoyland J 44	Campbell N 3 + 8	Brodie S 43	Milbourne I 2 + 14	Tate C 18 + 7	Williams G 17	Russell M 20 + 17	Radigan N 4 + 5	Kay J 23 + 1	Robinson L 17 + 12	McNaughton M 22 + 9	Carr G 5 + 5	Dabelsteen T 5	Weaver L 6	Greenacre C 10 + 2	Renshaw I — + 1	Rennison S 15	Mountfield D 5 + 1	Rainford D — + 2	Naisbett P 2	Hodges G 1	Goodlad M 3	Todd A — + 1	Roberts D 18	Porter G 11 + 2	Parks T 15	Atkinson G 15	Saville A — + 9	McAuley S 6 + 1	Jones N 8 + 1	Match No.
1	2	3	4	5	6	7[1]	8	9	10	11	12																										1
1	2	3[2]	4	5	6	7[1]	8	9	10[3]		12	11	13	14																							2
1	3	4[1]	5	6[3]	7	8	14		10		12	11	13			2	9[2]																				3
1	3	12	4	5	6	7[1]	8		10[3]		13	9	14			2	11[2]																				4
1	3	4[1]	5	6		7	8		10		12	9	13			2	11[2]																				5
1	3[3]	14	4	5	6	7	8		10[1]		12	9	13			2	11[2]																				6
1	3	4	5	6		7[1]	8	14	10[2]		13	9	12			2	11[3]																				7
1	3[2]	4[1]	5	6		7	8	12	10			9	13			2	11																				8
1	3	12	5	6		7[1]	8	13	10[2]			9	14			2	11[3]																				9
1	8	3		5	6	7[2]			10		12		14	4[3]		2	11[1]	9	13																		10
1	3	12	5	6		7[2]	8		10		14	9	13	4[1]		2	11[3]																				11
1	3[1]	4[2]	5	6	7	8		10			12	13	9			2	11																				12
1	3	4[2]	5	6	7[3]	8		10		11[1]		9	13			2		12	14																		13
1	3	12	5	6		7[1]	8		10		13	9		4[3]		2	11[2]	14																			14
1	3	4[1]	5	6	12	7[2]	8		10		13	9				2	11																				15
1	3[2]	4[1]	5	6		7	8	13	10			9	12			2	11[2]	14																			16
1	3[1]	4	5	6		7[3]	8	12	10[2]			9	13			2	11	14																			17
1	3	4	5			7	8		9[1]	11					6	2	12	10																			18
1	3	4	5			7	8		9	11					6	2	12	10[1]																			19
1	12	3[3]	4	5		7[1]	8	13	9						6	2	10[2]	14		11																	20
	2	3		5	6	7	8	12	9			13		4[2]	14		11[1]		1		10[3]																21
	2	3[2]	5	6		7	8		9		13			4[1]		12	11		1		10[3]	14															22
	2	3				7[1]	8	9[2]			12	13	4		6		11		1		10			5													23
	2	3	4[3]		12	7[1]	8	9			13		14		6[2]		11		1		10			5													24
	2[3]	6	5			7[1]	8		9	11[2]		13	12		4				1		10									3	14						25
	3	12		5	6		8		9	11		13	7[2]			2			1		10									4[1]							26
	3[3]				6	7	8	9[1]		11		13	12			2	11[2]	14			10		4[2]			1											27
	3			5	6	7	8		9			13	12			2	11[2]				10		4[1]			1											28
	3	4		5		7	8		9				12			2		6[1]			10[2]							1	13	11							29
	2[2]	4[1]				7	8		9			13	12			3		14			10		6	5[3]				1		11							30
	3					7[2]	8		9			13	12			2					10		6	5						11[1]		4	1				31
		12				7	8[1]		9			13				2					10		6	5						3	11[2]	4	1				32
						7	8[1]		9			13	12								10		6	5						3	11[2]	4	1				33
						7	8		9				12			2[1]							6	5						3	11[2]	4	1	13			34
						7	8		9							2					10[1]		6	5	12					3	11	4	1				35
						7	8		9[1]							2					10		6	5[2]						3	11	4	1	13	12		36
	8[2]	12				7			9			13				2							6							3	11[3]	4[1]	1	14	5	10	37
	8	12				7			9[3]			13				2							6[1]							3	11[2]	4	1	14	5	10	38
		13				7			9				12			2[1]					10		6							3	11[3]	4[2]	1	14	5	8	39
		12				7			9[3]			13				2					10		6							3	11	4[2]	1	14	5	8[1]	40
		4				7	8		9			13	12			2[2]					10		6							3[3]	11[1]		1	14	5		41
						7	8		9			13	12			2[1]	2[2]				10		6	5						3	11	4[2]	1		5		42
		4[1]				7			9				12			2					10		6	5						3	11		1			8	43
		4				7			9			13				2					10[1]		6	5	12					3	11[2]		1			8	44
		4				7			9[2]							2[1]					10		6	5	12					3	11		1	13		8	45
		4				7			9			13				2[1]					10		6	5	12					3	11[2]		1	14		8[3]	46

Worthington Cup
First Round   Barnsley   (h) 0-1
             (a) 0-3

FA Cup
First Round   Rochdale   (h) 1-1
             (a) 0-2

Division 2 SCUNTHORPE UNITED

FOUNDATION

The year of foundation for Scunthorpe United has often been quoted as 1910, but the club can trace its history back to 1899 when Brumby Hall FC, who played on the Old Showground, consolidated their position by amalgamating with some other clubs and changing their name to Scunthorpe United. The year 1910 was when that club amalgamated with North Lindsey United as Scunthorpe and Lindsey United. The link is Mr W. T. Lockwood whose chairmanship covers both years.

Glanford Park, Scunthorpe, North Lincolnshire DN15 8TD.

Telephone: (01724) 848077.

Fax: (01724) 857986.

Ground Capacity: 9183.

Record Attendance: Old Showground: 23,935 v Portsmouth, FA Cup 4th rd, 30 January 1954. Glanford Park: 8775 v Rotherham U, Division 4, 1 May 1989.

Record Receipts: £44,481.50 v Leeds U, Rumbelows Cup 2nd rd lst leg, 24 September 1991.

Pitch Measurements: 110yd × 71yd.

Vice-Presidents: I. T. Botham, G. Johnson, A. Harvey, R. Ashman, K. Waters, J. Brownsword, B. Heywood, Dr J. Zacarias.

Chairman: K. Wagstaff.

Vice-Chairman: R. Garton.

Directors: J. B. Borrill, J. S. Wharton, B. Collen, J. A. C. Godfrey CBE, D. Comerford.

Team Manager: Brian Laws.

Chief Executive/Secretary: A. D. Rowing.

Commercial Manager: A. D. Rowing.

LATEST SEQUENCES

Longest Sequence of League Wins: 6, 18.10.69 – 25.11.69.

Longest Sequence of League Defeats: 8, 29.11.97 – 20.1.98.

Longest Sequence of League Draws: 6, 2.1.84 – 25.2.84.

Longest Sequence of Unbeaten League Matches: 15, 13.11.71 – 26.2.72.

Longest Sequence Without a League Win: 14, 22.3.75 – 6.9.75.

HONOURS

Football League: Division 2 best season: 4th, 1961–62; Division 3 (N) – Champions 1957–58. Promoted from Division 3 1998–99 (play-offs).

FA Cup: best season: 5th rd, 1958, 1970.

Football League Cup: never past 3rd rd.

Colours
Sky blue and claret halved shirts, white shorts, white stockings with claret trim.

Change Colours
Navy and yellow shirts, navy shorts, navy and yellow stockings.

Year Formed: 1899.

Turned Professional: 1912.

Ltd Co.: 1912.

Club Nickname: 'The Iron'.

Previous Names: Amalgamated first with Brumby Hall then North Lindsey United to become Scunthorpe & Lindsey United, 1910; dropped '& Lindsey' in 1958.

Previous ground: 1899, Old Showground; 1988, Glanford Park.

First Football League Game: 19 August 1950, Division 3 (N), v Shrewsbury T (h) D 0–0 – Thompson; Barker, Brownsword; Allen, Taylor, McCormick; Mosby, Payne, Gorin, Rees, Boyes.

Record League Victory: 8–1 v Luton T, Division 3, 24 April 1965 – Sidebottom; Horstead, Hemstead; Smith, Neale, Lindsey; Bramley (1), Scott, Thomas (5), Mahy (1), Wilson (1). 8–1 v Torquay U (a), Division 3, 28 October 1995 – Samways; Housham, Wilson, Ford (1), Knill (1), Hope (Nicholson), Thornber, Bullimore (Walsh), McFarlane (4) (Young), Eyre (2), Paterson.

Record Cup Victory: 9–0 v Boston U, FA Cup 1st rd, 21 November 1953 – Malan; Hubbard, Brownsword; Sharpe, White, Bushby; Mosby (1), Haigh (3), Whitfield (2), Gregory (1), Mervyn Jones (2).

Record Defeat: 0–8 v Carlisle U, Division 3 (N), 25 December 1952.

Most League Points (2 for a win): 66, Division 3 (N), 1956–57, 1957–58.

Most League Points (3 for a win): 83, Division 4, 1982–83.

Most League Goals: 88, Division 3 (N), 1957–58.

Highest League Scorer in Season: Barrie Thomas, 31, Division 2, 1961–62.

Most League Goals in Total Aggregate: Steve Cammack, 110, 1979–81, 1981–86.

Most League Goals in One Match: 5, Barrie Thomas v Luton T, Division 3, 24 April 1965.

Most Capped Player: None.

Most League Appearances: Jack Brownsword, 595, 1950–65.

Youngest League Player: Mike Farrell, 16 years 240 days v Workington, 8 November 1975.

Record Transfer Fee Received: £350,000 from Aston Villa for Neil Cox, February 1991.

Record Transfer Fee Paid: £80,000 to York C for Ian Helliwell, August 1991.

Football League Record: 1950 Elected to Division 3 (N); 1958–64 Division 2; 1964–68 Division 3; 1968–72 Division 4; 1972–73 Division 3; 1973–83 Division 4; 1983–84 Division 3; 1984–92 Division 4; 1992–99 Division 3; 1999– Division 2.

MANAGERS

Harry Allcock 1915–53
(Secretary-Manager)
Tom Crilly 1936–37
Bernard Harper 1946–48
Leslie Jones 1950–51
Bill Corkhill 1952–56
Ron Suart 1956–58
Tony McShane 1959
Bill Lambton 1959
Frank Soo 1959–60
Dick Duckworth 1960–64
Fred Goodwin 1964–66
Ron Ashman 1967–73
Ron Bradley 1973–74
Dick Rooks 1974–76
Ron Ashman 1976–81
John Duncan 1981–83
Allan Clarke 1983–84
Frank Barlow 1984–87
Mick Buxton 1987–91
Bill Green 1991–93
Richard Money 1993–94
David Moore 1994–96
Mick Buxton 1996–97
Brian Laws February 1997–

TEN YEAR LEAGUE RECORD

		P	W	D	L	F	A	Pts	Pos
1988-89	Div 4	46	21	14	11	77	57	77	4
1989-90	Div 4	46	17	15	14	69	54	66	11
1990-91	Div 4	46	20	11	15	71	62	71	8
1991-92	Div 4	42	21	9	12	64	59	72	5
1992-93	Div 3	42	14	12	16	57	54	54	14
1993-94	Div 3	42	15	14	13	64	56	59	11
1994-95	Div 3	42	18	8	16	68	63	62	7
1995-96	Div 3	46	15	15	16	67	61	60	12
1996-97	Div 3	46	18	9	19	59	62	63	13
1997-98	Div 3	46	19	12	15	56	52	69	8

DID YOU KNOW ❓

In the 1954–55 season, Gordon Brown and John Gregory scored 45 of Scunthorpe United's 81 League goals between them; Brown scoring just one more than Gregory. The team finished third in Division Three (North).

SCUNTHORPE UNITED 1998–99 LEAGUE RECORD

Match No.	Date	Venue	Opponents	Result	H/T Score	Lg. Pos.	Goalscorers	Attendance
1	Aug 8	A	Shrewsbury T	L	1-2	0-0	—	Forrester [71]	2649
2	15	H	Carlisle U	W	3-1	2-0	6	Hope [38], Eyre [43], Gayle [83]	2810
3	22	A	Hartlepool U	W	2-1	1-0	4	Calvo-Garcia [3], Logan [90]	2697
4	29	H	Plymouth Arg	L	0-2	0-1	8		2868
5	31	A	Swansea C	W	2-1	0-0	7	Eyre (pen) [81], Forrester [86]	4024
6	Sept 5	H	Torquay U	W	2-0	2-0	4	Hope [43], Gayle [45]	2421
7	8	H	Cambridge U	W	3-2	1-1	—	Forrester 2 [31, 74], Logan [58]	2431
8	12	A	Rochdale	D	2-2	1-1	2	Forrester [8], Stamp [89]	1929
9	19	H	Mansfield T	W	3-2	2-2	2	Forrester [8], Eyre 2 [44, 71]	3554
10	26	A	Brighton & HA	W	3-1	1-0	1	Stamp 2 [2, 59], Eyre [47]	2625
11	Oct 3	H	Halifax T	L	0-4	0-0	1		4989
12	10	H	Southend U	D	1-1	1-0	2	Calvo-Garcia [35]	3747
13	17	A	Exeter C	D	2-2	2-0	2	Forrester [8], Hope [44]	2885
14	20	A	Brentford	L	1-2	1-0	—	Forrester [27]	4700
15	24	H	Rotherham U	W	4-3	2-0	1	Wilcox [12], Eyre (pen) [33], Knill (og) [54], Logan [59]	4783
16	31	A	Leyton Orient	L	0-1	0-0	2		3919
17	Nov 7	H	Chester C	W	2-1	2-0	2	Forrester [11], Logan [39]	3160
18	10	A	Barnet	L	0-1	0-0	—		1314
19	21	H	Hull C	W	3-2	2-1	2	Gayle [11], Forrester [43], Marshall [77]	5633
20	28	A	Peterborough U	L	1-2	1-1	5	Calvo-Garcia [39]	5160
21	Dec 12	H	Cardiff C	L	0-2	0-1	9		3200
22	19	H	Darlington	L	1-3	0-1	9	Brumwell (og) [83]	2465
23	26	H	Hartlepool U	W	1-0	0-0	7	Forrester [65]	3621
24	28	A	Scarborough	W	4-1	2-0	5	Hope [17], Calvo-Garcia [21], Forrester 2 [47, 52]	2300
25	Jan 9	A	Shrewsbury T	W	3-0	1-0	5	Forrester [39], Eyre [54], Gayle [85]	2860
26	16	A	Carlisle U	W	1-0	0-0	2	Eyre [60]	3044
27	30	H	Scarborough	W	5-1	2-0	3	Logan [14], Calvo-Garcia 2 [26, 63], Eyre (pen) [57], Hope [59]	3779
28	Feb 6	A	Torquay U	L	0-1	0-1	3		2071
29	13	A	Cambridge U	D	0-0	0-0	3		5596
30	20	H	Rochdale	L	0-1	0-0	4		3749
31	27	A	Mansfield T	L	1-2	1-1	6	Forrester [9]	3208
32	Mar 6	H	Brighton & HA	W	3-1	2-0	5	Eyre 3 (1 pen) [9, 43 (p), 90]	4148
33	13	A	Chester C	W	2-0	1-0	5	Calvo-Garcia [23], Forrester [69]	2115
34	20	H	Leyton Orient	W	2-0	0-0	4	Calvo-Garcia [55], Forrester [68]	4163
35	23	H	Swansea C	L	1-2	1-1	—	Walker [11]	3631
36	27	A	Rotherham U	D	0-0	0-0	4		4939
37	30	A	Plymouth Arg	L	0-5	0-2	—		3589
38	Apr 3	H	Exeter C	W	2-0	0-0	4	Eyre [57], Logan [77]	3419
39	5	A	Southend U	W	1-0	1-0	4	Sheldon [29]	4814
40	10	H	Brentford	D	0-0	0-0	4		5604
41	13	H	Peterborough U	D	1-1	1-0	—	Forrester [14]	3296
42	17	A	Hull C	W	3-2	2-0	4	Forrester [14], Stamp [24], Eyre [77]	9835
43	24	A	Barnet	W	3-1	2-0	4	Calvo-Garcia [6], Eyre [28], Forrester [68]	3930
44	27	A	Halifax T	L	0-1	0-0	—		3486
45	May 1	A	Cardiff C	D	0-0	0-0	4		12,455
46	8	H	Darlington	L	0-1	0-0	4		4238

Final League Position: 4

GOALSCORERS

League (69): Forrester 20, Eyre 15 (4 pens), Calvo-Garcia 9, Logan 6, Hope 5, Gayle 4, Stamp 4, Marshall 1, Sheldon 1, Walker 1, Wilcox 1, own goals 2.
Worthington Cup (1): Forrester 1.
FA Cup (6): Eyre 2 (1 pen), Forrester 2, Harsley 1, Housham 1.

Clarke T 22	Fickling A 28 + 1	McAuley S 16 + 1	Harsley P 32 + 2	Marshall L 5 + 14	Hope C 46	Walker J 40 + 1	Forrester J 46	Eyre J 41	Gayle J 36 + 1	Calvo-Garcia A 42 + 1	Wilcox R 24 + 4	Logan R 38 + 3	Bull G 4 + 20	Stamp D 5 + 20	Housham S 11 + 5	Stanton N 3 + 1	Atkinson G — + 1	Dawson A 24	Evans T 24	Sheldon G 5 + 6	Witter T 14	Match No.
1	2	3	4	5	6	7	8	9	10	11												1
1	2	3	4^2		6	7	8^3	9	10^1	11	5	13	14	12								2
1	2	3	4^2		6	7	8^3	9	10^1	11	5	13	14	12								3
1	2	3	4		6	7^2	8^1	9	10	11	5	12	13	14								4
1	2	3		12	6	7	8	9	10^2	11^1	5	4		13								5
1	2	3		12	6	7	8	9^2	10	11^1	5	4	13									6
1	2	3		12	6	7	8	9	10	11^1	5	4										7
1	2	3		12	6	7	8	9	10^1	11^2	5^3	4	14	13								8
1	2	3			6	7	8	9	10^1	11	5	4		12								9
1	2	3			6	7	8	9^1		11	5	4		12	10							10
1	2^1	3		12	6	7	10^2	9	8^3	11	5	4	14	13								11
1	2				6	7	8	9	10^1	11	5	4		12	3							12
1	2			12	6	7	8^1	9	10^2	11	5	4	13		3							13
1	2	12			6	7	8^1	9	10	11	5	4			3							14
1	2		12		6	7	8	9^3	10^2	11	5	4	14	13	3							15
1	2		12		6	7	8	9^2	10	11^1	5	4		13	3							16
1	2	3			6	7	8	9		11	5	4		10								17
1		3	12	13	6	7	8^2	9^3	10	11^1	5	4	14		2							18
1		3	7	12	6		8	9^1	10	11	5	4	13		2^1							19
1		3	7	12	6	13	8	9^1	10	11^2	5	4			2							20
1	2	3^3	10	4	6	7	8^1	9			5			12	11^2	14	13					21
1	2	3	12		6	7	8	9	10^1	13	5	4^2			11							22
	2	5	12		6	7	8	9^1	10	11		4						3	1			23
	2	5			6	7	8	9	10^1	11		4		12				3	1			24
	2	5			6	7	8	9	10	11		4						3	1			25
	2	5	12		6	7	8	9^1	10	11		4						3	1			26
		5			6	7	8	9		11		4		10^1		2		3	1	12		27
	4		5		6	7	8^1	9		11^2	10	12	13			2		3	1			28
	2		5		6	7	8	9			10	11						3	1		4	29
	2		5^3	11	6	7	8^1	9		13	12	10^2	14					3	1		4	30
	2	10	5		6	7	8	9		11	5		12	4				3^1	1			31
		5			6	7	8^1	9	10^2	11		4	12	13				3	1		2	32
		5			6	7	8		10^1			4	12					3	1	9	2	33
		5			6	7	8^1	9	10	11	2	4	12	13	14			3	1			34
		5			6	7	8^1	9^3	10^3	11	2	4	12	13	14			3	1			35
		5			6	7	8	9	10	11		4						3	1	12	2	36
		5	12		6	7^1	8	9	10^2	11^3		4	14	13				3	1		2	37
		5	7		6		8^1	9	10	11		4	12					3	1		2	38
		5	7^1	6			8		10	11	12	4						3	1	9	2	39
		5			6		8^2		10	11		4	13	12	7^1			3	1	9	2	40
		5			6		8^1	9	10^2	11		4	12	13				3	1	7	2	41
		5			6	7	8^1	9^2		11		4	12	10				3	1	13	2	42
	3	5			6	7	8	9	10	11^1		4							1	12	2	43
		5			6	7	8	9	10^1	11^2	12	4						3	1	13	2	44
		5			6	7	8^1	9	13	11	14	4	12					3	1	10^2	2^3	45
	12	5			6	7^1	8^2	9^3	10	11	2	4	13					3	1	14		46

Worthington Cup
First Round   Blackpool   (a)   0-1
                                     (h)   1-1

FA Cup
First Round   Woking   (a)   1-0
Second Round   Bedlington T   (h)   2-0
Third Round   Wrexham   (a)   3-4

Division 1   **SHEFFIELD UNITED**

FOUNDATION

In March 1889, Yorkshire County Cricket Club formed Sheffield United six days after an FA Cup semi-final between Preston North End and West Bromwich Albion had finally convinced Charles Stokes, a member of the cricket club, that the formation of a professional football club would prove successful at Bramall Lane. The United's first secretary, Mr J. B. Wostinholm was also secretary of the cricket club.

Bramall Lane Ground, Sheffield S2 4SU.
Telephone: (0114) 221 5757.
Fax: (0114) 272 3030.
Website: http://www.sheffutd.co.uk.
Email: info@sufc.co.uk.
ISDN: (0114) 221 3148.
Ticket Office: (0114) 221 1889.
Pools Office: (0114) 221 3131.
Club Shop: (0114) 221 3132.
Executive Suite: (0114) 221 3195.
Football in the Community: (0114) 276 9314
Ticket Info Line: (0645) 202020
Clubcall: 0891 888650.
Ground Capacity: 30,370.
Record Attendance: 68,287 v Leeds U, FA Cup 5th rd, 15 February 1936.
Record Receipts: £298,364 v Coventry C, FA Cup 6th rd replay, 17 March 1998.
Pitch Measurements: 112yd × 72yd.
Chairman: K. McCabe.
Directors: B. Proctor, S. White, P. Wood.
Manager: Adrian Heath.
Youth Team Managers: Russell Slade, Steve Myles.
Physio: Denis Pettitt.
Sales and Marketing Manager: Sean O'Toole.
Stadium Manager: Roy Mitchell.
Community Programme Organiser: Tony Currie,
Tel: (0114) 2769314.

LATEST SEQUENCES
Longest Sequence of League Wins: 8, 14.9.60 – 22.10.60.
Longest Sequence of League Defeats: 7, 19.8.75 – 20.9.75.
Longest Sequence of League Draws: 5, 16.12.95 – 20.1.96.
Longest Sequence of Unbeaten League Matches: 22, 2.9.1899 – 13.1.1900.
Longest Sequence Without a League Win: 19, 27.9.75 – 7.2.76.

HONOURS

Football League: Division 1 – Champions 1897–98; Runners-up 1896–97, 1899–1900; Division 2 – Champions 1952–53; Runners-up 1892–93, 1938–39, 1960–61, 1970–71, 1989–90; Division 4 – Champions 1981–82.

FA Cup: Winners 1899, 1902, 1915, 1925; Runners-up 1901, 1936.

Football League Cup: best season: 5th rd, 1962, 1967, 1972.

Colours
Red and white striped shirts with black trim, black shorts and stockings with red trim.

Change Colours
All white with red trim.

Year Formed: 1889.

Turned Professional: 1889.

Ltd Co.: 1899.

Club Nickname: 'The Blades'.

First Football League Game: 3 September 1892, Division 2, v Lincoln C (h) W 4–2 – Lilley; Witham, Cain; Howell, Hendry, Needham (1); Wallace, Dobson, Hammond (3), Davies, Drummond.

Record League Victory: 10–0 v Burslem Port Vale (a), Division 2, 10 December 1892 – Howlett; Witham, Lilley; Howell, Hendry, Needham; Drummond (1), Wallace (1), Hammond (4), Davies (2), Watson (2).

Record Cup Victory: 5–0 v Newcastle U (a), FA Cup 1st rd, 10 January 1914 – Gough; Cook, English; Brelsford, Howley, Sturgess; Simmons (2), Gillespie (1), Kitchen (1), Fazackerley, Revill (1). 5–0 v Corinthians, FA Cup 1st rd, 10 January 1925 – Sutcliffe; Cook, Milton; Longworth, King, Green; Partridge, Boyle (1), Johnson (4), Gillespie, Tunstall. 5–0 v Barrow, FA Cup 3rd rd, 7 January 1956 – Burgin; Coldwell, Mason; Fountain, Johnson, Iley; Hawksworth (1), Hoyland (2), Howitt, Wragg (1), Grainger (1).

Record Defeat: 0–13 v Bolton W, FA Cup 2nd rd, 1 February 1890.

Most League Points (2 for a win): 60, Division 2, 1952–53.

Most League Points (3 for a win): 96, Division 4, 1981–82.

Most League Goals: 102, Division 1, 1925–26.

Highest League Scorer in Season: Jimmy Dunne, 41, Division 1, 1930–31.

Most League Goals in Total Aggregate: Harry Johnson, 205, 1919–30.

Most League Goals in One Match: 5, Harry Hammond v Bootle, Division 2, 26 November 1892; 5, Harry Johnson v West Ham U, Division 1, 26 December 1927.

Most Capped Player: Billy Gillespie, 25, Northern Ireland.

Most League Appearances: Joe Shaw, 629, 1948–66.

Youngest League Player: Julian Broddle, 17 years 62 days v Halifax T, 2 January 1982.

Record Transfer Fee Received: £2,700,000 from Leeds U for Brian Deane, July 1993.

Record Transfer Fee Paid: £1,200,000 to West Ham U for Don Hutchison, January 1996.

Football League Record: 1892 Elected to Division 2; 1893–1934 Division 1; 1934–39 Division 2; 1946–49 Division 1; 1949–53 Division 2; 1953–56 Division 1; 1956–61 Division 2; 1961–68 Division 1; 1968–71 Division 2; 1971–76 Division 1; 1976–79 Division 2; 1979–81 Division 3; 1981–82 Division 4; 1982–84 Division 3; 1984–88 Division 2; 1988–89 Division 3; 1989–90 Division 2; 1990–92 Division 1; 1992–94 FA Premier League; 1994– Division 1.

MANAGERS

J. B. Wostinholm 1889–1899 *(Secretary-Manager)*
John Nicholson 1899–1932
Ted Davison 1932–52
Reg Freeman 1952–55
Joe Mercer 1955–58
Johnny Harris 1959–68 *(continued as General Manager to 1970)*
Arthur Rowley 1968–69
Johnny Harris *(General Manager resumed Team Manager duties)* 1969–73
Ken Furphy 1973–75
Jimmy Sirrel 1975–77
Harry Haslam 1978–81
Martin Peters 1981
Ian Porterfield 1981–86
Billy McEwan 1986–88
Dave Bassett 1988–95
Howard Kendall 1995–97
Nigel Spackman 1997–98
Steve Bruce 1998–99
Adrian Heath June 1999–

TEN YEAR LEAGUE RECORD

		P	W	D	L	F	A	Pts	Pos
1988-89	Div 3	46	25	9	12	93	54	84	2
1989-90	Div 2	46	24	13	9	78	58	85	2
1990-91	Div 1	38	13	7	18	36	55	46	13
1991-92	Div 1	42	16	9	17	65	63	57	9
1992-93	PR Lge	42	14	10	18	54	53	52	14
1993-94	PR Lge	42	8	18	16	42	60	42	20
1994-95	Div 1	46	17	17	12	74	55	68	8
1995-96	Div 1	46	16	14	16	57	54	62	9
1996-97	Div 1	46	20	13	13	75	52	73	5
1997-98	Div 1	46	19	17	10	69	54	74	6

DID YOU KNOW ?

On 12 January 1935, Sheffield United made their first trip to Southend United in an FA Cup third round tie. The Kursaal ground – a stone's throw from the beach – was a muddy mixture of sand and cockleshells. But the visitors won 4-0.

SHEFFIELD UNITED 1998–99 LEAGUE RECORD

Match No.	Date	Venue	Opponents	Result	H/T Score	Lg. Pos.	Goalscorers	Attendance
1	Aug 8	H	Swindon T	W 2-1	2-0	—	Stuart [9], Borbokis [45]	15,977
2	15	A	WBA	L 1-4	1-2	9	Saunders [38]	16,901
3	22	H	Birmingham C	L 0-2	0-0	13		17,528
4	29	A	Bolton W	D 2-2	0-2	14	Saunders [64], Taylor [90]	18,263
5	31	H	Crewe Alex	W 3-1	1-1	9	Hunt [45], Hamilton D [51], Woodhouse [85]	15,922
6	Sept 5	A	Huddersfield T	L 0-1	0-0	11		12,192
7	8	H	Grimsby T	W 3-2	0-1	—	Marker 2 [57, 68], McDermott (og) [89]	12,293
8	12	A	Bradford C	D 2-2	1-2	10	Saunders [11], Stuart [49]	13,169
9	19	H	Norwich C	W 2-1	1-0	6	Marcelo 2 [27, 72]	16,155
10	27	A	Crystal Palace	L 0-1	0-0	10		20,370
11	29	A	Watford	D 1-1	0-1	—	Marker [84]	9090
12	Oct 3	H	Portsmouth	W 2-1	1-0	7	Saunders [5], Dellas [85]	15,386
13	17	H	Barnsley	D 1-1	0-1	7	Quinn [48]	23,180
14	20	H	Stockport Co	D 1-1	0-1	—	Marcelo [71]	12,657
15	24	A	Oxford U	W 2-0	1-0	7	Saunders [12], Katchuro [60]	6586
16	31	A	Port Vale	W 3-2	1-0	6	Stuart [24], Katchuro [51], Saunders [87]	6737
17	Nov 7	H	Tranmere R	D 2-2	1-1	6	Saunders [45], Borbokis [61]	15,844
18	10	A	Wolverhampton W	L 1-2	1-0	—	Stuart [44]	20,804
19	14	H	Bury	W 3-1	0-1	6	Katchuro 3 [57, 71, 80]	14,164
20	21	A	QPR	W 2-1	2-0	4	Stuart [12], Katchuro [30]	12,558
21	28	H	Sunderland	L 0-4	0-3	6		25,612
22	Dec 5	A	Bristol C	L 0-2	0-1	9		11,134
23	11	A	Bury	D 3-3	1-1	—	Woodhouse [26], Marcelo 2 [53, 62]	5002
24	20	H	Ipswich T	L 1-2	0-0	11	Devlin [78]	12,944
25	26	A	Birmingham C	L 0-1	0-1	11		22,005
26	28	H	Huddersfield T	W 2-0	0-0	11	Gray (og) [49], Twiss [90]	17,359
27	Jan 9	A	Swindon T	D 2-2	1-1	12	Stuart [44], Holdsworth [88]	7583
28	16	H	Bolton W	L 1-2	1-1	12	Campbell [33]	15,787
29	30	A	Crewe Alex	W 2-1	0-1	12	Marcelo [52], Devlin [90]	5243
30	Feb 6	H	WBA	W 3-0	2-0	10	Morris [28], Marcelo 2 [36, 50]	16,566
31	19	H	Bradford C	D 2-2	1-1	—	Woodhouse [16], Marcelo [66]	14,675
32	27	A	Norwich C	D 1-1	0-1	11	Devlin [55]	14,224
33	Mar 2	H	Crystal Palace	D 1-1	0-1	—	Morris [90]	12,896
34	6	H	Watford	W 3-0	2-0	10	Devlin [38], Morris [44], Hamilton I [50]	15,943
35	9	A	Portsmouth	L 0-1	0-0	—		10,287
36	13	A	Tranmere R	W 3-2	0-2	9	Morris [67], Dellas 2 [68, 90]	6588
37	20	H	Port Vale	W 3-0	0-0	7	Devlin [72], Marcelo [78], Hunt [90]	15,515
38	26	A	Oxford U	L 1-2	1-1	—	Marcelo [28]	14,115
39	Apr 3	A	Barnsley	L 1-2	0-1	8	Marcelo [86]	17,566
40	5	H	Wolverhampton W	D 1-1	0-0	8	Marcelo [62]	21,761
41	10	A	Stockport Co	L 0-1	0-0	8		7551
42	17	H	QPR	W 2-0	1-0	8	Marcelo 2 (1 pen) [38 (p), 61]	14,341
43	20	A	Grimsby T	W 2-1	1-0	—	Campbell 2 [22, 59]	5109
44	24	A	Sunderland	D 0-0	0-0	8		41,179
45	May 1	H	Bristol C	W 3-1	1-0	8	Marcelo [44], Morris 2 [55, 64]	17,310
46	9	A	Ipswich T	L 1-4	0-3	8	Donis [63]	21,689

Final League Position: 8

GOALSCORERS

League (71): Marcelo 16 (1 pen), Saunders 7, Katchuro 6, Morris 6, Stuart 6, Devlin 5, Campbell 3, Dellas 3, Marker 3, Woodhouse 3, Borbokis 2, Hamilton I 2, Hunt 2, Donis 1, Holdsworth 1, Quinn 1, Taylor 1, Twiss 1, own goals 2.
Worthington Cup (7): Saunders 3, Borbokis 1, Ford 1, Hamilton I 1, Taylor 1.
FA Cup (10): Marcelo 3, Holdsworth 2, Morris 2, Borbokis 1, Devlin 1, Stuart 1.

Kelly A 22	Borbokis V 19	Quinn W 41+3	Bruce S 10	Nilsen R 14+3	Holdsworth D 16	Saunders D 19	Hamilton I 27+3	Taylor G 7+5	Stuart G 25	Woodhouse C 31+2	Devlin P 23+10	Tracey S 17+1	Ford B 27+3	Sandford L 34+1	Hunt J 12+1	Marcelo 26+9	Wilder C 4	Marker N 17+1	Goram A 7	Dallas T 9+8	Twiss M 2+10	Hamilton D 6	Katchuro P 8+8	Henry N 3+3	Derry S 23+3	O'Connor J 2	Campbell A 11	Morris L 14+6	Cullen J —+2	Jacobsen A 8+4	Kozluk R 10	Tebily O 7+1	Donis G 5+2	Match No.
1	2	3	4	5	6	7	8	9	10	11¹	12																							1
1	2	3	4	5	6	7	8	9	10	11¹	12																							2
	2	3			6	7	8	12	10		9		4	5	11¹																			3
	2	3²			6	7	8¹	12	10¹	13	9	1	4	5	11	14																		4
	2	3			6	7²	8	9	10	12	13	1	4	5	11¹																			5
		3			6²			9	10	8¹	7	1	4	5	11	12	2	13																6
	2¹	3						7	10	9²	11		4	5	12	13		6	1	8														7
	2	3	4					7	10	9	11				6			8	1	5														8
	2	3			12			7	10		13		4	6		9²		8	1	5¹														9
	2	3	4³	14				7	10	12	11		13	6	5²	9¹			1	8														10
	2³	3			6			7	10	12	11		13	4²	5	9¹		14	1	8														11
		3	4					7	10	12	11		13	2³	5	9¹		14	1	8		6²												12
		3			6			7		9	11	10		5			2	8	1			4												13
		3	4		6			7		11	10¹	12		5²	13		2	9¹	1	8														14
		3	4	5				7	10		11	6	12				2	9¹	1	8														15
		3¹	4	5				7	10		11	6	12				2	9²	1	8														16
1	2		4³	5				7	10²		11	3			6	12				8	9¹	14												17
	2	3		5				7	12		11	10	1			13		8		6¹	14	4³	9²											18
	2	3		5				7	4	11	10	1						8		9	6													19
	2	3	4					7	6	11	10	1						8		9	5													20
	2	3	4	12				6		11	10	1	7²			13		8¹		9³	14	5												21
		3					8			11	10¹	1	7	6		9		12		4	5	2												22
	2	3						10		7		1	4¹	6		9	8			12	11													23
1	2	3					10²			7	12		4¹			9	8				5	6	11	13										24
1		3	4				11			7	10			6		9¹	8²			2	12		5	13										25
1		3	4				12			7²	10		8	6		9³				2¹	13		11	5	14									26
1	2	3			6					11	10		4	5		8¹				7²	9		12	13										27
1	2	3	4¹	6						11	7	13		5		9				8²			10	12										28
1		3			6						7	10	4	5		9				12			2		8	11¹								29
1			3	6					11¹	4	10		12	5		9³		13					2		8	7²	14							30
1		3			6		8		11	4	10			5		9							2			7								31
1		3¹			6					4	10		11	5		9				12			2			7	8							32
1		3			6		8¹			4	10		11	5		9				12			2			7								33
1⁶		3			6		8			4	10	15	11¹	5		9				12			2			7								34
1		3			6		8			4²	10	1	11¹			9				12			2			7	13	5						35
1		3					8			4	10	1	11¹	6	9					12						7		5	2					36
		3			6		8²			4	10	1	12	5	11	9		13³					14			7¹			2					37
		3								4³	10	1	8	5²	11	9		13		12			6	7¹					2	14				38
1		3								4	10	12	5			9							8¹		11	7³		13	2²	6	14			39
1		3								4³	10		5	11		9				12			13		8¹	7³	14	2	6					40
1		3									10		7	6	11	9				4²			12			8¹		5	2			13		41
1		3									10	5	11²	9				13		12			14		8³			4	2	6		7¹		42
1		3									10	5		9¹				11		12²			2		8	13		4		6		7		43
1	12									4	10		8³	5				14		13			2			9²		3¹	11	6		7		44
1	12										10		5³	8¹	9²			4		13			2			11		14	3	6		7		45
1	12					13					10³		8	9			4			14			2²			11		5¹	3	6		7		46

Worthington Cup

First Round	Darlington	(h)	3-1
		(a)	2-2
Second Round	Grimsby T	(h)	2-1
		(a)	0-2

FA Cup

Third Round	Notts Co	(h)	1-1
		(a)	4-3
Fourth Round	Cardiff C	(h)	4-1
Fifth Round	Arsenal	(a)	1-2

FA Premiership   **SHEFFIELD WEDNESDAY**

FOUNDATION

Sheffield, being one of the principal centres of early Association Football, this club was formed as long ago as 1867 by the Sheffield Wednesday Cricket Club (formed 1825) and their colours from the start were blue and white. The inaugural meeting was held at the Adelphi Hotel and the original committee included Charles Stokes who was subsequently a founder member of Sheffield United.

Hillsborough, Sheffield S6 1SW.

Telephone: (0114) 221 2121.

Fax: (0114) 221 2122.

Website: www.swfc.co.uk.

Email: enquiries@swfc.co.uk.

Ticket Office: (0114) 221 2400.

Clubcall: 0891 121186.

Ground Capacity: 39,859.

Record Attendance: 72,841 v Manchester C, FA Cup 5th rd, 17 February 1934.

Record Receipts: £533,918 Sunderland v Norwich C, FA Cup semi-final, 5 April 1992.

Pitch Measurements: 115yd × 74yd.

President: K. T. Addy.

Chairman: D. G. Richards.

Vice-Chairman: K. T. Addy.

Directors: G. K. Hulley, R. M. Grierson FCA, J. Ashton MP, G. A. Thorpe, H. E. Culley.

Manager: Danny Wilson.

Assistant Manager: Peter Shreeves.

Physio: David Galley.

Secretary: Alan D. Sykes.

Commercial Manager: Sean O'Toole.

Stadium Manager: Trevor Grayson.

LATEST SEQUENCES

Longest Sequence of League Wins: 9, 23.4.04 – 15.10.04.

Longest Sequence of League Defeats: 7, 7.1.1893 – 18.3.1893.

Longest Sequence of League Draws: 5, 24.10.92 – 28.11.92.

Longest Sequence of Unbeaten League Matches: 19, 10.12.60 – 8.4.61.

Longest Sequence Without a League Win: 20, 11.1.75 – 30.8.75.

HONOURS

Football League: Division 1 – Champions 1902–03, 1903–04, 1928–29, 1929–30; Runners-up 1960–61; Division 2 – Champions 1899–1900, 1925–26, 1951–52, 1955–56, 1958–59; Runners-up 1949–50, 1983–84.

FA Cup: Winners 1896, 1907, 1935; Runners-up 1890, 1966, 1993.

Football League Cup: Winners 1991; Runners-up 1993.

European Competitions: *European Fairs Cup:* 1961–62, 1963–64. *UEFA Cup:* 1992–93.

Colours
Blue and white striped shirts, black shorts, black stockings.

Change Colours
Yellow shirts, navy shorts, yellow/navy stockings.

Year Formed: 1867 (fifth oldest League club).

Turned Professional: 1887.

Ltd Co.: 1899.

Former Names: The Wednesday until 1929.

Club Nickname: 'The Owls'.

Previous Grounds: 1867, Highfield; 1869, Myrtle Road; 1877, Sheaf House; 1887, Olive Grove; 1899, Owlerton (since 1912 known as Hillsborough). Some games were played at Endcliffe in the 1880s. Until 1895 Bramall Lane was used for some games.

First Football League Game: 3 September 1892, Division 1, v Notts Co (a) W 1–0 – Allan; Tom Brandon (1), Mumford; Hall, Betts, Harry Brandon; Spiksley, Brady, Davis, R. N. Brown, Dunlop.

Record League Victory: 9–1 v Birmingham, Division 1, 13 December 1930 – Brown; Walker, Blenkinsop; Strange, Leach, Wilson; Hooper (3), Seed (2), Ball (2), Burgess (1), Rimmer (1).

Record Cup Victory: 12–0 v Halliwell, FA Cup 1st rd, 17 January 1891 – Smith; Thompson, Brayshaw; Harry Brandon (1), Betts, Cawley (2); Winterbottom, Mumford (2), Bob Brandon (1), Woolhouse (5), Ingram (1).

Record Defeat: 0–10 v Aston Villa, Division 1, 5 October 1912.

Most League Points (2 for a win): 62, Division 2, 1958–59.

Most League Points (3 for a win): 88, Division 2, 1983–84.

Most League Goals: 106, Division 2, 1958–59.

Highest League Scorer in Season: Derek Dooley, 46, Division 2, 1951–52.

Most League Goals in Total Aggregate: Andy Wilson, 199, 1900–20.

Most League Goals in One Match: 6, Doug Hunt v Norwich C, Division 2, 19 November 1938.

Most Capped Player: Nigel Worthington, 50 (66), Northern Ireland.

Most League Appearances: Andy Wilson, 502, 1900–20.

Youngest League Player: Peter Fox, 15 years 269 days v Orient, 31 March 1973.

Record Transfer Fee Received: £2,650,000 from Blackburn R for Paul Warhurst, September 1993.

Record Transfer Fee Paid: £4,700,000 to Celtic for Paolo Di Canio, August 1997.

Football League Record: 1892 Elected to Division 1; 1899–1900 Division 2; 1900–20 Division 1; 1920–26 Division 2; 1926–37 Division 1; 1937–50 Division 2; 1950–51 Division 1; 1951–52 Division 2; 1952–55 Division 1; 1955–56 Division 2; 1956–58 Division 1; 1958–59 Division 2; 1959–70 Division 1; 1970–75 Division 2; 1975–80 Division 3; 1980–84 Division 2; 1984–90 Division 1; 1990–91 Division 2; 1991–92 Division 1; 1992– FA Premier League.

MANAGERS

Arthur Dickinson 1891–1920
(Secretary-Manager)
Robert Brown 1920–33
Billy Walker 1933–37
Jimmy McMullan 1937–42
Eric Taylor 1942–58
(continued as General Manager to 1974)
Harry Catterick 1958–61
Vic Buckingham 1961–64
Alan Brown 1964–68
Jack Marshall 1968–69
Danny Williams 1969–71
Derek Dooley 1971–73
Steve Burtenshaw 1974–75
Len Ashurst 1975–77
Jackie Charlton 1977–83
Howard Wilkinson 1983–88
Peter Eustace 1988–89
Ron Atkinson 1989–91
Trevor Francis 1991–95
David Pleat 1995–97
Ron Atkinson 1997–98
Danny Wilson July 1998–

TEN YEAR LEAGUE RECORD

		P	W	D	L	F	A	Pts	Pos
1988-89	Div 1	38	10	12	16	34	51	42	15
1989-90	Div 1	38	11	10	17	35	51	43	18
1990-91	Div 2	46	22	16	7	80	51	82	3
1991-92	Div 1	42	21	12	9	62	49	75	3
1992-93	PR Lge	42	15	14	13	55	51	59	7
1993-94	PR Lge	42	16	16	10	76	54	64	7
1994-95	PR Lge	42	13	12	17	49	57	51	13
1995-96	PR Lge	38	10	10	18	48	61	40	15
1996-97	PR Lge	38	14	15	9	50	51	57	7
1997-98	PR Lge	38	12	8	18	52	67	44	16

DID YOU KNOW ?

For long-serving Redfern Froggatt's Benefit Match on 17 October 1962, Sheffield Wednesday drew 2–2 with Ajax before a crowd of 21,810. Froggatt, who had left the year before, played in the first half.

SHEFFIELD WEDNESDAY 1998–99 LEAGUE RECORD

Match No.	Date	Venue	Opponents	Result	H/T Score	Lg. Pos.	Goalscorers	Attendance
1	Aug 15	H	West Ham U	L	0-1	0-0	—	30,236
2	22	A	Tottenham H	W	3-0	2-0	8	Atherton [27], Di Canio [35], Hinchcliffe [78]	32,075
3	29	H	Aston Villa	L	0-1	0-1	12		25,989
4	Sept 9	A	Derby Co	L	0-1	0-1	—		26,209
5	12	H	Blackburn R	W	3-0	2-0	10	Atherton [18], Hinchcliffe [33], Di Canio [87]	20,846
6	19	A	Wimbledon	L	1-2	0-1	13	Di Canio [84]	13,163
7	26	H	Arsenal	W	1-0	0-0	10	Briscoe [89]	27,949
8	Oct 3	A	Middlesbrough	L	0-4	0-2	15		34,163
9	18	A	Coventry C	L	0-1	0-0	16		16,003
10	24	H	Everton	D	0-0	0-0	16		26,592
11	31	H	Southampton	D	0-0	0-0	16		30,078
12	Nov 8	A	Leeds U	L	1-2	1-1	16	Booth [3]	30,012
13	14	A	Newcastle U	D	1-1	0-1	16	Rudi [80]	36,698
14	21	H	Manchester U	W	3-1	1-1	15	Alexandersson 2 [14, 73], Jonk [55]	39,475
15	28	A	Chelsea	D	1-1	0-1	16	Booth [67]	34,451
16	Dec 7	H	Nottingham F	W	3-2	1-0	—	Alexandersson [22], Carbone 2 [53, 58]	19,321
17	12	H	Charlton Ath	W	3-0	1-0	13	Booth [13], Carbone [64], Rudi [77]	26,010
18	19	A	Liverpool	L	0-2	0-2	14		40,003
19	26	H	Leicester C	L	0-1	0-1	15		33,513
20	28	A	Aston Villa	L	1-2	1-1	15	Carbone [8]	39,217
21	Jan 9	H	Tottenham H	D	0-0	0-0	15		28,204
22	16	A	West Ham U	W	4-0	2-0	13	Hinchcliffe [26], Rudi [31], Humphreys [68], Carbone (pen) [73]	25,642
23	30	H	Derby Co	L	0-1	0-0	14		24,440
24	Feb 6	A	Leicester C	W	2-0	0-0	14	Jonk [48], Carbone [78]	20,113
25	20	A	Blackburn R	W	4-1	3-0	12	Sonner [20], Rudi 2 [40, 43], Booth [82]	24,643
26	27	H	Middlesbrough	W	3-1	1-0	10	Booth 2 [11, 80], Sonner [77]	24,534
27	Mar 3	H	Wimbledon	L	1-2	0-2	—	Emerson [60]	24,116
28	9	A	Arsenal	L	0-3	0-0	—		37,792
29	13	H	Leeds U	L	0-2	0-1	13		28,142
30	20	A	Southampton	L	0-1	0-1	13		15,201
31	Apr 3	H	Coventry C	L	1-2	0-1	14	Rudi [51]	28,136
32	5	A	Everton	W	2-1	0-1	13	Carbone 2 [52, 68]	35,270
33	17	A	Manchester U	L	0-3	0-2	14		55,270
34	21	H	Newcastle U	D	1-1	0-1	—	Scott [52]	21,545
35	25	H	Chelsea	D	0-0	0-0	14		21,652
36	May 1	A	Nottingham F	L	0-2	0-2	14		20,480
37	8	H	Liverpool	W	1-0	0-0	13	Cresswell [87]	27,383
38	16	A	Charlton Ath	W	1-0	0-0	12	Sonner [79]	20,043

Final League Position: 12

GOALSCORERS

League (41): Carbone 8 (1 pen), Booth 6, Rudi 6, Alexandersson 3, Di Canio 3, Hinchcliffe 3, Sonner 3, Atherton 2, Jonk 2, Briscoe 1, Cresswell 1, Emerson 1, Humphreys 1, Scott 1.
Worthington Cup (1): own goal 1.
FA Cup (6): Humphreys 2, Carbone 1, Emerson 1, Rudi 1, Stefanovic 1.

Pressman K 14 + 1	Cobian J 7 + 2	Hinchcliffe A 32	Atherton P 38	Emerson 38	Walker D 37	Jonk W 38	Carbone B 31	Booth A 34	Rudi P 33 + 1	Di Canio P 5 + 1	Barrett E — + 5	Hyde G — + 1	Briscoe L 5 + 11	Whittingham G 1 + 1	Sanetti F — + 3	Newsome J 2 + 3	Quinn A 1	Magilton J 1 + 5	Alexandersson N 31 + 1	Humphreys R 10 + 9	Oakes S — + 1	Sonner D 24 + 2	Srnicek P 24	Stefanovic D 8 + 3	Morrison O — + 1	Agogo M — + 1	Scott P — + 4	Cresswell R 1 + 6	McKeever M 1 + 2	Haslam N 2	Match No.
1	2	3	4	5	6	7	8	9	10	11																					1
1	2[1]	3	4	5	6	7	8[2]	9	10	11[3]	12	13	14																		2
1	2[1]	3	4	5	6	7	8	9	10	11	12																				3
1	2[2]	3	4	5	6	7	8	9	10			13	12		11[1]																4
1	2[1]	3	4	5	6	7	8	9	10	11[2]	12					13															5
1		3	4	5	6	7	8	9			12				11[2]			2	10[1]	13											6
1	2	3	4	5	6	7[2]		9[3]	10	11	12								13	8[1]	14										7
1	2[1]	3	4	5	6	7			10[3]		12					13		11[2]	8	9	14										8
1		2	5	6	4	8[1]	9							3	12				7	11		10									9
1		3	4	5	6	7	9										2		11	8		10									10
1		3	4	5	6	7	9	12							2[1]	13			11	8		10[2]									11
1		3	2	5	6	4[1]	9	10								13		12	7	8[2]		11									12
		3	2	5	6	4	8[1]	9	10							13			7	12		11[2]	1								13
		3	2	5	6	4	8[1]	9	10										7			11[1]	1								14
		3	2	5	6	4	8	9[1]	10							13			7	12		11[2]	1								15
		3	2	5	6	4	8[2]	9	10[1]							12			7			11	1	13							16
		3	2	5	6	4	8	9	10[2]							12			7[1]			11	1	13							17
		3	2	5	6	4	8	9	10[1]							13			7[2]	12		11	1								18
		3	2	5	6	7	9	10								12			11[1]	8[2]			1	4	13						19
		3	2	5	6	7	8	9	10[1]							13			11[2]	12			1	4							20
		3	2	5	6	7	8		10										11	9			1	4							21
		3[1]	2	5	6	4	8		10							12			7	9		11	1								22
15		3	2	5	6	7[2]	8	9[1]	10							13			11[6]	12			1	4							23
		3	2	5	6	4	8	9[1]	10										7	12		11	1								24
1	12	3	2	5	6[2]	4	8	9	10							13			7			11[1]									25
1		3	2	5	6	4	8	9	10										7			11									26
		3	2	5	6	4	8	9	10										7	12		11[1]	1								27
		3	2	5	6	4	8	9	10										7			11	1								28
		3	2	5	6	4	9	10								12			7	8[2]		11[1]	1		13						29
		3[1]	2	5	6	4[1]	8	9	10										7	12		11	1	13							30
			2	5	6[3]	4[2]	8		10					3		14			7	11[1]		12						13	9		31
		3	2	5		4	8[2]	9	10						6				7[1]			11	1	3			12	13			32
		3	2	5	6	4	8	9[2]	10										7[1]			11	1	3			12	13			33
		3	2	5	6	4[1]	8	9	10										7			11	1	3			12				34
			2	5	6	4	8	9[1]											7			11	1	3			12		10		35
	12		2	5[1]	6	4	8	9	10[1]										7[2]			11	1	3				13	14		36
		4	5	6	7	8	9[2]	10[3]								12			11				1	3				13	14	2[1]	37
		4	5	6	7	8[1]	9	10											11			12	1	3				13		2[2]	38

Worthington Cup
Second Round   Cambridge U   (h)   0-1
  (a)   1-1

FA Cup
Third Round   Norwich C   (h)   4-1
Fourth Round   Stockport Co   (h)   2-0
Fifth Round   Chelsea   (h)   0-1

Division 3

SHREWSBURY TOWN

FOUNDATION

Shrewsbury School having provided a number of the early England and Wales international players it is not surprising that there was a Town club as early as 1876 which won the Birmingham Senior Cup in 1879. However, the present Shrewsbury Town club was formed in 1886 and won the Welsh FA Cup as early as 1891.

Gay Meadow, Shrewsbury SY2 6AB.
Telephone: (01743) 360111.
Fax: (01743) 236384.
Commercial Dept: (01743) 356316.
Clubcall: 0891 121194.
Community Officer: Derek Mann (01743) 356623.
Ground Capacity: 8000.
Record Attendance: 18,917 v Walsall, Division 3, 26 April 1961.
Record Receipts: £80,610 v Arsenal, FA Cup 5th rd, 27 February 1991.
Pitch Measurements: 114yd × 74yd.
President: F. C. G. Fry.
Vice-President: Dr J. Millard Bryson.
Chairman: R. Wycherley.
Directors: R. Bailey, A. Hopkins, M. J. Starkey, K. R. Woodhouse.
Associate Directors: M. R. Ashton, H. J. Wilson, K. J. Sayfritz.
Manager: Jake King.
Commercial Manager: M. Thomas.
Physio: Malcolm Musgrove.
Coaches: Mark Kearney, Roger Preece.
Secretary: M. J. Starkey.
Operations Manager: M. R. Ashton.

LATEST SEQUENCES

Longest Sequence of League Wins: 7, 28.10.95 – 16.12.95.
Longest Sequence of League Defeats: 7, 17.10.87 – 14.11.87.
Longest Sequence of League Draws: 6, 30.10.63 – 14.12.63.
Longest Sequence of Unbeaten League Matches: 16, 30.10.93 – 26.2.94.
Longest Sequence Without a League Win: 17, 25.1.92 – 11.4.92.

HONOURS

Football League: Division 2 best season: 8th, 1983–84, 1984–85; Division 3 – Champions 1978–79, 1993–94; Division 4 – Runners-up 1974–75.

FA Cup: best season: 6th rd, 1979, 1982.

Football League Cup: Semi-final 1961.

Welsh Cup: Winners 1891, 1938, 1977, 1979, 1984, 1985; Runners-up 1931, 1948, 1980.

Auto Windscreens Shield: Runners-up 1996

Colours
Blue shirts with white trim, blue shorts, blue stockings with white trim.

Change Colours
Yellow shirts, navy blue sleeves, yellow shorts, yellow stockings with navy blue tops.

Year Formed: 1886.

Turned Professional: 1896.

Ltd Co.: 1936.

Club Nickname: 'Town', 'Blues' or 'Salop'. The name 'Salop' is a colloquialism for the county of Shropshire. Since Shrewsbury is the only club in Shropshire, cries of 'Come on Salop' are frequently used!

Previous Ground: Old Shrewsbury Racecourse.

First Football League Game: 19 August 1950, Division 3 (N), v Scunthorpe U (a) D 0–0 – Egglestone; Fisher, Lewis; Wheatley, Depear, Robinson; Griffin, Hope, Jackson, Brown, Barker.

Record League Victory: 7–0 v Swindon T, Division 3 (S), 6 May 1955 – McBride; Bannister, Skeech; Wallace, Maloney, Candlin; Price, O'Donnell (1), Weigh (4), Russell, McCue (2).

Record Cup Victory: 11–2 v Marine, FA Cup 1st rd, 11 November 1995 – Edwards, Seabury (Dempsey (1)), Withe (1), Evans (1), Whiston (2), Scott (1), Woods, Stevens (1), Spink (3) (Anthrobus), Walton, Berkley, (1 og).

Record Defeat: 1–8 v Norwich C, Division 3 (S), 13 September 1952. 1–8 v Coventry C, Division 3, 22 October 1963.

Most League Points (2 for a win): 62, Division 4, 1974–75.

Most League Points (3 for a win): 79, Division 3, 1993–94.

Most League Goals: 101, Division 4, 1958–59.

Highest League Scorer in Season: Arthur Rowley, 38, Division 4, 1958–59.

Most League Goals in Total Aggregate: Arthur Rowley, 152, 1958–65 (thus completing his League record of 434 goals).

Most League Goals in One Match: 5, Alf Wood v Blackburn R, Division 3, 2 October 1971.

Most Capped Player: Jimmy McLaughlin, 5 (12), Northern Ireland; Bernard McNally, 5, Northern Ireland.

Most League Appearances: Colin Griffin, 406, 1975–89.

Youngest League Player: Gerry Nardiello, 17 years 9 days v Blackburn R, 14 May 1983

Record Transfer Fee Received: £500,000 from Crew Alex for Dave Walton, October 1997.

Record Transfer Fee Paid: £100,000 to Aldershot for John Dungworth, November 1979 and £100,000 to Southampton for Mark Blake, August 1990.

Football League Record: 1950 Elected to Division 3 (N); 1951–58 Division 3 (S); 1958–59 Division 4; 1959–74 Division 3; 1974–75 Division 4; 1975–79 Division 3; 1979–89 Division 2; 1989–94 Division 3; 1994– Division 2.

MANAGERS

W. Adams 1905–12
(Secretary-Manager)
A. Weston 1912–34
(Secretary-Manager)
Jack Roscamp 1934–35
Sam Ramsey 1935–36
Ted Bousted 1936–40
Leslie Knighton 1945–49
Harry Chapman 1949–50
Sammy Crooks 1950–54
Walter Rowley 1955–57
Harry Potts 1957–58
Johnny Spuhler 1958
Arthur Rowley 1958–68
Harry Gregg 1968–72
Maurice Evans 1972–73
Alan Durban 1974–78
Richie Barker 1978
Graham Turner 1978–84
Chic Bates 1984–87
Ian McNeill 1987–90
Asa Hartford 1990–91
John Bond 1991–93
Fred Davies 1994–97
(previously Caretaker-Manager 1993–94)
Jake King May 1997–

TEN YEAR LEAGUE RECORD

		P	W	D	L	F	A	Pts	Pos
1988-89	Div 2	46	8	18	20	40	67	42	22
1989-90	Div 3	46	16	15	15	59	54	63	11
1990-91	Div 3	46	14	10	22	61	68	52	18
1991-92	Div 3	46	12	11	23	53	68	47	22
1992-93	Div 3	42	17	11	14	57	52	62	9
1993-94	Div 3	42	22	13	7	63	39	79	1
1994-95	Div 2	46	13	14	19	54	62	53	18
1995-96	Div 2	46	13	14	19	58	70	53	18
1996-97	Div 2	46	11	13	22	49	74	46	22
1997-98	Div 3	46	16	13	17	61	62	61	13

DID YOU KNOW ❓

Jack Roscamp, scorer of two Blackburn Rovers goals in the 1928 FA Cup Final, cost Shrewsbury Town £350 when signed from Bradford City in 1934. He scored 13 goals including two 4s and a hat-trick.

SHREWSBURY TOWN 1998–99 LEAGUE RECORD

Match No.	Date	Venue	Opponents	Result		H/T Score	Lg. Pos.	Goalscorers	Atten- dance
1	Aug 8	H	Scunthorpe U	W	2-1	0-0	—	Fickling (og) [82], Evans [88]	2649
2	15	A	Southend U	L	1-2	1-1	10	Berkley [28]	3734
3	21	H	Cardiff C	L	0-3	0-2	—		3003
4	28	A	Halifax T	L	0-2	0-1	—		3424
5	31	H	Barnet	L	0-2	0-0	23		2369
6	Sept 5	A	Rochdale	L	0-1	0-1	24		1660
7	9	A	Scarborough	L	0-2	0-2	—		1910
8	12	H	Peterborough U	D	1-1	0-0	24	Seabury [60]	2225
9	19	A	Darlington	L	0-1	0-1	24		4484
10	26	H	Carlisle U	D	1-1	0-0	24	Kerrigan [90]	2180
11	Oct 3	A	Rotherham U	W	1-0	1-0	23	Steele [6]	3639
12	10	A	Hartlepool U	D	1-1	0-0	23	Gayle [58]	1897
13	17	H	Plymouth Arg	W	2-1	1-0	23	Berkley [23], Seabury [55]	2778
14	20	H	Swansea C	W	1-0	1-0	—	Berkley [41]	2328
15	24	A	Cambridge U	D	0-0	0-0	20		3127
16	31	A	Chester C	D	1-1	0-0	20	Evans (pen) [65]	3699
17	Nov 7	H	Brentford	W	2-0	2-0	18	Kerrigan [33], Berkley [45]	2799
18	10	H	Leyton Orient	D	1-1	1-0	—	Berkley [45]	2485
19	21	A	Exeter C	W	1-0	0-0	18	Jobling [67]	3510
20	28	H	Brighton & HA	L	1-3	0-2	18	Browne T (og) [86]	3168
21	Dec 11	A	Mansfield T	L	0-1	0-1	—		2865
22	18	L	Torquay U	L	1-2	0-1	—	Evans [74]	1934
23	26	A	Cardiff C	L	0-3	0-1	22		12,452
24	28	H	Hull C	W	3-2	2-1	20	Berkley [38], Steele [40], Kerrigan [80]	2879
25	Jan 2	H	Halifax T	D	2-2	1-1	20	Preece [23], Kerrigan [48]	2806
26	9	A	Scunthorpe U	L	0-3	0-1	21		2860
27	16	H	Southend U	W	3-1	1-1	20	Kerrigan [19], Berkley [73], Brown [80]	2132
28	23	A	Barnet	D	2-2	1-1	20	Steele 2 [23, 47]	2029
29	30	A	Hull C	D	1-1	0-0	20	Evans [50]	7331
30	Feb 6	H	Rochdale	W	3-2	2-1	17	Steele 2 [36, 43], Brown [72]	2561
31	13	H	Scarborough	W	3-1	1-0	15	Steele [27], Kerrigan [65], Preece [85]	2378
32	20	A	Peterborough U	D	2-2	1-1	17	Evans [3], Kerrigan [67]	4608
33	27	H	Darlington	W	3-0	1-0	15	Evans (pen) [11], Steele 2 [52, 90]	2624
34	Mar 6	A	Carlisle U	L	1-2	1-1	15	Berkley [32]	2501
35	13	A	Brentford	D	0-0	0-0	16		5082
36	20	H	Chester C	W	2-0	1-0	15	Steele 2 [7, 88]	2903
37	26	H	Cambridge U	D	1-1	0-0	—	Seabury [90]	3247
38	Apr 3	A	Plymouth Arg	L	0-2	0-1	16		5749
39	6	H	Hartlepool U	L	0-1	0-0	—		3187
40	9	A	Swansea C	D	1-1	1-0	—	Seabury [10]	5113
41	13	A	Brighton & HA	L	0-1	0-1	—		2207
42	17	H	Exeter C	D	1-1	0-0	19	Rees (og) [63]	2419
43	20	H	Rotherham U	L	2-3	1-1	20	Steele [13], Jagielka [79]	1620
44	24	A	Leyton Orient	L	1-6	0-4	20	Seabury [81]	4957
45	May 1	H	Mansfield T	W	1-0	0-0	18	Kerrigan [64]	2553
46	8	A	Torquay U	W	3-0	3-0	15	Kerrigan 2 [6, 25], Steele [43]	2800

Final League Position: 15

GOALSCORERS
League (52): Steele 13, Kerrigan 10, Berkley 8, Evans 6 (2 pens), Seabury 5, Brown 2, Preece 2, Gayle 1, Jagielka 1, Jobling 1, own goals 3.
Worthington Cup (4): Evans 3 (2 pens), Jobling 1.
FA Cup (0).

Edwards P 43	Jobling K 41	Hanmer G 46	Wilding P 42	Seabury K 44	Gayle B 43	Craven D 6 + 4	Kerrigan S 32 + 5	Steele L 33 + 5	Evans P 32	Preece R 16 + 4	White D 7 + 4	Jagielka S 13 + 18	Brown M 15 + 19	Berkley A 41	Herbert C 6 + 2	Hayfield M + 1	Rutherford M — + 3	Winstanley M 8	Tretton A 22 + 1	Whelan S 8 + 1	Beavers P 2	Cooksey S 2	Drysdale L 2	Thompson G 1	Jones M — + 1	Match No.
1	2	3	4	5	6	7	8^1	9	10	11^2	12	13														1
1	2	3		5	6	12	8	9	10	11		13	4^2	7^1												2
1	11	3	4	2	6	7^2	8	9	10			12	13		5^1											3
1	11	3	4	2	6	12		9^1	10	5^1		8	13	7												4
1	11	3	5	2	6	12	8^2	9^1	10			13	4	7												5
1	4	3	5	2	6			9	10	11^1	12	8		7												6
1	4	3	5^2	2	6			9^1	10	11^3	12	8		7		13	14									7
1	4	3		5	6	12		9^1	10	11^2		8		7	2		13									8
1	11	3	4	2	6		8	9^1	10					7			12	5								9
1	11	3	4	2	6	12		9^1	10			8^1	13	7				5								10
1	11	3	4	2	6		8	9	10					7				5								11
1	11	3	4	2^1	6		8	9	10			12		7				5								12
1	11	3	4	2	6		8^1	9	10			12		7				5								13
1	11	3	4	2	6		8^2	9^1	10			12	13	7				5								14
1	11	3	4	2	6		8	9	10					7				5								15
1	11	3	4^2	2	6		8^1	9	10			12	13	7				5								16
1		3	4	2	5	12		9	10	11^2		8^1	13	7					6							17
1	11^2	3	4	2	5		8	9^1	10		12		13	7					6							18
1	11	3	4	2	5		8	9^1	10		12^2		13	7					6							19
1	11	3		2	5		8	9^1	10		12		13	7					6^2	4						20
1	11	3	5	2	6			9^1	10		12			7					4	8						21
1^2	11	3	4		6		8^1	9	10		12		2	7					13	5						22
	11^1	3	4	2		12	8		10			9^2	13	7					6	5	1					23
		3	4	2	6		8	9	10	11				7						5	1					24
1		3	4	2	6		8		10	11		9		7						5						25
1		3	4	2	6		8^1		10	11	12	9	13	7^2						5						26
1		3	4	2	5^2		8^1	9	10	11	12		13	7					6							27
1	11	3	4	2	5			9	10		12	8^1		7					6							28
1	11	3	4	2	5			9	10			8		7					6							29
1	11	3	4	2	5	7^1		9	10		12		13		8^2				6							30
1	11	3	4	2	5	7^1	8^2	9	10		12		13						6							31
1	11	3		2	5	7^1	8	9	10		12				4				6							32
1	11	3	4	2	5		8	9	10^2		12		13	7^1					6							33
1	11^1	3	4	2	5^3		8^2	9	10		12		13	7					6	14						34
1	11	3	4	2			8	9^1	10		12		13	7					6	5^2						35
1	11	3	4	2			8^1	9	10		12			7	5				6							36
1	11	3	4	2	5^1		8	9	10		12			7					6							37
1	11^1	3	4	2	5		8	9	10		12			7					6							38
1	11	3	4	2	5		8	9	10					7					6							39
1	11	3	4	2	5		8	9^1	10	12				7					6							40
1	11	3	4	2	5	12	8^2	9	10				13	7^1					6							41
1	11	3	4	2	5		8^1	9	10		12			7					6							42
1	11	3	4		5^1		8	9	10		12			7					6				2			43
1	11	3	4	8	5^1	12		9^2	10				13	7	14				6				2^3			44
1	11	3	4	2	5		8	9	10					7					6							45
	11	3	4	2	5		8	9^1	10		12			7^2					6					1	13	46

Worthington Cup
First Round   Bristol C   (a)   0-4
                                             (h)   4-3

FA Cup
First Round   Rushden & D   (a)   0-1

FA Premiership

SOUTHAMPTON

The Dell, Milton Road, Southampton SO15 2XH.

Telephone: (01703) 220505.

Fax: (01703) 330360.

Website: www.soton.ac.uk/saints.

Email: sfc@tcp.co.uk.

Recorded Ticket Information: (01703) 228575.

Clubcall: 0891 121178.

Ground Capacity: 15,000.

Record Attendance: 31,044 v Manchester U, Division 1, 8 October 1969.

Record Receipts: £215,450 v Portsmouth, FA Cup 3rd rd, 7 January 1996.

Pitch Measurements: 110yd × 72yd.

Chairman: R. J. G. Lowe.

Vice-Chairman: B. H. D. Hunt.

Directors: I. L. Gordon, K. St. J. Wiseman, M. R. Richards FCA, A. Cowen.

President: E. T. Bates.

Manager: Dave Jones.

Joint Assistant Managers: John Sainty, John Mortimore, Terry Cooper.

Physios: Don Taylor, Jim Joyce.

Secretary: Brian Truscott.

LATEST SEQUENCES

Longest Sequence of League Wins: 6, 3.3.92 – 4.4.92.

Longest Sequence of League Defeats: 5, 16.8.98 – 12.9.98.

Longest Sequence of League Draws: 7, 28.12.94 – 11.2.95.

Longest Sequence of Unbeaten League Matches: 19, 5.9.21 – 31.12.21.

Longest Sequence Without a League Win: 20, 30.8.69 – 27.12.69.

HONOURS

Football League: Division 1 – Runners-up 1983–84; Division 2 – Runners-up 1965–66, 1977–78; Division 3 (S) – Champions 1921–22; Runners-up 1920–21; Division 3 – Champions 1959–60.

FA Cup: Winners 1976; Runners-up 1900, 1902.

Football League Cup: Runners-up 1979.

Zenith Data Systems Cup: Runners-up 1992.

European Competitions: European Fairs Cup: 1969–70. *UEFA Cup:* 1971–72, 1981–82, 1982–83, 1984–85. *European Cup-Winners' Cup:* 1976–77.

Colours
Red and white striped shirts, black shorts, black stockings with red trim.

Change Colours
Dark navy shirts, dark navy shorts, yellow stockings.

Year Formed: 1885.

Turned Professional: 1894.

Ltd Co.: 1897.

Previous Name: 1885, Southampton St Mary's; 1897, Southampton.

Club Nickname: 'The Saints'.

Previous Grounds: 1885, Antelope Ground; 1897, County Cricket Ground; 1898, The Dell.

First Football League Game: 28 August 1920, Division 3, v Gillingham (a) D 1–1 – Allen; Parker, Titmuss; Shelley, Campbell, Turner; Barratt, Dominy (1), Rawlings, Moore, Foxall.

Record League Victory: 9–3 v Wolverhampton W, Division 2, 18 September 1965 – Godfrey; Jones, Williams; Walker, Knapp, Huxford; Paine (2), O'Brien (1), Melia, Chivers (4), Sydenham (2).

Record Cup Victory: 7–1 v Ipswich T, FA Cup 3rd rd, 7 January 1961 – Reynolds; Davies, Traynor; Conner, Page, Huxford; Paine (1), O'Brien (3 incl. 1p), Reeves, Mulgrew (2), Penk (1).

Record Defeat: 0–8 v Tottenham H, Division 2, 28 March 1936. 0–8 v Everton, Division 1, 20 November 1971.

Most League Points (2 for a win): 61, Division 3 (S), 1921–22 and Division 3, 1959–60.

Most League Points (3 for a win): 77, Division 1, 1983–84.

Most League Goals: 112, Division 3 (S), 1957–58.

Highest League Scorer in Season: Derek Reeves, 39, Division 3, 1959–60.

Most League Goals in Total Aggregate: Mike Channon, 185, 1966–77, 1979–82.

Most League Goals in One Match: 5, Charlie Wayman v Leicester C, Division 2, 23 October 1948.

Most Capped Player: Peter Shilton, 49 (125), England.

Most League Appearances: Terry Paine, 713, 1956–74.

Youngest League Player: Danny Wallace, 16 years 313 days v Manchester U, 29 November 1980.

Record Transfer Fee Received: £7,250,000 from Blackburn R, for Kevin Davies, June 1998.

Record Transfer Fee Paid: £2,000,000 to Sheffield Wednesday for David Hirst, October 1997.

Football League Record: 1920 Original Member of Division 3; 1921–22 Division 3 (S); 1922–53 Division 2; 1953–58 Division 3 (S); 1958–60 Division 3; 1960–66 Division 2; 1966–74 Division 1; 1974–78 Division 2; 1978–92 Division 1; 1992– FA Premier League.

MANAGERS

Cecil Knight 1894–95
  (Secretary-Manager)
Charles Robson 1895–97
E. Arnfield 1897–1911
  (Secretary-Manager)
  (continued as Secretary)
George Swift 1911–12
Ernest Arnfield 1912–19
Jimmy McIntyre 1919–24
Arthur Chadwick 1925–31
George Kay 1931–36
George Gross 1936–37
Tom Parker 1937–43
J. R. Sarjantson stepped down
  from the board to act as
  Secretary-Manager 1943–47
  with the next two listed being
  team Managers during this
  period
Arthur Dominy 1943–46
Bill Dodgin Snr 1946–49
Sid Cann 1949–51
George Roughton 1952–55
Ted Bates 1955–73
Lawrie McMenemy 1973–85
Chris Nicholl 1985–91
Ian Branfoot 1991–94
Alan Ball 1994–95
Dave Merrington 1995–96
Graeme Souness 1996–97
Dave Jones June 1997–

TEN YEAR LEAGUE RECORD

		P	W	D	L	F	A	Pts	Pos
1988-89	Div 1	38	10	15	13	52	66	45	13
1989-90	Div 1	38	15	10	13	71	63	55	7
1990-91	Div 1	38	12	9	17	58	69	45	14
1991-92	Div 1	42	14	10	18	39	55	52	16
1992-93	PR Lge	42	13	11	18	54	61	50	18
1993-94	PR Lge	42	12	7	23	49	66	43	18
1994-95	PR Lge	42	12	18	12	61	63	54	10
1995-96	PR Lge	38	9	11	18	34	52	38	17
1996-97	PR Lge	38	10	11	17	50	56	41	16
1997-98	PR Lge	38	14	6	18	50	55	48	12

DID YOU KNOW ?

When Southampton beat Rotherham United 6–1 on 21 November 1964, Martin Chivers and George O'Brien scored hat-tricks. It was the first such 'double' since Vic Watson and Arthur Holt in 1936 against Nottingham Forest.

SOUTHAMPTON 1998–99 LEAGUE RECORD

Match No.	Date	Venue	Opponents	Result		H/T Score	Lg. Pos.	Goalscorers	Attendance
1	Aug 16	H	Liverpool	L	1-2	1-1	—	Ostenstad [36]	15,202
2	22	A	Charlton Ath	L	0-5	0-1	20		16,488
3	29	H	Nottingham F	L	1-2	0-0	20	Le Tissier (pen) [89]	14,942
4	Sept 8	A	Leeds U	L	0-3	0-1	—		30,637
5	12	A	Newcastle U	L	0-4	0-2	20		36,454
6	19	H	Tottenham H	D	1-1	0-1	20	Le Tissier [64]	15,204
7	28	A	West Ham U	L	0-1	0-0	—		23,153
8	Oct 3	H	Manchester U	L	0-3	0-1	20		15,251
9	17	A	Arsenal	D	1-1	0-1	20	Howells [67]	38,027
10	24	H	Coventry C	W	2-1	2-0	20	Le Tissier [23], Ostenstad [44]	15,152
11	31	A	Sheffield W	D	0-0	0-0	20		30,078
12	Nov 7	H	Middlesbrough	D	3-3	0-0	20	Monkou [61], Beattie [82], Ostenstad [85]	15,202
13	14	H	Aston Villa	L	1-4	0-1	20	Le Tissier [53]	15,242
14	21	A	Blackburn R	W	2-0	1-0	19	Oakley [4], Basham [89]	22,812
15	28	H	Derby Co	L	0-1	0-1	19		14,762
16	Dec 5	A	Leicester C	L	0-2	0-0	20		18,423
17	12	A	Everton	L	0-1	0-1	20		32,073
18	19	H	Wimbledon	W	3-1	1-0	19	Ostenstad 2 [11, 68], Kachloul [64]	14,354
19	26	H	Chelsea	L	0-2	0-1	19		15,253
20	28	A	Nottingham F	D	1-1	0-0	19	Kachloul [48]	23,456
21	Jan 9	A	Charlton Ath	W	3-1	1-1	18	Kachloul [8], Colleter [52], Beattie [89]	15,222
22	16	A	Liverpool	L	1-7	0-3	19	Ostenstad [59]	44,011
23	30	H	Leeds U	W	3-0	1-0	18	Kachloul [31], Oakley [62], Ostenstad [86]	15,236
24	Feb 6	A	Chelsea	L	0-1	0-1	18		34,920
25	20	A	Newcastle U	W	2-1	2-0	19	Beattie [16], Dodd (pen) [43]	15,244
26	27	H	Manchester U	L	1-2	0-0	19	Le Tissier [90]	55,316
27	Mar 2	A	Tottenham H	L	0-3	0-1	—		28,580
28	6	H	West Ham U	W	1-0	1-0	19	Kachloul [10]	15,240
29	14	A	Middlesbrough	L	0-3	0-2	19		33,387
30	20	H	Sheffield W	W	1-0	1-0	18	Le Tissier [41]	15,201
31	Apr 3	H	Arsenal	D	0-0	0-0	18		15,255
32	5	A	Coventry C	L	0-1	0-0	19		21,404
33	10	A	Aston Villa	L	0-3	0-1	19		32,203
34	17	H	Blackburn R	D	3-3	1-2	19	Marsden [22], Hughes M [61], Pakhar [85]	15,209
35	24	A	Derby Co	D	0-0	0-0	19		26,557
36	May 1	H	Leicester C	W	2-1	1-1	17	Marsden [36], Beattie [74]	15,228
37	8	A	Wimbledon	W	2-0	0-0	17	Beattie [72], Le Tissier [84]	24,068
38	16	H	Everton	W	2-0	1-0	17	Pakhar 2 [24, 68]	15,254

Final League Position: 17

GOALSCORERS

League (37): Le Tissier 7 (1 pen), Ostenstad 7, Beattie 5, Kachloul 5, Pakhar (Pahars) 3, Marsden 2, Oakley 2, Basham 1, Colleter 1, Dodd 1 (pen), Howells 1, Hughes M 1, Monkou 1.
Worthington Cup (1): Beattie 1.
FA Cup (1): Ostenstad 1.

Jones P 31	Dodd J 27+1	Hiley S 27+2	Palmer C 18+1	Lundekvam C 30+3	Dryden R 4	Ripley S 16+6	Oakley M 21+1	Ostenstad E 27+7	Hughes M 32	Beresford J 1+3	Beattie J 22+13	Le Tissier M 20+10	Bridge W 15+8	Howells D 8+1	Monkou K 22	Moss N 7	Warner P 5	Marshall S 2	Gibbens K 2+2	Benali F 19+4	Williams A —+1	Basham S —+4	Kachloul H 18+4	Monk G 4	Bradley S —+3	Colleter P 16	Marsden C 14	Hughes D 6+3	Hirst D —+2	Pakhar (Pahars) M 4+2	Match No.
1	2	3	4	5	6	7[1]	8	9[2]	10	11[3]	12	13	14																		1
1	2	3	4	5	6	7	8[3]	9[1]	10		12	13	11[2]	14																	2
1	2	3[1]	4		6	11[2]		9	10		12	7	13	8	5																3
	2	3	4	5	6	7	8[3]	9[1]	10	11[2]	12	13	14			1															4
1	5	2	4	12		7	13	10[2]	9[1]		14	11[3]		8	6					3											5
1	2[1]	5	4	12		7		9	10	11		13		8[2]	6					3											6
1	2		4	5		7		9	10	11	12			8[1]	6					3											7
1	2		4	5[2]		7[1]	8	9	10	11	12	13			6					3											8
1	2[1]	12	4	5		7	8[2]	9	10	11		13			6					3											9
1	2	12	4[1]	5		7	8[2]	9[3]	10	11		13	14		6					3											10
1	2		4	5		7	8	9	10	11					6					3											11
1	2		4	5		7	8	9	10	11	12				6					3[1]											12
1	11	2	4	5[1]		7	8	9	10[2]		12				6					3			13								13
1	5	2	4		6	7	8[1]	9[3]	10	11[2]					3								14	13							14
1	5	2	4			7[1]	8		10	9		12			3								13	11[2]	6						15
1	6	2	4	5		7[1]	8	9	10[2]		12	11			3								13								16
1	2	3		5		12	4	9	10	11[2]		8											7[1]	6	13						17
1		2	4	5			9	10	11	8[1]	3											12	7	6							18
1	12	2	4	5		13[3]	8[1]	9	10	11[2]					6								14	7		3					19
1	4	2	8	5		11		9	10						6								7			3					20
1	2		4	5		11		9	10	8					6								7			3					21
1	2			5		12		9	10	8	13	11[2]	4[1]										7	6		3					22
1	4	2		5		12[2]	6	9	10	11		8[1]	13										7			3					23
1	4	2[1]		5			8	9	10[2]	11		12											7	13	3	3	6				24
1	2			5		7[1]	8	9	10[2]		12	6	11[3]										13	13	3	4	14				25
1	2			5		8		9[1]	11	12	7	6[2]			13											3	4	10			26
1	2			5		8	12	10	9[1]	13	7[3]									6			14			3	4	11[2]			27
1	2			5		12	8	10	9	11[1]										6			7			3	4				28
1	2			5		12	8[1]	13	10	9[2]	11									6			7			3	4				29
1	2			5		8[1]	9	10	12	11					6					13			7			3[4]	4				30
	4	2		5		7[2]		9	10	12	11				6	1				13						3		8			31
	2	7		5				10	9[3]	12	11[1]				6	1				13						3	4	8[2]		14	32
	11	2		5		12		9	10[2]	7					6	1				13			3[2]			3	4	8	14		33
	8	2[1]		5				9	10	12	7				1					6			11			3[2]	4	13	14		34
	5	2		8[2]			12	10	13	11					6	1				3			7[1]			4		14	9[3]		35
	5	2[1]		12			13	10		8	7[3]				6	1				3			11			4	14		9[2]		36
1	2	12		5				10	13	11	14				6					3			7[1]			4[2]	8[3]	9			37
1	2			5			12	10	13	11	8[1]				6					3			7			4	9[2]				38

Worthington Cup
Second Round Fulham (a) 1-1
(h) 0-1

FA Cup
Third Round Fulham (h) 1-1
(a) 0-1

Division 3

SOUTHEND UNITED

FOUNDATION

The leading club in Southend around the turn of the century was Southend Athletic, but they were an amateur concern. Southend United was a more ambitious professional club when they were founded in 1906, employing Bob Jack as secretary-manager and immediately joining the Second Division of the Southern League.

Roots Hall Football Ground, Victoria Avenue, Southend-on-Sea SS2 6NQ.
Telephone: (01702) 304050.
Fax: (01702) 330164.
Commercial: (01702) 304050.
Soccerline: 0839 664444.
Ticket Office: (01702) 304090.
Infoline: 0839 664443.
Ground Capacity: 12,306.
Record Attendance: 31,090 v Liverpool, FA Cup 3rd rd, 10 January 1979.
Record Receipts: £83,999 v West Ham U, Division 1, 7 April 1993.
Pitch Measurements: 110yd × 74yd.
President: N. J. Woodcock.
Chairman and Chief Executive: J. J. W. R. Main.
Deputy-Chairman: G. King.
Secretary: Miss H. Giles.
Directors: J. A. Bridge, B. R. Gunner, W. R. Kelleway, D. M. Markscheffel, R. J. Osborne, J. W. Adams, P. Robinson, D. A. J. Wilshire.
Manager: Alan Little.
Assistant Manager: Mick Gooding.
Physio: John Gowens.
Commercial Manager: David Comley.
Safety Officer: George Wright.
Club Nickname: 'The Blues' or 'The Shrimpers'.

LATEST SEQUENCES

Longest Sequence of League Wins: 7, 27.4.90 – 18.9.90.
Longest Sequence of League Defeats: 6, 29.8.87 – 19.9.87.
Longest Sequence of League Draws: 6, 30.1.82 – 19.2.82.
Longest Sequence of Unbeaten League Matches: 16, 20.2.32 – 29.8.32.
Longest Sequence Without a League Win: 17, 31.12.83 – 14.4.84.

HONOURS

Football League: Division 1 best season: 13th, 1994–95. Division 3 – Runners-up 1990–91; Division 4 – Champions 1980–81; Runners-up 1971–72, 1977–78.
FA Cup: best season: old 3rd rd, 1921; 5th rd, 1926, 1952, 1976, 1993.
Football League Cup: never past 3rd rd.

Colours
Royal blue/white.

Change Colours
All yellow.

Year Formed: 1906.

Turned Professional: 1906.

Ltd Co.: 1919.

Previous Grounds: 1906, Roots Hall, Prittlewell; 1920, Kursaal; 1934, Southend Stadium; 1955, Roots Hall Football Ground.

First Football League Game: 28 August 1920, Division 3, v Brighton & HA (a) W 2–0 – Capper; Reid, Newton; Wileman, Henderson, Martin; Nicholls, Nuttall, Fairclough (2), Myers, Dorsett.

Record League Victory: 9–2 v Newport Co, Division 3 (S), 5 September 1936 – McKenzie; Nelson, Everest (1); Deacon, Turner, Carr; Bolan, Lane (1), Goddard (4), Dickinson (2), Oswald (1).

Record Cup Victory: 10–1 v Golders Green, FA Cup 1st rd, 24 November 1934 – Moore; Morfitt, Kelly; Mackay, Joe Wilson, Carr (1); Lane (1), Johnson (5), Cheesmuir (2), Deacon (1), Oswald. 10–1 v Brentwood, FA Cup 2nd rd, 7 December 1968 – Roberts; Bentley, Birks; McMillan (1) Beesley, Kurila; Clayton, Chisnall, Moore (4), Best (5), Hamilton. 10–1 v Aldershot, Leyland Daf Cup Prel rd, 6 November 1990 – Sansome; Austin, Powell, Cornwell, Prior (1), Tilson (3), Cawley, Butler, Ansah (1), Benjamin (1), Angell (4).

Record Defeat: 1–9 v Brighton & HA, Division 3, 27 November 1965.

Most League Points (2 for a win): 67, Division 4, 1980–81.

Most League Points (3 for a win): 85, Division 3, 1990–91.

Most League Goals: 92, Division 3 (S), 1950–51.

Highest League Scorer in Season: Jim Shankly, 31, 1928–29; Sammy McCrory, 1957–58, both in Division 3 (S).

Most League Goals in Total Aggregate: Roy Hollis, 122, 1953–60.

Most League Goals in One Match: 5, Jim Shankly v Merthyr T, Division 3S, 1 March 1930.

Most Capped Player: George Mackenzie, 9, Eire.

Most League Appearances: Sandy Anderson, 451, 1950–63.

Youngest League Player: Ray White, 16 years 101 days v Reading, 25 April 1964.

Record Transfer Fee Received: £3,570,000 from Nottingham F, for Stan Collymore, June 1993.

Record Transfer Fee Paid: £750,000 to Crystal Palace for Stan Collymore, November 1992.

Football League Record: 1920 Original Member of Division 3; 1921–58 Division 3 (S); 1958–66 Division 3; 1966–72 Division 4; 1972–76 Division 3; 1976–78 Division 4; 1978–80 Division 3; 1980–81 Division 4; 1981–84 Division 3; 1984–87 Division 4; 1987–89 Division 3; 1989–90 Division 4; 1990–91 Division 3; 1991–92 Division 2; 1992–97 Division 1; 1997–98 Division 2; 1998– Division 3.

MANAGERS

Bob Jack 1906–10
George Molyneux 1910–11
O. M. Howard 1911–12
Joe Bradshaw 1912–19
Ned Liddell 1919–20
Tom Mather 1920–21
Ted Birnie 1921–34
David Jack 1934–40
Harry Warren 1946–56
Eddie Perry 1956–60
Frank Broome 1960
Ted Fenton 1961–65
Alvan Williams 1965–67
Ernie Shepherd 1967–69
Geoff Hudson 1969–70
Arthur Rowley 1970–76
Dave Smith 1976–83
Peter Morris 1983–84
Bobby Moore 1984–86
Dave Webb 1986–87
Dick Bate 1987
Paul Clark 1987–88
Dave Webb *(General Manager)* 1988–92
Colin Murphy 1992–93
Barry Fry 1993
Peter Taylor 1993–95
Steve Thompson 1995
Ronnie Whelan 1995–97
Alvin Martin 1997–99
Alan Little March 1999–

TEN YEAR LEAGUE RECORD

		P	W	D	L	F	A	Pts	Pos
1988-89	Div 3	46	13	15	18	56	75	54	21
1989-90	Div 4	46	22	9	15	61	48	75	3
1990-91	Div 3	46	26	7	13	67	51	85	2
1991-92	Div 2	46	17	11	18	63	63	62	12
1992-93	Div 1	46	13	13	20	54	64	52	18
1993-94	Div 1	46	17	8	21	63	67	59	15
1994-95	Div 1	46	18	8	20	54	73	62	13
1995-96	Div 1	46	15	14	17	52	61	59	14
1996-97	Div 1	46	8	15	23	42	86	39	24
1997-98	Div 2	46	11	10	25	47	79	43	24

DID YOU KNOW ?

Billy Hick scored in seven successive League matches for Southend United from 15 October 1927 to 3 December in Division Three (South). His total of League goals from 1925 to 1928 was 69 in 106 games.

SOUTHEND UNITED 1998–99 LEAGUE RECORD

Match No.	Date	Venue	Opponents	Result	H/T Score	Lg. Pos.	Goalscorers	Attendance
1	Aug 8	A	Scarborough	W 2-1	0-1	—	Coleman [60], Hails [77]	2298
2	15	H	Shrewsbury T	W 2-1	1-1	2	Clarke [7], Burns [90]	3734
3	22	A	Peterborough U	D 1-1	0-0	3	Coleman [50]	5323
4	29	H	Chester C	L 0-1	0-0	7		4241
5	Sept 1	A	Carlisle U	L 0-3	0-0	—		2638
6	5	H	Rotherham U	W 3-0	1-0	9	Newman [22], Fitzpatrick 2 [80, 83]	3479
7	8	H	Halifax T	D 0-0	0-0	—		3620
8	12	A	Brighton & HA	W 2-0	1-0	8	Conlon [43], Whyte [46]	3840
9	19	H	Cambridge U	L 0-1	0-0	10		5009
10	26	A	Swansea C	L 1-3	1-1	12	Newman [42]	3890
11	Oct 3	H	Rochdale	D 1-1	0-1	14	Maher [73]	3686
12	10	A	Scunthorpe U	D 1-1	0-1	13	Burns [82]	3747
13	17	H	Leyton Orient	D 2-2	0-1	13	Clarke [49], Fitzpatrick [74]	6700
14	20	H	Mansfield T	L 1-2	1-1	—	Whyte [9]	3250
15	24	A	Hull C	D 1-1	0-0	16	Conlon [59]	3551
16	31	H	Darlington	W 2-1	1-1	11	Maher [13], Newman [65]	3527
17	Nov 7	A	Exeter C	L 1-2	1-0	16	Burns [27]	3085
18	10	A	Brentford	L 1-4	0-2	—	Burns [65]	4285
19	21	H	Plymouth Arg	W 1-0	0-0	14	Newman [88]	3814
20	28	A	Cardiff C	L 0-2	0-2	16		4638
21	Dec 12	H	Barnet	L 2-3	1-2	18	Coleman [20], Burns [90]	4311
22	19	A	Hartlepool U	W 4-2	3-1	16	Houghton [16], Newman [27], Fitzpatrick [34], Conlon [80]	1889
23	26	H	Peterborough U	W 2-0	1-0	15	Fitzpatrick [4], Newman [70]	6159
24	28	A	Torquay U	L 0-2	0-1	16		3228
25	Jan 2	A	Chester C	D 1-1	0-0	16	Newman [90]	2574
26	9	H	Scarborough	W 1-0	0-0	14	Livett [81]	3453
27	16	A	Shrewsbury T	L 1-3	1-1	15	Maher [40]	2132
28	23	H	Carlisle U	L 0-1	0-1	17		4120
29	30	A	Torquay U	D 0-0	0-0	16		3567
30	Feb 6	A	Rotherham U	D 2-2	0-2	15	Rapley 2 [58, 82]	3895
31	13	A	Halifax T	L 1-3	0-0	19	Rapley [55]	2302
32	20	H	Brighton & HA	W 3-0	2-0	18	Hunter 2 [18, 24], Rapley [66]	6066
33	27	A	Cambridge U	L 0-3	0-1	18		5013
34	Mar 6	H	Swansea C	W 2-0	1-0	18	Roach [16], Conlon [86]	3713
35	13	H	Exeter C	D 0-0	0-0	18		3695
36	20	A	Darlington	L 1-2	0-1	19	Conlon [75]	2516
37	26	H	Hull C	L 0-1	0-0	—		4149
38	30	A	Rochdale	L 0-1	0-1	—		1344
39	Apr 3	A	Leyton Orient	W 3-0	2-0	19	Campbell 2 [3, 40], Coleman [69]	6537
40	5	H	Scunthorpe U	L 0-1	0-1	19		4814
41	10	A	Mansfield T	D 0-0	0-0	21		2624
42	13	H	Cardiff C	L 0-1	0-0	—		4076
43	17	A	Plymouth Arg	W 3-0	2-0	18	Conlon 2 [12, 90], Houghton [42]	3949
44	24	H	Brentford	L 1-4	0-1	19	Clarke [85]	5248
45	May 1	A	Barnet	W 2-0	0-0	17	Houghton [50], Hodges [66]	2704
46	8	H	Hartlepool U	D 1-1	1-0	18	Maher [29]	4865

Final League Position: 18

GOALSCORERS

League (52): Conlon 7, Newman 7, Burns 5, Fitzpatrick 5, Coleman 4, Maher 4, Rapley 4, Clarke 3, Houghton 3, Campbell 2, Hunter 2, Whyte 2, Hails 1, Hodges 1, Livett 1, Roach 1.
Worthington Cup (2): Clarke 1, Newman 1.
FA Cup (0).

Margetson M 32	Hails J 11	Stimson M 17	Coleman S 41 + 1	Newman R 36	Roget L 11 + 3	Maher K 34	Beard M 36 + 1	Burns A 26 + 5	Whyte D 14 + 4	Clarke A 14 + 10	Dublin K 6 + 3	Livett S 19 + 4	De Souza M 2	Fitzpatrick T 7 + 16	Jones N 5 + 12	Morley D 26 + 1	Gooding M 19 + 4	Conlon B 28 + 6	Capleton M 14	Rapley K 9	Houghton S 26 + 1	Booty M 18 + 2	Iorfa D — + 2	Campbell N 9 + 3	McGavin S 4 + 7	Hunter B 5	Unger L 14	Harris A 1	Roach N 7 + 1	Hodges L 10	Patterson M 5	Coyne C — + 1	Match No.
1	2	3	4	5	6^1	7	8^2	9	10	11	12	13																					1
1	2	3	6	5		7		9	10^1	11				4^2	8	13	12																2
1	2	3	6^1	5	4	7	8	9	10^3	11^2	12					14	13																3
1	2	3^2		5	6	7	8^3	9	12	11^1					10	13	4	14															4
1	2	3		5		7	8^3	9^1	10	11^2	6					13	12	4	14														5
1	2	3		5		7		9^2	10	11	6					13	12	4	8^1														6
1	2	3^1		5		7			11	10		6				12		4	8	9													7
1	2	3	6	5		7			11	10						12		4	8	9^1													8
1	2	3^3	6	5		7			11	10^2	12					13	14	4	8	9													9
1	2	3	6	5		7				10^1		11				12		4	8	9													10
1	2	3	6	5		7				10^1		11				12		4	8	9													11
1		3^1	6	5		7		2	10	12				8^1		11	13	4		9													12
			6	5		7		2	10	11	12			8	13	3^1		4		9^2													13
1		3^1	6	5			8	2^1	10	11				12		13	7	4	9														14
1		3	6	5		7		2	10			11			4			8	9		1												15
1		3	6	5		7		2		10^1				11^2	4	12	13	8	9														16
1		3	6	5		7		2	10^1	12	13				4		11^2	8	9														17
1		3	6	5		7		2	10	12	13				4		11^2	8	9														18
1			6	5		7		2^2	9^1					8		12	3	4	13	9	10	11											19
1			6	5		7		12	9^2					8		3	4	2^1	13		10	11											20
1			6	5		7		2	10					8^1		12	13	4	3		9^2	11											21
1			6	5^2	13	7		2	3^1					8		10		4		9		11											22
1			6	5	4^2	7		2	12	3				8		10	13	9				11^1											23
1			6	5		7		2^2	12	3				8^1		10	13	4		9		11											24
1			6	5		7	4	10	12	3				8^1	2^1	13		9				11											25
1			6	5	4^1	7^2		2	10					12	13			8		9		11	3										26
1			6	5		7		2		4^1						8		9			10	11	3	12									27
1			6	5		7		2						8^1		4		9			10	11	3	12	9								28
1			6	5	12	7		2				13		8^1		4					10	11	3	9^2									29
1			6	5		7		2						4^2		8	12				10	11^1	3	9	13								30
1			6					2	12							4^1	13				10	11	3	9^2	7	5	8						31
1			6	5		7			12							9		10	11^1	3				4	8	2							32
1			6^1	5		7		2	12					13				9		11	3			4	8	10^2							33
			6	5		7		2								9			1	11	3			4	8	10							34
			6	5		7		2	12							9^2		1		11	3	13		4	8	10^1							35
			6	5	4	7^1		2								9		1		11	3	12	13		8	10^1							36
12			5	6	7^1			2^2						13		9		1		3	14	4		8	10^3	11							37
			6	5				2	12							9^1	1	13		3	10^1	14	8			7^3	11						38
			6	5				2						12		10	4	13	1	3^3	14	9^2			8	7	11^1						39
			6	5				2								10^1	4	12	1	3	13	9			8^2	7	11						40
			6					2						12		10^1	4	13	1	3	5	9^2	14		8	7^3	11						41
			6					2								10	4		1	3	5	9^2	12		8	7	11						42
			6					2					11			4			1	3	5	9			8	7							43
			6	5^3				2				12	11			4			1	3			9^2		8^1		13	7	14				44
			6			8	2	9					11			4			1	3	5		12				10^1	7					45
			6		13	8^1	2	9^3				12	11			4			1	3	5		14				10^2	7					46

Worthington Cup

First Round	Gillingham	(h)	1-0
		(a)	1-0
Second Round	Coventry C	(a)	0-1
		(h)	0-4

FA Cup

First Round	Doncaster R	(h)	0-1

Division 1   **STOCKPORT COUNTY**

FOUNDATION

Formed at a meeting held at Wellington Road South by members of Wycliffe Congregational Chapel in 1883, they called themselves Heaton Norris Rovers until changing to Stockport County in 1890, a year before joining the Football Combination.

Edgeley Park, Hardcastle Road, Stockport, Cheshire SK3 9DD.
Telephone: (0161) 286 8888.
Fax: (0161) 286 8900.
Club Shop: (0161) 286 8899.
Clubcall: 0891 121638.
Ground Capacity: 11,540.
Record Attendance: 27,833 v Liverpool, FA Cup 5th rd, 11 February 1950.
Record Receipts: £181,449 v Middlesbrough, Coca-Cola Cup Semi-final 1st leg, 26 February 1997.
Pitch Measurements: 111yd × 72yd.
Hon. Vice-Presidents: Freddie Pye, Andrew Barlow.
Chairman: Brendan Elwood.
Vice-Chairman: Grahame White.
Directors: Mike Baker, Michael Rains, Brian Taylor, David Jolley.
Secretary: Gary Glendenning BA (HONS), FCCA.
Manager: Andy Kilner.
Assistant Manager: Mike Phelan.
Physio: Rodger Wylde.
Assistant Secretary: Andrea Dawson.
Commercial Manager: John Rutter.
Marketing Manager/Programme Editor: Steve Bellis.
Year Formed: 1883.
Turned Professional: 1891.
Ltd Co.: 1908.
Previous Names: 1883, Heaton Norris Rovers; 1888, Heaton Norris; 1890, Stockport County.
Club Nicknames: 'County' or 'Hatters'.

LATEST SEQUENCES
Longest Sequence of League Wins: 8, 26.12.27 – 28.1.28.
Longest Sequence of League Defeats: 9, 19.12.08 – 13.2.09.
Longest Sequence of League Draws: 7, 17.3.89 – 14.4.89.
Longest Sequence of Unbeaten League Matches: 18, 28.1.33 – 28.8.33.
Longest Sequence Without a League Win: 15, 17.3.89 – 1.9.89.

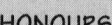

HONOURS

Football League: Division 1 best season: 8th, 1997–98; Division 2 – Runners-up 1996–97; Division 3 (N) – Champions 1921–22, 1936–37; Runners-up 1928–29, 1929-30; Division 4 – Champions 1966–67; Runners-up 1990–91.

FA Cup: best season: 5th rd, 1935, 1950.

Football League Cup: Semi-final 1997.

Autoglass Trophy: Runners-up 1992, 1993.

Colours
Blue shirts with vertical white chest band, blue shorts, blue stockings.

Change Colours
Black shirts with vertical tangerine chest band and sleeves, black shorts, tangerine and black stockings.

Previous Grounds: 1883 Heaton Norris Recreation Ground; 1884 Heaton Norris Wanderers Cricket Ground; 1885 Chorlton's Farm, Chorlton's Lane; 1886 Heaton Norris Cricket Ground; 1887 Wilkes' Field, Belmont Street; 1889 Nursery Inn, Green Lane; 1902 Edgeley Park.

First Football League Game: 1 September 1900, Division 2, v Leicester Fosse (a) D 2–2 – Moores; Earp, Wainwright; Pickford, Limond, Harvey; Stansfield, Smith (1), Patterson, Foster, Betteley (1).

Record League Victory: 13–0 v Halifax T, Division 3 (N), 6 January 1934 – McGann; Vincent (1p), Jenkinson; Robinson, Stevens, Len Jones; Foulkes (1), Hill (3), Lythgoe (2), Stevenson (2), Downes (4).

Record Cup Victory: 5–0 v Lincoln C, FA Cup 1st rd, 11 November 1995 – Edwards; Connelly, Todd, Bennett, Flynn, Gannon (Dinning), Beaumont, Oliver, Ware, Eckhardt (3), Armstrong (1) (Mike), Chalk, (1 og).

Record Defeat: 1–8 v Chesterfield, Division 2, 19 April 1902.

Most League Points (2 for a win): 64, Division 4, 1966–67.

Most League Points (3 for a win): 85, Division 2, 1993–94.

Most League Goals: 115, Division 3 (N), 1933–34.

Highest League Scorer in Season: Alf Lythgoe, 46, Division 3 (N), 1933–34.

Most League Goals in Total Aggregate: Jack Connor, 132, 1951–56.

Most League Goals in One Match: 5, Joe Smith v Southport, Division 3N, 7 January 1928; 5, Joe Smith v Lincoln C, Division 3N, 15 September 1928; 5, Frank Newton v Nelson, Division 3N, 21 September 1929; 5, Alf Lythgoe v Southport, Division 3N, 25 August 1934; 5, Billy McNaughton v Mansfield T, Division 3N, 14 December 1935; 5, Jack Connor v Workington, Division 3N, 8 November 1952; 5, Jack Connor v Carlisle U, Division 3N, 7 April 1956.

Most Capped Player: Martin Nash, 8, Canada.

Most League Appearances: Andy Thorpe, 489, 1978–86, 1988–92.

Youngest League Player: David Herd, 17 years 51 days v Hartlepools U, 5 May 1951.

Record Transfer Fee Received: £1,600,000 from Middlesbrough for Alun Armstrong, February 1998.

Record Transfer Fee Paid: £800,000 to Nottingham F for Ian Moore, July 1998.

Football League Record: 1900 Elected to Division 2; 1904 Failed re-election; 1905–21 Division 2; 1921–22 Division 3 (N); 1922–26 Division 2; 1926–37 Division 3 (N); 1937–38 Division 2; 1938–58 Division 3 (N); 1958–59 Division 3; 1959–67 Division 4; 1967–70 Division 3; 1970–91 Division 4; 1991–92 Division 3; 1992–97 Division 2; 1997– Division 1.

MANAGERS

Fred Stewart 1894–1911
Harry Lewis 1911–14
David Ashworth 1914–19
Albert Williams 1919–24
Fred Scotchbrook 1924–26
Lincoln Hyde 1926–31
Andrew Wilson 1932–33
Fred Westgarth 1934–36
Bob Kelly 1936–38
George Hunt 1938–39
Bob Marshall 1939–49
Andy Beattie 1949–52
Dick Duckworth 1952–56
Billy Moir 1956–60
Reg Flewin 1960–63
Trevor Porteous 1963–65
Bert Trautmann
    (General Manager) 1965–66
Eddie Quigley *(Team
    Manager)* 1965–66
Jimmy Meadows 1966–69
Wally Galbraith 1969–70
Matt Woods 1970–71
Brian Doyle 1972–74
Jimmy Meadows 1974–75
Roy Chapman 1975–76
Eddie Quigley 1976–77
Alan Thompson 1977–78
Mike Summerbee 1978–79
Jimmy McGuigan 1979–82
Eric Webster 1982–85
Colin Murphy 1985
Les Chapman 1985–86
Jimmy Melia 1986
Colin Murphy 1986–87
Asa Hartford 1987–89
Danny Bergara 1989–95
Dave Jones 1995–97
Gary Megson 1997–99
Andy Kilner July 1999–

TEN YEAR LEAGUE RECORD

		P	W	D	L	F	A	Pts	Pos
1988-89	Div 4	46	10	21	15	54	52	51	20
1989-90	Div 4	46	21	11	14	68	62	74	4
1990-91	Div 4	46	23	13	10	84	47	82	2
1991-92	Div 3	46	22	10	14	75	51	76	5
1992-93	Div 2	46	19	15	12	81	57	72	6
1993-94	Div 2	46	24	13	9	74	44	85	4
1994-95	Div 2	46	19	8	19	63	60	65	11
1995-96	Div 2	46	19	13	14	61	47	70	9
1996-97	Div 2	46	23	13	10	59	41	82	2
1997-98	Div 1	46	19	8	19	71	69	65	8

DID YOU KNOW ?

Jack Connor and his wife were in a Bradford cinema on 19 October 1951 when a message was flashed on the screen for him to go to the foyer. There he was promptly transferred from City for £2,500.

STOCKPORT COUNTY 1998–99 LEAGUE RECORD

Match No.	Date	Venue	Opponents		Result	H/T Score	Lg. Pos.	Goalscorers	Attendance
1	Aug 8	A	Bradford C	W	2-1	1-0	—	Dinning 2 (2 pens) [39, 87]	14,360
2	15	H	Norwich C	L	0-2	0-1	12		6538
3	21	A	Barnsley	D	1-1	0-1	—	Branch [65]	16,377
4	29	H	Crystal Palace	D	1-1	0-1	11	Byrne C [65]	7739
5	31	A	Wolverhampton W	D	2-2	1-2	14	Angell 2 [44, 53]	22,217
6	Sept 5	H	Grimsby T	W	2-0	0-0	8	Angell 2 [78, 90]	6199
7	8	A	Birmingham C	L	0-2	0-1	—		16,429
8	12	H	Crewe Alex	D	1-1	0-1	12	Flynn [79]	7302
9	19	A	QPR	L	0-2	0-0	15		8205
10	26	H	WBA	D	2-2	0-2	16	McIntosh [51], Byrne C [72]	8804
11	29	H	Huddersfield T	D	1-1	1-1	—	Moore [45]	8023
12	Oct 3	A	Swindon T	W	3-2	2-1	14	McIntosh [38], Branch [43], Moore [47]	7691
13	17	A	Bury	D	1-1	0-0	17	Branch [60]	5732
14	20	A	Sheffield U	D	1-1	1-0	—	Moore [18]	12,657
15	24	H	Ipswich T	L	0-1	0-0	19		7432
16	31	A	Tranmere R	D	1-1	0-0	18	Angell [87]	6597
17	Nov 8	H	Port Vale	W	4-2	2-1	14	Angell 3 [20, 41, 87], Grant [90]	7612
18	14	H	Watford	D	1-1	1-1	14	Dinning (pen) [38]	8019
19	21	A	Bristol C	D	1-1	0-1	17	Angell [53]	11,032
20	24	H	Bolton W	L	0-1	0-0	—		8520
21	28	H	Portsmouth	W	2-0	0-0	15	Cooper [47], Dinning (pen) [48]	7504
22	Dec 5	A	Sunderland	L	0-1	0-1	16		36,040
23	12	A	Watford	L	2-4	0-2	16	Connelly [89], Angell [90]	9250
24	19	H	Oxford U	W	2-0	1-0	15	Matthews [44], Dinning (pen) [66]	6500
25	26	H	Barnsley	L	0-1	0-1	17		10,263
26	28	A	Grimsby T	L	0-1	0-0	17		8058
27	Jan 9	H	Bradford C	L	1-2	0-1	18	Angell [61]	8975
28	16	A	Crystal Palace	D	2-2	2-1	18	Angell 2 [4, 23]	15,517
29	30	A	Wolverhampton W	L	1-2	0-0	20	Angell [56]	8654
30	Feb 6	H	Norwich C	W	2-0	2-0	17	Angell [9], Wilson (og) [36]	14,675
31	13	H	Birmingham C	W	1-0	1-0	16	Angell [10]	9056
32	20	A	Crewe Alex	W	2-0	1-0	15	Woodthorpe [45], Ellis [79]	5473
33	27	H	QPR	D	0-0	0-0	16		7694
34	Mar 2	A	WBA	L	1-3	0-1	—	McIntosh [75]	11,801
35	6	A	Huddersfield T	L	0-3	0-0	16		11,914
36	9	H	Swindon T	W	2-1	2-0	—	Angell [12], Ellis (pen) [25]	6048
37	13	A	Port Vale	D	1-1	1-0	15	Smith [21]	6456
38	20	A	Tranmere R	D	0-0	0-0	15		7589
39	Apr 3	H	Bury	D	0-0	0-0	16		7483
40	5	A	Bolton W	W	2-1	1-0	16	Ellis [22], Woodthorpe [75]	18,587
41	10	H	Sheffield U	W	1-0	0-0	15	Matthews [46]	7551
42	17	H	Bristol C	D	2-2	0-0	14	Ellis 2 [58, 69]	7602
43	20	A	Ipswich T	L	0-1	0-1	—		17,056
44	24	A	Portsmouth	L	1-3	0-2	16	Ellis [89]	11,212
45	May 1	H	Sunderland	L	0-1	0-0	16		10,548
46	9	A	Oxford U	L	0-5	0-3	16		6830

Final League Position: 16

GOALSCORERS

League (49): Angell 17, Ellis 6 (1 pen), Dinning 5 (5 pens), Branch 3, McIntosh 3, Moore 3, Byrne C 2, Matthews 2, Woodthorpe 2, Connelly 1, Cooper 1, Flynn 1, Grant 1, Smith 1, own goal 1.
Worthington Cup (2): Byrne C 1, Moore 1.
FA Cup (3): Angell 1, Woodthorpe 1, own goal 1.

Nash C 43	Connelly S 33 + 2	Woodthorpe C 37	Dinning T 35 + 6	Flynn M 46	McIntosh M 41	Phillips W 7 + 2	Byrne C 11	Angell B 42	Moore I 32 + 6	Cooper K 27 + 11	Gannon J 28 + 10	Wilbraham A 8 + 18	Alsaker P 1	Cook P 23 + 1	Branch G 10 + 4	Travis S 1 + 8	Grant S 1 + 12	Matthews R 19 + 4	McInnes D 13	Hughes P 7	Byrne D 2	Smith D 17	Ellis T 16	Mannion S —+ 1	Bennett T 3 + 4	Gray I 3	Match No.
1	2	3	4	5	6^1	7	8	9	10^2	11	12	13															1
1		3	4	5		2^1	8	9	10	11	6			7^2	12	13											2
1		3	2	5			8	9	10^1	7	6	12		4	11^2	13											3
1	2	3		5	6		8	9	10^2	7	12	13		4	11^1												4
1	2	3	12	5	6		8^1	9	10	13	7^3	11^2		4	14												5
1	2	3	12	5	6		8	9	10	11^1	7^2	13		4													6
1	2	3		5	6^1		8	9	10	11	12	7		4													7
1	2	3	7	5	6		8	9	10	11^1		12		4													8
1	2	3	7	5	6	12	8^1	9	10	11^2				4				13									9
1	2	3	7	5	6		8	9	10					4	11^1	12											10
1	2	3	7	5	6	12	8^1	9	10	13				4	11^2												11
1	2	3	7^1	5	6		8		10	12		9^2		4	11			13									12
1	2	3	7	5	6		8		10	12		9^1		4	11												13
1	2	3	7	5	6		8		10^1	12	13	9^3		4	11^2			14									14
1	2		7	5	6			9	10	8	3	12		4	11^1												15
1	2	3	7	5	6		8^1	9	10	12	13			4	11^2												16
1	2^1	3	7^2	5				9	10	6		11^3		4	14	13	12	8									17
1		3	2	5	6			9		12		7^2		4	11^3	14	13	8^1	10								18
1	2	3	12	5	6			9		13		7^2		14	4^1		11	8^3	10								19
1	2	3	12	5	6			9^3		11^2	13	7		4	14			8^1	10								20
1	2	3		5	6			9^2	10	11^1		12		4	13			7	8								21
1	2	3		5	6			9	10	11		12		4				7^1	8								22
1	2			5	6			9	10	11	3	12		4				7^1	8								23
1	2	3		5	6			9^2	10	11		12					13	7^1	8			4					24
1	2	3		5	6			9	10	11^1	12	13						7^2	8			4					25
1	2	11	3^1	5	6			10		12		13					9	7^2	8			4					26
1		3		5	6			9	10	12		7^1				2^3	13	14	8					4^2	11		27
1	2	11	3	5	6			9	10	12					14		13^3	7^2	8						4^1		28
1		3		5	6			9	10	11^1		2		12	4		13	7^2	8								29
1	11			5	6			9		2	12							7^1	8	3		4	10				30
1	11	3		5	6			9		2	12							7^1	8			4	10				31
1	2	11	3	5		8		9		6	12							7^1				4	10				32
1	12	11^2	3	5	6			9		13	2							8^1		14		4	10				33
1	11		3^1	5	6			9		12	2						8^3	13	7^2			4	10		14		34
1	2	3		5	6			9	7	11^1		8										4	10		12		35
1	2	3	12	5	6			9^3	7^2	11^1		8						13				4	10		14		36
1	2	3	12	5	6^1			9	7	11^2		8^2						13				4	10		14		37
1	2	3	8	5	6			9	7^1	11^2		12										4	10		13		38
1	11^1	3		5	6			9	10	12	2						13	7^2				4			8		39
1	11	3		5	6			9^1		12	2	7										4	10		8		40
1	12	11	3	5	6			9		13	2	7						8^2				4	10^1				41
1	11	3		5	6			9		12	2	7						8^1				4	10				42
1	11	3		5	6			9		12	2	7^1						13				4	10		8^2		43
2	11	3		5				9^1	8	7		6						12				4	10			1	44
8	11	3^1		5	6			9		12	2	7										4	10			1	45
8	11	3		5^1	6			9		12	2	7						13				4	10^2			1	46

Worthington Cup
First Round Hull C (h) 2-2 (a) 0-0

FA Cup
Third Round Bury (a) 3-0
Fourth Round Sheffield W (a) 0-2

Divison 2

STOKE CITY

FOUNDATION

The date of the formation of this club has long been in doubt. The year 1863 was claimed, but more recent research by Wade Martin has uncovered nothing earlier than 1868, when a couple of Old Carthusians, who were apprentices at the local works of the old North Staffordshire Railway Company, met with some others from that works, to form Stoke Ramblers. It should also be noted that the old Stoke club went bankrupt in 1908 when a new club was formed.

Britannia Stadium, Stoke-on-Trent ST4 4EG.

Telephone: (01782) 592222.

Fax: (01782) 592221.

Commercial Dept: (01782) 592211.

Soccerline Information: 0891 121040.

Football in the Community: (01782) 592255.

Ground Capacity: 24,054.

Record Attendance: 51,380 v Arsenal, Division 1, 29 March 1937.

Record Receipts: £160,000 v Newcastle U, Coca-Cola Cup 3rd rd, 25 October 1995.

Pitch Measurements: 116yd × 72yd.

Vice-President: J. A. M. Humphries.

Chairman: K. A. Humphreys.

Directors: D. J. Edwards, P. Coates.

Manager: Gary Megson.

Physio: R. Ryles.

Stadium Manager/Safety Officer: J. Alcock.

Chief Executive: J. Moxey.

LATEST SEQUENCES

Longest Sequence of League Wins: 8, 30.3.1895 – 21.9.1895.

Longest Sequence of League Defeats: 11, 6.4.85 – 17.8.85.

Longest Sequence of League Draws: 5, 21.3.87 – 11.4.87.

Longest Sequence of Unbeaten League Matches: 25, 5.9.92 – 20.2.93.

Longest Sequence Without a League Win: 17, 22.4.89 – 14.10.89.

HONOURS

Football League: Division 1 best season: 4th, 1935–36, 1946–47; Division 2 – Champions 1932–33, 1962–63, 1992–93; Runners-up 1921–22; Promoted 1978–79 (3rd); Division 3 (N) – Champions 1926–27.

FA Cup: Semi-finals 1899, 1971, 1972.

Football League Cup: Winners 1972.

Autoglass Trophy: Winners: 1992.

European Competitions: UEFA Cup: 1972–73, 1974–75.

Colours

Red and white striped shirts, white shorts, red and white hooped stockings.

Change Colours

White and royal blue shirts, blue shorts, blue stockings.

Year Formed: 1863 *(see Foundation).*

Turned Professional: 1885.

Ltd Co.: 1908.

Previous Names: 1868, Stoke Ramblers; 1870, Stoke; 1925, Stoke City.

Club Nickname: 'The Potters'.

Previous Grounds: 1875, Sweeting's Field; 1878, Victoria Ground (previously known as the Athletic Club Ground); 1997, Britannia Stadium.

First Football League Game: 8 September 1888, Football League, v WBA (h) L 0–2 – Rowley; Clare, Underwood; Ramsey, Shutt, Smith; Sayer, McSkimming, Staton, Edge, Tunnicliffe.

Record League Victory: 10–3 v WBA, Division 1, 4 February 1937 – Doug Westland; Brigham, Harbot; Tutin, Turner (1p), Kirton; Matthews, Antonio (2), Freddie Steele (5), Jimmy Westland, Johnson (2).

Record Cup Victory: 7–1 v Burnley, FA Cup 2nd rd (replay), 20 February 1896 – Clawley; Clare, Eccles; Turner, Grewe, Robertson; Willie Maxwell, Dickson, A. Maxwell (3), Hyslop (4), Schofield.

Record Defeat: 0–10 v Preston NE, Division 1, 14 September 1889.

Most League Points (2 for a win): 63, Division 3 (N), 1926–27.

Most League Points (3 for a win): 93, Division 2, 1992–93.

Most League Goals: 92, Division 3 (N), 1926–27.

Highest League Scorer in Season: Freddie Steele, 33, Division 1, 1936–37.

Most League Goals in Total Aggregate: Freddie Steele, 142, 1934–49.

Most League Goals in One Match: 7, Neville Coleman v Lincoln C, Division 2, 23 February 1957.

Most Capped Player: Gordon Banks, 36 (73), England.

Most League Appearances: Eric Skeels, 506, 1958–76.

Youngest League Player: Peter Bullock, 16 years 163 days v Swansea C, 19 April 1958.

Record Transfer Fee Received: £2,750,000 from QPR for Mike Sheron, July 1997.

Record Transfer Fee Paid: £580,000 to Birmingham C for Paul Peschisolido, July 1994.

Football League Record: 1888 Founder Member of Football League; 1890 Not re-elected; 1891 Re-elected; relegated in 1907, and after one year in Division 2, resigned for financial reasons; 1919 re-elected to Division 2; 1922–23 Division 1; 1923–26 Division 2; 1926–27 Division 3 (N); 1927–33 Division 2; 1933–53 Division 1; 1953–63 Division 2; 1963–77 Division 1; 1977–79 Division 2; 1979–85 Division 1; 1985–90 Division 2; 1990–92 Division 3; 1992–93 Division 2; 1993–98 Division 1; 1998– Division 2.

MANAGERS

Tom Slaney 1874–83
 (Secretary-Manager)
Walter Cox 1883–84
 (Secretary-Manager)
Harry Lockett 1884–90
Joseph Bradshaw 1890–92
Arthur Reeves 1892–95
William Rowley 1895–97
H. D. Austerberry 1897–1908
A. J. Barker 1908–14
Peter Hodge 1914–15
Joe Schofield 1915–19
Arthur Shallcross 1919–23
John 'Jock' Rutherford 1923
Tom Mather 1923–35
Bob McGrory 1935–52
Frank Taylor 1952–60
Tony Waddington 1960–77
George Eastham 1977–78
Alan A'Court 1978
Alan Durban 1978–81
Richie Barker 1981–83
Bill Asprey 1984–85
Mick Mills 1985–89
Alan Ball 1989–91
Lou Macari 1991–93
Joe Jordan 1993–94
Lou Macari 1994–97
Chic Bates 1997–98
Chris Kamara 1998
Brian Little 1998–99
Gary Megson July 1999–

TEN YEAR LEAGUE RECORD

		P	W	D	L	F	A	Pts	Pos
1988-89	Div 2	46	15	14	17	57	72	59	13
1989-90	Div 2	46	6	19	21	35	63	37	24
1990-91	Div 3	46	16	12	18	55	59	60	14
1991-92	Div 3	46	21	14	11	69	49	77	4
1992-93	Div 2	46	27	12	7	73	34	93	1
1993-94	Div 1	46	18	13	15	57	59	67	10
1994-95	Div 1	46	16	15	15	50	53	63	11
1995-96	Div 1	46	20	13	13	60	49	73	4
1996-97	Div 1	46	18	10	18	51	57	64	12
1997-98	Div 1	46	11	13	22	44	74	46	23

DID YOU KNOW ?

Lucien Emile Boullimier was a Stoke City wing-half in 1896–97. He was also accomplished in many other fields as an opera singer, actor and artist. He was the son of the famous Parisien ceramic artist Anton Boullimier.

STOKE CITY 1998–99 LEAGUE RECORD

Match No.	Date	Venue	Opponents	Result	H/T Score	Lg. Pos.	Goalscorers	Attendance
1	Aug 8	A	Northampton T	W 3-1	1-1	—	Kavanagh G (pen) [7], Thorne [63], Crowe [83]	6661
2	15	H	Macclesfield T	W 2-0	2-0	1	Crowe [25], Thorne [36]	13,981
3	22	A	Preston NE	W 4-3	0-2	1	Crowe 2 [50, 85], Kavanagh G 2 (1 pen) [69, 72 (p)]	11,587
4	29	H	Oldham Ath	W 2-0	1-0	1	Keen [22], Lightbourne [90]	12,306
5	31	H	Colchester U	W 1-0	0-0	1	Kavanagh G [78]	4728
6	Sept 5	H	Bournemouth	W 2-0	0-0	1	Thorne [70], Crowe [76]	13,443
7	8	A	Fulham	L 0-1	0-0	—		12,055
8	12	H	Millwall	W 1-0	0-0	1	Lightbourne [90]	12,307
9	19	A	Wrexham	W 1-0	0-0	1	Wallace [78]	7290
10	26	H	Blackpool	L 1-3	0-2	1	Crowe (pen) [69]	15,002
11	Oct 3	A	Reading	L 1-2	0-1	1	Whittle [69]	13,089
12	12	H	Chesterfield	D 0-0	0-0	—		10,557
13	17	A	Lincoln C	W 2-1	0-1	1	Robinson [49], Sigurdsson [52]	6159
14	20	A	Bristol R	L 0-1	0-1	—		6752
15	24	H	Wigan Ath	W 2-1	0-0	1	Kavanagh G [52], Griffiths (og) [53]	11,480
16	31	A	Notts Co	L 0-1	0-1	1		8546
17	Nov 7	H	Luton T	W 3-1	2-0	1	Oldfield [5], Forsyth [37], Lightbourne [90]	12,964
18	10	A	Burnley	W 2-0	0-0	—	Lightbourne [47], Thorne [62]	10,575
19	21	H	York C	W 2-0	2-0	1	Forsyth [30], Oldfield [35]	11,795
20	28	A	Wycombe W	W 1-0	0-0	1	Kavanagh G [79]	6023
21	Dec 12	H	Gillingham	D 0-0	0-0	1		17,233
22	19	A	Walsall	L 0-1	0-1	3		9056
23	26	H	Preston NE	L 0-1	0-1	3		23,272
24	28	A	Manchester C	L 1-2	1-0	3	Sigurdsson [31]	30,478
25	Jan 9	A	Northampton T	W 3-1	2-0	3	Wallace [56], Thorne [74], Lightbourne [84]	11,180
26	23	H	Colchester U	D 3-3	3-2	4	Gregory D (og) [30], Lightbourne [34], Sigurdsson [42]	12,507
27	29	H	Manchester C	L 0-1	0-1	—		13,679
28	Feb 6	A	Bournemouth	L 0-4	0-2	6		7637
29	20	A	Millwall	L 0-2	0-1	7		7855
30	27	H	Wrexham	L 1-3	0-1	9	Sigurdsson [82]	10,765
31	Mar 6	A	Blackpool	W 1-0	1-0	7	Lightbourne [34]	5504
32	10	H	Reading	L 0-4	0-0	—		8218
33	13	A	Luton T	W 2-1	2-0	7	Kavanagh G 2 (1 pen) [10 (p), 17]	5221
34	16	A	Fulham	L 0-1	0-1	—		12,298
35	20	H	Notts Co	L 2-3	0-0	9	Oldfield [68], Keen [90]	9565
36	27	A	Wigan Ath	W 3-2	0-0	8	Thorne [54], Kavanagh G [80], Strong [88]	4133
37	Apr 3	H	Lincoln C	W 2-0	1-0	7	Thorne 2 [21, 65]	12,845
38	5	A	Chesterfield	D 1-1	1-1	8	Oldfield [32]	5290
39	10	H	Bristol R	L 1-4	1-0	8	Thorne [41]	17,823
40	14	H	Wycombe W	D 2-2	1-1	—	Wallace [38], Oldfield [61]	6569
41	17	A	York C	D 2-2	1-0	7	Kavanagh G 2 (1 pen) [10 (p), 85]	4142
42	24	A	Burnley	L 1-4	1-2	8	Crowe [31]	10,965
43	27	A	Macclesfield T	W 2-1	1-1	—	Oldfield [31], Crowe [50]	3825
44	May 1	A	Gillingham	L 0-4	0-3	8		8289
45	4	A	Oldham Ath	L 0-1	0-0	—		5015
46	8	H	Walsall	W 2-0	1-0	8	Connor 2 [24, 50]	12,091

Final League Position: 8

GOALSCORERS

League (59): Kavanagh G 11 (4 pens), Thorne 9, Crowe 8 (1 pen), Lightbourne 7, Oldfield 6, Sigurdsson 4, Wallace 3, Connor 2, Forsyth 2, Keen 2, Robinson 1, Strong 1, Whittle 1, own goals 2.
Worthington Cup (2): Kavanagh G 1, Thorne 1.
FA Cup (1): Lightbourne 1.

Muggleton C 40	Robinson P 39 +1	Small B 35 +2	Sigurdsson L 38	Woods S 33	Whittle J 9 +5	Keen K 43 +1	Kavanagh G 36	Thorne P 33 +1	Lightbourne K 28 +8	Oldfield D 43 +3	Short C 19 +2	Crowe D 19 +19	Pickering A — +1	Wallace R 11 +20	Tweed S — +1	Heath R 7 +3	Mackenzie N 3 +3	Forsyth R 13 +5	Petty B 9 +2	Sturridge S 1 +2	Collins L 4	Ward G 6	Taaffe S 1 +2	O'Connor J 4	Mohan N 15	Kavanagh J 8	Strong G 5	Connor P 2 +1	Clarke C 2	Fraser S — +1	Woolliscroft A — +1	Match No.
1	2	3	4	5	6[1]	7	8	9	10[2]	11	12	13																				1
1	5[1]	3	4	6	12	7	8	9		11[2]	2	10	13																			2
1	5[2]	3	4[1]	6	12	7	8	9	13	11		2	10[3]	14																		3
1	5	3	4	6		7	8[2]	9	12	11	2	10[1]	13																			4
1	5	3	4	6		7[2]	8	9	12	11	2	10[1]	13																			5
1	5	3[2]		6	4	7		9	10	11[1]	2	12				8[3]	13	14														6
1	5	4		6	12	7	8[2]	9	10	11	2[1]	13						3														7
1	5	4		6	2	7	8	9	10	11		12						3[1]														8
1	2[1]	4	3	5		7	8	9	10	6		11[2]		13		12																9
1	2	4	6	5		7	8[1]	9	10	11		12				3																10
1	2	3[1]	4	5	6	7	8	9	10	11		12																				11
1	5	3	6	4		7	8	9[1]	10	11[2]		13	12	2																		12
1	5	3	4	6		7	8	9	10	11	2																					13
1	5	3	4	6[1]	12	7	8[2]	9	10	11[3]	2		14			13																14
1	5	3	6	4		7	8[2]	9	12	11	2	10[1]	13				14															15
1	5	3	4	6		7[2]	8	9	12	11[1]	2	10	13																			16
1	5	3[1]	4	6	12	7		9	10	11	2[3]	13				14		8[2]														17
1	5	3	4	2		7	8	9	10	11									6													18
1	5	3	4	2		7	8	9	10[1]	11		12							6													19
1	5	3	4	6		7	8[1]			11		12		9[2]				10	2	13												20
1	5	3	4	6		7			10	11	2[1]	13		12				8		9[2]												21
1	5	3	4	6[3]		7	8	9	10[1]	11[2]		12		13				2	14													22
1	5	3	4	6[1]		7	8	9	10[1]	11		12						2														23
1	5	3	4	6		7	8	9	10[1]	11		12						2		12												24
1	5		6			7	8	9[1]	12	11[1]		13		4		3	10[3]	14	2													25
1	5	3[1]	4	6		7	8	9	10[2]	12		13		2[1]				11	14													26
1	5	3	4	6		7	8[1]	10	12			9		13				2		11[2]												27
1	5	3	4	6[2]		7	8		12	11	2[3]	9				14		10[1]	13													28
1	3[1]			6[2]		7			12	11	2	9		8		13	10	5	4													29
		3	4			7[3]		9		11	2	12		8[1]		13		5[2]			6	1	14	10								30
12		3	4			7		9		11	2	10[2]				13		8				6[1]		1	5							31
4[3]	12		3			7[2]		9	13	11	2[1]	10				14		8				1			5	6						32
7		4	3		12	8	11	6	10[1]			13		9[2]								1			5	2						33
7[2]		4	3		10	8		9[1]		11	6	12				13						1			5	2						34
	5	4	3			7	8			11				9		10						1				6		2				35
1		3	4			7	8	9[2]	11[1]			10		12		13									5	2		6				36
1	12	3	4			7	8	9[2]	10	11[3]		13		14											5	2[1]		6				37
1	2	3	4			7	8	9	10	11															5			6				38
1	2[1]	3	4			7	8	9	10	11		12													5			6				39
1	2	3	4			7	8	9	12	11		10													5			6[1]				40
1	2	3	4			7	8	9	10	11[2]		12							6			13			5							41
1	2	3	4			7	8	9	6[1]	10		11													5				12			42
1	6	3	4			7		9	11	10		8[1]		12											5		2					43
1	2	3	4			7	8	9	11	10									6						5							44
1								11		10				8		6					4		12	7	5	2[1]		9	3			45
1[1]	11							8		10				14		2						4[2]		7	6	5		9	3	12	13[3]	46

Worthington Cup

First Round   Macclesfield T   (a)   1-3
                                          (h)   1-0

FA Cup

First Round   Reading   (a)   1-0
Second Round   Swansea C   (a)   0-1

FA Premiership

SUNDERLAND

FOUNDATION

A Scottish schoolmaster named James Allan, working at Hendon Boarding School, took the initiative in the foundation of Sunderland in 1879 when they were formed as The Sunderland and District Teachers' Association FC at a meeting in the Adults School, Norfolk Street. Due to financial difficulties, they quickly allowed members from outside the teaching profession and so became Sunderland AFC in October 1880.

Sunderland Stadium of Light, Sunderland, Tyne and Wear SR5 1SU.
Telephone: (0191) 551 5000.
Fax: (0191) 551 5123.
Website: www.sunderland-afc.com.
Ticket Office: (0191) 551 5151.
Club Shop: (0191) 551 5050.
Tour Hotline: (0191) 551 5055.
Ground Capacity: 42,000.
Record Attendance: 41,634 v Birmingham C, Division 1, 9 May 1999.
Roker Park: 75,118 v Derby Co, FA Cup 6th rd replay, 8 March 1933.
Record Receipts: £605,310 v Sheffield U, Division 1 play-off semi-final, 13 May 1998.
Pitch Measurements: 115yd × 75yd.
Chairman: R. S. Murray.
Chief Executive: John Fickling.
Directors: G. McDonnell, D. C. Stonehouse.
Associate Directors: J. R. Featherstone, G. S. Wood, J. G. Wood.
Manager: Peter Reid.
Assistant Manager: Bobby Saxton.
Physio: Gordon Ellis.
Academy Director: Ian Branfoot.
Youth Team Coaches: Bryan Robson, Ricky Sbragia.
Community Programme Officer: Bob Oates.
Secretary: Mark Blackbourne.
Commercial Director: Grahame McDonnell.
Stadium Manager: Dave Nicholson.
Safety Officer: John Davidson.

LATEST SEQUENCES
Longest Sequence of League Wins: 13, 14.11.1891 – 2.4.1892.
Longest Sequence of League Defeats: 9, 23.11.76 – 15.1.77.
Longest Sequence of League Draws: 6, 26.3.49 – 19.4.49.
Longest Sequence of Unbeaten League Matches: 19, 3.5.98 – 14.11.98.
Longest Sequence Without a League Win: 14, 16.4.85 – 14.9.85.

HONOURS

Football League: Division 1 – Champions 1891–92, 1892–93, 1894–95, 1901–02, 1912–13, 1935–36, 1995–96, 1998–99; Runners-up 1893–94, 1897–98, 1900–01, 1922–23, 1934–35; Division 2 – Champions 1975–76; Runners-up 1963–64, 1979–80; Division 3 – Champions 1987–88.

FA Cup: Winners 1937, 1973; Runners-up 1913, 1992.

Football League Cup: Runners-up 1985.

European Competitions: European Cup-Winners' Cup: 1973–74.

Colours
Red and white striped shirts, black shorts, black stockings, red turnover.

Change Colours
Navy blue shirts with red and white hoop across chest, navy shorts and stockings with red and white trim.

Year Formed: 1879.

Turned Professional: 1886.

Ltd Co.: 1906.

Previous Name: 1879, Sunderland and District Teacher's AFC; 1880, Sunderland.

Previous Grounds: 1879, Blue House Field, Hendon; 1882, Groves Field, Ashbrooke; 1883, Horatio Street; 1884, Abbs Field, Fulwell; 1886, Newcastle Road; 1898, Roker Park; 1997, Stadium of Light.

First Football League Game: 13 September 1890, Football League, v Burnley (h) L 2–3 – Kirtley; Porteous, Oliver; Wilson, Auld, Gibson; Spence (1), Miller, Campbell (1), Scott, D. Hannah.

Record League Victory: 9–1 v Newcastle U (a), Division 1, 5 December 1908 – Roose; Forster, Melton; Daykin, Thomson, Low; Mordue, Hogg (4), Brown, Holley (3), Bridgett (2).

Record Cup Victory: 11–1 v Fairfield, FA Cup 1st rd, 2 February 1895 – Doig; McNeill, Johnston; Dunlop, McCreadie (1), Wilson; Gillespie (1), Millar (5), Campbell, Hannah (3), Scott (1).

Record Defeat: 0–8 v West Ham U, Division 1, 19 October 1968. 0–8 v Watford, Division 1, 25 September 1982.

Most League Points (2 for a win): 61, Division 2, 1963–64.

Most League Points (3 for a win): 105, Division 1, 1998–99 (Football League Record).

Most League Goals: 109, Division 1, 1935–36.

Highest League Scorer in Season: Dave Halliday, 43, Division 1, 1928–29.

Most League Goals in Total Aggregate: Charlie Buchan, 209, 1911–25.

Most League Goals in One Match: 5, Charlie Buchan v Liverpool, Division 1, 7 December 1919; 5, Bobby Gurney v Bolton W, Division 1, 7 December 1935; 5, Dominic Sharkey v Norwich C, Division 2, 20 February 1962.

Most Capped Player: Charlie Hurley, 38 (40), Republic of Ireland.

Most League Appearances: Jim Montgomery, 537, 1962–77.

Youngest League Player: Derek Forster, 15 years 184 days v Leicester C, 22 August 1964.

Record Transfer Fee Received: £3,000,000 from Fulham for Lee Clark, July 1999.

Record Transfer Fee Paid: £3,500,000 to Valencia for Stefan Schwarz, July 1999.

Football League Record: 1890 Elected to Division 1; 1958–64 Division 2; 1964–70 Division 1; 1970–76 Division 2; 1976–77 Division 1; 1977–80 Division 2; 1980–85 Division 1; 1985–87 Division 2; 1987–88 Division 3; 1988–90 Division 2; 1990–91 Division 1; 1991–92 Division 2; 1992–96 Division 1; 1996–97 FA Premier League; 1997– 99 Division 1; 1999– FA Premier League.

MANAGERS

Tom Watson 1888–96
Bob Campbell 1896–99
Alex Mackie 1899–1905
Bob Kyle 1905–28
Johnny Cochrane 1928–39
Bill Murray 1939–57
Alan Brown 1957–64
George Hardwick 1964–65
Ian McColl 1965–68
Alan Brown 1968–72
Bob Stokoe 1972–76
Jimmy Adamson 1976–78
Ken Knighton 1979–81
Alan Durban 1981–84
Len Ashurst 1984–85
Lawrie McMenemy 1985–87
Denis Smith 1987–91
Malcolm Crosby 1992–93
Terry Butcher 1993
Mick Buxton 1993–95
Peter Reid March 1995–

TEN YEAR LEAGUE RECORD

		P	W	D	L	F	A	Pts	Pos
1988-89	Div 2	46	16	15	15	60	60	63	11
1989-90	Div 2	46	20	14	12	70	64	74	6
1990-91	Div 1	38	8	10	20	38	60	34	19
1991-92	Div 2	46	14	11	21	61	65	53	18
1992-93	Div 1	46	13	11	22	50	64	50	21
1993-94	Div 1	46	19	8	19	54	57	65	12
1994-95	Div 1	46	12	18	16	41	45	54	20
1995-96	Div 1	46	22	17	7	59	33	83	1
1996-97	PR Lge	38	10	10	18	35	53	40	18
1997-98	Div 1	46	26	12	8	86	50	90	3

DID YOU KNOW ?

On 10 April 1999, Sunderland set a post-War record of 12 successive home League victories when they beat Huddersfield T 2–0 at the Stadium of Light. It was also the 52nd first team fixture at the new ground.

SUNDERLAND 1998–99 LEAGUE RECORD

Match No.	Date	Venue	Opponents	Result	H/T Score	Lg. Pos.	Goalscorers	Atten- dance
1	Aug 8	H	QPR	W 1-0	0-0	—	Phillips (pen) 75	41,008
2	15	A	Swindon T	D 1-1	0-1	6	Phillips 60	10,207
3	22	H	Tranmere R	W 5-0	2-0	6	Phillips 17, Dichio 2 45, 79, Mullin 48, Butler 84	34,155
4	25	H	Watford	W 4-1	3-1	—	Johnston 26, Summerbee 41, Dichio 45, Melville 63	36,587
5	29	A	Ipswich T	W 2-0	2-0	1	Mullin 12, Phillips 36	15,813
6	Sept 8	H	Bristol C	D 1-1	1-0	—	Phillips 13	34,111
7	12	A	Wolverhampton W	D 1-1	0-0	3	Phillips 90	26,816
8	19	H	Oxford U	W 7-0	3-0	2	Bridges 2 3, 55, Gray 6, Dichio 2 (1 pen) 35 (p), 66, Rae 2 53, 82	34,567
9	26	A	Portsmouth	D 1-1	0-1	1	Johnston 83	17,022
10	29	A	Norwich C	D 2-2	1-2	—	Quinn 2, Marshall A (og) 47	17,504
11	Oct 3	H	Bradford C	D 0-0	0-0	2		37,828
12	18	A	WBA	W 3-2	0-2	2	Melville 67, Bridges 80, Ball 86	14,746
13	21	A	Huddersfield T	D 1-1	1-1	—	Ball 42	20,741
14	24	H	Bury	W 1-0	0-0	1	Dichio 79	38,049
15	Nov 1	A	Bolton W	W 3-0	2-0	1	Johnston 27, Quinn 34, Bridges 83	21,676
16	3	A	Crewe Alex	W 4-1	3-0	—	Dichio 11, Gray 28, Quinn 45, Bridges 61	5361
17	7	H	Grimsby T	W 3-1	0-0	1	Smith 2 65, 69, Quinn 81	40,077
18	14	A	Port Vale	W 2-0	1-0	1	Aspin (og) 28, Quinn 65	8839
19	21	H	Barnsley	L 2-3	0-1	1	Scott (pen) 63, Quinn 72	40,231
20	28	A	Sheffield U	W 4-0	3-0	1	Quinn 2 7, 75, Bridges 2 13, 35	25,612
21	Dec 5	H	Stockport Co	W 1-0	1-0	1	Summerbee 30	36,040
22	12	H	Port Vale	W 2-0	2-0	1	Smith 24, Butler 44	37,583
23	15	H	Crystal Palace	W 2-0	1-0	—	Scott (pen) 33, Dichio 88	33,870
24	19	A	Birmingham C	D 0-0	0-0	1		22,095
25	26	A	Tranmere R	L 0-1	0-0	1		14,248
26	28	H	Crewe Alex	W 2-0	1-0	1	Dichio 15, Bridges 78	41,433
27	Jan 9	A	QPR	D 2-2	1-1	1	Phillips 32, Quinn 90	17,444
28	17	H	Ipswich T	W 2-1	2-1	1	Quinn 2 26, 32	39,835
29	30	A	Watford	L 1-2	1-1	1	Quinn 36	20,188
30	Feb 6	H	Swindon T	W 2-0	2-0	1	Quinn 28, Phillips 30	41,304
31	13	A	Bristol C	W 1-0	0-0	1	Phillips (pen) 69	15,736
32	20	H	Wolverhampton W	W 2-1	1-1	1	Johnston 10, Quinn 90	41,268
33	27	A	Oxford U	D 0-0	0-0	1		9044
34	Mar 2	H	Portsmouth	W 2-0	1-0	—	Dichio 9, Phillips 60	37,656
35	6	H	Norwich C	W 1-0	1-0	1	Phillips 7	39,004
36	9	A	Bradford C	W 1-0	0-0	—	Quinn 71	15,124
37	13	A	Grimsby T	W 2-0	0-0	1	Phillips 50, Clark 79	9528
38	20	H	Bolton W	W 3-1	2-0	1	Phillips 23, Johnston 2 28, 55	41,505
39	Apr 3	A	WBA	W 3-0	2-0	1	Phillips 2 22, 48, Clark 26	41,135
40	5	A	Crystal Palace	D 1-1	1-1	1	Phillips 23	22,096
41	10	H	Huddersfield T	W 2-0	0-0	1	Quinn 28, Johnston 41	41,074
42	13	A	Bury	W 5-2	4-1	—	Phillips 4 (1 pen) 10 (p), 31, 33, 90, Quinn 24	8669
43	16	A	Barnsley	W 3-1	1-0	—	Summerbee 45, Clark 63, Phillips 90	17,390
44	24	H	Sheffield U	D 0-0	0-0	1		41,179
45	May 1	A	Stockport Co	W 1-0	0-0	1	Phillips 56	10,548
46	9	H	Birmingham C	W 2-1	0-1	1	Phillips 62, Quinn 71	41,634

Final League Position: 1

GOALSCORERS

League (91): Phillips 23 (3 pens), Quinn 18, Dichio 10 (1 pen), Bridges 8, Johnston 7, Clark 3, Smith 3, Summerbee 3, Ball 2, Butler 2, Gray 2, Melville 2, Mullin 2, Rae 2, Scott 2 (2 pens), own goals 2.
Worthington Cup (16): Bridges 4, Quinn 3, Dichio 2, Phillips 2, Johnston 1, McCann 1, Scott 1, Smith 1, own goal 1.
FA Cup (1): McCann 1.

Sorensen T 45	Gray M 36 + 1	Scott M 14 + 2	Clark L 26 + 1	Craddock J 3 + 3	Butler P 44	Ball K 42	Summerbee N 36	Quinn N 36 + 3	Phillips K 26	Johnston A 40	Bridges M 13 + 17	Williams D 16 + 9	Melville A 44	Mullin J 8 + 1	Dichio D 16 + 20	Thirlwell P 1 + 1	Smith M 4 + 4	Wainwright N — + 2	Makin C 37 + 1	Rae A 12 + 3	Alston S — + 1	McCann G 5 + 6	Holloway D 1 + 5	Marriott A 1	Match No.
1	2	3	4¹	5	6	7²	8	9	10	11	12	13													1
1	2	3			6	7¹	8	9²	10	11	12		4	5	13										2
1	3				6	7	4¹		10²	11³		2	5	8	9	12	13	14							3
1	3				6	7	4		10	11		2	5	8	9¹	12									4
1	3			12	6¹	7	4		10	11		2	5	8	9										5
1	3				6	7	4		10	11		2	5	8	9										6
1	3	8			6	7	4		10	11¹	12	2	5		9										7
1	3²				6	7	4	12	10	11		2	5	8²	9¹		13	14							8
1	3				6	7	4	12	10²	11		2	5	8¹	9		13								9
1	3				6	7	4		10	11			5		9				2	8					10
1	3				6	7	4		10	11			5		9				2	8					11
1	3¹		12		6	7	4	9		11²	14	13	5		10³				2	8					12
1	3				6	7	4	9	10¹	11			5		12				2	8					13
1	3				6	7	4	9	10¹	11			5		12				2	8					14
1	3	12			6		4	9¹	10²	11	13	14	5	7	8³				2						15
1	3¹	12			6		4	9	10²	11	13	8	5	7					2						16
1	3				6		4	9²	10¹	11		8	5			7	12		2		13				17
1	3	8¹			6	7	4	9	10²	11			5		13	12			2						18
1	3	8			6¹	7	4	12	10	11			5		9				2						19
1	3	8	12		6	7	4³	9²	10	11			5¹		13				2			14			20
1	3	8			6	7¹	4	9	10²	11³	12		5		13				2			14			21
1	3	8			6		4	9	10¹	11			5		12				2	7²		13			22
1	12	3	4		6			9²	10	11³		14	5		13		8¹		2	7					23
1	11³	3	8		6		4	9¹	10			13	5		12				2	7²		14			24
1	11²	3	8		6		4	9	10¹				5		12				2	7		13			25
1	11²	3	8		6		4	9¹			12	13	5		10				2	7³		14			26
1		8			6		4	9	10	11¹	12		5		13		2²		2²	7			3		27
1	3	8			6		4	9	10¹	11		13	5		12				2	7²					28
1	3				6	7	4	9	10	11²		13	5¹		12				2			8			29
1	3	8			6	7	4	9²	10	11¹	12		5		13				2						30
1	3	8			6	7	4	9¹	10	11			5		12				2						31
1	3	8			6	7	4	9	10	11			5						2						32
1					6	7		9¹	10	11		4	5		12				2			8	3		33
1	3	8²			6	7	4		10	11	12	13	5		9¹				2						34
1	3				6	7	4¹	9	10	11		8¹	5						2			12			35
1	3		12		6	7	4	9	10	11		8¹	5						2						36
	3	8			6	7	4	9²	10¹	11	12		5						2					1	37
1	3	8³	5		6	7	4	9¹	10²	11	13	14			12				2						38
1	3	8	5		6	7	4³	9¹	10	11²	13				12				2			14			39
1	3	8			6	7	4	9	10	11			5						2¹			12			40
1	3	8			6	7²	4³	9¹	10	11	13		5		12				2			14			41
1	3	8			6	7	4³	9¹	10	11²	13		5		12				2			14			42
1	3	8			6	7	4	9	10	11			5						2						43
1	3	8			6	7	4¹			11			5		9	10			2			12			44
1	3	8			6	7		9	10	11			5						2			4			45
1	3	8			6	7	4	9	10	11			5						2						46

Worthington Cup

First Round	York C	(a)	2-0
		(h)	2-1
Second Round	Chester C	(h)	3-0
		(a)	1-0
Third Round	Grimsby T	(h)	2-1
Fourth Round	Everton	(a)	1-1
Fifth Round	Luton T	(h)	3-0
Semi-Final	Leicester C	(h)	1-2
		(a)	1-1

FA Cup

Third Round	Lincoln C	(a)	1-0
Fourth Round	Blackburn R	(a)	0-1

Division 3

SWANSEA CITY

FOUNDATION

The earliest Association Football in Wales was played in the Northern part of the country and no international took place in the South until 1894, when a local paper still thought it necessary to publish an outline of the rules and an illustration of the pitch markings. There had been an earlier Swansea club, but this has no connection with Swansea Town (now City) formed at a public meeting in June 1912.

Vetch Field, Swansea SA1 3SU.
Telephone: (01792) 474114. *Fax:* (01792) 646120.
Website: www.swansfc.co.uk. *Email:* swans.prom@btinternet.com.
Club Shop: (01792) 462584.
Clubcall: 0891 543123.
Commercial Department: (01792) 465087.
Youth Development: (01792) 465610.
Ground Capacity: 10,402.
Record Attendance: 32,796 v Arsenal, FA Cup 4th rd, 17 February 1968.
Record Receipts: £36,477.42 v Liverpool, Division 1, 18 September 1982.
Pitch Measurements: 112yd × 74yd.
President: I. C. Pursey MBE.
Chairman: Steve Hamer. *Vice-Chairman:* Neil McClure.
Directors: Professor D. H. Farmer, R. G. Hamill, Mike Lewis.
Chief Executive: Peter Day.
Commercial Director: Mike Lewis.
Manager: John Hollins MBE.
Assistant Manager: Alan Curtis.
Director of Youth Development: Malcolm Elias.
Physio: Richard Evans.
Centre of Excellence Director: Jeremy Charles.
Football Development Officer: Lyndon Jones.
Club Secretary: Victoria Townsend.
Safety Officer: Don Goss.
Programme Editor: Major Reg Pike (01792) 474114.

LATEST SEQUENCES
Longest Sequence of League Wins: 8, 4.2.61 – 18.3.61.
Longest Sequence of League Defeats: 9, 26.1.91 – 19.3.91.
Longest Sequence of League Draws: 5, 5.1.93 – 5.2.93.
Longest Sequence of Unbeaten League Matches: 19, 19.10.70 – 9.3.71.
Longest Sequence Without a League Win: 15, 25.3.89 – 2.9.89.

HONOURS

Football League: Division 1 best season: 6th, 1981–82; Division 2 – Promoted 1980–81 (3rd); Division 3 (S) – Champions 1924–25, 1948–49; Division 3 – Promoted 1978–79 (3rd); Division 4 – Promoted 1969–70 (3rd), 1977–78 (3rd), 1987–88 (play-offs).

FA Cup: Semi-finals 1926, 1964.

Football League Cup: best season: 4th rd, 1965, 1977.

Welsh Cup: Winners 9 times; Runners-up 8 times.

Autoglass Trophy: Winners 1994.

European Competitions: European Cup-Winners' Cup: 1961–62, 1966–67, 1981–82, 1982–83, 1983–84, 1989–90, 1991–92.

Colours
White shirts with maroon and black facing, white shorts with maroon and black trim, white stockings with maroon ring top.

Change Colours
Maroon shirts with black and white facings, maroon shorts with black and white trim, maroon stockings with white band.

Year Formed: 1912.

Turned Professional: 1912.

Ltd Co.: 1912.

Previous Name: Swansea Town until February 1970.

Club Nickname: 'The Swans'.

First Football League Game: 28 August 1920, Division 3, v Portsmouth (a) L 0–3 – Crumley; Robson, Evans; Smith, Holdsworth, Williams; Hole, I. Jones, Edmundson, Rigsby, Spottiswood.

Record League Victory: 8–0 v Hartlepool U, Division 4, 1 April 1978 – Barber; Evans, Bartley, Lally (1) (Morris), May, Bruton, Kevin Moore, Robbie James (3 incl. 1p), Curtis (3), Toshack (1), Chappell.

Record Cup Victory: 12–0 v Sliema W (Malta), ECWC 1st rd 1st leg, 15 September 1982 – Davies; Marustik, Hadziabdic (1), Irwin (1), Kennedy, Rajkovic (1), Loveridge (2) (Leighton James), Robbie James, Charles (2), Stevenson (1), Latchford (1) (Walsh (3)).

Record Defeat: 0–8 v Liverpool, FA Cup 3rd rd, 9 January 1990. 0–8 v Monaco, ECWC, 1st rd 2nd leg, 1 October 1991.

Most League Points (2 for a win): 62, Division 3 (S), 1948–49.

Most League Points (3 for a win): 73, Division 2, 1992–93.

Most League Goals: 90, Division 2, 1956–57.

Highest League Scorer in Season: Cyril Pearce, 35, Division 2, 1931–32.

Most League Goals in Total Aggregate: Ivor Allchurch, 166, 1949–58, 1965–68.

Most League Goals in One Match: 5, Jack Fowler v Charlton Ath, Division 3S, 27 December 1924.

Most Capped Player: Ivor Allchurch, 42 (68), Wales.

Most League Appearances: Wilfred Milne, 585, 1919–37.

Youngest League Player: Nigel Dalling, 15 years 289 days v Southport, 6 December 1974.

Record Transfer Fee Received: £400,000 from Bristol C for Steve Torpey, August 1997.

Record Transfer Fee Paid: £340,000 to Liverpool for Colin Irwin, August 1981.

Football League Record: 1920 Original Member of Division 3; 1921–25 Division 3 (S); 1925–47 Division 2; 1947–49 Division 3 (S); 1949–65 Division 2; 1965–67 Division 3; 1967–70 Division 4; 1970–73 Division 3; 1973–78 Division 4; 1978–79 Division 3; 1979–81 Division 2; 1981–83 Division 1; 1983–84 Division 2; 1984–86 Division 3; 1986–88 Division 4; 1988–92 Division 2; 1992–96 Division 2; 1996– Division 3.

MANAGERS

Walter Whittaker 1912–14
William Bartlett 1914–15
Joe Bradshaw 1919–26
Jimmy Thomson 1927–31
Neil Harris 1934–39
Haydn Green 1939–47
Bill McCandless 1947–55
Ron Burgess 1955–58
Trevor Morris 1958–65
Glyn Davies 1965–66
Billy Lucas 1967–69
Roy Bentley 1969–72
Harry Gregg 1972–75
Harry Griffiths 1975–77
John Toshack 1978–83
  (resigned October re-appointed in December) 1983–84
Colin Appleton 1984
John Bond 1984–85
Tommy Hutchison 1985–86
Terry Yorath 1986–89
Ian Evans 1989–90
Terry Yorath 1990–91
Frank Burrows 1991–95
Kevin Cullis 1996
Jan Molby 1996–97
Micky Adams 1997
Alan Cork 1997–98
John Hollins July 1998–

TEN YEAR LEAGUE RECORD

		P	W	D	L	F	A	Pts	Pos
1988-89	Div 3	46	15	16	15	51	53	61	12
1989-90	Div 3	46	14	12	20	45	63	54	17
1990-91	Div 3	46	13	9	24	49	72	48	20
1991-92	Div 3	46	14	14	18	55	65	56	19
1992-93	Div 2	46	20	13	13	65	47	73	5
1993-94	Div 2	46	16	12	18	56	58	60	13
1994-95	Div 2	46	19	14	13	57	45	71	10
1995-96	Div 2	46	11	14	21	43	79	47	22
1996-97	Div 3	46	21	8	17	62	58	71	5
1997-98	Div 3	46	13	11	22	49	62	50	20

DID YOU KNOW ?

Jack Fowler scored nine hat-tricks for Swansea Town between 1924 and 1927. Signed from Plymouth Argyle for £1,280 he had scored on his debut against Southend United. He was capped on six occasions by Wales.

SWANSEA CITY 1998–99 LEAGUE RECORD

Match No.	Date	Venue	Opponents	Result		H/T Score	Lg. Pos.	Goalscorers	Attendance
1	Aug 8	H	Exeter C	W	2-0	1-0	—	Thomas [45], Watkin [47]	5809
2	15	A	Cambridge U	L	1-2	1-1	8	Casey [6]	3074
3	22	H	Leyton Orient	D	1-1	0-0	12	Bird [90]	4629
4	29	A	Mansfield T	L	0-1	0-1	16		2421
5	31	H	Scunthorpe U	L	1-2	0-0	17	Alsop [63]	4024
6	Sept 5	A	Brighton & HA	L	0-1	0-1	23		2931
7	8	A	Carlisle U	W	2-1	2-1	—	Howard [12], Watkin [25]	2816
8	12	H	Scarborough	W	2-0	1-0	14	Watkin (pen) [35], Price [49]	3360
9	19	A	Torquay U	D	1-1	0-1	17	Smith [65]	2527
10	26	H	Southend U	W	3-1	1-1	11	Alsop [31], Watkin [72], Bird [90]	3890
11	Oct 3	A	Darlington	D	2-2	1-0	12	Watkin [34], Price [86]	3046
12	9	H	Rotherham U	D	1-1	0-1	—	Thomas [58]	5180
13	17	A	Chester C	D	1-1	1-1	12	Alsop [29]	3926
14	20	A	Shrewsbury T	L	0-1	0-1	—		2328
15	31	A	Halifax T	L	0-2	0-1	19		2383
16	Nov 7	H	Peterborough U	D	0-0	0-0	20		3771
17	10	A	Plymouth Arg	W	2-1	1-0	—	Watkin [17], Alsop [81]	4517
18	22	H	Cardiff C	W	2-1	0-1	15	Thomas [69], Bound [89]	7757
19	28	A	Hartlepool U	W	2-1	0-1	13	Alsop 2 [69, 79]	2051
20	Dec 12	A	Rochdale	D	1-1	0-1	12	Alsop [52]	4010
21	19	H	Hull C	W	2-0	2-0	12	Appleby [35], Watkin [40]	4280
22	26	A	Leyton Orient	D	1-1	0-0	12	Alsop [83]	5343
23	28	H	Barnet	W	2-1	2-0	11	Smith [16], Watkin [30]	6514
24	Jan 9	A	Exeter C	L	0-4	0-2	12		3213
25	30	A	Barnet	W	1-0	0-0	12	Appleby [66]	2259
26	Feb 5	H	Brighton & HA	D	2-2	1-0	—	Jones S [27], Watkin [71]	6563
27	13	H	Carlisle U	D	1-1	0-0	14	Roberts [55]	4753
28	16	H	Brentford	W	2-1	1-1	—	Appleby [12], Watkin [84]	5109
29	20	A	Scarborough	L	1-2	1-2	13	Smith [45]	1512
30	23	H	Mansfield T	W	1-0	0-0	—	Alsop [90]	4361
31	27	H	Torquay U	D	0-0	0-0	11		5594
32	Mar 6	A	Southend U	L	0-2	0-1	11		3713
33	9	H	Darlington	W	2-0	2-0	—	O'Leary [20], Watkin [39]	4078
34	13	A	Peterborough U	W	1-0	1-0	7	Roberts [2]	4182
35	20	H	Halifax T	L	1-2	1-0	9	Cusack [17]	4974
36	23	A	Scunthorpe U	W	2-1	1-1	—	Watkin 2 [25, 87]	3631
37	Apr 3	H	Chester C	D	1-1	1-0	9	Roberts [5]	5994
38	5	A	Rotherham U	L	0-1	0-0	9		4257
39	9	H	Shrewsbury T	D	1-1	0-1	—	Bound [68]	5113
40	13	H	Hartlepool U	W	1-0	0-0	—	Smith [56]	4429
41	18	A	Cardiff C	D	0-0	0-0	8		10,809
42	24	A	Plymouth Arg	L	2-3	2-0	10	O'Leary [23], Jones S [44]	5660
43	May 1	A	Rochdale	W	3-0	1-0	9	Price 2 [13, 66], Alsop [49]	1654
44	4	A	Brentford	L	1-4	0-1	—	Bird [89]	7156
45	6	H	Cambridge U	W	2-0	1-0	—	Watkin 2 (1 pen) [15, 59 (p)]	6086
46	8	H	Hull C	W	2-0	1-0	7	Watkin 2 [21, 68]	9226

Final League Position: 7

GOALSCORERS

League (56): Watkin 17 (2 pens), Alsop 10, Price 4, Smith 4, Appleby 3, Bird 3, Roberts 3, Thomas 3, Bound 2, Jones S 2, O'Leary 2, Casey 1, Cusack 1, Howard 1.
Worthington Cup (1): Cusack 1.
FA Cup (6): Thomas 2, Alsop 1, Appleby 1, Price 1, Smith 1.

Freestone R 38	Price J 25+3	Howard M 38+1	Cusack N 42+1	Smith J 42	Bound M 45	Appleby R 36+3	Thomas M 26+4	Newhouse A 5+1	Watkin S 40+3	Coates J 30+3	O'Gorman D 2+3	Alsop J 37+4	Casey R 5+5	Roberts S 15+17	Walker K 1	Jenkins L 6+6	Bird T 8+21	Jones S 31+1	O'Leary K 17+2	Clode M 2	Jones J 3	Lacey D 7+5	Davies J —+1	Gregg M 5	Phillips G —+1	Match No.
1	2	3	4	5	6	7^{1}	8	9^{2}	10	11	12	13														1
1	2	3	4	5	6		8		10	11		9	7^{1}	12												2
1	2	3^{2}	4		6	7	8		10^{3}	11^{1}		9		12	5		13	14								3
1	2	3^{2}	4	5	6	11	8^{1}		10	12		9^{2}		13			7	14								4
1	2	3	4	5	6	11	12	8^{2}				9		13			7	10^{1}								5
1		3	4^{3}	5	6	11	8		10			12	13	7^{2}		14	9^{1}		2							6
1	7	3	4	5	6	11	8		10			9							2							7
1	7	3	4	5	6	11	8		10			9							2							8
1	7	3	4	5	6	11	8^{1}		10^{2}			9		13			12		2							9
1	7	3	4	5	6	11	8^{3}		10^{2}		12	9		14			13		2^{1}							10
1	7	3	4	5	6	11^{1}	8		10		12	9							2							11
1		3	4	5	6	11	8		10		12	9	7^{1}						2							12
1	7	3	4	5	6				10		12	11^{1}		9			8		2							13
1	7^{2}	3^{1}	4	5	6	13			10	11		9		14		8^{2}	12		2							14
1	7^{2}	3			6	11	8		10			9		13	4		12		2		5^{1}					15
1	7^{2}	3	4	5	6	11	8	12	10					13			9^{1}		2							16
1	7^{2}	3	4	5	6	11	8	9^{1}	10		12						13		2							17
1	7	3	4	5	6	11	8	9^{1}	10		12								2							18
1	7^{1}	3	4	5	6	11	8	10^{2}				9		13			12		2							19
1	7^{2}	3	4	5	6	11	8	12				9		13			10^{1}		2							20
1		3	4	5	6	11^{1}	8		10	7		9		12					2							21
1	12	3^{2}	4	5	6	11	8		10	7^{1}		9					13		2							22
1	12	3	4	5	6		8		10^{2}	7		9		11^{1}			13		2							23
1	12		4	5	6		8^{3}		10	11		9^{1}		7		14	13		2	3						24
		3	4		6		12		10^{2}	11		9		7^{1}			13		2		5	8		1		25
		3	4	5	6		12		10	11		9		7^{1}					2			8		1		26
		3		5	6	10		9^{1}		11			12	7		4^{1}			2^{2}	13		8	14	1		27
	2	3	4	5	6	8			10	11^{1}		9	13	7^{2}								12			1	28
	2	3	4	5^{2}	6	8			10	12		7					9	13				11			1	29
	2	3	4		6	8			10	11		9	7^{1}	12							5				1	30
	2^{3}	3	4		6	8			10^{1}	11		9	7^{2}	13			12				5	14			1	31
		3	4	9	6	8			10	11		7^{1}					12		5		2^{2}				1	32
1		3	4	5	6	8			10	11		9^{1}		7				12	2							33
1		3	4	5	6	8			10	11		9		7					2							34
1		3	4	5	6				10^{1}	11		9	8^{2}	7				12	2			13				35
1	7^{1}	3	4	5	6	8			10	11		9		12					2							36
1			4	5	6	8			10^{2}	11		9		7^{1}		13	12		2	3						37
1		3^{2}	4	5	6	8			10^{1}	11		9		7		13	12		2							38
1			4	5	6	8		13	10	3		9^{1}		11^{2}			12		2			7				39
1	12			5	6	7	8^{1}		10	3		9					2		4			11				40
1	11			5	6	7	8^{1}		10^{2}	3		9					12		2		4	13				41
1				5	6	7^{2}	8	12		3		9	14	13			10^{1}		2		4	11^{3}				42
1	8^{2}	11		5	6	7^{1}	13		10^{3}	3		9		14			12		2		4					43
1	8^{1}	12	11	5	6	7		13		3		9^{2}		14			10		2		4^{3}					44
1		3	4	5	6		8		10	11		9		7					2							45
1		3	4	5^{3}	6	12	8		10	11		9^{2}		7^{1}			13		2			14				46

Worthington Cup

First Round Norwich C   (h) 1-1
                         (a) 0-1

FA Cup

First Round	Millwall	(h)	3-0
Second Round	Stoke C	(h)	1-0
Third Round	West Ham U	(a)	1-1
		(h)	1-0
Fourth Round	Derby Co	(h)	0-1

Division 1   **SWINDON TOWN**

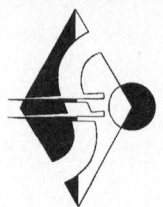

County Ground, Swindon, Wiltshire SN1 2ED.
Telephone: (01793) 333700. *Fax:* (01793) 333703.
Marketing: (01793) 333718. *Fax:* (01793) 333719.
Superstore: (01793) 333778. *Fax:* (01793) 333780.
Community Office: (01793) 421303.
Clubcall: 0891 121640.
Ground Capacity: 15,728.
Record Attendance: 32,000 v Arsenal, FA Cup 3rd rd, 15 January 1972.
Record Receipts: £149,371 v Bolton W, Coca-Cola Cup semi-final, 1st leg, 12 February 1995.
Pitch Measurements: 110yd × 70yd.
President: C. J. Green.
Chairman: Rikki Hunt.
Vice-Chairman: Cliff Puffett.
Directors: Sir Seton Wills Bt, P. R. Godwin CBE, J. M. Spearman, P. T. Archer, J. Wills, W. Carson OBE (Associate).
Manager: Jimmy Quinn.
Assistant Manager: Mike Walsh.
Coach: Alan McDonald.
Physios: Dave Moore and Dick Mackey.
Director of Finance/Company Secretary: Steve Jonas.
Football Secretary: David Norris.
Youth Team Manager: Tom Jones.
Director of Sales: Sandra Jones.
Community Officers: Clive Maguire and Jon Holloway.

LATEST SEQUENCES

Longest Sequence of League Wins: 8, 12.1.86 – 15.3.86.
Longest Sequence of League Defeats: 6, 2.5.93 – 25.8.93.
Longest Sequence of League Draws: 6, 22.11.91 – 28.12.91.
Longest Sequence of Unbeaten League Matches: 22, 12.1.86 – 23.8.86.
Longest Sequence Without a League Win: 19, 17.4.93 – 20.11.93.

Colours

Red shirts, white shorts, red stockings.

Change Colours

Light blue/dark blue panelled shirts and shorts, light blue stockings.

Year Formed: 1881* (*see Foundation*).

Turned Professional: 1894.

Ltd Co.: 1894.

Club Nickname: 'Robins'.

Previous Ground: 1881, The Croft; 1896, County Ground.

First Football League Game: 28 August 1920, Division 3, v Luton T (h) W 9–1 – Nash; Kay, Macconachie; Langford, Hawley, Wareing; Jefferson (1), Fleming (4), Rogers, Batty (2), Davies (1), (1 og).

Record League Victory: 9–1 v Luton T, Division 3 (S), 28 August 1920 – Nash; Kay, Macconachie; Langford, Hawley, Wareing; Jefferson (1), Fleming (4), Rogers, Batty (2), Davies (1), (1 og).

Record Cup Victory: 10–1 v Farnham U Breweries (away), FA Cup 1st rd (replay), 28 November 1925 – Nash; Dickenson, Weston, Archer, Bew, Adey; Denyer (2), Wall (1), Richardson (4), Johnson (3), Davies.

Record Defeat: 1–10 v Manchester C, FA Cup 4th rd (replay), 25 January 1930.

Most League Points (2 for a win): 64, Division 3, 1968–69.

Most League Points (3 for a win): 102, Division 4, 1985–86 (League record).

Most League Goals: 100, Division 3 (S), 1926–27.

Highest League Scorer in Season: Harry Morris, 47, Division 3 (S), 1926–27.

Most League Goals in Total Aggregate: Harry Morris, 216, 1926–33.

Most League Goals in One Match: 5, Harry Morris v QPR, Division 3S, 18 December 1926; 5, Harry Morris v Norwich C, Division 3S, 26 April 1930; 5, Keith East v Mansfield T, Division 3, 20 November 1965.

Most Capped Player: Rod Thomas, 30 (50), Wales.

Most League Appearances: John Trollope, 770, 1960–80.

Youngest League Player: Paul Rideout, 16 years 107 days v Hull C, 29 November 1980.

Record Transfer Fee Received: £1,500,000 from Manchester C for Kevin Horlock, January 1997.

Record Transfer Fee Paid: £800,000 to West Ham U for Joey Beauchamp, August 1994.

Football League Record: 1920 Original Member of Division 3; 1921–58 Division 3 (S); 1958–63 Division 3; 1963–65 Division 2; 1965–69 Division 3; 1969–74 Division 2; 1974–82 Division 3; 1982–86 Division 4; 1986–87 Division 3; 1987–92 Division 2; 1992–93 Division 1; 1993–94 FA Premier League; 1994–95 Division 1; 1995–96 Division 2; 1996– Division 1.

MANAGERS

Sam Allen 1902–33
Ted Vizard 1933–39
Neil Harris 1939–41
Louis Page 1945–53
Maurice Lindley 1953–55
Bert Head 1956–65
Danny Williams 1965–69
Fred Ford 1969–71
Dave Mackay 1971–72
Les Allen 1972–74
Danny Williams 1974–78
Bobby Smith 1978–80
John Trollope 1980–83
Ken Beamish 1983–84
Lou Macari 1984–89
Ossie Ardiles 1989–91
Glenn Hoddle 1991–93
John Gorman 1993–94
Steve McMahon 1994–99
Jimmy Quinn October 1999–

TEN YEAR LEAGUE RECORD

		P	W	D	L	F	A	Pts	Pos
1988-89	Div 2	46	20	16	10	68	53	76	6
1989-90	Div 2	46	20	14	12	79	59	74	4
1990-91	Div 2	46	12	14	20	65	73	50	21
1991-92	Div 2	46	18	15	13	69	55	69	8
1992-93	Div 1	46	21	13	12	74	59	76	5
1993-94	PR Lge	42	5	15	22	47	100	30	22
1994-95	Div 1	46	12	12	22	54	73	48	21
1995-96	Div 2	46	25	17	4	71	34	92	1
1996-97	Div 1	46	15	9	22	52	71	54	19
1997-98	Div 1	46	14	10	22	42	73	52	18

DID YOU KNOW ?

John Walker was considered to be one of the finest left-backs in the Southern League prior to the First World War. He joined Swindon Town from Rangers and won 11 full international caps for Scotland.

SWINDON TOWN 1998–99 LEAGUE RECORD

Match No.	Date	Venue	Opponents	Result		H/T Score	Lg. Pos.	Goalscorers	Atten- dance
1	Aug 8	A	Sheffield U	L	1-2	0-2	—	Holdsworth (og) [60]	15,977
2	15	H	Sunderland	D	1-1	1-0	18	Onuora [4]	10,207
3	22	A	Wolverhampton W	L	0-1	0-1	21		21,537
4	29	H	Port Vale	D	1-1	0-1	19	Barnett (og) [56]	7800
5	31	A	Bury	L	0-3	0-0	20		4513
6	Sept 5	H	Bristol C	W	3-2	3-0	18	Walters (pen) [2], Ndah [5], Onuora [8]	8537
7	9	H	Oxford U	W	4-1	1-1	—	Ndah 2 [8, 86], Onuora 2 [72, 75]	8305
8	12	A	Portsmouth	L	2-5	0-2	15	Onuora [65], Ndah [75]	10,105
9	19	H	Watford	L	1-4	1-2	16	Ndah [29]	8781
10	25	A	Tranmere R	D	0-0	0-0	—		5501
11	29	A	Bolton W	L	1-2	0-0	—	Onuora [88]	16,497
12	Oct 3	A	Stockport Co	L	2-3	1-2	22	Onuora [23], Walters [49]	7691
13	9	H	Huddersfield T	W	3-0	3-0	—	Onuora [1], Walters [14], Bullock [38]	8316
14	17	A	Ipswich T	L	0-1	0-1	21		13,212
15	20	A	Birmingham C	D	1-1	1-0	—	Gooden [74]	19,485
16	24	H	WBA	D	2-2	2-1	21	Hall [11], Walters [37]	8967
17	31	H	QPR	W	3-1	1-1	19	Walters 2 (1 pen) [45 (pl), 90], Onuora [79]	8500
18	Nov 7	A	Crewe Alex	W	2-0	1-0	17	Onuora 2 [19, 90]	4489
19	14	A	Bradford C	L	0-3	0-0	18		14,897
20	21	H	Crystal Palace	W	2-0	1-0	15	Ndah [22], Walters (pen) [46]	11,718
21	28	A	Grimsby T	L	0-1	0-1	17		5657
22	Dec 5	H	Norwich C	D	1-1	1-1	19	Walters [41]	9262
23	12	H	Bradford C	L	1-4	1-1	19	Onuora [3]	7447
24	19	A	Barnsley	W	3-1	3-0	17	Onuora 2 [15, 26], Hay [28]	15,342
25	26	H	Wolverhampton W	W	1-0	0-0	15	Onuora [89]	11,627
26	28	A	Bristol C	L	1-3	0-1	15	Ndah [46]	16,257
27	Jan 9	H	Sheffield U	D	2-2	1-1	15	Ndah [10], Onuora [47]	7583
28	16	A	Port Vale	W	1-0	0-0	15	Ndah [9]	5405
29	30	H	Bury	D	1-1	0-0	15	West (og) [86]	7797
30	Feb 6	A	Sunderland	L	0-2	0-2	15		41,304
31	13	A	Oxford U	L	0-2	0-1	17		8179
32	20	H	Portsmouth	D	3-3	3-1	17	Hay 2 [31, 40], Onuora [44]	10,230
33	26	A	Watford	W	1-0	1-0	—	Howe [45]	8692
34	Mar 3	H	Tranmere R	L	2-3	1-0	—	Reeves 2 [44, 67]	5765
35	6	H	Bolton W	D	3-3	1-0	15	Howe [17], Hay [48], Walters [68]	8392
36	9	A	Stockport Co	L	1-2	0-2	—	Walters [61]	6048
37	13	H	Crewe Alex	L	1-2	0-2	18	Hay [55]	7434
38	20	A	QPR	L	0-4	0-0	18		11,184
39	Apr 3	H	Ipswich T	L	0-6	0-4	19		10,337
40	5	A	Huddersfield T	W	2-1	0-0	17	Howe [19], Hay [67]	11,719
41	10	H	Birmingham C	L	0-1	0-0	18		8896
42	13	A	WBA	D	1-1	1-1	—	Ndah [32]	9601
43	17	A	Crystal Palace	W	1-0	0-0	17	Onuora [51]	18,660
44	24	H	Grimsby T	W	2-0	1-0	17	Onuora [3], Ndah [47]	7197
45	May 1	A	Norwich C	L	1-2	0-0	17	Onuora (pen) [47]	17,306
46	9	H	Barnsley	L	1-3	1-2	17	Griffin [7]	8182

Final League Position: 17

GOALSCORERS

League (59): Onuora 20 (1 pen), Ndah 11, Walters 10 (3 pens), Hay 6, Howe 3, Reeves 2, Bullock 1, Gooden 1, Griffin 1, Hall 1, own goals 3.
Worthington Cup (2): Ndah 1, Reeves 1.
FA Cup (1): Walters 1.

Talia F 43	Robinson M 25+4	Hall G 39+2	Gooden T 36+2	Reeves A 23+1	Borrows B 40	Watters M 31+7	Hay C 16+11	Onuora I 40+3	Bullock D 17+5	Ndah G 40+1	Davis S 21+4	Leitch S 23+1	Cuervo P 2+4	Kerslake D 12+2	Hulbert R 7+9	Glass J 3	Taylor C 18+3	Cowe S 2+3	Howe B 20+3	Willis A 11	Watson K 9+9	Campagna S —+2	Fenn N 4	Griffin C 1+4	Collins L 2+2	Davies G 6	Linton D 7+1	Bradley S 6+1	Williams J 1+2	McAreavey P —+1	McHugh F 1	Match No.
1	2	3	4	5	6	7	8¹	9	10	11	12																					1
1	2	3	11	5	6	7		9	10	8		4¹	12																			2
1		3	11	5	6	7	9	12	10	8¹	4²	13	2																			3
1		3	11	5	6	7		9	10	8		12	2	4¹																		4
1		3¹¹	5	6	7		9	10	8	12		2	4																			5
1		3	11	5	6¹	7		9	10	8	12	4²		2	13																	6
		3	11	5	6	7		9	10	8		4		2	1																	7
1	12	3	11	5	6	7		9	10¹	8		4		2																		8
1		3	11	5	6	7		10	8		4	2¹		12	9²	13																9
1	2		11	5	6	7		10	8	4		9¹		12		3																10
1	2		11	5	6	7	12	10	3		9¹			8²	13	4																11
1	2		11	5	6	7		9	10¹	3	4	12		8																		12
1	2	3	11	5	6	7		9	10	8	4																					13
1	2	3	11		6	7	12	9¹	10³	8	13	4²				5	14															14
1	2	3	11		6	7	12	9¹	10	8	4					5²	13															15
1	2	3	11	5	6	7	12	9		8¹		10				4																16
1	2	3	11	5²	6	7		9	12	8³	4	10¹	13			14																17
1	2	3	11		6		8¹	9	10	4		7²	12			5	13															18
1		3	11	6¹	7²		9		4	12		2		5	8	13	10															19
1	2	3	11¹²	6	7	9	12	13	4		14	5	8¹	10³																		20
1	2	3	6²	7	9	11	4	12		13	14	5	8³	10¹																		21
1	2	3²	6	7¹	14	9	12		11	4		13		5	8	10³																22
1	2¹	3	6²	7	9	12	10	11	4		13	5	8																			23
1	2	3	12	8¹	9	13	10	11	4	6²	5	7																				24
1	2	3	6	12	8	9	10	7²	11	4¹	5	13																				25
1	2¹	3	12	7	8²	9³	10	6	11	4	5	13	14																			26
1	2	3	10	6	9	8	11	4		5	7																					27
1	2¹	3	10	6	9	8	11	4	12	5	7																					28
1		3	10¹	5	7	12	9	8	11	4	2	6																				29
1	12	3²	13	6	7	10	9²	8	11¹	2	5	4	14																			30
1	12	3	11	6	7	13	9	8	4²	2³	14	5¹	10																			31
1	2	3	12	6	10	9	8	11¹	4	13	5	7²																				32
1	2¹	11	3	6	10	9	8	4	12	5	7²	13																				33
1	11	3	6	10	9	8	4¹	12	5	7	2																					34
1	12	11	3	6¹	9	10	8²	4	7	13	2	5																				35
1	12	11	3	6	9	10	13	8	4³	2¹	7	14	5²																			36
1	5	11	3	6¹	4	10	9	8	2	7	12																					37
1	5	11²	3	6	2	10¹	9	8	4		1	7	12	13																		38
	5	11	3	6³	12	13	9	8²		14	1	4	7	2	10¹																	39
1	5	11		12	13	9²	8	6¹	4	7¹	6	3	2	10²																		40
1	5	11		12	13	9²	8	4	7¹	6	3	2	10																			41
1	5	11		12	13	9²	8	4	7	6³	3¹	2	10	14																		42
1	12	5	11	6	13	4²	9	8	7	14	3¹	2	10³																			43
1	5	3	11	6	4²	12	9	8	7	13	2³	10¹	14																			44
1	5	3		6	10¹	9	8	11	7²	4	2	12	13																			45
1	5	3		6²	9	8	11	7¹	12	13	10	2	4																			46

Worthington Cup
First Round   Wycombe W   (h) 2-1   (a) 0-2

FA Cup
Third Round   Barnsley   (h) 0-0   (a) 1-3

Division 3

TORQUAY UNITED

FOUNDATION

The idea of establishing a Torquay club was agreed by old boys of Torquay College and Torbay College, while sitting in Princess Gardens listening to the band. A proper meeting was subsequently held at Tor Abbey Hotel at which officers were elected. This was on 1 May 1899 and the club's first competition was the Eastern League (later known as the East Devon League). As an amateur club it played at Teignmouth Road, Torquay Recreation Ground and Cricket Field Road before settling down for four years at Torquay Cricket Ground where the rugby club now plays. They became Torquay United in 1921 after merging with Babbacombe FC.

Plainmoor Ground, Torquay, Devon TQ1 3PS.

Telephone: (01803) 328666.

Fax: (01803) 323976.

Ground Capacity: 6003.

Record Attendance: 21,908 v Huddersfield T, FA Cup 4th rd, 29 January 1955.

Record Receipts: £26,205 v Exeter C, Division 3, 1 January 1992.

Pitch Measurements: 112yd × 74yd.

Chairman: M. Benney.

Managing Director: Miss H. Kindeleit.

Directors: M. Bateson, Mrs S. Bateson, I. Hayman, B. Palk.

Manager: Wes Saunders.

Physio: Norman Medhurst.

Company Secretary: Miss H. Kindeleit.

LATEST SEQUENCES

Longest Sequence of League Wins: 8, 24.1.98 – 3.3.98.

Longest Sequence of League Defeats: 8, 30.9.95 – 18.11.95.

Longest Sequence of League Draws: 8, 25.10.69 – 13.12.69.

Longest Sequence of Unbeaten League Matches: 15, 5.5.90 – 3.11.90.

Longest Sequence Without a League Win: 17, 5.3.38 – 10.9.38.

HONOURS

Football League: Division 3 best season: 4th, 1967–68; Division 3 (S) – Runners-up 1956–57; Division 4 – Promoted 1959–60 (3rd), 1965–66 (3rd), 1990–91 (play-offs).

FA Cup: best season: 4th rd, 1949, 1955, 1971, 1983, 1990.

Football League Cup: never past 3rd rd.

Sherpa Van Trophy: Runners-up 1989.

Colours
Yellow and white striped shirts, navy shorts, yellow stockings.

Change Colours
White shirts, white shorts, white stockings.

Year Formed: 1899.

Turned Professional: 1921.

Ltd Co.: 1921.

Previous Name: 1910, Torquay Town; 1921, Torquay United.

Club Nickname: 'The Gulls'.

Previous Grounds: 1899, Teignmouth Road; 1900, Torquay Recreation Ground; 1904, Cricket Field Road; 1906, Torquay Cricket Ground; 1910, Plainmoor Ground.

First Football League Game: 27 August 1927, Division 3 (S), v Exeter C (h) D 1–1 – Millsom; Cook, Smith; Wellock, Wragg, Connor, Mackey, Turner (1), Jones, McGovern, Thomson.

Record League Victory: 9–0 v Swindon T, Division 3 (S), 8 March 1952 – George Webber; Topping, Ralph Calland; Brown, Eric Webber, Towers; Shaw (1), Marchant (1), Northcott (2), Collins (3), Edds (2).

Record Cup Victory: 7–1 v Northampton T, FA Cup 1st rd, 14 November 1959 – Gill; Penford, Downs; Bettany, George Northcott, Rawson; Baxter, Cox, Tommy Northcott (1), Bond (3), Pym (3).

Record Defeat: 2–10 v Fulham, Division 3 (S), 7 September 1931. 2–10 v Luton T, Division 3 (S), 2 September 1933.

Most League Points (2 for a win): 60, Division 4, 1959–60.

Most League Points (3 for a win): 77, Division 4, 1987–88.

Most League Goals: 89, Division 3 (S), 1956–57.

Highest League Scorer in Season: Sammy Collins, 40, Division 3 (S), 1955–56.

Most League Goals in Total Aggregate: Sammy Collins, 204, 1948–58.

Most League Goals in One Match: 5, Robin Stubbs v Newport Co, Division 4, 19 October 1963.

Most Capped Player: Rodney Jack, St Vincent.

Most League Appearances: Dennis Lewis, 443, 1947–59.

Youngest League Player: David Byng, 16 years 36 days v Walsall, 14 August 1993.

Record Transfer Fee Received: £500,000 from Crewe Alex for Rodney Jack, July 1998.

Record Transfer Fee Paid: £70,000 to Barry T for Eifion Williams, March 1999.

Football League Record: 1927 Elected to Division 3 (S); 1958–60 Division 4; 1960–62 Division 3; 1962–66 Division 4; 1966–72 Division 3; 1972–91 Division 4; 1991– Division 3.

MANAGERS

Percy Mackrill 1927–29
A. H. Hoskins 1929 *(Secretary-Manager)*
Frank Womack 1929–32
Frank Brown 1932–38
Alf Steward 1938–40
Billy Butler 1945–46
Jack Butler 1946–47
John McNeil 1947–50
Bob John 1950
Alex Massie 1950–51
Eric Webber 1951–65
Frank O'Farrell 1965–68
Alan Brown 1969–71
Jack Edwards 1971–73
Malcolm Musgrove 1973–76
Mike Green 1977–81
Frank O'Farrell 1981–82
(continued as General Manager to 1983)
Bruce Rioch 1982–84
Dave Webb 1984–85
John Sims 1985
Stuart Morgan 1985–87
Cyril Knowles 1987–89
Dave Smith 1989–91
John Impey 1991–92
Ivan Golac 1992
Paul Compton 1992–93
Don O'Riordan 1993–95
Eddie May 1995–96
Kevin Hodges *(Head Coach)* 1996–98
Wes Saunders July 1998–

TEN YEAR LEAGUE RECORD

		P	W	D	L	F	A	Pts	Pos
1988-89	Div 4	46	17	8	21	45	60	59	14
1989-90	Div 4	46	15	12	19	53	66	57	15
1990-91	Div 4	46	18	18	10	64	47	72	7
1991-92	Div 3	46	13	8	25	42	68	47	23
1992-93	Div 3	42	12	7	23	45	67	43	19
1993-94	Div 3	42	17	16	9	64	56	67	6
1994-95	Div 3	42	14	13	15	54	57	55	13
1995-96	Div 3	46	5	14	27	30	84	29	24
1996-97	Div 3	46	13	11	22	46	62	50	21
1997-98	Div 3	46	21	11	14	68	59	74	5

DID YOU KNOW ?

Torquay United won the Southern League in 1926–27 by .002 of a goal from Bristol City reserves and were elected to the Football League by a seven-vote margin after a tie with Aberdare Athletic who were seeking re-election.

TORQUAY UNITED 1998–99 LEAGUE RECORD

Match No.	Date	Venue	Opponents	Result		H/T Score	Lg. Pos.	Goalscorers	Attendance
1	Aug 8	H	Cambridge U	L	0-1	0-0	—		2428
2	15	A	Rochdale	W	2-0	1-0	12	Partridge 2 [14, 52]	1713
3	22	H	Exeter C	W	1-0	0-0	8	Partridge [85]	3739
4	29	A	Brighton & HA	L	0-2	0-0	11		2703
5	Sept 1	H	Leyton Orient	D	1-1	0-1	—	Tully [51]	2384
6	5	A	Scunthorpe U	L	0-2	0-2	17		2421
7	8	H	Brentford	W	3-1	0-1	—	Hill [71], Partridge [77], McFarlane [79]	2340
8	12	A	Chester C	L	0-2	0-1	16		1729
9	19	H	Swansea C	D	1-1	1-0	18	Hill [6]	2527
10	26	A	Halifax T	D	1-1	0-0	19	McFarlane [84]	2753
11	Oct 3	H	Plymouth Arg	D	1-1	0-0	18	Partridge [57]	5719
12	9	A	Mansfield T	L	1-2	0-1	—	Partridge [84]	3573
13	17	H	Carlisle U	D	2-2	2-2	20	McGorry [9], Bedeau [44]	2211
14	20	H	Darlington	D	2-2	1-0	—	Gurney [44], Tully [58]	1775
15	24	A	Hartlepool U	L	1-4	0-1	21	Bedeau [52]	1593
16	31	A	Scarborough	D	1-1	0-0	21	Bedeau [85]	1365
17	Nov 7	H	Cardiff C	D	0-0	0-0	21		3342
18	10	A	Rotherham U	D	2-2	1-0	—	Partridge [8], Hill [62]	3708
19	21	H	Peterborough U	L	0-1	0-0	22		2093
20	28	A	Barnet	L	1-3	0-1	23	Thomas [82]	1665
21	Dec 12	H	Hull C	W	2-0	2-0	22	Leadbitter [15], Partridge [39]	2033
22	18	A	Shrewsbury T	W	2-1	1-0	—	Partridge 2 [33, 89]	1934
23	26	A	Exeter C	D	1-1	0-0	20	Lee [55]	5575
24	28	H	Southend U	W	2-0	1-0	18	Lee [44], Partridge [88]	3228
25	Jan 2	A	Brighton & HA	D	1-1	1-0	18	Hill [11]	3663
26	9	A	Cambridge U	L	0-2	0-0	19		3936
27	16	H	Rochdale	W	2-1	1-0	19	Bedeau [16], Partridge [70]	2205
28	30	A	Southend U	D	0-0	0-0	19		3567
29	Feb 6	H	Scunthorpe U	W	1-0	1-0	16	Bedeau [39]	2071
30	13	A	Brentford	L	2-3	1-1	20	Healy [24], McFarlane [81]	4299
31	20	H	Chester C	L	0-3	0-1	20		2384
32	27	A	Swansea C	D	0-0	0-0	20		5594
33	Mar 2	A	Leyton Orient	L	0-2	0-0	—		4099
34	6	H	Halifax T	W	4-0	1-0	19	Robinson [43], Donaldson [49], Hill [54], Bedeau [67]	1715
35	9	A	Plymouth Arg	D	0-0	0-0	—		7856
36	13	A	Cardiff C	D	2-2	1-1	20	Bedeau 2 [34, 65]	6956
37	20	H	Scarborough	L	0-1	0-0	20		1891
38	27	H	Hartlepool U	W	3-0	1-0	18	Williams 3 [37, 58, 73]	1927
39	Apr 3	A	Carlisle U	L	0-3	0-2	20		3765
40	5	H	Mansfield T	D	0-0	0-0	20		2897
41	10	A	Darlington	W	2-0	2-0	17	Bedeau [6], Williams [45]	2248
42	13	H	Barnet	D	1-1	0-0	—	Healy (pen) [58]	2132
43	17	A	Peterborough U	L	0-4	0-1	20		4162
44	24	H	Rotherham U	W	2-0	0-0	17	Williams [60], Simb [89]	2296
45	May 1	A	Hull C	L	0-1	0-1	19		7789
46	8	H	Shrewsbury T	L	0-3	0-3	20		2800

Final League Position: 20

GOALSCORERS

League (47): Partridge 12, Bedeau 9, Hill 5, Williams 5, McFarlane 3, Healy 2 (1 pen), Lee 2, Tully 2, Donaldson 1, Gurney 1, Leadbitter 1, McGorry 1, Robinson 1, Simb 1, Thomas 1.
Worthington Cup (2): Bedeau 1, Thomas 1.
FA Cup (1): Partridge 1.

Gregg M 11	Gurney A 20	Herrera R 39 + 1	Robinson J 29	Thomas W 44	Watson A 8	Clayton G 15	McGorry B 31 + 3	Bedeau A 28 + 8	McFarlane A 5 + 10	Hill K 22 + 13	Tully S 31 + 6	Partridge S 29	Hapgood L 11 + 6	Leadbitter C 37	Donaldson O 7 + 5	Monk G 6	Waddle C 7	Veysey K 10	Hadley S — + 2	Aggrey J 22 + 3	Witter T 4	Lee A 6 + 1	Southall N 25	Healy B 16 + 3	Forrester M 1 + 4	Harries P 5	Nichols J 5 + 1	Jermyn M — + 1	Worthington M — + 1	Platts M 7 + 1	Neil G 6 + 1	Russell L 9	Simb J 3 + 6	Williams E 7	Match No.
1	2	3	4	5	6	7	8	9¹	10	11	12																								1
1	2	3	4	5	6	7	8	9¹	12	11				10																					2
1		3	4	5	6	7	8	9				2	10	11																					3
1	2	3³	4	5²	6	7		9		12	11¹	13	10	14	8																				4
1	2		4		6	7		8¹		9	12	11	5	10	3																				5
1	2	3	4	5	6¹	7		9²		13	12	8	10		11																				6
1	2		4	5		7		9		11		6	10		8¹	3	12																		7
1	2		4	5		7			12	9		11	6¹		8²	3	13																		8
1	2	3¹	4	5		7			12			11	6	10		8	9																		9
1	2	3	4	5		7²	13			12			10		8	9¹	6		11																10
1	2	3	4			7				5	10		8		9	6	11																		11
	2	3¹	4	5		7				12	13		10		8²	9	6	11		1															12
	2	3	4	5			8	9²		12			10		7¹	6	11	1	13																13
	2	3	4¹	5			8	9		12		10			7	6	11	1																	14
	2	3		5			8	9		12	6¹	10			7	4	11	1																	15
	2	3		5	6		8	9				10			7	11		1		4															16
	2	3		5		7	8	9		11		10				1				4	6														17
	2	3		5		7	8	9		11		10				1				4	6														18
	2	3		5		7	8²	9¹		11	13	10				1	12			4	6														19
	2	3		5		7		9²		12	10	8¹	11			1				4	6	13													20
		3	4	5			8			11	2	10		6						7				9	1										21
		3	4	5			8	12		11	2	10		7						6				9¹	1										22
		3	4	5			8			11	2	10		6						7				9	1										23
		3	4	5			8	12		11²	2	10		6						7				9¹	1	13									24
		3	4	5			8	12		11	2²	10¹		6						7				9	1	13									25
	2	3⁴	4	5	7		8			11²	12	10		6¹						9				1	13	14									26
		3²	4	5	6		8	9¹	12	11	2	10								13				1	7										27
		3	4	5			8²	9	12	13	2	10¹	14	6²						7				1	11										28
		3	4	5			8	9¹	12	13	2	10		6¹						11				1	7										29
		3²	4	5			8	9	12	13	2	10		6¹						11				1	7										30
			4	5			8¹	9	10	11	2		12	3	13					6²				1	7										31
		3	4	5			8	10¹	7	2			6	12						11				1		9									32
			4	5			8	12		7²	2		13	6	10					11¹				1		9	3								33
			4	5				9		11³	2²		8	6	10¹					7				1	7	13		12	3	13	14				34
	12		4	5			13	9			2		8²	6						7				1		14	10	3¹		11³					35
		3		5			8	9					6							4				1	7		10¹			11					36
		3		5			8	9		2			6	12						4				1	7					11					37
		3		5			8			12	2		13	9³										1	7					11¹	4	6	14	10²	38
		3		5			8²	12		13	2		11³						14					1	7						4	6	9	10¹	39
		3		5				9¹		11	2		8											1	7						4	6	12	10	40
		3		5				9¹		12	2		8²	11										1	7		13			13	4	6	14	10³	41
		3		5			12	9			2		8¹	11										1	7	13					4	6		10²	42
		3		5			8			2²	12	4							1	11					7	9³	13			10¹		6	14		43
		3		5				9¹		12	2		8							4²				1	7¹					11	13	6	14	10	44
		3		5				9²		12	2		8¹	4										1	7¹					11		6	13	10	45
		3		5						12	13		8²	4					14					1	7¹		2			11³		6	9	10	46

Worthington Cup

First Round	Crystal Palace	(h)	1-1	
		(a)	1-2	

FA Cup

First Round	Worcester C	(a)	1-0	
Second Round	Bournemouth	(h)	0-1	

FA Premiership **TOTTENHAM HOTSPUR**

FOUNDATION

The Hotspur Football Club was formed from an older cricket club in 1882. Most of the founders were old boys of St John's Presbyterian School and Tottenham Grammar School. The Casey brothers were well to the fore as the family provided the club's first goalposts (painted blue and white) and their first ball. They soon adopted the local YMCA as their meeting place, but after a couple of moves settled at the Red House, which is still their headquarters, although now known simply as 748 High Road.

Bill Nicholson Way, 748 High Rd, Tottenham, London N17 0AP.
Telephone: (0181) 365 5000. *Fax:* (0181) 365 5005.
Commercial Dept: (0181) 365 5010. *Ticketline:* 0891 100505.
Ticket Office: (0181) 365 5050.
Spurs Line: 0891 100500. *Members Ticketline:* (0181) 365 5100.
Ground Capacity: 36,236.
Record Attendance: 75,038 v Sunderland, FA Cup 6th rd, 5 March 1938.
Record Receipts: £336,702 v Manchester U, Division 1, 28 September 1991.
Pitch Measurements: 110yd × 73yd.
Directors: A. M. Sugar (Chairman), J. Sedgwick (Finance Director), David Pleat (Director of Football).
Non-Executive Directors: A. G. Berry (Deputy Chairman), D. A. Alexiou, I. Yawetz, C. T. Sandy.
President: W. E. Nicholson OBE.
Vice-President: N. Solomon.
Manager: George Graham.
Assistant Manager: Stewart Houston.
Reserve Team Manager: Theo Foley.
Physio: Alasdair Beattie.
Club Secretary: Peter Barnes.
Commercial Manager: Mike Rollo.
PRO: John Fennelly.

LATEST SEQUENCES

Longest Sequence of League Wins: 13, 23.4.60 – 1.10.60.
Longest Sequence of League Defeats: 7, 1.1.94 – 27.2.94.
Longest Sequence of League Draws: 6, 9.1.99 – 27.2.99.
Longest Sequence of Unbeaten League Matches: 22, 31.8.49 – 31.12.49.
Longest Sequence Without a League Win: 16, 29.12.34 – 13.4.35.

HONOURS

Football League: Division 1 – Champions 1950–51, 1960–61; Runners-up 1921–22, 1951–52, 1956–57, 1962–63; Division 2 – Champions 1919–20, 1949–50; Runners-up 1908–09, 1932–33; Promoted 1977–78 (3rd).

FA Cup: Winners 1901 (as non-League club), 1921, 1961, 1962, 1967, 1981, 1982, 1991; Runners-up 1987.

Football League Cup: Winners 1971, 1973, 1999; Runners-up 1982.

European Competitions: European Cup: 1961–62. European Cup-Winners' Cup: 1962–63 (winners), 1963–64, 1967–68, 1981–82, 1982–83, 1991–92. UEFA Cup: 1971–72 (winners), 1972–73, 1973–74 (runners-up), 1983–84 (winners), 1984–85.

Colours
White shirts, navy blue shorts, navy blue stockings.

Change Colours
Gold and navy shirts, white shorts, white stockings.

Year Formed: 1882.

Turned Professional: 1895.

Ltd Co.: 1898.

Previous Name: 1882–84, Hotspur Football Club.

Club Nickname: 'Spurs'.

Previous Grounds: 1882, Tottenham Marshes; 1888, Northumberland Park; 1899, White Hart Lane.

First Football League Game: 1 September 1908, Division 2, v Wolverhampton W (h) W 3–0 – Hewitson; Coquet, Burton; Morris (1), D. Steel, Darnell; Walton, Woodward (2), Macfarlane, R. Steel, Middlemiss.

Record League Victory: 9–0 v Bristol R, Division 2, 22 October 1977 – Daines; Naylor, Holmes, Hoddle (1), McAllister, Perryman, Pratt, McNab, Moores (3), Lee (4), Taylor (1).

Record Cup Victory: 13–2 v Crewe Alex, FA Cup 4th rd (replay), 3 February 1960 – Brown; Hills, Henry; Blanchflower, Norman, Mackay; White, Harmer (1), Smith (4), Allen (5), Jones (3 incl. 1p).

Record Defeat: 0–8 v Cologne, UEFA Inter Toto Cup, 22 July 1995.

Most League Points (2 for a win): 70, Division 2, 1919–20.

Most League Points (3 for a win): 77, Division 1, 1984–85.

Most League Goals: 115, Division 1, 1960–61.

Highest League Scorer in Season: Jimmy Greaves, 37, Division 1, 1962–63.

Most League Goals in Total Aggregate: Jimmy Greaves, 220, 1961–70.

Most League Goals in One Match: 5, Ted Harper v Reading, Division 2, 30 August 1930; 5, Alf Stokes v Birmingham C, Division 1, 18 September 1957; 5, Bobby Smith v Aston Villa, Division 1, 29 March 1958.

Most Capped Player: Pat Jennings, 74 (119), Northern Ireland.

Most League Appearances: Steve Perryman, 655, 1969–86.

Youngest League Player: Ally Dick, 16 years 301 days v Manchester C, 20 February 1982.

Record Transfer Fee Received: £5,500,000 from Lazio for Paul Gascoigne, May 1992.

Record Transfer Fee Paid: £6,000,000 to Newcastle U for Les Ferdinand, July 1997.

Football League Record: 1908 Elected to Division 2; 1909–15 Division 1; 1919–20 Division 2; 1920–28 Division 1; 1928–33 Division 2; 1933–35 Division 1; 1935–50 Division 2; 1950–77 Division 1; 1977–78 Division 2; 1978–92 Division 1; 1992– FA Premier League.

MANAGERS

Frank Brettell 1898–99
John Cameron 1899–1906
Fred Kirkham 1907–08
Peter McWilliam 1912–27
Billy Minter 1927–29
Percy Smith 1930–35
Jack Tresadern 1935–38
Peter McWilliam 1938–42
Arthur Turner 1942–46
Joe Hulme 1946–49
Arthur Rowe 1949–55
Jimmy Anderson 1955–58
Bill Nicholson 1958–74
Terry Neill 1974–76
Keith Burkinshaw 1976–84
Peter Shreeves 1984–86
David Pleat 1986–87
Terry Venables 1987–91
Peter Shreeves 1991–92
Ossie Ardiles 1993–94
Gerry Francis 1994–97
Christian Gross *(Head Coach)* 1997–98
George Graham October 1998–

TEN YEAR LEAGUE RECORD

		P	W	D	L	F	A	Pts	Pos
1988-89	Div 1	38	15	12	11	60	46	57	6
1989-90	Div 1	38	19	6	13	59	47	63	3
1990-91	Div 1	38	11	16	11	51	50	49	10
1991-92	Div 1	42	15	7	20	58	63	52	15
1992-93	PR Lge	42	16	11	15	60	66	59	8
1993-94	PR Lge	42	11	12	19	54	59	45	15
1994-95	PR Lge	42	16	14	12	66	58	62	7
1995-96	PR Lge	38	16	13	9	50	38	61	8
1996-97	PR Lge	38	13	7	18	44	51	46	10
1997-98	PR Lge	38	11	11	16	44	56	44	14

DID YOU KNOW ?

Tottenham Hotspur were not only the first British club to win a European trophy, but their 5–1 Cup-Winners' Cup success over Atletico Madrid in 1963 remains the biggest British victory in any of the three major finals.

TOTTENHAM HOTSPUR 1998–99 LEAGUE RECORD

Match No.	Date	Venue	Opponents	Result	H/T Score	Lg. Pos.	Goalscorers	Attendance
1	Aug 15	A	Wimbledon	L	1-3	0-0	—	Fox [74]	23,031
2	22	H	Sheffield W	L	0-3	0-2	19		32,075
3	29	A	Everton	W	1-0	1-0	14	Ferdinand [5]	39,378
4	Sept 9	H	Blackburn R	W	2-1	1-1	—	Ferdinand [26], Nielsen [50]	28,338
5	13	H	Middlesbrough	L	0-3	0-2	12		30,437
6	19	A	Southampton	D	1-1	1-0	12	Fox [25]	15,204
7	26	H	Leeds U	D	3-3	1-2	13	Vega [14], Iversen [71], Campbell [90]	35,535
8	Oct 3	A	Derby Co	W	1-0	0-0	12	Campbell [60]	30,083
9	19	A	Leicester C	L	1-2	1-1	—	Ferdinand [12]	20,787
10	24	H	Newcastle U	W	2-0	1-0	8	Iversen 2 [40, 76]	36,047
11	Nov 2	H	Charlton Ath	D	2-2	0-1	—	Nielsen [50], Armstrong [57]	32,202
12	7	A	Aston Villa	L	2-3	0-2	14	Anderton (pen) [65], Vega [76]	39,241
13	14	A	Arsenal	D	0-0	0-0	14		38,278
14	21	H	Nottingham F	W	2-0	0-0	10	Armstrong [59], Nielsen [69]	35,832
15	28	H	West Ham U	L	1-2	0-1	12	Armstrong [72]	26,044
16	Dec 5	H	Liverpool	W	2-1	1-0	11	Fox [26], Carragher (og) [50]	36,125
17	12	H	Manchester U	D	2-2	0-2	11	Campbell 2 [70, 90]	36,058
18	19	A	Chelsea	L	0-2	0-0	13		34,881
19	26	A	Coventry C	D	1-1	1-0	13	Campbell [17]	23,091
20	28	H	Everton	W	4-1	1-1	12	Ferdinand [24], Armstrong 3 [63, 76, 81]	36,053
21	Jan 9	A	Sheffield W	D	0-0	0-0	12		28,204
22	16	H	Wimbledon	D	0-0	0-0	11		32,422
23	30	A	Blackburn R	D	1-1	0-1	11	Iversen [61]	29,643
24	Feb 6	H	Coventry C	D	0-0	0-0	11		34,376
25	20	A	Middlesbrough	D	0-0	0-0	13		34,687
26	27	H	Derby Co	D	1-1	0-0	12	Sherwood [69]	35,392
27	Mar 2	H	Southampton	W	3-0	1-0	—	Armstrong [19], Iversen [68], Dominguez [90]	28,580
28	10	A	Leeds U	L	0-2	0-1	—		34,561
29	13	A	Aston Villa	W	1-0	0-0	10	Sherwood [88]	35,963
30	Apr 3	H	Leicester C	L	0-2	0-1	12		35,415
31	5	A	Newcastle U	D	1-1	0-0	12	Anderton (pen) [50]	36,655
32	17	A	Nottingham F	W	1-0	0-0	10	Iversen [62]	25,181
33	20	A	Charlton Ath	W	4-1	0-1	—	Iversen [57], Campbell [79], Dominguez [89], Ginola [90]	20,043
34	24	H	West Ham U	L	1-2	0-1	10	Ginola [73]	36,089
35	May 1	A	Liverpool	L	2-3	2-0	10	Carragher (og) [13], Iversen [35]	44,007
36	5	H	Arsenal	L	1-3	1-2	—	Anderton [43]	36,019
37	10	H	Chelsea	D	2-2	1-1	—	Iversen [38], Ginola [64]	35,878
38	16	A	Manchester U	L	1-2	1-1	11	Ferdinand [24]	55,189

Final League Position: 11

GOALSCORERS

League (47): Iversen 9, Armstrong 7, Campbell 6, Ferdinand 5, Anderton 3 (2 pens), Fox 3, Ginola 3, Nielsen 3, Dominguez 2, Sherwood 2, Vega 2, own goals 2.
Worthington Cup (17): Armstrong 5, Nielsen 3, Campbell 2, Iversen 2, Carr 1, Dominguez 1, Ginola 1, Scales 1, Vega 1.
FA Cup (13): Ginola 3, Nielsen 3, Anderton 2 (1 pen), Iversen 2, Fox 1, Sherwood 1, Sinton 1.

Walker I 25	Carr S 37	Tramezzani P 6	Berti N 4	Vega R 13 + 3	Campbell S 37	Anderton D 31 + 1	Fox R 17 + 3	Armstrong C 24 + 10	Ferdinand L 22 + 2	Ginola D 30	Nielsen A 24 + 4	Saib M — + 4	Dominguez J 2 + 11	Baardsen E 12	Calderwood C 11 + 1	Clemence S 9 + 9	Sinton A 12 + 10	Segers H 1	Edinburgh J 14 + 2	Iversen S 22 + 5	Scales J 7	Allen R — + 5	Young L 14 + 1	Freund S 17	Taricco M 12 + 1	Sherwood T 12 + 2	Nilsen R 3	King L — + 1	Match No.
1	2	3	4[1]	5	6	7[2]	8	9	10	11	12	13																	1
1	2	3[2]		5[1]	6	7	8	9	10	11	4	12	13																2
	2	3		5	6	7	8	12	9[1]	11	10			1	4														3
	2	3	4	5			10	9		11[2]	8	12		1	6	7[1]	13												4
	2	3	4		6	7[3]	12	9		11	8[2]	13		1	5	10[1]	14												5
	2	3	8[1]	4	6	7		9		11			12		5	10		1											6
	2[1]			5	6	7	8	9	10[3]		4		13	1	12	11[2]			3	14									7
	2		4		6	7	10[2]	12	9	11[1]	8			1	5		13		3										8
	2		4		6	7	8	12	9	11[1]	13			1	5	10[2]			3										9
	2				6	7		9	10[2]	11[1]	8			1	5	12			3	13	4								10
	2				6	7		10[2]	9		8			1	5	12	11[1]		3		4	13							11
	2			12	6	7		10[2]		11	8			1	5[2]	13			3[1]	9	4	14							12
	2			5	6	7		9			8			1	11[1]	12			3	10	4								13
	2				6	7		9[3]		11	8			1	5[1]	12	13		3[2]	10	4	14							14
	2				6	7	12	9		11	8			1	4[1]				3	10			5						15
1	2				6	7	8	9	12	11	4								3	10[1]			5						16
1	2				6	7	8[1]			11	4								3		12		5						17
1	2				6	7	8[3]	9	10	11[1]	4					12			3[2]		13	14	5						18
1	2				6	7	8	9	10[2]	11	4					12			3		13		5						19
1	2				6	7	8	9[3]	10	11	4[1]					12			3				5						20
1	2				6	7[2]	12		10	11[3]	8						13		3	14	9		5	4					21
1	2			12	6		13	9		11					5[1]	8[3]	7[2]		3	10	4	14							22
1	2			5	6	7	12	10		11[1]	8								3	9	4								23
1	2				6	7	12	10		11	8									9[1]	4	13	5		3[2]				24
1	2			5	6	7	12	9		11										10[1]				4	3	8			25
1				5	6	7		9[1]	12	11										10				4	3	8	2		26
1	2			12	6	7		9		11[2]							13			10			5[1]	4	3	8			27
1	2				6	7[2]		9	12	11[3]										10[1]		13	5	4	3	8		14	28
1	2			5	6			9	10	11[3]	4					12	13					14			3[1]	8			29
1	2				6	7[1]	12		10	11	8						13			9			5	4	3[2]				30
1	2				6	7		9		11										10			5	4	3	8			31
1	2			12	6	7		9	10[1]	11													5	4	3	8			32
1	2				6	7		9[2]	12	11							13			10			5	4[1]	3	8			33
1	2				6	7[2]	12	9[1]		11							13			10			5	4	3	8			34
1	2				6	7	12	9		11[1]					8[3]					10		13	5	4[2]	3			14	35
1	2				6	7		9	12	11[2]							13			10			5	4	3[1]	8			36
1	2				6	7		9	12	11[2]							13			10			5	4[1]	3	8			37
1	2				6	7			10	11[1]	12[2]						13		3	9		14	5[3]	4		8			38

Worthington Cup

Second Round	Brentford	(a)	3-2
		(h)	3-2
Third Round	Northampton T	(a)	3-1
Fourth Round	Liverpool	(a)	3-1
Fifth Round	Manchester U	(h)	3-1
Semi-Final	Wimbledon	(h)	0-0
		(a)	1-0
Final	Leicester C		1-0
	(at Wembley)		

FA Cup

Third Round	Watford	(h)	5-2
Fourth Round	Wimbledon	(a)	1-1
		(h)	3-0
Fifth Round	Leeds U	(a)	1-1
		(h)	2-0
Sixth Round	Barnsley	(a)	1-0
Semi-Final	Newcastle U		0-2
	(at Old Trafford)		

Division 1 **TRANMERE ROVERS**

FOUNDATION

Formed in 1884 as Belmont they adopted their present title the following year and eventually joined their first league, the West Lancashire League in 1889–90, the same year as their first success in the Wirral Challenge Cup. The club almost folded in 1899–1900 when all the players left en bloc to join a rival club, but they survived the crisis and went from strength to strength winning the 'Combination' title in 1907–08 and the Lancashire Combination in 1913–14. They joined the Football League in 1921 from the Central League.

Prenton Park, Prenton Road West, Birkenhead CH42 9PY.
Telephone: (0151) 608 4194.
Fax: (0151) 608 4385.
Shop: (0151) 608 0438.
Ticket Office: (0151) 609 0137.
Ground Capacity: 16,789 (all seated).
Record Attendance: 24,424 v Stoke C, FA Cup 4th rd, 5 February 1972.
Record Receipts: £130,541 v Sunderland, FA Cup 4th rd, 24 January 1998.
Pitch Measurements: 110yd × 70yd.
Chief Executive: Lorraine Rogers.
Directors: Lorraine Rogers, Mick Horton, Richard Hughes.
Secretary: Mick Horton.
General Manager: Janet Ratcliffe.
Manager: John Aldridge.
Assistant Manager: Kevin Sheedy.
Youth Development Officer: Warwick Rimmer.
Reserve Team Manager: Dave Philpotts.
Physio: Les Parry.

LATEST SEQUENCES

Longest Sequence of League Wins: 9, 9.2.90 – 19.3.90.
Longest Sequence of League Defeats: 8, 29.10.38 – 17.12.38.
Longest Sequence of League Draws: 5, 26.12.97 – 31.1.98.
Longest Sequence of Unbeaten League Matches: 18, 16.3.70 – 4.9.70.
Longest Sequence Without a League Win: 16, 8.11.69 – 14.3.70.

HONOURS

Football League Division 1 best season: 4th, 1992–93; Promoted from Division 3 1990–91 (play-offs); Division 3 (N) – Champions 1937–38; Promotion to 3rd Division: 1966–67, 1975–76; Division 4 – Runners-up 1988–89.

FA Cup: best season: 5th rd, 1968.

Football League Cup: Semi-final 1994.

Welsh Cup: Winners 1935; Runners-up 1934.

Leyland Daf Cup: Winners 1990; Runners-up 1991.

Colours
White shirts, blue shorts.

Change Colours
Navy and sky blue.

Year Formed: 1884.

Turned Professional: 1912.

Ltd Co.: 1920.

Previous Name: 1884, Belmont AFC; 1885, Tranmere Rovers.

Club Nickname: 'The Rovers'.

Previous Grounds: 1884, Steeles Field; 1887, Ravenshaws Field/Old Prenton Park; 1912, Prenton Park.

First Football League Game: 27 August 1921, Division 3 (N), v Crewe Alex (h) W 4–1 – Bradshaw; Grainger, Stuart (1); Campbell, Milnes (1), Heslop; Moreton, Groves (1), Hyam, Ford (1), Hughes.

Record League Victory: 13–4 v Oldham Ath, Division 3 (N), 26 December 1935 – Gray; Platt, Fairhurst; McLaren, Newton, Spencer; Eden, MacDonald (1), Bell (9), Woodward (2), Urmson (1).

Record Cup Victory: 13–0 v Oswestry U, FA Cup 2nd prel rd, 10 October 1914 – Ashcroft; Stevenson, Bullough, Hancock, Taylor, Holden (1), Moreton (1), Cunningham (2), Smith (5), Leck (3), Gould (1).

Record Defeat: 1–9 v Tottenham H, FA Cup 3rd rd (replay), 14 January 1953.

Most League Points (2 for a win): 60, Division 4, 1964–65.

Most League Points (3 for a win): 80, Division 4, 1988–89 and Division 3, 1989–90.

Most League Goals: 111, Division 3 (N), 1930–31.

Highest League Scorer in Season: Bunny Bell, 35, Division 3 (N), 1933–34.

Most League Goals in Total Aggregate: Ian Muir, 142, 1985–95.

Most League Goals in One Match: 9, Bunny Bell v Oldham Ath, Division 3N, 26 December 1935.

Most Capped Player: John Aldridge, 30 (69), Republic of Ireland.

Most League Appearances: Harold Bell, 595, 1946–64 (incl. League record 401 consecutive appearances).

Youngest League Player: Dixie Dean, 16 years 355 days v Rotherham Co, 12 January 1924.

Record Transfer Fee Received: £3,300,000 from Everton for Steve Simonsen, September 1998.

Record Transfer Fee Paid: £450,000 to Aston Villa for Shaun Teale, August 1995.

Football League Record: 1921 Original Member of Division 3 (N): 1938–39 Division 2; 1946–58 Division 3 (N); 1958–61 Division 3; 1961–67 Division 4; 1967–75 Division 3; 1975–76 Division 4; 1976–79 Division 3; 1979–89 Division 4; 1989–91 Division 3; 1991–92 Division 2; 1992– Division 1.

MANAGERS

Bert Cooke 1912–35
Jackie Carr 1935–36
Jim Knowles 1936–39
Bill Ridding 1939–45
Ernie Blackburn 1946–55
Noel Kelly 1955–57
Peter Farrell 1957–60
Walter Galbraith 1961
Dave Russell 1961–69
Jackie Wright 1969–72
Ron Yeats 1972–75
John King 1975–80
Bryan Hamilton 1980–85
Frank Worthington 1985–87
Ronnie Moore 1987
John King 1987–96
John Aldridge April 1996–

TEN YEAR LEAGUE RECORD

		P	W	D	L	F	A	Pts	Pos
1988-89	Div 4	46	21	17	8	62	43	80	2
1989-90	Div 3	46	23	11	12	86	49	80	4
1990-91	Div 3	46	23	9	14	64	46	78	5
1991-92	Div 2	46	14	19	13	56	56	61	14
1992-93	Div 1	46	23	10	13	72	56	79	4
1993-94	Div 1	46	21	9	16	69	53	72	5
1994-95	Div 1	46	22	10	14	67	58	76	5
1995-96	Div 1	46	14	17	15	64	60	59	13
1996-97	Div 1	46	17	14	15	63	56	65	11
1997-98	Div 1	46	14	14	18	54	57	56	14

DID YOU KNOW ?

The first match played under the name of Tranmere Rovers was on 19 September 1885 away against Birkenhead Argyle at Chester Street and ended in a 1–1 draw. Tranmere wore the blue shirts of Belmont.

TRANMERE ROVERS 1998–99 LEAGUE RECORD

Match No.	Date	Venue	Opponents	Result		H/T Score	Lg. Pos.	Goalscorers	Attendance
1	Aug 8	A	Wolverhampton W	L	0-2	0-1	—		20,203
2	15	H	Portsmouth	D	1-1	1-1	21	Mellon [13]	6714
3	22	A	Sunderland	L	0-5	0-2	23		34,155
4	29	H	Bristol C	D	1-1	1-1	22	Parkinson [7]	5960
5	Sept 8	A	QPR	D	0-0	0-0	—		8070
6	11	H	Huddersfield T	L	2-3	0-2	—	Parkinson [66], Koumas [70]	5770
7	19	A	Bury	D	0-0	0-0	24		5030
8	25	H	Swindon T	D	0-0	0-0	—		5501
9	29	H	Ipswich T	L	0-2	0-1	—		5072
10	Oct 3	A	Birmingham C	D	2-2	1-1	24	Irons [31], Jones G [89]	17,189
11	10	A	Oxford U	W	2-1	1-1	24	Allen [42], Jones G [69]	5862
12	17	H	Watford	W	3-2	2-1	22	Irons 2 [5, 37], Mahon [73]	6753
13	20	H	Barnsley	W	3-0	2-0	—	Mahon [5], Jones G [39], Taylor [79]	5194
14	24	A	Crewe Alex	W	4-1	4-0	17	Irons [5], Jones G [6], Taylor [12], Mahon [14]	5080
15	31	H	Stockport Co	D	1-1	0-0	17	Taylor [88]	6597
16	Nov 7	A	Sheffield U	D	2-2	1-1	19	Jones G [26], Hill [72]	15,844
17	10	H	Bradford C	L	0-1	0-1	—		6002
18	14	A	Bolton W	D	2-2	1-0	15	Irons 2 (2 pens) [32, 67]	16,564
19	21	H	Norwich C	L	1-3	0-2	19	Irons [50]	6319
20	28	A	Port Vale	D	2-2	0-1	19	Allen [57], Irons [79]	5216
21	Dec 5	A	Grimsby T	L	1-2	1-1	21	Hill [18]	4937
22	8	A	Crystal Palace	D	1-1	0-0	—	Thompson [66]	12,919
23	12	H	Bolton W	D	1-1	0-1	20	Irons [90]	6959
24	19	A	WBA	W	2-0	0-0	18	Challinor [50], Irons (pen) [68]	13,966
25	26	H	Sunderland	W	1-0	0-0	16	Taylor [64]	14,248
26	28	A	Bradford C	L	0-2	0-1	16		14,076
27	Jan 8	H	Wolverhampton W	L	1-2	1-2	—	Santos [20]	6179
28	16	A	Bristol C	D	1-1	1-1	16	Mahon [8]	13,217
29	30	H	Crystal Palace	W	3-1	2-1	16	Jones L [31], Allen [45], Taylor [69]	6017
30	Feb 6	A	Portsmouth	D	1-1	1-1	16	Taylor [44]	10,597
31	13	H	QPR	W	3-2	1-1	13	Challinor [28], Jones L [67], Allen [70]	5896
32	20	A	Huddersfield T	D	0-0	0-0	14		11,411
33	27	H	Bury	W	4-0	1-0	13	Allen [23], O'Brien [56], Taylor [66], Koumas [79]	6002
34	Mar 3	A	Swindon T	W	3-2	0-1	—	Taylor [57], Kelly [78], Koumas [84]	5765
35	6	A	Ipswich T	L	0-1	0-0	13		15,929
36	9	H	Birmingham C	L	0-1	0-0	—		7184
37	13	H	Sheffield U	L	2-3	2-0	14	Hill [10], Mahon [42]	6588
38	20	A	Stockport Co	D	0-0	0-0	14		7589
39	26	H	Crewe Alex	W	3-0	2-0	—	Taylor [10], O'Brien [43], Irons [53]	9359
40	Apr 3	A	Watford	L	1-2	0-0	15	Kelly [53]	8682
41	5	H	Oxford U	D	2-2	2-0	15	Irons 2 (2 pens) [4, 24]	7837
42	10	A	Barnsley	D	1-1	1-0	16	Irons [29]	15,133
43	17	A	Norwich C	D	2-2	1-1	15	Kelly [9], Hill [75]	14,735
44	24	H	Port Vale	D	1-1	1-0	15	Mahon (pen) [45]	7770
45	May 1	A	Grimsby T	L	0-1	0-1	15		5916
46	9	H	WBA	W	3-1	2-0	15	Van Blerk (og) [17], Irons (pen) [19], Kelly [86]	10,540

Final League Position: 15

GOALSCORERS

League (63): Irons 15 (6 pens), Taylor 9, Mahon 6 (1 pen), Allen 5, Jones G 5, Hill 4, Kelly 4, Koumas 3, Challinor 2, Jones L 2, O'Brien 2, Parkinson 2, Mellon 1, Santos 1, Thompson 1, own goal 1.
Worthington Cup (8): Irons 3 (2 pens), Kelly 2, Jones L 1, Koumas 1, Parkinson 1.
FA Cup (0).

Simonsen S 5	Frail S 5	Thompson A 37	McGreal J 36	Hill C 33	Irons K 43	Morrissey J 5 + 19	Santos G 37	Kelly D 16 + 11	Russell C 3 + 1	Mellon M 21 + 3	Jones G 15 + 11	Parkinson A 20 + 9	Jones L 18 + 12	Morgan A 4 + 2	Sharps I — + 1	Koumas J 11 + 12	Coyne D 17	Allen G 41	O'Brien L 18 + 5	Mahon A 34 + 5	Challinor D 29 + 5	Achterberg J 24	Taylor S 31 + 5	Gibson N — + 1	Shepherd P — + 1	Williams R 2 + 3	Hinds R 1 + 1	Match No.
1	2	3	4	5	6	7^1	8	9	10^2	11	12	13																1
1	2	3	4	5	6	7	8^1	9^2		11	12	10	13															2
1	2	3	4^2		6	12		9^1	10	8	7	11	5	13^3	14													3
		3		5	6	7^2	12			14	9	10	11^1			2^3	1	4	13	8								4
		3		5	6		12	8		7	9	10	11^1				1	2	4									5
1		3		5	6	7^2	8^1			10^3	9	11	12			13		2	4	14								6
1		4	3		6	12	8^2				13	9	14			7^1		2	10	11^3	5							7
		4	3		6	12	8				13	9^1	11^3			7		2	10^2	14	5	1						8
		3	4	7^1	6	12	8^2				10	13	11			9^3		2	14	5	1							9
		3^1	4	8	6	12					10	9	13			7^2		2	11	5	1							10
2				5	6		8				10	9	12			7	3		4	1			11^1					11
2^1		4			6	12	8				10	9	13			7^3	3		14	5	1		11^2					12
		3	4	5	6	12	8	13			10	9^2	14			2		7^1		1			11^3					13
		3	4	5	6	12	8	13			10	9^1				2		7^2		1			11					14
		3^1	4	5^3	6	12	8	13			10^2	9				2		7^2	14	1			11					15
		3	4	5^3	6	12	8^1	13			10	9				2		7^2	14	1			11					16
		3^1		5	6	12	8	13			10	9				2		7^2	4	1			11					17
		3		5	6	12	8	13			10	9^2				2		7^1	4	1			11					18
		3			6	7^2	8	9			10^1	12				2		4	5	1			11	13				19
		3		5	6	12		9			10	13	8^1			14		2	7^3	4	1		11^2					20
		3	4		6	8^2	9				10^1	11				7		2	12	5	1		13					21
		3	4		6	12	8	9			13		11^3			7^2		2	10^1	5	14							22
		3	4	2^2	6	12	8	9^3			13	14				7^1	1		10	5	11							23
		3	4		6		8	9^1			7	12				1	2	10		5	11							24
		3	4	5	6^1		8				10	9	12			1	2	7			11							25
		3	4	5	6^2	12	8				10	9	14			13	1	2	7^3		11^1							26
		3	4		6	12	8	9^2			13		14			1	2	11^3	7	5			10^1					27
		3	4	10	6			12			9^2	13				1	2	8^1	7	5			11					28
			4		6	8		12			3^1	11				13	1	2	9^2	7	5		10					29
		3	4	9	6^2		8				12	14	11^3			1	2	13	7^1	5			10					30
		3	4	6^2			8				9^1	11				12	1	2	13	7^1	5		10					31
		3	4		6		8				11					12	1	2	9	7^1	5		10					32
		3	4	5	6	12		13			8	11^3	14			1	2	9^2	7				10^1					33
		3	4	5^2	6	12					8	11^1	13			1	2	9^3	7	14			10					34
		3	4	5^2	6	12					8	11^1	13			1	2	9^2	7	14			10					35
		3	4	5^2	6	12					8	11^2	13			1	2	9^1	7	14			10					36
		3	4	5	6		8	12			9	13	11^2			2		7		1			10^1					37
		3	4			8	9				2^1	11^2				6	7	5		1			10	12	13			38
		3	4		6		8	9^1				12				2	11	7	5		1		10^1					39
		3	4	11	6		8	9								2	7	5		1			10^1		12			40
		3	4		6		8	9			12	13				2	11^1	7	5		1		10^2					41
		3	4	11	6		8	9^2				2				12	7	5		1		13	10^1					42
		4	3	6			8	9			12	11^2				2	13	7	5		1		10^1					43
			4			8	9	3^1	12	11						2	6	7	5		1		10^2			13		44
			4		6	8	9		12	11^3			2	13		7^2	5	1		14			10^1			10^1	3	45
			4	6^1	12	8	9				10	11^2	3^3			2	7	5		1			13				14	46

Worthington Cup

First Round	Carlisle U	(h)	3-0
		(a)	1-0
Second Round	Blackpool	(a)	1-2
		(h)	3-1
Third Round	Newcastle U	(h)	0-1

FA Cup

| Third Round | Ipswich T | (h) | 0-1 |

Division 1 **WALSALL**

FOUNDATION

Two of the leading clubs around Walsall in the 1880s were Walsall
Swifts (formed 1877) and Walsall Town (formed 1879). The Swifts
were winners of the Birmingham Senior Cup in 1881, while the
Town reached the 4th round (5th round modern equivalent) of the
FA Cup in 1883. These clubs amalgamated as Walsall Town Swifts
in 1888, becoming simply Walsall in 1895.

Bescot Stadium, Bescot Crescent, Walsall WS1 4SA.
Telephone: (01922) 622791.
Fax: (01922) 613202.
Commercial Dept: (01922) 651412.
Saddlers Hotline: 0891 555800.
Ground Capacity: 9000.
Record Attendance: 10,628 B International, England v Switzerland, 20 May 1991.
Record Receipts: £98,828 v Leeds U, FA Cup 3rd rd, 7 January 1995.
Pitch Measurements: 110yd × 73yd.
Chairman and Managing Director: M. Lloyd.
Directors: K. R. Whalley, C. Welch, R. M. Tisdale, J. W. Conser.
Manager: Ray Graydon.
General Manager: Paul Taylor.
Physio: Tom Bradley.
Secretary/Commercial Manager: Roy Whalley.
Year Formed: 1888.
Turned Professional: 1888.
Ltd Co.: 1921.
Previous Names: Walsall Swifts (founded 1877) and Walsall Town (founded 1879) amalgamated in
1888 and were known as Walsall Town Swifts until 1895.
Club Nickname: 'The Saddlers'.

LATEST SEQUENCES
Longest Sequence of League Wins: 7, 10.10.59 – 21.11.59.
Longest Sequence of League Defeats: 15, 29.10.88 – 4.2.89.
Longest Sequence of League Draws: 5, 7.5.88 – 17.9.88.
Longest Sequence of Unbeaten League Matches: 21,
6.11.79 – 22.3.80.
Longest Sequence Without a League Win: 18, 15.10.88 –
4.2.89.

HONOURS
Football League: Division 2: Runners-
up, 1998–99; Division 3 – Runners-up
1960–61, 1994–95; Division 4 –
Champions 1959–60; Runners-up
1979–80.

FA Cup: best season: 5th rd, 1939,
1975, 1978, 1987 and last 16 1889.

Football League Cup: Semi-final 1984.

Colours
Red shirts with black shoulder panel, black shorts with white trim, red
stockings with white band.

Change Colours
Royal blue shirts with yellow side panel, royal blue shorts with yellow side
panel, royal blue stockings with white band.

Previous Grounds: 1888, Fellows Park; 1990, Bescot Stadium.

First Football League Game: 3 September 1892, Division 2, v Darwen (h) L 12 – Hawkins; Withington, Pinches; Robinson, Whitrick, Forsyth; Marshall, Holmes, Turner, Gray (1), Pangbourn.

Record League Victory: 10–0 v Darwen, Division 2, 4 March 1899 – Tennent; E. Peers (1), Davies; Hickinbotham, Jenkyns, Taggart; Dean (3), Vail (2), Aston (4), Martin, Griffin.

Record Cup Victory: 7–0 v Macclesfield T (a), FA Cup 2nd rd, 6 December 1997 – Walker; Evans, Marsh, Viveash (1), Ryder, Peron, Boli (2 incl. 1p) (Ricketts), Porter (2), Keates, Watson (Platt), Hodge (2 incl. 1p).

Record Defeat: 0–12 v Small Heath, 17 December 1892. 0–12 v Darwen, 26 December 1896, both Division 2.

Most League Points (2 for a win): 65, Division 4, 1959–60.

Most League Points (3 for a win): 87, Division 2, 1998–99.

Most League Goals: 102, Division 4, 1959–60.

Highest League Scorer in Season: Gilbert Alsop, 40, Division 3 (N), 1933–34 and 1934–35.

Most League Goals in Total Aggregate: Tony Richards, 184, 1954–63; Colin Taylor, 184, 1958–63, 1964–68, 1969–73.

Most League Goals in One Match: 5, Gilbert Alsop v Carlisle U, Division 3N, 2 February 1935; 5, Bill Evans v Mansfield T, Division 3N, 5 October 1935; 5, Johnny Devlin v Torquay U, Division 3S, 1 September 1949.

Most Capped Player: Mick Kearns, 15 (18), Republic of Ireland.

Most League Appearances: Colin Harrison, 467, 1964–82.

Youngest League Player: Geoff Morris, 16 years 218 days v Scunthorpe U, 14 September 1965.

Record Transfer Fee Received: £600,000 from West Ham U for David Kelly, July 1988.

Record Transfer Fee Paid: £175,000 to Birmingham C for Alan Buckley, June 1979.

Football League Record: 1892 Elected to Division 2; 1895 Failed re-election; 1896–1901 Division 2; 1901 Failed re-election; 1921 Original Member of Division 3 (N); 1927–31 Division 3 (S); 1931–36 Division 3 (N); 1936–58 Division 3 (S); 1958–60 Division 4; 1960–61 Division 3; 1961–63 Division 2; 1963–79 Division 3; 1979–80 Division 4; 1980–88 Division 3; 1988–89 Division 2; 1989–90 Division 3; 1990–92 Division 4; 1992–95 Division 3; 1995–99 Division 2; 1999– Division 1.

MANAGERS

H. Smallwood 1888–91
(Secretary-Manager)
A. G. Burton 1891–93
J. H. Robinson 1893–95
C. H. Ailso 1895–96
(Secretary-Manager)
A. E. Parsloe 1896–97
(Secretary-Manager)
L. Ford 1897–98
(Secretary-Manager)
G. Hughes 1898–99
(Secretary-Manager)
L. Ford 1899–1901
(Secretary-Manager)
J. E. Shutt 1908–13
(Secretary-Manager)
Haydn Price 1914–20
Joe Burchell 1920–26
David Ashworth 1926–27
Jack Torrance 1927–28
James Kerr 1928–29
Sid Scholey 1929–30
Peter O'Rourke 1930–32
Bill Slade 1932–34
Andy Wilson 1934–37
Tommy Lowes 1937–44
Harry Hibbs 1944–51
Tony McPhee 1951
Brough Fletcher 1952–53
Major Frank Buckley 1953–55
John Love 1955–57
Billy Moore 1957–64
Alf Wood 1964
Reg Shaw 1964–68
Dick Graham 1968
Ron Lewin 1968–69
Billy Moore 1969–72
John Smith 1972–73
Doug Fraser 1973–77
Dave Mackay 1977–78
Alan Ashman 1978
Frank Sibley 1979
Alan Buckley 1979–86
Neil Martin *(Joint Manager with Buckley)* 1981–82
Tommy Coakley 1986–88
John Barnwell 1989–90
Kenny Hibbitt 1990–94
Chris Nicholl 1994–97
Jan Sorensen 1997–98
Ray Graydon May 1998–

TEN YEAR LEAGUE RECORD

		P	W	D	L	F	A	Pts	Pos
1988-89	Div 2	46	5	16	25	41	80	31	24
1989-90	Div 3	46	9	14	23	40	72	41	24
1990-91	Div 4	46	12	17	17	48	51	53	16
1991-92	Div 4	42	12	13	17	48	58	49	15
1992-93	Div 3	42	22	7	13	76	61	73	5
1993-94	Div 3	42	17	9	16	48	53	60	10
1994-95	Div 3	42	24	11	7	75	40	83	2
1995-96	Div 2	46	19	12	15	60	45	69	11
1996-97	Div 2	46	19	10	17	54	53	67	12
1997-98	Div 2	46	14	12	20	43	52	54	19

DID YOU KNOW ?

Walsall beat Notts County 4–0 in an FA Cup fourth round replay on 26 January 1939 after a goalless draw, to reach the fifth round for the first time. Gilbert Alsop scored all four for them on the occasion.

WALSALL 1998–99 LEAGUE RECORD

Match No.	Date		Venue	Opponents	Result		H/T Score	Lg. Pos.	Goalscorers	Atten- dance
1	Aug	8	A	Gillingham	W	1-0	1-0	—	Carr (og) [33]	5712
2		15	H	Northampton T	D	0-0	0-0	8		4360
3		22	A	Wycombe W	W	2-1	0-0	4	McCarthy (og) [56], Rammell [59]	4102
4		29	H	Burnley	W	3-1	1-0	3	Brissett [34], Wrack 2 (1 pen) [88, 90 (p)]	4599
5	Sept	2	A	Manchester C	L	1-3	0-1	—	Rammell [79]	24,291
6		8	H	York C	L	2-3	1-2	—	Rammell [24], Wrack (pen) [49]	3098
7		12	A	Chesterfield	W	1-0	0-0	8	Rammell [70]	4169
8		18	H	Notts Co	W	3-2	1-0	—	Simpson [38], Rammell [62], Brissett [72]	3991
9		26	A	Luton T	W	1-0	0-0	5	Rammell [86]	5530
10		30	H	Reading	L	0-2	0-1	—		3729
11	Oct	3	H	Preston NE	W	1-0	1-0	2	Rammell [16]	5802
12		10	A	Wrexham	L	1-2	1-2	2	Watson [13]	3842
13		17	H	Blackpool	W	1-0	1-0	3	Wrack [39]	4728
14		20	H	Colchester U	D	1-1	0-0	—	Platt [47]	3319
15		24	A	Fulham	L	1-4	0-1	5	Marsh [71]	8452
16		31	A	Bristol R	W	4-3	2-2	4	Larusson 2 [29, 89], Smith (og) [44], Rammell [80]	5753
17	Nov	7	H	Millwall	W	3-0	2-0	4	Green [19], Wrack [38], Rammell [79]	4237
18		10	H	Lincoln C	W	2-1	0-1	—	Wrack [70], Otta [90]	3698
19		21	A	Macclesfield T	D	1-1	1-0	3	Otta [45]	3183
20		28	H	Bournemouth	W	1-0	0-0	2	Wrack [67]	3895
21	Dec	12	A	Oldham Ath	W	2-0	2-0	3	Otta [4], Rammell [34]	4195
22		19	H	Stoke C	W	1-0	1-0	2	Rammell [41]	9056
23		26	H	Wycombe W	D	2-2	1-0	2	Rammell 2 [21, 64]	6258
24		28	A	Wigan Ath	L	0-2	0-0	2		4579
25	Jan	2	A	Burnley	D	0-0	0-0	2		10,892
26		9	H	Gillingham	W	2-1	1-0	2	Wrack [44], Rammell [50]	5495
27		23	H	Manchester C	D	1-1	0-0	3	Watson [67]	9517
28		30	H	Wigan Ath	L	1-2	0-1	3	Keates [52]	5473
29	Feb	6	A	Reading	W	1-0	1-0	3	Keates [44]	9481
30		13	A	York C	W	2-1	1-0	3	Wrack [3], Watson [51]	2969
31		20	H	Chesterfield	D	1-1	1-1	3	Rammell [45]	5268
32		23	A	Northampton T	W	1-0	0-0	—	Mavrack [65]	5631
33		27	A	Notts Co	L	1-2	1-0	3	Rammell [35]	6172
34	Mar	6	H	Luton T	W	1-0	0-0	3	Wrack [70]	4508
35		13	A	Millwall	W	2-1	2-1	3	Cramb 2 (1 pen) [27 (p), 38]	6248
36		20	H	Bristol R	D	3-3	2-0	3	Rammell [2], Cramb 2 (1 pen) [38 (p), 67]	4967
37	Apr	3	A	Blackpool	W	2-0	1-0	3	Mavrack [7], Larusson [53]	5432
38		6	H	Wrexham	W	1-0	0-0	—	Steiner [65]	5763
39		10	A	Colchester U	L	0-1	0-1	2		4082
40		13	A	Bournemouth	W	1-0	1-0	—	Wrack [14]	8390
41		17	H	Macclesfield T	W	2-0	0-0	2	Steiner [54], Rammell [59]	6256
42		20	A	Preston NE	L	0-1	0-0	—		13,337
43		24	A	Lincoln C	W	1-0	0-0	2	Wrack [72]	4588
44	May	1	H	Oldham Ath	W	3-1	2-0	2	Wrack [22], Marsh [34], Eyjolfsson [76]	9184
45		4	H	Fulham	D	2-2	1-1	—	Steiner [40], Roper [70]	8326
46		8	A	Stoke C	L	0-2	0-1	2		12,091

Final League Position: 2

GOALSCORERS

League (63): Rammell 18, Wrack 13 (2 pens), Cramb 4 (2 pens), Larusson 3, Otta 3, Steiner 3, Watson 3, Brissett 2, Keates 2, Marsh 2, Mavrak 2, Eyjolfsson 1, Green 1, Platt 1, Roper 1, Simpson 1, own goals 3.
Worthington Cup (1): Rammell 1.
FA Cup (1): Roper 1.

Walker J 46	Marsh C 43	Pointon N 43	Keister J 2	Roper I 29 + 3	Viveash A 40	Wrack D 46	Brissett J 27 + 8	Rammell A 39	Porter G 14 + 1	Keates D 38 + 5	Watson A 12 + 9	Davis N — + 1	Ricketts M 2 + 6	Green R 22 + 6	Platt C 6 + 1	Gadsby M 3 + 3	Dyer W — + 1	Evans W 6 + 5	Thomas W 1 + 11	Simpson P 10	Larusson B 33 + 3	Lambert J 4 + 2	Otta W 6 + 2	Mavrak D 12 + 1	Eyjolfsson S — + 10	Cramb C 4	Henry N 8	Steiner R 10	Carter A — + 1	Match No.
1	2	3	4	5	6	7[1]	8[2]	9	10	11[3]	12	13	14																	1
1	2	3	4[1]		6	7	11	9	10[3]	13	8[2]			12	5	14														2
1	2[3]	3			6	7	11	9	10	4[2]	8[1]			12	5			14	13											3
1	2	3			6	7	8	9	10	4				11	5															4
1	2[1]	3			6	7	8	9	10	4	12			11[2]	5			13												5
1	11	3			6	7	8	9	10	4[1]				5				2	12											6
1	11[1]	3			6	7	8	9	10	4				5				2	12											7
1		3			6	7	8	9	10[1]	4				5				2	12	11										8
1	2	3			6	7	8[1]	9		4	12			5						11	10									9
1	2				6	7[1]	8	9		4	12			5		3				11	10									10
1	2[2]	3			6	7	8	9[1]		4	12			5			13			11	10									11
1	2	3	12		6	7	8			4	9			5						11[1]	10									12
1	2	3	12		6	7			8	4	9[2]			5[1]						11	10				13					13
1	2	3			6	7	11		8[1]	4				5	9						10				12					14
1	2	3	5		6	7	8			4	12				9					11[1]	10									15
1	2	3			6	7	8	9		4				5						11	10									16
1	2	3	6			7[2]	8[1]	9	10	4	12			5			13			11[3]					14					17
1	2	3	12		6[1]	7	8	9		4				5							10			11[2]	13					18
1	2	3	6			7	11[1]	9		4	12			5							10		8							19
1	2	3	6			7				4	11[1]			5	9			12			10		8							20
1	2[3]	3	6			7			9	12	4[1]	13						5	14	11	10		8[2]							21
1	2	3	6			7	12	9		4				5						11	10		8[1]							22
1	2	3			6	7				9	4			5						11	10		8							23
1	2	3	6			7	12	9		4	13			5						11	10[2]		8[1]							24
1	2	3	6			7				9	4		8	5						11	10									25
1		3		6	5	7		9		4	8[1]							2	12	11	10									26
1	2	3		6	5	7	11			4	8			12				9[1]			10[2]				13					27
1	2	3		6	5	7	11	9		4	8										10									28
1	2	3		6	5	7	12	9		4	8[2]							14	13		10[3]				11[1]					29
1	2	3		6	5	7	12	9		4	8[2]								13		10				11[1]					30
1	2	3		6	5	7	12	9		4	8[1]										10				11					31
1	2	3		6	5	7	8[1]	9		4									13		10				11	12[2]				32
1	2	3		6	5	7		9		4	12							13			10[2]				11[1]	14	8[3]			33
1	2	3[2]		6	5	7	12	9		4								14	13		10[2]				11[1]		8			34
1	2			6	5	7		9		4[1]			13			3		12			10				11[2]		8			35
1		3		6	5[1]	7	11	9										12			10						8			36
1	2	3		6	5	7[1]		9			12							13			10				11[3]	14		4	8[2]	37
1	2[1]	3		6	5	7	12	9			13										10[2]				11	14		4	8[3]	38
1	2	3[4]		6	5	7	12	9			13							14			10[2]				11[1]			4	8	39
1	2	3		6	5	7	11	9		10																		4	8	40
1	2	3		6	5	7	11	9[2]		10											12					13		4	8[1]	41
1	2[1]	3		6	5	7	11	9		10											12					13		4	8[2]	42
1		3		6[3]	5	7		9		10			14			2					11[1]			12	13			4	8[3]	43
1	2	3		6	5	7	11	9[2]		10[1]			13								12					14		4	8[3]	44
1	2	3		6	5	7[3]		9		10			12								4				11[1]	13		8[3]	14	45
1	2[2]	3		6	5	7		9		10			12	13							4[1]				11	14		8[3]		46

Worthington Cup
First Round   QPR   (h) 0-0
    (a) 1-3

FA Cup
First Round   Gresley R   (h) 1-0
Second Round   Preston NE   (a) 0-2

FA Premiership

WATFORD

<table>
<tr><td></td></tr>
</table>

FOUNDATION

The club was formed as Watford Rovers in 1881. The name was changed to West Herts in 1893 and then the name Watford was adopted after rival club Watford St Mary's was absorbed in 1898.

Vicarage Road Stadium, Watford WD1 8ER.
Telephone: (01923) 496000. *Fax:* (01923) 496001.
Ticket and Prizeline: 0891 400401. *Ticket Office:* (01923) 496010. *Ticket Office Fax:* (01923) 351145.
Club Shop: (01923) 496005. *Club Shop Fax:* (01923) 496238.
Catering: (01923) 252323. *Football in the Community:* (01923) 440449.
Junior Hornets Club: (01923) 496256.
Marketing: (01923) 496006. *Press Office:* (01923) 496234.
Ground Capacity: 22,000.
Record Attendance: 34,099 v Manchester U, FA Cup 4th rd (replay), 3 February 1969.
Record Receipts: £229,679.12 v Sunderland, Divison 1, 30 January 1999.
Pitch Measurements: 113yd × 73yd.
Life Presidents: Sir Elton John CBE, Geoff Smith.
Chairman: Sir Elton John CBE.
Vice Chairman: Charles Lissack, Haig Oundjian
Directors: B. Anderson, D. Meller.
Chief Executive: Howard Wells.
Secretary: John Alexander.
Football Manager: Graham Taylor.
Coach: Luther Blissett.
Reserve Team Manager: Tom Walley.
Academy Director: Gary Johnson.
Academy Assistant Directors: Jimmy Gilligan, Chris Cummins.
Press and Publications Officer: Andrew French.
Director of Sales and Marketing: Mark Jones.
Safety Officer: Martin Girvan.

LATEST SEQUENCES

Longest Sequence of League Wins: 7, 26.12.77 – 28.1.78.
Longest Sequence of League Defeats: 9, 26.12.72 – 27.2.73.
Longest Sequence of League Draws: 7, 30.11.96 – 27.1.97.
Longest Sequence of Unbeaten League Matches: 22, 1.10.96 – 1.3.97.
Longest Sequence Without a League Win: 19, 27.11.71 – 8.4.72.

HONOURS

Football League: Division 1 – Runners-up 1982–83, promoted from Division 1 1998–99 (play-offs); Division 2 – Champions 1997–98; Runners-up 1981–82; Division 3 – Champions 1968–69; Runners-up 1978–79; Division 4 – Champions 1977–78; Promoted 1959–60 (4th).

FA Cup: Runners-up 1984.

Football League Cup: Semi- final 1979.

European Competitions: UEFA Cup: 1983–84.

Colours

Yellow shirts with red sleeves and black collar and cuffs, red shorts, red stockings with yellow tops and two black hoops.

Change Colours

Blue and silver striped shirts with red pinstripes, blue shorts, blue stockings with red tops and two black hoops.

Year Formed: 1881.

Turned Professional: 1897.

Ltd Co.: 1909.

Club Nickname: 'The Hornets'.

Previous Names: 1881, Watford Rovers; 1893, West Herts; 1898, Watford.

Previous Grounds: 1883, Vicarage Meadow, Rose and Crown Meadow; 1889, Colney Butts; 1890, Cassio Road; 1922, Vicarage Road.

First Football League Game: 28 August 1920, Division 3, v QPR (a) W 2–1 – Williams; Horseman, F. Gregory; Bacon, Toone, Wilkinson; Bassett, Ronald (1), Hoddinott, White (1), Waterall.

Record League Victory: 8–0 v Sunderland, Division 1, 25 September 1982 – Sherwood; Rice, Rostron, Taylor, Terry, Bolton, Callaghan (2), Blissett (4), Jenkins (2), Jackett, Barnes.

Record Cup Victory: 10–1 v Lowestoft T, FA Cup 1st rd, 27 November 1926 – Yates; Prior, Fletcher (1); F. Smith, 'Bert' Smith, Strain; Stephenson, Warner (3), Edmonds (3), Swan (1), Daniels (1), (1 og).

Record Defeat: 0–10 v Wolverhampton W, FA Cup 1st rd (replay), 24 January 1912.

Most League Points (2 for a win): 71, Division 4, 1977–78.

Most League Points (3 for a win): 88, Division 2, 1997–98.

Most League Goals: 92, Division 4, 1959–60.

Highest League Scorer in Season: Cliff Holton, 42, Division 4, 1959–60.

Most League Goals in Total Aggregate: Luther Blissett, 148, 1976–83, 1984–88, 1991–92.

MANAGERS

John Goodall 1903–10
Harry Kent 1910–26
Fred Pagnam 1926–29
Neil McBain 1929–37
Bill Findlay 1938–47
Jack Bray 1947–48
Eddie Hapgood 1948–50
Ron Gray 1950–51
Haydn Green 1951–52
Len Goulden 1952–55
    (General Manager to 1956)
Johnny Paton 1955–56
Neil McBain 1956–59
Ron Burgess 1959–63
Bill McGarry 1963–64
Ken Furphy 1964–71
George Kirby 1971–73
Mike Keen 1973–77
Graham Taylor 1977–87
Dave Bassett 1987–88
Steve Harrison 1988–90
Colin Lee 1990
Steve Perryman 1990–93
Glenn Roeder 1993–96
Kenny Jackett 1996–97
Graham Taylor May 1997–
    (General Manager since February 1996)

Most League Goals in One Match: 5, Eddie Mummery v Newport Co, Division 3S, 5 January 1924.

Most Capped Player: John Barnes, 31 (79), England and Kenny Jackett, 31, Wales.

Most League Appearances: Luther Blissett, 415, 1976–83, 1984–88, 1991–92.

Youngest League Player: Keith Mercer, 16 years 125 days v Tranmere R, 16 February 1973.

Record Transfer Fee Received: £2,300,000 from Chelsea for Paul Furlong, May 1994.

Record Transfer Fee Paid: £550,000 to AC Milan for Luther Blissett, August 1984.

Football League Record: 1920 Original Member of Division 3; 1921–58 Division 3 (S); 1958–60 Division 4; 1960–69 Division 3; 1969–72 Division 2; 1972–75 Division 3; 1975–78 Division 4; 1978–79 Division 3; 1979–82 Division 2; 1982–88 Division 1; 1988–92 Division 2; 1992–96 Division 1; 1996–98 Division 2; 1998–99 Division 1; 1999– FA Premier League.

TEN YEAR LEAGUE RECORD

		P	W	D	L	F	A	Pts	Pos
1988-89	Div 2	46	22	12	12	74	48	78	4
1989-90	Div 2	46	14	15	17	58	60	57	15
1990-91	Div 2	46	12	15	19	45	59	51	20
1991-92	Div 2	46	18	11	17	51	48	65	10
1992-93	Div 1	46	14	13	19	57	71	55	16
1993-94	Div 1	46	15	9	22	66	80	54	19
1994-95	Div 1	46	19	13	14	52	46	70	7
1995-96	Div 1	46	10	18	18	62	70	48	23
1996-97	Div 2	46	16	19	11	45	38	67	13
1997-98	Div 2	46	24	16	6	67	41	88	1

DID YOU KNOW ?

On 2 December 1967 in a Division Three match, Watford beat a Grimsby Town team which included Graham Taylor at left-back 7–1 at Vicarage Road. Watford finished sixth, Grimsby were relegated that season.

WATFORD 1998–99 LEAGUE RECORD

Match No.	Date	Venue	Opponents	Result	H/T Score	Lg. Pos.	Goalscorers	Attendance
1	Aug 8	A	Portsmouth	W 2-1	0-1	—	Thomson (og) [80], Lee [84]	15,275
2	15	H	Bradford C	W 1-0	0-0	3	Ngonge [63]	10,731
3	22	A	Bristol C	W 4-1	1-0	3	Johnson 2 [8, 61], Yates [58], Hazan [79]	13,063
4	25	A	Sunderland	L 1-4	1-3	—	Smart [11]	36,587
5	28	H	Wolverhampton W	L 0-2	0-1	—		12,016
6	Sept 8	H	Huddersfield T	L 0-2	0-2	—		9811
7	12	H	QPR	W 2-1	1-0	9	Millen [5], Smart [85]	14,251
8	19	A	Swindon T	W 4-1	2-1	5	Smart 2 [37, 58], Wright [44], Hazan [50]	8781
9	26	H	Ipswich T	W 1-0	1-0	3	Kennedy (pen) [5]	13,109
10	29	H	Sheffield U	D 1-1	1-0	—	Noel-Williams [45]	9090
11	Oct 4	A	WBA	L 1-4	1-2	6	Kennedy (pen) [32]	11,840
12	10	H	Birmingham C	D 1-1	0-1	5	Rowett (og) [68]	10,096
13	17	A	Tranmere R	L 2-3	1-2	6	Smart [15], Noel-Williams [80]	6753
14	20	A	Bolton W	W 2-1	1-1	—	Noel-Williams [42], Kennedy [87]	15,921
15	24	H	Port Vale	D 2-2	1-1	5	Gudmundsson 2 [27, 53]	8750
16	31	A	Bury	W 3-1	2-1	5	Bazeley [26], Ngonge [42], Smart [84]	4342
17	Nov 3	H	Norwich C	D 1-1	1-1	—	Jackson (og) [8]	10,011
18	7	H	Oxford U	W 2-0	1-0	4	Palmer [25], Noel-Williams [77]	10,137
19	14	A	Stockport Co	D 1-1	1-1	3	Johnson [9]	8019
20	21	H	Crewe Alex	W 4-2	3-0	2	Noel-Williams 2 [39, 69], Bazeley [44], Wright [45]	9405
21	28	A	Crystal Palace	D 2-2	2-1	3	Wright [23], Kennedy [26]	19,521
22	Dec 5	H	Barnsley	D 0-0	0-0	3		10,165
23	12	A	Stockport Co	W 4-2	2-0	3	Johnson [8], Wright [17], Noel-Williams 2 [65, 87]	9250
24	19	A	Grimsby T	L 1-2	0-0	4	Noel-Williams [73]	6679
25	26	H	Bristol C	W 1-0	0-0	3	Smart [57]	15,081
26	29	A	Norwich C	D 1-1	0-0	—	Palmer [81]	19,259
27	Jan 9	A	Portsmouth	D 0-0	0-0	6		12,057
28	16	A	Wolverhampton W	D 0-0	0-0	7		23,408
29	23	H	WBA	L 0-2	0-1	7		11,664
30	30	H	Sunderland	W 2-1	1-1	6	Wright [19], Noel-Williams [53]	20,188
31	Feb 6	A	Bradford C	L 0-2	0-1	6		14,142
32	16	H	Huddersfield T	D 1-1	0-0	—	Mooney [70]	10,303
33	20	A	QPR	W 2-1	1-1	6	Wright [16], Smith [70]	14,918
34	26	H	Swindon T	L 0-1	0-1	—		8692
35	Mar 2	A	Ipswich T	L 2-3	0-2	—	Smith [82], Mooney [84]	18,818
36	6	A	Sheffield U	L 0-3	0-2	7		15,943
37	13	A	Oxford U	D 0-0	0-0	7		8137
38	20	H	Bury	D 0-0	0-0	8		9336
39	Apr 3	H	Tranmere R	W 2-0	1-0	7	Kennedy [67], Ngonge [87]	8682
40	5	A	Birmingham C	W 2-1	1-0	7	Mooney [26], Daley [58]	24,877
41	10	H	Bolton W	W 2-0	1-0	7	Hyde [24], Mooney [53]	13,001
42	17	A	Crewe Alex	W 1-0	1-0	7	Mooney [24]	5461
43	24	H	Crystal Palace	W 2-1	1-0	7	Hyde [6], Mooney [53]	15,590
44	27	A	Port Vale	W 2-1	1-1	—	Mooney 2 [24, 60]	7126
45	May 1	A	Barnsley	D 2-2	1-0	5	Ngonge [43], Mooney [67]	17,098
46	9	H	Grimsby T	W 1-0	1-0	5	Kennedy [42]	20,303

Final League Position: 5

GOALSCORERS
League (65): Noel-Williams 10, Mooney 9, Smart 7, Kennedy 6 (2 pens), Wright 6, Johnson 4, Ngonge 4, Bazeley 2, Gudmundsson 2, Hazan 2, Hyde 2, Palmer 2, Smith 2, Daley 1, Lee 1, Millen 1, Yates 1, own goals 3.
Worthington Cup (1): Ngonge 1.
FA Cup (2): Johnson 1, Kennedy 1.

Chamberlain A 46	Hazan A 8 + 15	Kennedy P 46	Page R 37 + 2	Palmer S 40 + 1	Mooney T 20 + 16	Smart A 34 + 1	Hyde M 43 + 1	Lee J 1	Easton C 7	Rosenthal R 1 + 4	Millen K 10 + 1	Bazeley D 36 + 4	Yates D 9	Ngonge M 13 + 9	Robinson P 26 + 3	Daley T 6 + 6	Johnson R 40	Noel-Williams G 19 + 7	Gibbs N 9 + 1	Wright N 31 + 2	Gudmundsson J 6 + 7	Iroha B 8 + 2	Bonnot A 1 + 3	Smith T 3 + 5	Ward D 1	Perpetuini D 1	Whittingham G 4 + 1	Match No.
1	2	3	4	5¹	6	7²	8	9	10	11	12	13																1
1	2¹	3	13	4		7³	8		10	12	5		6	9²	11		14											2
1	12	3	4			7²	8				5¹	2	6	9²	11	13	10	14										3
1	12	3	5	4		7²	8³					2¹	6	9	11	14	10	13										4
1		3	5	4		7¹	8		11	12		2	6	9²			10	13										5
1	12	3	4			7	8				5		6	9			10		2	11¹								6
1	12	3	6			7	8				5	4		9²			10	13	2	11¹								7
1	12	3	13	6		7	8				5²	4		9²			10	14	2	11¹								8
1		3	6			7	8				5	4		9¹			10	12	2	11								9
1		3	12	6		7	8				5	4					10	9	2	11¹								10
1	9²	3	4		6	7	8³				5	12			14		10	13	2	11¹								11
1		3	4		6	7	8				5	12					10	9	2	11¹								12
1		3	4		6¹	7	8				5	12		11			10	9	2									13
1		3	4	5	12	7¹	8					6		11			10	9		2²	13							14
1		3	4	5	12	7	8					6		11			10	9¹		13	2²							15
1	12	3	4	5	6	7¹	8					2		9²			10			11	13							16
1	7²	3	4	5	12		8					2		6			10	9		11¹	13							17
1		3	4	5			8					2		6			10	9		11	7							18
1		3	4	5	12	7	8					2		6¹			10	9		11								19
1		3	4	5	6	7¹	8					2		12			10	9		11								20
1		3	4	5	12	7¹	8					2		13	6		10	9¹		11								21
1		3	5	4	12		8					2		7¹	6		10	9		11²	13							22
1		3	4	5		7¹	8					2		12	6		10	9		11								23
1		3	4	5	12	7¹	8					2		6			10	9		11²	13							24
1		3	4	5		7	8					2					10	9		11	6							25
1		3	4	5	12	7²	8			13		2		14			10	9		11¹	6³							26
1		3	4	5	12	7¹	8					2		13			10	9		11²	6³	14						27
1		3	4	5	12	7¹	8	10				2		13				9		11²	6							28
1		3	4	5	12	7	8			13		2		11¹	10		9²				6							29
1	12	3	4	5	13							2		11¹	10		9²			7	6							30
1	12	3	4	5		9	8²					2		13	11³	10				7	14	6¹						31
1		3	4	5	9		8					2	12	11¹	10		7				6²	13						32
1	8¹	3	4	5	9					11		2		6	10		7							12				33
1	12	3²	4	5	13	9				11²		2		6	14	10	7							8¹				34
1	10	3	4	5	12	9¹	8			11³		2		6			7²					14						35
1	10²	3		5	9	7³	8					2		6			12	11¹		13		14	4					36
1		3	4	5	9²		8					2		12	6		10			11¹	13			7				37
1	12	3	4	5	13		8¹					2		10				14	11		7³	6²					9	38
1		3	4	5	12	7	8³					2		13	6		10			11²	14						9¹	39
1	8¹	3	4	5	9	7	12					2		6			11²	10				13						40
1	12	3	4	5	9²	7¹	8					2		13	6		10			11³				14				41
1	12	3	4	5	9		8					2		13	6					11¹	10			7²				42
1		3	4	5	9		8					2		12	6		10			11²		13		7¹				43
1	12	3	4	5	9		8					2		7	6		10			11³								44
1	12	3	4	5	9	13	8					2		7¹	6		10			11²								45
1	12	3	4	5	9		8					2		7	6		10			11¹								46

Worthington Cup
First Round   Cambridge U   (a)   0-1
                                        (h)   1-1

FA Cup
Third Round   Tottenham H   (a)   2-5

Division 1   **WEST BROMWICH ALBION**

FOUNDATION

There is a well known story that when employees of Salter's Spring Works in West Bromwich decided to form a football club, they had to send someone to the nearby Association Football stronghold of Wednesbury to purchase a football. A weekly subscription of 2d (less than 1p) was imposed and the name of the new club was West Bromwich Strollers.

The Hawthorns, West Bromwich B71 4LF.

Telephone: (0121) 525 8888 (all Depts).

Fax: (0121) 553 6634.

Registered Office: 'The Tom Silk Building', Halfords Lane, West Bromwich, West Midlands B71 4BR.

Ground Capacity: 25,396 (all seated).

Record Attendance: 64,815 v Arsenal, FA Cup 6th rd, 6 March 1937.

Record Receipts: £270,000 v Nottingham F, Div 1, 3 May 1998.

Pitch Measurements: 115yd × 74yd.

President: Sir F. A. Millichip.

Vice-President: John G. Silk LL.B (Lond).

Chairman: A. B. Hale.

Directors: J. W. Brandrick, B. Hurst, R. E. McGing, J. D. Wile (Chief Executive).

Manager: Denis Smith.

First Team Coach: Malcolm Crosby.

Coaches: John Trewick, Cyrille Regis, Richard O'Kelly.

Secretary: Dr John J. Evans BA, PHD. (Wales).

Club Statistician: Tony Matthews.

Commercial Executive: Tom Cardall.

LATEST SEQUENCES

Longest Sequence of League Wins: 11, 5.4.30 – 8.9.30.

Longest Sequence of League Defeats: 11, 28.10.95 – 26.12.95.

Longest Sequence of League Draws: 5, 20.4.91 – 11.5.91.

Longest Sequence of Unbeaten League Matches: 17, 7.9.57 – 7.12.57.

Longest Sequence Without a League Win: 14, 28.10.95 – 3.2.96.

HONOURS

Football League: Division 1 – Champions 1919–20; Runners-up 1924–25, 1953–54; Division 2 – Champions 1901–02, 1910–11; Runners-up 1930–31, 1948–49; Promoted to Division 1 1975–76 (3rd).

FA Cup: Winners 1888, 1892, 1931, 1954, 1968; Runners-up 1886, 1887, 1895, 1912, 1935.

Football League Cup: Winners 1966; Runners-up 1967, 1970.

European Competitions: *European Cup-Winners' Cup:* 1968–69. *European Fairs Cup:* 1966–67. *UEFA Cup:* 1978–79, 1979–80, 1981–82.

Colours

Navy blue and white striped shirts, white shorts, blue and white stockings.

Change Colours

Yellow shirts with navy blue band, blue shorts with yellow stripe, yellow stockings.

Year Formed: 1878.

Turned Professional: 1885.

Ltd Co.: 1892.

Plc: 1996.

Previous Name: 1878, West Bromwich Strollers; 1871, West Bromwich Albion.

Club Nicknames: 'Throstles', 'Baggies', 'Albion'.

Previous Grounds: 1878, Coopers Hill; 1879, Dartmouth Park; 1881, Bunns Field, Walsall Street; 1882, Four Acres (Dartmouth Cricket Club); 1885, Stoney Lane; 1900, The Hawthorns.

First Football League Game: 8 September 1888, Football League, v Stoke (a) W 2–0 – Roberts; J. Horton, Green; E. Horton, Perry, Bayliss; Bassett, Woodhall (1), Hendry, Pearson, Wilson (1).

Record League Victory: 12–0 v Darwen, Division 1, 4 April 1892 – Reader; J. Horton, McCulloch; Reynolds (2), Perry, Groves; Bassett (3), McLeod, Nicholls (1), Pearson (4), Geddes (1), (1 og).

Record Cup Victory: 10–1 v Chatham (away), FA Cup 3rd rd, 2 March 1889 – Roberts; J. Horton, Green; Timmins (1), Charles Perry, E. Horton; Bassett (2), Perry (1), Bayliss (2), Pearson, Wilson (3), (1 og).

Record Defeat: 3–10 v Stoke C, Division 1, 4 February 1937.

Most League Points (2 for a win): 60, Division 1, 1919–20.

Most League Points (3 for a win): 85, Division 2, 1992–93.

Most League Goals: 105, Division 2, 1929–30.

Highest League Scorer in Season: William 'Ginger' Richardson, 39, Division 1, 1935–36.

Most League Goals in Total Aggregate: Tony Brown, 218, 1963–79.

Most League Goals in One Match: 6, Jimmy Cookson v Blackpool, Division 2, 17 September 1927.

Most Capped Player: Stuart Williams, 33 (43), Wales.

Most League Appearances: Tony Brown, 574, 1963–80.

Youngest League Player: Charlie Wilson, 16 years 73 days v Oldham Ath, 1 October 1921.

Record Transfer Fee Received: £1,500,000 from Manchester U for Bryan Robson, October 1981.

Record Transfer Fee Paid: £1,250,000 to Preston NE for Kevin Kilbane, June 1997.

Football League Record: 1888 Founder Member of Football League; 1901–02 Division 2; 1902–04 Division 1; 1904–11 Division 2; 1911–27 Division 1; 1927–31 Division 2; 1931–38 Division 1; 1938–49 Division 2; 1949–73 Division 1; 1973–76 Division 2; 1976–86 Division 1; 1986–91 Division 2; 1991–92 Division 3; 1992–93 Division 2; 1993– Division 1.

MANAGERS

Louis Ford 1890–92
  (Secretary-Manager)
Henry Jackson 1892–94
  (Secretary-Manager)
Edward Stephenson 1894–95
  (Secretary-Manager)
Clement Keys 1895–96
  (Secretary-Manager)
Frank Heaven 1896–1902
  (Secretary-Manager)
Fred Everiss 1902–48
Jack Smith 1948–52
Jesse Carver 1952
Vic Buckingham 1953–59
Gordon Clark 1959–61
Archie Macaulay 1961–63
Jimmy Hagan 1963–67
Alan Ashman 1967–71
Don Howe 1971–75
Johnny Giles 1975–77
Ronnie Allen 1977
Ron Atkinson 1978–81
Ronnie Allen 1981–82
Ron Wylie 1982–84
Johnny Giles 1984–85
Ron Saunders 1986–87
Ron Atkinson 1987–88
Brian Talbot 1988–91
Bobby Gould 1991–92
Ossie Ardiles 1992–93
Keith Burkinshaw 1993–94
Alan Buckley 1994–97
Ray Harford 1997
Denis Smith December 1997–

TEN YEAR LEAGUE RECORD

		P	W	D	L	F	A	Pts	Pos
1988-89	Div 2	46	18	18	10	65	41	72	9
1989-90	Div 2	46	12	15	19	67	71	51	20
1990-91	Div 2	46	10	18	18	52	61	48	23
1991-92	Div 3	46	19	14	13	64	49	71	7
1992-93	Div 2	46	25	10	11	88	54	85	4
1993-94	Div 1	46	13	12	21	60	69	51	21
1994-95	Div 1	46	16	10	20	51	57	58	19
1995-96	Div 1	46	16	12	18	60	68	60	11
1996-97	Div 1	46	14	15	17	68	72	57	16
1997-98	Div 1	46	16	12	17	50	56	61	10

DID YOU KNOW ?

Right-back Billy Williams declined to play for the Football League against the Irish League in November 1897, preferring to turn out for the Albion. For his loyalty the club struck a special medal.

WEST BROMWICH ALBION 1998–99 LEAGUE RECORD

Match No.	Date	Venue	Opponents	Result	H/T Score	Lg. Pos.	Goalscorers	Attendance
1	Aug 8	A	Barnsley	D 2-2	2-1	—	Sneekes 13, Quinn 45	18,114
2	15	H	Sheffield U	W 4-1	2-1	4	Carbon 24, Kilbane 29, Hughes 2 49, 50	16,901
3	22	A	Port Vale	W 3-0	0-0	5	Hughes 3 58, 77, 80	8146
4	29	H	Norwich C	W 2-0	0-0	3	De Freitas 2 59, 72	17,401
5	31	A	Grimsby T	L 1-5	0-4	4	Sneekes 49	7931
6	Sept 8	H	Bolton W	L 2-3	1-2	—	Flynn 40, Kilbane 60	15,789
7	13	A	Bristol C	W 3-1	2-0	6	Hughes 2 11, 33, Quinn 52	13,761
8	20	H	Bradford C	L 0-2	0-2	9		12,426
9	26	A	Stockport Co	D 2-2	2-0	9	Hughes 2 23, 45	8804
10	29	A	Oxford U	L 0-3	0-2	—		7437
11	Oct 4	H	Watford	W 4-1	2-1	9	Kilbane 16, Hughes 2 37, 84, De Freitas 72	11,840
12	18	H	Sunderland	L 2-3	2-0	11	Hughes 2 26, 44	14,746
13	21	H	QPR	W 2-0	0-0	—	Evans 66, Murphy 82	11,842
14	24	A	Swindon T	D 2-2	1-2	9	Hughes 22, Flynn 57	8967
15	31	A	Ipswich T	L 0-2	0-0	11		15,568
16	Nov 3	H	Crystal Palace	W 3-2	1-1	—	Hughes 3 (1 pen) 1, 84, 90 (p)	11,606
17	7	H	Birmingham C	L 1-3	0-3	11	Carbon 80	19,472
18	14	H	Huddersfield T	W 3-1	1-1	10	Hughes 3 (2 pens) 28 (p), 75 (p), 84	13,626
19	21	A	Portsmouth	L 1-2	1-1	11	Hughes 1	11,144
20	29	H	Wolverhampton W	W 2-0	0-0	11	Kilbane 46, Murphy 61	22,682
21	Dec 5	A	Bury	L 0-2	0-2	12		5007
22	8	A	Crewe Alex	D 1-1	1-0	—	Hughes (pen) 35	5007
23	12	A	Huddersfield T	W 3-0	0-0	10	Quinn 2 74, 79, Hughes 80	11,947
24	19	H	Tranmere R	L 0-2	0-0	10		13,966
25	26	H	Port Vale	W 3-2	1-0	10	Murphy 5, Bortolazzi 54, Hughes (pen) 75	14,929
26	28	A	Crystal Palace	D 1-1	0-1	10	Hughes 61	19,137
27	Jan 9	H	Barnsley	W 2-0	0-0	9	Murphy 66, Hughes 69	15,029
28	16	A	Norwich C	D 1-1	0-0	8	Bortolazzi 50	15,411
29	23	A	Watford	W 2-0	1-0	8	Sneekes 15, Angel 90	11,664
30	30	H	Grimsby T	D 1-1	1-0	8	Hughes 74	17,843
31	Feb 6	A	Sheffield U	L 0-3	0-2	8		16,566
32	13	A	Bolton W	L 1-2	1-1	9	De Freitas 27	20,657
33	20	A	Bristol C	D 2-2	1-0	9	Hughes 2 32, 90	16,490
34	27	A	Bradford C	L 0-1	0-1	9		14,278
35	Mar 2	H	Stockport Co	W 3-1	1-0	—	Kilbane 18, De Freitas 52, Hughes 60	11,801
36	6	H	Oxford U	W 2-0	1-0	6	Quinn 38, Maresca 78	13,875
37	13	A	Birmingham C	L 0-4	0-1	8		29,060
38	20	H	Ipswich T	L 0-1	0-1	10		15,552
39	Apr 3	A	Sunderland	L 0-3	0-2	11		41,135
40	5	H	Crewe Alex	L 1-5	0-2	11	Sneekes 63	12,308
41	10	A	QPR	L 1-2	1-1	12	Kilbane 44	11,158
42	13	H	Swindon T	D 1-1	1-1	—	Hughes 31	9601
43	17	H	Portsmouth	D 2-2	0-2	12	Maresca 67, Quinn 78	12,750
44	25	A	Wolverhampton W	D 1-1	1-1	13	Evans 18	27,038
45	May 1	H	Bury	W 1-0	0-0	12	De Freitas 80	12,918
46	9	A	Tranmere R	L 1-3	0-2	12	De Freitas 75	10,540

Final League Position: 12

GOALSCORERS

League (69): Hughes 31 (5 pens), De Freitas 7, Kilbane 6, Quinn 6, Murphy 4, Sneekes 4, Bortolazzi 2, Carbon 2, Evans 2, Flynn 2, Maresca 2, Angel 1.
Worthington Cup (2): Evans 1, Hughes 1.
FA Cup (0).

Miller A 20	Mardon P 12+6	Van Blerk J 30	Flynn S 33+5	Murphy S 30+7	Carbon M 38+1	Quinn J 39+4	Sneekes R 35+5	Evans M 17+3	Hughes L 42	Kilbane K 44	Bortolazzi M 25+10	De Freitas F 22+15	Burgess D 15+5	Angel M 4+18	Raven P 6+1	McDermott A 20	Maresca E 9+13	Potter G 19+3	Holmes P 17	Whitehead P 26	Gabbidon D 2	Richards J —+1	Qualley B 1+1	Oliver A —+1	Match No.
1	2	3	4	5	6	7	8	9	10	11															1
1	2	3	4[1]	5	6	7	8	9	10	11	12														2
1	2	3	4	5	6	7	8		10[1]	11	9	12													3
1	2	3	4	5[3]	6	7[1]	8	9[2]	10	11	12	13	14												4
1	2	3	4[3]	5	6	7	8	9[1]	10[2]		12	13	14	11											5
1	2	3	4		6	7	8	9[1]	10	11	12				5										6
1	12	3	4		6	7	11	9[1]	10	13	8[2]				5	2									7
1	12	3	4[3]		6[1]	7	8		10	11	9[2]	13			5	2	14								8
1	6	3	4	12		7[1]	8		10	11	13	9[2]			5	2									9
1	6[3]		12	3		7	8[2]		10	11	4	9			5[1]	2	13	14							10
1		3	4	5	6	7			10	11	8[2]	9[1]	12			2	13								11
1	12	3	4	5	6	7	13		10	11	8[2]	9[1]				2									12
1		3	4	5	6	7	12		10	11	8	9[1]				2									13
1		3	4	5	6	7		9[1]	10	11	8	12				2									14
1		3	4[2]	5	6	7		9[1]	10	11	8	12				2	13								15
1	12	3	4[3]	5	6	7		9[2]	10	11	8	13				2[1]	14								16
1	12	3	4	5	6	7[3]		9[2]	10	11	8	13				2[1]	14								17
1		3	4	5	6	7[2]	12		10	11	8	9[1]	13			2									18
1		3	4	5	6	7[3]	12		10	11[1]	8[2]	9	14	13		2									19
1		3	4	5	6	7[1]	12	9[2]	10	11	8	13				2									20
12			4	5	6	7[2]	13	9[1]	10	11	8[3]		14					3	2	1					21
		3	4	5	6	7[1]		9	10	11	8[2]		12				13		2	1					22
	6		4[2]	5	12		8		10	11		9[1]	13				7	3	2	1					23
	6		4	5	12		8	13	10	11[1]		9[2]		14			7[2]	3	2	1					24
			4	5	6		8	9[1]	10	11	12						7	3	2	1					25
	2	12	4	5	6		8	9	10	11							7[1]	3		1					26
		12	4[1]	5	6		8	9	10	11[3]		13		14			7[2]	3	2	1					27
			4[1]	5	6	7	8		10	11[2]		12					13	3	2	1					28
		12	4	5	6	7	8[2]	9[1]	10	11		13						3	2	1					29
	13	12	4[1]	5[2]	6	7	8	9[1]	10	11				14				3	2	1					30
		12	4	5[1]	6	7	8	9	10	11[2]		13						3	2	1					31
			4	5	6[3]	7	8	9[2]	10	11[1]		12		14			13	3	2	1					32
	12	3	4[2]	5		7	8	9[1]	10	11				13	6				2	1					33
		3	4[2]	5			8	9[1]	10	11	12					6	7	13	2	1					34
			4	5	6	7[1]	8		10	11	12[2]	9				2	13	3		1					35
			4	5	6	7	8		10[1]	11		13		9		2	12[2]	3		1					36
	12		4	5	6	7[3]	8			11		13	14	9			10[2]	3[1]		1					37
	12		4	5	6	7[3]	8		10	11[2]				9			13	3[1]		1	2	14			38
			4	5	6	7[2]	8[1]		10	11		12		9			13	3		1	2				39
	12	3	4[3]	5	6		8		10[1]	11				9[2]			7	13	2	1		14			40
		3	4	5	6[3]	7	8			11	12			9[1]		2	13	14		1		10[2]			41
			4	5	6	7[1]	8	9	10	11			12			2	13	3		1					42
			4	5	6	7[2]	8	9[1]	10	11			12			2	13	3		1					43
			4	5	6	7	8	9[1]	10	11			12			2		3		1					44
		3	4	5	6	7[2]	8	9[1]	10	11[1]	12		14			2	13			1					45
		3	4[3]	5	6	7[1]	8	9[2]	10	11	12					2	13			1				14	46

Worthington Cup
First Round   Brentford   (h)   2-1
                                           (a)   0-3

FA Cup
Third Round   Bournemouth   (a)   0-1

FA Premiership

WEST HAM UNITED

FOUNDATION

Thames Ironworks FC was formed by employees of this shipbuilding yard in 1895 and entered the FA Cup in their initial season at Chatham and the London League in their second. Short of funds, the club was wound up in June 1900 and relaunched a month later as West Ham United. Connection with the Ironworks was not finally broken until four years later.

Boleyn Ground, Green Street, Upton Park, London E13 9AZ.
Telephone General Office: (0208) 548 2748.
Ticket Office: (0208) 548 2700.
Merchandise Shop: (0208) 548 2722.
Fax: (0208) 548 2758.
Membership Office: (0208) 548 2727.
Promotions: (0208) 548 2777.
Dial-a-seat: (0208) 548 2700.
Football in the Community: (0208) 548 2707.
Clubcall: 0891 121165.
Ground Capacity: 26,054.
Record Attendance: 42,322 v Tottenham H, Division 1, 17 October 1970.
Record Receipts: £339,420 gross v Liverpool, FA Premier League, 22 November 1995.
Pitch Measurements: 112yd × 72yd.
Chairman: T. W. Brown FCIS, AII, FCCA.
Vice-Chairman: M. W. Cearns ACIB.
Directors: C. J. Warner, N. Igoe, P. Aldridge.
Manager: Harry Redknapp.
Assistant Manager: Frank Lampard.
Coaches: Roger Cross, Tony Carr.
Physio: John Green BSC, MCSP, SRP.
Company Secretary: Graham Mackrell FCCA.
Football Secretary: Alison O'Dowd.
Stadium Manager: John Ball.

LATEST SEQUENCES

Longest Sequence of League Wins: 9, 19.10.85 – 14.12.85.
Longest Sequence of League Defeats: 9, 28.3.32 – 29.8.32.
Longest Sequence of League Draws: 5, 7.9.68 – 5.10.68.
Longest Sequence of Unbeaten League Matches: 27, 27.12.80 – 10.10.81.
Longest Sequence Without a League Win: 17, 31.1.76 – 21.8.76.

HONOURS

Football League: Division 1 best season: 3rd, 1985–86; Division 2 – Champions 1957–58, 1980–81; Runners-up 1922–23, 1990–91.

FA Cup: Winners 1964, 1975, 1980; Runners-up 1923.

Football League Cup: Runners-up 1966, 1981.

European Competitions: European Cup-Winners' Cup: 1964–65 (winners), 1965–66, 1975–76 (runners-up), 1980–81.

Colours
Claret shirts with blue sleeves, white shorts, light blue with claret hooped stockings.

Change Colours
All white.

Year Formed: 1895.

Turned Professional: 1900.

Ltd Co.: 1900.

Previous Name: Thames Iron Works FC, 1895–1900.

Club Nickname: 'The Hammers'.

Previous Grounds: 1895, Memorial Recreation Ground, Canning Town; 1904, Boleyn Ground.

First Football League Game: 30 August 1919, Division 2, v Lincoln C (h) D 1–1 – Hufton; Cope, Lee; Lane, Fenwick, McCrae; D. Smith, Moyes (1), Puddefoot, Morris, Bradshaw.

MANAGERS
Syd King 1902–32
Charlie Paynter 1932–50
Ted Fenton 1950–61
Ron Greenwood 1961–74
(continued as General Manager to 1977)
John Lyall 1974–89
Lou Macari 1989–90
Billy Bonds 1990–94
Harry Redknapp August 1994–

Record League Victory: 8–0 v Rotherham U, Division 2, 8 March 1958 – Gregory; Bond, Wright; Malcolm, Brown, Lansdowne; Grice, Smith (2), Keeble (2), Dick (4), Musgrove. 8–0 v Sunderland, Division 1, 19 October 1968 – Ferguson; Bonds, Charles; Peters, Stephenson, Moore (1); Redknapp, Boyce, Brooking (1), Hurst (6), Sissons.

Record Cup Victory: 10–0 v Bury, League Cup 2nd rd (2nd leg), 25 October 1983 – Parkes; Stewart (1), Walford, Bonds (Orr), Martin (1), Devonshire (2), Allen, Cottee (4), Swindlehurst, Brooking (2), Pike.

Record Defeat: 2–8 v Blackburn R, Division 1, 26 December 1963.

Most League Points (2 for a win): 66, Division 2, 1980–81.

Most League Points (3 for a win): 88, Division 1, 1992–93.

Most League Goals: 101, Division 2, 1957–58.

Highest League Scorer in Season: Vic Watson, 42, Division 1, 1929–30.

Most League Goals in Total Aggregate: Vic Watson, 298, 1920–35.

Most League Goals in One Match: 6, Vic Watson v Leeds U, Division 1, 9 February 1929; 6, Geoff Hurst v Sunderland, Division 1, 19 October 1968.

Most Capped Player: Bobby Moore, 108, England.

Most League Appearances: Billy Bonds, 663, 1967–88.

Youngest League Player: Neil Finn, 17 years 3 days v Manchester C, 1 January 1996.

Record Transfer Fee Received: £7,500,000 from Wimbledon for John Hartson, January 1999.

Record Transfer Fee Paid: £4,200,000 to Lens for Marc-Vivien Foe, January 1999.

Football League Record: 1919 Elected to Division 2; 1923–32 Division 1; 1932–58 Division 2; 1958–78 Division 1; 1978–81 Division 2; 1981–89 Division 1; 1989–91 Division 2; 1991–93 Division 1; 1993– FA Premier League.

TEN YEAR LEAGUE RECORD

		P	W	D	L	F	A	Pts	Pos
1988-89	Div 1	38	10	8	20	37	62	38	19
1989-90	Div 2	46	20	12	14	80	57	72	7
1990-91	Div 2	46	24	15	7	60	34	87	2
1991-92	Div 1	42	9	11	22	37	59	38	22
1992-93	Div 1	46	26	10	10	81	41	88	2
1993-94	PR Lge	42	13	13	16	47	58	52	13
1994-95	PR Lge	42	13	11	18	44	48	50	14
1995-96	PR Lge	38	14	9	15	43	52	51	10
1996-97	PR Lge	38	10	12	16	39	48	42	14
1997-98	PR Lge	38	16	8	14	56	57	56	8

DID YOU KNOW ?

West Ham United's fourth round FA Cup games against Tottenham Hotspur in 1939 drew an aggregate of 143,982 spectators. After a 3–3 draw at Upton Park and a 1–1 stalemate at White Hart Lane, West Ham won 2–1 at Highbury.

WEST HAM UNITED 1998–99 LEAGUE RECORD

Match No.	Date	Venue	Opponents	Result	H/T Score	Lg. Pos.	Goalscorers	Attendance
1	Aug 15	A	Sheffield W	W 1-0	0-0	—	Wright [84]	30,236
2	22	H	Manchester U	D 0-0	0-0	7		25,912
3	29	A	Coventry C	D 0-0	0-0	8		20,818
4	Sept 9	H	Wimbledon	L 3-4	3-1	—	Hartson [7], Wright 2 [14, 27]	24,601
5	12	H	Liverpool	W 2-1	1-0	8	Hartson [4], Berkovic [51]	26,010
6	19	A	Nottingham F	D 0-0	0-0	8		26,463
7	28	H	Southampton	W 1-0	0-0	—	Wright [61]	23,153
8	Oct 3	A	Blackburn R	L 0-3	0-1	9		25,213
9	17	H	Aston Villa	D 0-0	0-0	8		26,002
10	24	A	Charlton Ath	L 2-4	2-1	14	Rufus (og) [18], Berkovic [41]	20,043
11	31	A	Newcastle U	W 3-0	0-0	8	Wright 2 [56, 90], Sinclair [76]	36,744
12	Nov 8	H	Chelsea	D 1-1	1-0	9	Ruddock [4]	26,023
13	14	H	Leicester C	W 3-2	1-1	6	Kitson [37], Lomas [56], Lampard [76]	25,642
14	22	A	Derby Co	W 2-0	1-0	6	Hartson [7], Keller [72]	31,366
15	28	H	Tottenham H	W 2-1	1-0	3	Sinclair 2 [39, 46]	26,044
16	Dec 5	A	Leeds U	L 0-4	0-1	5		36,315
17	12	A	Middlesbrough	L 0-1	0-1	7		34,623
18	19	H	Everton	W 2-1	1-0	7	Keller [19], Sinclair [75]	25,998
19	26	A	Arsenal	L 0-1	0-1	7		38,098
20	28	H	Coventry C	W 2-0	1-0	6	Wright [7], Hartson [68]	25,662
21	Jan 10	A	Manchester U	L 1-4	0-2	8	Lampard [89]	55,180
22	16	H	Sheffield W	L 0-4	0-2	8		25,642
23	30	A	Wimbledon	D 0-0	0-0	9		23,035
24	Feb 6	H	Arsenal	L 0-4	0-2	9		26,042
25	13	H	Nottingham F	W 2-1	2-0	8	Pearce [35], Lampard [39]	25,458
26	20	A	Liverpool	D 2-2	1-2	8	Lampard (pen) [24], Keller [74]	44,511
27	27	H	Blackburn R	W 2-0	2-0	6	Pearce [28], Di Canio [31]	25,529
28	Mar 6	A	Southampton	L 0-1	0-1	7		15,240
29	13	A	Chelsea	W 1-0	0-0	7	Kitson [75]	34,765
30	20	H	Newcastle U	W 2-0	1-0	5	Di Canio [17], Kitson [82]	25,997
31	Apr 2	A	Aston Villa	D 0-0	0-0	—		36,813
32	5	H	Charlton Ath	L 0-1	0-0	5		26,041
33	10	A	Leicester C	D 0-0	0-0	6		20,402
34	17	H	Derby Co	W 5-1	2-0	6	Di Canio [19], Berkovic [28], Wright [55], Ruddock [64], Sinclair [68]	25,485
35	24	A	Tottenham H	W 2-1	1-0	6	Wright [5], Keller [66]	36,089
36	May 1	H	Leeds U	L 1-5	0-2	6	Di Canio [48]	25,997
37	8	A	Everton	L 0-6	0-3	6		40,029
38	16	H	Middlesbrough	W 4-0	2-0	5	Lampard [4], Keller [26], Sinclair 2 [75, 78]	25,902

Final League Position: 5

GOALSCORERS
League (46): Wright 9, Sinclair 7, Keller 5, Lampard 5 (1 pen), Di Canio 4, Hartson 4, Berkovic 3, Kitson 3, Pearce 2, Ruddock 2, Lomas 1, own goal 1.
Worthington Cup (1): Lampard 1.
FA Cup (1): Dicks 1.

Hislop S 37	Impey A 6+2	Lazaridis S 11+4	Pearce I 33	Ferdinand R 31	Ruddock N 27	Lampard F 38	Berkovic E 28+2	Sinclair T 36	Wright I 20+2	Lomas S 30	Moncur J 6+8	Hartson J 16+1	Abou S 2+1	Margas J 3	Potts S 11+8	Breacker T 2+1	Keller M 17+4	Omoyinmi E —+3	Dicks J 9	Hodges L —+1	Kitson P 13+4	Cole J 2+6	Minto S 14+1	Di Canio P 12+1	Foe M 13	Holligan G —+1	Forrest C 1+1	Coyne C —+1	Match No.
1	2	3	4	5	6	7	8^1	9	10	11	12																		1
1	2	3	4	5	6	7	8^1	9		11		10	12																2
1	2	3		5	6	7	8		10	11^1	12	9		4															3
1	12	3	4		6	7	8^1	2	10		11	9		5															4
1		3		5	6	7	8^1	2	10		11	9^2			4	12	13												5
1	3		6	5		7	8	2	10			9^1			4		11		12										6
1	12		4	5	6	7	8^2	2	10^3	13		9	14				11^1		3										7
1	2		6	5^2		7			11	10	8	9			4^1		12		3	13									8
1	12		4	5	6^1	7	8	2	10^2	11		9							3	13									9
1			4	5	6	7	8^1	2	10^2	11	12	9							3	13									10
1	3^2		4	5	6	7		2	10	11	12			13	8						9^1								11
1			4	5	6	7	8^1	2	10	11	12	9							3										12
1			4	5		7	8	2	10	11	12						6				9								13
1			4	5	6	7	8	2	11	10	12								3^1		9								14
1	3		4	5	6	7	8^1	2	11	10	12										9								15
1	3^1		4		6	7	8	2	10		12				5		11				9								16
1	3^1		4	5		7		2	10	11	12				8^1		6			13	9								17
1			4	5		7	8	2	10	11							6		3		9								18
1	12		4	5		7	8	2	10	11							6		3^1		9								19
1	3		4	5		7	8^1	2	10^2	11	12						6		13		9								20
1	3		4	5	6	7	8		10^1	11	12				2						9								21
1			4	5	6^2	7	8^1		10	11					2						9	12	3						22
1			5	4	8	7									2		6				9	12	3	10^1	11				23
1			4	5	8	7					12				2^1		6				9		3	10	11				24
1	3^1		4	5	6	7	8^1	2		11											9	12	13	10					25
1	12		4^1	5		7	8	2	11								6				13	9^1	3^2	10	14				26
1			4	5		7	8								2		6				9		3	10	11				27
1			4	5	6	7	8								2						9	12	3	10	11^1				28
1			4	5	6	7	8	2													9	12	3	10	11^1				29
1			4	5	6	7		2							8						9		3	10	11				30
1			4	5^1	6	7	8	2													9	12	3	10	11				31
1			4	5	6	7		2			12				4						9^1		3	10	11				32
1			4	5	6	7	8	2			12									13	9^1		3	10^2	11				33
1			4^1	5	6	7	8	2^2	9		12									13			3	10	11				34
1	12		4	5	6	7	8	2	10^1												9		3		11				35
1			4	5	6	7	8^6	2^1	10		12										9^2		3		11	15	13		36
1			4	5	6	7	8	2	10^1		12										9		3		11				37
			4	5	6	7	8	2			12										9^1		3	10	11		1		38

Worthington Cup
Second Round   Northampton T   (a) 0-2
                                 (h) 1-0

FA Cup
Third Round   Swansea   (h) 1-1
                          (a) 0-1

Division 2   **WIGAN ATHLETIC**

FOUNDATION

Following the demise of Wigan Borough and their resignation from the Football League in 1931, a public meeting was called in Wigan at the Queen's Hall in May 1932 at which a new club Wigan Athletic, was founded in the hope of carrying on in the Football League. With this in mind, they bought Springfield Park for £2,250, but failed to gain admission to the Football League until 46 years later.

JJB Stadium, Robin Park, Newtown, Wigan WN5.
Ticket Office: (08451) 473227.
Telephone: (01942) 774000.
Fax: (01942) 494654.
Commercial Dept: (01942) 243067.
Latics Clubcall: 0891 121655.
Football in the Community: (01942) 824599.
Ground Capacity: 7290 (to be 25,000 after redevelopment).
Record Attendance: 27,526 v Hereford U, 12 December 1953.
Record Receipts: £40,577 v Leeds U, FA Cup 6th rd, 15 March 1987.
Pitch Measurements: 115yd × 75yd.
President: S. Jackson.
Chairman: David Whelan.
Directors: D. Whelan, J. Winstanley, D. Sharpe, P. Williams, B. Ashcroft.
Chief Executive/Secretary: Mrs Brenda Spencer.
Assistant Secretary: Stuart Hayton.
Football Co-Ordinator: Frank Lord.
General Manager: John Benson.
Physio/Coach: Alex Cribley.
Safety Officer: David Johnson.
Groundsman: David Pinch.

LATEST SEQUENCES

Longest Sequence of League Wins: 6, 26.12.87 – 23.1.88.
Longest Sequence of League Defeats: 7, 6.4.93 – 4.5.93.
Longest Sequence of League Draws: 4, 9.5.89 – 19.8.89.
Longest Sequence of Unbeaten League Matches: 21, 24.10.81 – 12.3.82.
Longest Sequence Without a League Win: 14, 9.5.89 – 17.10.89.

HONOURS

Football League: Division 3 Champions, 1996–97; Division 4 – Promoted (3rd) 1981–82.
FA Cup: best season: 6th rd, 1987.
Football League Cup: best season: 4th rd, 1982.
Freight Rover Trophy: Winners 1985.
Auto Windscreens Shield: Winners 1999.

Colours
Blue shirts with white side panel, blue shorts and stockings.

Change Colours
Gold shirts with blue side panel, gold shorts and stockings.

Year Formed: 1932.

Club Nickname: 'The Latics'.

First Football League Game: 19 August 1978, Division 4, v Hereford U (a) D 0–0 – Brown; Hinnigan, Gore, Gillibrand, Ward, Davids, Corrigan, Purdie, Houghton, Wilkie, Wright.

Record League Victory: 7–1 v Scarborough, Division 3, 11 March 1997 – Butler L, Butler J, Sharp (Morgan), Greenall, McGibbon (Biggins (1)), Martinez (1), Diaz (2), Jones (Lancashire (1)), Lowe (2), Rogers, Kilford.

Record Cup Victory: 6–0 v Carlisle U (away), FA Cup 1st rd, 24 November 1934 – Caunce; Robinson, Talbot; Paterson, Watson, Tufnell; Armes (2), Robson (1), Roberts (2), Felton, Scott (1).

Record Defeat: 1–6 v Bristol R, Division 3, 3 March 1990.

Most League Points (2 for a win): 55, Division 4, 1978–79 and 1979–80.

Most League Points (3 for a win): 91, Division 4, 1981–82.

Most League Goals: 84, Division 3, 1996–97.

Highest League Scorer in Season: Graeme Jones, 31, Division 3, 1996–97.

Most League Goals in Total Aggregate: David Lowe, 66, 1982–87 and 1995–99.

Most League Goals in One Match: Not more than three goals by one player.

Most Capped Player: Roy Carroll, 2, Northern Ireland.

Most League Appearances: Kevin Langley, 317, 1981–86, 1990–94.

Youngest League Player: Steve Nugent, 16 years 132 days v Leyton Orient, 16 September 1989.

Record Transfer Fee Received: £329,000 from Coventry C for Peter Atherton, August 1991.

Record Transfer Fee Paid: £600,000 to Coventry C for Simon Haworth, October 1998.

Football League Record: 1978 Elected to Division 4; 1982–92 Division 3; 1992–93 Division 2; 1993–97 Division 3; 1997– Division 2.

MANAGERS

Charlie Spencer 1932–37
Jimmy Milne 1946–47
Bob Pryde 1949–52
Ted Goodier 1952–54
Walter Crook 1954–55
Ron Suart 1955–56
Billy Cooke 1956
Sam Barkas 1957
Trevor Hitchen 1957–58
Malcolm Barrass 1958–59
Jimmy Shirley 1959
Pat Murphy 1959–60
Allenby Chilton 1960
Johnny Ball 1961–63
Allan Brown 1963–66
Alf Craig 1966–67
Harry Leyland 1967–68
Alan Saunders 1968
Ian McNeill 1968–70
Gordon Milne 1970–72
Les Rigby 1972–74
Brian Tiler 1974–76
Ian McNeill 1976–81
Larry Lloyd 1981–83
Harry McNally 1983–85
Bryan Hamilton 1985–86
Ray Mathias 1986–89
Bryan Hamilton 1989–93
Dave Philpotts 1993
Kenny Swain 1993–94
Graham Barrow 1994–95
John Deehan 1995–98
Ray Mathias 1998–99
John Benson June 1999–

TEN YEAR LEAGUE RECORD

		P	W	D	L	F	A	Pts	Pos
1988-89	Div 3	46	14	14	18	55	53	56	17
1989-90	Div 3	46	13	14	19	48	64	53	18
1990-91	Div 3	46	20	9	17	71	54	69	10
1991-92	Div 3	46	15	14	17	58	64	59	15
1992-93	Div 2	46	10	11	25	43	72	41	23
1993-94	Div 3	42	11	12	19	51	70	45	19
1994-95	Div 3	42	14	10	18	53	60	52	14
1995-96	Div 3	46	20	10	16	62	56	70	10
1996-97	Div 3	46	26	9	11	84	51	87	1
1997-98	Div 2	46	17	11	18	64	66	62	11

DID YOU KNOW ?

On 4 February 1970, when Wigan Athletic beat Darwen 11–1 in a Lancashire FA Challenge Trophy second round tie, Tony McLoughlin scored an impressive seven times: 13, 18, 23, 50, 58, 64 and 90 minutes.

WIGAN ATHLETIC 1998–99 LEAGUE RECORD

Match No.	Date	Venue	Opponents	Result	H/T Score	Lg. Pos.	Goalscorers	Attendance
1	Aug 8	H	Millwall	L	0-1	0-1	—	4285
2	15	A	Lincoln C	L	0-1	0-0	23	3355
3	22	H	Blackpool	W	3-0	2-0	16	Barlow 2 [9, 29], Lee [85]	4853
4	29	A	Bristol R	L	2-3	0-1	17	Barlow [47], McGibbon [84]	6140
5	31	H	Luton T	L	1-3	0-1	18	Barlow [62]	3778
6	Sept 5	A	Notts Co	W	1-0	1-0	18	Barlow [25]	4445
7	8	H	Colchester U	D	1-1	0-0	—	Lee [86]	2784
8	12	A	Bournemouth	L	0-1	0-0	19		5151
9	19	H	Macclesfield T	W	2-0	1-0	17	Lee [24], Barlow (pen) [46]	3839
10	26	A	Burnley	D	1-1	0-0	17	McGibbon [90]	10,183
11	Oct 3	H	Northampton T	W	1-0	0-0	16	Dobson (og) [67]	4396
12	9	A	Oldham Ath	W	3-2	1-0	—	Bradshaw [14], Barlow [55], Warne [73]	5499
13	17	A	Manchester C	L	0-1	0-0	14		6700
14	24	A	Stoke C	L	1-2	0-0	17	Barlow [74]	11,480
15	31	H	York C	W	5-0	2-0	13	Jones (og) [30], Greenall [35], Haworth 2 [56, 83], Liddell [75]	3583
16	Nov 7	A	Gillingham	L	0-2	0-1	17		5869
17	11	A	Reading	W	1-0	1-0	—	Bradshaw (pen) [9]	9317
18	21	H	Wycombe W	D	0-0	0-0	13		3349
19	28	A	Preston NE	D	2-2	1-0	13	Greenall [7], Porter [54]	11,562
20	Dec 1	H	Fulham	W	2-0	0-0	—	McGibbon [51], Lowe [62]	3951
21	12	A	Wrexham	D	1-1	0-0	11	Lee [70]	3440
22	19	A	Chesterfield	D	1-1	1-1	10	Greenall [15]	3896
23	26	A	Blackpool	D	1-1	0-0	10	Liddell [64]	5147
24	28	H	Walsall	W	2-0	0-0	8	Barlow 2 [61, 83]	4579
25	Jan 9	A	Millwall	L	1-3	0-1	12	Jones [89]	5625
26	23	A	Luton T	W	4-0	2-0	11	McGibbon [15], Liddell [29], Jones [64], Haworth [77]	4934
27	30	A	Walsall	W	2-1	1-0	10	Jones [36], Barlow [80]	5473
28	Feb 12	A	Colchester U	L	1-2	0-2	—	Sharp [70]	3934
29	16	H	Notts Co	W	3-0	0-0	—	Bradshaw (pen) [60], Barlow [69], Liddell [89]	2971
30	20	H	Bournemouth	W	2-1	0-0	8	Liddell [54], Barlow [79]	4144
31	27	A	Macclesfield T	W	1-0	1-0	7	Lee [6]	3706
32	Mar 13	H	Gillingham	W	4-1	2-1	9	Rogers [14], Haworth 2 [20, 66], Barlow [87]	4248
33	20	A	York C	W	3-1	3-1	9	Lee [32], Sharp [34], Greenall [36]	3356
34	27	H	Stoke C	L	2-3	0-0	9	Liddell [49], Barlow [51]	4133
35	30	H	Bristol R	W	1-0	1-0	—	Bradshaw (pen) [35]	3568
36	Apr 3	A	Manchester C	L	0-1	0-0	8		31,058
37	5	H	Oldham Ath	W	2-0	1-0	7	Haworth [27], Bradshaw (pen) [90]	4754
38	10	A	Fulham	L	0-2	0-0	7		12,140
39	13	H	Preston NE	D	2-2	2-2	—	Liddell [2], Haworth [38]	5396
40	24	H	Reading	W	4-1	3-0	7	Rogers [6], Barlow 2 [15, 24], Greenall [69]	3885
41	27	H	Lincoln C	W	3-1	0-0	—	Greenall [48], Liddell [62], Bradshaw (pen) [65]	3728
42	29	A	Northampton T	D	3-3	1-1	—	Haworth [9], Barlow (pen) [47], Balmer [78]	5404
43	May 1	A	Wrexham	W	2-0	1-0	7	Barlow [4], Haworth [82]	4172
44	3	H	Burnley	D	0-0	0-0	—		5528
45	5	A	Wycombe W	L	1-2	1-1	—	Haworth [38]	5410
46	8	H	Chesterfield	W	3-1	1-1	6	Liddell 2 [45, 50], McGibbon [65]	5858

Final League Position: 6

GOALSCORERS

League (75): Barlow 19 (2 pens), Haworth 10, Liddell 10, Bradshaw 6 (5 pens), Greenall 6, Lee 6, McGibbon 5, Jones 3, Rogers 2, Sharp 2, Balmer 1, Lowe 1, Porter 1, Warne 1, own goals 2.
Worthington Cup (4): Barlow 1, Griffiths 1, Lee 1, own goal 1.
FA Cup (5): Lowe 2, Barlow 1, Greenall 1, Haworth 1.

Carroll R 43	Green S 32 + 5	Bradshaw G 39	Griffiths G 20	McGibbon P 35 + 1	Rogers P 42	Lee D 20 + 16	Lowe D 5 + 11	Jones G 8 + 12	Kilford I 16 + 7	Jenkinson L 3 + 4	Warne P 8 + 3	Martinez R 3 + 7	Sharp K 25 + 6	Barlow S 39 + 2	Porter A 6 + 10	Greenall C 40	Balmer S 36	O'Neill M 35 + 1	Smeets J — + 1	Haworth S 19 + 1	Nixon E 3	Liddell A 28	Fitzhenry N 1	Match No.
1	2	3	4	5	6	7	8¹	9	10	11	12													1
1	2	3	4	5	6	7	12	9	10²	11³	8¹	13	14											2
1	2	3	4	5	6	7	12	9¹	10²				8³	13	11	14								3
1	2	3	4	5	6	7	9¹		10			12	8²	13	11									4
1	2	3	4	5	6	7	12		10				9¹	8²	13	11								5
1	2	3	4¹	5	6		13		10		12²		9	7		11	8							6
1	2	3	4	5¹	6	12	13		10		9²		7	11		8								7
1	2	3	4	5	6	12		10¹	9²		14		7³	11		8								8
1	2	3¹	4		6	7	9	12	13				11²			8	5	10						9
1	2		4		6¹	7		3²	10		12		11			8	5	9	13					10
1	2	3	4		6	7							11			8	5	10		9				11
	2	3	4		6	7			10				11			8	5	9			1			12
1	2	3	4		6¹	7²	12				14	13	8³	5	10	9				11				13
1	2	3	4		6	12	7					13	8¹	5	10	9				11²				14
1	2	3	4		6¹	13			12				11²	8	5	10	9			7				15
1		3	4	12	6¹	13		2				14	11	8³	5	10	9			7²				16
1	2	3	4		6								11	8	5	10	9							17
1	2²	3	4¹		6	13	9		7			14	12	11	8	5	10³							18
1	2	3	4			7	12				11	6		8	5	10	9¹							19
1	2	3	4		6	9¹	7				11	12	8	5	10									20
1	2	3	4		6	7	12	13	9¹		11²	8	5	10										21
1	2	3	4		7	12					11¹	6	8	5	10					9				22
1	2	3	4		12	7			6		11³	8	5	10					9					23
1	2	3	4		6	12	7	13			11	8	5	10²	9¹									24
1	2		4		6	7²	12	13	3		14	11¹	8	5	10	9								25
1	2		4		6	12	9¹	13		3	11³	8	5²10		14	7								26
1	2	10	4		6	12	9¹			3	11	8	5			7								27
1	2	10	4		6	9	12			3	11¹	13	8²	5		7								28
1	2		4		6	9				3	11	12	8	5	10¹	7								29
1	12	2	4		6	9¹				3	11	8	5	10		7								30
1	2		4		6	9				3	11	8	5	10		7								31
1	2		4		6	12	13			3	11¹²	14	8	5	10³	9¹		7						32
1	2		4		6²	11¹	12			3	13	8	5	10	9	7								33
	2		4		6	9¹	12			3	11	8	5	10						1	7			34
	2		4		6	9¹				3	11	12	8	5	10					1	7			35
	2		4		7²	12	9¹	13		3	11	6	8	5	10									36
1	2		4		6					3	11	8	5	10	9	7								37
1	12	2	4¹		6	13				3	11²	8	5	10	9	7								38
1	2	8			6	13	12²			3	11	5	10	9	7								4¹	39
1	12	2	4		6¹	13	14			3	11²	8	5	10	9³	7								40
1	12	2¹	4		6	13	14			3	11	8	5	10	9	7²								41
1	2		4		6	12				3	11¹	13	8	5	10	9	7²							42
1	4	2			6	12	13			3	11¹	14	8	5	10³	9²	7							43
1	12	2¹	4		6	13	14			3	11	8	5²10		9	7²								44
1	2	5	4		6	12	13			3	11²	10³	8		14	9	7¹							45
1	2	5	4		6	12	13			3	11³	14	8		10¹	9	7²							46

Worthington Cup

First Round	Rochdale	(h)	1-0
		(a)	1-0
Second Round	Norwich C	(a)	0-1
		(h)	2-3

FA Cup

First Round	Blackpool	(h)	4-3
Second Round	Notts Co	(a)	1-1
		(h)	0-0

FA Premiership

WIMBLEDON

FOUNDATION

Old boys from Central School formed this club as Wimbledon Old Centrals in 1889. Their earliest successes were in the Clapham League before switching to the Southern Suburban League in 1902.

Selhurst Park, South Norwood, London SE25 6PY.
Telephone: (0181) 771 2233.
Fax: (0181) 768 0641.
Website: www.wimbledon-fc.co.uk.
Box Office: (0181) 771 8841.
Ground Capacity: 26,297.
Record Attendance: 30,115 v Manchester U, FA Premier League, 9 May 1993.
Record Receipts: £531,976 v Tottenham H, Worthington Cup semi-final, 2nd leg, 16 February 1999.
Pitch Measurements: 110yd × 74yd.
Governor: Sam Hammam.
Chairman: S. G. Reed.
Deputy Chairman: J. H. Lelliott.
Directors: S. G. N. Hammam, K. I. Røkke, B. R. Gjelsten, J. P. Storetvedt, P. Cork, P. R. Lloyd Cooper, N. N. Hammam, P. Miller.
Chief Executive: David Barnard.
Manager: Egil Olsen.
Coaches: David Kemp, Mick Harford.
Club Secretary: Steve Rooke.
Marketing Manager: Sharon Sillitoe.
Press and PR Manager: Reg Davis.
Academy Director: Terry Burton.
Chief Scout: Ron Suart.
Physio: Steve Allen.
Stadium Manager: Vic Worrall.
Safety Officer: Bob Morrison.

LATEST SEQUENCES

Longest Sequence of League Wins: 7, 4.9.96 – 19.10.96.
Longest Sequence of League Defeats: 7, 16.9.95 – 6.11.95.
Longest Sequence of League Draws: 4, 26.10.96 – 23.11.96.
Longest Sequence of Unbeaten League Matches: 22, 15.1.83 – 14.5.83.
Longest Sequence Without a League Win: 14, 16.9.95 – 23.12.95.

HONOURS

FA Premier League: best season: 6th, 1993–94.
Football League: Division 3 – Runners-up 1983–84; Division 4 – Champions 1982–83.
FA Cup: Winners 1988.
Football League Cup: Semi-final 1996–97, 1998–99.
League Group Cup: Runners-up 1982.
Amateur Cup: Winners 1963; Runners-up 1935, 1947.

Colours
All navy blue with yellow trim.

Change Colours
All white with black trim.

Year Formed: 1889.

Turned Professional: 1964.

Ltd Co.: 1964.

Previous Name: Wimbledon Old Centrals, 1899–1905.

Previous Ground: 1899, Plough Lane; 1991, Selhurst Park.

Club Nickname: 'The Dons', 'The Crazy Gang'.

First Football League Game: 20 August 1977, Division 4, v Halifax T (h) D 3–3 – Guy; Bryant (1), Galvin, Donaldson, Aitken, Davies, Galliers, Smith, Connell (1), Holmes, Leslie (1).

Record League Victory: 6–0 v Newport Co, Division 3, 3 September 1983 – Beasant; Peters, Winterburn, Galliers, Morris, Hatter, Evans (2), Ketteridge (1), Cork (3 incl. 1p), Downes, Hodges (Driver).

Record Cup Victory: 7–2 v Windsor & Eton, FA Cup 1st rd, 22 November 1980 – Beasant; Jones, Armstrong, Galliers, Mick Smith (2), Cunningham (1), Ketteridge, Hodges, Leslie, Cork (1), Hubbick (3).

Record Defeat: 0–8 v Everton, League Cup 2nd rd, 29 August 1978.

Most League Points (2 for a win): 61, Division 4, 1978–79.

Most League Points (3 for a win): 98, Division 4, 1982–83.

Most League Goals: 97, Division 3, 1983–84.

Highest League Scorer in Season: Alan Cork, 29, 1983–84.

Most League Goals in Total Aggregate: Alan Cork, 145, 1977–92.

Most League Goals in One Match: 4, Alan Cork v Torquay U, Division 4, 28 February 1979.

Most Capped Player: Kenny Cunningham, 23, Republic of Ireland.

Most League Appearances: Alan Cork, 430, 1977–92.

Youngest League Player: Kevin Gage, 17 years 15 days v Bury, 2 May 1981.

Record Transfer Fee Received: £4,000,000 from Newcastle U for Warren Barton, June 1995.

Record Transfer Fee Paid: £7,500,000 to West Ham U for John Hartson, January 1999.

Football League Record: 1977 Elected to Division 4; 1979–80 Division 3; 1980–81 Division 4; 1981–82 Division 3; 1982–83 Division 4; 1983–84 Division 3; 1984–86 Division 2; 1986–92 Division 1; 1992– FA Premier League.

MANAGERS

Les Henley 1955–71
Mike Everitt 1971–73
Dick Graham 1973–74
Allen Batsford 1974–78
Dario Gradi 1978–81
Dave Bassett 1981–87
Bobby Gould 1987–90
Ray Harford 1990–91
Peter Withe 1991
Joe Kinnear 1992–99
Egil Olsen July 1999–

TEN YEAR LEAGUE RECORD

		P	W	D	L	F	A	Pts	Pos
1988-89	Div 1	38	14	9	15	50	46	51	12
1989-90	Div 1	38	13	16	9	47	40	55	8
1990-91	Div 1	38	14	14	10	53	46	56	7
1991-92	Div 1	42	13	14	15	53	53	53	13
1992-93	PR Lge	42	14	12	16	56	55	54	12
1993-94	PR Lge	42	18	11	13	56	53	65	6
1994-95	PR Lge	42	15	11	16	48	65	56	9
1995-96	PR Lge	38	10	11	17	55	70	41	14
1996-97	PR Lge	38	15	11	12	49	46	56	8
1997-98	PR Lge	38	10	14	14	34	46	44	15

DID YOU KNOW

Wimbledon were 3–0 down after only 26 minutes play on 9 September 1998 in a Premier League game at West Ham United's Upton Park ground. They eventually ran out 4–3 winners, the winning goal coming in the 81st minute.

WIMBLEDON 1998–99 LEAGUE RECORD

Match No.	Date	Venue	Opponents	Result	H/T Score	Lg. Pos.	Goalscorers	Attendance
1	Aug 15	H	Tottenham H	W 3-1	0-0	—	Earle [48], Ekoku 2 [59, 90]	23,031
2	22	A	Derby Co	D 0-0	0-0	4		25,710
3	29	H	Leeds U	D 1-1	0-0	5	Hughes M [72]	16,473
4	Sept 9	A	West Ham U	W 4-3	1-3	—	Gayle 2 [30, 77], Euell [64], Ekoku [81]	24,601
5	12	A	Aston Villa	L 0-2	0-1	7		32,959
6	19	H	Sheffield W	W 2-1	1-0	4	Euell 2 [1, 50]	13,163
7	27	A	Leicester C	D 1-1	0-0	3	Earle [74]	17,725
8	Oct 3	H	Everton	L 1-2	1-1	8	Roberts [8]	16,054
9	17	A	Manchester U	L 1-5	1-2	11	Euell [39]	55,265
10	24	H	Middlesbrough	D 2-2	1-2	13	Gayle 2 [26, 76]	14,114
11	31	H	Blackburn R	D 1-1	0-0	12	Earle [76]	12,526
12	Nov 7	A	Nottingham F	W 1-0	1-0	10	Gayle [23]	21,362
13	14	A	Chelsea	L 0-3	0-1	10		34,800
14	21	H	Arsenal	W 1-0	0-0	8	Ekoku [77]	26,003
15	28	A	Newcastle U	L 1-3	1-1	10	Gayle [34]	36,623
16	Dec 5	H	Coventry C	W 2-1	0-0	8	Euell 2 [71, 83]	11,717
17	13	H	Liverpool	W 1-0	0-0	8	Earle [48]	26,080
18	19	A	Southampton	L 1-3	0-1	8	Gayle [76]	14,354
19	26	H	Charlton Ath	W 2-1	1-1	8	Euell [33], Hughes M [51]	19,106
20	29	A	Leeds U	D 2-2	1-1	—	Earle [41], Cort [83]	39,901
21	Jan 9	A	Derby Co	W 2-1	1-0	6	Euell [8], Roberts [83]	12,732
22	16	A	Tottenham H	D 0-0	0-0	7		32,422
23	30	H	West Ham U	D 0-0	0-0	7		23,035
24	Feb 8	A	Charlton Ath	L 0-2	0-1	—		20,002
25	21	H	Aston Villa	D 0-0	0-0	9		15,582
26	27	A	Everton	D 1-1	1-0	9	Ekoku [14]	32,574
27	Mar 3	A	Sheffield W	W 2-1	2-0	—	Ekoku [8], Gayle [31]	24,116
28	6	H	Leicester C	L 0-1	0-1	6		11,801
29	13	A	Nottingham F	L 1-3	0-1	8	Gayle [79]	12,149
30	20	A	Blackburn R	L 1-3	0-3	8	Euell [65]	21,754
31	Apr 3	H	Manchester U	D 1-1	1-1	10	Euell [5]	26,121
32	5	A	Middlesbrough	L 1-3	0-3	11	Cort [75]	33,999
33	11	H	Chelsea	L 1-2	0-1	11	Gayle [90]	21,577
34	19	A	Arsenal	L 1-5	0-1	—	Cort [70]	37,982
35	24	H	Newcastle U	D 1-1	1-1	13	Hartson [24]	21,325
36	May 1	A	Coventry C	L 1-2	0-2	13	Hartson [74]	21,198
37	8	H	Southampton	L 0-2	0-0	15		24,068
38	16	A	Liverpool	L 0-3	0-1	16		41,902

Final League Position: 16

GOALSCORERS
League (40): Euell 10, Gayle 10, Ekoku 6, Earle 5, Cort 3, Hartson 2, Hughes M 2, Roberts 2.
Worthington Cup (11): Ardley 3, Ekoku 3, Earle 1, Gayle 1, Hughes M 1 (pen), Kennedy 1, Leaburn 1.
FA Cup (2): Earle 1, Cort 1.

Sullivan N 38	Cunningham K 35	Kimble A 22 + 4	Roberts A 23 + 5	Blackwell D 27 + 1	Perry C 34	Ardley N 16 + 7	Earle R 35	Ekoku E 11 + 11	Euell J 31 + 2	Hughes M 28 + 2	Fear P — + 2	Gayle M 31 + 4	Jupp D 3 + 3	Kennedy M 7 + 10	Leaburn C 14 + 8	Thatcher B 31	Cort C 6 + 10	Ainsworth G 5 + 3	Hughes C 8 + 6	Hartson J 12 + 2	Goodman J — + 1	Castledine S 1	Match No.
1	2	3	4	5	6	7^1	8	9	10^2	11^3		12	13	14									1
1	2	3	4	5^2	6	7^1	8	9^3	10^1	11		12	13	14									2
1	2	3	4	5	6	7^1	8	9^2	10	11		12				13							3
1	5	3	4		6		8^1	12	10	11		7	2	9									4
1	2	3	4^3		6		8	12	10	7^2	14	11^1		13	9	5							5
1	2	3	4		6		8^3	12	10	7		11^1	13		9^2	5	14						6
1	2	3	4		6	12	8^1	9^1	10	7		11				5	13						7
1	2	3	4		6		8		10	7		11^1		12	9^1	5							8
1	2	3^1	4	5	6	12	8		10	11		13			9^2	7							9
1	2		4	5	6		8		10^1	7		11		12	9^2	3	13						10
1	2	12		5^1	6	4^3	8		10	7		11		13	9^2	3	14						11
1	2	3	12		6	13	8		10	4^2		11			9^1	5		7					12
1	2	3^1	4	12	6		8	13		10^2		9^2		11	14	5		7					13
1	2		5	6	12	8	13	10	4			11^2			9	3		7^1					14
1	2	12	5	6	13	8	14	10				11			4^2	9^3	3	7^1					15
1	2		5	6	4	8	9	10	7			11^1				3	12						16
1	2	12	5	6	4	8	13	10	7			11^1				9^2	3						17
1	2	10^3	5	6	4^1	8	9^2		7			11	13			3	12	14					18
1	2	12		5^1	6	4^2	8		10	7		11			9	3	13						19
1	2	3^2			6	4	8		10	7		11		13	9^1	5	12						20
1		3	4	5	6		12	10	7^2			9		13	14	2	8^3		11^1				21
1	2		4	5	6	7^2	8	12		11		10^1		13	14	3			9^3				22
1	2	3			6		8	9^1	7	11^2				13	12	5		4	10				23
1	2		4	5	6	7		10^2				11			3	8^1		12	9	13			24
1	2	12	4	5	6	7	8	9^2	10			11		13	3^1								25
1	2		4	5	6	12	8	9	10^1	7		11			3								26
1	2	3	4	5	6	7^1	8	9	12	11^2		10				13							27
1	2	3	4		6		8	9^2	10	7^1		11			5			12	13				28
1	2	3	4^2		6^1	7	8	12	13	14		10		11^3	5				9				29
1	2	3		5		4^2	8	12	10	7		11			6			13	9^1				30
1		3^2	12	5	6	13	8		10	7		11			2	14		4^1	9^3				31
1		12	5	6	2^2	8		10	13			11			3	14	7^1	4	9^3				32
1	2		4	5	6			10	7^3			11		12		3^1	13	14	8	9^2			33
1	2	3		5		8		11^1		9			6	10	12	4	13			7^2			34
1	4	12		5		8		7		11	2		3	10		6	9^1						35
1	4			5		8		10		11	2	7	12	3		6^1	9						36
1	2	3	4	5	6		8			7^1	11			10			9						37
1	2	3	4	5	6		8			11	7			10^1			12	9					38

Worthington Cup

Second Round	Portsmouth	(a)	1-2
		(h)	4-1
Third Round	Birmingham C	(a)	2-1
Fourth Round	Bolton W	(a)	2-1
Fifth Round	Chelsea	(h)	2-1
Semi-Final	Tottenham H	(a)	0-0
		(h)	0-1

FA Cup

Third Round	Manchester C	(h)	1-0
Fourth Round	Tottenham H	(h)	1-1
		(a)	0-3

Division 1 **WOLVERHAMPTON WANDERERS**

**Wolverhampton
Wanderers FC**

FOUNDATION

Another club where precise details of information are confused,
due in part to the existence of an earlier Wolverhampton club
which played rugby. However, it is now considered likely that it
came into being in 1879 when players from St Luke's (founded
1877) and Wanderers Cricket Club joined forces to form
Wolverhampton Wanderers FC.

Molineux Grounds, Wolverhampton WV1 4QR.

Telephone: (01902) 655000.

Fax: (01902) 687006.

Ground Capacity: 28,525.

Record Attendance: 63,315 v Liverpool, FA Cup 5th rd, 11 February 1939.

Record Receipts: £319,141 v Arsenal, FA Cup 4th rd, 24 January 1999.

Pitch Measurements: 110yd × 75yd.

President: Sir Jack Hayward.

Chairman: Sir Jack Hayward.

Managing Director: John Richards.

Directors: Jack Harris, John Harris, Rachael Heyhoe
Flint, Rick Hayward.

Manager: Colin Lee.

Assistant Manager: John Ward.

Stadium Manager: Clive Mountford.

Coach: Terry Connor.

Physio: Barry Holmes.

Secretary: Richard Skirrow.

LATEST SEQUENCES

Longest Sequence of League Wins: 8, 15.10.88 – 26.11.88.

Longest Sequence of League Defeats: 8, 5.12.81 – 13.2.82.

Longest Sequence of League Draws: 6, 22.4.95 – 20.8.95.

Longest Sequence of Unbeaten League Matches: 20,
24.11.23 – 5.4.24.

Longest Sequence Without a League Win: 19, 1.12.84 –
6.4.85.

HONOURS

Football League: Division 1 –
Champions 1953–54, 1957–58,
1958–59; Runners-up 1937–38,
1938–39, 1949–50, 1954–55, 1959–60;
Division 2 – Champions 1931–32,
1976–77; Runners-up 1966–67,
1982–83; Division 3 (N) – Champions
1923–24; Division 3 – Champions
1988–89; Division 4 – Champions
1987–88.

FA Cup: Winners 1893, 1908, 1949,
1960; Runners-up 1889, 1896, 1921,
1939.

Football League Cup: Winners 1974,
1980.

Texaco Cup: Winners 1971.

Sherpa Van Trophy: Winners 1988.

European Competitions: *European
Cup:* 1958–59, 1959–60. *European
Cup-Winners' Cup:* 1960–61. *UEFA
Cup:* 1971–72 (runners-up), 1973–74,
1974–75, 1980–81.

Colours
Gold shirts, black shorts, gold stockings.

Change Colours
White shirts, white shorts.

Year Formed: 1877* (*see Foundation*).

Turned Professional: 1888.

Ltd Co.: 1982.

Previous Names: 1879, St Luke's combined with Wanderers Cricket Club to become Wolverhampton Wanderers (1923) Ltd until 1982.

Club Nickname: 'Wolves'.

Previous Grounds: 1877, Goldthorn Hill; 1879, John Harper's Field; 1881, Dudley Road; 1889, Molineux.

First Football League Game: 8 September 1888, Football League, v Aston Villa (h) D 1–1 – Baynton; Baugh, Mason; Fletcher, Allen, Lowder; Hunter, Cooper, Anderson, White, Cannon, (1 og).

Record League Victory: 10–1 v Leicester C, Division 1, 15 April 1938 – Sidlow; Morris, Dowen; Galley, Cullis, Gardiner; Maguire (1), Horace Wright, Westcott (4), Jones (1), Dorsett (4).

Record Cup Victory: 14–0 v Cresswell's Brewery, FA Cup 2nd rd, 13 November 1886 – I. Griffiths; Baugh, Mason; Pearson, Allen (1), Lowder; Hunter (4), Knight (2), Brodie (4), B. Griffiths (2), Wood. Plus one goal 'scrambled through'.

Record Defeat: 1–10 v Newton Heath, Division 1, 15 October 1892.

Most League Points (2 for a win): 64, Division 1, 1957–58.

Most League Points (3 for a win): 92, Division 4, 1988–89.

Most League Goals: 115, Division 2, 1931–32.

Highest League Scorer in Season: Dennis Westcott, 38, Division 1, 1946–47.

Most League Goals in Total Aggregate: Steve Bull, 250, 1986–99.

Most League Goals in One Match: 5, Joe Butcher v Accrington, Division 1, 19 November 1892; 5, Tom Phillipson v Barnsley, Division 2, 26 April 1926; 5, Tom Phillipson v Bradford C, Division 2, 25 December 1926; 5, Billy Hartill v Notts Co, Division 2, 12 October 1929; 5, Billy Hartill v Aston Villa, Division 1, 3 September 1934.

Most Capped Player: Billy Wright, 105, England (70 consecutive).

Most League Appearances: Derek Parkin, 501, 1967–82.

Youngest League Player: Jimmy Mullen, 16 years 43 days v Leeds U, 18 February 1939.

Record Transfer Fee Received: £2,000,000 from Crystal Palace for Neil Emblen, August 1997.

Record Transfer Fee Paid: £1,850,000 to Bradford C for Dean Richards, May 1995.

Football League Record: 1888 Founder Member of Football League: 1906–23 Division 2; 1923–24 Division 3 (N); 1924–32 Division 3; 1932–65 Division 1; 1965–67 Division 2; 1967–76 Division 1; 1976–77 Division 2; 1977–82 Division 1; 1982–83 Division 2; 1983–84 Division 1; 1984–85 Division 2; 1985–86 Division 3; 1986–88 Division 4; 1988–89 Division 3; 1989–92 Division 2; 1992– Division 1.

MANAGERS

George Worrall 1877–85
   (*Secretary-Manager*)
John Addenbrooke 1885–1922
George Jobey 1922–24
Albert Hoskins 1924–26
   (*had been Secretary since 1922*)
Fred Scotchbrook 1926–27
Major Frank Buckley 1927–44
Ted Vizard 1944–48
Stan Cullis 1948–64
Andy Beattie 1964–65
Ronnie Allen 1966–68
Bill McGarry 1968–76
Sammy Chung 1976–78
John Barnwell 1978–81
Ian Greaves 1982
Graham Hawkins 1982–84
Tommy Docherty 1984–85
Bill McGarry 1985
Sammy Chapman 1985–86
Brian Little 1986
Graham Turner 1986–94
Graham Taylor 1994–95
Mark McGhee 1995–98
Colin Lee November 1998–

TEN YEAR LEAGUE RECORD

		P	W	D	L	F	A	Pts	Pos
1988-89	Div 3	46	26	14	6	96	49	92	1
1989-90	Div 2	46	18	13	15	67	60	67	10
1990-91	Div 2	46	13	19	14	63	63	58	12
1991-92	Div 2	46	18	10	18	61	54	64	11
1992-93	Div 1	46	16	13	17	57	56	61	11
1993-94	Div 1	46	17	17	12	60	47	68	8
1994-95	Div 1	46	21	13	12	77	61	76	4
1995-96	Div 1	46	13	16	17	56	62	55	20
1996-97	Div 1	46	22	10	14	68	51	76	3
1997-98	Div 1	46	18	11	17	57	53	65	9

DID YOU KNOW ?

Wolverhampton Wanderers pre-war full-back pairing of the brothers Jack and Frank Taylor later managed League clubs within eight days of each other in 1952, Jack with Queens Park Rangers, Frank at Stoke City.

**Wolverhampton
Wanderers FC**

WOLVERHAMPTON WANDERERS 1998–99 LEAGUE RECORD

Match No.	Date	Venue	Opponents	Result	H/T Score	Lg. Pos.	Goalscorers	Attendance
1	Aug 8	H	Tranmere R	W 2-0	1-0	—	Keane [19], Curle (pen) [88]	20,203
2	15	A	Oxford U	W 2-0	1-0	1	Bull [45], Osborn [80]	7521
3	22	H	Swindon T	W 1-0	1-0	4	Curle (pen) [29]	21,537
4	28	A	Watford	W 2-0	1-0	—	Bull [44], Keane [46]	12,016
5	31	H	Stockport Co	D 2-2	2-1	2	Richards [6], Fernando [37]	22,217
6	Sept 8	A	Port Vale	L 1-2	0-1	—	Keane [67]	8087
7	12	H	Sunderland	D 1-1	0-0	5	Keane [68]	26,816
8	19	A	Huddersfield T	L 1-2	0-1	7	Keane [89]	13,854
9	26	H	Bury	W 1-0	0-0	4	Bull [66]	20,155
10	29	H	QPR	L 1-2	0-2	—	Foley [75]	20,201
11	Oct 3	A	Crewe Alex	D 0-0	0-0	8		5759
12	17	A	Portsmouth	L 0-1	0-0	10		13,681
13	20	A	Crystal Palace	L 2-3	0-1	—	Sedgley 2 [63, 96]	16,417
14	24	H	Grimsby T	W 2-0	2-0	12	Foley [21], Curle (pen) [36]	18,480
15	31	H	Barnsley	D 1-1	1-0	—	Muscat (pen) [5]	20,714
16	Nov 3	A	Ipswich T	L 0-2	0-1	—		14,680
17	7	A	Bristol C	W 6-1	2-1	8	Whittingham [19], Connolly 4 [22, 57, 67, 77], Robinson [79]	15,432
18	10	H	Sheffield U	W 2-1	0-1	—	Connolly [50], Robinson [55]	20,804
19	14	A	Norwich C	D 0-0	0-0	7		17,275
20	22	H	Birmingham C	W 3-1	0-1	5	Naylor [72], Robinson 2 [80, 89]	23,037
21	29	A	WBA	L 0-2	0-1	8		22,682
22	Dec 5	H	Bolton W	D 1-1	0-0	10	Emblen [72]	22,537
23	12	H	Norwich C	D 2-2	0-1	12	Keane 2 [84, 89]	21,014
24	19	A	Bradford C	L 1-2	0-1	12	Keane [67]	13,846
25	26	A	Swindon T	L 0-1	0-0	12		11,627
26	28	H	Ipswich T	W 1-0	0-0	12	Muscat [88]	24,636
27	Jan 8	A	Tranmere R	W 2-1	2-1	—	Keane [1], Fernando [12]	6179
28	16	H	Watford	D 0-0	0-0	11		23,408
29	30	A	Stockport Co	W 2-1	0-0	9	Richards [54], Robinson [74]	8654
30	Feb 6	H	Oxford U	D 1-1	1-1	9	Keane [36]	20,811
31	13	H	Port Vale	W 3-1	2-1	7	Simpson [2], Keane [32], Curle (pen) [89]	20,952
32	20	A	Sunderland	L 1-2	1-1	8	Melville (og) [23]	41,268
33	27	H	Huddersfield T	D 2-2	1-0	7	Robinson [10], Gray (og) [64]	21,778
34	Mar 6	A	QPR	W 1-0	0-0	9	Sedgley [84]	13,150
35	13	H	Bristol C	W 3-0	1-0	6	Flo 2 [14, 84], Sebok (og) [53]	25,237
36	16	A	Bury	D 0-0	0-0	—		5204
37	20	A	Barnsley	W 3-2	1-2	6	Emblen [41], Connolly [78], Richards [90]	16,587
38	30	H	Crewe Alex	W 3-0	2-0	6	Robinson [14], Flo [25], Muscat (pen) [78]	24,197
39	Apr 3	H	Portsmouth	W 2-0	0-0	6	Muscat [71], Flo [76]	23,262
40	5	A	Sheffield U	D 1-1	0-0	5	Osborn [86]	21,761
41	10	H	Crystal Palace	D 0-0	0-0	5		23,643
42	17	A	Birmingham C	W 1-0	1-0	6	Corica [13]	28,143
43	25	H	WBA	D 1-1	1-1	6	Robinson [37]	27,038
44	30	A	Bolton W	D 1-1	0-1	—	Corica [52]	20,208
45	May 4	H	Grimsby T	D 0-0	0-0	—		7009
46	9	H	Bradford C	L 2-3	1-2	7	Flo [12], Simpson [81]	27,589

Final League Position: 7

GOALSCORERS

League (64): Keane 11, Robinson 8, Connolly 6, Flo 5, Curle 4 (4 pens), Muscat 4 (2 pens), Bull 3, Richards 3, Sedgley 3, Corica 2, Emblen 2, Fernando 2, Foley 2, Osborn 2, Simpson 2, Naylor 1, Whittingham 1, own goals 3.
Worthington Cup (8): Bull 3, Keane 3, Ferguson 1, Osborn 1.
FA Cup (3): Keane 2, Flo 1.

Stowell M 46	Muscat K 37	Froggatt S 8	Richards D 40 + 1	Emblen N 30 + 3	Curle K 44	Corica S 20 + 11	Robinson C 29 + 5	Bull S 11 + 4	Keane R 30 + 3	Osborn S 36 + 1	Sedgley S 41 + 3	Naylor L 17 + 6	Fernando 17 + 2	Connolly D 18 + 14	Gilkes M 25 + 5	Foley D 2 + 3	Atkins M 15	Ferguson D 2 + 2	Whittingham G 9 + 1	Jones M — + 2	Green R 1	Niestroj R 2 + 3	Flo H 18 + 1	Simpson P 8 + 3	Match No.
1	2	3	4	5	6	7[1]	8	9	10	11	12														1
1	2	7	4		6			9	10	11	5	3	8												2
1	2	7	4		6			9	10[1]	11	5	3	8	12											3
1	2	7	4		6			9	10[1]	11	5	3	8	12											4
1	2	7	4		6			9	10	11	5	3[1]	8	12											5
1	2	7	4		6			9	10	11	5	3[1]	8	12											6
1	2	7	4		6			9	10[1]	11	5	3	8	12											7
1	2	7	4		6			9	10	11	5	3[1]	8	12											8
1	2		4	8	6			9	10	11[1]	5	3		12	7[2]	13									9
1	2		4	8	6			9	10		5	3[1]	11	12	7[2]	13									10
1	2		4		6	7	8	9	10	11	5	3													11
1			4		6	7	8	9	10		5	3[1]	11	12			2								12
1	2		4[1]		6	7	8	9[2]	10		5	3	11	12		13									13
1	2		4		6	7	8	9	10		5	3	11												14
1	2		4		6	7	8	9		11	5	3	10												15
1	2		4		6	7[2]	8[1]	9		11	5	3		12		13			10						16
1	2[2]		4		6	7	13			11	5	3	8[1]	9[2]	12				10	14					17
1			4		6	7				11	5	3	8[1]	9	12	13			10			2[2]			18
1			4	5	6	7	8			11		3		12	9		2		10[1]						19
1	2		4		6	7[1]	8			11	5	3		12	9				10						20
1	3		4		6	7[1]	8[2]			11	5			12	9		2		10			13			21
1	2		4		6	7[1]	8		10	11	5	3		12					9[2]			13			22
1	2		4		6	7	8		10	11[1]	5[3]	3		12					9[2]	14		13			23
1			4[2]		6	7[1]	8		10	11	5	3			9		2		12			13			24
1			4		6	7	8		10	11	5	3			9		2								25
1	3		4	10	6		8			11[2]	5[3]			13	12		2	9		14		7[1]			26
1	3		4[1]	5	6		8		10	11	12			13	9[2]		2			14		7[3]			27
1	3		4[1]	5	6		8		10	11					12		2					7	9		28
1	3		4[1]	5	6		8		10	11					12		2					7	9		29
1	3		4	5	6		8[1]		10	11					12		2					7[2]	9	13	30
1	3		4	5	6		8[1]		10	11	12			13			2[2]			14		7	9[3]		31
1	3		4	5	6		8		10	11							2					7	9		32
1			5	8	6	7			10[1]	11	4	3			12		2						9		33
1			5	8	6				10[2]	11	4	3		13	12		2						9	7[1]	34
1			5	8[2]	6				10	11[1]	4	3		13	12		2			14			9	7[3]	35
1			5	8	6				10[2]	11	4	3		13	12		2						9	7[1]	36
1	2		5	8	6	7[1]			10[2]	11	4	3		13					12				9[3]		37
1	2		5	8	6	7[2]			10	11	4	3[1]			12					14		13	9[3]		38
1	2		5	8	6	7			10	11	4[1]	3			12								9		39
1	2		5	8	6	7			10[1]	11	4	3			12								9		40
1	2		5	8	6	7			10[1]	11	4	3[2]		13	12								9		41
1	2		5	10	6	7	8			11	4	3			12								9[1]		42
1	2		5	8	6	7			10[2]		4	3		13	12					14			9[1]	11[3]	43
1	2		5	8	6	7		9	10[1]	11	4	3							12						44
1	2		5	8	6	7[3]			10[1]	11	4	3		13	12					14			9[2]		45
1	2		5	8	6				10[1]	11[2]	4	3		13	12					14			9[3]	7	46

Worthington Cup

First Round   Barnet   (a) 1-2   (h) 5-0

Second Round   Bournemouth   (a) 1-1   (h) 1-2

FA Cup

Third Round   Bolton W   (a) 2-1

Fourth Round   Arsenal   (h) 1-2

Division 2

WREXHAM

Racecourse Ground, Mold Road, Wrexham LL11 2AH.
Telephone: (01978) 262129.
Fax: (01978) 357821.
Commercial Dept: (01978) 352536.
Community Office: (01978) 358545.
Clubcall: 0891 121642.
Ground Capacity: 15,500.
Record Attendance: 34,445 v Manchester U, FA Cup 4th rd, 26 January 1957.
Record Receipts: £126,012 v West Ham U, FA Cup 4th rd, 4 February 1992.
Pitch Measurements: 111yd × 71yd.
Chairman: W. P. Griffiths.
Managing Director: D. L. Rhodes.
Directors: C. Griffiths (Vice-Chairman), B. Williams.
Manager: Brian Flynn.
Assistant Manager: Kevin Reeves.
Secretary: D. L. Rhodes.
Player-Coach: Joey Jones.
Commercial Manager: Allan Thomas.
Physio: Mel Pejic.

LATEST SEQUENCES

Longest Sequence of League Wins: 7, 4.3.78 – 27.3.78.
Longest Sequence of League Defeats: 9, 2.10.63 – 30.10.63.
Longest Sequence of League Draws: 5, 29.10.66 – 19.11.66.
Longest Sequence of Unbeaten League Matches: 16, 3.9.66 – 19.11.66.
Longest Sequence Without a League Win: 14, 4.3.50 – 26.8.50.

HONOURS

Football League: Division 2 best
season: 7th, 1997–98; Division 3 –
Champions 1977–78; Runners-up
1992–93; Division 3 (N) – Runners-up
1932–33; Division 4 – Runners-up
1969–70.

FA Cup: best season: 6th rd, 1974,
1978, 1997.

Football League Cup: best season:
5th rd, 1961, 1978.

Welsh Cup: Winners 23 times
(record); Runners-up 22 times
(record).

FAW Premier Cup: Winners 1998.

*European Competition: European
Cup-Winners' Cup:* 1972–73, 1975–76,
1978–79, 1979–80, 1984–85, 1986–87,
1990–91, 1995–96.

Colours
Red shirts, white shorts, red stockings.

Change Colours
Gold shirts, navy blue shorts, navy blue stockings.

Year Formed: 1872 (oldest club in Wales).

Turned Professional: 1912.

Ltd Co.: 1912.

Club Nickname: 'Robins'.

Previous Grounds: 1872, Racecourse Ground; 1883, Rhosddu Recreation Ground; 1887, Racecourse Ground.

First Football League Game: 27 August 1921, Division 3 (N), v Hartlepools U (h) L 0–2 – Godding; Ellis, Simpson; Matthias, Foster, Griffiths; Burton, Goode, Cotton, Edwards, Lloyd.

Record League Victory: 10–1 v Hartlepool U, Division 4, 3 March 1962 – Keelan; Peter Jones, McGavan; Tecwyn Jones, Fox, Ken Barnes; Ron Barnes (3), Bennion (1), Davies (3), Ambler (3), Ron Roberts.

Record Cup Victory: 11–1 v New Brighton, Football League Northern Section Cup 1st rd, 3 January 1934 – Foster; Alfred Jones, Hamilton, Bulling, McMahon, Lawrence, Bryant (3), Findlay (1), Bamford (5), Snow, Waller (1), (o.g. 1).

Record Defeat: 0–9 v Brentford, Division 3, 15 October 1963.

Most League Points (2 for a win): 61, Division 4, 1969–70 and Division 3, 1977–78.

Most League Points (3 for a win): 80, Division 3, 1992–93.

Most League Goals: 106, Division 3 (N), 1932–33.

Highest League Scorer in Season: Tom Bamford, 44, Division 3 (N), 1933–34.

Most League Goals in Total Aggregate: Tom Bamford, 175, 1928–34.

Most League Goals in One Match: 5, Tom Lewis v Crewe Alex, Division 3N, 20 September 1930; 5, Tom Bamford v Carlisle U, Division 3N, 17 March 1934.

Most Capped Player: Joey Jones, 29 (72), Wales.

Most League Appearances: Arfon Griffiths, 592, 1959–61, 1962–79.

Youngest League Player: Ken Roberts, 15 years 158 days v Bradford PA, 1 September 1951.

Record Transfer Fee Received: £800,000 from Birmingham C for Bryan Hughes, March 1997.

Record Transfer Fee Paid: £210,000 to Liverpool for Joey Jones, October 1978.

Football League Record: 1921 Original Member of Division 3 (N); 1958–60 Division 3; 1960–62 Division 4; 1962–64 Division 3; 1964–70 Division 4; 1970–78 Division 3; 1978–82 Division 2; 1982–83 Division 3; 1983–92 Division 4; 1992–93 Division 3; 1993– Division 2.

MANAGERS

Selection Committee 1872–1924
Charlie Hewitt 1924–25
Selection Committee 1925–1929
Jack Baynes 1929–31
Ernest Blackburn 1932–37
James Logan 1937–38
Arthur Cowell 1938
Tom Morgan 1938–42
Tom Williams 1942–49
Les McDowell 1949–50
Peter Jackson 1950–55
Cliff Lloyd 1955–57
John Love 1957–59
Cliff Lloyd 1959–60
Billy Morris 1960–61
Ken Barnes 1961–65
Billy Morris 1965
Jack Rowley 1966–67
Alvan Williams 1967–68
John Neal 1968–77
Arfon Griffiths 1977–81
Mel Sutton 1981–82
Bobby Roberts 1982–85
Dixie McNeil 1985–89
Brian Flynn November 1989–

TEN YEAR LEAGUE RECORD

		P	W	D	L	F	A	Pts	Pos
1988-89	Div 4	46	19	14	13	77	63	71	7
1989-90	Div 4	46	13	12	21	51	67	51	21
1990-91	Div 4	46	10	10	26	48	74	40	24
1991-92	Div 4	42	14	9	19	52	73	51	14
1992-93	Div 3	42	23	11	8	75	52	80	2
1993-94	Div 2	46	17	11	18	66	77	62	12
1994-95	Div 2	46	16	15	15	65	64	63	13
1995-96	Div 2	46	18	16	12	76	55	70	8
1996-97	Div 2	46	17	18	11	54	50	69	8
1997-98	Div 2	46	18	16	12	55	51	70	7

DID YOU KNOW ❓

It was not a white Christmas Day in 1933, but Wrexham opened the scoring away to Tranmere Rovers through George Snow, going on to win this Third Division (North) match 2–1. Wrexham finished sixth, one place above Tranmere.

WREXHAM 1998–99 LEAGUE RECORD

Match No.	Date	Venue	Opponents	Result	H/T Score	Lg. Pos.	Goalscorers	Attendance
1	Aug 8	H	Reading	W 3-0	1-0	—	Connolly [35], Legg (og) [50], Ward [61]	6671
2	15	H	Colchester U	L 2-4	0-2	10	Roberts [61], Connolly (pen) [79]	4157
3	22	A	Manchester C	D 0-0	0-0	10		27,677
4	29	A	Northampton T	W 1-0	0-0	7	Ward [52]	3534
5	Sept 1	A	Gillingham	L 0-4	0-2	—		5349
6	5	H	Macclesfield T	W 2-1	1-0	6	Owen [5], Spink [61]	3384
7	8	H	Luton T	D 1-1	1-1	—	Skinner [42]	2951
8	12	A	York C	D 1-1	1-0	9	Spink [8]	2856
9	19	H	Stoke C	L 0-1	0-0	13		7290
10	26	A	Chesterfield	L 1-2	0-2	15	Skinner [90]	3681
11	Oct 3	H	Lincoln C	W 2-1	1-1	12	Brammer [11], Roberts [77]	3048
12	10	H	Walsall	W 2-1	2-1	10	Connolly [28], Russell [34]	3842
13	17	A	Bristol R	D 0-0	0-0	10		6072
14	20	A	Wycombe W	L 0-3	0-2	—		3361
15	24	H	Millwall	D 0-0	0-0	13		2766
16	31	A	Burnley	L 1-2	0-1	16	Ridler [46]	10,109
17	Nov 7	H	Blackpool	D 1-1	0-0	15	Connolly [84]	3511
18	10	H	Fulham	L 0-2	0-2	—		3485
19	21	A	Oldham Ath	L 2-3	1-1	17	Roberts [32], Carey [71]	4446
20	28	H	Notts Co	W 1-0	1-0	14	Russell [14]	2811
21	Dec 12	A	Wigan Ath	D 1-1	0-0	14	Connolly [72]	3440
22	19	A	Bournemouth	L 0-1	0-1	17		2716
23	26	H	Manchester C	L 0-1	0-0	17		9048
24	28	A	Preston NE	L 1-3	0-1	19	Gregan (og) [60]	12,106
25	Jan 9	A	Reading	L 0-4	0-2	19		8087
26	15	H	Colchester U	W 3-1	3-1	—	Whitley [9], Haydon (og) [11], Griffiths [24]	3491
27	30	H	Preston NE	L 0-5	0-3	19		6394
28	Feb 6	A	Macclesfield T	W 2-0	1-0	19	Connolly [6], Griffiths [90]	2578
29	13	A	Luton T	W 2-1	0-0	17	Edwards [57], Griffiths [67]	4759
30	20	H	York C	D 1-1	1-0	17	Thompson (og) [13]	2980
31	27	A	Stoke C	W 3-1	1-0	14	McGregor [8], Owen [54], Connolly [67]	10,765
32	Mar 2	A	Northampton T	W 2-0	0-0	—	Whitley [78], Gibson [83]	4710
33	6	H	Chesterfield	D 0-0	0-0	12		3224
34	13	A	Blackpool	D 1-1	0-0	12	Connolly [56]	3905
35	20	H	Burnley	D 1-1	1-0	12	Brammer [14]	4151
36	27	A	Millwall	L 0-3	0-1	14		7390
37	Apr 3	H	Bristol R	W 1-0	1-0	12	Owen [16]	3087
38	6	A	Walsall	L 0-1	0-0	—		5763
39	10	H	Wycombe W	L 0-2	0-0	15		2450
40	13	A	Notts Co	D 1-1	0-0	—	Connolly [88]	3294
41	17	H	Oldham Ath	L 1-2	1-0	16	Spink [35]	3267
42	20	H	Gillingham	W 2-1	1-0	—	Connolly (pen) [38], Carey [88]	1871
43	24	A	Fulham	D 1-1	1-1	13	Connolly (pen) [18]	11,754
44	May 1	H	Wigan Ath	L 0-2	0-1	18		4172
45	4	A	Lincoln C	L 0-1	0-0	—		2926
46	8	A	Bournemouth	D 0-0	0-0	17		8439

Final League Position: 17

GOALSCORERS

League (43): Connolly 11 (3 pens), Griffiths 3, Owen 3, Roberts 3, Spink 3, Brammer 2, Carey 2, Russell 2, Skinner 2, Ward 2, Whitley 2, Edwards 1, Gibson 1, McGregor 1, Ridler 1, own goals 4.
Worthington Cup (2): Connolly 1 (pen), Roberts 1.
FA Cup (9): Connolly 5, Brammer 1, Roberts 1 (pen), Russell 1, own goal 1.

Cartwright M 30	McGregor M 43	Brace D 15 + 2	Owen G 35	Humes T 10 + 2	Carey B 36	Chalk M 19 + 9	Russell K 25 + 6	Connolly K 43 + 1	Rush I 12 + 5	Ward P 25	Brammer D 31 + 3	Roberts N 11 + 11	Hardy P 31 + 2	Ridler D 35 + 1	Skinner C 12	Spink D 26 + 8	Rishworth S —+ 4	Thomas S 1 + 4	Cooke T 10	Edwards J 4 + 5	Whitley J 9	Griffiths C 4	Gibson R 3 + 4	Wright T 16	Morrell A 4 + 3	Elliott S 8 + 1	Barrett P 8 + 2	Match No.
1	2	3	4	5	6	7	8[1]	9[2]	10	11	12	13																1
1	2	3	4	5	6	7	8[2]	9	10	11	12	13																2
1	2		8		6		12	9		11	4[1]	10[2]	3	5	7	13												3
1	2	3[1]	8	12	6			9		11	4	10		5	7													4
1	2		8[1]	3	6			9	10	11	4			5	7[2]	12	13											5
1	2	3	8	12	6[1]	13			11[2]	4	10			5	7	9[3]	14											6
1	2	3	8		6		11	12			4	10[1]		5	7[2]	9	13											7
1	2	3	8		6[1]		11	9			4	12		5	7[2]	10	13											8
1	2	3	8		6		4[2]	9		11		12		5	7	10[1]		13										9
1	2	3	8[2]		6		4	9		11	13	12		5	7	10[1]												10
1	2		8		6		12	9		11[1]	4	10	3	5	7[2]	13												11
1	2		8		6		12	9	10[2]	11	4		3	5	7[1]													12
1	2		8		6		12	9	10	11	4		3	5	7[1]													13
1	2		8		6		12	9	10[3]	11[1]	4	13	3	5	7[2]	14												14
1	2		8		6		10	9	12	11[1]	4	7	3	5														15
1	2[2]		8[1]		6		12	9	10[2]	11	4	13	3	5			14		7									16
1	2		8		6			9	10	11[1]	4	12	3	5					7									17
1	2		8		6			9	10	11[1]	4	12	3	5					7									18
1	2				6		8	9[1]	12	11	4	10	3	5					7									19
1	2				6		8	9	12	11	4	10[2]	3	5		13			7[1]									20
1	2						12	8	9	11	4[1]	10	3	5		6			7									21
1	2						12	8[1]	9	11	4	10[2]	3	5		6			7	13								22
1	2		8[1]				12	9	10	11	4		3	5		6			7									23
1	2		8[1]		6		12	9	10	11	4		3	5					7									24
1	2				6		12	9	10	11	4	8[1]	3	5					7									25
1	2				6	7		9		11	4		3	5							8	10						26
1	2				6	7[2]	8	9	12		4		3	5							11	10[1]	13					27
1	2				6	7	8	9[2]			4		3	5						13	11[1]	10	12					28
1	2				6	7	8				4	12	3	5							9	11	10[1]					29
1	2				6		8	9[1]			4	12	3	5		13				10[2]	11	7						30
	2		10		6	7	8	9			4		3	5							11			1				31
	2				6[1]	7[2]	8	9		11	4	12	3	5						10	13			1				32
	2		10		6		8	9[1]			4		3	5						12	11	7		1				33
	2		11		6		8[1]	9			4		3	5						12	10	7		1				34
	2		11[1]			7	8	9			4		3	5		6				10[2]	12			1	13			35
	2		11		6	7	8[2]	9[1]					3	5						12	10	4	13	1				36
	2		11		6	7		9					3	5							10	4	8	1				37
	2	12	11[2]		6	7		9					3[1]	5		13					10	4	8	1				38
	2		11		6	7		9[1]	12			13	3	5[2]		14					10	4[3]	8	1				39
	2		11		6	7	8	9					3	5		10[1]					12	4		1				40
	2	12	11		6	7		9				13	3[1]	5		10				8[2]		4[3]	14	1				41
	2	3[1]	11		6	7		9			12	8		5		10						4		1				42
	2	3	11		6	7		9				8		5		10[1]					12	4		1				43
	2	3	11		6	7[2]		9				8		5		10		13				4[1]		1	12			44
	2	3	11		6	7		9						5		10								1		8	4	45
	2	3	11		6	12		9				13		5		10		7[1]						1		8[2]	4	46

Worthington Cup
First Round   Halifax T   (h)   0-2
                                     (a)   2-0

FA Cup
First Round   Peterborough U   (h)   1-0
Second Round   York C   (h)   2-1
Third Round   Scunthorpe U   (h)   4-3
Fourth Round   Huddersfield T   (h)   1-1
                                     (a)   1-2

Division 2   **WYCOMBE WANDERERS**

Founded 1884

FOUNDATION

In 1887 a group of young furniture trade workers called a meeting at the Steam Engine public house with the aim of forming a football club and entering junior football. It is thought that they were named after the famous FA Cup winners, The Wanderers who had visited the town in 1877 for a tie with the original High Wycombe club. It is also possible that they played informally before their formation, although there is no proof of this.

Adams Park, Hillbottom Road, Sands, High Wycombe HP12 4HJ.
Telephone: (01494) 472100.
Fax: (01494) 527633.
Credit Card Hotline: (01494) 441118.
Information Line: 0891 446855.
Ground Capacity: 10,000 new stand; now seats 7250.
Record Attendance: 9007 v West Ham U, FA Cup 3rd rd, 7 January 1995.
Record Receipts: £61,221 (net of VAT) v West Ham U, FA Cup 3rd rd, 7 January 1995.
Pitch Measurements: 115yd × 75yd.
Patron: J. Adams.
President: M. E. Seymour.
Chairman: I. L. Beeks.
Directors: G. Peart (Financial), G. Richards, B. R. Lee, A. Parry, A. Thibault, G. Cox.
Associate Director: J. Goldsworthy.
Secretary: Ian Moat.
Manager: Lawrie Sanchez.
Assistant Manager: Terry Gibson.
Physio: David Jones.
Youth Team Manager: Gary Goodchild.
Youth Development Officer: Adrian Cole.
Youth Physio: Terry Evans.
Marketing Manager: Mark Austin.
Promotions Manager: Mike Phillips.

LATEST SEQUENCES
Longest Sequence of League Wins: 4, 26.2.94 – 19.3.94.
Longest Sequence of League Defeats: 3, 19.11.96 – 30.11.96.
Longest Sequence of League Draws: 4, 16.9.95 – 7.10.95.
Longest Sequence of Unbeaten League Matches: 14, 29.8.95 – 18.11.95.
Longest Sequence Without a League Win: 12, 8.8.98 – 10.10.98.

HONOURS

Football League: Division 2 best season: 6th, 1994–95.
FA Amateur Cup: Winners 1931.
FA Trophy: Winners 1991, 1993.
GM Vauxhall Conference: Winners 1992–93.
FA Cup: best season: 3rd rd 1975, 1986, 1994, 1995.
Football League Cup: never beyond 2nd rd.

Colours
Light & dark blue quartered shirts, light blue shorts, light blue stockings.
Change Colours
All yellow.

Year Formed: 1887.

Turned Professional: 1974.

Club Nicknames: 'Chairboys' (after High Wycombe's tradition of furniture making), 'The Blues'.

Previous Grounds: 1887, The Rye; 1893, Spring Meadow; 1895, Loakes Park; 1899, Daws Hill Park; 1901, Loakes Park; 1990, Adams Park.

First Football League Game: 14 August 1993, Division 3 v Carlisle U (a) D 2–2: Hyde; Cousins, Horton (Langford), Kerr, Crossley, Ryan, Carroll, Stapleton, Thompson, Scott, Guppy (1) (Hutchinson), (1 og).

Record League Victory: 5–0 v Burnley, Division 2, 15 April 1997 – Parkin; Cousins, Bell, Kavanagh, McCarthy, Forsyth, Carroll (2p) (Simpson), Scott (Farrell), Stallard (1), McGavin (1) (Read (1)), Brown.

Record Cup Victory: 5–0 v Hitchin T (a), FA Cup 2nd rd, 3 December 1994 – Hyde; Cousins, Brown, Crossley, Evans, Ryan (1), Carroll, Bell (1), Thompson, Garner (3) (Hemmings), Stapleton (Langford).

Record Defeat: 0–5 v Walsall, Auto Windscreens Shield 1st rd, 7 November 1995.

Most League Points: 70, Division 3, 1993–94.

Most League Goals: 66, Division 3, 1993–94.

Highest League Goalscorer in Season: Miguel De Souza 18, 1995–96.

Most League Goals in Total Aggregate: Dave Carroll, 37, 1993–99.

Most League Goals in One Match: 3, Miguel Desouza v Bradford C, Division 2, 26 March 1996; 3, Mark Stallard v Walsall, Division 2, 21 October 1997.

Most Capped Player: None.

Most League Appearances: Dave Carroll, 242, 1993–99.

Youngest League Player: Maurice Harkin, 17 years 183 days v Preston NE, 15 February 1997.

Record Transfer Fee Received: £375,000 from Swindon T for Keith Scott, November 1993.

Record Transfer Fee Paid: £220,000 to Barnet for Sean Devine, 15 April 1999.

Football League Record: Promoted to Division 3 from GMVC in 1993; 1993–94 Division 3; 1994– Division 2.

MANAGERS

First coach appointed 1951.
Prior to Brian Lee's appointment in 1969 the team was selected by a Match Committee which met every Monday evening.

James McCormack 1951–52
Sid Cann 1952–61
Graham Adams 1961–62
Don Welsh 1962–64
Barry Darvill 1964–68
Brian Lee 1969–76
Ted Powell 1976–77
John Reardon 1977–78
Andy Williams 1978–80
Mike Keen 1980–84
Paul Bence 1984–86
Alan Gane 1986–87
Peter Suddaby 1987–88
Jim Kelman 1988–90
Martin O'Neill 1990–95
Alan Smith 1995–96
John Gregory 1996–98
Neil Smillie 1998–99
Lawrie Sanchez February 1999–

TEN YEAR LEAGUE RECORD

		P	W	D	L	F	A	Pts	Pos
1988-89	Conf	40	20	11	9	68	52	71	4
1989-90	Conf	42	17	10	15	64	56	61	10
1990-91	Conf	42	21	11	10	75	46	74	5
1991-92	Conf	42	30	4	8	84	35	94	2
1992-93	Conf	42	24	11	7	84	37	83	1
1993-94	Div 3	42	19	13	10	67	53	70	4
1994-95	Div 2	46	21	15	10	60	46	78	6
1995-96	Div 2	46	15	15	16	63	59	60	12
1996-97	Div 2	46	15	10	21	51	56	55	18
1997-98	Div 2	46	14	18	14	51	53	60	14

DID YOU KNOW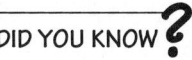

Dannie Bulman blocked a clearance to score a last minute equaliser for Wycombe Wanderers against Bristol Rovers on 31 August 1998 less than 30 seconds after coming on as a substitute for the team.

Founded 1884

WYCOMBE WANDERERS 1998–99 LEAGUE RECORD

Match No.	Date	Venue	Opponents	Result	H/T Score	Lg. Pos.	Goalscorers	Atten- dance
1	Aug 8	H	Luton T	L	0-1	0-1	—	5252
2	15	A	Millwall	L	1-2	0-0	20	Read [64]	7492
3	22	H	Walsall	L	1-2	0-0	24	Mohan [75]	4102
4	29	A	York C	L	0-3	0-1	24		2775
5	31	H	Bristol R	D	1-1	0-0	24	Bulman [90]	4318
6	Sept 8	H	Preston NE	L	0-1	0-0	—		3800
7	12	A	Burnley	D	1-1	1-1	24	Stallard [37]	9120
8	19	H	Bournemouth	L	0-2	0-2	24		4267
9	26	A	Colchester U	L	1-2	0-0	24	Stallard [60]	4205
10	29	A	Fulham	L	0-2	0-1	—		7447
11	Oct 3	H	Notts Co	D	1-1	1-0	24	Simpson [21]	4164
12	10	A	Gillingham	L	0-3	0-2	24		4575
13	17	H	Macclesfield T	W	3-0	2-0	24	Baird [12], Simpson [26], Scott [68]	4012
14	20	H	Wrexham	W	3-0	2-0	—	Scott 2 [7, 75], Brown [40]	3361
15	24	A	Oldham Ath	D	0-0	0-0	24		4337
16	31	H	Reading	L	2-3	1-2	24	Lawrence [32], Cousins [80]	6373
17	Nov 7	A	Northampton T	D	1-1	1-1	23	Mohan [38]	6248
18	10	H	Manchester C	W	1-0	1-0	—	Simpson (pen) [34]	8129
19	21	A	Wigan Ath	D	0-0	0-0	23		3349
20	28	H	Stoke C	L	0-1	0-0	23		6023
21	Dec 12	A	Blackpool	D	0-0	0-0	23		2990
22	19	H	Lincoln C	W	4-1	2-0	22	Brown [19], Carroll [45], McSporran 2 [79, 84]	4731
23	26	A	Walsall	D	2-2	0-1	23	McSporran [53], Brown [63]	6258
24	28	H	Chesterfield	W	1-0	0-0	21	Scott [65]	5391
25	Jan 2	A	York C	L	1-2	0-0	21	Ryan [71]	4612
26	9	A	Luton T	L	1-3	0-1	22	Carroll (pen) [89]	5063
27	16	H	Millwall	L	0-1	0-0	22		5510
28	30	A	Chesterfield	L	0-2	0-1	23		4248
29	Feb 6	H	Fulham	D	1-1	1-1	23	Baird [25]	7538
30	13	A	Preston NE	L	1-2	1-1	23	Cornforth (pen) [17]	10,686
31	20	H	Burnley	W	2-0	0-0	22	Simpson [51], Scott [52]	5195
32	27	A	Bournemouth	L	0-2	0-2	23		6693
33	Mar 6	A	Colchester U	D	2-2	0-1	23	Baird [57], Scott [76]	4670
34	13	H	Northampton T	L	1-2	0-1	24	Baird [68]	4861
35	20	A	Reading	L	1-2	0-1	24	Devine [80]	10,298
36	23	A	Bristol R	W	2-0	1-0	—	Cousins [8], Devine [82]	4833
37	27	H	Oldham Ath	W	3-0	3-0	22	Carroll 2 [16, 34], McCarthy [42]	4083
38	Apr 3	H	Macclesfield T	W	3-1	2-1	21	Lawrence [41], Baird [45], Devine [49]	3183
39	5	H	Gillingham	L	0-2	0-0	21		6688
40	10	A	Wrexham	W	2-0	0-0	20	Carroll [70], McSporran [88]	2450
41	14	A	Stoke C	D	2-2	1-1	—	Devine 2 [29, 89]	6569
42	24	A	Manchester C	W	2-1	2-1	22	Baird [15], Devine [30]	29,337
43	27	A	Notts Co	L	0-1	0-0	—		4721
44	May 1	H	Blackpool	D	2-2	2-1	21	Devine [2], Carroll [16]	5286
45	5	H	Wigan Ath	W	2-1	1-1	—	Devine [44], Emblen [48]	5410
46	8	A	Lincoln C	W	1-0	0-0	19	Emblen [83]	8145

Final League Position: 19

GOALSCORERS

League (52): Devine 8, Baird 6, Carroll 6 (1 pen), Scott 5, McSporran 4, Simpson 4 (1 pen), Brown 3, Cousins 2, Emblen 2, Lawrence 2, Mohan 2, Stallard 2, Bulman 1, Cornforth 1 (pen), McCarthy 1, Read 1, Ryan 1.
Worthington Cup (4): Brown 2, Read 1, Stallard 1.
FA Cup (4): Baird 1, Carroll 1 (pen), Reid 1, Scott 1.

Taylor M 44	Kavanagh J 14+4	Vinnicombe C 39+2	Ryan K 26+2	Cousins J 34	McCarthy P 26+3	Carroll D 27+5	Scott K 23+2	Stallard M 12+3	Harkin M 1+1	Brown S 34+4	Cornforth J 9+4	Read P 11+5	Mohan N 25	Baird A 25+3	Beeton A 11+5	Simpson M 31+2	McGavin S 1+4	Emblen P 28+7	Bulman D 5+6	Westhead M 2	Wraight G 6	Lawrence M 34	Robson M 1+3	McSporran J 11+15	Lee M 2+1	Devine S 11+1	Bates J 9	Senda D —+6	Forsyth M 4	Holsgrove L —+1	Match No.
1	2[1]	3	4	5	6	7	8	9	10[2]	11	12	13																			1
1	2	3	4	5	6	7	12[2]	9[1]	13	8	11	10																			2
1	2[1]	3	7[3]	5	4	11		9		8				10	6	12[2]	13	14													3
1	2[1]			5	4	11		9		8				10	6	3	12	7													4
1	12	3	4[1]	5[1]	2	7		9		8				10[2]	6	13	11	14													5
1	2[3]	3	4	5[1]		7		9		8	12			10[2]	6	13	11	14													6
1	2	3		5	4	7		9		8				10[1]	6	12	11														7
1	2	3		5	4	7	12	9		8				10[1]	6		11														8
1	2	3	7[1]	5	4			9		8				10	6	12	11														9
1	12	3		5		7		9[1]		8				10[3]	6	4[2]	13	14				2		11							10
1		3		5				9		8				10	6	4[2]		7				2		11							11
1	12	3[1]		5		7		9[1]		8		13		10	6	4[2]	14					2		11							12
1		3	4	5		7				8		13		10	6[3]	12[2]		9[1]				2		11					14		13
1	12	3[1]	4	5		7				8		13		10	6			9[2]				2		11[3]					14		14
1		3	4	5		7[1]				8	12	13		10	6			9[2]				2		11							15
1		3	4[1]	5		7				8	12	13		10	6			9[2]				2		11							16
1		3	4	5		7					12			10	6			9[1]			2	2		11							17
1		3	4	5		7				8[1]	12			10	6			9[2]				2		11		13					18
1		3	4	5		7				8	12			10	6			9[2]				2		11[1]		13					19
1		3[1]	4	5		7				8				10	6	12						2		11		9					20
1		3	4	5		7				8		11		10	6							2		9							21
1	12	3[1]	4	5		7				8	13	11		10	6[2]	14						2		9[3]							22
1		3	4	5	6[1]	7				8		11		10		12						2		9							23
1	12	3	4	5	6	7				8[1]		11		10								2		9							24
1		3	4	5	6	7[1]				8		11[2]		10		12						2		9					13		25
		3	4	5	6	7				8		11		10							1	2		9							26
1		3	4	5	6	7		8[1]				11		10				9[2]				2		12		13					27
1	4	3		5	6	7		9[1]		8				10		12		11[2]	13			2									28
1	7[1]	3	4		6	12		9		8			5	10				11[2]	13			2									29
1	11	3	4		6	7		8[1]			12		5	10				9[2]	13			2									30
1	11	3	4		6	7[1]		9		8	12		5	10					13			2									31
1	11	3	4[1]		6	7	12	9[2]		8			5	10[3]					13			2		14							32
1	3[?]	3	4	5	6	7		9[2]		11[1]	12	13										2	2								33
1	3	3	4	5	6	7		9[2]		11	12					13						2[1]	2								34
1	3[1]		4	5	6	7[2]		9		11				10		8						2		12		13					35
1	3	12	5[1]	6	7	4		9		11[2]				10		8						2		13		10					36
1	3	2	4	7[2]				9		11[1]	8					6						2		14	12	10[3]	5				37
1	3	6	4	7			12	9[2]		11[1]	13					8						2		14		10[2]	5	13			38
1	3	2	4	7			12	9[1]		11						6								14		10[3]	5				39
1	3	6	4	7			12	9[1]		11[2]	13					8						2		14		10	5				40
1	3	6	4	7[1]				9[2]		11	12					8						2		13		10	5				41
1	3	6	2					8		11	12		9			4								7[1]		10[2]	5	13	5		42
1	3	6	4					8[3]		11	12					9[2]						2		13		7[1]	10	5	14		43
1	3	6		7[2]				8		11[1]			9									2		12		11	10	5	13	4	44
1	3	6		7				8		9[1]												2		11[2]		10	5	12	4	13	45
1	3	6		7			12	8[1]		9						11[2]						2		13		10	5	4			46

Worthington Cup

First Round	Swindon T	(a)	1-2
		(h)	2-0
Second Round	Middlesbrough	(a)	0-2
		(h)	1-1

FA Cup

First Round	Chesterfield	(h)	1-0
Second Round	Plymouth Arg	(h)	1-1
		(a)	2-3

Division 3

YORK CITY

FOUNDATION

Although there was a York City club formed in 1903 by a soccer enthusiast from Darlington, this has no connection with the modern club because it went out of existence during World War I. Unlike many others of that period who restarted in 1919, York City did not re-form until 1922 and the tendency now is to ignore the modern club's pre-1922 existence.

Bootham Crescent, York YO30 7AQ.

Telephone: (01904) 624447.

Fax: (01904) 631457.

Ground Capacity: 9534.

Record Attendance: 28,123 v Huddersfield T, FA Cup 6th rd, 5 March 1938.

Record Receipts: £63,680 v Manchester U, Coca-Cola Cup 2nd rd, 2nd leg, 3 October 1995.

Pitch Measurements: 115yd × 74yd.

Chairman: D. M. Craig OBE, JP, BSC, FICE, FI, MUN E, FCI ARB, M CONS E.

Directors: C. Webb, E. B. Swallow, J. E. H. Quickfall FCA.

Manager: Neil Thompson.

First Team Coach: Adie Shaw.

Secretary: Keith Usher.

Commercial Manager: Mrs Maureen Leslie.

Physio: Jeff Miller.

Hon. Orthopaedic Surgeon: Mr Peter De Boer MA, FRCS.

Medical Officer: Dr R. Porter.

LATEST SEQUENCES

Longest Sequence of League Wins: 7, 31.10.64 – 26.12.64.

Longest Sequence of League Defeats: 8, 14.11.66 – 31.12.66.

Longest Sequence of League Draws: 6, 26.12.92 – 22.1.93.

Longest Sequence of Unbeaten League Matches: 21, 10.9.73 – 12.1.74.

Longest Sequence Without a League Win: 17, 4.5.87 – 24.10.87.

HONOURS

Football League: Division 3 – Promoted 1973–74 (3rd); Division 4 – Champions 1983–84.

FA Cup: Semi-finals 1955, when in Division 3.

Football League Cup: best season: 5th rd, 1962.

Colours
Red shirts, navy shorts, red stockings.

Change Colours
All green and white.

Year Formed: 1922.

Turned Professional: 1922.

Ltd Co.: 1922.

Club Nickname: 'Minstermen'.

Previous Grounds: 1922, Fulfordgate; 1932, Bootham Crescent.

First Football League Game: 31 August 1929, Division 3 (N), v Wigan Borough (a) W 2–0 – Farmery; Archibald, Johnson; Beck, Davis, Thompson; Evans, Gardner, Cowie (1), Smailes, Stockhill (1).

Record League Victory: 9–1 v Southport, Division 3 (N), 2 February 1957 – Forgan; Phillips, Howe; Brown (1), Cairney, Mollatt; Hill, Bottom (4 incl. 1p), Wilkinson (2), Wragg (1), Fenton (1).

Record Cup Victory: 6–0 v South Shields (away), FA Cup 1st rd, 16 November 1968 – Widdowson; Baker (1p), Richardson; Carr, Jackson, Burrows; Taylor, Ross (3), MacDougall (2), Hodgson, Boyer.

Record Defeat: 0–12 v Chester, Division 3 (N), 1 February 1936.

Most League Points (2 for a win): 62, Division 4, 1964–65.

Most League Points (3 for a win): 101, Division 4, 1983–84.

Most League Goals: 96, Division 4, 1983–84.

Highest League Scorer in Season: Bill Fenton, 31, Division 3 (N), 1951–52; Arthur Bottom, 31, Division 3 (N), 1954–55 and 1955–56.

Most League Goals in Total Aggregate: Norman Wilkinson, 125, 1954–66.

Most League Goals in One Match: 5, Alf Patrick v Rotherham U, Division 3N, 20 November 1948.

Most Capped Player: Peter Scott, 7 (10), Northern Ireland.

Most League Appearances: Barry Jackson, 481, 1958–70.

Youngest League Player: Reg Stockill, 15 years 281 days v Wigan Borough, 31 August 1929.

Record Transfer Fee Received: £1,000,000 from Manchester U for Jonathan Greening, March 1998.

Record Transfer Fee Paid: £140,000 to Burnley for Adrian Randall, December 1995.

Football League Record: 1929 Elected to Division 3 (N); 1958–59 Division 4; 1959–60 Division 3; 1960–65 Division 4; 1965–66 Division 3; 1966–71 Division 4; 1971–74 Division 3; 1974–76 Division 2; 1976–77 Division 3; 1977–84 Division 4; 1984–88 Division 3; 1988–92 Division 4; 1992–93 Division 3; 1993–99 Division 2; 1999– Division 3.

MANAGERS

Bill Sherrington 1924–60
(was Secretary for most of this time but virtually Secretary-Manager for a long pre-war spell)
John Collier 1929–36
Tom Mitchell 1936–50
Dick Duckworth 1950–52
Charlie Spencer 1952–53
Jimmy McCormick 1953–54
Sam Bartram 1956–60
Tom Lockie 1960–67
Joe Shaw 1967–68
Tom Johnston 1968–75
Wilf McGuinness 1975–77
Charlie Wright 1977–80
Barry Lyons 1980–81
Denis Smith 1982–87
Bobby Saxton 1987–88
John Bird 1988–91
John Ward 1991–93
Alan Little 1993–99
Neil Thompson March 1999–

TEN YEAR LEAGUE RECORD

		P	W	D	L	F	A	Pts	Pos
1988-89	Div 4	46	17	13	16	62	63	64	11
1989-90	Div 4	46	16	16	14	55	53	64	13
1990-91	Div 4	46	11	13	22	45	57	46	21
1991-92	Div 4	42	8	16	18	42	58	40	19
1992-93	Div 3	42	21	12	9	72	45	75	4
1993-94	Div 2	46	21	12	13	64	40	75	5
1994-95	Div 2	46	21	9	16	67	51	72	9
1995-96	Div 2	46	13	13	20	58	73	52	20
1996-97	Div 2	46	13	13	20	47	68	52	20
1997-98	Div 2	46	14	17	15	52	58	59	16

DID YOU KNOW

On 19 December 1998, Andrew Dawson, eleven days after his 19th birthday and making his League debut as a substitute, scored the winning goal against Manchester City within two minutes of his appearance in a 2–1 win.

YORK CITY 1998–99 LEAGUE RECORD

Match No.	Date	Venue	Opponents	Result		H/T Score	Lg. Pos.	Goalscorers	Atten- dance
1	Aug 8	A	Preston NE	L	0-3	0-2	—		8656
2	15	H	Gillingham	D	1-1	1-1	19	Cresswell [4]	2634
3	22	A	Burnley	W	1-0	1-0	13	Connelly [32]	9715
4	29	A	Wycombe W	W	3-0	1-0	8	Thompson 2 (1 pen) [21, 89 (p)], Cresswell [70]	2775
5	Sept 5	H	Colchester U	L	1-2	0-1	15	Thompson (pen) [75]	2699
6	8	A	Walsall	W	3-2	2-1	—	Cresswell 2 [1, 22], Tinkler [84]	3098
7	12	H	Wrexham	D	1-1	1-0	10	Cresswell [83]	2856
8	19	A	Fulham	D	3-3	1-2	11	Agnew 2 [29, 85], Tolson [49]	9071
9	26	H	Bristol R	W	1-0	0-0	9	Tolson [51]	3305
10	Oct 3	A	Blackpool	W	2-1	1-0	9	Thompson (pen) [25], Jordan [71]	5633
11	10	H	Luton T	D	3-3	2-2	8	Connelly [1], Cresswell 2 [10, 64]	3780
12	17	A	Chesterfield	L	1-2	1-1	9	Cresswell [4]	4113
13	21	A	Millwall	L	1-3	0-1	—	Cresswell (pen) [77]	4249
14	31	A	Wigan Ath	L	0-5	0-2	17		3583
15	Nov 4	A	Reading	L	0-1	0-1	—		7914
16	7	H	Notts Co	D	1-1	0-0	16	Connelly [47]	3391
17	10	H	Macclesfield T	L	0-2	0-2	—		2713
18	21	A	Stoke C	L	0-2	0-2	18		11,795
19	28	H	Northampton T	D	1-1	0-0	18	Cresswell [71]	2656
20	Dec 8	H	Lincoln C	W	2-1	1-1	16	Tolson [16], Holmes (og) [49]	2075
21	12	A	Bournemouth	L	1-2	1-0	16	Cresswell [8]	4863
22	19	H	Manchester C	W	2-1	1-1	14	Connelly [2], Dawson [86]	7527
23	26	H	Burnley	D	3-3	0-1	14	Hall [54], Rowe 2 [61, 72]	5630
24	28	A	Oldham Ath	W	2-0	1-0	13	Cresswell [34], Jones [60]	5343
25	Jan 2	A	Wycombe W	W	2-1	0-0	9	Cresswell [63], Jones [76]	4612
26	9	H	Preston NE	L	0-1	0-0	11		5744
27	16	A	Gillingham	L	1-3	0-1	11	Rowe [62]	6242
28	23	H	Reading	D	1-1	0-0	12	Rowe [71]	3274
29	30	A	Oldham Ath	L	0-1	0-1	13		3760
30	Feb 5	A	Colchester U	L	1-2	0-2	—	Cresswell (pen) [74]	3982
31	13	H	Walsall	L	1-2	0-1	14	Cresswell [73]	2969
32	20	A	Wrexham	D	1-1	0-1	15	Pouton [57]	2980
33	27	H	Fulham	L	0-3	0-2	17		6169
34	Mar 6	A	Bristol R	L	0-2	0-1	17		5749
35	13	A	Notts Co	L	2-4	1-3	19	Rowe [2], Cresswell (pen) [87]	5400
36	20	H	Wigan Ath	L	1-3	1-3	19	Jordan [41]	3356
37	28	A	Lincoln C	W	2-1	0-0	17	Williams 2 [73, 80]	5504
38	Apr 3	H	Chesterfield	L	1-2	0-1	18	Jordan [86]	3356
39	6	A	Luton T	L	1-2	1-0	—	Thompson [29]	4667
40	10	H	Millwall	W	2-1	0-0	19	Rowe [87], Thompson [90]	2572
41	13	A	Northampton T	D	2-2	1-1	19	Williams [19], Jordan [55]	5220
42	17	A	Stoke C	D	2-2	0-1	20	Garratt [51], Jordan [67]	4142
43	24	A	Macclesfield T	W	2-1	2-0	19	Rowe [4], Tinkler [45]	3077
44	27	H	Blackpool	W	1-0	1-0	—	Williams [7]	2971
45	May 1	H	Bournemouth	L	0-1	0-0	19		3503
46	8	A	Manchester C	L	0-4	0-1	21		32,471

Final League Position: 21

GOALSCORERS

League (56): Cresswell 16 (3 pens), Rowe 7, Thompson 6 (3 pens), Jordan 5, Connelly 4, Williams 4, Tolson 3, Agnew 2, Jones 2, Tinkler 2, Dawson 1, Garratt 1, Hall 1, Pouton 1, own goal 1.
Worthington Cup (1): Thompson 1.
FA Cup (5): Cresswell 3, Jordan 2.

Warrington A 11	McMillan A 33	Hall W 2B + 1	Jones B 44 + 1	Reed M 8 + 4	Tinkler M 36 + 1	Thompson N 24	Pouton A 24 + 3	Woods N 5 + 3	Cresswell R 36	Garratt M 33 + 5	Rowe R 24 + 15	Mimms B 35	Connelly G 28	Prendergast R 1 + 2	Agnew S 19 + 1	Jordan S 27 + 5	Tolson N 17 + 11	Barras T 24	Himsworth G 12 + 1	Dawson A 7 + 4	Carruthers M 3 + 3	Fairclough C 11	Williams M 11	Hocking M 4 + 2	Skinner C 3 + 2	Match No.
1	2	3	4	5	6	7	8	9¹	10	11	12															1
	2	3	5	4	6	8	12	9²	11	10¹		1	7	13												2
	2	3	5	4	6	8	10	9	12			1	7		11¹											3
	2	3	5	12	4¹	6	8	10³	9	11		1	7²			13	14									4
	2	3²	5	12	4	6	8	10³	9	11¹		1	7			13	14									5
	2	3	5	4	6	8			9			1	7		11	10										6
	2		5	4	3	8			9		12	1	7		11	10¹		6								7
	2		5	4	3	8			9²		12	1	7¹	13	11	10³		6								8
	2		5	4	3	8			9		12	1	7		11	10¹		6								9
	2		5		3	8¹			9		12	1	7	13	11	4²		6	10²							10
	2		5	12	3	8¹			9			1	7	13	11	4²	14	6	10³							11
	2	3	5			8			9		12	1	7		11	4		6	10¹							12
	2	3²	5	4		8			9		12	1	7¹	13	11	10		6								13
	2	3	5	4	6	8²			9		12	1	7	13	11	10¹										14
1	2		5	4	3	8			9				7		11	10		6								15
1	2		5	4	3	8			9		12		7		11	10¹		6								16
1	2	3²	5	4		8			9		12		7		11¹	10		6				13				17
1	2	3	5	4	6	8			9		12		7		11¹	10										18
	2		5	4	6	8			9	10¹	12	1	7		11	3										19
	2		5	4	3	8			9			1	7		11	10		6								20
	2		5	4	3	8			9		12	1	7		11¹	10		6								21
	2	3	5	4		8			9		12	1	7²			10¹		6	11			13				22
	2	3	5	4		8			9			1	7			10		6	11							23
	2	3	5	4		8			9			1	7			10		6	11							24
	2	3	5	4		8			9			1	7			10		6	11							25
	2	3	5	4		8			9		12	1	7²		11	10¹		6	13							26
	2	3	5	4		8			9		12	1	7¹		11	10		6								27
	2	3¹	5			8			9		12	1	7		11	10		6								28
	2	3¹	5			8			9		12	1	7²		11	10		6								29
	2²	3	5	4		8			9		12	1	7		11	10		6¹	13							30
	2	3	5	4		8			9		12	1	7		11¹	10		6								31
		3	5	4		8			9			1	7		11	10		6		2						32
1	2	3	5	4		8			9		12		7		11¹	10		6								33
1	2	3¹	5		6	8²			9	11	12		7			10³	14		13							34
1	2	3	5	4	6¹	8			9	11	12		7			10			10³							35
1	2²	3	5	4		8			9	11	12		7			10¹		6	13							36
1	2	3	5	4		8				11¹	12		7			10		6					9			37
1	2	3	5³	4		8				11²	12		7			10	14	6	13				9¹			38
	2	3	5	4		8				11	12	1	7			10¹		6					9			39
	2	3	5	4		8				11¹	12	1	7			10		6					9			40
	2	3	5	4		8				11		1	7			10		6					9			41
	2	3	5	4		8				11	12	1	7¹			10		6					9			42
	2	3	5	4³		8				11²	12	1	7			10¹		6					9	14	13	43
	2	3	5	4		8				11	12	1	7			10¹		6					9			44
	2¹	3	5	4²		8				11	12	1	7			10		6					9		13	45
	2	3¹	5	4		8				11	12	1	7²			10		6	13				9			46

Worthington Cup
First Round　　Sunderland　　(h)　0-2
　　　　　　　　　　　　　　　　(a)　1-2

FA Cup
First Round　　Enfield　　(a)　2-2
　　　　　　　　　　　　　　(h)　2-1
Second Round　Wrexham　　(a)　1-2

ENGLISH LEAGUE PLAYERS DIRECTORY

*Free transfer, †Non-contract, ‡Registration cancelled, §Trainee/Schoolboy
#Players over age 24, out of contract but who have been made an offer of re-engagement

Player	Ht	Wt	Pos	Birth Date	Place	Source	Clubs	League App	Gls
						ARSENAL			
Adams Tony	6 3	13 11	D	10 10 66	London	Apprentice	Arsenal	447	31
Anelka Nicolas	5 11	12 03	F	14 3 79	Versailles		Paris St Germain	10	1
							Arsenal	65	23
Barrett Graham			F	6 10 81	Dublin	Trainee	Arsenal	—	—
Bergkamp Dennis	6 0	12 05	F	18 5 69	Amsterdam		Ajax	185	103
							Internazionale	52	11
							Arsenal	119	51
Black Michael*	5 8	11 08	M	6 10 76	Chigwell	Trainee	Arsenal	—	—
							Millwall (loan)	13	2
Black Tommy			M	26 11 79	Chigwell	Trainee	Arsenal	—	—
Boa Morte Luis	5 10	11 05	F	4 8 77	Lisbon	Sporting Lisbon	Arsenal	23	—
Bould Steve	6 4	14 02	D	16 11 62	Stoke	Apprentice	Stoke C	183	6
							Torquay U (loan)	9	—
							Arsenal	287	5
Caballero Fabian*			F	31 1 78	Argentina	Cerro Porteno	Arsenal	1	—
Canoville Lee			D	14 3 81	Ealing	Trainee	Arsenal	—	—
Cole Ashley			D	20 12 80	Stepney	Trainee	Arsenal	—	—
Crowe Jason	5 9	10 09	D	30 9 78	Sidcup	Trainee	Arsenal	—	—
							Crystal Palace (loan)	8	—
Diawara Kaba			F	16 12 75	Toulon	Toulon	Bordeaux	43	9
							Rennes	12	3
							Bordeaux	17	5
							Arsenal	12	—
Dixon Lee	5 8	11 08	D	17 3 64	Manchester	Local	Burnley	4	—
							Chester C	16	1
							Chester	41	—
							Bury	45	5
							Stoke C	71	5
							Arsenal	388	20
Garde Remi*	5 9	11 07	M	3 4 66	L'Arbresle		Lyon	145	22
							Strasbourg	68	3
							Arsenal	31	—
Gray Julian			M	21 9 79	Lewisham	Trainee	Arsenal	—	—
Grimandi Gilles	6 0	12 07	D	11 11 70	Gap	FC Gap	Monaco	90	3
							Arsenal	30	1
Grondin David			D	8 5 80	Paris	St Etienne	Arsenal	1	—
Hughes Stephen	6 0	12 05	M	18 9 76	Wokingham	Trainee	Arsenal	47	4
Kanu Nwankwo	6 5	13 00	F	1 8 76	Owerri		Federation Works	30	9
							Iwanyanwu	30	6
							Ajax	54	25
							Internazionale	12	1
							Arsenal	12	6
Keown Martin	6 1	12 04	D	24 7 66	Oxford	Apprentice	Arsenal	22	—
							Brighton & HA (loan)	16	—
							Brighton & HA (loan)	7	1
							Aston Villa	112	3
							Everton	96	—
							Arsenal	199	3
Lincoln Greg			M	23 3 80	Cheshunt	Trainee	Arsenal	—	—
Livermore David			D	20 5 80	Edmonton	Trainee	Arsenal	—	—
Ljungberg Frederik			M	16 4 77	Sweden		Halmstad	79	10
							Arsenal	16	1
Lukic John	6 4	13 07	G	11 12 60	Chesterfield	Apprentice	Leeds U	146	—
							Arsenal	223	—
							Leeds U	209	—
							Arsenal	15	—
MacDonald James	6 0	12 05	M	21 2 79	Inverness	Trainee	Arsenal	—	—
Manninger Alex	6 2	13 03	G	4 6 77	Salzburg		Vorwaerts Steyr	5	—
							Salzburg	1	—
							Graz	23	—
							Arsenal	13	—
McGovern Brian			D	28 4 80	Dublin		Arsenal	—	—
McLeod Allan			D	19 4 80	Islington	Trainee	Arsenal	—	—
Mendez Alberto	5 11	11 09	M	24 10 74	Nuremberg	FC Feucht	Arsenal	4	—
(On loan to AEK Athens)									
Overmars Marc	5 8	11 04	F	29 3 73	Emst		Go Ahead	11	1
							Willem II	31	1
							Ajax	135	36
							Arsenal	69	18

Name	Ht	Wt	Pos	Born	Birthplace	From	Club	Apps	Gls
Parlour Ray	5 10	11 12	M	7 3 73	Romford	Trainee	Arsenal	205	17
Pennant Jermaine			M	15 1 83	Nottingham		Notts Co	—	—
							Arsenal	—	—
Petit Emmanuel	6 1	12 07	M	22 9 70	Dieppe	ES Arques	Monaco	222	4
							Arsenal	59	6
Platt David‡	5 10	11 12	M	10 6 66	Chadderton	Chadderton	Manchester U		
							Crewe Alex	134	55
							Aston Villa	121	50
							Bari	29	11
							Juventus	16	3
							Sampdoria	55	17
							Arsenal	88	13
Riza Omer			F	8 11 79	Edmonton	Trainee	Arsenal	—	—
(On loan to ADO Den Haag)									
Seaman David	6 4	14 10	G	19 9 63	Rotherham	Apprentice	Leeds U	—	—
							Peterborough U	91	—
							Birmingham C	75	—
							QPR	141	—
							Arsenal	312	—
Taylor Stuart			G	28 11 80	Romford	Trainee	Arsenal	—	—
Upson Matthew	6 1	11 05	D	18 4 79	Eye	Trainee	Luton T	1	—
							Arsenal	10	—
Vernazza Paulo			M	1 11 79	Islington	Trainee	Arsenal	1	—
							Ipswich T (loan)	2	—
Vieira Patrick	6 4	13 00	M	23 6 76	Dakar		Cannes	49	2
							AC Milan	2	—
							Arsenal	98	7
Vivas Nelson			D	18 10 69	San Nicolas	Lugano	Arsenal	23	—
Winterburn Nigel	5 8	11 04	D	11 12 63	Coventry	Local	Birmingham C	—	—
							Oxford U	—	—
							Wimbledon	165	8
							Arsenal	412	8
Wreh Christopher	5 8	11 13	F	14 5 75	Liberia		Monaco	13	3
(On loan to AEK Athens)							Guincamp	33	10
							Arsenal	28	3

Trainees/Scholars
Beale, David; Bothroyd, Jay; Chilvers, Liam C; English, Thomas D; Fahey, Keith D; Field, Declan R L; Halls, John; Harper, James A J; Noble, David J; Norbert, Guillaume; Oates, Greg W; Osei-Kuffour, Jonathan; Stack, Graham; Weston, Rhys D

ASTON VILLA

Name	Ht	Wt	Pos	Born	Birthplace	From	Club	Apps	Gls
Barry Gareth	5 11	12 06	D	23 2 81	Hastings	Trainee	Aston Villa	34	2
Blackwood Michael	5 10	11 07	F	30 9 79	Birmingham	Trainee	Aston Villa	—	—
Bosnich Mark	6 1	14 07	G	13 1 72	Fairfield	Croatia Sydney	Manchester U	3	—
							Aston Villa	179	1
Byfield Darren	5 11	11 11	F	29 9 76	Sutton Coldfield	Trainee	Aston Villa	7	—
							Preston NE (loan)	5	1
Calderwood Colin	6 0	13 00	D	20 1 65	Glasgow	Amateur	Mansfield T	100	1
							Swindon T	330	20
							Tottenham H	163	6
							Aston Villa	8	—
Charles Gary	5 9	11 06	D	13 4 70	London	Trainee	Nottingham F	56	1
(Transferred to Benfica, January 1999)							Leicester C (loan)	8	—
							Derby Co	61	3
							Aston Villa	79	3
Collymore Stan	6 2	14 04	F	22 1 71	Stone	Stafford R	Crystal Palace	20	1
							Southend U	30	15
							Nottingham F	65	41
							Liverpool	61	26
							Aston Villa	45	7
Curtolo David	5 9	11 00	M	30 9 80	Stockholm		Aston Villa	—	—
Delaney Mark	6 1	11 07	M	13 5 76	Haverfordwest	Carmarthen T	Cardiff C	28	—
							Aston Villa	2	—
Draper Mark	5 10	12 04	F	11 11 70	Long Eaton	Trainee	Notts Co	222	40
							Leicester C	39	5
							Aston Villa	119	7
Dublin Dion	6 2	12 04	F	22 4 69	Leicester		Norwich C	—	—
							Cambridge U	156	52
							Manchester U	12	2
							Coventry C	145	61
							Aston Villa	24	11
Ehiogu Ugo	6 2	14 10	D	3 11 72	Hackney	Trainee	WBA	2	—
							Aston Villa	204	11
Enckelman Peter	6 2	12 05	G	10 3 77	Turku	TPS Turku	Aston Villa	—	—
Evans Graham			F	16 6 80	Wrexham	Caersws	Aston Villa	—	—
Ferraresi Fabio	5 9	11 02	M	24 5 79	Fano	Cesena	Aston Villa	—	—
Ghent Matthew	6 3	14 01	G	5 10 80	Burton	Trainee	Aston Villa	—	—
Grayson Simon	6 0	13 04	D	16 12 69	Ripon	Trainee	Leeds U	2	—
							Leicester C	188	4
							Aston Villa	48	—
Hazell Reuben*	5 11	11 11	D	24 4 79	Birmingham	Trainee	Aston Villa	—	—

Name							Club	Apps	Gls
Hendrie Lee	5 10	11 00	F	18 5 77	Birmingham	Trainee	Aston Villa	56	6
Hughes David	6 4	14 02	D	1 2 78	Wrexham	Trainee	Aston Villa	7	—
							Carlisle U (loan)	1	—
Jaszczun Tommy	5 11	11 02	D	16 9 77	Kettering	Trainee	Aston Villa	—	—
Joachim Julian	5 6	12 00	M	20 9 74	Boston	Trainee	Leicester C	99	25
							Aston Villa	88	26
Lee Alan	6 2	13 09	F	21 8 78	Galway	Trainee	Aston Villa	—	—
							Torquay U (loan)	7	2
							Port Vale (loan)	11	2
Lescott Aaron	5 8	10 09	M	2 12 78	Birmingham	Trainee	Aston Villa	—	—
Melaugh Gavin	5 7	9 07	M	9 7 81	Derry	Trainee	Aston Villa	—	—
Merson Paul	6 0	13 02	F	20 3 68	Northolt	Apprentice	Arsenal	327	78
							Brentford (loan)	7	—
							Middlesbrough	48	11
							Aston Villa	26	5
Milosevic Savo	6 1	13 08	F	2 9 73	Bijelina		Partizan Belgrade	98	64
(Transferred to Zaragoza, July 1998)							Aston Villa	90	28
Mulhulland Brian			D	22 8 81	Alexandria	Trainee	Aston Villa	—	—
Nelson Fernando	5 11	11 08	D	5 11 71	Oporto		Sporting	115	3
(Transferred to Porto, August 1998)							Aston Villa	59	—
Nkubi Isaac			M	5 3 81	Uganda	Vasteras	Aston Villa	—	—
Oakes Michael	6 2	14 07	G	30 10 73	Northwich	Trainee	Aston Villa	51	—
							Scarborough (loan)	1	—
							Tranmere R (loan)	—	—
Rachel Adam	5 11	12 08	G	10 12 76	Birmingham	Trainee	Aston Villa	1	—
Ridley Martin*	6 0	11 09	D	30 3 80	Leicester	Trainee	Aston Villa	—	—
Samuel J Lloyd	5 11	11 04	D	29 3 81	Trinidad	Charlton Ath	Aston Villa	—	—
Scimeca Riccardo	6 0	13 11	D	13 6 75	Leamington Spa	Trainee	Aston Villa	73	2
Southgate Gareth	6 0	12 06	M	3 9 70	Watford	Trainee	Crystal Palace	152	15
							Aston Villa	129	3
Standing Michael	5 10	10 05	M	20 3 81	Shoreham	Trainee	Aston Villa	—	—
Stone Steve	5 8	12 02	M	20 8 71	Gateshead	Trainee	Nottingham F	193	23
							Aston Villa	10	—
Tarrant Neil	6 0	12 00	M	24 6 79	Darlington	Trainee	Darlington	—	—
							Shamrock R	2	—
							Ross Co	44	20
							Aston Villa	—	—
Taylor Ian	6 1	12 00	M	4 6 68	Birmingham	Moor Green	Port Vale	83	28
							Sheffield W	14	1
							Aston Villa	146	16
Thompson Alan	6 0	13 11	M	22 12 73	Newcastle	Trainee	Newcastle U	16	—
							Bolton W	157	33
							Aston Villa	25	2
Vassell Darius	5 7	12 00	F	13 6 80	Birmingham	Trainee	Aston Villa	6	—
Walker Richard	6 0	12 04	F	8 11 77	Sutton Coldfield	Trainee	Aston Villa	1	—
							Cambridge U (loan)	21	3
Watson Steve	6 1	12 07	D	1 4 74	North Shields	Trainee	Newcastle U	208	12
							Aston Villa	27	—
Wright Alan	5 4	9 09	D	28 9 71	Ashton-under-Lyme	Trainee	Blackpool	98	—
							Blackburn R	74	1
							Aston Villa	159	3

Trainees/Scholars
Berks, David; Evans, Stephen G; Folds, Liam J; Harding, David M; Haynes, Daniel; Johnson, Karl; Kearns, James; Marfell, Andrew K; McSeveney, Gary; Price, Michael; Prince, Luke; Smith, Jay A; Thornley, Stuart; Walters, Gregory

BARNET

Name							Club	Apps	Gls
Adams Kieran‡	5 11	11 06	M	20 10 77	St Ives	Trainee	Barnet	19	1
Arber Mark	6 1	12 11	D	8 10 77	Johannesburg	Trainee	Tottenham H	—	—
							Barnet	35	2
Barnes Steve	5 4	10 09	M	5 1 76	Harrow	Welling U	Birmingham C	3	—
							Brighton & HA (loan)	12	—
							Barnet	12	—
Basham Mike	6 2	13 09	D	27 9 73	Barking	Trainee	West Ham U	—	—
							Colchester U (loan)	1	—
							Swansea C	29	1
							Peterborough U	19	1
							Barnet	52	2
Brady Matthew‡	6 0	10 04	F	27 10 77	Barnet	Trainee	Barnet	10	—
Charlery Ken	6 1	13 12	F	28 11 64	Stepney	Beckton U	Maidstone U	59	11
							Peterborough U	51	19
							Watford	48	13
							Peterborough U	70	24
							Birmingham C	17	4
							Southend U (loan)	3	—
							Peterborough U	56	12
							Stockport Co	10	—
							Barnet	74	21

Currie Darren	5 10	12 07	M	29 11 74	Hampstead	Trainee	West Ham U	—	—
							Shrewsbury T (loan)	17	2
							Leyton Orient (loan)	10	—
							Shrewsbury T	66	8
							Plymouth Arg	7	—
							Barnet	38	4
Devito Claudio‡	5 9	11 02	M	21 7 78	Peterborough	Trainee	Northampton T	—	—
							Barnet	1	—
Doolan John	6 1	13 00	M	7 5 74	Liverpool	Trainee	Everton	—	—
							Mansfield T	131	10
							Barnet	59	2
Ford John‡	6 1	13 04	D	12 4 68	Birmingham	Cradley T	Swansea C	160	7
							Bradford C	19	—
							Gillingham	4	—
							Barnet	47	2
Gledhill Lee§	5 10	11 02	D	7 11 80	Bury	Trainee	Barnet	1	—
Goodhind Warren	5 11	11 02	D	16 8 77	Johannesburg	Trainee	Barnet	53	2
Hackett Warren	6 0	12 05	D	16 12 71	Plaistow	Tottenham H	Leyton Orient	72	3
							Doncaster R	46	2
							Mansfield T	117	5
							Barnet	7	—
Harle Mike‡	6 0	12 06	D	31 10 72	Lewisham	Sittingbourne	Millwall	21	1
							Bury (loan)	1	—
							Barnet	54	2
Harrison Lee	6 2	12 07	G	12 9 71	Billericay	Trainee	Charlton Ath	—	—
							Fulham (loan)	—	—
							Gillingham (loan)	2	—
							Fulham (loan)	—	—
							Fulham	12	—
							Barnet	110	—
Heald Greg	6 1	13 01	D	26 9 71	Enfield	Enfield	Peterborough U	105	6
							Barnet	62	5
Howarth Lee‡	6 3	13 09	D	3 1 68	Bolton	Chorley	Peterborough U	62	—
							Mansfield T	57	2
							Barnet	102	5
King Marlon	6 1	12 03	F	26 4 80	Dulwich	Trainee	Barnet	22	6
Manuel Billy‡	5 8	12 00	M	28 6 69	Hackney	Apprentice	Tottenham H	—	—
							Gillingham	87	5
							Brentford	94	1
							Cambridge U	10	—
							Peterborough U	27	2
							Gillingham	21	—
							Barnet	29	1
McGleish Scott	5 10	11 07	F	10 2 74	Camden Town	Edgware T	Charlton Ath	6	—
							Leyton Orient (loan)	6	1
							Peterborough U	13	—
							Colchester U (loan)	15	6
							Cambridge U (loan)	10	7
							Leyton Orient	36	7
							Barnet	73	21
Mustafa Tarkan‡	5 10	11 07	D	28 8 73	London	Kettering T	Barnet	11	—
Onwere Udo*	6 0	11 07	M	9 11 71	Hammersmith	Trainee	Fulham	85	7
							Lincoln C	43	4
							Blackpool	9	—
							Barnet	36	2
Rust Nicky‡	6 1	13 01	G	25 9 74	Ely	Arsenal	Brighton & HA	177	—
							Barnet	2	—
Samuels Dean‡	6 2	12 06	F	29 3 73	Hackney	Boreham Wood	Barnet	39	4
Sawyers Robert	5 10	11 03	D	20 11 78	Dudley	Wolverhampton W	Barnet	23	—
Searle Stevie	5 10	11 08	M	7 3 77	Lambeth	Sittingbourne	Barnet	65	5
Simpson Phil‡	5 8	11 12	M	19 10 69	Lambeth	Stevenage Bor	Barnet	100	7
Stockley Sam	6 0	12 00	D	5 9 77	Tiverton	Trainee	Southampton	—	—
							Barnet	103	—
Strevens Ben			M	24 5 80	Edgware		Barnet	—	—
Wilson Paul#	5 9	12 00	M	26 9 64	Forest Gate	Barking	Barnet	244	23

Trainees
Bell, Leon E; Butterfield, John P; Chapman, Danny P; Gledhill, Lee; Hall, Fitz; Lovatt, Scott C; McCann, Peter; Obili, Shaun; Pluck, Lee K; Taylor, Mark J; White, Ross A

BARNSLEY

Appleby Matty	5 10	11 08	D	16 4 72	Middlesbrough	Trainee	Newcastle U	20	—
							Darlington (loan)	10	1
							Darlington	79	7
							Barnsley	84	—
Bagshaw Paul	5 10	12 02	M	29 5 79	Sheffield	Trainee	Barnsley	1	—
							Carlisle U (loan)	9	—
Barker Christopher	6 0	11 08	D	2 3 80	Sheffield	Alfreton	Barnsley	—	—
Barnard Darren	5 9	12 03	D	30 11 71	Rinteln	Wokingham T	Chelsea	29	2
							Reading (loan)	4	—
							Bristol C	78	15
							Barnsley	61	6

Bassinder Gavin	5 8	11 01	D	24 9 79	Mexborough	Trainee	Barnsley	—	—
Bernard Curtis§	5 7	12 00	F	3 7 80	Leeds	Trainee	Barnsley	—	—
Blackmore Clayton*	5 7	12 01	M	23 9 64	Neath	Apprentice	Manchester U	186	19
							Middlesbrough	53	4
							Bristol C (loan)	5	1
							Barnsley	7	—
Bullock Martin#	5 6	9 04	M	5 3 75	Derby	Eastwood T	Barnsley	163	3
Bullock Tony	6 1	14 01	G	18 2 72	Warrington	Leek T	Barnsley	32	—
Butler Ian‡	5 8	11 05	D	9 11 79	Barnsley	Trainee	Barnsley	—	—
Cataroche David§	5 7	11 07	M	13 12 80	Leeds	Trainee	Barnsley	—	—
Crookes Dale	5 9	12 03	M	10 3 80	Sheffield	Trainee	Barnsley	—	—
Cross Matthew‡	5 6	12 03	D	25 3 80	Bury	Trainee	Barnsley	—	—
De Zeeuw Arjan#	6 3	13 03	D	16 4 70	Castricum	Vitesse 22	Telstar	102	5
							Barnsley	138	7
Dyer Bruce	5 11	12 06	F	13 4 75	Ilford	Trainee	Watford	31	6
							Crystal Palace	135	37
							Barnsley	28	7
Eaden Nicky	5 9	12 02	D	12 12 72	Sheffield	Trainee	Barnsley	251	9
Fallon Rory	6 2	11 09	F	20 3 82	Gisbourne	North Shore U	Barnsley	—	—
Fjortoft Jan Aage	6 4	13 12	F	10 1 67	Aalesund		Hamar	22	10
(Transferred to Eintracht Frankfurt, November 1998)							Lillestrom	35	20
							Rapid Vienna	128	62
							Swindon T	72	28
							Middlesbrough	41	9
							Sheffield U	34	19
							Barnsley	34	9
Fumaca Jose Antunes	6 0	11 08	M	15 7 76	Belem	Catunese	Birmingham C	—	—
							Colchester U	1	—
							Barnsley	—	—
Goodman Don‡	5 10	12 12	F	9 5 66	Leeds	School	Bradford C	70	14
(Transferred to Motherwell, March 1999)							WBA	158	60
							Sunderland	116	40
							Wolverhampton W	125	33
						Hiroshima	Barnsley (loan)	8	—
							Motherwell	8	1
Goodyear Craig§	5 7	12 01	M	7 11 80	Barnsley	Trainee	Barnsley	—	—
Gregory Andrew	5 10	11 04	M	8 10 76	Barnsley	Trainee	Barnsley	—	—
Heckingbottom Marc*	5 7	12 01	M	21 2 80	Barnsley	Trainee	Barnsley	—	—
Hendrie John‡	5 7	12 02	F	24 10 63	Lennoxtown	Apprentice	Coventry C	21	2
							Hereford U (loan)	6	—
							Bradford C	173	46
							Newcastle U	34	4
							Leeds U	27	5
							Middlesbrough	192	44
							Barnsley	65	17
Hignett Craig	5 9	11 03	F	12 1 70	Whiston	Liverpool	Crewe Alex	121	42
							Middlesbrough	156	33
							Aberdeen	13	2
							Barnsley	24	9
Hristov Georgi	6 0	12 09	F	30 1 76	Bitola		Partizan Belgrade	37	12
							Barnsley	26	4
Jones Scott	5 10	12 01	D	1 5 75	Sheffield	Trainee	Barnsley	63	4
							Mansfield T (loan)	6	—
							Notts Co (loan)	—	—
Kennedy Paul*	5 9	12 02	D	8 10 79	Stockport	Trainee	Barnsley	—	—
Krizan Ales	5 9	12 09	D	25 7 71	Maribor		Branik Maribor	159	—
							Barnsley	13	—
Leese Lars*	6 5	14 07	G	18 8 69	Cologne	Leverkusen	Barnsley	17	—
Marcelle Clint	5 5	9 09	M	9 11 68	Port of Spain	Rio Ave	Falgueiras	51	3
							Barnsley	69	8
Markstedt Peter	6 2	13 05	D	11 1 72	Vasteras		Vasteras	23	4
							Barnsley	9	—
McClare Sean	5 11	11 08	M	12 1 78	Rotherham	Trainee	Barnsley	30	3
Morgan Chris	6 1	12 08	D	9 11 77	Barnsley	Trainee	Barnsley	30	—
Moses Adrian	6 0	12 07	D	4 5 75	Doncaster	School	Barnsley	125	3
O'Callaghan Brian	6 1	12 12	D	24 2 81	Limerick	Pike Rovers	Barnsley	—	—
Parkin Jonathan	6 4	13 07	F	30 12 81	Barnsley	Scholarship	Barnsley	2	—
Pirri‡			M	10 11 70	Caneas de Onis		Merida	19	1
							Barnsley	2	—
Richardson Kevin	5 9	11 08	M	4 12 62	Newcastle	Apprentice	Everton	109	16
							Watford	39	2
							Arsenal	96	5
							Real Sociedad	37	—
							Aston Villa	143	13
							Coventry C	78	—
							Southampton	28	—
							Barnsley	26	—
Rose Karl	5 10	11 00	F	12 10 78	Barnsley		Barnsley	4	—
							Mansfield T (loan)	1	—
Sadler Adam‡	5 11	12 01	G	9 1 80	North Shields	Manchester U	Barnsley	—	—

Sheridan Darren#	5 6	11 03	M	8 12 67	Manchester	Winsford U	Barnsley	171	5
Sheron Mike	5 10	12 07	F	11 1 72	Liverpool	Trainee	Manchester C	100	24
							Bury (loan)	5	1
							Norwich C	28	2
							Stoke C	69	34
							QPR	63	19
							Barnsley	15	2
Siddall Richard	6 1	11 06	G	24 1 82	Sheffield	Scholarship	Barnsley	—	—
Smith Andrew	5 5	11 08	M	13 1 80	Blackpool	Trainee	Barnsley	—	—
Tinkler Eric	6 2	12 06	M	30 7 70	Roodepoort		Vitoria Setubal	57	1
							Cagliari	20	—
							Barnsley	50	5
Turner Mike	6 2	13 03	F	2 4 76	Stoke	Bilston T	Barnsley	13	1
Van der Laan Robin	5 11	13 08	M	5 9 68	Schiedam	Wageningen	Port Vale	176	24
							Derby Co	65	8
							Wolverhampton W (loan)	7	—
							Barnsley	17	1
Watson David	6 0	12 09	G	10 11 73	Barnsley	Trainee	Barnsley	178	—

Trainees
Bernard, Curtis J; Cataroche, David; Dudgeon, James F; Goodyear, Craig; Ravenhill, Richard J; Sidebottom, Frazer

Scholars
Barrowclough, Carl; Mulligan, David; Richards, Duncan; Welch, Michael F

Non-Contract
Hendrie, John G; Shirtliff, Peter A

Associated Schoolboys who have accepted the Club's offer of a Traineeship/Scholarship/Contract
Austin, Neil J; Jackson, Paul S; Kay, Anthony R; Reece, Gary L

BIRMINGHAM CITY

Ablett Gary#	6 2	11 04	D	19 11 65	Liverpool	Apprentice	Liverpool	109	1
							Derby Co (loan)	6	—
							Hull C (loan)	5	—
							Everton	128	5
							Sheffield U (loan)	12	—
							Birmingham C	104	1
Adebola Dele	6 3	12 08	F	23 6 75	Lagos	Trainee	Crewe Alex	124	39
							Birmingham C	56	20
Bass Jonathan	6 0	12 02	D	1 1 76	Weston-Super-Mare	Trainee	Birmingham C	59	—
							Carlisle U (loan)	3	—
Bennett Ian	6 0	12 10	G	10 10 71	Worksop	Newcastle U	Peterborough U	72	—
							Birmingham C	187	—
Charlton Simon	5 8	11 10	D	25 10 71	Huddersfield	Trainee	Huddersfield T	124	1
							Southampton	114	2
							Birmingham C	52	—
Dyson James	6 2	12 00	D	20 4 79	Wordsley	Trainee	Birmingham C	—	—
Forinton Howard	5 11	11 00	F	18 9 75	Boston	Yeovil T	Birmingham C	4	1
							Plymouth Arg (loan)	9	3
Forster Nicky	5 9	11 05	F	8 9 73	Caterham	Horley T	Gillingham	67	24
							Brentford	109	39
							Birmingham C	68	11
Furlong Paul	6 0	11 00	F	1 10 68	London	Enfield	Coventry C	37	4
							Watford	79	37
							Chelsea	64	13
							Birmingham C	97	38
Gardner Lee‡			D	18 5 78	Doncaster		Birmingham C	—	—
Gill Jeremy	5 11	11 00	D	8 9 70	Clevedon	Yeovil T	Birmingham C	6	—
Grainger Martin	5 10	11 07	D	23 8 72	Enfield	Trainee	Colchester U	46	7
							Brentford	101	12
							Birmingham C	104	9
Haarhoff James			M	27 5 81	Lusaka	Trainee	Birmingham C	—	—
Hey Tony	5 9	11 07	M	19 9 70	Berlin		Fortuna Cologne	32	9
							Birmingham C	9	—
Holdsworth David	6 1	12 10	D	8 11 68	Walthamstow	Trainee	Watford	258	10
							Sheffield U	93	4
							Birmingham C	8	1
Holland Chris	5 9	11 05	M	11 9 76	Whalley	Trainee	Preston NE	1	—
							Newcastle U	3	—
							Birmingham C	56	—
Hughes Bryan	5 9	10 00	M	19 6 76	Liverpool	Trainee	Wrexham	94	12
							Birmingham C	79	8
Hyde Graham	5 8	12 04	M	10 11 70	Doncaster	Trainee	Sheffield W	172	11
							Birmingham C	13	—
Johnson Andrew	5 6	10 00	F	10 2 81	Bedford	Trainee	Birmingham C	4	—
Johnson Michael	5 11	11 00	D	4 7 73	Nottingham	Trainee	Notts Co	107	—
							Birmingham C	151	8
Marsh Simon	5 11	12 00	D	29 1 77	Ealing	Trainee	Oxford U	56	3
							Birmingham C	7	—

Name			Pos	DOB	Birthplace	Source	Club	Apps	Gls
McCarthy Jon	5 9	11 05	M	18 8 70	Middlesbrough		Hartlepool U	1	—
						Shepshed	York C	199	31
							Port Vale	94	11
							Birmingham C	84	4
McKeown Francis	5 9	11 07	M	11 2 81	Belfast	Trainee	Sunderland	—	—
							Birmingham C	—	—
Ndlovu Peter	5 8	10 02	F	25 2 73	Zimbabwe	Highlanders	Coventry C	177	37
							Birmingham C	82	19
O'Connor Martin	5 8	10 08	M	10 12 67	Walsall	Bromsgrove R	Crystal Palace	2	—
							Walsall (loan)	10	1
							Walsall	94	21
							Peterborough U	18	3
							Birmingham C	94	9
Poole Kevin	5 10	11 11	G	21 7 63	Bromsgrove	Apprentice	Aston Villa	28	—
							Northampton T (loan)	3	—
							Middlesbrough	34	—
							Hartlepool U (loan)	12	—
							Leicester C	163	—
							Birmingham C	37	—
Purse Darren	6 2	13 08	D	14 2 76	Stepney	Trainee	Leyton Orient	55	3
							Oxford U	59	5
							Birmingham C	28	—
Rea Simon	6 1	13 00	D	20 9 76	Coventry	Trainee	Birmingham C	1	—
Robinson Steve	5 9	11 00	M	17 10 75	Nottingham	Trainee	Birmingham C	71	—
							Peterborough U (loan)	5	—
Rowett Gary	6 0	12 10	D	6 3 74	Bromsgrove	Trainee	Cambridge U	63	9
							Everton	4	—
							Blackpool (loan)	17	—
							Derby Co	105	2
							Birmingham C	42	5
Wassall Darren	6 0	12 07	D	27 6 68	Edgbaston		Nottingham F	27	—
							Hereford U (loan)	5	—
							Bury (loan)	7	1
							Derby Co	98	—
							Manchester C (loan)	15	—
							Birmingham C (loan)	8	—
							Birmingham C	17	—

Trainees
Capaldi, Anthony C; Scheppel, Daniel J

Scholars
Burns, Robert J; Diamond, Ross; Hart, Steven; Hider, Allan J; Hutchinson, Jonathan; Jameseon, Michael; Kennedy, Michael J; Wood, Paul A

Associated Schoolboys
Carter, Darren; Chisholm, Kelvin S; Hipkiss, Robert J; Holyoak, Daniel; Tarrant, Paul P

Associated Schoolboys who have accepted the Club's offer of a Traineeship/Scholarship/Contract
Fagan, Craig A; Parker, Sonny; Robertson, Daniel

BLACKBURN ROVERS

Name			Pos	DOB	Birthplace	Source	Club	Apps	Gls
Andersson Anders *(On loan to Aalborg)*	5 9	11 09	M	15 3 74	Tomelilla		Malmo	126	19
							Blackburn R	4	—
Baldacchino Ryan	5 9	12 03	F	13 1 81	Leicester	Trainee	Blackburn R	—	—
Bingham Michael	6 0	12 05	G	21 5 81	Preston	Trainee	Blackburn R	—	—
Blake Nathan	6 0	12 08	F	27 1 72	Cardiff	Chelsea	Cardiff C	131	35
							Sheffield U	69	34
							Bolton W	107	38
							Blackburn R	11	3
Broomes Marlon	6 1	12 12	D	28 11 77	Meriden	Trainee	Blackburn R	17	—
							Swindon T (loan)	12	1
Brown Keith	6 0	11 00	D	24 12 79	Edinburgh		Blackburn R	—	—
Burgess Ben	6 3	14 04	F	9 11 81	Buxton	Trainee	Blackburn R	—	—
Carsley Lee	5 9	12 00	M	28 2 74	Birmingham	Trainee	Derby Co	138	5
							Blackburn R	8	—
Connolly Patrick*			M	3 3 80	Preston	Trainee	Blackburn R	—	—
Corbett James	5 10	10 12	M	6 7 80	Hackney	Trainee	Gillingham	16	2
							Blackburn R	—	—
Coughlan Graham‡	6 3	14 00	D	18 11 74	Dublin	Bray Wanderers	Blackburn R	—	—
							Swindon T (loan)	3	—
Croft Gary	5 8	10 08	D	17 2 74	Stafford	Trainee	Grimsby T	149	3
							Blackburn R	40	1
Dahlin Martin *(On loan to Hamburg)*	6 1	13 03	F	16 4 68	Lund	Lund BK	Malmo	79	39
							Moenchengladbach	106	50
							Roma	3	—
							Blackburn R	26	4
Dailly Christian	6 0	12 05	D	23 10 73	Dundee		Dundee U	141	18
							Derby Co	67	4
							Blackburn R	17	—
Davidson Callum	5 10	11 00	D	26 6 76	Stirling		St Johnstone	44	4
							Blackburn R	35	1
Davies Kevin	6 0	13 11	F	26 3 77	Sheffield	Trainee	Chesterfield	129	22
							Southampton	25	9
							Blackburn R	21	1

Player	Ht	Wt	Pos	Date of Birth	Birthplace	From	Club	Apps	Gls
Doyle Robert			M	15 4 82	Dublin	Trainee	Blackburn R	—	—
Duff Damien	5 8	9 07	F	2 3 79	Ballyboden		Blackburn R	55	5
Dunn David	5 10	12 00	M	27 12 79	Blackburn	Trainee	Blackburn R	15	1
Dunning Darren	5 6	11 12	M	8 1 81	Scarborough	Trainee	Blackburn R	—	—
Dunning Richard	5 7	11 10	D	8 1 81	Scarborough	Trainee	Blackburn R	—	—
Fettis Alan	6 2	13 00	G	1 2 71	Newtownards	Ards	Hull C	135	2
							WBA (loan)	3	—
							Nottingham F	4	—
							Blackburn R	10	—
Filan John	6 2	14 04	G	8 2 70	Sydney	Budapest St George	Cambridge U	68	—
							Nottingham F (loan)	—	—
							Coventry C	16	—
							Blackburn R	33	—
Fitzpatrick Lee	5 10	11 07	M	31 10 78	Manchester	Trainee	Blackburn R	—	—
Flitcroft Garry	6 0	11 08	M	6 11 72	Bolton	Trainee	Manchester C	115	13
							Bury (loan)	12	—
							Blackburn R	72	5
Flitcroft Steven	5 10	11 01	M	17 10 81	Bolton	Trainee	Blackburn R	—	—
Flowers Tim	6 3	14 04	G	3 2 67	Kenilworth	Apprentice	Wolverhampton W	63	—
							Southampton (loan)	—	—
							Southampton	192	—
							Swindon T (loan)	2	—
							Swindon T (loan)	5	—
							Blackburn R	177	—
Forsyth Paul	5 8	10 05	F	11 4 81	Dublin	Trainee	Blackburn R	—	—
Foster Steve	5 9	13 01	F	30 12 81	Manchester	Trainee	Blackburn R	—	—
Gallacher Kevin	5 8	11 03	F	23 11 66	Clydebank	Duntocher BC	Dundee U	131	27
							Coventry C	100	28
							Blackburn R	139	46
Gill Wayne	5 9	11 00	M	28 11 75	Chorley	Trainee	Blackburn R	—	—
							Dundee U	2	—
							Blackburn R	—	—
Gillespie Keith	5 9	11 05	M	18 2 75	Larne	Trainee	Manchester U	9	1
							Wigan Ath (loan)	8	4
							Newcastle U	113	11
							Blackburn R	16	1
Hamilton Gary			F	6 10 80	Bambridge	Trainee	Blackburn R	—	—
Hawe Steven			F	23 12 80	Machbrafelt	Trainee	Blackburn R	—	—
Henchoz Stephane	6 2	12 08	D	7 9 74	Billens	Bulle	Neuchatel Xamax	91	1
							Hamburg	49	2
							Blackburn R	70	—
Hendry Colin	6 1	12 07	D	7 12 65	Keith	Islavale	Dundee	41	2
(Transferred to Rangers, August 1998)							Blackburn R	102	22
							Manchester C	63	5
							Blackburn R	234	12
							Rangers	19	—
Jansen Matt	5 11	11 03	F	20 10 77	Carlisle	Trainee	Carlisle U	42	10
							Crystal Palace	26	10
							Blackburn R	11	3
Johnson Damien	5 10	11 02	M	18 11 78	Lisburn	Trainee	Blackburn R	21	1
							Nottingham F (loan)	6	—
Kenna Jeff	5 11	12 03	D	27 8 70	Dublin	Trainee	Southampton	114	4
							Blackburn R	138	1
Konde Oumar	6 2	13 00	M	19 8 79	Basle	Binningen	Basle	35	—
							Blackburn R	—	—
Lawless Michael	5 6	10 13	M	15 8 81	Dublin	Trainee	Blackburn R	—	—
Marcolin Dario*	5 10	11 07	M	28 10 71	Brescia		Cremonese	60	5
							Lazio	19	—
							Cagliari	18	—
							Genoa	22	2
							Lazio	51	2
							Blackburn R	10	1
McAteer Jason	5 11	11 10	M	18 6 71	Birkenhead	Marine	Bolton W	114	8
							Liverpool	100	3
							Blackburn R	13	1
McAvoy Andy	6 0	12 00	M	28 8 79	Middlesbrough	Trainee	Blackburn R	—	—
McCann Peter	5 6	10 13	D	18 8 81	Dublin	Trainee	Blackburn R	—	—
McKinlay Billy	5 8	11 06	M	22 4 69	Glasgow	Hamilton Th	Dundee U	222	23
							Blackburn R	90	3
McNamee David	5 11	10 07	D	10 10 80	Glasgow	St Mirren BC	St Mirren	31	—
							Blackburn R	—	—
Murphy Peter	5 10	12 03	D	27 10 80	Dublin	Trainee	Blackburn R	—	—
Murray Frederick§			M	22 5 82	Clonmel	Trainee	Blackburn R	—	—
O'Brien Burton	5 11	10 07	F	10 6 81	South Africa	S Form	St Mirren	22	1
							Blackburn R	—	—
Peacock Darren	6 1	12 12	D	3 2 68	Bristol	Apprentice	Newport Co	28	—
							Hereford U	59	4
							QPR	126	6
							Newcastle U	133	2
							Blackburn R	30	1

Name	Ht	Wt	Pos	Date of Birth	Birthplace	Signed from	Club	Apps	Gls
Pedersen Per	5 11	13 00	F	30 3 69	Aalborg		Odense	44	16
(On loan to Moenchengladbach)							Lyngby	96	38
							Odense	49	27
							Blackburn R	11	1
Pedersen Tore‡			D	29 9 69	Fredrikstad	Fredrikstad	IFK Gothenburg	64	—
							Brann	22	—
							Oldham Ath	10	—
							Brann	1	—
						Sanfrecce	St Pauli	37	—
							Blackburn R	5	—
Perez Sebastian	5 10	12 00	D	24 11 73	Saint-Chamond		St Etienne	55	2
(On loan to Bastia)							Bastia	63	10
							Blackburn R	5	1
Richards Ian*	5 8	11 04	D	5 10 79	Barnsley	Trainee	Blackburn R	—	—
Richardson Leam			D	19 11 79	Leeds	Trainee	Blackburn R	—	—
Ryan Ciaran*	5 8	11 00	D	3 9 79	Dublin	Trainee	Blackburn R	—	—
Scates Garth			M	27 8 79	Dundonald	Trainee	Blackburn R	—	—
Stewart Gareth*	6 0	12 08	G	3 2 80	Preston	Trainee	Blackburn R	—	—
Sutton Chris	6 3	13 07	F	10 3 73	Nottingham	Trainee	Norwich C	102	35
							Blackburn R	130	47
Taylor Martin	6 4	14 00	D	9 11 79	Ashington	Trainee	Blackburn R	3	—
Thomas James	6 0	13 00	F	16 1 79	Swansea	Trainee	Blackburn R	—	—
							WBA (loan)	3	—
Topley Jonathan*			F	12 7 80	Craigavon	Trainee	Blackburn R	—	—
Valery Patrick‡	5 8	13 04	D	3 7 69	Brignoles	AS Brignoles	Monaco	210	—
							Blackburn R	15	—
Ward Ashley	6 1	12 02	F	24 11 70	Manchester	Trainee	Manchester C	1	—
							Wrexham (loan)	4	2
							Leicester C	10	—
							Blackpool (loan)	2	1
							Crewe Alex	61	25
							Norwich C	53	18
							Derby Co	40	9
							Barnsley	46	20
							Blackburn R	17	5
Whittle Christopher*			M	31 7 80	Preston	Trainee	Blackburn R	—	—
Wilcox Jason	6 0	11 00	F	15 7 71	Bolton	Trainee	Blackburn R	249	31
Williams Anthony	6 1	13 08	G	20 9 77	Ogwr	Trainee	Blackburn R	—	—
							QPR (loan)	—	—
							Macclesfield T (loan)	4	—
							Huddersfield T (loan)	—	—
							Bristol R (loan)	9	—
Woodfield Craig*			M	4 9 79	Coventry	Trainee	Blackburn R	—	—
Worrell David	5 11	12 04	D	12 1 78	Dublin	Trainee	Blackburn R	—	—
(Transferred to Dundee U, March 1999)							Dundee U	4	—

Trainees/Scholars
Chamberlain, Robert B; Derbyshire, Robert W; Douglas, Jonathan; Hardy, Lee; Hind, Matthew; Howson, Stuart L; Murray, Frederick A; Nutter, John R W; Richards, Marc J; Taylor, Stuart

BLACKPOOL

Name	Ht	Wt	Pos	Date of Birth	Birthplace	Signed from	Club	Apps	Gls
Aldridge Martin	5 11	12 02	F	4 12 74	Northampton	Trainee	Northampton T	70	17
							Oxford U	72	19
							Southend U (loan)	11	1
							Blackpool	22	7
Bardsley David	5 10	11 07	D	11 9 64	Manchester	Apprentice	Blackpool	45	—
							Watford	100	7
							Oxford U	74	7
							QPR	253	4
							Blackpool	29	—
Barnes Kevin‡	6 0	12 05	F	12 9 75	Fleetwood	Lancaster C	Blackpool	4	—
Barnes Phil	6 1	11 01	G	2 3 79	Rotherham	Trainee	Rotherham U	2	—
							Blackpool	2	—
Bent Junior	5 5	10 06	F	1 3 70	Huddersfield	Trainee	Huddersfield T	36	6
							Burnley (loan)	9	3
							Bristol C	183	20
							Stoke C (loan)	1	—
							Shrewsbury T (loan)	1	—
							Blackpool	75	4
Blunt Jason‡	5 8	10 01	M	16 8 77	Penzance	Trainee	Leeds U	4	—
							Blackpool	2	—
Bryan Marvin	6 0	12 02	D	2 8 75	Paddington	Trainee	QPR	—	—
							Doncaster R (loan)	5	1
							Blackpool	164	4
Bushell Steve	5 9	11 06	M	28 12 72	Manchester	Trainee	York C	174	10
							Blackpool	31	3
Caig Tony	6 1	12 00	G	11 4 74	Whitehaven	Trainee	Carlisle U	223	—
							Blackpool	10	—
Carlisle Clarke	6 1	12 07	D	14 10 79	Preston	Trainee	Blackpool	50	3

Name	Ht	Wt	Pos	DOB	Birthplace	Source	Club	Apps	Gls
Clarkson Phil	5 10	12 08	M	13 11 68	Garstang	Fleetwood T	Crewe Alex	98	27
							Scunthorpe U	52	19
							Blackpool	106	27
Coid Daniel§	5 11	11 07	M	3 10 81	Liverpool	Trainee	Blackpool	1	—
Conroy Mike	6 0	13 03	F	31 12 65	Glasgow	Apprentice	Coventry C	—	—
							Clydebank	114	38
							St Mirren	10	1
							Reading	80	7
							Burnley	77	30
							Preston NE	57	22
							Fulham	94	32
							Blackpool	14	—
							Chester C (loan)	15	3
Couzens Andy	5 10	11 11	M	4 6 75	Shipley	Trainee	Leeds U	28	1
							Carlisle U	42	2
							Blackpool	6	—
Garvey Steve	5 9	11 01	M	22 11 73	Stalybridge	Trainee	Crewe Alex	108	8
							Chesterfield (loan)	3	—
							Blackpool	15	1
Hills John	5 8	10 08	D	21 4 78	St Annes-on-Sea	Trainee	Blackpool	—	—
							Everton	3	—
							Swansea C (loan)	11	—
							Swansea C (loan)	7	1
							Blackpool	47	2
Hughes Ian	5 10	12 08	M	2 8 74	Bangor	Trainee	Bury	175	1
							Blackpool	54	1
Jarrett Jason‡	6 0	12 04	M	14 9 79	Bury	Trainee	Blackpool	2	—
Jones David‡	5 7	9 10	M	17 11 78	Goole	Goole T	Blackpool	—	—
Longworth Steve*	5 9	11 00	F	6 2 80	Leyland	Trainee	Blackpool	2	—
Malkin Chris*	6 3	12 09	F	4 6 67	Hoylake	Overpool	Tranmere R	232	60
							Millwall	52	14
							Blackpool	64	6
Nowland Adam	5 11	11 06	F	6 7 81	Preston	Trainee	Blackpool	38	2
Ormerod Brett	5 11	11 04	F	18 10 76	Blackburn	Accrington S	Blackpool	53	10
Robinson Phil	5 9	11 00	D	28 9 80	Manchester	Trainee	Blackpool	5	—
Rogan Anton*	6 0	13 00	D	25 3 66	Belfast	Distillery	Celtic	127	4
							Sunderland	46	1
							Oxford U	58	3
							Millwall	36	8
							Blackpool	15	—
Shuttleworth Barry	5 8	11 00	D	9 7 77	Accrington	Trainee	Bury	—	—
							Rotherham U	—	—
							Blackpool	14	1
Thompson Phil	5 11	12 00	D	1 4 81	Blackpool	Trainee	Blackpool	23	2
Worthington Nigel	5 11	12 06	D	4 11 61	Ballymena	Ballymena U	Notts Co	67	4
							Sheffield W	338	12
							Leeds U	43	1
							Stoke C	12	—
							Blackpool	9	—

Trainees
Bamber, Michael J; Byrne, Tamas; Coid, Daniel J; Connell, Darren S; Dickinson, Ian J; Ellis, Christopher A; Ellison, Gavin; Fahey, Mark A; Gilmore, Gavin; Lambert, Rickie L; Lazenby, Mark; Lynch, Patrick A; Manchester, Brian N; Sidebotham, Paul G; Smith, Robert J; Sugden, Scott I

Associated Schoolboys
Grand, Simon; Hone, James; Mallord, Simon J; Morgan, Nicholas S; Watson, David L; Zammit, Daniel S R

Associated Schoolboys who have accepted the Club's offer of a Traineeship/Scholarship/Contract
Carroll, John D; Connors, John J; Maden, Wayne T; Smyth, Marc

BOLTON WANDERERS

Name	Ht	Wt	Pos	DOB	Birthplace	Source	Club	Apps	Gls
Aljofree Hasney	6 0	12 03	D	11 7 78	Manchester	Trainee	Bolton W	6	—
Banks Steve	5 11	12 04	G	9 2 72	Hillingdon	Trainee	West Ham U	—	—
							Gillingham	67	—
							Blackpool	150	—
							Bolton W	9	—
Bergsson Gudni	6 1	12 03	D	21 7 65	Reykjavik	Valur	Tottenham H	71	2
							Bolton W	127	9
Branagan Keith	6 0	13 02	G	10 7 66	Fulham		Cambridge U	110	—
							Millwall	46	—
							Brentford (loan)	2	—
							Gillingham (loan)	1	—
							Fulham (loan)	—	—
							Bolton W	203	—
Corrigan Noel*	5 10	11 00	M	29 12 79	Belfast	Trainee	Bolton W	—	—
Cox Neil	6 0	13 02	D	8 10 71	Scunthorpe	Trainee	Scunthorpe U	17	1
							Aston Villa	42	3
							Middlesbrough	106	3
							Bolton W	65	5
Dawson Chris	5 10	10 02	D	22 8 79	Coventry	Trainee	Bolton W	—	—
Doherty Martin*	6 1	12 02	M	17 10 78	Urmston	Trainee	Bolton W	—	—

Name	Ht	Wt	Pos	Date	Birthplace	Source	Club	Apps	Gls
Elliott Robbie	5 10	10 13	D	25 12 73	Gosforth	Trainee	Newcastle U	79	9
							Bolton W	26	—
Evans James			M	27 1 82	Glasgow	Scholarship	Bolton W	—	—
Fish Mark	6 4	12 11	D	14 3 74	Cape Town	Arcadia Shepherds	Jomo Cosmos	55	2
							Orlando Pirates	75	6
							Lazio	15	1
							Bolton W	58	3
Frandsen Per	6 1	12 06	M	6 2 70	Copenhagen		B 1903	25	15
							Lille	109	19
							FC Copenhagen	55	19
							Bolton W	123	15
Gardner Ricardo	5 9	11 00	M	25 9 78	St Andrews	Harbour View	Bolton W	30	2
Giallanza Gaetano‡	6 0	11 03	F	6 6 74	Dornach		Basle	32	19
							Nantes	12	2
							Bolton W	3	—
Glennon Matthew	6 2	13 11	G	8 10 78	Stockport	Trainee	Bolton W	—	—
Gudjohnsen Eidur	6 0	13 00	F	15 9 78	Reykjavik		Valur	17	7
							PSV Eindhoven	13	3
							KR	—	—
							Bolton W	14	5
Hansen Bo	5 10	11 00	F	16 6 72	Jutland		Brondby	102	43
							Bolton W	8	—
Holden Dean	6 0	11 00	D	15 9 79	Salford		Bolton W	—	—
Holdsworth Dean	5 11	11 13	F	8 11 68	Walthamstow	Trainee	Watford	16	3
							Carlisle U (loan)	4	1
							Port Vale (loan)	6	2
							Swansea C (loan)	5	1
							Brentford (loan)	7	1
							Brentford	110	53
							Wimbledon	169	58
							Bolton W	52	15
Jaaskelainen Jussi	6 3	12 10	G	19 4 75	Mikkeli		MP	64	—
							VPS	54	—
							Bolton W	34	—
Jensen Claus	5 11	12 00	M	29 4 77	Nykobing		Naestved	4	—
							Lyngby	62	14
							Bolton W	44	2
Johansen Michael	5 6	10 05	M	22 7 72	Glostrup		KB Copenhagen	15	1
							B 1903	26	1
							FC Copenhagen	114	17
							Bolton W	92	13
Morrison Peter	5 11	10 00	M	29 6 80	Manchester	Trainee	Bolton W	—	—
Phillips Jimmy	6 0	12 07	D	8 2 66	Bolton	Apprentice	Bolton W	108	2
							Rangers	25	—
							Oxford U	79	8
							Middlesbrough	139	6
							Bolton W	198	2
Potter Lee	5 11	12 10	F	3 9 78	Salford	Trainee	Bolton W	—	—
Power Alan			M	18 9 80	Dublin	Trainee	Bolton W	—	—
Pryers Lee*	5 6	10 00	D	23 2 80	Bolton	Trainee	Bolton W	—	—
Sellars Scott*	5 8	10 00	M	27 11 65	Sheffield	Apprentice	Leeds U	76	12
							Blackburn R	202	35
							Leeds U	7	—
							Newcastle U	61	5
							Bolton W	111	15
Smith Gordon			M	18 12 80	Glasgow	Trainee	Bolton W	—	—
Snorrason Olafur			F	22 4 82	Reykjavik		Bolton W	—	—
Spooner Nicky*	5 10	11 09	D	5 6 71	Manchester	Trainee	Bolton W	23	2
							Oldham Ath (loan)	2	—
Staton Luke	5 7	10 07	M	10 3 79	Doncaster	Trainee	Blackburn R	—	—
							Bolton W	—	—
Strong Greg	6 2	11 12	D	5 9 75	Bolton	Trainee	Wigan Ath	35	3
							Bolton W	6	1
							Blackpool (loan)	11	1
							Stoke C (loan)	5	1
Taylor Bob	5 11	11 09	F	3 2 67	Easington	Horden CW	Leeds U	42	9
							Bristol C	106	50
							WBA	238	96
							Bolton W (loan)	12	3
							Bolton W	38	15
Todd Andy	5 10	10 11	D	21 9 74	Derby	Trainee	Middlesbrough	8	—
							Swindon T (loan)	13	—
							Bolton W	72	2
Trueman Kevin*	5 6	10 11	F	8 8 79	Downpatrick	Trainee	Bolton W	—	—
Warhurst Paul	6 1	12 01	D	26 9 69	Stockport	Trainee	Manchester C	—	—
							Oldham Ath	67	2
							Sheffield W	66	6
							Blackburn R	57	4
							Crystal Palace	27	4
							Bolton W	20	—
Whitlow Mike	6 1	11 06	D	13 1 68	Northwich	Witton Alb	Leeds U	77	4
							Leicester C	147	8
							Bolton W	41	—
Xiourouppa Costas*	5 11	11 00	F	11 9 79	Dudley	Trainee	Bolton W	—	—

Trainees
Bell, Philip S; O'Malley, Carl

Scholars
Astle, Brook M; Buchanan, Wayne B; Laidlaw, Simon G; Nolan, Kevin A J; O'Connor, Kieran J; O'Hare, Alan P J; Stephan, Matthew P; Tagoe, Darrel J

Associated Schoolboys who have accepted the Club's offer of a Traineeship/Scholarship/Contract
Downey, Christopher A; Flanagan, Daniel J

AFC BOURNEMOUTH

Name	Ht	Wt	Pos	Born	Birthplace	From	Club	Apps	Gls
Bailey John	5 8	10 02	M	6 5 69	London	Enfield	Bournemouth	148	6
Beardsmore Russell	5 8	10 04	M	28 10 69	Wigan	Apprentice	Manchester U	56	4
							Blackburn R (loan)	2	—
							Bournemouth	178	4
Berthe Mohamed	6 2	15 02	M	12 9 72	Conakry	Gaz Ajaccio	West Ham U	—	—
(Transferred to Hearts, March 1999)							Bournemouth	15	2
							Hearts	1	—
Boli Roger	5 8	10 12	F	26 9 65	Adjame	Lille	Lens	164	40
							Le Havre	26	4
							Walsall	41	12
							Dundee U	3	—
							Bournemouth	6	—
Broadhurst Karl	6 1	11 07	D	18 3 80	Portsmouth	Trainee	Bournemouth	—	—
Colgan Nick	6 1	13 06	G	19 9 73	Drogheda	Drogheda	Chelsea	1	—
							Crewe Alex (loan)	—	—
							Grimsby T (loan)	—	—
							Millwall (loan)	—	—
							Brentford (loan)	5	—
							Reading (loan)	5	—
							Bournemouth	—	—
Cox Ian	6 0	12 00	D	25 3 71	Croydon	Carshalton Ath	Crystal Palace	15	—
							Bournemouth	144	16
Day Jamie	5 10	11 04	M	13 9 79	Sidcup	Trainee	Arsenal	—	—
							Bournemouth	2	—
Dean Michael	5 9	11 10	M	9 3 78	Weymouth	Trainee	Bournemouth	34	—
Fletcher Carl	5 10	11 07	M	7 4 80	Camberley	Trainee	Bournemouth	2	—
Fletcher Steve	6 2	14 09	F	26 6 72	Hartlepool	Trainee	Hartlepool U	32	4
							Bournemouth	230	44
Griffin Anthony	5 11	11 02	D	22 3 79	Bournemouth	Trainee	Bournemouth	6	—
Hayter James	5 9	10 13	F	9 4 79	Newport (IW)	Trainee	Bournemouth	27	2
Howe Eddie	5 9	11 02	D	29 11 77	Amersham	Trainee	Bournemouth	103	3
Huck Willie	5 10	11 09	M	17 3 79	Paris	Monaco	Arsenal	—	—
							Bournemouth	8	—
Hughes Richard	6 2	12 0	D	25 6 79	Glasgow	Atalanta	Arsenal	—	—
							Bournemouth	44	2
Jenkins Jamie*	5 8	10 07	D	1 1 79	Pontypool	Trainee	Bournemouth	1	—
Lovell Stephen§			F	6 12 80	Amersham	Trainee	Bournemouth	7	—
O'Neill Jon	5 11	12 00	F	2 1 74	Glasgow	Queen's Park BC	Queen's Park	91	30
							Celtic	1	—
							Bournemouth	91	7
Ovendale Mark	6 2	13 10	G	22 11 73	Leicester	Wisbech T	Northampton T	6	—
							Barry T		
							Bournemouth	46	—
Rawlinson Mark	5 10	11 04	M	9 6 75	Bolton	Trainee	Manchester U	—	—
							Bournemouth	76	2
Robinson Steve	5 9	11 02	F	10 12 74	Crumlin	Trainee	Tottenham H	2	—
							Leyton Orient (loan)	—	—
							Bournemouth	200	42
Seydi Elhadji‡	6 3	13 04	D	25 12 75	Dakar	Le Mans	Bournemouth	—	—
Stein Mark	5 6	11 07	F	29 1 66	Capetown		Luton T	54	19
							Aldershot (loan)	2	1
							QPR	33	4
							Oxford U	82	18
							Stoke C	94	50
							Chelsea	50	21
							Stoke C (loan)	11	4
							Ipswich T (loan)	7	2
							Bournemouth (loan)	11	4
							Bournemouth	43	15
Tindall Jason	6 1	12 01	M	15 11 77	Stepney	Trainee	Charlton Ath	—	—
							Bournemouth	17	1
Town David	5 7	11 13	F	9 12 76	Bournemouth	Trainee	Bournemouth	56	2
Warren Christer	5 10	11 12	F	10 10 74	Poole	Cheltenham T	Southampton	8	—
							Brighton & HA (loan)	3	—
							Fulham (loan)	11	1
							Bournemouth	62	11
Young Neil	5 9	12 00	D	31 8 73	Harlow	Trainee	Tottenham H	—	—
							Bournemouth	205	3

Trainees
Birmingham, David P; Ford, James A; Lattimer, James D; Lovell, Stephen W H; Smith, Daniel L; Stock, Brian B

Associated Schoolboys
Nunn, Anthony D; O'Connor, Paul; Palmer, Paul; Tchupan, Daniel; Watts, Darren

BRADFORD CITY

Player							Club	Apps	Gls
Beagrie Peter	5 8	12 00	F	28 11 65	Middlesbrough	Local	Middlesbrough	33	2
							Sheffield U	84	11
							Stoke C	54	7
							Everton	114	11
							Sunderland (loan)	5	1
							Manchester C	52	3
							Bradford C	77	12
							Everton (loan)	6	—
Blake Robbie	5 8	11 00	F	4 3 76	Middlesbrough	Trainee	Darlington	68	21
							Bradford C	78	24
Bower Mark	5 10	10 11	D	23 1 80	Bradford	Trainee	Bradford C	3	—
Donaldson David‡	5 7	9 08	M	17 12 78	Gravesend	Arsenal	Bradford C	—	—
Dreyer John#	6 1	13 02	D	11 6 63	Alnwick	Wallingford T	Oxford U	60	2
							Torquay U (loan)	5	—
							Fulham (loan)	12	2
							Luton T	214	13
							Stoke C	49	3
							Bolton W (loan)	2	—
							Bradford C	66	1
Edinho	5 8	12 12	F	21 2 67	Brazil		Chaves	32	14
(Transferred to Dunfermline Ath, November 1998)							Guimaraes	32	15
							Bradford C	59	15
							Dunfermline Ath	9	1
Grant Gareth	5 10	10 04	F	6 9 80	Leeds	Trainee	Bradford C	8	—
							Halifax T (loan)	3	—
Jacobs Wayne	5 8	11 02	D	3 2 69	Sheffield	Apprentice	Sheffield W	6	—
							Hull C	129	4
							Rotherham U	42	2
							Bradford C	185	9
Jewell Paul†	5 8	12 01	F	28 9 64	Liverpool	Apprentice	Liverpool	—	—
							Wigan Ath	137	35
							Bradford C	269	56
							Grimsby T (loan)	5	1
Lawrence Jamie	6 0	12 06	M	8 3 70	Balham	Cowes	Sunderland	4	—
							Doncaster R	25	3
							Leicester C	47	1
							Bradford C	78	5
McCall Stuart	5 9	11 04	M	10 6 64	Leeds		Bradford C	238	37
							Everton	103	6
							Rangers	194	14
							Bradford C	43	3
Mills Lee	6 2	12 09	F	10 7 70	Mexborough	Stocksbridge PS	Wolverhampton W	25	2
							Derby Co	16	7
							Port Vale	109	35
							Bradford C	44	23
Moore Darren	6 3	15 08	D	22 4 74	Birmingham	Trainee	Torquay U	103	8
							Doncaster R	76	7
							Bradford C	62	3
O'Brien Andrew	5 10	10 06	D	29 6 79	Harrogate	Trainee	Bradford C	79	2
Patterson Andrew	5 10	10 04	F	26 11 80	Kirklady	Trainee	Bradford C	—	—
Pepper Nigel	5 10	11 13	M	25 4 68	Rotherham	Apprentice	Rotherham U	45	1
(Transferred to Aberdeen, November 1998)							York C	235	39
							Bradford C	52	11
							Aberdeen	10	—
Prudhoe Mark	6 0	14 00	G	8 11 63	Washington	Apprentice	Sunderland	7	—
							Hartlepool U (loan)	3	—
							Birmingham C	1	—
							Walsall	26	—
							Doncaster R (loan)	5	—
							Sheffield W (loan)	—	—
							Grimsby T (loan)	8	—
							Hartlepool U (loan)	13	—
							Bristol C (loan)	3	—
							Carlisle U	34	—
							Darlington	146	—
							Stoke C	82	—
							Peterborough U (loan)	6	—
							Liverpool (loan)	—	—
							York C (loan)	2	—
							Bradford C	8	—
Ramage Craig*	5 9	11 08	M	30 3 70	Derby	Trainee	Derby Co	42	4
							Wigan Ath (loan)	10	2
							Watford	104	27
							Peterborough U (loan)	7	—
							Bradford C	35	1
Rankin Isiah	5 10	11 00	F	22 5 78	London	Trainee	Arsenal	1	—
							Colchester U (loan)	11	5
							Bradford C	27	4
Steiner Rob	6 2	13 00	F	20 6 73	Finsprong		Norrkoping	41	14
							Bradford C	15	4
							Norrkoping	6	1
							Bradford C	37	10
							QPR (loan)	12	3
							Walsall (loan)	10	3

Todd Lee	5 7	11 01	D	7 3 72	Hartlepool	Hartlepool U	Stockport Co	225	2
							Southampton	10	—
							Bradford C	15	—
Verity Daniel*	5 11	10 12	D	19 4 80	Bradford	Trainee	Bradford C	1	—
Walsh Gary	6 3	14 11	G	21 3 68	Wigan	Apprentice	Manchester U	50	—
							Airdrieonians (loan)	3	—
							Oldham Ath (loan)	6	—
							Middlesbrough	44	—
							Bradford C	81	—
Watson Gordon#	5 10	12 08	F	20 3 71	Sidcup	Trainee	Charlton Ath	31	7
							Sheffield W	66	15
							Southampton	52	8
							Bradford C	21	5
Westwood Ashley	5 11	11 02	D	31 8 76	Bridgnorth	Trainee	Manchester U	—	—
							Crewe Alex	98	9
							Bradford C	19	2
Whalley Gareth	5 10	11 06	M	19 12 73	Manchester	Trainee	Crewe Alex	180	9
							Bradford C	45	2
Windass Dean	5 10	12 06	F	1 4 69	Hull	N. Ferriby	Hull C	176	57
							Aberdeen	73	21
							Oxford U	33	15
							Bradford C	12	3
Wright Stephen#	5 10	11 09	D	27 8 71	Bellshill		Aberdeen	147	2
							Rangers	7	—
							Wolverhampton W (loan)	3	—
							Bradford C	22	—

Trainees
Brown, Liam M; Meehan, Mark; Smith, Steven L

Scholars
Jordan, James E; Kerr, Scott A; Taylor, Edward D; Whiteley, Oliver S

Non-Contract
Jewell, Paul

Players who do not hold a current contract but their registrations have been retained by the Club
Hutton, Peter; Tomlinson, Paul; Holmes, Richard

Associated Schoolboys
Emanuel, Lewis J; Heap, Alex J; Lloyd, Matthew; McGahey, Phillip M; Sayers, Joseph J; Smith, Christopher P

Associated Schoolboys who have accepted the Club's offer of a Traineeship/Scholarship/Contract
Dufton, Jack P; Fishlock, Craig C; Hardy, Adam N; Hatton, Damian; Jones, Benjamin; Lee, Andrew J; Lopiccolo, Giuseppe M W; Rutherford, James; Tyson, Garry W; Worsnop, Jon

BRENTFORD

Anderson Ijah	5 8	10 06	D	30 12 75	Hackney	Tottenham H	Southend U	—	—
							Brentford	126	4
Boxall Danny	5 8	10 05	D	24 8 77	Croydon	Trainee	Crystal Palace	8	—
							Oldham Ath (loan)	18	—
							Brentford	38	1
Bryan Derek	5 10	11 05	F	11 11 74	London	Hampton	Brentford	31	6
Clark Dean	5 10	12 06	M	31 3 80	Hillingdon	Trainee	Brentford	4	—
Cullip Danny	6 1	12 07	D	17 9 76	Bracknell	Trainee	Oxford U	—	—
							Fulham	50	2
							Brentford	15	—
Dearden Kevin	5 11	13 12	G	8 3 70	Luton	Trainee	Tottenham H	—	—
							Cambridge U (loan)	15	—
							Hartlepool U (loan)	10	—
							Oxford U (loan)	—	—
							Swindon T (loan)	1	—
							Peterborough U (loan)	7	—
							Hull C (loan)	3	—
							Rochdale (loan)	2	—
							Birmingham C (loan)	12	—
							Portsmouth (loan)	—	—
							Brentford	205	—
							Barnet (loan)	1	—
							Huddersfield T (loan)	—	—
Dennis Kevin*	5 10	12 00	F	14 12 76	Islington	Arsenal	Brentford	17	—
Denys Ryan‡	5 6	11 02	F	16 8 78	Brentford	Trainee	Brentford	19	1
Evans Paul	5 7	12 00	M	1 9 74	Oswestry	Trainee	Shrewsbury T	198	26
							Brentford	14	3
Folan Tony	6 0	11 00	F	18 9 78	Lewisham	Trainee	Crystal Palace	1	—
							Brentford	29	4
Freeman Darren	5 11	13 00	F	22 8 73	Brighton	Horsham T	Gillingham	12	—
							Fulham	46	9
							Brentford	22	6
Hebel Dirk‡	5 10	12 01	M	24 11 72	Cologne	Cologne	Tranmere R	—	—
							Brentford	15	—
Hreidarsson Hermann	6 0	13 01	D	11 7 74	Iceland		IBV	66	5
							Crystal Palace	37	2
							Brentford	33	4

Name	Ht	Wt	Pos	DOB	Birthplace	Source	Club	Apps	Gls
Mahon Gavin	5 11	12 07	M	2 1 77	Birmingham	Trainee	Wolverhampton W	—	—
							Hereford U	11	1
							Brentford	29	4
McGhee David‡	5 11	12 05	D	19 6 76	Sussex	Trainee	Brentford	117	8
Oatway Charlie	5 7	10 10	M	28 11 73	Hammersmith	Yeading	Cardiff C	32	—
							Torquay U	67	1
							Brentford	57	—
							Lincoln C (loan)	3	—
Owusu Lloyd			F	12 12 76	Slough	Slough T	Brentford	46	22
Partridge Scott	5 9	11 02	F	13 10 74	Leicester	Trainee	Bradford C	5	—
							Bristol C	57	7
							Torquay U (loan)	5	2
							Plymouth Arg (loan)	7	2
							Scarborough (loan)	7	—
							Cardiff C	37	2
							Torquay U	34	12
							Brentford	14	7
Pearcey Jason	6 1	13 12	G	23 7 71	Leamington Spa	Trainee	Mansfield T	77	—
							Grimsby T	49	—
							Brentford	17	—
Powell Darren			D	10 3 76	Hammersmith	Hampton	Brentford	33	2
Quinn Robert	5 11	11 02	M	8 11 76	Sidcup	Trainee	Crystal Palace	23	1
							Brentford	43	2
Rowlands Martin			M	8 2 79	Ealing	Farnborough T	Brentford	36	4
Scott Andy	6 1	11 05	F	2 8 72	Epsom	Sutton U	Sheffield U	75	6
							Chesterfield (loan)	5	3
							Bury (loan)	8	—
							Brentford	60	12
Thompson Niall‡	5 11	11 00	F	16 4 74	Birmingham	Trainee	Crystal Palace	—	—
							Colchester U	13	5
						Zulte VV	Brentford	8	—
Townley Leon	6 2	13 06	D	16 2 76	Loughton	Trainee	Tottenham H	—	—
							Brentford	16	2
Walker Andrew*			M	20 4 80	Eastbourne		Brentford	—	—
Watson Paul	5 8	10 10	D	4 1 75	Hastings	Trainee	Gillingham	62	2
							Fulham	50	4
							Brentford	37	—
Woodman Andy	6 3	13 07	G	11 8 71	Camberwell	Apprentice	Crystal Palace	—	—
							Exeter C	6	—
							Northampton T	163	—
							Brentford	22	—

Trainees
Coleman, Danny; Courtnage, James M; Dobson, Michael W; James, Clement J; King, Daryl; Muldowney, Jamie J; O'Connor, Kevin P; Patel, Neerav R; Procter, Sebastian J; Saroya, Nevin; Smith, Jay; Taggart, Anthony C; Williams, Mark R; Woodhouse, Paul

Associated Schoolboys who have accepted the Club's offer of a Traineeship/Scholarship/Contract
Johnson, Lee; Windell, Gavin

BRIGHTON & HOVE ALBION

Name	Ht	Wt	Pos	DOB	Birthplace	Source	Club	Apps	Gls
Allan Derek*	5 11	12 05	D	24 12 74	Irvine	Ayr U BC	Ayr U	5	—
							Southampton	1	—
							Brighton & HA (loan)	8	—
							Brighton & HA	72	2
Andrews Ben	6 1	12 13	D	18 11 80	Burton-on-Trent	Trainee	Brighton & HA	4	—
Ansah Andy*	5 7	10 07	F	19 3 69	Lewisham	Crystal Palace	Brentford	8	2
							Southend U	157	33
							Brentford (loan)	3	1
							Brentford (loan)	6	1
							Peterborough U	2	1
							Gillingham	2	—
							Leyton Orient	2	—
							Brighton & HA	25	3
Armstrong Paul	5 10	10 09	M	5 10 78	Dublin	Trainee	Brighton & HA	48	2
Arnott Andy	6 0	12 02	M	18 10 73	Chatham	Trainee	Gillingham	73	12
							Manchester U (loan)	—	—
							Leyton Orient	50	6
							Fulham	1	—
							Brighton & HA	27	2
Barker Richard*	6 0	14 03	F	30 5 75	Sheffield	Trainee	Sheffield W	—	—
							Doncaster R (loan)	6	—
						Linfield	Brighton & HA	60	12
Bennett Mickey*	5 10	11 11	M	22 7 69	Camberwell	Apprentice	Charlton Ath	35	2
							Wimbledon	18	2
							Brentford	46	4
							Charlton Ath	24	1
							Millwall	2	—
							Cardiff C	14	1
						Cambridge C	Leyton Orient	2	—
							Brighton & HA	38	—
Browne Stafford‡				4 1 72	Cuckfield	Hastings T	Brighton & HA	3	—
Browne Tony*			D	12 2 77	Isle of Sheppey	West Ham U	Brighton & HA	13	—

Culverhouse Ian	5 10	11 02	D	22 9 64	Bishop's Stortford	Apprentice	Tottenham H	2	—
							Norwich C	296	—
							Swindon T	97	—
						Kingstonian	Brighton & HA	35	—
Davies Lawrence‡	6 1	11 11	F	3 9 77	Abergavenny	Trainee	Leeds U	—	—
							Bradford C	4	—
							Darlington (loan)	2	—
							Hartlepool U (loan)	3	—
							Brighton & HA	8	—
Davis Danny§	5 10	11 04	M	3 10 80	Brighton	Trainee	Brighton & HA	1	—
Doherty Lee*			D	6 2 80	Camden Town	Arsenal	Charlton Ath	—	—
							Brighton & HA	3	—
Hart Gary	5 9	12 08	F	6 11 75	Harlow	Stansted	Brighton & HA	44	12
Hinshelwood Danny‡	5 9	11 00	D	12 2 75	Bromley	Trainee	Nottingham F	—	—
							Portsmouth	5	—
							Torquay U (loan)	9	—
							Brighton & HA	4	—
Hobson Gary	6 2	13 02	D	12 11 72	North Ferriby	Trainee	Hull C	142	—
							Brighton & HA	92	1
Holsgrove Paul	6 2	13 03	M	26 8 69	Wellington	Trainee	Aldershot	3	—
(Transferred to Hibernian, July 1998)							Wimbledon (loan)	—	—
							WBA (loan)	—	—
						Wokingham T	Luton T	2	—
						Heracles	Millwall	11	—
							Reading	70	6
							Grimsby T (loan)	10	—
							Crewe Alex	8	1
							Stoke C	12	1
							Brighton & HA	—	—
							Hibernian	17	1
Johnson Ross	6 0	13 00	D	2 1 76	Brighton	Trainee	Brighton & HA	123	2
King Phil‡	5 11	12 07	D	28 12 67	Bristol	Apprentice	Exeter C	27	—
							Torquay U	24	3
							Swindon T	116	4
							Sheffield W	129	2
							Notts Co (loan)	6	—
							Aston Villa	16	—
							WBA (loan)	4	—
							Swindon T	5	—
							Blackpool (loan)	6	—
							Brighton & HA	3	—
Mayo Kerry	5 8	11 07	D	21 9 77	Cuckfield	Trainee	Brighton & HA	93	7
McArthur Duncan§			M	6 5 81	Brighton	Trainee	Brighton & HA	3	—
McPherson Keith‡	5 11	11 10	D	11 9 63	Greenwich	Apprentice	West Ham U	1	—
							Cambridge U (loan)	11	1
							Northampton T	182	8
							Reading	271	8
							Brighton & HA	10	—
Mills Danny*	5 11	11 07	M	13 2 75	Sidcup	Trainee	Charlton Ath	—	—
							Barnet	27	—
							Brighton & HA	2	—
Minton Jeffrey*	5 6	11 11	M	28 12 73	Hackney	Trainee	Tottenham H	2	1
							Brighton & HA	174	31
Moralee Jamie*	5 11	11 00	F	2 12 71	Wandsworth	Trainee	Crystal Palace	6	—
							Millwall	67	19
							Watford	49	7
							Crewe Alex	16	—
							Brighton & HA	31	3
Ormerod Mark	6 0	11 06	G	5 2 76	Bournemouth	Trainee	Brighton & HA	78	—
Ryan Darragh*	5 10	10 10	F	21 5 80	Cuckfield	Trainee	Brighton & HA	9	2
Smith Peter*	6 2	12 10	D	12 7 69	Stone	Alma Swanley	Brighton & HA	140	5
Storer Stuart*	5 11	12 12	F	16 1 67	Rugby	Local	Mansfield T	1	—
							Birmingham C	8	—
							Everton	—	—
							Wigan Ath (loan)	12	—
							Bolton W	123	12
							Exeter C	77	8
							Brighton & HA	142	11
Streeter Terry*			M	26 10 79	Brighton	Trainee	Brighton & HA	2	—
Sturgess Paul*	5 11	12 05	D	4 8 75	Dartford	Trainee	Charlton Ath	51	—
							Millwall	14	—
							Brighton & HA	30	—
Thomas Glen‡	6 0	14 00	D	6 10 67	Hackney	Apprentice	Fulham	251	6
							Peterborough U	8	—
							Barnet	23	—
							Gillingham	28	—
							Brighton & HA	3	—
Thomas Rod	5 6	11 11	F	10 10 70	London	Trainee	Watford	84	9
							Gillingham (loan)	8	1
							Carlisle U	146	16
							Chester C	44	7
							Brighton & HA	12	3
Tuck Stuart‡	5 10	11 10	D	1 10 74	Brighton	Trainee	Brighton & HA	93	1

Name	Ht	Wt	Pos	DOB	Birthplace	Source	Club	Apps	Gls
Walton Mark	6 4	15 08	G	1 6 69	Merthyr	Swansea C	Luton T	—	—
							Colchester U	40	—
							Norwich C	22	—
							Wrexham (loan)	6	—
							Dundee	—	—
							Bolton W	3	—
						Fakenham T	Fulham	40	—
							Gillingham (loan)	1	—
							Norwich C (loan)	—	—
							Brighton & HA	19	—
Westcott John	5 9	10 03	F	31 5 79	Eastbourne	Trainee	Brighton & HA	38	—
Woolsey Jeff‡	5 11	12 03	D	8 11 77	Upminster	Trainee	Arsenal	—	—
							QPR	—	—
							Brighton & HA	3	—
Wormull Simon	5 10	12 03	M	1 12 76	Crawley	Trainee	Tottenham H	—	—
							Brentford	5	—
							Brighton & HA	—	—

Trainees
Burke, Alan P; Davis, Daniel J S; Francis, Niel Giovanni; McArthur, Duncan E; Ottley, Matthew J; Packham, William J; Ramsay, Scott A; Winter, Neil D

Scholars
Beech, Andrew P; Dallaway, Steven J; Davis, Adam R; Marney, Daniel G; McCurdy, Conor M; Wilkinson, Shaun F

BRISTOL CITY

Name	Ht	Wt	Pos	DOB	Birthplace	Source	Club	Apps	Gls
Akinbiyi Ade	6 1	13 09	F	10 10 74	Hackney	Trainee	Norwich C	49	3
							Hereford U (loan)	4	2
							Brighton & HA (loan)	7	4
							Gillingham	63	28
							Bristol C	44	19
Andersen Braastrup			G	26 3 76	Slagelse		Lyngby	120	—
							Bristol C	10	—
Andersen Soren	5 11	12 06	F	31 1 70	Denmark		Vejle	59	22
							Aarhus	12	11
							Rayo Vallecano	10	1
							Norrkoping	10	4
							Aalborg	67	30
							Bristol C	39	10
Ashton Lee			M	8 11 79	Yeovil	Trainee	Bristol C	—	—
Badman Mark*			M	21 12 79	Bath	Trainee	Bristol C	—	—
Bell Mickey	5 8	11 13	D	15 11 71	Newcastle	Trainee	Northampton T	153	10
							Wycombe W	118	6
							Bristol C	77	15
Betterton Anthony*			M	24 10 79	Swindon	Trainee	Bristol C	—	—
Brennan Jim	5 9	11 06	D	8 5 77	Toronto	Sora Lazio	Bristol C	43	1
Brown Aaron	5 10	11 12	M	14 3 80	Bristol	Trainee	Bristol C	14	—
Carey Louis	5 10	12 05	D	20 1 77	Bristol	Trainee	Bristol C	144	—
Cramb Colin	6 0	12 09	F	23 6 74	Lanark	Hamilton A BC	Hamilton A	48	10
							Southampton	1	—
							Falkirk	8	1
							Hearts	6	1
							Doncaster R	62	25
							Bristol C	53	9
							Walsall (loan)	4	4
Doherty Tom	5 8	11 07	M	17 3 79	Bristol	Trainee	Bristol C	53	3
Dyche Sean	6 0	13 05	D	28 6 71	Kettering	Trainee	Nottingham F	—	—
							Chesterfield	231	8
							Bristol C	17	—
							Luton T (loan)	14	1
Edwards Robert#	6 0	12 07	D	1 7 73	Kendal	Trainee	Carlisle U	48	5
							Bristol C	216	5
Evans James‡			M	3 10 78	Epsom	Trainee	Tottenham H	—	—
							Bristol C	—	—
Goodridge Greg	5 6	11 02	F	10 7 71	Barbados	Lambada	Torquay U	38	4
							QPR	7	1
							Bristol C	89	14
Hale Matt‡	5 6	10 01	D	2 2 79	Bristol	Trainee	Bristol C	—	—
Hewlett Matthew	6 2	12 12	M	25 2 76	Bristol	Trainee	Bristol C	120	9
							Burnley (loan)	2	—
Hill Matthew			D	26 3 81	Bristol	Trainee	Bristol C	3	—
Hussey Stuart			M	4 12 80	Southampton	Portsmouth	Bristol C	—	—
Hutchings Carl	6 1	12 00	M	24 9 74	Hammersmith	Trainee	Brentford	162	7
							Bristol C	21	2
Jordan Andrew	6 0	13 01	D	14 12 79	Manchester	Trainee	Bristol C	1	—
Langan Kevin	5 11	11 02	D	7 4 78	Jersey	Trainee	Bristol C	4	—
Locke Adam#	5 11	12 07	M	20 8 70	Croydon	Trainee	Crystal Palace	—	—
							Southend U	73	4
							Colchester U (loan)	4	—
							Colchester U	79	8
							Bristol C	65	4
Meechan Alex			F	29 1 80	Plymouth	Trainee	Swindon T	1	—
							Bristol C	1	—

Name	Ht	Wt	Pos	No	DOB	Birthplace	From	Club	Apps	Gls
Morrison Scott‡			M	1	8 80	Bristol	Trainee	Bristol C	—	—
Muntasser Jehad	5 10	9 11	M	26	7 78	Tripoli	Prosesto	Arsenal	—	—
								Bristol C	—	—
Murray Scott	5 8	11 00	M	26	5 74	Aberdeen	Fraserburgh	Aston Villa	4	—
								Bristol C	55	3
Phillips Steve	6 1	12 07	G	6	5 78	Bath	Paulton R	Bristol C	15	—
Pinamonte Lorenzo	6 3	13 04	F	9	5 78	Foggia	Foggia	Bristol C	1	1
Plummer Dwayne‡	5 9	10 12	F	12	5 78	Bristol	Trainee	Bristol C	14	—
Sebok Vilmos			D	13	6 73	Hungary	Ujpesti	Bristol C	12	—
Shail Mark	6 1	12 06	D	15	10 66	Sweden	Yeovil T	Bristol C	127	4
Sloan Christopher‡			M	21	2 80	Gillingham	Trainee	Bristol C	—	—
Spiller Richard*			M	5	9 79	Enfield	Trainee	Bristol C	—	—
Stowell Matt	5 10	11 06	D	1	3 77	Reading	Trainee	Reading	—	—
							Slough T	Bristol C	—	—
Taylor Shaun#	6 1	12 10	D	26	2 63	Plymouth	Bideford	Exeter C	200	16
								Swindon T	212	30
								Bristol C	80	3
Testimitanu Ivan			M	27	4 74	Moldova		Zimbru Chisinau	79	24
								Bristol C	8	—
Thorpe Tony	5 8	12 06	F	10	4 74	Leicester	Leicester C	Luton T	120	50
								Fulham	13	3
								Bristol C	16	2
								Reading (loan)	6	1
								Luton T (loan)	8	4
Tinnion Brian	5 11	12 13	M	23	3 68	Stanley	Apprentice	Newcastle U	32	2
								Bradford C	145	22
								Bristol C	228	17
Tisdale Paul‡	5 9	10 09	M	14	1 73	Malta	School	Southampton	16	1
								Northampton T (loan)	5	—
								Huddersfield T (loan)	2	—
								Bristol C	5	—
								Exeter C (loan)	10	1
Torpey Steve	6 3	13 06	F	8	12 70	Islington	Trainee	Millwall	7	—
								Bradford C	96	22
								Swansea C	162	44
								Bristol C	50	12
								Notts Co (loan)	6	1
Watts Julian	6 2	13 06	D	17	3 71	Sheffield	Trainee	Rotherham U	20	1
								Sheffield W	16	1
								Shrewsbury T (loan)	9	—
								Leicester C	38	1
								Crewe Alex (loan)	5	—
								Huddersfield T (loan)	8	—
								Bristol C	17	1
								Lincoln C (loan)	2	—
								Blackpool (loan)	9	—
Welch Keith#	6 2	13 13	G	3	10 68	Bolton	Trainee	Bolton W	—	—
								Rochdale	205	—
								Bristol C	271	—
Wilmot Ellis			M	2	11 79	Bournemouth	Trainee	Bristol C	—	—
Wright Ben			M	1	7 80	Munster	Kettering T	Bristol C	—	—
Zwijnenberg Clemens†			M	18	5 70	Enschede	Aalborg	Bristol C	3	—

Trainees
Ball, Alex I; Burnell, Joseph M; Farmer, Christopher; Rai, Adam K B; Sammut, Benjamin A; Thompson, Phillip W; Watts, Leigh G; Whittington, Geoffrey

Scholars
Amankwaah, Kevin; Burnett, Michael A; Claridge, Jamie L; Cleverley, Benjamin R; Coles, Daniel R; Harrison, Jamie; Jordan, Thomas M; King, Rohan; McLay, Steven; Reynolds, Nicholas; Shorey, Adam C; Spencer, Damian M; Williams, Paul J; Wilson, Martin J

Non-Contract
Hobson, Graeme; Malessa, Antony G

Associated Schoolboys
Beck, Daniel G; Gibbs, Stuart J; Harrty, Nick; Hawkins, Darren; Lowe, Oliver; Platt, Daniel; Reid, Andrew K; Rosenior, Liam; Sandell, Andrew; Simpson, Sekani; Stickland, Ross; Trace, Ben; Turner, Michael J; Williams, Lee

Associated Schoolboys who have accepted the Club's offer of a Traineeship/Scholarship/Contract
Blake, David J; Brown, Marvin R; Dew, Simon J; Horseman, David J; Jones, Darren; Walters, James; Woodman, Craig A

BRISTOL ROVERS

Name	Ht	Wt	Pos	No	DOB	Birthplace	From	Club	Apps	Gls
Andreasson Marcus	6 4	13 02	D	13	7 78	Liberia		Osters	12	—
								Bristol R	5	—
Andrews Bradley*	5 11	10 12	M	8	12 79	Bristol	Trainee	Norwich C	—	—
								Bristol R	3	—
Basford Luke	5 6	9 02	D	6	1 80	Lambeth	Trainee	Bristol R	16	—
Bater Geraint	5 8	10 08	D	26	7 80	Bristol		Bristol R	—	—
Bennett Frankie#	5 7	12 10	F	13	1 69	Birmingham	Halesowen T	Southampton	19	1
								Shrewsbury T (loan)	4	3
								Bristol R	34	4

Name	Ht	Wt	Pos	DOB	Birthplace	Source	Club	Apps	Gls
Bokoto Mommainais†	5 11	11 13	F	20 10 74	France	Maria Aalter	Bristol C	—	—
							Bristol R	—	—
Challis Trevor	5 8	11 06	D	23 10 75	Paddington	Trainee	QPR	13	—
							Bristol R	38	—
Claridge Rob	6 0	11 10	F	13 3 80	Bristol	Trainee	Bristol R	—	—
Collett Andy*	5 11	12 10	G	28 10 73	Middlesbrough	Trainee	Middlesbrough	2	—
							Bristol R	107	—
Cureton Jamie	5 7	11 00	F	28 8 75	Bristol	Trainee	Norwich C	29	6
							Bournemouth (loan)	5	—
							Bristol R	127	49
Ellington Nathan	5 10	12 10	F	2 7 81	Bradford	Walton & Hersham	Bristol R	10	1
Foster Stephen	6 1	13 00	D	3 12 74	Mansfield	Trainee	Mansfield T	5	—
						Woking	Bristol R	77	1
French James	6 1	12 02	F	24 10 79	Germany	Trainee	Bristol R	—	—
Hillier David	5 10	12 07	M	19 12 69	Blackheath	Trainee	Arsenal	104	2
							Portsmouth	67	4
							Bristol R	13	—
Holloway Ian	5 7	10 10	M	12 3 63	Kingswood	Apprentice	Bristol R	111	14
							Wimbledon	19	2
							Brentford (loan)	13	2
							Brentford	17	—
							Torquay U (loan)	5	—
							Bristol R	179	26
							QPR	147	4
							Bristol R	107	1
Ipoua Guy*	6 1	13 10	F	14 1 76	Douala	Novelda	Bristol R	24	3
Johnston Ray§	6 1	13 13	G	5 5 81	Bristol	Trainee	Bristol R	1	—
Jones Lee	6 3	15 10	G	9 8 70	Pontypridd	Porth	Swansea C	6	—
							Crewe Alex (loan)	—	—
							Bristol R	40	—
Kite Phil*	6 2	15 04	G	26 10 62	Bristol	Apprentice	Bristol R	96	—
							Tottenham H (loan)	4	—
							Southampton	4	—
							Middlesbrough (loan)	2	—
							Gillingham	70	—
							Bournemouth	7	—
							Sheffield U	11	—
							Mansfield T (loan)	11	—
							Plymouth Arg (loan)	2	—
							Rotherham U (loan)	1	—
							Crewe Alex (loan)	5	—
							Stockport Co (loan)	5	—
							Cardiff C	18	—
							Bristol C	6	—
							Bristol R	—	—
Kuipers Michels	6 2	14 03	G	26 6 74	Amsterdam		Bristol R	1	—
Lee David#	6 3	14 10	D	26 11 69	Kingswood	Trainee	Chelsea	151	11
							Reading (loan)	5	5
							Plymouth Arg (loan)	9	1
							Portsmouth (loan)	5	—
							Sheffield U (loan)	5	—
							Bristol R	11	1
Leoni Stephane	5 9	13 00	D	1 9 76	Metz		Bristol R	30	—
Low Josh	6 0	14 00	M	15 2 79	Bristol	Trainee	Bristol R	22	—
Meaker Michael	5 11	12 12	M	18 8 71	Greenford	Trainee	QPR	34	1
							Plymouth Arg (loan)	4	—
							Reading	67	2
							Bristol R	20	2
Penrice Gary*	5 8	12 10	F	23 3 64	Bristol	Bristol C	Bristol R	188	54
							Watford	43	18
							Aston Villa	20	1
							QPR	82	20
							Watford	39	2
							Bristol R	66	6
Pethick Robbie	5 10	12 07	D	8 9 70	Tavistock	Weymouth	Portsmouth	189	3
							Bristol R	9	—
Pritchard David#	5 7	12 00	D	27 5 72	Wolverhampton	Telford U	WBA	5	—
						Telford U	Bristol R	137	—
Roberts Jason	6 1	13 06	F	25 1 78	Park Royal	Hayes	Wolverhampton W	14	6
							Torquay U (loan)	3	1
							Bristol C (loan)	37	16
							Bristol R		
Shore Jamie	5 9	12 05	M	1 9 77	Bristol	Trainee	Norwich C	—	—
							Bristol R	24	2
Smith Mark	6 0	13 07	D	13 9 79	Bristol	Trainee	Bristol R	14	—
Thompson Garry†	6 1	14 07	F	7 10 59	Birmingham	Apprentice	Coventry C	134	38
							WBA	91	39
							Sheffield W	36	7
							Aston Villa	60	17
							Watford	34	8
							Crystal Palace	20	3
							QPR	19	1
							Cardiff C	43	5
							Northampton T	50	6
							Bristol R	—	—

Name							Club	Apps	Gls
Thomson Andy	6 3	14 03	D	28 3 74	Swindon	Trainee	Swindon T	22	—
							Portsmouth	93	3
							Bristol R	21	1
Tillson Andy	6 2	13 05	D	30 6 66	Huntingdon	Kettering T	Grimsby T	105	5
							QPR	29	2
							Grimsby T (loan)	4	—
							Bristol R	210	10
Trees Robert	5 10	12 07	M	18 12 77	Manchester	Trainee	Manchester U	—	—
						Witton Alb	Bristol R	36	—
Trought Michael	6 2	14 03	D	19 10 80	Bristol	Trainee	Bristol R	9	—
White Tom	5 11	14 03	D	26 1 76	Bristol	Trainee	Bristol R	51	1
Zabek Lee	6 0	13 08	M	13 10 78	Bristol	Trainee	Bristol R	25	1

Trainees
Adams, Michael J; Hines, Alistair; Johnston, Ray; Pendry, Dean; Zamora, Bobby

Scholars
Clarke, Ryan J; Cozens, Leon; Crowley, Jonathan; Pope, Mark; Powell, Gary N; Shore, Andrew J; Watts, David J; Zabek, James K

Non-Contract
Thompson, Garry L

Associated Schoolboys
Arndale, Neil D; Clarke, Thomas W; Davis, Anthony; Gosling, Ian J; Graydon, Neil

Associated Schoolboys who have accepted the Club's offer of a Traineeship/Scholarship/Contract
Bryant, Simon; Chambers, Andrew J; Gilroy, David; Hardcastle, Mark; Hogg, Lewis J; Scott, Robert T

BURNLEY

Name							Club	Apps	Gls
Armstrong Gordon	6 0	13 04	D	15 7 67	Newcastle	Apprentice	Sunderland	349	50
							Bristol C (loan)	6	—
							Northampton T (loan)	4	1
							Bury	71	4
							Burnley	40	2
Branch Graham	6 2	12 02	M	12 2 72	Liverpool	Heswall	Tranmere R	102	10
							Bury (loan)	4	1
							Wigan Ath (loan)	3	—
							Stockport Co	14	3
							Burnley	20	1
Brass Chris	5 9	12 06	D	24 7 75	Easington	Trainee	Burnley	127	1
							Torquay U (loan)	7	—
Carr-Lawton Colin‡	5 10	11 06	F	5 9 78	South Shields	Trainee	Burnley	5	—
Cooke Andy	5 11	12 08	F	20 1 74	Stoke	Newtown	Burnley	124	43
Cowan Tom#	5 8	11 10	D	28 8 69	Bellshill	Netherdale BC	Clyde	16	2
							Rangers	12	—
							Sheffield U	45	—
							Stoke C (loan)	14	—
							Huddersfield T (loan)	10	—
							Huddersfield T	127	8
							Burnley	12	—
Cowans Gordon†	5 7	9 07	M	27 10 58	Durham	Apprentice	Aston Villa	286	42
							Bari	94	3
							Aston Villa	117	7
							Blackburn R	50	2
							Aston Villa	11	—
							Derby Co	36	—
							Wolverhampton W	37	—
							Sheffield U	20	—
							Bradford C	24	—
							Stockport Co	7	—
							Burnley	6	—
Crichton Paul	6 1	13 08	G	3 10 68	Pontefract	Apprentice	Nottingham F		—
							Notts Co (loan)	5	—
							Darlington (loan)	5	—
							Peterborough U (loan)	4	—
							Darlington (loan)	3	—
							Swindon T (loan)	4	—
							Rotherham U (loan)	6	—
							Torquay U (loan)	13	—
							Peterborough U	47	—
							Doncaster R	77	—
							Grimsby T	133	—
							WBA	32	—
							Aston Villa (loan)	—	—
							Burnley	29	—
Davis Steve	6 2	14 07	D	30 10 68	Hexham	Trainee	Southampton	7	—
							Burnley (loan)	9	—
							Notts Co (loan)	2	—
							Burnley	162	22
							Luton T	138	21
							Burnley	19	4
Devenney Michael	5 8	10 05	D	8 2 80	Bolton	Trainee	Burnley	—	—
Eastwood Philip*	5 10	12 02	F	6 4 78	Blackburn	Trainee	Burnley	16	1
Ford Mark*	5 7	10 08	M	10 10 75	Pontefract	Trainee	Leeds U	29	1
							Burnley	48	1

Name	Ht	Wt	Pos	DOB	Birthplace	Source	Club	Apps	Gls
Graham Paul*	5 9	10 09	M	28 7 80	Sefton North	Trainee	Burnley	—	—
Henderson Kevin*	5 10	12 04	F	8 6 74	Ashington	Morpeth T	Burnley	14	1
Heywood Matthew	6 3	14 00	D	26 8 79	Chatham	Trainee	Burnley	13	—
Jepson Ronnie#	6 0	14 00	F	12 5 63	Stoke	Nantwich T	Port Vale	22	—
							Peterborough U (loan)	18	5
							Preston NE	38	8
							Exeter C	54	21
							Huddersfield T	107	36
							Bury	47	9
							Oldham Ath	9	4
							Burnley	15	1
Johnrose Lenny	5 11	12 06	M	27 11 69	Preston	Trainee	Blackburn R	42	11
							Preston NE (loan)	3	1
							Hartlepool U	66	11
							Bury	188	18
							Burnley	12	1
Kval Frank*	6 0	13 00	G	17 7 74	Bergen		Burnley	—	—
Little Glen	6 3	13 00	M	15 10 75	Wimbledon	Trainee	Crystal Palace	—	—
							Glentoran	6	2
							Burnley	67	9
Mawson Craig	6 2	13 04	G	16 5 79	Keighley	Trainee	Burnley	—	—
Maylett Bradley			F	24 12 80	Manchester	Trainee	Burnley	17	—
Mellon Micky	5 10	12 11	D	18 3 72	Paisley	Trainee	Bristol C	35	1
							WBA	45	6
							Blackpool	124	14
							Tranmere R	57	3
							Burnley	20	2
Moore Neil*	6 1	12 07	D	21 9 72	Liverpool	Trainee	Everton	5	—
							Blackpool (loan)	7	—
							Oldham Ath (loan)	5	—
							Carlisle U (loan)	13	—
							Rotherham U (loan)	11	—
							Norwich C	2	—
							Burnley	52	3
Morgan Steve*	6 0	13 00	D	19 9 68	Oldham	Apprentice	Blackpool	144	10
							Plymouth Arg	121	6
							Coventry C	68	2
							Bristol R (loan)	5	—
							Wigan Ath	36	2
							Bury (loan)	5	—
							Burnley	17	—
Payton Andy	5 9	11 13	F	23 10 67	Burnley	Apprentice	Hull C	143	55
							Middlesbrough	19	3
							Celtic	36	15
							Barnsley	108	41
							Huddersfield T	43	17
							Burnley	59	28
Pickering Ally*	5 9	11 07	D	22 6 67	Manchester	Buxton	Rotherham U	88	2
							Coventry C	65	—
							Stoke C	83	1
							Burnley	21	1
Reid Brian*	6 3	13 08	D	15 6 70	Paisley		Burnley	31	3
Robertson Mark	5 9	11 09	M	6 4 77	Sydney	Marconi	Burnley	35	1
Scott Christopher	5 11	12 05	D	12 2 80	Burnley	Trainee	Burnley	14	—
Smith Carl‡	5 8	11 00	D	15 1 79	Sheffield	Trainee	Burnley	11	—
Smith Paul	6 0	13 03	M	22 7 76	Leeds	Trainee	Burnley	74	4
Swan Peter#	6 2	14 02	D	28 9 66	Leeds	Local	Leeds U	49	11
							Hull C	80	24
							Port Vale	111	5
							Plymouth Arg	27	2
							Burnley	49	7
							Bury	37	6
							Burnley	17	—
Vindheim Rune	5 11	12 04	D	18 5 72	Hoyancuer		Burnley	8	2
Weller Paul	5 8	11 02	M	6 3 75	Brighton	Trainee	Burnley	96	5
West Gareth*	6 1	11 10	D	1 8 78	Oldham	Trainee	Burnley	—	—
Williamson John§				3 3 81	Derby	Trainee	Burnley	1	—

Trainees
Berry, Shaun D; Collins, David W; Gardiner, Marc A; Gregson, Gareth C; Kelly, Eamonn P; Kevan, Alexander; McCoy, James J; McDonald, Christopher N; Williamson, John B; Woods, Ben

Scholars
Bowden, Anthony; Clark, Christopher; Paxton, Andrew J; Robertshaw, Duncan; Savage, David R; Shandran, Anthony M

Associated Schoolboys
Barrett, Paul J; Licastri, Dominic; Park, Deon S

Associated Schoolboys who have accepted the Club's offer of a Traineeship/Scholarship/Contract
Davis, Earl A; Waine, Andrew P

BURY

Name	Ht	Wt	Pos	DOB	Birthplace	Source	Club	Apps	Gls
Avdiu Kemajl	5 10	12 08	M	22 12 76	Yugoslavia	Esbjerg	Bury	6	1
							Partick T (loan)	6	1
Barnes Paul	5 11	13 00	F	16 11 67	Leeds	Apprentice	Notts Co	53	14
							Stoke C	24	3
							Chesterfield (loan)	1	—
							York C	148	76
							Birmingham C	15	7
							Burnley	65	30
							Huddersfield T	30	2
							Bury	8	—
Barrick Dean	5 8	12 00	D	30 9 69	Hemsworth	Trainee	Sheffield W	11	2
							Rotherham U	99	7
							Cambridge U	91	3
							Preston NE	109	1
							Bury	20	1
							Ayr U (loan)	11	—
Billy Chris	5 11	12 06	D	2 1 71	Huddersfield	Trainee	Huddersfield T	94	4
							Plymouth Arg	118	9
							Notts Co	6	—
							Bury	37	—
Borg John	5 7	10 07	M	22 2 80	Salford	Trainee	Doncaster R	1	—
							Bury	—	—
Buggie Lee			F	11 2 81	Bury	Trainee	Bolton W	—	—
							Bury	—	—
Bullock Darren	5 9	12 10	M	12 2 69	Worcester	Nuneaton Bor	Huddersfield T	128	16
							Swindon T	66	2
							Bury	12	1
Crossland Mark‡	5 11	12 02	M	14 12 78	Ashton-under-Lyne	Lincoln C	Bury	—	—
D'Jaffo Laurent	6 0	13 05	F	5 11 70	France		Ayr U	24	10
							Bury	37	8
Daws Nick	5 11	12 13	M	15 3 70	Salford	Altrincham	Bury	282	11
Debenham Rob	5 8	10 07	D	28 11 79	Doncaster	Trainee	Doncaster R	6	—
							Bury	—	—
Denney Phil*	6 1	13 04	F	6 1 79	Bury	Trainee	Bury	—	—
Donnelly Mark	6 1	12 07	D	22 12 79	Leeds	Trainee	Doncaster R	11	1
							Bury	—	—
Forrest Martyn	5 10	12 02	M	2 1 79	Bury	Trainee	Bury	1	—
Foster John*	5 11	12 13	D	19 9 73	Blackley	Trainee	Manchester C	19	—
							Carlisle U	7	—
							Bury	7	—
Green Alex‡	6 0	12 05	M	4 1 80	Bolton	Trainee	Bury	—	—
Hoggeth Gary	6 0	11 07	G	7 10 79	South Shields	Trainee	Doncaster R	8	—
							Bury	—	—
James Lutel	5 8	11 00	F	2 6 72	Manchester		Scarborough	6	—
						Hyde U	Bury	17	2
Jemson Nigel	5 11	13 00	F	10 8 69	Preston	Trainee	Preston NE	32	8
							Nottingham F	47	13
							Bolton W (loan)	5	—
							Preston NE (loan)	9	2
							Sheffield W	51	9
							Grimsby T (loan)	6	2
							Notts Co	14	1
							Watford (loan)	4	—
							Coventry C (loan)	—	—
							Rotherham U (loan)	16	5
							Oxford U	68	27
							Bury	29	1
Kenny Patrick	6 1	14 06	G	17 5 78	Halifax	Bradford PA	Bury	—	—
Kiely Dean	6 0	12 13	G	10 10 70	Salford	WBA	Coventry C	—	—
							Ipswich T (loan)	—	—
							York C (loan)	—	—
							York C	210	—
							Bury	137	—
Linighan Brian	6 4	11 04	D	2 11 73	Hartlepool	Trainee	Sheffield W	1	—
							Bury	—	—
Littlejohn Adrian	5 10	11 00	M	26 9 71	Wolverhampton	WBA	Walsall	44	1
							Sheffield U	69	12
							Plymouth Arg	110	29
							Oldham Ath	21	5
							Bury	20	1
Lucketti Chris	6 2	13 06	D	28 9 71	Littleborough	Trainee	Rochdale	1	—
							Stockport Co	—	—
							Halifax T	78	2
							Bury	235	8
Messer Gary	6 1	13 00	F	22 9 79	Consett	Trainee	Doncaster R	14	1
							Bury	—	—
Preece Andy	6 1	12 00	F	27 3 67	Evesham	Evesham U	Northampton T	1	—
						Worcester C	Wrexham	51	7
							Stockport Co	97	42
							Crystal Palace	20	4
							Blackpool	126	35
							Bury	39	3

Name	Ht	Wt	Pos	DOB	Birthplace	Source	Club	Apps	Gls
Randall Adrian‡	5 11	12 04	M	10 11 68	Salisbury	Apprentice	Bournemouth	3	—
							Aldershot	107	12
							Burnley	125	8
							York C	32	2
							Bury	34	3
Redmond Steve#	5 11	13 00	D	2 11 67	Liverpool	Apprentice	Manchester C	235	7
							Oldham Ath	205	4
							Bury	26	—
Reed John†	5 10	10 11	M	27 8 72	Rotherham	Trainee	Sheffield U	15	2
							Scarborough (loan)	14	6
							Scarborough (loan)	6	—
							Darlington (loan)	10	2
							Mansfield T (loan)	13	2
							Blackpool	3	—
							Bury	—	—
Rigby Tony*	5 10	13 12	M	10 8 72	Ormskirk	Barrow	Bury	166	19
							Scarborough (loan)	5	1
Souter Ryan	5 10	12 00	M	5 2 78	Bedford	Weston-Super-Mare	Bury	1	—
Swailes Chris	6 2	13 07	D	19 10 70	Gateshead	Bridlington T	Doncaster R	49	—
							Ipswich T	33	1
							Bury	56	4
Swailes Danny	6 3	12 06	D	1 4 79	Bolton	Trainee	Bury	—	—
Tedaldi Domenico	5 11	12 00	M	22 10 80	Aberystwyth	Trainee	Doncaster R	2	1
							Bury	—	—
Watson Richard*			M	2 11 78	Salford	Manchester U	Bury	—	—
West Dean#	5 10	11 07	D	5 12 72	Wakefield	Leeds U	Lincoln C	119	20
							Bury	110	7
Wilcox Rob*	5 9	12 06	M	7 11 79	Bury	Trainee	Bury	—	—
Wilkinson Steve‡	6 1	13 05	M	7 12 79	Rochdale	Trainee	Bury	—	—
Williams Paul	5 7	11 07	M	11 9 69	Leicester	Trainee	Leicester C	—	—
							Stockport Co	70	4
							Coventry C	14	—
							WBA (loan)	5	—
							Huddersfield T (loan)	9	—
							Plymouth Arg	131	4
							Gillingham	10	1
							Bury	15	1
Woodward Andy	6 0	13 06	D	23 9 73	Stockport	Trainee	Crewe Alex	20	—
							Bury	101	1

Trainees
Ball, Nicholas C; Barrass, Matthew R; Beal, Phillip L; Bury, Daniel J; Connell, Lee A; Halford, Stephen P; Hill, Nicholas D; Hutchinson, Ian P A; Ridley, Marc D; Smith, Paul A; Sturtivant, David M; Watson, Steven

Scholars
Armstrong, Christopher; Gaynor John; Gleaves, Carl M; Martin, Adam T; O'Shaughnessy, Paul J; Thompson, Nicholas A

Non-Contract
Blackwell, Kevin P; Radcliffe, Matthew S

Associated Schoolboys
Chapman, Neil D; Gidley, Stuart; Kennedy, Matthew; McIlduff, Paul A; Thompson, David J; Veitch, Tom D

CAMBRIDGE UNITED

Name	Ht	Wt	Pos	DOB	Birthplace	Source	Club	Apps	Gls
Armstrong Dean	5 8	9 13	M	7 9 79	Chiswick	Trainee	Cambridge U	—	—
Ashbee Ian	6 1	13 04	M	6 9 76	Birmingham	Trainee	Derby Co	1	—
							Cambridge U	76	5
Benjamin Trevor	6 2	13 07	F	8 2 79	Kettering	Trainee	Cambridge U	79	15
Butler Martin	5 11	11 12	F	15 9 74	Wordsley	Trainee	Walsall	74	8
							Cambridge U	77	27
Campbell Jamie	6 1	12 07	D	21 10 72	Birmingham	Trainee	Luton T	36	1
							Mansfield T (loan)	3	1
							Cambridge U (loan)	12	—
							Barnet	67	5
							Cambridge U	91	6
Chenery Ben	6 1	11 11	D	28 1 77	Ipswich	Trainee	Luton T	2	—
							Cambridge U	80	2
Cockrill Darren†	6 1	13 00	F	28 2 80	Great Yarmouth	Trainee	Cambridge U	—	—
Duncan Andy	5 11	13 04	D	20 10 77	Hexham	Trainee	Manchester U	—	—
							Cambridge U	64	1
Eustace Scott†	6 1	13 06	D	13 6 75	Leicester	Trainee	Leicester C	1	—
							Mansfield T	98	6
							Cambridge U	16	—
Gibson Mark§			M	24 8 81	Hitchin	Trainee	Cambridge U	—	—
Ingham Andrew			M	21 8 81	Leeds	Trainee	Cambridge U	—	—
Joseph Marc	6 1	12 12	D	10 11 76	Leicester	Trainee	Cambridge U	90	—
Kyd Michael	5 8	12 08	F	21 5 77	Hackney	Trainee	Cambridge U	106	20
Marshall Shaun	6 2	12 12	G	3 10 78	Fakenham	Trainee	Cambridge U	22	—
McAvoy Larry	5 8	11 00	D	7 9 79	Lambeth	Trainee	Cambridge U	1	—

McMahon Sam*	5 10	11 09	M	10 2 76	Newark	Trainee	Leicester C	5	1
							Cambridge U	3	—
McNeil Martin			D	28 9 80	Rutherglen	Trainee	Cambridge U	6	—
Mustoe Neil	5 8	12 00	M	5 11 76	Gloucester	Trainee	Manchester U	—	—
							Cambridge U	34	3
Newby Keith‡	5 8	11 00	M	27 9 79	Grimsby	Trainee	Cambridge U	—	—
Nyamah Kofi†	5 10	11 07	D	20 6 75	Islington	Trainee	Cambridge U	23	2
						Kettering T	Stoke C	17	—
							Luton T	—	—
							Cambridge U	—	—
Preece David	5 6	11 01	M	28 5 63	Bridgnorth	Apprentice	Walsall	111	5
							Luton T	336	21
							Derby Co	13	1
							Birmingham C (loan)	6	—
							Swindon T (loan)	7	1
							Cambridge U	61	2
Russell Alex	5 8	11 10	M	17 3 73	Crosby	Burscough	Rochdale	102	14
							Cambridge U	37	6
Smith Tommy†	5 9	13 00	M	25 11 77	Northampton	Trainee	Manchester U	—	—
							Cambridge U	1	—
Taylor John	6 2	14 00	F	24 10 64	Norwich	Local	Colchester U	—	—
						Sudbury T	Cambridge U	160	46
							Bristol R	95	44
							Bradford C	36	11
							Luton T	37	3
							Lincoln C (loan)	5	2
							Colchester U (loan)	8	5
							Cambridge U	95	31
Van Heusden Arjan	6 4	14 07	G	11 12 72	Alphen	Noordwijk	Port Vale	27	—
							Oxford U (loan)	11	—
							Cambridge U	27	—
Wanless Paul	6 1	13 11	M	14 12 73	Banbury	Trainee	Oxford U	32	—
							Lincoln C	8	—
							Cambridge U (loan)	14	1
							Cambridge U	117	19
Webb Darren‡	5 9	11 00	M	24 10 79	Brighton	Trainee	Cambridge U	—	—
Wilde Adam†	5 9	11 11	M	22 5 79	Southampton	Trainee	Cambridge U	4	—
Youngs Tom	5 9	10 07	F	31 8 79	Bury St Edmunds	Trainee	Cambridge U	14	—

Trainees
Barrows, Michael R D; Fox, Karl; Gibson, Mark A; Mills, Jonathan; Steward, Michael J

Scholars
Chillingworth, Daniel T; Cox, Darren M; Haniver, Matthew G; Kamara, Alim S; Mercer, James F; Nacca, Francesco; Tann, Adam J

Non-Contract
Cockrill, Darren P; Eustace, Scott D; Hill, Leighton J; Wilde, Adam

CARDIFF CITY

Bonner Mark	5 8	11 00	M	7 6 74	Ormskirk	Trainee	Blackpool	178	14
							Cardiff C	25	1
							Hull C (loan)	1	1
Bowen Jason	5 8	11 02	M	24 8 72	Merthyr	Trainee	Swansea C	124	26
							Birmingham C	48	7
							Southampton (loan)	3	—
							Reading	15	1
							Cardiff C	17	2
Cadette Nathan	5 8	11 11	M	6 1 80	Cardiff	Trainee	Cardiff C	4	—
Carpenter Richard	6 0	13 01	M	30 9 72	Sheppey	Trainee	Gillingham	122	4
							Fulham	58	7
							Cardiff C	42	1
Earnshaw Robert	5 6	9 09	F	6 4 81	Zambia	Trainee	Cardiff C	10	1
							Middlesbrough (loan)	—	—
Eckhardt Jeff	6 0	12 01	D	7 10 65	Sheffield		Sheffield U	74	2
							Fulham	249	25
							Stockport Co	62	7
							Cardiff C	91	13
Ford Mike	6 0	12 12	D	9 2 66	Bristol	Apprentice	Leicester C	—	—
						Devizes T	Cardiff C	145	13
							Oxford U	289	18
							Cardiff C	25	—
Fowler Jason	6 3	12 04	M	20 8 74	Bristol	Trainee	Bristol C	25	—
							Cardiff C	112	13
Hallworth Jon	6 3	14 08	G	26 10 65	Stockport	School	Ipswich T	45	—
							Swindon T (loan)	—	—
							Fulham (loan)	—	—
							Bristol R (loan)	2	—
							Oldham Ath	174	—
							Cardiff C	84	—

Hill Danny	5 8	11 08	M	1 10 74	Edmonton	Trainee	Tottenham H	10	—
							Birmingham C (loan)	5	—
							Watford (loan)	1	—
							Cardiff C (loan)	7	—
							Oxford U	9	—
							Cardiff C	26	2
Jarman Lee	6 3	14 01	D	16 12 77	Cardiff	Trainee	Cardiff C	93	1
Kelly Seamus	6 1	13 13	G	6 5 74	Tullamore	UCD	Cardiff C	5	—
Legg Andy	5 8	10 12	M	28 7 66	Swansea	Briton Ferry	Swansea C	163	29
							Notts Co	89	9
							Birmingham C	45	5
							Ipswich T (loan)	6	1
							Reading	12	—
							Peterborough U (loan)	5	—
							Cardiff C	24	2
Loveless Ian†	6 2	14 05	G	1 11 79	Cardiff	Trainee	Cardiff C	—	—
Middleton Craig	5 11	12 00	M	10 9 70	Nuneaton	Trainee	Coventry C	3	—
							Cambridge U	59	10
							Cardiff C	109	8
Mitchell Graham	6 1	13 01	D	16 2 68	Shipley	Apprentice	Huddersfield T	244	2
							Bournemouth (loan)	4	—
							Bradford C	65	1
							Raith R	23	—
							Cardiff C	46	—
Nugent Kevin	6 2	13 00	F	10 4 69	Edmonton	Trainee	Leyton Orient	94	20
							Plymouth Arg	131	32
							Bristol C	70	14
							Cardiff C	45	15
O'Sullivan Wayne#	5 7	10 11	M	25 2 74	Akrotiri	Trainee	Swindon T	89	3
							Cardiff C	85	4
Penney David‡	5 9	12 04	M	17 8 64	Wakefield	Pontefract	Derby Co	19	—
							Oxford U	110	15
							Swansea C (loan)	12	3
							Swansea C (loan)	11	2
							Swansea C	108	18
							Cardiff C	35	5
Phillips Lee	6 0	12 10	D	18 3 79	Aberdare	Trainee	Cardiff C	13	—
Ramasut Tom‡	5 10	11 00	M	30 8 77	Cardiff		Norwich C	—	—
							Bristol R	42	6
							Cardiff C	—	—
Roberts Chris	5 10	12 03	F	22 10 79	Cardiff	Trainee	Cardiff C	15	3
Thomas Dai	5 11	13 07	F	26 9 75	Caerphilly	Trainee	Swansea C	56	10
							Watford	16	3
							Cardiff C	24	4
Williams John	6 2	13 08	F	11 5 68	Birmingham	Cradley T	Swansea C	39	11
							Coventry C	80	11
							Notts Co (loan)	5	2
							Stoke C (loan)	4	—
							Swansea C (loan)	7	2
							Wycombe W	48	9
							Hereford U	11	3
							Walsall	1	—
							Exeter C	36	4
							Cardiff C	43	12
Young Scott	6 1	13 02	D	14 1 76	Llwynypia	Trainee	Cardiff C	165	5

Trainees
Buttery, Paul A; Darbyshire, Jonathan R; Davis, Craig A; George, Stephen A; Givans, Warren A L; Harris, Adrian E; Higginson, Matthew; Kelly, Philip J; Owen, Philip N R; Parnell, Blake L; Phillips, Darryl J; Skelly, Lee

Non-Contract
Loveless, Ian C

Associated Schoolboys who have accepted the Club's offer of a Traineeship/Scholarship/Contract
Evans, Gari

CARLISLE UNITED

Anthony Graham	5 7	11 02	M	9 8 75	South Shields	Trainee	Sheffield U	3	—
							Scarborough (loan)	2	—
							Swindon T	3	—
							Plymouth Arg	5	—
							Carlisle U	51	3
Barr Billy	5 11	11 02	D	21 1 69	Halifax	Trainee	Halifax T	196	13
						Halifax T	Crewe Alex	85	7
							Carlisle U	62	3
Bass David#	5 11	12 03	M	29 11 74	Frimley	Trainee	Reading	11	—
							Rotherham U	18	—
							Carlisle U	9	—
Bowman Rob*	6 1	12 10	D	21 11 75	Durham	Trainee	Leeds U	7	—
							Rotherham U	13	—
							Carlisle U	31	2

Name	Ht	Wt	Pos	DOB	Birthplace	Source	Club	Apps	Gls
Brightwell David	6 2	12 09	D	7 1 71	Lutterworth	Trainee	Manchester C	43	1
							Chester C (loan)	6	—
							Lincoln C (loan)	5	—
							Stoke C (loan)	1	—
							Bradford C	24	—
							Blackpool (loan)	2	—
							Northampton T	35	1
							Carlisle U	41	4
Clark Peter	6 1	12 04	D	10 12 79	Romford	Arsenal	Carlisle U	36	—
Dixon George‡	6 0	14 02	G	24 10 78	Whitehaven	Trainee	Carlisle U	—	—
Dobie Scott	6 2	12 09	F	10 10 78	Workington	Trainee	Carlisle U	58	7
							Clydebank (loan)	6	—
Douglas Andrew	5 9	10 05	F	27 5 80	Penrith	Trainee	Carlisle U	1	—
Harrison Edward‡			M	14 2 80	Carlisle	Trainee	Carlisle U	10	—
Heritage Paul	6 1	13 06	G	17 4 79	Sheffield	Trainee	Sheffield U	—	—
							Barnsley	—	—
							Carlisle U	—	—
Hopper Tony	5 11	12 08	M	31 5 76	Carlisle	Trainee	Carlisle U	73	1
McAlindon Gareth*	5 9	11 10	F	6 4 77	Hexham	Newcastle U	Carlisle U	59	5
Mendes Junior	5 8	10 00	M	15 9 76	Balham	Trainee	Chelsea	—	—
							St Mirren	22	4
							Carlisle U (loan)	6	1
Paterson Scott*	5 11	11 09	D	13 5 72	Aberdeen	Cove Rangers	Liverpool	—	—
							Bristol C	50	1
							Cardiff C (loan)	5	—
							Carlisle U	19	1
Prokas Richard	5 9	11 05	M	22 1 76	Penrith	Trainee	Carlisle U	140	2
Reid Paul	6 2	11 08	D	18 2 82	Carlisle	Trainee	Carlisle U	—	—
Sandwith Kevin‡	5 11	12 05	D	30 4 78	Workington	Trainee	Carlisle U	3	—
Searle Damon	5 10	11 00	M	26 10 71	Cardiff	Trainee	Cardiff C	234	3
							Stockport Co	41	—
							Carlisle U	45	2
Stevens Ian*	5 10	12 07	F	21 10 69	Malta	Trainee	Preston NE	11	2
							Stockport Co	2	—
						Lancaster C	Bolton W	47	7
							Bury	110	38
							Shrewsbury T	111	37
							Carlisle U	78	26
Thorpe Jeff	5 11	12 08	M	17 11 72	Cockermouth	Trainee	Carlisle U	163	6
Thurston Mark	6 2	11 08	M	10 2 80	Carlisle	Trainee	Carlisle U	—	—
Tracey Richard	5 11	12 04	F	9 7 79	Muirfield	Trainee	Sheffield U	—	—
							Rotherham U	3	—
							Carlisle U	11	3
Varty Will	6 0	12 00	D	1 10 76	Workington	Trainee	Carlisle U	82	1
							Rotherham U (loan)	14	—
Whitehead Stuart	6 0	12 02	D	17 7 76	Bromsgrove	Bromsgrove R	Bolton W	—	—
							Carlisle U	37	—

Trainees
Antony, Paul, M; Ballantyne, Paul; Benson, Jon K; Clark, Barry J; Graham, Ricky; Heath, Jamie; Heggie, John A; Hetherington, Philip M; Hodgson, Alan; Hore, John; Irving, Michael J; Skelton, Gavin R; Stevens, Barry J; Swann, Michael; Thwaites, Adam

Non-Contract
Dalton, Neil J; Wilkes, David A

Associated Schoolboys
Hewson, David L

Associated Schoolboys who have accepted the Club's offer of a Traineeship/Scholarship/Contract
Allan, Jonathan M; Andrews, Lee; Brain, Jonathan R; Hoolikin, Lee; Jack, Michael L; Johnston, Craig; Lewis, Craig; May, Kyle; Rooke, Steven

CHARLTON ATHLETIC

Name	Ht	Wt	Pos	DOB	Birthplace	Source	Club	Apps	Gls
Allen Bradley*	5 7	10 07	F	13 9 71	Harold Wood	School	QPR	81	27
							Charlton Ath	40	9
							Colchester U (loan)	4	1
Allman Anthony	5 9	10 07	D	14 12 80	Sidcup	Trainee	Charlton Ath	—	—
Barnes John*	5 11	12 07	M	7 11 63	Jamaica	Sudbury Court	Watford	233	65
							Liverpool	314	84
							Newcastle U	27	6
							Charlton Ath	12	—
Barness Anthony	5 11	12 01	D	25 3 73	Lewisham	Trainee	Charlton Ath	27	1
							Chelsea	14	—
							Middlesbrough (loan)	—	—
							Southend U (loan)	5	—
							Charlton Ath	77	3
Beale Michael*	6 1	11 06	M	4 9 80	Sidcup	Trainee	Charlton Ath	—	—
Bowen Mark*	5 8	11 11	D	7 12 63	Neath	Apprentice	Tottenham H	17	2
							Norwich C	320	24
							West Ham U	17	1
						Shimizu	Charlton Ath	42	—

Name			Pos	Born			Club	Apps	Gls
Bright Mark*	6 2	13 00	F	6 6 62	Stoke	Leek T	Port Vale	29	10
							Leicester C	42	6
							Crystal Palace	227	92
							Sheffield W	133	48
							Millwall (loan)	3	1
							Sion	—	—
							Charlton Ath	28	10
Brown Steve	6 1	13 10	D	13 5 72	Brighton	Trainee	Charlton Ath	160	5
Curbishley Alan	5 10	11 07	M	8 11 57	Forest Gate	Apprentice	West Ham U	85	5
							Birmingham C	130	11
							Aston Villa	36	1
							Charlton Ath	63	6
							Brighton & HA	116	13
							Charlton Ath	28	—
Fortune Jonathan	6 2	11 00	D	23 8 80	Islington	Trainee	Charlton Ath	—	—
Hales Lee	5 10	11 00	F	1 5 81	Gillingham	Trainee	Charlton Ath	—	—
Hockley David§	5 11	11 05	M	23 2 81	Gillingham	Trainee	Charlton Ath	—	—
Holmes Matty	5 7	11 00	M	1 8 69	Luton	Trainee	Bournemouth	114	8
							Cardiff C (loan)	1	—
							West Ham U	76	4
							Blackburn R	9	1
							Charlton Ath	16	1
Hunt Andy	6 0	11 12	F	9 6 70	Thurrock	Kettering T	Newcastle U	43	11
							WBA (loan)	10	9
							WBA	202	67
							Charlton Ath	34	7
Ifejiagwa Emeka	6 3	14 00	D	30 10 77	Nigeria	Udoji U	Charlton Ath	—	—
							Brighton & HA (loan)	2	1
Ilic Sasa	6 4	14 00	G	18 7 72	Melbourne	St Leonards Stamcroft	Charlton Ath	37	—
Izzet Kemal	5 8	10 05	M	29 9 80	Whitechapel	Trainee	Charlton Ath	—	—
James Kevin	5 9	10 07	F	3 1 80	Southwark	Trainee	Charlton Ath	—	—
Jones Keith	5 9	10 11	M	14 10 65	Dulwich	Apprentice	Chelsea	52	7
							Brentford	169	13
							Southend U	90	11
							Charlton Ath	141	5
Jones Steve	5 11	12 00	F	17 3 70	Cambridge	Billericay T	West Ham U	16	4
							Bournemouth	74	26
							West Ham U	8	—
							Charlton Ath	50	8
							Bournemouth (loan)	5	4
Kinsella Mark	5 9	11 05	M	12 8 72	Dublin	Home Farm	Colchester U	180	27
							Charlton Ath	121	14
Konchesky Paul	5 10	10 05	D	15 5 81	Barking	Trainee	Charlton Ath	5	—
Lee Matt*	5 10	11 00	D	13 5 79	Farnborough	Trainee	Charlton Ath	—	—
Lisbie Kevin	5 9	11 00	F	17 10 78	Hackney	Trainee	Charlton Ath	43	2
							Gillingham (loan)	7	4
MacDonald Charles	5 9	11 00	F	13 2 81	Southwark	Trainee	Charlton Ath	—	—
McCammon Mark	6 2	12 00	F	7 8 78	Barnet		Cambridge U	4	—
							Charlton Ath	—	—
Mendonca Clive	5 10	10 07	F	9 9 68	Islington	Apprentice	Sheffield U	13	4
							Doncaster R (loan)	2	—
							Rotherham U	84	27
							Sheffield U	10	1
							Grimsby T (loan)	10	3
							Grimsby T	156	56
							Charlton Ath	65	31
Mills Danny	5 11	11 09	D	18 5 77	Norwich	Trainee	Norwich C	66	—
							Charlton Ath	45	3
Mortimer Paul*	5 11	11 03	M	8 5 68	Kensington	Fulham	Charlton Ath	113	17
							Aston Villa	12	1
							Crystal Palace	22	2
							Brentford (loan)	6	—
							Charlton Ath	86	15
Newton Shaun	5 8	11 00	F	20 8 75	Camberwell	Trainee	Charlton Ath	188	15
Nicholls Kevin	5 11	11 12	M	2 1 79	Newham	Trainee	Charlton Ath	12	1
							Brighton & HA (loan)	4	1
Parker Scott	5 9	11 00	M	13 10 80	Lambeth	Trainee	Charlton Ath	7	—
Petterson Andy*	6 2	14 12	G	29 9 69	Fremantle		Luton T	19	—
							Swindon T (loan)	—	—
							Ipswich T (loan)	—	—
							Ipswich T (loan)	1	—
							Charlton Ath	72	—
							Bradford C (loan)	3	—
							Ipswich T (loan)	1	—
							Plymouth Arg (loan)	6	—
							Colchester U (loan)	5	—
							Portsmouth (loan)	13	—
Poole Gary*	6 0	11 00	D	11 9 67	Stratford	Arsenal	Tottenham H	—	—
							Cambridge U	43	—
						Barnet	Barnet	40	2
							Plymouth Arg	39	5
							Southend U	44	2
							Birmingham C	72	—
							Charlton Ath	16	1

Name							Club	Apps	Gls
Powell Chris	5 10	11 07	D	8 9 69	Lambeth	Trainee	Crystal Palace	3	—
							Aldershot (loan)	11	—
							Southend U	248	3
							Derby Co	91	1
							Charlton Ath	38	—
Pringle Martin	6 2	12 00	F	18 11 70	Gothenburg	Stenungsund	Helsingborg	64	15
							Benfica	41	6
							Charlton Ath	18	3
Redfearn Neil	5 8	12 00	M	20 6 65	Dewsbury	Nottingham F	Bolton W	35	1
							Lincoln C (loan)	10	1
							Lincoln C	90	12
							Doncaster R	46	14
							Crystal Palace	57	10
							Watford	24	3
							Oldham Ath	62	16
							Barnsley	292	71
							Charlton Ath	30	3
Robinson John	5 10	11 02	F	29 8 71	Bulawayo	Apprentice	Brighton & HA	62	6
							Charlton Ath	217	25
Royce Simon	6 2	12 10	G	9 9 71	Forest Gate	Heybridge Swifts	Southend U	149	—
							Charlton Ath	8	—
Rufus Richard	6 1	10 05	D	12 1 75	Lewisham	Trainee	Charlton Ath	172	1
Salmon Mick†	6 2	12 12	G	14 6 64	Leyland	Local	Blackburn R	1	—
							Chester C (loan)	16	—
							Stockport Co	118	—
							Bolton W	26	—
							Wrexham (loan)	17	—
							Wrexham	83	—
							Charlton Ath	148	—
							Oxford U (loan)	1	—
Smith Paul*	6 3	12 04	G	17 12 79	Epsom		Charlton Ath	—	—
							Bramet (loan)	—	—
Stuart Graham	5 8	11 11	M	24 10 70	Tooting	Trainee	Chelsea	87	14
							Everton	136	22
							Sheffield U	53	11
							Charlton Ath	9	4
Tiler Carl	6 2	13 10	D	11 2 70	Sheffield	Trainee	Barnsley	71	3
							Nottingham F	69	1
							Swindon T (loan)	2	—
							Aston Villa	12	1
							Sheffield U	23	2
							Everton	21	1
							Charlton Ath	27	1
Toms Frazer*	6 1	11 00	M	13 9 79	Ealing	Trainee	Charlton Ath	—	—
Turner John§	6 1	12 05	G	9 9 80	Pontypool	Trainee	Charlton Ath	—	—
Youds Eddie	6 1	13 00	D	3 5 70	Liverpool	Trainee	Everton	8	—
							Cardiff C (loan)	1	—
							Wrexham (loan)	20	2
							Ipswich T	50	1
							Bradford C	85	8
							Charlton Ath	30	2

Trainees/Scholars
Brown, Jason R; Collis, David J; Day, Aaron; Ford, Simon G; Hockley, David C E; McCarthy, Paul D; Pacey, Ryan J; Piper, Chrisopher C; Tambue, Joe; Turner, John S; Watson, Kevin M

Non-Contract
Salmon, Michael B

CHELSEA

Name							Club	Apps	Gls
Babayaro Celestine	5 9	10 12	D	29 8 78	Kaduna		Anderlecht	75	8
							Chelsea	36	3
Broad Stephen	6 2	12 00	D	10 6 80	Epsom	Trainee	Chelsea	—	—
Casiraghi Pierluigi	5 11	12 02	F	4 3 69	Milan		Monza	94	28
							Juventus	98	20
							Lazio	140	41
							Chelsea	10	1
Clement Neil	6 0	12 03	D	3 10 78	Reading	Trainee	Chelsea	1	—
							Reading (loan)	11	1
							Preston NE (loan)	4	—
Crittenden Nick	5 10	11 00	D	11 11 78	Ascot	Trainee	Chelsea	2	—
							Plymouth Arg (loan)	2	—
Dalla Bona Samuele	6 1	12 00	D	6 2 81	S. Dona di Piave		Atalanta	—	—
							Chelsea	—	—
De Goey Ed	6 6	15 04	G	20 12 66	Gouda		Sparta	145	—
							Feyenoord	201	—
							Chelsea	63	—
Desailly Marcel	6 2	12 06	D	17 9 68	Accra		Nantes	164	5
							Marseille	46	1
							AC Milan	137	5
							Chelsea	31	—

Name		Height	Weight	Pos	DOB	Birthplace	From	Club	Apps	Goals
Di Matteo Roberto		5 10	12 00	M	29 5 70	Schaffhausen		Schaffhausen	50	2
								Zurich	34	6
								Aarau	32	1
								Lazio	88	7
								Chelsea	94	13
Duberry Michael		6 1	14 00	D	14 10 75	Enfield	Trainee	Chelsea	86	1
								Bournemouth (loan)	7	—
Evans Rhys		6 1	12 01	G	27 1 82	Swindon	Trainee	Chelsea	—	—
Ferrer Albert		5 9	11 00	D	6 6 70	Barcelona		Tenerife	17	—
								Barcelona	205	1
								Chelsea	30	—
Flo Tore Andre		6 4	13 08	F	15 6 73	Strin		Sogndal	22	5
								Tromso	26	18
								Brann	40	28
								Chelsea	64	21
Forssell Mikael		5 10	10 10	F	15 3 81	Steinfurt		HJK Helsinki	17	1
								Chelsea	10	1
Goldbaek Bjarne		5 10	11 06	M	6 10 68	Denmark		Kaiserslautern	55	7
								Tennis Borussia	24	5
								Cologne	30	2
								FC Copenhagen	74	16
								Chelsea	23	5
Hampshire Steve		5 10	10 10	F	17 10 79	Edinburgh	Trainee	Chelsea	—	—
Harley Jon		5 10	11 10	M	26 9 79	Maidstone	Trainee	Chelsea	3	—
Hitchcock Kevin		6 1	13 00	G	5 10 62	Custom House	Barking	Nottingham F	—	—
								Mansfield T (loan)	14	—
								Mansfield T	168	—
								Chelsea	96	—
								Northampton T (loan)	17	—
								West Ham U (loan)	—	—
Hughes Paul		5 11	12 06	M	19 4 76	Hammersmith	Trainee	Chelsea	21	2
								Stockport Co (loan)	7	—
								Norwich C (loan)	4	1
Kharine Dmitri*		6 2	13 11	G	16 8 68	Moscow		Torpedo Moscow	63	—
								Dynamo Moscow	40	—
								CSKA Moscow	34	—
								Chelsea	118	—
Lambourde Bernard		6 1	12 06	D	11 5 71	Pointe-A-Pitre		Cannes	13	1
								Angers	36	1
								Cannes	28	1
								Bordeaux	28	1
								Chelsea	24	—
Laudrup Brian *(Transferred to FC Copenhagen, November 1998)*		6 0	13 02	F	22 2 69	Vienna		Brondby	49	13
								Uerdingen	34	6
								Bayern Munich	53	11
								Fiorentina	31	5
								AC Milan	9	1
								Rangers	116	33
								Chelsea	7	—
Le Saux Graeme		5 10	11 09	D	17 10 68	Jersey	St Pauls	Chelsea	90	8
								Blackburn R	129	7
								Chelsea	57	1
Leboeuf Franck		6 0	12 00	D	22 1 68	Marseille		Hyeres	14	1
								Meaux	39	3
								Laval	69	10
								Strasbourg	189	49
								Chelsea	91	15
Morris Jody		5 5	10 11	M	22 12 78	Hammersmith	Trainee	Chelsea	43	2
Myers Andy		5 10	13 11	D	3 11 73	Hounslow	Trainee	Chelsea	84	2
Newton Eddie*		6 0	12 11	M	13 12 71	Hammersmith	Trainee	Chelsea	165	8
								Cardiff C (loan)	18	4
Nicholls Mark		5 10	10 04	F	30 5 77	Hillingdon	Trainee	Chelsea	36	3
Parkin Sam		6 1	12 06	F	14 3 81	Roehampton	School	Chelsea	—	—
Percassi Luca		5 9	11 00	M	25 8 80	Milan		Atalanta	—	—
								Chelsea	—	—
Petrescu Dan		5 10	11 07	D	22 12 67	Bucharest		Steaua	95	26
								FC Olt (loan)	24	—
								Foggia	55	7
								Genoa	24	1
								Sheffield W	37	3
								Chelsea	121	14
Poyet Gustavo		6 1	13 01	M	15 11 67	Montevideo	Bella Vista	Zaragoza	239	63
								Chelsea	42	15
Richardson Jay		5 9	11 00	M	14 11 79	Keston	Trainee	Chelsea	—	—
Sheerin Joe		6 1	13 09	F	1 2 79	Hammersmith	Trainee	Chelsea	1	—
Slatter Danny		5 8	11 01	M	15 11 80	Cardiff	Trainee	Chelsea	—	—
Terry John		6 0	11 11	D	7 12 80	Barking	Trainee	Chelsea	2	—
Vialli Gianluca		5 10	13 06	F	9 7 64	Cremona		Cremonese	105	23
								Sampdoria	223	85
								Juventus	102	38
								Chelsea	58	21
Wise Dennis		5 6	10 11	F	16 12 66	Kensington	Southampton	Wimbledon	135	27
								Chelsea	266	46
Wolleaston Robert		5 11	11 10	F	21 12 79	Perivale	Trainee	Chelsea	—	—

Zola Gianfranco	5 6	10 10	F	5 7 66	Oliena		Nuorese	31	10
							Torres	88	21
							Napoli	105	32
							Parma	102	49
							Chelsea	87	29

Trainees/Scholars
Baxter, Darren L; Byle, Leslie D; Cummings, Warren; Demetrious, Shayne; Hajgato, Geza; Hook, Mark; King, John S; Nicholls, Paul D; Pitt, Courtney; Rattray, John W; Royal, Mark

CHELTENHAM TOWN

Banks Chris	5 11	12 02	D	22 11 65	Stone		Port Vale	65	1
							Exeter C	45	1
						Bath C	Cheltenham T	—	—
Bloomer Bob	5 10	12 07	M	21 6 66	Sheffield		Chesterfield	141	15
							Bristol R	22	—
							Cheltenham T	—	—
Book Steve	5 11	11 01	G	7 7 69	Bournemouth		Brighton & HA	—	—
							Lincoln C	—	—
						Forest Green R	Cheltenham T	—	—
Brough John	6 0	12 11	D	8 1 73	Heanor	Trainee	Notts Co	—	—
							Shrewsbury T	16	1
						Telford U	Hereford U	79	3
Casey Ross	5 10	10 09	M	7 8 79	Stroud	Trainee	Cheltenham T	—	—
Duff Michael	6 1	11 08	D	11 1 78	Belfast	Trainee	Cheltenham T	—	—
Eaton Jason	5 10	11 09	F	29 1 69	Bristol	Apprentice	Bristol R	3	0
							Bristol C	13	1
						Gloucester C	Cheltenham T	—	—
Freeman Mark	6 2	13 08	D	27 1 70	Walsall	Bilston T	Wolverhampton W	—	—
						Gloucester C	Cheltenham T	—	—
Gannaway Ryan	5 11	13 02	G	28 8 73	Gloucester	Shortwood U	Cheltenham T	—	—
Grayson Neil	5 10	12 09	F	1 11 64	York	Rowntree	Doncaster R	29	6
						Mackintosh	York C	1	—
							Chesterfield	15	—
						Boston U	Northampton T	120	31
Hopkins Gareth	6 2	13 08	F	14 6 80	Cheltenham	Trainee	Cheltenham T	—	—
Howells Lee	5 11	11 12	M	14 10 68	Fremantle	Apprentice	Bristol R	—	—
						Brisbane U	Cheltenham T	—	—
Jackson Michael	5 7	10 10	M	26 6 80	Cheltenham	Trainee	Cheltenham T	—	—
Knight Keith	5 7	11 07	M	16 2 69	Cheltenham	Cheltenham T	Reading	43	8
						Halesowen T	Cheltenham T	—	—
Milton Russell	5 8	12 01	M	12 1 69	Folkestone	Trainee	Arsenal	—	—
						Dover Ath	Cheltenham T	—	—
Murphy Stephen	6 0	10 11	D	31 8 79	Middlesbrough	Trainee	Cheltenham T	—	—
Norton David	5 10	11 10	M	3 3 65	Cannock	Apprentice	Aston Villa	44	2
							Notts Co	27	1
							Rochdale (loan)	9	—
							Hull C (loan)	15	—
							Hull C	134	5
							Northampton T	82	—
							Hereford U	45	—
Smith Jimmy	5 9	10 04	F	22 11 69	Johnstone	Trainee	Torquay U	45	5
						Salisbury C	Cheltenham T	—	—
Victory Jamie	5 11	12 02	D	14 11 75	London	Trainee	West Ham U	—	—
							Bournemouth	16	1
Walker Clive	5 8	11 12	F	25 6 57	Oxford	Apprentice	Chelsea	198	60
							Sunderland	50	10
							QPR	21	1
							Fulham	109	29
							Brighton & HA	106	8
						Woking	Brentford	—	—
							Cheltenham T	—	—
Walker Richard	5 10	11 09	D	9 11 71	Derby	Trainee	Notts Co	67	4
							Mansfield T (loan)	4	—
Watkins Dale	5 8	11 12	F	4 11 71	Peterborough	Trainee	Peterborough U	10	—
						Gloucester C	Cheltenham T	—	—
Yates Mark	5 11	13 02	M	24 1 70	Birmingham	Trainee	Birmingham C	54	6
							Burnley	18	1
							Lincoln C (loan)	14	—
							Doncaster R	34	4
						Kidderminster H	Cheltenham T	—	—

CHESTER CITY

Alsford Julian‡	6 2	13 07	D	24 12 72	Poole	Trainee	Watford	13	1
							Chester C	141	6
							Dundee U	3	—
							Chester C	10	1
							Barnet (loan)	9	1
Beckett Luke	5 11	11 06	F	25 11 76	Sheffield	Trainee	Barnsley	—	—
							Chester C	28	11

Name	Ht	Wt	Pos	Born	Birthplace	From	Club	Apps	Gls
Bennett Gary	5 11	12 00	F	20 9 62	Kirby	Kirby T	Wigan Ath	20	3
							Chester C	126	36
							Southend U	42	6
							Chester C	80	15
							Wrexham	121	77
							Tranmere R	29	9
							Preston NE	24	4
							Wrexham	15	5
							Chester C	48	13
Brown Wayne	6 1	11 06	G	14 1 77	Southampton	Trainee	Bristol C	1	—
						Weston-Super-Mare	Chester C	38	—
Carson Danny§	5 6	10 07	M	2 2 81	Huyton	Trainee	Chester C	2	—
Clench Philip‡			M	23 3 79	Chester	Trainee	Chester C	—	—
Crosby Andy	6 2	13 07	D	3 3 73	Rotherham	Leeds U	Doncaster R	51	—
							Darlington	181	3
							Chester C	41	4
Cross Jonathan#	5 10	11 07	M	2 3 75	Wallasey	Trainee	Wrexham	119	12
							Hereford U (loan)	5	1
							Tranmere R (loan)	—	—
							Chester C	35	1
Cutler Neil	6 1	12 00	G	3 9 76	Birmingham	Trainee	WBA	—	—
							Coventry C (loan)	—	—
							Chester C (loan)	1	—
							Crewe Alex	—	—
							Chester C (loan)	5	—
							Chester C	23	—
Davidson Ross#	5 9	12 04	D	13 11 73	Chertsey	Walton & Hersham	Sheffield U	2	—
							Chester C	123	5
Fisher Neil†	5 10	11 00	M	7 11 70	St Helens	Trainee	Bolton W	24	1
							Chester C	116	4
Flitcroft David#	5 11	13 05	M	14 1 74	Bolton	Trainee	Preston NE	8	2
							Lincoln C (loan)	2	—
							Chester C	167	18
Jones Jon	5 11	11 05	F	27 10 78	Wrexham	Trainee	Chester C	32	2
Lancaster Martin	6 0	12 07	D	10 11 80	Wigan	Trainee	Chester C	11	—
Moss Darren§	5 10	11 00	M	24 5 81	Wrexham	Trainee	Chester C	7	—
Murphy John	6 1	14 00	F	18 10 76	Whiston	Trainee	Chester C	103	20
Priest Chris#	5 10	10 10	M	18 10 73	Leigh	Trainee	Everton	—	—
							Chester C	167	26
Reid Shaun#	5 8	12 02	M	13 10 65	Huyton	Local	Rochdale	133	4
							Preston NE (loan)	3	—
							York C	106	7
							Rochdale	107	10
							Bury	21	—
							Chester C	49	2
Richardson Nick#	6 1	12 06	M	11 4 67	Halifax	Local	Halifax T	101	17
							Cardiff C	111	13
							Wrexham (loan)	4	2
							Chester C (loan)	6	1
							Bury	5	—
							Chester C	133	9
Shelton Andy	5 10	12 00	M	19 6 80	Sutton Coldfield	Trainee	Chester C	24	1
Shelton Gary	5 7	11 02	M	21 3 58	Nottingham	Apprentice	Walsall	24	—
							Aston Villa	24	7
							Notts Co (loan)	8	—
							Sheffield W	198	18
							Oxford U	65	1
							Bristol C	150	24
							Rochdale (loan)	3	—
							Chester C	69	6
Thompson Scott*	6 3	13 00	D	28 6 80	Warrington	Trainee	Chester C	—	—
Woods Matt	6 1	12 03	D	9 9 76	Gosport	Trainee	Everton	—	—
							Chester C	93	4
Wright Darren	5 6	10 00	F	7 9 79	Warrington	Trainee	Chester C	23	1

Trainees
Carson, Daniel; Conkie, Matthew J; Lloyd, David; Moss, Darren M; Pendleton, David J; Rendell, Carl

Scholars
Blackburn, Christopher R; Donnelly, Christopher; Doughty, Matthew L; Kilgannon, Wesley M; Lloyd-Hughes, Lee A; Roberts, Paul

Non-Contract
Fisher, Neil J

Associated Schoolboys who have accepted the Club's offer of a Traineeship/Scholarship/Contract
Cooper, Joseph D; Hopwood, Christopher P; Williams, Michael

CHESTERFIELD

Name	Ht	Wt	Pos	Born	Birthplace	From	Club	Apps	Gls
Beaumont Chris	5 11	11 12	M	5 12 65	Sheffield	Denaby U	Rochdale	34	7
							Stockport Co	258	39
							Chesterfield	111	4
Blatherwick Steve	6 1	15 00	D	20 9 73	Nottingham	Notts Co	Nottingham F	10	—
							Wycombe W (loan)	2	—
							Hereford U (loan)	10	1
							Reading (loan)	7	—
							Burnley	24	—
							Chesterfield	14	1

Name					Birthplace	Source	Club	Apps	Gls
Breckin Ian	5 11	11 07	D	24 2 75	Rotherham	Trainee	Rotherham U	132	6
							Chesterfield	87	3
Carss Tony	5 10	11 08	M	31 3 76	Alnwick	Bradford C	Blackburn R	—	—
							Darlington	57	2
							Cardiff C	42	1
							Chesterfield	4	—
Curtis Tom	5 8	10 08	M	1 3 73	Exeter	School	Derby Co	—	—
							Chesterfield	222	12
Dunn Iain‡	5 10	10 07	M	1 4 70	Derwent	School	York C	77	11
							Chesterfield	13	1
						Goole T	Huddersfield T	120	14
							Scunthorpe U (loan)	3	—
							Chesterfield	18	—
Ebdon Marcus	5 10	11 02	M	17 10 70	Pontypool	Trainee	Everton	—	—
							Peterborough U	147	15
							Chesterfield	85	4
Hewitt Jamie#	5 10	10 08	M	17 5 68	Chesterfield	School	Chesterfield	249	14
							Doncaster R	33	—
							Chesterfield	216	12
Holland Paul	5 11	12 10	M	8 7 73	Lincoln	School	Mansfield T	149	25
							Sheffield U	18	1
							Chesterfield	110	11
Howard Jonathan	5 11	11 07	F	7 10 71	Sheffield	Trainee	Rotherham U	36	5
							Chesterfield	149	27
Jules Mark*	5 7	10 09	D	5 9 71	Bradford	Trainee	Bradford C	—	—
							Scarborough	77	16
							Chesterfield	186	4
Leaning Andy#	6 2	13 00	G	18 5 63	York	Rowntree	York C	69	—
						Mackintosh	Sheffield U	21	—
							Bristol C	75	—
							Lincoln C	36	—
							Chesterfield	16	—
Lee Jason	6 3	13 03	F	9 5 71	Newham	Trainee	Charlton Ath	1	—
							Stockport Co (loan)	2	—
							Lincoln C	93	21
							Southend U	24	3
							Nottingham F	76	14
							Charlton Ath (loan)	8	3
							Grimsby T (loan)	7	1
							Watford	37	11
							Chesterfield	22	1
Lenagh Steve	5 11	10 09	D	21 3 79	Durham	Sheffield W	Chesterfield	13	1
Lomas Jamie	5 11	10 09	M	18 10 77	Chesterfield	Trainee	Chesterfield	13	—
Mercer Billy	6 1	11 00	G	22 5 69	Liverpool	Trainee	Liverpool	—	—
							Rotherham U	104	—
							Sheffield U	4	—
							Nottingham F (loan)	—	—
							Chesterfield	149	—
Nicholson Shane#	5 10	11 10	D	3 6 70	Newark	Trainee	Lincoln C	133	6
							Derby Co	74	1
							WBA	52	—
							Chesterfield	24	—
Pearce Greg	5 9	10 09	M	26 5 80	Bolton	Trainee	Chesterfield	1	—
Perkins Chris#	5 11	10 09	M	9 1 74	Nottingham	Trainee	Mansfield T	8	—
							Chesterfield	147	3
Reeves David	6 0	12 06	F	19 11 67	Birkenhead	Heswall	Sheffield W	17	2
							Scunthorpe U (loan)	4	2
							Scunthorpe U (loan)	6	4
							Burnley (loan)	16	8
							Bolton W	134	29
							Notts Co	13	2
							Carlisle U	127	48
							Preston NE	47	12
							Chesterfield	66	15
Simpkins James‡	6 0	11 11	M	28 11 78	Sheffield	Trainee	Sheffield W	—	—
							Chesterfield	—	—
Simpkins Mike	6 0	11 11	D	28 11 78	Sheffield	Trainee	Sheffield W	—	—
							Chesterfield	1	—
Wilkinson Steve	5 11	11 11	F	1 9 68	Lincoln	Apprentice	Leicester C	9	1
							Rochdale (loan)	—	—
							Crewe Alex (loan)	5	2
							Mansfield T	232	83
							Preston NE	52	13
							Chesterfield	53	12
Williams Mark#	6 0	12 04	D	28 9 70	Stalybridge	Newtown	Shrewsbury T	102	3
							Chesterfield	168	12
Willis Roger	6 0	12 00	M	17 6 67	Islington		Grimsby T	9	—
						Barnet	Barnet	44	13
							Watford	36	2
							Birmingham C	19	5
							Southend U	31	7
							Peterborough U	40	6
							Chesterfield	51	8

Trainees
Barrett, Daniel T; Bowler, Paul S; Danysz, Lee J; Dooley, James; Hawke, Richard J; Newton, Lee R; Reynolds, Steven J; Robinson, Scott A; Williams, Daniel J; Wilson, Jonathan S

Scholars
Armstrong, Joel; Mitchell, Alistair; Renshaw, Lee; Rushbury, Ian D; Wilding, Craig

COLCHESTER UNITED

Player			Pos	Born	Birthplace	Source	Club	Apps	Gls
Abrahams Paul*	5 10	11 00	F	31 10 73	Colchester	Trainee	Colchester U	55	8
							Brentford	35	8
							Colchester U (loan)	8	2
							Colchester U	81	16
Adcock Tony*	5 11	11 11	F	27 3 63	Bethnal Green	Apprentice	Colchester U	210	98
							Manchester C	15	5
							Northampton T	72	30
							Bradford C	38	6
							Northampton T	35	10
							Peterborough U	111	35
							Luton T	2	—
							Colchester U	108	28
Aspinall Warren	5 9	11 12	M	13 9 67	Wigan	Apprentice	Wigan Ath	10	1
							Everton	7	—
							Wigan Ath (loan)	41	21
							Aston Villa	44	14
							Portsmouth	132	21
							Swansea C (loan)	5	—
							Bournemouth	33	9
							Carlisle U (loan)	7	1
							Carlisle U	100	11
							Brentford	43	5
							Colchester U	15	3
Betts Simon*	5 7	11 06	D	3 3 73	Middlesbrough	Trainee	Ipswich T	—	—
							Scarborough	—	—
							Colchester U	191	11
Buckle Paul#	5 8	11 10	M	16 12 70	Welwyn	Trainee	Brentford	57	1
							Torquay U	59	9
							Exeter C	22	2
							Northampton T	—	—
							Wycombe W	—	—
							Colchester U	105	7
Dozzell Jason#	6 2	13 07	M	9 12 67	Ipswich	School	Ipswich T	332	52
							Tottenham H	84	13
							Ipswich T	8	1
							Northampton T	21	4
							Colchester U	29	4
Duguid Karl	5 11	11 00	F	21 3 78	Letchworth	Trainee	Colchester U	90	11
Dunne Joe*	5 9	11 08	D	25 5 73	Dublin	Trainee	Gillingham	115	1
							Colchester U	101	3
Emberson Carl#	6 2	14 10	G	13 7 73	Epsom	Trainee	Millwall	—	—
							Colchester U (loan)	13	—
							Colchester U	179	—
Fernandes Tamer*	6 3	14 05	G	7 12 74	Paddington	Trainee	Brentford	12	—
							Peterborough U (loan)	—	—
							Colchester U	8	—
Forbes Steve	6 1	13 03	M	24 12 75	Hackney	Sittingbourne	Millwall	5	—
							Colchester U	51	4
							Peterborough U (loan)	3	—
Germain Steve			F	22 6 81	Cannes		Colchester U	6	—
Goss Jeremy†	5 9	11 08	M	11 5 65	Oekolia	Amateur	Norwich C	188	14
							Hearts	10	—
							Colchester U	—	—
Greene David	6 3	14 03	D	26 10 73	Luton	Trainee	Luton T	19	—
							Colchester U (loan)	14	1
							Brentford (loan)	11	—
							Colchester U	124	14
Gregory David	5 10	12 03	M	23 1 70	Polstead	Trainee	Ipswich T	32	2
							Hereford U (loan)	2	—
							Peterborough U	3	—
							Colchester U	136	17
Gregory Neil	6 0	12 10	F	7 10 72	Ndola	Trainee	Ipswich T	45	9
							Chesterfield (loan)	3	1
							Scunthorpe U (loan)	10	7
							Torquay U (loan)	5	—
							Peterborough U (loan)	3	1
							Colchester U	53	11
Hathaway Ian‡	5 6	10 12	M	22 8 68	Wordsley	Bedworth U	Mansfield T	44	2
							Rotherham U	13	1
							Torquay U	140	14
							Colchester U	12	—
Haydon Nicky*	5 9	11 07	M	10 8 78	Barking	Trainee	Colchester U	31	2
Heuvel Arafath‡	6 0	12 00	M	13 10 75	Amsterdam		Colchester U	—	—
Hodson Matthew†			M	20 9 79	Derby	Trainee	Wycombe W	—	—
							Colchester U	—	—
Lock Tony*	6 0	12 04	F	3 9 76	Harlow	Trainee	Colchester U	64	9
Lua-Lua Lomano			F	28 12 80	Zaire		Colchester U	13	1
Okafor Samuel‡			M	17 3 82	Xtian		Colchester U	1	—
Opara Chris-Santos‡			F	21 12 81	Oweri Imo State		Colchester U	1	—
Pounewatchy Stephane#	6 0	15 00	D	10 2 68	Paris		Martigues	44	2
							Gueugnon	30	—
							Carlisle U	81	3
							Dundee	3	—
							Port Vale	2	—
							Colchester U	15	1

Name	Ht	Wt	Pos	Born	Birthplace	Source	Club	Apps	Gls
Rainford David‡	6 0	12 04	M	21 4 79	Stepney	Trainee	Colchester U	1	—
							Scarborough (loan)	2	—
Reeve Daniel‡			M	10 2 80	Pontefract		Colchester U	—	—
Richard Fabrice			D	16 8 73	Saintes		Colchester U	10	—
Rogers Joel‡			F	7 1 80	Wimbledon	Trainee	Colchester U	—	—
Sale Mark	6 5	14 09	F	27 2 72	Burton-on-Trent	Trainee	Stoke C	2	—
							Cambridge U	—	—
							Birmingham C	21	—
							Torquay U	44	8
							Preston NE	13	7
							Mansfield T	45	12
							Colchester U	80	12
							Plymouth Arg (loan)	8	1
Skelton Aaron#	6 0	12 08	M	22 11 74	Welwyn	Trainee	Luton T	8	—
							Colchester U	48	7
Stamps Scott*	5 11	11 09	D	20 3 75	Edgbaston	Trainee	Torquay U	86	5
							Colchester U	56	1
Walker Andy‡			G	30 9 81	Bexley		Colchester U	1	—
Wiles Ian	6 0	11 13	D	28 4 80	Epping	Trainee	Colchester U	1	—
Wilkins Richard	6 0	12 04	M	25 5 65	Streatham	Haverhill R	Colchester U	152	22
							Cambridge U	81	7
							Hereford U	77	5
							Colchester U	103	9
Williams Geraint#	5 8	13 00	M	5 1 62	Cwmpare	Apprentice	Bristol R	141	8
							Derby Co	277	9
							Ipswich T	217	3
							Colchester U	39	—

Trainees
Burch, Michael; Gallant, Paul K; Grace, Daniel J; Taylor, Andrew D; Watkins, John; Willis, David A

Scholars
Delaney, Paul M; Gyoury, Nicky D; Heighway, Gregg; Hillier, Sean E; Okafor, Samuel A; Opara, Kelechi C; Taylor, Andrew C; Walker, Andrew W; Warriner, Mark J; Wignall, Jack D

Associated Schoolboys
Hearn, Matthew J; Morgan, Dean; Swindells, Adam C

COVENTRY CITY

Name	Ht	Wt	Pos	Born	Birthplace	Source	Club	Apps	Gls
Aloisi John	6 1	12 06	F	5 2 76	Adelaide		Cremonese	26	2
							Portsmouth	60	25
							Coventry C	16	5
Barnett Christopher	5 11	12 00	M	20 12 78	Derby	Trainee	Coventry C	—	—
Betts Robert	5 10	11 00	M	21 12 81	Doncaster	School	Doncaster R	3	—
							Coventry C	—	—
Boateng George	5 9	10 12	M	5 9 75	Nkawkaw		Excelsior	9	—
							Feyenoord	68	1
							Coventry C	47	5
Boland Willie	5 9	11 02	M	6 8 75	Ennis	Trainee	Coventry C	63	—
Breen Gary	6 1	11 12	D	12 12 73	London	Charlton Ath	Maidstone U	19	—
							Gillingham	51	—
							Peterborough U	69	1
							Birmingham C	40	2
							Coventry C	64	1
Brightwell Ian	5 9	12 05	M	9 4 68	Lutterworth	Congleton T	Manchester C	321	18
							Coventry C	—	—
Burrows David	5 8	11 08	D	25 10 68	Dudley	Apprentice	WBA	46	1
							Liverpool	146	3
							West Ham U	29	1
							Everton	19	—
							Coventry C	96	—
Burrows Mark	6 3	12 08	D	14 8 80	Kettering	Trainee	Coventry C	—	—
Clement Philippe	6 2	13 00	M	22 3 74	Antwerp		Genk	53	2
							Coventry C	12	—
Colwell Richard	5 9	11 02	D	2 9 79	Wordsley	Trainee	Coventry C	—	—
Daish Liam*	6 2	13 05	D	23 9 68	Portsmouth	Apprentice	Portsmouth	1	—
							Cambridge U	139	4
							Birmingham C	73	3
							Coventry C	31	2
Delorge Laurent	5 10	11 12	M	21 7 79	Leuven	Gent	Coventry C	—	—
Devaney Martin*	5 10	11 12	M	1 6 80	Cheltenham	Trainee	Coventry C	—	—
Donlevy Andrew‡	5 11	10 12	D	13 4 81	Hong Kong	Trainee	Coventry C	—	—
Doyle Daire	5 10	11 06	M	18 10 80	Dublin	Cherry Orchard	Coventry C	—	—
Ducros Andrew*	5 6	9 08	F	16 9 77	Evesham	Trainee	Coventry C	8	—
Edworthy Marc	5 11	10 03	D	24 12 72	Barnstaple	Trainee	Plymouth Arg	69	1
							Crystal Palace	126	—
							Coventry C	22	—
Eribenne Chukkie	5 10	11 12	F	2 11 80	London	Trainee	Coventry C	—	—
Eustace John	5 11	11 12	M	3 11 79	Solihull	Trainee	Coventry C	—	—
(On loan to Dundee U, February 1999)							Dundee U	11	1
Faulconbridge Craig	6 1	13 00	F	20 4 78	Nuneaton	Trainee	Coventry C	—	—
							Dunfermline Ath	13	1
							Coventry C	—	—
							Hull C (loan)	10	—

Name	Ht	Wt	Pos	Born	Birthplace	Source	Clubs	Apps	Gls
Ferguson Barry	6 3	13 00	D	7 9 79	Dublin	Home Farm	Coventry C	—	—
Froggatt Steve	5 11	11 00	F	9 3 73	Lincoln	Trainee	Aston Villa	35	2
							Wolverhampton W	106	7
							Coventry C	23	1
Gioacchini Stefano			F	25 11 76	Rome		Perugia	5	—
(On loan from Venezia)							Cosenza	43	3
							Venezia	21	1
							Coventry C	3	—
Grant Martin			M	16 1 82	Kirkcaldy	Trainee	Coventry C	—	—
Hall Daniel			M	29 12 81	Rugby	Trainee	Coventry C	—	—
Hall Marcus	6 1	12 02	D	24 3 76	Coventry	Trainee	Coventry C	73	1
Hall Paul	5 8	10 02	F	3 7 72	Manchester	Trainee	Torquay U	93	1
							Portsmouth	188	37
							Coventry C	9	—
							Bury (loan)	7	—
Hedman Magnus	6 3	14 00	G	19 3 73	Stockholm		AIK Stockholm	127	—
							Coventry C	50	—
Huckerby Darren	5 11	11 04	F	23 4 76	Nottingham	Trainee	Lincoln C	28	5
							Newcastle U	1	—
							Millwall (loan)	6	3
							Coventry C	93	28
Johansen Martin‡	5 8	11 01	M	22 7 72	Glostrup		KB Copenhagen	20	4
							B1903	25	8
							FC Copenhagen	116	31
							Coventry C	2	—
Kirkland Christopher	6 3	11 07	G	2 5 81	Leicester	Trainee	Coventry C	—	—
Konjic Muhamed	6 3	13 00	D	14 5 70	Tulsa		Tuzla	8	—
							Belisce	18	—
							Zagreb	63	5
							Zurich	36	5
							Monaco	37	2
							Coventry C	4	—
McAllister Gary	6 1	11 11	M	25 12 64	Motherwell	Fir Park BC	Motherwell	59	6
							Leicester C	201	47
							Leeds U	231	31
							Coventry C	81	9
McPhee Gary	6 0	12 00	F	18 4 80	Glasgow		Coventry C	—	—
McPhee Stephen	5 7	10 08	M	5 6 81	Glasgow		Coventry C	—	—
McSheffrey Gary§			F	13 8 81	Coventry	Trainee	Coventry C	1	—
Miller Robert*	5 8	11 00	M	28 3 80	Bedford	West Ham U	Coventry C	—	—
Moldovan Viorel	5 9	11 08	F	8 7 72	Bistrita		Gloria	84	22
(Transferred to Fenerbahce, July 1998)							Dynamo Bucharest	60	19
							Neuchatel Xamax	32	19
							Grasshoppers	51	44
							Coventry C	10	1
Mooney Gerard	5 9	11 00	D	28 8 80	Glasgow	Trainee	Coventry C	—	—
Nilsson Roland*	5 10	11 10	D	27 11 63	Helsingborg		Helsingborg	38	3
							IFK Gothenburg	124	7
							Sheffield W	151	2
							Helsingborg	64	6
							Coventry C	60	—
Ogrizovic Steve*	6 3	15 00	G	12 9 57	Mansfield	ONRYC	Chesterfield	16	—
							Liverpool	4	—
							Shrewsbury T	84	—
							Coventry C	504	1
Pead Craig	5 9	11 06	M	15 9 81	Bromsgrove	Trainee	Coventry C	—	—
Prenderville Barry	6 0	12 08	D	16 10 76	Dublin	Trainee	Coventry C	—	—
							Hibernian (loan)	13	2
Quinn Barry	6 0	12 02	M	9 5 79	Dublin	Trainee	Coventry C	7	—
Scope Tynan*	6 2	13 09	G	30 7 79	Sydney		Coventry C	—	—
Shaw Richard	5 9	12 08	D	11 9 68	Brentford	Apprentice	Crystal Palace	207	3
							Hull C (loan)	4	—
							Coventry C	126	—
Shilton Sam	5 11	11 06	M	21 7 78	Nottingham	Schoolboy	Plymouth Arg	3	—
							Coventry C	7	—
Soltvedt Trond Egil	6 1	12 08	M	15 2 67	Voss		Viking	65	10
							Brann	64	34
							Rosenborg	60	18
							Coventry C	57	3
Strachan Gavin	5 10	11 07	M	23 12 78	Aberdeen	Trainee	Coventry C	9	—
							Dundee (loan)	6	—
Telfer Paul	5 9	11 06	M	21 10 71	Edinburgh	Trainee	Luton T	144	19
							Coventry C	130	6
Wallemme Jean-Guy	6 0	13 00	D	10 8 67	Naubeuge		Lens	378	12
(Transferred to Sochaux, January 1999)							Coventry C	6	—
Whelan Noel	6 2	12 03	F	30 12 74	Leeds	Trainee	Leeds U	48	7
							Coventry C	108	30
Williams Jamie‡	5 9	12 00	D	3 1 80	Bedworth	Trainee	Coventry C	—	—
Williams Paul	5 11	12 10	D	26 3 71	Burton	Trainee	Derby Co	160	26
							Lincoln C (loan)	3	—
							Coventry C	106	4

Trainees/Scholars
Castro-Pearson, David; Cudworth, Thomas J S; Ford, Brian; Graham, Mark A; Lewis, David M J; McSheffrey, Gary; Mehmet, Adam; Muir, Richard A D; Parkinson, Simon A; Strachan, Craig; Thompson, Nathan

CREWE ALEXANDRA

Name							Club	Apps	Goals
Anthrobus Steve*	6 2	12 06	F	10 11 68	Lewisham		Millwall	21	4
							Southend U (loan)	—	—
							Wimbledon	28	—
							Peterborough U (loan)	2	—
							Chester C (loan)	7	—
							Shrewsbury T	72	16
							Crewe Alex	61	9
Bignot Marcus	5 9	11 00	D	28 8 74	Birmingham	Kidderminster H	Crewe Alex	68	—
Chadwick Gareth*			M	23 9 79	Warrington	Trainee	Crewe Alex	—	—
Charnock Phil	5 10	11 03	M	14 2 75	Southport	Trainee	Liverpool	—	—
							Blackpool (loan)	4	—
							Crewe Alex	109	6
Collins James	5 8	10 00	M	28 5 78	Liverpool	Trainee	Crewe Alex	7	1
Critchley Neil			M	18 10 78	Crewe	Trainee	Crewe Alex	—	—
Foran Mark	6 3	13 04	D	30 10 73	Aldershot	Trainee	Millwall	—	—
							Sheffield U	11	1
							Rotherham U (loan)	3	—
							Wycombe W (loan)	5	—
							Peterborough U	25	1
							Lincoln C (loan)	2	—
							Oldham Ath (loan)	1	—
							Crewe Alex	18	1
Foster Stephen	5 11	11 00	D	10 9 80	Warrington	Trainee	Crewe Alex	1	—
Hulse Robert			M	25 10 79	Crewe	Trainee	Crewe Alex	—	—
Jack Rodney	5 7	10 07	F	28 9 72	Kingston, Jamaica	Lambada	Torquay U	87	24
							Crewe Alex	39	9
Johnson Seth	5 10	11 00	M	12 3 79	Birmingham	Trainee	Crewe Alex	93	6
Kearton Jason	6 1	12 03	G	9 7 69	Ipswich (Aus)	Brisbane Lions	Everton	6	—
							Stoke C (loan)	16	—
							Blackpool (loan)	14	—
							Notts Co (loan)	10	—
							Preston NE (loan)	—	—
							Crewe Alex	119	—
Lightfoot Chris#	6 1	12 00	D	1 4 70	Penketh	Trainee	Chester C	277	32
							Wigan Ath	14	1
							Crewe Alex	66	3
Little Colin	5 10	11 00	F	4 11 72	Wythenshaw	Hyde U	Crewe Alex	106	24
Lovelock Andrew*	6 0	12 08	F	20 12 76	Swindon	Trainee	Coventry C	—	—
						Southam U	Crewe Alex	—	—
Lunt Kenny	5 10	10 00	M	20 11 79	Runcorn	Trainee	Crewe Alex	59	3
Macauley Steve	6 1	12 03	D	4 3 69	Lytham	Fleetwood T	Crewe Alex	185	21
Morse Peter*			M	5 3 79	Stoke	Trainee	Crewe Alex	—	—
Newell Mike‡	6 0	13 00	F	27 1 65	Liverpool	Liverpool	Crewe Alex	3	—
							Wigan Ath	72	25
							Luton T	63	18
							Leicester C	81	21
							Everton	68	15
							Blackburn R	130	28
							Birmingham C	15	1
							West Ham U (loan)	7	—
							Bradford C (loan)	7	—
							Aberdeen	44	6
							Crewe Alex	4	—
Norris Richard*			M	5 1 78	Birkenhead	Marine	Crewe Alex	—	—
Pemberton John‡	5 11	11 09	D	18 11 64	Oldham	Chadderton	Rochdale	1	—
							Crewe Alex	121	1
							Crystal Palace	78	2
							Sheffield U	68	—
							Leeds U	53	—
							Crewe Alex	1	—
Rivers Mark	5 10	11 00	F	26 11 75	Crewe	Trainee	Crewe Alex	138	29
Smith Peter	5 10	10 00	F	15 9 78	Rhuddlan	Trainee	Crewe Alex	11	—
							Macclesfield T (loan)	12	3
Smith Shaun	5 10	11 00	D	9 4 71	Leeds	Trainee	Halifax T	7	—
							Crewe Alex	284	34
Street Kevin	5 10	10 08	M	25 11 77	Crewe	Trainee	Crewe Alex	55	6
Unsworth Lee	5 11	11 02	D	25 2 73	Eccles	Ashton U	Crewe Alex	118	—
Walton David	6 2	14 07	D	10 4 73	Bellingham	Trainee	Sheffield U	—	—
							Shrewsbury T	128	10
							Crewe Alex	65	1
Webster Colin*			M	10 9 79	Chester	Trainee	Crewe Alex	—	—
Welsby Kevin	6 0	10 06	G	27 8 80	Crewe	Trainee	Crewe Alex	—	—
Whittaker David*			M	13 8 78	Stockport	Trainee	Crewe Alex	—	—
Williamson Michael‡			M	29 12 78	Liverpool	Trainee	Crewe Alex	—	—
Wright David	5 11	10 09	D	1 5 80	Warrington	Trainee	Crewe Alex	23	1
Wright Jermaine	5 10	11 09	M	21 10 75	Greenwich	Trainee	Millwall	—	—
							Wolverhampton W	20	—
							Doncaster R (loan)	13	—
							Crewe Alex	49	5

Trainees
Arrowsmith, Paul; Beeston, Mark A; Grant, John A C; Hoult, Stephen R; Laurie, Carl A; Walker, Richard S

Scholars
Baylis, Philip; Blake, Mathew L; Bostock, Andrew M; Harris, Paul J; Liddle, Gareth J C; Lunt, Gary T; Marrow, James F J; Marsh, Nicholas J; McCready, Christopher J; Swiggs, Craig B; Whiting, Louie A

Associated Schoolboys
Ashton, Dean; Bell, Lee; Betts, Thomas G; Booth, Martin T; Davies, Clark W; Eaton, George; Edwards, Paul; Frost, Carl R; Hall, Simon G; Higdon, Michael; Jeffs, Ian D; Jenkins, Byron K; Johnson, Mark E; Jones, Robert A; Malbon, Craig D; Malpass, John; Mead, John M; Morris, Alexander S; Platt, Matthew; Rix, Benjamin; Roberts, Mark A; Robinson, James G; Spooner, Mark S; Vaughan, David O; Westwood, Lee K; Wilcock, James W; Yates, Adam P

CRYSTAL PALACE

Name	Ht	Wt	Pos	DOB	Birthplace	From	Clubs	Apps	Gls
Amsalem David	6 1	12 01	D	4 9 71	Israel		Hapoel Tel Aviv	27	4
							Beitar Jerusalem	85	5
							Crystal Palace	10	—
Austin Dean	5 11	11 11	D	26 4 70	Hemel Hempstead	St. Albans C	Southend U	96	2
							Tottenham H	124	—
							Crystal Palace	20	1
Bradbury Lee	6 2	13 10	F	3 7 75	Isle of Wight	Cowes	Portsmouth	54	15
							Exeter C (loan)	14	5
							Manchester C	40	10
							Crystal Palace	22	4
							Birmingham C (loan)	7	—
Burton Sagi	6 2	13 06	D	25 11 77	Birmingham	Trainee	Crystal Palace	25	1
Carlisle Wayne	6 0	11 06	M	9 9 79	Lisburn	Trainee	Crystal Palace	6	—
Cook Aaron*	6 0	11 10	D	6 12 79	Caerphilly	Trainee	Portsmouth	1	—
							Crystal Palace	—	—
Curcic Sasa	5 9	11 00	M	14 2 72	Belgrade		OFK Belgrade	49	5
							Partizan Belgrade	74	16
							Bolton W	28	4
							Aston Villa	29	—
							Crystal Palace	23	5
Del Rio Walter	6 0	12 06	D	16 6 76	Buenos Aires	Boca Juniors	Crystal Palace	2	—
Digby Fraser	6 1	12 12	G	23 4 67	Sheffield	Apprentice	Manchester U	—	—
							Oldham Ath (loan)	—	—
							Swindon T (loan)	—	—
							Swindon T	417	—
							Manchester U (loan)	—	—
							Crystal Palace	18	—
Evans Stephen	5 11	11 02	M	25 9 80	Caerphilly	Trainee	Crystal Palace	4	—
Foster Craig	5 11	12 00	M	15 4 69	Melbourne	Marconi	Portsmouth	16	2
							Crystal Palace	32	2
Frampton Andrew	5 11	10 10	D	3 9 79	Wimbledon	Trainee	Crystal Palace	6	—
Fullarton Jamie	5 9	10 09	M	20 7 74	Bellshill		St Mirren	102	3
							Bastia	17	—
							Crystal Palace	32	1
							Bolton W (loan)	1	—
Graham Gareth	5 7	10 02	M	6 12 78	Belfast	Trainee	Crystal Palace	1	—
Gregg Matt	5 11	12 00	G	30 11 78	Cheltenham	Trainee	Torquay U	32	—
							Crystal Palace	—	—
							Swansea C (loan)	5	—
Harries Paul*	6 1	13 00	F	19 11 77	Sydney	NSWSF	Portsmouth	1	—
							Crystal Palace	—	—
							Torquay U (loan)	5	—
Harris Richard	5 11	10 09	D	23 10 80	Croydon	Trainee	Crystal Palace	1	—
Hibburt James	6 0	12 08	D	30 10 79	Ashford	Trainee	Crystal Palace	2	—
Ismael Valerien‡	6 2	13 01	D	28 9 75	Strasbourg		Strasbourg	85	1
							Crystal Palace	13	—
Jihai Sun	5 10	10 07	D	30 9 77	Dalian	Dalian Wanda	Crystal Palace	23	—
Kendall Lee	5 10	10 05	G	8 1 81	Newport	Trainee	Crystal Palace	—	—
Linighan Andy	6 4	13 10	D	18 6 62	Hartlepool	Smiths BC	Hartlepool U	110	4
							Leeds U	66	3
							Oldham Ath	87	6
							Norwich C	86	8
							Arsenal	118	5
							Crystal Palace	65	2
							QPR (loan)	7	—
Lombardo Attilio	5 11	11 07	M	6 1 66	St. Maria La Fossa		Pergocrema	38	9
(Transferred to Lazio, January 1999)							Cremonese	141	17
							Sampdoria	201	34
							Juventus	35	2
							Crystal Palace	43	8
Loughran Kieran*	5 10	10 05	M	26 8 80	Ballymena	Trainee	Crystal Palace	—	—
Martin Andrew	6 0	10 12	F	28 2 80	Cardiff	Trainee	Crystal Palace	3	—
McKenzie Leon	5 10	10 03	F	17 5 78	Croydon	Trainee	Crystal Palace	52	3
							Fulham (loan)	3	—
							Peterborough U (loan)	14	8
Miller Kevin	6 1	13 00	G	15 3 69	Falmouth	Newquay	Exeter C	163	—
							Birmingham C	24	—
							Watford	128	—
							Crystal Palace	66	—

Name	Ht	Wt	Pos	Date of Birth	Birthplace	Signed from	Clubs	Apps	Gls
Moore Craig	6 1	12 00	D	12 12 75	Canterbury, Australia		Rangers	74	5
(Transferred to Rangers, March 1999)							Crystal Palace	23	3
Morrison Clinton	6 1	11 02	F	14 5 79	Tooting	Trainee	Crystal Palace	38	13
Mullins Hayden	6 0	11 12	M	27 3 79	Reading	Trainee	Crystal Palace	40	5
Ormshaw Gareth	6 0	12 10	G	8 7 79	Durban	Ramblers	Crystal Palace	—	—
Padovano Michele	5 10	11 00	F	28 8 66	Turin		Asti	24	5
(Transferred to Metz, October 1998)							Cosenza	103	25
							Pisa	30	11
							Napoli	27	7
							Genoa	27	9
							Reggiana	29	10
							Genoa	2	—
							Reggiana	19	7
							Juventus	42	12
							Crystal Palace	12	1
Petric Gordan	6 1	12 03	D	30 7 69	Belgrade		Dundee U	60	3
							Rangers	65	3
							Crystal Palace	18	1
Rizzo Nicky	5 10	12 00	M	9 6 79	Sydney	Sydney Olympic	Liverpool	—	—
							Crystal Palace	19	1
Rodger Simon#	5 9	11 09	M	3 10 71	Shoreham	Trainee	Crystal Palace	173	8
							Manchester C (loan)	8	1
							Stoke C (loan)	5	—
Sharpling Christopher			F	21 4 81	Bromley	Trainee	Crystal Palace	—	—
Smith Jamie	5 8	11 02	D	17 9 74	Birmingham	Trainee	Wolverhampton W	87	—
							Crystal Palace	44	—
							Fulham (loan)	9	1
Svensson Mathias	6 0	12 06	F	24 9 74	Boras		Elfsborg	22	15
							Portsmouth	45	10
						Tirol	Crystal Palace	8	1
Thomson Steve	5 8	10 04	M	23 1 78	Glasgow	Trainee	Crystal Palace	16	—
Tuttle David	6 2	12 10	D	6 2 72	Reading	Trainee	Tottenham H	13	—
							Peterborough U (loan)	7	—
							Sheffield U	63	1
							Crystal Palace	80	5
							Charlton Ath (loan)	—	—
Woozley David	6 0	12 10	D	6 12 79	Berkshire	Trainee	Crystal Palace	7	—
Wright David*			M	24 11 79	Portsmouth	Portsmouth	Crystal Palace	—	—
Zhiyi Fan	6 0	12 01	M	22 1 70	Shanghai	Shanghai Shenhua	Crystal Palace	29	2

Trainees
Boardman, Jonathan G; Dsane, Roscoe; Fowler, Michael D; Hankin, Sean A; Hunt, Stephen; Kabba, Steven; Wilde, Bobby

Scholars
Gooding, Scott O; Jones, Adrian S; Leacock, Jamie H; Nicholas, Mark P; Walsh, Ronald M; Williams, Ryan

Associated Schoolboys
Allen-Page, Danny L; Awbery, Jason; Lock, Christopher; Tabb, Jay A

Associated Schoolboys who have accepted the Club's offer of a Traineeship/Scholarship/Contract
Dimond, Kristian; Elsegood, Christopher J; Hunt, David; Smith, Robert; Surey, Ben

DARLINGTON

Name	Ht	Wt	Pos	Date of Birth	Birthplace	Signed from	Clubs	Apps	Gls
Atkinson Brian#	5 10	12 10	M	19 1 71	Darlington	Trainee	Sunderland	141	4
							Carlisle U (loan)	2	—
							Darlington	105	6
Barnard Mark*	5 11	11 10	D	27 11 75	Sheffield	Trainee	Rotherham U	—	—
							Darlington	143	4
Bennett Gary	6 2	12 01	D	4 12 61	Manchester	Amateur	Manchester C	—	—
							Cardiff C	87	11
							Sunderland	369	23
							Carlisle U	26	5
							Scarborough	88	18
							Darlington	29	4
Brumwell Phil	5 8	11 00	M	8 8 75	Darlington	Trainee	Sunderland	—	—
							Darlington	138	1
Campbell Paul	6 1	11 00	M	29 1 80	Middlesbrough	Trainee	Darlington	15	2
Carruthers Martin	5 11	11 07	F	7 8 72	Nottingham	Trainee	Aston Villa	4	—
							Hull C (loan)	13	6
							Stoke C	91	13
							Peterborough U	67	21
							York C (loan)	6	—
							Darlington	11	2
Carter Michael§			F	13 11 80	Darlington	Trainee	Darlington	1	1
Costa Riccardo†	5 7	10 08	F	10 1 73	Lisbon		Darlington	3	—
Devos Jason	6 4	13 07	D	2 1 74	Ontario	Montreal Impact	Darlington	44	5
(Transferred to Dundee U, October 1999)							Dundee U	25	—
Dorner Mario	5 10	13 02	F	21 3 70	Baden	Modling	Motherwell	2	—
							Darlington	49	13

Name	Ht	Wt	Pos	Date	Birthplace	Source	Club	Apps	Gls
Duffield Peter	5 6	10 04	F	4 2 69	Middlesbrough		Middlesbrough	—	—
							Sheffield U	58	14
							Halifax T (loan)	12	6
							Rotherham U (loan)	17	4
							Blackpool (loan)	5	1
							Bournemouth (loan)	—	—
							Stockport Co (loan)	7	4
							Crewe Alex (loan)	2	—
							Hamilton A	72	39
							Airdrieonians	24	6
							Raith R	42	10
							Darlington	14	2
Ellison Lee*	5 11	12 06	F	13 1 73	Darlington	Trainee	Darlington	72	17
							Hartlepool U (loan)	4	1
							Leicester C	—	—
							Crewe Alex	4	2
							Hereford U	1	—
							Mansfield T	—	—
					Bishop Auckland		Darlington	28	3
Gabbiadini Marco	5 10	13 04	F	21 1 68	Nottingham	Apprentice	York C	60	14
							Sunderland	157	74
							Crystal Palace	15	5
							Derby Co	188	50
							Birmingham C (loan)	2	—
							Oxford U (loan)	5	1
							Stoke C	8	—
							York C	7	1
							Darlington	40	23
Gaughan Steve	5 11	11 04	M	14 4 70	Doncaster	Hatfield Main	Doncaster R	67	3
							Sunderland	—	—
							Darlington	171	15
							Chesterfield	20	—
							Darlington	47	3
Himsworth Gary	5 8	11 00	M	19 12 69	York	Trainee	York C	88	8
							Scarborough	92	6
							Darlington	94	8
							York C	69	3
							Darlington	14	1
Hunt David	5 10	12 00	D	5 3 80	Durham	Trainee	Darlington	1	
Kilty Mark§			M	24 6 81	Sunderland	Trainee	Darlington	2	—
Kubicki Dariusz†	5 10	12 05	D	6 6 63	Kozuchow	Legia Warsaw	Aston Villa	25	—
							Sunderland (loan)	15	—
							Sunderland	121	—
							Wolverhampton W	12	—
							Tranmere R (loan)	12	—
							Carlisle U	7	—
							Darlington	3	—
Leah John	5 9	12 00	M	3 8 78	Shrewsbury	Newtown	Darlington	7	1
Liddle Craig	5 11	12 07	D	21 10 71	Chester-le-Street	Blyth Spartans	Middlesbrough	25	—
							Darlington (loan)	15	—
							Darlington	44	3
Naylor Glenn#	5 10	11 10	F	11 8 72	York	Trainee	York C	111	30
							Darlington (loan)	4	1
							Darlington	121	28
Oliver Michael	5 10	11 04	M	2 8 75	Middlesbrough	Trainee	Middlesbrough	—	—
							Stockport Co	22	1
							Darlington	114	12
Pepper Carl	5 11	11 00	D	26 7 80	Darlington	Trainee	Darlington	6	—
Preece David	6 2	11 11	G	26 8 76	Sunderland	Trainee	Sunderland	—	—
							Darlington	91	—
Reed Adam	6 1	11 00	D	18 2 75	Bishop Auckland	Trainee	Darlington	52	1
							Blackburn R	—	—
							Darlington (loan)	14	—
							Rochdale (loan)	10	—
							Darlington	29	2
Samways Mark	6 2	14 01	G	11 11 68	Doncaster	Trainee	Doncaster R	121	—
							Scunthorpe U (loan)	8	—
							Scunthorpe U	172	—
							York C (loan)	—	—
							York C	29	—
							Darlington	—	—
Shutt Carl*	5 10	12 10	F	10 10 61	Sheffield	Spalding U	Sheffield W	40	16
							Bristol C	46	10
							Leeds U	79	17
							Birmingham C	26	4
							Manchester C (loan)	6	—
							Bradford C	88	15
							Darlington	53	9
Stephenson Ashlyn‡	6 2	11 05	G	6 7 74	Manchester		Birmingham C	—	—
							Darlington	1	—
Tutill Steve	5 10	12 06	D	1 10 69	Derwent	Trainee	York C	301	6
							Darlington	43	—

Trainees
Carter, Michael D; Keegan, Justin; Kilty, Mark T; Pomford, Paul J; Skelton, Craig E; Smith, Martin; Wells, David J

Scholars
Birrell, Adam P; Bowes, Michael G; Finch, Keith J; Jackson, Neil P; Liddle, Graham B; Scroggins, Lee P; Williamson, Garry

Non-Contract
Heckingbottom, Paul

Associated Schoolboys
Foster, Stephen M; Gordon, Steven M

Associated Schoolboys who have accepted the Club's offer of a Traineeship/Scholarship/Contract
Ellenden, John

DERBY COUNTY

Name	Ht	Wt	Pos	DOB	Birthplace	Source	Club	Apps	Gls
Baiano Francesco	5 6	10 07	F	24 2 68	Naples		Napoli	4	—
							Empoli	26	2
							Napoli	1	—
							Parma	25	4
							Empoli	38	14
							Avellino	32	6
							Foggia	69	38
							Fiorentina	118	29
							Derby Co	55	16
Bate Christopher*			M	30 1 81	Derby	Trainee	Derby Co	—	—
Beck Mikkel	6 1	13 05	F	4 5 73	Aarhus	Kolding	B 1909	13	2
							Fortuna Cologne	79	26
							Middlesbrough	91	24
							Derby Co	7	1
Boertien Paul	5 10	11 11	D	21 1 79	Carlisle	Trainee	Carlisle U	17	1
							Derby Co	1	—
Bohinen Lars	6 1	13 00	M	8 9 69	Vadso		Valerengen	33	5
							Viking	10	—
							Young Boys	58	6
							Nottingham F	64	7
							Blackburn R	58	7
							Derby Co	41	1
Borbokis Vassilis	5 9	12 02	D	10 2 69	Serres		Apollon	29	2
							AEK Athens	86	9
							Sheffield U	55	4
							Derby Co	4	—
Bridge-Wilkinson Marc	5 6	10 08	M	16 3 79	Nuneaton	Trainee	Derby Co	1	—
							Carlisle U (loan)	7	—
Burton Deon	5 9	11 10	F	25 10 76	Reading	Trainee	Portsmouth	62	10
							Cardiff C (loan)	5	2
							Derby Co	50	12
							Barnsley (loan)	3	—
Carbonari Horace Angel	6 3	13 02	D	2 5 73	Rosario	Rosario Central	Derby Co	29	5
Christie Malcolm	6 0	11 00	F	11 4 79	Peterborough	Nuneaton B	Derby Co	2	—
Delap Rory	6 0	13 00	D	6 7 76	Sutton Coldfield	Trainee	Carlisle U	65	7
							Derby Co	36	—
Doherty Gerard			M	24 8 81	Derry	Derry C	Derby Co	—	—
Dorigo Tony	5 9	11 03	D	31 12 65	Adelaide	Apprentice	Aston Villa	111	1
							Chelsea	146	11
							Leeds U	171	5
							Torino	30	2
							Derby Co	18	1
Elliott Steve	6 1	13 12	D	29 10 78	Derby	Trainee	Derby Co	14	—
Eranio Stefano	5 10	12 00	M	29 12 68	Genoa		Genoa	213	13
							AC Milan	98	6
							Derby Co	48	5
Evatt Ian			D	19 11 81	Coventry	Trainee	Derby Co	—	—
Harper Kevin	5 7	12 00	F	15 1 76	Oldham		Hibernian	96	15
							Derby Co	27	1
Hoult Russell	6 4	14 07	G	22 11 72	Ashby	Trainee	Leicester C	10	—
							Lincoln C (loan)	2	—
							Blackpool (loan)	—	—
							Bolton W (loan)	4	—
							Lincoln C (loan)	15	—
							Derby Co (loan)	15	—
							Derby Co	98	—
Hutchinson James*			M	24 3 80	Nottingham		Derby Co	—	—
Jackson Richard	5 9	9 07	D	18 4 80	Whitby	Trainee	Scarborough	22	—
							Derby Co	—	—
Knight Richard	6 1	14 00	G	3 8 79	Burton	Burton Alb	Derby Co	—	—
							Carlisle U (loan)	6	—
Launders Brian*	5 8	11 10	M	8 1 76	Dublin	Trainee	Crystal Palace	4	—
							Oldham Ath (loan)	—	—
							Crewe Alex	9	—
						Veendam	Derby Co	1	—
							Colchester U (loan)	1	—
Laursen Jacob	5 11	12 11	D	6 10 71	Vejle		Vejle	55	1
							Silkeborg	125	8
							Derby Co	101	2
Le Geyt Sinclair			M	10 7 80	Port Elizabeth		Derby Co	—	—
Lyons Michael			M	24 7 81	Derby	Trainee	Derby Co	—	—
McDonald Jamie*			M	29 1 80	Luton	Trainee	Derby Co	—	—

Name			Pos	Born	Birthplace	From	Club	Apps	Gls
Murphy Leroy‡			M	26 12 78	Birmingham	Trainee	Derby Co	—	—
Murray Adam	5 9	10 00	M	30 9 81	Birmingham	Trainee	Derby Co	4	—
Poom Mart	6 5	13 05	G	3 2 72	Tallinn		Flora Tallinn	22	—
						FC Wil	Portsmouth	4	—
							Flora Tallinn	7	—
							Portsmouth	—	—
							Flora Tallinn	12	—
							Derby Co	57	—
Porter Daniel			M	23 1 79	Portsmouth		Derby Co	—	—
Powell Darryl	6 0	13 00	M	15 11 71	Lambeth	Trainee	Portsmouth	132	16
							Derby Co	126	6
Prior Spencer	6 1	13 00	D	22 4 71	Rochford	Trainee	Southend U	135	3
							Norwich C	74	1
							Leicester C	64	—
							Derby Co	34	1
Radzki Lee‡			M	14 11 78	Mansfield	Trainee	Derby Co	—	—
Riggott Chris			D	1 9 80	Derby	Trainee	Derby Co	—	—
Robinson Marvin	5 11	12 09	F	11 4 80	Crewe	Trainee	Derby Co	1	—
Schnoor Stefan	6 1	12 04	D	24 4 71	Neumunster		Hamburg	131	8
							Derby Co	23	2
Sidhu Amrit			F	16 12 81	Coventry	Trainee	Derby Co	—	—
Solis Mauricio‡	5 8	12 00	M	13 12 72	Costa Rica	Herediano	Derby Co	11	—
Stimac Igor	6 2	13 00	D	6 9 67	Metkovic	Hajduk Split	Cadiz	62	4
							Hajduk Split	21	2
							Derby Co	84	3
Sturridge Dean	5 8	12 06	F	27 7 73	Birmingham	Trainee	Derby Co	151	46
							Torquay U (loan)	10	5
Wall James*			D	21 3 80	Carshalton	Trainee	Derby Co	—	—
Wanchope Paulo	6 3	12 05	F	31 7 76	Heredia	Herediano	Derby Co	72	23
Willems Ron‡	6 1	12 05	F	20 9 66	Epe		PEC Zwolle	43	7
							Twente	85	16
							Ajax	47	15
							Grasshoppers	56	18
							Derby Co	59	13

Trainees/Scholars
Betteridge, Thomas D; Brown, Karl E; Gummer, Sean M; Hanson, Craig P; Hunt, Lewis J; Morton, Colin; Phillips, Thomas G; Rickards, Scott

EVERTON

Name			Pos	Born	Birthplace	From	Club	Apps	Gls
Bakayoko Ibrahima			F	31 12 76	Seguela	Stade Abidjan	Montpellier	76	24
							Everton	23	4
Ball Michael	6 1	11 09	M	2 10 79	Liverpool	Trainee	Everton	67	4
Barmby Nick	5 6	11 04	F	11 2 74	Hull	Trainee	Tottenham H	87	20
							Middlesbrough	42	8
							Everton	79	9
Bilic Slaven	6 3	14 03	D	11 9 68	Split		Hajduk Split	109	13
							Karlsruhe	54	5
							West Ham U	48	2
							Everton	28	—
Branch Michael	5 10	11 07	F	18 10 78	Liverpool	Trainee	Everton	41	3
							Manchester C (loan)	4	—
Cadamarteri Danny	5 8	12 11	F	12 10 79	Bradford	Trainee	Everton	57	8
Campbell Kevin*	6 1	13 08	F	4 2 70	Lambeth	Trainee	Arsenal	166	46
							Leyton Orient (loan)	16	9
							Leicester C (loan)	11	5
							Nottingham F	80	32
							Trabzonspor	17	5
							Everton	8	9
Clarke Peter	6 0	12 00	D	3 1 82	Southport	Trainee	Everton	—	—
Cleland Alec	5 9	11 10	D	10 12 70	Glasgow		Dundee U	151	8
							Rangers	96	4
							Everton	18	—
Collins John	5 8	10 06	M	30 1 68	Galashiels		Hibernian	163	16
							Celtic	217	47
							Monaco	53	7
							Everton	20	1
Dacourt Olivier	5 9	11 00	M	25 9 74	Montreuil		Strasbourg	127	4
							Everton	30	2
Degn Peter	5 10	13 04	M	6 4 77	Denmark		Aarhus	76	5
							Everton	4	—
Delany Dean			G	15 9 80	Dublin		Everton	—	—
Dempsey Gary			M	15 1 81	Wexford	Trainee	Everton	—	—
Dunne Richard	6 2	15 10	D	21 9 79	Dublin	Trainee	Everton	26	—
Eaton Adam			D	2 5 80	Wigan	Trainee	Everton	—	—
Farley Adam			D	12 1 80	Liverpool	Trainee	Everton	1	—
Farrelly Gareth	6 1	13 07	M	28 8 75	Dublin	Home Farm	Aston Villa	8	—
							Rotherham U (loan)	10	2
							Everton	27	1
Gemmill Scot	5 11	11 06	M	2 1 71	Paisley	School	Nottingham F	245	21
							Everton	7	1

Name			Pos	Born	Birthplace	Source	Clubs	Apps	Goals
Gerrard Paul	6 2	14 04	G	22 1 73	Heywood	Trainee	Oldham Ath	119	1
							Everton	9	—
							Oxford U (loan)	16	—
Grant Tony	5 10	10 10	M	14 11 74	Liverpool	Trainee	Everton	59	2
							Swindon T (loan)	3	1
Hibbert Anthony	5 8	11 01	M	20 2 81	Liverpool	Trainee	Everton	—	—
Hutchison Don	6 2	12 04	M	9 5 71	Gateshead	Trainee	Hartlepool U	24	2
							Liverpool	45	7
							West Ham U	35	11
							Sheffield U	78	5
							Everton	44	4
Jeffers Francis	5 10	10 02	F	25 1 81	Liverpool	Trainee	Everton	16	6
Jevons Phillip	5 11	11 07	M	1 8 79	Liverpool	Trainee	Everton	1	—
Madar Mikael‡	6 1	13 01	F	8 5 68	Paris		Sochaux	46	6
							Cannes	54	26
							Monaco	52	14
							La Coruna	24	4
							Everton	19	6
Materazzi Marco	6 4	14 00	D	19 8 73	Perugia		Messina	—	—
						Tor di Quinto	Marsala	25	4
							Trapani	13	2
							Perugia	1	—
							Carpi	18	7
							Perugia	46	7
							Everton	27	1
McAlpine Joseph			D	12 9 81	Glasgow		Everton	—	—
McDermott Wayne*			M	30 10 79	Liverpool	Trainee	Everton	—	—
McKay Matthew	6 0	11 08	M	21 1 81	Warrington	Trainee	Chester C	5	—
							Everton	—	—
McLeod Kevin	5 11	11 00	M	12 9 80	Liverpool	Trainee	Everton	—	—
Milligan Jamie			F	3 1 80	Blackpool	Trainee	Everton	3	—
Myhre Thomas	6 2	13 00	G	16 10 73	Sarpsborg		Viking	94	—
							Everton	60	—
O'Brien Michael*			M	25 9 79	Liverpool	Trainee	Everton	—	—
O'Kane John	5 10	12 06	D	15 11 74	Nottingham	Trainee	Manchester U	2	—
							Wimbledon (loan)	—	—
							Bury (loan)	13	3
							Bradford C (loan)	7	—
							Everton	14	—
							Burnley (loan)	8	—
Osman Leon	5 8	9 11	M	17 5 81	Billinge	Trainee	Everton	—	—
Oster John	5 9	10 12	F	8 12 78	Boston	Trainee	Grimsby T	24	3
							Everton	40	1
Parkinson Joe	6 0	15 05	M	11 6 71	Eccles	Trainee	Wigan Ath	119	6
							Bournemouth	30	1
							Everton	90	3
Phelan Terry	5 8	10 04	D	16 3 67	Manchester	Trainee	Leeds U	14	—
							Swansea C	45	—
							Wimbledon	159	1
							Manchester C	103	1
							Chelsea	15	—
							Everton	24	—
Pilkington George	5 11	11 00	D	7 11 81	Rugeley	Trainee	Everton	—	—
Poppleton David*			M	19 12 79	Doncaster	Trainee	Everton	—	—
Regan Carl			D	9 9 80	Liverpool	Trainee	Everton	—	—
Short Craig	6 0	14 01	D	25 6 68	Bridlington	Pickering T	Scarborough	63	7
							Notts Co	128	6
							Derby Co	118	9
							Everton	99	4
Simonsen Steve	6 3	13 02	G	3 4 79	South Shields	Trainee	Tranmere R	35	—
							Everton	—	—
Southern Keith§			M	24 4 81	Gateshead	Trainee	Everton	—	—
Spencer John	5 6	11 11	F	11 9 70	Glasgow	Rangers BC	Rangers	13	2
(Transferred to Motherwell, October 1998)							Morton (loan)	4	1
							Chelsea	103	36
							QPR	48	22
							Everton	9	—
							Motherwell	21	7
Thomas Tony	5 11	13 00	D	12 7 71	Liverpool	Trainee	Tranmere R	257	12
(Transferred to Motherwell, December 1998)							Everton	8	—
							Motherwell	10	—
Tynan Robert‡	5 9	11 00	M	13 1 78	Birkenhead	Trainee	Everton	—	—
Unsworth Dave	6 0	15 00	D	16 10 73	Chorley	Trainee	Everton	116	11
							West Ham U	32	2
							Aston Villa	—	—
							Everton	34	1
Ward Mitch	5 8	11 13	M	19 6 71	Sheffield	Trainee	Sheffield U	154	11
							Crewe Alex (loan)	4	1
							Everton	14	—
Watson Dave	5 11	11 12	D	20 11 61	Liverpool	Amateur	Liverpool	—	—
							Norwich C	212	11
							Everton	417	23

	Ht	Wt	Pos	DOB	Birthplace	Source	Club	Apps	Gls
Weir David	6 2	13 07	D	10 5 70	Falkirk		Falkirk	133	8
							Hearts	92	8
							Everton	14	—
Williamson Danny	5 11	13 13	M	5 12 73	West Ham	Trainee	West Ham U	51	5
							Doncaster R (loan)	13	1
							Everton	15	—

Trainees/Scholars
Curran, Damien M; Eaton, David F; Hogg, Craig A; Howarth, Carl J; Kearney, Thomas J; Knowles, David J; Logan, Damian G; O'Brien, Edward; Price, Michael D; Southern, Keith W; Tuft, Kevin D; Valentine, Ryan D; Woodcock, Colin; Wright, John G

Non-Contract
Lester, John; Penman, Craig; Woods, Christopher C

EXETER CITY

	Ht	Wt	Pos	DOB	Birthplace	Source	Club	Apps	Gls
Baddeley Lee*	6 1	12 07	D	2 7 74	Cardiff	Trainee	Cardiff C	133	1
							Exeter C	66	1
Bayes Ashley*	6 1	13 05	G	19 4 72	Lincoln	Trainee	Brentford	4	—
							Torquay U	97	—
							Exeter C	127	—
Birch Paul‡	5 6	10 04	M	20 11 62	West Bromwich	Apprentice	Aston Villa	173	16
							Wolverhampton W	142	15
							Preston NE (loan)	11	2
							Doncaster R	27	2
							Exeter C	35	5
Blake Noel	6 2	14 02	D	12 1 62	Jamaica	Sutton Coldfield T	Aston Villa	4	—
							Shrewsbury T (loan)	6	—
							Birmingham C	76	5
							Portsmouth	144	10
							Leeds U	51	4
							Stoke C	75	3
							Bradford C (loan)	6	—
							Bradford C	39	3
							Dundee	54	2
							Exeter C	135	9
Breslan Geoff	5 9	10 02	M	4 6 80	Torbay	Trainee	Exeter C	35	4
Chesterfield Gavin‡	5 10	11 12	D	18 8 79	Neath	Trainee	Exeter C	—	—
Clark Billy*	6 0	12 03	M	19 5 67	Christchurch	Trainee	Bournemouth	4	—
							Bristol R	248	14
							Exeter C	41	3
Curran Chris	5 11	11 09	D	17 9 71	Birmingham	Trainee	Torquay U	152	4
							Plymouth Arg	30	—
							Exeter C	43	4
Flack Steve	6 1	11 04	F	29 5 71	Cambridge	Cambridge C	Cardiff C	11	1
							Exeter C	112	29
Fox Peter†	5 11	13 10	G	5 7 57	Scunthorpe	Apprentice	Sheffield W	49	—
							West Ham U (loan)	—	—
							Barnsley (loan)	1	—
							Stoke C	409	—
							Wrexham (loan)	—	—
							Exeter C	108	—
Fry Chris*	5 10	10 07	M	23 10 69	Cardiff	Trainee	Cardiff C	55	1
							Hereford U	90	10
							Colchester U	130	16
							Exeter C	60	3
Gale Shaun	6 1	12 02	D	8 10 69	Reading	Trainee	Portsmouth	3	—
							Barnet	114	5
							Exeter C	70	4
Gardner Jimmy*	5 11	11 08	M	27 9 67	Dunfermline	Ayresome North	Queen's Park	2	—
							Motherwell	16	—
							St Mirren	41	1
							Scarborough	6	1
							Cardiff C	63	5
							Exeter C	50	1
Gittens Jon	5 11	12 10	D	22 1 64	Moseley	Paget R	Southampton	18	—
							Swindon T	126	6
							Southampton	19	—
							Middlesbrough (loan)	12	1
							Middlesbrough	13	—
							Portsmouth	83	2
							Torquay U	78	9
							Exeter C	44	2
Harris Danny‡	5 11	11 07	D	18 12 79	Exeter	Trainee	Exeter C	—	—
Holloway Chris	5 10	11 10	M	5 2 80	Swansea	Trainee	Exeter C	40	1
MacDiarmid Philip†			M	17 6 80	Liverpool	Swindon T	Bristol C	—	—
							Exeter C	—	—
McConnell Barry	5 11	10 03	F	1 1 77	Exeter	Trainee	Exeter C	80	11
Potter Danny	5 11	13 00	G	18 3 79	Ipswich	Chelsea	Colchester U	—	—
							Exeter C	5	—
Power Graeme	5 11	10 10	D	7 3 77	Northwick Park	Trainee	QPR	—	—
							Bristol R	26	—
							Exeter C	40	—

Rees Jason	5 5	10 00	M	22 12 69	Aberdare	Trainee	Luton T	82	—
							Mansfield T (loan)	15	1
							Portsmouth	43	3
							Exeter C (loan)	7	—
							Cambridge U	20	—
							Exeter C	44	1
Richardson Jon	6 1	12 05	D	29 8 75	Nottingham	Trainee	Exeter C	212	7
Rowbotham Darren	5 10	12 13	F	22 10 66	Cardiff	Trainee	Plymouth Arg	46	2
							Exeter C	118	47
							Torquay U	14	3
							Birmingham C	36	6
							Hereford U (loan)	8	2
							Mansfield T (loan)	4	—
							Crewe Alex	61	21
							Shrewsbury T	40	9
							Exeter C	100	35
Smith Peter§			M	31 10 80	Skemsdale	Trainee	Exeter C	1	—
Speakman Robert§			D	5 12 80	Swansea	Trainee	Exeter C	1	—
Tosh Paul	6 0	11 10	F	18 10 73	Arbroath		Arbroath	42	13
							Dundee	106	19
							Hibernian	6	1
							Hibernain	16	1
							Exeter C (loan)	10	2
Vinnicombe Luke†	6 1	11 07	D	7 3 80	Paignton	Trainee	Exeter C	—	—
Walker Scott†	5 8	11 00	M	17 3 80	Exeter	Trainee	Exeter C	—	—
Waugh Warren§	6 0	12 02	F	9 10 80	Harlesden	Trainee	Exeter C	7	—
Wilkinson John	5 8	10 12	M	24 8 79	Exeter	Trainee	Exeter C	19	2

Trainees
Baines, Simon A; Butterworth, Adam L; Cooper, Michael E C; Cronin, Glenn; Hensor, Stephen J; Jee, Russell; Kent, Stephen; Parry, Ian; Pointing, Neil T; Smith, Peter E; Speakman, Robert; Watts, Shaun S; Waugh, Warren A

Non-Contract
Fox, Peter D; Stacey, Steven J; Stansfield, Adam; Vinnicombe, Luke

Associated Schoolboys
Ash, Jacob W H; Carpenter, Perry S; Clemoes, Joseph G; Conibere, Brett D; Hayes, Gary J; Hunt, Ben S; McDonough, Matthew F; Orchard, Jack F; Ovey, Simon F; Quigley, Dean C; Rampaul, Steven R; Schamroth, Daniel S; Wainwright, Thomas W

Associated Schoolboys who have accepted the Club's offer of a Traineeship/Scholarship/Contract
Breslan, Gavin A C; Casey, Ross E; Gross, Marcus J; Hallam, Robin S; Mudge, James R M

FULHAM

Arendse Andre	6 4	11 05	G	27 6 67	Cape Town	Cape Town S	Fulham	6	—
Betsy Kevin	6 1	11 12	F	20 3 78	Seychelles	Woking	Fulham	7	1
Blake Mark‡	6 0	12 06	D	17 12 67	Portsmouth	Apprentice	Southampton	18	2
							Colchester U (loan)	4	1
							Shrewsbury T (loan)	10	—
							Shrewsbury T	132	3
							Fulham	140	17
Bracewell Paul	5 9	12 03	M	19 7 62	Heswall	Apprentice	Stoke C	129	5
							Sunderland	38	4
							Everton	95	7
							Sunderland	113	2
							Newcastle U	73	3
							Sunderland	77	—
							Fulham	62	1
Brazier Matthew	5 8	11 08	M	2 7 76	Whipps Cross	Trainee	QPR	49	2
							Fulham	9	1
							Cardiff C (loan)	11	2
Brevett Rufus	5 8	11 08	D	24 9 69	Derby	Trainee	Doncaster R	109	3
							QPR	152	1
							Fulham	56	1
Brooker Paul	5 8	10 01	F	25 11 76	Hammersmith	Trainee	Fulham	56	4
Coleman Chris	6 2	14 04	D	10 6 70	Swansea	Apprentice	Swansea C	160	2
							Crystal Palace	154	13
							Blackburn R	28	—
							Fulham	71	5
Collins Wayne	6 0	11 07	M	4 3 69	Manchester	Winsford U	Crewe Alex	117	14
							Sheffield W	31	6
							Fulham	34	3
Cornwall Luke	5 11	11 00	F	23 7 80	Lambeth	Trainee	Fulham	4	1
							QPR (loan)	—	—
Davis Sean	5 11	12 09	M	20 9 79	Clapham	Trainee	Fulham	7	—
Finnan Steve	5 10	12 00	M	20 4 76	Limerick	Welling U	Birmingham C	15	1
							Notts Co (loan)	17	2
							Notts Co	80	5
							Fulham	22	2
Hayles Barry	5 9	13 00	F	17 4 72	London	Stevenage Bor	Bristol R	62	32
							Fulham	30	8
Hayward Steve	5 11	12 07	M	8 9 71	Walsall	Trainee	Derby Co	26	1
							Carlisle U	90	13
							Fulham	77	7

Name	Ht	Wt	Pos	DOB	Birthplace	Prev	Club	Apps	Gls
Horsfield Geoff	6 0	11 07	F	1 11 73	Barnsley		Scarborough	12	1
						Witton Alb	Halifax T	10	7
							Fulham	28	15
Hudson Mark			M	30 3 82	Guilford	Trainee	Fulham	—	—
Hutchinson Thomas			M	23 2 82	Kingston		Fulham	—	—
Keller Francois*	6 0	12 00	M	27 10 73	Colmar		Strasbourg	35	1
							Fulham	1	—
Knight Zatyiah			M	2 5 80	Solihull		Fulham	—	—
Lehmann Dirk*	6 0	11 06	F	16 8 71	Aachen	Energie Cottbus	Fulham	26	2
Maher Shaun‡	6 2	12 03	D	10 6 78	Dublin	Bohemians	Fulham	—	—
Marshall John†	5 10	12 04	D	18 8 64	Surrey	Apprentice	Fulham	411	28
McAnespie Steve	5 9	10 08	D	1 2 72	Kilmarnock	Vasterhauringe	Raith R	40	—
							Bolton W	24	—
							Fulham	7	—
							Bradford C (loan)	7	—
McAree Rod‡	5 7	11 00	M	10 8 74	Dungannon	Trainee	Liverpool	—	—
							Bristol C	6	—
							Fulham	28	3
McGuckin Ian	6 2	14 02	D	24 4 73	Middlesbrough	Trainee	Hartlepool U	152	8
							Fulham	—	—
							Hartlepool U (loan)	8	—
Moody Paul	6 3	14 08	F	13 6 67	Portsmouth	Waterlooville	Southampton	12	—
							Reading (loan)	5	1
							Oxford U	136	49
							Fulham	40	19
Morgan Simon	5 10	12 05	D	5 9 66	Birmingham	Trainee	Leicester C	160	3
							Fulham	324	48
Neilson Alan	5 11	12 08	D	26 9 72	Wegburg	Trainee	Newcastle U	42	1
							Southampton	55	—
							Fulham	21	1
Palmer Ryan*	6 1	11 02	D	2 2 80	Dulwich	Trainee	Fulham	—	—
Peschisolido Paul	5 7	11 02	F	25 5 71	Canada	Toronto Blizzard	Birmingham C	43	16
							Stoke C	66	19
							Birmingham C	9	1
							WBA	45	18
							Fulham	65	20
Salako John	5 9	11 10	F	11 2 69	Nigeria	Trainee	Crystal Palace	215	22
							Swansea C (loan)	13	3
							Coventry C	72	4
							Bolton W	7	—
							Fulham	10	1
Selley Ian	5 9	11 05	M	14 6 74	Chertsey	Trainee	Arsenal	41	—
							Southend U (loan)	4	—
							Fulham	3	—
Smith Neil	5 8	12 02	M	30 9 71	Lambeth	Trainee	Tottenham H	—	—
							Gillingham	212	10
							Fulham	73	1
Symons Kit	6 1	13 07	D	8 3 71	Basingstoke	Trainee	Portsmouth	161	10
							Manchester C	124	4
							Fulham	45	11
Taylor Maik	6 3	13 09	G	4 9 71	Hildeshein	Farnborough T	Barnet	70	—
							Southampton	18	—
							Fulham	74	—
Trollope Paul	6 0	12 01	M	3 6 72	Swindon	Trainee	Swindon T	—	—
							Torquay U (loan)	10	—
							Torquay U	96	16
							Derby Co	65	5
							Grimsby T (loan)	7	1
							Crystal Palace (loan)	9	—
							Fulham	44	5
Uhlenbeek Gus	5 10	12 06	M	20 8 70	Paramaribo		Ajax	2	—
							Cambuur	39	—
							TOPS SV	22	3
							Ipswich T	89	4
							Fulham	23	1

Trainees
Hammond, Elvis Z; Keevil, Sam A; Tucker, Anthony

Scholars
Browning, Robert; Clark, Darren; Hunter, Jermaine A; Johnson, Michael; Lampton, Neil J; McCracken, Gary W; Pomroy, John S; Rafis, Daniel; Read, Paul; Upsher, Tom P; Yhdego, Esayes Y

Non-Contract
Marshall, John P

GILLINGHAM

Name	Ht	Wt	Pos	DOB	Birthplace	Prev	Club	Apps	Gls
Asaba Carl	6 2	13 00	F	28 1 73	London	Dulwich Hamlet	Brentford	54	25
							Colchester U (loan)	12	2
							Reading	33	8
							Gillingham	41	20
Ashby Barry	6 2	13 08	D	2 11 70	London	Trainee	Watford	114	3
							Brentford	121	4
							Gillingham	81	1

Player	Ht	Wt	Pos	DOB	Birthplace	Source	Club	Apps	Gls
Bartram Vince	6 2	13 04	G	8 8 68	Birmingham	Local	Wolverhampton W	5	—
							Blackpool (loan)	9	—
							WBA (loan)	—	—
							Bournemouth	132	—
							Arsenal	11	—
							Wolverhampton W (loan)	—	—
							Huddersfield T (loan)	12	—
							Gillingham	53	—
Brown Kenny†	5 9	11 06	D	11 7 67	Upminster	Apprentice	Norwich C	25	—
							Plymouth Arg	126	4
							West Ham U	63	5
							Huddersfield T (loan)	5	—
							Reading (loan)	12	1
							Southend U (loan)	6	—
							Crystal Palace (loan)	6	2
							Reading (loan)	5	—
							Birmingham C	11	—
							Millwall	45	—
							Gillingham	4	—
Browning Marcus	6 0	12 10	M	22 4 71	Bristol	Trainee	Bristol R	174	13
							Hereford U (loan)	7	5
							Huddersfield T	33	—
							Gillingham	4	—
Bryant Matthew	6 1	13 01	D	21 9 70	Bristol	Trainee	Bristol C	203	7
							Walsall (loan)	13	—
							Gillingham	97	—
Butters Guy	6 3	13 12	D	30 10 69	Hillingdon	Trainee	Tottenham H	35	1
							Southend U (loan)	16	3
							Portsmouth	154	6
							Oxford U (loan)	3	1
							Gillingham	84	10
Carr Darren	6 2	13 07	D	4 9 68	Bristol	Trainee	Bristol R	30	—
							Newport Co	9	—
							Sheffield U	13	1
							Crewe Alex	104	5
							Chesterfield	86	4
							Gillingham	30	2
Edge Roland	5 10	11 10	D	25 11 78	Gillingham	Trainee	Gillingham	8	—
Galloway Mick	5 11	12 05	M	13 10 74	Nottingham	Trainee	Notts Co	21	—
							Gillingham (loan)	9	1
							Gillingham	64	4
Hessenthaler Andy	5 7	11 05	M	17 6 65	Gravesend	Redbridge Forest	Watford	195	11
							Gillingham	119	9
Hodge John	5 7	11 06	F	1 4 69	Skelmersdale	Exmouth	Exeter C	65	10
							Swansea C	112	10
							Walsall	76	12
							Gillingham	34	1
Masters Neil*	6 1	14 02	D	25 5 72	Lisburn	Trainee	Bournemouth	38	2
							Wolverhampton W	12	—
							Gillingham	11	—
Nosworthy Nayron	6 1	12 07	M	11 10 80	London	Trainee	Gillingham	3	—
O'Connor Mark‡	5 8	11 03	M	10 3 63	Rochdale	Apprentice	QPR	3	—
							Exeter C (loan)	38	1
							Bristol R	80	10
							Bournemouth	128	12
							Gillingham	116	8
							Bournemouth	58	3
							Gillingham	40	1
Osborne Tommy‡	5 8	11 00	M	5 9 79	Dartford	Trainee	Gillingham	—	—
Patterson Mark	5 9	12 04	D	13 9 68	Leeds	Trainee	Carlisle U	22	—
							Derby Co	51	3
							Plymouth Arg	134	3
							Gillingham	65	2
Pennock Adrian	6 1	13 05	M	27 3 71	Ipswich	Trainee	Norwich C	1	—
							Bournemouth	131	9
							Gillingham	86	2
Pinnock James	5 9	11 05	F	1 8 78	Dartford	Trainee	Gillingham	7	—
Ratcliffe Simon‡	6 0	12 13	M	6 2 67	Davyhulme	Apprentice	Manchester U	—	—
							Norwich C	9	—
							Brentford	214	14
							Gillingham	105	10
Saunders Mark	5 11	11 12	M	23 7 71	Reading	Tiverton	Plymouth Arg	72	11
							Gillingham	34	4
Smith Paul	5 11	12 08	M	18 9 71	East Ham	Trainee	Southend U	20	1
							Brentford	159	11
							Gillingham	91	9
Southall Nicky#	5 10	12 12	M	28 1 72	Middlesbrough	Trainee	Hartlepool U	138	24
							Grimsby T	72	5
							Gillingham	65	6
Stannard Jim#	6 2	16 00	G	16 10 62	London	Local	Fulham	41	—
							Charlton Ath (loan)	1	—
							Southend U (loan)	17	—
							Southend U	92	—
							Fulham	348	1
							Gillingham	106	—

Statham Brian	5 7	11 06	D	21 5 69	Zimbabwe	Apprentice	Tottenham H	24	—
							Reading (loan)	8	—
							Bournemouth (loan)	2	—
							Brentford (loan)	18	—
							Brentford	148	1
							Gillingham	20	—
Taylor Robert	6 1	13 08	F	30 4 71	Norwich	Trainee	Norwich C	—	—
							Leyton Orient (loan)	3	1
							Birmingham C	—	—
							Leyton Orient	73	20
							Brentford	173	56
							Gillingham	43	16

Trainees
Ampofo, Russell S; Austin, Simon; Carter, James F W; Chamberlain, Dean; Collis, Adam M; Morris, Dean; Neal, Jon; Sinclair, Barry; Spiller, Daniel; Watts, Luke; White, Ben

Non-Contract
Bremner, Kevin J; Scally, Paul D P

GRIMSBY TOWN

Ashcroft Lee	5 9	12 00	F	7 9 72	Preston	Trainee	Preston NE	91	13
							WBA	90	17
							Notts Co (loan)	6	—
							Preston NE	64	22
							Grimsby T	27	3
Black Kingsley	5 10	12 00	M	22 6 68	Luton	School	Luton T	127	26
							Nottingham F	98	14
							Sheffield U (loan)	11	2
							Millwall (loan)	3	1
							Grimsby T	105	6
Bloomer Matthew	6 0	12 00	D	3 11 78	Cleethorpes	Trainee	Grimsby T	4	—
Buckley Adam	5 9	11 00	M	2 8 79	Nottingham		Grimsby T	2	—
Burnett Wayne	5 10	12 00	M	4 9 71	Lambeth	Trainee	Leyton Orient	40	—
							Blackburn R	—	—
							Plymouth Arg	70	3
							Bolton W	2	—
							Huddersfield T	50	—
							Grimsby T	41	3
Butterfield Danny	5 9	11 00	D	21 11 79	Boston	Trainee	Grimsby T	19	—
Chapman Ben§	5 6	11 00	D	2 3 79	Scunthorpe	Trainee	Grimsby T	1	—
Clare Daryl	5 9	12 00	F	1 8 78	Jersey	Trainee	Grimsby T	45	6
Coldicott Stacy	5 8	12 00	M	29 4 74	Redditch	Trainee	WBA	104	3
							Cardiff C (loan)	6	—
							Grimsby T	37	—
Croudson Steve	6 0	12 00	G	14 9 79	Grimsby	Trainee	Grimsby T	2	—
Davison Aidan*	6 2	14 00	G	11 5 68	Sedgefield	Billingham Syn	Notts Co	1	—
							Leyton Orient (loan)	—	—
							Bury	—	—
							Chester C (loan)	—	—
							Blackpool (loan)	—	—
							Millwall	34	—
							Bolton W	37	—
							Ipswich T (loan)	—	—
							Hull C (loan)	9	—
							Bradford C	10	—
							Grimsby T	77	—
Dobbin Jim*	5 9	11 07	M	17 9 63	Dunfermline	Whitburn BC	Celtic	2	—
							Motherwell (loan)	2	—
							Doncaster R	64	13
							Barnsley	129	12
							Grimsby T	164	21
							Rotherham U	19	—
							Doncaster R	31	—
							Scarborough	1	—
							Grimsby T	6	—
Donovan Kevin	5 8	12 12	F	17 12 71	Halifax	Trainee	Huddersfield T	20	1
							Halifax T (loan)	6	—
							WBA	168	19
							Grimsby T	74	16
Gallimore Tony	5 11	13 00	D	21 2 72	Crewe	Trainee	Stoke C	11	—
							Carlisle U (loan)	16	—
							Carlisle U (loan)	8	1
							Carlisle U	116	8
							Grimsby T	130	4
Groves Paul	5 11	13 00	M	28 2 66	Derby	Burton Alb	Leicester C	16	1
							Lincoln C (loan)	8	1
							Blackpool	107	21
							Grimsby T	184	38
							WBA	29	4
							Grimsby T	92	21
Handyside Peter	6 1	13 03	D	31 7 74	Dumfries	Trainee	Grimsby T	171	3
Lester Jack	5 10	11 10	F	8 10 75	Sheffield	Trainee	Grimsby T	107	13
							Doncaster R (loan)	11	1
Lever Mark	6 3	14 00	D	29 3 70	Beverley	Trainee	Grimsby T	326	8

Livingstone Steve	6 1	14 00	F	8 9 68	Middlesbrough	Trainee	Coventry C	31	5
							Blackburn R	30	10
							Chelsea	1	—
							Port Vale (loan)	5	—
							Grimsby T	195	33
Love Andrew	6 1	14 00	G	28 3 79	Grimsby	Trainee	Grimsby T	12	—
McDermott John	5 7	11 02	D	3 2 69	Middlesbrough	Trainee	Grimsby T	411	7
McKenzie Mat	6 0	13 00	D	3 4 79	Sheffield	Dunkerque	Grimsby T	—	—
Nogan Lee#	5 8	11 04	F	21 5 69	Cardiff	Apprentice	Oxford U	64	10
							Brentford (loan)	11	2
							Southend U (loan)	6	1
							Watford	105	26
							Southend U (loan)	5	—
							Reading	91	26
							Notts Co (loan)	6	—
							Grimsby T	74	10
Oswin Matthew			M	2 10 79	Grimsby	Trainee	Grimsby T	—	—
Smith David	5 8	11 04	M	29 3 68	Stonehouse		Coventry C	154	19
							Bournemouth (loan)	1	—
							Birmingham C	38	3
							WBA	102	2
							Grimsby T	48	6
Smith Richard	6 0	13 07	D	3 10 70	Lutterworth	Trainee	Leicester C	98	1
							Cambridge U (loan)	4	—
							Grimsby T	62	—
Widdrington Tommy*	5 8	11 00	M	1 10 71	Newcastle	Trainee	Southampton	75	3
							Wigan Ath (loan)	6	—
							Grimsby T	89	8
							Port Vale (loan)	9	1

Trainees
Blake, Kirk A; Chapman, Ben; Cocksworth, Matthew R; Crew, Lee N; Darby, Stuart; Goodhand, Paul A; McPherson, Lee; Partner, Dean R; Pritchard, Gareth J; Rowan, Jonathan R; Steadman, Daniel M; Teanby, Jonathan H; Thompson, Mark S

Associated Schoolboys
Tatari, Yaman; Ward, Iain

Associated Schoolboys who have accepted the Club's offer of a Traineeship/Scholarship/Contract
Gibson, Thomas W; Smithson, Luke R

HALIFAX TOWN

Bradshaw Mark#	5 10	11 00	D	7 9 69	Ashton-under-Lyne		Blackpool	42	1
							York C (loan)	1	—
						Macclesfield T	Halifax T	41	4
Brown Jon*	5 11	11 03	M	8 9 66	Barnsley		Exeter C	164	3
							Halifax T	40	—
Butler Peter	5 9	11 01	M	27 8 66	Halifax	Apprentice	Huddersfield T	5	—
							Cambridge U (loan)	14	1
							Bury	11	—
							Cambridge U	55	9
							Southend U	142	9
							Huddersfield T (loan)	7	—
							West Ham U	70	3
							Notts Co	20	—
							Grimsby T (loan)	3	—
							WBA (loan)	9	—
							WBA	51	—
							Halifax T	33	1
Carter Tim*	6 2	12 08	G	5 10 67	Bristol	Apprentice	Bristol R	47	—
							Newport Co (loan)	1	—
							Carlisle U (loan)	4	—
							Sunderland	37	—
							Bristol C (loan)	3	—
							Birmingham C (loan)	2	—
							Hartlepool U	18	—
							Millwall	4	—
							Oxford U	12	—
							Millwall	62	—
							Halifax T	10	—
Duerden Ian‡	5 10	12 07	F	27 3 78	Burnley	Trainee	Burnley	1	—
							Halifax T	2	—
Hamlet Gareth*	6 0	13 06	F	10 1 80	Huddersfield	Trainee	Halifax T	—	—
Hanson Dave‡	6 0	13 07	F	19 11 68	Huddersfield	Farsley Celtic	Bury	1	—
						Hednesford T	Leyton Orient	48	5
							Chesterfield (loan)	3	1
							Halifax T	31	2
Hulme Kevin#	5 10	13 07	M	7 12 67	Farnworth		Bury	110	21
							Chester C (loan)	4	—
							Doncaster R	34	8
							Bury	29	—
							Lincoln C	5	—
						Macclesfield T	Halifax T	30	4
Jackson Justin	5 11	11 06	F	10 12 74	Nottingham	Woking	Notts Co	25	1
							Rotherham U (loan)	2	1
							Halifax T	16	4

Name							Club	Apps	Gls
Lucas Richard#	5 10	12 06	D	22 9 70	Chapeltown	Trainee	Sheffield U	10	—
							Preston NE	50	—
							Lincoln C (loan)	4	—
							Scarborough	116	—
							Hartlepool U	49	2
							Halifax T	36	—
Martin Lee*	6 0	13 00	G	9 9 68	Huddersfield	Trainee	Huddersfield T	54	—
							Blackpool	98	—
							Bradford C (loan)	—	—
							Rochdale	—	—
							Halifax T	37	—
Murphy Jamie	6 1	13 00	D	25 2 73	Manchester	Trainee	Blackpool	55	1
							Doncaster R	54	—
							Cambridge U	—	—
							Halifax T	23	1
Murphy Stephen	5 11	11 06	M	5 4 78	Dublin	Belvedere	Huddersfield T	—	—
							Halifax T	12	—
Newton Chris	6 0	11 02	M	5 11 79	Leeds	Huddersfield T	Halifax T	14	1
O'Regan Kieran	5 8	10 12	M	9 11 63	Cork		Brighton & HA	86	2
							Swindon T	26	1
							Huddersfield T	199	25
							WBA	25	2
							Halifax T	19	2
Paterson Jamie	5 3	10 02	M	26 4 73	Dumfries	Trainee	Halifax T	86	18
							Falkirk	4	—
							Scunthorpe U	55	2
							Halifax T	24	10
Place Damien‡	5 9	10 07	M	31 12 78	Halifax		Halifax T	—	—
Power Lee	6 0	11 10	F	30 6 72	Lewisham	Trainee	Norwich C	44	10
							Charlton Ath (loan)	5	—
							Sunderland (loan)	3	—
							Portsmouth (loan)	2	—
							Bradford C	30	5
							Millwall (loan)	—	—
							Peterborough U	38	6
							Hibernian	11	2
							Plymouth Arg	16	—
							Halifax T	18	4
Sertori Mark	6 2	14 02	D	1 9 67	Manchester		Stockport Co	4	—
							Lincoln C	50	9
							Wrexham	110	3
							Bury	13	1
							Scunthorpe U	83	2
							Halifax T	40	—
Stansfield James†	6 1	13 06	D	18 9 78	Dewsbury	Trainee	Huddersfield T	—	—
							Halifax T	12	1
Stoneman Paul	6 0	12 07	D	26 2 73	Whitley Bay		Blackpool	43	—
							Colchester U (loan)	3	1
							Halifax T	40	4
Thackeray Andy*	5 9	11 00	D	13 2 68	Huddersfield	School	Manchester C	—	—
							Huddersfield T	2	—
							Newport Co	54	4
							Wrexham	152	14
							Rochdale	165	13
							Halifax T	38	5
Wills David†	5 5	9 04	F	9 3 79	Manchester	Trainee	Manchester C	—	—
							Halifax T	—	—

Trainees
Ayscough, Martin L; Gradon, Christopher; Mitchell, Adam J

Scholars
Lawler, Alex; Liversidge, Gareth J; Moores, Andrew M; Speight, Simon; Tyrell-Nestor, James A; Underwood, Steven

Non-Contract
Stansfield, James E; Wills, David J

HARTLEPOOL UNITED

Name							Club	Apps	Gls
Baker Paul*	6 2	14 04	F	5 1 63	Newcastle	Bishop Auckland	Southampton	—	—
							Carlisle U	71	11
							Hartlepool U	197	67
							Motherwell	9	1
							Gillingham	62	16
							York C	48	18
							Torquay U	30	8
							Scunthorpe U	21	9
							Hartlepool U	35	9
Barron Michael	5 11	11 06	D	22 12 74	Lumley	Trainee	Middlesbrough	3	—
							Hartlepool U (loan)	16	—
							Hartlepool U	71	1

Name	Ht	Wt	Pos	DOB	Birthplace	From	Club	Apps	Gls
Beardsley Peter*	5 8	13 00	M	18 1 61	Newcastle	Wallsend BC	Carlisle U	104	22
						Vancouver Whitecaps	Manchester U	—	—
						Vancouver Whitecaps	Newcastle U	147	61
							Liverpool	131	46
							Everton	81	25
							Newcastle U	129	46
							Bolton W	17	2
							Manchester C (loan)	6	—
							Fulham (loan)	8	1
							Fulham (loan)	13	3
							Hartlepool U	22	2
Bradley Russell*	6 2	13 02	D	28 3 66	Birmingham	Dudley T	Nottingham F	—	—
							Hereford U (loan)	12	1
							Hereford U	77	3
							Halifax T	56	3
							Scunthorpe U	119	5
							Hartlepool U (loan)	12	1
							Hartlepool U	43	1
Briggs John	5 11	10 10	M	9 11 79	Stockton	Trainee	Hartlepool U	—	—
Brightwell Stuart*	5 5	11 01	M	31 1 79	Easington	Trainee	Manchester U	—	—
							Hartlepool U	17	1
Clark Ian	5 10	11 02	M	23 10 74	Stockton	Stockton	Doncaster R	45	3
							Hartlepool U	63	9
Di Lella Gus	5 9	11 09	M	6 10 73	Buenos Aires		Darlington	5	—
						Blyth S	Hartlepool U	28	4
Dibble Andy	6 3	16 10	G	8 5 65	Cwmbran	Apprentice	Cardiff C	62	—
							Luton T	30	—
							Sunderland (loan)	12	—
							Huddersfield T (loan)	5	—
							Manchester C	115	—
							Aberdeen (loan)	5	—
							Middlesbrough (loan)	19	—
							Bolton W (loan)	13	—
							WBA (loan)	9	—
							Oldham Ath (loan)	—	—
							Rangers	7	—
							Luton T	1	—
							Middlesbrough	2	—
						Altrincham	Hartlepool U	—	—
Downey Glen	6 1	12 07	D	20 9 78	Newcastle		Hartlepool U	—	—
Dunwell Michael	5 11	12 02	F	6 1 80	Stockton	Trainee	Hartlepool U	1	—
Evans Nicky	5 8	12 05	M	12 5 80	Carmarthen	Trainee	Hartlepool U	1	—
Freestone Chris	5 10	12 00	F	4 9 71	Nottingham	Arnold T	Middlesbrough	9	1
							Carlisle U (loan)	5	2
							Northampton T	57	13
							Hartlepool U	10	3
Halliday Stephen‡	5 10	12 07	F	3 5 76	Sunderland	Charlton Ath	Hartlepool U	140	25
							Motherwell	4	—
Hollund Martin	6 0	12 05	G	11 8 74	Stord		Brann	24	—
							Hartlepool U	69	—
Hughes Danny	5 10	13 00	M	13 2 80	Bangor	Trainee	Wolverhampton W	—	—
							Hartlepool U	8	—
Hutt Stephen*	6 2	12 00	M	19 2 79	Middlesbrough	Trainee	Hartlepool U	9	—
Ingram Denny	5 11	12 02	D	27 6 76	Sunderland	Trainee	Hartlepool U	192	10
Irvine Stuart*	5 9	11 07	F	1 3 79	Hartlepool	Trainee	Hartlepool U	31	2
Jones Gary	6 1	13 00	F	6 4 69	Huddersfield	Rossington Main	Doncaster R	20	2
						Boston U	Southend U	70	16
							Lincoln C (loan)	4	2
							Notts Co	117	38
							Scunthorpe U (loan)	11	5
							Hartlepool U	12	1
Knowles Darren	5 6	11 01	D	8 10 70	Sheffield	Trainee	Sheffield U	—	—
							Stockport Co	63	—
							Scarborough	144	2
							Hartlepool U	99	1
Lake Craig	5 11	10 02	D	10 2 80	Stockton	Trainee	Hartlepool U	—	—
Lee Graeme	6 2	13 00	D	31 5 78	Middlesbrough	Trainee	Hartlepool U	91	6
McDonald Chris‡	6 0	13 04	D	14 10 75	Edinburgh	Trainee	Arsenal	—	—
							Hartlepool U	20	—
McKinnon Rob	5 11	11 01	D	31 7 66	Glasgow	Rutherglen			
						...airn	Newcastle U	1	—
							Hartlepool U	247	7
							Manchester U (loan)	—	—
							Motherwell	152	8
							Twente	50	1
							Hearts	16	—
							Hartlepool U (loan)	7	—
Midgley Craig	5 7	11 00	F	24 5 76	Bradford	Trainee	Bradford C	11	1
							Scarborough (loan)	16	1
							Scarborough (loan)	6	2
							Darlington (loan)	1	—
							Hartlepool U	38	10
Miller Tommy	6 1	12 00	D	8 1 79	Easington	Trainee	Hartlepool U	47	5
Miotto Simon‡	6 1	13 03	G	5 9 69	Tasmania	Riverside Olympic	Blackpool	—	—
							Hartlepool U	5	—

Moss Paul*	5 11	12 10	D	4 5 80	Easington	Trainee	Hartlepool U	—	—
Nash Marc‡	5 9	11 07	F	13 5 78	Newcastle	Benfield Park	Hartlepool U	1	—
Pemberton Martin‡	5 11	11 08	M	1 2 76	Bradford	Trainee	Oldham Ath	5	—
							Doncaster R	35	2
							Scunthorpe U	6	—
							Hartlepool U	4	—
Rush David‡	5 9	11 02	F	15 5 71	Sunderland	Trainee	Sunderland	59	12
							Hartlepool U (loan)	8	2
							Peterborough U (loan)	4	1
							Cambridge U (loan)	2	—
							Oxford U	92	21
							York C	5	—
							Hartlepool U	10	—
Smith Jeff	5 10	11 01	M	28 6 80	Middlesbrough	Trainee	Hartlepool U	3	—
Stephenson Paul	5 10	12 07	F	2 1 68	Wallsend	Apprentice	Newcastle U	61	1
							Millwall	98	6
							Gillingham (loan)	12	2
							Brentford	70	2
							York C	97	8
							Hartlepool U	30	2
Stokoe Graham*	6 0	13 03	M	17 12 75	Newcastle-under-Lyme	Birmingham C	Stoke C	2	—
							Hartlepool U (loan)	8	—
							Hartlepool U	20	—
Strodder Gary	6 2	13 04	D	1 4 65	Mirfield	Apprentice	Lincoln C	132	6
							West Ham U	65	2
							WBA	140	8
							Notts Co	121	10
							Rotherham U (loan)	3	—
							Hartlepool U	13	—
Sullivan Wayne‡	5 7	11 01	F	20 5 80	Hartlepool	Trainee	Hartlepool U	—	—
Tait Mick‡	5 11	14 05	D	30 9 56	Wallsend	Apprentice	Oxford U	64	23
							Carlisle U	106	20
							Hull C	33	3
							Portsmouth	240	30
							Reading	99	9
							Darlington	79	2
							Hartlepool U	139	3
Timmons Darren*	6 1	11 02	M	3 2 80	North Shields	Trainee	Hartlepool U	—	—
Westwood Chris	5 11	12 10	D	13 2 77	Dudley	Trainee	Wolverhampton W	4	1
							Hartlepool U	4	—

Trainees
Cooper, Paul; Downey, Gareth; Forster, Richard J; Hay, Andrew J; Jones, Francis; McCabe, Christopher; Nicholson, Mark; Robinson, Mark; Walton, Phillip

Scholars
Davison, Craig T; Dunkerley, Mark G; Hill, Terence; Lawlor, Terence S; Lines, Craig; McLean, Stephen; Nesbit, Mark A

Associated Schoolboys who have accepted the Club's offer of a Traineeship/Scholarship/Contract
Provett, Robert J; Ross, Brian S; Sheeran, Mark J; Skilbeck, Lee R

HUDDERSFIELD TOWN

Allison Wayne	6 0	14 07	F	16 10 68	Huddersfield		Halifax T	84	23
							Watford	7	—
							Bristol C	195	48
							Swindon T	101	31
							Huddersfield T	71	15
Armstrong Craig	5 11	12 10	D	23 5 75	South Shields	Trainee	Nottingham F	40	—
							Burnley (loan)	4	—
							Bristol R (loan)	14	—
							Gillingham (loan)	10	—
							Watford (loan)	15	—
							Huddersfield T	13	1
Baldry Simon	5 11	12 00	M	12 2 76	Huddersfield	Trainee	Huddersfield T	66	3
							Bury (loan)	5	—
Beech Chris	5 9	11 03	M	16 9 74	Blackpool	Trainee	Blackpool	82	4
							Hartlepool U	94	22
							Huddersfield T	17	2
Beresford David	5 5	11 00	F	11 11 76	Manchester	Trainee	Oldham Ath	64	2
							Swansea C (loan)	6	—
							Huddersfield T	33	3
Brennan Damien			D	30 8 80	Dublin	Belvedere	Huddersfield T	—	—
Collins Sam	6 2	14 04	D	5 6 77	Pontefract	Trainee	Huddersfield T	37	—
Crossley Ryan	6 0	12 00	D	23 7 80	Halifax	Trainee	Huddersfield T	—	—
Cuss Paul	6 1	13 07	G	19 4 79	Minden	Trainee	Huddersfield T	—	—
Dalton Paul	6 0	13 00	F	25 4 67	Middlesbrough	Brandon U	Manchester U	—	—
							Hartlepool U	151	37
							Plymouth Arg	98	25
							Huddersfield T	98	25
Dyson Jon	6 0	12 12	D	18 12 71	Mirfield	School	Huddersfield T	155	4
Edmondson Darren	6 0	12 10	D	4 11 71	Ulverston	Trainee	Carlisle U	214	9
							Huddersfield T	32	—
							Plymouth Arg (loan)	4	—

Name	Ht		Pos	Born	Birthplace	Signed from	Club	Apps	Gls
Edwards Rob	5 8	12 04	M	23 2 70	Manchester	Trainee	Crewe Alex	155	44
							Huddersfield T	129	13
Facey Delroy	5 10	14 10	F	22 4 80	Huddersfield	Trainee	Huddersfield T	26	3
Gray Kevin	5 11	14 02	D	7 1 72	Sheffield	Trainee	Mansfield T	141	3
							Huddersfield T	151	3
Heary Thomas	5 10	10 06	M	14 2 78	Dublin	Trainee	Huddersfield T	11	—
Hessey Sean*	6 0	12 03	D	19 9 78	Liverpool	Liverpool	Wigan Ath	—	—
							Leeds U	—	—
							Huddersfield T	11	—
Horne Barry#	5 9	12 07	M	18 5 62	St Asaph	Rhyl	Wrexham	136	17
							Portsmouth	70	7
							Southampton	112	6
							Everton	123	3
							Birmingham C	33	—
							Huddersfield T	50	1
Hurst Chris*	5 11	11 06	M	3 10 73	Barnsley	Emley	Huddersfield T	3	—
Jenkins Steve	6 0	12 08	D	16 7 72	Merthyr	Trainee	Swansea C	165	1
							Huddersfield T	129	3
Johnson Grant	5 11	11 03	M	24 3 72	Dundee	Dundee	Dundee U	85	7
							Huddersfield T	65	5
Lawson Ian	5 11	11 00	F	4 11 77	Huddersfield	Trainee	Huddersfield T	42	5
							Blackpool (loan)	9	3
Mattis Dwayne§	6 1	10 09	M	31 7 81	Huddersfield	Trainee	Huddersfield T	2	—
Richardson Lee J	5 10	12 07	M	12 3 69	Halifax		Halifax T	56	2
							Watford	41	1
							Blackburn R	62	3
							Aberdeen	64	6
							Oldham Ath	88	21
							Stockport Co (loan)	6	—
							Huddersfield T	36	3
Schofield Danny	5 10	11 02	F	10 4 80	Doncaster		Huddersfield T	1	—
Scott Paul	6 0	11 11	D	5 11 79	Wakefield	Trainee	Huddersfield T	—	—
Stewart Marcus	5 10	11 08	F	7 11 72	Bristol	Trainee	Bristol R	171	57
							Huddersfield T	104	44
Thornley Ben	5 7	11 07	F	21 4 75	Bury	Trainee	Manchester U	9	—
							Stockport Co (loan)	10	1
							Huddersfield T (loan)	12	2
							Huddersfield T	35	4
Vaesen Nico	6 4	13 01	G	28 9 69	Hasselt		CS Brugge	16	—
							Aalst	34	—
							Huddersfield T	43	—
Vincent Jamie	5 10	11 09	D	18 6 75	London	Trainee	Crystal Palace	25	—
							Bournemouth (loan)	8	—
							Bournemouth	105	5
							Huddersfield T	7	—

Trainees
Atkinson, Robert F; Brown, Nathaniel, L; Cartwright, Christopher R A; Gledhill, James G; Horsley, Jamie L; Mattis, Dwayne; Senior, Michael G

Scholars
Clarke, Doni J; Fowler, Adam M; Hay, Nathan A; Senior, Christopher M; Simpson, Neil

Associated Schoolboys
Atkins, Oliver D; Batchelor, Alistair A; Clapham, Daniel D; Gibbons, James M; Kelly, Gregory; Lloyd, Anthony F; Smith, Timothy K

Associated Schoolboys who have accepted the Club's offer of a Traineeship/Scholarship/Contract
Austin, Ben; Brown, Christopher; Clarke, Nathan; Greaves, Robert; Senior, Philip A; Stead, Jonathan; Trueman, Daniel; Worthington, Jonathan

HULL CITY

Name	Ht		Pos	Born	Birthplace	Signed from	Club	Apps	Gls
Alcide Colin	6 2	13 11	F	14 4 72	Huddersfield	Emley	Lincoln C	121	26
							Hull C	17	3
Baker Matthew	6 0	12 08	G	18 12 79	Claro	Trainee	Hull C	—	—
Bolder Adam	5 9	10 08	M	25 10 80	Hull	Trainee	Hull C	1	—
Brabin Gary	5 11	14 08	M	9 12 70	Liverpool	Trainee	Stockport Co	2	—
						Runcorn	Doncaster R	59	11
							Bury	5	—
							Blackpool	63	5
							Lincoln C (loan)	4	—
							Hull C	21	4
Brown David	5 10	12 08	F	2 10 78	Bolton	Trainee	Manchester U	—	—
							Hull C (loan)	7	2
							Hull C	42	11
D'Auria David	5 8	12 00	M	26 3 70	Swansea	Trainee	Swansea C	45	6
						Barry T	Scarborough	52	8
							Scunthorpe U	107	18
							Hull C	42	4
Dewhurst Rob*	6 3	14 00	D	10 9 71	Keighley	Trainee	Blackburn R	13	—
							Darlington (loan)	11	1
							Huddersfield T (loan)	7	—
							Hull C	138	13
Edwards Michael	6 0	12 10	D	25 4 80	North Ferriby	Trainee	Hull C	51	—
Ellington Lee	5 10	11 07	F	3 7 80	Bradford	Trainee	Hull C	15	2

Fidler Richard	5 9	10 09	M	26 10 76	Sheffield	Leeds U	Hull C	1	—
French Jon	5 10	10 10	M	25 9 76	Bristol	Trainee	Bristol R	17	1
							Hull C	15	—
Gage Kevin‡	5 9	12 11	D	21 4 64	Chiswick	Apprentice	Wimbledon	168	15
							Aston Villa	115	8
							Sheffield U	112	7
							Preston NE	23	—
							Hull C	13	—
Greaves Mark	6 1	13 00	D	22 1 75	Hull	Brigg Town	Hull C	80	4
Hateley Mark	6 2	13 00	F	7 11 61	Liverpool	Apprentice	Coventry C	93	25
							Portsmouth	38	22
							AC Milan	66	17
							Monaco	59	22
							Rangers	165	85
							QPR	27	3
							Leeds U (loan)	6	—
							Rangers	4	1
							Hull C	21	3
Hawes Steve	5 8	12 04	M	17 7 78	High Wycombe	Trainee	Sheffield U	4	—
							Doncaster R (loan)	11	—
							Hull C	19	—
Hocking Matthew	5 11	12 00	D	30 1 78	Boston	Trainee	Sheffield U	—	—
							Hull C	57	2
							York C (loan)	6	—
Joyce Warren	5 9	12 01	M	20 1 65	Oldham	School	Bolton W	184	17
							Preston NE	177	34
							Plymouth Arg	30	3
							Burnley	70	9
							Hull C (loan)	9	3
							Hull C	119	11
Mann Neil	5 10	12 01	M	19 11 72	Nottingham	Grantham T	Hull C	160	9
McGinty Brian*	6 1	12 01	M	10 12 76	East Kilbride		Rangers	3	—
							Hull C	53	6
Morley Ben	5 9	10 11	D	22 12 80	Hull	Trainee	Hull C	20	—
O'Keeffe Darren			M	29 8 78	Dublin	Trainee	Huddersfield T	—	—
							Hull C	—	—
Oakes Andy			G	11 1 77	Crewe		Bury	—	—
						Winsford U	Hull C	19	—
Perry Jason	5 11	11 12	D	2 4 70	Caerphilly	Trainee	Cardiff C	281	5
							Bristol R	25	—
							Lincoln C	12	—
							Hull C	8	—
Quigley Michael†	5 7	11 04	M	2 10 70	Manchester	Trainee	Manchester C	12	—
							Wrexham (loan)	4	—
							Hull C	51	3
Rioch Greg*	5 11	12 10	D	24 6 75	Sutton Coldfield	Trainee	Luton T	—	—
							Barnet (loan)	3	—
							Peterborough U	18	—
							Hull C	91	6
Sharman Sam‡	5 10	12 01	D	7 11 77	Hull	Sheffield W	Hull C	4	—
Swales Steve	5 9	10 03	D	26 12 73	Scarborough	Trainee	Scarborough	54	1
							Reading	43	1
							Hull C	22	—
Thomson Scott Y‡	6 0	11 09	G	8 11 66	Edinburgh		Dundee U	6	—
							Forfar Ath	88	—
							Raith R	123	—
							Hull C	9	—
							Motherwell	1	—
							Hull C	—	—
Tucker Dexter	6 1	12 02	F	22 9 79	Pontefract	Trainee	Hull C	7	—
Whitney Jon	5 10	13 08	D	23 12 70	Nantwich	Winsford U	Huddersfield T	18	—
							Wigan Ath (loan)	12	—
							Lincoln C	101	8
							Hull C	21	1
Whittle Justin	6 1	13 09	D	18 3 71	Derby	Celtic	Stoke C	79	1
							Hull C	24	1
Whitworth Neil	6 0	12 13	D	12 4 72	Ince		Wigan Ath	2	—
							Manchester U	1	—
							Preston NE (loan)	6	—
							Barnsley (loan)	11	—
							Rotherham U (loan)	8	1
							Blackpool (loan)	3	—
							Kilmarnock	76	3
							Wigan Ath	4	—
							Hull C	18	2
Williams Gareth	6 0	12 02	M	12 3 67	Newport (IW)	Gosport Bor	Aston Villa	12	—
							Barnsley	34	6
							Hull C (loan)	4	—
							Hull C (loan)	16	2
							Bournemouth	1	—
							Northampton T	50	1
							Scarborough	105	27
							Hull C	25	1
Wilson Steve#	5 10	10 12	G	24 4 74	Hull	Trainee	Hull C	154	—

Wright Ian	6 1	13 04	D	10 3 72	Lichfield	Trainee	Stoke C	6	—
							Bristol R	54	1
							Hull C	73	2

Trainees
Blythe, Michael; Bolder, Adam P; Brown, Daniel P; Dixon, Steven M; Flanagan, Lee M; Thacker, Martin; Wilson, Paul A

Scholars
Bolder, Christopher J; Flower, Clayton J; Lafferty, Mark A; McIntosh, Neil G; Poole, Philip J; Waslin, Daniel; Woodward, Oliver

Non-Contract
Quigley, Michael A

Associated Schoolboys who have accepted the Club's offer of a Traineeship/Scholarship/Contract
Bonsley, Anthony; Burton, Steven; Peat, Nathan N M

IPSWICH TOWN

Bowes Terry*	5 9	11 00	M	13 9 79	London	Arsenal	Ipswich T	—	—
Bracey Lee#	6 2	13 02	G	11 9 68	Barking	Trainee	West Ham U	—	—
							Swansea C	99	—
							Halifax T	73	—
							Bury	67	—
							Ipswich T (loan)	—	—
							Ipswich T	—	—
Bramble Titus	6 1	13 10	D	21 7 81	Ipswich	Trainee	Ipswich T	4	—
Brown Wayne	6 0	12 00	D	20 8 77	Barking	Trainee	Ipswich T	2	—
							Colchester U (loan)	2	—
Burgess Mark‡	5 11	11 09	D	3 2 79	Ipswich	Trainee	Ipswich T	—	—
Clapham Jamie	5 9	11 08	D	7 12 75	Lincoln	Trainee	Tottenham H	1	—
							Leyton Orient (loan)	6	—
							Bristol R (loan)	5	—
							Ipswich T	68	3
Cowell Claydon			M	3 9 80	Colchester	Arsenal	Ipswich T	—	—
Cundy Jason*	6 0	13 10	D	12 11 69	Wimbledon	Trainee	Chelsea	41	1
							Tottenham H (loan)	10	—
							Tottenham H	16	1
							Crystal Palace (loan)	4	—
							Bristol C (loan)	6	1
							Ipswich T	58	5
Delany Derek*			M	23 9 80	Drogheda		Ipswich T	—	—
Dyer Kieron	5 8	10 01	M	29 12 78	Ipswich	Trainee	Ipswich T	91	9
Friars Sean	5 8	10 07	F	15 5 79	Derry	Trainee	Liverpool	—	—
							Ipswich T	—	—
Holland Matt	5 10	11 10	M	11 4 74	Bury	Trainee	West Ham U	—	—
							Bournemouth	104	18
							Ipswich T	92	15
Holster Marco	5 6	10 11	M	4 12 71	Weesp	Huizen	AZ	90	17
							Heracles	28	6
							Heracles*	—	—
							Ipswich T	10	—
Inglis Kevin			M	26 8 80	Glasgow	Trainee	Ipswich T	—	—
Johnson David	5 6	12 00	F	15 8 76	Kingston, Jam	Trainee	Manchester U	—	—
							Bury	97	18
							Ipswich T	73	33
Keeble Chris	5 9	11 00	M	17 9 78	Colchester	Trainee	Ipswich T	1	—
Kennedy John	5 8	10 07	D	19 8 78	Cambridge	Trainee	Ipswich T	8	—
Logan Richard	6 0	12 05	F	4 1 82	Bury St Edmunds	Trainee	Ipswich T	2	—
Magilton Jim	6 0	14 00	M	6 5 69	Belfast	Apprentice	Liverpool	—	—
							Oxford U	150	34
							Southampton	130	13
							Sheffield W	27	1
							Ipswich T	19	3
Mason Paul‡	5 9	12 01	M	3 9 63	Liverpool	Groningen	Aberdeen	158	27
							Ipswich T	113	25
Mathie Alex	5 10	11 13	F	20 12 68	Bathgate	Celtic BC	Celtic	11	—
(Transferred to Dundee U, October 1998)							Morton	74	31
							Port Vale (loan)	3	—
							Newcastle U	25	4
							Ipswich T	109	38
							Dundee U	22	1
Midgley Neil	5 11	11 08	F	21 10 78	Cambridge	Trainee	Ipswich T	—	—
Mowbray Tony	6 1	13 07	D	22 11 63	Saltburn	Apprentice	Middlesbrough	348	25
							Celtic	78	6
							Ipswich T	92	4
Naylor Richard	6 0	13 07	F	28 2 77	Leeds	Trainee	Ipswich T	62	11
Niven Stuart	5 11	12 08	M	24 12 78	Glasgow	Trainee	Ipswich T	2	—
Petta Bobby#	5 7	11 05	M	6 8 74	Rotterdam		Ipswich T	70	9
Scowcroft James	6 2	14 02	F	15 11 75	Bury St Edmunds	Trainee	Ipswich T	127	30
Stewart Colin*	6 3	12 07	G	10 1 80	Cleveland	Trainee	Ipswich T	0	—
Stockwell Mick	5 7	11 07	M	14 2 65	Chelmsford	Apprentice	Ipswich T	471	33
Tanner Adam	6 0	13 00	M	25 10 73	Maldon	Trainee	Ipswich T	73	7
Theobald David*	6 3	11 00	D	15 12 78	Cambridge	Trainee	Ipswich T	0	—

Thetis Manuel	6 3	14 13	D	5 11 71	France	Sevilla	Ipswich T	31	2
Venus Mark	6 1	12 12	D	6 4 67	Hartlepool		Hartlepool U	4	—
							Leicester C	61	1
							Wolverhampton W	287	7
							Ipswich T	58	10
Wilnis Fabian	5 8	12 06	D	23 8 70	Paramaribo	Sparta	NAC	134	3
							De Graafschap	107	1
							Ipswich T	18	1
Wright Richard	6 2	13 07	G	5 11 77	Ipswich	Trainee	Ipswich T	158	—

Trainees
Dixon, Matthew F; Farrington, Louie M; Supple, Michael J; Woolnough, Benjamin S; Wright, Carl A J

Scholars
Asiamah, Justin; Miller, Adam E; Moffat, Steven J; Niemi, Tomi J; O'Neill, Lee G; Riley, Dominic M

Associated Schoolboys
Ambrose, Darren P F; Beevers, Lee-Jon; Burton, Steven P; Senior, James C; Wasylyczyn, Wayne M

Associated Schoolboys who have accepted the Club's offer of a Traineeship/Scholarship/Contract
Artun, Erdem K; Barker, Rory; Hulyer, Lee A; Kinsella, Sean I; Tunnicliffe, Andrew J

LEEDS UNITED

Batty David	5 8	11 10	M	2 12 68	Leeds	Trainee	Leeds U	211	4
							Blackburn R	54	1
							Newcastle U	83	3
							Leeds U	10	—
Beeney Mark‡	6 4	14 10	G	30 12 67	Pembury		Gillingham	2	—
							Maidstone U	50	—
							Aldershot (loan)	7	—
							Brighton & HA	69	—
							Leeds U	35	—
Bowyer Lee	5 9	10 09	M	3 1 77	London	Trainee	Charlton Ath	46	8
							Leeds U	92	16
Boyle Wesley	5 10	11 01	F	30 3 79	Portadown	Trainee	Leeds U	1	—
Cawley Alan	6 2	10 01	M	3 1 82	Sligo	Belvedere	Leeds U	—	—
Crawford Dale	5 9	11 01	F	14 9 81	Sunderland	Trainee	Leeds U	—	—
Dixon Kevin	5 9	12 03	M	27 6 80	Easington	Trainee	Leeds U	—	—
Donnelly Paul*	5 10	11 07	D	31 8 79	Dublin	Trainee	Leeds U	—	—
Doyle Kevin‡	5 11	12 02	M	13 10 80	Wexford	Trainee	Leeds U	—	—
Evans Gareth	6 0	11 11	D	15 2 81	Leeds	Trainee	Leeds U	—	—
Evans Kevin	6 2	12 10	D	16 12 80	Carmarthen	Trainee	Leeds U	—	—
Feeney Warren	5 10	11 00	F	17 1 81	Belfast	Trainee	Leeds U	—	—
Granville Danny	6 1	12 11	D	19 1 75	Islington	Trainee	Cambridge U	99	7
							Chelsea	18	—
							Leeds U	9	—
Haaland Alf-Inge	6 1	12 06	M	23 11 72	Stavanger	Bryne	Nottingham F	75	7
							Leeds U	61	8
Hackworth Tony	6 1	13 07	F	19 5 80	Durham	Trainee	Leeds U	—	—
Halle Gunnar	6 0	12 07	D	11 8 65	Larvik	Lillestrom	Oldham Ath	188	17
							Leeds U	70	4
Harte Ian	6 0	12 04	D	31 8 77	Drogheda	Trainee	Leeds U	65	6
Hasselbaink Jimmy Floyd	6 0	13 08	F	27 3 72	Paramaribo		Campomairorense	31	12
							Boavista	29	20
							Leeds U	69	34
Hiden Martin	6 1	12 00	D	11 3 73	Stainz		Sturm Graz	53	5
							Salzburg	58	2
							Sturm Graz	28	3
							Rapid Vienna	20	—
							Leeds U	25	—
Hopkin David	6 1	13 13	M	21 8 70	Greenock	Pt Glasgow R BC	Morton	18	—
							Chelsea	40	1
							Crystal Palace	83	21
							Leeds U	59	5
Jackson Mark	6 0	12 10	D	30 9 77	Barnsley	Trainee	Leeds U	19	—
							Huddersfield T (loan)	5	—
Jones Matthew	5 11	11 09	M	1 9 80	Llanelli	Trainee	Leeds U	8	—
Kelly Gary	5 8	11 00	D	9 7 74	Drogheda	Home Farm	Leeds U	190	2
Kennedy Alan	5 8	11 00	F	17 10 81	Dublin	Trainee	Leeds U	—	—
Kewell Harry	6 0	12 10	F	22 9 78	Sydney	NSW Academy	Leeds U	70	11
Knarvik Tommy	5 8	11 00	M	1 11 79	Bergen	Skjerjard	Leeds U	—	—
Korsten Willem*	6 4	13 04	F	21 1 75	Boxtel	Geen	NEC	4	—
							Vitesse	71	12
							Leeds U	7	2
Lagan Brian	5 5	10 00	M	3 10 80	Magherafelt	Trainee	Leeds U	—	—
Lanns Jason	5 8	10 07	D	2 11 81	Birmingham	Birmingham C	Leeds U	—	—
Lennon Anthony§			M	16 5 82	Leeds	Trainee	Leeds U	—	—
Lilley Derek	5 10	12 08	F	9 2 74	Paisley	Everton BC	Morton	180	57
							Leeds U	21	1
							Bury (loan)	5	1
							Hearts (loan)	4	1

Name			Pos	DOB	Birthplace	From	Club	Apps	Gls
Loughran Anthony	6 0	11 12	D	11 11 81	Liverpool	Trainee	Leeds U	—	—
Lynch Damien	5 10	11 00	D	31 7 79	Dublin		Leeds U	—	—
Martin Alan	5 10	11 05	D	21 11 81	Dublin	Trainee	Leeds U	—	—
Martyn Nigel	6 2	14 10	G	11 8 66	St Austell	St Blazey	Bristol R	101	—
							Crystal Palace	272	—
							Leeds U	108	—
Matthews Lee	6 2	13 05	F	6 1 79	Middlesbrough	Trainee	Leeds U	3	—
							Notts Co (loan)	5	—
Maybury Alan	5 9	10 04	D	8 8 78	Dublin	Trainee	Leeds U	13	—
							Reading (loan)	8	—
McChrystal Brian	6 3	13 01	D	20 1 81	Dundalk	Bellurgan U	Leeds U	—	—
McPhail Stephen	5 10	11 06	M	9 12 79	London	Trainee	Leeds U	21	—
Molenaar Robert	6 2	14 09	D	27 2 69	Zaandam		Volendam	124	3
							Leeds U	51	5
O'Brien Carl	5 9	10 10	M	6 11 81	Dublin	Trainee	Leeds U	—	—
Porter Graeme	5 6	10 00	F	24 11 81	Liverpool	Trainee	Leeds U	—	—
Quinn Andrew‡			M	1 9 79	Halifax		Leeds U	—	—
Radebe Lucas	6 1	12 04	D	12 4 69	Johannesburg	Kaiser Chiefs	Leeds U	113	—
Ribeiro Bruno	5 8	12 07	M	22 10 75	Setubal		Setubal	39	4
							Leeds U	42	4
Robertson David	5 11	13 01	D	17 10 68	Aberdeen		Aberdeen	135	2
							Rangers	183	15
							Leeds U	26	—
Robinson Paul	6 4	14 04	G	15 10 79	Beverley	Trainee	Leeds U	5	—
Santos Nuno	6 1	13 00	G	20 4 73	Setubal		Setubal	42	—
							Leeds U	—	—
Sharpe Lee	6 0	12 10	F	27 5 71	Halesowen	Trainee	Torquay U	14	3
							Manchester U	193	21
							Leeds U	30	5
							Bradford C (loan)	9	2
							Sampdoria	3	—
Shepherd Paul	5 11	12 00	D	17 11 77	Leeds	Trainee	Leeds U	1	—
							Ayr U (loan)	6	1
							Tranmere R (loan)	1	—
Singh Harpal	5 7	10 02	F	15 9 81	Bradford	Trainee	Leeds U	—	—
Smith Alan	5 9	10 13	F	28 10 80	Leeds	Trainee	Leeds U	22	7
Wallace Rod	5 7	11 03	F	2 10 69	Lewisham	Trainee	Southampton	128	45
(Transferred to Rangers, July 1998)							Leeds U	212	53
							Rangers	34	18
Watson Simon	5 9	10 00	M	22 9 80	Strabane	Trainee	Leeds U	—	—
Wetherall David	6 4	13 05	D	14 3 71	Sheffield	School	Sheffield W	—	—
							Leeds U	202	12
Wijnhard Clyde	5 11	13 06	F	9 11 73	Paramaribo		Ajax	4	2
							Groningen	23	3
							Ajax	—	—
							RKC	50	18
							Willem II	29	14
							Leeds U	18	3
Woodgate Jonathan	6 2	12 09	D	22 1 80	Middlesbrough		Leeds U	25	2
Wright Andy	5 8	9 06	M	21 10 78	Leeds	Trainee	Leeds U	—	—
							Reading (loan)	2	—

Trainees/Scholars
Cramer, Martin; Hackett, Kristian S; Lennon, Anthony C; McMaster, Jamie; Powell, Graham; Ross, Neil J; Travers, Mervyn

LEICESTER CITY

Name			Pos	DOB	Birthplace	From	Club	Apps	Gls
Allen Lee	5 10	10 08	F	12 3 79	Islington		Leicester C	—	—
Andrews Ian‡	6 2	14 01	G	1 12 64	Nottingham	Apprentice	Leicester C	126	—
							Swindon T (loan)	1	—
							Celtic	5	—
							Leeds U (loan)	1	—
							Southampton	10	—
							Bournemouth	64	—
							Leicester C (loan)	—	—
							Leicester C	—	—
Arphexad Pegguy	6 2	13 07	G	18 5 73	Abymes		Lens	3	—
							Leicester C	10	—
Ashley Neil*	5 10	10 10	M	16 9 80	Chesterfield	Nottingham F	Leicester C	—	—
Boateng Daniel			M	14 11 80	London	Arsenal	Leicester C	—	—
Branston Guy	6 1	13 11	D	9 1 79	Leicester		Leicester C	—	—
						Trainee	Colchester U (loan)	12	1
							Colchester U (loan)	1	—
							Plymouth Arg (loan)	7	1
Brennan Karl	5 6	11 00	M	19 3 81	Leicester	Trainee	Leicester C	—	—
Browne Bevan*			M	29 3 80	Wellingborough	Nottingham F	Leicester C	—	—
Campbell Stuart	5 10	10 08	M	9 12 77	Corby	Trainee	Leicester C	33	—
Cottee Tony	5 8	11 05	F	11 7 65	West Ham	Apprentice	West Ham U	212	92
							Everton	184	72
							West Ham U	67	23
						Selangor	Leicester C	50	14
							Birmingham C (loan)	5	1

Dudfield Lawrie	6 0	11 05	F	7 5 80	London	Kettering T	Leicester C	—	—
Elliott Matt	6 3	14 05	D	1 11 68	Wandsworth	Epsom & Ewell	Charlton Ath	—	—
							Torquay U	124	15
							Scunthorpe U (loan)	8	1
							Scunthorpe U	53	7
							Oxford U	148	21
							Leicester C	90	14
Emerson Paul	6 1	11 06	D	29 8 78	Newtonards	Trainee	Leicester C	—	—
Fenton Graham	5 10	11 09	F	22 5 74	Wallsend	Trainee	Aston Villa	32	3
							WBA (loan)	7	3
							Blackburn R	27	7
							Leicester C	32	3
Fox Martin	5 8	11 02	D	21 4 79	Sutton-in-Ashfield	Trainee	Leicester C	—	—
Goodwin Tommy	6 0	12 02	D	8 11 79	Leicester	Trainee	Leicester C	—	—
Gunnlaugsson Arnar	5 10	11 06	F	6 3 73	Akranes		IA Akranes	12	3
							IA Akranes*	—	—
							IA Akranes	18	15
							Feyenoord	9	—
							Nuremberg	28	8
							IA Akranes	9	16
							Bolton W	42	13
							Leicester C	9	—
Guppy Steve	5 11	12 00	M	29 3 69	Winchester	Southampton	Wycombe W	41	8
							Newcastle U	—	—
							Port Vale	105	12
							Leicester C	88	6
Heskey Emile	6 2	13 12	F	11 1 78	Leicester	Trainee	Leicester C	131	33
Hodges John	6 0	11 05	G	22 1 80	Leicester	Trainee	Leicester C	—	—
Impey Andrew	5 8	11 06	M	13 9 71	Hammersmith	Yeading	QPR	187	13
							West Ham U	27	—
							Leicester C	18	—
Izzet Muzzy	5 10	11 02	M	31 10 74	Mile End	Trainee	Chelsea	—	—
							Leicester C (loan)	9	1
							Leicester C	102	12
Jaffa Graeme‡	5 6	9 08	F	8 5 79	Falkirk	Trainee	Leicester C	—	—
Kamark Pontus*	5 11	12 02	D	5 4 69	Vasteras		Vasteras	55	6
							IFK Gothenburg	144	4
						IFK Gothenburg	Leicester C	65	—
Keller Kasey*	6 2	13 12	G	27 11 69	Washington	Portland University	Millwall	176	—
							Leicester C	99	—
Lennon Neil	5 9	13 02	M	25 6 71	Lurgan	Trainee	Manchester C	1	—
							Crewe Alex	147	15
							Leicester C	124	5
Marshall Ian*	6 2	13 09	F	20 3 66	Liverpool	Apprentice	Everton	15	1
							Oldham Ath	170	36
							Ipswich T	84	32
							Leicester C	62	18
McCann Tim	5 9	11 05	M	22 3 80	Belfast	Trainee	Leicester C	—	—
Mitchell Ross‡	5 11	10 13	M	24 8 78	Halifax	Trainee	Leicester C	—	—
Oakes Stefan	5 11	12 04	M	6 9 78	Leicester	Trainee	Leicester C	3	—
Parker Garry*	6 0	13 03	M	7 9 65	Oxford	Apprentice	Luton T	42	3
							Hull C	84	8
							Nottingham F	103	17
							Aston Villa	95	13
							Leicester C	114	10
Ramm Daniel*			M	21 9 79	Norwich	Trainee	Leicester C	—	—
Savage Robbie	5 11	10 07	M	18 10 74	Wrexham	Trainee	Manchester U	—	—
							Crewe Alex	77	10
							Leicester C	69	3
Sinclair Frank	5 10	12 07	D	3 12 71	Lambeth	Trainee	Chelsea	169	7
							WBA (loan)	6	1
							Leicester C	31	1
Taggart Gerry	6 2	14 00	D	18 10 70	Belfast	Trainee	Manchester C	12	1
							Barnsley	212	16
							Bolton W	69	4
							Leicester C	15	—
Taylor Scott*	5 9	11 05	M	23 11 70	Portsmouth	Trainee	Reading	207	24
							Leicester C	64	6
Thomas Danny	5 7	10 07	D	1 5 81	Leamington Spa	Trainee	Nottingham F	—	—
							Leicester C	—	—
Ullathorne Robert	5 8	10 10	D	11 10 71	Wakefield	Trainee	Norwich C	94	7
							Osasuna	18	—
							Leicester C	31	1
Walsh Steve	6 3	14 09	D	3 11 64	Fulwood	Local	Wigan Ath	126	4
							Leicester C	357	53
Wenlock Steve*	5 7	11 01	D	11 3 78	Peterborough	Trainee	Leicester C	—	—
Wilson Stuart	5 8	9 12	F	16 9 77	Leicester	Trainee	Leicester C	22	3
Zagorakis Theo	5 9	11 08	M	27 10 71	Kavala	PAOK Salonika	Leicester C	33	2

Trainees/Scholars
Bacon, Carl R; Heath, Matthew P; Miller, James C; Neckles, Ainsley M B; Noble, Craig P; Nurse, Matthew J; Orme, Richard P B; Padmore, Stephen R; Piper, Matthew J; Reeves, Martin L; Ridgway, David J; Saddington, David; Salter, Alex; Savage, Michael J; Steane, Ben; Stewart, Jordan B; Walker, Liam J; Weale, Richard J

LEYTON ORIENT

Name	Ht	Wt	Pos	DOB	Birthplace	Source	Club	Apps	Gls
Ampadu Kwame	5 10	11 10	M	20 12 70	Bradford	Belvedere	Arsenal	2	—
							Plymouth Arg (loan)	6	1
							WBA (loan)	7	1
							WBA	42	3
							Swansea C	147	12
							Leyton Orient	29	1
Baker Joe	5 8	10 07	F	9 4 77	London	Charlton Ath	Leyton Orient	75	3
Barrett Scott#	5 11	13 00	G	2 4 63	Ilkeston	Ilkeston T	Wolverhampton W	30	—
							Stoke C	51	—
							Colchester U (loan)	13	—
							Stockport Co (loan)	10	—
							Colchester U	—	—
							Gillingham	51	—
							Cambridge U	119	—
							Leyton Orient	20	—
Beall Billy	5 6	12 00	M	4 12 77	Enfield	Trainee	Cambridge U	81	7
							Leyton Orient	23	2
Brown Daniel	6 0	12 06	M	12 9 80	Bethnal Green	Trainee	Leyton Orient	—	—
Canham Scott	5 10	11 08	M	5 11 74	London	Trainee	West Ham U	—	—
							Torquay U (loan)	3	—
							Brentford (loan)	14	—
							Brentford	35	1
							Leyton Orient	8	—
Clark Paul†	5 9	13 13	M	14 9 58	Benfleet	Apprentice	Southend U	33	1
							Brighton & HA	79	9
							Reading (loan)	2	—
							Southend U	276	3
							Gillingham	90	1
							Cambridge U	2	—
							Leyton Orient		
Clark Simon	6 0	12 10	D	12 3 67	Boston	Stevenage Bor	Peterborough U	107	4
							Leyton Orient	79	8
Curran Danny§			M	13 6 81	Essex	Trainee	Leyton Orient	1	—
Downer Simon§			M	19 10 81	Romford	Trainee	Leyton Orient	1	—
Finney Steve*	5 11	12 08	F	31 10 73	Hexham	Trainee	Preston NE	6	1
							Manchester C	—	—
							Swindon T	73	18
							Cambridge U (loan)	7	2
							Carlisle U	33	6
							Leyton Orient	5	—
Hicks Stuart	6 1	13 03	D	30 5 67	Peterborough	Wisbech T	Colchester U	64	—
							Scunthorpe U	67	1
							Doncaster R	36	—
							Huddersfield T	22	1
							Preston NE	12	—
							Scarborough	85	2
							Leyton Orient	64	1
Hyde Paul‡	6 1	14 09	G	7 4 63	Hayes	Hayes	Wycombe W	105	—
							Leicester C	—	—
							Leyton Orient	41	—
Inglethorpe Alex	5 11	11 04	M	14 11 71	Epsom	School	Watford	12	2
							Barnet (loan)	6	3
							Leyton Orient	107	30
Joseph Matt	5 7	10 02	D	30 9 72	Bethnal Green	Trainee	Arsenal	—	—
							Gillingham	—	—
							Cambridge U	159	6
							Leyton Orient	48	1
Joseph Roger	5 11	11 10	D	24 12 65	Paddington	Juniors	Brentford	104	2
							Wimbledon	162	—
							Millwall (loan)	5	—
							Leyton Orient	15	—
							WBA	2	—
							Leyton Orient	49	—
Ling Martin	5 7	10 08	M	15 7 66	West Ham	Apprentice	Exeter C	116	14
							Swindon T	2	—
							Southend U	138	31
							Mansfield T (loan)	3	—
							Swindon T (loan)	1	—
							Swindon T	149	10
							Leyton Orient	134	7
Lockwood Matt	5 9	10 12	D	17 10 76	Rochford	Trainee	QPR	—	—
							Bristol R	63	1
							Leyton Orient	37	3
MacKenzie Chris*	6 0	12 06	G	14 5 72	Northampton	Corby T	Hereford U	60	1
							Leyton Orient	30	—
Martin John	5 5	10 00	M	15 7 81	Bethnal Green		Leyton Orient	2	—
Maskell Craig*	5 10	11 10	F	10 4 68	Aldershot	Apprentice	Southampton	6	1
							Swindon T (loan)	—	—
							Huddersfield T	87	43
							Reading	72	26
							Swindon T	47	22
							Southampton	17	1
							Bristol C (loan)	5	1
							Brighton & HA	69	20
						Happy Valley	Leyton Orient	23	2

Name							Club	Apps	Gls
McCormick Stephen	6 4	11 04	F	14 8 69	Dumbarton		Queen's Park	58	15
							Stirling A	72	33
							Dundee	15	5
							Leyton Orient (loan)	4	—
McDougald Junior†	5 9	11 00	F	12 1 75	Big Spring	Trainee	Tottenham H	—	—
							Brighton & HA	78	14
							Chesterfield (loan)	9	3
							Rotherham U	18	2
							Millwall	1	—
							Leyton Orient	8	—
Morrison Dave#	5 11	12 10	M	30 11 74	Waltham Forest	Chelmsford C	Peterborough U	77	12
							Leyton Orient	33	3
Raynor Paul‡	5 11	12 03	M	29 4 66	Nottingham	Apprentice	Nottingham F	3	—
							Bristol R (loan)	8	—
							Huddersfield T	50	9
							Swansea C	191	27
							Wrexham (loan)	6	—
							Cambridge U	49	2
							Preston NE	80	9
							Cambridge U	79	7
						Guang Deong	Leyton Orient	15	—
Reinelt Robbie‡	5 11	11 11	F	11 3 74	Epping	Trainee	Aldershot	5	—
							Gillingham	52	5
							Colchester U	48	10
							Brighton & HA	44	7
							Leyton Orient	7	—
Richards Tony	6 0	13 06	F	17 9 73	Newham	Sudbury T	Cambridge U	42	5
							Leyton Orient	46	9
Richardson Craig‡			D	8 10 79	Newham	Trainee	Leyton Orient	1	—
Simba Amara#	6 1	13 00	F	23 12 61	Paris		Paris St Germain	40	7
							Cannes	28	10
							Paris St Germain	38	10
							Monaco	32	4
							Caen	37	12
							Lille	39	4
						Lyon	Leyton Orient	24	10
Simpson Colin*	6 1	11 05	F	30 4 76	Oxford	Trainee	Watford	1	—
						Hendon	Leyton Orient	14	3
Smith Dean	6 0	13 00	D	19 3 71	West Bromwich	Trainee	Walsall	142	2
							Hereford U	117	19
							Leyton Orient	80	18
Stimson Mark*	5 10	12 02	D	27 12 67	Plaistow	Trainee	Tottenham H	2	—
							Leyton Orient (loan)	10	—
							Gillingham (loan)	18	—
							Newcastle U	86	2
							Portsmouth (loan)	4	—
							Portsmouth	58	2
							Barnet (loan)	5	—
							Southend U	56	—
							Leyton Orient	2	—
Walschaerts Wim	5 11	12 00	M	5 11 72	Antwerp	FC Tielen	Leyton Orient	44	3
Watts Steve	6 1	13 00	F	11 7 76	Lambeth	Fisher Ath	Leyton Orient	28	6

Trainees

Akontoh, Raymond; Crowe, Michael W; Curran, Danny; Dorrian, Chris S; Downer, Simon; Gough, Neil; Marwa, Ranbir B; McElholm, Brendan A; McKay, Darren G; Murray, Jade A; Parsons, David; Shorey, Nicholas; White, Lee

---

LINCOLN CITY

Name							Club	Apps	Gls
Austin Kevin#	6 1	14 00	D	12 2 73	Hackney	Saffron Walden	Leyton Orient	109	3
							Lincoln C	129	2
Bailey Dennis‡	5 10	11 08	F	13 11 65	Lambeth	Farnborough T	Crystal Palace	5	1
							Bristol R (loan)	17	9
							Birmingham C	75	23
							Bristol R (loan)	6	1
							QPR	39	10
							Charlton Ath (loan)	4	—
							Watford (loan)	8	4
							Brentford (loan)	6	3
							Gillingham	88	11
							Lincoln C	5	1
Barnett Jason	5 9	10 10	D	21 4 76	Shrewsbury	Trainee	Wolverhampton W	—	—
							Lincoln C	130	3
Battersby Tony	6 0	12 09	F	30 8 75	Doncaster	Trainee	Sheffield U	10	1
							Southend U (loan)	8	1
							Notts Co	39	8
							Bury (loan)	11	2
							Bury	37	6
							Lincoln C	39	7
Bimson Stuart	5 11	11 08	D	29 9 69	Liverpool	Macclesfield T	Bury	36	—
							Lincoln C	58	3
Brown Grant	6 0	11 12	D	19 11 69	Sunderland	Trainee	Leicester C	14	—
							Lincoln C	325	13
Finnigan John	5 8	10 11	M	29 3 76	Wakefield	Trainee	Nottingham F	—	—
							Lincoln C (loan)	6	—
							Lincoln C	37	1

Name	Ht	Wt	Pos	Date of Birth	Birthplace	Source	Club	Apps	Goals
Fleming Terry	5 9	10 01	M	5 1 73	Marston Green	Trainee	Coventry C	13	—
							Northampton T	31	1
							Preston NE	32	2
							Lincoln C	142	3
Gain Peter	6 1	11 00	M	2 11 76	Hammersmith	Trainee	Tottenham H	—	—
							Lincoln C	4	—
Gordon Gavin	6 1	12 00	F	24 6 79	Manchester	Trainee	Hull C	38	9
							Lincoln C	40	8
Grobbelaar Bruce‡	6 1	12 08	G	6 10 57	Durban	Vancouver Whitecaps	Crewe Alex	24	1
							Liverpool	440	—
							Stoke C (loan)	4	—
							Southampton	32	—
							Plymouth Arg	36	—
							Oxford U	—	—
							Oldham Ath	4	—
						Chesham U	Bury	1	—
							Lincoln C	2	—
Holmes Steve	6 2	13 00	D	13 1 71	Middlesbrough	Guisborough T	Preston NE	13	1
							Hartlepool U (loan)	5	2
							Lincoln C	134	16
Miller Paul	6 0	11 07	M	31 1 68	Bisley	Trainee	Wimbledon	80	10
							Newport Co (loan)	6	2
							Bristol C (loan)	3	—
							Bristol R	105	22
							Lincoln C	56	4
Peacock Richard	5 10	11 05	M	29 10 72	Sheffield	Sheffield FC	Hull C	174	21
							Lincoln C	10	—
Phillips Dave	5 9	12 04	D	29 7 63	Wegberg	Apprentice	Plymouth Arg	73	15
							Manchester C	81	13
							Coventry C	100	8
							Norwich C	152	18
							Nottingham F	126	5
							Huddersfield T	52	3
							Lincoln C	9	—
Philpott Lee	5 9	11 08	M	21 2 70	Barnet	Trainee	Peterborough U	4	—
							Cambridge U	134	17
							Leicester C	75	3
							Blackpool	71	5
							Lincoln C	24	—
Reeson Nick*			M	5 5 80	Boston	Trainee	Lincoln C	—	—
Richardson Barry	6 1	12 01	G	5 8 69	Wallsend	Trainee	Sunderland	—	—
							Scunthorpe U	—	—
							Scarborough	30	—
							Northampton T	96	—
							Preston NE	20	—
							Lincoln C	109	—
Smith Paul	5 11	11 07	M	25 1 76	Hastings	Hastings T	Nottingham F	—	—
							Lincoln C (loan)	17	3
							Lincoln C	28	2
Stant Phil†	6 1	12 07	F	13 10 62	Bolton	Camberley	Reading	4	2
						Army	Hereford U	89	38
							Notts Co	22	6
							Blackpool (loan)	12	5
							Lincoln C (loan)	4	—
							Huddersfield T (loan)	5	1
							Fulham	19	5
							Mansfield T	57	32
							Cardiff C	79	34
							Mansfield T (loan)	4	1
							Bury	62	23
							Northampton T (loan)	5	2
							Lincoln C	46	17
Stones Craig			M	31 5 80	Scunthorpe	Trainee	Lincoln C	18	—
Thorpe Lee	6 0	11 06	F	14 12 75	Wolverhampton	Trainee	Blackpool	12	—
							Lincoln C	82	22
Vaughan John	5 10	13 01	G	26 6 64	Isleworth	Apprentice	West Ham U	—	—
							Charlton Ath (loan)	6	—
							Bristol R (loan)	6	—
							Wrexham (loan)	4	—
							Bristol C (loan)	2	—
							Fulham	44	—
							Bristol C (loan)	3	—
							Cambridge U	178	—
							Charlton Ath	6	—
							Preston NE	66	—
							Lincoln C	60	—
							Colchester U (loan)	5	—
Walling Dean	6 0	10 08	D	17 4 69	Leeds	Apprentice	Leeds U	—	—
							Rochdale	65	8
						Guiseley	Carlisle U	236	22
							Lincoln C	38	5
Wilkins Ian			D	3 4 80	Lincoln	Trainee	Lincoln C	2	—

Trainees
Banks, Steven J; Bridge, James; Carmody, Ryan D; Clarke, Justin A; Crowfoot, Benjamin G; Gray, Darren K; Lewis, Graham; Nower, Benjamin E; Pitter, Dominic J; Reeve, David T; Walshe, Liam R

Non-Contract
Stant, Philip

Associated Schoolboys who have accepted the Club's offer of a Traineeship/Scholarship/Contract
Bent, Daniel

LIVERPOOL

Name	Ht	Wt	Pos	Born	Birthplace	Status	Club	Apps	Gls
Armstrong Ian			F	16 11 81	Fazackerley	Trainee	Liverpool	—	—
Babb Phil	6 0	12 03	D	30 11 70	Lambeth	Trainee	Millwall	—	—
							Bradford C	80	14
							Coventry C	77	3
							Liverpool	128	1
Berger Patrik	6 1	12 06	M	10 11 73	Prague		Slavia Prague	89	24
							Borussia Dortmund	25	4
							Liverpool	77	16
Bjornebye Stig Inge	5 10	11 09	D	11 12 69	Elverum		Strammen	19	—
							Kongsvinger	62	3
							Rosenborg	21	3
							Liverpool	139	2
Boardman John			D	6 9 80	Liverpool	Trainee	Liverpool	—	—
Byrne Niall*	5 8	11 00	F	3 9 79	Dublin	Trainee	Liverpool	—	—
Carragher James	6 1	13 00	M	28 1 78	Liverpool	Trainee	Liverpool	56	2
Cassidy Jamie*	5 9	10 08	M	21 11 77	Liverpool	Trainee	Liverpool	—	—
Culshaw Thomas*	5 10	12 02	D	10 10 78	Liverpool	Trainee	Liverpool	0	—
Doherty Kevin			M	18 4 80	Dublin		Liverpool	—	—
Dunbavin Ian			G	27 5 80	Knowsley	Trainee	Liverpool	—	—
Dundee Sean	6 1	13 00	F	7 12 72	Durban	D'Alberton Carries	Stuttgart Kickers	7	—
						Ditzingen	Karlsruhe	85	36
							Liverpool	3	—
Ferri Jean-Michel	6 0	12 00	M	7 2 69	Lyon		Nantes	290	21
						Istanbul	Liverpool	2	—
Fowler Robbie	5 11	11 10	F	9 4 75	Liverpool	Trainee	Liverpool	185	106
Friedel Brad	6 3	14 00	G	18 5 71	Lakewood		Liverpool	23	—
Gerrard Steven	6 1	13 00	M	30 5 80	Whiston	Trainee	Liverpool	12	—
Gudnason Haukar	5 10	12 00	F	8 9 78	Keflavik		Keflavik	34	11
							Liverpool	—	—
Harkness Steve	5 10	11 02	D	27 8 71	Carlisle	Trainee	Carlisle U	13	—
(Transferred to Benfica, March 1999)							Liverpool	102	2
							Huddersfield T (loan)	5	—
							Southend U (loan)	6	—
Heggem Vegard	5 11	12 00	D	13 7 75	Trondheim		Rosenborg	52	5
							Liverpool	29	2
Ince Paul	5 10	12 02	M	21 10 67	Ilford	Trainee	West Ham U	72	7
							Manchester U	206	24
							Internazionale	54	9
							Liverpool	65	14
James David	6 5	14 02	G	1 8 70	Welwyn	Trainee	Watford	89	—
							Liverpool	214	—
Jones Eifion	6 3	13 00	D	28 9 80	Llanrug	Trainee	Liverpool	—	—
Jones Rob*	5 8	11 00	D	5 11 71	Wrexham	Trainee	Crewe Alex	75	2
							Liverpool	183	—
Kippe Frode			D	17 1 78	Oslo		Lillestrom	34	2
							Liverpool	—	—
Kvarme Bjorn	5 11	12 04	D	17 6 72	Trondheim		Rosenborg	88	2
							Liverpool	45	—
Leonhardsen Oyvind	5 10	11 02	M	17 8 70	Kristiansund	Clausenengen	Molde	64	9
							Rosenborg	63	20
							Wimbledon	76	13
							Liverpool	37	7
Matteo Dominic	6 1	11 10	D	24 4 74	Dumfries	Trainee	Liverpool	95	1
							Sunderland (loan)	1	—
Maxwell Leyton	5 8	11 00	M	3 10 79	St Asaph	Trainee	Liverpool	—	—
McManaman Steve	6 0	10 06	M	11 2 72	Liverpool	School	Liverpool	272	46
Miles John			F	28 9 81	Fazackerley	Trainee	Liverpool	—	—
Murphy Danny	5 9	10 08	M	18 3 77	Chester	Trainee	Crewe Alex	134	27
							Liverpool	17	—
							Crewe Alex (loan)	16	1
Murphy Neil	5 9	11 00	D	19 5 80	Liverpool	Trainee	Liverpool	—	—
Navarro Alan			D	31 5 81	Liverpool	Trainee	Liverpool	—	—
Newby John	6 0	12 00	F	28 11 78	Warrington	Trainee	Liverpool	—	—
Nielsen Jorgen	6 0	13 00	G	6 5 71	Nykobing		Naestved	2	—
							Hvidovre*	—	—
							Liverpool	—	—
							Wolverhampton W (loan)	—	—
O'Brien Chris			M	13 1 82	Liverpool	Trainee	Liverpool	—	—
O'Mara Paul	5 9	11 00	D	23 11 80	Dublin	Trainee	Liverpool	—	—
Owen Michael	5 8	11 00	F	14 12 79	Chester	Trainee	Liverpool	68	37
Partridge Richie	5 8	10 10	M	12 9 80	Dublin	Trainee	Liverpool	—	—
Redknapp Jamie	6 0	12 10	M	25 6 73	Barton-on-Sea	Trainee	Bournemouth	13	—
							Liverpool	211	26

Name	Ht	Wt	Pos	Date	Place	Source	Club	Apps	Gls
Riedle Karlheinz	5 11	12 00	F	16 9 65	Weiler	Augsburg	Blau-Weiss 90	34	10
							Werder Bremen	86	38
							Lazio	84	30
							Borussia Dortmund	87	24
							Liverpool	59	11
Roberts Gareth‡	5 8	11 00	D	6 2 78	Wrexham	Trainee	Liverpool	—	—
Song Rigobert	6 0	13 00	D	1 7 76	Nkanglicock	Tonnerre	Metz	123	3
							Salernitana	4	1
							Liverpool	13	—
Staunton Steve	6 1	12 11	D	19 1 69	Drogheda	Dundalk	Liverpool	65	—
							Bradford C (loan)	8	—
							Aston Villa	208	16
							Liverpool	31	—
Thomas Michael	5 9	12 06	M	24 8 67	Lambeth	Apprentice	Arsenal	163	24
(Transferred to Benfica, December 1998)							Portsmouth (loan)	3	—
							Liverpool	124	9
							Middlesbrough (loan)	10	—
Thompson David	5 7	10 00	M	12 9 77	Birkenhead	Trainee	Liverpool	21	2
							Swindon T (loan)	10	—
Torpey Steve			M	16 9 81	Fazackerley	Trainee	Liverpool	—	—
Traore Djimi	6 3	13 10	D	1 3 80	Saint Ouen	Laval	Liverpool	—	—
Warner Tony*	6 4	13 09	G	11 5 74	Liverpool	School	Liverpool	—	—
							Swindon T (loan)	2	—
							Celtic (loan)	3	—
							Aberdeen (loan)	6	—
Warnock Stephen			M	12 12 81	Ormskirk	Trainee	Liverpool	—	—
Wright Mark‡	6 2	13 03	D	1 8 63	Dorchester	Amateur	Oxford U	10	—
							Southampton	170	7
							Derby Co	144	10
							Liverpool	158	5
Wright Stephen			D	8 2 80	Liverpool	Trainee	Liverpool	—	—

Trainees/Scholars
Bishop, David S; Boggan, Jonathan R; Cavanagh, Peter J; Crookes, Peter; Culshaw, Paul R; Foley, Michael P; Gregson, Neil R; Harkin, Bryan; Olsen, James P; Park, Stephen M; Porter, Stephen P; Roberts, John P; Thompson, Christopher M

LUTON TOWN

Name	Ht	Wt	Pos	Date	Place	Source	Club	Apps	Gls
Abbey Nathan*	6 1	11 13	G	11 7 78	Islington	Trainee	Luton T	2	—
Augustine Steve*	6 0	13 07	F	13 12 78	Hammersmith		Luton T	—	—
Ayres James	6 3	13 00	D	18 9 80	Luton	Trainee	Luton T	—	—
Bacque Herve			F	13 7 76	Bordeaux	Monaco	Luton T	7	—
(Transferred to Motherwell, January 1999)							Motherwell	1	—
Boyce Emmerson	5 11	11 02	D	24 9 79	Aylesbury	Trainee	Luton T	1	—
Clarke Richard*	5 11	10 10	D	15 2 80	Enfield	Trainee	Luton T	—	—
Cox Jimmy*	5 6	10 07	F	11 4 80	Gloucester	Trainee	Luton T	8	—
Davis Kelvin	6 1	13 11	G	29 9 76	Bedford	Trainee	Luton T	92	—
							Torquay U (loan)	2	—
							Hartlepool U (loan)	2	—
Doherty Gary	6 1	13 00	D	31 1 80	Donegal	Trainee	Luton T	30	6
Douglas Stuart	5 8	11 05	F	9 4 78	London	Trainee	Luton T	76	11
Fotiadis Andrew	5 11	11 07	F	6 9 77	Hitchin	School	Luton T	53	6
Fraser Stuart	5 9	10 06	D	9 1 80	Edinburgh	Trainee	Luton T	9	—
George Liam	5 9	11 04	F	2 2 79	Luton	Trainee	Luton T	13	—
Gray Phil	5 9	12 07	F	2 10 68	Belfast	Apprentice	Tottenham H	9	—
							Barnsley (loan)	3	—
							Fulham (loan)	3	—
							Luton T	59	22
							Sunderland	115	34
							Luton T	52	10
James Julian*	5 10	12 06	D	22 3 70	Tring	Trainee	Luton T	282	13
							Preston NE (loan)	6	—
Johnson Marvin	6 1	13 00	D	29 10 68	Wembley	Apprentice	Luton T	302	6
Kandol Tresor	6 1	11 07	F	30 8 81	Banga	Trainee	Luton T	4	—
Lawes Russell*	5 10	11 00	D	16 1 80	Bedford	Trainee	Luton T	—	—
Lough Lee‡	5 10	12 06	M	18 7 79	London	Ashford T	Luton T	—	—
McGowan Gavin	5 10	12 06	D	16 1 76	Blackheath	Trainee	Arsenal	6	—
							Luton T (loan)	2	—
							Luton T (loan)	8	—
							Luton T	31	—
McIndoe Michael	5 8	10 06	M	2 12 79	Edinburgh	Trainee	Luton T	22	—
McKinnon Ray*	5 10	11 08	M	5 8 70	Dundee		Dundee U	53	6
							Nottingham F	6	1
							Aberdeen	26	—
							Dundee U	44	6
							Luton T	30	2
McLaren Paul	6 1	13 00	M	17 11 76	High Wycombe	Trainee	Luton T	103	1
Moses Jerry	5 9	11 05	M	22 2 81	Kampala	Trainee	Luton T	—	—
Scarlett Andre	5 4	9 12	M	11 1 80	Brent	Trainee	Luton T	6	1

Name	Ht	Wt	Pos	DOB	Birthplace	Previous	Club	Apps	Gls
Showler Paul*	5 10	11 00	M	10 10 66	Doncaster	Altrincham	Barnet	71	12
							Bradford C	88	15
							Luton T	27	6
Spring Matthew	5 11	11 07	M	17 11 79	Harlow	Trainee	Luton T	57	3
Tate Daniel	5 11	11 12	G	12 11 80	Bedford	Trainee	Luton T	—	—
Taylor Matthew	5 10	11 08	D	27 11 81	Oxford	Trainee	Luton T	—	—
Thomas Mitchell*	6 2	14 00	D	2 10 64	Luton	Apprentice	Luton T	107	1
							Tottenham H	157	6
							West Ham U	38	3
							Luton T	185	5
Ward Scott	6 2	13 00	G	5 10 81	Brent	Trainee	Luton T	—	—
White Alan	6 1	13 07	D	22 3 76	Darlington	Derby Co	Middlesbrough	—	—
							Luton T	61	2
Willmott Chris	6 2	11 13	D	30 9 77	Bedford	Trainee	Luton T	14	—
Zahana-Oni Landry	5 9	10 09	M	8 8 76	Ivory Coast	Bromley	Luton T	8	—

Trainees
Akurang, Cliff D; Harrington, Joseph; Howe, Darren M; Hudson, Anthony P; McKoy, Delroy N B; Minton, Alex; Moran, Ryan J; Stirling, Jude B

Associated Schoolboys who have accepted the Club's offer of a Traineeship/Scholarship/Contract
Carroll, John M; Clarke, Duane; Dogbe, Steven; James-Barriteau, Rene W; Mansell, Lee R; Mentore, Ezra; Mortara, Dean P; Thomas, Jerome W; Wraight, Graham D

MACCLESFIELD TOWN

Name	Ht	Wt	Pos	DOB	Birthplace	Previous	Club	Apps	Gls
Askey John	6 0	12 02	F	4 11 64	Stoke	Port Vale	Macclesfield T	77	10
Barclay Dominic*	6 0	11 10	F	5 9 76	Bristol	Trainee	Bristol C	12	—
							Macclesfield T	9	1
Brown Greg	5 10	12 04	D	31 7 78	Wythenshawe	Trainee	Chester C	4	—
							Macclesfield T	7	—
Brown Steve	6 0	13 10	F	6 12 73	Rochford	Trainee	Southend U	10	2
							Scunthorpe U	—	—
							Colchester U	62	17
							Gillingham	9	2
							Lincoln C	72	8
							Macclesfield T	2	—
Chambers Leroy‡	5 11	11 08	F	25 10 72	Sheffield	Trainee	Sheffield W	—	—
							Chester C	21	1
							Chesterfield	—	—
						Boston U	Macclesfield T	21	4
Clyde Glynn*	6 2	11 07	G	16 1 79	Derby	Barnsley	Macclesfield T	—	—
Da Costa Nelson‡	5 10	12 03	D	8 12 78	Angola	Belenenses	Stockport Co	—	—
							Macclesfield T	—	—
Davenport Peter†	5 11	12 10	M	24 3 61	Birkenhead	Everton	Nottingham F	118	54
							Manchester U	92	22
							Middlesbrough	59	7
							Sunderland	99	15
							Airdrie	38	9
							St Johnstone	22	4
							Stockport Co	6	1
						Southport	Macclesfield T	5	1
Davies Simon	5 11	12 04	M	23 4 74	Davenham	Trainee	Manchester U	11	—
							Exeter C (loan)	6	1
							Huddersfield T (loan)	3	—
							Luton T	22	1
							Macclesfield T	12	2
Durkan Kieron	5 10	12 09	M	1 12 73	Chester	Trainee	Wrexham	50	3
							Stockport Co	64	4
							Macclesfield T	30	3
Griffiths Peter	5 9	11 06	M	13 3 80	St Helier	Trainee	Macclesfield T	4	1
Hitchen Steve	5 8	11 07	D	28 11 76	Salford	Trainee	Blackburn R	—	—
							Macclesfield T	37	—
Howarth Neil‡	6 3	13 07	D	15 11 71	Bolton	Trainee	Burnley	1	—
						Macclesfield T	Macclesfield T	60	3
Ingram Rae	5 11	12 02	D	6 12 74	Manchester	Trainee	Manchester C	23	—
							Macclesfield T (loan)	5	—
							Macclesfield T	29	—
Landon Richard*	6 2	13 10	F	22 3 70	Worthing	Bedworth U	Plymouth Arg	30	12
							Stockport Co	13	5
							Rotherham U (loan)	8	—
							Macclesfield T	32	9
Lomax Michael	5 10	10 12	D	7 12 79	Whithington		Macclesfield T	1	—
Lonergan Darren*	6 0	13 04	D	28 1 74	Cork	Waterford	Oldham Ath	2	—
							Bury	—	—
							Macclesfield T	—	—
Mason Michael	5 9	11 11	F	7 8 79	Walsall		Macclesfield T	—	—
Matias Pedro†	6 0	12 00	F	11 10 73	Madrid		Logrones	12	—
							Macclesfield T	22	2
McDonald Martin‡	5 11	11 12	M	4 12 73	Irvine	Southport	Doncaster R	48	4
							Macclesfield T	45	3
Pates Bradley	5 9	11 02	M	21 12 79	Burnley		Macclesfield T	—	—

Payne Steve	5 11	12 05	D	1 8 75	Castleford	Trainee	Huddersfield T	—	—
							Macclesfield T	77	2
Price Ryan	6 6	14 00	G	13 3 70	Wolverhampton	Stafford R	Birmingham C	—	—
							Macclesfield T	88	—
Sedgemore Ben	6 0	12 08	M	5 8 75	Wolverhampton	Trainee	Birmingham C	—	—
							Northampton T (loan)	1	—
							Mansfield T (loan)	9	—
							Peterborough U	17	—
							Mansfield T	67	6
							Macclesfield T	40	2
Sodje Efetobar#	6 1	12 00	D	5 10 72	Greenwich	Stevenage Bor	Macclesfield T	83	6
Sorvel Neil‡	6 0	12 09	M	2 3 73	Whiston	Trainee	Crewe Alex	9	—
							Macclesfield T	86	7
Tinson Darren	6 0	14 04	D	15 11 69	Birmingham	Northwich V	Macclesfield T	81	—
Tomlinson Graeme	5 10	12 04	F	10 12 75	Watford	Trainee	Bradford C	17	6
							Manchester U	—	—
							Luton T (loan)	7	—
							Bournemouth (loan)	7	1
							Millwall (loan)	3	1
							Macclesfield T	28	4
Whittaker Stuart	5 7	10 06	M	2 1 75	Liverpool	Liverpool	Bolton W	3	—
							Wigan Ath (loan)	3	—
							Macclesfield T	58	5
Wood Steve#	5 9	10 10	M	23 6 63	Oldham	Ashton U	Macclesfield T	85	17
Wright Andy*	6 0	11 04	F	12 9 79	Bristol		Macclesfield T	—	—

Trainees
Buckley, Matthew T H; Cain, Philip; Leonard, Christopher; O'Neill, Paul D

Non-Contract
Davenport, Peter; Matias, Pedro M M

MANCHESTER CITY

Allsopp Danny	6 0	12 08	F	10 8 78	Melbourne	Port Melbourne	Manchester C	24	4
Bailey Alan	5 11	12 03	F	1 1 78	Macclesfield	Trainee	Manchester C	—	—
							Macclesfield T (loan)	10	1
Bishop Ian	5 10	12 00	M	29 5 65	Liverpool	Apprentice	Everton	1	—
							Crewe Alex (loan)	4	—
							Carlisle U	132	14
							Bournemouth	44	2
							Manchester C	19	2
							West Ham U	254	12
							Manchester C	31	—
Brannan Ged	6 0	12 05	D	15 1 72	Liverpool	Trainee	Tranmere R	238	20
(Transferred to Motherwell, October 1998)							Manchester C	43	4
							Norwich C (loan)	11	1
							Motherwell	25	5
Brown Michael*	5 9	10 07	G	6 11 79	Stranraer	Trainee	Manchester C	—	—
Brown Michael R	5 9	10 07	M	25 1 77	Hartlepool	Trainee	Manchester C	89	2
							Hartlepool U (loan)	6	1
Clough Nigel‡	5 10	12 03	M	19 3 66	Sunderland	AC Hunters	Nottingham F	311	101
							Liverpool	39	7
							Manchester C	38	4
							Nottingham F (loan)	13	1
							Sheffield W (loan)	1	—
Cooke Terry	5 8	10 03	F	5 8 76	Marston Green	Trainee	Manchester U	4	—
							Sunderland (loan)	6	—
							Birmingham C (loan)	4	—
							Wrexham (loan)	10	—
							Manchester C	21	7
Crooks Lee	6 1	12 09	D	14 1 78	Wakefield	Trainee	Manchester C	54	1
Dickov Paul	5 5	11 09	F	1 11 72	Glasgow	Trainee	Arsenal	21	3
							Luton T (loan)	15	1
							Brighton & HA (loan)	8	5
							Manchester C	94	24
Dunfield Terry	5 7	10 03	M	20 2 82	Canada	Trainee	Manchester C	—	—
Edghill Richard	5 9	11 00	D	23 9 74	Oldham	Trainee	Manchester C	123	—
Fenton Nick	6 1	11 08	D	23 11 79	Preston	Trainee	Manchester C	15	—
Goater Shaun	6 0	12 10	F	25 2 70	Bermuda		Manchester U	—	—
							Rotherham U	209	70
							Notts Co (loan)	1	—
							Bristol C	75	40
							Manchester C	50	20
Greenacre Chris	5 11	10 06	F	23 12 77	Halifax	Trainee	Manchester C	8	1
							Cardiff C (loan)	11	2
							Blackpool (loan)	4	—
							Scarborough (loan)	12	2
							Northampton T (loan)	—	—
Heaney Neil	5 9	11 07	F	3 11 71	Middlesbrough	Trainee	Arsenal	7	—
							Hartlepool U (loan)	3	—
							Cambridge U (loan)	13	4
							Southampton	61	5
							Manchester C	18	1
							Charlton Ath (loan)	6	—
							Bristol C (loan)	3	—

Name	Ht	Wt	Pos	DOB	Birthplace	Source	Club	Apps	Gls
Hodgson Steven	5 11	11 00	G	23 12 81	Macclesfield	Scholarship	Manchester C	—	—
Holmes Shaun	5 9	10 07	D	27 12 80	Derry	Trainee	Manchester C	—	—
Horlock Kevin	6 0	12 00	M	1 11 72	Erith	Trainee	West Ham U	—	—
							Swindon T	163	22
							Manchester C	80	18
Jobson Richard	6 2	12 12	D	9 5 63	Holderness	Burton Alb	Watford	28	4
							Hull C	221	17
							Oldham Ath	189	10
							Leeds U	22	1
							Southend U (loan)	8	1
							Manchester C	6	1
Jordan Stephen			M	6 3 82	Warrington	Scholarship	Manchester C	—	—
Kavelashvili Mikhail*	5 11	12 01	M	22 7 71	Tbilisi	Spartak Vladikavkaz	Manchester C	28	3
Kelly Ray‡	5 11	12 00	F	29 12 76	Ballinasloe	Athlone T	Manchester C	1	—
							Wrexham (loan)	10	1
Killen Chris	5 11	11 03	F	8 10 81	Wellington	Miramar R	Manchester C	—	—
Kinkladze Georgiou	5 8	10 09	M	6 7 73	Tbilisi	Dynamo Tbilisi	Manchester C	106	20
(Transferred to Ajax, June 1998)									
Laycock David	5 10	10 07	M	1 10 80	Hull	Trainee	Manchester C	—	—
Mason Gary	5 8	10 01	M	15 10 79	Edinburgh	Trainee	Manchester C	19	—
McGoldrick Eddie*	5 10	11 07	M	30 4 65	London	Nuneaton Bor, Kettering T	Northampton T	107	9
							Crystal Palace	147	11
							Arsenal	38	—
							Manchester C	40	—
							Stockport Co (loan)	2	—
Mike Leon	6 0	12 02	F	4 9 81	Manchester	Scholarship	Manchester C	—	—
Morley Neil*	5 8	10 02	M	16 11 78	Warrington	Trainee	Manchester C	—	—
Morrison Andy	5 11	12 12	D	30 7 70	Inverness	Trainee	Plymouth Arg	113	6
							Blackburn R	5	—
							Blackpool	47	3
							Huddersfield T	45	2
							Manchester C	22	4
Pollock Jamie	6 0	13 03	M	16 2 74	Stockton	Trainee	Middlesbrough	155	17
							Osasuna	—	—
							Bolton W	46	5
							Manchester C	34	2
Porteous Andrew*	5 11	10 11	M	13 9 79	Edinburgh	Trainee	Nottingham F	—	—
							Manchester C	—	—
Reilly Alan	5 11	12 01	M	22 8 80	Dublin	Trainee	Manchester C	—	—
Rimmer Stephen*	6 3	13 02	D	23 5 79	Liverpool	Trainee	Manchester C	—	—
Robins Mark*	5 8	11 11	F	22 12 69	Ashton-under-Lyne	Apprentice	Manchester U	48	11
							Norwich C	67	20
							Leicester C	56	12
							Reading (loan)	5	—
						Panionios	Manchester C	2	—
Russell Craig	5 10	12 07	F	4 2 74	Jarrow	Trainee	Sunderland	150	31
							Manchester C	31	2
							Tranmere R (loan)	4	—
							Port Vale (loan)	8	1
Shelia Murtaz	6 0	13 02	D	7 9 68	Georgia		Dynamo Tbilisi	10	2
							Alania	62	9
							Manchester C	15	2
Taylor Gareth	6 1	12 02	F	25 2 73	Weston-Super-Mare	Southampton	Bristol R	47	16
							Crystal Palace	20	1
							Sheffield U	84	25
							Manchester C	26	4
Tiatto Danny	5 8	11 01	D	22 5 73	Melbourne	Baden	Stoke C	15	—
							Manchester C	17	—
Tskhadadze Kakhabor	6 1	12 04	D	7 9 68	Rustavi		Dynamo Tbilisi	41	1
							Sundsvall*	—	—
							Sundsvall	4	—
							Spartak Moscow	7	—
							Eintracht Frankfurt	64	1
							Eintracht Frankfurt*	—	—
							Alania	17	1
							Manchester C	12	2
Vaughan Tony	6 1	12 10	D	11 10 75	Manchester	Trainee	Ipswich T	67	3
							Manchester C	57	2
Weaver Nick	6 3	13 01	G	2 3 79	Sheffield	Trainee	Mansfield T	1	—
							Manchester C	45	—
Whitley Jeff	5 9	10 10	M	28 1 79	Zambia	Trainee	Manchester C	48	3
							Wrexham (loan)	9	2
Whitley Jim	5 9	10 12	M	14 4 75	Zambia	Trainee	Manchester C	37	—
Wiekens Gerard	6 0	12 06	D	25 2 73	Tolhuiswyk		Veendam	33	1
							Manchester C	79	7
Wright-Phillips Shaun	5 6	10 01	F	25 10 81	London		Manchester C	—	—
Wright Tommy	6 1	14 05	G	29 8 63	Belfast	Linfield	Newcastle U	73	—
							Hull C (loan)	6	—
							Nottingham F	11	—
							Reading (loan)	17	—
							Manchester C	32	—
							Wrexham (loan)	16	—

Trainees
Allcock, Adam M; Daly, Lee C; Duff, Gregory J; Garfield, Darren J S; Julien, Michael F; Kneen, Jason; O'Keefe, Gerald J

Scholars
Day, Rhys; Etuhu, Dixon P; Parkhouse, Stephen; Pavey, Andrew; Shuker, Christopher A

Associated Schoolboys
Anderson-Hodgson, David; Ashton, Stephen D J; Barton, Joseph; Egerton, Mark; Fenlon, Thomas; Furnival, Gary R; Hughes, Lee S; Knowles, Alexander; McDowall, Ryan; Mears, Tyrone; Orr, Adrian; Pheonix, Jamie; Richards, Leonard R; Watkins, Kenneth W; Waugh, Peter M

MANCHESTER UNITED

Beckham David	6 0	11 09	M	2 5 75	Leytonstone	Trainee	Manchester U	144	29
							Preston NE (loan)	5	2
Berg Henning	6 0	12 01	D	1 9 69	Eidsvoll	Lillestrom	Blackburn R	159	4
							Manchester U	43	1
Best Russell‡			M	1 9 79	Nottingham		Manchester U	—	—
Blomqvist Jesper	5 9	11 03	F	5 2 74	Tavelsjo		Umea	38	8
							IFK Gothenburg	71	19
							AC Milan	20	1
							Parma	28	1
							Manchester U	25	1
Brown Wes	6 1	11 11	D	13 10 79	Manchester	Trainee	Manchester U	16	—
Butt Nicky	5 10	11 05	M	21 1 75	Manchester	Trainee	Manchester U	146	13
Chadwick Luke	5 11	10 09	F	18 11 80	Cambridge	Trainee	Manchester U	—	—
Clegg Michael	5 8	11 10	D	3 7 77	Ashton-under-Lyne	Trainee	Manchester U	7	—
Cole Andy	5 10	12 04	F	15 10 71	Nottingham	Trainee	Arsenal	1	—
							Fulham (loan)	13	3
							Bristol C (loan)	12	8
							Bristol C	29	12
							Newcastle U	70	55
							Manchester U	137	61
Cosgrove Stephen	5 9	10 05	M	29 12 80	Glasgow	Trainee	Manchester U	—	—
Cruyff Jordi	6 1	10 12	F	9 2 74	Amsterdam	Ajax	Barcelona	41	11
(On loan to Celta Vigo)							Manchester U	26	4
Culkin Nick	6 2	13 05	G	6 7 78	York	York C	Manchester U	—	—
Curtis John	5 10	11 07	D	3 9 78	Nuneaton	Trainee	Manchester U	12	—
Djordjic Bojan			M	6 2 82	Belgrade		Manchester U	—	—
(On loan to Brommapojkarna)									
Evans Wayne	5 9	9 12	M	23 10 80	Carmarthen	Trainee	Manchester U	—	—
Fitzpatrick Ian	5 9	10 00	F	22 9 80	Manchester	Trainee	Manchester U	—	—
Ford Ryan	5 9	10 04	M	3 9 80	Worksop	Trainee	Manchester U	—	—
Giggs Ryan	5 11	10 10	F	29 11 73	Cardiff	School	Manchester U	260	53
Greening Jonathan	6 0	11 03	F	2 1 79	Scarborough	Trainee	York C	25	2
							Manchester U	3	—
Healy David	5 8	10 09	F	5 8 79	Downpatrick	Trainee	Manchester U	—	—
Higginbotham Danny	6 1	12 03	D	29 12 78	Manchester	Trainee	Manchester U	1	—
(On loan to Antwerp)									
Irwin Denis	5 8	10 10	D	31 10 65	Cork	Apprentice	Leeds U	72	1
							Oldham Ath	167	4
							Manchester U	310	19
Johnsen Ronny	6 3	13 02	D	10 6 69	Sandefjord	Eik	Lyn	31	7
							Lillestrom	23	4
							Besiktas	22	1
							Manchester U	75	5
Keane Roy	5 11	12 01	M	10 8 71	Cork	Cobh Ramb	Nottingham F	114	22
							Manchester U	156	19
May David	6 0	13 05	D	24 6 70	Oldham	Trainee	Blackburn R	123	3
							Manchester U	79	6
McDermott Alan	6 1	11 13	D	22 1 82	Dublin	Trainee	Manchester U	—	—
Neville Gary	5 11	12 07	D	18 2 75	Bury	Trainee	Manchester U	149	2
Neville Philip	5 11	11 11	D	21 1 77	Bury	Trainee	Manchester U	102	1
Nevland Erik	5 10	11 12	F	10 11 77	Stavanger		Viking	14	5
(On loan to IFK Gothenburg)							Manchester U	1	—
Notman Alex	5 7	10 11	F	10 12 79	Edinburgh	Trainee	Manchester U	—	—
							Aberdeen (loan)	2	—
O'Shea John	6 3	11 12	D	30 4 81	Waterford	Waterford	Manchester U	—	—
Roche Lee	5 10	10 11	D	28 10 80	Bolton	Trainee	Manchester U	—	—
Schmeichel Peter	6 4	16 00	G	18 11 63	Gladsaxe		Hvidovre	88	6
							Brondby	119	2
							Manchester U	292	—
Scholes Paul	5 7	11 08	M	16 11 74	Salford	Trainee	Manchester U	129	32
Sheringham Teddy	6 0	13 00	F	2 4 66	Highams Park	Apprentice	Millwall	220	93
							Aldershot (loan)	5	—
							Nottingham F	42	14
							Tottenham H	166	75
							Manchester U	48	11
Solskjaer Ole Gunnar	5 10	11 06	F	26 2 73	Kristiansund		Molde	42	31
							Manchester U	74	35

Stam Jaap	6 3	13 09	D	17 7 72	Kampen		Zwolle	32	1
							Cambuur	66	3
							Willem II	19	1
							PSV Eindhoven	76	12
							Manchester U	30	1
Stewart Michael	5 11	11 06	M	26 2 81	Edinburgh	Trainee	Manchester U	—	—
Strange Gareth	5 9	10 09	M	3 10 81	Bolton	Trainee	Manchester U	—	—
Teather Paul	6 0	11 08	D	28 12 77	Rotherham	Trainee	Manchester U	—	—
							Bournemouth (loan)	10	—
Thorrington John*	5 7	10 05	F	17 10 79	Johannesburg	US College	Manchester U	—	—
Twiss Michael	5 11	12 00	M	18 12 77	Salford	Trainee	Manchester U	—	—
							Sheffield U (loan)	12	1
Van der Gouw Raimond	6 3	13 07	G	24 3 63	Oldenzaal		Go Ahead	97	—
							Vitesse	258	—
							Manchester U	12	—
Wallwork Ronnie	5 10	12 12	D	10 9 77	Manchester	Trainee	Manchester U	1	—
(On loan to Antwerp)							Carlisle U (loan)	10	1
							Stockport Co (loan)	7	—
Webber Danny	5 9	10 03	F	28 12 81	Manchester	Trainee	Manchester U	—	—
Wellens Richard	5 9	11 05	M	26 3 80	Manchester	Trainee	Manchester U	—	—
Wheatcroft Paul	5 8	9 09	F	22 11 80	Manchester	Trainee	Manchester U	—	—
Wilson Mark	6 0	13 02	M	9 2 79	Scunthorpe	Trainee	Manchester U	—	—
							Wrexham (loan)	13	4
Wood Jamie*	5 10	12 11	F	21 9 78	Salford	Trainee	Manchester U	—	—
Yorke Dwight	5 10	12 04	F	3 11 71	Canaan	St Clair's	Aston Villa	231	73
							Manchester U	32	18

Trainees/Scholars
Clegg, George G; Davis, James R W; Dodd, Ashley M; Gaff, Gerard A; Grogan, Kevin M; Hickson, Jason M; Hilton, Kirk; Howard, Joshua L; Jones, Rhodri G; Lynch, Mark J; Marsh, Allan S; Molloy, Eric; Rachubka, Paul S; Rose, Michael; Rose, Stephen D; Studley, Dominic P; Studley, Mark L; Szmid, Marek A; Walker, Joshua G; Whiteley, Lee A

MANSFIELD TOWN

Allardyce Craig#	6 2	14 00	D	9 6 75	Bolton	Trainee	Preston NE	1	—
							Blackpool	1	—
						Chorley	Chesterfield	1	—
							Peterborough U	4	—
							Mansfield T	6	—
Bowling Ian	6 3	13 11	G	27 7 65	Sheffield	Gainsborough T	Lincoln C	59	—
							Hartlepool U (loan)	1	—
							Bradford C (loan)	7	—
							Bradford C	29	—
							Mansfield T	160	—
Carruthers Matt‡			F	22 7 76	Dover	Dover Ath	Mansfield T	5	—
Christie Iyseden	5 10	12 02	F	14 11 76	Coventry	Trainee	Coventry C	1	—
							Bournemouth (loan)	4	—
							Mansfield T (loan)	8	—
							Mansfield T	81	18
Clarke Darrell	5 10	10 11	M	16 12 77	Mansfield	Trainee	Mansfield T	90	11
Ford Tony	5 9	13 00	M	14 5 59	Grimsby	Apprentice	Grimsby T	355	55
							Sunderland (loan)	9	1
							Stoke C	112	13
							WBA	114	14
							Grimsby T	68	3
							Bradford C (loan)	5	—
							Scunthorpe U	76	9
						Barrow	Mansfield T	103	7
Harper Steve*	5 10	11 12	M	3 2 69	Newcastle-under-Lyme	Trainee	Port Vale	28	2
							Preston NE	77	10
							Burnley	69	8
							Doncaster R	65	11
							Mansfield T	160	18
Hassell Bobby	5 10	11 13	D	4 6 80	Derby	Trainee	Mansfield T	12	—
Kerr David#	5 11	12 01	M	6 9 74	Dumfries	Trainee	Manchester C	6	—
							Mansfield T (loan)	5	—
							Mansfield T	62	4
L'Helgoualch Cyrille†			D	25 9 70	Saint Nazaire		Mansfield T	4	1
Linighan David#	6 2	13 12	D	9 1 65	Hartlepool	Local	Hartlepool U	91	5
							Leeds U (loan)	—	—
							Derby Co	—	—
							Shrewsbury T	65	—
							Ipswich T	277	12
							Blackpool	100	5
							Dunfermline Ath	1	—
							Mansfield T	10	—
Lormor Tony	6 2	13 13	F	29 10 70	Ashington	Trainee	Newcastle U	8	3
							Norwich C (loan)	—	—
							Lincoln C	100	30
							Peterborough U	5	—
							Chesterfield	113	35
							Preston NE	12	3
							Notts Co (loan)	7	—
							Mansfield T	41	11

Name	Ht	Wt	Pos	Born	Birthplace	Source	Clubs	Apps	Gls
Milner Jonathan§	5 8	11 07	F	30 3 81	Mansfield	Trainee	Mansfield T	7	—
Parkin Steve	5 6	11 01	D	7 11 65	Mansfield	Apprentice	Stoke C	113	5
							WBA	48	2
							Mansfield T	87	3
Peacock Lee	6 1	13 12	F	9 10 76	Paisley	Trainee	Carlisle U	76	11
							Mansfield T	77	22
Peters Mark*	6 0	11 03	D	6 7 72	St Asaph	Trainee	Manchester C	—	—
							Norwich C	—	—
							Peterborough U	19	—
							Mansfield T	108	9
Ryder Stuart*	6 0	12 09	D	6 11 73	Sutton Coldfield	Trainee	Walsall	101	5
							Mansfield T	22	2
Schofield Jon*	5 10	11 03	D	16 5 65	Barnsley	Gainsborough T	Lincoln C	231	11
							Doncaster R	110	12
							Mansfield T	86	—
Sedlan Jason*	5 10	10 11	M	5 8 79	Peterborough	Trainee	Mansfield T	6	—
Sisson Michael	5 9	10 11	M	24 11 78	Sutton-in-Ashfield	Trainee	Mansfield T	2	—
Tallon Gary#	5 9	12 09	M	5 9 73	Drogheda	Trainee	Blackburn R	—	—
							Kilmarnock	4	—
							Chester C (loan)	1	—
							Mansfield T	62	2
Walker John*	5 7	11 00	M	12 12 73	Glasgow	Clydebank BC	Rangers	—	—
							Clydebank	27	2
							Grimsby T	3	1
							Mansfield T	74	4
Watkiss Stuart‡	6 2	13 06	D	8 5 66	Wolverhampton	Apprentice Rushall Olympic	Wolverhampton W	2	—
							Walsall	62	2
							Hereford U	19	—
							Mansfield T	41	1
Wilkins Christopher*	5 6	11 00	D	25 2 80	Walsall	Trainee	Mansfield T	—	—
Williams Lee	5 8	11 13	D	3 2 73	Edgbaston	Trainee	Aston Villa	—	—
							Shrewsbury T (loan)	3	—
							Peterborough U	91	1
							Tranmere R	—	—
							Mansfield T	88	5

Trainees
Archbold, Shaun J; Asher, Alistair A; Bacon, Daniel S; Disley, Craig E; Gibbons, Scott P; Jervis, David J; Jones, Adam L; Lawrence, Liam; Milner, Jonathan R; Mitchell, Dean J; Overton, Paul D; Preston, Richard J; Sweeney, Dean; Tye, Kevin; Williamson, Lee T

Associated Schoolboys
Hemingray, Ryan

Associated Schoolboys who have accepted the Club's offer of a Traineeship/Scholarship/Contract
Elliott, Dominic S; Stringfellow, Daniel J; Swinscoe, Craig A; Williams, Ryan A

MIDDLESBROUGH

Name	Ht	Wt	Pos	Born	Birthplace	Source	Clubs	Apps	Gls
Armstrong Alun	6 0	13 08	F	22 2 75	Gateshead	School	Newcastle U	—	—
							Stockport Co	159	48
							Middlesbrough	17	8
Baker Steve	6 0	12 06	D	8 9 78	Pontefract		Middlesbrough	8	—
Beresford Marlon	6 1	13 08	G	2 6 69	Lincoln	Trainee	Sheffield W	—	—
							Bury (loan)	1	—
							Ipswich T (loan)	—	—
							Northampton T (loan)	13	—
							Crewe Alex (loan)	3	—
							Northampton T (loan)	15	—
							Burnley	240	—
							Middlesbrough	7	—
Branca Marco‡	6 0	12 09	F	6 1 65	Grosseto		Grosseto	—	—
							Cagliari	52	4
							Udinese	18	2
							Sampdoria	9	1
							Udinese	55	13
							Sampdoria	20	5
							Fiorentina	23	5
							Udinese	58	22
							Parma	25	7
							Roma	7	2
							Internazionale	52	23
							Middlesbrough	12	9
Burdock Gary‡			F	9 3 80	Dublin	Trainee	Middlesbrough	—	—
Campbell Andy	6 0	11 13	F	18 4 79	Middlesbrough	Trainee	Middlesbrough	20	—
							Sheffield U (loan)	11	3
Canavan Michael	6 1	12 02	F	17 9 80	South Shields	Trainee	Middlesbrough	—	—
Connor Paul*	6 2	11 05	F	12 1 79	Bishop Auckland	Trainee	Middlesbrough	—	—
							Hartlepool U (loan)	5	—
							Stoke C (loan)	3	2
Cooper Colin	5 11	11 11	D	28 2 67	Sedgefield		Middlesbrough	188	6
							Millwall	77	6
							Nottingham F	180	20
							Middlesbrough	32	1
Cronin Gary‡	5 10	10 00	M	16 3 79	Dublin	Stella Maris	Middlesbrough	—	—

Cummins Michael	6 0	12 08	M	1 6 78	Dublin	Trainee	Middlesbrough	1	—
Deane Brian	6 3	14 00	F	7 2 68	Leeds	Apprentice	Doncaster R	66	12
							Sheffield U	197	82
							Leeds U	138	32
							Sheffield U	24	11
						Benfica	Middlesbrough	26	6
Dunn Thomas‡	5 10	12 00	D	21 12 79	Hartlepool	Trainee	Middlesbrough	—	—
Festa Gianluca	5 11	13 00	D	15 3 69	Cagliari		Cagliari	156	—
							Fersuicis (loan)	26	2
							Internazionale	66	3
							Roma (loan)	21	1
							Middlesbrough	76	5
Fleming Curtis	5 10	12 05	D	8 10 68	Manchester	St Patrick's Ath	Middlesbrough	201	3
Gascoigne Paul	5 10	12 09	M	27 5 67	Gateshead		Newcastle U	92	21
							Tottenham H	92	19
							Lazio	41	6
							Rangers	74	30
							Middlesbrough	33	3
Gavin Jason	6 0	11 12	D	14 3 80	Dublin	Trainee	Middlesbrough	2	—
Gordon Dean	6 0	13 08	D	10 2 73	Thornton Heath	Trainee	Crystal Palace	201	20
							Middlesbrough	38	3
Hanson Christian	6 1	11 05	D	3 8 81	Middlesbrough	Trainee	Middlesbrough	—	—
Harrison Craig	6 0	11 08	D	10 11 77	Gateshead	Trainee	Middlesbrough	24	—
							Preston NE (loan)	6	—
Jackson John‡	6 1	11 10	G	30 6 80	Stockton	Trainee	Middlesbrough	—	—
Jones Bradley	6 3	12 01	G	19 3 82	Armadale	Trainee	Middlesbrough	—	—
Jones Thomas	5 10	11 02	F	26 3 80	Middlesbrough	Trainee	Middlesbrough	—	—
Kell Richard			M	15 9 79	Bishop Auckland	Trainee	Middlesbrough	—	—
Kelly Brian			M	6 2 81	Dublin	Trainee	Middlesbrough	—	—
Kinder Vladimir	5 9	12 03	D	9 3 69	Bratislava	Karlovy Vary	Slovan Bratislava	161	22
							Middlesbrough	37	5
Lombardi Gustavo‡	5 10	11 05	D	10 9 75	Buenos Aires	River Plate	Middlesbrough	—	—
Maddison Neil	5 10	11 10	M	2 10 69	Darlington	Trainee	Southampton	169	19
							Middlesbrough	43	4
Middleton James‡	6 1	10 10	D	2 10 79	Stockton	Trainee	Middlesbrough	—	—
Moore Alan	5 10	11 02	M	25 11 74	Dublin	Rivermount	Middlesbrough	118	14
							Barnsley (loan)	5	—
Mustoe Robbie	6 0	12 03	M	28 8 68	Oxford		Oxford U	91	10
							Middlesbrough	276	23
Naylor Gavin‡	5 6	11 01	M	30 5 79	Hartlepool	Trainee	Manchester U	—	—
							Middlesbrough	—	—
O'Brien Ronnie‡	5 10	11 08	M	15 1 79	Dublin	St Joseph's BC	Middlesbrough	—	—
O'Loughlin John	5 8	10 12	M	31 1 79	Letterkenny	Bruncrana Hearts	Middlesbrough	—	—
O'Neill Keith	6 2	12 07	F	16 2 76	Dublin	Trainee	Norwich C	73	9
							Middlesbrough	6	—
Ormerod Anthony	5 11	12 00	M	31 3 79	Middlesbrough	Trainee	Middlesbrough	18	3
							Carlisle U (loan)	5	—
Pallister Gary	6 5	15 02	D	30 6 65	Ramsgate	Billingham T	Middlesbrough	156	5
							Darlington (loan)	7	—
							Manchester U	317	12
							Middlesbrough	26	—
Pearson Nigel*	6 1	14 01	D	21 8 63	Nottingham	Heanor T	Shrewsbury T	153	5
							Sheffield W	180	14
							Middlesbrough	116	5
Prunty Sean	5 9	10 11	M	10 7 80	Dublin	Belvedere	Middlesbrough	—	—
Reeve Chris‡	5 11	11 05	F	1 10 79	Darlington	Trainee	Middlesbrough	—	—
Ricard Hamilton	6 1	13 12	F	12 1 74	Colombia	Deportivo Cali	Middlesbrough	45	17
Roberts Ben	6 1	12 11	G	2 5 75	Bishop Auckland	Trainee	Middlesbrough	16	—
							Hartlepool U (loan)	4	—
							Wycombe W (loan)	15	—
							Bradford C (loan)	2	—
							Millwall (loan)	11	—
Schwarzer Mark	6 5	15 01	G	6 10 72	Sydney	Dynamo Dresden	Kaiserslautern	4	—
							Bradford C	13	—
							Middlesbrough	76	—
Stamp Phil	5 11	14 09	M	12 12 75	Middlesbrough	Trainee	Middlesbrough	75	5
Stockdale Robbie	6 0	12 03	D	30 11 79	Redcar	Trainee	Middlesbrough	20	—
Summerbell Mark	5 9	11 01	M	30 10 76	Durham	Trainee	Middlesbrough	25	—
Swalwell Andrew*	5 9	10 06	M	29 3 79	Middlesbrough	Trainee	Middlesbrough	—	—
Townsend Andy	6 0	13 05	M	27 7 63	Maidstone	Weymouth	Southampton	83	5
							Norwich C	71	8
							Chelsea	110	12
							Aston Villa	134	8
							Middlesbrough	72	3
Trevor Kris‡	5 9	11 08	F	15 5 79	South Shields	Trainee	Middlesbrough	—	—
Vickers Steve	6 2	13 01	D	13 10 67	Bishop Auckland	Spennymoor U	Tranmere R	311	11
							Middlesbrough	195	8
Walklate Steve	5 11	12 00	M	27 9 79	Durham	Trainee	Middlesbrough	—	—
Wiltshire Luke			M	2 10 81	Australia		Middlesbrough	—	—

Trainees/Scholars
Allon, Wayne; Bennion, Chrisopher; Burton, Andrew; Cuthbertson, Andrew; Greenwood, David; Hudson, Mark; Huntley, James A; Kilgannon, Sean; McStea, Anthony C; Moat, David J; Newham, Stephen J C; Parnaby, Stuart; Pickover, Matthew G; Robinson, Gerard; Stephenson, Paul; Taylor, Andrew A

Non-Contract
McMahon, Adam

MILLWALL

Name	Ht	Wt	Pos	DOB	Birthplace	Source	Club	Apps	Gls
Barnard Richard			G	27 12 80	Frimley	Trainee	Millwall	—	—
Bibbo Sal‡	6 2	14 00	G	24 8 74	Basingstoke	Bournemouth	Sheffield U	—	—
							Chesterfield (loan)	1	—
							Reading	7	—
							Millwall	—	—
Bircham Marc	5 10	10 12	D	11 5 78	Wembley	Trainee	Millwall	38	—
Bowry Bobby	5 9	10 08	M	19 5 71	Croydon		Crystal Palace	50	1
							Millwall	134	5
Bubb Byron			M	17 12 81	Harrow	Scholarship	Millwall	3	—
Bull Ronnie			D	26 12 80	Hackney		Millwall	1	—
Cahill Tim	5 10	10 11	M	6 12 79	Sydney	Sydney U	Millwall	37	6
Canoville Dean‡	6 0	11 10	M	30 11 78	Perivale	Trainee	Millwall	2	—
Carter Jimmy*	5 10	11 02	M	9 11 65	Hammersmith	Apprentice	Crystal Palace	—	—
							QPR	—	—
							Millwall	110	10
							Liverpool	5	—
							Arsenal	25	2
							Oxford U (loan)	5	—
							Oxford U (loan)	4	—
							Portsmouth	72	5
							Millwall	16	—
Cook Andy	5 9	12 00	M	10 8 69	Romsey	Apprentice	Southampton	16	1
							Exeter C	70	1
							Swansea C	62	—
							Portsmouth	9	—
							Millwall	5	—
Cort Leon			D	11 7 79	Southwark	Dulwich H	Millwall	—	—
Dolan Joe	6 3	12 12	D	27 5 80	Harrow	Chelsea	Millwall	9	1
Fitzgerald Scott	6 0	12 12	D	13 8 69	Westminster	Trainee	Wimbledon	106	1
							Sheffield U (loan)	6	—
							Millwall (loan)	7	—
							Millwall	50	1
Grant Kim	5 10	11 05	F	25 9 72	Ghana	Trainee	Charlton Ath	123	18
							Luton T	35	5
							Millwall	55	11
							Notts Co (loan)	6	1
Gray Andy‡	5 11	14 04	M	22 2 64	Lambeth		Crystal Palace	98	27
							Aston Villa	37	4
							QPR	11	2
							Crystal Palace	90	12
							Tottenham H (loan)	14	1
							Tottenham H	19	2
							Swindon T (loan)	3	—
						Marbella	Falkirk	16	—
							Bury	21	1
							Millwall	12	1
Harris Neil	5 11	12 08	F	12 7 77	Orsett	Cambridge C	Millwall	42	15
Hicks Mark			F	24 7 81	Belfast		Millwall	1	—
Hockton Danny	6 0	11 11	F	7 2 79	Barking	Trainee	Millwall	36	4
Ifill Paul			F	20 10 79	Brighton	Trainee	Millwall	15	1
Lavin Gerard*	5 10	11 00	D	5 2 74	Corby	Trainee	Watford	126	3
							Millwall	74	—
Law Brian*	6 2	13 07	D	1 1 70	Merthyr	Apprentice	QPR	20	—
							Wolverhampton W	31	1
							Millwall	45	4
Markey Brendan‡	5 10	12 00	F	19 5 76	Dublin	Bohemians	Millwall	—	—
McLeary Alan#	5 11	11 09	D	6 10 64	Lambeth	Apprentice	Millwall	307	5
							Sheffield U (loan)	3	—
							Wimbledon (loan)	4	—
							Charlton Ath	66	3
							Bristol C	34	—
							Millwall	36	—
Mead Billy			D	7 1 81	London		Millwall	—	—
Neill Lucas	6 1	12 00	M	9 3 78	Sydney	NSW Academy	Millwall	93	9
Nethercott Stuart	6 0	13 08	D	21 3 73	Ilford	Trainee	Tottenham H	54	—
							Maidstone U (loan)	13	1
							Barnet (loan)	3	—
							Millwall	47	2
Newman Ricky	5 10	12 06	M	5 8 70	Guildford	Trainee	Crystal Palace	48	3
							Maidstone U (loan)	10	1
							Millwall	136	5
Odunsi Leke			M	5 12 80	Walworth	Trainee	Millwall	3	—
Reid Steven	5 11	11 10	F	10 3 81	Kingston	Trainee	Millwall	26	—

Name	Ht	Wt	Pos	Born	Birthplace	Source	Clubs	Apps	Gls
Roberts Tony‡	6 0	13 11	G	4 8 69	Holyhead	Trainee	QPR	122	—
							Millwall	8	—
Robertson Graham‡	5 10	11 11	M	12 11 76	Edinburgh	Balgorie Colts	Raith R	—	—
							Millwall	2	—
Roche Stephen‡	5 11	11 02	D	2 10 78	Dublin	Belvedere	Millwall	11	—
Ryan Robbie	5 10	12 00	D	16 5 77	Dublin	Belvedere	Huddersfield T	15	—
							Millwall	42	—
Sadlier Richard	6 2	12 10	F	14 1 79	Dublin	Belvedere	Millwall	45	8
Shaw Paul	5 11	12 04	F	4 9 73	Burnham	Trainee	Arsenal	12	2
							Burnley (loan)	9	4
							Cardiff C (loan)	6	—
							Peterborough U (loan)	12	5
							Millwall	74	21
Smith Phil	6 1	13 00	G	14 12 79	Harrow	Trainee	Millwall	5	—
Spink Nigel#	6 2	14 06	G	8 8 58	Chelmsford	Chelmsford C	Aston Villa	361	—
							WBA	19	—
							Millwall	43	—
Stevens Keith#	6 0	12 12	D	21 6 64	Merton	Apprentice	Millwall	462	9
Stuart Jamie	5 10	11 00	D	15 10 76	Southwark	Trainee	Charlton Ath	50	3
							Millwall	35	—
Tyne Thomas			F	2 3 81	Lambeth		Millwall	—	—
Veart Carl‡	5 10	11 05	M	21 5 70	Whyalla	Adelaide C	Sheffield U	66	15
							Crystal Palace	57	6
							Millwall	8	1

Trainees
Davies, Robert M; Fermie, Jason W; Little, Joseph G; Maguire, Patrick; Powell, Terry M

Scholars
Alderton, Rio; Alimi, Bashiru; Deegan, Darren S; Dunne, Alan J; Karaiskos, Andreas; Mullin, Patrick J; Phillips, Mark

Associated Schoolboys
Booth, Stuart; Hearn, Charley; Idaewor, Ambrose; Jaganjac, Ernest; Lombardo, Daniel C R; Ngonda, Petit; Redmond, Gary; Robinson, Paul M J

Associated Schoolboys who have accepted the Club's offer of a Traineeship/Scholarship/Contract
Campbell-Rye, Jamal; Honey, Christopher M; Kevin, Joseph S; Rees, Matthew R; Taylor, Billy

NEWCASTLE UNITED

Name	Ht	Wt	Pos	Born	Birthplace	Source	Clubs	Apps	Gls
Albert Philippe	6 3	12 04	D	10 8 67	Bouillon		Charleroi	65	7
							Mechelen	87	5
							Anderlecht	50	9
							Newcastle U	96	8
							Fulham (loan)	13	2
Ameobi Foluwashola	6 2	12 00	F	12 10 81	Zaria	Trainee	Newcastle U	—	—
Andersson Andreas	6 1	12 01	F	10 4 74	Osterhoninge	Hova	Tidaholm	9	6
							Degerfors	40	16
							IFK Gothenburg	39	32
							AC Milan	13	1
							Newcastle U	27	4
Arnison Paul	5 10	10 12	D	18 9 77	Hartlepool	Trainee	Newcastle U	—	—
Barton Warren	5 11	12 00	D	19 3 69	Stoke Newington	Leytonstone/Ilford	Maidstone U	42	—
							Wimbledon	180	10
							Newcastle U	96	4
Beharall David	6 0	11 07	D	8 3 79	Newcastle	Trainee	Newcastle U	4	—
Boyd Mark	5 9	11 02	M	22 10 81	Carlisle	Trainee	Newcastle U	—	—
Brady Garry	5 10	10 09	M	7 9 76	Glasgow	Trainee	Tottenham H	9	—
							Newcastle U	9	—
Broadbent David*	5 9	10 06	F	26 9 79	Pembury	Trainee	Newcastle U	—	—
Burghall Terry*	6 0	11 06	F	25 9 78	Liverpool	Liverpool	Newcastle U	—	—
Burt David*	5 9	10 11	M	5 2 78	Newcastle	Trainee	Newcastle U	—	—
Caldwell Gary	5 11	11 10	D	12 4 82	Stirling	Trainee	Newcastle U	—	—
Caldwell Stephen	6 0	11 05	D	12 9 80	Stirling	Trainee	Newcastle U	—	—
Charvet Laurent	5 11	12 10	D	8 5 73	Beziers		Cannes	99	19
							Chelsea	11	2
							Newcastle U	31	1
Clarke Steve†	5 10	12 07	D	29 8 63	Saltcoats	Beith Jun	St Mirren	151	6
							Chelsea	330	7
							Newcastle U	—	—
Coppinger James	5 7	10 03	M	10 1 81	Middlesbrough	Darlington	Newcastle U	—	—
Dabizas Nikos	6 0	11 11	D	3 8 73	Amypeo		Olympiakos	104	8
							Newcastle U	41	4
Dalglish Paul	5 9	10 10	F	18 2 77	Glasgow	X Form	Celtic	—	—
							Liverpool	—	—
							Newcastle U	11	1
							Bury (loan)	12	—
							Norwich C (loan)	5	—
Domi Didier	5 10	11 04	D	2 5 79	Sarcelles		Paris St Germain	48	—
							Newcastle U	14	—

Name	Ht	Wt	Pos	Born	Birthplace	From	Club	Apps	Gls
Elliott Stuart	5 8	11 05	D	27 8 77	London	Trainee	Newcastle U	—	—
							Hull C (loan)	3	—
							Swindon T (loan)	2	—
							Gillingham (loan)	5	—
							Hartlepool U (loan)	5	—
							Wrexham (loan)	9	—
Ferguson Duncan	6 4	14 06	F	27 12 71	Stirling	Carse T	Dundee U	77	28
							Rangers	14	2
							Everton	116	37
							Newcastle U	7	2
Gall Kevin	5 9	11 01	F	4 2 82	Merthyr	Trainee	Newcastle U	—	—
Georgiadis George	5 8	10 11	M	8 3 72	Kavala		Doxa	55	10
							Panathinaikos	176	59
							Newcastle U	10	—
Given Shay	6 0	11 08	G	24 4 76	Lifford	Celtic	Blackburn R	2	—
							Swindon T (loan)	—	—
							Swindon T (loan)	5	—
							Sunderland (loan)	17	—
							Newcastle U	55	—
Glass Stephen	5 8	10 11	M	23 5 76	Dundee		Aberdeen	106	7
							Newcastle U	22	3
Griffin Andy	5 8	10 10	D	17 3 79	Wigan	Trainee	Stoke C	57	2
							Newcastle U	18	—
Gudjonsson Bjarni‡	5 8	10 10	F	26 2 79	Akranes		IA Akranes	25	15
							Newcastle U	—	—
Guivarc'h Stephane	6 0	13 00	F	6 9 70	Concarneau	Guingamp	Auxerre	23	3
(Transferred to Rangers, November 1998)							Rennes	36	22
							Auxerre	32	21
							Newcastle U	4	1
							Rangers	14	5
Hamann Dietmar	6 3	12 06	M	27 8 73	Waldsasson	Wacker Munich	Bayern Munich	105	6
							Newcastle U	23	4
Hamilton Des	5 11	12 13	D	15 8 76	Bradford	Trainee	Bradford C	88	5
							Newcastle U	12	—
							Sheffield U (loan)	6	—
							Huddersfield T (loan)	10	1
Harper Steve	6 1	13 09	G	3 2 74	Easington	Seaham Red Star	Newcastle U	8	—
							Bradford C (loan)	1	—
							Stockport Co (loan)	—	—
							Hartlepool U (loan)	15	—
							Huddersfield T (loan)	24	—
Harris Michael			D	6 12 80	Liverpool	Trainee	Newcastle U	—	—
Howey Steve	6 1	11 12	D	26 10 71	Sunderland	Trainee	Newcastle U	182	6
Hughes Aaron	6 0	11 02	D	8 11 79	Magherafelt	Trainee	Newcastle U	18	—
Keen Peter*	6 0	11 10	G	16 11 76	Middlesbrough	Trainee	Newcastle U	—	—
Keidal Ralf*	5 8	10 12	M	6 3 77	Wurzburg	Schweinfurt	Newcastle U	—	—
Kelly Paddy*	6 0	11 07	D	26 4 78	Kirkcaldy		Celtic	1	—
							Newcastle U	—	—
							Reading (loan)	3	—
Kerr Brian	5 8	11 00	M	12 10 81	Motherwell	Trainee	Newcastle U	—	—
Ketsbaia Temuri	5 8	10 12	F	18 3 68	Gale	Dynamo Sukhumi	Dynamo Tbilisi	54	8
							Anorthosis	76	36
							AEK Athens	84	24
							Newcastle U	57	8
Knight Paul	5 7	10 07	F	16 10 80	Dublin	Trainee	Newcastle U	—	—
Lee Robert	5 10	11 03	M	1 2 66	Hornchurch	Hornchurch	Charlton Ath	298	59
							Newcastle U	235	43
Macklin Gareth*	5 8	10 06	D	27 8 80	Belfast	Trainee	Newcastle U	—	—
Maric Silvio	5 10	11 02	M	20 3 75	Zagreb	Croatia Zagreb	Newcastle U	10	—
McClen Jamie	5 8	10 07	M	13 5 79	Newcastle	Trainee	Newcastle U	1	—
McMahon David	6 1	11 05	F	17 1 81	Dublin	Trainee	Newcastle U	—	—
Muir Karl*			D	4 9 79	North Shields	Trainee	Newcastle U	—	—
Pearce Stuart	5 10	12 06	D	24 4 62	Shepherd's Bush	Wealdstone	Coventry C	51	4
							Nottingham F	401	63
							Newcastle U	37	—
Perez Lionel	5 11	13 04	G	24 4 67	Bagnols Coze		Nimes	111	—
							Bordeaux	16	—
							Sunderland	75	—
							Newcastle U	—	—
Pinas Brian‡	5 8	10 12	M	29 12 78	Rotterdam	Feyenoord	Newcastle U	—	—
Pistone Alessandro	5 11	11 05	D	27 7 75	Milan		Vicenza	—	—
(On loan to Venezia)							Solbiatese	20	1
							Crevalcore	29	4
							Vicenza	6	—
							Internazionale	45	1
							Newcastle U	31	—
Reed Matthew*	5 10	11 10	G	7 4 80	Stanford-Le-Hope	Trainee	Newcastle U	—	—
Robinson Paul	5 10	10 12	F	20 11 78	Sunderland	Trainee	Darlington	26	3
							Newcastle U	—	—
Saha Louis	5 11	11 06	F	8 8 78	Paris		Metz	24	1
							Newcastle U	11	1

Serrant Carl	5 11	11 02	D	12 9 75	Bradford	Trainee	Oldham Ath	90	1
							Newcastle U	4	—
							Bury (loan)	15	—
Shearer Alan	5 11	12 06	F	13 8 70	Newcastle	Trainee	Southampton	118	23
							Blackburn R	138	112
							Newcastle U	78	41
Solano Nolberto	5 9	11 06	M	12 12 74	Callao		Sporting Cristal	75	32
							Boca Juniors	32	5
							Newcastle U	29	6
Speed Gary	5 10	10 12	M	8 9 69	Mancot	Trainee	Leeds U	248	39
							Everton	58	16
							Newcastle U	51	5
Tait Jordan*			D	27 9 79	Berwick	Trainee	Newcastle U	—	—
Talbot Paul	5 10	10 09	D	11 8 79	Gateshead	Trainee	Newcastle U	—	—
Tomasson Jon Dahl	6 0	11 02	F	29 8 76	Copenhagen	Koge	Heerenveen	78	37
(Transferred to Feyenoord, August 1998)							Newcastle U	23	3
Walker Andrew			M	2 1 81	Salford	Trainee	Newcastle U	—	—
Woodcock Chris*	5 7	10 08	F	7 5 80	Bradford	Trainee	Newcastle U	—	—

Trainees/Scholars
Charlton, Craig D; Collins, Shaun T; Cowan, David R; Cunningham, David; Gordon, Roy M; Green, Stuart; Grindlay, Stephen J; Hogg, Graham; Leighton, Kris; Martin, Ian; Parry, Anthony; Warwick, Stephen J; Wealleans, Kevin; Wright, Peter D

NORTHAMPTON TOWN

Bishop Charlie‡	6 0	13 07	D	16 2 68	Nottingham	Stoke C	Watford	—	—
							Bury	114	6
							Barnsley	130	1
							Preston NE (loan)	4	—
							Burnley (loan)	9	—
							Wigan Ath	28	—
							Northampton T	11	—
Clarkson Ian*	5 11	12 00	D	4 12 70	Solihull	Trainee	Birmingham C	136	—
							Stoke C	75	—
							Northampton T	92	1
Corazzin Carlo	5 10	12 07	F	25 12 71	Canada	Vancouver 86ers	Cambridge U	105	39
							Plymouth Arg	74	22
							Northampton T	39	16
Dobson Tony	6 1	12 06	D	5 2 69	Coventry	Apprentice	Coventry C	54	1
							Blackburn R	41	—
							Portsmouth	53	2
							Oxford U (loan)	5	—
							Peterborough U (loan)	4	—
							WBA	11	—
							Gillingham (loan)	2	—
							Northampton T	11	—
Frain John	5 9	11 09	D	8 10 68	Birmingham	Apprentice	Birmingham C	274	23
							Northampton T	99	1
Francis Steve*	6 0	14 00	G	29 5 64	Billericay	Apprentice	Chelsea	71	—
							Reading	216	—
							Huddersfield T	186	—
							Northampton T	3	—
Gibb Ali	5 9	11 07	F	17 2 76	Salisbury	Trainee	Norwich C	—	—
							Northampton T	117	4
Heggs Carl‡	6 1	12 10	F	11 10 70	Leicester	Paget R	WBA	40	3
							Bristol R (loan)	5	1
							Swansea C	46	7
							Northampton T	46	5
Hendon Ian	6 0	12 10	D	5 12 71	Ilford	Trainee	Tottenham H	4	—
							Portsmouth (loan)	4	—
							Leyton Orient (loan)	6	—
							Barnsley (loan)	6	—
							Leyton Orient	131	5
							Birmingham C (loan)	4	—
							Notts Co	82	6
							Northampton T	7	—
Hill Colin*	6 0	12 11	D	12 11 63	Uxbridge	Apprentice	Arsenal	46	1
						Maritimo	Brighton & HA (loan)	—	—
							Colchester U	69	—
							Sheffield U	82	1
							Leicester C (loan)	10	—
							Leicester C	135	—
							Trelleborg	11	—
							Northampton T	54	—
Hodgson Dougie	6 2	13 10	D	27 2 69	Frankston	Heidelberg	Sheffield U	30	—
							Plymouth Arg (loan)	5	—
							Burnley (loan)	1	—
							Oldham Ath	41	4
							Northampton T	8	1
Hope Richard	6 2	12 06	D	22 6 78	Stockton	Trainee	Blackburn R	—	—
							Darlington	63	1
							Northampton T	19	—
Howard Steve	6 2	14 06	F	10 5 76	Durham	Tow Law T	Hartlepool U	142	27
							Northampton T	12	—

Name					Birthplace	From	Club	Apps	Gls
Howey Lee	6 2	13 09	D	1 1 69	Sunderland	AC Hemptinne	Sunderland	69	8
							Burnley	26	—
							Northampton T	25	6
Hughes Garry	6 1	11 09	D	19 11 79	Birmingham	Trainee	Northampton T	—	—
Hunt James	5 8	10 03	M	17 12 76	Derby	Trainee	Notts Co	19	1
							Northampton T	56	2
Hunter Roy	5 10	12 08	M	29 10 73	Saltburn	Trainee	WBA	9	1
							Northampton T	116	10
Lee Christian	6 2	11 07	F	8 10 76	Aylesbury	Doncaster R	Northampton T	59	8
Matthew Damian	5 11	10 10	M	23 9 70	Islington	Trainee	Chelsea	21	—
							Luton T (loan)	5	—
							Crystal Palace	24	1
							Bristol R (loan)	8	—
							Burnley	59	7
							Northampton T	1	—
Morrow Andrew	5 8	9 07	F	5 10 80	Bangor	Trainee	Northampton T	—	—
Newell Paul†	6 1	14 07	G	23 2 69	Woolwich	Trainee	Southend U	15	—
							Leyton Orient	61	—
							Colchester U (loan)	14	—
							Barnet	16	—
							Darlington	41	—
							Colchester U	—	—
							Northampton T	—	—
Parrish Sean	5 10	11 08	M	14 3 72	Wrexham	Trainee Telford U	Shrewsbury T	3	—
							Doncaster R	66	8
							Northampton T	84	10
Peer Dean*	6 2	12 04	M	8 8 69	Stourbridge	Trainee	Birmingham C	120	8
							Mansfield T (loan)	10	—
							Walsall	45	8
							Northampton T	119	5
Sampson Ian	6 2	13 03	D	14 11 68	Wakefield	Goole T	Sunderland	17	1
							Northampton T (loan)	8	—
							Northampton T	199	15
Savage Dave	6 1	12 07	M	30 7 73	Dublin	Longford T	Millwall	132	6
							Northampton T	27	5
Seal David*	5 11	12 04	F	26 1 72	Penrith	Aalst	Bristol C	51	10
							Northampton T	43	12
Spedding Duncan	6 1	11 01	D	7 9 77	Frimley	Trainee	Southampton	7	—
							Northampton T	24	1
Turley Billy	6 4	14 10	G	15 7 73	Wolverhampton	Evesham U	Northampton T	28	—
							Leyton Orient (loan)	14	—
Warburton Ray‡	6 0	12 13	D	7 10 67	Rotherham	Apprentice	Rotherham U	4	—
							York C	90	9
							Northampton T (loan)	17	1
							Northampton T	169	11
Warner Michael*	5 9	10 10	M	17 1 74	Harrogate	Tamworth	Northampton T	28	—
Wilkinson Paul	6 1	12 04	F	30 10 64	Louth	Apprentice	Grimsby T	71	27
							Everton	31	7
							Nottingham F	34	5
							Watford	134	52
							Middlesbrough	166	49
							Oldham Ath (loan)	4	1
							Watford (loan)	4	—
							Luton T (loan)	3	—
							Barnsley	49	9
							Millwall	30	3
							Northampton T	15	1
Wilson Kevin*	5 8	11 04	F	18 4 61	Banbury	Banbury U	Derby Co	122	30
							Ipswich T	98	34
							Chelsea	152	42
							Notts Co	69	3
							Bradford C (loan)	5	—
							Walsall	125	38
							Northampton T	17	1

Trainees
Binder, Paul M; Burt, Ian C J; Butcher, Richard T; Carolan, Philip; Chamberlain, Stephen; Dickson, Mark S; Finlay, Mathew D; Gould, James R; Hancock, Adam; Hough, Paul D; Piercewright, Brad; Silvestri, Lorenzo; Thompson, Ryan J D; Woods, Scott

Non-Contract
Atkins, Ian L

Associated Schoolboys who have accepted the Club's offer of a Traineeship/Scholarship/Contract
Champlovier, Neil M; Nash, Ryan M

NORWICH CITY

Name					Birthplace	From	Club	Apps	Gls
Adams Neil*	5 9	11 04	M	23 11 65	Stoke	Local	Stoke C	32	4
							Everton	20	—
							Oldham Ath (loan)	9	—
							Oldham Ath	129	23
							Norwich C	182	25
Allen Alex*	6 0	11 12	D	12 2 80	Doncaster	Trainee	Norwich C	—	—

Name	Ht	Wt	Pos	DOB	Birthplace	From	Club	Apps	Gls
Anselin Cedric	5 7	11 00	M	24 7 77	Lens		Bordeaux	8	—
							Lille	14	1
							Bordeaux	1	—
							Norwich C	7	1
Bellamy Craig	5 8	10 05	F	13 1 79	Cardiff	Trainee	Norwich C	79	30
Carey Shaun	5 10	11 03	M	13 5 76	Kettering	Trainee	Norwich C	47	—
Coote Adrian	6 1	12 00	F	30 9 78	Gt Yarmouth	Trainee	Norwich C	29	2
Eadie Darren	5 9	11 03	F	10 6 75	Chippenham	Trainee	Norwich C	155	34
Fleming Craig	5 11	13 00	D	6 10 71	Halifax	Trainee	Halifax T	57	—
							Oldham Ath	164	1
							Norwich C	59	4
Forbes Adrian	5 7	11 02	F	23 1 79	Greenford	Trainee	Norwich C	58	4
Fuglestad Erik	5 9	11 02	D	13 8 74	Randaberg		Viking	74	4
							Norwich C	48	2
Grant Peter	5 10	11 08	M	30 8 65	Bellshill		Celtic	363	15
							Norwich C	68	3
Green Robert	6 3	12 12	G	18 1 80	Chertsey	Trainee	Norwich C	2	—
Henderson Tommy*	5 6	10 10	M	9 10 79	Bury St Edmunds	Trainee	Norwich C	—	—
Jackson Matt	6 0	13 00	D	19 10 71	Leeds	School	Luton T	9	—
							Preston NE (loan)	4	—
							Everton	138	4
							Charlton Ath (loan)	8	—
							QPR (loan)	7	—
							Birmingham C (loan)	10	—
							Norwich C	97	6
Kenton Darren	5 11	11 10	D	13 9 78	Wandsworth	Trainee	Norwich C	33	1
Llewellyn Chris	6 0	11 07	F	28 8 79	Merthyr	Trainee	Norwich C	46	6
MacKay Malcolm	6 3	13 06	D	19 2 72	Bellshill		Queen's Park	70	6
							Celtic	37	4
							Norwich C	27	1
Marshall Andy	6 2	14 00	G	14 4 75	Bury	Trainee	Norwich C	110	—
							Bournemouth (loan)	11	—
							Gillingham (loan)	5	—
Marshall Lee	6 2	12 06	M	21 1 79	Islington	Enfield	Norwich C	48	3
Milligan Mike	5 10	11 06	M	20 2 67	Manchester	Trainee	Oldham Ath	162	17
							Everton	17	1
							Oldham Ath	117	6
							Norwich C	113	5
Mulryne Philip	5 8	11 02	M	1 1 78	Belfast	Trainee	Manchester U	1	—
							Norwich C	7	2
Roberts Iwan	6 3	13 06	F	26 6 68	Bangor	Trainee	Watford	63	9
							Huddersfield T	142	50
							Leicester C	100	41
							Wolverhampton W	33	12
							Norwich C	76	24
Russell Darel	6 0	12 00	M	22 10 80	Mile End	Trainee	Norwich C	14	1
Scott Kevin	6 3	14 03	D	17 12 66	Easington	Middlesbrough	Newcastle U	227	8
							Tottenham H	18	1
							Port Vale (loan)	17	1
							Charlton Ath (loan)	4	—
							Norwich C	33	—
							Darlington (loan)	4	—
Segura Victor*	6 0	12 00	D	13 3 73	Zaragoza	Lleida	Norwich C	29	—
Sutch Daryl	5 11	12 09	D	11 9 71	Lowestoft	Trainee	Norwich C	201	7
Watt Michael*	6 2	13 05	G	27 11 70	Aberdeen		Aberdeen	79	—
							Blackburn R	—	—
							Norwich C	8	—
Way Darren	5 6	10 09	M	21 11 79	Plymouth	Trainee	Norwich C	—	—
Wilson Che	5 11	11 04	D	17 1 79	Ely	Trainee	Norwich C	17	—

Trainees
Belgrave, Barrington; Carr, Shaun L; Elridge, Martin; Goreham, Paul M; Joynson, Matthew; Murray, David S; Parker, Kevin J; Smith, Robert S

Scholars
Bilham, Neil; Blois, Lewis P; Gay, Daniel K; Gilman, Lee D; Ngopwani, Pitshou M; Parry, Matthew G; Thompson, Ian R

Associated Schoolboys
Brown, Lee; Lucas, Ben; Mundy, Mathew; Pacey, Gary; Ringer, Daniel P; Rudd, Bradley; Scullion, Steven; Thompson, Ben

Associated Schoolboys who have accepted the Club's offer of a Traineeship/Scholarship/Contract
Edwards, Julian; Goodchild, Richard; Oxby, Andrew

NOTTINGHAM FOREST

Name	Ht	Wt	Pos	DOB	Birthplace	From	Club	Apps	Gls
Allou Bernard	5 8	11 00	M	19 6 75	Cocody		Paris St Germain	41	3
						Grampas 8	Nottingham F	2	—
Bart-Williams Chris	5 11	12 07	M	16 6 74	Freetown	Trainee	Leyton Orient	36	2
							Sheffield W	124	16
							Nottingham F	106	8

Name					Birthplace	Source	Club	Apps	Gls
Beasant Dave*	6 4	14 02	G	20 3 59	Willesden	Edgware T	Wimbledon	340	—
							Newcastle U	20	—
							Chelsea	133	—
							Grimsby T (loan)	6	—
							Wolverhampton W (loan)	4	—
							Southampton	88	—
							Nottingham F	67	—
Bonalair Thierry	5 9	10 08	D	14 6 66	Paris		Nantes	145	2
							Auxerre	25	1
							Lille	69	5
							Neuchatel Xamax	68	9
							Nottingham F	59	3
Burns John	5 10	11 02	M	4 12 77	Dublin	Belvedere	Nottingham F	—	—
Carter Nicky	5 11	11 07	F	29 11 81	Stoke	Trainee	Nottingham F	—	—
Chettle Steve	6 1	13 04	D	27 9 68	Nottingham	Apprentice	Nottingham F	404	10
Cooper Richard	5 9	10 07	D	27 9 79	Nottingham	Trainee	Nottingham F	—	—
Cowling Lee*	5 9	11 00	D	22 9 77	Doncaster	Trainee	Nottingham F	—	—
Crossley Mark	6 0	15 09	G	16 6 69	Barnsley	Trainee	Nottingham F	283	—
							Manchester U (loan)	—	—
							Millwall (loan)	13	—
Darcheville Jean-Claude*	5 8	13 09	F	25 7 75	French Guyana		Rennes	43	5
							Nottingham F	16	2
Dawson Kevin	6 0	10 07	D	18 6 81	Northallerton	Trainee	Nottingham F	—	—
Doig Chris	6 2	12 06	D	13 2 81	Dumfries	Trainee	Nottingham F	2	—
Edds Gareth	5 11	10 12	M	3 2 81	Sydney	Trainee	Nottingham F	—	—
Edwards Christian	6 2	12 03	D	23 11 75	Caerphilly	Trainee	Swansea C	115	4
							Nottingham F	12	—
							Bristol C (loan)	3	—
Fitchett Scott*	5 8	9 06	M	20 1 79	Manchester	Trainee	Nottingham F	—	—
Follett Richard*	5 9	10 02	D	29 8 79	Leamington Spa	Trainee	Nottingham F	—	—
							Scunthorpe U (loan)	—	—
Foy Keith	5 11	12 03	M	30 12 81	Crumlin	Trainee	Nottingham F	—	—
Freedman Dougie	5 9	12 05	F	21 1 74	Glasgow	Trainee	QPR	—	—
							Barnet	47	27
							Crystal Palace	90	31
							Wolverhampton W	29	10
							Nottingham F	31	9
Freeman David	5 10	11 07	F	25 11 79	Dublin	Cherry Orchard	Nottingham F	—	—
Goodlad Mark	6 0	13 02	G	9 9 80	Barnsley	Trainee	Nottingham F	—	—
							Scarborough (loan)	3	—
Gough Richard*	6 2	11 09	D	5 4 62	Stockholm		Dundee U	165	23
							Tottenham H	49	2
							Rangers	318	26
						San Jose Clash	Nottingham F	7	—
Gough Steven‡	5 11	11 10	M	16 9 80	Burton	Trainee	Nottingham F	—	—
Gray Andy	6 0	13 00	M	15 11 77	Harrogate	Trainee	Leeds U	22	—
							Bury (loan)	6	1
							Nottingham F	8	—
							Preston NE (loan)	5	—
							Oldham Ath (loan)	4	—
Guinan Stephen	6 1	13 06	F	24 12 75	Birmingham	Trainee	Nottingham F	6	—
							Darlington (loan)	3	1
							Burnley (loan)	6	—
							Crewe Alex (loan)	3	—
							Halifax T (loan)	12	2
							Plymouth Arg (loan)	11	7
Harewood Marlon	6 1	13 03	F	25 8 79	Hampstead	Trainee	Nottingham F	24	1
							Ipswich T (loan)	6	1
Harkes John‡	5 10	12 03	M	8 3 67	New Jersey	USSF	Sheffield W	81	7
							Derby Co	74	2
							West Ham U	11	—
						DC United	Nottingham F	3	—
Higgins Paul‡	5 7	10 02	D	6 1 81	Ilkeston	Trainee	Nottingham F	—	—
Hjelde Jon Olav	6 2	13 05	D	30 7 72	Levanger		Rosenborg	27	1
							Nottingham F	45	2
Hodgson Richard	5 10	11 06	F	1 10 79	Sunderland	Trainee	Nottingham F	—	—
Howarth Paul‡	5 6	10 01	D	21 11 80	Nottingham	Trainee	Nottingham F	—	—
Hudson Niall	5 10	10 02	M	7 1 82	Ilkeston	Trainee	Nottingham F	—	—
Jerkan Nikola‡	6 2	12 07	D	8 12 64	Sinj	Hajduk Split	Oviedo	203	1
							Nottingham F	14	—
Johnson Andy	6 1	13 03	M	2 5 74	Bristol	Trainee	Norwich C	66	13
							Nottingham F	62	4
Louis-Jean Mathieu	5 9	10 08	D	22 2 76	Mont-St-Aignan		Le Havre	78	—
							Nottingham F	16	—
Lyttle Des*	5 8	13 02	D	24 9 71	Wolverhampton	Worcester C	Swansea C	46	1
							Nottingham F	185	3
							Port Vale (loan)	7	—
Mattsson Jesper	6 1	13 01	D	18 4 68	Visby		Hacken	24	3
							Halmstad	101	8
							Nottingham F	6	—
McNamara Niall	5 11	11 09	F	26 1 82	Eire	Trainee	Nottingham F	—	—
Melton Steve	5 11	12 03	M	3 10 78	Lincoln	Trainee	Nottingham F	1	—

Name	Ht	Wt	Pos	Born	Birthplace	Signed from	Club	Apps	Gls
Merino Carlos*	5 8	10 04	M	15 3 80	Bilbao	Urdaneta	Nottingham F	—	—
Palmer Carlton	6 2	13 00	M	5 12 65	Oldbury	Trainee	WBA	121	4
							Sheffield W	205	14
							Leeds U	102	5
							Southampton	45	3
							Nottingham F	13	—
Pascolo Marco	6 2	14 04	G	2 5 66	Sion		Sion	17	1
(On loan to Zurich)							Neuchatel Xamax	52	—
							Servette	163	—
							Cagliari	14	—
							Nottingham F	5	—
Porfirio Hugo*	5 8	10 05	M	28 9 73	Lisbon		Sporting	11	—
							Tirsense (loan)	19	—
							Uniao Leiria (loan)	28	8
							West Ham U	23	2
							Santander	20	1
							Benfica	3	—
							Nottingham F	9	1
Prutton David	6 1	11 06	D	12 9 81	Hull	Trainee	Nottingham F	—	—
Quashie Nigel	5 9	12 08	M	20 7 78	Nunhead	Trainee	QPR	57	3
							Nottingham F	16	—
Rogers Alan	5 10	12 08	D	3 1 77	Liverpool	Trainee	Tranmere R	57	2
							Nottingham F	80	5
Shipperley Neil	6 1	14 01	F	30 10 74	Chatham	Trainee	Chelsea	37	7
							Watford (loan)	6	1
							Southampton	66	12
							Crystal Palace	61	20
							Nottingham F	20	1
Stensaas Stale	5 11	12 01	D	7 7 71	Trondheim		Rosenborg	85	2
							Rangers	21	1
							Nottingham F	7	—
Thomas Geoff*	6 1	13 07	M	5 8 64	Manchester	Local	Rochdale	11	1
							Crewe Alex	125	20
							Crystal Palace	195	26
							Wolverhampton W	46	8
							Nottingham F	25	4
Turner Matthew*	5 9	10 00	F	29 12 81	Nottingham	Trainee	Nottingham F	—	—
Van Hooijdonk Pierre	6 4	13 07	F	29 11 69	Steenbergen		RBC	69	33
							NAC	99	71
							Celtic	69	44
							Nottingham F	71	36
Williams Gareth	5 11	11 08	M	16 12 81	Glasgow	Trainee	Nottingham F	—	—
Woan Ian	5 10	12 07	F	14 12 67	Wirral	Runcorn	Nottingham F	210	31

Trainees/Scholars
Cash, Brian D; Dell, Richard T; Gill, Robert; Kearney, Martin R; Mayo, Paul; Reid, Andrew M; Roche, Barry; Shevlin, Anthony

Non-Contract
Sherwood, Benjamin D

NOTTS COUNTY

Name	Ht	Wt	Pos	Born	Birthplace	Signed from	Club	Apps	Gls
Beadle Peter	6 1	13 07	F	13 5 72	Lambeth	Trainee	Gillingham	67	14
							Tottenham H	—	—
							Bournemouth (loan)	9	2
							Southend U (loan)	8	1
							Watford	23	1
							Bristol R	109	39
							Port Vale	23	6
							Notts Co	14	3
Beattie Damien*	6 1	13 00	G	24 10 78	Melbourne	Moorrabbin	Notts Co	—	—
Bolland Paul	5 10	10 12	M	23 12 79	Bradford	Trainee	Bradford C	12	—
							Notts Co	13	—
Creaney Gerry†	5 11	13 07	F	13 4 70	Coatbridge	Celtic BC	Celtic	113	36
							Portsmouth	60	32
							Manchester C	21	4
							Oldham Ath (loan)	9	2
							Ipswich T (loan)	6	1
							Burnley (loan)	10	8
							Chesterfield (loan)	4	—
							Notts Co	16	3
Darby Duane	5 11	12 06	F	17 10 73	Birmingham	Trainee	Torquay U	108	26
							Doncaster R	17	4
							Hull C	78	27
							Notts Co	—	—
							Hull C (loan)	8	—
Diuk Wayne‡	5 9	11 00	M	26 5 80	Nottingham	Trainee	Notts Co	2	—
Dyer Alex	5 11	12 00	M	14 11 65	Forest Gate	Watford	Blackpool	108	19
							Hull C	60	14
							Crystal Palace	17	2
							Charlton Ath	78	13
							Oxford U	76	6
							Lincoln C	1	—
							Barnet	35	2
							Huddersfield T	12	1
							Notts Co	39	—

Name	Ht	Wt	Pos	DOB	Birthplace	Source	Club	App	Gls
Fairclough Chris	5 11	11 07	D	12 4 64	Nottingham	Apprentice	Nottingham F	107	1
							Tottenham H	60	5
							Leeds U	193	21
							Bolton W	90	8
							Notts Co	16	1
							York C (loan)	11	—
Farrell Sean	6 1	13 07	F	28 2 69	Watford	Apprentice	Luton T	25	1
							Colchester U (loan)	9	1
							Northampton T (loan)	4	1
							Fulham	94	31
							Peterborough U	66	20
							Notts Co	60	19
Garcia Tony‡	6 0	12 00	F	18 3 72	Pierre Patte		Notts Co	19	2
Gibson Paul	6 2	13 06	G	1 11 76	Sheffield	Trainee	Manchester U	—	—
							Mansfield T (loan)	13	—
							Hull C (loan)	4	—
							Notts Co	1	—
Henshaw Terrence*	5 10	10 10	D	29 2 80	Nottingham	Trainee	Notts Co	—	—
Holmes Richard			D	7 11 80	Grantham	Trainee	Notts Co	8	—
Hughes Andy	6 0	11 00	M	2 1 78	Manchester	Trainee	Oldham Ath	33	1
							Notts Co	45	5
Liburd Richard	5 9	11 01	D	26 9 73	Nottingham	Forest Ath	Middlesbrough	41	1
							Bradford C	78	3
							Carlisle U	9	—
							Notts Co	35	1
Marshall Ben‡	6 0	12 00	M	5 9 79	Sutton	Trainee	Notts Co	—	—
Murray Shaun	5 8	11 02	M	7 12 70	Newcastle	Trainee	Tottenham H	—	—
							Portsmouth	34	1
							Millwall (loan)	—	—
							Scarborough	29	5
							Bradford C	130	8
							Notts Co	35	3
Owers Gary	5 11	12 07	M	3 10 68	Newcastle	Apprentice	Sunderland	268	25
							Bristol C	126	9
							Notts Co	39	3
Parkin Brian‡	6 4	14 02	G	12 10 65	Birkenhead	Local	Oldham Ath	6	—
							Crewe Alex (loan)	12	—
							Crewe Alex	86	—
							Crystal Palace (loan)	—	—
							Crystal Palace	20	—
							Bristol R	241	—
							Wycombe W	25	—
							Notts Co	1	—
Pearce Dennis	5 9	11 00	D	10 9 74	Wolverhampton	Trainee	Aston Villa	—	—
							Wolverhampton W	9	—
							Notts Co	71	3
Quayle Mark*	5 9	11 04	F	2 10 78	Liverpool	Trainee	Everton	—	—
							Notts Co	5	—
Rapley Kevin	5 9	10 08	F	21 9 77	Reading	Trainee	Brentford	51	12
							Southend U (loan)	9	4
							Notts Co	16	2
Redmile Matthew	6 4	14 10	D	12 11 76	Nottingham	Trainee	Notts Co	98	6
Richardson Ian	5 11	11 01	M	22 10 70	Barking	Dagenham & Redbridge	Birmingham C	7	—
							Notts Co	87	10
Robson Mark	5 7	10 02	F	22 5 69	Newham	Trainee	Exeter C	26	7
							Tottenham H	8	—
							Reading (loan)	7	—
							Watford (loan)	1	—
							Plymouth Arg (loan)	7	—
							Exeter C (loan)	8	1
							West Ham U	47	8
							Charlton Ath	105	9
							Notts Co	30	4
							Wycombe W (loan)	4	—
Samuels Jerome‡			M	8 3 76	Jamaica		Notts Co	—	—
Stallard Mark	6 0	12 10	F	24 10 74	Derby	Trainee	Derby Co	27	2
							Fulham (loan)	4	3
							Bradford C	43	10
							Preston NE (loan)	4	1
							Wycombe W	70	23
							Notts Co	14	4
Tierney Fran	5 10	11 00	M	9 10 75	Liverpool	Trainee	Crewe Alex	87	10
							Notts Co	20	3
Ward Darren	5 11	12 09	G	11 5 74	Worksop	Trainee	Mansfield T	81	—
							Notts Co	171	—
Warren Mark	6 0	12 02	D	12 11 74	Clapton	Trainee	Leyton Orient	152	5
							West Ham U (loan)	—	—
							Oxford U (loan)	4	—
							Notts Co	18	—
Webster Adam			M	3 7 80	Leicester		Notts Co	—	—

Trainees

Brough, Michael; Cockerill, Colin P; Cooke, Russell; Howell, Dean G; Lindley, James D; Norwood, Andrew M; Osborne, Matthew A; Wigginton, Steven

Scholars
Briggs, Andrew; Davies, Andrew M; Housley, Craig; Skevington, Matthew

Associated Schoolboys
Clarke, Ryan; Darby, Thomas W; Ferguson, Alex; Hartshorn, Michael; Holtham, Michael; Jeffries, Alan B; Lewis, Carl; Reid, Dwayne; Rogers, Gareth; Screaton, Iain; Winch, Thomas D

Associated Schoolboys who have accepted the Club's offer of a Traineeship/Scholarship/Contract
McCaul, Matthew; Osborne, Calum; Poznanski, Lee; Riley, Paul

OLDHAM ATHLETIC

Name	Ht	Wt	Pos	Birthdate	Birthplace	Source	Club	Apps	Gls
Allott Mark	5 11	10 12	F	16 3 78	Middleton	Trainee	Oldham Ath	68	10
Battersby Richard*	5 8	10 03	M	13 6 79	York	Trainee	Oldham Ath	—	—
Boshell Daniel			M	30 5 81	Bradford	Trainee	Oldham Ath	—	—
Campbell Jamie			M	2 12 80	Glasgow	Trainee	Oldham Ath	—	—
Cherry Steve†	6 1	13 00	G	5 8 60	Nottingham	Apprentice	Derby Co	77	—
							Port Vale (loan)	4	—
							Walsall	71	—
							Plymouth Arg	73	—
							Chesterfield (loan)	10	—
							Notts Co	266	—
							Watford	4	—
							Plymouth Arg (loan)	16	—
							Rotherham U	20	—
							Notts Co	—	—
							Mansfield T	1	—
							Oldham Ath	—	—
Clitheroe Lee	5 10	10 07	F	18 11 78	Chorley	Trainee	Oldham Ath	5	—
Dudley Craig	5 11	11 02	F	12 9 79	Ollerton	Trainee	Notts Co	31	3
							Shrewsbury T (loan)	4	—
							Hull C (loan)	7	2
							Oldham Ath	—	—
Duxbury Lee	5 10	10 07	M	7 10 69	Keighley	Trainee	Bradford C	209	25
							Rochdale (loan)	10	—
							Huddersfield T	29	2
							Bradford C	63	7
							Oldham Ath	91	12
Earnshaw Mark*	5 9	11 02	M	11 11 78	Leeds	Trainee	Oldham Ath	—	—
Fairhurst Scott*	5 11	10 12	D	29 11 78	Manchester	Trainee	Oldham Ath	—	—
Garnett Shaun	6 2	13 01	D	22 11 69	Wallasey	Trainee	Tranmere R	112	5
							Chester C (loan)	9	—
							Preston NE (loan)	10	2
							Wigan Ath (loan)	13	1
							Swansea C	15	—
							Oldham Ath	94	6
Graham Richard	6 2	12 09	D	28 11 74	Dewsbury	Trainee	Oldham Ath	133	12
Holt Andy	6 1	11 02	D	21 5 78	Manchester	Trainee	Oldham Ath	58	6
Hotte Mark	5 11	11 00	M	27 9 78	Bradford	Trainee	Oldham Ath	2	—
Innes Mark	5 10	12 04	D	27 9 78	Bellshill	Trainee	Oldham Ath	17	1
Kelly Gary	5 11	12 08	G	3 8 66	Fulwood	Apprentice	Newcastle U	53	—
							Blackpool (loan)	5	—
							Bury	236	—
							West Ham U (loan)	—	—
							Oldham Ath	113	—
McGinlay John	5 10	12 02	F	8 4 64	Inverness	Elgin C	Shrewsbury T	60	27
							Bury	25	9
							Millwall	34	10
							Bolton W	192	87
							Bradford C	17	3
							Oldham Ath	7	1
McLean Ian	5 10	11 04	D	13 9 78	Leeds	Trainee	Bradford C	—	—
							Oldham Ath	5	—
McNiven David	5 10	12 00	F	27 5 78	Leeds	Trainee	Oldham Ath	22	1
McNiven Scott	5 10	10 08	D	27 5 78	Leeds	Trainee	Oldham Ath	97	2
Miskelly David	6 0	12 02	G	3 9 79	Ards	Trainee	Oldham Ath	1	—
Murphy Ged*	5 10	11 03	D	19 12 78	Manchester	Trainee	Oldham Ath	—	—
Orlygsson Toddy*	5 11	11 02	M	2 8 66	Odense	FC Akureyi	Nottingham F	37	2
							Stoke C	90	16
							Oldham Ath	76	1
Philliskirk Tony	6 2	12 12	F	10 2 65	Sunderland	Amateur	Sheffield U	80	20
							Rotherham U (loan)	6	1
							Oldham Ath	10	1
							Preston NE	14	6
							Bolton W	141	51
							Peterborough U	43	15
							Burnley	40	9
							Carlisle U (loan)	3	1
							Cardiff C	61	5
							Macclesfield T (loan)	10	1
							Oldham Ath	—	—
Prendergast Rory†	5 8	12 00	M	6 4 78	Pontefract	Rochdale	Barnsley	—	—
							York C	3	—
							Oldham Ath	—	—

Name					Birthplace	Status	Clubs	Apps	Goals
Reid Paul#	5 10	10 12	M	19 1 68	Oldbury	Apprentice	Leicester C	162	21
							Bradford C (loan)	7	—
							Bradford C	82	15
							Huddersfield T	77	6
							Oldham Ath	93	6
Rickers Paul	5 10	10 07	M	9 5 75	Dewsbury	Trainee	Oldham Ath	158	13
Ritchie Andy#	5 11	11 09	F	28 11 60	Manchester	Apprentice	Manchester U	33	13
							Brighton & HA	89	23
							Leeds U	136	40
							Oldham Ath	217	82
							Scarborough	68	17
							Oldham Ath	26	2
Rush Matthew*	5 11	12 05	F	6 8 71	Dalston	Trainee	West Ham U	48	5
							Cambridge U (loan)	10	—
							Swansea C (loan)	13	—
							Norwich C	3	—
							Northampton T (loan)	14	3
							Oldham Ath	24	3
Salt Philip	5 10	11 02	M	2 3 79	Huddersfield	Trainee	Oldham Ath	11	—
Selfe Oliver*	5 9	10 02	M	1 10 79	Warrington	Trainee	Oldham Ath	—	—
Sheridan John	5 10	12 01	M	1 10 64	Stretford	Local	Leeds U	230	47
							Nottingham F	—	—
							Sheffield W	197	25
							Birmingham C (loan)	2	—
							Bolton W	32	2
							Oldham Ath	30	2
Sinnott Lee*	6 1	13 01	D	12 7 65	Pelsall	Apprentice	Walsall	40	2
							Watford	78	2
							Bradford C	173	6
							Crystal Palace	55	—
							Bradford C	34	1
							Huddersfield T	87	1
							Oldham Ath	31	—
							Bradford C (loan)	7	—
Sugden Ryan			M	26 12 80	Bradford	Trainee	Oldham Ath	2	—
Swan Iain	6 2	11 03	D	4 7 80	Glasgow	Trainee	Oldham Ath	1	—
Thom Stuart	6 2	11 10	D	27 12 76	Dewsbury	Trainee	Nottingham F	—	—
							Mansfield T (loan)	5	—
							Oldham Ath	25	1
Tipton Matthew	5 10	11 02	F	29 6 80	Bridgend	Trainee	Oldham Ath	31	2
Walsh Danny	5 9	12 03	D	16 9 78	Manchester	Trainee	Oldham Ath	1	—
Wardle Darren			M	2 1 81	Bury	Trainee	Oldham Ath	—	—
Whitehall Steve	5 11	11 07	F	8 12 66	Bromborough	Southport	Rochdale	238	75
							Mansfield T	43	24
							Oldham Ath	36	4

Trainees
Fielding, Dale A F; Futcher, Benjamin P; Gardiner, Gareth J-R; Johnston, Patrick P; Lush, Simon; McLaughlin, Gerard J; Pashley, Adam C; Roberts, Glen R; Spurr, Jonathan T; Wharton, Nathan B

Scholars
Clark, Liam J; Froggatt, Jonathon P; Hall, Colin A R; McLean, Michael J; Oliver, Alun M; Robertson, Benjamin A; Robinson, Thomas J; Rock, Alexander P; Saunders, John J; Smith, Benjamin; Wright, Matthew

Non-Contract
Tranter, Carl

Associated Schoolboys
Chadderton, Daniel; Davenport, Michael J; Hall, Daniel; Harris, Chad; Holt, Mark; Lavery, Carl; Robinson, Christopher; Wademan, Gareth

Associated Schoolboys who have accepted the Club's offer of a Traineeship/Scholarship/Contract
Donnelly, Mark; Doran, Joseph; Duncan, Kevin; O'Grady, Paul; Otto, Alastair; Sutcliffe, Arren; Thompson, Darren

OXFORD UNITED

Name					Birthplace	Status	Clubs	Apps	Goals
Banger Nicky*	5 8	11 10	F	25 2 71	Southampton	Trainee	Southampton	55	8
							Oldham Ath	64	10
							Oxford U	60	8
Beauchamp Joey	5 10	12 07	M	13 3 71	Oxford	Trainee	Oxford U	124	20
							Swansea C (loan)	5	2
							West Ham U	—	—
							Swindon T	45	3
							Oxford U	158	31
Cook Jamie	5 10	10 10	F	2 8 79	Oxford	Trainee	Oxford U	39	3
Davis Steve	6 1	13 05	D	26 7 65	Birmingham	Stoke C	Crewe Alex	145	1
							Burnley	147	11
							Barnsley	107	10
							York C (loan)	2	1
							Oxford U	18	2
Folland Robbie	5 9	10 07	F	16 9 79	Swansea	Trainee	Oxford U	2	—
Francis Kevin	6 7	16 12	F	6 12 67	Moseley	Mile Oak R	Derby Co	10	—
							Stockport Co	152	88
							Birmingham C	73	13
							Oxford U	33	8

Gilchrist Phil	6 0	13 04	D	25 8 73	Stockton	Trainee	Nottingham F	—	—
							Middlesbrough	—	—
							Hartlepool U	82	—
							Oxford U	176	10
Gray Martin	5 9	11 04	M	17 8 71	Stockton	Trainee	Sunderland	64	1
							Aldershot (loan)	5	—
							Fulham (loan)	6	—
							Oxford U	121	4
Jackson Elliott*	6 3	14 06	G	27 8 77	Swindon	Trainee	Oxford U	7	—
Lewis Mickey*	5 8	12 04	M	15 2 65	Birmingham	School	WBA	24	—
							Derby Co	43	1
							Oxford U	300	7
Lundin Paul	6 4	14 00	G	21 11 64	Osby		Osters*	—	—
							Osters	144	—
							Umea	7	—
							Osters	38	—
							Oxford U	7	—
Murphy Matt*	6 0	12 02	M	20 8 71	Northampton	Corby T	Oxford U	160	21
							Scunthorpe U (loan)	3	—
Powell Paul	5 8	11 01	M	30 6 78	Wallingford	Trainee	Oxford U	68	4
Remy Christophe*	5 9	12 06	D	6 8 71	Besancon		Auxerre	22	—
							Derby Co	—	—
							Oxford U	28	1
Robinson Les	5 9	12 02	D	1 3 67	Shirebrook	Local	Mansfield T	15	—
							Stockport Co	67	3
							Doncaster R	82	12
							Oxford U	338	3
Rose Andrew*	5 9	10 13	D	9 8 78	Ascot	Trainee	Oxford U	5	—
Tait Paul	5 11	11 10	M	31 7 71	Sutton Coldfield	Trainee	Birmingham C	170	14
							Millwall (loan)	—	—
							Northampton T (loan)	3	—
							Oxford U	17	—
Thomson Andy	5 10	11 05	F	1 4 71	Motherwell	Jerviston BC	Q of S	175	93
							Southend U	122	28
							Oxford U	38	7
Watson Mark	6 0	12 04	D	8 9 70	Vancouver		Watford	18	—
							Osters	24	—
							Oxford U	23	—
Weatherstone Simon	5 10	12 04	F	26 1 80	Reading	Trainee	Oxford U	24	2
Whelan Phil	6 3	13 05	D	7 3 72	Stockport		Ipswich T	82	2
							Middlesbrough	22	1
							Oxford U	23	—
							Rotherham U (loan)	13	4
Williams Michael*	5 10	12 00	M	21 11 69	Bradford	Maltby MW	Sheffield W	23	1
							Halifax T (loan)	9	1
							Huddersfield T (loan)	2	—
							Peterborough U (loan)	6	—
							Burnley	16	1
							Oxford U	2	—
Wilsterman Brian*	6 1	13 03	D	19 11 66	Surinam	Beerschot	Oxford U	42	2
Wright Tony‡	5 7	11 01	M	1 9 79	Swansea	Trainee	Oxford U	7	—

Trainees
Bennett, Oliver J; Brennan, Aaron A; Davies, Alex S; Hamp, Adam R M; Henshaw, Benjamin A; Nix, Lee E; Richards, Andrew K; Ricketts, Sam D; Shepheard, Jonathan T; Simms, Ian M; Townsend, Jon R; Weatherstone, Ross; Whitehead, Dean

Player who does not hold a current contract but his registration has been retained by the Club
Wickens, Gary J

Associated Schoolboys
Costelloe, Michael W; Kershaw, Richard J; Lovegrove, Robert T; Mills, Jonathan P; Stalcup, Gregory M; Wallace, Stuart S; Zappi, Daniel

Associated Schoolboys who have accepted the Club's offer of a Traineeship/Scholarship/Contract
Brooks, Jamie P; Hackett, Christopher; Holder, Jorden A; Jones, Brynmor R; King, Simon; McIntosh, Kelvin; Newton, Andrew J; Spence, Brynley J; Wilson, Philip

PETERBOROUGH UNITED

Bodley Mick‡	6 1	13 01	D	14 9 67	Hayes	Apprentice	Chelsea	6	1
							Northampton T	20	—
							Barnet	69	3
							Southend U	67	2
							Gillingham (loan)	7	—
							Birmingham C (loan)	3	—
							Peterborough U	86	1
Boothroyd Aidy‡	5 9	11 07	D	8 2 71	Bradford	Trainee	Huddersfield T	10	—
							Bristol R	16	—
							Hearts	4	—
							Mansfield T	102	3
							Peterborough U	26	1
Broughton Drewe	6 3	12 01	F	25 10 78	Hitchin	Trainee	Norwich C	9	1
							Wigan Ath (loan)	4	—
							Brentford	1	—
							Peterborough U	25	7

Name	Ht	Wt	Pos	DOB	Birthplace	From	Clubs	Apps	Gls
Butler Steve	6 1	12 02	F	21 1 62	Birmingham	Wokingham T	Brentford	21	3
						Maidstone U	Maidstone U	76	41
							Watford	62	9
							Bournemouth (loan)	1	—
							Cambridge U	109	51
							Gillingham	108	20
							Peterborough U	14	2
Campbell James	6 2	11 12	D	16 11 79	Kent	Trainee	Peterborough U	—	—
Castle Steve	5 11	11 07	M	17 5 66	Ilford	Apprentice	Orient	243	55
							Plymouth Arg	101	35
							Birmingham C	23	1
							Gillingham (loan)	6	1
							Leyton Orient (loan)	4	1
							Peterborough U	63	7
Chapple Phil	6 2	13 01	D	21 11 66	Norwich	Apprentice	Norwich C	—	—
							Cambridge U	187	19
							Charlton Ath	142	15
							Peterborough U	1	—
Clarke Andy	5 10	11 07	F	22 7 67	Islington	Barnet	Wimbledon	170	17
							Port Vale (loan)	6	—
							Northampton T (loan)	4	—
							Peterborough U	—	—
Cleaver Chris	5 10	11 07	F	24 3 79	Hitchin	Trainee	Peterborough U	29	3
Connor Dan	6 2	12 09	G	31 1 81	Dublin	Trainee	Peterborough U	2	—
Danielsson Helgi	5 11	10 10	M	13 7 81	Reykjavik	Fylkir	Peterborough U	—	—
Davies Simon	5 10	12 03	M	23 10 79	Haverfordwest	Trainee	Peterborough U	49	4
De Souza Miguel‡	5 11	13 08	F	11 2 70	Newham	Dagenham	Birmingham C	15	—
							Bury (loan)	3	—
							Wycombe W	83	29
							Peterborough U	35	5
							Southend U (loan)	2	—
							Rochdale (loan)	5	—
Drury Adam	5 10	11 06	D	29 8 78	Cottenham	Trainee	Peterborough U	77	1
Edwards Andy	6 2	12 00	D	17 9 71	Epping	Trainee	Southend U	147	5
							Birmingham C	40	1
							Peterborough U	112	4
Etherington Matthew	5 10	10 07	F	14 8 81	Truro	School	Peterborough U	32	3
Farrell Dave	5 9	11 07	F	11 11 71	Birmingham	Redditch U	Aston Villa	6	—
							Scunthorpe U (loan)	5	1
							Wycombe W	60	8
							Peterborough U	79	10
French Daniel	5 11	11 01	M	25 11 79	Peterborough	Trainee	Peterborough U	—	—
Gill Matthew	5 11	11 10	M	8 11 80	Cambridge	Trainee	Peterborough U	28	—
Grazioli Guiliano#	5 11	12 00	F	23 3 75	London	Wembley	Peterborough U	41	16
Green Francis	5 9	11 04	F	23 4 80	Derby	Ilkeston T	Peterborough U	11	2
Griemink Bart	6 3	15 04	G	29 3 72	Holland	WKE	Birmingham C	20	—
							Barnsley (loan)	—	—
							Peterborough U	44	—
Haley Grant	5 8	10 02	D	20 9 79	Bristol	Trainee	Peterborough U	—	—
Hanlon Ritchie	5 10	11 12	M	25 5 78	Kenton	Chelsea	Southend U	2	—
						Rushden & D	Peterborough U	4	1
Hann Matthew	5 9	10 04	M	6 9 80	Saffron Walden	Trainee	Peterborough U	4	—
Haxthausen Michael‡	5 10	11 00	G	23 10 79	Helsingor	Trainee	Peterborough U	—	—
Hooper Dean	5 10	12 12	D	13 4 71	Harefield	Hayes	Swindon T	4	—
							Peterborough U (loan)	4	—
						Kingstonian	Peterborough U	38	2
Inman Niall	5 9	11 06	M	6 2 78	Wakefield	Trainee	Peterborough U	11	2
Jelleyman Gareth	5 10	10 02	D	14 11 80	Holywell	Trainee	Peterborough U	—	—
Kenna Warren	6 1	13 06	D	18 5 80	Southampton	Trainee	Peterborough U	—	—
Koogi Anders	5 10	10 11	M	8 9 79	Roskilde	Trainee	Peterborough U	1	—
Lewis Neil	5 8	10 05	D	28 6 74	Wolverhampton	Trainee	Leicester C	67	1
							Peterborough U	34	—
Linton Des*	6 1	13 10	D	5 9 71	Birmingham	Trainee	Leicester C	11	—
							Luton T	83	1
							Peterborough U	46	—
							Swindon T (loan)	8	—
Lyttle Gerard	5 7	11 01	D	27 11 77	Belfast	Star of the Stea	Celtic	—	—
							Peterborough U	—	—
Martin Jae	5 11	11 00	M	5 2 76	London	Trainee	Southend U	8	—
							Leyton Orient (loan)	4	—
							Birmingham C	7	—
							Lincoln C	41	5
							Peterborough U	4	—
McMenamin Chris‡	5 10	11 10	D	27 12 73	Donegal	Hitchin T	Coventry C	—	—
							Peterborough U	33	—
Neal Ashley‡	6 1	14 10	D	16 12 74	Northampton	Trainee	Liverpool	—	—
							Brighton & HA (loan)	8	—
							Huddersfield T	—	—
							Peterborough U	8	—
Payne Derek‡	5 6	10 08	M	26 4 67	Edgware	Hayes	Barnet	51	6
							Southend U	35	—
							Watford	36	1
							Peterborough U	82	4

Rennie David*	6 0	13 00	D	29 8 64	Edinburgh	Apprentice	Leicester C	21	1
							Leeds U	101	5
							Bristol C	104	8
							Birmingham C	35	4
							Coventry C	82	3
							Northampton T	48	3
							Peterborough U	27	—
Rowe Zeke	5 10	11 08	F	30 10 73	Stoke Newington	Trainee	Chelsea		
							Barnet (loan)	10	2
							Brighton & HA (loan)	9	3
							Peterborough U	35	3
							Doncaster R (loan)	6	2
Scott Richard	5 9	10 10	M	29 9 74	Dudley	Trainee	Birmingham C	12	
							Shrewsbury T	105	18
							Peterborough U	27	4
Shearer Peter‡	6 0	11 00	M	4 2 67	Birmingham	Apprentice	Birmingham C	4	
							Rochdale	1	—
						Cheltenham T	Bournemouth	85	10
							Birmingham C	25	7
							Peterborough U	—	—
Shields Tony	5 8	10 01	M	4 6 80	Derry	Trainee	Peterborough U	10	—
Tyler Mark	5 11	12 00	G	2 4 77	Norwich	Trainee	Peterborough U	81	—
Vickers Ashley‡	6 3	13 10	D	14 6 72	Sheffield	Heybridge S	Peterborough U	1	—
Wicks Matthew	6 2	13 05	D	8 9 78	Reading	Manchester U	Arsenal	—	—
							Crewe Alex	6	—
							Peterborough U	11	—

Trainees
Blowers, Robert; Cable, Aaron P; Foster, Ozie L; Sadler, Christopher J

Scholars
Byrne, Matthew J; Duncliffe, John P; Evans, Louie; Hardy, Luke; Murray, Daniel; Rusk, Simon; Vaughan, Jonathan R

Player who does not hold a current contract but his registration has been retained by the Club
McCormick, Charlie

Associated Schoolboys who have accepted the Club's offer of a Traineeship/Scholarship/Contract
Brewster, Jorden; Lang, Adam B

PLYMOUTH ARGYLE

Ashton Jon	6 0	13 00	D	4 8 79	Plymouth	Trainee	Plymouth Arg	26	—
Barlow Martin	5 7	10 03	M	25 6 71	Barnstable	Trainee	Plymouth Arg	307	24
Barrett Adam†			M	29 11 79	Dagenham		Plymouth Arg	1	—
Bastow Darren			M	22 12 81	Torquay	Trainee	Plymouth Arg	29	2
Beswetherick John	5 11	11 04	D	15 1 78	Liverpool	Trainee	Plymouth Arg	24	—
Collins Simon#	6 0	12 05	M	16 12 73	Pontefract	Trainee	Huddersfield T	52	3
							Plymouth Arg	84	5
Crowe Glen*	5 10	13 01	F	25 12 77	Dublin	Trainee	Wolverhampton W	10	1
							Exeter C (loan)	10	5
							Cardiff C (loan)	8	1
							Exeter C (loan)	9	—
							Plymouth Arg	11	1
Dobson Warren‡	6 1	13 08	G	5 11 78	North Shields	QPR	Hartlepool U	1	—
							Plymouth Arg	—	—
Dungey James†	5 8	12 00	G	7 2 78	Plymouth	Trainee	Plymouth Arg	10	—
							Exeter C	1	—
						Bodmin T	Plymouth Arg	7	—
Flash Richard‡	5 11	12 00	D	8 4 76	Birmingham	Trainee	Manchester U	—	—
							Wolverhampton W	—	—
							Watford	1	—
							Lincoln C (loan)	5	—
							Plymouth Arg	5	—
Ford Liam	5 7	10 03	F	8 9 79	Bradford	Trainee	Plymouth Arg	1	—
Gibbs Paul	5 10	11 09	D	26 10 72	Gorleston	Diss T	Colchester U	53	3
							Torquay U	41	7
							Plymouth Arg	27	3
Gritton Martin†	6 1	12 02	F	1 6 78	Glasgow	Porthleven	Plymouth Arg	2	—
Hargreaves Chris	5 11	12 02	M	12 5 72	Cleethorpes	Trainee	Grimsby T	51	5
							Scarborough (loan)	3	—
							Hull C	49	—
							WBA	1	—
							Hereford U (loan)	17	2
							Hereford U	44	4
						Hereford U	Plymouth Arg	32	2
Heathcote Mike	6 2	12 08	D	10 9 65	Durham	Spennymoor U	Sunderland	9	—
							Halifax T (loan)	7	1
							York C (loan)	3	—
							Shrewsbury T	44	6
							Cambridge U	128	13
							Plymouth Arg	165	12
Jean Earl‡	5 7	11 00	F	9 10 71	St Lucia	Felgueiras	Ipswich T	1	—
							Rotherham U	18	6
							Plymouth Arg	65	7

Name			Pos	DOB	Birthplace	From	Club	Apps	Gls
Lloyd Kevin‡	6 0	12 03	D	26 9 70	Llanidloes	Caersws	Hereford U	51	3
							Cardiff C	33	1
							Oldham Ath	—	—
							Plymouth Arg	—	—
Marshall Dwight‡	6 1	11 02	F	3 10 65	Lucea	Grays Ath	Plymouth Arg	99	27
							Middlesbrough (loan)	3	—
							Luton T	128	28
							Plymouth Arg	28	12
Mauge Ronnie*	5 10	10 06	M	10 3 69	Islington	Trainee	Charlton Ath	—	—
							Fulham	50	2
							Bury	108	10
							Manchester C (loan)	—	—
							Plymouth Arg	135	14
McCall Steve	5 11	12 10	M	15 10 60	Carlisle	Apprentice	Ipswich T	257	7
							Sheffield W	29	2
							Carlisle U (loan)	6	—
							Plymouth Arg	100	5
							Torquay U	51	2
							Plymouth Arg	17	—
McCarthy Sean	6 1	12 05	F	12 9 67	Bridgend	Bridgend	Swansea C	91	25
							Plymouth Arg	70	19
							Bradford C	131	60
							Oldham Ath	140	42
							Bristol C (loan)	7	1
							Plymouth Arg	16	3
McGovern Brendan	5 10	12 07	M	9 2 80	Camborne	Trainee	Plymouth Arg	2	—
Parsons Matthew‡	6 1	12 07	D	29 2 80	Truro	Trainee	Plymouth Arg	—	—
Phillips Lee	5 10	12 00	F	16 9 80	Penzance	School	Plymouth Arg	27	1
Rodosthenous Michael‡	5 11	11 02	F	25 8 76	Islington	Trainee	WBA	1	—
							Cambridge U	2	—
							Plymouth Arg	—	—
Rowbotham Jason	5 9	11 09	D	3 1 69	Cardiff	Trainee	Plymouth Arg	9	—
							Shrewsbury T	—	—
							Hereford U	5	1
							Raith R	56	1
							Wycombe W	27	—
							Plymouth Arg	40	—
Sheffield Jon	5 11	11 06	G	1 2 69	Bedworth	Apprentice	Norwich C	1	—
							Aldershot (loan)	11	—
							Ipswich T (loan)	—	—
							Aldershot (loan)	15	—
							Cambridge U (loan)	2	—
							Cambridge U	54	—
							Colchester U (loan)	6	—
							Swindon T (loan)	2	—
							Hereford U (loan)	8	—
							Peterborough U	62	—
							Watford (loan)	—	—
							Oldham Ath (loan)	—	—
							Plymouth Arg	85	—
Sweeney Terry*	5 9	11 10	M	26 1 79	Paisley	Trainee	Luton T	—	—
							Plymouth Arg	13	1
Wills Kevin§	5 7	10 04	F	15 10 80	Torbay	Trainee	Plymouth Arg	2	—
Wotton Paul	5 11	11 08	M	17 8 77	Plymouth	Trainee	Plymouth Arg	87	3

Trainees
Adams, Stephen M; Berry, Stuart; Broad, Joseph R; Cusack, Aaron; Gill, James O; Hampton, Andrew J; Mallett, Neil; Morrison-Hill, Jamie S; Nevin, Fergus P; Parnell, Simon R; Prosser, Owain M; Wesson, Gareth; Wills, Kevin M

Non-Contract
Barrett, Adam N; Dungey, James A; Hodges, Kevin

Associated Schoolboys
Moore, Jude

Associated Schoolboys who have accepted the Club's offer of a Traineeship/Scholarship/Contract
Baker, Paul M; Bance, Daniel; Curtis, Karl G; Edwards, Darren P; McGowan, Jamie; McGowan, Matthew; Sundercombe, Thomas

PORTSMOUTH

Name			Pos	DOB	Birthplace	From	Club	Apps	Gls
Allen Martin‡	5 11	12 06	M	14 8 65	Reading	School	QPR	136	16
							West Ham U	190	25
							Portsmouth	45	4
							Southend U (loan)	5	—
Andreasson Svein‡			M	3 7 68	Hadsel		Lillestrom	15	4
							Portsmouth	2	—
Awford Andy	5 9	11 02	D	14 7 72	Worcester	Worcester C	Portsmouth	277	2
Bundy Scott‡	6 3	12 00	F	20 10 77	Southampton	Trainee	Portsmouth	—	—
Claridge Steve	5 9	13 00	F	10 4 66	Portsmouth	Fareham T	Bournemouth	7	1
						Weymouth	Crystal Palace	—	—
							Aldershot	62	19
							Cambridge U	79	28
							Luton T	16	2
							Cambridge U	53	18
							Birmingham C	88	35
							Leicester C	63	16
							Portsmouth (loan)	10	2
							Wolverhampton W	5	—
							Portsmouth	39	9

Name							Club	Apps	Gls
Durnin John	5 10	11 10	M	18 8 65	Liverpool	Waterloo Dock	Liverpool	—	—
							WBA (loan)	5	2
							Oxford U	161	44
							Portsmouth	179	31
Fenton Anthony†	5 10	10 02	D	23 11 79	Preston	Trainee	Manchester C	—	—
							Portsmouth	—	—
Flahavan Aaron	6 1	11 12	G	15 12 75	Southampton	Trainee	Portsmouth	63	—
Hawley Jon‡	6 1	12 08	D	25 1 78	Lincoln	Trainee	Portsmouth	—	—
Holbrook Adam	5 9	11 04	M	17 10 80	Newport (IW)	Trainee	Portsmouth	—	—
Igoe Sammy	5 6	9 07	M	30 9 75	Spelthorne	Trainee	Portsmouth	134	10
Jukes Nathan‡	5 11	11 13	M	10 4 79	Worcester	Trainee	Portsmouth	—	—
Knight Alan*	6 1	13 11	G	3 7 61	Balham	Apprentice	Portsmouth	682	—
Kyzeridis Nicos‡	5 6	11 07	M	20 4 71	Salonika		Naoussa	24	2
							Naoussa*	—	—
							Paniliakos	82	17
							Portsmouth	4	—
MacDonald Gary*	6 1	12 00	M	25 10 79	Germany	Trainee	Portsmouth	—	—
McLoughlin Alan	5 8	10 10	M	20 4 67	Manchester	Local	Manchester U	—	—
							Swindon T	9	—
							Torquay U	24	4
							Swindon T	97	19
							Southampton	24	1
							Aston Villa (loan)	—	—
							Portsmouth	290	49
McNab Joe	5 4	9 00	M	29 10 80	Brighton	Manchester C	Portsmouth	—	—
McNab Neil	5 6	10 03	M	29 10 80	Brighton	Manchester C	Portsmouth	—	—
Miglioranzi Stefani	6 0	11 12	M	20 9 77	Pacos de Caldas	St Johns Univ	Portsmouth	7	—
Nightingale Luke	5 10	12 05	F	22 12 80	Portsmouth	Trainee	Portsmouth	19	3
Peron Jean-Francois	5 8	10 04	M	11 10 65	St Omer	Caen	Walsall	38	1
							Portsmouth	38	1
Perrett Russell	6 2	13 00	D	18 6 73	Barton-on-Sea	AFC Lymington	Portsmouth	72	2
Pettefer Carl	5 6	10 11	M	22 3 81	Taplow	Trainee	Portsmouth	—	—
Phillips Martin	5 9	10 03	M	13 3 76	Exeter	Trainee	Exeter C	52	5
							Manchester C	15	—
							Scunthorpe U (loan)	3	—
							Exeter C (loan)	8	—
							Portsmouth	17	1
							Bristol R (loan)	2	—
Robinson Matthew	5 11	11 04	D	23 12 74	Exeter	Trainee	Southampton	14	—
							Portsmouth	44	1
Russell Lee*	5 10	11 09	D	3 9 69	Southampton	Trainee	Portsmouth	123	3
							Bournemouth (loan)	3	—
							Torquay U (loan)	9	—
Simpson Fitzroy	5 8	12 00	M	26 2 70	Trowbridge	Trainee	Swindon T	105	9
							Manchester C	71	4
							Bristol C (loan)	4	—
							Portsmouth	131	10
Simpson Robbie	5 10	11 06	F	3 3 76	Luton	Trainee	Tottenham H	—	—
							Portsmouth	2	—
Soley Steve	5 11	12 08	M	22 4 71	Widnes	Leek T	Portsmouth	8	—
							Macclesfield T (loan)	10	—
Tardif Chris	6 0	12 05	G	19 9 79	Guernsey	Trainee	Portsmouth	—	—
Thogersen Thomas	6 1	13 00	D	2 4 68	Copenhagen		Frem	57	7
							Brondby	111	22
							Portsmouth	34	—
Vlachos Michalis	5 11	12 08	D	20 9 67	Athens		Apollon	80	10
							Olympiakos	47	2
							AEK Athens	105	3
							Portsmouth	45	—
Waterman David	5 10	13 02	D	16 5 77	Guernsey	Trainee	Portsmouth	29	—
Whitbread Adrian	6 1	13 00	D	22 10 71	Epping	Trainee	Leyton Orient	125	2
							Swindon T	36	1
							West Ham U	10	—
							Portsmouth (loan)	13	—
							Portsmouth	95	1
Wyatt Nicky‡	5 6	10 00	F	22 10 79	Portsmouth	Trainee	Portsmouth	—	—

Trainees
Barnett, Phillip; Connolly, Gary M; Dodd, Jonathon; Eastman, Wayne; Fisher, Daniel; Griffiths, Ben; Hannon, Robert J; Hawkins, David J; Jones, Gavin J; Linpow, Steven J; Osborne, Benjamin H; Riddington, Charles A T; Stoner, Craig J; White, Thomas; Wilson, Michael A

Non-Contract
Fenton, Anthony B

Associated Schoolboys
Boyle, Ashley D; Breslin, Neil J; Buxton, Lewis E; Cole, James; Cooper, Shaun D; Hunt, Warren D; Parker, Terry J; Stacey, Daniel L T; Thorogood, Jonathan T

Associated Schoolboys who have accepted the Club's offer of a Traineeship/Scholarship/Contract
Molyneaux, Lee A; O'Neil, Gary P; Pook, Robbie J; Vine, Rowan L

PORT VALE

Allen Chris*	5 11	12 04	M	18 11 72	Oxford	Trainee	Oxford U	150	12
							Nottingham F (loan)	3	1
							Nottingham F	25	—
							Luton T (loan)	14	1
							Cardiff C (loan)	4	—
							Port Vale	5	1
Aspin Neil*	6 0	13 02	D	12 4 65	Gateshead	Apprentice	Leeds U	207	5
							Port Vale	348	3
Barker Simon#	5 8	11 07	M	4 11 64	Farnworth	Apprentice	Blackburn R	182	35
							QPR	315	33
							Port Vale	27	2
Barnett Dave	6 1	12 08	D	16 4 67	Birmingham	Windsor & Eton	Colchester U	20	—
							WBA	—	—
							Walsall	5	—
					Kidderminster H	Barnet	59	3
							Birmingham C	46	—
							Dunfermline Ath	21	1
							Port Vale	36	1
Beesley Paul*	6 1	12 06	D	21 7 65	Liverpool	Marine	Wigan Ath	155	3
							Leyton Orient	32	1
							Sheffield U	168	7
							Leeds U	22	—
							Manchester C	13	—
							Port Vale (loan)	5	—
							WBA (loan)	8	—
							Port Vale	35	3
Bent Marcus	6 2	12 04	F	19 5 78	Hammersmith	Trainee	Brentford	70	8
							Crystal Palace	28	5
							Port Vale	15	—
Berntsen Robin‡			F	10 7 70	Tromso	Tromso	Port Vale	1	—
Bogie Ian	5 7	11 10	M	6 12 67	Newcastle	Apprentice	Newcastle U	14	—
							Preston NE	79	12
							Millwall	51	1
							Leyton Orient	65	5
							Port Vale	145	9
Brammer Dave	5 10	12 00	M	28 2 75	Bromborough	Trainee	Wrexham	137	12
							Port Vale	9	—
Brisco Neil	6 0	11 05	M	26 1 78	Billinge	Trainee	Manchester C	—	—
							Port Vale	1	—
Burns Liam	6 0	13 03	D	30 10 78	Belfast	Trainee	Port Vale	5	—
Butler Tony	6 2	12 03	D	28 9 72	Stockport	Trainee	Gillingham	148	5
							Blackpool	99	—
							Port Vale	4	—
Carragher Matthew	5 9	11 06	D	14 1 76	Liverpool	Trainee	Wigan Ath	119	—
							Port Vale	36	—
Corden Wayne	5 10	11 05	M	1 11 75	Leek	Trainee	Port Vale	64	1
Eyre Richard	5 8	11 08	M	15 9 76	Poynton	Trainee	Port Vale	12	—
Foyle Martin#	5 10	12 00	F	2 5 63	Salisbury	Amateur	Southampton	12	1
							Blackburn R (loan)	—	—
							Aldershot	98	35
							Oxford U	126	36
							Port Vale	274	77
Gardner Anthony	6 5	13 00	D	19 9 80	Staffordshire	Trainee	Port Vale	15	1
Griffiths Carl	5 10	11 05	F	15 7 71	Oswestry	Trainee	Shrewsbury T	143	54
							Manchester C	18	4
							Portsmouth	14	2
							Peterborough U	16	2
							Leyton Orient	70	32
							Wrexham (loan)	4	3
							Port Vale	3	1
Horlaville Christopher‡			F	1 3 69	Rouen		Rouen	102	42
							Cannes	71	23
							Guincamp	13	—
							Le Havre	26	3
							Port Vale	2	—
Jansson Jan‡	5 11	13 00	M	26 1 68	Kalmar		Norrkoping	73	9
							Port Vale	51	6
Koordes Rogier‡	6 1	13 06	M	13 6 72	Holland		Telstar	12	—
							Port Vale	38	—
McGill Derek‡	5 11	11 04	F	14 10 75	Lanark		Dunfermline Ath	—	—
							Hamilton A	23	4
							Falkirk	—	—
							Raith R	9	—
							Port Vale	3	—
McGlinchey Brian*	5 8	10 05	D	26 10 77	Derry	Trainee	Manchester C	—	—
							Port Vale	15	1
McQuade John‡	5 8	12 02	F	8 7 70	Glasgow		Port Vale	3	—
Musselwhite Paul	6 2	14 04	G	22 12 68	Portsmouth		Portsmouth	—	—
							Scunthorpe U	132	—
							Port Vale	282	—
Naylor Tony	5 7	10 07	F	29 3 68	Manchester	Droylsden	Crewe Alex	122	45
							Port Vale	175	51

O'Callaghan George	6 1	10 05	M	5 9 79	Cork	Trainee	Port Vale	4	—
Pilkington Kevin	6 1	13 00	G	8 3 74	Hitchin	Trainee	Manchester U	6	—
							Rochdale (loan)	6	—
							Rotherham U (loan)	17	—
							Port Vale	8	—
Rougier Tony	5 10	14 07	F	17 7 71	Trinidad		Raith R	56	2
							Hibernian	35	4
							Port Vale	13	—
Smith Alex	5 9	9 09	M	15 2 76	Liverpool	Trainee	Everton	—	—
							Swindon T	31	1
							Chester C	32	2
							Port Vale	8	—
Snijders Mark	6 2	14 04	D	12 3 72	Alkmaar		Port Vale	34	2
Talbot Stuart	5 11	13 07	M	14 6 73	Birmingham	Moor Green	Port Vale	131	10
Tankard Allen	5 10	13 04	D	21 5 69	Fleet	Trainee	Southampton	5	—
							Wigan Ath	209	4
							Port Vale	207	6
Walsh Michael	6 0	12 08	D	5 8 77	Rotherham	Trainee	Scunthorpe U	103	1
							Port Vale	19	1

Trainees
Blount, Ivan G W; Clitheroe, Stewart; Croft, Steven; Donnelly, Paul M; Green, Christopher R; Tarr, Lee A; Taylor, Paul S; Wallace, Carl L

Scholars
Carrigan, Benjamin D; Farr, David J; Maye, Daniel P; Rowland, Stephen J; Simpson, Benjamin J

Associated Schoolboys
Birchall, Christopher; Clewlow, Matthew; Eldershaw, Simon; Gettings, James A; Goldthorpe, Ben; Goodwin, Mark; Hill, Jason M; Jennings, Simon; Jones, Darren P; Kirkham, Shane; Lightfoot, Philip A; Myatt, Andrew P; Orme, Matthew J; Parker, Matthew J; Paynter, William; Price, Andrew; Reid, Levi S J; Roberts, Dafydd; Seward, Adam; Sneade, Adam; Stevenson, Matthew; Travis, Michael; Whitehead, Kevin I T; Woodward, Karl C

Associated Schoolboys who have accepted the Club's offer of a Traineeship/Scholarship/Contract
Barker, Philip; Byrne, Paul; Dolapo, Olaoye; Fairbrother, Craig; Taylor, Andrew

PRESTON NORTH END

Alexander Graham	5 10	12 02	D	10 10 71	Coventry	Trainee	Scunthorpe U	159	18
							Luton T	150	15
							Preston NE	10	—
Appleton Michael	5 8	11 00	M	4 12 75	Salford	Trainee	Manchester U	—	—
							Lincoln C (loan)	4	—
							Grimsby T (loan)	10	3
							Preston NE	63	4
Cartwright Lee	5 8	10 06	F	19 9 72	Rossendale	Trainee	Preston NE	259	20
Darby Julian*	6 0	11 04	M	3 10 67	Bolton	Trainee	Bolton W	270	36
							Coventry C	55	5
							WBA	39	1
							Preston NE	32	1
							Rotherham U (loan)	3	—
Davey Simon*	5 10	11 02	M	1 10 70	Swansea	Trainee	Swansea C	49	4
							Carlisle U	105	18
							Preston NE	106	21
							Darlington (loan)	11	—
Eyres David	5 11	11 05	F	26 2 64	Liverpool	Rhyl	Blackpool	158	38
							Burnley	175	37
							Preston NE	62	12
Gregan Sean	6 2	12 03	M	29 3 74	Stockton	Trainee	Darlington	136	4
							Preston NE	97	6
Harris Jason	6 1	11 10	F	24 11 76	Sutton	Trainee	Crystal Palace	2	—
							Bristol R (loan)	6	2
							Lincoln C (loan)	1	—
							Leyton Orient	37	7
							Preston NE	34	6
Jackson Michael	5 11	11 09	D	4 12 73	Chester	Trainee	Crewe Alex	5	—
							Bury	125	9
							Preston NE	91	10
Kidd Ryan	5 11	10 08	D	16 10 71	Radcliffe	Trainee	Port Vale	1	—
							Preston NE	209	9
King Stuart			M	20 3 81	Derry	Trainee	Preston NE	—	—
Lucas David	6 1	11 06	G	23 11 77	Preston		Preston NE	40	—
							Darlington (loan)	6	—
							Darlington (loan)	7	—
							Scunthorpe U (loan)	6	—
Ludden Dominic	5 7	10 09	D	30 3 74	Basildon	Trainee	Leyton Orient	58	1
							Watford	33	—
							Preston NE	32	—
Macken Jonathan	5 10	12 00	F	7 9 77	Manchester	Trainee	Manchester U	—	—
							Preston NE	71	14
McDonald Neil†	6 0	13 10	D	2 11 65	Wallsend	Wallsend BC	Newcastle U	180	24
							Everton	90	4
							Oldham Ath	24	1
							Bolton W	4	—
							Preston NE	33	—

McGregor Paul*	5 10	11 06	F	17 12 74	Liverpool	Trainee	Nottingham F	30	3
							Carlisle U (loan)	10	3
							Preston NE	4	—
McKenna Paul	5 8	11 11	M	20 10 77	Chorley	Trainee	Preston NE	46	1
Moilanen Teuvo	6 5	12 06	G	12 12 73	Oulu		Ilves	63	—
							Jaro	26	—
							Preston NE	61	—
							Scarborough (loan)	4	—
							Darlington (loan)	16	—
Morgan Paul	6 0	11 03	D	23 10 78	Belfast	Trainee	Preston NE	—	—
Moyes David†	6 1	12 12	D	25 4 63	Glasgow	Drumchapel Amat	Celtic	24	—
							Cambridge U	79	1
							Bristol C	83	6
							Shrewsbury T	96	11
							Dunfermline Ath	105	13
							Hamilton A	5	—
							Preston NE	143	15
Murdock Colin	6 1	12 00	D	2 7 75	Ballymena	Trainee	Manchester U	—	—
							Preston NE	60	2
Nogan Kurt	5 10	11 01	F	9 9 70	Cardiff	Trainee	Luton T	33	3
							Peterborough U	—	—
							Brighton & HA	97	49
							Burnley	92	33
							Preston NE	71	23
O'Hanlon Kelham†	6 1	13 12	G	16 5 62	Saltburn		Middlesbrough	87	—
							Rotherham U	248	—
							Carlisle U	83	—
							Preston NE	23	—
							Dundee U	30	—
							Preston NE	13	—
Parkinson Gary	5 10	11 08	D	10 1 68	Middlesbrough	Everton	Middlesbrough	202	5
							Southend U (loan)	6	—
							Bolton W	3	—
							Burnley	135	4
							Preston NE	72	6
Rankine Mark	5 9	11 06	M	30 9 69	Doncaster	Trainee	Doncaster R	164	20
							Wolverhampton W	132	1
							Preston NE	100	4
Winstanley Mark#	6 1	12 08	D	22 1 68	St Helens	Trainee	Bolton W	220	3
							Burnley	152	5
							Shrewsbury T (loan)	8	—
							Scunthorpe U (loan)	—	—
							Preston NE	—	—
Wright Mark	5 10	11 04	F	4 9 81	Chorley	Schoolboy	Preston NE	1	—

Trainees
Bates, Gavin R; Beckett, Grant M; Beesley, Mark A; Bridgwater, David J; Clare, Gregory J; Connolly, James M; Little, Thomas E S; Rhodes, Tristan M; Turnbull, David

Scholars
Hollis, John; Lin, Paul; McLetchie, Ross; McMillan, Antony T; Underwood, Jeffrey H; Wright, Ronnie M

Non-Contract
McDonald, Neil R; Moyes, David W; O'Hanlon, Kelham G

Associated Schoolboys
Hallam, Anthony T; Lonergan, Andrew; Mercer, Richard M; Porter, Christopher; Rimmer, Courtney; Walsh, Matthew

QUEENS PARK RANGERS

Bankole Ademola	6 3	12 08	G	9 9 69	Lagos	Leyton Orient	Crewe Alex	6	—
							QPR	—	—
							Grimsby T (loan)	—	—
Baraclough Ian	6 1	12 02	D	4 12 70	Leicester	Trainee	Leicester C	—	—
							Wigan Ath (loan)	9	2
							Grimsby T (loan)	4	—
							Grimsby T	1	—
							Lincoln C	73	10
							Mansfield T	47	5
							Notts Co	111	10
							QPR	51	1
Breacker Tim	5 11	13 00	D	2 7 65	Bicester	Apprentice	Luton T	210	3
							West Ham U	240	8
							QPR	18	1
Brown Carlos	5 11	10 06	M	22 4 81	Edmonton	Trainee	QPR	—	—
Bruce Paul	5 10	12 01	F	18 2 78	London	Trainee	QPR	5	1
							Cambridge U (loan)	4	—
Bubb Alvin	5 5	10 00	M	11 10 80	Paddington	Trainee	QPR	—	—
Cass Matthew	5 7	10 05	D	16 12 79	Liverpool	Trainee	QPR	—	—
Currie Michael	5 10	11 00	F	19 10 79	Westminster	Trainee	QPR	—	—

Darlington Jermaine	5 10	12 05	D	11 4 74	London	Aylesbury U	QPR	4	—
Dowie Iain	6 1	13 07	F	9 1 65	Hatfield	Hendon	Luton T	66	16
							Fulham (loan)	5	1
							West Ham U	12	4
							Southampton	122	30
							Crystal Palace	19	6
							West Ham U	68	8
							QPR	30	2
Gallen Kevin	5 11	12 10	F	21 9 75	Hammersmith	Trainee	QPR	140	32
Graham Mark*	5 7	10 08	M	24 10 74	Newry	Trainee	QPR	18	—
Graham Richard	5 8	10 06	M	5 8 79	Newry	Trainee	QPR	2	—
Harper Lee	6 1	13 11	G	30 10 71	Chelsea	Sittingbourne	Arsenal	1	—
							QPR	51	—
Heinola Antti	5 7	10 05	D	20 3 73	Helsinki		HJK Helsinki	80	5
							Emmen	19	—
							Heracles	31	3
							QPR	33	—
Hurst Richard*	6 0	13 01	G	23 12 76	Hammersmith	Trainee	QPR	—	—
Jeanne Leon	5 6	10 00	M	17 11 80	Cardiff	Trainee	QPR	10	—
Jones Vinnie	6 0	11 12	M	5 1 65	Watford	Wealdstone	Wimbledon	77	9
							Leeds U	46	5
							Sheffield U	35	2
							Chelsea	42	4
							Wimbledon	177	12
							QPR	9	1
Kiwomya Chris*	5 9	10 07	F	2 12 69	Huddersfield	Trainee	Ipswich T	225	51
							Arsenal	14	3
							Le Havre (loan)	7	—
							QPR	16	6
Kulcsar George	6 1	13 08	M	12 8 67	Budapest		Antwerp	66	1
							Bradford C	26	1
							QPR	29	1
Langley Richard	5 10	11 04	M	27 12 79	London	Trainee	QPR	8	1
Lopez Rik	5 10	11 04	F	25 12 79	Northwick Park	Arsenal	QPR	—	—
Lusardi Mario	5 9	10 02	F	27 9 79	Islington	Trainee	QPR	—	—
Maddix Danny*	5 11	12 00	D	11 10 67	Ashford	Apprentice	Tottenham H	—	—
							Southend U (loan)	2	—
							QPR	275	12
Mahoney-Johnson Michael	5 10	12 10	F	6 11 76	Paddington	Trainee	QPR	3	—
							Wycombe W (loan)	4	2
							Brighton & HA (loan)	4	—
McFlynn Terry	5 9	10 05	M	27 3 81	Magherafelt	Trainee	QPR	—	—
Miklosko Ludek	6 5	14 00	G	9 12 61	Protesov	Banik Ostrava	West Ham U	315	—
							QPR	31	—
Morrow Steve	6 0	11 03	D	2 7 70	Bangor	Trainee	Arsenal	62	1
							Reading (loan)	10	—
							Watford (loan)	8	—
							Reading (loan)	3	—
							Barnet (loan)	1	—
							QPR	60	2
Murray Paul	5 8	10 05	M	31 8 76	Carlisle	Trainee	Carlisle U	41	1
							QPR	104	7
Ord Richard	6 2	12 08	D	3 3 70	Murton	Trainee	Sunderland	243	7
							York C (loan)	3	—
							QPR	—	—
Owen Karl	5 10	10 06	D	12 10 79	Coventry	Trainee	QPR	—	—
Peacock Gavin	5 8	11 08	M	18 11 67	Eltham	Apprentice	QPR	17	1
							Gillingham	70	11
							Bournemouth	56	8
							Newcastle U	105	35
							Chelsea	103	17
							QPR	108	22
Perry Mark	5 11	12 09	M	19 10 78	Perivale	Trainee	QPR	11	1
Plummer Chris	6 2	12 12	D	12 10 76	Isleworth	Trainee	QPR	16	—
Purser Wayne	5 9	11 04	F	13 4 80	Basildon	Trainee	QPR	—	—
Ready Karl	6 1	12 10	D	14 8 72	Neath	Trainee	QPR	170	8
Rose Matthew	5 11	11 01	D	24 9 75	Dartford	Trainee	Arsenal	5	—
							QPR	45	—
Rowland Keith	5 10	10 00	D	1 9 71	Portadown	Trainee	Bournemouth	72	2
							Coventry C (loan)	2	—
							West Ham U	80	1
							QPR	37	3
Scully Tony	5 7	11 05	F	12 6 76	Dublin	Trainee	Crystal Palace	3	—
							Bournemouth (loan)	10	—
							Cardiff C (loan)	14	—
							Manchester C	9	—
							Stoke C (loan)	7	—
							QPR	30	2
Slade Steve	6 0	10 13	F	6 10 75	Hackney	Trainee	Tottenham H	5	—
							QPR	59	5
							Brentford (loan)	4	—
Weare Ross	6 2	13 05	F	19 3 77	Perivale	East Ham U	QPR	—	—
Whittle David	5 10	12 07	M	2 12 78	Waterford	Trainee	QPR	—	—

Wright Daniel	5 8	10 06	F	24 9 81	London	Trainee	QPR	—	—
Yates Steve*	5 10	12 02	D	29 1 70	Bristol	Trainee	Bristol R	197	—
							QPR	134	2

Trainees
Anderson, Peter M; Andrews, Barry D F; Meeking, Scott A; Newall, John F

Scholars
Browne, Ricky D; Bull, Nikki; Burgess, Oliver D; Cochrane, Justin V; Rustem, Adam R

Associated Schoolboys
Bean, Marcus; Egan, Richard L; Pilgrim, Wayne M; Spackman, Perry E

Associated Schoolboys who have accepted the Club's offer of a Traineeship/Scholarship/Contract
Brady, Richard L; D'Austin, Ryan A; Daly, Wesley J P; Dick, Alex R; Duncan, Lyndon E; Fitzgerald, Brian M; Gradley, Patrick; Mills, Danny W; Murphy, Danny T; Nugent, Marcel; Pacquette, Richard; Walshe, Ben; Wattley, David A

READING

Barras Tony	6 0	13 00	D	29 3 71	Stockton	Trainee	Hartlepool U	12	—
							Stockport Co	99	5
							Rotherham U (loan)	5	1
							York C	171	11
							Reading	6	1
Bernal Andy	5 10	12 05	D	16 7 66	Canberra	Sporting Gijon	Ipswich T	9	—
						Sydney Olympic	Reading	164	2
Brayson Paul	5 6	10 10	F	16 9 77	Newcastle	Trainee	Newcastle U	—	—
							Swansea C (loan)	11	5
							Reading	34	1
Brebner Grant	5 10	11 11	M	6 12 77	Edinburgh	Trainee	Manchester U	—	—
							Cambridge U (loan)	6	1
							Hibernian (loan)	9	1
							Reading	39	9
Bristow Jason*	6 2	11 00	D	23 4 80	Basingstoke	Trainee	Reading	—	—
Caskey Darren	5 8	11 09	M	21 8 74	Basildon	Trainee	Tottenham H	32	4
							Watford (loan)	6	1
							Reading	115	9
Casper Chris	6 0	12 02	D	28 4 75	Burnley	Trainee	Manchester U	2	—
							Bournemouth (loan)	16	1
							Swindon T (loan)	9	1
							Reading	32	
Crawford Jimmy	5 11	11 06	M	1 5 74	Chicago	Bohemians	Newcastle U	2	—
							Rotherham U (loan)	11	—
							Dundee U (loan)	2	—
							Reading	17	—
Evers Sean	5 9	9 11	M	10 10 77	Hitchin	Trainee	Luton T	52	6
							Reading	1	—
Fleck Robert‡	5 7	11 09	F	11 8 65	Glasgow	Possil YM	Partick T	2	1
							Rangers	85	29
							Norwich C	143	40
							Chelsea	40	3
							Bolton W (loan)	7	1
							Bristol C (loan)	10	1
							Norwich C	104	16
							Reading	9	1
Glasgow Byron	5 6	10 11	M	18 2 79	Tooting	Trainee	Reading	39	1
Gray Stuart	5 11	11 02	D	18 12 73	Harrogate		Celtic	28	1
							Reading	34	2
Gurney Andy	5 11	12 02	D	25 1 74	Bristol	Trainee	Bristol R	108	9
							Torquay U	64	10
							Reading	8	—
Hammond Nicky	6 0	11 13	G	7 9 67	Hornchurch	Apprentice	Arsenal	—	—
							Bristol R (loan)	3	—
							Peterborough U (loan)	—	—
							Aberdeen (loan)	—	—
							Swindon T	67	—
							Plymouth Arg	4	—
							Reading	25	—
Harrison Ross‡	5 9	10 04	F	28 12 79	Leamington Spa	Trainee	Reading	—	—
Hodges Lee	6 0	12 00	F	4 9 73	Epping	Trainee	Tottenham H	4	—
							Plymouth Arg (loan)	7	2
							Wycombe W (loan)	4	—
							Barnet	105	26
							Reading	25	6
Houghton Ray*	5 7	10 10	M	9 1 62	Glasgow	Amateur	West Ham U	1	—
							Fulham	129	16
							Oxford U	83	10
							Liverpool	153	28
							Aston Villa	95	6
							Crystal Palace	72	7
							Reading	43	1
Howie Scott	6 3	13 07	G	4 1 72	Motherwell		Clyde	55	—
							Norwich C	2	—
							Motherwell	69	—
							Reading	49	—

Name	Ht	Wt	Pos	Birth date	Birthplace	Source	Club	Apps	Gls
Hunter Barry#	6 3	13 02	D	18 11 68	Coleraine	Crusaders	Wrexham	91	4
							Reading	30	2
							Southend U (loan)	5	2
Kromheer Elroy	6 4	12 07	D	15 1 70	Amsterdam		Volendam	72	6
							Motherwell	12	—
							Volendam	53	2
							Zwolle	30	5
							Reading	11	—
Lambert James‡	5 7	11 02	M	14 9 73	Henley	School	Reading	125	16
							Walsall (loan)	6	—
Lockwood Adam	5 11	11 08	D	26 10 81	Wakefield	Trainee	Reading	—	—
Mautone Steve#	6 2	13 02	G	10 8 70	Myrtleford	Canberra Cosmos	West Ham U	1	—
							Crewe Alex (loan)	3	—
							Reading	29	—
McIntyre Jim	5 11	12 00	F	24 5 72	Alexandria		Bristol C	1	—
							Exeter C (loan)	15	3
							Airdrieonians	54	10
							Kilmarnock	46	9
							Reading	38	6
McLaren Andy	5 10	10 06	M	5 6 73	Glasgow		Dundee U	165	12
							Reading	7	1
Murty Graeme	5 10	11 10	M	13 11 74	Saltburn	Trainee	York C	117	7
							Reading	9	—
Parkinson Phil	6 0	12 09	M	1 12 67	Chorley	Apprentice	Southampton	—	—
							Bury	145	5
							Reading	257	13
Polston John	5 11	11 12	D	10 6 68	Walthamstow	Apprentice	Tottenham H	24	1
							Norwich C	215	8
							Reading	4	—
Primus Linvoy	6 0	13 07	D	14 9 73	Forest Gate	Trainee	Charlton Ath	4	—
							Barnet	127	7
							Reading	67	1
Reilly Mark	5 7	11 00	M	3 3 69	Bellshill		Motherwell	4	—
(Transferred to Kilmarnock, November 1998)							Kilmarnock	205	8
							Reading	6	—
							Kilmarnock	18	—
Sarr Mass	5 8	11 13	F	6 2 73	Monrovia		Hajduk Split	59	17
							Reading	28	3
Scott Keith	6 2	14 07	F	9 6 67	Westminster	Leicester U	Lincoln C	16	2
						Wycombe W	Wycombe W	15	10
							Swindon T	51	12
							Stoke C	25	3
							Norwich C	25	5
							Bournemouth (loan)	8	1
							Watford (loan)	6	2
							Wycombe W (loan)	9	3
							Wycombe W	54	17
							Reading	9	2
Smith Grant‡			M	5 5 80	Irvine	Wycombe W	Reading	—	—
Stamp Neville§	5 10	11 08	D	7 7 81	Reading	Trainee	Reading	1	—
Van der Kwaak Peter	6 4	13 12	G	12 10 68	Haarlem	Ajax	Dordrecht	50	—
							Reading	3	—
Williams Martin	5 9	11 12	F	12 7 73	Luton	Leicester C	Luton T	40	2
							Colchester U (loan)	3	—
							Reading	99	21

Trainees
Arkins, Stephen F; Ashdown, Jamie L; Beasley, Adam; Etunmu, Anayo S; Haddow, Alexander; Hadland, Phillip J; Henderson, Darius A; Hill, Emlyn R; Martin, Paul; Masters, Daniel E; McDonald, Marcus; Osborne, Steven J; Rodgers, Declan J; Smith, Christopher A; Stamp, Neville; Sumner, Toby; Tyson, Nathan

Associated Schoolboys who have accepted the Club's offer of a Traineeship/Scholarship/Contract
Allaway, Ricky; Allaway, Shaun; Campion, Adam J; Kurton, Stuart; Williams, Scott

---

ROCHDALE

Name	Ht	Wt	Pos	Birth date	Birthplace	Source	Club	Apps	Gls
Bailey Mark*	5 9	11 11	M	12 8 76	Stoke	Trainee	Stoke C	—	—
							Rochdale	67	1
Barlow Andy*	5 8	11 12	D	24 11 65	Oldham		Oldham Ath	261	5
							Bradford C (loan)	2	—
							Blackpool	80	2
							Rochdale	67	1
Bayliss Dave	5 11	12 00	D	8 6 76	Liverpool	Trainee	Rochdale	107	3
Bryson Ian*	5 11	12 07	M	26 11 62	Kilmarnock		Kilmarnock	215	40
							Sheffield U	155	36
							Barnsley	16	3
							Preston NE	151	19
							Rochdale	54	1
Carden Paul	5 9	11 10	M	29 3 79	Liverpool	Trainee	Blackpool	1	—
							Rochdale	32	—
Diaz Isidro‡	5 7	9 03	M	15 5 72	Valencia	Balaguer	Wigan Ath	76	16
							Wolverhampton W	1	—
							Wigan Ath	2	—
							Rochdale	14	2
Edghill Phil‡	6 0	9 08	M	13 9 79	Oldham	Trainee	Rochdale	—	—

Name	Ht	Wt	Pos	DOB	Birthplace	Source	Club	Apps	Gls
Edwards Neil	5 8	11 02	G	5 12 70	Aberdare	Trainee	Leeds U	—	—
							Huddersfield T (loan)	—	—
							Stockport Co	164	—
							Rochdale	72	—
Farrell Andy*	5 11	12 00	M	7 10 65	Colchester	School	Colchester U	105	5
							Burnley	257	19
							Wigan Ath	54	1
							Rochdale	118	6
Gray David*	6 2	13 07	F	19 1 80	Rossendale		Rochdale	3	—
Hicks Graham			D	17 2 81	Oldham	Trainee	Rochdale	1	—
Hill Keith#	6 1	12 07	D	17 5 69	Bolton	Apprentice	Blackburn R	96	3
							Plymouth Arg	123	2
							Rochdale	113	6
Holt Michael	5 10	11 03	F	28 7 77	Barnoldswick	Trainee	Blackburn R	—	—
							Preston NE	36	5
							Macclesfield T (loan)	4	1
							Rochdale	24	7
Johnson Alan*	6 0	14 02	D	19 2 71	Wigan	Trainee	Wigan Ath	180	13
							Lincoln C	63	—
							Preston NE (loan)	2	—
							Rochdale	62	4
Jones Gary	5 11	11 07	M	3 6 77	Birkenhead	Caernarfon Town	Swansea C	8	—
							Rochdale	37	2
Key Lance‡	6 3	15 00	G	13 5 68	Kettering	Histon	Sheffield W	—	—
							York C (loan)	—	—
							Oldham Ath (loan)	2	—
							Portsmouth (loan)	—	—
							Oxford U (loan)	6	—
							Lincoln C (loan)	5	—
							Hartlepool U (loan)	1	—
							Rochdale (loan)	14	—
							Dundee U	4	—
							Sheffield U	—	—
							Rochdale	19	—
Lancashire Graham	5 9	12 04	F	19 10 72	Blackpool	Trainee	Burnley	31	8
							Halifax T (loan)	2	—
							Chester C (loan)	11	7
							Preston NE	23	2
							Wigan Ath	30	12
							Rochdale	38	12
Leonard Mark‡	6 1	13 03	F	27 9 62	Whiston	Witton Alb	Everton	—	—
							Tranmere R (loan)	7	—
							Crewe Alex	54	15
							Stockport Co	73	24
							Bradford C	157	29
							Rochdale	9	1
							Preston NE	22	1
							Chester C	32	8
							Wigan Ath	64	12
							Rochdale	80	6
Monington Mark#	6 1	13 07	D	21 10 70	Mansfield	School	Burnley	84	5
							Rotherham U	79	3
							Rochdale	37	3
Morris Andy	6 4	14 07	F	17 11 67	Sheffield	School	Rotherham U	7	—
							Chesterfield	266	56
							Exeter C (loan)	7	2
							Rochdale	25	7
Painter Rob#	5 10	12 02	F	26 1 71	Wigan	Trainee	Chester C	84	8
							Maidstone U	30	5
							Burnley	26	2
							Darlington	115	28
							Rochdale	112	30
Peake Jason	5 11	12 13	M	29 9 71	Leicester	Trainee	Leicester C	8	1
							Hartlepool U (loan)	6	1
							Halifax T	33	1
							Rochdale	95	6
							Brighton & HA	30	1
							Bury	6	—
							Rochdale	38	5
Pender John*	6 2	13 05	D	19 11 63	Luton	Apprentice	Wolverhampton W	117	3
							Charlton Ath	41	—
							Bristol C	83	3
							Burnley	171	8
							Wigan Ath	70	1
							Rochdale	14	—
Priestley Phil			G	30 3 76	Wigan	Atherton LR	Rochdale	1	—
Robson Glen‡	5 10	10 04	F	25 9 77	Sunderland	Murton	Rochdale	10	—
Sparrow Paul*	6 0	11 00	D	24 3 75	London	Trainee	Crystal Palace	1	—
							Preston NE	20	—
							Rochdale	25	2
Stoker Gareth	5 9	11 04	M	22 2 73	Bishop Auckland	Leeds U	Hull C	30	2
							Hereford U	70	6
							Cardiff C	37	4
							Rochdale	12	1
Stokes Dean	5 8	11 02	D	23 5 70	Birmingham	Halesowen T	Port Vale	60	—
							Rochdale	11	—

Stuart Mark*	5 11	11 12	M	15 12 66	Hammersmith	QPR	Charlton Ath	107	28
							Plymouth Arg	57	11
							Ipswich T (loan)	5	2
							Bradford C	29	5
							Huddersfield T	15	3
							Rochdale	202	41
Williams Scott‡	6 0	12 05	M	7 8 74	Bangor	Trainee	Wrexham	32	—
							Rochdale	—	—

Trainees
Loft, Paul; Taylor, Carl D; Wilkinson, James; Wilson, Scott A

Scholars
Cantello, Stuart L; Crowe, Alex; Duffy, Lee; Gilks, Matthew; Manousios, Nicholas G; Rudd, Paul G; Taylor, Daniel J

Non-Contract
Fielding, David P; Hampson, James J S; Taylor, Andrew; Westmorland, Darren P

Player who does not hold a current contract but his registration has been retained by the Club
Robson, Glen A

Associated Schoolboys who have accepted the Club's offer of a Traineeship/Scholarship/Contract
Bell, Colin; Walsh, David

ROTHERHAM UNITED

Bagshaw Neil‡	6 2	12 08	D	24 12 79	Doncaster	Trainee	Rotherham U	—	—
Beech Chris	5 9	12 09	D	5 11 75	Congleton	Trainee	Manchester C	—	—
							Cardiff C	46	1
							Rotherham U	24	—
Berry Trevor	5 6	11 00	M	1 8 74	Haslemere	Bournemouth	Aston Villa	—	—
							Rotherham U	126	16
Bos Gijsbert‡	6 4	12 09	F	22 2 73	Spakenburg	Ijsselmeervogels	Lincoln C	34	6
							Rotherham U	18	4
							Walsall (loan)	—	—
Clark Martin*	5 9	10 12	D	12 9 70	Accrington	Accrington S	Crewe Alex	—	—
						Southport	Rotherham U	29	—
Dillon Paul	5 9	10 11	D	22 10 78	Limerick	Trainee	Rotherham U	55	2
Fortune-West Leo	6 4	13 01	F	9 4 71	Stratford	Stevenage Bor	Gillingham	67	18
							Leyton Orient (loan)	5	—
							Lincoln C	9	1
							Brentford	11	—
							Rotherham U	20	12
Garner Darren	5 9	12 07	M	10 12 71	Plymouth	Trainee	Plymouth Arg	27	1
						Dorchester T	Rotherham U	141	10
Glover Lee	5 11	11 09	F	24 4 70	Kettering	Trainee	Nottingham F	76	9
							Leicester C (loan)	5	1
							Barnsley (loan)	8	—
							Luton T (loan)	1	—
							Port Vale	52	7
							Rotherham U	78	28
							Huddersfield T (loan)	11	—
Hudson Danny	5 8	10 03	M	25 6 79	Mexborough	Trainee	Rotherham U	36	4
Hurst Paul	5 4	90	D	25 9 74	Sheffield	Trainee	Rotherham U	149	6
Ingledow Jamie	5 7	11 01	M	23 8 80	Barnsley	Trainee	Rotherham U	21	2
Knill Alan*	6 4	13 00	D	8 10 64	Slough	Apprentice	Southampton	—	—
							Halifax T	118	6
							Swansea C	89	3
							Bury	144	8
							Cardiff C (loan)	4	—
							Scunthorpe U	131	8
							Rotherham U	74	6
Martindale Gary	6 1	11 13	F	24 6 71	Liverpool	Burscough	Bolton W	—	—
							Peterborough U	31	15
							Notts Co	66	13
							Mansfield T (loan)	5	2
							Rotherham U	18	4
Monkhouse Andy	6 0	13 09	F	23 10 80	Leeds	Trainee	Rotherham U	5	1
Pettinger Paul	6 0	13 00	G	1 10 75	Sheffield	Barnsley	Leeds U		
							Torquay U (loan)	3	—
							Rotherham U (loan)	1	—
							Gillingham		
							Carlisle U	—	—
							Rotherham U	3	—
Pollitt Mike	6 3	14 12	G	29 2 72	Farnworth	Trainee	Manchester U	—	—
							Oldham Ath (loan)	—	—
							Bury	—	—
							Lincoln C	57	—
							Darlington	55	—
							Notts Co	10	—
							Oldham Ath (loan)	16	—
							Gillingham (loan)	6	—
							Brentford (loan)	5	—
							Sunderland	—	—
							Rotherham U	46	—

Player	Ht	Wt	Pos	DOB	Birthplace	Source	Club	Apps	Gls
Richardson Neil*	6 0	13 00	D	3 3 68	Sunderland	Brandon U	Rotherham U	184	9
							Exeter C (loan)	14	—
Roscoe Andy*	5 10	11 08	M	4 6 73	Liverpool	Trainee	Liverpool	—	—
							Bolton W	3	—
							Rotherham U	202	18
Scott Gary*	5 8	10 09	D	2 3 78	Liverpool	Trainee	Tranmere R	—	—
							Rotherham U	20	—
Scott Rob	6 1	12 04	F	15 8 73	Epsom	Sutton U	Sheffield U	6	1
							Scarborough (loan)	8	3
							Northampton T (loan)	5	—
							Fulham	84	17
							Carlisle U (loan)	7	3
							Rotherham U	6	1
Sedgwick Chris	5 11	10 10	F	28 4 80	Sheffield	Trainee	Rotherham U	37	4
Thompson Steve#	5 11	13 00	M	2 11 64	Oldham	Apprentice	Bolton W	335	49
							Luton T	5	—
							Leicester C	127	18
							Burnley	49	1
							Rotherham U	72	8
Warne Paul	5 8	11 01	F	8 5 73	Norwich	Wroxham	Wigan Ath	36	3
							Rotherham U	19	8
Warner Vance	6 0	13 04	D	3 9 74	Leeds	Trainee	Nottingham F	5	—
							Grimsby T (loan)	3	—
							Rotherham U	44	1
White Jason	6 1	12 12	F	19 10 71	Meriden	Derby Co	Scunthorpe U	68	16
							Darlington (loan)	4	1
							Scarborough	63	20
							Northampton T	77	18
							Rotherham U	53	18
Williams Mark	6 0	11 02	D	10 11 78	Liverpool	Trainee	Rochdale	14	1
							Rotherham U	11	—

Trainees
Allen, Paul C; Artell, David J; Beesley, Darren K; Beeton, Lee J; Merris, David A; Nixon, Adam R C; Roden, Craig L; Towey, Christopher J

Scholars
Capill, Stephen L; Connor, Gareth A; Hensman, Matthew D; Sandland, Guy; Shelton, Lee M

Associated Schoolboys
Barker, Damien J; Colliver, James L; Hanson, Christopher; Johnson, Mark I; Laycock, Joseph; Lees, Scott; Parker, Daniel; Ring, Andrew I

Associated Schoolboys who have accepted the Club's offer of a Traineeship/Scholarship/Contract
Alabi, Stephen; Barraclough, Simon D; Beggs, John A; Boyd, Darren; Holmes, Ian; Holyer, Ian D

SCARBOROUGH

Player	Ht	Wt	Pos	DOB	Birthplace	Source	Club	Apps	Gls
Atkinson Graeme#	5 8	11 05	D	11 11 71	Hull	Trainee	Hull C	149	23
							Preston NE	79	6
							Rochdale (loan)	6	—
							Brighton & HA	16	—
							Scunthorpe U	1	—
							Scarborough	15	1
Atkinson Paddy*	5 10	11 06	D	22 5 70	Singapore	Sheffield U	Hartlepool U	21	3
						Workington	York C	41	—
							Scarborough	27	—
Bazelya Eammon*	5 9	11 00	F	25 10 78	London	Trainee	Scarborough	—	—
Brodie Steve	5 7	10 08	F	14 1 73	Sunderland	Trainee	Sunderland	12	—
							Doncaster R (loan)	5	1
							Scarborough	111	27
Bullimore Wayne*	5 10	12 00	M	12 9 70	Mansfield	Trainee	Manchester U	—	—
							Barnsley	35	1
							Stockport Co	—	—
							Scunthorpe U	67	11
							Bradford C	2	—
							Doncaster R (loan)	4	—
							Peterborough U	21	1
							Scarborough	35	1
Buxton Nick‡	6 0	13 00	G	6 9 76	Doncaster		Bury	—	—
						Goole T	Scarborough	3	—
Carr Graeme	5 10	11 00	M	28 10 78	Chester-le-Street	Trainee	Scarborough	10	—
Dabelsteen Thomas†			M	6 3 73	Copenhagen		Scarborough	5	1
Elliott Tony*	6 0	13 06	G	30 11 69	Nuneaton		Birmingham C	—	—
							Hereford U	75	—
							Huddersfield T	15	—
							Carlisle U	22	—
							Cardiff C	39	—
							Scarborough	35	—
Hodges Glynt†	6 0	12 10	M	30 4 63	Streatham	Apprentice	Wimbledon	232	49
							Newcastle U	7	—
							Watford	86	15
							Crystal Palace	7	—
							Sheffield U	147	19
							Derby Co	9	—
						Sin Tao	Hull C	18	4
							Nottingham F	5	—
							Scarborough	1	—

Hoyland Jamie	6 0	14 07	M	23 1 66	Sheffield	Apprentice	Manchester C	2	—
							Bury	172	35
							Sheffield U	89	6
							Bristol C (loan)	6	—
							Burnley	87	3
							Carlisle U (loan)	5	—
							Scarborough	44	3
Kay John*	5 10	11 08	D	29 1 64	Sunderland	Apprentice	Arsenal	14	—
							Wimbledon	63	2
							Middlesbrough (loan)	8	—
							Sunderland	199	—
							Shrewsbury T (loan)	7	—
							Preston NE	7	—
							Scarborough	98	—
Lydiate Jason*	6 0	13 00	D	29 10 71	Manchester	Trainee	Manchester U	—	—
							Bolton W	30	—
							Blackpool	86	2
							Scarborough	27	1
							Rochdale (loan)	14	1
Marinkov Alex	6 2	13 00	D	2 12 67	Grenoble		Scarborough	22	4
(Transferred to Hibernian, February 1999)							Hibernian	10	1
Martin Kevin	6 1	12 05	G	22 6 76	Bromsgrove	Trainee	Scarborough	23	—
McNaughton Michael	6 2	14 00	D	29 1 80	Blackpool	Trainee	Scarborough	31	1
Milbourne Ian	5 9	11 02	F	21 1 79	Hexham	Trainee	Newcastle U	—	—
							Scarborough	16	—
Mountfield Derek†	6 1	13 08	D	2 11 62	Liverpool	Apprentice	Tranmere R	26	1
							Everton	106	19
							Aston Villa	90	9
							Wolverhampton W	83	4
							Carlisle U	31	3
							Northampton T	4	—
							Walsall	97	2
						Bromsgrove R	Scarborough	6	—
Naisbett Philip†			G	2 1 79	Easington	Trainee	Sunderland	—	—
							Scarborough	2	—
Parks Tony#	5 10	11 05	G	28 1 63	Hackney		Tottenham H	37	—
							Oxford U (loan)	5	—
							Gillingham (loan)	2	—
							Brentford	71	—
							QPR (loan)	—	—
							Fulham	2	—
							West Ham U	6	—
							Stoke C	2	—
							Falkirk	112	—
							Blackpool	—	—
							Burnley	—	—
							Doncaster R (loan)	6	—
						Barrow	Scarborough	15	—
Porter Gary*	5 6	10 13	M	6 3 66	Sunderland	Apprentice	Watford	400	47
							Walsall	44	1
							Scarborough	13	—
Radigan Neil‡	5 9	11 00	M	4 7 80	Middlesbrough	Trainee	Scarborough	9	—
Rennison Shaun				23 11 80	Northallerton	Trainee	Scarborough	15	1
Renshaw Ian‡			D	14 4 78	Chelmsford		Scarborough	1	—
Roberts Darren	6 0	12 04	F	12 10 69	Birmingham	Burton Alb	Wolverhampton W	21	5
							Hereford U (loan)	6	5
							Doncaster R	—	—
							Chesterfield	25	1
							Darlington	96	33
							Peterborough U (loan)	3	—
							Scarborough	18	3
Robinson Liam*	5 7	12 07	F	29 12 65	Bradford	Nottingham F	Huddersfield T	21	2
							Tranmere R (loan)	4	3
							Bury	262	89
							Bristol C	41	4
							Burnley	63	9
							Scarborough	65	7
Rockett Jason*	6 1	13 04	D	26 9 69	London		Rotherham U	—	—
							Scarborough	172	11
Russell Matthew	6 0	11 05	M	17 1 78	Leeds	Trainee	Scarborough	44	3
							Doncaster R (loan)	5	—
Saville Andy‡	6 0	12 09	F	12 12 64	Hull	Local	Hull C	101	18
							Walsall	38	5
							Barnsley	82	21
							Hartlepool U	37	13
							Birmingham C	59	17
							Burnley (loan)	4	1
							Preston NE	56	30
							Wigan Ath	25	4
							Cardiff C	35	12
							Hull C (loan)	3	—
							Scarborough	9	—
Tate Chris	6 0	12 00	F	27 12 77	York	York C	Sunderland	—	—
							Scarborough	49	13
Todd Andrew‡	6 0	11 03	M	22 2 79	Nottingham	Trainee	Nottingham F	—	—
							Scarborough	1	—

Worrall Ben	5 5	10 00	M	7 12 75	Swindon	Trainee	Swindon T	3	—
							Scarborough	67	3

Trainees
Brunton, Daniel J; Darcy, Richard A; Gildea, Alex; Grant, Leigh; Hunter, Darren T; Morris, Stewart I; Newton, Paul A; Tremble, David G; Wilson, Dean P

Scholars
Atkinson, Paul R; Bell, Steven G; Brown, James; Ferguson, Anthony; Jewell, Adam R; Pounder, David; Toone, Leigh S

Associated Schoolboys
Ball, Jason; Burns, Dean; Crawford, Richard E H; Fitzsimmons, Peter; Gildea, Daniel; Hammond, Kevin M; Jowsey, James R; Marley, Karl N; Taylor, Dean R

Associated Schoolboys who have accepted the Club's offer of a Traineeship/Scholarship/Contract
Baxter, Nicholas P

SCUNTHORPE UNITED

Bull Gary*	5 10	12 02	F	12 6 66	Tipton	Swindon T	Southampton	—	—
							Cambridge U	19	4
						Barnet	Barnet	83	37
							Nottingham F	12	1
							Birmingham C (loan)	10	6
							Brighton & HA (loan)	10	2
							Birmingham C (loan)	6	—
							York C	83	11
							Scunthorpe U	24	—
Calvo-Garcia Alexander	5 11	11 10	M	1 1 72	Ordizia	Eibar	Scunthorpe U	100	16
Clarke Tim	6 3	15 12	G	19 9 68	Stourbridge	Halesowen T	Coventry C	—	—
							Huddersfield T	70	—
							Rochdale (loan)	2	—
							Shrewsbury T	31	—
						Witton Alb	York C	17	—
							Scunthorpe U	78	—
Dawson Andrew	5 10	11 02	D	20 10 78	Northallerton	Trainee	Nottingham F	—	—
							Scunthorpe U	24	—
Evans Tom	6 1	13 02	G	31 12 76	Doncaster	Trainee	Sheffield U	—	—
							Crystal Palace	—	—
							Coventry C (loan)	—	—
							Scunthorpe U	29	—
Eyre John#	5 11	13 00	F	9 10 74	Hull	Trainee	Oldham Ath	10	1
							Scunthorpe U (loan)	9	8
							Scunthorpe U	164	43
Featherstone James‡	6 0	12 12	F	12 11 79	Wharfedale	Blackburn R	Scunthorpe U	1	—
Fickling Ashley#	5 10	11 08	D	15 11 72	Sheffield	Trainee	Sheffield U	—	—
							Darlington (loan)	14	—
							Darlington (loan)	1	—
							Grimsby T	39	2
							Darlington (loan)	8	—
							Scunthorpe U	29	—
Forrester Jamie#	5 6	10 12	F	1 11 74	Bradford	Auxerre	Leeds U	9	—
							Southend U (loan)	5	—
							Grimsby T (loan)	9	1
							Grimsby T	41	6
							Scunthorpe U	101	37
Gayle John	6 3	15 00	F	30 7 64	Bromsgrove	Burton Alb	Wimbledon	20	2
							Birmingham C	44	10
							Walsall (loan)	4	1
							Coventry C	3	—
							Burnley	14	3
							Stoke C	26	4
							Gillingham (loan)	9	3
							Northampton T	48	7
							Scunthorpe U	37	4
Graves Wayne	5 8	10 07	M	18 9 80	Scunthorpe	Trainee	Scunthorpe U	3	—
Harsley Paul	5 10	11 03	M	29 5 78	Scunthorpe	Trainee	Grimsby T	—	—
							Scunthorpe U	49	1
Hope Chris	6 1	12 08	D	14 11 73	Sheffield	Darlington	Nottingham F	—	—
							Scunthorpe U	243	16
Housham Steven	5 10	12 03	M	24 2 76	Gainsborough T	Trainee	Scunthorpe U	106	4
Laws Brian#	5 9	12 04	D	14 10 61	Wallsend	Apprentice	Burnley	125	12
							Huddersfield T	56	1
							Middlesbrough	107	12
							Nottingham F	147	4
							Grimsby T	46	2
							Darlington	10	—
							Scunthorpe U	18	—
Logan Richard	6 0	13 03	M	24 5 69	Barnsley	Gainsborough T	Huddersfield T	45	1
							Plymouth Arg	86	12
							Scunthorpe U	41	6
Marshall Lee	5 10	10 08	M	1 8 75	Nottingham	Trainee	Nottingham F	—	—
						Grantham T	Stockport Co	1	—
						Eastwood T	Scunthorpe U	40	2

Name	Ht	Wt	Pos	Birthdate	Birthplace	Source	Club	Apps	Gls
McAuley Sean	5 11	12 02	D	23 6 72	Sheffield	Trainee	Manchester U	—	—
							St Johnstone	62	—
							Chesterfield (loan)	1	1
							Hartlepool U	84	1
							Scunthorpe U	61	1
							Scarborough (loan)	7	—
Neil Jim‡	5 8	12 01	D	28 2 76	Bury St Edmunds	Trainee	Grimsby T	2	—
							Scunthorpe U	7	—
Nottingham Steve‡			D	21 2 80	Peterborough	Trainee	Scunthorpe U	1	—
Shakespeare Craig‡	5 10	13 06	M	26 10 63	Birmingham	Apprentice	Walsall	284	45
							Sheffield W	17	—
							WBA	112	12
							Grimsby T	106	10
							Scunthorpe U	4	—
Sheldon Gareth	5 11	11 10	F	31 1 80	Birmingham	Trainee	Scunthorpe U	12	1
Stamp Darryn	6 1	11 10	F	21 9 78	Beverley		Scunthorpe U	35	5
Stanton Nathan	5 11	12 00	D	6 5 81	Nottingham	Trainee	Scunthorpe U	5	—
Walker Justin#	6 0	13 03	M	6 9 75	Nottingham	Trainee	Nottingham F	—	—
							Scunthorpe U	90	2
Wilcox Russ	6 0	12 13	D	25 3 64	Hemsworth	Apprentice	Doncaster R	1	—
						Frickley Ath	Northampton T	138	9
							Hull C	100	7
							Doncaster R	81	6
							Preston NE	62	1
							Scunthorpe U	59	3
Witter Tony†	6 1	13 00	D	12 8 65	London	Grays Ath	Crystal Palace	—	—
							QPR	1	—
							Millwall (loan)	—	—
							Plymouth Arg (loan)	3	1
							Reading (loan)	4	—
							Millwall	102	2
							Northampton T	4	—
							Torquay U	4	—
						Welling U	Scunthorpe U	14	—

Trainees
Fielding, Jonathan; Shirtliff, Philip

Scholars
Anderson, Mark J; Cotterill, James M; Herrick, Leigh; Marsh, Craig; Ridley, Lee; Sparrow, Matthew

Associated Schoolboy
Singh, Sean

SHEFFIELD UNITED

Name	Ht	Wt	Pos	Birthdate	Birthplace	Source	Club	Apps	Gls
Bettney Chris*	5 10	11 00	F	27 10 77	Chesterfield	Trainee	Sheffield U	1	—
							Hull C (loan)	30	1
Bruce Steve*	6 0	13 00	D	31 12 60	Corbridge	Apprentice	Gillingham	205	29
							Norwich C	141	14
							Manchester U	309	36
							Birmingham C	72	2
							Sheffield U	10	—
Capper David‡	6 1	12 02	D	8 9 78	Stoke	Trainee	Sheffield U	—	—
Cullen Jon	6 0	11 10	M	10 1 73	Durham	Trainee	Doncaster R	9	—
						Morpeth T	Hartlepool U	34	12
							Sheffield U	4	—
Davies Kevin	6 0	12 00	M	15 11 78	Sheffield	Trainee	Sheffield U	—	—
Dellas Traianos	6 4	15 00	D	31 1 76	Salonika	Aris Salonika	Sheffield U	26	3
Derry Shaun	5 10	10 13	M	6 12 77	Nottingham	Trainee	Notts Co	79	4
							Sheffield U	38	—
Devlin Paul	5 8	11 05	F	14 4 72	Birmingham	Stafford R	Notts Co	141	25
							Birmingham C	76	28
							Sheffield U	43	6
							Notts Co (loan)	5	—
Doane Ben	5 10	12 00	D	22 12 79	Sheffield	Trainee	Sheffield U	—	—
Donis George#	6 0	12 00	M	29 10 69	Greece		Yannina	22	3
							Panathinaikos	136	34
							Blackburn R	22	2
						AEK Athens	Sheffield U	7	1
Ebbrell John‡	5 10	11 11	M	1 10 69	Bromborough		Everton	217	13
							Sheffield U	1	—
Ford Bobby	5 8	11 00	M	22 9 74	Bristol	Trainee	Oxford U	116	7
							Sheffield U	53	1
Goram Andy	5 11	11 06	G	13 4 64	Bury		Oldham Ath	195	—
(Transferred to Motherwell, January 1999)							Hibernian	138	1
							Rangers	184	—
							Notts Co	1	—
							Sheffield U	7	—
							Motherwell	13	—
Hamilton Ian	5 10	12 03	M	14 12 67	Stevenage	Apprentice	Southampton	—	—
							Cambridge U	24	1
							Scunthorpe U	145	18
							WBA	240	23
							Sheffield U	38	3

Hunt Jonathan	5 10	11 13	M	2 11 71	London	Slough T	Barnet	33	—
							Southend U	49	6
							Birmingham C	77	18
							Derby Co	25	2
							Sheffield U	13	2
							Ipswich T (loan)	6	—
Jacobsen Anders#	6 3	13 07	D	18 4 68	Oslo	Start	Sheffield U	12	—
James Owen	5 11	12 00	D	1 9 78	Derby	Trainee	Sheffield U	—	—
Johnson David*			G	18 3 80	Bolton	Trainee	Sheffield U	—	—
Katchuro Petr#	6 0	12 06	F	2 8 72	Minsk		Dynamo 93	15	7
							Dynamo Minsk	60	52
							Sheffield U	72	18
Kelly Alan	6 3	14 02	G	11 8 68	Preston	Trainee	Preston NE	142	—
							Sheffield U	216	—
Kozluk Robert	5 8	10 12	D	5 8 77	Sutton-in-Ashfield	Trainee	Derby Co	16	—
							Sheffield U	10	—
Lehtinen Ville‡	5 11	11 10	M	17 12 78	Toijala		JJK	22	1
							HJK Helsinki	2	—
							Sheffield U	—	—
Ludlam Ryan*	5 9	11 00	M	12 5 79	Carlisle	Trainee	Sheffield U	—	—
Macari Paul	5 8	11 06	F	23 8 76	Manchester	Trainee	Stoke C	3	—
							Sheffield U	—	—
Marcelo	6 0	13 08	F	11 10 69	Niteroi	Alaves	Sheffield U	56	22
Marker Nicky	6 0	13 00	D	3 5 65	Exeter	Apprentice	Exeter C	202	3
							Plymouth Arg	202	13
							Blackburn R	54	1
							Sheffield U	61	5
							Plymouth Arg (loan)	4	—
Meacci Francesco*			M	19 9 79	Florence		Sheffield U	—	—
Morris Lee	5 10	10 06	F	30 4 80	Driffield	Trainee	Sheffield U	25	6
O'Connor Jon	6 0	11 00	D	29 10 76	Darlington	Trainee	Everton	5	—
							Sheffield U	4	—
Quinn Wayne	5 10	11 11	M	19 11 76	Truro		Sheffield U	72	3
Sandford Lee#	6 0	13 07	D	22 4 68	Basingstoke	Apprentice	Portsmouth	72	1
							Stoke C	258	8
							Sheffield U	80	2
							Reading (loan)	5	—
Saunders Dean	5 8	10 06	F	21 6 64	Swansea	Apprentice	Swansea C	49	12
(Transferred to Benfica, December 1998)							Cardiff C (loan)	4	—
							Brighton & HA	72	21
							Oxford U	59	22
							Derby Co	106	42
							Liverpool	42	11
							Aston Villa	112	37
							Galatasaray	27	15
							Nottingham F	43	5
							Sheffield U	43	17
Tebily Oliver	6 0	13 00	D	19 12 75	Abidjan	Chateauroux	Sheffield U	8	—
Tracey Simon	6 0	13 12	G	9 12 67	Woolwich	Apprentice	Wimbledon	1	—
							Sheffield U	206	—
							Manchester C (loan)	3	—
							Norwich C (loan)	1	—
							Wimbledon (loan)	1	—
Vonk Michael‡	6 3	13 03	D	28 10 68	Alkmaar		AZ	112	8
							SVV/Dordrecht	29	1
							Manchester C	91	3
							Oldham Ath (loan)	5	1
							Sheffield U	37	2
Walker Andy‡	5 8	11 05	F	6 4 65	Glasgow	Baillieston Jun	Motherwell	76	17
							Celtic	108	30
							Newcastle U (loan)	2	—
							Bolton W	67	44
							Celtic	42	9
							Sheffield U	52	20
							Hibernian (loan)	8	3
							Raith R (loan)	7	2
White David‡	6 1	13 09	M	30 10 67	Manchester		Manchester C	285	79
							Leeds U	42	9
							Sheffield U	66	13
Whitehouse Dane#	5 10	12 08	M	14 10 70	Sheffield	Trainee	Sheffield U	231	39
Wilder Chris*	5 11	12 07	D	23 9 67	Stocksbridge	Apprentice	Southampton	—	—
							Sheffield U	93	1
							Walsall (loan)	4	—
							Charlton Ath (loan)	1	—
							Charlton Ath (loan)	2	—
							Leyton Orient (loan)	16	1
							Rotherham U	132	11
							Notts Co	46	—
							Bradford C	42	—
							Sheffield U	12	—
							Northampton T (loan)	1	—
							Lincoln C (loan)	3	—
Woodhouse Curtis	5 8	11 00	M	17 4 80	Driffield	Trainee	Sheffield U	42	3

Trainees
Burke, Paul; Burley, Adam G; Camm, Mark L; Henderson, Ewan; McAughtrie, Craig J; Mosley, Matthew J; Parkin, Andrew T; Walker, Leigh D

Scholars
Adams, Carl; Anderson, Michael; Clarke, Stuart; Crutchley, Wayne; Cryan, Colin; Dempsey, Paul; Hayden, John; Jagielka, Philip N; Kendrick, Scott; Lopez, Richard; Montgomery, Nicholas A; Spencer, Steven L; Thompson, Tyrone; Thornley, Carl

Associated Schoolboys who have accepted the Club's offer of a Traineeship/Scholarship/Contract
Adam, Chris; Featherstone, Lee; Killeen, Lewis K; Mallon, Ryan; Morgan, Robert D

SHEFFIELD WEDNESDAY

Name		Ht	Wt	Pos	Date of birth	Birthplace	Prev club	Clubs	Apps	Gls
Agogo	Manuel	5 9	11 07	M	1 8 79	Accra	Willesden	Sheffield W	2	—
Alexandersson	Niclas	6 2	11 07	M	29 12 71	Halmstad		Halmstad	114	18
								IFK Gothenburg	52	13
								Sheffield W	38	3
Atherton	Peter	5 11	13 13	D	6 4 70	Wigan	Trainee	Wigan Ath	149	1
								Coventry C	114	—
								Sheffield W	179	8
Barrett	Earl*	5 10	11 02	D	28 4 67	Rochdale	Apprentice	Manchester C	3	—
								Chester C (loan)	12	—
								Oldham Ath	183	7
								Aston Villa	119	1
								Everton	74	—
								Sheffield U (loan)	5	—
								Sheffield W	15	—
Bennett	Neil	6 1	11 13	G	29 10 80	Dewsbury	Trainee	Sheffield W	—	—
Bettney	Scott	5 9	12 06	D	12 3 80	Hull	Trainee	Sheffield W	—	—
Billington	David	5 7	10 07	D	15 10 80	Oxford	Trainee	Peterborough U	5	—
								Sheffield W	—	—
Booth	Andy	6 1	13 00	F	6 12 73	Huddersfield	Trainee	Huddersfield T	123	54
								Sheffield W	92	23
Brennan	Dean	5 9	11 04	M	17 6 80	Dublin		Sheffield W	—	—
Briscoe	Lee	5 11	11 13	F	30 9 75	Pontefract	Trainee	Sheffield W	62	1
								Manchester C (loan)	5	1
Bromby	Leigh	6 0	11 05	D	2 6 80	Dewsbury		Sheffield W	—	—
Carbone	Benito	5 6	10 09	F	14 8 71	Begnara		Torino	8	—
								Reggina	31	5
								Casert	31	4
								Ascoli	28	6
								Torino	28	3
								Napoli	29	5
								Internazionale	32	2
								Sheffield W	89	23
Clarke	Matthew	6 4	13 10	G	3 11 73	Sheffield	Trainee	Rotherham U	124	—
								Sheffield W	4	—
Cobian	Juan*	5 6	10 10	D	11 9 75	Buenos Aires	Boca Juniors	Sheffield W	9	—
Coubrough	James			M	4 10 80	Bradford	Trainee	Sheffield W	—	—
Cresswell	Richard	6 1	11 07	F	20 9 77	Bridlington	Trainee	York C	95	21
								Mansfield T (loan)	5	1
								Sheffield W	7	1
Davis	Ryan*	5 7	10 02	D	16 11 79	Stoke	Trainee	Sheffield W	—	—
Douglas	Andrew	5 7	10 09	F	7 2 80	Edmonton	Arsenal	Sheffield W	—	—
Emerson		6 1	14 07	D	30 3 72	Porto Alegre	Benfica	Sheffield W	44	1
Geary	Derek	5 6	10 08	D	19 6 80	Dublin		Sheffield W	—	—
Hamshaw	Matthew			M	1 1 82	Rotherham	Trainee	Sheffield W	—	—
Haslam	Nathan			M	13 1 81	Middlesbrough	Trainee	Sheffield W	—	—
Haslam	Steven	5 11	11 00	M	6 9 79	Sheffield	Trainee	Sheffield W	2	—
Hibbins	John	6 2	12 09	M	17 11 79	Sheffield	Trainee	Sheffield W	—	—
Higgins	Alex	5 9	10 12	M	22 7 81	Sheffield	Trainee	Sheffield W	—	—
Hinchcliffe	Andy	5 10	12 10	D	5 2 69	Manchester	Apprentice	Manchester C	112	8
								Everton	182	7
								Sheffield W	47	4
Hiner	Daniel			M	4 10 78	Sheffield	Trainee	Sheffield W	—	—
Holmes	Peter	5 11	10 05	M	18 11 80	Bishop Auckland	Trainee	Sheffield W	—	—
Humphreys	Richie	5 11	14 07	F	30 11 77	Sheffield	Trainee	Sheffield W	60	4
Hutton	John	5 10	11 12	F	23 9 80	Easington	Trainee	Sheffield W	—	—
Jones	Stuart	6 1	13 11	G	24 10 77	Bristol	Weston-Super-Mare	Sheffield W	—	—
								Crewe Alex (loan)	—	—
Jonk	Wim	6 1	12 02	M	12 10 66	Volendam		Volendam	59	28
								Ajax	96	18
								Internazionale	54	8
								PSV Eindhoven	89	20
								Sheffield W	38	2
King	Christopher*	5 11	10 12	D	1 10 79	Sheffield	Trainee	Sheffield W	—	—
Kotylo	Krystof*	5 10	11 02	M	28 9 77	Sheffield	School	Sheffield W	—	—
McKeever	Mark	5 9	11 08	M	16 11 78	Derry	Trainee	Peterborough U	3	—
								Sheffield W	3	—
								Bristol R (loan)	7	—
								Reading (loan)	7	2

Name	Ht	Wt	Pos	DOB	Birthplace	Source	Club	Apps	Gls
Morrison Owen			F	8 12 81	Derry	Trainee	Sheffield W	1	—
Newsome Jon	6 3	13 10	D	6 9 70	Sheffield	Trainee	Sheffield W	7	—
							Leeds U	76	3
							Norwich C	62	7
							Sheffield W	48	4
							Bolton W (loan)	6	—
Nicholson Kevin	5 8	11 05	D	2 10 80	Derby	Trainee	Sheffield W	—	—
Nolan Ian	5 11	12 02	D	9 7 70	Liverpool	Marine	Tranmere R	88	1
							Sheffield W	136	4
Oakes Scott	5 11	11 12	M	5 8 72	Leicester	Trainee	Leicester C	3	—
							Luton T	173	27
							Sheffield W	24	1
Pembridge Mark	5 7	12 03	M	28 11 70	Merthyr Tydfil	Trainee	Luton T	60	6
(Transferred to Benfica, July 1998)							Derby Co	110	28
							Sheffield W	93	11
Powell Vill*	5 11	12 05	F	2 10 79	Sheffield	Trainee	Sheffield W	—	—
Pressman Kevin	6 1	15 05	G	6 11 67	Fareham	Apprentice	Sheffield W	247	—
							Stoke C (loan)	4	—
Quinn Alan	5 9	10 05	F	13 6 79	Dublin		Sheffield W	2	—
Rudi Petter	6 3	12 11	D	17 9 73	Kristiansund		Molde	116	7
							Sheffield W	56	6
Sanetti Francesco	5 11	12 07	F	11 1 79	Rome	Genoa	Sheffield W	5	1
Scott Philip	5 9	11 01	M	14 11 74	Perth		St Johnstone	134	27
							Sheffield W	4	1
Sedloski Goce	6 2	13 00	D	10 4 74	Golemo Konjari		Sheffield W	4	—
(Transferred to Croatia Zagreb, February 1999)									
Siddall Christopher*	5 10	11 05	D	11 12 79	Sheffield	Trainee	Sheffield W	—	—
Sonner Danny	6 0	12 08	M	9 1 72	Wigan	Wigan Ath	Burnley	6	—
							Bury (loan)	5	3
						Erzgebirge Aue	Ipswich T	56	3
							Sheffield W	26	3
Srnicek Pavel	6 2	14 07	G	10 3 68	Bohumin	Banik Ostrava	Newcastle U	149	—
						Banik Ostrava	Sheffield W	24	—
Staniforth Thomas			M	15 12 80	Carlisle	Trainee	Sheffield W	—	—
Stefanovic Dejan*	6 2	13 00	D	28 10 74	Yugoslavia	Red Star Belgrade	Sheffield W	66	4
Wainwright Jody*	6 1	14 07	G	22 2 80	Dewsbury	Trainee	Sheffield W	—	—
Walker Des	5 11	11 12	D	26 11 65	Hackney	Apprentice	Nottingham F	264	1
							Sampdoria	30	—
							Sheffield W	227	—
Whittingham Guy*	5 8	12 02	F	10 11 64	Evesham	Yeovil T, Army	Portsmouth	160	88
							Aston Villa	25	5
							Wolverhampton W (loan)	13	8
							Sheffield W	113	22
							Wolverhampton W (loan)	10	1
							Portsmouth (loan)	9	7
							Watford (loan)	5	—
Woodward Jonathan*			G	16 6 79	Sheffield	Trainee	Sheffield W	—	—

Trainees/Scholars
Barton, Paul; Fraser, Andrew J; Hindley, Ryan P; Houlahan, Martin J; McNutt, Martin P; Nelson, Craig M; Rand, Craig I

SHREWSBURY TOWN

Name	Ht	Wt	Pos	DOB	Birthplace	Source	Club	Apps	Gls
Berkley Austin	5 9	10 10	M	28 1 73	Gravesend	Trainee	Gillingham	3	—
							Swindon T	1	—
							Shrewsbury T	139	12
Blamey Nathan‡	5 10	11 05	D	10 6 77	Plymouth	Trainee	Southampton	—	—
							Shrewsbury T	15	1
Briscoe Anthony*	6 0	11 01	F	16 8 78	Birmingham	Trainee	Shrewsbury T	1	—
Brown Mickey#	5 9	10 12	F	8 2 68	Birmingham	Apprentice	Shrewsbury T	190	9
							Bolton W	33	3
							Shrewsbury T	67	11
							Preston NE	16	1
							Rochdale (loan)	5	—
							Shrewsbury T	83	5
Cooksey Scott	6 3	13 10	G	24 6 72	Birmingham	Bromsgrove R	Peterborough U	15	—
						Hednesford T	Shrewsbury T	2	—
Corns Stuart‡	5 11	12 00	F	1 7 79	Shrewsbury	Trainee	Shrewsbury T	—	—
Craven Dean	5 6	10 10	M	17 2 79	Shrewsbury	WBA	Shrewsbury T	11	—
Dignam Michael‡			M	10 8 78	Havering	Trainee	Shrewsbury T	—	—
Doyle Maurice‡	5 8	10 07	M	17 10 69	Ellesmere Port	Trainee	Crewe Alex	8	2
							QPR	6	—
							Crewe Alex (loan)	7	2
							Wolverhampton W (loan)	—	—
							Millwall	66	1
							Shrewsbury T	—	—
Drysdale Leon§	5 9	10 12	D	3 2 81	Walsall	Trainee	Shrewsbury T	2	—
Edwards Paul	6 0	11 05	G	22 2 65	Liverpool	St. Helens T	Crewe Alex	29	—
							Shrewsbury T	246	—

Name	Ht	Wt	Pos	Born	Birthplace	Signed from	Club	Apps	Gls
Gayle Brian#	6 2	13 12	D	6 3 65	Kingston		Wimbledon	83	3
							Manchester C	55	3
							Ipswich T	58	4
							Sheffield U	117	9
							Exeter C	10	—
							Rotherham U	20	—
							Bristol R (loan)	7	—
							Bristol R	16	—
							Shrewsbury T	66	1
Hanmer Gary	5 6	10 02	D	12 10 73	Shrewsbury	Newtown	WBA	—	—
							Shrewsbury T	85	1
Hayfield Matt‡	5 10	11 07	M	8 8 75	Bristol	Trainee	Bristol R	41	—
							Shrewsbury T	2	—
Herbert Craig	5 10	11 00	D	9 11 75	Coventry	Torquay U	WBA	8	—
							Shrewsbury T	32	—
Jagielka Steve	5 8	11 03	F	10 3 78	Manchester	Trainee	Stoke C	—	—
							Shrewsbury T	47	2
Jobling Kevin	5 8	12 00	M	1 1 68	Sunderland	Apprentice	Leicester C	9	—
							Grimsby T	285	10
							Scunthorpe U (loan)	—	—
							Shrewsbury T	41	1
Jones Matthew§	6 0	11 03	F	11 10 80	Shrewsbury	Trainee	Shrewsbury T	1	—
Kerrigan Steve	6 1	12 04	F	9 10 72	Bailleston	Newmains J	Albion R	53	14
							Clydebank	30	—
							Stranraer	21	5
							Ayr U	33	17
							Shrewsbury T	51	12
Naylor Martyn‡	5 9	10 02	D	2 8 77	Walsall	Telford U	Shrewsbury T	2	—
Pountney Craig*	5 5	9 00	F	23 11 79	Bromsgrove	Trainee	Shrewsbury T	1	—
Preece Roger	5 8	10 13	M	9 6 69	Much Wenlock	Coventry C	Wrexham	110	12
							Chester C	170	4
							Shrewsbury T	47	3
Rutherford Mark‡			F	25 3 72	Birmingham	Trainee	Birmingham C	5	—
						Shelbourne	Shrewsbury T	3	—
Seabury Kevin#	5 9	11 06	M	24 11 73	Shrewsbury	Trainee	Shrewsbury T	186	7
Steele Lee	5 8	12 05	F	7 12 73	Liverpool	Northwich V	Shrewsbury T	76	26
Thompson Glyn	6 3	11 03	G	24 2 81	Shrewsbury	Trainee	Shrewsbury T	1	—
Tretton Andrew	6 0	12 08	D	9 10 76	Derby	Trainee	Derby Co	—	—
							Chesterfield	—	—
							Shrewsbury T	37	1
Whelan Spencer	6 2	13 00	D	17 9 71	Liverpool	Liverpool	Chester C	215	8
							Shrewsbury T	9	—
White Devon*	6 3	14 00	F	2 3 64	Nottingham	Arnold T	Lincoln C	29	4
						Boston U	Bristol R	202	53
							Cambridge U	22	4
							QPR	26	9
							Notts Co	40	15
							Watford	38	7
							Notts Co	15	4
							Shrewsbury T	43	10
Wilding Peter	6 1	12 09	D	28 11 68	Shrewsbury	Telford U	Shrewsbury T	76	1
Williams Mark*	5 11	12 07	F	10 12 73	Bangor	Trainee	Shrewsbury T	8	—

Trainees
Drysdale, Leon A; Howarth, Paul A; Impey, Daniel E; Jones, Matthew N; Leydon, Scott A; Murray, Karl A; Neville, Mark J; Northwood, Sean; Rodgers, Luke J; Woodley, Frederick R

Player who does not hold a current contract but his registration has been retained by the Club
Nielson, Thomas

Associated Schoolboy
Murphy, Gareth A

SOUTHAMPTON

Name	Ht	Wt	Pos	Born	Birthplace	Signed from	Club	Apps	Gls
Atzeni Allessandro*			M	1 1 80	Italy		Fiorentina	2	—
							Southampton	—	—
Basham Steve	5 11	12 04	F	2 12 77	Southampton	Trainee	Southampton	19	1
							Wrexham (loan)	5	—
							Preston NE (loan)	17	10
Beattie James	6 0	13 03	F	27 2 78	Lancaster	Trainee	Blackburn R	4	—
							Southampton	35	5
Benali Francis	5 9	11 03	M	30 12 68	Southampton	Apprentice	Southampton	276	1
Beresford John	5 7	12 00	M	4 9 66	Sheffield	Apprentice	Manchester C	—	—
							Barnsley	88	5
							Portsmouth	107	8
							Newcastle U	179	3
							Southampton	14	—
Bevan Scott	6 6	15 03	G	16 9 79	Southampton	Trainee	Southampton	—	—
Blake Dean‡	5 8	10 01	M	20 2 80	Portsmouth	Trainee	Southampton	—	—
Bradley Shayne	6 0	13 06	F	8 12 79	Gloucester	Trainee	Southampton	3	—
							Swindon T (loan)	7	—
Bridge Wayne	5 10	12 04	F	5 8 80	Southampton	Trainee	Southampton	23	—

Colleter Patrick	5 8	11 04	D	6 11 65	Brest		Brest	127	8
							Montpellier	31	—
							Paris St Germain	157	1
							Bordeaux	30	1
							Marseille	41	—
							Southampton	16	1
Collins Chris	6 0	13 01	D	26 9 79	Chatham	Trainee	Southampton	—	—
Dodd Jason	5 9	12 08	D	2 11 70	Bath	Bath C	Southampton	259	8
Dryden Richard	6 0	14 09	D	14 6 69	Stroud	Trainee	Bristol R	13	—
							Exeter C	51	7
							Manchester C (loan)	—	—
							Notts Co	31	1
							Plymouth Arg (loan)	5	—
							Birmingham C	48	—
							Bristol C	37	2
							Southampton	46	1
Gibbens Kevin	5 10	13 02	M	4 11 79	Southampton	Trainee	Southampton	6	—
Hiley Scott	5 9	11 12	D	27 9 68	Plymouth	Trainee	Exeter C	210	12
							Birmingham C	49	—
							Manchester C	9	—
							Southampton	29	—
Hirst David	5 11	14 10	F	7 12 67	Cudworth	Apprentice	Barnsley	28	9
							Sheffield W	294	106
							Southampton	30	9
Howells David	6 0	12 03	M	15 12 67	Guildford	Trainee	Tottenham H	277	22
							Southampton	9	1
							Bristol C (loan)	8	1
Hughes David	5 11	11 07	M	30 12 72	St Albans	Trainee	Southampton	54	3
Hughes Mark	5 9	13 04	F	1 11 63	Wrexham	Apprentice	Manchester U	89	37
							Barcelona	28	4
							Bayern Munich (loan)	18	6
							Manchester U	256	82
							Chelsea	95	25
							Southampton	32	1
James Kevin‡	5 8	10 05	F	26 3 80	Merthyr	Trainee	Southampton	—	—
Jenkins Steve*	6 2	13 10	D	2 1 80	Bristol	Trainee	Southampton	—	—
							Brentford (loan)	1	—
Johansen Stig‡	5 9	12 05	F	13 6 72	Norway		Bodo Glimt	70	45
							Southampton	6	—
							Bristol C (loan)	3	—
Jones Paul	6 2	15 03	G	18 4 67	Chirk	Kidderminster H	Wolverhampton W	33	—
							Stockport Co	46	—
							Southampton	69	—
Kachloul Hassan	6 1	12 09	M	19 2 73	Agadir		Nimes	86	26
							Dunkerque	28	6
							Metz	7	—
							St Etienne	16	—
							Southampton	22	5
Le Tissier Matthew	6 0	14 01	F	14 10 68	Guernsey	Trainee	Southampton	413	158
Lundekvam Claus	6 3	13 03	D	22 2 73	Austevoll		Brann	53	1
							Southampton	93	—
Marsden Chris	6 0	12 07	M	3 10 69	Sheffield	Trainee	Sheffield U	16	1
							Huddersfield T	121	9
							Coventry C (loan)	7	—
							Wolverhampton W	8	—
							Notts Co	10	—
							Stockport Co	65	3
							Birmingham C	52	3
							Southampton	14	2
Marshall Scott *(On loan to Celtic)*	6 1	12 13	D	1 5 73	Edinburgh	Trainee	Arsenal	24	1
							Rotherham U (loan)	10	1
							Oxford U (loan)	—	—
							Sheffield U (loan)	17	—
							Southampton	2	—
							Celtic	2	—
Monk Gary	6 1	13 05	D	6 3 79	Bedford	Trainee	Torquay U	5	—
							Southampton	4	—
							Torquay U (loan)	6	—
Monkou Ken	6 3	14 11	D	29 11 64	Surinam	Feyenoord	Chelsea	94	2
							Southampton	198	10
Moss Neil	6 2	13 07	G	10 5 75	New Milton	Trainee	Bournemouth	22	—
							Southampton	10	—
							Gillingham (loan)	10	—
Oakley Matthew	5 10	12 06	M	17 8 77	Peterborough	Trainee	Southampton	94	6
Ostenstad Egil	5 11	13 00	F	2 1 72	Haugesund		Viking	128	54
							Southampton	93	27
Pakhar (Pahars) Marian	5 8	10 09	F	5 8 76	Latvia		Pardaugava Riga	17	3
							Skonto/Metals Riga	16	4
							Skonto Riga	85	44
							Southampton	6	3
Paul Mark	5 6	10 10	F	3 1 79	Peterborough	Kings Lynn	Southampton	—	—
Pelanti Simone‡			M	21 1 81	Italy	Fiorentina	Southampton	—	—
Ripley Stuart	5 11	13 05	F	20 11 67	Middlesbrough	Apprentice	Middlesbrough	249	26
							Bolton W (loan)	5	1
							Blackburn R	187	13
							Southampton	22	—

Name	Ht	Wt	Pos	DOB	Birthplace	Previous	Club	Apps	Gls
Rodrigues Danny	5 10	11 07	F	3 3 80	Madeira	Farense	Bournemouth	5	—
							Southampton	—	—
Sarli Cosimo‡	5 10	12 07	F	13 3 79	Conigliano Calabro		Torino	—	—
							Southampton	—	—
Stensgaard Michael	6 2	13 11	G	1 9 74	Denmark	Hvidovre	Liverpool	—	—
							FC Copenhagen	17	—
							Southampton	—	—
Warner Phil	5 10	11 09	D	2 2 79	Southampton	Trainee	Southampton	6	—
Williams Andy	5 9	10 12	F	8 10 77	Bristol	Trainee	Southampton	21	—

Trainees/Scholars
Ashford, Ryan M; Baird, Chrisopher P; Blayney, Alan; Cleife, Lloyd R; Davies, Mathew D; Grimshaw, Steven; Huxley, Matthew S; Liddon, Paul G; Madgwick, Benjamin; Sims, Adam D; Wallace, Adam J; Waller, Andrew P; Webber, Lloyd E; Wilson, Richard S

Non-Contract
Gray, Steven

SOUTHEND UNITED

Name	Ht	Wt	Pos	DOB	Birthplace	Previous	Club	Apps	Gls
Beard Mark	5 10	10 12	M	8 10 74	Roehampton	Trainee	Millwall	45	2
							Sheffield U	38	—
							Southend U (loan)	8	—
							Southend U	37	—
Boere Jeroen‡	6 3	13 02	F	18 11 67	Arnheim	Go Ahead	West Ham U	25	6
							Portsmouth (loan)	5	—
							WBA (loan)	5	—
							Crystal Palace	8	1
							Southend U	73	25
Booty Martyn	5 9	12 06	D	30 5 71	Kirby Muxloe	Trainee	Coventry C	5	—
							Crewe Alex	96	5
							Reading	64	1
							Southend U	20	—
Burns Alex	5 9	12 09	F	4 8 73	Bellshill		Motherwell	76	8
						Heracles	Southend U	31	5
Byrne Paul	5 11	13 00	M	30 6 72	Dublin	Trainee	Oxford U	6	—
						Bangor	Celtic	28	4
							Brighton & HA (loan)	8	1
							Southend U	83	6
Campbell Neil	6 2	13 10	F	26 1 77	Middlesbrough	Trainee	York C	12	1
							Scarborough	45	7
							Southend U	12	2
Capleton Mel†	6 0	13 03	G	24 10 73	London	Trainee	Southend U	—	—
							Blackpool	11	—
							Leyton Orient	—	—
						Grays Ath	Southend U	14	—
Clarke Adrian#	5 9	11 00	M	28 9 74	Cambridge	Trainee	Arsenal	7	—
							Rotherham U (loan)	2	—
							Southend U (loan)	7	—
							Southend U	69	8
Coleman Simon	6 0	12 03	D	13 6 68	Worksop	Apprentice	Mansfield T	96	7
							Middlesbrough	55	2
							Derby Co	70	2
							Sheffield W	16	1
							Bolton W	34	5
							Wolverhampton W (loan)	4	—
							Southend U	56	4
Conlon Barry	6 2	13 07	F	1 10 78	Drogheda	QPR	Manchester C	7	—
							Plymouth Arg (loan)	13	2
							Southend U	34	7
Dublin Keith*	6 0	12 10	D	29 1 66	Brent	Apprentice	Chelsea	51	—
							Brighton & HA	132	5
							Watford	168	2
							Southend U	179	9
							Colchester U (loan)	2	—
Fitzpatrick Trevor	6 1	12 10	F	19 2 80	Surrey	Trainee	Southend U	26	5
Gooding Mick*	5 8	10 10	M	12 4 59	Newcastle	Bishop Auckland	Rotherham U	102	10
							Chesterfield	12	—
							Rotherham U	156	33
							Peterborough U	47	21
							Wolverhampton W	44	4
							Reading	314	26
							Southend U	23	—
Gridelet Phil‡	5 11	13 00	M	30 4 67	Edgware	Barnet	Barnsley	6	—
							Rotherham U (loan)	9	—
							Southend U	176	10
Hails Julian	5 10	11 02	M	20 11 67	Lincoln	Hemel Hempstead	Fulham	109	12
							Southend U	160	7
Harris Andrew*	5 10	12 02	D	26 2 77	Springs	Trainee	Liverpool	—	—
							Southend U	72	—
Henriksen Tony‡	6 3	13 09	G	25 4 73	Hammel	Randers Freja	Southend U	—	—

Houghton Scott	5 7	12 03	M	22 10 71	Hitchin	Trainee	Tottenham H	10	2
							Ipswich T (loan)	8	1
							Cambridge U (loan)	—	—
							Gillingham (loan)	3	—
							Charlton Ath (loan)	6	—
							Luton T	16	1
							Walsall	78	14
							Peterborough U	70	13
							Southend U	27	3
Iorfa Dominic‡	6 0	12 12	F	1 10 68	Lagos	Antwerp	QPR	8	—
							Peterborough U	60	9
							Southend U	10	1
							Falkirk	4	1
						Billericay T	Southend U	2	—
Jones Mark‡			M	4 8 79	Havering	Trainee	Southend U	1	—
Jones Nathan	5 7	10 12	D	28 5 73	Rhondda	Merthyr T	Luton T	—	—
						Numaicia	Southend U	56	—
							Scarborough (loan)	9	—
Leggatt Philip‡	5 8	10 04	M	7 10 78	Harlow	Trainee	Southend U	—	—
Livett Simon	5 10	12 07	M	8 1 69	Plaistow	Trainee	West Ham U	1	—
							Leyton Orient	24	—
							Cambridge U	12	—
						Billericay T	Southend U	23	1
Maher Kevin	5 11	12 08	M	17 10 76	Ilford	Trainee	Tottenham H	—	—
							Southend U	52	5
Margetson Martyn	6 0	14 00	G	8 9 71	West Neath	Trainee	Manchester C	51	—
							Bristol R (loan)	3	—
							Bolton W (loan)	—	—
							Luton T (loan)	—	—
							Southend U	32	—
McGavin Steve‡	5 11	12 07	F	24 1 69	North Walsham	Sudbury T	Colchester U	58	17
							Birmingham C	23	2
							Wycombe W	120	15
							Southend U	11	—
Morley David	6 2	13 02	D	25 9 77	St Helens	Trainee	Manchester C	3	1
							Ayr U (loan)	4	—
							Southend U	27	—
Morrish Adam			M	28 6 80	Greenwich	Trainee	Southend U	—	—
Newman Rob	6 1	13 10	D	13 12 63	Bradford-on-Avon	Apprentice	Bristol C	394	52
							Norwich C	205	14
							Motherwell (loan)	11	—
							Wigan Ath (loan)	8	—
							Southend U	36	7
Nielsen John‡	5 9	11 12	M	7 4 72	Aarhus		Ikast	19	—
							Southend U	29	3
Nzamba Guy†			F	13 7 70	Gabon	Trieste	Southend U	1	—
Patterson Mark‡	5 8	11 07	M	24 5 65	Darwen	Apprentice	Blackburn R	101	20
							Preston NE	55	19
							Bury	42	10
							Bolton W	169	11
							Sheffield U	74	4
							Southend U (loan)	4	—
							Bury	31	2
							Blackpool (loan)	7	—
							Southend U	5	—
Perkins Chris	5 11	12 11	D	1 3 80	Stepney	Trainee	Southend U	5	—
Roach Neville	5 10	11 12	F	29 9 78	Reading	Trainee	Reading	16	1
							Southend U	8	1
Roget Leo	6 1	12 02	D	1 8 77	Ilford	Trainee	Southend U	58	1
Unger Lars*	6 2	13 09	M	30 9 72	Eutin		Southend U	14	—
Whyte David	5 8	12 00	F	20 4 71	Greenwich	Greenwich Bor	Crystal Palace	27	4
							Charlton Ath (loan)	8	2
							Charlton Ath	85	28
							Ipswich T	2	—
							Bristol R	4	—
							Southend U	26	3

Trainees
Abiodun, Ayodeji O; Cross, Garry R; Doyle, Jonathan L; Fisher, Matthew J; McDonald, Thomas; Spittle, Stephen D

Scholars
Ayres, Kevin C; Hunter, Leon D; Johnson, Leon D; Kerrigan, Daniel A; McSweeney, David; Pitts, Daniel J

Non-Contract
Capleton, Melvin D; Nzamba, Guy R

Players who do not hold a current contract but their registrations have been retained by the Club
Byrne, Paul; Roche, David

Associated Schoolboys
Biddlecombe, James A; Cumberworth, Peter J; Watson, John M

Associated Schoolboys who have accepted the Club's offer of a Traineeship/Scholarship/Contract
Boot, Tony D; Davey, Thomas; Fisher, James; Harding, Dean J; Simmons, Michael; Wray, Matthew K

STOCKPORT COUNTY

Name							Club	Apps	Goals
Alsaker Paul‡	5 9	10 10	M	6 11 73	Bergen	Flora Tallinn	Stockport Co	1	—
Angell Brett	6 2	13 10	F	20 8 68	Marlborough	Cheltenham T	Derby Co	—	—
							Stockport Co	70	28
							Southend U	115	47
							Everton (loan)	1	—
							Everton	19	1
							Sunderland	10	—
							Sheffield U (loan)	6	2
							WBA (loan)	3	—
							Stockport Co	121	50
Bennett Tom	5 11	11 08	M	12 12 69	Falkirk	Trainee	Aston Villa	—	—
							Wolverhampton W	115	2
							Stockport Co	101	5
Byrne Chris	5 9	10 02	M	9 2 75	Hulme	Macclesfield T	Sunderland	8	—
							Stockport Co	37	9
Byrne Des‡			D	10 4 81	Dublin	Trainee	Stockport Co	2	—
Connelly Sean	5 10	11 10	D	26 6 70	Sheffield	Hallam	Stockport Co	246	3
Cook Paul	5 11	11 00	M	22 6 67	Liverpool	Marine	Wigan Ath	83	14
							Norwich C	6	—
							Wolverhampton W	193	19
							Coventry C	37	3
							Tranmere R	60	4
							Stockport Co	49	3
							Burnley (loan)	12	1
Cooper Kevin	5 8	10 07	F	8 2 75	Derby	Trainee	Derby Co	2	—
							Stockport Co (loan)	12	3
							Stockport Co	76	9
Dinning Tony	6 0	12 00	D	12 4 75	Wallsend	Trainee	Newcastle U	—	—
							Stockport Co	141	13
Ellis Tony	5 11	11 00	F	20 10 64	Salford	Northwich Vic	Oldham Ath	8	—
							Preston NE	86	26
							Stoke C	77	19
							Preston NE	72	48
							Blackpool	146	54
							Bury	38	8
							Stockport Co	16	6
Fish David*	6 1	11 07	G	4 8 80	Ashton-under-Lyne	Trainee	Stockport Co	—	—
Flood James*	5 9	11 02	F	21 9 79	Stockport	Trainee	Stockport Co	—	—
Flynn Mike	6 0	11 02	D	23 2 69	Oldham	Trainee	Oldham Ath	40	1
							Norwich C	—	—
							Preston NE	136	7
							Stockport Co	271	13
Gannon Jim	6 2	13 00	D	7 9 68	Southwark	Dundalk	Sheffield U	—	—
							Halifax T (loan)	2	—
							Stockport Co	354	52
							Notts Co (loan)	2	—
Grant Stephen*	6 1	12 00	F	14 4 77	Birr	Athlone T	Sunderland	—	—
							Shamrock R		
							Stockport Co	29	4
Gray Ian	6 2	13 00	G	25 2 75	Manchester	Trainee	Oldham Ath	—	—
							Rochdale (loan)	12	—
							Rochdale	66	—
							Stockport Co	6	—
Mannion Sean	5 8	11 05	M	3 3 80	Dublin	Stella Maris	Stockport Co	1	—
Matthews Rob	6 0	12 05	F	14 10 70	Slough	Loughborough Univ	Notts Co	43	11
							Luton T	11	—
							York C	17	1
							Bury	74	11
							Stockport Co	23	2
McInnes Derek	5 7	11 04	M	5 7 71	Paisley		Greenock Morton	221	19
							Rangers	34	1
							Stockport Co (loan)	13	—
McIntosh Martin	6 3	12 05	D	19 3 71	East Kilbride	Tottenham H	St Mirren	4	—
							Clydebank	65	10
							Hamilton A	99	12
							Stockport Co	79	5
Moore Ian	5 11	12 02	F	26 8 76	Birkenhead	Trainee	Tranmere R	58	12
							Bradford C (loan)	6	—
							Nottingham F	15	1
							West Ham U (loan)	1	—
							Stockport Co	38	3
Nash Carlo	6 5	14 01	G	13 9 73	Bolton	Clitheroe	Crystal Palace	21	—
							Stockport Co	43	—
Phelan Mike†	5 11	11 01	D	24 9 62	Nelson	Apprentice	Burnley	168	9
							Norwich C	156	9
							Manchester U	102	2
							WBA	21	—
							Blackpool	—	—
							Stockport Co	—	—
Phillips Wayne	5 11	11 00	M	15 12 70	Bangor	Trainee	Wrexham	207	16
							Stockport Co	22	—
Smith David	5 10	12 11	M	26 12 70	Liverpool	Trainee	Norwich C	18	—
							Oxford U	198	2
							Stockport Co	17	1

Travis Simon	5 7	10 00	D	22 3 77	Preston	Trainee Holywell T	Torquay U Stockport Co	8 22	— 2
Turkington Eddie*	6 1	13 00	M	15 5 78	Merseyside	Trainee	Liverpool Stockport Co	— —	— —
Vaughan Francis*	5 10	11 00	M	8 9 79	Salford	Trainee	Stockport Co	—	—
Wilbraham Aaron	6 3	12 04	F	21 10 79	Knutsford	Trainee	Stockport Co	33	1
Woodthorpe Colin	6 0	11 08	D	13 1 69	Ellesmere Pt		Chester C Norwich C Aberdeen Stockport Co	155 43 48 69	6 1 1 3

Trainees
Abel, Graeme F; Briggs, Keith; Daly, Jonathan M; Evans, Lee; Hancock, Glynn R; Hennessy, Michael P; Hooper, Daniel J; Hussain Rafaqat; Johnson, Ben; Lillis, Adam D; McConnell, Darren P; Mudd, Lee C; Salmons, Adam L; Smythe, Ben; Thomas, Marc; Villers, Lee W; Woolley, Matthew D; Wright, Paul S

Non-Contract
Megson, Gary J; Phelan, Michael C

Player who does not hold a current contract but his registration has been retained by the Club
Byrne, Desmond

Associated Schoolboys who have accepted the Club's offer of a Traineeship/Scholarship/Contract
Andrews, Martyn; McLachlan, Fraser M; Rowley, Paul; Thomas, Andrew; Wild, Peter

STOKE CITY

Bullock Matthew	5 8	11 00	M	1 11 80	Stoke	Trainee	Stoke C	—	—
Burgess Richard†	5 8	11 00	F	18 8 78	Bromsgrove	Trainee	Aston Villa Stoke C	— —	— —
Cartwright Jamie	5 7	9 06	M	11 10 79	Lichfield	Trainee	Stoke C	—	—
Clarke Clive	6 1	12 05	D	14 1 80	Dublin	Trainee	Stoke C	2	—
Collins Lee	6 2	13 05	D	10 9 77	Bellshill	Trainee	Aston Villa Stoke C	— 4	— —
Crowe Dean	5 5	11 02	F	6 6 79	Stockport	Trainee	Stoke C	54	12
Dixon Calvin			M	20 10 80	Walsall	Trainee	Stoke C	—	—
Forsyth Richard*	5 10	13 01	M	3 10 70	Dudley	Kidderminster H	Birmingham C Stoke C	26 95	2 17
Fraser Stuart	6 0	12 00	G	1 8 78	Cheltenham		Stoke C	1	—
Godbold Jamie	5 4	9 0	M	10 1 80	Great Yarmouth	Trainee	Stoke C	—	—
Goodfellow Marc			M	20 9 81	Burton		Stoke C	—	—
Heath Robert	5 9	10 07	M	31 8 78	Newcastle-Under-Lyme		Stoke C	16	—
Kavanagh Graham	5 10	12 06	M	2 12 73	Dublin	Home Farm	Middlesbrough Darlington (loan) Stoke C	35 5 118	3 — 20
Kavanagh Jason	5 8	12 09	D	23 11 71	Meriden	Birmingham C	Derby Co Wycombe W Stoke C	99 90 8	1 1 —
Keen Kevin*	5 7	10 10	M	25 2 67	Amersham	Apprentice	West Ham U Wolverhampton W Stoke C	219 42 154	21 7 9
Lightbourne Kyle	6 2	12 00	F	29 9 68	Bermuda		Scarborough Walsall Coventry C Fulham (loan) Stoke C	19 165 7 4 49	3 65 — 2 9
MacKenzie Neil	6 2	12 05	M	15 4 76	Birmingham		Stoke C Cambridge U (loan)	40 4	1 1
McGeough David			M	10 11 80	Drogheda		Stoke C	—	—
McNally Mark *(Transferred to Dundee U, July 1998)*	5 11	12 02	D	10 3 71	Bellshill	Celtic BC	Celtic Southend U Stoke C Dundee U	123 54 7 5	3 2 — —
Mohan Nicky	6 0	13 07	D	6 10 70	Middlesbrough	Trainee	Middlesbrough Hull C (loan) Leicester C Bradford C Wycombe W Stoke C	99 5 23 83 58 15	4 1 — 4 2 —
Muggleton Carl	6 2	13 03	G	13 9 68	Leicester	Apprentice	Leicester C Chesterfield (loan) Blackpool (loan) Hartlepool U (loan) Stockport Co (loan) Liverpool (loan) Stoke C (loan) Sheffield U (loan) Celtic Stoke C Rotherham U (loan) Sheffield U (loan)	46 17 2 8 4 — 6 — 12 137 6 1	— — — — — — — — — — — —

Name					Birthplace	Source	Clubs	Apps	Gls
Neal Lewis			M	14 7 81	Leicester		Stoke C	—	—
O'Connor James	5 8	11 00	M	1 9 79	Dublin	Trainee	Stoke C	4	—
Oldfield David	6 1	13 04	M	30 5 68	Perth (Aus)	Apprentice	Luton T	29	4
							Manchester C	26	6
							Leicester C	188	26
							Millwall (loan)	17	6
							Luton T	117	18
							Stoke C	46	6
Petty Ben	6 1	13 03	D	22 3 77	Solihull	Trainee	Aston Villa	—	—
							Stoke C	11	—
Robinson Phil	5 10	11 06	M	6 1 67	Stafford	Apprentice	Aston Villa	3	1
							Wolverhampton W	71	8
							Notts Co	66	5
							Birmingham C (loan)	9	—
							Huddersfield T	75	5
							Northampton T (loan)	14	—
							Chesterfield	61	17
							Notts Co	77	5
							Stoke C	40	1
Scheuber Stuart			M	3 4 81	Rhuddlan	Trainee	Stoke C	—	—
Short Chris	5 10	12 03	D	9 5 70	Munster	Pickering T	Scarborough	43	1
							Manchester U (loan)	—	—
							Notts Co	94	2
							Huddersfield T (loan)	6	—
							Sheffield U	44	—
							Stoke C	21	—
Sigurdsson Kris	5 11	11 11	D	7 10 80	Akureyri		KA	15	—
							Stoke C	—	—
Sigurdsson Larus	6 0	13 11	D	4 6 73	Akureyri	Thor	Stoke C	195	6
Sinclair Ronnie	5 11	12 09	G	19 11 64	Stirling	Apprentice	Nottingham F	—	—
							Wrexham (loan)	11	—
							Derby Co (loan)	—	—
							Sheffield U (loan)	—	—
							Leeds U (loan)	—	—
							Leeds U	8	—
							Halifax T (loan)	4	—
							Halifax T (loan)	10	—
							Bristol C	44	—
							Walsall (loan)	10	—
							Stoke C	80	—
							Bradford C (loan)	—	—
							Chester C	70	—
							Cardiff C	—	—
							Stoke C	—	—
Small Bryan	5 9	11 09	D	15 11 71	Birmingham	Trainee	Aston Villa	36	—
							Birmingham C (loan)	3	—
							Bolton W	12	—
							Luton T (loan)	15	—
							Bradford C (loan)	5	—
							Bury	18	1
							Stoke C	37	—
Stewart Paul‡	6 0	14 01	F	7 10 64	Manchester	Apprentice	Blackpool	201	56
							Manchester C	51	26
							Tottenham H	131	28
							Liverpool	32	1
							Crystal Palace (loan)	18	3
							Wolverhampton W (loan)	8	2
							Burnley (loan)	6	—
							Sunderland	36	5
							Stoke C	22	3
Sturridge Simon*	5 6	11 10	F	9 12 69	Birmingham	Trainee	Birmingham C	150	30
							Stoke C	71	14
							Blackpool (loan)	5	1
Taaffe Steven	5 5	9 08	F	10 9 79	Stoke	Trainee	Stoke C	6	—
Thorne Peter	6 0	13 07	F	21 6 73	Manchester	Trainee	Blackburn R	—	—
							Wigan Ath (loan)	11	—
							Swindon T	77	27
							Stoke C	70	21
Tweed Steven	6 3	13 02	D	8 8 72	Edinburgh		Hibernian	108	3
(Transferred to Dundee, December 1998)							Ionikos	2	—
							Stoke C	39	—
							Dundee	10	1
Wallace Ray*	5 7	11 05	M	2 10 69	Lewisham	Trainee	Southampton	35	—
							Leeds U	7	—
							Swansea C (loan)	2	—
							Reading (loan)	3	—
							Stoke C	179	15
							Hull C (loan)	7	—
Ward Gavin	6 2	13 06	G	30 6 70	Sutton Coldfield	Aston Villa	Shrewsbury T	—	—
							WBA	—	—
							Cardiff C	59	—
							Leicester C	38	—
							Bradford C	36	—
							Bolton W	22	—
							Burnley (loan)	17	—
							Stoke C	6	—
Woods Stephen*	5 11	11 13	D	15 12 76	Davenham	Trainee	Stoke C	34	—
							Plymouth Arg (loan)	5	—
Wooliscroft Ashley	5 10	11 02	D	28 12 79	Stoke	Trainee	Stoke C	1	—

Trainees
Evans, Jamie M

Scholars
Alexander, Daniel J; Gibson, Alexander J; Shaw, Martyn P

Non-Contract
Burgess, Richard D

Associated Schoolboys who have accepted the Club's offer of a Traineeship/Scholarship/Contract
Henry, Karl L D; Owen, Gareth D

SUNDERLAND

Name							Club	Apps	Gls
Aiston Sam	6 0	12 01	F	21 11 76	Newcastle	Newcastle U	Sunderland	20	—
							Chester C (loan)	14	—
							Chester C (loan)	11	—
Ball Kevin	5 9	11 06	M	12 11 64	Hastings	Apprentice	Portsmouth	105	4
							Sunderland	328	21
Beavers Paul	6 0	12 05	F	2 10 78	Blackpool	Trainee	Sunderland	—	—
							Shrewsbury T (loan)	2	—
							Oldham Ath (loan)	7	2
Bridges Michael	6 1	11 00	F	5 8 78	North Shields	Trainee	Sunderland	79	16
Butler Paul	6 0	13 05	D	2 11 72	Manchester	Trainee	Rochdale	158	10
							Bury	84	4
							Sunderland	44	2
Butler Thomas	5 8	10 07	M	25 4 81	Ballymun	Trainee	Sunderland	—	—
Clark Lee	5 8	11 07	M	27 10 72	Wallsend	Trainee	Newcastle U	195	23
							Sunderland	73	16
Convery Mark	5 6	10 05	F	29 5 81	Newcastle	Trainee	Sunderland	—	—
Coton Tony‡	6 2	13 07	G	19 5 61	Tamworth	Mile Oak R	Birmingham C	94	—
							Hereford U (loan)	—	—
							Watford	233	—
							Manchester C	164	—
							Manchester U	—	—
							Sunderland	10	—
Craddock Jody	6 0	11 01	D	25 7 75	Bromsgrove	Christchurch	Cambridge U	145	4
							Sunderland	38	—
Dichio Daniele	6 3	12 08	F	19 10 74	Hammersmith	Trainee	QPR	75	20
							Barnet (loan)	9	2
							Sampdoria	—	—
							Lecce	4	1
							Sunderland	49	10
Dickman Elliott‡	5 8	9 08	D	11 10 78	Hexham	Trainee	Sunderland	—	—
Dickman Jonjo	5 8	10 05	D	22 9 81	Hexham		Sunderland	—	—
Duke David	5 10	11 00	M	7 11 78	Inverness	Redby CA	Sunderland	—	—
Frampton Kevin‡	5 11	11 00	M	18 3 80	Carlisle	Trainee	Sunderland	—	—
Gray Michael	5 7	10 08	D	3 8 74	Sunderland	Trainee	Sunderland	226	14
Harrison Gerry	5 8	12 05	D	15 4 72	Lambeth	Trainee	Watford	9	—
							Bristol C	38	1
							Cardiff C (loan)	10	1
							Hereford U (loan)	6	—
							Huddersfield T	—	—
							Burnley	124	3
							Sunderland	—	—
							Luton T (loan)	14	—
							Hull C (loan)	8	—
Heckingbottom Paul‡	6 0	12 03	D	17 7 77	Barnsley	Manchester U	Sunderland	—	—
							Scarborough (loan)	29	—
							Hartlepool U (loan)	5	1
							Darlington (loan)	10	—
Holloway Darren	6 0	12 04	D	3 10 77	Bishop Auckland	Trainee	Sunderland	38	—
							Carlisle U (loan)	5	—
Ingram Stuart‡	6 1	11 07	F	7 11 79	Stockton	Trainee	Sunderland	—	—
Johnston Allan	5 7	9 07	F	14 12 73	Glasgow		Hearts	84	12
							Rennes	23	2
							Sunderland	86	19
Kyle Kevin	5 8	12 00	F	7 6 81	Stranraer		Sunderland	—	—
Lamb Kris‡	5 10	10 10	M	22 9 79	Gateshead	Trainee	Sunderland	—	—
Lumsdon Chris	5 11	10 03	M	15 12 79	Newcastle	Trainee	Sunderland	1	—
Lynch Finbar	5 8	10 01	F	24 1 82	Dublin		Sunderland	—	—
Makin Chris	5 10	12 10	D	8 5 73	Manchester	Trainee	Oldham Ath	94	4
							Wigan Ath (loan)	15	2
							Marseille	29	—
							Sunderland	63	—
Maley Mark	5 8	12 00	D	26 1 81	Newcastle	Trainee	Sunderland	—	—
Marriott Andy	6 2	10 10	G	11 10 70	Sutton-in-Ashfield	Trainee	Arsenal	—	—
							Nottingham F	11	—
							WBA (loan)	3	—
							Blackburn R (loan)	2	—
							Colchester U (loan)	10	—
							Burnley (loan)	15	—
							Wrexham	213	—
							Sunderland	1	—

Name					Birthplace	Source	Club	Apps	Gls
McCann Gavin	5 11	11 00	M	10 1 78	Blackpool	Trainee	Everton	11	—
							Sunderland	11	—
McCartney George	6 0	12 06	D	29 4 81	Belfast	Trainee	Sunderland	—	—
McGill Brendan	5 9	10 05	M	22 3 81	Dublin		Sunderland	—	—
Melville Andy*	6 1	12 06	D	29 11 68	Swansea	School	Swansea C	175	22
							Oxford U	135	13
							Sunderland	204	14
							Bradford C (loan)	6	1
Mullin John*	6 0	11 05	F	11 8 75	Bury	School	Burnley	18	2
							Sunderland	35	4
							Preston NE (loan)	7	—
							Burnley (loan)	6	—
Phillips Kevin	5 7	11 00	F	25 7 73	Hitchin	Baldock T	Watford	59	24
							Sunderland	69	52
Pitts Matthew‡	5 11	12 06	D	25 12 79	Middlesbrough	Trainee	Sunderland	—	—
Porter Christopher			M	10 11 79	Sunderland	Trainee	Sunderland	—	—
Proctor Michael	5 11	12 00	F	3 10 80	Sunderland	Trainee	Sunderland	—	—
Quinn Niall	6 4	12 04	F	6 10 66	Dublin		Arsenal	67	14
							Manchester C	203	66
							Sunderland	86	34
Rae Alex	5 8	11 08	M	30 9 69	Glasgow	Bishopbriggs	Falkirk	83	20
							Millwall	218	63
							Sunderland	67	7
Scott Martin*	5 9	11 00	D	7 1 68	Sheffield	Apprentice	Rotherham U	94	3
							Nottingham F (loan)	—	—
							Bristol C	171	14
							Sunderland	106	9
Shannon Greg	6 0	11 00	G	15 2 81	Maghreafelt	Trainee	Sunderland	—	—
Smith Martin*	5 11	12 00	F	13 11 74	Sunderland	Trainee	Sunderland	119	25
Sorensen Thomas	6 3	12 05	G	12 6 76	Fredericia	Odense	Sunderland	45	—
Summerbee Nicky	5 8	11 08	F	26 8 71	Altrincham	Trainee	Swindon T	112	6
							Manchester C	131	6
							Sunderland	61	6
Thirlwell Paul	5 11	11 04	M	13 2 79	Newcastle	Trainee	Sunderland	2	—
Wainwright Neil	5 10	10 02	F	4 11 77	Warrington	Trainee	Wrexham	11	3
							Sunderland	2	—
Weaver Luke	6 2	13 02	G	26 6 79	Woolwich	Trainee	Leyton Orient	9	—
							West Ham U (loan)	—	—
							Sunderland	—	—
							Scarborough (loan)	6	—
Williams Darren	5 9	11 00	D	28 4 77	Middlebrough	Trainee	York C	20	—
							Sunderland	72	4

Trainees
Byrne, Clifford; Harte, Shane P; Rice, Dominic A; Robson, Michael

Scholars
Harrison, Stephen; Marchant, Ross A; McGhie, Gareth; Morgan, David; Ramsden, Simon P; Vickers, Thomas A F

Associated Schoolboys
Cogdon, Gavin; Cronin, Christopher P; Dowell, Adam; Hand, Mark; Hope, Shaun; James, Craig; Jolly, Nathan; McConville, Christopher; Redford, Lee; Rowland, Nicholas; Straker, Phillip; Taylor, Alan; Turns, Craig; Williamson, Darren

SWANSEA CITY

Name					Birthplace	Source	Club	Apps	Gls
Alsop Julian	6 5	14 08	F	28 5 73	Nuneaton	Halesowen T	Bristol R	33	4
							Swansea C	53	13
Appleby Ritchie	5 9	11 03	M	18 9 75	Stockton	Trainee	Newcastle U	—	—
							Darlington (loan)	—	—
							Ipswich T	3	—
							Swansea C	85	7
Barwood Danny§	5 9	11 00	F	25 2 81	Caerphilly	Trainee	Swansea C	3	1
Bird Tony	5 11	12 10	F	1 9 74	Cardiff	Trainee	Cardiff C	75	13
						Barry T	Swansea C	70	17
Bound Matthew	6 2	14 00	D	9 11 72	Bradford-on-Avon	Trainee	Southampton	5	—
							Hull C (loan)	7	1
							Stockport Co	44	5
							Lincoln C (loan)	4	—
							Swansea C	73	2
Casey Ryan	6 0	10 12	M	3 1 79	Coventry	Trainee	Swansea C	26	1
Clode Mark‡	5 10	10 10	D	24 2 73	Plymouth	Trainee	Plymouth Arg	—	—
							Swansea C	119	3
Coates Jonathan	5 8	10 04	M	27 5 75	Swansea	Trainee	Swansea C	144	11
Cusack Nick	6 0	12 05	M	24 12 65	Rotherham	Alvechurch	Leicester C	16	1
							Peterborough U	44	10
							Motherwell	77	17
							Darlington	21	6
							Oxford U	61	10
							Wycombe W (loan)	4	—
							Fulham	116	14
							Swansea C	75	1
Davies Jamie	6 0	11 09	F	12 2 80	Swansea	Trainee	Swansea C	1	

Freestone Roger	6 3	14 06	G	19 8 68	Newport	Trainee	Newport Co	13	—
							Chelsea	42	—
							Swansea C (loan)	14	—
							Hereford U (loan)	8	—
							Swansea C	350	3
Harris Jamie‡	6 3	13 06	F	28 6 79	Swansea	Mumbles R	Swansea C	6	—
Hartfield Charlie	6 0	13 08	M	4 9 71	London	Trainee	Arsenal	—	—
							Sheffield U	56	1
							Fulham (loan)	2	—
							Swansea C	22	2
							Lincoln C (loan)	3	1
Howard Mike	5 9	11 13	D	2 12 78	Birkenhead	Tranmere R	Swansea C	42	1
Jenkins Lee	5 9	10 00	M	28 6 79	Pontypool	Trainee	Swansea C	56	2
Jones Jason	6 2	12 10	G	10 5 79	Wrexham	Liverpool	Swansea C	4	—
Jones Steve	5 10	12 02	D	25 12 70	Bristol	Cheltenham T	Swansea C	95	3
Lacey Damien	5 9	11 03	D	3 8 77	Bridgend	Trainee	Swansea C	44	1
Mainwaring Carl‡	5 11	12 07	F	15 3 80	Swansea	Trainee	Swansea C	3	—
Munroe Karl‡	6 0	10 08	D	23 9 79	Manchester	Trainee	Swansea C	1	—
Newhouse Aidan‡	6 2	13 10	F	23 5 72	Wallasey	Trainee	Chester C	44	6
							Wimbledon	23	2
							Tranmere R (loan)		—
							Port Vale (loan)	2	—
							Portsmouth (loan)	6	1
							Torquay U (loan)	4	2
							Fulham	8	1
							Swansea C	14	—
O'Gorman Dave‡	6 0	13 00	F	20 6 72	Chester	School	Wrexham	17	—
						Barry T	Swansea C	39	5
O'Leary Kristian	6 0	13 04	D	30 8 77	Port Talbot	Trainee	Swansea C	61	3
Phillips Gareth	5 7	11 02	M	19 8 79	Church Village	Trainee	Swansea C	8	—
Price Jason	6 0	11 05	D	12 4 77	Aberdare	Aberaman Ath	Swansea C	64	7
Roberts Stuart	5 6	9 8	M	22 7 80	Carmarthen	Trainee	Swansea C	32	3
Smith Jason	6 1	13 06	D	6 9 74	Bromsgrove	Tiverton	Coventry C	—	—
						Tiverton T	Swansea C	42	4
Thomas Martin	5 8	11 06	M	12 9 73	Lyndhurst	Trainee	Southampton	—	—
							Leyton Orient	5	2
							Fulham	90	8
							Swansea C	30	3
Walker Keith	6 0	12 08	D	17 4 66	Edinburgh	ICI Juveniles	Stirling Albion	91	17
							St Mirren	43	6
							Swansea C	270	9
Watkin Steve	5 10	11 10	F	16 6 71	Wrexham	School	Wrexham	200	55
							Swansea C	75	20

Trainees

Barwood, Daniel D; Cleverley, Richard J T; De-Vulgt, Leigh S; Gregson, Lyndon; Howard, Martin G; James, Grant R; James, Robert K; Keegan, Michael J; Kern, Jamie T; Mazurczak, Ross P; Morgan, David B R; Morgan, Ian K; Mounty, Carl T; Thomas, Carl I; Todd, Christopher; Watkins, David J

SWINDON TOWN

Borrows Brian*	5 10	11 12	D	20 12 60	Liverpool	Amateur	Everton	27	—
							Bolton W	95	—
							Coventry C	409	11
							Bristol C (loan)	6	—
							Swindon T	80	—
Campagna Sam§			M	19 11 80	Worcester	Trainee	Swindon T	2	—
Collins Lee	5 9	11 02	M	3 2 74	Bellshill	Possil U	Albion R	45	1
							Swindon T	39	1
Cowe Steve	5 7	10 02	F	29 9 74	Gloucester	Trainee	Aston Villa	—	—
							Swindon T	71	9
Cuervo Philippe	5 11	11 03	M	13 8 69	Ris-oranges		St Etienne	21	—
							Swindon T	29	—
Davies Gareth	6 1	11 03	D	11 12 73	Hereford	Trainee	Hereford U	95	1
							Crystal Palace	27	2
							Cardiff C (loan)	6	2
							Reading	19	—
							Swindon T	6	—
Davis Sol	5 7	11 00	D	4 9 79	Cheltenham	Trainee	Swindon T	31	—
Elkins Gary‡	5 9	13 04	D	4 5 66	Wallingford	Apprentice	Fulham	104	2
							Exeter C (loan)	5	—
							Wimbledon	110	3
							Swindon T	23	1
Glass Jimmy	6 1	13 04	G	1 8 73	Swindon	Trainee	Crystal Palace	—	—
							Portsmouth (loan)	3	—
							Bournemouth	94	—
							Swindon T	3	—
							Carlisle U (loan)	3	1
Gooden Ty	5 8	12 06	M	23 10 72	Canvey Island	Wycombe W	Swindon T	136	9
Griffin Charlie			F	25 6 79	Bath	Bristol R	Swindon T	5	1
Hall Gareth	5 8	12 00	D	12 3 69	Croydon	Apprentice	Chelsea	138	4
							Sunderland	48	—
							Brentford (loan)	6	—
							Swindon T	41	1

Name							Club		
Hay Chris	6 0	12 05	F	28 8 74	Glasgow		Celtic	25	4
							Swindon T	63	20
Holcroft Peter*	5 9	11 07	M	3 1 76	Liverpool	Trainee	Everton	—	—
							Swindon T	3	—
							Exeter C (loan)	6	—
Howe Bobby	5 7	10 06	M	6 11 73	Annitsford	Trainee	Nottingham F	14	2
							Ipswich T (loan)	3	—
							Swindon T	33	3
Hulbert Robin			M	14 3 80	Plymouth	Trainee	Swindon T	17	—
							Newcastle U (loan)	—	—
Kerslake David*	5 9	12 04	D	19 6 66	Stepney	Apprentice	QPR	58	6
							Swindon T	135	1
							Leeds U	8	—
							Tottenham H	37	—
							Swindon T (loan)	8	—
							Ipswich T	7	—
							Wycombe W (loan)	10	—
							Swindon T	24	—
Leitch Scott	5 10	12 00	M	6 10 69	Motherwell	Shettleston Jun	Dunfermline Ath	89	16
							Hearts	55	2
							Swindon T	93	1
McAreavey Paul§			M	3 12 80	Belfast	Trainee	Swindon T	2	—
McDonald Alan*	6 3	13 10	D	12 10 63	Belfast	Apprentice	QPR	402	13
							Charlton Ath (loan)	9	—
							Swindon T	33	1
McHugh Frazer§			M	14 7 81	Nottingham	Trainee	Swindon T	1	—
Mildenhall Steve	6 4	14 01	G	13 5 78	Swindon	Trainee	Swindon T	5	—
Ndah George	6 1	11 04	F	23 12 74	Dulwich	Trainee	Crystal Palace	78	8
							Bournemouth (loan)	12	2
							Gillingham (loan)	4	—
							Swindon T	55	13
Onuora Iffy	6 0	13 01	F	28 7 67	Glasgow	British Univ	Huddersfield T	165	30
							Mansfield T	28	8
							Gillingham	62	23
							Swindon T	49	21
Quinn Jimmy†	6 1	13 10	F	18 11 59	Belfast	Oswestry T	Swindon T	49	10
							Blackburn R	71	17
							Swindon T	64	30
							Leicester C	31	6
							Bradford C	35	14
							West Ham U	47	18
							Bournemouth	43	19
							Reading	182	71
							Peterborough U	49	25
							Swindon T	—	—
Reeves Alan	6 0	12 00	D	19 11 67	Birkenhead	Heswall	Norwich C	—	—
							Gillingham (loan)	18	—
							Chester C	40	2
							Rochdale	121	9
							Wimbledon	57	4
							Swindon T	24	2
Robinson Mark	5 9	12 04	D	21 11 68	Rochdale	Trainee	WBA	2	—
							Barnsley	137	6
							Newcastle U	25	—
							Swindon T	185	3
Talia Frank	6 1	13 06	G	20 7 72	Melbourne	Sunshine GC	Blackburn R	—	—
							Hartlepool U (loan)	14	—
							Swindon T	76	—
Taylor Craig	6 1	12 03	D	24 1 74	Plymouth	Dorchester T	Swindon T	53	2
							Plymouth Arg (loan)	6	1
Walters Mark	5 9	11 05	M	2 6 64	Birmingham	Apprentice	Aston Villa	181	39
							Rangers	106	32
							Liverpool	94	14
							Stoke C (loan)	9	2
							Wolverhampton W (loan)	11	3
							Southampton	5	—
							Swindon T	99	23
Watson Kevin*	5 9	12 08	M	3 1 74	Hackney	Trainee	Tottenham H	5	—
							Brentford (loan)	3	—
							Bristol C (loan)	2	—
							Barnet (loan)	13	—
							Swindon T	63	1
Williams James§			M	15 7 82	Liverpool	Trainee	Swindon T	3	—
Willis Adam	6 1	13 02	D	21 9 76	Nuneaton	Trainee	Coventry C	—	—
							Swindon T	11	—
							Mansfield T (loan)	10	—

Trainees
Bitner, James; Burke, Nicholas P; Cairns, Peter A; Campagna, Sam P P; Culbertson, Richard D J; Donlan, Jason A; Evans, Scott; Flanagan, Alan; Jeffery, Danny; Martin, Lee; McAreavey, Paul; McHugh, Frazer; McRobie, Craig; McSherry, Ian G R; Mills, Jamie M; Peters, Bradley S; Ratcliffe, David F; Robinson, Karl J; Williams, James

Non-Contract
Jones, Tom; Quinn, James M

Associated Schoolboys
Horrix, Terence; Hughes, Alun T; Murdoch, Jordan

Associated Schoolboys who have accepted the Club's offer of a Traineeship/Scholarship/Contract
Andersen, Paul A; Bishop, Leslie M; Collier, Adam; Collins, Christopher J; Edwards, Nathan M; Fenwick, Mark T; Halliday, Kevin J; Kitchen, Luke F; Reed, Paul S; Scarlett, Philip J; Smith, Bryan J; Young, Alan J

TORQUAY UNITED

Name	Ht	Wt	Pos	Born	Birthplace	Prev Club	Club	Apps	Gls
Aggrey Jimmy	6 3	13 06	D	26 10 78	London	Chelsea	Fulham	—	—
							Torquay U	25	—
Bedeau Anthony	5 10	11 00	F	24 3 79	Hammersmith	Trainee	Torquay U	82	15
Clayton Gary‡	5 10	12 08	M	2 2 63	Sheffield	Burton Alb	Doncaster R	35	5
							Cambridge U	179	17
							Peterborough U (loan)	4	—
							Huddersfield T	19	1
							Plymouth Arg	38	2
							Torquay U	56	2
Donaldson O'Neill	6 0	12 04	F	24 11 69	Birmingham	Hinckley	Shrewsbury T	28	4
							Doncaster R	9	2
							Mansfield T (loan)	4	6
							Sheffield W	14	3
							Oxford U (loan)	6	2
							Stoke C	2	—
							Torquay U	12	1
Forrester Mark§	5 8	10 02	F	15 4 81	Stockton	Trainee	Torquay U	5	—
Hadley Shaun‡	5 8	10 05	M	6 2 80	Birmingham	Trainee	Torquay U	2	—
Hapgood Leon	5 6	10 00	F	7 8 79	Torbay	Trainee	Torquay U	40	3
Healy Brian	6 1	13 02	M	27 12 68	Glasgow	Morecambe	Torquay U	19	2
Herrera Robbie	5 7	10 06	D	12 6 70	Torbay	Trainee	QPR	6	—
							Torquay U (loan)	11	—
							Torquay U (loan)	5	—
							Fulham	145	1
							Torquay U	40	—
Hill Kevin	5 8	10 03	M	6 3 76	Exeter	Torrington	Torquay U	72	12
Jermyn Mark§	5 11	12 00	D	16 4 81	West Germany	Trainee	Torquay U	1	—
Leadbitter Chris#	5 9	10 06	M	17 10 67	Middlesbrough	Apprentice	Grimsby T	—	—
							Hereford U	36	1
							Cambridge U	176	18
							Bournemouth	54	3
							Plymouth Arg	52	1
							Torquay U	63	2
McFarlane Andy*	6 3	12 08	F	30 11 66	Wolverhampton	Cradley T	Portsmouth	2	—
							Swansea C	55	8
							Scunthorpe U	60	19
							Torquay U	56	11
McGorry Brian*	5 10	12 08	M	16 4 70	Liverpool	Weymouth	Bournemouth	61	11
							Peterborough U	52	6
							Wycombe W	4	—
							Cardiff C (loan)	7	—
							Hereford U	7	1
						Hereford U	Torquay U	34	1
Neil Gary	6 0	12 10	F	16 8 78	Glasgow	Trainee	Leicester C	—	—
							Torquay U	7	—
Newell Justin‡	6 1	10 07	F	8 2 80	Germany	Trainee	Torquay U	1	—
Nichols Jon§	6 0	11 10	D	10 9 80	Plymouth	Trainee	Torquay U	6	—
Platts Mark	5 8	11 12	F	23 5 79	Sheffield	Trainee	Sheffield W	2	—
							Torquay U	8	—
Robinson Jamie*	6 1	12 08	D	26 2 72	Liverpool	Trainee	Liverpool	—	—
							Barnsley	9	—
							Carlisle U	57	4
							Torquay U	75	1
Simb Jean-Pierre	6 1	11 05	F	4 9 74	Paris	FC Paris	Torquay U	9	1
Southall Neville†	6 1	13 00	G	16 9 58	Llandudno	Winsford U	Bury	39	—
							Everton	578	—
							Port Vale (loan)	9	—
							Southend U (loan)	9	—
							Stoke C	12	—
							Torquay U	25	—
Thomas Wayne	5 11	11 02	D	17 5 79	Gloucester	Trainee	Torquay U	83	2
Tully Stephen	5 7	10 04	M	10 2 80	Paignton	Trainee	Torquay U	46	2
Veysey Kenneth*	5 11	12 07	G	8 6 67	Hackney	Arsenal	Torquay U	72	—
							Oxford U	57	—
							Sheffield U (loan)	—	—
							Exeter C	12	—
						Dorchester T	Torquay U	37	—
Waddle Chris‡	6 0	13 07	M	14 12 60	Hedworth	Tow Law T	Newcastle U	170	46
							Tottenham H	138	33
							Marseille	107	22
							Sheffield W	109	10
							Falkirk	4	1
							Bradford C	25	5
							Sunderland	7	1
							Burnley	31	1
							Torquay U	7	—

Watson Alex	6 1	12 00	D	5 4 68	Liverpool	Apprentice	Liverpool	4	—
							Derby Co (loan)	5	—
							Bournemouth	151	5
							Gillingham (loan)	10	1
							Torquay U	129	4
Williams Eifion	5 11	11 00	F	15 11 75	Bangor	Barry T	Torquay U	7	5
Worthington Martin§	5 10	11 11	F	25 1 81	Torquay	Trainee	Torquay U	1	—

Trainees
Douglin, Troy-Alexander; Ennis, Robert; Forrester, Mark; Grinsill, Justin A; Guttridge, Luke; Hall, Jonathan P; Higgins, Dean R J; Hockley, Matthew; Jermyn, Mark S; Law, Gareth M; Legg, Scott G; Nichols, Jonathan A; Northmore, Ryan; Patterson, Jamie; Tomkinson, David J; Worthington, Martin P

Non-Contract
Southall, Neville

Associated Schoolboys who have accepted the Club's offer of a Traineeship/Scholarship/Contract
Ashington, Ryan; Benefield, Jimm

TOTTENHAM HOTSPUR

Allen Rory	5 11	11 02	F	17 10 77	Beckenham	Trainee	Tottenham H	21	2
							Luton T (loan)	8	6
Anderton Darren	6 1	12 05	F	3 3 72	Southampton	Trainee	Portsmouth	62	7
							Tottenham H	179	25
Armstrong Chris	6 0	12 10	F	19 6 71	Newcastle	Llay Welfare	Wrexham	60	13
							Millwall	28	5
							Crystal Palace	118	45
							Tottenham H	101	32
Baardsen Espen	6 5	13 03	G	7 12 77	San Rafael	San Francisco AB	Tottenham H	23	—
Berti Nicola	6 1	12 02	M	14 4 67	Salsomaggiore		Parma	28	—
(Transferred to Alaves, December 1998)					Terme		Fiorentina	80	8
							Internazionale	229	29
							Tottenham H	21	3
Brown Simon*	6 2	15 01	G	3 12 76	Chelmsford	Trainee	Tottenham H	—	—
							Lincoln C (loan)	1	—
							Fulham (loan)	—	—
Bunn James‡			F	12 1 78	Tottenham	Trainee	Tottenham H	—	—
Campbell Sol	6 21	14 04	D	18 9 74	Newham	Trainee	Tottenham H	205	8
Carr Stephen	5 9	12 04	D	29 8 76	Dublin	Trainee	Tottenham H	102	—
Clemence Stephen	5 11	11 07	M	31 3 78	Liverpool	Trainee	Tottenham H	35	—
Crouch Peter	6 2	11 12	F	30 1 81	Macclesfield	Trainee	Tottenham H	—	—
Darcy Ross	6 0	12 02	D	21 3 78	Balbriggan	Trainee	Tottenham H	—	—
Dominguez Jose	5 3	10 00	F	16 2 74	Lisbon	Benfica	Birmingham C	35	3
							Sporting Lisbon	62	4
							Tottenham H	31	4
Edinburgh Justin	5 10	12 01	D	18 12 69	Basildon	Trainee	Southend U	37	—
							Tottenham H (loan)	—	—
							Tottenham H	205	1
Fenn Neale	5 10	12 08	F	18 1 77	Edmonton	Trainee	Tottenham H	8	—
							Leyton Orient (loan)	3	—
							Norwich C (loan)	7	1
							Swindon T (loan)	4	—
							Lincoln C (loan)	4	—
Ferdinand Les	5 11	13 05	F	18 12 66	Acton	Hayes	QPR	163	80
							Brentford (loan)	3	—
							Besiktas (loan)	24	14
							Newcastle U	68	41
							Tottenham H	45	10
Fox Ruel	5 6	10 05	F	14 1 68	Ipswich	Apprentice	Norwich C	172	22
							Newcastle U	58	12
							Tottenham H	103	13
Freund Steffen	5 11	12 06	M	19 1 70	Brandenburg		Brandenburg	31	—
							Schalke	53	3
							Borussia Dortmund	117	6
							Tottenham H	17	—
Ginola David	5 11	11 10	F	25 1 67	Gassin		Toulon	81	4
							Racing Paris	61	8
							Brest	50	10
							Paris St Germain	115	32
							Newcastle U	58	6
							Tottenham H	64	9
Gower Mark			M	5 10 78	Edmonton	Trainee	Tottenham H	—	—
(On loan to Motherwell)							Motherwell	9	1
Grodas Frode	6 2	14 07	G	24 10 64	Volda		Lillestrom	182	1
(Transferred to Schalke, July 1998)							Chelsea	21	—
							Tottenham H	—	—
Hillier Ian	5 11	11 05	D	26 12 79	Neath	Trainee	Tottenham H	—	—
Iversen Steffen	6 1	11 08	F	10 11 76	Oslo		Rosenborg	25	10
							Tottenham H	56	15
Kersey Lee*	5 11	13 02	D	12 8 79	Harlow	Trainee	Tottenham H	—	—
King Ledley	6 2	13 08	D	12 10 80	London	Trainee	Tottenham H	1	—
Lee David	5 11	11 08	M	28 3 80	Basildon	Trainee	Tottenham H	—	—
Marriott Alan*	6 1	12 05	G	3 9 78	Bedford	Trainee	Tottenham H	—	—
McVeigh Paul	5 6	10 05	F	6 12 77	Belfast	Trainee	Tottenham H	3	1

Name	Ht	Wt	Pos	Date	Birthplace	From	Club	Apps	Gls
Nielsen Allan	5 8	11 02	M	13 3 71	Esbjerg	Esbjerg	Bayern Munich	1	—
							Sion	—	—
							Odense	55	9
							FC Copenhagen	26	3
							Brondby	42	11
							Tottenham H	83	12
Nilsen Roger*	5 11	12 06	D	8 8 69	Tromso	Viking Stavanger	Sheffield U	166	—
							Tottenham H	3	—
O'Brien Kevin‡	5 11	11 08	D	14 8 80	Waterford	Trainee	Tottenham H	—	—
Piercy John	5 11	11 12	M	18 9 79	Forest Gate	Trainee	Tottenham H	—	—
Saib Moussa	5 9	11 08	M	5 3 69	Theniet-El-Had		Auxerre	134	23
							Valencia	14	—
							Tottenham H	13	1
Scales John	6 2	13 05	D	4 7 66	Harrogate		Leeds U	—	—
							Bristol R	72	2
							Wimbledon	240	11
							Liverpool	65	2
							Tottenham H	29	—
Segers Hans*	5 11	12 12	G	30 10 61	Eindhoven	PSV Eindhoven	Nottingham F	58	—
							Stoke C (loan)	1	—
							Sheffield U (loan)	10	—
							Dunfermline Ath (loan)	4	—
							Wimbledon	267	—
							Wolverhampton W	11	—
							Tottenham H	1	—
Sherwood Tim	6 1	12 09	M	2 2 69	St Albans	Trainee	Watford	32	2
							Norwich C	71	10
							Blackburn R	246	25
							Tottenham H	14	2
Sinton Andy*	5 8	11 01	M	19 3 66	Newcastle	Apprentice	Cambridge U	93	13
							Brentford	149	28
							QPR	160	22
							Sheffield W	60	3
							Tottenham H	83	6
Stone Gavin‡			M	9 1 80	Staffordshire		Tottenham H	—	—
Taricco Mauricio	5 8	11 05	D	10 3 73	Buenos Aires		Argentinos Juniors	21	—
							Ipswich T	137	4
							Tottenham H	13	—
Thelwell Alton			D	5 9 80	London	Trainee	Tottenham H	—	—
Tramezzani Paolo	6 1	13 06	D	30 7 70	Reggio-Emilia		Internazionale	—	—
							Prato	29	—
							Cosenza	15	—
							Lucchese	30	1
							Internazionale	26	—
							Venezia	25	—
							Cesena	19	2
							Piacenza	57	2
							Tottenham H	6	—
Vaughan Wayne			M	18 2 80	Barking	Trainee	Tottenham H	—	—
Vega Ramon	6 3	13 00	D	14 6 71	Olten	Trimbach	Grasshoppers	156	13
							Cagliari	14	—
							Tottenham H	49	6
Walker Ian	6 2	13 01	G	31 10 71	Watford	Trainee	Tottenham H	217	—
							Oxford U (loan)	2	—
							Ipswich T (loan)	—	—
Webb Simon	5 11	12 03	M	19 1 78	Castle Bar	Trainee	Tottenham H	—	—
Wilson Clive*	5 7	11 04	D	13 11 61	Manchester	Local	Manchester C	98	9
							Chester (loan)	21	2
							Chelsea	81	5
							Manchester C (loan)	11	—
							QPR	172	12
							Tottenham H	70	1
Young Luke			M	19 7 79	Harlow	Trainee	Tottenham H	15	—

Trainees/Scholars

Attwell, Jamie W; Bernard, Narada M; Clist, Simon J; Ellis, Paul D; Fitzsimon, Ross J; Gray, Matthew J; Hunt, Nicholas G; Jackson, Johnnie; Kelly, Gavin R; Lacy, Neil D; Makumbu, Destin; Mapes, Charles E; Mills, Stephen J; Morley, Wayne; Poole, Glenn S; Saker, Blake M; Stonebridge, Ian R; Tait, Allan D; Thurgood, Stuart A; Toner, Ciaran; Wood, Paul T

TRANMERE ROVERS

Name	Ht	Wt	Pos	Date	Birthplace	From	Club	Apps	Gls
Achterberg John	6 1	13 00	G	8 7 71	Utrecht	Utrecht	NAC	9	—
							Eindhoven	32	—
						Utrecht	Tranmere R	24	—
Allen Graham	6 0	12 00	D	8 4 77	Bolton	Trainee	Everton	6	—
							Tranmere R	41	5
Challinor Dave	6 1	12 00	D	2 10 75	Chester	Bromborough Pool	Tranmere R	71	3
Coyne Danny*	5 11	12 05	G	27 8 73	Prestatyn	Trainee	Tranmere R	111	—
Crowe Barry‡	5 4	10 05	D	15 6 80	Liverpool	Trainee	Tranmere R	—	—
Fairclough David‡	6 1	11 08	D	26 4 78	Drogheda		Tranmere R	—	—
Frail Stephen	5 11	12 03	D	10 8 69	Glasgow		Dundee	101	1
							Hearts	54	4
							Tranmere R	11	—
Gibson Neil	5 11	11 08	M	10 10 79	St Asaph	Trainee	Tranmere R	1	—

English League Players – Walsall

Player	Ht	Wt	Pos	DOB	Birthplace	From	Club	Apps	Gls
Hill Clint	6 0	11 06	D	19 10 78	Liverpool	Trainee	Tranmere R	47	4
Hinds Richard	6 2	12 00	D	22 8 80	Sheffield	Schoolboy	Tranmere R	2	—
Holmes Tommy	6 0	12 06	D	1 9 79	Bevington	Trainee	Tranmere R	—	—
Irons Kenny	5 10	11 02	M	4 11 70	Liverpool	Trainee	Tranmere R	351	54
Jones Gary	6 3	13 05	F	10 5 75	Chester	Trainee	Tranmere R	147	25
Jones Lee	5 8	10 06	F	29 5 73	Wrexham	Trainee	Wrexham	39	10
							Liverpool	3	—
							Crewe Alex (loan)	8	1
							Wrexham (loan)	20	9
							Wrexham (loan)	6	—
							Tranmere R (loan)	8	5
							Tranmere R	64	11
Joy Ian	5 10	11 00	M	14 7 81	San Diego	Trainee	Tranmere R	—	—
Kelly David	5 11	11 10	F	25 11 65	Birmingham	Alvechurch	Walsall	147	63
							West Ham U	41	7
							Leicester C	66	22
							Newcastle U	70	35
							Wolverhampton W	83	26
							Sunderland	34	2
							Tranmere R	56	15
Koumas Jason	5 10	11 06	M	25 9 79	Wrexham	Trainee	Tranmere R	23	3
Mahon Alan	5 9	11 05	M	4 4 78	Dublin	Crumplin U	Tranmere R	84	9
Mauro‡	6 1	12 12	M	16 6 76	Portugal	Casapia	Tranmere R	—	—
McGreal John	6 1	11 06	D	2 6 72	Birkenhead	Trainee	Tranmere R	195	1
McIntyre Kevin‡	6 0	11 10	M	23 12 77	Liverpool	Trainee	Tranmere R	2	—
Moran Andy	5 11	11 02	F	7 10 79	Wigan	Trainee	Tranmere R	—	—
Morgan Alan	5 9	11 00	D	2 11 73	Aberystwyth	Trainee	Tranmere R	30	1
Morrissey John*	5 8	11 09	F	8 3 65	Liverpool	Apprentice	Everton	1	—
							Wolverhampton W	10	1
							Tranmere R	470	50
O'Brien Liam*	6 1	11 10	M	5 9 64	Dublin	Shamrock R	Manchester U	31	2
							Newcastle U	151	19
							Tranmere R	181	12
Parkinson Andy	5 8	10 12	F	27 5 79	Liverpool	Liverpool	Tranmere R	47	3
Powell Gareth‡	6 1	12 00	G	23 3 80	Newcastle	Trainee	Tranmere R	—	—
Santos Georges	6 3	14 08	D	15 8 70	Marseille	Toulon	Tranmere R	37	1
Sharps Ian§	6 3	13 05	M	23 10 80	Warrington	Trainee	Tranmere R	1	—
Taylor Perry	5 11	12 02	M	29 1 81	Birkenhead	Trainee	Tranmere R	—	—
Taylor Scott	5 10	11 06	F	5 5 76	Chertsey	Staines	Millwall	28	—
							Bolton W	12	1
							Rotherham U (loan)	10	3
							Blackpool (loan)	5	1
							Tranmere R	36	9
Thompson Andy	5 5	10 06	D	9 11 67	Cannock	Apprentice	WBA	24	1
							Wolverhampton W	376	43
							Tranmere R	81	4
Williams Ryan	5 4	11 02	F	31 8 78	Chesterfield	Trainee	Mansfield T	26	3
							Tranmere R	5	—

Trainees
Davies, Kevin M; Holmes, Jamie; Murphy, Joseph; Rogers, Peter N; Sharps, Ian W; Sutcliffe, Steven O

Scholars
Aldridge, Paul J; Costello, Michael R; Farren, Mark J; Garry, Spencer D; Hay, Alexander; Taylor, Craig; Walsham, Paul J; Wright, Kevin

Associated Schoolboys
Baker, Phillip; Ewers, Delwyn G; Linwood, Paul A; McGregor, Andrew; Mortin, Alan J; Roberts, Paul; Thurston, Dean; Williams, Ashley L

Associated Schoolboys who have accepted the Club's offer of a Traineeship/Scholarship/Contract
Climo, Daniel; Dreves, Thomas; Evans, Dylan; Harrison, Daniel; Naylor, Stuart; Taylor, Michael

WALSALL

Player	Ht	Wt	Pos	DOB	Birthplace	From	Club	Apps	Gls
Birch Gary			M	8 10 81	Birmingham	Trainee	Walsall	—	—
Brissett Jason	5 10	12 05	F	7 9 74	Redbridge	Arsenal	Peterborough U	35	—
							Bournemouth	124	8
							Walsall	35	2
Carter Alfonso			M	23 8 80	Birmingham	Trainee	Walsall	1	—
Davis Neil‡	5 10	11 07	F	15 8 73	Bloxwich	Redditch U	Aston Villa	2	—
							Wycombe W (loan)	13	—
							Walsall	1	—
Dyer Wayne‡	6 1	11 07	M	24 11 77	Birmingham	Trainee	Birmingham C	—	—
						Trainee	Oxford U	—	—
						Barry T	Walsall	1	—
Evans Wayne*	5 10	12 03	D	25 8 71	Welshpool	Welshpool	Walsall	183	1
Eyjolfsson Siggi	6 2	12 09	F	1 12 73	Reykjavik	From IA Akranes	Walsall	10	1
Gadsby Matthew	6 1	11 12	D	6 9 79	Sutton Coldfield	Trainee	Walsall	7	—
Green Richard	6 2	14 00	D	22 11 67	Wolverhampton	Apprentice	Shrewsbury T	125	5
							Swindon T	—	—
							Gillingham	216	16
							Walsall	30	1

Henry Nick#	5 6	10 12	M	21 2 69	Liverpool	Trainee	Oldham Ath	273	19
							Sheffield U	16	—
							Walsall	8	—
Keates Dean	5 5	10 07	M	30 6 78	Walsall	Trainee	Walsall	78	3
Keister John#	5 7	10 10	M	11 11 70	Manchester	Faweh FC	Walsall	105	2
Larkin James‡			G	23 10 75	Canada		Cambridge U	1	—
							Walsall	—	—
Larusson Bjarni			M	11 3 76	Iceland		IBV	60	5
							Hibernian	7	1
							Walsall	36	3
Marsh Chris	5 10	13 04	D	14 1 70	Dudley	Trainee	Walsall	345	23
Mavrak Darko			M	19 1 69	Mostar		Norrkoping	26	1
							Walsall	13	2
Naisbitt Daniel†	6 1	11 12	G	25 11 78	Bishop Auckland	Trainee	Walsall	—	—
Naylor Stuart#	6 4	14 01	G	6 12 62	Wetherby	Yorkshire Amat	Lincoln C	49	—
							Peterborough U (loan)	8	—
							Crewe Alex (loan)	38	—
							Crewe Alex (loan)	17	—
							WBA	355	—
							Bristol C	37	—
							Mansfield T (loan)	6	—
							Walsall	—	—
Otta Walter‡			M	20 12 73	Cordova	Puerto Montt	Walsall	8	3
Platt Clive	6 3	13 04	F	27 10 77	Wolverhampton	Trainee	Walsall	32	4
Pointon Neil#	5 10	12 11	D	28 11 64	Warsop Vale	Apprentice	Scunthorpe U	159	2
							Everton	102	5
							Manchester C	74	2
							Oldham Ath	94	3
							Hearts	67	3
							Walsall	43	—
Rammell Andy	6 1	14 00	F	10 2 67	Nuneaton	Atherstone U	Manchester U	—	—
							Barnsley	185	44
							Southend U	69	13
							Walsall	39	18
Ricketts Michael	6 1	12 05	F	4 12 78	Birmingham	Trainee	Walsall	44	3
Roper Ian	6 3	13 09	D	20 6 77	Nuneaton	Trainee	Walsall	69	1
Thomas Wayne	5 8	12 02	M	28 8 78	Walsall	Trainee	Walsall	37	—
Viveash Adrian	6 1	13 05	D	30 9 69	Swindon	Trainee	Swindon T	54	2
							Reading (loan)	5	—
							Reading (loan)	6	—
							Barnsley (loan)	2	1
							Walsall	159	12
Walker James	5 10	13 01	G	9 7 73	Sutton-in-Ashfield	Trainee	Notts Co	—	—
							Walsall	189	—
Watson Andy*	5 8	12 06	F	1 4 67	Leeds	Harrogate T	Halifax T	83	15
							Swansea C	14	1
							Carlisle U	56	22
							Blackpool	115	43
							Walsall	84	15
Wrack Darren	5 10	12 02	M	5 5 76	Cleethorpes	Trainee	Derby Co	26	1
							Grimsby T	13	1
							Shrewsbury T (loan)	4	—
							Walsall	46	13

Trainees
Bowen, Adam P; Edwards, Gary S; Gozzard, Paul J; Osbourne, Lee M; Scott, Dion E; Smith, Richard D L; Turner, Andrew J

Scholars
Bate, Ross; Birch, Gary S; Gaunt, Ian T F; Hawley, Carl L; Hunt, David T; Wright, Mark

Non-Contract
Naisbitt, Daniel J

Associated Schoolboys who have accepted the Club's offer of a Traineeship/Scholarship/Contract
Bishop, Andrew J; Bissell, James; Jones, Craig R; Smith, Nicholas A

WATFORD

Andrews Wayne*	5 10	11 09	F	25 11 77	Paddington	Trainee	Watford	28	4
							Cambridge U (loan)	2	—
							Peterborough U (loan)	10	5
Bakalli Adrian			M	22 11 76	Brussels	Molenbeek	Watford	—	—
Bazeley Darren#	5 10	12 00	D	5 10 72	Northampton	Trainee	Watford	240	21
Bonnot Alexandre#	5 8	11 05	M	31 7 73	Boissy	Angers	Watford	4	—
Boyce Mark*	5 7	10 00	D	11 8 80	Hammersmith	Trainee	Watford	—	—
Chamberlain Alec	6 2	13 10	G	20 6 64	March	Ramsey T	Ipswich T	—	—
							Colchester U	184	—
							Everton	—	—
							Tranmere R (loan)	15	—
							Luton T	138	—
							Chelsea (loan)	—	—
							Sunderland	90	—
							Liverpool (loan)	—	—
							Watford	96	—

Cornock Grant*	6 3	12 06	M	2 2 80	Watford	Trainee	Watford	—	—
Daley Tony#	5 9	11 00	M	18 11 67	Birmingham	Apprentice	Aston Villa	233	31
							Wolverhampton W	21	3
							Watford	12	1
Day Chris	6 3	13 06	G	28 7 75	Walthamstow	Trainee	Tottenham H	—	—
							Crystal Palace	24	—
							Watford	—	—
Easton Clint	5 11	10 04	M	1 10 77	Barking	Trainee	Watford	36	1
Gibbs Nigel	5 7	11 06	D	20 11 65	St Albans	Apprentice	Watford	384	5
Grieves Danny*	5 11	11 06	M	21 9 78	Watford	Trainee	Watford	—	—
Gudmundsson Johann	6 0	12 00	M	5 12 77	Reykjavik		Keflavik	49	13
							Watford	13	2
Hazan Alon	6 1	13 08	M	14 9 67	Ashdod	Ironi Ashdod	Watford	33	2
Hyde Micah	5 10	11 12	M	10 11 74	Newham	Trainee	Cambridge U	107	13
							Watford	84	6
Iroha Ben	5 8	11 06	M	29 11 69	Calabar	San Jose Clash	Bristol R	—	—
							Watford	10	—
Johnson Lee	5 6	10 07	M	7 6 81	Newmarket	Trainee	Watford	—	—
Johnson Richard	5 10	12 07	M	27 4 74	Kurri Kurri	Trainee	Watford	204	17
Kennedy Peter	5 10	11 05	D	10 9 73	Lisburn	Portadown	Notts Co	22	—
							Watford	80	17
Langston Matthew	6 2	12 04	M	2 4 81	Brighton	Trainee	Watford	—	—
Lowndes Nathan	5 11	10 11	F	2 6 77	Salford	Trainee	Leeds U	—	—
(Transferred to St Johnstone, August 1998)							Watford	7	—
							St Johnstone	29	2
Millen Keith	6 2	13 00	D	26 9 66	Croydon	Juniors	Brentford	305	17
							Watford	165	5
Mooney Tommy	5 11	13 10	D	11 8 71	Teesside North	Trainee	Aston Villa	—	—
							Scarborough	107	30
							Southend U	14	5
							Watford (loan)	10	2
							Watford	189	37
Ngonge Michel	6 0	12 08	F	10 1 67	Huy		Harelbeke	31	14
							Samsunspor	52	1
							Watford	22	4
Noel-Williams Gifton	6 1	13 09	F	21 1 80	Islington	Trainee	Watford	89	19
Page Robert	6 0	12 13	D	3 9 74	Llwynipia	Trainee	Watford	144	—
Palmer Steve	6 1	13 05	M	31 3 68	Brighton	Cambridge University	Ipswich T	111	2
							Watford	158	7
Panayi James	6 1	13 12	D	24 1 80	Hammersmith	Trainee	Watford	—	—
Perpetuini David	5 9	10 07	M	26 9 79	Hitchin	Trainee	Watford	1	—
Pluck Colin	6 0	12 05	D	6 9 78	London	Trainee	Watford	1	—
Robinson Paul	5 9	11 10	D	14 12 78	Watford	Trainee	Watford	63	2
Rosenthal Ronny	5 11	13 04	F	4 10 63	Haifa	Standard Liege	Luton T (loan)	—	—
							Liverpool (loan)	8	7
							Liverpool	66	14
							Tottenham H	88	4
							Watford	30	8
Slater Stuart*	5 9	10 13	M	27 3 69	Sudbury	Apprentice	West Ham U	141	11
							Celtic	43	3
							Ipswich T	72	4
							Leicester C	—	—
							Watford	30	1
Smart Allan	6 2	12 11	F	8 7 74	Perth		Caledonian Th	4	—
							Preston NE	21	6
							Carlisle U (loan)	4	—
							Northampton T (loan)	1	—
							Carlisle U	44	16
							Watford	35	7
Smith Tommy	5 9	10 11	F	22 5 80	Hemel Hempstead	Trainee	Watford	9	2
Squires Oliver*	5 9	12 09	M	15 9 80	Harrow	Trainee	Watford	—	—
Ward Darran	6 0	14 02	D	13 9 78	Kenton	Trainee	Watford	9	—
Wright Nick	5 9	11 13	F	15 10 75	Derby	Trainee	Derby Co	—	—
							Carlisle U	25	5
							Watford	33	6
Yates Dean	6 2	12 06	D	26 10 67	Leicester	Apprentice	Notts Co	314	33
							Derby Co	68	3
							Watford	9	1

Trainees
Brooker, Stephen M L; Collis, Stephen P; Farley, Craig; Maynard, Stuart A C; Murphy, Mitchell E; Ougham, James B; Tipton, Daniel P

Scholars
Andrews, Christopher I; Brathwaite, Daniel S; Dickie, James P; Ettienne, Leon A; Fisken, Gary S; Forde, Fabian W; Gilder, Robert J; Neill, Thomas E

Associated Schoolboys
Blizzard, Dominic J; Bonner, Jason; Buxton, Nicholas J; Cracknell, Dean P; Grant, Gavin R; Gruar, Danny; Hand, Jamie; Hopton, Matthew; Hughes, Bradley R; Norville, Jason; Smith, Jack D

Associated Schoolboys who have accepted the Club's offer of a Traineeship/Scholarship/Contract
Deamer, William D; Doyley, Lloyd; Francis, Anthony N; Goldsmith, Lee F; Lee, Richard A; Lonergan, Sean; Saunders, Neil C; Sinclair, Steve; Swannell, Sam A

WEST BROMWICH ALBION

Name	Ht	Wt	Pos	Born	Birthplace	From	Club	Apps	Gls
Adamson Christopher	5 11	11 00	G	4 11 78	Ashington	Trainee	WBA	3	—
							Mansfield T (loan)	2	—
Angel Mark	5 8	11 02	M	23 8 75	Newcastle	Trainee	Sunderland	—	—
							Oxford U	73	4
							WBA	22	1
Blake Marvin‡			M	22 8 79	Leicester	Trainee	WBA	—	—
Bortolazzi Mario#	5 9	11 04	M	10 1 65	Verona		Mantova	27	—
							Fiorentina	11	—
							AC Milan	7	—
							Parma	34	7
							AC Milan	13	1
							Verona	33	4
							Atalanta	20	2
							Genoa	250	16
							WBA	35	2
Burgess Daryl	5 11	11 04	D	24 1 71	Birmingham	Trainee	WBA	303	9
Carbon Matt	6 2	12 05	D	8 6 75	Nottingham	Trainee	Lincoln C	69	10
							Derby Co	20	—
							WBA	55	3
Chambers Adam	5 10	11 08	D	20 11 80	Sandwell	Trainee	WBA	—	—
Chambers James	5 10	11 08	D	20 11 80	Sandwell	Trainee	WBA	—	—
Cooper James‡			M	6 2 80	Wordsley	Trainee	WBA	—	—
Cunningham Darren‡			M	23 8 79	Telford		WBA	—	—
De Freitas Fabian	6 0	12 00	F	28 7 72	Paramaribo	Volendam	Bolton W	40	7
							Osasuna	25	4
							WBA	37	7
Evans Micky	6 0	12 03	F	1 1 73	Plymouth	Trainee	Plymouth Arg	163	38
							Blackburn R (loan)	—	—
							Southampton	22	4
							WBA	30	3
Flynn Sean	5 8	11 09	M	13 3 68	Birmingham	Halesowen T	Coventry C	97	9
							Derby Co	59	3
							Stoke C (loan)	5	—
							WBA	73	4
Gabbidon Daniel	5 10	11 02	D	8 8 79	Cwmbran	Trainee	WBA	2	—
Garrity Michael*			M	6 5 80	Liverpool	Trainee	WBA	—	—
Holmes Paul	5 10	11 00	D	18 2 68	Stocksbridge	Apprentice	Doncaster R	47	1
							Torquay U	138	4
							Birmingham C	12	—
							Everton	21	—
							WBA	103	1
Hughes Lee	5 10	11 06	F	22 5 76	Birmingham	Kidderminster H	WBA	79	45
Ince James‡			M	27 3 80	Chelmsford	Trainee	WBA	—	—
Kilbane Kevin	6 0	12 07	F	1 2 77	Preston	Trainee	Preston NE	47	3
							WBA	87	10
Mardon Paul	6 0	11 10	D	14 9 69	Bristol	Trainee	Bristol C	42	—
							Doncaster R (loan)	3	—
							Birmingham C	64	—
							WBA	139	3
							Oldham Ath (loan)	12	3
Maresca Enzo	5 11	12 00	M	10 2 80	Salerno		WBA	22	2
McDermott Andy	5 9	11 03	D	24 3 77	Sydney	Aust Inst of Sport	QPR	6	2
							WBA	39	—
Miller Alan	6 3	14 06	G	29 3 70	Epping	Trainee	Arsenal	8	—
							Plymouth Arg (loan)	13	—
							WBA (loan)	3	—
							Birmingham C (loan)	15	—
							Middlesbrough	57	—
							Huddersfield T (loan)	—	—
							Grimsby T (loan)	3	—
							WBA	73	—
Murphy Shaun‡	6 1	12 00	D	5 5 70	Sydney	Perth Italia	Notts Co	109	5
							WBA	71	7
Oliver Adam	5 9	11 02	M	25 10 80	Sandwell	Trainee	WBA	1	—
Potter Graham	6 1	11 12	D	20 5 75	Solihull	Trainee	Birmingham C	25	2
							Wycombe W (loan)	3	—
							Stoke C	45	1
							Southampton	8	—
							WBA	33	—
							Northampton T (loan)	4	—
Quailey Brian	6 1	13 11	F	21 3 78	Leicester	Nuneaton B	WBA	7	—
							Exeter C (loan)	12	2
Quinn James	6 1	12 10	F	15 12 74	Coventry	Trainee	Birmingham C	4	—
							Blackpool	151	37
							Stockport Co (loan)	1	—
							WBA	56	8
Raven Paul	6 1	12 11	D	28 7 70	Salisbury	School	Doncaster R	52	4
							WBA	227	14
							Doncaster R (loan)	7	—
							Rotherham U (loan)	11	2
Richards Justin	6 0	11 10	F	16 10 80	Sandwell	Trainee	WBA	1	—

Player	Ht	Wt	Pos	Born	Birthplace	From	Club	Apps	Gls
Sneekes Richard	5 11	12 03	M	30 10 68	Amsterdam		Ajax	3	—
							Volendam	31	7
							Fortuna Sittard	126	20
						Locarno	Bolton W	55	7
							WBA	140	25
Van Blerk Jason*	6 1	13 00	D	16 3 68	Sydney	Go Ahead	Millwall	73	2
							Manchester C	19	—
							WBA	38	—
Whitehead Phil	6 3	15 04	G	17 12 69	Halifax	Trainee	Halifax T	42	—
							Barnsley	16	—
							Halifax T (loan)	9	—
							Scunthorpe U (loan)	8	—
							Scunthorpe U (loan)	8	—
							Bradford C (loan)	6	—
							Oxford U	207	—
							WBA	26	—

Trainees
Abercrombie, Garry B; Ball, Richard; Joynson, Dean; Morris, Elliott J; Porter, Karl

Scholars
Ball, Jamie C; Blake, Mosiah N; Briggs, Mark J; Collins, Matthew J; McFarlane, Dwaine W; Scott, Mark; Watson, Anthony C

Associated Schoolboys
Hadley, Darren; James, Dale J; Russell, Christopher M; Turton, Adam P

WEST HAM UNITED

Player	Ht	Wt	Pos	Born	Birthplace	From	Club	Apps	Gls
Abou Samassi	6 1	12 08	F	4 4 73	Gagnoa		Cannes	37	5
							West Ham U	22	5
							Ipswich T (loan)	5	1
Alexander Gary			F	15 8 79	South London	Trainee	West Ham U	—	—
Bartley Danny*			F	11 9 79	Lincoln	Trainee	West Ham U	—	—
Berkovic Eyal	5 7	10 02	M	2 4 72	Haifa		Maccabi Haifa	128	25
							Southampton	28	4
							West Ham U	65	10
Boylan Lee*			F	2 9 78	Witham	Trainee	West Ham U	1	—
Bullard Jimmy	5 10	11 07	M	23 10 78	Newham	Gravesend & N	West Ham U	—	—
Bywater Steve			G	7 6 81	Manchester	Trainee	Rochdale	—	—
							West Ham U	—	—
Carrick Michael			F	28 7 81	Wallsend	Trainee	West Ham U	—	—
Cole Joe	5 9	11 00	M	8 11 81	North London	Trainee	West Ham U	8	—
Coyne Chris	6 1	13 10	D	20 12 78	Brisbane	Perth SC	West Ham U	1	—
							Brentford (loan)	7	—
							Southend U (loan)	1	—
Di Canio Paolo	5 9	11 07	F	9 7 68	Rome		Lazio	—	2
							Ternana	27	2
							Lazio	54	4
							Juventus	78	6
							Napoli	26	5
							Juventus	—	—
							AC Milan	37	6
							Celtic	26	12
							Sheffield W	41	15
							West Ham U	13	4
Dicks Julian	5 10	13 00	D	8 8 68	Bristol	Apprentice	Birmingham C	89	1
							West Ham U	159	29
							Liverpool	24	3
							West Ham U	103	21
Etherington Craig			M	16 9 79	Basildon	Trainee	West Ham U	—	—
						Trainee	Halifax T (loan)	4	—
Ferdinand Rio	6 2	12 00	D	8 11 78	Peckham	Trainee	West Ham U	82	2
							Bournemouth (loan)	10	—
Ferrante Michael			M	28 4 81	Melbourne	Australia IOS	West Ham U	—	—
Foe Marc Vivien	6 2	13 06	M	1 5 75	Yaounde	Canon Yaounde	Lens	85	11
							West Ham U	13	—
Forrest Craig	6 4	14 04	G	20 9 67	Vancouver	Apprentice	Ipswich T	263	—
							Colchester U (loan)	11	—
							Chelsea (loan)	3	—
							West Ham U	15	—
Garcia Richard			F	4 9 81	Perth	Trainee	West Ham U	—	—
Hall Richard‡	6 2	13 11	D	14 3 72	Ipswich	Trainee	Scunthorpe U	22	3
							Southampton	126	12
							West Ham U	7	—
Henry Anthony*			D	13 9 79	London	Trainee	West Ham U	—	—
Hislop Shaka	6 4	14 04	G	22 2 69	Hackney	Howard Univ	Reading	104	—
							Newcastle U	53	—
							West Ham U	37	—
Hodges Lee	5 5	10 02	M	2 3 78	Newham	Trainee	West Ham U	3	—
							Exeter C (loan)	17	—
							Leyton Orient (loan)	3	—
							Plymouth Arg (loan)	9	—
							Ipswich T (loan)	4	—
							Southend U (loan)	10	1
Holligan Gavin	6 0	13 00	F	13 6 80	Lambeth	Kingstonian	West Ham U	1	—
Iriekpen Ezomo§			D	14 5 82	Nigeria	Trainee	West Ham U	—	—

Name			Pos	Born	Birthplace	Source	Club	Apps	Gls
Keith Joseph*			D	1 10 78	London	Trainee	West Ham U	—	—
Keller Marc	5 9	12 03	M	14 1 68	Colmar		Mulhouse	88	11
							Strasbourg*	—	
							Strasbourg	115	24
							Karlsruhe	61	13
							West Ham U	21	5
Kitson Paul	5 11	10 12	F	9 1 71	Murton	Trainee	Leicester C	50	6
							Derby Co	105	36
							Newcastle U	36	10
							West Ham U	44	15
Lampard Frank	6 0	11 12	M	20 6 78	Romford	Trainee	West Ham U	84	9
							Swansea C (loan)	9	1
Lazaridis Stan	5 9	12 00	D	16 8 72	Perth	West Adelaide	West Ham U	69	3
Lomas Steve	6 0	12 08	M	18 1 74	Hanover	Trainee	Manchester C	111	8
							West Ham U	70	3
Margas Javier			D	10 5 69	Chile	Univ Catolica	West Ham U	3	—
McCann Grant			M	14 4 80	Belfast	Trainee	West Ham U	—	—
Mean Scott*	5 11	13 08	M	13 12 73	Crawley	Trainee	Bournemouth	74	8
							West Ham U	3	—
							Port Vale (loan)	1	—
Minto Scott	5 10	12 04	D	6 8 71	Cheshire	Trainee	Charlton Ath	180	7
							Chelsea	54	4
							Benfica	31	—
							West Ham U	15	—
Moncur John	5 7	9 10	M	22 9 66	Mile End	Apprentice	Tottenham H	21	1
							Cambridge U (loan)	4	—
							Doncaster R (loan)	4	—
							Portsmouth (loan)	7	—
							Brentford (loan)	5	1
							Ipswich T (loan)	6	—
							Nottingham F (loan)	—	—
							Swindon T	58	5
							West Ham U	111	5
O'Reilly Alex			G	15 9 79	Epping	Trainee	West Ham U	—	—
Omoyimni Emmanuel	5 6	10 07	F	28 12 77	Nigeria	Trainee	West Ham U	9	2
							Bournemouth (loan)	7	—
							Dundee U (loan)	4	—
							Leyton Orient (loan)	4	1
Partridge David			M	26 11 78	Westminster	Trainee	West Ham U	—	—
(Transferred to Dundee U, March 1999)							Dundee U	1	—
Pearce Ian	6 3	14 04	D	7 5 74	Bury St Edmunds	Schoolboy	Chelsea	4	—
							Blackburn R	62	2
							West Ham U	63	3
Potts Steve	5 7	10 11	D	7 5 67	Hartford (USA)	Apprentice	West Ham U	374	1
Purces Stephen			M	14 1 80	Essex	Trainee	West Ham U	—	—
Ruddock Neil	6 2	12 12	D	9 5 68	South London	Apprentice	Millwall	—	—
							Tottenham H	9	—
							Millwall	2	1
							Southampton	107	9
							Tottenham H	38	3
							Liverpool	115	11
							QPR (loan)	7	—
							West Ham U	27	2
Sealey Les‡	6 1	13 06	G	29 11 57	Bethnal Green	Apprentice	Coventry C	158	—
							Luton T	207	—
							Plymouth Arg (loan)	6	—
							Manchester U (loan)	2	—
							Manchester U	31	—
							Aston Villa	18	—
							Coventry C (loan)	2	—
							Birmingham C (loan)	12	—
							Manchester U	—	—
							Blackpool	7	—
							West Ham U	2	—
							Leyton Orient	12	—
							West Ham U	2	—
							Bury (loan)	—	—
Sinclair Trevor	5 10	12 05	F	2 3 72	Dulwich	Trainee	Blackpool	112	15
							QPR	167	16
							West Ham U	50	14
Wright Ian	5 10	11 08	F	3 11 63	Woolwich	Greenwich Bor	Crystal Palace	225	89
							Arsenal	221	128
							West Ham U	22	9

Trainees/Scholars
Angus, Stevland D; Birch, Francis A; Brayley, Albert P; Briggs, Ryan D; Byrne, Shaun R; Clark, Steven T; Cooper, Ashley D; Forbes, Terrell; Foyewa, Amos; Iriekpen, Ezomo; Newton, Adam L; Omonua, Stephen; Richards, Lee J; Taylor, Sam A J; Uddin, Anwar

WIGAN ATHLETIC

Name			Pos	Born	Birthplace	Source	Club	Apps	Gls
Balmer Stuart	6 0	12 11	D	20 9 69	Falkirk	Celtic BC	Celtic	—	—
							Charlton Ath	227	8
							Wigan Ath	36	1

Name				DOB	Birthplace	Source	Club	Apps	Gls
Barlow Stuart	5 10	11 01	F	16 7 68	Liverpool	School	Everton	71	10
							Rotherham U (loan)	—	—
							Oldham Ath	93	31
							Wigan Ath	50	22
Bradshaw Carl	5 10	11 08	D	2 10 68	Sheffield	Apprentice	Sheffield W	32	4
							Barnsley (loan)	6	1
							Manchester C	5	—
							Sheffield U	147	8
							Norwich C	65	2
							Wigan Ath	67	7
Butler Lee	6 2	13 00	G	30 5 66	Sheffield	Haworth Colliery	Lincoln C	30	—
(Transferred to Dunfermline Ath, July 1998)							Aston Villa	8	—
							Hull C (loan)	4	—
							Barnsley	120	—
							Scunthorpe U (loan)	2	—
							Wigan Ath	63	—
							Dunfermline Ath	35	—
Carroll Roy	6 2	13 05	G	30 9 77	Enniskillen	Trainee	Hull C	46	—
							Wigan Ath	72	—
Fitzhenry Neil	6 0	12 02	D	24 9 78	Billinge	Trainee	Wigan Ath	4	—
Furlong Lee‡			M	9 8 79	Liverpool		Wigan Ath	—	—
Green Scott	5 10	13 04	D	15 1 70	Walsall	Trainee	Derby Co		
							Bolton W	220	25
							Wigan Ath	75	1
Greenall Colin†	5 11	12 12	D	30 12 63	Billinge	Apprentice	Blackpool	183	9
							Gillingham	62	4
							Oxford U	67	2
							Bury (loan)	3	—
							Bury	68	5
							Preston NE	29	1
							Chester C	42	1
							Lincoln C	43	3
							Wigan Ath	162	14
Griffiths Gareth	6 4	14 01	D	10 4 70	Winsford	Rhyl	Port Vale	94	4
							Shrewsbury T (loan)	6	—
							Wigan Ath	20	—
Haworth Simon	6 1	13 01	F	30 3 77	Cardiff	Trainee	Cardiff C	37	9
							Coventry C	11	—
							Wigan Ath	20	10
Jenkinson Leigh	6 0	14 01	M	9 7 69	Thorne	Trainee	Hull C	130	13
(Transferred to Hearts, December 1998)							Rotherham U (loan)	7	—
							Coventry C	32	1
							Birmingham C (loan)	3	—
							St Johnstone	67	10
							Wigan Ath	7	—
							Hearts	5	—
Jones Graeme	6 0	14 04	F	13 3 70	Gateshead	Bridlington T	Doncaster R	92	26
							Wigan Ath	93	43
Kilford Ian	5 10	11 03	M	6 10 73	Bristol	Trainee	Nottingham F	1	—
							Wigan Ath (loan)	8	3
							Wigan Ath	148	26
Lee David	5 7	11 01	F	5 11 67	Whitefield	Blackburn Schools	Bury	208	35
							Southampton	20	—
							Bolton W	155	17
							Wigan Ath	79	11
Liddell Andy	5 6	11 06	F	28 6 73	Leeds	Trainee	Barnsley	198	34
							Wigan Ath	28	10
Lloyd Neil‡	5 10	11 08	F	19 7 79	Knowsley	Trainee	Wigan Ath	—	—
Lowe David*	5 10	11 10	F	30 8 65	Liverpool	Apprentice	Wigan Ath	188	40
							Ipswich T	134	37
							Port Vale (loan)	9	2
							Leicester C	94	22
							Port Vale (loan)	19	5
							Wigan Ath	108	26
Martinez Roberto	5 11	12 03	M	13 7 73	Balaguer	Balaguer	Wigan Ath	128	14
McGibbon Pat	6 2	14 01	D	6 9 73	Lurgan	Portadown	Manchester U	—	—
							Swansea C (loan)	1	—
							Wigan Ath (loan)	10	1
							Wigan Ath	71	5
Mills Leon‡	5 11	11 10	M	17 11 79	Manchester	Manchester U	Wigan Ath	—	—
Nixon Eric	6 4	14 00	G	4 10 62	Manchester	Curzon Ashton	Manchester C	58	—
							Wolverhampton W (loan)	16	—
							Bradford C (loan)	3	—
							Southampton (loan)	4	—
							Carlisle U (loan)	16	—
							Tranmere R (loan)	8	—
							Tranmere R	333	—
							Blackpool (loan)	20	—
							Bradford C (loan)	12	—
							Stockport Co	43	—
							Wigan Ath	3	—
O'Connell Brendan‡	5 9	12 01	M	12 11 66	London		Portsmouth	—	—
							Exeter C	81	19
							Burnley	64	17
							Huddersfield T (loan)	11	1
							Barnsley	240	35
							Charlton Ath	38	2

							Wigan Ath	17	5
O'Neill Michael	5 11	10 10	M	5 7 69	Portadown	Coleraine	Newcastle U	48	15
							Dundee U	64	11
							Hibernian	98	19
							Coventry C	5	—
							Reading (loan)	9	1
							Wigan Ath	36	—
Porter Andy	5 9	12 03	M	17 9 68	Holmes Chapel	Trainee	Port Vale	357	22
							Wigan Ath	16	1
Rogers Paul*	6 0	13 02	M	21 3 65	Portsmouth	Sutton U	Sheffield U	125	10
							Notts Co	22	2
							Wigan Ath	100	5
Sharp Kevin#	5 9	11 04	D	19 9 74	Ontario	Auxerre	Leeds U	17	—
							Wigan Ath	124	10
Smeets Jorg	5 6	10 04	F	5 11 70	Bussum		Heracles	8	2
							Wigan Ath	24	3
							Chester C (loan)	3	—

Trainees
Addison, Carl W; Court, Mark; Coyne, John; Critchley, Craig J; Culshaw, Louis; Dann, John J; Field, Dean T; Greenwood, Stephen; Haley, Danny; Jones, Philip A; McMahon, Francis; Mitchell, Paul A; Morris, Andrew; Pitfield, John M; Rhead, Michael; Smith, David; Willis, Scott L

Non-Contract
Greenall, Colin A

Associated Schoolboys
Beardall, Dean M; Clegg, Michael J; Fitzhenry, Paul J; Lee, Paul K; Robinson, Nigel T

Associated Schoolboys who have accepted the Club's offer of a Traineeship/Scholarship/Contract
Johnson, Ian R; Kay, Stephen B; Peoples, Victor; Pitts, Douglas J; Speakman, Craig

WIMBLEDON

Agyemang Patrick	6 1	12 00	F	29 9 80	London	Trainee	Wimbledon	—	—
Ainsworth Gareth	5 8	13 02	M	10 5 73	Blackburn	Blackburn R	Preston NE	5	—
							Cambridge U	4	1
							Preston NE	82	12
							Lincoln C	83	37
							Port Vale	55	10
							Wimbledon	8	—
Ardley Neal	5 11	11 09	M	1 9 72	Epsom	Trainee	Wimbledon	162	10
Bakke Morten‡			M	16 12 68	Gonefoff	Molde	Wimbledon	—	—
Blackwell Dean	6 1	12 10	D	5 12 69	Camden	Trainee	Wimbledon	182	1
							Plymouth Arg (loan)	7	—
Castledine Stewart	6 1	12 00	M	22 1 73	Wandsworth	Trainee	Wimbledon	28	4
							Wycombe W (loan)	7	3
Cort Carl	6 4	12 07	F	1 11 77	Southwark		Wimbledon	39	7
							Lincoln C (loan)	6	1
Cunningham Kenny	5 11	11 02	D	28 6 71	Dublin	Tolka R	Millwall	136	1
							Wimbledon	164	—
Earle Robbie	5 9	10 10	M	27 1 65	Newcastle-under-Lyme	Stoke C	Port Vale	294	77
							Wimbledon	259	56
Ekoku Efan	6 2	12 00	F	8 6 67	Manchester	Sutton U	Bournemouth	62	21
							Norwich C	37	15
							Wimbledon	123	37
Euell Jason	5 11	11 02	F	6 2 77	Lambeth	Trainee	Wimbledon	68	18
Favata Sebastian	5 10	11 07	D	18 10 80	Carshalton	Trainee	Wimbledon	—	—
Fear Peter*	5 10	11 07	M	10 9 73	Sutton	Trainee	Wimbledon	73	4
Francis Damien	6 0	10 10	M	27 2 79	Wandsworth	Trainee	Wimbledon	2	—
Futcher Andy*	5 7	10 07	D	10 2 78	Enfield	Trainee	Wimbledon	0	—
Gayle Marcus	6 1	12 09	F	27 9 70	Hammersmith	Trainee	Brentford	156	22
							Wimbledon	168	27
Gier Robert	5 9	11 07	M	6 1 81	Bracknell	Trainee	Wimbledon	—	—
Goodman Jon	6 0	12 03	F	2 6 71	Walthamstow	Bromley	Millwall	109	35
							Wimbledon	60	11
Gray Wayne	5 10	12 07	F	7 11 80	London	Trainee	Wimbledon	—	—
Halliwell Bryn	5 11	12 00	G	1 10 80	Epsom	Trainee	Wimbledon	—	—
Hartson John	6 0	13 00	F	5 4 75	Swansea	Trainee	Luton T	54	11
							Arsenal	53	14
							West Ham U	60	24
							Wimbledon	14	2
Hawkins Peter	6 0	11 04	D	19 9 78	Maidstone	Trainee	Wimbledon	—	—
Heald Paul	6 2	12 05	G	20 9 68	Wath-on-Dearne	Trainee	Sheffield U	—	—
							Leyton Orient	176	—
							Coventry C (loan)	2	—
							Crystal Palace (loan)	—	—
							Swindon T (loan)	2	—
							Wimbledon	20	—
Hinds Leigh	5 8	10 10	F	17 8 78	Beckenham	Trainee	Wimbledon	—	—
Hodges Danny*	6 0	12 07	D	14 9 76	Greenwich	Trainee	Wimbledon	—	—
Hughes Ceri	5 10	12 07	M	26 2 71	Pontypridd	Trainee	Luton T	175	17
							Wimbledon	31	1

Hughes Michael	5 6	10 08	M	2 8 71	Larne	Carrick R	Manchester C	26	1
							Strasbourg	83	9
							West Ham U (loan)	17	2
							West Ham U (loan)	28	—
							West Ham U	38	3
							Wimbledon	59	6
Jupp Duncan	6 0	12 11	D	25 1 75	Guildford	Trainee	Fulham	105	2
							Wimbledon	15	—
Kennedy Mark	5 11	11 00	F	15 5 76	Dublin	Belvedere	Millwall	43	9
							Liverpool	16	—
							QPR (loan)	8	2
							Wimbledon	21	—
Kimble Alan	5 10	12 04	D	6 8 66	Poole		Charlton Ath	6	—
							Exeter C (loan)	1	—
							Cambridge U	299	24
							Wimbledon	153	—
Leaburn Carl	6 3	13 00	F	30 3 69	Lewisham	Apprentice	Charlton Ath	322	53
							Northampton T (loan)	9	—
							Wimbledon	38	4
McAllister Brian	5 11	12 05	D	30 11 70	Glasgow	Trainee	Wimbledon	85	—
							Plymouth Arg (loan)	8	—
							Crewe Alex (loan)	13	1
Murphy Brendan*	5 11	11 12	G	19 8 75	Wexford	Bradford C	Wimbledon	—	—
O'Connor Richard*	5 9	10 07	F	30 8 78	Wandsworth	Trainee	Wimbledon	—	—
Odlum Gary*	5 11	11 04	D	19 10 78	Beckenham	Trainee	Wimbledon	—	—
Owusu Ansah	5 11	11 02	M	22 11 79	Hackney	Trainee	Wimbledon	—	—
Pearce Andy*	6 4	14 11	D	20 4 66	Bradford-on-Avon	Halesowen T	Coventry C	71	4
							Sheffield W	69	3
							Wimbledon	7	—
Perry Chris	5 8	10 08	D	26 4 73	Carshalton	Trainee	Wimbledon	167	2
Renner Victor*	6 0	11 02	F	18 4 79	Sierra Leone	Trainee	Wimbledon	—	—
Roberts Andy	5 10	13 00	M	20 3 74	Dartford	Trainee	Millwall	138	5
							Crystal Palace	108	2
							Wimbledon	40	3
Sullivan Neil	6 0	12 01	G	24 2 70	Sutton	Trainee	Wimbledon	144	—
							Crystal Palace (loan)	1	—
Thatcher Ben	5 11	12 07	D	30 11 75	Swindon	Trainee	Millwall	90	1
							Wimbledon	66	—
Thurgood Sean	6 2	12 09	D	11 2 80	Hayling Island	Alton T	Wimbledon	—	—
Vella Simon*	6 2	11 11	D	19 9 79	Westminster	Trainee	Wimbledon	—	—
Williamson Russell	5 4	8 10	D	17 3 80	Epping	Trainee	Wimbledon	—	—
Willy Mark	5 11	12 00	M	5 8 80	Sidcup	Trainee	Wimbledon	—	—

Trainees/Scholars
Correia, Artur B; Daly, Thomas F; Flinn, Stephen G; Gore, Shane S; Jenkins, Neil; Jones, Mark C; Lewington, Craig J; McAnuff, Joel J; Mensing, Simon R; Oflynn, Stephen J; Okikiolu, Samuel K; Shirley, Mark D; Tapp, Alexander N G; Unal, Mehmet

WOLVERHAMPTON WANDERERS

Andrews Keith	5 11	11 05	M	13 9 80	Dublin	Trainee	Wolverhampton W	—	—
Atkins Mark*	6 1	12 00	M	14 8 68	Doncaster		Scunthorpe U	48	2
							Blackburn R	257	35
							Wolverhampton W	126	9
Bray Justin*	5 11	11 00	G	1 11 79	Great Yarmouth	Trainee	Wolverhampton W	—	—
Bull Steve	5 11	11 04	F	28 3 65	Tipton	Apprentice	WBA	4	2
							Wolverhampton W	474	250
Connolly David*	5 8	12 00	F	6 6 77	Willesden	Trainee	Watford	26	10
							Wolverhampton W	32	6
Corica Steve	5 8	10 10	M	24 3 73	Cairns	Marconi	Leicester C	16	2
							Wolverhampton W	85	4
Crowe Seamie	5 7	11 07	M	18 11 80	Galway	Trainee	Wolverhampton W	—	—
Curle Keith#	6 0	12 07	D	14 11 63	Bristol	Apprentice	Bristol R	32	4
							Torquay U	16	5
							Bristol C	121	1
							Reading	40	—
							Wimbledon	93	3
							Manchester C	171	11
							Wolverhampton W	105	7
Dixon Alan‡	5 8	11 02	M	9 10 79	Dublin	Trainee	Wolverhampton W	—	—
Emblen Neil	6 1	13 03	M	19 6 71	Bromley	Sittingbourne	Millwall	12	—
							Wolverhampton W	95	9
							Crystal Palace	13	—
							Wolverhampton W	33	2
Ferguson Darren‡	5 10	10 04	M	9 2 72	Glasgow	Trainee	Manchester U	27	—
							Wolverhampton W	117	4
Fernando*	5 10	13 00	M	11 9 65	Valencia	Valencia	Wolverhampton W	19	2
Flo Havard	6 2	13 08	F	4 4 70	Volda	Sogndal	Aarhus	53	27
							Werder Bremen	55	5
							Wolverhampton W	19	5
Foley Dominic*	6 1	12 08	F	7 7 76	Cork	St James Gate	Wolverhampton W	20	3
							Watford (loan)	8	1
							Notts Co (loan)	2	—

Name							Club	Apps	Gls
Gilkes Michael*	5 8	10 10	M	20 7 65	Hackney	Leicester C	Reading	393	43
							Chelsea (loan)	1	—
							Southampton (loan)	6	—
							Wolverhampton W	38	1
Green Ryan	5 8	10 10	D	20 10 80	Cardiff	Danes Court	Wolverhampton W	1	—
Hackett Stephen			D	17 9 80	Dublin	Trainee	Wolverhampton W	—	—
Jones Mark	5 9	12 06	F	7 9 79	Walsall	Trainee	Wolverhampton W	2	—
Keane Robbie	5 9	11 07	F	8 7 80	Dublin	Trainee	Wolverhampton W	71	22
Lamey Nathan*			F	14 10 80	Leeds	Trainee	Wolverhampton W	—	—
Larkin Colin			M	27 4 82	Dundalk	Trainee	Wolverhampton W	—	—
Loughlin Paul			M	5 10 81	Dublin	Stella Maris	Wolverhampton W	—	—
Middleton Darren	6 1	11 13	F	28 12 78	Lichfield	Trainee	Aston Villa	—	—
							Wolverhampton W	—	—
Murray Matthew	6 4	13 11	G	2 5 81	Solihull	Trainee	Wolverhampton W	—	—
Muscat Kevin	5 11	11 07	D	7 8 73	Crawley	South Melbourne	Crystal Palace	53	2
							Wolverhampton W	61	7
Naylor Lee	5 8	11 08	D	19 3 80	Bloxwich	Trainee	Wolverhampton W	39	1
Niestroj Robert	5 10	11 03	M	2 12 74	Oppeln	Fortuna Dusseldorf	Wolverhampton W	5	—
Osborn Simon	5 8	11 04	M	9 1 72	New Addington	Apprentice	Crystal Palace	55	5
							Reading	32	5
							QPR	9	1
							Wolverhampton W	117	11
Paatelainen Mixu	6 0	13 10	F	3 2 67	Helsinki	Valkeakosken Haka	Dundee U	133	33
(Transferred to Hibernian, September 1998)							Aberdeen	75	23
							Bolton W	69	15
							Wolverhampton W	23	—
							Hibernian	26	12
Richards Dean*	6 2	13 07	D	9 6 74	Bradford	Trainee	Bradford C	86	4
							Wolverhampton W (loan)	10	2
							Wolverhampton W	112	5
Robinson Carl	5 10	11 10	M	13 10 76	Llandrindod Wells	Trainee	Wolverhampton W	68	11
							Shrewsbury T (loan)	4	—
Sedgley Steve	6 1	13 13	D	26 5 68	Enfield	Apprentice	Coventry C	84	3
							Tottenham H	164	9
							Ipswich T	105	15
							Wolverhampton W	63	3
Simms Gordon	6 1	12 06	D	23 3 81	Larne	Trainee	Wolverhampton W	—	—
Simpson Paul*	5 8	11 11	M	26 7 66	Carlisle	Apprentice	Manchester C	121	18
							Oxford U	144	43
							Derby Co	186	48
							Sheffield U (loan)	6	—
							Wolverhampton W	39	6
							Walsall (loan)	10	1
Slater Robbie‡	5 10	13 03	D	22 11 64	Ormskirk	Anderlecht	Lens	81	4
							Blackburn R	18	—
							West Ham U	25	2
							Southampton	41	2
							Wolverhampton W	6	—
Stowell Mike	6 2	13 10	G	19 4 65	Portsmouth	Leyland Motors	Preston NE	—	—
							Everton	—	—
							Chester C (loan)	14	—
							York C (loan)	6	—
							Manchester C (loan)	14	—
							Port Vale (loan)	7	—
							Wolverhampton W (loan)	7	—
							Preston NE (loan)	2	—
							Wolverhampton W	359	—
Turner Andy#	5 10	11 10	F	23 3 75	Woolwich	Trainee	Tottenham H	20	3
							Wycombe W (loan)	4	—
							Doncaster R (loan)	4	1
							Huddersfield T (loan)	5	1
							Southend U (loan)	6	—
							Portsmouth	40	3
							Crystal Palace	2	—
							Wolverhampton W	—	—
Williams Adrian	6 2	12 06	D	16 8 71	Reading	Trainee	Reading	196	14
							Wolverhampton W	26	—

Trainees
Barrett, Shane J; Clarke, Christopher E; Clarke, Matthew P; Clegg, Dean R; Easter, Jermaine M; Eccleston, Neil G; Hagan, Conor; Haveron, Gary S; Jones, Kenny R; Lee, Marc C W; Leonard, Gerard; Lescott, Jolean P; McQuade, Scott; Melligan, John J; Mitchell, Patrick J; Proudlock, Adam D; Tudor, Shane

Player who does not hold a current contract but his registration has been retained by the Club
Clark, David

Associated Schoolboys
Bampfield, Steve D; Bonser, John; Cash, Ryan; Clark, David; Clark, Nicholas; Danks, Mark; Jones, Jimmi L; Renton, Michell J; Rollins, Mark; Slater, Christopher; Solly, Lewis; Taylor, Paul; Walker, Richard; Webb, Mark; Wesley, Robert; Woolerton, Stephen

Associated Schoolboys who have accepted the Club's offer of a Traineeship/Scholarship/Contract
Dickson, Andrew; Downes, Lee; Gilmore, Craig C; Kerr, Aaron G; Morrow, Andrew J; Tower, Andrew R; Willis, James R

WREXHAM

Player	Ht	Wt	Pos	DOB	Birthplace	Source	Club	Apps	Gls
Barrett Paul	5 9	11 04	M	13 4 78	Newcastle	Trainee	Newcastle U	—	—
							Wrexham	10	
Brace Deryn	5 7	10 12	D	15 3 75	Haverfordwest	Trainee	Norwich C	—	—
							Wrexham	82	2
Carey Brian	6 3	13 02	D	31 5 68	Cork	Cork C	Manchester U	—	—
							Wrexham (loan)	3	—
							Wrexham (loan)	13	1
							Leicester C	58	1
							Wrexham	117	3
Cartwright Mark	6 2	13 06	G	13 1 73	Chester	York C	Wrexham	37	—
Chalk Martyn	5 6	11 03	F	30 8 69	Swindon	Louth U	Derby Co	7	1
							Stockport Co	43	6
							Wrexham	116	6
Connolly Karl	5 10	11 01	F	9 2 70	Prescot	Napoli (Liverpool)	Wrexham	317	79
Cooper Steve	5 9	11 03	D	10 12 79	Pontypridd		Wrexham	—	—
Edwards Jake	6 1	12 08	F	11 5 76	Manchester	USA College	Wrexham	9	1
Gibson Robin	5 7	10 07	F	15 11 79	Crewe	Trainee	Wrexham	7	1
Griffiths Andy*	5 10	11 04	M	21 11 78	Wirral	Trainee	Wrexham	—	—
Hardy Phil	5 7	11 08	D	9 4 73	Chester	Trainee	Wrexham	298	—
Hopkins Steve*	5 10	11 04	D	12 4 80	St Asaph		Wrexham	—	—
Humes Tony	6 0	12 00	D	19 3 66	Blyth	Apprentice	Ipswich T	120	10
							Wrexham	199	8
Mazzarella Paul*	6 0	11 05	M	8 8 80	Wrexham	Trainee	Wrexham	—	—
McGregor Mark	5 10	11 05	D	16 2 77	Chester	Trainee	Wrexham	156	5
Morrell Andy	5 11	11 06	F	28 9 74	Doncaster		Wrexham	7	—
Owen Gareth	5 8	12 00	M	21 10 71	Chester	Trainee	Wrexham	289	31
Ridler Dave	6 0	12 02	D	12 3 76	Liverpool	Prescot T	Wrexham	67	1
Rishworth Steve†	5 11	11 09	M	8 6 80	Chester	Schoolboy	Wrexham	4	—
Roberts Neil	5 10	11 02	F	7 4 78	Wrexham	Trainee	Wrexham	56	11
Roberts Paul‡	5 11	11 09	F	29 7 77	Bangor	Porthmadog	Wrexham	1	—
Roberts Steve	6 2	11 06	D	24 2 80	Wrexham	Trainee	Wrexham	—	—
Rush Ian#	6 0	12 06	F	20 10 61	St Asaph	Apprentice	Chester C	34	14
							Liverpool	224	139
							Juventus	29	7
							Liverpool	245	90
							Leeds U	36	3
							Newcastle U	10	—
							Sheffield U (loan)	4	—
							Wrexham	17	—
Russell Kevin	5 9	10 12	M	6 12 66	Portsmouth	Brighton & HA	Portsmouth	4	1
							Wrexham	84	43
							Leicester C	43	10
							Peterborough U (loan)	7	3
							Cardiff C (loan)	3	—
							Hereford U (loan)	3	1
							Stoke C (loan)	5	1
							Stoke C	40	5
							Burnley	28	6
							Bournemouth	30	1
							Notts Co	11	—
							Wrexham	128	9
Ryan Michael†	5 9	11 00	D	3 10 79	Stockport	Trainee	Manchester U	—	—
							Wrexham	—	—
Spink Dean	6 1	12 12	D	22 1 67	Halesowen	Halesowen T	Aston Villa	—	—
							Scarborough (loan)	3	2
							Bury (loan)	6	1
							Shrewsbury T	273	52
							Wrexham	70	9
Thomas Steve	5 10	11 07	M	23 6 79	Hartlepool	Trainee	Wrexham	4	—
Walsh Dave	6 1	12 05	G	29 4 79	Wrexham	Trainee	Wrexham	—	—
Ward Peter*	6 0	12 01	M	15 10 64	Durham	Chester-le-Street	Huddersfield T	37	2
							Rochdale	84	10
							Stockport Co	142	10
							Wrexham	120	14
Williams Danny	6 1	13 00	M	12 7 79	Wrexham	Trainee	Liverpool	—	—
							Wrexham	—	—

Trainees
Hughes, Gareth J; Jones, Thomas A; Owen, Adam L; Whitley, John S

Scholars
Cocks, Ian T; Harrison, David; Horan, George J; Johnson, Darran M; Lee, Kenneth; Pybus, David A; Sweet, David; Whitfield, Paul M

Non-Contract
Digwood, Jamie; Hannon, Kevin M; Jones, David A; Rawlins, Richard P; Rigg, Michael; Rishworth, Stephen P; Rogers, Kristian R J; Ryan, Michael S P; Stanhope, Jonpaul

Associated Schoolboys
Bates, Matthew J; Brand, Benjamin J; Cargill, Gary S; Dabbs, Matthew S; Entwistle, Mark R; Graham, Adam; Jones, Adam; O'Toole, Dominic; Simons, Dean D; Taylor, Michael J; Williams, David P; Williams, Gavin P

WYCOMBE WANDERERS

Player	Ht	Wt	Pos	Born	Birthplace	From	Club	Apps	Gls
Baird Andy	5 8	11 13	D	18 1 79	East Kilbride	Trainee	Wycombe W	30	6
Bates Jamie	5 11	14 06	D	24 2 68	Croydon	Trainee	Brentford	419	18
							Wycombe W	9	—
Beeton Alan	5 11	11 13	D	4 10 78	Watford	Trainee	Wycombe W	36	—
Brown Steve	5 11	11 12	M	6 7 66	Northampton		Northampton T	158	19
							Wycombe W	199	14
Bulman Dannie	5 9	11 12	M	24 1 79	Ashford	Ashford T	Wycombe W	11	1
Carroll Dave	6 0	11 12	M	20 9 66	Paisley	Ruislip Manor	Wycombe W	242	36
Cornforth John‡	5 11	14 06	M	7 10 67	Whitley Bay	Apprentice	Sunderland	32	2
							Doncaster R (loan)	7	3
							Shrewsbury T (loan)	3	—
							Lincoln C (loan)	9	1
							Swansea C	149	16
							Birmingham C	8	—
							Wycombe W	47	6
							Peterborough U (loan)	4	—
Cousins Jason	5 10	12 07	D	4 10 70	Hayes	Trainee	Brentford	21	—
						Wycombe W	Wycombe W	208	5
Devine Sean	5 11	13 00	F	6 9 72	Lewisham	Omonia	Barnet	126	47
							Wycombe W	12	8
Emblen Paul	5 11	12 12	F	3 4 76	Bromley	Tonbridge A	Charlton Ath	4	—
							Brighton & HA (loan)	15	4
							Wycombe W	35	2
Forsyth Mike‡	5 11	12 07	D	20 3 66	Liverpool	Apprentice	WBA	29	—
							Northampton T (loan)	—	—
							Derby Co	325	8
							Notts Co	7	—
							Hereford U (loan)	12	—
							Wycombe W	52	2
Harkin Maurice	5 9	11 05	F	16 8 79	Derry	Trainee	Wycombe W	41	2
Holsgrove Lee	6 1	12 06	D	13 12 79	Wendover	Trainee	Millwall	—	—
							Wycombe W	1	—
Kennedy Richard‡	5 10	10 05	M	28 8 78	Waterford	Trainee	Crystal Palace	—	—
							Wycombe W	—	—
Lawrence Matthew	6 1	12 12	D	19 6 74	Northampton	Grays Ath	Wycombe W	16	1
							Fulham	59	—
							Wycombe W	34	2
Lee Martyn	5 7	9 00	M	10 9 80	Guilford	Trainee	Wycombe W	3	—
McCarthy Paul	5 10	13 10	D	4 8 71	Cork	Trainee	Brighton & HA	181	6
							Wycombe W	100	2
McSporran Jermaine	5 7	10 12	F	1 1 77	Manchester		Wycombe W	26	4
Osborn Mark			M	18 6 81	Bletchley	Trainee	Wycombe W	—	—
Patton Aaron‡	5 7	12 11	M	27 2 79	London	Trainee	Wycombe W	1	—
Read Paul‡	5 8	12 06	F	25 9 73	Harlow	Trainee	Arsenal	—	—
							Leyton Orient (loan)	11	—
							Southend U (loan)	4	1
							Wycombe W	57	9
Rogers Mark	6 1	12 12	D	3 11 75	Geulph		Wycombe W	—	—
Rolling Frank	6 2	13 00	D	23 8 68	Colmar	FC Pau	Ayr U	35	2
							Leicester C	18	—
							Bournemouth	30	4
							Gillingham	1	—
							Wycombe W	—	—
Ryan Keith	5 11	12 06	M	25 6 70	Northampton	Berkhamsted T	Wycombe W	157	13
Senda Daniel	5 9	10 02	F	17 4 81	Harrow	Southampton	Wycombe W	6	—
Simpson Michael	5 6	11 07	M	28 2 74	Nottingham	Trainee	Notts Co	49	3
							Plymouth Arg (loan)	12	—
							Wycombe W	74	5
Taylor Martin	5 11	13 11	G	9 12 66	Tamworth	Mile Oak R	Derby Co	97	—
							Carlisle U (loan)	10	—
							Scunthorpe U (loan)	8	—
							Crewe Alex (loan)	6	—
							Wycombe W (loan)	4	—
							Wycombe W	89	—
Thompson Richard	5 7	12 02	F	2 5 74	Lambeth	Crawley T	Wycombe W	—	—
Vinnicombe Chris	5 8	10 12	D	20 10 70	Exeter		Exeter C	39	1
							Rangers	23	1
							Burnley	95	3
							Wycombe W	41	—
Westhead Mark	6 2	14 05	G	19 7 75	Blackpool		Bolton W	—	—
						Telford U	Wycombe W	2	—
Wraight Gary	5 9	11 13	D	5 3 79	Epping	Trainee	Wycombe W	7	—

Trainees
Copeman, Nathan J; Gray, Edward; Hendry, Iain K; James, Matthew; Johnson, Lee P; Leach, Nicholas P; Williams, Warren R

Scholars
Gostick, Ryan J; Holsgrove, Peter; Johnson, Paul M; Powell, Kevin; Reeks, Stuart J; Townsend, Ben

Associated Schoolboys
Cook, Lewis L; Dixon, Jonathan J; Simpemba, Ian F

YORK CITY

Name	Height	Weight	Pos	Born	Birthplace	Previous	Club	App	Gls
Agnew Steve	5 10	10 06	M	9 11 65	Shipley	Apprentice	Barnsley	194	29
							Blackburn R	2	—
							Portsmouth (loan)	5	—
							Leicester C	56	4
							Sunderland	63	9
							York C	20	2
Connelly Gordon	6 0	11 07	M	1 11 76	Glasgow		York C	28	4
Dawson Andrew	6 0	12 00	D	8 12 79	York	Trainee	York C	11	1
Garratt Martin	5 10	11 00	M	22 2 80	York		York C	38	1
Hall Wayne	5 9	10 06	D	25 10 68	Rotherham	Darlington	York C	331	9
Jones Barry	5 10	11 07	D	20 6 70	Prescot	Prescot T	Liverpool	0	—
							Wrexham	195	5
							York C	68	4
Jordan Scott	5 9	11 02	M	19 7 75	Newcastle	Trainee	York C	127	10
McMillan Andy	5 11	11 09	D	22 6 68	Bloemfontein		York C	421	5
Mimms Bobby	6 2	14 01	G	12 10 63	York	Halifax T	Rotherham U	83	—
							Everton	29	—
							Notts Co (loan)	2	—
							Sunderland (loan)	4	—
							Blackburn R (loan)	6	—
							Manchester C (loan)	3	—
							Tottenham H	37	—
							Aberdeen (loan)	6	—
							Blackburn R	128	—
							Crystal Palace	1	—
							Preston NE	27	—
							Rotherham U	43	—
							York C	35	—
Pouton Alan	6 0	12 02	M	1 2 77	Newcastle	Newcastle U	Oxford U	—	—
							York C	90	7
Reed Martin	5 11	11 07	D	10 1 78	Scarborough	Trainee	York C	36	—
Rennison Graham	6 1	12 00	D	2 10 78	Northallerton	Trainee	York C	1	—
Rowe Rodney	5 8	12 08	F	30 7 75	Plymouth	Trainee	Huddersfield T	34	2
							Scarborough (loan)	14	1
							Bury (loan)	3	—
							York C	90	20
Sharples John‡	6 0	11 03	D	26 1 73	Bury	Manchester U	Hearts	—	—
							Ayr U	53	4
							York C	38	1
Skinner Craig	5 8	11 00	M	21 10 70	Bury	Trainee	Blackburn R	16	—
							Plymouth Arg	53	4
							Wrexham	87	10
							York C	5	—
Thompson Neil*	6 0	13 08	D	2 10 63	Beverley	Nottingham F	Hull C	31	—
						Scarborough	Scarborough	87	15
							Ipswich T	206	19
							Barnsley	27	5
							Oldham Ath (loan)	8	—
							York C	36	8
Tinkler Mark	5 11	11 04	M	21 10 74	Bishop Auckland	Trainee	Leeds U	25	—
							York C	90	8
Tolson Neil*	6 3	11 05	F	25 10 73	Wordley	Trainee	Walsall	9	1
							Oldham Ath	3	—
							Bradford C	63	12
							Chester C (loan)	4	—
							York C	84	18
Warrington Andy*	6 3	12 13	G	10 6 76	Sheffield	Trainee	York C	61	—
Williams Marc	5 9	11 07	F	8 2 73	Bangor	Bangor C	Stockport Co	18	1
							Halifax T	24	6
							York C	11	4
Woods Neil	6 0	12 11	F	30 7 66	York	Apprentice	Doncaster R	65	16
							Rangers	3	—
							Ipswich T	27	5
							Bradford C	14	2
							Grimsby T	226	42
							Wigan Ath (loan)	1	—
							Scunthorpe U (loan)	2	—
							Mansfield T (loan)	6	—
							York C	8	—

Trainees
Batchelor, Peter J; Bullock, Lee; Dibie, Michael; Dufton, Thomas S; Farley, Michael C; Fox, Christian; Mohan, John; Turley, James; Urwin, Jonathan G; Walters, Steven K

Scholars
Fielding, John R; Hakami, Darren R; Howarth, Russell M; Keegan, John K P; Marshall, Christopher; Thompson, Marc; Whitfield, Richard

Associated Schoolboys
Barry, Daniel; Hellens, Lee; Paxton, James M; Pollock, Matthew W; Sadler, Adam; Stuart, Cameron; Surtees, Andrew

Associated Schoolboys who have accepted the Club's offer of a Traineeship/Scholarship/Contract
Darlow, Kieran B; Gowen, Christopher J; Rhodes, Benjamin; Russell, Adam J; Vasey, Peter W J; Wood, Leigh

THE FOREIGN (INTERNATIONAL) LEGION

The following full international players born outside the UK played in the FA Premier League and Nationwide Football League in 1997-98.

	Player	Club	From	Fee £s
ALGERIA	Moussa Saib	Tottenham H	Valencia	2,300,000
ARGENTINA	Nelson Vivas	Arsenal	Lugano	1,600,000
AUSTRALIA	John Aloisi	Coventry C	Portsmouth	650,000
	Andy Bernal	Reading	Syndey Olympic	30,000
	Mark Bosnich	Aston Villa	Croatia Sydney	Free
	Steve Corica	Wolverhampton W	Leicester C	1,100,000
	John Filan	Blackburn R	Coventry C	700,000
	Harry Kewell	Leeds U	NSW Soccer Academy	Free
	George Kulcsar	QPR	Bradford C	250,000
	Stan Lazaridis	West Ham U	West Adelaide	300,000
	Shaun Murphy	WBA	Notts Co	500,000
	Kevin Muscat	Wolverhampton W	Crystal Palace	exch.
	Lucas Neill	Millwall	NSW Soccer Academy	Free
	Mark Schwarzer	Middlesbrough	Bradford C	1,500,000
	Jason Van Blerk	WBA	Manchester C	50,000
AUSTRIA	Martin Hiden	Leeds U	Rapid Vienna	1,300,000
BARBADOS	Greg Goodridge	Bristol C	QPR	50,000
BELARUS	Petr Katchuro	Sheffield U	Dynamo Minsk	650,000
BELGIUM	Philippe Albert	Newcastle U	Anderlecht	2,650,000
BERMUDA	Shaun Goater	Manchester C	Bristol C	500,000
	Kyle Lightbourne	Stoke C	Coventry C	500,000
BOSNIA	Muhamed Konjic	Coventry C	Monaco	2,000,000
CAMEROON	Marc-Vivien Foe	West Ham U	Lens	4,200,000
	Rigobert Song	Liverpool	Salernitana	2,720,000
CANADA	Marc Bircham	Millwall	Trainee	No fee
	Jim Brennan	Bristol C	Sora Lazio	undisclosed
	Carlo Corazzin	Northampton T	Plymouth Arg	Free
	Jason Devos	Darlington	Montreal Impact	undisclosed
	Craig Forrest	West Ham U	Ipswich T	500,000
	Paul Peschisolido	Fulham	WBA	1,100,000
	Mark Watson	Oxford U	Osters	Free
CHILE	Javier Margas	West Ham U	Univ Catolica	2,000,000
CHINA	Sun Jihai	Crystal Palace	Dalian Wanda	500,000
	Fan Zhiyi	Crystal Palace	Shanghai	500,000
COLOMBIA	Hamilton Ricard	Middlesbrough	Deportivo Cali	200,000
COSTA RICA	Paulo Wanchope	Derby Co	Heridiano	600,000
CROATIA	Slaven Bilic	Everton	West Ham U	4,500,000
	Silvio Maric	Newcastle U	Croatia Zagreg	3,650,000
	Igor Stimac	Derby Co	Hajduk Split	1,500,000
CZECH REPUBLIC	Patrik Berger	Liverpool	Borussia Dortmund	3,250,000
	Ludek Miklosko	QPR	West Ham U	50,000
	Pavel Srnicek	Sheffield W	Banik Ostrava	undisclosed
DENMARK	Soren Andersen	Bristol C	Aalborg	410,000
	Mikkel Beck	Derby Co	Middlesbrough	500,000
	Per Frandsen	Bolton W	FC Copenhagen	1,250,000
	Bjarni Goldbaek	Chelsea	FC Copenhagen	350,000
	Brian Laudrup	Chelsea	Rangers	Free
	Jacob Laursen	Derby Co	Silkeborg	500,000
	Allan Nielsen	Tottenham H	Brondby	1,650,000
	Peter Schmeichel	Manchester U	Brondby	550,000
ESTONIA	Mart Poom	Derby Co	Flora	500,000
FINLAND	Mikael Forssell	Chelsea	HJK Helsinki	Free
	Jussi Jaaskelainen	Bolton W	VPS Vaasa	100,000
	Teuvo Molianen	Preston NE	Jaro	undisclosed

FRANCE	Nicolas Anelka	Arsenal	Paris St Germain	500,000
	Marcel Desailly	Chelsea	AC Milan	4,600,000
	Jean-Michel Ferri	Liverpool	Istanbul	1,500,000
	Remy Garde	Arsenal	Strasbourg	Free
	David Ginola	Tottenham H	Newcastle U	2,000,000
	Stephane Guivarc'h	Newcastle U	Auxerre	3,500,000
	Marc Keller	West Ham U	Karlsruhe	Free
	Frank Leboeuf	Chelsea	Strasbourg	2,500,000
	Mikael Madar	Everton	La Coruna	Free
	Emmanuel Petit	Arsenal	Monaco	3,500,000
	Amara Simba	Leyton Orient	Leon	Free
	Patrick Vieira	Arsenal	AC Milan	3,500,000
GEORGIA	Temuri Ketsbaia	Newcastle U	AEK Athens	Free
	Murtaz Shelia	Manchester C	Alania	500,000
	Kakhabor Tskhadadze	Manchester C	Alania	300,000
GERMANY	Steffen Freund	Tottenham H	Borussia Dortmund	750,000
	Dietmar Hamann	Newcastle U	Bayern Munich	5,250,000
	Karlheinz Riedle	Liverpool	Borussia Dortmund	1,600,000
GHANA	Kim Grant	Millwall	Luton T	undisclosed
GREECE	Vassilis Borbokis	Derby Co	Sheffield U	600,000
	Nikos Dabizas	Newcastle U	Olympiakos	2,000,000
	George Donis	Sheffield U	AEK Athens	Free
	George Georgiadis	Newcastle U	Panathinaikos	420,000
	Michalis Vlachos	Portsmouth	AEK Athens	undisclosed
	Theo Zagorakis	Leicester C	PAOK Salonika	750,000
HOLLAND	Dennis Bergkamp	Arsenal	Inter Milan	7,500,000
	Jordi Cruyff	Manchester U	Barcelona	1,400,000
	Ed De Goey	Chelsea	Feyenoord	2,250,000
	Jimmy Hasselbaink	Leeds U	Boavista	2,000,000
	Wim Jonk	Sheffield W	PSV Eindhoven	2,500,000
	Marc Overmars	Arsenal	Ajax	5,000,000
	Jaap Stam	Manchester U	PSV Eindhoven	10,500,000
	Pierre Van Hooijdonk	Nottingham F	Celtic	3,500,000
HUNGARY	Vilmos Sebok	Bristol C	Ujpest	200,000
ICELAND	Gudni Bergsson	Bolton W	Tottenham H	65,000
	Eidur Gudjohnsen	Bolton W	PSV Eindhoven	Free
	Arnar Gunnlaugsson	Leicester C	Bolton W	2,000,000
	Hermann Hreidarsson	Brentford	Crystal Palace	850,000
	Thorvaldur Orlygsson	Oldham Ath	Stoke C	180,000
	Larus Sigurdsson	Stoke C	Thor	undisclosed
ISRAEL	David Amsalem	Crystal Palace	Beitar Jerusalem	800,000
	Eyal Berkovic	West Ham U	Maccabi Haifa	1,700,000
	Alon Hazan	Watford	Ironi Ashdod	200,000
	Ronny Rosenthal	Watford	Tottenham H	undisclosed
ITALY	Francesco Baiano	Derby Co	Fiorentina	650,000
	Nicola Berti	Tottenham H	Internazionale	Free
	Pierluigi Casiraghi	Chelsea	Lazio	5,400,000
	Roberto Di Matteo	Chelsea	Lazio	4,900,000
	Stefano Eranio	Derby Co	AC Milan	Free
	Attilio Lombardo	Crystal Palace	Juventus	1,600,000
	Michele Padovano	Crystal Palace	Juventus	1,700,000
	Gianluca Vialli	Chelsea	Juventus	Free
	Gianfranco Zola	Chelsea	Parma	4,500,000
IVORY COAST	Ibrahim Bakayoko	Everton	Montpellier	4,500,000
JAMAICA	Deon Burton	Derby Co	Portsmouth	1,500,000
	Robbie Earle	Wimbledon	Port Vale	775,000
	Ricardo Gardner	Bolton W	Harbour View	1,000,000
	Marcus Gayle	Wimbledon	Brentford	250,000
	Paul Hall	Coventry C	Portsmouth	300,000
	Darryl Powell	Derby Co	Portsmouth	750,000
	Fitzroy Simpson	Portsmouth	Manchester C	200,000
	Frank Sinclair	Leicester C	Chelsea	2,000,000
LATVIA	Marian Pakhar (Pahars)	Southampton	Skonto Riga	800,000
MACEDONIA	Georgi Hristov	Barnsley	Partizan Belgrade	1,500,000
MOROCCO	Hassan Kachloul	Southampton	St Etienne	Free
NIGERIA	Celestine Babayaro	Chelsea	Anderlecht	2,250,000
	Efan Ekoku	Wimbledon	Norwich C	900,000
	Ben Iroha	Watford	Bristol R	Non contract
	Nwankwo Kanu	Arsenal	Internazionale	4,500,000

NORWAY	Espen Baardsen	Tottenham H	San Francisco	Free
	Henning Berg	Manchester U	Blackburn R	5,000,000
	Stig Inge Bjornebye	Liverpool	Rosenborg	600,000
	Lars Bohinen	Derby Co	Blackburn R	1,450,000
	Jan-Aage Fjortoft	Barnsley	Sheffield U	800,000
	Harvard Flo	Wolverhampton W	Werder Bremen	370,000
	Tore Andre Flo	Chelsea	Brann	300,000
	Alf Inge Haaland	Leeds U	Tottenham H	1,600,000
	Gunnar Halle	Leeds U	Oldham Ath	400,000
	Vegard Heggem	Liverpool	Rosenborg	3,500,000
	Steffen Iversen	Tottenham H	Rosenborg	2,600,000
	Ronny Johnsen	Manchester U	Besiktas	1,200,000
	Bjorn Kvarme	Liverpool	Rosenborg	undisclosed
	Oyvind Leonhardsen	Liverpool	Wimbledon	3,500,000
	Claus Lundekvam	Southampton	Brann	400,000
	Thomas Myhre	Everton	Viking Stavanger	800,000
	Roger Nilsen	Tottenham H	Sheffield U	Free
	Egil Ostenstad	Southampton	Viking Stavanger	800,000
	Petter Rudi	Sheffield W	Molde	800,000
	Ole Gunnar Solskjaer	Manchester U	Molde	1,500,000
	Trond Egil Soltvedt	Coventry C	Rosenborg	500,000
PERU	Nolberto Solano	Newcastle U	Boca Juniors	2,500,000
POLAND	Dariusz Kubicki	Darlington	Carlisle U	Free
PORTUGAL	Jose Dominguez	Tottenham H	Sporting Lisbon	1,600,000
	Hugo Porfirio	West Ham U	Benfica	Loan
ROMANIA	Dan Petrescu	Chelsea	Sheffield W	2,300,000
RUSSIA	Dmitri Kharine	Chelsea	CSKA Moscow	200,000
SLOVAKIA	Vladimir Kinder	Middlesbrough	Slovan Bratislava	1,000,000
SLOVENIA	Ales Krizan	Barnsley	Branik Maribor	500,000
SOUTH AFRICA	Mark Fish	Bolton W	Lazio	2,000,000
	Lucas Radebe	Leeds U	Kaiser Chiefs	250,000
	Eric Tinkler	Barnsley	Cagliari	650,000
SPAIN	Albert Ferrer	Chelsea	Barcelona	2,200,000
ST LUCIA	Earl Jean	Plymouth Arg	Rotherham U	Free
ST VINCENT	Rodney Jack	Crewe Alex	Torquay U	500,000
SWEDEN	Niclas Alexandersson	Sheffield W	IFK Gothenburg	750,000
	Andreas Andersson	Newcastle U	AC Milan	3,600,000
	Jesper Blomqvist	Manchester U	Parma	4,400,000
	Martin Dahlin	Blackburn R	Roma	2,500,000
	Magnus Hedman	Coventry C	AIK Stockholm	500,000
	Jan Jansson	Port Vale	Norrkoping	200,000
	Pontus Kamark	Leicester C	IFK Gothenburg	840,000
	Fredrik Ljungberg	Arsenal	Halmstad	3,000,000
	Jesper Mattson	Nottingham F	Halmstad	300,000
	Roland Nilsson	Coventry C	Helsingborg	200,000
	Martin Pringle	Charlton Ath	Benfica	Loan
	Robert Steiner	Bradford C	Norrkoping	600,000
	Mathias Svensson	Crystal Palace	Tirol	100,000
SWITZERLAND	Stephane Henchoz	Blackburn R	Hamburg	3,000,000
	Ramon Vega	Tottenham H	Cagliari	3,750,000
TRINIDAD & TOBAGO	Clint Marcelle	Barnsley	Felgueiras	Free
	Dwight Yorke	Manchester U	Aston Villa	12,600,000
URUGUAY	Gustavo Poyet	Chelsea	Zaragoza	Free
USA	Brad Friedel	Liverpool	Columbus Crew	1,000,000
	John Harkes	Nottingham F	DC United	Loan
	Kasey Keller	Leicester C	Millwall	900,000
YUGOSLAVIA	Sasa Curcic	Crystal Palace	Aston Villa	1,000,000
	Sasa Ilic	Charlton Ath	St Leonards Stamcroft	undisclosed
	Dejan Stefanovic	Sheffield W	Red Star Belgrade	2,000,000
ZIMBABWE	Bruce Grobbelaar	Lincoln C	Bury	Non contract
	Peter Ndlovu	Birmingham C	Coventry C	1,600,000

TRANSFERS 1998–99

May 1998	From	To	Fee in £
22 Corbett, James J.	Gillingham	Blackburn Rovers	525,000

June 1998			
11 Abbott, Gary	Slough Town	Aldershot Town	8000
11 Beckett, Luke J.	Barnsley	Chester	Free
10 Bradley, Russell	Hartlepool United	Hednesford Town	undisclosed
16 Brebner, Grant I.	Manchester United	Reading	300,000
2 Davies, Kevin C.	Southampton	Blackburn Rovers	7,250,000
12 Finnigan, John F.	Nottingham Forest	Lincoln City	50,000
24 Glass, James R.	AFC Bournemouth	Swindon Town	Free
18 Hercules, Cliff N.	Slough Town	Aylesbury United	undisclosed
9 Milsom, Paul J.	Trowbridge Town	Clevedon Town	undisclosed
23 Reeves, Alan	Wimbledon	Swindon Town	Free
15 Richardson, Stephen J.	Dorchester Town	Bashley	undisclosed
18 Stowell, Matthew D.	Slough Town	Bristol City	15,000
12 Thompson, Alan	Bolton Wanderers	Aston Villa	4,500,000
23 Thorpe, Anthony	Fulham	Bristol City	1,000,000
15 Wicks, Matthew	Arsenal	Crewe Alexandra	100,000
15 Wray, Shaun	Stafford Rangers	Nuneaton Borough	undisclosed

July 1998			
4 Angel, Mark	Oxford United	West Bromwich Albion	Free
1 Angus, Terence	Slough Town	Nuneaton Borough	undisclosed
15 Barclay, Dominic A.	Bristol City	Macclesfield Town	Free
17 Beattie, James S.	Blackburn Rovers	Southampton	1,000,000
8 Bennett, Gary E.	Scarborough	Darlington	Free
10 Berthe, Mohamed	West Ham United	AFC Bournemouth	Free
1 Bolt, Daniel A.	Slough Town	Woking	undisclosed
9 Boxall, Daniel J.	Crystal Palace	Brentford	Free
15 Brady, Garry	Tottenham Hotspur	Newcastle United	undisclosed
8 Brady, Jon E.A.	Hayes	Rushden & Diamonds	undisclosed
22 Bruce, Stephen R.	Birmingham City	Sheffield United	200,000
27 Butler, Paul J.	Bury	Sunderland	600,000
29 Carpenter, Richard	Fulham	Cardiff City	35,000
15 Challis, Trevor	Queens Park Rangers	Bristol Rovers	Free
3 Dandy, Richard	Hednesford Town	Blakenall	undisclosed
17 Gordon, Dean D.	Crystal Palace	Middlesbrough	900,000
8 Granville, Daniel P.	Chelsea	Leeds United	1,600,000
14 Huckerby, Scott	Ilkeston Town	Telford United	undisclosed
31 Holsgrove, Paul	Brighton & Hove Albion	Hibernian	Free
15 Hughes, Leslie M.	Chelsea	Southampton	650,000
15 Liddle, Craig	Middlesbrough	Darlington	Free
16 Lormor, Anthony	Preston North End	Mansfield Town	20,000
31 Moore, Ian R.	Nottingham Forest	Stockport County	800,000
18 Murty, Graeme S.	York City	Reading	700,000
9 Mustoe, Neil J.	Wigan Athletic	Cambridge United	Free
24 Ord, Richard J.	Sunderland	Queens Park Rangers	650,000
30 Owers, Gary	Bristol City	Notts County	15,000
28 Owusu, Lloyd	Slough Town	Brentford	25,000
24 Pallister, Gary A.	Manchester United	Middlesbrough	2,500,000
1 Powell, Christopher G.	Derby County	Charlton Athletic	825,000
9 Quinn, Robert J.	Crystal Palace	Brentford	40,000
1 Redfearn, Neil D.	Barnsley	Charlton Athletic	1,000,000
17 Richardson, Kevin	Southampton	Barnsley	300,000
10 Ripley, Stuart E.	Blackburn Rovers	Southampton	1,500,000
15 Romasz, Anton	Fareham Town	Hastings Town	undisclosed
31 Ruddock, Neil	Liverpool	West Ham United	100,000
20 Scott, Richard P.	Shrewsbury Town	Peterborough United	Trib.
9 Serrant, Carl	Oldham Athletic	Newcastle United	500,000
3 Smart, Alan A.C.	Carlisle United	Watford	75,000
21 Smith, Robert L.	Slough Town	Yeovil Town	undisclosed
17 Spedding, Duncan	Southampton	Northampton Town	60,000
30 Thomson, Peter	Chorley	Lancaster City	undisclosed
3 Thornley, Benjamin L.	Manchester United	Huddersfield Town	Trib.
28 Unsworth, David G.	West Ham United	Aston Villa	3,000,000
17 Van der Laan, Robertus P.	Derby County	Barnsley	325,000
9 Wainwright, Neil	Wrexham	Sunderland	100,000
30 Walsh, Michael S.	Scunthorpe United	Port Vale	100,000
15 Walton, Mark A.	Fulham	Brighton & Hove Albion	25,000
24 Whalley, Gareth	Crewe Alexandra	Bradford City	600,000
10 Whitehall, Steven C.	Mansfield Town	Oldham Athletic	50,000
30 Wright, Darren J.	Cheltenham Town	Stafford Rangers	undisclosed
27 Wright, Ian E.	Arsenal	West Ham United	750,000
7 Wright, Nicholas J.	Carlisle United	Watford	100,000

August 1998			
27 Armstrong, Gordon I.	Bury	Burnley	Free
12 Ashcroft, Lee	Preston North End	Grimsby Town	400,000
14 Battersby, Anthony	Bury	Lincoln City	75,000
6 Beadle, Peter C.	Bristol Rovers	Port Vale	300,000
28 Beesley, Paul	Manchester City	Port Vale	Free
6 Butler, Peter J.F.	West Bromwich Albion	Halifax Town	Free
7 Carr, Darren J.	Chesterfield	Gillingham	75,000
10 Claridge, Stephen E.	Wolverhampton Wanderers	Portsmouth	200,000
6 Coldicott, Stacy	West Bromwich Albion	Grimsby Town	125,000
22 Cooper, Colin T.	Nottingham Forest	Middlesbrough	2,500,000
22 Dailly, Christian	Derby County	Blackburn Rovers	5,300,000
20 Daly, Jonathan P.	St Albans City	Hendon	undisclosed
12 Delisser, Andre	Yeading	Hayes	undisclosed
28 Edworthy, Marc	Crystal Palace	Coventry City	800,000
12 Freedman, Douglas A.	Wolverhampton Wanderers	Nottingham Forest	950,000

	From	To	Fee in £
10 Hall, Paul A.	Portsmouth	Coventry City	300,000
4 Herrera, Roberto	Fulham	Torquay United	30,000
24 Hiley, Scott P.	Manchester City	Southampton	Free
6 Hooper, Dean R.	Kingstonian	Peterborough United	undisclosed
12 Hughes, Richard D.	Arsenal	AFC Bournemouth	20,000
14 Jack, Rodney A.	Torquay United	Crewe Alexandra	500,000
20 Kirkby, Martin J.	Penrith	Workington	undisclosed
28 Lee, Jason B.	Watford	Chesterfield	250,000
20 Lowndes, Nathan P.	Watford	St Johnstone	50,000
20 McCarthy, Sean C.	Oldham Athletic	Plymouth Argyle	undisclosed
7 Mills, Lee	Port Vale	Bradford City	1,000,000
28 Morley, David T.	Manchester City	Southend United	undisclosed
18 O'Brien, Paul J.	Ashford Town	Margate	undisclosed
18 Payne, Stephen R.	Hastings Town	Ashford Town	undisclosed
27 Phillips, Martin J.	Manchester City	Portsmouth	50,000
22 Prior, Spencer	Leicester City	Derby County	700,000
25 Quashie, Nigel F.	Queens Park Rangers	Nottingham Forest	2,500,000
14 Rankin, Isaiah	Arsenal	Bradford City	1,300,000
12 Rizzo, Nicholas A.	Liverpool	Crystal Palace	undisclosed
7 Roberts, Jason A.D.	Wolverhampton Wanderers	Bristol Rovers	250,000
17 Rowett, Gary	Derby County	Birmingham City	900,000
5 Rowlands, Martin C.	Farnborough Town	Brentford	45,000
20 Savage, Robert	Crewe Alexandra	Leicester City	undisclosed
21 Simpson, Wayne W.	Hednesford Town	Nuneaton Borough	undisclosed
14 Sinclair, Frank M.	Chelsea	Leicester City	2,000,000
19 Skelly, Richard B.	Basingstoke Town	Sutton United	undisclosed
28 Swan, Peter H.	Bury	Burnley	Free
6 Taylor, Robert A.	Brentford	Gillingham	500,000
20 Thomas, David J.	Watford	Cardiff City	50,000
6 Todd, Lee	Southampton	Bradford City	250,000
22 Unsworth, David G.	Aston Villa	Everton	3,000,000
20 Vickers, Ashley J.	Peterborough United	St Albans City	10,000
11 Whalley, Gareth	Crewe Alexandra	Bradford City	600,000
17 Williams, Dean	Gateshead	Telford United	undisclosed
20 Williams, Gary L.	Morecambe	Ashton United	undisclosed
6 Windass, Dean	Aberdeen	Oxford United	475,000
6 Wrack, Darren	Grimsby Town	Walsall	Free
22 Yorke, Dwight	Aston Villa	Manchester United	12,600,000

Temporary transfers

	From	To	
28 Allen, Graham	Everton	Tranmere Rovers	
17 Arnott, Andrew J.	Fulham	Rushden & Diamonds	
28 Asaba, Carl E.	Reading	Gillingham	
18 Barrett, Scott	Cambridge United	Kingstonian	
10 Battersby, Anthony	Bury	Lincoln City	
7 Beardsley, Peter A.	Bolton Wanderers	Fulham	
21 Brannan, Gerard D.	Manchester City	Norwich City	
7 Branston, Guy P.B.	Leicester City	Colchester United	
28 Brazier, Matthew R.	Fulham	Cardiff City	
13 Brooker, Paul	Fulham	Stevenage Borough	
4 Brown, Simon J.	Tottenham Hotspur	Fulham	
28 Clarke, Andrew W.	Wimbledon	Port Vale	
22 Clark, Paul D.	Sutton United	Bishops Stortford	
21 Coyne, Christopher	West Ham United	Brentford	
7 Crichton, Paul A.	West Bromwich Albion	Burnley	
6 Crowe, Glen M.	Wolverhampton Wanderers	Exeter City	
11 De Souza, Juan M.I.	Peterborough United	Southend United	
28 Emblen, Paul D.	Charlton Athletic	Wycombe Wanderers	
10 Green, Richard E.	Gillingham	Walsall	
28 Harris, Jason A.S.	Leyton Orient	Preston North End	
4 Hiley, Scott	Manchester City	Southampton	
5 Hughes, Richard	Arsenal	AFC Bournemouth	
20 Hunt, Jonathan R.	Derby County	Sheffield United	
28 Kenny, Patrick	Bradford Park Avenue	Bury	
7 McCarthy, Sean C.	Oldham Athletic	Plymouth Argyle	
14 McIntyre, Kevin	Tranmere Rovers	Doncaster Rovers	
13 McKenzie, Leon M.	Crystal Palace	Peterborough United	
17 Marriott, Andrew	Wrexham	Sunderland	
21 Mean, Scott	West Ham United	Port Vale	
14 Mimms, Robert A.	Rotherham United	York City	
30 Naylor, Martin P.	Shrewsbury Town	Telford United	
28 Nixon, Eric W.	Stockport County	Wigan Athletic	
20 Roach, Neville	Kingstonian	Slough Town	
7 Russell, Craig S.	Manchester City	Tranmere Rovers	
18 Scott, Robert	Fulham	Carlisle United	
26 Simpson, Colin R.	Leyton Orient	Hendon	
29 Soares, Clifton J.	Newport (IW)	Weston-Super-Mare	
7 Torpey, Stephen D.J.	Bristol City	Notts County	
7 Twiss, Michael J.	Manchester United	Sheffield United	
14 Ward, Gavin J.	Bolton Wanderers	Burnley	
22 Wood, Robert M.	Nuneaton Borough	Bedworth United	

September 1998

	From	To	Fee in £
23 Allen, Graham	Everton	Tranmere Rovers	Free
2 Asaba, Carl E.	Reading	Gillingham	600,000
18 Balmer, Stuart M.	Charlton Athletic	Wigan Athletic	200,000
16 Betsy, Kevin	Woking	Fulham	80,000
18 Clark, Paul D.	Sutton United	Bishops Stortford	undisclosed
11 Dobson, Anthony J.	West Bromwich Albion	Northampton Town	25,000
18 Emblen, Paul D.	Charlton Athletic	Wycombe Wanderers	60,000
22 Folan, Anthony S.	Crystal Palace	Brentford	100,000
2 Gray, Andrew D.	Leeds United	Nottingham Forest	175,000
11 Green, Richard E.	Gillingham	Walsall	undisclosed
10 Harlow, David S.	Farnborough Town	Sutton United	undisclosed
24 Harris, Jason A.S.	Leyton Orient	Preston North End	undisclosed

	From	To	Fee in £
23 Hollingdale, Robert	Boreham Wood	Woking	undisclosed
24 Hreidarsson, Hermann	Crystal Palace	Brentford	850,000
3 Kenny, Patrick J.	Bradford Park Avenue	Bury	10,000
11 Martin, Craig A.	Hinckley United	Sutton Coldfield Town	undisclosed
14 McGrath, Stephen M.	Enfield	Yeovil Town	undisclosed
21 Mackay, Malcolm	Celtic	Norwich City	350,000
10 Merson, Paul C.	Middlesbrough	Aston Villa	6,750,000
9 Mustafa, Tarkan	Barnet	Kingstonian	Free
18 O'Neill, Michael A.	Coventry City	Wigan Athletic	Free
3 Peron, Jean F.	Walsall	Portsmouth	150,000
23 Priestley, Philip A.	Atherton LR	Rochdale	undisclosed
8 Samuels, Dean	Barnet	Stevenage Borough	undisclosed
22 Shipperley, Neil J.	Crystal Palace	Nottingham Forest	1,500,000
23 Simonsen, Steven P.A.	Tranmere Rovers	Everton	3,300,000
21 Taylor, Stephen C.	Bromsgrove Rovers	Kidderminster Harriers	undisclosed
30 Tiler, Carl	Everton	Charlton Athletic	700,000

Temporary transfers

7 Adams, Kieran C.	Barnet	Dover Athletic	
17 Alsford, Julian	Dundee United	Barnet	
18 Arber, Mark A.	Tottenham Hotspur	Barnet	
8 Baldry, Simon	Huddersfield Town	Bury	
7 Beardsley, Peter A.	Bolton Wanderers	Fulham	
2 Beckett, Darren	Nuneaton Borough	Moor Green	
3 Birkby, Dean	Yeovil Town	Weymouth	
18 Blatherwick, Steven S.	Burnley	Chesterfield	
4 Bowder, Stanley R.	Wealdstone	Yeading	
7 Brady, Matthew J.	Barnet	Dover Athletic	
21 Brannan, Gerard D.	Manchester City	Norwich City	
4 Broadhurst, Neil O.	Hednesford Town	Belper Town	
18 Brown, Simon J.	Tottenham Hotspur	Kingstonian	
5 Campbell, David J.	Whitby Town	Spennymoor United	
25 Campbell, Neil A.	Scarborough	Telford United	
16 Casper, Christopher M.	Manchester United	Reading	
30 Celaire, Mario	Wealdstone	Aveley	
7 Conlon, Barry J.	Manchester City	Southend United	
11 Connor, John J.	Winsford United	Radcliffe Borough	
12 Creed, James	Hastings Town	Folkestone Invicta	
11 Crowe, Glen	Wolverhampton Wanderers	Exeter City	
11 Davies, Lawrence	Bradford City	Hartlepool United	
7 Dent, Nicholas W.	Hastings Town	Folkestone Invicta	
4 Dobson, Anthony J.	West Bromwich Albion	Gillingham	
11 Edmondson, Darren S.	Huddersfield Town	Plymouth Argyle	
1 Evans, Richard W.	St Albans City	Uxbridge	
7 Francis, Delton M.	Hednesford Town	Halesowen Town	
18 Hale, Matthew J.	Bristol City	Dorchester Town	
17 Hartfield, Charles J.	Swansea City	Lincoln City	
25 Hathaway, Ian A.	Colchester United	Aldershot Town	
18 Haynes, Junior L.A.	Sutton United	Carshalton Athletic	
25 Heckingbottom, Paul	Sunderland	Hartlepool United	
18 Hodson, Simeon P.	Telford United	Altrincham	
25 Holt, Michael A.	Preston North End	Macclesfield Town	
25 Jones, Mark C.	Aylesbury United	Brackley Town	
25 Kemp, Steven	Farnborough Town	Staines Town	
11 Knowles, Michael	Morecambe	Chorley	
11 Lake, Stuart J.	Hednesford Town	Burton Albion	
25 Larusson, Bjarnolfur	Hibernian	Walsall	
18 Mackay, Malcolm	Celtic	Norwich City	
4 Martin, Dean S.	Stalybridge Celtic	Lancaster City	
24 Matthews, Lee J.	Leeds United	Notts County	
8 McCormick, Steven	Dundee	Leyton Orient	
26 McDonnell, Matthew T.	Whitney Town	Marlow	
25 McGregor, Paul A.	Nottingham Forest	Carlisle United	
14 McIntyre, Kevin	Tranmere Rovers	Doncaster Rovers	
13 Mimms, Robert A.	Rotherham United	York City	
25 Monk, Garry A.	Southampton	Torquay United	
25 Norbury, Michael S.	Telford United	Gateshead	
17 Parks, Anthony	Burnley	Barrow	
4 Reeve, Daniel J.	Colchester United	Heybridge Swifts	
28 Robinson, Anthony A.	Kidderminster Harriers	Moor Green	
18 Saville, Andrew V.	Cardiff City	Hull City	
17 Simpson, Paul D.	Wolverhampton Wanderers	Walsall	
25 Smith, Peter L.	Crewe Alexandra	Macclesfield Town	
15 Statham, Brian	Gillingham	Woking	
15 Sturgess, Paul C.	Millwall	Brighton & Hove Albion	
25 Venables, David	Cambridge City	Stamford AFC	
15 Ward, Gavin J.	Bolton Wanderers	Burnley	
17 Winstanley, Mark A.	Burnley	Shrewsbury Town	

October 1998

23 Arnott, Andrew J.	Fulham	Brighton & Hove Albion	20,000
23 Barnes, Steven L.	Birmingham City	Barnet	Free
26 Beall, Matthew J.	Cambridge United	Leyton Orient	Trib
30 Blake, Nathan A.	Bolton Wanderers	Blackburn Rovers	4,250,000
21 Boli, Roger Z.	Dundee United	AFC Bournemouth	50,000
28 Brannan, Gerald D.	Manchester City	Motherwell	378,000
30 Broughton, Drewe O.	Norwich City	Brentford	100,000
29 Butler, Stephen	Gillingham	Peterborough United	Free
2 Caffel, Jason R.	Oxford City	Whitney Town	undisclosed
9 Conlon, Barry J.	Manchester City	Southend United	90,000
22 Cooksey, Scott A.	Hednesford Town	Shrewsbury Town	20,000
6 Dent, Nicholas W.	Hastings Town	Folkestone Invicta	undisclosed
23 Dyer, Bruce A.	Crystal Palace	Barnsley	700,000
29 Forbes, Scott	Bishops Stortford	Braintree Town	undisclosed
26 Francis, Delton M.	Hednesford Town	Halesowen Town	undisclosed

	From	To	Fee in £
1 Froggatt, Stephen J.	Wolverhampton Wanderers	Coventry City	1,900,000
24 Gregg, Matthew S.	Torquay United	Crystal Palace	400,000
23 Harford, Paul	Welling United	Sutton United	undisclosed
23 Hathaway, Ian A.	Colchester United	Aldershot Town	Free
2 Haworth, Simon O.	Coventry City	Wigan Athletic	600,000
5 Haynes, Junior L.	Sutton United	Carshalton Athletic	undisclosed
23 Heggs, Carl S.	Northampton Town	Rushden & Diamonds	65,000
12 Hodgson, Douglas J.	Oldham Athletic	Northampton Town	20,000
12 Horsfield, Geoffrey M.	Halifax Town	Fulham	325,000
9 Jones, David J.	Blackpool	Doncaster Rovers	undisclosed
2 Lawrence, Matthew J.	Fulham	Wycombe Wanderers	undisclosed
15 Liddell, Andrew M.	Barnsley	Wigan Athletic	350,000
5 Marriott, Andrew	Wrexham	Sunderland	undisclosed
16 Mathie, Alexander	Ipswich Town	Dundee United	700,000
16 Mimms, Robert A.	Rotherham United	York City	undisclosed
23 Morgan, Philip J.	Macclesfield Town	Hednesford Town	Free
21 Perkins, Steven W.	Stevenage Borough	Woking	undisclosed
7 Savage, David T.	Millwall	Northampton Town	100,000
15 Sonner, Daniel J.	Ipswich Town	Sheffield Wednesday	75,000
9 Taylor, Scott J.	Bolton Wanderers	Tranmere Rovers	undisclosed
8 Thomas, Roderick C.	Chester City	Brighton & Hove Albion	25,000
30 Vercesi, Richard	Welling United	Ashford Town	undisclosed
23 Warburton, Raymond	Northampton Town	Rushden & Diamonds	35,000
15 Watson, Stephen C.	Newcastle United	Aston Villa	4,000,000
14 Watts, Stephen	Fisher Athletic	Leyton Orient	Free

Temporary transfers

	From	To	
22 Allen, Christopher A.	Nottingham Forest	Cardiff City	
2 Andrews, Wayne M.H.	Watford	Cambridge United	
20 Arber, Mark A.	Tottenham Hotspur	Barnet	
11 Beardsley, Peter A.	Bolton Wanderers	Fulham	
16 Bee, Christopher	Ilkeston Town	Alfreton Town	
29 Bradbury, Lee M.	Manchester City	Crystal Palace	
29 Branch, Paul M.	Everton	Manchester City	
2 Breacker, Timothy S.	West Ham United	Queens Park Rangers	
6 Broadhurst, Neil O.	Hednesford Town	Belper Town	
18 Casper, Christopher M.	Manchester United	Reading	
30 Cooke, Terence J.	Manchester United	Wrexham	
19 Crittenden, Nicholas J.	Chelsea	Plymouth Argyle	
31 Cuggy, Michael S.	Folkestone Invicta	Tonbridge Angels	
23 Dennis, Kevin J.	Brentford	Chesham United	
29 Desouza, Juan M.I.	Peterborough United	Rochdale	
23 Devlin, Paul J.	Sheffield United	Notts County	
16 Earnshaw, Mark W.	Oldham Athletic	Blyth Spartans	
23 Elliott, Stuart T.	Newcastle United	Gillingham	
30 Excell, Nathan C.	Altrincham	Flixton	
8 Fortune-West, Leo O.	Lincoln City	Rotherham United	
16 Guinan, Stephen	Nottingham Forest	Halifax Town	
19 Hale, Matthew	Bristol City	Dorchester Town	
16 Hamilton, Derick V.	Newcastle United	Sheffield United	
30 Hawtin, Dale C.	Leek Town	Witton Albion	
2 Hayward, Andrew	Hednesford Town	Doncaster Rovers	
9 Hodgson, Douglas J.H.	Oldham Athletic	Northampton Town	
31 Holding, Scott	Enfield	Witham Town	
20 Hunt, Jonathan R.	Derby County	Ipswich Town	
23 Ifejiagwa, Emeka	Charlton Athletic	Brighton & Hove Albion	
29 Jackson, Mark G.	Leeds United	Huddersfield Town	
12 Knowles, Michael	Morecambe	Chorley	
16 Lambert, Christopher J.P.	Reading	Walsall	
23 Landon, Richard J.	Macclesfield Town	Nuneaton Borough	
15 Legg, Andrew	Reading	Peterborough United	
16 Lough, Lee A.	Luton Town	Ashford Town	
16 Lunt, Andrew P.	Stourbridge	Redditch United	
26 McDonnell, Matthew T.	Whitney Town	Marlow	
16 McGregor, Marc R.	Forest Green Rovers	Cirencester Town	
29 McKenzie, Leon M.	Crystal Palace	Peterborough United	
2 Miklosko, Ludek	West Ham United	Queens Park Rangers	
7 Miles, Benjamin D.	Slough Town	Chesham United	
30 Moore, Alan	Middlesbrough	Barnsley	
30 Morrish, Adam	Southend United	Dartford	
29 Morrison, Andrew C.	Huddersfield Town	Manchester City	
8 Nixon, Eric W.	Stockport County	Wigan Athletic	
21 Oatway, Anthony	Brentford	Lincoln City	
31 O'Kane, John A.	Everton	Burnley	
31 Ormshaw, Gareth D.	Crystal Palace	Maidenhead United	
30 Perkins, Christopher P.	Southend United	Purfleet	
27 Plummer, Dwane J.	Bristol City	Stevenage Borough	
29 Raven, Paul D.	West Bromwich Albion	Rotherham United	
5 Reeve, Daniel J.	Colchester United	Wivenhoe Town	
17 Robson, Mark A.	Notts County	Wycombe Wanderers	
16 Rollo, James S.	Forest Green Rovers	Cirencester Town	
6 Simpson, Colin N.	Leyton Orient	Boreham Wood	
26 Smith, Peter L.	Crewe Alexandra	Macclesfield Town	
30 Smith, Philip A.	Millwall	Bromley	
30 Spooner, Nicholas M.	Bolton Wanderers	Oldham Athletic	
18 Sturgess, Paul C.	Millwall	Brighton & Hove Albion	
16 Taylor, Craig	Swindon Town	Plymouth Argyle	
21 Thom, Stuart P.	Nottingham Forest	Oldham Athletic	
9 Thompson, Christopher	Ilkeston Town	Matlock Town	
2 Vernazza, Paolo A.	Arsenal	Ipswich Town	
16 Whittaker, David A.	Crewe Alexandra	Belper Town	
16 Williams, Anthony S.	Blackburn Rovers	Macclesfield Town	
6 Williams, Steven R.	Kings Lynn	Gainsborough Trinity	
9 Wilson, Paul R.	Barnet	Aldershot Town	

	From	To	Fee in £
18 Winstanley, Mark A.	Burnley	Shrewsbury Town	
30 Whitney, Scott	St Albans City	Romford	

November 1998

	From	To	Fee in £
24 Adams, Darren S.	Dover Athletic	Welling United	undisclosed
3 Ainsworth, Gareth	Port Vale	Wimbledon	2,000,000
19 Arber, Mark A.	Tottenham Hotspur	Barnet	75,000
4 Bradbury, Lee M.	Manchester City	Crystal Palace	1,500,000
17 Broughton, Drewe O.	Brentford	Peterborough United	15,000
4 Casper, Christopher M.	Manchester United	Reading	300,000
10 Creed, James	Hastings Town	Tonbridge Angels	undisclosed
19 Crichton, Paul A.	West Bromwich Albion	Burnley	100,000
5 Emerson, Dean	Hinckley United	Stafford Rangers	undisclosed
12 Endersby, Lee A.	Aldershot Town	Slough Town	undisclosed
12 Evans, Richard W.	St Albans City	Chertsey Town	undisclosed
25 Ferguson, Duncan	Everton	Newcastle United	7,000,000
13 Finnan, Stephen J.	Notts County	Fulham	600,000
17 Fortune-West, Leopold O.	Lincoln City	Brentford	60,000
1 Green, Marc	Bamber Bridge	Workington	undisclosed
6 Harding, Alexander J.	Dorking	Southall	undisclosed
17 Hayles, Barrington E.	Bristol Rovers	Fulham	2,000,000
25 Impey, Andrew R.	West Ham United	Leicester City	1,600,000
6 Keeling, Darren K.	Gloucester City	Yeovil Town	undisclosed
13 Littlejohn, Adrian S.	Oldham Athletic	Bury	75,000
12 Matthews, Robert D.	Bury	Stockport County	120,000
27 McCann, Gavin P.	Everton	Sunderland	500,000
5 McSporran, Jermaine	Oxford City	Wycombe Wanderers	undisclosed
6 Morrison, Andrew C.	Huddersfield Town	Manchester City	undisclosed
13 O'Connor, Joseph N.	Hednesford Town	Nuneaton Borough	undisclosed
26 Pepper, Colin N.	Bradford City	Aberdeen	300,000
11 Petric, Gordon	Rangers	Crystal Palace	300,000
18 Plummer, Dwayne	Bristol City	Stevenage Borough	Free
13 Reed, Jason D.	Worthing	Bognor Regis Town	undisclosed
5 Reilly, Mark	Reading	Kilmarnock	70,000
20 Scott, Robert	Fulham	Rotherham United	50,000
13 Steel, Paul	Chippenham Town	Yeovil Town	undisclosed
6 Sturgess, Paul C.	Millwall	Brighton & Hove Albion	Free
26 Taylor, Gareth K.	Sheffield United	Manchester City	400,000
6 Thom, Stuart P.	Nottingham Forest	Oldham Athletic	45,000
6 Whelan, Spencer R.	Chester City	Shrewsbury Town	undisclosed
10 Whittaker, Andrew	Southport	Bamber Bridge	undisclosed
27 Whittle, Justin P.	Stoke City	Hull City	Free
27 Williams, Gareth J.	Scarborough	Hull City	Free

Temporary transfers

	From	To
7 Adams, Kieran C.	Barnet	Chesham United
27 Aiston, Sam J.	Sunderland	Chester City
12 Amaral, Neto (Edinho)	Bradford City	Dunfermline Athletic
27 Akers, Lee	Dulwich Hamlet	Carshalton Athletic
26 Allan, Jamie	Ilkeston Town	Alfreton Town
10 Allcock, John P.	Hucknall Town	Hinckley United
27 Beech, Christopher S.	Hartlepool United	Huddersfield Town
26 Bee, Christopher	Ilkeston Town	Alfreton Town
13 Blackman, Barry G.	Sutton United	Croydon
20 Branston, Guy P.B.	Leicester City	Plymouth Argyle
27 Brookes, Darren P.	Doncaster Rovers	Worksop Town
6 Brown, Greg J.	Macclesfield Town	Chorley
26 Brown, Simon J.	Tottenham Hotspur	Gravesend & Northfleet
11 Brown, Stephen R.	Macclesfield Town	Waterford
20 Browning, Marcus T.	Huddersfield Town	Gillingham
26 Bunn, James T.	Tottenham Hotspur	Gravesend & Northfleet
6 Byfield, Darren	Aston Villa	Preston North End
24 Catley, Andrew	Forest Green Rovers	Cirencester Town
19 Clement, Neil	Chelsea	Reading
25 Coombs, Paul A.	Basingstoke Town	Purfleet
14 Cooper, William	Bishop's Stortford	Witham Town
10 Crowe, Jason W.R.	Arsenal	Crystal Palace
28 Cuggy, Michael S.	Folkestone Invicta	Tonbridge Angels
23 Dandy, Richard	Blakenall	Stourbridge
29 Devlin, Paul J.	Sheffield United	Notts County
13 Dobie, Robert S.	Carlisle United	Clydebank
6 Domingos, Alfredo A.	Hayes	Maidenhead United
9 Dublin, Keith B.L.	Southend United	Colchester United
10 Dudley, Craig B.	Notts County	Hull City
19 Earnshaw, Mark W.	Oldham Athletic	Blyth Spartans
27 Edwards, Matthew	Hucknall Town	Sutton United
20 Elliott, Stuart T.	Newcastle United	Gillingham
27 Fearon, Dean A.	Ilkeston Town	Emley
13 Fenn, Neale M.C.	Tottenham Hotspur	Swindon Town
21 Follett, Richard J.	Nottingham Forest	Kings Lynn
26 Gibson, Paul R.	Manchester United	Hull City
16 Guinan, Stephen	Nottingham Forest	Halifax Town
27 Hewlett, Paul M.	Bristol City	Burnley
20 Hodges, Lee L.	West Ham United	Ipswich Town
26 Holsgrove, Lee	Wycombe Wanderers	Aldershot Town
16 Holt, Michael A.	Preston North End	Rochdale
20 Houghton, Scott A.	Peterborough United	Southend United
6 Howey, Lee M.	Burnley	Northampton Town
6 Jackson, Justin J.	Notts County	Morecambe
12 Jones, Stuart C.	Sheffield Wednesday	Crewe Alexandra
13 Knowles, Michael	Morecambe	Chorley
6 Lawson, Ian J.	Huddersfield Town	Blackpool
27 Lee, Alan D.	Aston Villa	Torquay United

	From	To	Fee in £
25 Linighan, Brian	Bury	Cambridge City	
30 Lovelock, Andrew J.	Crewe Alexandra	Witton Albion	
27 Low, Joshua D.	Bristol Rovers	Farnborough Town	
20 Lyttle, Desmond	Nottingham Forest	Port Vale	
27 McDonnell, Matthew T.	Whitney Town	Marlow	
20 McGregor, Paul A.	Nottingham Forest	Carlisle United	
5 McInnes, Derek	Rangers	Stockport County	
27 McIntyre, Kevin	Tranmere Rovers	Barrow	
30 McKenzie, Leon M.	Crystal Palace	Peterborough United	
18 Mendes, Junior	St Mirren	Carlisle United	
24 Miklosko, Ludek	West Ham United	Queens Park Rangers	
28 Moore, Michael T.	Stourbridge	Tamworth	
30 Morrish, Adam	Southend United	Dartford	
18 Newsome, Jon	Sheffield Wednesday	Bolton Wanderers	
6 Niblett, Nigel	Kidderminster Harriers	Atherstone United	
26 O'Kane, John A.	Everton	Burnley	
29 Ormshaw, Gareth D.	Crystal Palace	Maidenhead United	
27 Peel, Nathan J.	Winsford United	Stevenage Borough	
13 Petterson, Andrew K.	Charlton Athletic	Portsmouth	
16 Puckett, David C.	Havant Town	Wokingham Town	
20 Rapley, Kevin J.	Brentford	Southend United	
30 Raven, Paul D.	West Bromwich Albion	Rotherham United	
27 Simpson, Colin R.	Leyton Orient	Sutton United	
24 Smith, Peter L.	Crewe Alexandra	Macclesfield Town	
6 Steiner, Robert H.	Bradford City	Queens Park Rangers	
12 Theobald, David J.	Ipswich Town	Braintree Town	
25 Warhurst, Paul	Crystal Palace	Bolton Wanderers	
5 Warne, Paul	Wigan Athletic	Kettering Town	
3 Whittingham, Guy	Sheffield Wednesday	Wolverhampton Wanderers	
6 Wilder, Christopher J.	Sheffield United	Northampton Town	
3 Wilkins, Ian J.	Lincoln City	Grantham Town	
5 Williams, Paul R.C.	Gillingham	Bury	
30 Witney, Scott	St Albans City	Romford	

December 1998

	From	To	Fee in £
18 Aloisi, John	Portsmouth	Coventry City	650,000
9 Batty, David	Newcastle United	Leeds United	4,400,000
1 Blatherwick, Steven S.	Burnley	Chesterfield	undisclosed
31 Branch, Graham	Stockport County	Burnley	Free
17 Davies, Simon I.	Luton Town	Macclesfield Town	undisclosed
31 Davis, Stephen M.	Luton Town	Burnley	800,000
9 De Souza, Juan M.	Peterborough United	Rushden & Diamonds	exch.
18 Gillespie, Keith R.	Newcastle United	Blackburn Rovers	2,250,000
30 Gutzmore, Leon	Billericay Town	Aldershot Town	11,000
9 Hanlon, Ritchie K.	Rushden & Diamonds	Peterborough United	exch.
16 Healy, Brian	Morecambe	Torquay United	25,000
24 Hope, Richard P.	Darlington	Northampton Town	undisclosed
23 Houghton, Scott A.	Peterborough United	Southend United	undisclosed
30 Jenkinson, Leigh	Wigan Athletic	Heart of Midlothian	50,000
18 Kelly, Raymond	Manchester City	Bohemians	undisclosed
11 Law, Nicholas	Stourbridge	Stafford Rangers	undisclosed
11 Leeding, Stuart	Stourbridge	Stafford Rangers	undisclosed
10 Marsh, Simon T.	Oxford United	Birmingham City	250,000
30 Miklosko, Ludek	West Ham United	Queens Park Rangers	50,000
18 Niblett, Nigel	Kidderminster Harriers	Gloucester City	undisclosed
9 Norfolk, Lee R.	Bishop's Stortford	Sudbury Wanderers	undisclosed
16 Oakes, Andrew M.	Winsford United	Hull City	undisclosed
18 Perry, Jason	Lincoln City	Hull City	undisclosed
17 Pickering, Albert G.	Stoke City	Burnley	Free
16 Richardson, Stephen J.	Bashley	Weymouth	undisclosed
31 Swailes, Matthew	Chorley	Workington	undisclosed
4 Taricco, Mauricio R.	Ipswich Town	Tottenham Hotspur	1,800,000
14 Turner, Graham M.	Telford United	Kings Lynn	undisclosed
18 Tweed, Steven	Stoke City	Dundee	150,000
31 Ward, Ashley S.	Barnsley	Blackburn Rovers	4,250,000
14 White, Christopher J.	Farnborough Town	Slough Town	undisclosed
1 Whitehead, Philip M.	Oxford United	West Bromwich Albion	250,000
18 Whitney, John D.	Lincoln City	Hull City	undisclosed
12 Wilkes, Timothy C.	Kettering Town	Telford United	undisclosed
10 Williams, Paul R.C.	Gillingham	Bury	50,000

Temporary transfers

	From	To	Fee in £
3 Abou, Samassi	West Ham United	Ipswich Town	
11 Adams, Kieran C.	Barnet	Chesham United	
27 Aiston, Sam J.	Sunderland	Chester City	
11 Allcock, John P.	Hucknall Town	Hinckley United	
23 Allen, Lee S.	Leicester City	Kings Lynn	
4 Anderson, Dale R.	Hednesford Town	Blakenall	
11 Anderson, Luke	Dulwich Hamlet	Welling United	
7 Beavers, Paul M.	Sunderland	Shrewsbury Town	
11 Bignall, Michael G.	Kidderminster Harriers	Hednesford Town	
12 Blackman, Barry G.	Sutton United	Croydon	
17 Boylan, Lee M.	West Ham United	Kingstonian	
11 Brabin, Gary	Blackpool	Lincoln City	
22 Branston, Guy	Leicester City	Plymouth Argyle	
27 Brookes, Darren P.	Doncaster Rovers	Worksop Town	
4 Brown, Greg J.	Macclesfield Town	Chorley	
28 Buglione, Martin	Hayes	Gravesend & Northfleet	
4 Burton, Deon J.	Derby County	Barnsley	
4 Byfield, Darren	Aston Villa	Preston North End	
10 Campbell, Andrew P.	Middlesbrough	Sheffield United	
12 Conroy, Michael K.	Blackpool	Chester City	
26 Coombs, Paul A.	Basingstoke Town	Purfleet	

	From	To	Fee in £
28 Davidson, Daniel	Burton Albion	Belper Town	
18 Dawson, Andrew	Nottingham Forest	Scunthorpe United	
18 Dobbin, James	Grimsby Town	Southport	
10 Dudley, Craig B.	Notts County	Hull City	
18 Earnshaw, Mark W.	Oldham Athletic	Blyth Spartans	
11 Edwards, Christian N.H.	Nottingham Forest	Bristol City	
31 Ejiofor, Emeke	Burton Albion	Moor Green	
27 Emsden, Nigel G.	Basingstoke Town	Oxford City	
18 Faulconbridge, Craig M.	Coventry City	Hull City	
31 Fenn, Neale M.C.	Tottenham Hotspur	Lincoln City	
8 Foley, Dominic J.	Wolverhampton Wanderers	Notts County	
23 Follett, Richard J.	Nottingham Forest	Kings Lynn	
18 Forinton, Howard L.	Birmingham City	Plymouth Argyle	
24 French, James R.	Bristol Rovers	Newport AFC	
31 Gain, Peter	Tottenham Hotspur	Lincoln City	
18 Gerrard, Paul W.	Everton	Oxford United	
20 Gibson, James R.	Carshalton Athletic	Egham Town	
1 Graham, Gareth L.	Crystal Palace	Merthyr Tydfil	
24 Grant, Kim T.	Millwall	Notts County	
22 Gray, David	Rochdale	Chorley	
11 Greenacre, Christopher M.	Manchester City	Scarborough	
15 Guinan, Stephen	Nottingham Forest	Halifax Town	
24 Harrison, Gerald R.	Sunderland	Luton Town	
18 Hayter, James E.	AFC Bournemouth	Salisbury City	
24 Henderson, Damien N.	Blyth Spartans	Grantham Town	
29 Holsgrove, Lee	Wycombe Wanderers	Aldershot Town	
16 Holt, Michael A.	Preston North End	Rochdale	
18 Hope, Richard P.	Darlington	Northampton Town	
6 Howey, Lee M.	Burnley	Northampton Town	
17 Hughes, John P.	Chelsea	Stockport County	
15 Hunwick, Colin J.	Worthing	St Leonards	
4 Jackson, Leon	Hednesford Town	Evesham United	
17 Jelleyman, Gareth A.	Peterborough United	Boston United	
12 Jones, Stuart C.	Sheffield Wednesday	Crewe Alexandra	
18 Key, Lance W.	Rochdale	Northwich Victoria	
7 Landon, Richard J.	Macclesfield Town	Atherstone United	
27 Lee, Alan D.	Aston Villa	Torquay United	
23 Linighan, Brian	Bury	Cambridge City	
23 Lyttle, Desmond	Nottingham Forest	Port Vale	
4 Mason, Philip	Aylesbury United	Oxford City	
24 McConnell, Barry	Exeter City	Weston-Super-Mare	
18 McGuckin, Thomas I.	Fulham	Hartlepool United	
31 McIntyre, Kevin	Tranmere Rovers	Doncaster Rovers	
11 McKeever, Mark	Sheffield Wednesday	Bristol Rovers	
1 Martin, Andrew P.	Crystal Palace	Merthyr Tyfil	
4 Morrisey, Terence	Oxford City	Abingdon Town	
10 Morrison, David E.	Leyton Orient	St Albans City	
31 Nartey, Joseph H.	Aldershot Town	Billericay Town	
11 Naylor, Stuart W.	Bristol City	Mansfield Town	
9 Norbury, Michael S.	Telford United	Gainsborough Trinity	
8 Oakes, Andrew M.	Winsford United	Hull City	
11 Patterson, Mark A.	Bury	Blackpool	
11 Perkins, Christopher P.	Southend United	Dartford	
14 Petterson, Andrew K.	Charlton Athletic	Portsmouth	
11 Pierce, David E.	Ashton United	Congleton Town	
11 Power, Lee M.	Plymouth Argyle	Halifax Town	
23 Quailey, Brian S.	West Bromwich Albion	Exeter City	
31 Rainford, David J.	Colchester United	Scarborough	
22 Rapley, Kevin J.	Brentford	Southend United	
11 Salmon, Michael B.	Charlton Athletic	Oxford United	
28 Simpson, Colin	Leyton Orient	Sutton United	
11 Simpson, Paul D.	Wolverhampton Wanderers	Walsall	
19 Springett, Mitchell	Dagenham & Redbridge	Witham Town	
4 Steiner, Robert	Bradford City	Queens Park Rangers	
23 Thompson, Paul Z.	Stevenage Borough	Kettering Town	
30 Walker, Richard M.	Aston Villa	Cambridge United	
24 Warren, Mark W.	Leyton Orient	Oxford United	
18 Watts, Julian	Bristol City	Lincoln City	
11 Weaver, Luke D.S.	Sunderland	Scarborough	
31 Webster, Colin J.L.	Crewe Alexandra	Congleton Town	
2 Whittingham, Guy	Sheffield Wednesday	Wolverhampton Wanderers	
24 Winstanley, Mark A.	Burnley	Scunthorpe United	
8 Wright, Andrew J.	Leeds United	Reading	

January 1999

	From	To	Fee in £
8 Archer, Lee	Rushden & Diamonds	Slough Town	undisclosed
27 Beech, Christopher S.	Hartlepool United	Huddersfield Town	Trib
29 Bennett, Dean A.	Bromsgrove Rovers	Kidderminster Harriers	undisclosed
15 Bent, Marcus N.	Crystal Palace	Port Vale	375,000
8 Brabin, Gary	Blackpool	Hull City	Free
22 Campbell, Neil A.	Scarborough	Southend United	15,000
28 Di Canio, Paolo	Sheffield Wednesday	West Ham United	1,700,000
27 Druce, Mark A.	Hereford United	Kidderminster Harriers	undisclosed
29 Fitzpatrick, Gary G.	Hednesford Town	Telford United	undisclosed
28 Francis, Stephen S.	Huddersfield Town	Northampton Town	undisclosed
29 Griffin, Charles	Chippenham Town	Swindon Town	undisclosed
15 Gurney, Andrew R.	Torquay United	Reading	100,000
22 Hall, Mark A.	Hayes	Slough Town	undisclosed
15 Hartson, John	West Ham United	Wimbledon	3,000,000
16 Holt, Michael A.	Preston North End	Rochdale	undisclosed
22 Jackson, Kirk S.	Grantham Town	Worksop Town	undisclosed
11 Jansen, Matthew B.	Crystal Palace	Blackburn Rovers	4,100,000
28 McAteer, Jason W.	Liverpool	Blackburn Rovers	4,000,000
19 McIntyre, Kevin	Tranmere Rovers	Doncaster Rovers	undisclosed

	From	To	Fee in £
22 McKimm, Steven	Dulwich Hamlet	Farnborough	undisclosed
8 Mellon, Michael J.	Tranmere Rovers	Burnley	350,000
21 Palmer, Carlton L.	Southampton	Nottingham Forest	1,100,000
29 Payne, Stuart	Bromsgrove Rovers	Kidderminster Harriers	undisclosed
21 Peacock, Richard J.	Hull City	Lincoln City	Free
14 Pennant, Jermaine	Notts County	Arsenal	1,500,000
14 Power, Lee M.	Plymouth Argyle	Halifax Town	undisclosed
4 Rougier, Anthony L.	Hibernian	Port Vale	undisclosed
22 Samuels, Dean	Stevenage Borough	Slough Town	undisclosed
27 Sheron, Michael N.	Queens Park Rangers	Barnsley	1,500,000
8 Souter, Ryan J.	Weston-Super-Mare	Bury	undisclosed
4 Staton, Luke R.	Blackburn Rovers	Bolton Wanderers	undisclosed
21 Strouts, James G.	Dover Athletic	Stevenage Borough	undisclosed
15 Tait, Paul	Birmingham City	Oxford United	Free
15 Thomson, Andrew J.	Portsmouth	Bristol Rovers	60,000
7 Warhurst, Paul	Crystal Palace	Bolton Wanderers	800,000
15 Warne, Paul	Wigan Athletic	Rotherham United	Free
28 Warren, Mark W.	Leyton Orient	Notts County	undisclosed
28 Woodman, Andrew J.	Northampton Town	Brentford	undisclosed
28 Yates, Mark J.	Kidderminster Harriers	Cheltenham Town	undisclosed
4 Zahana-Oni, Landry	Bromley	Luton Town	35,000

Temporary transfers

	From	To
14 Adams, Kieran C.	Barnet	Billericay Town
25 Albert, Philippe	Newcastle United	Fulham
29 Allen, Lee S.	Leicester City	Kings Lynn
1 Anderson, Dale R.	Hednesford Town	Blakenall
29 Bailey, Alan	Manchester City	Macclesfield Town
22 Ball, Darren	Ilkeston Town	Stafford Rangers
29 Beckett, Duane L.	Doncaster Rovers	Spennymoor United
16 Blackman, Barry G.	Sutton United	Croydon
22 Boateng, Desmond	Woking	Yeading
14 Bolland, Paul G.	Bradford City	Notts County
8 Bonner, Mark	Cardiff City	Hull City
7 Booty, Martyn J.	Reading	Southend United
20 Branston, Guy	Leicester City	Plymouth Argyle
28 Brookes, Darren P.	Doncaster Rovers	Worksop Town
4 Brown, Greg J.	Macclesfield Town	Chorley
13 Campbell, Andrew P.	Middlesbrough	Sheffield United
13 Campbell, James R.	Peterborough United	Wisbech Town
9 Canoville, Dean	Millwall	Walton & Hersham
29 Carruthers, Martin G.	Peterborough United	York City
22 Catlin, Neil	Hayes	Marlow
29 Claridge, Robert R.	Bristol Rovers	Weston-Super-Mare
15 Clarke, Andrew W.	Wimbledon	Northampton Town
29 Cleaver, Christopher W.	Peterborough United	Grantham Town
18 Clement, Neil	Chelsea	Reading
11 Conroy, Michael K.	Blackpool	Chester City
15 Cooke, Terence J.	Manchester United	Manchester City
29 Cooper, Mark D.	Welling United	Bishop's Stortford
17 Dawson, Andrew	Nottingham Forest	Scunthorpe United
22 Dillnutt, James	Stevenage Borough	Bishop's Stortford
15 Duffield, Peter	Falkirk	Darlington
4 Dyche, Sean M.	Bristol City	Luton Town
29 Elliott, Stuart T.	Newcastle United	Hartlepool United
19 Forinton, Howard L.	Birmingham City	Plymouth Argyle
29 Gerrard, Paul W.	Everton	Oxford United
24 Grant, Kim T.	Millwall	Notts County
20 Gray, David	Rochdale	Chorley
12 Greenacre, Christopher	Manchester City	Scarborough
13 Griffiths, Carl B.	Leyton Orient	Wrexham
28 Harewood, Marlon A.	Nottingham Forest	Ipswich Town
15 Harrison, Craig	Middlesbrough	Preston North End
24 Harrison, Gerald R.	Sunderland	Luton Town
18 Hayter, James E.	AFC Bournemouth	Salisbury City
7 Howey, Lee M.	Burnley	Northampton Town
12 Hughes, John P.	Chelsea	Stockport County
23 Humphreys, Delwyn J.	Stafford Rangers	Bromsgrove Rovers
8 Jackson, John	Middlesbrough	Bishop Auckland
21 Jackson, Justin J.	Notts County	Rotherham United
8 Lawson, Ian J.	Huddersfield Town	Blackpool
22 Longworth, Steven P.	Blackpool	Lancaster City
9 Lovelock, Andrew J.	Crewe Alexandra	Witton Albion
15 Magilton, James	Sheffield Wednesday	Ipswich Town
8 Mardon, Paul J.	West Bromwich Albion	Oldham Athletic
15 McGuckin, Thomas I.	Fulham	Hartlepool United
11 McKeever, Mark	Sheffield Wednesday	Bristol Rovers
21 Miles, Benjamin D.	Slough Town	Wokingham Town
1 Morrish, Adam	Southend United	Dartford
15 Naylor, Stuart W.	Bristol City	Mansfield Town
19 Ormerod, Anthony	Middlesbrough	Carlisle United
1 Ormshaw, Gareth D.	Crystal Palace	Maidenhead United
11 Patterson, Mark A.	Bury	Blackpool
15 Perkins, Christopher P.	Southend United	Dartford
14 Petterson, Andrew K.	Charlton Athletic	Portsmouth
27 Quailey, Brian S.	West Bromwich Albion	Exeter City
27 Rapley, Kevin J.	Brentford	Southend United
12 Reed, Jason D.	Bognor Regis Town	Lewes
19 Rimmer, Stephen A.	Manchester City	Doncaster Rovers
11 Rollo, James S.	Forest Green Rovers	Bath City
29 Russell, Craig S.	Manchester City	Port Vale
29 Scott, Kevin W.	Norwich City	Darlington
29 Simpson, Philip M.	Barnet	Farnborough Town
29 Strodder, Gary J.	Notts County	Rotherham United

	From	To	Fee in £
18 Swailes, Daniel	Bury	Gainsborough Trinity	
22 Tucker, Mark J.	Kettering Town	Wisbech Town	
12 Weaver, Luke D.S.	Sunderland	Scarborough	
14 Whitley, Jeffrey	Manchester City	Wrexham	
28 Whittingham, Guy	Sheffield Wednesday	Portsmouth	
22 Wilkes, Timothy C.	Telford United	Gainsborough Trinity	
7 Williams, Anthony S.	Blackburn Rovers	Macclesfield Town	
15 Williamson, Michael P.	Crewe Alexandra	Congleton Town	
22 Woodman, Andrew J.	Northampton Town	Brentford	

February 1999

	From	To	Fee in £
26 Armstrong, Steven C.	Nottingham Forest	Huddersfield Town	750,000
16 Arnold, Ian	Kidderminster Harriers	Southport	undisclosed
18 Beadle, Peter C.	Port Vale	Notts County	250,000
10 Breacker, Timothy S.	West Ham United	Queens Park Rangers	Free
15 Bullock, Darren J.	Swindon Town	Bury	150,000
19 Collins, Lee D.	Aston Villa	Stoke City	Free
4 Crowe, Glen M.	Wolverhampton Wanderers	Plymouth Argyle	undisclosed
5 Ejiofor, Emeke	Burton Albion	Moor Green	undisclosed
18 Ellington, Nathan	Walton & Hersham	Bristol Rovers	150,000
3 Ellis, Anthony J.	Bury	Stockport County	25,000
26 Fortune-West, Leo O.	Brentford	Rotherham United	35,000
12 Francis, Delton M.	Halesowen Town	Kingstonian	undisclosed
5 Gunnlaugsson, Arnar B.	Bolton Wanderers	Leicester City	2,000,000
24 Hillier, David	Portsmouth	Bristol Rovers	15,000
24 Howard, Steven J.	Hartlepool United	Northampton Town	120,000
19 Howey, Lee M.	Burnley	Northampton Town	50,000
5 Hyde, Graham	Sheffield Wednesday	Birmingham City	Free
11 Jackson, Justin J.	Notts County	Halifax Town	undisclosed
12 Johnrose, Leonard	Bury	Burnley	225,000
26 Leadbeater, Richard P.	Hereford United	Stevenage Borough	undisclosed
17 Marinkov, Alexandre	Scarborough	Hibernian	25,000
2 Marsden, Christopher	Birmingham City	Southampton	800,000
19 McNamee, David	St Mirren	Blackburn Rovers	300,000
25 Morris, Mark J.	Hastings Town	Dorchester Town	undisclosed
19 O'Brien, Burton	St Mirren	Blackburn Rovers	300,000
19 Partridge, Scott M.	Torquay United	Brentford	100,000
19 Pethick, Robert J.	Portsmouth	Bristol Rovers	15,000
25 Rapley, Kevin J.	Brentford	Notts County	50,000
5 Roberts, Darren A.	Darlington	Scarborough	undisclosed
5 Sherwood, Tim A.	Blackburn Rovers	Tottenham Hotspur	3,800,000
19 Simpson, Philip M.	Barnet	Yeovil Town	7500
25 Strodder, Gary J.	Notts County	Hartlepool United	25,000
25 Ward, Gavin J.	Bolton Wanderers	Stoke City	Free

Temporary transfers

	From	To	Fee in £
15 Adams, Kieran C.	Barnet	Billericay Town	
13 Aiston, Sam J.	Sunderland	Chester City	
22 Albert, Phillipe	Newcastle United	Fulham	
4 Alcide, Colin J.	Lincoln City	Hull City	
24 Allen, Bradley J.	Charlton Athletic	Colchester United	
26 Allen, Lee S.	Leicester City	Kings Lynn	
5 Andrews, Wayne M.H.	Watford	Peterborough United	
10 Aspinall, Warren	Brentford	Colchester United	
21 Ball, Darren	Ilkeston Town	Stafford Rangers	
27 Bankole, Ademola	Queens Park Rangers	Grimsby Town	
19 Barrick, Dean	Bury	Ayr United	
5 Basham, Steven	Southampton	Preston North End	
19 Bass, David	Rotherham United	Farnborough Town	
20 Benstead, Graham M.	Basingstoke Town	Chertsey Town	
22 Boateng, Desmond	Woking	Yeading	
14 Bolland, Paul G.	Bradford City	Notts County	
19 Brown, Simon J.	Tottenham Hotspur	Aylesbury United	
19 Brown, Stephen R.	Macclesfield Town	Dover Athletic	
26 Bytheway, Matthew	Telford United	Bromsgrove Rovers	
12 Campbell, James R.	Peterborough United	Cambridge City	
15 Canoville, Dean	Millwall	Walton & Hersham	
11 Catley, Paul D.	Braintree Town	Chelmsford City	
15 Cowe, Steven M.	Swindon Town	Hereford United	
27 Cramb, Colin	Bristol City	Walsall	
22 Crawford, Michael G.	Tamworth	Rothwell Town	
26 Critchley, Neil	Crewe Alexandra	Winsford United	
17 Dawson, Andrew	Nottingham Forest	Scunthorpe United	
5 Dearden, Kevin C.	Brentford	Barnet	
5 Dennis, Kevin J.	Brentford	Welling United	
26 Denys, Ryan H.	Brentford	Carshalton Athletic	
7 Dyche, Sean M.	Bristol City	Luton Town	
15 Earnshaw, Robert	Cardiff City	Middlesbrough	
10 Eastwood, Philip J.	Burnley	Kettering Town	
12 Edwards, Matthew D.	Carshalton Athletic	Molesey	
4 Etherington, Craig	West Ham United	Halifax Town	
17 Falana, Wade R.	Harlow Town	Braintree Town	
12 Fearon, Dean A.	Ilkeston Town	Emley	
19 Franklin, Damien M.	Yeovil Town	Hampton	
5 Goodlad, Mark	Nottingham Forest	Scarborough	
12 Grant, Gareth M.	Bradford City	Halifax Town	
23 Gray, Andrew D.	Nottingham Forest	Preston North End	
12 Gregg, Matthew S.	Crystal Palace	Swansea City	
12 Greenacre, Christopher	Manchester City	Scarborough	
26 Hailstone, Ricky	Kettering Town	Stamford	
18 Hall, Paul A.	Coventry City	Bury	
15 Hamilton, Derick V.	Newcastle United	Huddersfield Town	
26 Harding, Paul J.	Halesowen Town	Harrow Borough	

	From	To	Fee in £
26 Harries, Paul G.	Crystal Palace	Torquay United	
23 Howard, Steven J.	Hartlepool United	Northampton Town	
12 Hunter, Barry V.	Reading	Southend United	
25 Jones, Mark C.	Aylesbury United	Oxford City	
26 Longworth, Steven P.	Blackpool	Accrington Stanley	
12 Lydiate, Jason L.	Scarborough	Rochdale	
11 McKinnon, Robert	Heart of Midlothian	Hartlepool United	
18 Magilton, James	Sheffield Wednesday	Ipswich Town	
13 Mahoney-Johnson, Michael A.	Queens Park Rangers	Aylesbury United	
7 Mardon, Paul	West Bromwich Albion	Oldham Athletic	
26 Marker, Nicholas R.T.	Sheffield United	Plymouth Argyle	
18 Mason, Michael	Macclesfield Town	Burton Albion	
20 Miles, Benjamin D.	Slough Town	Wokingham Town	
26 Mitten, Paul J.	Stalybridge Celtic	Trafford	
5 Morgan, John R.	Enfield	Romford	
19 Morrish, Adam	Southend United	Witham Town	
12 Murphy, Daniel B.	Liverpool	Crewe Alexandra	
26 Nicholls, Kevin J.R.	Charlton Athletic	Brighton & Hove Albion	
27 O'Connor, Derek P.	Bradford Park Avenue	Frickley Athletic	
12 Perkins, Christopher P.	Southend United	Dartford	
24 Phillips, Martin J.	Portsmouth	Bristol Rovers	
19 Quayle, Mark L.	Notts County	Grantham Town	
23 Rapley, Kevin J.	Brentford	Notts County	
12 Reed, Jason D.	Bognor Regis Town	Lewes	
26 Roach, Neville	Reading	Southend United	
12 Roberts, Ben J.	Middlesbrough	Millwall	
18 Serrant, Carl	Newcastle United	Bury	
23 Shepherd, Paul	Leeds United	Tranmere Rovers	
11 Simpson, Colin R.	Leyton Orient	Farnborough Town	
12 Statham, Brian	Gillingham	Stevenage Borough	
16 Stoker, Gareth	Cardiff City	Rochdale	
2 Strevens, Benjamin J.	Barnet	Wingate & Finchley	
17 Swailes, Daniel	Bury	Gainsborough Trinity	
26 Telemaque, Errol	Stevenage Borough	Bromley	
5 Thorpe, Anthony L.	Bristol City	Reading	
26 Tosh, Paul J.	Hibernian	Exeter City	
19 Tucker, Mark J.	Kettering Town	Wisbech Town	
5 Vaughan, Wayne S.	Tottenham Hotspur	Witham Town	
1 Webster, Colin J.	Crewe Alexandra	Congleton Town	
26 Whittaker, David A.	Crewe Alexandra	Winsford United	
18 Witney, Scott	St Albans City	Bishop's Stortford	
26 Wright, Thomas J.	Manchester City	Wrexham	
12 Young, Roy E.	Aldershot Town	Billericay Town	

March 1999

	From	To	Fee in £
31 Adams, Kieran C.	Barnet	Billericay Town	undisclosed
10 Alcide, Colin J.	Lincoln City	Hull City	Free
25 Alexander, Graham	Luton Town	Preston North End	50,000
15 Anderson, Dale R.	Hednesford Town	Burton Albion	undisclosed
19 Andrews, Bradley J.	Norwich City	Bristol Rovers	undisclosed
25 Banks, Steven	Blackpool	Bolton Wanderers	50,000
15 Barnes, Paul L.	Huddersfield Town	Bury	40,000
25 Barras, Anthony	York City	Reading	20,000
26 Beck, Mikkel	Middlesbrough	Derby County	500,000
26 Beevor, Stuart	Stevenage Borough	Aylesbury United	undisclosed
19 Berthe, Mohamed	AFC Bournemouth	Heart of Midlothian	Free
9 Bignall, Michael G.	Kidderminster Harriers	Aylesbury United	undisclosed
25 Boertien, Paul	Carlisle United	Derby County	250,000
12 Borbokis, Vassilis	Sheffield United	Derby County	600,000
24 Brammer, David	Wrexham	Port Vale	350,000
25 Browning, Marcus T.	Huddersfield Town	Gillingham	175,000
25 Butler, Philip A.	Blackpool	Port Vale	115,000
25 Caig, Antony	Carlisle United	Blackpool	40,000
24 Calderwood, Colin	Tottenham Hotspur	Aston Villa	225,000
25 Carruthers, Martin G.	Peterborough United	Darlington	undisclosed
23 Carsley, Lee K.	Derby County	Blackburn Rovers	3,375,000
24 Couzens, Andrew J.	Carlisle United	Blackpool	Free
17 Cowan, Thomas	Huddersfield Town	Burnley	20,000
26 Cresswell, Richard P.W.	York City	Sheffield Wednesday	950,000
25 Darlington, Jermaine C.	Aylesbury United	Queens Park Rangers	25,000
19 Dawson, Andrew	Nottingham Forest	Scunthorpe United	50,000
3 Day, James R.	Arsenal	AFC Bournemouth	20,000
10 Delaney, Mark A.	Cardiff City	Aston Villa	250,000
25 Dudley, Craig B.	Notts County	Oldham Athletic	undisclosed
3 Evans, Paul D.	Shrewsbury Town	Brentford	110,000
25 Evers, Sean A.	Luton Town	Reading	500,000
25 Finney, Stephen K.	Carlisle United	Leyton Orient	Free
26 Freestone, Christopher M.	Northampton Town	Hartlepool United	undisclosed
26 Gain, Peter	Tottenham Hotspur	Lincoln City	undisclosed
25 Gemmill, Scot	Nottingham Forest	Everton	250,000
25 Gibson, Paul R.	Manchester United	Notts County	Free
25 Griffiths, Carl B.	Leyton Orient	Port Vale	100,000
23 Grocutt, Darren	Burton Albion	Tamworth	undisclosed
26 Hendon, Ian M.	Notts County	Northampton Town	30,000
5 Himsworth, Gary P.	York City	Darlington	undisclosed
23 Holdsworth, David G.	Sheffield United	Birmingham City	1,200,000
26 Huck, William R.F.	Arsenal	AFC Bournemouth	50,000
2 Hughes, Daniel P.	Wolverhampton Wanderers	Hartlepool United	undisclosed
12 Hunt, Jonathan R.	Derby County	Sheffield United	exch.
25 Jackson, Richard	Scarborough	Derby County	30,000
10 Jones, Gary	Notts County	Hartlepool United	undisclosed
8 Kavanagh, Jason C.	Wycombe Wanderers	Stoke City	Free
31 Keeble, Shaun R.	Wisbech Town	Kings Lynn	undisclosed

	From	To	Fee in £
12 Kozluk, Robert	Derby County	Sheffield United	exch.
23 Magilton, James	Sheffield Wednesday	Ipswich Town	682,500
24 McGregor, Paul A.	Nottingham Forest	Preston North End	Free
25 McLaren, Andrew	Dundee United	Reading	undisclosed
3 Mohan, Nicholas	Wycombe Wanderers	Stoke City	Free
31 Moore, Craig A.	Crystal Palace	Rangers	800,000
26 Mulryne, Philip P.	Manchester United	Norwich City	500,000
12 Mutchell, Robert D.	Kettering Town	Tamworth	undisclosed
19 O'Neill, Keith P.	Norwich City	Middlesbrough	700,000
25 Phillips, David O.	Huddersfield Town	Lincoln City	Free
25 Randall, Adrian J.	Salisbury City	Forest Green Rovers	25,000
1 Roach, Neville	Reading	Southend United	30,000
24 Scott, Keith	Wycombe Wanderers	Reading	50,000
26 Scott, Philip C.	St Johnstone	Sheffield Wednesday	75,000
30 Sills, Timothy	Camberley Town	Basingstoke Town	undisclosed
25 Smith, Alexander P.	Chester City	Port Vale	75,000
3 Stallard, Mark	Wycombe Wanderers	Notts County	10,000
6 Stoker, Gareth	Cardiff City	Rochdale	Free
12 Stone, Steven B.	Nottingham Forest	Aston Villa	5,500,000
24 Stuart, Graham C.	Sheffield United	Charlton Athletic	1,100,000
31 Talbot, Gary P.	Winsford United	Altrincham	undisclosed
31 Thompson, Christopher	Matlock Town	Ilkeston Town	undisclosed
25 Tracey, Richard S.	Rotherham United	Carlisle United	Free
25 Vincent, Jamie R.	AFC Bournemouth	Huddersfield Town	440,000
12 Watson, Andrew	Garforth Town	Doncaster Rovers	undisclosed
25 Weare, Ross	East Ham United	Queens Park Rangers	undisclosed
3 Wicks, Matthew J.	Crewe Alexandra	Peterborough United	Free
22 Williams, Daniel I.L.	Liverpool	Wrexham	Free
19 Williams, Marc L.	Halifax Town	York City	30,000
5 Windass, Dean	Oxford United	Bradford City	950,000
10 Wright, Benjamin	Kettering Town	Bristol City	30,000

Temporary transfers

	From	To
18 Adams, Kieran C.	Barnet	Billericay Town
26 Adcock, Anthony C.	Colchester United	Heybridge Swifts
25 Albert, Philippe	Newcastle United	Fulham
9 Alcide, Colin J.	Lincoln City	Hull City
11 Aspinall, Warren	Brentford	Colchester United
30 Avdiu, Kemasl	Bury	Partick Thistle
25 Bagshaw, Paul J.	Barnsley	Carlisle United
30 Bailey, Alan	Manchester City	Macclesfield Town
31 Ball, Darren	Ilkeston Town	Atherstone United
19 Berkeley, Dominic A.	Macclesfield Town	Kettering Town
19 Barras, Anthony	York City	Reading
31 Bartley, Daniel R.	West Ham United	Dorchester Town
7 Basham, Steven	Southampton	Preston North End
25 Beavers, Paul M.	Sunderland	Oldham Athletic
21 Benstead, Graham M.	Basingstoke Town	Chertsey Town
3 Berthe, Mohamed	AFC Bournemouth	Brentford
6 Blackman, Barry G.	Sutton United	Dulwich Hamlet
17 Bolland, Paul G.	Bradford City	Notts County
25 Bradbury, Lee M.	Crystal Palace	Birmingham City
25 Bradley, Shayne	Southampton	Swindon Town
18 Branston, Guy	Leicester City	Rushden & Diamonds
5 Bridge-Wilkinson, Marc	Derby County	Carlisle United
31 Briscoe, Anthony M.	Shrewsbury Town	Tamworth
5 Brodrick, Darren	Gravesend & Northfleet	Walton & Hersham
5 Brown, Greg J.	Macclesfield Town	Morecambe
22 Brown, Simon J.	Tottenham Hotspur	Aylesbury United
25 Bruce, Paul M.	Queens Park Rangers	Cambridge United
19 Butler, Stephen	Peterborough United	Stevenage Borough
25 Cadette, Nathan D.	Cardiff City	Merthyr Tydfil
25 Campbell, Andrew P.	Middlesbrough	Sheffield United
1 Carroll, Anthony	Radcliffe Borough	Chorley
1 Carruthers, Martin G.	Peterborough United	York City
10 Catley, Paul D.	Braintree Town	Chelmsford City
2 Claridge, Robert R.	Bristol Rovers	Weston-Super-Mare
1 Cleaver, Christopher W.	Peterborough United	Grantham Town
25 Clement, Neil	Chelsea	Preston North End
2 Collett, Andrew A.	Bristol Rovers	Rushden & Diamonds
25 Connor, Paul	Middlesbrough	Stoke City
25 Conroy, Michael K.	Blackpool	Chester City
12 Cook, Paul A.	Stockport County	Burnley
25 Cornwall, Lucas C.	Fulham	Queens Park Rangers
5 Couzens, Andrew J.	Carlisle United	Blackpool
12 Cowan, Thomas	Huddersfield Town	Burnley
14 Cowe, Steven M.	Swindon Town	Hereford United
25 Coyne, Christopher	West Ham United	Southend United
28 Critchley, Neil	Crewe Alexandra	Winsford United
25 Dalglish, Paul	Newcastle United	Norwich City
25 Darby, Duane A.	Notts County	Hull City
11 Dearden, Kevin C.	Brentford	Huddersfield Town
8 Dennis, Kevin J.	Brentford	Welling United
26 Denys, Ryan H.	Brentford	Carshalton Athletic
18 Devine, Sean T.	Barnet	Wycombe Wanderers
31 Douglas, Andrew R.	Sheffield Wednesday	Slough Town
3 Dublin, Keith B.L.	Southend United	Canvey Island
17 Dudley, Craig B.	Notts County	Telford United
25 Dyche, Sean M.	Bristol City	Luton Town
22 Elliott, Stuart T.	Newcastle United	Wrexham
12 Evans, Keith	Leigh RMI	Lancaster City
3 Excell, Nathan C.	Altrincham	Witton Albion
17 Fairclough, Courtney H.	Notts County	York City

	From	To	Fee in £
25 Follett, Richard J.	Nottingham Forest	Scunthorpe United	
3 Forbes, Steven D.	Colchester United	Peterborough United	
25 French, James R.	Bristol Rovers	Merthyr Tydfil	
25 Fullarton, Jamie	Crystal Palace	Bolton Wanderers	
2 Gerrard, Paul W.	Everton	Oxford United	
25 Gray, Andrew D.	Nottingham Forest	Oldham Athletic	
25 Greenacre, Christopher M.	Manchester City	Northampton Town	
8 Grime, Nicholas	Hitchen Town	Boreham Wood	
24 Guinan, Stephen	Nottingham Forest	Plymouth Argyle	
26 Hailstone, Ricky	Kettering Town	Stamford	
24 Hamilton, Derick	Newcastle United	Huddersfield Town	
25 Hanlon, Ritchie K.	Peterborough United	Welling United	
2 Harrison, Gerald R.	Sunderland	Luton Town	
25 Harrison, Gerald R.	Sunderland	Hull City	
5 Haydon, Nicholas	Colchester United	Kettering Town	
12 Heaney, Neil	Manchester City	Bristol City	
31 Henshaw, Terrence R.	Notts County	Burton Albion	
26 Hocking, Matthew J.	Hull City	York City	
25 Hodges, Lee L.	West Ham United	Southend United	
25 Howells, David	Southampton	Bristol City	
24 Hughes, John P.	Chelsea	Norwich City	
19 Hurdle, Agustus A.	Basingstoke Town	Carshalton Athletic	
25 Hurst, Richard A.	Queens Park Rangers	Aylesbury United	
5 Hutt, Stephen	Hartlepool United	Bishop Auckland	
19 Jackson, Elliott	Oxford United	Stevenage Borough	
25 Jenkins, Stephen M.	Southampton	Brentford	
26 Jones, Mark C.	Aylesbury United	Oxford City	
26 Jones, Nathan J.	Southend United	Scarborough	
31 Kelly, Gavin J.	Whitby Town	Frickley Athletic	
25 Kenny, Patrick J.	Bury	Whitby Town	
26 Knight, Richard	Derby County	Carlisle United	
25 Launders, Brian T.	Derby County	Colchester United	
2 Lee, Alan D.	Aston Villa	Port Vale	
25 Lilley, Derek	Leeds United	Bury	
25 Linighan, Andrew	Crystal Palace	Queens Park Rangers	
19 Linton, Desmond M.	Peterborough United	Swindon Town	
5 Lisbie, Kevin A.	Charlton Athletic	Gillingham	
31 Lovelock, Andrew J.	Crewe Alexandra	Altrincham	
12 Lydidate, Jason L.	Scarborough	Rochdale	
5 Mackenzie, Christopher N.	Leyton Orient	Nuneaton Borough	
24 Mackenzie, Neil D.	Stoke City	Cambridge United	
25 McAuley, Sean	Scunthorpe United	Scarborough	
8 McKeever, Mark A.	Sheffield Wednesday	Reading	
19 Magilton, James	Sheffield Wednesday	Ipswich Town	
8 Mardon, Paul	West Bromwich Albion	Oldham Athletic	
8 Martin, Jae A.	Peterborough United	Grantham Town	
25 Maybury, Alan	Leeds United	Reading	
18 Miles, Benjamin D.	Slough Town	Wokingham Town	
26 Miller, Charles	Rangers	Leicester City	
27 Mitten, Paul J.	Stalybridge Celtic	Trafford	
2 Mohan, Nicholas	Wycombe Wanderers	Stoke City	
13 Mokler, Stephen J.	Gloucester City	Moor Green	
11 Morgan, John R.	Enfield	Romford	
29 Morrish, Adam	Southend United	Witham Town	
16 Murphy, Daniel B.	Liverpool	Crewe Alexandra	
25 Neil, Gary D.C.	Leicester City	Torquay United	
25 Nielsen, Jorgen T.	Liverpool	Wolverhampton Wanderers	
12 Norman, Steven D.	St Leonards	Dover Athletic	
19 Omoyimni, Emmanuel	West Ham United	Leyton Orient	
15 Pitt, Ian	Gresley Rovers	Burton Albion	
9 Platts, Mark A.	Sheffield Wednesday	Torquay United	
1 Quailey, Brian S.	West Bromwich Albion	Exeter City	
19 Quayle, Mark	Notts County	Grantham Town	
25 Randall, Adrian J.	Forest Green Rovers	Salisbury City	
12 Randall, Dean	Ilkeston Town	Alfreton Town	
16 Read, David	Telford United	Stafford Rangers	
9 Reed, Jason D.	Bognor Regis Town	Lewes	
31 Rigby, Anthony A.	Bury	Altrincham	
12 Roberts, Ben J.	Middlesbrough	Millwall	
25 Roberts, Christian J.	Cardiff City	Hereford United	
26 Rose, Karl B.	Barnsley	Mansfield Town	
12 Rowe, Ezekiel B.	Peterborough United	Welling United	
1 Russell, Craig S.	Manchester City	Port Vale	
25 Russell, Lee	Portsmouth	Torquay United	
25 Sale, Mark D.	Colchester United	Plymouth Argyle	
23 Serrant, Carl	Newcastle United	Bury	
26 Sharpe, Lee S.	Leeds United	Bradford City	
30 Simpson, Colin R.	Leyton Orient	Bromley	
25 Smeets, Jorg	Wigan Athletic	Chester City	
25 Smith, James J.A.	Crystal Palace	Fulham	
25 Smith, Paul D.	Charlton Athletic	Barnet	
19 Soley, Stephen	Portsmouth	Macclesfield Town	
31 Spiller, Richard B.	Bristol City	Weymouth	
2 Steiner, Robert H.	Bradford City	Queens Park Rangers	
25 Steiner, Robert H.	Bradford City	Walsall	
4 Strevens, Benjamin J.	Barnet	Wingate & Finchley	
25 Strong, Greg	Bolton Wanderers	Stoke City	
25 Stuart, Mark R.	Rochdale	Southport	
9 Sturridge, Simon A.	Stoke City	Blackpool	
24 Thompson, Paul Z.	Stevenage Borough	Gateshead	
30 Thompson, Scott R.	Chester City	Witton Albion	
25 Thorpe, Anthony L.	Bristol City	Luton Town	

		From	To	Fee in £
31	Timothy, David	Woking	Hampton	
12	Tracey, Richard S.	Rotherham United	Carlisle United	
2	Tucker, Dexter C.	Hull City	Gainsborough Trinity	
19	Tucker, Mark J.	Kettering Town	Wisbech Town	
26	Tuttle, David P.	Crystal Palace	Charlton Athletic	
12	Varty, John W.	Carlisle United	Rotherham United	
10	Vaughan, Wayne S.	Tottenham Hotspur	Witham Town	
31	Vines, Frances G.	Sutton United	Staines Town	
25	Watts, Julian	Bristol City	Blackpool	
12	Whelan, Philip J.	Oxford United	Rotherham United	
5	White, Thomas M.	Bristol Rovers	Kingstonian	
25	Whittaker, David A.	Crewe Alexandra	Winsford United	
1	Whittingham, Guy	Sheffield Wednesday	Portsmouth	
18	Whittingham, Guy	Sheffield Wednesday	Watford	
24	Widdrington, Thomas	Grimsby Town	Port Vale	
25	Wilder, Christopher J.	Sheffield United	Lincoln City	
4	Wilkes, Timothy C.	Telford United	Rothwell Town	
5	Williams, Anthony S.	Blackburn Rovers	Huddersfield Town	
24	Williams, Anthony S.	Blackburn Rovers	Bristol Rovers	
15	Williams, Jamie L.	Coventry City	Hinckley United	
31	Williamson, Michael P.	Crewe Alexandra	Nantwich Town	
25	Willis, Adam P.	Swindon Town	Mansfield Town	
31	Winston, Samuel A.	Chesham United	Sutton United	
16	Young, Roy E.	Aldershot Town	Bognor Regis Town	

April 1999

16	Bolland, Paul G.	Bradford City	Notts County	undisclosed
27	Buggie, Lee D.	Bolton Wanderers	Bury	undisclosed
22	Cooke, Terence J.	Manchester United	Manchester City	undisclosed
16	Coombs, Paul A.	Basingstoke Town	Purfleet	undisclosed
17	Cooper, William	Bishop's Stortford	Bedford Town	undisclosed
16	Devine, Sean T.	Barnet	Wycombe Wanderers	undisclosed
9	Duffield, Peter	Falkirk	Darlington	undisclosed
6	Romasz, Anton	Hastings Town	Chichester City	undisclosed

Temporary transfers

30	Adamson, Christopher	West Bromwich Albion	Mansfield Town	
7	Basham, Steven	Southampton	Preston North End	
4	Blackman, Barry G.	Sutton United	Dulwich Hamlet	
28	Connor, Paul	Middlesbrough	Stoke City	
13	Cook, Paul A.	Stockport County	Burnley	
30	Cowe, Steven M.	Swindon Town	Hereford United	
21	Cryer, Lee	Leigh RMI	Radcliffe Borough	
4	Dublin, Keith B.L.	Southend United	Canvey Island	
22	Glass, James R.	Swindon Town	Carlisle United	
1	Hamlet, Gareth	Halifax Town	Farsley Celtic	
7	Hanlon, Ritchie K.	Peterborough United	Welling United	
29	Hodges, Lee L.	West Ham United	Southend United	
2	Hutt, Stephen	Hartlepool United	Bishop Auckland	
6	Lee, Alan D.	Aston Villa	Port Vale	
3	Lisbie, Kevin	Charlton Athletic	Gillingham	
11	Mokler, Stephen J.	Gloucester City	Moor Green	
7	Nielsen, Jorgen T.	Liverpool	Wolverhampton Wanderers	
16	Russell, Lee E.	Portsmouth	Torquay United	
13	Smith, James A.	Crystal Palace	Fulham	
19	Soley, Steven	Portsmouth	Macclesfield Town	
6	Strevens, Benjamin J.	Barnet	Wingate & Finchley	
22	Stuart, Mark R.	Rochdale	Southport	
1	Thompson, Scott R.	Chester City	Witton Albion	
1	Tucker, Dexter C.	Hull City	Gainsborough Trinity	
14	Varty, John W.	Carlisle United	Rotherham United	
8	Wilkes, Timothy C.	Telford United	Rothwell Town	
15	Williams, Jamie L.	Coventry City	Hinckley United	

May 1999

25	Brown, Daniel	Leyton Orient	Barnet	
28	Burton, Sagi	Crystal Palace	Colchester United	
13	Eaton, Jason	Cheltenham Town	Yeovil Town	undisclosed
26	Hocking, Matthew J.	Hull City	York City	
21	Johnson, Seth A.M.	Crewe Alexandra	Derby County	
27	Kiely, Dean L.	Bury	Charlton Athletic	
27	Low, Joshua D.	Bristol Rovers	Leyton Orient	
27	Read, David	Telford United	Stafford Rangers	undisclosed
27	Spiller, Lee M.	Margate	Gravesend & Northfleet	undisclosed
29	Walling, Dean A.	Lincoln City	Doncaster Rovers	

Temporary transfers

8	Varty, John W.	Carlisle United	Rotherham United	
8	Whelan, Philip J.	Oxford United	Rotherham United	

June 1999

11	Dalglish, Paul	Newcastle United	Norwich City	
29	Eaton, Adam P.	Everton	Preston North End	
25	Forster, Nicholas	Birmingham City	Reading	
4	Gray, Martin	Oxford United	Darlington	
11	Halle, Gunnar	Leeds United	Bradford City	
21	Higgs, Shane P.	Worcester City	Cheltenham Town	undisclosed
17	Irons, Kenneth	Tranmere Rovers	Huddersfield Town	
23	James, David B.	Liverpool	Aston Villa	
14	Lucketti, Christopher	Bury	Huddersfield Town	
21	Nicholls, Kevin J.	Charlton Athletic	Wigan Athletic	
7	Oakes, Andrew M.	Hull City	Derby County	
5	Town, David	AFC Bournemouth	Rushden & Diamonds	undisclosed
15	Turley, William L.	Northampton Town	Rushden & Diamonds	undisclosed
19	Varty, John W.	Carlisle United	Rotherham United	

THE THINGS THEY SAID ...

Ray Harford, after resigning as manager of Queens Park Rangers:
"We lost 4-1 at Oxford and then I found my car had been broken into for the third time. There I was, window smashed, driving round the M25 with the rain soaking me and feeling miserable as sin, after a bad defeat. I thought to myself, maybe someone is trying to tell me something here."

West Ham United's Eyal Berkovic, after being kicked in the head by team mate John Hartson during a training session:
"If my head had been a ball, it would have been in the top corner of the net."

West Ham manager Harry Redknapp with the response to those who had called for Hartson to be sacked:
"Sack him? Oh Yeah, it would be a good idea to sack him. Every Premiership club would take him tomorrow morning if I sack him and give him a £5m signing-on fee because he is worth £10m of anyone's money."

Dermot Keely, coach of Shelbourne who were 3-0 up against Rangers in the UEFA Cup, before losing 5-3:
"I saw Dick Advocaat (Rangers manager) sitting with his head in his hands when it was 3-0 and that was worth the admission money alone."

West Ham defender Julian Dicks with thoughts of becoming a professional golfer once his playing career has ended:
"I definitely don't want to stay in football as a coach and although I always felt golf was a poof's game, I now like it more than football."

Terry Venables on claims in Glenn Hoddle's World Cup Diary that the former England coach wanted his old job back:
"Maybe he knows something. He's supposed to be able to look into the future, isn't he?"

Blackburn manager Roy Hodgson when asked whether an injury and illness situation at Ewood Park constituted a crisis:
"The only crises I can remember were Suez and the Bay of Pigs, when I thought my life might come to an end because of a nuclear war."

Wimbledon's Kenny Cunningham after winning the Republic of Ireland Player of the Year Award:
"My first Award? Goodness, no. I was voted the Worst Dressed Player at Wimbledon for two successive years. I also once won the Young Player of the Year Award at Millwall. Mind you, the average age of the side was 34."

Ron Atkinson on his virtually impossible task of keeping Nottingham Forest from relegation:
"I feel we have to win every game and I feel we also need a few snookers."

Aston Villa manager John Gregory talking about the Brighton & Hove Albion chairman who had criticised Villa for not paying an instalment of Gareth Barry's transfer fee:
"Dick Knight wouldn't recognise Barry if he stood on Brighton beach in an Albion shirt with a ball tucked under his arm and a seagull on his head."

Coventry City manager Gordon Strachan on the touchline fracas which led to his dismissal at Chelsea:
"There was nothing going on apart from a Monty Python sketch with people pushing each other in the chest."

Sir Jack Hayward, the Wolverhampton Wanderers chairman, looking forward to the FA Cup tie with Arsenal:
"I hope Tony Adams is playing because he is the only name I know. All these Viallis, Vieiras and Viagras."

Wolverhampton Wanderers manager Colin Lee, talking about his star attraction, Robbie Keane:
"Talk of £5m is a joke. That wouldn't even buy one of his arms and its his legs which are supposed to be valuable."

West Ham manager, Harry Redknapp after an unexpected victory at Chelsea:
"We could have sat on a 0-0 but last night, I was lying in bed with my wife - if you have a husband as ugly as me, you want to talk about football - and she said 'Harry, if you are drawing, push Trevor Sinclair up'. So I gambled and it worked a treat."

Derby County manager Jim Smith extolling the virtues of his Italian player, Francesco Baiano while making an oblique reference to Stan Collymore:
"The Italians are very used to going to places and playing a different formation. They are not like the Englishmen who might go to clinics when they are left out of the team."

Lee Dixon, questioned by his nine year old daughter Olivia after learning that he had been recalled to the England team to face France at the age of 34:
"Does that mean you won't play for Arsenal any more?"

Nottingham Forest goalkeeper Dave Beasant following his team's 8-1 thrashing by Manchester United:
"It's the lowest I have ever felt after a game. There have been games where I haven't performed but at the end, I was shaking with anger. It was very frustrating. There were so many goals that a ten year old could have put it in from six yards."

Ron Atkinson Nottingham Forest manager after his team was beaten 8-1 at home by Manchester United:
"They murdered us."

Alex Ferguson Manchester United manager speaking of the same match in which Ole Gunnar Solskjaer scored four goals in 13 minutes 46 seconds:
"Four goals for a substitute, I don't think that's happened before either. He's a terrific sub: he picks up the pace of the game straightaway."

Gordon Strachan Coventry manager denied the opportunity to seek absolution from PFA Chief Executive Gordon Taylor:
"Getting hold of him on the telephone is more difficult than getting hold of the Pope."

Martin Neil, captain of Berwick Rangers describing life in the Scottish Third Division:
"I have even taken drugs twenty minutes before a match. It was a few years ago and I paid the price. I started the match on speed and ended it on crutches."

Alex Ferguson, following the 3-2 win over Juventus in Turin:
"Late in the game, I had a real go at Andy Cole for shooting when he had Nicky Butt in a better position. The next thing he scores and he's the greatest thing since sliced bread. I told him that this morning – one minute I was slaughtering him and the next I wanted to give him a kiss!"

Alex Ferguson discussing Blackburn's situation after the draw:
"They're down? They needed a win tonight? I thought they needed a point."

Alex Ferguson at half-time in the European Cup Final:
"The Cup will only be six feet away from you at the end of the night. If you lose, you can't even touch it."

Howard Wilkinson, after taking over temporary charge of England for the friendly international with France:
"I have religious beliefs. Fortunately, I keep them to the dinner table. My specific thoughts about reincarnation are that I don't have any. That might change at half-time on Wednesday."

Ken Bates, Chelsea chairman, suggesting that Eileen Drewery is omnipotent:
"The silly woman said that she ensured that Wright hit the post instead of scoring in Italy to avoid trouble on the terraces. Well, if she's that good, why didn't she ensure that somebody put the ball in the net in Sweden and helping with qualifying rather than hitting the post?"

West Ham United manager Harry Redknapp talking about the club's entry into the Inter Toto Cup:
"This competition will only be worthwhile if we get a UEFA Cup place at the end of it."

Arsenal manager Arsène Wenger discussing his want-away striker Nicolas Anelka:
"We have got to defend our interests and the laws of football or else contracts will no longer have any meaning. Nicolas is leaving for financial reasons, but he is making a bit mistake – he wasn't exactly on the minimum wage with us."

Chris Sutton after his £10 million move from Blackburn Rovers to Chelsea:
"Chelsea are going to create a lot of chances. They scored from every position last season and I just hope I can get on the end of a few myself."

Manchester United striker Teddy Sheringham, before the players were banned from speaking on the subject of the club's withdrawal from the FA Cup:
"Maybe we should even field a stronger team in the Worthington Cup and try to capture all four trophies next season."

Gordon Taylor, Chief Executive of the Professional Footballers' Association, discussing the problems associated with Manchester United and defending the FA Cup:
"Every player I have spoken to has made it clear they want to take part in the FA Cup. I can't name names because the players are obviously in a difficult position. They don't want to be seen criticising a decision made by the club's bosses."

UEFA General Secretary Gerhard Aigner on the same subject:
"The Committee regrets the negative trend which leads to a situation that the holders of the oldest cup competition in the world are not in that competition."

Kevin Keegan after his appointment as England Manager:
"I promise the fans I'll give them everything I've got. I want exactly the same thing for an England side that they want. I've had tremendous support from an awful lot of people to get this job and not least from the fans and I appreciate that."

FIFA President Joseph S. Blatter quoted in FIFA News, May 1999:
"Time and again we hear that football is rolling in money. Television, sponsors, merchandising take-over bids ... never before has the game been the subject of so much commercial activity. Never before have so many financial resources been available to the sport. But available to whom, exactly? Not to everybody, it seems. Try to tell the coach of a local league team that the game has more money than it knows what to do with."

Gerhard Aigner quoted in the May 1999 edition of UEFA Flash:
"The disappearance of the Cup-Winners' Cup – or to be more precise – its incorporation into the UEFA Cup, has not come totally out of the blue. It is not a brutal consequence of the restructuring of UEFA's club competitions, but rather the logical result of the disinterest – in some countries at least – in the domestic cup competitions."

Michel Zen-Ruffinen, General Secretary of FIFA:
"The legal problems facing football are a challenge that suits my training and my personality."

Lawrie Sanchez on his appointment as Wycombe Wanderers manager:
"It's a lovely stadium and a well-run club – just in a bit of bother right now."

Glenn Hoddle revealing that his biggest World Cup mistake was leaving faith-healer Eileen Drewery at home:
"Jesus was a normal, run-of-the-mill sort of guy who had a genuine gift, just as Eileen has."

Glenn Hoddle on the subject of whether he was correctly reported or misquoted:
"It was not what I said and not what I believe – that disabled people are being punished. In the last two years I have issued twenty writs."

Asked how many candidates were under consideration for the England job, the FA's acting Chief Executive David Davies:
"Well, there isn't a queue stretching down Lancaster Gate."

Marc Bircham of Millwall, who qualified to play for Canada because of his French Canadian grandfather:
"I haven't been there yet, but I've seen it on the map."

Germany's national team coach Erich Ribbeck:
"When we lost the friendly in America, you would think from the reaction at home it was bigger than the Second World War."

Alan Shearer discussing his new international striking partner Kevin Phillips, who used to clean the England Captain's boots:
"I don't remember a lot about him at Southampton, except that he told me where to go when I said the boots weren't good enough."

The then Sheffield Wednesday striker Paolo Di Canio, following his altercation with referee Paul Alcock:
"I acted badly towards the referee, but it was just a slight push and he took two or three paces back and fell over, just like a player does when he wants a free-kick. It was a bit of play acting."

FA CHARITY SHIELD WINNERS 1908–98

1908	Manchester U v QPR	4-0 after 1-1 draw	1961	Tottenham H v FA XI	3-2
1909	Newcastle U v Northampton T	2-0	1962	Tottenham H v Ipswich T	5-1
1910	Brighton v Aston Villa	1-0	1963	Everton v Manchester U	4-0
1911	Manchester U v Swindon T	8-4	1964	Liverpool v West Ham U	2-2*
1912	Blackburn R v QPR	2-1	1965	Manchester U v Liverpool	2-2*
1913	Professionals v Amateurs	7-2	1966	Liverpool v Everton	1-0
1920	WBA v Tottenham H	2-0	1967	Manchester U v Tottenham H	3-3*
1921	Tottenham H v Burnley	2-0	1968	Manchester C v WBA	6-1
1922	Huddersfield T v Liverpool	1-0	1969	Leeds U v Manchester C	2-1
1923	Professionals v Amateurs	2-0	1970	Everton v Chelsea	2-1
1924	Professionals v Amateurs	3-1	1971	Leicester C v Liverpool	1-0
1925	Amateurs v Professionals	6-1	1972	Manchester C v Aston Villa	1-0
1926	Amateurs v Professionals	6-3	1973	Burnley v Manchester C	1-0
1927	Cardiff C v Corinthians	2-1	1974	Liverpool† v Leeds U	1-1
1928	Everton v Blackburn R	2-1	1975	Derby Co v West Ham U	2-0
1929	Professionals v Amateurs	3-0	1976	Liverpool v Southampton	1-0
1930	Arsenal v Sheffield W	2-1	1977	Liverpool v Manchester U	0-0*
1931	Arsenal v WBA	1-0	1978	Nottingham F v Ipswich T	5-0
1932	Everton v Newcastle U	5-3	1979	Liverpool v Arsenal	3-1
1933	Arsenal v Everton	3-0	1980	Liverpool v West Ham U	1-0
1934	Arsenal v Manchester C	4-0	1981	Aston Villa v Tottenham H	2-2*
1935	Sheffield W v Arsenal	1-0	1982	Liverpool v Tottenham H	1-0
1936	Sunderland v Arsenal	2-1	1983	Manchester U v Liverpool	2-0
1937	Manchester C v Sunderland	2-0	1984	Everton v Liverpool	1-0
1938	Arsenal v Preston NE	2-1	1985	Everton v Manchester U	2-0
1948	Arsenal v Manchester U	4-3	1986	Everton v Liverpool	1-1*
1949	Portsmouth v Wolverhampton W	1-1*	1987	Everton v Coventry C	1-0
1950	World Cup Team v Canadian Touring Team	4-2	1988	Liverpool v Wimbledon	2-1
1951	Tottenham H v Newcastle U	2-1	1989	Liverpool v Arsenal	1-0
1952	Manchester U v Newcastle U	4-2	1990	Liverpool v Manchester U	1-1*
1953	Arsenal v Blackpool	3-1	1991	Arsenal v Tottenham H	0-0*
1954	Wolverhampton W v WBA	4-4*	1992	Leeds U v Liverpool	4-3
1955	Chelsea v Newcastle U	3-0	1993	Manchester U† v Arsenal	1-1
1956	Manchester U v Manchester C	1-0	1994	Manchester U v Blackburn R	2-0
1957	Manchester U v Aston Villa	4-0	1995	Everton v Blackburn R	1-0
1958	Bolton W v Wolverhampton W	4-1	1996	Manchester U v Newcastle U	4-0
1959	Wolverhampton W v Nottingham F	3-1	1997	Manchester U† v Chelsea	1-1
1960	Burnley v Wolverhampton W	2-2*			

Each club retained shield for six months.   † *Won on penalties.*

AXA FA CHARITY SHIELD 1998

Arsenal (1) 3, Manchester U (0) 0

At Wembley, 9 August 1998, attendance 67,342

Arsenal: Seaman; Dixon, Winterburn, Vieira (Grimandi), Keown, Adams (Bould), Parlour, Anelka, Petit (Boa Morte), Bergkamp (Wreh), Overmars (Hughes).

Scorers: Overmars 33, Wreh 56, Anelka 71.

Manchester U: Schmeichel; Neville G, Irwin, Johnsen, Keane (Berg), Stam, Beckham, Butt (Solskjaer), Cole (Sheringham), Scholes (Neville P), Giggs (Cruyff).

Referee: G. Poll (Tring).

ENGLISH LEAGUE HONOURS 1888-89 to 1998-99

FA PREMIER LEAGUE
Maximum points: a 126; *b* 114.

	First	Pts	Second	Pts	Third	Pts
1992–93*a*	Manchester U	84	Aston Villa	74	Norwich C	72
1993–94*a*	Manchester U	92	Blackburn R	84	Newcastle U	77
1994–95*a*	Blackburn R	89	Manchester U	88	Nottingham F	77
1995–96*a*	Manchester U	82	Newcastle U	78	Liverpool	71
1996–97*b*	Manchester U	75	Newcastle U*	68	Arsenal*	68
1997–98*b*	Arsenal	78	Manchester U	77	Liverpool	65
1998–99*b*	Manchester U	79	Arsenal	78	Chelsea	75

FIRST DIVISION
Maximum points: 138

1992–93	Newcastle U	96	West Ham U*	88	Portsmouth††	88
1993–94	Crystal Palace	90	Nottingham F	83	Millwall††	74
1994–95	Middlesbrough	82	Reading††	79	Bolton W	77
1995–96	Sunderland	83	Derby Co	79	Crystal Palace††	75
1996–97	Bolton W	98	Barnsley	80	Wolverhampton W††	76
1997–98	Nottingham F	94	Middlesbrough	91	Sunderland††	90
1998–99	Sunderland	105	Bradford C	87	Ipswich T††	86

SECOND DIVISION
Maximum points: 138

1992–93	Stoke C	93	Bolton W	90	Port Vale††	89
1993–94	Reading	89	Port Vale	88	Plymouth Arg*††	85
1994–95	Birmingham C	89	Brentford††	85	Crewe Alex††	83
1995–96	Swindon T	92	Oxford U	83	Blackpool††	82
1996–97	Bury	84	Stockport Co	82	Luton T††	78
1997–98	Watford	88	Bristol C	85	Grimsby T	72
1998–99	Fulham	101	Walsall	87	Manchester C	82

THIRD DIVISION
Maximum points: a 126; *b* 138.

1992–93*a*	Cardiff C	83	Wrexham	80	Barnet	79
1993–94*a*	Shrewsbury T	79	Chester C	74	Crewe Alex	73
1994–95*a*	Carlisle U	91	Walsall	83	Chesterfield	81
1995–96*a*	Preston NE	86	Gillingham	83	Bury	79
1996–97*b*	Wigan Ath*	87	Fulham	87	Carlisle U	84
1997–98*b*	Notts Co	99	Macclesfield T	82	Lincoln C	72
1998–99*b*	Brentford	85	Cambridge U	81	Cardiff C	80

††*Not promoted after play-offs.*

FOOTBALL LEAGUE
Maximum points: a 44; *b* 60

	First	Pts	Second	Pts	Third	Pts
1888–89*a*	Preston NE	40	Aston Villa	29	Wolverhampton W	28
1889–90*a*	Preston NE	33	Everton	31	Blackburn R	27
1890–91*a*	Everton	29	Preston NE	27	Notts Co	26
1891–92*b*	Sunderland	42	Preston NE	37	Bolton W	36

FIRST DIVISION to 1991–92
Maximum points: a 44; *b* 52; *c* 60; *d* 68; *e* 76; *f* 84; *g* 126; *h* 120; *k* 114.

1892–93*c*	Sunderland	48	Preston NE	37	Everton	36
1893–94*c*	Aston Villa	44	Sunderland	38	Derby Co	36
1894–95*c*	Sunderland	47	Everton	42	Aston Villa	39
1895–96*c*	Aston Villa	45	Derby Co	41	Everton	39
1896–97*c*	Aston Villa	47	Sheffield U*	36	Derby Co	36
1897–98*c*	Sheffield U	42	Sunderland	37	Wolverhampton W*	35
1898–99*d*	Aston Villa	45	Liverpool	43	Burnley	39
1899–1900*d*	Aston Villa	50	Sheffield U	48	Sunderland	41
1900–01*d*	Liverpool	45	Sunderland	43	Notts Co	40
1901–02*d*	Sunderland	44	Everton	41	Newcastle U	37
1902–03*d*	The Wednesday	42	Aston Villa*	41	Sunderland	41
1903–04*d*	The Wednesday	47	Manchester C	44	Everton	43
1904–05*d*	Newcastle U	48	Everton	47	Manchester C	46
1905–06*e*	Liverpool	51	Preston NE	47	The Wednesday	44
1906–07*e*	Newcastle U	51	Bristol C	48	Everton*	45
1907–08*e*	Manchester U	52	Aston Villa*	43	Manchester C	43
1908–09*e*	Newcastle U	53	Everton	46	Sunderland	44
1909–10*e*	Aston Villa	53	Liverpool	48	Blackburn R*	45
1910–11*e*	Manchester U	52	Aston Villa	51	Sunderland*	45
1911–12*e*	Blackburn R	49	Everton	46	Newcastle U	44
1912–13*e*	Sunderland	54	Aston Villa	50	Sheffield W	49
1913–14*e*	Blackburn R	51	Aston Villa	44	Middlesbrough*	43
1914–15*e*	Everton	46	Oldham Ath	45	Blackburn R*	43
1919–20*f*	WBA	60	Burnley	51	Chelsea	49
1920–21*f*	Burnley	59	Manchester C	54	Bolton W	52
1921–22*f*	Liverpool	57	Tottenham H	51	Burnley	49

Won or placed on goal average (ratio), goal difference or most goals scored.

	First	Pts	Second	Pts	Third	Pts
1922–23*f*	Liverpool	60	Sunderland	54	Huddersfield T	53
1923–24*f*	Huddersfield T*	57	Cardiff C	57	Sunderland	53
1924–25*f*	Huddersfield T	58	WBA	56	Bolton W	55
1925–26*f*	Huddersfield T	57	Arsenal	52	Sunderland	48
1926–27*f*	Newcastle U	56	Huddersfield T	51	Sunderland	49
1927–28*f*	Everton	53	Huddersfield T	51	Leicester C	48
1928–29*f*	Sheffield W	52	Leicester C	51	Aston Villa	50
1929–30*f*	Sheffield W	60	Derby Co	50	Manchester C*	47
1930–31*f*	Arsenal	66	Aston Villa	59	Sheffield W	52
1931–32*f*	Everton	56	Arsenal	54	Sheffield W	50
1932–33*f*	Arsenal	58	Aston Villa	54	Sheffield W	51
1933–34*f*	Arsenal	59	Huddersfield T	56	Tottenham H	49
1934–35*f*	Arsenal	58	Sunderland	54	Sheffield W	49
1935–36*f*	Sunderland	56	Derby Co*	48	Huddersfield T	48
1936–37*f*	Manchester C	57	Charlton Ath	54	Arsenal	52
1937–38*f*	Arsenal	52	Wolverhampton W	51	Preston NE	49
1938–39*f*	Everton	59	Wolverhampton W	55	Charlton Ath	50
1946–47*f*	Liverpool	57	Manchester U*	56	Wolverhampton W	56
1947–48*f*	Arsenal	59	Manchester U*	52	Burnley	52
1948–49*f*	Portsmouth	58	Manchester U*	53	Derby Co	53
1949–50*f*	Portsmouth*	53	Wolverhampton W	53	Sunderland	52
1950–51*f*	Tottenham H	60	Manchester U	56	Blackpool	50
1951–52*f*	Manchester U	57	Tottenham H*	53	Arsenal	53
1952–53*f*	Arsenal*	54	Preston NE	54	Wolverhampton W	51
1953–54*f*	Wolverhampton W	57	WBA	53	Huddersfield T	51
1954–55*f*	Chelsea	52	Wolverhampton W*	48	Portsmouth*	48
1955–56*f*	Manchester U	60	Blackpool*	49	Wolverhampton W	49
1956–57*f*	Manchester U	64	Tottenham H*	56	Preston NE	56
1957–58*f*	Wolverhampton W	64	Preston NE	59	Tottenham H	51
1958–59*f*	Wolverhampton W	61	Manchester U	55	Arsenal*	50
1959–60*f*	Burnley	55	Wolverhampton W	54	Tottenham H	53
1960–61*f*	Tottenham H	66	Sheffield W	58	Wolverhampton W	57
1961–62*f*	Ipswich T	56	Burnley	53	Tottenham H	52
1962–63*f*	Everton	61	Tottenham H	55	Burnley	54
1963–64*f*	Liverpool	57	Manchester U	53	Everton	52
1964–65*f*	Manchester U*	61	Leeds U	61	Chelsea	56
1965–66*f*	Liverpool	61	Leeds U*	55	Burnley	55
1966–67*f*	Manchester U	60	Nottingham F*	56	Tottenham H	56
1967–68*f*	Manchester C	58	Manchester U	56	Liverpool	55
1968–69*f*	Leeds U	67	Liverpool	61	Everton	57
1969–70*f*	Everton	66	Leeds U	57	Chelsea	55
1970–71*f*	Arsenal	65	Leeds U	64	Tottenham H*	52
1971–72*f*	Derby Co	58	Leeds U*	57	Liverpool*	57
1972–73*f*	Liverpool	60	Arsenal	57	Leeds U	53
1973–74*f*	Leeds U	62	Liverpool	57	Derby Co	48
1974–75*f*	Derby Co	53	Liverpool*	51	Ipswich T	51
1975–76*f*	Liverpool	60	QPR	59	Manchester U	56
1976–77*f*	Liverpool	57	Manchester C	56	Ipswich T	52
1977–78*f*	Nottingham F	64	Liverpool	57	Everton	55
1978–79*f*	Liverpool	68	Nottingham F	60	WBA	59
1979–80*f*	Liverpool	60	Manchester U	58	Ipswich T	52
1980–81*f*	Aston Villa	60	Ipswich T	56	Arsenal	53
1981–82*g*	Liverpool	87	Ipswich T	83	Manchester U	78
1982–83*g*	Liverpool	82	Watford	71	Manchester U	70
1983–84*g*	Liverpool	80	Southampton	77	Nottingham F*	74
1984–85*g*	Everton	90	Liverpool*	77	Tottenham H	77
1985–86*g*	Liverpool	88	Everton	86	West Ham U	84
1986–87*g*	Everton	86	Liverpool	77	Tottenham H	71
1987–88*h*	Liverpool	90	Manchester U	81	Nottingham F	73
1988–89*k*	Arsenal*	76	Liverpool	76	Nottingham F	64
1989–90*k*	Liverpool	79	Aston Villa	70	Tottenham H	63
1990–91*k*	Arsenal†	83	Liverpool	76	Crystal Palace	69
1991–92*g*	Leeds U	82	Manchester U	78	Sheffield W	75

No official competition during 1915–19 and 1939–46; Regional Leagues operated.
†2 pts deducted

SECOND DIVISION to 1991–92
Maximum points: a 44; b 56; c 60; d 68; e 76; f 84; g 126; h 132; k 138.

	First	Pts	Second	Pts	Third	Pts
1892–93*a*	Small Heath	36	Sheffield U	35	Darwen	30
1893–94*b*	Liverpool	50	Small Heath	42	Notts Co	39
1894–95*c*	Bury	48	Notts Co	39	Newton Heath*	38
1895–96*c*	Liverpool*	46	Manchester C	46	Grimsby T*	42
1896–97*c*	Notts Co	42	Newton Heath	39	Grimsby T	38
1897–98*c*	Burnley	48	Newcastle U	45	Manchester C	39
1898–99*d*	Manchester C	52	Glossop NE	46	Leicester Fosse	45
1899–1900*d*	The Wednesday	54	Bolton W	52	Small Heath	46
1900–01*d*	Grimsby T	49	Small Heath	48	Burnley	44
1901–02*d*	WBA	55	Middlesbrough	51	Preston NE*	42
1902–03*d*	Manchester C	54	Small Heath	51	Woolwich A	48

Won or placed on goal average (ratio)/goal difference.

	First	Pts	Second	Pts	Third	Pts
1903–04d	Preston NE	50	Woolwich A	49	Manchester U	48
1904–05d	Liverpool	58	Bolton W	56	Manchester U	53
1905–06e	Bristol C	66	Manchester U	62	Chelsea	53
1906–07e	Nottingham F	60	Chelsea	57	Leicester Fosse	48
1907–08e	Bradford C	54	Leicester Fosse	52	Oldham Ath	50
1908–09e	Bolton W	52	Tottenham H*	51	WBA	51
1909–10e	Manchester C	54	Oldham Ath*	53	Hull C*	53
1910–11e	WBA	53	Bolton W	51	Chelsea	49
1911–12e	Derby Co*	54	Chelsea	54	Burnley	52
1912–13e	Preston NE	53	Burnley	50	Birmingham	46
1913–14e	Notts Co	53	Bradford PA*	49	Woolwich A	49
1914–15e	Derby Co	53	Preston NE	50	Barnsley	47
1919–20f	Tottenham H	70	Huddersfield T	64	Birmingham	56
1920–21f	Birmingham*	58	Cardiff C	58	Bristol C	51
1921–22f	Nottingham F	56	Stoke C*	52	Barnsley	52
1922–23f	Notts Co	53	West Ham U*	51	Leicester C	51
1923–24f	Leeds U	54	Bury*	51	Derby Co	51
1924–25f	Leicester C	59	Manchester U	57	Derby Co	55
1925–26f	Sheffield W	60	Derby Co	57	Chelsea	52
1926–27f	Middlesbrough	62	Portsmouth*	54	Manchester C	54
1927–28f	Manchester C	59	Leeds U	57	Chelsea	54
1928–29f	Middlesbrough	55	Grimsby T	53	Bradford PA*	48
1929–30f	Blackpool	58	Chelsea	55	Oldham Ath	53
1930–31f	Everton	61	WBA	54	Tottenham H	51
1931–32f	Wolverhampton W	56	Leeds U	54	Stoke C	52
1932–33f	Stoke C	56	Tottenham H	55	Fulham	50
1933–34f	Grimsby T	59	Preston NE	52	Bolton W*	51
1934–35f	Brentford	61	Bolton W*	56	West Ham U	56
1935–36f	Manchester U	56	Charlton Ath	55	Sheffield U*	52
1936–37f	Leicester C	56	Blackpool	55	Bury	52
1937–38f	Aston Villa	57	Manchester U*	53	Sheffield U	53
1938–39f	Blackburn R	55	Sheffield U	54	Sheffield W	53
1946–47f	Manchester C	62	Burnley	58	Birmingham C	55
1947–48f	Birmingham C	59	Newcastle U	56	Southampton	52
1948–49f	Fulham	57	WBA	56	Southampton	55
1949–50f	Tottenham H	61	Sheffield W*	52	Sheffield U*	52
1950–51f	Preston NE	57	Manchester C	52	Cardiff C	50
1951–52f	Sheffield W	53	Cardiff C*	51	Birmingham C	51
1952–53f	Sheffield U	60	Huddersfield T	58	Luton T	52
1953–54f	Leicester C*	56	Everton	56	Blackburn R	55
1954–55f	Birmingham C*	54	Luton T*	54	Rotherham U	54
1955–56f	Sheffield W	55	Leeds U	52	Liverpool*	48
1956–57f	Leicester C	61	Nottingham F	54	Liverpool	53
1957–58f	West Ham U	57	Blackburn R	56	Charlton Ath	55
1958–59f	Sheffield W	62	Fulham	60	Sheffield U*	53
1959–60f	Aston Villa	59	Cardiff C	58	Liverpool*	50
1960–61f	Ipswich T	59	Sheffield U	58	Liverpool	52
1961–62f	Liverpool	62	Leyton Orient	54	Sunderland	53
1962–63f	Stoke C	53	Chelsea*	52	Sunderland	52
1963–64f	Leeds U	63	Sunderland	61	Preston NE	56
1964–65f	Newcastle U	57	Northampton T	56	Bolton W	50
1965–66f	Manchester C	59	Southampton	54	Coventry C	53
1966–67f	Coventry C	59	Wolverhampton W	58	Carlisle U	52
1967–68f	Ipswich T	59	QPR*	58	Blackpool	58
1968–69f	Derby Co	63	Crystal Palace	56	Charlton Ath	50
1969–70f	Huddersfield T	60	Blackpool	53	Leicester C	51
1970–71f	Leicester C	59	Sheffield U	56	Cardiff C*	53
1971–72f	Norwich C	57	Birmingham C	56	Millwall	55
1972–73f	Burnley	62	QPR	61	Aston Villa	50
1973–74f	Middlesbrough	65	Luton T	50	Carlisle U	49
1974–75f	Manchester U	61	Aston Villa	58	Norwich C	53
1975–76f	Sunderland	56	Bristol C*	53	WBA	53
1976–77f	Wolverhampton W	57	Chelsea	55	Nottingham F	52
1977–78f	Bolton W	58	Southampton	57	Tottenham H*	56
1978–79f	Crystal Palace	57	Brighton & HA*	56	Stoke C	56
1979–80f	Leicester C	55	Sunderland	54	Birmingham C*	53
1980–81f	West Ham U	66	Notts Co	53	Swansea C*	50
1981–82g	Luton T	88	Watford	80	Norwich C	71
1982–83g	QPR	85	Wolverhampton W	75	Leicester C	70
1983–84g	Chelsea*	88	Sheffield W	88	Newcastle U	80
1984–85g	Oxford U	84	Birmingham C	82	Manchester C	74
1985–86g	Norwich C	84	Charlton Ath	77	Wimbledon	76
1986–87g	Derby Co	84	Portsmouth	78	Oldham Ath††	75
1987–88h	Millwall	82	Aston Villa*	78	Middlesbrough	78
1988–89k	Chelsea	99	Manchester C	82	Crystal Palace	81
1989–90k	Leeds U*	85	Sheffield U	85	Newcastle U††	80
1990–91k	Oldham Ath	88	West Ham U	87	Sheffield W	82
1991–92k	Ipswich T	84	Middlesbrough	80	Derby Co	78

No official competition during 1915–19 and 1939–46; Regional Leagues operated.
*Won or placed on goal average (ratio)/goal difference.
††Not promoted after play-offs.

THIRD DIVISION to 1991–92
Maximum points: 92; 138 from 1981–82.

	First	Pts	Second	Pts	Third	Pts
1958–59	Plymouth Arg	62	Hull C	61	Brentford*	57
1959–60	Southampton	61	Norwich C	59	Shrewsbury T*	52
1960–61	Bury	68	Walsall	62	QPR	60
1961–62	Portsmouth	65	Grimsby T	62	Bournemouth*	59
1962–63	Northampton T	62	Swindon T	58	Port Vale	54
1963–64	Coventry C*	60	Crystal Palace	60	Watford	58
1964–65	Carlisle U	60	Bristol C*	59	Mansfield T	59
1965–66	Hull C	69	Millwall	65	QPR	57
1966–67	QPR	67	Middlesbrough	55	Watford	54
1967–68	Oxford U	57	Bury	56	Shrewsbury T	55
1968–69	Watford*	64	Swindon T	64	Luton T	61
1969–70	Orient	62	Luton T	60	Bristol R	56
1970–71	Preston NE	61	Fulham	60	Halifax T	56
1971–72	Aston Villa	70	Brighton & HA	65	Bournemouth*	62
1972–73	Bolton W	61	Notts Co	57	Blackburn R	55
1973–74	Oldham Ath	62	Bristol R*	61	York C	61
1974–75	Blackburn R	60	Plymouth Arg	59	Charlton Ath	55
1975–76	Hereford U	63	Cardiff C	57	Millwall	56
1976–77	Mansfield T	64	Brighton & HA	61	Crystal Palace*	59
1977–78	Wrexham	61	Cambridge U	58	Preston NE*	56
1978–79	Shrewsbury T	61	Watford*	60	Swansea C	60
1979–80	Grimsby T	62	Blackburn R	59	Sheffield W	58
1980–81	Rotherham U	61	Barnsley*	59	Charlton Ath	59
1981–82	Burnley*	80	Carlisle U	80	Fulham	78
1982–83	Portsmouth	91	Cardiff C	86	Huddersfield T	82
1983–84	Oxford U	95	Wimbledon	87	Sheffield U*	83
1984–85	Bradford C	94	Millwall	90	Hull C	87
1985–86	Reading	94	Plymouth Arg	87	Derby Co	84
1986–87	Bournemouth	97	Middlesbrough	94	Swindon T	87
1987–88	Sunderland	93	Brighton & HA	84	Walsall	82
1988–89	Wolverhampton W	92	Sheffield U*	84	Port Vale	84
1989–90	Bristol R	93	Bristol C	91	Notts Co	87
1990–91	Cambridge U	86	Southend U	85	Grimsby T*	83
1991–92	Brentford	82	Birmingham C	81	Huddersfield T	78

FOURTH DIVISION (1958–1992)
Maximum points: 92; 138 from 1981–82.

	First	Pts	Second	Pts	Third	Pts	Fourth	Pts
1958–59	Port Vale	64	Coventry C*	60	York C	60	Shrewsbury T	58
1959–60	Walsall	65	Notts Co*	60	Torquay U	60	Watford	57
1960–61	Peterborough U	66	Crystal Palace	64	Northampton T*	60	Bradford PA	60
1961–62†	Millwall	56	Colchester U	55	Wrexham	53	Carlisle U	52
1962–63	Brentford	62	Oldham Ath*	59	Crewe Alex	59	Mansfield T*	57
1963–64	Gillingham*	60	Carlisle U	60	Workington	59	Exeter C	58
1964–65	Brighton & HA	63	Millwall*	62	York C	62	Oxford U	61
1965–66	Doncaster R*	59	Darlington	59	Torquay U	58	Colchester U*	56
1966–67	Stockport Co	64	Southport*	59	Barrow	59	Tranmere R	58
1967–68	Luton T	66	Barnsley	61	Hartlepools U	60	Crewe Alex	58
1968–69	Doncaster R	59	Halifax T	57	Rochdale*	56	Bradford C	56
1969–70	Chesterfield	64	Wrexham	61	Swansea C	60	Port Vale	59
1970–71	Notts Co	69	Bournemouth	60	Oldham Ath	59	York C	56
1971–72	Grimsby T	63	Southend U	60	Brentford	59	Scunthorpe U	57
1972–73	Southport	62	Hereford U	58	Cambridge U	57	Aldershot*	56
1973–74	Peterborough U	65	Gillingham	62	Colchester U	60	Bury	59
1974–75	Mansfield T	68	Shrewsbury T	62	Rotherham U	59	Chester*	57
1975–76	Lincoln C	74	Northampton T	68	Reading	60	Tranmere R	58
1976–77	Cambridge U	65	Exeter C	62	Colchester U*	59	Bradford C	59
1977–78	Watford	71	Southend U	60	Swansea C*	56	Brentford	56
1978–79	Reading	65	Grimsby T*	61	Wimbledon*	61	Barnsley	61
1979–80	Huddersfield T	66	Walsall	64	Newport Co	61	Portsmouth*	60
1980–81	Southend U	67	Lincoln C	65	Doncaster R	56	Wimbledon	55
1981–82	Sheffield U	96	Bradford C*	91	Wigan Ath	91	Bournemouth	88
1982–83	Wimbledon	98	Hull C	90	Port Vale	88	Scunthorpe U	83
1983–84	York C	101	Doncaster R	85	Reading*	82	Bristol C	82
1984–85	Chesterfield	91	Blackpool	86	Darlington	85	Bury	84
1985–86	Swindon T	102	Chester C	84	Mansfield T	81	Port Vale	79
1986–87	Northampton T	99	Preston NE	90	Southend U	80	Wolverhampton W††	79
1987–88	Wolverhampton W	90	Cardiff C	85	Bolton W	78	Scunthorpe U††	77
1988–89	Rotherham U	82	Tranmere R	80	Crewe Alex	78	Scunthorpe U††	77
1989–90	Exeter C	89	Grimsby T	79	Southend U	75	Stockport Co††	74
1990–91	Darlington	83	Stockport Co*	82	Hartlepool U	82	Peterborough U	80
1991–92†*	Burnley	83	Rotherham U*	77	Mansfield T	77	Blackpool	76

* Won or placed on goal average (ratio)/goal difference.

†*Maximum points:* 88 owing to Accrington Stanley's resignation.   ††*Not promoted after play-offs.*

†**Maximum points:* 126 owing to Aldershot being expelled.

THIRD DIVISION—SOUTH (1920–1958)
1920–21 season as Third Division.
Maximum points: a 84; b 92.

	First	Pts	Second	Pts	Third	Pts
1920–21a	Crystal Palace	59	Southampton	54	QPR	53
1921–22a	Southampton*	61	Plymouth Arg	61	Portsmouth	53
1922–23a	Bristol C	59	Plymouth Arg*	53	Swansea T	53
1923–24a	Portsmouth	59	Plymouth Arg	55	Millwall	54
1924–25a	Swansea T	57	Plymouth Arg	56	Bristol C	53
1925–26a	Reading	57	Plymouth Arg	56	Millwall	53
1926–27a	Bristol C	62	Plymouth Arg	60	Millwall	56
1927–28a	Millwall	65	Northampton T	55	Plymouth Arg	53
1928–29a	Charlton Ath*	54	Crystal Palace	54	Northampton T*	52
1929–30a	Plymouth Arg	68	Brentford	61	QPR	51
1930–31a	Notts Co	59	Crystal Palace	51	Brentford	50
1931–32a	Fulham	57	Reading	55	Southend U	53
1932–33a	Brentford	62	Exeter C	58	Norwich C	57
1933–34a	Norwich C	61	Coventry C*	54	Reading*	54
1934–35a	Charlton Ath	61	Reading	53	Coventry C	51
1935–36a	Coventry C	57	Luton T	56	Reading	54
1936–37a	Luton T	58	Notts Co	56	Brighton & HA	53
1937–38a	Millwall	56	Bristol C	55	QPR*	53
1938–39a	Newport Co	55	Crystal Palace	52	Brighton & HA	49
1939–46	Competition cancelled owing to war. Regional Leagues operated.					
1946–47a	Cardiff C	66	QPR	57	Bristol C	51
1947–48a	QPR	61	Bournemouth	57	Walsall	51
1948–49a	Swansea T	62	Reading	55	Bournemouth	52
1949–50a	Notts Co	58	Northampton T*	51	Southend U	51
1950–51b	Nottingham F	70	Norwich C	64	Reading*	57
1951–52b	Plymouth Arg	66	Reading*	61	Norwich C	61
1952–53b	Bristol R	64	Millwall*	62	Northampton T	62
1953–54b	Ipswich T	64	Brighton & HA	61	Bristol C	56
1954–55b	Bristol C	70	Leyton Orient	61	Southampton	59
1955–56b	Leyton Orient	66	Brighton & HA	65	Ipswich T	64
1956–57b	Ipswich T*	59	Torquay U	59	Colchester U	58
1957–58b	Brighton & HA	60	Brentford*	58	Plymouth Arg	58

THIRD DIVISION—NORTH (1921–1958)
Maximum points: a 76; b 84; c 80; d 92.

	First	Pts	Second	Pts	Third	Pts
1921–22a	Stockport Co	56	Darlington*	50	Grimsby T	50
1922–23a	Nelson	51	Bradford PA	47	Walsall	46
1923–24b	Wolverhampton W	63	Rochdale	62	Chesterfield	54
1924–25b	Darlington	58	Nelson*	53	New Brighton	53
1925–26b	Grimsby T	61	Bradford PA	60	Rochdale	59
1926–27b	Stoke C	63	Rochdale	58	Bradford PA	55
1927–28b	Bradford PA	63	Lincoln C	55	Stockport Co	54
1928–29g	Bradford C	63	Stockport Co	62	Wrexham	52
1929–30b	Port Vale	67	Stockport Co	63	Darlington*	50
1930–31b	Chesterfield	58	Lincoln C	57	Wrexham*	54
1931–32c	Lincoln C*	57	Gateshead	57	Chester	50
1932–33b	Hull C	59	Wrexham	57	Stockport Co	54
1933–34b	Barnsley	62	Chesterfield	61	Stockport Co	59
1934–35b	Doncaster R	57	Halifax T	55	Chester	54
1935–36b	Chesterfield	60	Chester*	55	Tranmere R	55
1936–37b	Stockport Co	60	Lincoln C	57	Chester	53
1937–38b	Tranmere R	56	Doncaster R	54	Hull C	53
1938–39b	Barnsley	67	Doncaster R	56	Bradford C	52
1939–46	Competition cancelled owing to war. Regional Leagues operated.					
1946–47b	Doncaster R	72	Rotherham U	60	Chester	56
1947–48b	Lincoln C	60	Rotherham U	59	Wrexham	50
1948–49b	Hull C	65	Rotherham U	62	Doncaster R	50
1949–50b	Doncaster R	55	Gateshead	53	Rochdale*	51
1950–51d	Rotherham U	71	Mansfield T	64	Carlisle U	62
1951–52d	Lincoln C	69	Grimsby T	66	Stockport Co	59
1952–53d	Oldham Ath	59	Port Vale	58	Wrexham	56
1953–54d	Port Vale	69	Barnsley	58	Scunthorpe U	57
1954–55d	Barnsley	65	Accrington S	61	Scunthorpe U*	58
1955–56d	Grimsby T	68	Derby Co	63	Accrington S	59
1956–57d	Derby Co	63	Hartlepools U	59	Accrington S*	58
1957–58d	Scunthorpe U	66	Accrington S	59	Bradford C	57

* Won or placed on goal average (ratio).

PROMOTED AFTER PLAY-OFFS
(Not accounted for in previous section)

1986–87	Aldershot to Division 3.
1987–88	Swansea C to Division 3.
1988–89	Leyton Orient to Division 3.
1989–90	Cambridge U to Division 3; Notts Co to Division 2; Sunderland to Division 1.
1990–91	Notts Co to Division 1; Tranmere R to Division 2; Torquay U to Division 3.
1991–92	Blackburn R to Premier League; Peterborough U to Division 1.
1992–93	Swindon T to Premier League; WBA to Division 1; York C to Division 2.

1993–94   Leicester C to Premier League; Burnley to Division 1; Wycombe W to Division 2.
1994–95   Huddersfield T to Division 1.
1995–96   Leicester C to Premier League; Bradford C to Division 1; Plymouth Arg to Division 2.
1996–97   Crystal Palace to Premier League; Crewe Alex to Division 1; Northampton T to Division 2.
1997–98   Charlton Ath to Premier League; Colchester U to Division 2.
1998–99   Watford to Premier League; Scunthorpe U to Division 2.

LEAGUE TITLE WINS

FA PREMIER LEAGUE – Manchester U 5, Arsenal 1, Blackburn R 1.

LEAGUE DIVISION 1 – Liverpool 18, Arsenal 10, Everton 9, Sunderland 8, Manchester U 7, Aston Villa 7, Newcastle U 5, Sheffield W 4, Huddersfield T 3, Leeds U 3, Wolverhampton W 3, Blackburn R 2, Portsmouth 2, Preston NE 2, Burnley 2, Manchester C 2, Nottingham F 2, Tottenham H 2, Derby Co 2, Bolton W, Chelsea, Crystal Palace, Sheffield U, WBA, Ipswich T, Middlesbrough 1 each.

LEAGUE DIVISION 2 – Leicester C 6, Manchester C 6, Sheffield W 5, Birmingham C (one as Small Heath) 5, Derby Co 4, Liverpool 4, Ipswich T 3, Leeds U 3, Notts Co 3, Preston NE 3, Middlesbrough 3, Stoke C 3, Bury 2, Grimsby T 2, Norwich C 2, Nottingham F 2, Tottenham H 2, WBA 2, Aston Villa 2, Burnley 2, Chelsea 2, Manchester U 2, West Ham U 2, Wolverhampton W 2, Bolton W 2, Fulham 2, Swindon T, Huddersfield T, Bristol C, Brentford, Bradford C, Everton, Sheffield U, Newcastle U, Coventry C, Blackpool, Blackburn R, Sunderland, Crystal Palace, Luton T, QPR, Oxford U, Millwall, Oldham Ath, Reading 1, Watford 1 each.

LEAGUE DIVISION 3 – Portsmouth 2, Oxford U 2, Shrewsbury T 2, Carlisle U 2, Preston NE 2, Brentford 2, Plymouth Arg, Southampton, Northampton T, Coventry C, Hull C, QPR, Watford, Leyton Orient, Aston Villa, Bolton W, Oldham Ath, Blackburn R, Hereford U, Mansfield T, Wrexham, Grimsby T, Rotherham U, Burnley, Bradford C, Bournemouth, Reading, Sunderland, Wolverhampton W, Bristol R, Cambridge U, Cardiff C, Wigan Ath 1, Notts Co 1 each.

LEAGUE DIVISION 4 – Chesterfield 2, Doncaster R 2, Peterborough U 2, Port Vale, Walsall, Millwall, Brentford, Gillingham, Brighton & HA, Stockport Co, Luton T, Notts Co, Grimsby T, Southport, Mansfield T, Lincoln C, Cambridge U, Watford, Reading, Huddersfield T, Southend U, Sheffield U, Wimbledon, York C, Swindon T, Northampton T, Wolverhampton W, Rotherham U, Exeter C, Darlington, Burnley 1 each.

To 1957–58

DIVISION 3 (South) – Bristol C 3; Charlton Ath, Ipswich T, Millwall, Notts Co, Plymouth Arg, Swansea T 2 each; Brentford, Bristol R, Cardiff C, Crystal Palace, Coventry C, Fulham, Leyton Orient, Luton T, Newport Co, Nottingham F, Norwich C, Portsmouth, QPR, Reading, Southampton, Brighton & HA 1 each.

DIVISION 3 (North) – Barnsley, Doncaster R, Lincoln C 3 each; Chesterfield, Grimsby T, Hull C, Port Vale, Stockport Co 2 each; Bradford PA, Bradford C, Darlington, Derby Co, Nelson, Oldham Ath, Rotherham U, Stoke C, Tranmere R, Wolverhampton W, Scunthorpe U 1 each.

RELEGATED CLUBS

1891–92 League extended. Newton Heath, Sheffield W and Nottingham F admitted. *Second Division formed* including Darwen.
1892–93 In Test matches, Sheffield U and Darwen won promotion in place of Notts Co and Accrington S.
1893–94 In Tests, Liverpool and Small Heath won promotion. Newton Heath and Darwen relegated.
1894–95 After Tests, Bury promoted, Liverpool relegated.
1895–96 After Tests, Liverpool promoted, Small Heath relegated.
1896–97 After Tests, Notts Co promoted, Burnley relegated.
1897–98 Test system abolished after success of Stoke C and Burnley. League extended. Blackburn R and Newcastle U elected to First Division. *Automatic promotion and relegation introduced.*

FA PREMIER LEAGUE TO DIVISION 1

1992–93 Crystal Palace, Middlesbrough, Nottingham F
1993–94 Sheffield U, Oldham Ath, Swindon T
1994–95 Crystal Palace, Norwich C, Leicester C, Ipswich T
1995–96 Manchester C, QPR, Bolton W

1996–97 Sunderland, Middlesbrough, Nottingham F
1997–98 Bolton W, Barnsley, Crystal Palace
1998–99 Charlton Ath, Blackburn R, Nottingham F

DIVISION 1 TO DIVISION 2

1898–99 Bolton W and Sheffield W
1899–1900 Burnley and Glossop
1900–01 Preston NE and WBA
1901–02 Small Heath and Manchester C
1902–03 Grimsby T and Bolton W
1903–04 Liverpool and WBA
1904–05 League extended. Bury and Notts Co, two bottom clubs in First Division, re-elected.
1905–06 Nottingham F and Wolverhampton W
1906–07 Derby Co and Stoke C
1907–08 Bolton W and Birmingham C
1908–09 Manchester C and Leicester Fosse
1909–10 Bolton W and Chelsea
1910–11 Bristol C and Nottingham F
1911–12 Preston NE and Bury
1912–13 Notts Co and Woolwich Arsenal
1913–14 Preston NE and Derby Co
1914–15 Tottenham H and Chelsea*
1919–20 Notts Co and Sheffield W
1920–21 Derby Co and Bradford PA
1921–22 Bradford C and Manchester U
1922–23 Stoke C and Oldham Ath
1923–24 Chelsea and Middlesbrough
1924–25 Preston NE and Nottingham F
1925–26 Manchester C and Notts Co

1926–27 Leeds U and WBA
1927–28 Tottenham H and Middlesbrough
1928–29 Bury and Cardiff C
1929–30 Burnley and Everton
1930–31 Leeds U and Manchester U
1931–32 Grimsby T and West Ham U
1932–33 Bolton W and Blackpool
1933–34 Newcastle U and Sheffield U
1934–35 Leicester C and Tottenham H
1935–36 Aston Villa and Blackburn R
1936–37 Manchester U and Sheffield W
1937–38 Manchester C and WBA
1938–39 Birmingham C and Leicester C
1946–47 Brentford and Leeds U
1947–48 Blackburn R and Grimsby T
1948–49 Preston NE and Sheffield U
1949–50 Manchester C and Birmingham C
1950–51 Sheffield W and Everton
1951–52 Huddersfield T and Fulham
1952–53 Stoke C and Derby Co
1953–54 Middlesbrough and Liverpool
1954–55 Leicester C and Sheffield W
1955–56 Huddersfield T and Sheffield U
1956–57 Charlton Ath and Cardiff C
1957–58 Sheffield W and Sunderland

1958–59 Portsmouth and Aston Villa
1959–60 Luton T and Leeds U
1960–61 Preston NE and Newcastle U
1961–62 Chelsea and Cardiff C
1962–63 Manchester C and Leyton Orient
1963–64 Bolton W and Ipswich T
1964–65 Wolverhampton W and Birmingham C
1965–66 Northampton T and Blackburn R
1966–67 Aston Villa and Blackpool
1967–68 Fulham and Sheffield U
1968–69 Leicester C and QPR
1969–70 Sunderland and Sheffield W
1970–71 Burnley and Blackpool
1971–72 Huddersfield T and Nottingham F
1972–73 Crystal Palace and WBA
1973–74 Southampton, Manchester U, Norwich C
1974–75 Luton T, Chelsea, Carlisle U
1975–76 Wolverhampton W, Burnley, Sheffield U
1976–77 Sunderland, Stoke C, Tottenham H
1977–78 West Ham U, Newcastle U, Leicester C
1978–79 QPR, Birmingham C, Chelsea

1979–80 Bristol C, Derby Co, Bolton W
1980–81 Norwich C, Leicester C, Crystal Palace
1981–82 Leeds U, Wolverhampton W, Middlesbrough
1982–83 Manchester C, Swansea C, Brighton & HA
1983–84 Birmingham C, Notts Co, Wolverhampton W
1984–85 Norwich C, Sunderland, Stoke C
1985–86 Ipswich T, Birmingham C, WBA
1986–87 Leicester C, Manchester C, Aston Villa
1987–88 Chelsea**, Portsmouth, Watford, Oxford U
1988–89 Middlesbrough, West Ham U, Newcastle U
1989–90 Sheffield W, Charlton Ath, Millwall
1990–91 Sunderland and Derby Co
1991–92 Luton T, Notts Co, West Ham U
1992–93 Brentford, Cambridge U, Bristol R
1993–94 Birmingham C, Oxford U, Peterborough U
1994–95 Swindon T, Burnley, Bristol C, Notts Co
1995–96 Millwall, Watford, Luton T
1996–97 Grimsby T, Oldham Ath, Southend U
1997–98 Manchester C, Stoke C, Reading
1998–99 Bury, Oxford U, Bristol C

***Relegated after play-offs.*
**Subsequently re-elected to Division 1 when League was extended after the War.*

DIVISION 2 TO DIVISION 3

1920–21 Stockport Co
1921–22 Bradford PA and Bristol C
1922–23 Rotherham Co and Wolverhampton W
1923–24 Nelson and Bristol C
1924–25 Crystal Palace and Coventry C
1925–26 Stoke C and Stockport Co
1926–27 Darlington and Bradford C
1927–28 Fulham and South Shields
1928–29 Port Vale and Clapton Orient
1929–30 Hull C and Notts Co
1930–31 Reading and Cardiff C
1931–32 Barnsley and Bristol C
1932–33 Chesterfield and Charlton Ath
1933–34 Millwall and Lincoln C
1934–35 Oldham Ath and Notts Co
1935–36 Port Vale and Hull C
1936–37 Doncaster R and Bradford C
1937–38 Barnsley and Stockport Co
1938–39 Norwich C and Tranmere R
1946–47 Swansea T and Newport Co
1947–48 Doncaster R and Millwall
1948–49 Nottingham F and Lincoln C
1949–50 Plymouth Arg and Bradford PA
1950–51 Grimsby T and Chesterfield
1951–52 Coventry C and QPR
1952–53 Southampton and Barnsley
1953–54 Brentford and Oldham Ath
1954–55 Ipswich T and Derby Co
1955–56 Plymouth Arg and Hull C
1956–57 Port Vale and Bury
1957–58 Doncaster R and Notts Co
1958–59 Barnsley and Grimsby T
1959–60 Bristol C and Hull C
1960–61 Lincoln C and Portsmouth
1961–62 Brighton & HA and Bristol R
1962–63 Walsall and Luton T
1963–64 Grimsby T and Scunthorpe U
1964–65 Swindon T and Swansea T

1965–66 Middlesbrough and Leyton Orient
1966–67 Northampton T and Bury
1967–68 Plymouth Arg and Rotherham U
1968–69 Fulham and Bury
1969–70 Preston NE and Aston Villa
1970–71 Blackburn R and Bolton W
1971–72 Charlton Ath and Watford
1972–73 Huddersfield T and Brighton & HA
1973–74 Crystal Palace, Preston NE, Swindon T
1974–75 Millwall, Cardiff C, Sheffield W
1975–76 Oxford U, York C, Portsmouth
1976–77 Carlisle U, Plymouth Arg, Hereford U
1977–78 Blackpool, Mansfield T, Hull C
1978–79 Sheffield U, Millwall, Blackburn R
1979–80 Fulham, Burnley, Charlton Ath
1980–81 Preston NE, Bristol C, Bristol R
1981–82 Cardiff C, Wrexham, Orient
1982–83 Rotherham U, Burnley, Bolton W
1983–84 Derby Co, Swansea C, Cambridge U
1984–85 Notts Co, Cardiff C, Wolverhampton W
1985–86 Carlisle U, Middlesbrough, Fulham
1986–87 Sunderland**, Grimsby T, Brighton & HA
1987–88 Huddersfield T, Reading, Sheffield U**
1988–89 Shrewsbury T, Birmingham C, Walsall
1989–90 Bournemouth, Bradford C, Stoke C
1990–91 WBA and Hull C
1991–92 Plymouth Arg, Brighton & HA, Port Vale
1992–93 Preston NE, Mansfield T, Wigan Ath, Chester C
1993–94 Fulham, Exeter C, Hartlepool U, Barnet
1994–95 Cambridge U, Plymouth Arg, Cardiff C,
         Chester C, Leyton Orient
1995–96 Carlisle U, Swansea C, Brighton & HA, Hull C
1996–97 Peterborough U, Shrewsbury T, Rotherham U,
         Notts Co
1997–98 Brentford, Plymouth Arg, Carlisle U, Southend U
1998–99 York C, Northampton T, Lincoln C,
         Macclesfield T

DIVISION 3 TO DIVISION 4

1958–59 Rochdale, Notts Co, Doncaster R, Stockport Co
1959–60 Accrington S, Wrexham, Mansfield T, York C
1960–61 Chesterfield, Colchester U, Bradford C,
         Tranmere R
1961–62 Newport Co, Brentford, Lincoln C, Torquay U
1962–63 Bradford PA, Brighton & HA, Carlisle U,
         Halifax T
1963–64 Millwall, Crewe Alex, Wrexham, Notts Co
1964–65 Luton T, Port Vale, Colchester U, Barnsley
1965–66 Southend U, Exeter C, Brentford, York C
1966–67 Doncaster R, Workington, Darlington, Swansea T
1967–68 Scunthorpe U, Colchester U, Grimsby T,
         Peterborough U (demoted)
1968–69 Oldham Ath, Crewe Alex, Hartlepool,
         Northampton T
1969–70 Bournemouth, Southport, Barrow, Stockport Co

1970–71 Reading, Bury, Doncaster R, Gillingham
1971–72 Mansfield T, Barnsley, Torquay U, Bradford C
1972–73 Rotherham U, Brentford, Swansea C,
         Scunthorpe U
1973–74 Cambridge U, Shrewsbury T, Southport,
         Rochdale
1974–75 Bournemouth, Tranmere R, Watford,
         Huddersfield T
1975–76 Aldershot, Colchester U, Southend U, Halifax T
1976–77 Reading, Northampton T, Grimsby T, York C
1977–78 Port Vale, Bradford C, Hereford U, Portsmouth
1978–79 Peterborough U, Walsall, Tranmere R, Lincoln C
1979–80 Bury, Southend U, Mansfield T, Wimbledon
1980–81 Sheffield U, Colchester U, Blackpool, Hull C
1981–82 Wimbledon, Swindon T, Bristol C, Chester
1982–83 Reading, Wrexham, Doncaster R, Chesterfield

1983–84 Scunthorpe U, Southend U, Port Vale, Exeter C	1987–88 Doncaster R, York C, Grimsby T, Rotherham U**
1984–85 Burnley, Orient, Preston NE, Cambridge U	1988–89 Southend U, Chesterfield, Gillingham, Aldershot
1985–86 Lincoln C, Cardiff C, Wolverhampton W,	1989–90 Cardiff C, Northampton T, Blackpool, Walsall
Swansea C	1990–91 Crewe Alex, Rotherham U, Mansfield T
1986–87 Bolton W**, Carlisle U, Darlington, Newport Co	1991–92 Bury, Shrewsbury T, Torquay U, Darlington

** *Relegated after play-offs.*

APPLICATIONS FOR RE-ELECTION
FOURTH DIVISION

Eleven: Hartlepool U.
Seven: Crewe Alex.
Six: Barrow (lost League place to Hereford U 1972), Halifax T, Rochdale, Southport (lost League place to Wigan Ath 1978), York C.
Five: Chester C, Darlington, Lincoln C, Stockport Co, Workington (lost League place to Wimbledon 1977).
Four: Bradford PA (lost League place to Cambridge U 1970), Newport Co, Northampton T.
Three: Doncaster R, Hereford U.
Two: Bradford C, Exeter C, Oldham Ath, Scunthorpe U, Torquay U.
One: Aldershot, Colchester U, Gateshead (lost League place to Peterborough U 1960), Grimsby T, Swansea C, Tranmere R, Wrexham, Blackpool, Cambridge U, Preston NE.
Accrington S resigned and Oxford U were elected 1962.
Port Vale were forced to re-apply following expulsion in 1968.
Aldershot expelled March 1992. Maidstone U resigned August 1992.

THIRD DIVISIONS NORTH & SOUTH

Seven: Walsall.
Six: Exeter C, Halifax T, Newport Co.
Five: Accrington S, Barrow, Gillingham, New Brighton, Southport.
Four: Rochdale, Norwich C.
Three: Crystal Palace, Crewe Alex, Darlington, Hartlepool U, Merthyr T, Swindon T.
Two: Aberdare Ath, Aldershot, Ashington, Bournemouth, Brentford, Chester, Colchester U, Durham C, Millwall, Nelson, QPR, Rotherham U, Southend U, Tranmere R, Watford, Workington.
One: Bradford C, Bradford PA, Brighton & HA, Bristol R, Cardiff C, Carlisle U, Charlton Ath, Gateshead, Grimsby T, Mansfield T, Shrewsbury T, Torquay U, York C.

LEAGUE STATUS FROM 1986–87

RELEGATED FROM LEAGUE		PROMOTED TO LEAGUE
1986–87	Lincoln C	Scarborough
1987–88	Newport Co	Lincoln C
1988–89	Darlington	Maidstone U
1989–90	Colchester U	Darlington
1990–91	—	Barnet
1991–92	—	Colchester U
1992–93	Halifax T	Wycombe W
1993–94	—	—
1994–95	—	—
1995–96	—	—
1996–97	Hereford U	Macclesfield T
1997–98	Doncaster R	Halifax T
1998–99	Scarborough	Cheltenham T

Micah Hyde of Watford gets high above Bolton Wanderers' Per Frandsen in the play-off at Wembley, which shot Watford back to the top division. (Colorsport)

LEAGUE ATTENDANCES SINCE 1946–47

Season	Matches	Total	Div. 1	Div. 2	Div. 3 (S)	Div. 3 (N)
1946–47	1848	35,604,606	15,005,316	11,071,572	5,664,004	3,863,714
1947–48	1848	40,259,130	16,732,341	12,286,350	6,653,610	4,586,829
1948–49	1848	41,271,414	17,914,667	11,353,237	6,998,429	5,005,081
1949–50	1848	40,517,865	17,278,625	11,694,158	7,104,155	4,440,927
1950–51	2028	39,584,967	16,679,454	10,780,580	7,367,884	4,757,109
1951–52	2028	39,015,866	16,110,322	11,066,189	6,958,927	4,880,428
1952–53	2028	37,149,966	16,050,278	9,686,654	6,704,299	4,708,735
1953–54	2028	36,174,590	16,154,915	9,510,053	6,311,508	4,198,114
1954–55	2028	34,133,103	15,087,221	8,988,794	5,996,017	4,051,071
1955–56	2028	33,150,809	14,108,961	9,080,002	5,692,479	4,269,367
1956–57	2028	32,744,405	13,803,037	8,718,162	5,622,189	4,601,017
1957–58	2028	33,562,208	14,468,652	8,663,712	6,097,183	4,332,661

					Div. 3	Div. 4
1958–59	2028	33,610,985	14,727,691	8,641,997	5,946,600	4,276,697
1959–60	2028	32,538,611	14,391,227	8,399,627	5,739,707	4,008,050
1960–61	2028	28,619,754	12,926,948	7,033,936	4,784,256	3,874,614
1961–62	2015	27,979,902	12,061,194	7,453,089	5,199,106	3,266,513
1962–63	2028	28,885,852	12,490,239	7,792,770	5,341,362	3,261,481
1963–64	2028	28,535,022	12,486,626	7,594,158	5,419,157	3,035,081
1964–65	2028	27,641,168	12,708,752	6,984,104	4,436,245	3,512,067
1965–66	2028	27,206,980	12,480,644	6,914,757	4,779,150	3,032,429
1966–67	2028	28,902,596	14,242,957	7,253,819	4,421,172	2,984,648
1967–68	2028	30,107,298	15,289,410	7,450,410	4,013,087	3,354,391
1968–69	2028	29,382,172	14,584,851	7,382,390	4,339,656	3,075,275
1969–70	2028	29,600,972	14,868,754	7,581,728	4,223,761	2,926,729
1970–71	2028	28,194,146	13,954,337	7,098,265	4,377,213	2,764,331
1971–72	2028	28,700,729	14,484,603	6,769,308	4,697,392	2,749,426
1972–73	2028	25,448,642	13,998,154	5,631,730	3,737,252	2,081,506
1973–74	2027	24,982,203	13,070,991	6,326,108	3,421,624	2,163,480
1974–75	2028	25,577,977	12,613,178	6,955,970	4,086,145	1,992,684
1975–76	2028	24,896,053	13,089,861	5,798,405	3,948,449	2,059,338
1976–77	2028	26,182,800	13,647,585	6,250,597	4,152,218	2,132,400
1977–78	2028	25,392,872	13,255,677	6,474,763	3,332,042	2,330,390
1978–79	2028	24,540,627	12,704,549	6,153,223	3,374,558	2,308,297
1979–80	2028	24,623,975	12,163,002	6,112,025	3,999,328	2,349,620
1980–81	2028	21,907,569	11,392,894	5,175,442	3,637,854	1,701,379
1981–82	2028	20,006,961	10,420,793	4,750,463	2,836,915	1,998,790
1982–83	2028	18,766,158	9,295,613	4,974,937	2,943,568	1,552,040
1983–84	2028	18,358,631	8,711,448	5,359,757	2,729,942	1,557,484
1984–85	2028	17,849,835	9,761,404	4,030,823	2,667,008	1,390,600
1985–86	2028	16,488,577	9,037,854	3,551,968	2,490,481	1,408,274
1986–87	2028	17,379,218	9,144,676	4,168,131	2,350,970	1,715,441
1987–88	2030	17,959,732	8,094,571	5,341,599	2,751,275	1,772,287
1988–89	2036	18,464,192	7,809,993	5,887,805	3,035,327	1,791,067
1989–90	2036	19,445,442	7,883,039	6,867,674	2,803,551	1,891,178
1990–91	2036	19,508,202	8,618,709	6,285,068	2,835,759	1,768,666
1991–92	2064*	20,487,273	9,989,160	5,809,787	2,993,352	1,694,974

		Total	FA Premier	Div. 1	Div. 2	Div. 3
1992–93	2028	20,657,327	9,759,809	5,874,017	3,483,073	1,540,428
1993–94	2028	21,683,381	10,644,551	6,487,104	2,972,702	1,579,024
1994–95	2028	21,856,020	11,213,168	6,044,293	3,037,752	1,560,807
1995–96	2036	21,844,416	10,469,107	6,566,349	2,843,652	1,965,308
1996–97	2036	22,783,163	10,804,762	6,931,539	3,195,223	1,851,639
1997–98	2036	24,692,608	11,092,106	8,330,018	3,503,264	1,767,220
1998–99						

Figures include matches played by Aldershot.

ENGLISH LEAGUE ATTENDANCES 1998–99

FA CARLING PREMIERSHIP ATTENDANCES

	Average Gate			Season 1998/99	
	1997/98	1998/99	+/– %	Highest	Lowest
Arsenal	38,053	38,024	–0.08	38,308	37,323
Aston Villa	36,137	36,937	+2.21	39,241	29,559
Blackburn Rovers	25,253	25,773	+2.06	30,436	21,754
Charlton Athletic	13,275	19,816	+49.27	20,048	16,488
Chelsea	32,901	34,754	+5.63	35,017	34,000
Coventry City	19,718	20,773	+5.35	23,091	16,003
Derby County	29,105	29,193	+0.30	32,913	25,710
Everton	35,376	36,202	+2.34	40,185	30,357
Leeds United	34,725	35,773	+3.02	40,255	30,012
Leicester City	20,615	20,469	–0.71	22,091	17,725
Liverpool	40,628	43,321	+6.63	44,852	36,019
Manchester United	55,168	55,188	+0.04	55,316	55,052
Middlesbrough	29,994	34,386	+14.64	34,687	33,387
Newcastle United	36,680	36,690	+0.03	36,784	36,352
Nottingham Forest	20,584	24,415	+18.61	30,025	20,480
Sheffield Wednesday	28,709	26,745	–6.84	39,475	19,321
Southampton	15,159	15,140	–0.13	15,255	14,354
Tottenham Hotspur	29,143	34,149	+17.18	36,125	28,338
West Ham United	24,967	25,639	+2.69	26,044	23,153
Wimbledon	16,675	18,207	+9.19	26,121	11,717

TOTAL ATTENDANCES: 11,620,326 (380 games)
Average 30,580 (+4.76%)
HIGHEST: 55,316 Manchester United v Southampton
LOWEST: 11,717 Wimbledon v Coventry C
HIGHEST AVERAGE: 55,188 Manchester United
LOWEST AVERAGE: 15,140 Southampton

NATIONWIDE FOOTBALL LEAGUE: DIVISION ONE ATTENDANCES

	Average Gate			Season 1998/99	
	1997/98	1998/99	+/– %	Highest	Lowest
Barnsley	18,449	16,269	–11.8	18,114	14,733
Birmingham City	18,708	20,794	+11.2	29,060	15,935
Bolton Wanderers	24,352	18,240	–25.1	24,625	13,324
Bradford City	15,564	14,298	–8.1	15,887	12,595
Bristol City	11,846	12,860	+8.6	16,257	9,810
Bury	6,177	5,476	–11.3	8,669	3,436
Crewe Alexandra	5,243	5,269	+0.5	5,759	4,489
Crystal Palace	21,983	17,123	–22.1	22,096	12,919
Grimsby Town	5,601	6,681	+19.3	9,528	4,789
Huddersfield Town	12,145	12,976	+6.8	20,741	9,717
Ipswich Town	14,973	16,920	+13.0	22,162	11,596
Norwich City	14,444	15,761	+9.1	19,511	11,137
Oxford United	7,512	7,040	–6.3	9,434	5,587
Port Vale	8,432	6,991	–17.1	10,465	4,980
Portsmouth	11,149	11,973	+7.4	17,022	8,180
Queens Park Rangers	13,083	11,793	–9.9	18,498	8,070
Sheffield United	17,942	16,243	–9.5	25,612	12,293
Stockport County	8,322	7,900	–5.1	10,548	6,048
Sunderland	33,492	38,745	+15.7	41,634	33,870
Swindon Town	10,298	8,651	–16.0	11,718	5,765
Tranmere Rovers	7,999	6,930	–13.4	14,248	4,937
Watford	11,532	11,822	+2.5	20,303	8,682
West Bromwich Albion	16,662	14,585	–12.5	22,682	9,601
Wolverhampton Wanderers	23,281	22,620	–2.8	27,589	18,480

TOTAL ATTENDANCES: 7,543,369 (552 games)
Average 13,666 (–9.4%)
HIGHEST: 41,634 Sunderland v Birmingham C
LOWEST: 3,436 Bury v Oxford U
HIGHEST AVERAGE: 38,745 Sunderland
LOWEST AVERAGE: 5,269 Crewe Alexandra

NATIONWIDE FOOTBALL LEAGUE: DIVISION TWO ATTENDANCES

	Average Gate			Season 1998/99	
	1997/98	1998/99	+/−%	Highest	Lowest
AFC Bournemouth	4,732	7,117	+50.4	10,964	4,863
Blackpool	5,220	5,116	−2.0	10,868	2,990
Bristol Rovers	6,413	6,263	−2.3	8,033	4,833
Burnley	10,481	10,605	+1.2	17,251	8,526
Chesterfield	4,756	4,564	−4.0	8,245	2,621
Colchester United	3,137	4,479	+44.2	6,554	3,228
Fulham	9,018	11,387	+26.3	17,176	7,447
Gillingham	6,450	6,339	−1.7	10,400	4,575
Lincoln City	3,968	4,654	+17.3	8,145	2,518
Luton Town	6,501	5,527	−15.0	9,070	4,021
Macclesfield Town	2,913	3,311	+13.7	6,381	1,868
Manchester City	28,196	28,261	+0.2	32,471	24,291
Millwall	7,023	6,958	−0.9	12,726	4,249
Northampton Town	6,389	6,073	−4.9	7,557	4,710
Notts County	5,711	5,617	−1.6	10,316	3,294
Oldham Athletic	5,586	5,628	+0.8	12,976	3,913
Preston North End	9,460	11,926	+26.1	20,857	8,656
Reading	9,676	11,265	+16.4	20,055	7,914
Stoke City	15,025	12,732	−15.3	23,272	6,569
Walsall	4,062	5,457	+34.3	9,517	3,098
Wigan Athletic	3,968	4,250	+7.1	6,700	2,784
Wrexham	4,090	3,948	−3.5	9,048	1,871
Wycombe Wanderers	5,415	5,121	−5.4	8,129	3,361
York City	3,853	3,646	−5.4	7,527	2,075

TOTAL ATTENDANCES: 4,169,697 (552 games)
Average 7,554 (+18.7%)
HIGHEST: 32,471 Manchester City v York C
LOWEST: 1,868 Macclesfield Town v Gillingham
HIGHEST AVERAGE: 28,261 Manchester City
LOWEST AVERAGE: 3,311 Macclesfield Town

NATIONWIDE FOOTBALL LEAGUE: DIVISION THREE ATTENDANCES

	Average Gate			Season 1998/99	
	1997/98	1998/99	+/−%	Highest	Lowest
Barnet	2,254	2,107	−6.5	3,129	1,314
Brentford	5,029	5,444	+8.3	9,535	3,674
Brighton & Hove Albion	2,329	3,253	+39.7	4,838	1,793
Cambridge United	2,898	4,583	+58.1	8,936	2,385
Cardiff City	3,610	7,131	+97.5	12,455	3,742
Carlisle United	5,381	3,319	−38.3	7,599	2,273
Chester City	2,255	2,562	+13.6	3,926	1,729
Darlington	2,314	3,181	+37.5	5,899	2,085
Exeter City	3,988	3,154	−20.9	6,746	1,929
Halifax Town	3,002	2,541	+18.1	4,455	1,906
Hartlepool United	2,258	2,690	+19.1	5,098	1,593
Hull City	4,684	6,051	+29.2	13,949	3,433
Leyton Orient	4,374	4,672	+6.8	6,537	3,186
Mansfield Town	2,720	2,963	+8.9	4,095	2,292
Peterborough United	6,192	5,306	−14.3	10,168	3,785
Plymouth Argyle	5,323	5,323	n/c	11,936	3,589
Rochdale	1,847	2,125	+15.1	5,374	1,344
Rotherham United	3,648	3,988	+9.3	5,943	2,696
Scarborough	2,489	2,211	−11.2	4,769	1,056
Scunthorpe United	3,006	3,741	+24.5	5,633	2,421
Shrewsbury Town	2,403	2,575	+7.2	3,247	1,620
Southend United	4,148	4,317	+4.1	6,700	3,250
Swansea City	3,443	5,225	+51.8	9,226	3,360
Torquay United	2,679	2,600	−2.9	5,719	1,715

TOTAL ATTENDANCES: 2,102,150 (552 games)
Average 3,808 (+19.0%)
HIGHEST: 13,949 Hull City v Scarborough
LOWEST: 1,056 Scarborough v Barnet
HIGHEST AVERAGE: 7,131 Cardiff City
LOWEST AVERAGE: 2,107 Barnet

LEAGUE CUP FINALISTS 1961–99

Played as a two-leg final until 1966. All subsequent finals at Wembley.

Year	Winners	Runners-up	Score
1961	Aston Villa	Rotherham U	0-2, 3-0 (aet)
1962	Norwich C	Rochdale	3-0, 1-0
1963	Birmingham C	Aston Villa	3-1, 0-0
1964	Leicester C	Stoke C	1-1, 3-2
1965	Chelsea	Leicester C	3-2, 0-0
1966	WBA	West Ham U	1-2, 4-1
1967	QPR	WBA	3-2
1968	Leeds U	Arsenal	1-0
1969	Swindon T	Arsenal	3-1 (aet)
1970	Manchester C	WBA	2-1 (aet)
1971	Tottenham H	Aston Villa	2-0
1972	Stoke C	Chelsea	2-1
1973	Tottenham H	Norwich C	1-0
1974	Wolverhampton W	Manchester C	2-1
1975	Aston Villa	Norwich C	1-0
1976	Manchester C	Newcastle U	2-1
1977	Aston Villa	Everton	0-0, 1-1 (aet), 3-2 (aet)
1978	Nottingham F	Liverpool	0-0 (aet), 1-0
1979	Nottingham F	Southampton	3-2
1980	Wolverhampton W	Nottingham F	1-0
1981	Liverpool	West Ham U	1-1 (aet), 2-1

MILK CUP

Year	Winners	Runners-up	Score
1982	Liverpool	Tottenham H	3-1 (aet)
1983	Liverpool	Manchester U	2-1 (aet)
1984	Liverpool	Everton	0-0 (aet), 1-0
1985	Norwich C	Sunderland	1-0
1986	Oxford U	QPR	3-0

LITTLEWOODS CUP

Year	Winners	Runners-up	Score
1987	Arsenal	Liverpool	2-1
1988	Luton T	Arsenal	3-2
1989	Nottingham F	Luton T	3-1
1990	Nottingham F	Oldham Ath	1-0

RUMBELOWS LEAGUE CUP

Year	Winners	Runners-up	Score
1991	Sheffield W	Manchester U	1-0
1992	Manchester U	Nottingham F	1-0

COCA-COLA CUP

Year	Winners	Runners-up	Score
1993	Arsenal	Sheffield W	2-1
1994	Aston Villa	Manchester U	3-1
1995	Liverpool	Bolton W	2-1
1996	Aston Villa	Leeds U	3-0
1997	Leicester C	Middlesbrough	1-1 (aet), 1-0 (aet)
1998	Chelsea	Middlesbrough	2-0 (aet)

WORTHINGTON CUP

Year	Winners	Runners-up	Score
1999	Tottenham H	Leicester C	1-0

LEAGUE CUP WINS
Aston Villa 5, Liverpool 5, Nottingham F 4, Tottenham H 3, Arsenal 2, Chelsea 2, Leicester C 2, Manchester C 2, Norwich C 2, Wolverhampton W 2, Birmingham C 1, Leeds U 1, Luton T 1, Manchester U 1, Oxford U 1, QPR 1, Sheffield W 1, Stoke C 1, Swindon T 1, WBA 1.

APPEARANCES IN FINALS
Aston Villa 7, Liverpool 7, Nottingham F 6, Arsenal 5, Leicester C 4, Manchester U 4, Norwich C 4, Tottenham H 4, Chelsea 3, Manchester C 3, WBA 3, Everton 2, Leeds U 2, Luton T 2, Middlesbrough 2, QPR 2, Sheffield W 2, Stoke C 2, West Ham U 2, Wolverhampton W 2, Birmingham C 1, Bolton W 1, Newcastle U 1, Oldham Ath 1, Oxford U 1, Rochdale 1, Rotherham U 1, Southampton 1, Sunderland 1, Swindon T 1.

APPEARANCES IN SEMI-FINALS
Aston Villa 10, Liverpool 10, Arsenal 9, Tottenham H 9, Manchester U 7, West Ham U 7, Chelsea 6, Nottingham F 6, Leeds U 5, Manchester C 5, Norwich C 5, Leicester C 4, Middlesbrough 4, WBA 4, Birmingham C 3, Burnley 3, Everton 3, QPR 3, Sheffield W 3, Sunderland 3, Swindon T 3, Wolverhampton W 3, Blackburn R 2, Bolton W 2, Bristol C 2, Coventry C 2, Crystal Palace 2, Ipswich T 2, Luton T 2, Oxford U 2, Plymouth Arg 2, Southampton 2, Stoke C 2, Wimbledon 2, Blackpool 1, Bury 1, Cardiff C 1, Carlisle U 1, Chester C 1, Derby Co 1, Huddersfield T 1, Newcastle U 1, Oldham Ath 1, Peterborough U 1, Rochdale 1, Rotherham U 1, Shrewsbury T 1, Stockport Co 1, Tranmere R 1, Walsall 1, Watford 1.

WORTHINGTON CUP 1998–99

FIRST ROUND, FIRST LEG

11 AUG

Barnet (0) 2 *(McGleish 68, Currie 90)*
Wolverhampton W (0) 1 *(Osborn 77)*   3181
Barnet: Harrison; Stockley, Sawyers, Goodhind, Ford, Simpson, Wilson (Doolan), Charlery, Currie, McGleish, Onwere.
Wolverhampton W: Stowell; Muscat, Naylor (Froggatt), Richards, Emblen, Curle, Osborn, Robinson (Atkins), Bull, Keane, Simpson.

Birmingham C (0) 2 *(Adebola 70, Johnson M 87)*
Millwall (0) 0   14,133
Birmingham C: Bennett; Gill, Charlton, Marsden, Ablett, Johnson M, McCarthy (Holland), O'Connor, Adebola, Ndlovu, Forster (Hughes).
Millwall: Spink; Lavin, Stuart, Bowry, Law, Fitzgerald, Neill (Bircham), Newman, Sadlier, Shaw, Carter.

Blackpool (1) 1 *(Conroy 14)*
Scunthorpe U (0) 0   1873
Blackpool: Banks; Bardsley, Hills, Butler, Hughes, Brabin, Bent, Clarkson, Aldridge (Malkin), Bushell, Conroy.
Scunthorpe U: Clarke; Wilcox, McAuley, Harsley, Hope, Fickling, Walker, Calvo-Garcia, Eyre (Bull), Gayle, Forrester (Stamp).

Bolton W (0) 1 *(Taylor B 49)*
Hartlepool U (0) 0   6429
Bolton W: Jaaskelainen; Cox, Whitlow, Strong, Bergsson, Fish, Jensen, Gunnlaugsson, Taylor B, Holdsworth (Taylor S), Sellars (Johansen).
Hartlepool U: Hollund; Knowles, Ingram, Barron, Lee, Beech, Miller, Di Lella (Stephenson), Irvine (Howard), Midgley (Pemberton), Clark.

Bournemouth (1) 2 *(Robinson 15, Howe 88)*
Colchester U (0) 0   3745
Bournemouth: Ovendale; Young, Vincent, Howe, Berthe (Tindall), Bailey, Cox, Robinson, Stein, Fletcher S (Town), Hughes.
Colchester U: Emberson; Betts, Stamps, Williams, Greene, Buckle, Haydon, Gregory D, Sale, Gregory N (Duguid), Abrahams (Adcock).

Bradford C (0) 1 *(Beagrie 89)*
Lincoln C (0) 1 *(Battersby 87)*   4481
Bradford C: Walsh; Wright, Todd (Dreyer), Bolland, Moore, O'Brien, Lawrence, Steiner (Watson), Mills (Grant), Whalley, Beagrie.
Lincoln C: Vaughan; Perry, Whitney, Fleming, Brown, Austin, Smith, Finnigan, Fortune-West, Battersby, Alcide.

Bristol C (3) 4 *(Hutchings 13, Akinbiyi 14, 54, Andersen 21)*
Shrewsbury T (0) 0   3585
Bristol C: Welch; Locke, Bell, Hewlett, Watts (Dyche), Carey, Goodridge (Murray), Hutchings, Akinbiyi, Andersen (Thorpe), Tinnion.
Shrewsbury T: Edwards; Seabury, Hanmer, Jobling, Wilding, Gayle, Craven, Kerrigan (White), Steele (Jagielka), Evans, Preece (Williams).

Bury (1) 1 *(Matthews 17)*
Burnley (1) 1 *(Cooke 29)*   3927
Bury: Kiely; Woodward, Barrick, Daws, Lucketti, Redmond, Swailes C, Ellis (Rigby) (Armstrong), Matthews (D'Jaffo), Johnrose, Preece.
Burnley: Parks; Brass, Morgan, Smith P, Blatherwick, Howey, Little, Williams (Moore), Cooke (Robertson), Jepson (Henderson), Smith C.

Cambridge U (1) 1 *(Benjamin 21)*
Watford (0) 0   3073
Cambridge U: Van Heusden; Chenery, Ashbee, Duncan, Joseph, Campbell, Wanless, Benjamin, Butler, Kyd (Taylor), Russell.
Watford: Chamberlain; Hazan, Kennedy, Page, Palmer, Mooney (Millen), Bazeley (Daley), Hyde, Lee, Easton (Robinson), Rosenthal.

Exeter C (0) 1 *(Richardson 90)*
Ipswich T (1) 1 *(Holland 13)*   3233
Exeter C: Bayes; Gale, Power, Curran, Richardson, Gittens, Rowbotham, Rees, Crowe (Flack), Clark, Breslan (Fry).
Ipswich T: Wright; Stockwell, Taricco, Clapham, Mowbray, Venus, Dyer (Sonner), Holland, Johnson, Naylor, Petta.

Fulham (1) 2 *(Beardsley 43, Lehmann 48)*
Cardiff C (1) 1 *(Williams 8)*   4305
Fulham: Taylor; Morgan, Brevett, Collins (Lawrence), Coleman, Symons, Beardsley, Bracewell, Lehmann, Trollope (Hayward), Salako.
Cardiff C: Hallworth; Delaney, Phillips, Mitchell (Eckhardt), Young, Carpenter, Bonner (Penney), Williams, Saville (Nugent), Roberts, O'Sullivan.

Huddersfield T (1) 3 *(Johnson 18, Allison 74, Dalton 81 (pen))*
Mansfield T (2) 2 *(Christie 2, Peters 27)*   3988
Huddersfield T: Vaesen; Jenkins, Edwards, Browning (Dalton), Morrison, Collins, Johnson, Horne, Stewart (Barnes), Allison, Thornley.
Mansfield T: Bowling; Williams, Harper, Peters, Ford, Hackett, Schofield, Clarke, Peacock, Christie, Tallon.

Leyton Orient (1) 1 *(Richards 32)*
Bristol R (0) 1 *(Cureton 62)*   2663
Leyton Orient: MacKenzie; Walschaerts, Lockwood, Smith, Raynor, Clark (Reinelt), Ling, Ampadu, Richards (Griffiths), Maskell, Martin (Morrison).
Bristol R: Jones; Smith, Challis, Zabek, Foster, Andreasson (Trees), Holloway, Meaker, Roberts, Ipoua (Cureton), Hayles.

Luton T (0) 2 *(Alexander 60 (pen), 63 (pen))*
Oxford U (2) 3 *(Murphy 43, 45, Weatherstone 88)*   3165
Luton T: Davis K; Alexander, Thomas (McLaren), Spring, Davis S, Johnson, McGowan, Evers, Bacque, Gray (McIndoe), Marshall (George).
Oxford U: Whitehead; Robinson, Marsh, Gray, Wilsterman, Gilchrist, Banger (Weatherstone), Windass (Smith), Rose (Powell), Murphy, Beauchamp.

Macclesfield T (1) 3 *(Wood 2, Askey 76, 85)*
Stoke C (1) 1 *(Kavanagh 19)*   2963
Macclesfield T: Price; Tinson, Ingram, Payne, McDonald, Sodje, Askey, Wood (Sorvel), Tomlinson (Barclay), Sedgemore (Durkan), Whittaker.
Stoke C: Muggleton; Short, Small, Sigurdsson, Robinson, Woods, Keen, Kavanagh, Thorne, Lightbourne, Oldfield.

Northampton T (1) 2 *(Heggs 39, Freestone 53)*
Brighton & HA (0) 1 *(Storer 47)*   3390
Northampton T: Woodman; Matthew (Hunt), Frain, Hill, Warburton, Bishop, Gibb, Freestone, Heggs, Corazzin, Spedding (Clarkson).
Brighton & HA: Walton; Smith, Tuck, Minton, Johnson, Hobson (Thomas), Storer, Mayo, Moralee, Hart (Barker), Bennett.

Notts Co (0) 0
Manchester C (0) 2 *(Tskhadadze 72, Allsop 90)*   5795
Notts Co: Ward; Hendon (Torpey), Pearce (Liburd), Redmile, Fairclough, Strodder (Dyer), Billy, Owers, Farrell, Jones, Murray.
Manchester C: Weaver; Edghill, Horlock, Tskhadadze, Wiekens, Vaughan, Mason, Pollock, Jim Whitley, Dickov, Bradbury (Allsop).

Oldham Ath (3) 3 *(Littlejohn 20, Reid 23 (pen), Allott 31)*
Crewe Alex (1) 2 *(Little 40, 78)*   3766
Oldham Ath: Kelly; McNiven S, Holt, Sinnott, Graham, Duxbury (Salt), Rickers (Whitehall), Orlygsson, Allott, Littlejohn, Reid.
Crewe Alex: Kearton; Bignot, Smith S, Unsworth, Walton, Charnock (Lunt), Wright J, Collins, Rivers, Little, Smith P (Lovelock).

Peterborough U (0) 0 *(Carruthers 50)*
Reading (0) 1 *(Asaba 79)*   2187
Peterborough U: Tyler; Hooper (Little), Drury, Gill, Bodley, Edwards, Davies, Scott (Farrell), Carruthers, Quinn, Houghton (Castle).
Reading: Van der Kwaak; Booty, Legg, Brebner, Parkinson, Kromheer, Bowen (Houghton), Caskey, McIntyre, Gray, Williams (Asaba).

Plymouth Arg (1) 1 *(McCarthy 20)*
Portsmouth (3) 3 *(McLoughlin 38 (pen), Vlachos 40, Aloisi 45)*   4380
Plymouth Arg: Sheffield; Collins, Gibbs, Mauge, Heathcote, Wotton, Barlow, McCarthy, Jean, Power (McCall), Hargreaves.
Portsmouth: Flahavan (Knight); Pethick, Simpson F, McLoughlin, Whitbread, Awford, Vlachos (Soley), Kyzeridis, Aloisi, Durnin (Claridge), Thomson.

Port Vale (0) 1 *(Ainsworth 48)*
Chester C (2) 2 *(Beckett 24, 28)*   3478
Port Vale: Musselwhite; Carragher (Walsh), Tankard, Bogie (Koordes), Aspin, Snijders, Ainsworth, Talbot, Beadle (Naylor), Foyle, Jansson.
Chester C: Brown; Davidson, Cross, Richardson, Crosby, Woods, Flitcroft, Priest, Murphy, Beckett (Bennett), Smith.

Rotherham U (0) 0
Chesterfield (1) 1 *(Holland 26)*   3142
Rotherham U: Pollitt; Ingledow, Beech, Warner, Knill, Dillon, Garner (Hudson), Compton, White (Martindale), Glover, Roscoe.
Chesterfield: Mercer; Beaumont, Perkins, Curtis, Williams, Breckin, Willis, Holland, Reeves, Wilkinson, Howard.

Sheffield U (1) 3 *(Borbokis 21, Saunders 49, Taylor 60)*
Darlington (0) 1 *(Roberts 90)*   5035
Sheffield U: Kelly; Borbokis, Quinn, Bruce (Sandford), Nilsen, Holdsworth, Saunders, Hamilton I (Devlin), Taylor, Stuart, Woodhouse.
Darlington: Preece; Pepper, Barnard, Liddle, Tutill, Devos, Gaughan (Shutt), Naylor, Dorner (Roberts), Gabbiadini, Atkinson.

Southend U (0) 1 *(Newman 86)*
Gillingham (0) 0   2509
Southend U: Margetson; Hails, Stimson (Jones), Dublin, Newman, Coleman, Maher, Livett, Burns, Whyte (Fitzpatrick), Clarke (De Souza).
Gillingham: Bartram; Patterson (Bryant), Pennock, Smith, Ashby, Carr, Hessenthaler (Southall), Hodge (Pinnock), Galloway, Taylor, Williams.

Stockport Co (1) 2 *(Moore 41, Byrne 83)*
Hull C (2) 2 *(Brown 10, McGinty 16)*   3134
Stockport Co: Nash; Connelly, Woodthorpe (Gannon), Dinning, Flynn, McIntosh, Phillips (Cook), Byrne, Angell, Moore, Cooper.
Hull C: Wilson; Hocking, Gage, Hawes, Whitworth, McGinty, French (Edwards), D'Auria (Peacock), Brown, Ellington, Mann.

Swansea C (0) 1 *(Cusack 88)*
Norwich C (0) 1 *(Bellamy 76)*   3803
Swansea C: Freestone; Price, Howard, Cusack, Smith, Bound, O'Gorman (Casey), Thomas, Alsop, Watkin, Coates (Roberts).
Norwich C: Marshall A; Marshall L, Kenton, Grant, Fleming (Scott), Jackson, Adams (Llewellyn), Bellamy, Carey, Eadie (Roberts), O'Neill.

Torquay U (1) 1 *(Bedeau 3)*
Crystal Palace (1) 1 *(Lombardo 34)*   3042
Torquay U: Gregg; Gurney, Herrera, Robinson, Thomas, Watson, Clayton, McGorry, Bedeau, Partridge, Hill.
Crystal Palace: Miller; Austin, Smith, Curcic (Edworthy), Tuttle (Linighan), Hreidarsson, Lombardo, Warhurst, Dyer (Morrison), Jansen, Mullins.

Tranmere R (1) 3 *(Irons 24, Kelly 82, 89)*
Carlisle U (0) 0   5116
Tranmere R: Simonsen; Frail, Thompson, McGreal, Hill, Irons, Morrissey (Jones L), Santos (Jones G), Kelly, Parkinson, Mellon.
Carlisle U: Caig; Kubicki (Varty), Searle, Whitehead, Patterson, Brightwell, Barr, Prokas (Skelton), Stevens (Finney), McAlindon, Dobie.

Walsall (0) 0
QPR (0) 0   3691
Walsall: Walker; Marsh, Pointon, Keister, Green, Viveash, Wrack, Brissett, Rammell, Porter, Keates (Watson).
QPR: Harper; Heinola, Baraclough, Yates, Ready, Maddix, Murray, Peacock, Sheron, Gallen (Slade), Scully.

WBA (2) 2 *(Evans 35, Hughes 43)*
Brentford (0) 1 *(Rapley 89)*   8460
WBA: Crichton; Mardon (Burgess), Van Blerk, Flynn, Murphy, Carbon, Quinn (Angel), Sneekes, Evans, Hughes, Kilbane (Oliver).
Brentford: Dearden; Boxall, Anderson, Cullip, Watson, Bates, Freeman (Owusu), Aspinall (Oatway), Quinn, Rowlands, Scott (Rapley).

Wigan Ath (0) 0 *(Hill 55 (og))*
Rochdale (0) 0   2252
Wigan Ath: Carroll; Green, Bradshaw, Griffiths, McGibbon, Rogers, Lee, Jenkinson, Jones, Kilford (Porter), Lowe.
Rochdale: Edwards; Sparrow, Stokes, Hill, Bayliss, Johnson (Bailey), Jones (Lancashire), Farrell, Leonard, Peake, Bryson.

Wrexham (0) 0
Halifax T (1) 2 *(Horsfield 12, Hanson 81)*   2655
Wrexham: Cartwright; McGregor, Brace, Owen, Humes, Carey, Chalk (Skinner), Russell (Brammer), Connolly, Rush, Ward.
Halifax T: Martin; Thackeray, Bradshaw, Sertori, Lucas, Stoneman, Murphy S, Hulme, Hanson (Duerden), Horsfield (Overson), Brown.

York C (0) 0
Sunderland (2) 2 *(Dichio 14, 29)*   6277
York C: Warrington; McMillan, Hall, Tinkler, Jones, Thompson, Connelly, Pouton, Cresswell, Rowe, Garratt (Prendergast).
Sunderland: Sorensen; Gray, Scott, Williams, Craddock, Melville, Summerbee, Ball (Mullin), Dichio, Phillips, Johnston (Wainwright).

12 AUG

Grimsby T (0) 0
Preston NE (0) 0   3008
Grimsby T: Davison; McDermott, Gallimore (Smith D), Handyside, Smith R, Widdrington (Burnett), Coldicott, Black, Nogan, Lester, Groves.
Preston NE: Moilanen; Parkinson, Ludden, Murdock, Jackson, Gregan, Appleton, Rankine, Nogan, Macken, Eyres.

Scarborough (0) 0
Barnsley (1) 1 *(Ward 30)*   3064
Scarborough: Elliott; Jackson, Atkinson, Williams, Lydiate, Mirankov (Radigan), Bullimore, Hoyland, Campbell (Worrell), Brodie, Milbourne (Tate).
Barnsley: Watson; Eaden, Morgan, Richardson (Sheridan), Moses, De Zeeuw, Bullock M (Liddell), Van der Laan, Ward (Hendrie), Fjortoft, Barnard.

Swindon T (1) 2 *(Reeves 44, Ndah 69)*
Wycombe W (0) 1 *(Read 60)* 4626
Swindon T: Glass; Robinson, Hall (McHugh), Gooden, Reeves, Borrows, Walters, Hay (Watson), Onuora, Bullock, Ndah.
Wycombe W: Taylor; Kavanagh, Vinnicombe, Ryan, Cousins, McCarthy, Carroll, Brown, Stallard (Baird), Read (Scott), Cornforth (Harkin).

FIRST ROUND, SECOND LEG

18 AUG

Barnsley (2) 3 *(Fjortoft 35, Van der Laan 42, Eaden 56)*
Scarborough (0) 0 7978
Barnsley: Watson; Eaden, Morgan, Richardson (Sheridan), Moses (Markstedt), De Zeeuw, McClare, Van der Laan, Ward, Liddell (Fjortoft), Barnard.
Scarborough: Elliott; Jackson (Russell), Atkinson (Milbourne), Worrall, Lydiate, Mirankov, Williams, Hoyland, Campbell (Radigan), Brodie, Robinson.
Barnsley won 4-0 on aggregate.

Brentford (0) 3 *(Bates 57, Oatway 59, Owusu 89)*
WBA (0) 0 4664
Brentford: Pearcey; Boxall, Powell, Cullip (Oatway), Watson, Bates, Freeman (Rapley), Aspinall, Quinn, Rowlands, Scott (Owusu).
WBA: Miller; Mardon, Van Blerk, Flynn, Murphy, Carbon, Quinn, Sneekes, Evans (Quailey) (Potter), Hughes, Kilbane.
Brentford won 4-2 on aggregate.

Bristol R (1) 1 *(Hayles 32)*
Leyton Orient (1) 2 *(Inglethorpe 29, Warren 119)* 4235
Bristol R: Jones; Trees, Challis (Leoni), Zabek (Penrice), Foster, Andreasson, Holloway (Ipoua), Meaker, Roberts, Cureton, Hayles.
Leyton Orient: MacKenzie; Walschaerts, Lockwood, Smith, Hicks, Clark, Ling, Ampadu, Griffiths (Warren), Maskell, Inglethorpe (Morrison) (Reinelt).
aet; Leyton Orient won 3-2 on aggregate.

Burnley (1) 1 *(Payton 42)*
Bury (1) 4 *(D'Jaffo 45, Daws 51, Armstrong 70, Matthews 78)* 5453
Burnley: Parks; Brass, Morgan (Henderson), Moore, Blatherwick, Howey (Carr-Lawton), Little, Weller, Jepson (Robertson), Payton, Smith P.
Bury: Kiely; Woodward, Barrick, Daws, Lucketti, Redmond, Swailes C, Patterson (Armstrong), D'Jaffo (Matthews), Johnrose, Preece.
Bury won 5-2 on aggregate.

Cardiff C (0) 1 *(Eckhardt 86)*
Fulham (2) 4 *(Salako 22, Morgan 37)* 4768
Cardiff C: Hallworth; Delaney, Phillips (Eckhardt), Mitchell, Young, Carpenter, Bonner, Williams (Earnshaw), Roberts (O'Sullivan), Nugent, Fowler.
Fulham: Taylor; Uhlenbeek, Brevett, Morgan, Coleman, Symons, Beardsley (Peschisolido), Bracewell, Lehmann (Moody), Hayward, Salako.
Fulham won 4-2 on aggregate.

Carlisle U (0) 0
Tranmere R (0) 1 *(Irons 57 (pen))* 2106
Carlisle U: Caig; Kubicki (Couzens), Searle, Whitehead, Paterson, Brightwell, Anthony, Barr (Dobie), Stevens, Finney, Thorpe (Hopper).
Tranmere R: Simonsen; Morgan, Thompson, McGreal, Hill, Irons, Mahon (Koumas), Mellon, Jones G, Parkinson (Morrissey), Jones L.
Tranmere R won 4-0 on aggregate.

Chester C (0) 2 *(Smith 52, Snijders 82 (og))*
Port Vale (1) 2 *(Naylor 21, 67)* 2461
Chester C: Brown; Davidson, Cross, Richardson, Crosby, Woods, Bennett (Thomas), Priest, Murphy, Flitcroft, Smith.
Port Vale: Musselwhite; Carragher, Tankard (McQuade), Bogie, Walsh, Snijders, Ainsworth, Talbot, Beadle (Foyle), Naylor, Corden (McGlinchey).
Chester C won 4-3 on aggregate.

Chesterfield (0) 2 *(Reeves 51, Holland 82)*
Rotherham U (0) 0 3487
Chesterfield: Mercer; Hewitt, Perkins, Curtis (Ebdon), Williams, Breckin, Willis, Holland, Reeves (Beaumont), Wilkinson (Jules), Howard.
Rotherham U: Pollitt; Ingledow, Beech, Richardson, Knill (Martindale), Dillon, Garner (Sedgwick), Thompson (Hudson), White, Glover, Roscoe.
Chesterfield won 3-0 on aggregate.

Colchester U (1) 3 *(Gregory D 12 (pen), 90 (pen), Abrahams 66)*
Bournemouth (2) 2 *(Stein 23, Fletcher S 28)* 2550
Colchester U: Emberson; Betts (Dunne), Stamps, Williams, Greene, Buckle, Haydon, Gregory D, Sale, Gregory N (Forbes), Abrahams.
Bournemouth: Ovendale; Young, Vincent, Howe, Berthe (O'Neill), Bailey, Cox, Robinson (Tindall), Stein, Fletcher S, Hughes.
Bournemouth won 4-3 on aggregate.

Crewe Alex (1) 2 *(Jack 31, 76)*
Oldham Ath (0) 0 3428
Crewe Alex: Kearton; Bignot, Smith S, Lightfoot, Walton, Charnock, Wright J, Johnson, Jack, Little, Smith P.
Oldham Ath: Kelly; McNiven S, Holt, Graham, Sinnott, Duxbury, Rickers, Orlygsson, Allott, Littlejohn (Whitehall), Reid.
Crewe Alex won 4-3 on aggregate.

Darlington (0) 2 *(Holdsworth 62 (og), Devos 84)*
Sheffield U (0) 2 *(Saunders 103, 105)* 3756
Darlington: Preece; Pepper, Barnard (Brumwell), Liddle, Hope, Devos, Gaughan, Naylor, Dorner (Shutt), Gabbiadini (Roberts), Atkinson.
Sheffield U: Kelly; Borbokis (Wilder), Quinn, Sandford, Nilsen (Devlin), Holdsworth, Saunders, Marker, Taylor, Hamilton I, Stuart.
aet; Sheffield U won 5-3 on aggregate.

Gillingham (0) 0
Southend U (0) 1 *(Clarke 90)* 3417
Gillingham: Bartram; Patterson, Bryant, Smith, Ashby, Carr, Hodge, Hessenthaler, Pinnock, Williams, Butler.
Southend U: Margetson; Hails, Stimson, Roget, Newman, Coleman, Maher, Beard, Burns, De Souza, Clarke.
Southend U won 2-0 on aggregate.

Halifax T (0) 0
Wrexham (1) 2 *(Roberts 27, Connolly 78 (pen))* 2692
Halifax T: Martin; Thackeray, Lucas, Butler, Sertori, Stoneman, Murphy J, Hulme, Hanson, Horsfield (O'Regan), Brown.
Wrexham: Cartwright; McGregor, Hardy (Skinner), Brammer, Ridler, Carey, Roberts, Owen, Connolly, Rush (Spink), Ward (Russell).
aet; Halifax T won 4-2 on penalties.

Hull C (0) 0
Stockport Co (0) 0 3480
Hull C: Wilson; Greaves, Edwards, Hocking, Whitworth, Hawes, Morley (Mann), McGinty, Brown (Ellington), D'Auria, Peacock (Hateley).
Stockport Co: Nash; Dinning, Woodthorpe, Cook, Flynn, Gannon, Alsaker (Cooper), Byrne, Angell (Wilbraham), Moore, Branch (Travis).
aet; Hull C won on away goals.

Ipswich T (3) 5 *(Taricco 30, Holland 31, Stockwell 43, Mathie 80, Mason 87)*
Exeter C (1) 1 *(Richardson 44)* 7952
Ipswich T: Wright; Stockwell (Mason), Taricco, Clapham, Mowbray, Venus, Dyer (Holster), Holland, Johnson, Mathie, Petta (Naylor).
Exeter C: Bayes; Gale, Power (Gardner), Curran (Holloway), Richardson, Gittens, Rowbotham, Rees, Flack, Clark, Breslan (Fry).
Ipswich T won 6-2 on aggregate.

Lincoln C (0) 0
Bradford C (0) 1 *(Rankin 74)* 3066
Lincoln C: Vaughan; Perry, Whitney, Fleming, Brown, Austin, Smith (Thorpe), Finnigan, Fortune-West (Philpott), Battersby, Alcide.
Bradford C: Walsh; Bolland, Dreyer, Grant, Moore, O'Brien, Lawrence, Rankin, Mills, Whalley, Beagrie.
Bradford C won 2-1 on aggregate.

Mansfield T (0) 1 *(Clarke 77)*
Huddersfield T (1) 1 *(Stewart 26)* 2936
Mansfield T: Bowling; Williams, Harper, Peters, Ford (Kerr), Hackett, Schofield, Clarke (Walker), Peacock (Lormor), Christie, Tallon.
Huddersfield T: Vaesen; Jenkins (Gray), Edwards, Johnson, Morrison, Collins, Dalton (Browning), Horne, Stewart (Barnes), Allison, Thornley.
Huddersfield T won 4-3 on aggregate.

Norwich C (0) 1 *(Roberts 91)*
Swansea C (0) 0 13,146
Norwich C: Marshall A; Sutch, Kenton, Grant, Fleming, Jackson, Marshall L, Bellamy, Llewellyn, Eadie, O'Neill (Roberts).
Swansea C: Freestone; Price, Howard, Cusack, Smith, Bound, Casey (Jenkins), Thomas (Bird), Alsop, Watkin (Roberts), Coates.
aet; Norwich C won 2-1 on aggregate.

Oxford U (1) 1 *(Whelan 25)*
Luton T (1) 3 *(Gray 37, Evers 48, McLaren 70)* 5099
Oxford U: Whitehead; Robinson, Marsh, Smith, Whelan, Gilchrist, Banger (Hill), Windass, Thomson (Cook), Murphy (Weatherstone), Beauchamp.
Luton T: Davis K; Alexander, McGowan, Spring, Davis S, Johnson, McLaren, Evers, Douglas (George), Gray, Marshall (McKinnon).
Luton T won 5-4 on aggregate.

Portsmouth (2) 3 *(Hillier 11, McLoughlin 25 (pen), Aloisi 53)*
Plymouth Arg (1) 2 *(Jean 3, McCarthy 66)* 5479
Portsmouth: Knight; Thomson, Simpson F, McLoughlin (Igoe), Whitbread, Awford, Hillier, Claridge, Aloisi, Durnin (Robinson), Kyzeridis (Soley).
Plymouth Arg: Sheffield; Flash, Gibbs, McCall (Ashton), Heathcote, Wotton, Barlow, McCarthy, Jean (Power), Mauge, Hargreaves.
Portsmouth won 6-3 on aggregate.

Preston NE (0) 0
Grimsby T (0) 0 5650
Preston NE: Moilanen; Parkinson, Kidd, McKenna, Jackson, Gregan, Appleton, Rankine, Nogan, Macken (Holt), Eyres (Cartwright).
Grimsby T: Davison; McDermott, Gallimore, Handyside, Smith R, Burnett (Widdrington), Coldicott, Smith D, Nogan (Livingstone), Lester (Clare), Groves.
aet; Grimsby T won 7-6 on penalties.

Rochdale (0) 0
Wigan Ath (0) 1 *(Lee 62)* 1697
Rochdale: Edwards; Bayliss, Stokes, Hill, Farrell, Johnson, Diaz, Painter, Lancashire, Bailey, Peake.
Wigan Ath: Carroll; Breen, Bradshaw, Griffiths, McGibbon, Rogers, Lee, Martinez (Porter), Jones, Kilford, Jenkinson (Sharp).
Wigan Ath won 2-0 on aggregate.

Scunthorpe U (1) 1 *(Forrester 45)*
Blackpool (1) 1 *(Bent 10)* 2211
Scunthorpe U: Clarke; Fickling, McAuley, Harsley (Marshall), Wilcox, Hope, Walker, Forrester, Eyre, Gayle, Calvo-Garcia.
Blackpool: Banks; Bardsley, Hills, Butler (Carlisle), Hughes, Brabin, Bent, Clarkson, Conroy, Bushell, Malkin.
Blackpool won 2-1 on aggregate.

Shrewsbury T (2) 4 *(Evans 38 (pen), 43, 46 (pen), Jobling 69)*
Bristol C (2) 3 *(Thorpe 4, Akinbiyi 31, Doherty 88)* 1011
Shrewsbury T: Edwards; Seabury, Hanmer, Herbert, Wilding, Gayle, Craven, Jagielka, White, Evans, Jobling.
Bristol C: Welch; Locke, Brennan, Hewlett, Dyche, Carey, Murray (Watts), Doherty, Akinbiyi (Cramb), Thorpe (Edwards), Tinnion.
Bristol C won 7-4 on aggregate.

Sunderland (0) 2 *(Phillips 65, Smith 88)*
York C (0) 1 *(Thompson 86)* 22,695
Sunderland: Sorensen; Maley, Gray, Harrison (Thirlwell), Butler, Williams, Wainwright, Mullin, Smith, Phillips (Johnston), Bridges.
York C: Mimms; McMillan, Hall (Garratt), Tinkler, Jones, Thompson, Connelly, Pouton, Cresswell, Woods (Tolson), Agnew.
Sunderland won 4-1 on aggregate.

Watford (0) 1 *(Ngonge 48)*
Cambridge U (0) 1 *(Butler 80 (pen))* 6817
Watford: Chamberlain; Daley (Bazeley), Kennedy (Hazan), Palmer, Millen, Yates, Rosenthal (Smart), Hyde, Ngonge, Easton, Robinson.
Cambridge U: Van Heusden; Chenery, Ashbee, Duncan, Joseph, Campbell, Wanless, Benjamin, Butler, Kyd, Russell.
Cambridge U won 2-1 on aggregate.

Wolverhampton W (3) 5 *(Bull 14, 35, 79, Keane 45, 74)*
Barnet (0) 0 15,296
Wolverhampton W: Stowell; Muscat, Naylor (Gilkes), Richards, Sedgley, Curle, Froggatt, Fernando, Bull (Jones), Keane, Osborn.
Barnet: Harrison; Stockley, Basham, Goodhind, Ford, Doolan, Simpson (Manuel), Devine, Currie (Harle), McGleish (Charlery), Onwere.
Wolverhampton W won 6-2 on aggregate.

Wycombe W (1) 2 *(Brown 20, Stallard 52)*
Swindon T (0) 0 2478
Wycombe W: Taylor; Kavanagh, Vinnicombe, McCarthy, Cousins, Mohan, Ryan, Brown, Stallard, Read, Cornforth (Carroll).
Swindon T: Talia; Robinson, Hall, Watson (Hay), Reeves, Borrows, Walters, Ndah, Onuora, Bullock, Gooden (Cuervo).
Wycombe W won 3-2 on aggregate.

19 AUG

Brighton & HA (0) 1 *(Barker 48)*
Northampton T (0) 1 *(Heggs 97)* 1291
Brighton & HA: Walton; Smith, Atkinson, Minton, Allan, Thomas, Culverhouse, Mayo, Moralee (Hart), Barker, Bennett.
Northampton T: Woodman; Clarkson, Frain, Bishop, Warburton, Hunt, Gibb (Warner), Peer (Spedding), Heggs, Corazzin, Hill.
aet; Northampton T won 3-2 on aggregate.

Manchester C (4) 7 *(Mason 6, Dickov 16, 58, Bradbury 21, Goater 38, 90, Jim Whitley 69)*
Notts Co (0) 1 *(Torpey 86)* 10,063
Manchester C: Weaver; Edghill, Horlock (Jim Whitley), Fenton, Wiekens, Vaughan, Mason, Pollock, Goater, Dickov (Allsop), Bradbury (Conlon).
Notts Co: Ward; Hughes, Liburd, Redmile, Fairclough, Owers, Billy (Dudley), Murray, Torpey, Jones (Henshaw), Robson (Dyer).
Manchester C won 9-1 on aggregate.

Millwall (1) 1 *(Shaw 26)*
Birmingham C (1) 1 *(Adebola 45)* 4478
Millwall: Spink; Lavin, Stuart, Bowry, Law, Fitzgerald, Neill (Reid), Newman (Cahill), Sadlier, Shaw, Carter.
Birmingham C: Bennett; Rowett, Grainger, Marsden, Ablett (Purse), Johnson M, McCarthy, O'Connor, Adebola, Hughes (Forster), Ndlovu (Holland).
Birmingham C won 3-1 on aggregate.

Stoke C (0) 1 *(Thorne 78)*
Macclesfield T (0) 0 6152
Stoke C: Muggleton; Short (Tweed), Small (Wallace), Whittle, Robinson, Woods, Pickering, Kavanagh, Thorne, Crowe (Sturridge), Oldfield.
Macclesfield T: Price; Tinson, Ingram, Payne, McDonald, Sodje, Askey (Tomlinson), Wood, Durkan, Sorvel, Whittaker (Howarth).
Macclesfield T won 3-2 on aggregate.

25 AUG

Crystal Palace (1) 2 *(Lombardo 18, Hreidarsson 99)*
Torquay U (0) 1 *(Thomas 70)* 6872
Crystal Palace: Digby; Austin, Smith, Curcic (Morrison), Rodger (Bent), Linighan, Lombardo, Hreidarsson, Dyer, Jansen (Amsalem), Mullins.
Torquay U: Veysey; Gurney, Herrera, Robinson, Thomas, Watson, Leadbitter (Tully), McGorry (Hapgood), Bedeau, Partridge, Hill (McFarlane).
aet; Crystal Palace won 3-2 on aggregate.

Hartlepool U (0) 0
Bolton W (0) 3 *(Blake 55, 59, 71)* 3185
Hartlepool U: Hollund; Knowles, Ingram, Barron, Lee, Beech, Miller (Brightwell), Midgley (Irvine), McDonald, Howard, Clark.
Bolton W: Jaaskelainen; Cox, Phillips (Whitlow), Todd, Strong, Fish, Jensen, Frandsen, Blake, Holdsworth (Taylor B), Gunnlaugsson (Gardner).
Bolton W won 4-0 on aggregate.

26 AUG

QPR (0) 3 *(Sheron 68, Maddix 99, Slade 114)*
Walsall (0) 1 *(Rammell 80)* 5052
QPR: Harper; Rose, Baraclough, Yates (Slade), Ready, Maddix, Murray, Peacock, Sheron, Gallen, Scully (Kulcsar).
Walsall: Walker; Marsh, Pointon (Roper), Keates (Dyer), Green, Viveash, Wrack, Watson (Ricketts), Rammell, Porter, Brissett.
aet; QPR won 3-1 on aggregate.

Reading (1) 2 *(Caskey 40 (pen), Brebner 88)*
Peterborough U (0) 0 9151
Reading: Howey; Booty, Gray, Brebner, Parkinson, Primus, Houghton, Caskey, Fleck (Williams), Reilly, Sarr (Asaba).
Peterborough U: Griemink; Hooper, Drury, Gill (Scott), Bodley, Edwards, Davies, Castle (Inman), Carruthers (Etherington), Quinn, Grazioli.
Reading won 3-1 on aggregate.

SECOND ROUND, FIRST LEG

15 SEPT

Barnsley (1) 3 *(Barnard 22, Fjortoft 59, 86)*
Reading (0) 0 7840
Barnsley: Leese; McClare, De Zeeuw, Richardson, Moses, Appleby, Bullock M (Marcelle), Sheridan, Ward, Fjortoft, Barnard.
Reading: Hammond; Booty, Gray, Brebner, Primus, McPherson, Crawford, Caskey, Glasgow, Reilly, Sarr (Williams).

Blackpool (1) 2 *(Aldridge 24, 54)*
Tranmere R (1) 1 *(Parkinson 16)* 3954
Blackpool: Banks; Bryan, Shuttleworth, Hughes, Carlisle, Ormerod (Nowland), Thompson, Clarkson, Aldridge, Bushell, Malkin (Brabin).
Tranmere R: Simonsen; McGreal, Thompson, O'Brien, Hill, Irons, Koumas (Morrissey), Santos, Jones G (Jones L), Parkinson, Mellon (Mahon).

Bolton W (1) 3 *(Phillips 45, Gunnlaugsson 61, Frandsen 89)*
Hull C (0) 1 *(Brown 80)* 7544
Bolton W: Jaaskelainen; Cox, Phillips, Jensen, Bergsson, Strong, Johansen, Frandsen, Taylor B, Gunnlaugsson, Gardner.
Hull C: Wilson; Greaves (Morley), Mann, Hocking, Whitworth, Hawes, Peacock, McGinty, Brown, D'Auria, French.

Bournemouth (1) 1 *(Stein 17)*
Wolverhampton W (0) 1 *(Ferguson 83)* 7096
Bournemouth: Ovendale; Young, Vincent, Howe, Berthe (Warren) (Town), Bailey (O'Neill), Cox, Robinson, Stein, Fletcher S, Hughes.
Wolverhampton W: Stowell; Muscat, Naylor (Ferguson), Richards, Sedgley, Williams, Froggatt, Corica (Emblen), Connolly, Keane (Jones), Osborn.

Brentford (1) 2 *(Scott 28, Freeman 66)*
Tottenham H (1) 3 *(Carr 44, Dominguez 53, Vega 82)* 11,831
Brentford: Pearcey; Boxall, Anderson, Coyne, Powell, Bates, Freeman (Rapley), Aspinall, Quinn, Rowlands, Scott (Owusu).
Tottenham H: Baardsen; Carr, Tramezzani (Dominguez), Vega, Calderwood, Campbell, Ginola, Clemence, Armstrong, Allen (Gower), Sinton.

Bury (2) 3 *(Johnrose 9, 58, Matthews 23)*
Crystal Palace (0) 0 2780
Bury: Kiely; Woodward (Swailes D), Barrick, Dawes, Lucketti, Patterson, Swailes C, Matthews (Jemson), D'Jaffo (Ellis), Johnrose, Preece.
Crystal Palace: Digby; Austin, Smith, Jihai (Bent), Rodger, Zhiyi, Lombardo, Hreidarsson, Shipperley, Jansen, Mullins.

Fulham (0) 1 *(Coleman 54)*
Southampton (0) 1 *(Beattie 62)* 10,222
Fulham: Taylor; Collins, Brevett, Morgan, Coleman, Symons, Beardsley, Bracewell, Lehmann, Hayward, Cornwall (Davis).
Southampton: Jones; Dodd, Benali, Palmer, Warner, Gibbens, Le Tissier, Howells (Lundekvam), Ostenstad (Beattie), Hughes, Ripley.

Halifax T (0) 1 *(Hanson 57)*
Bradford C (1) 2 *(Moore 32, Beagrie 68)* 5714
Halifax T: Martin; Thackeray, Bradshaw, Sertori, Lucas, Stoneman, O'Regan (Paterson), Hulme, Hanson, Horsfield, Brown.
Bradford C: Walsh; Wright, Jacobs, McCall, Moore, Dreyer, Pepper, Blake (Watson), Mills, Whalley, Beagrie.

Huddersfield T (1) 1 *(Allison 45)*
Everton (1) 1 *(Watson 37)* 15,395
Huddersfield T: Vaesen; Jenkins, Edwards, Johnson (Browning), Gray, Collins, Dalton, Horne, Stewart, Allison, Thornley (Beresford).
Everton: Myhre; Cleland, Ball, Materazzi, Watson, Unsworth, Collins, Barmby (Cadamarteri), Ferguson, Dacourt (Madar), Hutchison.

Ipswich T (0) 2 *(Scowcroft 48, Thetis 79)*
Luton T (0) 1 *(Douglas 60)* 9032
Ipswich T: Wright; Stockwell, Taricco, Clapham, Thetis, Venus (Tanner), Dyer, Holland, Johnson, Scowcroft, Petta.
Luton T: Davis K; Alexander, McGowan, Spring, Davis S, Johnson, Cox (Bacque), Evers, Douglas (Fotiadis), Gray, McIndoe.

Leyton Orient (0) 1 *(Reinelt 87)*
Nottingham F (4) 5 *(Johnson 4, Freedman 14, 17, Stone 44, Harewood 84)* 4906
Leyton Orient: MacKenzie; Walschaerts, Warren, Smith, Hicks (Joseph R), Joseph M, Ling (Baker), Ampadu, Griffiths, McCormick (Reinelt), Morrison.
Nottingham F: Beasant (Crossley); Lyttle, Rogers (Louis-Jean), Stone, Chettle, Armstrong, Quashie, Johnson A, Darcheville (Harewood), Freedman, Bonalair.

Macclesfield T (0) 0
Birmingham C (0) 3 *(Forster 66, Marsden 70, Rowett 89)* 2275
Macclesfield T: Price; Tinson (Hitchen), Howarth, Payne, McDonald (Durkan), Sodje, Askey (Brown), Wood, Barclay, Sorvel, Whittaker.
Birmingham C: Bennett; Rowett, Grainger, Marsden, Ablett, Johnson M, McCarthy, O'Connor, Adebola (Forinton), Forster (Johnson A), Robinson (Holland).

Northampton T (0) 2 *(Freestone 77, 85)*
West Ham U (0) 0 7254
Northampton T: Woodman; Gibb, Parrish, Sampson, Warburton, Peer, Hunter (Hunt), Spedding, Freestone (Heggs), Corazzin (Wilkinson), Hill.
West Ham U: Hislop; Sinclair, Lazaridis, Potts, Pearce, Ruddock (Breacker), Lampard, Berkovic, Hartson, Wright, Moncur.

Portsmouth (2) 2 *(Aloisi 9, McLoughlin 25)*
Wimbledon (1) 1 *(Ekoku 35)* 7010
Portsmouth: Knight; Thorgersen, Simpson F, McLoughlin, Whitbread, Awford, Perrett, Peron, Aloisi, Durnin (Phillips), Igoe (Soley).
Wimbledon: Heald; Jupp, Thatcher, Francis, McAllister, Perry (Cunningham), Ardley (Euell), Fear (Leaburn), Ekoku, Cort, Kennedy.

Sheffield U (1) 2 *(Hamilton I 28, Ford 69)*
Grimsby T (0) 1 *(Ashcroft 51)* 4689
Sheffield U: Goram; Borbokis, Quinn, Ford, Sandford, Dellas, Saunders, Marker, Taylor (Marcello), Hamilton I, Stuart.
Grimsby T: Davison; McDermott, Gallimore (Smith D), Livingstone, Smith R, Burnett, Widdrington, Black (Butterfield), Ashcroft, Lester (Nogan), Groves.

Sunderland (2) 3 *(Scott 32, Phillips 39, Bridges 58)*
Chester C (0) 0 20,618
Sunderland: Sorensen; Makin, Scott, Rae, Craddock, Williams (Butler), Wainwright, Mullin, Dichio, Phillips (Bridges), Smith.
Chester C: Cutler; Richardson, Cross, Reid, Davidson, Woods, Flitcroft, Priest, Murphy, Wright (Thomas), Smith.

16 SEPT

Bristol C (1) 1 *(Akinbiyi 15)*
Crewe Alex (1) 1 *(Rivers 21)* 3082
Bristol C: Welch; Locke, Bell, Goodridge (Murray), Watts, Carey (Edwards), Brennan, Hutchings, Akinbiyi, Andersen, Tinnion.
Crewe Alex: Kearton; Bignot (Wright D), Smith S, Wicks, Charnock (Lunt), Unsworth, Rivers, Street, Little (Foster), Wright J, Smith P.

Coventry C (0) 1 *(Hall P 64)*
Southend U (0) 0 6631
Coventry C: Hedman; Shaw (Shilton), Burrows, Breen, Wallemme (Williams), Boateng, Telfer, Hall P, Dublin, Clement (Soltvedt), Huckerby.
Southend U: Margetson; Hails, Stimson, Morley, Newman, Coleman, Maher, Gooding, Burns, Whyte (Fitzpatrick), Jones.

Derby Co (1) 1 *(Delap 9)*
Manchester C (1) 1 *(Tiatto 27)* 22,986
Derby Co: Poom; Eranio, Delap, Laursen, Stimac, Elliott (Harper), Carsley, Sturridge, Baiano, Wanchope, Powell.
Manchester C: Weaver; Edghill, Tiatto, Fenton, Wiekens, Vaughan, Jim Whitley, Pollock, Goater, Dickov (Jeff Whitley), Bradbury (Brown M R).

Leicester C (1) 3 *(Heskey 41, 51, Taggart 61)*
Chesterfield (0) 0 13,480
Leicester C: Keller; Savage (Zagorakis), Guppy, Elliott, Taggart, Sinclair, Lennon (Ullathorne), Parker, Cottee (Wilson), Campbell, Heskey.
Chesterfield: Leaning; Hewitt, Perkins, Beaumont, Williams (Eustace), Breckin, Willis, Holland, Howard, Ebdon, Jules.

Middlesbrough (1) 2 *(Ricard 37, Festa 90)*
Wycombe W (0) 0 11,531
Middlesbrough: Beresford; Stockdale, Gordon (Harrison), Vickers, Festa, Kinder, Campbell, Gascoigne, Ricard, Stamp, Moore (Ormerod).
Wycombe W: Westhead; Kavanagh, Beeton, Cornforth, Cousins, Mohan, Carroll (Wraight), Vinnicombe, Stallard, McGavin (Bulman), Emblen.

Norwich C (1) 1 *(Bradshaw 22 (og))*
Wigan Ath (0) 0 11,426
Norwich C: Marshall A; Sutch, Kenton, Grant, Fleming, Segura, Marshall L, Bellamy, Roberts (Coote), Eadie, Llewellyn (Forbes).
Wigan Ath: Carroll; Green, Bradshaw, Griffiths, McGibbon, Rogers, Lee, Greenall, Lowe, Martinez, Barlow (Warne).

QPR (0) 0
Charlton Ath (2) 2 *(Newton 15, Redfearn 45)* 6497
QPR: Harper; Heinola, Baraclough, Murray, Ready, Maddix, Slade, Peacock, Scully (Kulcsar), Gallen, Rowland (Sheron).
Charlton Ath: Ilic; Mills, Powell, Redfearn, Rufus (Jones S), Youds, Newton, Jones K, Hunt, Mendonca (Brown), Robinson (Mortimer).

Sheffield W (0) 0
Cambridge U (1) 1 *(Benjamin 3)* 8921
Sheffield W: Pressman; Cobian, Hinchliffe, Atherton, Emerson, Walker, Jonk, Carbone, Booth (Whittingham), Rudi (Sanetti), Di Canio.
Cambridge U: Van Heusden; Chenery, Mustoe, Duncan, Joseph, Campbell, Wanless, Taylor, Butler, Benjamin, Russell.

SECOND ROUND, SECOND LEG

22 SEPT

Birmingham C (3) 6 *(Ndlovu 7, 19, Askey 37 (og),*
Marsden 57, Rowett 66, Johnson M 89)
Macclesfield T (0) 0 3443
Birmingham C: Bennett; Rowett, Charlton, Hurst, Marsden, Johnson M, McCarthy (Grainger), O'Connor (Holland), Forinton, Robinson, Ndlovu (Johnson A).
Macclesfield T: Price; Tinson, Hitchen, Payne, McDonald, Sodje, Askey (Barclay), Wood, Brown, Sedgemore (Griffiths), Whittaker.
Birmingham C won 9-0 on aggregate.

Bradford C (0) 3 *(Blake 56, Beagrie 77 (pen), Pepper 82)*
Halifax T (0) 1 *(Paterson 54)* 6237
Bradford C: Walsh; Wright, Jacobs, McCall (Ramage), Moore, O'Brien, Pepper (Dreyer), Blake, Watson (Edinho), Whalley, Beagrie.
Halifax T: Martin; Thackeray, Bradshaw, Sertori, Butler, Stoneman, Paterson, Hulme, Hanson, Horsfield, O'Regan (Williams).
Bradford won 5-2 on aggregate.

Cambridge U (0) 1 *(Benjamin 74)*
Sheffield W (0) 1 *(Campbell 69 (og))* 8502
Cambridge U: Van Heusden; Chenery, Mustoe, Duncan, Joseph, Campbell, Wanless, Taylor, Butler, Benjamin, Russell.
Sheffield W: Pressman; Briscoe, Hinchliffe, Newsome (Sanetti), Emerson, Walker, Atherton, Carbone (Alexandersson), Booth, Jonk (Barrett), Di Canio.
Cambridge U won 2-1 on aggregate.

Charlton Ath (1) 1 *(Youds 18)*
QPR (0) 0 11,726
Charlton Ath: Ilic; Mills, Powell, Jones K, Rufus (Brown), Youds, Mortimer, Redfearn, Jones S, Mendonca (Allen), Robinson (Newton).
QPR: Harper; Heinola, Baraclough, Yates, Ready, Maddix, Slade (Kiwomya), Peacock, Murray (Sheron), Gallen, Scully (Dowie).
Charlton Ath won 3-0 on aggregate.

Chester C (0) 0
Sunderland (1) 1 *(Johnston 12)* 2738
Chester C: Brown; Davidson, Cross, Reid, Crosby, Woods, Flitcroft, Shelton, Murphy, Thomas (Jones), Smith.
Sunderland: Sorensen; Makin, Scott, Rae, Melville (Smith), Butler, Summerbee, Mullin, Dichio, Bridges, Johnston (Craddock).
Sunderland won 4-0 on aggregate.

Chesterfield (1) 1 *(Howard 28)*
Leicester C (0) 3 *(Heskey 57, Fenton 87, Wilson 90)* 4565
Chesterfield: Leaning; Hewitt, Perkins, Lomas, Beaumont, Breckin, Willis, Holland, Reeves, Howard, Jules.
Leicester C: Arphexad; Kamark, Guppy, Elliott, Taggart, Wilson, Lennon (Campbell), Parker, Zagorakis, Ullathorne (Savage), Heskey (Fenton).
Leicester C won 6-1 on aggregate.

Crewe Alex (0) 2 *(Rivers 64, 65)*
Bristol C (0) 0 3089
Crewe Alex: Kearton; Bignot, Smith S, Unsworth, Walton, Charnock, Wright J, Johnson, Anthrobus, Little (Street), Rivers.
Bristol C: Welch; Murray, Bell, Doherty (Hutchings), Zwijnenberg, Watts, Goodridge, Edwards R, Akinbiyi, Cramb (Andersen), Tinnion.
Crewe Alex won 3-1 on aggregate.

Grimsby T (0) 2 *(Groves 56, Clare 101)*
Sheffield U (0) 0 4287
Grimsby T: Davison; McDermott, Gallimore, Livingstone, Smith R, Widdrington (Donovan), Black, Smith D (Dobbin), Ashcroft (Clare), Lester, Groves.
Sheffield U: Goram; Borbokis, Nilsen (Devlin), Ford, Sandford, Dellas (Woodhouse), Saunders, Marker, Marcello, Hamilton I (Taylor), Stuart.
aet; Grimsby T won 3-2 on aggregate.

Hull C (1) 2 *(Brown 42, Rioch 47 (pen))* 4226
Bolton W (1) 3 *(Jensen 26, Johansen 72, Gardner 79)*
Hull C: Wilson; Edwards, Mann, Hocking, Whitworth, Hawes, Peacock, D'Auria, Brown, Rioch (French), McGinty.
Bolton W: Jaaskelainen; Cox, Whitlow (Phillips), Jensen, Strong, Fish, Johansen, Frandsen, Taylor (Gudjohnson), Gardner, Gunnlaugsson (Blake).
Bolton W won 6-3 on aggregate.

Luton T (0) 4 *(Fotiadis 52, Douglas 84, Davis S 98, Johnson 119)*
Ipswich T (1) 2 *(Johnson 35, Davis S 118 (og))* 5655
Luton T: Davis K; Alexander, McGowan, Spring, Davis S, Johnson, McKinnon (White), Evers, Douglas, Fotiadis (Bacque), Marshall (Cox).
Ipswich T: Wright; Stockwell (Mathie), Taricco (Sonner), Tanner, Thetis, Venus, Dyer, Holland, Johnson, Scowcroft, Petta (Clapham).
aet; Luton T won 5-4 on aggregate.

Nottingham F (0) 0
Leyton Orient (0) 0 6382
Nottingham F: Crossley; Louis-Jean, Rogers, Bonalair (Darchville) (Harewood), Hjelde, Armstrong, Johnson, Quashie (Burns), Freedman, Dawson, Gray.
Leyton Orient: Capleton; Walschaerts, Joseph R, Smith, Hicks, Joseph M, Ling, Ampadu, Griffiths (Reinelt), McCormick (Raynor), Martin (Morrison).
Nottingham F won 5-1 on aggregate.

Southend U (0) 0
Coventry C (3) 4 *(Boateng 6, Dublin 27, Whelan 44, Soltvedt 83)* 6292
Southend U: Margetson; Hails, Stimson, Morley, Newman, Coleman, Maher, Gooding, Fitzpatrick (Dublin), Whyte, Clarke.
Coventry C: Hedman; Wallemme, Burrows, Williams (Clement), Shaw, Boateng (Strachan), Quinn (Soltvedt), Shilton, Dublin, Whelan, Boland.
Coventry C won 5-0 on aggregate.

Tranmere R (1) 3 *(Koumas 33, Jones L 63, Irons 82 (pen))*
Blackpool (1) 1 *(Malkin 1)* 5765
Tranmere R: Simonsen; Allen, Hill, McGreal, Challinor, Irons, Koumas, Santos (Jones G), Parkinson, O'Brien, Mahon (Jones L).
Blackpool: Banks; Bryan, Shuttleworth, Bardsley, Carlisle, Ormerod (Bent), Thompson (Robinson), Clarkson, Hughes, Bushell, Malkin.
Tranmere R won 4-3 on aggregate.

West Ham U (0) 1 *(Lampard 90)*
Northampton T (0) 0 25,435
West Ham U: Hislop; Impey, Dicks, Potts, Ferdinand, Pearce, Keller, Lampard, Abou (Omoyimni), Wright, Sinclair.
Northampton T: Woodman; Gibb, Frain, Sampson, Warburton, Peer, Hunter (Spedding) (Dobson), Wilkinson, Freestone (Corazzin), Parrish, Hill.
Northampton T won 2-1 on aggregate.

Wigan Ath (0) 2 *(Griffiths 78, Barlow 89)*
Norwich C (2) 3 *(Bellamy 10, Roberts 37, 66)* 3402
Wigan Ath: Carroll; Green, Jenkinson (Smeets), Griffiths, Balmer, Rogers, Lee, Greenall, Lowe, O'Neill, Barlow.
Norwich C: Marshall A; Sutch, Kenton, Grant, Fleming, Mackay, Marshall L (Forbes), Bellamy, Roberts, Eadie, Brannan.
Norwich C won 4-2 on aggregate.

Wimbledon (1) 4 *(Ardley 26, Ekoku 55, 112, Leaburn 104)*
Portsmouth (1) 1 *(Whitbread 19)* 3756
Wimbledon: Heald; Cunningham, Jupp (Kimble), Francis (Roberts), Thatcher, Perry, Ardley, Cort (Euell), Ekoku, Leaburn, Kennedy.
Portsmouth: Flahavan; Thorgersen, Simpson F (Phillips), McLoughlin, Whitbread, Awford, Perrett, Peron (Soley), Aloisi, Claridge, Igoe.
aet; Wimbledon won 5-3 on aggregate.

Wolverhampton W (0) 1 *(Keane 57)*
Bournemouth (1) 2 *(Stein 21, 60)* 15,431
Wolverhampton W: Stowell; Muscat, Naylor, Richards, Sedgley (Ferguson), Curle, Emblen, Fernando (Corica), Connolly, Keane, Osborn.
Bournemouth: Ovendale; Young, Vincent, Howe, O'Neill, Bailey (Warren), Cox, Tindall, Stein, Fletcher, Hughes.
Bournemouth won 3-2 on aggregate.

Wycombe W (1) 1 *(Brown 24)*
Middlesbrough (0) 1 *(Ricard 53)* 5698
Wycombe W: Taylor; Kavanagh (Wraight), Beeton, Cornforth, Cousins, Mohan (McCarthy), Vinnicombe, Brown, Stallard (Baird), Bulman, Emblen.
Middlesbrough: Beresford; Stockdale, Harrison, Vickers, Cooper, Blackmore, Maddison, Gascoigne (Summerbell), Ricard, Stamp, Beck (Campbell).
Middlesbrough won 3-1 on aggregate.

23 SEPT

Crystal Palace (1) 2 *(Morrison 8, Zhiyi 77)*
Bury (1) 1 *(Morrison 25 (og))* 3546
Crystal Palace: Digby; Austin (Linighan), Amsalem (Dyer), Zhiyi, Tuttle, Burton (Del Rio), Lombardo, Rizzo, Morrison, Jansen, Mullins.
Bury: Kiely; Patterson, Barrick, Daws, Lucketti, Redmond, Swailes C, Matthews (Jemson), D'Jaffo (Ellis), Johnrose (Swailes D), Preece.
Bury won 4-2 on aggregate.

Everton (2) 2 *(Dacourt 29, Materazzi 42)*
Huddersfield T (1) 1 *(Stewart 1)* 18,718
Everton: Myhre; Cleland, Ball, Unsworth, Materazzi, Tiler, Cadamarteri (Barmby), Oster (Collins), Ferguson, Dacourt, Hutchison.
Huddersfield T: Vaesen; Jenkins, Edwards, Johnson, Gray, Collins, Dalton (Beresford), Horne, Stewart, Morrison (Barnes), Thornley.
Everton won 3-2 on aggregate.

Manchester C (0) 0
Derby Co (0) 1 *(Wanchope 28)* 19,622
Manchester C: Wright; Edghill, Horlock, Fenton, Wiekens, Vaughan, Mason (Allsop), Pollock, Goater, Jim Whitley, Bradbury (Dickov).
Derby Co: Poom; Kozluk, Schnoor, Delap, Laursen, Prior, Eranio (Carsley), Sturridge, Baiano, Wanchope (Harper), Powell.
Derby Co won 2-1 on aggregate.

Reading (0) 1 *(Caskey 90 (pen))*
Barnsley (0) 1 *(Ward 85)* 6983
Reading: Howey; Booty, Gray, McPherson, Primus, Houghton (Caskey), Parkinson, Glasgow, Williams, Hadland (Brayson), Casper.
Barnsley: Leese; Eaden, De Zeeuw (Marcelle), Richardson, Moses, Krizan, Bullock M (Bagshaw), McClare, Ward, Fjortoft (Hendrie), Barnard.
Barnsley won 4-1 on aggregate.

Southampton (0) 0
Fulham (1) 1 *(Lehmann 10)* 11,645
Southampton: Jones; Dodd, Benali, Palmer, Lundekvam, Gibbens, Le Tissier, Beattie (Basham), Ostenstad, Hughes, Bridge.
Fulham: Taylor; Collins (Trollope), Brevett, Morgan, Coleman, Symons, Beardsley, Bracewell, Lehmann, Hayward, Uhlenbeek (Neilson).
Fulham won 2-1 on aggregate.

Tottenham H (1) 3 *(Nielsen 24, Campbell 46, Armstrong 53)*
Brentford (1) 2 *(Scott 1, Owusu 74)* 22,980
Tottenham H: Segers; Carr, Edinburgh, Nielsen, Calderwood, Campbell, Anderton, Fox, Armstrong, Clemence (Gower), Ginola (Dominguez).
Brentford: Pearcey; Boxall, Anderson, Oatway (Rapley), Powell, Bates, Freeman (Owusu), Aspinall, Quinn, Rowlands, Scott (Folan).
Tottenham H won 6-4 on aggregate.

THIRD ROUND

27 OCT

Barnsley (1) 2 *(Ward 42 (pen), Fjortoft 47)*
Bournemouth (0) 1 *(Stein 87)* 8560
Barnsley: Bullock T; Moses, De Zeeuw, Jones, Tinkler, Eaden, Bullock M, McClare, Ward, Fjortoft, Barnard (Sheridan).
Bournemouth: Ovendale; Young, Vincent, Howe, Berthe (Boli), Bailey, Cox, Robinson (Warren) (Town), Stein, O'Neill, Hughes.

Charlton Ath (0) 1 *(Mortimer 56)*
Leicester C (0) 2 *(Cottee 51, 60)* 19,671
Charlton Ath: Petterson; Mills (Parker), Powell, Jones K (Lisbie), Rufus, Youds, Robinson, Kinsella, Hunt (Bright), Mendonca, Mortimer.
Leicester C: Keller; Savage, Guppy, Elliott, Ullathorne, Sinclair, Lennon, Izzet, Cottee, Zagorakis, Heskey.

Liverpool (0) 3 *(Morgan 53 (og), Fowler 66 (pen), Ince 76)*
Fulham (0) 1 *(Peschisolido 60)* 22,296
Liverpool: Friedel; McAteer, Bjornebye, Thompson, Carragher, Staunton, Murphy, Ince, Fowler, Owen (Dundee), Berger.
Fulham: Taylor; Uhlenbeek, Brevett, Morgan, Coleman, Symons, Collins, Davis (Smith), Lehmann (Betsy), Peschisolido (Beardsley), Hayward.

Luton T (0) 2 *(Gray 50, Davis S 78)*
Coventry C (0) 0 9051
Luton T: Davis K; Alexander, Thomas, Spring, Davis S, Johnson, McKinnon, Evers, Douglas (Fotiadis), Gray, McGowan.
Coventry C: Hedman; Brightwell, Hall M, Breen, Shaw, Boateng, Telfer, Whelan, Huckerby, McAllister, Hall P (Soltvedt).

Northampton T (1) 1 *(Parrish 30)*
Tottenham H (1) 3 *(Armstrong 39, 83, Campbell 47)* 7422
Northampton T: Woodman; Gibb, Frain, Sampson, Hodgson, Hill (Witter), Hunt, Wilkinson (Warner), Corazzin, Freestone, Parrish.
Tottenham H: Baardsen; Carr, Edinburgh, Scales, Calderwood, Campbell, Anderton, Nielsen, Iversen, Armstrong (Allen), Ginola (Clemence).

Norwich C (0) 1 *(O'Neill 104)*
Bolton W (0) 1 *(Elliott 96)* 14,189
Norwich C: Marshall A; Kenton, Fuglestad, Sutch, Fleming, Jackson (McKay), Marshall L, Bellamy, Roberts, Eadie (Milligan), Adams (O'Neill).
Bolton W: Branagan; Aljofree, Phillips, Todd, Bergsson, Fish, Johansen, Jensen, Blake (Taylor B), Elliott, Gunnlaugsson (Holdsworth).
aet; Bolton W won 3-1 on penalties.

Nottingham F (2) 3 *(Freedman 22, Armstrong 45, Harewood 46)*
Cambridge U (0) 3 *(Benjamin 68, Butler 72, Taylor 84 (pen))* 9192
Nottingham F: Beasant; Bonalair, Rogers, Stone, Chettle, Hjelde, Armstrong, Gemmill (Gray), Freedman (Lyttle), Harewood (Darcheville), Bart-Williams.
Cambridge U: Marshall; Chenery, Mustoe, Duncan, McNeil, Campbell (Kyd), Wanless, Taylor (Preece), Butler, Benjamin, Russell.
aet; Nottingham F won 4-3 on penalties.

Sunderland (0) 2 *(Bridges 66, Quinn 115)*
Grimsby T (1) 1 *(Nogan 11)* 18,676
Sunderland: Sorensen; Macken, Gray, Thirlwell, Craddock, Scott, Summerbee, Mullin, Dichio (Quinn), Bridges (Aiston), Smith (Lumsdon).
Grimsby T: Davison; McDermott, Gallimore, Smith R (Widdrington), Lever, Livingstone, Butterfield (Handyside), Black, Nogan, Lester, Groves.

Tranmere R (0) 0
Newcastle U (1) 1 *(Dalglish 31)* 12,017
Tranmere R: Achterberg; Allen, Thompson (Challinor), McGreal, Hill, Irons, Koumas (Parkinson), Santos, Jones G, Mellon (O'Brien), Kelly.
Newcastle U: Given; Griffin, Pearce, Dabizas, Charvet, Glass (Gillespie), Dalglish, Batty, Shearer, Solano, Speed.

28 OCT

Birmingham C (1) 1 *(Marsden 34)*
Wimbledon (1) 2 *(Ardley 35, 46)* 11,845
Birmingham C: Poole; Rowett, Charlton, Purse, Ablett, Marsden, McCarthy, Adebola (Forster), Furlong, Holland, Ndlovu.
Wimbledon: Sullivan; Cunningham, Thatcher, Ardley, Blackwell, Perry, Kennedy (Kimble) (Earle), Leaburn, Euell, Gayle (Cort).

Chelsea (1) 4 *(Vialli 32, 67, 85, Flo 71)*
Aston Villa (1) 1 *(Draper 10)* 26,790
Chelsea: Kharine; Petrescu (Terry), Babayaro, Morris, Duberry, Nicholls (Clement), Poyet, Lambourde, Vialli (Harley), Flo, Wise.
Aston Villa: Oakes; Charles (Vassell), Wright (Jaszczun), Grayson, Ehiogu, Scimeca (Thompson), Taylor, Draper, Joachim, Watson, Byfield.

Crewe Alex (0) 0
Blackburn R (0) 1 *(Sutton 47)* 5403
Crewe Alex: Kearton; Bignot, Smith S, Lightfoot (Anthrobus), Walton, Charnock, Wright J, Johnson (Lunt), Jack, Little, Rivers.
Blackburn R: Flowers; Kenna, Davidson, Sherwood, Peacock, Henchoz, McKinlay, Johnson, Sutton, Davies, Duff.

Derby Co (0) 1 *(Sturridge 83)*
Arsenal (1) 2 *(Carsley 21 (og), Vivas 55)* 25,621
Derby Co: Poom; Schnoor, Dorigo, Delap, Laursen, Prior (Elliott), Powell, Sturridge, Baiano (Wanchope), Burton (Harper), Carsley.
Arsenal: Manninger; Vivas, Grondin, Garde, Grimandi, Upson (Crowe), Ljungberg, Mendez, Hughes, Wreh (Riza), Boa Morte.

Leeds U (1) 1 *(Kewell 28)*
Bradford C (0) 0   27,561
Leeds U: Robinson; Halle, Granville, Woodgate, Radebe, Molenaar, Hopkin, McPhail, Hasselbaink, Kewell, Bowyer.
Bradford C: Walsh; Todd, Jacobs, McCall, Moore, Dreyer (Lawrence), Rankin (Watson), Blake, Mills, Whalley, Beagrie.

Manchester U (0) 2 *(Solskjaer 106, Nevland 115)*
Bury (0) 0   52,495
Manchester U: Van der Gouw; Clegg (Brown), Curtis, Berg, Neville P, May, Wilson (Scholes), Mulryne (Nevland), Greening, Solskjaer, Cruyff.
Bury: Kiely; Woodward, Barrick, Daws, Lucketti, Redmond, Swailes C, Patterson (Matthews), D'Jaffo (Preece), Johnrose, Ellis (James).

Middlesbrough (0) 2 *(Summerbell 64, Ricard 117)*
Everton (0) 3 *(Ferguson 67, Bakayoko 102, Hutchison 108)*   20,748
Middlesbrough: Beresford; Stockdale (Campbell), Gordon, Vickers, Festa, Fleming, Mustoe (Summerbell), Stamp, Ricard, Townsend, Beck (Deane).
Everton: Gerrard; Short, Ward (Collins), Unsworth, Dunne, Materazzi, Grant (Ball), Cadamarteri, Ferguson, Dacourt (Hutchison), Bakayoko.

FOURTH ROUND

10 NOV

Bolton W (0) 1 *(Jensen 52)*
Wimbledon (1) 2 *(Gayle 16, Kennedy 63)*   7868
Bolton W: Jaaskelainen; Cox, Whitlow, Jensen, Todd, Fish, Johansen (Taylor B), Frandsen, Holdsworth, Sellars, Gunnlaugsson.
Wimbledon: Sullivan; Cunningham, Kimble, Roberts, Thatcher, Perry, Hughes M (Leaburn), Earle, Gayle, Euell, Kennedy.

Liverpool (0) 1 *(Owen 81)*
Tottenham H (2) 3 *(Iversen 2, Scales 20, Nielsen 62)*   20,772
Liverpool: Friedel; Heggem, Bjornebye, McAteer, Carragher, Staunton, Thompson, Ince, Fowler, Owen (Murphy), Leonhardsen (Riedle).
Tottenham H: Baardsen; Carr, Campbell, Scales, Vega, Calderwood, Anderton, Nielsen, Iversen, Sinton (Wilson), Ginola (Allen) (Fox).

Luton T (0) 1 *(Gray 81)*
Barnsley (0) 0   8435
Luton T: Davis K; Alexander, McGowan, Spring, Davis S, Johnson, McKinnon (McLaren), Evers, Douglas (White), Gray, McIndoe (Nyamah).
Barnsley: Bullock T; Morgan, De Zeeuw, Jones, Tinkler (McClare), Appleby, Bullock M (Hendrie), Sheridan, Ward, Fjortoft, Barnard.

11 NOV

Arsenal (0) 0
Chelsea (1) 5 *(Leboeuf 34 (pen), Vialli 49, 73, Poyet 65, 80)*   37,562
Arsenal: Manninger; Grondin, Upson, Vivas, Grimandi, Garde (Mendez), Ljungberg, Wreh, Hughes, Bergkamp (Caballero), Boa Morte.
Chelsea: Kharine; Petrescu, Goldbaek (Percassi), Duberry, Leboeuf (Lambourde), Babayaro, Poyet, Di Matteo, Vialli, Flo, Nicholls (Clement).

Everton (0) 1 *(Collins 74)*
Sunderland (1) 1 *(Bridges 29)*   28,132
Everton: Myhre; Short, Ball, Dunne, Materazzi, Hutchison (Oster), Collins, Cadamarteri (Grant), Ferguson, Dacourt (Cleland), Bakayoko.
Sunderland: Sorensen; Makin, Scott, Thirlwell (Clark), Melville, Butler (Craddock), Smith, Williams, Quinn, Bridges (Proctor), Johnston.
aet; Sunderland won 5-4 on penalties.

Leicester C (0) 2 *(Izzet 88, Parker 90 (pen))*
Leeds U (1) 1 *(Kewell 17)*   20,161
Leicester C: Keller; Savage, Guppy, Elliott, Walsh, Sinclair, Lennon, Izzet, Heskey (Wilson), Zagorakis (Parker), Ullathorne.
Leeds U: Martyn; Hiden, Harte, Ribeiro, Molenaar, Woodgate, Hopkin, Wijnhard, Hasselbaink, Kewell, Bowyer.

Manchester U (0) 2 *(Solskjaer 57, 60)*
Nottingham F (0) 1 *(Stone 68)*   37,237
Manchester U: Van der Gouw; Clegg, Curtis, May (Wallwork), Berg, Wilson, Greening, Butt, Solskjaer, Mulryne, Cruyff.
Nottingham F: Beasant; Louis-Jean, Rogers, Stone, Chettle, Armstrong, Gray, Gemmill, Freedman, Harewood (Van Hooijdonk), Bart-Williams.

Newcastle U (1) 1 *(Shearer 9)*
Blackburn R (1) 1 *(Sherwood 30)*   34,702
Newcastle U: Given; Barton, Pearce, Dabizas, Hughes, Glass (Speed), Georgiadis, Batty, Shearer, Hamann, Dalglish.
Blackburn R: Filan; Kenna, Croft, Sherwood, Peacock, Henchoz, Dailly, Johnson, Marcolin (Dunn), Davies, Duff (Davidson).
aet; Blackburn R won 4-2 on penalties.

FIFTH ROUND

1 DEC

Sunderland (1) 3 *(Johnson 40 (og), Bridges 89, Quinn 90)*
Luton T (0) 0   35,742
Sunderland: Sorensen; Makin, Scott, Ball, Melville, Butler, Summerbee, Clark, Quinn, Bridges, Johnston.
Luton T: Davis K; Alexander, Thomas, Spring, Davis S, Johnson, McKinnon (McLaren), Evers, Douglas (Doherty), Gray, McGowan (White).

Wimbledon (1) 2 *(Earle 20, Hughes M 75 (pen))*
Chelsea (0) 1 *(Vialli 85)*   19,286
Wimbledon: Sullivan; Cunningham, Thatcher, Ardley, Blackwell, Perry, Hughes M, Earle, Leaburn (Ekoku), Euell, Gayle.
Chelsea: Kharine; Petrescu, Babayaro, Duberry (Ferrer), Leboeuf, Goldbaek (Flo), Poyet, Morris (Di Matteo), Vialli, Lambourde, Wise.

2 DEC

Leicester C (0) 1 *(Lennon 67)*
Blackburn R (0) 0   19,442
Leicester C: Keller; Savage, Guppy, Elliott, Walsh, Sinclair, Lennon, Parker, Fenton (Taggart), Ullathorne, Heskey (Wilson).
Blackburn R: Filan; Kenna, Davison, Marcolin, Dailly, Henchoz, Johnson, Gallacher, Dunn, Davies, Duff.

Tottenham H (0) 3 *(Armstrong 48, 55, Ginola 86)*
Manchester U (0) 1 *(Sheringham 71)*   35,702
Tottenham H: Walker; Carr, Sinton, Calderwood (Fox), Young, Campbell, Anderton, Nielsen, Armstrong (Ferdinand), Iversen, Ginola.
Manchester U: Van der Gouw; Clegg, Curtis (Blomqvist), Berg, Neville P, Johnsen, Greening (Beckham), Butt (Notman), Solskjaer, Sheringham, Giggs.

SEMI-FINALS, FIRST LEG

26 JAN

Sunderland (0) 1 *(McCann 75)*
Leicester C (1) 2 *(Cottee 30, 62)*   38,332
Sunderland: Sorensen; Makin, Gray, Ball, Melville, Butler, McCann, Clark (Summerbee), Quinn, Phillips, Johnston (Smith).
Leicester C: Keller; Sinclair (Kamark), Guppy, Elliott, Walsh, Taggart, Lennon, Izzet, Cottee, Ullathorne, Heskey (Wilson).

27 JAN

Tottenham H (0) 0
Wimbledon (0) 0 35,997

Tottenham H: Walker; Carr, Edinburgh, Freund, Vega, Campbell, Anderton, Nielsen, Armstrong (Ferdinand), Iversen, Ginola (Sinton).
Wimbledon: Sullivan; Cunningham, Thatcher, Roberts, Blackwell, Perry, Ardley (Hughes C), Earle, Ekoku, Euell (Leaburn), Hughes M.

SEMI-FINALS, SECOND LEG

16 FEB

Wimbledon (0) 0
Tottenham H (1) 1 *(Iversen 39)* 25,204

Wimbledon: Sullivan; Cunningham, Thatcher, Roberts, Blackwell, Perry, Hughes M, Earle, Ekoku (Leaburn), Euell (Kennedy), Gayle.
Tottenham H: Walker; Carr, Edinburgh (Sinton), Freund, Vega, Campbell, Anderton, Nielsen, Iversen, Ferdinand, Ginola (Young).
Tottenham H won 1-0 on aggregate.

17 FEB

Leicester C (0) 1 *(Cottee 54)*
Sunderland (1) 1 *(Quinn 34)* 21,231

Leicester C: Keller; Sinclair, Guppy, Elliott, Walsh, Taggart (Savage), Lennon, Izzet, Cottee, Ullathorne, Heskey.
Sunderland: Sorensen; Makin, Gray, Ball, Melville, Butler, Summerbee (Dichio), Clark, Quinn, Phillips (Bridges), Johnston.
Leicester C won 3-2 on aggregate.

FINAL (at Wembley)

21 MAR

Leicester C (0) 0
Tottenham H (0) 1 *(Nielsen 90)* 77,892

Leicester C: Keller; Ullathorne, Guppy, Elliott, Walsh, Taggart, Lennon, Izzet, Cottee, Savage (Zagorakis), Heskey (Marshall).
Tottenham H: Walker; Carr, Edinburgh, Freund, Vega, Campbell, Anderton, Nielsen, Iversen, Ferdinand, Ginola (Sinton).
Referee: T. Heilbron (Newton Aycliffe).

An injury time diving header from Allan Nielsen (white shirt), gives Tottenham Hotspur a 1-0 win over Leicester City in the Worthington Cup Final at Wembley. (Actionimages)

FOOTBALL LEAGUE COMPETITION ATTENDANCES

LEAGUE CUP ATTENDANCES

Season	Attendances	Games	Average
1960/61	1,204,580	112	10,755
1961/62	1,030,534	104	9,909
1962/63	1,029,893	102	10,097
1963/64	945,265	104	9,089
1964/65	962,802	98	9,825
1965/66	1,205,876	106	11,376
1966/67	1,394,553	118	11,818
1967/68	1,671,326	110	15,194
1968/69	2,064,647	118	17,497
1969/70	2,299,819	122	18,851
1970/71	2,035,315	116	17,546
1971/72	2,397,154	123	19,489
1972/73	1,935,474	120	16,129
1973/74	1,722,629	132	13,050
1974/75	1,901,094	127	14,969
1975/76	1,841,735	140	13,155
1976/77	2,236,636	147	15,215
1977/78	2,038,295	148	13,772
1978/79	1,825,643	139	13,134
1979/80	2,322,866	169	13,745
1980/81	2,051,576	161	12,743
1981/82	1,880,682	161	11,681
1982/83	1,679,756	160	10,498
1983/84	1,900,491	168	11,312
1984/85	1,876,429	167	11,236
1985/86	1,579,916	163	9,693
1986/87	1,531,498	157	9,755
1987/88	1,539,253	158	9,742
1988/89	1,552,780	162	9,585
1989/90	1,836,916	168	10,934
1990/91	1,675,496	159	10,538
1991/92	1,622,337	164	9,892
1992/93	1,558,031	161	9,677
1993/94	1,744,120	163	10,700
1994/95	1,530,478	157	9,748
1995/96	1,776,060	162	10,963
1996/97	1,529,321	163	9,382
1997/98	1,484,297	153	9.701

WORTHINGTON CUP 1998–99

Round	Aggregate	Games	Average
One	343,480	72	4,771
Two	417,923	48	8,707
Three	290,919	16	18,182
Four	194,706	8	24,338
Five	110,172	4	27,543
Semi-finals	120,764	4	30,191
Final	77,892	1	77,892
Total	1,555,856	153	10,169

AUTO WINDSCREENS SHIELD 1998–99

FIRST ROUND

5 DEC

Colchester U (1) 1 *(Gregory D 23 (pen))*
Gillingham (4) 5 *(Asaba 22, Pennock 29, Taylor 34, 67, Smith 37)* 1742
Colchester U: Emberson; Dunne, Betts, Williams, Greene, Buckle, Forbes (Stamps), Gregory D, Sale (Dozzell), Gregory N (Lock), Abrahams.
Gillingham: Bartram; Bryant, Butters, Smith, Ashby, Pennock, Hodge, Southall, Asaba (Nosworthy), Galloway, Taylor (Pinnock).

8 DEC

Blackpool (0) 0
Stoke C (1) 2 *(Kavanagh 10 (pen), Thorne 76)* 1759
Blackpool: Barnes; Bryan, Hills, Bardsley, Carlisle, Hughes, Bent (Conroy), Clarkson, Longworth, Blunt, Jarrett.
Stoke C: Muggleton; Petty, Small, Sigurdsson, Tweed, Woods, Wallace (Keen), Kavanagh (O'Connor), Thorne, Sturridge, Heath (Forsyth).

Burnley (0) 0
Preston NE (0) 1 *(Macken 57)* 3366
Burnley: Crichton; Brass, Vindheim (Devenney), Ford, Heywood, Reid, Maylett, Hewlett, Cooke (Henderson), Carr-Lawton, Eastwood.
Preston NE: Lucas; Parkinson, Kidd, Murdock, Jackson, Darby, Cartwright, Byfield, Macken, Harris (Wright), McKenna.

Chester C (1) 1 *(Shelton 13)*
Hartlepool U (0) 2 *(Howard 46, Brightwell 102)* 960
Chester C: Cutler; Richardson, Cross, Reid, Crosby, Woods, Flitcroft, Shelton (Lancaster), Murphy, Aiston, Smith.
Hartlepool U: Hollund; Knowles, Clark, Barron, Lee, Ingram, Stokoe, Miller (Baker), Howard, Midgley (Rush), Stephenson (Brightwell).
aet; Hartlepool U won in sudden death.

Macclesfield T (0) 0
Wrexham (0) 1 *(Edwards 48)* 804
Macclesfield T: Price; Tinson (Lonergan), Ingram, Payne, Wood, Howarth, Griffiths, Tomlinson, Smith (Wright), Sedgemore, Whittaker (Durkan).
Wrexham: Cartwright; McGregor, Hardy, Brammer (Owen), Ridler, Spink, Cooke, Russell, Connolly (Edwards), Roberts, Chalk.

Manchester C (0) 1 *(Allsop 74)*
Mansfield T (0) 2 *(Peacock 52 (pen), 56)* 3007
Manchester C: Wright; Jeff Whitley, Tiatto, Fenton, Rimmer, Vaughan, Brown, Pollock (Jim Whitley), Allsop, Taylor (Bailey), Heaney.
Mansfield T: Bowling; Ford (Williams), Harper, Peters, Kerr, Hackett (Ryder), Schofield, Christie, Lormor, Peacock, Tallon.

Oldham Ath (0) 0
Darlington (0) 1 *(Gabbiadini 95)* 2133
Oldham Ath: Kelly; McNiven S, Holt, Garnett, Rickers, Duxbury (Allott), McGinlay (Tipton), Salt, Thom, Whitehall, Reid.
Darlington: Samways; Brumwell, Barnard, Liddle, Tutill, Leah (Oliver), Campbell (Ellison), Naylor (Kubicki), Dorner, Gabbiadini, Atkinson.
aet; Darlington won in sudden death.

Rotherham U (0) 0
Wigan Ath (1) 3 *(Barlow 24 (pen), Warne 49, Balmer 60)* 1225
Rotherham U: Pollitt; Warner (Thompson), Hurst, Garner, Knill, Dillon, Berry (Sedgwick), Ingledow, Scott R, Glover, Monkhouse.
Wigan Ath: Carroll; Green, Sharp, McGibbon, Balmer, Porter, Lee, Greenall (Jenkinson), Warne, Martinez, Barlow.

Bournemouth (1) 2 *(Fletcher 9, Cox 76)*
Reading (0) 0 2666
Bournemouth: Ovendale; Young, Vincent, Howe, Warren (Berthe), Bailey, Cox, Robinson (Rodrigues), Stein, Fletcher (O'Neill), Hughes.
Reading: Howie; Crawford (Roach), Clement, Parkinson, Primus, Casper, Glasgow, Caskey, McIntyre, Brayson, Wright (Sarr).

Brentford (1) 2 *(Hreidarsson 42, Rowlands 49)*
Plymouth Arg (0) 0 1580
Brentford: Pearcey; Bryan, Folan, Hreidarsson, Quinn, Bates, Hebel, Mahon, Owusu, Rowlands, Fortune-West.
Plymouth Arg: Dungey; Ashton, Beswetherick, Branston, Heathcote (Adams), Bastow, Barlow (Gill), Mauge, Phillips, Jean (Power), Sweeney.

Peterborough U (3) 3 *(Broughton 21, McKenzie 38, Edwards 40)*
Leyton Orient (0) 0 1801
Peterborough U: Tyler; Hooper, Drury, Davies, Chapple, Edwards, Farrell, Castle, Broughton, McKenzie (Grazioli), Etherington (Scott).
Leyton Orient: MacKenzie; Canham, Morrison (Curran), Warren, Downer, Brown, Martin, Inglethorpe, Watts, Maskell, Baker.

Shrewsbury T (0) 0
Wycombe W (0) 1 *(McSporran 110)* 1033
Shrewsbury T: Cooksey; Seabury, Hanmer, Whelan, Wilding, Tretton, Berkley, Beavers (Brown), Steele (Jagielka), Evans, Jobling.
Wycombe W: Taylor; Lawrence, Vinnicombe, Cousins, McCarthy, Mohan, Simpson, Brown, Baird (McSporran), Scott, Carroll.
aet; Wycombe W won in sudden death.

Swansea C (2) 4 *(Appleby 12, Smith 21, Bird 84, 90)*
Barnet (0) 1 *(McGleish 82)* 1017
Swansea C: Freestone; Price (O'Leary), Howard, Cusack, Smith, Bound, Roberts (Coates), Jenkins, Alsop (Newhouse), Bird, Appleby.
Barnet: Harrison; Stockley, Manuel, Alsford, Ford, Arber, Searle (Wilson), Doolan, King (McGleish), Devine, Currie (Onwere).

Walsall (0) 2 *(Larusson 84 (pen), Otta 78)*
Bristol R (0) 2 *(Cureton 53, Shore 62)* 2210
Walsall: Walker; Marsh, Pointon (Porter), Keates, Green (Gadsby), Roper, Wrack, Otta, Rammell, Larusson, Garrault (Platt).
Bristol R: Jones; Leoni, Challis, Zabek, Foster, Trought, Shore, Trees, Ipoua, Cureton (Pritchard), Roberts.
aet; Walsall won 5-4 on penalties.

9 DEC

Millwall (2) 2 *(Shaw 26, Harris 28)*
Cardiff C (0) 0 1858
Millwall: Spink; Lavin, Ryan, Cahill (Odunsi), Nethercott, Fitzgerald, Reid, Newman, Harris, Shaw (Sadlier), Roche (Neill).
Cardiff C: Hallworth; Eckhardt, Allen, Mitchell, Jarman, Bonner, Hill (Cadette), O'Sullivan, Williams (Roberts), Thomas, Middleton.

22 DEC

Notts Co (0) 0
Hull C (1) 1 *(D'Auria 22)* 1109
Notts Co: Ward; Hughes, Jackson (Quayle), Henshaw, Strodder, Pearce, Tierney, Garcia (Samuels), Foley (Pennant), Jones, Rabat.
Hull C: Wilson; Hocking, Swales, Edwards, Perry, Whitney, McGinty, D'Auria, Brown (Ellington), Faulconbridge (Hawes), Peacock (French).

SECOND ROUND

5 JAN

Halifax T (1) 4 *(Lucas 16, Williams 61, 83, Hanson 63)*
York C (1) 2 *(Rowe 45, Tolson 77)* 1446
Halifax T: Carter; Wills, Lucas, Sertori, Murphy J, Stansfield, O'Regan, Hulme (Murphy S), Williams, Hanson, Butler.
York C: Mimms; McMillan, Hall, Tinkler, Jones, Barras, Connelly (Garratt), Jordan, Cresswell, Rowe, Himsworth (Tolson).

Hull C (0) 1 *(Williams 75)*
Wrexham (1) 2 *(Roberts N 25, 53)* 2331
Hull C: Oakes; Hocking, Rioch, Perry, Edwards (Greaves), McGinty, Joyce, D'Auria, Williams, Brown (Faulconbridge), Peacock (Morley).
Wrexham: Cartwright; McGregor, Ridler, Brammer (Ward), Spink (Roberts S), Carey, Gibson, Owen, Roberts N, Russell (Morrell), Chalk.

Lincoln C (1) 1 *(Bimson 26)*
Mansfield T (0) 0 2289
Lincoln C: Richardson; Barnett, Bimson, Stones, Watts, Brown, Smith, Brabin, Fenn (Stant), Alcide (Gordon), Philpott (Wilkins).
Mansfield T: Bowling; Ford, Harper, Peters, Lormor, Ryder, Schofield, Walker, Christie (Sedlan), Peacock, Tallon.

Bournemouth (3) 5 *(Fletcher 20, Stein 24, 28, 49, Robinson 68)*
Peterborough U (1) 1 *(Butler 16)* 3398
Bournemouth: Ovendale; Young, Vincent, Howe, Warren (O'Neill), Bailey (Rodrigues), Cox, Robinson, Stein, Fletcher, Hughes (Boli).
Peterborough U: Tyler; Scott, Drury, Rennie (Gill), Edwards, Hanlon, Hann (Grazioli), Davies, Butler, Carruthers, Etherington (Broughton).

Brighton & HA (1) 1 *(Moralee 15)*
Millwall (2) 5 *(Harris 39, 76, Lavin 42, Shaw 60, Hockton 90)* 2003
Brighton & HA: Ormerod; Browne T, Sturgess, Minton, Johnson, Arnott (Mayo), Storer, Bennett, Hart, Moralee, Culverhouse (Ansah).
Millwall: Spink; Lavin, Stuart, Cahill, Nethercott, Fitzgerald, Reid, Bowry, Harris (Hockton), Shaw, Neill.

Cambridge U (1) 3 *(Walker 18, Benjamin 57, Butler 60)*
Northampton T (1) 2 *(Corazzin 11, Freestone 56)* 2391
Cambridge U: Van Heusden; Chenery, Ashbee, Duncan, Joseph, Campbell, Preece (Butler), Walker, Kyd (Youngs), Benjamin, Russell.
Northampton T: Turley; Warner (Hunt), Frain, Sampson, Howey, Spedding, Peer, Hope, Freestone, Corazzin, Savage (Hill).

Exeter C (1) 3 *(Quailey 5, Clark 85, Flack 90)*
Southend U (0) 1 *(Maher 87)* 1143
Exeter C: Bayes; Fry (Wilkinson), Powell (Gale), Holloway, Richardson, Gittens, Quailey (Waugh), Clark, Flack, Curran, Breslan.
Southend U: Margetson; Beard, Dublin, Gooding, Newman, Coleman, Maher, Livett (Jones), Conlon, Burns, Houghton.

Luton T (0) 0
Walsall (1) 3 *(Watson 6, Wrack 47, Keates 80)* 1870
Luton T: Abbey; Boyce, Fraser, Evers, White, Dyche, McLaren (Scarlett), Harrison, Bacque (Kandol), McIndoe, Fotiadis (Doherty).
Walsall: Walker; Evans, Pointon, Keates, Viveash, Roper (Gadsby), Wrack, Watson, Rammell (Platt), Larusson (Thomas), Brissett.

Swansea C (0) 0
Gillingham (0) 1 *(Hessenthaler 76)* 5126
Swansea C: Freestone; Jones, Clode, Lacey, O'Leary, Bound, Coates, Jenkins, Alsop (Bird), Watkin, Price (Roberts).
Gillingham: Bartram; Southall, Edge, Butters, Bryant (Statham), Carr (Pinnock), Hodge, Hessenthaler, Asaba, Galloway, Saunders.

Torquay U (0) 2 *(Partridge 88, Lee 107)*
Fulham (0) 1 *(Trollope 47)* 2596
Torquay U: Southall; Tully (Hapgood), Herrera, Robinson, Thomas, Watson, Healy, McGorry (Bedeau), Lee, Partridge, Hill (Leadbitter).
Fulham: Arendse; Uhlenbeek, Brazier, Keller, Neilson, Trollope, Finnan, Betsy (Brooker), Lehmann, Collins, Salako.
aet; Torquay U won on sudden death.

Wycombe W (0) 1 *(Ryan 58)*
Brentford (2) 4 *(Fortune-West 16, Scott 39, 51, Quinn 50)* 2010
Wycombe W: Westhead; Lawrence, Kavanagh, Emblen, Ryan, Mohan, Simpson (Cornforth), Brown, McSporran, Read (McGavin), Carroll.
Brentford: Dearden; Boxall, Anderson, Hreidarsson, Quinn, Mahon, Freeman (Bryan), Aspinall (Watson), Fortune-West, Rowlands, Scott (Owusu).

12 JAN

Darlington (0) 0
Chesterfield (0) 2 *(Wilkinson 60, Perkins 85)* 1391
Darlington: Preece; Brumwell (Ellison), Barnard, Liddle, Tutill, Bennett (Reed), Gaughan (Costa), Oliver, Roberts, Naylor, Atkinson.
Chesterfield: Mercer; Perkins, Jules, Curtis (Lomas), Blatherwick, Breckin, Howard (Willis), Beaumont, Reeves (Lee), Ebdon, Wilkinson.

NORTHERN QUARTER-FINALS

19 JAN

Wrexham (1) 3 *(Connolly 11, Griffiths 65 (pen), Owen 70)*
Chesterfield (0) 2 *(Williams 53, Hewitt 89)* 1572
Wrexham: Cartwright; McGregor, Hardy (Ridler), Brammer, Spink, Carey, Chalk, Russell, Connolly (Edwards), Griffiths, Owen (Gibson).
Chesterfield: Mercer; Hewitt, Nicholson, Blatherwick, Williams, Breckin, Howard (Lee), Beaumont (Lomas), Reeves, Lenagh (Jules), Wilkinson.

SECOND ROUND

19 JAN

Hartlepool U (0) 2 *(Miller 72, 90)*
Preston NE (0) 2 *(Darby 77, Parkinson 85 (pen))* 1205
Hartlepool U: Hollund; Knowles, Clark, Barron, Hutt, Di Lella, Beardsley, Miller, Howard, Midgley, Ingram (Irvine).
Preston NE: Lucas; Parkinson, Harrison, Murdock, Jackson, Gregan, McKenna (Nogan), Darby, Macken, Harris, Appleton (King).
aet; Hartlepool U won 4-3 on penalties.

Scunthorpe U (1) 1 *(Walker 4)*
Carlisle U (0) 1 *(Searle 53)* 1507
Scunthorpe U: Evans; Fickling, Dawson, Logan, Harsley (Housham), Hope, Walker, Forrester (Sheldon), Eyre, Gayle (Bull), Calvo-Garcia.
Carlisle U: Caig; Bowman, Clark, Whitehead, Brightwell (Searle), Hopper, Dobie, Prokas, Finney, McGregor (Ormerod), Couzens (Anthony).
aet; Carlisle U won 4-3 on penalties.

Wigan Ath (1) 3 *(O'Neill 41, Jones 79, Lee 89)*
Scarborough (0) 0 1693
Wigan Ath: Carroll; Green, Sharp, McGibbon (Porter), Balmer, Rogers, Kilford, Greenall, Jones (Lowe), O'Neill, Barlow (Lee).
Scarborough: Naisbett; Russell, Atkinson, Rainford, McNaughton, Rennison, Lydiate, Hoyland (Milbourne), Greenacre, Tate, Bullimore.

SOUTHERN QUARTER-FINALS

19 JAN

Brentford (0) 0
Walsall (0) 0 2048
Brentford: Dearden; Boxall, Anderson, Hreidarsson, Quinn (Oatway), Bates, Mahon, Folan, Owusu, Rowlands (Powell), Scott (Fortune-West).
Walsall: Walker; Marsh (Evans), Pointon, Keates, Viveash, Roper, Wrack, Watson, Rammell (Platt), Larusson (Thomas), Brissett.
aet; Walsall won 4-3 on penalties.

Cambridge U (1) 1 *(Benjamin 9)*
Exeter C (0) 1 *(Flack 65)* 2758
Cambridge U: Van Heusden; Chenery, Mustoe (Ashbee) (Youngs), Duncan, Joseph, Campbell, Wanless, Taylor (Walker), Butler, Benjamin, Russell.
Exeter C: Bayes; Gale, Power, Breslan, Clark, Gittens, Quailey, Rees, Flack, Curran, Gardner (Wilkinson).
aet; Cambridge U won 5-3 on penalties.

23 JAN

Torquay U (0) 0
Gillingham (1) 1 *(Taylor 31)* 3121
Torquay U: Southall; Tully, Herrera, Aggrey, Thomas, Leadbitter (Bedeau), Healy, McGorry, Lee (McFarlane), Partridge, Hill.
Gillingham: Bartram; Southall, Ashby, Smith, Butters, Pennock, Patterson, Edge, Asaba, Saunders, Taylor.

NORTHERN QUARTER-FINALS

26 JAN

Carlisle U (0) 0
Wigan Ath (1) 3 *(Haworth 45, Barlow 76,*
Kilford 90) 2383
Carlisle U: Caig; Barr, Clark, Whitehead, Searle, Hopper, Dobie, Prokas, Finney, Ormerod, Anthony (Paterson).
Wigan Ath: Carroll; Green, Sharp, McGibbon, Kilford, Rogers, Liddell, Greenall, Jones, O'Neill (Porter), Haworth (Barlow).

Hartlepool U (0) 0
Lincoln C (0) 3 *(Miller 76, Battersby 83, Thorpe 88)* 1370
Hartlepool U: Hollund; Knowles, Clark, Barron, Ingram, Miller, Stephenson (Irvine), Beardsley, Lee, Midgley, Smith.
Lincoln C: Vaughan; Barnett, Bimson, Fleming, Holmes, Austin (Brown), Gain (Thorpe), Finnigan, Battersby, Gordon (Philpott), Miller.

SECOND ROUND

2 FEB

Rochdale (2) 2 *(Morris 1, Holt 5)*
Stoke C (0) 1 *(Crowe 88)* 7361
Rochdale: Edwards; Jones, Barlow (Sparrow), Hill (Bayliss), Monington, Farrell, Carden, Painter, Morris, Peake, Holt.
Stoke C: Muggleton; Heath, Small, Sigurdsson, Forsyth, Woods, Keen, Kavanagh, Crowe, Lightbourne (MacKenzie), Oldfield.
at Stoke.

SOUTHERN QUARTER-FINALS

2 FEB

Bournemouth (1) 1 *(Stein 5)*
Millwall (1) 1 *(Shaw 38)* 5339
Bournemouth: Ovendale; Young, Vincent, Howe, O'Neill, Bailey, Cox, Robinson, Stein, Fletcher, Hughes.
Millwall: Spink; Lavin, Ryan, Cahill, Nethercott, Stuart, Reid, Bowry, Sadlier, Shaw, Neill.
aet; Millwall won 4-3 on penalties.

NORTHERN SEMI-FINALS

16 FEB

Lincoln C (0) 1 *(Holmes 81 (pen))*
Wrexham (1) 2 *(Ridler 45, Bimson 103 (og))* 3490
Lincoln C: Vaughan; Barnett, Bimson, Fleming, Holmes, Austin, Thorpe, Wilkins (Philpott), Battersby, Gordon, Miller.
Wrexham: Cartwright; McGregor, Ridler, Brammer, Spink, Carey, Chalk, Russell (Gibson), Connolly, Edwards (Roberts), Owen.
aet; Wrexham won on sudden death.

SOUTHERN SEMI-FINALS

16 FEB

Millwall (0) 1 *(Sadlier 97)*
Gillingham (0) 0 11,555
Millwall: Roberts B; Lavin, Stuart, Bircham, Nethercott, Dolan, Reid, Bowry, Harris, Sadlier, Neill.
Gillingham: Bartram; Southall, Bryant, Smith, Butters, Pennock, Carr, Hessenthaler, Asaba, Saunders (Hodge), Taylor.
aet; Millwall won on sudden death.

Walsall (1) 1 *(Rammell 1)*
Cambridge U (0) 1 *(Taylor 56)* 5087
Walsall: Walker; Marsh, Pointon (Evans), Keates, Viveash, Roper, Wrack, Watson, Rammell, Larusson (Thomas), Mavrak (Brissett).
Cambridge U: Van Heusden; Chenery, Mustoe, Duncan, Joseph, Campbell, Wanless, Kyd (Walker), Butler, Benjamin (Taylor), Ashbee.
aet; Walsall won 4-3 on penalites.

NORTHERN QUARTER-FINALS

23 FEB

Rochdale (0) 2 *(Jones 57 (pen), Monington 94)*
Halifax T (0) 1 *(Bradshaw 77 (pen))* 2327
Rochdale: Edwards, Sparrow, Stokes (Jones), Bayliss, Monington, Farrell, Stoker, Carden, Morris, Peake, Holt (Painter).
Halifax T: Martin; Thackeray, Lucas (Grant), Sertori, Stansfield (Newton), Stoneman (Brown), Etherington, Hulme, Williams, Hanson, Bradshaw.
aet; Rochdale won on sudden death.

NORTHERN SEMI-FINALS

8 MAR

Rochdale (0) 0
Wigan Ath (1) 2 *(Barlow 30, O'Neill 70)* 2484
Rochdale: Edwards; Bailey (Painter), Barlow, Bayliss, Monington, Farrell, Carden, Stoker, Morris (Lancashire), Peake, Holt.
Wigan Ath: Carroll; Bradshaw, Sharp, McGibbon, Griffiths, Rogers, Liddell, Greenall, Lee (Porter), O'Neill, Barlow.

SOUTHERN FINAL, FIRST LEG

9 MAR

Millwall (1) 1 *(Cahill 4)*
Walsall (0) 0 11,626
Millwall: Roberts B; Lavin, Stuart, Cahill, Nethercott, Stevens, Reid (Hockton), Newman, Harris (Ifill), Sadlier, Neill.
Walsall: Walker; Marsh, Pointon, Keates, Viveash, Roper, Wrack, Cramb, Rammell (Brissett), Larusson, Mavrak.

NORTHERN FINAL, FIRST LEG

16 MAR

Wigan Ath (0) 2 *(Sharp 59, Barlow 71)*
Wrexham (0) 0 4938
Wigan Ath: Carroll; Bradshaw, Sharp, McGibbon, Balmer, Rogers, Liddell, Greenall, Haworth, O'Neill, Barlow.
Wrexham: Cartwright; McGregor, Hardy, Spink, Ridler, Carey (Rush), Gibson (Edwards), Russell, Connolly, Brammer, Owen.

SOUTHERN FINAL, SECOND LEG

16 MAR

Walsall (0) 1 *(Eyjolfsson 89)*
Millwall (1) 1 *(Sadlier 37)* 9158
Walsall: Walker; Marsh, Pointon (Evans), Keates (Thomas), Viveash, Roper, Wrack, Cramb, Brissett, Larusson, Mavrak (Eyjolfsson).
Millwall: Roberts B; Lavin, Stuart, Bowry, Nethercott, Dolan, Ifill (Grant), Newman, Harris (Bircham), Sadlier, Neill.
Millwall won 2-1 on aggregate.

NORTHERN FINAL, SECOND LEG

23 MAR

Wrexham (1) 2 *(Brammer 37, Edwards 59)*
Wigan Ath (1) 3 *(Haworth 2, 52, O'Neill 88)* 4941
Wrexham: Cartwright; McGregor, Hardy (Gibson) (Edwards), Brammer, Ridler, Carey, Chalk, Russell (Spink), Connolly, Elliott, Owen.
Wigan Ath: Carroll; Bradshaw, Kilford, McGibbon, Balmer, Rogers, Liddell, Greenall, Haworth, O'Neill, Barlow.
Wigan Ath won 5-2 on aggregate.

FINAL (at Wembley)

18 APR

Millwall (0) 0
Wigan Ath (0) 1 *(Rogers 90)* 55,349
Millwall: Roberts B; Lavin, Stuart, Cahill, Nethercott, Dolan, Newman, Ifill, Harris, Sadlier, Neill.
Wigan Ath: Carroll; Bradshaw, Sharp, McGibbon, Balmer, Rogers, Liddell, Greenall, Haworth, O'Neill, Barlow (Lee).
Referee: C. Wilkes (Gloucester).

AUTO WINDSCREENS SHIELD 1998–99

Attendances

Round	Aggregate	Games	Average
One	28,270	16	1,766
Two	39,760	16	2,485
Area Quarter-finals	20,918	8	2,614
Area Semi-finals	22,616	4	5,654
Area finals	30,663	4	7,665
Final	55,349	1	55,349
Total	197,576	49	4,032

FA CUP FINALS 1872–1999

1872 and 1874–92	Kennington Oval	1911	Replay at Old Trafford
1873	Lillie Bridge	1912	Replay at Bramall Lane
1886	Replay at Derby (Racecourse Ground)		
1893	Fallowfield, Manchester	1915	Old Trafford, Manchester
1894	Everton	1920–22	Stamford Bridge
1895–1914	Crystal Palace	1923 to date	Wembley
1901	Replay at Bolton	1970	Replay at Old Trafford
1910	Replay at Everton		

Year	Winners	Runners-up	Score
1872	Wanderers	Royal Engineers	1-0
1873	Wanderers	Oxford University	2-0
1874	Oxford University	Royal Engineers	2-0
1875	Royal Engineers	Old Etonians	2-0 (after 1-1 draw aet)
1876	Wanderers	Old Etonians	3-0 (after 1-1 draw aet)
1877	Wanderers	Oxford University	2-1 (aet)
1878	Wanderers*	Royal Engineers	3-1
1879	Old Etonians	Clapham R	1-0
1880	Clapham R	Oxford University	1-0
1881	Old Carthusians	Old Etonians	3-0
1882	Old Etonians	Blackburn R	1-0
1883	Blackburn Olympic	Old Etonians	2-1 (aet)
1884	Blackburn R	Queen's Park, Glasgow	2-1
1885	Blackburn R	Queen's Park, Glasgow	2-0
1886	Blackburn R†	WBA	2-0 (after 0-0 draw)
1887	Aston Villa	WBA	2-0
1888	WBA	Preston NE	2-1
1889	Preston NE	Wolverhampton W	3-0
1890	Blackburn R	Sheffield W	6-1
1891	Blackburn R	Notts Co	3-1
1892	WBA	Aston Villa	3-0
1893	Wolverhampton W	Everton	1-0
1894	Notts Co	Bolton W	4-1
1895	Aston Villa	WBA	1-0
1896	Sheffield W	Wolverhampton W	2-1
1897	Aston Villa	Everton	3-2
1898	Nottingham F	Derby Co	3-1
1899	Sheffield U	Derby Co	4-1
1900	Bury	Southampton	4-0
1901	Tottenham H	Sheffield U	3-1 (after 2-2 draw)
1902	Sheffield U	Southampton	2-1 (after 1-1 draw)
1903	Bury	Derby Co	6-0
1904	Manchester C	Bolton W	1-0
1905	Aston Villa	Newcastle U	2-0
1906	Everton	Newcastle U	1-0
1907	Sheffield W	Everton	2-1
1908	Wolverhampton W	Newcastle U	3-1
1909	Manchester U	Bristol C	1-0
1910	Newcastle U	Barnsley	2-0 (after 1-1 draw)
1911	Bradford C	Newcastle U	1-0 (after 0-0 draw)
1912	Barnsley	WBA	1-0 (aet, after 0-0 draw)
1913	Aston Villa	Sunderland	1-0
1914	Burnley	Liverpool	1-0
1915	Sheffield U	Chelsea	3-0
1920	Aston Villa	Huddersfield T	1-0 (aet)
1921	Tottenham H	Wolverhampton W	1-0
1922	Huddersfield T	Preston NE	1-0
1923	Bolton W	West Ham U	2-0
1924	Newcastle U	Aston Villa	2-0
1925	Sheffield U	Cardiff C	1-0
1926	Bolton W	Manchester C	1-0
1927	Cardiff C	Arsenal	1-0
1928	Blackburn R	Huddersfield T	3-1
1929	Bolton W	Portsmouth	2-0
1930	Arsenal	Huddersfield T	2-0
1931	WBA	Birmingham	2-1
1932	Newcastle U	Arsenal	2-1
1933	Everton	Manchester C	3-0
1934	Manchester C	Portsmouth	2-1
1935	Sheffield W	WBA	4-2
1936	Arsenal	Sheffield U	1-0
1937	Sunderland	Preston NE	3-1
1938	Preston NE	Huddersfield T	1-0 (aet)
1939	Portsmouth	Wolverhampton W	4-1
1946	Derby Co	Charlton Ath	4-1 (aet)
1947	Charlton Ath	Burnley	1-0 (aet)
1948	Manchester U	Blackpool	4-2
1949	Wolverhampton W	Leicester C	3-1
1950	Arsenal	Liverpool	2-0
1951	Newcastle U	Blackpool	2-0
1952	Newcastle U	Arsenal	1-0

Year	Winners	Runners-up	Score
1953	Blackpool	Bolton W	4-3
1954	WBA	Preston NE	3-2
1955	Newcastle U	Manchester C	3-1
1956	Manchester C	Birmingham C	3-1
1957	Aston Villa	Manchester U	2-1
1958	Bolton W	Manchester U	2-0
1959	Nottingham F	Luton T	2-1
1960	Wolverhampton W	Blackburn R	3-0
1961	Tottenham H	Leicester C	2-0
1962	Tottenham H	Burnley	3-1
1963	Manchester U	Leicester C	3-1
1964	West Ham U	Preston NE	3-2
1965	Liverpool	Leeds U	2-1 (aet)
1966	Everton	Sheffield W	3-2
1967	Tottenham H	Chelsea	2-1
1968	WBA	Everton	1-0 (aet)
1969	Manchester C	Leicester C	1-0
1970	Chelsea	Leeds U	2-1 (aet)
		(after 2-2 draw, after extra time)	
1971	Arsenal	Liverpool	2-1 (aet)
1972	Leeds U	Arsenal	1-0
1973	Sunderland	Leeds U	1-0
1974	Liverpool	Newcastle U	3-0
1975	West Ham U	Fulham	2-0
1976	Southampton	Manchester U	1-0
1977	Manchester U	Liverpool	2-1
1978	Ipswich T	Arsenal	1-0
1979	Arsenal	Manchester U	3-2
1980	West Ham U	Arsenal	1-0
1981	Tottenham H	Manchester C	3-2
		(after 1-1 draw, after extra time)	
1982	Tottenham H	QPR	1-0
		(after 1-1 draw, after extra time)	
1983	Manchester U	Brighton & HA	4-0
		(after 2-2 draw, after extra time)	
1984	Everton	Watford	2-0
1985	Manchester U	Everton	1-0 (aet)
1986	Liverpool	Everton	3-1
1987	Coventry C	Tottenham H	3-2 (aet)
1988	Wimbledon	Liverpool	1-0
1989	Liverpool	Everton	3-2 (aet)
1990	Manchester U	Crystal Palace	1-0
		(after 3-3 draw, after extra time)	
1991	Tottenham H	Nottingham F	2-1 (aet)
1992	Liverpool	Sunderland	2-0
1993	Arsenal	Sheffield W	2-1 (aet)
		(after 1-1 draw, after extra time)	
1994	Manchester U	Chelsea	4-0
1995	Everton	Manchester U	1-0
1996	Manchester U	Liverpool	1-0
1997	Chelsea	Middlesbrough	2-0
1998	Arsenal	Newcastle U	2-0
1999	Manchester U	Newcastle U	2-0

* *Won outright, but restored to the Football Association.*
† *A special trophy was awarded for third consecutive win.*

FA CUP WINS

Manchester U 10, Tottenham H 8, Arsenal 7, Aston Villa 7, Blackburn R 6, Newcastle U 6, Everton 5, Liverpool 5, The Wanderers 5, WBA 5, Bolton W 4, Manchester C 4, Sheffield U 4, Wolverhampton W 4, Sheffield W 3, West Ham U 3, Bury 2, Chelsea 2, Nottingham F 2, Old Etonians 2, Preston NE 2, Sunderland 2, Barnsley 1, Blackburn Olympic 1, Blackpool 1, Bradford C 1, Burnley 1, Cardiff C 1, Charlton Ath 1, Clapham R 1, Coventry C 1, Derby Co 1, Huddersfield T 1, Ipswich T 1, Leeds U 1, Notts Co 1, Old Carthusians 1, Oxford University 1, Portsmouth 1, Royal Engineers 1, Southampton 1, Wimbledon 1.

APPEARANCES IN FINALS

Manchester U 15, Arsenal 13, Newcastle U 13, Everton 12, Liverpool 11, Newcastle U 12, WBA 10, Aston Villa 9, Tottenham H 9, Blackburn R 8, Manchester C 8, Wolverhampton W 8, Bolton W 7, Preston NE 7, Old Etonians 6, Sheffield U 6, Sheffield W 6, Chelsea 5, Huddersfield T 5, *The Wanderers 5, Derby Co 4, Leeds U 4, Leicester C 4, Oxford University 4, Royal Engineers 4, Sunderland 4, West Ham U 4, Blackpool 3, Burnley 3, Nottingham F 3, Portsmouth 3, Southampton 3, Barnsley 2, Birmingham C 2, *Bury 2, Cardiff C 2, Charlton Ath 2, Clapham R 2, Notts Co 2, Queen's Park (Glasgow) 2, *Blackburn Olympic 1, *Bradford C 1, Brighton & HA 1, Bristol C 1, *Coventry C 1, Crystal Palace 1, Fulham 1, *Ipswich T 1, Luton T 4, Middlesbrough 1, *Old Carthusians 1, QPR 1, Watford 1, *Wimbledon 1.
* *Denotes undefeated.*

APPEARANCES IN SEMI-FINALS

Everton 23, Manchester U 22, Arsenal 20, Liverpool 20, WBA 19, Aston Villa 18, Blackburn R 16, Sheffield W 16, Tottenham H 16, Newcastle U 15, Wolverhampton W 14, Chelsea 13, Derby Co 13, Bolton W 12, Nottingham F 12, Sheffield U 12, Sunderland 11, Manchester C 10, Preston NE 10, Southampton 10, Birmingham C 9, Burnley 8, Leeds U 8, Leicester C 8, Huddersfield T 7, Old Etonians 6, Oxford University 6, West Ham U 6, Fulham 5, Notts Co 5, Portsmouth 5, The Wanderers 5, Luton T 4, Queen's Park (Glasgow) 4, Royal Engineers 4, Blackpool 3, Cardiff C 3, Clapham R 3, Crystal Palace (professional club) 3, Ipswich T 3, Millwall 3, Norwich C 3, Old Carthusians 3, Oldham Ath 3, Stoke C 3, The Swifts 3, Watford 3, Barnsley 2, Blackburn Olympic 2, Bristol C 2, Bury 2, Charlton Ath 2, Grimsby T 2, Swansea T 2, Swindon T 2, Wimbledon 2, Bradford C 1, Brighton & HA 1, Cambridge University 1, Chesterfield 1, Coventry C 1, Crewe Alex 1, Crystal Palace (amateur club) 1, Darwen 1, Derby Junction 1, Glasgow R 1, Hull C 1, Marlow 1, Old Harrovians 1, Middlesbrough 1, Orient 1, Plymouth Arg 1, Port Vale 1, QPR 1, Reading 1, Shropshire W 1, York C 1.

Manchester United forward Teddy Sheringham is congratulated by colleague David Beckham, after scoring the first goal in the 1999 FA Cup Final against Newcastle United at Wembley. (Colorsport)

Newcastle United fans *en masse* at Wembley in the Cup Final. (ASP)

FA CUP 1998–99
SPONSORED BY LITTLEWOODS POOLS

PRELIMINARY AND QUALIFYING ROUNDS

PRELIMINARY ROUND

Ashton United v Willington	5-2
Thackley v Hebburn	2-1
Atherton Collieries v Armthorpe Welfare	1-2
Stockton v Liversedge	1-4
Rossendale United v Brigg Town	0-3
Ashington v Horden CW	2-1
Sheffield v Atherton LR	2-4
at Ossett Town FC	
Trafford v Peterlee Newtown	4-1
Ramsbottom United v Maine Road	0-0, 2-1
Harrogate Town v Burscough	1-2
Tadcaster Albion v Ossett Town	1-0
Guisborough Town v Rossington Main	1-3
Shotton Comrades v Jarrow Roofing Boldon CA	1-2
Flixton v Northallerton Town	3-0
Marske United v Billingham Synthonia	1-1, 0-3
Oldham Town v Warrington Town	0-2
Bacup Borough w.o. v Blackpool (Wren) Rovers	
withdrew	
Bradford Park Avenue v Easington Colliery	4-1
Yorkshire Amateur v Witton Albion	1-3
Durham City v Dunston FB	2-0
Sandwell Borough v Blakenall	0-3
Boston Town v Blackstone	2-0
Shepshed Dynamo v Barwell	1-1, 3-3
Shepshed Dynamo won 7-6 on penalties	
Sutton Coldfield Town v VS Rugby	1-0
Hinckley United v Rushall Olympic	2-0
Lye Town v Racing Club Warwick	0-1
Oldbury United v Shifnal Town	2-0
Stafford Rangers v Boldmere St Michaels	3-0
Matlock Town v Redditch United	4-1
Halesowen Harriers v Stourport Swifts	2-1
Bridgnorth Town v Borrowash Victoria	3-3, 2-0
Corby Town v Leek CSOB	0-4
Chelmsford City v Fakenham Town	6-0
Canvey Island v Stansted	6-1
Eynesbury Rovers v Southall	3-3, 0-6
Tring Town v Waltham Abbey	0-2
Waltham Abbey disqualified for fielding player	
under suspension	
Bowers United v Wootton Blue Cross	5-3
Felixstowe Port & Town v Ford Sports Daventry	1-2
Leyton Pennant v Wembley	2-1
Stotfold v Sudbury Town	2-2, 1-2
Harpenden Town v Burnham	3-2
Potton United v Baldock Town	0-3
Hornchurch v London Colney	1-1, 0-1
Marlow v Hemel Hempstead Town	2-1
Bury Town v Tilbury	1-1, 2-3
Kingsbury Town v Grays Athletic	4-4, 0-7
Stowmarket Town v Gorleston	5-1
Potters Bar Town v Wealdstone	2-2, 3-5
Witney Town v Northwood	3-0
Arlesey Town v Barking	0-2
Welwyn Garden City v East Thurrock United	6-1
Ford United v Wellingborough Town	2-0
Burnham Ramblers v Soham Town Rangers	2-1
Halstead Town v Flackwell Heath	3-0
Wisbech Town v Bedford Town	2-3
Desborough Town v Cheshunt	1-0
Farnham Town v Hailsham Town	1-1, 2-3
Molesey v Oxford City	1-4
Deal Town v Hillingdon Borough	4-1
Egham Town v Fisher Athletic	2-2, 0-6
St Leonards v Wick	2-1
Cowes Sports v Dorking	1-2
Godalming & Guildford v Banstead Athletic	1-2
Dartford v Reading Town	0-0, 3-0
Folkestone Invicta v Tonbridge Angels	2-3
abandoned after 54 minutes; flooded pitch, 1-0	
Ashford Town v Margate	1-1, 2-1
Littlehampton Town v Fleet Town	1-4

Fareham Town v Croydon	0-2
Portfield v Eastleigh	1-1, 2-1
Abingdon Town v Maidenhead United	0-3
Ashford Town (Middlesex) v Erith & Belvedere	1-3
Bashley v Ramsgate	4-2
Chatham Town v Horsham	1-1, 1-3
Eastbourne Town v Herne Bay	1-0
at Herne Bay FC	
Wokingham Town v Camberley Town	0-2
Burgess Hill Town v Thame United	1-0
Torrington v Melksham Town	0-1
Cirencester Town v Chippenham Town	3-2
Falmouth Town v Devizes Town	1-0
Newport AFC v Weston-Super-Mare	0-0, 0-1
Elmore v Yate Town	1-0
Paulton Rovers v Bemerton Heath Harlequins	2-1
Minehead Town v Frome Town	4-0
Backwell United v Calne Town	2-1
Bideford v Barnstaple Town	1-2
Bridgwater Town v Welton Rovers	5-0

FIRST QUALIFYING ROUND

Billingham Town v Denaby United	7-3
Ashington v Louth United	0-2
Atherton LR v Chester-Le-Street Town	0-4
Prescot Cables v Liversedge	5-2
Crook Town v Farsley Celtic	1-4
Eccleshill United v Penrith	2-2, 0-6
Brigg Town v Garforth Town	1-0
Tadcaster Albion v Armthorpe Welfare	1-1, 0-0
Tadcaster Albion won 4-3 on penalties	
Seaham Red Star v Netherfield Kendal	2-2, 1-8
Warrington Town v North Ferriby United	0-4
Bootle v Bradford Park Avenue	2-3
Glasshoughton Welfare v Salford City	3-1
Tie awarded to Salford City as Glasshoughton	
Welfare fielding an ineligible player	
Consett v Newcastle Blue Star	1-2
West Auckland Town v Rossington Main	5-0
Chadderton v Ryhope CA	1-1, 1-2
St Helens Town v Brandon United	3-1
Radcliffe Borough v Clitheroe	2-1
Evenwood Town v Durham City	4-1
Droylsden v Maltby Main	2-2, 2-0
Flixton v Brodsworth	3-0
Ossett Albion v Workington	1-1, 2-2
Ossett Albion won 4-2 on penalties	
Ashton United v Tow Law Town	2-1
Great Harwood Town v Whitley Bay	3-3, 2-1
South Shields v Witton Albion	0-2
Morpeth Town v Skelmersdale United	2-0
Parkgate v Cheadle Town	4-2
Ramsbottom United v Shildon	3-0
Trafford v Mossley	3-0
Bedlington Terriers v Pickering Town	11-1
Billingham Synthonia v Darwen	7-0
Gretna v Harrogate Railway	0-0, 1-2
Whickham v Stocksbridge Park Steels	2-0
Thackley v Bacup Borough	2-0
Selby Town v Curzon Ashton	6-0
Burscough v Jarrow Roofing Boldon CA	2-0
Staveley MW v Leek CSOB	1-3
Racing Club Warwick v Willenhall Town	1-0
Boston Town v Eastwood Town	0-5
Stapenhill v Spalding United	1-0
Belper Town v Alfreton Town	3-0
Rocester v Holbeach United	3-0
Shepshed Dynamo v Bloxwich Town	4-1
Glapwell v Matlock Town	1-2
Lincoln United v Wednesfield	3-0
Halesowen Harriers v Nantwich Town	1-2
West Midlands Police v Stratford Town	1-0
Blakenall v Hinckley United	1-0

Congleton Town v Bilston Town	5-3
Moor Green v Pelsall Villa	6-1
Bourne Town v Glossop North End	1-2
Sutton Coldfield Town v Kidsgrove Athletic	2-1
Arnold Town v Knypersley Victoria	3-1
Stamford v Buxton	2-3
Newcastle Town v Chasetown	1-3
Paget Rangers v Solihull Borough	1-1, 2-4
Oldbury United v Stourbridge	1-6
Bridgnorth Town v Hucknall Town	0-4
Stafford Rangers v Bedworth United	1-1, 2-1
Wroxham v Stewarts & Lloyds	3-0
Chalfont St Peter v St Neots Town	3-3, 3-0
Beaconsfield SYCOB v Concord Rangers	2-1
London Colney v Braintree Town	1-3
Banbury United v Harpenden Town	3-1
Hertford Town v Barkingside	0-0, 2-3
Leighton Town v Ford Sports Daventry	1-2
Canvey Island v Histon	5-3
Edgware Town v Grays Athletic	2-3
Northampton Spencer v Chelmsford City	1-4
Bowers United v Halstead Town	1-3
Burnham Ramblers v Basildon United	2-2, 0-2
Marlow v Tiptree United	1-2
Woodbridge Town v Southall	4-2
Buckingham Town v Wealdstone	0-1
Bedford United v Royston Town	0-3
Ford United v Barton Rovers	1-1, 1-0
Yaxley v Berkhamsted Town	2-5
Clapton v Tilbury	2-0
Harlow Town v Diss Town	5-0
Sudbury Town v Ruislip Manor	4-0
Barking v Warboys Town	3-2
Newmarket Town v Great Yarmouth Town	0-0, 2-2
Newmarket Town won 4-2 on penalties	
Ware v Leyton Pennant	3-2
Ely City v Harwich & Parkeston	0-4
Brook House v Aveley	1-3
Yeading v Welwyn Garden City	1-2
Staines Town v Lowestoft Town	1-1, 2-2
Lowestoft Town won 3-1 on penalties	
Stowmarket Town v Romford	0-1
Desborough Town v Raunds Town	1-2
Tring Town v Wingate & Finchley	0-1
Clacton Town v Bedford Town	1-1, 0-2
Long Buckby v Witney Town	1-2
Sudbury Wanderers v Uxbridge	0-0, 2-3
Witham Town v Hitchin Town	1-0
Brackley Town v Wivenhoe Town	0-2
Baldock Town v Great Wakering Rovers	1-3
Sheppey United v Lymington & New Milton	0-0, 2-1
East Preston v Peacehaven & Telscombe	6-0
Thatcham Town v Ashford Town	3-4
Oxford City v Chertsey Town	3-2
Bedfont v Whitstable Town	5-2
Fisher Athletic v BAT Sports	4-0
Corinthian-Casuals v Worthing	1-2
Havant & Waterlooville v Hassocks	1-0
Thamesmead Town v Horsham YMCA	3-0
Burgess Hill Town v Saltdean United	1-3
Arundel v Camberley Town	0-7
Horsham v Bracknell Town	2-2, 4-3
Gosport Borough v Croydon	0-2
Slade Green v Hungerford Town	2-4
Fleet Town v Dartford	3-2
Chipstead v Redhill	2-0
Langney Sports v Hailsham Town	3-1
Newbury AFC v Tooting & Mitcham United	1-2
Eastbourne Town v Tunbridge Wells	2-2, 4-2
Metropolitan Police v Canterbury City	2-2, 1-1
Canterbury City won 4-3 on penalties	
Leatherhead v Whitehawk	5-0
Viking Sports v Bashley	1-5
Sandhurst Town v Tonbridge Angels	0-1
Bognor Regis Town v Newport (IW)	2-4
Andover v Deal Town	2-5
Epsom & Ewell v Shoreham	2-1
Windsor & Eton v Chichester City	1-1, 4-0
Portsmouth Royal Navy v Raynes Park Vale	4-2
Whyteleafe v Banstead Athletic	2-2, 2-1
Maidenhead United v Selsey	2-1
Brockenhurst v Dorking	1-7
Ash United v Pagham	7-1
Hythe United v Croydon Athletic	2-1
Portfield v Sittingbourne	1-2
Lewes v Erith & Belvedere	1-2

St Leonards v Erith Town	2-0
Ringmer v Didcot Town	1-0
Falmouth Town v Wimborne Town	3-1
Tuffley Rovers v Minehead Town	0-3
Mangotsfield United v Melksham Town	2-1
Tiverton Town v Weston-Super-Mare	2-0
Paulton Rovers v Glastonbury	8-1
Taunton Town v Bournemouth	4-0
Barnstaple Town v Evesham United	1-0
Bridgwater Town v Bridport	1-0
Cirencester Town v Odd Down	2-2, 2-0
St Blazey v EFC Cheltenham	3-2
Brislington v Pershore Town	3-3, 2-4
Westbury United v Elmore	3-3, 0-4
Backwell United v Downton	10-1
Clevedon Town v Cinderford Town	1-1, 0-0
Cinderford Town won 5-4 on penalties	

SECOND QUALIFYING ROUND

Selby Town v Frickley Athletic	1-2
Colwyn Bay v Emley	0-1
Whitby Town v Accrington Stanley	4-2
Radcliffe Borough v Ryhope CA	2-0
Billingham Synthonia v Mossley	0-0, 0-1
Louth United v Brigg Town	0-2
Ashton United v Altrincham	1-0
Flixton v Spennymoor United	4-0
Thackley v Guiseley	1-1, 1-2
Netherfield Kendal v Lancaster City	1-3
Bradford Park Avenue v Stocksbridge Park Steels	1-0
Runcorn v Blyth Spartans	0-0, 4-2
Hyde United v Gainsborough Trinity	4-0
Morpeth Town v Ossett Albion	0-0, 2-2
Morpeth Town won 3-2 on penalties	
Gateshead v Bishop Auckland	3-0
Droylsden v St Helens Town	6-0
Bedlington Terriers v Bamber Bridge	1-1, 4-4
Bedlington Terriers won 4-3 on penalties	
Penrith v Chorley	1-1, 0-1
Stalybridge Celtic v Worksop Town	1-2
Great Harwood Town v Marine	1-3
Witton Albion v Salford City	7-2
Ramsbottom United v Billingham Town	3-0
North Ferriby United v Newcastle Blue Star	5-3
Burscough v Evenwood Town	2-2, 6-0
Leigh RMI v Winsford United	1-0
Tadcaster Albion v Farsley Celtic	1-2
Harrogate Railway v Prescot Cables	1-1, 0-2
Chester-Le-Street Town v West Auckland Town	1-1, 0-2
Grantham Town v West Midlands Police	4-0
Cambridge City v Glossop North End	1-1, 1-1
Glossop North End won 5-4 on penalties	
Congleton Town v Boston United	1-0
Parkgate v Sutton Coldfield Town	0-3
Racing Club Warwick v Stourbridge	0-1
Arnold Town v Matlock Town	1-1, 2-0
Belper Town v Stafford Rangers	1-2
Blakenall v Lincoln United	1-0
Shepshed Dynamo v Gresley Rovers	1-2
Nantwich Town v Raunds Town	1-1, 0-2
Stapenhill v Rothwell Town	0-4
Ilkeston Town v Moor Green	2-0
Atherstone United v Nuneaton Borough	0-0, 0-3
Solihull Borough v Hucknall Town	0-1
Halesowen Town v Eastwood Town	2-2, 1-0
Chasetown v Buxton	0-1
Leek CSOB v Tamworth	2-3
Rocester v Burton Albion	0-1
Bromsgrove Rovers v Kings Lynn	1-1, 1-2
Dorking v Carshalton Athletic	0-5
Sheppey United v Leatherhead	0-0, 1-3
Witney Town v Wroxham	1-1, 3-2
Grays Athletic v Ashford Town	2-0
Sudbury Town v Sittingbourne	0-0, 2-1
Bedfont v Chipstead	0-2
Dagenham & Redbridge v Eastbourne Town	4-0
Welwyn Garden City v Great Wakering Rovers	2-2, 4-3
Ash United v Walton & Hersham	1-5
Clapton v Purfleet	0-1
Bishop's Stortford v Aldershot Town	0-2
Banbury United v Epsom & Ewell	2-2, 1-0
Tooting & Mitcham United v Lowestoft Town	2-3
Wivenhoe Town v Harlow Town	1-3
Fisher Athletic v Halstead Town	1-2
Hendon v Chelmsford City	1-1, 3-2

Slough Town v Fleet Town	1-1, 2-0	Ilkeston Town v Kings Lynn	1-2
Romford v St Albans City	1-2	Hucknall Town v Stourbridge	0-0, 0-3
Ware v Braintree Town	1-1, 1-4	Hastings Town v Yeovil Town	0-3
Boreham Wood v Saltdean United	4-0	Hereford United v Newport (IW)	2-3
Berkhamsted Town v Langney Sports	1-1, 0-0	Crawley Town v Billericay Town	1-0
Langney Sports won 4-3 on penalties		Worcester City v Falmouth Town	2-1
Tiptree United v Royston Town	0-1	Gravesend & Northfleet v Dover Athletic	0-0, 2-3
Barking v Beaconsfield SYCOB	1-0	Farnborough Town v Heybridge Swifts	2-0
Witham Town v Hythe United	5-2	Basingstoke Town v Chalfont St Peter	2-0
Whyteleafe v Bedford Town	2-1	Taunton Town v Kettering Town	4-3
Aylesbury United v Horsham	3-1	Dulwich Hamlet v Purfleet	2-2, 3-1
St Leonards v Sutton United	0-1	Welling United v Weymouth	3-2
East Preston v Worthing	0-2	Barnstaple Town v Cheltenham Town	0-1
Croydon v Enfield	0-4	Dagenham & Redbridge v Chipstead	2-0
Billericay Town v Tonbridge Angels	4-0	Rushden & Diamonds v Forest Green Rovers	2-0
Basildon United v Barkingside	2-2, 3-3	Welwyn Garden City v Ford United	2-2, 2-4
Basildon United won 4-2 on penalties		Hayes v Bromley	1-0
Ford Sports Daventry v Aveley	2-1	Maidenhead United v Kingstonian	2-4
Crawley Town v Canterbury City	5-0	Royston Town v Boreham Wood	0-2
Wingate & Finchley v Canvey Island	0-5	Minehead Town v Woking	1-5
Heybridge Swifts v Bashley	3-1	Witney Town v Stevenage Borough	1-2
Uxbridge v Maidenhead United	0-5	Gloucester City v Sudbury Town	10-0
Dulwich Hamlet v Deal Town	1-0	Slough Town v Halstead Town	3-1
Bromley v Chesham United	2-1	Braintree Town v Camberley Town	1-3
Wealdstone v Newport (IW)	0-0, 2-3	Langney Sports v Harrow Borough	4-1
Hungerford Town v Portsmouth Royal Navy	6-0	Worthing v Whyteleafe	0-2
Havant & Waterlooville v Hampton	5-1	Leatherhead v Windsor & Eton	2-0
Harwich & Parkeston v Chalfont St Peter	0-2	Grays Athletic v Aldershot Town	0-1
Erith & Belvedere v Windsor & Eton	0-1	Walton & Hersham v Bath City	2-2, 0-3
Ford United v Woodbridge Town	1-1, 2-1	Aylesbury United v Carshalton Athletic	0-1
Harrow Borough v Thamesmead Town	3-0	St Albans City v Basildon United	3-0
Gravesend & Northfleet v Oxford City	3-1	Lowestoft Town v Canvey Island	4-2
Newmarket Town v Hastings Town	1-1, 1-2	Banbury United v Enfield	0-4
Camberley Town v Ringmer	2-1	Hungerford Town v Salisbury City	1-1, 2-3
Bath City v Cirencester Town	3-1	Ford Sports Daventry v Sutton United	2-2, 0-3
Dorchester Town v Salisbury City	0-3	Havant & Waterlooville v Witham Town	0-0, 4-0
Mangotsfield United v Worcester City	0-1	Harlow Town v Hendon	2-4
Taunton Town v Cinderford Town	3-1	St Blazey v Barking	1-0
Pershore Town v St Blazey	1-3		
Minehead Town v Bridgwater Town	0-0, 1-0		
Elmore v Barnstaple Town	0-1	**FOURTH QUALIFYING ROUND**	
Backwell United v Basingstoke Town	1-1, 0-1	Runcorn v Ashton United	5-3
Falmouth Town v Tiverton Town	1-0	Kings Lynn v West Auckland Town	0-1
Merthyr Tydfil v Weymouth	0-2	Tamworth v Grantham Town	2-1
Gloucester City v Paulton Rovers	2-1	Droylsden v Leigh RMI	1-2
		Southport v Stourbridge	4-0
		Leek Town v Lancaster City	0-3
THIRD QUALIFYING ROUND		Telford United v Burscough	2-1
West Auckland Town v Hyde United	2-0	Doncaster Rovers v Guiseley	3-1
Mossley v Lancaster City	0-1	Morpeth Town v Burton Albion	0-1
Whitby Town v Bedlington Terriers	1-1, 1-1	Frickley Athletic v Gresley Rovers	0-0, 1-2
Bedlington Terriers won 4-3 on penalties		Morecambe v Hednesford Town	1-2
Doncaster Rovers v Flixton	2-0	Emley v Gateshead	1-1, 3-0
Runcorn v North Ferriby United	1-1, 2-1	Stafford Rangers v Bedlington Terriers	1-2
Gateshead v Barrow	2-1	Aldershot Town v Woking	0-0, 1-2
Bradford Park Avenue v Ashton United	0-1	St Albans City v Kingstonian	1-1, 1-1
Emley v Marine	0-0, 4-1	*Kingstonian won 5-4 on penalties*	
Morpeth Town v Prescot Cables	1-0	Enfield v Raunds Town	2-0
Morecambe v Farsley Celtic	4-2	Havant & Waterlooville v Hayes	2-2, 1-1
Frickley Athletic v Witton Albion	1-0	*Hayes won 4-3 on penalties*	
Guiseley v Chorley	1-1, 2-1	Dagenham & Redbridge v Stevenage Borough	0-3
Droylsden v Northwich Victoria	2-0	Lowestoft Town v Ford United	1-3
Worksop Town v Leigh RMI	1-2	Hendon v Bath City	4-0
Radcliffe Borough v Burscough	0-1	Basingstoke Town v Dover Athletic	2-2, 2-1
Ramsbottom United v Southport	0-5	Boreham Wood v Sutton United	1-0
Kidderminster Harriers v Blakenall	3-1	Worcester City v Langney Sports	7-0
Halesowen Town v Gresley Rovers	1-2	Welling United v Whyteleafe	3-1
Sutton Coldfield Town v Telford United	1-1, 0-1	Leatherhead v Rushden & Diamonds	1-1, 0-4
Congleton Town v Hednesford Town	1-1, 0-1	Kidderminster Harriers v Gloucester City	2-1
Buxton v Leek Town	0-0, 0-3	Farnborough Town v Yeovil Town	1-3
Stafford Rangers v Arnold Town	5-1	Carshalton Athletic v Salisbury City	0-6
Burton Albion v Nuneaton Borough	2-1	Dulwich Hamlet v Newport (IW)	3-2
Glossop North End v Grantham Town	2-3	Cheltenham Town v Taunton Town	3-2
Brigg Town v Tamworth	0-2	St Blazey v Camberley Town	0-2
Raunds Town v Rothwell Town	2-2, 1-0	Crawley Town v Slough Town	0-0, 2-3

FA CUP 1998–99
SPONSORED BY LITTLEWOODS POOLS

COMPETITION PROPER

FIRST ROUND

13 NOV

Manchester C (2) 3 *(Russell 7, 35, Goater 65)*
Halifax T (0) 0 11,106
Manchester C: Weaver; Crooks, Vaughan, Morrison, Wiekens, Horlock (Brown), Bishop (Pollock), Mason, Goater, Dickov, Russell.
Halifax T: Martin; Thackeray, Bradshaw, Sertori, Murphy J, Stoneman, Paterson, Lucas (Murphy S), Williams, Butler, Brown.

Swansea C (2) 3 *(Price 5, Thomas 25, Alsop 90)*
Millwall (0) 0 5728
Swansea C: Freestone; Jones S, Howard, Cusack, Smith, Bound, Price, Thomas, Newhouse (Alsop), Watkin, Appleby.
Millwall: Spink; Lavin, Stuart, Bowry, Nethercott, Fitzgerald, Ryan (Carter), Bircham, Sadlier (Harris), Shaw, Neill.

14 NOV

Basingstoke T (0) 1 *(Mancey 57)*
Bournemouth (1) 2 *(O'Neill 37, Stein 66)* 3830
Basingstoke T: Benstead; Marshall, Redwood, Richardson (Coombs), Harris (Cleeve), Lisk, Wilkinson, Simpson, Mancey, Killick, Hurdle.
Bournemouth: Ovendale; Young, Vincent, Howe, Berthe (O'Neill), Bailey, Cox, Robinson, Stein, Warren, Hughes.

Bedlington T (2) 4 *(Ditchburn 16, Milner 22, 85 (pen), Cross 59)*
Colchester U (0) 1 *(Adcock 86)* 1600
Bedlington T: O'Connor; Sokoluk, Pike, Teasdale, Ditchburn, Melrose, Cross, Bond, Gibb, Milner, Middleton.
Colchester U: Emberson; Dunne, Stamps (Duguid), Williams, Greene, Buckle, Dozzell (Haydon), Gregory D, Sale, Lock, Forbes (Adcock).

Brentford (2) 5 *(Bates 30, Quinn 42, Folan 63, 74, Hreidarsson 66)*
Camberley T (0) 0 4783
Brentford: Pearcey; Boxall, Watson, Hreidarsson, Quinn (Rapley), Bates, Freeman (Bryan), Aspinall (Hebel), Owusu, Rowlands, Folan.
Camberley T: Gray; Tippins, Heath, Sills J, Powell, Xiberras, Todd (Ross), Jopling (Tomsett), Lloyd, Sills T, Harkness (Garrod).

Bristol R (0) 3 *(Roberts 51, 70, 71)*
Welling U (0) 0 5381
Bristol R: Jones; Trees, Challis, Penrice, Foster, Smith, Holloway, Meaker, Ipoua (Shore), Cureton, Roberts.
Welling U: Knight; Powell, Dolby, Allardyce, Copley (Hynes), Skiverton, Linger, Rutherford, Appiah (Riviere), Browne S, Brown D (Watts S).

Cardiff C (3) 6 *(Fowler 10, 40, Middleton 12, Williams 55, 71, Delaney 63)*
Chester C (0) 0 4220
Cardiff C: Hallworth; Delaney, Ford, Mitchell, Young, Carpenter, Fowler (Cadette), O'Sullivan, Williams (Roberts), Nugent, Middleton.
Chester C: Cutler; Davidson, Cross (Lancaster), Richardson, Crosby, Woods, Flitcroft, Priest, Murphy, Reid (Jones), Wright.

Cheltenham T (0) 0
Lincoln C (0) 1 *(Thorpe 79)* 3589
Cheltenham T: Book; Duff, Victory, Banks, Freeman, Brough, Howells (Milton), Bloomer, Eaton (Knight), Grayson (Smith), Norton.
Lincoln C: Richardson; Holmes, Bimson, Fleming, Brown, Austin, Smith, Finnigan, Alcide, Thorpe, Perry.

Dulwich H (0) 0
Southport (0) 1 *(Houghton 56 (og))* 1835
Dulwich H: Cleevely; Humphrey, Cyrus (Anderson), Hewitt, Edwards, Garland M (Gorman), Griggs, McKimm, Bartley, Thompson, Houghton.
Southport: Stewart; Farley, Ryan, Gouck (Formby), Guyett, Horner, Quinn (Thompson), Butler, Ross (Furlong), Gamble, O'Reilly.

Enfield (0) 2 *(Dunwell 61, Richardson 66)*
York C (2) 2 *(Cresswell 16, 35)* 1634
Enfield: Pape; Annon, Naylor, Cooper G, Terry, Jones, Penn, Bentley, Richardson, Dunwell, Cooper S (Deadman).
York C: Warrington; McMillan, Garratt, Tinkler (Himsworth), Jones, Barras (Reed), Connelly, Jordan, Cresswell, Tolson (Rowe), Agnew.

Hartlepool U (1) 2 *(Howard 43, Miller 64)*
Carlisle U (0) 1 *(Stevens 57)* 2845
Hartlepool U: Hollund; Knowles, Clark, Ingram, Lee, Di Lella, Brightwell (Rush), Miller (Stokoe), Howard, Midgley, Stephenson.
Carlisle U: Caig; Bowman, Searle, Whitehead, Brightwell, Prokas, Hopper, Clark, Stevens, Douglas (Thorpe), Finney.

Hednesford T (0) 3 *(Davis 71, Kimmins 79, Carty 90)*
Barnet (0) 1 *(Currie 47)* 1436
Hednesford T: Morgan; Sedgemore, Colkin, Comyn, Brindley, Bradley, Ware, Lake, Davis (Hayward), Carty, Kimmins.
Barnet: Harrison; Stockley, Harle, Goodhind (Simpson) (King), Alsford, Ford, Wilson, Doolan, Charlery, McGleish, Currie.

Kingstonian (0) 1 *(Holligan 65)*
Burton A (0) 0 1505
Kingstonian: Farrelly; Mustafa, Luckett, Crossley, Stewart, Harris, Patterson, Pitcher, Rattray, Holligan (Leworthy), Akuamoah.
Burton A: Goodwin; Davies, Ashby (Francis), Marsden, Blount, Grocutt, Lyons, Stride, Holmes, Garner, Spooner.

Leyton Orient (1) 4 *(Richards 26, 47, 76, Walschaerts 68)*
Brighton & HA (1) 2 *(Barker 22, Mayo 82)* 7406
Leyton Orient: MacKenzie; Walschaerts, Lockwood, Smith, Hicks, Clark, Ling, Ampadu (Joseph M), Griffiths, Richards (Simba), Beall (Joseph R).
Brighton & HA: Ormerod; Browne T, Sturgess, Armstrong (Moralee), Storer, Johnson, Bennett, Arnott (Mayo), Hart, Barker, Culverhouse.

Macclesfield T (0) 2 *(Tomlinson 72, Sodje 87)*
Slough T (2) 2 *(Pierson 24, Deaner 38)* 2114
Macclesfield T: Price; Hitchen, Ingram (Howarth), Payne, Wood, Sodje, Askey, Sorvel, Tomlinson, Sedgemore (Durkan), Whittaker.
Slough T: Wilkerson; Channing, Hughes (Hardyman), Roberts, Pierson, Thorp (Bicknell), Denton, Kemp, Deaner (Holzman), Hamment, Browne.

Mansfield T (1) 2 *(Clarke 8, Lormor 71)*
Hayes (0) 1 *(Flynn 74)*   2613
Mansfield T: Bowling; Ford (Williams), Harper, Peters, Clarke, Hackett, Schofield, Walker (Kerr), Lormor, Peacock (Christie), Tallon.
Hayes: Meara; Goodliffe, Flynn, Watts, Bunce, Sparks (Catlin), Metcalfe, Hall (Dellisser), Hodson (Booth), Randall, Wilkinson.

Northampton T (0) 2 *(Thomson 55 (og), Sampson 56)*
Lancaster C (1) 1 *(Thomson 30)*   4545
Northampton T: Turley; Savage, Frain, Sampson, Hodgson (Freestone), Hill, Gibb, Seal, Corazzin (Hunt), Wilkinson, Parrish.
Lancaster C: Thornley; Curwen (Lang), Graham (Lavelle), Udall, Baldwin, Gelling, Martin, Flannery, Diggle (Cheal), Thomson, Parkinson.

Oldham Ath (2) 2 *(Salt 33, McNiven S 37)*
Gillingham (0) 0   3173
Oldham Ath: Kelly; McNiven S, Holt, Garnett, Rickers, Duxbury, Salt, Sheridan, Tipton (Allott), Whitehall (Ritchie), Reid.
Gillingham: Stannard; Edge, Carr, Smith, Ashby (Bryant), Pennock (Hodge), Patterson, Hessenthaler (Galloway), Asaba, Southall, Taylor.

Plymouth Arg (0) 0
Kidderminster H (0) 0   4284
Plymouth Arg: Sheffield; Collins, Beswetherick, McCall, Heathcote, Wotton, Barlow, Mauge, McCarthy, Marshall (Phillips), Hargreaves.
Kidderminster H: Brock; Hinton, Hines, Weir (Wolsey), Smith, Yates, Webb, Taylor, Hadley, Arnold, Willetts.

Preston NE (1) 3 *(Rankine 31, Harris 53, Darby 90)*
Ford U (0) 0   10,167
Preston NE: Lucas; Parkinson, Ludden, Murdock, Kidd, Gregan, Cartwright, Rankine (Darby), Nogan (Macken), Harris, Appleton.
Ford U: Chapman; Devereux, Fowler, Beck, Gardner (Hughes), Willis, Munday (Bly), Reilly (Waites), Wood, Parish, Lord.

Reading (0) 0
Stoke C (1) 1 *(Lightbourne 27)*   10,095
Reading: Howey; Bernal, McPherson, Crawford (Roach), Primus, Casper, Glasgow, Caskey, Williams, Brayson (Sarr), Brebner.
Stoke C: Muggleton; Woods, Small, Sigurdsson, Robinson, Forsyth, Keen, Kavanagh, Thorne, Lightbourne (Wallace), Oldfield.

Runcorn (0) 1 *(McNally 85)*
Stevenage B (0) 1 *(Alford 58)*   1114
Runcorn: Morris; Ward (Carragher), Oliver (Callaghan), Warder, Ellis, Ruffer, Salt, McNally, Rose, Nolan (Randles), Watson.
Stevenage B: Taylor; Harvey, Naylor, Smith, Howarth, Beevor, Reinelt, Berry, Alford, Love, Samuels.

Rushden & D (1) 1 *(Underwood 19)*
Shrewsbury T (0) 0   4121
Rushden & D: Gayle; Wooding, Bradshaw, Mison, Warburton, Heggs, McElhatton, Butterworth, West, Collins (Rawle), Underwood.
Shrewsbury T: Edwards; Seabury, Hanmer, Wilding, Gayle, Tretton, Berkley, Kerrigan (Steele), Jagielka, Evans, Brown.

Salisbury C (0) 0
Hull C (0) 2 *(Rioch 55, McGinty 79)*   2570
Salisbury C: Matthews; Braybrook, Ferrett (Bright), Rofe, Emms, Randall, Bowers, Sales, Harbut, Chalk, Housley.
Hull C: Wilson; Joyce, Mann, Hocking, Whitworth, Hawes, Greaves, Edwards, Brown (Ellington), Rioch (Gage), McGinty.

Scarborough (0) 1 *(Williams 47)*
Rochdale (0) 1 *(Bryson 75)*   1860
Scarborough: Elliott; Kay, Atkinson, Worrall, Lydiate, Mirankov, Bullimore (Russell), Hoyland, Robinson (Campbell), Brodie, Williams.

Rochdale: Edwards; Williams, Sparrow, Hill, Monington, Farrell, Jones (Diaz), Painter, Stuart, Bryson, Peake.

Southend U (0) 0
Doncaster R (1) 1 *(Penney 12)*   3740
Southend U: Margetson; Beard, Stimson (Jones), Livett, Newman, Coleman (Fitzpatrick), Maher, Burns, Conlon, Whyte (Morley), Clarke.
Doncaster R: Woods; Ibarra, Shaw, Snodin, Warren, Nicol, Maamria, Penney, Duerden (Hume), Kirkwood, Wright.

Tamworth (1) 2 *(Shaw 28, Smith 52)*
Exeter C (1) 2 *(Gittens 15, Richardson 90)* 2485
Tamworth: McNamara; Warner, Shaw, Steele, Batchelor, Howard, Crawford, Walker, Smith, Dixon, Haughton.
Exeter C: Bayes; Wilkinson (McConnell), Power, Baddeley, Richardson, Gittens, Rowbotham, Rees, Flack, Holloway (Gardner), Breslan (Fry).

Telford U (0) 0
Cambridge U (1) 2 *(Benjamin 22, Butler 66)* 1818
Telford U: Williams; Turner, Lyne, Fowler, Bentley, Shakespeare, Doyle, Jones, Norbury (Gray), Huckerby, Palmer (Murphy).
Cambridge U: Marshall; Chenery, Ashbee, Duncan, McNeil, Campbell, Wanless, Kyd (Taylor), Butler, Benjamin, Russell.

Walsall (0) 1 *(Roper 79)*
Gresley R (0) 0   4274
Walsall: Walker; Marsh, Pointon, Keates, Green, Roper, Wrack, Otta (Thomas), Rammell, Larusson (Porter), Brissett (Watson).
Gresley R: Ford; Wardle, Kearns, Fitzpatrick (Fowkes), Carvell, Faulkner, Smith (Lonergon), Simpson, Pitt, Rowland, Orton.

Wigan Ath (2) 4 *(Greenall 8, Haworth 44, Barlow 49, Lowe 67)*
Blackpool (1) 3 *(Blunt 16, Ormerod 53, Aldridge 90)* 4640
Wigan Ath: Carroll; Green, Bradshaw, Griffiths, Balmer, Rogers, Kilford, Greenall, Haworth (Lowe) (Lee), O'Neill, Barlow.
Blackpool: Banks; Bryan, Hills, Butler, Robinson, Shuttleworth (Jarrett), Blunt (Bent), Clarkson, Aldridge, Bushell, Ormerod.

Woking (0) 0
Scunthorpe U (1) 1 *(Forrester 35)*   3399
Woking: Batty; Payne, Hollingdale, Saunders, Smith, Danzey, Girdler, Perkins (Bolt), Steele, West, Hay.
Scunthorpe U: Clarke; Housham, McAuley, Logan, Wilcox, Hope, Walker (Harsley), Forrester, Marshall, Stamp, Calvo-Garcia.

Worcester C (0) 0
Torquay U (0) 1 *(Partridge 77)*   3023
Worcester C: Higgs; Sandeman, Burnham, Greenman, Talbot (Woods), Cottrill, Wells, Chenoweth, Bowen (Owen), Griffiths, Hillman.
Torquay U: Veysey; Gurney, Herrera, Aggrey, Robinson, Witter, Clayton, McGorry, Bedeau, Partridge, Hill.

Wrexham (0) 1 *(Brammer 89)*
Peterborough U (0) 0   2592
Wrexham: Cartwright; McGregor, Hardy, Brammer, Ridler, Carey, Roberts, Owen, Connolly, Rush (Spink), Russell (Chalk).
Peterborough U: Tyler; Linton, Drury, Scott (Hooper), Bodley, Edwards, Davies, Castle (Etherington), Butler (Cleaver), Rowe, Farrell.

Wycombe W (0) 1 *(Scott 73)*
Chesterfield (0) 0   3102
Wycombe W: Taylor; Wraight, Vinnicombe, Lawrence, Cousins, McCarthy, Simpson, Brown, Baird, Scott, Emblen (Bulman).
Chesterfield: Mercer; Hewitt, Jules (Wilkinson), Curtis, Williams, Breckin, Howard, Holland (Lee), Reeves, Ebdon, Perkins.

Yeovil T (1) 2 *(Patmore 39, Hannigan 90)*
West Auckland T (2) 2 *(Milroy 9, Adamson 35)*   3203
Yeovil T: Pennock; Piper (Smith B), Fishlock, Brown, Hannigan, Cousins, Thompson, Stott, Patmore, Dale (Pounder), Hayfield (Franklin).
West Auckland T: Sams; Bainbridge, Stout, Sinclair, Jackson, Fleming, Wheldon, Innes (Johnson), Milroy, Adamson (Gorman), Hornsby.

15 NOV

Boreham Wood (0) 2 *(Nisbet 54, Xavier 81)*
Luton T (1) 3 *(Gray 33, 53, Davis S 76)*   1772
Boreham Wood: Taylor; Sanders, McCarthy, Shaw, Nisbet, Brown (Daly), Grime, Heffer, Dixon, Samuels (Xavier), Brady (Ireland).
Luton T: Davis K; Alexander, McGowan, McLaren, Davis S, Johnson, McKinnon (Spring), Evers, Douglas (Doherty), Gray, Nyamah (McIndoe).

Emley (1) 1 *(Bambrook 14)*
Rotherham U (0) 1 *(Hudson 80)*   6062
Emley: Rhodes; Nicholson (Wood), Jones, Thompson, Lacey, David, Banks, Hurst, Thorpe (Calcutt), Bambrook, Reynolds.
Rotherham U: Pollitt; Ingledow, Hurst, Garner, Richardson, Warner, Sedgwick, Hudson, Tracey (Glover), Berry, Roscoe.

Fulham (1) 1 *(Lehmann 36)*
Leigh RMI (1) 1 *(Whealing 20)*   7965
Fulham: Taylor; Uhlenbeek, Brevett, Hayward, Coleman, Symons, Collins, Davis (Trollope), Lehmann, Peschisolido, Salako (Horsfield).
Leigh RMI: Felgate; Locke, Whealing, Hill, Prescott, Turpin, Monk (Cryer), Ridings, Matthews, Evans, Smyth.

Hendon (0) 0
Notts Co (0) 0   1627
Hendon: McCann; Howard, Clarke, Daly, Bateman, Cox, Pye (Heard), Hyatt, Whitmarsh (Maran), Fitzgerald, Lewis.
Notts Co: Ward; Hendon, Pearce, Redmile, Fairclough, Richardson, Owers, Jackson, Farrell (Liburd), Jones, Murray.

17 NOV

Darlington (0) 3 *(Atkinson 81, Dorner 87, Barnard 90)*
Burnley (1) 2 *(Payton 37, 55 (pen))*   5059
Darlington: Preece; Reed, Barnard, Liddle, Tutill, Bennett (Oliver), Gaughan, Naylor, Roberts (Dorner), Gabbiadini, Atkinson.
Burnley: Kval; Scott, Eastwood, Vindheim, Heywood, Reid, Little, Brass, Payton, Ford, Morgan.
at Middlesbrough.

FIRST ROUND REPLAYS

23 NOV

Stevenage B (0) 2 *(Love 48, Awford 74)*
Runcorn (0) 0   3252
Stevenage B: Taylor; Harvey, Naylor, Smith, Trott, Beevor (Meah), Reinelt (Thompson), Berry, Awford (Samuels), Love, Kean.
Runcorn: Morris; Ward, Carragher (Brooks), Warder (Whalley), Ellis, Ruffer, Salt, McNally, Rose (Irving), Nolan, Watson.

24 NOV

Exeter C (3) 4 *(Rowe 15 (og), Rowbotham 31, 45, Flack 51)*
Tamworth (0) 1 *(Smith 75)*   3152
Exeter C: Bayes; Gale, Power, Baddeley (Clark), Richardson, Fry, Rowbotham, Rees, Flack, Curran, Gardner (Wilkinson).
Tamworth: Rowe; Warner, Shaw, Steele, Batchelor, Howard, Crawford, Walker (Hatton), Smith, Dixon (Yates), Haughton.

Kidderminster H 0
Plymouth Arg 0
Abandoned at half-time; fog.

Leigh RMI (0) 0
Fulham (2) 2 *(Peschisolido 32 (pen), 41)*   7125
Leigh RMI: Felgate; Locke, Whealing, Hill, Prescott, Turpin, Monk, Ridings, Matthews (Cryer), Evans, Smyth.
Fulham: Taylor; Uhlenbeek, Brevett, Morgan, Coleman, Symons, Smith (Brazier), Bracewell, Horsfield (Hayward), Peschisolido (Salako), Trollope.

Rochdale (1) 2 *(Monington 8, Bryson 89)*
Scarborough (0) 0   1850
Rochdale: Edwards; Williams, Sparrow, Hill, Monington, Bryson, Diaz (Bayliss), Painter, Carden, Peake (Jones), Stuart (Farrell).
Scarborough: Elliott; Kay, Atkinson, Worrall, Lydiate, Russell (Morris), Bullimore, Hoyland, Brodie, McNaughton, Williams.

Rotherham U (1) 3 *(Glover 28, Hurst 82, Garner 85)*
Emley (1) 1 *(Bambrook 1)*   5077
Rotherham U: Pollitt; Ingledow, Hurst, Garner (Thompson), Richardson, Dillon, Sedgwick (Tracey), Hudson, Berry, Glover, Roscoe (Monkhouse).
Emley: Rhodes; Tonks (Calcutt), Jones, Thompson, Lacey, David, Wilson, Hurst, Bambrook, Wood, Reynolds.

Slough T (1) 1 *(Hughes 16)*
Macclesfield T (1) 1 *(Sedgemore 7)*   2010
Slough T: Wilkerson; Channing (Holzman), Hughes, Roberts (Hardyman), Pierson, Thorp, Denton, Kemp (Line), Deaner, Hamment, Browne.
Macclesfield T: Price; Hitchen, Ingram, Payne, Tinson (Griffiths), Sodje, Askey, Sorvel, Tomlinson, Sedgemore (Clyde), Whittaker (Howarth).
aet; Macclesfield T won 9-8 on penalties.

West Auckland T (0) 1 *(Milroy 61)*
Yeovil T (0) 1 *(Dale 72)*   2164
West Auckland T: Sams; Bainbridge, Stout, Sinclair, Jackson, Fleming, Wheldon, Johnson (Cowell), Milroy (Gorman), Adamson (Innes), Hornsby.
Yeovil T: Pennock; Piper (Pitman), Fishlock, Brown, Hannigan, Cousins, Thompson, Stott, Patmore, Dale, Pounder.
aet; Yeovil T won 5-3 on penalties.

York C (2) 2 *(Jordan 18, Cresswell 45)*
Enfield (1) 1 *(Dunwell 27)*   2131
York C: Warrington; McMillan, Himsworth (Prendergast), Tinkler, Jones, Garratt, Connelly, Jordan, Cresswell (Rowe), Woods (Tolson), Agnew.
Enfield: Pape; Annon, Protheroe, Cooper G, Terry, Jones (Clarke), Penn, Bentley, Richardson, Dunwell (Hall), Cooper S (Morgan).

1 DEC

Kidderminster H (0) 0
Plymouth Arg (0) 0   4471
Kidderminster H: Brock; Hinton, Hines, Webb, Smith, Yates, Cunnington (Willetts), Hadley (Deakin), May, Arnold, Taylor.
Plymouth Arg: Sheffield; Ashton, Beswetherick, Bastow, Heathcote, Wotton, Barlow, McCall (Adams), McCarthy, Jean, Hargreaves (Phillips).
aet; Plymouth Arg won 5-4 on penalties.

Notts Co (0) 3 *(Owers 60, Jones 75, 82)*
Hendon (0) 0   2230
Notts Co: Ward; Hendon, Pearce, Redmile, Jackson (Quayle), Richardson, Owers, Garcia (Dyer), Hughes (Liburd), Jones, Murray.
Hendon: McCann; Howard, Clarke, Daly, Bateman, Cox (Heard), Pye (Warmington), Hyatt, Whitmarsh (Kelly T), Fitzgerald, Lewis.

SECOND ROUND
4 DEC

Darlington (1) 1 *(Bennett 16)*
Manchester C (0) 1 *(Dickov 77)* 7250
Darlington: Preece; Reed, Barnard, Liddle, Tutill, Bennett (Brumwell), Gaughan, Naylor, Dorner (Oliver), Gabbiadini, Atkinson.
Manchester C: Weaver; Edghill, Vaughan, Morrison, Wiekens, Crooks, Mason (Dickov), Pollock, Goater, Taylor, Russell.

5 DEC

Cardiff C (1) 3 *(Middleton 45, Fowler 59, Williams 82)*
Hednesford T (0) 1 *(Carty 87)* 5638
Cardiff C: Hallworth; Delaney, Ford, Mitchell, Young, Carpenter (Hill), Fowler, O'Sullivan, Williams (Earnshaw), Nugent (Thomas), Middleton.
Hednesford T: Morgan; Sedgemore, Culkin, Comyn, Brindley, Bradley, Ware, Beeston (Blades), Davis (Kelly), Carty, Kimmins (Hayward).

Doncaster R (0) 0
Rushden & D (0) 0 5396
Doncaster R: Woods; Shaw, Warren, Snodin (Beckett), Nicol, Sutherland, Penney, Goodwin, Duerden (Hume), Kirkwood, Wright.
Rushden & D: Gayle; Wooding, Bradshaw, Mison, Warburton, Heggs, McElhatton, Butterworth, West, Archer, Underwood.

Exeter C (1) 2 *(Flack 36, Gardner 49)*
Bristol R (1) 2 *(Penrice 43, Cureton 76)* 4352
Exeter C: Bayes; Fry (Breslan), Power, Clark, Richardson, Gittens, Rowbotham (McConnell), Rees, Flack, Curran, Gardner.
Bristol R: Jones; Leoni, Challis, Trees, Foster, Smith, Holloway, Meaker (Zabek), Penrice, Cureton, Ipoua.

Fulham (1) 4 *(Horsfield 6, 84, Di Lella 47 (og), Morgan 81)*
Hartlepool U (1) 2 *(Midgley 41, Howard 58)* 6358
Fulham: Taylor; Uhlenbeek, Brazier, Morgan, Coleman, Symons, Hayward, Bracewell (Smith), Horsfield, Peschisolido, Hayles (Salako).
Hartlepool U: Hollund; Knowles, Clark, Barron, Ingram, Di Lella (Hutt), Stokoe, Miller, Howard, Midgley, Stephenson (Brightwell).

Lincoln C (1) 4 *(Battersby 22, Alcide 49, Finnigan 66, Holmes 69)*
Stevenage B (0) 1 *(Alford 90)* 4375
Lincoln C: Richardson; Miller (Stones), Bimson, Fleming, Holmes, Austin, Smith, Finnigan, Battersby, Thorpe, Alcide (Whitney).
Stevenage B: Taylor; Harvey, Naylor, Smith, Howarth, Beevor (Kean), Plummer, Berry, Alford, Love, Reinelt (Samuels).

Luton T (1) 1 *(Davis S 36)*
Hull C (1) 2 *(Morley 29, Dewhurst 63)* 5021
Luton T: Davis K; Alexander, McGowan, Spring, Davis S, White, McKinnon (McIndoe), Evers, Doherty (Douglas), Gray, McLaren (Scarlett).
Hull C: Wilson; Greaves, Edwards, Hocking, Whittle, Dewhurst, French, D'Auria, Brown (Ellington), Morley, McGinty.

Macclesfield T (1) 4 *(Askey 35, Tomlinson 60, 65, 71)*
Cambridge U (0) 1 *(Campbell 55)* 2650
Macclesfield T: Price; Tinson, Hitchen, Payne, Wood, Sodje (Ingram), Askey, Sorvel, Tomlinson, Sedgemore, Whittaker (Davenport).
Cambridge U: Marshall; Chenery, Ashbee, Duncan, McNeil (Joseph), Campbell, Wanless, Taylor (Mustoe), Butler, Benjamin, Russell.

Mansfield T (0) 1 *(Lormor 72)*
Southport (1) 2 *(Gamble 25 (pen), Ross 46)* 3210
Mansfield T: Bowling; Ford, Harper, Peters, Clarke, Hackett, Schofield, Walker (Christie), Lormor, Peacock, Tallon.

Southport: Stewart; Farley, Ryan, Butler (Futcher), Guyett, Horner, Thompson (Furlong), Gouck (Bolland), Ross, Gamble, Formby.

Notts Co (1) 1 *(Jones 27)*
Wigan Ath (0) 1 *(Lowe 57)* 3591
Notts Co: Ward; Hendon, Pearce, Redmile, Dyer, Richardson, Owers, Garcia (Quayle), Liburd, Jones, Murray.
Wigan Ath: Carroll; Green, Bradshaw, McGibbon, Balmer, Rogers (Lee), Kilford, Greenall, Lowe, O'Neill, Barlow.

Oldham Ath (0) 1 *(McGinlay 74 (pen))*
Brentford (1) 1 *(Freeman 35 (pen))* 4217
Oldham Ath: Kelly; McNiven S, Holt, Garnett, Rickers, Duxbury, Graham (Allott), Sheridan, Tipton (McGinlay), Whitehall, Reid.
Brentford: Pearcey; Anderson, Watson, Hebel, Quinn, Bates, Freeman (Bryan), Oatway, Owusu, Rowlands, Folan.

Preston NE (0) 2 *(Nogan 58, McKenna 69)*
Walsall (0) 0 8488
Preston NE: Lucas; Parkinson, Ludden, Kidd, Jackson, Gregan, Cartwright, Rankine, Nogan, Harris (Wright), McKenna.
Walsall: Walker; Evans (Garrault), Pointon, Keates, Green, Roper, Wrack, Otta (Watson), Rammell, Larusson, Marsh.

Rochdale (0) 0
Rotherham U (0) 0 3346
Rochdale: Key (Edwards); Williams (Diaz), Sparrow, Hill, Monington, Johnson, Carden, Painter, Stuart, Bryson, Peake.
Rotherham U: Pollitt; Ingledow, Hurst, Garner, Richardson, Dillon, Berry (Sedgewick), Hudson, Scott R, Glover, Roscoe.

Scunthorpe U (0) 2 *(Eyre 54 (pen), Forrester 81)*
Bedlington T (0) 0 4719
Scunthorpe U: Clarke; Fickling, McAuley, Logan, Wilcox, Hope, Harsley, Forrester, Eyre, Stamp (Bull), Calvo-Garcia (Marshall).
Bedlington T: O'Connor; Sokoluk, Pike, Teasdale, Ditchburn, Melrose, Cross (Ludlow), Bond (Boon), Gibb, Milner, Middleton (Renforth).

Swansea C (1) 1 *(Appleby 41)*
Stoke C (0) 0 7460
Swansea C: Freestone; Jones S, Howard, Cusack, Smith, Bound, Price, Thomas, Alsop, Bird (Jenkins), Appleby.
Stoke C: Muggleton; Petty (Sturridge), Small, Sigurdsson, Robinson, Woods, Keen, Kavanagh, Thorne, Forsyth, Oldfield.

Torquay U (0) 0
Bournemouth (1) 1 *(Robinson 22)* 2929
Torquay U: Veysey; Gurney, Herrera, Robinson, Aggrey (Bedeau), Witter, Leadbitter, McGorry, Thomas, Partridge, Hill (Hapgood).
Bournemouth: Ovendale; Young, Vincent, Howe, Warren (O'Neill), Bailey, Cox, Robinson, Stein, Fletcher, Hughes.

Wrexham (1) 2 *(Roberts 33 (pen), Connolly 72)*
York C (1) 1 *(Jordan 25)* 2836
Wrexham: Cartwright; McGregor, Hardy, Brammer, Ridler, Spink, Chalk, Russell, Connolly, Roberts (Owen), Ward.
York C: Mimms; Bullock (Rennison), Garratt, Tinkler, Jones, Reed, Connelly, Jordan, Cresswell, Tolson, Agnew (Rowe).

Wycombe W (1) 1 *(Baird 31)*
Plymouth Arg (0) 1 *(McCarthy 76 (og))* 3493
Wycombe W: Taylor; Lawrence, Vinnicombe, McCarthy, Cousins, Mohan, Simpson, Carroll, Baird, Scott, Emblen (Bulman).
Plymouth Arg: Dungey; Ashton, Beswetherick, Bastow, Heathcote, Wotton, Barlow, Sweeney, McCarthy, Jean, Phillips.

Yeovil T (1) 2 *(Thompson 14, Patmore 82)*
Northampton T (0) 0   5218
Yeovil T: Pennock; Piper, Fishlock, Brown, Hannigan, Cousins, Thompson, Stott, Patmore, Dale (Smith B), Pitman (Pounder).
Northampton T: Turley; Hill, Frain, Sampson, Hunter (Freestone), Hunt (Warner), Gibb, Savage, Wilkinson, Corazzin, Lee (Hughes).

6 DEC

Kingstonian (0) 0
Leyton Orient (0) 0   3495
Kingstonian: Farrelly; Mustafa, Luckett, Stewart, Crossley, Harris, Pitcher, Rattray, Akuamoah, Leworthy (Holligan), Patterson.
Leyton Orient: MacKenzie; Morrison (Inglethorpe), Walschaerts, Hicks, Smith, Clark, Ling, Joseph M, Griffiths (Maskell), Simba, Beall.

SECOND ROUND REPLAYS

15 DEC

Brentford (1) 2 *(Owusu 10, Freeman 67)*
Oldham Ath (1) 2 *(McGinlay 20, Duxbury 72)*   4375
Brentford: Dearden; Boxall (Aspinall), Folan, Hreidarsson, Quinn, Bates, Freeman (Fortune-West), Oatway, Owusu, Rowlands, Hebel (Anderson).
Oldham Ath: Kelly; McNiven S (Tipton), Sinnott (Holt), Garnett, Rickers, Duxbury (Miskelly), McGinlay, Sheridan, Graham, Whitehall, Reid.
aet; Oldham Ath won 4-2 on penalties.

Bristol R (1) 5 *(Zabek 9, Shore 53, 61, Cureton 63, Roberts 77)*
Exeter C (0) 0   5093
Bristol R: Jones; Leoni (Pritchard), Challis, Zabek, Foster, Trought (Smith), Shore, Trees, Ipoua, Cureton, Roberts (Meaker).
Exeter C: Bayes; Clark, Power, Blake (Breslan), Richardson, Gittens, Rowbotham, Rees, Flack, Curran, Gardner.

Leyton Orient (1) 2 *(Walschaerts 12, Simba 48)*
Kingstonian (0) 1 *(Holligan 74)*   3652
Leyton Orient: MacKenzie; Walschaerts, Lockwood, Smith, Hicks, Clark, Ling, Joseph M, Inglethorpe (Warren), Simba (Maskell), Beall.
Kingstonian: Farrelly; Mustafa, Luckett, Crossley, Stewart (Holligan), Harris, Patterson, Pitcher, Rattray (Corbett), Leworthy (John), Akuamoah.

Manchester C (0) 1 *(Brown 108)*
Darlington (0) 0   8595
Manchester C: Weaver; Crooks, Edghill, Morrison (Bishop), Wiekens, Horlock, Brown, Pollock, Goater (Dickov), Taylor, Russell (Tiatto).
Darlington: Preece; Brumwell, Barnard, Liddle, Tutill, Bennett, Gaughan, Leah (Carter) (Campbell), Naylor, Gabbiadini, Oliver.
aet.

Plymouth Arg (2) 3 *(Wotton 27 (pen), Heathcote 39, Sweeney 83)*
Wycombe W (0) 2 *(Read 71, Carroll 90 (pen))*   4304
Plymouth Arg: Sheffield; Ashton, Hargreaves, Bastow, Heathcote, Wotton, Barlow, Mauge, McCarthy, Jean (Sweeney), Phillips (Marshall).
Wycombe W: Taylor; Lawrence, Vinnicombe (Beeton), McCarthy, Cousins, Mohan, Simpson (Emblen), Brown, Baird (Read), Scott, Carroll.

Rotherham U (1) 4 *(Garner 39, Berry 47, Glover 59, Scott R 65)*
Rochdale (0) 0   3424
Rotherham U: Pollitt; Scott G (Thompson), Dillon, Garner, Warner, Richardson (Berry), Sedgwick, Ingledow, Scott R, Glover (White), Hurst.
Rochdale: Edwards; Williams, Sparrow, Hill, Monington, Farrell, Carden, Painter (Bayliss), Stuart, Bryson (Jones), Peake (Barlow).

Rushden & D (1) 4 *(Hamsher 6 (pen), West 63, 84, Brady 68)*
Doncaster R (1) 2 *(Sutherland 17, Maamria 89)*   5564
Rushden & D: Gayle; Wooding, Bradshaw, Hamsher, Warburton, Heggs, Brady, Butterworth, West, Collins (Mison), Underwood.
Doncaster R: Woods; Warren, Maxfield, Nicol, Penney, Sutherland (George), Beckett (Duerden), Goodwin, Hume, Kirkwood (Maamria), Wright.

Wigan Ath (0) 0
Notts Co (0) 0   3292
Wigan Ath: Carroll; Green, Sharp (Jenkinson), McGibbon, Balmer, Porter, Lee, Greenall, Warne (Martinez), O'Neill, Kilford (Smeets).
Notts Co: Ward; Hendon, Pearce, Redmile, Dyer (Tierney), Richardson, Owers, Liburd, Strodder (Garcia), Jackson, Murray.
aet; Notts Co won 4-2 on penalties.

THIRD ROUND

2 JAN

Aston Villa (1) 3 *(Collymore 45, 67, Joachim 51)*
Hull C (0) 0   39,217
Aston Villa: Oakes; Watson (Charles), Wright, Southgate, Ehiogu, Barry, Draper (Grayson), Hendrie (Lescott), Joachim, Collymore, Scimeca.
Hull C: Wilson; Whittle, Hocking, Edwards, Greaves (Peacock), Rioch, Joyce (Hawes), D'Auria, Brown (McGinty), Faulconbridge, Morley.

Blackburn R (1) 2 *(Davies 45, Wilcox 88)*
Charlton Ath (0) 0   16,631
Blackburn R: Filan; Perez, Croft, Marcolin (Dunne), Broomes, Henchoz, McKinlay, Gillespie, Gallacher (Duff), Davies, Wilcox.
Charlton Ath: Ilic; Mills (Newton), Powell, Tiler (Holmes), Rufus, Youds, Kinsella, Redfearn, Hunt, Parker (Bright), Robinson.

Bolton W (0) 1 *(Sellars 57)*
Wolverhampton W (1) 2 *(Keane 8, 65)*   18,269
Bolton W: Jaaskelainen; Cox, Whitlow, Frandsen, Bergsson, Fish, Johansen, Jensen (Gardner), Holdsworth (Gunnlaugsson), Taylor, Sellars.
Wolverhampton W: Stowell; Atkins, Muscat, Fernando, Emblen, Curle, Niestroj, Robinson, Corica, Keane, Gilkes.

Bournemouth (1) 1 *(Howe 34)*
WBA (0) 0   10,881
Bournemouth: Ovendale; Young, Vincent, Howe, O'Neill, Bailey, Warren, Robinson, Stein (Boli), Fletcher, Hughes.
WBA: Whitehead; Holmes, Potter, Bortolazzi (Angel), Murphy, Carbon, Maresca (De Freitas), Sneekes, Quinn (Flynn), Hughes, Kilbane.

Bradford C (1) 2 *(Mills 30, Lawrence 67)*
Grimsby T (0) 1 *(McDermott 79)*   13,870
Bradford C: Walsh; Wright, Jacobs, McCall, Moore, O'Brien, Lawrence, Blake (Westwood), Mills, Whalley, Beagrie.
Grimsby T: Davison; McDermott, Gallimore, Handyside, Smith R, Coldicott (Lever), Donovan (Widdrington), Smith D (Black), Livingstone, Lester, Groves.

Bristol C (0) 0
Everton (0) 2 *(Bakayoko 86, 88)*   19,608
Bristol C: Phillips; Locke (Goodridge), Bell, Murray, Shail, Carey, Hewlett (Hutchings), Testimetanu, Akinbiyi, Torpey, Andersen.
Everton: Myhre; Dunne, Ball, Bilic, Watson, Unsworth, Cadamarteri (Branch), Barmby (Oster), Bakayoko, Dacourt (Grant), Hutchison.

Bury (0) 0
Stockport Co (3) 3 *(Angell 5, Lucketti 13 (og),*
Woodthorpe 26) 5325
Bury: Kiely; Woodward, Williams, Daws, Lucketti, West, Swailes D (Jemson), Billy (Forrest), D'Jaffo (Preece), Johnrose, Littlejohn.
Stockport Co: Nash; Connelly, Dinning, Gannon (Travis), Flynn, McIntosh, Matthews, McInnes, Angell (Grant), Moore, Woodthorpe.

Cardiff C (0) 1 *(Nugent 84)*
Yeovil T (0) 1 *(Dale 54)* 12,561
Cardiff C: Hallworth; Delaney, Ford, Mitchell, Eckhardt, Fowler, Hill (Legg), O'Sullivan, Williams (Roberts), Nugent, Middleton.
Yeovil T: Pennock; Piper, Pounder (Pitman), Brown, Hayfield, Cousins, Thompson, Stott, Patmore, Dale (Appleton), Smith.

Coventry C (3) 7 *(Froggatt 28, Whelan 36, Payne 45 (og),*
Huckerby 60, 71, 90, Boateng 88)
Macclesfield T (0) 0 14,197
Coventry C: Hedman; Nilsson (Telfer), Burrows (Shilton), Williams, Shaw, Boateng, Soltvedt, Whelan (Aloisi), Huckerby, McAllister, Froggatt.
Macclesfield T: Price; Hitchen, Howarth, Payne, Wood (Lonergan), Sodje (Durkan), Askey, Sedgemore, Davies, Matias (Whittaker), Tomlinson.

Crewe Alex (0) 1 *(Johnson 47)*
Oxford U (2) 3 *(Windass 19, Murphy 45, 66)* 4207
Crewe Alex: Kearton; Bignot (Lunt), Smith S, Unsworth (Street), Foran, Charnock, Wright J, Johnson, Jack, Little (Smith P), Rivers.
Oxford U: Jackson; Robinson, Powell, Wright (Smith), Wilsterman, Watson, Remy, Murphy, Banger (Thomson), Windass, Beauchamp.

Leicester C (2) 4 *(Sinclair 20, Ullathorne 26, Cottee 51,*
Guppy 70)
Birmingham C (1) 2 *(Robinson 35, Adebola 89)* 19,846
Leicester C: Keller; Campbell, Guppy, Elliott, Taggart, Sinclair, Lennon (Zagorakis), Izzet (Parker), Cottee (Marshall), Ullathorne, Heskey.
Birmingham C: Poole; Rowett, Marsh (Grainger), Robinson, Ablett, Johnson M, McCarthy (Hughes), Adebola, Furlong (Forster), O'Connor, Ndlovu.

Lincoln C (0) 0
Sunderland (1) 1 *(McCann 16)* 10,408
Lincoln C: Vaughan; Barnett, Bimson, Fleming (Philpott), Holmes, Brown, Smith (Alcide), Finnigan, Battersby (Stant), Thorpe, Miller.
Sunderland: Sorensen; Makin, Scott (McCann), Ball, Melville, Butler, Williams, Clark, Quinn, Dichio, Gray.

Newcastle U (0) 2 *(Speed 48, Shearer 69)*
Crystal Palace (1) 1 *(Bradbury 18)* 36,536
Newcastle U: Given; Charvet, Barton (Georgiadis), Dabizas, Hughes, Solano, Glass (Harper), Hamann, Shearer, Anderson, Speed.
Crystal Palace: Miller; Jihai, Smith, Moore, Mullins, Foster (Jansen), Tuttle, Zhiyi (Linighan), Bradbury (Bent), Morrison, Rodger.

Nottingham F (0) 0
Portsmouth (1) 1 *(Claridge 17)* 10,092
Nottingham F: Beasant; Louis-Jean, Lyttle (Gray), Stone, Chettle, Hjelde, Johnson (Quashie), Gemmill, Freedman (Harewood), Shipperley, Bart-Williams.
Portsmouth: Knight; Robinson, Simpson, McLoughlin, Waterman, Andreasson (Nightingale), Thomson, Peron, Vlachos, Claridge, Igoe.

Oldham Ath (0) 0
Chelsea (0) 2 *(Vialli 68, 75)* 12,770
Oldham Ath: Kelly; McNiven S, Holt (Tipton), Garnett (Swan), Rickers, Duxbury, Thom, Sheridan, Allott, Whitehall, Reid.
Chelsea: De Goey; Terry, Le Saux, Goldbaek (Di Matteo), Duberry, Desailly, Babayaro, Morris, Vialli, Zola (Flo) (Nicholls), Wise.

Plymouth Arg (0) 0
Derby Co (2) 3 *(Burton 15, 82, Eranio 21 (pen))* 16,730
Plymouth Arg: Sheffield; Ashton, Beswetherick (McCall), Mauge, Heathcote, Wotton, Barlow, Hargreaves, McCarthy, Jean, Phillips (Marshall).
Derby Co: Poom; Kozluk, Laursen, Elliott, Carbonari, Prior, Eranio (Harper), Sturridge, Burton, Bohinen (Hunt), Carsley.

QPR (0) 0
Huddersfield T (1) 1 *(Allison 42)* 11,685
QPR: Miklosko; Heinola, Baraclough, Morrow, Ready, Rowland, Rose, Peacock, Slade (Kiwomya), Gallen, Murray (Dowie).
Huddersfield T: Vaesen; Jenkins (Edmondson), Edwards, Johnson, Hessey, Gray, Collins, Phillips, Stewart, Allison, Cowan.

Rotherham U (0) 0
Bristol R (1) 1 *(Leoni 45)* 6056
Rotherham U: Pollitt; Ingledow, Hurst, Garner (Sedgwick), Knill, Dillon, Warner, Thompson, White, Glover (Berry), Roscoe.
Bristol R: Jones; Leoni, Challis, Holloway (Trought), Foster, Lee, Shore, Meaker, Trees, Cureton, Roberts (Ipoua) (Penrice).

Rushden & D (0) 0
Leeds U (0) 0 6431
Rushden & D: Feuer; Bradshaw, Rodwell, Underwood, Wooding, McElhatton, Butterworth, Hamsher, De Souza, Foster, Heggs.
Leeds U: Martyn; Halle, Granville, Woodgate, Haaland, Harte, Hopkin, Wijnhard (Smith), Hasselbaink, Kewell, Bowyer.

Sheffield U (1) 1 *(Marcello 36)*
Notts Co (0) 1 *(Jones 71)* 12,264
Sheffield U: Kelly; Borbokis, Quinn, Ford (Morris), Derry, Sandford, Woodhouse, Marker (Stuart), Marcello, Devlin, Henry (Twiss).
Notts Co: Ward; Hendon, Pearce, Redmile, Tierney (Pennant), Richardson, Owers, Hughes (Jackson), Garcia (Liburd), Jones, Murray.

Southampton (0) 1 *(Ostenstad 89)*
Fulham (1) 1 *(Haywood 9)* 12,549
Southampton: Jones; Hiley, Colleter, Dodd, Lundekvam (Monk), Monkou, Kachloul, Palmer, Ostenstad, Beattie, Oakley (Hughes).
Fulham: Taylor; Finnan, Brevett, Neilson, Coleman, Symons, Hayward, Bracewell (Collins), Horsfield (Trollope), Smith, Hayles (Lehmann).

Southport (0) 0
Leyton Orient (0) 2 *(Smith 60 (pen), Griffiths 71)* 4950
Southport: Bagnall; Farley, Ryan, Bolland, Guyett, Horner, Quinn (Newman), Futcher (Furlong), Gouck, Gamble, Thompson.
Leyton Orient: MacKenzie; Walschaerts, Lockwood, Smith, Joseph M, Clark, Ling (Inglethorpe), McDougald, Griffiths (Simba), Richards (Ampadu), Beall.

Swindon T (0) 0
Barnsley (0) 0 8016
Swindon T: Talia; Robinson, Hall, Hulbert, Taylor, Howe, Walters (Onuora), Hay (Cowe), Ndah, Bullock, Gooden.
Barnsley: Bullock T; Eaden, Moses, De Zeeuw, Tinkler, Appleby (Jones), McClare, Hignett, Goodman, Marcelle (Bullock M), Barnard.

Tottenham H (4) 5 *(Iversen 11, 20, Anderton 14 (pen),*
Nielsen 43, Fox 87)
Watford (2) 2 *(Johnson 1, Kennedy 34)* 36,022
Tottenham H: Walker; Carr, Sinton (Edinburgh), Nielsen, Young, Campbell, Anderton (Clemence), Fox, Iversen, Ferdinand, Ginola.
Watford: Chamberlain; Bazeley, Kennedy, Palmer, Page, Iroha, Smart (Wright), Hyde (Rosenthal), Noel-Williams, Johnson, Robinson.

Tranmere R (0) 0
Ipswich T (0) 1 *(McGreal 46 (og))* 7223
Tranmere R: Coyne; Allen, Thompson (Morrissey), McGreal, Challinor, Irons, Mahon, Santos, Jones G, Mellon (Jones L), Taylor (Parkinson).
Ipswich T: Wright; Kennedy, Thetis, Clapham, Mowbray, Venus, Dyer, Holland, Johnson, Naylor, Petta (Holster).

West Ham U (0) 1 *(Dicks 87)*
Swansea C (0) 1 *(Smith 61)* 26,039
West Ham U: Hislop; Sinclair, Lazaridis (Omoyimni), Pearce, Ruddock, Dicks, Potts, Berkovic (Cole), Hartson (Abou), Wright, Lomas.
Swansea C: Freestone; Jones, Howard, Cusack, Smith, Bound, Coates, Thomas, Alsop, Watkin, Roberts.

Wimbledon (0) 1 *(Cort 62)*
Manchester C (0) 0 11,226
Wimbledon: Sullivan; Cunningham, Kimble, Ardley, Thatcher, Kennedy (Hughes C), Hughes M, Earle (Roberts), Leaburn (Cort), Euell, Gayle.
Manchester C: Weaver; Jim Whitley, Vaughan, Wiekens, Morrison, Horlock, Brown, Pollock (Russell), Taylor, Goater, Dickov.

Wrexham (1) 4 *(Logan 22 (og), Connolly 47, 56, 90)*
Scunthorpe U (0) 3 *(Housham 50, Eyre 71,*
Harsley 85) 4429
Wrexham: Cartwright; McGregor, Ridler, Brammer, Spink, Carey, Chalk, Roberts (Russell), Connolly, Rush, Ward.
Scunthorpe U: Evans; Fickling, McAuley (Housham), Logan, Harsley, Hope, Walker, Forrester, Eyre, Gayle (Marshall), Calvo-Garcia.

3 JAN

Manchester U (0) 3 *(Cole 68, Irwin 82 (pen), Giggs 90)*
Middlesbrough (0) 1 *(Townsend 52)* 52,232
Manchester U: Schmeichel; Brown (Neville P), Irwin, Berg, Keane, Stam, Blomqvist (Solskjaer), Butt, Cole, Yorke (Sheringham), Giggs.
Middlesbrough: Schwarzer; Fleming, Gordon, Maddison, Cooper, Pallister, Mustoe (Stamp), Gascoigne (Beck), Ricard, Deane, Townsend.

Port Vale (0) 0
Liverpool (2) 3 *(Owen 34 (pen), Ince 38,*
Fowler 90) 16,557
Port Vale: Pilkington; Walsh, Tankard, Beesley (Horlaville), Barnett, Aspin, Brisco (O'Callaghan), Bogie, Beadle, Naylor, McGlinchey (Corden).
Liverpool: James; McAteer, Bjornebye (Harkness), Babb, Carragher, Staunton, Redknapp, Ince, Riedle (Fowler), Owen, Berger.

Sheffield W (3) 4 *(Humphreys 18, 33, Rudi 40, Stefanovic 73)*
Norwich C (1) 1 *(Roberts 45)* 18,737
Sheffield W: Srnicek; Atherton, Hinchcliffe, Stefanovic, Emerson (Briscoe), Walker, Jonk (Sonner), Carbone, Humphreys, Rudi, Alexandersson.
Norwich C: Watt; Sutch, Fuglestad, Grant, MacKay (Fleming), Jackson, Adams, Marshall L (Forbes), Roberts, Eadie, Llewellyn.

4 JAN

Preston NE (2) 2 *(Nogan 17, 21)*
Arsenal (1) 4 *(Boa Morte 44, Petit 60, 79,*
Overmars 81) 21,099
Preston NE: Lucas; Parkinson, Kidd, Murdock, Jackson, Gregan (Appleton), Cartwright, Rankine, Nogan (Harris), Macken (McKenna), Eyres.
Arsenal: Manninger; Dixon, Vivas, Vieira, Keown, Bould, Parlour, Mendez (Caballero), Petit, Boa Morte, Overmars (Garde).

THIRD ROUND REPLAYS

12 JAN

Yeovil T (0) 1 *(Hayfield 86)*
Cardiff C (1) 2 *(Eckhardt 43, Nugent 91)* 8101
Yeovil T: Pennock; Piper (Hayfield), Fishlock, Brown, Hannigan, Cousins, Thompson, Stott, Patmore (Pickard), Dale (Pounder), Smith B.
Cardiff C: Hallworth; Delaney, Ford, Mitchell, Eckhardt, Carpenter, Fowler (Legg), O'Sullivan, Williams (Thomas), Nugent, Middleton.
aet.

13 JAN

Fulham (0) 1 *(Hayles 85)*
Southampton (0) 0 17,448
Fulham: Taylor; Neilson, Brazier, Finnan, Coleman, Symons, Horsfield (Smith), Bracewell (Uhlenbeek), Peschisolido (Lehmann), Hayward, Hayles.
Southampton: Jones; Dodd, Colleter, Oakley (Le Tissier), Lundekvam, Monkou, Kachloul, Howells (Ripley), Ostenstad, Hughes, Beattie.

Leeds U (1) 3 *(Smith 22, 51, Hasselbaink 67)*
Rushden & D (1) 1 *(Heggs 11)* 39,159
Leeds U: Martyn; Harte, Granville, Woodgate, Radebe, Wetherall, Hopkin, Smith (Haaland), Hasselbaink, Kewell, Bowyer.
Rushden & D: Feuer; Wooding, Bradshaw, Hamsher (Brady), Rodwell, Heggs, McElhatton, Butterworth, Foster (West), De Souza (Whyte), Underwood.

Swansea C (1) 1 *(Thomas 29)*
West Ham U (0) 0 10,116
Swansea C: Freestone; Jones S, Howard, Cusack, Smith, Bound, Coates, Thomas, Alsop, Watkin, Roberts.
West Ham U: Hislop; Breacker (Hall), Lazaridis, Ruddock, Ferdinand, Dicks, Lampard, Omoyimni (Berkovic), Hartson, Lomas, Sinclair.

19 JAN

Barnsley (0) 3 *(McClare 56, Bullock M 82, Hignett 90)*
Swindon T (0) 1 *(Walters 85)* 10,510
Barnsley: Bullock T; Eaden, Moses, Richardson, De Zeeuw, Appleby, McClare, Hignett, Hendrie (Bullock M), Rose, Jones.
Swindon T: Talia; Hulbert, Hall, Leitch, Taylor, Borrows (Cowe), Howe (Watson), Ndah, Onuora, Gooden, Davis (Walters).

23 JAN

Notts Co (1) 3 *(Jones 19, 83, Murray 57)*
Sheffield U (1) 4 *(Borbokis 40, Holdsworth 85, Marcelo 89, 94)* 7489
Notts Co: Ward; Hendon, Pearce (Tierney), Redmile, Liburd, Richardson, Owers, Hughes (Garcia), Dyer (Strodder), Jones, Murray.
Sheffield U: Kelly; Borbokis, Quinn, Henry (Morris), Sandford, Holdsworth, Woodhouse, O'Connor (Ford), Marcelo (Jacobsen), Twiss, Stuart.
aet.

FOURTH ROUND

Aston Villa (0) 0
Fulham (2) 2 *(Morgan 8, Hayward 43)* 35,260
Aston Villa: Oakes; Watson, Wright (Vassell), Southgate, Ehiogu, Barry, Taylor, Hendrie, Joachim, Merson, Scimeca.
Fulham: Taylor; Finnan, Brevett, Morgan, Symons, Coleman, Collins, Bracewell, Horsfield, Peschisolido (Smith), Hayward.

Barnsley (1) 3 *(Sheridan 14, Hignett 65, Bullock M 88)*
Bournemouth (0) 1 *(Howe 51)* 11,982
Barnsley: Bullock T; Eaden, Moses, Richardson, De Zeeuw, Appleby, McClare, Hignett, Hendrie (Bullock M), Goodman (Rose), Sheridan.
Bournemouth: Ovendale; Vincent (Boli), Young, Howe, Warren (O'Neill), Bailey, Cox, Robinson, Stein, Fletcher, Hughes.

Blackburn R (0) 1 *(Gillespie 67)*
Sunderland (0) 0 30,125
Blackburn R: Filan (Flowers); Kenna, Davidson, Henchoz, Peacock (Blake), Broomes, Gillespie, Dunn, Ward, Duff (Croft), Wilcox.
Sunderland: Sorensen; Makin, Gray, Clark, Melville, Butler (Smith), Rae (Summerbee), McCann, Quinn (Dichio), Phillips, Johnston.

Bristol R (0) 3 *(Roberts 76, 85, Lee 80)*
Leyton Orient (0) 0 9274
Bristol R: Jones; Pritchard, Challis, Trees, Foster, Trought, Holloway, Meaker (Penrice), Lee, Cureton, Roberts.
Leyton Orient: MacKenzie; Walschaerts, Lockwood (McDougald), Smith, Joseph M, Clark, Ling, Ampadu (Curran), Inglethorpe, Simba, Beall.

Everton (1) 1 *(Barmby 39)*
Ipswich T (0) 0 28,854
Everton: Myhre; Ward, Ball, Cleland (O'Kane), Materazzi, Unsworth, Grant, Barmby, Cadamarteri (Branch), Oster, Hutchison.
Ipswich T: Wright; Wilnis, Thetis (Tanner), Clapham, Mowbray, Venus, Dyer, Holland, Johnson, Stockwell (Bramble), Petta (Naylor).

Leicester C (0) 0
Coventry C (1) 3 *(Whelan 16, Telfer 89,*
Froggatt 90) 21,207
Leicester C: Keller; Impey, Guppy, Elliott, Walsh, Sinclair, Lennon, Izzet, Zagorakis (Parker), Ullathorne (Taggart), Heskey.
Coventry C: Hedman; Edworthy, Burrows, Williams, Shaw, Boateng, Soltvedt, Whelan, Huckerby (Telfer), McAllister (Clement), Froggatt.

Newcastle U (1) 3 *(Hamann 33, Shearer 52, Ketsbaia 86)*
Bradford C (0) 0 36,698
Newcastle U: Given; Griffin, Domi, Dabizas, Charvet, Solano (Glass), Brady, Hamann, Shearer, Ketsbaia, Speed.
Bradford C: Walsh; Jacobs, Wright (Rankine), McCall, Moore, Westwood, Lawrence, Blake, Mills, Whalley, Beagrie.

Portsmouth (1) 1 *(Nightingale 10)*
Leeds U (2) 5 *(Wetherall 11, Harte 17, Kewell 50, Ribeiro 73, Wijnhard 82)* 18,864
Portsmouth: Knight; Robinson, Simpson F, McLoughlin, Whitbread, Waterman (Phillips), Nightingale (Thogersen), Peron, Vlachos, Claridge, Igoe.
Leeds U: Martyn; Halle (Knarvik), Granville (Jones), Harte, Wetherall, Woodgate, Hopkin, Ribeiro, Hasselbaink, Kewell, Korsten (Wijnhard).

Sheffield W (1) 2 *(Emerson 17, Carbone 57)*
Stockport Co (0) 0 20,984
Sheffield W: Srnicek; Atherton, Hinchcliffe, Jonk, Emerson, Walker (Newsome), Alexandersson, Carbone, Humphreys (Booth), Rudi, Sonner.
Stockport Co: Nash; Connelly, Dinning (Gannon), Cook, Flynn, McIntosh, Phillips (Matthews), McInnes, Angell, Moore, Woodthorpe.

Swansea C (0) 0
Derby Co (0) 1 *(Harper 81)* 11,383
Swansea C: Freestone; Jones S, Howard, Cusack, O'Leary (Bird), Bound, Roberts, Lacey, Alsop, Watkin, Coates (Appleby).
Derby Co: Poom; Schnoor, Dorigo, Laursen, Carbonari, Prior, Bohinen (Kozluk), Sturridge, Baiano (Elliott), Burton (Harper), Carsley.

Wimbledon (0) 1 *(Earle 61)*
Tottenham H (0) 1 *(Ginola 72)* 22,229
Wimbledon: Sullivan; Cunningham, Thatcher, Roberts, Blackwell, Perry, Ardley (Cort), Earle, Leaburn, Euell (Hughes C), Hughes M.
Tottenham H: Walker; Carr, Edinburgh, Freund, Vega, Campbell, Anderton, Fox (Ferdinand), Armstrong, Iversen, Ginola.

Wrexham (1) 1 *(Connolly 6)*
Huddersfield T (1) 1 *(Allison 22)* 8714
Wrexham: Cartwright; McGregor, Hardy, Brammer, Spink, Carey, Chalk, Russell, Connolly, Rush, Ward.
Huddersfield T: Vaesen; Jenkins, Edwards, Johnson, Collins, Gray, Barnes, Phillips, Stewart, Allison, Cowan (Beresford).

24 JAN

Manchester U (0) 2 *(Yorke 88, Solskjaer 90)*
Liverpool (1) 1 *(Owen 3)* 54,591
Manchester U: Schmeichel; Neville G, Irwin (Solskjaer), Berg (Johnsen), Keane, Stam, Beckham, Butt (Scholes), Cole, Yorke, Giggs.
Liverpool: James; Heggem, Bjornebye, Matteo, Carragher, Harkness, Redknapp, Ince (McAteer), Fowler, Owen, Berger.

Wolverhampton W (1) 1 *(Flo 37)*
Arsenal (1) 2 *(Overmars 10, Bergkamp 69)* 27,511
Wolverhampton W: Stowell; Atkins (Connolly), Muscat, Emblen, Richards, Curle, Gilkes (Sedgley), Robinson (Simpson), Flo, Keane, Osborn.
Arsenal: Manninger; Dixon, Winterburn, Garde (Vivas), Upson, Adams, Parlour, Anelka (Grimandi), Petit, Bergkamp, Overmars (Hughes).

25 JAN

Oxford U (0) 1 *(Windass 52)*
Chelsea (0) 1 *(Leboeuf 90 (pen))* 9059
Oxford U: Jackson; Robinson, Powell, Gray, Watson, Gilchrist, Banger (Remy), Tait, Murphy (Francis), Windass, Cook.
Chelsea: De Goey; Terry, Le Saux, Duberry, Leboeuf, Desailly (Goldbaek), Petrescu (Babayaro), Di Matteo, Vialli, Zola (Nicholls), Wise.

27 JAN

Sheffield U (1) 4 *(Devlin 13, Holdsworth 52, Morris 58, Stuart 68)*
Cardiff C (1) 1 *(Nugent 19)* 13,296
Sheffield U: Kelly; Borbokis (Ford), Quinn, Derry, Sandford, Holdsworth, Woodhouse (Henry), Twiss (Morris), Marcelo, Devlin, Stuart.
Cardiff C: Hallworth; Delaney, Ford, Mitchell, Eckhardt, Carpenter, Fowler, O'Sullivan (Legg), Williams (Bowen), Nugent, Middleton (Hill).

FOURTH ROUND REPLAYS

2 FEB

Tottenham H (1) 3 *(Sinton 3, Nielsen 56, 85)*
Wimbledon (0) 0 24,049
Tottenham H: Walker; Carr, Edinburgh, Freund (Young), Vega, Campbell, Anderton (Armstrong), Nielsen, Iversen, Ferdinand (Taricco), Sinton.
Wimbledon: Sullivan; Jupp (Cort), Kimble, Roberts (Hughes C), Blackwell, Perry, Ardley, Earle, Leaburn, Euell, Kennedy.

3 FEB

Chelsea (2) 4 *(Wise 13, Zola 40, Forssell 46, 53)*
Oxford U (1) 2 *(Gilchrist 5, Windass 77 (pen))* 32,106
Chelsea: De Goey; Petrescu, Le Saux, Morris, Leboeuf (Terry), Desailly, Babayaro, Di Matteo (Goldbaek), Forssell (Nicholls), Zola, Wise.
Oxford U: Jackson; Robinson, Powell, Gray, Watson, Gilchrist, Banger (Remy), Tait, Murphy (Francis), Windass, Cook (Beauchamp).

Huddersfield T (2) 2 *(Stewart 20, Thornley 28)*
Wrexham (1) 1 *(Russell 27)* 15,427
Huddersfield T: Vaesen; Jenkins, Edwards, Johnson, Collins, Gray, Beresford (Barnes), Phillips, Stewart, Allison, Thornley.
Wrexham: Cartwright; McGregor, Hardy, Brammer, Spink, Ridler, Chalk (Gibson), Russell, Connolly, Rush, Owen.

FIFTH ROUND

13 FEB

Arsenal (1) 2 *(Vieira 28, Overmars 76)*
Sheffield U (0) 1 *(Marcelo 48)* 38,020
Arsenal: Seaman; Vivas, Winterburn, Vieira, Grimandi, Bould, Adams, Garde (Hughes), Diawara (Kanu), Bergkamp, Overmars.
Sheffield U: Kelly; Derry, Quinn, Woodhouse, Sandford, Holdsworth, Devlin (Twiss), Morris (Ford), Marcelo, Hamilton I, Stuart.
Match void after Arsenal's plea for replay was accepted by F.A.

Barnsley (2) 4 *(Hignett 38, 44, 71, Dyer 63)*
Bristol R (0) 1 *(Roberts 83)* 17,508
Barnsley: Bullock T; Eaden, Jones, Tinkler (Appleby), Moses (Richardson), De Zeeuw, McClare, Hignett, Sheron (Bullock M), Dyer, Sheridan.
Bristol R: Jones; Pritchard, Challis, Trees (Low), Foster, Trought, Shore, Lee (Penrice), Leoni, Cureton, Roberts.

Everton (1) 2 *(Jeffers 20, Oster 77)*
Coventry C (0) 1 *(McAllister 84)* 33,907
Everton: Myhre; Ward (O'Kane), Ball, Oster (Bakayoko), Watson, Dunne, Grant, Barmby, Jeffers (Cadamarteri), Dacourt, Hutchison.
Coventry C: Hedman; Nilsson, Burrows, Breen, Shaw, Boateng (Telfer), Clement (Soltvedt), Whelan, Huckerby, McAllister, Froggatt (Aloisi).

Huddersfield T (1) 2 *(Beech 42, Stewart 71)*
Derby Co (0) 2 *(Burton 55, Dorigo 59 (pen))* 22,129
Huddersfield T: Vaesen; Edmondson (Facey), Edwards, Johnson, Dyson, Gray, Baldry, Phillips, Stewart, Beech, Thornley.
Derby Co: Hoult; Laursen, Dorigo, Stimac, Carbonari (Powell), Prior, Eranio, Sturridge (Harper), Baiano (Hunt), Burton, Carsley.

Leeds U (0) 1 *(Harte 73)*
Tottenham H (0) 1 *(Sherwood 53)* 39,696
Leeds U: Martyn; Haaland (Korsten), Harte, Woodgate, Radebe, Wetherall, Hopkin, Smith, Hasselbaink, Kewell, Bowyer.
Tottenham H: Walker; Carr, Edinburgh, Freund, Young, Campbell, Anderton (Nielsen), Sherwood, Iversen, Ferdinand, Ginola (Sinton).

Sheffield W (0) 0
Chelsea (0) 1 *(Di Matteo 85)* 29,410
Sheffield W: Pressman; Atherton, Stefanovic, Jonk, Emerson, Walker, Alexandersson, Carbone, Booth, Rudi (Briscoe), Sonner (Agogo).
Chelsea: De Goey; Ferrer (Di Matteo), Le Saux, Morris (Goldbaek), Leboeuf, Desailly, Petrescu, Babayaro, Vialli, Zola, Wise.

14 FEB

Manchester U (1) 1 *(Cole 26)*
Fulham (0) 0 54,798
Manchester U: Schmeichel; Neville G, Irwin (Greening), Berg, Neville P, Stam, Beckham, Butt, Cole (Johnsen), Yorke, Solskjaer (Blomqvist).
Fulham: Taylor; Finnan, Brevett, Smith, Coleman, Symons, Hayward, Salako (Trollope), Lehmann (Betsy), Collins (Uhlenbeek), Hayles.

Newcastle U (0) 0
Blackburn R (0) 0 36,295
Newcastle U: Given; Barton, Domi, Charvet, Howey, Solano, Glass, Hamann, Shearer, Ketsbaia, Speed (Brady).
Blackburn R: Filan; Kenna, Croft, Marcolin, Peacock, Broomes, Dunn (Konde), Gillespie, Sutton, Ward, Duff (Blake).

23 FEB

Arsenal (2) 2 *(Overmars 15, Bergkamp 37)*
Sheffield U (0) 1 *(Morris 86)* 37,161
Arsenal: Seaman; Vivas, Winterburn, Vieira, Bould, Adams, Parlour, Anelka (Kanu), Hughes, Bergkamp (Diawara), Overmars (Garde).
Sheffield U: Kelly; Derry, Quinn, Woodhouse, Sandford, Holdsworth, Morris, Hamilton I, Marcelo, Devlin (Twiss), Stuart (Ford).

FIFTH ROUND REPLAYS

24 FEB

Blackburn R (0) 0
Newcastle U (1) 1 *(Saha 37)* 27,483
Blackburn R: Filan; Kenna (Croft), Davidson, Marcolin, Peacock, Broomes, Duff (Ward), Gillespie, Blake, Davies, Wilcox.
Newcastle U: Given; Charvet, Barton, Dabizas, Howey, Solano, Brady, Hamann, Saha, Ketsbaia, Speed.

Derby Co (1) 3 *(Dorigo 34, Baiano 73, 82)*
Huddersfield T (1) 1 *(Beech 15)* 28,704
Derby Co: Hoult; Eranio, Dorigo, Stimac (Delap), Carbonari, Schnoor, Bohinen, Burton, Baiano, Wanchope, Carsley.
Huddersfield T: Vaesen; Edmondson, Edwards, Johnson, Dyson, Gray, Phillips (Baldry), Beech, Stewart, Allison, Thornley (Facey).

Tottenham H (0) 2 *(Anderton 60, Ginola 68)*
Leeds U (0) 0 32,307
Tottenham H: Walker; Carr, Edinburgh, Freund, Vega (Young), Campbell, Anderton, Sherwood, Iversen, Ferdinand (Armstrong), Ginola (Sinton).
Leeds U: Martyn; Haaland, Harte, Woodgate, Radebe, Wetherall (Halle), Hopkin, Korsten (Smith), Hasselbaink, Kewell, Bowyer.

SIXTH ROUND

6 MAR

Arsenal (0) 1 *(Kanu 89)*
Derby Co (0) 0 38,046
Arsenal: Seaman; Dixon, Winterburn, Ljungberg (Kanu), Keown, Adams, Parlour, Anelka, Hughes (Vivas), Bergkamp, Overmars (Diawara).
Derby Co: Hoult; Laursen, Schnoor (Hunt), Powell, Stimac, Prior, Eranio, Sturridge, Burton, Wanchope, Carsley.

7 MAR

Manchester U (0) 0
Chelsea (0) 0 54,587
Manchester U: Schmeichel; Neville G, Irwin, Berg, Neville P (Yorke), Brown, Beckham, Keane, Solskjaer (Sheringham), Scholes, Blomqvist (Cole).
Chelsea: De Goey; Ferrer, Le Saux, Goldbaek, Lambourde, Desailly, Petrescu (Newton), Di Matteo, Flo (Forssell), Zola (Myers), Morris.

Newcastle U (1) 4 *(Ketsbaia 21, 73, Georgiadis 61, Shearer 81)*
Everton (0) 1 *(Unsworth 57)* 36,504
Newcastle U: Given; Barton, Domi, Dabizas, Howey, Solano, Lee, Hamann, Shearer, Ketsbaia, Maric (Georgiadis).
Everton: Myhre; Weir, O'Kane, Materazzi, Watson, Unsworth, Grant, Barmby, Cadamarteri (Bakayoko), Jeffers (Oster), Hutchison.

SIXTH ROUND REPLAY

10 MAR

Chelsea (0) 0
Manchester U (1) 2 *(Yorke 4, 59)* 33,075
Chelsea: De Goey; Lambourde, Le Saux, Babayaro, Leboeuf (Myers), Desailly, Morris (Goldbaek), Di Matteo, Flo (Forssell), Zola, Wise.
Manchester U: Schmeichel; Neville G, Irwin, Berg, Keane, Stam, Beckham, Scholes, Cole (Neville P), Yorke (Solskjaer), Giggs (Blomqvist).

SIXTH ROUND

16 MAR

Barnsley (0) 0
Tottenham H (0) 1 *(Ginola 68)* 18,793
Barnsley: Bullock T; Eaden, De Zeeuw, Moses, Tinkler, Morgan, McClare (Van der Laan), Hignett, Blackmore (Bullock M), Dyer (Sheron), Jones.
Tottenham H: Walker; Carr, Taricco, Freund, Vega, Campbell, Anderton, Sherwood, Armstrong, Ferdinand (Iversen), Ginola (Sinton).

SEMI-FINALS

11 APR

Newcastle U (0) 2 *(Shearer 109 (pen), 118)*
Tottenham H (0) 0 53,609
Newcastle U: Given; Griffin, Barton, Dabizas, Howey (Hughes), Solano (Ferguson), Lee, Hamann, Shearer, Ketsbaia (Maric), Speed.
Tottenham H: Walker; Carr, Taricco, Freund, Young, Campbell, Anderton (Sinton) (Nielsen), Sherwood, Armstrong, Ferdinand, Ginola (Iversen).
aet.

Manchester U (0) 0
Arsenal (0) 0 39,217
Manchester U: Schmeichel; Neville G, Irwin (Neville P), Johnsen, Keane, Stam, Beckham, Butt, Cole (Scholes), Yorke, Giggs (Solskjaer).
Arsenal: Seaman; Dixon, Winterburn, Vieira, Keown, Adams, Parlour, Anelka (Kanu), Vivas, Bergkamp, Overmars (Ljungberg).
aet.

SEMI-FINAL REPLAY

14 APR

Manchester U (1) 2 *(Beckham 17, Giggs 109)*
Arsenal (0) 1 *(Bergkamp 69)* 30,223
Manchester U: Schmeichel; Neville G, Neville P, Johnsen, Keane, Stam, Beckham, Butt, Solskjaer (Yorke), Sheringham (Scholes), Blomqvist (Giggs).
Arsenal: Seaman; Dixon, Winterburn, Vieira, Keown, Adams, Parlour (Kanu), Anelka, Petit (Bould), Bergkamp, Ljungberg (Overmars).
aet.

FINAL (at Wembley)

22 MAY

Manchester U (1) 2 *(Sheringham 11, Scholes 53)*
Newcastle U (0) 0 79,101
Manchester U: Schmeichel; Neville G, Neville P, May, Keane (Sheringham), Johnsen, Beckham, Scholes (Stam), Cole (Yorke), Solskjaer, Giggs.
Newcastle U: Harper; Griffin, Domi, Dabizas, Charvet, Solano (Maric), Lee, Hamann (Ferguson), Shearer, Ketsbaia (Glass), Speed.
Referee: P. Jones (Loughborough).

Happy Manchester United players celebrate victory at Wembley, in what was the second leg of their unique treble.
(Actionimages)

FA CUP ATTENDANCES 1967–99

	1st Round	2nd Round	3rd Round	4th Round	5th Round	6th Round	Semi-Finals & Final	Total	No. of matches	Average per match
1997–98	204,803	130,261	629,127	455,557	341,290	192,651	172,007	2,125,696	165	12,883
1998–99	191,954	132,341	609,486	431,613	359,398	181,005	202,150	2,107,947	155	13,599
1996-97	209,521	122,324	651,139	402,293	199,873	67,035	191,813	1,843,998	151	12,211
1995-96	185,538	115,669	748,997	391,218	274,055	174,142	156,500	2,046,199	167	12,252
1994-95	219,511	125,629	640,017	438,596	257,650	159,787	174,059	2,015,249	161	12,517
1993-94	190,683	118,031	691,064	430,234	172,196	134,705	228,233	1,965,146	159	12,359
1992-93	241,968	174,702	612,494	377,211	198,379	149,675	293,241	2,047,670	161	12,718
1991-92	231,940	117,078	586,014	372,576	270,537	155,603	201,592	1,935,340	160	12,095
1990-91	194,195	121,450	594,592	530,279	276,112	124,826	196,434	2,038,518	162	12,583
1989-90	209,542	133,483	683,047	412,483	351,423	123,065	277,420	2,190,463	170	12,885
1988-89	212,775	121,326	690,199	421,255	206,781	176,629	167,353	1,966,318	164	12,173
1987-88	204,411	104,561	720,121	443,133	281,461	119,313	177,585	2,050,585	155	13,229
1986-87	209,290	146,761	593,520	349,342	263,550	119,396	195,533	1,877,400	165	11,378
1985-86	171,142	130,034	486,838	495,526	311,833	184,262	192,316	1,971,951	168	11,738
1984-85	174,604	137,078	616,229	320,772	269,232	148,690	242,754	1,909,359	157	12,162
1983-84	192,276	151,647	625,965	417,298	181,832	185,382	187,000	1,941,400	166	11,695
1982-83	191,312	150,046	670,503	452,688	260,069	193,845	291,162	2,209,625	154	14,348
1981-82	236,220	127,300	513,185	356,987	203,334	124,308	279,621	1,840,955	160	11,506
1980-81	246,824	194,502	832,578	534,402	320,530	288,714	339,250	2,756,800	169	16,312
1979-80	267,121	204,759	804,701	507,725	364,209	157,530	355,541	2,661,416	163	16,328
1978-79	243,773	185,343	880,345	537,748	243,683	263,213	249,897	2,604,002	166	15,687
1977-78	258,248	178,930	881,406	540,164	400,751	137,059	198,020	2,594,578	160	16,216
1976-77	379,230	192,159	942,523	631,265	373,330	205,379	258,216	2,982,102	174	17,139
1975-76	255,533	178,099	867,880	573,843	471,925	206,851	205,810	2,759,941	161	17,142
1974-75	283,956	170,466	914,994	646,434	393,323	268,361	291,369	2,968,903	172	17,261
1973-74	214,236	125,295	840,142	747,909	346,012	233,307	273,051	2,779,952	167	16,646
1972-73	259,432	169,114	938,741	735,825	357,386	241,934	226,543	2,928,975	160	18,306
1971-72	277,726	236,127	986,094	711,399	486,378	230,292	248,546	3,158,562	160	19,741
1970-71	329,687	230,942	956,683	757,852	360,687	304,937	279,644	3,220,432	162	19,879
1969-70	345,229	195,102	925,930	651,374	319,893	198,537	390,700	3,026,765	170	17,805
1968-69	331,858	252,710	1,094,043	883,675	464,915	188,121	216,232	3,431,554	157	21,857
1967-68	322,121	236,195	1,229,519	771,284	563,779	240,095	223,831	3,586,824	160	22,418

Manchester United supporters at Wembley were in no doubt that the treble was more than a possibility.
(Colorsport)

THE SCOTTISH SEASON 1998–99

Quite a season!

The new Premier League soon caused many talking points, but the pattern was not long in settling, more or less as usual: Rangers and Celtic at the top; a couple of clubs fighting for the third place, and a go at Europe; and the rest running from the darkness and banishment of bottom place, and the resulting financial disasters. Then, in the First Division of the SFL, a group of clubs all desperate to reach the upper level.

Looking at the four tables in January, there was the extraordinary sight of the leaders all ten points ahead of the field: Rangers clear in the SPL; Hibernian almost out of sight in the First Division; Livingston and Inverness well clear in the Second Division; and Ross County (at last!) cruising at the top of the Third Division. By mid-April, much was already fixed at the top of the Divisions, but what had happened in the SPL? Rangers had three results in succession which did not look like those of champions: two losses and a draw. Celtic licked their lips, and reduced the deficit from ten points to four, with an Old Firm game at Celtic Park to come. Was the impossible going to happen? In third place, Kilmarnock – and they looked clear enough of St Johnstone, who had slipped a bit. Dunfermline at the other end, and points down on the next team; but none of the last six could feel completely clear of the spectre of relegation with five games to go. There was an undertone of finance in most clubs: to be in the SPL, they had to have grounds up to standard, and it had cost them money. That meant having to sell some of the best players, it meant having less for the purchase of new players, to cut down the thumping overdrafts. Dundee, keeping just clear of the immediate relegation zone, had trouble enough trying to see that Dens Park was going to be ready for the next season. There were ominous rumbles from SPL headquarters.

The monster TV who held many purse strings demanded that games be played exactly when they wanted, and little thought went to the loyal fans. The last insult to them was that all the final games in the SPL had to be played on the Sunday evening. Rangers scarcely had a Sunday at home during the last weeks; it was no surprise when Dick Advocaat voiced disapproval. In the end these final games *were* all played on the Sunday, but at least at an earlier time. By this stage Rangers, who had beaten Celtic conclusively to clinch the League, were coasting. Celtic were sure of second place. Dunfermline were relegated. The remaining point to be decided was the third spot: Kilmarnock or St Johnstone? On this last afternoon, Killie managed a draw at Ibrox; but it was not enough: Saints won at home against a Dundee team which had annexed fifth place after a good late run, and took the third place. It was the end of a fine season for the Perth team and manager Sandy Clark, who had taken over a going concern from Paul Sturrock and had maintained the success with great enthusiasm. Bobby Williamson, another inspiring manager, was disappointed; happily for him the powers-that-be awarded Scotland another place in Europe as a result of good behaviour, so that Kilmarnock have their reward for a rousing season.

In the First Division, Hibernian, after an unconvincing start to the season, soon put their poor form aside and steamed ahead. They were too good for the rest, and had a long series of wins broken only by the odd draw and – with respect to Clydebank – an extraordinary loss at Boghead in inclement conditions. As there was only one promotion place, the rest of the teams at the top had kudos to be gained, but not much else. It will be very different next season when the SPL is due to increase to twelve teams. Falkirk, Ayr United and Airdrieonians all looked to have what it needs, and Greenock Morton had some good moments. Clydebank, with much uncertainty about their future, did remarkably well. St Mirren kept clear of danger. Raith Rovers had an unhappy time, and Jimmy Nicholl did well in the circumstances to keep clear of the drop. It was Hamilton Accies who could not quite cope, and who join an ever-struggling Stranraer in an excursion into the lower division.

Two ambitious and forward-looking teams ran away with the Second Division. They were rarely seriously challenged, though Clyde had a spell when they looked to be in the hunt. Livingston, with the old war-horse John Robertson scoring many a useful goal, had a team of mixed experience, but with promotion as a clear target; and they never relented.

Inverness, too, have sights set upwards. They lost the final battle with Livingston in a thriller and finished as runners-up, but they are a formidable team with a mission. Finishing in mid-table, Queen of the South made a remarkable run which took them from near the bottom place to respectability with a run of six wins in a row. Again, in this division there were several teams worried that they might join Forfar in a move down. Partick and Stirling drew away, and left East Fife going down; but it was close till the end.

A seasoned critic pronounced before the season began that nothing could stop Ross County from winning the Third Division. He was quite right. The team from Dingwall stuttered a little at times, but their overall performance was impressive, and they should do well next season once they have settled. Second place was more of a problem, and it was fitting that the two contenders met head on on the last afternoon.

Stenhousemuir won, and that was that: for the first time in their history they are promoted. Brechin will have to try again, but will rue one or two of the later results which they could easily have avoided. For the rest, Dumbarton had a much better season despite some difficulties with their ground; and Berwick, though inconsistent, could hold their own against the best; Queen's Park, with a modest place in the league, had a good cup run.

Until ten years ago, Scottish international teams and club teams did extraordinarily well for a small country. Nowadays they tend to have the unenviable reputation outwith Scotland of being easy pushovers. It is a reputation which fans long to dispute, but the day has not yet dawned. Perhaps there are some hopeful signs, though often hope is aroused only to be shattered by the next result. Craig Brown has done magnificently on a shoe-string – and a shoestring which often has pieces missing; he is a great student of tactics, and can instil enthusiasm. Sometimes one wishes that there might be a few more Scots in the international teams, and more of those who value Scottish football and a Scottish shirt.

The season started with a Bang and the League Cup. As soon as the SPL joined in, there were some shocks: Dundee went out to Alloa and Dunfermline to Livingston straight away; Motherwell and Dundee United survived extra time, with the latter on penalties. Both these survivors left in the next round, the former to Ayr United and the latter to Ross County; also out went Aberdeen (to Hibs); Airdrieonians celebrated the opening of their new stadium by defeating Celtic – a notable scalp. In the quarter-finals, Ross County lost to Hearts on penalties, whilst Airdrie beat Kilmarnock to reach the semi-finals. St Johnstone reached their first final for nearly thirty years, but they could not quite get the better of a steady Rangers.

The Tennent's Scottish Cup had its moments, too: Livingston accounted for Aberdeen in the third round, and Ayr United again were the downfall of Kilmarnock, and they nearly took Dundee United, failing with a late penalty which would have seen them through. Dundee United had a troubled advance indeed to the semi-final: replays were needed against Queen's Park and Clydebank as well as, finally, Ayr. Then they lost to Celtic, whilst Rangers, in the other semi-final, put St Johnstone out of this cup as well. The final was an occasion in the new Hampden Park, a worthy opening; though the game itself was not all that much of a spectacle. Rangers won with the only goal, and thus made a clean sweep of the season's trophies. That signalled the end of the road for Dr Jozef Venglos as the Celtic Head Coach, a cultivated and unpretentious gentleman who had had a difficult row to hoe, but who had done it with dignity.

Next season the League Cup becomes the CIS Insurance Cup; the League Challenge Cup returns as the Bell's Challenge Cup; and the SFL, with its three divisions, as from now is the Bell's Scottish Football League. It is good to see confidence from sponsors in this way

It is too soon to judge whether the SPL is going to help raise standards generally. What is needed is a stronger thrust for the top. The Old Firm will always be there or there-abouts, but there must be more of the Kilmarnocks and St Johnstones. It is time for a revival on the east coast. With a larger SPL, perhaps this may come. Meantime, next season is going to see some hard effort in that league itself, and also in the First Division, where the top three places matter more than usual.

Have we too many now playing in Scottish teams who come from abroad? Perhaps, but we may still look hopefully for the good old traditional values of Scottish football, namely skill, entertainment, and character.

ALAN ELLIOTT

ABERDEEN   Premier League

Year Formed: 1903. *Ground & Address:* Pittodrie Stadium, Pittodrie St, Aberdeen AB24 5QH. *Telephone:* 01224 650400.
Ground Capacity: all seated: 22,199. *Size of Pitch:* 110yd × 72yd.
Chairman: Stewart Milne. *Secretary:* Richard A. M. Ramsay. *Operations Manager:* David Johnston.
Manager: Ebbe Skovdahl. *Assistant Manager:* Tommy Moller Nielsen. *Physios:* David Wylie, John Sharp.
Managers since 1975: Ally MacLeod; Billy McNeill; Alex Ferguson; Ian Porterfield; Alex Smith and Jocky Scott; Willie Miller; Roy Aitken; Alex Miller; Paul Hegarty. *Club Nicknames(s):* The Dons. *Previous Grounds:* None.
Record Attendance: 45,061 v Hearts, Scottish Cup 4th rd; 13 Mar, 1954.
Record Transfer Fee received: £1.75 million for Eoin Jess to Coventry City (February 1996).
Record Transfer Fee paid: £1m+ for Paul Bernard from Oldham Athletic (September 1995).
Record Victory: 13-0 v Peterhead, Scottish Cup; 9 Feb, 1923.
Record Defeat: 0-8 v Celtic, Division 1; 30 Jan, 1965.
Most Capped Players: Alex McLeish, 77, Scotland.
Most League Appearances: 556: Willie Miller, 1973-90.
Most League Goals in Season (Individual): 38: Benny Yorston, Division I; 1929-30.
Most Goals Overall (Individual): 199: Joe Harper.

ABERDEEN 1998–99 LEAGUE RECORD

Match No.	Date		Venue	Opponents	Result	H/T Score	Lg. Pos.	Goalscorers	Attendance
1	Aug	1	A	Dundee	W 2-0	1-0	—	Jess [21], Hignett [25]	7816
2		16	H	Celtic	W 3-2	1-0	1	Perry [35], Blinker (og) [56], Hignett [59]	16,640
3		22	A	Hearts	L 0-2	0-2	4		14,416
4		29	A	Dunfermline Ath	D 1-1	0-0	5	Perry [74]	6510
5	Sept	12	H	Motherwell	D 1-1	1-1	4	Jess [8]	11,260
6		19	A	St Johnstone	L 0-2	0-1	5		5814
7		23	H	Rangers	D 1-1	1-0	—	Jess [4]	17,862
8		27	H	Kilmarnock	L 0-1	0-1	6		13,048
9	Oct	4	A	Dundee U	L 0-1	0-1	6		8933
10		17	H	Dundee	D 2-2	1-0	6	Jess 2 [11, 61]	10,004
11		24	A	Celtic	L 0-2	0-1	7		59,963
12		31	A	Motherwell	D 2-2	1-0	9	Newell [31], Winters [47]	8146
13	Nov	7	H	Dunfermline Ath	W 2-1	1-0	8	Jess 2 [2, 84]	10,293
14		14	A	Rangers	L 1-2	0-1	9	Jess [56]	49,479
15		21	H	St Johnstone	L 0-1	0-1	9		10,044
16		28	H	Dundee U	L 0-3	0-1	9		11,964
17	Dec	5	A	Kilmarnock	L 0-4	0-3	10		9785
18		12	H	Hearts	W 2-0	2-0	9	Winters [31], Jess [37]	11,137
19		19	A	Dundee	W 2-1	1-1	8	Winters 2 [44, 82]	6340
20		26	A	Dunfermline Ath	W 2-1	0-0	7	Inglis [53], Jess [75]	7873
21		29	H	Motherwell	D 1-1	1-0	—	Jess [32]	15,269
22	Jan	2	A	St Johnstone	L 1-4	1-1	7	Buchan [24]	8971
23		30	H	Rangers	L 2-4	1-2	7	Newell [34], Jess [50]	19,507
24	Feb	6	H	Kilmarnock	W 2-1	1-0	6	Jess [44], Mayer [46]	9299
25		20	A	Dundee U	L 0-3	0-1	6		8309
26		27	A	Hearts	W 2-0	0-0	6	Bernard [53], Wyness [71]	13,957
27	Mar	14	H	Celtic	L 1-5	0-1	6	Winters [79]	16,825
28		20	A	Motherwell	D 1-1	0-0	6	Winters [60]	6963
29	Apr	3	H	Dunfermline Ath	W 3-1	0-1	6	Winters 3 [46, 56, 68]	11,361
30		10	A	Kilmarnock	L 2-4	1-2	6	Winters [2], Hamilton [52]	9048
31		17	H	Dundee U	L 0-4	0-1	6		11,603
32		25	A	Rangers	L 1-3	1-1	7	Perry [19]	49,145
33	May	1	H	St Johnstone	W 1-0	0-0	7	Winters [67]	9561
34		8	H	Dundee	L 1-2	0-1	7	Winters [89]	9790
35		15	A	Celtic	L 2-3	0-1	8	Mayer [55], Perry [81]	59,138
36		23	H	Hearts	L 2-5	1-1	8	Buchan [7], Jess [61]	13,042

Final League Position: 8   1997–98 6

Honours
League Champions: Division I 1954-55. Premier Division 1979-80, 1983-84, 1984-85; *Runners-up:* Division I 1910-11, 1936-37, 1955-56, 1970-71, 1971-72. Premier Division 1977-78, 1980-81, 1981-82, 1988-89, 1989-90, 1990-91, 1992-93, 1993-94.
Scottish Cup Winners: 1947, 1970, 1982, 1983, 1984, 1986, 1990; *Runners-up:* 1937, 1953, 1954, 1959, 1967, 1978, 1993.
League Cup Winners: 1955-56, 1976-77, 1985-86, 1989-90, (Coca Cola cup) 1995-96; *Runners-up:* 1946-47, 1978-79, 1979-80, 1987-88, 1988-89, 1992-93.
Drybrough Cup Winners: 1971, 1980.

European: *European Cup:* 12 matches (1980-81, 1984-85, 1985-86); *Cup Winners' Cup:* 39 matches (1967-68, 1970-71, 1978-79, 1982-83 winners, 1983-84 semi-finals, 1986-87, 1990-91, 1993-94); *UEFA Cup:* 42 matches (*Fairs Cup:* 1968-69. *UEFA Cup:* 1971-72, 1972-73, 1973-74, 1977-78, 1979-80, 1981-82, 1987-88, 1988-89, 1989-90, 1991-92, 1994-95, 1996-97).

Club colours: Shirt, Shorts, Stockings: Red with white trim.

Goalscorers: *League (43):* Jess 14, Winters 12, Perry 4, Buchan 2, Hignett 2, Mayer 2, Newell 2, Bernard 1, Hamilton 1, Inglis 1, Wyness 1, own goal 1. *Scottish Cup (0).* League Cup (3): Dodds 3.

Leighton J 22	Perry M 32	Smith G 30	Whyte D 35	Inglis J 16+1	Anderson R 13+3	Hignett C 13	Jess E 36	Dodds W 6	Kinakov I 17+5	Newell M 14+9	Rowson D 18+4	Gillies R 4+7	Buchan J 19+4	Dow A 22+3	Young Dere —+4	Hart M 5+9	Wyness D 6+8	Winters R 28	Young Darr 11	Bett B 1	Pepper N 7+3	Good I —+1	Stillie D 8	Mayer A 13	Notman A —+2	Bernard P 8+1	Hamilton J 6+1	Warner A 6	Match No.
1	2	3	4	5	6	7	8	9¹	10	11¹	12	13																	1
1	2	3	4	5	6	7	8¹	9	10				11	12															2
1	2²	3	4	5		7	8	9	12				11¹	6		10	13												3
1	2		4	5	6	7	8	9	13		10		12	3²		11¹													4
1	2	3	4	5			8	9	12	11²	7	13	6³	10¹		14													5
1		3	4	12	2	6	8	9	10¹	11²	7³	13	5			14													6
1	2	3¹	4	5		7	8		12	13	11	14	6	10³		9²													7
1	2		4	5¹	13	7	8		12	10	11	6	3¹			9													8
1	2	3	4		6	7	8		11¹	12	10	5				9													9
1	2	3	4		6		8		10	13	12	11²	5¹			14	9³	7											10
1	2	3	4		6	7	8		14		11	13	5³	12			9²	10¹											11
1	2	3	4		6		8		10	11	7	12	5¹	13			9²												12
1	2	3	4	5	6		8		10	11	7							9											13
1	2	3	4	5	6¹		8		10	11	7		12					9											14
1	2	3	4		5		8		10¹	11	7	13	14	12		9²		6³											15
1	2	3	4				8		10¹	11	7		5	12		9		6											16
1		3	4	5	12	8		13	11		6²	2	10¹	9		7³	14												17
1	2	3	4	5			8¹	10	12	11	6		9			7													18
1	2		4	5			8	10		11	6	3	9			7													19
	2		4	5			8	10	12	11	6	3	9			7¹							1						20
	2		4	5			8	10	12	11	6²	3	13	9		7¹							1						21
	2		4	5			8	10	12	11	6¹	3	13	9		7²							1						22
1	2	3	4	5			8	10¹	11		12		9	6				7											23
1	2	3	4	5			8	10¹	11	12		13	9²	6				7											24
1	2	3	4	5¹			8	10	9	12		11	6			7²		13											25
	2	3	4				8	9¹		5	12	11	6					1	7					10					26
	2	3	4				8	10¹		6²	5	7	11	9		12		1			13			10					27
	2	3	4	14			8³	12		5	13	11	9¹	6²				1						10					28
	2	3	4				8	12	5		9	6				1	7¹							10	11				29
	2	3	4				8		5	12	9	6				1	7¹							10	11				30
	2	3	4				8		5	12	9	6	13	7¹		10²	11											1	31
	2	3	4				8		5		9	6	7	10	11													1	32
		3	4	2			8		6	5	11³	9	13	7		10¹	12											1	33
		3	4	2			8		6³	5	13	12	10²	9		7	14	11¹										1	34
		4	3	2			8		5	12	6¹	13	9	7		10	11¹											1	35
	2	3	4	6			8		11	5²	12	10	13	9		7¹												1	36

AIRDRIEONIANS

First Division

Year Formed: 1878. *Ground & Address:* Shyberry Excelsior Stadium, Broomfield Park, Craigneuk Avenue, Airdrie ML6 8QZ. *Telephone:* 01236 622000.
Ground Capacity: all seated: 10,000. *Size of Pitch:* 112yd × 76yd.
Chairman: Campbell Craig. *Secretary:* George W. Peat CA.
Manager: Gary Mackay. *Assistant Manager:* Walter Kidd. *Physio:* Peter Salila. *Coach:* Andy Smith.
Managers since 1975: I. McMillan; J. Stewart; R. Watson; W. Munro; A. MacLeod; D. Whiteford; G. McQueen; J. Bone; A. MacDonald. *Club Nickname(s):* The Diamonds or The Waysiders. *Previous Grounds:* Mavisbank, Broomfield Park.
Record Attendance: 26,000 v Hearts, Scottish Cup; 8 Mar, 1952 (at Broomfield Park). 8762 v Celtic, League Cup 3rd rd, 19 Aug 1998 (at Shyberry Excelsior Stadium).
Record Transfer Fee received: £200,000 for Sandy Clark to West Ham U (May 1982).
Record Transfer Fee paid: £175,000 for Owen Coyle from Clydebank (February 1990).
Record Victory: 15-1 v Dundee Wanderers, Division II; 1 Dec, 1894.
Record Defeat: 1-11 v Hibernian, Division I; 24 Oct, 1959.
Most Capped Player: Jimmy Crapnell, 9, Scotland.
Most League Appearances: 523: Paul Jonquin, 1962-79.
Most League Goals in Season (Individual): 53, Hugh Baird, Division II, 1954-55. *Most Goals Overall (Individual):* —

AIRDRIEONIANS 1998–99 LEAGUE RECORD

Match No.	Date		Venue	Opponents	Result	H/T Score	Lg. Pos.	Goalscorers	Attendance
1	Aug	4	H	Clydebank	D 0-0	0-0	—		2716
2		15	A	Hamilton A	D 1-1	1-1	7	Cooper [44]	1137
3		22	H	St Mirren	W 1-0	0-0	4	Sissoko [86]	3073
4		29	H	Raith R	L 0-1	0-0	6		2297
5	Sept	5	A	Stranraer	W 2-1	1-0	4	Moore [2], Taylor [79]	687
6		12	H	Greenock Morton	L 0-1	0-1	5		2243
7		19	A	Falkirk	W 1-0	1-0	5	Cooper [27]	4157
8		26	A	Ayr U	W 2-1	0-1	2	Evans 2 [77, 89]	2392
9	Oct	3	H	Hibernian	L 1-3	0-2	5	Black [62]	4301
10		6	H	Hamilton A	W 3-2	2-0	—	Black (pen) [24], Cooper 2 [32, 79]	1945
11		17	A	Clydebank	W 1-0	0-0	2	Cooper [70]	571
12		31	H	Stranraer	W 3-2	1-0	3	Cooper [12], McCann 2 [66, 80]	1988
13	Nov	3	A	Raith R	W 3-1	2-1	—	Cooper [4], McCann [23], Black [61]	1406
14		7	H	Falkirk	L 0-3	0-0	3		3570
15		14	A	Greenock Morton	D 0-0	0-0	3		1935
16		21	H	Ayr U	L 0-2	0-1	4		2632
17		28	H	Hibernian	L 0-1	0-0	4		9732
18	Dec	5	H	Clydebank	W 2-0	1-0	4	McLaughlin (og) [12], Farrell G [62]	1641
19		12	A	St Mirren	W 5-1	4-1	4	Evans [10], McCann [19], Wilson [43], Black [45], McGrillen [54]	2306
20		19	A	Stranraer	W 2-1	0-0	4	Cooper [53], Wilson [55]	635
21		26	H	Raith R	D 2-2	2-1	3	Evans [6], Black (pen) [40]	2077
22	Jan	2	A	Falkirk	D 1-1	0-1	4	McCormick [72]	4518
23		16	A	Ayr U	W 1-0	0-0	3	McCormick [47]	2387
24		19	H	Greenock Morton	L 0-2	0-1	—		1801
25		30	H	Hibernian	L 1-4	1-1	3	Black (pen) [30]	4809
26	Feb	6	A	Hamilton A	W 2-0	2-0	4	Johnston [7], Moore [24]	814
27		23	H	St Mirren	L 0-3	0-1	—		1860
28		27	A	Raith R	W 1-0	0-0	3	Evans [55]	1896
29	Mar	13	H	Stranraer	W 2-0	1-0	3	McKeown [23], Black (pen) [80]	1341
30		20	A	Hibernian	L 0-3	0-2	3		9991
31	Apr	3	H	Ayr U	L 0-2	0-0	4		1868
32		10	H	Falkirk	L 1-2	1-2	4	Taylor (pen) [44]	1957
33		17	A	Greenock Morton	W 2-0	1-0	4	Evans [23], Moore [58]	1442
34		24	A	Clydebank	W 1-0	0-0	4	Moore [87]	296
35	May	1	H	Hamilton A	W 1-0	0-0	4	Farrell D [57]	2257
36		8	A	St Mirren	L 0-3	0-1	4		2078

Final League Position: 4   1997–98 4

Honours
League Champions: Division II 1902-03, 1954-55, 1973-74; *Runners-up:* Division I 1922-23, 1923-24, 1924-25, 1925-26.
First Division 1979-80, 1989-90, 1990-91, 1996–97. Division II 1900-01, 1946-47, 1949-50, 1965-66.
Scottish Cup Winners: 1924; *Runners-up:* 1975, 1992, 1995. *Scottish Spring Cup Winners:* 1976.
League Cup semi-finalists: 1991-92, 1994-95, 1998-99.
B&Q Cup Winners: 1994-95.

European: *Cup Winners' Cup:* 2 matches (1992-93).

Club colours: Shirt: White with red diamond. Shorts: White. Stockings: Red.

Goalscorers: *League (42):* Cooper 8, Black 7 (4 pens), Evans 6, McCann 4, Moore 4, McCormick 2, Taylor 2 (1 pen), Wilson 2, Farrell D 1, Farrell G 1, Johnston 1, McGrillen 1, McKeown 1, Sissoko 1, own goal 1. *Scottish Cup (1):* Cooper 1. *League Cup (4):* Moore 2, Wilson 2.

Martin J 28	Stewart A 31+1	Johnston F 26+5	Sandison J 33+1	Farrell D 20+4	Smith A 23+2	Farrell G 6+12	Wilson M 31	Cooper S 25+2	Evans G 21+5	McGrillen P 20+3	Taylor S 8+4	Black K 30+1	McCann A 27+4	Jack P 21+1	McCloy B 2+2	Moore A 21+7	Sissoko H —+1	Mackay G 4+6	McKeown S 2+11	McCormick S 4+8	Thomson S 8	McGuire D 2+1	Brady D —+1	Easton S 3+4	Greacen S —+1	Match No.
1	2	3	4	5	6	7	8	9	10²	11¹	12	13														1
1			4	5	11	2²	8	9		7¹	10	6	3	12	13											2
1			4	5	11	13	8	9	10¹	6	2	3²		7	12											3
1	13	12	4	5	11¹	14	8	9	10²	6	2	3³		7												4
1		12	4	5¹	10	8	9²	14	11	13	6	2	3	7³												5
1	2	12	4	5	8	9	14	10	13	6²	11¹	3³		7												6
1	2	5	4	11	13	8	9	10²		6	12	3¹		7												7
1	2	5²	4	14	10	13	8	9	12	11		6	3³	7¹												8
1	2	3³	4	5²	11	13	8	9	12	10		6	14	7¹												9
1	2	12	4	5		8³	9	10		6	11	3²		7¹		13	14									10
1	2	5	4	12	8	9	10²		6	11	3¹		7			13										11
1	2	5¹	4	12	13	8	9	10³		6	11	3		7²		14										12
1	2		4	5	13	12	8	9	10¹		6	11	3²	7³		14										13
1	2		4	12	5²	8³	9	11		6	10	3		7¹		14	13									14
1	2	3²	4	5	13	8	9	10³		6	11		7¹	14		12										15
1	2	7	4	5²	14		9	10²		6	11	3		12		8¹	13									16
1	2	8	4²	5		9	13	10		6	11	3		7¹		12										17
1	2	8	4	5	7	9	10¹	11²		6	3		12			13										18
1	2	7³	4	5	14	8	9²	10	11¹	6	3		12	13												19
1	2	7	4	5	13	8	9	10¹	11²	6	3		12													20
1	2	5	4	11	8	9	10²	7¹		6	3		12			13										21
1	2	5	4	14	8	9²	10³	7¹		6	11	3		12			13									22
1	2	5	4	11		10	12		6	3		7		8	9¹											23
1	2	5	4	7	8	12		11²		6	13	3		10¹	14	9³										24
1	2	7	4	5	8	9	10	12		6	11	3¹														25
1	2	5	4	11	8	9¹	10		6	3		7		12												26
1	2	5²	4	13	11	8		10		6	3		7³		14	12	9¹									27
	2	14	4	5	7	8		9²	11³	6	3		12		13		1	10¹								28
		5	3		8	9		10²		6	11	2	4	7¹	12	1		13								29
5²	2	6		11	8	9		12		10	13	3		7			1							4¹		30
5	2	14	3		8	9		12	10³	6		11²	13	1	7¹			4								31
	2	4	6²	3	11	8³	12	9		7		5	13	10¹		1		14								32
	2	7	6	5	11	4		9¹		8²	3		10	12		1		13								33
	2	7	6	5	11	4²	9		8¹	3		10		12		1		13								34
1	2	7	6	5	11	4¹	9³	8²	3		10		13		14	12										35
	2	7		5	6²		9	8¹	3		4	10		1	12		11	13								36

ALBION ROVERS   Third Division

Year Formed: 1882. *Ground & Address:* Cliftonhill Stadium, Main St, Coatbridge ML5 3RB. *Telephone/Fax:* 01236 606334.
Ground capacity: total: 2496, seated: 538. *Size of Pitch:* 110yd × 72yd.
Chairman: Andrew Dick, *Company Secretary:* David Shanks BSc. *General Manager:* John Reynolds.
Commercial Manager: Dennis Newall.
Manager: Mark Shanks. *Assistant Manager and Youth Development:* Jimmy Lindsay. *Physio:* Derek Kelly.
Managers since 1975: G. Caldwell; S. Goodwin; H. Hood; J. Baker; D. Whiteford; M. Ferguson; W. Wilson; B. Rooney;
A. Ritchie; T. Gemmell; D. Provan; M. Oliver; B. McLaren; T. Gemmell; T Spence; J. Crease; V. Moore; B. McLaren.
Club Nickname(s): The Wee Rovers. *Previous Grounds:* Cowheath Park, Meadow Park, Whifflet.
Record Attendance: 27,381 v Rangers, Scottish Cup 2nd rd; 8 Feb, 1936.
Record Transfer Fee received: £40,000 from Motherwell for Bruce Cleland.
Record Transfer Fee paid: £7000 for Gerry McTeague to Stirling Albion, September 1989.
Record Victory: 12-0 v Airdriehill, Scottish Cup; 3 Sept, 1887.
Record Defeat: 1-11 v Partick T, League Cup, 11 August 1993.
Most Capped Player: Jock White, 1 (2), Scotland.
Most League Appearances: 399, Murdy Walls, 1921-36.
Most League Goals in Season (Individual): 41: Jim Renwick, Division II; 1932-33.
Most Goals Overall (Individual): 105: Bunty Weir, 1928-31.

ALBION ROVERS 1998–99 LEAGUE RECORD

Match No.	Date		Venue	Opponents	Result	H/T Score	Lg. Pos.	Goalscorers	Atten- dance
1	Aug	4	A	Dumbarton	L 0-2	0-1	—		291
2		15	H	Ross Co	L 0-8	0-5	—		302
3		22	A	Berwick R	L 1-2	1-1	10	Melvin [26]	374
4		29	H	Queen's Park	W 2-1	1-1	8	Donaldson [44], Shaw [72]	419
5	Sept	5	A	Montrose	W 2-1	0-0	6	Lorimer (pen) [52], Bruce [61]	244
6		12	A	East Stirling	W 1-0	0-0	6	Lorimer [61]	237
7		19	H	Brechin C	L 1-4	1-1	6	McStay [20]	507
8		26	H	Cowdenbeath	L 0-1	0-0	6		403
9	Oct	3	A	Stenhousemuir	L 1-4	0-3	8	Ross [57]	410
10		10	A	Ross Co	W 2-1	0-1	6	Diack [52], Lorimer [68]	1385
11		17	H	Berwick R	D 1-1	0-0	6	Diack [47]	360
12		27	A	Queen's Park	D 0-0	0-0	—		336
13		31	H	Montrose	W 4-1	2-1	5	Melvin 2 [33, 60], Donaldson [42], Diack [80]	302
14	Nov	7	A	Brechin C	L 0-1	0-0	5		307
15		14	H	East Stirling	W 3-1	2-1	5	Diack [16], McLees [38], McStay [74]	304
16		21	A	Cowdenbeath	W 3-2	2-0	5	McLees 2 [16, 23], Lorimer [87]	161
17		28	H	Stenhousemuir	L 1-3	0-0	5	Lorimer [89]	337
18	Dec	12	H	Dumbarton	L 0-2	0-0	6		324
19		19	A	Berwick R	D 1-1	0-1	6	Melvin [67]	307
20		26	H	Queen's Park	W 1-0	0-0	5	Melvin [83]	322
21	Jan	9	A	Montrose	W 3-2	1-1	4	Lorimer [13], Meldrum (og) [48], Murphy [59]	342
22		30	A	Stenhousemuir	W 2-1	1-0	4	Murphy [32], McLees [62]	382
23	Feb	6	H	Brechin C	W 4-1	1-1	3	Lorimer 2 (1 pen) [23 (pl, 58)], Donaldson [61], Bottiglieri [69]	259
24		13	A	East Stirling	L 1-4	0-2	—	McLees [59]	244
25		23	H	Cowdenbeath	D 1-1	0-1	—	Lorimer [52]	240
26		27	H	Ross Co	D 3-3	1-2	5	Donaldson 2 [12, 49], McStay [73]	432
27	Mar	9	A	Dumbarton	D 1-1	0-1	—	Blair [57]	230
28		13	A	Queen's Park	D 0-0	0-0	4		492
29		16	H	Montrose	D 0-0	0-0	—		258
30		20	H	Stenhousemuir	L 1-2	1-0	5	McLees [4]	326
31	Apr	3	A	Cowdenbeath	W 2-0	1-0	5	Lorimer [14], Blair [69]	161
32		10	A	Brechin C	L 1-3	0-2	5	Hamilton [61]	291
33		17	H	East Stirling	L 0-2	0-1	5		304
34		24	H	Berwick R	L 0-3	0-2	6		308
35	May	1	A	Ross Co	L 0-2	0-1	6		1837
36		8	H	Dumbarton	L 0-2	0-1	7		256

Final League Position: 7   1997–98 5

Honours
League Champions: Division II 1933-34, Second Division 1988-89; *Runners-up:* Division II 1913-14, 1937-38, 1947-48. *Scottish Cup Runners-up:* 1920. *League Cup:* —.

Club colours: Shirt: Yellow with black trim. Shorts: Black. Stockings: Black.

Goalscorers: *League (43):* Lorimer 10 (2 pens), McLees 6, Donaldson 5, Melvin 5, Diack 4, McStay 3, Blair 2, Murphy 2, Bottiglieri 1, Bruce 1, Hamilton 1, Ross 1, Shaw 1, own goal 1. *Scottish Cup (7):* Lorimer 2, Murphy 2, Diack 1, Hamilton 1, Melvin 1. *League Cup (1):* Donaldson 1.

McLean M 35	Greenock R 15+7	McGowan N 33	Melvin M 33+1	Shaw M 9+12	Docherty R 6	Sinclair C 2+2	Ross A 5	Bruce D 6+1	Harty M 8+13	Donaldson E 35+1	Lorimer D 31+5	McLees J 29+2	Duncan G 26	Mitchell C 1	McIlhatton L —+2	McColm R 1	McStay J 32	Limond W 3+2	Diack I 14+5	McGowan C —+2	Goldie G —+1	Sturrock G 10+12	Hamilton J 23	McQuade K —+2	McBride M —+1	McBride K 1+3	Bottiglieri E 10	Murphy J 11+3	Blair P 12	Silvestro C 4+1	Smith J 1	Match No.
1	2	3	4	5²	6	7	8	9	10¹	11	12	13																				1
1		3	5	7	6	11²		13	9	10	8					2	4¹	12														2
	2	3²	8	7¹		12		10	9	11	6		5			13	1	4														3
1		3	2	7¹	10	12		9		6	8		5				4	11														4
1	12	3	2	7¹	10			9	13	6	8		5				4	11²														5
1	2	3	5	7	10			9	12	6	8						4	11¹														6
1	2	3	5		10			9	11²	6	8	7¹					4	12	13	14												7
1	2	3	5	7¹				9²	10²	6	8	14					4	11	13	12												8
1		3	5¹	12				9²	7	11	8	6	2				4	13	10													9
1	2	3	8					9	12	11	6	7	5				4	10¹														10
1	2	3	6					9¹	13	11	8	7	5				4	10²			12											11
1	7	3	4	13				12	11	8²	6	5					9¹		10	2												12
1	7	3	6²					9¹	11	13	8	2					4		12		10	5										13
1	7	3	5	14				13	11	12	8²	2					4		9¹		10	6³										14
1		3	8	12				13	7	9	6	2					4		10²		11¹	5										15
1		3	8	12				11	9	6	2						4		10¹		7	5										16
1	13	3	8³	12				11	10	6	2						4		9¹		7³	5	14									17
1	4	3	5	7				12	11	8	6³	2					9¹		10²			13	14									18
1	12	3	8					11	10	6	2						4		9¹		13	5				7²						19
1		3	8					12	11	10	6	2					4		9¹		5		7									20
1	13	3	8	12				11	10	6	2						4				5²		7¹	9								21
1	12	3	8¹					11	10²	6	2						4				13	5		7	9							22
1	8	3		14				13	11	10¹	6	2					4				5³	12		7	9²							23
1	5	3	8	13				11¹	10²	6	2						4				12			7	9							24
1		3	8					11	12	6¹	2						4				13	5		7	9¹	10						25
1		6						11²	10	3	2						4		12		13	5		7	9¹	8						26
1		3		14				11	8	6	2¹						4				10¹	5		7²	12	9	13					27
1		3	2	13				11	8	6							4				12	5		7²	10¹	9						28
1		3	7					9	10	6²	2						4		13		11¹	5			12	8						29
1	14	3	7					11	12	6	2						4		9¹		13	5³			10²	8						30
1	12	3	8³					13	11	10²	6	2					4		9¹		12	5	14			7						31
1	2	3	6					12	11	10	8						4					5			9¹	7						32
1		3	6¹					9²	11	10	5						4				13	2			12	7	8					33
	2	14						13	12	9	6³						4				11²	5		3	8	7	10¹					34
1		3	2					11	9¹	8²	4						12				14	5		13	10³	7	6					35
1	2¹	3	12					11	9	8²	4											13	6			7	10	5				36

ALLOA ATHLETIC   Second Division

Year Formed: 1883. *Ground & Address:* Recreation Park, Clackmannan Rd, Alloa FK10 1RR. *Telephone:* 01259 722695.
Ground Capacity: total: 3142, seated: 414. *Size of Pitch:* 110yd × 75yd.
Chairman: William McKie. *Secretary:* E. G. Cameron. *Commercial Manager:* Pat McAuley.
Manager: Terry Christie. *Assistant Manager:* John Coughlin. *Physio:* Alan Anderson.
Managers since 1975: H. Wilson; A. Totten; W. Garner; J. Thomson; D. Sullivan; G. Abel; B. Little; H. McCann; W. Lamont; P. McAuley; T. Hendrie. *Club Nickname(s):* The Wasps. *Previous Grounds:* None.
Record Attendance: 13,000 v Dunfermline Athletic, Scottish Cup 3rd rd replay; 26 Feb, 1939.
Record Transfer Fee received: £60,000 for Paul Sheerin to Southampton (1992).
Record Transfer Fee paid: £10,000 for Douglas Lawrie from Stirling Albion.
Record Victory: 9-2 v Forfar Ath, Division II; 18 Mar, 1933.
Record Defeat: 0-10 v Dundee, Division II; 8 Mar, 1947: v Third Lanark, League Cup, 8 Aug, 1953.
Most Capped Player: Jock Hepburn, 1, Scotland.
Most League Appearances: —.
Most League Goals in Season (Individual): 49: William 'Wee' Crilley, Division II; 1921-22.
Most Goals Overall (Individual): —.

ALLOA ATHLETIC 1998–99 LEAGUE RECORD

Match No.	Date	Venue	Opponents	Result	H/T Score	Lg. Pos.	Goalscorers	Attendance
1	Aug 4	H	Forfar Ath	L	1-2	0-2	—	Simpson [49]	495
2	15	A	East Fife	D	2-2	1-2	6	McKechnie [31], Irvine [80]	737
3	22	H	Inverness CT	D	1-1	0-1	7	Simpson [64]	616
4	29	H	Stirling A	W	7-0	2-0	4	Simpson [13], Pew [20], McKechnie 2 [34, 68], Cowan [76], Irvine [77], Mackay [87]	1272
5	Sept 5	A	Partick Th	L	0-1	0-0	6		1655
6	12	H	Clyde	W	3-0	1-0	4	Cowan [38], Ramsay [48], Irvine [59]	755
7	19	A	Arbroath	W	2-0	1-0	4	Irvine (pen) [10], Simpson [68]	687
8	26	H	Livingston	L	3-4	1-2	5	Simpson [2], Irvine 2 (1 pen) [48 (p), 69]	978
9	Oct 3	A	Queen of the S	L	1-2	1-2	6	Irvine [35]	1038
10	10	H	East Fife	W	5-1	2-0	5	Cameron 2 [7, 39], Simpson [58], Irvine 2 (1 pen) [80 (p), 88]	526
11	17	A	Forfar Ath	W	2-1	1-0	4	Cameron [1], McAneny [73]	401
12	24	A	Stirling A	L	2-4	0-2	5	Simpson [50], Wilson M [77]	1085
13	31	H	Partick Th	W	3-1	3-1	5	Irvine [12], Simpson [20], Cameron [44]	1469
14	Nov 7	A	Arbroath	D	1-1	1-1	5	Cameron [25]	653
15	14	A	Clyde	L	1-2	0-1	6	Mackay [60]	908
16	21	A	Livingston	L	1-2	0-2	6	Irvine [72]	1992
17	28	H	Queen of the S	W	2-1	0-0	5	Cameron [64], McKechnie [85]	592
18	Dec 16	H	Inverness CT	L	2-3	1-1	—	Cowan [34], Cameron [55]	1323
19	19	H	Forfar Ath	W	3-1	2-0	5	McKechnie 2 [15, 40], Irvine (pen) [61]	466
20	29	H	Stirling A	D	2-2	1-1	—	Cameron 2 [15, 52]	971
21	Jan 13	A	Partick Th	L	1-2	1-1	—	Cameron [39]	1502
22	16	H	Livingston	L	1-3	1-1	6	Simpson [8]	774
23	30	A	Queen of the S	D	0-0	0-0	6		1201
24	Feb 6	A	Arbroath	W	2-1	2-0	5	McKechnie [31], McAneny [36]	603
25	16	H	Clyde	W	1-0	0-0	5	Irvine [76]	508
26	20	H	Inverness CT	L	1-4	1-1	4	McKechnie [8]	595
27	27	A	East Fife	W	4-0	4-0	4	Irvine [7], Cameron 3 [12, 13, 23]	768
28	Mar 6	H	Partick Th	L	0-1	0-1	4		996
29	13	A	Stirling A	D	1-1	1-0	4	Duthie [22]	1225
30	20	H	Queen of the S	L	3-5	1-2	4	Clark [40], Cameron 2 [57, 77]	523
31	Apr 3	A	Livingston	L	0-1	0-0	5		1892
32	10	H	Arbroath	L	1-2	1-0	6	Simpson [38]	505
33	17	A	Clyde	W	1-0	1-0	4	Wilson S [12]	800
34	24	A	Forfar Ath	L	1-3	0-1	6	Duthie [57]	440
35	May 1	H	East Fife	W	3-0	0-0	5	Irvine [65], McKechnie [69], Beaton [85]	806
36	8	A	Inverness CT	D	1-1	0-0	5	Clark [85]	2662

Final League Position: 5   1997–98 DIV 3 1

Honours
League Champions: Division II 1921-22; Third Division 1997–98. *Runners-up:* Division II 1938-39. Second Division 1976-77, 1981-82, 1984-85, 1988-89.
Scottish Cup: —.
League Cup: —.

Club colours: Shirt: Gold with black trim. Shorts: Black. Stockings: Gold.

Goalscorers: *League (65):* Cameron 15, Irvine 15 (4 pens), Simpson 10, McKechnie 9, Cowan 3, Clark 2, Duthie 2, McAneny 2, Mackay 2, Beaton 1, Pew 1, Ramsay 1, Wilson M 1, Wilson S 1. *Scottish Cup (1):* Cameron 1. *League Cup (5):* McKechnie 2, Cameron 1, Simpson 1, Wilson M 1.

Cairns M 36	Valentine C 34	Nelson M 19+7	McAneny P 33+1	McCulloch K 6	Pew D 21+8	Wilson M 22+3	Wilson S 27+1	Simpson P 25+8	Irvine W 33	McKechnie G 20+5	Ramsay S 15+4	McLeod K —+2	Cowan M 18	Mackay S 6+13	Cameron M 21+7	Gilmour J —+1	Haddow L 12+1	Donaghy M 10+1	Sharp R 15+2	Clark D 9+5	Duthie M 5+3	Armstrong G 1+1	Allan G 2+1	Beaton D 6	Match No.
1	2	3	4	5	6	7	8¹	9	10	11²	12	13													1
1²	2	3	4		6	7	8¹	9	10	11		13	5		12										2
1	2	3	4		6³	7	8²	9	10	11¹			5	13	12	14									3
																									4
1	2	3⁴	4		6	7	8	9	10	11³			5	14	12	13									5
1	2		4		6²	7	8	9	10	11¹	13		5		12	3									6
1	2	12	4		11²	7¹	8	9	10		6		5	14	13³	3									7
1	2	7	4		11¹			6	9	10	8		5		12	3									8
1	2	12	4		6²	7		9	10	8³	13		5	14	11¹	3									9
1	2	7	4		12		8	9	10		6		5		11¹	3									10
1	2	7	4		6		8	9	10				5		11	3									11
1	2	7	4		13	14	8²	9	10	12			5		11¹	3⁹	6								12
1	2	7	4		12	13	8	9	10	14			5		11³	3²	6¹								13
1	2	7	4		12	8		10	11				5	13	9¹	3	6²								14
1	2	7¹			6	8		9	10	11²	13		5		12		3		4						15
1	2	12			7²			9	10	14	6		5	8	11		3¹	13³	4						16
1	2	7	4		12			9	10	13	6¹		5	8	11²			3							17
1	2	13	4		8		7²	12	10	9	6		5		11¹			3							18
1	2	7	4		6	8²	12		10	9	13		5¹		11			3							19
1			5		6	4	2	12	10	11	7²			8¹	9			3	13						20
1	2		4		6¹	7	8³	5	10	11	12			13	9²			3	14						21
1	2		4		6	5	9	10	12	7²			8		11¹			3	13						22
1	2		4	5	12		8	11¹	10		6				9			3							23
1	2		4	5	6	7	8¹	13	10	11²				12	9			3							24
1	2	13	4	5²	6	7	8³	14	10	11				12	9			3¹							25
1	2	5	4		6	7		8¹	10	11					9				12	3					26
1	2	5	4¹		6	7		13	10	11²					9		8		3						27
1	2	5			6²	7	4	11	10					13			8	3	12		9¹				28
1	2	3¹	4	5	12	7		6	13	10							8		11	9²					29
1	2	12	4	5¹		6									9		8	3	11	10	13	7²			30
1	2	5			7¹	6	12								9	3	8		11	10				4	31
1	2	5		13	7	6	11								9		8²	12	3	10¹				4	32
1	2	5			7	6	8	10	9¹								3	11	12					4	33
1	2	12	5		7	6	8	10	9²								3¹	11³	13		14			4	34
1	2	13	5		7	6²	8	10	9		3							11	12					4	35
1		3	5		7		12	10	9¹					8			6	13	11			2²		4	36

ARBROATH
Second Division

Year Formed: 1878. *Ground & Address:* Gayfield Park, Arbroath DD11 1QB. *Telephone and Fax:* 01241 872157.
Ground Capacity: 6488, seated: 715. *Size of Pitch:* 115yd × 71yd.
President: John D. Christison. *Secretary:* Charles Kinnear. *Commercial Manager:* Bill Thompson.
Manager: David Baikie. *Assistant Manager:* Graeme Irons. *Physio:* Marie Thomson. *Coaches:* John Martin, Tom Fairweather.
Managers since 1975: A. Henderson; I. J. Stewart; G. Fleming; J. Bone; J. Young; W. Borthwick; M. Lawson, D. McGrain MBE, J. Scott, J. Brogan, T. Campbell, G. Mackie.
Club Nickname(s): The Red Lichties. *Previous Grounds:* None.
Record Attendance: 13,510 v Rangers, Scottish Cup 3rd rd; 23 Feb, 1952.
Record Transfer Fee received: £120,000 for Paul Tosh to Dundee (Aug 1993).
Record Transfer Fee paid: £20,000 for Douglas Robb from Montrose (1981).
Record Victory: 36-0 v Bon Accord, Scottish Cup 1st rd; 12 Sept, 1885.
Record Defeat: 1-9 v Celtic, League Cup 3rd rd; 25 Aug 1993.
Most Capped Player: Ned Doig, 2 (5), Scotland.
Most League Appearances: 445: Tom Cargill, 1966-81.
Most League Goals in Season (Individual): 45: Dave Easson, Division II; 1958-59.
Most Goals Overall (Individual): 120: Jimmy Jack; 1966-71.

ARBROATH 1998–99 LEAGUE RECORD

Match No.	Date	Venue	Opponents	Result	H/T Score	Lg. Pos.	Goalscorers	Attendance
1	Aug 4	H	East Fife	L 0-2	0-0	—		807
2	15	A	Queen of the S	D 0-0	0-0	9		1104
3	22	H	Stirling A	L 0-3	0-0	10		805
4	29	H	Forfar Ath	W 2-1	1-1	8	Cooper (pen) [20], Mann (og) [90]	905
5	Sept 5	A	Inverness CT	L 1-2	0-1	9	Gallagher [89]	1836
6	12	A	Livingston	L 1-2	0-2	9	Peters [89]	2725
7	19	H	Alloa Ath	L 0-2	0-1	10		687
8	26	A	Partick Th	L 0-2	0-1	10		2006
9	Oct 3	H	Clyde	D 0-0	0-0	10		710
10	10	H	Queen of the S	W 2-1	1-1	9	McGlashan J [19], McGlashan C [88]	603
11	17	A	East Fife	W 3-0	0-0	8	Gallagher 2 [64, 69], McGlashan C [85]	719
12	26	A	Forfar Ath	W 3-1	0-0	—	Gallagher [49], Mercer [81], McGlashan C [86]	800
13	31	H	Inverness CT	L 0-1	0-0	7		934
14	Nov 7	A	Alloa Ath	D 1-1	1-1	7	Sellars [35]	653
15	14	H	Livingston	D 2-2	1-1	8	McGlashan J [1], Arbuckle [61]	810
16	21	H	Partick Th	W 1-0	0-0	7	Sellars [60]	1121
17	28	A	Clyde	L 0-3	0-1	7		918
18	Dec 12	A	Stirling A	W 1-0	0-0	7	McGlashan C [89]	824
19	19	H	East Fife	W 2-1	0-1	7	Sellars 2 [70, 86]	701
20	Jan 9	A	Inverness CT	L 0-2	0-2	7		1795
21	16	A	Partick Th	D 0-0	0-0	7		2105
22	19	A	Forfar Ath	D 2-2	0-2	—	Tindal [70], Arbuckle [89]	767
23	30	H	Clyde	L 0-3	0-2	7		777
24	Feb 6	H	Alloa Ath	L 1-2	0-2	8	McGlashan C [80]	603
25	16	A	Livingston	L 0-1	0-1	—		888
26	20	H	Stirling A	W 1-0	1-0	8	McGlashan C [30]	610
27	27	A	Queen of the S	L 0-3	0-0	8		1020
28	Mar 6	H	Inverness CT	W 3-1	0-1	7	McGlashan C 2 [54, 74], Tindal [88]	705
29	13	A	Forfar Ath	L 2-5	2-4	8	McGlashan C (pen) [20], Tindal [25]	864
30	20	A	Clyde	D 1-1	1-1	9	McGlashan C [10]	694
31	Apr 3	H	Partick Th	W 2-1	1-1	7	Arbuckle [27], Crawford [74]	1301
32	10	A	Alloa Ath	W 2-1	0-1	5	Arbuckle [55], Sellars [62]	505
33	17	H	Livingston	D 1-1	1-0	6	Crawford [44]	729
34	24	A	East Fife	W 2-1	0-1	5	Devine [75], McGlashan C [78]	837
35	May 1	H	Queen of the S	L 0-2	0-0	6		976
36	8	A	Stirling A	L 1-2	1-1	7	McGlashan C [17]	1005

Final League Position: 7   1997–98 DIV 3 2

Honours
League Champions Runners-up: Division II 1934-35, 1958-59, 1967-68, 1971-72; Third Division 1997–98.
Scottish Cup: Quarter-finals: 1993.
League Cup: —.

Club colours: Shirt: Maroon with white and sky blue trim. Shorts: White. Stockings: Maroon with white and sky blue hooped tops.

Goalscorers: *League (37):* McGlashan C 12 (1 pen), Sellars 5, Arbuckle 4, Gallagher 4 (2 pens), Tindal 3, Crawford 2, McGlashan J 2, Cooper 1 (pen), Devine 1, Mercer 1, Peters 1, own goal 1. *Scottish Cup (1):* Gallagher 1 (pen). *League Cup (0).*

Hinchcliffe C 25	Mitchell B 2	Tindal K 23+8	McAulay J 34+1	Jones K 22+1	Crawford J 35	Cooper C 13+4	Thomson N 14+9	Grant B 2+6	Spence W 5+6	Scott W 15+5	Mercer J 22+7	Florence S 24	Sellars B 22+8	McWalter M 3+2	Gallagher J 31+1	Peters S 10+2	Scott S 1+2	Burns K —+1	Wight C 11	O'Driscoll J 3+1	McGlashan J 14	Arbuckle D 23+5	McGlashan C 27	Elliott J 8+3	Devine C 5+1	Donnachie B 2+1	Match No.
1	2	3	4	5	6	7	8	9^1	10	11	12																1
1	5	2	4		6		8^2	13	9^1	11	10	3	7	12													2
1		7	4		6	8	12		11^2	9^1	2^2	10	3	5	13	14											3
	13	4	5	6	7	12		2	9^1	3	8^2				1	10	11										4
	12	4		6	13	9^2	11	2	7^1	3	5				1	10	8										5
	12	4	14	6^3	7		11^1	13	2	3	5	9			1	10^2	8										6
	8^1	4	5	6	12	9	10^2	7	3	2	13				1		11										7
1	2	4	5	6	7	12	9^1	10	3		11		8														8
1	2^1	4	5	6	7^2	12	9^1	11	10	14	3				8	13											9
1	2^1	4	5	6	7^2		10^3	3	14	11					13	8	12	9									10
1	2^2	4	5	6	7^1	14	10^3	3	13	11					8	12	9										11
1	2^1	4	5	6	12		10	3	13	11					8	7^1	9										12
1	2^1	4	5	6			10	3	12	11					8	7	9										13
1	12	4	5	6	13		10	3	2	11^1					8	7^2	9										14
1		4		6	7	12	13	10^2	3	2					8	5^1	9										15
1		4		6	7		10	3	2						8	5	9										16
1	12	4	5^2	6	7	13		3	2	11^1					8	10	9										17
1	12		5	6	7^1	13	3	10^2	2	4	11^3	14			8	9											18
1	12	14	5	6	13	7^1	3^2	10	2	4	11				8	9^3											19
1		4	5	6	7		12	3^1	10	2	11				8	9											20
1	2	4		6	5	12	10^1	3	7		11				8	9											21
1	12	4		6	7	5	13	10^1	3	2	11^2				8	9											22
1	11	4	5	7	6	12	10^1	2	8	3^2					13	9											23
1	3	4	5	6		13	10^1	2	11	12					8^2	9	7										24
1		4	2	5	6	12	10^1	3	13	11					8^2	9	7										25
1		4	2	5	6	7	12	3		11	11^2				8	9^1	10										26
1		8	2	5	6	7	13	3^1			12		11^2		4	9	10										27
		4^2	2	5	6	12		13	14	7	10^3	3				1						8^1	9	11			28
		4	2	5	6	12		14	13	7	10^2	3^3				1						8^1	9	11			29
		4	2		6	7^2	12	8	11	10^1	3	5				1						14	9^3	13			30
1		8^2	2	5	6	7		11		10^1	3	13										4	9	12			31
1		8	4		6	7^1		11	13	12		3	2									5	9^2	14	10^3		32
		8	4		6			12	7			3	2			1						5	9^{11}	11	10^2	13	33
		4		6	13		14	11^1		7^3	3	2				1						5	9	12	10	8^2	34
		4		6			12	7				3	2			1						5	9	11	10	8^1	35
		8	4		6	11^1		3		7	12		2			1						5	9			10	36

AYR UNITED
First Division

Year Formed: 1910. *Ground & Address:* Somerset Park, Tryfield Place, Ayr KA8 9NB. *Telephone:* 01292 263435.
Ground Capacity: 12,178, seated: 1500. *Size of Pitch:* 110yd × 72yd.
Chairman: W. J. Barr. *Administrator:* Brian Caldwell. *Secretary:* J. E. Eyley. *Lottery Manager:* Andrew Downie.
Manager: Gordon Dalziel. *Coach:* Iain Munro.
Managers since 1975: Alex Stuart; Ally MacLeod; Willie McLean; George Caldwell; Ally MacLeod; George Burley;
Simon Stainrod. *Club Nickname(s):* The Honest Men. *Previous Grounds:* None.
Record Attendance: 25,225 v Rangers, Division I; 13 Sept, 1969.
Record Transfer Fee received: £300,000 for Steven Nicol to Liverpool (Oct 1981).
Record Transfer Fee paid: £80,000 for Mark Campbell from Stranraer (March 1999).
Record Victory: 11-1 v Dumbarton, League Cup; 13 Aug, 1952.
Record Defeat: 0-9 in Division I v Rangers (1929); v Hearts (1931); B Division v Third Lanark (1954).
Most Capped Player: Jim Nisbet, 3, Scotland.
Most League Appearances: 459, John Murphy, 1963–78.
Most League League and Cup Goals in Season (Individual): 66, Jimmy Smith, 1927-28.
Most League and Cup Goals Overall (Individual): 213, Peter Price, 1955–61.

AYR UNITED 1998–99 LEAGUE RECORD

Match No.	Date	Venue	Opponents	Result	H/T Score	Lg. Pos.	Goalscorers	Attendance
1	Aug 4	A	Falkirk	L 0-1	0-1	—		3127
2	15	H	Greenock Morton	W 1-0	1-0	6	Davies [33]	2329
3	22	A	Raith R	D 0-0	0-0	7		2010
4	29	A	Hibernian	L 2-4	0-2	7	Hurst [49], Findlay (pen) [57]	9231
5	Sept 5	H	Hamilton A	L 2-3	1-2	8	Lyons [36], Hurst [46]	1917
6	12	A	Clydebank	W 1-0	0-0	6	Ferguson [68]	569
7	19	H	Stranraer	W 7-1	3-1	6	Walker 2 (1 pen) [22, 86 (p)], Hurst [27], Ferguson 3 (1 pen) [28, 55 (p), 67], Robertson [58]	1917
8	26	H	Airdrieonians	L 1-2	1-0	7	Davies [11]	2392
9	Oct 3	A	St Mirren	W 2-0	1-0	6	Lyons [31], Ferguson [67]	2673
10	11	A	Greenock Morton	W 2-1	1-0	3	Kelly [16], Lyons [55]	2156
11	17	H	Falkirk	W 4-2	2-2	3	Teale [23], Walker 2 [42, 75], Burns [87]	2731
12	24	H	Hibernian	D 3-3	2-1	2	Hurst 2 [3, 70], Walker (pen) [25]	4684
13	31	A	Hamilton A	W 3-1	1-1	2	Millen [30], Walker [55], Ferguson [84]	1267
14	Nov 7	A	Stranraer	W 1-0	0-0	2	Hurst [89]	1390
15	14	H	Clydebank	W 4-1	1-0	1	Hurst 2 [43, 56], Lyons [84], Walker [87]	2450
16	21	A	Airdrieonians	W 2-0	1-0	1	Teale [3], Hurst [80]	2632
17	28	H	St Mirren	D 1-1	1-0	2	Walker [44]	3640
18	Dec 5	A	Falkirk	L 0-3	0-1	3		4010
19	12	H	Raith R	L 0-2	0-2	3		2245
20	19	H	Hamilton A	W 5-0	2-0	3	Hurst 3 [13, 31, 60], Walker 2 [85, 88]	2102
21	26	A	Hibernian	L 0-3	0-2	4		14,106
22	Jan 2	H	Stranraer	W 4-0	2-0	3	Findlay [3], Hurst 2 [40, 86], Walker [69]	2722
23	16	A	Airdrieonians	L 0-1	0-0	4		2387
24	30	A	St Mirren	L 0-1	0-0	4		2670
25	Feb 6	H	Greenock Morton	W 1-0	0-0	4	Craig [74]	2222
26	20	A	Raith R	W 4-2	1-2	2	Ferguson [11], Lyons 2 [46, 88], Craig [52]	1873
27	27	H	Hibernian	L 1-3	1-2	4	Ferguson (pen) [5]	5010
28	Mar 20	H	St Mirren	D 2-2	1-1	4	Lyons [33], Hurst [61]	2436
29	24	A	Hamilton A	W 2-0	0-0	—	Lyons [62], Teale [64]	769
30	Apr 3	A	Airdrieonians	W 2-0	0-0	3	Teale (pen) [74], Reynolds [81]	1868
31	10	A	Stranraer	W 2-0	1-0	3	Hurst 2 [20, 86]	990
32	18	H	Clydebank	D 0-0	0-0	3		2113
33	24	A	Falkirk	L 1-2	1-0	3	Walker [44]	2496
34	27	A	Clydebank	L 1-2	1-1	—	Bradford [18]	305
35	May 1	A	Greenock Morton	W 4-1	3-1	3	Hurst [6], Walker 2 [22, 44], Davies [79]	2337
36	8	H	Raith R	W 1-0	1-0	3	Walker (pen) [30]	1886

Final League Position: 3   1997–98 7

Honours
League Champions: Division II 1911-12, 1912-13, 1927-28, 1936-37, 1958-59, 1965-66. Second Division 1987-88, 1996–97; *Runners-up:* Division II 1910-11, 1955-56, 1968-69.
Scottish Cup: —. *League Cup:* —.
B&Q Cup Runners-up: 1990-91, 1991-92.

Club colours: Shirt: White with black trim. Shorts: Black. Stockings: Black and white.

Goalscorers: *League (66):* Hurst 18, Walker 15 (3 pens), Ferguson 8 (2 pens), Lyons 8, Teale 4 (1 pen), Davies 3, Craig 2, Findlay 2 (1 pen), Bradford 1, Burns 1, Kelly 1, Millen 1, Reynolds 1, Robertson 1. *Scottish Cup (5):* Walker 3 (2 pens), Lyons 1, Teale 1. *League Cup (8):* Hurst 2, Armstrong 1, Davies 1, Lyons 1, Walker 1, Welsh 1, own goal 1.

The following table records the shirt numbers worn by each player in each league match (superscripts indicate goals scored).

Castilla D 21	Robertson J 21	Miller C 4+2	Millen A 34	Welsh C 25+1	Burns G 4+6	Hurst G 34	Agnew P 1+2	Walker A 31+2	Findlay W 15+7	Lyons A 31+1	Traynor J 22+7	Duthie M —+5	Armstrong G —+2	Craig D 22	Davies J 27+2	Kelly R 7+11	Ferguson I 9+13	Nelson C 15	Dick J 1+3	Crilly M —+3	Teale G 23	Winnie D 12	Reynolds M 11+7	Horace A —+4	Scally N 2	Barrick D 11	Campbell M 9	Hamilton B 2+1	Bowman G —+4	Bradford J 2+3	Stewart D —+1	Nolan V —+1	Match No.
1	2	3	4	5	6^1	8^2		9	10^3	11	12	13	14																				1
1	2	3	4	5		7		9^3	10^1	11^2		13		6	8	12	14																2
1	2	3	4	5		7		9	10	11				6	8^1	12																	3
1	2	3	4	5		7		9	10	11				6	8^1	12																	4
1	2	12	4	5		7		11	10	3				6^1	8		9																5
	2	13	4	5		7		11^1	10	3^2				6	8	14	9	1			12^3												6
	2^3		4^2	5^1	14	7			10	11	3	12		6	8		9	1			13												7
	2		4	5		7			10	11	3	12		6	8		9^1	1															8
	2		4	5		7		9		11	12^3			6^1	8	3	13	1					10^2	14									9
	2		4	5	14	7		12	9	11				6	8^1		3^3	1			13		10^2										10
	2		4	5	14	7^3		9^2		11	12			8	3^1		13	1			10		6										11
	2		5			4^2		7	13	9^1	11	6		8	3	12		1			10												12
	2		4	5		7		9		11^1	6			8	12	13		1			10^2		3										13
	2		4	5		7		9		11	6			12	8^1			1			10		3										14
	2		4			7		9	6^2	11				5	8	13	12	1					10^1	3									15
	2		4	5		7		9^1	14	11^3	12			6	8		13	1					10^2	3									16
			4	5		7		9^1	12	11	2			6	8		13	1					10^2	3									17
			4	5	2^3	7		9		11	6			8	12		13	1			14		10^2	3^1									18
			4	5^3				9	13	11	2			6	8	14		1					10^1	3			7^2	12					19
1			4	5	14	7^2		9	10		2^1	13		6	8		3										11^3	12					20
1			4	5	12	7		9^2	10		2^3	14		6	8		3										11^1	13					21
1			4^3			7		9	6			14		5	8	13							10^1	3^2	11		12	2					22
1	2		4	5^2	14			9			13			6	11^1	12					10		3			7			8^3				23
1		4	3	2^2	7			9^3	8^1	11	5			6	13	14					10		12										24
1	2^1					7		9^2		11	5			6	8	12	4				10		3	13									25
1	2		4			7				11	5			6	8		9				10^1		12		3								26
1	2		4^3			7		12		11^2				6	8		9^1				10		13		3	5	14						27
	2		4			7		14		11							9^3	1		13	6^1		10		3		5^2	8	12				28
1			4			7		9^2	12	11	5			6	13	14					10^2		8		3		2^1						29
1			4	13		7			6	11^1	2				10	9^2					3		5		12								30
1			4			7		13	8	11	2			6	12						10^3		14		3	5^1	9^2						31
1			4			7		9^1	8	12	2										10^2		11		3	5	6	13					32
1		4	6			7		9^2	12	11	2			8^1							10		13		3	5							33
1		6^1	4			7		9	13	11^3	2	14		8											3	5		12	10^2				34
1			4			7		9^5	6	11^1	2			8							10^2		12		3	5		13	14				35
1		4	5			7		9^1	6^2	2				8^3							10		11		3			13	12		14		36

BERWICK RANGERS — Third Division

Year Formed: 1881. *Ground & Address:* Shielfield Park, Tweedmouth, Berwick-upon-Tweed TD15 2EF. *Telephone:* 01289 307424. *Fax (to Secretary):* 01289 307424. Club 24 hour hotline 01891 800697. *Ground Capacity:* 4131, seated: 1366. *Size of Pitch:* 110yd × 70yd.
Chairman: Tom Davidson. *Vice-chairman:* Moray McLaren. *Club Secretary:* Dennis McCleary.
Manager: Paul Smith. *Assistant Manager:* John Clark. *Physio:* Ian Oliver. *Coaches:* Ian Oliver, Ian Smith
Managers since 1975: H. Melrose; G. Haig; W. Galbraith; D. Smith; F. Connor; J. McSherry; E. Tait; J. Thomson; J. Jefferies; J. Anderson, J. Crease, T. Hendrie, I. Ross, J. Thomson.
Club Nickname(s): The Borderers. *Previous Grounds:* Bull Stob Close, Pier Field, Meadow Field, Union Park, Old Shielfield.
Record Attendance: 13,365 v Rangers, Scottish Cup 1st rd; 28 Jan, 1967.
Record Victory: 8-1 v Forfar Ath. Division II; 25 Dec, 1965: v Vale of Leithen, Scottish Cup; Dec, 1966.
Record Defeat: 1-9 v Hamilton A, First Division; 9 Aug, 1980.
Most Capped Player: —.
Most League Appearances: 435: Eric Tait, 1970-87.
Most League Goals in Season (Individual): 38: Ken Bowron, Division II; 1963-64.
Most Goals Overall (Individual): 115: Eric Tait, 1970-87.

BERWICK RANGERS 1998–99 LEAGUE RECORD

Match No.	Date	Venue	Opponents	Result	Score	H/T Pos.	Lg.	Goalscorers	Attendance
1	Aug 4	H	Queen's Park	L	0-3	0-1	—		448
2	15	A	Montrose	D	1-1	0-1	—	Shaw [51]	269
3	22	H	Albion R	W	2-1	1-1	6	Shaw [34], McNicoll [67]	374
4	29	A	Dumbarton	D	0-0	0-0	6		303
5	Sept 5	H	Ross Co	L	0-2	0-0	8		453
6	12	A	Cowdenbeath	D	1-1	1-1	8	Forrester [16]	242
7	19	H	East Stirling	L	1-2	0-1	8	Rafferty [55]	328
8	26	H	Stenhousemuir	L	1-2	0-1	9	Rafferty [79]	358
9	Oct 3	A	Brechin C	D	1-1	1-1	9	Rafferty [42]	404
10	11	H	Montrose	D	1-1	1-0	9	Neil M [5]	921
11	17	A	Albion R	D	1-1	0-0	9	Neill A [90]	360
12	24	H	Dumbarton	W	3-1	1-0	9	Ramage [3], Leask 2 [60, 65]	303
13	31	A	Ross Co	L	1-3	0-0	9	Forrester [87]	1546
14	Nov 7	A	East Stirling	D	0-0	0-0	9		277
15	14	H	Cowdenbeath	W	3-1	0-1	7	Forrester 2 [46, 63], Neil M [57]	296
16	21	A	Stenhousemuir	W	2-1	2-0	6	Leask [2], Watt [13]	389
17	28	A	Brechin C	W	3-0	1-0	6	Watt [40], Leask [52], Forrester [71]	344
18	Dec 12	A	Queen's Park	D	1-1	0-1	5	Forrester [87]	389
19	19	H	Albion R	D	1-1	1-0	5	Leask [34]	307
20	Jan 16	H	Stenhousemuir	W	2-1	1-0	6	Forrester [9], Watt [46]	349
21	27	A	Ross Co	D	2-2	1-1	—	Watt [39], Hunter [71]	319
22	30	A	Brechin C	W	3-0	2-0	6	Watt 2 [6, 9], Forrester [46]	273
23	Feb 2	A	Dumbarton	D	1-1	0-0	—	Watt [74]	242
24	6	H	East Stirling	L	1-2	1-1	6	Leask [7]	351
25	13	A	Cowdenbeath	W	2-1	1-0	5	Hunter [43], Leask [61]	328
26	20	H	Queen's Park	L	0-2	0-0	5		330
27	Feb 27	A	Montrose	W	3-0	1-0	4	Smith D [5], Leask 2 [56, 65]	301
28	Mar 6	A	Ross Co	L	0-6	0-2	4		1732
29	13	H	Dumbarton	L	0-1	0-0	6		321
30	20	H	Brechin C	L	2-3	0-1	6	Baigrie [78], Ramage [83]	256
31	Apr 3	A	Stenhousemuir	D	1-1	0-0	6	Shaw [59]	424
32	10	A	East Stirling	D	3-3	2-2	6	Leask [3], Smith D 2 [8, 66]	252
33	18	H	Cowdenbeath	W	2-1	0-1	6	Shaw [60], Leask [89]	404
34	24	A	Albion R	W	3-0	2-0	5	Rafferty 2 [13, 75], Forrester [43]	308
35	May 1	H	Montrose	W	4-1	3-0	5	Leask [2], Smith D 3 [33, 36, 89]	606
36	8	A	Queen's Park	D	1-1	0-0	5	Smith D [79]	473

Final League Position: 5   1997–98 6

Honours
League Champions: Second Division 1978-79; *Runners-up:* Second Division 1993-94.
Scottish Cup: Quarter-finals: 1953-54, 1979-80.
League Cup: Semi-finals: 1963-64.

Club colours: Shirt: Black with 2 inch gold stripes. Shorts: Black, gold trim. Stockings: Black with gold trim.

Goalscorers: *League (53):* Leask 12, Forrester 9, Smith D 7, Watt 7, Rafferty 5, Shaw 4, Hunter 2, Neil M 2, Ramage 2, Baigrie 1, McNicoll 1, Neill A 1. *Scottish Cup (0). League Cup (2):* Forrester 1, Laidlaw 1.

O'Connor G 35	Cunningham T 1	Neill A 35	Clark J 2	Beaton D 28	Campbell C 25+1	Rafferty K 24+8	Watt D 28+2	Laidlaw S 2+2	Forrester P 28+2	Ramage I 20+9	Fraser G 26+3	Shaw G 14+7	Baigrie J 1+7	McNicoll G 34	Irvine N 2	Smith S —+3	McLeod J 7+1	Dixon A —+4	Ritchie I 9	Seaton S 4+5	Neil M 19+1	Leask M 24+6	Quinn B —+11	Burgess M 1	Smith D 9+6	Hunter M 12+3	Haddow L 3	Sinclair C 2	Reilly D 1+1	Buglass K —+1	McCole D —+1	Match No.
1	2	3	4^3	5	6	7^1	8	9	10	11^2	12	13	14																			1
1		3	4	5	6	7	8	9	10^1	11	12			2																		2
1		3	4	5	6	7	8^2	9	10	11^1	12	13		2																		3
1		3	4	5	6^1	7	8	9^1	10	11^2	12	13	14	2																		4
1		3^3	4^1	5	6	7	8	9	10	11^2	12	13	14	2																		5
1		3	4	5	6	7	8	9	10	11^1	12			2																		6
1		3	4^1	5	6	7	8		10	11	12	13		2					9^2													7
1		3	4	5	6	7	8		10^2	11^1	12	13	14	2					9^3													8
1		3	4	5	6	7	8^1		10^2	11	12	13		2					9													9
1		3	4	5	6	7	8		10^2	11	12	13		2					9^1													10
1		3	4^1	5^2	6^2	7	8		10	11	12	13	14	2					9													11
1		3^3	4	5	6	7	8		10	11^1	12	13	14	2					9^2													12
1		3	4	5	6	7^3	8		10	11^1	12	13	14	2					9^2													13
		3	4	5	6		8			11	12			2							7	10		1		9^1						14
1		3	4	5	6		8			11	12			2							7	10				9^1						15
1		3	4	5	6		8			11	12			2							7	10^1			13	9^2						16
1		3	4	5^1	6		8			11^2	12			2							7	10^3	14		13	9						17
1		3	4	5	6		8^2			11^1	12			2							7	10			13	9						18
1		3^2	4	5	6		8			11	12			2							7	10^1			13	9						19
1		3	4	5	6		8			11^1	12			2							7	10			13	9^2						20
1		3	4	5	6		8			11	12			2							7	10^1				9						21
1		3	4	5	6		8			11^1	12			2							7^3	10^2	14		13	9						22
1		3	4	5	6		8^1			11	12			2							7	10			13	9^2						23
1		3	4^3	5^1	6		8			11^2	12			2							7	10	14		13	9						24
1		3	4	5^1	6		8			11^2	12			2							7	10^3	14		13	9						25
1		3	4	5	6		8			11^1	12			2							7	10^2			13	9						26
1			4	5			8			11	12			2						6^1	7	10	14		13	9^1	3^2					27
1		3	4	5			8			11^2	12			2						6	7^1	10^3	14		13	9						28
1		3	4^1	5			8			11^2	12			2						6	7	10			13	9						29
1			4	5			8			11	12			2						6	7	10^3	14		13	9^1	3^2					30
1		3	4		6					11	12			2							7^2	10			13	9^1	8	5				31
1		3	4	5	6		8^2			11	12			2							7	10			13	9^1						32
1		3	4	5	6		8			11^1	12			2							7	10			13	9^2						33
1		3	4	5	6^1		8^2			11	12			2							7	10			13	9^3			14			34
1		3	4^3	5	6^2		8^1			11	12			2							7	10	14		13	9						35
1		3	4^2	5	6		8			11^3	12			2								10			13	9			7^1	13	14	36

BRECHIN CITY   Third Division

Year Formed: 1906. *Ground & Address:* Glebe Park, Trinity Rd, Brechin, Angus DD9 6BJ. *Telephone:* 01356 622856.
Fax (to Secretary): 01356 625524.
Ground Capacity: total: 3980, seated: 1518. *Size of Pitch:* 110yd × 67yd.
Chairman: David Birse. *Vice-Chairman:* Hugh Campbell Adamson. *Secretary:* Ken Ferguson.
Manager: John Young. *Assistant Manager:* Jake Ferrier. *Youth Coach:* Eddie Wolecki. *Physio:* Tom Gilmartin.
Managers since 1975: Charlie Dunn; Ian Stewart; Doug Houston; Ian Fleming; John Ritchie, Ian Redford. *Club Nickname(s):* The City. *Previous Grounds:* Nursery Park.
Record Attendance: 8122 v Aberdeen, Scottish Cup 3rd rd; 3 Feb, 1973.
Record Transfer Fee received: £100,000 for Scott Thomson to Aberdeen (1991).
Record Transfer Fee paid: £16,000 for Sandy Ross from Berwick Rangers (1991).
Record Victory: 12-1 v Thornhill, Scottish Cup 1st rd; 28 Jan, 1926.
Record Defeat: 0-10 v Airdrieonians, Albion R and Cowdenbeath, all in Division II; 1937-38.
Most Capped Player: —.
Most League Appearances: 459: David Watt, 1975-89.
Most League Goals in Season (Individual): 26: W. McIntosh, Division II; 1959-60.
Most Goals Overall (Individual): 131: Ian Campbell.

BRECHIN CITY 1998–99 LEAGUE RECORD

Match No.	Date	Venue	Opponents	Result	H/T Score	Lg. Pos.	Goalscorers	Atten-dance
1	Aug 4	H	Stenhousemuir	W 1-0	0-0	—	Hutcheon [81]	286
2	15	A	East Stirling	D 1-1	1-0	—	Smart [20]	263
3	22	H	Queen's Park	D 2-2	1-0	4	Dickson [36], Dailly [89]	300
4	29	H	Montrose	W 3-0	0-0	3	Dickson 2 (1 pen) [62 (p), 78], Bain [63]	452
5	Sept 5	A	Cowdenbeath	W 1-0	1-0	2	Dickson [24]	206
6	12	H	Dumbarton	D 0-0	0-0	2		355
7	19	A	Albion R	W 4-1	1-1	2	Dickson 2 (1 pen) [1, 79 (p)], Sorbie [67], Black [90]	507
8	26	A	Ross Co	W 1-0	0-0	1	Campbell [85]	1512
9	Oct 3	H	Berwick R	D 1-1	1-1	2	Dickson [20]	404
10	10	H	East Stirling	D 0-0	0-0	2		364
11	17	A	Queen's Park	D 1-1	0-1	4	Dickson [48]	446
12	27	A	Montrose	W 2-1	0-1	—	Sorbie [49], Black [66]	340
13	31	H	Cowdenbeath	W 2-1	0-1	2	Sorbie [66], Kerrigan [85]	291
14	Nov 7	H	Albion R	W 1-0	0-0	2	Sorbie [72]	307
15	14	A	Dumbarton	W 2-1	1-1	2	Dickson [45], Sorbie [54]	357
16	21	H	Ross Co	L 0-1	0-1	2		826
17	28	A	Berwick R	L 0-3	0-1	2		344
18	Dec 15	A	Stenhousemuir	W 1-0	0-0	—	Sorbie [51]	294
19	19	H	Queen's Park	W 1-0	0-0	2	Bain [61]	328
20	Jan 26	A	Cowdenbeath	W 2-0	0-0	2	Sorbie [51], Kerrigan [72]	117
21	30	H	Berwick R	L 0-3	0-2	2		273
22	Feb 6	A	Albion R	L 1-4	1-1	2	Campbell [16]	259
23	13	H	Dumbarton	D 3-3	0-1	2	McKellar [55], Sorbie [60], Dickson [80]	360
24	16	H	Montrose	L 2-3	1-1	—	Sorbie 2 [42, 84]	317
25	20	H	Stenhousemuir	L 0-2	0-1	2		265
26	27	A	East Stirling	L 1-4	1-1	3	Kerrigan [27]	219
27	Mar 6	H	Cowdenbeath	D 1-1	0-1	3	Kerrigan [85]	269
28	9	A	Ross Co	L 1-2	1-2	—	Christie [25]	1537
29	13	A	Montrose	W 3-1	1-1	3	Sorbie 2 [27, 61], Dickson [47]	404
30	20	A	Berwick R	W 3-2	1-0	3	Smith [24], Dickson 2 (1 pen) [67 (p), 81]	256
31	Apr 3	H	Ross Co	L 0-1	0-1	3		698
32	10	A	Albion R	W 3-1	2-0	3	Bain 2 [1, 44], Dickson [47]	291
33	17	A	Dumbarton	L 0-2	0-0	3		562
34	24	A	Queen's Park	W 2-0	1-0	3	Dickson (pen) [44], McKellar [51]	503
35	May 1	H	East Stirling	W 1-0	0-0	3	Bain [52]	344
36	8	A	Stenhousemuir	L 0-1	0-0	3		1654

Final League Position: 3   1997–98 DIV 2 10

Honours
League Champions: Second Division 1982-83. C Division 1953-54. Second Division 1989-90. *Runners-up:* 1992-93. Third Division Runners-up 1995-96.
Scottish Cup: —.
League Cup: —.

Club colours: Shirt, Shorts, Stockings: Red with white trimmings.

Goalscorers: *League (47):* Dickson 15 (3 pens), Sorbie 12, Bain 5, Kerrigan 4, Black 2, Campbell 2, McKellar 2, Christie 1, Dailly 1, Hutcheon 1, Smart 1, Smith 1. *Scottish Cup (5):* Dickson 2, Sorbie 2, Kerrigan 1. *League Cup (2):* Hutcheon 2.

Garden S 33	Smith G 26	Black R 32 + 1	Cairney H 34	Brown R 13 + 3	Bain K 31	Hutcheon A 6 + 15	Smart C 11 + 1	Sorbie S 31	Dailly M 10 + 6	Campbell S 27 + 1	Williamson K 12 + 1	Dickson J 34 + 2	Kerrigan S 14 + 12	McKellar J 22 + 7	Buick G 15 + 7	MacLeod I — + 3	Christie G 11 + 5	Laing K 5	Butter J 3	Riley P 12	Boyle S 8	Boylan P 6	Match No.
1	2	3	4	5^1	6	7	8^2	9	10^3	11	12	13	14										1
1	6	3	4	14	5	7^1	2	8	10^3	11^2	9	12	13										2
1	6	3	4	5^1		12	8		10	9^1		2^2	7	13	11	14							3
1	6	3	4	12	5	10^2	8		11			2^1	9	13	7								4
1	6	3	4	2^2	5	10^1	8		11	14		9	12	7^3	13								5
1	6	3^2	4		5	12	2	9	8	11		10			7^1		13						6
1	6	10	4		5^2			2^1	9	8	11		7	13		12	3						7
	6	10	4		5			2	9	8^1	11	7	12				3	1					8
1	6^1	10	4			12	2	9	8	11		7		13	5		3^2						9
1	6	10	4			14	2^3	9^2	12	3		7	13	11	8^1	5							10
1	6	10	4		5			9	8^1	3	2	7		11	12								11
1	6	10	4		5			9		3	2	7		11	8								12
1	6	10	4		5			9		3	2^1	7	13	11	8^2		12						13
1	6	10	4		5			9		3		7		11	2		8						14
1	5^1	6	4	12				9		3	2	7	13	11^2	8		10						15
1	10	4	6	5	12			9		3		7		11^1	2		8						16
1	10	4	6	5	12			9		3		7		11^1	2		8						17
1	6	10	4		5			9		3		7	11		2		8						18
1	6	10	4		5	13	12	9		3		7	11^2		2		8^1						19
1	6	10	4^2		5			9	12		2^1	7	11	13	8		3						20
1	10		6	13		9	14		2	7	11^2	12	4		5	3^1	8^3						21
1	10	4	6	5		9	12	3^3	2^1	7^2	11	13	8	14									22
1	2	10	4	6^1	5		8		3	11	9	7	12										23
1	10	4	6	5	13		8		3	11	9^1	7^2	2	12									24
1	10	4	6	5	11^3	2^1	9		3	7^2	13	8	14	12									25
1	2	10	4	6^1	5	13	8	14	3	11^3	9	7^2	12										26
1	6	10	4		5			9	12	3^1		13	14	7^3	8		2^2			11			27
1	3	6			5	13		9		2	10^2	8	7^1	12	4					11			28
1	3	10	4		5	12		8		2	11	9^1	7		6								29
1	3	10	4		5			9		2	8	7			6					11			30
	3	10	4	6	5			9			8	12	7^1					1		11		2	31
	3	10	4	6	5	12		8			7	9^1						1	11			2	32
1		12	4		5		8		3		7	9	13		6					10^1	11^2	2^2	33
1		4			5	13	8		3		7	9^1	12	14	6					10	11^2	2^3	34
1		4			5	9			3		8	7			6					10	11	2	35
1		4			5	12	8		3		9	7^1			6					10	11	2	36

CELTIC

Premier League

Year Formed: 1888. *Ground & Address:* Celtic Park, Glasgow G40 3RE. *Telephone:* 0141 556 2611.
Ground Capacity: all seated: 60,506. *Size of Pitch:* 110m × 68m.
Chairman: Frank O'Callaghan. *Chief Executive:* Allan MacDonald. *Secretary:* Heather-Anne Barton.
Director Football Operations: Kenny Dalglish. *Head Coach:* John Barnes. *Assistant Head Coach:* Eric Black.
Head Youth Coach: Willie McStay. *Kit Manager:* John Clark. *Physio:* Brian Scott. *Assistant Physio:* Neil McLeod.
Managers since 1975: Jock Stein, Billy McNeill, David Hay, Billy McNeill, Liam Brady, Lou Macari, Tommy Burns,
Wim Jansen; Dr Jozef Venglos. *Club Nickname(s):* The Bhoys. *Previous Grounds:* None.
Record Attendance: 92,000 v Rangers, Division I; 1 Jan, 1938.
Record Transfer Fee received: £4,700,000 for Paolo Di Canio to Sheffield W (August 1997).
Record Transfer Fee paid: £4,500,000 for Alan Stubbs from Bolton W (July 1996).
Record Victory: 11-0 Dundee, Division I; 26 Oct, 1895.
Record Defeat: 0-8 v Motherwell, Division I; 30 Apr, 1937.
Most Capped Player: Paddy Bonner, 80, Republic of Ireland.
Most League Appearances: 486: Billy McNeill 1957-75.
Most League Goals in Season (Individual): 50: James McGrory, Division I; 1935-36.
Most Goals Overall (Individual): 397: James McGrory; 1922-39.

CELTIC 1998–99 LEAGUE RECORD

Match No.	Date		Venue	Opponents	Result	H/T Score	Lg. Pos.	Goalscorers	Attendance
1	Aug	1	H	Dunfermline Ath	W 5-0	0-0	—	Donnelly [38], Burley 3 [46, 84, 89], Mackay [83]	59,377
2		16	A	Aberdeen	L 2-3	0-1	4	Larsson 2 (1 pen) [58, 90 (p)]	16,640
3		22	H	Dundee U	W 2-1	0-1	2	Burley [80], Burchill [82]	59,133
4		29	A	Dundee	D 1-1	0-0	2	Burley [69]	9853
5	Sept	12	H	Kilmarnock	D 1-1	1-0	2	Blinker [29]	58,567
6		20	A	Rangers	D 0-0	0-0	2		50,026
7		23	H	St Johnstone	L 0-1	0-1	—		55,745
8		26	H	Hearts	D 1-1	1-0	5	Donnelly [32]	59,283
9	Oct	3	A	Motherwell	W 2-1	2-0	3	Brattbakk [30], Lambert [45]	12,103
10		17	A	Dunfermline Ath	D 2-2	2-2	4	Larsson [16], Brattbakk [36]	10,968
11		24	H	Aberdeen	W 2-0	1-0	3	Donnelly 2 [12, 70]	59,963
12		31	A	Kilmarnock	L 0-2	0-0	3		16,695
13	Nov	7	H	Dundee	W 6-1	3-1	3	Larsson 3 (2 pens) [8 (p), 19 (p), 58], Burchill 2 [27, 54], Donnelly [66]	58,974
14		14	A	St Johnstone	L 1-2	0-1	3	Larsson [50]	9762
15		21	H	Rangers	W 5-1	1-0	3	Moravcik 2 [12, 50], Larsson 2 [53, 57], Burchill [85]	59,783
16		28	H	Motherwell	W 2-0	1-0	3	Larsson [40], O'Donnell [47]	59,227
17	Dec	6	A	Hearts	L 1-2	0-1	3	O'Donnell [74]	17,334
18		12	A	Dundee U	D 1-1	0-0	3	Larsson [85]	11,612
19		19	H	Dunfermline Ath	W 3-0	0-0	3	Larsson 2 (1 pen) [56, 58 (p)], Mjallby [61], Moravcik 2 [64, 72]	59,024
20		27	A	Dundee	W 3-0	2-0	3	Burchill [3], Riseth [11], Larsson [56]	10,043
21	Jan	3	A	Rangers	D 2-2	1-1	3	Stubbs [39], Larsson [65]	50,059
22		31	H	St Johnstone	W 5-0	3-0	3	Brattbakk 3 [6, 75, 76], Moravcik [19], Larsson [31]	59,746
23	Feb	6	H	Hearts	W 3-0	2-0	3	Larsson 3 (1 pen) [21, 25, 66 (p)]	59,844
24		17	H	Kilmarnock	W 1-0	0-0	—	Riseth [49]	59,220
25		21	A	Motherwell	W 7-1	2-1	2	Larsson 4 (1 pen) [21 (p), 65, 85, 87], Moravcik [30], Burley [74], Burchill [84]	11,963
26		27	H	Dundee U	W 2-1	0-1	2	Burley [75], Larsson [80]	59,902
27	Mar	14	A	Aberdeen	W 5-1	1-0	2	Viduka 2 [27, 47], Larsson 2 [70, 74], Burley [88]	16,825
28		21	A	Kilmarnock	D 0-0	0-0	2		14,472
29	Apr	3	H	Dundee	W 5-0	3-0	—	Larsson 2 (1 pen) [7, 57 (p)], Burley [32], Viduka [41], Blinker [70]	59,269
30		14	A	Hearts	W 4-2	3-1	—	Riseth [2], Blinker [8], Viduka 2 [28, 51]	16,388
31		17	H	Motherwell	W 1-0	0-0	2	Larsson (pen) [63]	59,588
32		24	A	St Johnstone	L 0-1	0-0	2		10,393
33	May	2	H	Rangers	L 0-3	0-2	2		59,918
34		8	A	Dunfermline Ath	W 2-1	2-0	2	Johnson 2 [2, 44]	8848
35		15	A	Aberdeen	W 3-2	1-0	2	Blinker [1], Johnson [60], Burchill [87]	59,138
36		23	A	Dundee U	W 2-1	2-0	2	Burchill 2 [34, 36]	10,062

Final League Position: 2   1997–98 1

Honours
League Champions: (36 times) Division I 1892-93, 1893-94, 1895-96, 1897-98, 1904-05, 1905-06, 1906-07, 1907-08, 1908-09, 1909-10, 1913-14, 1914-15, 1915-16, 1916-17, 1918-19, 1921-22, 1925-26, 1935-36, 1937-38, 1953-54, 1965-66, 1966-67, 1967-68, 1968-69, 1969-70, 1970-71, 1971-72, 1972-73, 1973-74. Premier Division 1976-77, 1978-79, 1980-81, 1981-82, 1985-86, 1987-88, 1997-98. *Runners-up:* 25 times.
Scottish Cup Winners: (30 times) 1892, 1899, 1900, 1904, 1907, 1908, 1911, 1912, 1914, 1923, 1925, 1927, 1931, 1933, 1937, 1951, 1954, 1965, 1967, 1969, 1971, 1972, 1974, 1975, 1977, 1980, 1985, 1988, 1989, 1995; *Runners-up:* 17 times.
League Cup Winners: (10 times) 1956-57, 1957-58, 1965-66, 1966-67, 1967-68, 1968-69, 1969-70, 1974-75, 1982-83, 1997-98; *Runners-up:* 10 times.

European: *European Cup:* 82 matches (1966-67 winners, 1967-68, 1968-69, 1969-70 runners-up, 1970-71, 1971-72 semi-finals, 1972-73, 1973-74 semi-finals, 1974-75, 1977-78, 1979-80, 1981-82, 1982-83, 1986-87, 1988-89, 1998-99). *Cup Winners' Cup:* 39 matches (1963-64 semi-finals, 1965-66 semi-finals, 1975-76, 1980-81, 1984-85, 1985-86, 1989-90, 1995-96). *UEFA Cup:* 42 matches (*Fairs Cup:* 1962-63, 1964-65. *UEFA Cup:* 1976-77, 1983-84, 1987-88, 1991-92, 1992-93, 1993-94, 1996-97, 1997-98, 1998-99).

Club colours: Shirt: Green and white hoops. Shorts: White. Stockings: White.

Goalscorers: *League (84):* Larsson 29 (7 pens), Burchill 9, Burley 9, Moravcik 6, Brattbakk 5, Donnelly 5, Viduka 5, Blinker 4, Johnson 3, Riseth 3, O'Donnell 2, Lambert 1, Mackay 1, Mjallby 1, Stubbs 1. *Scottish Cup (12):* Larsson 5, Viduka 3, Blinker 1, Brattbakk 1, O'Donnell 1, own goal 1. *League Cup (0).*

Gould J 28	Boyd T 31	Mackay M 1	McNamara J 15 + 1	Stubbs A 22 + 1	Donnelly S 20 + 3	Lambert P 33	Burley C 20 + 1	Brattbakk H 16 + 8	Larsson H 35	Blinker R 13 + 2	Jackson D 4 + 2	Annoni E 9 + 5	Rieper M 7	Mahe S 24	McKinlay T 11 + 7	Burchill M 5 + 16	O'Donnell P 13 + 2	Hannah D 5 + 4	Riseth V 26 + 1	McCondichie A 1	Moravcik L 14	McBride J — + 1	Warner A 3	Mjallby J 17	Viduka M 8 + 1	Wieghorst M 5 + 2	Corr B — + 1	Kerr S 4	Marshall S 1 + 1	Healy C 2 + 1	Johnson T 3	Match No.
1	2	3	4	5	6	7	8	9¹	10	11	12																					1
1	2		5		6¹	7	8	12	10	11	9	3	4																			2
1	2			5	11	7	8	9¹	10			4	3	6	12																	3
1	2			5	11¹	7	8	12	10	6	9	4	3																			4
1	2			5	11	7	8	9¹	10	6²	12	4	3	13																		5
1	2			5	11		8		10	9	13	4	3	12		6¹	10²															6
1	2¹			5	6²	7	8	9	10	11	12	3	13	14		4³																7
1				5	11	7	8	9	10			4	3		12		6	2¹														8
1	2			5	11	7¹	8	9	10			4	3			12	6															9
1	2			5¹	11	7	8	9	10			4	12			6	3															10
1	2	6			11	7	8	9	10			4⁵			5		13	12	3²													11
1	2	4			11	7	8¹	9²	10			3	6	13	12		5															12
	2	4		6	7				10				3	11	8		5	1	9¹	12												13
	2	4		6					10			3¹	12	11	8	10	5		9	1												14
	2			5	11¹	7			10			3		13	8	12	6		9²		1	4										15
	2			5¹	11	7		14	10			12		3	13	8	6³		9²		1	4										16
1	2			5	11	7			10					3	12	8	6		9¹			4										17
1	2			5	11	7			10					3	12	8	6¹		9			4										18
1	2			5	6²	7		14	10			12		3	11	8³		13	9			4¹										19
1	2	12	5			7		13	10					3	11²	8	6¹		9			4										20
1	2	11	5		7				10					3		8	6		9			4										21
1	2			5	14	7			9	10	13			3¹			8²	12	6³		11		4									22
1	2			5¹		7			9	10	13	12		3		14	8²		6		11³		4									23
1		6			7				9	10	11			3	2				5		8		4									24
1	2	6			7	12	9²	10	11					3²	13	14			5		8¹		4									25
1	2	6			7	8	9¹	10	11					3					5				4	12								26
1	2	6			7	8		10	11					3	12				5				4	9¹								27
1	2	6			7	8		10	11					3					5				4	9								28
1	2	6			7	8	12	10	11³					3	14				5				4²	9¹	13							29
1⁶	2	6			7	8		10	11	4				3					5					9		15						30
	2				7¹	8	13	10³	11	6				3	14				5				4²	9	12		1				31
	2	6	13	12	7	8³		10		4				3¹	14				5				9	11²			1				32
		6	12	7		11¹	10			4	3								5				9	8²			1	2	13		33
		2²	6	7		12	10			4					14	8¹			5				9	3			1	13	5	11³	34
1			2	7			10	11		4			6		12			5					3				8	9¹			35
1	2		5				8¹	11					3	12	7			10			4		6						9		36

CLYDE

Second Division

Year Formed: 1878. *Ground & Address:* Broadwood Stadium, Cumbernauld, G68 9NE. *Telephone:* 01236 451511.
Ground Capacity: all seated: 8200. *Size of Pitch:* 112yd × 76yd.
Chairman: W. B. Carmichael. *Secretary:* John D. Taylor. *General Manager:* Ronnie MacDonald.
Manager: Allan Maitland. *First Team Coach:* Denis McDaid. *Physio:* John Watson.
Managers since 1975: S. Anderson; C. Brown; J. Clark; A. Smith; G. Speirs. *Club Nickname(s):* The Bully Wee. *Previous Grounds:* Barrowfield & Shawfield Stadium.
Record Attendance: 52,000 v Rangers, Division I, 21 Nov, 1908.
Record Transfer Fee received: £175,000 for Scott Howie to Norwich City (Aug 1993).
Record Transfer Fee paid: £14,000 for Harry Hood from Sunderland (1966).
Record Victory: 11-1 v Cowdenbeath, Division II; 6 Oct, 1951.
Record Defeat: 0-11 v Dumbarton, Scottish Cup 4th rd, 22 Nov, 1879; v Rangers, Scottish Cup 4th rd, 13 Nov, 1880.
Most Capped Player: Tommy Ring, 12, Scotland.
Most League Appearances: 428: Brian Ahern.
Most League Goals in Season (Individual): 32: Bill Boyd, 1932-33.
Most Goals Overall (Individual): —.

CLYDE 1998–99 LEAGUE RECORD

Match No.	Date	Venue	Opponents	Result	H/T Score	Lg. Pos.	Goalscorers	Attendance
1	Aug 4	H	Queen of the S	W 2-0	1-0	—	McGraw [15], O'Brien [90]	631
2	15	A	Stirling A	W 2-1	1-1	1	McGraw [6], O'Brien [82]	1059
3	22	H	East Fife	D 0-0	0-0	1		806
4	29	H	Partick Th	L 1-2	0-1	2	McHarg [56]	2621
5	Sept 5	A	Forfar Ath	D 2-2	0-0	3	Spittal [68], Convery (pen) [75]	494
6	12	A	Alloa Ath	L 0-3	0-1	5		755
7	19	H	Livingston	D 1-1	1-0	5	McCusker [39]	1044
8	26	H	Inverness CT	W 4-1	3-0	4	Grant [40], McCusker [44], Convery [45], Barratt [56]	969
9	Oct 3	A	Arbroath	D 0-0	0-0	4		710
10	10	H	Stirling A	W 2-1	0-1	4	Convery 2 (1 pen) [65 (p)], [85]	1008
11	17	A	Queen of the S	L 1-2	0-1	5	McHarg [65]	1139
12	24	A	Partick Th	W 2-0	0-0	4	McCusker [80], Keogh [87]	2627
13	31	H	Forfar Ath	W 3-1	0-0	3	Convery [55], McCusker 2 [62, 72]	918
14	Nov 7	A	Livingston	L 0-2	0-2	3		2556
15	14	H	Alloa Ath	W 2-1	1-0	3	McCusker (pen) [45], Convery [83]	908
16	21	A	Inverness CT	D 1-1	0-1	3	McCusker [80]	2268
17	28	A	Arbroath	W 3-0	1-0	3	Carrigan [31], McCusker (pen) [61], Convery [89]	918
18	Dec 12	A	East Fife	D 0-0	0-0	3		804
19	19	H	Queen of the S	W 2-1	1-1	3	Carrigan [37], Convery [80]	794
20	26	H	Partick Th	L 0-1	0-1	3		2673
21	Jan 16	H	Inverness CT	D 1-1	1-1	3	Convery [42]	1105
22	30	A	Arbroath	W 3-0	2-0	3	McLay [37], Keogh [44], Convery [75]	777
23	Feb 2	A	Forfar Ath	L 1-3	1-1	—	McCusker [1]	419
24	6	H	Livingston	L 0-3	0-1	3		1366
25	16	A	Alloa Ath	L 0-1	0-0	—		508
26	20	H	East Fife	W 1-0	0-0	3	O'Brien [87]	768
27	27	A	Stirling A	W 3-2	1-1	3	Convery 2 [11, 67], Carrigan [57]	888
28	Mar 6	H	Forfar Ath	W 1-0	1-0	3	Keogh [38]	815
29	13	A	Partick Th	W 1-0	0-0	3	Keogh [59]	3342
30	20	H	Arbroath	D 1-1	1-1	3	Cranmer [22]	694
31	Apr 3	A	Inverness CT	L 0-3	0-1	3		3019
32	10	A	Livingston	L 0-2	0-0	3		1925
33	17	H	Alloa Ath	L 0-1	0-1	3		800
34	24	A	Queen of the S	L 1-2	0-0	3	Barratt [85]	1218
35	May 1	H	Stirling A	W 4-1	3-0	3	Keogh [30], Barratt [40], McCusker [43], Grant [80]	1107
36	8	A	East Fife	L 1-2	0-2	3	Keogh [61]	845

Final League Position: 3   1997–98 8

Honours
League Champions: Division II 1904-05, 1951-52, 1956-57, 1961-62, 1972-73. Second Division 1977-78, 1981-82, 1992-93.
Runners-up: Division II 1903-04, 1905-06, 1925-26, 1963-64.
Scottish Cup Winners: 1939, 1955, 1958; *Runners-up:* 1910, 1912, 1949.
League Cup: —

Club colours: Shirt: White with red and black trim. Shorts: Black. Stockings: Black with red and white tops.

Goalscorers: *League (46):* Convery 12 (2 pens), McCusker 10 (2 pens), Keogh 6, Barratt 3, Carrigan 3, O'Brien 3, Grant 2, McGraw 2, McHarg 2, Cranmer 1, McLay 1, Spittal 1. *Scottish Cup (11):* McCusker 3 (1 pen), Carrigan 2, Convery 2, McHarg 2, Grant 1, McLay 1. *League Cup (1):* McPhee 1.

McIntyre G 2	Smith B 35	Cranmer C 23 + 5	Spittal I 35	Murray D 25 + 4	McCusker R 35	Convery S 30	Keogh P 34 + 2	McGraw M 5	Rice B 8 + 10	Grant A 28 + 6	McHarg S 7 + 9	O'Brien A 1 + 15	Sexton D 1	Campbell P — + 4	Balfour R 3	McLay A 29	McMillan A 9	Carrigan B 19 + 12	Barratt J 13 + 7	Dillon J — + 2	Wylie D — + 2	Peters S 1 + 1	McPhee G 2 + 2	Brownlie P — + 1	McDonald I 14 + 4	Hay P 6 + 5	Mitchell J 2 + 4	McGhee G — + 1	Match No.
1	2	3	4	5	6	7	8	9¹	10	11²	12	13																	1
	5	3	4	2	6	7¹	8	9³	10¹	14	11	13	1	12															2
	5	3	4	2	6	7¹	8²	9³		12	11	14	13	1		10													3
1	5	3	4	2	6	9	8		13	11	7²	12		10															4
	5	3	4	2	10	9	8		11²		12		1			7	6¹	13											5
	5	3	4	2	10	7	8		11¹		12⁴	1				6	13	9²	14										6
	5	13	4	2	6	7	10			14						8		9¹	11¹	12	1	3²							7
	5	3	4¹	2	10	7¹			11		13					8	6	14	9²	1									8
	5	3²	4	2	10	7	14		11²		13					8	6¹	9		1	12								9
	5		4	2	10	7	3		11²		12					8	6	13	9¹	1									10
	5	3¹	4	2	10	7¹			11		14	12				8	6	13	9²	1									11
	5	13	4¹	2	10	7²	3		12	11		9³				8	6	14		1									12
	14		4	2	10	7²	5		3²	11		9¹				8	6	13	12	1									13
	5		4	2	10	7¹	3		11							8	6	12	9	1									14
	5	3	1		10	7	2¹		6³	11						8		9²	14	12		4	13						15
	5	3¹	4	2	10	7²	6		12	11	14					8		9¹	13	1									16
	5		4	2	10	9	6		3¹	11	12					8		7		1									17
	5	3¹	4		10	7¹	2		6²	11	14					8		9	12	1			13						18
	5		4	2¹	10	7	6		3¹	11	13					8		9²	12	1			14						19
	5		4	2	10	7	8		13	11	12					6²		9¹		1			3						20
	5		4	2	10	7	6¹		14	11²	13					8		12	9	1			3³						21
	5	14	4	2³	10	7²	6		12	11¹	9					8		13		1			3						22
	5²		4	2	10	7	6		13	11¹	9					8		12	14	1			3²						23
	5	12	4	2	10	7²	6		13	11	14					8²		9¹		1			3						24
	5	2	4¹		10	7	6		13	11	14					8		9²		1			3³	12					25
	5	4			10	7	2		11		12					8		9¹		1			3	6²	13				26
	5	2	4		10	7¹	9		13		12					8		11²		1			3	6					27
	5	2	4	13	10	7¹	9		12	8¹	14					11				1			3	6²					28
	5	2	4	6	10	7	9		11¹							8				1			3	12					29
	5	2	4		7¹	10	9¹	12	11		13					8		6		1			3¹	14					30
	5	2¹	4	14	10²		11	9¹	7							8		6		1			3	13	12				31
	5	2¹	4	7	10³	3			13		12					8		11¹²	9	1			14	6					32
	5	2	4²	13	10	9				14						8		7	11³	1			3¹	6	12				33
	5		4	2	10	8			11							7		9¹	12	1			14	3²	6²	13			34
	5²	2	4	14	10	3			11							8		9		1			6³		12	13	7¹		35
	5	3	4³		10	2			6¹	11						8		12	9²	1				13			7	14	36

CLYDEBANK

First Division

Year Formed: 1965. *Club Address:* c/o West of Scotland RFC, Burnbrae, Milngavie, G62 6HX. *Telephone:* 0141 955 9048.
Fax: 0141 955 9049. *Telephone (Match days only):* 01475 723571. *Ground:* (sharing with Morton) Cappielow Park, Sinclair
St, Greenock PA15 2TY. *Ground Capacity:* total: 14,891, seated: 5741. *Size of Pitch:* 110yd × 71yd.
Chairman: Dr John Hall. *Secretary:* Billy Hall.
Player-Manager: Ian McCall. *First Team Coach:* Stephen Morrison.
Club Nickname(s): The Bankies. *Previous Ground:* Kilbowie Park.
Record Attendance: 14,900 v Hibernian, Scottish Cup 1st rd; 10 Feb, 1965.
Record Transfer Fee received: £175,000 for Owen Coyle from Airdrieonians (Feb 1990).
Record Transfer Fee paid: £50,000 for Gerry McCabe from Clyde.
Record Victory: 8-1 Arbroath, First Division; 3 Jan 1977.
Record Defeat: 1-9 v Gala Fairydean, Scottish Cup qual rd; 15 Sept, 1965.
Most Capped Player: —.
Most League Appearances: 620: Jim Fallon; 1968-86.
Most League Goals in Season (Individual): 29: Ken Eadie, First Division, 1990-91.
Most League Goals Overall (Individual): 138, Ken Eadie 1988-95.

CLYDEBANK 1998–99 LEAGUE RECORD

Match No.	Date		Venue	Opponents	Result		H/T Score	Lg. Pos.	Goalscorers	Atten- dance
1	Aug	4	A	Airdrieonians	D	0-0	0-0	—		2716
2		15	H	Falkirk	L	0-1	0-1	8		928
3		22	A	Stranraer	W	2-0	0-0	5	Gardner [60], Smith [75]	570
4		29	A	Greenock Morton	D	2-2	2-1	5	McLaughlin [16], McWilliams [26]	1382
5	Sept	5	H	Hibernian	D	2-2	0-0	6	Smith [73], Brannigan [90]	1828
6		12	H	Ayr U	L	0-1	0-0	7		569
7		19	A	Hamilton A	W	2-1	2-1	7	Miller [1], Teale [6]	648
8		26	H	St Mirren	W	1-0	0-0	6	Teale [57]	1462
9	Oct	3	A	Raith R	W	1-0	0-0	4	McDonald [60]	1661
10		11	A	Falkirk	D	2-2	1-1	5	McDonald 2 [20, 70]	4316
11		17	H	Airdrieonians	L	0-1	0-0	6		571
12		27	H	Greenock Morton	W	2-1	1-0	—	Taggart [17], McLaughlin [47]	452
13		31	A	Hibernian	L	1-2	0-1	6	Brown [88]	10,172
14	Nov	7	H	Hamilton A	D	0-0	0-0	6		451
15		14	A	Ayr U	L	1-4	0-1	6	Robertson [70]	2450
16		21	A	St Mirren	D	0-0	0-0	6		2847
17		28	H	Raith R	D	1-1	1-1	6	Smith [33]	417
18	Dec	5	A	Airdrieonians	L	0-2	0-1	6		1641
19		12	H	Stranraer	W	2-1	1-0	6	McLaughlin [22], Miller [58]	207
20		19	A	Hibernian	L	0-3	0-1	6		9064
21		26	A	Greenock Morton	D	1-1	0-1	6	Docherty (pen) [85]	1947
22	Jan	12	A	Hamilton A	W	1-0	1-0	—	McDonald [24]	651
23		16	H	St Mirren	D	2-2	0-1	6	Nicholls [75], McDonald [88]	934
24		30	A	Raith R	L	1-2	1-1	7	McDonald [18]	1803
25	Feb	20	A	Stranraer	W	2-0	2-0	7	Elliot [17], Anthony (pen) [35]	452
26	Mar	10	H	Falkirk	L	1-2	1-1	—	McDonald [33]	289
27		13	H	Hibernian	W	2-0	1-0	6	Elliot [45], Love [58]	1695
28		20	H	Raith R	D	0-0	0-0	7		300
29	Apr	3	A	St Mirren	D	1-1	0-1	7	Gardner [62]	1756
30		10	H	Hamilton A	D	0-0	0-0	7		262
31		18	A	Ayr U	D	0-0	0-0	7		2113
32		21	H	Greenock Morton	L	1-2	1-0	—	McDonald [8]	402
33		24	H	Airdrieonians	L	0-1	0-0	7		296
34		27	H	Ayr U	W	2-1	1-1	—	Miller [30], Brannigan [50]	305
35	May	1	A	Falkirk	W	2-0	1-0	7	McDonald [30], Docherty [80]	2737
36		8	H	Stranraer	L	1-2	0-1	7	Taggart [48]	269

Final League Position: 7   1997–98 DIV 2 2

Honours
League Champions: Second Division 1975-76; *Runners-up:* 1997-98; *Runners-up:* First Division 1976-77, 1984-85.
Scottish Cup: Semi-finalists 1990. *League Cup:* —.

Club colours: Shirt: Vertical red and white stripes. Shorts: Black. Stockings: Black.

Goalscorers: *League (36):* McDonald 9, McLaughlin 3, Miller 3, Smith 3, Brannigan 2, Docherty 2 (1 pen), Elliot 2, Gardner 2, Taggart 2, Teale 2, Anthony 1 (pen), Brown 1, Love 1, McWilliams 1, Nicholls 1, Robertson 1. *Scottish Cup (6):* Nicholls 3, Gardner 1, McMillan 1, Ritchie 1. *League Cup (1):* McDonald 1.

Scott C 28	Wishart F 32	Lovering P 12	Teale G 7+1	McLaughlin J 32	Brannigan K 31	Nicholls D 34	McDonald C 22+8	Taggart C 25+10	Robertson A 7+4	McWilliams D 5+4	Gardner L 24+11	Smith T 20+1	Miller S 28+4	Inglis N 1	Docherty S 17+11	Brown A 1+14	McKelvie D —+9	Murdoch S 13+3	Ritchie I 11+2	Dobie S 6	Callaghan S 5	Anthony M 9+4	Naker R 1	McMillan A 1+1	Newlands R 1	Love G 7	Ross S 3	McKinstrey J 7+2	Elliot B 4	Morrison S 2+1	Match No.
1	2	3	4^3	5	6	7	8	9	10^1	11^2	12	13	14																		1
	2	3	9	5	6	7	8^3	10^1		11^2	12	4	13	1	14																2
1	2	3	13	5	6	7	8^1	9		11	10^2	4	12																		3
1	2	3	8	5	6	7		9^1	12	11	10^2	4	13																		4
1	2	3	9	5	6	7	13	12	8^1		10^2	4	11																		5
1	2	3	9	5	6	7	14	12	8^1	13	10^2	4^3	11																		6
1	2	3	9^2	5	6	7	13	12	8^1		10	4	11																		7
1	2	3	9^3	5	6	7	14	12	8^1		10^2	4	11		13																8
1	2	3		5	6	7	9^3	13	8^1		10^2	4	11		12	14															9
1	2	3		5	6	7	9	8			10^1	4	11		12																10
1	2	3		5	6	7	9	8		13	10^2	4	11^1		12																11
1	2	3		5	6	7	9	8^2			10^1	4			11		12	13													12
1	2			5	6	7	9	8^3	12		10^1	4			11^2	14	13	3													13
1	2		5^1	6	7		9^3	8			10^2	13	4		11	14		3	12												14
1	2					7	14	12		10	4		9^3		8^1	13	3	5	6^2	11											15
1			9	7	8^2	12		10	4		9^1	13			2		5	11	3												16
1				5	6	7	13	8^1			10	4	9^2		14		2^1	12	11	3											17
1^1	2			5	6	7	13	12			10	4	11					9^2	3	8											18
	2			5	6	7	14	10^2			4		11		12			9^3	3	8^1	1	13									19
	2			5	6	7		10^1			12	4	11		13			9		8			1			3^2					20
	2			5	6	7		9			12	4	11		10					8^1						3	1				21
	2			5	6	7	9^1	13			12		11		10					8^2						3	1	4			22
	2			5		7	9	13			12		11		10	14		6^1		8^3						3^2	1	4			23
1	2			5	6	7	9	8^1			13				10^2	14				12						3		4	11^3		24
1	2			5		7	13	6			10		11			12		4^1				8^2		3				14	9^1		25
1	2			5		7	9	6			10^2		11		13	12	14	4^2				8^1						3			26
1	2			5		7	9^1	6			12		11		10^3	13		4				14				3			8^2		27
1	2			5	6	7	9^2				14		11		12		13	4				10^1				3			8^3		28
1				5	6	7	9^1	2			8		11^2		10	13		4	3			12									29
	2			5	6	7	9^1	3			8		11		10^2	12		4				13									30
	2			5	6	7		3			8^2		11		10	13	12	4^1										9			31
	2			5	6	7	9	3			8^1		11		10	12	13	4^2													32
	2			5^2	6	7	9^2	3	14	12	11		10		13		8^1	4												1	33
	2				6	7^2		3	14	8	11^3		10	9^1	12	13	4										5		1	34
1	2				6		9^2	3	12		8^3		11		10	14	13	7	4^1								5				35
1				5	6		9^2	3		7^1	8		11		10		12	2^2	4								13		14		36

COWDENBEATH

Third Division

Year Formed: 1881. *Ground & Address:* Central Park, Cowdenbeath KY4 9EY. *Telephone:* 01383 610166. *Fax:* 01383 512132.
Ground Capacity: total: 5268, seated: 1622. *Size of Pitch:* 107yd × 66yd.
Chairman: Gordon McDougall. *Secretary:* Tom Ogilvie. *Commercial Manager:* Joe McNamara.
Manager: Craig Levein. *Assistant Manager:* Gary Kirk. *Physios:* Oliver Finlay, Wendy McDonald.
Managers since 1975: D. McLindon; F. Connor; P. Wilson; A. Rolland; H. Wilson; W. McCulloch; J. Clark; J. Craig; R.
Campbell; J. Blackley; J. Brownlie, A. Harrow, J. Reilly, P Dolan, T. Steven, S. Conn. *Previous Grounds:* North End
Park, Cowdenbeath.
Record Attendance: 25,586 v Rangers, League Cup quarter-final; 21 Sept, 1949.
Record Transfer Fee received: £30,000 for Nicky Henderson to Falkirk (March 1994).
Record Transfer Fee paid: —
Record Victory: 12-0 v Johnstone, Scottish Cup 1st rd; 21 Jan, 1928.
Record Defeat: 1-11 v Clyde, Division II; 6 Oct, 1951.
Most Capped Player: Jim Paterson, 3, Scotland.
Most League and Cup Appearances: 491 Ray Allan 1972-75, 1979-89.
Most League Goals in Season (Individual): 54, Rab Walls, Division II, 1938-39.
Most Goals Overall (Individual): 127, Willie Devlin, 1922-26, 1929-30.

COWDENBEATH 1998–99 LEAGUE RECORD

Match No.	Date	Venue	Opponents	Result	H/T Score	Lg. Pos.	Goalscorers	Attendance
1	Aug 4	H	Montrose	W 4-1	2-0	—	Brown 2 [12, 55], Stewart [43], Snedden [60]	161
2	15	A	Stenhousemuir	W 2-1	1-0	—	Winter [28], Graham [76]	306
3	22	H	East Stirling	W 2-1	1-1	2	Brown [29], Robertson [59]	220
4	29	A	Ross Co	L 0-2	0-2	2		1553
5	Sept 5	H	Brechin C	L 0-1	0-1	4		206
6	12	H	Berwick R	D 1-1	1-1	5	Stewart [20]	242
7	19	A	Dumbarton	L 0-5	0-1	5		348
8	26	A	Albion R	W 1-0	0-0	5	Welsh [66]	403
9	Oct 3	H	Queen's Park	L 0-3	0-0	5		280
10	9	H	Stenhousemuir	L 0-2	0-2	5		320
11	17	A	East Stirling	D 1-1	0-0	5	Dair [56]	230
12	28	H	Ross Co	L 1-2	0-2	—	Bowsher [89]	212
13	31	A	Brechin C	L 1-2	1-0	7	Thomson [1]	291
14	Nov 7	H	Dumbarton	L 0-2	0-0	8		228
15	14	A	Berwick R	L 1-3	1-0	9	Hamilton [3]	296
16	21	H	Albion R	L 2-3	0-2	9	Milne [57], Stewart [80]	161
17	28	A	Queen's Park	L 0-2	0-1	9		439
18	Dec 12	A	Montrose	D 1-1	0-0	9	Hunter [54]	324
19	19	H	East Stirling	W 3-2	1-0	8	Milne [26], Thomson [46], Bradley [80]	108
20	26	A	Ross Co	L 0-1	0-0	9		1842
21	Jan 26	H	Brechin C	L 0-2	0-0	—		117
22	30	H	Queen's Park	D 0-0	0-0	9		198
23	Feb 13	H	Berwick R	L 1-2	0-1	10	Milne [70]	328
24	20	H	Montrose	W 1-0	1-0	10	Milne [28]	234
25	23	A	Albion R	D 1-1	1-0	—	Winter [10]	240
26	27	A	Stenhousemuir	L 1-4	1-1	9	Bradley [15]	361
27	Mar 6	A	Brechin C	D 1-1	1-0	9	Stewart [22]	269
28	13	H	Ross Co	L 2-3	2-1	9	Brown [19], Stewart [34]	316
29	20	A	Queen's Park	L 1-2	0-1	10	Hamilton [85]	336
30	Apr 3	H	Albion R	L 0-2	0-1	10		161
31	5	A	Dumbarton	L 1-6	0-1	—	Brown [78]	650
32	10	H	Dumbarton	W 2-1	1-0	10	Stewart [26], Milne [84]	245
33	18	A	Berwick R	L 1-2	1-0	10	Stewart [33]	404
34	24	A	East Stirling	D 0-0	0-0	10		208
35	May 1	H	Stenhousemuir	L 0-2	0-0	10		300
36	8	A	Montrose	W 2-1	0-1	9	Milne [70], Snedden [87]	293

Final League Position: 9   1997–98 8

Honours

League Champions: Division II 1913-14, 1914-15, 1938-39; *Runners-up:* Division II 1921-22, 1923-24, 1969-70. Second Division 1991-92.
Scottish Cup: Quarter-finals: 1931.
League Cup: Semi-finals: 1959-60, 1970-71.

Club colours: Shirt: Royal blue with white stripe down shoulder and sleeve; white round neck with one Royal blue stripe. Shorts: White with Royal blue stripe on side. Stockings: Royal blue with one white leg hoop.

Goalscorers: *League (34):* Stewart 7, Milne 6, Brown 5, Bradley 2, Hamilton 2, Snedden 2, Thomson 2, Winter 2, Bowsher 1, Dair 1, Graham 1, Hunter 1, Robertson 1, Welsh 1. *Scottish Cup (2):* Burns 1, Snedden 1. *League Cup (0).*

Hutchison S 27	Urquhart M 11+2	Cuthbert L 15+2	Bowsher C 7+1	Snedden S 29+1	Hamilton A 22+4	Winter C 25	Robertson M 13+4	Burns J 23+4	Brown G 23+12	Stewart W 26+3	Graham C 11+4	Dinse R 2	Ritchie A 4+3	Murray D 7+1	Lakie J 1	Humphreys M 10+3	Pryde D 2+3	Bannatyne P —+2	Paterson G 1	Welsh B 4+8	Ward M —+3	Lynch J 1	Blair D 2+1	Milne K 23	Dair L 3	Melvin A —+6	Thomson R 21+1	McKenzie J 5	Godfrey R 9	Smith P —+1	Malcolm S 4	Findlay G 5	Hunter G 2	Bradley M 19	Martin A —+1	Mitchell W 13+2	Millar P 1+2	McMillan C 7+6	Bruno P 1	Horn R 8	McMillan A 1	Carnie G 8	Match No.
1	2	3	4	5	6	7	8	9	10	11																																	1
1	2	3	4	5	8	7	6	9	10¹	11	12																																2
1	2	3¹	4	5	8	7	6	11	9	10			12																														3
1	2²		4³	5	8	7	6	11	9¹	10			3	12		13	14																										4
1	2	3		5¹	6	7	8	10	9²	11³		13	14			12	4																										5
1	2			5	8	7¹	6²	11	10	9			3	4		12	13																										6
1	2²			5	10	11	12	7	9	14			3	4					6¹	8²		13																					7
1		4		5	7	8		10¹	12	9	11		3	6			2																										8
1		4		5	7³			11¹	12	14	9	10	3	13	6					8	2²																						9
1	2³			5	8	7	6	12	9¹	11			4	14										3	10²	13																	10
1				5	7	10	8	9	12	11¹			4										3	6	2																		11
1	3¹	13		5	7	8	11	12	9¹				4										10	6	2																		12
	6¹	5³	3	7	10	12	11	9²					2	14									13	4	8	1																	13
2				13	7	8	6¹	14	9³	10			3²			12							5	11	1	4																	14
2				7²	6	12	10	9					5			8¹							13	4	11	1	3																15
14				8²	7	6¹	9	10³	12				5			13							3	2	11	1	4																16
1				4	14	8	12	9	13	10			11³							7²			3¹	2				5	6														17
1				5		7		9	10¹				6							12			3	2				8¹	4	11													18
1				5	12	7		11	9²				2							13			3	6				8¹	4	10													19
1				4	2	7	12³	9	10¹				3	14		13							11	8				6²	5														20
1				4	6	7		9	13	10¹	11²		3	2									5					8³	12	14													21
1				5	8	7		10	9	11¹			3							12			2					6	4														22
1	12	6²		5				11¹	10	9			3										2					8	4	13													23
1	8²	6		5	2	7		12	9	10¹			3										6					8²	4	13	14												24
1	11			5	2	7		12	10¹	9³			3										6					8²	4	13	14												25
1	6¹			5	12			7²	14	9	10		3										2					11	4	8³	13												26
1	3		5		8			13	9	10¹	13												11	12	2²				6	4	7												27
1	12							14	9	10²	13												3					8³	4			2	5¹	6	7	11							28
1	4¹			5	14			12	9	11	13												3					10	6		2²	8	7³		29
1				5	7			8²	11¹	12	10	9											3		2³				6	14	13	4											30
	12			5	2²			13								9²	10						3					7¹	1		6	4		14	11		8						31
				5	8			11	9														3					12	1		10	6		2	4		7¹					32
					7			11¹	9														3					12	6	1		10	5		2	4		8				33
	3							9¹	10							11²		2		12		13	8						1		6	4		7				5				34
	4							9²	11											13		12	3²					8		1	14		10	6¹		2			5		7	35
1	4	8						9²	10	11¹										12			3					2			7		13			6			5			36

DUMBARTON   Third Division

Year Formed: 1872. *Ground & Address:* Boghead Park, Miller St, Dumbarton G82 2JA. *Telephone:* 01389 762569/767864. *Fax:* 01389 762629
Ground Capacity: total: 5503, seated: 303. *Size of Pitch:* 110yd × 68yd.
Chairman: D. Dalglish. *Club Secretary:* Colin J. Hosie. *Company Secretary:* John Benn.
Manager: Jimmy Brown. *Assistant Manager:* Tom Carson. *Coach:* Ringo Watts. *Physio:* David Stobie.
Managers since 1975: A. Wright; D. Wilson; S. Fallon; W. Lamont; D. Wilson; D. Whiteford; A. Totten; M. Clougherty; R. Auld; J. George; W. Lamont; M. MacLeod; J. Fallon; I. Wallace. *Club Nickname(s):* The Sons. *Previous Grounds:* Broadmeadow, Ropework Lane, Townend Ground.
Record Attendance: 18,000 v Raith Rovers, Scottish Cup; 2 Mar, 1957.
Record Transfer Fee received: £125,000 for Graeme Sharp to Everton (March 1982).
Record Transfer Fee paid: £50,000 for Charlie Gibson from Stirling Albion (1989).
Record Victory: 13-1 v Kirkintilloch Central. 1st Rd; 1 Sept, 1888.
Record Defeat: 1-11 v Albion Rovers, Division II; 30 Jan, 1926: v Ayr United, League Cup; 13 Aug, 1952.
Most Capped Player: James McAulay, 9, Scotland.
Most League Appearances: 297: Andy Jardine, 1957-67.
Most Goals in Season (Individual): 38: Kenny Wilson, Division II; 1971-72. *(League and Cup):* 46 Hughie Gallacher, 1955-56.

DUMBARTON 1998–99 LEAGUE RECORD

Match No.	Date	Venue	Opponents	Result	H/T Score	Lg. Pos.	Goalscorers	Attendance
1	Aug 4	H	Albion R	W 2-0	1-0	—	McKinnon [42], Flannery [46]	291
2	15	A	Queen's Park	W 1-0	0-0	—	Sharp [55]	656
3	22	H	Stenhousemuir	L 0-2	0-1	3		378
4	29	H	Berwick R	D 0-0	0-0	4		303
5	Sept 5	A	East Stirling	W 2-1	1-1	3	Robertson [18], King [58]	217
6	12	A	Brechin C	D 0-0	0-0	3		355
7	19	H	Cowdenbeath	W 5-0	1-0	3	McKinnon [30], Melvin W 2 [58, 75], Flannery [63], Sharp [67]	348
8	26	A	Montrose	D 1-1	1-0	4	Flannery [38]	318
9	Oct 3	H	Ross Co	L 1-2	1-2	4	Flannery [45]	538
10	10	H	Queen's Park	W 1-0	0-0	4	Flannery [69]	343
11	17	A	Stenhousemuir	W 3-0	0-0	3	Flannery [48], Mooney [84], Glancy [90]	456
12	24	A	Berwick R	L 1-3	0-1	4	Robertson [89]	303
13	31	H	East Stirling	D 2-2	1-0	4	Flannery [17], Robertson [79]	309
14	Nov 7	A	Cowdenbeath	W 2-0	0-0	4	Flannery 2 [54, 72]	228
15	14	H	Brechin C	L 1-2	1-1	4	Flannery [37]	357
16	25	H	Montrose	L 0-2	0-1	—		240
17	28	A	Ross Co	L 0-2	0-0	4		1759
18	Dec 12	A	Albion R	W 2-0	0-0	4	Mooney [46], Flannery [80]	324
19	19	H	Stenhousemuir	L 1-4	0-4	4	Wilson [81]	283
20	Jan 16	A	Montrose	L 2-4	1-2	5	Flannery 2 [44, 76]	326
21	26	A	East Stirling	W 2-1	0-0	—	Melvin W [79], Brittain [83]	204
22	30	H	Ross Co	D 0-0	0-0	5		400
23	Feb 2	H	Berwick R	D 1-1	0-0	—	Flannery [60]	242
24	13	A	Brechin C	D 3-3	1-0	6	Mooney [28], Gow [82], Grace [90]	360
25	27	A	Queen's Park	D 1-1	1-0	6	Bradford [7]	516
26	Mar 6	H	East Stirling	L 0-2	0-2	6		246
27	9	H	Albion R	D 1-1	1-0	—	McKinnon [28]	230
28	13	A	Berwick R	W 1-0	0-0	5	Flannery [58]	321
29	20	A	Ross Co	W 2-1	0-1	4	Bradford [55], Robertson (pen) [59]	2374
30	Apr 3	H	Montrose	W 2-1	0-1	4	Robertson 2 (2 pens) [73, 86]	541
31	5	H	Cowdenbeath	W 6-1	1-0	—	Stewart [23], Jack [51], King 2 [55, 58], Flannery [61], Smith [65]	650
32	10	A	Cowdenbeath	L 1-2	0-1	4	Smith [75]	245
33	17	H	Brechin C	W 2-0	0-0	4	Smith [46], Robertson (pen) [74]	562
34	24	A	Stenhousemuir	W 2-0	1-0	4	Flannery [72], Mooney (pen) [85]	629
35	May 1	H	Queen's Park	L 0-1	0-0	4		762
36	8	A	Albion R	W 2-0	1-0	4	Bruce [10], Robertson [73]	256

Final League Position: 4   1997–98 10

Most Goals Overall (Individual): 169: Hughie Gallacher, 1954-62 (including C Division 1954-55). *(League and Cup):* 202 Hughie Gallacher, 1954-62

Honours
League Champions: Division I 1890-91 (shared with Rangers), 1891-92. Division II 1910-11, 1971-72. Second Division 1991-92; *Runners-up:* First Division 1983-84. Division II 1907-08.
Scottish Cup Winners: 1883; *Runners-up:* 1881, 1882, 1887, 1891, 1897. *League Cup:* —.
Club colours: Shirt: White with yellow horizontal band between two black bands. Shorts: White. Stockings: White with black and gold hooped tops.

Goalscorers: *League (53):* Flannery 17, Robertson 8 (4 pens), Mooney 4 (1 pen), King 3, McKinnon 3, Melvin W 3, Smith 3, Bradford 2, Sharp 2 (1 pen), Brittain 1, Bruce 1, Glancy 1, Gow 1, Grace 1, Jack 1, Stewart 1, Wilson 1. *Scottish Cup (1):* Flannery 1. *League Cup (0).*

Dennison P 2	Wilson W 35	Brittain C 22+1	Sharp L 17	Reid D 9+1	Jack S 35	Melvin W 24+6	McKinnon C 27	Glancy M 5+5	Flannery P 33	Grace A 18+2	Melvin M 2+9	Brown A 2+5	Meechan K 33	King T 29	Mooney M 28+4	Gow S 6+3	Robertson J 21+5	Smith C 3+6	Harvey P 7+2	Wilkinson B 4+2	Miller K 2+7	Barnes D 1	Stewart D 9+1	Bruce J 17	Bradford J 4	Finnegan P 1+2	Match No.
1	2	3	4	5	6	7[1]	8	9[2]	10	11	12	13															1
	2	3	4	5	6	7[1]	8	9	10[1]		13		1	11	12												2
	2	3[1]	4	5[1]	6	7[2]	8	9	10		13		1	11	12	14											3
	2	3	4		6	7[1]		9	12				1	8	10	5[2]	11	13									4
	2	3[1]	4	12	5	11	7		10[2]				1	6	8		9	13									5
	2	4	3	5	11	7			10[1]				1	6	8		9	12									6
	2[1]	4	3	5	11	7		12	10				1	6	8		9										7
	2	4	3	5	11	7[1]			10	12			1	6	8		9										8
	2	4	3	5	11	7		13	10				1	6[1]	8	12	9[2]										9
	2	4	3		6	7	8	9	12				1	10		5[2]	11[1]	13									10
	2	4	3[1]	5		7	8	11	9				1	10	6	12											11
	2		4	5		7[2]	8		9	11[1]			1	3	10	13	6	12									12
	2[1]		4	5		12	8	13	9				1	6	10[2]	11	7	3									13
	2		4	5			8		9				1	6	10	11	7	3									14
	2		4	5	14		8	13	9	12			1[3]	6	10	11[2]	7[1]	3									15
	2		4	5			8		9[1]	7	13		1	6	10		3	12									16
	2	3	4	5			8		9	11[1]				6	7	12	13	10[2]				1					17
	2	3		5	11	7			9				1	6	10		4	8									18
	2	3		5	11	7			9		13		1	6[1]	10		4[2]	12	8								19
	2				6		8	11[1]	9	7			1	10		5	12						3	4			20
	2	11		5		7	8	9	10					6									3	4			21
	2	11		5		7[1]	8		9		13		1	6	10	12							3[1]	4			22
	2	3		5	11[1]	7	8		9				1	6	10	12								4			23
	2	3		5			8[2]		9	11	13	14	1	6	10[1]	7[1]	12							4			24
	2	11		5		7	8		10[1]		13		1	6	12								3	4	9[2]		25
	2	3		5	11[1]	7	8		9[2]		13		1	12	6	10								4			26
	2	3		5	11[1]	7	8		9				1	6	12									4	10		27
	2	3		5			8		9	12			1	6	11[1]									4	10		28
	2	3		5		7[1]	8		9[2]				1	6	11	13								4	10	12	29
	2	3		5		7	8		9	11			1	6	10[1]						12			4			30
1	2	3		5	6	7[2]	8	9[1]							14	11					12	13	10[3]	4			31
	2	3		5		7[1]	8		9				1	6	11						12		10	4			32
	2			5			8	9		12			1	6	7[1]	11	10[2]				13		3	4			33
	2	13		5	14		8		9				1	6	7[3]	11[2]	10[1]						3	4	12		34
		12		5			8	9					1	6	7	11	10[1]						3	4		2	35
	2	3		5			8[2]	9	10[3]	12	13		1	6	7	11[1]	14							4			36

DUNDEE

Premier League

Year Formed: 1893. *Ground & Address:* Dens Park Stadium, Sandeman St, Dundee DD3 7JY. *Telephone:* 01382 889966. *Fax:* 01382 832284.
Ground Capacity: all seated: 10,531 (increases to 12,371 after further reconstruction). *Size of Pitch:* 101m × 66m.
Chairman: John Marr. *Chief Executive:* Peter Marr.
Manager: John Scott. *Assistant Manager:* Jimmy Bone. *Youth Coach:* Ray Farningham. *Physio:* Jim Crosby. *Youth Development:* Kenny Cameron. *Coach:* Billy Thomson.
Managers since 1975: David White; Tommy Gemmell; Donald Mackay; Archie Knox; Jocky Scott; Dave Smith; Gordon Wallace; Iain Munro; Simon Stainrod; Jim Duffy, John McCormack. *Club Nickname(s):* The Dark Blues or The Dee.
Previous Grounds: Carolina Port 1893-98.
Record Attendance: 43,024 v Rangers, Scottish Cup; 1953.
Record Transfer Fee received: £500,000 for Tommy Coyne to Celtic (March 1989).
Record Transfer Fee paid: £200,000 for Jim Leighton (Feb 1992).
Record Victory: 10-0 Division II v Alloa; 9 Mar, 1947 and v Dunfermline Ath; 22 Mar, 1947.
Record Defeat: 0-11 v Celtic, Division I; 26 Oct, 1895.
Most Capped Player: Alex Hamilton, 24, Scotland.
Most League Appearances: 341: Doug Cowie 1945-61.
Most League Goals in Season (Individual): 52: Alan Gilzean, 1963-64.
Most Goals Overall (Individual): 113: Alan Gilzean.

DUNDEE 1998–99 LEAGUE RECORD

Match No.	Date	Venue	Opponents	Result	H/T Score	Lg. Pos.	Goalscorers	Attendance
1	Aug 1	H	Aberdeen	L	0-2	0-1	—	7816
2	15	A	Dunfermline Ath	L	0-2	0-1	10	5279
3	23	H	St Johnstone	L	0-1	0-0	10	3641
4	29	H	Celtic	D	1-1	0-0	10	Annand (pen) 90	9853
5	Sept 12	A	Hearts	W	2-0	0-0	9	Adamczuk 2 48, 84	13,117
6	19	H	Dundee U	D	2-2	0-0	9	Annand 69, Adamczuk 90	12,081
7	23	A	Kilmarnock	L	1-2	1-1	—	Annand 10	7069
8	26	H	Motherwell	W	1-0	1-0	8	Irvine 9	5655
9	Oct 4	A	Rangers	L	0-1	0-0	10		48,348
10	17	A	Aberdeen	D	2-2	0-1	9	Annand 2 59, 69	10,004
11	28	H	Dunfermline Ath	W	1-0	0-0	—	Falconer 61	4619
12	31	H	Hearts	W	1-0	0-0	5	Weir (og) 76	6142
13	Nov 7	A	Celtic	L	1-6	1-3	6	Annand 21	58,974
14	14	H	Kilmarnock	D	1-1	1-1	7	Annand 29	4249
15	22	A	Dundee U	W	1-0	0-0	6	Grady 82	11,230
16	Dec 12	A	St Johnstone	D	1-1	0-0	6	Adamczuk 74	6033
17	16	A	Motherwell	L	1-2	1-1	—	Adamczuk 37	5840
18	19	H	Aberdeen	L	1-2	1-1	7	Rae 18	6340
19	27	H	Celtic	L	0-3	0-2	8		10,043
20	30	A	Hearts	W	2-1	2-1	—	Sharp 17, Falconer 42	13,383
21	Jan 2	H	Dundee U	L	1-3	1-2	8	McSkimming 28	11,751
22	27	H	Rangers	L	0-4	0-3	—		10,043
23	30	A	Kilmarnock	D	0-0	0-0	8		7677
24	Feb 6	H	Motherwell	W	1-0	1-0	7	Tweed 2	4187
25	20	A	Rangers	L	1-6	1-2	7	Adamczuk 26	49,462
26	27	H	St Johnstone	L	0-1	0-1	7		7245
27	Mar 13	A	Dunfermline Ath	L	0-2	0-0	7		6980
28	20	H	Hearts	W	2-0	0-0	7	Annand 2 52, 65	5500
29	Apr 3	A	Celtic	L	0-5	0-3	7		59,269
30	10	A	Motherwell	W	2-1	0-1	7	Falconer 64, Grady 75	5717
31	18	H	Rangers	D	1-1	1-0	5	Anderson 23	11,070
32	24	H	Kilmarnock	W	2-1	1-0	5	Anderson 44, McSkimming 74	4296
33	May 1	A	Dundee U	W	2-0	0-0	5	Irvine 78, Grady 89	12,280
34	8	A	Aberdeen	W	2-1	1-0	5	Boyack 41, Anderson 84	9790
35	15	H	Dunfermline Ath	W	3-1	1-0	5	Irvine 22, Boyack 50, Falconer 61	4179
36	23	A	St Johnstone	L	0-1	0-0	5		10,575

Final League Position: 5   1997–98 DIV 1 1

Honours
League Champions: Division I 1961-62. First Division 1978-79, 1991-92, 1997-98. Division II 1946-47; *Runners-up:* Division I 1902-03, 1906-07, 1948-49, 1980-81.
Scottish Cup Winners: 1910; *Runners-up:* 1925, 1952, 1964.
League Cup Winners: 1951-52, 1952-53, 1973-74; *Runners-up:* 1967-68, 1980-81. *(Coca-Cola Cup):* 1995–96.
B&Q (Centenary) Cup Winners: 1990-91; *Runners-up:* 1994-95.

European: *European Cup:* 8 matches (1962-63 semi-finals). *Cup Winners' Cup:* 2 matches: (1964-65).
UEFA Cup: 18 matches: (*Fairs Cup:* 1967-68 semi-finals. *UEFA Cup:* 1971-72, 1973-74, 1974-75).

Club colours: Shirt: Dark blue with red and white trim. Shorts: White. Stockings: Blue and white.

Goalscorers: *League (36):* Annand 9, Adamczuk 6, Falconer 4, Anderson 3, Grady 3, Irvine 3, Boyack 2, McSkimming 2, Rae 1, Sharp 1, Tweed 1, own goal 1. *Scottish Cup (1):* Annand 1. *League Cup (0).*

Douglas R 35	Miller W 26	Smith B 29 + 4	Irvine B 33	McSkimming S 25 + 4	Maddison L 21	Garcin E 2 + 1	Adamczuk D 24 + 2	Coyne T 8 + 8	Grady J 20 + 6	Falconer W 31 + 2	Pounewatchy S 2 + 1	McCormick S — + 1	Magee D 1 + 1	McInally J 14 + 1	O'Driscoll J — + 1	Raeside R 19 + 2	Annand E 19 + 10	Grant B — + 4	Rae G 23 + 7	Rogers D 7 + 4	Anderson I 17 + 11	Langfield J 1 + 1	Hunter G 3	Fleming D 1	Sharp L 4 + 2	Tweed S 10	Robertson H 9 + 1	Strachan G 4 + 2	Boyack S 8	Bayne G — + 2	Match No.
1	2	3	4	5	6^1	7^2	8	9	10^3	11	12	13	14																		1
1	2	13	4	3^1			8	9	10	11				5		6^2	7	12													2
1	2	3		6^2	12		8	9^1	10	11	4			7		5	13														3
1	2	3	4	6	7^1		8	10	9	11						5^2	14	12^2	13												4
1	2	3	4	11^3	6		8	10^1	9							5^2	12		7	13	14										5
1	2	3^3	4	11^2	6		8	10^1	9					14		5	12		7	13											6
1	2	3	4	10			8			11						5	9		7	6^1	12										7
1	2	3	4	10	6^2		8	13		11						5	9^1		7	12											8
1	2	3	4	10	6^2		8	12		11						5	9^1		7	13											9
1	2	3^1	4	10			8^2			11				7		5	9		13	6	12										10
1	2	3	4	10						11						8	9	12	6	7^1	5										11
1	2	3	4	10			12			11						8	13	9^1	6	7	5^2										12
1	2	3	4	10						11				8		12	9	13	6^2	7^1	5										13
	2		4	6			8^3		10^2	11				14		5	9	13	12		7	1	3^1								14
1	2		4	6			8^2	9^1								12	7	5	10	13	3	11									15
1	2	12	4	6			8	13	10								7	5	9^2		3^1	11									16
1		3	4	6^2			8	13	10	9						5	2	12			11						7^1				17
1	2	3	4	6			8			11									10^1	9	7				12	5					18
1		3	4	6			8		10	9						7^3	12		14	2^1	11^2				13	5					19
1		3	4	14			8		10	9^2						2	13		7		12					6^2	5	11^1			20
1		3	4	7			8	14	10	11^2						12	2		9		13						6^1	5			21
1	12		4^1	14	3		8		10							7	9		2		11^2					5	6^3	13			22
1		3	4	6^2			8		10^1	9							2	12			13				5	7	11				23
1	12		4				8	9^2	10					14		13	2		11		3					5^1	6^2	7			24
1		3	4	6			8	9^1	10	11						12	13		2							5	7				25
1		3	4	7^3			8	14	10	9							2		13		6^2	12				5^1	11				26
1	2		4	7^2	3		8	13	9							10					6^1		11			5	12				27
1	2	3	4	6					10							5	9				8				12	7			11^1		28
1	2	3	4	7	6				10							5	9				8					11					29
1	2^1	3	4	14	6			13	10							5	9^3				11				12		7^2		8		30
1	2	3	4	7	5												9^1	10	12		6						11		8		31
1		3	4	5	2			9	10^1								7	12			6						11		8		32
1	2	3	4	7^1	5			13	10								9^2				6						11	12	8		33
1	2	3	4	5^1	12			13	10								9^2				6						11	7	8		34
1	2	3	4	5			12	14								9^2	10^3				6						11	7	8^1	13	35
1	2	3	4	13	5												9	10			6						11^1	7^2	8	12	36

DUNDEE UNITED   Premier League

Year Formed: 1909 (1923). *Ground & Address:* Tannadice Park, Tannadice St, Dundee DD3 7JW. *Telephone:* 01382 833166. *Fax:* 01382 889398. *Ground Capacity:* total: 14,209 all seated: stands: east 2868, west 2096, south 2201, Fair Play 1601, George Fox 5151, executive boxes 292.
Size of Pitch: 110yd × 72yd.
Chairman: James Y. McLean. *Company Secretary:* Miss Priti Trivedi. *Commercial Manager:* Bill Campbell.
Manager: Paul Sturrock. *Assistant Manager:* John Blackley. *Coaches:* Terry Butcher, Maurice Malpas. *Physio:* David Rankine.
Managers since 1975: J. McLean; I. Golac; W. Kirkwood; T. McLean. *Club Nickname(s):* The Terrors. *Previous Grounds:* None.
Record Attendance: 28,000 v Barcelona, Fairs Cup; 16 Nov, 1966.
Record Transfer Fee received: £4,000,000 for Duncan Ferguson from Rangers (July 1993).
Record Transfer Fee paid: £750,000 for Steven Pressley from Coventry C (July 1995).
Record Victory: 14-0 v Nithsdale Wanderers, Scottish Cup 1st rd; 17 Jan, 1931.
Record Defeat: 1-12 v Motherwell, Division II; 23 Jan, 1954.
Most Capped Player: Maurice Malpas, 55, Scotland.
Most League Appearances: 612, Dave Narey; 1973-94.
Most Appearances in European Matches: 76, Dave Narey (record for Scottish player).
Most League Goals in Season (Individual): 41: John Coyle, Division II; 1955-56.
Most Goals Overall (Individual): 158: Peter McKay.

DUNDEE UNITED 1998–99 LEAGUE RECORD

Match No.	Date	Venue	Opponents	Result	H/T Score	Lg. Pos.	Goalscorers	Attendance
1	Aug 1	A	Kilmarnock	L 0-2	0-1	—		8137
2	16	H	Hearts	D 0-0	0-0	9		9629
3	22	A	Celtic	L 1-2	1-0	9	Winters [31]	59,133
4	30	A	Motherwell	L 0-1	0-1	9		11,201
5	Sept 12	H	Rangers	D 0-0	0-0	10		12,088
6	19	A	Dundee	D 2-2	0-0	10	McSwegan [53], Olofsson [67]	12,081
7	23	H	Dunfermline Ath	D 1-1	1-1	—	McSwegan [27]	6957
8	26	A	St Johnstone	W 3-1	2-0	10	Dodds 3 (1 pen) [16, 34 (p), 83]	6655
9	Oct 4	H	Aberdeen	W 1-0	1-0	8	McSwegan [23]	8933
10	17	H	Kilmarnock	L 0-2	0-1	7		8137
11	24	A	Hearts	W 1-0	0-0	5	Dodds [83]	13,124
12	31	A	Rangers	L 1-2	1-0	6	Dodds [25]	49,503
13	Nov 7	H	Motherwell	D 2-2	0-1	7	Dodds [48], Jonsson [60]	6616
14	15	A	Dunfermline Ath	L 1-2	1-2	8	Mathie [3]	10,704
15	22	H	Dundee	L 0-1	0-0	8		11,230
16	28	A	Aberdeen	W 3-0	1-0	8	Olofsson [17], Miller [49], Easton [56]	11,964
17	Dec 5	H	St Johnstone	D 1-1	0-0	7	Dodds [53]	7293
18	12	H	Celtic	D 1-1	0-0	7	Zetterlund [51]	11,612
19	20	A	Kilmarnock	L 0-2	0-1	9		13,538
20	26	A	Motherwell	L 0-2	0-0	9		6001
21	30	H	Rangers	L 1-2	1-1	—	Dodds [42]	11,707
22	Jan 2	A	Dundee	W 3-1	2-1	9	Dodds [11], Thompson [16], Olofsson [70]	11,751
23	30	A	Dunfermline Ath	D 1-1	1-0	9	Olofsson [32]	7646
24	Feb 6	A	St Johnstone	L 0-1	0-1	9		5771
25	20	H	Aberdeen	W 3-0	1-0	8	Olofsson [34], Dodds [48], Hannah [66]	8309
26	27	A	Celtic	L 1-2	1-0	8	Dodds [25]	59,902
27	Mar 20	A	Rangers	W 1-0	1-0	8	Olofsson [44]	49,164
28	Apr 3	H	Motherwell	L 0-3	0-2	8		8110
29	6	H	Hearts	L 1-3	1-2	—	Dodds [3]	10,648
30	17	A	Aberdeen	W 4-0	1-0	8	Dodds 2 [35, 56], Miller [53], Olofsson [54]	11,603
31	20	A	St Johnstone	L 0-1	0-1	—		6741
32	24	A	Dunfermline Ath	D 2-2	2-0	8	Dodds 2 (1 pen) [12, 20 (p)]	6227
33	May 1	H	Dundee	L 0-2	0-0	8		12,280
34	8	H	Kilmarnock	D 0-0	0-0	9		7190
35	15	A	Hearts	L 1-4	0-1	9	Eustace [90]	13,187
36	23	H	Celtic	L 1-2	0-2	9	Dodds (pen) [59]	10,062

Final League Position: 9   1997–98 7

Honours
League Champions: Premier Division 1982-83. Division II 1924-25, 1928-29; *Runners-up:* Division II 1930-31, 1959-60. First Division Runners-up 1995-96.
Scottish Cup Winners: 1994; *Runners-up:* 1974, 1981, 1985, 1987, 1988, 1991.
League Cup Winners: 1979-80, 1980-81; *Runners-up:* 1981-82, 1984-85, 1997-98.
Summer Cup Runners-up: 1964-65. *Scottish War Cup Runners-up:* 1939-40.

European: *European Cup:* 8 matches (1983-84, semi-finals). *Cup Winners' Cup:* 10 matches (1974-75, 1988-89, 1994-95). *UEFA Cup:* 84 matches (*Fairs Cup:* 1966-67, 1969-70, 1970-71. *UEFA Cup:* 1975-76, 1977-78, 1978-79, 1979-80, 1980-81, 1981-82, 1982-83, 1984-85, 1985-86, 1986-87 runners-up, 1987-88, 1989-90, 1990-91, 1993-94, 1997-98).

Club colours: Tangerine and black shirt, black shorts, tangerine and black hoops.

Goalscorers: *League (37):* Dodds 17 (3 pens), Olofsson 7, McSwegan 3, Miller 2, Easton 1, Eustace 1, Hannah 1, Jonsson 1, Mathie 1, Thompson 1, Winters 1, Zetterlund 1. *Scottish Cup (8):* Olofsson 3, Dodds 1, Duffy 1, Murray 1, Patterson D 1, Skoldmark 1. *League Cup (2):* Boli 1, McSwegan 1.

Dijkstra S 26 + 1	Skoldmark M 22 + 3	Jenkins J 5 + 1	Malpas M 31	Jonsson S 12 + 2	Zetterlund L 20 + 1	Miller J 14 + 10	Mols T 11	Olofsson K 32 + 2	Easton C 28 + 2	Boli R 3	Valeriani J — + 1	Thompson S 5 + 10	McNally M 4 + 1	Pascual B 16	Patterson D 17 + 2	McLaren A 3 + 5	Winters R 1 + 2	Duffy C 12 + 3	Paterson J 8 + 7	McSwegan G 5	Dodds W 29 + 1	Mathie A 13 + 9	De Vos J 23 + 2	Combe A 10	Dolan J 4 + 1	Pedersen E 6	Hannah D 13	Eustace J 8 + 3	McCulloch S 9	McLaughlin B 1 + 2	Murray N 2 + 1	Worrall D 3 + 1	McConalogue S — + 1	Partridge D — + 1	Match No.
1	2	3	4	5³	6²	7	8	9	10¹	11	12	13	14																						1
1	3		4	7²	6¹	10	8	9		12		11³	14								2	5	13												2
1	7		4		6¹		8	9	10			13			3	2		5	11²12																3
1	3	12	4	7¹	6²		8	9	10	11			5	2³				13		14															4
1	5	3	4		6		8	9						11		2	7	10																	5
1	5	3	4		6		9³	14				12					11²13		2	7	10³														6
1		2	4		6		8	9						5	11¹		3	7	10	12															7
1	3	2	4		6			11	8					7	5				10	9															8
1	3		4		6	11¹			8					2	5	12		7	10	9															9
1			4		6		11	8				13	3¹		5³	12		2	7	9	10²14														10
1	2		4		6	12	11	8						5				7	9	10¹	3														11
1	3¹		4	7	6	13	11¹	8					14	2	5			12	9	10²															12
1	3¹		4	7	6	12	11	8						2	5				9	10															13
1	3¹		4	7	6²13		11³	8					14	2	5				9	10	12														14
	4	5	6	7		12	8							2				11¹	9	10	3	1													15
	4		6	12		11²	8							2	5	13			9	10¹	3	1	7											16
	4		6	12		11¹	8					13		2	5				9	10²	3	1	7											17
5	4		6			11	8							2					9	10	3	1	7											18
			6	13	8²11							12		2	5			14	9	10¹	3	1	7	4³										19
14	4³		7¹	13		11	8							2	5				9	10	3	1	12	6²										20
	4		7	11			8							2	5				9	10	3	1	6											21
1	12		4	7²	6	11	8		10¹					2	5				9	13	3													22
1			4	5	13	7³	8²11		10					2	14				9¹	12	3		6											23
1	2		4	5		12		11¹	8³			13		14					9	10²	3		6	7										24
1			4	13		7³	11	8				14		2				12	9		3		5¹	10	6²									25
1	12		4¹			7¹	11	8				13		2	5				9	14	3		10	6²										26
1	5		4			11²	8							12					2		9	13	3		10	6¹	7								27
1			4	7¹		11	8¹							2					9		13	3		10	6	5	12							28
1	5		4¹	12		13	11	8						2³					9	14	3		10	6²	7									29
1	5		4	2²	6		11	8				13							9		3		10	7¹	12									30
1	2		4	7			11	8¹					5		14				9	13	3		10³12	6²										31
1	5		4	2	6		11	8¹				12							9		3		10	13	7²									32
1	5		4¹	2		10¹	11	8										2	9	13	3		6²12	7²				14						33
	5						11	8	10¹										9		3	1			6	7	4	12			2				34
	5						12		10	5									9	13	3	1			6	7	4	11¹	8²		2				35
15	5						11		10¹					6					9		3	1⁰			8	7	4²			2	12	13			36

DUNFERMLINE ATHLETIC First Division

Year Formed: 1885. *Ground & Address:* East End Park, Halbeath Rd, Dunfermline KY12 7RB. *Telephone:* 01383 724295. *Fax:* 01383 723468.
Ground Capacity: all seated: 12,500. *Size of Pitch:* 115yd × 71yd.
Chairman: John Yorkston. *Secretary:* P. A. M. D'Mello. *Commercial Manager:* Miss Audrey Bastianelli.
Manager: Dick Campbell.
Physio: Philip Yeates, MCSP. *Coach and Youth Development Officer:* John Ritchie.
Managers since 1975: G. Miller; H. Melrose; P. Stanton; T. Forsyth; J. Leishman; I. Munro; J. Scott; B. Paton. *Club Nickname(s):* The Pars. *Previous Grounds:* None.
Record Attendance: 27,816 v Celtic, Division I, 30 April, 1968.
Record Transfer Fee received: £650,000 for Jackie McNamara to Celtic (Oct 1995).
Record Transfer Fee paid: £540,000 for Istvan Kozma from Bordeaux (Sept 1989).
Record Victory: 11-2 v Stenhousemuir, Division II, 27 Sept, 1930.
Record Defeat: 1-11 v Hibernian, Scottish Cup, 3rd rd replay, 26 Oct, 1889.
Most Capped Player: Colin Miller 15(59), Canada.
Most League Appearances: 497: Norrie McCathie; 1981-96.
Most League Goals in Season (Individual): 53: Bobby Skinner, Division II, 1925-26.
Most Goals Overall (Individual): 154: Charles Dickson.

DUNFERMLINE ATHLETIC 1998–99 LEAGUE RECORD

Match No.	Date		Venue	Opponents	Result		H/T Score	Lg. Pos.	Goalscorers	Atten-dance
1	Aug	1	A	Celtic	L	0-5	0-0	—		59,377
2		15	H	Dundee	W	2-0	1-0	7	Smith [45], Shaw [46]	5279
3		22	A	Motherwell	D	0-0	0-0	8		9858
4		29	H	Aberdeen	D	1-1	0-0	7	French [89]	6510
5	Sept	12	A	St Johnstone	D	1-1	0-1	7	Smith (pen) [51]	5997
6		20	H	Hearts	D	1-1	1-0	8	Smith [12]	5963
7		23	A	Dundee U	D	1-1	1-1	—	Squires [41]	6957
8		26	H	Rangers	L	0-2	0-1	9		11,507
9	Oct	3	A	Kilmarnock	D	0-0	0-0	9		8346
10		17	H	Celtic	D	2-2	2-2	8	Britton (pen) [12], French [27]	10,968
11		28	A	Dundee	L	0-1	0-0	—		4619
12		31	H	St Johnstone	D	1-1	1-0	10	Smith [22]	8126
13	Nov	7	A	Aberdeen	L	1-2	0-1	10	Squires [82]	10,293
14		15	H	Dundee U	W	2-1	2-1	10	Tod [26], McCulloch [35]	10,704
15		21	A	Hearts	L	1-2	1-0	10	Edinho [18]	13,268
16		28	H	Kilmarnock	L	0-3	0-1	10		5608
17	Dec	5	A	Rangers	D	1-1	0-1	9	Petrie [76]	47,465
18		12	H	Motherwell	D	1-1	0-0	10	Smith [79]	5182
19		19	A	Celtic	L	0-5	0-0	10		59,024
20		26	H	Aberdeen	L	1-2	0-0	10	Shaw [54]	7873
21		29	A	St Johnstone	D	1-1	0-0	—	Smith (pen) [69]	6070
22	Jan	2	H	Hearts	D	0-0	0-0	10		9227
23		30	A	Dundee U	D	1-1	0-1	10	Smith [46]	7646
24	Feb	7	H	Rangers	L	0-3	0-0	10		10,360
25		27	A	Motherwell	D	1-1	0-0	10	Britton [86]	7324
26	Mar	6	A	Kilmarnock	D	0-0	0-0	10		8032
27		13	H	Dundee	W	2-0	0-0	—	Thomson [64], Graham [89]	6980
28		20	H	St Johnstone	W	1-0	0-0	9	Petrie [62]	5504
29	Apr	3	A	Aberdeen	L	1-3	1-0	9	Graham [6]	11,361
30		14	A	Rangers	L	0-1	0-1	—		46,220
31		17	H	Kilmarnock	L	0-6	0-1	10		5585
32		24	H	Dundee U	D	2-2	0-2	10	Millar (pen) [46], Smith [54]	6227
33	May	3	A	Hearts	L	0-2	0-0	10		15,176
34		8	H	Celtic	L	1-2	0-2	10	Coyle [82]	8848
35		15	A	Dundee	L	1-3	0-1	10	Thomson [49]	4179
36		23	H	Motherwell	L	1-2	1-0	10	Boyle [20]	3532

Final League Position: 10   1997–98 PREM 8

Honours
League Champions: First Division 1988-89, 1995-96. Division II 1925-26. Second Division 1985-86; *Runners-up:* First Division 1986-87, 1993-94, 1994-95. Division II 1912-13, 1933-34, 1954-55, 1957-58, 1972-73. Second Division 1978-79.
Scottish Cup Winners: 1961, 1968; *Runners-up:* 1965.
League Cup Runners-up: 1949-50, 1991-92.

European: *Cup Winners' Cup:* 14 matches (1961-62, 1968-69 semi-finals). *UEFA Cup:* 28 matches (*Fairs Cup:* 1962-63, 1964-65, 1965-66, 1966-67, 1969-70).

Club colours: Shirt: Black and white vertical stripes, stippled with red dots. Shorts: Black with white side panel. Stockings: White with red chevrons.

Goalscorers: *League (28):* Smith 8 (2 pens), Britton 2, French 2, Graham 2, Petrie 2, Shaw 2, Squires 2, Thomson 2, Boyle 1, Coyle 1, Edinho 1, McCulloch 1, Millar 1 (pen), Tod 1. *Scottish Cup (2):* Smith 2. *League Cup (0).*

Westwater 1 1	Linighan D 1	Ireland C 21+2	Shields G 36	Tod A 24+1	Huxford R 22+3	Millar M 13+8	French H 15+6	Smith A 29+6	Shaw G 10+8	Thomson S 20+1	Faulconbridge C 1+5	Den Bieman I —+2	Ferguson D 18+3	Butler L 35	Squires J 19+2	Johnson G 18	Fraser J 2+4	Templeman C 5+7	Britton G 13+8	McCulloch S 19	Petrie S 19+11	Edinho 5+4	Graham D 14+7	Martin C 2+1	MacDonald W —+1	McGroarty C 3+1	Nish C —+2	Dolan J 10	Dair J 9+1	Coyle O 11	Boyle S 1	Match No.
1	2	3^{2}	4	5	6	7	8^{3}	9^{1}	10	11	12	13	14																			1
		6	4	5			12	9	10^{3}				13	8	1	2		3	7^{2}	11^{1}	14											2
		6	4	5^{1}	12			13	9	10	14			8	1	2			7^{2}	11^{3}	3											3
			5	4		7	12	14	9	13	8^{1}				1	2		6		11^{1}	10^{3}	3										4
			5	4		7		13	9	14	11^{2}		8		1	2		6^{1}			10	3^{1}	12									5
			5	4		7	13	8^{1}	9		11	14			1	2		6^{2}			10^{3}	3	12									6
			5	4		7		8^{1}	9	11					1	2		6			10	3	12									7
			5	4		7	12	8^{9}	9	11	14				1	2		6			10^{2}	3^{1}	13									8
			5	4		3		8^{2}	9	12	10	14			1	2		6^{3}			7^{1}	13		11								9
		6	4	13	7	14	8		9^{1}		12				1	2		2^{3}			10^{3}	5	11									10
		6	4	5	7^{3}	14	8	13				9^{2}			12	1		2^{1}			10	3	11									11
		6	4	5	13	7		9		8			14		1	2		11^{2}	10^{3}	3^{2}	12											12
		6^{1}	4	5	8^{2}	12		9							10	1	2	3	14	13	7	11^{3}										13
		6	4	5	13			9^{1}							10	1	2	3^{2}	14		7	12	8^{1}	11								14
		6	4	5			13	9							10	1	2	3			7	12	8^{1}	11^{2}								15
		6	4	5			12	9							10	1	2	3^{2}			7	13	8	11^{1}								16
	4	5	6	12	8	9									10^{3}	1			3	14		2	13	7^{1}	11^{2}							17
	4	5	6	12	8	9									10^{3}	1		3^{1}		14		2	7	13	11^{2}							18
	4		3	8	9	12									10^{3}	1			13		5	7	6^{2}	11^{1}	14							19
	5	4	6		8	9	11									1	2				10^{1}	3	7	12								20
	4		3		8	9	6								10^{1}	1			11	2	7		12	5								21
	4	5	3		8	9	6								1				10^{1}	2	7	12	11^{2}		13							22
	4	5	6		8	9	10^{3}								1	2	3	14	13			12	11^{2}			7^{1}						23
	4	5	2		8	9	10^{2}								7	1		3	13			11				6^{1}	12					24
	4	5	2		9		7^{2}				6	1			3				12	13	11^{1}						8	10				25
	4	5	2		13		7				6^{1}	1			3					9^{2}	10^{3}	14					8	12	11			26
	4	5		2	13		7					1			3^{2}	14		9^{1}	10^{3}		12						8	6	11			27
	4	5^{1}	3	12		7				1	2				13	14	10^{2}		9^{3}							8	6	11				28
	4		3^{2}	9	14	7				1	2	12			13				10^{1}		8^{3}						5	6	11			29
	4	5	2	3	12	7				1	14								10		9^{1}						8	6	11			30
12	4	5	2^{1}	3^{2}	12	7				1	14								10		9^{2}				13	8	6	11			31
12	4	5		9	13	7^{2}				1									10^{3}	14	2^{1}					8	6	11			32
2	4	5		9	13	7				1									10^{1}	12						8	6^{2}	11			33
2	4	5	8^{1}	6	9	13	7			1						12			10							3^{2}	11					34
2	5	4	6		9^{1}	10	7				3				14	8^{1}	13		12								11^{2}					35
2^{1}	4	5		9	7					1	12	3			13	14			10		8	11^{3}	6^{2}									36

EAST FIFE   Third Division

Year Formed: 1903. *Ground & Address:* Bayview Stadium, Harbour View, Methil, Fife KY8 3RW. *Telephone:* 01333 426323. *Fax:* 01333 426376.
Ground Capacity: all seated: 2000. *Size of Pitch:* 115yd × 75yd.
Chairman: Julian Danskin. *Secretary:* Kenneth R. MacKay.
Manager: Steve Kirk. *Assistant Managers:* Dave Clarke, Dave Gorman. *Stadium Controller:* Jai Paragreen. *Physio:* John Cooper.
Managers since 1975: Frank Christie; Roy Barry; David Clarke; Gavin Murray, Alex Totten, Steve Archibald, James Bone. *Club Nickname(s):* The Fifers. *Previous Ground:* Bayview Park.
Record Attendance: 22,515 v Raith Rovers, Division I; 2 Jan, 1950.
Record Transfer Fee received: £150,000 for Paul Hunter from Hull C (March 1990).
Record Transfer Fee paid: £70,000 for John Sludden from Kilmarnock (July 1991).
Record Victory: 13-2 v Edinburgh City, Division II; 11 Dec, 1937.
Record Defeat: 0-9 v Hearts, Division I; 5 Oct, 1957.
Most Capped Player: George Aitken, 5 (8), Scotland.
Most League Appearances: 517: David Clarke, 1968-86.
Most League Goals in Season (Individual): 41: Jock Wood, Division II; 1926-27 and Henry Morris, Division II; 1947-48.
Most Goals Overall (Individual): 225: Phil Weir (215 in League).

EAST FIFE 1998–99 LEAGUE RECORD

Match No.	Date	Venue	Opponents	Result	H/T Score	Lg. Pos.	Goalscorers	Atten- dance
1	Aug 4	A	Arbroath	W 2-0	0-0	—	Brown [57], Allan [73]	807
2	15	H	Alloa Ath	D 2-2	2-1	3	Moffat [28], Allan [45]	737
3	22	A	Clyde	D 0-0	0-0	3		806
4	29	H	Inverness CT	L 1-5	0-2	6	Gartshore [75]	814
5	Sept 5	A	Livingston	L 1-3	1-2	8	Moffat [21]	3002
6	12	A	Forfar Ath	W 2-1	1-1	6	Brown [2], Kirk [64]	451
7	19	H	Partick Th	L 1-3	1-1	6	Cusick [13]	1314
8	27	H	Queen of the S	W 2-0	0-0	6	Kirk [69], Moffat [73]	803
9	Oct 3	A	Stirling A	L 2-3	1-1	7	Moffat [41], Kirk [88]	748
10	10	A	Alloa Ath	L 1-5	0-2	7	Kirk [66]	526
11	17	H	Arbroath	L 0-3	0-0	9		719
12	24	A	Inverness CT	L 2-4	2-2	9	Dyer [11], Moffat [31]	1547
13	31	H	Livingston	L 2-3	1-1	9	Brown [12], McManus (og) [61]	1008
14	Nov 7	A	Partick Th	W 1-0	1-0	8	Dair [19]	1870
15	14	H	Forfar Ath	W 1-0	0-0	7	Moffat [84]	1462
16	21	A	Queen of the S	D 0-0	0-0	8		937
17	28	H	Stirling A	L 2-3	1-2	8	Martin [31], Gibb [58]	1003
18	Dec 12	H	Clyde	D 0-0	0-0	8		804
19	19	A	Arbroath	L 1-2	1-0	8	Martin [44]	701
20	27	H	Inverness CT	W 3-2	1-0	8	Allan [45], Dair [75], Martin [88]	1101
21	Jan 17	H	Queen of the S	L 0-1	0-0	8		797
22	20	A	Livingston	L 0-1	0-1	—		1554
23	30	A	Stirling A	W 1-0	1-0	8	Dair [37]	806
24	Feb 6	A	Partick Th	W 1-0	1-0	7	Moffat [38]	1241
25	16	A	Forfar Ath	W 4-2	4-1	—	Dair [17], Moffat 3 [26, 40, 43]	420
26	20	A	Clyde	L 0-1	0-0	7		768
27	27	H	Alloa Ath	L 0-4	0-4	7		768
28	Mar 6	H	Livingston	D 1-1	1-0	8	Dair [34]	995
29	13	A	Inverness CT	L 0-4	0-1	9		1797
30	20	H	Stirling A	W 1-0	1-0	8	Moffat [12]	641
31	Apr 3	A	Queen of the S	L 0-2	0-2	9		1411
32	10	A	Partick Th	D 2-2	0-1	9	Kirk [72], Robertson [86]	1811
33	17	H	Forfar Ath	W 2-1	1-0	9	Ramsay [24], Moffat [86]	605
34	24	H	Arbroath	L 1-2	1-0	9	Moffat [3]	837
35	May 1	A	Alloa Ath	L 1-3	0-0	9	Lawrie [87]	806
36	8	H	Clyde	W 2-1	2-0	9	Honeyman 2 [2, 45]	845

Final League Position: 9   1997–98 DIV 2 6

Honours
League Champions: Division II 1947-48; *Runners-up:* Division II 1929-30, 1970-71. Second Division 1983-84, 1995-96.
Scottish Cup Winners: 1938; *Runners-up:* 1927, 1950.
League Cup Winners: 1947-48, 1949-50, 1953-54.

Club colours: Shirt: Amber and black diamonds. Shorts: Black with two amber stripes. Stockings: Amber with 3 black stripes on top.

Goalscorers: *League (42):* Moffat 13, Dair 5, Kirk 5, Allan 3, Brown 3, Martin 3, Honeyman 2, Cusick 1, Dyer 1, Gartshore 1, Gibb 1, Lawrie 1, Ramsay 1, Robertson 1, own goal 1. *Scottish Cup (2):* Coyle 1, Moffat 1. *League Cup (3):* Coyle 1, Cusick 1, Kirk 1.

McCulloch W 34	Strathdee J 7+4	Gibb R 28+3	Cusick J 32	Johnston G 17	Coyle R 25+1	Munro K 36	Brown G 13+4	Martin J 11+9	Moffat B 35	Allan G 21+2	Kirk S 17+10	Abercromby M 7+3	McNeil J 4+7	Gartshore P 1+5	Fisher D —+3	MacFarlane C —+1	Butter J 2	McPherson G 3+6	Dyer M 4+2	Dixon A 1	Findlay M 1	Skeldon K 18+4	Dair L 13+3	Harrison T 17	Peters S 5+2	Venables R 12+1	Archibald E —+2	Lawrie A 13	Robertson G 7	Ramsay S 7	Honeyman B 2+1	Mooney R 3+2	Match No.
1	2	3	4	5	6	7	8	9	10	11																							1
1		4¹	5	6		7	8	9	10²	11		2	12	13																			2
1	2	3	4	5	6	7	8²	9¹	10	11			13	12																			3
1	2	3²	4	5	6	7	8¹			11	10		9³	12	13	14																	4
1		3	4	5	6	2	8²		10	11	9	13	7¹	12																			5
1		3	4	5	6	2	8¹		10³	11	9²	7	13	12				1	14														6
		3²	4	5	6	2¹	12		10	11	9	8³	13	14				1	7														7
1		3²	4	5	6	2	14		10	11	13	8³	12					9	7²														8
1		3	4	5	6	2	13		10	11³	14	8	7¹					9²	12														9
1		3		5	6	4	2		10	9	8	12						7	11¹														10
1		5		6	2	4¹		10	11	9	8	7²		13				3	12														11
1		3	4		6	7	2²	12	10	11	5		13					9¹				8											12
1		3	4		6	2	9²		10	11	5¹							12	13			8	7										13
1		3	4	5	6	2	9¹	13	10	11								12				8	7²										14
1		3	4²	5	6	2	9¹	14	10	11	13							12				8	7³										15
1	13	3	4	5	6	2	7²	9	10¹	11	12							8															16
1	7³	3	4	5	6	2¹		9	10	11	13							14				8²	12										17
1	2³	3	4	5		7	14	9²	10	11	13											8¹	12	6									18
1	13	3	4			2		9	10	11	8²											12	7¹	6	5								19
1		3	4	5		2		9	10³	11¹²	13							14				7¹	12	6	8								20
1				5	6	2		9	10			13	3¹					4				12			11	8	7²						21
1	3			5	6	2		9²	10			13										12	11¹	4	8	7							22
1	2	3				6		12	10	11	5²											7	9¹		4	8	13						23
1	12	11	6			3			10	8¹	5											7	9	4		2							24
1	11²	2		6	3				10		9¹											7	8	4	13	12	5						25
1	12	11	2		6	3			10													7¹	9	8	4		5						26
1	9¹	2		6	3			13	10	12												7	8²	4	11		5						27
1		2	4	3				10		6								9	11	8		7		5									28
1	13	3			2			10	12	6								9	11²	8		7¹		5	4								29
1	4				2			10²	6									7¹	11	8				5	9	3	12	13					30
1	13	2			3			10²	6									8¹		4	12			5	7	11							31
1	14	2			3			13	10	12								11¹				4³	6	5	7	9	8²						32
1	11	2	6¹	3²				13	10	12									14			7	5	9	4	8²							33
1	3	6			2			12	10	9¹								8		7	5	11	4										34
1	3	6	14	2				9²	10¹	13								4	7	5	8³	11	12										35
1	3			6	2			12	10¹									4	7	5	8	11	9										36

EAST STIRLINGSHIRE Third Division

Year Formed: 1880. *Ground & Address:* Firs Park, Firs St, Falkirk FK2 7AY. *Telephone:* 01324 623583. *Fax:* 01324 637 862
Ground Capacity: total: 1880, seated: 200. *Size of Pitch:* 112yd × 72yd.
Chairman: Leslie G. Thomson. *Vice Chairman:* Tom Kirk. *Secretary:* Margaret Thomson.
Manager: Hugh McCann. *Physio:* Paul Green.
Managers since 1975: I. Ure; D. McLinden; W. P. Lamont; A. Ferguson; W. Little; D. Whiteford; D. Lawson; J. D.
Connell; A. Mackin; Dom Sullivan; Bobby McCulley; Billy Little; John Brownlie. *Club Nickname(s):* The Shire.
Previous Grounds: Burnhouse, Randyford Park, Merchiston Park, New Kilbowie Park.
Record Attendance: 12,000 v Partick T, Scottish Cup 3rd rd; 21 Feb 1921.
Record Transfer Fee received: £35,000 for Jim Docherty to Chelsea (1978).
Record Transfer Fee paid: £6,000 for Colin McKinnon from Falkirk (March 1991).
Record Victory: 11-2 v Vale of Bannock, Scottish Cup 2nd rd; 22 Sept, 1888.
Record Defeat: 1-12 v Dundee United, Division II; 13 Apr, 1936.
Most Capped Player: Humphrey Jones, 5 (14), Wales.
Most League Appearances: 379: Gordon Simpson, 1968-80.
Most League Goals in Season (Individual): 36: Malcolm Morrison, Division II; 1938-39.
Most Goals Overall (Individual): —.

EAST STIRLINGSHIRE 1998-99 LEAGUE RECORD

Match No.	Date	Venue	Opponents	Result	H/T Score	Lg. Pos.	Goalscorers	Attendance
1	Aug 4	A	Ross Co	L 0-1	0-0	—		1021
2	15	H	Brechin C	D 1-1	0-1	—	McNeill [72]	263
3	22	A	Cowdenbeath	L 1-2	1-1	8	McNeill [4]	220
4	29	A	Stenhousemuir	L 0-1	0-1	9		357
5	Sept 5	H	Dumbarton	L 1-2	1-1	9	McNeill [42]	217
6	12	H	Albion R	L 0-1	0-0	9		237
7	19	A	Berwick R	W 2-1	1-0	9	McNeill [7], Smith [83]	328
8	26	A	Queen's Park	W 4-0	3-0	8	McGoldrick 2 [17, 44], McNeill [29], Ward [65]	526
9	Oct 3	H	Montrose	W 3-1	1-1	7	McNeill [27], Patterson [61], Muirhead [81]	243
10	10	A	Brechin C	D 0-0	0-0	7		364
11	17	H	Cowdenbeath	D 1-1	0-0	7	McNeill [48]	230
12	26	H	Stenhousemuir	D 1-1	0-0	—	Barr [62]	387
13	31	A	Dumbarton	D 2-2	0-1	6	Muirhead [51], Wilkinson (og) [85]	309
14	Nov 7	H	Berwick R	D 0-0	0-0	7		277
15	14	A	Albion R	L 1-3	1-2	8	Barr [41]	304
16	21	H	Queen's Park	D 1-1	1-0	8	Patterson [32]	247
17	28	A	Montrose	L 0-2	0-1	8		271
18	Dec 12	H	Ross Co	D 2-2	1-0	8	Kennedy [12], Walker [51]	338
19	19	A	Cowdenbeath	L 2-3	0-1	9	Walker [54], Humphreys (og) [85]	108
20	26	A	Stenhousemuir	D 2-2	0-2	8	Walker [60], Barr [79]	979
21	Jan 16	H	Queen's Park	D 1-1	1-1	8	Smith [44]	224
22	26	H	Dumbarton	L 1-2	0-0	—	Muirhead [85]	204
23	30	H	Montrose	W 2-1	1-1	8	Ward [8], Laidlaw [89]	209
24	Feb 6	A	Berwick R	W 2-1	1-1	8	Laidlaw [22], Hardie [59]	351
25	13	H	Albion R	W 4-1	2-0	—	Ward [7], Muirhead [25], Laidlaw [70], Hardie [76]	244
26	27	H	Brechin C	W 4-1	1-1	7	Laidlaw [21], Ward [52], Smith [67], Kennedy [83]	219
27	Mar 2	A	Ross Co	L 2-4	1-3	—	Muirhead (pen) [36], McNeill [59]	1021
28	6	A	Dumbarton	W 2-0	2-0	7	Patterson [27], Muirhead (pen) [28]	246
29	13	H	Stenhousemuir	D 1-1	0-1	7	Kennedy [85]	391
30	20	A	Montrose	L 0-1	0-0	7		249
31	Apr 3	A	Queen's Park	L 1-2	1-2	8	Ward [45]	455
32	10	H	Berwick R	D 3-3	2-2	8	Laidlaw [6], Patterson [25], Walker [85]	252
33	17	A	Albion R	W 2-0	1-0	8	Hardie [18], Laidlaw [80]	304
34	24	H	Cowdenbeath	D 0-0	0-0	7		208
35	May 1	A	Brechin C	L 0-1	0-0	8		344
36	8	H	Ross Co	L 1-2	0-2	8	Patterson [57]	356

Final League Position: 8   1997-98 4

Honours
League Champions: Division II 1931-32; C Division 1947-48. *Runners-up:* Division II 1962-63. Second Division 1979-80. Division Three 1923-24.
Scottish Cup: —.
League Cup: —.

Club colours: Shirt: Black and white stripes. Shorts: Black and white. Stockings: Black with 3 tangerine bands on top.

Goalscorers: *League (50):* McNeill 8, Laidlaw 6, Muirhead 6, Patterson 5, Ward 5, Walker 4, Barr 3, Hardie 3, Kennedy 3, Smith 3, McGoldrick 2, own goals 2. *Scottish Cup (2):* Walker 2. *League Cup (0).*

McDougall G 13	Barr A 23+3	Millar D 1	Ross B 32	Smith J 28	Walker S 25	Ferguson B 16+2	Muirhead D 34	McNeill W 22+6	Patterson P 36	McGoldrick K 19+1	Sime A —+5	McBeth P —+3	Brown M 21+6	Hardie M 20+3	Hoxley P 1+2	Starrar A 21+8	Ward H 26+5	Hunter S —+4	Russell G 13+1	Kennedy K 7+11	Bruce G 4	Thompson B 19	Laidlaw S 14	Scott A —+4	Lepper N 1+1	Abdulraham K —+1	Match No.
1	2	3	4	5	6	7	8^2	9^1	10	11	12	13															1
1			4	5	6	2	8	9	10^1	11		12	3^2	7	13	12											2
1			4	5	6	2^1	8	9	10	11^2	13		3	7		12											3
1	7		4	5	6	2	8	9	10	11			3^1			12											4
1	11		4	5	6^2	2	8	9	10	3^1				7		12	13										5
		2	5	4^2	7^1	6		9	11		12		3		14	8	10^3	13									6
1	8^2		4	5			6	9	7	11	12		3			2	10^1	13									7
1	8^2		4	5			6	9	7	11	12		3			2	10^1	13									8
1	8		4	5			6	9	7	11			3			2	10										9
1	8		4	5		2	6	9	7	11			3				10										10
1	8^1		4	5		2	6	9	7	11			3	12			10^2		13								11
1	8^1		4	5		2	6	9	7	11	14		3^2	12		13	10^3										12
1^2	14		4	5		2^1	6	9^3	7	11			3	8		12	10			13							13
	8		4	5			6	9	7	11^1			3			2	10			12			1				14
	8		4	5			6	9	7^1	11			3			2	10			12			1				15
	8^1		4	5			6	9^2	7	11			3	12			10			13			1				16
			4	5	12		6	9	7	11			3	8		2^1	10^2			13			1				17
10^1			4	5	8		6		7	11			3			2	13	12		9^2				1			18
10			4	5	8		6	12	7	11			3			2^1	13			9^2				1			19
2			4	5	3		6	9^1	7^2	13			11^1	8		12	10			14				1			20
			4	5	6			11	10^1	7			3	8		2	12			9				1			21
			4	5	6		8		10				3	11		2	12			7				1	9^1		22
	4^1		5	6	2		8	13	7^2				11				10		3	12				1	9		23
	4^1		5	6	2		8		7				11				10		3					1	9		24
12			5	4	2	6			7^2				14	11		13	10		3^3	12				1	9		25
8^1			5	4		6	12		7				11			2	10^1		3	13				1	9		26
8			5	4	12		6	13	7^3				11			2^1	10^2		3	14				1	9		27
12			5^1	4	2		6	13	7				11				10^2		3	8				1	9		28
2	5			4			6		7				11			12	10^1		3	8				1	9		29
7	5			4				11					12	6		2	10		3	8^1				1	9		30
8	5^1			4			13	7					3^3	6	11^2	2	10							1	9	14	31
	5			4		6	8^1	7					11			2	10	3					1	9		32
	4		5			6	8^1	7					12	11		2	10^3		3				1	9		33
	4		5			6	8^1	7					13	11		2	10^3		3	12^2			1	9	14	34
8	5		4^3	2^2	6	9	11^1						14			7	10		3			1		12	13	35
11	4^1			6	2	8	10						12			7^2			3		1	9	13	5		36

FALKIRK

First Division

Year Formed: 1876. *Ground & Address:* Brockville Park, Hope St, Falkirk FK1 5AX. *Telephone:* 01324 624121. *Fax:* 01324 612418.
Ground Capacity: total: 9706, seated: 2661. *Size of Pitch:* 110yd × 72yd.
Chairman: Martin Ritchie. *Secretary:* Alex Blackwood. *General Manager:* Crawford Baptie.
Manager: Alex Totten. *Assistant Manager:* Kevin McAllister. *Physio:* A. McQueen.
Managers since 1975: J. Prentice; G. Miller; W. Little; J. Hagart; A. Totten; G. Abel; W. Lamont; D. Clarke; J. Duffy; W. Lamont; J. Jefferies; J. Lambie E. Bannon; A. Totten. *Club Nickname(s):* The Bairns. *Previous Grounds:* Randyford 1876–81; Blinkbonny Grounds 1881–83; Brockville Park 1883 to present.
Record Attendance: 23,100 v Celtic, Scottish Cup 3rd rd; 21 Feb, 1953.
Record Transfer Fee received: £380,000 for John Hughes to Celtic (Aug 1995).
Record Transfer Fee paid: £225,000 to Chelsea for Kevin McAllister (Aug 1991).
Record Victory: 12-1 v Laurieston, Scottish Cup 2nd rd; 23 Sept, 1893.
Record Defeat: 1-11 v Airdrieonians, Division I; 28 Apr, 1951.
Most Capped Player: Alex Parker, 14 (15), Scotland.
Most League Appearances: (post-war): 353, George Watson, 1975–87.
Most League Goals in Season (Individual): 43: Evelyn Morrison, Division I; 1928-29.
Most Goals Overall (Individual): Dougie Moran, 86, 1957–61 and 1964–67.

FALKIRK 1998–99 LEAGUE RECORD

Match No.	Date	Venue	Opponents	Result	H/T Score	Lg. Pos.	Goalscorers	Attendance
1	Aug 4	H	Ayr U	W 1-0	1-0	—	Crabbe [17]	3127
2	15	A	Clydebank	W 1-0	1-0	2	Keith [35]	928
3	22	H	Hibernian	D 1-1	1-0	2	Keith [21]	5748
4	29	H	Stranraer	W 1-0	0-0	1	Keith [60]	2741
5	Sept 5	A	St Mirren	W 2-0	0-0	1	McKenzie [72], Keith [73]	2390
6	12	H	Raith R	D 1-1	1-1	1	Duffield [35]	3072
7	19	H	Airdrieonians	L 0-1	0-1	1		4157
8	26	H	Greenock Morton	W 2-1	2-0	1	Crabbe (pen) [26], Keith [40]	3047
9	Oct 3	A	Hamilton A	L 1-2	0-2	1	Henry [57]	878
10	11	H	Clydebank	D 2-2	1-1	2	Hutchison [48], Corrigan [67]	4316
11	17	A	Ayr U	L 2-4	2-2	5	Keith [28], McAllister [31]	2731
12	28	A	Stranraer	W 2-1	1-0	—	Keith [12], Crabbe [85]	502
13	31	H	St Mirren	D 1-1	1-0	4	Hutchison [38]	3848
14	Nov 7	A	Airdrieonians	W 3-0	0-0	4	Keith 2 [66, 79], Duffield [82]	3570
15	14	H	Raith R	D 1-1	1-1	4	Keith [20]	3611
16	21	A	Greenock Morton	W 3-0	1-0	3	Henry [43], Hamilton [76], Duffield [90]	1843
17	28	H	Hamilton A	W 2-1	0-0	3	Henry [59], Hutchison [85]	3325
18	Dec 5	A	Ayr U	W 3-0	1-0	2	Hamilton [15], Henry [60], Hutchison [67]	4010
19	12	A	Hibernian	L 1-2	0-1	2	Crabbe (pen) [79]	12,572
20	19	A	St Mirren	W 3-0	2-0	2	Crabbe [28], Henry [34], McAllister [65]	2137
21	26	H	Stranraer	W 3-2	1-1	2	Hutchison [32], Keith 2 [55, 80]	3260
22	Jan 2	A	Airdrieonians	D 1-1	1-0	2	Moss [35]	4518
23	9	A	Raith R	L 1-2	1-0	2	Crabbe [1]	3390
24	16	H	Greenock Morton	L 1-2	0-0	2	Keith [85]	2824
25	30	A	Hamilton A	W 2-0	1-0	2	Moss [34], Keith [77]	1106
26	Feb 20	H	Hibernian	L 1-2	0-1	3	Keith [52]	6086
27	27	A	Stranraer	W 1-0	1-0	2	Keith [3]	709
28	Mar 10	A	Clydebank	W 2-1	1-1	—	Hutchison [44], Moss [56]	289
29	13	H	St Mirren	W 1-0	0-0	2	Corrigan [75]	3237
30	20	H	Hamilton A	W 6-1	2-1	2	Crabbe (pen) [3], McAllister 2 [45, 50], Moss 2 [47, 77], McStay [75]	2206
31	Apr 3	A	Greenock Morton	L 2-3	1-1	2	McCart [42], Crabbe [71]	1914
32	10	A	Airdrieonians	W 2-1	2-1	2	Keith [12], Corrigan [26]	1957
33	17	H	Raith R	W 1-0	0-0	2	Crabbe (pen) [59]	2532
34	24	A	Ayr U	W 2-1	0-1	2	McAllister 2 [68, 79]	2496
35	May 1	H	Clydebank	L 0-2	0-1	2		2737
36	8	A	Hibernian	L 1-2	0-1	2	Crabbe [72]	14,801

Final League Position: 2   1997–98 2

Honours
League Champions: Division II 1935-36, 1969-70, 1974-75. First Division 1990-91, 1993-94. Second Division 1979-80; *Runners-up:* Division I 1907-08, 1909-10. First Division 1985-86, 1988-89. Division II 1904-05, 1951-52, 1960-61. *Scottish Cup Winners:* 1913, 1957; *Runners-up:* 1997. *League Cup Runners-up:* 1947-48. *B&Q Cup Winners:* 1993-94. *League Challenge Cup Winners:* 1997-98.

Club colours: Shirt: Navy blue. Shorts: White. Stockings: Navy blue.

Goalscorers: *League (60):* Keith 17, Crabbe 10 (4 pens), Hutchison 6, McAllister 6, Henry 5, Moss 5, Corrigan 3, Duffield 3, Hamilton 2, McCart 1, McKenzie 1, McStay 1. *Scottish Cup (6):* Moss 3, Crabbe 1 (pen), McAllister 1, own goal 1. *League Cup (5):* McKee 2, Crabbe 1, Keith 1, Oliver 1.

Mathers P 31	Corrigan M 21+3	McQuilken J 21+1	Oliver N 7+1	McCart C 12+2	Hagen D 9+3	McAllister K 35	Hamilton B 12+4	Crabbe S 36	Keith M 27+2	McKee C 2+2	James K 11+2	McKenzie S 33+2	Seaton A 16+8	Hutchison G 24+9	Duffield P 10+7	O'Hara G 2	Henry J 11+1	McStay G 4+6	Sinclair D 23	Den Bieman I 24	Moss D 16+1	Morrison S —+1	Hogarth M 5	Rennie S 3	Kerr M 1+1	Match No.
1	2	3	4	5	6	7	8	9	10	11																1
1	2	3	4		6	7	8	9	10²	11¹	5	12	13													2
1	2	3	4	5	6³	7	12	9	10			13	8¹	14	11²											3
1	2	3	4	5		7	13	9	8			12	6²	11¹	10											4
1	2	3	4	5		7	10	9	8²			6	13	12	11¹											5
1	2	3		5	11²	7		9	8			6	12	13	10	4¹										6
1	2	3	4	5	11	7	13	9	8				6²	12	10¹											7
1	2			5	11	7	13	9	8	4	3	10¹	12				6²									8
1	2			5	11	7	4¹	9	8	12	3	13	10²				6									9
1	2			5	11	7	9¹		8	3	10	12	4²				6	13								10
1		4			11	7		9	10	2	3	6	8					5								11
1						7	6	9	10	2	3	11	8¹					12	4	5						12
1						7	6	9	10	2	3	11						8	4	5						13
1			12			7	6	9¹	10	2	3	11¹	13					8	4	5						14
1			12			7	6¹	9	10	2	3	11²	13					8	4	5						15
1	12						6	9	10¹	2	3	7	11					8	4	5						16
1						7	6	9		12	2	3¹	11	10				8	4	5						17
1	3					7	6	9		2		11	10¹					8	4	5	12					18
1	3					7	6¹	9	12	2		11²	13					8	4	5	10					19
1	2	12	6			7		9			8	3					11		4	5	10¹					20
1	11²					7		9	8	5¹	2	3	12	13					4	6	10					21
1						7		9	8	5	2	3	11¹	12					4	6	10					22
1	2	12				7		9		5	8	3	11						4	6	10¹					23
1	12	6¹				7		9	8	5	2	3	11²						4		10	13				24
1	12	3				7		9	8	5	2		11						4¹	6	10					25
1	2¹					7		9	8	5	10	3	11				12		4	6						26
1	2	3	13			7		9	8¹	5²	10		11				12		4	6						27
1	2	3				7		9	8¹	5		11	13	12					4	6	10²					28
1	2	3	14			7		9	12	5	4	13	11¹				8²			6	10³					29
1	2	3²				7		9¹	8	5	11¹	13	14				12		4	6	10					30
1	2	3	5			7		9	8		4	11¹	12							6	10					31
	2	3				7		9	8		4	11¹	12							6	10		1	5		32
	2	3				7		9²	8		4	13	12	11¹					5	6	10		1			33
	2	3				7		9	8¹		4		12	11					5	6	10		1			34
		3				7		9	12		4		11						5	6	10	1		2¹	8	35
		3				7		9			4		11²	8¹					5	6	10	1		2	13	36

FORFAR ATHLETIC   Third Division

Year Formed: 1885. *Ground & Address:* Station Park, Carseview Road, Forfar. *Telephone:* 01307 463576/462259. *Fax:* 01307 466956.
Ground Capacity: total: 8732, seated: 739. *Size of Pitch:* 115yd × 69yd.
Chairman and Secretary: David McGregor.
Manager: Ian McPhee. *Assistant Manager:* Billy Bennett. *Physio:* Jim Peacock. *Coaches:* Jim Moffat, Malcolm Lowe.
Managers since 1975: Jerry Kerr; Archie Knox; Alex Rae; Doug Houston; Henry Hall; Bobby Glennie; Paul Hegarty; Tommy Campbell. *Club Nickname(s):* Loons. *Previous Grounds:* None.
Record Attendance: 10,780 v Rangers, Scottish Cup 2nd rd; 2 Feb, 1970.
Record Transfer Fee received: £65,000 for David Bingham to Dunfermline Ath (September 1995).
Record Transfer Fee paid: £50,000 for Ian McPhee from Airdrieonians (1991).
Record Victory: 14-1 v Lindertis, Scottish Cup 1st rd; 1 Sept 1988.
Record Defeat: 2-12 v King's Park, Division II; 2 Jan, 1930.
Most Capped Player: —.
Most League Appearances: 484: Ian McPhee, 1978–88 and 1991–98.

FORFAR ATHLETIC 1998–99 LEAGUE RECORD

Match No.	Date	Venue	Opponents	Result	H/T Score	Lg. Pos.	Goalscorers	Atten- dance
1	Aug 4	A	Alloa Ath	W 2-1	2-0	—	Honeyman 2 [39, 44]	495
2	15	H	Partick Th	L 0-1	0-1	4		1053
3	22	A	Livingston	D 1-1	0-1	5	Brand [88]	1193
4	29	A	Arbroath	L 1-2	1-1	7	Mann (pen) [30]	905
5	Sept 5	H	Clyde	D 2-2	0-0	7	Mann (pen) [80], Brand [89]	494
6	12	H	East Fife	L 1-2	1-1	8	Gibson [25]	451
7	19	A	Queen of the S	L 0-3	0-0	9		916
8	26	H	Stirling A	L 1-2	1-0	9	Honeyman [39]	427
9	Oct 3	A	Inverness CT	D 2-2	1-1	9	Honeyman [31], Brand [81]	1925
10	11	A	Partick Th	L 0-2	0-1	10		2870
11	17	H	Alloa Ath	L 1-2	0-1	10	Honeyman [84]	401
12	26	H	Arbroath	L 1-3	0-0	—	Brand [84]	800
13	31	A	Clyde	L 1-3	0-0	10	McLean [70]	918
14	Nov 7	H	Queen of the S	W 1-0	0-0	10	Nairn [65]	389
15	14	A	East Fife	L 0-1	0-0	10		1462
16	21	A	Stirling A	L 1-3	0-1	10	Brand [47]	731
17	28	H	Inverness CT	D 2-2	0-1	10	Cargill 2 [56, 89]	511
18	Dec 12	H	Livingston	L 1-2	0-0	10	Craig [47]	502
19	19	A	Alloa Ath	L 1-3	0-2	10	McLean [73]	466
20	Jan 16	H	Stirling A	D 3-3	1-1	10	McLauchlan 2 [21, 51], Rattray [83]	445
21	19	A	Arbroath	D 2-2	2-0	—	McLauchlan [15], McLean [35]	767
22	30	A	Inverness CT	L 0-2	0-1	10		2018
23	Feb 2	H	Clyde	W 3-1	1-1	—	Rattray [5], McIllravey [47], Brand [72]	419
24	6	A	Queen of the S	W 3-0	2-0	10	Cargill 2 [32, 79], McIllravey [38]	968
25	16	H	East Fife	L 2-4	1-4	—	Tully [40], McLauchlan [86]	420
26	20	A	Livingston	L 0-5	0-4	10		1534
27	27	H	Partick Th	W 2-1	1-1	10	Honeyman [9], Brand [61]	662
28	Mar 6	A	Clyde	L 0-1	0-1	10		815
29	13	H	Arbroath	W 5-2	4-2	10	Brand 2 [1, 31], Cargill [9], McLauchlan [40], McCheyne [89]	864
30	20	H	Inverness CT	L 0-3	0-1	10		504
31	Apr 3	A	Stirling A	D 2-2	2-0	10	McCheyne [9], Brand [19]	820
32	10	H	Queen of the S	W 2-1	1-0	10	Nairn [5], McLean [68]	416
33	17	A	East Fife	L 1-2	0-1	10	McLean [56]	605
34	24	H	Alloa Ath	W 3-1	1-0	10	McLean [17], Cargill 2 [85, 89]	440
35	May 1	A	Partick Th	L 0-1	0-0	10		2539
36	8	H	Livingston	L 1-2	0-1	10	McLauchlan (pen) [84]	1395

Final League Position: 10   1997–98 DIV 2 7

Most League Goals in Season (Individual): 45: Dave Kilgour, Division II; 1929–30.
Most Goals Overall (Individual): 124, John Clark.

Honours
League Champions: Second Division 1983–84. Third Division 1994–95; *Runners-up:* 1996–97. C Division 1948–49.
Scottish Cup: Semi-finals 1982.
League Cup: Semi-finals 1977–78.

Club colours: Shirt: Sky blue with navy chest panel. Shorts: Navy. Stockings: Sky blue.

Goalscorers: *League (48):* Brand 10, Cargill 7, Honeyman 6, McLauchlan 6 (1 pen), McLean 6, McCheyne 2, McIllravey 2, Mann 2 (2 pens), Nairn 2, Rattray 2, Craig 1, Gibson 1, Tully 1. *Scottish Cup (3):* Brand 2, Craig 1. *League Cup (0).*

Robertson D 25	McCheyne G 27 + 1	Ferguson G 19	Hamilton J 5	Mann R 18	Raynes S 27 + 5	Gibson A 8 + 1	Gillies K 17 + 4	Brand R 24 + 10	Honeyman B 17 + 6	Cargill A 30 + 3	McLauchlan M 24 + 9	Allison J 19 + 8	Gray A — + 2	Watson G 19	Moffat J 11	Sharp R 9	Bowes M — + 1	Nairn J 22 + 1	McLean B 12 + 8	Craig D 26 + 2	Rattray A 20	McIllravey P 6 + 3	Tully C 6	Christie S 1 + 3	Johnston G 4 + 2	Glennie S — + 1	Match No.
1	2	3	4	5	6	7	8	9[1]	10[3]	11[2]	12	13	14														1
1	2	3	4	5	11		8	9[1]	10	7	12			6													2
1	2	6	4[2]	5	11		7	12	13	10	8[1]	9[3]	14	3													3
1	2	6	4	5	11		8	7	12	10[2]	13	9[1]		3													4
	2	6	4	5	11[3]		9	8	14	10[2]	7[1]	13	12	1	3												5
1	2	6		5	12	10	8	9		7	11[1]			4	3												6
1	2	6		5	9	10	8	12		7[3]	11[1]			4[2]	3	13	14										7
1		6		5	11[3]	8	7	9[2]	10	13	12	2		3		4[1]	14										8
1		6[2]		5	11[1]		7	9	10	12		8		2	3		4	13									9
1	13			5	11		7	9	10[3]	14	12	8[2]		2	3		4[1]	6									10
1	2			5	11		7[1]	9	10	8				3		4	12	6									11
1	2			5	11	12	7[1]	9	10	8	13			3		4[2]	6										12
1					11[2]		7	9	10[1]	8	12			2	3		4	13	6	5							13
1	2			5	11		7[1]	9		8	10	12					4			3	6						14
1				5	11			9[1]	12	8	10	2[2]		7			4	13	3	6							15
1	2			5	11			9		8	10			7			4		3	6							16
1	6			5	11			9	10[1]	8	7	4		2				12	3								17
1	2	6		5	11			9		10	7[1]	8		4			12	3[2]	13								18
1	2	6[2]		5	11[1]		14	9[1]		10	7	8		3			4	12	13								19
							13	9[1]	10	11	7	2[2]		4	1		8	12	3	6	5						20
1							12	13	10	11	7[2]	2		4	8		9[1]	3	6	5							21
1	2				11[2]		8	13	12	10	7			4			9[1]	3	6	5							22
1					11		8[3]	12	13	10	7[2]	2		6				3	4	9[1]	5	14					23
1					11		8	12		10	7	2[2]		6				3	4	9[1]	5	13					24
1	6[2]	4			11		8	12	13	10	7	2						9[1]	5								25
1	2	5[1]			11		8[2]	13	12	10	9	7		6			3	4									26
1	2	5					9[1]	11	10	7		6		8			3	4	12								27
	2	5			12		9	11	10	7	13				1		6	8[2]	3	4[1]							28
	2	5			12		9	11[2]	10	7	13				1		6	8[1]	3	4							29
	2	5			11		9		10	7	12				1		6[1]	8[2]	3	4	13						30
	2	5			11		9[1]		10	8	6				1		6	7	3	4		12					31
	2				11		9		10		8				1		6	7	3	4			5				32
	2	5[1]			6[3]		9		10	13	14				1		8	7	3	4		11[2]	12				33
	2							10	11[1]	8					1		6	7	3	4	9	12	5				34
	2				12		13		10	11	8				1		6	7	3	4[1]	9[2]		5				35
	2				13		11		10	12	8				1		6[3]	7	3	4[2]	9[1]		5	14			36

HAMILTON ACADEMICAL   Second Division

Year Formed: 1874. *Ground:* Firhill Stadium, 80 Firhill Road, Glasgow G20 7AL. *Telephone (match days only):* 0141 579 1971. *(Weekdays):* 01698 286103. *Club Address:* Enable Building, Prospect House, New Park St, Hamilton ML3 0BN. *Telephone:* 01698 286103.
Ground Capacity: total: 14,538, seated: 8397. *Size of Pitch:* 110yd × 75yd.
Secretary: Scott A. Struthers BA. *Commercial Manager:* Gary Clark
Manager: Colin Miller. *Physio:* Jim Fallon.
Managers since 1975: J. Eric Smith; Dave McParland; John Blackley; Bertie Auld; John Lambie; Jim Dempsey; John Lambie; Billy McLaren; Iain Munro; Sandy Clark. *Club Nickname(s):* The Accies. *Previous Grounds:* Bent Farm, South Avenue, South Haugh.
Record Attendance: 28,690 v Hearts, Scottish Cup 3rd rd; 3 Mar, 1937.
Record Transfer Fee received: £380,000 for Paul Hartley to Millwall (July 1996).
Record Transfer Fee paid: £60,000 for Paul Martin from Kilmarnock (Oct 1988) and for John McQuade from Dumbarton (Aug 1993).
Record Victory: 11-1 v Chryston, Lanarkshire Cup; 28 Nov, 1885.
Record Defeat: 1-11 v Hibernian, Division I; 6 Nov, 1965.
Most Capped Player: Colin Miller, 29, Canada, 1988-94.
Most League Appearances: 452: Rikki Ferguson, 1974-88.

HAMILTON ACADEMICAL 1998–99 LEAGUE RECORD

Match No.	Date		Venue	Opponents	Result		H/T Score	Lg. Pos.	Goalscorers	Atten- dance
1	Aug	4	A	Raith R	W	2-0	1-0	—	Geraghty [10], Wales [73]	2316
2		15	H	Airdrieonians	D	1-1	1-1	3	Geraghty [32]	1137
3		22	A	Greenock Morton	W	2-1	0-1	1	Wales 2 [63, 78]	1691
4		29	H	St Mirren	D	0-0	0-0	2		1575
5	Sept	5	A	Ayr U	W	3-2	2-1	2	Geraghty 2 [15, 66], Wales [37]	1917
6		12	A	Stranraer	L	1-2	0-1	2	Renicks [47]	666
7		19	H	Clydebank	L	1-2	1-2	4	Cunnington [45]	648
8		26	A	Hibernian	D	0-0	0-0	5		9696
9	Oct	3	H	Falkirk	W	2-1	2-0	3	Geraghty [10], Wales [20]	878
10		6	A	Airdrieonians	L	2-3	0-2	—	Henderson D [56], Wales [90]	1945
11		17	H	Raith R	W	3-2	0-2	4	McCormick 2 [58, 59], Wales [69]	790
12		24	A	St Mirren	L	2-3	2-0	5	Wales 2 (1 pen) [6, 13 (p)]	2312
13		31	H	Ayr U	L	1-3	1-1	7	Wales (pen) [35]	1267
14	Nov	7	A	Clydebank	D	0-0	0-0	7		451
15		14	H	Stranraer	L	1-2	1-1	7	McFarlane D [36]	609
16		21	H	Hibernian	D	2-2	0-1	7	Moore [75], Henderson D [87]	2288
17		28	A	Falkirk	L	1-2	0-0	7	Henderson D [57]	3325
18	Dec	8	A	Raith R	D	1-1	1-0	—	Tait [11]	1929
19		12	H	Greenock Morton	D	0-0	0-0	7		1012
20		19	A	Ayr U	L	0-5	0-2	7		2102
21		26	H	St Mirren	D	0-0	0-0	7		1450
22	Jan	9	A	Stranraer	D	2-2	0-2	7	McCormick [50], Berry [61]	565
23		12	H	Clydebank	L	0-1	0-1	—		651
24		16	A	Hibernian	L	0-4	0-1	8		10,233
25		30	H	Falkirk	L	0-2	0-1	9		1106
26	Feb	6	H	Airdrieonians	L	0-2	0-2	9		814
27		20	A	Greenock Morton	L	0-3	0-0	9		1914
28		27	A	St Mirren	L	0-1	0-0	9		2130
29	Mar	20	A	Falkirk	L	1-6	1-2	9	Wales [7]	2206
30		24	H	Ayr U	L	0-2	0-0	—		769
31	Apr	3	H	Hibernian	L	0-2	0-1	9		4350
32		10	A	Clydebank	D	0-0	0-0	9		262
33		17	H	Stranraer	W	1-0	1-0	9	Thomson [19]	525
34		24	H	Raith R	L	1-2	0-1	9	McCormick [59]	1398
35	May	1	A	Airdrieonians	L	0-1	0-0	9		2257
36		8	H	Greenock Morton	L	0-2	0-1	9		744

Final League Position: 9   1997–98 DIV 1 8

Most League Goals in Season (Individual): 35: David Wilson, Division I; 1936-37.
Most Goals Overall (Individual): 246: David Wilson, 1928-39.

Honours
League Champions: First Division 1985-86, 1987-88; *Runners-up:* Second Division 1996–97. Division II 1903-04; *Runners-up:* Division II 1952-53, 1964-65.
Scottish Cup Runners-up: 1911, 1935. *League Cup:* Semi-finalists three times.
B&Q Cup Winners: 1991-92, 1992-93.

Club colours: Shirt: Red and white hoops. Shorts: White. Stockings: White.

Goalscorers: *League (30):* Wales 11 (2 pens), Geraghty 5, McCormick 4, Henderson D 3, Berry 1, Cunnington 1, McFarlane D 1, Moore 1, Renicks 1, Tait 1, Thomson 1. *Scottish Cup (2):* Clark 1, Wales 1. *League Cup (3):* Geraghty 1, McFarlane D 1, Renicks 1.

Reid C 6	Renicks S 32	Cunnington E 33	Hillcoat C 25	Berry N 14+1	Thomson S 33+1	McAulay I 21+3	Tait T 21+1	Geraghty M 18+5	Wales G 28+2	Henderson N 24+4	Clark G 14+11	MacLaren R 12+3	McFarlane D 5+10	MacFarlane I 15	McKenzie P 13+5	Henderson D 25	Robertson S 6	McCormick S 12+9	Miller C 7+1	Moore M 3+9	Krivokapic M —+1	McGill D 3	Hillcoat J 9	Bonnar M —+1	Davidson W 3+1	Rajamaki M 4+3	Martin M 2+1	Kerr A 1+1	Oliver N 6	Lynn G 1	Muir D —+1	Kelly R —+1	Match No
1^1	2^2	3	4	5	6	7	8	9	10	11^3	12	13	14																				1
	2	3	4	5	6	7	8	9	10^1	11					12	1																	2
	2	3	4	5	6		8	9	10^1	11	7^2			12	1	13																	3
	2	3	4	5^1	6	7	8	9	10	11				12	1																		4
	2	3	4	5	6	7^2	8	9	10^1		13	12	1		11																		5
	2	3		5	6	7	8	9	10^1		4				11	1	12																6
	2	3^1	4		6	7^2	8	9	10	13	5^1				12	11	1	14															7
	2	3	4		6	8^1		9	10^2	12	7				5	11	1	13															8
	2	3	4		6	13		9	10	8^2	7				5	11	1	12															9
	2	3	4		6	13			10	8^2	7	12			5	11	1	9^1															10
		3	4		6	2			10	8	7		9^1		5	11	1	12															11
	2	3^1	4		6	13			10	8	7^2	12	1		5	11		9															12
	2	3			6	7			10	8	4	12	1		5	11		9^1															13
	2	3	4		6	7	5		10	8^2	13	12	1			11		9^1															14
	2		4		6	7^2	5		10	8^1	13	9	1			11	12	3															15
	2		4		6	7	5			8^1	12	10^2	1			11		9^3	3	13	14												16
	2	3	4		6	7	8^2		13	9		10^1	1	5		11		12															17
		3	4^3	14	6	7^1	8	13	10	12		9^2	1	5		11		2															18
7^1	3	4	5	6		8		9		12	13	1				11		2		10													19
	2		4	5	6	8		9		7		1				11	12	3		10^1													20
	2	3	4	5	6	8		9^1	11	7^2	13					12			10	1													21
	2	3	4	5	6	8		9^1	13	11	7^1					12		10^3		1	14												22
	2	3	4	5		8		9	12	11	13			6^2				10^1		1	7												23
	2	3	4	5			7	8		9	11^2	12		6					13	1	10^1												24
	2	3	4	5^2	13		8	9^1		11	7^3			6		10		12		1	14												25
	2	3	4		6	13		9^1	10	11^3	7^2	5			8	14		12		1													26
	2	3	4	5	6			10							8		9^1	7	12	1				11									27
	2	3		5		6	13	9		12	4					11			7	10^2		1		8^1									28
		3			6	4		12	10	13	15	5			8	11		9^1					1^6			7^2	2						29
		3			5	4		13	9	7^3		14		1	6	10		9^1							8^2	11	2^1	12					30
	2	3			6	8^3			9	10		5		1	13	11^2			14						12			7^1	4				31
1	2	3			6	8		9^1	10	7^2		5			11				12							13		4					32
1	2	3			6	8			10	7^1		5			11		9									12		4					33
1	2	3			6	8^1			10	7	12	5			11		9									12		4					34
1	2	3			6	8^2		12	10	7	11^2	5					9^1	14	13									4					35
1	2^2	3			6			9	10	7^3	5				8^1											13		4	11	12	14		36

HEART OF MIDLOTHIAN   Premier League

Year Formed: 1874. *Ground & Address:* Tynecastle Stadium, Gorgie Rd, Edinburgh EH11 2NL. *Telephone:* 0131 200 7200. *Fax:* 0131 346 0699. *Website:* www.heartsfc.co.uk.
Ground Capacity: 18,000. *Size of Pitch:* 108yd × 73yd.
Chairman: Douglas Smith. *Chief Executive:* Christopher Robinson. *Sales and Marketing Manager:* Kenny Wittmann.
Manager: Jim Jefferies. *Assistant Manager:* Billy Brown.
Physio: Alan Rae. *Coach:* Peter Houston.
Managers since 1975: J. Hagart; W. Ormond; R. Moncur; T. Ford; A. MacDonald; A. MacDonald & W. Jardine; A. MacDonald; J. Jordan, S. Clark, T. McLean.
Club Nickname(s): Hearts, Jambo's. *Previous Grounds:* The Meadows 1874, Powderhall 1878, Old Tynecastle 1881, (Tynecastle Park, 1886).
Record Attendance: 53,396 v Rangers, Scottish Cup 3rd rd; 13 Feb, 1932.
Record Transfer Fee received: £2,100,000 for Alan McLaren from Rangers (October 1994).
Record of Transfer paid: £750,000 for Derek Ferguson to Rangers (July 1990).
Record Victory: 21-0 v Anchor, EFA Cup 30th October 1880.
Record Defeat: 1-8 v Vale of Leven, Scottish Cup, 1888.
Most Capped Player: Bobby Walker, 29, Scotland.
Most League Appearances: 515: Gary Mackay, 1980-97.
Most League Goals in Season (Individual): 44: Barney Battles.
Most Goals Overall (Individual): 214: John Robertson, 1983-98.

HEART OF MIDLOTHIAN 1998–99 LEAGUE RECORD

Match No.	Date	Venue	Opponents	Result	H/T Score	Lg. Pos.	Goalscorers	Attendance
1	Aug 2	H	Rangers	W 2-1	2-1	—	Adam [9], Hamilton [11]	15,272
2	16	A	Dundee U	D 0-0	0-0	3		9629
3	22	H	Aberdeen	W 2-0	2-0	1	Fulton [6], Pressley [12]	14,416
4	30	A	Kilmarnock	L 0-3	0-1	3		10,376
5	Sept 12	H	Dundee	L 0-2	0-0	6		13,117
6	20	A	Dunfermline Ath	D 1-1	0-1	6	Hamilton [58]	5963
7	23	H	Motherwell	W 3-0	0-0	—	Weir [70], McCann 2 [87, 89]	12,323
8	26	A	Celtic	D 1-1	0-1	3	Hamilton [52]	59,283
9	Oct 4	H	St Johnstone	D 1-1	0-0	4	Makel [79]	13,121
10	17	H	Rangers	L 0-3	0-0	5		49,749
11	24	H	Dundee U	L 0-1	0-0	6		13,124
12	31	A	Dundee	L 0-1	0-0	7		6142
13	Nov 7	H	Kilmarnock	W 2-1	1-0	5	Adam [7], Fulton [86]	14,363
14	14	A	Motherwell	L 2-3	0-1	6	Hamilton (pen) [69], Guerin [85]	8912
15	21	H	Dunfermline Ath	W 2-1	0-1	5	Flögel [60], McCann [89]	13,268
16	Dec 6	H	Celtic	W 2-1	1-0	5	Adam 2 [37, 50]	17,334
17	9	A	St Johnstone	D 1-1	1-1	—	Hamilton [11]	4808
18	12	A	Aberdeen	L 0-2	0-2	5		11,137
19	19	H	Rangers	L 2-3	1-1	5	Locke [2], Hamilton [69]	17,134
20	26	A	Kilmarnock	L 0-1	0-1	6		10,668
21	30	H	Dundee	L 1-2	1-2	—	Lilley [24]	13,383
22	Jan 2	A	Dunfermline Ath	D 0-0	0-0	6		9227
23	30	H	Motherwell	L 0-2	0-0	6		12,821
24	Feb 6	A	Celtic	L 0-3	0-2	8		59,844
25	20	H	St Johnstone	L 0-2	0-0	9		12,229
26	27	H	Aberdeen	L 0-2	0-0	9		13,957
27	Mar 20	A	Dundee	L 0-2	0-0	10		5500
28	Apr 3	H	Kilmarnock	D 2-2	2-0	10	McSwegan 2 [17, 43]	14,689
29	6	A	Dundee U	W 3-1	2-1	—	McSwegan [23], Adam [44], Cameron [62]	10,648
30	14	H	Celtic	L 2-4	1-3	—	Adam 2 [28, 47]	16,388
31	17	A	St Johnstone	D 0-0	0-0	9		6154
32	24	A	Motherwell	W 4-0	1-0	9	Jackson [22], Adam 2 [47, 58], Cameron [89]	8926
33	May 3	H	Dunfermline Ath	W 2-0	0-0	—	Cameron 2 [63, 83]	15,176
34	9	A	Rangers	D 0-0	0-0	8		49,495
35	15	H	Dundee U	W 4-1	1-0	6	Ritchie [42], McSwegan [51], Adam [68], Cameron [77]	13,187
36	23	A	Aberdeen	W 5-2	1-1	6	McSwegan 3 [2, 47, 49], Cameron [52], Flögel [64]	13,042

Final League Position: 6   1997–98 3

Honours
League Champions: Division I 1894-95, 1896-97, 1957-58, 1959-60. First Division 1979-80; *Runners-up:* Division I 1893-94, 1898-99, 1903-04, 1905-06, 1914-15, 1937-38, 1953-54, 1956-57, 1958-59, 1964-65. Premier Division 1985-86, 1987-88, 1991-92. First Division 1977-78, 1982-83.
Scottish Cup Winners: 1891, 1896, 1901, 1906, 1956, 1998; *Runners-up:* 1903, 1907, 1968, 1976, 1986, 1996.
League Cup Winners: 1954-55, 1958-59, 1959-60, 1962-63; *Runners-up:* 1961-62, 1996-97.

European: *European Cup:* 4 matches (1958-59, 1960-61). *Cup Winners' Cup:* 10 matches (1976-77, 1996-97, 1998-99). *UEFA Cup:* 33 matches (*Fairs Cup:* 1961-62, 1963-64, 1965-66. *UEFA Cup:* 1984-85, 1986-87, 1988-89, 1990-91, 1992-93, 1993-94).

Club colours: Shirt: Maroon. Shorts: White. Stockings: Maroon with white tops.

Goalscorers: *League (44):* Adam 10, McSwegan 7, Cameron 6, Hamilton 6 (1 pen), McCann 3, Flögel 2, Fulton 2, Guerin 1, Jackson 1, Lilley 1, Locke 1, Makel 1, Pressley 1, Ritchie 1, Weir 1. *Scottish Cup (1):* Hamilton 1. *League Cup (5):* Adam 1, Fulton 1, Hamilton 1, Holmes 1, McKinnon 1.

Rousset G 26	Locke G 22+3	Naysmith G 23+3	Weir D 23	Salvatori S 11+1	Ritchie P 29	McCann N 8	Fulton S 27	Adam S 28+1	Hamilton J 20+5	Flögel T 18+2	Murray G 18+3	Pressley S 29+1	McKinnon R 14+2	Quitongo J 5+7	Holmes D 1+5	Makel L 6+8	Murie D —+4	McKenzie R 10	McPherson D 17+1	Guerin V 9+10	McSwegan G 17+4	Carricondo J 1+10	O'Neill K —+3	Jenkinson L 3+2	Lilley D 3+1	Callaghan S 2	Cameron C 10+1	Kirk A —+5	Berthe M 1	Jackson D 9	James K 1+3	Severin S 5+2	Match No.
1	2	3	4	5	6	7	8	9¹	10	11	12																						1
1	2	3	4	5	6	7	8	9	10	11																							2
1	7	3	4	13	6		8	9¹	10²			2	5³	11	12	14																	3
1	3		4		6	7	8	9¹	10¹	11		2	5²	12	14	13																	4
1	5²	3	4		6	7	8	12		13		2		11	9	10¹																	5
1		3	4	5	6	7	8¹	9	10		13	2							11²	12													6
	8¹	3	4	5	6	7		9	10			2						1	11	12	1												7
	8	3	4	5	6	7		9²	10			2						1	11	12	1	13											8
1		3	4	5	6			9	10			2	7¹					11	13		8²	12											9
1		3	4	5	6		8		10	11²		2						12³	13	9	7¹	14											10
1			4	5	6		8		10			2	3	11¹					7	9²	12	13											11
1	7	12	4				8	9²	13	6³	2	3¹	11					5	14	10													12
1	7	3	4				8	9²	12	6	2		14					5	11¹	10²	13												13
1	7³	3	4				8	9²	12	6²	2		13					5	11	10¹	14												14
	3	4		6	7	8	9²	10	11	2								1	5			12											15
1	13	3	4		6		8	9²	10¹	11	2			12				5	7²		14												16
1	7¹	3	4		6		8	9	10³	11	2	13	14					5²		12													17
1	14	3¹	4		6		8	9	10	11	2	12		13				5	7¹														18
1	7³	3	4		6		8	9²	10	11	2¹		3					5		13													19
1	7		4				8	10³	11	6²	2	3	12	14	13			5	9¹														20
1	13		4				8	12	11³		2	3		6				5	9²	14							7¹	10					21
6							8	10	11	4	2	3						1	5	12							7¹	9					22
	3	4	5	6		8		9¹	10	11		2		13	1			8³				14	7²	12									23
	3	4	5	6	8			11		7	2		12		1		13			9¹	10²												24
4	3					8³	9¹	10	11	2		14		1	5	6²	13								7	12							25
	3¹		4	6		8	9¹	10	11	2			1	5	13	12									7²	14							26
1	4	3		6		8	13	11²		2			5	7¹	9		14								12	10³							27
1	4¹			6	8	9		2	3	13		5	10		7²											11	12					28
1			6		8	9		4	2¹	3		5	14	10		7²									11³	12	13					29
1	4²		6		8	9		13	2	3³		5¹	14	10		7									11	12						30
1			6		8	9		4	2	3¹			10		7										11	5²	13					31
1	5		6		9³			4	2	3		12	10²		7	13									11¹		8					32
1	5	12		6		9³		4	2	3¹		13	10²		7	14	11										8					33
1	6	5		3		9¹		4	2			13	10²		7	12	11										8					34
6¹	5		3		9	12	4	2			1	13	10³	14		7		11²									8					35
5			3		9³	8	4	2			1	10²	13	14		7		11¹									6					36

HIBERNIAN   Premier League

Year Formed: 1875. *Ground & Address:* Easter Road Stadium, Albion Rd, Edinburgh EH7 5QG. *Telephone:* 0131 661 2159. *Fax:* 0131 659 6488.
Ground Capacity: total: 16,032. *Size of Pitch:* 112yd × 74yd.
Chairman: Malcolm McPherson. *Secretary:* Mary Anne McAdam. *Commercial Manager:* T. Dickson.
Manager: Alex McLeish. *Assistant Manager:* Andrew Watson.
Physio: Malcolm Colquhoun. *Coach:* D. Park.
Managers since 1975: Eddie Turnbull; Willie Ormond; Bertie Auld; Pat Stanton; John Blackley, Alex Miller, Jim Duffy.
Club Nickname(s): Hibees. *Previous Grounds:* Meadows 1875-78, Powderhall 1878-79, Mayfield 1879-80, First Easter Road 1880-92, Second Easter Road 1892-.
Record Attendance: 65,860 v Hearts, Division I; 2 Jan, 1950.
Record Transfer Fee received: £1,000,000 for Andy Goram to Rangers (June 1991).
Record Transfer Fee paid: £420,000 for Keith Wright from Dundee.
Record Victory: 22-1 v 42nd Highlanders; 3 Sept, 1881.
Record Defeat: 0-10 v Rangers; 24 Dec, 1898.
Most Capped Player: Lawrie Reilly, 38, Scotland.
Most League Appearances: 446: Arthur Duncan.
Most League Goals in Season (Individual): 42: Joe Baker.
Most Goals Overall (Individual): 364: Gordon Smith.

HIBERNIAN 1998–99 LEAGUE RECORD

Match No.	Date	Venue	Opponents	Result	H/T Score	Lg. Pos.	Goalscorers	Atten- dance
1	Aug 4	A	Greenock Morton	W 1-0	0-0	—	Lavety 90	5747
2	15	H	Stranraer	L 1-2	0-0	4	Skinner 85	9489
3	22	A	Falkirk	D 1-1	0-1	6	Dennis 70	5748
4	29	H	Ayr U	W 4-2	2-0	3	Guggi 15, Crawford 2 (1 pen) 17, 70 (p), Lovell 64	9231
5	Sept 5	A	Clydebank	D 2-2	0-0	3	Harper 70, Crawford 89	1828
6	12	A	St Mirren	L 0-2	0-1	4		3638
7	19	H	Raith R	W 3-1	0-0	3	Crawford 2 (1 pen) 68 (p), 89, Guggi 78	8853
8	26	H	Hamilton A	D 0-0	0-0	4		9696
9	Oct 3	A	Airdrieonians	W 3-1	2-0	2	McGinlay 2 26, 50, Paatelainen 33	4301
10	10	A	Stranraer	W 1-0	0-0	1	Lovell 87	1832
11	17	H	Greenock Morton	W 2-1	1-0	1	Prenderville 15, McGinlay 85	9524
12	24	A	Ayr U	D 3-3	1-2	1	Hughes J 2 42, 89, Paatelainen 86	4684
13	31	H	Clydebank	W 2-1	1-0	1	McGinlay 39, Paatelainen 85	10,172
14	Nov 7	A	Raith R	W 3-1	0-0	1	McGinlay 59, Crawford (pen) 62, Paatelainen 77	4925
15	21	A	Hamilton A	D 2-2	1-0	2	Paatelainen 2 33, 60	2288
16	24	H	St Mirren	W 4-1	3-1	—	Lovell 2 28, 34, Prenderville 42, McGinlay 75	9153
17	28	H	Airdrieonians	W 1-0	0-0	1	Lovell 85	9732
18	Dec 5	A	Greenock Morton	W 3-1	1-0	1	Crawford 5, Lovell 96, Rougier 90	3150
19	12	H	Falkirk	W 2-1	1-0	1	Hughes J 6, Crawford 76	12,572
20	19	A	Clydebank	W 3-0	1-0	1	McGinlay 2 5, 88, Latapy 86	9064
21	26	H	Ayr U	W 3-0	2-0	1	McGinlay 26, Paatelainen 2 42, 63	14,106
22	Jan 2	H	Raith R	W 5-1	4-1	1	Lovell 1, McGinlay 2 12, 43, Latapy 30, McEwan (og) 72	14,703
23	9	A	St Mirren	W 2-1	0-0	1	Paatelainen 56, Hartley 82	6674
24	16	H	Hamilton A	W 4-0	1-0	1	Paatelainen 2 38, 53, Lavety 63, McGinlay 89	10,233
25	30	A	Airdrieonians	W 4-1	1-1	1	Paatelainen 40, Skinner 46, Lovell 2 57, 87	4809
26	Feb 6	H	Stranraer	W 2-0	2-0	1	Crawford 2 31, 35	8659
27	20	A	Falkirk	W 2-1	1-0	1	Hartley 45, Den Bieman (og) 68	6086
28	27	A	Ayr U	W 3-1	2-1	1	Crawford 3 (1 pen) 20 (p), 45, 78	5010
29	Mar 13	A	Clydebank	L 0-2	0-1	1		1695
30	20	A	Airdrieonians	W 3-0	2-0	1	Dennis 6, Holsgrove 14, Lovering 90	9991
31	Apr 3	A	Hamilton A	W 2-0	1-0	1	Latapy 2 25, 53	4350
32	10	A	Raith R	W 3-1	1-1	1	Latapy 14, Dennis 56, Marinkov 88	5730
33	17	H	St Mirren	W 2-1	0-1	1	Hartley 70, Latapy 85	8959
34	24	H	Greenock Morton	W 2-1	2-1	1	Lovell 11, Shauzee 42	8865
35	May 1	A	Stranraer	W 4-0	1-0	1	Lovell 20, Crawford 56, Miller 77, Hartley 80	1597
36	8	H	Falkirk	W 2-1	1-0	1	Sauzee 45, Hartley 47	14,801

Final League Position: 1   1997–98 PREM 10

Honours
League Champions: Division I 1902-03, 1947-48, 1950-51, 1951-52. First Division 1980-81, 1998-99. Division II 1893-94, 1894-95, 1932-33; *Runners-up:* Division I 1896-97, 1946-47, 1949-50, 1952-53, 1973-74, 1974-75.
Scottish Cup Winners: 1887, 1902; *Runners-up:* 1896, 1914, 1923, 1924, 1947, 1958, 1972, 1979.
League Cup Winners: 1972-73, 1991-92; *Runners-up:* 1950-51, 1968-69, 1974-75, 1993-94.

European: *European Cup:* 6 matches (1955-56 semi-finals). *Cup Winners' Cup:* 6 matches (1972-73). *UEFA Cup:* 59 matches (*Fairs Cup:* 1960-61 semi-finals, 1961-62, 1962-63, 1965-66, 1967-68, 1968-69, 1970-71. *UEFA Cup:* 1973-74, 1974-75, 1975-76, 1976-77, 1978-79, 1989-90, 1992-93).

Club colours: Shirt: Green with white sleeves. Shorts: White. Stockings: Green with white trim.

Goalscorers: *League (84):* Crawford 14 (4 pens), McGinlay 12, Paatelainen 12, Lovell 11, Latapy 6, Hartley 5 (4 pens), Dennis 3, Hughes J 3, Guggi 2, Lavety 2, Prenderville 2, Sauzee 2, Skinner 2, Harper 1, Holsgrove 1, Lovering 1, Marenko 1, Miller 1, Rougier 1, own goals 2. *Scottish Cup (2):* Latapy 1, Lovering 1. *League Cup (3):* Crawford 1 (pen), Lovell 1, Skinner 1.

Gottskalksson O 36	Renwick M 15 + 1	Elliot D 8	Holsgrove P 9 + 8	Hughes J 22 + 1	Dennis S 29 + 2	Lovell S 26 + 5	Skinner J 24	Crawford S 28 + 7	Lavety B 9 + 17	McGinlay P 29 + 1	Rougier A 10 + 5	Bannerman S 2 + 10	Guggi P 7 + 1	Paton E 1 + 3	Harper K — + 2	Shannon R 1	Tosh P 1	Prenderville B 13	Dietrich C 1	Paatelainen M 25 + 1	Anderson D 6	Miller K 5 + 2	Latapy R 23	Lovering P 17	Collins D 16	Dempsie M 5 + 3	Hartley P 6 + 6	Smith T 3 + 2	Marinkov A 10	Sauzee F 9	Reid A — + 1	Bottiglieri E — + 1	McManus T — + 1	*Match No.*
1	2	3	4	5	6	7¹	8	9	10	11²	12	13																						1
1	2	3²	4³	5	6	9	8	12	10¹	11	7		13	14																				2
1	2	3	13	5	6	12	8²	9	10¹	11	7		4																					3
1	2²	3	13	5	6	12	8	9	10¹	11	7³		4		14																			4
1		3	12	5	6	10	8¹	9	14	11			4³		13	2	7²																	5
1		3		5	6¹	14	8³	9	13	11			4²	12				2	7	10														6
1	7		6²	5		13		9	10	11			4¹	12				2			3	8												7
1		3	8³	5	14			9	10²	11	13		4					2		12	6	7¹												8
1	3		4	5		9	8	12		11	7¹							2		10	6													9
1	3		4¹	5		9		13	10	11	7	12		8²				2			6													10
1	3			5		9	8	12		11	7¹	13	4²					2		10	6													11
1	3			5	12	9²	8	13		11	7³	14						2		10	6¹		4											12
1	3		12	5	6	9²	8¹	13		11	7³	14						2		10			4											13
1			4²	5	6	13		8	14	11	7	12						2		9³			10	3¹										14
1				5	6		4	8		11	7¹	12						2		9			10	3										15
1				5	6	10	4	8²	13	11	12	7¹						2		9				3										16
1				5	6	7	4	8¹	12	11								2		9			10	3										17
1				5	6	7²	4	8	13	11	12							2		9			10¹	3										18
1				5	6	7	4	8		11	12									9			10¹	3	2²	13								19
1				5	6	7²	4	8¹	12	11		13								9			10	3	2									20
1				5	6	7	4³	8²	13	11										9			10¹	3	2	14	12							21
1			12	5	6	7²	4¹	8	13	11										9			10³	3	2		14							22
1		3			6	7¹	4	8	13	11										9			10²			5	12	2						23
1			12		6		4¹		8	11		13								9			10	3²		5	7	2						24
1			14		6	7	4³	8	12	11										9¹			10²	3	2	5	13							25
1					6	7	4	8		11										9			10	3	2	5								26
1					6		4	9		11													10	3	2		7		5	8				27
1	13				6		4	9¹	7	11		12											10	3²	2				5	8				28
1					6	4		7	12											9¹		11	10	3	2				5	8				29
1			7		6	11		8												9		13	10²	3¹	2				5	4	12			30
1			7		6	11		8²	13											9			10¹	3	2		12		5	4				31
1	3		12		6	7¹		8³	13	11										9²			10		2		14		5	4				32
1	3				6	11		8	14											9³		12	10		2²		7¹	13	5	4				33
1	3				6	11		12												9		8¹	10²		2³	14	7	13	5	4				34
1	3					11		8³	13			10										9			2¹	4	7	6²	5			12	14	35
1	3			13	6	11		8	14	12										9			10		2		7³		5²	4¹				36

INVERNESS CALEDONIAN THISTLE
First Division

Year Formed: 1994. *Ground & Address:* Caledonian Stadium, East Longman, Inverness IV1 1FF. *Telephone:* 01463 222880.
Ground Capacity: 5600, seated: 2200. *Size of Pitch:* 115yd × 75yd.
Chairman: Dugald McGilvray. *Hon. Presidents:* John S. McDonald and Norman Miller. *Secretary:* Jim Falconer.
Manager: Steven W. Paterson. *Assistant Manager:* Alex Caldwell. *Physio:* Ian Manning. *Coach:* Alex Young. *Youth Development Officer:* Duncan Shearer.
Record Attendance: 5821 v Dundee United, Scottish Cup 4th rd replay, 18 February 1998.
Record Victory: 8-1, v Annan Ath, Scottish Cup 3rd rd, 24 January 1998.
Record Defeat: 0-4, v Queen's Park, Third Division, 20 August 1994 and v Montrose, Third Division, 14 February 1995.
Most League Appearances: 136, Charlie Christie, 1995-99.
Most League Goals in Season: 27, Ian Stewart, 1996-97.
Most Goals Overall (Individual): 68, Ian Stewart, 1995-99.

INVERNESS CALEDONIAN THISTLE 1998–99 LEAGUE RECORD

Match No.	Date	Venue	Opponents	Result	H/T Score	Lg. Pos.	Goalscorers	Atten- dance
1	Aug 4	A	Partick Th	W 1-0	0-0	—	Wilson [56]	1905
2	15	H	Livingston	W 2-1	0-0	2	Shearer [57], Wilson [62]	1897
3	22	A	Alloa Ath	D 1-1	1-0	2	Tokely [39]	616
4	29	A	East Fife	W 5-1	2-0	1	Sheerin (pen) [28], Shearer [37], Cherry [85], Bavidge [87], Teasdale [89]	814
5	Sept 5	H	Arbroath	W 2-1	1-0	1	Crawford (og) [44], Shearer [56]	1836
6	12	H	Queen of the S	W 3-2	0-1	1	Sheerin [46], McLean [48], Wilson [67]	1812
7	19	A	Stirling A	W 1-0	1-0	1	Shearer [38]	915
8	26	A	Clyde	L 1-4	0-3	2	Cherry [51]	969
9	Oct 3	H	Forfar Ath	D 2-2	1-1	1	McLean [10], Wilson [83]	1925
10	10	A	Livingston	L 1-2	0-1	3	McLean [86]	4100
11	17	H	Partick Th	W 3-2	2-1	2	Sheerin [1], McLean 2 [24, 73]	2598
12	24	H	East Fife	W 4-2	2-2	2	Shearer [9], Christie [27], Sheerin (pen) [72], McLean [74]	1547
13	31	A	Arbroath	W 1-0	0-0	2	Cherry [47]	934
14	Nov 7	H	Stirling A	W 3-1	1-0	2	McLean 2 [19, 58], Wilson [88]	2026
15	14	A	Queen of the S	D 2-2	1-1	2	Sheerin [32], McLean [74]	1021
16	21	H	Clyde	D 1-1	1-0	2	Wilson [25]	2268
17	28	A	Forfar Ath	D 2-2	1-0	2	Shearer [40], McLean [77]	511
18	Dec 16	H	Alloa Ath	W 3-2	1-1	—	Robertson [29], McCulloch [67], McLean [90]	1323
19	19	A	Partick Th	L 1-2	0-2	2	Wilson (pen) [67]	2141
20	27	A	East Fife	L 2-3	0-1	2	Teasdale [63], McLean [69]	1101
21	Jan 9	H	Arbroath	W 2-0	2-0	2	Wilson [33], Sheerin (pen) [36]	1795
22	16	A	Clyde	D 1-1	1-1	2	Glancy [43]	1105
23	30	H	Forfar Ath	W 2-0	1-0	2	Wilson [17], Christie [67]	2018
24	Feb 6	A	Stirling A	W 5-1	3-0	2	Sheerin (pen) [10], McCulloch [15], Teasdale [35], Glancy 2 [46, 67]	890
25	13	H	Queen of the S	W 1-0	0-0	2	Rowe (og) [73]	2204
26	20	A	Alloa Ath	W 4-1	1-1	2	Shearer 2 [14, 63], Wilson [81], Christie [88]	595
27	27	H	Livingston	W 3-1	2-1	2	McLean [24], Wilson [31], Shearer [70]	3279
28	Mar 6	A	Arbroath	L 1-3	1-0	2	McLean [42]	705
29	13	H	East Fife	W 4-0	1-0	2	McLean [32], Wilson [59], Sheerin [82], Teasdale [84]	1797
30	20	A	Forfar Ath	W 3-0	1-0	1	McLean 2 [14, 88], Sheerin [89]	504
31	Apr 3	H	Clyde	W 3-0	1-0	1	Wilson [3], Sheerin [56], Shearer [86]	3019
32	10	A	Stirling A	D 2-2	0-0	2	Shearer 2 [78, 88]	1778
33	17	A	Queen of the S	D 1-1	1-0	2	Wilson [17]	1214
34	24	H	Partick Th	W 3-2	2-1	1	McLean 2 [29, 34], McCulloch [85]	3246
35	May 1	A	Livingston	L 3-4	1-4	2	McCulloch [37], Christie [62], Stewart [67]	5316
36	8	H	Alloa Ath	D 1-1	0-0	2	Stewart [84]	2662

Final League Position: 2   1997–98 DIV 2 5

Honours
Scottish Cup: Quarter-finals 1996.
League Champions: Third Division 1996–97; *Runners-up:* Second Division 1998-99.

Club colours: Shirts: Royal blue with white and red chest panels. Shorts: Royal blue with red side stripe. Stockings: White.

Goalscorers: *League (80):* McLean 19, Wilson 14 (1 pen), Shearer 12, Sheerin 10 (5 pens), Christie 4, McCulloch 4, Teasdale 4, Cherry 3, Glancy 3, Stewart 2, Bavidge 1, Robertson 1, Tokely 1, own goals 2. *Scottish Cup (1):* own goal 1.
League Cup (4): Cherry 1, McLean 1, Shearer 1, Sheerin 1.

Calder J 22	Cherry P 24 + 3	Sheerin P 34 + 2	McCulloch M 32 + 1	Teasdale M 36	Farquhar G 9 + 3	Wilson B 35 + 1	Shearer D 21 + 9	McLean S 34 + 1	Christie C 33 + 1	Robson B 4 + 11	Bavidge M 1 + 7	Hastings R 23	Tokely R 23 + 1	MacArthur I 1 + 3	Allan A 9 + 4	Stewart I 1 + 5	Robertson H 12	Addicoat W 5 + 4	Fridge L 14	Glancy M 9 + 4	Craig D — + 1	Mann R 13	Nicol G 1 + 3	Match No.
1	2	3	4	5	6	7	8¹	9	10	11	12													1
1	2	11	4	5	6	7	8¹	9	10		12	3												2
1	11	4	2	6¹		7	8²	9	10	12	13	3	5											3
1	6	11	4	2		7	8²	9¹	10		13	3		5³	12	14								4
1	6	11	4	10		7	8	9				3	5	2										5
1	6	11	4	2		7²	8¹	9	10		13	3	5	12										6
1	6	11	4	2		7	8²	9¹	10		13	3	5				12							7
1	6	11	4	2		7		9	10	8²	3¹	5	12				13							8
1	6	11	4	2		7		9	10		5		8¹	3			12							9
1	6	11	4	2	12	7¹		9	10		5		3	8										10
1	6	11	4	2		7	8	9	10		5		3											11
1	6	11	4	2		7	8	9	10		5		3											12
1	6	11	4¹	2	12	7		9	10		5		3	8										13
1	2	11		4	6	7		9	10	12	5		3	8¹										14
1	2	11		4	6	7		9	10	12	5		3	8¹										15
1	2	11		4	6	7¹	13	9	10³	12	14	5		3	8²									16
1	6¹	11	12	4	8	7	10²	9		2	5		3	13										17
1	6¹	11²	2	5	12	7	8	9	10	13	4		3											18
1	12	2	5	6		7	8²	9	10	11¹	13	4	3											19
1	6	11	4	2		7²	8¹	9	10		5	12	3	13										20
	2	11	6	5		7	12	9²	10	13		3	4						1	8¹				21
	11²		6	5		7	12	9¹	10			3	4	2					1	8		13		22
1	11		6	4		7	12	9	10			3	5	2			13			8²				23
	11		6	4		7	12	9	10	13		3²		2					1	8¹		5		24
	11		6	4		7	8	9¹	10	12		3		2					1			5		25
	12	11²	6	4		7		9	10	13		3		2					1	8¹		5		26
	12	11	6	4		7³	8²	9¹	10	14		3		2					1		13	5		27
1	12	11²	6	4		7	8	9³	10	13		3		2¹							14	5		28
	13		6	4		7²	14	9³	10	11		3		2	12				1	8¹		5		29
	2	6	7	4		13	12	9	10	11²		3							1	8¹		5		30
	2	11	6	4		7	12	9²	10			3							1	8¹		5	13	31
	2	11	6	4		7	13	9¹	10			3							1	8¹		5	12	32
	2	11	6	4	10	7		9²	12	13		3							1			5	8¹	33
	2	11	6	4		7²	8¹	9	10			3					12		1			5	13	34
		11	6	4		7	8¹	9¹	10			3	2				12		1	13		5		35
		11	6	4		7³	8²	9¹	10			3	2	14	12				1	13		5		36

KILMARNOCK

Premier League

Year Formed: 1869. *Ground & Address:* Rugby Park, Kilmarnock KA1 2DP. *Telephone:* 01563 525184. *Fax:* 01563 522181. *Website:* www.kilmarnockfc.co.uk.
Ground Capacity: all seated: 18,128. *Size of Pitch:* 114yd × 72yd.
Chairman: W. Costley. *Chief Executive:* I. Welsh. *Secretary:* Kevin Collins. *Commercial Manager:* J. McSherry. *Stadium Manager:* A. Hollas.
Manager: Bobby Williamson. *Assistant Managers:* Jim Clark, Gerry McCabe. *Physio:* A. MacFie.
Managers since 1975: W. Fernie; D. Sneddon; J. Clunie; E. Morrison; J. Fleeting; T. Burns; A. Totten. *Club Nickname(s):* Killie. *Previous Grounds:* Rugby Park (Dundonald Road); The Grange; Holm Quarry; Present ground since 1899.
Record Attendance: 35,995 v Rangers, Scottish Cup; 10 March, 1962.
Record Transfer Fee received: £300,000 for Shaun McSkimming to Motherwell (1995).
Record Transfer Fee paid: £300,000 for Paul Wright from St Johnstone (1995).
Record Victory: 11-1 v Paisley Academical, Scottish Cup; 18 Jan, 1930 (15-0 v Lanemark, Ayrshire Cup; 15 Nov, 1890).
Record Defeat: 1-9 v Celtic, Division I; 13 Aug, 1938.
Most Capped Player: Joe Nibloc, 11, Scotland.
Most League Appearances: 481: Alan Robertson, 1972-88.
Most League Goals in Season (Individual): 34: Harry 'Peerie' Cunningham 1927-28 and Andy Kerr 1960-61.
Most Goals Overall (Individual): 148: W. Culley; 1912-23.

KILMARNOCK 1998–99 LEAGUE RECORD

Match No.	Date		Venue	Opponents	Result		H/T Score	Lg. Pos.	Goalscorers	Attendance
1	Aug	1	H	Dundee U	W	2-0	1-0	—	Wright [31], Nevin [71]	8137
2		15	A	St Johnstone	D	0-0	0-0	2		6210
3		22	H	Rangers	L	1-3	0-2	5	Wright [51]	17,608
4		30	H	Hearts	W	3-0	1-0	4	McCoist 3 [8, 61, 86]	10,376
5	Sept	12	A	Celtic	D	1-1	0-1	3	Vareille [49]	58,567
6		19	A	Motherwell	D	0-0	0-0	3		9063
7		23	H	Dundee	W	2-1	1-1	—	McCoist [21], McGowne [89]	7069
8		27	A	Aberdeen	W	1-0	1-0	2	Wright (pen) [13]	13,048
9	Oct	3	H	Dunfermline Ath	D	0-0	0-0	2		8346
10		17	A	Dundee U	W	2-0	1-0	2	McGowne [10], Vareille [77]	8137
11		24	H	St Johnstone	D	2-2	0-1	2	Roberts [77], Kernaghan (og) [83]	9336
12		31	H	Celtic	W	2-0	0-0	2	Roberts [54], Mitchell [69]	16,695
13	Nov	7	A	Hearts	L	1-2	0-1	2	Wright [87]	14,363
14		14	A	Dundee	D	1-1	1-1	2	Vareille [44]	4249
15		21	H	Motherwell	D	0-0	0-0	2		10,176
16		28	A	Dunfermline Ath	W	3-0	1-0	2	Durrant 2 [33, 56], Holt [77]	5608
17	Dec	5	A	Aberdeen	W	4-0	3-0	2	Mitchell 2 [6, 33], Vareille [38], Wright (pen) [66]	9785
18		12	A	Rangers	L	0-1	0-1	2		49,781
19		20	H	Dundee U	W	2-0	1-0	2	Wright [31], Durrant (pen) [86]	13,538
20		26	H	Hearts	W	1-0	1-0	2	Holt [26]	10,668
21	Jan	1	A	Motherwell	W	2-1	1-1	2	McCoist [15], McGowne [86]	8532
22		30	H	Dundee	D	0-0	0-0	2		7677
23	Feb	6	A	Aberdeen	L	1-2	0-1	2	Mahood [66]	9299
24		17	A	Celtic	L	0-1	0-0	—		59,220
25		28	A	Rangers	L	0-5	0-1	4		16,242
26	Mar	6	H	Dunfermline Ath	D	0-0	0-0	3		8032
27		13	A	St Johnstone	W	1-0	1-0	3	Holt [18]	5461
28		21	H	Celtic	D	0-0	0-0	3		14,472
29	Apr	3	A	Hearts	D	2-2	0-2	3	Henry [70], McCoist [80]	14,689
30		10	H	Aberdeen	W	4-2	2-1	3	Mahood [9], MacPherson [19], McCutcheon 2 [88, 90]	9048
31		17	A	Dunfermline Ath	W	6-0	1-0	3	Henry 2 [26, 74], Durrant [54], Mitchell [55], Vareille [68], McCoist [88]	5585
32		24	A	Dundee	L	1-2	0-1	3	Innes [53]	4296
33	May	1	H	Motherwell	L	0-1	0-0	3		15,300
34		8	A	Dundee U	D	0-0	0-0	3		7190
35		15	H	St Johnstone	D	1-1	1-0	3	Roberts [8]	15,086
36		23	A	Rangers	D	1-1	1-1	4	McGowne [41]	48,835

Final League Position: 4   1997–98 4

Honours
League Champions: Division I 1964-65. Division II 1897-98, 1898-99; *Runners-up:* Division I 1959-60, 1960-61, 1962-63, 1963-64. First Division 1975-76, 1978-79, 1981-82, 1992-93. Division II 1953-54, 1973-74. Second Division 1989-90.
Scottish Cup Winners: 1920, 1929, 1997; *Runners-up:* 1898, 1932, 1938, 1957, 1960.
League Cup Runners-up: 1952-53, 1960-61, 1962-63.

European: *European Cup:* 4 matches (1965-66). *Cup Winners' Cup:* 4 matches (1997-98). *UEFA Cup:* 16 matches (*Fairs Cup:* 1964-65, 1966-67, 1969-70, 1970-71, *UEFA Cup:* 1998-99).

Club colours: Shirt: Blue and white vertical stripes. Shorts: Blue. Stockings: Blue.

Goalscorers: *League (47):* McCoist 7, Wright 6 (2 pens), Vareille 5, Durrant 4 (1 pen), McGowne 4, Mitchell 4, Henry 3, Holt 3, Roberts 3, McCutcheon 2, Mahood 2, Innes 1, MacPherson 1, Nevin 1, own goal 1. *Scottish Cup (0). League Cup (3):* Wright 2 (1 pen), McCoist 1.

Marshall G 36	MacPherson A 31	Baker M 23	Lauchlan J 14	McGowne K 32	Holt G 33	Nevin P 2+1	Mahood A 16+12	Wright P 25+8	Durrant J 36	Mitchell A 27+5	Roberts M 9+13	Burke A 2+17	Henry J 7+4	Vareille J 20+3	McCoist A 16+10	Kerr D 16	Montgomerie R 22	Bagan D 1+4	McCutcheon G 2+11	Hamilton S 5	Innes C 4	Reilly M 17+1	Match No.
1	2	3	4	5	6	7^2	8	9^1	10	11^3	12	13	14										1
1	2	3	4	5	6	11	8^1	9^2	10	7					12	13							2
1	2		4	5	6	14	13	9	10	7^2		12		11^1	8^3	3							3
1	2			5	6^1		8	9	10	12		13		7^2	11^3	3	4		14				4
1	2^1	11		5	6		8	14	10^3	7				9^1	13	3	4		12				5
1	2	11^2		5	6		13	9	10	7				8^1	12	3	4						6
1	2	11^1		5	6			9^2	10	7		12		13	8	3	4						7
1	2			5	6			9^1	10	7	13	12		11^1	8^2	3	4		14				8
1	2			5	6			9	10	8	12			7	11^1	3	4						9
1	2	3		5	6		12	9	10^1	8	11^2	14		7^3			4		13				10
1		3			6		13	9^1	10^2	8	11	12		7^1			4		14	2	5		11
1		3		5	6		8	12	10^2	7	9			11^1			4		13	2			12
1		3		5	6		8	13	10^2	7^3	9			11			4			2		12	13
1	2	3		5	6			9	10	7	8			11			4						14
1	2	3		5	6		14	11^3	10	7		9^1	12	8^2			4		13				15
1	2	3		5	6		12	9	10^1	7				8^2	13		4					11	16
1	2	3		5	6		13	9^3	10^2	7	14			11^1	12		4					8	17
1	2	3		5	6		12	9^2	10	7^3	14			11^1	13		4					8	18
1	2	3		5	6		14	9^2	10^3	7	12			11^1			4	13				8	19
1	2	3		5	6		13	9^3	10^2	7	12		14	11^1			4					8	20
1	2	3		5	6			9	10	7				11			4					8	21
1	2	3		5	6	8^1		10			12			9			4		11			7	22
1	2	3		5			8	14	10		12	13		9^3			4	6^2	11^1			7	23
1	2	3		5	6		8^9	12	10		14	11^2	13	9^1			4					7	24
1		3		5	6			9	10	12	13	8		11^2			4		2^1			7	25
1			4	5	6		8^2	9^1	10	12	14	13		11^3	3				2			7	26
1	2		4	5	6^2	13		9	10	8	12			11^1	3							7	27
1	2		4	5	6	14		9^2	10	8	12	13		11^1	3							7	28
1	2^1		4	5	6	8		9^2	10	11		14	12	13	3							7^2	29
1	2		4		6^1		8	9^2	10^3	11		14	7	12		3		13		5			30
1	2		4			8	13		10^2	11^3			7	9^1	14	3		12		5		6	31
1	2		4			8	13		10	11^2			7	9^3	12	3		14		5		6^1	32
1	2	3	4	5	6			9^2	10	12			14	7	8^2	11^1			13				33
1	2	3	4	5	6			10			11^2	12	7	9^1				13				8	34
1	2		4	5	6^1		8	13	10	12	11			7^3	9^2	3		14					35
1	2		4	5	6		8		10	9^1	11^1	14	7^2	12		3		13					36

LIVINGSTON

First Division

Year Formed: 1974. *Ground:* Almondvale Stadium, Almondvale Stadium Road, Livingston EH54 7DN. *Telephone:* 01506 417000. *Fax:* 01506 418888. *Email:* livingstonfc@btinternet.com.
Ground Capacity: total: 6100. Main stand only used 7500. *Size of Pitch:* 105yd × 72yd.
Chairman: Dominic Keane. *Secretary:* J. R. S. Renton. *General Manager:* Jim Leishman. *Head Coach:* Ray Stewart.
Assistant Player/Coach: John Robertson. *Physios:* Michael McBride and Arthur Duncan.
Managers since 1975: John Bain; Alec Ness; Willie MacFarlane; Terry Christie; Michael Lawson. *Club Nickname:* Livvy
Lions. *Previous Grounds:* None.
Record Attendance: 4000 v Albion Rovers, League Cup 1st rd; 9 Sept, 1974.
Record Transfer Fee received: £115,000 for John Inglis to St Johnstone (1990).
Record Transfer Fee paid: £28,000 for Victor Kasule from Albion Rovers (1987).
Record Victory: 6-0 v Raith R, Second Division, 1986-87.
Record Defeat: 0-8 v Hamilton A. Division II; 14 Dec, 1974.
Most Capped Player (under 18): I. Little.
Most League Appearances: 446: Walter Boyd, 1979-89.
Most League Goals in Season (Individual): 21: John McGachie, 1986-87. *(Team):* 69; Second Division, 1986-87.
Most Goals Overall (Individual): 64: David Roseburgh, 1986-93.

LIVINGSTON 1998–99 LEAGUE RECORD

Match No.	Date	Venue	Opponents	Result		H/T Score	Lg. Pos.	Goalscorers	Atten- dance
1	Aug 4	H	Stirling A	D	1-1	1-1	—	McCormick [1]	1496
2	15	A	Inverness CT	L	1-2	0-0	7	Millar [83]	1897
3	22	H	Forfar Ath	D	1-1	1-0	8	Bingham (pen) [40]	1193
4	29	A	Queen of the S	W	1-0	0-0	5	Robertson [86]	1281
5	Sept 5	H	East Fife	W	3-1	2-1	4	Bingham 2 (1 pen) [6, 80 (p)], Robertson [35]	3002
6	12	H	Arbroath	W	2-1	2-0	3	McPhee [20], Sherry [39]	2725
7	19	A	Clyde	D	1-1	0-1	3	Bingham (pen) [69]	1044
8	26	A	Alloa Ath	W	4-3	2-1	3	Deas [8], Sherry 2 [34, 88], Robertson [54]	978
9	Oct 3	H	Partick Th	W	1-0	1-0	3	Deas [14]	5200
10	10	H	Inverness CT	W	2-1	1-0	2	Robertson [34], McPhee [76]	4100
11	17	A	Stirling A	W	3-1	3-0	1	Robertson [3], Bingham [11], McManus [42]	909
12	24	H	Queen of the S	W	2-0	2-0	1	Bingham 2 [20, 23]	2005
13	31	A	East Fife	W	3-2	1-1	1	Robertson [12], Bingham [61], McCormick [81]	1008
14	Nov 7	H	Clyde	W	2-0	2-0	1	Deas [34], Watson [40]	2556
15	14	A	Arbroath	D	2-2	1-1	1	Deas [44], Bingham [50]	810
16	21	H	Alloa Ath	W	2-1	2-0	1	Millar [42], King [44]	1992
17	28	A	Partick Th	W	3-1	1-0	1	Fleming [40], Sherry [60], Robertson [84]	2341
18	Dec 12	A	Forfar Ath	W	2-1	0-0	1	King [46], Bingham [66]	502
19	19	H	Stirling A	D	0-0	0-0	1		1996
20	27	A	Queen of the S	D	2-2	0-1	1	Millar [46], Bingham [75]	1221
21	Jan 16	A	Alloa Ath	W	3-1	1-1	1	Robertson [16], McPhee [75], Feroz [79]	774
22	20	H	East Fife	W	1-0	1-0	—	Millar [26]	1554
23	30	H	Partick Th	D	1-1	0-1	1	McPhee [79]	3293
24	Feb 6	A	Clyde	W	3-0	1-0	1	Robertson [43], King [76], McPhee [84]	1366
25	16	H	Arbroath	W	1-0	1-0	—	Fleming [43]	888
26	20	H	Forfar Ath	W	5-0	4-0	1	Robertson 2 [6, 39], McCormick [8], King 2 [20, 65]	1534
27	27	A	Inverness CT	L	1-3	1-2	1	McCormick [9]	3279
28	Mar 6	A	East Fife	D	1-1	0-1	1	Fleming [60]	995
29	13	H	Queen of the S	L	1-2	0-2	1	Boyle [87]	2300
30	20	A	Partick Th	D	1-1	1-1	2	Little [12]	2112
31	Apr 3	A	Alloa Ath	W	1-0	0-0	2	McPhee [60]	1892
32	10	H	Clyde	W	2-0	0-0	1	McPhee [46], King [70]	1925
33	17	A	Arbroath	D	1-1	0-1	1	Robertson [89]	729
34	24	A	Stirling A	D	0-0	0-0	2		1404
35	May 1	H	Inverness CT	W	4-3	4-1	1	King 2 [9, 11], Deas [17], McPhee [24]	5316
36	8	A	Forfar Ath	W	2-1	1-0	1	McPhee [4], King [66]	1395

Final League Position: 1   1997–98 DIV 2 3

Honours
League Champions: Second Division 1986-87, 1998–99. Third Division 1995-96; *Runners-up:* Second Division 1982-83. First Division 1987-88.
Scottish Cup: —. *League Cup:* Semi-finals 1984-85. *B&Q Cup:* Semi-finals 1992-93, 1993-94.

Club colours: Shirt: Black with yellow trim. Shorts: Black. Stockings: Black.

Goalscorers: *League (66):* Robertson 12, Bingham 11 (3 pens), King 9, McPhee 9, Deas 5, McCormick 4, Millar 4, Sherry 4, Fleming 3, Boyle 1, Feroz 1, Little 1, McManus 1, Watson 1. *Scottish Cup (8):* Bingham 2 (1 pen), Robertson 2, Fleming 1, McCormick 1, Millar 1, own goal 1. *League Cup (4):* Bingham 2 (1 pen), Millar 1, Robertson 1.

McCaldon I 15	Boyle J 34	Deas P 35	Conway F 10 + 2	Watson G 26 + 1	Millar J 30	Rajamaki M 3 + 2	Bennett N 13 + 7	Bingham D 29	Robertson J 30 + 6	McCormick J 10 + 22	Little I 7 + 7	Feroz C 1 + 10	McManus A 31	Sherry J 20 + 2	McPhee B 9 + 19	Magee K 2 + 1	Sweeney S 10	King C 29	Alexander N 21	McMartin G —+ 4	Forrest G 2 + 3	Fleming D 14 + 1	Harvey P 1 + 3	Coutts T —+ 1	Macdonald W 5	Coughlan G 6	Ferguson I 3 + 1	Match No.
	2	3	4	5	6	7	8^2	9	10	11^1	12	13																1
1	7^1	3	2	5	8	11^3	6^2	10	9	14	13	12	4															2
1	2	3	6	5	7			10^1	11	9	8	12	4															3
1	2	3	6^1	5	7^3	11^2	14	10	9	12		8	4	13														4
1	2	3	6	5	7		13	11	9				4		8^2	10^1	12											5
		3	4^2		7		12	11		13			2		8			10	6^1	5								6
1		3	4^2		7		12	14	11	9	13		2		8			10^1	6^3	5								7
1	2	3			6			10^1	11	9^2	12		4		8			13	5	7								8
	2	3			6			10^3	11	9^1	14		4		8			12	5	7^2	1	13						9
	2^2	3			6			10^1	11	9^3	14		4		8			12	5	7	1	13						10
	2	3			6			10	11^2	9^3	14		4		8			13	5	7^1	1	12						11
	2	3			6			10^1	11	9			4					13	5	7	1	12	8^2					12
	2^2	3			6			10^1	11	9	13		4		8			12	5	7	1							13
	2	3	12		6			10	11^2	9	13		4^1		8			14	5	7^1	1							14
	2	3	14	4	6			10^2	11	9^1	13				8			12	5^3	7	1							15
	2	3		5	6			10^1	11^2	9	13		4		8					7	1	12						16
	2	3		5	6			9	12	13			4		8	11^1				7	1	10^2						17
	2	3		5	6			11^2	9^1	12			4		8			13		7	1	10						18
	2	3		5	6^1			11	9	12	13		4		8					7	1	10^2						19
	2	3	8	5	6			11^3	9^2	12	14		4	13						7^2		10						20
	2	3		5^1	6			11	9^2	10	13		4		8			14		7^2	1	12						21
	2	3		5	6			11^1	12	9	13		4		8			10		7^2	1							22
	2^2	3		5	6			9	10^4		14		4		8^1			13		7	1	12	11					23
	2	3		5				9^1	13	11^2			4					12		7	1	8	10^3	6	14			24
	2	3		5	6			9^1	10				4		8			12		7	1	11						25
	2	3		5	6^2			9	10^3	13			4		8			14		7	1	11	12					26
	2^2	3	8^1	5	6			9^3	10	14			4					13		7	1	11	12					27
	2			5	6			9^3	10	11^2	14		4		8^1			13		7	1	12	3					28
	2	3		5	6		8^3	13	9		14		4					10		7	1	11^2	12					29
1	2	3	14	5				10	9	12	8	13	4							7		11^3				6^2		30
1	2	3		5		13	11	10^1	6^2						12					7					8	4	9	31
1	2	3		5		12	11	14	13	8^1					10^2					7					6	4	9^3	32
1	2	3		5	6		11	14	10^3		13				12					7^2					8	4	9^1	33
1	2	3		5			11^3	9^2	13	10		6			12					7^1					8	4	14	34
1	2	3		5			8	14	9^1	13	12	6			10^2					7		11^3				4		35
1	2	3		5			8	14	9	13	12	6			10^2					7		11^3				4		36

MONTROSE

Third Division

Year Formed: 1879. *Ground & Address:* Links Park, Wellington St, Montrose DD10 8QD. *Telephone:* 01674 673200.
Ground Capacity: total: 4338, seated: 1338. *Size of Pitch:* 113yd × 70yd.
Chairman: John F. Paton. *Secretary:* Malcolm J. Watters.
Manager: Kevin Drinkell. *Assistant Manager:* John Sheran. *Physio:* Allan Borthwick.
Managers since 1975: A. Stuart; K. Cameron; R. Livingstone; S. Murray; D. D'Arcy; I. Stewart; C. McLelland; D. Rougvie;
J. Leishman, J Holt, A. Dornan, D. Smith; T. Campbell.
Club Nickname(s): The Gable Endies. *Previous Grounds:* None.
Record Attendance: 8983 v Dundee, Scottish Cup 3rd rd; 17 Mar, 1973.
Record Transfer Fee received: £50,000 for Gary Murray to Hibernian (Dec 1980).
Record Transfer Fee paid: £17,500 for Jim Smith from Airdrieonians (Feb 1992).
Record Victory: 12-0 v Vale of Leithen, Scottish Cup 2nd rd; 4 Jan, 1975.
Record Defeat: 0-13 v Aberdeen; 17 Mar, 1951.
Most Capped Player: Alexander Keillor, 2 (6), Scotland.
Most League Appearances: 426: David Larter, 1987-98.
Most League Goals in Season (Individual): 28: Brian Third, Division II; 1972-73.

MONTROSE 1998–99 LEAGUE RECORD

Match No.	Date	Venue	Opponents	Result	H/T Score	Lg. Pos.	Goalscorers	Atten- dance
1	Aug 4	A	Cowdenbeath	L	1-4	0-2	—	Higgins [75]	161
2	15	H	Berwick R	D	1-1	1-0	—	Taylor [1]	269
3	22	A	Ross Co	L	1-3	0-2	9	Higgins [76]	1266
4	29	A	Brechin C	L	0-3	0-0	10		452
5	Sept 5	H	Albion R	L	1-2	0-0	10	Farnan [60]	244
6	12	A	Stenhousemuir	L	0-4	0-2	10		283
7	19	H	Queen's Park	W	1-0	0-0	10	Farnan [47]	310
8	26	H	Dumbarton	D	1-1	0-1	10	Coulston [71]	318
9	Oct 3	A	East Stirling	L	1-3	1-1	10	McGlashan (pen) [32]	243
10	11	A	Berwick R	D	1-1	0-1	10	Taylor [87]	921
11	17	H	Ross Co	L	3-6	2-3	10	Hutton [7], Farnan [41], Andrew [82]	339
12	27	H	Brechin C	L	1-2	1-0	—	Andrew [10]	340
13	31	A	Albion R	L	1-4	1-2	10	Coulston [6]	302
14	Nov 7	A	Queen's Park	L	0-3	0-2	10		385
15	14	H	Stenhousemuir	D	0-0	0-0	10		271
16	25	A	Dumbarton	W	2-0	1-0	—	Paterson [2], Niddrie [57]	240
17	28	H	East Stirling	W	2-0	1-0	10	Taylor [25], Loney [47]	271
18	Dec 12	H	Cowdenbeath	D	1-1	0-0	10	Taylor (pen) [57]	324
19	19	A	Ross Co	L	0-3	0-1	10		1571
20	Jan 9	H	Albion R	L	2-3	1-1	10	Shand [28], Lyon [77]	342
21	16	H	Dumbarton	W	4-2	2-1	10	Craig 2 [2, 14], Duffy [72], Lyon [90]	326
22	30	A	East Stirling	L	1-2	1-1	10	Paterson [40]	209
23	Feb 6	H	Queen's Park	W	3-0	1-0	9	Magee [3], Craig (pen) [75], McWilliam [86]	260
24	16	A	Brechin C	W	3-2	1-1	—	Magee [31], Taylor [50], Coulston [82]	317
25	20	A	Cowdenbeath	L	0-1	0-1	9		234
26	23	A	Stenhousemuir	L	1-3	1-2	—	Paterson [7]	276
27	Feb 27	H	Berwick R	L	0-3	0-1	10		301
28	Mar 13	H	Brechin C	L	1-3	1-1	10	Craig [25]	404
29	16	A	Albion R	D	0-0	0-0	—		258
30	20	H	East Stirling	W	1-0	0-0	9	Paterson [85]	249
31	Apr 3	A	Dumbarton	L	1-2	1-0	9	Craig (pen) [37]	541
32	10	A	Queen's Park	W	2-1	2-0	9	Mailer [10], Magee [41]	363
33	17	H	Stenhousemuir	L	1-2	1-1	9	Magee [6]	354
34	24	H	Ross Co	L	2-3	1-1	9	Taylor [34], Magee [84]	394
35	May 1	A	Berwick R	L	1-4	0-3	10	Taylor [55]	606
36	8	H	Cowdenbeath	L	1-2	1-0	10	Andrew [44]	293

Final League Position: 10   1997–98 9

Honours
League Champions: Second Division 1984-85; *Runners-up:* 1990-91. Third Division, *Runners-up:* 1994-95.
Scottish Cup: Quarter-finals 1973, 1976.
League Cup: Semi-finals 1975-76.
B&Q Cup: Semi-finals 1992-93.
League Challenge Cup: Semi-finals 1996-97.

Club colours: Shirt: Royal blue with white sleeves. Shorts: White. Stockings: Royal blue.

Goalscorers: *League (42):* Taylor 7 (1 pen), Craig 5 (1 pen), Magee 5, Paterson 4, Andrew 3, Coulston 3, Farnan 3, Higgins 2, Lyon 2, Duffy 1, Hutton 1, Loney 1, McGlashan 1 (pen), McWilliam 1, Mailer 1, Niddrie 1, Shand 1. *Scottish Cup (1):* Taylor 1. *League Cup (1):* Andrew 1.

Murray M 15	Mailer C 32	Watt J 13+5	Craib M 31	Wylie R 4+1	Meldrum G 35	Andrew B 13+11	Farnan C 30+1	McGlashan C 8	Higgins G 7	Loney J 14+2	Taylor S 30+2	Henry J 3+5	Winiarski S 5+2	McWilliam R 4+13	Niddrie K 21+1	Hutton D 3+3	Coulston D 19	Irvine B —+1	Lyon M 6+3	Fitzpatrick F 21+1	Duffy K 21	Paterson G 14	Shand M 9+4	Craig M 15	Magee K 13	O'Driscoll J 9	Stevenson C 1+4	Match No.
1	2^2	3	4	5	6	7^1	8	9	10	11	12	13																1
1	5	6	4		3	12	2	9	10^1	11		7	8															2
1	5		4		3		2	9	10	11		7	8	6														3
1	5	13	4	6	3	12	8^2		10^1	11		9	7	2														4
1	5		4	6	3	12	8	9	10	11	7		2^1															5
1	5	12	4	6	3	2	8	9	10^1	11	7																	6
1	5		4	12	3	13	8	9	10	11	7^2		2^1	6														7
1	5	13	4			12	8	9		11	7		2^1	6		3^2	10											8
1	5	3	4	6		2^1	8	9		11	7		12				10											9
1	2	6	4		3	11	8			9			7^1		5	13	10^2	12										10
1	2	6^2	4		3	10	8			11	9	13			12		5^1	7										11
1	2	4	6		3	10	8^2			11^1	9	13	14		5	12	7^3											12
1	2	4	6		3	10^1	8^2			11	9	13			12	5	14	7^3										13
1	2	4^1	6		3		8			9		13			12	5	11^2	7	10									14
	2	4	6		3		11			12	9					5^1	7		10	1	8							15
	4	2	3				11				9				12	5	7		10^1	1	8	6						16
	4	2	3				11				10	9				5	7			1	8	6						17
	2	4	6		3		11				10^1	9				5	7		12	1	8							18
	2	4			3		11				12	9				5	7		10^1	1	8	6						19
	13	6	3		2						9^1		14		5		4^2		12	1	8		7^3	10	11			20
	2		3		4						9^2					5^1	7	13		1	8	6	12	10	11^1			21
4	2		3		12										5		7		9^2	1	8	6	13	10	11^1			22
2		6	3		4									12			7		10	1	8	5		9^1	11			23
6		2	3		4					10			12				8			1		5	7^1	9	11			24
6		2	3	12	4					10^2		13					8			1	11	5	7^1	9				25
4		2	3	12		11^1					10					6	7			1	8	5		9				26
	4	14	2		3^3	12	11^2				10	13			5					1	8	6	7^1	9				27
	2		6		3	13	4^1				10	12								1	8	5		9	11		7^2	28
	2		6		3	12					10^1	4								1	8	5	13	9^2	11	7		29
	2				3	12					10				6					1	8	5	4^1	9	11	7		30
	2				3	10^1	6						4	12						1	8	5	11	9		7		31
	2				3	10	6						12	5^2						1	8^1		7	9	11	4	13	32
	2				3	10^3	6				14		13	5						1	8^2		7^1	9	11	4	12	33
	2	6			3	10					7			5^1						1	8			9	11	4	12	34
	2	6			3	9^2					10			12	5^1					1	8		7		11	4	13	35
1^6	4		5		3	7					9			2						15	8		12		11	6	10^1	36

MORTON

First Division

Year Formed: 1874. *Ground & Address:* Cappielow Park, Sinclair St, Greenock. *Telephone:* 01475 723571.
Ground Capacity: total: 14,891, seated: 5741. *Size of Pitch:* 110yd × 71yd.
Chairman: Hugh Scott. *Club Secretary:* Gary W. Miller.
Manager: Billy Stark. *Assistant Manager:* Frank Connor. *Physio:* Ian Cardle. *Youth Coach:* Peter Weir.
Managers since 1975: Joe Gilroy; Benny Rooney; Alex Miller; Tommy McLean; Willie McLean, Allan McGraw. *Club Nickname(s):* The Ton. *Previous Grounds:* Grant Street 1874, Garvel Park 1875, Cappielow Park 1879, Ladyburn Park 1882, (Cappielow Park 1883).
Record Attendance: 23,500 v Celtic; 29 April, 1922.
Record Transfer Fee received: £350,000 for Neil Orr to West Ham U.
Record Transfer Fee paid: £150,000 for Allan Mahood from Nottingham Forest.
Record Victory: 11-0 v Carfin Shamrock, Scottish Cup 1st rd; 13 Nov, 1886.
Record Defeat: 1-10 v Port Glasgow Ath, Division II; 5 May, 1894 and v St Bernards, Division II; 14 Oct, 1933.
Most Capped Player: Jimmy Cowan, 25, Scotland.
Most League Appearances: 358: David Hayes, 1969-84.
Most League Goals in Season (Individual): 58: Allan McGraw, Division II; 1963-64.

GREENOCK MORTON 1998–99 LEAGUE RECORD

Match No.	Date		Venue	Opponents	Result		H/T Score	Lg. Pos.	Goalscorers	Atten- dance
1	Aug	4	H	Hibernian	L	0-1	0-0	—		5747
2		15	A	Ayr U	L	0-1	0-1	9		2329
3		22	H	Hamilton A	L	1-2	1-0	10	Fenwick [29]	1691
4		29	H	Clydebank	D	2-2	1-2	10	Curran [27], Anderson J [75]	1382
5	Sept	5	A	Raith R	D	0-0	0-0	10		1880
6		12	A	Airdrieonians	W	1-0	1-0	10	Hawke [70]	2243
7		19	H	St Mirren	L	0-1	0-0	10		4108
8		26	A	Falkirk	L	1-2	0-2	10	Fenwick [69]	3047
9	Oct	3	H	Stranraer	W	3-0	0-0	8	Twaddle [58], Matheson [72], Blakie [89]	1444
10		11	A	Ayr U	L	1-2	0-1	9	Hawke [76]	2156
11		17	A	Hibernian	L	1-2	0-1	9	Twaddle [59]	9524
12		27	A	Clydebank	L	1-2	0-1	—	Fenwick [68]	452
13		31	H	Raith R	W	2-0	2-0	8	McCormick [3], Hawke [44]	1468
14	Nov	7	A	St Mirren	L	0-1	0-1	8		4776
15		14	A	Airdrieonians	D	0-0	0-0	8		1935
16		21	H	Falkirk	L	0-3	0-1	10		1843
17		28	A	Stranraer	W	3-2	2-2	8	Fenwick [7], Twaddle [8], Anderson J [90]	795
18	Dec	5	H	Hibernian	L	1-3	0-1	8	Fenwick [89]	3150
19		12	A	Hamilton A	D	0-0	0-0	9		1012
20		19	A	Raith R	W	3-1	3-1	8	Thomas [3], Curran 2 [17, 27]	2721
21		26	H	Clydebank	D	1-1	1-0	8	Anderson J [41]	1947
22	Jan	5	H	St Mirren	D	0-0	0-0	—		2936
23		16	A	Falkirk	W	2-1	0-0	7	McPherson [50], Thomas [73]	2824
24		19	A	Airdrieonians	W	2-0	1-0	—	Twaddle [25], (og) [60]	1801
25		30	H	Stranraer	W	1-0	1-0	6	Twaddle [26]	1581
26	Feb	6	A	Ayr U	L	0-1	0-0	6		2222
27		20	H	Hamilton A	W	3-0	0-0	6	Wright 2 [55, 89], Curran [74]	1914
28	Mar	13	H	Raith R	D	1-1	0-0	7	Thomas [18]	1795
29		20	A	Stranraer	W	1-0	1-0	6	Thomas [15]	563
30	Apr	3	H	Falkirk	W	3-2	1-1	6	Anderson J [27], Curran [52], Wright [66]	1914
31		10	A	St Mirren	W	5-1	2-1	6	Thomas 3 (1 pen) [13, 41, 84 (p)], Wright 2 [58, 73]	3538
32		17	H	Airdrieonians	L	0-2	0-1	6		1442
33		21	A	Clydebank	W	2-1	0-1	—	Anderson J [56], Thomas [80]	402
34		24	A	Hibernian	L	1-2	1-2	6	Anderson D [7]	8865
35	May	1	A	Ayr U	L	1-4	1-3	6	Anderson J [41]	2337
36		8	A	Hamilton A	W	2-0	1-0	6	Thomas [6], Wright [64]	744

Final League Position: 6　　　　1997–98 5

Honours
League Champions: First Division 1977-78, 1983-84, 1986-87. Division II 1949-50, 1963-64, 1966-67. Second Division 1994-95. *Runners-up:* Division 1 1916-17, Division II 1899-1900, 1928-29, 1936-37.
Scottish Cup Winners: 1922; *Runners-up:* 1948. *League Cup Runners-up:* 1963-64.
B&Q Cup Runners-up: 1992-93.

European: *UEFA Cup:* 2 matches (*Fairs Cup:* 1968-69).

Club colours: Shirt: Royal blue and white 4" Hoops. Shorts: White with royal blue panel down side. Stockings: Royal blue and white hoops.

Goalscorers: *League (45):* Thomas 9 (1 pen), Anderson J 6, Wright 6, Curran 5, Fenwick 5, Twaddle 5, Hawke 3, Anderson D 1, Blaikie 1, McCormick 1, McPherson 1, Matheson 1, own goal 1. *Scottish Cup (8):* Archdeacon 2, Thomas 2, Twaddle 2, Matheson 1, own goal 1. *League Cup (0).*

Wylie D 6	Collins D 18	Archdeacon O 33	Curran H 34	Anderson J 33	Fenwick P 30	George M 1+2	Matheson R 17+14	Hawke W 27+4	Duffield P 2+1	Twaddle K 31	Blaikie A 3+9	Blair P —+2	Aitken S 19+3	Foster M 14+5	Morrow J 4+1	McPherson C 20+13	Juttla J 4+5	Maxwell A 30	McCormick S 3+2	Thomas K 22	Wright K 10+6	Slavin B 11+4	Tweedie G 2+2	Anderson D 16	Whalen S —+1	Murie D 6+1	McDonald S —+1	Match No.
1	2	3	4	5	6	7	8¹	9	10	11²	12	13																1
1	2	3	4	5	6			9	10	11			7¹	8		12												2
1	2	3	4	5	6			9	12	11	13		7¹	8²		10												3
1	2	3	4	5	6			9		11			8	7		10												4
1	2	3	4	5	6			9		11	10¹		8	7		12												5
1	2	3	4	5	6			9		11	12		8	7²		10¹	13											6
	2	3	4	5	6		13	9		11²	12		8	7		10¹		1										7
	2	3	4	5	6¹		7	9		11			8			10	12	1										8
	2	3	4	5	6	12	7²	9		11	13		8			10¹		1										9
	2	3	4	5	6		7	9		11			8			12		1		10¹								10
	2	3	4	5	6		7	9		11¹	13		8			10²		1		12								11
	2	3	4	5	6		7	9		11	12		8²			10¹		1		13								12
	2	3	4	5	6		7	9		11²	13	14	8¹			12		1		10²								13
	2	3	4²	5	6		7	9		11	12	13	8					1		10¹								14
	2	3	4¹	5	6		7	9		11	12		8²					1		10								15
	2³	3	4	5	6		7			11	13	14	8¹			12		1		10	9²							16
	2	3	4	5	6		13	9		11			7¹	8		12		1		10²								17
	2	3		5	6		12	9		11			4	7				1	8¹	10								18
		3		5	6		12	9		11			4	7¹				1	8	10			2					19
		3	4	5	6		12	9		11²			8	13		14		1		10³	7¹		2					20
		3	4	5			12	9		11	13		8	7²				1		10¹			2	6				21
		3	4	5			12	9		11			8	7¹		13		1		10²			2	6				22
		3		5	6		7¹	9		11	12					13		1	8	10²			2	4				23
		3	4	5	6		7³	9		11¹			8²			12	14	1		10			2	13				24
		3	4	5	6		7³	9		11¹			8²			12	14	1		10			2	13				25
		3	2	5	6		7¹	9		11	12		8³			13	14	1		10²				4				26
		3	8	5	6²		14	9¹		11			7³	13		12		1		10			2	4				27
	8		5	6			11			7			2	12		3¹		1		10	9²			4	13			28
		3	8	5	6		12			7			2			11		1		10¹	9			4				29
		3	8	5	6		12			7²			2			11¹		1		10³	9	13		4			14	30
		3	8	5	6		7¹	14		12						11³		1		10	9	13		4		2		31
		3	8				12	13		7³			6²			11¹	14	1		10	9	5		4		2		32
		3	8¹	5	6		11	9²		7				13		10²		1		12	14			4		2		33
		3	8²	5	6		12	13		11			7³	14		10		1		9¹				4		2		34
			8	5			12	11		7			6	13		10¹		1		9	3			4		2³		35
			8¹	5	6		13	12		7				11²		10²		1		9	3			4		2	14	36

MOTHERWELL

Premier League

Year Formed: 1886. *Ground & Address:* Fir Park Stadium, Motherwell ML1 2QN. *Telephone:* 01698 333333. *Fax:* 01698 338001. *Ground Capacity:* all seated: 13,742. *Size of Pitch:* 110yd × 75yd.
Chairman: John Boyle. *General Manager/Secretary:* Alisdair Barron. *Commercial Manager:* John Swinburne.
Manager: Billy Davies. *Assistant Manager:* Jim Griffin. *Physio:* John Porteous. *Director of Football:* Willie McLean.
Managers since 1975: Ian St. John; Willie McLean; Rodger Hynd; Ally MacLeod; David Hay; Jock Wallace; Bobby Watson; Tommy McLean; Alex McLeish; Harri Kampman.
Club Nickname(s): The Well. *Previous Grounds:* Roman Road, Dalziel Park.
Record Attendance: 35,632 v Rangers, Scottish Cup 4th rd replay; 12 Mar, 1952.
Record Transfer Fee received: £1,750,000 for Phil O'Donnell to Celtic (September 1994).
Record Transfer Fee paid: £500,000 for John Spencer from Everton (Jan 1999).
Record Victory: 12-1 v Dundee U, Division II; 23 Jan, 1954.
Record Defeat: 0-8 v Aberdeen, Premier Division; 26 Mar, 1979.
Most Capped Player: Tommy Coyne, 13, Republic of Ireland.
Most League Appearances: 626: Bobby Ferrier, 1918-37.
Most League Goals in Season (Individual): 52: Willie McFadyen, Division I; 1931-32.
Most Goals Overall (Individual): 283: Hugh Ferguson, 1916-25.

MOTHERWELL 1998–99 LEAGUE RECORD

Match No.	Date	Venue	Opponents	Result	H/T Score	Lg. Pos.	Goalscorers	Atten- dance
1	Aug 1	H	St Johnstone	W 1-0	0-0	—	Stirling [49]	5686
2	15	A	Rangers	L 1-2	0-1	6	Coyle [50]	49,275
3	22	H	Dunfermline Ath	D 0-0	0-0	6		9858
4	30	H	Dundee U	W 1-0	1-0	6	Nyyssonen [43]	11,201
5	Sept 12	A	Aberdeen	D 1-1	1-1	5	Coyle [34]	11,260
6	19	H	Kilmarnock	D 0-0	0-0	4		9063
7	23	A	Hearts	L 0-3	0-0	—		12,323
8	26	A	Dundee	L 0-1	0-1	7		5655
9	Oct 3	H	Celtic	L 1-2	0-2	7	Adams [90]	12,103
10	17	A	St Johnstone	L 0-5	0-0	10		4062
11	28	H	Rangers	W 1-0	0-0	—	Spencer [55]	11,777
12	31	H	Aberdeen	D 2-2	0-1	8	Spencer [57], McGowan [69]	8146
13	Nov 7	A	Dundee U	D 2-2	1-0	9	Coyle 2 [4, 50]	6616
14	14	H	Hearts	W 3-2	1-0	5	Spencer [40], Coyle 2 [68, 84]	8912
15	21	A	Kilmarnock	D 0-0	0-0	7		10,176
16	28	A	Celtic	L 0-2	0-1	7		59,227
17	Dec 12	A	Dunfermline Ath	D 1-1	0-0	8	Spencer [47]	5182
18	16	H	Dundee	W 2-1	1-1	—	Coyle [34], McMillan [77]	5840
19	19	H	St Johnstone	L 1-2	1-1	6	Adams [28]	5686
20	26	H	Dundee U	W 2-0	0-0	5	McMillan [55], Brannan [57]	6001
21	29	A	Aberdeen	D 1-1	0-1	—	McCulloch [66]	15,269
22	Jan 1	H	Kilmarnock	L 1-2	1-1	5	Brannan [27]	8532
23	30	A	Hearts	W 2-0	0-0	5	McCulloch [48], Adams [71]	12,821
24	Feb 6	A	Dundee	L 0-1	0-1	5		4187
25	21	H	Celtic	L 1-7	1-2	5	Brannan [26]	11,963
26	27	H	Dunfermline Ath	D 1-1	0-0	5	McCulloch [46]	7324
27	Mar 13	A	Rangers	L 1-2	0-1	6	Gower [69]	49,483
28	20	H	Aberdeen	D 1-1	0-0	5	Teale (pen) [90]	6963
29	Apr 3	A	Dundee U	W 3-0	2-0	5	Brannan [7], Spencer 2 [38, 60]	8110
30	10	H	Dundee	L 1-2	1-0	5	Spencer [2]	5717
31	17	A	Celtic	L 0-1	0-0	6		59,588
32	24	H	Hearts	L 0-4	0-1	6		8926
33	May 1	A	Kilmarnock	W 1-0	0-0	6	Brannan (pen) [53]	15,300
34	8	A	St Johnstone	D 0-0	0-0	6		4599
35	15	H	Rangers	L 1-5	0-2	7	Nicholas [75]	11,078
36	23	A	Dunfermline Ath	W 2-1	0-1	7	Goodman [76], Ramsay [90]	3532

Final League Position: 7   1997–98 9

Honours

League Champions: Division I 1931-32. First Division 1981-82, 1984-85. Division II 1953-54, 1968-69; *Runners-up:* Premier Division 1994-95. Division I 1926-27, 1929-30, 1932-33, 1933-34. Division II 1894-95, 1902-03. *Scottish Cup:* 1952, 1991; *Runners-up:* 1931, 1933, 1939, 1951.
League Cup: 1950-51. *Runners-up:* 1954-55. *Scottish Summer Cup:* 1944, 1965.

Club colours: Shirt: Amber with claret hoop and trimmings. Shorts: White. Stockings: Claret.

European: *Cup Winners' Cup:* 2 matches (1991-92). *UEFA Cup:* 6 matches (1994-95, 1995-96).

Goalscorers: *League (35):* Coyle 7, Spencer 7, Brennan 5 (1 pen), Adams 3, McCulloch 3, McMillan 2, Goodman 1, Gower 1, McGowan 1, Nicholas 1, Nyyssonen 1, Ramsay 1, Stirling 1, Teale 1 (pen). *Scottish Cup (5):* Brannan 1, Coyle 1, McCulloch 1, Thomas 1, own goal 1. *League Cup (1):* Halliday 1.

Kaven M 16	Doesburg M 29+1	McMillan S 30	McGowan J 32	Stirling J 4+1	Valakari S 35	Matthaei R 14+3	Michels J 7+3	Ross I 8+4	McClair B 8+3	Coyle O 26	Denham G —+1	Halliday S 2+2	McCulloch L 14+12	Woods S 7	Teale S 29	Nyyssonen K 3	Miller G 1+3	Shivute E —+1	Nevin P 14+16	Adams D 11+15	Craigan S 6+4	Christie K 4+1	Brannan G 25	Spencer J 21	May E 10+2	Thomas A 10	Goram A 13	Bacque H —+1	Ramsay D —+4	Gower M 8+1	Nicholas S 1+6	Goodman D 8	Match No.
1	2[1]	3	4	5	6	7	8	9[3]	10	11[2]	12	13	14																				1
	2		4	5	6[1]	7	8[2]		10	11	13	12		1	3	9																	2
1	2	3	4		6	7	8[2]	10	11		12			5	9[1]	13																	3
1	2	3	4		6	7		8	10	11				5	9[1]	12																	4
1	2	3	4	13	6	7	8[1]	9	10	11[2]				5						12													5
1	2	3	4		6	7	8[1]	9	10[3]	11[2]		14		5						12	13												6
1	2	3	4		6	7	8[1]	10[3]	14	11	13			5						12	9[2]												7
1	2	3	4		6	8[2]	14	13	10	11	12			5						7[2]	9[1]												8
	2	3	4	8[2]	6	7		9	10[1]	11	1			5						12	13												9
	2	4[3]	3[2]	8	12		6	10[1]	11	13	1			5					7	9	14												10
1	2	3	4		8					11	12			5					13	9[1]		6	7	10[2]									11
1	2	3	4		8					11[3]				5		9[2]	14		12	13		6[1]	7	10									12
1	2	3	4		8					11[3]				5		9			12	14	13		7	10[1]	6[2]								13
1	2	3	4		8		12			11				5		9[2]				7	10			6[1]									14
1	2	3	4		8			12	11					5		9[2]				13	7	10			6[1]								15
1	2	3	4[2]		8			13	11					5		9[1]				7	10	6											16
1	2	3			8					11[3]				5		9			12		6	7	10	4									17
1		3	4		8	13				11				5		9[1]			7	12		2	10		6[2]								18
1	2	3	4[3]		8			14		11				5		9[1]			5	10		6[2]	7										19
	2[1]	3			8					11				5		9[3]	1		7[2]	14		12	4	10	13	6							20
	2	3			8					11				5		9[3]	1		12	14		7[1]	4	10[2]	13	6							21
	2		4		8	10	6			11				9		1			7	12		3[1]		5									22
	2[1]		4		8	7[2]				11				9		5			13	12	3	10	6	1									23
	2		4		8					11				10[1]		5			7[2]	9	6	3				1	12	13					24
	2	3	4		8					14				11[2]		9			5	12	13	7[1]	3	10	6[3]			1	14				25
	2	3	4		8			13		11				9[1]		5			10[3]	12		7	6[2]			1		14					26
	2	3	4		8			14						9[2]		5			13	12		10	7	6			1		11[3]				27
	2	3			8									5		10[2]			13	14		7	9	6	4[3]		1		11[1]	12			28
		3	4		8									5		10[1]			2	9		6		1	7				12	11			29
12		3	4		8									5		10[1]			2	9		6		1	7[2]				13	11			30
	2[1]	3	4		8									5		13	12[2]		6	10		1	7[3]					14	11				31
	2	3	4[2]		8[3]	13								12		5[1]			14	7		9	6	1					11	10			32
		3	4		6						12							12	7[1]	11	5	2	9	1		8[2]			13	10			33
		3	4		8	6					12								7[1]	11	5	2	9	1						10			34
		3	4		8	11							14		6[2]		5		7	9	6	1					12		7[1]	13	10[2]		35
		3[1]	4		8	5				9									7[2]	6	2	1					12		13	11	10		36

PARTICK THISTLE   Second Division

Year Formed: 1876. *Ground & Address:* Firhill Stadium, 80 Firhill Rd, Glasgow G20 7AL. *Telephone:* 0141 579 1971. *Fax:* 0141 945 1525
Ground Capacity: total: 14,538, seated: 8397. *Size of Pitch:* 110yd × 75yd.
Chairman: T. Brown McMaster. *Secretary:* Alan C. Dick. *Commercial Manager:* George Carson.
Manager: John Lambie. *Assistant Manager:* Gerry Collins. *Physio:* Walter Cannon. *Player/Coach:* Kenny Brannigan.
Managers since 1975: R. Auld; P. Cormack; B. Rooney; R. Auld; D. Johnstone; W. Lamont; S. Clark; J. Lambie; M. MacLeod; J. McVeigh; T. Bryce. *Club Nickname(s):* The Jags. *Previous Grounds:* Jordanvale Park; Muirpark; Inchview; Meadowside Park.
Record Attendance: 49,838 v Rangers, Division I; 18 Feb, 1922. *Ground Record:* 54,723, Scotland v Ireland, 25 Feb 1928.
Record Transfer Fee received: £200,000 for Mo Johnston to Watford.
Record Transfer Fee paid: £85,000 for Andy Murdoch from Celtic (Feb 1991).
Record Victory: 16-0 v Royal Albert, Scottish Cup 1st rd; 17 Jan, 1931.
Record Defeat: 0-10 v Queen's Park, Scottish Cup; 3 Dec, 1881.
Most Capped Player: Alan Rough, 51 (53), Scotland.
Most League Appearances: 410: Alan Rough, 1969-82.
Most League Goals in Season (Individual): 41: Alec Hair, Division I; 1926-27.

PARTICK THISTLE 1998–99 LEAGUE RECORD

Match No.	Date	Venue	Opponents	Result	H/T Score	Lg. Pos.	Goalscorers	Attendance
1	Aug 4	H	Inverness CT	L	0-1	0-0	—	1905
2	15	A	Forfar Ath	W	1-0	1-0	5	Lauchlan [30]	1053
3	22	H	Queen of the S	D	2-2	1-1	6	Morgan (pen) [29], Dunn [72]	1963
4	29	A	Clyde	W	2-1	1-0	3	Morgan 2 (1 pen) [30 (p), 85]	2621
5	Sept 5	H	Alloa Ath	W	1-0	0-0	2	Morgan [68]	1655
6	12	H	Stirling A	W	1-0	1-0	2	Bryce [30]	1998
7	19	A	East Fife	W	3-1	1-1	2	Dunn 2 [17, 53], Lauchlan [66]	1314
8	26	H	Arbroath	W	2-0	1-0	1	Bryce [28], Morgan (pen) [46]	2006
9	Oct 3	A	Livingston	L	0-1	0-1	2		5200
10	11	H	Forfar Ath	W	2-0	1-0	1	Morgan [22], Bryce [46]	2870
11	17	A	Inverness CT	L	2-3	1-2	3	McDonald [44], Archibald [87]	2598
12	24	H	Clyde	L	0-2	0-0	3		2627
13	31	A	Alloa Ath	L	1-3	1-3	4	Flannigan [20]	1469
14	Nov 7	H	East Fife	L	0-1	0-1	4		1870
15	14	A	Stirling A	L	0-2	0-1	4		1513
16	21	A	Arbroath	L	0-1	0-0	5		1121
17	28	H	Livingston	L	1-3	0-1	6	Dunn [77]	2341
18	Dec 12	A	Queen of the S	D	0-0	0-0	6		1731
19	19	H	Inverness CT	W	2-1	2-0	6	Tosh [16], Connell [19]	2141
20	26	A	Clyde	W	1-0	1-0	4	McDonald [12]	2673
21	Jan 13	H	Alloa Ath	W	2-1	1-1	—	Dunn [41], Simpson (og) [79]	1502
22	16	H	Arbroath	D	0-0	0-0	4		2105
23	30	A	Livingston	D	1-1	1-0	4	Dunn [1]	3293
24	Feb 6	A	East Fife	L	0-1	0-1	4		1241
25	17	H	Stirling A	L	0-1	0-0	—		1203
26	20	H	Queen of the S	L	1-3	1-2	5	Dunn [38]	1510
27	27	A	Forfar Ath	L	1-2	1-1	5	Jamieson [43]	662
28	Mar 6	A	Alloa Ath	W	1-0	1-0	5	Lauchlan [42]	996
29	13	H	Clyde	L	0-1	0-0	5		3342
30	20	H	Livingston	D	1-1	1-1	5	Dunn [43]	2112
31	Apr 3	A	Arbroath	L	1-2	1-1	6	Dunn [24]	1301
32	10	H	East Fife	D	2-2	1-0	7	Houston [32], Avdiu [71]	1811
33	17	A	Stirling A	L	0-3	0-2	8		1664
34	24	A	Inverness CT	L	2-3	1-2	8	Dunn [27], Jamieson [55]	3246
35	May 1	H	Forfar Ath	D	0-0	0-0	7	McDonald (pen) [79]	2539
36	8	A	Queen of the S	D	2-2	2-1	8	Lauchlan 2 (1 pen) [4 (p), 10]	2335

Final League Position: 8   1997–98 DIV 1 9

Honours

League Champions: First Division 1975-76. Division II 1896-97, 1899-1900, 1970-71; *Runners-up:* First Division 1991-92. Division II 1901-02.
Scottish Cup Winners: 1921; *Runners-up:* 1930.
League Cup Winners: 1971-72; *Runners-up:* 1953-54, 1956-57, 1958-59.

European: *Fairs Cup:* 4 matches (1963-64). *UEFA Cup:* 2 matches (1972-73).

Club colours: Shirt: Red and yellow hoops. Shorts: Black. Stockings: Red with two yellow leg bands, tops red with one broad yellow band.

Goalscorers: *League (36):* Dunn 10, Morgan 6 (3 pens), Lauchlan 5 (1 pen), Bryce 3, McDonald 3 (1 pen), Jamieson 2, Archibald 1, Ardiu 1, Connell 1, Flannigan 1, Houston 1, Tosh 1, own goal 1. *Scottish Cup (8):* Dunn 4 (1 pen), Tosh 4. *League Cup (2):* Lauchlan 1, Morgan 1.

Arthur K 28	Kennedy D 24	McArthur S 8 + 1	Jamieson W 25	Archibald A 33	Connell G 32 + 1	Lauchlan M 22 + 5	Bryce T 18 + 1	Morgan A 12 + 1	Callaghan T 14 + 11	Donaghy M 1	Johnston S 4 + 11	Dunn R 26 + 8	Martin A — + 1	Callaghan W 7 + 6	Gaughan K 22 + 4	McDonald P 29 + 2	McKeown D 30	Ross S 8	McKenzie J 3 + 4	Flannigan C 8 + 8	Bonar S 7 + 7	Tosh P 10	Dair L 1	Frame A 4 + 3	Hood G 6	McHarg S 1 + 1	Houston S — + 2	Burns G 6	Avdiu K 6	McCann K 1	Howie W — + 1	Match No.
1	2	3	4	5	6	7	8²	9	10	11¹	12	13																				1
1	2	3	4	5	6	7	10	9	11		8¹	12																				2
1	2	3	4	5	6	7	8	9²	11		12				10¹	13																3
1	2	3	4¹	5	6	7	8	9	11²				14	10³	12	13																4
1	2	3			6	7	8²	9	13		12			10¹	4	11																5
1	2		5	6	7	8²		9	13		12			10¹	4	11	3															6
1	2		5	6	7¹	8		9²	12		10			13	4	11	3															7
1	2		5	6	7	8		9¹	12		10²			13	4	11	3															8
	2		5	6²	7	8		9	13		12			10¹	4	11	3	1														9
	2		5	6	7	8		9						10	4	11	3	1														10
	2		5	6²	7	8		9	7		12			10¹	4	11	3	1	13													11
	2	12	5	6	7³	8		9	14					10²	4	11	3¹	1	13													12
	2¹		5	6	8²	7		12	9		14			10²	4	11	3¹	1				10										13
			4	5	6³	8	12²	7	14		13			9¹	2	11	3	1				10										14
			5¹	4	6	8³	12		14		13			10²	2	11	3	1						7	9							15
			4	5	6		8²				13	12		10¹	11		3	1						2	9	7						16
1	2		5	4	7		14				13	10			6	11	3		8²	12		9³										17
1	2		4	5	7							10			6	11	3		8	12		9										18
1	2		4	5	7							10³			6	11	3		8²	12	14	9¹		13								19
1	2		4	5	7				13			10²			6	11	3			12	14	9¹		8³								20
1	2²		4	5	7	12						10⁵			6		3		11	13	9	8										21
1	2		4	5	7	13						10			6	12³	3			11²	9¹	8										22
1	2		5	4		12			8			10¹			6	11	3				7	9										23
1	2			4		12			7		13	10			5	11	3				6¹	9		8²								24
1	2³		4	5	6²	7			8¹			9				11	3		12	10	14				13							25
1			5	6	4	8	7					9		14	11	3³					12	10²	6¹			13		2				26
1			5	4	6	7	8				12	9			11						2¹					3	10					27
1¹	2			4	6	7	8				10²	9			11	3					13	12				5³	14					28
1	2¹		5	6	8	11	9²		13			4³	10			7	3				14	12										29
1	3		5	6	2	11					8¹	10²			7	4			12	9							13					30
1	3³		5	6	4	7²					12	13			9				11¹		14					2			8	10		31
1			5	6		7			8			12			9¹	13	11	3		2							12²		4	10		32
1			5	6	2	12			7¹			9			4	11²	3		13										8	10		33
1			5		8			7¹				12			9	6	11	3						2					4	10		34
1			5	13		7			4²			14			9¹	6	11	3	12					2					8	10⁹		35
1	3		5	6¹		8			7			12					11					9²						2	10	4	13	36

QUEEN OF THE SOUTH   Second Division

Year Formed: 1919. *Ground & Address:* Palmerston Park, Dumfries DG2 9BA. *Telephone and Fax:* 01387 254853.
Ground Capacity: total: 8352, seated: 3549. *Size of Pitch:* 112yd × 73yd.
Chairman: Norman Blount. *Secretary:* Richard Shaw MBE. *Commercial Manager:* Robert McKinnell.
First Team Coaches: George Rowe, Ken Eadie.
Managers since 1975: M. Jackson; W. Hunter; B. Little; G. Herd; H. Hood; A. Busby; R. Clark; M. Jackson; D. Wilson;
W. McLaren; F. McGarvey; A. MacLeod; D. Frye; W. McLaren; M. Shanks; R. Alexander. *Club Nickname(s):* The
Doonhamers. *Previous Grounds:* None.
Record Attendance: 24,500 v Hearts, Scottish Cup 3rd rd; 23 Feb, 1952.
Record Transfer Fee received: £250,000 for Andy Thomson to Southend U (1994).
Record Transfer Fee paid: £30,000 for Jim Butter from Alloa Athletic (1995).
Record Victory: 11-1 v Stranraer, Scottish Cup 1st rd; 16 Jan, 1932.
Record Defeat: 2-10 v Dundee, Division I; 1 Dec, 1962.
Most Capped Player: Billy Houliston, 3, Scotland.
Most League Appearances: 731: Allan Ball, 1963–82.
Most League Goals in Season (Individual): 37: Jimmy Gray, Division II; 1927-28.
Most Goals in Season: 41: Jimmy Rutherford, 1931–32.
Most Goals Overall (Individual): 250: Jim Patterson, 1949–63.

QUEEN OF THE SOUTH 1998–99 LEAGUE RECORD

Match No.	Date		Venue	Opponents	Result	H/T Score	Lg. Pos.	Goalscorers	Atten- dance
1	Aug	4	A	Clyde	L	0-2	0-1	—	631
2		15	H	Arbroath	D	0-0	0-0	10	1104
3		22	A	Partick Th	D	2-2	1-1	9	Potts 38, Eadie 51	1963
4		29	H	Livingston	L	0-1	0-0	10		1281
5	Sept	5	A	Stirling A	L	0-1	0-0	10		640
6		12	A	Inverness CT	L	2-3	1-0	10	Rowe 21, Mallan 85	1812
7		19	H	Forfar Ath	W	3-0	0-0	8	Townsley 2 54, 55, Eadie 85	916
8		27	A	East Fife	L	0-2	0-0	8		803
9	Oct	3	H	Alloa Ath	W	2-1	2-1	8	Mallan 31, Townsley 38	1038
10		10	A	Arbroath	L	1-2	1-1	8	Mallan 32	603
11		17	H	Clyde	W	2-1	1-0	7	Eadie 32, Mallan 79	1139
12		24	A	Livingston	L	0-2	0-2	7		2005
13		31	H	Stirling A	L	2-3	1-2	8	Nesovic 36, Townsley 90	1128
14	Nov	7	A	Forfar Ath	L	0-1	0-0	9		389
15		14	H	Inverness CT	D	2-2	1-1	9	Eadie (pen) 34, Bailey 76	1021
16		21	A	East Fife	D	0-0	0-0	9		937
17		28	A	Alloa Ath	L	1-2	0-0	9	Mallan 53	592
18	Dec	12	H	Partick Th	D	0-0	0-0	9		1731
19		19	A	Clyde	L	1-2	1-1	9	Rowe 23	794
20		27	H	Livingston	D	2-2	1-0	9	Eadie 1, Mallan 87	1221
21	Jan	17	A	East Fife	W	1-0	0-0	9	Nesovic 64	797
22		26	A	Stirling A	W	3-1	1-0	—	Nesovic 22, Armstrong 80, Caldwell 88	643
23		30	A	Alloa Ath	D	0-0	0-0	9		1201
24	Feb	6	H	Forfar Ath	L	0-3	0-2	9		968
25		13	A	Inverness CT	L	0-1	0-0	9		2204
26		20	A	Partick Th	W	3-1	2-1	9	Mallan 2 21, 71, Rowe 43	1510
27		27	A	Arbroath	W	3-0	0-0	9	Leslie 49, Townsley 2 58, 78	1020
28	Mar	6	H	Stirling A	W	3-0	3-0	9	Townsley 6, Adams 21, Cleeland 38	1014
29		13	A	Livingston	W	2-1	2-0	7	Townsley 29, Adams 41	2300
30		20	A	Alloa Ath	W	5-3	2-1	6	Townsley 16, Adams 44, Mallan 2 47, 75, Rowe 74	523
31	Apr	3	H	East Fife	W	2-0	2-0	4	Adams 12, Rowe 32	1411
32		10	A	Forfar Ath	L	1-2	0-1	4	Rowe 82	416
33		17	H	Inverness CT	D	1-1	0-1	5	Rowe 88	1214
34		24	H	Clyde	W	2-1	0-0	4	Mallan 2 (1 pen) 61 (p), 73	1218
35	May	1	A	Arbroath	W	2-0	1-0	4	Mallan 2 30, 80	976
36		8	H	Partick Th	D	2-2	1-2	4	Townsley 23, Mallan 84	2335

Final League Position: 4   1997–98 4

Honours

League Champions: Division II 1950-51; *Runners-up:* Division II 1932-33, 1961-62, 1974-75. Second Division 1980-81, 1985-86.

Scottish Cup: semi-finalists 1949-50.

League Cup: semi-finalists 1950-51, 1960-61.

B&Q Cup: semi-finalists 1991-92. *League Challenge Cup:* runners-up 1997-98.

Club colours: Shirt: Royal blue. Shorts: White. Stockings: Royal blue with white tops.

Goalscorers: *League (50):* Mallan 15 (1 pen), Townsley 10, Rowe 7, Eadie 5 (1 pen), Adams 4, Nesovic 3, Armstrong 1, Bailey 1, Caldwell 1, Cleeland 1, Leslie 1, Potts 1. *Scottish Cup (1):* Nesovic 1. *League Cup (1):* Eadie 1.

Mathieson D 36	Milligan R 1	Love G 9	Rowe G 28 + 2	Thomson J 18	Cleeland M 26 + 2	McAllister J 25 + 2	Leslie S 21 + 1	Eadie K 15 + 5	Nesovic A 20 + 3	Bailey L 16 + 10	Boyle D 6 + 5	Mallan S 24 + 7	Lilley D 27	Townsley D 21 + 6	Potts C 5	Aitken A 27 + 2	Doig K 9	Adams C 18 + 9	MacLeod J 4	Caldwell B 2 + 13	Weir M 17 + 2	McKee C 2	Turner T 5	Armstrong G 4 + 3	Russell G 5 + 1	McCaig J 1 + 1	Bryce T 1 + 5	Moffat A 2	McGuffie R 1	Match No.
1	2	3	4	5	6²	7¹	8	9	10	11	12	13																		1
1		3	4	5	6		8	10²	13		14	9	2¹	7	11³	12														2
1		3	4	5			8	9	10¹	11			2	7		6	12													3
1		3	4	5		13	8	9	10	11			2²	12	7¹	6														4
1		3	4	5	2¹		8	9²	10	11			12	7		6	13													5
1		6	5		12		14	10	8²		9		7³	11¹	3	4	13	2												6
1		3	6	5	2	11²		12	10		13	9¹		7		4	8													7
1		3	6	5	2	11²		12	10			9		7¹		4	8	13												8
1		3		5	6	11²		10		12		9¹	2	8	13	4	7													9
1		3	13	5	6¹	11³		10	12	14		9	2	8²		4	7													10
1			4	5	6		14	9	10	8²		13³	2	12		3	7¹				11									11
1			4	5¹	6			10	8			9	2	12		3	7²			13	11									12
1		5	4				8	10	13			12	2	6		3	7¹				11		9²							13
1			4		3		8		10			11¹	9	2		6		12		5	11		7							14
1			5	6	11¹		8	9	10²	7³		14		4		3				2	12	13								15
1			5	4	11¹		8	9	10²			13		6		3				2	12		7							16
1		12	5	6	11		8		10²			9		4		3		2¹		13			7							17
1			4	5	6			12	10	13		9²		2		3		8¹			11		7							18
1			4	5	6			9²	10	14	12	13		2		3					11¹		7	8¹						19
1			5	6	3			9¹	10	6²		11		13		2		4		12			7	8						20
1			4		3			10		6		12		9		2		5		13	11²			7¹	8					21
1			4	14	3			10¹		7		9		2		5		6³		13	11²			12	8					22
1			4		3			10		7		9		2		5		6¹		13	11²			12	8					23
1			4	11	3		7¹	10²		6		9³		2		12		5		14				13	8					24
1			4	5	14		3	12		11³		9		2		7²		6		13				10¹	8					25
1			4		8		3	6		9		11¹		10		2		7			5			12						26
1			4		6		3	8		9				10		2		7			5			12	11					27
1			4		6		3	8		9²		12		14		2		7¹			5	10		13	11					28
1			4		6		3	8		9³		12				2		7¹			5	10	14		11²		13			29
1			4		6		3	8						10		7¹		5			9				11		2	12		30
1			4¹		6³		3	8		12		10				2		7			5	9²	13		11²	14	13			31
1			4		6		3	8						10		2		7¹			5	9			12		11			32
1			4		6		3	8						10		2					5	9			12		11	7¹		33
1			4		6		3²	8						10		2		7			5	9			12	11¹	13			34
1			6²		3		13	8						10		2		7			5	9³			12	11¹	14	4		35
1			6		13		8¹	10						2		7		5			9²				11	14	12	4³	3	36

QUEEN'S PARK   Third Division

Year Formed: 1867. *Ground & Address:* Hampden Park, Mount Florida, Glasgow G42 9BA. *Telephone:* 0141 632 1275.
Fax: 0141 636 1612.
Ground Capacity: all seated: 52,000. *Size of Pitch:* 115yd × 75yd.
President: James Nicholson. *Secretary:* Alistair Mackay. *Commercial Director:* Kenneth Harvey. *Coach:* John McCormack.
Physio: R.C.Findlay.
Coaches since 1975: D. McParland, J. Gilroy, E. Hunter, H. McCann. *Club Nickname(s):* The Spiders. *Previous Grounds:* 1st Hampden (Recreation Ground); (Titwood Park was used as an interim measure between 1st & 2nd Hampdens); 2nd Hampden (Cathkin); 3rd Hampden.
Record Attendance: 95,772 v Rangers, Scottish Cup, 18 Jan, 1930.
Record for Ground: 149,547 Scotland v England, 1937.
Record Transfer Fee received: Not applicable due to amateur status.
Record Transfer Fee paid: Not applicable due to amateur status.
Record Victory: 16-0 v St. Peters, Scottish Cup 1st rd; 29 Aug, 1885.
Record Defeat: 0-9 v Motherwell, Division I; 26 Apr, 1930.
Most Capped Player: Walter Arnott, 14, Scotland.
Most League Appearances: 473: J. B. McAlpine.

QUEEN'S PARK 1998–99 LEAGUE RECORD

Match No.	Date	Venue	Opponents	Result	H/T Score	Lg. Pos.	Goalscorers	Atten-dance
1	Aug 4	A	Berwick R	W 3-0	1-0	—	Little [40], Graham 2 [62, 87]	448
2	15	H	Dumbarton	L 0-1	0-0	—		656
3	22	A	Brechin C	D 2-2	0-1	5	Black (og) [75], Orr [89]	300
4	29	A	Albion R	L 1-2	1-1	7	Edgar [2]	419
5	Sept 5	H	Stenhousemuir	D 0-0	0-0	7		499
6	12	H	Ross Co	W 4-2	0-0	7	McGill (pen) [63], Caven [65], Martin P [77], Edgar [84]	688
7	19	A	Montrose	L 0-1	0-0	7		310
8	26	H	East Stirling	L 0-4	0-3	7		526
9	Oct 3	A	Cowdenbeath	W 3-0	0-0	6	Carmichael 2 [63, 90], Martin P [74]	280
10	10	A	Dumbarton	L 0-1	0-0	8		343
11	17	H	Brechin C	D 1-1	1-0	8	Edgar [27]	446
12	27	H	Albion R	D 0-0	0-0	—		336
13	31	A	Stenhousemuir	L 1-2	0-2	8	Carmichael [56]	387
14	Nov 7	H	Montrose	W 3-0	2-0	6	Edgar [41], Finlayson K [42], Elder [88]	385
15	14	A	Ross Co	L 1-5	1-2	6	Carmichael [18]	1433
16	21	A	East Stirling	D 1-1	0-1	7	Carmichael [51]	247
17	28	H	Cowdenbeath	W 2-0	1-0	7	Carmichael [8], Parks [86]	439
18	Dec 12	H	Berwick R	D 1-1	1-0	7	Edgar [13]	389
19	19	A	Brechin C	L 0-1	0-0	7		328
20	26	A	Albion R	L 0-1	0-0	7		322
21	Jan 16	A	East Stirling	D 1-1	1-1	7	Martin P [12]	224
22	26	H	Stenhousemuir	W 4-1	1-0	—	Edgar 2 [31, 46], Ferry [53], Finlayson K [80]	333
23	30	A	Cowdenbeath	D 0-0	0-0	7		198
24	Feb 6	A	Montrose	L 0-3	0-1	7		260
25	13	H	Ross Co	L 0-3	0-1	7		581
26	20	A	Berwick R	W 2-0	0-0	7	Campbell (og) [48], Brown [68]	330
27	27	H	Dumbarton	D 1-1	0-1	8	Martin P [98]	516
28	Mar 6	A	Stenhousemuir	L 1-4	0-3	8	Martin P [75]	425
29	13	H	Albion R	D 0-0	0-0	8		492
30	20	H	Cowdenbeath	W 2-1	1-0	8	Finlayson K [7], Brown [47]	336
31	Apr 3	H	East Stirling	W 2-1	2-1	7	Martin P [14], Finlayson K [30]	455
32	10	H	Montrose	L 1-2	0-2	7	Finlayson K [49]	363
33	17	A	Ross Co	W 2-1	0-1	7	Brown [53], Finlayson K [96]	3758
34	24	H	Brechin C	L 0-2	0-1	8		503
35	May 1	A	Dumbarton	W 1-0	0-0	7	McGuffie [85]	762
36	8	H	Berwick R	D 1-1	0-0	6	Whelan [80]	473

Final League Position: 6   1997–98 7

Most League Goals in Season (Individual): 30: William Martin, Division I; 1937-38.
Most Goals Overall (Individual): 163: J. B. McAlpine.

Honours
League Champions: Division II 1922-23. B Division 1955-56. Second Division 1980-81.
Scottish Cup Winners: 1874, 1875, 1876, 1880, 1881, 1882, 1884, 1886, 1890, 1893; *Runners-up:* 1892, 1900.
League Cup: —.
FA Cup runners-up: 1884, 1885.

Club colours: Shirt: White and black hoops. Shorts: White. Stockings: White with black hoops.

Goalscorers: *League (41):* Edgar 7, Carmichael 6, Finlayson K 6, Martin P 6, Brown 3, Graham 2, Caven 1, Elder 1, Ferry 1, Little 1, McGill 1 (pen), McGuffie 1, Orr 1, Parks 1, Whelan 1, own goals 2. *Scottish Cup (6):* Edgar 2, Brown 1, Finlayson K 1, Graham 1, Parks 1. *League Cup (1):* Graham 1.

Monaghan M 2	Alexander D 24 + 2	Connaghan D 26 + 4	Ferguson P 11 + 3	Martin P 28	Caven R 27	Ferry D 31 + 4	Graham D 19 + 1	Edgar S 29 + 7	Parks G 7 + 13	Little T 13 + 9	Finlayson K 26 + 9	Rossiter B 26 + 1	Cooke B 6	Agostini D 5 + 4	Orr G 4 + 2	Hamilton W — + 3	Inglis N 11	McGill D 4	Carmichael D 12 + 1	McGhee D 3	Elder G 11 + 2	Reid A 7 + 3	McColl B 2 + 9	Tyrrell P 15 + 4	Chalmers J 17	Finlayson R — + 1	Brown J 13 + 1	McGuffie R 5 + 6	Martin A 4 + 5	Whelan J 8	Match No.
1	2	3	4	5	6	7	8	9	10¹	11	12																				1
1	4		2	5	6	7	8¹	9	10	11	12	3																			2
	4²	3	6	5		7		9	10¹	11³	12	8	1	2	13	14															3
10	3	6²	4		2²	8	9		11	14	7		5	13	12	1															4
2³	3		5		7	8	9		11²	12	6		14	4	13	1	10¹														5
4	3¹	12	5	6		8³			11²	13	2		14	7		1	10														6
2¹		3	5³	6²	13	8	9		11		4		12	7		1	10	14													7
2		3		6	13	8²	9	14		12	4			7		1	10²	11¹	5												8
2	3	6	5	8	7		9		12	11¹	4					1	10														9
2	3	6¹	5	8	7		9³	14	13	11	4					1	10²		12												10
2	3	6²	5		13		9		11¹	12	4					1	10		8	7											11
2	3		5	4	7		9	13	11²	12						1	10¹		8	6											12
2	3¹		5	4	7		13		11²	9	12					1	10		6	8³	14										13
2	14		5	3	7³		9	12	13	11²	4					1	10¹		6	8											14
2	14		5	3	7		9	12	13	11¹	4³	1					10		6		8²										15
2	3		5		7		9			11	4	1					10		6		8										16
	3	14	5	2	7	4³	9²	13	12	11¹		1					10		6		8										17
	3	4¹	5	2	7	12	9²	13	14	11		1					10³		6		8										18
13	3		5	2²	7	6	12	10³	14	11	4						9¹				8		1								19
2	3		5		7	6²	9¹	10	12	11									4		13	8	1								20
2	3	13	5		7		9	10¹		11	4								6			8	1	12²							21
5		3²		2	10	6	9	12	11¹	7	4	1									14	8³		13							22
2	12		5	6	10	9	13	11²	7	4											14	8¹	1	3³							23
5	3		2	8	6¹	9	13	11²	7	4												12	1	10							24
5			2	8		9²	11¹	14	7	4	3									6	12		1	10³	13						25
			2	6		13	12	7		3					4				10³	14	8	1	5	11¹	9²						26
2	14		5	6		12		7		4								13	8	3³	1	10	11¹	9²							27
2¹	3		5	13		9		7		14					4				6²	8	1	10	11³	12							28
	3		5	2	8		9²	14		7	4									12	1	6³	11¹	13	10						29
	3		5	2	8		12			7²	4								9¹		11		10³	13	14	6					30
	3		5	2	8	11²	12			7	4										13	1	10³	14	9¹	6					31
	3		5	2	8	6³	12			7	4						14		13	1			10¹	9²	11						32
	3		5	2	8	6¹	9³			7	4								12	14	13	1	10²			11					33
	3		5	2	8	11²	9¹	12		7							4		13				10	14		6²					34
14	3		2	8³	5	9²				7	4										11	1	10¹	12	13	6					35
	3		2	8	5²	9³				7	4							14			11	1	10¹	12	13	6					36

RAITH ROVERS
First Division

Year Formed: 1883. *Ground & Address:* Stark's Park, Pratt St, Kirkcaldy KY1 1SA. *Telephone:* 01592 263514. *Fax:* 01592 642833.
Ground Capacity: all seated: 10,271. *Size of Pitch:* 113yd × 70yd.
Chairman: William Gray. *Office Manager:* Keri Gooding.
Manager: John McVeigh. *Assistant Manager:* Peter Hetherston. *Youth Coach:* Kenny Black. *Physio:* John McCreadie.
Managers since 1975: R. Paton; A. Matthew; W. McLean; G. Wallace; R. Wilson; F. Connor; J. Nicholl; J. Thomson; T. McLean; I. Munro; J. Nicholl. *Club Nickname:* Rovers. *Previous Grounds:* Robbie's Park.
Record Attendance: 31,306 v Hearts, Scottish Cup 2nd rd; 7 Feb, 1953.
Record Transfer Fee received: £900,000 for S. McAnespie to Bolton Wanderers (Sept 1995).
Record Transfer Fee paid: £225,000 for Paul Harvey from Airdrieonians (1996).
Record Victory: 10-1 v Coldstream, Scottish Cup 2nd rd; 13 Feb, 1954.
Record Defeat: 2-11 v Morton, Division II; 18 Mar, 1936.
Most Capped Player: David Morris, 6, Scotland.
Most League Appearances: 430: Willie McNaught.
Most League Goals in Season (Individual): 38: Norman Haywood, Division II; 1937-38.
Most Goals Overall (Individual): 154: Gordon Dalziel (League), 1987-94.

RAITH ROVERS 1998–99 LEAGUE RECORD

Match No.	Date	Venue	Opponents	Result	H/T Score	Lg. Pos.	Goalscorers	Atten- dance
1	Aug 4	H	Hamilton A	L 0-2	0-1	—		2316
2	15	A	St Mirren	L 1-2	1-1	10	Cameron [7]	2106
3	22	H	Ayr U	D 0-0	0-0	9		2010
4	29	A	Airdrieonians	W 1-0	0-0	8	Hartley [78]	2297
5	Sept 5	H	Greenock Morton	D 0-0	0-0	7		1880
6	12	H	Falkirk	D 1-1	1-1	8	Dargo [45]	3072
7	19	A	Hibernian	L 1-3	0-0	8	Wright [60]	8853
8	26	A	Stranraer	L 0-2	0-1	8	Hartley [48], Dair J [69]	618
9	Oct 3	H	Clydebank	L 0-1	0-0	9		1661
10	11	H	St Mirren	W 1-0	0-0	8	Wright [77]	1963
11	17	A	Hamilton A	L 2-3	2-0	8	Tosh 2 [12, 34]	790
12	31	A	Greenock Morton	L 0-2	0-2	9		1468
13	Nov 3	H	Airdrieonians	L 1-3	1-2	—	Tosh [25]	1406
14	7	H	Hibernian	L 1-3	0-0	9	Dargo [86]	4925
15	14	A	Falkirk	D 1-1	1-1	9	Dargo [24]	3611
16	21	H	Stranraer	W 2-0	1-0	8	Hartley (pen) [20], Dargo [90]	1938
17	28	A	Clydebank	D 1-1	1-1	9	Hartley (pen) [41]	417
18	Dec 8	A	Hamilton A	D 1-1	0-1	—	Britton [80]	1929
19	12	A	Ayr U	W 2-0	2-0	8	Welsh (og) [12], Dair J [45]	2245
20	19	H	Greenock Morton	L 1-3	1-3	9	Cameron [13]	2721
21	26	A	Airdrieonians	D 2-2	1-2	9	Cameron [10], Stein [75]	2077
22	Jan 2	A	Hibernian	L 1-5	1-4	9	Dargo [39]	14,703
23	9	H	Falkirk	W 2-1	0-1	8	Cameron [85], Holmes [90]	3390
24	16	A	Stranraer	L 0-2	0-0	9		575
25	30	H	Clydebank	W 2-1	1-1	8	Dair J [9], Tosh [49]	1803
26	Feb 6	A	St Mirren	L 1-3	1-1	8	Andrews [22]	1621
27	20	A	Ayr U	L 2-4	2-1	8	Holmes 2 [3, 8]	1873
28	27	H	Airdrieonians	L 0-1	0-0	8		1896
29	Mar 13	A	Greenock Morton	D 1-1	0-1	8	Dargo (pen) [61]	1795
30	20	A	Clydebank	D 0-0	0-0	8		300
31	Apr 3	H	Stranraer	W 3-2	2-1	8	Fotheringham K [19], McQuade [37], Dargo [90]	1883
32	10	H	Hibernian	L 1-3	1-1	8	Holmes [29]	5730
33	17	A	Falkirk	L 0-1	0-0	8		2532
34	24	A	Hamilton A	W 2-1	1-0	8	Dargo [31], Holmes [89]	1398
35	May 1	H	St Mirren	D 1-1	1-0	8	Holmes [26]	2380
36	8	A	Ayr U	L 0-1	0-1	8		1886

Final League Position: 8   1997–98 3

Honours

League Champions: First Division: 1992-93, 1994-95. Division II 1907-08, 1909-10 (shared), 1937-38, 1948-49; *Runners-up:* Division II 1908-09, 1926-27, 1966-67. Second Division 1975-76, 1977-78, 1986-87. *Scottish Cup Runners-up:* 1913. *League Cup Winners: (Coca-Cola Cup):* 1994-95. *Runners-up:* 1948-49.

European: *UEFA Cup:* 6 matches (1995-96).

Club colours: Shirt: Navy blue, white trim. Shorts: White. Stockings: White.

Goalscorers: *League (37):* Dargo 8 (1 pen), Holmes 6, Cameron 4, Hartley 4 (2 pens), Tosh 4, Dair J 3, Wright 2, Andrews 1, Britton 1, Fotheringham K 1, McQuade 1, Stein 1, own goal 1. *Scottish Cup (0).* *League Cup (4):* Dair J 1, Hartley 1, Shields 1, Wright 1.

Van De Kamp G 33	McEwan C 23+3	McPherson D 3+1	McCulloch G 23+8	Browne P 31+1	Fotheringham K 26	Hartley P 18	Bowman D 23	Wright K 8+4	Tosh S 23+2	Dair J 27	Stein J 6+14	Dair L —+2	Venables R 2	Cameron I 26+2	Smart C 3+2	Shields P 6+8	Robertson G 3+3	Dargo C 21+1	Andrews M 19+5	Lennon D 21+4	Grant C —+1	Byers K 10+5	Fotheringham G 1+4	Britton G 5	Ellis L 4+5	Brownlie P 2+7	Holmes D 13+1	Kirkwood D 5+1	McGeown M 3	Cormack P 1	McQuade J 3+3	McLeish K 1+1	Maughan R 1	Nicol K 1+1	McInally D 1	Clark A —+1	Match No.
1	2	3²	4¹	5	6	7	8	9	10	11	12	13																									1
1	3¹	12	5	6	7	8	9	10³	2²				14	4	11	13																					2
1	2	13	5	6	7	4	9¹	10	3					11²	14	8³	12																				3
1	2	13	5	6	7	8			10	3				4²	11			12	9¹																		4
1	2		5	6	7	8	13	10	3		12			11				9¹	4²																		5
1	2	8¹	13	5	6	7	4		10³	3				11				12	14	9²																	6
1	2		4²	5		7	8¹	12	10	3				11			13	9	6																		7
1	2		5		4	7	8	9²	10¹	3				11				6	12	13																	8
1	2¹	14	4	6	7	8	12	13	3					11²				9	5	10³																	9
1	2		5	6	7		9		3	11²						10¹	13	4	8	12																	10
1	12	2	6		7	4	9	8	3	13							10¹	5	11²																		11
1	2²		5		7	4	10	3		12				8¹	14			9²	6	11	13																12
1		12	5		7	2	8	10	3					11				9³	6¹	4²	13	14															13
1	2²		5	6³	7	8	13		3					14				11	9	12	10	4¹															14
1	2	13	5	6			11	8²	3	12				10				9		7		4¹															15
1	2		5	6	7				12	3				11				9	8		4¹	10															16
1	12	2		6	7¹	4			3	13				11				5	8	10²	9																17
1	13	2		6	7	4			3	11¹				9				5²	8	12	10																18
1	2	4	5	6	7	10			3	12				8				11¹	9																		19
1	2		5	6	10				3	12				11¹	7²	13		8	4¹	9	14																20
1	2	6	5		4				3	13				11	10²	14	9¹	8	7¹	12																	21
1	2	4	5						3	11				10¹	12	6³	9	8	7²	14	13																22
1	2	4¹	6		7	11²	3							13				9	5	8³							12	10	14								23
1	2	13	6		4				3	11				9				5	8								12	10²	7¹								24
	2¹	6	8	4	7²	3	13			11				9¹				5	12			14					10			1							25
	2	6	4	7	3¹	11¹	10	9²	5								14	13	12	8										1							26
	5	11	7¹	4³	2	10	14	9²	6	12				13	8												3	14	10	4							27
1	2	6	14	3		4	13	11¹	9	12	5	8³						7	10²																		28
1	2	4	5	3		7	8²	14	11³	9	6	13						10¹	12																		29
1	2	4	5	3		7	8	11¹	10	12	6	9																									30
1	13	7	4	3		2	11¹	6²	9	5	8			10							12																31
1	2	7²	5	3		4	11¹	9	6	8³			13	10						12	14																32
1	2	7	5	6		9	14	8	12	3³	13	10	4²	11¹																							33
1	2	7	5	6		12	9²	14	8¹	13	3	10	4	11²																							34
1		6	5			11	9¹	13	3	14	10	4	12	8	2²	7³																					35
1	2¹	6		12	5	8	7	3	10³	4	9²	14	11	13																							36

RANGERS   Premier League

Year Formed: 1873. *Ground & Address:* Ibrox Stadium, 150 Edmiston Drive, Glasgow G51 2XD.
Telephone: 0141 427 8500. *Fax:* 0141 419 0600.
Ground Capacity: all seated: 50,403. *Size of Pitch:* 115yd × 76yd.
Chairman: David Murray. *Secretary:* R. C. Ogilvie. *Commercial & Marketing Manager:* Martin Bain.
Manager: Dick Advocaat. *Assistant Manager:* Bert Van Lingen. *Physio:* Grant Downie. *Reserve team coaches:* John McGregor, John Brown.
Managers since 1975: Jock Wallace; John Greig; Jock Wallace; Graeme Souness. *Club Nickname(s):* The Gers.
Previous Grounds: Flesher's Haugh, Burnbank, Kinning Park, Old Ibrox.
Record Attendance: 118,567 v Celtic, Division I; 2 Jan, 1939.
Record Transfer Fee received: £5,580,000 for Trevor Steven to Marseille (Aug 1991).
Record Transfer Fee paid: £5.5 million for Andrei Kanchelskis from Fiorentina (July 1998).
Record Victory: 14-2 v Blairgowrie, Scottish Cup 1st rd; 20 Jan, 1934.
Record Defeat: 2-10 v Airdrieonians; 1886.
Most Capped Player: Ally McCoist, 60, Scotland.
Most League Appearances: 496: John Greig, 1962-78.
Most League Goals in Season (Individual): 44: Sam English, Division I; 1931–32.
Most Goals Overall (Individual): 355: Ally McCoist; 1985–98.

RANGERS 1998–99 LEAGUE RECORD

Match No.	Date	Venue	Opponents	Result	H/T Score	Lg. Pos.	Goalscorers	Atten-dance
1	Aug 2	A	Hearts	L	1-2	1-2	—	Wallace [28]	15,272
2	15	H	Motherwell	W	2-1	1-0	5	Wallace [14], Albertz (pen) [90]	49,275
3	22	A	Kilmarnock	W	3-1	2-0	3	Wallace [25], Albertz (pen) [28], Miller [88]	17,608
4	29	H	St Johnstone	W	4-0	2-0	1	Kanchelskis [26], Van Bronckhorst [44], Wallace [55], Albertz (pen) [85]	48,732
5	Sept 12	A	Dundee U	D	0-0	0-0	' 1		12,088
6	20	H	Celtic	D	0-0	0-0	1		50,026
7	23	A	Aberdeen	D	1-1	0-1	—	Wallace [78]	17,862
8	26	A	Dunfermline Ath	W	2-0	1-0	1	Johansson [11], Ferguson B [50]	11,507
9	Oct 4	H	Dundee	W	1-0	0-0	1	Albertz (pen) [80]	48,348
10	17	H	Hearts	W	3-0	0-0	1	Johansson [49], Wallace 2 [61, 88]	49,749
11	28	A	Motherwell	L	0-1	0-0	—		11,777
12	31	H	Dundee U	W	2-1	0-1	1	Wallace [62], Amoruso [84]	49,503
13	Nov 8	A	St Johnstone	W	7-0	3-0	1	Wallace [9], Johansson [28], Albertz 2 [31, 81], Kanchelskis [64], Guivarc'h 2 [69, 79]	9660
14	14	H	Aberdeen	W	2-1	1-0	1	Van Bronckhorst [8], Kanchelskis [82]	49,479
15	21	A	Celtic	L	1-5	0-1	1	Van Bronckhorst [54]	59,783
16	Dec 5	H	Dunfermline Ath	D	1-1	1-0	1	Van Bronckhorst [16]	47,465
17	12	H	Kilmarnock	W	1-0	1-0	1	Wallace [11]	49,781
18	19	A	Hearts	W	3-2	1-0	1	Guivarc'h 2 [15, 62], Kanchelskis [59]	17,134
19	26	A	St Johnstone	W	1-0	0-0	1	Porrini [72]	49,479
20	30	A	Dundee U	W	2-1	1-1	—	Wilson [32], Wallace [88]	11,707
21	Jan 3	H	Celtic	D	2-2	1-1	1	Amato [44], Wallace [58]	50,059
22	27	A	Dundee	W	4-0	3-0	—	Miller 2 [8, 42], Guivarc'h [11], Johansson [76]	10,043
23	30	A	Aberdeen	W	4-2	2-1	1	Porrini [10], Wallace [12], Albertz (pen) [96], Kanchelskis [89]	19,507
24	Feb 7	A	Dunfermline Ath	W	3-0	0-0	1	Kanchelskis [56], Johansson 2 [59, 89]	10,360
25	20	H	Dundee	W	6-1	2-1	1	Albertz 3 (1 pen) [24 (p), 38, 57], McCann 2 [51, 72], Van Bronckhorst [87]	49,462
26	28	A	Kilmarnock	W	5-0	1-0	1	McCann [5], Wallace 3 [75, 87, 89], Johansson [85]	16,242
27	Mar 13	H	Motherwell	W	2-1	1-0	1	Wallace [31], Johansson [59]	49,483
28	20	H	Dundee U	L	0-1	0-1	1		49,164
29	Apr 4	A	St Johnstone	L	1-3	0-1	1	Moore [57]	9742
30	14	H	Dunfermline Ath	W	1-0	1-0	—	Van Bronckhorst [34]	46,220
31	18	A	Dundee	D	1-1	0-1	1	Vidmar [48]	11,070
32	25	H	Aberdeen	W	3-1	1-1	1	Amato [27], Kanchelskis [55], Wallace [60]	49,145
33	May 2	A	Celtic	W	3-0	2-0	1	McCann 2 [13, 76], Albertz (pen) [43]	59,918
34	9	H	Hearts	D	0-0	0-0	1		49,495
35	15	A	Motherwell	W	5-1	2-0	1	Amato 3 (1 pen) [16, 51, 53 (p)], Van Bronckhorst [37], Kanchelskis [65]	11,078
36	23	H	Kilmarnock	D	1-1	1-1	1	Amato [5]	48,835
Final League Position: 1				1997–98 2				

Honours
League Champions: (48 times) Division I 1890-91 (shared), 1898-99, 1899-1900, 1900-01, 1901-02, 1910-11, 1911-12, 1912-13, 1917-18, 1919-20, 1920-21, 1922-23, 1923-24, 1924-25, 1926-27, 1927-28, 1928-29, 1929-30, 1930-31, 1932-33, 1933-34, 1934-35, 1936-37, 1938-39, 1946-47, 1948-49, 1949-50, 1952-53, 1955-56, 1956-57, 1958-59, 1960-61, 1962-63, 1963-64, 1974-75. Premier Division: 1975-76, 1977-78, 1986-87, 1988-89, 1989-90, 1990-91, 1991-92, 1992-93, 1993-94, 1994-95, 1995-96, 1996-97, 1998-99; *Runners-up:* 24 times.
Scottish Cup Winners: (28 times) 1894, 1897, 1898, 1903, 1928, 1930, 1932, 1934, 1935, 1936, 1948, 1949, 1950, 1953, 1960, 1962, 1963, 1964, 1966, 1973, 1976, 1978, 1979, 1981, 1992, 1993, 1996, 1999; *Runners-up:* 17 times.
League Cup Winners: (21 times) 1946-47, 1948-49, 1960-61, 1961-62, 1963-64, 1964-65, 1970-71, 1975-76, 1977-78, 1978-79, 1981-82, 1983-84, 1984-85, 1986-87, 1987-88, 1988-89, 1990-91, 1992-93, 1993-94, 1996-97, 1998-99; *Runners-up:* 7 times.

European: *European Cup:* 91 matches (1956-57, 1957-58, 1959-60 semi-finals, 1961-62, 1963-64, 1975-76, 1976-77, 1978-79, 1987-88, 1989-90, 1990-91, 1991-92, 1992-93 final pool, 1993-94, 1994-95, 1995-96; 1996-97, 1997-98). *Cup Winners' Cup:* 54 matches (1960-61 runners-up, 1962-63, 1966-67 runners-up, 1969-70, 1971-72 winners, 1973-74, 1977-78, 1979-80, 1981-82, 1983-84). *UEFA Cup:* 1967-68, 1968-69 semi-finals, 1970-71. *UEFA Cup:* 1982-83, 1984-85, 1985-86, 1986-87, 1988-89, 1997-98, 1998-99).

Club colours: Shirt: Royal blue with red and blue panels. Shorts: White with red and blue panels. Stockings: Red with black tops.

Goalscorers: *League (78):* Wallace 18, Albertz 11 (7 pens), Johansson 8, Kanchelskis 8, Van Bronckhorst 7, Amato 6 (1 pen), Guivarc'h 5, McCann 5, Miller 3, Porrini 2, Amoruso 1, Ferguson B 1, Moore 1, Vidmar 1, Wilson 1. *Scottish Cup (15):* Johansson 3, McCann 3, Wallace 3, Albertz 1 (pen), Amoruso 1, Guivarc'h 1, Kanchelskis 1, Van Bronckhorst 1, Vidmar 1. *League Cup (13):* Albertz 3, Wallace 2, Amato 1, Amoruso 1, Durie 1, Ferguson B 1, Ferguson I 1, Guivarc'h 1, Johansson 1, Miller 1.

Niemi A 7	Porrini S 35	Numan A 8+2	Moore C 8	Thern J	Albertz J 33+1	Van Bronckhorst G 35	Ferguson I 4+9	Gattuso G 3+2	Durie G 1+4	Wallace R 34	Kanchelskis A 29+1	Amato G 13+7	Charbonnier L 11	Amoruso L 33	Hendry C 16+3	Ferguson B 23	Johansson J 13+12	Graham D —+3	Miller C 2+14	Vidmar A 26+2	Rozental S —+3	Wilson S 7+5	Guivarc'h S 11+3	Stensaas S 1	McCann N 15+4	Klos S 18	Nicholson B 3+3	Feeney L —+1	McInnes D —+7	Reyna C 6	Riccio L —+1	Match No.
1	2	3	4	5[1]	6	7[2]	8	9	10	11	12	13																				1
	2	3			6		8	9[1]		10	11[2]		1	4	5	7	12	13														2
	2	3		5	6		8	9[2]		10	11[1]	13	1	4		7	12															3
	2			5	6		8	9	14	10	11[1]		1	4		7[3]	12	13		3[2]												4
	2			5	6		8	9		10	11[1]		1	4		7	12			3												5
	2	3			6		8	9[2]		10	11[1]		1	4	5	7	12	13														6
	2			5	6		8			10	11[3]	13	1	4		7	12		14	3[1]			9[2]									7
	2			5[3]	6		8	9		10[2]	11[1]		1	4		7	12	13	14	3												8
	2				6		8	9[1]	14	10[2]	11[2]		1	4	5	7	12	13		3												9
	2				6		8	9[2]		10[3]	11[1]		1	4	5	7	12	13	14	3												10
	2				6[1]		8	9	14	10	11[3]	13	1	4	5	7	12			3[2]												11
	2				6		8	9		10	11[2]	12	1	4	5	7		13		3[1]												12
1	2	3[1]			6	7	8	9		10	11[2]			4	5[1]		12	13	14													13
1	2	3			6[2]		8	9		10	11[1]	13		4	5	7	12															14
1	2	3			6[1]		8	9[2]		10	11			4	5	7[3]	12	13	14													15
1	2	3			6		8	9		10	11[1]			4	5	7	12															16
1	2	3[1]			6		8	9		10	11[2]			4	5	7[3]	12	13	14													17
1	2				6		8	9		10	11			4	5	7	12[2]	13		3[1]												18
	2				6		8	9[1]		10[3]				4	5	7	12	13	14	3					11[2]	1						19
	2				6[2]		8			10				4	5	7	12	13	14	3			9[3]		11[1]	1						20
	2				6[2]		8			10				4	5	7	12	13		3			9[1]		11	1						21
	2				6		8			10				4		7	12			3		5	9		11[1]	1	8[2]		13			22
	2				6[3]		8			10				4	5	7[2]	12	13	14	3			9		11[1]	1						23
	2				6		8			10				4		7	12	13		3		5[1]	9[2]		11	1						24
	2				6					10[3]				4	5	7[2]	12	13	14	3			9		11[1]	1	8					25
	2[3]				6[1]					10				4	5	7	12	13	14	3			9		11[2]	1	8					26
	2				6					10				4	5	7[1]	12	13	14	3			9[2]		11	1	8[3]					27
	2				6					10				4	5[1]	7	12	13		3[2]			9		11	1	8					28
	2				6					10				4	5	7	12			3[1]			9		11	1	8					29
	2				6					10				4		7							9		11[1]	1	8					30
	2				6					10				4		7	12		14	3		5[2]	9[3]		11[1]	1	8		13			31
	2									10				4	5	7	12	13	14	3			9[2]		11[1]	1	8			6[1]		32
	2				6					10				4	5	7[2]	12			3			9		11[1]	1	8		13			33
	2				6					10				4	5	7	12		14	3[1]			9[2]		11[3]	1	8		13			34
	2									10				4		7	12	13	14	3		5[1]	9		11	1	8[2]			6[1]		35
	2						8			10[1]				4		7	12			3		5[2]	9		11	1			13	6		36

ROSS COUNTY

Second Division

Year Formed: 1929. *Ground & Address:* Victoria Park, Dingwall IV15 9QW. *Telephone:* 01349 862253. *Fax:* 01349 866277.
Ground Capacity: total 5400, seated 1520. *Size of Ground:* 110×75yd.
Chairman: Roy McGregor. *Secretary:* Donnie MacBean. *Facilities Manager:* Brian Campbell.
Manager: Neale Cooper. *Assistant Manager:* Jim Kelly. *Physio:* Douglas Sim. *Record Attendance:* 6600, benefit match v Celtic, 31 August 1970.
Record Transfer Fee Received: £200,000 for Neil Tarrant to Aston Villa (April 1999).
Record Transfer Fee Paid: £25,000 for Barry Wilson from Southampton (Oct.1992).
Record Victory: 11-0 v St Cuthbert Wanderers, Scottish Cup, Dec.1993.
Record Defeat: 1-10 v Inverness Thistle, Highland League.
Most League Appearances: 124: W. Herd, 1995–98.
Most League Goals in Season: 22: D. Adams, 1996–97.
Most League Goals (Overall): 38: D. Adams, 1996–98.

ROSS COUNTY 1998–99 LEAGUE RECORD

Match No.	Date		Venue	Opponents	Result	H/T Score	Lg. Pos.	Goalscorers	Attendance
1	Aug	4	H	East Stirling	W 1-0	0-0	—	McBain [66]	1021
2		15	A	Albion R	W 8-0	5-0	—	Ross [8], Tarrant 3 [19, 23, 76], Escalon [33], Ferguson 2 [37, 61], McBain [87]	302
3		22	H	Montrose	W 3-1	2-0	1	Ferguson [18], Craib (og) [30], Wood [71]	1266
4		29	H	Cowdenbeath	W 2-0	2-0	1	Ferguson [8], Adams [41]	1553
5	Sept	5	A	Berwick R	W 2-0	0-0	1	Adams 2 [52, 89]	453
6		12	A	Queen's Park	L 2-4	0-0	1	Tarrant 2 [52, 57]	688
7		19	H	Stenhousemuir	L 0-1	0-0	1		2105
8		26	H	Brechin C	L 0-1	0-0	3		1512
9	Oct	3	A	Dumbarton	W 2-1	2-1	3	McBain [9], Ferries [21]	538
10		10	H	Albion R	L 1-2	1-0	3	Wood [43]	1385
11		17	A	Montrose	W 6-3	3-2	2	Wood 4 [11, 21, 23, 75], Ferguson [80], McBain [90]	339
12		28	A	Cowdenbeath	W 2-1	2-0	—	Wood 2 [22, 26]	212
13		31	H	Berwick R	W 3-1	0-0	1	Ferguson 2 [46, 55], Tarrant [63]	1546
14	Nov	7	A	Stenhousemuir	W 4-2	2-0	1	Ferguson 3 [8, 80, 90], Taylor [24]	510
15		14	H	Queen's Park	W 5-1	2-1	1	Tarrant 3 (2 pens) [17 (pl, 48 (pl), 59], Ferries [34], Ferguson (pen) [85]	1433
16		21	A	Brechin C	W 1-0	1-0	1	Tarrant [21]	826
17		28	H	Dumbarton	W 2-0	0-0	1	Taylor [59], Ferguson [63]	1759
18	Dec	12	A	East Stirling	D 2-2	0-1	1	McGlashan [52], Golabek [78]	338
19		19	H	Montrose	W 3-0	1-0	1	Ferries [33], Tarrant [64], Taylor [87]	1571
20		26	H	Cowdenbeath	W 1-0	0-0	1	Golabek [63]	1842
21	Jan	27	A	Berwick R	D 2-2	1-1	—	Ferguson [21], McBain [80]	319
22		30	A	Dumbarton	D 0-0	0-0	1		400
23	Feb	6	H	Stenhousemuir	D 2-2	1-1	1	Maxwell [6], McGlashan [69]	1837
24		13	A	Queen's Park	W 3-0	1-0	1	Agostini (og) [21], Maxwell [53], Ferries [75]	581
25		27	A	Albion R	D 3-3	2-1	1	Ferguson [4], Wood [35], McStay (og) [59]	432
26	Mar	2	H	East Stirling	W 4-2	3-1	—	Ferguson 2 [10, 54], Wood [20], Tarrant [39]	1021
27		6	H	Berwick R	W 6-0	2-0	1	Tarrant 2 [2, 57], McGlashan 2 [8, 52], Taylor [55], Ross [62]	1732
28		9	H	Brechin C	W 2-1	2-1	—	Ferguson [22], Tarrant (pen) [40]	1537
29		13	A	Cowdenbeath	W 3-2	1-2	1	Tarrant [37], Mitchell (og) [48], Maxwell [73]	316
30		20	H	Dumbarton	L 1-2	1-0	1	Tarrant (pen) [32]	2374
31	Apr	3	A	Brechin C	W 1-0	1-0	1	Haro [42]	698
32		10	A	Stenhousemuir	L 2-3	1-0	1	Kinnaird [30], Wood [75]	492
33		17	H	Queen's Park	L 1-2	1-0	1	McGlashan [18]	3758
34		24	A	Montrose	W 3-2	1-1	1	Ross 2 [29, 82], McGlashan [50]	394
35	May	1	H	Albion R	W 2-0	1-0	1	Ross 2 [16, 77]	1837
36		8	A	East Stirling	W 2-1	2-0	1	Ross [26], Wood [38]	356

Final League Position: 1   1997–98 DIV 3 3

Honours
League Champions: Third Division: 1998-99.

Club colours: Shirt: Dark blue with white centre band. Shorts: White. Stockings: Blue.

Goalscorers: *League (87):* Ferguson 17 (1 pen), Tarrant 17 (4 pens), Wood 12, Ross 7, McGlashan 6, McBain 5, Ferries 4, Taylor 4, Adams 3, Maxwell 3, Golabek 2, Escalon 1, Haro 1, Kinnaird 1, own goals 4. *Scottish Cup (6):* Tarrant 5 (1 pen), McBain 1. *League Cup (8):* Adams 5, Tarrant 2, McBain 1.

Walker J 31	Mackay D 16 + 4	McBain R 33	Furphy W 6 + 4	Maxwell I 36	Gilbert K 25	Escalon F 17 + 1	Adams D 4	Tarrant N 27 + 6	Taylor A 24 + 8	Ross D 19 + 9	Hunter M 3 + 3	Ferguson M 3 + 3	Campbell C 1 + 7	Herd W 5 + 2	Wood G 12 + 15	Hart R 1	Golabek S 18 + 5	Den Bieman I 2	Ferries K 15 + 7	Higgins G 1 + 2	Haro M 26	Matheson D 7	Williamson R 1 + 2	McGlashan J 16 + 1	Meldrum C 2	Tully C 8	McKee C — + 1	Kinnaird P 10	Mackay S — + 2	Ewing G 1 + 2	McLeod B 1 + 2	Stewart G 1	Munro G 1	Match No.
1	2	3	4	5	6	7	8	9^1	10	11	12																							1
1	2	3	4	5	6	7^1		9^2	10^1	11	12		8	13	14																			2
1	2	3		5	6	7	8	9	10^2	13			4	11^3	14	12																		3
1	2^1	3		5	6	7^2	8	9	10	13			4	11		12																		4
1		3		5	6	10	8	9^2	12	11^1	13	7	4	2																				5
1		3	8^3	5	6	10			13	11^1	2	9^2	7	12	4	14																		6
1		3	13	5	6	2^3		9	10^3			7	14	4	12	8^1	11																	7
1		3	4	5	6	10^2		11	13			9^1	7				2	8	12															8
1		3	4^1	5	6			13	10			9^2	7	14	12		2	8	11^3															9
1		3	2^2	5	6	12		13	11^1				8	10	9			7	4															10
1		3		4	6	10		12	14			8			9^3		11^2		7^1	5	2	13												11
1		3		5	6	10		12	13			8			9		11		7^1	4	2^2													12
1		3		5	6	10^1		13	12			8			9^2		11		7^3	4	2	14												13
1		3		5	6			9	10	12		8					11		7^1	4	2													14
1		3		5	6			9^2	10	12		8					11		7	13	4^1	2												15
1		3		5	6			9	10	12		8					11		7^1	4	2													16
1		3		5	6			9	10	13		8^1	12				11		7^2	4	2													17
1	12	3		5	6			9^2	10^1	13		8	14				11		7^2	2				4										18
1	2	3		5	6			9^2	10	12		8			13		11		7^1	4				8										19
1	2	3^2		5	6			9	10	7^1					13		11	12	4					8										20
1	2	3		5	6			9					8				12	11	7^1	4				10										21
1	2	3		5	6	11^2		9	7^3			8^1			14		12	13		4				10										22
1	2	3		5	6	10^1		9^3		13		8			14		11		7^2	4				12										23
1	2	3		5		10^2		9	13	7		8			6^1		11	12	4															24
	2	3		5				9		7		6			8^1		11	12	4					10	1									25
	3			5				9	10^1	7		6			11^2		12		4					8	1	2	13							26
1	13	3		5				9	10^1	7		6			14		12		4^2					8		2		11^3						27
1		3		5				9	10	7^1		6			13		12		4					8		2		11						28
1		3		5				9	10	7^1		6			13		12		4					8		2		11^2						29
1	14			5	6			9	10	7					12		3		4^3					8^2		2		11^1	13					30
1	3			5	6	10^3		9	13	11					12				7^1			4^2	2					8		14				31
	2			5		10		11	8^1	1					9		3				4			6				7			12			32
	2	3^2		5		10^1		9	12	7					14		6		13		4			8				11^3				1		33
	2	3	14	5					10^3	7					9				13		4			6			1	8^2		11^1	12			34
1	12	3	14	5					10	7					9^3				13		4^1			6			2	8			11^2			35
1	2	3	13	5					10	7					9^3									8^2			4	11	14	12			6^1	36

ST JOHNSTONE Premier League

Year Formed: 1884. *Ground & Address:* McDiarmid Park, Crieff Road, Perth PH1 2SJ. *Telephone:* 01738 459090. *Fax:* 01738 625 771. *Clubcall:* 0898 121559.
Ground Capacity: all seated: 10,673. *Size of Pitch:* 115yd × 75yd.
Chairman: G.S.Brown. *Secretary and Managing Director:* Stewart Duff.
Manager: Sandy Clark. *Sales Executive:* Helen Harcus. *Physio:* Nick Summersgill. *Coach:* Billy Kirkwood. *Youth Development Coach:* Alistair Stevenson.
Managers since 1975: J. Stewart; J. Storrie; A. Stuart; A. Rennie; I. Gibson; A. Totten, J. McClelland, P. Sturrock. *Club Nickname(s):* Saints. *Previous Grounds:* Recreation Grounds, Muirton Park.
Record Attendance: (McDiarmid Park): 10,504 v Rangers, Premier Division; 20 Oct, 1990.
Record Transfer Fee received: £1,750,000 for Calum Davidson to Blackburn R (March 1998).
Record Transfer Fee paid: £300,000 for Billy Dodds from Dundee (1994).
Record Victory: 9-0 v Albion R, League Cup; 9 March, 1946.
Record Defeat: 1-10 v Third Lanark, Scottish Cup; 24 January, 1903.
Most Capped Player: George O'Boyle, 10, Northern Ireland.
Most League Appearances: 298: Drew Rutherford.
Most League Goals in Season (Individual): 36: Jimmy Benson, Division II; 1931-32.
Most Goals Overall (Individual): 140: John Brogan, 1977-83.

ST JOHNSTONE 1998–99 LEAGUE RECORD

Match No.	Date	Venue	Opponents	Result	H/T Score	Lg. Pos.	Goalscorers	Attendance
1	Aug 1	A	Motherwell	L 0-1	0-0	—		5686
2	15	H	Kilmarnock	D 0-0	0-0	8		6210
3	23	A	Dundee	W 1-0	0-0	7	Scott 58	3641
4	29	A	Rangers	L 0-4	0-2	8		48,732
5	Sept12	H	Dunfermline Ath	D 1-1	1-0	8	Squires (og) 37	5997
6	19	H	Aberdeen	W 2-0	1-0	7	Lowndes 17, McMahon 66	5814
7	23	A	Celtic	W 1-0	1-0	—	Dasovic 15	55,745
8	26	H	Dundee U	L 1-3	0-2	4	Grant 84	6655
9	Oct 4	A	Hearts	D 1-1	0-0	5	Preston 56	13,121
10	17	H	Motherwell	W 5-0	1-0	3	O'Boyle 2 39, 85, Kernaghan 53, Simao 62, Dods 88	4062
11	24	A	Kilmarnock	D 2-2	1-0	4	Dods 38, Lowndes 62	9336
12	31	A	Dunfermline Ath	D 1-1	0-1	4	McQuillan 54	8126
13	Nov 8	H	Rangers	L 0-7	0-3	4		9660
14	14	H	Celtic	W 2-1	1-0	4	Simao 45, McAnespie 78	9762
15	21	A	Aberdeen	W 1-0	1-0	4	Simao 38	10,044
16	Dec 5	A	Dundee U	D 1-1	0-0	4	Grant (pen) 55	7293
17	9	H	Hearts	D 1-1	1-1	—	Kernaghan 8	4808
18	12	H	Dundee	D 1-1	0-0	4	Bollan 85	6033
19	19	A	Motherwell	W 2-1	1-1	4	Connolly 31, Grant 72	5686
20	26	A	Rangers	L 0-1	0-0	4		49,479
21	29	H	Dunfermline Ath	D 1-1	0-0	—	Kane 81	6070
22	Jan 2	H	Aberdeen	W 4-1	1-1	4	Bollan (pen) 44, Kernaghan 50, O'Neil 2 74, 82	8971
23	31	A	Celtic	L 0-5	0-3	4		59,746
24	Feb 6	H	Dundee U	W 1-0	1-0	4	Bollan (pen) 9	5771
25	20	A	Hearts	W 2-0	0-0	4	Scott 59, Kane 63	12,229
26	27	A	Dundee	W 1-0	1-0	3	Grant 6	7245
27	Mar 13	H	Kilmarnock	L 0-1	0-1	4		5461
28	20	A	Dunfermline Ath	L 0-1	0-0	4		5504
29	Apr 4	H	Rangers	W 3-1	1-0	4	Weir 13, Simao 72, McAnespie 90	9742
30	17	H	Hearts	D 0-0	0-0	4		6154
31	20	A	Dundee U	W 1-0	1-0	—	Griffin 41	6741
32	24	H	Celtic	W 1-0	0-0	4	O'Halloran 54	10,393
33	May 1	A	Aberdeen	L 0-1	0-0	4		9561
34	8	H	Motherwell	D 0-0	0-0	4		4599
35	15	A	Kilmarnock	D 1-1	0-1	4	Bollan 66	15,086
36	23	H	Dundee	W 1-0	0-0	3	Kane 72	10,575

Final League Position: 3   1997–98 5

Honours
League Champions: First Division 1982–83, 1989–90, 1996–97. Division II 1923–24, 1959–60, 1962–63; *Runners-up:* Division II 1931–32. Second Division 1987–88.
Scottish Cup: Semi-finals 1934, 1968, 1989, 1991.
League Cup Runners-up: 1969, 1998.
League Challenge Cup Runners-up: 1996–97.

European: *UEFA Cup:* 6 matches (1971–72).

Club colours: Shirt: Royal blue with white trim. Shorts: White. Stockings: Royal blue with white hoops.

Goalscorers: *League (39):* Bollan 4 (2 pens), Grant 4 (1 pen), Simao 4, Kane 3, Kernaghan 3, Dods 2, Lowndes 2, McAnespie 2, O'Boyle 2, O'Neil 2, Scott 2, Connolly 1, Dasovic 1, Griffin 1, McMahon 1, McQuillan 1, O'Halloran 1, Preston 1, Weir 1, own goal 1. *Scottish Cup (6):* Grant 2, Dods 1, O'Neil 1, Scott 1, Simao 1. *League Cup (12):* Dasovic 2, Lowndes 2, O'Boyle 2, Connolly 1, Kane 1, McMahon 1, O'Halloran 1, O'Neil 1, Preston 1.

Ferguson A 2+1	McQuillan J 27+1	Dods D 34	Preston A 8+7	Griffin D 14+5	McMahon G 13+6	O'Neil J 33	Kane P 33+1	McAnespie K 8+10	Dasovic N 31	O'Boyle G 12+1	O'Halloran K 10+6	Scott P 14+2	Connolly P 6+3	Main A 34	Bollan G 32+1	Grant R 14+11	Simao M 20+6	Lowndes N 12+17	Kernaghan A 26	McCluskey S 5+2	Whiteford A —+1	McBride J 2+1	Weir D 6+1	Parker K —+2	Match No.
1	2	3	4	5	6[3]	7[2]	8	9[1]	10	11	12	13	14												1
1	2	3	4	5	6	7	13	12	10	11	8[2]		9[1]												2
	2	3	4		6	7	8			11	12	10[1]		1	5	9									3
	2	3	4[3]	5	13	7	8			6[2]	10			1		14	9	11[1]	12						4
		3	12	2	6	7			10	11[2]	8[1]			1	5	13	9		4						5
		3	13	12	6	7[2]	8			10[1]	11[3]			1	5	14	9		4	2					6
		3	14	13	6[2]	7	8			10	11[1]			1	5	12	9[2]		4	2					7
		3	12		6[1]	7[2]	8			10	11			1	5	14	9[4]		4	2		13			8
	2	3			6	7	8		10	11[1]				1	5		9[1]	13	4						9
	2	3	6	12		7[2]	8		10	11				1	5		9[1]	13	4						10
	2	3	6	13		7[2]	8		10	11				1	5		9[1]	12	4						11
	2	3	6[1]	12		7	8		10	11[3]				1	5	14	9[2]	13	4						12
	2	3		12	6[2]	7	8		10	11[3]				1	5	14	9	13	4						13
	2	3			6	7	8[1]		10		12			1	5	13	9[2]	11	4						14
	2	3			6	7[2]	8	13	10				14	1	5	12	9[1]	11[1]	4						15
	2	3			6	7	8	13	10					1	5	12	9[2]	11[1]	4						16
	2	3			6	7	8	13	10					1	5	12	9[2]	11[1]	4						17
	2	3				7	8		10				6	1	5	9	11		4						18
	2	3	5	6		7	8		10			13		1		12	9[2]	11[1]	4						19
	2	3			6[3]	7	8		10	11[2]				1	5	12	9[1]	13	4			14			20
	2	3			6[2]	7	8		10		11	13		1	5	12	9[1]		4						21
	2	3			6[3]	7	8		10				14	1	5	13	9[1]	11[2]	4						22
	2	3	13		9[1]	7	8[2]		10		12		6	1	5			11	4						23
	2	3	6	13		7	8		10					1	5	12	9[2]	11	4						24
	2	3				7	8		10				6	1	5	12	9	11[1]	4						25
	2	3				7[1]	8		10	6[3]	12			1	5	13	9	11[1]	4		14				26
	2	3		12			8		10	6[1]	7[2]			1	5	13	9	11	4						27
	2	3	7[1]		6		8		10					1	5	14	9[2]	13	4			11[1]	12		28
		3	13			7[2]	8		10		11			1	5	12	9[1]	14	4			6[1]	2		29
15	2	3				7[1]	8		10	12			6	1[5]	5	13	9[1]	11	4				2		30
		3	12	4		7[2]	8		10			13	6	1	5		9[1]	11					2		31
12		3	13	4		7	8		10	11[3]			6[1]	1	5	14	9[2]						2		32
		3	14	4		7	8		10	11[3]			6[1]	1	5	13	9[2]	12					2		33
	2	3			6[2]	7	8		10	11[3]		13		1	5	12	9					14	4[1]		34
	2		4			7[2]	8	13	10				6	1	5		9	11[1]				3		12	35
	2		4			7	8	12	10			13	6[1]	1	5		9	11[2]				3			36

ST MIRREN

First Division

Year Formed: 1877. *Ground & Address:* St Mirren Park, Love St, Paisley PA3 2EJ. *Telephone:* 0141 889 2558/0141 840 1337. *Fax:* 0141 848 6444.
Ground Capacity: total: 14,950, seated 8935. *Size of Pitch:* 112yd × 73yd.
Chairman: Stewart Gilmour. *Vice-Chairman:* George Campbell. *Secretary:* Allan Marshall.
Manager: Tom Hendrie. *Physio:* Colin Brow. *Youth Development Officer:* Joe Hughes.
Managers since 1975: Alex Ferguson; Jim Clunie; Rikki MacFarlane; Alex Miller; Alex Smith; Tony Fitzpatrick; David Hay; Jimmy Bone; Tony Fitzpatrick. *Club Nickname(s):* The Buddies. *Previous Grounds:* Short Roods 1877-79, Thistle Park Greenhill 1879-83, Westmarch 1883-94.
Record Attendance: 47,438 v Celtic, League Cup, 20 Aug, 1949.
Record Transfer Fee received: £850,000 for Ian Ferguson to Rangers (1988).
Record Transfer Fee paid: £400,000 for Thomas Stickroth from Bayer Uerdingen (1990).
Record Victory: 15-0 v Glasgow University, Scottish Cup 1st rd; 30 Jan, 1960.
Record Defeat: 0-9 v Rangers, Division I; 4 Dec, 1897.
Most Capped Player: Godmundor Torfason, 29, Iceland.
Most League Appearances: 351: Tony Fitzpatrick, 1973-88.
Most League Goals in Season (Individual): 45: Dunky Walker, Division I; 1921-22.
Most Goals Overall (Individual): 221: David McCrae, 1923-24.

ST MIRREN 1998–99 LEAGUE RECORD

Match No.	Date	Venue	Opponents	Result	H/T Score	Lg. Pos.	Goalscorers	Attendance
1	Aug 5	A	Stranraer	W 1-0	0-0	—	Nicolson [50]	1058
2	15	H	Raith R	W 2-1	1-1	1	Brown [14], Nicolson [50]	2106
3	22	A	Airdrieonians	L 0-1	0-0	3		3073
4	29	A	Hamilton A	D 0-0	0-0	4		1575
5	Sept 5	H	Falkirk	L 0-2	0-0	5		2390
6	12	H	Hibernian	L 2-0	1-0	3	Yardley [38], Nicolson [82]	3638
7	19	A	Greenock Morton	W 1-0	0-0	2	McGarry [66]	4108
8	26	A	Clydebank	L 0-1	0-0	3		1462
9	Oct 3	H	Ayr U	L 0-2	0-1	7		2673
10	11	A	Raith R	L 0-1	0-0	7		1963
11	17	H	Stranraer	W 1-0	0-0	7	Yardley (pen) [75]	2884
12	24	H	Hamilton A	W 3-2	0-2	4	McGarry [54], Creaney 2 (1 pen) [57 (p), 75]	2312
13	31	A	Falkirk	D 1-1	0-1	5	Yardley [87]	3848
14	Nov 7	H	Greenock Morton	W 1-0	1-0	5	McGarry [17]	4776
15	21	H	Clydebank	D 0-0	0-0	5		2847
16	24	A	Hibernian	L 1-4	1-3	—	Yardley [20]	9153
17	28	A	Ayr U	D 1-1	0-1	5	Yardley [68]	3640
18	Dec 5	A	Stranraer	W 2-1	1-1	5	Brown [24], McGarry [56]	890
19	12	H	Airdrieonians	L 1-5	1-4	5	Creaney (pen) [38]	2306
20	19	H	Falkirk	L 0-3	0-2	5		2137
21	26	A	Hamilton A	D 0-0	0-0	5		1450
22	Jan 5	A	Greenock Morton	D 0-0	0-0	—		2936
23	9	H	Hibernian	L 1-2	0-0	5	Kerr [84]	6674
24	16	A	Clydebank	D 2-2	1-0	5	Love (og) [37], Brown (pen) [72]	934
25	30	H	Ayr U	W 1-0	0-0	5	Mendes [54]	2670
26	Feb 6	H	Raith R	W 3-1	1-1	5	McLaughlan [17], McGarry [49], Yardley [60]	1621
27	23	A	Airdrieonians	W 3-0	1-0	—	Mendes [18], McGarry [96], Cameron [89]	1860
28	27	H	Hamilton A	W 1-0	0-0	5	O'Brien [60]	2130
29	Mar 13	A	Falkirk	L 0-1	0-0	5		3237
30	20	A	Ayr U	D 2-2	1-1	5	Yardley [15], Brown (pen) [70]	2436
31	Apr 3	H	Clydebank	D 1-1	1-0	5	Kerr [44]	1756
32	10	H	Greenock Morton	L 1-5	1-2	5	Yardley [37]	3538
33	17	A	Hibernian	L 1-2	1-0	5	McGarry [32]	8959
34	24	H	Stranraer	W 5-1	1-0	5	Yardley 2 [34, 76], McGarry [53], Watson (og) [75], Mendes [81]	2210
35	May 1	A	Raith R	D 1-1	0-1	5	Mendes [74]	2380
36	8	H	Airdrieonians	W 3-0	1-0	5	Yardley [35], Nicolson [57], Cameron [85]	2078

Final League Position: 5   1997–98 6

Honours
League Champions: First Division 1976-77. Division II 1967-68; *Runners-up:* 1935-36.
Scottish Cup Winners: 1926, 1959, 1987. *Runners-up:* 1908, 1934, 1962.
League Cup Runners-up: 1955-56.
B&Q Cup Runners-up: 1993-94. *Victory Cup:* 1919-20. *Summer Cup:* 1943-44. *Anglo-Scottish Cup:* 1979-80.

European: *Cup Winners' Cup:* 4 matches (1987-88). *UEFA Cup:* 10 matches (1980-81, 1983-84, 1985-86).

Club colours: Shirt: Black and white vertical stripes. Shorts: Black. Stockings: Black with white trim. Change colours: Predominantly red.

Goalscorers: *League (42):* Yardley 11 (1 pen), McGarry 8, Brown 4 (2 pens), Mendes 4, Nicolson 4, Creaney 3 (2 pens), Cameron 2, Kerr 2, McLaughlin 1, O'Brien 1, own goals 2. *Scottish Cup (1):* Mendes 1. *League Cup (1):* Brown 1.

Scrimgour D 19	McNamee D 30+1	Nicolson I 24+6	Rodden P 18+8	McQuilter R 29	McLaughlan B 23	Murray H 27+2	Drew C 15+1	McGarry S 27+7	Mendes J 13+9	Brown T 23+3	Yardley M 22+13	Prentice A 1+5	Milne D 7+2	McWhirter N 24+1	Kerr C 24+4	O'Brien B 17+5	Turner T 13+1	Creaney G 11+1	Roy L 17	Walker P —+1	Innes C 9	Cameron D 3+8	Robinson R —+1	Match No.
1	2	3	4	5	6	7²	8	9¹	10	11	12	13												1
1	3	8	6	5	2	7	4	9¹	12	11¹	13		10											2
1	3	8	6	5	2	7¹	4	9¹	13	11	12		10											3
1	3²	8	6	5	2	7¹		9¹	12	11	14		10	4	13									4
1	3¹	8²	6	5	2			9	13		14		11	4	12	10²								5
1	2	12	6	5	8	7²		9³		11			10¹	4	3	14	13							6
1	2	10	6	5	8	7		9¹		11				4	3	12								7
1	2	10¹	6	5	8	7		9		11				4	3	12								8
1	2	6³		5	7		11	12	10¹	9	13		14	4	3	8²								9
1	2¹	10	6	5	3		8	9³	13	11	14		7²	4	12									10
1	3	6	2³	5	7	14	8	9¹	12	11	13			4				10²						11
1	2	11¹	14	5	6	7³	8	12	9		13			4	3			10²						12
1	2	7	3¹	5	6		8	9³	13	11	14			4²	12			10						13
1	2	12		5	6	7	8	9²	13	11¹	14			4	3			10³						14
1	13	6	5	2	7³	8		9	11²		12	14		4	3			10¹						15
1	3	12	6³	5	2	7	8	13			14	11		9¹	4²			10						16
1	2		5	6¹	7		13	9²	11			8	12	4	3			10						17
1	8		5	6	12	2	9¹		7	11				4	3			10						18
1	12	3¹	2¹	5	6	7	4	9	8	11²	13	14						10						19
	2	8	5	6	7		9			11¹				4	3	12		10	1					20
	2	8	5	6	7		9¹				13			4	3	11		10²	1	12				21
	2	12		6¹	7	5		9	10	11					3	8	4		1					22
	2	14		5		7³		9²	10	11¹	13				3	8	4	12	1		6			23
	2			5	7			12	10	9	11¹				3	8	4		1		6			24
	3²	13		5	7		2	12	10	9¹	11					8	4		1		6			25
	2		6²		7		13	12	10¹	9³	11				3	8	4		1		5	14		26
	2¹	12		5	7			9	10²	11					4	8	3		1		6	13		27
	2	7		5				9	10	11¹					3	8	4		1		6	12		28
	2	13		5	7²			9¹	10³	14	11				4	3	8		1		6	12		29
	2	12		5	7				10	11					4¹	3	8		1		6	9		30
	2	13		5²	7			9	10¹	11					4	3	8		1		6	12		31
	3	2²	14		7³			9	10	11	13				4¹	5	8	6	1			12		32
	3	2¹	7²					9	10³	11	14				4	5	8	6	1			12	13	33
	3	2	12		7			9¹	14	10²	11				4¹	5	8	6	1			13		34
	3	2¹	5					9	10	7	12				6	8	4		1			11		35
	7	2	5					10	3	11					6	8	4		1			9		36

STENHOUSEMUIR Second Division

Year Formed: 1884. *Ground & Address:* Ochilview Park, Gladstone Rd, Stenhousemuir FK5 5QL. *Telephone:* 01324 562992. *Fax:* 01324 562980.
Ground Capacity: total: 2374, seated: 626. *Size of Pitch:* 110yd × 72yd.
Chairman: A Terry Bulloch. *Secretary:* David O.Reid. *Commercial Manager:* John Sharp.
Manager: Graeme Armstrong. *Assistant Manager:* Gordon Buchanan. *Physio:* Lee Campbell.
Managers since 1975: H. Glasgow; J. Black; A. Rose; W. Henderson; A. Rennie; J. Meakin; D. Lawson; T. Christie.
Club Nickname(s): The Warriors. *Previous Grounds:* Tryst Ground 1884-86, Goschen Park 1886-90.
Record Attendance: 12,500 v East Fife, Scottish Cup 4th rd; 11 Mar, 1950.
Record Transfer Fee received: £70,000 for Euan Donaldson to St Johnstone (May 1995).
Record Transfer Fee paid: £20,000 to Livingston for Ian Little (June 1995).
Record Victory: 9-2 v Dundee U, Division II; 19 Apr, 1937.
Record Defeat: 2-11 v Dunfermline Ath. Division II; 27 Sept, 1930.
Most Capped Player: —.
Most League Appearances: 360: Archie Rose.
Most League Goals in Season (Individual): 32: Robert Taylor, Division II; 1925-26.
Most Goals Overall (Individual): —.

STENHOUSEMUIR 1998–99 LEAGUE RECORD

Match No.	Date	Venue	Opponents	Result		H/T Score	Lg. Pos.	Goalscorers	Atten-dance
1	Aug 4	A	Brechin C	L	0-1	0-0	—		286
2	15	H	Cowdenbeath	L	1-2	0-1	—	Hamilton R [81]	306
3	22	A	Dumbarton	W	2-0	1-0	7	Hamilton R 2 [18, 87]	378
4	29	H	East Stirling	W	1-0	1-0	5	Sprott [16]	357
5	Sept 5	A	Queen's Park	D	0-0	0-0	5		499
6	12	H	Montrose	W	4-0	2-0	4	Graham 2 [15, 89], Craig 2 [30, 56]	283
7	19	A	Ross Co	W	1-0	0-0	4	Graham [60]	2105
8	26	A	Berwick R	W	2-1	1-0	2	Lawrence [6], Watters [89]	358
9	Oct 3	H	Albion R	W	4-1	3-0	1	Craig [3], Lawrence 3 [6, 34, 69]	410
10	9	A	Cowdenbeath	W	2-0	2-0	1	Hamilton R [20], Sprott [41]	320
11	17	H	Dumbarton	L	0-3	0-0	1		456
12	26	A	East Stirling	D	1-1	0-0	—	Craig [70]	387
13	31	H	Queen's Park	W	2-1	2-0	3	Lawrence [16], Hamilton R [31]	387
14	Nov 7	H	Ross Co	L	2-4	0-2	3	Hamilton R [62], Lawrence [70]	510
15	14	A	Montrose	D	0-0	0-0	3		271
16	21	H	Berwick R	L	1-2	0-2	3	Armstrong (pen) [60]	389
17	28	A	Albion R	W	3-1	0-0	3	Armstrong (pen) [53], Miller 2 [57, 65]	337
18	Dec 15	H	Brechin C	L	0-1	0-0	—		294
19	19	A	Dumbarton	W	4-1	4-0	3	Gibson [15], Baptie [20], Christie [24], Hamilton R [44]	283
20	26	H	East Stirling	D	2-2	2-0	3	Miller 2 [20, 44]	979
21	Jan 16	A	Berwick R	L	1-2	0-1	3	Watters [75]	349
22	26	A	Queen's Park	L	1-4	0-1	—	Watters [70]	333
23	30	H	Albion R	L	1-2	0-1	3	Watters [70]	382
24	Feb 6	A	Ross Co	D	2-2	1-1	4	Lawrence [20], Gibson [82]	1837
25	20	A	Brechin C	W	2-0	1-0	3	Miller 2 [45, 74]	265
26	23	H	Montrose	W	3-1	2-1	—	Miller 2 [2, 13], Watters [56]	276
27	27	H	Cowdenbeath	W	4-1	1-1	2	Hamilton R [9], Watters [60], Craig 2 [75, 83]	361
28	Mar 6	H	Queen's Park	W	4-1	3-0	2	Hamilton R 2 [19, 27], Watters [42], Sprott [87]	425
29	13	A	East Stirling	D	1-1	1-0	2	McKinnon [18]	391
30	20	A	Albion R	W	2-1	0-0	2	Huggon [79], McKinnon [85]	326
31	Apr 3	H	Berwick R	D	1-1	0-0	2	Watters [55]	424
32	10	H	Ross Co	W	3-2	0-1	2	Gibson [70], Banks [86], Watters [89]	492
33	17	A	Montrose	W	2-1	1-1	2	Graham [38], Lawrence [90]	354
34	24	H	Dumbarton	L	0-2	0-0	2		629
35	May 1	A	Cowdenbeath	W	2-0	0-0	2	Craig [73], Wood [79]	300
36	8	H	Brechin C	W	1-0	0-0	2	Hamilton R [73]	1654

Final League Position: 2   1997–98 DIV 3 9

Honours

League Champions: Third Division runners-up: 1998-99. *Scottish Cup:* Semi-finals 1902-03. Quarter-finals 1948–49, 1949–50, 1994-95. *League Cup:* Quarter-finals 1947-48, 1960-61, 1975-76. *League Challenge Cup:* Winners 1995-96.

Club colours: Shirt: Maroon. Shorts: White. Stockings: Maroon.

Goalscorers: *League (62):* Hamilton R 11, Watters 9, Lawrence 8, Miller 8, Craig 7, Graham 4, Gibson 3, Sprott 3, Armstrong 2 (2 pens), McKinnon 2, Banks 1, Baptie 1, Christie 1, Huggon 1, Wood 1. *Scottish Cup (6):* Craig 2, Miller 2, Hall 1, Watters 1. *League Cup (1):* Watters 1.

Hamilton L 34	Sprott A 17+13	Banks A 20+7	Armstrong G 35	Graham T 22+2	Baptie C 25+2	Kane K 3+3	Lansdowne A 10+7	Watters W 18+11	Hutchison G 2	Gibson J 17+5	Middlemist R —+1	Brown S —+1	Fisher J 29	Hamilton R 34+1	Davidson G 23+1	Craig A 32	Lawrence A 33	Budinaukas K 2	Hall M 15+3	Hunter P —+2	Miller K 11	Christie M 3	Huggon R —+2	McKinnon C 6+1	Wood D 5+3	Match No.
1	2	3[2]	4	5	6	7[1]	8	9	10	11	12	13														1
1	2[2]	13	4	5	6	12	7[1]	9	10	3			8	11												2
1		3	4		5	11[1]	6		9		12		8	7	2	10										3
1	11[1]	3	4	14	5		6[3]	13		12			8	7	2	10	9[2]									4
1	11	3	4	14	5		13	12		6[1]			8	7	2	10[2]	9[3]									5
1	11	3	4	6	5			12					8	7[1]	2	10	9									6
1	11	3	4	6	5								8	7	2	10	9									7
1	11	3	4	6	5			12					8	7	2	10	9[1]									8
1	11		4	6	5		3	12					8	7[1]	2	10	9									9
1	11		4	6	5		3						8	7	2	10	9									10
1	11		4	6	5	13	3[2]	12					8	7[1]	2	10	9									11
	11	3[1]	4	6[2]	5	12	13						8	7[1]	2	10	9	1	14							12
1	11	3	4	6	5	8[1]	13							7	2[2]	10	9		12							13
1	11	3	4	6[1]	5			12					8	7	2	10	9									14
1		3	4	2[1]	5		8[2]		11				6	7		10	9		12	13						15
1		3[2]	4	6[1]	5		12	13	11				8	7	2	10	9									16
1			4		5		6	12		3			8	7[1]	2	10	9				11					17
1	12		4		5		6[2]			3			8[1]	7	2		9		13	11	10					18
1			4		5		12			3				7	2	10[1]	9		11		8	6				19
1	12		4							3			8	7	2	10[1]	9		5		11	6				20
1	13		4		5			12		6			8[2]	7	2	10	9		3[1]		11					21
	3[3]	14	4		5		12	13		6			8	7[2]	2[1]	10	9	1			11					22
1	13	3[2]	4		5		6[1]	7					8	12		10	9		2		11					23
1	13	3[1]	4		5			9		12			8	6		10	7		2		11[2]					24
1	13	3[2]	4		5			9[1]		12			8	6		10	7		2		11					25
1	12	3	4					9[1]		8				6	5	10	7		2		11					26
1	12		4		5			9[1]		8			3	6		10	7		2		11					27
1	11	3[1]	4	5			13	9[2]		8				6		10	7		2			12				28
1	11	3	4	5				9						6[2]	12	10[1]	7		2					8	13	29
1	11[3]	12	4	5[1]				9		3[2]				6		10	7		2				14	8	13	30
1	12	14	4[3]	5				9		3[1]			11	6		10	7		2[2]					8	13	31
1	12	14		5	13			9		8[2]			3	6	4	10	7[1]		2[3]						11	32
1		12	4	5				9					3	6	2	10[1]	7							8	11	33
1	13	3	4	5	12			9					10	6	2[1]		7							8	11[2]	34
1	14	12	4	5				9			13		10	7[2]		6	2		3[2]					8[1]	11	35
1	13	8[1]	4	5				9					10	7		6	2		3					12	11[2]	36

STIRLING ALBION

Second Division

Year Formed: 1945. *Ground & Address:* Forthbank Stadium, Springkerse Industrial Estate, Stirling FK7 7UJ. *Telephone:* 01786 450399. *Fax:* 01786 448592.
Ground Capacity: 3808, seated: 2508. *Size of Pitch:* 110yd × 74yd.
Chairman: Peter McKenzie. *Secretary:* Mrs Marlyn Hallam.
Manager: John Philliben. *Physio:* George Cameron.
Managers since 1975: A. Smith; G. Peebles; J. Fleeting; J. Brogan; K. Drinkell. *Club Nickname(s):* The Binos.
Previous Grounds: Annfield 1945–92.
Record Attendance: 26,400 (at Annfield) v Celtic, Scottish Cup 4th rd; 14 Mar, 1959. 3808 v Aberdeen, Scottish Cup 4th rd, 15 February 1996 (Forthbank).
Record Transfer Fee received: £70,000 for John Philliben to Doncaster R (Mar 1984).
Record Transfer Fee paid: £25,000 for Craig Taggart from Falkirk (Aug 1994).
Record Victory: 20-0 v Selkirk, Scottish Cup 1st rd; 8 Dec, 1984.
Record Defeat: 0-9 v Dundee U, Division I; 30 Dec, 1967.
Most Capped Player: —.
Most League Appearances: 504: Matt McPhee, 1967-81.

STIRLING ALBION 1998–99 LEAGUE RECORD

Match No.	Date	Venue	Opponents	Result	H/T Score	Lg. Pos.	Goalscorers	Attendance
1	Aug 4	A	Livingston	D	1-1	1-1	—	Donald [12]	1496
2	15	H	Clyde	L	1-2	1-1	8	Bone [35]	1059
3	22	A	Arbroath	W	3-0	0-0	4	Hendry 2 [65, 78], Bone [70]	805
4	29	A	Alloa Ath	L	0-7	0-2	9		1272
5	Sept 5	H	Queen of the S	W	1-0	0-0	5	Nicholas [66]	640
6	12	H	Partick Th	L	0-1	0-1	7		1998
7	19	H	Inverness CT	L	0-1	0-1	7		915
8	26	A	Forfar Ath	W	2-1	0-1	7	Martin [89], Bone [90]	427
9	Oct 3	H	East Fife	W	3-2	1-1	5	Bone 2 (1 pen) [22, 49 (p)], Wood [47]	748
10	10	A	Clyde	L	1-2	1-0	6	Nicholas [39]	1008
11	17	H	Livingston	L	1-3	0-3	6	McCallum [90]	909
12	24	H	Alloa Ath	W	4-2	2-0	6	Bone 3 (1 pen) [5 (p), 53, 74], Nicholas [41]	1085
13	31	A	Queen of the S	W	3-2	2-1	6	Paterson [25], Nicholas [44], Bone [56]	1128
14	Nov 7	A	Inverness CT	L	1-3	0-1	6	Graham [72]	2026
15	14	H	Partick Th	W	2-0	1-0	5	Graham [37], Bone [76]	1513
16	21	H	Forfar Ath	W	3-1	1-0	4	Nicholas [26], Bone 2 (1 pen) [83 (p), 88]	731
17	28	A	East Fife	W	3-2	2-1	4	Bone 3 (1 pen) [20, 38 (p), 69]	1003
18	Dec 12	H	Arbroath	L	0-1	0-0	4		824
19	19	A	Livingston	D	0-0	0-0	4		1996
20	29	A	Alloa Ath	D	2-2	1-1	—	Graham [41], Bone [64]	971
21	Jan 16	A	Forfar Ath	D	3-3	1-1	5	Bone [37], Jackson [74], Watson (og) [75]	445
22	26	H	Queen of the S	L	1-3	0-1	—	Graham [86]	643
23	30	H	East Fife	L	0-1	0-1	5		806
24	Feb 6	H	Inverness CT	L	1-5	0-3	6	Woods [79]	890
25	17	A	Partick Th	W	1-0	0-0	—	Paterson [73]	1203
26	20	A	Arbroath	L	0-1	0-1	6		610
27	27	A	Clyde	L	2-3	1-1	6	Price 2 [40, 56]	888
28	Mar 6	A	Queen of the S	L	0-3	0-3	6		1014
29	13	H	Alloa Ath	D	1-1	0-1	6	Grant [53]	1225
30	20	A	East Fife	L	0-1	0-1	7		641
31	Apr 3	H	Forfar Ath	D	2-2	0-2	8	Paterson [68], Donald [87]	820
32	10	A	Inverness CT	D	2-2	0-0	8	Bone 2 [49, 90]	1778
33	17	H	Partick Th	W	3-0	2-0	7	Provan [8], Donald [25], Bone [68]	1664
34	24	H	Livingston	D	0-0	0-0	7		1404
35	May 1	A	Clyde	L	1-4	0-3	8	Price [59]	1107
36	8	H	Arbroath	W	2-1	1-1	6	Bone [29], Graham [59]	1005

Final League Position: 6 1997–98 DIV 1 10

Most League Goals in Season (Individual): 27: Joe Hughes, Division II; 1969-70.
Most Goals Overall (Individual): 129: Billy Steele, 1971-83.

Honours
League Champions: Division II 1952-53, 1957-58, 1960-61, 1964-65. Second Division 1976-77, 1990-91, 1995-96; *Runners-up:* Division II 1948-49, 1950-51.
Scottish Cup: —. *League Cup:* —.

Club colours: Shirt: Red and white halves. Shorts: Red and white halves. Stockings: Red.

Goalscorers: *League (50):* Bone 21 (4 pens), Graham 5, Nicholas 5, Donald 3, Paterson 3, Price 3, Hendry 2, Wood 2, Grant 1, Jackson 1, McCallum 1, Martin 1, Provan 1, own goal 1. *Scottish Cup (5):* Graham 2, Jackson 1, McCallum 1, Nicholas 1. *League Cup (3):* Bone 2, Price 1.

McGeown M 9	Paterson A 36	McCallum D 28 + 2	Clark P 30 + 3	Martin B 33	Phillben J 20 + 2	Bone A 27 + 1	Donald G 18 + 4	Price G 14 + 5	Mortimer P 15 + 8	Nicholas S 27	Bell D 1 + 16	Hendry J 6 + 1	Forrest E 24 + 3	Bradley M 4 + 3	Provan A 8 + 10	Wood C 10 + 14	McCallion K — + 2	Jackson C 21 + 1	Gow G 27	Graham A 23	Grant B 7	Aitken A — + 1	McKee C 1 + 1	Cormack B 6	Jaffa G 1 + 2	Match No.
1	2	3	4	5	6	7	8	9^{1}	10	11	12															1
1	2	3	4	5	6	7	8	9	10^{1}	11			12													2
1	2	3	4	5	6	7	8		10	11^{1}	12	9														3
1	2		4	5	6	7	8^{1}			11	10^{2}	9	3	12	13											4
1	2	6^{1}	4	5		7		9^{1}	10	11^{2}	12	8	3	13	14											5
1	2	9^{1}	4	5	6					11	12^{3}	10	3	8	7^{2}	13	14									6
1	2	13	4	5	6	7				11		8	3	12	9^{1}	10^{2}										7
1	2	10^{1}	4	5	6	7				11		8	3	9		12										8
1	2	3	4	5	6	7				11	12		9^{1}			10		8								9
	2	3^{1}	4	5	6	7				11			12	9		10		8	1							10
	2^{1}	3	4	5		7	8^{2}		12	11	13		6^{3}	14	10			9	1							11
	2	3^{1}	4	5		7	13		10^{2}	11			6		12			8	1	9						12
	2	3	4	5^{1}		7	12		10^{3}	11	13		6		14			8	1	9^{2}						13
	2	3^{1}	4	5	14	7	12		10^{1}	11			6^{2}		13			8	1	9						14
	2	13	4	5	3^{1}	7	6		10^{2}	11			12					8	1	9						15
	2^{1}	3	4	5		7	6		10^{2}	11^{3}	14		12		13			8	1	9						16
	2	10^{2}	4	5		7	6	14	12	11^{1}			3		13			8	1	9^{4}						17
	2	10^{1}	4	5		7	6	14	12	11^{2}			3^{3}					8	1	9						18
	2	10	4	5		7	6		12	11			3					8	1	9^{1}						19
	2^{1}	10^{2}	4		14	7	6	13	5	11^{2}			3		12			8	1	9						20
	2			5	7	6^{1}	10	4^{2}		11	13		3		12			8	1	9						21
	2	10	14	5	4^{3}	7^{1}				11^{2}	12		3	13	6			8	1	9						22
	2	10	6	5^{2}		7							3	13	11^{1}	12		8	1	9	4					23
	2	10^{2}	12	5	6^{1}	7				11^{3}			3	14	13			8	1	9	4					24
	2	10^{2}	6	5		7	14			11^{1}	13		3		12			8	1	9^{1}	4					25
	2	10	6^{1}	8				9	12	11	13		3		7^{2}			8	1		4					26
	2	10^{1}	8^{2}	5				9	7^{3}	11	14		3	13	6				1		4	12				27
	2	6^{1}	5^{3}	13	12	7	8			11	14		3		10				1	9	4^{2}					28
	2		5		7	6		10	8^{1}	11			3						1	9	4		12			29
	2^{2}	14	5	4			6	7		12			3	13	11^{1}	8^{3}			1	9			10			30
	2	10		5^{1}		4	8	13		3			7^{2}	12					1	9				6	11	31
	2	11^{1}	4	5	6	7	8	10	12										1	9				3		32
	2	11^{1}	4	5	6	7	8^{3}	13	10^{2}	12									1	9				3	14	33
	2	11^{1}	4	5	6	7	8^{3}		10^{2}	12	14								1	9				3	13	34
	2	11^{1}	4^{3}	5	6	7	12	14	10^{1}	13								8	1	9				3		35
	2		4	5	6	7		10		11								8	1	9				3		36

STRANRAER   Second Division

Year Formed: 1870. *Ground & Address:* Stair Park, London Rd, Stranraer DG9 8BS. *Telephone:* 01776 703271.
Ground Capacity: total: 6100, seated: 1800. *Size of Pitch:* 110yd × 70yd.
Chairman/Secretary: Graham Rodgers. *Commercial Manager:* T. L. Sutherland.
Manager: Billy McLaren.
Managers since 1975: J. Hughes; N. Hood; G. Hamilton; D. Sneddon; J. Clark; R. Clark; A. McAnespie; C. Money. *Club Nickname(s):* The Blues. *Previous Grounds:* None.
Record Attendance: 6500 v Rangers, Scottish Cup 1st rd; 24 Jan, 1948.
Record Transfer Fee received: £30,000 for Duncan George to Ayr Utd.
Record Transfer Fee paid: £15,000 for Colin Harkness from Kilmarnock (Aug 1989).
Record Victory: 7-0 v Brechin C, Division II; 6 Feb, 1965.
Record Defeat: 1-11 v Queen of the South, Scottish Cup 1st rd; 16 Jan, 1932.
Most Capped Player: —.
Most League Appearances: 256: Danny McDonald.
Most League Goals in Season (Individual): 27: Derek Frye, Second Division; 1977-78.
Most Goals Overall (Individual): —.

STRANRAER 1998–99 LEAGUE RECORD

Match No.	Date	Venue	Opponents	Result	H/T Score	Lg. Pos.	Goalscorers	Atten- dance
1	Aug 5	H	St Mirren	L 0-1	0-0	—		1058
2	15	A	Hibernian	W 2-1	0-0	5	Black (pen) [48], Young J [58]	9489
3	22	H	Clydebank	L 0-2	0-0	8		570
4	29	A	Falkirk	L 0-1	0-0	9		2741
5	Sept 5	H	Airdrieonians	L 1-2	0-1	9	Ronald [75]	687
6	12	H	Hamilton A	W 2-1	1-0	9	George [28], Ronald [90]	666
7	19	A	Ayr U	L 1-7	1-3	9	Friels [9]	1917
8	26	H	Raith R	W 2-0	1-0	9	Campbell [34], Young J [66]	618
9	Oct 3	A	Greenock Morton	L 0-3	0-0	10		1444
10	10	H	Hibernian	L 0-1	0-0	10		1832
11	17	A	St Mirren	L 0-1	0-0	10		2884
12	28	H	Falkirk	L 1-2	0-1	—	Young G [49]	502
13	31	A	Airdrieonians	L 2-3	0-1	10	George [65], Black [70]	1988
14	Nov 7	H	Ayr U	L 0-1	0-0	10		1390
15	14	A	Hamilton A	W 2-1	1-1	10	Harty [10], Young G [58]	609
16	21	H	Raith R	L 0-2	0-1	10		1938
17	28	H	Greenock Morton	L 2-3	2-2	10	Skilling [4], Ronald [14]	795
18	Dec 5	H	St Mirren	L 1-2	1-1	10	Campbell [45]	890
19	12	A	Clydebank	L 1-2	0-1	10	Ronald [69]	207
20	19	H	Airdrieonians	L 1-2	0-0	10	Campbell [54]	635
21	26	A	Falkirk	L 2-3	1-1	10	Bell [19], Ronald [68]	3260
22	Jan 2	A	Ayr U	L 0-4	0-2	10		2722
23	9	H	Hamilton A	D 2-2	2-0	10	Young G [7], Kinnaird (pen) [38]	565
24	16	H	Raith R	W 2-0	0-0	10	Young G 2 [68, 84]	575
25	30	A	Greenock Morton	L 0-1	0-1	10		1581
26	Feb 6	A	Hibernian	L 0-2	0-2	10		8659
27	20	H	Clydebank	L 0-2	0-2	10		452
28	27	H	Falkirk	L 0-1	0-1	10		709
29	Mar 13	A	Airdrieonians	L 0-2	0-1	10		1341
30	20	H	Greenock Morton	L 0-1	0-1	10		563
31	Apr 3	A	Raith R	L 2-3	1-2	10	Knox (pen) [36], Harty [53]	1883
32	10	H	Ayr U	L 0-2	0-1	10		990
33	17	A	Hamilton A	L 0-1	0-1	10		525
34	24	A	St Mirren	L 1-5	0-1	10	Knox (pen) [69]	2210
35	May 1	H	Hibernian	L 0-4	0-1	10		1597
36	8	A	Clydebank	W 2-1	1-0	10	Walker [10], Jenkins [71]	269

Final League Position: 10   1997–98 DIV 2 1

Honours
League Champions: Second Division 1993-94, 1997-98.
Scottish Cup: —.
League Cup: —.
Qualifying Cup Winners: 1937.
League Challenge Cup Winners: 1996-97.

Club colours: Shirt: Blue. Shorts: White. Stockings: Blue with red tops.

Goalscorers: *League (29):* Ronald 5, Young G 5, Campbell 3, Black 2 (1 pen), George 2, Harty 2, Knox 2 (pens), Young J 2, Bell 1, Friels 1, Jenkins 1, Kinnaird 1 (pen), Skilling 1, Walker 1. *Scottish Cup (2):* Friels 1, Knox 1. *League Cup (1):* Ronald 1.

Matthews G 18	Knox K 25 + 1	Black T 26	Archdeacon P 4	Campbell M 26	Johnstone D 21 + 3	Watson P 36	McIntyre P 22 + 1	Young G 17 + 10	Young J 13 + 2	Skilling M 25 + 3	Bell R 12 + 8	Galloway G 4 + 4	Harty I 13 + 8	Jenkins A 9 + 10	Ronald P 25 + 4	Wright F — + 2	Brownlie P 2	Friels G 9 + 10	George D 17 + 1	Kinnaird P 21	Meldrum C 7	McMartin G 13	Adams M — + 2	Bruce G 11	Hamilton B 1	O'Neill M 1	Walker P 8 + 1	Abbott S 2 + 2	Blakie A 4 + 1	Smith J 4	Match No.
1	2²	3	4	5	6¹	7	8	9	10	11	12⁹	13	14																		1
1		3	8	5		6	2	13	10²	4			11¹	7	9	12															2
1		3		5		6	2	12	10	7			13	8¹	4²	9		11													3
1		3	10	5		6	4	9		2			11	7¹	8					12											4
1		3	10²	5		6	4	9		2			12	7³	8			11¹	14	13											5
1		3		5		6	8	13	9	2			11¹	12		10		7²	4												6
1		3		5		6	8		10	2²	13		11¹	12	9			7	4												7
1		3		5		6	7	2		9			12		10			8¹	4	11											8
1		3		5	6	7	2		9²			13		8	10¹			12	4	11											9
1		3		5	6	7	2	12	9¹					10			8	4	11												10
1	12	3		5	6	7	2	13	9					10¹			8²	4	11												11
1	8	3		5	6	7²	2	10¹	9			13					12	4	11												12
	2	3		5	6	7	8	10	9									4	11	1											13
	3		5	6	7	2¹	10³	14	12	8		9²	13						4	11	1										14
8	3		5	6	7		10²	12	2			9¹		13					4	11	1										15
8	3		5	6	7		10		2¹			9		12					4	11	1										16
2	3		5	6		10	8					9¹		7			12		4	11	1										17
2	3		5	6		9		8¹	12				10					4	11	1	7										18
1	2	3		5	14	6		9¹		8²	13		10					4³	11		7	12									19
	2	3		5	6	7		12	8			9						13	4	11²	1	10¹									20
1	2	3		5	6	10		12		8¹	4			9					11		7										21
1	2	3		5	6		12		8	4²		14	13	9			10¹		11³		7										22
	2	3		5	12	6		9		8	4¹		14	10²			13		11³		7		1								23
	2	3		5	6		9		8	4¹			12	10			11				7		1								24
	2	3²		5	13	6	8¹	9		4			12	10			11				7		1								25
	2			5		6	10	9²	3	4			13	12			13	4³	11		7		1	8¹							26
	2			5	10	6		8¹	12	3		9²	14				13	4³	11		7		1								27
	6			5	3			2¹						9²	4	11			7	13	1			8	10	12					28
1	6			5	3		12	2	10				13	4	9¹			8²			7				11						29
1	6			5	3	12	9	2		4³		13	14	10			8¹				7²				11						30
1	6			5	3	4	10¹	2	13				11³	12	8			14							7²			9			31
	6			5	3	2	13	12	8				11	4¹	10²	14							1		7			9³			32
	4			3	2	10			13				11¹	7²	8								1		12	6	9		5	33
	6			3	2	10			4	8¹			11	12									1		7		9		5	34
	4			6	3	2	14		10		12	13	11²	9³									1		7	8¹			5	35
	4	3		6	10	2			11²				8	9¹		14							1		7³	13	12	5		36

SCOTTISH LEAGUE TABLES 1998–99

Premier Division

	P	W	D	L	F	A	W	D	L	F	A	Pts	GD
		Home			*Goals*		*Away*			*Goals*			
Rangers	36	12	5	1	32	11	11	3	4	46	20	77	+47
Celtic	36	14	2	2	49	12	7	6	5	35	23	71	+49
St Johnstone	36	8	7	3	24	18	7	5	6	15	20	57	+1
Kilmarnock	36	8	7	3	24	15	6	7	5	23	14	56	+18
Dundee	36	7	4	7	18	23	6	3	9	18	33	46	−20
Hearts	36	8	2	8	27	26	3	7	8	17	24	42	−6
Motherwell	36	6	5	7	20	31	4	6	8	15	23	41	−19
Aberdeen	36	6	4	8	24	35	4	3	11	19	36	37	−28
Dundee U	36	2	8	8	13	22	6	2	10	24	26	34	−11
Dunfermline Ath	36	4	7	7	18	29	0	9	9	10	30	28	−31

First Division

	P	W	D	L	F	A	W	D	L	F	A	Pts	GD
		Home			*Goals*		*Away*			*Goals*			
Hibernian	36	16	1	1	45	13	12	4	2	39	20	89	+51
Falkirk	36	9	5	4	28	18	11	1	6	32	20	66	+22
Ayr U	36	8	4	6	38	23	11	1	6	28	19	62	+24
Airdrieonians	36	6	2	10	17	29	12	3	3	25	14	59	−1
St Mirren	36	10	2	6	26	25	4	8	6	16	18	52	−1
Greenock Morton	36	5	5	8	20	24	9	2	7	25	17	49	+4
Clydebank	36	5	6	7	17	18	6	7	5	19	20	46	−2
Raith R	36	5	5	8	19	27	3	6	9	18	30	35	−20
Hamilton A	36	3	5	10	13	26	3	5	10	17	36	28	−32
Stranraer	36	2	2	14	14	31	3	0	15	15	43	17	−45

Second Division

	P	W	D	L	F	A	W	D	L	F	A	Pts	GD
		Home			*Goals*		*Away*			*Goals*			
Livingston	36	13	4	1	32	12	9	7	2	34	23	77	+31
Inverness CT	36	14	4	0	44	20	7	5	6	36	28	72	+32
Clyde	36	10	4	4	28	16	5	4	9	18	26	53	+4
Queen of the S	36	7	8	3	26	17	6	1	11	24	28	48	+5
Alloa Ath	36	8	3	7	41	30	5	4	9	24	26	46	+9
Stirling A	36	7	3	8	27	28	5	5	8	23	35	44	−13
Arbroath	36	7	4	7	19	25	5	4	9	18	27	44	−15
Partick T	36	7	4	7	18	19	5	3	10	18	26	43	−9
East Fife	36	7	3	8	22	31	5	3	10	20	33	42	−22
Forfar Ath	36	6	3	9	31	34	2	4	12	17	36	31	−22

Third Division

	P	W	D	L	F	A	W	D	L	F	A	Pts	GD
		Home			*Goals*		*Away*			*Goals*			
Ross Co	36	12	1	5	39	16	12	4	2	48	26	77	+45
Stenhousemuir	36	9	2	7	34	26	10	5	3	28	16	64	+20
Brechin C	36	7	6	5	21	19	10	2	6	26	24	59	+4
Dumbarton	36	6	5	7	25	21	10	4	4	28	19	57	+13
Berwick R	36	7	3	8	28	27	5	11	2	25	22	50	+4
Queen's Park	36	6	7	5	22	21	5	4	9	19	25	44	−5
Albion R	36	5	4	9	22	36	7	4	7	21	27	44	−20
East Stirlingshire	36	4	10	4	27	22	5	3	10	23	26	40	+2
Cowdenbeath	36	5	2	11	19	30	3	5	10	15	35	31	−31
Montrose	36	5	4	9	26	31	3	2	13	16	43	30	−32

SCOTTISH LEAGUE HONOURS 1890–91 to 1998–99

*On goal average (ratio)/difference. †Held jointly after indecisive play-off. ‡Won on deciding match.
††Held jointly. ¶Two points deducted for fielding ineligible player.
Competition suspended 1940–45 during war; Regional Leagues operating. ‡‡Two points deducted for registration irregularities.

PREMIER LEAGUE

Maximum points: 108

	First	Pts	Second	Pts	Third	Pts
1998–99	Rangers	77	Celtic	71	St Johnstone	57

PREMIER DIVISION

Maximum points: 72

	First	Pts	Second	Pts	Third	Pts
1975–76	Rangers	54	Celtic	48	Hibernian	43
1976–77	Celtic	55	Rangers	46	Aberdeen	43
1977–78	Rangers	55	Aberdeen	53	Dundee U	40
1978–79	Celtic	48	Rangers	45	Dundee U	44
1979–80	Aberdeen	48	Celtic	47	St Mirren	42
1980–81	Celtic	56	Aberdeen	49	Rangers*	44
1981–82	Celtic	55	Aberdeen	53	Rangers	43
1982–83	Dundee U	56	Celtic*	55	Aberdeen	55
1983–84	Aberdeen	57	Celtic	50	Dundee U	47
1984–85	Aberdeen	59	Celtic	52	Dundee U	47
1985–86	Celtic*	50	Hearts	50	Dundee U	47

Maximum points: 88

1986–87	Rangers	69	Celtic	63	Dundee U	60
1987–88	Celtic	72	Hearts	62	Rangers	60

Maximum points: 72

1988–89	Rangers	56	Aberdeen	50	Celtic	46
1989–90	Rangers	51	Aberdeen*	44	Hearts	44
1990–91	Rangers	55	Aberdeen	53	Celtic*	41

Maximum points: 88

1991–92	Rangers	72	Hearts	63	Celtic	62
1992–93	Rangers	73	Aberdeen	64	Celtic	60
1993–94	Rangers	58	Aberdeen	55	Motherwell	54

Maximum points: 108

1994–95	Rangers	69	Motherwell	54	Hibernian	53
1995–96	Rangers	87	Celtic	83	Aberdeen*	55
1996–97	Rangers	80	Celtic	75	Dundee U	60
1997–98	Celtic	74	Rangers	72	Hearts	67

FIRST DIVISION

Maximum points: 52

	First	Pts	Second	Pts	Third	Pts
1975–76	Partick T	41	Kilmarnock	35	Montrose	30

Maximum points: 78

1976–77	St Mirren	62	Clydebank	58	Dundee	51
1977–78	Morton*	58	Hearts	58	Dundee	57
1978–79	Dundee	55	Kilmarnock*	54	Clydebank	54
1979–80	Hearts	53	Airdrieonians	51	Ayr U*	44
1980–81	Hibernian	57	Dundee	52	St Johnstone	51
1981–82	Motherwell	61	Kilmarnock	51	Hearts	50
1982–83	St Johnstone	55	Hearts	54	Clydebank	50
1983–84	Morton	54	Dumbarton	51	Partick T	46
1984–85	Motherwell	50	Clydebank	48	Falkirk	45
1985–86	Hamilton A	56	Falkirk	45	Kilmarnock	44

Maximum points: 88

1986–87	Morton	57	Dunfermline Ath	56	Dumbarton	53
1987–88	Hamilton A	56	Meadowbank T	52	Clydebank	49

Maximum points: 78

1988–89	Dunfermline Ath	54	Falkirk	52	Clydebank	48
1989–90	St Johnstone	58	Airdrieonians	54	Clydebank	44
1990–91	Falkirk	54	Airdrieonians	53	Dundee	52

Maximum points: 88

1991–92	Dundee	58	Partick T*	57	Hamilton A	57
1992–93	Raith R	65	Kilmarnock	54	Dunfermline Ath	52
1993–94	Falkirk	66	Dunfermline Ath	65	Airdrieonians	54

Maximum points: 108

1994–95	Raith R	69	Dunfermline Ath*	68	Dundee	68
1995–96	Dunfermline Ath	71	Dundee U*	67	Morton	67
1996–97	St Johnstone	80	Airdrieonians	60	Dundee*	58
1997–98	Dundee	70	Falkirk	65	Raith R*	60
1998–99	Hibernian	89	Falkirk	66	Ayr U	62

SECOND DIVISION

Maximum points: 52

	First	Pts	Second	Pts	Third	Pts
1975–76	Clydebank*	40	Raith R	40	Alloa	35

Maximum points: 78

	First	Pts	Second	Pts	Third	Pts
1976–77	Stirling A	55	Alloa	51	Dunfermline Ath	50
1977–78	Clyde*	53	Raith R	53	Dunfermline Ath	48
1978–79	Berwick R	54	Dunfermline Ath	52	Falkirk	50
1979–80	Falkirk	50	East Stirling	49	Forfar Ath	46
1980–81	Queen's Park	50	Queen of the S	46	Cowdenbeath	45
1981–82	Clyde	59	Alloa*	50	Arbroath	50
1982–83	Brechin C	55	Meadowbank T	54	Arbroath	49
1983–84	Forfar Ath	63	East Fife	47	Berwick R	43
1984–85	Montrose	53	Alloa	50	Dunfermline Ath	49
1985–86	Dunfermline Ath	57	Queen of the S	55	Meadowbank T	49
1986–87	Meadowbank T	55	Raith R*	52	Stirling A*	52
1987–88	Ayr U	61	St Johnstone	59	Queen's Park	51
1988–89	Albion R	50	Alloa	45	Brechin C	43
1989–90	Brechin C	49	Kilmarnock	48	Stirling A	47
1990–91	Stirling A	54	Montrose	46	Cowdenbeath	45
1991–92	Dumbarton	52	Cowdenbeath	51	Alloa	50
1992–93	Clyde	54	Brechin C*	53	Stranraer	53
1993–94	Stranraer	56	Berwick R	48	Stenhousemuir*	47

Maximum points: 108

	First	Pts	Second	Pts	Third	Pts
1994–95	Morton	64	Dumbarton	60	Stirling A	58
1995–96	Stirling A	81	East Fife	67	Berwick R	60
1996–97	Ayr U	77	Hamilton A	74	Livingston	64
1997–98	Stranraer	61	Clydebank	60	Livingston	59
1998–99	Livingston	77	Inverness CT	72	Clyde	53

THIRD DIVISION

Maximum points: 108

	First	Pts	Second	Pts	Third	Pts
1994–95	Forfar Ath	80	Montrose	67	Ross Co	60
1995–96	Livingston	72	Brechin C	63	Caledonian T	57
1996–97	Inverness CT	76	Forfar Ath*	67	Ross Co	67
1997–98	Alloa Ath	76	Arbroath	68	Ross Co	67
1998–99	Ross Co	77	Stenhousemuir	64	Brechin C	59

FIRST DIVISION to 1974–75

Maximum points: a 36; b 44; c 40; d 52; e 60; f 68; g 76; h 84.

	First	Pts	Second	Pts	Third	Pts
1890–91*a*	Dumbarton††	29	Rangers††	29	Celtic	21
1891–92*b*	Dumbarton	37	Celtic	35	Hearts	34
1892–93*a*	Celtic	29	Rangers	28	St Mirren	20
1893–94*a*	Celtic	29	Hearts	26	St Bernard's	23
1894–95*a*	Hearts	31	Celtic	26	Rangers	22
1895–96*a*	Celtic	30	Rangers	26	Hibernian	24
1896–97*a*	Hearts	28	Hibernian	26	Rangers	25
1897–98*a*	Celtic	33	Rangers	29	Hibernian	22
1898–99*a*	Rangers	36	Hearts	26	Celtic	24
1899–1900*a*	Rangers	32	Celtic	25	Hibernian	24
1900–01*c*	Rangers	35	Celtic	29	Hibernian	25
1901–02*a*	Rangers	28	Celtic	26	Hearts	22
1902–03*b*	Hibernian	37	Dundee	31	Rangers	29
1903–04*d*	Third Lanark	43	Hearts	39	Celtic*	38
1904–05*d*	Celtic‡	41	Rangers	41	Third Lanark	35
1905–06*e*	Celtic	49	Hearts	43	Airdrieonians	38
1906–07*f*	Celtic	55	Dundee	48	Rangers	45
1907–08*f*	Celtic	55	Falkirk	51	Rangers	50
1908–09*f*	Celtic	51	Dundee	50	Clyde	48
1909–10*f*	Celtic	54	Falkirk	52	Rangers	46
1910–11*f*	Rangers	52	Aberdeen	48	Falkirk	44
1911–12*f*	Rangers	51	Celtic	45	Clyde	42
1912–13*f*	Rangers	53	Celtic	49	Hearts*	41
1913–14*g*	Celtic	65	Rangers	59	Hearts*	54
1914–15*g*	Celtic	65	Hearts	61	Rangers	50
1915–16*g*	Celtic	67	Rangers	56	Morton	51
1916–17*g*	Celtic	64	Morton	54	Rangers	53
1917–18*f*	Rangers	56	Celtic	55	Kilmarnock*	43
1918–19*f*	Celtic	58	Rangers	57	Morton	47
1919–20*h*	Rangers	71	Celtic	68	Motherwell	57
1920–21*h*	Rangers	76	Celtic	66	Hearts	50
1921–22*h*	Celtic	67	Rangers	66	Raith R	51
1922–23*g*	Rangers	55	Airdrieonians	50	Celtic	46
1923–24*g*	Rangers	59	Airdrieonians	50	Celtic	46
1924–25*g*	Rangers	60	Airdrieonians	57	Hibernian	52
1925–26*g*	Celtic	58	Airdrieonians*	50	Hearts	50
1926–27*g*	Rangers	56	Motherwell	51	Celtic	49

	First	Pts	Second	Pts	Third	Pts
1927–28g	Rangers	60	Celtic*	55	Motherwell	55
1928–29g	Rangers	67	Celtic	51	Motherwell	50
1929–30g	Rangers	60	Motherwell	55	Aberdeen	53
1930–31g	Rangers	60	Celtic	58	Motherwell	56
1931–32g	Motherwell	66	Rangers	61	Celtic	48
1932–33g	Rangers	62	Motherwell	59	Hearts	50
1933–34g	Rangers	66	Motherwell	62	Celtic	47
1934–35g	Rangers	55	Celtic	52	Hearts	50
1935–36g	Celtic	66	Rangers*	61	Aberdeen	61
1936–37g	Rangers	61	Aberdeen	54	Celtic	52
1937–38g	Celtic	61	Hearts	58	Rangers	49
1938–39g	Rangers	59	Celtic	48	Aberdeen	46
1946–47e	Rangers	46	Hibernian	44	Aberdeen	39
1947–48e	Hibernian	48	Rangers	46	Partick T	36
1948–49e	Rangers	46	Dundee	45	Hibernian	39
1949–50e	Rangers	50	Hibernian	49	Hearts	43
1950–51e	Hibernian	48	Rangers*	38	Dundee	38
1951–52e	Hibernian	45	Rangers	41	East Fife	37
1952–53e	Rangers*	43	Hibernian	43	East Fife	39
1953–54e	Celtic	43	Hearts	38	Partick T	35
1954–55e	Aberdeen	49	Celtic	46	Rangers	41
1955–56f	Rangers	52	Aberdeen	46	Hearts*	45
1956–57f	Rangers	55	Hearts	53	Kilmarnock	42
1957–58f	Hearts	62	Rangers	49	Celtic	46
1958–59f	Rangers	50	Hearts	48	Motherwell	44
1959–60f	Hearts	54	Kilmarnock	50	Rangers*	42
1960–61f	Rangers	51	Kilmarnock	50	Third Lanark	42
1961–62f	Dundee	54	Rangers	51	Celtic	46
1962–63f	Rangers	57	Kilmarnock	48	Partick T	46
1963–64f	Rangers	55	Kilmarnock	49	Celtic*	47
1964–65f	Kilmarnock*	50	Hearts	50	Dunfermline Ath	49
1965–66f	Celtic	57	Rangers	55	Kilmarnock	45
1966–67f	Celtic	58	Rangers	55	Clyde	46
1967–68f	Celtic	63	Rangers	61	Hibernian	45
1968–69f	Celtic	54	Rangers	49	Dunfermline Ath	45
1969–70f	Celtic	57	Rangers	45	Hibernian	44
1970–71f	Celtic	56	Aberdeen	54	St Johnstone	44
1971–72f	Celtic	60	Aberdeen	50	Rangers	44
1972–73f	Celtic	57	Rangers	56	Hibernian	45
1973–74f	Celtic	53	Hibernian	49	Rangers	48
1974–75f	Rangers	56	Hibernian	49	Celtic	45

SECOND DIVISION to 1974–75

Maximum points: a 76; b 72; c 68; d 52; e 60; f 36; g 44.

	First	Pts	Second	Pts	Third	Pts
1893–94f	Hibernian	29	Cowlairs	27	Clyde	24
1894–95f	Hibernian	30	Motherwell	22	Port Glasgow	20
1895–96f	Abercorn	27	Leith Ath	23	Renton	21
1896–97f	Partick T	31	Leith Ath	27	Kilmarnock*	21
1897–98f	Kilmarnock	29	Port Glasgow	25	Morton	22
1898–99f	Kilmarnock	32	Leith Ath	27	Port Glasgow	25
1899–1900f	Partick T	29	Morton	28	Port Glasgow	20
1900–01f	St Bernard's	25	Airdrieonians	23	Abercorn	21
1901–02g	Port Glasgow	32	Partick T	31	Motherwell	26
1902–03g	Airdrieonians	35	Motherwell	28	Ayr U*	27
1903–04g	Hamilton A	37	Clyde	29	Ayr U	28
1904–05g	Clyde	32	Falkirk	28	Hamilton A	27
1905–06g	Leith Ath	34	Clyde	31	Albion R	27
1906–07g	St Bernard's	32	Vale of Leven*	27	Arthurlie	27
1907–08g	Raith R	30	Dumbarton*‡‡	27	Ayr U	27
1908–09g	Abercorn	31	Raith R*	28	Vale of Leven	28
1909–10g	Leith Ath‡	33	Raith R	33	St Bernard's	27
1910–11g	Dumbarton	31	Ayr U	27	Albion R	25
1911–12g	Ayr U	35	Abercorn	30	Dumbarton	27
1912–13d	Ayr U	34	Dunfermline Ath	33	East Stirling	32
1913–14g	Cowdenbeath	31	Albion R	27	Dunfermline Ath*	26
1914–15d	Cowdenbeath*	37	St Bernard's*	37	Leith Ath	37
1921–22a	Alloa	60	Cowdenbeath	47	Armadale	45
1922–23a	Queen's Park	57	Clydebank¶	50	St Johnstone¶	45
1923–24a	St Johnstone	56	Cowdenbeath	55	Bathgate	44
1924–25a	Dundee U	50	Clydebank	48	Clyde	47
1925–26a	Dunfermline Ath	59	Clyde	53	Ayr U	52
1926–27a	Bo'ness	56	Raith R	49	Clydebank	45
1927–28a	Ayr U	54	Third Lanark	45	King's Park	44
1928–29b	Dundee U	51	Morton	50	Arbroath	47
1929–30a	Leith Ath*	57	East Fife	57	Albion R	54
1930–31a	Third Lanark	61	Dundee U	50	Dunfermline Ath	47
1931–32a	East Stirling*	55	St Johnstone	55	Raith R*	46
1932–33c	Hibernian	54	Queen of the S	49	Dunfermline Ath	47

	First	Pts		Second	Pts		Third	Pts
1933–34c	Albion R	45		Dunfermline Ath*	44		Arbroath	44
1934–35c	Third Lanark	52		Arbroath	50		St Bernard's	47
1935–36c	Falkirk	59		St Mirren	52		Morton	48
1936–37c	Ayr U	54		Morton	51		St Bernard's	48
1937–38c	Raith R	59		Albion R	48		Airdrieonians	47
1938–39c	Cowdenbeath	60		Alloa*	48		East Fife	48
1946–47d	Dundee	45		Airdrieonians	42		East Fife	31
1947–48e	East Fife	53		Albion R	42		Hamilton A	40
1948–49e	Raith R*	42		Stirling A	42		Airdrieonians*	41
1949–50e	Morton	47		Airdrieonians	44		Dunfermline Ath*	36
1950–51e	Queen of the S*	45		Stirling A	45		Ayr U*	36
1951–52e	Clyde	44		Falkirk	43		Ayr U	39
1952–53e	Stirling A	44		Hamilton A	43		Queen's Park	37
1953–54e	Motherwell	45		Kilmarnock	42		Third Lanark*	36
1954–55e	Airdrieonians	46		Dunfermline Ath	42		Hamilton A	39
1955–56b	Queen's Park	54		Ayr U	51		St Johnstone	49
1956–57b	Clyde	64		Third Lanark	51		Cowdenbeath	45
1957–58b	Stirling A	55		Dunfermline Ath	53		Arbroath	47
1958–59b	Ayr U	60		Arbroath	51		Stenhousemuir	46
1959–60b	St Johnstone	53		Dundee U	50		Queen of the S	49
1960–61b	Stirling A	55		Falkirk	54		Stenhousemuir	50
1961–62b	Clyde	54		Queen of the S	53		Morton	44
1962–63b	St Johnstone	55		East Stirling	49		Morton	48
1963–64b	Morton	67		Clyde	53		Arbroath	46
1964–65b	Stirling A	59		Hamilton A	50		Queen of the S	45
1965–66b	Ayr U	53		Airdrieonians	50		Queen of the S	47
1966–67a	Morton	69		Raith R	58		Arbroath	57
1967–68b	St Mirren	62		Arbroath	53		East Fife	49
1968–69b	Motherwell	64		Ayr U	53		East Fife*	48
1969–70b	Falkirk	56		Cowdenbeath	55		Queen of the S	50
1970–71b	Partick T	56		East Fife	51		Arbroath	46
1971–72b	Dumbarton*	52		Arbroath	52		Stirling A	50
1972–73b	Clyde	56		Dumfermline Ath	52		Raith R*	47
1973–74b	Airdrieonians	60		Kilmarnock	58		Hamilton A	55
1974–75a	Falkirk	54		Queen of the S*	53		Montrose	53

Elected to First Division: 1894 Clyde; 1895 Hibernian; 1896 Abercorn; 1897 Partick T; 1899 Kilmarnock; 1900 Morton and Partick T; 1902 Port Glasgow and Partick T; 1903 Airdrieonians and Motherwell; 1905 Falkirk and Aberdeen; 1906 Clyde and Hamilton A; 1910 Raith R; 1913 Ayr U and Dumbarton.

RELEGATED FROM PREMIER LEAGUE

1998–99 Dunfermline Ath

RELEGATED FROM PREMIER DIVISION

1974–75 *No relegation due to League reorganization*
1975–76 Dundee, St Johnstone
1976–77 Hearts, Kilmarnock
1977–78 Ayr U, Clydebank
1978–79 Hearts, Motherwell
1979–80 Dundee, Hibernian
1980–81 Kilmarnock, Hearts
1981–82 Partick T, Airdrieonians
1982–83 Morton, Kilmarnock
1983–84 St Johnstone, Motherwell
1984–85 Dumbarton, Morton
1985–86 *No relegation due to League reorganization*
1986–87 Clydebank, Hamilton A
1987–88 Falkirk, Dunfermline Ath, Morton
1988–89 Hamilton A
1989–90 Dundee
1990–91 *None*
1991–92 St Mirren, Dunfermline Ath
1992–93 Falkirk, Airdrieonians
1993–94 *See footnote*
1994–95 Dundee U
1995–96 Partick T, Falkirk
1996–97 Raith R
1997–98 Hibernian

RELEGATED FROM DIVISION 1

1974–75 *No relegation due to League reorganization*
1975–76 Dunfermline Ath, Clyde
1976–77 Raith R, Falkirk
1977–78 Alloa Ath, East Fife
1978–79 Montrose, Queen of the S
1979–80 Arbroath, Clyde
1980–81 Stirling A, Berwick R
1981–82 East Stirling, Queen of the S
1982–83 Dunfermline Ath, Queen's Park
1983–84 Raith R, Alloa
1984–85 Meadowbank T, St Johnstone
1985–86 Ayr U, Alloa
1986–87 Brechin C, Montrose
1987–88 East Fife, Dumbarton
1988–89 Kilmarnock, Queen of the S
1989–90 Albion R, Alloa
1990–91 Clyde, Brechin C
1991–92 Montrose, Forfar Ath
1992–93 Meadowbank T, Cowdenbeath
1993–94 *See footnote*
1994–95 Ayr U, Stranraer
1995–96 Hamilton A, Dumbarton
1996–97 Clydebank, East Fife
1997–98 Partick T, Stirling A
1998–99 Hamilton A, Stranraer

RELEGATED FROM DIVISION 2

1994–95 Meadowbank T, Brechin C
1995–96 Forfar Ath, Montrose
1996–97 Dumbarton, Berwick R

1997–98 Stenhousemuir, Brechin C
1998–99 East Fife, Forfar Ath

RELEGATED FROM DIVISION 1 (TO 1973–74)

1921–22 *Queen's Park, Dumbarton, Clydebank	1951–52 Morton, Stirling A
1922–23 Albion R, Alloa Ath	1952–53 Motherwell, Third Lanark
1923–24 Clyde, Clydebank	1953–54 Airdrieonians, Hamilton A
1924–25 Third Lanark, Ayr U	1954–55 *No clubs relegated*
1925–26 Raith R, Clydebank	1955–56 Stirling A, Clyde
1926–27 Morton, Dundee U	1956–57 Dunfermline Ath, Ayr U
1927–28 Dunfermline Ath, Bo'ness	1957–58 East Fife, Queen's Park
1928–29 Third Lanark, Raith R	1958–59 Queen of the S, Falkirk
1929–30 St Johnstone, Dundee U	1959–60 Arbroath, Stirling A
1930–31 Hibernian, East Fife	1960–61 Ayr U, Clyde
1931–32 Dundee U, Leith Ath	1961–62 St Johnstone, Stirling A
1932–33 Morton, East Stirling	1962–63 Clyde, Raith R
1933–34 Third Lanark, Cowdenbeath	1963–64 Queen of the S, East Stirling
1934–35 St Mirren, Falkirk	1964–65 Airdrieonians, Third Lanark
1935–36 Airdrieonians, Ayr U	1965–66 Morton, Hamilton A
1936–37 Dunfermline Ath, Albion R	1966–67 St Mirren, Ayr U
1937–38 Dundee, Morton	1967–68 Motherwell, Stirling A
1938–39 Queen's Park, Raith R	1968–69 Falkirk, Arbroath
1946–47 Kilmarnock, Hamilton A	1969–70 Raith R, Partick T
1947–48 Airdrieonians, Queen's Park	1970–71 St Mirren, Cowdenbeath
1948–49 Morton, Albion R	1971–72 Clyde, Dunfermline Ath
1949–50 Queen of the S, Stirling A	1972–73 Kilmarnock, Airdrieonians
1950–51 Clyde, Falkirk	1973–74 East Fife, Falkirk

*Season 1921–22 – only 1 club promoted, 3 clubs relegated.

Scottish League championship wins: Rangers 48 (including one Premier League), Celtic 36, Aberdeen 4, Hearts 4, Hibernian 4, Dumbarton 2, Dundee 1, Dundee U 1, Kilmarnock 1, Motherwell 1, Third Lanark 1.

At the end of the 1993–94 season four divisions were created assisted by the admission of two new clubs Ross County and Caledonian Thistle. Only one club was promoted from Division 1 and Division 2. The three relegated from the Premier joined with teams finishing second to seventh in Division 1 to form the new Division 1. Five relegated from Division 1 combined with those who finished second to sixth to form a new Division 2 and the bottom eight in Division 2 linked with the two newcomers to form a new Division 3. At the end of the 1997–98 season the nine clubs remaining in the Premier Division plus the promoted team from Division 1 formed a breakaway Premier League.

Neil McCann responds to the crowd's applause, after Rangers clinched the first Scottish Premier League title. On the right is Jonatan Johansson. (Colorsport)

SCOTTISH LEAGUE CUP FINALS 1946–99

Season	Winners	Runners-up	Score
1946–47	Rangers	Aberdeen	4-0
1947–48	East Fife	Falkirk	4-1 after 0-0 draw
1948–49	Rangers	Raith R	2-0
1949–50	East Fife	Dunfermline Ath	3-0
1950–51	Motherwell	Hibernian	3-0
1951–52	Dundee	Rangers	3-2
1952–53	Dundee	Kilmarnock	2-0
1953–54	East Fife	Partick T	3-2
1954–55	Hearts	Motherwell	4-2
1955–56	Aberdeen	St Mirren	2-1
1956–57	Celtic	Partick T	3-0 after 0-0 draw
1957–58	Celtic	Rangers	7-1
1958–59	Hearts	Partick T	5-1
1959–60	Hearts	Third Lanark	2-1
1960–61	Rangers	Kilmarnock	2-0
1961–62	Rangers	Hearts	3-1 after 1-1 draw
1962–63	Hearts	Kilmarnock	1-0
1963–64	Rangers	Morton	5-0
1964–65	Rangers	Celtic	2-1
1965–66	Celtic	Rangers	2-1
1966–67	Celtic	Rangers	1-0
1967–68	Celtic	Dundee	5-3
1968–69	Celtic	Hibernian	6-2
1969–70	Celtic	St Johnstone	1-0
1970–71	Rangers	Celtic	1-0
1971–72	Partick T	Celtic	4-1
1972–73	Hibernian	Celtic	2-1
1973–74	Dundee	Celtic	1-0
1974–75	Celtic	Hibernian	6-3
1975–76	Rangers	Celtic	1-0
1976–77	Aberdeen	Celtic	2-1
1977–78	Rangers	Celtic	2-1
1978–79	Rangers	Aberdeen	2-1
1979–80	Dundee U	Aberdeen	3-0 after 0-0 draw
1980–81	Dundee U	Dundee	3-0
1981–82	Rangers	Dundee U	2-1
1982–83	Celtic	Rangers	2-1
1983–84	Rangers	Celtic	3-2
1984–85	Rangers	Dundee U	1-0
1985–86	Aberdeen	Hibernian	3-0
1986–87	Rangers	Celtic	2-1
1987–88	Rangers	Aberdeen	3-3
		(Rangers won 5-3 on penalties)	
1988–89	Rangers	Aberdeen	3-2
1989–90	Aberdeen	Rangers	2-1
1990–91	Rangers	Celtic	2-1
1991–92	Hibernian	Dunfermline Ath	2-0
1992–93	Rangers	Aberdeen	2-1
1993–94	Rangers	Hibernian	2-1
1994–95	Raith R	Celtic	2-2
		(Raith R won 6-5 on penalties)	
1995–96	Aberdeen	Dundee	2-0
1996–97	Rangers	Hearts	4-3
1997–98	Celtic	Dundee U	3-0
1998–99	Rangers	St Johnstone	2-1

SCOTTISH LEAGUE CUP WINS

Rangers 21, Celtic 10, Aberdeen 5, Hearts 4, Dundee 3, East Fife 3, Dundee U 2, Hibernian 2, Motherwell 1, Partick T 1, Raith R 1.

APPEARANCES IN FINALS

Rangers 27, Celtic 22, Aberdeen 11, Hibernian 7, Dundee 6, Hearts 6, Dundee U 5, Partick T 4, East Fife 3, Kilmarnock 3, Dunfermline Ath 2, Motherwell 2, Raith R 2, St Johnstone 2, Falkirk 1, Morton 1, St Mirren 1, Third Lanark 1.

SCOTTISH COCA-COLA CUP 1998–99

FIRST ROUND

1 AUG

Arbroath (0) 0
Clydebank (0) 1 *(McDonald 65)* 649
Arbroath: Hinchcliffe; Mitchell (Sellars), Gallagher, McAulay, Jones, Crawford, Cooper, Tindal, Grant (Mercer), Spence, Thomson (Scott).
Clydebank: Scott; Wishart, Lovering, Smith (Teale), McLaughlin, Brannigan, Nicholls, McDonald (Miller), Taggart, Robertson, McWilliams (Gardner).

Brechin C (0) 2 *(Hutcheon 65, 106)*
Hamilton A (1) 2 *(Renicks 39, Geraghty 120)* 349
Brechin C: Garden; Smith (Williamson), Christie (Brown), Cairney, Bain, Black, Hutcheon, Smart, Sorbie, Dailly (Kerrigan), Campbell.
Hamilton A: MacFarlane I; Renicks, Cunnington, Tait, Berry, Thomson, Henderson N (Clark), McAulay, Geraghty, Wales (McFarlane D), Henderson D.
aet (Hamilton A won 3-2 on penalties)

Clyde (0) 1 *(McPhee 84)*
Berwick R (0) 1 *(Laidlaw 83)* 594
Clyde: McIntyre; Smith, Cranmer, Spittal, Murray (Dillon), Carrigan, Convery (McPhee), McCusker, McHarg, Brownlie (McGraw), Grant.
Berwick R: O'Connor; Cunningham (Laidlaw), Neill A, Clark, Beaton, Campbell, Neil M, Watt, Shaw (Rafferty), Forrester, Ramage (Smith).
aet (Berwick R won 4-3 on penalties)

Cowdenbeath (0) 0
Livingston (1) 2 *(Millar 16, Bingham 56)* 507
Cowdenbeath: Hutchison; Urquhart, Cuthbert, Bowsher, Snedden, Robertson, Winter, Ritchie (Brown), Stewart, Graham, Hamilton.
Livingston: McCaldon; Boyle, Deas, Sweeney, Watson, Bennett, Millar, Bingham, Robertson J, McPhee (McCormick), Rajamaki (Little).

Dumbarton (0) 0
Alloa Athletic (2) 4 *(Wilson M 25, Simpson 39,*
McKechnie 75, Cameron 87) 352
Dumbarton: Meechan; Wilson, Brittain, Gow, Currie, Sharp, Grace (Reid), Jack, Smith (Brown), McKinnon, Melvin W (Melvin M).
Alloa Athletic: Cairns; Valentine, Nelson, McAneny, McCulloch, Ramsay (Pew), Wilson M, Wilson S, Simpson (Cameron), Irvine (Haddow), McKechnie.

East Fife (1) 3 *(Cusick 36, Coyle 83, Kirk 97)*
Partick T (2) 2 *(Lauchlan 14, Morgan 19)* 1231
East Fife: McCulloch; Strathdee, Gibb, Cusick (Gartshore), Johnston, Coyle, Munro, Fisher (Brown), Martin, Moffat (Kirk), Allan.
Partick T: Arthur; Kennedy, McArthur, Jamieson, Archibald, Connell, Lauchlan, Bryce (Donaghy), Morgan, Callaghan W (Dunn), Johnston (Callaghan T).
aet

Forfar Ath (0) 0
Stirling Albion (0) 1 *(Price 65)* 524
Forfar Ath: Robertson; McCheyne, Ferguson, Hamilton, Mann, Raynes, Gibson, Gillies (Allison), Brand, McLauchlan (Honeyman), Cargill (Watson).
Stirling Albion: McGeown; Donald, McCallum, Clark, Martin, Philliben, Bone, Bell (Price), Nicholas (McCallion), Mortimer, Angus.

Queen of the S (0) 1 *(Eadie 89)*
Inverness CT (2) 4 *(Sheerin 6, McLean 28,*
Shearer 73, Cherry 75) 1227
Queen of the S: Mathieson; Cleeland, Love, Rowe, Thomson, Boyle (Aitken), Weir, Leslie, Mallan, Adams (Nesovic), Bailey (Eadie).
Inverness CT: Calder; Teasdale, Hastings (Robson), McCulloch, Tokely, Cherry, Wilson (Farquhar), Shearer (Bavidge), McLean, Christie, Sheerin.

Queen's Park (1) 1 *(Graham 41)*
Ayr U (1) 3 *(Davies 37, Armstrong 53, Welsh 72)* 1016
Queen's Park: Monaghan; Alexander, Connaghan, Elder, Martin, Caven, Ferry, Graham (Ferguson), Edgar, Parks (Agostini), Little.
Ayr U: Castilla; Traynor (Robertson), Miller, Millen, Welsh, Lyons, Hurst, Davies (Agnew), Armstrong (Burns), Findlay, Duthie.

Ross Co (1) 4 *(Adams 38, 58, 70, Tarrant 57)*
Montrose (0) 1 *(Andrew 67)* 923
Ross Co: Walker; Mackay D, McBain, Furphy, Maxwell, Gilbert, Escalon (Herd), Adams, Tarrant (Hunter), Taylor, Ross (Ferries).
Montrose: Murray; Mailer, Watt, Craib, Wylie, Meldrum, Andrew, Farnan (Henry), McGlashan, Higgins (Taylor), Loney.

Stenhousemuir (0) 1 *(Watters 65)*
East Stirling (0) 0 348
Stenhousemuir: Hamilton L; Sprott, Hall, Armstrong, Graham, Lansdowne, Kane, Fisher, Lawrence (Watters), Hutchison, Gibson.
East Stirling: McDougall; Barr, Brown (Hoxley), Ross, Smith, Walker, Hardie, Muirhead, McNeill (Sime), Patterson, McGoldrick.

Stranraer (0) 1 *(Ronald 53)*
Albion R (0) 1 *(Ross 50)* 516
Stranraer: Matthews; Knox, Black, George, Campbell, Johnstone, Watson, McIntyre, Ronald (Young G), Young J (Harty), Skilling (Bell).
Albion R: McLean; Mitchell (Bruce), McGowan, Melvin, Duncan (McLees), Docherty, Sinclair, Shaw, Harty (Greenock), Ross, Donaldson.
aet (Stranraer won 4-3 on penalties)

SECOND ROUND

8 AUG

Berwick R (0) 1 *(Forrester 60)*
Falkirk (3) 5 *(Crabbe 17, McKee 35, 50, Oliver 44,*
Keith 75) 1015
Berwick R: O'Connor; McNicoll (Ramage), Neill A, Campbell, Beaton, Rafferty (Baigrie), Neil M (Clark), Fraser, Forrester, Watt, Laidlaw.
Falkirk: Mathers; Corrigan, Seaton, Oliver, James (McCart), Hagen (McQuilken), McAllister (McStay), Hamilton, Crabbe, Keith, McKee.

Dundee (0) 0
Alloa Ath (1) 1 *(McKechnie 38)* 2057
Dundee: Douglas; Smith, Pounewatchy, Adamczuk, Irvine, Falconer, Miller, Garcin, Annand (McCormick), Coyne, McSkimming (Grady).
Alloa Ath: Cairns; Valentine, Nelson, McAneny, McCulloch, Pew (Ramsay), Wilson M, Wilson S, Simpson, Irvine, McKechnie (Cameron).

Dundee U (2) 2 *(McSwegan 24, Boli 35)*
Stirling Albion (1) 2 *(Bone 25, 71)*   4957
Dundee U: Dijkstra; Jenkins, Malpas, Mols (Dolan), McNally (Skoldmark), Pascual, Olofsson, Zetterlund, Boli, McSwegan, Miller (McLaren).
Stirling Albion: McGeown; Paterson, McCallum, Clark, Martin, Philliben, Bone, Donald, Price, Mortimer (Bell), Nicholas.
aet (Dundee U won 3-0 on penalties)

East Fife (0) 0
Motherwell (0) 1 *(Halliday 97)*   1592
East Fife: McCulloch; Strathdee, Gibb, Cusick (Fisher), Johnston, Coyle, Munro, Brown, Martin (Gartshore), Moffat (Kirk), Allan.
Motherwell: Kaven; McGowan, Valakari, Halliday, McClair (Shivute), McCulloch, Doesburg, Matthaei, Stirling, Teale, Nyyssonen (Miller).
aet

Greenock Morton (0) 0
Ross Co (0) 1 *(Tarrant 83)*   1619
Greenock Morton: Wylie; Collins, Archdeacon, Curran, Anderson J, Fenwick, George (Morrow), Blair (Blaikie), Hawke, Duffield, Twaddle.
Ross Co: Walker; Mackay, McBain, Furphy (Herd), Maxwell, Gilbert, Escalon (Ferguson), Adams, Tarrant (Hunter), Taylor, Ross.

Hamilton A (0) 1 *(McFarlane D 66)*
Hibernian (1) 2 *(Skinner 18, Lovell 90)*   3063
Hamilton A: MacFarlane I; Renicks, Cunnington, Hillcoat C, Berry, Thomson, McAulay, Tait, Geraghty (McFarlane D), Wales, Henderson N.
Hibernian: Gottskalksson; Renwick, Elliot, Holsgrove, Hughes, Dennis, Rougier (Harper), Skinner, Crawford (Lovell), Lavety, McGinlay.

Inverness CT (0) 0
Aberdeen (1) 3 *(Dodds 1, 79, 82)*   5164
Inverness CT: Calder; Teasdale, Hastings, McCulloch, Tokely, Farquhar, Wilson (Bavidge), Shearer (MacArthur), McLean, Christie, Sheerin.
Aberdeen: Leighton; Perry, Whyte, Anderson (Gillies), Inglis, Smith, Hignett, Jess, Derek Young (Rowson), Dodds, Kiriakov (Dow).

Livingston (0) 1 *(Robertson 94)*
Dunfermline Ath (0) 0   3038
Livingston: McCaldon; Conway, Deas, Sweeney, Watson, Bennett, Rajamaki (Feroz), Millar (Little), Robertson, McPhee, Bingham (McCormick).
Dunfermline Ath: Butler; Shields, McCulloch, Tod, Linighan (Shaw), Millar, French (Faulconbridge), Huxford, Smith, Ferguson, Thomson (Ireland).
aet

Raith R (0) 2 *(Dair J 50, Wright 63)*
Clydebank (0) 0   1556
Raith R: Van De Kamp; McEwan, McPherson, Venables, Browne, Fotheringham K, Hartley, Bowman, Wright (Robertson), Tosh, Dair J (Smart).
Clydebank: Scott (Smith); Wishart, Lovering, Teale, McLaughlin, Brannigan, Nicholls (Brown), McDonald, Taggart, Gardner (Miller), McWilliams.

St Johnstone (0) 3 *(O'Halloran 67, Connolly 77, O'Boyle 84)*
Stranraer (0) 0   2679
St Johnstone: Ferguson; McQuillan, Dods (Whiteford), Griffin, Bollan, Dasovic, O'Neil, McMahon, O'Boyle, Connolly, O'Halloran.
Stranraer: Matthews; McIntyre, Black, George, Campbell, Watson, Skilling, Young J, Ronald, Archdeacon, Galloway (Harty).

St Mirren (0) 1 *(Brown 70)*
Ayr U (2) 3 *(Walker 40, Lyons 43, Hurst 65)* 2556
St Mirren: Scrimgour; McNamee (Prentice), Nicolson, Rudden (Yardley), McQuilter, McLaughlin, Murray, Drew, McGarry (McWhirter), Mendes, Brown.
Ayr U: Castilla; Robertson, Miller, Millen (Traynor), Welsh, Craig, Hurst, Davies, Walker (Armstrong), Kelly (Findlay), Lyons.

Stenhousemuir (0) 0
Airdrieonians (1) 2 *(Moore 25, 66)*   801
Stenhousemuir: Hamilton L; Sprott, Hall (Kane), Armstrong, Graham, Baptie, Lansdowne, Fisher, Watters, Hutchison, Gibson (Hamilton R).
Airdrieonians: Martin; Stewart (Black), Johnston (McCann), Sandison, Farrell D, Smith, Farrell G, Wilson, Cooper, Moore, McGrillen (Taylor).

THIRD ROUND

18 AUG
Falkirk (0) 0
St Johnstone (0) 1 *(Kane 89)*   3749
Falkirk: Mathers; Corrigan, McQuilken, Oliver, James, Hagen (Seaton), McAllister, Hamilton, Crabbe, Keith, McKee (McKenzie).
St Johnstone: Main; McQuillan, Preston, Dods, Griffin, Dasovic, O'Neil, Kane, Grant, O'Boyle, McMahon (O'Halloran).

Kilmarnock (1) 3 *(Wright 25 (pen), 116, McCoist 92)*
Livingston (1) 1 *(Bingham 50 (pen))*   6565
Kilmarnock: Marshall; MacPherson, Kerr, McGowne, Lauchlan, Holt, Nevin (McCoist), Durrant, Mahood (Vareille), Wright, Mitchell (Burke).
Livingston: McCaldon; Boyle, Deas, Sweeney, Watson, Conway (Rajamaki), Millar, Little (Feroz), Robertson, McPhee (McCormick), Bingham.
aet

Motherwell (0) 0
Ayr U (1) 2 *(Hurst 1, Teale 70 (og))*   4893
Motherwell: Woods; May, Denham (Stirling), Halliday, McClair, Coyle, Michels, Christie, Davies (Miller), McCulloch (Craigan), Teale.
Ayr U: Castilla; Robertson, Miller, Millen, Welsh, Craig, Hurst (Traynor), Davies, Walker, Findlay, Lyons.

Rangers (2) 4 *(Amoruso 2, Ferguson B 41, Albertz 60, 82)*
Alloa Ath (0) 0   42,368
Rangers: Charbonnier; Porrini, Numan, Amoruso, Hendry (Moore), Albertz, Van Bronckhorst, Ferguson B, Gattuso, Wallace (Miller), Amato.
Alloa Ath: Cairns; Valentine, Nelson, McAneny, McCulloch (Haddow), Pew, Wilson S, Ramsay (Mackay), Simpson, Irvine, McKechnie (Cameron).

19 AUG
Airdrieonians (1) 1 *(Wilson 15)*
Celtic (0) 0   8762
Airdrieonians: Martin; Stewart (Black), Jack, Sandison, Farrell D, Smith, Moore, Wilson, Cooper (McGrillen), Taylor, McCann.
Celtic: Gould; Boyd, Mahe, McNamara (Annoni), Mackay, Lambert, O'Donnell (McKinlay), Burley, Donnelly, Jackson, Blinker (Burchill).

Hearts (2) 4 *(Hamilton 4, Adam 23, McKinnon 109, Fulton 120)*
Raith R (1) 2 *(Shields 4, Hartley 87)*   11,653
Hearts: Rousset; Locke (Flögel), Naysmith, Weir, Salvatori (McKinnon), Pressley, McCann, Fulton, Adam (Quitongo), Makel, Hamilton.
Raith R: Van De Kamp; McEwan (McCulloch), Dair J, Bowman, Browne, Fotheringham K, Hartley, Shields (Robertson), Wright, Tosh (Venables), Cameron.
aet

Hibernian (0) 1 *(Crawford 82 (pen))*
Aberdeen (0) 0 8020
Hibernian: Gottskalksson; Renwick, Elliot, Guggi, Hughes, Dennis, Rougier, Skinner, Crawford, Lavety (Lovell), McGinlay.
Aberdeen: Leighton; Perry (Dow), Whyte, Anderson, Inglis, Smith, Hignett, Jess, Rowson, Dodds, Kiriakov (Gillies).

Ross Co (0) 2 *(Adams 106, 118)*
Dundee U (0) 0 3206
Ross Co: Walker; Mackay D, McBain, Furphy (Herd), Maxwell, Gilbert, Escalon (Hunter), Ferguson, Tarrant, Taylor (Adams), Ross.
Dundee U: Dijkstra; Pascual, Malpas, Dolan, Patterson D, Skoldmark, Winters (Olofsson), Easton, Boli (McSwegan), Mols, Miller.
aet

QUARTER-FINALS

8 SEPT

Ayr U (0) 0
Rangers (1) 2 *(Amato 14, Miller 84)* 11,198
Ayr U: Nelson; Robertson, Miller, Millen, Welsh, Craig, Hurst, Davies, Walker (Ferguson), Findlay, Lyons.
Rangers: Charbonnier; Porrini, Vidmar, Amoruso, Moore (Hendry), Albertz (Miller), Ferguson B, Van Bronckhorst, Johansson, Wallace, Amato (Ferguson I).

Kilmarnock (0) 0
Airdrieonians (0) 1 *(Wilson 114)* 7835
Kilmarnock: Marshall; MacPherson, Kerr, Montgomerie, McGowne, Holt, Wright, Durrant (Mitchell), McCoist (Roberts), Mahood, Vareille.
Airdrieonians: Martin; Stewart, Jack, Sandison, Johnston (Taylor), Black, Moore (Farrell G), Wilson, Cooper, McGrillen, McCann.
aet

St Johnstone (3) 4 *(Lowndes 11, 32, McMahon 24, O'Neil 57)*
Hibernian (0) 0 8165
St Johnstone: Main; McQuillan (Griffin), Dods, Kernaghan, Bollan, McMahon, O'Neil, Kane, O'Boyle (Grant), Dasovic (Preston), Lowndes.
Hibernian: Gottskalksson; Renwick, Elliot, Guggi, Hughes, Dennis, Rougier (Dietrich), Holsgrove (Tosh), Crawford, Lovell (Miller), McGinlay.

9 SEPT

Hearts (0) 1 *(Holmes 73)*
Ross Co (1) 1 *(McBain 41)* 11,672
Hearts: Rousset; Naysmith, Pressley, Weir, Ritchie, Locke, McCann (Makel), Fulton, Adam, Hamilton (Holmes), Flögel (Quitongo).
Ross Co: Walker; Golabek (Campbell), McBain, Herd, Maxwell, Gilbert, Ferguson, Adams, Tarrant (Wood), Taylor (Ross), Escalon.
aet (Hearts won 3-0 on penalties)

SEMI-FINALS

25 OCT

Rangers (2) 5 *(Johansson 6, Ferguson I 35, Wallace 74, 78, Durie 89)*
Airdrieonians (0) 0 21,171
Rangers: Charbonnier; Porrini, Vidmar, Wilson, Hendry, Albertz (Ferguson I), Ferguson B, Van Bronckhorst (Numan), Kanchelskis, Wallace, Johansson.
Airdrieonians: Martin; Stewart, Jack (Evans), Sandison, Smith, Black, Moore (Johnston), Wilson, Cooper, McCann, McGrillen.

27 OCT

St Johnstone (2) 3 *(Dasovic 41, Preston 45, O'Boyle 87)*
Hearts (0) 0 12,027
St Johnstone: Main; McQuillan, Dods, Kernaghan, Bollan, Preston (McMahon), O'Neil, Kane, O'Boyle (Grant), Dasovic, Simao (Lowndes).
Hearts: Rousset; McKinnon, McPherson, Weir, Salvatori (Flögel), Ritchie, Fulton, Locke, Adam, Hamilton, Guerin (Quitongo).

FINAL

29 NOV (at Celtic Park)
Rangers (2) 2 *(Guivarc'h 6, Albertz 36)*
St Johnstone (1) 1 *(Dasovic 8)* 45,533
Rangers: Niemi; Porrini, Numan, Amoruso, Hendry, Albertz (Ferguson I), Ferguson B, Van Bronckhorst, Kanchelskis, Wallace, Guivarc'h (Durie).
St Johnstone: Main; McQuillan, Dods, Kernaghan, Bollan, Scott, O'Neil (Preston), Kane, O'Boyle (Lowndes), Dasovic, Simao (Grant).
Referee: H. Dallas (Motherwell).

Rodney Wallace, the Rangers leading goalscorer, darts between two St Johnstone defenders in the Scottish Coca-Cola Cup Final. (Actionimages)

SCOTTISH CUP FINALS 1874–1999

Year	Winners	Runners-up	Score
1874	Queen's Park	Clydesdale	2-0
1875	Queen's Park	Renton	3-0
1876	Queen's Park	Third Lanark	2-0 after 1-1 draw
1877	Vale of Leven	Rangers	3-2 after 0-0 and 1-1 draws
1878	Vale of Leven	Third Lanark	1-0
1879	Vale of Leven*	Rangers	
1880	Queen's Park	Thornlibank	3-0
1881	Queen's Park†	Dumbarton	3-1
1882	Queen's Park	Dumbarton	4-1 after 2-2 draw
1883	Dumbarton	Vale of Leven	2-1 after 2-2 draw
1884	Queen's Park‡	Vale of Leven	
1885	Renton	Vale of Leven	3-1 after 0-0 draw
1886	Queen's Park	Renton	3-1
1887	Hibernian	Dumbarton	2-1
1888	Renton	Cambuslang	6-1
1889	Third Lanark§	Celtic	2-1
1890	Queen's Park	Vale of Leven	2-1 after 1-1 draw
1891	Hearts	Dumbarton	1-0
1892	Celtic¶	Queen's Park	5-1
1893	Queen's Park	Celtic	2-1
1894	Rangers	Celtic	3-1
1895	St Bernard's	Renton	2-1
1896	Hearts	Hibernian	3-1
1897	Rangers	Dumbarton	5-1
1898	Rangers	Kilmarnock	2-0
1899	Celtic	Rangers	2-0
1900	Celtic	Queen's Park	4-3
1901	Hearts	Celtic	4-3
1902	Hibernian	Celtic	1-0
1903	Rangers	Hearts	2-0 after 1-1 and 0-0 draws
1904	Celtic	Rangers	3-2
1905	Third Lanark	Rangers	3-1 after 0-0 draw
1906	Hearts	Third Lanark	1-0
1907	Celtic	Hearts	3-0
1908	Celtic	St Mirren	5-1
1909	••		
1910	Dundee	Clyde	2-1 after 2-2 and 0-0 draws
1911	Celtic	Hamilton A	2-0 after 0-0 draw
1912	Celtic	Clyde	2-0
1913	Falkirk	Raith R	2-0
1914	Celtic	Hibernian	4-1 after 0-0 draw
1920	Kilmarnock	Albion R	3-2
1921	Partick T	Rangers	1-0
1922	Morton	Rangers	1-0
1923	Celtic	Hibernian	1-0
1924	Airdrieonians	Hibernian	2-0
1925	Celtic	Dundee	2-1
1926	St Mirren	Celtic	2-0
1927	Celtic	East Fife	3-1
1928	Rangers	Celtic	4-0
1929	Kilmarnock	Rangers	2-0
1930	Rangers	Partick T	2-1 after 0-0 draw
1931	Celtic	Motherwell	4-2 after 2-2 draw
1932	Rangers	Kilmarnock	3-0 after 1-1 draw
1933	Celtic	Motherwell	1-0
1934	Rangers	St Mirren	5-0
1935	Rangers	Hamilton A	2-1
1936	Rangers	Third Lanark	1-0
1937	Celtic	Aberdeen	2-1
1938	East Fife	Kilmarnock	4-2 after 1-1 draw
1939	Clyde	Motherwell	4-0
1947	Aberdeen	Hibernian	2-1
1948	Rangers	Morton	1-0 after 1-1 draw
1949	Rangers	Clyde	4-1
1950	Rangers	East Fife	3-0
1951	Celtic	Motherwell	1-0
1952	Motherwell	Dundee	4-0
1953	Rangers	Aberdeen	1-0 after 1-1 draw
1954	Celtic	Aberdeen	2-1
1955	Clyde	Celtic	1-0 after 1-1 draw
1956	Hearts	Celtic	3-1
1957	Falkirk	Kilmarnock	2-1 after 1-1 draw
1958	Clyde	Hibernian	1-0
1959	St Mirren	Aberdeen	3-1
1960	Rangers	Kilmarnock	2-0
1961	Dunfermline Ath	Celtic	2-0 after 0-0 draw
1962	Rangers	St Mirren	2-0
1963	Rangers	Celtic	3-0 after 1-1 draw
1964	Rangers	Dundee	3-1
1965	Celtic	Dunfermline Ath	3-2
1966	Rangers	Celtic	1-0 after 0-0 draw

Year	Winners	Runners-up	Score
1967	Celtic	Aberdeen	2-0
1968	Dunfermline Ath	Hearts	3-1
1969	Celtic	Rangers	4-0
1970	Aberdeen	Celtic	3-1
1971	Celtic	Rangers	2-1 after 1-1 draw
1972	Celtic	Hibernian	6-1
1973	Rangers	Celtic	3-2
1974	Celtic	Dundee U	3-0
1975	Celtic	Airdrieonians	3-1
1976	Rangers	Hearts	3-1
1977	Celtic	Rangers	1-0
1978	Rangers	Aberdeen	2-1
1979	Rangers	Hibernian	3-2 after 0-0 and 0-0 draws
1980	Celtic	Rangers	1-0
1981	Rangers	Dundee U	4-1 after 0-0 draw
1982	Aberdeen	Rangers	4-1 (aet)
1983	Aberdeen	Rangers	1-0 (aet)
1984	Aberdeen	Celtic	2-1 (aet)
1985	Celtic	Dundee U	2-1
1986	Aberdeen	Hearts	3-0
1987	St Mirren	Dundee U	1-0 (aet)
1988	Celtic	Dundee U	2-1
1989	Celtic	Rangers	1-0
1990	Aberdeen	Celtic	0-0 (aet)
		(Aberdeen won 9-8 on penalties)	
1991	Motherwell	Dundee U	4-3 (aet)
1992	Rangers	Airdrieonians	2-1
1993	Rangers	Aberdeen	2-1
1994	Dundee U	Rangers	1-0
1995	Celtic	Airdrieonians	1-0
1996	Rangers	Hearts	5-1
1997	Kilmarnock	Falkirk	1-0
1998	Hearts	Rangers	2-1
1999	Rangers	Celtic	1-0

*Vale of Leven awarded cup, Rangers failing to appear for replay after 1-1 draw.
†After Dumbarton protested the first game, which Queen's Park won 2-1.
‡Queen's Park awarded cup, Vale of Leven failing to appear.
§Replay by order of Scottish FA because of playing conditions in first match, won 3-0 by Third Lanark.
¶After mutually protested game which Celtic won 1-0.
••Owing to riot, the cup was withheld after two drawn games – between Celtic and Rangers 2-2 and 1-1.

SCOTTISH CUP WINS

Celtic 30, Rangers 28, Queen's Park 10, Aberdeen 7, Hearts 6, Clyde 3, Kilmarnock 3, St Mirren 3, Vale of Leven 3, Dunfermline Ath 2, Falkirk 2, Hibernian 2, Motherwell 2, Renton 2, Third Lanark 2, Airdrieonians 1, Dumbarton 1, Dundee 1, Dundee U 1, East Fife 1, Morton 1, Partick T 1, St Bernard's 1.

APPEARANCES IN FINAL

Celtic 48, Rangers 45, Aberdeen 14, Queen's Park 12, Hearts 12, Hibernian 10, Kilmarnock 8, Vale of Leven 7, Clyde 6, Dumbarton 6, Dundee U 7, Motherwell 6, St Mirren 6, Third Lanark 6, Renton 5, Airdrieonians 4, Dundee 4, Dunfermline Ath 3, East Fife 3, Falkirk 3, Hamilton A 2, Morton 2, Partick T 2, Albion R 1, Cambuslang 1, Clydesdale 1, Raith R 1, St Bernard's 1, Thornlibank 1.

Regi Blinker (hooped shirt) of Celtic attempts to weave his way through Lorenzo Amoroso (left) and Giovanni Van Bronckhorst, the Rangers defenders in the Scottish Cup Final. But in the end, his team lost 1-0. (Colorsport)

TENNENT'S SCOTTISH CUP 1998-99

FIRST ROUND

5 DEC

Arbroath (1) 1 *(Gallagher (pen) 37)*
Partick T (2) 2 *(Tosh 7, Dunn 43)*   1333
Arbroath: Hinchcliffe; Florence (Tindal), Gallagher, Sellars, Jones, Crawford, Cooper, Arbuckle, McGlashan C, Mercer, Scott D.
Partick T: Arthur; Kennedy, McKeown, Jamieson, Archibald, Gaughan, Connell, McKenzie, Tosh, Dunn (Flannigan), McDonald.

Dumbarton (0) 1 *(Flannery 84)*
Livingston (0) 1 *(Millar 58)*   530
Dumbarton: Barnes; Wilson, Brittain, Gow, Jack, King, Harvey, McKinnon, Flannery, Miller (Melvin W), Grace (Robertson J).
Livingston: Alexander; Boyle, Deas, McManus, Watson, Millar, Little (Conway), Sherry, Robertson (McPhee), Fleming, Bingham (McCormick).

Queen's Park (0) 2 *(Parks 77, Edgar 81)*
Berwick R (0) 0   559
Queen's Park: Cook; Caven, Connaghan, Ferguson, Martin, Elder, Ferry, Tyrell, Edgar, Carmichael (Little), Finlayson K (Parks).
Berwick R: O'Connor; McNicoll, Neill A, Fraser, Beaton, Watt, Neil M, Rafferty, Forrester, Leask, Ramage (Quinn).

Stenhousemuir (1) 1 *(Craig 39)*
Alloa Ath (1) 1 *(Cameron 7)*   566
Stenhousemuir: Hamilton L; Davidson, Gibson, Armstrong, Baptie, Lansdowne, Hamilton R, Fisher, Lawrence, Craig, Sprott.
Alloa Ath: Cairns; Valentine, Nelson, McAneny, Cowan, Ramsay, Wilson S, Mackay (Pew), Simpson, Irvine, Cameron (McKechnie).

FIRST ROUND REPLAYS

8 DEC

Livingston (1) 3 *(Wilson W (og) 15, Fleming 71, Bingham 90)*
Dumbarton (0) 0   449
Livingston: Alexander; Boyle, Deas, McManus, Watson, Millar, Conway, McCormick (Little), Robertson (McPhee), Fleming (Bennett), Bingham.
Dumbarton: Barnes; Wilson W, Brittain, Gow (Wilkinson), Jack, King, Miller (Robertson), McKinnon, Flannery, Grace (Melvin W), Harvey.

12 DEC

Alloa Ath (0) 0
Stenhousemuir (0) 2 *(Hall 64, Watters 79)*   643
Alloa Ath: Cairns; Valentine, Sharp, McAneny, Cowan, Pew, Wilson M, Wilson S (Mackay), Simpson, Irvine, McKechnie (Cameron).
Stenhousemuir: Hamilton L; Davidson, Gibson, Armstrong, Baptie, Lansdowne, Hamilton R, Fisher (Watters), Lawrence, Christie, Hall (Sprott).

SECOND ROUND

2 JAN

Civil Service Stroll (0) 0
Albion R (2) 3 *(Hamilton 36, Melvin 39, Diack 55)*   322
Civil Service Stroll: Tomassi P; Weatherston, Hemingway, Wood, Dallas, Wright (Lynch), Given (Davies), Scott, Smith, Temple (Tomassi M), Curran.
Albion R: McLean; Duncan, McGowan, McStay, Hamilton, McLees, Bottiglieri, Melvin, Diack (Harty), Lorimer, Donaldson.

Dalbeattie Star (1) 1 *(Glendinning 18)*
East Stirling (1) 2 *(Walker 19, 75)*   1268
Dalbeattie Star: McKinnon; McMinn, Campbell D, Aitchison, Campbell A, Glendinning (Wykes), Pearson, McMillan (McGaw), Johnston, Black (Burns).

East Stirling: Thompson; Barr, Walker, Ross, Smith, Muirhead, Patterson, Hardie, Kennedy (Storrar), Ward (McNeill), Brown (McGoldrick).

Forfar Ath (0) 2 *(Craig 57, Brand 69)*
East Fife (2) 2 *(Coyle 4, Moffat 10)*   657
Forfar Ath: Robertson; Watson, Craig, McCheyne, Mann, Nairn, Gillies (McLauchlan), Allison, Brand, Cargill, McLean (Honeyman).
East Fife: McCulloch; Munro, Gibb (Kirk), Cusick (Skeldon), Johnston, Coyle, Dair, Peters, Martin, Moffat, Allan.

Huntly (3) 3 *(Grant 11, 24, Whyte 31)*
Peterhead (0) 0   1137
Huntly: Morgan; Black, Allan, Murphy, Paterson (McRonald), Morland, De Barros (Smith), Copland, Grant B, Whyte (Wolecki), Wilson.
Peterhead: Pirie; Clark S, Morrison, King, Simpson, Yule (Clark G), Yates, Smith (Paterson), Milne, Brown, Livingston.

Inverness CT (1) 1 *(McManus (og) 44)*
Livingston (1) 2 *(Bingham 10, McCormick 63)*   3367
Inverness CT: Calder; Teasdale, Sheerin, Allan, Tokely, McCulloch, Wilson, Shearer (Munro), McLean (Addicoat), Christie, Robson (Craig).
Livingston: Alexander; Boyle, Deas, McManus, Watson, Millar, King (Robertson), Conway, McCormick, Fleming (Feroz), Bingham (Forrest).

Keith (0) 0
Brechin C (0) 0   539
Keith: Thain; McKenzie M, Paterson, Murray, Watt, McKenzie K, Still, Brown, McRitchie (Hendry), Nichol, Simmers (Maver).
Brechin C: Garden; Buick, Campbell, Cairney, Bain, Smith, Dickson, Riley, Sorbie, Black, Kerrigan (McKellar).

Montrose (0) 0
Stirling Albion (0) 0   633
Montrose: Fitzpatrick; Craib, Meldrum, Mailer, Niddrie, Paterson, Shand (McWilliam), Duffy, Taylor, Loney (Lyon), Farnan.
Stirling Albion: Gow; Paterson, Forrest, Clark, Mortimer, Donald, Bone, Jackson, Graham (Price), McCallum (Philliben), Nicholas (Bell).

Partick T (2) 5 *(Tosh 9, 15, 54, Dunn 65, 82)*
Cowdenbeath (1) 2 *(Burns 22, Snedden 58)*   3019
Partick T: Arthur; Bonar, McDonald, Archibald, Jamieson, Gaughan, Connell, Frame (Callaghan T), Tosh, Dunn, Flannigan.
Cowdenbeath: Hutchison; Hamilton, Milne, Hunter, Snedden, Bradley, Winter, Welsh, Stewart, Humphreys (Graham), Burns.

Spartans (1) 1 *(Hobbins 8)*
Clyde (1) 1 *(McCusker 44)*   737
Spartans: Oliver; Cowie P (Burns), Munro, Findlay, Thomson, McKeating, Bannon, Ettles, Hobbins (Cowie S), Johnston, Middlemist (Knowles).
Clyde: Wylie; Murray (Rice), McDonald, Spittal, Smith, Keogh, Convery, McLay, McHarg, McCusker, Grant.

Whitehill Welfare (1) 1 *(Jardine 9)*
Stenhousemuir (0) 1 *(Craig 51)*   901
Whitehill Welfare: Cantley; McLaren (Manson), Gowrie, Purvis, Martin, Bennett, Jardine (Bird), Samuel, Cameron, McGovern (Millar), Thorburn.
Stenhousemuir: Hamilton L; Davidson, Gibson, Armstrong, Baptie, Christie, Hamilton R, Fisher (Watters), Lawrence, Craig, Hall (Sprott).

9 JAN

Queen of the S (0) 1 *(Nesovic 85)*

Ross Co (3) 3 *(Tarrant 30, 37, 39 (pen))* 1194

Queen of the S: Mathieson; Lilley, Aitken, Rowe, Thomson (Townsley), Leslie, Bailey, Armstrong, Adams (Mallan), Nesovic, Boyle (Weir).
Ross Co: Walker; Mackay, McBain, Haro, Maxwell, Gilbert, Ferries, Ferguson, Tarrant, McGlashan, Golabek (Wood).

18 JAN

Queen's Park (0) 1 *(Edgar 72)*

Clachnacuddin (0) 1 *(MacPherson 57)* 441

Queen's Park: Chalmers; Alexander (Parks), Connaghan, Rossiter, Martin, Elder (Ferguson), Ferry, Tyrrell, Edgar, Little, Finlayson K.
Clachnacuddin: Rae; Skinner, Douglas, Bennett, Sinclair, Mackay (Holmes), Brennan, Lewis, MacPherson (Hercher), McCraw, Richardson.

SECOND ROUND REPLAYS

6 JAN

Clyde (2) 5 *(McHarg 21, Convery 29, McLay 64, Carrigan 71, Grant 73)*

Spartans (0) 0 939

Clyde: Wylie; Murray (Cranmer), McDonald (Rice), Spittal, Smith, Keogh, Convery, McLay, McHarg (Carrigan), McCusker, Grant.
Spartans: Oliver; Cowie P (McClory), Ettles, Findlay, Thomson, McKeating, Bannon (Burns), Knox, Hobbins (Nott), Johnston, Middlemist.

9 JAN

Brechin C (1) 3 *(Sorbie 29, Dickson 57, Kerrigan 80)*

Keith (0) 1 *(Still 81)* 688

Brechin C: Garden; Buick, Campbell, Cairney, Bain, Smith, Dickson, Riley, Sorbie, Black (McKellar), Kerrigan (Hutcheon).
Keith: Thain; McKenzie M (Simmers), Paterson, Murray (Maver), Watt, McKenzie K, Still, Brown (Hendry), McRitchie, Nichol, McPherson.

East Fife (0) 0

Forfar Ath (1) 1 *(Brand 16)* 860

East Fife: McCulloch; Munro, Gibb, Brown (McPherson), Johnston, Coyle, Dair, Peters (Skeldon), Martin, Moffat, Allan (McNeil).
Forfar Ath: Moffat; McCheyne (McLean), Craig, Watson, Mann, Rattray, McLauchlan, Nairn, Brand, Honeyman, Cargill.

Stenhousemuir (0) 2 *(Miller 50, 82)*

Whitehill Welfare (0) 0 1066

Stenhousemuir: Hamilton L; Davidson, Gibson, Armstrong, Baptie, Christie (Sprott), Hamilton R (Watters), Fisher, Lawrence, Craig, Miller.
Whitehill Welfare: Cantley; McLaren (Tulloch), Bird, Purvis, Millar (McGovern), Gowrie, Thorburn, Samuel, Cameron, Jardine, Manson (Steel).

18 JAN

Stirling Albion (1) 2 *(Graham 36, 78)*

Montrose (0) 1 *(Taylor 57)* 625

Stirling Albion: Gow; Paterson, Forrest, Clark, Philliben, Mortimer (Wood), Bone, Jackson, Graham, Price, Nicholas.
Montrose: Fitzpatrick; Craib, Meldrum, Mailer, Niddrie, Paterson, Shand (Coulston), Duffy, Taylor (Loney), Lyon (Watt), Farnan.

23 JAN

Clachnacuddin (0) 2 *(Bennett 52, Sinclair 68)*

Queen's Park (1) 3 *(Graham 52, Brown 84, Finlayson K 87)* 1129

Clachnacuddin: Rae; Skinner, Douglas (Hercher), Bennett, Sinclair, Mackay (McCuish), Brennan, Holmes,

MacPherson (Keddie), McCraw, Richardson.
Queen's Park: Chalmers; Caven, Ferguson (Tyrrell), Rossiter, Martin, Ferry, Finlayson K, Alexander, Edgar, Graham (Brown), Little (Parks).

THIRD ROUND

23 JAN

Aberdeen (0) 0

Livingston (0) 1 *(Robertson 59)* 10,311

Aberdeen: Stillie; Perry, Dow, Whyte, Smith, Hart (Inglis), Rowson (Buchan), Jess, Winters, Kiriakov, Newell.
Livingston: Alexander; Boyle, Deas, McManus, Watson, Millar, King, Sherry, Robertson (McPhee), McCormick (Forrest), Bingham (Little).

Ayr U (1) 3 *(Lyons 30, Walker 81 (pen), 83 (pen))*

Kilmarnock (0) 0 10,153

Ayr U: Castilla; Robertson, Winnie, Millen, Traynor, Craig, Hurst, Davies, Walker, Teale, Lyons (Reynolds).
Kilmarnock: Marshall; MacPherson, Baker, Montgomerie, McGowne, Roberts, Reilly, Holt (Mahood), McCoist, Durrant, Mitchell.

Brechin C (0) 1 *(Sorbie 63)*

Albion R (0) 1 *(Lorimer 47 (pen))* 463

Brechin C: Garden; Williamson, Laing, Cairney, Bain, Smith (McKellar), Dickson, Buick (Hutcheon), Sorbie, Black, Kerrigan.
Albion R: McLean; Duncan, McGowan, McStay, Hamilton (Greenock), McLees, Bottiglieri, Melvin, Murphy, Lorimer (Sturrock), Donaldson.

Celtic (1) 3 *(Larsson 3, Stewart 49 (og), O'Donnell 51)*

Airdrieonians (1) 1 *(Cooper 23)* 43,609

Celtic: Gould; Boyd, Mahe, Mjallby (Hannah), Riseth, Stubbs, Lambert, O'Donnell, Moravcik (Blinker), Larsson, Donnelly (Burchill).
Airdrieonians: Martin; Stewart, McCann, Sandison, Johnston, Black, Jack, Wilson, Cooper, Evans (Moore), Smith (McGrillen).

Falkirk (0) 3 *(Paterson 52 (og), Crabbe 75 (pen), McAllister 87)*

Huntly (0) 0 3018

Falkirk: Mathers; Corrigan, McQuilken, Sinclair, James, Den Bieman, McAllister, Keith, Crabbe, McKenzie, Hutchison.
Huntly: Morgan; Black, Allan, Murphy, Paterson, Morland, Wilson (Grant N), Copland, Grant B (Wolecki), Whyte, McRonald (Stewart).

Greenock Morton (2) 2 *(Archdeacon 30, Matheson 38)*

Dundee (1) 1 *(Annand 41)* 2823

Greenock Morton: Maxwell; Slavin, Archdeacon, Anderson D, Anderson J, Fenwick, Matheson (Twaddle), Curran, McPherson (Wright), Hawke, Thomas (Aitken).
Dundee: Douglas; Smith (Grady), Miller, Tweed, Raeside, Maddison, Robertson, Adamczuk, Annand, Falconer, Grant (Anderson).

Hibernian (0) 1 *(Lovering 76)*

Stirling Albion (1) 1 *(Nicholas 20)* 9306

Hibernian: Gottskalksson; Smith (Lovell), Lovering, Skinner, Dempsie, Dennis, Hartley, Lavety (Crawford), Paatelainen, Latapy, McGinlay.
Stirling Albion: Gow; Paterson, Forrest, Philliben, Martin, Wood, Bone, Jackson, Graham, McCallum, Nicholas (Price).

Partick T (1) 1 *(Dunn 43 (pen))*

Dunfermline Ath (2) 2 *(Smith 17, 31)* 4650

Partick T: Arthur; Kennedy, McKeown, Archibald, Gaughan, Connell, Boyar, Callaghan T (Frame), Tosh, Dunn, Flannigan (Lauchlan).
Dunfermline Ath: Butler; Shields, McCulloch (Johnson), Tod, Shaw, Millar, French, Huxford, Smith, Graham (Edinho), Petrie.

Raith R (0) 0

Clyde (2) 4 *(Convery 7, McCusker 16 (pen), McHarg 70, Carrigan 87)*　　　2581
Raith R: Van De Kamp; McEwan, Dair J, Bowman, Browne, Fotheringham, Byers (Andrews), Lennon (McCulloch), Dargo, Robertson (Stein), Cameron.
Clyde: Wylie; Murray, McDonald, Spittal, Smith, Keogh, Convery (Carrigan), McLay, McHarg (Rice), McCusker, Grant (Barratt).

Rangers (2) 2 *(Guivarc'h 5, Wallace 38)*

Stenhousemuir (0) 0　　　37,759
Rangers: Klos; Porrini, Vidmar, Wilson, Hendry, Albertz (Van Bronckhorst), McCann (Ferguson B), Miller, Kanchelskis, Wallace, Guivarc'h (Amato).
Stenhousemuir: Hamilton L; Davidson, Sprott (Banks), Armstrong, Baptie, Gibson (Lansdowne), Hamilton R, Fisher, Lawrence, Craig, Miller (Watters).

St Johnstone (0) 1 *(O'Neil 63)*

Forfar Ath (0) 0　　　3717
St Johnstone: Main; McQuillan, Griffin, Dods, Bollan, O'Halloran, O'Neil, Kane, McMahon (McAnespie), Connolly (Grant), Simao (Preston).
Forfar Ath: Robertson; Watson (Raynes), Craig, Tully, Mann, Rattray, Nairn, McCheyne, Brand, Honeyman (McLean), Cargill.

St Mirren (1) 1 *(Mendes 4)*

Hamilton A (0) 1 *(Clark 90)*　　　2361
St Mirren: Roy; Drew, Nicolson, Turner, McLaughlin, McQuilter, Murray (Rudden), O'Brien, Brown (McGarry), Mendes, Yardley.
Hamilton A: Hillcoat J; Renicks, Cunnington, Hillcoat C, Berry (MacLaren), McKenzie, Davidson (McCormick), Tait (Clark), Geraghty, Henderson D, Henderson N.

Stranraer (1) 1 *(Knox 42 (pen))*

East Stirling (0) 0　　　579
Stranraer: Bruce; Knox, Black, George, Campbell, Watson, McMartin, Bell (Jenkins), Young G, Ronald (McIntyre), Harty (Friels).
East Stirling: Thompson; Storrar, Brown, Ross, Smith, Walker, Patterson (Ferguson), Hardie, Kennedy, Muirhead, Ward (McNeill).

24 JAN

Motherwell (1) 3 *(Brannan 13, Coyle 65, Thomas 75)*

Hearts (0) 1 *(Hamilton 57)*　　　9372
Motherwell: Goram; Doesburg, McMillan, Brannan, Teale, Thomas, Valakari, Nevin (Adams), Spencer, McCulloch (Matthaei), Coyle.
Hearts: Rousset; Pressley, Naysmith, Weir, Locke (Makel), Ritchie, Lilley (McSwegan), Fulton (Jenkinson), Adam, Hamilton, Flögel.

2 FEB

Queen's Park (0) 0

Dundee U (0) 0　　　1953
Queen's Park: Chalmers; Caven, Connaghan, Rossiter, Martin, Graham, Finlayson K, Ferry (Alexander), Edgar, Brown (Tyrrell), Little (Parks).
Dundee U: Dijkstra; de Vos, Jonsson, Malpas, Duffy (Skoldmark), Pedersen, Zetterlund, Paterson J (Olofsson), Dodds, Mathie, Thompson (Miller).

3 FEB

Clydebank (0) 1 *(Nicholls 76)*

Ross Co (0) 1 *(Tarrant 65)*　　　420
Clydebank: Scott; Wishart, McMillan, McKinstrey (Gardner), McLaughlin, Ritchie, Nicholls, Anthony, McDonald, Docherty (Taggart), Brown.
Ross Co: Walker; Mackay, McBain, Haro, Maxwell, Gilbert, Ross, Ferguson, Tarrant (Wood), Escalon (Ferries), Golabek.

THIRD ROUND REPLAYS

2 FEB

Albion R (1) 3 *(Murphy 24, 80, Lorimer 89)*

Brechin C (1) 1 *(Dickson 29)*　　　457
Albion R: McLean; Duncan, McGowan, McStay, Hamilton, McLees, Bottiglieri, Greenock, Murphy, Lorimer, Donaldson.
Brechin C: Garden; Williamson, Laing (McLeod), Campbell, Christie, Black, Dickson, Buick, McKellar, Riley, Kerrigan (Dailly).

Hamilton A (0) 1 *(Wales 73)*

St Mirren (0) 0　　　3050
Hamilton A: Hillcoat J; Renicks, Cunnington, Hillcoat C, MacLaren, Thomson, Clark (McAulay), Henderson D, Geraghty (Moore), Wales, Henderson N.
St Mirren: Roy; McNamee (Drew), Kerr, Turner, Innes, McLaughlin, Murray, O'Brien, Brown (McGarry), Mendes, Yardley.

Stirling Albion (1) 2 *(McCallum 14, Jackson 58)*

Hibernian (1) 1 *(Latapy 37)*　　　3643
Stirling Albion: Gow; Paterson, Forrest, Philliben, Martin, Wood, Bone, Jackson, Price, McCallum, Nicholas.
Hibernian: Gottskalksson; Collins (Hartley), Lovering, Skinner, Dempsie, Dennis, Lovell, Crawford, Paatelainen, Latapy, McGinlay.

9 FEB

Dundee U (1) 1 *(Dodds 38)*

Queen's Park (0) 0　　　4973
Dundee U: Dijkstra; de Vos, Jonsson, Malpas, Pedersen, Dolan, Miller, Mathie (Thompson) (Paterson J), Dodds, Olofsson, Easton.
Queen's Park: Chalmers; Caven, Connaghan, Rossiter, Alexander, Ferguson (Tyrrell), Finlayson K, Ferry, Edgar, Brown (Agostini), Parks (Little).

15 FEB

Ross Co (1) 2 *(Tarrant 31, McBain 70)*

Clydebank (0) 3 *(Nicholls 50, Ritchie 52, McMillan 110)*　　　1391
Ross Co: Walker; Mackay, McBain, Haro, Maxwell, Ross, Ferries (Escalon)(Taylor), Ferguson, Tarrant, McGlashan, Golabek.
Clydebank: Scott; Wishart, Ritchie, McKinstrey (McMillan), McLaughlin, Brannigan, Nicholls, Anthony (Taggart), McDonald (Miller), Gardner, Brown.
aet

FOURTH ROUND

13 FEB

Ayr U (0) 1 *(Teale 78)*

Albion R (0) 0　　　3229
Ayr U: Castilla; Robertson, Winnie, Millen, Traynor (Reynolds), Craig, Hurst, Davies, Walker (Ferguson), Teale, Lyons.
Albion R: McLean; Duncan, McGowan, McStay, Hamilton (Sturrock), McLees, Greenock, Melvin, Murphy (Shaw), Lorimer, Donaldson.

Celtic (4) 4 *(Larsson 23, 32, 40, Brattbakk 38)*

Dunfermline Ath (0) 0　　　46,887
Celtic: Gould; McKinlay, Mahe, Riseth, Mjallby, McNamara, Lambert, O'Donnell (Blinker), Brattbakk, Larsson (Burchill), Moravcik.
Dunfermline Ath: Butler; Millar (McGroarty), Shaw (Nish), Shields, Tod, French, Ferguson (Huxford), Graham, Smith, Thomson, Petrie.

Livingston (0) 1 *(Robertson 85)*
St Johnstone (2) 3 *(Grant 19, 60, Scott 42)*   5788
Livingston: Alexander; Boyle (McCormick), Deas, McManus, Watson, Millar, King, Conway (Forrest), Robertson, McPhee (Little), Fleming.
St Johnstone: Main; McQuillan, Dods, Bollan, Kernaghan, Scott, O'Neil (McMahon), Kane, Grant, Dasovic (Griffin), Lowndes (Simao).

Motherwell (0) 2 *(McCulloch 63, Forrest 86 (og))*
Stirling Albion (0) 0   7244
Motherwell: Goram; Doesburg, McGowan, Teale, McMillan (Craigan), Valakari, Brannan, Nevin, Spencer, McCulloch (Adams), Coyle.
Stirling Albion: Gow; Paterson (Bell), Forrest, Clark, Martin, Philliben, Bone, Jackson, Graham, McCallum, Nicholas.

Stranraer (0) 1 *(Friels 87)*
Falkirk (1) 2 *(Moss 27, 62)*   1757
Stranraer: Bruce; Knox, Skilling, George, Campbell, Watson, McMartin, McIntyre, Bell (Jenkins), Ronald (Friels), Kinnaird.
Falkirk: Mathers; McKenzie, McQuilken, Sinclair, James, Den Bieman, McAllister, Keith, Crabbe, Moss, Hutchison (Seaton).

Greenock Morton (3) 6 *(Rice 13 (og), Thomas 26, 53, Archdeacon 40, Twaddle 71, 74)*
Clyde (0) 1 *(McCusker 56)*   3005
Greenock Morton: Maxwell; Slavin (Aitken), Archdeacon, Anderson D, Anderson J, Fenwick, Twaddle (Matheson), Curran, Hawke (Wright), Thomas, McPherson.
Clyde: Wylie; Murray, McDonald (Cranmer), Spittal, Smith, Rice, Convery (Carrigan), McLay, Keogh, McCusker, Grant.

14 FEB
Hamilton A (0) 0
Rangers (2) 6 *(Johansson 4, 73, Albertz 43 (pen), Vidmar 56, Kanchelskis 65, McCann 75)*   7339
Hamilton A: Hillcoat J; Renicks, Cunnington, Hillcoat C, Berry, Thomson, McAulay (Clark), Henderson N (Moore), McCormick, Wales, Henderson D
Rangers: Klos; Porrini, Vidmar (Wilson), Amoruso, Van Bronckhorst, Albertz (Miller), Ferguson B, McCann, Kanchelskis, Wallace (Guivarc'h), Johansson.

3 MAR
Clydebank (1) 2 *(Nicholls 13, Gardner 68)*
Dundee U (0) 2 *(Olofsson 51, Patterson D 80)*   320
Clydebank: Scott; Wishart, Love, Ritchie, McLaughlin, Brannigan, Nicholls (Docherty), Anthony (Taggart), McDonald (Brown), Gardner, Miller.
Dundee U: Dijkstra; Patterson D, Paterson J, Mols, de Vos, Duffy, Miller (Skoldmark), Zetterlund (Mathie), Dodds, Easton, Olofsson.

FOURTH ROUND REPLAY
6 MAR
Dundee U (1) 3 *(Duffy 14, Olofsson 61, 65)*
Clydebank (0) 0   5570
Dundee U: Dijkstra; Patterson D, Paterson J, Mols, de Vos, Duffy, Miller (Skoldmark), Mathie, Dodds (Thompson), Easton, Olofsson (McLaren).
Clydebank: Scott; Wishart, Love (Murdoch), Ritchie, Taggart, Brannigan, Nicholls, Anthony, McDonald (Brown), Gardner (Docherty), Miller.

QUARTER-FINALS
6 MAR
Motherwell (0) 0
St Johnstone (0) 2 *(Dods 73, Simao 80)*   7660
Motherwell: Goram; Doesburg (May), McMillan, McGowan, Teale, Brannan, Valakari, Ross (Nevin), Adams, McCulloch, Spencer.
St Johnstone: Main; McQuillan, Dods, Bollan, Kernaghan, Griffin (O'Halloran), Kane, Dasovic, Grant (McBride), Scott, Lowndes (Simao).

7 MAR
Rangers (0) 2 *(McCann 52, Amoruso 75)*
Falkirk (0) 1 *(Moss 60)*   39,250
Rangers: Klos; Porrini, Vidmar (Amato), Amoruso, Albertz, Ferguson B, Kanchelskis, Van Bronckhorst, Guivarc'h (Johansson), Wallace, McCann (Wilson).
Falkirk: Mathers; Corrigan, McQuilken, Sinclair, James, Den Bieman, McAllister, Keith, Crabbe (Hutchison), Moss, McKenzie.

8 MAR
Greenock Morton (0) 0
Celtic (1) 3 *(Viduka 9, 83, Larsson 58)*   12,062
Greenock Morton: Maxwell; Aitken, Archdeacon, Anderson D, Anderson J, Fenwick, Twaddle (Wright), Curran, Matheson, Thomas, McPherson.
Celtic: Gould; Boyd, Mahe (McKinlay), Mjallby, Stubbs, Riseth, Lambert, Burley, Viduka (Brattbakk), Larsson, Blinker.

13 MAR
Ayr U (0) 0
Dundee U (0) 0   5508
Ayr U: Castilla; Robertson, Barrick, Millen, Traynor, Craig, Hurst, Davies (Ferguson), Walker, Teale, Lyons.
Dundee U: Dijkstra; Patterson D, Paterson J (Skoldmark), Mols, de Vos, Duffy, Miller (McLaren), Eustace, Olofsson (Mathie), Dodds, Easton.

QUARTER-FINAL REPLAY
16 MAR
Dundee U (1) 2 *(Murray 41, Skoldmark 52)*
Ayr U (0) 1 *(Walker 47)*   7313
Dundee U: Dijkstra; Skoldmark, Malpas, Murray, Duffy, Jonsson, Miller (McLaren), Eustace, Olofsson, Dodds, Easton.
Ayr U: Castilla; Robertson, Barrick, Millen, Traynor (Reynolds), Craig, Hurst, Davies, Walker, Teale, Lyons (Ferguson).

SEMI-FINALS
10 APR
Celtic (2) 2 *(Blinker 29, Viduka 39)*
Dundee U (0) 0   43,491
Celtic: Gould; Boyd, Mahe (Wieghorst), McNamara, Annoni, McKinlay, Lambert, Burley, Viduka (Donnelly), Larsson, Blinker.
Dundee U: Dijkstra; Skoldmark, Malpas, Murray, de Vos, Jonsson, Miller, Easton, Mathie (Thompson), Dodds, Olofsson.

11 APR
St Johnstone (0) 0
Rangers (2) 4 *(Wallace 15, Van Bronckhorst 33, Johansson 62, McCann 71)*   20,664
St Johnstone: Main; Weir, Dods, Kernaghan, Bollan, O'Halloran, McBride (Simao), Kane, Grant (Lowndes), Dasovic (Griffin), McAnespie.
Rangers: Klos; Porrini, Vidmar, Amoruso, Hendry (Wilson), Van Bronckhorst, Albertz, McCann, Kanchelskis (McInnes), Wallace, Guivarc'h (Johansson).

FINAL (at Hampden Park)
29 MAY
Rangers (0) 1 *(Wallace 48)*
Celtic (0) 0   51,746
Rangers: Klos; Porrini (Kanchelskis), Amoruso, Hendry, Vidmar, McCann (Ferguson I), McInnes, Van Bronckhorst, Wallace, Amato (Wilson), Albertz.
Celtic: Gould; Boyd, Mahe (O'Donnell), Mjallby, Stubbs, Annoni (Johnson), Lambert, Wieghorst, Larsson, Moravcik, Blinker.
Referee: H. Dallas (Motherwell).

WELSH FOOTBALL 1998–99

Twelve months ago, I declined to pass judgment on Bobby Gould's performance as Welsh manager.

He was guiding his adopted country through a transitional period and I felt it would be unfair to criticise him – even though results indicated that the former Coventry and Wimbledon manager was struggling to come to terms with the demands of international football. The jury, I suggested, was still out.

After a humiliating 4-0 drubbing in Bologna in June, Bobby Gould decided not to wait for their verdict. He pleaded guilty and resigned on the spot 'in the best interests of Welsh football'.

At a stroke, Gould managed to achieve something he had patently failed to do during his four years in charge – he united a nation. It seemed that everybody welcomed his decision to stand down. Having talked himself into the job ahead of Howard Kendall, Ron Atkinson, Mike Walker and Brian Flynn, Gould had been unable to turn rhetoric into results.

Under him, Wales won just seven of their 24 games and are no nearer to reaching the finals of a major tournament. Indeed, some critics claim that Welsh football has taken at least one step backwards under Gould.

So what went wrong? It was always going to be difficult for an Englishman to run the Welsh national team. In his first spell in charge, Mike Smith had managed it through his deep knowledge of the game. Despite his managerial experience – remember he won the FA Cup with Wimbledon in 1988 – Gould always had problems in gaining respect – especially from the players.

After Mike Smith's second ill-fated spell in charge, Gould promised to put a smile back on the face of Welsh football but in doing so he became a figure of fun. It was a role he appeared to relish – once attending a news conference wearing a Max Wall mask – as he courted publicity on a regular basis. There was the series of run-ins with leading players like Ian Rush, the race row with Nathan Blake and the infamous reprimand of Robbie Savage after the Leicester midfielder lightheartedly threw away an Italian shirt in a television interview.

With only sporadic success, Gould became more and more sensitive to criticism. He was involved in a very public slanging match with one of his predecessors John Toshack after the 6-4 defeat in Turkey and resented former Welsh internationals questioning his team selections and rather naïve tactics. To all the world, Gould looked out of his depth on the international stage and his strange reluctance to appoint an experienced assistant didn't help. The recruitment of the former Welsh full-back Graham Williams was well-meaning but far too late and he was sacked three weeks after Gould resigned.

After two unexpected wins over Denmark and Belarus in the space of four days in October 1998, Gould failed to capitalise on his extremely fortunate stay of execution. The resultant wave of public enthusiasm was allowed to ebb away and, by declining to play a friendly match before the next Euro 2000 tie, Gould lost the momentum as well as the plot. Wales were humbled by a mediocre Swiss side and when Italy tore apart his spiritless team in Bologna, there was no alternative. Gould resigned – but only after negotiating a healthy settlement of the remaining seven months of his contract.

As one former international observed after the manager's departure, Bobby Gould had been appointed on his ability to talk. The special six-man committee set up by the Welsh FA to find his successor would do well to remember that actions speak louder than words.

The administrators had a lot of explaining to do themselves following their involvement in the Football Association's 'cash-for-votes' scandal. Like Gould, Graham Kelly and eventually Keith Wiseman decided to fall on their swords but the FAW secretary-general David Collins didn't even bother looking for his scabbard. The explanation that the switch of support from Scotland to England in a FIFA executive election was unconnected with a £3.2 million grant to the Welsh FA was laughable. Despite FIFA clearing both bodies of 'incorrect or improper actions', those men running Welsh football hardly covered themselves in glory. Positions may have remained intact but reputations lay in tatters. The whole grubby affair did nothing to strengthen the fight against the plan to create a single United Kingdom team.

The Welsh FA also caught a cold after a pitifully low crowd of 10,000 turned up to see Denmark win 2-0 at Anfield in the first post-Gould qualifier. The game was crying out to be played at Cardiff's Ninian Park but the deal had been done and UEFA rejected a late appeal to change the venue. So no big bucks or Euro 2000 points either.

On the domestic front, Welsh football looks to be in much better shape. Cardiff City are back in Division Two after a season which saw them top the table for long periods before their promotion push petered out during April. Manager Frank Burrows and a largely local board are ambitiously aiming towards the First Division and, after one or two new signings, their squad looks strong enough to mount a serious challenge during their centenary season.

Swansea City flattered to deceive by reaching the Third Division play-offs after a season dogged by inconsistency. John Hollins, having succeeded Alan Cork as manager, worked wonders at the Vetch Field but unless the purse strings are loosened, the Swans are unlikely to begin their new life at the Morfa Stadium in a new division.

The long-overdue development of the Racecourse sadly coincided with Wrexham's unexpected decline. After three promotion play-off near-misses, they struggled for much of the season and manager Brian Flynn's rebuilding programme is now well underway. It surely won't be long before they have a team to match their improved ground.

Wrexham's season ended on a decidedly disappointing note when they lost 2-1 to the League of Wales champions Barry Town in the final of the FAW Premier Cup. Barry again pulled off a hat-trick – they won the Gilbert League Cup too – but missed out on the Welsh Cup where an appalling final was settled on penalties as Inter Cable-Tel overcame plucky Carmarthen Town. Inter Cable-Tel, reverting to their former name of Inter Cardiff next season, will represent Wales in the UEFA Cup – along with Cwmbran Town and Barry.

For the second successive season, Barry had the misfortune to be drawn against Dynamo Kiev, one of the strongest teams in the Champions League. After being heavily beaten, the League of Wales champions took some comfort from watching the Ukranians progress to the semi-finals where they lost to Bayern Munich. Newtown, Bangor City and the now-defunct Ebbw Vale could only muster a single draw between them in six matches in the UEFA and Inter-Toto Cups.

GRAHAME LLOYD

LEAGUE OF WALES

	Aberystwyth Town	Afan Lido	Bangor City	Barry Town	Caernarfon Town	Caersws	Carmarthen Town	Connah's Quay Nomads	Conwy United	Cwmbran Town	Haverfordwest County	Holywell Town	Inter Cable-Tel	Newtown	Rhayader Town	Rhyl	Total Network Solutions
Aberystwyth Town	—	2-1	3-0	1-1	1-1	0-5	3-2	2-1	3-1	1-3	2-1	0-0	1-1	5-0	2-1	2-1	0-1
Afan Lido	2-2	—	0-2	0-0	1-3	0-1	1-1	1-3	0-1	0-4	0-2	2-0	0-2	0-2	2-0	2-1	3-3
Bangor City	1-2	0-1	—	0-3	1-1	0-1	4-0	0-2	1-3	2-2	3-0	5-2	1-0	2-3	0-1	4-1	2-1
Barry Town	5-1	0-2	4-2	—	3-0	5-2	6-2	1-0	1-1	2-1	2-0	4-0	1-1	1-0	7-1	2-0	2-0
Caernarfon Town	2-0	2-0	1-0	0-4	—	2-2	3-2	1-1	1-1	2-4	2-0	2-2	1-1	3-1	2-0	3-0	2-1
Caersws	2-3	2-1	1-2	2-4	3-2	—	1-2	2-0	0-3	1-3	4-4	3-2	0-2	1-1	0-0	3-1	3-1
Carmarthen Town	2-5	1-1	1-2	2-1	0-0	0-1	—	6-2	2-1	1-1	3-1	3-0	0-1	1-0	1-1	1-2	1-0
Connah's Quay Nomads	0-0	2-0	1-1	0-3	2-2	0-1	0-2	—	1-2	1-0	3-1	4-2	1-2	3-0	4-1	6-2	2-3
Conwy United	1-1	2-0	3-1	1-3	2-1	2-1	1-2	1-3	—	2-4	4-2	2-1	3-0	1-0	1-1	6-1	3-3
Cwmbran Town	0-1	0-4	2-4	0-4	6-0	2-1	2-0	2-1	3-0	—	4-0	4-0	0-0	3-0	3-6	6-1	0-4
Haverfordwest County	2-6	1-1	0-0	0-0	0-2	1-1	1-2	1-0	1-3	2-1	—	7-2	0-1	2-0	1-0	5-2	1-4
Holywell Town	3-6	0-0	1-1	2-3	1-2	0-0	1-1	0-0	4-3	0-4	4-0	—	1-2	0-3	2-2	0-3	3-3
Inter Cable-Tel	6-1	0-1	3-0	1-2	3-0	6-0	1-2	1-1	3-0	0-1	1-0	5-1	—	0-2	1-0	3-2	1-1
Newtown	1-1	4-0	3-1	0-0	1-1	4-0	0-0	1-0	2-1	0-0	1-1	4-0	1-3	—	3-0	2-1	0-0
Rhayader Town	0-2	1-1	0-0	0-0	2-0	1-3	1-0	2-0	2-2	1-1	2-2	1-3	0-5	0-2	—	1-2	0-0
Rhyl	1-0	2-0	1-2	0-6	0-1	1-1	1-2	1-2	0-3	1-4	1-2	5-1	1-2	3-3	3-1	—	0-3
Total Network Solutions	0-0	1-1	1-2	1-2	2-0	2-1	1-1	2-0	1-4	2-2	0-2	2-0	1-3	1-1	1-0	6-0	—

LEAGUE OF WALES

		Home			Goals		Away			Goals			
	P	W	D	L	F	A	W	D	L	F	A	GD	Pts
Barry Town	32	13	2	1	46	13	10	5	1	36	10	+59	76
Inter Cable-Tel	32	9	2	5	35	14	10	4	2	26	12	+35	63
Cwmbran Town	32	9	1	6	38	26	8	5	3	35	18	+29	57
Aberystwyth Town	32	9	4	3	28	20	7	5	4	31	28	+11	57
Caernarfon Town	32	9	5	2	29	19	4	6	6	16	27	−1	50
Newtown	32	8	7	1	25	9	5	3	8	20	26	+10	49
Conwy United	32	7	4	5	26	24	7	3	6	29	25	+6	49
Total Network Solutions	32	7	5	4	28	19	5	6	5	27	23	+13	47
Carmarthen Town	32	7	4	5	25	19	6	4	6	21	27	0	47
Caersws	32	7	3	6	29	29	5	5	6	20	26	−6	44
Bangor City	32	6	2	8	26	23	5	4	7	18	26	−5	39
Connah's Quay Nomads	32	6	5	5	28	23	4	3	9	16	24	−3	38
Haverfordwest County	32	6	4	6	25	24	3	3	10	18	36	−17	34
Afan Lido	32	3	4	9	14	27	4	6	6	14	19	−18	31
Rhayader Town	32	3	7	6	14	23	2	4	10	15	31	−25	26
Rhyl	32	4	2	10	21	33	3	0	13	20	48	−40	23
Holywell Town	32	2	7	7	22	33	1	2	13	16	53	−48	18

WELSH CUP 1998–99

First Round

Aberaman Athletic v Porthcawl	2-1
Ammanford Town v Blaenrhondda	3-2
Bridgend Town v Cardiff Civil Service	3-1
Caerleon v Briton Ferry Athletic	4-1
Chirk AAA v British Aerospace	2-3
Flexys Cefn Druids v Mostyn	4-0
Grange Harlequins v Maesteg Park Athletic	2-1
Halkyn United v Brymbo Broughton	0-1
Hoover Sports v Penrhiwceiber Rangers	2-1
Lex XI v Rhydymwyn	3-4
Morriston Town v Pontyclun	4-3
Penycae v Castell Alun Colts	1-1
Pontlottyn Blast Furnace v Garw Athletic	2-1
Risca United v Ely Rangers	1-2
UWIC v Llandridnod Wells	6-1
AFC Rhondda v Caerau	7-1
BP Llandarcy v Cardiff Corinthians	4-2
Buckley Town v Ruthin Town	0-3
Chepstow Town v Llanwern	5-2
Corwen Amateurs v Denbigh Town	0-5
Goytre United v Caldicot Town	4-1
Guilsfield v Llanidloes Town	2-0
Holyhead Hotspurs v Bala Town	6-0
Knighton Town v Penrhyncoch	1-2
Llandyrnog United v Llangefni Town	2-5
Oswestry Town v Rhos Aelwyd	2-1
Pontardawe Town v Skewen Athletic	4-1
Porth Tywyn Suburbs v Caerau Ely	2-1
Taffs Well v Tredegar Town	1-2

Replay

Castell Alun Colts v Penycae	1-0

Second Round

Aberaman Athletic v Llanelli	2-3
AFC Rhondda v Ammanford Town (aet & pens)	2-3
Caernarfon Town v Llangefni Town	3-0
Chepstow Town v Morriston Town	4-0
Flexys Cefn Druids v Cemaes Bay	2-1
Guilsfield v Caersws	0-5
Haverfordwest County v Bridgend Town	6-0
Penrhyncoch v Oswestry Town	3-2
Porthmadog v Holywell Town	0-2
Port Talbot Athletic v Grange Harlequins	7-0
Rhydymwyn v Conwy United	2-2
Ruthin Town v Colwyn Bay YMCA	0-1
Treowen Stars v Ely Rangers	5-0
Afan Lido v Caerleon	5-1
British Aerospace v Brymbo Broughton	5-1
Carmarthen Town v Hoover Sports	2-1
Cwmbran Town v Goytre United	2-0
Flint Town United v Castell Alun Colts	6-2
Gwynfi United v BP Llandarcy	0-2
Owens Corning v Holyhead Hotspurs	1-4
Pontlottyn Blast Furnace v Tredegar Town	0-3

Porth Tywyn Suburbs v Ton Pentre	2-1
Rhayader Town v Welshpool Town	3-1
Rhyl v Denbigh Town	5-4
Total Network Solutions v Aberystwyth Town	2-2
UWIC v Pontardawe Town	1-1

Replays

Aberystwyth Town v Total Network Solutions	2-3
Pontardawe Town v UWIC	4-3
Conwy United v Rhydymwyn	2-1

Third Round

Barry Town v Haverfordwest County	2-0
Caersws v Cwmbran Town	3-4
Connah's Quay Nomads v Newtown	2-2
Holyhead Hotspurs v Conwy United	1-3
Llanelli v Tredegar Town	2-1
Porth Tywyn Suburbs v Port Talbot Athletic	1-1
Rhyl v Flint Town United	2-2
Treowen Stars v Pontardawe Town	1-2
British Aerospace v BP Llandarcy	2-2
Camarthen Town v Chepstow Town	2-2
Flexys Cefn Druids v Caernarfon Town	1-5
Inter Cable-Tel v Holywell Town	1-0
Penrhyncoch v Colwyn Bay YMCA	2-4
Rhayader Town v Bangor City	3-0
Total Network Solutions v Afan Lido	2-0
Ammanford Town w.o. Ebbw Vale defunct	

Replays

BP Llandarcy v British Aerospace	3-2
Flint Town United v Rhyl (aet & pens)	5-4
Port Talbot Athletic v Porth Tywyn Suburbs	1-0
Chepstow Town v Carmarthen Town	2-5
Newtown v Connah's Quay Nomads	0-1

Fourth Round

Ammanford Town v Colwyn Bay YMCA	1-0
Carmarthen Town v Caernarfon Town	2-0
Inter Cable-Tel v Pontardawe Town	1-1
Port Talbot Athletic v Flint Town United	2-0
Barry Town v Connah's Quay Nomads	0-1
Conwy United v BP Llandarcy	7-0
Llanelli v Cwmbran Town	1-2
Total Network Solutions v Rhayader Town	2-1

Replay

Pontardawe Town v Inter Cable-Tel	0-3

Round Five

Ammanford Town v Conwy United	0-0
Connah's Quay Nomads v Inter Cable-Tel	1-1
Carmarthen Town v Port Talbot Athletic	1-0
Total Network Solutions v Cwmbran Town	1-2

Replays

Conwy United v Ammanford Town		1-0
Inter Cable-Tel v Connah's Quay Nomads		3-1

Semi-finals

Cwmbran Town v Inter Cable-Tel		3-4
Carmarthen Town v Conwy United		1-0

Final

Inter Cable-Tel (0) 1 Carmarthen Town (0) 1

(at Penydarren Park, Merthyr 9 May 1999)

(aet; Inter Cable-Tel won 4-2 on penalties)

Inter Cable-Tel: Wager; Parselle, Wile, Brazil, Richards, Dyson, Davies, Poretta, Mardenborough, Evans (Tyler 108), Dyer (Misbah 63).
Scorer: Poretta 115.
Carmarthen Town: Fitzgerald; Nicholas (Burrows 91), Jones, Barnhouse, Cable, Thomas, Rees (Vaughan 98), Rossiter, Williams, Meredith.
Scorer: Meredith 113.
Referee: K. Burge (Tonypandy).
Attendance: 1008.

FAW PREMIER CUP

Group A	P	W	D	L	F	A	GD	Pts
Cardiff City	6	3	2	1	13	6	+7	11
Merthyr Tydfil	6	2	4	0	7	5	+2	10
Bangor City	6	2	1	3	7	9	−2	7
Rhyl	6	1	1	4	7	14	−7	4

Group B	P	W	D	L	F	A	GD	Pts
Barry Town	6	4	1	1	10	5	+5	13
Swansea City	6	3	2	1	9	5	+4	11
Wrexham	6	3	1	2	7	7	0	10
Caernarfon Tn	6	0	0	6	1	10	−9	0

Group C	P	W	D	L	F	A	GD	Pts
Inter Cable	6	4	0	2	12	6	+6	12
Newtown	6	4	0	2	7	10	−3	12
Cwmbran Tn	6	2	2	2	11	8	+3	8
Connah's Q	6	0	2	4	7	13	−6	2

Quarter-finals

Inter Cable-Tel v Cwmbran Town	4-0
Newtown v Wrexham	0-1
Cardiff City v Swansea City	3-2
Barry Town v Merthyr Tydfil	1-0

Semi-finals (two-legs)

Barry Town v Inter Cable-Tel	2-0
Inter Cable-Tel v Barry Town	1-3
Wrexham v Cardiff City	3-1
Cardiff City v Wrexham	2-1

Final

Wrexham v Barry Town	1-2

CC SPORTS WELSH LEAGUE

Division One

	P	W	D	L	F	A	Pts
Ton Pentre	34	25	5	4	79	32	80
Llanelli*	34	21	5	8	79	45	68
AFC Rhondda	34	19	7	8	78	46	64
BP	34	19	4	11	69	47	61
UWIC	34	15	8	11	49	44	53
Pontardawe	34	15	8	11	55	54	53
Bridgend Town	34	14	10	10	76	48	52
Maesteg Park	34	13	12	9	51	43	51
Port Talbot	34	15	4	15	54	56	49
Treowen	34	12	10	12	57	52	46
Goytre	34	13	5	16	50	50	44
Cardiff Civil Service	34	12	4	18	41	64	40
Aberaman	34	10	7	17	53	74	37
Briton Ferry	34	9	9	16	46	66	36
Cardiff Corries	34	9	8	17	51	70	35
Porth Tywyn	34	7	11	16	57	66	32
Grange Harlequins	34	6	10	17	46	83	28
Porthcawl	34	6	5	23	35	86	23

*Promoted in place of champions who declined place in League of Wales for second successive season.

NORTH WALES JOINERY CYMRU ALLIANCE

	P	W	D	L	F	A	Pts
Flexsys Cefn Druids	30	22	3	5	105	36	69
Rhydymwyn	30	17	6	7	66	36	57
Flint Town United	30	14	6	10	60	44	48
Oswestry Town	30	15	3	12	67	53	48
Glantraeth	30	13	7	10	57	47	46
Cemaes Bay	30	12	9	9	53	48	45
Porthmadog	30	12	7	11	52	49	43
Welshpool Town	30	11	9	10	47	39	42
Llandudno	30	11	7	12	49	48	40
Lex XI	30	11	7	12	48	62	40
Holyhead Hotspur	30	11	6	13	49	62	39
Denbigh Town	30	11	4	15	52	65	37
Ruthin Town	30	7	15	8	36	37	36
Buckley	30	9	6	15	48	75	33
Brymbo Broughton	30	8	7	15	28	43	31
Mostyn	30	1	8	21	26	99	11

NORTHERN IRISH FOOTBALL 1998–99

Northern Ireland football now finds itself at the crossroads – both internationally and domestically. The future looks precarious and uncertain with the prospect of a 12-club Irish Premier League being formed under the auspices of the Irish Football Association.

International manager Lawrie McMenemy, his assistant Joe Jordan and Pat Jennings, the goalkeeping coach, have experienced mixed fortunes since taking over – four wins, three draws and three defeats – by Germany, Spain and Turkey. The 1-0 win over the Republic of Ireland in a May charity match for the Omagh Bomb Disaster Fund with a team missing 10 regulars was, however, a major morale boost.

Further European championship games are scheduled against Germany, Turkey and Finland while world champions France have agreed to play at Windsor Park in August – a major coup which will generate record receipts from attendance, track advertising and television.

This management team has brought professionalism and discipline to the squad which, primarily, is lacking in top-drawer quality. Biggest disappointments were the home and away draws with Moldova, an emerging nation like so many others after the fragmentation of the Soviet Union.

Much success has been obtained with the Under-21 squad, managed by Chris Nicholl, the former Northern Ireland defender, especially in the European Championship in which they are competing for the first time at this level.

This is an encouraging aspect but, alas, too many of the players are a long way from senior level. What concerns the dedicated McMenemy most is their inability to get regular first team football at club level, especially in the Premiership.

With the constant import of foreigners to the British game the prospect of them making the breakthrough appears remote. An outstanding example is Philip Mulryne who was a member of Manchester United's European squad but remained a constant reserve and eventually moved to Norwich for regular first team football. Others with glamour clubs may follow a similar route.

Domestically, it was an indifferent season with an over abundance of internecine strife among administrators and, of course, the climax was the fiasco of the abandoned Portadown–Cliftonville Bass Irish Cup Final at Windsor Park.

Cliftonville were dismissed from the competition for using an ineligible player, Simon Gribben, in the semi-final against Linfield; he had played for a junior club in an earlier round and, under the IFA regulations, there was no alternative but elimination from the series. Portadown were awarded the trophy and also given entry into the European Cup.

Glentoran proved the team of the year winning the Irish League Premiership with consistent performances of high class football which earned Roy Coyle the Manager of the Year Trophy while John Devine, centre-back and captain, was named Ulster Footballer of the Year by sports writers and also the independent panel who judge the Castlreagh Glentoran Trophy which was inaugurated in 1951.

Irish FA general secretary David Bowen, who revealed a near £1m profit at the annual meeting, also introduced The Way Forward Plan in which he advocated the formation of the new league, improved sponsorship, better facilities, more involvement by clubs at coaching youth and a general overhaul of the game.

Premier League chairmen after a series of meetings gave it the green light but the Irish FA Council has still to approve. Target date for its introduction is 2000–2001 season but there are many hurdles yet to be overcome – perhaps some insurmountable.

A major drive against sectarian chanting at certain matches has also been undertaken by the soccer authorities who are determined to stamp it out. Their task won't be easy.

MALCOLM BRODIE

COCA-COLA FLOODLIT CUP

Semi-finals

Cliftonville v Linfield (at Windsor Park)	1-2
Glentoran v Carrick Rangers (at Seaview)	1-0

Final

Linfield 2 Glentoran 1 (at Windsor Park) – aet
Linfield: Robinson; McDonald (Shaw), McShane, Young I, Murphy, Cleland (Semple), Morgan (Larmour), Gorman, Ferguson, Marks, Bailie.
Glentoran: Russell; Nixon, Kennedy, Walker, Devine, Leeman, McCann, Hamill, Elliott, Batey (Young), McBride (Rainey).
Referee: M. Ross (Carrickfergus).
Scorers: Linfield: Ferguson (2).
  Glentoran: Hamill.
Attendance: 6500.

SMIRNOFF IFL

Premiership

	P	W	D	L	F	A	GD	Pts
Glentoran	36	24	6	6	74	35	+39	78
Linfield	36	20	10	6	68	39	+29	70
Crusaders	36	18	8	10	48	39	+9	62
Newry Town	36	17	9	10	52	46	+6	60
Glenavon	36	13	12	11	49	35	+14	51
Ballymena United	36	11	8	17	40	42	−2	41
Coleraine	36	10	9	17	34	53	−19	39
Portadown	36	9	10	17	41	47	−6	37
Cliftonville	36	7	14	15	31	47	−16	35
Omagh Town	36	5	6	25	25	79	−54	21

First Division

	P	W	D	L	F	A	GD	Pts
Distillery	28	17	4	7	44	30	+14	55
Ards	28	16	1	11	47	34	+13	49
Bangor	28	15	3	10	37	35	+2	48
Ballyclare Comrades	28	11	5	12	55	44	+11	38
Dungannon Swifts	28	11	5	12	36	46	−10	38
Carrick Rangers	28	10	4	14	41	41	0	34
Larne	28	9	5	14	28	32	−4	32
Limavady United	28	6	7	15	37	63	−26	25

Irish League leading scorers:

31 Darren Armour (Distillery) **26** Vinny Arkins (Portadown) **23** Davy Larmour (Linfield) **22** Stephen Baxter (Glenavon); Glenn Ferguson (Linfield) **21** Dessie Gorman (Newry Town) **20** Alan Gough (Dungannon Swifts); Graeme Arthur (Carrick Rangers) **19** Andy Kirk (Glentoran) **18** Crawford McRae (Crusaders); Rory Hamill (Glentoran); Gavin Treanor (Carrick Rangers) **17** Glenn Hunter (Ballymena Utd) **16** Chris Morgan (Linfield); Kevin Bates (Dungannon Swifts); **15** Paul Stokes (Coleraine); Justin McBride (Glentoran); Tony Grant (Glenavon); Paul Leeman (Glentoran); Phillip Dykes (Ards) **14** Gavin Arthur (Glenavon); Tony Gorman (Linfield); David Rainey (Glentoran); Stuart Elliott (Glentoran); **13** Darren Erskine (Ards) **12** Jim McCloskey (Distillery); Dessie Loughrey (Ballymena Utd); Tim McCann (Glentoran) **11** Davy Patton (Larne); Paul Cullen (Bangor); Gavin McCrystal (Ballyclare Comrades).

IRISH LEAGUE CHAMPIONSHIP WINNERS

1891	Linfield	1910	Cliftonville	1934	Linfield	1961	Linfield	1981	Glentoran
1892	Linfield	1911	Linfield	1935	Linfield	1962	Linfield	1982	Linfield
1893	Linfield	1912	Glentoran	1936	Belfast Celtic	1963	Distillery	1983	Linfield
1894	Glentoran	1913	Glentoran	1937	Belfast Celtic	1964	Glentoran	1984	Linfield
1895	Linfield	1914	Linfield	1938	Belfast Celtic	1965	Derry City	1985	Linfield
1896	Distillery	1915	Belfast Celtic	1939	Belfast Celtic	1966	Linfield	1986	Linfield
1897	Glentoran	1920	Belfast Celtic	1940	Belfast Celtic	1967	Glentoran	1987	Linfield
1898	Linfield	1921	Glentoran	1948	Belfast Celtic	1968	Glentoran	1988	Glentoran
1899	Distillery	1922	Linfield	1949	Linfield	1969	Linfield	1989	Linfield
1900	Belfast Celtic	1923	Linfield	1950	Linfield	1970	Glentoran	1990	Portadown
1901	Distillery	1924	Queen's Island	1951	Glentoran	1971	Linfield	1991	Portadown
1902	Linfield	1925	Glentoran	1952	Glenavon	1972	Glentoran	1992	Glentoran
1903	Distillery	1926	Belfast Celtic	1953	Glentoran	1973	Crusaders	1993	Linfield
1904	Linfield	1927	Belfast Celtic	1954	Linfield	1974	Coleraine	1994	Linfield
1905	Glentoran	1928	Belfast Celtic	1955	Linfield	1975	Linfield	1995	Crusaders
1906	Cliftonville	1929	Belfast Celtic	1956	Linfield	1976	Crusaders	1996	Portadown
	Distillery	1930	Linfield	1957	Glentoran	1977	Glentoran	1997	Crusaders
1907	Linfield	1931	Glentoran	1958	Ards	1978	Linfield	1998	Cliftonville
1908	Linfield	1932	Linfield	1959	Linfield	1979	Linfield	1999	Glentoran
1909	Linfield	1933	Belfast Celtic	1960	Glenavon	1980	Linfield		

FIRST DIVISION

1996	Coleraine
1997	Ballymena United
1998	Newry Town
1999	Distillery

ULSTER CUP FINAL TABLE

	P	W	D	L	F	A	Gd	Pts
Distillery	7	4	1	2	10	6	+4	13
Ards*	7	4	0	3	14	10	+4	12
Bangor	7	3	3	1	9	6	+3	12
Limavady United	7	3	1	3	6	9	−3	10
Dungannon Swifts	7	2	3	2	14	8	+6	9
Ballyclare Comrades**	7	3	0	4	9	18	−9	9
Carrick Rangers	7	2	1	4	9	12	−3	7
Larne	7	1	3	3	8	10	−2	6

Ards forfeited 3 points for playing an ineligible player v Bangor on 15th August 1998 and a scoreline of 1-0 recorded in favour of Bangor.

**Ballyclare Comrades forfeited 3 points for playing an ineligible player v Limavady United on 15th August 1998 and a scoreline of 1-0 recorded in favour of Limavady United.*

ULSTER CUP WINNERS

1949	Linfield	1960	Linfield	1970	Linfield	1980	Ballymena U	1990	Portadown
1950	Larne	1961	Ballymena U	1971	Linfield	1981	Glentoran	1991	Bangor
1951	Glentoran	1962	Linfield	1972	Coleraine	1982	Glentoran	1992	Linfield
1952		1963	Crusaders	1973	Ards	1983	Glentoran	1993	Crusaders
1953	Glentoran	1964	Linfield	1974	Linfield	1984	Linfield	1994	Bangor
1954	Crusaders	1965	Coleraine	1975	Coleraine	1985	Coleraine	1995	Portadown
1955	Glenavon	1966	Glentoran	1976	Glentoran	1986	Coleraine	1996	Portadown
1956	Linfield	1967	Linfield	1977	Linfield	1987	Larne	1997	Coleraine
1957	Linfield	1968	Coleraine	1978	Linfield	1988	Glentoran	1998	Ballyclare Comrades
1958	Distillery	1969	Coleraine	1979	Linfield	1989	Glentoran	1999	Distillery
1959	Glenavon								

IRISH LEAGUE 'B' DIVISION—SECTION 1

	P	W	D	L	F	A	GD	Pts
Chimney Corner	26	19	4	3	47	23	+24	61
RUC	26	19	3	4	62	23	+39	60
Dundela	26	14	10	2	76	27	+49	52
Institute	26	14	6	6	51	28	+23	48
Loughgall	26	13	5	8	49	41	+8	44
Armagh City	26	10	9	7	51	39	+12	39
Tobermore Utd	26	9	7	10	35	39	−4	34
H&W Welders	26	9	4	13	45	43	+2	31
Brantwood	26	8	6	12	40	49	−9	30
Banbridge Town	26	8	4	14	29	44	−15	28
Moyola Park	26	7	6	13	40	51	−11	27
Ballymoney Utd	26	7	3	16	43	77	−34	24
Ballinamallard Utd	26	6	5	15	20	50	−30	23
Cookstown Utd	26	2	2	22	18	71	−53	8

IRISH LEAGUE 'B' DIVISION—SECTION 2

	P	W	D	L	F	A	GD	Pts
Linfield Swifts	32	27	2	3	93	27	+66	83
Cliftonville Olympic	32	18	9	5	67	49	+18	63
Dungannon Sw Res	32	18	5	9	67	51	+16	59
Glenavon Res	32	17	5	10	63	36	+27	56
Distillery II	32	15	10	7	59	34	+25	55
Coleraine Res	32	17	4	11	59	45	+14	55
Glentoran II	32	15	7	10	53	35	+18	52
Ballymena Utd Res	32	12	9	11	54	49	+5	45
Crusaders Res	32	11	12	9	42	39	+3	45
Portadown Res	32	13	5	14	59	55	+4	44
Larne Olympic	32	10	8	14	48	55	−7	38
Bangor Res	32	10	8	14	37	45	−8	38
Ards II	32	8	10	14	43	50	−7	34
Carrick Rngrs Res	32	6	7	19	36	77	−41	25
Newry Town Res	32	7	2	23	37	90	−53	23
Limavady Utd Res	32	5	6	21	47	83	−36	21
Ballyclare Com Res	32	4	9	19	24	68	−44	21

BASS IRISH CUP 1998–99

Fifth Round

Linfield v Crumlin United	6-0
Crusaders v Newry Town	1-1, 3-2
Cliftonville v Crewe United	6-1
Glentoran v Tobermore	3-0
Distillery v H&W Welders	4-0
Carrick Rangers v Dungannon Swifts	2-2, 4-3
Portadown v Ballymoney United	1-0
Omagh Town v Ballyclare Comrades	1-2
Ballymena United v Larne	3-1
Loughgall v Dundela	2-1
Brantwood v Drummond United	3-1
Ards v Ards Rangers	1-0
Drumaness Mills v Lurgan Celtic	0-2
Institute v Chimney Corner	0-1
Bangor v Glenavon	0-3
Coleraine v Limavady United	1-1, 1-0

Sixth Round

Linfield v Chimney Corner	3-1
Portadown v Lurgan Celtic	3-0

Carrick Rangers v Ards	2-0
Distillery v Brantwood	5-0
Cliftonville v Glentoran	2-1
Ballymena United v Ballyclare Comrades	3-0
Coleraine v Loughgall	2-1
Glenavon v Crusaders	3-0

Quarter-finals

Coleraine v Portadown	1-2
Linfield v Glenavon	0-0, 2-1
Distillery v Ballymena United	1-1, 1-2
Carrick Rangers v Cliftonville	1-2

Semi-finals

Cliftonville v Linfield	1-1, 1-0
Ballymena United v Portadown	0-2

Final

Not played: Cliftonville dismissed under Irish FA rules from competition for using ineligible player in earlier round. Trophy awarded to Portadown who also qualified for Europe.

IRISH CUP FINALS (from 1946–47)

1946–47	Belfast Celtic 1, Glentoran 0	1974–75	Coleraine 1:0:1, Linfield 1:0:0
1947–48	Linfield 3, Coleraine 0	1975–76	Carrick Rangers 2, Linfield 1
1948–49	Derry City 3, Glentoran 1	1976–77	Coleraine 4, Linfield 1
1949–50	Linfield 2, Distillery 1	1977–78	Linfield 3, Ballymena U 1
1950–51	Glentoran 3, Ballymena U 1	1978–79	Cliftonville 3, Portadown 2
1951–52	Ards 1, Glentoran 0	1979–80	Linfield 2, Crusaders 0
1952–53	Linfield 5, Coleraine 0	1980–81	Ballymena U 1, Glenavon 0
1953–54	Derry City 1, Glentoran 0	1981–82	Linfield 2, Coleraine 1
1954–55	Dundela 3, Glenavon 0	1982–83	Glentoran 1:2, Linfield 1:1
1955–56	Distillery 1, Glentoran 0	1983–84	Ballymena U 4, Carrick Rangers 1
1956–57	Glenavon 2, Derry City 0	1984–85	Glentoran 1:1, Linfield 1:0
1957–58	Ballymena U 2, Linfield 0	1985–86	Glentoran 2, Coleraine 1
1958–59	Glenavon 2, Ballymena U 0	1986–87	Glentoran 1, Larne 0
1959–60	Linfield 5, Ards 1	1987–88	Glentoran 1, Glenavon 0
1960–61	Glenavon 5, Linfield 1	1988–89	Ballymena U 1, Larne 0
1961–62	Linfield 4, Portadown 0	1989–90	Glentoran 3, Portadown 0
1962–63	Linfield 2, Distillery 1	1990–91	Portadown 2, Glenavon 1
1963–64	Derry City 2, Glentoran 0	1991–92	Glenavon 2, Linfield 1
1964–65	Coleraine 2, Glenavon 1	1992–93	Bangor 1:1:1, Ards 1:1:0
1965–66	Glentoran 2, Linfield 0	1993–94	Linfield 2, Bangor 0
1966–67	Crusaders 3, Glentoran 1	1994–95	Linfield 3, Carrick Rangers 1
1967–68	Crusaders 2, Linfield 0	1995–96	Glentoran 1, Glenavon 0
1968–69	Ards 4, Distillery 2	1996–97	Glenavon 1, Cliftonville 0
1969–70	Linfield 2, Ballymena U 1	1997–98	Glentoran 1, Glenavon 0
1970–71	Distillery 3, Derry City 0	1998–99	*Portadown awarded trophy after*
1971–72	Coleraine 2, Portadown 1		*Cliftonville were eliminated for using an*
1972–73	Glentoran 3, Linfield 2		*ineligible player in semi-final.*
1973–74	Ards 2, Ballymena U 1		

NATIONWIDE GOLD CUP

Section 1	P	W	D	L	F	A	GD	Pts
Ballymena United	5	3	1	1	7	6	+1	10
Coleraine	5	2	3	0	9	5	+4	9
Cliftonville	5	2	2	1	8	6	+2	8
Distillery	5	1	4	0	10	6	+4	7
Bangor	5	1	1	3	7	7	0	4
Carrick Rangers	5	0	1	4	4	15	−11	1

Section 2	P	W	D	L	F	A	GD	Pts
Linfield	5	4	0	1	11	4	+7	12
Glenavon	5	3	1	1	15	6	+9	10
Newry Town	5	3	1	1	15	10	+5	10
Limavady United	5	2	0	3	8	14	−6	6
Dungannon Swifts	5	1	0	4	6	17	−11	3
Crusaders	5	0	2	3	6	10	−4	2

Section 3	P	W	D	L	F	A	GD	Pts
Glentoran	5	4	1	0	17	4	+13	13
Portadown*	5	3	1	1	9	5	+4	10
Ards	5	2	1	2	6	10	−4	7
Omagh Town	5	2	0	3	4	8	−4	6
Larne**	5	1	1	3	4	7	−3	4
Ballyclare Com	5	1	0	4	5	11	−6	3

Portadown forfeited 3 points for playing two in-eligible players v Omagh Town on Tuesday 13th October 1998; and these points were awarded to their opponents and a scoreline of 1-0 recorded in Omagh Town's favour.

**Larne forfeited 1 point for playing an unregistered player in their drawn game v Omagh Town on 27th October 1998; and as a result 3 points were awarded to their opponents and a scoreline of 1-0 recorded in Omagh Town's favour.*

Quarter-finals

Newry Town v Glentoran	1-3
Coleraine v Linfield (*aet*)	1-2
Cliftonville v Glenavon	2-3
Portadown v Ballymena United	1-0

Semi-finals

Linfield v Portadown (*at The Oval*)	0-3
Glenavon v Glentoran (*at Windsor Park*)	1-4

Final

Glentoran 3 Portadown 1 (*at Windsor Park*)

Glentoran: Russell; Leeman, Ferguson, Walker, Devine, Quigley, Elliott, Hamill, Kirk, Batey, Young.

Portadown: Dalton; McKeown, Davidson (Bowman), Casey, Strain, Major, Clarke, Byrne, Millar, Arkins, Fulton.

Scorers: Glentoran: Hamill, Kirk, Devine.
Portadown: Arkins.

Referee: D. Malcolm (Bangor).
Attendance: 2670.

WHERE THE TROPHIES WENT

	Winners	Runners-up
Smirnoff Irish League		
Premier Division	Glentoran	Linfield
First Division	Distillery	Ards
Bass Irish Cup	Portadown awarded trophy; Glentoran eliminated for using ineligible player, Simon Gribben, in semi-final replay 1-0 win over Linfield	
Nationwide Gold Cup	Glentoran	Portadown
Coca-Cola Irish League Floodlit Cup	Linfield	Glentoran
Ulster Cup	Distillery	Ards
Calor County Antrim Shield	Glentoran	Cliftonville
Calor County Antrim Junior Shield	Lisburn Rangers	Rathfern Rangers
Belfast Telegraph Intermediate Cup	Dundela	Comber Rec
Silverwood Mid Ulster Cup	Glenavon	Ards
Mid Ulster Shield	St Marys	Carnlough Rovers
North West Senior Cup	Limavady United	Dyford United Stars
Warner Services Bob Radcliffe Mem Cup	Loughgall	Armagh City
Smirnoff Knock Out Cup	Ballymoney United	Institute
Irish News Cup	Finn Harps	Ballymena United
Calor Steel & Sons Cup	Dunmurry Rec	RUC
Harry Cavan Coca-Cola Youth Cup	Cliftonville Strollers	Linfield Rangers
Irish Youth League Cup	Linfield Rangers	Glentoran Colts
George Wilson Cup	Linfield Swifts	Glentoran Colts
Irish League B Division		
Section One	Chimney Corner	RUC
Section Two	Linfield Swifts	Cliftonville Olympic
Sunday Mirror Irish Junior Cup Final	Enniskillen Rangers	Lisburn Rangers
Calor County Antrim Shield	Lisburn Rangers	Rathfern Rangers
Charity Shield	Glentoran	Cliftonville

EUROPEAN CUP

EUROPEAN CUP FINALS 1956–99

Year	Winners		Runners-up		Venue	Attendance	Referee
1956	Real Madrid	4	Reims	3	Paris	38,000	Ellis (E)
1957	Real Madrid	2	Fiorentina	0	Madrid	124,000	Horn (Ho)
1958	Real Madrid	3	AC Milan	2 *(aet)*	Brussels	67,000	Alsteen (Bel)
1959	Real Madrid	2	Reims	0	Stuttgart	80,000	Dutsch (WG)
1960	Real Madrid	7	Eintracht Frankfurt	3	Glasgow	135,000	Mowat (S)
1961	Benfica	3	Barcelona	2	Berne	28,000	Dienst (Sw)
1962	Benfica	5	Real Madrid	3	Amsterdam	65,000	Horn (Ho)
1963	AC Milan	2	Benfica	1	Wembley	45,000	Holland (E)
1964	Internazionale	3	Real Madrid	1	Vienna	74,000	Stoll (A)
1965	Internazionale	1	Benfica	0	Milan	80,000	Dienst (Sw)
1966	Real Madrid	2	Partizan Belgrade	1	Brussels	55,000	Kreitlein (WG)
1967	Celtic	2	Internazionale	1	Lisbon	56,000	Tschenscher (WG)
1968	Manchester U	4	Benfica	1 *(aet)*	Wembley	100,000	Lo Bello (I)
1969	AC Milan	4	Ajax	1	Madrid	50,000	Ortiz (Sp)
1970	Feyenoord	2	Celtic	1 *(aet)*	Milan	50,000	Lo Bello (I)
1971	Ajax	2	Panathinaikos	0	Wembley	90,000	Taylor (E)
1972	Ajax	2	Internazionale	0	Rotterdam	67,000	Helies (F)
1973	Ajax	1	Juventus	0	Belgrade	93,500	Guglovic (Y)
1974	Bayern Munich	1	Atletico Madrid	1	Brussels	49,000	Loraux (Bel)
Replay	Bayern Munich	4	Atletico Madrid	0	Brussels	23,000	Delcourt (Bel)
1975	Bayern Munich	2	Leeds U	0	Paris	50,000	Kitabdjian (F)
1976	Bayern Munich	1	St Etienne	0	Glasgow	54,864	Palotai (H)
1977	Liverpool	3	Moenchengladbach	1	Rome	57,000	Wurtz (F)
1978	Liverpool	1	FC Brugge	0	Wembley	92,000	Corver (Ho)
1979	Nottingham F	1	Malmo	0	Munich	57,500	Linemayr (A)
1980	Nottingham F	1	Hamburg	0	Madrid	50,000	Garrido (P)
1981	Liverpool	1	Real Madrid	0	Paris	48,360	Palotai (H)
1982	Aston Villa	1	Bayern Munich	0	Rotterdam	46,000	Konrath (F)
1983	Hamburg	1	Juventus	0	Athens	80,000	Rainea (R)
1984	Liverpool	1	Roma	1	Rome	69,693	Fredriksson (Se)
	(aet; Liverpool won 4–2 on penalties)						
1985	Juventus	1	Liverpool	0	Brussels	58,000	Daina (Sw)
1986	Steaua Bucharest	0	Barcelona	0	Seville	70,000	Vautrot (F)
	(aet; Steaua won 2–0 on penalties)						
1987	Porto	2	Bayern Munich	1	Vienna	59,000	Ponnet (Bel)
1988	PSV Eindhoven	0	Benfica	0	Stuttgart	70,000	Agnolin (I)
	(aet; PSV won 6–5 on penalties)						
1989	AC Milan	4	Steaua Bucharest	0	Barcelona	97,000	Tritschler (WG)
1990	AC Milan	1	Benfica	0	Vienna	57,500	Kohl (A)
1991	Red Star Belgrade	0	Marseille	0	Bari	56,000	Lanese (I)
	(aet; Red Star won 5–3 on penalties)						
1992	Barcelona	1	Sampdoria	0 *(aet)*	Wembley	70,827	Schmidhuber (G)
1993	Marseille*	1	AC Milan	0	Munich	64,400	Rothlisberger (Sw)
1994	AC Milan	4	Barcelona	0	Athens	70,000	Don (E)
1995	Ajax	1	AC Milan	0	Vienna	49,730	Craciunescu (Ro)
1996	Juventus	1	Ajax	1	Rome	67,000	Vega (Sp)
	(aet; Juventus won 4–2 on penalties)						
1997	Borussia Dortmund	3	Juventus	1	Munich	59,000	Puhl (H)
1998	Real Madrid	1	Juventus	0	Amsterdam	47,500	Krug (G)
1999	Manchester U	2	Bayern Munich	1	Barcelona	90,000	Collina (I)

Subsequently stripped of title.

EUROPEAN CUP 1998-99

FIRST QUALIFYING ROUND, FIRST LEG

Beitar Jerusalem (3) 4 *(Shitrit 2, Salloi 9, 45, 78)*,	
B36 Torshavn (0) 1 *(Petersen 73 (pen))*	11,000
Celtic (0) 0, St Patrick's Athletic (0) 0	56,864
Cliftonville (1) 1 *(Flynn 45)*, Kosice (3) 5	
(Zvara 22, 29, Nemeth 35, Lubarsky 59,	
Prohaszka 71)	1500
Dynamo Kiev (4) 8 *(Rebrov 9, 16, 37, 82,*	
Shevchenko 33, 59, Gerasimenko 48, Belkevich 65),	
Barry Town (0) 0	15,500
Dynamo Tbilisi (0) 1 *(Khomeriki 53)*,	
Vllaznia (0) 0	10,000
UEFA declared the match to be 3-0	
Grasshoppers (3) 6 *(N'Kufo 6, 55, Kavelashvili 29,*	
Cabanas 41, Tikva 65, Magnin 90),	
Jeunesse Esch (0) 0	5000
HJK Helsinki (0) 2 *(Wiss 50, Kugi 85)*, Erevan (0) 0	2300
Kareda (0) 0, Branik Maribor (1) 3 *(Gajser 43, 87,*	
Filipovic 71)	3500
Litets (1) 2 *(Bushi 7, Yurukov 89)*, Halmstad (0) 0	5000
LKS Lodz (1) 4 *(Cebula 16, Trzeciak 50 (pen),*	
76 (pen), Wieszczycki 73), Kapaz (0) 1	
(Suleimanov 83)	2000
Obilic (1) 2 *(Juskic 18, Grozdic 65)*, IBV (0) 0	1500
Sileks (0) 0, FC Brugge (0) 0	5000
Skonto Riga (0) 0, Dynamo Minsk (0) 0	3000
Steaua (2) 4 *(Ciocoiu 12, 39, Serban 78 (pen),*	
Danciulescu 89), Flora Tallinn (1) 1	
(Terenkov 40)	5000
Valletta (0) 0, Anorthosis (0) 2 *(Palashkeva 52,*	
Okkas 80)	2500
Zimbru Chisinau (1) 1 *(Kulik 10 (pen))*,	
Ujpest (0) 0	8000

FIRST QUALIFYING ROUND, SECOND LEG

Anorthosis (3) 6 *(Civic 16, Charalambous 18,*	
Andreou 45 (pen), Sotiriou 51, 90, Okkas 71),	
Valletta (0) 0	5000
B36 Torshavn (0) 0, Beitar Jerusalem (0) 1	
(Hamar 68)	285
Barry Town (1) 1 *(Williams 30)*, Dynamo Kiev (1) 2	
(Mikhailenko 11, Venglinski 50)	1500
Branik Maribor (0) 1 *(Balajic 78)*, Kareda (0) 0	4000
Dynamo Minsk (1) 1 *(Osipovich 27)*,	
Skonto Riga (1) 2 *(Astafyev 45, Novikov 72)*	3500
Erevan (0) 0, HJK Helsinki (2) 3 *(Lehkosuo 1, 79,*	
Ilola 28)	4000
FC Brugge (2) 2 *(Vermant 14, Claessens 30)*,	
Sileks (0) 1 *(Bozinov 76)*	6000
Flora Tallinn (1) 3 *(Smirnov 42, Zelinski 46, Oper 81)*,	
Steaua (0) 1 *(Danciulescu 72)*	1100
Halmstad (2) 2 *(Sakiri 38, Arvidsson 42)*, Litets (0) 1	
(Yorolkov 76)	3438
IBV (1) 1 *(Haflidason 26)*, Obilic (0) 2 *(Vesiljevic 60,*	
Grozdic 89)	1000
Jeunesse Esch (0) 0, Grasshoppers (2) 2 *(Esposito 34,*	
Turkyilmaz 43)	1000
Kapaz (0) 1 *(Smirnov 53)*, LKS Lodz (1) 3 *(Jak 45, 49,*	
Niesgucki 81)	12,000
Kosice (3) 8 *(Kozak J 4, Janocko 14, 54, Nemeth 32,*	
Prohaszka 58, 72, Lubarsky 67, Kozlej 86),	
Cliftonville (0) 0	1948
St Patrick's Athletic (0) 0, Celtic (1) 2 *(Brattbakk 12,*	
Larsson 72)	9500
Ujpest (3) 3 *(Niriuta 17, Kovacs 73, 90)*, Zimbru	
Chisinau (1) 1 *(Kulyk 28)*	8000
Vllaznia (1) 3 *(Cungu 12, Miloti 87, Noga 90 (pen))*,	
Dynamo Tbilisi (0) 1 *(Melkadze 89)*	5000

SECOND QUALIFYING ROUND, FIRST LEG

Bayern Munich (0) 4 *(Effenberg 59, Elber 63,*	
Zickler 65, Fink 76), Obilic (0) 0	37,000
Benfica (2) 6 *(Pembridge 25, 82, Deane 29,*	
Calado 64 (pen), Shelach 79 (og),	
Nuno Gomes 86 (pen)), Beitar Jerusalem (0) 0	60,000
Branik Maribor (1) 2 *(Filipovic 11, Breznik 87)*,	
PSV Eindhoven (0) 1 *(Marcos dos Santos 61)*	7200
Celtic (0) 1 *(Jackson 50)*, Croatia Zagreb (0) 0	59,397
Dynamo Kiev (0) 0, Sparta Prague (1) 1	
(Baranek 5)	15,000
Dynamo Tbilisi (2) 2 *(Khomeriki 14, Tskitishvili 30)*,	
Athletic Bilbao (0) 1 *(Imaz 46)*	17,000

Galatasaray (0) 2 *(Hagi 58 (pen), Hakan Sukur 67)*,	
Grasshoppers (0) 1 *(Vogel J 86 (pen))*	22,000
HJK Helsinki (0) 1 *(Stasser 72 (og))*, Metz (0) 0	8087
Internazionale (3) 4 *(Zamorano 4, Simeone 10,*	
Ventola 21, Roberto Baggio 59), Skonto	
Riga (0) 0	16,166
Kosice (0) 0, Brondby (0) 2 *(Daugaard 54,*	
Thygesen 90)	4725
Litets (0) 0, Spartak Moscow (0) 5 *(Pisarev 54, 86,*	
Titov 62, Samaroni 77, Tsymbalar 90)	25,000
Manchester United (1) 2 *(Giggs 16, Cole 81)*,	
LKS Lodz (0) 0	50,906
Olympiakos (2) 2 *(Yannakopoulos 12, De Souza L 32)*,	
Anorthosis (0) 1 *(Mihajlovic 65)*	40,000
Rosenborg (0) 2 *(Rushfeldt 60, Skammelsrud 80)*,	
FC Brugge (0) 0	2919
Steaua (1) 2 *(Serban 12, Szekely 75)*, Panathinaikos (1) 2	
(Asanovic 9, Liberopoulos 67)	19,000
Sturm Graz (1) 4 *(Vastic 7, 70, Neukirchner 82, Haas 88)*,	
Ujpest (0) 0	12,500

SECOND QUALIFYING ROUND, SECOND LEG

Anorthosis (1) 2 *(Mihajlovic 35, Krcmarevic 75)*,	
Olympiakos (0) 4 *(Georgakos 47, Gejordjevic 57, 80,*	
Gogic 90)	10,000
(in Larnaca).	
Athletic Bilbao (0) 1 *(Etxeberria J 53)*,	
Dynamo Tbilisi (0) 0	40,000
Beitar Jerusalem (2) 4 *(Hamar 25, Salloi 27 (pen),*	
Shitrit 51, Abuksis 81), Benfica (1) 2	
(Nuno Gomes 18 (pen), Pringle 90)	4000
Brondby (0) 0, Kosice (1) 1 *(Lapsansky 39)*	16,967
FC Brugge (1) 4 *(Fadiga 23, Claessens 46, 84, Schockaert*	
77), Rosenborg (1) 2 *(Rushfeldt 43, 71)*	9700
Croatia Zagreb (2) 3 *(Maric 23, Prosinecki 44 (pen), 68)*,	
Celtic (0) 0	27,000
Grasshoppers (2) 3 *(Turkyilmaz 45, Vogel J 70 (pen))*,	
Galatasaray (2) 3 *(Hakan Sukur 17, 45,*	
Hagi 65 (pen))	15,000
LKS Lodz (0) 0, Manchester United (0) 0	8000
Metz (0) 1 *(Meyrieu 79 (pen))*, HJK Helsinki (0) 1	
(Vasara 69)	8000
Obilic (0) 1 *(Sarac 67)*, Bayern Munich (0) 1	
(Matthaus 89)	11,000
Panathinaikos (3) 6 *(Milovevic 8 (pen), Linkar 27 (og),*	
Liberopoulos 35, Warzycha 58, 66, Asanovic 89),	
Steaua (2) 3 *(Rachita 12, Liberopoulos 16 (og),*	
Belodedici 61)	55,000
PSV Eindhoven (1) 4 *(Van Nistelrooy 8, Bruggink 69,*	
Rommedahl 100, De Bilde 102), Branik Maribor (1) 1	
(Filipovic 5)	11,000
Skonto Riga (1) 1 *(Miholap 23)*, Internazionale (1) 3	
(Zamorano 8, Galante 54, Djorkaeff 71)	5600
Sparta Prague (0) 0, Dynamo Kiev (1) 1	
(Shevchenko 88)	10,000
(Dynamo Kiev won 3-1 on penalties.)	
Spartak Moscow (3) 6 *(Tikhonov 7, 30, Titov 34,*	
Tsymbalar 49, Robson 54, 90), Litets (1) 2	
(Beljakov 28, Bushi 71)	8000
Ujpest (1) 2 *(Kovacs 36, Jenei 72)*, Sturm Graz (1) 3	
(Haas 8, Reinmayr 50, 56)	3000

CHAMPIONS LEAGUE

GROUP A

Croatia Zagreb (0) 0, Ajax (0) 0	28,000
Porto (0) 2 *(Zahovic 64, Jardel 85)*, Olympiakos (0) 2	
(Yannakopoulos 85, Gogic 90)	37,000
Ajax (0) 2 *(Rudy 62, Litmanen 89 (pen))*, Porto (0) 1	
(Zahovic 68)	41,000
Olympiakos (1) 2 *(Alexandris 22, Gogic 80)*,	
Croatia Zagreb (0) 0	60,000
Olympiakos (1) 1 *(Alexandris 42)*, Ajax (0) 0	74,700
Porto (2) 3 *(Doriva 32, Zahovic 42, 75)*,	
Croatia Zagreb (0) 0	20,000
Ajax (1) 2 *(Witschge 33, Gorre 88)*,	
Olympiakos (0) 0	45,000
Croatia Zagreb (2) 3 *(Mikic 7, Rukavina 37, Mujcin 60)*,	
Porto (1) 1 *(Jardel 39)*	10,000
Ajax (0) 0, Croatia Zagreb (0) 1 *(Simic J 68)*	47,000
Olympiakos (1) 2 *(Gogic 18, Djordjevic 54)*, Porto (0) 1	
(Zahovic 76)	70,000

Croatia Zagreb (1) 1 *(Jelicic 35)*, Olympiakos (0) 1
  (Yannakopoulos 64) 23,000
Porto (0) 3 *(Zahovic 54, 73, Drulovic 79)*,
  Ajax (0) 0 20,000

FINAL TABLE

	P	W	D	L	F	A	Pts
Olympiakos	6	3	2	1	8	6	11
Croatia Zagreb	6	2	2	2	5	7	8
Porto	6	2	1	3	11	9	7
Ajax	6	2	1	3	4	6	7

GROUP B

Athletic Bilbao (1) 1 *(Etxeberria J 5)*, Rosenborg (0) 1
  (Strand 66) 35,000
Juventus (1) 2 *(Inzaghi 17, Birindelli 68)*, Galatasaray (1)
  2 *(Hakan Sukur 42, Umit 63)* 37,912
Galatasaray (1) 2 *(Okan 15, Hagi 90)*,
  Athletic Bilbao (1) 1 *(Urzaiz 16)* 31,000
Rosenborg (0) 1 *(Skammelsrud 69)*, Juventus (1) 1
  (Inzaghi 27) 15,385
Athletic Bilbao (0) 0, Juventus (0) 0 40,000
Rosenborg (0) 3 *(Rushfeldt 68, 86, 90)*,
  Galatasaray (0) 0 17,372
Galatasaray (0) 3 *(Hakan Sukur 55, 74, Arif 66)*,
  Rosenborg (0) 0 23,700
Juventus (0) 1 *(Montero 69)*, Athletic Bilbao (1) 1
  (Guerrero 45) 25,000
Galatasaray (0) 1 *(Suat 90)*, Juventus (0) 1
  (Amoruso 78) 25,000
Rosenborg (1) 2 *(Sorensen 2, 50)*, Athletic Bilbao (0) 1
  (Perez 90) 15,450
Athletic Bilbao (1) 1 *(Guerrero 43)*,
  Galatasaray (0) 0 25,000
Juventus (2) 2 *(Inzaghi 16, Amoruso 35)*,
  Rosenborg (0) 0 30,000

FINAL TABLE

	P	W	D	L	F	A	Pts
Juventus	6	1	5	0	7	5	8
Galatasaray	6	2	2	2	8	8	8
Rosenborg	6	2	2	2	7	8	8
Athletic Bilbao	6	1	3	2	5	6	6

GROUP C

Real Madrid (0) 2 *(Hierro 79 (pen), Seedorf 90)*,
  Internazionale (0) 0 40,000
Sturm Graz (0) 0, Spartak Moscow (0) 2 *(Titov 62,
  Tsymbalar 64)* 11,000
Internazionale (0) 1 *(Djorkaeff 90)*, Sturm
  Graz (0) 0 25,000
Spartak Moscow (0) 2 *(Tsymbalar 72, Titov 78)*,
  Real Madrid (0) 1 *(Raul 64)* 60,000
Internazionale (1) 2 *(Ventola 32, Ronaldo 59)*,
  Spartak Moscow (0) 1 *(Tsymbalar 65)* 44,000
Real Madrid (2) 6 *(Savio 13, 90, Raul 22, Jarni 60, 79,
  Popovic 66 (og))*, Sturm Graz (1) 1 *(Vastic 8)* 12,000
Spartak Moscow (0) 1 *(Tikhonov 68)*,
  Internazionale (0) 1 *(Simeone 89)* 70,000
Sturm Graz (1) 1 *(Haas 4)*, Real Madrid (2) 5 *(Panucci 8,
  62, Mijatovic 35, Seedorf 57, Suker 74)* 15,000
Internazionale (0) 3 *(Zamorano 51, Roberto Baggio
  90)*, Real Madrid (0) 1 *(Seedorf 59)* 77,829
Spartak Moscow (0) 0, Sturm Graz (0) 0 36,200
Real Madrid (1) 2 *(Raul 34, Savio 65)*,
  Spartak Moscow (0) 1 *(Khlestov 89)* 60,000
Sturm Graz (0) 0, Internazionale (0) 2 *(Zanetti 64,
  Roberto Baggio 80)* 14,000

FINAL TABLE

	P	W	D	L	F	A	Pts
Internazionale	6	4	1	1	9	5	13
Real Madrid	6	4	0	2	17	8	12
Spartak Moscow	6	2	2	2	7	6	8
Sturm Graz	6	0	1	5	2	16	1

GROUP D

Brondby (0) 2 *(Helmer 88 (og), Ravn 90)*, Bayern Munich
  (0) 1 *(Babbel 75)* 30,378
Manchester United (2) 3 *(Giggs 17, Scholes 24, Beckham
  64)*, Barcelona (0) 3 *(Anderson 47, Giovanni 60 (pen),
  Luis Enrique 71 (pen))* 53,601
Barcelona (1) 2 *(Anderson 42, 85)*, Brondby (0) 0 70,000

Bayern Munich (1) 2 *(Elber 11, Sheringham 90 (og))*,
  Manchester United (1) 2 *(Yorke 29, Scholes 48)* 57,000
Bayern Munich (1) 1 *(Effenberg 45)*,
  Barcelona (0) 0 55,000
Brondby (1) 2 *(Daugaard 35, Sand 90)*, Manchester
  United (3) 6 *(Giggs 2, 21, Cole 27, Keane 55, Yorke 60,
  Solskjaer 63)* 40,530
Barcelona (1) 1 *(Giovanni 29 (pen))*, Bayern
  Munich (0) 2 *(Zickler 48, Salihamidzic 87)* 90,000
Manchester United (4) 5 *(Beckham 7, Cole 13, Neville P
  15, Yorke 27, Scholes 63)*, Brondby (0) 0 53,250
Barcelona (1) 3 *(Anderson 1, Rivaldo 57, 73)*,
  Manchester United (1) 3 *(Yorke 25, 68, Cole 53)* 67,650
Bayern Munich (0) 2 *(Jancker 51, Basler 57)*,
  Brondby (0) 0 34,000
Brondby (0) 0, Barcelona (2) 2 *(Figo 4,
  Rivaldo 35)* 40,892
Manchester U (1) 1 *(Keane 43)*, Bayern Munich (0) 1
  (Salihamidzic 56) 54,434

FINAL TABLE

	P	W	D	L	F	A	Pts
Bayern Munich	6	3	2	1	9	6	11
Manchester United	6	2	4	0	20	11	10
Barcelona	6	2	2	2	11	9	8
Brondby	6	1	0	5	4	18	3

GROUP E

Lens (0) 1 *(Vairelles 90)*, Arsenal (0) 1 *(Overmars 51)*
  36,000
Panathinaikos (0) 2 *(Mykland 57, Liberopoulos 69)*,
  Dynamo Kiev (1) 1 *(Rebrov 31)* 35,000
Arsenal (0) 2 *(Adams 64, Keown 72)*, Panathinaikos (0) 1
  (Mauro 87) 73,455 *at Wembley.*
Dynamo Kiev (0) 1 *(Shevchenko 61)*, Lens (0) 1
  (Vairelles 62) 40,000
Arsenal (0) 1 *(Bergkamp 74)*, Dynamo Kiev (0) 1
  (Rebrov 90) 73,256 *at Wembley.*
Lens (0) 1 *(Eloi 80)*, Panathinaikos (0) 0 31,000
Dynamo Kiev (1) 3 *(Rebrov 26 (pen), Golovko 61,
  Shevchenko 72)*, Arsenal (0) 1 *(Hughes 84)* 80,000
Panathinaikos (0) 1 *(Vokolos 53)*, Lens (0) 0 52,000
Arsenal (0) 0, Lens (0) 1 *(Debeve 72)* 73,207 *at Wembley.*
Dynamo Kiev (0) 2 *(Rebrov 72, Basinas 80 (og))*,
  Panathinaikos (1) 1 *(Lagonikas 36)* 35,000
Lens (0) 1 *(Smicer 77)*, Dynamo Kiev (1) 3 *(Kaladze 60,
  Vaschuk 75, Shevchenko 85)* 42,000
Panathinaikos (0) 1 *(Sypniewski 74)*, Arsenal (1) 3
  (Mendez 66, Anelka 79, Boa Morte 86) 45,000

FINAL TABLE

	P	W	D	L	F	A	Pts
Dynamo Kiev	6	3	2	1	11	7	11
Lens	6	2	2	2	5	6	8
Arsenal	6	2	2	2	8	8	8
Panathinaikos	6	2	0	4	6	9	6

GROUP F

PSV Eindhoven (0) 2 *(Ooijer 59, Bruggink 90)*,
  HJK Helsinki (1) 1 *(Kottila 31)* 15,000
Kaiserslautern (1) 1 *(Wagner 41)*, Benfica (0) 0 31,112
Benfica (0) 2 *(Nuno Gomes 47, Joao Pinto 79)*,
  PSV Eindhoven (0) 1 *(Rommedahl 70)* 35,000
HJK Helsinki (0) 0, Kaiserslautern (0) 0 21,217
HJK Helsinki (1) 2 *(Lehkosuo 20 (pen), Kottila 70)*,
  Benfica (0) 0 27,000
PSV Eindhoven (0) 1 *(Khokhlov 78)*, Kaiserslautern (0) 2
  (Riedl 67, Rische 80) 22,500
Benfica (0) 2 *(Nuno Gomes 78, Calado 81)*, HJK Helsinki
  (1) 2 *(Minto 5 (og), Luiz Antonio 86)* 35,000
Kaiserslautern (0) 3 *(Rische 68, Reich 75, Hristov 90)*,
  PSV Eindhoven (1) 1 *(Van Nistelrooy 18)* 31,444
Benfica (1) 2 *(Nuno Gomes 31, Joao Pinto 69)*,
  Kaiserslautern (0) 1 *(Rische 90)* 25,000
HJK Helsinki (0) 1 *(Lehkosuo 70 (pen))*,
  PSV Eindhoven (1) 3 *(Van Nistelrooy 30, 67,
  82 (pen))* 34,146
Kaiserslautern (1) 5 *(Rosler 43, 61, 80, Marschall 49,
  Rische 85)*, HJK Helsinki (1) 2 *(Ilola 29,
  Moraes 68)* 25,000
PSV Eindhoven (1) 2 *(Khokhlov 41, Van Nistelrooy 89)*,
  Benfica (0) 2 *(Nuno Gomes 47 (pen), 62)* 23,000

FINAL TABLE

	P	W	D	L	F	A	Pts
Kaiserslautern	6	4	1	1	12	6	13
Benfica	6	2	2	2	8	9	8
PSV Eindhoven	6	2	1	3	10	11	8
HJK Helsinki	6	1	2	3	8	12	5

QUARTER-FINALS, FIRST LEG

Bayern Munich (2) 2 *(Elber 31, Effenberg 35)*,
  Kaiserslautern (0) 0   54,000
Juventus (1) 2 *(Inzaghi 38, Conte 79)*, Olympiakos (0) 1
  (Niniadis 90 (pen))   33,761
Manchester United (2) 2 *(Yorke 6, 45)*,
  Internazionale (0) 0   54,430
Real Madrid (0) 1 *(Mijatovic 67)*, Dynamo Kiev (0) 1
  (Shevchenko 56)   40,000

QUARTER-FINALS, SECOND LEG

Dynamo Kiev (0) 2 *(Shevchenko 63 (pen), 80)*,
  Real Madrid (0) 0   80,000

Internazionale (0) 1 *(Ventola 63)*,
  Manchester United (0) 1 *(Scholes 88)*   79,528
Kaiserslautern (0) 0, Bayern Munich (3) 4 *(Effenberg 9*
  (pen), Jancker 22, 39, Basler 56)   31,400
Olympiakos (1) 1 *(Gogic 12)*, Juventus (0) 1 *(Conte 85)*
     70,000

SEMI-FINALS, FIRST LEG

Dynamo Kiev (2) 3 *(Shevchenko 16, Kaladze 43,*
  Kossovsky 49), Bayern Munich (1) 3 *(Tarnat 45,*
  Effenberg 78, Jancker 90)   82,000
Manchester United (0) 1 *(Giggs 90)*, Juventus (1) 1
  (Conte 25)   54,487

SEMI-FINALS, SECOND LEG

Bayern Munich (1) 1 *(Basler 35)*, Dynamo
  Kiev (0) 0   59,000
Juventus (2) 2 *(Inzaghi 6, 10)*, Manchester United (2) 3
  (Keane 24, Yorke 34, Cole 84)   65,500

FINAL

Manchester U (0) 2, Bayern Munich (1) 1

(in Barcelona, 26 May 1999, 90,000)

Manchester U: Schmeichel; Neville G, Irwin, Johnsen, Butt, Stam, Beckham, Blomqvist (Sheringham 66), Cole
  (Solskjaer 80), Yorke, Giggs.
Scorers: Sheringham 89, Solskjaer 90.
Bayern Munich: Kahn; Babbel, Tarnat, Linke, Matthaus (Fink 80), Kuffour, Basler (Salihamidzic 89), Effenberg,
  Jancker, Zickler (Scholl 70), Jeremies.
Scorer: Basler 6.
Referee: Collina (Italy).

Manchester United manager Alex Ferguson joins his triumphant players after their 1999 European Cup success in Barcelona. (ASP)

EUROPEAN CUP 1998–99 – BRITISH AND IRISH CLUBS

FIRST QUALIFYING ROUND, FIRST LEG

22 JULY

Celtic (0) 0
St Patrick's Ath (0) 0 56,864
Celtic: Gould; Boyd, Mahe, McNamara (Donnelly 67), Rieper (Annoni 83), Stubbs, Larsson, Burley, Lambert, Blinker, Brattbakk (Jackson 46).
St Patrick's Ath: Wood; Clarke, Campbell, Lynch, Hawkins, Osam, Gormley, Russell, Molloy (Reilly 72), Braithwaite (Crolly 82), Gilzean.

Cliftonville (1) 1 *(Flynn 45)*
Kosice (3) 5 *(Zvara 22, 29, Nemeth 35, Lubarsky 59, Prohaszka 71)* 1500
Cliftonville: Reece; Small, Flynn (Kerr 65), Tabb, McCallion, Sliney, McCann T, Collins (McDonagh 86), Tolan, McCann M, Donnelly.
Kosice: Seman; Toth (Jambor 63), Kozak I, Dzurik (Kral 72), Spilar, Sovic, Nemeth, Sehenik, Zvara (Kozak J 52), Prohaszka, Lubarsky.

Dynamo Kiev (4) 8 *(Rebrov 9, 16, 37, 82, Shevchenko 33, 59, Gerasimenko 48, Belkevich 65)*
Barry Town (0) 0 15,500
Dynamo Kiev: Shovkovski; Horovko, Vashchuk, Dmitrulin, Kaladze, Kalitv (Venglinski 69), Shevchenko, Rebrov, Gusin (Belkevich 56), Khatskevich, Gerasimenko.
Barry Town: Nurse; Lloyd, Jones, York, Barrow, Barnett, Carter, Williams (Evans C 59), Dempsey, Thorpe, Evans T.

FIRST QUALIFYING ROUND, SECOND LEG

29 JULY

Barry Town (1) 1 *(Williams 30)*
Dynamo Kiev (1) 2 *(Mikhailenko 11, Venglinski 50)* 1500
Barry Town: Mountain; Evans T, Lloyd, Jones, York, Barrow, Barnett, Carter, Evans C, Williams, Dempsey.
Dynamo Kiev: Kernozenko; Luzhny, Khatskevich, Kaladze, Vashchuk, Shevchenko (Gerasimenko 70), Federov, Milhailenko, Konovalov (Rebrov 46), Belkevich (Kossovsky 76), Venglinski.

Kosice (3) 8 *(Kozak J 4, Janocko 14, 54, Nemeth 32, Prohaszka 58, 72, Lubarsky 67, Kozlej 86)*
Cliftonville (0) 0 1948
Kosice: Seman; Gerich, Kozak I (Toth 46), Sovic (Lubarsky 58), Nemeth (Prohaszka 46), Kozlej, Sehenik, Jambor, Kral, Kozak J, Janocko.
Cliftonville: Reece; Small, Flynn, Tabb, McCallion, Sliney (McMahon 72), McCann T, Collins (Davey 72), Tolan, McCann M (McDonagh 72), Donnelly.

St Patrick's Ath (0) 0
Celtic (1) 2 *(Brattbakk 12, Larsson 72)* 9500
St Patrick's Ath: Wood; Clarke, Campbell (Doyle 46), Lynch, Hawkins, Osam, Gormley, Morgan (Russell 46), Braithwaite, Gilzean (Reilly 75), Molloy.
Celtic: Gould; Boyd, McNamara, Stubbs, Larsson, Burley, Brattbakk, Lambert, Jackson (Donnelly 68), Mackay, Blinker (McKinlay 75).

SECOND QUALIFYING ROUND, FIRST LEG

12 AUG

Celtic (0) 1 *(Jackson 50)*
Croatia Zagreb (0) 0 59,397
Celtic: Gould; McNamara, Boyd, Burley, Rieper, Stubbs, Blinker, Lambert, Brattbakk (Jackson 46), Larsson, Donnelly.
Croatia Zagreb: Ladic; Simic D, Juric, Tokic, Rukavina, Prosinecki, Jurcic, Jelicic (Mujcin 76), Cvitanovic, Maric (Simic J 82), Viduka.

Manchester U (1) 2 *(Giggs 16, Cole 81)*
LKS Lodz (0) 0 50,906
Manchester U: Schmeichel; Neville G, Irwin, Johnsen, Keane, Stam, Beckham, Butt, Cole, Scholes (Solskjaer 80), Giggs.
LKS Lodz: Wyparlo; Bendkowski, Pawlak, Krysiak, Omodiagbe (Jakubowski 85), Kos, Cebula, Wyciskiewicz, Zuberek (Paszulewicz 72), Niznik (Carbone 56), Wieszczycki.

SECOND QUALIFYING ROUND, SECOND LEG

26 AUG

Croatia Zagreb (2) 3 *(Maric 23, Prosinecki 44 (pen), 68)*
Celtic (0) 0 27,000
Croatia Zagreb: Ladic; Simic D, Juric, Tokic, Rukavina, Jurcic, Prosinecki, Cvitanovic, Jelicic (Mujcin 60), Maric (Saric 83), Viduka (Sokota 73).
Celtic: Gould; McNamara, Boyd, Burley, Rieper, Stubbs, Blinker (Brattbakk 63), Lambert, Mahe, Jackson (Donnelly 76), Larsson.

LKS Lodz (0) 0
Manchester U (0) 0 8000
LKS Lodz: Wyparlo; Jakubowski (Bugaj 85), Lenart (Pluciennik 82), Pawlak, Bendkowski, Krysiak, Wieszczycki, Kos, Zuberek (Matys 61), Wyciszkiewicz, Niznik.
Manchester U: Schmeichel; Irwin, Neville P, Johnsen, Keane, Stam, Beckham, Butt, Scholes, Sheringham, Giggs (Solskjaer 65).

CHAMPIONS LEAGUE
GROUP D
16 SEPT

Manchester U (2) 3 *(Giggs 17, Scholes 24, Beckham 64)*
Barcelona (0) 3 *(Anderson 47, Giovanni 60 (pen), Luis Enrique 71 (pen))* 53,601
Manchester U: Schmeichel; Neville G, Irwin (Neville P 78), Berg, Keane, Stam, Beckham, Solskjaer (Butt 54), Yorke, Scholes, Giggs (Blomqvist 82).
Barcelona: Hesp; Luis Enrique, Abelardo, Reiziger, Sergi, Giovanni (Xavi 68), Cocu, Rivaldo, Figo, Anderson, Zenden.

30 SEPT

Bayern Munich (1) 2 *(Elber 11, Sheringham 90 (og))*
Manchester U (1) 2 *(Yorke 29, Scholes 48)* 57,000
Bayern Munich: Kahn; Babbel, Matthaus, Linke, Strunz, Effenberg, Jeremies (Fink 83), Salihamidzic (Goktan 63), Lizarazu, Elber, Jancker (Daei 63).
Manchester U: Schmeichel; Neville P, Irwin, Neville G, Keane, Stam, Beckham, Scholes, Yorke, Sheringham, Blomqvist (Cruyff 68).

21 OCT

Brondby (1) 2 *(Daugaard 35, Sand 90)*
Manchester U (3) 6 *(Giggs 2, 21, Cole 27, Keane 55, Yorke 60, Solskjaer 63)* 40,530
Brondby: Krogh; Colding, Nielsen (Jensen M 30), Rasmussen, Jensen B (Da Silva 27), Bjur, Ravn, Daugaard, Lindrup, Hansen (Bagger 66), Sand.
Manchester U: Schmeichel; Brown, Neville P, Neville G, Keane, Stam, Scholes, Blomqvist, Cole (Solskjaer 60), Yorke (Wilson 64), Giggs (Cruyff 60).

4 NOV

Manchester U (4) 5 *(Beckham 7, Cole 13, Neville P 15, Yorke 27, Scholes 63)*
Brondby (0) 0 53,250
Manchester U: Schmeichel; Neville P (Brown 31), Irwin, Neville G, Keane, Stam, Beckham, Blomqvist (Cruyff 46), Cole (Solskjaer 56), Yorke, Scholes.
Brondby: Andersen; Colding, Rasmussen, Nielsen P, Skarbalius, Bjur (Krogh 74), Daugaard, Ravn, Jensen, Bagger (Thygesen 70), Sand (Hansen 75).

25 NOV

Barcelona (1) 3 *(Anderson 1, Rivaldo 57, 73)*
Manchester U (1) 3 *(Yorke 25, 68, Cole 53)* 67,650
Barcelona: Hesp; Celades, Okunowo, Reiziger, Sergi, Xavi, Rivaldo, Giovanni, Figo, Anderson, Zenden.
Manchester U: Schmeichel; Brown, Irwin, Neville G, Keane, Stam, Beckham (Butt 81), Blomqvist, Cole, Yorke, Scholes.

9 DEC

Manchester U (1) 1 *(Keane 43)*
Bayern Munich (0) 1 *(Salihamidzic 56)* 54,434
Manchester U: Schmeichel; Brown, Irwin (Johnsen 46), Neville G, Keane, Stam, Beckham, Scholes, Cole, Yorke (Butt 64), Giggs.
Bayern Munich: Kahn; Babbel, Matthaus (Linke 61), Kuffour, Strunz, Jeremies, Effenberg, Lizarazu, Zickler (Basler 82), Elber (Jancker 82), Salihamidzic.

GROUP E

16 SEPT

Lens (0) 1 *(Vairelles 90)*
Arsenal (0) 1 *(Overmars 51)* 36,000
Lens: Warmuz; Sikora, Meride (Rool 76), Dehu, Etchi (Sankhare 82), Nyarko, Debeve, Dalmat, Smicer, Nouma (Moreira 70), Vairelles.
Arsenal: Seaman; Dixon, Winterburn, Vieira, Keown, Adams, Parlour, Anelka, Petit (Hughes 72), Bergkamp (Garde 89), Overmars.

30 SEPT

Arsenal (0) 2 *(Adams 64, Keown 72)*
Panathinaikos (0) 1 *(Mauro 87)* 73,455
Arsenal: Seaman; Dixon, Winterburn, Vieira, Keown, Adams, Garde (Vivas 79), Anelka, Petit, Bergkamp, Overmars.
Panathinaikos: Wandzik; Goumas, Milojevic, Konstantinidis, Kiassos (Kola 71), Mykland, Apostolakis, Asanovic, Lagonikakis, Liberopoulos (Sypniewski 84), Strandli (Mauro 84).
(at Wembley)

21 OCT

Arsenal (0) 1 *(Bergkamp 74)*
Dynamo Kiev (0) 1 *(Rebrov 90)* 73,256
Arsenal: Seaman; Dixon, Winterburn, Garde, Keown, Adams, Parlour, Anelka (Vivas 84), Hughes, Bergkamp, Overmars.
Dynamo Kiev: Shovkovskyi; Luzhny, Golovko, Vashchuk, Dmitrulin, Kaladze, Gusin (Kardash 82), Kossovski V, Belkevich, Rebrov, Shevchenko.
(at Wembley)

4 NOV

Dynamo Kiev (1) 3 *(Rebrov 26 (pen), Golovko 61, Shevchenko 72)*
Arsenal (0) 1 *(Hughes 84)* 80,000
Dynamo Kiev: Shovkovskyi; Luzhny, Golovko, Vashchuk, Dmitrulin, Kardash, Belkevich (Kalitvintsev 90), Gusin, Kossovski V, Rebrov, Shevchenko.
Arsenal: Seaman; Dixon, Winterburn, Vieira, Keown, Bould, Parlour, Vivas (Garde 83), Petit (Grimandi 46), Wreh, Boa Morte (Hughes 67).

25 NOV

Arsenal (0) 0
Lens (0) 1 *(Debeve 72)* 73,207
Arsenal: Seaman; Dixon, Winterburn, Garde (Vivas 68), Keown, Adams (Bould 46), Parlour, Anelka, Hughes, Wreh (Boa Morte 68), Overmars.
Lens: Warmuz; Sikora, Magnier, Dehu, Lachor, Debeve, Nyarko, Rool, Smicer (Moreira 80), Vairelles, Nouma (Eloi 59).
(at Wembley)

9 DEC

Panathinaikos (0) 1 *(Sypniewski 74)*
Arsenal (0) 3 *(Asanovic 66 (og), Anelka 79, Boa Morte 86)* 45,000
Panathinaikos: Wandzik; Apostolakis, Goumas, Milojevic, Basinas (Vokolos 78), Liberopoulos, Asanovic, Konstantinidis (Strandli 69), Lagonikakis, Kola (Sypniewski 56), Warzycha.
Arsenal: Seaman; Vivas, Grondin, Grimandi, Bould, Upson, Vernazza, Mendez (Black 77), Anelka, Wreh, Boa Morte.

QUARTER-FINALS, FIRST LEG

3 MAR

Manchester U (2) 2 *(Yorke 6, 45)*
Internazionale (0) 0 54,430
Manchester U: Schmeichel; Neville G, Irwin, Johnsen (Berg 46), Keane, Stam, Beckham, Scholes (Butt 68), Cole, Yorke, Giggs.
Internazionale: Pagliuca; Galante, Colonnese, Zanetti, Bergomi, Cauet, Simeone, Winter, Zamorano (Ventola 69), Djorkaeff, Roberto Baggio (Pirlo 79).

QUARTER-FINALS, SECOND LEG

17 MAR

Internazionale (0) 1 *(Ventola 63)*
Manchester U (0) 1 *(Scholes 88)*
Internazionale: Pagliuca; West, Colonnese, Zanetti, Bergomi (Moriero 70), Cauet, Simeone (Ze Elias 32), Silvestre, Zamorano, Ronaldo (Ventola 60), Roberto Baggio.
Manchester U: Schmeichel; Neville G, Irwin, Berg, Johnsen (Scholes 77), Stam, Beckham, Keane, Cole, Yorke, Giggs (Neville P).

SEMI-FINALS, FIRST LEG

7 APR

Manchester U (0) 1 *(Giggs 90)*   54,487
Juventus (1) 1 *(Conte 25)*
Manchester U: Schmeichel; Neville G, Irwin, Berg
(Johnsen 46), Keane, Stam, Beckham, Scholes, Cole,
Yorke (Sheringham 79), Giggs.
Juventus: Peruzzi; Mirkovic, Montero (Ferrara 68),
Iuliano, Pessotto, Conte, Deschamps, Davids, Di Livio
(Tacchinardi 77), Zidane, Inzaghi (Esnaider 88).

SEMI-FINALS, SECOND LEG

21 APR

Juventus (2) 2 *(Inzaghi 6, 10)*   65,500
Manchester U (2) 3 *(Keane 24, Yorke 34, Cole 84)*
Juventus: Peruzzi; Birindelli (Montero 46), Iuliano,
Ferrara, Pessotto, Conte, Deschamps, Davids, Di Livio
(Fonseca 80), Zidane, Inzaghi.
Manchester U: Schmeichel; Neville G, Irwin, Johnsen,
Keane, Stam, Beckham, Butt, Cole, Yorke, Blomqvist
(Scholes 68).

FINAL

(in Barcelona, 26 May 1999, 90,000)

Manchester U (0) 2 *(Sheringham 89, Solskjaer 90)*
Bayern Munich (1) 1 *(Basler 6)*
Manchester U: Schmeichel; Neville G, Irwin, Johnsen, Butt, Stam, Beckham, Blomqvist (Sheringham 66), Cole
(Solskjaer 80), Yorke, Giggs.
Bayern Munich: Kahn; Babbel, Tarnat, Linke, Matthaus (Fink 80), Kuffour, Basler (Salihamidzic 89), Effenberg,
Jancker, Zickler (Scholl 70), Jeremies.
Referee: Collina (Italy).

An injury time stab at the ball by Ole Gunnar Solskjaer provides Manchester United with a dramtic last gasp win over
Bayern Munich. (Actionimages)

EUROPEAN CUP-WINNERS' CUP

EUROPEAN CUP-WINNERS' CUP FINALS 1961–99

Year	Winners		Runners-up		Venue	Attendance	Referee
1961	Fiorentina	2	Rangers	0 *(1st Leg)*	Glasgow	80,000	Steiner (A)
	Fiorentina	2	Rangers	1 *(2nd Leg)*	Florence	50,000	Hernadi (H)
1962	Atletico Madrid	1	Fiorentina	1	Glasgow	27,389	Wharton (S)
Replay	Atletico Madrid	3	Fiorentina	0	Stuttgart	38,000	Tschenscher (WG)
1963	Tottenham Hotspur	5	Atletico Madrid	1	Rotterdam	49,000	Van Leuwen (Ho)
1964	Sporting Lisbon	3	MTK Budapest	3 *(aet)*	Brussels	3000	Van Nuffel (Bel)
Replay	Sporting Lisbon	1	MTK Budapest	0	Antwerp	19,000	Versyp (Bel)
1965	West Ham U	2	Munich 1860	0	Wembley	100,000	Szolt (H)
1966	Borussia Dortmund	2	Liverpool	1 *(aet)*	Glasgow	41,657	Schwinte (F)
1967	Bayern Munich	1	Rangers	0 *(aet)*	Nuremberg	69,480	Lo Bello (I)
1968	AC Milan	2	Hamburg	0	Rotterdam	53,000	Ortiz (Sp)
1969	Slovan Bratislava	3	Barcelona	2	Basle	19,000	Van Ravens (Ho)
1970	Manchester C	2	Gornik Zabrze	1	Vienna	8,000	Schiller (A)
1971	Chelsea	1	Real Madrid	1 *(aet)*	Athens	42,000	Scheurer (Sw)
Replay	Chelsea	2	Real Madrid	1 *(aet)*	Athens	35,000	Bucheli (Sw)
1972	Rangers	3	Moscow Dynamo	2	Barcelona	24,000	Ortiz (Sp)
1973	AC Milan	1	Leeds U	0	Salonika	45,000	Mihas (Gr)
1974	Magdeburg	2	AC Milan	0	Rotterdam	4000	Van Gemert (Ho)
1975	Dynamo Kiev	3	Ferencvaros	0	Basle	13,000	Davidson (S)
1976	Anderlecht	4	West Ham U	2	Brussels	58,000	Wurtz (F)
1977	Hamburg	2	Anderlecht	0	Amsterdam	65,000	Partridge (E)
1978	Anderlecht	4	Austria/WAC	0	Paris	48,679	Adlinger (WG)
1979	Barcelona	4	Fortuna Dusseldorf	3 *(aet)*	Basle	58,000	Palotai (H)
1980	Valencia	0	Arsenal	0	Brussels	36,000	Christov (Cz)
	(aet; Valencia won 5-4 on penalties)						
1981	Dynamo Tbilisi	2	Carl Zeiss Jena	1	Dusseldorf	9000	Lattanzi (I)
1982	Barcelona	2	Standard Liege	1	Barcelona	100,000	Eschweiler (WG)
1983	Aberdeen	2	Real Madrid	1 *(aet)*	Gothenburg	17,804	Menegali (I)
1984	Juventus	2	Porto	1	Basle	60,000	Prokop (EG)
1985	Everton	3	Rapid Vienna	1	Rotterdam	50,000	Casarin (I)
1986	Dynamo Kiev	3	Atletico Madrid	0	Lyon	39,300	Wohrer (A)
1987	Ajax	1	Lokomotiv Leipzig	0	Athens	35,000	Agnolin (I)
1988	Mechelen	1	Ajax	0	Strasbourg	39,446	Pauly (WG)
1989	Barcelona	2	Sampdoria	0	Berne	45,000	Courtney (E)
1990	Sampdoria	2	Anderlecht	0	Gothenburg	20,103	Galler (Sw)
1991	Manchester U	2	Barcelona	1	Rotterdam	42,000	Karlsson (Se)
1992	Werder Bremen	2	Monaco	0	Lisbon	16,000	D'Elia (I)
1993	Parma	3	Antwerp	1	Wembley	37,393	Assenmacher (G)
1994	Arsenal	1	Parma	0	Copenhagen	33,765	Krondl (Czr)
1995	Zaragoza	2	Arsenal	1	Paris	42,424	Ceccarini (I)
1996	Paris St Germain	1	Rapid Vienna	0	Brussels	37,500	Pairetto (I)
1997	Barcelona	1	Paris St Germain	0	Rotterdam	45,000	Merk (G)
1998	Chelsea	1	Stuttgart	0	Stockholm	30,216	Braschi (I)
1999	Lazio	2	Mallorca	1	Villa Park	33,021	Benko (A)

EUROPEAN CUP-WINNERS' CUP 1998-99

QUALIFYING ROUND, FIRST LEG
Amica (1) 4 *(Kryszalowicz 38, Sobocinski 62, 75, Przerada 56)*, Hibernians (0) 0
Apolonia (1) 1 *(Zeqo 25)*, Genk (3) 5 *(Strupar 30, Olivieri 35, Beniamin 40, Oulare 65, Horvas 79)* 4250
Bangor City (0) 0, Haka (1) 2 *(Niemi 40, Salli 59)* 1429
FC Copenhagen (4) 4 *(Nielsen M 2, Thorninger 6, Nielsen P 13, 40)*, Karabakh (2) 2 *(Goldbaek 20 (og), Falch 26)* 8750
Cork City (2) 2 *(Flanagan 20 (pen), Coughlan 42)*, CSKA Kiev (0) 1 *(Revut 90)* 4500
Ekranas (1) 1 *(Stumbrys 38)*, Apollon (1) 2 *(Spoljaric 17, Charalambos 90)* 1000
Glentoran (0) 0, Maccabi Haifa (1) 1 *(Mizrahi 23)* 2150
GI Gotu (1) 1 *(Olsen S 8)*, MTK Budapest (2) 3 *(Kenesei 17, Preisinger 19, Szekeres 90)* 800
Grevenmacher (1) 2 *(Krahen 38, 72)*, Rapid Bucharest (1) 6 *(Sabau 13, Pancu 64, Dulca 66, Stanci 69, Lupu 77 (pen), Mutica 82)* 1260
Lantana (0) 0, Hearts (1) 1 *(Makel 21)* 1000
Lausanne (1) 5 *(Celestini 28 (pen), 47, 59, 70, Cavin 87)*, Tsement (1) 1 *(Hovhanessian 36)* 4500
Levski (5) 8 *(Ivanov G 8, 32, Borisov 23, 44, 88, Donev 42, Radukanov 52, Todorov N 85)*, Lokomotiv 96 (0) 1 *(Demenkovets 49 (pen))* 9000
Metalurgs (0) 4 *(Bulders 61, 87, 88, Magdishauskas 90)*, IBK Keflavik (0) 2 *(Tanasik 60, Gilfason 90)* 2000
Partizan Belgrade (2) 2 *(Bjekovic N 17, Ilic 33)*, Dynamo Batumi (0) 0 12,000
Rudar (1) 2 *(Vidojevic 32, Sumnik 90)*, Constructorul (0) 0 3000
Vaduz (0) 0, Helsingborg (1) 2 *(Stavrum 9, Wibran 67)* 500
Vardar (0) 0, Spartak Trnava (1) 1 *(Urlaki 76)* 11,000

QUALIFYING ROUND, SECOND LEG
Apollon (0) 3 *(Spoljaric 52 (pen), 89 (pen), Kavazis 60)*, Ekranas (2) 3 *(Kalinisevas 6, Vileniskis 9, Varnas 90)* 6000
Constructorul (0) 0, Rudar (0) 0 8000
CSKA Kiev (1) 2 *(Tsykhmeistruk 42, Leonenko 56)*, Cork City (0) 0 5000
Dynamo Batumi (1) 1 *(Sichinava 28)*, Partizan Belgrade (0) 0 12,000
Genk (1) 4 *(Oulare 4, N'Sumbu 83, Strupar 85, 90)*, Apolonia (0) 0 6400
Haka (1) 1 *(Ruhanen 28)*, Bangor City (0) 0 2431
Hearts (3) 5 *(Hamilton 18, Fulton 29, McCann 41, Flogel 75, Holmes 89)*, Lantana (0) 0 15,053
Helsingborg (1) 3 *(Wibram 43, Edman 57, Powell 67)*, Vaduz (0) 0 3600
Hibernians (0) 0, Amica (0) 1 *(Kryszalowicz 70)* 2500
IBK Keflavik (1) 1 *(Jonsson M 29)*, Metalurgs (0) 0 1000
Karabakh (0) 0, FC Copenhagen (0) 4 *(Jensen 64, 70, Newson 75, 84)* 10,000
Lokomotiv 96 (0) 1 *(Sivkov 90)*, Levski (0) 1 *(Lazorev 50)* 2000
Maccabi Haifa (1) 2 *(Harazi 16 (pen), Mizrahi 80 (pen))*, Glentoran (1) 1 *(Batey 42)* 5000
MTK Budapest (3) 7 *(Kenesei 16, 71, 76, Preisinger 34, Halmai 37, Ilies 62, Balasko 73)*, GI Gotu (0) 0 1500
Rapid Bucharest (0) 2 *(Pancu 53, 88)*, Grevenmacher (0) 0 7000
Spartak Trnava (0) 2 *(Tittel 83, Fabio Luis Gomes 85)*, Vardar (0) 0 10,014
Tsement (1) 1 *(Asatryan 39)*, Lausanne (0) 2 *(Douglas 66, Hottinger 89)* 1500

FIRST ROUND, FIRST LEG
Apollon (1) 2 *(Kavazis 45, Kirstia 68)*, Jablonec (1) 1 *(Fukal 38)* 2000
Besiktas (2) 3 *(Mehmet 9, Oktay 21, Ohen 49)*, Spartak Trnava (0) 0 20,580
Chelsea (1) 1 *(Leboeuf 43)*, Helsingborg (0) 0 17,714
CSKA Kiev (0) 0, Lokomotiv Moscow (1) 2 *(Charlasjev 24, Janashia 51)* 6500
Duisburg (0) 1 *(Wedau 83)*, Genk (0) 1 *(Reini 61)* 10,602
Hearts (0) 0, Mallorca (1) 1 *(Marcelino 17)* 13,573
Heerenveen (2) 3 *(Talan 38, Mitrita 45, Pahlplatz 66)*, Amica (0) 1 *(Krol 63)* 12,100

Lazio (1) 1 *(Nedved 37)*, Lausanne (0) 1 *(Douglas 55)* 22,659
Levski (0) 0, FC Copenhagen (1) 2 *(Goldbaek 35 (pen), Thorninger 74)* 2500
Metalurgs (0) 0, Braga (0) 0 6000
Newcastle U (1) 2 *(Shearer 12, Dabizas 71)*, Partizan Belgrade (0) 1 *(Rasovic 69 (pen))* 26,599
Panionios (1) 2 *(Haylock 35, Robins 54)*, Haka (0) 0 3500
Paris St Germain (0) 1 *(Simone 83 (pen))*, Maccabi Haifa (0) 1 *(Benayoun 86)* 30,000
Rapid Bucharest (0) 2 *(Sumidica 51, Bundea 75)*, Valerengen (0) 2 *(Carew 52, 88)* 2350
Ried (1) 2 *(Strafner 20, Brunmayr 64)*, MTK Budapest (0) 0 4500
Rudar (0) 0, Varteks (0) 1 *(Matas 90)* 850

FIRST ROUND, SECOND LEG
Amica (0) 0, Heerenveen (1) 1 *(Dennis de Nooijer 30)* 3000
Braga (2) 4 *(Bruno 12 (pen), 60, Karoglan 35, Silva 84)*, Metalurgs (0) 0 8000
FC Copenhagen (1) 4 *(Nielsen M 18, Hoyer-Nielsen 49, Thorninger 59, 79), Duisburg (0) 0* 17,200
Genk (2) 5 *(Oulare 13, 49, Strupar 32, Gudjonsson 73, 79)*, Duisburg (0) 0 17,200
Haka (0) 1 *(Salli 75)*, Panionios (2) 3 *(Fryssas 32, Kouvalis 45, Sapountis 56)* 1700
Helsingborg (0) 0, Chelsea (0) 0 12,348
Jablonec (2) 2 *(Prochazka 24, 45)*, Apollon (0) 1 *(Themistocleous 59) Apollon won 4-3 on penalties* 3100
Lausanne (1) 2 *(Douglas 9, Rehn 84)*, Lazio (2) 2 *(Salas 7, Conseicao 26)* 12,000
Lokomotiv Moscow (1) 3 *(Boelikin 19, 51, Janashia 70)*, CSKA Kiev (1) 1 *(Bezhenar 13)* 5000
Maccabi Haifa (0) 3 *(Keysi 58, Mizrahi 77, 90)*, Paris St Germain (0) 2 *(Ouedec 72, Okocha 86)* 14,000
Mallorca (0) 1 *(Lopez 49)*, Hearts (0) 0 *(Hamilton 75)* 12,218
MTK Budapest (0) 0, Ried (1) 1 *(Strafner 10)* 5000
Partizan Belgrade (0) 1 *(Rasovic 53 (pen))*, Newcastle U (0) 0 26,000
Spartak Trnava (0) 2 *(Formanko 49, Timko 71)*, Besiktas (1) 1 *(Oktay 45)* 6546
Valerengen (0) 0, Rapid Bucharest (0) 0 6257
Varteks (1) 1 *(Kamberovic 7)*, Rudar (0) 0 5000

SECOND ROUND, FIRST LEG
Chelsea (0) 1 *(Desailly 90)*, FC Copenhagen (0) 1 *(Goldbaek 80)* 21,207
Genk (0) 1 *(Oulare 71)*, Mallorca (0) 1 *(Dani 56)* 24,046
Heerenveen (0) 2 *(Dennis de Nooijer 56, Hansma 90)*, Varteks (0) 1 *(Mumlek 63)* 12,200
Lazio (0) 0, Partizan Belgrade (0) 0 45,000
Lokomotiv Moscow (2) 3 *(Boelikin 22, 35, Chugainov 68)*, Braga (0) 1 *(Odair 46)* 12,000
Panionios (2) 3 *(Sapountis 25, Haylock 40, Robins 58)*, Apollon (2) 2 *(Spoljaric 14, 43)* 5000
Ried (1) 2 *(Sliwowski 22, Strafner 88)*, Maccabi Haifa (1) 1 *(Mizrahi 13)* 5000
Valerengen (0) 1 *(Levemes 48)*, Besiktas (0) 0 6284

SECOND ROUND, SECOND LEG
Apollon (0) 0, Panionios (1) 1 *(Sapountis 18)* 8000
Besiktas (3) 3 *(Derelioglu 7, 42, Havutcu 38)*, Valerengen (0) 3 *(Haraldsen 62, Kaasa 66, Carew 72)* 25,000
Braga (1) 1 *(Karoglan 11)*, Lokomotiv Moscow (0) 0 14,000
FC Copenhagen (0) 0, Chelsea (1) 1 *(Laudrup 32)* 25,188
Maccabi Haifa (1) 4 *(Mizrahi 35, Keyse 62, Benayoun 75, Duro 90)*, Ried (0) 1 *(Anicic 70)* 17,100
Mallorca (0) 0, Genk (0) 0 15,000
Partizan Belgrade (1) 2 *(Kristajic 18, Iliev 85)*, Lazio (1) 3 *(Salas 43 (pen), 76, Stankovic 67)* 32,000
Varteks (0) 4 *(Mumiek 65, 117, Kamberovic 80, 99)*, Heerenveen (1) 2 *(Samardzic 18, De Visser 114)* 6000

QUARTER-FINALS, FIRST LEG
Chelsea (2) 3 *(Babayaro 10, Zola 30, Wise 85)*,
  Valerengen (0) 0   34,177
Lokomotiv Moscow (0) 3 *(Janashia 47, 77, 89)*,
  Maccabi Haifa (0) 0   23,000
Panionios (0) 0, Lazio (2) 4 *(Stankovic 3, 60,*
  Gazis 14 (og), Nedved 63)   11,000
Varteks (0) 0, Mallorca (0) 0   10,000

QUARTER-FINALS, SECOND LEG
Lazio (0) 3 *(Nedved 69, Stankovic 72, De la Pena 81)*,
  Panionios (0) 0   20,448
Maccabi Haifa (0) 0, Lokomotiv Moscow (0) 1
  (Chugainov 72 (pen))   16,000

Mallorca (0) 3 *(Ibagaza 53, Paunovic 55, Dani 75)*,
  Varteks (0) 1 *(Kamberovic 90)*   15,000
Valerengen (2) 2 *(Kjolner 27, Carew 41)*, Chelsea (3) 3
  (Vialli 11, Lambourde 15, Flo 33) 17,936

SEMI-FINALS, FIRST LEG
Chelsea (0) 1 *(Flo 50)*, Mallorca (1) 1 *(Dani 31)* 35,524
Lokomotiv Moscow (0) 1 *(Janashia 60)*, Lazio (0) 1
  (Boksic 76)   20,000

SEMI-FINALS, SECOND LEG
Lazio (0) 0, Lokomotiv Moscow (0) 0   25,000
Mallorca (1) 1 *(Biagini 15)*, Chelsea (0) 0 18,848

FINAL

Mallorca (1) 1, Lazio (1) 2

(at Villa Park, 19 May 1999, 33,021)

Mallorca: Roa; Olaizola, Soler M, Lauren, Marcelino, Siviero, Engonga, Ibagaza, Biagini (Paunovic 73), Dani,
  Stankovic.
Scorer: Dani 11.
Lazio: Marchegiani; Pancaro, Favalli, Almeyda, Mihajlovic, Nesta, Stankovic (Conceicao 56), Mancini (Fernando
  Couto 89), Vieri, Salas, Nedved (Lombardo 84).
Scorers: Vieri 7, Nedved 81.
Referee: Benko (Austria).

Christian Vieri, the most expensive player in the world, is tackled by the Mallorca defender Siviero, but Lazio won the
1999 European Cup-Winners' Cup Final 2-1 at Villa Park. (ASP)

EUROPEAN CUP-WINNERS' CUP 1998-99 – BRITISH AND IRISH CLUBS

QUALIFYING ROUND, FIRST LEG

13 AUG

Bangor City (0) 0
Haka (1) 2 *(Niemi 40, Salli 59)*   1429
Bangor City: Williams L; Williams G, Fox, Allen, McLoughlin, Horner, Hilditch, Taylor (Langley 83), Ayorinde, Garnell, McGoona (Wenham 53).
Haka: Vilnrotter; Heikkinen, Karjalainen, Salli, Rasanen, Makela, Ivanov (Okkonen 76), Harewood (Torkkeli 82), Popovitch, Ylonen, Niemi (Ruhanen 71).

Cork City (2) 2 *(Flanagan 20 (pen), Coughlan 42)*
CSKA Kiev (0) 1 *(Revut 90)*   4500
Cork City: Mooney; Daly, Coughlan, Hill, Cronin, O'Halloran (Caulfield 81), Flanagan, Freyne (Herrick 74), Murphy, Cahill, Hartigan (Kabia 72).
CSKA Kiev: Reva; Levchenko, Revut, Daraselia (Korvenev 57), Semchuk, Bezhenar, Oliynuk, Shkapenko, Zakarlyuka (Olexiyenko 33), Leonenko (Koriaka 46), Tsykhmeistruk.

Glentoran (0) 0
Maccabi Haifa (1) 1 *(Mizrahi 23)*   2150
Glentoran: Russell; Nixon, Kennedy, Walker, Devine, Leeman, Mitchell (Quigley 80), Hamill (Rainey 90), Kirk (McCallen 65), Batey, Elliott.
Maccabi Haifa: Davidovitch; Balanchuk, Harazi, Benado, Keise, Elkayan, Kopel, Duro (Silvas 84), Mizrahi (Vilner 90), Hromadko (Benayouan 62), Zano.

Lantana (0) 0
Hearts (1) 1 *(Makel 21)*   1000
Lantana: Ussoltsev; Krasnopgrov, Kalimullin, Kolotsei, Bahmatski, Mitjunov, Borissov, Leitan (Tselnokov 78), Valuiski, Gorjatsov (Kulikov 80), Koulitchenko.
Hearts: Rousset; Naysmith, Weir, Salvatori, Ritchie, McCann, Adam (Murray 86), Hamilton (Quitongo 86), Locke, Flogel, Makel.

QUALIFYING ROUND, SECOND LEG

27 AUG

CSKA Kiev (1) 2 *(Tsykhmeistruk 42, Leonenko 56)*
Cork City (0) 0   5000
CSKA Kiev: Reva; Hrehul, Revut, Ulyanytsky, Semchuk, Bezhenar, Koriaka (Koryenev 33), Shkapenko, Zakarlyuka, Leonenko (Daraselia 64), Tsykhmeistruk.
Cork City: Mooney; Daly, Coughlan, Hill, Cronin, O'Halloran, Flanagan (Caulfield 82), Freyne, Murphy B (Dobbs 57), Cahill, Hartigan (Kabia 57).

Haka (1) 1 *(Ruhanen 28)*
Bangor City (0) 0   2431
Haka: Vilnrotter; Heikkinen (Okkonen 78), Karjalainen, Salli, Rasanen, Makela, Ivanov, Ruhanen (Torkkeli 66), Popovitch, Ylonen, Niemi (Rantala 85).
Bangor City: Williams L; Mooney (Gibney 90), Fox, Allen, Horner, Hilditch, Lloyd, Taylor, Ayorinde, Garnell, Langley.

Hearts (3) 5 *(Hamilton 18, Fulton 29, McCann 41, Flogel 75, Holmes 89)*
Lantana (0) 0   15,053
Hearts: Rousset; Weir, Ritchie, McCann, Fulton, Adam (Quitongo 60), Hamilton (Flogel 60), Locke, Makel (Holmes 76), McKinnon, Pressley.
Lantana: Ussoltsev; Krasnopgrov, Kolotsei, Bahmatski, Mitjunov, Leitan, Valuiski (Tselnokov 80), Gorjatsov, Koulitchenko, Tjunin, Kulikov.

Maccabi Haifa (1) 2 *(Harazi 16 (pen), Mizrahi 80 (pen))*
Glentoran (1) 1 *(Batey 42)*   5000
Maccabi Haifa: Davidovitch; Balanchuk, Harazi, Benado, Keise, Elkayan, Kopel (Silvas 63), Duro (Benayouan 78), Mizrahi, Hromadko, Zano.
Glentoran: Russell; Nixon, Kennedy, Walker, Devine, Leeman, Mitchell, Hamill, Rainey (Elliott 77), Batey (Livingstone 83), McBridge (Kirk 83).

FIRST ROUND, FIRST LEG

17 SEPT

Chelsea (1) 1 *(Leboeuf 43)*
Helsingborg (0) 0   17,714
Chelsea: Kharine; Ferrer, Le Saux, Babayaro (Poyet 62), Leboeuf, Desailly, Laudrup, Di Matteo, Vialli (Nicholls 86), Flo (Casiraghi 55), Wise.
Helsingborg: Andersson S; Nilsson, Jakobsson, Jovanovski, Edman, Stavrum (Wahlstedt 66), Wibran, Lantz, Strovik (Ljung 90), Johansen (Jonsson 73), Powell.

Hearts (0) 0
Mallorca (1) 1 *(Marcelino 17)*   13,573
Hearts: Rousset; McPherson, Naysmith, Weir, Salvatori, Ritchie, McCann, Adam, Hamilton (Holmes 82), Locke, Pressley.
Mallorca: Roa; Soler, Siviero, Marcelino, Garcia, Stankovic (Carreras 85), Bisa, Olaizola, Arpon (Nino 87), Engonga, Lopez (Dominguez 70).

Newcastle U (1) 2 *(Shearer 12, Dabizas 71)*
Partizan Belgrade (0) 1 *(Rasovic 69 (pen))*   26,599
Newcastle U: Given; Watson, Pearce, Glass, Charvet, Dabizas, Lee, Andersson (Solano 46), Shearer, Ketsbaia, Speed.
Partizan Belgrade: Damjanac; Savic, Stojanoski, Rasovic, Krstajic, Trobok, Ivic (Pazin 74), Ilic, Tomic, Bjekovic (Stojisavljevic 86), Obradovic.

FIRST ROUND, SECOND LEG

1 OCT

Helsingborg (0) 0
Chelsea (0) 0   12,348
Helsingborg: Andersson S; Nilsson, Jovanovski, Jacobsen, Edman (Andersson C 83), Wibran, Lantz, Storvik, Stavrum (Johansen 62), Powell, Jonsson (Wahlstedt 72).
Chelsea: De Goey; Ferrer, Le Saux, Duberry, Leboeuf, Desailly, Poyet, Di Matteo, Vialli (Casiraghi 90), Flo, Babayaro.

Mallorca (0) 1 *(Lopez 49)*
Hearts (0) 1 *(Hamilton 75)*   12,218
Mallorca: Galvez; Soler M, Siviero, Marcelino, Dani (Nino 80), Stankovic, Etame Mayer, Olaizola, Soler F (Carreras 85), Arpon, Lopez (Biagini 81).
Hearts: Rousset; Naysmith, Weir, Salvatori, Ritchie, McCann (Holmes 52), Adam, Hamilton, Locke, Makel (McPherson 78), Pressley.

Partizan Belgrade (0) 0 *(Rasovic 53 (pen))*
Newcastle U (0) 0   26,000
Partizan Belgrade: Damjanac; Savic, Stojanoski, Rasovic, Krstajic (Stojisavljevic 46), Trobok, Ivic, Ilic, Tomic, Bjekovic (Tesovic 79), Kezman (Pazin 64).
Newcastle U: Given; Griffin (Albert 73), Pearce, Batty, Charvet, Dabizas, Glass, Solano, Shearer, Ketsbaia, Speed.

SECOND ROUND, FIRST LEG

22 OCT

Chelsea (0) 1 *(Desailly 90)*

FC Copenhagen (0) 1 *(Goldbaek 80)*   21,207

Chelsea: De Goey; Ferrer (Petrescu 69), Le Saux, Di Matteo, Leboeuf, Desailly, Laudrup, Poyet, Zola, Casiraghi (Flo 69), Wise.
FC Copenhagen: Stensgaard; Rytter (Madsen 65), Michael Nielsen, Haren, Jensen, Goldbaek, Hemmingsen, Nielsen L (Falch 84), Thorninger (Jonsson 72), Nielsen P, Nielsen D.

SECOND ROUND, SECOND LEG

5 NOV

FC Copenhagen (0) 0

Chelsea (1) 1 *(Laudrup 32)*   25,118

FC Copenhagen: Stensgaard; Rytter, Michael Nielsen, Haren (Larsson M 88), Jensen, Goldbaek, Hemmingsen, Nielsen L, Thorninger (Jonsson 57), Nielsen P, Nielsen D.
Chelsea: De Goey; Ferrer, Le Saux, Babayaro, Leboeuf, Desailly, Laudrup (Petrescu 67), Di Matteo, Zola (Flo 76), Casiraghi (Poyet 89), Wise.

QUARTER-FINALS, FIRST LEG

4 MAR

Chelsea (2) 3 *(Babayaro 10, Zola 30, Wise 85)*

Valerengen (0) 0   34,177

Chelsea: De Goey; Ferrer, Le Saux, Babayaro, Lambourde, Desailly, Petrescu, Di Matteo, Vialli, Zola (Flo 46), Wise.
Valerengen: Kaven; Berntsen, Haraldsen, Kjolner, Tran, Haug (Kaasa 58), Walltin, Levernes (Simpson 85), Hovi, Riisnaes, Carew.

QUARTER-FINALS, SECOND LEG

18 MAR

Valerengen (2) 2 *(Kjolner 27, Carew 41)*

Chelsea (3) 3 *(Vialli 11, Lambourde 15, Flo 33)*   17,936

Valerengen: Kaven; Berntsen, Haraldsen, Knolner, Tran, Hovi (Haug 75), Walltin, Levernes, Simpson (Thorsen 69), Riisnaes, Carew (Museus 84).
Chelsea: De Goey; Terry, Le Saux, Babayaro (Myers 46), Lambourde, Duberry, Petrescu, Di Matteo, Vialli, Flo (Nicholls 46), Wise (Newton 46).

SEMI-FINALS, FIRST LEG

8 APR

Chelsea (0) 1 *(Flo 50)*

Mallorca (1) 1 *(Dani 31)*   35,524

Chelsea: De Goey; Ferrer (Lambourde 81), Le Saux, Babayaro (Flo 46), Leboeuf, Desailly, Petrescu, Morris, Vialli, Zola (Poyet 60), Wise.
Mallorca: Roa; Olaizola, Marcelino, Siviero, Soler M, Lauren, Ibagaza (Carreras 62), Engonga, Paunovic, Dani, Biagini (Soler F 75).

SEMI-FINALS, SECOND LEG

22 APR

Mallorca (1) 1 *(Biagini 15)*

Chelsea (0) 0   18,848

Mallorca: Roa; Olaizola, Marcelino, Siviero (Carreras 46), Soler M, Lauren, Engonga, Paunovic, Stankovic (Arpon 80), Dani, Biagini (Soler F 67).
Chelsea: De Goey; Ferrer, Le Saux (Babayaro 46), Di Matteo, Leboeuf, Desailly, Petrescu (Morris 78), Poyet, Flo, Zola, Wise.

Chelsea's challenge in the Cup-Winners' Cup took them creditably to the semi-final. Here, Tore Andre Flo attempts to get the better of the Valerengen defender Fredrik Kjolner. (Colorsport)

INTER-CITIES FAIRS & UEFA CUP

FAIRS CUP FINALS 1958–71
(Winners in italics)

Year	First Leg	Attendance	Second Leg	Attendance
1958	London 2 Barcelona 2	45,466	*Barcelona* 6 London 0	62,000
1960	Birmingham C 0 Barcelona 0	40,500	*Barcelona* 4 Birmingham C 1	70,000
1961	Birmingham C 2 Roma 2	21,005	*Roma* 2 Birmingham C 0	60,000
1962	Valencia 6 Barcelona 2	65,000	Barcelona 1 *Valencia* 1	60,000
1963	Dynamo Zagreb 1 Valencia 2	40,000	*Valencia* 2 Dynamo Zagreb 0	55,000
1964	*Zaragoza* 2 Valencia 1	50,000	(in Barcelona)	
1965	*Ferencvaros* 1 Juventus 0	25,000	(in Turin)	
1966	Barcelona 0 Zaragoza 1	70,000	Zaragoza 2 *Barcelona* 4	70,000
1967	Dynamo Zagreb 2 Leeds U 0	40,000	Leeds U 0 *Dynamo Zagreb* 0	35,604
1968	Leeds U 1 Ferencvaros 0	25,368	Ferencvaros 0 *Leeds U* 0	70,000
1969	Newcastle U 3 Ujpest Dozsa 0	60,000	Ujpest Dozsa 2 *Newcastle U* 3	37,000
1970	Anderlecht 3 Arsenal 1	37,000	*Arsenal* 3 Anderlecht 0	51,612
1971	Juventus 0 Leeds U 0 *(abandoned 51 minutes)*	42,000		
	Juventus 2 Leeds U 2	42,000	*Leeds U* 1* Juventus 1	42,483

UEFA CUP FINALS 1972–97
(Winners in italics)

Year	First Leg	Attendance	Second Leg	Attendance
1972	Wolverhampton W 1 Tottenham H 2	45,000	*Tottenham H* 1 Wolverhampton W 1	48,000
1973	Liverpool 0 Moenchengladbach 0			
	(abandoned 27 minutes)	44,967		
	Liverpool 3 Moenchengladbach 0	41,169	Moenchengladbach 2 *Liverpool* 0	35,000
1974	Tottenham H 2 Feyenoord 2	46,281	*Feyenoord* 2 Tottenham H 0	68,000
1975	Moenchengladbach 0 Twente 0	45,000	Twente 1 *Moenchengladbach* 5	24,500
1976	Liverpool 3 FC Brugge 2	56,000	FC Brugge 1 *Liverpool* 1	32,000
1977	Juventus 1 Athletic Bilbao 0	75,000	Athletic Bilbao 2 *Juventus* 1*	43,000
1978	Bastia 0 PSV Eindhoven 0	15,000	*PSV Eindhoven* 3 Bastia 0	27,000
1979	Red Star Belgrade 1 Moenchengladbach 1	87,500	*Moenchengladbach* 1 Red Star Belgrade 0	45,000
1980	Moenchengladbach 3 Eintracht Frankfurt 2	25,000	*Eintracht Frankfurt* 1* Moenchengladbach 0	60,000
1981	Ipswich T 3 AZ 67 Alkmaar 0	27,532	AZ 67 Alkmaar 4 *Ipswich T* 2	28,500
1982	Gothenburg 1 Hamburg 0	42,548	Hamburg 0 *Gothenburg* 3	60,000
1983	Anderlecht 1 Benfica 0	45,000	Benfica 1 *Anderlecht* 1	80,000
1984	Anderlecht 1 Tottenham H 1	40,000	*Tottenham H* 1[1] Anderlecht 1	46,258
1985	Videoton 0 Real Madrid 3	30,000	*Real Madrid* 0 Videoton 1	98,300
1986	Real Madrid 5 Cologne 1	80,000	Cologne 2 *Real Madrid* 0	15,000
1987	Gothenburg 1 Dundee U 0	50,023	Dundee U 1 *Gothenburg* 1	20,911
1988	Espanol 3 Bayer Leverkusen 0	42,000	*Bayer Leverkusen* 3[2] Espanol 0	22,000
1989	Napoli 2 Stuttgart 1	83,000	Stuttgart 3 *Napoli* 3	67,000
1990	Juventus 3 Fiorentina 1	45,000	Fiorentina 0 *Juventus* 0	32,000
1991	Internazionale 2 Roma 0	68,887	Roma 1 *Internazionale* 0	70,901
1992	Torino 2 Ajax 2	65,377	*Ajax* 0* Torino 0	40,000
1993	Borussia Dortmund 1 Juventus 3	37,000	*Juventus* 3 Borussia Dortmund 0	62,781
1994	Salzburg 0 Internazionale 1	47,500	*Internazionale* 1 Salzburg 0	80,326
1995	Parma 1 Juventus 0	23,000	Juventus 1 *Parma* 1	80,750
1996	Bayern Munich 2 Bordeaux 0	62,000	Bordeaux 1 *Bayern Munich* 3	36,000
1997	Schalke 1 Internazionale 0	56,824	Internazionale 1 *Schalke* 0[3]	81,670

*won on away goals   [1]*Tottenham H won 4-3 on penalties aet*   [2]*Bayer Leverkusen won 3-2 on penalties aet*
[3]*Schalke won 4-1 on penalties aet*

UEFA CUP FINALS 1998–99

Year	Winners	Runners-up	Venue	Attendance	Referee
1998	Internazionale 3	Lazio 0	Paris	42,938	Nieto (Sp)
1999	Parma 3	Marseille 0	Moscow	61,000	Dallas (S)

UEFA CUP 1998–99

FIRST QUALIFYING ROUND, FIRST LEG
Arges (2) 5 *(Emirbakan 3 (og), Barbu 5, 82 (pen),*
  Birdes 26, Jilaveanu 89), Dynamo Baku (1) 1
  (Aliev 37 (pen)) 5000
Belshina (0) 0, CSKA Sofia (0) 0 4000
Donetsk (0) 2 *(Seleznyov 62, Kriventsov 66 (pen)),*
  Birkirkara (0) 1 *(Zammit 77)* 10,000
Ekeren (3) 4 *(Van Ankeren 26, Morhaye 29, 90,*
  Kovac 34), Sarajevo (0) 1 *(Feratovic 59)* 5000
Ferencvaros (2) 6 *(Fulop 25, Selimi 42, Schultz 48, 75,*
  Vamosi 63, Matyus 90), Principat (0) 0 4000
Hapoel Tel Aviv (1) 3 *(Simerotic 30 (pen), Tubi 53,*
  Tikva 64), FinnPa (1) 1 *(Hautala 45)* 6000
HB Torshavn (1) 2 *(Johannesen S F 28, 71),*
  VPS Vaasa (0) 0 430
IA Akranes (1) 3 *(Adolfsson 46, Eyjolfsson 61, Ivsic 86),*
  Zalgiris (1) 2 *(Skinderis 11, Vasiliauskas 72)* 980
Inter Bratislava (1) 2 *(Suchancok 14, Miklos 58),*
  SK Tirana (0) 0 1798
Kolkheti (0) 0, Red Star Belgrade (1) 4 *(Ognjenovic 20,*
  Acimovic 55, 75, Pantelic 63) (in Poti) 10,000
Mura (5) 6 *(Cifer 6, 32, Lukic 17, 88, Sipot 30, Galic 39),*
  Daugava (0) 1 *(Ridnyi 75)* 2500
Newtown (0) 0, Wisla (0) 0 1475
Omonia (2) 5 *(Kitanov 40, 60, Rauffman 43 (pen),*
  Panayiotou 65, Kontolefteros 88), Linfield (0) 1
  (Ferguson 79) 5000
Otelul (2) 3 *(Stefan 30, Mihalache 41, Males 88 (pen)),*
  Sloga (0) 0 5000
Sadam (0) 0, Polonia (1) 2 *(Olisadebe 34, Bak 80)* 750
Shelbourne (2) 3 *(Porrini 7 (og), Rutherford 41,*
  Morley 58), Rangers (0) 5 *(Albertz 59 (pen), 85 (pen),*
  Amato 74, 82, Van Bronckhorst 75) (at Tranmere) 6047
Shirak (0) 0, Malmo (0) 2 *(Pavlovic 55, Ohlsson 68)*
  (in Erevan) 2000
Tiligul (0) 0, Anderlecht (0) 1 *(Staelens 51)* 6000
Union Luxembourg (0) 0, IFK Gothenburg (0) 3
  (Ekstrom 58, Nilsson M 63 (pen), Hermansson 86) 500
Zeljeznicar (0) 1 *(Vazda 66),* Kilmarnock (0) 2
  (McGowne 55) 15,000

FIRST QUALIFYING ROUND, SECOND LEG
Anderlecht (2) 5 *(Stoica 31, De Boeck 42, Dheedene 55,*
  Taument 59, Aarst 77), Tiligul (0) 0 5000
Birkirkara (0) 0, Donetsk (1) 4 *(Seleznyov 39,*
  Kriventsov 48, Kovalev 81 (pen), 90) 4800
CSKA Sofia (2) 3 *(Petrov 5, Naidenov 37, Stanchev 90),*
  Belshina (0) 1 *(Balashov 50)* 8000
Daugava (0) 1 *(Sharando 69),* Mura (0) 2
  (Vogrinchich 59, Ristich 66) 1000
Dynamo Baku (0) 0, Arges (0) 2 *(Mutu 51,*
  Jilavianu 90) 3000
FinnPa (0) 1 *(Geagea 88),* Hapoel Tel Aviv (2) 3
  (Tikva 5, 18, Tobi 74) 671
IFK Gothenburg (1) 4 *(Ekstrom 17, 50, 79, Henriksson*
  71), Union Luxembourg (0) 0 3073
Kilmarnock (0) 0 *(Mahood 31),* Zeljeznicar (0) 0 14,512
Linfield (3) 5 *(Feeney 19, Gorman 35, 48, McDonald 45,*
  Ferguson 72), Omonia (3) 3 *(Marantos 2, Kitanov 15,*
  Ioakim 23) 2000
Malmo (3) 5 *(Thylander 19, Kindvall 33, 45, 77,*
  Gudmundsson 68), Shirak (0) 0 2091
Polonia (3) 3 *(Moskal 8, Wedzynski 16, Bak 21),*
  Sadam (1) 1 *(Krylov 3)* 1000
Principat (1) 1 *(Pasqui 24),* Ferencvaros (2) 8
  (Selimi 18, 74, Kovacs 23, 83, Kriston 51, Nagy 52,
  Jagodics 58, Schultz 84) 500
Rangers (1) 2 *(Johansson 4, 89),* Shelbourne (0) 0 46,906
Red Star Belgrade (2) 7 *(Pantelic 28,Ognjenovic 45 (pen),*
  47, Gojkovic 54, Micic 57, 69, 90),
  Kolkheti (0) 0 7000
Sarajevo (0) 0, Ekeren (0) 0 12,000
SK Tirana (0) 0, Inter Bratislava (0) 2 *(Balonic 55,*
  Miklos 82) 3000
Sloga (1) 1 *(Stankovski 41),* Otelul (1) 1
  (Mihalache 58) 2000
VPS Vaasa (2) 4 *(Suoste 3, 17, Tarkkio 72, Nygard 90),*
  HB Torshavn (0) 0 2500
Wisla (2) 7 *(Kulawik 28, 47, Sunday 35, Kaliciak 51,*
  Dubicki 54, Pater 61, 66), Newtown (0) 0 7500
Zalgiris (1) 1 *(Steshko 11),* IA Akranes (0) 0 2000

SECOND QUALIFYING ROUND, FIRST LEG
Arges (2) 2 *(Mutu 33, Barbu 45),* Istanbul (0) 0 11,000
Brann (0) 1 *(Kvisvik 75),* Zalgiris (0) 0 7250
Ekeren (0) 1 *(Morhaye 85),* Servette (2) 4 *(Rey 21 (pen),*
  51, Wolf 36, Durix 79) 5000
Ferencvaros (2) 4 *(Selimi 10, Lendval 29, Nyilasi 55,*
  Vincze 83), AEK Athens (0) 2 *(Nikolaidis 89,*
  Sebwe 90) 8000
Hajduk Split (1) 1 *(Brajkovic 44),* Malmo (0) 1
  (Bjarnason 72) 13,000
Hapoel Tel Aviv (0) 1 *(Tubi 75),*
  Stromsgodset (0) 0 11,250
IFK Gothenburg (1) 2 *(Hermansson 37, Persson 74),*
  Fenerbache (0) 1 *(Kemaletin 49)* 15,000
Molde (0) 0, CSKA Sofia (0) 0 2500
Mura (0) 0, Silkeborg (0) 0 9000
Olomouc (1) 2 *(Krohmer 26, Konig 78),*
  Kilmarnock (0) 0 4200
Omonia (1) 3 *(Rauffman 42, 57, Malekos 47),*
  Rapid Vienna (1) 1 *(Wagner R)* 6000
Osijek (1) 3 *(Krpan 29, Prisc 54, Vranjes 81),*
  Anderlecht (0) 1 *(Claeys 80)* 17,000
Polonia (0) 0, Dynamo Moscow (0) 1 *(Guseyev 54)* 8000
Rangers (0) 2 *(Kanchelskis 55, Wallace 68),*
  PAOK Salonika (0) 0 35,392
Red Star Belgrade (0) 2 *(Skoric 60, Ognjenovic 90 (pen)),*
  Volgograd (0) 1 *(Abramov 66)* 20,000
Slavia Prague (1) 4 *(Vagner 23, 90, Kozel 55, Skala 72),*
  Inter Bratislava (0) 0 16,000
Vejle (2) 3 *(Wael 31, 41, Soegaard 62),* Otelul (0) 0 4000
VPS Vaasa (0) 0, Graz (0) 0 2500
Wisla (2) 5 *(Dubicki 3, Kowalik 33, 71, 80, Zajac 89),*
  Trabzonspor (0) 1 *(Vugrinec 66)* 9000
Zurich (1) 4 *(Sant'Anna 1, Djordjevic 61, Chassot 71,*
  Tarone 88), Donetsk (0) 0 5000

SECOND QUALIFYING ROUND, SECOND LEG
AEK Athens (3) 4 *(Nikolaidis 8 (pen), 13 (pen), 26 (pen),*
  Donis 63), Ferencvaros (0) 0 24,000
Anderlecht (1) 2 *(Aarst 4, Stoica 85),* Osijek (0) 0 13,000
CSKA Sofia (1) 2 *(Petkov 39, Stanchev 60),*
  Molde (0) 0 8000
Donetsk (1) 3 *(Orbu 25, 69, Shtolkers 90),* Zurich (2) 2
  (Bartlett 19, 28) 10,000
Dynamo Moscow (0) 1 *(Terekhin 89),* Polonia (0) 0 4000
Fenerbahce (0) 1 *(Balgic 64),* IFK
  Gothenburg (0) 0 25,000
Graz (0) 3 *(Luhovy 51, Grimm 54, Drechsel 90),*
  VPS Vaasa (0) 0 5000
Inter Bratislava (1) 2 *(Babnic 12, Ovad 52),*
  Slavia Prague (0) 0 3474
Istanbul (2) 4 *(Saffet 14, Sergen 20, Mehmet 78,*
  Aykut 86), Arges (0) 2 *(Mutu 53, Barbu 73)* 25,000
Kilmarnock (0) 0, Olomouc (2) 2 *(Heinz 13,*
  Mucha 90) 11,140
Malmo (0) 1 *(Ohlsson 90),* Hajduk Split (1) 2
  (Vucko 41, 55) 4453
Otelul (0) 0, Vejle (2) 3 *(Jung 21, Graulund 35,*
  Wael 53) 12,000
PAOK Salonika (0) 0, Rangers (0) 0 32,000
Rapid Vienna (1) 2 *(Heraf 9, Wagner 70),*
  Omonia (0) 0 14,500
Servette (0) 1 *(Rey 83 (pen)),* Ekeren (2) 2
  (Karlen 6 (og), Karagiannis 43) 5853
Silkeborg (0) 2 *(Sorensen 63, Larsen 64),* Mura (0) 0 2550
Stromsgodset (1) 1 *(Michelsen 42),* Hapoel Tel
  Aviv (0) 0 2160
Stromsgodset won 4-2 on penalties.
Trabzonspor (0) 1 *(Huseyin 67),* Wisla (0) 2
  (Sunday 53, Kulawik 62) 20,000
Volgograd (0) 1 *(Zernov 59),* Red Star Belgrade (0) 2
  (Ognjenovic 70, Dudic 80) 10,000
Zalgiris (0) 0, Brann (0) 0 1100

FIRST ROUND, FIRST LEG
Anderlecht (0) 0, Grasshoppers (0) 2 *(Comisetti 51,*
  Tikva 85) 10,000
Arges (0) 0, Celta Vigo (1) 1 *(Sanchez 25)* 12,000
Aston Villa (0) 3 *(Charles 83, Vassell 89, 90),*
  Stromsgodset (2) 2 *(Michelsen 21, George 23)* 28,893
Atletico Madrid (1) 2 *(Juninho 15, Jose Mari 52),*
  Obilic (0) 0 22,000

Beitar Jerusalem (1) 1 *(Abukasis 16 (pen))*, Rangers (0) 1
  (Albertz 84) 14,000
Blackburn Rovers (0) 0, Lyon (0) 1 *(Bak 85)* 13,646
Bordeaux (1) 1 *(Hatz 23 (og))*, Rapid Vienna (0) 1
  (Freund 65) 13,000
Branik Maribor (0) 0, Wisla (2) 2 *(Frankowski 22,*
  Pater 45) 6500
Brann (1) 2 *(Moen 29, Lovvik 48)*, Werder
  Bremen (0) 0 5281
Dynamo Moscow (1) 2 *(Golovskoi 2, Ostrovski 69)*,
  Skonto Riga (1) 2 *(Mikholop 39, Pakhar 49)* 6200
Fenerbahce (1) 1 *(Moldovan 23)*, Parma (0) 0 25,000
Fiorentina (0) 2 *(Edmundo 50, 81)*, Hajduk Split (1) 1
  (Vucko 45) 10,000
Guimaraes (0) 1 *(Geraldo 86)*, Celtic (1) 2 *(Larsson 1,*
  Donnelly 70) 8000
Kosice (0) 0, Liverpool (2) 3 *(Berger 18, Riedle 23,*
  Owen 59) 4500
Leeds United (0) 1 *(Hasselbaink 84)*,
  Maritimo (0) 0 38,033
Litets (0) 1 *(Stoilov 60)*, Graz (0) 1 *(Lipa 56)* 4000
LKS Lodz (1) 1 *(Metys 10)*, Monaco (0) 3
  (Bendowski 58 (og), Trezeguet 68 (pen),
  Spehar 82) 1000
Olomouc (2) 2 *(Heinz 37, 40)*, Marseille (1) 2
  (Ravanelli 26, Roy 85) 6558
Red Star Belgrade (2) 2 *(Ognjenovic 3, Drulic 12)*,
  Metz (0) 1 *(Rodriguez 90)* 45,000
Schalke (1) 1 *(Wilmots 40)*, Slavia Prague (0) 0 55,000
Servette (0) 2 *(Pizzinat 84, Melunovic 88)*,
  CSKA Sofia (1) 1 *(Stantsjev 45)* 5208
Silkeborg (0) 0, Roma (0) 2 *(Totti 62, Alenichev 70)* 4500
Sparta Prague (2) 2 *(Cizek 31, Lokvenc 39)*,
  Real Sociedad (1) 4 *(Kovacevic 8, 58, Aldeondo 48,*
  Adepoju 83) 8100
Sporting Lisbon (0) 0, Bologna (1) 2 *(Nervo 15,*
  Eriberto 90) 47,000
Steaua (1) 3 *(Lincar 30, Rosa 60, Dumitrescu 84)*,
  Valencia (2) 4 *(Ilie A 11, 24, Angulo 78, 86)* 17,000
Stuttgart (1) 1 *(Bobic 31)*, Feyenoord (3) 3
  (Van Gastel 19, Tomasson 21, 32) 24,000
Udinese (0) 1 *(Walem 81)*, Leverkusen (1) 1
  (Kirsten 12) 38,000
Ujpest (0) 0, FC Brugge (3) 5 *(Jankauskas 12, Ilic 20,*
  Vermant 42, Anic 50, Ekakia 90) 1500
Vejle (0) 1 *(Graulund 86)*, Betis (0) 0 6035
Vitesse (0) 3 *(Laros 50, Perovic 53, Machlas 90)*,
  AEK Athens (0) 0 20,000
Willem II (0) 3 *(Ramzi 76, Arts 80, Schenning 86)*,
  Dynamo Tbilisi (0) 0 10,000
Zurich (1) 4 *(Nixon 35, Hodel 54, Bartlett 69, Chassot 81)*,
  Anorthosis (0) 0 4100

FIRST ROUND, SECOND LEG
AEK Athens (1) 3 *(Nikolaidis 14, 75, Kopitsis 69)*,
  Vitesse (2) 3 *(Machlas 11, 27, Reuser 55)* 23,000
Anorthosis (1) 2 *(Mihajlovic 44, Krcmarevic 72)*,
  Zurich (2) 3 *(Sant'Anna 12, Bartlett 38, 63)* 1500
Betis (2) 5 *(Ivan 1, 20, 89, Finidi George 71, Galvez 72)*,
  Vejle (0) 0 7900
Bologna (0) 2 *(Nervo 77, Signori 89)*,
  Sporting Lisbon (0) 1 *(Leandro 64)* 3680
Celta Vigo (4) 7 *(Penev 7, 13, 27, Mazinho 17, Sanchez*
  70, Cadete 78, Tomas 90), Arges (0) 0 18,000
Celtic (1) 2 *(Stubbs 38, Larsson 90)*, Guimaraes (0) 1
  (Soderstrom 87) 38,076
CSKA Sofia (1) 1 *(Stanchev 10)*, Servette (0) 0 15,000
Dynamo Tbilisi (0) 0, Willem II (1) 3 *(Valk 19, Ceesay 89,*
  Ramzi 90) 14,000
FC Brugge (2) 2 *(Borkelmans 32, Vermant 70)*,
  Ujpest (0) 2 *(Kopunovics 50, Szanyo 90)* 4000
Feyenoord (0) 0, Stuttgart (1) 3 *(Balakov 34,*
  Djordjevic 69, Bobic 89) 34,387
Grasshoppers (0) 0, Anderlecht (0) 0 7300
Graz (1) 2 *(Golombek 7, Akwuegbu 82)*, Litets (0) 0 7536
Hajduk Split (0) 0, Fiorentina (0) 0 38,000
Leverkusen (0) 1 *(Beinlich 76)*, Udinese (0) 0 22,500
Liverpool (1) 5 *(Redknapp 23, 55, Ince 52, Fowler 53, 90)*,
  Kosice (0) 0 23,792
Lyon (2) 2 *(Caveglia 2, Grassi 35 (pen))*,
  Blackburn Rovers (1) 2 *(Perez 26, Flitcroft 56)* 24,558
Maritimo (1) 1 *(Soares 45)*, Leeds United (0) 0
  aet; Leeds U won 4-1 on penalties. 10,000
Marseille (2) 4 *(Dugarry 19, 75, Pires 23, 86)*,
  Olomouc (0) 0 17,000

Metz (1) 2 *(Kastendeuch 39, Meyrieu 68)*,
  Red Star Belgrade (1) 1 *(Marinovic 17)* 11,000
Red Star Belgrade won 4-3 on penalties
Monaco (0) 0, LKS Lodz (0) 0 5200
Obilic (0) 0, Atletico Madrid (0) 1 *(Kiko 55)* 11,000
Parma (2) 3 *(Saffet 22 (og), Crespo 44, Boghossian 72)*,
  Fenerbahce (0) 1 *(Balic 58)* 10,519
Rangers (2) 4 *(Gattuso 1, Porrini 25, Johansson 60,*
  Wallace 65), Beitar Jerusalem (1) 2 *(Salloi 34,*
  Ohana 80 (pen)) 45,610
Rapid Vienna (1) 1 *(Wagner 43)*, Bordeaux (1) 2
  (Alicarte 28, Diabate 86) 24,500
Real Sociedad (0) 1 *(Kovacevic 51)*, Sparta
  Prague (0) 0 23,000
Roma (1) 1 *(Delvecchio 53)*, Silkeborg (0) 0 21,247
Skonto Riga (0) 2 *(Pakhar 75, 88)*,
  Dynamo Moscow (1) 3 *(Goussev 17, Golovskoi 51,*
  Terekhine 76) 4500
Slavia Prague (1) 1 *(Dostalek 17)*, Schalke (0) 0 8896
aet; Slavia Prague won 5-4 on penalties.
Stromsgodset (0) 0, Aston Villa (2) 3
  (Collymore 11, 23, 64) 4835
Valencia (0) 3 *(Roche 53, Lopez 56, Lucarelli 86)*,
  Steaua (0) 0 33,000
Werder Bremen (1) 4 *(Wicky 32, Wiedener 69,*
  Maximov 107, Flo 110), Brann (0) 0 17,374
Wisla (0) 3 *(Zajac 85, 89, Kulawik 90)*,
  Branik Maribor (0) 0 4093

SECOND ROUND, FIRST LEG
Bologna (0) 2 *(Signori 51, Ingesson 85)*,
  Slavia Prague (0) 1 *(Dostalek 68)* 4795
Celta Vigo (0) 0, Aston Villa (1) 1 *(Joachim 15)* 25,000
Celtic (1) 1 *(Brattbakk 23)*, Zurich (0) 1
  (Fischer 75) 44,121
CSKA Sofia (0) 2 *(Guentchev 52, Petrov 74)*, Atletico
  Madrid (2) 4 *(Torrisi 41, Kiko 43, 87,*
  Roberto 75) 21,000
Dynamo Moscow (0) 2 *(Nekrassov 72, 73)*,
  Real Sociedad (3) 3 *(Kovacevic 3, 11,*
  De Pedro 36 (pen)) 8000
Grasshoppers (0) 0, Fiorentina (1) 2 *(Batistuta 20,*
  Robbiati 48) 16,000
Graz (1) 3 *(Akwuegbu 28, 56, Luhovy 64)*, Monaco (1) 3
  (Spehar 17, 60, Giuly 77) 15,400
Leverkusen (0) 1 *(Reichenberger 90)*, Rangers (1) 2
  (Van Bronckhorst 45, Johanssen 63) 22,000
Liverpool (0) 0, Valencia (0) 0 26,004
Red Star Belgrade (0) 1 *(Skoric 59)*, Lyon (0) 2
  (Grassi 69, Kanoute 84) 11,000
Roma (1) 1 *(Delvecchio 17)*, Leeds United (0) 0 41,892
Stuttgart (1) 1 *(Akpoborie 7)*, FC Brugge (0) 1
  (Vermant 71) 11,750
Vitesse (0) 0, Bordeaux (1) 1 *(Wilford 44)* 19,000
Werder Bremen (0) 1 *(Herzog 68)*, Marseille (0) 1
  (Maurice 67) 22,086
Willem II (0) 1 *(Bombarda 86)*, Betis (0) 1
  (Alexis 85) 14,500
Wisla (0) 1 *(Kulawik 68)*, Parma (1) 1 *(Chiesa 2)* 10,000

SECOND ROUND, SECOND LEG
Aston Villa (1) 1 *(Collymore 30 (pen))*, Celta Vigo (2) 3
  (Sanchez 26, Mostovoi 34, Penev 48) 29,910
Atletico Madrid (1) 1 *(Juninho 45 (pen))*,
  CSKA Sofia (0) 0 28,000
Betis (1) 3 *(Finidi George 29, Zarandona 56, Sanchez 89)*,
  Willem II (0) 0 28,500
Bordeaux (1) 2 *(Micoud 9, Wilford 65)*, Vitesse (1) 1
  (Jochemsen 8) 15,000
FC Brugge (0) 3 *(De Kock 60, Claessens 105, Ilic 116)*,
  Stuttgart (0) 2 *(Verlaat 76, Bobic 110)* 11,384
Fiorentina 2, Grasshoppers 1 *(in Salerno) (match*
  abandoned at half-time following an explosion which
  injured the fourth referee official; tie awarded to
  Grasshoppers).
Leeds United (0) 0, Roma (0) 0 39,161
Lyon (3) 3 *(Caveglia 17, 42, Cocard 40)*,
  Red Star Belgrade (2) 2 *(Bunjevcevic 37,*
  Acimovic 90) 22,508
Marseille (3) 3 *(Maurice 35, Issa 52, Dugarry 78)*,
  Werder Bremen (0) 2 *(Eilts 47, Herzog 83)* 43,490
Monaco (2) 4 *(Gava 8, 67, Spehar 16, Diawara 55)*,
  Graz (0) 0 6810
Parma (1) 2 *(Fiore 20, Zajac 46 (og))*, Wisla (0) 1
  (Zajac 90) 7438
Rangers (0) 1 *(Johansson 56)*, Leverkusen (0) 1
  (Kirsten 79) 50,012

Real Sociedad (0) 3 *(Kovacevic 55, 75, De Paula 70)*,
    Dynamo Moscow (0) 0   22,855
Slavia Prague (0) 0, Bologna (0) 2 *(Signori 80,*
    Cappioli 85)   8827
Valencia (1) 2 *(Lopez 45, James 90 (og))*, Liverpool (0) 2
    (McManaman 81, Berger 86)   53,000
Zurich (0) 4 *(Del Signore 51, Chassot 56, Bartlett 61,*
    Sant'Anna 75), Celtic (0) 2 *(O'Donnell 57, Larsson 72)*
                                            14,500

THIRD ROUND, FIRST LEG
Bologna (1) 4 *(Fontolan 25, 74, Kolyvanov 52,*
    Eriberto 58), Betis (0) 1 *(Benjamin 63)*   15,000
Celta Vigo (0) 3 *(Mostovoi 49, Karpin 56, Gudel 90)*,
    Liverpool (1) 1 *(Owen 35)*   24,600
Grasshoppers (2) 3 *(Kavelashvili 21, Turkyilmaz 33,*
    Comisetti 53), Bordeaux (2) 3 *(Wilford 6, 74,*
    Micoud 20)   7200
Lyon (1) 1 *(Bak 45)*, FC Brugge (0) 0   20,178
Monaco (1) 2 *(Trezeguet 17 (pen), Giuly 56)*,
    Marseille (2) 2 *(Pires 9, Camara 39)* 15,500
Rangers (0) 1 *(Wallace 69)*, Parma (0) 1 *(Balbo 51)* 49,514
Real Sociedad (1) 2 *(Kovacevic 45, Roberto 85 (og))*,
    Atletico Madrid (1) 1 *(Juninho 3)*   24,431
Zurich (0) 0, Roma (0) 1 *(Totti 90 (pen))* 19,375

THIRD ROUND, SECOND LEG
Atletico Madrid (2) 4 *(Jugovic 17, 45 (pen), Santi 94,*
    Jose Mari 97), Real Sociedad (0) 1 *(Gracia 50)* 30,000
Betis (1) 1 *(Alvarez 3)*, Bologna (0) 0   20,000
Bordeaux (0) 0, Grasshoppers (0) 0   19,407
FC Brugge (0) 3 *(De Brul 64, De Kock 70, Anic 73)*,
    Lyon (1) 4 *(Caveglia 16, 55, 71, Dhorasoo 76)* 14,500
Liverpool (0) 0, Celta Vigo (0) 1 *(Revivo 57)* 30,289

Marseille (0) 1 *(Camara 71)*, Monaco (0) 0   55,000
Parma (0) 3 *(Balbo 47, Fiore 63, Chiesa 66 (pen))*,
    Rangers (1) 1 *(Albertz 29)*   17,000
Roma (1) 2 *(Delvecchio 14, Totti 90)*, Zurich (0) 2
    (Bartlett 60, 79)   15,300

QUARTER-FINALS, FIRST LEG
Atletico Madrid (1) 2 *(Jose Mari 13, Roberto 46)*, Roma
    (0) 1 *(Di Biagio 76)*   57,000
Bologna (1) 3 *(Signori 8, 50, Binotto 54)*,
    Lyon (0) 0   19,545
Bordeaux (2) 2 *(Micoud 39, Wilford 45)*, Parma (0) 1
    (Crespo 84)   33,000
Marseille (1) 2 *(Maurice 33, 67)*, Celta Vigo (0) 1
    (Mostovoi 63)   54,137

QUARTER-FINALS, SECOND LEG
Celta Vigo (0) 0, Marseille (0) 0   35,000
Lyon (2) 2 *(Caveglia 16, Job 39)*, Bologna (0) 0 38,000
Parma (2) 6 *(Crespo 36, 62, Chiesa 43, 59, Veron 48,*
    Balbo 89 (pen)), Bordeaux (0) 0   16,400
Roma (1) 1 *(Delvecchio 32)*, Atletico Madrid (0) 2
    (Aguilera 57, Roberto 89)   64,485

SEMI-FINALS, FIRST LEG
Atletico Madrid (1) 1 *(Juninho 21 (pen))*, Parma (2) 3
    (Chiesa 13, 40, Crespo 63)   52,000
Marseille (0) 0, Bologna (0) 0   60,000

SEMI-FINALS, SECOND LEG
Bologna (1) 1 *(Paramatti 18)*, Marseille (0) 1
    (Blanc 87 (pen))   39,000
Parma (1) 2 *(Balbo 35, Chiesa 82)*, Atletico Madrid (0) 1
    (Roberto 64)   18,000

FINAL

Parma (2) 3, Marseille (0) 0

(in Moscow, 12 May 1999, 61,000)

Parma: Buffon; Fuser, Vanoli, Thuram, Sensini, Cannavaro, Dino Baggio, Boghossian, Crespo (Asprilla 82), Chiesa
    (Balbo 72), Veron (Fiore 78).
Scorers: Crespo 26, Vanoli 36, Chiesa 55.
Marseille: Porato; Blondeau, Edson (Camara 46), Issa, Blanc, Domoraud, Pires, Brando, Maurice, Gourvennec, Bravo.
Referee: Dallas (Scotland).

Frederic Brando (8) the Marseille midfield player is closely watched by Parma's Dino Baggio in the 1999 UEFA Cup
Final. Parma won 3-0. (Actionimages)

UEFA CUP 1998–99 – BRITISH AND IRISH CLUBS

FIRST QUALIFYING ROUND, FIRST LEG

22 JULY

Newtown (0) 0
Wisla (0) 0   1475

Newtown: Barton; Thomas S (Line 82), Evans G, Reynolds, Thomas A, Roberts, Evans M, Wickham, Williams, Yates, Ruscoe.
Wisla: Sarnat; Kaluzny, Zajac B, Wegrzyn (Nowak 85), Pater, Kaliciak, Czerwiec, Kulawik, Sunday, Zajac M, Nicinski (Dubicki 46).

Omonia (2) 5 *(Kitanov 40, 60, Rauffman 43 (pen), Panayiotou 65, Kontolefteros 88)*
Linfield (0) 1 *(Ferguson 79)*   5000

Omonia: Christofi; Kaiafas, Georgiou, Ioakim, Panayiotou, Constandinides, Andreou, Kitanov (Kontolefteros 85), Arangos, Malekos, Rauffman.
Linfield: Geddes; McDonald, Easton, McCoosh, Murphy, Beatty, Marks, Gorman, Ferguson, Feeney, Bailie.

Shelbourne (2) 3 *(Porrini 7 (og), Rutherford 41, Morley 58)*
Rangers (0) 5 *(Albertz 59 (pen), 85 (pen), Amato 74, 82, Van Bronckhorst 75)*   6047

Shelbourne: Gough; Geoghegan, McCartney, Scully, Baker D, Rutherford, Smith, Fenlon, Fitzgerald, Morley (Sheridan 78), Kelly.
Rangers: Niemi; Porrini, Amoruso, Petric, Van Bronckhorst, Gattuso (Amato 46), Ferguson B, Thern (Ferguson I 63), Albertz, Graham (Johansson 46), Durie. *(at Tranmere).*

Zeljeznicar (0) 1 *(Vazda 66)*
Kilmarnock (0) 1 *(McGowne 55)*   15,000

Zeljeznicar: Guso; Biocevic, Mulmuic, Kunic (Pehliravic 88), Greolic (Ceman 81), Falic, Vazola, Muharemonic, Mulaosmanovic, Burek, Zeric (Selinonic 46).
Kilmarnock: Marshall; MacPherson, Montgomerie, McGowne, Baker, Holt, Wright (Roberts 79), Durrant, Mitchell, Mahood, Lauchlan.

FIRST QUALIFYING ROUND, SECOND LEG

29 JULY

Kilmarnock (0) 1 *(Mahood 31)*
Zeljeznicar (0) 0   14,512

Kilmarnock: Marshall; MacPherson, McGowne, Holt, Wright, Durrant, Mitchell, Mahood (Henry 89), Baker, Lauchlan, Burke (Nevin 74).
Zeljeznicar: Guso; Biocevic, Mulaosmanovic, Kunic, Mulmuic, Burek, Fulimovic, Greolic (Zeric 46), Muharemonic, Vazola, Satic (Edin 51).

Linfield (3) 5 *(Feeney 19, Gorman 35, 48, McDonald 45, Ferguson 72)*
Omonia (3) 3 *(Marantos 2, Kitanov 15, Ioakim 23)*   2000

Linfield: Geddes; McDonald (Marks 70), Easton, Semple (Campbell 80), Murphy, Beatty, Larmour (Cleland 80), Gorman, Ferguson, Feeney, Bailie.
Omonia: Christofi; Kaiafas, Nicolaou N, Ioakim, Panayiotou, Constandinides (Pontikos 41), Andreou, Kitanov (Kontolefteros 79), Arangos, Malekos, Rauffman (Nicolaou C 62).

Rangers (1) 2 *(Johansson 4, 89)*
Shelbourne (0) 0   46,906

Rangers: Niemi; Porrini, Moore, Amoruso, Numan, Kanchelskis (Amato 46), Ferguson B, Van Bronckhorst (Ferguson I 74), Albertz, Durie (Gattuso 62), Johansson.
Shelbourne: Gough; Geoghegan, McCartney, Scully, Baker D, Rutherford, Smith, Fenlon, Fitzgerald, Morley (Sheridan 67), Kelly.

Wisla (2) 7 *(Kulawik 28, 47, Sunday 35, Kaliciak 51, Dubicki 54, Pater 61, 66)*
Newtown (0) 0   7500

Wisla: Sarnat; Zajac B, Wegrzyn, Matyja, Dubicki, Pater, Kulawik (Piszczek 70), Czerwiec (Nowak 53), Sunday, Nicinski (Skrzinski 81), Kaliciak.
Newtown: Barton; Line, Evans G, Reynolds, Thomas A, Roberts, Wickham (Clifford 59), Williams, Yates (Commerford 76), Evans M, Ruscoe (Davies 79).

SECOND QUALIFYING ROUND, FIRST LEG

11 AUG

Olomouc (1) 2 *(Krohmer 26, Konig 78)*
Kilmarnock (0) 0   4200

Olomouc: Skacel; Kouar, Ujfalusi, Krohmer, Mucha (Steska 85), Barborik (Ryska 81), Drulak, Machala (Cupak 66), Konig, Kotulek, Heinz.
Kilmarnock: Marshall; MacPherson, Baker, Lauchlan, Montgomerie, McGowne, Mitchell, Mahood (Burke 74), Wright (Varielle 63), Durrant, Holt.

Rangers (0) 2 *(Kanchelskis 55, Wallace 68)*
PAOK Salonika (0) 0   35,392

Rangers: Niemi; Porrini, Moore, Amoruso, Numan, Kanchelskis, Ferguson B (Albertz 67), Ferguson I, Van Bronckhorst (Gattuso 78), Wallace, Durie (Amato 6).
PAOK Salonika: Mihopoulos; Bantovic, Olivares, Kapetanopoulos, Toursounidis (Zafiriou 46), Vrizas, Frantzeskos, Nagbe, Katsiatis, Komtamtimibis, Maxaritis.

SECOND QUALIFYING ROUND, SECOND LEG

25 AUG

Kilmarnock (0) 0
Olomouc (2) 2 *(Heinz 13, Mucha 19)*   11,140

Kilmarnock: Marshall; MacPherson, Kerr, McGowne, Nevin (McCutcheon 64), Holt (Mahood 46), Wright (Roberts 76), Durrant, Varielle, Lauchlan, Burke.
Olomouc: Skacel; Kouar, Ujfalusi, Mucha (Ryska 81), Barborik (Steska 84), Drulak, Balcarek, Konig, Kucera, Kotulek, Heinz (Vivek 70).

PAOK Salonika (0) 0
Rangers (0) 0   32,000

PAOK Salonika: Mihopoulos; Bantovic, Olivares, Zafiriou (Uafes 72), Kapetanopoulos, Srdatzeskos, Vrizas (Cominges 52), Toursounidis (Marifalieu 66), Nagbe, Koulakiotis, Katsiatis.
Rangers: Charbonnier; Porrini, Amoruso (Petric 77), Numan, Ferguson B, Kanchelskis (Gattuso 81), Van Bronckhorst, Albertz (Amato 61), Ferguson I, Wallace, Moore.

FIRST ROUND, FIRST LEG

15 SEPT

Aston Villa (0) 3 *(Charles 83, Vassell 89, 90)*
Stromsgodset (2) 2 *(Michelsen 21, George 23)*   28,893

Aston Villa: Bosnich; Charles, Wright, Southgate, Grayson (Taylor 37), Barry, Draper (Scimeca 66), Hendrie, Joachim, Byfield (Vassell 80), Thompson.
Stromsgodset: Hansen; Granas, Karlsen, Waehler, Skistad, Solberg, Nyan, Odegaard H (George 11) (Strom 70), Kihle, Hagen, Michelsen (Olsen 87).

Beitar Jerusalem (1) 1 *(Abukasis 16 (pen))*
Rangers (0) 1 *(Albertz 84)*   14,000

Beitar Jerusalem: Korrfein; Domb, Dery, Levy, Abukasis, Pelesnikov, Shelah, Shitrit, Hamar, Santor, Reuven (Reichman 35).
Rangers: Charbonnier; Porrini, Vidmar (Stensaas 41), Ferguson B, Amoruso, Muir, Kanchelskis, Ferguson I, Johansson (Albertz 78), Wallace (Graham 90), Van Bronckhorst.

Blackburn R (0) 0
Lyon (0) 1 *(Bak 85)*   13,646
Blackburn R: Flowers; Dailly, Davidson, Sherwood, Peacock, Henchoz, Flitcroft, Perez (Dahlin 69), Sutton, Davies, Wilcox.
Lyon: Coupet; Carteron, Fournier, Laville, Delmotte, Bak, Violeau, Bassila, Dhorasoo, Caveglia (Linares 69), Grassi.

Guimaraes (0) 1 *(Geraldo 86)*
Celtic (1) 2 *(Larsson 1, Donnelly 70)*   8000
Guimaraes: Espinha; Carlos, Alexandre, Auri, Berto, Paneira, Costa (Riva 38), Rocha, Geraldo, Edmilson (Neno 80), Gilmar.
Celtic: Gould; Burley, Boyd (Annoni 21), Mahe, Rieper, Stubbs, Lambert, Donnelly, Jackson (Hannah 90), Larsson, O'Donnell.

Kosice (0) 0
Liverpool (2) 3 *(Berger 18, Riedle 23, Owen 59)*   4500
Kosice: Molnar; Dzurik, Semenik, Spilar, Toth (Ljubarski 67), Sovic, Nemeth, Zvara, Kozak I, Kozlej (Prohaska 67), Kral (Kozak J 58).
Liverpool: Friedel; Heggem, Staunton, Harkness, Carragher, Babb, McManaman (McAteer 78), Berger, Riedle (Fowler 58), Owen, Redknapp (Leonhardsen 82).

Leeds U (0) 1 *(Hasselbaink 84)*
Maritimo (0) 0   38,033
Leeds U: Martyn; Hiden, Harte, Haaland (Riberio 61), Radebe, Molenaar, Hopkin (Sharpe 76), Wijnhard (Lilley 61), Hasselbaink, Kewell, Bowyer.
Maritimo: Van der Straeten; Rui Oscar, Paulo Silva, Carlos Jorge, Soares, Eusebio, Duveau (Moreira 55), Antonio M, Jorge Silva, Bunbury, Lopes (Cruz 55).

FIRST ROUND, SECOND LEG

29 SEPT
Celtic (1) 2 *(Stubbs 38, Larsson 90)*
Guimaraes (0) 1 *(Soderstrom 87)*   38,076
Celtic: Gould; Mahe, Burley, Rieper, Stubbs, McKinlay, Brattbakk (Jackson 85), Donnelly, Hannah, Larsson, Lambert.
Guimaraes: Ferreira; Medeiros, Souza, Machado, Costa, Espevan (Almida 78), Milovanovic (Lucena 61), Soderstrom, Kabre, Silva, Junior.

Liverpool (1) 5 *(Redknapp 23, 55, Ince 52, Fowler 53, 90)*
Kosice (0) 0   23,792
Liverpool: James; McAteer (Heggem 66), Bjornebye, Leonhardsen, Carragher, Babb (Matteo 62), Redknapp, Ince (Staunton 71), Fowler, Owen, Berger.
Kosice: Molnar; Kozak I, Semenik, Spilar, Sovic (Lapsansky 62), Kral (Jambor 56), Dzurik, Kozak J, Gerich, Zvara, Nemeth (Kozlej 56).

Lyon (2) 2 *(Caveglia 2, Grassi 35 (pen))*
Blackburn R (1) 2 *(Perez 26, Flitcroft 56)*   24,558
Lyon: Coupet; Carteron, Fournier, Laville, Delmotte, Bak, Violeau, Linares, Dhorasoo, Caveglia (Cocard 27), Grassi (Bassila 67).
Blackburn R: Flowers; Dailly, Kenna (Davidson 67), Sherwood, Peacock, Henchoz, McKinlay (Taylor 84), Perez (Johnson 46), Duff, Flitcroft, Wilcox.

Maritimo (1) 1 *(Soares 45)*
Leeds U (0) 0   10,000
Maritimo: Van der Straeten; Carlos Jorge, Soares, Rui Oscar, Jorge Silva, Jokanovic (Paulo Silva 62), Antonio M, Eusebio, Lopes (Antonio P 85), Bunbury, Nelson (Cruz 64).
Leeds U: Martyn; Hiden, Harte, Halle, Radebe, Molenaar, Hopkin (Granville 120), Haaland, Hasselbaink, Kewell (Sharpe 77), Bowyer (Wijnhard 75).
aet; Leeds U won 4-1 on penalties.

Stromsgodset (0) 0
Aston Villa (2) 3 *(Collymore 11, 23, 64)*   4835
Stromsgodset: Hansen; Granaas, Johnsen, Waehler, Skistad, George (Odegaard H 67), Nyan, Solberg (Strom 85), Hagen E, Hagen R (Olsen 67), Flo.
Aston Villa: Bosnich; Charles (Scimeca 51), Wright, Southgate, Ehiogu, Grayson, Taylor (Ferraresi 71), Draper, Joachim (Vassell 67), Collymore, Thompson.

1 OCT
Rangers (2) 4 *(Gattuso 1, Porrini 25, Johansson 60, Wallace 65)*
Beitar Jerusalem (1) 2 *(Salloi 34, Ohana 80 (pen))* 45,610
Rangers: Charbonnier; Porrini, Vidmar, Ferguson B, Moore (Hendry 89), Amoruso, Gattuso, Wallace, Johansson (Miller 80), Albertz, Van Bronckhorst.
Beitar Jerusalem: Kornfein; Levi (Ohana 66), Shelah, Bedi, Pelesnikov, Abukasis, Mizrahi, Salloi, Hammar, Samdor, Shitrit.

SECOND ROUND, FIRST LEG

20 OCT
Celta Vigo (0) 0
Aston Villa (1) 1 *(Joachim 15)*   25,000
Celta Vigo: Dutruel; Salgado, Caceres, Djorovic, Josema (Tomas 62), Karpin (Cadete 82), Makelele, Mazinho, Revivo (Sanchez), Mostovoi, Penev.
Aston Villa: Oakes; Charles, Wright, Southgate, Ehiogu, Barry, Draper, Hendrie, Joachim, Collymore, Scimeca.

Celtic (1) 1 *(Brattbakk 23)*
Zurich (0) 1 *(Fischer 75)*   44,121
Celtic: Gould; McNamara, McKinlay, Burley, Mahe, Boyd, Donnelly, Lambert, Brattbakk (Jackson 75), Larsson, O'Donnell.
Zurich: Pascolo; Tarone, Fischer, Hodel, Di Jorio, Sant'Anna (Castillo 84), Del Signore, Lima, Nixon (Wiederkehr 46), Chassot, Bartlett.

Liverpool (0) 0
Valencia (0) 0   26,004
Liverpool: James; Heggem, Bjornebye, McAteer, Carragher, Staunton, McManaman, Ince, Fowler (Owen 72), Riedle, Berger (Leonhardsen 75).
Valencia: Canizares; Bjorklund, Roche, Djukic, Angulo, Milla (Farinos 81), Popescu (Soria 86), Mendieta, Carboni, Lopez, Ilie (Lucarelli 84).

Roma (1) 1 *(Delvecchio 17)*
Leeds U (0) 0   41,892
Roma: Chimenti; Cafu, Zago, Aldair, Candela, Frau (Bartelt 60), Tommassi, Di Biagio, Di Francesco, Totti, Delvecchio.
Leeds U: Martyn; Hiden, Halle, McPhail, Radebe, Molenaar, Hopkin, Ribeiro, Hasselbaink (Wijnhard 80), Kewell (Haaland 69), Bowyer.

22 OCT
Leverkusen (0) 1 *(Reichenberger 90)*
Rangers (1) 2 *(Van Bronckhorst 45, Johansson 63)* 22,000
Leverkusen: Matysek; Kovac R, Happe (Reichenberger 76), Nowotny, Beinlich, Ramelow (Heintze 58), Ze Roberto, Emerson (Kovac N 58), Reeb, Meijer, Rink.
Rangers: Charbonnier; Porrini, Vidmar, Ferguson B, Hendry, Wilson, Kanchelskis, Wallace (Durie 86), Johansson (Ferguson I 79), Albertz, Van Bronckhorst.

SECOND ROUND, SECOND LEG

3 NOV
Aston Villa (1) 1 *(Collymore 30 (pen))*
Celta Vigo (2) 3 *(Sanchez 26, Mostovoi 34, Penev 48)*   29,910
Aston Villa: Oakes; Charles (Draper 46), Wright, Southgate, Ehiogu, Barry (Vassell 64), Taylor, Hendrie, Joachim, Collymore, Thompson (Grayson 82).
Celta Vigo: Dutruel; Michel, Caceres, Djorovic, Berges, Karpin (Hervas 69), Mostovoi, Mazinho, Makelele, Sanchez (Eggen 56), Penev (Cadete 77).

Leeds U (0) 0
Roma (0) 0   39,161
Leeds U: Martyn; Hiden, Harte, Hopkin, Woodgate, Molenaar, Sharpe (Wijnhard 60), McPhail, Hasselbaink, Kewell, Bowyer.
Roma: Chimenti; Aldair, Petruzzi, Zago, Wome, Tommassi, Tomic, Di Francesco, Sergio (Candela 46), Delvecchio, Totti (Cafu 86).

Valencia (1) 2 *(Lopez 45, James 90 (og))*
Liverpool (0) 2 *(McManaman 81, Berger 86)*   53,000
Valencia: Canizares; Bjorklund, Carboni, Djukic, Angulo, Soria, Popescu, Mendieta, Schwarz, Lopez, Ilie (Lucarelli 75).
Liverpool: James; Heggem (Dundee 78), Bjornebye (Harkness 90), Redknapp, Carragher, Staunton, McManaman, Ince, Fowler (McAteer 83), Owen, Berger.

Zurich (0) 4 *(Del Signore 51, Chassot 56, Bartlett 61, Sant'Anna 75)*
Celtic (0) 2 *(O'Donnell 57, Larsson 72)*   14,500
Zurich: Pascolo; Tarone, Hodel, Fischer, Di Jorio, Sant'Anna, Del Signore (Nixon 77), Lima F, Wiederkehr (Opango 64), Chassot (Castillo 77), Bartlett.
Celtic: Gould (Kerr 63); McNamara, McKinlay, Donnelly, Hannah, Mahe, O'Donnell, Brattbakk, Jackson, Larsson, Lambert.

5 NOV

Rangers (0) 1 *(Johansson 56)*
Leverkusen (0) 1 *(Kirsten 79)*   50,012
Rangers: Charbonnier (Niemi 67); Porrini, Numan, Ferguson B (Wilson 90), Hendry, Amoruso, Kanchelskis (Ferguson I 67), Wallace, Johansson, Albertz, Van Bronckhorst.
Leverkusen: Matysek; Kovac R (Emerson 39), Happe, Nowotny, Reeb, Ramelow, Heintze (Reichenberger 66), Ze Roberto, Beinlich, Meijer (Kovac N 77), Kirsten.

THIRD ROUND, FIRST LEG

24 NOV

Celta Vigo (0) 3 *(Mostovoi 49, Karpin 56, Gudel 90)*
Liverpool (1) 1 *(Owen 35)*   24,600
Celta Vigo: Dutruel; Salgado, Caceres, Djorovic, Tomas, Karpin (Caires 86), Mazinho, Makelele, Mostovoi (Lopez 88), Penev (Gudelj 86), Sanchez.
Liverpool: James; Heggem, Bjornebye, Kvarme, Carragher, Staunton, Redknapp, Thompson (Riedle 82), Fowler, Owen, Berger (Babb 87).

Rangers (0) 1 *(Wallace 69)*
Parma (0) 1 *(Balbo 51)*   49,514
Rangers: Niemi; Porrini (Durie 57), Numan, Ferguson B, Hendry, Amoruso, Kanchelskis, Wallace, Johansson (Amato 46), Ferguson I, Albertz.
Parma: Buffon; Sartor, Thuram, Cannavaro, Benarrivo, Stanic, Boghossian, Dino Baggio, Veron (Fiore 69), Crespo (Orlandini 89), Balbo.

THIRD ROUND, SECOND LEG

8 DEC

Liverpool (0) 0
Celta Vigo (0) 1 *(Revivo 57)*   30,289
Liverpool: James (Friedel 62); McAteer, Matteo, Babb (Murphy 46), Carragher, Staunton, Gerrard, Thompson (Riedle 59), Fowler, Owen, Berger.
Celta Vigo: Dutruel; Salgado, Caceres, Djorovic, Berges, Karpin, Mazinho, Makelele, Mostovoi, Sanchez, Revivo (Tomas 70).

Parma (0) 3 *(Balbo 47, Fiore 63, Chiesa 66 (pen))*
Rangers (1) 1 *(Albertz 29)*   17,000
Parma: Buffon; Thuram, Sensini, Cannavaro, Fuser (Mussi 84), Boghossian (Fiore 58), Dino Baggio, Benarrivo, Veron, Chiesa (Crespo 77), Balbo.
Rangers: Niemi; Porrini, Numan, Ferguson B (Miller 80), Hendry, Amoruso, Ferguson I, Wallace (Amato 72), Durie (Vidmar 54), Albertz, Van Bronckhorst.

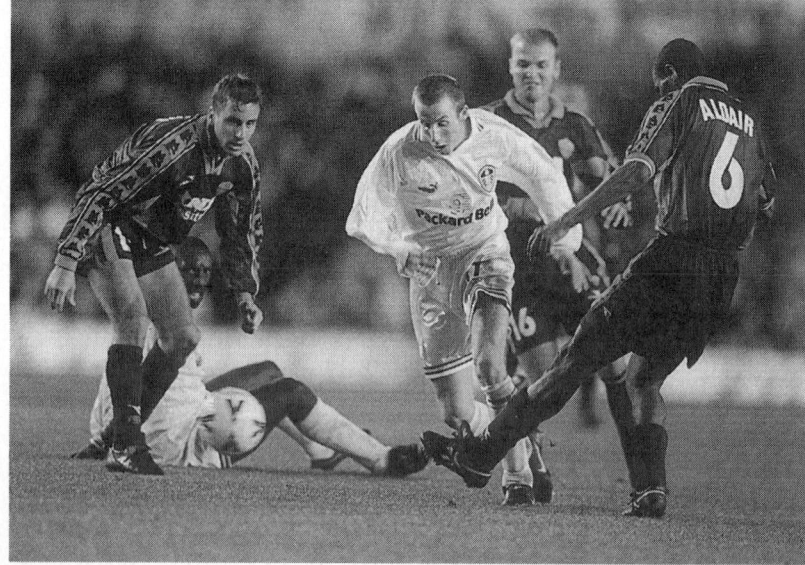

In the UEFA Cup, Leeds United's progress was ended by Roma. Here, Lee Bowyer is surrounded by Italian players, including Aldair (6). (Colorsport)

Summary of Appearances

EUROPEAN CUP (1955–99)

English clubs
12 Liverpool
10 Manchester U
3 Nottingham F, Leeds U, Arsenal
2 Derby Co, Wolverhampton W, Everton, Aston Villa
1 Burnley, Tottenham H, Ipswich T, Manchester C, Blackburn R, Newcastle U

Scottish clubs
19 Rangers
16 Celtic
3 Aberdeen
2 Hearts
1 Dundee, Dundee U, Kilmarnock, Hibernian

Welsh clubs
2 Barry T
1 Cwmbran T

Northern Ireland clubs
18 Linfield
8 Glentoran
3 Crusaders
2 Portadown
1 Glenavon, Ards, Distillery, Derry C, Coleraine, Cliftonville

Eire clubs
7 Shamrock R, Dundalk
6 Waterford
3 Drumcondra
2 Bohemians, Limerick, Athlone T, Shelbourne, Derry C*, St Patrick's Ath
1 Cork Hibs, Cork Celtic, Cork City, Sligo R

Winners: Celtic 1966–67; Manchester U 1967–68, 1998–99; Liverpool 1976–77, 1977–78, 1980–81, 1983–84; Nottingham F 1978–79, 1979–80; Aston Villa 1981–82

Finalists: Celtic 1969–70; Leeds U 1974–75; Liverpool 1984–85

EUROPEAN CUP-WINNERS' CUP (1960–99)

English clubs
6 Tottenham H
5 Manchester U, Liverpool, Chelsea
4 West Ham U
3 Arsenal, Everton
2 Manchester C
1 Wolverhampton W, Leicester C, WBA, Leeds U, Sunderland, Southampton, Ipswich T, Newcastle U

Scottish clubs
10 Rangers
8 Aberdeen, Celtic
3 Hearts
2 Dunfermline Ath, Dundee U
1 Dundee, Hibernian, St Mirren, Motherwell, Airdrieonians, Kilmarnock

Welsh clubs
14 Cardiff C
8 Wrexham
7 Swansea C
3 Bangor C
1 Borough U, Newport Co, Merthyr Tydfil, Barry T, Llansantfraid, Cwmbran T

Northern Ireland clubs
9 Glentoran
5 Glenavon
4 Ballymena U, Coleraine
3 Crusaders, Linfield
2 Ards, Bangor
1 Derry C, Distillery, Portadown, Carrick Rangers, Cliftonville

Eire clubs
6 Shamrock R
4 Shelbourne
3 Limerick, Waterford, Dundalk, Bohemians
2 Cork Hibs, Galway U, Sligo R, Derry C*, Cork City
1 Cork Celtic, St Patrick's Ath, Finn Harps, Home Farm, University College Dublin, Bray W

Winners: Tottenham H 1962–63; West Ham U 1964–65; Manchester C 1969–70; Chelsea 1970–71, 1997–98; Rangers 1971–72; Aberdeen 1982–83; Everton 1984–85; Manchester U 1990–91; Arsenal 1993–94

Finalists: Rangers 1960–61, 1966–67; Liverpool 1965–66; Leeds U 1972–73; West Ham U 1975–76; Arsenal 1979–80, 1994–95

EUROPEAN FAIRS CUP & UEFA CUP (1955–99)

English clubs
10 Leeds U
9 Liverpool, Aston Villa
8 Ipswich T, Arsenal
7 Manchester U
6 Everton, Newcastle U
5 Southampton, Tottenham H, Nottingham F
4 Manchester C, Birmingham C, Wolverhampton W, WBA
3 Chelsea, Sheffield W
2 Stoke C, Derby Co, QPR, Blackburn R
1 Burnley, Coventry C, Norwich C, London Rep XI, Watford, Leicester C

Scottish clubs
18 Dundee U
14 Hibernian
13 Aberdeen
12 Celtic
10 Rangers
9 Hearts
5 Dunfermline Ath, Kilmarnock
4 Dundee
3 St Mirren
2 Partick T, Motherwell
1 Morton, St Johnstone, Raith R

Welsh Clubs
2 Bangor C, Newtown
1 Inter Cardiff, Afan Lido, Barry T, Inter Cable-Tel

Northern Ireland clubs
11 Glentoran
7 Coleraine
6 Linfield
4 Glenavon, Portadown
3 Crusaders
1 Ards, Ballymena U, Bangor

Eire clubs
10 Bohemians
5 Dundalk
4 Shamrock R, Shelbourne
3 Finn Harps, St Patrick's Ath
2 Drumcondra, Derry C*, Cork City
1 Cork Hibs, Athlone T, Limerick, Drogheda U, Galway U

Winners: Leeds U 1967–68, 1970–71; Newcastle U 1968–69; Arsenal 1969–70; Tottenham H 1971–72, 1983–84; Liverpool 1972–73, 1975–76; Ipswich T 1980–81

Finalists: London 1955–58, Birmingham C 1958–60, 1960–61; Leeds U 1966–67; Wolverhampton W 1971–72; Tottenham H 1973–74; Dundee U 1986–87

* Now play in League of Ireland

INTER-TOTO CUP 1998

FIRST ROUND
Altay v Shamrock Rovers 3-1, 2-3
Dinaburg v Trencin 1-1, 1-4
TPS Turku v Sion 0-1, 3-2
Makedonia v Olimpija 4-2, 1-1
Inkaras v Baki 1-0, 0-1
Kutaisi v Homenmen 6-0, 1-1
Sobota v Omagh 1-0, 2-2
National v Hapoel Haifa 3-1, 2-1
Dnepr v Debrecen 2-4, 0-6
Hobscheid v Kralove 0-0, 1-2
Diosgyor v Sliema 2-0, 3-2
Hrvatski v Lyngby 1-4, 1-0
Ethnikos v Orgryte 2-1, 0-4
St Gallen v Tulevik 3-2, 6-1
FK Austria v Ruch 0-1, 2-2
Baltika v Varna 4-0, 1-1
Stabaek v Vojvodina 1-2, 2-3
Vagur v Boby Brno 0-3, 1-3
Ebbw Vale v Kongsvinger 1-6, 0-3
Leiftur v Vorskla 0-3, 0-3

SECOND ROUND
Iraklis v National 3-1, 0-3
Samsun v Lyngby 3-0, 1-3
TPS Turku v Shinnik 0-2, 2-3
Debrecen v Kralove 0-0, 1-1
Boby Brno v Espanyol 5-3, 0-2
Twente v Kongsvinger 2-0, 0-0
Salzburg v St Gallen 3-1, 0-1
Werder Bremen v Inkaras 4-1, 1-0
Akademisk v Vorskla 2-2, 1-1
Lommel v Kutaisi 0-1. 2-1
Orgryte v Ruch 2-1, 0-1
Sampdoria v Sobota 2-0, 0-1

Altay v Diosgyor 1-1, 1-0
Vojvodina v Orebro 2-0, 2-0
Makedonia v Bastia 1-0, 0-7
Trencin v Baltika 0-1, 0-0

THIRD ROUND
Harelbeke v Sampdoria 0-1, 0-3
Crystal Palace v Samsun 0-2, 0-2
Valencia v Shinnik 4-1, 0-1
Bologna v National 2-0, 1-3
Bastia v Altay 2-0, 2-3
Auxerre v Espanyol 1-1, 0-1
Lommel v Werder Bremen 1-3, 1-2
Vojvodina v Baltika 4-1, 0-1
Sittard v Vorskla 3-0, 2-2
Twente v Salzburg 2-2, 1-3
Debrecen v Hansa 1-1, 2-1
Ruch v Amadora 1-1, 1-1
(Ruch won on penalties).

SEMI-FINALS
Espanyol v Valencia 0-1, 0-2
Bastia v Vojvodina 2-0, 0-4
Bologna v Sampdoria 3-1, 0-1
Sittard v Salzburg 2-1, 1-3
Werder Bremen v Samsun 3-0, 3-0
Ruch v Debrecen 1-0, 3-0

FINALS
Bologna v Ruch 1-0, 2-0
Werder Bremen v Vojvodina 1-0, 1-1
Salzburg v Valencia 0-2, 1-2
Bologna, Werder Bremen and Valencia qualified for 1998-99 UEFA Cup.

EUROPEAN CUP DRAWS 1999–2000

EUROPEAN CUP

FIRST QUALIFYING ROUND
Barry Town v Valletta
Litets v Glentoran
St Patrick's Ath v Zimbru

SECOND QUALIFYING ROUND
Rapid Vienna v Barry Town or Valletta
Litets or Glentoran v Widzew Lodz
Haka or HB Torshavn v Rangers
Dynamo Tbilisi v St Patrick's Ath or Zimbru

Draw British and Irish Clubs only

UEFA CUP

QUALIFYING ROUND

GROUP 1
Gorica v Inter Cardiff

GROUP 3
Vaasa v St Johnstone
Portadown v CSKA Sofia

GROUP 4
Grasshoppers v Bray Wanderers

GROUP 5
IFK Gothenburg v Cork City
KR Reykjavik v Kilmarnock
Lokomotiv Tbilisi v Linfield

GROUP 6
Cwmbran Town v Celtic

Matches played August 12 and August 26.

WORLD CLUB CHAMPIONSHIP

Played annually up to 1974 and intermittently since then between the winners of the European Cup and the winners of the South American Champions Cup — known as the Copa Libertadores. In 1980 the winners were decided by one match arranged in Tokyo in February 1981 and the venue has been the same since. AC Milan replaced Marseille who had been stripped of their European Cup title in 1993.

1960	Real Madrid beat Penarol 0-0, 5-1
1961	Penarol beat Benfica 0-1, 5-0, 2-1
1962	Santos beat Benfica 3-2, 5-2
1963	Santos beat AC Milan 2-4, 4-2, 1-0
1964	Inter-Milan beat Independiente 0-1, 2-0, 1-0
1965	Inter-Milan beat Independiente 3-0, 0-0
1966	Penarol beat Real Madrid 2-0, 2-0
1967	Racing Club beat Celtic 0-1, 2-1, 1-0
1968	Estudiantes beat Manchester United 1-0, 1-1
1969	AC Milan beat Estudiantes 3-0, 1-2
1970	Feyenoord beat Estudiantes 2-2, 1-0
1971	Nacional beat Panathinaikos* 1-1, 2-1
1972	Ajax beat Independiente 1-1, 3-0
1973	Independiente beat Juventus* 1-0
1974	Atlético Madrid* beat Independiente 0-1, 2-0
1975	Independiente and Bayern Munich could not agree dates; no matches.
1976	Bayern Munich beat Cruzeiro 2-0, 0-0
1977	Boca Juniors beat Borussia Moenchengladbach* 2-2, 3-0
1978	Not contested
1979	Olimpia beat Malmö* 1-0, 2-1
1980	Nacional beat Nottingham Forest 1-0

1981	Flamengo beat Liverpool 3-0
1982	Penarol beat Aston Villa 2-0
1983	Gremio Porto Alegre beat SV Hamburg 2-1
1984	Independiente beat Liverpool 1-0
1985	Juventus beat Argentinos Juniors 4-2 on penalties after a 2-2 draw
1986	River Plate beat Steaua Bucharest 1-0
1987	FC Porto beat Penarol 2-1 after extra time
1988	Nacional (Uru) beat PSV Eindhoven 7-6 on penalties after 1-1 draw
1989	AC Milan beat Atletico Nacional (Col) 1-0 after extra time
1990	AC Milan beat Olimpia 3-0
1991	Red Star Belgrade beat Colo Colo 3-0
1992	Sao Paulo beat Barcelona 2-1
1993	Sao Paulo beat AC Milan 3-2
1994	Velez Sarsfield beat AC Milan 2-0
1995	Ajax beat Gremio Porto Alegre 4-3 on penalties after 0-0 draw
1996	Juventus beat River Plate 1-0
1997	Borussia Dortmund beat Cruzeiro 2-0

*European Cup runners-up; winners declined to take part.

1998

1 December in Tokyo

Real Madrid (1) 2

Vasco da Gama (0) 1   51,514

Real Madrid: Illgner; Panucci, Sanchis, Sanz, Hierro, Roberto Carlos, Raul, Redondo, Seedorf, Savio (Suker 90), Mijatovic (Jarni 81).
Scorers: Naza 26 (og), Raul 83.
Vasco da Gama: Germano; Mauro Galvao, Odvan, Felipe, Luizinho (Guilherme 85), Naza, Ramon (Valver 88), Vagner (Vitor 81), Juninho, Donizete, Luizao.
Scorer: Juninho 57.
Referee: Yanten (Chile).

EUROPEAN SUPER CUP

Played annually between the winners of the European Champions' Cup and the European Cup-Winners' Cup. AC Milan replaced Marseille in 1993-94.

1972	Ajax beat Rangers 3-1, 3-2
1973	Ajax beat AC Milan 0-1, 6-0
1974	Not contested
1975	Dynamo Kiev beat Bayern Munich 1-0, 2-0
1976	Anderlecht beat Bayern Munich 4-1, 1-2
1977	Liverpool beat Hamburg 1-1, 6-0
1978	Anderlecht beat Liverpool 3-1, 1-2
1979	Nottingham F beat Barcelona 1-0, 1-1
1980	Valencia beat Nottingham F 1-0, 1-2
1981	Not contested
1982	Aston Villa beat Barcelona 0-1, 3-0
1983	Aberdeen beat Hamburg 0-0, 2-0
1984	Juventus beat Liverpool 2-0
1985	Juventus v Everton not contested due to UEFA ban on English clubs
1986	Steaua Bucharest beat Dynamo Kiev 1-0
1987	FC Porto beat Ajax 1-0, 1-0
1988	KV Mechelen beat PSV Eindhoven 3-0, 0-1
1989	AC Milan beat Barcelona 1-1, 1-0
1990	AC Milan beat Sampdoria 1-1, 2-0
1991	Manchester U beat Red Star Belgrade 1-0
1992	Barcelona beat Werder Bremen 1-1, 2-1

1993	Parma beat AC Milan 0-1, 2-0
1994	AC Milan beat Arsenal 0-0, 2-0
1995	Ajax beat Zaragoza 1-1, 4-0
1996	Juventus beat Paris St. Germain 6-1, 3-1
1997	Barcelona beat Borussia Dortmund 2-0, 1-1

1998

28 August 1998, Monaco

Real Madrid (0) 0

Chelsea (0) 1 *(Poyet 83)*   9762

Real Madrid: Illgner; Panucci, Sanchis, Hierro, Roberto Carlos, Karembeu (Morientes 58), Seedorf, Redondo, Savio, Mijatovic (Jarni 74), Raul.
Chelsea: De Goey; Ferrer, Le Saux, Duberry, Leboeuf, Desailly, Babayaro, Di Matteo (Poyet 63), Casiraghi (Flo 90), Zola (Laudrup 83), Wise.
Referee: Batta (France).

INTERNATIONAL DIRECTORY

The latest available information has been given regarding numbers of clubs and players registered with FIFA, the world governing body. Where known, official colours are listed. With European countries, League tables show a number of signs. * indicates relegated teams, + play-offs, *+ relegated after play-offs, ++ promoted.

There are 197 member associations and one provisional member, Palestine. The four home countries, England, Scotland, Northern Ireland and Wales, are dealt with elsewhere in the Yearbook; but basic details appear in this directory.

EUROPE

ALBANIA

The Football Association of Albania, Rruga Dervish Hima Nr. 31, Tirana.
Founded: 1930; *Number of Clubs:* 49; *Number of Players:* 5,192; *National Colours:* All red.
Telephone: 00–355–42 27 877; *Cable:* ALBSPORT TIRANA; *Telex:* 2228 bfssh ab. *Fax:* 00 355–42 50 275.

International matches 1998
Turkey (a) 4-1, Malta (a) 1-1, Latvia (a) 2-2, Cyprus (a) 2-3, Georgia (a) 0-1, Norway (a) 2-2, Greece (h) 0-0.

League Championship wins (1930–37; 1945–99)
Dinamo Tirana 15; Partizani Tirana 15; SK Tirana 10; 17 Nentori 8; Vllaznia 8; Flamurtari 1; Labinoti 1; Skenderbeu 1, Teuta 1.

Cup wins (1948–99)
Partizani Tirana 14; Dinamo Tirana 12; 17 Nentori 6; Vllaznia 5; SK Tirana 3; Flamurtari 2; Labinoti 1; Elbasan 1; Teuta 1; Apolonia 1.

Final League Table 1998–99

	P	W	D	L	F	A	Pts
SK Tirana	30	18	7	5	48	20	61
Vllaznia	30	18	6	6	57	18	60
Bylis	30	18	5	7	51	20	59
Tomori	30	13	7	10	31	25	46
Lushnja	30	14	2	14	52	40	44
Dinamo	30	11	7	12	37	37	40
Shkumbini	30	12	4	14	30	38	40
Teuta	30	12	4	14	28	48	40
Elbasan	30	11	6	13	30	30	39
Partizani	30	10	9	11	37	46	39
Flamurtari	30	11	5	14	40	47	38
Skenderbeu	30	12	2	16	44	53	38
Apolonia	30	10	7	13	32	42	37
Besa*	30	10	6	14	25	40	36
Laci*	30	9	6	15	36	55	33
Burrel*	30	8	3	19	40	60	27

Top scorer: Bano (Lushnja) 22.
Cup Final: SK Tirana 0, Vllaznia 0.
SK Tirana won 3-0 on penalties.

ANDORRA

Federacio Andorrana de Futbol, C/Sant Salvador, 10-2-5, Edifici Galerias Plaza, Andorra la Vella, Principat d'Andorra.
Founded: 1994; *Number of Clubs:* 12; *Number of Players:* 300; *National Colours:* Yellow shirts, red shorts, yellow stockings.
Telephone: 00376 862003; *Fax:* 00376 862006.

International matches 1998
Brazil (a) 0-3, Estonia (a) 1-2, Azerbaijan (a) 0-0, Latvia (a) 0-2, Lithuania (a) 0-4, Armenia (a) 1-3, Ukraine (h) 0-2, France (a) 0-2.

League Championship wins (1996–99)
Principat 3; Dicoansa 1.

Cup wins (1996–99)
Principat 4.

ALBANIA

Final League Table 1998–99

	P	W	D	L	F	A	Pts
Principat	22	20	2	0	110	10	62
Don Pernil	22	17	3	2	64	19	54
Dicoansa	22	13	4	5	62	30	43
Construccions	22	12	5	5	46	22	41
Constelacio	22	11	2	9	52	32	35
Matecosa	22	10	5	7	50	42	35
Cava Benito	22	9	4	9	33	29	31
Sporting	22	7	5	10	29	44	26
Francfurt	22	5	1	16	23	83	16
Engolasters	22	4	5	13	24	49	14
Deportivo	22	3	2	17	22	82	11
Gimnastic	22	1	2	19	23	96	5

Top scorer: Imbernon (Principat) 27.
Cup Final: Principat 3, Don Pernil 1.

ARMENIA

Football Federation of Armenia, 9, Abovian Str. 375001 Erevan, Armenia.
Founded: 1992; *Number of Clubs:* 32; *Number of Players:* 15,000; *National Colours:* Red shirts, blue shorts, orange stockings.
Telephone: 00374 2/589480; *Telex:* 243337 minor su; *Fax:* 00374 2/151573.

International matches 1998
Libya (h) 1-0, Andorra (h) 3-1, Iceland (h) 0-0, Ukraine (a) 0-2, Estonia (h) 2-1.

League Championship wins (1992–98)
Shirak Gyumri 3*; Pyunik 2; Ararat Erevan 2*; Homenmen 1; FC Erevan 1; Tsement 1.
*Includes one unofficial title.

Cup wins (1992–99)
Ararat Erevan 4; Tsement 2; Banants 1; Pyunik 1.

Final League Table 1998

	P	W	D	L	F	A	Pts
Tsement	26	20	4	2	70	22	64
Shirak	26	19	4	3	72	25	61
FC Erevan	26	15	3	8	47	30	48
Ararat	26	10	5	11	35	36	35
Erebouni	26	9	4	13	38	42	31
Pyunik	26	6	3	17	27	68	21
Relegation							

	P	W	D	L	F	A	Pts
Dvinn	20	8	5	7	41	36	29
Karabach	20	4	5	11	24	37	17
Shirak 2	20	0	1	19	10	68	1

Play-Off
Shirak 2 - Lori 3-2
Top scorer: Akopyan (Dvinn) 20.
Cup Final: Tsement 3, Shirak 2.

AUSTRIA

Oesterreichischer Fussball-Bund, Ernst-Happel Stadion, Postfach 340, Meierestrasse, A-1021 Wien.
Founded: 1904; *Number of Clubs:* 2,081; *Number of Players:* 253,576; *National Colours:* White shirts, black shorts, white stockings.
Telephone: 0043 1 727 180; *Cable:* FOOTBALL WIEN; *Telex:* 111919 oefb a; *Fax:* 0043 1 728 1632.

International matches 1998
Hungary (h) 2-3, USA (h) 0-3, Tunisia (h) 2-1, Liechtenstein (h) 6-2, Cameroon (n) 1-1, Chile (n) 1-1,

Italy (n) 1-2, France (h) 2-2, Israel (h) 1-1, Cyprus (a) 3-0, San Marino (a) 4-1.

League Championship wins (1912–99)
Rapid Vienna 30; FK Austria 22; Admira-Energie-Wacker 9; First Vienna 6; Tirol-Svarowski-Innsbruck 7; Wiener Sportklub 3; Austria Salzburg 3; Sturm Graz 2; FAC 1; Hakoah 1; Linz ASK 1; WAF 1; Voest Linz 1.

Cup wins (1919–99)
FK Austria 25; Rapid Vienna 14; TS Innsbruck (prev. Wacker Innsbruck) 7; Admira-Energie-Wacker (prev. Sportklub Admira & Admira-Energie) 5; First Vienna 3; Sturm Graz 3; Linz ASK 1; Wacker Vienna 1; WAF 1; Wiener Sportklub 1; Graz 1; Stockerau 1; Ried 1.

Final League Table 1998–99

	P	W	D	L	F	A	Pts
Sturm Graz	36	23	4	9	72	32	73
Rapid	36	19	13	4	50	25	70
Graz	36	20	5	11	46	29	65
Austria Salzburg	36	15	12	9	55	40	57
Linz ASK	36	17	6	13	53	44	57
Innsbruck	36	15	10	11	49	41	55
FK Austria	36	13	11	12	41	44	50
Ried	36	8	8	20	25	47	32
Lustenau	36	4	11	21	24	61	23
Steyr* (-3)	36	3	6	27	29	81	12

Top scorer: Glieder (Austria Salzburg) 22.
Cup Final: Sturm Graz 1, Linz ASK 1.
Sturm Graz won 4-2 on penalties.

AZERBAIJAN

Association of Football Federations of Azerbaijan, Husu Haciyev kuc., 42, 370009 Baku, Azerbaijan.
Founded: 1992; *Number of Clubs:* 1,500; *Number of Players:* 95,000; *National Colours:* White shirts with blue stripes, blue shorts, white stockings.
Telephone: 00994 12 94 49 16; *Cable:* FOOTBALL ASSOCIATION, AZ; *Fax:* 00994 12 98 93 93.

International matches 1998
Moldovo (h) 1-0, Estonia (a) 0-0, Andorra (h) 0-0, Lithuania (a) 2-1, Georgia (h) 1-0, Slovakia (a) 0-3, Hungary (h) 0-4, Liechtenstein (a) 1-2, Estonia (h) 2-1.

League Championship wins (1992–99)
Kopaz 3; Karabach 2; Neftchi 2; Turan 1.

Cup wins (1992–99)
Kopaz 3; Neftchi 3; Karabach 1; Inshatchi 1.

Qualifying Table 1998–99

	P	W	D	L	F	A	Pts
Kopaz	26	18	4	4	76	14	58
Karabach	26	17	3	6	40	16	54
Dinamo Baku	26	16	4	6	36	16	52
Neftchi	26	15	7	4	47	17	52
Shamkir	26	16	2	8	39	23	50
Pivani	26	15	5	6	37	21	50
Turan	26	14	7	5	41	20	49
Vilash	26	14	4	8	31	20	46
Bakili	26	7	7	12	14	27	28
SKA Baku	26	6	8	12	18	24	26
Kimyachi	26	5	1	20	19	58	16
Shafa	26	3	5	18	19	49	14
Shahdag	26	2	4	20	17	81	10
Neftegaz	26	2	3	21	13	61	9

Final Table 1998–99

	P	W	D	L	F	A	Pts
Kopaz	10	8	1	1	17	7	25
Shankir	10	5	1	4	10	10	16
Neftchi	10	4	3	3	11	7	15
Karabach	10	3	3	4	5	8	12
Pivani	10	2	3	5	5	8	9
Dinamo Baku	10	2	1	7	6	14	7

Places 7–10

	P	W	D	L	F	A	Pts
Turan	6	4	2	0	17	6	14
Vilash	6	2	3	1	16	12	9
SKA Baku	6	2	3	1	8	7	9
Bakili	6	0	0	6	0	16	0

Promotion/Relegation Table 1998–99

	P	W	D	L	F	A	Pts
Shafa	4	3	1	0	12	3	10
Kimyachi	4	1	2	1	9	9	5
Neftegaz	4	0	1	3	3	12	1

Top scorer: Bahramov (Vilash) 24.
Cup Final: Neftchi 0, Shamkir 0.
Neftchi won on penalties.

BELARUS

Belarus Football Association, 8–2 Kyrov Str. 220600 Minsk, Belarus.
Founded: 1989; Number of Clubs: 455; *Number of Players:* 120,000; *National Colours:* All green.
Telephone: 007 0172 375 272325; *Telex:* 252175 athlet su; *Fax:* 007 0172 27 29 20.

International matches 1998
Lithuania (h) 3-0, Denmark (h) 0-0, Wales (a) 2-3.

League Championship wins (1992–98)
Dynamo Minsk 6; MPKC Mozyr 1; Dnepr Mogilev 1.

Cup wins (1992–99)
Dynamo Minsk 2; Belshina 2; Neman 1; Dynamo 93 Minsk 1; MPKC Mozyr 1; Lokomotiv 96 1.

Final League Table 1998

	P	W	D	L	F	A	Pts
Dnepr Mogilev	28	21	4	3	55	14	67
BATE Borisov	28	18	4	6	50	25	58
Belshina	28	17	6	5	47	17	57
Lokomotiv 96	28	14	6	8	35	24	48
Gomel	28	12	9	7	36	30	45
Slavia	28	12	9	7	41	36	45
Torpedo Minsk	28	12	8	8	44	22	44
Dynamo Minsk	28	11	6	11	39	38	39
Dynamo Brest	28	12	2	14	40	40	38
Neman	28	8	7	13	27	44	31
Shakhter	28	8	6	14	33	54	30
Torpedo Mogilev	28	7	8	13	30	40	29
Naftan	28	7	4	17	33	47	25
Molodechno	28	4	4	20	21	51	16
Kommunalnik*	28	3	5	20	14	63	14

Top scorer: Jaromko (Torpedo Minsk) 19.
Cup Final: Belshina 1, Slavia Mozyr 1.
Belshina won 4-2 on penalties.

BELGIUM

Union Royale Belge Des Societes De Football Association, 145 Avenue Houba de Strooper, B-1020 Bruxelles.
Founded: 1895; *Number of Clubs:* 2,120; *Number of Players:* 390,468; *National Colours:* All red.
Telephone: 0032 2 477 12 11; *Cable:* URBSFA BRUX-ELLES; *Telex:* 23257 bvbfbf b; *Fax:* 0032 2 478 23 91.

International matches 1998
USA (h) 2-0, Norway (h) 2-2, Romania (h) 1-1, France (a) 0-1, England (h) 0-0, Colombia (h) 2-0, Paraguay (h) 1-0, Holland (n) 0-0, Mexico (n) 2-2, South Korea (n) 1-1, Luxemborg (a) 0-0.

League Championship wins (1896–1999)
Anderlecht 24; Union St Gilloise 11; FC Brugge 11; Standard Liege 8; Beerschot 7; RC Brussels 6; FC Liege 5; Daring Brussels 5; Antwerp 4; Mechelen 4; Lierse SK 4; SV Brugge 3; Beveren 2; RWD Molenbeek 1; Genk 1.

Cup wins (1954–99)
Anderlecht 8; FC Brugge 7; Standard Liege 5; Beerschot 2; Waterschei 2; Beveren 2; Gent 2; Antwerp 2; Lierse SK 2; Racing Doornik 1; Waregem 1; SV Brugge 1; Mechelen 1; FC Liege 1; Ekeren 1; Genk 1.

Final League Table 1998–99

	P	W	D	L	F	A	Pts
Genk	34	22	7	5	74	38	73
FC Brugge	34	22	5	7	65	38	71
Anderlect	34	21	7	6	76	39	70
Mouscron	34	19	9	6	76	47	66
Lokeren	34	17	6	11	69	61	57
Lierse	34	16	6	12	72	47	54
Standard Liege	34	17	3	14	55	47	54
Gent	34	14	10	10	55	59	52
St Truiden	34	14	9	11	52	46	51
Ekeren	34	14	7	13	48	46	49
Harelbeke	34	10	11	13	44	46	41
Westerlo	34	11	7	16	56	62	40
Aalst	34	9	8	17	48	66	35
Charleroi	34	7	11	16	40	54	32
Beveren	34	8	6	20	33	60	30
Lommel	34	7	7	20	33	56	28
Kortrijk*	34	6	7	21	49	81	25
Ostend*	34	4	10	20	27	79	22

Top scorer: Koller (Lokeren) 24.
Cup Final: Lierse 3, Standard Liege 1.

BOSNIA HERZEGOVINA

Bosnia & Herzegovina Football Federation, Sime Milutinovico, 12/1 71000 Sarajevo.
Founded: 1992; *National Colours:* White shirts, blue shorts, white stockings.
Telephone: 00387 71/213881; *Fax:* 00387 71/444332.

International matches 1998
Argentina (a) 0-5, Macedonia (a) 1-1, Faeroes (h) 1-0, Estonia (h) 1-1, Czech Republic (h) 1-3, Lithuania (a) 2-4.

League Championship wins (1996–99)
Celik 2; Zeljeznicar 1; Sarajevo 1.

Cup wins (1996–99)
Sarajevo 2; Bosna 1; Celik 1.

Final League Table 1998–99

	P	W	D	L	F	A	Pts
Sarajevo	30	22	2	6	55	21	68
Bosna	30	18	2	10	50	21	56
Rudar	30	15	7	8	39	26	52
Velez	30	15	7	8	46	37	52
Sloboda	30	15	6	9	45	32	51
Jedinstvo	30	13	6	11	37	39	45
Zeljeznicar	30	12	8	10	43	30	44
Lukavac	30	13	4	13	36	32	43
Celik	30	13	3	14	47	42	42
Buducnost	30	12	6	12	23	27	42
Drina	30	8	10	12	28	34	34
Gradina	30	7	12	11	24	32	33
Iskra	30	8	8	14	29	39	32
Zenica	30	7	8	18	27	54	29
Zmajod*	30	7	5	18	34	57	26
Vrbanjusa*	30	5	6	19	22	57	21

Top scorer: Vazda (Zeljeznicar) 19.
Cup Final: Bosna 1, Sarajevo 0.

BULGARIA

Bulgarian Football Union, Karnigradska 19, BG-1000 Sofia.
Founded: 1923; *Number of Clubs:* 376; *Number of Players:* 48,240; *National Colours:* White shirts, green shorts, white stockings.
Telephone: 00359 2 987 74 90; *Cable:* BULFUTBOL SOFIA; *Telex:* 23145 bfs bg; *Fax:* 00359 2 986 2538.

International matches 1998
Argentina (a) 0-2, Macedonia (a) 0-1, Morocco (h) 2-1, Algeria (h) 2-0, Paraguay (n) 0-0, Nigeria (n) 2-3, Spain (n) 1-6, Poland (h) 0-3, England (a) 0-0, Sweden (h) 0-1, Algeria (h) 0-0.

League Championship wins (1925–99)
CSKA Sofia 28; Levski Sofia 19; Slavia Sofia 7; Vladislav Varna 3; Lokomotiv Sofia 3; Litets 2; Trakia Plovdiv 2; AC 23 Sofia 1; Botev Plovdiv 1; SC Sofia 1; Sokol Varna 1; Spartak Plovdiv 1; Tichka Varna 1; JSZ Sofia 1; Beroe Stara Zagora 1; Etur 1.

Cup wins (1946–99)
Levski Sofia 19; CSKA Sofia 16; Slavia Sofia 7; Lokomotiv Sofia 4; Botev Plovdiv 1; Spartak Plovdiv 1; Spartak Sofia 1; Marek Stanke 1; Trakia Plovdiv 1; Spartak Varna 1; Sliven 1.

Final League Table 1998–99

	P	W	D	L	F	A	Pts
Litets	30	24	4	2	83	25	76
Levski Sofia	30	23	5	2	55	11	74
Levski Kustendil	30	18	4	8	57	29	57
Lokomotiv Sofia	30	17	4	9	46	30	55
CSKA Sofia	30	15	6	9	54	39	50
Neftochimik	30	15	4	11	52	38	49
Slavia Sofia	30	11	8	11	47	36	41
Mineur	30	11	7	12	44	46	40
Dobrudja	30	11	3	16	45	55	36
Metalurg	30	11	2	17	33	46	35
Spartak Varna	30	10	4	16	39	50	34
Pirin	30	10	4	16	35	58	34
Botev Plovdiv	30	9	5	16	34	55	32
Chumen*	30	8	8	14	36	56	32
Lokomotiv Plovdiv*	30	4	5	21	26	73	17
Septemvri Sofia*	30	4	5	21	34	73	17

Top scorer: Beliakov (Litets) 21.
Cup Final: CSKA Sofia 1, Litets 0.

CROATIA

Croatian Football Federation, Illica 31, CRO-10000 Zagreb, Croatia.
Founded: 1912; *Number of Clubs:* 1,221; *Number of Players:* 78,127; *National Colours:* Red/white shirts, white shorts, blue stockings.
Telephone: 00385 1/4554100. *Fax:* 00385 1 42 46 39.

International matches 1998
Poland (h) 4-1, Slovakia (a) 2-1, Iran (h) 2-0, Australia (h) 7-0, Jamaica (n) 3-1, Japan (n) 1-0, Argentina (n) 0-1, Romania (n) 1-0, Germany (n) 3-0, France (n) 1-2, Holland (n) 2-1, Eire (a) 0-2, Malta (a) 4-1, Macedonia (h) 3-2.

League Championship wins (1941–44; 1992–99)
Croatia Zagreb 5; Hajduk Split 3; Gradanski 3; Concordia 1.

Cup wins (1993–99)
Croatia Zagreb 4, Hajduk Split 2, Osijek 1.

Final League Table 1998–99

	P	W	D	L	F	A	Pts
Croatia Zagreb	22	17	2	3	44	14	53
Rijeka	22	17	1	4	35	18	52
Hajduk Split	22	12	6	4	38	17	42
Osijek	22	11	3	8	37	23	36
Varteks	22	9	3	10	40	36	30
Hrvatski	22	6	7	9	17	23	25
Sibenik	22	7	3	12	27	45	24
Cibalia	22	6	5	11	28	29	23
Zagreb	22	5	8	9	38	37	23
Zadarcommerce	22	5	6	11	27	40	21
Slaven	22	5	6	11	24	37	21
Mladost 127	22	4	13	22	42	19	

Top scorer: Popovic (Sibenik) 21.
Cup Final: Osijek 2, Cibalia 1.

CYPRUS

Cyprus Football Association, 1 Stasinos Str., Engomi, P.O. Box 5071, CY-2404 Nicosia.
Founded: 1934; *Number of Clubs:* 85; *Number of Players:* 6,000; *National Colours:* Blue shirts, white shorts, blue stockings.
Telephone: 00357 2 /352341; *Cable:* FOOTBALL CYPRUS; *Telex:* 3880 football cy; *Fax:* 00357 2/590544.

International matches 1998
Finland (h) 1-1, Slovenia (h) 1-0, Albania (h) 3-2, Spain (h) 3-2, Austria (h) 0-3, San Marino (a) 1-0.

League Championship wins (1935–99)
Omonia 17; Apoel 16; Anorthosis 10; AEL 5; EPA 3; Olympiakos 3; Apollon 2; Pezoporikos 2; Chetin Kayal 1; Trast 1.

Cup wins (1935–99)
Apoel 17; Omonia 10; AEL 6; EPA 5; Anorthosis 5; Apollon 4; Trast 3; Chetin Kayal 2; Olympiakos 1; Pezoporikos 1; Salamina 1.

Final League Table 1998–99

	P	W	D	L	F	A	Pts
Anorthosis	26	21	4	1	95	28	67
Omonia	26	21	4	1	81	25	67
Apoel	26	19	2	5	70	29	59
AEK	26	14	3	9	63	45	45
AEL	26	13	5	8	55	39	44
Ethnikos	26	12	6	8	49	43	42
Apollon	26	13	2	11	51	45	41
ENP	26	8	8	10	55	64	32
Olympiakos	26	8	5	13	40	49	29
Salamina	26	8	4	14	46	53	28
Alki	26	7	4	15	37	70	25
Evagoras*	26	6	4	16	30	66	22
Doxa*	26	2	3	21	27	79	9
Aris*	26	3	0	23	32	96	9

Top scorer: Rauffmann (Omonia) 35.
Cup Final: Apoel 2, Anorthosis 0.

CZECH REPUBLIC

Football Association of Czech Republic, Diskarska 100, 169 00 Prague 6 - Strahov, Czech Republic.
Founded: 1901; *Number of Clubs:* 3,836; *Number of Players:* 319,500; *National Colours:* Red shirts, white shorts, blue stockings.
Telephone: 00422 20513575; *Cable:* SPORTSVAZ PRAHA; *Telex:* 122650 cstv c; *Fax:* 004202 3335 3107.

International matches 1998
Eire (h) 2-1, Slovenia (a) 3-1, Paraguay (a) 1-0, Japan (a) 0-0, South Korea (a) 2-2, Denmark (h) 1-0, Faeroes (a) 1-0, Bosnia (a) 3-1, Estonia (h) 4-1, England (a) 0-2.

League Championship wins (1926–93)
Sparta Prague 20; Slavia Prague 12; Dukla Prague (prev. UDA) 11; Slovan Bratislava 7; Spartak Trnava 5; Banik Ostrava 3; Inter-Bratislava 3; Spartak Hradec Kralove 1; Viktoria Zizkov 1; Zbrojovka Brno 1; Bohemians 1; Vitkovice 1.

Cup wins (1961–93)
Dukla Prague 8; Sparta Prague 8; Slovan Bratislava 5; Spartak Trnava 4; Banik Ostrava 3; Lokomotiv Kosice 3; TJ Gottwaldov 1; Dunajska Streda 1.
From 1993–94, there were two separate countries; the Czech Republic and Slovakia.

League Championship wins (1993–99)
Sparta Prague 6; Slavia Prague 1.

Cup wins (1994–99)
Slavia Prague 2; Viktoria Zizkov 1; Spartak Hradec Kralove 1; Sparta Prague 1; Jablonec 1.

Final League Table 1998–99

	P	W	D	L	F	A	Pts
Sparta Prague	30	17	9	4	62	23	60
Teplice	30	16	7	7	55	30	55
Slavia Prague	30	15	10	5	51	31	55
Sigma Olomouc	30	12	11	7	42	34	47
Banik Ostrava	30	10	15	5	39	26	45
Chmel Bisany	30	12	6	12	48	44	42
Boby Brno	30	11	8	11	37	33	41
Hradec Kralove	30	11	6	13	33	40	39
Slovan Liberec	30	9	11	10	33	34	38
Viktoria Zizkov	30	11	5	14	31	47	38
Petra Drnovice	30	9	10	11	35	44	37
Jablonec	30	9	8	13	37	46	35
Dukla Prague	30	8	9	13	28	41	33
Kaucuk Opava	30	8	8	14	40	54	32
Viktoria Plzen*	30	8	8	14	26	43	32
Karvina*	30	6	5	19	28	55	23

Top scorer: Siegl (Sparta Prague) 18.
Cup Final: Slavia Prague 1, Slovan Liberec 0.

DENMARK

Danish Football Association, Idraettens Hus, Brondby Stadion 20, DK-2605, Brondby.
Founded: 1889; *Number of Clubs:* 1,555; *Number of Players:* 268,517; *National Colours:* Red shirts, white shorts, red stockings.
Telephone: 0045 43/262222; *Cable:* DANSKBOLDSPIL COPENHAGEN; *Telex:* 15545 dbu dk; *Fax:* 0045 43/262245.

International matches 1998
Scotland (a) 1-0, Norway (h) 0-2, Sweden (a) 0-3, Cameroon (h) 1-2, Saudi Arabia (n) 1-0, South Africa (n) 1-1, France (n) 1-2, Nigeria (n) 4-1, Brazil (n) 2-3, Denmark (h) 1-0, Belarus (a) 0-0, Wales (h) 1-2, Switzerland (a) 1-1.

League Championship wins (1913–99)
KB Copenhagen 15; B 93 Copenhagen 10; AB (Akademisk) 9; Brondby 8; B 1903 Copenhagen 7; Frem 6; Esbjerg BK 5; Vejle BK 5; AGF Aarhus 5; Hvidovre 3; Odense BK 3; AaB Aalborg 2; B 1909 Odense 2; Koge BK 2; Lyngby 2; FC Copenhagen 1; Silkeborg 1.

Cup wins (1955–99)
Aarhus GF 9; Vejle BK 6; Randers Freja 3; Lyngby 3; OB Odense 3; Brondby 3; B1909 Odense 2; Aalborg BK 2; Esbjerg BK 2; Frem 2; B 1903 Copenhagen 2; FC Copenhagen 2; B 93 Copenhagen 1; KB Copenhagen 1; Vanlose 1; Hvidovre 1; B1913 Odense 1, AB Copenhagen 1.

Final League Table 1998–99

	P	W	D	L	F	A	Pts
Aalborg	33	17	13	3	65	37	64
Brondby	33	19	4	10	73	37	61
AB Copenhagen	33	17	5	11	49	36	56
Lyngby	33	14	10	9	55	60	52
Herfolge	33	12	11	10	44	36	47
Vejle	33	14	5	14	54	48	47
FC Copenhagen	33	12	10	11	55	52	46
Viborg	33	13	5	15	61	59	44
Silkeborg	33	10	14	9	52	53	44
Aarhus	33	11	10	12	45	55	43
Fremad*	33	7	8	18	51	73	29
B1893*	33	3	3	27	22	80	12

Top scorer: Fernandez (Viborg) 23.
Cup Final: AB Copenhagen 2, Aalborg 1.

ENGLAND

The Football Association, 16 Lancaster Gate, London W2 3LW.
Founded: 1863; *Number of Clubs:* 42,000; *Number of Players:* 2,250,000; *National Colours:* White shirts with navy blue collar, navy blue shorts, white stockings with light blue top.
Telephone: 0171 262 4542, 0171 402 7151; *Cable:* FOOTBALL ASSOCIATION LONDON W2; *Telex:* 261110 faldn g; *Fax:* 0171 402 0486.

ESTONIA

Estonian Football Association, Voidu 16, Tallinn EE 0012.
Founded: 1921; *Number of Clubs:* 40; *Number of Players:* 12,000; *National Colours:* Blue shirts, black shorts, white stockings.
Telephone: 00372 6/542715, 542716, 542717; *Fax:* 00372 6/542719.

International matches 1998
Mexico (a) 0-5, Azerbaijan (h) 0-0, Faeroes (h) 5-0, Andorra (h) 2-1, Latvia (h) 0-2, Lithuania (h) 0-0, Moldova (h) 0-1, Bosnia (a) 1-1, Egypt (h) 2-2, Scotland (a) 2-3, Czech Republic (a) 1-4, Georgia (n) 1-3, Armenia (a) 1-2, Azerbaijan (a) 1-2.

League Championship wins (1922–40; 1992–99)
Sport 8; Estonia 5; Flora Tallinn 4; Norma Tallinn 2; Tallinn JK 2; Kalev 2; LFLS 1; Olimpia 1; Lantana 1.

Cup wins (1992–99)
Sadam 2; VMV Tallinn 1; Nikol Tallinn 1; Norma Tallinn 1, Lantana 1; Flora Tallinn 1; Levadia 1.

Final League Table 1998–99

	P	W	D	L	F	A	Pts
Flora	14	11	2	1	46	13	35
Sadam	14	11	1	2	48	10	34
Lantana	14	7	4	3	27	20	25
Trans	14	6	5	3	28	20	23
Tulevik	14	5	3	6	15	25	18
VMK	14	3	4	7	15	27	13
Johvi	14	2	0	12	10	44	6
Lelle*	14	0	3	11	10	39	3

Lelle reprieved from relegation following the amalgamation of Sadam with Levadia, the promoted club. Johvi remained in Division One after a play-off with Second Division Vigri.
Top scorers: Oper (Flora), Zelinski (Flora), Krolov (Sadam) 10.
Cup Final: Levadia 3, Tulevik 2.

FAEROE ISLANDS

Fotboltssamband Foroya, The Faeroes' Football Assn., Gundalur, P.O. Box 3028, FR-110, Torshavn.
Founded: 1979; *Number of Clubs:* 16; *Number of Players:* 1,014; *National Colours:* White shirts, blue shorts, white stockings.
Telephone: 00298 31 6707/457607; *Telex:* 81328 nspkkl fa; *Fax:* 00298 31 9079.

International matches 1998
Estonia (a) 0-5, Bosnia (a) 0-1, Czech Republic (h) 0-1, Lithuania (a) 0-0, Scotland (a) 1-2.

League Championship wins (1942–98)
KI Klaksvik 15; HB Torshavn 15; TB Tvoroyri 7; GI Gotu 7; B36 Torshavn 6; B68 Toftir 3; SI Sorvag 1; IF Fuglafjordur 1; B71 Sandur 1.

Cup wins (1955–98)
HB Torshavn 25; TB Tvoroyri 4; KI Klaksvik 4; GI Gotu 4; B36 Torshavn 1; VB Vagur 1; NSI Runavik 1; B71 Sandur 1.

Final League Table 1998

	P	W	D	L	F	A	Pts
HB	18	14	3	1	57	19	45
KI	18	11	5	2	54	24	38
B36	18	11	4	3	59	24	37
GI	18	8	4	6	48	30	28
NSI	18	8	4	6	37	28	28
B68	18	6	4	8	39	39	22
VB	18	5	6	9	27	40	21
IF	18	1	8	9	25	47	11
Sumba+	18	2	3	13	18	73	9
TB*	18	1	5	12	21	61	8

Top scorer: Borg A (B36) 20.
Cup Final: HB 2, KI 1 0.

FINLAND

Suomen Palloliitto Finlands Bollfoerbund, Lantinen Brahenkatu 2, P.O. Box 179, SF-00511 Helsinki.
Founded: 1907; *Number of Clubs:* 1,135; *Number of Players:* 66,100; *National Colours:* White shirts, blue shorts, white stockings.
Telephone: 00358 0 9701 01 01; *Cable:* SUOMIFOT-BOLL HELSINKI; *Telex:* 126033 spl sf; *Fax:* 00358 0 9701 01 099.

International matches 1998
Cyprus (a) 1-1, Slovakia (a) 0-2, Malta (a) 2-0, Scotland (a) 1-1, Germany (h) 0-0, France (h) 0-1, Slovakia (a) 0-0, Moldova (h) 3-2, N Ireland (a) 0-1, Turkey (a) 3-1.

League Championship wins (1949–98)
HJK Helsinki 10; Valkeakosken Haka 6; Turun Palloseura 5; Kuopion Palloseura 5; Kuusysi 4; Lahden Reipas 3; IF Kamraterna 3; Ilves-Kissat 2; Jazz Pori 2; Kotkan TP 2; OPS Oulu 2; Torun Pyrkiva 1; IF Kronohagens 1; Helsinki PS 1; Kokkolan PV 1; Vasa 1; TPV Tampere 1.

Cup wins (1955–98)
Valkeakosken Haka 10; Lahden Reipas 7; HJK Helsinki 6; Kotkan TP 4; Mikkeli 2; Kuusysi 2; Kuopion Palloseura 2; Ilves Tampere 2; TPS Turku 2; ; MyPa 2; IFK Abo 1; Drott 1; Helsinki PS 1; Pallo-Peikot 1; Rovaniemi PS 1.

Final League Table 1998

	P	W	D	L	F	A	Pts
Haka	27	13	9	5	46	31	48
VPS	27	12	9	6	42	27	45
PK-35	27	11	11	5	36	24	44
HJK Helsinki	27	9	11	7	33	31	38
Jazz Pori	27	9	8	10	37	36	35
TPS Turku	27	8	10	9	25	31	34
MyPa	27	8	8	11	35	39	32
RoPS Rovaniemi	27	6	14	7	27	31	32
FinnPa+	27	5	11	11	37	43	26
Jaro*	27	4	9	14	25	50	21

Top scorer: Hiukka (RoPS Rovaniemi) 11.
Cup Final: HJK Helsinki 3, PK-35 2.

FRANCE

Federation Francaise De Football, 60 Bis Avenue D'Iena, F-75783 Paris, Cedex 16.
Founded: 1919; *Number of Clubs:* 21,629; *Number of Players:* 1,692,205; *National Colours:* Blue shirts, white shorts, red stockings.
Telephone: 0033 1 44 31 73 00; *Cable:* CEFI PARIS 034; *Telex:* 640000 fedfoot f; *Fax:* 0033 1 47 20 82 96.

International matches 1998
Spain (h) 1-0, Norway (h) 3-3, Russia (a) 0-1, Sweden (a) 0-0, Belgium (h) 1-0, Morocco (a) 2-2, Finland (a) 1-0, South Africa (h) 3-0, Saudi Arabia (h) 4-0, Denmark (h) 2-1, Paraguay (h) 1-0, Italy (h) 0-0, Croatia (h) 2-1, Brazil (h) 3-0, Austria (a) 2-2, Iceland (a) 1-1, Russia (a) 3-2, Andorra (h) 2-0.

League Championship wins (1933–99)
Saint Etienne 10; Olympique Marseille 8; Nantes 7; Stade de Reims 6; AS Monaco 6; Girondins Bordeaux 5; OGC Nice 4; Lille OSC 3; Paris St Germain 2; FC Sete 2; Sochaux 2; Racing Club Paris 1; Roubaix-Tourcoing 1; Strasbourg 1; Auxerre 1; Lens 1.

Cup wins (1918–99)
Olympique Marseille 10; Saint Etienne 6; Lille OSC 5; Racing Club Paris 5; Red Star 5; AS Monaco 5; Olympique Lyon 4; Paris St Germain 4; Girondins Bordeaux 3; OGC Nice 3; CAS Genereaux 2; Nancy 2; Racing Club Strasbourg 2; Sedan 2; FC Sete 2; Stade de Reims 2; SO Montpellier 2; Stade Rennes 2; Auxerre 2; Nantes 2; AS Cannes 1; Club Français 1; Excelsior Roubaix 1; Le Havre 1; Olympique de Pantin 1; CA Paris 1; Sochaux 1; Toulouse 1; Bastia 1; Metz 1.

Final League Table 1998–99

	P	W	D	L	F	A	Pts
Bordeaux	34	22	6	6	66	29	72
Marseille	34	21	8	5	56	28	71
Lyon	34	18	9	7	51	31	63
Monaco	34	18	8	8	52	32	62
Rennes	34	17	8	9	45	38	59
Lens	34	14	7	13	46	43	49
Nantes	34	12	12	10	40	34	48
Montpellier	34	11	10	13	53	50	43
Paris St Germain	34	10	9	15	34	35	39
Metz	34	9	12	13	28	37	39
Nancy	34	10	9	15	35	45	39
Strasbourg	34	8	14	12	30	36	38
Bastia	34	10	8	16	37	46	38
Auxerre	34	9	10	15	40	45	37
Le Havre	34	8	11	15	23	38	35
Lorient*	34	8	11	15	33	49	35
Sochaux*	34	6	15	13	30	54	33
Toulouse*	34	6	11	17	24	53	29

Top scorer: Wiltord (Bordeaux) 22.
Cup Final: Nantes 1, Sedan 0.

GEORGIA

Georgian Football Federation, 5 Shota Iamanidze Str, Tbilisi 380012, Georgia.
Founded: 1990; *Number of Clubs:* 4050. *Number of Players:* 115,000; *National Colours:* White shirts, black shorts, cherry stockings.
Telephone: 00995 32/960750; *Fax:* 00995 32/001128.

International matches 1998
Latvia (h) 2-1, Albania (h) 3-0, Malta (a) 3-1, Tunisia (a) 1-1, Russia (h) 1-1, Azerbaijan (a) 0-1, Ukraine (a) 0-4, Albania (h) 1-0, Latvia (a) 0-1, Greece (a) 0-3, Estonia (h) 3-1.

League Championship wins (1990–99)
Dynamo Tbilisi 10.

Cup wins (1992–1999)
Dynamo Tbilisi 7; Dynamo Batumi 1, Torpedo Kutaisi 1.

Final League Table 1998–99

	P	W	D	L	F	A	Pts
Dynamo Tbilisi	30	24	5	1	91	17	77
Torpedo Kutaisi	30	21	4	5	73	27	67
Lokomotivi	30	18	10	2	43	14	64
Kolkheti	30	15	7	8	57	36	52
Dynamo Batumi	30	13	11	6	49	22	50
Merani 91	30	12	9	9	38	31	45
WIT (-3)	30	14	5	11	44	30	44
Samtredia	30	11	5	14	45	48	38
Arsenali	30	9	11	10	34	44	38
Dila Gori	30	10	5	15	37	54	35
Samgurali	30	10	3	17	32	57	33
Gorda	30	7	11	12	28	26	32
Sioni+	30	7	7	16	27	52	28
TSU+	30	6	9	15	28	46	27
Odishi*	30	6	2	22	21	70	20
Guria*	30	3	4	23	34	87	13

Top Scorer: Ashvetia (Dynamo Tbilisi) 26.
Cup Final: Torpedo Kutaisi 0, Samgurali 0.
Torpedo Kutaisi won 4-2 on penalties.

GERMANY

Deutsche Fussball-Bund, Postfach 710265, D-60492, Frankfurt Am Main.
Founded: 1900; *Number of Clubs:* 26,760; *Number of Players:* 5,260,320; *National Colours:* White shirts, black shorts, white stockings.
Telephone: 0049 69 678 80; *Telex:* 416815 dfb d; *Fax:* 0049 69 678 82 66.

International matches 1998
Oman (a) 2-0, Saudi Arabia (a) 3-0, Brazil (h) 1-2, Nigeria (h) 1-0, Finland (a) 0-0, Colombia (h) 3-1, Luxemborg (h) 7-0, USA (n) 2-0, Yugoslavia (n) 2-2, Iran (n) 2-0, Mexico (n) 2-1, Croatia (n) 0-3, Malta (a) 2-1, Romania (h) 1-1, Turkey (a) 0-1, Moldova (a) 3-1, Holland (h) 1-1.

League Championship wins (1903–99)
Bayern Munich 15; IFC Nuremberg 9; Schalke 04 7; SV Hamburg 6; Borussia Moenchengladbach 5; Borussia Dortmund 5; VfB Stuttgart 4; IFC Kaiserslautern 4; VfB Leipzig 3; Sp Vgg Furth 3; IFC Cologne 3; Werder Bremen 3; Viktoria Berlin 2; Hertha Berlin 2; Hanover 96 2; Dresden SC 2; Munich 1860 1; Union Berlin 1; FC Freiburg 1; Phoenix Karlsruhe 1; Karlsruher FV 1; Holsten Kiel 1; Fortuna Dusseldorf 1; Rapid Vienna 1; VfB Mannheim 1; Rot-Weiss Essen 1; Eintracht Frankfurt 1; Eintracht Brunswick 1.

Cup wins (1935–99)
Bayern Munich 9; IFC Cologne 4; Eintracht Frankfurt 4; Werder Bremen 4; IFC Nuremberg 3; SV Hamburg 3; Moenchengladbach 3; VfB Stuttgart 3; Dresden SC 2; Fortuna Dusseldorf 2; Karlsruhe SC 2; Munich 1860 2; Schalke 04 2; Borussia Dortmund 2; Kaiserslautern 2; First Vienna 1; VfB Leipzig 1; Kickers Offenbach 1; Rapid Vienna 1; Rot-Weiss Essen 1; SW Essen 1; Bayer Uerdingen 1; Hannover 96 1; Leverkusen 1.

Final League Table 1998–99

	P	W	D	L	F	A	Pts
Bayern Munich	34	24	6	4	76	28	78
Leverkusen	34	17	12	5	61	30	63
Hertha	34	18	8	8	59	32	62
Borussia Dortmund	34	16	9	9	48	34	57
Kaiserslautern	34	17	6	11	51	47	57
Wolfsburg	34	15	10	9	54	49	55
Hamburg	34	13	11	10	47	46	50
Duisburg	34	13	10	11	48	45	49
Munich 1860	34	11	8	15	49	56	41
Schalke	34	10	11	13	41	54	41
Stuttgart	34	9	12	13	41	48	39
Freiburg	34	10	9	15	36	44	39
Werder Bremen	34	10	8	16	41	47	38
Hansa Rostock	34	9	11	14	49	58	38
Eintracht Frankfurt	34	9	10	15	44	54	37
Nuremberg*	34	7	16	11	40	50	37
Bochum*	34	7	8	19	40	65	29
Moenchengladbach*	34	4	9	21	41	79	21

Top scorer: Preetz (Hertha) 23.
Cup Final: Werder Bremen 1, Bayern Munich 1.
Werder Bremen won 5-4 on penalties.

GREECE

Federation Hellenique De Football, Singrou Avenue 137, 17121 Athens.
Founded: 1926; *Number of Clubs:* 4,050; *Number of Players:* 180,000; *National Colours:* White shirts, blue shorts, white stockings.
Telephone: 0030 1 933 88 50; *Cable:* FOOTBALL ATHENS; *Telex:* 215328 epo gr; *Fax:* 0030 1 935 96 66.

International matches 1998
Russia (h) 1-1, Romania (a) 1-2, Slovenia (h) 2-2, Georgia (h) 3-0, Albania (a) 0-0.

League Championship wins (1928–99)
Olympiakos 28; Panathinaikos 18; AEK Athens 11; Aris Salonika 3; PAOK Salonika 2; Larissa 1.

Cup wins (1932–99)
Olympiakos 21; Panathinaikos 16; AEK Athens 11; PAOK Salonika 2; Panionios 2; Aris Salonika 1; Ethnikos 1; Iraklis 1; Kastoria 1; Larissa 1; Ofi Crete 1.

Final League Table 1998–99

	P	W	D	L	F	A	Pts
Olympiakos	34	27	4	3	82	21	85
AEK Athens	34	23	6	5	71	27	75
Panathinaikos	34	23	6	6	66	36	74
PAOK Salonika	34	19	5	10	51	31	62
Ionikos	34	17	9	8	64	36	60
Aris	34	19	3	12	53	43	60
Xanthi	34	16	8	10	44	33	56
Ofi Crete	34	16	3	15	50	44	51
Iraklis	34	13	8	13	54	45	47
Kavala	34	12	6	16	46	62	42
Astir	34	11	7	16	40	58	40
Proodeftiki	34	10	9	15	28	37	39
Paniliakos	34	11	5	18	37	54	38
Apollon	34	9	9	16	42	62	36
Panionios	34	9	5	20	42	58	32
Panelefsiniakos*	34	7	11	16	25	49	32
Veria*	34	6	5	23	20	55	23
Ethnikos*	34	0	8	26	17	81	8

Top scorer: Nikolaidis (AEK Athens) 22.
Cup Final: Olympiakos 2, Panathinaikos 0.

HOLLAND

Koninklijke Nederlandsche Voetbalbond, Woudenbergseweg 56-58, Postbus 515, NL-3700 AM, Zeist.
Founded: 1889; *Number of Clubs:* 3,097; *Number of Players:* 962,397; *National Colours:* Orange shirts, white shorts, orange stockings.
Telephone: 0031343 499211; *Cable:* VOETBAL ZEIST; *Telex:* 40497 knvb nl; *Fax:* 0031343 499189.

International matches 1998
USA (a) 2-0, Mexico (a) 3-2, Cameroon (h) 0-0, Paraguay (h) 5-1, Nigeria (h) 5-1, Belgium (n) 0-0, South

Korea (n) 5-0, Mexico (n) 2-2, Yugoslavia (n) 2-1, Argentina (n) 2-1, Brazil (n) 1-1, Croatia (n) 1-2, Peru (h) 2-0, Ghana (h) 0-0, Germany (a) 1-1.

League Championship wins (1898–1999)
Ajax Amsterdam 27; Feyenoord 15; PSV Eindhoven 14; HVV The Hague 8; Sparta Rotterdam 6; Go Ahead Deventer 4; HBS The Hague 3; Willem II Tilburg 3; RCH Haarlem 2; RAP 2; Heracles 2; ADO The Hague 2; Quick The Hague 1; BVV Schiedam 1; NAC Breda 1; Eindhoven 1; Enschede 1; Volewijckers Amsterdam 1; Limburgia 1; Rapid JC Haarlem 1; DOS Utrecht 1; DWS Amsterdam 1; Haarlem 1; Be Quick Groningen 1; SVV Schiedam 1; AZ 67 Alkmaar 1.

Cup wins (1899–1999)
Ajax Amsterdam 14; Feyenoord 10; PSV Eindhoven 8; Quick The Hague 4; AZ 67 Alkmaar 3; Rotterdam 3; DFC 2; Fortuna Geleen 2; Haarlem 2; HBS The Hague 2; RCH 2; VOC 2; Wageningen 2; Willem II Tilburg 2; FC Den Haag 2; Concordia Rotterdam 1; CVV 1; Eindhoven 1; HVV The Hague 1; Longa 1; Quick Nijmegen 1; RAP 1; Roermond 1; Schoten 1; Velocitas Breda 1; Velocitas Groningen 1; VSV 1; VUC 1; VVV Groningen 1; ZFC 1; NAC Breda 1; Twente Enschede 1; Utrecht 1; Roda 1.

Final League Table 1997–99

	P	W	D	L	F	A	Pts
Feyenoord	34	25	5	4	76	38	80
Willem II	34	20	5	9	69	46	65
PSV Eindhoven	34	17	10	7	87	55	61
Vitesse	34	18	7	9	61	44	61
Roda JC	34	17	9	8	59	40	60
Ajax	34	16	9	9	73	41	57
Heerenveen	34	14	12	8	53	41	54
Twente	34	13	13	8	51	45	52
AZ	34	12	12	10	52	60	48
Fortuna Sittard	34	12	8	14	49	56	44
NEC Nijmegen	34	10	9	15	42	56	39
Utrecht	34	10	8	16	54	64	38
De Graafschap	34	8	12	14	40	57	36
Maastricht	34	7	11	16	42	63	32
Cambuur	34	7	11	16	37	64	32
RKC Waalwijk+	34	6	9	19	41	62	27
Sparta+	34	7	5	22	37	71	26
NAC Breda*	34	4	11	19	41	61	23

Top scorer: Van Nistelrooy (PSV Eindhoven) 31.
Cup Final: Ajax 2, Fortuna Sittard 0.

HUNGARY

Hungarian Football Federation, Magyar Labdarugo Szovetseg, Istvanmezei ut. 3-5, Nepstadion (Toronyepulet), H-1146 Budapest. For correspondence: Pf. 106H-1581 Budapest.
Founded: 1901; *Number of Clubs:* 1944; *Number of Players* 95,986; *National Colours:* Red shirts, white shorts, green stockings.
Telephone: 0036 1 222 0343; *Telex:* 225782 misz h; *Fax:* 0036 1 222 0324/222 0344.

International matches 1998
Austria (a) 3-2, Iran (a) 2-0, Macedonia (h) 0-0, Lithuania (h) 1-0, Slovenia (h) 2-1, Portugal (h) 1-3, Azerbaijan (a) 4-0, Romania (h) 1-1, Switzerland (h) 2-0.

League Championship wins (1901–99)
Ferencvaros 26; MTK-VM Budapest 21; Ujpest Dozsa 20; Honved 13; Vasas Budapest 6; Csepel 4; Raba Gyor 3; BTC 2; Nagyvarad 1; Vac 1.

Cup wins (1910–99)
Ferencvaros 17; MTK-VM Budapest 11; Ujpest Dozsa 8; Raba Gyor 4; Kispest Honved 4; Vasas Budapest 3; Diösgyör 2; Bocskai 1; III Ker 1; Kispesti AC 1; Soroksar 1; Szolnoki MAV 1; Siofok Banyasz 1; Bekescsaba 1; Pecs 1; Debrecen 1.
Cup not regularly held until 1964.

Final League Table 1998–99

	P	W	D	L	F	A	Pts
MTK	34	27	2	5	77	26	83
Ferencvaros	34	19	7	8	61	40	64
Ujpest	34	20	3	11	58	40	63
Gyori	34	16	11	7	53	39	59
Dunaferr	34	17	6	11	54	46	57
Vasas	34	15	10	9	51	44	55
Zalaegerszeg	34	15	8	11	43	37	53
Diosgyor	34	14	9	11	56	54	51
Debrecen	34	14	7	13	53	39	49
Vac	34	13	10	11	51	49	49
Gazszer	34	11	11	12	37	40	44
Kispest Honved	34	11	9	14	38	50	42
Nyiregyhaza	34	10	9	15	46	52	39
Haladas	34	10	6	18	39	54	36
Siofok	34	7	9	18	32	49	30
Videoton*	34	7	9	18	36	54	30
BVSC*	34	7	6	21	34	53	27
TVE*	34	4	6	24	40	93	18

Top scorer: Illes (MTK) 22.
Cup Final: Debrecen 2, Tatabanya 1.

ICELAND

Knattspyrnusamband Island, Laugardal, 104 Reykjavik.
Founded: 1929; *Number of Clubs:* 73; *Number of Players:* 23,673; *National Colours;* All blue.
Telephone: 00354 5102900; *Cable* KSI REYKJAVIK; *Telex:* 2314 isi is; *Fax:* 00354 75689793.

International matches 1998
Slovenia (a) 2-3, Slovakia (a) 1-2, Saudi Arabia (a) 1-1, South Africa (a) 1-1, Latvia (h) 4-1, France (h) 1-1, Armenia (a) 0-0, Russia (h) 1-0.

League Championship wins (1912–98)
KR 20; Valur 19; Fram 18; IA Akranes 17; Vikingur 5; IBV Vestmann 4; IBK Keflavik 3; KA Akureyri 1.

Cup wins (1960–98)
KR 9; Valur 8; Fram 7; IA Akranes 6; IBV Vestmann 4; IBK Keflavik 2; IBA Akureyri 1; Vikingur 1.

Final League Table 1998

	P	W	D	L	F	A	Pts
IBV	18	12	2	4	40	15	38
KR	18	9	6	3	25	9	33
IA	18	8	6	4	27	22	30
IBK	18	8	4	6	19	23	28
Leiftur	18	7	4	7	21	21	25
Fram	18	5	5	8	21	23	20
Grindavik	18	5	4	9	24	34	19
Valur	18	4	6	8	25	33	18
Trottur*	18	4	6	8	27	39	18
IR*	18	4	5	9	20	30	17

Top scorer: Johannesson (IBV) 16.
Cup Final: IBV 2, Leiftur 0.

REPUBLIC OF IRELAND

The Football Association of Ireland, (Cumann Peile Na H-Eireann), 80 Merrion Square, South Dublin 2.
Founded: 1921; *Number of Clubs:* 3,190; *Number of Players:* 124,615; *National Colours:* Green shirts, white shorts, green and white stockings.
Telephone: 00353 1 676 68 64; *Telex:* 91397 fai ei; *Fax:* 00353 1 661 09 31.

International matches 1998
Czech Republic (a) 1-2, Argentina (h) 0-2, Mexico (h) 0-0, Croatia (h) 2-0, Malta (h) 5-0, Yugoslavia (a) 0-1.

League Championship wins (1922–99)
Shamrock Rovers 15; Dundalk 9; Shelbourne 8; St Patrick's Athletic 8; Bohemians 7; Waterford 6; Cork United 5; Drumcondra 5; St James's Gate 2; Cork Athletic 2; Sligo Rovers 2; Limerick 2; Athlone Town 2; Derry City 2; Dolphin 1; Cork Hibernians 1; Cork Celtic 1; Cork City 1.

Cup wins (1922–99)
Shamrock Rovers 24; Dundalk 8; Drumcondra 5; Bohemians 5; Shelbourne 5; Cork Athletic 2; Cork United 2; St James's Gate 2; St Patrick's Athletic 2; Cork Hibernians 2; Limerick 2; Waterford 2; Derry City 2; Athlone Town 2; Sligo 2; Bray Wanderers 2; Alton United 1; Cork 1; Fordsons 1; Transport 1; Finn Harps 1; Home Farm 1; UCD 1; Galway United 1; Cork City 1.

Final League Table 1998–99

	P	W	D	L	F	A	Pts
St Patrick's Ath	33	22	7	4	58	21	73
Cork City	33	21	7	5	62	25	70
Shelbourne	33	13	8	12	37	35	47
Finn Harps	33	12	10	11	38	39	46
Derry City	33	12	9	12	34	32	45
UCD	33	10	12	11	31	32	42
Waterford United	33	11	9	13	21	37	42
Shamrock Rovers	33	9	13	11	34	40	40
Sligo Rovers	33	9	11	13	37	50	38
Bohemians	33	10	7	16	28	37	37
Bray Wanderers*	33	8	8	17	30	45	32
Dundalk*	33	6	9	18	23	40	27

Top scorer: Molloy (St Patrick's Ath) 15.
Cup Final: Finn Harps 0, 2, 1, Bray Wanderers 0, 2, 2.

ISRAEL

Israel Football Association, Ramat-Gan Stadium, 299 Aba Hilell Street, Ramat-Gan 52594.
Founded: 1948; *Number of Clubs:* 544; *Number of Players:* 30,449; *National Colours:* Blue shirts, white shorts, blue stockings.
Telephone: 00972 3 570 59 99; *Cable:* CADUREGEL RAMAT-GAN; *Telex:* 361353 fa; *Fax:* 00972 3 570 20 44.

International matches 1998
Turkey (h) 4-0, Poland (h) 2-0, Romania (a) 1-0, Argentina (h) 2-1, Latvia (a) 5-1, Poland (a) 0-2, Austria (a) 1-1, San Marino (a) 5-0, Spain (h) 1-2, Portugal (a) 0-2, Yugoslavia (h) 2-0.

League Championship wins (1932–99)
Maccabi Tel Aviv 18; Hapoel Tel Aviv 12; Hapoel Petah Tikva 6; Maccabi Haifa 5; Maccabi Netanya 5; Beitar Jerusalem 4; Hakoah Ramat Gan 2; Hapoel Beersheba 2; Bnei Yehouda 1; British Police 1; Hapoel Kfar Sava 1; Hapoel Ramat Gan 1; Hapoel Haifa 1.

Cup wins (1928–99)
Maccabi Tel Aviv 19; Hapoel Tel Aviv 10; Beitar Jerusalem 5; Maccabi Haifa 5; Hapoel Haifa 3; Hapoel Kfar Sava 3; Beitar Tel Aviv 2; Bnei Yehouda 2; Hakoah Ramat Gan 2; Hapoel Petah Tikva 2; Maccabi Petah Tikva 2; British Police 1; Hapoel Jerusalem 1; Hapoel Lod 1; Maccabi Netanya 1; Hapoel Beersheba 1.

Final League Table 1998–99

	P	W	D	L	F	A	Pts
Hapoel Haifa	30	22	5	3	66	23	71
Maccabi Tel Aviv	30	20	3	7	72	32	63
Maccabi Haifa	30	19	3	8	62	24	60
Beitar Jerusalem	30	17	6	7	67	33	57
Hapoel Tel Aviv	30	15	7	8	45	26	52
Hapoel Petah Tikva	30	13	7	10	54	47	46
Rishon Le Zion	30	12	6	12	58	61	42
Hapoel Kfar Sabah	30	11	6	13	47	66	39
Hapoel Jerusalem	30	11	5	14	35	52	38
Maccabi Petah Tikva	30	10	7	13	45	45	37
Bnei Yehuda	30	10	6	14	43	51	36
Ironi Ashdod	30	9	9	12	40	49	36
Maccabi Herzliya	30	10	5	15	31	42	35
Zafirim Holon*	30	8	10	12	35	38	34
Hapoel Beit Shean*	30	5	3	22	25	83	18
Maccabi Jaffa*	30	2	4	24	15	73	10

Top scorer: Kubicka (Maccabi Tel Aviv) 21.
Cup Final: Hapoel Tel Aviv 1, Beitar Jerusalem 1.
Hapoel Tel Aviv won 3-1 on penalties.

ITALY

Federazione Italiana Giuoco Calcio, Via Gregorio Allegri 14, C.P. 2450, 1-00198, Roma.

Founded: 1898; *Number of Clubs:* 20,961; *Number of Players:* 1,420,160; *National Colours:* Blue shirts, white shorts, blue stockings with white trim.
Telephone: 0039 6 849 11; *Cable:* FEDERCALCIO ROMA; *Telex:* 624132 calcio i; *Fax:* 0039 6 849 12 526.

International matches 1998
Slovakia (h) 3-0, Paraguay (h) 3-1, Sweden (a) 0-1, Chile (n) 2-2, Cameroon (n) 3-0, Austria (n) 2-1, Norway (n) 1-0, France (n) 0-0, Wales (a) 2-0, Switzerland (h) 2-0, Spain (h) 2-2.

League Championship wins (1898–1999)
Juventus 25; AC Milan 16; Inter-Milan 13; Genoa 9; Torino 8; Pro Vercelli 7; Bologna 7; Fiorentina 2; Napoli 2; AS Roma 2; Casale 1; Novese 1; Cagliari 1; Lazio 1; Verona 1; Sampdoria 1.

Cup wins (1922–99)
Juventus 9; AS Roma 8; Fiorentina 5; Torino 4; AC Milan 4; Sampdoria 4; Inter-Milan 3; Napoli 3; Bologna 2; Lazio 2; Parma 2; Atalanta 1; Genoa 1; Vado 1; Venezia 1; Vicenza 1.

Final League Table 1998–99

	P	W	D	L	F	A	Pts
AC Milan	34	20	10	4	59	34	70
Lazio	34	20	9	5	65	31	69
Fiorentina	34	16	8	10	55	41	56
Parma	34	15	10	9	55	36	55
Roma	34	15	9	10	69	49	54
Juventus	34	15	9	10	42	36	54
Udinese	34	16	6	12	52	52	54
Internazionale	34	13	7	14	59	54	46
Bologna	34	11	11	12	44	47	44
Bari	34	9	15	10	39	44	42
Venezia	34	11	9	14	38	45	42
Cagliari	34	11	8	15	49	50	41
Piacenza	34	11	8	15	48	49	41
Perugia	34	11	6	17	43	61	39
Salernitana*	34	10	8	16	37	51	38
Sampdoria*	34	9	10	15	38	55	37
Vicenza*	34	8	9	17	27	47	33
Empoli*	34	4	10	20	26	63	20

Top scorer: Amoroso (Udinese) 22.
Cup Final: Parma 1, 2, Fiorentina 1, 2.
Parma won on away goals.

LATVIA

Latvian Football Federation, Augsiela, 1, LV-1009, Riga.
Founded: 1921; *Number of Clubs:* 50; *Number of Players:*12,000; *National Colours:* Carmine red shirts, white shorts, carmine red stockings.
Telephone: 00371 2 29 29 88; *Fax:* 00371 7828331.

International matches 1998
Georgia (a) 1-2, Malta (h) 1-2, Albania (h) 2-2, Lithuania (h) 1-2, Israel (h) 1-5, Estonia (a) 2-0, Andorra (h) 2-0, Iceland (a) 1-4, Norway (a) 3-1, Georgia (h) 1-0, Slovenia (a) 0-1, Tunisia (h) 0-3.

League Championship wins (1922–98)
ASK Riga 9; RFK Riga 8; Skonto Riga 8; Olympia Liepaya 7; Sarkanais Metalurgs Liepaya 7; VEF Riga 6; Energija Riga 4; Elektrons Riga 3; Torpedo Riga 3; Daugava Liepaya 2; ODO Riga 2; Khimikis Daugavpils 2; RAF Yelgava 2; Keisermezhs Riga 2; Dinamo Riga 1; Zhmilyeva Team 1; Darba Rezervi 1; REZ Riga 1; Start Brotseni 1; Venta Ventspils 1; Yurnieks Riga 1; Alfa Riga 1; Gauya Valmiera 1.

Cup wins (1937–99)
Elektrons Riga 7; Sarkanais Metalurgs Liepaya 5; Skonto Riga 4; ODO Riga 3; VEF Riga 3; ASK Riga 3; Tseltnieks Riga 3; RAF Yelgava 3; RFK Riga 2; Daugava Liepaya 2; Start Brotseni 2; Selmash Liepaya 2; Yurnieks Riga 2; Khimikis Daugavpils 2; Rigas Vilki 1; Dinamo Liepaya 1; Dinamo Riga 1; REZ Riga 1; Voulkan Kouldiga 1; Baltija Liepaya 1; Venta Ventspils 1; Pilot Riga 1; Lielupe Yurmala 1; Energija Riga 1; Torpedo Riga 1; Daugava SKIF Riga 1; Tseltnieks Daugavpils 1; Olympia Riga 1; FK Riga 1.

Final League Table 1998

	P	W	D	L	F	A	Pts
Skonto Riga	28	21	4	3	98	27	67
Metalurgs Liepaya	28	17	6	5	62	25	57
FK Ventspils	28	16	6	6	56	23	54
Dinaburg Daugavpils	28	11	10	7	49	31	43
FK Valmiera	28	10	7	11	39	59	37
Daugava Riga	28	7	9	12	42	42	30
FK Rezekne	28	2	5	21	22	80	11
Ranto/Miks Riga	28	2	5	21	25	106	11

Top scorer: Dobretsov (Metalurgs Liepaya) 23.
Cup Final 1998: Skonto Riga 1, Metalurgs Liepaya 0.
Cup Final 1999: Skonto Riga 1, FK Riga 1.
FK Riga won 6-5 on penalties.

LIECHTENSTEIN

Liechtensteiner Fussball-Verband, Malbuner Huus Altenbach 11, Postfach 165, 9490 Vaduz.
Founded: 1934; *Number of Clubs:* 7; *Number of Players:* 1,247; *National Colours:* Blue shirts, red shorts, blue stockings.
Telephone: 004175 237 4747; *Cable:* FUSSBALLVER-BAND VADUZ; *Fax:* 004175 237 4748.

International matches 1998
Austria (a) 0-6, Romania (a) 0-7, Slovakia (h) 0-4, Azerbaijan (h) 2-1.
Liechtenstein has no national league. Teams compete in Swiss regional leagues.

Cup wins (1946–99)
Vaduz 28; Balzers 11; Triesen 8; Eschen/Mauren 4; Schaan 3.
Cup Final: Vaduz 3, Balzers 2.

LITHUANIA

Lithuanian Football Federation, Seimyniskiu str. 15, 2005 Vilnius.
Founded: 1922; *Number of Clubs:* 152; *Number of Players:* 16,600; *National Colours:* Yellow shirts, green shorts, yellow stockings.
Telephone: 00370 2/723654; *Fax:* 00370 2/723651.

International matches 1998
Latvia (a) 2-1, Chile (a) 0-1, Hungary (a) 0-1, Azerbaijan (h) 1-2, Estonia (a) 0-0, Andorra (h) 4-0, Moldova (h) 1-1, Belarus (a) 0-3, Scotland (h) 0-0, Faeroes (h) 0-0, Bosnia (h) 4-2.

League Championship wins (1922–99)
Kovas Kaunas 6; KSS Klaipeda 6; LFLS Kaunas 4; Zalgiris Vilnius 4; LGSF Kaunas 2; Kareda 2; MSK Kaunas 1; Ekranas Panevezys 1; Romar Mazeikiai 1; Inkaras Grifas 1.

Cup wins (1992–99)
Zalgiris Vilnius 3; Kareda 2; Inkaras 1; Ekranas 1.

Final League Table 1998–99

	P	W	D	L	F	A	Pts
Zalgiris	23	18	5	0	68	8	59
Kareda	23	18	4	1	67	11	58
FBK	23	18	3	2	57	14	57
Ekranas	23	12	5	6	45	20	41
Inkaras	23	11	4	8	34	27	37
Atlantas	23	8	4	11	34	33	28
Banga	23	7	5	11	18	30	26
Nevezis	23	7	4	12	17	36	25
Dainava	23	8	1	14	24	53	25
Zalgiris 2*	23	6	3	14	25	60	21
Kauno*	23	6	2	15	22	48	20
Lokomotyvas+	23	4	0	19	12	47	12
Mastis	12	1	0	3	4	40	3

Mastis did not complete the season.

Promotion/Relegation Play-Offs
Lokomotyvas 0, 5, Lietava 3, 1.
Top scorer: Fomenka (Kareda) 14.
Cup Final: Kareda 3, FBK 0.

LUXEMBOURG

Federation Luxembourgeoise De Football, (F.L.F.), 50, Rue De Strasbourg, L-2560, Luxembourg.
Founded: 1908; *Number of Clubs:* 126; *Number of Players:* 21,684; *National Colours:* All red.
Telephone: 00352 48 86 65; *Cable:* FOOTBALL LUX-EMBOURG; *Telex:* 2426 flf l; *Fax:* 00352 40 02 01.

International matches 1998
Cameroon (h) 0-2, Germany (a) 0-7, Poland (a) 0-3, Argentina (h) 0-3, Belgium (h) 0-0.

League Championship wins (1910–99)
Jeunesse Esch 26; Spora Luxembourg 11; Stade Dudelange 10; Avenir Beggen 7; Red Boys Differdange 6; US Hollerich-Bonnevoie 5; Fola Esch 5; US Luxembourg 5; Aris Bonnevoie 3; Progres Niedercorn 3.

Cup wins (1922–99)
Red Boys Differdange 16; Jeunesse Esch 11; US Luxembourg 10; Spora Luxembourg 8; Avenir Beggen 6; Stade Dudelange 4; Progres Niedercorn 4; Fola Esch 3; Alliance Dudelange 2; US Rumelange 2; Grevenmacher 2; Aris Bonnevoie 1; US Dudelange 1; Jeunesse Hautcharage 1; National Schiffige 1; Racing Luxembourg 1; SC Tetange 1; Hesperange 1.

Final Table 1998–99

	P	W	D	L	F	A	Pts
Jeunesse Esch	22	16	3	3	56	13	51
F91 Dudelange	22	14	5	3	40	18	47
Avenir Beggen	22	14	3	5	65	21	45
Union	22	12	7	3	46	18	43
Grevenmacher	22	13	2	7	50	26	41
Sporting Mertzig	22	10	5	7	51	34	37
Mondercange	22	6	6	10	26	40	24
Aris	22	7	3	12	26	51	24
Hobscheid	22	7	2	13	43	50	23
FC Wiltz 71	22	6	2	14	25	54	20
Petange*	22	4	2	16	16	71	14
Spora*	22	2	2	18	17	63	8

Top scorer: Cicchirillo (Sporting Mertzig) 25.
Cup Final: Jeunesse Esch 3, Monnerich 0.

MACEDONIA

Football Association of the Former Yugoslav Republic of Macedonia, VIII-ma Udarna Brigada 31A, PO Box 84, MAC-91000 Skopje.
Founded: 1948; *Number of Clubs:* 598; *Number of Players:* 15,165; *National Colours:* All red.
Telephone: 00389 1 22 90 42; *Fax:* 00389 1 23 54 48.

International matches 1998
Bulgaria (h) 1-0, South Korea (h) 2-2, Jamaica (h) 2-1, Hungary (a) 0-0, USA (a) 0-0, Bosnia (h) 1-1, Malta (h) 4-0, Croatia (a) 2-3, Malta (a) 2-1.

League Championship wins (1993–99)
Vardar 3; Sileks 3; Sloga 1.

Cup wins (1993–99)
Vardar 4; Sileks 1.

Final Table 1998–99

	P	W	D	L	F	A	Pts
Sloga	26	19	3	4	41	12	60
Sileks	26	17	6	3	63	22	57
Pobeda	26	17	2	7	51	18	53
Vardar	26	15	4	7	61	32	49
Cement	26	14	2	10	47	37	44
Makedonia	26	10	7	9	44	40	37
Tikves	26	10	6	10	34	37	36
Borec	26	8	8	10	31	35	32
Rabotnicki	26	9	5	12	38	46	32
Pelister	26	7	8	11	30	50	29
Sasa	26	7	5	14	28	38	26
Osogovo	26	7	4	15	27	47	25
Skopje*	26	5	2	19	25	59	17
Balkan*	26	4	4	18	14	61	16

Top scorer: Oliveira (Pobeda) 22.
Cup Final: Vardar 2, Sloga 0.

MALTA

Malta Football Association, 280 St. Paul Street, Valletta VLT07.
Founded: 1900; *Number of Clubs:* 252; *Number of Players:* 5,544; *National Colours:* Red shirts, white shorts, red stockings.
Telephone: 00356 22 26 97; *Cable:* FOOTBALL MALTA VALLETTA; *Fax:* 00356 24 51 36.

International matches 1998
Albania (h) 1-1, Latvia (h) 2-1, Georgia (h) 1-3, Finland (h) 0-2, Wales (h) 0-3, Germany (h) 1-2, Macedonia (a) 0-4, Croatia (h) 1-4, Eire (a) 0-5, Macedonia (h) 1-2.

League Championship wins (1910–99)
Floriana 25; Sliema Wanderers 23; Valletta 17; Hibernians 8; Hamrun Spartans 7; Rabat Ajax 2; St George's 1; KOMR 1.

Cup wins (1935–99)
Floriana 18; Sliema Wanderers 17; Valletta 9; Hamrun Spartans 6; Hibernians 6; Gzira United 1; Melita 1; Zurrieq 1; Rabat Ajax 1.

Final League Table 1998–99

	P	W	D	L	F	A	Pts
Valletta	27	23	1	3	71	23	70
Birkirkara	27	21	5	1	69	20	68
Silema Wanderers	27	14	5	8	54	32	47
Hibernians	27	12	6	9	47	33	42
Floriana	27	10	6	11	47	50	36
Naxxar Lions	27	7	8	12	32	46	29
Pieta Hotspurs	27	7	6	14	39	39	27
Rabat Ajax	27	7	6	14	37	67	27
St Patrick*	27	3	8	16	29	71	17
Hamrun Spartans*	27	4	3	20	26	70	15

Top scorer: Agius (Valletta) 20.
Cup Final: Valletta 1, Birkirkara 0.

MOLDOVA

Moldavian Football Federation, 39 Tricolorului Str, 2012, Chisinau.
Founded: 1990; *Number of Clubs:* 143; *Number of Players:* 75,000; *National Colours:* Blue shirts, red shorts, yellow stockings.
Telephone: 00373 2 247878. *Fax:* 00373 2 247890.

International matches 1998
Azerbaijan (a) 0-1, Romania (a) 1-5, Lithuania (a) 1-1, Estonia (a) 1-0, Finland (a) 2-3, Romania (h) 0-0, Germany (h) 1-3, N Ireland (a) 2-2.

League Championship wins (1992–99)
Zimbru Chisinau 7; Constructorul 1.

Cup wins (1992–99)
Tiligul 4; Zimbru Chisinau 2; Combat 1, Serif 1.

Qualifying Table 1998–99

	P	W	D	L	F	A	Pts
Zimbru Chisinau	18	14	3	1	31	4	45
Constructorul	18	10	4	4	20	9	34
Tiligul	18	9	4	5	22	19	31
Serif	18	7	7	4	30	17	28
Olimpia	18	7	6	5	13	10	27
Agro	18	4	6	8	13	24	18
Moldova-Gaz	18	5	3	10	15	29	18
Otaci	18	5	4	9	17	18	18
Roma	18	5	1	12	11	25	16
Unisport	18	3	4	11	12	29	13

Final Table 1998–99

	P	W	D	L	F	A	Pts
Zimbru Chisinau	26	18	7	1	43	9	61
Constructorul	26	15	6	5	30	13	51
Tiligul	26	11	6	9	26	27	39
Serif	26	9	10	7	39	24	37
Olimpia	26	7	9	10	14	22	30

Promotion/Relegation Table 1998–99

	P	W	D	L	F	A	Pts
Moldova-Gaz	24	9	4	11	24	33	31
Roma	24	6	5	13	17	27	23
Agro	24	4	9	11	15	31	21
Unisport	24	5	6	13	16	37	21
Nistru*	18	5	4	9	17	18	18

Nistru expelled for failing to fulfill a fixture.
Top scorer: Rogaciov (Serif) 21.
Cup Final: Constructorul 1, Serif 2.

NORTHERN IRELAND

Irish Football Association Ltd, 20 Windsor Avenue, Belfast BT9 6EG.
Founded: 1880; *Number of Clubs:* 1,555; *Number of Players:* 24,558; *National Colours:* Green shirts, white shorts, green stockings.
Telephone: 01232 66 94 58; *Cable:* FOOTBALL BELFAST; *Telex:* 747317 ifa ni g; *Fax:* 01232 66 76 20.

NORWAY

Norges Fotballforbund Ulleval Stadion, Postboks 3823, Ulleval Hageby, 0805 Oslo 8.
Founded: 1902; *Number of Clubs:* 1,810; *Number of Players:* 300,000; *National Colours:* Red shirts, white shorts, blue stockings.
Telephone: 0047 22/024500 ; *Cable* FOTBALLFOR-BUND OSLO; *Telex:* 71722 nff n; *Fax:* 0047 22 95 10 10.

International matches 1998
France (a) 3-3, Belgium (a) 2-2, Denmark (a) 2-0, Mexico (h) 5-2, Saudi Arabia (h) 6-0, Morocco (n) 2-2, Scotland (n) 1-1, Brazil (n) 2-1, Italy (n) 0-1, Romania (h) 0-0, Latvia (h) 1-3, Slovenia (a) 2-1, Albania (h) 2-2, Egypt (a) 1-1.

League Championship wins (1938–98)
Rosenborg Trondheim 12; Fredrikstad 9; Viking Stavanger 8; Lillestroem 6; Valerengen 4; Larvik Turn 3; Brann Bergen 2; Lyn Oslo 2; IK Start 2; Friedig 1; Fram 1; Skeid Oslo 1; Strömsgodset Drammen 1; Moss 1.

Cup wins (1902–98)
Odds Bk Skien 11; Fredrikstad 10; Lyn Oslo 8; Skeid Oslo 8; Sarpsborg FK 6; Rosenborg Trondheim 6; Brann Bergen 5; Orn F Horten 4; Lillestroem 4; Viking Stavanger 4; Strömsgodset Drammen 4; Frigg 3; Mjondalens F 3; Bodo-Glimt 2; Mercantile 2; Tromso 2; Valerengen 2; Grane Nordstrand 1; Kvik Halden 1; Sparta 1; Gjovik 1; Moss 1; Byrne 1; Molde 1; Stabaek 1.
(*Known as the Norwegian Championship for HM The King's Trophy.*)

Final League Table 1998

	P	W	D	L	F	A	Pts
Rosenborg	26	20	3	3	79	23	63
Molde	26	16	6	4	70	34	54
Stabaek	26	16	5	5	63	29	53
Viking	26	14	4	8	66	44	46
Bodo-Glimt	26	9	9	8	47	47	36
Brann	26	9	8	9	44	39	35
Valerengen	26	10	3	13	44	48	33
Lillestrom	26	9	6	11	41	49	33
Moss	26	10	2	14	36	55	32
Stromsgodset	26	9	5	12	40	61	32
Tromso	26	7	7	12	39	48	28
Kongsvinger+	26	7	5	14	35	59	26
Haugesund*	26	6	5	15	41	55	23
Sogndal*	26	4	4	18	26	80	16

Top scorer: Rushfeldt (Rosenborg) 27.
Cup Final: Rosenborg 1, Stabaek 3 aet.

POLAND

Federation Polonaise De Foot-Ball, Al. Ujazdowskie 22, 00-478 Warszawa.
Founded: 1919; *Number of Clubs:* 5,881; *Number of Players:* 317,442; *National Colours:* White shirts, red shorts, white & red stockings.
Telephone: 0048 22 6223398; *Cable:* PEZETPEEN WARSZAWA; *Telex:* 825320 pzpn pl; *Fax:* 0048 22 629 24 89.

International matches 1998
Paraguay (a) 0-4, Israel (a) 0-2, Slovenia (h) 2-0, Croatia (a) 1-4, Russia (h) 3-1, Ukraine (a) 2-1, Israel (h) 2-0, Bulgaria (a) 3-0, Luxemborg (h) 3-0, Slovakia (a) 3-1.

League Championship wins (1921–99)
Gornik Zabrze 14; Ruch Chorzow 13; Wisla Krakow 7; Legia Warsaw 6; Widzew Lodz 6; Lech Poznan 5; Pogon Lwow 4; Cracovia 3; Warta Poznan 2; Polonia Bytom 2; Stal Mielec 2; LKS Lodz 2; Garbarnia Krakow 1; Polonia Warsaw 1; Slask Wroclaw 1; Szombierki Bytom 1; Zaglebie Lubin 1.

Cup wins (1951–99)
Legia Warsaw 12; Gornik Zabrze 6; Zaglebie Sosnowiec 4; Lech Poznan 3; GKS Katowice 3; Ruch Chorzow 3; Slask Wroclaw 2; Amica Wronki 2; Gwardia Warsaw 1; LKS Lodz 1; Polonia Warsaw 1; Wisla Krakow 1; Stal Rzeszow 1; Arka Gdynia 1; Lechia Gdansk 1; Widzew Lodz 1; Miedz Legnica 1.

Final League Table 1998–99

	P	W	D	L	F	A	Pts
Wisla	30	23	4	3	75	23	73
Widzew	30	18	2	10	50	33	56
Legia	30	16	8	6	41	25	56
Lech	30	17	3	10	55	36	54
Polonia	30	13	7	10	38	31	46
Radzionkow	30	10	11	9	40	35	41
Gornik Zabrze	30	9	12	9	34	31	39
Zaglebie Lubin	30	9	11	10	42	44	38
Stomil	30	10	7	13	29	38	37
Ruch	30	9	9	12	23	36	36
Amica	30	9	7	14	31	39	34
LKS Lodz	30	8	10	12	33	45	34
Pogon	30	9	6	15	33	54	33
Odra	30	8	8	14	33	41	32
Belchatow*	30	7	7	16	26	48	28
Katowice*	30	5	8	17	25	49	23

Top scorer: Frankowski (Wisla) 21.
Cup Final: Amica 1, Belchatow 0.

PORTUGAL

Federacao Portuguesa De Futebol, Praca De Alegria N.25, Apartado 21.100, P-1127, Lisboa Codex.
Founded: 1914; *Number of Clubs:* 204; *Number of Players:* 79,235; *National Colours:* Red shirts, green shorts, red stockings.
Telephone: 00351 1 342 8207/8/9/0; *Cable:* FUTEBOL LISBOA; *Telex:* 13489 fpf p; *Fax:* 00351 1 346 72 31.

International matches 1998
England (a) 0-3, Mozambique (h) 2-1, Hungary (a) 3-1, Romania (h) 0-1, Slovakia (a) 3-0, Israel (h) 2-0.

League Championship wins (1935–99)
Benfica 30; FC Porto 18; Sporting Lisbon 16; Belenenses 1.

Cup wins (1939–99)
Benfica 23; Sporting Lisbon 12; FC Porto 9; Boavista 5; Belenenses 3; Vitoria Setubal 2; Academica Coimbra 1; Leixoes Porto 1; Sporting Braga 1; Amadora 1; Beira Mar 1.

Final League Table 1998–99

	P	W	D	L	F	A	Pts
Porto	34	27	7	3	85	26	79
Boavista	34	20	11	3	57	29	71
Benfica	34	19	8	7	71	29	65
Sporting Lisbon	34	17	12	5	64	32	63
Setubal	34	15	8	11	37	38	53
Uniao Leiria	34	14	10	10	36	29	52
Guimaraes	34	14	8	12	53	41	50
Amadora	34	11	12	11	33	40	45
Braga	34	10	12	12	38	50	42
Maritimo	34	10	11	13	44	45	41
Farense	34	10	9	15	39	54	39
Salgueiros	34	7	17	10	45	55	38
Campomaiorense	34	10	7	17	41	51	37
Alverca	34	8	11	15	36	50	35
Rio Ave	34	8	11	15	26	47	35
Beira Mar*	34	6	15	13	36	53	33
Chaves*	34	5	10	19	39	70	25
Academica*	34	4	9	21	30	71	21

Top scorer: Jardel (Porto) 36.
Cup Final: Beira Mar 1, Campomaiorense 0.

ROMANIA

Federatia Romana De Fotbal, Str. Poligrafiei 3, Sector 1, 71556 Bucharest.
Founded: 1909; *Number of Clubs:* 414; *Number of Players:* 22,920; *National Colours:* All yellow.
Telephone: 0040 1 224 1993/224 2983; *Cable:* SPORTROM BUCURESTI-FOTBAL; *Telex:* 10097 frf r; *Fax:* 0040 1 224 0661.

International matches 1998
Argentina (a) 1-2, Israel (h) 0-1, Greece (h) 2-1, Belgium (a) 1-1, Paraguay (h) 3-2, Moldova (h) 5-1, Colombia (n) 1-0, England (n) 2-1, Tunisia (n) 1-1, Croatia (n) 0-1, Norway (a) 0-0, Liechtenstein (h) 7-0, Moldova (a) 0-0, Portugal (a) 1-0, Hungary (a) 1-1.

League Championship wins (1910–99)
Steaua Bucharest 20; Dinamo Bucharest 14; Venus Bucharest 8; Chinezul Timisoara 6; UT Arad 6; Ripensia Temesvar 4; Uni Craiova 4; Petrolul Ploesti 3; Olimpia Bucharest 2; Colentina Bucharest 2; Arges Pitesti 2; ICO Oradea 2; ; Rapid Bucharest 2; Soc RA Bucharest 1; Prahova Ploesti 1; Coltea Brasov 1; Juventus Bucharest 1; Metalochimia Resita 1; Ploesti United 1; Unirea Tricolor 1.

Cup wins (1934–99)
Steaua Bucharest 20; Rapid Bucharest 10; Dinamo Bucharest 7; Uni Craiova 6; UT Arad 2; Ripensia Temesvar 2; Politehnica Timisoara 2; Petrolul Ploesti 2; ICO Oradeo 1; Metalochimia Resita 1; Stinta Cluj 1; CFR Turnu Severin 1; Chimia Ramnicu Vilcea 1; Jiul Petroseni 1; Progresul Bucharest 1; Progresul Oradea 1; Gloria Bistrita 1.

Final League Table 1998–99

	P	W	D	L	F	A	Pts
Rapid	34	28	5	1	79	18	89
Dinamo	34	26	4	4	95	27	82
Steaua	34	19	9	6	62	33	66
Arges	34	20	4	10	57	37	64
Bacau	34	18	8	8	46	35	62
Otelul	34	17	4	13	47	33	55
National	34	18	1	15	61	51	55
Petrolul	34	16	5	13	50	46	53
Ceahlaul	34	15	4	15	54	53	49
Astra	34	13	7	14	40	38	46
Gloria	34	12	7	15	55	60	43
Farul	34	12	4	18	37	54	40
Uni Craiova	34	11	6	17	43	50	39
Onesti	34	12	3	19	56	67	39
Resita	34	8	11	15	34	59	35
Foresta*	34	6	6	22	31	61	24
Uni Cluj*	34	4	4	26	19	92	16
Olimpia*	34	3	4	27	22	74	13

Top scorer: Ganea (Rapid) 28.
Cup Final: Steaua 2, Rapid 2.
Steaua won 4-2 on penalties.

RUSSIA

Football Union of Russia; Luzhnetskaya Naberezyhnaja, 8. SU-119871 Moscow.
Founded: 1912; *Number of Clubs:* 43,700; *Number of Players:* 785,000; *National Colours:* White shirts, blue shorts, red stockings.
Telephone: 0070 95 2011637; *Telex:* 411287 priz su; *Fax:* 0070 95 2011303.

International matches 1998
Greece (a) 1-1, France (h) 1-0, Turkey (h) 1-0, Poland (a) 1-3, Georgia (a) 1-1, Sweden (a) 0-1, Ukraine (a) 2-3, Spain (a) 0-1, France (h) 2-3, Iceland (a) 0-1, Brazil (a) 1-5.

League Championship wins (1945–98)
Spartak Moscow 17; Dynamo Kiev 13; Dynamo Moscow 11; CSKA Moscow 7; Torpedo Moscow 3; Dynamo Tbilisi 2; Dnepr Dnepropetrovsk 2; Saria Voroshilovgrad 1; Ararat Erevan 1; Dynamo Minsk 1; Zenit Leningrad 1; Spartak Vladikavkaz 1.

Cup wins (1936–99)
Spartak Moscow 12; Dynamo Kiev 10; Torpedo Moscow 7; Dynamo Moscow 7; CSKA Moscow 5; Donetsk Shaktyor 4; Lokomotiv Moscow 4; Dynamo Tbilisi 2; Ararat Erevan 2; Zenit Leningrad 2; Karpaty Lvov 1; SKA Rostov 1; Metallist Kharkov 1; Dnepr 1.

Final League Table 1998

	P	W	D	L	F	A	Pts
Spartak Moscow	30	17	8	5	58	27	59
CSKA Moscow	30	17	5	8	50	22	56
Lokomotiv Moscow	30	16	7	7	45	28	55
Volgograd	30	12	12	6	52	37	48
Zenit	30	12	11	7	42	25	47
Rostov	30	11	11	8	42	38	44
Uralan	30	12	6	12	39	41	42
Vladikavkaz	30	11	7	12	46	39	40
Dynamo Moscow	30	8	15	7	31	30	39
Chernomorets	30	9	11	10	38	38	38
Torpedo Moscow	30	9	10	11	38	34	37
Krylia Sovekov	30	9	8	13	25	37	35
Sotchi	30	9	8	13	31	48	35
Shinnik	30	9	8	13	30	40	35
Baltika*	30	7	11	12	32	43	32
Tyumen*	30	2	2	26	17	89	8

Top scorer: Veretennikov (Volgograd) 22.
Cup Final: Zenit 3, Dynamo Moscow 1.

SAN MARINO

Federazione Sammarinese Giuoco Calcio, Viale Campo dei Giudei, 14; 47031-Rep. San Marino.
Founded: 1931; *Number of Clubs:* 17; *Number of Players:* 1,033; *National Colours:* All light blue.
Telephone: 00378 9990515; *Telex:* 0505284 cosmar so; *Fax:* 00378 9992348.

International matches 1998
Israel (h) 0-5, Austria (h) 1-4, Cyprus (h) 0-1.

League Championship wins (1986–99)
Tre Fiori 4; Faetano 3; Fiorita 2; Folgore 2; Domagnano 1; Montevito 1, Libertas 1.

Cup wins (1986–99)
Domagnano 4; Libertas 3; Cosmos 2; Faetano 2, Fiorita 1, Tre Fiori 1; Murata 1.

Final League Table 1998–99
Group A

	P	W	D	L	F	A	Pts
Folgore	22	12	7	3	52	30	43
Domagnano	22	12	6	4	44	28	42
Cosmos	22	12	5	5	38	22	41
Tre Fiori	22	10	6	6	45	34	36
Fiorita	22	10	4	8	29	32	34
Pennarossa	22	8	5	9	42	50	29
Montevito	22	7	6	9	32	37	27
San Giovanni	22	3	6	12	21	47	15

Top scorer: Gualtieri (Pennarossa) 21.

Group B

	P	W	D	L	F	A	Pts
Murata	22	17	2	3	61	34	53
Tre Penne	22	11	6	5	51	41	39
Faetano	22	11	5	6	32	16	38
Virtus	22	8	4	10	46	37	28
Dogana	22	5	6	11	21	33	21
Juvenes	22	4	5	13	20	40	17
Libertas	22	2	6	14	25	57	12
Callungo	22	2	5	15	22	43	11

Top scorer: Renzi (Tre Penne) 22.

Championship play-offs
Domagnano 1, Faetano 0; Tre Penne 1, Cosmos 3; Volgore 2, Cosmos 1; Murata 2, Domagnano 3; Murata 2, Tre Penne 3; Cosmos 1, Faetano 2.

Semi-finals
Domagnano 3, Folgor 3 (Folgor won 7-6 on penalties); Tre Penne 1, Faetano 2.

Final
Faetano 1, Folgor 0.
Cup Final: Cosmos 5, Domagnano 1.

SCOTLAND

The Scottish Football Association Ltd, 6 Park Gardens, Glasgow G3 7YF.
Founded: 1873; *Number of Clubs:* 6,148; *Number of Players:* 135,474; *National Colours:* Dark blue shirts, white shorts, red stockings with dark blue tops.
Telephone: 0141 332 6372; *Cable:* EXECUTIVE GLASGOW; *Telex:* 778904 sfa g; *Fax:* 0141 332 7559.

SLOVAKIA

Slovak Football Association, Junacka 6, 83280 Bratislava, Slovakia.
Founded: 1993; *Number of Clubs:* 2,140; *Number of Players:* 141,000; *National Colours:* All blue.
Telephone: 00421 75049151/5; *Fax:* 00421 75 049554.

International matches 1998
Italy (a) 0-3, Slovenia (a) 1-1, Iceland (h) 2-1, Finland (h) 2-0, N Ireland (a) 0-1, South Korea (h) 0-0, Croatia (h) 1-2, Finland (h) 0-0, Azerbaijan (h) 3-0, Liechtenstein (a) 4-0, Portugal (h) 0-3, Poland (h) 1-3.

League Championship wins (1939–44; 1994–99)
Slovan Bratislava 8; Kosice 2; Bystrica 1; OAP Bratislava 1.

Cup wins (1994–99)
Slovan Bratislava 2; Tatran Presov 1; Inter 1; Humenne 1; Spartak Trnava 1.

Final League Table 1998–99

	P	W	D	L	F	A	Pts
Slovan Bratislava	30	21	7	2	56	11	70
Inter	30	21	5	4	64	15	68
Spartak Trnava	30	19	7	4	59	20	64
Kosice	30	19	4	7	51	26	61
Odu Trencin	30	15	8	7	53	25	53
Zilina	30	15	3	12	36	42	48
Ruzomberok	30	12	10	8	31	31	46
Tatran Presov	30	11	10	9	38	35	43
Petrzalka	30	11	6	13	37	42	39
Humenne	30	10	5	15	24	37	35
Dukla Bystrica	30	8	10	12	34	46	34
Nitra	30	7	7	16	28	48	28
Dubnica	30	8	4	18	28	60	28
Prievidza	30	6	6	18	34	56	24
Tauris*	30	5	7	18	29	56	22
Bardejov*	30	2	1	27	14	66	7

Top scorer: Fabus (Odu Trencin) 19.
Cup Final: Slovan Bratislava 3, Dukla Bystrica 0.

SLOVENIA

Football Association of Slovenia, P.P. 3986, 1001 Ljubljana, Slovenia.
Founded: 1920; *Number of Clubs:* 375; *Number of Players:* 20,117; *National Colours:* White shirts, green shorts, white stockings.
Telephone: 00386 61 1611500; *Fax:* 00386 61 612220.

International matches 1998
Iceland (h) 3-2, Slovakia (h) 1-1, Cyprus (a) 0-1, Poland (a) 0-2, Czech Republic (h) 1-3, Hungary (a) 1-2, Greece (a) 2-2, Norway (h) 1-2, Latvia (h) 1-0.

League Championship wins (1992–99)
SCT Olimpija 4; Maribor 3; Gorica 1.

Cup wins (1992–99)
Maribor 4; SCT Olimpija 2; Mura 1; Rudar 1.

Final League Table 1998–99

	P	W	D	L	F	A	Pts
Maribor Teatanic	33	19	9	5	72	29	66
Gorica	33	18	8	7	55	31	62
Rudar	33	16	8	9	43	33	56
Mura	33	16	5	12	53	35	53
Korotan	33	14	6	13	44	45	48
Olimpija	33	12	8	13	54	50	44
Publikum	33	10	12	11	30	35	42
Primorje	33	11	7	15	39	45	40
Domzale	33	10	10	13	39	49	40
Beltinci	33	11	5	17	41	61	38
Koper*	33	8	8	17	34	61	32
Zivila*	33	5	10	18	28	58	25

Top scorer: Nikcevic (Gorica) 17.
Cup Final: Olimpija 2, 0, Maribor Teatanic 3, 2.

SPAIN

Real Federacion Espanola De Futbol, Calle Alberto Bosch 13, Apartado Postal 347, E-28014 Madrid.
Founded: 1913; *Number of Clubs:* 10,240; *Number of Players:* 408,135; *National Colours:* Red shirts, blue shorts, blue stockings with red, blue & yellow border.
Telephone: 0034 91 420 1362; *Cable:* FUTBOL MADRID; *Fax:* 0034 91 420 2094.

International matches 1998
France (a) 0-1, Sweden (h) 4-0, N Ireland (h) 4-1, Nigeria (n) 2-3, Paraguay (n) 0-0, Bulgaria (n) 6-1, Cyprus (a) 2-3, Russia (h) 1-0, Israel (a) 2-1, Italy (a) 2-2.

League Championship wins (1929–36; 1940–99)
Real Madrid 27; Barcelona 16; Atletico Madrid 9; Athletic Bilbao 8; Valencia 4; Real Sociedad 2; Real Betis 1; Seville 1.

Cup wins (1902–99)
Barcelona 24; Athletic Bilbao 23; Real Madrid 17; Atletico Madrid 9; Valencia 6; Real Zaragoza 4; Real Union de Irun 3; Seville 3; Espanol 2; Arenas 1; Ciclista Sebastian 1; Racing de Irun 1; Vizcaya Bilbao 1; Real Betis 1; Real Sociedad 1, La Coruna 1.

Final League Table 1998–99

	P	W	D	L	F	A	Pts
Barcelona	38	24	7	7	87	43	79
Real Madrid	38	21	5	12	77	62	68
Mallorca	38	20	6	12	48	31	66
Valencia	38	19	8	11	63	39	65
Celta	38	17	13	8	69	41	64
La Coruna	38	17	12	9	55	43	63
Espanyol	38	16	13	9	49	38	61
Athletic Bilbao	38	17	9	12	53	47	60
Zaragoza	38	16	9	13	57	46	57
Real Sociedad	38	14	12	12	47	43	54
Betis	38	14	7	17	47	58	49
Valladolid	38	13	9	16	35	44	48
Atletico Madrid	38	12	10	16	54	50	46
Oviedo	38	11	12	15	41	57	45
Santander	38	10	12	16	41	53	42
Alaves	38	11	7	20	36	63	40
Extremadura+	38	9	12	17	27	53	39
Villarreal+	38	8	12	18	47	63	36
Tenerife*	38	7	13	18	41	63	34
Salamanca*	38	7	6	25	29	66	27

Top scorer: Raul (Real Madrid) 25.
Cup Final: Valencia 3, Atletico Madrid 0.

SWEDEN

Svenska Fotbollfoerbundet, Box 1216, S-17123 Solna.
Founded: 1904; *Number of Clubs:* 3,250; *Number of Players:* 485,000; *National Colours:* Yellow shirts, blue shorts, yellow stockings.
Telephone: 0046 8 735 09 00; *Cable:* FOOTBALL-S; *Fax:* 0046 8 27 51 47.

International matches 1998
USA (a) 0-1, Jamaica (a) 0-0, Spain (a) 0-4, France (h) 0-0, Denmark (h) 3-0, Italy (h) 1-0, Russia (h) 1-0, England (h) 2-1, Bulgaria (a) 1-0.

League Championship wins (1896–1998)
IFK Gothenburg 18; Oergryte IS Gothenburg 14; Malmo FF 14; IFK Norrköping 11; AIK Stockholm 10; Djurgaarden 8; GAIS Gothenburg 6; IF Helsingborg 5; Boras IF Elfsborg 4; Oster Vaxjo 4; Halmstad 3; Atvidaberg 2; IFK Ekilstune 1; IF Gavic Brynas 1; IF Gothenburg 1; Fassbergs 1; Norrköping IK Sleipner 1.

Cup wins (1941–98)
Malmo FF 13; AIK Stockholm 7; IFK Norrköping 6; IFK Gothenburg 4; Atvidaberg 2; Kalmar 2; Helsingborg 2; GAIS Gothenburg 1; IF Raa 1; Landskrona 1; Oster Vaxjo 1; Djurgaarden 1; Degerfors 1, Halmstad 1.

Final League Table 1998

	P	W	D	L	F	A	Pts
AIK	26	11	13	2	25	15	46
Helsingborg	26	12	8	6	43	28	44
Hammarby	26	11	9	6	39	34	42
Halmstad	26	12	5	9	42	40	41
Vastra	26	10	8	8	29	31	38
Orebro	26	10	6	10	35	38	36
Norrköping	26	9	8	9	43	35	35
IFK Gothenburg	26	9	8	9	27	29	35
Malmo	26	9	6	11	35	30	33
Elfsborg	26	8	9	9	36	33	33
Trelleborg+	26	8	8	10	31	35	32
Orgryte*	26	7	7	12	35	36	28
Hacken*	26	7	6	13	27	46	27
Osters*	26	5	7	14	26	43	22

Top scorer: Stravum (Helsingborg) 18.
Cup Final: AIK Stockholm 1, IFK Gothenburg 0.

SWITZERLAND

Schweizerisher Fussballverband, Postfach 3000 Berne 15.
Founded: 1895; *Number of Clubs:* 1,473; *Number of Players:* 185,286; *National Colours:* Red shirts, white shorts, red stockings.
Telephone: 0041 31 950 81 11; *Cable:* SWISSFOOT BERNE; *Fax:* 0041 31 950 81 81.

International matches 1998
England (h) 1-1, N Ireland (a) 0-1, Yugoslavia (h) 1-1, Yugoslavia (a) 0-1, Italy (a) 0-2, Denmark (h) 1-1, Hungary (a) 0-2.

League Championship wins (1898–1999)
Grasshoppers 24; Servette 17; Young Boys Berne 11; FC Zurich 9; FC Basle 8; Lausanne 7; La Chaux-de-Fonds 3; FC Lugano 3; Winterthur 3; FX Aarau 3; Neuchatel Xamax 3; Sion 2; FC Anglo-American 1; St Gallen 1; FC Brühl 1; Cantonal-Neuchatel 1; Biel 1; Bellinzona 1; FC Etoile Le Chaux-de-Fonds 1; Lucerne 1.

Cup wins (1926–99)
Grasshoppers 18; FC Sion 9; Lausanne 9; La Chaux-de-Fonds 6; Young Boys Berne 6; Servette 6; FC Basle 5; FC Zurich 5; Lucerne 2; FC Lugano 2; FC Granges 1; St Gallen 1; Urania Geneva 1; Young Fellows Zurich 1; Aarau 1.

Qualifying Table 1998–99

	P	W	D	L	F	A	Pts
Servette	22	12	8	2	38	24	44
Grasshoppers	22	11	5	6	37	25	38
Zurich	22	10	8	4	33	21	38
Lausanne	22	10	8	4	36	33	38
Neuchatel Xamax	22	7	11	4	30	23	32
Basle	22	8	4	10	21	34	28
Lucerne	22	6	9	7	26	25	27
St Gallen	22	7	6	9	31	31	27
Sion	22	5	8	9	22	36	23
Lugano	22	5	7	10	35	43	22
Young Boys	22	4	7	11	33	34	19
Aarau	22	3	7	12	28	41	16

Final Table 1998–99

	P	W	D	L	F	A	Pts
Servette	14	7	3	4	19	14	46
Grasshoppers	14	8	3	3	31	11	46
Lausanne	14	8	2	4	28	20	45
Zurich	14	7	2	5	24	15	42
Basle	14	5	4	5	18	19	33
Neuchatel Xamax	14	2	6	6	12	27	28
Lucerne	14	4	2	8	13	27	28
St Gallen	14	2	4	8	13	25	24

Teams take half points from qualifying table.

Promotion/Relegation Table 1998–99

	P	W	D	L	F	A	Pts
Lugano	14	9	2	3	19	10	29
Delemont	14	7	2	5	23	20	23
Yverdon	14	6	3	5	22	17	21
Aarau	14	6	2	6	24	24	20
Sion*	14	6	1	7	16	17	19
Young Boys*	14	5	2	7	25	31	17
Wil*	14	5	1	8	26	30	16
Etoile Carouge*	14	4	3	7	18	24	15

Top scorer: Rey (Servette) 19.
Cup Final: Lausanne 2, Grasshoppers 0.

TURKEY

Turkiye Futbol Federasyonu, Konaklar Mah. Ihlamurlu Sok. 9, 80620 4 Levent, Istanbul.
Founded: 1923; *Number of Clubs:* 230; *Number of Players:* 64,521; *National Colours:* White shirts, white shorts, red and white stockings.
Telephone: 0090 212 282 70 10; *Cable:* ISTANBUL FUTBOL SPOR; *Telex:* 46308 btff tr; *Fax:* 0090 212 282 70 15.

International matches 1998
Israel (a) 0-4, Russia (a) 0-1, N Ireland (h) 3-0, Germany (h) 1-0, Finland (h) 1-3.

League Championship wins (1960–99)
Fenerbahce 13; Galatasaray 13; Besiktas 10; Trabzonspor 6.

Cup wins (1963–99)
Galatasaray 12; Besiktas 6; Trabzonspor 5; Fenerbahce 4; Goztepe İzmir 2; Altay Izmir 2; Ankaragucu 2; Eskisehirspor 1; Bursapor 1; Genclerbirligi 1; Sakaryaspor 1; Kocaeli 1.

Final League Table 1998–99

	P	W	D	L	F	A	Pts
Galatasaray	34	23	9	2	85	30	78
Besiktas	34	23	8	3	58	27	77
Fenerbahce	34	22	6	6	84	29	72
Trabzonspor	34	17	7	10	48	37	58
Kocaeli	34	14	8	12	44	37	50
Antalya	34	14	7	13	46	47	49
Gaziantep	34	12	12	10	51	48	48
Genclerbirligi	34	12	10	12	49	47	46
Istanbul	34	12	7	15	48	55	43
Samsun	34	11	8	15	38	53	41
Altay	34	11	7	16	45	59	40
Bursa	34	11	6	17	51	69	39
Erzurum	34	10	9	15	40	64	39
Ankaragucu	34	10	8	16	45	55	38
Adana	34	10	8	16	37	53	38
Sakarya*	34	9	8	17	44	52	35
Dardanel*	34	8	8	15	35	49	32
Karabuk*	34	5	8	21	26	64	23

Top scorer: Hakan Sukur (Galatasaray) 19.
Cup Final: Galatasaray 0, 2, Besiktas 0, 0

UKRAINE

Football Federation of Ukraine, Ulianovyh Street 1, P.O. Box 503, 252150 Kiev, Ukraine.
Founded: 1991; *Number of Clubs:* 1500; *Number of Players:* 759,500; *National Colours:* Yellow and blue shirts, blue shorts, yellow stockings.
Telephone: 00380 44 2528498; *Fax:* 00380 44 2528513 (or) 2692550; *Telex:* 631461 uff ux.

International matches 1998
Poland (h) 1-2, Georgia (h) 4-0, Russia (h) 3-2, Andorra (a) 2-0, Armenia (h) 2-0.

League Championship wins (1992–99)
Dynamo Kiev 6; Tavria Simferopol 1.

Cup wins (1992–99)
Dynamo Kiev 4; Chernomorets 2; Shakhtjor Donetsk 2.

Final League Table 1998–99

	P	W	D	L	F	A	Pts
Dynamo Kiev	30	23	5	2	75	17	74
Shakhtjor Donetsk	30	20	5	5	70	25	65
Krivbas	30	16	11	3	43	18	59
Karpaty	30	15	10	5	54	34	55
Metalurg Mariupol	30	14	6	10	35	27	48
Metallist Charkov	30	14	5	11	31	32	47
CSKA	30	11	10	9	37	35	43
Metalurg Zapor	30	12	6	12	46	43	42
Simferopol	30	10	7	13	33	39	37
Vorskla	30	10	5	15	36	43	35
Kirovograd	30	9	7	14	31	40	34
Dnepr	30	9	5	16	28	46	32
Ternopol	30	8	7	15	29	41	31
Metalurg Donetsk	30	7	7	16	27	51	28
Prekarpate+	30	6	6	18	24	59	24
Nikolaiev*	30	2	6	22	18	67	12

Top scorer: Shevchenko (Dynamo Kiev) 18.
Cup Final: Dynamo Kiev 3, Karpaty 0.

WALES

The Football Association of Wales Limited, Plymouth Chambers, 3 Westgate Street, Cardiff, South Glamorgan CF1 1DD.
Founded: 1876; *Number of Clubs:* 2,326; *Number of Players:* 53,926; *National Colours:* All red.
Telephone: 01222 372325; *Telex:* 497 363 faw g; *Cable:* WELSOCCER CARDIFF; *Fax:* 01222 343961.

YUGOSLAVIA

Yugoslav Football Association, P.O. Box 263, Terazije 35, 11000 Beograd.
Founded: 1919; *Number of Clubs:* 6,532; *Number of Players:* 229,024; *National Colours:* Blue shirts, white shorts, red stockings.
Telephone: 00381 11 323 3447; *Cable:* JUGOFUDBAL BEOGRAD; *Telex:* 11666 fsj yu; *Fax:* 00381 11 323 3433.

International matches 1998
Tunisia (a) 3-0, Argentina (a) 1-3, Colombia (a) 0-0, South Korea (h) 3-1, Nigeria (h) 3-0, Japan (h) 1-0, Switzerland (a) 1-1, Iran (n) 1-0, Germany (n) 2-2, USA (n) 1-0, Holland (n) 1-2, Switzerland (h) 1-0, Brazil (a) 1-1, Libya (a) 1-0, Eire (h) 1-0, Israel (a) 0-2.

League Championship wins (1923–99)
Red Star Belgrade 20; Partizan Belgrade 16; Hajduk Split 9; Gradjanski Zagreb 5; BSK Belgrade 5; Dynamo Zagreb 4; Jugoslavija Belgrade 2; Concordia Zagreb 2; FC Sarajevo 2; Vojvodina Novi Sad 2; HASK Zagreb 1; Zeljeznicar 1; Obilic 1.

Cup wins (1947–99)
Red Star Belgrade 17; Hajduk Split 9; Dynamo Zagreb 8; Partizan Belgrade 8; BSK Belgrade 2; OFK Belgrade 2; Rijeka 2; Velez Mostar 2; Vardar Skopje 1; Borac Banjaluka 1.

Final League Table 1998–99

	P	W	D	L	F	A	Pts
Partizan Belgrade	24	21	3	0	59	11	66
Obilic	24	20	4	0	61	9	64
Red Star Belgrade	24	15	6	3	54	18	51
Vojvodina	24	13	3	8	45	22	42
Rad	24	11	7	6	26	26	40
Proleter	24	10	5	9	29	29	35
Hajduk Kula	24	9	5	10	27	28	32
OFK Belgrade	24	8	7	9	35	39	31
Sartid 1913	24	7	9	8	24	27	30
Radnicki Kragujevac	24	9	3	12	33	43	30
Milicionar	24	8	5	11	39	39	29
Zemun	24	9	1	14	30	47	28
Zeleznik	24	7	5	12	29	43	26
Buducnost	24	7	5	12	28	42	26
Mogren	24	4	8	12	18	42	20
Radnicki Nis	24	4	7	13	21	44	19
Pristina	24	5	3	16	25	49	18
Spartak	24	6	0	18	33	58	18

League ended for security reasons with ten matches to play.
Top scorer: Osmanovic (Hajduk Kula) 16.
Cup Final: Red Star Belgrade 4, Partizan Belgrade 2.

SOUTH AMERICA

ARGENTINA

Asociacion Del Futbol Argentina, Viamonte 1366/76, 1053 Buenos Aires.
Founded: 1893; *Number of Clubs:* 3,035; *Number of Players:* 306,365; *National Colours:* Light blue & white striped shirts, black shorts, white stockings.
Telephone: 00541 371 4276; *Cable:* FUTBOL BUENOS AIRES; *Telex:* 17848 AFA AR; *Fax:* 00541 375 4410.

International matches 1998
Romania (h) 2-1, Yugoslavia (h) 3-1, Bulgaria (h) 2-0, Israel (a) 1-2, Eire (a) 2-0, Brazil (a) 1-0, Bosnia (h) 5-0, Chile (h) 1-0, South Africa (h) 2-0, Japan (n) 1-0, Jamaica (n) 5-0, Croatia (n) 1-0, England (n) 2-2, Holland (n) 1-2.

BOLIVIA

Federacion Boliviana De Futbol, Av. Libertador Bolivar No. 1168, Casilla de Correo 484, Cochabamba, Bolivia.
Founded: 1925; *Number of Clubs:* 305; *Number of Players:* 15,290; *National Colours:* Green shirts with white borders, white shorts with green borders, green stockings.
Telephone: 0059142 44982; *Cable:* FEDFUTBOL COCHABAMBA; *Telex:* 6239 FEDBOL; *Fax:* 0059142 82132.

International matches 1998
None played.

BRAZIL

Confederacao Brasileira De Futebol, Rua Da Alfandega, 70, P.O. Box 1078, 20.070 Rio De Janeiro.
Founded: 1914; *Number of Clubs:* 12,987; *Number of Players:* 551,358; *National Colours:* Yellow shirts with green collar/cuffs, blue shorts, white stockings with green-yellow border.
Telephone: 005521 509 5937; *Cable:* DESPORTOS RIO DE JANEIRO; *Telex:* 21509 CBDS BR; *Fax:* 005521 252 9294.

International matches 1998
Jamaica (h) 0-0, Guatemala (h) 1-1, El Salvador (a) 4-0, USA (a) 0-1, Jamaica (h) 1-0, Germany (a) 2-1, Argentina (h) 0-1, Andorra (h) 3-0, Scotland (n) 2-1, Morocco (n) 3-0, Norway (n) 1-2, Chile (n) 4-1, Denmark (n) 3-2, Holland (n) 1-1, France (n) 0-3, Yugoslavia (h) 1-1, Ecuador (a) 5-1, Russia (h) 5-1.

CHILE

Federacion De Futbol De Chile, Avda. Quillin No. 5635, Casilla postal 3733, Correo Central, Santiago de Chile.
Founded: 1895; *Number of Clubs:* 4,598; *Number of Players:* 609,724; *National Colours:* Red shirts with white collar & cuffs, blue shorts, white stockings.
Telephone: 00562 2849000; *Cable:* FEDFUTBOL SANTIAGO DE CHILE; *Fax:* 00562 2843510.

International matches 1998
Iran (a) 1-1, New Zealand (a) 0-0, Australia (a) 1-0, England (a) 2-0, Colombia (h) 2-2, Lithuania (h) 1-0, Argentina (a) 0-1, Uruguay (h) 2-2, Tunisia (a) 3-2, Morocco (a) 1-1, Italy (n) 2-2, Austria (n) 1-1, Cameroon (n) 1-1, Brazil (n) 1-4.

COLOMBIA

Federacion Colombiana De Futbol, Avenida 32, No. 16-22 piso 40. Apartado Aereo 17602, Santafe de Bogota.
Founded: 1924; *Number of Clubs:* 3,685; *Number of Players:* 188,050; *National Colours:* Yellow shirts with tricolour borders, blue shorts, Red stockings with tricolour borders.
Telephone: 00571 2853320; *Cable:* COLFUTBOL BOGOTA; *Fax:* 00571 2889740.

International matches 1998
Yugoslavia (h) 0-0, Paraguay (h) 1-1, Chile (a) 2-2, Scotland (h) 2-2, Germany (a) 1-3, Belgium (a) 0-2, Romania (n) 0-1, Tunisia (n) 1-0, England (n) 0-2.

ECUADOR

Federacion Ecuatoriana del Futbol, km 4 via a la Costa (Avda. del Bombero), Guayaquil.
Founded: 1925; *Number of Clubs:* 170; *Number of Players:* 15,700; *National Colours:* Yellow shirts with blue and red fringes, blue shorts, red stockings.
Telephone: 005934 352 372/3; *Cable:* ECUAFUTBOL GUAYAQUIL; *Fax:* 005934 352 116.

International matches 1998
Brazil (a) 1-5.

PARAGUAY

Asociacion Paraguaya de Futbol, Estadio De Sajonia, Calles Mayor Martinez Y Alejo Garcia, Asuncion.
Founded: 1906; *Number of Clubs:* 1,500; *Number of Players:* 140,000; *National Colours:* Red & white shirts, blue shorts, blue stockings.
Telephone: 0059521 480120; *Telex:* 38009 PY FUTBOL; *Fax:* 0059521 480124.

International matches 1998
Colombia (a) 1-1, Italy (a) 1-3, Japan (a) 1-1, Czech Republic (a) 0-1, Holland (a) 1-5, Romania (a) 2-3, Belgium (a) 0-1, Bulgaria (n) 0-0, Spain (n) 0-0, Nigeria (n) 3-1, France (n) 0-1.

PERU

Federacion Peruana De Futbol, Av. Aviacion Cdra. 20 s/n, San Luis, Lima.
Founded: 1922; *Number of Clubs:* 10,000; *Number of Players:* 325,650; *National Colours:* White shirts with red stripe, white shorts with red lines, white stockings with red line.
Telephone: 00511 2258236-9; *Cable* FEPEFUTBOL LIMA; *Fax:* 00511 2258240; *Telex:* 20066 FEPEFUT PE.

International matches 1998
Mexico (a) 0-1, Holland (a) 0-2.

URUGUAY

Asociacion Uruguaya De Futbol, Guayabo 1531, 11200 Montevideo.
Founded: 1900; *Number of Clubs:* 1,091; *Number of Players:* 134,310; *National Colours:* Sky blue shirts with white collar/cuffs, black shorts, black stockings with sky blue borders.
Telephone: 005982 4007101/06; *Cable:* FOOTBALL MONTEVIDEO; *Fax:* 005982 4007873; *Telex:* AUF UY 22607.

International matches 1998
Chile (a) 2-2.

VENEZUELA

Federacion Venezolana De Futbol, Avda S. Erminy, Torre Mega II Pent House B, e/Sabana Gr. y la Solano, Parroquia el Recreo, Caracas.
Founded: 1926; *Number of Clubs:* 1,753; *Number of Players:* 63,175; *National Colours:* Dark red shirts, white shorts, white stockings with black border.
Telephone: 00582 7620362; *Cable:* FEVEFUTBOL CARACAS; *Telex:* 26140 FVFCS VC; *Fax:* 00582 7620596.

International matches 1998
None played.

ASIA

AFGHANISTAN

Afghanistan Football Federation, c/o Afghanistan Olympic Committee, P.O. Box 1824, Kabul.
Founded: 1933; Number of Clubs: 30; Number of Players: 3,300; National Colours: All white with red lines.
Telephone: 0093 11420579; *Cable:* OLYMPIC KABUL.

BAHRAIN

Bahrain Football Association, P.O. Box 5464, Manama.
Founded: 1957; *Number of Clubs:* 25; *Number of Players:* 2,030; *National Colours:* All red.
Telephone: 00973 252929; *Cable:* BAHKORA BAHRAIN; *Telex:* 9040 FAB BN; *Fax:* 00973 255560.

BANGLADESH

Bangladesh Football Federation, National Stadium-1, Dhaka 1000.
Founded: 1972; *Number of Clubs:* 1,265; *Number of Players:* 30,385; *National Colours:* Orange shirts, white shorts, green stockings.

Telephone: 008802 9556072; *Cable:* FOOTBALFED DHAKA; *Fax:* 008802 9563419.

BRUNEI

The Football Association of Brunei Darussalam, P.O. Box 2010, 1920 Bandar Seri Begawan.
Founded: 1959; *Number of Clubs:* 22; *Number of Players:* 830; *National Colours:* Yellow shirts, black shorts, yellow stockings.
Telephone: 006732 383883; *Cable:* BAFA BRUNEI; *Telex:* BU 2575 Attn: BAFA; *Fax:* 006732 382900.

CAMBODIA

Cambodian Football Federation, PO Box 2327 PTT, Phnom-Penh 3.
Founded: 1933; *Number of Clubs:* 30; *Number of Players:* 650; *National Colours:* Blue, red and white shirts, white and blue shorts, red, white and blue stockings.
Telephone: 0085523 364889; *Cable:* CFF PHNOM PENH; *Fax:* 0088523 367191.

CHINA PR

Football Association of The People's Republic of China, 9 Tiyuguan Road, Beijing 100763.
Founded: 1924; *Number of Clubs:* 1,045; *Number of Players:* 2,250,000; *National Colours:* All white.
Telephone: 008610 67117019; *Cable:* SPORTSCHINE BEIJING; *Telex:* 22034 ACSF CN; *Fax:* 008610 67142533.

CHINA TAIPEI

Chinese Taipei Football Association, 100, Kuang-Fu South Road, Taipei, Taiwan.
Founded: 1936; *Number of Players:* 17,000; *National Colours:* Blue shirts, white shorts, red stockings.
Telephone: 008862 27117710; *Cable:* CTFA Taipei; *Fax:* 008862 27117713.

GUAM

Guam Soccer Association, P.O.Box 5093, Agana, Guam 96932.
Founded: 1975; *National Colours:* Blue shirts, white shorts, blue stockings.
Telephone: 00671 472 1824, 646 9609; *Fax:* 00671 4775424.

HONG KONG

The Hong Kong Football Association Ltd, 55 Fat Kwong Street, Homantin, Kowloon, Hong Kong.
Founded: 1914; *Number of Clubs:* 69; *Number of Players:* 3,274; *National Colours:* All Red.
Telephone: 00852 27129122; *Cable:* FOOTBALL HONG KONG; *Telex:* 40518 FAHKG HX; *Fax:* 00852 27604303.

INDIA

All India Football Federation , Mr KN Mour, Gen. Secretary, Youth Hostel Complex, Paltan Bazar, Guwahati - 781 008, Assam.
Founded: 1937; *Number of Clubs:* 2,000; *Number of Players:* 56,000; *National Colours:* Orange shirts, white shorts, green stockings.
Telephone: 0091361 525109; *Fax:* 0091 361525110.

INDONESIA

All Indonesia Football Federation, Wisma Karsa Pemuda, Jl.Gerbang Pemuda No. 3, PO Box 2305, Jakarta 10023.
Founded: 1930; *Number of Clubs:* 2,880; *Number of Players:* 97,000; *National Colours:* Red shirts, white shorts, red and white stockings.
Telephone: 006221 5722948; *Cable:* PSSI JAKARTA; *Telex:* 65739 PSSI IA; *Fax:* 006221 5734386.

IRAN

IR Iran Football Federation, Shahid Keshvari Sports Complex, Mirdamad Ave., Razan Jonoobi Str., PO Box 15875-6967 Tehran 15875.
Founded: 1920; *Number of Clubs:* 6,326; *Number of Players:* 306,000; *National Colours:* All white.
Telephone: 009821 2258116; *Cable:* FOOTBALL IRAN - TEHRAN; *Telex:* 212691 NOC IR; *Fax:* 009821 2258123.

IRAQ

Iraqi Football Association, Olympic Committee Building, Palestine Street, PO Box 484, Baghdad.
Founded: 1948; *Number of Clubs:* 155; *Number of Players:* 4,400; *National Colours:* All black.
Telephone: 009641 7729990; *Cable:* BALL BAGHDAD; *Telex:* 213409 IRFA IK; *Fax:* 009641 7744475.

JAPAN

Japan Football Association, 2nd Floor, Gotoh Ikueikai Bldg, 1-10-7 Dogenzaka, Shibuya-Ku, Tokyo 150, Japan.
Founded: 1921; *Number of Clubs:* 13,047; *Number of Players:* 358,989; *National Colours:* Blue shirts, white shorts, blue stockings.
Telephone: 00813 34762011; *Cable:* SOCCERJAPAN TOKYO; *Telex:* 2422975 FOTJPN J; *Fax:* 00813 34762291.

JORDAN

Jordan Football Association, P.O. Box 1054, Amman.
Founded: 1949; *Number of Clubs:* 98; *Number of Players:* 4,305; *National Colours:* All white and red.
Telephone: 009626 825450; *Cable:* JORDAN FOOTBALL ASSN AMMAN; *Fax:* 009626 861530.

KAZAKHSTAN

The Football Association of the Republic of Kazakhstan, 44 Abai Street, 480072 Almaty, Kazakhstan.
Founded: 1914; *Number of Clubs:* 5,793; *Number of Players:* 260,000.
Telephone: 0073272 671885; *Telex:* 251347 TREK SU; *Fax:* 0073272 671885.

KOREA, NORTH

Football Association of The Democratic People's Rep. of Korea, Kumsong-dong 2, Mangyongdae Distr, Pyongyang.
Founded: 1945; *Number of Clubs:* 90; *Number of Players:* 3,420; *National Colours:* All white.
Telephone: 008502 3814164; *Cable:* DPR KOREA FOOTBALL PYONGYANG; *Telex:* 5472 KP; *Fax:* 008502 3814403.

KOREA, SOUTH

Korea Football Association, 110-39, Kyeonji-Dong, Chongro-Ku, Seoul.
Founded: 1928; *Number of Clubs:* 476; *Number of Players:* 2,047; *National Colours:* Red shirts, black shorts, red stockings.
Telephone: 00822 7336764; *Cable:* FOOTBALLKOREA SEOUL; *Telex:* KFASEL K 25373; *Fax:* 00822 7352755.

KUWAIT

Kuwait Football Association, P.O. Box 2029 Safat, 13021 Safat.
Founded: 1952; *Number of Clubs:* 14 (senior); *Number of Players:* 1,526; *National Colours:* Blue shirts, white shorts, blue stockings.
Telephone: 00965 2555851; *Cable:* FOOT KUWAIT; *Fax:* 00965 2549955.

KYRGYZSTAN

Football Association of Kyrgyz Republic, Frunze Street, 503 Bishkek 720040, Kyrgyzstan.
Founded: 1992; *Number of Players:* 20,000; *National Colours:* Red shirts, white shorts, red stockings.
Telephone: 00331 2223507; *Fax:* 00331 2225492.

LAOS

Federation Lao de Football, National Stadium, Vientiane, Laos.
Founded: 1951; *Number of Clubs:* 76; *Number of Players:* 2,060; *National Colours:* Red shirts, white shorts, blue stockings.
Telephone: 0085621 216008/9; *Cable:* FOOTBALL VIEN-TIANE; *Fax:* 0085621 216008.

LEBANON

Federation Libanaise De Football-Association, P.O. Box 4732, Verdun Street, Bristol, Radwan Centre Building, Beirut.
Founded: 1933; *Number of Clubs:* 105; *Number of Players:* 8,125; *National Colours:* Red shirts, white shorts, red stockings.
Telephone: 009611 347157; *Cable:* FOOTBALL BEIRUT; *Telex:* 21404 LIBALL; *Fax:* 009611 349529; *Internet:*

http://www.lebanon-online.com/lfa; E-mail: lfa@lebanon-online.com.lb.

MACAO

Associacao De Futebol De Macau (AFM), P.O. Box 920, Macau.
Founded: 1939; *Number of Clubs:* 52; *Number of Players:* 800; *National Colours:* Green shirts, black shorts, green stockings.
Telephone: 00853 71996; *Cable:* FOOTBALL MACAU; *Fax:* 00853 260148.

MALAYSIA

Football Association of Malaysia, Wisma Fam, Tingkat 3, Jalan SS5A/9, Kelana Jaya, 47301 Petaling Jaya, Selangor.
Founded: 1933; *Number of Clubs:* 450; *Number of Players:* 11,250; *National Colours:* All yellow and black.
Telephone: 00603 7763766; *Cable:* FOOTB. PETALING JAYA SELANGO; *Telex:* FAM PJ MA 36701; *Fax:* 00603 7757984.

MALDIVES REPUBLIC

Football Association of Maldives, National Stadium Ghalolhu, Male 20-04.
Founded: 1982; *Number of Clubs: Number of Players: National Colours:* Green shirts, white shorts, red stockings.
Telephone: 0096031 7006; *Fax:* 0096031 7005.

MONGOLIA

Mongolia Football Federation, R413, Mongolia Youth Association Building, Baga Toiruu 10, Ulaanbaatar 10.
Telephone & fax: 009761 313145.

MYANMAR

Myanmar Football Federation, Attn Maj. Naw Tawng, Gen. Secr. Youth Training Centre, Thuwunna, Yangon.
Founded: 1947; *Number of Clubs:* 600; *Number of Players:* 21,000; *National Colours:* Red shirts, white shorts, red stockings.
Telephone: 00951 577366; *Cable:* FOOTBALL YANGON; *Telex:* 21253 SPED BM; *Fax:* 00951 571253.

NEPAL

All-Nepal Football Association, Dasharath Rangashala, Tripureshwor, PO Box 2090, Kathmandu.
Founded: 1951; *Number of Clubs:* 85; *Number of Players:* 2,550; *National Colours:* All red.
Telephone: 009771 241367; *Cable:* ANFA KATHMANDU; *Telex:* 2390 NSC NP; *Fax:* 009771 241365.

OMAN

Oman Football Association, P.O. Box 3462, Ruwi Postal Code 112.
Founded: 1978; *Number of Clubs:* 47; *Number of Players:* 2,340; *National Colours:* Red shirts with white sleeves, red/white shorts and stockings.
Telephone: 00968 787638/9; *Cable:* FOOTBALL MUSCAT; *Telex:* FOOTBALL 3223 ON; *Fax:* 00968 787632/33.

PAKISTAN

Pakistan Football Federation, 183, Abu Bakar Block, New Garden Town, Lahore, Pakistan.
Founded: 1948; *Number of Clubs:* 882; *Number of Players:* 21,000; *National Colours:* Green shirts, white shorts, green stockings.
Telephone: 009242 5832786; *Cable:* FOOTBALL LAHORE; *Telex:* 47643 PFF PK; *Fax:* 009242 7281541.

PALESTINE

Palestinian Football Federation, Al-Yarmouk, Gaza.
Telephone: 009727 829433; *Fax:* 009727 857020.

PHILIPPINES

Philippine Football Federation, Room 207 PSC, Administration Building, Rizal Memorial Sports Complex, P. Ocampo Street, Manila.
Founded: 1907; *Number of Clubs:* 650; *Number of Players:* 45,000; *National Colours:* Blue and red shirts, blue shorts, white stockings.
Telephone: 00632 5256502; *Cable:* FOOTBALL MANILA;

Telex: 65014 POC PACA PN; *Fax:* 00632 5233741.

QATAR

Qatar Football Association, P.O. Box 5333, Doha.
Founded: 1960; *Number of Clubs:* 8 (senior); *Number of Players:* 1,380; *National Colours:* All white.
Telephone: 00974 434455; *Cable:* FOOTQATAR DOHA; *Telex:* 4749 QATFOT DH; *Fax:* 00974 411660.

SAUDI ARABIA

Saudi Arabian Football Federation, Al Mather Quarter (Olympic Complex), P.O. Box 5844, Riyadh 11432.
Founded: 1959; *Number of Clubs:* 120; *Number of Players:* 9,600; *National Colours:* White shirts, green shorts, white stockings.
Telephone: 009661 4822240; *Cable:* KURA RIYADH; *Telex:* 404300 SAFOTB SJ; *Fax:* 009661 4821215.

SINGAPORE

Football Association of Singapore, Jalan Besar Stadium, Tyrwhitt Road, Singapore 207542.
Founded: 1892; *Number of Clubs:* 250; *Number of Players:* 8,000; *National Colours:* All red.
Telephone: 0065 2931477; *Fax:* 0065 2933728.

SRI LANKA

Football Federation of Sri Lanka, No. 2, Old Grand Stand, Race Course, Reid Avenue, Colombo 7.
Founded: 1939; *Number of Clubs:* 600; *Number of Players:* 18,825; *National Colours:* Maroon and gold shirts, white shorts and stockings.
Telephone: 00941 696179; *Cable:* SOCCER COLOMBO; *Telex:* 21537 METALIX CE; *Fax:* 00941 682471.

SYRIA

Syrian Football Federation, Maysaloon St., PO Box 421, Damascus.
Founded: 1936; *Number of Clubs:* 102; *Number of Players:* 30,600; *National Colours:* All white.
Telephone: 0096311 3335866; *Cable:* FOOTBALL DAMASCUS; *Telex:* 411578 SPOFED SY; *Fax:* 0096311 3331511.

TAJIKISTAN

Tajikistan National Football Federation, 44, Rudaki Ave., PO Box 26, 734025 Dushanbe, Tajikistan.
Founded: 1991; *Number of Clubs:* 1,804; *Number of Players:* 71,400; *National Colours:* Green shirts, white shorts, green stockings.
Telephone: 0073772 212363; *Telex:* 116286 SHAKH; *Fax:* 0073772 212447.

THAILAND

The Football Association of Thailand, National Stadium, Rama I Road, Bangkok.
Founded: 1916; *Number of Clubs:* 168; *Number of Players:* 15,000; *National Colours:* All red.
Telephone: 00662 2141058; *Cable:* FOOTBALL BANGKOK; *Telex:* 20211 FAT TH; *Fax:* 00662 2154494.

TURKMENISTAN

Turkmenistan Football Federation, 10 Turkmenbashi Avenue, 744005 Ashgabat, Turkmenistan.
Founded: 1992; *Number of Players:* 75,000; *National Colours:* Green shirts, white shorts, green stockings.
Telephone: 00363 2353739; *Fax:* 00363 2355327; *Telex:* 116175 TINTO SU.

UNITED ARAB EMIRATES

United Arab Emirates Football Association, P.O. Box 916, Abu Dhabi.
Founded: 1971; *Number of Clubs:* 23 (senior); *Number of Players:* 1,787; *National Colours:* All white.
Telephone: 00971 2445600; *Cable:* FOOTBALL EMIRATES ABU DHABI; *Telex:* 22121 UAEFA EM; *Fax:* 00971 2448558.

UZBEKISTAN

Uzbekistan Football Federation, Massiv Almazar Furkat Street 15/1, 700003 Tashkent, Uzbekistan.

Founded: 1946; *Number of Clubs:* 15,000; *Number of Players:* 217,000; *National Colours:* Blue shirts, white shorts, green stockings.
Telephone: 0073712 457106; *Telex:* 116108 PTB SU; *Fax:* 0073712 454948.

VIETNAM

Vietnam Football Federation, 141 Nguyen Thai Hoc Str., Dis Dongda, Hanoi.
Founded: 1962; *Number of Clubs:* 55 (senior); *Number of*

Players: 16,000; *National Colours:* All red.
Telephone: 008448 452480; *Cable:* AFBVN, 141 NGUYEN THAI HOC STR.; *Fax:* 008448 233119.

YEMEN

Yemen Football Association, P.O. Box 908, Sana'a.
Founded: 1962; *Number of Clubs:* 26; *Number of Players:* 1750; *National Colours:* All green.
Telephone: 009671 264159. *Cable:* SANA'A FOOTBALL; *Telex:* 2710 YOUTH YE; *Fax:* 009671 263182.

CONCACAF

ANGUILLA

Anguilla Football Association, P.O. Box 608, The Valley, Anguilla, BWI.
National Colours: All blue.
Telephone: 001264 4975214/4972416; *Fax:* 001264 4972326.

ANTIGUA & BARBUDA

The Antigua Football Association, P.O. Box 773, St. John's.
Founded: 1928; *Number of Clubs:* 60; *Number of Players:* 1,008; *National Colours:* Gold shirts, black shorts and stockings.
Telephone: 001268 4624863; *Cable:* AFA ANTIGUA; *Fax:* 001268 4624864.

ARUBA

Arubaanse Voetbal Bond, PO Box 376, Oranjestad, Aruba.
Founded: 1932; *Number of Clubs:* 50; *Number of Players:* 1,000; *National Colours:* Yellow shirts, blue shorts, yellow and blue stockings.
Telephone: 00297 829550; *Cable:* AVB ARUBA; *Fax:* 00297 820624.

BAHAMAS

Bahamas Football Association, P.O. Box N 8434, Nassau, N.P.
Founded: 1967; *Number of Clubs:* 14; *Number of Players:* 700; *National Colours:* Yellow shirts, black shorts, yellow stockings.
Telephone: 001809 3233426; *Cable:* BAHSOCA NASSAU; *Fax:* 001809 3288006.

BARBADOS

Barbados Football Association, P.OI. Box 1362, Bridgetown, Barbados.
Physical address: Hadley Court, Upper Collymore Rock, St. Michael.
Founded: 1910; *Number of Clubs:* 92; *Number of Players:* 1,100; *National Colours;* Royal blue and gold shirts, gold shorts, white, gold and blue stockings.
Tel: 001246 2281707; *Cable:* FOOTBALL BRIDGETOWN; *Fax:* 001246 2286484.

BELIZE

Belize National Football Association, P.O. Box 1742, Belize City.
Founded: 1980; *National Colours:* Red, white and blue shirts and shorts, red stockings.
Telephone: 005012 36563; *Fax:* 005012 36564.

BERMUDA

The Bermuda Football Association, P.O. Box HM 745, Hamilton HM CX.
Founded: 1928; *Number of Clubs:* 30; *Number of Players:* 1,947; *National Colours:* Royal blue shirts, white shorts and stockings.
Telephone: 001809 2952199; *Cable:* FOOTBALL BERMUDA; *Telex:* 3441 BFA BA; *Fax:* 001809 2950773.

BRITISH VIRGIN ISLANDS

British Virgin Islands Football Association, P.O. Box 29, Road Town, Tortola, BVI.
Telephone: 001284 4945655; *Fax:* 001284 4948968.

US VIRGIN ISLANDS

V.I. Soccer Federation, P.O. Box 2618, Kingshill, St. Croix, US.V.I. 00851-2618.
Telephone: 001 340 7737216; *Fax:* 001 340 7739686.

CANADA

The Canadian Soccer Association, Place Soccer Canada, 237 Metcalfe Street, Ottawa, ONT K2P 1R2.
Founded: 1912; *Number of Clubs:* 1,600; *Number of Players:* 224,290; *National Colours:* All red.
Telephone: 001613 2377678; *Cable:* SOCCANADA OTTAWA; *Fax:* 001613 2371516.

CAYMAN ISLANDS

Cayman Islands Football Association, PO Box 178 GT, George Town, Grand Cayman, Cayman Islands W1.
Founded: 1966; *Number of Clubs:* 25; *Number of Players:* 875; *National Colours:* Red shirts, blue shorts, white stockings.
Telephone: 001345 9497822328. *Fax:* 001345 945 7673.

COSTA RICA

Federacion Costarricense De Futbol, Apartado 670-1000, Calle 40, Avda CTL & I, San Jose.
Founded: 1921; *Number of Clubs:* 431; *Number of Players:* 12,429; *National Colours:* Red and white shirts, blue shorts, white stockings.
Telephone: 00506 2221544; *Cable:* FEDEFUTBOL SAN JOSE; *Telex:* 3394 DIDER CR; *Fax:* 00506 2552674.

CUBA

Federacion Cubana De Futbol, c/o Comite Olimpico Cubano, Calle 13 No. 601, Esq. C. Vedado, La Habana, ZP R2.
Founded: 1924; *Number of Clubs:* 70; *Number of Players:* 12,900; *National Colours:* White shirts with red collar & cuffs, dark blue shorts, white and red stockings.
Telephone: 00537 403581; *Cable:* FOOTBALL HABANA; *Telex:* 511332 INDER CU; *Fax:* 00537 409037.

DOMINICA

Dominica Football Association, P.O. Box 372, Roseau, Commonwealth of Dominica.
Founded: 1970; *Number of Clubs:* 30; *Number of Players:* 500; *National Colours:* Emerald green shirts, green shorts, yellow stockings.
Telephone & fax: 001767 4492173.

DOMINICAN REPUBLIC

Federacion Dominicana De Futbol, Apartado De Correos No. 1953, Santo Domingo.
Founded: 1953; *Number of Clubs:* 128; *Number of Players:* 10,706; *National Colours:* Navy blue shirts, white shorts, red stockings.
Telephone: 001809542 6923. *Cable:* FEDOFUTBOL SANTO DOMINGO; *Telex:* 817240; *Fax:* 001809547 5363.

EL SALVADOR

Federacion Salvadorena De Futbol, Av. J.M. Delgado, Col. Escalon, Frente Ctro Espanol, Apartado 1029, San Salvador.
Founded: 1935; *Number of Clubs:* 944; *Number of Players:* 21,294; *National Colours:* Blue shirts, white shorts, blue stockings.
Telephone: 00503 2637525/6; *Cable:* FESFUT SAN SALVADOR; *Fax:* 00503 2637583.

GRENADA

Grenada Football Association, P.O. Box 326, St. Juilles Street, St George's, Grenada, West Indies.
Founded: 1924; *Number of Clubs:* 15; *Number of Players:* 200; *National Colours:* Green & yellow striped shirts, red shorts, yellow stockings.

Telephone & fax: 001473 4401986; *Cable:* GRENBALL GRENADA; *Telex:* 3431 CW BUR.

GUATEMALA

Federacion Nacional De Futbol De Guatemala, Avenida Reforma 1-90 Zona 9, 11 Nivel, Edificio Masval, 01009 Ciudad Guatemala, C.A.
Founded: 1946; *Number of Clubs:* 1,611; *Number of Players:* 43,516; *National Colours:* Blue shirts, white shorts, blue stockings.
Telephone: 005023 314797; *Cable:* FEDFUTBOL GUATEMALA C.A.; *Fax:* 005023 600188.

GUYANA

Guyana Football Association, Lot 65 King Street, P.O. Box 10727 Georgetown.
Founded: 1902; *Number of Clubs:* 103; *Number of Players:* 1,665; *National Colours:* Green shirts and shorts, yellow stockings.
Telephone & fax: 005922 62641;*Telex:* 2266 RICEBRD GY.

HAITI

Federation Haitienne De Football, P.O. Box 2258, Port-Au-Prince.
Founded: 1904; *Number of Clubs:* 40; *Number of Players:* 4,000; *National Colours:* Blue and red shirts, blue shorts, blue and red stockings.
Telephone: 00509 464509; *Cable:* FEDHAFOOB PORT-AU-PRINCE; *Fax:* 00509 573001.

HONDURAS

Federacion Nacional Autonoma De Futbol De Honduras, Apartado Postal 827, Costa Oeste Del Est. Nac, Tegucigalpa, D. C.
Founded: 1951; *Number of Clubs:* 1,050; *Number of Players:* 15,300; *National Colours:* Blue shirts, white shorts, blue stockings.
Telephone: 00504 231 1432/231 1463/ 232 1897/239 8826; *Cable* FENAFUTH TEGUCIGALPA; *Fax:* 00504 231 1428.

JAMAICA

Jamaica Football Federation, General Secretariat, Room 8, Nat. Arena, Institue of Sports, Independence Park, Kingston 6.
Founded: 1910; *Number of Clubs:* 266; *Number of Players:* 45,200; *National Colours:* Gold shirts, black shorts, gold stockings.
Telephone: 001809 9290484; *Cable:* FOOTBALL JAMAICA KINGSTON; *Telex:* 2224 FEDLASCO JA; *Fax:* 001809 9290483.

MEXICO

Federacion Mexicana De Futbol Asociacion, A.C., Abraham Gonzales 74, Col. Juarez, C.P. 06600, Mexico 6, D.F.
Founded: 1927; *Number of Clubs:* 77 (senior); *Number of Players:* 1,402,270; *National Colours:* Green shirts with white collar, white shorts, red stockings.
Telephone: 00525 5662155; *Cable:* MEXFUTBOL MEXICO; *Fax:* 00525 5667580.

MONSERRAT

Monserrat Football Association, P.O. Box 46, Church Road, Plymouth, Monserrat.
Telephone: 001664 4912346; *Fax:* 001664 4912719.

NETHERLANDS ANTILLES

Nederlands Antiliaanse Voetbal Unie, P.O. Box 341, Curacao, N.A.
Founded: 1921; *Number of Clubs:* 85; *Number of Players:* 4,500; *National Colours:* white shirts with red and blue stripes, white shorts, red, white and blue stockings.
Telephone: 005999 4627222/4343862; *Cable:* NAVU CURA-CAO; *Telex:* 1046 ENNIA NA; *Fax:* 005999 4627087/4343837.

NICARAGUA

Federacion Nicaraguense De Futbol, Estadio Futbol Camilo Ortega (Cranshaw), Apdo Postal 976, Managua.
Founded: 1931; *Number of Clubs:* 31; *Number of Players:* 160 (senior); *National Colours:* Blue and white striped shirts, blue

shorts, blue and white striped stockings.
Telephone: 005052 680006/7/8; *Cable:* FENIFUT MANAGUA; *Fax:* 005052 664134.

PANAMA

Federacion Panamena De Futbol, Apartado Postal 8-391, Zona 8, Panama.
Founded: 1937; *Number of Clubs:* 65; *Number of Players:* 4,225; *National Colours:* Red shirts, blue shorts, white stockings.
Telephone & fax: 00507 2282238.

PUERTO RICO

Federacion Puertorriquena De Futbol, Coliseo Roberto Clemente, P.O. Box 1944355, Hato Rey, P.R. 00919-4355.
Founded: 1940; *Number of Clubs:* 175; *Number of Players:* 4,200; *National Colours:* Blue shirts, blue and white shorts and stockings.
Telephone & fax: 001787 7642025.

SAINT LUCIA

St Lucia National Football Association, PO Box 255, Castries, St Lucia.
Founded: 1979; *Number of Clubs:* 100; *Number of Players:* 4,000; *National Colours:* Blue and white shirts, black shorts, blue stockings.
Telephone: 001758 0689; *Cable:* NFU ST. LUCIA; *Telex:* 6394 FOR AFF LC; *Fax:* 001758 2506.

SAINT KITTS & NEVIS

St Kitts-Nevis Football Association, P.O. Box 465, Basseterre, St Kitts, W.I.
Founded: 1932; *Number of Clubs:* 36; *Number of Players:* 600; *National Colours:* Green and yellow shirts, red shorts, yellow stockings.
Telephone: 001869 465 6809; *Cable:* HORSFORD ST. KITTS; *Telex:* 6822 HORSFDSKB KC; *Fax:* 001869 465 1190; *Internet:* www.skbee.com/sknfa; *E-mail:* sknfa@skbee.com.

SAINT VINCENT & THE GRENADINES

St Vincent & The Grenadines Football Federation, PO Box 1278, Kingstown, St Vincent, W.I.
Founded: 1979; *Number of Clubs:* 500; *Number of Players:* 5,000; *National Colours:* Green shirts with yellow border, blue shorts, yellow stockings.
Telephone: 001784 4561659; *Fax:* 001784 4571659.

SURINAM

Surinaamse Voetbal Bond, Letitia Vriesde Laan 7, P.O. Box 1223, Paramaribo.
Founded: 1920; *Number of Clubs:* 168; *Number of Players:* 4,430; *National Colours:* Red green and white shirts, white or green shorts and stockings.
Telephone: 00597 473112; *Cable:* SVB Paramaribo; *Fax:* 00597 479718.

TRINIDAD AND TOBAGO

Trinidad & Tobago Football Federation, Petrotrin Savannah Building, 9 Queen's Park West, P.O. Box 400, Port of Spain.
Founded: 1908; *Number of Clubs:* 124; *Number of Players:* 5,050; *National Colours:* Red shirts, black shorts, white stockings.
Telephone: 001809 6271011; *Fax:* 001809 6271007.

TURKS & CAICOS

Turks & Caicos Football Association, P.O. Box 180, Providenciales, Turks & Caicos Islands, BWI.
Telephone: 001649 9464650; *Fax:* 001649 9464663.

USA

US Soccer, Soccer House, 1801-1811 S. Prairie Avenue, Chicago, Illinois 60616.
Founded: 1913; *Number of Clubs:* 7,000; *Number of Players:* 1,411,500; *National Colours:* All white.
Telephone: 001312 8081300; *Telex:* 450024 US SOCCER FED; *Fax:* 001312 8081301.

OCEANIA

AMERICAN SAMOA

American Samoa Football Association, P.O. Box 282, Pago Pago.
Telephone: 00684 6882290; *Fax:* 00684 6882291.

AUSTRALIA

Soccer Australia, Sydney Football Stadium, Driver Avenue, P.O. Box 175, Paddington NSW 2021.
Founded: 1961; *Number of Clubs:* 6,816; *Number of Players:* 433,957; *National Colours:* Gold shirts with green trim, gold shorts, gold and green stockings.
Telephone: 0061 293806099; *Cable:* FOOTBALL SYDNEY; *Fax:* 0061 293806155.

COOK ISLANDS

Cook Islands Football Federation, P.O. Box 29, Avarua, Rarotonga, Cook Islands.
Founded: 1971; *Number of Clubs:* 9; *National Colours:* Green shirts and shorts with golden stripes, gold and green stockings.
Telephone: 00682 21231; *Fax:* 00682 25912.

FIJI

Fiji Football Association, Bob S. Kumar, Hon. Secretary, Government Bldgs, P.O.Box 2514, Suva.
Founded: 1938; *Number of Clubs:* 140: *Number of Players:* 21,300; *National Colours:* White shirts, blue shorts and stockings.
Telephone: 00679 300453; *Fax:* 00679 304642.

NEW ZEALAND

Soccer New Zealand, 51 O'Rorke Road, Penrose, Auckland, New Zealand.
Founded: 1891; *Number of Clubs:* 312; *Number of Players:* 52,969; *National Colours:* White shirts with black trim, white shorts and stockings.
Telephone: 00649 5256120; *Fax:* 00649 5256123.

PAPUA NEW GUINEA

Papua New Guinea Football (Soccer) Association, c/o National Sports Institute, P.O. Box 337, Goroka, EHP 441.
Founded: 1962; *Number of Clubs:* 350; *Number of Players:* 8,250;

National Colours: Red shirts, black shorts, red stockings.
Telephone: 00675 7321699; *Telex:* TOTOTRA NE 23436; *Fax:* 00675 7321941.

SOLOMAN ISLANDS

Soloman Islands Football Federation, PO Box 854, Honiara, Soloman Islands.
Founded: 1978; *Number of Players:* 4,000; *National Colours:* Green, yellow and blue shirts and shorts, white stockings.
Telephone: 00677 26496; *Telex:* HQ 66349; *Fax:* 00677 26497.

TAHITI

Federation Tahitienne de Football (F.T.F.), B.P.50 358, Pirae, Tahiti, French Polynesia.
Founded: 1989; *National Colours:* White shirts, red shorts, white stockings.
Telephone: 00689 540954; *Cable:* FOOTBALL TAHITI; *Fax:* 00689 419629.

TONGA

Tonga Football Association, P.O. Box 852, Nuku'Alofa, Tonga.
Founded: 1965; *Number of Clubs:* 23; *Number of Players:* 350; *National Colours:* Red shirts, white shorts, red and white stockings.
Telephone: 00676 24442; *Cable:* SOCCER NUKU'ALOFA; *Fax:* 00676 23340; *E-mail:* tfa@kalianet.to.

VANUATU

Vanuatu Football Federation, P.O. Box 226, Port Vila, Vanuatu.
Founded: 1934; *National Colours:* Gold and black shirts, black shorts, gold and black stockings.
Telephone: 00678 25236; *Cable:* FUTBOL BLONG VANUATU; *Fax:* 00678 25236.

WESTERN SAMOA

Samoa Football (Soccer) Association, P.O. Box 960, Apia.
Founded: 1968; *National Colours:* Royal blue shirts, white shorts, royal blue and white stockings.
Telephone: 00685 22822; *Telex:* 233 TREASURY SX; *Fax:* 00685 21312.

AFRICA

ALGERIA

Federation Algerienne De Foot-ball, Chemin Ahmed Ouaked, Boite Postale No. 39, Dely-Ibrahim-Alger.
Founded: 1962; *Number of Clubs:* 780; *Number of Players:* 58,567; *National Colours:* Green shirts, white shorts, green stockings.
Telephone: 002132 365938; *Cable:* FAFOOT ALGER; *Telex:* 61378. *Fax:* 002132 365949.

ANGOLA

Federation Angolaise De Football, Compl. da Cidadela Desportiva, B.P. 3449, Luanda.
Founded: 1979; *Number of Clubs:* 276; *Number of Players:* 4,269; *National Colours:* Red shirts, black shorts, red stockings.
Telephone: 002442 364948; *Cable:* FUTANGOLA; *Telex:* 2580 PALANCA AN; *Fax:* 002442 333147.

BENIN

Federation Beninoise De Football, B.P. 965, Cotonou.
Founded: 1962; *Number of Clubs:* 117; *Number of Players:* 6,700; *National Colours:* Yellow shirts, green shorts, red stockings.
Telephone: 00229 330537; *Cable:* FEBEFOOT COTONOU; *Telex:* 5245 SONACOP COTONOU; *Fax:* 00229 312485.

BOTSWANA

Botswana Football Association, P.O. Box 1396, Gabarone.
Founded: 1970; *National Colours:* Blue and white shirts, blue, white and black shorts, blue, white and black striped stockings.
Telephone: 00267 300279; *Cable:* BOTSBALL GABARONE; *Telex:* 2977 BD; *Fax:* 00267 300280.

BURKINA FASO

Federation Burkinabe De Foot-Ball, 01 B.P. 57, Ouagadougou 01.

Founded: 1960; *Number of Clubs:* 57; *Number of Players:* 4,672; *National Colours:* Red shirts, green shorts with yellow star, red stockings.
Telephone: 00226 318815; *Cable:* FEDEFOOT OUA-GADOUGOU; *Fax:* 00226 318843.

BURUNDI

Federation De Football Du Burundi, B.P. 3426, Bujumbura.
Founded: 1948; *Number of Clubs:* 132; *Number of Players:* 3,930; *National Colours:* Red shirts, white shorts, green stockings.
Telephone & fax: 00257 212891; *Cable:* FFB BUJA.

CAMEROON

Federation Camerounaise De Football, B.P. 1116, Yaounde.
Founded: 1959; *Number of Clubs:* 200; *Number of Players:* 9,328; *National Colours:* Green shirts, red shorts, yellow stockings.
Telephone: 00237 216662; *Cable:* FECAFOOT YAOUNDE; *Telex:* 8568 JEUNESPO KN; *Fax:* 00237 217403/202784.

CAPE VERDE ISLANDS

Federacao Cabo-Verdiana De Futebol, P.O. Box 234, Praia.
Founded: 1982; *National Colours:* All green.
Telephone & fax: 00238 611362; *Cable:* FUTEBOL PRAIA CV; *Telex:* 6005 ACAS CV.

CENTRAL AFRICAN REPUBLIC

Federation Centrafricaine De Football Amateur, B.P. 344, Bangui.
Founded: 1937; *Number of Clubs:* 256; *Number of Players:* 7,200; *National Colours:* Grey & blue shirts with Nat. emblem and star, white shorts, red stockings with yellow trim.
Telephone: 00236 612433; *Cable:* FOOTBANGUI BANGUI; *Fax:* 00236 615660.

CHAD

Federation Tchadienne de Footbal, B.P. 886, N'Djamena.
Founded: 1962; *National Colours:* Blue shirts, yellow shorts, red stockings.
Telephone: 00235/519204; *Telex:* 5248 kd; *Fax:* 00235/518648.

CONGO

Federation Congolaise De Football, B.P. 4041, Brazzaville.
Founded: 1962; *Number of Clubs:* 250; *Number of Players:* 5,940; *National Colours:* All red.
Telephone: 00242 834885; *Cable:* FECOFOOT BRAZZAVILLE; *Telex:* 5210 KG; *Fax:* 00242 836199.

CONGO DR

Federation Congolaise De Football-Association (FECOFA), P.O. Box 1284, Av. De L'Enseignem. 210, Z/Kasa-Vubu, Kinshasa 1.
Founded: 1919; *Number of Clubs:* 3,800; *Number of Players:* 64,627; *National Colours:* Green shirts, yellow shorts, red stockings.
Telephone & fax: 001212 3769411; *Cable:* FECOFA KINSHASA.

DJIBOUTI

Federation Djiboutienne de Football, B.P. 2694, Djibouti.
Founded: 1977; *Number of Players:* 2,000; *National Colours:* Green shirts, white shorts, blue stockings.
Telephone: 00253 342049; *Fax:* 00253 356793.

EGYPT

Egyptian Football Association, 5, Shareh Gabalaya, Gueziza, Al Borg Post Office, Cairo.
Founded: 1921; *Number of Clubs:* 247; *Number of Players:* 19,735; *National Colours:* Red shirts, white shorts, black stockings.
Telephone: 00202 3401793; *Cable:* KORA CAIRO; *Telex:* 93506 KORA UN; *Fax:* 00202 3417817.

ERITREA

The Eritrean National Football Federation, P.O. Box 3665, Asmara.
Telephone & fax: 002911 126821.

ETHIOPIA

Ethiopia Football Federation, Addis Ababa Stadium, P.O. Box 1080, Addis Ababa.
Founded: 1943; *Number of Clubs:* 767; *Number of Players:* 20,594; *National Colours:* Green shirts, yellow shorts, red stockings.
Telephone: 002511 514453; *Cable:* FOOTBALL ADDIS ABABA; *Telex:* 21377 NESCO ET; *Fax:* 002511 513345.

GABON

Federation Gabonaise De Football, B.P. 181, Libreville.
Founded: 1962; *Number of Clubs:* 320; *Number of Players:* 10,000; *National Colours:* Green, yellow and blue shirts, blue and yellow shorts, white stockings with tricolour trims.
Telephone: 00241 730460; *Cable:* FEGAFOOT LIBREVILLE; *Telex:* 5526 GO; *Fax:* 00241 746047.

GAMBIA

Gambia Football Association, Independence Stadium, Bakau, P.O. Box 523, Banjul.
Founded: 1952; *Number of Clubs:* 30; *Number of Players:* 860; *National Colours:* White shirts with striped band, white shorts, white stockings with red tops.
Telephone: 00220 496980; *Cable:* SPORTS GAMBIA BANJUL; *Telex:* 2262 FISCO GV.

GHANA

Ghana Football Association, P.O. Box 1272, Accra.
Founded: 1957; *Number of Clubs:* 347; *Number of Players:* 11,275; *National Colours:* All yellow.
Telephone: 0023321 666697; *Cable:* GFA ACCRA; *Telex:* 2519 SPORTS GH; *Fax:* 0023321 668590.

GUINEA

Federation Guineenne De Football, P.O. Box 3645, Conakry.
Founded: 1959; *Number of Clubs:* 351; *Number of Players:* 10,000; *National Colours:* Red shirts, yellow shorts, green stockings.
Telephone: 00224 461159; *Cable:* GUINEFOOT CONAKRY; *Telex:* 22302 MJ GE; *Fax:* 00224 411926.

GUINEA-BISSAU

Federacao De Football Da Guinea-Bissau, Rua 4 No. 10-C,

Apartado 375, 1035 Bissau- Codex.
Founded: 1974; *National Colours:* All red..
Telephone & fax: 00245 201918; *Cable:* FUTEBOL BISSAU.

GUINEA, EQUATORIAL

Federacion Ecuatoguineana De Futbol, Malabo.
Founded: 1986; *National Colours:* All red.
Telephone: 002409 2392; *Cable:* FEGUIFUT MALABO; *Telex:* 9991111 EG; *Fax:* 002409 3353.

IVORY COAST

Federation Ivoirienne De Football, Av. 1 Treichville, 01 B.P. 1202, Abidjan 01.
Founded: 1960; *Number of Clubs:* 84 (senior); *Number of Players:* 3,655; *National Colours:* Orange shirts, white shorts, green stockings.
Telephone: 00225 242301; *Cable:* FIF ABIDJAN; *Telex:* 42344 FIF CI; *Fax:* 00225 257111.

KENYA

Kenya Football Federation, Nyayo National Stadium, P.O. Box 40234, Nairobi.
Founded: 1960; *Number of Clubs:* 351; *Number of Players:* 8,880; *National Colours:* Red, green and white shirts, red, green and black shorts and stockings.
Telephone: 002542 501825/35; *Cable:* KEFF NAIROBI; *Telex:* 24069 SPICERS KE; *Fax:* 002542 501120.

LESOTHO

Lesotho Football Association, P.O. Box 756, Maseru-100, Lesotho.
Founded: 1932; *Number of Clubs:* 88; *Number of Players:* 2,076; *National Colours:* Blue shirts, green shorts, white stockings.
Telephone: 00266 311879; *Cable:* LEFA MASERU; *Telex:* 4493, 4228; *Fax:* 00266 310586.

LIBERIA

Liberia Football Association, 110 Camp Johnson Road, P.O. Box 10-1066, 1000 Monrovia 10.
Founded: 1936; *National Colours:* Red shirts, white shorts, blue stockings.
Telephone: 00231 226284; *Cable:* LIBFOTASS MONROVIA; *Telex:* 44220 EXM IBR. *Fax:* 00231 225217.

LIBYA

Libyan Arab Football Federation, 7th October Stadium, P.O. Box 5137, Tripoli.
Founded: 1963; *Number of Clubs:* 89; *Number of Players:* 2,941; *National Colours:* Green shirts, white shorts, green stockings.
Telephone & fax: 0021821 4446610/3339150; *Telex:* 20896 LY.

MADAGASCAR

Federation Malagasy De Football, P. O. Box 4409, Antananarivo 101.
Founded: 1961; *Number of Clubs:* 775; *Number of Players:* 23,536; *National Colours:* Red shirts, white shorts, green stockings.
Telephone: 0026120 2228433; *Telex:* 22265 AROSUR MG; *Fax:* 0026120 2234464.

MALAWI

Football Association of Malawi, P.O. Box 865, Blantyre.
Founded: 1966; *Number of Clubs:* 465; *Number of Players:* 12,500; *National Colours:* Red shirts, red and green shorts, green stockings.
Telephone & fax: 00265 674290; *Cable:* FOOTBALL BLANTYRE; *Telex:* 4526 SPORTS MI.

MALI

Federation Malienne De Football, Stade Mamdou Konate, B.P. 1020, Bamako.
Founded: 1960; *Number of Clubs:* 128; *Number of Players:* 5,480; *National Colours:* Green shirts, yellow shorts, red stockings.
Telephone: 00223 224254; *Cable:* MALIFOOT BAMAKO; *Telex:* 0985 1200 MJ; *Fax:* 00356 245136.

MAURITANIA

Federation De Foot-Ball De La Rep. Islamique. De Mauritanie, B.P. 566, Nouakchott.
Founded: 1961; *Number of Clubs:* 59; *Number of Players:* 1,930; *National Colours:* Green and yellow shirts, yellow shorts, green stockings.
Telephone: 00222 291032 (or) 50424; *Cable:* FOOTRIM NOUAKCHOTT; *Telex:* 577 MTN NKTT RIM; *Fax:* 00222 291031 (or) 50424.

MAURITIUS

Mauritius Football Association, Chancery House, 2nd Floor Nos. 303-305, 14 Lislet Geoffroy Street, Port Louis.
Founded: 1952; *Number of Clubs:* 397; *Number of Players:* 29,375; *National Colours:* Red shirts, white shorts, red stockings with white tops.
Telephone: 00230 2121418; *Cable:* MFA PORT LOUIS; *Fax:* 00230 2084100.

MOROCCO

Federation Royale Marocaine De Football, Av. Ibn Sina, C.N.S. Bellevue, B.P. 51, Rabat.
Founded: 1955; *Number of Clubs:* 350; *Number of Players:* 19,768; *National Colours:* All red.
Telephone: 002127 672706/08; *Cable:* FERMAFOOT RABAT; *Telex:* 32940 FERMFOOT M. *Fax:* 002127 671070.

MOZAMBIQUE

Federacao Mocambicana De Futebol, Av. Samora Machel, 11-2, Caixa Postal 1467, Maputo.
Founded: 1978; *Number of Clubs:* 144; *National Colours:* Red shirts, black shorts, black and red stockings.
Telephone: 002581 300366; *Cable:* MOCAMBOLA MAPUTO; *Telex:* 6-747 MCID MO; *Fax:* 002581 300367.

NAMIBIA

Namibia Football Federation, Abraham Mashego Street 8521, Katurua Council of Churches in Namibia, PO Box 1345, Windhoek, Namibia.
Founded: 1990*Number of Clubs:* 244; *Number of Players:* 7320; *National Colours*: All blue, red, green, yellow and white.
Telephone & fax: 0026461 217621.

NIGER

Federation Nigerienne De Football (Fenifoot), Stade du 29 Juillet, B.P. 10299, Niamey.
Founded: 1967; *Number of Clubs:* 64; *Number of Players:* 1,525; *National Colours:* Orange shirts, white shorts, green stockings.
Telephone: 00227 725127/722147; *Cable:* FEDERFOOT NIGER NIAMEY; *Telex:* 5527; *Fax:* 00227 722147/ 734694.

NIGERIA

Nigeria Football Association, Plot 2033, Olusegun Obasanjo Way, Wuse Zone 7, Abuja, Nigeria.
Founded: 1945; *Number of Clubs:* 326; *Number of Players:* 80,190; *National Colours:* Green shirts, white shorts, green stockings.
Telephone: 002349 5237326; *Cable:* FOOTBALL ABUJA; *Telex:* 26570 NFA NG; *Fax:* 002349 5237327.

RWANDA

Federation Rwandaise De Football Amateur, B.P. 2000, Kigali.
Founded: 1972; *Number of Clubs:* 167; *National Colours:* Red, green and yellow shirts, green shorts, red stockings.
Telephone: 00250 84999; *Cable:* FERWAFA KIGALI; *Telex:* 22504 PUBLIC RW; *Fax:* 00250 76574.

SENEGAL

Federation Senegalaise De Football, Stade L.S. Senghor, Route De L'Aeroport De Yoff, B.P. 130 21, Dakar.
Founded: 1960; *Number of Clubs:* 75 (senior); *Number of Players:* 3,977; *National Colours:* Green shirts, yellow shorts, red stockings.
Telephone & fax: 00221 8273528; *Cable:* SENEFOOT DAKAR ; *Telex:* 13048 PUBLIDK SG.

SEYCHELLES

Seychelles Football Federation, P.O. Box 843, People's Stadium, Victoria-Mahe, Seychelles.
Founded: 1979; *National Colours:* Red and blue shirts, blue and red shorts, white stockings.
Telephone: 00248 323908 ext. 244; *Fax:* 00248 225468.

ST. THOMAS AND PRINCIPE

Federation Santomense De Futebol, P.O. Box 42, Sao Tome.
Founded: 1975; *National Colours:* All green and yellow.
Telephone: 0023912 23431; *Telex:* 213 PUBLICO STP; *Fax:* 0023912 21365.

SIERRA LEONE

Sierra Leone Football Association, P.O. Box 672, National Stadium, Brookfields, Freetown.
Founded: 1967; *Number of Clubs:* 104; *Number of Players:* 8,120; *National Colours:* Green, white and blue shirts, white shorts, blue stockings with white tops.
Telephone & fax: 00232 2224 1872.

SOMALIA

Somali Football Federation, c/o Conf. Afric. de Football, 5 Gabalaya Street, 11567, El Borg, Cairo, Egypt.
Founded: 1951; *Number of Clubs:* 46 (senior); *Number of Players:* 1,150; *National Colours:* All sky blue and white.
Telephone: 0020 2/3412497; *Cable:* SOMALIA FOOTBALL CAIRO; *Telex:* 93162 CAF UN; *Fax:* 0020 2/3420114 (CAF).

SOUTH AFRICA

South African Football Association, First National Bank Stadium, Nasrec/ PO Box 910, Johannesburg 2000; South Africa.
Founded: 1991; *Number of Teams:* 51,944; *Number of Players:* 1,039,880; *National Colours:* Gold and black shirts, green shorts, white stockings.
Telephone: 002711 4943522; *Fax:* 002711 4943013.

SUDAN

Sudan Football Association, P.O. Box 437, Khartoum.
Founded: 1936; *Number of Clubs:* 750; *Number of Players:* 42,200; *National Colours:* Green shirts, white shorts, green stockings.
Telephone & fax: 0024911 776633; *Cable:* ALKOURA KHARTOUM; *Telex:* 23007 KORA SD.

SWAZILAND

National Football Association of Swaziland, P.O. Box 641, Mbabane.
Founded: 1968; *Number of Clubs:* 136; *National Colours:* Blue shirts, gold shorts, white stockings.
Telephone: 00268 46852; *Telex:* 2245 EXP WD; *Fax:* 00268 46206.

TANZANIA

Football Association of Tanzania, Uhuru/Shaurimoyo Road, Karume Memorial Stadium, P.O. Box 1574, Ilala/Dar Es Salaam.
Founded: 1930; *Number of Clubs:* 51; *National Colours:* Yellow shirts with black stripes, yellow shorts, yellow and black stockings with horiz. stripe.
Telephone: 0025551 117931; *Cable:* FAT DAR- ES- SALAAM; *Telex:* 41873 TZ; *Fax:* 0025551 117930.

TOGO

Federation Togolaise De Football, C.P. 5, Lome.
Founded: 1960; *Number of Clubs:* 144; *Number of Players:* 4,346; *National Colours:* White shirts, green shorts, red and yellow stockings with green stripes.
Telephone: 00228 221412; *Cable:* TOGOFOOT LOME; *Telex:* 5015 CNOT TG. *Fax:* 00228 221413.

TUNISIA

Federation Tunisienne De Football, 16 Rue de la Ligue Arabe, El-Menzah VI, Tunis 1004.
Founded: 1956; *Number of Clubs:* 215; *Number of Players:* 18,300; *National Colours:* Red shirts, white shorts, red stockings.
Telephone: 002161 233303; *Cable:* FOOTBALL TUNIS; *Telex:* 14783 FTFOOT TN; *Fax:* 002161 767929.

UGANDA

Federation of Uganda Football Associations, P.O. Box 22518, Kampala, Uganda.
Founded: 1924; *Number of Clubs:* 400; *Number of Players:* 1,518; *National Colours:* Yellow shirts with black stripes, black shorts with yellow stripes, yellow and red stockings.
Telephone: 0025641 342731; *Cable:* FUFA LUGOGO STADIUM, KAMPALA; *Telex:* 61605; *Fax:* 0025641 342731.

ZAMBIA

Football Association of Zambia, P.O. Box 34751, Lusaka.
Founded: 1929; *Number of Clubs:* 20 (senior); *Number of Players:* 4,100; *National Colours:* Copper shirts, black shorts, copper stockings.
Telephone: 002601 750254; *Cable:* FOOTBALL LUSAKA; *Fax:* 002601 225046.

ZIMBABWE

Zimbabwe Football Association, P.O. Box CY 114, Causeway, Harare.
Founded: 1965; *National Colours:* Green shirts, gold shorts, green and gold stockings.
Telephone: 002634 731262; *Cable:* SOCCER HARARE; *Telex:* 22299 SOCCER ZW; *Fax:* 002634 731265.

THE WORLD CUP 1930–98

Year	Winners		Runners-up		Venue	Attendance	Referee
1930	Uruguay	4	Argentina	2	Montevideo	90,000	Langenus (B)
1934	Italy	2	Czechoslovakia	1	Rome	50,000	Eklind (Se)
	(after extra time)						
1938	Italy	4	Hungary	2	Paris	45,000	Capdeville (F)
1950	Uruguay	2	Brazil	1	Rio de Janeiro	199,854	Reader (E)
1954	West Germany	3	Hungary	2	Berne	60,000	Ling (E)
1958	Brazil	5	Sweden	2	Stockholm	49,737	Guigue (F)
1962	Brazil	3	Czechoslovakia	1	Santiago	68,679	Latychev (USSR)
1966	England	4	West Germany	2	Wembley	93,802	Dienst (Sw)
	(after extra time)						
1970	Brazil	4	Italy	1	Mexico City	107,412	Glockner (EG)
1974	West Germany	2	Holland	1	Munich	77,833	Taylor (E)
1978	Argentina	3	Holland	1	Buenos Aires	77,000	Gonella (I)
	(after extra time)						
1982	Italy	3	West Germany	1	Madrid	90,080	Coelho (Br)
1986	Argentina	3	West Germany	2	Mexico City	114,580	Filho (Br)
1990	West Germany	1	Argentina	0	Rome	73,603	Codesal (Mex)
1994	Brazil	0	Italy	0	Los Angeles	94,194	Puhl (H)
	(Brazil won 3-2 on penalties aet)						
1998	France	3	Brazil	0	St-Denis	75,000	Belqola (Mor)

GOALSCORING AND ATTENDANCES IN WORLD CUP FINAL ROUNDS

Venue	Matches	Goals (av)	Attendance (av)
1930, Uruguay	18	70 (3.9)	434,500 (24,138)
1934, Italy	17	70 (4.1)	395,000 (23,235)
1938, France	18	84 (4.6)	483,000 (26,833)
1950, Brazil	22	88 (4.0)	1,337,000 (60,772)
1954, Switzerland	26	140 (5.4)	943,000 (36,270)
1958, Sweden	35	126 (3.6)	868,000 (24,800)
1962, Chile	32	89 (2.8)	776,000 (24,250)
1966, England	32	89 (2.8)	1,614,677 (50,458)
1970, Mexico	32	95 (2.9)	1,673,975 (52,311)
1974, West Germany	38	97 (2.5)	1,774,022 (46,684)
1978, Argentina	38	102 (2.7)	1,610,215 (42,374)
1982, Spain	52	146 (2.8)	2,064,364 (38,816)
1986, Mexico	52	132 (2.5)	2,441,731 (46,956)
1990, Italy	52	115 (2.2)	2,515,168 (48,368)
1994, USA	52	141 (2.7)	3,567,415 (68,604)
1998, France	64	171 (2.6)	2,775,400 (43,366)

LEADING GOALSCORERS

Year	Player	Goals
1930	Guillermo Stabile (Argentina)	8
1934	Angelo Schiavio (Italy)	
	Oldrich Nejedly (Czechoslovakia)	
	Edmund Conen (Germany)	4
1938	Leonidas da Silva (Brazil)	8
1950	Ademir (Brazil)	9
1954	Sandor Kocsis (Hungary)	11
1958	Just Fontaine (France)	13
1962	Valentin Ivanov (USSR), Leonel Sanchez (Chile), Garrincha, Vava (both Brazil), Florian Albert (Hungary), Drazen Jerkovic (Yugoslavia)	4
1966	Eusebio (Portugal)	9
1970	Gerd Muller (West Germany)	10
1974	Grzegorz Lato (Poland)	7
1978	Mario Kempes (Argentina)	6
1982	Paolo Rossi (Italy)	6
1986	Gary Lineker (England)	6
1990	Salvatore Schillaci (Italy)	6
1994	Oleg Salenko (Russia)	
	Hristo Stoichkov (Bulgaria)	6
1998	Davor Suker (Croatia)	6

WOMEN'S WORLD CUP 1999

Played in the United States

GROUP A
USA 3, Denmark 0
North Korea 1, Nigeria 2
USA 7, Nigeria 1
North Korea 3, Denmark 1
USA 3, North Korea 0
Nigeria 2, Denmark 0

GROUP B
Brazil 7, Mexico 1
Germany 1, Italy 1
Brazil 2, Italy 0
Germany 6, Mexico 0
Brazil 3, Germany 3
Italy 2, Mexico 0

GROUP C
Japan 1, Canada 1
Norway 2, Russia 1
Norway 7, Canada 1
Japan 0, Russia 5
Russia 4, Canada 1
Norway 4, Japan 0

GROUP D
China 2, Sweden 1
Australia 1, Ghana 1

Australia 1, Sweden 3
China 7, Ghana 0
Sweden 2, Ghana 0
China 3, Australia 1

QUARTER-FINALS
China 2, Russia 0
Norway 3, Sweden 1
USA 3, Germany 2
Brazil 4, Nigeria 3 aet

SEMI-FINALS
USA 2, Brazil 0
Norway 0, China 5

MATCH FOR THIRD PLACE
Brazil 0, Norway 0
Brazil won 5-4 on penalties.

FINAL
USA 0, China 0
USA won 5-4 on penalties.

EURO 2000

GROUP 1

Minsk, 5 September 1998, 35,000

Belarus (0) 0
Denmark (0) 0

Belarus: Satsunkevich; Yakhimovic, Ostrovski, Shtanyuk, Romashchenko M (Geraschenko 40), Gurenko, Khatskevich, Baranov, Lavrik, Belkevich, Makovski V (Romashchenko M A 89).
Denmark: Schmeichel; Tobiasen, Rieper, Hogh, Heintze, Helveg, Nielsen A, Thomsen, Tomasson (Frederiksen 81), Jorgensen (Andersen 67), Moller (Gravesen 67).
Referee: Dardenne (Germany).

Anfield, 5 September 1998, 23,160

Wales (0) 0
Italy (1) 2 *(Fuser 19, Vieri 76)*

Wales: Jones P; Robinson, Barnard, Symons, Williams, Coleman, Speed, Johnson, Blake (Saunders 66), Hughes M (Savage 80), Giggs.
Italy: Peruzzi; Panucci, Pessotto, Albertini (Di Biagio 68), Cannavaro, Iuliano, Fuser, Dino Baggio, Vieri, Del Piero (Roberto Baggio 74), Di Francesco (Serena 82).
Referee: Hauge (Norway).

Copenhagen, 10 October 1998, 36,009

Denmark (0) 1 *(Frederiksen 57)*
Wales (0) 2 *(Williams 58, Bellamy 86)*

Denmark: Krogh; Tobiasen, Rieper, Hogh, Heintze, Helveg, Frandsen (Gravesen 76), Steen-Nielsen, Jorgensen, Frederiksen, Beck (Sand 65).
Wales: Jones P; Savage, Barnard, Williams, Symons, Coleman, Saunders (Robinson 81), Blake (Bellamy 69), Hughes M, Johnson (Pembridge 62), Speed.
Referee: Piller (Hungary).

Udine, 10 October 1998, 35,247

Italy (1) 2 *(Del Piero 19, 61)*
Switzerland (0) 0

Italy: Buffon; Panucci, Cannavaro, Maldini, Torricelli, Fuser, Dino Baggio, Albertini, Di Francesco (Bachini 63), Inzaghi, Del Piero (Totti 70).
Switzerland: Hilfiker; Wolf (Chassot 68), Vega, Henchoz, Vogel, Wicky (Celestini 86), Sforza, Rothenbuhler, Sesa, Chapuisat, Muller.
Referee: Sars (France).

Zurich, 14 October 1998, 12,500

Switzerland (0) 1 *(Chapuisat 58)*
Denmark (0) 1 *(Tobiasen 90)*

Switzerland: Hilfiker; Jeanneret (Rothenbuhler 76), Sforza, Henchoz, Vogel, Wicky, Sesa (Haas 89), Fournier, Celestini, Chapuisat, Muller (Di Jorio 78).
Denmark: Krogh; Tobiasen, Rieper, Hogh, Heintze, Helveg, Frandsen (Colding 59), Steen-Nielsen, Tomasson (Beck 78), Fredriksen (Sand 61), Jorgensen.
Referee: Radoman (Yugoslavia).

Cardiff, 14 October 1998, 11,975

Wales (1) 3 *(Robinson 15, Coleman 54, Symons 85)*
Belarus (1) 2 *(Gurenko 21, Belkevich 48)*

Wales: Jones P; Robinson, Barnard, Savage, Symons, Coleman, Saunders, Johnson, Blake, Hughes M, Pembridge.
Belarus: Satsunkevich; Yakhimovic, Ostrovski, Lavrik, Shtanyuk, Baranov (Gerasimets 70), Khatskevich, Geraschenko (Romashchenko M 88), Gurenko, Belkevich, Makovski V (Katchuro 73).
Referee: Sammut (Malta).

Minsk, 27 March 1999, 44,000

Belarus (0) 0
Switzerland (0) 1 *(Fournier 72)*

Belarus: Tumilovich; Lavrik, Lukhvich, Yakhimovic, Gurenko, Khatskevich, Belkevich, Geraschenko (Skripchenko 86), Baranov (Chaika 56), Romashchenko, Makovski (Ostrovski 87).
Switzerland: Brunner; Hodel, Henchoz, Vogel, Fournier, Jeanneret, Wicky (Muller 66), Sforza, Sesa (De Napoli 74), Chapuisat, Comisetti.
Referee: Sarvan (Turkey).

Copenhagen, 27 March 1999, 41,429

Denmark (0) 1 *(Sand 56)*
Italy (1) 2 *(Inzaghi 1, Conte 68)*

Denmark: Schmeichel; Helveg, Henriksen, Hogh, Heintze, Goldbaek (Colding 82), Thomsen, Nielsen A (Tofting 77), Gronkjaer (Molnar 53), Jorgensen, Sand.
Italy: Buffon; Panucci, Nesta, Cannavaro, Maldini, Fuser (Conte 46), Dino Baggio, Di Biagio, Di Francesco, Inzaghi, Chiesa (Totti 63).
Referee: Lopez (Spain).

Ancona, 31 March 1999, 20,735

Italy (1) 1 *(Inzaghi 31 (pen))*
Belarus (1) 1 *(Belkevich 24)*

Italy: Buffon; Panucci, Nesta, Cannavaro, Maldini, Conte, Dino Baggio, Di Biagio (Giannichedda 46), Totti (Di Francesco 46), Inzaghi, Chiesa (Roberto Baggio 64).
Belarus: Tumilovich; Lavrik, Lukhvich, Yakhimovic, Gurenko, Orlovski, Belkevich, Ostrovski, Baranov, Romashchenko, Makovski V.
Referee: Piraux (Belgium).

Zurich, 31 March 1999, 13,500

Switzerland (1) 2 *(Chapuisat 4, 70)*
Wales (0) 0

Switzerland: Brunner; Jeanneret, Henchoz, Wolf, Muller, Vogel, Sforza, Fournier, Wicky, Chapuisat, Comisetti (Buhlmann 67).
Wales: Jones P (Crossley 26); Robinson, Pembridge, Symons, Coleman, Johnson, Saunders, Savage, Blake (Hartson 63), Hughes M (Bellamy 73), Speed.
Referee: Liba (Czech Republic).

Copenhagen, 5 June 1999, 24,876

Denmark (1) 1 *(Heintze 22)*
Belarus (0) 0

Denmark: Schmeichel; Colding, Henriksen, Hogh, Heintze, Goldbaek, Nielsen A, Tofting (Steen-Nielsen 87), Gronkjaer, Jorgensen, Sand (Molnar 78).
Belarus: Tumilovich; Lavrik, Lukhvich, Yakhimovic, Gurenko, Orlovski, Belkevic, Yaskovich (Kulchi 70), Ostrovski (Romashchenko 46), Baranov, Makovski V (Ryndyuk 85).
Referee: Baptista (Portugal).

Bologna, 5 June 1999, 12,392

Italy (3) 4 *(Vieri 6, Inzaghi 36, Maldini 39, Chiesa 89)*
Wales (0) 0

Italy: Buffon; Panucci, Maldini, Fuser (Di Livio 68), Negro, Cannavaro, Conte, Albertini, Vieri (Montella 46), Inzaghi (Chiesa 80), Di Francesco.
Wales: Jones P; Robinson (Jenkins 77), Barnard, Page, Melville, Williams, Giggs, Bellamy (Pembridge 79), Saunders (Hartson 46), Hughes M, Speed.
Referee: Steinborn (Germany).

Lausanne, 9 June 1999, 15,800

Switzerland (0) 0
Italy (0) 0

Switzerland: Huber; Wicky (Haas 70), Muller, Hodel, Geanneret (Di Jorio 78), Vogel, Sforza, Rothenbuhler, Sesa, Chapuisat, Comisetti (Celestini 57).
Italy: Buffon; Panucci (Pancaro 72), Negro, Cannavaro, Maldini, Fuser (Di Livio 61), Albertini, Conte, Vieri (Chiesa 61), Inzaghi, Di Francesco.
Referee: Poll (England).

Liverpool, 9 June 1999, 10,000

Wales (0) 0

Denmark (0) 2 *(Tomasson 84, Tofting 90 (pen))*

Wales: Jones P; Jenkins, Barnard (Legg 90), Robinson (Pembridge 87), Melville, Coleman, Speed, Saunders, Hartson (Bellamy 89), Hughes M, Giggs.
Denmark: Schmeichel; Colding, Heintze, Gronkjaer, Hogh, Henriksen, Goldbaek, Nielsen A (Tofting 85), Jorgensen (Frandsen 90), Sand, Molnar (Tomasson 72).
Referee: Ancion (Belgium).

Group 1	P	W	D	L	F	A	Pts
Italy	6	4	2	0	11	2	14
Denmark	6	2	2	2	6	5	8
Switzerland	5	2	2	1	4	3	8
Wales	6	2	0	4	5	13	6
Belarus	5	0	2	3	3	6	2

GROUP 2
Tbilisi, 5 September 1998, 35,000

Georgia (0) 1 *(Arveladze A 65)*
Albania (0) 0

Georgia: Gvaramadze; Kaladze, Tskitishvili, Silagadze (Kiknadze 42), Tsereteli, Kobiashvili, Nemsadze, Jamarauli, Ketsbaia (Janashia 56), Kinkladze, Iashvili (Arveladze A 60).
Albania: Strakosha; Lala, Shulku, Xhumba, Vata, Pinari, Haxhi, Bushi (Galo 74), Kola, Rrakli, Tare (Peco 67) (Maxhuni 87).
Referee: Tetrucci (Switzerland).

Athens, 6 September 1998, 29,000

Greece (0) 2 *(Mahlas 56 (pen), Frantzeskos 58)*
Slovenia (1) 2 *(Zahovic 19, 73)*

Greece: Atmatsidis; Kalitzakis, Ouzounidis, Dabizas, Borbokis (Liberopoulos 83), Markos, Zagorakis, Tsartas (Frantzeskos 46), Kassapis (Georgatos 78), Mahlas, Nikolaidis.
Slovenia: Simeunovic; Milanic, Galic, Knavs, Novak, Ceh, Zahovic, Pavlin, Rudonja, Udovic (Englaro 46), Osterc (Siljak 68) (Acimovic 72).
Referee: Trentalange (Italy).

Oslo, 6 September 1998, 11,030

Norway (1) 1 *(Solbakken 17)*
Latvia (1) 3 *(Pakhar 11, Shtolcers 53, Zemlinsky 65 (pen))*

Norway: Baardsen; Heggem (Berg 61), Bjornebye, Johnsen, Hoftun, Rekdal, Rudi (Flo H 79), Solbakken, Strandli, Flo T, Solskjaer (Flo J 62).
Latvia: Karavayev; Laizans (Lukashevich 51), Lobanyov, Zemlinsky, Ivanov, Bleidelis, Zakreshevsky, Babichev, Sharando (Boulders 73), Pakhar (Isakov 81), Shtolcers.
Referee: Shmolik (Belarus).

Riga, 10 October 1998, 1900

Latvia (1) 1 *(Shtolcers 2)*
Georgia (0) 0

Latvia: Karavayev; Lukashevich, Zemlinsky, Lobanyov, Sharando, Ivanov, Astafyev (Isakov 75), Bleidelis (Laizans 51), Babichev, Pakhar (Boulders 89), Shtolcers.
Georgia: Gvaramadze; Kaladze, Shekiladze, Kavelashvili, Gakhokidze (Demetradze 60), Kobiashvili, Nemsadze, Jamarauli, Ketsbaia, Kinkladze, Arveladze S.
Referee: Zotta (Romania).

Ljubljana, 10 October 1998, 7000

Slovenia (1) 1 *(Zahovic 24)*
Norway (1) 2 *(Flo T 43, Rekdal 80)*

Slovenia: Simeunovic; Galic, Milanic, Knavs, Rudonja, Novak, Ceh, Zahovic, Pavlin, Osterc (Englaro 46), Udovic (Acimovic 65).
Norway: Grodas; Haaland, Berg, Hoftun, Bjornebye, Heggem (Riseth 86), Strand (Hestad 77), Rekdal, Solbakken, Flo J, Flo T (Rushfeldt 89).
Referee: Schluchter (Switzerland).

Maroussi, 14 October 1998, 15,000

Greece (3) 3 *(Mahlas 13, Liberopoulos 15, Ouzounidis 36)*
Georgia (0) 0

Greece: Atmatsidis; Kalitzakis, Ouzounidis, Dabizas, Zagorakis, Markos, Poursanidis, Frantzeskos (Tsartas 74), Georgatos, Liberopoulos (Yannakopoulos 67), Mahlas (Mavroyenidis 85).
Georgia: Togonidze; Kobiashvili, Kaladze, Shelia, Nemsadze, Shekiladze, Ketsbaia, Jamarauli, Kinkladze, Kavelashvili (Gakhokidze 59), Arveladze S.
Referee: Ouzounov (Bulgaria).

Oslo, 14 October 1998, 17,770

Norway (0) 2 *(Rekdal 80 (pen), Berg 87)*
Albania (1) 2 *(Bushi 38, Tare 53)*

Norway: Grodas; Haaland (Iversen 12), Berg, Hoftun, Bjornebye, Heggem, Strand, Rekdal, Solbakken (Rushfeldt 90), Flo J (Solskjaer 57), Flo T.
Albania: Strakosha; Shulku, Lala, Xhumba, Haxhi, Bushi (Halili 84), Vata, Kola (Dalipi 90), Fakaj, Tare, Rrakli.
Referee: Grabher (Austria).

Maribor, 14 October 1998, 4700

Slovenia (0) 1 *(Udovic 86)*
Latvia (0) 0

Slovenia: Simeunovic; Galic, Milanic, Knavs (Gliha 46), Novak, Istenic (Acimovic 65), Pavlin, Englaro, Zahovic, Udovic (Milinovic 88), Rudonja.
Latvia: Karavayev; Lukashevich, Zemlinsky, Ivanov (Rimkus 87), Lobanyov, Sharando, Bleidelis (Mikholap 51), Astafyev (Boulders 79), Isakov, Pakhar, Shtolcers.
Referee: Nalbandyan (Armenia).

Tirana, 18 November 1998, 14,000

Albania (0) 0
Greece (0) 0

Albania: Strakosha; Dalipi (Halili 52), Haxhi, Vata, Xhumba, Shulku, Fakaj, Kola, Bushi, Rrakli, Tare.
Greece: Atmatsidis; Dabizas (Vokolos 90), Ouzounidis, Kalitzakis, Zagorakis, Poursanidis, Frantzeskos (Liberopoulos 46), Georgatos, Mahlas, Nikolaidis (Konstantinidis 68), Markos.
Referee: Torres (Spain).

Tbilisi, 27 March 1999, 20,000

Georgia (1) 1 *(Janashia 42)*
Slovenia (0) 1 *(Zahovic 52)*

Georgia: Grishikashvili; Kaladze, Bashvili, Chkhaidze, Tsereteli, Aleksidze (Kinkladze 46), Nemsadze, Jamarauli (Daraselia 82), Kobiashvili, Janashia, Demetradze (Kavelashvili 74).
Slovenia: Simeunovic; Galic, Milanic, Knavs, Rudonja (Mitrakovic 89), Bulajic, Milinovic, Ceh, Pavlin (Istenic 78), Udovic (Acimovic 60), Zahovic.
Referee: Hamer (Luxembourg).

Athens, 27 March 1999, 42,571

Greece (0) 0
Norway (1) 2 *(Solskjaer 38, 87)*

Greece: Atmatsidis; Dabizas, Ouzounidis, Anatolikis, Zagorakis (Mavrogenidis 46), Yannakopoulos, Poursanidis, Markos (Mahlas 55), Georgatos, Liberopoulos (Frantzeskos 75), Nikolaidis.
Norway: Myhre; Heggem, Berg, Johnsen, Bergdolmo (Halle 65), Iversen, Strand (Bohinen 60), Solbakken, Mykland, Rudi, Solskjaer (Carew 88).
Referee: Irvine (Republic of Ireland).

Riga, 31 March 1999, 3200

Latvia (0) 0

Greece (0) 0

Latvia: Karavayev; Lukashevich, Astafyev, Zemlinsky, Lobanyov, Ivanov (Isakov 27), Sharando (Stepanov 62), Mikholap (Boulders 46), Blagonadezhdin, Pakhar, Shtolcers.

Greece: Atmatsidis; Kassapis, Ouzounidis, Dabizas, Poursanidis, Mavrogenidis, Zagorakis (Yannakopoulos 75), Liberopoulos, Georgatos (Frantzeskos 75), Mahlas (Anastasiou 81), Nikolaidis.

Referee: Fisker (Denmark).

Tbilisi, 28 April 1999, 20,000

Georgia (0) 1 *(Janashia 58)*

Norway (4) 4 *(Shekiladze 16 (og), Flo T 26, 38, Solskjaer 35)*

Georgia: Togonidze; Shekiladze (Popkhadze 46), Didava, Tsereteli, Kaladze, Nemsadze, Revazishvili (Kiknadze 81), Jamarauli, Kobiashvili, Janashia, Ketsbaia (Demetradze 46).

Norway: Myhre; Haaland, Pedersen, Hoftun, Bergdolmo, Solskjaer (Strand 46), Iversen, Solbakken, Mykland, Rudi (Riseth 82), Flo T (Carew 88).

Referee: Puhl (Hungary).

Riga, 28 April 1999, 2700

Latvia (0) 0

Albania (0) 0

Latvia: Karavayev; Stepanov (Sharando 84), Isakov, Lukashevich, Lobanyov, Blagonadezhdin, Ivanov, Boulders, Rubins, Mikholap (Dobretsov 70), Shtolcers (Laizans 60).

Albania: Strakosha; Lala, Shulku, Xhumba, Vata (Jupi 77), Fakaj, Haxhi, Bushi (Halili 87), Kola, Rrakli (Dalipi 82), Tare.

Referee: Romain (Belgium).

Oslo, 30 May 1999, 18,236

Norway (1) 1 *(Iversen 4)*

Georgia (0) 0

Norway: Olsen; Heggem, Pedersen, Hoftun, Bergdolmo, Iversen (Dahlum 85), Leonhardsen (Rudi 46), Solbakken, Mykland, Riseth (Rekdal 70), Flo T.

Georgia: Gvaramadze; Guchua (Tskitishvili 62), Kaladze, Didava (Popkhadze 46), Tsereteli, Tskitishvili, Nemsadze, Ketsbaia, Jamarauli, Kavelashvili, Demetradze (Ashvetia 77).

Referee: Huyghe (Belgium).

Tirana, 5 June 1999, 5000

Albania (1) 1 *(Tare 16)*

Norway (1) 2 *(Iversen 4, Flo T 83)*

Albania: Strakosha; Lala, Shulku, Xhumba, Vata, Haxhi, Bushi, Kola (Duro 69), Fakaj (Bellaj 62), Tare, Rrakli (Bogdani 80).

Norway: Olsen; Haaland, Pedersen (Bragstad 62), Hoftun, Bergdolmo, Iversen, Solbakken (Riseth 89), Rekdal, Mykland, Rudi (Dahlum 78), Flo T.

Referee: Stoica (Romania).

Tbilisi, 5 June 1999, 15,000

Georgia (0) 1 *(Ketsbaia 55)*

Greece (0) 2 *(Mavrogenidis 88, Mahlas 90)*

Georgia: Gvaramadze; Chichveishvili (Didava 10), Khizaneishvili O, Akhvlediani (Khizaneishvili Z 67), Tsereteli, Tskitishvili (Alexidze 56), Nemsadze, Ketsbaia, Jamarauli, Ashvetia, Kobiashvili.

Greece: Atmatsidis; Mavrogenidis, Ouzounidis, Anatolakis, Kassapis, Konstantinidis (Froussas 46), Poursanidis, Zagorakis (Frantzeskos 81), Niniadis, Georgatos (Anastasiou 61), Mahlas.

Referee: Young (Scotland).

Riga, 5 June 1999, 2500

Latvia (1) 1 *(Pakhar 18)*

Slovenia (2) 2 *(Zahovic 25, 38 (pen))*

Latvia: Kolinko; Lukashevich, Astafyev (Rubins 41), Zemlinsky, Lobanyov (Korablov 43), Sharando (Bleidelis 69), Laizans, Shtolcers, Pakhar, Babichev, Mikholap.

Slovenia: Simeunovic; Rudonja (Osterc 88), Milinovic, Karic, Galic (Acimovic 66), Knavs, Novak, Ceh, Udovic, Zahovic, Pavlin (Istenic 79).

Referee: Arceo (Spain).

Tirana, 9 June 1999, 8000

Albania (0) 0

Slovenia (1) 1 *(Zahovic 26 (pen))*

Albania: Strakosha; Lala, Shulku, Xhumba, Vata, Duro, Bushi, Bellaj, Bogdani (Dalipi 75), Rrakli (Halili 46), Tare.

Slovenia: Simeunovic; Galic, Knavs, Osterc (Tsentic 80), Milinovic, Karic, Novak, Ceh, Udovic (Acimovic 66), Rudonja, Zahovic.

Referee: Stoica (Romania).

Athens, 9 June 1999, 15,000

Greece (1) 1 *(Niniadis 38 (pen))*

Latvia (1) 2 *(Verpakovskis 24, Zemlinsky 90 (pen))*

Greece: Atmatsidis; Mavrogenidis, Ouzounidis, Anatolakis, Kassapis, Zikos, Zagorakis, Frantzeskos (Anastasiou 60), Niniadis (Froussos 79), Georgatos (Markos 73), Mahlas.

Latvia: Kolinko; Lukashevich, Astafyev (Bleidelis 54), Zemlinsky, Rubins (Sismannovs 64), Pakhar, Babichev, Laizans, Verpakovskis (Mikholap 46), Korablovs, Lobanyov.

Referee: Pucek (Czech Republic).

Group 2	P	W	D	L	F	A	Pts
Norway	7	5	1	1	14	8	16
Slovenia	6	3	2	1	8	6	11
Latvia	7	3	2	2	7	5	11
Greece	7	2	3	2	8	7	9
Georgia	7	1	1	5	4	12	4
Albania	6	0	3	3	3	6	3

GROUP 3

Helsinki, 5 September 1998, 18,716

Finland (2) 3 *(Kolkka 8, Johansson 44, Paatelainen 62)*

Moldova (2) 2 *(Oprea 10, 11)*

Finland: Niemi; Ylonen, Tuomela, Hyypia, Turpeinen (Reini 46), Wiss, Kautonen, Litmanen, Johansson (Sumiala 80), Paatelainen, Kolkka (Mahlio 73).

Moldova: Coselev; Fistican (Tabanov 76), Rebeja (Pusca 46), Testimitanu, Guzun, Stroenco, Oprea, Gaidamasciuc, Epureanu (Suharev 76), Curtianu, Clescenco.

Referee: Barber (England).

Istanbul, 5 September 1998, 26,500

Turkey (1) 3 *(Oktay 18, 58, Tayfur 49 (pen))*

Northern Ireland (0) 0

Turkey: Rustu; Saffet, Mert, Alpay, Okan (Arif 87), Sergen, Tayfur, Tugay (Oguz 75), Abdullah, Oktay (Hami 79), Hakan Sukur.

Northern Ireland: Fettis; Hughes A, Horlock, Mulryne, Hill, Morrow, Gillespie (Jim Whitley 78), Lennon, Dowie, Rowland (Quinn 46), Hughes M.

Referee: Wojcik (Poland).

Belfast, 10 October 1998, 10,002

Northern Ireland (1) 1 *(Rowland 31)*

Finland (0) 0

Northern Ireland: Fettis; Hughes A, Horlock, Mulryne, Morrow, Patterson, Gillespie (McCarthy 71), Lennon, Dowie (O'Boyle 80), Rowland (Quinn 89), Hughes M.

Finland: Niemi; Ylonen, Ilola, Hyypia, Kautonen, Reini, Riihilahti (Litmanen 75), Valakari, Kolkka, Paatelainen, Johansson.

Referee: Arsic (Yugoslavia).

Bursa, 10 October 1998, 20,000

Turkey (0) 1 *(Hakan Sukur 70)*

Germany (0) 0

Turkey: Rustu; Fatih, Ogun (Unsal 89), Alpay, Tayfun, Tugay, Tugay (Oktay 61), Abdullah, Mert, Sergen (Saffet 81), Hakan Sukur.
Germany: Kahn; Babbel, Nowotny, Rehmer, Ricken (Bode 81), Ramelow, Beinlich, Jeremies, Heinrich (Neuville 76), Bierhoff, Kirsten.
Referee: Dallas (Scotland).

Chisinau, 14 October 1998, 5000

Moldova (1) 1 *(Guzun 6)*

Germany (3) 3 *(Kirsten 20, 36, Bierhoff 38)*

Moldova: Coselev; Fistican, Stroenco, Testimitanu, Gaidamasciuc, Rebeja, Guzun, Oprea, Curtianu (Suharev 53), Clescenco, Epureanu.
Germany: Kahn; Babbel, Nowotny, Rehmer, Ricken (Neuville 53), Ramelow, Beinlich (Wosz 83), Nerlinger, Tarnat, Kirsten (Jancker 74), Bierhoff.
Referee: Marin (Spain).

Istanbul, 14 October 1998, 25,000

Turkey (0) 1 *(Ogun 73)*

Finland (1) 3 *(Paatelainen 5, Johansson 51, Litmanen 90)*

Turkey: Rustu; Alpay, Ogun, Fatih, Okan (Hami 46), Tugay (Mert 46), Sergen (Hasan Sas 83), Tayfur, Abdullah, Hakan Sukur, Oktay.
Finland: Niemi; Reini, Ylonen (Kolkka 61), Hyypia, Kautonen, Tuomela, Riihilahti (Valakari 76), Litmanen, Ilola, Johansson (Saastamoinen 90), Paatelainen.
Referee: Krondl (Czech Republic).

Belfast, 18 November 1998, 11,137

Northern Ireland (0) 2 *(Dowie 49, Lennon 63)*

Moldova (1) 2 *(Gaidamasciuc 22, Testimitanu 57)*

Northern Ireland: Fettis; Griffin, Kennedy, Lomas, Patterson, Morrow, Gillespie (McCarthy 88), Lennon, Dowie, Rowland (Gray 77), Hughes.
Moldova: Dinov; Fistican, Guzun, Stroenco, Rebeja, Curtian, Stratulat (Suharev 62), Testimitanu (Maeivic 86), Epureanu, Gaidamasciuc, Clescenco.
Referee: Hrinak (Slovakia).

Belfast, 27 March 1999, 14,270

Northern Ireland (0) 0

Germany (2) 3 *(Bode 11, 42, Hamann 62)*

Northern Ireland: Taylor; Patterson, Horlock, Lomas, Williams, Morrow, Gillespie (McCarthy 84), Lennon (Sonner 68), Dowie, Rowland (Kennedy 69), Hughes M.
Germany: Kahn; Babbel, Worns, Jeremies, Matthaus (Nowotny 46), Strunz, Heinrich, Hamann, Bierhoff, Neuville (Jancker 69), Bode (Preetz 79).
Referee: Cesari (Italy).

Istanbul, 27 March 1999, 30,000

Turkey (1) 2 *(Hakan Sukur 34, Sergen 90)*

Moldova (0) 0

Turkey: Rustu; Fatih, Ogun, Alpay, Okan, Tugay (Ayhan 85), Sergen, Tayfur, Abdullah, Hakan Sukur, Oktay (Hami 9) (Arif 74).
Moldova: Dinov; Fistican, Rebeja, Tabanov, Guzun, Stroenco, Sischin, Stratulat, Gaidamasciuc, Epureanu, Clescenco (Suharev 81).
Referee: Plautz (Austria).

Nuremberg, 31 March 1999, 40,758

Germany (2) 2 *(Jeremies 31, Neuville 37)*

Finland (0) 0

Germany: Kahn; Babbel, Matthaus, Worns, Strunz, Hamann (Nowotny 72), Jeremies, Heinrich, Neuville (Kirsten 65), Bierhoff, Bode (Jancker 76).
Finland: Niemi; Reini (Lehkosuo 89), Hyypia, Ylonen, Kautonen (Kolkka 72), Kinnunen, Riihilahti, Litmanen, Ilola, Johansson, Paatelainen (Saastamoinen 46).
Referee: Koussainov (Russia).

Chisinau, 31 March 1999, 9237

Moldova (0) 0

Northern Ireland (0) 0

Moldova: Dinov; Fistican, Stroenco, Sosnovsky, Oprea (Stratulat 90), Gaidamasciuc, Epureanu, Rebeja, Guzun, Clescenco, Suharev.
Northern Ireland: Taylor; Patterson (Hughes A 62), Horlock, Lomas, Williams M, Morrow, Gillespie, Lennon, Dowie, Robinson, Hughes M.
Referee: Trivkovic (Croatia).

Leverkusen, 4 June 1999, 21,000

Germany (3) 6 *(Bierhoff 2, 56, 82, Kirsten 27, Bode 38, Scholl 71)*

Moldova (0) 1 *(Stratulat 76)*

Germany: Kahn; Nowotny, Matthaus (Babbel 75), Strunz, Hamann, Jeremies (Scholl 46), Heinrich, Neuville, Bierhoff, Kirsten (Ramelow 54), Bode.
Moldova: Dinov; Fistican, Malevici (Stratulat 55), Storenco, Rebeja, Gaidamasciuc (Belous 74), Epureanu, Guzun, Curtianu, Oprea, Clescenco (Sischin 81).
Referee: Coroado (Portugal).

Helsinki, 5 June 1999, 36,042

Finland (2) 2 *(Tihinen 10, Paatelainen 14)*

Turkey (2) 4 *(Tayfur 25, 84, Hakan Sukur 34, 87)*

Finland: Niemi; Ylonen, Hyypia, Kuivasto, Tihinen, Riihilahti, Valakari, Litmanen, Kolkka, Paatelainen, Johansson.
Turkey: Rustu; Fatih, Ali Eren, Alpay, Saffet, Sergen (Daval 89), Tayfur, Abdullah (Hakan Unsal 90), Tayfun, Hakan Sukur, Ayhan (Tugay 74).
Referee: Jol (Holland).

Chisinau, 9 June 1999, 8000

Moldova (0) 0

Finland (0) 0

Moldova: Dinov; Fistican, Stratulat, Stroenco, Rebeja, Siskin (Belous 75), Guzun, Epureanu, Curtianu, Oprea (Gaidamascius 79), Suharev (Chirilov 89).
Finland: Niemi; Ylonen, Reini (Lehkosuo 85), Hyypia, Tininen (Kautonen 46), Riihilahti, Valakari, Paatelainen, Kolkka, Ilola, Johansson (Forssell 60).
Referee: Treossi (Italy).

Group 3	P	W	D	L	F	A	Pts
Germany	5	4	0	1	14	3	12
Turkey	5	4	0	1	11	5	12
Finland	6	2	1	3	8	10	7
N. Ireland	5	1	2	2	3	8	5
Moldova	7	0	3	4	6	16	3

GROUP 4

Erevan, 5 September 1998, 2300

Armenia (1) 3 *(Avalyan 40, Yessayan 71, 90)*

Andorra (0) 1 *(Lucendo 86 (pen))*

Armenia: Berezovski; Soukiassian, Krbachian, Hovsepian, Oganessian (Khodgoyan 83), Vardanian, Sarkissian, Arm Adamian (Gsepyan 86), Art Adamian, Shahgeldian, Avalyan (Yessayan 68).
Andorra: Koldo; Ramirez, Chema, Martin, Lima, Escurza, Garcia, Oscar, Sanchez, Lucendo, Justo.
Referee: O'Hanlon (Republic of Ireland).

Reykjavik, 5 September 1998, 10,500

Iceland (1) 1 *(Dadason 33)*

France (1) 1 *(Dugarry 36)*

Iceland: Kristinsson B; Helgason, Sigurdsson L, Sverrisson E, Marteinsson, Hreidarsson, Kolvidsson, Gudjonsson T, Kristinsson R, Dadason, Gunnlaugsson A (Thordarson 69).
France: Barthez; Karembeu, Thuram, Leboeuf, Lizarazu, Dugarry (Henry 66), Deschamps, Djorkaeff, Zidane, Pires, Laslandes.
Referee: Blareau (Belgium).

Kiev, 5 September 1998, 18,000

Ukraine (2) 3 *(Popov 14, Skachenko 24, Rebrov 74 (pen))*

Russia (0) 2 *(Varlamov 67, Onopko 87)*

Ukraine: Shovkovskyi; Gusin, Mikitin, Golovko, Vashchuk, Dmitrulin, Skachenko (Kalitvintsev 46), Popov, Kovalov (Kriventsov 87), Shevchenko, Rebrov.

Russia: Kharine; Minko, Chugainov, Kovtun, Yanovski, Semak (Cheryshev 72), Onopko, Alenichev (Mostovoi 64), Kanchelskis (Karpin 71), Kolyvanov, Varlamov.

Referee: Merk (Germany).

Andorra, 10 October 1998, 850

Andorra (0) 0

Ukraine (2) 2 *(Kossovski V 30, Rebrov 43)*

Andorra: Koldo; Ramirez, Chema, Martin, Lima A, Lima I, Pol, Oscar, Emiliano, Sanchez (Jimenez 87), Ruiz.

Ukraine: Shovkovskyi; Luzhny, Golovko, Vashchuk, Mikitin (Kovalov 46), Popov, Maximov (Kriventsov 51), Gusin, Kossovski V, Shevchenko (Mikhailenko 69), Rebrov.

Referee: Guetzov (Bulgaria).

Erevan, 10 October 1998, 6,000

Armenia (0) 0

Iceland (0) 0

Armenia: Berezovski; Soukiassian, Vardanian, Khachatrian, Hovsepian, Sarkissian, Art Petrossian (Oganessian 40), Arm Adamian, Shahgeldian, Mikaelian, Assadourian (Yessayan 25).

Iceland: Kristinsson B; Jonsson O, Hreidarsson, Adolfsson, Helgason, Kristinsson R, Kolvidsson, Gunnlaugsson A, Dadason, Gudjonsson T, Sigurdsson H.

Referee: Norman (Sweden).

Moscow, 10 October 1998, 32,500

Russia (1) 2 *(Yanovski 45, Mostovoi 55)*

France (2) 3 *(Anelka 12, Pires 28, Boghossian 81)*

Russia: Ovchinnikov; Kovtun, Onopko, Varlamov, Khlestov, Karpin, Yanovski, Alenichev (Semak 69), Mostovoi, Tikhonov, Bestchastnykh (Gerasimenko 62).

France: Lama; Thuram, Blanc, Desailly, Lizarazu, Deschamps, Petit (Boghossian 46), Pires, Zidane, Djorkaeff (Vieira 54), Anelka (Vairelles 88).

Referee: Ceccarini (Italy).

Saint-Denis, 14 October 1998, 75,000

France (0) 2 *(Candela 53, Djorkaeff 61)*

Andorra (0) 0

France: Lama; Candela, Leboeuf, Blanc, Lizarazu, Deschamps, Zidane, Djorkaeff (Boghossian 82), Dugarry (Pires 71), Trezeguet (Anelka 71), Vairelles.

Andorra: Koldo; Ramirez (Sanchez 80), Chema, Martin, Lima A, Lima I, Pol, Oscar, Lucendo (Jimenez 88), Ruiz, Emiliano.

Referee: Koren (Israel).

Reykjavik, 14 October 1998, 3500

Iceland (0) 1 *(Kovtun 88 (og))*

Russia (0) 0

Iceland: Kristinsson B; Jonsson S, Hreidarsson, Adolfsson, Helgason, Kristinsson R, Kolvidsson (Thordarson 85), Gunnlaugsson A, Dadason, Sigurdsson L, Gudjonsson T (Sigurdsson H 6).

Russia: Cherchesov; Kovtun, Onopko, Smertin, Yanovski, Shalimov, Varlamov (Solomatin 59), Mostovoi, Tikhonov (Igonin 12), Karpin (Khokhlov 59), Titov.

Referee: Temmink (Holland).

Kiev, 14 October 1998, 25,000

Ukraine (1) 2 *(Skachenko 31, Gusin 83)*

Armenia (0) 0

Ukraine: Shovkovskyi; Luzhny, Dmitrulin, Golovko, Vashchuk, Popov (Maximov 75), Skachenko (Kovalov 61), Gusin, Kossovski V, Shevchenko (Kriventsov 80), Rebrov.

Armenia: Berezovski; Soukiassian, Vardanian, Khachatrian, Hovsepian, Kropochian (Oganessian 85), Art Petrossian, Arm Adamian, Shahgeldian, Mikaelian (Avalyan 65), Assadourian (Yessayan 73).

Referee: Lica (Romania).

La Vella, 27 March 1999, 1400

Andorra (0) 0

Iceland (0) 2 *(Sverrisson E 58, Adolfsson 67.)*

Andorra: Alvarez; Ramirez (Gonzalez 77), Garcia, Martin, Lima T, Lima I, Pol, Sonejee, Jimenez (Sanchez 73), Lucendo, Ruiz (Imbernon 83).

Iceland: Kristinsson B; Jonsson, Gunnarsson B (Hreidarsson 70), Adolfsson, Helgason, Kristinsson R, Thordarsson, Gunnlaugsson A (Gudmundsson T 81), Sverrisson E (Gretarsson 70), Sigurdsson H, Gudjonsson T.

Referee: Agius (Malta).

Erevan, 27 March 1999, 20,000

Armenia (0) 0

Russia (1) 3 *(Karpin 7, 63 (pen), Bestchastnykh 89)*

Armenia: Berezovski; Mkrtichian, Hovsepian, Oganessian, Karbanian (Arotonian 65), Vardanian, Art Petrossian, Voskanian (Kakosian 78), Sarkissian, Shahgeldian, Mikalian (Yessayan 81).

Russia: Filimonov; Khlestov, Onopko, Drozdov, Tsymbalar, Karpin, Alenichev (Tikhonov 65), Yanovski, Titov, Yuran (Khokhlov 85), Panov (Bestchastnykh 46).

Referee: Hauge (Norway).

Saint-Denis, 27 March 1999, 78,500

France (0) 0

Ukraine (0) 0

France: Barthez; Thuram, Lizarazu, Deschamps, Blanc, Desailly, Pires (Dhorasoo 85), Djorkaeff, Petit (Boghossian 78), Anelka, Dugarry (Wiltord 69).

Ukraine: Shovkovskyi; Luzhny, Vashchuk, Golovko, Mikitin, Gusin (Skrypnyk 85), Popov, Kovalov (Kossovski 55), Rebrov, Skachenko (Maximov 69), Shevchenko.

Referee: Benko (Austria).

Saint-Denis, 31 March 1999, 78,852

France (2) 2 *(Wiltord 3, Dugarry 45)*

Armenia (0) 0

France: Barthez; Thuram (Karembeu 79), Blanc, Desailly, Deschamps, Vieira, Djorkaeff (Pires 69), Boghossian, Anelka, Wiltord, Dugarry (Trezeguet 46).

Armenia: Berezovski; Soukiassian (Khachatrian 40), Mkritician, Vardanian, Hovsepian, Oganessian, Art Petrossian, Voskanian (Hyropetian 77), Sarkissian, Shahgeldian (Yessayan 53), Mikaelian.

Referee: Bikas (Greece).

Moscow, 31 March 1999, 20,000

Russia (3) 6 *(Titov 8, Bestchastnykh 11, 62, Onopko 42, Tsymbalar 50, Alenichev 90)*

Andorra (0) 1 *(Sanchez 73)*

Russia: Filimonov; Khlestov, Smertin, Tsymbalar, Yevseyev (Tikhonov 46), Alenichev, Onopko, Karpin, Titov, Chirko, Bestchastnykh.

Andorra: Alvarez; Alonso (Gonzalez 57), Garcia, Martin, Lima T, Lima I, Pol, Sonejee, Jimenez, Lucendo (Sanchez 65), Ruiz.

Referee: Vuorela (Finland).

Kiev, 31 March 1999, 50,000

Ukraine (0) 1 *(Vashchuk 59)*

Iceland (0) 1 *(Sigurdsson L 66)*

Ukraine: Shovkovskyi; Luzhny, Vashchuk, Golovko, Mikitin, Gusin, Popov (Kalitvintsev 75), Kossovski V, Rebrov, Skachenko (Maximov 46), Shevchenko.

Iceland: Kristinsson B; Jonsson, Gunnarsson B, Adolfsson, Helgason, Kristinsson R (Kolvidsson 80), Sigurdsson L, Gunnlaugsson A, Sverrisson E, Sigurdsson H (Sverrisson S 86), Gudjonsson T.

Referee: Dani (Israel).

Saint-Denis, 5 June 1999, 78,000

France (0) 2 *(Petit 48, Wiltord 54)*

Russia (1) 3 *(Panov 40, 75, Karpin 85)*

France: Barthez; Thuram, Blanc, Desailly, Candela (Pires 88), Deschamps, Petit, Djorkaeff (Boghossian 90), Dugarry (Vieira 59), Anelka, Wiltord.
Russia: Filimonov; Khlestov, Onopko, Smertin, Varlamov, Karpin, Semak (Bestchastnykh 60), Mostovoi (Khokhlov 26), Titov, Tikhonov (Tsymbalar 71), Panov.
Referee: Durkin (England).

Reykjavik, 5 June 1999, 5565

Iceland (1) 2 *(Dadason 30, Gunnarsson B 46)*

Armenia (0) 0

Iceland: Kristinsson B; Helgason (Kolvidsson 72), Hreidarsson, Jonsson S, Marteinsson, Gunnarsson B, Kristinsson R, Sverrisson, Sigurdsson (Danielsson 81), Gudjonsson T, Dadason (Helguson 69).
Armenia: Berezovski; Soukiassian (Nkrchian 65), Khachatrian, Hovsepian, Voskanian (Gregorian 84), Vardanian, Art Petrossian (Hayrapepian 75), Harutyunian, Sarkissian, Shahgeldian, Mikaelian.
Referee: Peltola (Finland).

Kiev, 5 June 1999, 45,000

Ukraine (2) 4 *(Popov 38, Rebrov 41, Dmitrulin 56, Husin 89)*

Andorra (0) 0

Ukraine: Vorobyev; Luzhny, Mikitin (Mizin 72), Golovko, Vashchuk, Dmitrulin (Maximov 78), Tsykhmeistruk, Popov, Gusin, Shevchenko (Skachenko 67), Rebrov.
Andorra: Alvarez; Pol, Martin (Lucendo 53), Garcia, Lima T, Lima I, Gonzalez, Sonajee, Ramirez, Sanchez, Ruiz.
Referee: Georgiou (Cyprus).

Barcelona, 9 June 1999, 4000

Andorra (0) 0

France (0) 1 *(Leboeuf 85 (pen))*

Andorra: Alvarez; Pol, Ramirez, Lima T, Lima I, Chema (Jonas 70), Gonzalez, Sonejee, Ruiz, Jimenez (Genis 89), Lucendo (Martin 77).
France: Rame; Karembeu, Candela, Boghossian, Leboeuf, Desailly, Wiltord, Dugarry, Anelka, Petit (Vieira 56), Dhorasoo (Pires 60).
Referee: Ross (Northern Ireland).

Erevan, 9 June 1999, 10,000

Armenia (0) 0

Ukraine (0) 0

Armenia: Berezovski; Petrossian T (Gregorian 63), Khachatrian, Hovsepian, Oganessian (Harutiunian 46), Vardanian, Art Petrossian, Voskanian, Sarkissian, Shahgeldian, Mikaelian (Mkritichian 46).
Ukraine: Vorobyev; Luzhny, Mikitin, Golovko, Vashchuk, Dmitrulin, Tsykhmeistruk, Popov (Konovalov 34), Gusin, Shevchenko (Cardash 80), Rebrov (Skachenko 70).
Referee: Boggi (Italy).

Moscow, 9 June 1999, 36,000

Russia (1) 1 *(Karpin 44)*

Iceland (0) 0

Russia: Filimonov; Khlestov, Varlamov (Yanovski 56), Onopko, Semak (Bulatov 46), Smertin, Karpin, Khokhlov, Tikhonov, Bestchastnykh (Tsymbalar 71), Panov.
Iceland: Kristinsson B; Helgason, Hreidarsson (Adolfsson 60), Jonsson S (Kolvidsson 46), Marteinsson, Kristinsson R, Gunnarsson B (Helguson 82), Sverrisson, Sigurdsson L, Gudjonsson T, Dadason.
Referee: Tokat (Turkey).

Group 4	P	W	D	L	F	A	Pts
Ukraine	7	4	3	0	12	3	15
France	7	4	2	1	11	6	14
Russia	7	4	0	3	17	10	12
Iceland	7	3	3	1	7	3	12
Armenia	7	1	2	4	3	10	5
Andorra	7	0	0	7	2	20	0

GROUP 5

Stockholm, 5 September 1998, 35,394

Sweden (2) 2 *(Andersson A 30, Mjallby 32)*

England (1) 1 *(Shearer 2)*

Sweden: Hedman; Nilsson, Andersson P, Bjorklund, Kamark (Lucic 82), Schwarz, Andersson A (Andersson D 90), Mjallby, Ljungberg, Larsson, Pettersson.
England: Seaman; Anderton (Lee 42), Le Saux, Southgate, Adams, Campbell (Merson 74), Redknapp, Ince, Shearer, Owen, Scholes (Sheringham 85).
Referee: Collina (Italy).

Bourgas, 6 September 1998, 20,000

Bulgaria (0) 0

Poland (2) 3 *(Czereszewski 19, 45, Iwan 47)*

Bulgaria: Zdravkov; Ginchev, Zagorcic (Petkov I 50), Yordanov, Petkov M (Trendafilov 46), Sirakov, Kishishev, Bachev, Borimirov (Gruiev 46), Stoichkov, Donev.
Poland: Sidorczuk; Bak, Zielinski, Lapinski, Siadaczka, Hajto (Klos 68), Brzeczek, Czereszewski, Swierczewski (Michalski 76), Iwan, Trzeciak (Juskowiak 83).
Referee: Batta (France).

Wembley, 10 October 1998, 72,974

England (0) 0

Bulgaria (0) 0

England: Seaman; Anderton (Batty 67), Hinchcliffe (Le Saux 34), Neville G, Southgate, Campbell, Lee, Scholes (Sheringham 77), Shearer, Owen, Redknapp.
Bulgaria: Zdravkov; Yordanov, Zagorcic, Kirilov, Kishishev, Iliev (Gruiev 63), Yankov, Petkov M, Naidenov, Stoichkov (Bachev 60), Hristov (Ivanov G 90).
Referee: Vagner (Hungary).

Warsaw, 10 October 1998, 8000

Poland (2) 3 *(Brzeczek 18, Juskowiak 35, Trzeciak 65)*

Luxembourg (0) 0

Poland: Matysek; Zielinski, Lapinski, Ratajczyk (Siadaczka 69), Hajto (Majak 62), Czereszewski, Iwan, Brzeczek (Bak 75), Swierczewski, Juskowiak, Trzeciak.
Luxembourg: Koch; Ferron, Birsens, Funck, Strasser, Holtz (Afrika 69), Theis (Deville F 46), Saibene, Cardoni, Deville L, Christophe (Thill 63).
Referee: Pregia (Albania).

Bourgas, 14 October 1998, 12,000

Bulgaria (0) 0

Sweden (0) 1 *(Larsson 62)*

Bulgaria: Zdravkov; Zagorcic, Yordanov, Kirilov (Parushev 17), Naidenov (Ivanov G 69), Iliev (Bachev 61), Yankov, Petkov M, Petkov I, Stoichkov, Hristov.
Sweden: Hedman; Nilsson, Andersson P, Bjorklund, Lucic (Sundgren 76), Ljungberg, Mild, Mjallby, Schwarz, Larsson (Erlingmark 88), Aslund (Blomqvist 71).
Referee: Heynemann (Germany).

Luxembourg, 14 October 1998, 8000

Luxembourg (0) 0

England (2) 3 *(Owen 19, Shearer 40 (pen), Southgate 90)*

Luxembourg: Koch; Ferron, Deville L, Funck, Deville F, Theis (Holtz 62), Saibene, Strasser, Posing, Cardoni, Christophe.
England: Seaman; Anderton (Lee 64), Neville P, Southgate, Ferdinand, Campbell, Beckham, Batty, Shearer, Owen, Scholes (Wright 76).
Referee: Vorgias (Greece).

Wembley, 27 March 1999, 73,836

England (2) 3 *(Scholes 11, 21, 70)*

Poland (1) 1 *(Brzeczek 29)*

England: Seaman; Neville G, Le Saux, Sherwood, Keown, Campbell, Beckham (Neville P 77), Scholes (Redknapp 83), Shearer, Cole, McManaman (Parlour 69).

Poland: Matysek; Hajto, Zielinski, Lapinski, Ratajczyk, Swierczewski (Klos 46), Bak, Brzeczek, Siadaczka (Kowalczyk 87), Iwan, Trzeciak (Juskowiak 83).
Referee: Pereira (Portugal).

Gothenburg, 27 March 1999, 37,728

Sweden (1) 2 *(Mjallby 34, Larsson 87)*
Luxembourg (0) 0

Sweden: Hedman; Kamark (Lucic 68), Andersson P, Bjorklund, Sundgren, Schwarz, Alexandersson, Mjallby, Ljungberg (Andersson D 79), Larsson, Andersson K.
Luxembourg: Felgen; Ferron, Funck, Birsens, Strasser, Theis (Holtz 70), Vanek, Saibene (Deville F 89), Cardoni, Deville L, Christophe (Zaritski 81).
Referee: Melnitjuk (Ukraine).

Luxembourg, 31 March 1999, 3004

Luxembourg (0) 0

Bulgaria (2) 2 *(Stoichkov 18, Yordanov 38)*
Luxembourg: Felgen; Ferron (Holtz 75), Vanek, Strasser, Deville L, Saibene, Birsens, Theis (Deville F 88), Posing (Zaritski 46), Cardoni, Christophe.
Bulgaria: Zdravkov; Kishishev, Yankov, Stoianov (Petkov I 48), Petkov M, Markov, Yordanov, Petrov, Iliev, Jovov (Ivanov 79), Stoichkov (Todorov 71).
Referee: Mitrovic (Slovakia).

Chorzow, 31 March 1999, 32,000

Poland (0) 0

Sweden (1) 1 *(Ljungberg 36)*
Poland: Sidorczuk; Waldoch, Lapinski, Zielinski, Siadaczka (Adamczuk 82), Iwan, Michalski (Bak 87), Brzeczek, Majak (Kowalczyk 70), Juskowiak, Trzeciak.
Sweden: Hedman; Kamark, Andersson P, Bjorklund, Lucic, Mild (Andersson D 72), Schwarz, Mjallby, Ljungberg, Larsson (Pettersson 89), Andersson K.
Referee: Merk (Germany).

Warsaw, 4 June 1999, 8000

Poland (1) 2 *(Hajto 16, Iwan 62)*
Bulgaria (0) 0

Poland: Matysek; Waldoch, Lapinski, Zielinski, Hajto (Majak 80), Nowak (Brzeczek 73), Michalski, Iwan, Siadaczka, Wichniarek (Frankowski 64), Trzeciak.
Bulgaria: Ivankov; Kirilov, Zagorcic, Markov, Kishishev, Petrov, Stoilov, Petkov M, Petkov I (Iliev 80), Stoichkov (Ivanov 63), Jovov (Bachev 46).
Referee: Braschi (Italy).

Wembley, 5 June 1999, 75,824

England (0) 0

Sweden (0) 0

England: Seaman; Neville P, Le Saux (Gray 46), Batty, Keown (Ferdinand R 35), Campbell, Beckham (Parlour 76), Sherwood, Shearer, Cole, Scholes.
Sweden: Hedman; Nilsson R, Kamark, Schwarz, Andersson P, Bjorklund, Mild (Alexandersson 7), Mjallby (Andersson D 82), Andersson K, Larsson (Svensson 70), Ljungberg.
Referee: Aranda (Spain).

Sofia, 9 June 1999, 22,000

Bulgaria (1) 1 *(Markov 18)*

England (1) 1 *(Shearer 15)*
Bulgaria: Ivankov; Kirilov, Stoilov, Kishishev, Zagorcic, Markov, Petrov S, Iliev (Borimirov 61), Petkov M, Stoichkov (Bachev 75), Yovov (Petrov M 46).
England: Seaman; Neville P, Gray, Southgate, Woodgate (Parlour 65), Campbell, Redknapp, Batty, Shearer, Fowler (Heskey 81), Sheringham.
Referee: Van der Ende (Holland).

Luxembourg, 9 June 1999, 2806

Luxembourg (0) 2 *(Birsens 76, Vanek 82)*
Poland (2) 3 *(Siadaczka 22, Wichniarek 45, Iwan 68)*
Luxembourg: Felgen; Vanek, Funck, Birsens, Strasser, Saibene (Alverdi 80), Theis (Schneider 46), Deville F, Cardoni, Christophe, Zaritski (Posing 65).
Poland: Matysek; Waldoch, Lapinski, Klos, Hajto (Brzeczek 65), Novak, Michalski, Iwan, Siadaczka, Wichniarek (Majak 87), Trzeciak.
Referee: Ivanov (Russia).

Group 5	P	W	D	L	F	A	Pts
Sweden	5	4	1	0	6	1	13
Poland	6	4	0	2	12	6	12
England	6	2	3	1	8	4	9
Bulgaria	6	1	2	3	3	7	5
Luxembourg	5	0	0	5	2	13	0

GROUP 6

Vienna, 5 September 1998, 20,000

Austria (1) 1 *(Reinmayr 7)*

Israel (0) 1 *(Nimni 68 (pen))*
Austria: Wohlfahrt; Schottel (Hiden 73), Feiersinger, Pfeffer, Cerny (Stoger 74), Kuhbauer, Mahlich, Reinmayr, Amerhauser, Vastic, Haas (Mayrleb 73).
Israel: Cohen; Harazi A, Shelach (Nimni 46), Ben Shimon, Amsalem, Abuksis (Mizrahi 46), Berkovic, Revivo, Benado, Harazi R (Graiev 61), Badir.
Referee: Frisk (Sweden).

Larnaca, 5 September 1998, 3500

Cyprus (1) 3 *(Engomitis 44, Gogic 48, Spoljaric 77)*
Spain (0) 2 *(Raul 72, Morientes 85)*
Cyprus: Panayiotou; Costa, Ioannou D (Ioakim 84), Charalambous, Pittas, Melanarkitis, Spoljaric, Christodolou M, Engomitis, Gogic (Agathocleous 61), Malekos (Pounnas 55).
Spain: Canizares; Michel, Nadal (Amor 65), Alkorta, Sergi, Etxeberria J (Ezquerro 59), Hierro, Raul, Luis Enrique, Alfonso (Kiko 39), Morientes.
Referee: Guseinov (Russia).

Larnaca, 10 October 1998, 10,000

Cyprus (0) 0

Austria (0) 3 *(Cerny 53, 61, Reinmayr 74)*
Cyprus: Panayiotou; Engomitis, Ioannou D, Costa, Charalambous, Pittas (Georgiou 67), Spolianis, Melanarkitis (Okkas 67), Christodolou M, Agathocleous (Pounnas 46), Gogic.
Austria: Wohlfahrt; Hiden, Schottel, Pfeffer, Cerny, Kuhbauer, Mahlich, Reinmayr (Stoger 78), Wetl, Vastic (Glieder 82), Haas (Mayrleb 78).
Referee: Meese (Belgium).

Serravalle, 10 October 1998, 872

San Marino (0) 0

Israel (3) 5 *(Revivo 16, Nimni 19, Mizrahi 31, 64, Graiev 83)*
San Marino: Gasperoni F; Gennari, Guerra, Valentini M, Bacciocchi (Valentini V 55), Marani, Montagna (Gualtieri 78), Muccioli, Della Valle (Francini 67), Matteoni, Selva.
Israel: Cohen; Harazi A, Ben Shimon, Telasnikov, Badir, Benado (Shelach 68), Nimni (Banin 59), Graiev, Revivo, Berkovic (Shitrit 74), Mizrahi.
Referee: Khudiev (Azerbaijan).

Tel Aviv, 14 October 1998, 42,000

Israel (0) 1 *(Hazan 63)*

Spain (0) 2 *(Hierro 65, Etxeberria J 77)*
Israel: Cohen; Harazi A, Ben Shimon, Benado, Hazan (Banin 75), Badir, Telasnikov (Mizrahi 59), Graiev, Nimni, Revivo, Berkovic.
Spain: Canizares; Michel, Hierro, Alkorta, Aranzabal, Luis Enrique, Engonga, Alkiza, De Pedro (Etxeberria J 72), Kiko (Urzaiz 88), Raul (Marcos Vales 90).
Referee: Elleray (England).

Serravalle, 14 October 1998, 1000

San Marino (0) 1 *(Selva 80 (pen))*
Austria (0) 4 *(Vastic 58, Mayrleb 63, Hiden 68, Glieder 76)*

San Marino: Gasperoni F; Gennari, Guerra, Valentini M (Della Valle 80), Bacciocchi, Marani, Muccioli, Francini (Valentini S 69), Ugolini (Montagna 62), Matteoni, Selva.
Austria: Wohlfahrt; Hiden, Schottel, Pfeffer, Cerny, Kuhbauer, Heraf, Reinmayr (Mayrleb 46), Wetl, Vastic (Stoger 70), Haas (Glieder 66).
Referee: Onufer (Ukraine).

Serravalle, 18 November 1998, 600

San Marino (0) 0
Cyprus (1) 1 *(Spoljaric 41)*

San Marino: Gasperoni F; Gennari, Valentini M, Guerra, Valentini V, Marani, Gasperoni B, Muccioli (Mularoni 83), Matteoni (Francini 75), Montagna (Bacchiocchi 67), Ugolini.
Cyprus: Panayiotou N; Pittas, Panayiotou P, Charalambous, Sophocleous, Engomitis, Melanarkitis, Spoljaric, Agathocleous (Constandinou 73), Malekos (Ioannou D 73), Gogic (Okkas 86).
Referee: McDermott (Republic of Ireland).

Nicosia, 10 February 1999, 3000

Cyprus (3) 4 *(Melanarkitis 18, Constantinou 32, 45, Christodoulou 88)*
San Marino (0) 0

Cyprus: Panayiotou; Theodotou, Christodoulou, Ioachim, Charalambous, Pittas, Melanarkitis, Spoljaric, Gogic (Ioannou 80), Constantinou (Okkas 80), Malekos (Aristocleous 89).
San Marino: Gasperoni F; Gennari, Marani (Vanucci 84), Gobbi, Vittorio, Guerra, Zonzini, Della Valle (Manzaroli 70), Ugolini (Bacciocchi 46), Mularoni L, Selva.

Valencia, 27 March 1999, 40,000

Spain (5) 9 *(Raul 5, 17, 47, 74, Urzaiz 30, 44, Hierro 35 (pen), Wetl 76 (og), Fran 84)*
Austria (0) 0

Spain: Canizares; Michel, Hierro, Marcelino, Sergi, Etxeberria J (Dani 84), Guardiola, Valeron (Mendieta 71), Fran, Raul, Urzaiz (Munitis 61).
Austria: Wohlfahrt; Schottel, Feiersinger (Kogler 54), Pfeffer, Cerny, Mahlich, Neukirchner, Prosenik (Reinmayr 58), Wetl, Herzog, Haas (Mayrleb 69).
Referee: Veissiere (France).

Tel Aviv, 28 March 1999, 30,000

Israel (1) 3 *(Banin 11, Mizrahi 47, 53)*
Cyprus (0) 0

Israel: Davidovich; Harazi A, Graiev, Shelach, Badir (Talkar 46), Banin, Benado, Berkovic, Revivo (Tikva 85), Harazi R (Mizrahi 46), Nimni.
Cyprus: Panayiotou; Theodotou, Pittas, Ioannou, Charalambous, Constandinou (Okkas 65), Melanarkitis, Spoljaric (Agathocleous 79), Malekos (Nicolaou 46), Sophocleous, Christodolou.
Referee: Lica (Romania).

Serravalle, 31 March 1999, 1000

San Marino (0) 0
Spain (2) 6 *(Fran 20, Raul 45, 59, 66, Urzaiz 49, Etxeberria J 72)*

San Marino: Gasperoni F; Gennari, Marani, Valentini V, Zonzini, Valentini M, Manzaroli, Gasperoni B (Muccioli 75), Gobbi (Della Valle 51), Selva, Montagna (Gualtieri 60).
Spain: Canizares; Michel, Marcelino, Paco, Sergi, Etxeberria J, Guardiola (Engonga 68), Valeron (Helguera 78), Fran, Raul, Urzaiz (Dani 61).
Referee: Maric (Croatia).

Graz, 28 April 1999, 15,000

Austria (3) 7 *(Mayrleb 24, 53, Vastic 42, 44, 84, Amerhauser 71, Herzog 82 (pen))*
San Marino (0) 0

Austria: Wohlfahrt; Winklhofer (Rohseano 80), Feiersinger, Neukirchner, Cerny (Kitzbichler 71), Schopp (Glieder 71), Herzog, Prosenik, Amerhauser, Mayrleb, Vastic.
San Marino: Gasperoni F; Gennari (Bacciocchi S 46), Della Valle, Guerra, Gobbi, Vanucci, Gasperoni B (Manzaroli 15), Zonzini, Muccioli, Selva, Montagna (Bacciocchi N 78).
Referee: Vassaros (Greece).

Villarreal, 5 June 1999, 16,000

Spain (4) 9 *(Hierro 8 (pen), Luis Enrique 22, 67, 71, Etxeberria J 25, 45, Raul 56, Gennari 85 (og), Mendieta 90)*
San Marino (0) 0

Spain: Canizares; Michel (Munitis 60), Marcelino, Hierro, Aranzabal, Etxeberria J, Guardiola, Guerrero (Mendieta 74), Luis Enrique, Raul (Urzaiz 60), Morientes.
San Marino: Gasperoni F; Gennari (Vanucci 90), Marani, Della Balda, Gobbi, Guerra, Bacciocchi, Della Valle, Zonzini, Manzaroli (Valentini V 75), Montagna (Ugolini 58).
Referee: Perry (Republic of Ireland).

Tel Aviv, 6 June 1999, 43,000

Israel (2) 5 *(Berkovic 26, 47, Revivo 45, Mizrahi 54, Graiev 75)*
Austria (0) 0

Israel: Davidovich; Shelach, Benado, Harazi A, Graiev, Banin, Abuksis (Tal 82), Hazan, Mizrahi (Silivia 77), Berkovic (Tikva 79), Revivo.
Austria: Wohlfahrt; Winklhofer, Barisic, Kogler, Cerny, Mahlich, Herzog, Neukirchner, Amerhauser (Prosenik 46), Mayrleb (Haas 67), Vastic (Glieder 57).
Referee: Michel (Slovakia).

Group 6	P	W	D	L	F	A	Pts
Spain	5	4	0	1	28	4	12
Israel	5	3	1	1	15	3	10
Austria	6	3	1	2	15	16	10
Cyprus	5	3	0	2	8	8	9
San Marino	7	0	0	7	1	36	0

GROUP 7

Bucharest, 2 September 1998, 6000

Romania (4) 7 *(Gheorge Popescu 18, Munteanu C 30, Ilie A 32, 45, 51, Moldovan 56, Haas 60 (og))*
Liechtenstein (0) 0

Romania: Stelea (Lobont 80); Petrescu, Batranu, Gheorge Popescu, Contra, Petre, Galca, Munteanu C (Sabau 72), Munteanu D, Moldovan, Ilie A (Mihalcea 69).
Liechtenstein: Oehry M; Hefti, Hanselmann, Michael Stocklasa, Telser M (Ender 89), Ritter, Zech, Lingg (Buchel 62), Beck, Oehri R, Haas (Martin Stocklasa 63).
Referee: Prolic (Bosnia).

Kosice, 5 September 1998, 3243

Slovakia (3) 3 *(Fabus 17, Dubovsky 26 (pen), Moravcik 40)*
Azerbaijan (0) 0

Slovakia: Vencel; Varga, Tomaschek, Tittel, Spilar, Kinder, Sovic, Moravcik, Fabus (Jancula 62), Majoros (Ujlaky 46), Dubovsky (Zvara 62).
Azerbaijan: Kramarenko; Gaisumov, Abusev, Jabarov, Agayev, Lichkin (Rzayev 66), Kasumov (Guseynov 79), Asadov, Sirkhaev, Suleimanov (Kuliyev 46), Kurbanov K.
Referee: Snoddy (Northern Ireland).

Budapest, 6 September 1998, 50,000

Hungary (1) 1 *(Horvath 32)*

Portugal (0) 3 *(Sa Pinto 56, 76, Rui Costa 84)*

Hungary: Kiraly; Feher C (Korsos 78), Lakos, Hrutka, Matyus, Lisztes (Dardai 46), Halmai, Illes, Dombi (Kovacs Z 78), Horvath, Hamar.
Portugal: Vitor Baia; Secretario, Jorge Costa, Paulo Madeira, Dimas, Figo, Paulo Bento, Rui Costa, Paulinho Santos, Joao Pinto, Sa Pinto.
Referee: Meier (Switzerland).

Baku, 10 October 1998, 10,000

Azerbaijan (0) 0

Hungary (0) 4 *(Dardai 58, Illes 85 (pen), Pisont 87, Feher M 90)*

Azerbaijan: Kramarenko (Jidkov 59); Guseynov, Agayev, Abusev, Kerimov, Asadov, Lichkin, Sirkhaev, Rzayev, Kambarov (Kasumov 46), Kurbanov K.
Hungary: Kiraly; Sebok, Feher C, Hrutka, Matyus, Dardai, Pisont, Illes, Lisztes (Dombi 75), Horvath, Hamar (Feher M 46).
Referee: Bre (France).

Vaduz, 10 October 1998, 1900

Liechtenstein (0) 0

Slovakia (3) 4 *(Sovic 3, Dubovsky 13, Tomaschek 36, 61)*

Liechtenstein: Oehry M; Ritter, Hanselmann, Zech, Hefti (Lingg 76), Haas (Martin Stocklasa 33), Oehri R (Ospelt 46), Hasler, Michael Stocklasa, Frick M, Telser M.
Slovakia: Vencel; Varga (Timko 65), Tittel, Spilar, Sovic, Tomaschek, Moravcik, Dubovsky, Kinder (Kozak 30), Majoros, Fabus (Jancula 61).
Referee: Antonov (Moldova).

Porto, 10 October 1998, 40,000

Portugal (0) 0

Romania (0) 1 *(Munteanu D 90)*

Portugal: Vitor Baia; Abel Xavier (Dani 85), Jorge Costa, Fernando Couto, Dimas, Figo, Paulo Bento (Conceicao 70), Rui Costa, Paulinho Santos, Joao Pinto (Nuno Gomes 79), Sa Pinto.
Romania: Stelea; Petrescu (Contra 83), Filipescu, Gheorge Popescu, Ciobotariu, Petre, Munteanu C (Lupescu 61), Galca, Munteanu D, Rosu, Moldovan (Mihalcea 89).
Referee: Krug (Germany).

Budapest, 14 October 1998, 40,000

Hungary (0) 1 *(Hrutka 82)*

Romania (0) 1 *(Moldovan 51)*

Hungary: Kiraly; Feher C, Sebok, Hrutka, Matyus, Pisont, Dardai, Illes, Egressy (Lisztes 78), Feher M (Hamori 75), Hamar (Toth 70).
Romania: Stelea; Petrescu, Filipescu, Georghe Popescu, Ciobotariu, Petre (Serban 70), Galca, Lupescu, Munteanu D, Moldovan (Mihalcea 85), Craioveanu (Munteanu C 75).
Referee: Nielsen (Denmark).

Vaduz, 14 October 1998, 1900

Liechtenstein (0) 2 *(Frick M 47 (pen), Telser M 49)*

Azerbaijan (0) 1 *(Kurbanov K 59)*

Liechtenstein: Jehle; Ritter, Zech, Hasler, Martin Stocklasa, Bicker (Ospelt 67), Lingg, Michael Stocklasa, Beck (Buchel 74), Frick M, Telser M.
Azerbaijan: Jidkov; Jadulayev, Gaisumov, Agayev, Kerimov, Abusev (Kuliyev 76), Kurbanov M (Suleimanov 25), Rzayev, Kambarov, Kurbanov K (Mamedov 61), Sirkhaev.
Referee: Barr (N Ireland).

Bratislava, 14 October 1998, 22,059

Slovakia (0) 0

Portugal (2) 3 *(Joao Pinto 16, 31, Abel Xavier 72)*

Slovakia: Vencel; Spilar, Kinder, Tittel, Varga, Sovic (Pinte 82), Tomaschek, Fabus (Nemeth 57), Moravcik, Majoros, Dubovsky.

Portugal: Vitor Baia; Abel Xavier, Jorge Costa, Fernando Couto, Dimas, Figo (Capucho 89), Paulo Bento, Rui Costa (Costinha 67), Paulinho Santos, Joao Pinto (Conceicao 46), Sa Pinto.
Referee: Sarvan (Turkey).

Guimaraes, 26 March 1999, 20,000

Portugal (2) 7 *(Sa Pinto 28, Joao Pinto 36, 77, Paulo Madeira 67, Conceicao 75, Pauleta 82, 83)*

Azerbaijan (0) 0

Portugal: Vitor Baia (Espinha 83); Secretario, Paulo Madeira, Fernando Couto, Dimas, Paulo Sousa, Rui Costa (Pedro Barbosa 83), Conceicao, Figo (Pauleta 74), Sa Pinto, Joao Pinto.
Azerbaijan: Kramarenko; Agayev, Asadov, Akhmedov, Stukas, Abusev, Gambarov (Vasiliev 72), Musaev (Rzayev 69), Sirkhaev, Lichkin, Kurbanov G.
Referee: Granat (Poland).

Budapest, 27 March 1999, 9534

Hungary (3) 5 *(Sebok J 17, Sebok V 33, 41, 86, Illes 74)*

Liechtenstein (0) 0

Hungary: Kiraly; Hrutka (Simogyi 79), Sebok V, Korsos, Matyus, Halmai, Sebok J (Dombi 71), Pisont, Illes, Feher, Toth (Hamar 76).
Liechtenstein: Jehle; Hanselmann (Hefti 46), Martin Stocklasa, Lingg, Ritter, Michael Stocklasa, Wohlwend, Frick M, Hasler, Telser M, Beck (Ospelt J 78).
Referee: Kapitanis (Cyprus).

Bucharest, 27 March 1999, 15,000

Romania (0) 0

Slovakia (0) 0

Romania: Stelea; Petrescu, Batranu, Gheorge Popescu, Rosu, Petre, Galca, Munteanu C (Lupescu 66), Munteanu D, Moldovan (Craioveanu 64), Illie A.
Slovakia: Konig; Varga, Zeman, Karhan, Kratochvil, Zatek (Dzurik 75), Tomaschek, Balic, Labant, Dubovsky (Suchanok 78), Majoros (Slicho 62).
Referee: Barber (England).

Baku, 31 March 1999, 25,000

Azerbaijan (0) 0

Romania (0) 1 *(Petre 49)*

Azerbaijan: Magomedov; Gerimov, Pusuchatev, Asadov, Agayev (Kuliyev 75), Paki-Zadeh (Gambarov 69), Kurbanov M (Asaev 67), Akhmedov, Lichkin, Sirkhaev, Kurbanov K.
Romania: Lobont; Contra, Filipescu, Ciobotariu, Munteanu D, Petre, Galca, Lupescu, Rosu (Florea 75), Moldovan, Craioveanu (Mihalcea 89).
Referee: Luinge (Holland).

Vaduz, 31 March 1999, 3000

Liechtenstein (0) 0

Portugal (1) 5 *(Rui Costa 16 (pen), 79, Figo 49, Paulo Madeira 54, 60)*

Liechtenstein: Jehle; Lingg, Hasler, Zech, Hefti, Ritter (Ospelt 85), Telser, Frick C, Michael Stocklasa (Beck 66), Wohlwend (Burgmeier 83), Frick M.
Portugal: Vitor Baia; Secretario, Paulo Madeira, Fernando Couto, Dimas, Conceicao (Capucho 88), Paulo Sousa, Rui Costa, Figo, Sa Pinto (Pauleta 61), Joao Pinto (Nuno Gomes 79).
Referee: Orrason (Iceland).

Bratislava, 31 March 1999, 19,400

Slovakia (0) 0

Hungary (0) 0

Slovakia: Konig; Kratochvil, Zeman (Dzuric 13), Varga, Karhan, Balis, Tomaschek, Dubovsky, Zatek (Hrncar 79), Majoros, Pinte (Slicho 83).
Hungary: Kiraly; Korsos, Sebok V, Hrutka, Matyus, Pisont, Halmai, Illes, Sebok J (Dombi 56), Feher M (Hamar 64), Toth.
Referee: Colombo (France).

Baku, 5 June 1999, 8500

Azerbaijan (2) 4 *(Kurbanov G 16, Lichkin 42, Tagizade 60, Isajev 73)*

Liechtenstein (0) 0

Azerbaijan: Kramarenko; Agayev, Jadoelajev, Akhmedov, Kerimov, Kurbanov M, Tagizade (Isajev 68), Vasiljev (Khankishijev 61), Sirkhaev, Lichkin, Kurbanov G.
Liechtenstein: Jehle; Lingg, Hasler, Zech, Martin Stocklasa, Ritter, Telser, Michael Stocklasa (Wohlwend 74), Frick C, Bicker (Beck M 59), Benz (Beck T 46).
Referee: Stadskaar (Denmark).

Lisbon, 5 June 1999, 25,000

Portugal (0) 1 *(Capucho 62)*

Slovakia (0) 0

Portugal: Vitor Baia; Xavier (Conceicao 31), Fernando Couto, Paulo Madeira, Teixeira, Paulo Sousa, Paulo Bento, Rui Costa, Figo (Barbosa 89), Joao Pinto (Capucho 61), Sa Pinto.
Slovakia: Konig; Varga, Timko, Karhan, Kratochvil, Zvara (Valachovic 30), Tomaschek, Pinte (Slicho 64), Labant, Dubovsky, Majoros (Kosuch 83).
Referee: Larsen (Denmark).

Bucharest, 5 June 1999, 23,000

Romania (2) 2 *(Ilie 2, Munteanu D 15)*

Hungary (0) 0

Romania: Lobont; Petrescu, Filipescu, Gheorge Popescu, Nanu, Petre, Hagi (Lupescu 46), Galca, Munteanu D, Moldovan (Ganea 64), Ilie A (Craioveanu 86).
Hungary: Kiraly; Sebok V, Hrutka, Matyus, Korsos, Dardai, Halami, Illes (Preisinger 81), Egressy, Sebok J, Feher M (Pisont 46).
Referee: Pedersen (Norway).

Gyor, 9 June 1999, 16,500

Hungary (0) 0

Slovakia (0) 1 *(Fabus 53)*

Hungary: Kiraly; Sebok V, Hrutka, Matyus, Korsos G, Dardai, Halmai (Pisont 73), Illes, Egressy (Dombi 60), Sebok J, Somogyi (Preisinger 78).
Slovakia: Konig; Varga, Timko, Karhan, Kratochvil, Zvara (Dzurik 81), Valachovic, Pinte, Labant, Nemeth, Fabus.
Referee: Vega (Spain).

Coimbra, 9 June 1999, 25,000

Portugal (3) 8 *(Sa Pinto 28, 44, Joao Pinto 40, 59, 67, Ritter 52 (og), Rui Costa 80, 90 (pen))*

Liechtenstein (0) 0

Portugal: Vitor Baia; Secretario (Capucho 14), Fernando Couto, Paulo Madeira, Teixeira, Paulo Sousa (Barbosa 63), Conceicao, Rui Costa, Figo, Joao Pinto, Sa Pinto.
Liechtenstein: Jehle; Zech, Hasler, Ospelt, Ritter, Telser D (Lingg 53), Michael Stocklasa (Burgmeier 67), Wohlwend, Telser M (Buchel 73), Bicker, Beck T.
Referee: Drabek (Austria).

Bucharest, 9 June 1999, 8000

Romania (2) 4 *(Ganea 35, Munteanu D 44 (pen), Vladiou 50, Rosu 90)*

Azerbaijan (0) 0

Romania: Lobont; Petrescu, Filipescu, Gheorge Popescu, Nanu, Petre (Moldovan 68), Galca, Lupescu, Munteanu D, Ganea (Craioveanu 59), Vladiou (Rosu 79).
Azerbaijan: Kramarenko; Agayev (Getman 71), Jadulayev, Akhmedov, Isayev (Vasilyev 82), Kerimov, Kurbanov M (Musayev 59), Tagizade, Kurbanov G, Poshehontzev, Sirkhaev.
Referee: Siric (Croatia).

Group 7	P	W	D	L	F	A	Pts
Portugal	7	6	0	1	27	2	18
Romania	7	5	2	0	16	1	17
Slovakia	7	3	2	2	8	4	11
Hungary	7	2	2	3	11	7	8
Azerbaijan	7	1	0	6	5	21	3
Liechtenstein	7	1	0	6	2	34	3

GROUP 8

Dublin, 5 September 1998, 34,000

Republic of Ireland (2) 2 *(Irwin 4 (pen), Roy Keane 15)*

Croatia (0) 0

Republic of Ireland: Given; Irwin, Staunton, McAteer, Cunningham, Babb, Kinsella, Roy Keane, O'Neill (Cascarino 9), Robbie Keane (Carsley 62), Duff (Kenna 46).
Croatia: Ladic; Soldo (Tokic 77), Stimac, Simic, Tudor (Krpan 62), Jurcic, Boban, Asanovic, Jarni, Stanic, Maric (Panic 46).
Referee: Pereira (Portugal).

Skopje, 6 September 1998, 5000

Macedonia (1) 4 *(Bozinov 20, 48, Sakiri 75, 80)*

Malta (0) 0

Macedonia: Milosevski; Lazarevski, Stojkovski (Gosev 80), Nikolovski (Sainovski 78), Sedloski, Micevski, Stojanoski (Sakiri 70), Trenevski, Zaharievski, Stavrevski, Bozinov.
Malta: Muscat; Said, Overend, Debono, Chetcuti, Turner, Agius (Suda 70), Brincat, Zahra (Carabott 78), Busuttil, Camilleri.
Referee: Wegereef (Holland).

Ta'Qali, 10 October 1998, 8000

Malta (1) 1 *(Suda 28 (pen))*

Croatia (0) 4 *(Simic 54, Vugrinec 68, 74, Suker 85)*

Malta: Muscat; Buhagiar (Sixsmith 77), Overend, Debono, Chetcuti, Suda, Agius (Zammit 11), Brincat, Zahra (Turner 58), Busuttil, Camilleri.
Croatia: Ladic; Simic (Tokic 81), Soldo, Tudor, Saric, Maric, Boban, Asanovic, Jarni (Cvitanovic 87), Suker, Vucko (Vugrinec 60).
Referee: Benedik (Slovakia).

Zagreb, 14 October 1998, 20,000

Croatia (2) 3 *(Suker 16, Boban 45, 70)*

Macedonia (1) 2 *(Ciric 2, Sainovski 55)*

Croatia: Ladic; Tudor, Stimac, Simic, Stanic (Jurcic 81), Soldo, Boban, Asanovic (Saric 61), Jarni, Maric, Suker.
Macedonia: Milosevski; Sedloski, Stavrevski, Nikolovski (Stojanoski 77), Sainovski, Zaharievski, Micevski (Gosev 46), Lazarevski (Bozinov 60), Trenevski, Sakiri, Ciric.
Referee: Levnikov (Russia).

Dublin, 14 October 1998, 34,500

Republic of Ireland (2) 5 *(Robbie Keane 16, 18, Roy Keane 54, Quinn 63, Breen 82)*

Malta (0) 0

Republic of Ireland: Given; Kenna, Staunton, McAteer (Carsley 85), Cunningham, Breen, Kinsella, Roy Keane, Quinn (Cascarino 66), Robbie Keane (Kennedy 81), Duff.
Malta: Cini; Debono, Buttigieg, Spiteri, Carabott, Brincat, Zahra (Zammit 70), Sixsmith (Camilleri 66), Chetcuti, Turner, Suda (Agius 65).
Referee: Olsen (Norway).

Valletta, 18 November 1998, 4000

Malta (0) 1 *(Sixsmith 69)*

Macedonia (0) 2 *(Nikolovski 49, Zaharievski 62)*

Malta: Muscat; Sixsmith, Camilleri, Buttigieg, Spiteri, Debono, Busuttil, Saliba (Turner 67), Brincat, Nwoko (Carabott 54), Cutajar (Agius 59).
Macedonia: Milosevski; Lazarevski, Nikolovski, Sedloski, Babunski, Stavrevski, Zaharievski, Micevski, Sainovski, Bozinov (Trenevski 65), Sakiri.
Referee: Smolik (Belarus).

Belgrade, 18 November 1998, 44,000

Yugoslavia (0) 1 *(Mijatovic 65)*

Republic of Ireland (0) 0

Yugoslavia: Kralj; Djukic, Djorovic, Mihajlovic, Jokanovic, Jugovic (Grodzic 77), Stojkovic (Kovacevic 46), Stankovic J, Stankovic D, Mijatovic, Milosevic (Drulovic 77).
Republic of Ireland: Given; Cunningham, Irwin, McLoughlin (Connolly 72), Breen, Staunton, Kinsella, Roy Keane, Quinn (Cascarino 72), McAteer (O'Neill 83), Duff.
Referee: Nilsson (Sweden).

Valletta, 10 February 1999, 7000

Malta (0) 0

Yugoslavia (1) 3 *(Nadj 22, 55, Milosevic 90)*

Malta: Barry; Said, Turner, Spiteri, Camilleri (Sixsmith 73), Buttigieg, Busuttil, Saliba, Carabott, Nwoko (Cutajar 82), Agius (Bencini 59).

Yugoslavia: Kralj; Mirkovic, Djorovic, Jokanovic, Djukic, Mihajlovic, Stankovic (Tomic 75), Nadj, Stankovic (Grodzic 87), Mijatovic, Kovacevic (Milosevic 70).

Referee: Garibian (France).

Skopje, 5 June 1999, 14,000

Macedonia (0) 1 *(Hristov 80)*

Croatia (1) 1 *(Suker 19)*

Macedonia: Milosevski; Nikolovski, Stojanovski, Stavrevski, Babunski (Zaharievski 60), Sainovski, Micevski, Trenevski (Bozinov 46), Trajcov (Hristov 80), Sakiri, Ciric.

Croatia: Ladic; Juric, Simic, Soldo, Saric, Boban, Asanovic, Vugrinec (Vlaovic 19), Jarni, Suker, Boksic (Rapajic 19).

Referee: Dallas (Scotland).

Salonika, 8 June 1999, 2000

Yugoslavia (1) 4 *(Mijatovic 36, Milosevic 49, 90, Kovacevic 75)*

Malta (1) 1 *(Saliba 7)*

Yugoslavia: Kralj; Mirkovic, Djukic, Djorovic, Saveljic, Stojkovic (Drulovic 77), Nadj (Milosevic 46), Jokanovic, Stankovic D (Grozdic 63), Mijatovic, Kovacevic.

Malta: Barry; Buhagiar (Cutajar 80), Said, Debono, Chetcuti, Ruttieg, Saliba, Camilleri D (Brincat 64), Carabott, Busuttil, Nwoko (Sultana 83).

Referee: Stahl (Sweden).

Dublin, 9 June 1999, 28,108

Republic of Ireland (0) 1 *(Quinn 67)*

Macedonia (0) 0

Republic of Ireland: Kelly; Carr, Irwin, Duff (Kilbane 63), Cunningham, Breen, Kennedy, Kinsella, Quinn (Connolly 83), Robbie Keane (Cascarino 67), Carsley.

Macedonia: Milosevski; Stavrevski, Babunski, Stojanoski, Trajcev (Medmendi 46), Micevski, Trenevski (Hristov 75), Sainovski (Sedloski 70), Nikolovski, Ciric, Sakiri.

Referee: Meier (Switzerland).

Group 8	P	W	D	L	F	A	Pts
Yugoslavia	3	3	0	0	8	1	9
Republic of Ireland	4	3	0	1	8	1	9
Croatia	4	2	1	1	8	6	7
Macedonia	5	2	1	2	9	6	7
Malta	6	0	0	6	3	22	0

GROUP 9

Tallinn, 4 June 1998, 3500

Estonia (2) 5 *(Viikmae 13, Reim 43 (pen), Terehhov 76, Oper 87, Kirs 90)*

Faeroes (0) 0

Estonia: Poom; Lemsalu, Kirs, Hohlov-Simson, Meet, Viikmae (O'Konnel-Bronin 80), Terehhov, Oper, Kristal, Reim, Zelinski.

Faeroes: Knudsen; Dam, Hansen J, Thorsteinsson, Hansen O (Jarnskor H 83), Morkore A, Joensen, Johnsson, Petersen, Muller (Mikkelsen 41), Jonsson (Arge 83).

Sarajevo, 19 August 1998, 20,000

Bosnia (0) 1 *(Baljic 65)*

Faeroes (0) 0

Bosnia: Dedic; Kapetanovic, Barbarez (Mujdza 75), Konjic, Varesanovic, Hibic, Bolic (Mujcin 65), Halilovic, Kodro, Salihamidzic (Sabic 81), Baljic.

Faeroes: Mikkelsen; Hansen H, Hansen J, Thorsteinsson, Johannesen O, Jarnskor H, Joensen, Johnsson, Morkore A, Arge (Borg 77), Petersen.

Sarajevo, 5 September 1998, 21,000

Bosnia (0) 1 *(Barbarez 75 (pen))*

Estonia (1) 1 *(Hibic 28 (og))*

Bosnia: Dedic; Varesanovic, Konjic, Hibic, Kapetanovic, Salihamidzic, Katana (Mujcin 55), Halilovic (Bolic 77), Mujdza (Sabic 65), Barbarez, Baljic.

Estonia: Poom; Rooba U (Meet 81), Kirs, Hohlov-Simson, Reim, Smirnov, Terehov, Kristal, Alonen, Zelinski (Viikmae 81), Oper.

Referee: Agius (Malta).

Vilnius, 5 September 1998, 5112

Lithuania (0) 0

Scotland (0) 0

Lithuania: Stauce; Shugzda (Buitkus 61), Semberas, Zutautas R, Zvirgzdauskas, Mikulenas (Slekys 90), Skerla, Baltusnikas, Preitsaitis, Jankauskas, Skarbalius.

Scotland: Leighton; Dailly, Boyd, Elliott, Hendry, Calderwood (Davidson 70), Lambert, Gallacher, McCoist (McCann 82), Jackson (Ferguson B 56), Collins.

Referee: Zotta (Romania).

Toftir, 6 September 1998, 2000

Faeroes (0) 0

Czech Republic (0) 1 *(Smicer 84)*

Faeroes: Mikkelsen; Johannesen O, Hansen JK, Thorsteinsson, Hansen H, Jarnskor H, Leiftur (Jarnskor M 78), Johnsson, Morkore, Jonsson T, Petersen.

Czech Republic: Postulka; Rada, Bejbl (Latal 81), Suchoparek, Votava, Cizek (Berger 55), Nemec, Nedved, Lokvenc, Poborsky (Sloncik 81), Smicer.

Referee: Hirviniemi (Finland).

Sarajevo, 10 October 1998, 30,000

Bosnia (0) 1 *(Topic 88)*

Czech Republic (1) 3 *(Baranek 13, Smicer 59, Kuka 90)*

Bosnia: Dedic; Varesanovic, Konjic, Hibic, Kapetanovic, Salihamidzic (Demirovic 66), Katana, Halilovic, Mujcin (Topic 63), Barbarez, Baljic (Besirevic 71).

Czech Republic: Postulka; Baranek (Rada 71), Repka, Suchoparek, Latal, Votava, Nemec, Bejbl, Lokvenc (Kuka 80), Smicer (Sloncik 85), Berger.

Referee: Messina (Italy).

Vilnius, 10 October 1998, 1500

Lithuania (0) 0

Faeroes (0) 0

Lithuania: Stauce; Skerla, Mikalajunas (Zvingilas 74), Zutautas R, Baltusnikas, Zvirgzdauskas, Mikulenas (Buitkus 46), Ivanauskas, Skarbalius, Preitsaitis, Jankauskas.

Faeroes: Mikkelsen; Johannesen O, Hansen J, Thorsteinsson, Hansen H, Joensen, Jarnskor H, Johnsson, Arge (Borg 88), Jonsson T, Petersen.

Referee: Schaack (Luxembourg).

Edinburgh, 10 October 1998, 16,930

Scotland (0) 3 *(Dodds 70, 85, Hohlov-Simson 78 (og))*

Estonia (1) 2 *(Hohlov-Simson 35, Smirnov 76)*

Scotland: Leighton; Weir, Davidson, Calderwood (Donnelly 56), Hendry, Boyd, McKinlay W, Durrant, McCoist (Dodds 68), Gallacher (Jackson 17), Johnston.

Estonia: Poom; Kirs, Hohlov-Simson, Reim, Rooba U, Kristal, Smirnov, Alonen, Terehov, Zelinski (Viikmae 86), Oper.

Referee: Marques (Portugal).

Teplice, 14 October 1998, 13,123

Czech Republic (4) 4 *(Nedved 8, Berger 21, 41, Meet 44 (og))*

Estonia (0) 1 *(Arbeiter 90)*

Czech Republic: Postulka; Latal, Suchoparek, Repka, Votava (Rada 53), Nedved, Nemec, Bejbl (Cizek 80), Berger, Lokvenc (Kuka 61), Smicer.

Estonia: Poom; Smirnov (Nommik 46), Meet, Hohlov-Simson, Rooba U, Alonen, Terehov (O'Konnel-Bronin 63), Oper, Viikmae (Arbeiter 46), Reim, Zelinski.

Referee: Olafsson (Iceland).

Vilnius, 14 October 1998, 2000

Lithuania (0) 4 *(Ivanauskas 10, 67, 75, Baltusnikas 90)*

Bosnia (0) 2 *(Konjic 4, Baljic 68)*

Lithuania: Stauce; Skerla, Mikalajunas (Baltusnikas 87), Zutautas R, Gleveckas, Zvirgzdauskas, Semberas, Ivanauskas, Skarbalius (Zvingilas 62), Preitsatis, Jankauskas (Danilicevas 79).

Bosnia: Dedic; Varesanovic, Konjic, Ramcic, Kapetanovic (Mujdza 86), Salihamidzic, Katana (Topic 75), Halilovic, Mujcin, Barbarez, Baljic.

Referee: Schuttengruber (Austria).

Aberdeen, 14 October 1998, 18,517

Scotland (2) 2 *(Burley 22, Dodds 45)*

Faeroes (0) 1 *(Petersen 86 (pen))*

Scotland: Sullivan; Weir, Davidson, Elliott, Hendry, Boyd, McKinlay W (Durrant 46), Donnelly, Dodds, Burley, Johnston (Glass 79).

Faeroes: Mikkelsen; Hansen H, Johannesen O, Hansen JC, Thorsteinsson, Petersen, Joensen, Johnsson, Jarnskor H (Hansen J 80), Arge (Borg 69), Jonsson T.

Referee: Kapitanis (Cyprus).

Teplice, 27 March 1999, 14,658

Czech Republic (1) 2 *(Hornak 10, Berger 74 (pen))*

Lithuania (0) 0

Czech Republic: Srnicek; Repka, Suchoparek, Hornak, Poborsky (Kuka 63), Hasek, Nemec, Berger, Nedved, Lokvenc (Koller 71), Smicer (Baranek 80).

Lithuania: Stauce; Skerla, Zvirgzdauskas, Zutautas, Semberas, Vainoras, Preitsaitis, Skarbalius, Mikalajunas, Ivanauskas (Buitkas 83), Jankauskas (Zvingilas 67).

Referee: Juhos (Hungary).

Vilnius, 31 March 1999, 3000

Lithuania (0) 1 *(Fomenka 83)*

Estonia (0) 2 *(Terehov 49, 77)*

Lithuania: Stauce; Skerla, Zutautas, Zvirgzdauskas, Semberas, Vainoras, Preitsaitis, Mikalajunas, Skarbalius (Gleveckus 35) (Buitkus 52), Mikulenas (Fomenka 46).

Estonia: Poom; Lemsalu, Kirs, Hohlov-Simson, Saviauk, Svets (Kristal 69), Terehov, Oper (Zelinski 67), Viikmae, Smirnov (Alonen 90), Reim.

Referee: Trentalange (Italy).

Glasgow, 31 March 1999, 44,513

Scotland (0) 1 *(Jess 68)*

Czech Republic (2) 2 *(Elliott 27 (og), Smicer 35)*

Scotland: Sullivan; Hopkin, Davidson (Johnston 51), Elliott, Boyd, Weir, Burley, Lambert, McCann, McAllister (Hutchison 62), Jess.

Czech Republic: Srnicek; Hornak, Votava, Suchoparek, Poborsky (Rada 74), Hasek, Nedved, Berger, Nemec, Smicer (Baranek 82), Lokvenc (Kuka 69).

Referee: Nielsen (Denmark).

Sarajevo, 5 June 1999, 5000

Bosnia (1) 2 *(Kodro 26 (pen), Bolic 90)*

Lithuania (0) 0

Bosnia: Dedic; Smajic, Kapetanovic, Varesanovic, Hibic, Repuh (Bolic 87), Besirevic, Sabic, Topic (Turkovic 90), Kodro (Mujcin 79), Salihamidzic.

Lithuania: Leus; Skerla, Marius, Darius, Kancelskis, Mikalajunas, Zvirgzdauskas, Semberas (Grozveydos 71), Maciulevicius, Ivanauskas, Preitsatis.

Referee: Ibanez (Spain).

Tallin, 5 June 1999, 3000

Estonia (0) 0

Czech Republic (1) 2 *(Berger 45, Koller 83)*

Estonia: Poom; Lemsalu, Kirs, Hohlov-Simson, Saviauk, Alonen (Smirnov 65) (O'Konnel-Bronin 74), Terehov (Svets 80), Kristal, Oper, Reim, Viikmae.

Czech Republic: Srnicek; Suchoparek, Repka, Hornak, Poborsky, Hasek, Nedved (Galasek 85), Berger, Nemec, Smicer (Kuka 65), Lokvenc (Koller 70).

Referee: Roca (Spain).

Toftir, 5 June 1999, 4500

Faeroes (0) 1 *(Hansen H 90)*

Scotland (1) 1 *(Johnston 38)*

Faeroes: Mikkelsen; Johannesen O, Hansen H, Thorsteinsson, Hansen O (Hansen J 87), Johnsson J, Joensen J (Borg 73), Joensen S, Jonsson T, Morkore A, Petersen (Arge 82).

Scotland: Sullivan; Weir, Davidson, Elliott, Calderwood, Boyd, Durrant (Cameron 46), Gallacher (Jess 88), Dodds, Lambert, Johnston (Gemmill 85).

Referee: Kalt (France).

Prague, 9 June 1999, 22,000

Czech Republic (0) 3 *(Repka 65, Kuka 75, Koller 87)*

Scotland (1) 2 *(Ritchie 30, Johnston 62)*

Czech Republic: Srnicek; Poborsky (Kuka 68), Berger, Hornak, Suchoparek, Repka, Nedved, Hasek (Baranek 60), Nemec, Lokvenc (Koller 68), Smicer.

Scotland: Sullivan; Johnston, Davidson, Weir, Boyd, Ritchie, Lambert, Calderwood, Gallacher, Dodds, Durrant (Jess 70).

Referee: Krug (Germany).

Tallinn, 9 June 1999, 2500

Estonia (1) 1 *(Oper 10)*

Lithuania (0) 2 *(Bahelis 52, Maciulevicius 56)*

Estonia: Poom; Lemsalu, Kirs, Kaal, Viikmae, Alonen, Terehov (O'Konnel-Bronin 73), Kristal (Svets 80), Oper, Reim, Zelinski.

Lithuania: Leus; Skerla, Skinderis, Zutautas D (Maciulevicius 46), Zutautas R, Mikalajunas, Zvirgzdauskas, Bahelis, Bazanauskas, Skarbalius, Ivanauskas (Preitsaitis 87).

Referee: Albrecht (Germany).

Toftir, 9 June 1999, 4600

Faeroes (1) 2 *(Arge 38, 48)*

Bosnia (1) 2 *(Bolic 13, 50)*

Faeroes: Mikkelsen; Johannesen O, Joensen S, Thorsteinsson, Hansen O (Jarnskor H 65), Johnsson J, Hansen H, Arge (Joensen J 85), Morkore A, Jonsson T, Petersen.

Bosnia: Dedic; Smajic, Besirevic, Varesanovic, Hibic, Repuh (Osmanhodzic 78), Sabic, Topic, Turkovic (Joulic 63), Bolic, Mujcin (Muratovic 85).

Referee: Jones (England).

Group 9	P	W	D	L	F	A	Pts
Czech Republic	7	7	0	0	17	5	21
Scotland	6	2	2	2	9	9	8
Bosnia	6	2	2	2	9	10	8
Lithuania	7	2	2	3	7	9	8
Estonia	7	2	1	4	12	13	7
Faeroes	7	0	3	4	4	12	3

EURO 2000 – Remaining fixtures

GROUP 1
Italy, Denmark, Switzerland, Wales, Belarus
04.09.99 Denmark v Switzerland
04.09.99 Belarus v Wales
08.09.99 Italy v Denmark
08.09.99 Switzerland v Belarus
09.10.99 Wales v Switzerland
09.10.99 Belarus v Italy

GROUP 2
Norway, Greece, Georgia, Latvia, Slovenia, Albania
04.09.99 Norway v Greece

04.09.99 Latvia v Albania
04.09.99 Slovenia v Georgia
08.09.99 Greece v Albania
08.09.99 Norway v Slovenia
08.09.99 Georgia v Latvia
09.10.99 Albania v Georgia
09.10.99 Slovenia v Greece
09.10.99 Latvia v Norway

GROUP 3
Germany, Turkey, Finland, Northern Ireland, Moldova
04.09.99 Finland v Germany
04.09.99 Northern Ireland v Turkey

08.09.99 Germany v Northern Ireland
08.09.99 Moldova v Turkey
09.10.99 Germany v Turkey
09.10.99 Finland v Northern Ireland

GROUP 4
Russia, France, Ukraine, Iceland, Armenia, Andorra
04.09.99 Ukraine v France
04.09.99 Iceland v Andorra
04.09.99 Russia v Armenia
08.09.99 Andorra v Russia
08.09.99 Iceland v Ukraine
08.09.99 Armenia v France

EUROPEAN FOOTBALL CHAMPIONSHIP
(formerly EUROPEAN NATIONS' CUP)

Year	Winners		Runners-up		Venue	Attendance
1960	USSR	2	Yugoslavia	1	Paris	17,966
1964	Spain	2	USSR	1	Madrid	120,000
1968	Italy	2	Yugoslavia	0	Rome	60,000
	After 1-1 draw					75,000
1972	West Germany	3	USSR	0	Brussels	43,437
1976	Czechoslovakia	2	West Germany	2	Belgrade	45,000
	(Czechoslovakia won on penalties)					
1980	West Germany	2	Belgium	1	Rome	47,864
1984	France	2	Spain	0	Paris	48,000
1988	Holland	2	USSR	0	Munich	72,308
1992	Denmark	2	Germany	0	Gothenburg	37,800
1996	Germany	2	Czech Republic	1	Wembley	73,611
	(Germany won on sudden death)					

EURO 2000 Remaining fixtures – *continued*

09.10.99 France v Iceland
09.10.99 Russia v Ukraine
09.10.99 Andorra v Armenia

GROUP 5
England, Bulgaria, Sweden, Poland, Luxembourg
04.09.99 England v Luxembourg
05.09.99 Sweden v Bulgaria
08.09.99 Poland v England
08.09.99 Luxembourg v Sweden
09.10.99 Sweden v Poland
10.10.99 Bulgaria v Luxembourg

GROUP 6
Spain, Austria, Israel, Cyprus, San Marino
04.09.99 Austria v Spain
05.09.99 Cyprus v Israel
08.09.99 Israel v San Marino

08.09.99 Spain v Cyprus
09.10.99 Spain v Israel
10.10.99 Austria v Cyprus

GROUP 7
Romania, Portugal, Slovakia, Hungary, Liechtenstein, Azerbaijan
03.09.99 Azerbaijan v Portugal
04.09.99 Liechtenstein v Hungary
04.09.99 Slovakia v Romania
08.09.99 Hungary v Azerbaijan
08.09.99 Romania v Portugal
08.09.99 Slovakia v Liechtenstein
09.10.99 Liechtenstein v Romania
09.10.99 Azerbaijan v Slovakia
10.10.99 Portugal v Hungary

GROUP 8
Yugoslavia, Croatia, Rep. of Ireland, Macedonia, Malta

04.09.99 Croatia v Rep. of Ireland
08.09.99 Malta v Rep. of Ireland
08.09.99 Macedonia v Yugoslavia
10.10.99 Croatia v Yugoslavia
10.10.99 Rep. of Ireland v Macedonia

GROUP 9
Scotland, Czech Republic, Lithuania, Bosnia, Faeroes, Estonia
04.09.99 Bosnia v Scotland
04.09.99 Faeroes v Estonia
04.09.99 Lithuania v Czech Republic
08.09.99 Czech Republic v Bosnia
08.09.99 Faeroes v Lithuania
08.09.99 Estonia v Scotland
09.10.99 Estonia v Bosnia
09.10.99 Czech Republic v Faeroes
09.10.99 Scotland v Lithuania

Paul Scholes completes his hat-trick for England with a header against Poland at Wembley in the European Championship match. (Actionimages)

BRITISH AND IRISH INTERNATIONAL RESULTS 1872–1999

Note: In the results that follow, wc=World Cup, ec=European Championship, ui=Umbro International Trophy. tf = Tournoi de France. For Ireland, read Northern Ireland from 1921.

ENGLAND v SCOTLAND

Played: 108; England won 44, Scotland won 40, Drawn 24. *Goals:* England 190, Scotland 168.

Year	Date	Venue	E	S		Year	Date	Venue	E	S
1872	30 Nov	Glasgow	0	0		1931	28 Mar	Glasgow	0	2
1873	8 Mar	Kennington Oval	4	2		1932	9 Apr	Wembley	3	0
1874	7 Mar	Glasgow	1	2		1933	1 Apr	Glasgow	1	2
1875	6 Mar	Kennington Oval	2	2		1934	14 Apr	Wembley	3	0
1876	4 Mar	Glasgow	0	3		1935	6 Apr	Glasgow	0	2
1877	3 Mar	Kennington Oval	1	3		1936	4 Apr	Wembley	1	1
1878	2 Mar	Glasgow	2	7		1937	17 Apr	Glasgow	1	3
1879	5 Apr	Kennington Oval	5	4		1938	9 Apr	Wembley	0	1
1880	13 Mar	Glasgow	4	5		1939	15 Apr	Glasgow	2	1
1881	12 Mar	Kennington Oval	1	6		1947	12 Apr	Wembley	1	1
1882	11 Mar	Glasgow	1	5		1948	10 Apr	Glasgow	2	0
1883	10 Mar	Sheffield	2	3		1949	9 Apr	Wembley	1	3
1884	15 Mar	Glasgow	0	1		wc1950	15 Apr	Glasgow	1	0
1885	21 Mar	Kennington Oval	1	1		1951	14 Apr	Wembley	2	3
1886	31 Mar	Glasgow	1	1		1952	5 Apr	Glasgow	2	1
1887	19 Mar	Blackburn	2	3		1953	18 Apr	Wembley	2	2
1888	17 Mar	Glasgow	5	0		wc1954	3 Apr	Glasgow	4	2
1889	13 Apr	Kennington Oval	2	3		1955	2 Apr	Wembley	7	2
1890	5 Apr	Glasgow	1	1		1956	14 Apr	Glasgow	1	1
1891	6 Apr	Blackburn	2	1		1957	6 Apr	Wembley	2	1
1892	2 Apr	Glasgow	4	1		1958	19 Apr	Glasgow	4	0
1893	1 Apr	Richmond	5	2		1959	11 Apr	Wembley	1	0
1894	7 Apr	Glasgow	2	2		1960	9 Apr	Glasgow	1	1
1895	6 Apr	Everton	3	0		1961	15 Apr	Wembley	9	3
1896	4 Apr	Glasgow	1	2		1962	14 Apr	Glasgow	0	2
1897	3 Apr	Crystal Palace	1	2		1963	6 Apr	Wembley	1	2
1898	2 Apr	Glasgow	3	1		1964	11 Apr	Glasgow	0	1
1899	8 Apr	Birmingham	2	1		1965	10 Apr	Wembley	2	2
1900	7 Apr	Glasgow	1	4		1966	2 Apr	Glasgow	4	3
1901	30 Mar	Crystal Palace	2	2		ec1967	15 Apr	Wembley	2	3
1902	3 Mar	Birmingham	2	2		ec1968	24 Jan	Glasgow	1	1
1903	4 Apr	Sheffield	1	2		1969	10 May	Wembley	4	1
1904	9 Apr	Glasgow	1	0		1970	25 Apr	Glasgow	0	0
1905	1 Apr	Crystal Palace	1	0		1971	22 May	Wembley	3	1
1906	7 Apr	Glasgow	1	2		1972	27 May	Glasgow	1	0
1907	6 Apr	Newcastle	1	1		1973	14 Feb	Wembley	5	0
1908	4 Apr	Glasgow	1	1		1973	19 May	Wembley	1	0
1909	3 Apr	Crystal Palace	2	0		1974	18 May	Glasgow	0	2
1910	2 Apr	Glasgow	0	2		1975	24 May	Wembley	5	1
1911	1 Apr	Everton	1	1		1976	15 May	Glasgow	1	2
1912	23 Mar	Glasgow	1	1		1977	4 June	Wembley	1	2
1913	5 Apr	Chelsea	1	0		1978	20 May	Glasgow	1	0
1914	14 Apr	Glasgow	1	3		1979	26 May	Wembley	3	1
1920	10 Apr	Sheffield	5	4		1980	24 May	Glasgow	2	0
1921	9 Apr	Glasgow	0	3		1981	23 May	Wembley	0	1
1922	8 Apr	Aston Villa	0	1		1982	29 May	Glasgow	1	0
1923	14 Apr	Glasgow	2	2		1983	1 June	Wembley	2	0
1924	12 Apr	Wembley	1	1		1984	26 May	Glasgow	1	1
1925	4 Apr	Glasgow	0	2		1985	25 May	Glasgow	0	1
1926	17 Apr	Manchester	0	1		1986	23 Apr	Wembley	2	1
1927	2 Apr	Glasgow	2	1		1987	23 May	Glasgow	0	0
1928	31 Mar	Wembley	1	5		1988	21 May	Wembley	1	0
1929	13 Apr	Glasgow	0	1		1989	27 May	Glasgow	2	0
1930	5 Apr	Wembley	5	2		ec1996	15 June	Wembley	2	0

ENGLAND v WALES

Played: 97; England won 62, Wales won 14, Drawn 21. *Goals:* England 239, Wales 90.

Year	Date	Venue	E	W		Year	Date	Venue	E	W
1879	18 Jan	Kennington Oval	2	1		1882	13 Mar	Wrexham	3	5
1880	15 Mar	Wrexham	3	2		1883	3 Feb	Kennington Oval	5	0
1881	26 Feb	Blackburn	0	1		1884	17 Mar	Wrexham	4	0

Year	Date	Venue	E	W
1885	14 Mar	Blackburn	1	1
1886	29 Mar	Wrexham	3	1
1887	26 Feb	Kennington Oval	4	0
1888	4 Feb	Crewe	5	1
1889	23 Feb	Stoke	4	1
1890	15 Mar	Wrexham	3	1
1891	7 May	Sunderland	4	1
1892	5 Mar	Wrexham	2	0
1893	13 Mar	Stoke	6	0
1894	12 Mar	Wrexham	5	1
1895	18 Mar	Queen's Club, Kensington	1	1
1896	16 Mar	Cardiff	9	1
1897	29 Mar	Sheffield	4	0
1898	28 Mar	Wrexham	3	0
1899	20 Mar	Bristol	4	0
1900	26 Mar	Cardiff	1	1
1901	18 Mar	Newcastle	6	0
1902	3 Mar	Wrexham	0	0
1903	2 Mar	Portsmouth	2	1
1904	29 Feb	Wrexham	2	2
1905	27 Mar	Liverpool	3	1
1906	19 Mar	Cardiff	1	0
1907	18 Mar	Fulham	1	1
1908	16 Mar	Wrexham	7	1
1909	15 Mar	Nottingham	2	0
1910	14 Mar	Cardiff	1	0
1911	13 Mar	Millwall	3	0
1912	11 Mar	Wrexham	2	0
1913	17 Mar	Bristol	4	3
1914	16 Mar	Cardiff	2	0
1920	15 Mar	Highbury	1	2
1921	14 Mar	Cardiff	0	0
1922	13 Mar	Liverpool	1	0
1923	5 Mar	Cardiff	2	2
1924	3 Mar	Blackburn	1	2
1925	28 Feb	Swansea	2	1
1926	1 Mar	Crystal Palace	1	3
1927	12 Feb	Wrexham	3	3
1927	28 Nov	Burnley	1	2
1928	17 Nov	Swansea	3	2
1929	20 Nov	Chelsea	6	0
1930	22 Nov	Wrexham	4	0
1931	18 Nov	Liverpool	3	1
1932	16 Nov	Wrexham	0	0
1933	15 Nov	Newcastle	1	2
1934	29 Sept	Cardiff	4	0
1936	5 Feb	Wolverhampton	1	2
1936	17 Oct	Cardiff	1	2
1937	17 Nov	Middlesbrough	2	1
1938	22 Oct	Cardiff	2	4
1946	13 Nov	Manchester	3	0
1947	18 Oct	Cardiff	3	0
1948	10 Nov	Aston Villa	1	0
wc1949	15 Oct	Cardiff	4	1
1950	15 Nov	Sunderland	4	2
1951	20 Oct	Cardiff	1	1
1952	12 Nov	Wembley	5	2
wc1953	10 Oct	Cardiff	4	1
1954	10 Nov	Wembley	3	2
1955	27 Oct	Cardiff	1	2
1956	14 Nov	Wembley	3	1
1957	19 Oct	Cardiff	4	0
1958	26 Nov	Aston Villa	2	2
1959	17 Oct	Cardiff	1	1
1960	23 Nov	Wembley	5	1
1961	14 Oct	Cardiff	1	1
1962	21 Oct	Wembley	4	0
1963	12 Oct	Cardiff	4	0
1964	18 Nov	Wembley	2	1
1965	2 Oct	Cardiff	0	0
EC1966	16 Nov	Wembley	5	1
EC1967	21 Oct	Cardiff	3	0
1969	7 May	Wembley	2	1
1970	18 Apr	Cardiff	1	1
1971	19 May	Wembley	0	0
1972	20 May	Cardiff	3	0
wc1972	15 Nov	Cardiff	1	0
wc1973	24 Jan	Wembley	1	1
1973	15 May	Wembley	3	0
1974	11 May	Cardiff	2	0
1975	21 May	Wembley	2	2
1976	24 Mar	Wrexham	2	1
1976	8 May	Cardiff	1	0
1977	31 May	Wembley	0	1
1978	3 May	Cardiff	3	1
1979	23 May	Wembley	0	0
1980	17 May	Wrexham	1	4
1981	20 May	Wembley	0	0
1982	27 Apr	Cardiff	1	0
1983	23 Feb	Wembley	2	1
1984	2 May	Wrexham	0	1

ENGLAND v IRELAND

Played: 96; England won 74, Ireland won 6, Drawn 16. *Goals:* England 319, Ireland 80.

Year	Date	Venue	E	I
1882	18 Feb	Belfast	13	0
1883	24 Feb	Liverpool	7	0
1884	23 Feb	Belfast	8	1
1885	28 Feb	Manchester	4	0
1886	13 Mar	Belfast	6	1
1887	5 Feb	Sheffield	7	0
1888	31 Mar	Belfast	5	1
1889	2 Mar	Everton	6	1
1890	15 Mar	Belfast	9	1
1891	7 Mar	Wolverhampton	6	1
1892	5 Mar	Belfast	2	0
1893	25 Feb	Birmingham	6	1
1894	3 Mar	Belfast	2	2
1895	9 Mar	Derby	9	0
1896	7 Mar	Belfast	2	0
1897	20 Feb	Nottingham	6	0
1898	5 Mar	Belfast	3	2
1899	18 Feb	Sunderland	13	2
1900	17 Mar	Dublin	2	0
1901	9 Mar	Southampton	3	0
1902	22 Mar	Belfast	1	0
1903	14 Feb	Wolverhampton	4	0
1904	12 Mar	Belfast	3	1
1905	25 Feb	Middlesbrough	1	1
1906	17 Feb	Belfast	5	0
1907	16 Feb	Everton	1	0
1908	15 Feb	Belfast	3	1
1909	13 Feb	Bradford	4	0
1910	12 Feb	Belfast	1	1
1911	11 Feb	Derby	2	1
1912	10 Feb	Dublin	6	1
1913	15 Feb	Belfast	1	2
1914	14 Feb	Middlesbrough	0	3
1919	25 Oct	Belfast	1	1
1920	23 Oct	Sunderland	2	0
1921	22 Oct	Belfast	1	1
1922	21 Oct	West Bromwich	2	0
1923	20 Oct	Belfast	1	2
1924	22 Oct	Everton	3	1
1925	24 Oct	Belfast	0	0
1926	20 Oct	Liverpool	3	3
1927	22 Oct	Belfast	0	2

			E	I					E	I
1928	22 Oct	Everton	2	1		1962	20 Oct	Belfast	3	1
1929	19 Oct	Belfast	3	0		1963	20 Nov	Wembley	8	3
1930	20 Oct	Sheffield	5	1		1964	3 Oct	Belfast	4	3
1931	17 Oct	Belfast	6	2		1965	10 Nov	Wembley	2	1
1932	17 Oct	Blackpool	1	0		EC1966	20 Oct	Belfast	2	0
1933	14 Oct	Belfast	3	0		EC1967	22 Nov	Wembley	2	0
1935	6 Feb	Everton	2	1		1969	3 May	Belfast	3	1
1935	19 Oct	Belfast	3	1		1970	21 Apr	Wembley	3	1
1936	18 Nov	Stoke	3	1		1971	15 May	Belfast	1	0
1937	23 Oct	Belfast	5	1		1972	23 May	Wembley	0	1
1938	16 Nov	Manchester	7	0		1973	12 May	Everton	2	1
1946	28 Sept	Belfast	7	2		1974	15 May	Wembley	1	0
1947	5 Nov	Everton	2	2		1975	17 May	Belfast	0	0
1948	9 Oct	Belfast	6	2		1976	11 May	Wembley	4	0
wc1949	16 Nov	Manchester	9	2		1977	28 May	Belfast	2	1
1950	7 Oct	Belfast	4	1		1978	16 May	Wembley	1	0
1951	14 Nov	Aston Villa	2	0		EC1979	7 Feb	Wembley	4	0
1952	4 Oct	Belfast	2	2		1979	19 May	Belfast	2	0
wc1953	11 Nov	Everton	3	1		EC1979	17 Oct	Belfast	5	1
1954	2 Oct	Belfast	2	0		1980	20 May	Wembley	1	1
1955	2 Nov	Wembley	3	0		1982	23 Feb	Wembley	4	0
1956	10 Oct	Belfast	1	1		1983	28 May	Belfast	0	0
1957	6 Nov	Wembley	2	3		1984	24 Apr	Wembley	1	0
1958	4 Oct	Belfast	3	3		wc1985	27 Feb	Belfast	1	0
1959	18 Nov	Wembley	2	1		wc1985	13 Nov	Wembley	0	0
1960	8 Oct	Belfast	5	2		EC1986	15 Oct	Wembley	3	0
1961	22 Nov	Wembley	1	1		EC1987	1 Apr	Belfast	2	0

SCOTLAND v WALES

Played: 102; Scotland won 60, Wales won 19, Drawn 23. *Goals:* Scotland 238, Wales 112.

			S	W					S	W
1876	25 Mar	Glasgow	4	0		1921	12 Feb	Aberdeen	2	1
1877	5 Mar	Wrexham	2	0		1922	4 Feb	Wrexham	1	2
1878	23 Mar	Glasgow	9	0		1923	17 Mar	Paisley	2	0
1879	7 Apr	Wrexham	3	0		1924	16 Feb	Cardiff	0	2
1880	3 Apr	Glasgow	5	1		1925	14 Feb	Tynecastle	3	1
1881	14 Mar	Wrexham	5	1		1925	31 Oct	Cardiff	3	0
1882	25 Mar	Glasgow	5	0		1926	30 Oct	Glasgow	3	0
1883	12 Mar	Wrexham	4	1		1927	29 Oct	Wrexham	2	2
1884	29 Mar	Glasgow	4	1		1928	27 Oct	Glasgow	4	2
1885	23 Mar	Wrexham	8	1		1929	26 Oct	Cardiff	4	2
1886	10 Apr	Glasgow	4	1		1930	25 Oct	Glasgow	1	1
1887	21 Mar	Wrexham	2	0		1931	31 Oct	Wrexham	3	2
1888	10 Mar	Edinburgh	5	1		1932	26 Oct	Edinburgh	2	5
1889	15 Apr	Wrexham	0	0		1933	4 Oct	Cardiff	2	3
1890	22 Mar	Paisley	5	0		1934	21 Nov	Aberdeen	3	2
1891	21 Mar	Wrexham	4	3		1935	5 Oct	Cardiff	1	1
1892	26 Mar	Edinburgh	6	1		1936	2 Dec	Dundee	1	2
1893	18 Mar	Wrexham	8	0		1937	30 Oct	Cardiff	1	2
1894	24 Mar	Kilmarnock	5	2		1938	9 Nov	Edinburgh	3	2
1895	23 Mar	Wrexham	2	2		1946	19 Oct	Wrexham	1	3
1896	21 Mar	Dundee	4	0		1947	12 Nov	Glasgow	1	2
1897	20 Mar	Wrexham	2	2		wc1948	23 Oct	Cardiff	3	1
1898	19 Mar	Motherwell	5	2		1949	9 Nov	Glasgow	2	0
1899	18 Mar	Wrexham	6	0		1950	21 Oct	Cardiff	3	1
1900	3 Feb	Aberdeen	5	2		1951	14 Nov	Glasgow	0	1
1901	2 Mar	Wrexham	1	1		wc1952	18 Oct	Cardiff	2	1
1902	15 Mar	Greenock	5	1		1953	4 Nov	Glasgow	3	3
1903	9 Mar	Cardiff	1	0		1954	16 Oct	Cardiff	1	0
1904	12 Mar	Dundee	1	1		1955	9 Nov	Glasgow	2	0
1905	6 Mar	Wrexham	1	3		1956	20 Oct	Cardiff	2	2
1906	3 Mar	Edinburgh	0	2		1957	13 Nov	Glasgow	1	1
1907	4 Mar	Wrexham	0	1		1958	18 Oct	Cardiff	3	0
1908	7 Mar	Dundee	2	1		1959	4 Nov	Glasgow	1	1
1909	1 Mar	Wrexham	2	3		1960	20 Oct	Cardiff	0	2
1910	5 Mar	Kilmarnock	1	0		1961	8 Nov	Glasgow	2	0
1911	6 Mar	Cardiff	2	2		1962	20 Oct	Cardiff	3	2
1912	2 Mar	Tynecastle	1	0		1963	20 Nov	Glasgow	2	1
1913	3 Mar	Wrexham	0	0		1964	3 Oct	Cardiff	2	3
1914	28 Feb	Glasgow	0	0		EC1965	24 Nov	Glasgow	4	1
1920	26 Feb	Cardiff	1	1		EC1966	22 Oct	Cardiff	1	1

			S	W				S	W
1967	22 Nov	Glasgow	3	2	wc1977	12 Oct	Liverpool	2	0
1969	3 May	Wrexham	5	3	1978	17 May	Glasgow	1	1
1970	22 Apr	Glasgow	0	0	1979	19 May	Cardiff	0	3
1971	15 May	Cardiff	0	0	1980	21 May	Glasgow	1	0
1972	24 May	Glasgow	1	0	1981	16 May	Swansea	0	2
1973	12 May	Wrexham	2	0	1982	24 May	Glasgow	1	0
1974	14 May	Glasgow	2	0	1983	28 May	Cardiff	2	0
1975	17 May	Cardiff	2	2	1984	28 Feb	Glasgow	2	1
1976	6 May	Glasgow	3	1	wc1985	27 Mar	Glasgow	0	1
wc1976	17 Nov	Glasgow	1	0	wc1985	10 Sept	Cardiff	1	1
1977	28 May	Wrexham	0	0	1997	27 May	Kilmarnock	0	1

SCOTLAND v IRELAND

Played: 92; Scotland won 61, Ireland won 15, Drawn 16. *Goals:* Scotland 254, Ireland 81.

			S	I				S	I
1884	26 Jan	Belfast	5	0	1934	20 Oct	Belfast	1	2
1885	14 Mar	Glasgow	8	2	1935	13 Nov	Edinburgh	2	1
1886	20 Mar	Belfast	7	2	1936	31 Oct	Belfast	3	1
1887	19 Feb	Glasgow	4	1	1937	10 Nov	Aberdeen	1	1
1888	24 Mar	Belfast	10	2	1938	8 Oct	Belfast	2	0
1889	9 Mar	Glasgow	7	0	1946	27 Nov	Glasgow	0	0
1890	29 Mar	Belfast	4	1	1947	4 Oct	Belfast	0	2
1891	28 Mar	Glasgow	2	1	1948	17 Nov	Glasgow	3	2
1892	19 Mar	Belfast	3	2	1949	1 Oct	Belfast	8	2
1893	25 Mar	Glasgow	6	1	1950	1 Nov	Glasgow	6	1
1894	31 Mar	Belfast	2	1	1951	6 Oct	Belfast	3	0
1895	30 Mar	Glasgow	3	1	1952	5 Nov	Glasgow	1	1
1896	28 Mar	Belfast	3	3	1953	3 Oct	Belfast	3	1
1897	27 Mar	Glasgow	5	1	1954	3 Nov	Glasgow	2	2
1898	26 Mar	Belfast	3	0	1955	8 Oct	Belfast	1	2
1899	25 Mar	Glasgow	9	1	1956	7 Nov	Glasgow	1	0
1900	3 Mar	Belfast	3	0	1957	5 Oct	Belfast	1	1
1901	23 Feb	Glasgow	11	0	1958	5 Nov	Glasgow	2	2
1902	1 Mar	Belfast	5	1	1959	3 Oct	Belfast	4	0
1903	21 Mar	Glasgow	0	2	1960	9 Nov	Glasgow	5	2
1904	26 Mar	Dublin	1	1	1961	7 Oct	Belfast	6	1
1905	18 Mar	Glasgow	4	0	1962	7 Nov	Glasgow	5	1
1906	17 Mar	Dublin	1	0	1963	12 Oct	Belfast	1	2
1907	16 Mar	Glasgow	3	0	1964	25 Nov	Glasgow	3	2
1908	14 Mar	Dublin	5	0	1965	2 Oct	Belfast	2	3
1909	15 Mar	Glasgow	5	0	1966	16 Nov	Glasgow	2	1
1910	19 Mar	Belfast	0	1	1967	21 Oct	Belfast	0	1
1911	18 Mar	Glasgow	2	0	1969	6 May	Glasgow	1	1
1912	16 Mar	Belfast	4	1	1970	18 Apr	Belfast	1	0
1913	15 Mar	Dublin	2	1	1971	18 May	Glasgow	0	1
1914	14 Mar	Belfast	1	1	1972	20 May	Glasgow	2	0
1920	13 Mar	Glasgow	3	0	1973	16 May	Glasgow	1	2
1921	26 Feb	Belfast	2	0	1974	11 May	Glasgow	0	1
1922	4 Mar	Glasgow	2	1	1975	20 May	Glasgow	3	0
1923	3 Mar	Belfast	1	0	1976	8 May	Glasgow	3	0
1924	1 Mar	Glasgow	2	0	1977	1 June	Glasgow	3	0
1925	28 Feb	Belfast	3	0	1978	13 May	Glasgow	1	1
1926	27 Feb	Glasgow	4	0	1979	22 May	Glasgow	1	0
1927	26 Feb	Belfast	2	0	1980	17 May	Belfast	0	1
1928	25 Feb	Glasgow	0	1	wc1981	25 Mar	Glasgow	1	1
1929	23 Feb	Belfast	7	3	1981	19 May	Glasgow	2	0
1930	22 Feb	Glasgow	3	1	wc1981	14 Oct	Belfast	0	0
1931	21 Feb	Belfast	0	0	1982	28 Apr	Belfast	1	1
1931	19 Sept	Glasgow	3	1	1983	24 May	Glasgow	0	0
1932	12 Sept	Belfast	4	0	1983	13 Dec	Belfast	0	2
1933	16 Sept	Glasgow	1	2	1992	19 Feb	Glasgow	1	0

WALES v IRELAND

Played: 90; Wales won 42, Ireland won 27, Drawn 21. *Goals:* Wales 181, Ireland 126.

			W	I				W	I
1882	25 Feb	Wrexham	7	1	1886	27 Feb	Wrexham	5	0
1883	17 Mar	Belfast	1	1	1887	12 Mar	Belfast	1	4
1884	9 Feb	Wrexham	6	0	1888	3 Mar	Wrexham	11	0
1885	11 Apr	Belfast	8	2	1889	27 Apr	Belfast	3	1

			W	I
1890	8 Feb	Shrewsbury	5	2
1891	7 Feb	Belfast	2	7
1892	27 Feb	Bangor	1	1
1893	8 Apr	Belfast	3	4
1894	24 Feb	Swansea	4	1
1895	16 Mar	Belfast	2	2
1896	29 Feb	Wrexham	6	1
1897	6 Mar	Belfast	3	4
1898	19 Feb	Llandudno	0	1
1899	4 Mar	Belfast	0	1
1900	24 Feb	Llandudno	2	0
1901	23 Mar	Belfast	1	0
1902	22 Mar	Cardiff	0	3
1903	28 Mar	Belfast	0	2
1904	21 Mar	Bangor	0	1
1905	18 Apr	Belfast	2	2
1906	2 Apr	Wrexham	4	4
1907	23 Feb	Belfast	3	2
1908	11 Apr	Aberdare	0	1
1909	20 Mar	Belfast	3	2
1910	11 Apr	Wrexham	4	1
1911	28 Jan	Belfast	2	1
1912	13 Apr	Cardiff	2	3
1913	18 Jan	Belfast	1	0
1914	19 Jan	Wrexham	1	2
1920	14 Feb	Belfast	2	2
1921	9 Apr	Swansea	2	1
1922	4 Apr	Belfast	1	1
1923	14 Apr	Wrexham	0	3
1924	15 Mar	Belfast	1	0
1925	18 Apr	Wrexham	0	0
1926	13 Feb	Belfast	0	3
1927	9 Apr	Cardiff	2	2
1928	4 Feb	Belfast	2	1
1929	2 Feb	Wrexham	2	2
1930	1 Feb	Belfast	0	7
1931	22 Apr	Wrexham	3	2
1931	5 Dec	Belfast	0	4
1932	7 Dec	Wrexham	4	1
1933	4 Nov	Belfast	1	1
1935	27 Mar	Wrexham	3	1

			W	I
1936	11 Mar	Belfast	2	3
1937	17 Mar	Wrexham	4	1
1938	16 Mar	Belfast	0	1
1939	15 Mar	Wrexham	3	1
1947	16 Apr	Belfast	1	2
1948	10 Mar	Wrexham	2	0
1949	9 Mar	Belfast	2	0
wc1950	8 Mar	Wrexham	0	0
1951	7 Mar	Belfast	2	1
1952	19 Mar	Swansea	3	0
1953	15 Apr	Belfast	3	2
wc1954	31 Mar	Wrexham	1	2
1955	20 Apr	Belfast	3	2
1956	11 Apr	Cardiff	1	1
1957	10 Apr	Belfast	0	0
1958	16 Apr	Cardiff	1	1
1959	22 Apr	Belfast	1	4
1960	6 Apr	Wrexham	3	2
1961	12 Apr	Belfast	5	1
1962	11 Apr	Cardiff	4	0
1963	3 Apr	Belfast	4	1
1964	15 Apr	Cardiff	2	3
1965	31 Mar	Belfast	5	0
1966	30 Mar	Cardiff	1	4
EC1967	12 Apr	Belfast	0	0
EC1968	28 Feb	Wrexham	2	0
1969	10 May	Belfast	0	0
1970	25 Apr	Swansea	1	0
1971	22 May	Belfast	0	1
1972	27 May	Wrexham	0	0
1973	19 May	Everton	0	1
1974	18 May	Wrexham	1	0
1975	23 May	Belfast	0	1
1976	14 May	Swansea	1	0
1977	3 June	Belfast	1	1
1978	19 May	Wrexham	1	0
1979	25 May	Belfast	1	1
1980	23 May	Cardiff	0	1
1982	27 May	Wrexham	3	0
1983	31 May	Belfast	1	0
1984	22 May	Swansea	1	1

OTHER BRITISH INTERNATIONAL RESULTS 1908–1999

ENGLAND

v ALBANIA			E	A
wc1989	8 Mar	Tirana	2	0
wc1989	26 Apr	Wembley	5	0

v ARGENTINA			E	A
1951	9 May	Wembley	2	1
1953	17 May	Buenos Aires	0	0

(abandoned after 21 mins)

			E	A
wc1962	2 June	Rancagua	3	1
1964	6 June	Rio de Janeiro	0	1
wc1966	23 July	Wembley	1	0
1974	22 May	Wembley	2	2
1977	12 June	Buenos Aires	1	1
1980	13 May	Wembley	3	1
wc1986	22 June	Mexico City	1	2
1991	25 May	Wembley	2	2
wc1998	30 June	St Etienne	2	2

v AUSTRALIA			E	A
1980	31 May	Sydney	2	1
1983	11 June	Sydney	0	0
1983	15 June	Brisbane	1	0
1983	18 June	Melbourne	1	1
1991	1 June	Sydney	1	0

v AUSTRIA			E	A
1908	6 June	Vienna	6	1
1908	8 June	Vienna	11	1

			E	A
1909	1 June	Vienna	8	1
1930	14 May	Vienna	0	0
1932	7 Dec	Chelsea	4	3
1936	6 May	Vienna	1	2
1951	28 Nov	Wembley	2	2
1952	25 May	Vienna	3	2
wc1958	15 June	Boras	2	2
1961	27 May	Vienna	1	3
1962	4 Apr	Wembley	3	1
1965	20 Oct	Wembley	2	3
1967	27 May	Vienna	1	0
1973	26 Sept	Wembley	7	0
1979	13 June	Vienna	3	4

v BELGIUM			E	B
1921	21 May	Brussels	2	0
1923	19 Mar	Highbury	6	1
1923	1 Nov	Antwerp	2	2
1924	8 Dec	West Bromwich	4	0
1926	24 May	Antwerp	5	3
1927	11 May	Brussels	9	1
1928	19 May	Antwerp	3	1
1929	11 May	Brussels	5	1
1931	16 May	Brussels	4	1
1936	9 May	Brussels	2	3
1947	21 Sept	Brussels	5	2

			E	B
1950	18 May	Brussels	4	1
1952	26 Nov	Wembley	5	0
wc1954	17 June	Basle	4	4*
1964	21 Oct	Wembley	2	2
1970	25 Feb	Brussels	3	1
EC1980	12 June	Turin	1	1
wc1990	27 June	Bologna	1	0*
1998	29 May	Casablanca	0	0

*After extra time

		v BOHEMIA	E	B
1908	13 June	Prague	4	0

		v BRAZIL	E	B
1956	9 May	Wembley	4	2
wc1958	11 June	Gothenburg	0	0
1959	13 May	Rio de Janeiro	0	2
wc1962	10 June	Vina del Mar	1	3
1963	8 May	Wembley	1	1
1964	30 May	Rio de Janeiro	1	5
1969	12 June	Rio de Janeiro	1	2
wc1970	7 June	Guadalajara	0	1
1976	23 May	Los Angeles	0	1
1977	8 June	Rio de Janeiro	0	0
1978	19 Apr	Wembley	1	1
1981	12 May	Wembley	0	1
1984	10 June	Rio de Janeiro	2	0
1987	19 May	Wembley	1	1
1990	28 Mar	Wembley	1	0
1992	17 May	Wembley	1	1
1993	13 June	Washington	1	1
UI1995	11 June	Wembley	1	3
TF1997	10 June	Paris	0	1

		v BULGARIA	E	B
wc1962	7 June	Rancagua	0	0
1968	11 Dec	Wembley	1	1
1974	1 June	Sofia	1	0
EC1979	6 June	Sofia	3	0
EC1979	22 Nov	Wembley	2	0
1996	27 Mar	Wembley	1	0
EC1998	10 Oct	Wembley	0	0
EC1999	9 June	Sofia	1	1

		v CAMEROON	E	C
wc1990	1 July	Naples	3	2*
1991	6 Feb	Wembley	2	0
1997	15 Nov	Wembley	2	0

*After extra time

		v CANADA	E	C
1986	24 May	Burnaby	1	0

		v CHILE	E	C
wc1950	25 June	Rio de Janeiro	2	0
1953	24 May	Santiago	2	1
1984	17 June	Santiago	0	0
1989	23 May	Wembley	0	0
1998	11 Feb	Wembley	0	2

		v CHINA	E	C
1996	23 May	Beijing	3	0

		v CIS	E	C
1992	29 Apr	Moscow	2	2

		v COLOMBIA	E	C
1970	20 May	Bogota	4	0
1988	24 May	Wembley	1	1
1995	6 Sept	Wembley	0	0
wc1998	26 June	Lens	2	0

		v CROATIA	E	C
1996	24 Apr	Wembley	0	0

		v CYPRUS	E	C
EC1975	16 Apr	Wembley	5	0
EC1975	11 May	Limassol	1	0

		v CZECHOSLOVAKIA	E	C
1934	16 May	Prague	1	2
1937	1 Dec	Tottenham	5	4
1963	29 May	Bratislava	4	2
1966	2 Nov	Wembley	0	0
wc1970	11 June	Guadalajara	1	0
1973	27 May	Prague	1	1
EC1974	30 Oct	Wembley	3	0
EC1975	30 Oct	Bratislava	1	2
1978	29 Nov	Wembley	1	0
wc1982	20 June	Bilbao	2	0
1990	25 Apr	Wembley	4	2
1992	25 Mar	Prague	2	2

		v CZECH REPUBLIC	E	C
1998	18 Nov	Wembley	2	0

		v DENMARK	E	D
1948	26 Sept	Copenhagen	0	0
1955	2 Oct	Copenhagen	5	1
wc1956	5 Dec	Wolverhampton	5	2
wc1957	15 May	Copenhagen	4	1
1966	3 July	Copenhagen	2	0
EC1978	20 Sept	Copenhagen	4	3
EC1979	12 Sept	Wembley	1	0
EC1982	22 Sept	Copenhagen	2	2
EC1983	21 Sept	Wembley	0	1
1988	14 Sept	Wembley	1	0
1989	7 June	Copenhagen	1	1
1990	15 May	Wembley	1	0
EC1992	11 June	Malmo	0	0
1994	9 Mar	Wembley	1	0

		v ECUADOR	E	Ec
1970	24 May	Quito	2	0

		v EGYPT	E	Eg
1986	29 Jan	Cairo	4	0
wc1990	21 June	Cagliari	1	0

		v FIFA	E	FIFA
1938	26 Oct	Highbury	3	0
1953	21 Oct	Wembley	4	4
1963	23 Oct	Wembley	2	1

		v FINLAND	E	F
1937	20 May	Helsinki	8	0
1956	20 May	Helsinki	5	1
1966	26 June	Helsinki	3	0
wc1976	13 June	Helsinki	4	1
wc1976	13 Oct	Wembley	2	1
1982	3 June	Helsinki	4	1
wc1984	17 Oct	Wembley	5	0
wc1985	22 May	Helsinki	1	1
1992	3 June	Helsinki	2	1

		v FRANCE	E	F
1923	10 May	Paris	4	1
1924	17 May	Paris	3	1
1925	21 May	Paris	3	2
1927	26 May	Paris	6	0
1928	17 May	Paris	5	1
1929	9 May	Paris	4	1
1931	14 May	Paris	2	5
1933	6 Dec	Tottenham	4	1
1938	26 May	Paris	4	2
1947	3 May	Highbury	3	0
1949	22 May	Paris	3	1
1951	3 Oct	Highbury	2	2

			E	F
1955	15 May	Paris	0	1
1957	27 Nov	Wembley	4	0
EC1962	3 Oct	Sheffield	1	1
EC1963	27 Feb	Paris	2	5
wc1966	20 July	Wembley	2	0
1969	12 Mar	Wembley	5	0
wc1982	16 June	Bilbao	3	1
1984	29 Feb	Paris	0	2
1992	19 Feb	Wembley	2	0
EC1992	14 June	Malmo	0	0
TF1997	7 June	Montpellier	1	0
1999	10 Feb	Wembley	0	2

v GEORGIA			E	G
wc1996	9 Nov	Tbilisi	2	0
wc1997	30 Apr	Wembley	2	0

v GERMANY			E	G
1930	10 May	Berlin	3	3
1935	4 Dec	Tottenham	3	0
1938	14 May	Berlin	6	3
1991	11 Sept	Wembley	0	1
1993	19 June	Detroit	1	2
EC1996	26 June	Wembley	1	1*

v EAST GERMANY			E	EG
1963	2 June	Leipzig	2	1
1970	25 Nov	Wembley	3	1
1974	29 May	Leipzig	1	1
1984	12 Sept	Wembley	1	0

v WEST GERMANY			E	WG
1954	1 Dec	Wembley	3	1
1956	26 May	Berlin	3	1
1965	12 May	Nuremberg	1	0
1966	23 Feb	Wembley	1	0
wc1966	30 July	Wembley	4	2*
1968	1 June	Hanover	0	1
wc1970	14 June	Leon	2	3*
EC1972	29 Apr	Wembley	1	3
EC1972	13 May	Berlin	0	0
1975	12 Mar	Wembley	2	0
1978	22 Feb	Munich	1	2
wc1982	29 June	Madrid	0	0
1982	13 Oct	Wembley	1	2
1985	12 June	Mexico City	3	0
1987	9 Sept	Dusseldorf	1	3
wc1990	4 July	Turin	1	1*

*After extra time

v GREECE			E	G
EC1971	21 Apr	Wembley	3	0
EC1971	1 Dec	Athens	2	0
EC1982	17 Nov	Athens	3	0
EC1983	30 Mar	Wembley	0	0
1989	8 Feb	Athens	2	1
1994	17 May	Wembley	5	0

v HOLLAND			E	H
1935	18 May	Amsterdam	1	0
1946	27 Nov	Huddersfield	8	2
1964	9 Dec	Amsterdam	1	1
1969	5 Nov	Amsterdam	1	0
1970	14 Jun	Wembley	0	0
1977	9 Feb	Wembley	0	2
1982	25 May	Wembley	2	0
1988	23 Mar	Wembley	2	2
EC1988	15 June	Dusseldorf	1	3
wc1990	16 June	Cagliari	0	0
wc1993	28 Apr	Wembley	2	2
wc1993	13 Oct	Rotterdam	0	2
EC1996	18 June	Wembley	4	1

v HUNGARY			E	H
1908	10 June	Budapest	7	0
1909	29 May	Budapest	4	2
1909	31 May	Budapest	8	2
1934	10 May	Budapest	1	2
1936	2 Dec	Highbury	6	2
1953	25 Nov	Wembley	3	6
1954	23 May	Budapest	1	7
1960	22 May	Budapest	0	2
wc1962	31 May	Rancagua	1	2
1965	5 May	Wembley	1	0
1978	24 May	Wembley	4	1
wc1981	6 June	Budapest	3	1
wc1982	18 Nov	Wembley	1	0
EC1983	27 Apr	Wembley	2	0
EC1983	12 Oct	Budapest	3	0
1988	27 Apr	Budapest	0	0
1990	12 Sept	Wembley	1	0
1992	12 May	Budapest	1	0
1996	18 May	Wembley	3	0
1999	28 Apr	Budapest	1	1

v ICELAND			E	I
1982	2 June	Reykjavik	1	1

v REPUBLIC OF IRELAND			E	RI
1946	30 Sept	Dublin	1	0
1949	21 Sept	Everton	0	2
wc1957	8 May	Wembley	5	1
wc1957	19 May	Dublin	1	1
1964	24 May	Dublin	3	1
1976	8 Sept	Wembley	1	1
EC1978	25 Oct	Dublin	1	1
EC1980	6 Feb	Wembley	2	0
1985	26 Mar	Wembley	2	1
EC1988	12 June	Stuttgart	0	1
wc1990	11 June	Cagliari	1	1
EC1990	14 Nov	Dublin	1	1
EC1991	27 Mar	Wembley	1	1
1995	15 Feb	Dublin	0	1

(abandoned after 27 mins)

v ISRAEL			E	I
1986	26 Feb	Ramat Gan	2	1
1988	17 Feb	Tel Aviv	0	0

v ITALY			E	I
1933	13 May	Rome	1	1
1934	14 Nov	Highbury	3	2
1939	13 May	Milan	2	2
1948	16 May	Turin	4	0
1949	30 Nov	Tottenham	2	0
1952	18 May	Florence	1	1
1959	6 May	Wembley	2	2
1961	24 May	Rome	3	2
1973	14 June	Turin	0	2
1973	14 Nov	Wembley	0	1
1976	28 May	New York	3	2
wc1976	17 Nov	Rome	0	2
wc1977	16 Nov	Wembley	2	0
EC1980	15 June	Turin	0	1
1985	6 June	Mexico City	1	2
1989	15 Nov	Wembley	0	0
wc1990	7 July	Bari	1	2
wc1997	12 Feb	Wembley	0	1
TF1997	4 June	Nantes	2	0
wc1997	11 Oct	Rome	0	0

v JAPAN			E	J
UI1995	3 June	Wembley	2	1

v KUWAIT			E	K
wc1982	25 June	Bilbao	1	0

v LUXEMBOURG			E	L
1927	21 May	Luxembourg	5	2
wc1960	19 Oct	Luxembourg	9	0
wc1961	28 Sept	Highbury	4	1
wc1977	30 Mar	Wembley	5	0
wc1977	12 Oct	Luxembourg	2	0
EC1982	15 Dec	Wembley	9	0
EC1983	16 Nov	Luxembourg	4	0
EC1998	14 Oct	Luxembourg	3	0

v MALAYSIA			E	M
1991	12 June	Kuala Lumpur	4	2

v MALTA			E	M
EC1971	3 Feb	Valletta	1	0
EC1971	12 May	Wembley	5	0

v MEXICO			E	M
1959	24 May	Mexico City	1	2
1961	10 May	Wembley	8	0
wc1966	16 July	Wembley	2	0
1969	1 June	Mexico City	0	0
1985	9 June	Mexico City	0	1
1986	17 May	Los Angeles	3	0
1997	29 Mar	Wembley	2	0

v MOLDOVA			E	M
wc1996	1 Sept	Chisinau	3	0
wc1997	10 Sept	Wembley	4	0

v MOROCCO			E	M
wc1986	6 June	Monterrey	0	0
1998	27 May	Casablanca	1	0

v NEW ZEALAND			E	NZ
1991	3 June	Auckland	1	0
1991	8 June	Wellington	2	0

v NIGERIA			E	N
1994	16 Nov	Wembley	1	0

v NORWAY			E	N
1937	14 May	Oslo	6	0
1938	9 Nov	Newcastle	4	0
1949	18 May	Oslo	4	1
1966	29 June	Oslo	6	1
wc1980	10 Sept	Wembley	4	0
wc1981	9 Sept	Oslo	1	2
wc1992	14 Oct	Wembley	1	1
wc1993	2 June	Oslo	0	2
1994	22 May	Wembley	0	0
1995	11 Oct	Oslo	0	0

v PARAGUAY			E	P
wc1986	18 June	Mexico City	3	0

v PERU			E	P
1959	17 May	Lima	1	4
1962	20 May	Lima	4	0

v POLAND			E	P
1966	5 Jan	Everton	1	1
1966	5 July	Chorzow	1	0
wc1973	6 June	Chorzow	0	2
wc1973	17 Oct	Wembley	1	1
wc1986	11 June	Monterrey	3	0
wc1989	3 June	Wembley	3	0
wc1989	11 Oct	Katowice	0	0
EC1990	17 Oct	Wembley	2	0
EC1991	13 Nov	Poznan	1	1
wc1993	29 May	Katowice	1	1
wc1993	8 Sept	Wembley	3	0
wc1996	9 Oct	Wembley	2	0
wc1997	31 May	Katowice	2	0
EC1999	27 Mar	Wembley	3	1

v PORTUGAL			E	P
1947	25 May	Lisbon	10	0
1950	14 May	Lisbon	5	3
1951	19 May	Everton	5	2
1955	22 May	Oporto	1	3
1958	7 May	Wembley	2	1
wc1961	21 May	Lisbon	1	1
wc1961	25 Oct	Wembley	2	0
1964	17 May	Lisbon	4	3
1964	4 June	São Paulo	1	1
wc1966	26 July	Wembley	2	1
1969	10 Dec	Wembley	1	0
1974	3 Apr	Lisbon	0	0
EC1974	20 Nov	Wembley	0	0
EC1975	19 Nov	Lisbon	1	1
wc1986	3 June	Monterrey	0	1
1995	12 Dec	Wembley	1	1
1998	22 Apr	Wembley	3	0

v ROMANIA			E	R
1939	24 May	Bucharest	2	0
1968	6 Nov	Bucharest	0	0
1969	15 Jan	Wembley	1	1
wc1970	2 June	Guadalajara	1	0
wc1980	15 Oct	Bucharest	1	2
wc1981	29 April	Wembley	0	0
wc1985	1 May	Bucharest	0	0
wc1985	11 Sept	Wembley	1	1
1994	12 Oct	Wembley	1	1
wc1998	22 June	Toulouse	1	2

v SAN MARINO			E	SM
wc1992	17 Feb	Wembley	6	0
wc1993	17 Nov	Bologna	7	1

v SAUDI ARABIA			E	SA
1988	16 Nov	Riyadh	1	1
1998	23 May	Wembley	0	0

v SOUTH AFRICA			E	SA
1997	24 May	Old Trafford	2	1

v SPAIN			E	S
1929	15 May	Madrid	3	4
1931	9 Dec	Highbury	7	1
wc1950	2 July	Rio de Janeiro	0	1
1955	18 May	Madrid	1	1
1955	30 Nov	Wembley	4	1
1960	15 May	Madrid	0	3
1960	26 Oct	Wembley	4	2
1965	8 Dec	Madrid	2	0
1967	24 May	Wembley	2	0
EC1968	3 Apr	Wembley	1	0
EC1968	8 May	Madrid	2	1
1980	26 Mar	Barcelona	2	0
EC1980	18 June	Naples	2	1
1981	25 Mar	Wembley	1	2
wc1982	5 July	Madrid	0	0
1987	18 Feb	Madrid	4	2
1992	9 Sept	Santander	0	1
EC 1996	22 June	Wembley	0	0

v SWEDEN			E	S
1923	21 May	Stockholm	4	2
1923	24 May	Stockholm	3	1
1937	17 May	Stockholm	4	0
1947	19 Nov	Highbury	4	2
1949	13 May	Stockholm	1	3
1956	16 May	Stockholm	0	0
1959	28 Oct	Wembley	2	3
1965	16 May	Gothenburg	2	1
1968	22 May	Wembley	3	1
1979	10 June	Stockholm	0	0
1986	10 Sept	Stockholm	0	1
wc1988	19 Oct	Wembley	0	0
wc1989	6 Sept	Stockholm	0	0
EC1992	17 June	Stockholm	1	2
UI1995	8 June	Leeds	3	3
EC1998	5 Sept	Stockholm	1	2
EC1999	5 June	Wembley	0	0

v SWITZERLAND

			E	S
1933	20 May	Berne	4	0
1938	21 May	Zurich	1	2
1947	18 May	Zurich	0	1
1948	2 Dec	Highbury	6	0
1952	28 May	Zurich	3	0
wc1954	20 June	Berne	2	0
1962	9 May	Wembley	3	1
1963	5 June	Basle	8	1
EC1971	13 Oct	Basle	3	2
EC1971	10 Nov	Wembley	1	1
1975	3 Sept	Basle	2	1
1977	7 Sept	Wembley	0	0
wc1980	19 Nov	Wembley	2	1
wc1981	30 May	Basle	1	2
1988	28 May	Lausanne	1	0
1995	15 Nov	Wembley	3	1
EC1996	8 June	Wembley	1	1
1998	25 Mar	Berne	1	1

v TUNISIA

			E	T
1990	2 June	Tunis	1	1
wc1998	15 June	Marseilles	2	0

v TURKEY

			E	T
wc1984	14 Nov	Istanbul	8	0
wc1985	16 Oct	Wembley	5	0
EC1987	29 Apr	Izmir	0	0
EC1987	14 Oct	Wembley	8	0
EC1991	1 May	Izmir	1	0
EC1991	16 Oct	Wembley	1	0
wc1992	18 Nov	Wembley	4	0
wc1993	31 Mar	Izmir	2	0

v URUGUAY

			E	U
1953	31 May	Montevideo	1	2
wc1954	26 June	Basle	2	4
1964	6 May	Wembley	2	1
wc1966	11 July	Wembley	0	0
1969	8 June	Montevideo	2	1
1977	15 June	Montevideo	0	0
1984	13 June	Montevideo	0	2

			E	U
1990	22 May	Wembley	1	2
1995	29 Mar	Wembley	0	0

v USA

			E	USA
wc1950	29 June	Belo Horizonte	0	1
1953	8 June	New York	6	3
1959	28 May	Los Angeles	8	1
1964	27 May	New York	10	0
1985	16 June	Los Angeles	5	0
1993	9 June	Foxboro	0	2
1994	7 Sept	Wembley	2	0

v USSR

			E	USSR
1958	18 May	Moscow	1	1
wc1958	8 June	Gothenburg	2	2
wc1958	17 June	Gothenburg	0	1
1958	22 Oct	Wembley	5	0
1967	6 Dec	Wembley	2	2
EC1968	8 June	Rome	2	0
1973	10 June	Moscow	2	1
1984	2 June	Wembley	0	2
1986	26 Mar	Tbilisi	1	0
EC1988	18 June	Frankfurt	1	3
1991	21 May	Wembley	3	1

v YUGOSLAVIA

			E	Y
1939	18 May	Belgrade	1	2
1950	22 Nov	Highbury	2	2
1954	16 May	Belgrade	0	1
1956	28 Nov	Wembley	3	0
1958	11 May	Belgrade	0	5
1960	11 May	Wembley	3	3
1965	9 May	Belgrade	1	1
1966	4 May	Wembley	2	0
EC1968	5 June	Florence	0	1
1972	11 Oct	Wembley	1	1
1974	5 June	Belgrade	2	2
EC1986	12 Nov	Wembley	2	0
EC1987	11 Nov	Belgrade	4	1
1989	13 Dec	Wembley	2	1

SCOTLAND

v ARGENTINA

			S	A
1977	18 June	Buenos Aires	1	1
1979	2 June	Glasgow	1	3
1990	28 Mar	Glasgow	1	0

v AUSTRALIA

			S	A
wc1985	20 Nov	Glasgow	2	0
wc1985	4 Dec	Melbourne	0	0
1996	27 Mar	Glasgow	1	0

v AUSTRIA

			S	A
1931	16 May	Vienna	0	5
1933	29 Nov	Glasgow	2	2
1937	9 May	Vienna	1	1
1950	13 Dec	Glasgow	0	1
1951	27 May	Vienna	0	4
wc1954	16 June	Zurich	0	1
1955	19 May	Vienna	4	1
1956	2 May	Glasgow	1	1
1960	29 May	Vienna	1	4
1963	8 May	Glasgow	4	1
(abandoned after 79 mins)				
wc1968	6 Nov	Glasgow	2	1
wc1969	5 Nov	Vienna	0	2
EC1978	20 Sept	Vienna	2	3
EC1979	17 Oct	Glasgow	1	1
1994	20 Apr	Vienna	2	1
wc1996	31 Aug	Vienna	0	0
wc1997	2 Apr	Celtic Park	2	0

v BELARUS

			S	B
wc1997	8 June	Minsk	1	0
wc1997	7 Sept	Aberdeen	4	1

v BELGIUM

			S	B
1947	18 May	Brussels	1	2
1948	28 Apr	Glasgow	2	0
1951	20 May	Brussels	5	0
EC1971	3 Feb	Liège	0	3
EC1971	10 Nov	Aberdeen	1	0
1974	2 June	Brussels	1	2
EC1979	21 Nov	Brussels	0	2
EC1979	19 Dec	Glasgow	1	3
EC1982	15 Dec	Brussels	2	3
EC1983	12 Oct	Glasgow	1	1
EC1987	1 Apr	Brussels	1	4
EC1987	14 Oct	Glasgow	2	0

v BRAZIL

			S	B
1966	25 June	Glasgow	1	1
1972	5 July	Rio de Janeiro	0	1
1973	30 June	Glasgow	0	1
wc1974	18 June	Frankfurt	0	0
1977	23 June	Rio de Janeiro	0	2
wc1982	18 June	Seville	1	4
1987	26 May	Glasgow	0	2
wc1990	20 June	Turin	0	1
wc1998	10 June	Sant-Denis	1	2

v BULGARIA

			S	B
1978	22 Feb	Glasgow	2	1
EC1986	10 Sept	Glasgow	0	0
EC1987	11 Nov	Sofia	1	0
EC1990	14 Nov	Sofia	1	1
EC1991	27 Mar	Glasgow	1	1

		v CANADA	S	C
1983	12 June	Vancouver	2	0
1983	16 June	Edmonton	3	0
1983	20 June	Toronto	2	0
1992	21 May	Toronto	3	1

		v CHILE	S	C
1977	15 June	Santiago	4	2
1989	30 May	Glasgow	2	0

		v CIS	S	C
EC1992	18 June	Norrkoping	3	0

		v COLOMBIA	S	C
1988	17 May	Glasgow	0	0
1996	30 May	Miami	0	1
1998	23 May	New York	2	2

		v COSTA RICA	S	CR
wc1990	11 June	Genoa	0	1

		v CYPRUS	S	C
wc1968	17 Dec	Nicosia	5	0
wc1969	11 May	Glasgow	8	0
wc1989	8 Feb	Limassol	3	2
wc1989	26 Apr	Glasgow	2	1

		v CZECHOSLOVAKIA	S	C
1937	22 May	Prague	3	1
1937	8 Dec	Glasgow	5	0
wc1961	14 May	Bratislava	0	4
wc1961	26 Sept	Glasgow	3	2
wc1961	29 Nov	Brussels	2	4*
1972	2 July	Porto Alegre	0	0
wc1973	26 Sept	Glasgow	2	1
wc1973	17 Oct	Prague	0	1
wc1976	13 Oct	Prague	0	2
wc1977	21 Sept	Glasgow	3	1

*After extra time

		v CZECH REPUBLIC	S	C
EC1999	31 Mar	Glasgow	1	2
EC1999	9 June	Prague	2	3

		v DENMARK	S	D
1951	12 May	Glasgow	3	1
1952	25 May	Copenhagen	2	1
1968	16 Oct	Copenhagen	1	0
EC1970	11 Nov	Glasgow	1	0
EC1971	9 June	Copenhagen	0	1
wc1972	18 Oct	Copenhagen	4	1
wc1972	15 Nov	Glasgow	2	0
EC1975	3 Sept	Copenhagen	1	0
EC1975	29 Oct	Glasgow	3	1
wc1986	4 June	Nezahualcayotl	0	1
1996	24 Apr	Copenhagen	0	2
1998	25 Mar	Glasgow	0	1

		v ECUADOR	S	E
1995	24 May	Toyama	2	1

		v EGYPT	S	E
1990	16 May	Aberdeen	1	3

		v ESTONIA	S	E
wc1993	19 May	Tallinn	3	0
wc1993	2 June	Aberdeen	3	1
wc1997	11 Feb	Monaco	0	0
wc1997	29 Mar	Kilmarnock	2	0
EC1998	10 Oct	Edinburgh	3	2

		v FAEROES	S	F
EC1994	12 Oct	Glasgow	5	1
EC1995	7 June	Toftir	2	0
EC1998	14 Oct	Aberdeen	2	1
EC1999	5 June	Toftir	1	1

		v FINLAND	S	F
1954	25 May	Helsinki	2	1
wc1964	21 Oct	Glasgow	3	1
wc1965	27 May	Helsinki	2	1
1976	8 Sept	Glasgow	6	0

			S	F
1992	25 Mar	Glasgow	1	1
EC1994	7 Sept	Helsinki	2	0
EC1995	6 Sept	Glasgow	1	0
1998	22 Apr	Edinburgh	1	1

		v FRANCE	S	F
1930	18 May	Paris	2	0
1932	8 May	Paris	3	1
1948	23 May	Paris	0	3
1949	27 Apr	Glasgow	2	0
1950	27 May	Paris	1	0
1951	16 May	Glasgow	1	0
wc1958	15 June	Orebro	1	2
1984	1 June	Marseilles	0	2
wc1989	8 Mar	Glasgow	2	0
wc1989	11 Oct	Paris	0	3
1997	12 Nov	St Etienne	1	2

		v GERMANY	S	G
1929	1 June	Berlin	1	1
1936	14 Oct	Glasgow	2	0
EC1992	15 June	Norrkoping	0	2
1993	24 Mar	Glasgow	0	1
1998	28 Apr	Bremen	1	0

		v EAST GERMANY	S	EG
1974	30 Oct	Glasgow	3	0
1977	7 Sept	East Berlin	0	1
EC1982	13 Oct	Glasgow	2	0
EC1983	16 Nov	Halle	1	2
1985	16 Oct	Glasgow	0	0
1990	25 Apr	Glasgow	0	1

		v WEST GERMANY	S	WG
1957	22 May	Stuttgart	3	1
1959	6 May	Glasgow	3	2
1964	12 May	Hanover	2	2
wc1969	16 Apr	Glasgow	1	1
wc1969	22 Oct	Hamburg	2	3
1973	14 Nov	Glasgow	1	1
1974	27 Mar	Frankfurt	1	2
wc1986	8 June	Queretaro	1	2

		v GREECE	S	G
EC1994	18 Dec	Athens	0	1
EC1995	16 Aug	Glasgow	1	0

		v HOLLAND	S	H
1929	4 June	Amsterdam	2	0
1938	21 May	Amsterdam	3	1
1959	27 May	Amsterdam	2	1
1966	11 May	Glasgow	0	3
1968	30 May	Amsterdam	0	0
1971	1 Dec	Rotterdam	1	2
wc1978	11 June	Mendoza	3	2
1982	23 Mar	Glasgow	2	1
1986	29 Apr	Eindhoven	0	0
EC1992	12 June	Gothenburg	0	1
1994	23 Mar	Glasgow	0	1
1994	27 May	Utrecht	1	3
EC1996	10 June	Birmingham	0	0

		v HUNGARY	S	H
1938	7 Dec	Glasgow	3	1
1954	8 Dec	Glasgow	2	4
1955	29 May	Budapest	1	3
1958	7 May	Glasgow	1	1
1960	5 June	Budapest	3	3
1980	31 May	Budapest	1	3
1987	9 Sept	Glasgow	2	0

		v ICELAND	S	I
wc1984	17 Oct	Glasgow	3	0
wc1985	28 May	Reykjavik	1	0

		v IRAN	S	I
wc1978	7 June	Cordoba	1	1

		v REPUBLIC OF IRELAND	S	RI
wc1961	3 May	Glasgow	4	1
wc1961	7 May	Dublin	3	0
1963	9 June	Dublin	0	1
1969	21 Sept	Dublin	1	1
EC1986	15 Oct	Dublin	0	0
EC1987	18 Feb	Glasgow	0	1

		v ISRAEL	S	I
wc1981	25 Feb	Tel Aviv	1	0
wc1981	28 Apr	Glasgow	3	1
1986	28 Jan	Tel Aviv	1	0

		v ITALY	S	I
1931	20 May	Rome	0	3
wc1965	9 Nov	Glasgow	1	0
wc1965	7 Dec	Naples	0	3
1988	22 Dec	Perugia	0	2
wc1992	18 Nov	Glasgow	0	0
wc1993	13 Oct	Rome	1	3

		v JAPAN	S	J
1995	21 May	Hiroshima	0	0

		v LATVIA	S	L
wc1996	5 Oct	Riga	2	0
wc1997	11 Oct	Glasgow	2	0

		v LITHUANIA	S	L
EC1998	5 Sept	Vilnius	0	0

		v LUXEMBOURG	S	L
1947	24 May	Luxembourg	6	0
EC1986	12 Nov	Glasgow	3	0
EC1987	2 Dec	Esch	0	0

		v MALTA	S	M
1988	22 Mar	Valletta	1	1
1990	28 May	Valletta	2	1
wc1993	17 Feb	Glasgow	3	0
wc1993	17 Nov	Valletta	2	0
1997	1 June	Valletta	3	2

		v MOROCCO	S	M
wc1998	23 June	St Etienne	0	3

		v NEW ZEALAND	S	NZ
wc1982	15 June	Malaga	5	2

		v NORWAY	S	N
1929	28 May	Oslo	7	3
1954	5 May	Glasgow	1	0
1954	19 May	Oslo	1	1
1963	4 June	Bergen	3	4
1963	7 Nov	Glasgow	6	1
1974	6 June	Oslo	2	1
EC1978	25 Oct	Glasgow	3	2
EC1979	7 June	Oslo	4	0
wc1988	14 Sept	Oslo	2	1
wc1989	15 Nov	Glasgow	1	1
1992	3 June	Oslo	0	0
wc1998	16 June	Bordeaux	1	1

		v PARAGUAY	S	P
wc1958	11 June	Norrkoping	2	3

		v PERU	S	P
1972	26 Apr	Glasgow	2	0
wc1978	3 June	Cordoba	1	3
1979	12 Sept	Glasgow	1	1

		v POLAND	S	P
1958	1 June	Warsaw	2	1
1960	4 June	Glasgow	2	3
wc1965	23 May	Chorzow	1	1
wc1965	13 Oct	Glasgow	1	2
1980	28 May	Poznan	0	1
1990	19 May	Glasgow	1	1

		v PORTUGAL	S	P
1950	21 May	Lisbon	2	2
1955	4 May	Glasgow	3	0
1959	3 June	Lisbon	0	1
1966	18 June	Glasgow	0	1
EC1971	21 Apr	Lisbon	0	2
EC1971	13 Oct	Glasgow	2	1
1975	13 May	Glasgow	1	0
EC1978	29 Nov	Lisbon	0	1
EC1980	26 Mar	Glasgow	4	1
wc1980	15 Oct	Glasgow	0	0
wc1981	18 Nov	Lisbon	1	2
wc1992	14 Oct	Glasgow	0	0
wc1993	28 Apr	Lisbon	0	5

		v ROMANIA	S	R
EC1975	1 June	Bucharest	1	1
EC1975	17 Dec	Glasgow	1	1
1986	26 Mar	Glasgow	3	0
EC1990	12 Sept	Glasgow	2	1
EC1991	16 Oct	Bucharest	0	1

		v RUSSIA	S	R
EC1994	16 Nov	Glasgow	1	1
EC1995	29 Mar	Moscow	0	0

		v SAN MARINO	S	SM
EC1991	1 May	Serravalle	2	0
EC1991	13 Nov	Glasgow	4	0
EC1995	26 Apr	Serravalle	2	0
EC1995	15 Nov	Glasgow	5	0

		v SAUDI ARABIA	S	SA
1988	17 Feb	Riyadh	2	2

		v SPAIN	S	Sp
wc1957	8 May	Glasgow	4	2
wc1957	26 May	Madrid	1	4
1963	13 June	Madrid	6	2
1965	8 May	Glasgow	0	0
EC1974	20 Nov	Glasgow	1	2
EC1975	5 Feb	Valencia	1	1
1982	24 Feb	Valencia	0	3
wc1984	14 Nov	Glasgow	3	1
wc1985	27 Feb	Seville	0	1
1988	27 Apr	Madrid	0	0

		v SWEDEN	S	Sw
1952	30 May	Stockholm	1	3
1953	6 May	Glasgow	1	2
1975	16 Apr	Gothenburg	1	1
1977	27 Apr	Glasgow	3	1
wc1980	10 Sept	Stockholm	1	0
wc1981	9 Sept	Glasgow	2	0
wc1990	16 June	Genoa	2	1
1995	11 Oct	Stockholm	0	2
wc1996	10 Nov	Glasgow	1	0
wc1997	30 Apr	Gothenburg	1	2

		v SWITZERLAND	S	Sw
1931	24 May	Geneva	3	2
1948	17 May	Berne	1	2
1950	26 Apr	Glasgow	3	1
wc1957	19 May	Basle	2	1
wc1957	6 Nov	Glasgow	3	2
1973	22 June	Berne	0	1
1976	7 Apr	Glasgow	1	0

			S	Sw
EC1982	17 Nov	Berne	0	2
EC1983	30 May	Glasgow	2	2
EC1990	17 Oct	Glasgow	2	1
EC1991	11 Sept	Berne	2	2
wc1992	9 Sept	Berne	1	3
wc1993	8 Sept	Aberdeen	1	1
EC1996	18 June	Birmingham	1	0

		v TURKEY	S	T
1960	8 June	Ankara	2	4

		v URUGUAY	S	U
wc1954	19 June	Basle	0	7
1962	2 May	Glasgow	2	3
1983	21 Sept	Glasgow	2	0
wc1986	13 June	Nezahualcoyotl	0	0

		v USA	S	USA
1952	30 Apr	Glasgow	6	0
1992	17 May	Denver	1	0
1996	26 May	New Britain	1	2
1998	30 May	Washington	0	0

		v USSR	S	USSR
1967	10 May	Glasgow	0	2
1971	14 June	Moscow	0	1
wc1982	22 June	Malaga	2	2
1991	6 Feb	Glasgow	0	1

		v YUGOSLAVIA	S	Y
1955	15 May	Belgrade	2	2
1956	21 Nov	Glasgow	2	0
wc1958	8 June	Vasteras	1	1
1972	29 June	Belo Horizonte	2	2
wc1974	22 June	Frankfurt	1	1
1984	12 Sept	Glasgow	6	1
wc1988	19 Oct	Glasgow	1	1
wc1989	6 Sept	Zagreb	1	3

		v ZAIRE	S	Z
wc1974	14 June	Dortmund	2	0

WALES

		v ALBANIA	W	A
EC1994	7 Sept	Cardiff	2	0
EC1995	15 Nov	Tirana	1	1

		v ARGENTINA	W	A
1992	3 June	Tokyo	0	1

		v AUSTRIA	W	A
1954	9 May	Vienna	0	2
EC1955	23 Nov	Wrexham	1	2
EC1974	4 Sept	Vienna	1	2
1975	19 Nov	Wrexham	1	0
1992	29 Apr	Vienna	1	1

		v BELARUS	W	B
EC1998	14 Oct	Cardiff	3	2

		v BELGIUM	W	B
1949	22 May	Liège	1	3
1949	23 Nov	Cardiff	5	1
EC1990	17 Oct	Cardiff	3	1
EC1991	27 Mar	Brussels	1	1
wc1992	18 Nov	Brussels	0	2
wc1993	31 Mar	Cardiff	2	0
wc1997	29 Mar	Cardiff	1	2
wc1997	11 Oct	Brussels	2	3

		v BRAZIL	W	B
wc1958	19 June	Gothenburg	0	1
1962	12 May	Rio de Janeiro	1	3
1962	16 May	São Paulo	1	3
1966	14 May	Rio de Janeiro	1	3
1966	18 May	Belo Horizonte	0	1
1983	12 June	Cardiff	1	1
1991	11 Sept	Cardiff	1	0
1997	12 Nov	Brasilia	0	3

		v BULGARIA	W	B
EC1983	27 Apr	Wrexham	1	0
EC1983	16 Nov	Sofia	0	1
EC1994	14 Dec	Cardiff	0	3
EC1995	29 Mar	Sofia	1	3

		v CANADA	W	C
1986	10 May	Toronto	0	2
1986	20 May	Vancouver	3	0

		v CHILE	W	C
1966	22 May	Santiago	0	2

		v COSTA RICA	W	CR
1990	20 May	Cardiff	1	0

		v CYPRUS	W	C
wc1992	14 Oct	Limassol	1	0
wc1993	13 Oct	Cardiff	2	0

		v CZECHOSLOVAKIA	W	C
wc1957	1 May	Cardiff	1	0
wc1957	26 May	Prague	0	2
EC1971	21 Apr	Swansea	1	3
EC1971	27 Oct	Prague	0	1
wc1977	30 Mar	Wrexham	3	0
wc1977	16 Nov	Prague	0	2
wc1980	19 Nov	Cardiff	1	0
wc1981	9 Sept	Prague	0	2
EC1987	29 Apr	Wrexham	1	1
EC1987	11 Nov	Prague	0	2
wc1993	28 Apr	Ostrava†	1	1
wc1993	8 Sept	Cardiff†	2	2

†Czechoslovakia played as RCS (Republic of Czechs and Slovaks).

		v DENMARK	W	D
wc1964	21 Oct	Copenhagen	0	1
wc1965	1 Dec	Wrexham	4	2
EC1987	9 Sept	Cardiff	1	0
EC1987	14 Oct	Copenhagen	0	1
1990	11 Sept	Copenhagen	0	1
EC1998	10 Oct	Copenhagen	2	1
EC1999	9 June	Liverpool	0	2

		v ESTONIA	W	E
1994	23 May	Tallinn	2	1

		v FINLAND	W	F
EC1971	26 May	Helsinki	1	0
EC1971	13 Oct	Swansea	3	0
EC1987	10 Sept	Helsinki	1	1
EC1987	1 Apr	Wrexham	4	0
wc1988	19 Oct	Swansea	2	2
wc1989	6 Sept	Helsinki	0	1

		v FAEROES	W	F
wc1992	9 Sept	Cardiff	6	0
wc1993	6 June	Toftir	3	0

		v FRANCE	W	F
1933	25 May	Paris	1	1
1939	20 May	Paris	1	2
1953	14 May	Paris	1	6
1982	2 June	Toulouse	1	0

v GEORGIA		W	G
EC1994	16 Nov Tbilisi	0	5
EC1995	7 June Cardiff	0	1

v GERMANY		W	G
EC1995	26 Apr Dusseldorf	1	1
EC1995	11 Oct Cardiff	1	2

v EAST GERMANY		W	EG
wc1957	19 May Leipzig	1	2
wc1957	25 Sept Cardiff	4	1
wc1969	16 Apr Dresden	1	2
wc1969	22 Oct Cardiff	1	3

v WEST GERMANY		W	WG
1968	8 May Cardiff	1	1
1969	26 Mar Frankfurt	1	1
1976	6 Oct Cardiff	0	2
1977	14 Dec Dortmund	1	1
EC1979	2 May Wrexham	0	2
EC1979	17 Oct Cologne	1	5
wc1989	31 May Cardiff	0	0
wc1989	15 Nov Cologne	1	2
EC1991	5 June Cardiff	1	0
EC1991	16 Oct Nuremberg	1	4

v GREECE		W	G
wc1964	9 Dec Athens	0	2
wc1965	17 Mar Cardiff	4	1

v HOLLAND		W	H
wc1988	14 Sept Amsterdam	0	1
wc1989	11 Oct Wrexham	1	2
1992	30 May Utrecht	0	4
wc1996	5 Oct Cardiff	1	3
wc1996	9 Nov Eindhoven	1	7

v HUNGARY		W	H
wc1958	8 June Sanviken	1	1
wc1958	17 June Stockholm	2	1
1961	28 May Budapest	2	3
EC1962	7 Nov Budapest	1	3
EC1963	20 Mar Cardiff	1	1
EC1974	30 Oct Cardiff	2	0
EC1975	16 Apr Budapest	2	1
1985	16 Oct Cardiff	0	3

v ICELAND		W	I
wc1980	2 June Reykjavik	4	0
wc1981	14 Oct Swansea	2	2
wc1984	12 Sept Reykjavik	0	1
wc1984	14 Nov Cardiff	2	1
1991	1 May Cardiff	1	0

v IRAN		W	I
1978	18 Apr Teheran	1	0

v REPUBLIC OF IRELAND		W	RI
1960	28 Sept Dublin	3	2
1979	11 Sept Swansea	2	1
1981	24 Feb Dublin	3	1
1986	26 Mar Dublin	1	0
1990	28 Mar Dublin	0	1
1991	6 Feb Wrexham	0	3
1992	19 Feb Dublin	1	0
1993	17 Feb Dublin	1	2
1997	11 Feb Cardiff	0	0

v ISRAEL		W	I
wc1958	15 Jan Tel Aviv	2	0
wc1958	5 Feb Cardiff	2	0
1984	10 June Tel Aviv	0	0
1989	8 Feb Tel Aviv	3	3

v ITALY		W	I
1965	1 May Florence	1	4
wc1968	23 Oct Cardiff	0	1
wc1969	4 Nov Rome	1	4
1988	4 June Brescia	1	0
1996	24 Jan Terni	0	3
EC1998	5 Sept Liverpool	0	2
EC1999	5 June Bologna	0	4

v JAMAICA		W	J
1998	25 Mar Cardiff	0	0

v JAPAN		W	J
1992	7 June Matsuyama	1	0

v KUWAIT		W	K
1977	6 Sept Wrexham	0	0
1977	20 Sept Kuwait	0	0

v LUXEMBOURG		W	L
EC1974	20 Nov Swansea	5	0
EC1975	1 May Luxembourg	3	1
EC1990	14 Nov Luxembourg	1	0
EC1991	13 Nov Cardiff	1	0

v MALTA		W	M
EC1978	25 Oct Wrexham	7	0
EC1979	2 June Valletta	2	0
1988	1 June Valletta	3	2
1998	3 June Valletta	3	0

v MEXICO		W	M
wc1958	11 June Stockholm	1	1
1962	22 May Mexico City	1	2

v MOLDOVA		W	M
EC1994	12 Oct Kishinev	2	3
EC1995	6 Sept Cardiff	1	0

v NORWAY		W	N
EC1982	22 Sept Swansea	1	0
EC1983	21 Sept Oslo	0	0
1984	6 June Trondheim	0	1
1985	26 Feb Wrexham	1	1
1985	5 June Bergen	2	4
1994	9 Mar Cardiff	1	3

v POLAND		W	P
wc1973	28 Mar Cardiff	2	0
wc1973	26 Sept Katowice	0	3
1991	29 May Radom	0	0

v PORTUGAL		W	P
1949	15 May Lisbon	2	3
1951	12 May Cardiff	2	1

v ROMANIA		W	R
EC1970	11 Nov Cardiff	0	0
EC1971	24 Nov Bucharest	0	2
1983	12 Oct Wrexham	5	0
wc1992	20 May Bucharest	1	5
wc1993	17 Nov Cardiff	1	2

v SAN MARINO		W	SM
wc1996	2 June Serravalle	5	0
wc1996	31 Aug Cardiff	6	0

v SAUDI ARABIA		W	SA
1986	25 Feb Dahran	2	1

v SPAIN		W	S
wc1961	19 Apr Cardiff	1	2
wc1961	18 May Madrid	1	1
1982	24 Mar Valencia	1	1
wc1984	17 Oct Seville	0	3
wc1985	30 Apr Wrexham	3	0

		v SWEDEN	W	S
wc1958	15 June	Stockholm	0	0
1988	27 Apr	Stockholm	1	4
1989	26 Apr	Wrexham	0	2
1990	25 Apr	Stockholm	2	4
1994	20 Apr	Wrexham	0	2

		v SWITZERLAND	W	S
1949	26 May	Berne	0	4
1951	16 May	Wrexham	3	2
1996	24 Apr	Lugano	0	2
EC1999	31 Mar	Zurich	0	2

		v TUNISIA	W	T
1998	6 June	Tunis	0	4

		v TURKEY	W	T
EC1978	29 Nov	Wrexham	1	0
EC1979	21 Nov	Izmir	0	1
wc1980	15 Oct	Cardiff	4	0
wc1981	25 Mar	Ankara	1	0
wc1996	14 Dec	Cardiff	0	0
wc1997	20 Aug	Istanbul	4	6

		v REST OF UNITED KINGDOM	W	UK
1951	5 Dec	Cardiff	3	2
1969	28 July	Cardiff	0	1

		v URUGUAY	W	U
1986	21 Apr	Wrexham	0	0

		v USSR	W	USSR
wc1965	30 May	Moscow	1	2
wc1965	27 Oct	Cardiff	2	1
wc1981	30 May	Wrexham	0	0
wc1981	18 Nov	Tbilisi	0	3
1987	18 Feb	Swansea	0	0

		v YUGOSLAVIA	W	Y
1953	21 May	Belgrade	2	5
1954	22 Nov	Cardiff	1	3
EC1976	24 Apr	Zagreb	0	2
EC1976	22 May	Cardiff	1	1
EC1982	15 Dec	Titograd	4	4
EC1983	14 Dec	Cardiff	1	1
1988	23 Mar	Swansea	1	2

NORTHERN IRELAND

		v ALBANIA	NI	A
wc1965	7 May	Belfast	4	1
wc1965	24 Nov	Tirana	1	1
EC1982	15 Dec	Tirana	0	0
EC1983	27 Apr	Belfast	1	0
wc1992	9 Sept	Belfast	3	0
wc1993	17 Feb	Tirana	2	1
wc1996	14 Dec	Belfast	2	0
wc1997	10 Sept	Zurich	0	1

		v ALGERIA	NI	A
wc1986	3 June	Guadalajara	1	1

		v ARGENTINA	NI	A
wc1958	11 June	Halmstad	1	3

		v ARMENIA	NI	A
wc1996	5 Oct	Belfast	1	1
wc1997	30 Apr	Erevan	0	0

		v AUSTRALIA	NI	A
1980	11 June	Sydney	2	1
1980	15 June	Melbourne	1	1
1980	18 June	Adelaide	2	1

		v AUSTRIA	NI	A
wc1982	1 July	Madrid	2	2
EC1982	13 Oct	Vienna	0	2
EC1983	21 Sept	Belfast	3	1
EC1990	14 Nov	Vienna	0	0
EC1991	16 Oct	Belfast	2	1
EC1994	12 Oct	Vienna	2	1
EC1995	15 Nov	Belfast	5	3

		v BELGIUM	NI	B
wc1976	10 Nov	Liège	0	2
wc1977	16 Nov	Belfast	3	0
1997	11 Feb	Belfast	3	0

		v BRAZIL	NI	B
wc1986	12 June	Guadalajara	0	3

		v BULGARIA	NI	B
wc1972	18 Oct	Sofia	0	3
wc1973	26 Sept	Sheffield	0	0
EC1978	29 Nov	Sofia	2	0
EC1979	2 May	Belfast	2	0

		v CANADA	NI	C
1995	22 May	Edmonton	0	2
1999	27 Apr	Belfast	1	1

		v CHILE	NI	C
1989	26 May	Belfast	0	1
1995	25 May	Edmonton	1	2

		v COLOMBIA	NI	C
1994	4 June	Boston	0	2

		v CYPRUS	NI	C
EC1971	3 Feb	Nicosia	3	0
EC1971	21 Apr	Belfast	5	0
wc1973	14 Feb	Nicosia	0	1
wc1973	8 May	London	3	0

		v CZECHOSLOVAKIA	NI	C
wc1958	8 June	Halmstad	1	0
wc1958	17 June	Malmo	2	1*

*After extra time

		v DENMARK	NI	D
EC1978	25 Oct	Belfast	2	1
EC1979	6 June	Copenhagen	0	4
1986	26 Mar	Belfast	1	1
EC1990	17 Oct	Belfast	1	1
EC1991	13 Nov	Odense	1	2
wc1992	18 Nov	Belfast	0	1
wc1993	13 Oct	Copenhagen	0	1

		v FAEROES	NI	F
EC1991	1 May	Belfast	1	1
EC1991	11 Sept	Landskrona	5	0

		v FINLAND	NI	F
wc1984	27 May	Pori	0	1
wc1984	14 Nov	Belfast	2	1
EC1998	10 Oct	Belfast	1	0

		v FRANCE	NI	F
1951	12 May	Belfast	2	2
1952	11 Nov	Paris	1	3
wc1958	19 June	Norrkoping	0	4
1982	24 Mar	Paris	0	4
wc1982	4 July	Madrid	1	4
1986	26 Feb	Paris	0	0
1988	27 Apr	Belfast	0	0

		v GERMANY	NI	G
1992	2 June	Bremen	1	1
1996	29 May	Belfast	1	1
wc1996	9 Nov	Nuremberg	1	1

			NI	G
wc1997	20 Aug	Belfast	1	3
EC1999	27 Mar	Belfast	0	3

v WEST GERMANY			NI	WG
wc1958	15 June	Malmo	2	2
wc1960	26 Oct	Belfast	3	4
wc1961	10 May	Hamburg	1	2
1966	7 May	Belfast	0	2
1977	27 Apr	Cologne	0	5
EC1982	17 Nov	Belfast	1	0
EC1983	16 Nov	Hamburg	1	0

v GREECE			NI	G
wc1961	3 May	Athens	1	2
wc1961	17 Oct	Belfast	2	0
1988	17 Feb	Athens	2	3

v HOLLAND			NI	H
1962	9 May	Rotterdam	0	4
wc1965	17 Mar	Belfast	2	1
wc1965	7 Apr	Rotterdam	0	0
wc1976	13 Oct	Rotterdam	2	2
wc1977	12 Oct	Belfast	0	1

v HONDURAS			NI	H
wc1982	21 June	Zaragoza	1	1

v HUNGARY			NI	H
wc1988	19 Oct	Budapest	0	1
wc1989	6 Sept	Belfast	1	2

v ICELAND			NI	I
wc1977	11 June	Reykjavik	0	1
wc1977	21 Sept	Belfast	2	0

v REPUBLIC OF IRELAND			NI	RI
EC1978	20 Sept	Dublin	0	0
EC1979	21 Nov	Belfast	1	0
wc1988	14 Sept	Belfast	0	0
wc1989	11 Oct	Dublin	0	3
wc1993	31 Mar	Dublin	0	3
wc1993	17 Nov	Belfast	1	1
EC1994	16 Nov	Belfast	0	4
EC1995	29 Mar	Dublin	1	1
1999	29 May	Dublin	1	0

v ISRAEL			NI	I
1968	10 Sept	Jaffa	3	2
1976	3 Mar	Tel Aviv	1	1
wc1980	26 Mar	Tel Aviv	0	0
wc1981	18 Nov	Belfast	1	0
1984	16 Oct	Belfast	3	0
1987	18 Feb	Tel Aviv	1	1

v ITALY			NI	I
wc1957	25 Apr	Rome	0	1
1957	4 Dec	Belfast	2	2
wc1958	15 Jan	Belfast	2	1
1961	25 Apr	Bologna	2	3
1997	22 Jan	Palermo	0	2

v LATVIA			NI	L
wc1993	2 June	Riga	2	1
wc1993	8 Sept	Belfast	2	0
EC1995	26 Apr	Riga	1	0
EC1995	7 June	Belfast	1	2

v LIECHTENSTEIN			NI	L
EC1994	20 Apr	Belfast	4	1
EC1995	11 Oct	Eschen	4	0

v LITHUANIA			NI	L
wc1992	28 Apr	Belfast	2	2
wc1993	25 May	Vilnius	1	0

v MALTA			NI	M
wc1988	21 May	Belfast	3	0
wc1989	26 Apr	Valletta	2	0

v MEXICO			NI	M
1966	22 June	Belfast	4	1
1994	11 June	Miami	0	3

v MOLDOVA			NI	M
EC1998	18 Nov	Belfast	2	2
EC1999	31 Mar	Chisinau	0	0

v MOROCCO			NI	M
1986	23 Apr	Belfast	2	1

v NORWAY			NI	N
EC1974	4 Sept	Oslo	1	2
EC1975	29 Oct	Belfast	3	0
1990	27 Mar	Belfast	2	3
1996	27 Mar	Belfast	0	2

v POLAND			NI	P
EC1962	10 Oct	Katowice	2	0
EC1962	28 Nov	Belfast	2	0
1988	23 Mar	Belfast	1	1
1991	5 Feb	Belfast	3	1

v PORTUGAL			NI	P
wc1957	16 Jan	Lisbon	1	1
wc1957	1 May	Belfast	3	0
wc1973	28 Mar	Coventry	1	1
wc1973	14 Nov	Lisbon	1	1
wc1980	19 Nov	Lisbon	0	1
wc1981	29 Apr	Belfast	1	0
EC1994	7 Sept	Belfast	1	2
EC1995	3 Sept	Lisbon	1	1
wc1997	29 Mar	Belfast	0	0
wc1997	11 Oct	Lisbon	0	1

v ROMANIA			NI	R
wc1984	12 Sept	Belfast	3	2
wc1985	16 Oct	Bucharest	1	0
1994	23 Mar	Belfast	2	0

v SLOVAKIA			NI	S
1998	25 Mar	Belfast	1	0

v SPAIN			NI	S
1958	15 Oct	Madrid	2	6
1963	30 May	Bilbao	1	1
1963	30 Oct	Belfast	0	1
EC1970	11 Nov	Seville	0	3
EC1972	16 Feb	Hull	1	1
wc1982	25 June	Valencia	1	0
1985	27 Mar	Palma	0	0
wc1986	7 June	Guadalajara	1	2
wc1988	21 Dec	Seville	0	4
wc1989	8 Feb	Belfast	0	2
wc1992	14 Oct	Belfast	0	0
wc1993	28 Apr	Seville	1	3
1998	2 June	Santander	1	4

v SWEDEN			NI	S
EC1974	30 Oct	Solna	2	0
EC1975	3 Sept	Belfast	1	2
wc1980	15 Oct	Belfast	3	0
wc1981	3 June	Solna	0	1
1996	24 Apr	Belfast	1	2

v SWITZERLAND			NI	S
wc1964	14 Oct	Belfast	1	0
wc1964	14 Nov	Lausanne	1	2
1998	22 Apr	Belfast	1	0

v THAILAND			NI	T
1997	21 May	Bangkok	0	0

v TURKEY			NI	T
wc1968	23 Oct	Belfast	4	1
wc1968	11 Dec	Istanbul	3	0
EC1983	30 Mar	Belfast	2	1
EC1983	12 Oct	Ankara	0	1

			NI	T
wc1985	1 May	Belfast	2	0
wc1985	11 Sept	Izmir	0	0
EC1986	12 Nov	Izmir	0	0
EC1987	11 Nov	Belfast	1	0
EC1998	5 Sept	Istanbul	0	3

		v UKRAINE	NI	U
wc1996	31 Aug	Belfast	0	1
wc1997	2 Apr	Kiev	1	2

		v URUGUAY	NI	U
1964	29 Apr	Belfast	3	0
1990	18 May	Belfast	1	0

		v USSR	NI	USSR
wc1969	19 Sept	Belfast	0	0
wc1969	22 Oct	Moscow	0	2
EC1971	22 Sept	Moscow	0	1
EC1971	13 Oct	Belfast	1	1

		v YUGOSLAVIA	NI	Y
EC1975	16 Mar	Belfast	1	0
EC1975	19 Nov	Belgrade	0	1
wc1982	17 June	Zaragoza	0	0
EC1987	29 Apr	Belfast	1	2
EC1987	14 Oct	Sarajevo	0	3
EC1990	12 Sept	Belfast	0	2
EC1991	27 Mar	Belgrade	1	4

REPUBLIC OF IRELAND

		v ALBANIA	RI	A
wc1992	26 May	Dublin	2	0
wc1993	26 May	Tirana	2	1

		v ALGERIA	RI	A
1982	28 Apr	Algiers	0	2

		v ARGENTINA	RI	A
1951	13 May	Dublin	0	1
1979	29 May	Dublin	0	0*
1980	16 May	Dublin	0	1
1998	22 Apr	Dublin	0	2

* Not considered a full international

		v AUSTRIA	RI	A
1952	7 May	Vienna	0	6
1953	25 Mar	Dublin	4	0
1958	14 Mar	Vienna	1	3
1962	8 Apr	Dublin	2	3
EC1963	25 Sept	Vienna	0	0
EC1963	13 Oct	Dublin	3	2
1966	22 May	Vienna	0	1
1968	10 Nov	Dublin	2	2
EC1971	30 May	Dublin	1	4
EC1971	10 Oct	Linz	0	6
EC1995	11 June	Dublin	1	3
EC1995	6 Sept	Vienna	1	3

		v BELGIUM	RI	B
1928	12 Feb	Liège	4	2
1929	30 Apr	Dublin	4	0
1930	11 May	Brussels	3	1
wc1934	25 Feb	Dublin	4	4
1949	24 Apr	Dublin	0	2
1950	10 May	Brussels	1	5
1965	24 Mar	Dublin	0	2
1966	25 May	Liège	3	2
wc1980	15 Oct	Dublin	1	1
wc1981	25 Mar	Brussels	0	1
EC1986	10 Sept	Brussels	2	2
EC1987	29 Apr	Dublin	0	0
wc1997	29 Oct	Dublin	1	1
wc1997	16 Nov	Brussels	1	2

		v BOLIVIA	RI	B
1994	24 May	Dublin	1	0
1996	15 June	New Jersey	3	0

		v BRAZIL	RI	B
1974	5 May	Rio de Janeiro	1	2
1982	27 May	Uberlandia	0	7
1987	23 May	Dublin	1	0

		v BULGARIA	RI	B
wc1977	1 June	Sofia	1	2
wc1977	12 Oct	Dublin	0	0
EC1979	19 May	Sofia	0	1
EC1979	17 Oct	Dublin	3	0

			RI	B
wc1987	1 Apr	Sofia	1	2
wc1987	14 Oct	Dublin	2	0

		v CHILE	RI	C
1960	30 Mar	Dublin	2	0
1972	21 June	Recife	1	2
1974	12 May	Santiago	2	1
1982	22 May	Santiago	0	1
1991	22 May	Dublin	1	1

		v CHINA	RI	C
1984	3 June	Sapporo	1	0

		v CROATIA	RI	C
1996	2 June	Dublin	2	2
EC1998	5 Sept	Dublin	2	0

		v CYPRUS	RI	C
wc1980	26 Mar	Nicosia	3	2
wc1980	19 Nov	Dublin	6	0

		v CZECHOSLOVAKIA	RI	C
1938	18 May	Prague	2	2
EC1959	5 Apr	Dublin	2	0
EC1959	10 May	Bratislava	0	4
wc1961	8 Oct	Dublin	1	3
wc1961	29 Oct	Prague	1	7
EC1967	21 May	Dublin	0	2
EC1967	22 Nov	Prague	2	1
wc1969	4 May	Dublin	1	2
wc1969	7 Oct	Prague	0	3
1979	26 Sept	Prague	1	4
1981	29 Apr	Dublin	3	1
1986	27 May	Reykjavik	1	0

		v CZECH REPUBLIC	RI	C
1994	5 June	Dublin	1	3
1996	24 Apr	Prague	0	2
1998	25 Mar	Olomouc	1	2

		v DENMARK	RI	D
wc1956	3 Oct	Dublin	2	1
wc1957	2 Oct	Copenhagen	2	0
wc1968	4 Dec	Dublin	1	1
(abandoned after 51 mins)				
wc1969	27 May	Copenhagen	0	2
wc1969	15 Oct	Dublin	1	1
EC1978	24 May	Copenhagen	3	3
EC1979	2 May	Dublin	2	0
wc1984	14 Nov	Copenhagen	0	3
wc1985	13 Nov	Dublin	1	4
wc1992	14 Oct	Copenhagen	0	0
wc1993	28 Apr	Dublin	1	1

		v ECUADOR	RI	E
1972	19 June	Natal	3	2

		v EGYPT	*RI*	*E*
wc1990	17 June	Palermo	0	0

		v ENGLAND	*RI*	*E*
1946	30 Sept	Dublin	0	1
1949	21 Sept	Everton	2	0
wc1957	8 May	Wembley	1	5
wc1957	19 May	Dublin	1	1
1964	24 May	Dublin	1	3
1976	8 Sept	Wembley	1	1
EC1978	25 Oct	Dublin	1	1
EC1980	6 Feb	Wembley	0	2
1985	26 Mar	Wembley	1	2
EC1988	12 June	Stuttgart	1	0
wc1990	11 June	Cagliari	1	1
EC1990	14 Nov	Dublin	1	1
EC1991	27 Mar	Wembley	1	1
1995	15 Feb	Dublin	1	0
		(abandoned after 27 mins)		

		v FINLAND	*RI*	*F*
wc1949	8 Sept	Dublin	3	0
wc1949	9 Oct	Helsinki	1	1
1990	16 May	Dublin	1	1

		v FRANCE	*RI*	*F*
1937	23 May	Paris	2	0
1952	16 Nov	Dublin	1	1
wc1953	4 Oct	Dublin	3	5
wc1953	25 Nov	Paris	0	1
wc1972	15 Nov	Dublin	2	1
wc1973	19 May	Paris	1	1
wc1976	17 Nov	Paris	0	2
wc1977	30 Mar	Dublin	1	0
wc1980	28 Oct	Paris	0	2
wc1981	14 Oct	Dublin	3	2
1989	7 Feb	Dublin	0	0

		v GERMANY	*RI*	*G*
1935	8 May	Dortmund	1	3
1936	17 Oct	Dublin	5	2
1939	23 May	Bremen	1	1
1994	29 May	Hanover	2	0

		v WEST GERMANY	*RI*	*WG*
1951	17 Oct	Dublin	3	2
1952	4 May	Cologne	0	3
1955	28 May	Hamburg	1	2
1956	25 Nov	Dublin	3	0
1960	11 May	Dusseldorf	1	0
1966	4 May	Dublin	0	4
1970	9 May	Berlin	1	2
1975	1 Mar	Dublin	1	0†
1979	22 May	Dublin	1	3
1981	21 May	Bremen	0	3†
1989	6 Sept	Dublin	1	1
†v West Germany 'B'				

		v HOLLAND	*RI*	*N*
1932	8 May	Amsterdam	2	0
1934	8 Apr	Amsterdam	2	5
1935	8 Dec	Dublin	3	5
1955	1 May	Dublin	1	0
1956	10 May	Rotterdam	4	1
wc1980	10 Sept	Dublin	2	1
wc1981	9 Sept	Rotterdam	2	2
EC1982	22 Sept	Rotterdam	1	2
EC1983	12 Oct	Dublin	2	3
EC1988	18 June	Gelsenkirchen	0	1
wc1990	21 June	Palermo	1	1
1994	20 Apr	Tilburg	1	0
wc1994	4 July	Orlando	0	2
EC1995	13 Dec	Liverpool	0	2
1996	4 June	Rotterdam	1	3

		v HUNGARY	*RI*	*H*
1934	15 Dec	Dublin	2	4
1936	3 May	Budapest	3	3
1936	6 Dec	Dublin	2	3
1939	19 Mar	Cork	2	2
1939	18 May	Budapest	2	2
wc1969	8 June	Dublin	1	2
wc1969	5 Nov	Budapest	0	4
wc1989	8 Mar	Budapest	0	0
wc1989	4 June	Dublin	2	0
1991	11 Sept	Gyor	2	1

		v ICELAND	*RI*	*I*
EC1962	12 Aug	Dublin	4	2
EC1962	2 Sept	Reykjavik	1	1
EC1982	13 Oct	Dublin	2	0
EC1983	21 Sept	Reykjavik	3	0
1986	25 May	Reykjavik	2	1
wc1996	10 Nov	Dublin	0	0
wc1997	6 Sept	Reykjavik	4	2

		v IRAN	*RI*	*I*
1972	18 June	Recife	2	1

		v N. IRELAND	*RI*	*NI*
EC1978	20 Sept	Dublin	0	0
EC1979	21 Nov	Belfast	0	1
wc1988	14 Sept	Belfast	0	0
wc1989	11 Oct	Dublin	3	0
wc1993	31 Mar	Dublin	3	0
wc1993	17 Nov	Belfast	1	1
EC1994	16 Nov	Belfast	4	0
EC1995	29 Mar	Dublin	1	1
1999	29 May	Dublin	0	1

		v ISRAEL	*RI*	*I*
1984	4 Apr	Tel Aviv	0	3
1985	27 May	Tel Aviv	0	0
1987	10 Nov	Dublin	5	0

		v ITALY	*RI*	*I*
1926	21 Mar	Turin	0	3
1927	23 Apr	Dublin	1	2
EC1970	8 Dec	Rome	0	3
EC1971	10 May	Dublin	1	2
1985	5 Feb	Dublin	1	2
wc1990	30 June	Rome	0	1
1992	4 June	Foxboro	0	2
wc1994	18 June	New York	1	0

		v LATVIA	*RI*	*L*
wc1992	9 Sept	Dublin	4	0
wc1993	2 June	Riga	2	1
EC1994	7 Sept	Riga	3	0
EC1995	11 Oct	Dublin	2	1

		v LIECHTENSTEIN	*RI*	*L*
EC1994	12 Oct	Dublin	4	0
EC1995	3 June	Eschen	0	0
wc1996	31 Aug	Eschen	5	0
wc1997	21 May	Dublin	5	0

		v LITHUANIA	*RI*	*L*
wc1993	16 June	Vilnius	1	0
wc1993	8 Sept	Dublin	2	0
wc1997	20 Aug	Dublin	0	0
wc1997	10 Sept	Vilnius	2	1

		v LUXEMBOURG	*RI*	*I*
1936	9 May	Luxembourg	5	1
wc1953	28 Oct	Dublin	4	0
wc1954	7 Mar	Luxembourg	1	0
EC1987	28 May	Luxembourg	2	0
EC1987	9 Sept	Dublin	2	1

v MACEDONIA			RI	M
wc1996	9 Oct	Dublin	3	0
wc1997	2 Apr	Skopje	2	3
EC1999	9 June	Dublin	1	0

v MALTA			RI	M
EC1983	30 Mar	Valletta	1	0
EC1983	16 Nov	Dublin	8	0
wc1989	28 May	Dublin	2	0
wc1989	15 Nov	Valletta	2	0
1990	2 June	Valletta	3	0
EC1998	14 Oct	Dublin	5	0

v MEXICO			RI	M
1984	8 Aug	Dublin	0	0
wc1994	24 June	Orlando	1	2
1996	13 June	New Jersey	2	2
1998	23 May	Dublin	0	0

v MOROCCO			RI	M
1990	12 Sept	Dublin	1	0

v NORWAY			RI	N
wc1937	10 Oct	Oslo	2	3
wc1937	7 Nov	Dublin	3	3
1950	26 Nov	Dublin	2	2
1951	30 May	Oslo	3	2
1954	8 Nov	Dublin	2	1
1955	25 May	Oslo	3	1
1960	6 Nov	Dublin	3	1
1964	13 May	Oslo	4	1
1973	6 June	Oslo	1	1
1976	24 Mar	Dublin	3	0
1978	21 May	Oslo	0	0
wc1984	17 Oct	Oslo	0	1
wc1985	1 May	Dublin	0	0
1988	1 June	Oslo	0	0
wc1994	28 June	New York	0	0

v PARAGUAY			RI	P
1999	10 Feb	Dublin	2	0

v POLAND			RI	P
1938	22 May	Warsaw	0	6
1938	13 Nov	Dublin	3	2
1958	11 May	Katowice	2	2
1958	5 Oct	Dublin	2	2
1964	10 May	Kracow	1	3
1964	25 Oct	Dublin	3	2
1968	15 May	Dublin	2	2
1968	30 Oct	Katowice	0	1
1970	6 May	Dublin	1	2
1970	23 Sept	Dublin	0	2
1973	16 May	Wroclaw	0	2
1973	21 Oct	Dublin	1	0
1976	26 May	Poznan	2	0
1977	24 Apr	Dublin	0	0
1978	12 Apr	Lodz	0	3
1981	23 May	Bydgoszcz	0	3
1984	23 May	Dublin	0	0
1986	12 Nov	Warsaw	0	1
1988	22 May	Dublin	3	1
EC1991	1 May	Dublin	0	0
EC1991	16 Oct	Poznan	3	3

v PORTUGAL			RI	P
1946	16 June	Lisbon	1	3
1947	4 May	Dublin	0	2
1948	23 May	Lisbon	0	2
1949	22 May	Dublin	1	0
1972	25 June	Recife	1	2

			RI	P
1992	7 June	Boston	2	0
EC1995	26 Apr	Dublin	1	0
EC1995	15 Nov	Lisbon	0	3
1996	29 May	Dublin	0	1

v ROMANIA			RI	R
1988	23 Mar	Dublin	2	0
wc1990	25 June	Genoa	0	0*
wc1997	30 Apr	Bucharest	0	1
wc1997	11 Oct	Dublin	1	1

*After extra time

v RUSSIA			RI	R
1994	23 Mar	Dublin	0	0
1996	27 Mar	Dublin	0	2

v SCOTLAND			RI	S
wc1961	3 May	Glasgow	1	4
wc1961	7 May	Dublin	0	3
1963	9 June	Dublin	1	0
1969	21 Sept	Dublin	1	1
EC1986	15 Oct	Dublin	0	0
EC1987	18 Feb	Glasgow	1	0

v SPAIN			RI	S
1931	26 Apr	Barcelona	1	1
1931	13 Dec	Dublin	0	5
1946	23 June	Madrid	1	0
1947	2 Mar	Dublin	3	2
1948	30 May	Barcelona	1	2
1949	12 June	Dublin	1	4
1952	1 June	Madrid	0	6
1955	27 Nov	Dublin	2	2
EC1964	11 Mar	Seville	1	5
EC1964	8 Apr	Dublin	0	2
wc1965	5 May	Dublin	1	0
wc1965	27 Oct	Seville	1	4
wc1965	10 Nov	Paris	0	1
EC1966	23 Oct	Dublin	0	0
EC1966	7 Dec	Valencia	0	2
1977	9 Feb	Dublin	0	1
EC1982	17 Nov	Dublin	3	3
EC1983	27 Apr	Zaragoza	0	2
1985	26 May	Cork	0	0
wc1988	16 Nov	Seville	0	2
wc1989	26 Apr	Dublin	1	0
wc1992	18 Nov	Seville	0	0
wc1993	13 Oct	Dublin	1	3

v SWEDEN			RI	S
wc1949	2 June	Stockholm	1	3
wc1949	13 Nov	Dublin	1	3
1959	1 Nov	Dublin	3	2
1960	18 May	Malmo	1	4
EC1970	14 Oct	Dublin	1	1
EC1970	28 Oct	Malmo	0	1
1999	28 Apr	Dublin	2	0

v SWITZERLAND			RI	S
1935	5 May	Basle	0	1
1936	17 Mar	Dublin	1	0
1937	17 May	Berne	1	0
1938	18 Sept	Dublin	4	0
1948	5 Dec	Dublin	0	1
EC1975	11 May	Dublin	2	1
EC1975	21 May	Berne	0	1
1980	30 Apr	Dublin	2	0
wc1985	2 June	Dublin	3	0
wc1985	11 Sept	Berne	0	0
1992	25 Mar	Dublin	2	1

		v TRINIDAD & TOBAGO	*RI*	*TT*
1982	30 May	Port of Spain	1	2

		v TUNISIA	*RI*	*T*
1988	19 Oct	Dublin	4	0

		v TURKEY	*RI*	*T*
EC1966	16 Nov	Dublin	2	1
EC1967	22 Feb	Ankara	1	2
EC1974	20 Nov	Izmir	1	1
EC1975	29 Oct	Dublin	4	0
1976	13 Oct	Ankara	3	3
1978	5 Apr	Dublin	4	2
1990	26 May	Izmir	0	0
EC1990	17 Oct	Dublin	5	0
EC1991	13 Nov	Istanbul	3	1

		v URUGUAY	*RI*	*U*
1974	8 May	Montevideo	0	2
1986	23 Apr	Dublin	1	1

		v USA	*RI*	*USA*
1979	29 Oct	Dublin	3	2
1991	1 June	Boston	1	1
1992	29 Apr	Dublin	4	1
1992	30 May	Washington	1	3
1996	9 June	Boston	1	2

		v USSR	*RI*	*USSR*
wc1972	18 Oct	Dublin	1	2
wc1973	13 May	Moscow	0	1
EC1974	30 Oct	Dublin	3	0
EC1975	18 May	Kiev	1	2
wc1984	12 Sept	Dublin	1	0
wc1985	16 Oct	Moscow	0	2
EC1988	15 June	Hanover	1	1
1990	25 Apr	Dublin	1	0

		v WALES	*RI*	*W*
1960	28 Sept	Dublin	2	3
1979	11 Sept	Swansea	1	2
1981	24 Feb	Dublin	1	3
1986	26 Mar	Dublin	0	1
1990	28 Mar	Dublin	1	0
1991	6 Feb	Wrexham	3	0
1992	19 Feb	Dublin	0	1
1993	17 Feb	Dublin	2	1
1997	11 Feb	Cardiff	0	0

		v YUGOSLAVIA	*RI*	*Y*
1955	19 Sept	Dublin	1	4
1988	27 Apr	Dublin	2	0
EC1998	18 Nov	Belgrade	0	1

England's David Beckham tackled fiercely by Stefan Schwarz during the 0-0 draw against Sweden in the European Championship qualifier at Wembley. (Colorsport)

OTHER BRITISH AND IRISH INTERNATIONAL MATCHES 1998–99

FRIENDLIES

Wembley, 18 November 1998, 38,535

England (2) 2 *(Anderton 22, Merson 39)*

Czech Republic (0) 0

England: Martyn; Anderton, Le Saux, Keown, Ferdinand R, Campbell, Beckham, Butt, Dublin, Wright (Fowler 71), Merson (Hendrie 77).
Czech Republic: Kouba; Novotny (Baranek 46), Votava, Repka, Poborsky, Bejbl, Nemec (Kotulek 46), Berger, Latal (Vonasek 46), Smicer (Lokvenc 46), Kuka.
Referee: Meier (Switzerland).

Wembley, 10 February 1999, 74,111

England (0) 0

France (0) 2 *(Anelka 69, 76)*

England: Seaman (Martyn 46); Dixon (Ferdinand R 71), Le Saux, Keown (Wilcox 86), Adams, Redknapp (Scholes 85), Beckham, Ince, Shearer, Owen (Cole 65), Anderton.
France: Barthez; Thuram, Blanc (Leboeuf 46), Desailly, Lizarazu, Pires (Dugarry 46), Zidane, Deschamps (Candela 90), Petit, Djorkaeff (Wiltord 83), Anelka (Vieira 83).
Referee: Krug (Germany).

Dublin, 10 February 1999, 27,600

Republic of Ireland (1) 2 *(Irwin 37 (pen), Connolly 74)*

Paraguay (0) 0

Republic of Ireland: Given (Kelly A 66); Irwin, Harte (Babb 71), McAteer (McLoughlin 81), Cunningham, Breen, Kinsella (Carsley 66), Roy Keane, Quinn (Cascarino 69), Robbie Keane (Connolly 66), Duff.
Paraguay: Tavarelli; Rolon, Caniza, Ortiz, Valdez, Aguilera, Paredes, Acosta, Franco (Esquivel 79), Caballero (Britez 71), Roman (Peralta 63).
Referee: Orrason (Iceland).

Belfast, 27 April 1999, 7663

Northern Ireland (0) 1 *(Parker 90 (og))*

Canada (0) 1 *(Bircham 67)*

Northern Ireland: Taylor (Wright 46); Hughes A, Horlock, Williams M, Hunter, Lomas, McCarthy (Hamill 60), Mulryne (Sonner 81), Dowie (Ferguson 74), Coote (McVeigh 74), Rowland.
Canada: Forrest; Clark, Brennan, Watson, Parker, Devos, Xausa (Bircham 59), Dasovic, Staltari (Kusch 65), Peschisolido, Bent.
Referee: McCurry (Scotland).

Michael Owen opens the scoring for England in the European Championship qualifier in Luxembourg.
(Actionimages)

Bremen, 28 April 1999, 27,000

Germany (0) 0
Scotland (0) 1 *(Hutchison 66)*

Germany: Lehmann; Nowotny, Matthaus, Worns, Strunz (Jancker 88), Jeremies (Ramelow 46), Hamann (Ballack 59), Heinrich, Neuville, Bierhoff (Kirsten 59), Heldt.
Scotland: Sullivan; Weir, Davidson (Whyte 79), Boyd, Hendry (Ritchie 66), Lambert (Cameron 84), Gemmill (Jess 59), Durrant (Winters 72), Dodds, Hutchison, Johnston (O'Neil 88).
Referee: Meier (Switzerland).

Budapest, 28 April 1999, 20,000

Hungary (0) 1 *(Hrutka 76)*
England (1) 1 *(Shearer 21 (pen))*

Hungary: Kiraly; Korsos (Toth 65), Hrutka, Sebok, Matyus, Halmai, Pisont (Somogyi 46), Dardal, Dombi, Illes, Korsos.
England: Seaman; Brown (Gray 73), Neville P, Keown, Ferdinand R (Carragher 62), Batty, McManaman (Redknapp 85), Sherwood, Shearer, Phillips (Heskey 83), Butt.
Referee: Frohlick (Germany).

Dublin, 28 April 1999, 29,300

Republic of Ireland (0) 2 *(Kavanagh 75, Kennedy 77)*
Sweden (0) 0

Republic of Ireland: Given; Carr, Staunton, McAteer (Kilbane 46), Cunningham, Breen (Babb 46), Kinsella (Kavanagh 46), McLoughlin, Quinn (Robbie Keane 79), Connolly (Cascarino 71), Kennedy (Duff 79).
Sweden: Kihlstedt; Kamark, Lucic, Andersson P, Bjorklund (Jakobsson 46), Mild (Alexandersson 46), Andersson D, Schwarz, Pettersson (Jonsson M 81), Larsson, Blomqvist.
Referee: Garibian (France).

Dublin, 29 May 1999, 12,100

Republic of Ireland (0) 0
Northern Ireland (0) 1 *(Griffin 85)*

Republic of Ireland: Given; Carr, Maybury, Carsley (McLoughlin 46), Cunningham, Babb, Kinsella (Kavanagh 82), Robbie Keane (Connolly 56), Quinn (Cascarino 72), Duff (O'Neill 56), Kennedy.
Northern Ireland: Taylor (Carroll 46); Patterson, Hughes A, Williams M, Hunter, Lennon (Griffin 79), McCarthy, Robinson, Dowie (Coote 46), Quinn, Rowland (Johnson 73).
Referee: Richards (Wales).

Sol Campbell has proved to be one of the most consistent defenders in the England team in recent seasons.
(ASP)

INTERNATIONAL APPEARANCES 1872–1999

This is a list of full international appearances by Englishmen, Irishmen, Scotsmen and Welshmen in matches against the Home Countries and against foreign nations. It does not include unofficial matches against Commonwealth and Empire countries. The year indicated refers to the season; ie 1998 is the 1997-98 season.

Explanatory code for matches played by all five countries: A represents Austria; Alb, Albania; Alg, Algeria; An, Angola; Arg, Argentina; Arm, Armenia; Aus, Australia; B, Bohemia; Bel, Belgium; Bl, Belarus; Bol, Bolivia; Br, Brazil; Bul, Bulgaria; C,CIS; Ca, Canada; Cam, Cameroon; Ch, Chile; Chn, China; Co, Colombia; Cr, Costa Rica; Cro, Croatia; Cy, Cyprus; Cz, Czechoslovakia; CzR, Czech Republic; D, Denmark; E, England; Ec, Ecuador; Ei, Republic of Ireland; EG, East Germany; Eg, Egypt; Es, Estonia; F, France; Fa, Faeroes; Fi, Finland; G, Germany; Ge, Georgia; Gr, Greece; H, Hungary; Ho, Holland; Hon, Honduras; I, Italy; Ic, Iceland; Ir, Iran; Is, Israel; J, Japan; Jam, Jamaica; K, Kuwait; L, Luxembourg; La, Latvia; Li, Lithuania; Lie, Liechtenstein; M, Mexico; Ma, Malta; Mac, Macedonia; Mal, Malaysia; Mol, Moldova; Mor, Morocco; N, Norway; Ni, Ng, Nigeria; Ni, Northern Ireland; Nz, New Zealand; P, Portugal; Para, Paraguay; Pe, Peru; Pol, Poland; R, Romania; RCS, Republic of Czechs and Slovaks; R of E, Rest of Europe; R of UK, Rest of United Kingdom; R of W, Rest of World; Ru, Russia; S.Af, South Africa; S.Ar, Saudi Arabia; S, Scotland; Se, Sweden; Slo, Slovakia; Sm, San Marino; Sp, Spain; Sw, Switzerland; T, Turkey; Th, Thailand; Tr, Trinidad & Tobago; Tun, Tunisia; U, Uruguay; Uk, Ukraine; US, United States of America; USSR, Soviet Union; W, Wales; WG, West Germany; Y, Yugoslavia; Z, Zaire.
As at July 1999.

ENGLAND

Abbott, W. (Everton), 1902 v W (1)
A'Court, A. (Liverpool), 1958 v Ni, Br, A, USSR; 1959 v W (5)
Adams, T. A. (Arsenal), 1987 v Sp, T, Br; 1988 v WG, T, Y, Ho, H, S, Co, Sw, Ei, Ho, USSR; 1989 v D, Se, S.Ar.; 1991 v Ei (2); 1993 v N, T, Sm, T, Ho, Pol, N; 1994 v Pol, Ho, D, Gr, N; 1995 v US, R, Ei, U; 1996 v Co, N, Sw, P, Chn, Sw, S, Ho, Sp, G; 1997 v Ge (2); 1998 v I, Ch, P, S.Ar, Tun, R, Co, Arg; 1999 v Se, F (57)
Adcock, H. (Leicester C), 1929 v F, Bel, Sp; 1930 v Ni, W (5)
Alcock, C. W. (Wanderers), 1875 v S (1)
Alderson, J. T. (C Palace), 1923 v F (1)
Aldridge, A. (WBA), 1888 v Ni; (with Walsall Town Swifts), 1889 v Ni (2)
Allen, A. (Stoke C) 1960 v Se, W, Ni (3)
Allen, A. (Aston Villa), 1888 v Ni (1)
Allen, C. (QPR), 1984 v Br (sub), U, Ch; (with Tottenham H), 1987 v T; 1988 v Is (5)
Allen, H. (Wolverhampton W), 1888 v S, W, Ni; 1889 v S; 1890 v S (5)
Allen, J. P. (Portsmouth), 1934 v Ni, W (2)
Allen, R. (WBA), 1952 v Sw; 1954 v Y, S; 1955 v WG, W (5)
Alsford, W. J. (Tottenham H), 1935 v S (1)
Amos, A. (Old Carthusians), 1885 v S; 1886 v W (2)
Anderson, R. D. (Old Etonians), 1879 v W (1)
Anderson, S. (Sunderland), 1962 v A, S (2)
Anderson, V. (Nottingham F), 1979 v Cz, Se; 1980 v Bul, Sp; 1981 v N, R, W, S; 1982 v Ni, Ic; 1984 v Ni; (with Arsenal), 1985 v T, Ni, Ei, R, Fi, S, M, US; 1986 v USSR, M; 1987 v Se, Ni (2), Y, Sp, T; (with Manchester U), 1988 v WG, H, Co (30)
Anderton, D. R. (Tottenham H), 1994 v D, Gr, N; 1995 v US, Ei, U, J, Se, Br; 1996 v H, Chn, Sw, S, Ho, Sp, G; 1998 v S.Ar, Mor, Tun, R, Co, Arg; 1999 v Se, Bul, L, CzR, F (27)
Angus, J. (Burnley), 1961 v A (1)
Armfield, J. C. (Blackpool), 1959 v Br, Pe, M, US; 1960 v Y, Sp, H, S; 1961 v L, P, Sp, M, I, A, W, Ni, S; 1962 v A, Sw, Pe, W, Ni, S, L, P, H, Arg, Bul, Br; 1963 v I (2), Br, EG, Sw, Ni, W, S; 1964 v R of W, W, Ni, S; 1966 v Y, Fi (43)
Armitage, G. H. (Charlton Ath), 1926 v Ni (1)
Armstrong, D. (Middlesbrough), 1980 v Aus; (with Southampton), 1983 v WG; 1984 v W (3)
Armstrong, K. (Chelsea), 1955 v S (1)
Arnold, J. (Fulham), 1933 v S (1)
Arthur, J. W. H. (Blackburn R), 1885 v S, W, Ni; 1886 v S, W; 1887 v W, Ni (7)
Ashcroft, J. (Woolwich Arsenal), 1906 v Ni, W, S (3)
Ashmore, G. S. (WBA), 1926 v Bel (1)
Ashton, C. T. (Corinthians), 1926 v Ni (1)
Ashurst, W. (Notts Co), 1923 v Se (2); 1925 v S, W, Bel (5)
Astall, G. (Birmingham C), 1956 v Fi, WG (2)
Astle, J. (WBA), 1969 v W; 1970 v S, P, Br (sub), Cz (5)
Aston, J. (Manchester U), 1949 v S, W, D, Sw, Se, N, F; 1950 v S, W, Ni, Ei, I, P, Bel, Ch, US; 1951 v Ni (17)
Athersmith, W. C. (Aston Villa), 1892 v Ni, 1897 v S, W, Ni; 1898 v S, W, Ni; 1899 v S, W, Ni; 1900 v S, W (12)
Atyeo, P. J. W. (Bristol C), 1956 v Br, Se, Sp; 1957 v D, Ei (2) (6)
Austin, S. W. (Manchester C), 1926 v Ni (1)

Bach, P. (Sunderland), 1899 v Ni (1)

Bache, J. W. (Aston Villa), 1903 v W; 1904 v W, Ni; 1905 v S; 1907 v Ni; 1910 v Ni; 1911 v S (7)
Baddeley, T. (Wolverhampton W), 1903 v S, Ni; 1904 v S, W, Ni (5)
Bagshaw, J. J. (Derby Co), 1920 v Ni (1)
Bailey, G. R. (Manchester U), 1985 v Ei, M (2)
Bailey, H. P. (Leicester Fosse), 1908 v W, A (2), H, B (5)
Bailey, M. A. (Charlton Ath), 1964 v US; 1965 v W (2)
Bailey, N. C. (Clapham Rovers), 1878 v S; 1879 v S, W; 1880 v S; 1881 v S; 1882 v S, W; 1883 v S, W; 1884 v S, W, Ni; 1885 v S, W, Ni; 1886 v S, W; 1887 v S, W (19)
Baily, E. F. (Tottenham H), 1950 v Sp; 1951 v Y, Ni, W; 1952 v A (2), Sw, W; 1953 v Ni (9)
Bain, J. (Oxford University), 1887 v S (1)
Baker, A. (Arsenal), 1928 v W (1)
Baker, B. H. (Everton), 1921 v Bel; (with Chelsea), 1926 v Ni (2)
Baker, J. H. (Hibernian), 1960 v Y, Sp, H, Ni, S; (with Arsenal), 1966 v Sp, Pol, Ni (8)
Ball, A. J. (Blackpool), 1965 v Y, WG, Se; 1966 v S, Sp, Fi, D, U, Arg, P, WG (2), Pol (2); (with Everton), 1967 v W, S, Ni, A, Cz, Sp; 1968 v W, S, USSR, Sp (2), Y, WG; 1969 v Ni, W, S, R (2), M, Br, U; 1970 v P, Co, Ec, R, Br, Cz (sub), WG, W, S, Bel; 1971 v Ma, EG, Gr, Ma (sub), Ni, S; 1972 v Sw, Gr; (with Arsenal), WG (2), S; 1973 v W (3), Y, S (2), Cz, Ni, Pol; 1974 v P (sub); 1975 v WG, Cy (2), Ni, W, S (72)
Ball, J. (Bury), 1928 v Ni (1)
Balmer, W. (Everton), 1905 v Ni (1)
Bamber, J. (Liverpool), 1921 v W (1)
Bambridge, A. L. (Swifts), 1881 v W; 1883 v W; 1884 v Ni (3)
Bambridge, E. C. (Swifts), 1879 v S; 1880 v S; 1881 v S; 1882 v S, W, Ni; 1883 v W; 1884 v S, W, Ni; 1885 v S, W, Ni; 1886 v S, W; 1887 v S, W, Ni (18)
Bambridge, E. H. (Swifts), 1876 v S (1)
Banks, G. (Leicester C), 1963 v S, Br, Cz, EG; 1964 v W, Ni, S, R of W, U, P (2), US, Arg; 1965 v Ni, S, H, Y, WG, Se; 1966 v Ni, S, Sp, Pol (2), Y, Fi, U, M, F, Arg, P; 1967 v Ni, W, S, Cz; (with Stoke C), 1968 v W, Ni, S, USSR (2), Sp, WG, Y; 1969 v Ni, S, R (2), F, U, Br; 1970 v W, Ni, S, Ho, Bel, Co, Ec, R, Br, Cz; 1971 v Gr, Ma (2), Ni, S; 1972 v Sw, Gr, WG (2), W, S (73)
Banks, H. E. (Millwall), 1901 v Ni (1)
Banks, T. (Bolton W), 1958 v USSR (3), Br, A; 1959 v Ni (6)
Bannister, W. (Burnley), 1901 v W; (with Bolton W), 1902 v Ni (2)
Barclay, R. (Sheffield U), 1932 v S; 1933 v Ni; 1936 v S (3)
Bardsley, D. J. (QPR), 1993 v Sp (sub), Pol (2)
Barham, M. (Norwich C), 1983 v Aus (2) (2)
Barkas, S. (Manchester C), 1936 v Bel; 1937 v S; 1938 v W, Ni, Cz (5)
Barker, J. (Derby Co), 1935 v I, Ho, S, W, Ni; 1936 v G, A, S, W, Ni; 1937 v W (11)
Barker, R. (Herts Rangers), 1872 v S (1)
Barker, R. R. (Casuals), 1895 v W (1)
Barlow, R. J. (WBA), 1955 v Ni (1)
Barmby, N.J. (Tottenham H), 1995 v U (sub), Se (sub); (with Middlesbrough), 1996 v Co, N, P, Chn, Sw (sub), Ho (sub), Sp (sub); 1997 v Mol (10)

Barnes, J. (Watford), 1983 v Ni (sub), Aus (sub+2); 1984 v D, L (sub), F (sub), S, USSR, Br, U, Ch; 1985 v EG, Fi, T, Ni, R, Fi, S, I (sub), M, WG (sub), US (sub); 1986 v R (sub), Is (sub), M (sub), Ca (sub), Arg (sub); 1987 v Se, T (sub), Br; (with Liverpool), 1988 v WG, T, Y, Is, Ho, S, Co, Sw, Ei, Ho, USSR; 1989 v Se, Gr, Alb, Pol, D; 1990 v Se, I, Br, D, U, Tun, Ei, Ho, Eg, Bel, Cam; 1991 v H, Pol, Cam, Ei, T, USSR, Arg; 1992 v Cz, Fi; 1993 v Sm, T, Ho, Pol, US, G; 1995 v US, R, Ng, U, Se; 1996 v Co (sub) (79)
Barnes, P. S. (Manchester C), 1978 v I, WG, Br, W, S, H; 1979 v D, Ei, Cz, Ni (2), S, Bul, A; (with WBA), 1980 v D, W; 1981 v Sp (sub), Br, W, Sw (sub); (with Leeds U), 1982 v N (sub), Ho (sub) (22)
Barnet, H. H. (Royal Engineers), 1882 v Ni (1)
Barrass, M. W. (Bolton W), 1952 v W, Ni; 1953 v S (3)
Barrett, A. F. (Fulham), 1930 v Ni (1)
Barrett, E. D. (Oldham Ath), 1991 v Nz; 1993 v Br, G (3)
Barrett, J. W. (West Ham U), 1929 v Ni (1)
Barry, L. (Leicester C), 1928 v F, Bel; 1929 v F, Bel, Sp (5)
Barson, F. (Aston Villa), 1920 v W (1)
Barton, J. (Blackburn R), 1890 v Ni (1)
Barton, P. H. (Birmingham), 1921 v Bel; 1922 v Ni; 1923 v F; 1924 v Bel, S, W; 1925 v Ni (7)
Barton, W. D. (Wimbledon), 1995 v Ei; (with Newcastle U), Se, Br (sub) (3)
Bassett, W. I. (WBA), 1888 v Ni, 1889 v S, W; 1890 v S, W; 1891 v S, Ni; 1892 v S; 1893 v S, W; 1894 v S; 1895 v S, Ni; 1896 v S, W, Ni (16)
Bastard, S. R. (Upton Park), 1880 v S (1)
Bastin, C. S. (Arsenal), 1932 v W; 1933 v I, Sw; 1934 v S, Ni, W, H, Cz; 1935 v S, Ni, I; 1936 v S, W, G, A; 1937 v W, Ni; 1938 v S, G, Sw, F (21)
Batty, D. (Leeds U), 1991 v USSR (sub), Arg, Aus, Nz, Mal; 1992 v G, T, H (sub), F, Se; 1993 v N, Sm, US, Br; (with Blackburn R), 1994 v D (sub); 1995 v J, Br; (with Newcastle U), 1997 v Mol (sub), Ge, I, M, Ge, S.Af (sub), Pol (sub), F; 1998 v Mol, I, Ch, Sw (sub), P, S.Ar, Tun, R, Co (sub), Arg (sub); 1999 v Bul (sub), L; (with Leeds U), H, Se, Bul (40)
Baugh, R. (Stafford Road), 1886 v Ni; (with Wolverhampton W) 1890 v Ni (2)
Bayliss, A. E. J. M. (WBA), 1891 v Ni (1)
Baynham, R. L. (Luton T), 1956 v Ni, D, Sp (3)
Beardsley, P. A. (Newcastle U), 1986 v Eg (sub), Is, USSR, M, Ca (sub), P (sub), Pol, Para, Arg; 1987 v Ni (2), Y, Sp, Br, S; (with Liverpool), 1988 v WG, T, Y, Is, Ho, H, S, Co, Sw, Ei, Ho; 1989 v D, Se, S.Ar, Gr (sub), Alb (sub+1), Pol, D; 1990 v Se, Pol, I, Br, U (sub), Tun (sub), Ei, Eg (sub), Cam (sub), WG, I; 1991 v Pol (sub), Ei (2), USSR (sub); (with Newcastle U), 1994 v D, Gr, N; 1995 v Ng, Ei, U, J, Se; 1996 v P (sub), Chn (sub) (59)
Beasant, D. J. (Chelsea), 1990 v I (sub), Y (sub) (2)
Beasley, A. (Huddersfield T), 1939 v S (1)
Beats, W. E. (Wolverhampton W), 1901 v W; 1902 v S (2)
Beattie, T. K. (Ipswich T), 1975 v Cy (2), S; 1976 v Sw, P; 1977 v Fi, I (sub), Ho; 1978 v L (sub) (9)
Beckham, D. R. J. (Manchester U), 1997 v Mol, Pol, Ge, I, Ge, S.Af (sub), Pol, I, F; 1998 v Mol, I, Cam, P, S.Ar, Bel (sub), R (sub), Co, Arg; 1999 v L, CzR, F, Pol, Se (23)
Becton, F. (Preston NE), 1895 v Ni; (with Liverpool), 1897 v W (2)
Bedford, H. (Blackpool), 1923 v Se; 1925 v Ni (2)
Bell, C. (Manchester C), 1968 v Se, WG; 1969 v W, Bul, F, U, Br; 1970 v Ni (sub), Ho (2), P, Br (sub), Cz, WG (sub); 1972 v Gr, WG (2), W, Ni, S; 1973 v W (3), Y, S (2), Ni, Cz, Pol; 1974 v A, Pol, I, W, Ni, S, Arg, EG, Bul, Y; 1975 v Cz, P, WG, Cy (2), Ni, S; 1976 v Sw, Cz (48)
Bennett, W. (Sheffield U), 1901 v S, W (2)
Benson, R. W. (Sheffield U), 1913 v Ni (1)
Bentley, R. T. F. (Chelsea), 1949 v Se; 1950 v S, P, Bel, Ch, USA; 1953 v W, Bel; 1955 v W, WG, Sp, P (12)
Beresford, J. (Aston Villa), 1934 v Cz (1)
Berry, A. (Oxford University), 1909 v Ni (1)
Berry, J. J. (Manchester U), 1953 v Arg, Ch, U; 1956 v Se (4)
Bestall, J. G. (Grimsby T), 1935 v Ni (1)
Betmead, H. A. (Grimsby), 1937 v Fi (1)
Betts, M. P. (Old Harrovians), 1877 v S (1)
Betts, W. (Sheffield W), 1889 v W (1)
Beverley, J. (Blackburn R), 1884 v S, W, Ni (3)
Birkett, R. H. (Clapham Rovers), 1879 v S (1)
Birkett, R. J. E. (Middlesbrough), 1936 v Ni (1)
Birley, F. H. (Oxford University), 1874 v S; (with Wanderers), 1875 v S (2)
Birtles, G. (Nottingham F), 1980 v Arg (sub), I; 1981 v R (3)
Bishop, S. M. (Leicester C), 1927 v S, Bel, L, F (4)
Blackburn, F. (Blackburn R), 1901 v S; 1902 v Ni; 1904 v S (3)
Blackburn, G. F. (Aston Villa), 1924 v F (1)

Blenkinsop, E. (Sheffield W), 1928 v F, Bel; 1929 v S, W, Ni, F, Bel, Sp; 1930 v S, W, Ni, G, A; 1931 v S, W, Ni, F, Bel; 1932 v S, W, Ni, Sp; 1933 v S, W, Ni, A (26)
Bliss, H. (Tottenham H), 1921 v S (1)
Blissett, L. (Watford), 1983 v WG (sub), L, W, Gr (sub), H, Ni, S (sub), Aus (1+1 sub); (with AC Milan), 1984 v D (sub), H, W (sub), S, USSR (14)
Blockley, J. P. (Arsenal), 1973 v Y (1)
Bloomer, S. (Derby Co), 1895 v S, Ni; 1896 v W, Ni; 1897 v S, W, Ni; 1898 v S; 1899 v S, W, Ni; 1900 v S; 1901 v S, W; 1902 v S, W, Ni; 1904 v S; 1905 v S, W, Ni; (with Middlesbrough), 1907 v S, W (23)
Blunstone, F. (Chelsea), 1955 v W, S, F, P; 1957 v Y (5)
Bond, R. (Preston NE), 1905 v Ni, W; 1906 v S, W, Ni; (with Bradford C), 1910 v S, W, Ni (8)
Bonetti, P. P. (Chelsea), 1966 v D; 1967 v Sp, A; 1968 v Sp; 1970 v Ho, P, WG (7)
Bonsor, A. G. (Wanderers), 1873 v S; 1875 v S (2)
Booth, F. (Manchester C), 1905 v Ni (1)
Booth, T. (Blackburn R), 1898 v W; (with Everton), 1903 v S (2)
Bould, S. A. (Arsenal), 1994 v Gr, N (2)
Bowden, E. R. (Arsenal), 1935 v W, I; 1936 v W, Ni, A; 1937 v H (6)
Bower, A. G. (Corinthians), 1924 v Ni, Bel; 1925 v W, Bel; 1927 v W (5)
Bowers, J. W. (Derby Co), 1934 v S, Ni, W (3)
Bowles, S. (QPR), 1974 v P, W, Ni; 1977 v I, Ho (5)
Bowser, S. (WBA), 1920 v Ni (1)
Boyer, P. J. (Norwich C), 1976 v W (1)
Boyes, W. (WBA), 1935 v Ho; (with Everton), 1939 v W, R of É (3)
Boyle, T. W. (Burnley), 1913 v Ni (1)
Brabrook, P. (Chelsea), 1958 v USSR; 1959 v Ni; 1960 v Sp (3)
Bracewell, P. W. (Everton), 1985 v WG (sub), US; 1986 v Ni (3)
Bradford, G. R. W. (Bristol R), 1956 v D (1)
Bradford, J. (Birmingham), 1924 v Ni; 1925 v Bel; 1928 v S; 1929 v Ni, W, F, Sp; 1930 v S, Ni, G, A; 1931 v W (12)
Bradley, W. (Manchester U), 1959 v I, US, M (sub) (3)
Bradshaw, F. (Sheffield W), 1908 v A (1)
Bradshaw, T. H. (Liverpool), 1897 v Ni (1)
Bradshaw, W. (Blackburn R), 1910 v W, Ni; 1912 v Ni; 1913 v W (4)
Brann, G. (Swifts), 1886 v S, W; 1891 v W (3)
Brawn, W. F. (Aston Villa), 1904 v W, Ni (2)
Bray, J. (Manchester C), 1935 v W; 1936 v S, W, Ni, G; 1937 v S (6)
Brayshaw, E. (Sheffield W), 1887 v Ni (1)
Bridges, B. J. (Chelsea), 1965 v S, H, Y; 1966 v A (4)
Bridgett, A. (Sunderland), 1905 v S; 1908 v S, A (2), H, B; 1909 v Ni, W, H (2), A (11)
Brindle, T. (Darwen), 1880 v S, W (2)
Brittleton, J. T. (Sheffield W), 1912 v S, W, Ni; 1913 v S; 1914 v W (5)
Britton, C. S. (Everton), 1935 v S, W, Ni, I; 1937 v S, Ni, H, N, Se (9)
Broadbent, P. F. (Wolverhampton W), 1958 v USSR; 1959 v S, W, Ni, I, Br; 1960 v S (7)
Broadis, I. A. (Manchester C), 1952 v S, A, I; 1953 v S, Arg, Ch, U, US; (with Newcastle U), 1954 v S, H, Y, Bel, Sw, U (14)
Brockbank, J. (Cambridge University), 1872 v S (1)
Brodie, J. B. (Wolverhampton W), 1889 v S, Ni; 1891 v Ni (3)
Bromilow, T. G. (Liverpool), 1921 v W; 1922 v S, W; 1923 v Bel; 1926 v Ni (5)
Bromley-Davenport, W. E. (Oxford University), 1884 v S, W (2)
Brook, E. F. (Manchester C), 1930 v Ni; 1933 v Sw: 1934 v S, W, H, F, H, Cz; 1935 v S, W, Ni, I; 1936 v S, W, Ni; 1937 v H; 1938 v W, Ni (18)
Brooking, T. D. (West Ham U), 1974 v P, Arg, EG, Bul, Y; 1975 v Cz (sub); P; 1976 v P, W, Br, I, Fi; 1977 v Ei, Fi, I, Ho, Ni, W; 1978 v I, WG, Br (sub), H; 1979 v D, Ei, Ni, W (sub), S, Bul, Se (sub), A; 1980 v D, Ni, Arg (sub), W, Ni, S, Bel, Sp; 1981 v Sw, Sp, R, H; 1982 v H, S, Fi, Sp (sub) (47)
Brooks, J. (Tottenham H), 1957 v W, Y, D (3)
Broome, F. H. (Aston Villa), 1938 v G, Sw, F; 1939 v N, I, R, Y (7)
Brown, A. (Aston Villa), 1882 v S, W, Ni (3)
Brown, A. S. (Sheffield U), 1904 v W; 1906 v Ni (2)
Brown, A. (WBA), 1971 v W (1)
Brown, A. (Huddersfield T), 1927 v S, W, Ni, Bel, L, F; 1928 v W; 1929 v S; (with Aston Villa), 1933 v W (9)
Brown, J. (Blackburn R), 1881 v W; 1882 v Ni; 1885 v S, W, Ni (5)

Brown, J. H. (Sheffield W), 1927 v S, W, Bel, L, F; 1930 v Ni (6)
Brown, K. (West Ham U), 1960 v Ni (1)
Brown, W. (West Ham U), 1924 v Bel (1)
Brown, W. M. (Manchester U), 1999 v H (1)
Bruton, J. (Burnley), 1928 v F, Bel; 1929 v S (3)
Bryant, W. I. (Clapton), 1925 v F (1)
Buchan, C. M. (Sunderland), 1913 v Ni; 1920 v W; 1921 v W, Bel; 1923 v F; 1924 v S (6)
Buchanan, W. S. (Clapham R), 1876 v S (1)
Buckley, F. C. (Derby Co), 1914 v Ni (1)
Bull, S. G. (Wolverhampton W), 1989 v S (sub), D (sub); 1990 v Y, Cz, D (sub), U (sub), Tun (sub), Ei (sub), Ho (sub), Eg, Bel (sub); 1991 v H, Pol (13)
Bullock, F. E. (Huddersfield T), 1921 v Ni (1)
Bullock, N. (Bury), 1923 v Bel; 1926 v W; 1927 v Ni (3)
Burgess, H. (Manchester C), 1904 v S, W, Ni; 1906 v S (4)
Burgess, H. (Sheffield W), 1931 v S, Ni, F, Bel (4)
Burnup, C. J. (Cambridge University), 1896 v S (1)
Burrows, H. (Sheffield W), 1934 v H, Cz; 1935 v Ho (3)
Burton, F. E. (Nottingham F), 1889 v Ni (1)
Bury, L. (Cambridge University), 1877 v S; (with Old Etonians), 1879 v W (2)
Butcher, T. (Ipswich T), 1980 v Aus; 1981 v Sp; 1982 v W, S, F, Cz, WG, Sp; 1983 v D, WG, L, W, Gr, H, Ni, S, Aus (3); 1984 v D, H, L, F, Ni; 1985 v EG, Fi, T, Ni, Ei, R, Fi, S, I, WG, US; 1986 v Is, USSR, S, M, Ca, P, Mor, Pol, Para, Arg; (with Rangers), 1987 v Se, Ni (2), Y, Sp, Br, S; 1988 v T, Y; 1989 v D, Se, Gr, Alb (2), Ch, S, Pol, D; 1990 v Se, Pol, I, Y, Br, Cz, D, U, Tun, Ei, Ho, Bel, Cam, WG (77)
Butler, J. D. (Arsenal), 1925 v Bel (1)
Butler, W. (Bolton W), 1924 v S (1)
Butt, N. (Manchester U), 1997 v M (sub), S.Af (sub); 1998 v Mol (sub), I (sub), Ch, Bel; 1999 v CzR, H (8)
Byrne, G. (Liverpool), 1963 v S; 1966 v N (2)
Byrne, J. J. (C Palace), 1962 v Ni; (with West Ham U), 1963 v Sw; 1964 v S, U, P (2), Ei, Br, Arg; 1965 v W, S (11)
Byrne, R. W. (Manchester U), 1954 v S, H, Y, Bel, Sw, U; 1955 v S, W, Ni, WG, F, Sp, P; 1956 v S, W, Ni, Br, Se, Fi, WG, D, Sp; 1957 v S, W, Ni, Y, D (2), Ei (2); 1958 v W, Ni, F (33)

Callaghan, I. R. (Liverpool), 1966 v Fi, F; 1978 v Sw, L (4)
Calvey, J. (Nottingham F), 1902 v Ni (1)
Campbell, A. F. (Blackburn R), 1929 v W, Ni; (with Huddersfield T), 1931 v W, S, Ni; 1932 v W, Ni, Sp (8)
Campbell, S. (Tottenham H), 1996 v H (sub), S (sub); 1997 v Ge, I, Ge, S.Af (sub), Pol, F, Br; 1998 v Mol, I, Cam, Ch, P, Mor, Bel, Tun, R, Co, Arg; 1999 v Se, Bul, L, CzR, Pol, Se, Bul (27)
Camsell, G. H. (Middlesbrough), 1929 v F, Bel; 1930 v Ni, W; 1934 v F; 1936 v S, G, A, Bel (9)
Capes, A. J. (Stoke C), 1903 v S (1)
Carr, J. (Middlesbrough), 1920 v Ni; 1923 v W (2)
Carr, J. (Newcastle U), 1905 v Ni; 1907 v Ni (2)
Carr, W. H. (Owlerton, Sheffield), 1875 v S (1)
Carragher, J. L. (Liverpool), 1999 v H (sub) (1)
Carter, H. S. (Sunderland), 1934 v S, H; 1936 v G; 1937 v S, Ni, H; (with Derby Co), 1947 v S, W, Ni, Ei, Ho, F, Sw (13)
Carter, J. H. (WBA), 1926 v Bel; 1929 v Bel, Sp (3)
Catlin, A. E. (Sheffield W), 1937 v W, Ni, H, N, Se (5)
Chadwick, A. (Southampton), 1900 v S, W (2)
Chadwick, E. (Everton), 1891 v S, W; 1892 v S; 1893 v S; 1894 v S; 1896 v Ni; 1897 v S (7)
Chamberlain, M (Stoke C), 1983 v L (sub); 1984 v D (sub), S, USSR, Br, U, Ch; 1985 v Fi (sub) (8)
Chambers, H. (Liverpool), 1921 v S, W, Bel; 1923 v S, W, Ni, Bel; 1924 v Ni (8)
Channon, M. R. (Southampton), 1973 v Y, S (2), Ni, W, Cz, USSR, I; 1974 v A, Pol, I, P, W, Ni, S, Arg, EG, Bul, Y; 1975 v Cz, P, WG, Cy (2), Ni (sub), W, S; 1976 v Sw, Cz, P, W, Ni, S, Br, I, Fi; 1977 v Fi, I, L, Ni, W, S, Br (sub), Arg, U; (with Manchester C), 1978 v Sw (46)
Charles, G. A. (Nottingham F), 1991 v Nz, Mal (2)
Charlton, J. (Leeds U), 1965 v S, H, Y, WG, Se; 1966 v W, Ni, S, A, Sp, Pol (2), WG (2), Y, Fi, D, U, M, F, Arg, P; 1967 v W, S, Ni, Cz; 1968 v W, Sp; 1969 v W, R, F; 1970 v Ho (2), P, Cz (35)
Charlton, R. (Manchester U), 1958 v S, P, Y; 1959 v S, W, Ni, USSR, I, Br, Pe, M, US; 1960 v W, S, Se, Y, Sp, H; 1961 v Ni, W, S, L, P, Sp, M, I, A; 1962 v W, Ni, S, A, Sw, Pe, L, P, H, Arg, Bul, Br; 1963 v S, F, Br, Cz, EG, Sw; 1964 v S, W, Ni, R of W, U, P, Ei, Br, Arg, US (sub); 1965 v Ni, S, Ho; 1966 v W, Ni, S, A, Sp, WG (2), Y, Fi, N, Pol, U, M, F, Arg, P; 1967 v Ni, W, S, Cz; 1968 v W, Ni, S, USSR (2), Sp (2), Se, Y; 1969 v S, W, Ni, R (2), Bul, M, Br; 1970 v W, Ni, Ho (2), P, Co, Ec, Cz, R, Br, WG (106)

Charnley, R. O. (Blackpool), 1963 v F (1)
Charsley, C. C. (Small Heath), 1893 v Ni (1)
Chedgzoy, S. (Everton), 1920 v W; 1921 v W, S, Ni; 1922 v Ni; 1923 v S; 1924 v W; 1925 v Ni (8)
Chenery, C. J. (C Palace), 1872 v S; 1873 v S; 1874 v S (3)
Cherry, T. J. (Leeds U), 1976 v W, S (sub), Br, Fi; 1977 v Ei, I, L, Ni, S (sub), Br, Arg, U; 1978 v Sw, L, I, Br, W; 1979 v Cz, W, Se; 1980 v Ei, Arg (sub), W, Ni, S, Aus, Sp (sub) (27)
Chilton, A. (Manchester U), 1951 v Ni; 1952 v F (2)
Chippendale, H. (Blackburn R), 1894 v Ni (1)
Chivers, M. (Tottenham H), 1971 v Ma (2), Gr, Ni, S; 1972 v Sw (1+1 sub), Gr, WG (2), Ni (sub), S; 1973 v W (3), S (2), Ni, Cz, Pol, USSR, I; 1974 v A, Pol (24)
Christian, E. (Old Etonians), 1879 v S (1)
Clamp, E. (Wolverhampton W), 1958 v USSR (2), Br, A (4)
Clapton, D. R. (Arsenal), 1959 v W (1)
Clare, T. (Stoke C), 1889 v Ni; 1892 v Ni; 1893 v W; 1894 v S (4)
Clarke, A. J. (Leeds U), 1970 v Cz; 1971 v EG, Ma, Ni, W (sub), S (sub); 1973 v S (2), W, Cz, Pol, USSR, I; 1974 v A, Pol, I; 1975 v P; 1976 v Cz, P (sub) (19)
Clarke, H. A. (Tottenham H), 1954 v S (1)
Clay, T. (Tottenham H), 1920 v W; 1922 v W, S, Ni (4)
Clayton, R. (Blackburn R), 1956 v Ni, Br, Se, Fi, WG, Sp; 1957 v S, W, Ni, Y, D (2), Ei (2); 1958 v S, W, Ni, F, P, Y, USSR; 1959 v S, W, Ni, USSR, I, Br, Pe, M, US; 1960 v W, Ni, S, Se, Y (35)
Clegg, J. C. (Sheffield W), 1872 v S (1)
Clegg, W. E. (Sheffield W), 1873 v S; (with Sheffield Albion), 1879 v W (2)
Clemence, R. N. (Liverpool), 1973 v W (2); 1974 v EG, Bul, Y; 1975 v Cz, P, WG, Cy, Ni, W, S; 1976 v Sw, Cz, P, W (2), Ni, S, Br, Fi; 1977 v Ei, Fi, I, Ho, L, S, Br, Arg, U; 1978 v Sw, L, I, WG, Ni, S; 1979 v D, Ei, Ni (2), S, Bul, A (sub); 1980 v D, Bul, Ei, Arg, W, S, Bel, Sp; 1981 v R, Sp, Br, Sw, H; (with Tottenham H), 1982 v N, Ni, Fi; 1983 v L; 1984 v L (61)
Clement, D. T. (QPR), 1976 v W (sub+1), I; 1977 v I, Ho (5)
Clough, B. H. (Middlesbrough), 1960 v W, Se (2)
Clough, N. H. (Nottingham F), 1989 v Ch; 1991 v Arg (sub), Aus, Mal; 1992 v F, Cz, C; 1993 v Sp, T (sub), Pol (sub), N (sub), US, Br, G (14)
Coates, R. (Burnley), 1970 v Ni; 1971 v Gr (sub); (with Tottenham H), Ma, W (4)
Cobbold, W. N. (Cambridge University), 1883 v S, Ni; 1885 v S, Ni; 1886 v S, W; (with Old Carthusians), 1887 v S, W, Ni (9)
Cock, J. G. (Huddersfield T), 1920 v Ni; (with Chelsea), v S (2)
Cockburn, H. (Manchester U), 1947 v W, Ni, Ei; 1948 v S, I; 1949 v S, Ni, D, Sw, Se; 1951 v Arg, P; 1952 v F (13)
Cohen, G. R. (Fulham), 1964 v U, P, Ei, US, Br; 1965 v W, S, Ni, Bel, H, Ho, Y, WG, Se; 1966 v W, S, Ni, A, Sp, Pol (2), WG (2), N, D, U, M, F, Arg, P; 1967 v W, S, Ni, Cz, Sp; 1968 v W, Ni (37)
Cole, A. (Manchester U), 1995 v U (sub); 1997 v I (sub); 1999 v F (sub), Ho, Se (5)
Coleman, E. H. (Dulwich Hamlet), 1921 v W (1)
Coleman, J. (Woolwich Arsenal), 1907 v Ni (1)
Colclough, H. (C Palace), 1914 v W (1)
Collymore, S. V. (Nottingham F), 1995 v J, Br (sub); (with Aston Villa), 1998 v Mol (sub) (3)
Common, A. (Sheffield U), 1904 v W, Ni; (with Middlesbrough), 1906 v W (3)
Compton, L. H. (Arsenal), 1951 v W, Y (2)
Conlin, J. (Bradford C), 1906 v S (1)
Connelly, J. M. (Burnley), 1960 v W, N, S, Se; 1962 v W, A, Sw, P; 1963 v W, F; (with Manchester U), 1965 v H, Y, Se; 1966 v W, Ni, S, A, N, D, U (20)
Cook, T. E. R. (Brighton), 1925 v W (1)
Cooper, C. T. (Nottingham F), 1995 v Se, Br (2)
Cooper, N. C. (Cambridge University), 1893 v Ni (1)
Cooper, T. (Derby Co), 1928 v Ni; 1929 v W, Ni, S, F, Bel, Sp; 1931 v F; 1932 v W, Sp; 1933 v S; 1934 v S, H, Cz; 1935 v W (15)
Cooper, T. (Leeds U), 1969 v W, S, F, M; 1970 v Ho, Bel, Co, Ec, R, Cz, Br, WG; 1971 v EG, Ma, Ni, W, S; 1972 v Sw (2); 1975 v P (20)
Coppell, S. J. (Manchester U), 1978 v I, WG, Br, W, Ni, S, H; 1979 v D, Ei, Cz, Ni (2), W (sub), S, Bul, A; 1980 v D, Ni, Ei (sub), Sp, Arg, W, S, Bel, I; 1981 v R (sub), Sw, R, Br, W, S, Sw, H; 1982 v H, S, Fi, F, Cz, K, WG; 1983 v L, Gr (42)
Copping, W. (Leeds U), 1933 v I, Sw; 1934 v S, Ni, W, F; (with Arsenal), 1935 v Ni, I; 1936 v A, Bel; 1937 v N, Se, Fi; 1938 v S, W, Ni, Cz; 1939 v W, R of E; (with Leeds U), R (20)
Corbett, B. O. (Corinthians), 1901 v W (1)
Corbett, R. (Old Malvernians), 1903 v W (1)
Corbett, W. S. (Birmingham), 1908 v A, H, B (3)

Corrigan, J. T. (Manchester C), 1978 v I (sub), Br; 1979 v W; 1980 v Ni, Aus; 1981 v W, S; 1982 v W, Ic (9)
Cottee, A. R. (West Ham U), 1987 v Se (sub), Ni (sub); 1988 v H (sub); (with Everton), 1989 v D (sub), Se (sub), Ch (sub), S (7)
Cotterill, G. H. (Cambridge University), 1891 v Ni; (with Old Brightonians), 1892 v W; 1893 v S, Ni (4)
Cottle, J. R. (Bristol C), 1909 v Ni (1)
Cowan, S. (Manchester C), 1926 v Bel; 1930 v A; 1931 v Bel (3)
Cowans, G. (Aston Villa), 1983 v W, H, Ni, S, Aus (3); (with Bari), 1986 v Eg, USSR; (with Aston Villa), 1991 v Ei (10)
Cowell, A. (Blackburn R), 1910 v Ni (1)
Cox, J. (Liverpool), 1901 v Ni; 1902 v S; 1903 v S (3)
Cox, J. D. (Derby Co), 1892 v Ni (1)
Crabtree, J. W. (Burnley), 1894 v Ni; 1895 v Ni, S; (with Aston Villa), 1896 v W, S, Ni; 1899 v S, W, Ni; 1900 v S, W, Ni; 1901 v W; 1902 v W (14)
Crawford, J. F. (Chelsea), 1931 v S (1)
Crawford, R. (Ipswich T), 1962 v Ni, A (2)
Crawshaw, T. H. (Sheffield W), 1895 v Ni; 1896 v S, W, Ni; 1897 v S, W, Ni; 1901 v Ni; 1904 v W, Ni (10)
Crayston, W. J. (Arsenal), 1936 v S, W, G, A, Bel; 1938 v W, Ni, Cz (8)
Creek, F. N. S. (Corinthians), 1923 v F (1)
Cresswell, W. (South Shields), 1921 v W; (with Sunderland), 1923 v F; 1924 v Bel; 1925 v Ni; 1926 v W; 1927 v Ni; (with Everton), 1930 v Ni (7)
Crompton, R. (Blackburn R), 1902 v S, W, Ni; 1903 v S, W; 1904 v S, W, Ni; 1906 v S, W, Ni; 1907 v S, W, Ni; 1908 v S, W, Ni, A (2), H, B; 1909 v S, W, Ni, H (2), A; 1910 v S, W; 1911 v S, W, Ni; 1912 v S, W, Ni; 1913 v S, W, Ni; 1914 v S, W, Ni (41)
Crooks, S. D. (Derby Co), 1930 v S, G, A; 1931 v S, W, Ni, F, Bel; 1932 v S, W, Ni, Sp; 1933 v Ni, W, A; 1934 v S, Ni, W, F, H, Cz; 1935 v Ni; 1936 v S, W; 1937 v W, H (26)
Crowe, C. (Wolverhampton W), 1963 v F (1)
Cuggy, F. (Sunderland), 1913 v Ni; 1914 v Ni (2)
Cullis, S. (Wolverhampton W), 1938 v S, W, Ni, F, Cz; 1939 v S, Ni, R of E, N, I, R, Y (12)
Cunliffe, A. (Blackburn R), 1933 v Ni, W (2)
Cunliffe, D. (Portsmouth), 1900 v Ni (1)
Cunliffe, J. N. (Everton), 1936 v Bel (1)
Cunningham, L. (WBA), 1979 v W, Se, A (sub); (with Real Madrid), 1980 v Ei (sub), Sp (sub); 1981 v R (sub) (6)
Curle, K. (Manchester C), 1992 v C (sub), H, D (3)
Currey, E. S. (Oxford University), 1890 v S, W (2)
Currie, A. W. (Sheffield U), 1972 v Ni; 1973 v USSR, I; 1974 v A, Pol, I; 1976 v Sw; (with Leeds U), 1978 v Br, W (sub), Ni, S, H (sub); 1979 v Cz, Ni (2), W, Se (17)
Cursham, A. W. (Notts Co), 1876 v S; 1877 v S; 1878 v S; 1879 v W; 1883 v S, W (6)
Cursham, H. A. (Notts Co), 1880 v W; 1882 v S, W, Ni; 1883 v S, W, Ni; 1884 v Ni (8)

Daft, H. B. (Notts Co), 1889 v Ni; 1890 v S, W; 1891 v Ni; 1892 v Ni (5)
Daley, A. M. (Aston Villa), 1992 v Pol (sub), C, H, Br, Fi (sub), D (sub), Se (7)
Danks, T. (Nottingham F), 1885 v S (1)
Davenport, P. (Nottingham F), 1985 v Ei (sub) (1)
Davenport, J. K. (Bolton W), 1885 v W; 1890 v Ni (2)
Davis, G. (Derby Co), 1904 v W, Ni (2)
Davis, H. (Sheffield W), 1903 v S, W, Ni (3)
Davison, J. E. (Sheffield W), 1922 v W (1)
Dawson, J. (Burnley), 1922 v S, Ni (2)
Day, S. H. (Old Malvernians), 1906 v Ni, W, S (3)
Dean, W. R. (Everton), 1927 v S, W, F, Bel, L; 1928 v S, W, Ni, F, Bel; 1929 v S, W, Ni; 1931 v S; 1932 v Sp; 1933 v Ni (16)
Deane, B. C. (Sheffield U), 1991 v Nz (sub + 1); 1993 v Sp (sub) (3)
Deeley, N. V. (Wolverhampton W), 1959 v Br, Pe (2)
Devey, J. H. G. (Aston Villa), 1892 v Ni; 1894 v Ni (2)
Devonshire, A. (West Ham U), 1980 v Aus (sub), Ni; 1982 v Ho, Ic; 1983 v WG, W, Gr; 1984 v L (8)
Dewhurst, F. (Preston NE), 1886 v W, Ni; 1887 v S, W, Ni; 1888 v S, W, Ni; 1889 v W (9)
Dewhurst, G. P. (Liverpool Ramblers), 1895 v W (1)
Dickinson, J. W. (Portsmouth), 1949 v N, F; 1950 v S, W, Ei, P, Bel, Ch, US, Sp; 1951 v Ni, W, Y; 1952 v W, Ni, S, A (2), I, Sw; 1953 v W, Ni, S, Bel, Arg, Ch, U, US; 1954 v W, Ni, S, R of E, H (2), Y, Bel, Sw, U; 1955 v Sp, P; 1956 v W, Ni, S, D, Sp; 1957 v W, Y, D (48)
Dimmock, J. H. (Tottenham H), 1921 v S; 1926 v W, Bel (3)
Ditchburn, E. G. (Tottenham H), 1949 v Sw, Se; 1953 v US; 1957 v W, Y, D (6)

Dix, R. W. (Derby Co), 1939 v N (1)
Dixon, J. A. (Notts Co), 1885 v W (1)
Dixon, K. M. (Chelsea), 1985 v M (sub), WG, US; 1986 v Ni, Is, M (sub), Pol (sub); 1987 v Se (8)
Dixon, L. M. (Arsenal), 1990 v Cz; 1991 v H, Pol, Ei (2), Cam, T, Arg; 1992 v G, T, Pol, Cz (sub); 1993 v Sp, N, T, Sm, T, Ho, N, US; 1994 v Sm; 1999 v F (22)
Dobson, A. T. C. (Notts Co), 1882 v Ni; 1884 v S, W, Ni (4)
Dobson, C. F. (Notts Co), 1886 v Ni (1)
Dobson, J. M. (Burnley), 1974 v P, EG, Bul, Y; (with Everton), 1975 v Cz (5)
Doggart, A. G. (Corinthians), 1924 v Bel (1)
Dorigo, A. R. (Chelsea), 1990 v Y (sub), Cz (sub), D (sub), I; 1991 v H (sub), USSR; (with Leeds U), 1992 v G, Cz (sub), H, Br; 1993 v Sm, Pol, US, Br; 1994 v H (15)
Dorrell, A. R. (Aston Villa), 1925 v W, Bel, F; 1926 v Ni (4)
Douglas, B. (Blackburn R), 1958 v S, W, Ni, F, P, Y, USSR (2), Br, A; 1959 v S, USSR; 1960 v Y, H; 1961 v Ni, W, S, L, P, Sp, M, I, A; 1962 v W, Ni, S, Pe, L, P, H, Arg, Bul, Br; 1963 v S, Br, Sw (36)
Downs, R. W. (Everton), 1921 v Ni (1)
Doyle, M. (Manchester C), 1976 v W, S (sub); Br, I; 1977 v Ho (5)
Drake, E. J. (Arsenal), 1935 v Ni, I; 1936 v W; 1937 v H; 1938 v F (5)
Dublin, D. (Coventry C), 1998 v Ch, Mor, Bel (sub); (with Aston Villa), 1999 v CzR (4)
Ducat, A. (Woolwich Arsenal), 1910 v S, W, Ni; (with Aston Villa), 1920 v S, W; 1921 v Ni (6)
Dunn, A. T. B. (Cambridge University), 1883 v Ni; 1884 v Ni; (with Old Etonians), 1892 v S, W (4)
Duxbury, M. (Manchester U), 1984 v L, F, W, S, USSR, Br, U, Ch; 1985 v EG, Fi (10)

Earle, S. G. J. (Clapton), 1924 v F; (with West Ham U), 1928 v Ni (2)
Eastham, G. (Arsenal), 1963 v Br, Cz, EG; 1964 v W, Ni, S, R of W, U, P, Ei, US, Br, Arg; 1965 v H, WG, Se; 1966 v Sp, Pol, D (19)
Eastham, G. R. (Bolton W), 1935 v Ho (1)
Eckersley, W. (Blackburn R), 1950 v Sp; 1951 v S, Y, Arg, P; 1952 v A (2), Sw; 1953 v Ni, Arg, Ch, U, US; 1954 v W, Ni, R of E, H (17)
Edwards, D. (Manchester U), 1955 v S, F, Sp, P; 1956 v S, Br, Se, Fi, WG; 1957 v S, Ni, Ei (2), D (2); 1958 v W, Ni, F (18)
Edwards, J. H. (Shropshire Wanderers), 1874 v S (1)
Edwards, W. (Leeds U), 1926 v S, W; 1927 v W, Ni, S, F, Bel, L; 1928 v S, F, Bel; 1929 v S, W, Ni; 1930 v W, Ni (16)
Ehiogu, U. (Aston Villa), 1996 v Chn (sub) (1)
Ellerington, W. (Southampton), 1949 v N, F (2)
Elliott, G. W. (Middlesbrough), 1913 v Ni; 1914 v Ni; 1920 v W (3)
Elliott, W. H. (Burnley), 1952 v I, A; 1953 v Ni, W, Bel (5)
Evans, R. E. (Sheffield U), 1911 v S, W, Ni; 1912 v W (4)
Ewer, F. H. (Casuals), 1924 v F; 1925 v Bel (2)

Fairclough, P. (Old Foresters), 1878 v S (1)
Fairhurst, D. (Newcastle U), 1934 v F (1)
Fantham, J. (Sheffield W), 1962 v L (1)
Fashanu, J. (Wimbledon), 1989 v Ch, S (2)
Felton, W. (Sheffield W), 1925 v F (1)
Fenton, M. (Middlesbrough), 1938 v S (1)
Fenwick, T. (QPR), 1984 v W (sub), USSR, Br, U, Ch; 1985 v Fi, S, M, US; 1986 v R, T, Ni, Eg, M, P, Mor, Pol, Arg; (with Tottenham H), 1988 v Is (sub) (20)
Ferdinand, L. (QPR), 1993 v Sm, Ho, N, US; 1994 v Pol, Sm; 1995 v US (sub); (with Newcastle U), 1996 v P, Bul, H; 1997 v Pol, Ge, I (sub); (with Tottenham H), 1998 v Mol, S.Ar (sub), Mor (sub), Bel (17)
Ferdinand, R. G. (West Ham U), 1998 v Cam (sub), Sw, Bel (sub); 1999 v L, CzR, F (sub), H, Se (sub) (8)
Field, E. (Clapham Rovers), 1876 v S; 1881 v S (2)
Finney, T. (Preston NE), 1947 v W, Ni, Ei, Ho, F, P; 1948 v S, W, Ni, Bel, Se, I; 1949 v S, W, Ni, Se, N, F; 1950 v S, W, Ni, Ei, I, P, Bel, Ch, US, Sp; 1951 v W, S, Arg, P; 1952 v W, Ni, S, F, I, Sw, A; 1953 v W, Ni, S, Bel, Arg, Ch, U, US; 1954 v W, S, Bel, Sw, U, H, Y; 1955 v WG; 1956 v S, W, Ni, D, Sp; 1957 v S, W, Y, D (2), Ei (2); 1958 v W, S, F, P, Y, USSR (2); 1959 v Ni, USSR (76)
Fleming, H. J. (Swindon T), 1909 v S, H (2); 1910 v W, Ni; 1911 v W, Ni; 1912 v Ni; 1913 v S, W; 1914 v S (11)
Fletcher, A. (Wolverhampton W), 1889 v W; 1890 v W (2)
Flowers, R. (Wolverhampton W), 1955 v F; 1959 v S, W, I, Br, Pe, US, M (sub); 1960 v W, Ni, S, Se, Y, Sp, H; 1961 v Ni, W, S, L, P, Sp, M, I, A; 1962 v W, Ni, S, A, Sw, Pe, L, P, H, Arg, Bul, Br; 1963 v Ni, W, S, F (2); Sw; 1964 v Ei, US, P;

Hedley, G. A. (Sheffield U), 1901 v Ni (1)
Hegan, K. E. (Corinthians), 1923 v Bel, F; 1924 v Ni, Bel (4)
Hellawell, M. S. (Birmingham C), 1963 v Ni, F (2)
Hendrie, L. A. (Aston Villa), 1999 v CzR (sub) (1)
Henfrey, A. G. (Cambridge University), 1891 v Ni; (with Corinthians), 1892 v W; 1895 v W; 1896 v S, W (5)
Henry, R. P. (Tottenham H), 1963 v F (1)
Heron, F. (Wanderers), 1876 v S (1)
Heron, G. H. H. (Uxbridge), 1873 v S; 1874 v S; (with Wanderers), 1875 v S; 1876 v S; 1878 v S (5)
Heskey, E. W. (Leicester C), 1999 v H (sub), Bul (sub) (2)
Hibbert, W. (Bury), 1910 v S (1)
Hibbs, H. E. (Birmingham), 1930 v S, W, A, G; 1931 v S, W, Ni; 1932 v W, Ni, Sp; 1933 v S, W, Ni, A, I, Sw; 1934 v Ni, W, F; 1935 v S, W, Ni, Ho; 1936 v G, W (25)
Hill, F. (Bolton W), 1963 v Ni, W (2)
Hill, G. A. (Manchester U), 1976 v I; 1977 v Ei (sub), Fi (sub), L; 1978 v Sw (sub), L (6)
Hill, J. H. (Burnley), 1925 v W; 1926 v S; 1927 v S, Ni, Bel, F; 1928 v Ni, W; (with Newcastle U), 1929 v F, Bel, Sp (11)
Hill, R. (Luton T), 1983 v D (sub), WG; 1986 v Eg (sub) (3)
Hill, R. H. (Millwall), 1926 v Bel (1)
Hillman, J. (Burnley), 1899 v Ni (1)
Hills, A. F. (Old Harrovians), 1879 v S (1)
Hilsdon, G. R. (Chelsea), 1907 v Ni; 1908 v S, W, Ni, A, H, B; 1909 v Ni (8)
Hinchcliffe, A. G. (Everton), 1997 v Mol, Pol, Ge; 1998 v Cam; (with Sheffield W), Sw, S.Ar; 1999 v Bul (7)
Hine, E. W. (Leicester C), 1929 v W, Ni; 1930 v W, Ni; 1932 v W, Ni (6)
Hinton, A. T. (Wolverhampton W), 1963 v F; (with Nottingham F), 1965 v W, Bel (3)
Hirst, D. E. (Sheffield W), 1991 v Aus, Nz (sub); 1992 v F (3)
Hitchens, G. A. (Aston Villa), 1961 v M, I, A; (with Internazionale), 1962 v Sw, Pe, H, Br (7)
Hobbis, H. H. F. (Charlton Ath), 1936 v A, Bel (2)
Hoddle, G. (Tottenham H), 1980 v Bul, W, Aus, Sp; 1981 v Sp, W, S; 1982 v N, Ni, W, Ic, Cz (sub), K; 1983 v L (sub), Ni, S; 1984 v H, L, F; 1985 v Ei (sub), S, I (sub), M, WG, US; 1986 v R, T, Ni, Is, USSR, S, M, Ca, P, Mor, Pol, Para, Arg; 1987 v Se, Ni, Y, Sp, T, S; (with Monaco), 1988 v WG, T (sub), Y (sub), Ho (sub), H (sub), Co (sub), Ei (sub), Ho, USSR (53)
Hodge, S. B. (Aston Villa), 1986 v USSR (sub), S, Ca, P (sub), Mor (sub), Pol, Para, Arg; 1987 v Se, Ni, Y; (with Tottenham H), Sp. Ni, T, S; (with Nottingham F), 1989 v D; 1990 v I (sub), Y (sub), Cz, D, U, Tun; 1991 v Cam (sub), T (sub) (24)
Hodgetts, D. (Aston Villa), 1888 v S, W, Ni; 1892 v S, Ni; 1894 v Ni (6)
Hodgkinson, A. (Sheffield U), 1957 v S, Ei (2), D; 1961 v W (5)
Hodgson, G. (Liverpool), 1931 v S, Ni, W (3)
Hodkinson, J. (Blackburn R), 1913 v W, S; 1920 v Ni (3)
Hogg, W. (Sunderland), 1902 v S, W, Ni (3)
Holdcroft, G. H. (Preston NE), 1937 v W, Ni (2)
Holden, A. D. (Bolton W), 1959 v S, I, Br, Pe, M (5)
Holden, G. H. (Wednesbury OA), 1881 v S; 1884 v S, W, Ni (4)
Holden-White, C. (Corinthians), 1888 v W, S (2)
Holford, T. (Stoke), 1903 v Ni (1)
Holley, G. H. (Sunderland), 1909 v S, W, H (2), A; 1910 v W; 1912 v S, W, Ni; 1913 v S (10)
Holliday, E. (Middlesbrough), 1960 v W, Ni, Se (3)
Hollins, J. W. (Chelsea), 1967 v Sp (1)
Holmes, R. (Preston NE), 1888 v Ni; 1891 v S; 1892 v S; 1893 v S, W; 1894 v Ni; 1895 v Ni (7)
Holt, J. (Everton), 1890 v W; 1891 v S, W; 1892 v S, Ni; 1893 v S; 1894 v S, Ni; 1895 v S; (with Reading), 1900 v Ni (10)
Hopkinson, E. (Bolton W), 1958 v W, Ni, S, F, P, Y; 1959 v S, I, Br, Pe, M, US; 1960 v W, Se (14)
Hossack, A. H. (Corinthians), 1892 v W; 1894 v W (2)
Houghton, W. E. (Aston Villa), 1931 v Ni, W, F, Bel; 1932 v S, Ni; 1933 v A (7)
Houlker, A. E. (Blackburn R), 1902 v S; (with Portsmouth), 1903 v S, W; (with Southampton), 1906 v W, Ni (5)
Howarth, R. H. (Preston NE), 1887 v Ni; 1888 v S, W; 1891 v S; (with Everton), 1894 v Ni (5)
Howe, D. (WBA), 1958 v S, W, Ni, F, P, Y, USSR (3), Br, A; 1959 v S, W, Ni, USSR, I, Br, Pe, M, US; 1960 v W, Ni, Se (23)
Howe, J. R. (Derby Co), 1948 v I; 1949 v S, Ni (3)
Howell, L. S. (Wanderers), 1873 v S (1)
Howell, R. (Sheffield U), 1895 v Ni; (with Liverpool) 1899 v S (2)
Howey, S. N. (Newcastle U), 1995 v Ng; 1996 v Co, P, Bul (4)
Hudson, A. A. (Stoke C), 1975 v WG, Cy (2)

Hudson, J. (Sheffield), 1883 v Ni (1)
Hudspeth, F. C. (Newcastle U), 1926 v Ni (1)
Hufton, A. E. (West Ham U), 1924 v Bel; 1928 v S, Ni; 1929 v F, Bel, Sp (6)
Hughes, E. W. (Liverpool), 1970 v W, Ni, S, Ho, P, Bel; 1971 v EG, Ma (2), Gr, W; 1972 v Sw, Gr, WG (2), W, Ni, S; 1973 v W (3), S (2), Pol, USSR, I; 1974 v A, Pol, I, W, Ni, S, Arg, EG, Bul, Y; 1975 v Cz, P, Cy (sub), Ni; 1977 v I, L, W, S, Br, Arg, U; 1978 v Sw, L, I, WG, Ni, S, H; 1979 v D, Ei, Ni, W, Se; (with Wolverhampton W), 1980 v Sp (sub), Ni, S (sub) (62)
Hughes, L. (Liverpool), 1950 v Ch, US, Sp (3)
Hulme, J. H. A. (Arsenal), 1927 v S, Bel, F; 1928 v S, Ni, W; 1929 v Ni, W; 1933 v S (9)
Humphreys, P. (Notts Co), 1903 v S (1)
Hunt, G. S. (Tottenham H), 1933 v I, Sw, S (3)
Hunt, Rev K. R. G. (Leyton), 1911 v S, W (2)
Hunt, R. (Liverpool), 1962 v A; 1963 v EG; 1964 v S, US, P; 1965 v W; 1966 v S, Sp, Pol (2), WG (2), Fi, N, U, M, F, Arg, P; 1967 v Ni, W, Cz, Sp, A; 1968 v W, Ni, USSR (2), Sp (2), Se, Y; 1969 v R (2) (34)
Hunt, S. (WBA), 1984 v S (sub), USSR (sub) (2)
Hunter, J. (Sheffield Heeley), 1878 v S; 1880 v S, W; 1881 v S, W; 1882 v S, W (7)
Hunter, N. (Leeds U), 1966 v WG, Y, Fi, Sp (sub); 1967 v A; 1968 v Sp, Se, Y, WG, USSR; 1969 v R, W; 1970 v Ho, WG (sub); 1971 v Ma; 1972 v WG (2), W, Ni, S; 1973 v W (2) USSR (sub); 1974 v A, Pol, Ni (sub), S; 1975 v Cz (28)
Hurst, G. C. (West Ham U), 1966 v S, WG (2), Y, Fi, D, Arg, P; 1967 v Ni, W, S, Cz, Sp, A; 1968 v W, Ni, S, Se (sub), WG, USSR (2); 1969 v Ni, S, R (2), Bul, F, M, U, Br; 1970 v W, Ni, S, Ho (1+1 sub), Bel, Co, Ec, R, Br, WG; 1971 v EG, Gr, W, S; 1972 v Sw (2), Gr, WG (49)

Ince, P. E. C. (Manchester U), 1993 v Sp, N, T (2), Ho, Pol, US, Br, G; 1994 v Pol, Ho, Sm, D, N; 1995 v R, Ei; (with Internazionale), 1996 v Bul, Cro, H, Sw, S, Ho, G; 1997 v Mol, Pol, Ge, I, M, Ge, Pol, I, F (sub), Br; (with Liverpool), 1998 v I, Cam, Ch (sub), Sw, P, Mor, Tun, R, Co, Arg; 1999 v Se, F (45)
Iremonger, J. (Nottingham F), 1901 v S; 1902 v Ni (2)

Jack, D. N. B. (Bolton W), 1924 v S, W; 1928 v F, Bel; (with Arsenal), 1930 v S, G, A; 1933 v W, A (9)
Jackson, E. (Oxford University), 1891 v W (1)
James, D. B. (Liverpool), 1997 v M (1)
Jarrett, B. G. (Cambridge University), 1876 v S; 1877 v S; 1878 v S (3)
Jefferis, F. (Everton), 1912 v S, W (2)
Jezzard, B. A. G. (Fulham), 1954 v H; 1956 v Ni (2)
Johnson, D. E. (Ipswich T), 1975 v W, S; 1976 v Sw; (with Liverpool), 1980 v Ei, Arg, Ni, S, Bel (8)
Johnson, E. (Saltley College), 1880 v W; (with Stoke C), 1884 v Ni (2)
Johnson, J. A. (Stoke C), 1937 v N, Se, Fi, S, Ni (5)
Johnson, T. C. F. (Manchester C), 1926 v Bel; 1930 v W; (with Everton), 1932 v S, Sp; 1933 v Ni (5)
Johnson, W. H. (Sheffield U), 1900 v S, W, Ni; 1903 v S, W, Ni (6)
Johnston, H. (Blackpool), 1947 v S, Ho; 1951 v S; 1953 v Arg, Ch, U, US; 1954 v W, Ni, H (10)
Jones, A. (Walsall Swifts), 1882 v S, W; (with Great Lever), 1883 v S (3)
Jones, H. (Blackburn R), 1927 v S, Bel, L, F; 1928 v S, Ni (6)
Jones, H. (Nottingham F), 1923 v F (1)
Jones, M. D. (Sheffield U), 1965 v WG, Se; (with Leeds U), 1970 v Ho (3)
Jones, R. (Liverpool), 1992 v F; 1994 v Pol, Gr, N; 1995 v US, R, Ng, U (8)
Jones, W. (Bristol C), 1901 v Ni (1)
Jones, W. H. (Liverpool), 1950 v P, Bel (2)
Joy, B. (Casuals), 1936 v Bel (1)

Kail, E. I. L. (Dulwich Hamlet), 1929 v F, Bel, Sp (3)
Kay, A. H. (Everton), 1963 v Sw (1)
Kean, F. W. (Sheffield W), 1923 v S, Bel; 1924 v W; 1925 v Ni; 1926 v Ni, Bel; 1927 v L; (with Bolton W), 1929 v F, Sp (9)
Keegan, J. K. (Liverpool), 1973 v W (2); 1974 v W, Ni, Arg, EG, Bul, Y; 1975 v Cz, WG, Cy (2), Ni, S; 1976 v Sw, Cz, P, W (2), Ni, S, Br, Fi; 1977 v Ei, Fi, I, Ho, L; (with SV Hamburg), W, Br, Arg, U; 1978 v Sw, H, Br, H; 1979 v D, Ei, Cz, Ni, W, S, Bul, Se, A; 1980 v D, Ni, Ei, Sp (2), Arg, Bel, I; (with Southampton), 1981 v Sp, Sw, H; 1982 v N, H, Ni, S, Fi, Sp (sub) (63)
Keen, E. R. L. (Derby Co), 1933 v A; 1937 v W, Ni, H (4)
Kelly, R. (Burnley), 1920 v S; 1921 v S, W, Ni; 1922 v S, W;

1923 v S; 1924 v Ni; 1925 v W, Ni, S; (with Sunderland), 1926 v W; (with Huddersfield T), 1927 v L; 1928 v S (14)

Kennedy, A. (Liverpool), 1984 v Ni, W (2)

Kennedy, R. (Liverpool), 1976 v W (2), Ni, S; 1977 v L, W, S, Br (sub), Arg (sub); 1978 v Sw, L; 1980 v Bul, Sp, Arg, W, Bel (sub), I (17)

Kenyon-Slaney, W. S. (Wanderers), 1873 v S (1)

Keown, M. R. (Everton), 1992 v F, Cz, C, H, Br, Fi, D, Fe, Se; (with Arsenal), 1993 v Ho, G (sub); 1997 v M, S.Af, I, Br; 1998 v Sw, Mor, Bel; 1999 v CzR, F, Pol, H, Se (23)

Kevan, D. T. (WBA), 1957 v S; 1958 v W, Ni, S, P. Y, USSR (3), Br, A; 1959 v M, US; 1961 v M (14)

Kidd, B. (Manchester U), 1970 v Ni, Ec (sub) (2)

King, R. S. (Oxford University), 1882 v Ni (1)

Kingsford, R. K. (Wanderers), 1874 v S (1)

Kingsley, M. (Newcastle U), 1901 v W (1)

Kinsey, G. (Wolverhampton W), 1892 v W; 1893 v S; (with Derby Co), 1896 v W, Ni (4)

Kirchen, A. J. (Arsenal), 1937 v N, Se, Fi (3)

Kirton, W. J. (Aston Villa), 1922 v Ni (1)

Knight, A. E. (Portsmouth), 1920 v Ni (1)

Knowles, C. (Tottenham H), 1968 v USSR, Sp, Se, WG (4)

Labone, B. L. (Everton), 1963 v Ni, W, F; 1967 v Sp, A; 1968 v S, Sp, Se, Y, USSR, WG; 1969 v Ni, S, R, Bul, M, U, Br; 1970 v S, W, Bel, Co, Ec, R, Br, WG (26)

Lampard, F. R. G. (West Ham U), 1973 v Y; 1980 v Aus (2)

Langley, E. J. (Fulham), 1958 v S, P, Y (3)

Langton, R. (Blackburn R), 1947 v W, Ni, Ei, Ho, F, Sw; 1948 v Se; (with Preston NE), 1949 v D, Se; (with Bolton W), 1950 v S; 1951 v Ni (11)

Latchford, R. D. (Everton), 1978 v I, Br, W; 1979 v D, Ei, Cz (sub), Ni (2), W, S, Bul, A (12)

Latheron, E. G. (Blackburn R), 1913 v W; 1914 v Ni (2)

Lawler, C. (Liverpool), 1971 v Ma, W, S; 1972 v Sw (4)

Lawton, T. (Everton), 1939 v S, W, Ni, R of E, N, I, R, Y; (with Chelsea), 1947 v S, W, Ni, Ei, Ho, F, Sw, P; 1948 v W, Ni, Bel; (with Notts Co), 1948 v S, Se, I; 1949 v D (23)

Leach, T. (Sheffield W), 1931 v W, Ni (2)

Leake, A. (Aston Villa), 1904 v S, Ni; 1905 v S, W, Ni (5)

Lee, E. A. (Southampton), 1904 v W (1)

Lee, F. H. (Manchester C), 1969 v Ni, W, S, Bul, F, M, U; 1970 v W, Ho (2), P, Bel, Co, Ec, R, Br, WG; 1971 v EG, Gr, Ma, Ni, W, S; 1972 v Sw (2), Gr, WG (27)

Lee, J. (Derby Co), 1951 v Ni (1)

Lee, R. M. (Newcastle U), 1995 v R, Ng; 1996 v Co (sub), N, Sw, Bul (sub), H; 1997 v M, Ge, S.Af, Pol, F (sub), Br (sub); 1998 v Cam (sub), Ch, Sw, Bel, Co (sub); 1999 v Se (sub), Bul, L (sub) (21)

Lee, S. (Liverpool), 1983 v Gr, L, W, Gr, H, S, Aus; 1984 v D, H, L, F, Ni, W, Ch (sub) (14)

Leighton, J. E. (Nottingham F), 1886 v Ni (1)

Le Saux, G. P. (Blackburn R), 1994 v D, Gr, N; 1995 v US, R, Ng, Ei, U, Se, Br; 1996 v Co, P (sub); 1997 v I, M, Ge, S.Af, Pol, I, F, Br; (with Chelsea), 1998 v I, Ch (sub), P, Mor, Bel, Tun, Ro, Arg; 1999 v Se, Bul (sub), CzR, F, Pol, Se (35)

Le Tissier, M. P. (Southampton), 1994 v D (sub), Gr (sub), N (sub); 1995 v R, Ng (sub), Ei; 1997 v Mol (sub), I (8)

Lilley, H. E. (Sheffield U), 1892 v W (1)

Linacre, H. J. (Nottingham F), 1905 v W, S (2)

Lindley, T. (Cambridge University), 1886 v S, W, Ni; 1887 v S, W, Ni; 1888 v S, W, Ni; (with Nottingham F), 1889 v S; 1890 v S, W; 1891 v Ni (13)

Lindsay, A. (Liverpool), 1974 v Arg, EG, Bul, Y (4)

Lindsay, W. (Wanderers), 1877 v S (1)

Lineker, G. (Leicester C), 1984 v S (sub); 1985 v Ei, R (sub), S (sub), I (sub), WG, US; (with Everton), 1986 v R, T, Ni, Eg, USSR, Ca, P, Mor, Pol, Para, Arg; (with Barcelona), 1987 v Ni (2), Y, Sp, T, Br; 1988 v WG, T, Y, Ho, H, S, Co, Sw, Ei, Ho, USSR; 1989 v Se, S.Ar, Gr, Alb (2), Pol, D; (with Tottenham H), 1990 v Se, Pol, I, Y, Br, Cz, D, U, Tun, Ei, Ho, Eg, Bel, Cam, WG, I; 1991 v H, Pol, Ei (2), Cam, T, Arg, Aus, Nz, Mal; 1992 v G, T, Pol, F (sub), Cz (sub), C, H, Br, Fi, D, F, Se (80)

Lintott, E. H. (QPR), 1908 v S, W, Ni; (with Bradford C), 1909 v S, Ni, H (2) (7)

Lipsham, H. B. (Sheffield U), 1902 v W (1)

Little, B. (Aston Villa), 1975 v W (sub) (1)

Lloyd, L. V. (Liverpool), 1971 v W; 1972 v Sw, Ni; (with Nottingham F), 1980 v W (4)

Lockett, A. (Stoke C), 1903 v Ni (1)

Lodge, L. V. (Cambridge University), 1894 v W; 1895 v S, W; (with Corinthians), 1896 v S, Ni (5)

Lofthouse, J. M. (Blackburn R), 1885 v S, W, Ni; 1887 v S, W; (with Accrington), 1889 v Ni; (with Blackburn R), 1890 v Ni (7)

Lofthouse, N. (Bolton W), 1951 v Y; 1952 v W, Ni, S, A (2), I, Sw; 1953 v W, Ni, S, Bel, Arg, Ch, U, US; 1954 v W, Ni, R of E, Bel, U; 1955 v Ni, S, F, Sp, P; 1956 v W, S, Sp, D, Fi (sub); 1959 v W, USSR (33)

Longworth, E. (Liverpool), 1920 v S; 1921 v Bel; 1923 v S, W, Bel (5)

Lowder, A. (Wolverhampton W), 1889 v W (1)

Lowe, E. (Aston Villa), 1947 v F, Sw, P (3)

Lucas, T. (Liverpool), 1922 v Ni; 1924 v F; 1926 v Bel (3)

Luntley, E. (Nottingham F), 1880 v S, W (2)

Lyttelton, Hon. A. (Cambridge University), 1877 v S (1)

Lyttelton, Hon. E. (Cambridge University), 1878 v S (1)

McCall, J. (Preston NE), 1913 v S, W; 1914 v S; 1920 v S; 1921 v Ni (5)

McDermott, T. (Liverpool), 1978 v Sw, L; 1979 v Ni, W, Se; 1980 v D, Ni (sub), Ei, Ni, S, Bel (sub), Sp; 1981 v N, R, Sw, R (sub), Br, Sw (sub), H; 1982 v N, H, W (sub), Ho, S (sub), Ic (25)

McDonald, C. A. (Burnley), 1958 v USSR (3), Br, A; 1959 v W, Ni, USSR (8)

McFarland, R. L. (Derby Co), 1971 v Gr, Ma (2), Ni, S; 1972 v Sw, Gr, WG, W, S; 1973 v W (3), Ni, S, Cz, Pol, USSR, I; 1974 v A, Pol, I, W, Ni; 1976 v Cz, S; 1977 v Ei, I (28)

McGarry, W. H. (Huddersfield T), 1954 v Sw, U; 1956 v W, D (4)

McGuinness, W. (Manchester U), 1959 v Ni, M (2)

McInroy, A. (Sunderland), 1927 v Ni (1)

McMahon, S. (Liverpool), 1988 v Is, H, Co, USSR; 1989 v D (sub); 1990 v Se, Pol, I, Y (sub); Br, Cz (sub), D, Ei (sub), Eg, Bel, I; 1991 v Ei (17)

McManaman, S. (Liverpool), 1995 v Ng (sub), U (sub), J (sub); 1996 v Co, N, Sw, P (sub), Bul, Cro, Chn, Sw, S, Ho, Sp, G; 1997 v Pol, I, M; 1998 v Cam, Sw, Mor, Co (sub); 1999 v Pol, H (24)

McNab, R. (Arsenal), 1969 v Ni, Bul, R (1+1 sub) (4)

McNeal, R. (WBA), 1914 v S, W (2)

McNeil, M. (Middlesbrough), 1961 v W, Ni, S, L, P, Sp, M, I; 1962 v L (9)

Mabbutt, G. (Tottenham H), 1983 v WG, Gr, L, W, Gr, H, Ni, S (sub); 1984 v H; 1987 v Y, Ni, T; 1988 v WG; 1992 v T, Pol, Cz (16)

Macaulay, R. H. (Cambridge University), 1881 v S (1)

Macdonald, M. (Newcastle U), 1972 v W, Ni, S (sub); 1973 v USSR (sub); 1974 v P, S (sub), Y (sub); 1975 v WG, Cy (2), Ni; 1976 v Sw (sub), Cz, P (14)

Macrae, S. (Notts Co), 1883 v S, W, Ni; 1884 v S, Ni (5)

Maddison, F. B. (Oxford University), 1872 v S (1)

Madeley, P. E. (Leeds U), 1971 v Ni; 1972 v Sw (2), Gr, WG (2), W, S; 1973 v S, Cz, Pol, USSR, I; 1974 v A, Pol, I; 1975 v Cz, P, Cy; 1976 v Cz, P, Fi; 1977 v Ei, Ho (24)

Magee, T. P. (WBA), 1923 v W, Se; 1925 v S, Bel, F (5)

Makepeace, H. (Everton), 1906 v S; 1910 v S; 1912 v S, W (4)

Male, C. G. (Arsenal), 1935 v S, Ni, I, Ho; 1936 v S, W, Ni, G, A, Bel; 1937 v S, Ni, H, N, Se, Fi; 1939 v I, R, Y (19)

Mannion, W. J. (Middlesbrough), 1947 v S, W, Ni, Ei, Ho, F, Sw, P; 1948 v W, Ni, Bel, Se, I; 1949 v N, F; 1950 v S, Ei, P, Bel, Ch, US; 1951 v Ni, W, S, Y; 1952 v F (26)

Mariner, P. (Ipswich T), 1977 v L (sub), Ni; 1978 v L, W (sub), S; 1980 v W, Ni (sub), S, Aus, I (sub), Sp (sub); 1981 v N, Sw, Sp, Sw, H; 1982 v N, H, Ho, S, Fi, F, Cz, K, WG, Sp; 1983 v D, WG, Gr, W; 1984 v D, H, L; (with Arsenal), 1985 v EG, R (35)

Marsden, J. T. (Darwen), 1891 v Ni (1)

Marsden, W. (Sheffield W), 1930 v W, S, G (3)

Marsh, R. W. (QPR), 1972 v Sw (sub); (with Manchester C), WG (sub+1), W, Ni, S; 1973 v W (2), Y (9)

Marshall, T. (Darwen), 1880 v W; 1881 v W (2)

Martin, A. (West Ham U), 1981 v Br, S (sub); 1982 v H, Fi; 1983 v Gr, L, W, Gr, H; 1984 v H, L, W; 1985 v Ni; 1986 v Is, Ca, Para; 1987 v Se (17)

Martin, H. (Sunderland), 1914 v Ni (1)

Martyn, A. N. (C Palace), 1992 v C (sub), H; 1993 v G; (with Leeds U), 1997 v S.Af; 1998 v Cam, Ch, Bel; 1999 v CzR, F (sub) (9)

Marwood, B. (Arsenal), 1989 v S.Ar (sub) (1)

Maskrey, H. M. (Derby Co), 1908 v Ni (1)

Mason, C. (Wolverhampton W), 1887 v Ni; 1888 v W; 1890 v Ni (3)

Matthews, R. D. (Coventry C), 1956 v S, Br, Se, WG; 1957 v Ni (5)

Matthews, S. (Stoke C), 1935 v W, I; 1936 v G; 1937 v S; 1938 v S, W, Cz, G, Sw, F; 1939 v S, W, Ni, R of E, N, I, Y; 1947 v S; (with Blackpool), 1947 v Sw, P; 1948 v S, W, Ni, Bel, I; 1949 v S, W, Ni, D, Sw; 1950 v Sp; 1951 v Ni, S; 1954 v Ni, R of E, H, Bel, U; 1955 v Ni, W, S, F, WG, Sp, P; 1956 v W, Br; 1957 v S, W, Ni, Y, D (2), Ei (54)

Matthews, V. (Sheffield U), 1928 v F, Bel (2)
Maynard, W. J. (1st Surrey Rifles), 1872 v S; 1876 v S (2)
Meadows, J. (Manchester C), 1955 v S (1)
Medley, L. D. (Tottenham H), 1951 v Y, W; 1952 v F, A, W, Ni (6)
Meehan, T. (Chelsea), 1924 v Ni (1)
Melia, J. (Liverpool), 1963 v S, Sw (2)
Mercer, D. W. (Sheffield U), 1923 v Ni, Bel (2)
Mercer, J. (Everton), 1939 v S, Ni, I, R, Y (5)
Merrick, G. H. (Birmingham C), 1952 v Ni, S, A (2), I, Sw; 1953 v Ni, W, S, Bel, Arg, Ch, U; 1954 v W, Ni, S, R of E, H (2), Y, Bel, Sw, U (23)
Merson, P. C. (Arsenal), 1992 v G (sub), Cz, H, Br (sub), Fi (sub), D, Se (sub); 1993 v Sp (sub), N (sub), Ho (sub), Br (sub), G; 1994 v Ho, Gr; 1997 v I (sub); (with Middlesbrough), 1998 v Sw, P (sub), Bel, Arg (sub); 1999 v Se (sub); (with Aston Villa), CzR (21)
Metcalfe, V. (Huddersfield T), 1951 v Arg, P (2)
Mew, J. W. (Manchester U), 1921 v Ni (1)
Middleditch, B. (Corinthians), 1897 v Ni (1)
Milburn, J. E. T. (Newcastle U), 1949 v S, W, Ni, Sw; 1950 v W, P, Bel, Sp; 1951 v W, Arg, P; 1952 v F; 1956 v D (13)
Miller, B. G. (Burnley), 1961 v A (1)
Miller, H. S. (Charlton Ath), 1923 v Se (1)
Mills, G. R. (Chelsea), 1938 v W, Ni, Cz (3)
Mills, M. D. (Ipswich T), 1973 v Y; 1976 v W (2), Ni, S, Br, I (sub), Fi; 1977 v Fi (sub), I, Ni, W, S; 1978 v WG, Br, W, Ni, S, H; 1979 v D, Ei, Ni (2), S, Bul, A; 1980 v D, Ni, Sp (2); 1981 v Sw (2), H; 1982 v N, H, S, Fi, F, Cz, K, WG, Sp (42)
Milne, G. (Liverpool), 1963 v Br, Cz, EG; 1964 v W, Ni, S, R of W, U, P, Ei, Br, Arg; 1965 v Ni, Bel (14)
Milton, C. A. (Arsenal), 1952 v A (1)
Milward, A. (Everton), 1891 v S, W; 1897 v S, W (4)
Mitchell, C. (Upton Park), 1880 v W; 1881 v S; 1883 v S, W; 1885 v W (5)
Mitchell, J. F. (Manchester C), 1925 v Ni (1)
Moffat, H. (Oldham Ath), 1913 v W (1)
Molyneux, G. (Southampton), 1902 v S; 1903 v S, W, Ni (4)
Moon, W. R. (Old Westminsters), 1888 v S, W; 1889 v S, W; 1890 v S, W; 1891 v S (7)
Moore, H. T. (Notts Co), 1883 v Ni; 1885 v W (2)
Moore, J. (Derby Co), 1923 v Se (1)
Moore, R. F. (West Ham U), 1962 v Pe, H, Arg, Bul, Br; 1963 v W, Ni, S, F (2), Br, Cz, EG, Sw; 1964 v W, Ni, S, R of W, U, P (2), Ei, Br, Arg; 1965 v Ni, S, Bel, H, Y, WG, Se; 1966 v W, Ni, S, A, Sp, Pol (2), WG (2), N, D, U, M, F, Arg, P; 1967 v W, Ni, S, Cz, Sp, A; 1968 v W, Ni, S, USSR (2), Sp (2), Se, Y, WG; 1969 v Ni, W, S, R, Bul, F, M, U, Br; 1970 v W, Ni, S, Ho, P, Bel, Co, Ec, R, Br, Cz, WG; 1971 v EG, Gr, Ma, Ni, S; 1972 v Sw (2), Gr, WG (2), W, S; 1973 v W (3), Y, S (2), Ni, Cz, Pol, USSR, I; 1974 v I (108)
Moore, W. G. B. (West Ham U), 1923 v Se (1)
Mordue, J. (Sunderland), 1912 v Ni; 1913 v Ni (2)
Morice, C. J. (Barnes), 1872 v S (1)
Morley, A. (Aston Villa), 1982 v H (sub), Ni, W, Ic; 1983 v D, Gr (6)
Morley, H. (Notts Co), 1910 v Ni (1)
Morren, T. (Sheffield U), 1898 v Ni (1)
Morris, F. (WBA), 1920 v S; 1921 v Ni (2)
Morris, J. (Derby Co), 1949 v N, F; 1950 v Ei (3)
Morris, W. W. (Wolverhampton W), 1939 v S, Ni, R (3)
Morse, H. (Notts Co), 1879 v S (1)
Mort, T. (Aston Villa), 1924 v W, F; 1926 v S (3)
Morten, A. (C Palace), 1873 v S (1)
Mortensen, S. H. (Blackpool), 1947 v P; 1948 v W, S, Ni, Bel, Se, I; 1949 v S, W, Ni, Se, N; 1950 v S, W, Ni, I, P, Bel, Ch, US, Sp; 1951 v S, Arg; 1954 v R of E, H (25)
Morton, J. R. (West Ham U), 1938 v Cz (1)
Mosforth, W. (Sheffield W), 1877 v S; (with Sheffield Albion), 1878 v S; 1879 v S, W; 1880 v S, W; (with Sheffield W), 1881 v W; 1882 v S, W (9)
Moss, F. (Arsenal), 1934 v S, H, Cz; 1935 v I (4)
Moss, F. (Aston Villa), 1922 v S, Ni; 1923 v Ni; 1924 v S, Bel (5)
Mosscrop, E. (Burnley), 1914 v S, W (2)
Mozley, B. (Derby Co), 1950 v W, Ni, Ei (3)
Mullen, J. (Wolverhampton W), 1947 v S; 1949 v N, F; 1950 v Bel (sub), Ch, US; 1954 v W, Ni, S, R of E, Y, Sw (12)
Mullery, A. P. (Tottenham H), 1965 v Ho; 1967 v Sp, A; 1968 v W, Ni, S, USSR, Sp (2), Se, Y; 1969 v Ni, S, R, Bul, F, M, U, Br; 1970 v W, Ni, S (sub), Ho, P, Bel, Co, Ec, R, Cz, WG, Br; 1971 v Ma, EG, Gr; 1972 v Sw (35)

Neal, P. G. (Liverpool), 1976 v W, I; 1977 v W, S, Br, Arg, U; 1978 v Sw, I, WG, Ni, S, H; 1979 v D, Ei, Ni (2), S, Bul, A; 1980 v D, Ni, Sp, Arg, W, Bel, I; 1981 v R, Sw, Sp, Br, H;

1982 v N, H, W, Ho, Ic, F (sub), K; 1983 v D, Gr, L, W, Gr, H, Ni, S, Aus (2); 1984 v D (50)
Needham, E. (Sheffield U), 1894 v S; 1895 v S; 1897 v S, W, Ni; 1898 v S, W; 1899 v S, W, Ni; 1900 v S, Ni; 1901 v S, W, Ni; 1902 v W (16)
Neville, G. A. (Manchester U), 1995 v J, Br; 1996 v Co, N, Sw, P, Bul, Cro, H, Chn, Sw, S, Ho, Sp; 1997 v Mol, Pol, I, Ge, Pol, I (sub), F, Br (sub); 1998 v Mol, Ch, P, S.Ar, Bel, R, Co, Arg; 1999 v Bul, Pol (32)
Neville, P. J. (Manchester U), 1996 v Chn; 1997 v S.Af, Pol (sub), I, F, Br; 1998 v Mol, Cam, Ch, P (sub), S.Ar (sub), Bel; 1999 v L, Pol (sub), H, Se, Bul (17)
Newton, K. R. (Blackburn R), 1966 v S, WG; 1967 v Sp, A; 1968 v W, S, Sp, Se, Y, WG; 1969 v Ni, W, S, R, Bul, M, U, Br, F; (with Everton), 1970 v Ni, S, Ho, Co, Ec, R, Cz, WG (27)
Nicholls, J. (WBA), 1954 v S, Y (2)
Nicholson, W. E. (Tottenham H), 1951 v P (1)
Nish, D. J. (Derby Co), 1973 v Ni; 1974 v P, W, Ni, S (5)
Norman, M. (Tottenham H), 1962 v Pe, H, Arg, Bul, Br; 1963 v S, F, Br, Cz, EG; 1964 v W, Ni, S, R of W, U, P (2), US, Br, Arg; 1965 v Ni, Bel, Ho (23)
Nuttall, H. (Bolton W), 1928 v W, Ni; 1929 v S (3)

Oakley, W. J. (Oxford University), 1895 v W; 1896 v S, W, Ni; (with Corinthians), 1897 v S, W, Ni; 1898 v S, W, Ni; 1900 v S, W, Ni; 1901 v S, W, Ni (16)
O'Dowd, J. P. (Chelsea), 1932 v S; 1933 v Ni, Sw (3)
O'Grady, M. (Huddersfield T), 1963 v Ni; (with Leeds U), 1969 v F (2)
Ogilvie, R. A. M. M. (Clapham R), 1874 v S (1)
Oliver, L. F. (Fulham), 1929 v Bel (1)
Olney, B. A. (Aston Villa), 1928 v F, Bel (2)
Osborne, F. R. (Fulham), 1923 v Ni, F; (with Tottenham H), 1925 v Bel; 1926 v Bel (4)
Osborne, R. (Leicester C), 1928 v W (1)
Osgood, P. L. (Chelsea), 1970 v Bel, R (sub), Cz (sub); 1974 v I (4)
Osman, R. (Ipswich T), 1980 v Aus; 1981 v Sp, R, Sw; 1982 v N, Ic; 1983 v D, Aus (3); 1984 v D (11)
Ottaway, C. J. (Oxford University), 1872 v S; 1874 v S (2)
Owen, J. R. B. (Sheffield), 1874 v S (1)
Owen, M. J. (Liverpool), 1998 v Ch, Sw, P (sub), Mor (sub), Bel (sub), Tun (sub), R, Co, Arg; 1999 v Se, Bul, L, F (13)
Owen, S. W. (Luton T), 1954 v H, Y, Bel (3)

Page, L. A. (Burnley), 1927 v S, W, Bel, L, F; 1928 v W, Ni (7)
Paine, T. L. (Southampton), 1963 v Cz, EG; 1964 v W, Ni, S, R of W, U, US, P; 1965 v Ni, H, Y, WG, Se; 1966 v W, A, Y, N, M (19)
Pallister, G. A. (Middlesbrough), 1988 v H; 1989 v S.Ar; (with Manchester U), 1991 v Cam (sub), T; 1992 v G; 1993 v N, US, Br, G; 1994 v Pol, Ho, Sm, D; 1995 v US, R, Ei, U, Se; 1996 v N, Swr; 1997 v Mol, Pol (sub) (22)
Palmer, C. L. (Sheffield W), 1992 v C, H, Br, Fi (sub), D, F, Se; 1993 v Sp (sub), N (sub), T, Sm, T, Ho, Pol, N, US, Br (sub); 1994 v Ho (18)
Pantling, H. H. (Sheffield U), 1924 v Ni (1)
Paravacini, P. J. de (Cambridge University), 1883 v S, W, Ni (3)
Parker, P. A. (QPR), 1989 v Alb (sub), Ch, D; 1990 v Y, U, Ho, Eg, Bel, Cam, WG, I; 1991 v H, Pol, USSR, Aus, Nz; (with Manchester U), 1992 v G; 1994 v Ho, D (19)
Parker, T. R. (Southampton), 1925 v F (1)
Parkes, P. B. (QPR), 1974 v P (1)
Parkinson, J. (Liverpool), 1910 v S, W (2)
Parlour, R. (Arsenal), 1999 v Pol (sub), Se (sub), Bul (sub) (3)
Parr, P. C. (Oxford University), 1882 v W (1)
Parry, E. H. (Old Carthusians), 1879 v W; 1882 v W, S (3)
Parry, R. A. (Bolton W), 1960 v Ni, S (2)
Patchitt, B. C. A. (Corinthians), 1923 v Se (2) (2)
Pawson, F. W. (Cambridge University), 1883 v Ni; (with Swifts), 1885 v Ni (2)
Payne, J. (Luton T), 1937 v Fi (1)
Peacock, A. (Middlesbrough), 1962 v Arg, Bul; 1963 v Ni, W; (with Leeds U), 1966 v W, Ni (6)
Peacock, J. (Middlesbrough), 1929 v F, Bel, Sp (3)
Pearce, S. (Nottingham F), 1987 v Br, S; 1988 v WG (sub), Is, H; 1989 v D, Se, S.Ar, Gr, Alb (2), Ch, S, Pol, D; 1990 v Pol, I, Y, Br, Cz, D, U, Tun, Ho, Eg, Bel, Cam, WG; 1991 v H, Pol, Ei (2), Cam, T, Arg, Aus, Nz (2), Mal; 1992 v T, Pol, F, Cz, Br (sub), Fi, D, F, Se; 1993 v Sp, N, T; 1994 v Pol, Sm, Gr (sub); 1995 v R (sub), J, Br; 1996 v N, Sw, P, Bul, Cro, H, Sw, S, Ho, Sp, G; 1997 v Mol, Pol, I, M, S.Af, I (76)
Pearson, H. F. (WBA), 1932 v S (1)

Scott, W. R. (Brentford), 1937 v W (1)
Seaman, D. A. (QPR), 1989 v S.Ar, D (sub); 1990 v Cz (sub); (with Arsenal), 1991 v Cam, Ei, T, Arg; 1992 v Cz, H (sub); 1994 v Pol, Ho, Sm, D, N; 1995 v US, R, Ei; 1996 v Co, N, Sw, P, Bul, Cro, H, Sw, S, Ho, Sp, G; 1997 v Mol, Pol, Ge (2), Pol, F, Br; 1998 v Mol, I, P, S.Ar, Tun, R, Co, Arg; 1999 v Se, Bul, L, F, Pol, H, Se, Bul (52)
Seddon, J. (Bolton W), 1923 v F, Se (2); 1924 v Bel; 1927 v W; 1929 v S (6)
Seed, J. M. (Tottenham H), 1921 v Bel: 1923 v W, Ni, Bel; 1925 v S (5)
Settle, J. (Bury), 1899 v S, W, Ni; (with Everton), 1902 v S, Ni; 1903 v Ni (6)
Sewell, J. (Sheffield W), 1952 v Ni, A, Sw; 1953 v Ni; 1954 v H (2) (6)
Sewell, W. R. (Blackburn R), 1924 v W (1)
Shackleton, L. F. (Sunderland), 1949 v W, D; 1950 v W; 1955 v W, WG (5)
Sharp, J. (Everton), 1903 v Ni; 1905 v S (2)
Sharpe, L. S. (Manchester U), 1991 v Ei (sub); 1993 v T (sub), N, US, Br, G; 1994 v Pol, Ho (8)
Shaw, G. E. (WBA), 1932 v S (1)
Shaw, G. L. (Sheffield U), 1959 v S, W, USSR, I; 1963 v W (5)
Shea, D. (Blackburn R), 1914 v W, Ni (2)
Shearer, A. (Southampton), 1992 v F, C, F; (with Blackburn R), 1993 v Sp, N, T; 1994 v Ho, D, Gr, N; 1995 v US, R, Ng, Ei, J, Se, Br; 1996 v Co, N, Sw, P, H (sub), Chn, Sw, S, Ho, Sp, G; (with Newcastle U), 1997 v Mol, Pol, I, Ge, Pol, F, Br; 1998 v Ch (sub), Sw, P, S.Ar, Tun, R, Co, Arg; 1999 v Se, Bul, L, F, Pol, H, Se, Bul (51)
Shellito, K. J. (Chelsea), 1963 v Cz (1)
Shelton A. (Notts Co), 1889 v Ni; 1890 v S, W; 1891 v S, W; 1892 v S (6)
Shelton, C. (Notts Rangers), 1888 v Ni (1)
Shepherd, A. (Bolton W), 1906 v S; (with Newcastle U), 1911 v Ni (2)
Sherwood, T. A. (Tottenham H), 1999 v Pol, H, Se (3)
Sheringham, E. P. (Tottenham H), 1993 v Pol, N; 1995 v US, R (sub), Ng (sub), U, J (sub), Se, Br; 1996 v Co (sub), N (sub), Sw, Bul, Cro, H, Sw, S, Ho, Sp, G; 1997 v Ge, M, Ge, S.Af, Pol, I, F (sub), Br; (with Manchester U), 1998 v I, Ch, Sw (sub), P, S.Ar, Tun, R; 1999 v Se (sub), Bul (sub+1) (38)
Shilton, P. L. (Leicester C), 1971 v EG, W; 1972 v Sw, Ni; 1973 v Y, S (2), Ni, W, Cz, Pol, USSR, I; 1974 v A, Pol, I, W, Ni, S, Arg; (with Stoke C), 1975 v Cy; 1977 v Ni, W; (with Nottingham F), 1978 v W, H; 1979 v Cz, Se, A; 1980 v Ni, Sp, I; 1981 v N, Sw, R; 1982 v H, Ho, S, F, Cz, K, WG, Sp; (with Southampton), 1983 v D, WG, Gr, W, Gr, H, Ni, S, Aus (3); 1984 v D, H, F, Ni, W, S, USSR, Br, U, Ch; 1985 v EG, Fi, T, Ni, R, Fi, S, I, WG; 1986 v R, T, Ni, Eg, Is, USSR, S, M, Ca, P, Mor, Pol, Para, Arg; 1987 v Se, Ni (2), Sp, Br; (with Derby Co), 1988 v WG, T, Y, Ho, S, Co, Sw, Ei, Ho; 1989 v D, Se, Gr, Alb (2), Ch, S, Pol, D; 1990 v Se, Pol, I, Y, Br, Cz, D, U, Tun, Ei, Ho, Eg, Bel, Cam, WG, I (125)
Shimwell, E. (Blackpool), 1949 v Se (1)
Shutt, G. (Stoke C), 1886 v Ni (1)
Silcock, J. (Manchester U), 1921 v S, W; 1923 v Se (3)
Sillett, R. P. (Chelsea), 1955 v F, Sp, P (3)
Simms, E. (Luton T), 1922 v Ni (1)
Simpson, J. (Blackburn R), 1911 v S, W, Ni; 1912 v S, W, Ni; 1913 v S; 1914 v W (8)
Sinton, A. (QPR), 1992 v Pol, C, H (sub), Br, F, Se; 1993 v Sp, T, Br, G; (with Sheffield W), 1994 v Ho (sub), Sm (12)
Slater, W. J. (Wolverhampton W), 1955 v W, WG; 1958 v S, P, Y, USSR (3), Br, A; 1959 v USSR; 1960 v S (12)
Smalley, T. (Wolverhampton W), 1937 v W (1)
Smart, T. (Aston Villa), 1921 v S; 1924 v S, W; 1926 v Ni; 1930 v W (5)
Smith, A. (Nottingham F), 1891 v S, W; 1893 v Ni (3)
Smith, A. K. (Oxford University), 1872 v S (1)
Smith, A. M. (Arsenal), 1989 v S.Ar (sub), Gr, Alb (sub) Pol (sub); 1991 v T, USSR, Arg; 1992 v G, T, Pol (sub), H (sub), D, Se (sub) (13)
Smith, B. (Tottenham H), 1921 v S; 1922 v W (2)
Smith, C. E. (C Palace), 1876 v S (1)
Smith, G. O. (Oxford University), 1893 v Ni; 1894 v W, S; 1895 v W; 1896 v Ni, W, S; (with Old Carthusians), 1897 v Ni, W, S; 1898 v Ni, W, S; (with Corinthians), 1899 v Ni, W, S; 1899 v Ni, W, S; 1901 v S (20)
Smith, H. (Reading), 1905 v W, S; 1906 v W, Ni (4)
Smith, J. (WBA), 1920 v Ni; 1923 v Ni (2)
Smith, Joe (Bolton W), 1913 v Ni; 1914 v S, W; 1920 v W, Ni (5)
Smith, J. C. R. (Millwall), 1939 v Ni, N (2)
Smith, J. W. (Portsmouth), 1932 v Ni, W, Sp (3)
Smith, Leslie (Brentford), 1939 v R (1)

Smith, Lionel (Arsenal), 1951 v W; 1952 v W, Ni; 1953 v W, S, Bel (6)
Smith, R. A. (Tottenham H), 1961 v Ni, W, S, L, P, Sp; 1962 v S; 1963 v S, F, Br, Cz, EG; 1964 v W, Ni, R of W (15)
Smith, S. (Aston Villa), 1895 v S (1)
Smith, S. C. (Leicester C), 1936 v Ni (1)
Smith, T. (Birmingham C), 1960 v W, Se (2)
Smith, T. (Liverpool), 1971 v W (1)
Smith, W. H. (Huddersfield T), 1922 v W, S; 1928 v S (3)
Sorby, T. H. (Thursday Wanderers, Sheffield), 1879 v W (1)
Southgate, G. (Aston Villa), 1996 v P (sub), Bul, H (sub), Chn, Sw, S, Ho, Sp, G; 1997 v Mol, Pol, Ge, M, Ge (sub), S.Af, Pol, I, F, Br; 1998 v Mol, I, Cam, Sw, S.Ar, Mor, Tun, Arg (sub); 1999 v Se, Bul, L, Bul (31)
Southworth, J. (Blackburn R), 1889 v W; 1891 v W; 1892 v S (3)
Sparks, F. J. (Herts Rangers), 1879 v S; (with Clapham Rovers), 1880 v S, W (3)
Spence, J. W. (Manchester U), 1926 v Bel; 1927 v Ni (2)
Spence, R. (Chelsea), 1936 v A, Bel (2)
Spencer, C. W. (Newcastle U), 1924 v S; 1925 v W (2)
Spencer, H. (Aston Villa), 1897 v S, W; 1900 v W; 1903 v Ni; 1905 v W, S (6)
Spiksley, F. (Sheffield W), 1893 v S, W; 1894 v S, Ni; 1896 v Ni; 1898 v S, W (7)
Spilsbury, B. W. (Cambridge University), 1885 v Ni; 1886 v Ni, S (3)
Spink, N. (Aston Villa), 1983 v Aus (sub) (1)
Spouncer, W. A. (Nottingham F), 1900 v W (1)
Springett, R. D. G. (Sheffield W), 1960 v Ni, S, Y, Sp, H; 1961 v Ni, S, L, P, Sp, M, I, A; 1962 v W, Ni, S, A, Sw, Pe, L, P, H, Arg, Bul, Br; 1963 v Ni, W, F (2), Sw; 1966 v W, A, N (33)
Sproston, B. (Leeds U), 1937 v W; 1938 v S, W, Ni, Cz, G, Sw, F; (with Tottenham H), 1939 v W, R of E; (with Manchester C), N (11)
Squire, R. T. (Cambridge University), 1886 v S, W, Ni (3)
Stanbrough, M. H. (Old Carthusians), 1895 v W (1)
Staniforth, R. (Huddersfield T), 1954 v S, H, Y, Bel, Sw, U; 1955 v W, WG (8)
Starling, R. W. (Sheffield W), 1933 v S; (with Aston Villa), 1937 v S (2)
Statham, D. (WBA), 1983 v W, Aus (2) (3)
Steele, F. C. (Stoke C), 1937 v S, W, Ni, N, Se, Fi (6)
Stein, B. (Luton T), 1984 v F (1)
Stephenson, C. (Huddersfield T), 1924 v W (1)
Stephenson, G. T. (Derby Co), 1928 v F, Bel; (with Sheffield W), 1931 v F (3)
Stephenson, J. E. (Leeds U), 1938 v S; 1939 v Ni (2)
Stepney, A. C. (Manchester U), 1968 v Se (1)
Sterland, M. (Sheffield W), 1989 v S.Ar (1)
Steven, T. M. (Everton), 1985 v Ni, Ei, R, Fi, I, US (sub); 1986 v T (sub), Eg, USSR (sub), M (sub), Pol, Para, Arg; 1987 v Se, Y (sub), Sp (sub); 1988 v T, Y, Ho, H, S, Sw, Ho, USSR; 1989 v S; (with Rangers), 1990 v Cz, Cam (sub), WG (sub), I; 1991 v Cam; (with Marseille), 1992 v G, C, Br, Fi, D, F (36)
Stevens, G. A. (Tottenham H), 1985 v Fi (sub), T (sub), Ni; 1986 v S (sub), M (sub), Mor (sub), Para (sub) (7)
Stevens, M. G. (Everton), 1985 v I, WG; 1986 v R, T, Ni, Eg, Is, S, Ca, P, Mor, Pol, Para, Arg; 1987 v Br, S; 1988 v T, Y, Is, Ho, H (sub), S, Sw, Ei, Ho, USSR; (with Rangers), 1989 v D, Se, Gr, Alb (2), S, Pol; 1990 v Se, Pol, I, Br, D, Tun, Ei, I; 1991 v USSR; 1992 v C, H, Br, Fi (46)
Stewart, J. (Sheffield W), 1907 v S, W; (with Newcastle U), 1911 v S (3)
Stewart, P. A. (Tottenham H), 1992 v G (sub), Cz (sub), C (sub) (3)
Stiles, N. P. (Manchester U), 1965 v S, H, Y, Se; 1966 v W, Ni, S, A, Sp, Pol (2), WG (2), N, D, U, M, F, Arg, P; 1967 v Ni, W, S, Cz; 1968 v USSR; 1969 v R; 1970 v Ni, S (28)
Stoker, J. (Birmingham), 1933 v W; 1934 v S, H (3)
Stone, S. B. (Nottingham F), 1996 v N (sub), Sw (sub), P, Bul, Cro, Chn (sub), Sw (sub), G (sub), Sp (sub) (9)
Storer, H. (Derby Co), 1924 v F; 1928 v Ni (2)
Storey, P. E. (Arsenal), 1971 v Gr, Ni, S; 1972 v Sw, WG, W, Ni, S; 1973 v W (3), Y, S (2), Ni, Cz, Pol, USSR, I (19)
Storey-Moore, I. (Nottingham F), 1970 v Ho (1)
Strange, A. H. (Sheffield W), 1930 v S, A, G; 1931 v S, W, Ni, F, Bel; 1932 v S, W, Ni, Sp; 1933 v S, Ni, A, I, Sw; 1934 v Ni, W, F (20)
Stratford, A. H. (Wanderers), 1874 v S (1)
Streten, B. (Luton T), 1950 v Ni (1)
Sturgess, A. (Sheffield U), 1911 v Ni; 1914 v S (2)
Summerbee, M. G. (Manchester C), 1968 v S, Sp, WG; 1972 v Sw, WG (sub), W, Ni; 1973 v USSR (sub) (8)

Sunderland, A. (Arsenal), 1980 v Aus (1)
Sutcliffe, J. W. (Bolton W), 1893 v W; 1895 v S, Ni; 1901 v S; (with Millwall), 1903 v W (5)
Sutton, C. R. (Blackburn R), 1998 v Cam (sub) (1)
Swan, P. (Sheffield W), 1960 v Y, Sp, H; 1961 v Ni, W, S, L, P, Sp, M, I, A; 1962 v W, Ni, S, A, Sw, L, P (19)
Swepstone, H. A. (Pilgrims), 1880 v S; 1882 v S, W; 1883 v S, W, Ni (6)
Swift, F. V. (Manchester C), 1947 v S, W, Ni, Ei, Ho, F, Sw, P; 1948 v S, W, Ni, Bel, Se, I; 1949 v S, W, Ni, D, N (19)

Tait, G. (Birmingham Excelsior), 1881 v W (1)
Talbot, B. (Ipswich T), 1977 v Ni (sub), S, Br, Arg, U; (with Arsenal), 1980 v Aus (6)
Tambling, R. V. (Chelsea), 1963 v W, F; 1966 v Y (3)
Tate, J. T. (Aston Villa), 1931 v F, Bel; 1933 v W (3)
Taylor, E. (Blackpool), 1954 v H (1)
Taylor, E. H. (Huddersfield T), 1923 v S, W, Ni, Bel; 1924 v S, Ni, F; 1926 v S (8)
Taylor, J. G. (Fulham), 1951 v Arg, P (2)
Taylor, P. H. (Liverpool), 1948 v W, Ni, Se (3)
Taylor, P. J. (C Palace), 1976 v W (sub+1), Ni, S (4)
Taylor, T. (Manchester U), 1953 v Arg, Ch, U; 1954 v Bel, Sw; 1956 v S, Br, Se, Fi, WG; 1957 v Ni, Y (sub), D (2), Ei (2); 1958 v W, Ni, F (19)
Temple, D. W. (Everton), 1965 v WG (1)
Thickett, H. (Sheffield U), 1899 v S, W (2)
Thomas, D. (Coventry C), 1983 v Aus (1+1 sub) (2)
Thomas, D. (QPR), 1975 v Cz (sub), P, Cy (sub+1), W, S (sub); 1976 v Cz (sub), P (sub) (8)
Thomas, G. R. (C Palace), 1991 v T, USSR, Arg, Aus, Nz (2), Mal; 1992 v Pol, F (9)
Thomas, M. L. (Arsenal), 1989 v S.Ar; 1990 v Y (2)
Thompson, P. (Liverpool), 1964 v P (2), Ei, US, Br, Arg; 1965 v Ni, W, S, Bel, Ho; 1966 v Ni; 1968 v Ni, WG; 1970 v S, Ho (sub) (16)
Thompson, P. B. (Liverpool), 1976 v W (2), Ni, S, Br, I, Fi; 1977 v Fi; 1979 v Ei (sub), Cz, Ni, S, Bul, Se (sub), A; 1980 v D, Ni, Bul, Ei, Sp (2), W, S, Bel, I; 1981 v N, R, H; 1982 v N, H, W, Ho, S, Fi, F, Cz, K, WG, Sp; 1983 v WG, Gr (42)
Thompson T. (Aston Villa), 1952 v W; (with Preston NE), 1957 v S (2)
Thomson, R. A. (Wolverhampton W), 1964 v Ni, US, P, Arg; 1965 v Bel, Ho, Ni, W (8)
Thornewell, G. (Derby Co), 1923 v Se (2); 1924 v F; 1925 v F (4)
Thornley, I. (Manchester C), 1907 v W (1)
Tilson, S. F. (Manchester C), 1934 v H, Cz; 1935 v W; 1936 v Ni (4)
Titmuss, F. (Southampton), 1922 v W; 1923 v W (2)
Todd, C. (Derby Co), 1972 v Ni; 1974 v P, W, Ni, S, Arg, EG, Bul, Y; 1975 v P (sub), WG, Cy (2), Ni, W, S; 1976 v Sw, Cz, P, Ni, S, Br, Fi; 1977 v Ei, Fi, Ho (sub), Ni (27)
Toone, G. (Notts Co), 1892 v S, W (2)
Topham, A. G. (Casuals), 1894 v W (1)
Topham, R. (Wolverhampton W), 1893 v Ni; (with Casuals), 1894 v W (2)
Towers, M. A. (Sunderland), 1976 v W, Ni (sub), I (3)
Townley, W. J. (Blackburn R), 1889 v W; 1890 v Ni (2)
Townrow, J. E. (Clapton Orient), 1925 v S; 1926 v W (2)
Tremelling, D. R. (Birmingham), 1928 v W (1)
Tresadern, J. (West Ham U), 1923 v S, Se (2)
Tueart, D. (Manchester C), 1975 v Cy (sub), Ni; 1977 v Fi, Ni, W (sub), S (sub) (6)
Tunstall, F. E. (Sheffield U), 1923 v S; 1924 v S, W, Ni, F; 1925 v Ni, S (7)
Turnbull, R. J. (Bradford), 1920 v Ni (1)
Turner, A. (Southampton), 1900 v Ni; 1901 v Ni (2)
Turner, H. (Huddersfield T), 1931 v F, Bel (2)
Turner, J. A. (Bolton W), 1893 v W; (with Stoke C), 1895 v Ni; (with Derby Co), 1898 v Ni (3)
Tweedy, G. J. (Grimsby T), 1937 v H (1)

Ufton, D. G. (Charlton Ath), 1954 v R of E (1)
Underwood, A. (Stoke C), 1891 v Ni; 1892 v Ni (2)
Unsworth, D. G. (Everton), 1995 v J (1)
Urwin, T. (Middlesbrough), 1923 v Se (2); 1924 v Bel; (with Newcastle U), 1926 v W (4)
Utley, G. (Barnsley), 1913 v Ni (1)

Vaughton, O. H. (Aston Villa), 1882 v S, W, Ni; 1884 v S, W (5)
Veitch, C. C. M. (Newcastle U), 1906 v S, W, Ni; 1907 v S, W; 1909 v W (6)
Veitch, J. G. (Old Westminsters), 1894 v W (1)

Venables, T. F. (Chelsea), 1965 v Ho, Bel (2)
Venison, B. (Newcastle U), 1995 v US, U (2)
Vidal, R. W. S. (Oxford University), 1873 v S (1)
Viljoen, C. (Ipswich T), 1975 v Ni, W (2)
Viollet, D. S. (Manchester U), 1960 v H; 1962 v L (2)
Von Donop (Royal Engineers), 1873 v S; 1875 v S (2)

Wace, H. (Wanderers), 1878 v S; 1879 v S, W (3)
Waddle, C. R. (Newcastle U), 1985 v Ei, R (sub), Fi (sub), S (sub), I, M (sub), WG, US; (with Tottenham H), 1986 v R, T, Ni, Is, USSR, S, M, Ca, P, Mor, Pol (sub), Arg (sub); 1987 v Se (sub), Ni (2), Y, Sp, T, Br, S; 1988 v WG, Is, H, S (sub), Co, Sw (sub), Ei, Ho (sub); 1989 v Se, S.Ar, Alb (2), Ch, S, Pol, D (sub); (with Marseille), 1990 v Se, Pol, I, Y, Br, D, U, Tun, Ei, Ho, Eg, Bel, Cam, WG, I (sub); 1991 v H (sub), Pol (sub); 1992 v T (62)
Wadsworth, S. J. (Huddersfield T), 1922 v S; 1923 v S, Bel; 1924 v S, Ni; 1925 v S, Ni; 1926 v W; 1927 v Ni (9)
Wainscoat, W. R. (Leeds U), 1929 v S (1)
Waiters, A. K. (Blackpool), 1964 v Ei, Br; 1965 v W, Bel, Ho (5)
Walden, F. I. (Tottenham H), 1914 v S; 1922 v W (2)
Walker, D. S. (Nottingham F), 1989 v D (sub), Se (sub), Gr, Alb (2), Ch, S, Pol, D; 1990 v Se, Pol, I, Y, Br, Cz, D, U, Tun, Ei, Ho, Eg, Bel, Cam, WG, I; 1991 v H, Pol, Ei (2), Cam, T, Arg, Aus, Nz (2), Mal; 1992 v T, Pol, F, Cz, C, H, Br, Fi, D, F, Se; 1993 v Sp, N, T, Sm, T, Ho, Pol, N, US (sub), Br, G; (with Sheffield W), 1994 v Sm (59)
Walker, I. M. (Tottenham H), 1996 v H (sub), Chn (sub); 1997 v I (3)
Walker, W. H. (Aston Villa), 1921 v Ni; 1922 v Ni, W, S; 1923 v Se (2); 1924 v S; 1925 v Ni, W, S, Bel, F; 1926 v Ni, W, S; 1927 v Ni, W; 1933 v A (18)
Wall, G. (Manchester U), 1907 v W; 1908 v Ni; 1909 v S; 1910 v W, S; 1912 v S; 1913 v Ni (7)
Wallace, C. W. (Aston Villa), 1913 v W; 1914 v Ni; 1920 v S (3)
Wallace, D. L. (Southampton), 1986 v Eg (1)
Walsh, P. (Luton T), 1983 v Aus (2 + 1 sub); 1984 v F, W (5)
Walters, A. M. (Cambridge University), 1885 v S, N; 1886 v S; 1887 v S, W; (with Old Carthusians), 1889 v S, W; 1890 v S, W (9)
Walters, K. M. (Rangers), 1991 v Nz (1)
Walters, P. M. (Oxford University), 1885 v S, Ni; (with Old Carthusians), 1886 v S, W, Ni; 1887 v S, W; 1888 v S, Ni; 1889 v S, W; 1890 v S, W (13)
Walton, N. (Blackburn R), 1890 v Ni (1)
Ward, J. T. (Blackburn Olympic), 1885 v W (1)
Ward, P. (Brighton & HA), 1980 v Aus (sub) (1)
Ward, T. V. (Derby Co), 1948 v Bel; 1949 v W (2)
Waring, T. (Aston Villa), 1931 v F, Bel; 1932 v S, W, Ni (5)
Warner, C. (Upton Park), 1878 v S (1)
Warren, B. (Derby Co), 1906 v S, W, Ni; 1907 v S, W, Ni; 1908 v S, W, Ni, A (2), H, B; (with Chelsea), 1909 v S, Ni, W, H (2), A; 1911 v S, Ni, W (22)
Waterfield, G. S. (Burnley), 1927 v W (1)
Watson, D. (Norwich C), 1984 v Br, U, Ch; 1985 v M, US (sub); 1986 v S; (with Everton), 1987 v Ni; 1988 v Is, Ho, S, Sw (sub); USSR (12)
Watson, D. V. (Sunderland), 1974 v P, S (sub), Arg, EG, Bul, Y; 1975 v Cz, P, WG, Cy (2), Ni, W, S; (with Manchester C), 1976 v Sw, Cz (sub), P; 1977 v Ho, L, Ni, W, S, Br, Arg, U; 1978 v Sw, L, I, WG, Br, W, Ni, S, H; 1979 v D, Ei, Cz, Ni (2), W, S, Bul, Se, A; (with Werder Bremen), 1980 v D; (with Southampton), Ni, Bul, Ei, Sp (2), Arg, Ni, S, Bel, I; 1981 v N, R, Sw, R, W, S, Sw, H; (with Stoke C), 1982 v Ni, Ic (65)
Watson, V. M. (West Ham U), 1923 v W, S; 1930 v S, G, A (5)
Watson, W. (Burnley), 1913 v S; 1914 v Ni; 1920 v Ni (3)
Watson, W. (Sunderland), 1950 v Ni, I; 1951 v W, Y (4)
Weaver, S. (Newcastle U), 1932 v S, 1933 v S, Ni (3)
Webb, G. W. (West Ham U), 1911 v S, W (2)
Webb, N. J. (Nottingham F), 1988 v WG (sub), T, Y, Is, Ho, S, Sw, Ei, USSR (sub); 1989 v D, Se, Gr, Alb (2), Ch, S, Pol, D; (with Manchester U), 1990 v Se, I (sub); 1992 v F, H, Br (sub), Fi, D (sub), Se (26)
Webster, M. (Middlesbrough), 1930 v S, A, G (3)
Wedlock, W. J. (Bristol C), 1907 v S, Ni, W; 1908 v S, Ni, W, A (2), H, B; 1909 v S, W, Ni, H (2), A; 1910 v S, W, Ni; 1911 v S, W, Ni; 1912 v S, W, Ni; 1914 v W (26)
Weir, D. (Bolton W), 1889 v S, Ni (2)
Welch, R. de C. (Wanderers), 1872 v S; (with Harrow Chequers), 1874 v S (2)
Weller, K. (Leicester C), 1974 v Ni, S, Arg (4)
Welsh, D. (Charlton Ath), 1938 v G, Sw; 1939 v R (3)
West, G. (Everton), 1969 v W, Bul, M (3)

Westwood, R. W. (Bolton W), 1935 v S, W, Ho; 1936 v Ni, G; 1937 v W (6)
Whateley, O. (Aston Villa), 1883 v S, Ni (2)
Wheeler, J. E. (Bolton W), 1955 v Ni (1)
Wheldon, G. F. (Aston Villa), 1897 v Ni; 1898 v S, W, Ni (4)
White, D. (Manchester C), 1993 v Sp (1)
White, T. A. (Everton), 1933 v I (1)
Whitehead, J. (Accrington), 1893 v W; (with Blackburn R), 1894 v Ni (2)
Whitfeld, H. (Old Etonians), 1879 v W (1)
Whitham, M. (Sheffield U), 1892 v Ni (1)
Whitworth, S. (Leicester C), 1975 v WG, Cy, Ni, W, S; 1976 v Sw, P (7)
Whymark, T. J. (Ipswich T), 1978 v L (sub) (1)
Widdowson, S. W. (Nottingham F), 1880 v S (1)
Wignall, F. (Nottingham F), 1965 v W, Ho (2)
Wilcox, J. M. (Blackburn R), 1996 v H; 1999 v F (sub) (2)
Wilkes, A. (Aston Villa), 1901 v S, W; 1902 v S, W, Ni (5)
Wilkins, R. G. (Chelsea), 1976 v I; 1977 v Ei, Fi, Ni, Br, Arg, U; 1978 v Sw (sub), L, I, WG, W, Ni, S, H; 1979 v D, Ei, Cz, Ni, W, S, Bul, Se (sub), A; (with Manchester U), 1980 v D, Ni, Bul, Sp (2), Arg, W (sub), Ni, S, Bel, I; 1981 v Sp (sub), R, Br, W, S, Sw, H (sub); 1982 v Ni, W, Ho, S, Fi, F, Cz, K, WG, Sp; 1983 v D, WG; 1984 v D, Ni, W, S, USSR, Br, U, Ch; (with AC Milan), 1985 v EG, Fi, T, Ni, Ei, R, Fi, S, I, M; 1986 v T, Ni, Is, Eg, USSR, S, M, Ca, P, Mor; 1987 v Se, Y (sub) (84)
Wilkinson, B. (Sheffield U), 1904 v S (1)
Wilkinson, L. R. (Oxford University), 1891 v W (1)
Williams, B. F. (Wolverhampton W), 1949 v F; 1950 v S, W, Ei, I, P, Bel, Ch, US, Sp; 1951 v Ni, W, S, Y, Arg, P; 1952 v W, F; 1955 v S, WG, F, Sp, P; 1956 v W (24)
Williams, O. (Clapton Orient), 1923 v W, Ni (2)
Williams, S. (Southampton), 1983 v Aus (1+1 sub); 1984 v F; 1985 v EG, Fi, T (6)
Williams, W. (WBA), 1897 v Ni; 1898 v W, Ni, S; 1899 v W, Ni (6)
Williamson, E. C. (Arsenal), 1923 v Se (2) (2)
Williamson, R. G. (Middlesbrough), 1905 v Ni; 1911 v Ni, S, W; 1912 v S, W; 1913 v Ni (7)
Willingham, C. K. (Huddersfield T), 1937 v Fi; 1938 v S, G, Sw, F; 1939 v S, W, Ni, R of E, N, I, Y (12)
Willis, A. (Tottenham H), 1952 v F (1)
Wilshaw, D. J. (Wolverhampton W), 1954 v W, Sw, U; 1955 v S, F, Sp, P; 1956 v W, Ni, Fi, WG; 1957 v Ni (12)
Wilson, C. P. (Hendon), 1884 v S, W (2)
Wilson, C. W. (Oxford University), 1879 v W; 1881 v S (2)
Wilson, G. (Sheffield W), 1921 v S, W, Bel; 1922 v S, Ni; 1923 v S, W, Ni, Bel; 1924 v W, Ni, F (12)
Wilson, G. P. (Corinthians), 1900 v S, W (2)
Wilson, R. (Huddersfield T), 1960 v S, Y, Sp, H; 1962 v W, Ni, S, A, Sw, Pe, P, H, Arg, Bul, Br; 1963 v Ni, F, Br, Cz, EG, Sw; 1964 v W, S, R of W, U, P (2), Ei, Br, Arg; (with Everton), 1965 v S, H, Y, WG, Se; 1966 v WG (sub), W, Ni, A, Sp, Pol (2), Y, Fi, D, U, M, F, Arg, P, WG; 1967 v Ni, W, S, Cz, A; 1968 v Ni, S, USSR (2), Sp (2), Y (63)
Wilson, T. (Huddersfield T), 1928 v S (1)
Winckworth, W. N. (Old Westminsters), 1892 v W; 1893 v Ni (2)
Windridge, J. E. (Chelsea), 1908 v S, W, Ni, A (2), H, B; 1909 v Ni (8)
Wingfield-Stratford, C. V. (Royal Engineers), 1877 v S (1)
Winterburn, N. (Arsenal), 1990 v I (sub); 1993 v G (sub) (2)
Wise, D. F. (Chelsea), 1991 v T, USSR, Aus (sub), Nz (2); 1994 v N; 1995 v R (sub), Ng; 1996 v Co, N, P, H (sub) (12)
Withe, P. (Aston Villa), 1981 v Br, W, S; 1982 v N (sub), W, Ic; 1983 v H, Ni, S; 1984 v H (sub); 1985 v T (11)
Wollaston, C. H. R. (Wanderers), 1874 v S; 1875 v S; 1877 v S; 1880 v S (4)

Wolstenholme, S. (Everton), 1904 v S; (with Blackburn R), 1905 v W, Ni (3)
Wood, H. (Wolverhampton W), 1890 v S, W; 1896 v S (3)
Wood, R. E. (Manchester U), 1955 v Ni, W; 1956 v Fi (3)
Woodcock, A. S. (Nottingham F), 1978 v Ni; 1979 v Ei (sub), Cz, Bul (sub), Se; 1980 v Ni; (with Cologne), Bul, Ei, Sp (2), Arg, Bel, I; 1981 v N, R, Sw, R, W (sub), S; 1982 v Ni (sub), Ho, Fi (sub), WG (sub), Sp; (with Arsenal), 1983 v WG (sub), Gr, L, Gr; 1984 v L, F (sub), Ni, W, S, Br, U (sub); 1985 v EG, Fi, T, Ni; 1986 v R (sub), T (sub), Is (sub) (42)
Woodgate, J. S. (Leeds U), 1999 v Bul (1)
Woodger, G. (Oldham Ath), 1911 v Ni (1)
Woodhall, G. (WBA), 1888 v S, W (2)
Woodley, V. R. (Chelsea), 1937 v S, N, Se, Fi; 1938 v S, W, Ni, Cz, G, Sw, F; 1939 v S, W, Ni, R of E, N, I, R, Y (19)
Woods, C. C. E. (Norwich C), 1985 v US; 1986 v Eg (sub), Is (sub), Ca (sub); (with Rangers), 1987 v Y, Sp (sub), Ni (sub), T, S; 1988 v Is, H, Sw (sub), USSR; 1989 v D (sub); 1990 v Br (sub), D (sub); 1991 v H, Pol, Ei, USSR, Aus, Nz (2), Mal; (with Sheffield W), 1992 v G, T, Pol, F, C, Br, Fi, D, F, Se; 1993 v Sp, N, T, Sm, T, Ho, Pol, N, US (43)
Woodward, V. J. (Tottenham H), 1903 v S, W, Ni; 1904 v S, Ni; 1905 v S, W, Ni; 1907 v S; 1908 v S, W, Ni, A (2), H, B; 1909 v W, Ni, H (2), A; (with Chelsea), 1910 v Ni; 1911 v W (23)
Woosnam, M. (Manchester C), 1922 v W (1)
Worrall, F. (Portsmouth), 1935 v Ho; 1937 v Ni (2)
Worthington, F. S. (Leicester C), 1974 v Ni (sub), S, Arg, EG, Bul, Y; 1975 v Cz, P (sub) (8)
Wreford-Brown, C. (Oxford University), 1889 v Ni; (with Old Carthusians), 1894 v W; 1895 v W; 1898 v S (4)
Wright, E, G. D. (Cambridge University), 1906 v W (1)
Wright, I. E. (C Palace), 1991 v Cam, Ei (sub), USSR, Nz; (with Arsenal), 1992 v H (sub); 1993 v N, T (2), Pol (sub), N (sub), US (sub), Br, G (sub); 1994 v Pol, Ho (sub), Sm, Gr (sub), N (sub); 1995 v US (sub), R; 1997 v Ge (sub), I (sub), M (sub), S.Af, I, F, Br (sub); 1998 v Mol, I, S.Ar (sub), Mor; (with West Ham U), 1999 v L (sub), CzR (33)
Wright, J. D. (Newcastle U), 1939 v N (1)
Wright, M. (Southampton), 1984 v W; 1985 v EG, Fi, T, Ei, R, I, WG; 1986 v R, T, Ni, Eg, USSR; 1987 v Y, Ni, S; (with Derby Co), 1988 v Is, Ho (sub), Co, Sw, Ei, Ho; 1990 v Cz (sub), Tun (sub), Ho, Eg, Bel, Cam, WG, I; 1991 v H, Pol, Ei (2), Cam, USSR, Arg, Aus, Nz, Mal; (with Liverpool), 1992 v F, Fi; 1993 v Sp; 1996 v Cro, H (45)
Wright, T. J. (Everton), 1968 v USSR; 1969 v R (2), M (sub), U, Br; 1970 v W, Ho, Bel, R (sub), Br (11)
Wright, W. A. (Wolverhampton W), 1947 v S, W, Ni, Ei, Ho, F, Sw, P; 1948 v S, W, Ni, Bel, Se, I; 1949 v S, W, Ni, D, Sw, Se, N, F; 1950 v S, W, Ni, Ei, I, P, Bel, Ch, US, Sp; 1951 v Ni, S, Arg; 1952 v W, Ni, S, F, A (2), I, Sw; 1953 v Ni, W, S, Bel, Arg, Ch, U, US; 1954 v W, Ni, S, R of E, H (2), Y, Bel, Sw, U; 1955 v W, Ni, S, WG, F, Sp, P; 1956 v Ni, W, S, Br, Se, Fi, WG, D, Sp; 1957 v S, W, Ni, Y, D (2), Ei (2); 1958 v W, Ni, S, P, Y, USSR (3), Br, A, F; 1959 v W, Ni, S, USSR, I, Br, Pe, M, US (105)
Wylie, J. G. (Wanderers), 1878 v S (1)

Yates, J. (Burnley), 1889 v Ni (1)
York, R. E. (Aston Villa), 1922 v S; 1926 v S (2)
Young, A. (Huddersfield T), 1933 v W; 1937 v S, H, N, Se; 1938 v G, Sw, F; 1939 v W (9)
Young, G. M. (Sheffield W), 1965 v W (1)

R. E. Evans also played for Wales against E, Ni, S; J. Reynolds also played for Ireland against E, W, S.

NORTHERN IRELAND

Aherne, T. (Belfast C), 1947 v E; 1948 v S; 1949 v W; (with Luton T), 1950 v W (4)
Alexander, T. E. (Cliftonville), 1895 v S (1)
Allan, C. (Cliftonville), 1936 v E (1)
Allen, J. (Limavady), 1887 v E (1)
Anderson, T. (Manchester U), 1973 v Cy, E, S, W; 1974 v Bul, P; (with Swindon T), 1975 v S (sub); 1976 v Is; 1977 v Ho, Bel, WG, E, S, W, Ic; 1978 v Ic, Ho, Bel; (with Peterborough U), S, E, W; 1979 v D (sub) (22)
Anderson, W. (Linfield), 1898 v W, E, S; (with Cliftonville), 1899 v S (4)
Andrews, W. (Glentoran), 1908 v S; (with Grimsby T), 1913 v E, S (3)

Armstrong, G. J. (Tottenham H), 1977 v WG, E, W (sub), Ic (sub); 1978 v Bel, S, E, W; 1979 v Ei, D, Bul, E, Bul, E, S, W, D; 1980 v E, Ei, Is, S, E, Aus (3); 1981 v Se; (with Watford), P, S, P, S, Se; 1982 v S, Is, E, F, W, Y, Hon, Sp, A, F; 1983 v A, T, Alb, S, E, W; (with Real Mallorca), 1984 v A, W, E, W, Fi; 1985 v R, Fi, E, Sp; (with WBA), 1986 v T, R (sub), E (sub), F (sub); (with Chesterfield), D (sub), Br (sub) (63)

Baird, G. (Distillery), 1896 v S, E, W (3)
Baird, H. C. (Huddersfield T), 1939 v E (1)
Balfe, J. (Shelbourne), 1909 v E; 1910 v W (2)

Bambrick, J. (Linfield), 1929 v W, S, E; 1930 v W, S, E; 1932 v W; (with Chelsea), 1935 v W; 1936 v E, S; 1938 v W (11)
Banks, S. J. (Cliftonville), 1937 v W (1)
Barr, H. H. (Linfield), 1962 v E; (with Coventry C), 1963 v E, Pol (3)
Barron, J. H. (Cliftonville), 1894 v E, W, S; 1895 v S; 1896 v S; 1897 v E, W (7)
Barry, J. (Cliftonville), 1888 v W, S; 1889 v E (3)
Barry, J. (Bohemians), 1900 v S (1)
Baxter, R. A. (Distillery), 1887 v S (1)
Baxter, S. N. (Cliftonville), 1887 v W (1)
Bennett, L. V. (Dublin University), 1889 v W (1)
Berry, J. (Cliftonville), 1888 v S, W; 1889 v E (3)
Best, G. (Manchester U), 1964 v W, U; 1965 v E, Ho (2), S, Sw (2), Alb; 1966 v S, E, Alb; 1967 v E; 1968 v S; 1969 v E, S, W, T; 1970 v S, E, W, USSR; 1971 v Cy (2), Sp, E, S, W; 1972 v USSR, Sp; 1973 v Bul; 1974 v P; (with Fulham), 1977 v Ho, Bel, WG; 1978 v Ic, Ho (37)
Bingham, W. L. (Sunderland), 1951 v F; 1952 v E, S, W; 1953 v E, S, F, W; 1954 v E, S, W; 1955 v E, S, W; 1956 v E, S, W; 1957 v E, S, W, P (2), I; 1958 v S, E, W, I (2), Arg, Cz (2), WG, F; (with Luton T), 1959 v E, S, W, Sp; 1960 v S, E, W; (with Everton), 1961 v E, S, WG (2), Gr, I; 1962 v E, Gr; 1963 v E, S, Pol (2), Sp; (with Port Vale), 1964 v S, E, Sp (56)
Black, K. T. (Luton T), 1988 v Fr (sub), Ma (sub); 1989 v Ei, H, Sp (2), Ch (sub); 1990 v H, N, U; 1991 v Y (2), D, A, Pol, Fa; (with Nottingham F), 1992 v Fa, A, D, S, Li, G; 1993 v Sp, D (sub), Alb, Ei (sub), Sp; 1994 v D (sub), Ei (sub), R (sub) (30)
Black, T. (Glentoran), 1901 v E (1)
Blair, H. (Portadown), 1931 v S; 1932 v S; (with Swansea), 1934 v S (3)
Blair, J. (Cliftonville), 1907 v W, E, S; 1908 v E, S (5)
Blair, R. V. (Oldham Ath), 1975 v Se (sub), S (sub), W; 1976 v Se, Is (5)
Blanchflower, R. D. (Barnsley), 1950 v S, W; 1951 v E, S; (with Aston Villa), F; 1952 v W; 1953 v E, S, W, F; 1954 v E, S, W; 1955 v E, S; (with Tottenham H), W; 1956 v E, S, W; 1957 v E, S, W, I, P (2); 1958 v E, S, W, I (2), Cz (2), Arg, F, WG; 1959 v E, S, W, Sp; 1960 v E, S, W; 1961 v E, S, W, WG (2); 1962 v E, S, W, Gr, Ho; 1963 v E, S, Pol (2) (56)
Blanchflower, J. (Manchester U), 1954 v W; 1955 v E, S; 1956 v S, W; 1957 v S, E, P; 1958 v S, E, I (2) (12)
Bookman, L. J. O. (Bradford C), 1914 v W; (with Luton T), 1921 v S, W; 1922 v E (4)
Bothwell, A. W. (Ards), 1926 v S, E, W; 1927 v E, W (5)
Bowler, G. C. (Hull C), 1950 v E, S, W (3)
Boyle, P. (Sheffield U), 1901 v E; 1902 v E; 1903 v S, W; 1904 v E (5)
Braithwaite, R. M. (Linfield), 1962 v W; 1963 v P, Sp; (with Middlesbrough), 1964 v W, U; 1965 v E, S, Sw (2), Ho (10)
Breen, T. (Belfast C), 1935 v E, W; 1937 v E, S; (with Manchester U), 1937 v W; 1938 v E, S; 1939 v W, S (9)
Brennan, B. (Bohemians), 1912 v W (1)
Brennan, R. A. (Luton T), 1949 v W; (with Birmingham C), 1950 v E, S, W; (with Fulham), 1951 v E (5)
Briggs, W. R. (Manchester U), 1962 v W; (with Swansea T), 1965 v Ho (2)
Brisby, D. (Distillery), 1891 v S (1)
Brolly, T. H. (Millwall), 1937 v W; 1938 v W; 1939 v E, W (4)
Brookes, E. A. (Shelbourne), 1920 v S (1)
Brotherston, N. (Blackburn R), 1980 v S, E, W, Aus (3); 1981 v Se, P; 1982 v S, Is, E, F, S, W, Hon (sub), A (sub); 1983 v A (sub), WG, Alb, T, Alb, S (sub), E (sub), W; 1984 v T; 1985 v Is (sub), T (27)
Brown, J. (Glenavon), 1921 v W; (with Tranmere R), 1924 v E, W (3)
Brown, J. (Wolverhampton W), 1935 v E, W; 1936 v E; (with Coventry C), 1937 v E, W; 1938 v S, W; (with Birmingham C), 1939 v E, S, W (10)
Brown, N. M. (Limavady), 1887 v E (1)
Brown, W. G. (Glenavon), 1926 v W (1)
Browne, F. (Cliftonville), 1887 v E, S, W; 1888 v E, S (5)
Browne, R. J. (Leeds U), 1936 v E, W; 1938 v E, W; 1939 v E, S (6)
Bruce, W. (Glentoran), 1961 v S; 1967 v W (2)
Buckle, H. R. (Sunderland), 1904 v E; (with Bristol R), 1908 v W (2)
Buckle, J. (Cliftonville), 1882 v E (1)
Burnett, J. (Distillery), 1894 v E, W, S; (with Glentoran), 1895 v E, W (5)
Burnison, J. (Distillery), 1901 v E, W (2)
Burnison, S. (Distillery), 1908 v E; 1910 v E, S; (with Bradford), 1911 v E, S, W; (with Distillery), 1912 v E; 1913 v W (8)

Burns, J. (Glenavon), 1923 v E (1)
Butler, M. P. (Blackpool), 1939 v W (1)

Campbell, A. C. (Crusaders), 1963 v W; 1965 v Sw (2)
Campbell, D. A. (Nottingham F), 1986 v Mor (sub), Br; 1987 v E (2), T, Y; (with Charlton Ath), 1988 v Y, T (sub), Gr (sub), Pol (sub) (10)
Campbell, James (Cliftonville), 1897 v E, S, W; 1898 v E, S, W; 1899 v E; 1900 v E, S; 1901 v S, W; 1902 v S; 1903 v E; 1904 v S (14)
Campbell, John (Cliftonville), 1896 v W (1)
Campbell, J. P. (Fulham), 1951 v E, S (2)
Campbell, R. M. (Bradford C), 1982 v S, W (sub) (2)
Campbell, W. G. (Dundee), 1968 v S, E; 1969 v T; 1970 v S, W, USSR (6)
Carey, J. J. (Manchester U), 1947 v E, W; 1948 v E; 1949 v E, S, W (7)
Carroll, E. (Glenavon), 1925 v S (1)
Carroll, R. E. (Wigan Ath), 1997 v Th (sub); 1999 v Ei (sub) (2)
Casey, T. (Newcastle U), 1955 v W; 1956 v W; 1957 v E, S, W, I, P (2); 1958 v WG, F; (with Portsmouth), 1959 v E, Sp (12)
Caskey, W. (Derby Co), 1979 v Bul, E, Bul, E, S (sub), D (sub); 1980 v E (sub); (with Tulsa R), 1982 v F (sub) (8)
Cassidy, T. (Newcastle U), 1971 v E (sub); 1972 v USSR (sub); 1974 v Bul (sub), S, E, W; 1975 v N; 1976 v S, E, W; 1977 v WG (sub); 1980 v E, S (sub), Is, S, E, W, Aus (3); (with Burnley), 1981 v Se, P; 1982 v Is, Sp (sub) (24)
Caughey, M. (Linfield), 1986 v F (sub), D (sub) (2)
Chambers, R. J. (Distillery), 1921 v W; (with Bury), 1928 v E, S, W; 1929 v E, S, W; 1930 v S, W; (with Nottingham F), 1932 v E, S, W (12)
Chatton, H. A. (Partick T), 1925 v E, S; 1926 v E (3)
Christian, J. (Linfield), 1889 v S (1)
Clarke, C. J. (Bournemouth), 1986 v F, D, Mor, Alg (sub), Sp, Br; (with Southampton), 1987 v E, T, Y; 1988 v Y, T, Gr, Pol, F, Ma; 1989 v Ei, H, Sp (1+1 sub); (with QPR), Ma, Ch; 1990 v H, Ei, N; (with Portsmouth), 1991 v Y (sub), D, A, Pol, Y (sub), Fa; 1992 v Fa, D, S, G; 1993 v Alb, Sp, D (38)
Clarke, R. (Belfast C), 1901 v E, S (2)
Cleary, J. (Glentoran), 1982 v W; 1983 v W (sub); 1984 v T (sub); 1985 v Is (5)
Clements, D. (Coventry C), 1965 v W, Ho; 1966 v M; 1967 v S, W; 1968 v S, E; 1969 v T (2), S, W; 1970 v S, E, W, USSR (2); 1971 v Sp, E, S, W, Cy; (with Sheffield W), 1972 v USSR (2), Sp, E, S, W; 1973 v Bul, Cy (2), P, E, S, W; (with Everton), 1974 v Bul, P, S, E, W; 1975 v N, Y, E, S, W; 1976 v Se, Y; (with New York Cosmos), E, W (48)
Clugston, J. (Cliftonville), 1888 v W; 1889 v W, S, E; 1890 v E, S; 1891 v E, W; 1892 v E, S, W; 1893 v E, S, W (14)
Cochrane, D. (Leeds U), 1939 v E, W; 1947 v E, S, W; 1948 v E, S, W; 1949 v S, W; 1950 v S, E (12)
Cochrane, M. (Distillery), 1898 v S, W, E; 1899 v E; 1900 v E, S, W; (with Leicester Fosse), 1901 v S, W (8)
Cochrane, G. T. (Coleraine), 1976 v N (sub); (with Burnley), 1978 v S (sub), E (sub), W (sub); 1979 v Ei (sub); (with Middlesbrough), D, Bul, E, Bul, E; 1980 v Is, E (sub), W (sub), Aus (1+2 sub); 1981 v Se (sub), P (sub), S, P, S, Se; 1982 v E (sub), F; (with Gillingham), 1984 v S, Fi (sub) (26)
Collins, F. (Celtic), 1922 v S (1)
Condy, J. (Distillery), 1882 v W; 1886 v E, S (3)
Connell, T. E. (Coleraine), 1978 v W (sub) (1)
Connor, J. (Glentoran), 1901 v S, E; (with Belfast C), 1905 v E, S, W; 1907 v E, S; 1908 v E, S; 1909 v W; 1911 v S, E, W (13)
Connor, M. J. (Brentford), 1903 v S, W; (with Fulham), 1904 v E (3)
Cook, W. (Celtic), 1933 v E, W, S; (with Everton), 1935 v E; 1936 v S, W; 1937 v E, S, W; 1938 v E, S, W; 1939 v E, S, W (15)
Cooke, S. (Belfast YMCA), 1889 v E; (with Cliftonville), 1890 v E, S (3)
Coote, A. (Norwich C), 1999 v Ca, Ei (sub) (2)
Coulter, J. (Belfast C), 1934 v E, S, W; (with Everton), 1935 v E, S, W; 1937 v S, W; (with Grimsby T), 1938 v S, W; (with Chelmsford C), 1939 v S (11)
Cowan, J. (Newcastle U), 1970 v E (sub) (1)
Cowan, T. S. (Queen's Island), 1925 v W (1)
Coyle, F. (Coleraine), 1956 v E, S; 1957 v P; (with Nottingham F), 1958 v Arg (4)
Coyle, L. (Derry City), 1989 v Ch (sub) (1)
Coyle, R. I. (Sheffield W), 1973 v P, Cy (sub), W (sub); 1974 v Bul (sub), P (sub) (5)
Craig, A. B. (Rangers), 1908 v E, S, W; 1909 v S; (with Morton), 1912 v S, W; 1914 v E, S, W (9)

Craig, D. J. (Newcastle U), 1967 v W; 1968 v W; 1969 v T (2), E, S, W; 1970 v E, S, W, USSR; 1971 v Cy (2), Sp, S (sub); 1972 v USSR, S (sub); 1973 v Cy (2), E, S, W; 1974 v Bul, P; 1975 v N (25)

Crawford, A. (Distillery), 1889 v E, W; (with Cliftonville), 1891 v E, S, W; 1893 v E, W (7)

Croft, T. (Queen's Island), 1924 v E (1)

Crone, R. (Distillery), 1889 v S; 1890 v E, S, W (4)

Crone, W. (Distillery), 1882 v W; 1884 v E, S, W; 1886 v E, S, W; 1887 v E; 1888 v E, W; 1889 v S; 1890 v W (12)

Crooks, W. J. (Manchester U), 1922 v W (1)

Crossan, E. (Blackburn R), 1950 v S; 1951 v E; 1955 v W (3)

Crossan, J. A. (Sparta-Rotterdam), 1960 v E; (with Sunderland), 1963 v W, P, Sp; 1964 v E, S, W, U, Sp; 1965 v E, S, Sw (2); (with Manchester C), W, Ho (2), Alb; 1966 v S, E, Alb, WG; 1967 v E, S; (with Middlesbrough), 1968 v S (24)

Crothers, C. (Distillery), 1907 v W (1)

Cumming, L. (Huddersfield T), 1929 v W, S; (with Oldham Ath), 1930 v E (3)

Cunningham, W. (Ulster), 1892 v S, E, W; 1893 v E (4)

Cunningham, W. E. (St Mirren), 1951 v W; 1953 v E; 1954 v S; 1955 v S; (with Leicester C), 1956 v E, S, W; 1957 v E, S, W, I, P (2); 1958 v S, W, I, Cz (2), Arg, WG, F; 1959 v E, S, W; 1960 v E, S, W; (with Dunfermline Ath), 1961 v W; 1962 v W, Ho (30)

Curran, S. (Belfast C), 1926 v S, W; 1928 v S (3)

Curran, J. J. (Glenavon), 1922 v W; (with Pontypridd), 1923 v E, S; (with Glenavon), 1924 v E (4)

Cush, W. W. (Glenavon), 1951 v E, S; 1954 v S, E; 1957 v W, I, P (2); (with Leeds U), 1958 v I (2), W, Cz (2), Arg, WG, F; 1959 v E, S, W, Sp; 1960 v E, S, W; (with Portadown), 1961 v WG, Gr; 1962 v Gr (26)

Dalton, W. (YMCA), 1888 v S; (with Linfield), 1890 v S, W; 1891 v S, W; 1892 v E, S, W; 1894 v E, S, W (11)

D'Arcy, S. D. (Chelsea), 1952 v W; 1953 v E; (with Brentford), 1953 v S, W, F (5)

Darling, J. (Linfield), 1897 v E, S; 1900 v S; 1902 v E, S, W; 1903 v S, W; 1905 v E, S, W; 1906 v E, S, W; 1908 v W; 1909 v E; 1910 v E, S, W; 1912 v S (21)

Davey, H. H. (Reading), 1926 v E; 1927 v E, S; 1928 v E; (with Portsmouth), 1928 v W (5)

Davis, T. L. (Oldham Ath), 1937 v E (1)

Davison, A. J. (Bolton W), 1996 v Se; (with Bradford C), 1997 v Th; (with Grimsby T), 1998 v G (3)

Davison, J. R. (Cliftonville), 1882 v E, W; 1883 v E, W; 1884 v E, W, S; 1885 v E (8)

Dennison, R. (Wolverhampton W), 1988 v F, Ma; 1989 v H, Sp, Ch (sub); 1990 v Ei, U; 1991 v Y (2), A, Pol, Fa (sub); 1992 v Fa, A, D (sub); 1993 v Sp (sub); 1994 v Co (sub); 1997 v I (sub) (18)

Devine, A. O. (Limavady), 1886 v E, W; 1887 v W; 1888 v W (4)

Devine, J. (Glentoran), 1990 v U (sub) (1)

Dickson, D. (Coleraine), 1970 v S (sub), W; 1973 v Cy, P (4)

Dickson, T. A. (Linfield), 1957 v S (1)

Dickson, W. (Chelsea), 1951 v W, F; 1952 v E, S, W; 1953 v E, S, W, F; (with Arsenal), 1954 v E, W; 1955 v E (12)

Diffin, W. J. (Belfast C), 1931 v W (1)

Dill, A. H. (Knock), 1882 v E, W; (with Down Ath), 1883 v W; (with Cliftonville), 1884 v E, S, W; 1885 v E, S, W (9)

Doherty, I. (Belfast C), 1901 v E (1)

Doherty, J. (Cliftonville), 1933 v E, W (2)

Doherty, L. (Linfield), 1985 v Is; 1988 v T (sub) (2)

Doherty, M. (Derry C), 1938 v S (1)

Doherty, P. D. (Blackpool), 1935 v E, W; 1936 v E, S; (with Manchester C), 1937 v E, W; 1938 v E, S; 1939 v E, W; (with Derby Co), 1947 v E; (with Huddersfield T), 1948 v E, W; 1949 v S; (with Doncaster R), 1951 v S (16)

Donaghy, M. M. (Luton T), 1980 v S, E, W; 1981 v Se, P, S (sub); 1982 v S, Is, E, F, S, W, Y, Hon, Sp, F; 1983 v A, WG, Alb, T, Alb, S, E, W; 1984 v A, T, WG, S, E, W, Fi; 1985 v R, Fi, E, Sp, T; 1986 v T, R, E, F, D, Mor, Alg, Sp, Br; 1987 v E (2), T, Is, Y; 1988 v Y, T, Gr, Pol, F, Ma; 1989 v Ei, H; (with Manchester U), Sp (2), Ma, Ch; 1990 v Ei, N; 1991 v Y (2), D, A, Pol, Fa; 1992 v Fa, A, D, S, Li, G; (with Chelsea), 1993 v Alb, Sp, D, Alb, Ei, Sp, Li, La; 1994 v La, D, Ei, R, Lie, Co, M (91)

Donnelly, L. (Distillery), 1913 v W (1)

Doran, J. F. (Brighton), 1921 v E; 1922 v E, W (3)

Dougan, A. D. (Portsmouth), 1958 v Cz; (with Blackburn R), 1960 v S; 1961 v E, W, I, Gr; (with Aston Villa), 1963 v S, Pol (2); (with Leicester C), 1966 v S, E, W, M, Alb, WG; 1967 v E, S; (with Wolverhampton W), 1967 v W; 1968 v S, W; 1969 v Is, T (2), E, S, W; 1970 v S, E, USSR (2); 1971 v

Cy (2), Sp, E, S, W; 1972 v USSR (2), E, S, W; 1973 v Bul, Cy (43)

Douglas, J. P. (Belfast C), 1947 v E (1)

Dowd, H. O. (Glenavon), 1974 v W; (with Sheffield W), 1975 v N (sub), Se (3)

Dowie, I. (Luton T), 1990 v N (sub), U; 1991 v Y, D, A (sub), (with West Ham U), Y, Fa; (with Southampton), 1992 v Fa, A, D (sub), S (sub), Li; 1993 v Alb (2), Ei, Sp (sub), Li, La; 1994 v La, D, Ei (sub), R (sub), Lie, Co, M (sub); 1995 v A, Ei; (with C Palace), Ei, La, Ca, Ch, La; 1996 v P; (with West Ham U), A, N, G; 1997 v Uk, Arm, G, Alb, P, Uk, Arm, Th; 1998 v Alb, P; (with QPR), Slo, Sw, Sp; 1999 v T, Fi, Mol, G, Mol, Ca, Ei (56)

Duggan, H. A. (Leeds U), 1930 v E; 1931 v E, W; 1933 v E; 1934 v E; 1935 v S, W; 1936 v S (8)

Dunlop, G. (Linfield), 1985 v Is; 1987 v E, Y; 1990 v Ei (4)

Dunne, J. (Sheffield U), 1928 v W; 1931 v W, E; 1932 v E, S; 1933 v E, W (7)

Eames, W. L. E. (Dublin U), 1885 v E, S, W (3)

Eglington, T. J. (Everton), 1947 v S, W; 1948 v E, S, W; 1949 v E (6)

Elder, A. R. (Burnley), 1960 v W; 1961 v S, E, W, WG (2), Gr; 1962 v E, S, Gr; 1963 v E, S, W, Pol (2), Sp; 1964 v W, U; 1965 v E, S, W, Sw (2), Ho (2), Alb; 1966 v E, S, W, M, Alb; 1967 v E, S, W; (with Stoke C), 1968 v E, W; 1969 v E (sub), S, W; 1970 v USSR (40)

Elleman, A. R. (Cliftonville), 1889 v W; 1890 v E (2)

Elwood, J. H. (Bradford), 1929 v W; 1930 v E (2)

Emerson, M. (Glentoran), 1920 v E, S, W; 1921 v E; 1922 v E, S; (with Burnley), 1922 v W; 1923 v E, S, W; 1924 v E (11)

English, S. (Rangers), 1933 v W, S (2)

Enright, J. (Leeds C), 1912 v S (1)

Falloon, E. (Aberdeen), 1931 v S; 1933 v S (2)

Farquharson, T. G. (Cardiff C), 1923 v S, W; 1924 v E, S, W; 1925 v E, S (7)

Farrell, P. (Distillery), 1901 v S, W (2)

Farrell, P. (Hibernian), 1938 v W (1)

Farrell, P. D. (Everton), 1947 v S, W; 1948 v E, S, W; 1949 v E, W (7)

Feeney, J. M. (Linfield), 1947 v S; (with Swansea T), 1950 v E (2)

Feeney, W. (Glentoran), 1976 v Is (1)

Ferguson, G. (Glentoran), 1999 v Ca (sub) (1)

Ferguson, W. (Linfield), 1966 v M; 1967 v E (2)

Ferris, J. (Belfast C), 1920 v E, W; (with Chelsea), 1921 v S, E; (with Belfast C), 1928 v S (5)

Ferris, R. O. (Birmingham C), 1950 v S; 1951 v F; 1952 v S (3)

Fettis, A. W. (Hull C), 1992 v D, Li; 1993 v D; 1994 v M; 1995 v P, Ei, La, Ca, Ch, La; 1996 v P, Lie, A; (with Nottingham F), v N, G; 1997 v Uk, Arm (2); (with Blackburn R), 1998 v P, Slo, Sw, Sp; 1999 v T, Fi, Mol (25)

Finney, T. (Sunderland), 1975 v N, E (sub), S, W; 1976 v N, Y, S; (with Cambridge U), 1980 v E, Is, S, E, W, Aus (2) (14)

Fitzpatrick, J. C. (Bohemians), 1896 v E, S (2)

Flack, H. (Burnley), 1929 v S (1)

Fleming, J. G. (Nottingham F), 1987 v E (2), Is, Y; 1988 v T, Gr, Pol; 1989 v Ma, Ch; (with Manchester C), 1990 v H, Ei; (with Barnsley), 1991 v Y; 1992 v Li (sub), G; 1993 v Alb, Sp, D, Alb, Sp, Li, La; 1994 v La, D, Ei, R, Lie, Co, M; 1995 v P, A, Ei (31)

Forbes, G. (Limavady), 1888 v W; (with Distillery), 1891 v E, S (3)

Forde, J. T. (Ards), 1959 v Sp; 1961 v E, S, WG (4)

Foreman, T. A. (Cliftonville), 1899 v S (1)

Forsyth, J. (YMCA), 1888 v E, S (2)

Fox, W. T. (Ulster), 1887 v E, S (2)

Fulton, R. P. (Belfast C), 1930 v W; 1931 v E, S, W; 1932 v W, E; 1933 v E, S; 1934 v E, W, S; 1935 v E, W, S; 1936 v S, W; 1937 v E, S, W; 1938 v W (20)

Gaffikin, G. (Linfield Ath), 1890 v S, W; 1891 v S, W; 1892 v E, S; 1893 v E, S, W; 1894 v E, S, W; 1895 v E, W (15)

Galbraith, W. (Distillery), 1890 v W (1)

Gallagher, P. (Celtic), 1920 v E, S; 1922 v S; 1923 v S, W; 1924 v S, W; 1925 v S, W, E; (with Falkirk), 1927 v S (11)

Gallogly, C. (Huddersfield T), 1951 v E, S (2)

Gara, A. (Preston NE), 1902 v E, S, W (3)

Gardiner, A. (Cliftonville), 1930 v S, W; 1931 v S; 1932 v E, S (5)

Garrett, J. (Distillery), 1925 v W (1)

Gaston, R. (Oxford U), 1969 v Is (sub) (1)

Gaukrodger, G. (Linfield), 1895 v W (1)

Gaussen, A. D. (Moyola Park), 1884 v E, S; (with Magherafelt), 1888 v E, W; 1889 v E, W (6)

Geary, J. (Glentoran), 1931 v S; 1932 v S (2)
Gibb, J. T. (Wellington Park) 1884 v S, W; 1885 v S, E, W; 1886 v S; 1887 v S, E, W; (with Cliftonville), 1889 v S (10)
Gibb, T. J. (Cliftonville), 1936 v W (1)
Gibson W. K. (Cliftonville), 1894 v S, W, E; 1895 v S; 1897 v W; 1898 v S, W, E; 1901 v S, W, E; 1902 v S, W (13)
Gillespie, K.R. (Manchester U), 1995 v P, A, Ei; (with Newcastle U), Ei, La, Ca, Ch (sub), La (sub); 1996 v P, A, N, G; 1997 v Uk, Arm, Bel, P, Uk; 1998 v G, Alb, Slo, Sw; 1999 v T, Fi, Mol; (with Blackburn R), G, Mol (26)
Gillespie, S. (Hertford), 1886 v E, S, W; 1887 v E, S, W (6)
Gillespie, W. (Sheffield U), 1913 v E, S; 1914 v E, W; 1920 v S, W; 1921 v E; 1922 v E, S, W; 1923 v E, S, W; 1924 v E, S, W; 1925 v E, S; 1926 v S, W; 1927 v E, W; 1928 v E; 1929 v E; 1931 v E (25)
Gillespie, W. (West Down), 1889 v W (1)
Goodall, A. L. (Derby Co), 1899 v S, W; 1900 v E, W; 1901 v E; 1902 v S; 1903 v E, W; (with Glossop), 1904 v E, W (10)
Goodbody, M. F. (Dublin University), 1889 v E; 1891 v W (2)
Gordon, H. (Linfield), 1895 v E; 1896 v E, S (3)
Gordon R. W. (Linfield), 1891 v S; 1892 v W, E, S; 1893 v E, S, W (7)
Gordon, T. (Linfield), 1894 v W; 1895 v E (2)
Gorman, W. C. (Brentford), 1947 v E, S, W; 1948 v W (4)
Gowdy, J. (Glentoran), 1920 v E; (with Queen's Island), 1924 v W; (with Falkirk), 1926 v E, S; 1927 v E, S (6)
Gowdy, W. A. (Hull C), 1932 v S; (with Sheffield W), 1933 v S; (with Linfield), 1935 v E, S, W; (with Hibernian), 1936 v W (6)
Graham, W. G. L. (Doncaster R), 1951 v W, F; 1952 v E, S, W; 1953 v S, F; 1954 v E, W; 1955 v S, W; 1956 v E, S; 1959 v E (14)
Gray, P. (Luton T), 1993 v D (sub), Alb, Ei, Sp; (with Sunderland), 1994 v La, D, Ei, R, Lie (sub); 1995 v P, A, Ei, Ca, Ch (sub); 1996 v P (sub), Lie, A; (with Nancy), 1997 v Uk, Arm, G (sub); (with Luton T), 1999 v Mol (sub) (21)
Greer, W. (QPR), 1909 v E, S, W (3)
Gregg, H. (Doncaster R), 1954 v W; 1957 v E, S, W, I, P (2); 1958 v E, I; (with Manchester U), 1958 v Cz, Arg, WG, F, W; 1959 v E, W; 1960 v S, E, W; 1961 v E, S; 1962 v S, Gr; 1964 v S, E (25)
Griffin, D. J. (St Johnstone), 1996 v G; 1997 v Uk, I, Bel (sub), Th; 1998 v G (sub), Alb; 1999 v Mol, Ei (sub) (9)

Hall, G. (Distillery), 1897 v E (1)
Halligan, W. (Derby Co), 1911 v W; (with Wolverhampton W), 1912 v E (2)
Hamill, M. (Manchester U), 1912 v E; 1914 v E, S; (with Belfast C), 1920 v E, S, W; (with Manchester C), 1921 v S (7)
Hamill, R. (Glentoran), 1999 v Ca (sub) (1)
Hamilton, B. (Linfield), 1969 v T; 1971 v Cy (2), E, S, W; (with Ipswich T), 1972 v USSR (1+1 sub), Sp; 1973 v Bul, Cy (2), P, E, S, W; 1974 v Bul, S, E; 1975 v N, Se, Y, E; 1976 v Se, N, Y; (with Everton), Is, S, E, W; 1977 v Ho, Bel, WG, E, S, W, Ic; (with Millwall), 1978 v S, E, W; 1979 v Ei (sub); (with Swindon T), Bul (2), E, S, W, D; 1980 v Aus (2 sub) (50)
Hamilton, J. (Knock), 1882 v E, W (2)
Hamilton, R. (Rangers), 1928 v S; 1929 v E; 1930 v S, E; 1932 v S (5)
Hamilton, W. R. (QPR), 1978 v S (sub); (with Burnley), 1980 v S, E, W, Aus (2); 1981 v Se, P, S, P, Se; 1982 v S, Is, E, W, Y, Hon, Sp, A, F; 1983 v A, WG, Alb (2), S, E, W; 1984 v A, T, WG, S, E, W, Fi; (with Oxford U), 1985 v R, Sp; 1986 v Mor (sub), Alg, Sp (sub), Br (sub) (41)
Hamilton, W. D. (Dublin Association), 1885 v W (1)
Hamilton, W. J. (Distillery), 1908 v W (1)
Hamilton, W. J. (Dublin Association), 1885 v W (1)
Hampton, H. (Bradford C), 1911 v E, S, W; 1912 v E, W; 1913 v E, S, W; 1914 v E (9)
Hanna, J. (Nottingham F), 1912 v S, W (2)
Hanna, J. D. (Royal Artillery, Portsmouth), 1899 v W (1)
Hannon, D. J. (Bohemians), 1908 v E, S; 1911 v E, S; 1912 v W; 1913 v E (6)
Harkin, J. T. (Southport), 1968 v W; 1969 v T; (with Shrewsbury T), W (sub); 1970 v USSR; 1971 v Sp (5)
Harland, A. I. (Linfield), 1923 v E (1)
Harris, J. (Cliftonville), 1921 v W (1)
Harris, V. (Shelbourne), 1906 v E; 1907 v E, W; 1908 v E, W, S; (with Everton), 1909 v E, W, S; 1910 v E, S, W; 1911 v E, S, W; 1912 v E; 1913 v E, S; 1914 v S, W (20)
Harvey, M. (Sunderland), 1961 v I; 1962 v Ho; 1963 v W, Sp; 1964 v S, E, W, U, Sp; 1965 v E, S, W, Sw (2), Ho (2), Alb; 1966 v S, E, W, M, Alb, WG; 1967 v E, S; 1968 v E, W; 1969 v Is, T (2), E; 1970 v USSR; 1971 v Cy, W (sub) (34)
Hastings, J. (Knock), 1882 v E, W; (with Ulster), 1883 v W; 1884 v E, S; 1886 v E, S (7)

Hatton, S. (Linfield), 1963 v S, Pol (2)
Hayes, W. E. (Huddersfield T), 1938 v E, S; 1939 v E, S (4)
Healy, P, J. (Coleraine), 1982 v S, W, Hon (sub); (with Glentoran), 1983 v A (sub) (4)
Hegan, D. (WBA), 1970 v USSR; (with Wolverhampton W), 1972 v USSR, E, S, W; 1973 v Bul, Cy (7)
Henderson, J. (Ulster), 1885 v E, S, W (3)
Hewison, G. (Moyola Park), 1885 v E, S (2)
Hill, C. F. (Sheffield U), 1990 v N, U; 1991 v Pol, Y; 1992 v A, D; (with Leicester C), 1995 v Ei, La; 1996 v P, Lie, A, N, Se, G; 1997 v Uk, Arm, G, Alb, P, Uk, Arm, Th; (with Trelleborg), 1998 v G, Alb, P; (with Northampton T), Slo; 1999 v T (27)
Hill, M. J. (Norwich C), 1959 v W; 1960 v W; 1961 v WG; 1962 v S; (with Everton), 1964 v S, E, Sp (7)
Hinton, E. (Fulham), 1947 v S, W; 1948 v S, E, W; (with Millwall), 1951 v W, F (7)
Hopkins, J. (Brighton & HA), 1926 v E (1)
Horlock, K. (Swindon T), 1995 v La, Ca; 1997 v G, Alb, I; (with Manchester C), v Bel, Uk, Arm, Th; 1998 v G, Alb, P; 1999 v T, Fi, G, Mol, Ca (17)
Houston, J. (Linfield), 1912 v S, W; 1913 v W; (with Everton), 1913 v E, S; 1914 v S (6)
Houston, W. (Linfield), 1933 v W (1)
Houston, W. J. (Moyola Park), 1885 v E, S (2)
Hughes, A. W. (Newcastle U), 1998 v Slo, Sw, Sp (sub); 1999 v T, Fi, Mol (sub), Ca, Ei (8)
Hughes, M. E. (Manchester C), 1992 v D, S, Li, G; (with Strasbourg), 1993 v Alb, Sp, D, Ei, Sp, Li, La; 1994 v La, D, Ei, R, Lie, Co, M; 1995 v P, A, Ei (2) La, Ca, Ch, La; 1996 v P, Lie, A, N, G; (with West Ham U), 1997 v Uk, Arm, G, Alb, I, Uk; 1998 v G; (with Wimbledon), P, Slo, Sw, Sp; 1999 v T, Fi, Mol, G, Mol (47)
Hughes, P. A. (Bury), 1987 v E, T, Is (3)
Hughes, W. (Bolton W), 1951 v W (1)
Humphries, W. M. (Ards), 1962 v W; (with Coventry C), 1962 v Ho; 1963 v E, S, W, Pol, Sp; 1964 v S, E, Sp; 1965 v S, Ho; (with Swansea T), 1965 v W, Alb (14)
Hunter, A. (Distillery), 1905 v W; 1906 v W, E, S; (with Belfast C), 1908 v W; 1909 v W, E, S (8)
Hunter, A. (Blackburn R), 1970 v USSR; 1971 v Cy (2), E, S, W; (with Ipswich T), 1972 v USSR (2), Sp, E, S, W; 1973 v Bul, Cy (2), P, E, S, W; 1974 v Bul, S, E, W; 1975 v N, Se, Y, E, S, W; 1976 v Se, N, Y, Is, S, E, W; 1977 v Ho, Bel, WG, E, S, W, Ic; 1978 v Ic, Ho, Bel; 1979 v Ei, D, S, W, D; 1980 v E, Ei (53)
Hunter, B.V. (Wrexham), 1995 v La; 1996 v P, Lie, A, Se, G; (with Reading), 1997 v Arm, G, Alb, I, Bel; 1999 v Ca, Ei (13)
Hunter, R. J. (Cliftonville), 1884 v E, S, W (3)
Hunter, V. (Coleraine), 1962 v E; 1964 v Sp (2)

Irvine, R. J. (Linfield), 1962 v Ho; 1963 v E, S, W, Pol (2), Sp; (with Stoke C), 1965 v W (8)
Irvine, R. W. (Everton), 1922 v S; 1923 v E, W; 1924 v E, S; 1925 v E; 1926 v E; 1927 v E, W; 1928 v E, S; (with Portsmouth), 1929 v E; 1930 v S; (with Connah's Quay), 1931 v E (with Derry C), 1932 v W (15)
Irvine, W. J. (Burnley), 1963 v W, Sp; 1965 v S, W, Sw, Ho (2), Alb; 1966 v S, E, W, M, Alb; 1967 v E, S; 1968 v E, W; (with Preston NE), 1969 v Is, T, E; (with Brighton & HA), 1972 v E, S, W (23)
Irving, S, J. (Dundee), 1923 v S, W; 1924 v S, E, W; 1925 v S, E, W; 1926 v S, W; (with Cardiff C), 1927 v S, E, W; 1928 v S, E, W; (with Chelsea), 1929 v E; 1931 v W (18)

Jackson, T. A. (Everton), 1969 v Is, E, S, W; 1970 v USSR (1+1 sub); (with Nottingham F), 1971 v Sp; 1972 v E, S, W; 1973 v Cy, E, S, W; 1974 v Bul, P, S (sub), E (sub), W (sub); 1975 v N (sub), Se, N, Y, Is, S, W; (with Manchester U), 1976 v Se, N, Y; 1977 v Ho, Bel, WG, E, S, W, Ic (35)
Jamison, J. (Glentoran), 1976 v N (1)
Jenkins, I. (Chester C), 1997 v Arm, Th; 1998 v Slo; (with Dundee U), Sw, Sp (5)
Jennings, P. A. (Watford), 1964 v W, U; (with Tottenham H), 1965 v E, S, Sw (2), Ho, Alb; 1966 v S, E, W, Alb, WG; 1967 v E, S; 1968 v S, E, W; 1969 v Is, T (2), E, S, W; 1970 v S, W, Se, Y, E, S, W; 1971 v Cy (2), E, S, W; 1972 v USSR, Sp, S, E, W; 1973 v Bul, Cy, P, E, S, W; 1974 v P, S, E, W; 1975 v N, Se, Y, E, S, W; 1976 v Se, N, Y, Is, S, E, W; 1977 v Ho, Bel, WG, E, S, W, Ic; (with Arsenal), 1978 v Ic, Ho, Bel; 1979 v Ei, D, Bul, E, Bul, E, S, W, D; 1980 v E, Ei, Is; 1981 v S, P, S, Se; 1982 v S, Is, E, W, Y, Hon, Sp, F; 1983 v Alb, S, E, W; 1984 v A, T, WG, S, W, Alb v R, Fi, E, Sp, T; (with Tottenham H), 1986 v T, R, E, F, D; (with Everton), Mor; (with Tottenham H), Alg, Sp, Br (119)

Johnson, D. M. (Blackburn R), 1999 v Ei (sub) (1)
Johnston, H. (Portadown), 1927 v W (1)
Johnston, W (Oldpark), 1885 v S, W (2)
Johnston, R. S. (Distillery), 1882 v W; 1884 v E; 1886 v E, S (4)
Johnston, S. (Linfield), 1890 v W; 1893 v S, W; 1894 v E (4)
Johnston, R. S. (Distillery), 1905 v W (1)
Johnston, W. C. (Glenavon), 1962 v W; (with Oldham Ath), 1966 v M (sub) (2)
Jones, J. (Linfield), 1930 v S, W; 1931 v S, W, E; 1932 v S, E; 1933 v S, E, W; 1934 v S, E, W; 1935 v S, E, W; 1936 v E, S; (with Hibernian), 1936 v W; 1937 v E, W, S; (with Glenavon), 1938 v E (23)
Jones, J. (Glenavon), 1956 v W; 1957 v E, W (3)
Jones, S. (Distillery), 1934 v E; (with Blackpool), 1934 v W (2)
Jordan, T. (Linfield), 1895 v E, W (2)

Kavanagh, P. J. (Celtic), 1930 v E (1)
Keane, T. R. (Swansea T), 1949 v S (1)
Kearns, A. (Distillery), 1900 v E, S, W; 1902 v E, S, W (6)
Kee, P. V. (Oxford U), 1990 v N; 1991 v Y (2), D, A, Pol, Fa; (with Ards), 1995 v A, Ei (9)
Keith, R. M. (Newcastle U), 1958 v E, W, Cz (2), Arg, I, WG, F; 1959 v E, S, W, Sp; 1960 v S, E; 1961 v S, E, W, I, WG (2), Gr; 1962 v W, Ho (23)
Kelly, H. R. (Fulham), 1950 v E, W; (with Southampton), 1951 v E, S (4)
Kelly, J. (Glentoran), 1896 v E (1)
Kelly, J. (Derry C), 1932 v E, W; 1933 v E, W, S; 1934 v W; 1936 v E, S, W; 1937 v S, E (11)
Kelly, P. J. (Manchester C), 1921 v E (1)
Kelly, P. M. (Barnsley), 1950 v S (1)
Kennedy, A. L. (Arsenal), 1923 v W; 1925 v E (2)
Kennedy, P. H. (Watford), 1999 v Mol, G (sub) (2)
Kernaghan, N. (Belfast C), 1936 v W; 1937 v S; 1938 v E (3)
Kirkwood, H. (Cliftonville), 1904 v W (1)
Kirwan, J. (Tottenham H), 1900 v W; 1902 v E, W; 1903 v E, S, W; 1904 v E, S, W; 1905 v E, S, W; (with Chelsea), 1906 v E, S, W; 1907 v W; (with Clyde), 1909 v S (17)

Lacey, E. S., W; (Everton), 1909 v E, S, W; 1910 v E, S, W; 1911 v E, S, W; 1912 v E; (with Liverpool), 1913 v W; 1914 v E, S, W; 1920 v E, S, W; 1921 v E, S, W; 1922 v E, S; (with New Brighton), 1925 v E (23)
Lawther, R. (Glentoran), 1888 v E, S (2)
Lawther, W. I. (Sunderland), 1960 v W; 1961 v I; (with Blackburn R), 1962 v S, Ho (4)
Leatham, J. (Belfast C), 1939 v W (1)
Ledwidge, J. J. (Shelbourne), 1906 v S, W (2)
Lemon, J. (Glentoran), 1886 v W; (with Belfast YMCA), 1888 v S; 1889 v W (3)
Lennon, N. F. (Crewe Alex), 1994 v M (sub); 1995 v Ch; 1996 v P, Lie, A; (with Leicester C), v N; 1997 v Uk, Arm, G, Alb, Bel, P, Uk, Arm, Th; 1998 v G, Alb, P, Slo, Sw, Sp; 1999 v T, Fi, Mol, G, Mol, Ei (27)
Leslie, W. (YMCA), 1887 v E (1)
Lewis, J. (Glentoran), 1899 v S, E, W; (with Distillery), 1900 v S (4)
Lockhart, H. (Russell School), 1884 v W (1)
Lockhart, N. H. (Linfield), 1947 v E; (with Coventry C), 1950 v W; 1951 v W; 1952 v W; (with Aston Villa), 1954 v S, E; 1955 v W; 1956 v W (8)
Lomas, S. M. (Manchester C), 1994 v R, Lie, Co (sub); M; 1995 v P, A; 1996 v P, Lie, A, N, Se, G; 1997 v Uk, Arm, G, Alb, I, Bel; (with West Ham U), P, Uk, Arm, Th; 1998 v Alb, P, Slo, Sw; 1999 v Mol, G, Mol, Ca (30)
Loyal, J. (Clarence), 1891 v S (1)
Lutton, R. J. (Wolverhampton W), 1970 v S, E; (with West Ham U), 1973 v Cy (sub), S (sub), W (sub); 1974 v P (6)
Lyner, D. R. (Glentoran), 1920 v E, W; 1922 v S, W; (with Manchester U), 1923 v E; (with Kilmarnock), W (6)
Lytle, J. (Glentoran), 1898 W (1)

McAdams, W. J. (Manchester C), 1954 v W; 1955 v S; 1957 v E; 1958 v S, I; (with Bolton W), 1961 v E, S, W, I, WG (2), Gr; 1962 v E, Gr; (with Leeds U), Ho (15)
McAlery, J. M. (Cliftonville), 1882 v E, W (2)
McAlinden, J. (Belfast C), 1938 v S; 1939 v S; (with Portsmouth), 1947 v E; (with Southend U), 1949 v E (4)
McAllen, J. (Linfield), 1898 v E; 1899 v E, S, W; 1900 v E, S, W; 1901 v W; 1902 v S (9)
McAlpine, S. (Cliftonville), 1901 v S (1)
McArthur, A. (Distillery), 1886 v W (1)
McAuley, J. L. (Huddersfield T), 1911 v E, W; 1912 v E, S; 1913 v E, S (6)
McAuley, P. (Belfast C), 1900 v S (1)

McBride, S. D.(Glenavon), 1991 v D (sub), Pol (sub); 1992 v Fa (sub), D (4)
McCabe, J. J. (Leeds U), 1949 v S, W; 1950 v E; 1951 v W; 1953 v W; 1954 v S (6)
McCabe, W. (Ulster), 1891 v E (1)
McCambridge, J. (Ballymena), 1930 v S, W; (with Cardiff C), 1931 v W; 1932 v E (4)
McCandless, J. (Bradford), 1912 v W; 1913 v W; 1920 v W, S; 1921 v E (5)
McCandless, W. (Linfield), 1920 v E, W; 1921 v E; (with Rangers), 1921 v W; 1922 v S; 1924 v W, S; 1925 v S; 1929 v W (9)
McCann, P. (Belfast C), 1910 v E, S, W; 1911 v E; (with Glentoran), 1911 v S; 1912 v E; 1913 v W (7)
McCarthy, J. D. (Port Vale), 1996 v Se; 1997 v I, Arm, Th; (with Birmingham C), 1998 v P (sub), Slo (sub), Sp; 1999 v Fi (sub), Mol (sub), G (sub), Ca, Ei (12)
McCashin, J. (Cliftonville), 1896 v W; 1898 v S, W; 1899 v S (4)
McCavana, W. T. (Coleraine), 1955 v S; 1956 v E, S (3)
McCaw, D. (Malone), 1882 v E (1)
McCaw, J. H. (Linfield), 1927 v W; 1930 v S; 1931 v E, S, W (5)
McClatchey, J. (Distillery), 1886 v E, S, W (3)
McClatchey, T. (Distillery), 1895 v S (1)
McCleary, J. W. (Cliftonville), 1955 v W (1)
McCleery, W. (Linfield), 1930 v E, W; 1931 v E, S, W; 1932 v S, W; 1933 v E, W (9)
McClelland, J. T. (Arsenal), 1961 v W, I, WG (2), Gr; (with Fulham), 1966 v M (6)
McClelland, J. (Mansfield T), 1980 v S (sub), Aus (3); 1981 v Se, S; (with Rangers), S, Se (sub); 1982 v S, W, Y, Hon, Sp, A, F; 1983 v A, WG, Alb, T, Alb, S, E, W; 1984 v A, T, WG, S, E, W, Fi; 1985 v R, Is; (with Watford), Fi, E, Sp, T; 1986 v T, F (sub); 1987 v E (2), T, Is, Y; 1988 v T, Gr, F, Ma; 1989 v Ei, H, Sp (2), Ma; (with Leeds U), 1990 v N (53)
McCluggage, A. (Bradford), 1924 v E; (with Burnley), 1927 v S, W; 1928 v S, E, W; 1929 v S, E, W; 1930 v W; 1931 v E, W (12)
McClure, G. (Cliftonville), 1907 v S, W; 1908 v E; (with Distillery), 1909 v E (4)
McConnell, E. (Cliftonville), 1904 v S, W; (with Glentoran), 1905 v S; (with Sunderland), 1906 v E; 1907 v E; 1908 v S, W; (with Sheffield W), 1909 v S, W; 1910 v S, W, E (12)
McConnell, P. (Doncaster R), 1928 v W; (with Southport), 1932 v E (2)
McConnell, W. G. (Bohemians), 1912 v W; 1913 v E, S; 1914 v E, S, W (6)
McConnell, W. H. (Reading), 1925 v W; 1926 v E, W; 1927 v E, S, W; 1928 v E, W (8)
McCourt, F. J. (Manchester C), 1952 v E, W; 1953 v E, S, W, F (6)
McCoy, S. (Distillery), 1896 v W (1)
McCoy, R. K. (Coleraine), 1987 v Y (sub) (1)
McCracken, E (C Palace), 1921 v E; 1922 v E, S, W (4)
McCracken, W. R. (Distillery), 1902 v E, W; 1903 v E; 1904 v E, S, W; (with Newcastle U), 1905 v E, S, W; 1907 v E; 1920 v E; 1922 v E, S, W; (with Hull C), 1923 v S (15)
McCreery, D. (Manchester U), 1976 v S (sub), E, W; 1977 v Ho, Bel, WG, E, S, W, Ic; 1978 v Ic, Ho, Bel, S, E, W; 1979 v Ei, D, Bul, E, Bul, W, D; (with QPR), 1980 v E, Ei, S (sub), E (sub), W (sub), Aus (1+1 sub); 1981 v Se (sub), P (sub); (with Tulsa R), S, P, Se; 1982 v S, Is, E (sub), F, Y, Hon, Sp, A, F; (with Newcastle U), 1983 v A; 1984 v T (sub); 1985 v R, Sp (sub); 1986 v T (sub), R, E, F, D, Alg, Sp, Br; 1987 v T, E, Y; 1988 v Y; 1989 v Sp, Ma, Ch; (with Hearts), 1990 v H, Ei, N, U (sub) (67)
McCrory, S. (Southend U), 1958 v E (1)
McCullough, K. (Belfast C), 1935 v W; 1936 v E; (with Manchester C), 1936 v S; 1937 v E, S (5)
McCullough, W. J. (Arsenal), 1961 v I; 1963 v Sp; 1964 v S, E, W, U, Sp; 1965 v E, Sw; (with Millwall), 1967 v E (10)
McCurdy, C. (Linfield), 1980 v Aus (sub) (1)
McDonald, A. (QPR), 1986 v R, E, F, D, Mor, Alg, Sp, Br; 1987 v E (2), T, Is, Y; 1988 v Y, T, Pol, F, Ma; 1989 v Ei, H, Sp, Ch; 1990 v H, Ei, U, N; (with QPR), 1992 v Fa, S, Li, G; 1993 v Alb, Sp, D, Alb, Ei, Sp, Li, La; 1994 v D, Ei; 1995 v P, A, Ei, La, Ca, Ch, La; 1996 v A (sub), N (52)
McDonald, R. (Rangers), 1930 v S; 1932 v E (2)
McDonnell, J. (Bohemians), 1911 v E, S; 1912 v W; 1913 v W (4)
McElhinney, G. M. A. (Bolton W), 1984 v WG, S, E, W, Fi; 1985 v R (6)
McFaul, W. S. (Linfield), 1967 v E (sub); (with Newcastle U), 1970 v W; 1971 v Sp; 1972 v USSR; 1973 v Cy; 1974 v Bul (6)
McGarry, J. K. (Cliftonville), 1951 v W, F, S (3)
McGaughey, M. (Linfield), 1985 v Is (sub) (1)

McGibbon, P. C. G. (Manchester U), 1995 v Ca (sub), Ch, La; 1996 v Lie (sub); 1997 v Th; (with Wigan Ath), 1998 v Alb (6)

McGrath, R. C. (Tottenham H), 1974 v S, E, W; 1975 v N; 1976 v Is (sub); (with Manchester U), 1977 v Ho, Bel, WG, E, S, W, Ic; 1978 v Ic, Ho, Bel, S, E, W; 1979 v Bul (sub), E (2 sub) (21)

McGregor, S. (Glentoran), 1921 v S (1)

McGrillen, J. (Clyde), 1924 v S; (with Belfast C), 1927 v S (2)

McGuire, E. (Distillery), 1907 v S (1)

McIlroy, H. (Cliftonville), 1906 v E (1)

McIlroy, J. (Burnley), 1952 v E, S, W; 1953 v E, S, W; 1954 v E, S, W; 1955 v E, S, W; 1956 v E, S, W; 1957 v E, S, W, I, P (2); 1958 v E, S, W, I (2), Cz (2), Arg, WG, F; 1959 v E, S, W, Sp; 1960 v E, S, W; 1961 v E, W, WG (2), Gr; 1962 v E, S, Gr, Ho; 1963 v E, S, Pol (2); (with Stoke C), 1963 v W; 1966 v S, E, Alb (55)

McIlroy, S. B. (Manchester U), 1972 v Sp, S (sub); 1974 v S, E, W; 1975 v N, Se, Y, E, S, W; 1976 v Se, N, Y, S, E, W; 1977 v Ho, Bel, E, S, W, Ic; 1978 v Ic, Ho, Bel, S, E, W; 1979 v Ei, D, Bul, E, Bul, E, S, W, D; 1980 v E, Ei, Is, S, E, W; 1981 v Se, P, S, P, S, Se; 1982 v S, Is; (with Stoke C), E, F, S, W, Y, Hon, Sp, A, F; 1983 v A, WG, Alb, T, Alb, S, E, W; 1984 v A, T, S, E, W, Fi; 1985 v Fi, E, T; (with Manchester C), 1986 v T, R, E, F, D, Mor, Alg, Sp, Br; 1987 v E (sub) (88)

McIlvenny, R. (Distillery), 1890 v E; (with Ulster), 1891 v E (2)

McIlvenny, P. (Distillery), 1924 v W (1)

McKeag, W. (Glentoran), 1968 v S, W (2)

McKee, F. W. (Cliftonville), 1906 v S, W; (with Belfast C), 1914 v S, W (5)

McKelvey, H. (Glentoran), 1901 v W (1)

McKenna, J. (Huddersfield), 1950 v E, S, W; 1951 v E, S, F; 1952 v E (7)

McKenzie, H. (Distillery), 1923 v S (1)

McKenzie, R. (Airdrie), 1967 v W (1)

McKeown, N. (Linfield), 1892 v E, S, W; 1893 v S, W; 1894 v S, W (7)

McKie, H. (Cliftonville), 1895 v E, S, W (3)

McKinney, D. (Hull C), 1921 v S; (with Bradford C), 1924 v S (2)

McKinney, V. J. (Falkirk), 1966 v WG (1)

McKnight, A. D. (Celtic), 1988 v Y, T, Gr, Pol, F, Ma; (with West Ham U), 1989 v Ei, H, Sp (2) (10)

McKnight, J. (Preston NE), 1912 v S; (with Glentoran), 1913 v S (2)

McLaughlin, J. C. (Shrewsbury T), 1962 v E, S, W, Gr; 1963 v W; (with Swansea T), 1964 v W, U; 1965 v E, W, Sw (2); 1966 v W (12)

McLean, T. (Limavady), 1885 v S (1)

McMahon, G. J. (Tottenham H), 1995 v Ca (sub), Ch, La; 1996 v Lie, N (sub), Se, G; (with Stoke C), 1997 v Arm (sub), Alb (sub), Bel, P (sub), Uk (sub), Arm (sub), Th (sub); 1998 v G (sub), Alb (sub), P (sub) (17)

McMahon, J. (Bohemians), 1934 v S (1)

McMaster, G. (Glentoran), 1897 v E, S, W (3)

McMichael, A. (Newcastle U), 1950 v E, S; 1951 v E, S, F; 1952 v E, S, W; 1953 v E, S, W; 1954 v E, S, W; 1955 v E, W; 1956 v W; 1957 v E, S, W, I, P (2); 1958 v E, S, W, I (2), Cz (2), Arg, WG, F; 1959 v S, W, Sp; 1960 v E, S, W (40)

McMillan, G. (Distillery), 1903 v E; 1905 v W (2)

McMillan, S. T. (Manchester U), 1963 v E, S (2)

McMillen, W. S. (Manchester U), 1934 v E; 1935 v S; 1937 v S; (with Chesterfield), 1938 v S, W; 1939 v E, S (7)

McMordie, A. S. (Middlesbrough), 1969 v Is, T (2), E, S, W; 1970 v E, S, W, USSR; 1971 v Cy (2), E, S, W; 1972 v USSR, Sp, E, S, W; 1973 v Bul (21)

McMorran, E. J. (Belfast C), 1947 v E; (with Barnsley), 1951 v E, S, W; 1952 v E, S, W; 1953 v E, S, F; (with Doncaster R), 1953 v W; 1954 v E; 1956 v W; 1957 v I, P (15)

McMullan, D. (Liverpool), 1926 v E, W; 1927 v S (3)

McNally, B. A. (Shrewsbury T), 1986 v Mor; 1987 v T (sub); 1988 v Y, Gr, Ma (sub) (5)

McNinch, J. (Ballymena), 1931 v S; 1932 v S, W (3)

McParland, P. J. (Aston Villa), 1954 v W; 1955 v E, S; 1956 v E, S; 1957 v E, S, W, P; 1958 v E, S, W, I (2), Cz (2), Arg, WG, F; 1959 v E, S, W, Sp; 1960 v E, S, W; 1961 v E, S, W, I, WG (2), Gr; (with Wolverhampton W), 1962 v Ho (34)

McShane, J. (Cliftonville), 1899 v S; 1900 v E, S, W (4)

McVeigh, P. (Tottenham H), 1999 v Ca (sub) (1)

McVicker, J. (Linfield), 1888 v E, S; (with Glentoran), 1889 v S (2)

McWha, W. B. R. (Knock), 1882 v E, W; (with Cliftonville), 1883 v E, W; 1884 v E; 1885 v E, W (7)

McCartney, A. (Ulster), 1903 v S, W; (with Linfield), 1904 v S, W; (with Everton), 1905 v E, S; (with Belfast C), 1907 v E, S, W; 1908 v E, S, W; (with Glentoran), 1909 v E, S, W (15)

Mackie, J. (Arsenal), 1923 v W; (with Portsmouth), 1935 v S, W (3)

Madden, O. (Norwich C), 1938 v E (1)

Magee, G. (Wellington Park), 1885 v E, S, W (3)

Magill, E. J. (Arsenal), 1962 v E, S, Gr; 1963 v E, S, W, Pol (2); 1964 v E, S, W, U, Sp; 1965 v E, S, Sw (2), Ho, Alb; 1966 v S; (with Brighton & HA), E, Alb, W, WG, M (26)

Magilton, J. (Oxford U), 1991 v Pol, Y, Fa; 1992 v Fa, A, D, S, Li, G; 1993 v Alb, D, Alb, Ei, Li, La; 1994 v La, D, Ei;(with Southampton), R, Lie, Co, M; 1995 v P, A, Ei (2), Ca, Ch, La; 1996 v P, N, G; 1997 v Uk (sub), Arm (sub), Bel, P; 1998 v G; (with Sheffield W), P, Sp (39)

Maginnis, H. (Linfield), 1900 v E, S, W; 1903 v S, W; 1904 v E, S, W (8)

Mahood, J. (Belfast C), 1926 v S; 1928 v E, S, W; 1929 v E, S, W; 1930 v W; (with Ballymena), 1934 v S (9)

Manderson, R. (Rangers), 1920 v W, S; 1925 v S, E; 1926 v S (5)

Mansfield, J. (Dublin Freebooters), 1901 v E (1)

Martin, C. J. (Glentoran), 1947 v S; (with Leeds U), 1948 v E, S, W; (with Aston Villa), 1949 v E; 1950 v W (6)

Martin, C. (Bo'ness), 1925 v S (1)

Martin, C. (Cliftonville), 1882 v E, W; 1883 v E (3)

Martin, D. K. (Belfast C), 1934 v E, S, W; 1935 v S; (with Wolverhampton W), 1935 v E; 1936 v W; (with Nottingham F), 1937 v S; 1938 v E, S; 1939 v S (10)

Mathieson, A. (Luton T), 1921 v W; 1922 v E (2)

Maxwell, J. (Linfield), 1902 v W; 1903 v W, E; (with Glentoran), 1905 v W, S; (with Belfast C), 1906 v W; 1907 v S (7)

Meek, H. L. (Glentoran), 1925 v W (1)

Mehaffy, J. A. C. (Queen's Island), 1922 v W (1)

Meldon, P. A. (Dublin Freebooters), 1899 v S, W (2)

Mercer, H. V. A. (Linfield), 1908 v E (1)

Mercer, J. T. (Distillery), 1898 v E, S, W; 1899 v E; (with Linfield), 1902 v E, W; (with Distillery), 1903 v S, W; (with Derby Co), 1904 v E, W; 1905 v S (11)

Millar, W. (Barrow), 1932 v W; 1933 v S (2)

Miller, J. (Middlesbrough), 1929 v W, S; 1930 v E (3)

Milligan, D. (Chesterfield), 1939 v W (1)

Milne, R. G. (Linfield), 1894 v E, S, W; 1895 v E, W; 1896 v E, S, W; 1897 v E, S; 1898 v E, S, W; 1899 v E, W; 1901 v W; 1902 v E, S, W; 1903 v E, S; 1904 v E, S, W; 1906 v E, S, W (27)

Mitchell, E. J. (Cliftonville), 1933 v S; (with Glentoran), 1934 v W (2)

Mitchell, W. (Distillery), 1932 v E, W; 1933 v E, W; (with Chelsea), 1934 v W, S; 1935 v S, E; 1936 v S, E; 1937 v E, S, W; 1938 v E, S (15)

Molyneux, T. B. (Ligoniel), 1883 v E, W; (with Cliftonville), 1884 v E, S; 1885 v E, W; 1886 v E, W, S; 1888 v S (11)

Montgomery, F. J. (Coleraine), 1955 v E (1)

Moore, C. (Glentoran), 1949 v W (1)

Moore, R. (Linfield Ath), 1891 v E, S, W (3)

Moore, P. (Aberdeen), 1933 v E (1)

Moore, R. L. (Ulster), 1887 v S, W (2)

Moore, W. (Falkirk), 1923 v S (1)

Moorhead, F. W. (Dublin University), 1885 v E (1)

Moorhead, G. (Linfield), 1923 v S; 1928 v S; 1929 v S (3)

Moran, J. (Leeds C), 1912 v S (1)

Moreland, V. (Derby Co), 1979 v Bul (2 sub), E, S; 1980 v E, Ei (6)

Morgan, F. G. (Linfield), 1923 v E; (with Nottingham F), 1924 v S; 1927 v E; 1928 v E, S, W; 1929 v E (7)

Morgan, S. (Port Vale), 1972 v Sp; 1973 v Bul (sub), P, Cy, E, S, W; (with Aston Villa), 1974 v Bul, P, S, E; 1975 v Se; 1976 v Se (sub), N, Y; (with Brighton & HA), S, W (sub); (with Sparta Rotterdam), 1979 v D (18)

Morrison, R. (Linfield Ath), 1891 v E, W (2)

Morrison, T. (Glentoran), 1895 v E, S, W; (with Burnley), 1899 v W; 1900 v W; 1902 v E, S (7)

Morrogh, D. (Bohemians), 1896 v S (1)

Morrow, S. J. (Arsenal), 1990 v U (sub); 1991 v A (sub), Pol, Y; 1992 v Fa, S (sub), Sp (sub); 1993 v Sp (sub), Alb, Ei; 1994 v R, Co, M (sub); 1995 v P, Ei (2), La; 1996 v P, Se; 1997 v Uk, G, Alb, I, Bel; (with QPR), P, Uk, Arm; 1998 v G, P, Slo, Sw, Sp; 1999 v T, Fi, Mol, G, Mol (37)

Morrow, W. J. (Moyola Park), 1883 v E, W; 1884 v S (3)

Muir, R. (Oldpark), 1885 v S, W (2)

Mullan, G. (Glentoran), 1983 v S, E, W, Alb (sub) (4)

Mulholland, S. (Celtic), 1906 v S, E (2)

Mulligan, J. (Manchester C), 1921 v S (1)

Mulryne, P. P. (Manchester U), 1997 v Bel (sub), Arm (sub), Th; 1998 v Alb (sub), Sp (sub); 1999 v T, Fi; (with Norwich C), Ca (8)
Murphy, J. (Bradford C), 1910 v E, S, W (3)
Murphy, N. (QPR), 1905 v E, S, W (3)
Murray, J. M. (Motherwell), 1910 v E, S; (with Sheffield W), 1910 v W (3)

Napier, R. J. (Bolton W), 1966 v WG (1)
Neill, W. J. T. (Arsenal), 1961 v I, Gr, WG; 1962 v E, S, W, Gr; 1963 v E, W, Pol, Sp; 1964 v S, E, W, U, Sp; 1965 v E, S, W, Sw, Ho (2), Alb; 1966 v S, E, W, Alb, WG, M; 1967 v S, W; 1968 v S, E; 1969 v E, S, W, Is, T (2); 1970 v S, E, W, USSR (2); (with Hull C), 1971 v Cy, Sp; 1972 v USSR (2), Sp, S, E, W; 1973 v Bul, Cy (2), P, E, S, W (59)
Nelis, P. (Nottingham F), 1923 v E (1)
Nelson, S. (Arsenal), 1970 v W, E (sub); 1971 v Cy, Sp, E, S, W; 1972 v USSR (2), Sp, E, S, W; 1973 v Bul, Cy, P; 1974 v S, E; 1975 v Se, Y; 1976 v Se, N, Is, E; 1977 v Bel (sub), WG, W, Ic; 1978 v Ic, Ho, Bel; 1979 v Ei, D, Bul, E, Bul, E, S, W, D; 1980 v E, Ei, Is; 1981 v S, P, S, Se; (with Brighton & HA), 1982 v E, S, Sp (sub), A (51)
Nicholl, C. J. (Aston Villa), 1975 v Se, Y, E, S, W; 1976 v Se, N, Y, S, E, W; 1977 v W; (with Southampton), 1978 v Bel (sub), S, E, W; 1979 v Ei, Bul, E, Bul, E, W; 1980 v Ei, Is, S, E, W, Aus (3); 1981 v Se, P, S, P, S, Se; 1982 v S, Is, E, F, W, Y, Hon, Sp, A, F; 1983 v S (sub), E, W; (with Grimsby T), 1984 v A, T (51)
Nicholl, H. (Belfast C), 1902 v E, W; 1905 v E (3)
Nicholl, J. M. (Manchester U), 1976 v Is, W (sub); 1977 v Ho, Bel, E, S, W, Ic; 1978 v Ic, Ho, Bel, S, E, W; 1979 v Ei, D, Bul, E, Bul, E, S, W, D; 1980 v E, Ei, Is, S, E, W, Aus (3); 1981 v Se, P, S, P, S, Se; 1982 v S, Is, E; (with Toronto B), F, W, Y, Hon, Sp, A, F; (with Sunderland), 1983 v A, WG, Alb, T, Alb; (with Toronto B), S, E, W; 1984 v T; (with Rangers), WG, S, E; (with Toronto B), Fi; 1985 v R; (with WBA), Fi, E, Sp, T; 1986 v T, R, E, F, Alg, Sp, Br (73)
Nicholson, J. J. (Manchester U), 1961 v S, W; 1962 v E, W, Gr, Ho; 1963 v E, S, Pol (2); (with Huddersfield T), 1965 v W, Ho (2), Alb; 1966 v S, E, W, Alb, M; 1967 v S, W; 1968 v S, E, W; 1969 v S, E, W, T (2); 1970 v S, E, W, USSR (2); 1971 v Cy (2), E, S, W; 1972 v USSR (2) (41)
Nixon, R. (Linfield), 1914 v S (1)
Nolan, I.R. (Sheffield W), 1997 v Arm, G, Alb, P, Uk; 1998 v G, P (7)
Nolan-Whelan, J. V. (Dublin Freebooters), 1901 v E, W; 1902 v S, W (4)

O'Boyle, G. (Dunfermline Ath), 1994 v Co (sub), M; (with St Johnstone), 1995 v P (sub), La (sub), Ca (sub), Ch (sub); 1996 v Se (sub), G (sub); 1997 v I (sub), Bel (sub); 1998 v Slo (sub), Sw (sub); 1999 v Fi (sub) (13)
O'Brien, M. T. (QPR), 1921 v S; (with Leicester C), 1922 v S, W; 1924 v S, W; (with Hull C), 1925 v S, E, W; 1926 v W; (with Derby Co), 1927 v W (10)
O'Connell, P. (Sheffield W), 1912 v E, S; (with Hull C), 1914 v E, S, W (5)
O'Doherty, A. (Coleraine), 1970 v E, W (sub) (2)
O'Driscoll, J. F. (Swansea T), 1949 v E, S, W (3)
O'Hagan, C. (Tottenham H), 1905 v S, W; 1906 v S, W, E; (with Aberdeen), 1907 v S, W; 1908 v S, W; 1909 v E (11)
O'Hagan, W. (St Mirren), 1920 v E, W (2)
O'Hehir, J. C. (Bohemians), 1910 v W (1)
O'Kane, W. J. (Nottingham F), 1970 v E, W, S (sub); 1971 v Sp, E, S, W; 1972 v USSR (2); 1973 v P, Cy; 1974 v Bul, P, S, E, W; 1975 v N, Se, E, S (20)
O'Mahoney, M. T. (Bristol R), 1939 v S (1)
O'Neill, C. (Motherwell), 1989 v Ch (sub); 1990 v Ei (sub); 1991 v D (3)
O'Neill, J. (Sunderland), 1962 v W (1)
O'Neill, J. P. (Leicester C), 1980 v Is, S, E, W, Aus (3); 1981 v P, S, P, S, Se; 1982 v S, Is, E, F, S, F (sub); 1983 v A, WG, Alb, T, Alb, S; 1984 v S (sub); 1985 v Is, Fi, E, Sp, T; 1986 v T, R, E, F, D, Mor, Alg, Sp, Br (39)
O'Neill, M. A. M. (Newcastle U), 1988 v Gr, Pol, F, Ma; 1989 v Ei, H, Sp (sub), Sp (sub), Ma (sub), Ch; (with Dundee U), 1990 v H (sub), Ei; 1991 v Pol; 1992 v Fa (sub), S (sub), G (sub); 1993 v Alb (sub + 1), Ei, Sp, Li, La; (with Hibernian), 1994 v Lie (sub); 1995 v A (sub), Ei; 1996 v Lie, A, N, Se; (with Coventry C), 1997 v Uk (sub), Arm (sub) (31)
O'Neill, M. H. M. (Distillery), 1972 v USSR (sub); (with Nottingham F), Sp (sub), W (sub); 1973 v P, Cy, E, S, W; 1974 v Bul, P, E (sub), W; 1975 v Se, Y, E, S; 1976 v Y (sub); 1977 v E (sub), S; 1978 v Ic, Ho, S, E, W; 1979 v Ei, D, Bul, E, Bul, D; 1980 v Ei, Is, Aus (3); 1981 v Se, P; (with Norwich C), P, S, Se; (with Manchester C), 1982 v S (with

Norwich C), E, F, S, Y, Hon, Sp, A, F; 1983 v A, WG, Alb, T, Alb, S, E; (with Notts Co), 1984 v A, T, WG, E, W, Fi; 1985 v R, Fi (64)
O'Reilly, H. (Dublin Freebooters), 1901 v S, W; 1904 v S (3)

Parke, J. (Linfield), 1964 v S; (with Hibernian), 1964 v E, Sp; (with Sunderland), 1965 v Sw, S, W, Ho (2), Alb; 1966 v WG; 1967 v E, S; 1968 v S, E (14)
Patterson, D. J. (C Palace), 1994 v Co (sub), M (sub); 1995 v Ei (sub+1), La, Ca, Ch (sub), La (sub); (with Luton T), 1996 v N (sub), Se; 1998 v Sw, Sp; (with Dundee U), 1999 v Fi, Mol, G, Mol, Ei (17)
Peacock, R. (Celtic), 1952 v S; 1953 v F; 1954 v W; 1955 v E, S; 1956 v E, S; 1957 v W, I, P; 1958 v S, E, W, I (2), Arg, Cz (2), WG; 1959 v E, S, W; 1960 v S, E; 1961 v E, S, I, WG (2), Gr; (with Coleraine), 1962 v S (31)
Peden, J. (Distillery), 1887 v S, W; 1888 v W, E; 1889 v S, E; 1890 v W, S; 1891 v W, E; 1892 v W, E; 1893 v E, S, W; 1896 v W, E, S; 1897 v W, S; 1898 v W, E, S; 1899 v W (24)
Penney, S. (Brighton & HA), 1985 v Is; 1986 v T, R, E, F, D, Mor, Alg, Sp; 1987 v E, T, Is; 1988 v Pol, F, Ma; 1989 v Ei, Sp (17)
Percy, J. C. (Belfast YMCA), 1889 v W (1)
Platt, J. A. (Middlesbrough), 1976 v Is (sub); 1978 v S, E, W; 1980 v S, E, W, Aus (3); 1981 v Se, P; 1982 v F, S, W (sub), A; 1983 v A, WG, Alb, T; (with Ballymena U), 1984 v E, W (sub); (with Coleraine), 1986 v Mor (sub) (23)
Ponsonby, J. (Distillery), 1895 v S, W; 1896 v E, S, W; 1897 v E, S, W; 1899 v E (9)
Potts, R. M. C. (Cliftonville), 1883 v E, W (2)
Priestley, T. J. M. (Coleraine), 1933 v S; (with Chelsea), 1934 v E (2)
Pyper, Jas. (Cliftonville), 1897 v S, W; 1898 v S, E, W; 1899 v S; 1900 v E (7)
Pyper, John (Cliftonville), 1897 v E, S, W; 1899 v E, W; 1900 v E, W, S; 1902 v S (9)
Pyper, M. (Linfield), 1932 v W (1)

Quinn, J. M. (Blackburn R), 1985 v Is, Fi, E, Sp, T; 1986 v T, R, E, F, D (sub), Mor (sub); 1987 v E (sub), T; (with Swindon T), 1988 v Y (sub), T, Gr, Pol, F (sub), Ma; (with Leicester C), 1989 v Ei, H (sub), Sp (sub+1); (with Bradford C), Ma, Ch; 1990 v H, (with West Ham U), N; 1991 v Y (sub); (with Bournemouth), 1992 v Li; (with Reading), 1993 v Sp, D, Alb (sub), Ei (sub), La (sub); 1994 v La, D (sub), Ei, R, Lie, Co, M; 1995 v P, A (sub), La (sub); 1996 v Lie, A (sub) (46)
Quinn, S. J. (Blackpool), 1996 v Se (sub); 1997 v Alb (sub), I, Bel, P, Uk (sub), Arm, Th (sub); 1998 v G, Alb; (with WBA), Slo, Sw; 1999 v T (sub), Fi (sub), Ei (15)

Rafferty, P. (Linfield), 1980 v E (sub) (1)
Ramsey, P. C. (Leicester C), 1984 v A, WG, S; 1985 v Is, E, Sp, T; 1986 v T, Mor; 1987 v Is, E, Y (sub); 1988 v Y; 1989 v Sp (14)
Rankine, J. (Alexander), 1883 v E, W (2)
Rattray, D. (Avoniel), 1882 v E; 1883 v E, W (3)
Rea, R. (Glentoran), 1901 v E (1)
Redmond, R. (Cliftonville), 1884 v W (1)
Reid, G. H. (Cardiff C), 1923 v S (1)
Reid, F. (Ulster), 1883 v E; 1884 v W; 1887 v S; 1889 v W; 1890 v S, W (6)
Reid, S. E. (Derby Co), 1934 v E, W; 1936 v E (3)
Reid, W. (Hearts), 1931 v E (1)
Reilly, M. M. (Portsmouth), 1900 v E; 1902 v E (2)
Renneville, W. T. J. (Leyton), 1910 v S, E, W; (with Aston Villa), 1911 v W (4)
Reynolds, J. (Distillery), 1890 v E, W; (with Ulster), 1891 v E, S, W (5)
Reynolds, R. (Bohemians), 1905 v W (1)
Rice, P. J. (Arsenal), 1969 v Is; 1970 v USSR; 1971 v E, S, W; 1972 v USSR, Sp, E, S, W; 1973 v Bul, Cy, E, S, W; 1974 v Bul, P, S, E, W; 1975 v N, Y, E, S, W; 1976 v Se, N, Y, Is, S, E, W; 1977 v Ho, Bel, WG, E, S, Ic; 1978 v Ic, Ho, Bel; 1979 v Ei, D, E (2), S, W, D; 1980 v E (49)
Roberts, F. C. (Glentoran), 1931 v S (1)
Robinson, P. (Distillery), 1920 v S; (with Blackburn R), 1921 v W (2)
Robinson, S. (Bournemouth), 1997 v Th (sub); 1999 v Mol, Ei (3)
Rogan, A. (Celtic), 1988 v Y (sub), Gr, Pol (sub); 1989 v Ei (sub), H, Sp (2), Ma (sub), Ch; 1990 v H, N (sub), U; 1991 v Y (2), D, A; (with Sunderland), 1992 v Li (sub); (with Millwall), 1997 v G (sub) (18)
Rollo, D. (Linfield), 1912 v W; 1913 v W; 1914 v W, E; (with Blackburn R), 1920 v S, W; 1921 v E, S, W; 1922 v E; 1923 v E; 1924 v S, W; 1925 v W; 1926 v E; 1927 v E (16)

Roper, E. O. (Dublin University), 1886 v W (1)
Rosbotham, A. (Cliftonville), 1887 v E, S, W; 1888 v E, S, W; 1889 v E (7)
Ross, W. E. (Newcastle U), 1969 v Is (1)
Rowland, K. (West Ham U), 1994 v La (sub); 1995 v Ca, Ch, La; 1996 v P (sub), Lie (sub), N (sub), Se, G (sub); 1997 v Uk, Arm, I (sub); 1998 v Alb; (with QPR), 1999 v T, Fi, Mol, G, Ca, Ei (19)
Rowley, R. W. M. (Southampton), 1929 v S, W; 1930 v W, E; (with Tottenham H), 1931 v W; 1932 v S (6)
Russell, A. (Linfield), 1947 v E (1)
Russell, S. R. (Bradford C), 1930 v E, S; (with Derry C), 1932 v E (3)
Ryan, R. A. (WBA), 1950 v W (1)

Sanchez, L. P. (Wimbledon), 1987 v T (sub); 1989 v Sp, Ma (3)
Scott, E. (Liverpool), 1920 v S; 1921 v E, S, W; 1922 v E; 1925 v W; 1926 v E, S, W; 1927 v E, S, W; 1928 v E, S, W; 1929 v E, S, W; 1930 v E; 1931 v E; 1932 v W; 1933 v E, S, W; 1934 v E, S, W; (with Belfast C), 1935 v S; 1936 v E, S, W (31)
Scott, J. (Grimsby), 1958 v Cz, F (2)
Scott, J. E. (Cliftonville), 1901 v S (1)
Scott, L. J. (Dublin University), 1895 v S, W (2)
Scott, P. W. (Everton), 1975 v W; 1976 v Y; (with York C), Is, S, E (sub), W; 1978 v S, E, W; (with Aldershot), 1979 v S (sub) (10)
Scott, T. (Cliftonville), 1894 v E, S; 1895 v S, W; 1896 v S, E, W; 1897 v E, W; 1898 v E, S, W; 1900 v W (13)
Scott, W. (Linfield), 1903 v E, S, W; 1904 v E, S, W; (with Everton), 1905 v E, S; 1907 v E, S; 1908 v E, S, W; 1909 v E, S, W; 1910 v E, S; 1911 v E, S, W; 1912 v E; (with Leeds City), 1913 v E, S, W (25)
Scraggs, M. J. (Glentoran), 1921 v W; 1922 v E (2)
Seymour, H. C. (Bohemians), 1914 v W (1)
Seymour, J. (Cliftonville), 1907 v W; 1909 v W (2)
Shanks, T. (Woolwich Arsenal), 1903 v S; 1904 v W; (with Brentford), 1905 v E (3)
Sharkey, P. G. (Ipswich T), 1976 v S (1)
Sheehan, Dr G. (Bohemians), 1899 v S; 1900 v E, W (3)
Sheridan, J. (Everton), 1903 v W, E, S; 1904 v E, S; (with Stoke C), 1905 v E (6)
Sherrard, J. (Limavady), 1885 v S; 1887 v W; 1888 v W (3)
Sherrard, W. C. (Cliftonville), 1895 v E, W, S (3)
Sherry, J. J. (Bohemians), 1906 v E; 1907 v W (2)
Shields, R. J. (Southampton), 1957 v S (1)
Silo, M. (Belfast YMCA), 1888 v E (1)
Simpson, W. J. (Rangers), 1951 v W, F; 1954 v E, S; 1955 v E; 1957 v I, P; 1958 v S, E, W, I; 1959 v S (12)
Sinclair, J. (Knock), 1882 v E, W (2)
Slemin, J. C. (Bohemians), 1909 v W (1)
Sloan, A. S. (London Caledonians), 1925 v W (1)
Sloan, D. (Oxford U), 1969 v Is; 1971 v Sp (2)
Sloan, H. A. de B. (Bohemians), 1903 v E; 1904 v S; 1905 v E; 1906 v W; 1907 v E, W; 1908 v W; 1909 v S (8)
Sloan, J. W. (Arsenal), 1947 v W (1)
Sloan, T. (Cardiff C), 1926 v S, W, E; 1927 v W, S; 1928 v E, W; 1929 v E; (with Linfield), 1930 v W, S; 1931 v S (11)
Sloan, T. (Manchester U), 1979 v S, W (sub), D (sub) (3)
Small, J. M. (Clarence), 1887 v E; (with Cliftonville), 1893 v E, S, W (4)
Smith, E. E. (Cardiff C), 1921 v S; 1923 v W, E; 1924 v E (4)
Smith, J. E. (Distillery), 1901 v S, W (2)
Smyth, R. H. (Dublin University), 1886 v W (1)
Smyth, S. (Wolverhampton W), 1948 v E, S, W; 1949 v S, W; 1950 v E, S, W; (with Stoke C), 1952 v E (9)
Smyth, W. (Distillery), 1949 v E, S; 1954 v S, E (4)
Snape, A. (Airdrie), 1920 v E (1)
Sonner, D. J. (Ipswich T), 1998 v Alb (sub); (with Sheffield W), 1999 v G (sub), Ca (sub) (3)
Spence, D. W. (Bury), 1975 v Y, E, S, W; 1976 v Se, Is, E, W, S (sub); (with Blackpool), 1977 v Ho (sub), WG (sub), E (sub), S (sub), W (sub), Ic (sub); 1979 v Ei, D (sub), E (sub), Bul (sub), E (sub), N; D; 1980 v Ei; (with Southend U), Is (sub), Aus (sub); 1981 v S (sub), Se (sub); 1982 v F (sub) (29)
Spencer, S. (Distillery), 1890 v E, S; 1892 v E, S, W; 1893 v E (6)
Spiller, E. A. (Cliftonville), 1883 v E, W; 1884 v E, W, S (5)
Stanfield, O. M. (Distillery), 1887 v E, S, W; 1888 v E, S, W; 1889 v E, S, W; 1890 v E, S; 1891 v E, S, W; 1892 v E, S, W; 1893 v E, W; 1894 v E, S, W; 1895 v E, S; 1896 v E, S, W; 1897 v E, S, W (30)
Steele, A. (Charlton Ath), 1926 v W, S; (with Fulham), 1929 v W, S (4)

Stevenson, A. E. (Rangers), 1934 v E, S, W; (with Everton), 1935 v E, S; 1936 v S, W; 1937 v E, W; 1938 v E, W; 1939 v W; 1947 v S, W; 1948 v S (17)
Stewart, A. (Glentoran), 1967 v W; 1968 v S, E; (with Derby Co), 1968 v W; 1969 v Is, T (1+1 sub) (7)
Stewart, D. C. (Hull C), 1978 v Bel (1)
Stewart, I. (QPR), 1982 v F (sub); 1983 v A, WG, Alb, T, Alb, S, E, W; 1984 v A, T, WG, S, E, W, Fi; 1985 v R, Fi, Is, E, Sp, T; (with Newcastle U), 1986 v R, E, D, Mor, Alg (sub), Sp (sub), Br; 1987 v E, Is (sub) (31)
Stewart, R. K. (St Columb's Court), 1890 v E, S, W; (with Cliftonville), 1892 v E, S, W; 1893 v E, W; 1894 v E, S, W (11)
Stewart, T. C. (Linfield), 1961 v W (1)
Swan, M. (Linfield), 1899 v S (1)

Taggart, G. P. (Barnsley), 1990 v N, U; 1991 v Y, D, A, Pol, Fa; 1992 v Fa, A, D, S, Li, G; 1993 v Alb, Sp, D, Alb, Ei, Sp, Li, La; 1994 v La, D, Ei, R, Lie, Co, M; 1995 v P (sub), A, Ei (2), Ca, Ch, La; (with Bolton W), 1997 v G, Alb, I, Bel, P, Uk, Arm; 1998 v G, P, Sp (45)
Taggart, J. (Walsall), 1899 v W (1)
Taylor, M. S. (Fulham), 1999 v G, Mol, Ca, Ei (4)
Thompson, F. W. (Cliftonville), 1910 v E, S, W; (with Linfield), 1911 v W; (with Bradford C), 1911 v E; 1912 v E, W; 1913 v E, S, W; (with Clyde), 1914 v E, S (12)
Thompson, J. (Belfast Ath), 1889 v S (1)
Thompson, J. (Distillery), 1897 v S (1)
Thunder, P. J. (Bohemians), 1911 v W (1)
Todd, S. J. (Burnley), 1966 v M (sub); 1967 v E; 1968 v W; 1969 v E, S, W; 1970 v S, USSR; (with Sheffield W), 1971 v Cy (2), Sp (sub) (11)
Toner, J. (Arsenal), 1922 v W; 1923 v W; 1924 v W, E; 1925 v E, S; (with St Johnstone), 1927 v E, S (8)
Torrans, R. (Linfield), 1893 v S (1)
Torrans, S. (Linfield), 1889 v S; 1890 v S, W; 1891 v S, W; 1892 v E, S, W; 1893 v E, S; 1894 v E, S, W; 1895 v E; 1896 v E, S, W; 1897 v E, S, W; 1898 v E, S; 1899 v E, W; 1901 v S, W (26)
Trainor, D. (Crusaders), 1967 v W (1)
Tully, L. P. (Celtic), 1949 v E; 1950 v E; 1952 v S; 1953 v E, S, W, F; 1954 v S; 1956 v E; 1959 v Sp (10)
Turner, E. (Cliftonville), 1896 v E, W (2)
Turner, J. (Cliftonville), 1886 v E, S; 1888 v S (3)
Twoomey, J. F. (Leeds U), 1938 v W; 1939 v E (2)

Uprichard, W. N. M. C. (Swindon T), 1952 v E, S, W; 1953 v E, S; (with Portsmouth), 1953 v W, F; 1955 v E, S, W; 1956 v E, S, W; 1958 v S, I, Cz; 1959 v S, Sp (18)

Vernon, J. (Belfast C), 1947 v E, S; (with WBA), 1947 v W; 1948 v E, S, W; 1949 v E, S, W; 1950 v E, S; 1951 v E, S, W, F; 1952 v S, E (17)

Waddell, T. M. R. (Cliftonville), 1906 v S (1)
Walker, J. (Doncaster R), 1955 v W (1)
Walker, J. (Bury), 1911 v S (1)
Walsh, D. J. (WBA), 1947 v S, W; 1948 v E, S, W; 1949 v E, S, W; 1950 v W (9)
Walsh, W. (Manchester C), 1948 v E, S, W; 1949 v E, S (5)
Waring, J. (Cliftonville), 1899 v E (1)
Warren, P. (Shelbourne), 1913 v E, S (2)
Watson, J. (Ulster), 1883 v E, W; 1886 v E, S, W; 1887 v S, W; 1889 v E, W (9)
Watson, P. (Distillery), 1971 v Cy (sub) (1)
Watson, T. (Cardiff C), 1926 v S (1)
Wattie, J. (Distillery), 1899 v E (1)
Webb, C. G. (Brighton & HA), 1909 v S, W; 1911 v S (3)
Weir, C. (Clyde), 1939 v W (1)
Welsh, E. (Carlisle U), 1966 v W, WG, M; 1967 v W (4)
Whiteside, N. (Manchester U), 1982 v Y, Hon, Sp, A, F; 1983 v WG, Alb, T; 1984 v A, T, WG, S, E, W, Fi; 1985 v R, Fi, Is, E, Sp, T; 1986 v R, E, F, D, Mor, Alg, Sp, Br; 1987 v E (2), Is, Y; 1988 v T, Pol, F; (with Everton), 1990 v H, Ei (38)
Whiteside, T. (Distillery), 1891 v W (1)
Whitfield, E. R. (Dublin University), 1886 v W (1)
Whitley, Jeff (Manchester C), 1997 v Bel (sub), Th (sub); 1998 v Sp (sub) (3)
Whitley, Jim (Manchester C), 1998 v Sp; 1999 v T (sub) (2)
Williams, J. R. (Ulster), 1886 v E, S (2)
Williams, M. S. (Chesterfield), 1999 v G, Mol, Ca, Ei (4)
Williams, P. A. (WBA), 1991 v Fa (sub) (1)
Williamson, J. (Cliftonville), 1890 v E; 1892 v S; 1893 v S (3)
Willighan, T. (Burnley), 1933 v W; 1934 v S (2)
Willis, G. (Linfield), 1906 v S, W; 1907 v S; 1912 v S (4)

Wilson, D. J. (Brighton & HA), 1987 v T, Is, E (sub); (with Luton T), 1988 v Y, T, Gr, Pol, F, Ma; 1989 v Ei, H, Sp, Ma, Ch; 1990 v H, Ei, N, U; (with Sheffield W), 1991 v Y, D, A, Fa; 1992 v A (sub), S (24)

Wilson, H. (Linfield), 1925 v W (1)

Wilson, K. J. (Ipswich T), 1987 v Is, E, Y; (with Chelsea), 1988 v Y, T, Gr (sub), Pol (sub), F (sub); 1989 v H (sub), Sp (2), Ma, Ch; 1990 v Ei (sub), N, U; 1991 v Y (2), A, Pol, Fa; 1992 v Fa, A, D, S; (with Notts Co), Li, G; 1993 v Alb, Sp, D, Sp, Li, La; 1994 v La, D, Ei, R, Lie, Co, M; (with Walsall), 1995 v Ei (sub), La (42)

Wilson, M. (Distillery), 1884 v E, S, W (3)

Wilson, R. (Cliftonville), 1888 v S (1)

Wilson, S. J. (Glenavon), 1962 v S; 1964 v S; (with Falkirk), 1964 v E, W, U, Sp; 1965 v E, Sw; (with Dundee), 1966 v W, WG; 1967 v S; 1968 v E (12)

Wilton, J. M. (St Columb's Court), 1888 v E, W; 1889 v S, E; (with Cliftonville), 1890 v E; (with St Columb's Court); 1893 v W, S (7)

Wood, T. J. (Walsall), 1996 v Lie (sub) (1)

Worthington, N. (Sheffield W), 1984 v W, Fi (sub); 1985 v Is, Sp (sub); 1986 v T, R (sub), E (sub), D, Alg, Sp; 1987 v E (2), T, Is, Y; 1988 v Y, T, Gr, Pol, F, Ma; 1989 v Ei, H, Sp, Ma; 1990 v H, Ei, U; 1991 v Y, D, A, Fa; 1992 v A, D, S, Li, G; 1993 v Alb, Sp, D, Ei, Sp, Li, La; 1994 v La, D, Ei, Lie, Co, M; (with Leeds U), 1995 v P, A, Ei (2), La, Ca (sub), Ch, La; 1996 v P, Lie, A, N, Se, G; (with Stoke C), 1997 v I, Bel (sub) (66)

Wright, J. (Cliftonville), 1906 v E, S, W; 1907 v E, S, W (6)

Wright, T. J. (Newcastle U), 1989 v Ma, Ch; 1990 v H, U; 1992 v Fa, A, S, G; 1993 v Alb, Sp, Alb, Ei, Sp, Li, La; 1994 v La; (with Nottingham F), D, Ei, R, Lie, Co, M (sub); 1997 v G, Alb, I, Bel; (with Manchester C), P, Uk; 1998 v Alb; 1999 v Ca (sub) (30)

Young, S. (Linfield), 1907 v E, S; 1908 v E, S; (with Airdrie), 1909 v E; 1912 v S; (with Linfield), 1914 v E, S, W (9)

SCOTLAND

Adams, J. (Hearts), 1889 v Ni; 1892 v W; 1893 v Ni (3)

Agnew, W. B. (Kilmarnock), 1907 v Ni; 1908 v W, Ni (3)

Aird, J. (Burnley), 1954 v N (2), A, U (4)

Aitken, A. (Newcastle U), 1901 v E; 1902 v E; 1903 v E, W; 1904 v E; 1905 v E, W; 1906 v E; (with Middlesbrough), 1907 v E, W; 1908 v E; (with Leicester Fosse), 1910 v E; 1911 v E, Ni (14)

Aitken, G. G. (East Fife), 1949 v E, F; 1950 v W, Ni, Sw; (with Sunderland), 1953 v W, Ni; 1954 v E (8)

Aitken, R. (Dumbarton), 1886 v E; 1888 v Ni (2)

Aitken, R. (Celtic), 1980 v Pe (sub), Bel, W (sub), E, Pol; 1983 v Bel, Ca (1+1 sub); 1984 v Bel (sub), N, W (sub); 1985 v E, Ic; 1986 v W, EG, Aus (2), Is, R, E, D, WG, U; 1987 v Bul, Ei (2), L, Bel, E, Br; 1988 v H, Bel, Bul, L, S.Ar, Ma, Sp, Co, E; 1989 v N, Y, I, Cy, F, Cy, E, Ch; 1990 v Y, F, N; (with Newcastle U), Arg (sub), Pol, Ma, Cr, Se, Br; (with St Mirren), 1992 v R (sub) (57)

Aitkenhead, W. A. C. (Blackburn R), 1912 v Ni (1)

Albiston, A. (Manchester U), 1982 v Ni; 1984 v U, Bel, EG, W, E; 1985 v Y, Ic, Sp (2), W; 1986 v EG, Ho, U (14)

Alexander, D. (East Stirlingshire), 1894 v W, Ni (2)

Allan, D. S. (Queen's Park), 1885 v E, W; 1886 v W (3)

Allan, G. (Liverpool), 1897 v E (1)

Allan, H. (Hearts), 1902 v W (1)

Allan, J. (Queen's Park), 1887 v E, W (2)

Allan, T. (Dundee), 1974 v WG, N (2)

Ancell, R. F. D. (Newcastle U), 1937 v W, Ni (2)

Anderson, A. (Hearts), 1933 v E; 1934 v A, E, W, Ni; 1935 v E, W, Ni; 1936 v E, W, Ni; 1937 v G, E, W, Ni, A; 1938 v E, W, Ni, Cz, Ho; 1939 v W, H (23)

Anderson, F. (Clydesdale), 1874 v E (1)

Anderson, G. (Kilmarnock), 1901 v Ni (1)

Anderson, H. A. (Raith R), 1914 v W (1)

Anderson, J. (Leicester C), 1954 v Fi (1)

Anderson, K. (Queen's Park), 1896 v Ni; 1898 v E, Ni (3)

Anderson, W. (Queen's Park), 1882 v E; 1883 v E, W; 1884 v E; 1885 v E, W (6)

Andrews, P. (Eastern), 1875 v E (1)

Archibald, A. (Rangers), 1921 v W; 1922 v W, E; 1923 v Ni; 1924 v E, W; 1931 v E; 1932 v E (8)

Archibald, S. (Aberdeen), 1980 v P (sub); (with Tottenham H), Ni, Pol, H; 1981 v Se (sub), Is, Ni, Is, Ni, E; 1982 v Ni, P, Sp (sub), Ho, Nz (sub), Br, USSR; 1983 v EG, Sw (sub), Bel; 1984 v EG, E, F; (with Barcelona), 1985 v Sp, E, Ic (sub); 1986 v WG (27)

Armstrong, M. W. (Aberdeen), 1936 v W, Ni; 1937 v G (3)

Arnott, W. (Queen's Park), 1883 v W; 1884 v E, Ni; 1885 v E, W; 1886 v E; 1887 v E, W; 1888 v E; 1889 v E; 1890 v E; 1891 v E; 1892 v E; 1893 v E (14)

Auld, J. R. (Third Lanark), 1887 v E, W; 1889 v W (3)

Auld, R. (Celtic), 1959 v H, P; 1960 v W (3)

Baird, A. (Queen's Park), 1892 v Ni; 1894 v W (2)

Baird, D. (Hearts), 1890 v Ni; 1891 v E; 1892 v W (3)

Baird, H. (Airdrieonians), 1956 v A (1)

Baird, J. C. (Vale of Leven), 1876 v E; 1878 v W; 1880 v E (3)

Baird, S. (Rangers), 1957 v Y, Sp (2), Sw, WG; 1958 v F, Ni (7)

Baird, W. U. (St Bernards), 1897 v Ni (1)

Bannon, E. (Dundee U), 1980 v Bel; 1983 v Ni, W, E, Ca; 1984 v EG; 1986 v Is, R, E, D (sub), WG (11)

Barbour, A. (Renton), 1885 v Ni (1)

Barker, J. B. (Rangers), 1893 v W; 1894 v W (2)

Barrett, F. (Dundee), 1894 v Ni; 1895 v W (2)

Battles, B. (Celtic), 1901 v E, W, Ni (3)

Battles, B. jun. (Hearts), 1931 v W (1)

Bauld, W. (Hearts), 1950 v E, Sw, P (3)

Baxter, J. C. (Rangers), 1961 v Ni, Ei (2), Cz; 1962 v Ni, W, E, Cz (2), U; 1963 v W, Ni, E, A, N, Ei, Sp; 1964 v W, E, N, WG; 1965 v W, Ni, Fi; (with Sunderland), 1966 v P, Br, Ni, W, E, I; 1967 v W, E, USSR; 1968 v W (34)

Baxter, R. D. (Middlesbrough), 1939 v E, W, H (3)

Beattie, A. (Preston NE), 1937 v E, A, Cz; 1938 v E; 1939 v W, Ni, H (7)

Beattie, R. (Preston NE), 1939 v W (1)

Begbie, I. (Hearts), 1890 v Ni; 1891 v E; 1892 v W; 1894 v E (4)

Bell, A. (Manchester U), 1912 v Ni (1)

Bell, J. (Dumbarton), 1890 v Ni; 1892 v E; (with Everton), 1896 v E; 1897 v E; 1898 v E; (with Celtic), 1899 v E, W, Ni; 1900 v E, W (10)

Bell, M. (Hearts), 1901 v W (1)

Bell, W. J. (Leeds U), 1966 v P, Br (2)

Bennett, A. (Celtic), 1904 v W; 1907 v Ni; 1908 v W; (with Rangers), 1909 v W, Ni, E; 1910 v E, W; 1911 v E, W; 1913 v Ni (11)

Bennie, R. (Airdrieonians), 1925 v W, Ni; 1926 v Ni (3)

Bernard, P. R. J. (Oldham Ath), 1995 v J (sub), Ec (2)

Berry, D. (Queen's Park), 1894 v W; 1899 v W, Ni (3)

Berry, W. H. (Queen's Park), 1888 v E; 1889 v E; 1890 v E; 1891 v E (4)

Bett, J. (Rangers), 1982 v Ho; 1983 v Bel; (with Lokeren), 1984 v Bel, W, E, F; 1985 v Ic, Sp (2), W, E, Ic; (with Aberdeen), 1986 v W, Is, Ho; 1987 v Bel; 1988 v W (sub); 1989 v Y; 1990 v F (sub), N, Arg, Eg, Ma, Cr (25)

Beveridge, W. W. (Glasgow University), 1879 v E, W; 1880 v W (3)

Black, A. (Hearts), 1938 v Cz, Ho; 1939 v H (3)

Black, D. (Hurlford), 1889 v Ni (1)

Black, E. (Metz), 1988 v H (sub), L (sub) (2)

Black, I. H. (Southampton), 1948 v E (1)

Blackburn, J. E. (Royal Engineers), 1873 v E (1)

Blacklaw, A. S. (Burnley), 1963 v N, Sp; 1966 v I (3)

Blackley, J. (Hibernian), 1974 v Cz, E, Bel, Z; 1976 v Sw; 1977 v W, Se (7)

Blair, D. (Clyde), 1929 v W, Ni; 1931 v E, A, I; 1932 v W, Ni; (with Aston Villa), 1933 v W (8)

Blair, J. (Sheffield W), 1920 v E, Ni; (with Cardiff C), 1921 v E; 1922 v E; 1923 v E, W, Ni; 1924 v W (8)

Blair, J. (Motherwell), 1934 v W (1)

Blair, J. A. (Blackpool), 1947 v W (1)

Blair, W. (Third Lanark), 1896 v W (1)

Blessington, J. (Celtic), 1894 v E, Ni; 1896 v E, Ni (4)

Blyth, J. A. (Coventry C), 1978 v Bul, W (2)

Bone, J. (Norwich C), 1972 v Y (sub); 1973 v D (2)

Booth, S. (Aberdeen), 1993 v G (sub), Es (2 subs); 1994 v Sw, Ma (sub); 1995 v Fa, Ru; 1996 v Fi, Sm, Aus (sub), US, Ho, Sw (sub); (with Borussia Dortmund), 1998 v D, Fi, Co (sub), Mor (sub) (17)

Bowie, J. (Rangers), 1920 v E, Ni (2)

Bowie, W. (Linthouse), 1891 v Ni (1)

Bowman, D. (Dundee U), 1992 v Fi, US (sub); 1993 v G, Es; 1994 v Sw, I (6)

Bowman, G. A. (Montrose), 1892 v Ni (1)

Boyd, J. M. (Newcastle U), 1934 v Ni (1)

Boyd, R. (Mossend Swifts), 1889 v Ni; 1891 v W (2)

Boyd, T. (Motherwell), 1991 v R (sub), Sw, Bul, USSR; (with Chelsea), 1992 v Sw, R; (with Celtic), Fi, Ca, N, C; 1993 v Sw, P, I, Ma, G, Es (2); 1994 v I, Ma (sub), Ho (sub), A; 1995 v Fi, Fa, Ru, Gr, Ru, Sm; 1996 v Gr, Fi, Se, Sm, Aus, D, US, Co, Ho, E, Sw; 1997 v A, La, Se, Es (2), A, Se, W, Ma, Bl; 1998 v Bl, La, F, D, Fi (sub), Co, US, Br, N, Mor; 1999 v Li, Es, Fa, CzR, G, Fa, CzR (65)

Boyd, W. G. (Clyde), 1931 v I, Sw (2)

Breckenbridge, T. (Hearts), 1888 v Ni (1)

Bradshaw, T. (Bury), 1928 v E (1)

Brand, R. (Rangers), 1961 v Ni, Cz, Ei (2); 1962 v Ni, W, Cz, U (8)

Branden, T. (Blackburn R), 1896 v E (1)

Brazil, A. (Ipswich T), 1980 v Pol (sub), H; 1982 v Sp, Ho (sub), Ni, W, E, Nz, USSR (sub); 1983 v EG, Sw; (with Tottenham H), W, E (sub) (13)

Bremner, D. (Hibernian), 1976 v Sw (sub) (1)

Bremner, W. J. (Leeds U), 1965 v Sp; 1966 v E, Pol, P, Br, I (2); 1967 v W, Ni, E; 1968 v W, E; 1969 v W, E, Ni, D, A, WG, Cy (2); 1970 v Ei, WG, A; 1971 v W, E; 1972 v P, Bel, Ho, Ni, W, E, Y, Cz, Br; 1973 v D (2), E (2), Ni (sub), Sw, Br; 1974 v Cz, WG, Ni, W, E, Bel, N, Z, Br, Y; 1975 v Sp (2); 1976 v D (54)

Brennan, F. (Newcastle U), 1947 v W, Ni; 1953 v W, Ni, E; 1954 v Ni, E (7)

Breslin, B. (Hibernian), 1897 v W (1)

Brewster, G. (Everton), 1921 v E (1)

Brogan, J. (Celtic), 1971 v W, Ni, P, E (4)

Brown, A. (Middlesbrough), 1904 v E (1)

Brown, A. (St Mirren), 1890 v W; 1891 v W (2)

Brown, A. D. (East Fife), 1950 v Sw, P, F; (with Blackpool), 1952 v USA, D, Se; 1953 v W; 1954 v W, E, N (2), Fi, A, U (14)

Brown, G. C. P. (Rangers), 1931 v W; 1932 v E, W, Ni; 1933 v E; 1934 v A; 1935 v E, W; 1936 v E, W; 1937 v G, E, W, Ni, Cz; 1938 v E, W, Cz, Ho (19)

Brown, H. (Partick T), 1947 v W, Bel, L (3)

Brown, J. (Cambuslang), 1890 v W (1)

Brown, J. B. (Clyde), 1939 v W (1)

Brown, J. G. (Sheffield U), 1975 v R (1)

Brown, R. (Dumbarton), 1884 v W, Ni (2)

Brown, R. (Rangers), 1947 v Ni; 1949 v Ni; 1952 v E (3)

Brown, R. jun. (Dumbarton), 1885 v W (1)

Brown, W. D. F. (Dundee), 1958 v F; 1959 v E, W, Ni; (with Tottenham H), 1960 v W, Ni, Pol, A, H, T; 1962 v Ni, W, E, Cz; 1963 v W, Ni, E, A; 1964 v Ni, W, N; 1965 v E, Fi, Pol, Sp; 1966 v Ni, Pol, I (28)

Browning, J. (Celtic), 1914 v W (1)

Brownlie, J. (Hibernian), 1971 v USSR; 1972 v Pe, Ni, E; 1973 v D (2); 1976 v R (7)

Brownlie, J. (Third Lanark), 1909 v E, Ni; 1910 v E, W, Ni; 1911 v W, Ni; 1912 v W, Ni, E; 1913 v W, Ni, E; 1914 v W, Ni, E (16)

Bruce, D. (Vale of Leven), 1890 v W (1)

Bruce, R. F. (Middlesbrough), 1934 v A (1)

Buchan, M. M. (Aberdeen), 1972 v P (sub), Bel; (with Manchester U), W, Y, Cz, Br; 1973 v D (2), E; 1974 v WG, Ni, W, N, Br, Y; 1975 v EG, Sp, P; 1976 v D, R; 1977 v Fi, Cz, Ch, Arg, Br; 1978 v EG, W (sub), Ni, Pe, Ir, Ho; 1979 v A, N, P (34)

Buchanan, J. (Cambuslang), 1889 v Ni (1)

Buchanan, J. (Rangers), 1929 v E; 1930 v E (2)

Buchanan, P. S. (Chelsea), 1938 v Cz (1)

Buchanan, R. (Abercorn), 1891 v W (1)

Buckley, P. (Aberdeen), 1954 v N; 1955 v W, Ni (3)

Buick, A. (Hearts), 1902 v W, Ni (2)

Burley, C. W. (Chelsea), 1995 v J, Ec, Fa; 1996 v Gr, Se, Aus, D, US, Co (sub), Ho (sub), E (sub), Sw; 1997 v A, La, Se, Es, A, Se, Ma, Bl; (with Celtic), 1998 v Bl, La, F, Co, US (sub), Br, N, Mor; 1999 v Fa, CzR (30)

Burley, G. (Ipswich T), 1979 v W, Ni, E, Arg, N; 1980 v P, Ni, E (sub), Pol; 1982 v W (sub), E (11)

Burns, F. (Manchester U), 1970 v A (1)

Burns, K. (Birmingham C), 1974 v WG; 1975 v EG (sub), Sp (2); 1977 v Cz (sub), W, Se, W (sub); (with Nottingham F), 1978 v Ni (sub), W, E, Pe, Ir; 1979 v N; 1980 v Pe, A, Bel; 1981 v Is, Ni, W (20)

Burns, T. (Celtic), 1981 v Ni; 1982 v Ho (sub), W; 1983 v Bel (sub), Ni, Ca (1 + 1 sub); 1988 v E (sub) (8)

Busby, M. W. (Manchester C), 1934 v W (1)

Cairns, T. (Rangers), 1920 v W; 1922 v E; 1923 v E, W; 1924 v Ni; 1925 v W, E, Ni (8)

Calderhead, D. (Queen of the South), 1889 v Ni (1)

Calderwood, C. (Tottenham H), 1995 v Ru, Sm, J, Ec, Fa; 1996 v Gr, Fi, Se, Sm, US, Co, Ho, E, Sw; 1997 v A, La, Se, Es (2), A, Se; 1998 v Bl, La, F, D, Fi, Co, US, Br, N; 1999 v Li, Es; (with Aston Villa), Fa, CzR (34)

Calderwood, R. (Cartvale), 1885 v Ni, E, W (3)

Caldow, E. (Rangers), 1957 v Sp (2), Sw, WG, E; 1958 v Ni, W, Sw, Par, H, Pol, Y, F; 1959 v E, W, Ni, WG, Ho, P; 1960 v E, W, Ni, A, H, T; 1961 v E, W, Ni, Ei (2), Cz; 1962 v Ni, W, E, Cz (2), U; 1963 v W, Ni, E (40)

Callaghan, P. (Hibernian), 1900 v Ni (1)

Callaghan, W. (Dunfermline Ath), 1970 v Ei (sub), W (2)

Cameron, C. (Hearts), 1999 v G (sub), Fa (sub) (2)

Cameron, J. (Rangers), 1886 v Ni (1)

Cameron, J. (Queen's Park), 1896 v Ni (1)

Cameron, J. (St Mirren), 1904 v Ni; (with Chelsea), 1909 v E (2)

Campbell, C. (Queen's Park), 1874 v E; 1876 v W; 1877 v E, W; 1878 v E; 1879 v E; 1880 v E; 1881 v E; 1882 v E, W; 1884 v E; 1885 v E; 1886 v E (13)

Campbell, H. (Renton), 1889 v W (1)

Campbell, Jas (Sheffield W), 1913 v W (1)

Campbell, J. (South Western), 1880 v W (1)

Campbell, J. (Kilmarnock), 1891 v Ni; 1892 v W (2)

Campbell, John (Celtic), 1893 v E, Ni; 1898 v E, Ni; 1900 v E, Ni; 1901 v E, W, Ni; 1902 v W, Ni; 1903 v W (12)

Campbell, John (Rangers), 1899 v E, W, Ni; 1901 v Ni (4)

Campbell, K. (Liverpool), 1920 v E, W, Ni; (with Partick T), 1921 v W, Ni; 1922 v W, Ni, E (8)

Campbell, P. (Rangers), 1878 v W; 1879 v W (2)

Campbell, P. (Morton), 1898 v W (1)

Campbell, R. (Falkirk), 1947 v Bel, L; (with Chelsea), 1950 v Sw, P, F (5)

Campbell, W. (Morton), 1947 v Ni; 1948 v E, Bel, Sw, F (5)

Carabine, J. (Third Lanark), 1938 v Ho; 1939 v E, Ni (3)

Carr, W. M. (Coventry C), 1970 v Ni, W, E; 1971 v D; 1972 v Pe; 1973 v D (sub) (6)

Cassidy, J. (Celtic), 1921 v W, Ni; 1923 v Ni; 1924 v W (4)

Chalmers, S. (Celtic), 1965 v W, Fi; 1966 v P (sub), Br; 1967 v Ni (5)

Chalmers, W. (Rangers), 1885 v Ni (1)

Chalmers, W. S. (Queen's Park), 1929 v Ni (1)

Chambers, T. (Hearts), 1894 v W (1)

Chaplin, G. D. (Dundee), 1908 v W (1)

Cheyne, A. G. (Aberdeen), 1929 v E, N, G, Ho; 1930 v F (5)

Christie, A. J. (Queen's Park), 1898 v W; 1899 v E, Ni (3)

Christie, R. M. (Queen's Park), 1884 v E (1)

Clark, J. (Celtic), 1966 v Br; 1967 v W, Ni, USSR (4)

Clark, R. B. (Aberdeen), 1968 v W, Ho; 1970 v Ni; 1971 v W, Ni, E, D, P, USSR; 1972 v Bel Ni, W, E, Cz, Br; 1973 v D, E (17)

Clarke, S. (Chelsea), 1988 v H, Bel, Bul, S.Ar, Ma; 1994 v Ho (6)

Cleland, J. (Royal Albert), 1891 v Ni (1)

Clements, R. (Leith Ath), 1891 v Ni (1)

Clunas, W. L. (Sunderland), 1924 v E; 1926 v W (2)

Collier, W. (Raith R), 1922 v W (1)

Collins, J. (Hibernian), 1988 v S.Ar; 1990 v EG, Pol (sub), Ma (sub); (with Celtic), 1991 v Sw (sub), Bul (sub); 1992 v Ni (sub), Fi; 1993 v P, Ma, G, P, Es (2); 1994 v Sw, Ho (sub), A, Ho; 1995 v Fi, Fa, Ru, Gr, Ru, Sm, Fa; 1996 v Gr, Fi, Se, Sm, Aus, D, US (sub), Co, Ho, E, Sw; (with Monaco), 1997 v A, La, Se, Es, A, Se, Ma; 1998 v Bl, La, F, Fi, Co, US, Br, N, Mor; (with Everton), 1999 v Li (53)

Collins, R. Y. (Celtic), 1951 v W, Ni, A; 1955 v Y, A, H; 1956 v Ni, W; 1957 v E, W, Sp (2), Sw, WG; 1958 v Ni, W, Sw, H, Pol, Y, F, Par; (with Everton), 1959 v E, W, Ni, WG, Ho, P; (with Leeds U), 1965 v E, Pol, Sp (31)

Collins, T. (Hearts), 1909 v W (1)

Colman, D. (Aberdeen), 1911 v E, W, Ni; 1913 v Ni (4)

Colquhoun, E. P. (Sheffield U), 1972 v P, Ho, Pe, Y, Cz, Br; 1973 v D (2), E (9)

Colquhoun, J. (Hearts), 1988 v S.Ar (sub), Ma (sub) (2)

Combe, J. R. (Hibernian), 1948 v E, Bel, Sw (3)

Conn, A. (Hearts), 1956 v A (1)

Conn, A. (Tottenham H), 1975 v Ni (sub), E (2)

Connachan, E. D. (Dunfermline Ath), 1962 v Cz, U (2)

Connelly, G. (Celtic), 1974 v Cz, WG (2)

Connolly, J. (Everton), 1973 v Sw (1)

Connor, J. (Airdrieonians), 1886 v Ni (1)

Connor, J. (Sunderland), 1930 v F; 1932 v Ni; 1934 v E; 1935 v Ni (4)

Connor, R. (Dundee), 1986 v Ho; (with Aberdeen), 1988 v S.Ar (sub); 1989 v E; 1991 v R (4)

Cook, W. L. (Bolton W), 1934 v E; 1935 v W, Ni (3)

Cooke, C. (Dundee), 1966 v W, I; (with Chelsea), P, Br; 1968 v E, Ho; 1969 v W, Ni, A, WG (sub), Cy (2); 1970 v A; 1971 v Bel; 1975 v Sp, P (16)

Cooper, D. (Rangers), 1980 v Pe, A (sub); 1984 v W, E; 1985 v Y, Ic, Sp (2), W; 1986 v W (sub), EG, Aus (2), Ho, WG (sub), U (sub); 1987 v Bul, L, Ei, Br; (with Motherwell), 1990 v N, Eg (22)

Cormack, P. B. (Hibernian), 1966 v Br; 1969 v D (sub); 1970 v Ei, WG; (with Nottingham F), 1971 v D (sub), W, P, E; 1972 v Ho (sub) (9)

Cowan, J. (Aston Villa), 1896 v E; 1897 v E; 1898 v E (3)

Cowan, J. (Morton), 1948 v Bel, Sw; F; 1949 v E, W, F; 1950 v E, W, Ni, Sw, P, F; 1951 v E, W, Ni, A (2), D, F, Bel; 1952 v Ni, W, USA, D, Se (25)

Cowan, W. D. (Newcastle U), 1924 v E (1)

Cowie, D. (Dundee), 1953 v E, Se; 1954 v Ni, W, Fi, N, A, U; 1955 v W, Ni, A, H; 1956 v W, A; 1957 v Ni, W; 1958 v H, Pol, Y, Par (20)

Cox, C. J. (Hearts), 1948 v F (1)

Cox, S. (Rangers), 1949 v E, F; 1950 v E, F, W, Ni, Sw, P; 1951 v E, D, F, Bel, A; 1952 v Ni, W, USA, D, Se; 1953 v W, Ni, E; 1954 v W, Ni, E (24)

Craig, A. (Motherwell), 1929 v N, Ho; 1932 v E (3)

Craig, J. (Celtic), 1977 v Se (sub) (1)

Craig, J. P. (Celtic), 1968 v W (1)

Craig, T. (Rangers), 1927 v Ni; 1928 v Ni; 1929 v N, G, Ho; 1930 v Ni, E, W (8)

Craig, T. B. (Newcastle U), 1976 v Sw (1)

Crapnell, J. (Airdrieonians), 1929 v E, N, G; 1930 v F; 1931 v Ni, Sw; 1932 v E, F; 1933 v Ni (9)

Crawford, D. (St Mirren), 1894 v W, Ni; 1900 v W (3)

Crawford, J. (Queen's Park), 1932 v F, Ni; 1933 v E, W, Ni (5)

Crawford, S. (Raith R), 1995 v Ec (sub) (1)

Crerand, P. T. (Celtic), 1961 v Ei (2), Cz; 1962 v Ni, W, E, Cz (2), U; 1963 v W, Ni; (with Manchester U), 1964 v Ni; 1965 v E, Pol, Fi; 1966 v Pol (16)

Cringan, W. (Celtic), 1920 v W; 1922 v E, Ni; 1923 v W, E (5)

Crosbie, J. A. (Ayr U), 1920 v W; (with Birmingham), 1922 v E (2)

Croal, J. A. (Falkirk), 1913 v Ni; 1914 v E, W (3)

Cropley, A. J. (Hibernian), 1972 v P, Bel (2)

Cross, J. H. (Third Lanark), 1903 v Ni (1)

Cruickshank, J. (Hearts), 1964 v WG; 1970 v W, E; 1971 v D, Bel; 1976 v R (6)

Crum, J. (Celtic), 1936 v E; 1939 v Ni (2)

Cullen, M. J. (Luton T), 1956 v A (1)

Cumming, D. S. (Middlesbrough), 1938 v E (1)

Cumming, J. (Hearts), 1955 v E, H, P, Y; 1960 v E, Pol, A, H, T (9)

Cummings, G. (Partick T), 1935 v E; 1936 v W, Ni; (with Aston Villa), E; 1937 v G; 1938 v W, Ni, Cz; 1939 v E (9)

Cunningham, A. N. (Rangers), 1920 v Ni; 1921 v W, E; 1922 v Ni; 1923 v E, W; 1924 v E, Ni; 1926 v E, Ni; 1927 v E, W (12)

Cunningham, W. C. (Preston NE), 1954 v N (2), U, Fi, A; 1955 v W, E, H (8)

Curran, H. P. (Wolverhampton W), 1970 v A; 1971 v Ni, E, D, USSR (sub) (5)

Dailly, C. (Derby Co), 1997 v W, Ma, Bl; 1998 v Bl, La, F, D, Fi, Co, US, Br, N, Mor; (with Blackburn R), 1999 v Li (14)

Dalglish, K. (Celtic), 1972 v Bel (sub), Ho; 1973 v D (1+1 sub), E (2), W, Ni, Sw, Br; 1974 v Cz (2), WG (2), Ni, W, E, Bel, N (sub), Z, Br, Y; 1975 v EG, Sp (sub+1), Se, P, W, Ni, E, R; 1976 v D (2), R, Sw, Ni, E; 1977 v Fi, Cz, W (2), Se, Ni, E, Ch, Arg, Br; (with Liverpool), 1978 v EG, Cz, W, Bul, Ni (sub), W, E, Pe, Ir, Ho; 1979 v A, N, P, W, Ni, E, Arg, N; 1980 v Pe, A, Bel (2), P, Ni, W, E, Pol, H; 1981 v Se, P, Is; 1982 v Se, Ni, P (sub), Sp, Ho, Ni, W, E, Nz, Br (sub); 1983 v Bel, Sw; 1984 v U, Bel, EG; 1985 v Y, Ic, Sp, W; 1986 v EG, Aus, R; 1987 v Bul (sub), L (102)

Davidson, C. I. (Blackburn R), 1999 v Li (sub), Es, Fa, CzR, G, Fa, CzR (7)

Davidson, D. (Queen's Park), 1878 v W; 1879 v W; 1880 v W; 1881 v E, W (5)

Davidson, J. A. (Partick T), 1954 v N (2), A, U; 1955 v W, Ni, E, H (8)

Davidson, S. (Middlesbrough), 1921 v E (1)

Dawson, A. (Rangers), 1980 v Pol (sub), H; 1983 v Ni, Ca (2) (5)

Dawson, J. (Rangers), 1935 v Ni; 1936 v E; 1937 v G, E, W, Ni, A, Cz; 1938 v W, Ho, Ni; 1939 v E, Ni, H (14)

Deans, J. (Celtic), 1975 v EG, Sp (2)

Delaney, J. (Celtic), 1936 v W, Ni; 1937 v G, E, A, Cz; 1938 v Ni; 1939 v W, Ni; (with Manchester U), 1947 v E; 1948 v E, W, Ni (13)

Divine, A. (Falkirk), 1910 v W (1)

Dewar, G. (Dumbarton), 1888 v Ni; 1889 v E (2)

Dewar, N. (Third Lanark), 1932 v E, F; 1933 v W (3)

Dick, J. (West Ham U), 1959 v E (1)

Dickie, M. (Rangers), 1897 v Ni; 1899 v Ni; 1900 v W (3)

Dickson, W. (Dumbarton), 1888 v Ni (1)

Dickson, W. (Kilmarnock), 1970 v Ni, W, E; 1971 v D, USSR (5)

Divers, J. (Celtic), 1895 v W (1)

Divers, J. (Celtic), 1939 v Ni (1)

Docherty, T. H, (Preston NE), 1952 v W; 1953 v E, Se; 1954 v N (2), A, U; 1955 v W, E, H (3); 1957 v E, Y, Sp (2), Sw, WG; 1958 v W, Ni, E, Sw; (with Arsenal), 1959 v W, E, Ni (25)

Dodds, D. (Dundee U), 1984 v U (sub), Ni (2)

Dodds, J. (Celtic), 1914 v E, W, Ni (3)

Dodds, W. (Aberdeen), 1997 v La (sub), W, Bl (sub); 1998 v Bl (sub); (with Dundee U), 1999 v Es (sub), Fa, G, Fa, CzR (9)

Doig, J. E. (Arbroath), 1887 v Ni; 1889 v Ni; (with Sunderland), 1896 v E; 1899 v E; 1903 v E (5)

Donachie, W. (Manchester C), 1972 v Pe, Ni, E, Y, Cz, Br; 1973 v D, E, W, Ni; 1974 v Ni; 1976 v R, Ni, W, E; 1977 v Fi, Cz, W (2), Se, Ni, E, Ch, Arg, Br; 1978 v EG, W, Bul, W, E, Ir, Ho; 1979 v A, N, P (sub) (35)

Donaldson, A. (Bolton W), 1914 v E, Ni, W; 1920 v E, Ni; 1922 v Ni (6)

Donnachie, J. (Oldham Ath), 1913 v E; 1914 v E, Ni (3)

Donnelly, S. (Celtic), 1997 v W (sub), Ma (sub); 1998 v La (sub), F (sub), D (sub), Fi (sub), Co (sub), US (sub); 1999 v Es (sub), Fa (10)

Dougall, C. (Birmingham C), 1947 v W (1)

Dougall, J. (Preston NE), 1939 v E (1)

Dougan, R. (Hearts), 1950 v Sw (1)

Douglas, A. (Chelsea), 1911 v Ni (1)

Douglas, J. (Renfrew), 1880 v W (1)

Dowds, P. (Celtic), 1892 v Ni (1)

Downie, R. (Third Lanark), 1892 v W (1)

Doyle, D. (Celtic), 1892 v E; 1893 v W; 1894 v E; 1895 v E, Ni; 1897 v E; 1898 v E, Ni (8)

Doyle, J. (Ayr U), 1976 v R (1)

Drummond, J. (Falkirk), 1892 v Ni; (with Rangers), 1894 v Ni; 1895 v Ni, E; 1896 v E, Ni; 1897 v Ni; 1898 v E; 1900 v E; 1901 v E; 1902 v E, W, Ni; 1903 v Ni (14)

Dunbar, M. (Cartvale), 1886 v Ni (1)

Duncan, A. (Hibernian), 1975 v P (sub), W, Ni, E, R; 1976 v D (sub) (6)

Duncan, D. (Derby Co), 1933 v E, W; 1934 v A, W; 1935 v E, W; 1936 v W, Ni; 1937 v G, E, W, Ni, W (14)

Duncan, D. M. (East Fife), 1948 v Bel, Sw, F (3)

Duncan, J. (Alexandra Ath), 1878 v W; 1882 v W (2)

Duncan, J. (Leicester C), 1926 v W (1)

Duncanson, J. (Rangers), 1947 v Ni (1)

Dunlop, J. (St Mirren), 1890 v W (1)

Dunlop, W. (Liverpool), 1906 v E (1)

Dunn, J. (Hibernian), 1925 v W, Ni; 1927 v Ni; 1928 v Ni, E; (with Everton), 1929 v W (6)

Durie, G. S. (Chelsea), 1988 v Bul (sub); 1989 v I (sub), Cy; 1990 v Y, EG, Eg, Se; 1991 v Sw (sub), Bul (2), USSR (sub), Sm; (with Tottenham H), 1992 v Sw, R, Sm, Ni (sub), Fi, Ca, N (sub), Ho, G; 1993 v Sw, I; 1994 v Sw, I; (with Rangers), Ho (2); 1996 v US, Ho, E, Sw; 1997 v A (sub), Se (sub), Ma (sub), Bl; 1998 v Bl, La, F, Fi (sub), Co, Br, N, Mor (43)

Durrant, I. (Rangers), 1988 v H, Bel, Ma, Sp; 1989 v N (sub); 1993 v Sw (sub), P (sub), I, P (sub); 1994 v I (sub), Ma; (with Kilmarnock), 1999 v Es, Fa (sub), G, Fa, CzR (16)

Dykes, J. (Hearts), 1938 v Ho; 1939 v Ni (2)

Easson, J. F. (Portsmouth), 1931 v A, Sw; 1934 v W (3)

Ellis, J. (Mossend Swifts), 1892 v Ni (1)

Elliott, M. S. (Leicester C), 1998 v F (sub), D, Fi; 1999 v Li, Fa, CzR, Fa (7)

Evans, A. (Aston Villa), 1982 v Ho, Ni, E, Nz (4)

Evans, R. (Celtic), 1949 v E, W, Ni, F; 1950 v W, Ni, Sw, P; 1951 v A; 1952 v Ni; 1953 v Se; 1954 v Ni, W, E, N, Fi; 1955 v Ni, P, Y, A, H; 1956 v E, Ni, W, A; 1957 v WG, Sp; 1958 v Ni, W, E, Sw, H, Pol, Y, Par, F; 1959 v E, WG, Ho, P; 1960 v E, Ni, W, Pol; (with Chelsea), 1960 v A, H, T (48)

Ewart, J. (Bradford C), 1921 v E (1)

Ewing, T. (Partick T), 1958 v W, E (2)

Farm, G. N. (Blackpool), 1953 v W, Ni, E, Se; 1954 v Ni, W, E; 1959 v WG, Ho, P (10)

Ferguson, B. (Rangers), 1999 v Li (sub)(1)

Ferguson, D. (Rangers), 1988 v Ma, Co (sub) (2)

Ferguson, D. (Dundee U), 1992 v US (sub), Ca, Ho (sub); 1993 v G; (with Everton), 1995 v Gr; 1997 v A, Es (7)

Ferguson, I. (Rangers), 1989 v I, Cy (sub), F; 1993 v Ma (sub), Es; 1994 v Ma, A (sub), Ho (sub); 1997 v Es (sub) (9)

Ferguson, J. (Vale of Leven), 1874 v E; 1876 v E, W; 1877 v E, W; 1878 v W (6)
Ferguson, R. (Kilmarnock), 1966 v W, E, Ho, P, Br; 1967 v W, Ni (7)
Fernie, W. (Celtic), 1954 v Fi, A, U; 1955 v W, Ni; 1957 v E, Ni, W, Y; 1958 v W, Sw, Par (12)
Findlay, R. (Kilmarnock), 1898 v W (1)
Fitchie, T. T. (Woolwich Arsenal), 1905 v W; 1906 v W, Ni; (with Queen's Park), 1907 v W (4)
Flavell, R. (Airdrieonians), 1947 v Bel, L (2)
Fleck, R. (Norwich C), 1990 v Arg, Se, Br (sub); 1991 v USSR (4)
Fleming, C. (East Fife), 1954 v Ni (1)
Fleming, J. W. (Rangers), 1929 v G, Ho; 1930 v E (3)
Fleming, R. (Morton), 1886 v Ni (1)
Forbes, A. R. (Sheffield U), 1947 v Bel, L, E; 1948 v W, Ni; (with Arsenal), 1950 v E, P, F; 1951 v W, Ni, A; 1952 v W, D, Se (14)
Forbes, J. (Vale of Leven), 1884 v E, W, Ni; 1887 v W, E (5)
Ford, D. (Hearts), 1974 v Cz (sub), WG (sub), W (3)
Forrest, J. (Rangers), 1966 v W, I; (with Aberdeen), 1971 v Bel (sub), D, USSR (5)
Forrest, J. (Motherwell), 1958 v E (1)
Forsyth, A. (Partick T), 1972 v Y, Cz, Br; 1973 v D; (with Manchester U), E; 1975 v Sp, Ni (sub), R, EG; 1976 v D (10)
Forsyth, C. (Kilmarnock), 1964 v E; 1965 v W, Ni, Fi (4)
Forsyth, T. (Motherwell), 1971 v D; (with Rangers), 1974 v Cz; 1976 v Sw, Ni, W, E; 1977 v Fi, Se, W, Ni, E, Ch, Arg, Br; 1978 v Cz, W, Ni, W (sub), E, Pe, Ir (sub), Ho (22)
Foyers, R. (St Bernards), 1893 v W; 1894 v W (2)
Fraser, D. M. (WBA), 1968 v Ho; 1969 v Cy (2)
Fraser, J. (Moffat), 1891 v Ni (1)
Fraser, M. J. E. (Queen's Park), 1880 v W; 1882 v W, E; 1883 v W, E (5)
Fraser, J. (Dundee), 1907 v Ni (1)
Fraser, W. (Sunderland), 1955 v W, Ni (2)
Fulton, W. (Abercorn), 1884 v Ni (1)
Fyfe, J. H. (Third Lanark), 1895 v W (1)

Gabriel, J. (Everton), 1961 v W; 1964 v N (sub) (2)
Gallacher, H. K. (Airdrieonians), 1924 v Ni; 1925 v E, W, Ni; 1926 v W; (with Newcastle U), 1926 v E, Ni; 1927 v E, W, Ni; 1928 v E, W; 1929 v E, W, Ni; 1930 v W, Ni, F; (with Chelsea), 1934 v E; (with Derby Co), 1935 v E (20)
Gallacher, K. W. (Dundee U), 1988 v Co, E (sub); 1989 v N, I; (with Coventry C), 1991 v Sm; 1992 v R (sub), Sm (sub), Ni (sub), N (sub), Ho (sub), G (sub), C; 1993 v Sw (sub), P; (with Blackburn R), P, Es (2); 1994 v I, Ma; 1996 v Aus (sub), D, Co (sub), Ho; 1997 v Se (sub), Es (2), A, Se, W, Ma, Bl; 1998 v Bl, La, F, Fi (sub), US, Br, N, Mor; 1999 v Li, Es, Fa, CzR (43)
Gallacher, P. (Sunderland), 1935 v Ni (1)
Galloway, M. (Celtic), 1992 v R (1)
Galt, J. H. (Rangers), 1908 v W, Ni (2)
Gardiner, I. (Motherwell), 1958 v W (1)
Gardner, D. R. (Third Lanark), 1897 v W (1)
Gardner, R. (Queen's Park), 1872 v E; 1873 v E; (with Clydesdale), 1874 v E; 1875 v E; 1878 v E (5)
Gemmell, R. (St Mirren), 1955 v P, Y (2)
Gemmell, T. (Celtic), 1966 v E; 1967 v W, Ni, E, USSR; 1968 v Ni, E; 1969 v W, Ni, E, D, A, WG, Cy; 1970 v E, Ei, WG; 1971 v Bel (18)
Gemmill, A. (Derby Co), 1971 v Bel; 1972 v P, Ho, Pe, Ni, W, E; 1976 v D, R, Ni, W, E; 1977 v Fi, Cz, W (2), Ni (sub), E (sub), Ch (sub), Arg, Br; 1978 v EG (sub); (with Nottingham F), Bul, Ni, W, E (sub), Pe (sub), Ir, Ho; 1979 v A, N, P, N; (with Birmingham C), 1980 v A, P, Ni, W, E, H; 1981 v Se, P, Is, Ni (43)
Gemmill, S. (Nottingham F), 1995 v J, Ec, Fa (sub); 1996 v Sm, D (sub), US; 1997 v Es, Se (sub), W, Ma (sub), Bl (sub); 1998 v D, Fi; (with Everton), 1999 v G, Fa (sub) (15)
Gibb, W. (Clydesdale), 1873 v E (1)
Gibson, D. W. (Leicester C), 1963 v A, N, Ei, Sp; 1964 v Ni; 1965 v W, Fi (7)
Gibson, J. D. (Partick T), 1926 v E; 1927 v E, W, Ni; (with Aston Villa), 1928 v E, W; 1930 v W, Ni (8)
Gibson, N. (Rangers), 1895 v E, Ni; 1896 v E, Ni; 1897 v E, Ni; 1898 v E; 1899 v E, W, Ni; 1900 v E, Ni; 1901 v W; (with Partick T), 1905 v Ni (14)
Gilchrist, J. E. (Celtic), 1922 v E (1)
Gilhooley, M. (Hull C), 1922 v W (1)
Gillespie, G. (Rangers), 1880 v W; 1881 v E, W; 1882 v E; (with Queen's Park), 1886 v W; 1890 v W; 1891 v Ni (7)
Gillespie, G. T. (Liverpool), 1988 v Bel, Bul, Sp; 1989 v N, F, Ch; 1990 v Y, EG, Eg, Pol, Ma, Br (sub); 1991 v Bul (13)

Gillespie, Jas (Third Lanark), 1898 v W (1)
Gillespie, John (Queen's Park), 1896 v W (1)
Gillespie, R. (Queen's Park), 1927 v W; 1931 v W; 1932 v F; 1933 v E (4)
Gillick, T. (Everton), 1937 v A, Cz; 1939 v W, Ni, H (5)
Gilmour, J. (Dundee), 1931 v W (1)
Gilzean, A. J. (Dundee), 1964 v W, E, N, WG; 1965 v Ni, (with Tottenham H), Sp; 1966 v Ni, W, Pol, I; 1968 v W; 1969 v W, E, WG, Cy (2), A (sub); 1970 v Ni, E (sub), WG, A; 1971 v P (22)
Glass, S. (Newcastle U), 1999 v Fa (sub) (1)
Glavin, R. (Celtic), 1977 v Se (1)
Glen, A. (Aberdeen), 1956 v E, Ni (2)
Glen, R. (Renton), 1895 v W; 1896 v W; (with Hibernian), 1900 v Ni (3)
Goram, A. L. (Oldham Ath), 1986 v EG (sub), R, Ho; 1987 v Br; (with Hibernian), 1989 v Y, I; 1990 v EG, Pol, Ma; 1991 v R, Sw, Bul (2), USSR, Sm; (with Rangers), 1992 v Sw, R, Sm, Fi, N, Ho, G, C; 1993 v Sw, P, I, Ma, P; 1994 v Ho; 1995 v Fi, Fa, Ru, Gr; 1996 v Se (sub), D (sub), Co, Ho, E, Sw; 1997 v A, La, Es; 1998 v D (sub) (43)
Gordon, J. E. (Rangers), 1912 v E, Ni; 1913 v E, Ni, W; 1914 v E, Ni; 1920 v W, E, Ni (10)
Gossland, J. (Rangers), 1884 v Ni (1)
Goudie, J. (Abercorn), 1884 v Ni (1)
Gough, C. R. (Dundee U), 1983 v Sw, Ni, W, E, Ca (3); 1984 v U, Bel, EG, Ni, W, E, F; 1985 v Sp, E, Ic; 1986 v W, EG, Aus, Is, R, E, D, WG, U; (with Tottenham H), 1987 v Bul, L, Ei (2), Bel, E, Br; 1988 v H; (with Rangers), S.Ar, Sp, Co, E; 1989 v Y, I, Cy, F, Cy; 1990 v F, Arg, EG, Eg, Pol, Ma, Cr; 1991 v USSR, Bul; 1992 v Sm, Ni, Ca, N, Ho, G, C; 1993 v Sw, P (61)
Gourlay, J. (Cambuslang), 1886 v Ni; 1888 v W (2)
Govan, J. (Hibernian), 1948 v E, W, Bel, Sw, F; 1949 v Ni (6)
Gow, D. R. (Rangers), 1888 v E (1)
Gow, J. J. (Queen's Park), 1885 v E (1)
Gow, J. R. (Rangers), 1888 v Ni (1)
Graham, A. (Leeds U), 1978 v EG (sub); 1979 v A (sub), N, W, Ni, E, Arg, N; 1980 v A; 1981 v W (10)
Graham, G. (Arsenal), 1972 v P, Ho, Ni, Y, Cz, Br; 1973 v D (2); (with Manchester U), E, W, Ni, Br (sub) (12)
Graham, J. (Annbank), 1884 v Ni (1)
Graham, J. A. (Arsenal), 1921 v Ni (1)
Grant, J. (Hibernian), 1959 v W, Ni (2)
Grant, P. (Celtic), 1989 v E (sub), Ch (2)
Gray, A. (Hibernian), 1903 v Ni (1)
Gray, A. M. (Aston Villa), 1976 v R, Sw; 1977 v Fi, Cz; 1979 v A, N; (with Wolverhampton W), 1980 v P, E (sub); 1981 v Se, P, Is (sub), Ni; 1982 v US (sub), Ni (sub); 1983 v Ni, W, E, Ca (1+1 sub); (with Everton), 1985 v Ic (20)
Gray, D. (Rangers), 1929 v W, Ni, G, Ho; 1930 v W, E, Ni; 1931 v W; 1933 v W, Ni (10)
Gray, E. (Leeds U), 1969 v E, Cy; 1970 v WG, A; 1971 v W, Ni; 1972 v Bel, Ho; 1976 v W, E; 1977 v Fi, W (12)
Gray, F. T. (Leeds U), 1976 v Sw; 1979 v N, P, W, Ni, E, Arg (sub); (with Nottingham F), 1980 v Bel (sub); 1981 v Se, P, Is, Ni, Is, W; (with Leeds U), Ni, E; 1982 v Se, Ni, P, Sp, Ho, W, Nz, Br, USSR; 1983 v EG, Sw, Bel, Sw, W, E, Ca (32)
Gray, W. (Pollokshields Ath), 1886 v E (1)
Green, A. (Blackpool), 1971 v Bel (sub), P (sub), Ni, E; (with Newcastle U), 1972 v W, E (sub) (6)
Greig, J. (Rangers), 1964 v E, WG; 1965 v W, Ni, E, Fi (2), Sp, Pol; 1966 v W, E, Pol, I (2), P, Ho, Br; 1967 v W, Ni, E; 1968 v Ni, W, E, Ho; 1969 v W, Ni, E, D, A, WG, Cy (2); 1970 v W, E, Ei, WG, A; 1971 v D, Bel, W (sub), Ni, E; 1976 v D (44)
Groves, W. (Hibernian), 1888 v W; (with Celtic), 1889 v Ni; 1890 v E (3)
Guilliland, W. (Queen's Park), 1891 v W; 1892 v Ni; 1894 v E; 1895 v E (4)
Gunn, B. (Norwich C), 1990 v Eg; 1993 v Es (2); 1994 v Sw, I, Ho (sub) (6)

Haddock, H. (Clyde), 1955 v E, H (2), P, Y; 1958 v E (6)
Haddow, D. (Rangers), 1894 v E (1)
Haffey, F. (Celtic), 1960 v E; 1961 v E (2)
Hamilton, A. (Queen's Park), 1885 v E, W; 1886 v E; 1888 v E (4)
Hamilton, A. W. (Dundee), 1962 v Cz, U, W, E; 1963 v W, Ni, E, A, N, Ei; 1964 v Ni, W, E, N, WG; 1965 v Ni, W, E, Fi (2), Pol, Sp; 1966 v Pol, Ni (24)
Hamilton, G. (Aberdeen), 1947 v Ni; 1951 v Bel, A; 1954 v N (2) (5)
Hamilton, G. (Port Glasgow Ath), 1906 v Ni (1)
Hamilton, J. (Queen's Park), 1892 v Ni; 1893 v E, Ni (3)
Hamilton, J. (St Mirren), 1924 v Ni (1)

Hamilton, R. C. (Rangers), 1899 v E, W, Ni; 1900 v W; 1901 v E, Ni; 1902 v W, Ni; 1903 v E; 1904 v Ni; (with Dundee), 1911 v W (11)
Hamilton, T. (Hurlford), 1891 v Ni (1)
Hamilton, T. (Rangers), 1932 v E (1)
Hamilton, W. M. (Hibernian), 1965 v Fi (1)
Hannah, A. B. (Renton), 1888 v W (1)
Hannah, J. (Third Lanark), 1889 v W (1)
Hansen, A. D. (Liverpool), 1979 v W, Arg; 1980 v Bel, P; 1981 v Se, P, Is; 1982 v Se, Ni, P, Sp, Ni (sub), W, E, Nz, Br, USSR; 1983 v EG, Sw, Bel, Sw; 1985 v W (sub); 1986 v R (sub); 1987 v Ei (2), L (26)
Hansen, J. (Partick T), 1972 v Bel (sub), Y (sub) (2)
Harkness, J. D. (Queen's Park), 1927 v E, Ni; 1928 v E; (with Hearts), 1929 v W, E, Ni; 1930 v E, W; 1932 v W, F; 1934 v Ni (11)
Harper, J. M. (Aberdeen), 1973 v D (1+1 sub); (with Hibernian), 1976 v D; (with Aberdeen), 1978 v Ir (sub) (4)
Harper, W. (Hibernian), 1923 v E, Ni, W; 1924 v E, Ni, W; 1925 v E, Ni, W; (with Arsenal), 1926 v E, Ni (11)
Harris, J. (Partick T), 1921 v W, Ni (2)
Harris, N. (Newcastle U), 1924 v E (1)
Harrower, W. (Queen's Park), 1882 v E; 1884 v Ni; 1886 v W (3)
Hartford, R. A. (WBA), 1972 v Pe, W (sub), E, Y, Cz, Br; (with Manchester C), 1976 v D, R, Ni (sub); 1977 v Cz (sub), W (sub), Se, W, Ni, E, Ch, Arg, Br; 1978 v EG, Cz, W, Bul, W, E, Pe, Ir, Ho; 1979 v A, N, P, W, Ni, E, Arg, N; (with Everton), 1980 v Pe, Bel; 1981 v Ni (sub), Is, W, Ni, E; 1982 v Se; (with Manchester C), Ni, P, Sp, Ni, W, E, Br (50)
Harvey, D. (Leeds U), 1973 v D; 1974 v Cz, WG, Ni, W, E, Bel, Z, Br, Y; 1975 v EG, Sp (2); 1976 v D (2); 1977 v Fi (sub) (16)
Hastings, A. C. (Sunderland), 1936 v Ni; 1938 v Ni (2)
Haughney, M. (Celtic), 1954 v E (1)
Hay, D. (Celtic), 1970 v Ni, W, E; 1971 v D, Bel, W, P, Ni; 1972 v P, Bel, Ho; 1973 v W, Ni, E, Sw, Br; 1974 v Cz (2), WG, Ni, W, E, Bel, N, Z, Br, Y (27)
Hay, J. (Celtic), 1905 v Ni; 1909 v Ni; 1910 v W, Ni, E; 1911 v Ni, E; (with Newcastle U), 1912 v E, W; 1914 v E, Ni (11)
Hegarty, P. (Dundee U), 1979 v W, Ni, E, Arg, N (sub); 1980 v W, E; 1983 v Ni (8)
Heggie, C. (Rangers), 1886 v Ni (1)
Henderson, G. H. (Rangers), 1904 v Ni (1)
Henderson, J. G. (Portsmouth), 1953 v Se; 1954 v Ni, E, N; 1956 v W; (with Arsenal), 1959 v W, Ni (7)
Henderson, W. (Rangers), 1963 v W, Ni, E, A, N, Ei, Sp; 1964 v W, Ni, E, N, WG; 1965 v Fi, Pol, E, Sp; 1966 v Ni, W, Pol, I, Ho; 1967 v W, Ni; 1968 v Ho; 1969 v Ni, E, Cy; 1970 v Ei; 1971 v P (29)
Hendry, E. C. J. (Blackburn R), 1993 v Es (2); 1994 v Ma, Ho, A, Ho; 1995 v Fi, Fa, Gr, Ru, Sm; 1996 v Fi, Se, Sm, Aus, D, US, Co, Ho, E, Sw; 1997 v A, Se, Es (2), A, Se; 1998 v La, D, Fi, Co, US, Br, N, Mor; (with Rangers), 1999 v Li, Es, Fa, G (39)
Hepburn, J. (Alloa Ath), 1891 v W (1)
Hepburn, R. (Ayr U), 1932 v Ni (1)
Herd, A. C. (Hearts), 1935 v Ni (1)
Herd, D. G. (Arsenal), 1959 v E, W, Ni; 1961 v Ei, Cz (5)
Herd, G. (Clyde), 1958 v E; 1960 v H, T; 1961 v W, Ni (5)
Herriot, J. (Birmingham C), 1969 v Ni, E, D, Cy (2), W (sub); 1970 v Ei (sub), WG (8)
Hewie, J. D. (Charlton Ath), 1956 v E, A; 1957 v E, Ni, W, Y, Sp (2), Sw, WG; 1958 v H, Pol, Y, F; 1959 v Ho, P; 1960 v Ni, W, Pol (19)
Higgins, A. (Kilmarnock), 1885 v Ni (1)
Higgins, A. (Newcastle U), 1910 v E, Ni; 1911 v E, Ni (4)
Highet, T. C. (Queen's Park), 1875 v E; 1876 v E, W; 1878 v E (4)
Hill, D. (Rangers), 1881 v E, W; 1882 v W (3)
Hill, D. A. (Third Lanark), 1906 v Ni (1)
Hill, F. R. (Aberdeen), 1930 v F; 1931 v W, Ni (3)
Hill, J. (Hearts), 1891 v E; 1892 v W (2)
Hogg, G (Hearts), 1896 v E, Ni (2)
Hogg, J. (Ayr U), 1922 v W (1)
Hogg, R. M. (Celtic), 1937 v Cz (1)
Holm, A. H. (Queen's Park), 1882 v W; 1883 v E, W (3)
Holt, D. D. (Hearts), 1963 v A, N, Ei, Sp; 1964 v WG (sub) (5)
Holton, J. A. (Manchester U), 1973 v W, Ni, E, Sw, Br; 1974 v Cz, WG, Ni, W, E, N, Z, Br, Y; 1975 v EG (15)
Hope, R. (WBA), 1968 v Ho; 1969 v D (2)
Hopkin, D. (Crystal Palace), 1997 v Ma, Bl; (with Leeds U), 1998 v Bl (sub), F (sub); 1999 v CzR (5)
Houliston, W. (Queen of the South), 1949 v E, Ni, F (3)
Houston, S. M. (Manchester U), 1976 v D (1)
Howden, W. (Partick T), 1905 v Ni (1)

Howe, R. (Hamilton A), 1929 v N, Ho (2)
Howie, J. (Newcastle U), 1905 v E; 1906 v E; 1908 v E (3)
Howie, H. (Hibernian), 1949 v W (1)
Howieson, J. (St Mirren), 1927 v Ni (1)
Hughes, J. (Celtic), 1965 v Pol, Sp; 1966 v Ni, I (2); 1968 v E; 1969 v A; 1970 v Ei (8)
Hughes, W. (Sunderland), 1975 v Se (sub) (1)
Humphries, W. (Motherwell), 1952 v Se (1)
Hunter, A. (Kilmarnock), 1972 v Pe, Y; (with Celtic), 1973 v E; 1974 v Cz (4)
Hunter, J. (Dundee), 1909 v W (1)
Hunter, J. (Third Lanark), 1874 v E; (with Eastern), 1875 v E; (with Third Lanark), 1876 v E; 1877 v W (4)
Hunter, R. (St Mirren), 1890 v Ni (1)
Hunter, W. (Motherwell), 1960 v H, T; 1961 v W (3)
Husband, J. (Partick T), 1947 v W (1)
Hutchison, D. (Everton), 1999 v CzR (sub), G (2)
Hutchison, T. (Coventry C), 1974 v Cz (2), WG (2), Ni, W, Bel (sub), N, Z (sub), Y (sub); 1975 v EG, Sp (2), P, E (sub), R (sub); 1976 v D (17)
Hutton, J. (Aberdeen), 1923 v E, W, Ni; 1924 v Ni; 1926 v W, E, Ni; (with Blackburn R), 1927 v Ni; 1928 v W, Ni (10)
Hutton, J. (St Bernards), 1887 v Ni (1)
Hyslop, T. (Stoke C), 1896 v E; (with Rangers), 1897 v E (2)

Imlach, J. J. S. (Nottingham F), 1958 v H, Pol, Y, F (4)
Imrie, W. N. (St Johnstone), 1929 v N, G (2)
Inglis, J. (Kilmarnock Ath), 1884 v Ni (1)
Inglis, J. (Rangers), 1883 v E, W (2)
Irons, J. H. (Queen's Park), 1900 v W (1)
Irvine, B. (Aberdeen), 1991 v R; 1993 v G, Es (2); 1994 v Sw, I, Ma, A, Ho (9)

Jackson, A. (Cambuslang), 1886 v W; 1888 v Ni (2)
Jackson, A. (Aberdeen), 1925 v E, W, Ni; (with Huddersfield T), 1926 v E, W, Ni; 1927 v W, Ni; 1928 v E, W; 1929 v E, W, Ni; 1930 v E, W, Ni, F (17)
Jackson, C. (Rangers), 1975 v Se, P (sub), W; 1976 v D, R, Ni, W, E (8)
Jackson, D. (Hibernian), 1995 v Ru, Sm, J, Ec, Fa; 1996 v Gr, Fi (sub), Se (sub), Sm (sub), Aus (sub), D (sub), US; 1997 v La, Se, Es, A, Se, W, Ma, Bl; (with Celtic), 1998 v D, Fi, Co, US, Br, N; 1999 v Li, Es (sub) (28)
Jackson, J. (Partick T), 1931 v A, I, Sw; 1933 v E; (with Chelsea), 1934 v E; 1935 v E; 1936 v W, Ni (8)
Jackson, T. A. (St Mirren), 1904 v W, E, Ni; 1905 v W; 1907 v W, Ni (6)
James, A. W. (Preston NE), 1926 v W; 1928 v E; 1929 v E, Ni; (with Arsenal), 1930 v E, W, Ni; 1933 v W (8)
Jardine, A. (Rangers), 1971 v D (sub); 1972 v P, Bel, Ho; 1973 v E, Sw, Br; 1974 v Cz (2), WG (2), Ni, W, E, Bel, N, Z, Br, Y; 1975 v EG, Sp (2), Se, P, W, Ni, E; 1977 v Se (sub), Ch (sub), Br (sub); 1978 v Cz, W, Ni, Ir; 1980 v Pe, A, Bel (2) (38)
Jarvie, A. (Airdrieonians), 1971 v P (sub), Ni (sub), E (sub) (3)
Jenkinson, T. (Hearts), 1887 v Ni (1)
Jess, E. (Aberdeen), 1993 v I (sub), Ma; 1994 v Sw (sub), I, Ho (sub), A, Ho (sub); 1995 v Fi (sub); 1996 v Se (sub), Sm; (with Coventry C), US, Co (sub), E (sub); (with Aberdeen), 1998 v D (sub); 1999 v CzR, G (sub), Fa (sub), CzR (sub) (18)
Johnston, A. (Sunderland), 1999 v Es, Fa, CzR (sub), G, Fa, CzR (6)
Johnston, L. H. (Clyde), 1948 v Bel, Sw (2)
Johnston, M. (Watford), 1984 v W (sub), E (sub), F; 1985 v Y; (with Celtic), Ic, Sp (2), W; 1986 v EG; 1987 v Bul, Ei (2), L; (with Nantes), 1988 v H, Bel, L, S.Ar, Sp, Co, E; 1989 v N, Y, I, Cy, F, Cy, E, Ch (sub); (with Rangers), 1990 v F, N, EG, Pol, Ma, Cr, Se, Br; 1992 v Sw, Sm (sub) (38)
Johnston, R. (Sunderland), 1938 v Cz (1)
Johnston, W. (Rangers), 1966 v W, E, Pol, Ho; 1968 v W, E; 1969 v Ni (sub); 1970 v Ni; 1971 v D; (with WBA), 1977 v Se, W (sub), Ni, E, Ch, Arg, Br; 1978 v EG, Cz, W (2), E, Pe (22)
Johnstone, D. (Rangers), 1973 v W, Ni, E, Sw, Br; 1975 v EG (sub), Se (sub); 1976 v Sw, Ni (sub), E (sub); 1978 v Bul (sub), Ni, W; 1980 v Bel (14)
Johnstone, J. (Abercorn), 1888 v W (1)
Johnstone, J. (Celtic), 1965 v W, Fi; 1966 v E; 1967 v W, USSR; 1968 v W; 1969 v A, WG; 1970 v E, WG; 1971 v D, E; 1972 v P, Bel, Ho, Ni, E (sub); 1974 v W, E, Bel, N; 1975 v EG, Sp (23)
Johnstone, Jas (Kilmarnock), 1894 v W (1)
Johnstone, J. A. (Hearts), 1930 v W; 1933 v W, Ni (3)

Johnstone, R. (Hibernian), 1951 v E, D, F; 1952 v Ni, E; 1953 v E, Se; 1954 v W, E, N, Fi; 1955 v Ni, H; (with Manchester C), 1955 v E; 1956 v E, Ni, W (17)
Johnstone, W. (Third Lanark), 1887 v Ni; 1889 v W; 1890 v E (3)
Jordan, J. (Leeds U), 1973 v E (sub), Sw (sub), Br; 1974 v Cz (sub+1), WG (sub), Ni (sub), W, E, Bel, N, Z, Br, Y; 1975 v EG, Sp (2); 1976 v Ni, W, E; 1977 v Cz, W, Ni, E; 1978 v EG, Cz, W; (with Manchester U), Bul, Ni, E, Pe, Ir, Ho; 1979 v A, P, W (sub), Ni, E, Ni; 1980 v Bel, Ni (sub), W, E, Pol; 1981 v Is, W, E; (with AC Milan), 1982 v Se, Ho, W, E, USSR (52)

Kay, J. L. (Queen's Park), 1880 v E; 1882 v E, W; 1883 v E, W; 1884 v W (6)
Keillor, A. (Montrose), 1891 v W; 1892 v Ni; (with Dundee), 1894 v Ni; 1895 v W; 1896 v W; 1897 v W (6)
Keir, L. (Dumbarton), 1885 v W; 1886 v Ni; 1887 v E, W; 1888 v E (5)
Kelly, H. T. (Blackpool), 1952 v USA (1)
Kelly, J. (Renton), 1888 v E; (with Celtic), 1889 v E; 1890 v E; 1892 v E; 1893 v E, Ni; 1894 v W; 1896 v Ni (8)
Kelly, J. C. (Barnsley), 1949 v W, Ni (2)
Kelso, R. (Renton), 1885 v W, Ni; 1886 v W; 1887 v E, W; 1888 v E, Ni; (with Dundee), 1898 v Ni (8)
Kelso, T. (Dundee), 1914 v W (1)
Kennaway, J. (Celtic), 1934 v W, A (2)
Kennedy, A. (Eastern), 1875 v E; 1876 v E, W; (with Third Lanark), 1878 v E; 1882 v W; 1884 v W (6)
Kennedy, J. (Celtic), 1964 v W, E, WG; 1965 v W, Ni, Fi (6)
Kennedy, J. (Hibernian), 1897 v W (1)
Kennedy, S. (Aberdeen), 1978 v Bul, W, E, Pe, Ho; 1979 v A, P; 1982 v P (sub) (8)
Kennedy, S. (Partick T), 1905 v W (1)
Kennedy, S. (Rangers), 1975 v Se, P, W, Ni, E (5)
Ker, G. (Queen's Park), 1880 v E; 1881 v E, W; 1882 v W, E (5)
Ker, W. (Granville), 1872 v E; (with Queen's Park), 1873 v E (2)
Kerr, A. (Partick T), 1955 v A, H (2)
Kerr, P. (Hibernian), 1924 v Ni (1)
Key, G. (Hearts), 1902 v Ni (1)
Key, W. (Queen's Park), 1907 v Ni (1)
King, A. (Hearts), 1896 v E, W; (with Celtic), 1897 v Ni; 1898 v Ni; 1899 v Ni, W (6)
King, J. (Hamilton A), 1933 v Ni; 1934 v Ni (2)
King, W. S. (Queen's Park), 1929 v W (1)
Kinloch, J. D. (Partick T), 1922 v Ni (1)
Kinnaird, A. F. (Wanderers), 1873 v E (1)
Kinnear, D. (Rangers), 1938 v Cz (1)

Lambert, P. (Motherwell), 1995 v J, Ec (sub); (with Borussia Dortmund), 1997 v La (sub), Se (sub), A, Se, Bl; 1998 v Bl, La; (with Celtic), Fi (sub), Co, US, Br, N, Mor; 1999 v Li, CzR, G, Fa, CzR (20)
Lambie, J. A. (Queen's Park), 1886 v Ni; 1887 v Ni; 1888 v E (3)
Lambie, W. A. (Queen's Park), 1892 v Ni; 1893 v W; 1894 v E; 1895 v E, Ni; 1896 v E, Ni; 1897 v E, Ni (9)
Lamont, D. (Pilgrims), 1885 v Ni (1)
Lang, A. (Dumbarton), 1880 v W (1)
Lang, J. J. (Clydesdale), 1876 v W; (with Third Lanark), 1878 v W (2)
Latta, A. (Dumbarton), 1888 v W; 1889 v E (2)
Law, D. (Huddersfield T), 1959 v W, Ni, Ho, P; 1960 v Ni, W; (with Manchester C), 1960 v E, Pol, A; 1961 v E, Ni; (with Torino), 1962 v Cz (2), E; (with Manchester U), 1963 v W, Ni, E, A, N, Ei, Sp; 1964 v W, E, N, WG; 1965 v W, Ni, E, Fi (2), Pol, Sp; 1966 v Ni, E, Pol; 1967 v W, E, USSR; 1968 v Ni; 1969 v Ni, A, WG; 1972 v Pe, Ni, W, E, Y, Cz, Br; (with Manchester C), 1974 v Cz (2), WG (2), Ni, Z (55)
Law, G. (Rangers), 1910 v E, Ni, W (3)
Law, T. (Chelsea), 1928 v E; 1930 v E (2)
Lawrence, J. (Newcastle U), 1911 v E (1)
Lawrence, T. (Liverpool), 1963 v Ei; 1969 v W, WG (3)
Lawson, D. (St Mirren), 1923 v E (1)
Leckie, R. (Queen's Park), 1872 v E (1)
Leggat, G. (Aberdeen), 1956 v E; 1957 v W; 1958 v Ni, H, Pol, Y, Par; (with Fulham), 1959 v E, W, Ni, WG, Ho; 1960 v E, Ni, W, Pol, A, H (18)
Leighton, J. (Aberdeen), 1983 v EG, Sw, Bel, Sw, W, E, Ca (2); 1984 v U, Bel, Ni, W, E, F; 1985 v Y, Ic, Sp (2), W, E, Ic; 1986 v W, EG, Aus (2), Is, D, WG, U; 1987 v L, Bel, E; 1988 v H, Bel, Bul, L, S.Ar, Ma, Sp; (with Manchester U), Co, E; 1989 v N, Cy, F, Cy, E, Ch; 1990 v Y, F, N, Arg, Ma (sub), Cr, Se, Br; (with Hibernian), 1994 v

Ma, A, Ho; 1995 v Gr (sub), Ru, Sm, J, Ec, Fa; 1996 v Gr, Fi, Se, Sm, Aus, D, US; 1997 v Se, Es, A, Se, W (sub), Ma, Bl; (with Aberdeen), 1998 v Bl, La, D, Fi, US, Br, N, Mor; 1999 v Li, Es (91)
Lennie, W. (Aberdeen), 1908 v W, Ni (2)
Lennox, R. (Celtic), 1967 v Ni, E, USSR; 1968 v W, L; 1969 v D, A, WG, Cy (sub); 1970 v W (sub) (10)
Leslie, L. G. (Airdrieonians), 1961 v W, Ni, Ei (2), Cz (5)
Levein, C. (Hearts), 1990 v Arg, EG, Eg (sub), Pol, Ma (sub), Se; 1992 v R, Sm; 1993 v P, G, P; 1994 v Sw, Ho; 1995 v Fi, Fa, Ru (16)
Liddell, W. (Liverpool), 1947 v W, Ni; 1948 v E, W, Ni; 1950 v E, W, P, F; 1951 v W, Ni, E, A; 1952 v W, Ni, E, USA, D, Se; 1953 v W, Ni, E; 1954 v W; 1955 v P, Y, A, H; 1956 v Ni (28)
Liddle, D. (East Fife), 1931 v A, I, Sw (3)
Lindsay, D. (St Mirren), 1903 v Ni (1)
Lindsay, J. (Dumbarton), 1880 v W; 1881 v W, E; 1884 v W, E; 1885 v W, E; 1886 v E (8)
Lindsay, J. (Renton), 1888 v E; 1893 v E, Ni (3)
Linwood, A. B. (Clyde), 1950 v W (1)
Little, R. J. (Rangers), 1953 v Se (1)
Livingstone, G. T. (Manchester C), 1906 v E; (with Rangers), 1907 v W (2)
Lochhead, A. (Third Lanark), 1889 v W (1)
Logan, J. (Ayr U), 1891 v W (1)
Logan, T. (Falkirk), 1913 v Ni (1)
Logie, J. T. (Arsenal), 1953 v Ni (1)
Loney, W. (Celtic), 1910 v W, Ni (2)
Long, H. (Clyde), 1947 v Ni (1)
Longair, W. (Dundee), 1894 v Ni (1)
Lorimer, P. (Leeds U), 1970 v A (sub); 1971 v W, Ni; 1972 v Ni (sub), W, E; 1973 v D (2), E (2); 1974 v WG (sub), E, Bel, N, Z, Br, Y; 1975 v Sp (sub); 1976 v D (2), R (sub) (21)
Love, A. (Aberdeen), 1931 v A, I, Sw (3)
Low, A. (Falkirk), 1934 v Ni (1)
Low, T. P. (Rangers), 1897 v Ni (1)
Low, W. L. (Newcastle U), 1911 v E, W; 1912 v Ni; 1920 v E, Ni (5)
Lowe, J. (Cambuslang), 1891 v Ni (1)
Lowe, J. (St Bernards), 1887 v Ni (1)
Lundie, J. (Hibernian), 1886 v W (1)
Lyall, J. (Sheffield W), 1905 v E (1)

McAdam, J. (Third Lanark), 1880 v W (1)
McAllister, B. (Wimbledon), 1997 v W, Ma, Bl (sub) (3)
McAllister, G. (Leicester C), 1990 v EG, Pol, Ma (sub); (with Leeds U), 1991 v R, Sw, Bul, USSR (sub), Sm; 1992 v Sw (sub), Sm, Ni, Fi (sub), US, Ca, N, Ho, G, C; 1993 v Sw, P, I, Ma; 1994 v Sw, I, Ma, Ho, A, Ho; 1995 v Fi, Ru, Gr, Ru, Sm; 1996 v Gr, Fi, Se, Sm, Aus, D, US (sub), Co, Ho, E, Sw; (with Coventry C), 1997 v A, La, Es (2), A, Se, W, Ma, Bl; 1998 v Bl, La, F; 1999 v CzR (57)
McArthur, D. (Celtic), 1895 v E, Ni; 1899 v W (3)
McAtee, J. (Celtic), 1913 v W (1)
McAulay, J. (Arthurlie), 1884 v Ni (1)
McAulay, J. D. (Dumbarton), 1882 v W; 1883 v E, W; 1884 v E; 1885 v E, W; 1886 v E; 1887 v E, W (9)
McAuley, R. (Rangers), 1932 v Ni, W (2)
McAvennie, F. (West Ham U), 1986 v Aus (2), D (sub), WG (sub); (with Celtic), 1988 v S.Ar (5)
McBain, E. (St Mirren), 1894 v W (1)
McBain, N. (Manchester U), 1922 v E; (with Everton), 1923 v Ni; 1924 v W (3)
McBride, J. (Celtic), 1967 v W, Ni (2)
McBride, P. (Preston NE), 1904 v E; 1906 v E; 1907 v E, W; 1908 v E; 1909 v W (6)
McCall, J. (Renton), 1886 v W; 1887 v E, W; 1888 v E; 1890 v E (5)
McCall, S. M. (Everton), 1990 v Arg, EG, Eg (sub), Pol, Ma, Cr, Se, Br; 1991 v Sw, USSR, Sm; (with Rangers), 1992 v Sw, R, Sm, US, Ca, N, Ho, G, C; 1993 v Sw, P (2); 1994 v I, Ho, A (sub), Ho; 1995 v Fi (sub), Ru, Gr; 1996 v Gr, D, US (sub), Co, Ho, E, Sw; 1997 v A, La; 1998 v D (sub) (40)
McCalliog, J. (Sheffield W), 1967 v E, USSR; 1968 v Ni; 1969 v D; (with Wolverhampton W), 1971 v P (5)
McCallum, N. (Renton), 1888 v Ni (1)
McCann, N.D. (Hearts), 1999 v Li (sub); (with Rangers), CzR (2)
McCann, R. J. (Motherwell), 1959 v WG; 1960 v E, Ni, W; 1961 v E (5)
McCartney, W. (Hibernian), 1902 v Ni (1)
McClair, B. (Celtic), 1987 v L, Ei, E, Br (sub); (with Manchester U), 1988 v Bul, Ma (sub), Sp (sub); 1989 v N, Y, I (sub), Cy, F (sub); 1990 v N (sub), Arg (sub); 1991 v Bul (2), Sm; 1992 v Sw (sub), R, Ni, US, Ca (sub), N, Ho, G, C; 1993 v Sw, P (sub), Es (2) (30)

McClory, A. (Motherwell), 1927 v W; 1928 v Ni; 1935 v W (3)
McCloy, P. (Ayr U), 1924 v E; 1925 v E (2)
McCloy, P. (Rangers), 1973 v W, Ni, Sw, Br (4)
McCoist, A. (Rangers), 1986 v Ho; 1987 v L (sub), Ei (sub), Bel, E, Br; 1988 v H, Bel, Ma, Sp, Co, E; 1989 v Y (sub), F, Cy, E; 1990 v Y, F, N, EG (sub), Eg, Pol, Ma (sub), Cr (sub), Se (sub), Br; 1991 v R, Sw, Bul (2), USSR; 1992 v Sw, Sm, Ni, Fi (sub), US, Ca, N, Ho, G, C; 1993 v Sw, P, I, Ma, P; 1996 v Gr (sub), Fi (sub), Sm (sub), Aus, D (sub), Co, E (sub), Sw; 1997 v A, Se (sub), Es (sub), A (sub); 1998 v Bl (sub); (with Kilmarnock), 1999 v Li, Es (61)
McColl, A. (Renton), 1888 v Ni (1)
McColl, I. M. (Rangers), 1950 v E, F; 1951 v W, Ni, Bel; 1957 v E, Ni, W, Y, Sp, Sw, WG; 1958 v Ni, E (14)
McColl, R. S. (Queen's Park), 1896 v W, Ni; 1897 v Ni; 1898 v Ni; 1899 v Ni, E, W; 1900 v E, W; 1901 v E, W; (with Newcastle U), 1902 v E; (with Queen's Park), 1908 v Ni (13)
McColl, W. (Renton), 1895 v W (1)
McCombie, A. (Sunderland), 1903 v E, W; (with Newcastle U), 1905 v E, W (4)
McCorkindale, J. (Partick T), 1891 v W (1)
McCormick, R. (Abercorn), 1886 v W (1)
McCrae, D. (St Mirren), 1929 v N, G (2)
McCredie, A. (Rangers), 1893 v W; 1894 v E (2)
McCreadie, E. G. (Chelsea), 1965 v E, Sp, Fi, Pol; 1966 v P, Ni, W, Pol, I; 1967 v E, USSR; 1968 v Ni, W, E, Ho; 1969 v W, Ni, E, D, A, WG, Cy (2) (23)
McCulloch, D. (Hearts), 1935 v W; (with Brentford), 1936 v E; 1937 v W, Ni; 1938 v Cz; (with Derby Co), 1939 v H, W (7)
MacDonald, A. (Rangers), 1976 v Sw (1)
McDonald, J. (Edinburgh University), 1886 v E (1)
McDonald, J. (Sunderland), 1956 v W, Ni (2)
MacDougall, E. J. (Norwich C) 1975 v Se, P, W, Ni, E; 1976 v D, R (sub) (7)
McDougall, J. (Liverpool), 1931 v I, A (2)
McDougall, J. (Airdrieonians), 1926 v Ni (1)
McDougall, J. (Vale of Leven), 1877 v E, W; 1878 v E; 1879 v E, W (5)
McFadyen, W. (Motherwell), 1934 v A, W (2)
Macfarlane, A. (Dundee), 1904 v W; 1906 v W; 1908 v W; 1909 v Ni; 1911 v W (5)
McFarlane, R. (Greenock Morton), 1896 v W (1)
Macfarlane, W. (Hearts), 1947 v L (1)
McGarr, E. (Aberdeen), 1970 v Ei, A (2)
McGarvey, F. P. (Liverpool), 1979 v Ni (sub), Arg; (with Celtic), 1984 v U, Bel (sub), EG (sub), Ni, W (7)
McGeoch, A. (Dumbreck), 1876 v E, W; 1877 v E, W (4)
McGhee, J. (Hibernian), 1886 v W (1)
McGhee, M. (Aberdeen), 1983 v Ca (1+1 sub); 1984 v Ni (sub), E (4)
McGinlay, J. (Bolton W), 1994 v A, Ho; 1995 v Fa, Ru, Gr, Ru, Sm, Fa; 1996 v Se; 1997 v Se, Es (1 + sub), A (sub) (13)
McGonagle, W. (Celtic), 1933 v E; 1934 v A, E, Ni; 1935 v Ni, W (6)
McGrain, D. (Celtic), 1973 v W, Ni, E, Sw, Br; 1974 v Cz (2), WG, W (sub), E, Bel, N, Z, Br, Y; 1975 v Sp, W, N, Ni, E, R; 1976 v D (2), Sw, Ni, W, E; 1977 v Fi, Cz, W (2), Se, Ni, E, Ch, Arg, Br; 1978 v EG, Cz; 1980 v Bel, P, Ni, W, E, Pol, H; 1981 v Se, P, Is, Ni, Is, W (sub), Ni, E; 1982 v Se, Sp, Ho, Ni, E, Nz, USSR (sub) (62)
McGregor, J. C. (Vale of Leven), 1877 v E, W; 1878 v E; 1880 v E (4)
McGrory, J. E. (Kilmarnock), 1965 v Ni, Fi; 1966 v P (3)
McGrory, J. (Celtic), 1928 v Ni; 1931 v E; 1932 v Ni, W; 1933 v E, Ni; 1934 v Ni (7)
McGuire, W. (Beith), 1881 v E, W (2)
McGurk, F. (Birmingham), 1934 v W (1)
McHardy, H. (Rangers), 1885 v Ni (1)
McInally, A. (Aston Villa), 1989 v Cy (sub), Ch; (with Bayern Munich), 1990 v Y (sub), F (sub), Arg, Pol (sub), Ma, Cr (8)
McInally, J. (Dundee U), 1987 v Bel, Br; 1988 v Ma (sub); 1991 v Bul (2); 1992 v US (sub), N (sub), C (sub); 1993 v G, P (10)
McInally, T. B. (Celtic), 1926 v Ni; 1927 v W (2)
McInnes, T. (Cowlairs), 1889 v Ni (1)
McIntosh, W. (Third Lanark), 1905 v Ni (1)
McIntyre, A. (Vale of Leven), 1878 v E; 1882 v E (2)
McIntyre, H. (Rangers), 1880 v W (1)
McIntyre, J. (Rangers), 1884 v W (1)
MacKay, D. (Celtic), 1959 v E, WG, Ho, P; 1960 v E, Pol, A, H, T; 1961 v W, Ni; 1962 v Ni, Cz, U (sub) (14)
Mackay, D. C. (Hearts), 1957 v Sp; 1958 v F; 1959 v W, Ni; (with Tottenham H), 1959 v WG, E; 1960 v W, Ni, A, Pol, H, T; 1961 v W, Ni; 1963 v E, A, N; 1964 v Ni, W, N; 1966 v Ni (22)

Mackay, G. (Hearts), 1988 v Bul (sub), L (sub), S.Ar (sub), Ma (4)
McKay, J. (Blackburn R), 1924 v W (1)
McKay, R. (Newcastle U), 1928 v W (1)
McKean, R. (Rangers), 1976 v Sw (sub) (1)
McKenzie, D. (Brentford), 1938 v Ni (1)
Mackenzie, J. A. (Partick T), 1954 v W, E, N, Fi, A, U; 1955 v E, H; 1956 v A (9)
McKeown, M. (Celtic), 1889 v Ni; 1890 v E (2)
McKie, J. (East Stirling), 1898 v W (1)
McKillop, T. R. (Rangers), 1938 v Ho (1)
McKimmie, S. (Aberdeen), 1989 v E, Ch; 1990 v Arg, Eg, Cr (sub), Br; 1991 v R, Sw, Bul, Sm; 1992 v Sw, R, Ni, Fi, US, Ca (sub), N (sub), Ho, G, C; 1993 v P, Es (sub); 1994 v Sw, I, Ho, A, Ho; 1995 v Fi, Fa, Ru, Gr, Ru, Fa; 1996 v Gr, Fi, Se, D, Co, Ho, E (40)
McKinlay, D. (Liverpool), 1922 v W, Ni (2)
McKinlay, T. (Celtic), 1996 v Gr, Fi, D, Co, E, Sw; 1997 v A, La, Se, Es (sub + 1), A, Se, W, Ma, Bl; 1998 v Bl, La (sub), F (sub), US, Br (sub), Mor (sub) (22)
McKinlay, W. (Dundee U), 1994 v Ma, Ho (sub), A, Ho; 1995 v Fa (sub), Ru, Gr, Ru (sub), Sm (sub), J, Ec, Fa; 1996 v Fi (sub), Se (sub); (with Blackburn R), Sm (sub), Aus, D (sub), Ho (sub); 1997 v Se, Es (sub); 1998 v La (sub), F, D, Fi, Co (sub), US, Br (sub); 1999 v Es, Fa (29)
McKinnon, A. (Queen's Park), 1874 v E (1)
McKinnon, R. (Rangers), 1966 v W, E, I (2), Ho, Br; 1967 v W, Ni, E; 1968 v Ni, W, E, Ho; 1969 v D, A, WG, Cy; 1970 v Ni, W, E, Ei, WG, A; 1971 v D, Bel, P, USSR, D (28)
McKinnon, R. (Motherwell), 1994 v Ma; 1995 v J, Fa (3)
MacKinnon, W. (Dumbarton), 1883 v E, W; 1884 v E, W (4)
MacKinnon, W. W. (Queen's Park), 1872 v E; 1873 v E; 1874 v E; 1875 v E; 1876 v E, W; 1877 v E; 1878 v E; 1879 v E (9)
McLaren, A. (St Johnstone), 1929 v N, G, Ho; 1933 v W, Ni (5)
McLaren, A. (Preston NE), 1947 v E, Bel, L; 1948 v W (4)
McLaren, A. (Hearts), 1992 v US, Ca, N; 1993 v I, Ma, G, Es (sub + 1); 1994 v I, Ma, Ho, A; 1995 v Fi, Fa; (with Rangers), Ru, Gr, Ru, Sm, J, Ec, Fa; 1996 v Fi, Se, Sm (24)
McLaren, J. (Hibernian), 1888 v W; (with Celtic), 1889 v E; 1890 v E (3)
McLean, A. (Celtic), 1926 v W, Ni; 1927 v W, E (4)
McLean, D. (St Bernards), 1896 v W; 1897 v Ni (2)
McLean, D. (Sheffield W), 1912 v E (1)
McLean, G. (Dundee), 1968 v Ho (1)
McLean, T. (Kilmarnock), 1969 v D, Cy, W; 1970 v Ni, W; 1971 v D (6)
McLeish, A. (Aberdeen), 1980 v P, Ni, W, E, Pol, H; 1981 v Se, Is, Ni, Is, Ni, E; 1982 v Se, Sp, Ni, Br (sub); 1983 v Bel, Sw (sub), W, E, Ca (3); 1984 v U, Bel, EG, Ni, W, E, F; 1985 v Y, Ic, Sp (2), W, E, Ic; 1986 v W, EG, Aus (2), E, Ho, D; 1987 v Bel, E, Br; 1988 v Bel, Bul, L, S.Ar (sub), Ma, Sp, Co, E; 1989 v N, Y, I, Cy, F, Cy, E, Ch; 1990 v Y, F, N, Arg, EG, Eg, Cr, Se, Br; 1991 v R, Sw, USSR, Bul; 1993 v Ma (77)
McLeod, D. (Celtic), 1905 v Ni; 1906 v E, W, Ni (4)
McLeod, J. (Dumbarton), 1888 v Ni; 1889 v W; 1890 v Ni; 1892 v E; 1893 v W (5)
MacLeod, J. M. (Hibernian), 1961 v E, Ei (2), Cz (4)
MacLeod, M. (Celtic), 1985 v C (sub); 1987 v Ei, L, E, Br; (with Borussia Dortmund), 1988 v Co, E; 1989 v I, Ch; 1990 v Y, F, N (sub), Arg, EG, Pol, Se Br; (with Hibernian), 1991 v R, Sw, USSR (sub) (20)
McLeod, W. (Cowlairs), 1886 v Ni (1)
McLintock, A. (Vale of Leven), 1875 v E; 1876 v E; 1880 v E (3)
McLintock, F. (Leicester C), 1963 v N (sub), Ei, Sp; (with Arsenal), 1965 v Ni; 1967 v USSR; 1970 v Ni; 1971 v W, Ni, E (9)
McLuckie, J. S. (Manchester C), 1934 v W (1)
McMahon, A. (Celtic), 1892 v E; 1893 v E, Ni; 1894 v E; 1901 v Ni; 1902 v W (6)
McMenemy, J. (Celtic), 1905 v Ni; 1909 v Ni; 1910 v E, W; 1911 v Ni, W, E; 1912 v W; 1914 v W, Ni, E; 1920 v Ni (12)
McMenemy, J. (Motherwell), 1934 v W (1)
McMillan, J. (St Bernards), 1897 v W (1)
McMillan, I. L. (Airdrieonians), 1952 v E, USA, D; 1955 v E; 1956 v E; (with Rangers), 1961 v Cz (6)
McMillan, T. (Dumbarton), 1887 v Ni (1)
McMullan, J. (Partick T), 1920 v W; 1921 v W, Ni, E; 1924 v E, Ni; 1925 v E; 1926 v W; (with Manchester C), 1926 v E; 1927 v E, W; 1928 v E, W; 1929 v W, E, Ni (16)
McNab, A. (Morton), 1921 v E, Ni (2)
McNab, A. (Sunderland), 1937 v A; (with WBA), 1939 v E (2)
McNab, C. D. (Dundee), 1931 v E, W, A, I, Sw; 1932 v E (6)
McNab, J. S. (Liverpool), 1923 v W (1)

McNair, A. (Celtic), 1906 v W; 1907 v Ni; 1908 v E, W; 1909 v E; 1910 v W; 1912 v E, W, Ni; 1913 v E; 1914 v E, Ni; 1920 v E, W, Ni (15)

McNamara, J. (Celtic), 1997 v La (sub), Se, Es, W (sub); 1998 v D, Co, US (sub), N (sub), Mor (9)

McNaught, W. (Raith R), 1951 v A, W, Ni; 1952 v E; 1955 v Ni (5)

McNiel, H. (Queen's Park), 1874 v E; 1875 v E; 1876 v E, W; 1877 v W; 1878 v E; 1879 v E, W; 1881 v E, W (10)

McNiel, M. (Rangers), 1876 v W; 1880 v E (2)

McNeill, W. (Celtic), 1961 v E, Ei (2), Cz; 1962 v Ni, E, Cz, U; 1963 v Ei, Sp; 1964 v W, E, WG; 1965 v E, Fi, Pol, Sp; 1966 v Ni, Pol; 1967 v USSR; 1968 v E; 1969 v Cy, W, E, Cy (sub); 1970 v WG; 1972 v Ni, W, E (29)

McPhail, J. (Celtic), 1950 v W; 1951 v W, Ni, A; 1954 v Ni (5)

McPhail, R. (Airdrieonians), 1927 v E; (with Rangers), 1929 v W; 1931 v E, Ni; 1932 v W, Ni, F; 1933 v E, Ni; 1934 v A, Ni; 1935 v E; 1937 v G, E, Cz; 1938 v W, Ni (17)

McPherson, D. (Kilmarnock), 1892 v Ni (1)

McPherson, D. (Hearts), 1989 v Cy, E; 1990 v N, Ma, Cr, Se, Br; 1991 v Sw, Bul (2), USSR (sub), Sm; 1992 v Sw, R, Sm, Ni, Fi, US, Ca, N, Ho, G, C; (with Rangers), 1993 v Sw, I, Ma, P (27)

McPherson, J. (Clydesdale), 1875 v E (1)

McPherson, J. (Vale of Leven), 1879 v E, W; 1880 v E; 1881 v W; 1883 v E, W; 1884 v E; 1885 v Ni (8)

McPherson, J. (Kilmarnock), 1888 v W; (with Cowlairs), 1889 v E; 1890 v Ni, E; (with Rangers), 1892 v W; 1894 v E; 1895 v E, Ni; 1897 v Ni (9)

McPherson, J. (Hearts), 1891 v E (1)

McPherson, R. (Arthurlie), 1882 v E (1)

McQueen, G. (Leeds U), 1974 v Bel; 1975 v Sp (2), P, W, Ni, E, R; 1976 v D; 1977 v Cz, W (2), Ni, E; 1978 v EG, Cz, W; (with Manchester U), Bul, Ni, W; 1979 v A, N, P, Ni, E, N; 1980 v Pe, A, Bel; 1981 v W (30)

McQueen, M. (Leith Ath), 1890 v W; 1891 v W (2)

McRorie, D. M. (Morton), 1931 v W (1)

McSpadyen, A. (Partick T), 1939 v E, H (2)

McStay, P. (Celtic), 1984 v U, Bel, EG, Ni, W, E (sub); 1985 v Y, Ic, Sp (2); 1986 v EG (sub), Aus, Is, U; 1987 v Bul, Ei (1+1 sub), L (sub), Bel, E, Br; 1988 v H, Bel, Bul, L, S.Ar, Sp, Co, E; 1989 v N, Y, I, Cy, F, Cy, E, Ch; 1990 v Y, F, N, Arg, EG (sub), Eg, Pol (sub), Ma, Cr, Se (sub), Br; 1991 v R, USSR, Bul; 1992 v Sm, Fi, US, Ca, N, Ho, G, C; 1993 v Sw, P, I, Ma, P, Es (2); 1994 v I (sub), Ho; 1995 v Fi, Fa, Ru; 1996 v Aus; 1997 v Es (2), A (sub) (76)

McStay, W. (Celtic), 1921 v W, Ni; 1925 v E, Ni, W; 1926 v E, Ni, W; 1927 v E, Ni, W; 1928 v W, Ni (13)

McTavish, J. (Falkirk), 1910 v Ni (1)

McWattie, G. C. (Queen's Park), 1901 v W, Ni (2)

McWilliam, P. (Newcastle U), 1905 v E; 1906 v E; 1907 v E, W; 1909 v E, W; 1910 v E; 1911 v W (8)

Macari, L. (Celtic), 1972 v W (sub), E, Y, Cz, Br; 1973 v D; (with Manchester U), E (2), W (sub), Ni (sub); 1975 v Se, P (sub), W, E (sub), R; 1977 v Ni (sub), E (sub), Ch, Arg; 1978 v EG, W, Bul, Pe (sub), Ir (24)

Macauley, A. R. (Brentford), 1947 v E; (with Arsenal), 1948 v E, W, Ni, Bel, Sw, F (7)

Madden, J. (Celtic), 1893 v W; 1895 v W (2)

Main, F. R. (Rangers), 1938 v W (1)

Main, J. (Hibernian), 1909 v Ni (1)

Maley, W. (Celtic), 1893 v E, Ni (2)

Malpas, M. (Dundee U), 1984 v F; 1985 v E, Ic; 1986 v W, Aus (2), Is, R, E, Ho, D, WG; 1987 v Bul, Ei, Bel; 1988 v Bel, Bul, L, S.Ar, Ma; 1989 v N, Y, I, Cy, F, Cy, E, Ch; 1990 v Y, F, N, Eg, Pol, Ma, Cr, Se, Br; 1991 v R, Bul (2), USSR, Sm; 1992 v Sw, R, Sm, Ni, Fi, US, Ca (sub), N, Ho, G; 1993 v Sw, P, I (55)

Marshall, G. (Celtic), 1992 v US (1)

Marshall, H. (Celtic), 1899 v W; 1900 v Ni (2)

Marshall, J. (Middlesbrough), 1921 v E, W, Ni; 1922 v E, W, Ni; (with Llanelly), 1924 v W (7)

Marshall, J. (Third Lanark), 1885 v Ni; 1886 v W; 1887 v E, W (4)

Marshall, J. (Rangers), 1932 v E; 1933 v E; 1934 v E (3)

Marshall, R. W. (Rangers), 1892 v Ni; 1894 v Ni (2)

Martin, B. (Motherwell), 1995 v J, Ec (2)

Martin, F. (Aberdeen), 1954 v N (2), A, U; 1955 v E, H (6)

Martin, N. (Hibernian), 1965 v Fi, Pol; (with Sunderland), 1966 v I (3)

Martis, J. (Motherwell), 1961 v W (1)

Mason, J. (Third Lanark), 1949 v E, W, Ni; 1950 v Ni; 1951 v Ni, Bel, A (7)

Massie, A. (Hearts), 1932 v Ni, W, F; 1933 v Ni; 1934 v E, Ni; 1935 v E, Ni, W; 1936 v W, Ni; (with Aston Villa), 1936 v E; 1937 v G, E, W, Ni, A; 1938 v W (18)

Masson, D. S. (QPR), 1976 v Ni, W, E; 1977 v Fi, Cz, W, Ni, E, Ch, Arg, Br; 1978 v EG, Cz, W; (with Derby Co), Ni, E, Pe (17)

Mathers, D. (Partick T), 1954 v Fi (1)

Maxwell, W. S. (Stoke C), 1898 v E (1)

May, J. (Rangers), 1906 v W, Ni; 1908 v E, Ni; 1909 v W (5)

Meechan, P. (Celtic), 1896 v Ni (1)

Meiklejohn, D. D. (Rangers), 1922 v W; 1924 v W; 1925 v W, Ni, E; 1928 v W, Ni; 1929 v E, Ni; 1930 v E, Ni; 1931 v E; 1932 v W, Ni; 1934 v A (15)

Menzies, A. (Hearts), 1906 v E (1)

Mercer, R. (Hearts), 1912 v W; 1913 v Ni (2)

Middleton, R. (Cowdenbeath), 1930 v Ni (1)

Millar, A. (Hearts), 1939 v W (1)

Millar, J. (Rangers), 1897 v E; 1898 v E, W (3)

Millar, J. (Rangers), 1963 v A, Ei (2)

Miller, J. (St Mirren), 1931 v E, I, Sw; 1932 v F; 1934 v E (5)

Miller, P. (Dumbarton), 1882 v E; 1883 v E, W (3)

Miller, T. (Liverpool), 1920 v E; (with Manchester U), 1921 v E, Ni (3)

Miller, W. (Third Lanark), 1876 v E (1)

Miller, W. (Celtic), 1947 v E, W, Bel, L; 1948 v W, Ni (6)

Miller, W. (Aberdeen), 1975 v R; 1978 v Bul; 1980 v Bel, W, E, Pol, H; 1981 v Se, P, Is (sub), Ni, W, Ni, E; 1982 v Ni, P, Ho, Br, USSR; 1983 v EG, Sw (2), W, E, Ca (3); 1984 v U, Bel, EG, W, E, F; 1985 v Y, Ic, Sp (2), W, E, Ic; 1986 v W, EG, Aus (2), Is, R, E, Ho, D, WG, U; 1987 v Bul, E, Br; 1988 v H, L, S.Ar, Ma, Sp, Co, E; 1989 v N, Y; 1990 v Y, N (65)

Mills, W. (Aberdeen), 1936 v W, Ni; 1937 v W (3)

Milne, J. V. (Middlesbrough), 1938 v E; 1939 v E (2)

Mitchell, D. (Rangers), 1890 v Ni; 1892 v E; 1893 v E, Ni; 1894 v E (5)

Mitchell, J. (Kilmarnock), 1908 v Ni; 1910 v Ni, W (3)

Mitchell, R. C. (Newcastle U), 1951 v D, F (2)

Mochan, N. (Celtic), 1954 v N, A, U (3)

Moir, W. (Bolton W), 1950 v E (1)

Moncur, R. (Newcastle U), 1968 v Ho; 1970 v Ni, W, E, Ei; 1971 v D, Bel, W, P, Ni, E, D; 1972 v Pe, Ni, W, E (16)

Morgan, H. (St Mirren), 1898 v W; (with Liverpool), 1899 v E (2)

Morgan, W. (Burnley), 1968 v Ni; (with Manchester U), 1972 v Pe, Y, Cz, Br; 1973 v D (2), E (2), W, Ni, Sw, Br; 1974 v Cz (2), WG (2), Ni, Bel (sub), Br, Y (21)

Morris, D. (Raith R), 1923 v Ni; 1924 v E, Ni; 1925 v E, W, Ni (6)

Morris, H. (East Fife), 1950 v Ni (1)

Morrison, T. (St Mirren), 1927 v E (1)

Morton, A. L. (Queen's Park), 1920 v W, Ni; (with Rangers), 1921 v E; 1922 v E, W; 1923 v E, W, Ni; 1924 v E, W, Ni; 1925 v E, W, Ni; 1927 v E, Ni; 1928 v E, W, Ni; 1929 v E, W, Ni; 1930 v E, W, Ni; 1931 v E, W, Ni; 1932 v E, W, F (31)

Morton, H. A. (Kilmarnock), 1929 v G, Ho (2)

Mudie, J. K. (Blackpool), 1957 v W, Ni, E, Y, Sw, Sp (2), WG; 1958 v Ni, E, W, Sw, H, Pol, Y, Par, F (17)

Muir, W. (Dundee), 1907 v Ni (1)

Muirhead, T. A. (Rangers), 1922 v Ni; 1923 v E; 1924 v W; 1927 v Ni; 1928 v Ni; 1929 v W, Ni; 1930 v W (8)

Mulhall, G. (Aberdeen), 1960 v Ni; (with Sunderland), 1963 v Ni; 1964 v Ni (3)

Munro, A. D. (Hearts), 1937 v W, Ni; (with Blackpool), 1938 v Ho (3)

Munro, F. M. (Wolverhampton W), 1971 v Ni (sub), E (sub), D, USSR; 1975 v Se, W (sub), Ni, E, R (9)

Munro, I. (St Mirren), 1979 v Arg, N; 1980 v Pe, A, Bel, W, E (7)

Munro, N. (Abercorn), 1888 v W; 1889 v E (2)

Murdoch, J. (Motherwell), 1931 v Ni (1)

Murdoch, R. (Celtic), 1966 v W, E, I (2); 1967 v Ni; 1968 v Ni; 1969 v W, Ni, E, WG, Cy; 1970 v A (12)

Murphy, F. (Celtic), 1938 v Ho (1)

Murray, J. (Renton), 1895 v W (1)

Murray, J. (Hearts), 1958 v E, H, Pol, Y, F (5)

Murray, J. W. (Vale of Leven), 1890 v W (1)

Murray, P. (Hibernian), 1896 v Ni; 1897 v W (2)

Murray, S. (Aberdeen), 1972 v Bel (1)

Mutch, G. (Preston NE), 1938 v E (1)

Napier, C. E. (Celtic), 1932 v E; 1935 v E, W; (with Derby Co), 1937 v Ni, A (5)

Narey, D. (Dundee U), 1977 v Se (sub); 1979 v P, Ni (sub), Arg; 1980 v P, Ni, Pol, H; 1981 v W, E (sub); 1982 v Ho, W, E, Nz (sub), Br, USSR; 1983 v EG, Sw, Bel, Ni, W, E, Ca (3); 1986 v Is, R, Ho, WG, U; 1987 v Bul, E, Bel; 1989 v I, Cy (35)

Neil, R. G. (Hibernian), 1896 v W; (with Rangers), 1900 v W (2)

Neill, R. W. (Queen's Park), 1876 v W; 1877 v E, W; 1878 v W; 1880 v E (5)
Nellies, P. (Hearts), 1913 v Ni; 1914 v W (2)
Nelson, J. (Cardiff C), 1925 v W, Ni; 1928 v E; 1930 v F (4)
Nevin, P. K. F. (Chelsea), 1986 v R (sub), E (sub); 1987 v L, Ei, Bel (sub); 1988 v L; (with Everton), 1989 v Cy, E; 1991 v R (sub), Bul (sub), Sm (sub); 1992 v US, G (sub), C (sub); (with Tranmere R), 1993 v Ma, P (sub), Es; 1994 v Sw, Ma, Ho, A (sub), Ho; 1995 v Fa, Ru (sub), Sm; 1996 v Se (sub), Sm, Aus (sub) (28)
Niblo, T. D. (Aston Villa), 1904 v E (1)
Nibloe, J. (Kilmarnock), 1929 v E, N, Ho; 1930 v W; 1931 v E, Ni, A, I, Sw; 1932 v E, F (11)
Nicholas, C. (Celtic), 1983 v Sw, Ni, E, Ca (3); (with Arsenal), 1984 v Bel (sub); 1985 v Y (sub), Ic (sub), Sp (sub), W (sub); 1986 v Is, R (sub), E, D, U (sub); 1987 v Bul, E (sub); (with Aberdeen), 1989 v Cy (sub) (20)
Nicol, S. (Liverpool), 1985 v Y, Ic, Sp, W; 1986 v W, EG, Aus, E, D, WG, U; 1988 v H, Bul, S.Ar, Sp, Co, E; 1989 v N, Y, Cy, F; 1990 v Y, F; 1991 v Sw, USSR, Sm; 1992 v Sw (27)
Nisbet, J. (Ayr U), 1929 v N, G, Ho (3)
Niven, J. B. (Moffatt), 1885 v Ni (1)

O'Donnell, F. (Preston NE), 1937 v E, A, Cz; 1938 v W; (with Blackpool), E, Ho (6)
O'Donnell, P. (Motherwell), 1994 v Sw (sub) (1)
Ogilvie, D. H. (Motherwell), 1934 v A (1)
O'Hare, J. (Derby Co), 1970 v W, Ni, E; 1971 v D, Bel, W, Ni; 1972 v P, Bel, Ho (sub), Pe, Ni, W (13)
O'Neil, B. (Celtic), 1996 v Aus; (with Wolfsburg), 1999 v G (sub) (2)
Ormond, W. E. (Hibernian), 1954 v E, N, Fi, A, U; 1959 v E (6)
O'Rourke, F. (Airdrieonians), 1907 v Ni (1)
Orr, J. (Kilmarnock), 1892 v W (1)
Orr, R. (Newcastle U), 1902 v E; 1904 v E (2)
Orr, T. (Morton), 1952 v Ni, W (2)
Orr, W. (Celtic), 1900 v Ni; 1903 v Ni; 1904 v W (3)
Orrock, R. (Falkirk), 1913 v W (1)
Oswald, J. (Third Lanark), 1889 v E; (with St Bernards), 1895 v E; (with Rangers), 1897 v W (3)

Parker, A. H. (Falkirk), 1955 v P, Y, A; 1956 v E, Ni, W, A; 1957 v Ni, W, Y; 1958 v Ni, W, E, Sw; (with Everton), Par (15)
Parlane, D. (Rangers), 1973 v W, Sw, Br; 1975 v Sp (sub), Se, P, W, Ni, E, R; 1976 v D (sub); 1977 v W (12)
Parlane, R. (Vale of Leven), 1878 v W; 1879 v E, W (3)
Paterson, G. D. (Celtic), 1939 v Ni (1)
Paterson, J. (Leicester C), 1920 v E (1)
Paterson, J. (Cowdenbeath), 1931 v A, I, Sw (3)
Paton, A. (Motherwell), 1952 v D, Se (2)
Paton, D. (St Bernards), 1896 v W (1)
Paton, M. (Dumbarton), 1883 v E; 1884 v W; 1885 v W, E; 1886 v E (5)
Paton, R. (Vale of Leven), 1879 v E, W (2)
Patrick, J. (St Mirren), 1897 v E, W (2)
Paul, H. McD. (Queen's Park), 1909 v E, W, Ni (3)
Paul, W. (Partick T), 1888 v W; 1889 v W; 1890 v W (3)
Paul, W. (Dykebar), 1891 v Ni (1)
Pearson, T. (Newcastle U), 1947 v E, Bel (2)
Penman, A. (Dundee), 1966 v Ho (1)
Pettigrew, W. (Motherwell), 1976 v Sw, Ni, W; 1977 v W (sub), Se (5)
Phillips, J. (Queen's Park), 1877 v E, W; 1878 v W (3)
Plenderleith, J. B. (Manchester C), 1961 v Ni (1)
Porteous, W. (Hearts), 1903 v Ni (1)
Pringle, C. (St Mirren), 1921 v W (1)
Provan, D. (Rangers), 1964 v Ni, N; 1966 v I (2), Ho (5)
Provan, D. (Celtic), 1980 v Bel (2 sub), P (sub), Ni (sub); 1981 v Is, W, E; 1982 v Se, P, Ni (10)
Pursell, P. (Queen's Park), 1914 v W (1)

Quinn, J. (Celtic), 1905 v Ni; 1906 v Ni, W; 1908 v Ni, E; 1909 v E; 1910 v E, Ni, W; 1912 v E, W (11)
Quinn, P. (Motherwell), 1961 v E, Ei (2); 1962 v U (4)

Rae, J. (Third Lanark), 1889 v W; 1890 v Ni (2)
Raeside, J. S. (Third Lanark), 1906 v W (1)
Raisbeck, A. G. (Liverpool), 1900 v E; 1901 v E; 1902 v E; 1903 v E; 1904 v E; 1906 v E; 1907 v E (8)
Rankin, G. (Vale of Leven), 1890 v Ni; 1891 v E (2)
Rankin, R. (St Mirren), 1929 v N, G, Ho (3)
Redpath, W. (Motherwell), 1949 v W, Ni; 1951 v E, D, F, Bel, A; 1952 v Ni, E (9)
Reid, J. G. (Airdrieonians), 1914 v W; 1920 v W; 1924 v Ni (3)

Reid, R. (Brentford), 1938 v E, Ni (2)
Reid, W. (Rangers), 1911 v E, W, Ni; 1912 v Ni; 1913 v E, W, Ni; 1914 v E, Ni (9)
Reilly, L. (Hibernian), 1949 v E, W, F; 1950 v W, Ni, Sw, F; 1951 v W, E, D, F, Bel, A; 1952 v Ni, W, E, USA, D, Se; 1953 v W, Ni, E, Se; 1954 v W; 1955 v H (2), P, Y, A, E; 1956 v E, W, Ni, A; 1957 v E, Ni, W, Y (38)
Rennie, H. G. (Hearts), 1900 v E, Ni; (with Hibernian), 1901 v E; 1902 v E, Ni, W; 1903 v Ni, W; 1904 v Ni; 1905 v W; 1906 v Ni; 1908 v Ni, W (13)
Renny-Tailyour, H. W. (Royal Engineers), 1873 v E (1)
Rhind, A. (Queen's Park), 1872 v E (1)
Richmond, A. (Queen's Park), 1906 v W (1)
Richmond, J. T. (Clydesdale), 1877 v E; (with Queen's Park), 1878 v E; 1882 v W (3)
Ring, T. (Clyde), 1953 v Se; 1955 v W, Ni, E, H; 1957 v E, Sp (2), Sw, WG; 1958 v Ni, Sw (12)
Rioch, B. D. (Derby Co), 1975 v P, W, Ni, E, R; 1976 v D (2), R, Ni, W, E; 1977 v Fi, Cz, W; (with Everton), W, Ni, E, Ch, Br; 1978 v Cz; (with Derby Co), Ni, E, Pe, Ho (24)
Ritchie, A. (East Stirlingshire), 1891 v W (1)
Ritchie, H. (Hibernian), 1923 v W; 1928 v Ni (2)
Ritchie, J. (Queen's Park), 1897 v W (1)
Ritchie, P. S. (Hearts), 1999 v G (sub), CzR (2)
Ritchie, W. (Rangers), 1962 v U (sub) (1)
Robb, D. T. (Aberdeen), 1971 v W, E, P, D (sub), USSR (5)
Robb, W. (Rangers), 1926 v W; (with Hibernian), 1928 v W (2)
Robertson, A. (Clyde), 1955 v P, A, H; 1958 v Sw, Par (5)
Robertson, D. (Rangers), 1992 v Ni; 1994 v Sw, Ho (3)
Robertson, G. (Motherwell), 1910 v W; (with Sheffield W), 1912 v W; 1913 v E, Ni (4)
Robertson, G. (Kilmarnock), 1938 v Cz (1)
Robertson, H. (Dundee), 1962 v Cz (1)
Robertson, J. (Dundee), 1931 v A, I (2)
Robertson, J. (Hearts), 1991 v R, Sw, Bul (sub), Sm (sub); 1992 v Sm, Ni (sub), Fi; 1993 v I (sub), Ma (sub), G, Es; 1995 v J (sub), Ec, Fa (sub); 1996 v Gr (sub), Se (16)
Robertson, J. N. (Nottingham F), 1978 v Ni, W (sub), Ir; 1979 v P, N; 1980 v Pe, A, Bel (2), P; 1981 v Se, P, Is, Ni, Is, Ni, E; 1982 v Se, Ni (2), E (sub), Nz, Br, USSR; 1983 v EG, Sw; (with Derby Co), 1984 v U, Bel (28)
Robertson, J. G. (Tottenham H), 1965 v W (1)
Robertson, J. T. (Everton), 1898 v E; (with Southampton), 1899 v E; (with Rangers), 1900 v E, W; 1901 v W, Ni, E; 1902 v W, Ni, E; 1903 v E, W; 1904 v E, W, Ni; 1905 v W (16)
Robertson, P. (Dundee), 1903 v Ni (1)
Robertson, T. (Queen's Park), 1889 v Ni; 1890 v E; 1891 v W; 1892 v Ni (4)
Robertson, T. (Hearts), 1898 v Ni (1)
Robertson, W. (Dumbarton), 1887 v E, W (2)
Robinson, R. (Dundee), 1974 v WG (sub); 1975 v Se, Ni, R (sub) (4)
Rough, A. (Partick T), 1976 v Sw, Ni, W, E; 1977 v Fi, Cz, W (2), Se, Ni, E, Ch, Arg, Br; 1978 v Cz, W, Ni, E, Pe, Ir, Ho; 1979 v A, P, W, Arg, N; 1980 v Pe, A, Bel (2), P, W, E, Pol, H; 1981 v Se, P, Is, Ni, Is, W, E; 1982 v Se, Ni, Sp, Ho, W, E, Nz, Br, USSR; (with Hibernian), 1986 v W (sub), E (53)
Rougvie, A. (Aberdeen), 1984 v Ni (1)
Rowan, A. (Caledonian), 1880 v E; (with Queen's Park), 1882 v W (2)
Russell, D. (Hearts), 1895 v E, Ni; (with Celtic), 1897 v W; 1898 v Ni; 1901 v W, Ni (6)
Russell, J. (Cambuslang), 1890 v Ni (1)
Russell, W. F. (Airdrieonians), 1924 v W; 1925 v E (2)
Rutherford, E. (Rangers), 1948 v F (1)

St John, I. (Motherwell), 1959 v WG; 1960 v E, Ni, W, Pol, A; 1961 v E; (with Liverpool), 1962 v Ni, W, E, Cz (2), U; 1963 v W, Ni, E, N, Ei (sub), Sp; 1964 v Ni; 1965 v E (21)
Sawers, W. (Dundee), 1895 v W (1)
Scarff, P. (Celtic), 1931 v Ni (1)
Schaedler, E. (Hibernian), 1974 v WG (1)
Scott, A. S. (Rangers), 1957 v Ni, Y, WG; 1958 v W, Sw; 1959 v P; 1962 v Ni, W, E, Cz, U; (with Everton), 1964 v W, N; 1965 v Fi; 1966 v P, Br (16)
Scott, J. (Hibernian), 1966 v Ho (1)
Scott, J. (Dundee), 1971 v D (sub), USSR (2)
Scott, M. (Airdrieonians), 1898 v W (1)
Scott, R. (Airdrieonians), 1894 v Ni (1)
Scoular, J. (Portsmouth), 1951 v D, F, A; 1952 v E, USA, D, Se; 1953 v W, Ni (9)
Sellar, W. (Battlefield), 1885 v E; 1886 v E; 1887 v E, W; 1888 v E; (with Queen's Park), 1891 v E; 1892 v E; 1893 v E, Ni (9)

Waddell, W. (Rangers), 1947 v W; 1949 v E, W, Ni, F; 1950 v E, Ni; 1951 v E, D, F, Bel, A; 1952 v Ni, W; 1954 v Ni; 1955 v W, Ni (17)
Wales, H. M. (Motherwell), 1933 v W (1)
Walker, A. (Celtic), 1988 v Co (sub); 1995 v Fi, Fa (sub) (3)
Walker, F. (Third Lanark), 1922 v W (1)
Walker, G. (St Mirren), 1930 v F; 1931 v Ni, A, Sw (4)
Walker, J. (Hearts), 1895 v Ni; 1897 v W; 1898 v Ni; (with Rangers), 1904 v W, Ni (5)
Walker, J. (Swindon T), 1911 v E, W, Ni; 1912 v E, W, Ni; 1913 v E, W, Ni (9)
Walker, J. N. (Hearts), 1993 v G; (with Partick T), 1996 v US (sub) (2)
Walker, R. (Hearts), 1900 v E, Ni; 1901 v E, W; 1902 v E, W, Ni; 1903 v E, W, Ni; 1904 v E, W, Ni; 1905 v E, W, Ni; 1906 v Ni; 1907 v E, Ni; 1908 v E, W, Ni; 1909 v E, W; 1912 v E, W, Ni; 1913 v E, W (29)
Walker, T. (Hearts), 1935 v E, W; 1936 v E, W, Ni; 1937 v G, E, W, Ni, A, Cz; 1938 v E, W, Ni, Cz, Ho; 1939 v E, W, Ni, H (20)
Walker, W. (Clyde), 1909 v Ni; 1910 v Ni (2)
Wallace, I. A. (Coventry C), 1978 v Bul (sub); 1979 v P (sub), W (3)
Wallace, W. S. B. (Hearts), 1965 v Ni; 1966 v E, Ho; (with Celtic), 1967 v E, USSR (sub); 1968 v Ni; 1969 v E (sub) (7)
Wardhaugh, J. (Hearts), 1955 v H; 1957 v Ni (2)
Wark, J. (Ipswich T), 1979 v W, Ni, E, Arg, N (sub); 1980 v Pe, A, Bel (2); 1981 v Is, Ni; 1982 v Se, Sp, Ho, Ni, Nz, Br, USSR; 1983 v EG, Sw (2), Ni, E (sub); 1984 v U, Bel, EG; (with Liverpool), E, F; 1985 v Y (29)
Watson, A. (Queen's Park), 1881 v E, W; 1882 v E (3)
Watson, J. (Sunderland), 1903 v E, W; 1904 v E; 1905 v E; (with Middlesbrough), 1909 v E, Ni (6)
Watson, J. (Motherwell), 1948 v Ni; (with Huddersfield T), 1954 v Ni (2)
Watson, J. A. K. (Rangers), 1878 v W (1)
Watson, P. R. (Blackpool), 1934 v A (1)
Watson, R. (Motherwell), 1971 v USSR (1)
Watson, W. (Falkirk), 1898 v W (1)
Watt, F. (Kilbirnie), 1889 v W, Ni; 1890 v W; 1891 v E (4)
Watt, W. W. (Queen's Park), 1887 v Ni (1)
Waugh, A. (Hearts), 1938 v Cz (1)
Weir, A. (Motherwell), 1959 v WG; 1960 v E, P, A, H, T (6)
Weir, D. G. (Hearts), 1997 v W, Ma (sub); 1998 v F, D (sub), Fi (sub), N (sub), Mor; 1999 v Es, Fa; (with Everton) CzR, G, Fa, CzR (13)
Weir, J. (Third Lanark), 1887 v Ni (1)
Weir, J. B. (Queen's Park), 1872 v E; 1874 v E; 1875 v E; 1878 v W (4)
Weir, P. (St Mirren), 1980 v Ni, W, Pol (sub), H; (with Aberdeen), 1983 v Sw; 1984 v Ni (6)
White, John (Albion R), 1922 v W; (with Hearts), 1923 v Ni (2)
White, J. A. (Falkirk), 1959 v WG, Ho, P; 1960 v Ni; (with Tottenham H), 1960 v W, Pol, A, T; 1961 v W; 1962 v Ni, W, E, Cz (2); 1963 v W, Ni, E; 1964 v Ni, W, E, N, WG (22)

White, W. (Bolton W), 1907 v E; 1908 v E (2)
Whitelaw, A. (Vale of Leven), 1887 v Ni; 1890 v W (2)
Whyte, D. (Celtic), 1988 v Bel (sub), L; 1989 v Ch (sub); 1992 v US (sub); (with Middlesbrough), 1993 v P, I; 1995 v J (sub), Ec; 1996 v US; 1997 v La; (with Aberdeen), 1998 v Fi; 1999 v G (sub) (12)
Wilson, A. (Sheffield W), 1907 v E; 1908 v E; 1912 v E; 1913 v E, W; 1914 v Ni (6)
Wilson, A. (Portsmouth), 1954 v Fi (1)
Wilson, A. N. (Dunfermline), 1920 v E, W, Ni; 1921 v E, W, Ni; (with Middlesbrough), 1922 v E, W, Ni; 1923 v E, W, Ni (12)
Wilson, D. (Queen's Park), 1900 v W (1)
Wilson, D. (Oldham Ath), 1913 v E (1)
Wilson, D. (Rangers), 1961 v E, W, Ni, Ei (2), Cz; 1962 v Ni, W, E, Cz, U; 1963 v E, A, N, Ei, Sp; 1964 v E, WG; 1965 v Ni, E, Fi (22)
Wilson, G. W. (Hearts), 1904 v W; 1905 v E, Ni; 1906 v W; (with Everton), 1907 v E; (with Newcastle U), 1909 v E (6)
Wilson, Hugh (Newmilns), 1890 v W; (with Sunderland), 1897 v E; (with Third Lanark), 1902 v W; 1904 v Ni (4)
Wilson, I. A. (Leicester C), 1987 v E, Br; (with Everton), 1988 v Bel, Bul, L (5)
Wilson, J. (Vale of Leven), 1888 v W; 1889 v E; 1890 v E; 1891 v E (4)
Wilson, P. (Celtic), 1926 v Ni; 1930 v F; 1931 v Ni; 1933 v E (4)
Wilson, P. (Celtic), 1975 v Sp (sub) (1)
Wilson, R. P. (Arsenal), 1972 v P, Ho (2)
Winters, R. (Aberdeen), 1999 v G (sub) (1)
Wiseman, W. (Queen's Park), 1927 v W; 1930 v Ni (2)
Wood, G. (Everton), 1979 v Ni, E, Arg (sub); (with Arsenal), 1982 v Ni (4)
Woodburn, W. A. (Rangers), 1947 v E, Bel, L; 1948 v W, Ni; 1949 v E, F; 1950 v E, W, Ni, P, F; 1951 v E, W, Ni, A (2), D, F, Bel; 1952 v E, W, Ni, USA (24)
Wotherspoon, D. N. (Queen's Park), 1872 v E; 1873 v E (2)
Wright, K. (Hibernian), 1992 v Ni (1)
Wright, S. (Aberdeen), 1993 v G, Es (2)
Wright, T. (Sunderland), 1953 v W, Ni, E (3)
Wylie, T. G. (Rangers), 1890 v Ni (1)

Yeats, R. (Liverpool), 1965 v W; 1966 v I (2)
Yorston, B. C. (Aberdeen), 1931 v Ni (1)
Yorston, H. (Aberdeen), 1955 v W (1)
Young, A. (Hearts), 1960 v E, A (sub), H, T; 1961 v W, Ni; (with Everton), Ei; 1966 v P (8)
Young, A. (Everton), 1905 v E; 1907 v W (2)
Young, G. L. (Rangers), 1947 v E, Ni, Bel, L; 1948 v E, Ni, Bel, Sw, F; 1949 v E, W, Ni, F; 1950 v E, W, Ni, Sw, P, F; 1951 v E, W, Ni, A (2), D, F, Bel; 1952 v E, W, Ni, USA, D, Se; 1953 v W, E, Ni, Se; 1954 v Ni, W; 1955 v W, Ni, P, Y; 1956 v Ni, W, E, A; 1957 v E, Ni, W, Y, Sp, Sw (53)
Young, J. (Celtic), 1906 v Ni (1)
Younger, T. (Hibernian), 1955 v P, Y, A, H; 1956 v E, Ni, W, A; (with Liverpool), 1957 v E, Ni, W, Y, Sp (2), Sw, WG; 1958 v Ni, W, E, Sw, H, Pol, Y, Par (24)

WALES

Adams, H. (Berwyn R), 1882 v Ni, E; (with Druids), 1883 v Ni, E (4)
Aizlewood, M. (Charlton Ath), 1986 v S.Ar, Ca (2); 1987 v Fi; (with Leeds U), USSR, Fi (sub); 1988 v D (sub), Se, Ma, I; 1989 v Ho, Se (sub), WG; (with Bradford C), 1990 v Fi, WG, Ei, Cr; (with Bristol C), 1991 v D, Bel (2), L, Ei, Ic, Pol, WG; 1992 v Br, L, Ei, A, R, Ho, Arg, J; 1993 v Ei, Bel, Fa; 1994 v RCS, Cy; (with Cardiff C) 1995 v Bul (39)
Allchurch, I. J. (Swansea T), 1951 v E, Ni, P, Sw; 1952 v E, S, Ni, R of UK; 1953 v S, E, Ni, F, Y; 1954 v S, E, Ni, A; 1955 v S, E, Ni, Y; 1956 v E, S, Ni, A; 1957 v E, S; 1958 v Ni, Is (2), H (2), M, Sw, Br; (with Newcastle U), 1959 v E, S, Ni; 1960 v E, S; 1961 v Ni, H, Sp (2); 1962 v E, S, Br (2), M; (with Cardiff C), 1963 v S, E, Ni, H (2); 1964 v E; 1965 v S, E, Ni, Gr, I, USSR; (with Swansea T), 1966 v USSR, E, S, D, Br (2), Ch (68)
Allchurch, L. (Swansea T), 1955 v Ni; 1956 v A; 1958 v S, Ni, EG, Is; 1959 v S; (with Sheffield U), 1962 v S, Ni, Br; 1964 v E (11)
Allen, B. W. (Coventry C), 1951 v S, E (2)
Allen, M. (Watford), 1986 v S.Ar (sub), Ca (1 + 1 sub); (with Norwich C), 1989 v Is (sub); 1990 v Ho, WG; (with Millwall), Ei, Se, Cr (sub); 1991 v L (sub), Ei (sub); 1992 v A; 1993 v Ei (sub); (with Newcastle U), 1994 v R (sub) (14)
Arridge, S. (Bootle), 1892 v S, Ni; (with Everton), 1894 v Ni;

1895 v Ni; 1896 v E; (with New Brighton Tower), 1898 v E, Ni; 1899 v E (8)
Astley, D. J. (Charlton Ath), 1931 v Ni; (with Aston Villa), 1932 v E; 1933 v E, S, Ni; 1934 v E, S; 1935 v S; 1936 v E, Ni; (with Derby Co), 1939 v E, S; (with Blackpool), F (13)
Atherton, R. W. (Hibernian), 1899 v E, Ni; 1903 v E, S, Ni; (with Middlesbrough), 1904 v E, S, Ni; 1905 v Ni (9)

Bailiff, W. E. (Llanelly), 1913 v E, S, Ni; 1920 v Ni (4)
Baker, C. W. (Cardiff C), 1958 v M; 1960 v S, Ni; 1961 v S, E, Ei; 1962 v S (7)
Baker, W. G. (Cardiff C), 1948 v Ni (1)
Bamford, T. (Wrexham), 1931 v E, S, Ni; 1932 v Ni; 1933 v F (5)
Barnard, D. S. (Barnsley), 1998 v Jam; 1999 v I, D, Bl, I, D (6)
Barnes, W. (Arsenal), 1948 v E, S, Ni; 1949 v E, S, Ni; 1950 v E, S, Ni, Bel; 1951 v E, S, Ni, P; 1952 v E, S, Ni, R of UK; 1954 v E, S; 1955 v S, Y (22)
Bartley, T. (Glossop NE), 1898 v E (1)
Bastock, A. M. (Shrewsbury), 1892 v Ni (1)
Beadles, G. H. (Cardiff C), 1925 v E, S (2)
Bell, W. S. (Shrewsbury Engineers), 1881 v E, S; (with Crewe Alex), 1886 v E, S, Ni (5)
Bellamy, C. D. (Norwich C), 1998 v Jam (sub), Ma, Tun; 1999 v D (sub), Sw (sub), I, D (sub) (7)

Bennion, S. R. (Manchester U), 1926 v S; 1927 v S; 1928 v S, E, Ni; 1929 v S, E, Ni; 1930 v S; 1932 v Ni (10)

Berry, G. F. (Wolverhampton W), 1979 v WG; 1980 v Ei, WG (sub), T; (with Stoke C), 1983 v E (sub) (5)

Blackmore, C. G. (Manchester U), 1985 v N (sub); 1986 v S (sub), H (sub), S.Ar, Ei, U; 1987 v Fi (2), USSR, Cz; 1988 v D (2), Cz, Y, Se, Ma, I; 1989 v Ho, Fi, Is, WG; 1990 v F; Ho, WG, Cr; 1991 v Bel, L; 1992 v Ei (sub), A, R (sub), Ho, Arg, J; 1993 v Fa, Cy, Bel, RCS; 1994 v Se (sub); (with Middlesbrough), 1997 v Bel (39)

Blake, N. A. (Sheffield U), 1994 v N, Se (sub); 1995 v Alb, Mol; 1996 v G (with Bolton W), I (sub); 1998 v T; 1999 v I, D, Bl; (with Blackburn R) Sw (11)

Blew, H. (Wrexham), 1899 v E, S, Ni; 1902 v S, Ni; 1903 v E, S; 1904 v E, S, Ni; 1905 v S, Ni; 1906 v E, S, Ni; 1907 v S; 1908 v E, S, Ni; 1909 v E, S; 1910 v E (22)

Boden, T. (Wrexham), 1880 v E (1)

Bodin, P. J. (Swindon T), 1990 v Cr; 1991 v D, Bel, L, Ei; (with C Palace), Bel, Ic, Pol, WG; 1992 v Br, G, L (sub); (with Swindon T), Ei (sub), Ho, Arg; 1993 v Ei, Bel, RCS, Fa; 1994 v R, Se, Es (sub); 1995 v Alb (23)

Boulter, L. M. (Brentford), 1939 v Ni (1)

Bowdler, H. E. (Shrewsbury), 1893 v S (1)

Bowdler, J. C. H. (Shrewsbury), 1890 v Ni; (with Wolverhampton W), 1891 v S; 1892 v Ni; (with Shrewsbury), 1894 v E (4)

Bowen, D. L. (Arsenal), 1955 v S, Y; 1957 v Ni, Cz, EG; 1958 v E, S, Ni, EG, Is (2), H (2), M, Se, Br; 1959 v E, S, Ni (19)

Bowen, E. (Druids), 1880 v S; 1883 v S (2)

Bowen, J. P. (Swansea C), 1994 v Es; (with Birmingham C), 1997 v Ho (2)

Bowen, M. R. (Tottenham H), 1986 v Ca (2 sub); (with Norwich C), 1988 v Y (sub); 1989 v Fi (sub), Is, Se, WG (sub); 1990 v Fi (sub), Ho, WG, Se; 1992 v Br (sub), G, L, Ei, A, R, Ho (sub), J; 1993 v Fa, Cy, Bel (1 + sub), RCS (sub); 1994 v RCS, Se; 1995 v Mol, Ge, Bul (2), G, Ge; 1996 v Mol, G, Alb, Sw, Sm; (with West Ham U), 1997 v Sm, Ho (2), Ei (sub) (41)

Bowsher, S. J. (Burnley), 1929 v Ni (1)

Boyle, T. (C Palace), 1981 v Ei, S (sub) (2)

Britten, T. J. (Parkgrove), 1878 v S; (with Presteigne), 1880 v S (2)

Brookes, S. J. (Llandudno), 1900 v E, Ni (2)

Brown, A. I. (Aberdare Ath), 1926 v Ni (1)

Browning, M. T. (Bristol R), 1996 v I (sub), Sm; 1997 v Sm, Ho; (with Huddersfield T), S (sub) (5)

Bryan, T. (Oswestry), 1886 v E, Ni (2)

Buckland, T. (Bangor), 1899 v E (1)

Burgess, W. A. R. (Tottenham H), 1947 v E, S, Ni; 1948 v E, S; 1949 v S, Ni, P, Bel, Sw; 1950 v E, S, Ni, Bel; 1951 v S, Ni, P, Sw; 1952 v E, S, Ni, R of UK; 1953 v S, E, Ni, F, Y; 1954 v S, E, Ni, A (32)

Burke, T. (Wrexham), 1883 v E; 1884 v S; 1885 v E, S, Ni; (with Newton Heath), 1887 v E, S; 1888 v S (8)

Burnett, T. B. (Ruabon), 1877 v S (1)

Burton, A. D. (Norwich C), 1963 v Ni, H; (with Newcastle U), 1964 v S; 1969 v S, E, Ni, I, EG; 1972 v Cz (9)

Butler, J. (Chirk), 1893 v E, S, Ni (3)

Butler, W. T. (Druids), 1900 v S, Ni (2)

Cartwright, L. (Coventry C), 1974 v E (sub), S, Ni; 1976 v S (sub); 1977 v WG (sub); (with Wrexham), 1978 v Ir (sub); 1979 v Ma (7)

Carty, T. See McCarthy (Wrexham).

Challen, J. B. (Corinthians), 1887 v E, S; 1888 v E; (with Wellingborough GS), 1890 v E (4)

Chapman, T. (Newtown), 1894 v E, S, Ni; 1895 v S, Ni; (with Manchester C), 1896 v E; 1897 v E (7)

Charles, J. M. (Swansea C), 1981 v Cz, T (sub), S (sub), USSR (sub); 1982 v Ic; 1983 v N (sub), Y (sub), Bul (sub), S, Ni, Br; 1984 v Bul (sub); (with QPR), Y (sub), S; (with Oxford U), 1985 v Ic (sub), Sp, Ic; 1986 v Ei; 1987 v Fi (19)

Charles, M. (Swansea T), 1955 v Ni; 1956 v E, S, A; 1957 v E, Ni, Cz (2), EG; 1958 v E, S, EG, Is (2), H (2), M, Se, Br; 1959 v E, S; (with Arsenal), 1961 v Ni, H, Sp (2); 1962 v E, S; (with Cardiff C), 1962 v Br, Ni; 1963 v S, H (31)

Charles, W. J. (Leeds U), 1950 v Ni; 1951 v Sw; 1953 v Ni, F, Y; 1954 v E, S, Ni, A; 1955 v S, E, Ni, Y; 1956 v E, S, A, Ni; 1957 v E, S, Ni, Cz (2), EG; (with Juventus), 1958 v Is (2), H (2), M, Se; 1960 v S; 1962 v E, Br (2), M; (with Leeds U), 1963 v S; (with Cardiff C), 1964 v S; 1965 v S, USSR (38)

Clarke, R. J. (Manchester C), 1949 v E; 1950 v S, Ni, Bel; 1951 v E, S, Ni, P, Sw; 1952 v S, E, Ni, R of UK; 1953 v S, E; 1954 v E, S, Ni; 1955 v Y, S, E; 1956 v Ni (22)

Coleman, C. (C Palace), 1992 v A (sub); 1993 v Ei (sub); 1994 v N, Es; 1995 v Alb, Mol, Ge, Bul (2), G; 1996 v Mol; (with Blackburn R), I, Sw, Sm; 1997 v Sm; 1998 v Br; (with Fulham), Jam, Ma, Tun; 1999 v I, D, Bl, Sw, D (24)

Collier, D. J. (Grimsby T), 1921 v S (1)

Collins, W. S. (Llanelly), 1931 v S (1)

Conde, C. (Chirk), 1884 v E, S, Ni (3)

Cook, F. C. (Newport Co), 1925 v E, S; (with Portsmouth), 1928 v S; 1930 v E, S, Ni; 1932 v E (8)

Cornforth, J.M. (Swansea C), 1995 v Bul (sub), Ge (2)

Coyne, D. (Tranmere R), 1996 v Sw (1)

Crompton, W. (Wrexham), 1931 v E, S, Ni (3)

Cross, E. A. (Wrexham), 1876 v S; 1877 v S (2)

Crosse, K. (Druids), 1879 v S; 1881 v E, S (3)

Crossley, M. G. (Nottingham F), 1997 v Ei; 1999 v Sw (sub) (2)

Crowe, V. H. (Aston Villa), 1959 v E, Ni; 1960 v E, Ni; 1961 v S, E, Ni, Ei, H, Sp (2); 1962 v E, S, Br, M; 1963 v H (16)

Cumner, R. H. (Arsenal), 1939 v E, S, Ni (3)

Curtis, A. (Swansea C), 1976 v E, Y (sub), S, Ni, Y (sub), E; 1977 v WG, S (sub), Ni (sub); 1978 v WG, E, S; 1979 v WG, S; (with Leeds U), E, Ni, Ma; 1980 v Ei, WG, T; (with Swansea C), 1982 v Cz, Ic, USSR, Sp, E, S, Ni; 1983 v N; 1984 v R (sub); (with Southampton), S; 1985 v Sp, N (1 + 1 sub); 1986 v H; (with Cardiff C), 1987 v USSR (35)

Curtis, E. R. (Cardiff C), 1928 v S; (with Birmingham C), 1932 v S; 1934 v Ni (3)

Daniel, R. W. (Arsenal), 1951 v E, Ni, P; 1952 v E, S, Ni, R of UK; 1953 v S, E, Ni, F, Y; (with Sunderland), 1954 v E, S, Ni; 1955 v E, Ni; 1957 v S, E, Ni, Cz (21)

Darvell, S. (Oxford University), 1897 v S, Ni (2)

Davies, A. (Manchester U), 1983 v Ni, Br; 1984 v E, Ni; 1985 v Ic (2), N; (with Newcastle U), 1986 v H; (with Swansea C), 1988 v Ma, I; 1989 v Ho; (with Bradford C), 1990 v Fi, Ei (13)

Davies, A. (Wrexham), 1876 v S; 1877 v S (2)

Davies, A. (Druids), 1904 v S; (with Middlesbrough), 1905 v S (2)

Davies, A. O. (Barmouth), 1885 v Ni; 1886 v E, S; (with Swifts), 1887 v E, S; 1888 v E, Ni; (with Wrexham), 1889 v S; (with Crewe Alex), 1890 v E (9)

Davies, A. T. (Shrewsbury), 1891 v Ni (1)

Davies, C. (Charlton Ath), 1972 v R (sub) (1)

Davies, D. (Bolton W), 1904 v S, Ni; 1908 v E (sub) (3)

Davies, D. C. (Brecon), 1899 v Ni; (with Hereford), 1900 v Ni (2)

Davies, D. W. (Treharris), 1912 v Ni; (with Oldham Ath), 1913 v Ni (2)

Davies, E. Lloyd (Stoke C), 1904 v E; 1907 v E, S, Ni; (with Northampton T), 1908 v S; 1909 v Ni; 1910 v Ni; 1911 v E, S; 1912 v E, S; 1913 v E, S; 1914 v Ni, E, S (16)

Davies, E. R. (Newcastle U), 1953 v S, E; 1954 v E, S; 1958 v E, EG (6)

Davies, G. (Fulham), 1980 v T, Ic; 1982 v Sp (sub), F (sub); 1983 v E, Bul, S, Ni, Br; 1984 v R (sub), S (sub), E, Ni; 1985 v Ic; (with Manchester C), 1986 v S.Ar, Ei (16)

Davies, Rev. H. (Wrexham), 1928 v Ni (1)

Davies, Idwal (Liverpool Marine), 1923 v S (1)

Davies, J. E. (Oswestry), 1885 v E (1)

Davies, Jas (Wrexham), 1878 v S (1)

Davies, John (Wrexham), 1879 v S (1)

Davies, Jos (Newton Heath), 1888 v E, S, Ni; 1889 v S; 1890 v E; (with Wolverhampton W), 1892 v E; 1893 v E (7)

Davies, Jos (Everton), 1889 v S, Ni; (with Chirk), 1891 v Ni; (with Ardwick), v E, S; (with Sheffield U), 1895 v E, S, Ni; (with Manchester C), 1896 v E; (with Millwall), 1897 v E; (with Reading), 1900 v E (11)

Davies, J. P. (Druids), 1883 v E, Ni (2)

Davies, Ll. (Wrexham), 1907 v Ni; 1910 v Ni, S, E; (with Everton), 1911 v S, Ni; (with Wrexham), 1912 v Ni, S, E; 1913 v Ni, S, E; 1914 v Ni (13)

Davies, L. S. (Cardiff C), 1922 v E, S, Ni; 1923 v E, S, Ni; 1924 v E, S, Ni; 1925 v S, Ni; 1926 v E, Ni; 1927 v E, Ni; 1928 v S, Ni, E; 1929 v S, Ni, E; 1930 v E, S (23)

Davies, O. (Wrexham), 1890 v S (1)

Davies, R. (Wrexham), 1883 v Ni; 1884 v Ni; 1885 v Ni (3)

Davies, R. (Druids), 1885 v E (1)

Davies, R. O. (Wrexham), 1892 v Ni, E (2)

Davies, R. T. (Norwich C), 1964 v Ni; 1965 v E; 1966 v Br (2), Ch; (with Southampton), 1967 v S, E, Ni; 1968 v S, Ni, WG; 1969 v S, E, Ni, I, WG, R of UK; 1970 v E, S, Ni; 1971 v Cz, S, E, Ni; 1972 v R, E, S, N; (with Portsmouth), 1974 v E (29)

Davies, R. W. (Bolton W), 1964 v E; 1965 v E, S, Ni, D, Gr, USSR; 1966 v E, S, Ni, USSR, D, Br (2), Ch (sub); 1967 v S; (with Newcastle U), E; 1968 v S, Ni, WG; 1969 v S, E, Ni, I; 1970 v EG; 1971 v R, Cz; (with Manchester C), 1972 v E, S, Ni; (with Manchester U), 1973 v E, S (sub), Ni; (with Blackpool), 1974 v Pol (34)

Davies, S. I. (Manchester U), 1996 v Sw (sub) (1)

Davies, Stanley (Preston NE), 1920 v E, S, Ni; (with Everton), 1921 v E, S, Ni; (with WBA), 1922 v E, S, Ni; 1923 v S; 1925 v S, Ni; 1926 v S, E, Ni; 1927 v S; 1928 v S; (with Rotherham U), 1930 v Ni (18)

Davies, T. (Oswestry), 1886 v E (1)

Davies, T. (Druids), 1903 v E, Ni, S; 1904 v S (4)

Davies, W. (Wrexham), 1884 v Ni (1)

Davies, W. (Swansea T), 1924 v E, S, Ni; (with Cardiff C), 1925 v E, S, Ni; 1926 v E, S, Ni; 1927 v S; 1928 v Ni; (with Notts Co), 1929 v E, S, Ni; 1930 v E, S, Ni (17)

Davies, William (Wrexham), 1903 v Ni; 1905 v Ni; (with Blackburn R), 1908 v E, S; 1909 v E, S, Ni; 1911 v E, S, Ni; 1912 v Ni (11)

Davies, W. C. (C Palace), 1908 v S; (with WBA), 1909 v E; 1910 v S; (with C Palace), 1914 v E (4)

Davies, W. D. (Everton), 1975 v H, L, S, E, Ni; 1976 v Y (2), E, Ni; 1977 v WG, S (2), Cz, E, Ni; 1978 v K; (with Wrexham), S, Cz, WG, Ir, E, S, Ni; 1979 v Ma, T, WG, S, E, Ni, Ma; 1980 v Ei, WG, T, E, S, Ni, Ic; 1981 v T, Cz, Ei, T, S, E, USSR; (with Swansea C), 1982 v Cz, Ic, USSR, Sp, E, S, F; 1983 v Y (52)

Davies, W. H. (Oswestry), 1876 v S; 1877 v S; 1879 v E; 1880 v E (4)

Davies, W. O. (Millwall Ath), 1913 v E, S, Ni; 1914 v S, Ni (5)

Davis, G. (Wrexham), 1978 v Ir, E (sub), Ni (3)

Day, A. (Tottenham H), 1934 v Ni (1)

Deacy, N. (PSV Eindhoven), 1977 v Cz, S, E, Ni; 1978 v K (sub), S (sub), Cz (sub), WG, Ir, S (sub), Ni; (with Beringen), 1979 v T (12)

Dearson, D. J. (Birmingham), 1939 v S, Ni, F (3)

Derrett, S. C. (Cardiff C), 1969 v S, WG; 1970 v I; 1971 v Fi (4)

Dewey, F. T. (Cardiff Corinthians), 1931 v E, S (2)

Dibble, A. (Luton T), 1986 v Ca (1+1 sub); (with Manchester C), 1989 v Is (3)

Doughty, J. (Druids), 1886 v S; (with Newton Heath), 1887 v S, Ni; 1888 v E, S, Ni; 1889 v S; 1890 v E (8)

Doughty, R. (Newton Heath and Druids), 1888 v S, Ni (2)

Durban, A. (Derby Co), 1966 v Br (sub); 1967 v Ni; 1968 v E, S, Ni, WG; 1969 v EG, S, E, Ni, WG; 1970 v E, S, Ni, EG, I; 1971 v R, S, E, Ni, Cz, Fi; 1972 v Fi, Cz, E, S, Ni (27)

Dwyer, P. (Cardiff C), 1978 v Ir, E, S, Ni; 1979 v T, S, E, Ni, Ma (sub); 1980 v WG (10)

Edwards, C. (Wrexham), 1878 v S (1)

Edwards, C. N. H. (Swansea C), 1996 v Sw (sub) (1)

Edwards, G. (Birmingham C), 1947 v E, S, Ni; 1948 v E, S, Ni; (with Cardiff C), 1949 v Ni, P, Bel, Sw; 1950 v E, S (12)

Edwards, H. (Wrexham Civil Service), 1878 v S; 1880 v E, S; 1882 v S; 1883 v S; 1884 v Ni; 1887 v Ni (8)

Edwards, J. H. (Wanderers), 1876 v S (1)

Edwards, J. H. (Oswestry), 1895 v Ni; 1897 v E, Ni (3)

Edwards, J. H. (Aberystwyth), 1898 v Ni (1)

Edwards, L. T. (Charlton Ath), 1957 v Ni, EG (2)

Edwards, R. I. (Chester), 1978 v K (sub); 1979 v Ma, WG; (with Wrexham), 1980 v T (sub) (4)

Edwards, R. W. (Bristol C), 1998 v T (sub), Bel, Ma (sub), Tun (sub) (4)

Edwards, T. (Linfield), 1932 v S (1)

Egan, W. (Chirk), 1892 v S (1)

Ellis, B. (Motherwell), 1932 v E; 1933 v E, S; 1934 v S; 1936 v E; 1937 v S (6)

Ellis, E. (Nunhead), 1931 v S; (with Oswestry), E; 1932 v Ni (3)

Emanuel, W. J. (Bristol C), 1973 v E (sub), Ni (sub) (2)

England, H. M. (Blackburn R), 1962 v Ni, Br, M; 1963 v Ni, H; 1964 v E, S, Ni; 1965 v E, D, Gr (2), USSR, Ni, I; 1966 v E, S, Ni, USSR, D; (with Tottenham H), 1967 v S, E; 1968 v E, Ni, WG; 1969 v EG; 1970 v R of UK, EG, E, S, Ni, I; 1971 v R; 1972 v Fi, E, S, Ni; 1973 v E (3), S; 1974 v Pol; 1975 v H, L (44)

Evans, B. C. (Swansea C), 1972 v Fi, Cz; 1973 v E (2), Pol, S; (with Hereford U), 1974 v Pol (7)

Evans, D. G. (Reading), 1926 v Ni; 1927 v Ni, E; (with Huddersfield T), 1929 v S (4)

Evans, H. P. (Cardiff C), 1922 v E, S, Ni; 1924 v E, S, Ni (6)

Evans, I. (C Palace), 1976 v A, E, Y (2), E, Ni; 1977 v WG, S (2), Cz, E, Ni; 1978 v K (13)

Evans, J. (Oswestry), 1893 v Ni; 1894 v E, Ni (3)

Evans, J. (Cardiff C), 1912 v Ni; 1913 v Ni; 1914 v S; 1920 v S, Ni; 1922 v Ni; 1923 v E, Ni (8)

Evans, J. H. (Southend U), 1922 v E, S, Ni; 1923 v S (4)

Evans, Len (Aberdare Ath), 1927 v Ni; (with Cardiff C), 1931 v E, S; (with Birmingham), 1934 v Ni (4)

Evans, M. (Oswestry), 1884 v E (1)

Evans, R. (Clapton), 1902 v Ni (1)

Evans, R. E. (Wrexham), 1906 v E, S; (with Aston Villa), Ni; 1907 v E; 1908 v E, S; (with Sheffield U), 1909 v S; 1910 v E, S, Ni (10)

Evans, R. O. (Wrexham), 1902 v Ni; 1903 v E, S, Ni; (with Blackburn R), 1908 v Ni; (with Coventry C), 1911 v E, Ni; 1912 v E, S, Ni (10)

Evans, R. S. (Swansea T), 1964 v Ni (1)

Evans, T. J. (Clapton Orient), 1927 v S; 1928 v E, S; (with Newcastle U), Ni (4)

Evans, W. (Tottenham H), 1933 v Ni; 1934 v E, S; 1935 v E; 1936 v E, Ni (6)

Evans, W. A. W. (Oxford University), 1876 v S; 1877 v S (2)

Evans, W. G. (Bootle), 1890 v E; 1891 v E; (with Aston Villa), 1892 v E (3)

Evelyn, E. C. (Crusaders), 1887 v E (1)

Eyton-Jones, J. A. (Wrexham), 1883 v Ni; 1884 v Ni, E, S (4)

Farmer, G. (Oswestry), 1885 v E, S (2)

Felgate, D. (Lincoln C), 1984 v R (sub) (1)

Finnigan, R. J. (Wrexham), 1930 v Ni (1)

Flynn, B. (Burnley), 1975 v L (2 sub), H (sub), S, E, Ni; 1976 v A, E, Y (2), E, Ni; 1977 v WG (sub), S (2), Cz, E, Ni; 1978 v K (2), S; (with Leeds U), Cz, WG, Ir (sub), E, S, Ni; 1979 v Ma, T, S, E, Ni, Ma; 1980 v Ei, WG, T, E, S, Ni, Ic; 1981 v T, Cz, Ei, T, S, E, USSR; 1982 v Cz, USSR, E, S, Ni, F; 1983 v N; (with Burnley), Y, E, Bul, S, Ni, Br; 1984 v N, R, Bul, Y, S, N, Is (66)

Ford, T. (Swansea T), 1947 v S; (with Aston Villa), 1947 v Ni; 1948 v S, Ni; 1949 v E, S, Ni, P, Bel, Sw; 1950 v E, S, Ni, Bel; 1951 v S; (with Sunderland), 1951 v E, Ni, P, Sw; 1952 v E, S, Ni, R of UK; 1953 v E, Ni, F, Y; (with Cardiff C), 1954 v A; 1955 v S, E, Ni, Y; 1956 v S, Ni, E, A; 1957 v S (38)

Foulkes, H. E. (WBA), 1932 v Ni (1)

Foulkes, W. I. (Newcastle U), 1952 v E, S, Ni, R of UK; 1953 v E, S, F, Y; 1954 v E, S, Ni (11)

Foulkes, W. T. (Oswestry), 1884 v Ni; 1885 v S (2)

Fowler, J. (Swansea T), 1925 v E; 1926 v E, Ni; 1927 v S; 1928 v S; 1929 v E (6)

Garner, J. (Aberystwyth), 1896 v S (1)

Giggs, R. J. (Manchester U), 1992 v G (sub), L (sub), R (sub); 1993 v Fa (sub), Bel (sub + 1), RCS, Fa; 1994 v RCS, Cy, R; 1995 v Alb, Bul; 1996 v G, Alb, Sm; 1997 v Sm, T, Bel; 1998 v T, Bel; 1999 v I (2), D (24)

Giles, D. (Swansea C), 1980 v E, S, Ni, Ic; 1981 v T, Cz, T (sub), E (sub), USSR (sub); (with C Palace), 1982 v Sp (sub); 1983 v Ni (sub), Br (12)

Gillam, S. G. (Wrexham), 1889 v S (sub), Ni; (with Shrewsbury), 1890 v E, Ni; (with Clapton), 1894 v S (5)

Glascodine, G. (Wrexham), 1879 v E (1)

Glover, E. M. (Grimsby T), 1932 v S; 1934 v Ni; 1936 v S; 1937 v E, S, Ni; 1939 v Ni (7)

Godding, G. (Wrexham), 1923 v S, Ni (2)

Godfrey, B. C. (Preston NE), 1964 v Ni; 1965 v D, I (3)

Goodwin, U. (Ruthin), 1881 v E (1)

Goss, J. (Norwich C), 1991 v Ic, Pol (sub); 1992 v A; 1994 v Cy (sub), R (sub); Se; 1995 v Alb; 1996 v Sw (sub), Sm (sub) (9)

Gough, R. T. (Oswestry White Star), 1883 v S (1)

Gray, A. (Oldham Ath), 1924 v E, S, Ni; 1925 v E, S, Ni; 1926 v E, S; 1927 v S; (with Manchester C), 1928 v E, S; 1929 v E, S, Ni; (with Manchester Central), 1930 v S; (with Tranmere R), 1932 v E, S, Ni; (with Chester), 1937 v E, S, Ni; 1938 v E, S, Ni (24)

Green, A. W. (Aston Villa), 1901 v Ni; (with Notts Co), 1903 v E; 1904 v S, Ni; 1906 v Ni, E; (with Nottingham F), 1907 v E; 1908 v S (8)

Green, C. R. (Birmingham C), 1965 v USSR, I; 1966 v E, S, USSR, Br (2); 1967 v E; 1968 v E, S, Ni, WG; 1969 v S, I, Ni (sub) (15)

Green, G. H. (Charlton Ath), 1938 v Ni; 1939 v E, Ni, F (4)

Green, R. M. (Wolverhampton W), 1998 v Ma, Tun (2)

Grey, Dr W. (Druids), 1876 v S; 1878 v S (2)

Griffiths, A. T. (Wrexham), 1971 v Cz (sub); 1975 v A, H (2), L (2), E; Ni; 1976 v A, E, S, E (sub), Ni, Y (2); 1977 v WG, S (17)

Griffiths, F. J. (Blackpool), 1900 v E, S (2)

Griffiths, G. (Chirk), 1887 v Ni (1)

Griffiths, J. H. (Swansea T), 1953 v Ni (1)

Griffiths, L. (Wrexham), 1902 v S (1)

Jones, A. T. (Nottingham F), 1905 v E; (with Notts Co), 1906 v E (2)

Jones, Bryn (Wolverhampton W), 1935 v Ni; 1936 v E, S, Ni; 1937 v E, S, Ni; 1938 v E, S, Ni; (with Arsenal), 1939 v E, S, Ni; 1947 v S, Ni; 1948 v E; 1949 v S (17)

Jones, B. S. (Swansea T), 1963 v S, E, Ni, H (2); 1964 v S, Ni; (with Plymouth Arg), 1965 v D; (with Cardiff C), 1969 v S, E, Ni, I (sub), WG, EG, R of UK (15)

Jones, Charlie (Nottingham F), 1926 v E; 1927 v S, Ni; 1928 v E; (with Arsenal), 1930 v E, S; 1932 v E; 1933 v F (8)

Jones, Cliff (Swansea T), 1954 v A; 1956 v E, Ni, S, A; 1957 v E, S, Ni, Cz (2), EG; 1958 v EG, E, S, Is (2); (with Tottenham H), 1958 v Ni, H (2), M, Se, Br; 1959 v Ni; 1960 v E, S, Ni; 1961 v S, E, Ni, Sp, H, Ei; 1962 v E, Ni, S, Br (2), M; 1963 v S, Ni, H; 1964 v E, S, Ni; 1965 v E, S, Ni, D, Gr (2), USSR, I; 1967 v S, E; 1968 v E, S, WG; (with Fulham), 1969 v I, R of UK (59)

Jones, C. W. (Birmingham), 1935 v Ni; 1939 v F (2)

Jones, D. (Chirk), 1888 v S, Ni; (with Bolton W), 1889 v E, S, Ni; 1890 v E; 1891 v S; 1892 v Ni; 1893 v E; 1894 v E; 1895 v E; 1898 v S; (with Manchester C), 1900 v E, Ni (14)

Jones, D. E. (Norwich C), 1976 v S, E (sub); 1978 v S, Cz, WG, Ir, E; 1980 v E (8)

Jones, D. O. (Leicester C), 1934 v E, Ni; 1935 v E, S; 1936 v E, Ni; 1937 v Ni (7)

Jones, Evan (Chelsea), 1910 v S, Ni; (with Oldham Ath), 1911 v E, S; 1912 v E, S; (with Bolton W), 1914 v Ni (7)

Jones, F. R. (Bangor), 1885 v E, Ni; 1886 v S (3)

Jones, F. W. (Small Heath), 1893 v S (1)

Jones, G. P. (Wrexham), 1907 v S, Ni (2)

Jones, H. (Aberaman), 1902 v Ni (1)

Jones, Humphrey (Bangor), 1885 v E, Ni, S; 1886 v E, Ni, S; (with Queen's Park), 1887 v E; (with East Stirlingshire), 1889 v E, Ni; 1890 v E, S, Ni; (with Queen's Park), 1891 v E, S (14)

Jones, Ivor (Swansea T), 1920 v S, Ni; 1921 v Ni, E; 1922 v S, Ni; (with WBA), 1923 v E, Ni; 1924 v S; 1926 v Ni (10)

Jones, Jeffrey (Llandrindod Wells), 1908 v Ni; 1909 v Ni; 1910 v S (3)

Jones, J. (Druids), 1876 v S (1)

Jones, J. (Berwyn Rangers), 1883 v S, Ni; 1884 v S (3)

Jones, J. (Wrexham), 1925 v Ni (1)

Jones, J. L. (Sheffield U), 1895 v E, S, Ni; 1896 v Ni, S, E; 1897 v Ni, S, E; (with Tottenham H), 1898 v Ni, E, S; 1899 v S, Ni; 1900 v S; 1902 v E, S, Ni; 1904 v E, S, Ni (21)

Jones, J. Love (Stoke C), 1906 v S; (with Middlesbrough), 1910 v Ni (2)

Jones, J. O. (Bangor), 1901 v S, Ni (2)

Jones, J. P. (Liverpool), 1976 v A, E, S; 1977 v WG, S (2), Cz, E, Ni; 1978 v K (2), S, Cz, WG, Ir, E, S, Ni; (with Wrexham), 1979 v Ma, T, WG, S, E, Ni, Ma; 1980 v Ei, WG, T, E, S, Ni, Ic; 1981 v T, Ei, T, S, E, USSR; 1982 v Cz, Ic, USSR, Sp, E, S, Ni, F; 1983 v N; (with Chelsea), Y, E, Bul, S, Ni, Br; 1984 v N, R, Bul, Y, S, E, Ni, N, Is; 1985 v Ic, N, S, N; (with Huddersfield T), 1986 v S, H, Ei, U, Ca (2) (72)

Jones, J. T. (Stoke C), 1912 v E, S, Ni; 1913 v E, Ni; 1914 v S, Ni; 1920 v E, S, Ni; (with C Palace), 1921 v E, S; 1922 v E, S, Ni (15)

Jones, K. (Aston Villa), 1950 v S (1)

Jones, Leslie J. (Cardiff C), 1933 v F; (with Coventry C), 1935 v Ni; 1936 v S; 1937 v E, S, Ni; (with Arsenal), 1938 v E, S, Ni; 1939 v E, S (11)

Jones, P. L. (Liverpool), 1997 v S (sub); (with Tranmere R), 1998 v T (sub) (2)

Jones, P. S. (Stockport Co), 1997 v S (sub); (with Southampton), 1998 v T (sub), Br, Jam, Ma; 1999 v I, D, Bl, Sw, I, D (11)

Jones, P. W. (Bristol R), 1971 v Fi (1)

Jones, R. (Bangor), 1887 v S; 1889 v E; (with Crewe Alex), 1890 v E (3)

Jones, R. (Leicester Fosse), 1898 v S (1)

Jones, R. (Druids), 1899 v S (1)

Jones, R. (Bangor), 1900 v S, Ni (2)

Jones, R. (Millwall), 1906 v S, Ni (2)

Jones, R. A. (Druids), 1884 v E, Ni, S; 1885 v S (4)

Jones, R. A. (Sheffield W), 1994 v Es (1)

Jones, R. S. (Everton), 1894 v Ni (1)

Jones, S. (Wrexham), 1887 v Ni; (with Chester), 1890 v S (2)

Jones, S. (Wrexham), 1893 v S, Ni; (with Burton Swifts), 1895 v S; 1896 v E, Ni; (with Druids), 1899 v E (6)

Jones, T. (Manchester U), 1926 v Ni; 1927 v E, Ni; 1930 v Ni (4)

Jones, T. D. (Aberdare), 1908 v Ni (1)

Jones, T. G. (Everton), 1938 v Ni; 1939 v E, S, Ni; 1947 v E, S; 1948 v E, S, Ni; 1949 v E, Ni, P, Bel, Sw; 1950 v E, S, Bel (17)

Jones, T. J. (Sheffield W), 1932 v Ni; 1933 v F (2)

Jones, V. P. (Wimbledon), 1995 v Bul (2), G, Ge; 1996 v Sw; 1997 v Ho, T, Ei, Bel (9)

Jones, W. E. A. (Swansea T), 1947 v E, S; (with Tottenham H), 1949 v E, S (4)

Jones, W. J. (Aberdare), 1901 v E, S; (with West Ham U), 1902 v E, S (4)

Jones, W. Lot (Manchester C), 1905 v E, Ni; 1906 v E, S, Ni; 1907 v E, S, Ni; 1908 v S; 1909 v E, S, Ni; 1910 v E; 1911 v E; 1913 v E, S; 1914 v S, Ni; (with Southend U), 1920 v E, Ni (20)

Jones, W. P. (Druids), 1889 v E, Ni; (with Wynstay), 1890 v S, Ni (4)

Jones, W. R. (Aberystwyth), 1897 v S (1)

Keenor, F. C. (Cardiff C), 1920 v E, Ni; 1921 v E, Ni, S; 1922 v Ni; 1923 v E, Ni, S; 1924 v E, Ni, S; 1925 v E, Ni, S; 1926 v S; 1927 v E, Ni, S; 1928 v E, Ni, S; 1929 v E, Ni, S; 1930 v E, Ni, S; 1931 v E, Ni, S; (with Crewe Alex), 1933 v S (32)

Kelly, F. C. (Wrexham), 1899 v S, Ni; (with Druids), 1902 v Ni (3)

Kelsey, A. J. (Arsenal), 1954 v Ni, A; 1955 v S, Ni, Y; 1956 v E, Ni, S, A; 1957 v E, Ni, S, Cz (2), EG; 1958 v E, S, Ni, Is (2), H (2), M, Se, Br; 1959 v E, S; 1960 v E, Ni, S; 1961 v E, Ni, S, H, Sp (2); 1962 v E, S, Ni, Br (2) (41)

Kenrick, S. L. (Druids), 1876 v S; 1877 v S; (with Oswestry), 1879 v E, S; (with Shropshire Wanderers), 1881 v E (5)

Ketley, C. F. (Druids), 1882 v Ni (1)

King, J. (Swansea T), 1955 v E (1)

Kinsey, N. (Norwich C), 1951 v Ni, P, Sw; 1952 v E; (with Birmingham C), 1954 v Ni; 1956 v E, S (7)

Knill, A. R. (Swansea C), 1989 v Ho (1)

Krzywicki, R. L. (WBA), 1970 v EG, I; (with Huddersfield T), Ni, E, S; 1971 v R, Fi; 1972 v Cz (sub) (8)

Lambert, R. (Liverpool), 1947 v S; 1948 v E; 1949 v P, Bel, Sw (5)

Latham, G. (Liverpool), 1905 v E, S; 1906 v S; 1907 v E, S, Ni; 1908 v E; 1909 v Ni; (with Southport Central), 1910 v E; (with Cardiff C), 1913 v Ni (10)

Law, B. J. (QPR), 1990 v Se (1)

Lawrence, E. (Clapton Orient), 1930 v Ni; (with Notts Co), 1932 v S (2)

Lawrence, S. (Swansea T), 1932 v Ni; 1933 v F; 1934 v S, E, Ni; 1935 v E, S; 1936 v S (8)

Lea, A. (Wrexham), 1889 v E; 1891 v S, Ni; 1893 v Ni (4)

Lea, C. (Ipswich T), 1965 v Ni, I (2)

Leary, P. (Bangor), 1889 v Ni (1)

Leek, K. (Leicester C), 1961 v S, E, Ni, H, Sp (2); (with Newcastle U), 1962 v S; (with Birmingham C), v Br (sub), M; 1963 v E; 1965 v S, Gr; (with Northampton T), 1965 v Gr (13)

Legg, A. (Birmingham C), 1996 v Sw, Sm (sub); 1997 v Ho (sub), Ei; (with Cardiff C), 1999 v D (sub) (5)

Lever, A. R. (Leicester C), 1953 v S (1)

Lewis, B. (Chester), 1891 v Ni; (with Wrexham), 1892 v S, E, Ni; (with Middlesbrough), 1893 v S, E; (with Wrexham), 1894 v S, Ni; 1895 v S (10)

Lewis, D. (Arsenal), 1927 v E; 1928 v Ni; 1930 v E (3)

Lewis, D. (Swansea C), 1983 v Br (sub) (1)

Lewis, D. J. (Swansea T), 1933 v E, S (2)

Lewis, D. M. (Bangor), 1890 v Ni, S (2)

Lewis, J. (Bristol R), 1906 v E (1)

Lewis, J. (Cardiff C), 1926 v S (1)

Lewis, T. (Wrexham), 1881 v E, S (2)

Lewis, W. (Bangor), 1885 v E; 1886 v E, S; 1887 v E, S; 1888 v E; 1889 v E, Ni, S; (with Crewe Alex), 1890 v E; 1891 v E, S; 1892 v E, S, Ni; 1894 v E, S, Ni; (with Chester), 1895 v S, Ni, E; 1896 v E, S, Ni; (with Manchester C), 1897 v E, S; (with Chester), 1898 v Ni (27)

Lewis, W. L. (Swansea T), 1927 v E, Ni; 1928 v E, Ni; 1929 v S; (with Huddersfield T), 1930 v E (6)

Llewellyn, C. M. (Norwich C), 1998 v Ma (sub), Tun (sub) (2)

Lloyd, B. W. (Wrexham), 1976 v A, E, S (3)

Lloyd, J. W. (Wrexham), 1879 v S; (with Newtown), 1885 v S (2)

Lloyd, R. A. (Ruthin), 1891 v Ni; 1895 v S (2)

Lockley, A. (Chirk), 1898 v Ni (1)

Lovell, S. (C Palace), 1982 v USSR (sub); (with Millwall), 1985 v N; 1986 v S (sub), H (sub), Ca (1+1 sub) (6)

Lowrie, G. (Coventry C), 1948 v E, S, Ni; (with Newcastle U), 1949 v P (4)

Lowndes, S. (Newport Co), 1983 v S (sub), Br (sub); (with Millwall), 1985 v N (sub); 1986 v S.Ar (sub), Ei, U, Ca (2); (with Barnsley), 1987 v Fi (sub); 1988 v Se (sub) (10)

Lucas, P. M. (Leyton Orient), 1962 v Ni, M; 1963 v S, E (4)

Lucas, W. H. (Swansea T), 1949 v S, Ni, P, Bel, Sw; 1950 v E; 1951 v E (7)
Lumberg, A. (Wrexham), 1929 v Ni; 1930 v E, S; (with Wolverhampton W), 1932 v S (4)

McCarthy, T. P. (Wrexham), 1899 v Ni (1)
McMillan, R. (Shrewsbury Engineers), 1881 v E, S (2)
Maguire, G. T. (Portsmouth), 1990 v Fi (sub), Ho, WG, Ei, Se; 1992 v Br (sub), G (7)
Mahoney, J. F. (Stoke C), 1968 v E; 1969 v EG; 1971 v Cz; 1973 v E (3), Pol, S, Ni; 1974 v Pol, E, S, Ni; 1975 v A, H (2), L (2), S, E, Ni; 1976 v A, Y (2), E, Ni; 1977 v WG, Cz, S, E, Ni; (with Middlesbrough), 1978 v K (2), S, Cz, Ir, E (sub), S, Ni; 1979 v WG, S, E, Ni, Ma; (with Swansea C), 1980 v Ei, WG, T (sub); 1982 v Ic, USSR; 1983 v Y, E (51)
Mardon, P. J. (WBA), 1996 v G (sub) (1)
Marriott, A. (Wrexham), 1996 v Sw (sub); 1997 v S; 1998 v Bel, Br (sub), Tun (5)
Martin, T. J. (Newport Co), 1930 v Ni (1)
Marustik, C. (Swansea C), 1982 v Sp, E, S, Ni, F; 1983 v N (6)
Mates, J. (Chirk), 1891 v Ni; 1897 v E, S (3)
Mathews, R. W. (Liverpool), 1921 v Ni; (with Bristol C), 1923 v E; (with Bradford), 1926 v Ni (3)
Matthews, W. (Chester), 1905 v Ni; 1908 v E (2)
Matthias, J. S. (Brymbo), 1896 v S, Ni; (with Shrewsbury), 1897 v E, S; (with Wolverhampton W), 1899 v S (5)
Matthias, T. J. (Wrexham), 1914 v S, E; 1920 v Ni, S, E; 1921 v S, E, Ni; 1922 v S, E, Ni; 1923 v S (12)
Mays, A. W. (Wrexham), 1929 v Ni (1)
Medwin, T. C. (Swansea T), 1953 v Ni, F, Y; (with Tottenham H), 1957 v E, S, Ni, Cz (2), EG; 1958 v E, S, Ni, Is (2), H (2), M, Br; 1959 v E, S, Ni; 1960 v E, S, Ni; 1961 v S, Ei, E, Sp; 1963 v E, H (30)
Melville, A. K. (Swansea C), 1990 v WG, Ei, Se, Cr (sub); (with Oxford U), 1991 v Ic, Pol, WG; 1992 v Br, G, L, R, Ho, J (sub); 1993 v RCS, Fa (sub); (with Sunderland), 1994 v RCS (sub), R, N, Se, Es; 1995 v Alb, Mol (sub), Ge, Bul; 1996 v G, Alb, Sm; 1997 v Sm, Ho (2), T; 1998 v T; (with Fulham), 1999 v I, D (34)
Meredith, S. (Chirk), 1900 v S; 1901 v S, E, Ni; (with Stoke C), 1902 v E; 1903 v Ni; 1904 v E; (with Leyton), 1907 v E (8)
Meredith, W. H. (Manchester C), 1895 v E, Ni; 1896 v E, Ni; 1897 v Ni, S; 1898 v E, Ni; 1899 v E; 1900 v E, Ni; 1901 v E, Ni; 1902 v E, S; 1903 v E, S, Ni; 1904 v E; 1905 v E, S; (with Manchester U), 1907 v E, S, Ni; 1908 v E, Ni; 1909 v E, S, Ni; 1910 v E, S, Ni; 1911 v E, S, Ni; 1912 v E, S, Ni; 1913 v E, S, Ni; 1914 v E, S, Ni; 1920 v E, S, Ni (48)
Mielczarek, R. (Rotherham U), 1971 v Fi (1)
Millership, H. (Rotherham Co), 1920 v E, S, Ni; 1921 v E, S, Ni (6)
Millington, A. H. (WBA), 1963 v S, E, H; (with C Palace), 1965 v E, USSR; (with Peterborough U), 1966 v Ch, Br; 1967 v E, Ni; 1968 v Ni, WG; 1969 v I, EG; (with Swansea T), 1970 v E, S, Ni; 1971 v Cz, Fi; 1972 v Fi (sub), Cz, R (21)
Mills, T. J. (Clapton Orient), 1934 v E, Ni; (with Leicester C), 1935 v E, S (4)
Mills-Roberts, R. H. (St Thomas' Hospital), 1885 v E, S, Ni; 1886 v E; 1887 v E; (with Preston NE), 1888 v E, Ni; (with Llanberis), 1892 v E (8)
Moore, G. (Cardiff C), 1960 v E, S, Ni; 1961 v Ei, Sp; (with Chelsea), 1962 v Br; 1963 v Ni, H; (with Manchester U), 1964 v S, Ni; (with Northampton T), 1966 v Ni, Ch; (with Charlton Ath), 1969 v S, E, Ni, R of UK; 1970 v E, S, Ni, I; 1971 v R (21)
Morgan, J. R. (Cambridge University), 1877 v S; (with Swansea T), 1879 v S; (with Derby School Staff), 1880 v E, S; 1881 v E, S; 1882 v E, S, Ni; (with Swansea T), 1883 v E (10)
Morgan, J. T. (Wrexham), 1905 v Ni (1)
Morgan-Owen, H. (Oxford University), 1902 v S; 1906 v E, Ni; (with Welshpool), 1907 v S (5)
Morgan-Owen, M. M. (Oxford University), 1897 v S, Ni; 1898 v E, S; 1899 v S; 1900 v E; (with Corinthians), 1901 v S, E; 1903 v S; 1906 v S, E, Ni; 1907 v E (13)
Morley, E. J. (Swansea T), 1925 v E; (with Clapton Orient), 1929 v E, S, Ni (4)
Morris, A. G. (Aberystwyth), 1896 v E, Ni, S; (with Swindon T), 1897 v E; 1898 v S; (with Nottingham F), 1899 v E, S; 1903 v E, S; 1905 v E, S; 1907 v E, S; 1908 v E; 1910 v E, S, Ni; 1911 v E, S, Ni; 1912 v E (21)
Morris, C. (Chirk), 1900 v E, S, Ni; (with Derby Co), 1901 v E, S, Ni; 1902 v E, S; 1903 v E, S, Ni; 1904 v Ni; 1905 v E, S, Ni; 1906 v S; 1907 v S; 1908 v E, S; 1909 v E, S, Ni; 1910 v E, S, Ni; (with Huddersfield T), 1911 v E, S, Ni (27)
Morris, E. (Chirk), 1893 v E, S, Ni (3)

Morris, H. (Sheffield U), 1894 v S; (with Manchester C), 1896 v E; (with Grimsby T), 1897 v E (3)
Morris, J. (Oswestry), 1887 v S (1)
Morris, J. (Chirk), 1898 v Ni (1)
Morris, R. (Chirk), 1900 v E, Ni; 1901 v Ni; 1902 v S; (with Shrewsbury T), 1903 v E, Ni (6)
Morris, R. (Druids), 1902 v E, S; (with Newtown), Ni; (with Liverpool), 1903 v S, Ni; 1904 v E, S, Ni; (with Leeds C), 1906 v S; (with Grimsby T), 1907 v Ni; (with Plymouth Arg), 1908 v Ni (11)
Morris, S. (Birmingham), 1937 v E, S; 1938 v E, S; 1939 v F (5)
Morris, W. (Burnley), 1947 v Ni; 1949 v E; 1952 v S, Ni, R of UK (5)
Moulsdale, J. R. B. (Corinthians), 1925 v Ni (1)
Murphy, J. P. (WBA), 1933 v F, E, Ni; 1934 v E, S; 1935 v E, S, Ni; 1936 v E, S, Ni; 1937 v S, Ni; 1938 v E, S (15)

Nardiello, D. (Coventry C), 1978 v Cz, WG (sub) (2)
Neal, J. E. (Colwyn Bay), 1931 v E, S (2)
Neilson, A. B. (Newcastle U), 1992 v Ei; 1994 v Se, Es; 1995 v Ge; (with Southampton), 1997 v Ho (5)
Newnes, J. (Nelson), 1926 v Ni (1)
Newton, L. F. (Cardiff Corinthians), 1912 v Ni (1)
Nicholas, D. S. (Stoke C), 1923 v S; (with Swansea T), 1927 v E, Ni (3)
Nicholas, P. (C Palace), 1979 v S (sub), Ni (sub), Ma; 1980 v Ei, WG, T, E, S, Ni, Ic; 1981 v T, Cz, E; (with Arsenal), T, S, E, USSR; 1982 v Cz, Ic, USSR, Sp, E, S, Ni, F; 1983 v Y, Bul, S, Ni; 1984 v N, Bul, N, Is; (with C Palace), 1985 v Sp; (with Luton T), N, S, Sp, N; 1986 v S, H, S.Ar, Ei, U, Ca (2); 1987 v Fi (2) USSR, Cz; (with Aberdeen), 1988 v D (2), Cz, Y, Se; (with Chelsea), 1989 v Ho, Fi, Is, Se, WG; 1990 v Fi, Ho, WG, Ei, Se, Cr; 1991 v D (sub), Bel, L, Ei; (with Watford), Bel, Pol, WG; 1992 v L (73)
Nicholls, J. (Newport Co), 1924 v E, Ni; (with Cardiff C), 1925 v E, S (4)
Niedzwiecki, E. A. (Chelsea), 1985 v N (sub); 1988 v D (2)
Nock, W. (Newtown), 1897 v Ni (1)
Nogan, L. M. (Watford), 1992 v A (sub); (with Reading), 1996 v Mol (2)
Norman, A. J. (Hull C), 1986 v Ei (sub), U, Ca; 1988 v Ma, I (5)
Nurse, M. T. G. (Swansea T), 1960 v E, Ni; 1961 v S, E, H, Ni, Ei, Sp (2); (with Middlesbrough), 1963 v E, H; 1964 v S (12)

O'Callaghan, E. (Tottenham H), 1929 v Ni; 1930 v S; 1932 v S, E; 1933 v Ni, S, E; 1934 v Ni, S, E; 1935 v E (11)
Oliver, A. (Blackburn R), 1905 v E; (with Bangor), S (2)
O'Sullivan, P. A. (Brighton), 1973 v S (sub); 1976 v S; 1979 v Ma (sub) (3)
Oster, J. M. (Everton), 1998 v Br, Jam (2)
Owen, D. (Oswestry), 1879 v E (1)
Owen, E. (Ruthin Grammar School), 1884 v E, Ni, S (3)
Owen, G. (Chirk), 1888 v S; (with Newton Heath), 1889 v S, Ni; 1893 v Ni (4)
Owen, J. (Newton Heath), 1892 v E (1)
Owen, Trevor (Crewe Alex), 1899 v E, S (2)
Owen, T. (Oswestry), 1879 v E (1)
Owen, W. (Chirk), 1884 v E; 1885 v Ni; 1887 v E; 1888 v E; 1889 v E, Ni, S; 1890 v S, Ni; 1891 v E, S, Ni; 1892 v E, S; 1893 v S, Ni (16)
Owen, W. P. (Ruthin), 1880 v E, S; 1881 v E, S; 1882 v E, S, Ni; 1883 v E, S; 1884 v E, S, Ni (12)
Owens, J. (Wrexham), 1902 v S (1)

Page, M. E. (Birmingham C), 1971 v Fi; 1972 v S, Ni; 1973 v E (1+1 sub), Ni; 1974 v S, Ni; 1975 v H, L, S, E, Ni; 1976 v E, Y (2), E, Ni; 1977 v WG, S; 1978 v K (sub+1), WG, Ir, E, S; 1979 v Ma, WG (28)
Page, R. J. (Watford), 1997 v T, Bel, S; 1998 v T, Bel (sub), Br; 1999 v I (7)
Palmer, D. (Swansea T), 1957 v Cz; 1958 v E, EG (3)
Parris, J. E. (Bradford), 1932 v Ni (1)
Parry, B. J. (Swansea T), 1951 v S (1)
Parry, C. (Everton), 1891 v S; 1893 v E; 1894 v E; 1895 v E, S; (with Newtown), 1896 v E, S, Ni; 1897 v Ni; 1898 v E, S, Ni (13)
Parry, E. (Liverpool), 1922 v S; 1923 v E, Ni; 1925 v Ni; 1926 v Ni (5)
Parry, M. (Liverpool), 1901 v E, S, Ni; 1902 v E, S, Ni; 1903 v E, S; 1904 v E, Ni; 1906 v E; 1908 v E, S, Ni; 1909 v E, S (16)
Parry, T. D. (Oswestry), 1900 v E, S, Ni; 1901 v E, S, Ni; 1902 v E (7)
Parry, W. (Newtown), 1895 v Ni (1)
Pascoe, C. (Swansea C), 1984 v N, Is; (with Sunderland), 1989 v Fi, Is, WG (sub); 1990 v Ho (sub), WG (sub); 1991 v Ei, Ic (sub); 1992 v Br (10)

Paul, R. (Swansea T), 1949 v E, S, Ni, P, Sw; 1950 v E, S, Ni, Bel; (with Manchester C), 1951 v S, E, Ni, P, Sw; 1952 v E, S, Ni, R of UK; 1953 v S, E, Ni, F, Y; 1954 v E, S, Ni; 1955 v S, E, Y; 1956 v E, Ni, S, A (33)

Peake, E. (Aberystwyth), 1908 v Ni; (with Liverpool), 1909 v Ni, S, E; 1910 v S, Ni; 1911 v Ni; 1912 v E; 1913 v E, Ni; 1914 v Ni (11)

Peers, E. J. (Wolverhampton W), 1914 v Ni, S, E; 1920 v E, S; 1921 v S, Ni, E; (with Port Vale), 1922 v E, S, Ni; 1923 v E (12)

Pembridge, M. A. (Luton T), 1992 v Br, Ei, R; (with Derby Co), Ho, J (sub); 1993 v Bel (sub), Ei; 1994 v N (sub); 1995 v Alb (sub), Mol, Ge (sub); (with Sheffield W), 1996 v Mol, G, Alb, Sw, Sm; 1997 v Ho (2), T, Ei, Bel, S; 1998 v Bel, Br, Jam, Ma, Tun; (with Benfica), 1999 v D (sub), Bl, Sw, I (sub), D (sub) (33)

Perry, E. (Doncaster R), 1938 v E, S, Ni (3)

Perry, J. (Cardiff C), 1994 v N (1)

Phennah, E. (Civil Service), 1878 v S (1)

Phillips, C. (Wolverhampton W), 1931 v Ni; 1932 v E; 1933 v S; 1934 v E, S, Ni; 1935 v E, S, Ni; 1936 v S; (with Aston Villa), 1936 v E, Ni; 1938 v S (13)

Phillips, D. (Plymouth Arg), 1984 v E, Ni, N; (with Manchester C), 1985 v Sp, Ic, S, Sp, N; 1986 v S, H, S.Ar, Ei, U; (with Coventry C), 1987 v Fi, Cz; 1988 v D (2), Cz, Y, Se; 1989 v Se, WG; (with Norwich C), 1990 v Fi, Ho, WG, Ei, Se; 1991 v D, Bel, Ic, Pol, WG; 1992 v L, Ei, A, R, Ho (sub), Arg, J; 1993 v Fa, Cy, Bel, Ei, Bel, RCS, Fa; (with Nottingham F), 1994 v RCS, Cy, R, N, Se, Es; 1995 v Alb, Mol, Ge, Bul (2), G, Ge; 1996 v Mol (sub), Alb, I (62)

Phillips, L. (Cardiff C), 1971 v Cz, S, E, Ni; 1972 v Cz, R, S, Ni; 1973 v E; 1974 v Pol (sub), Ni; 1975 v A; (with Aston Villa), H (2), L (2), S, E, Ni; 1976 v A, E, Y (2), E, Ni; 1977 v WG, S (2), Cz, E; 1978 v K (2), S, Cz, WG, E, S; 1979 v Ma; (with Swansea C), T, WG, S, E, Ni, Ma; 1980 v Ei, WG, T, S (sub), Ni, Ic; 1981 v T, Cz, T, S, E, USSR; (with Charlton Ath), 1982 v Cz, USSR (58)

Phillips, T. J. S. (Chelsea), 1973 v E; 1974 v E; 1975 v H (sub); 1978 v K (4)

Phoenix, H. (Wrexham), 1882 v S (1)

Poland, G. (Wrexham), 1939 v Ni, F (2)

Pontin, K. (Cardiff C), 1980 v E (sub), S (2)

Powell, A. (Leeds U), 1947 v E, S; 1948 v E, S, Ni; (with Everton), 1949 v E; 1950 v Bel; (with Birmingham C), 1951 v S (8)

Powell, D. (Wrexham), 1968 v WG; (with Sheffield U), 1969 v S, E, Ni, I, WG; 1970 v E, S, Ni, EG; 1971 v R (11)

Powell, I. V. (QPR), 1947 v E; 1948 v E, S, Ni; (with Aston Villa), 1949 v Bel; 1950 v S, Bel; 1951 v S (8)

Powell, J. (Druids), 1878 v S; 1880 v E, S; 1882 v E, S, Ni; 1883 v E, S, Ni; (with Bolton W), 1884 v E; (with Newton Heath), 1887 v E, S; 1888 v E, S, Ni (15)

Powell, Seth (WBA), 1885 v S; 1886 v E, Ni; 1891 v E, S; 1892 v E, S (7)

Price, H. (Aston Villa), 1907 v S; (with Burton U), 1908 v Ni; (with Wrexham), 1909 v S, E, Ni (5)

Price, J. (Wrexham), 1877 v S; 1878 v S; 1879 v E; 1880 v E, S; 1881 v E, S; (with Druids), 1882 v S, E, Ni; 1883 v S, Ni (12)

Price, P. (Luton T), 1980 v E, S, Ni; 1981 v T, Cz, Ei, T, S, E, USSR; (with Tottenham H), 1982 v USSR, Sp, F; 1983 v N, Y, E, Bul, S, Ni; 1984 v N, R, Bul, Y, S (sub) (25)

Pring, K. D. (Rotherham U), 1966 v Ch, D; 1967 v Ni (3)

Pritchard, H. K. (Bristol C), 1985 v N (sub) (1)

Pryce-Jones, A. W. (Newtown), 1895 v E (1)

Pryce-Jones, W. E. (Cambridge University), 1887 v S; 1888 v S, E, Ni; 1890 v Ni (5)

Pugh, A. (Rhostyllen), 1889 v S (sub) (1)

Pugh, D. H. (Wrexham), 1896 v S, Ni; 1897 v S, Ni; (with Lincoln C), 1900 v S; 1901 v S, E (7)

Pugsley, J. (Charlton Ath), 1930 v Ni (1)

Pullen, W. J. (Plymouth Arg), 1926 v E (1)

Rankmore, F. E. J. (Peterborough), 1966 v Ch (sub) (1)

Ratcliffe, K. (Everton), 1981 v Cz, Ei, T, S, E, USSR; 1982 v Cz, Ic, USSR, Sp, E; 1983 v Y, E, Bul, S, Ni, Br; 1984 v N, R, Bul, Y, S, E, Ni, N, Is; 1985 v Ic, Sp, Ic, N, S, Sp; 1986 v S, H, S.Ar, U; 1987 v Fi (2), USSR, Cz; 1988 v D (2), Cz; 1989 v Fi, Is, Se, WG; 1990 v Fi; 1991 v D, Bel (2), L, Ei, Ic, Pol, WG; 1992 v Br, G; (with Cardiff C), 1993 v Bel (59)

Rea, J. C. (Aberystwyth), 1894 v Ni, S, E; 1895 v S; 1896 v S, Ni; 1897 v S, Ni; 1898 v Ni (9)

Ready, K. (QPR), 1997 v Ei; 1998 v Bel, Br, Ma, Tun (5)

Reece, G. I. (Sheffield U), 1966 v E, S, Ni, USSR; 1967 v S; 1969 v R of UK (sub); 1970 v I (sub); 1971 v S, E, Ni, Fi; 1972 v Fi, R, E (sub), S, Ni; (with Cardiff C), 1973 v E (sub), Ni; 1974 v Pol (sub), E, S, Ni; 1975 v A, H (2), L (2), S, Ni (29)

Reed, W. G. (Ipswich T), 1955 v S, Y (2)

Rees, A. (Birmingham C), 1984 v N (sub) (1)

Rees, J. M. (Luton T), 1992 v A (sub) (1)

Rees, R. R. (Coventry C), 1965 v S, E, Ni, D, Gr (2), I, R; 1966 v E, S, Ni, R, D, Br (2), Ch; 1967 v E, Ni; 1968 v E, S, Ni; (with WBA), WG; 1969 v I; (with Nottingham F), 1969 v WG, EG, S (sub), R of UK; 1970 v E, S, Ni, EG, I; 1971 v Cz, R, E (sub), Ni (sub), Fi; 1972 v Cz (sub), R (39)

Rees, W. (Cardiff C), 1949 v Ni, Bel, Sw; (with Tottenham H), 1950 v Ni (4)

Richards, A. (Barnsley), 1932 v S (1)

Richards, D. (Wolverhampton W), 1931 v Ni; 1933 v E, S, Ni; 1934 v E, S, Ni; 1935 v E, S, Ni; 1936 v S; (with Brentford), 1936 v E, Ni; 1937 v S, E; (with Birmingham), Ni; 1938 v E, S, Ni; 1939 v E, S (21)

Richards, G. (Druids), 1899 v E, S, Ni; (with Oswestry), 1903 v Ni; (with Shrewsbury), 1904 v S; 1905 v Ni (6)

Richards, R. W. (Wolverhampton W), 1920 v E, S; 1921 v Ni; 1922 v E, S; (with West Ham U), 1924 v E, S, Ni; (with Mold), 1926 v S (9)

Richards, S. V. (Cardiff C), 1947 v E (1)

Richards, W. E. (Fulham), 1933 v Ni (1)

Roach, J. (Oswestry), 1885 v Ni (1)

Robbins, W. W. (Cardiff C), 1931 v E, S; 1932 v Ni, E, S; (with WBA), 1933 v F, E, S, Ni; 1934 v S; 1936 v S (11)

Roberts, A. M. (QPR), 1993 v Ei (sub); 1997 v Sm (sub) (2)

Roberts, D. F. (Oxford U), 1973 v Pol, E (sub), Ni; 1974 v E, S; 1975 v A; (with Hull C), L, Ni; 1976 v S, Ni, Y; 1977 v E (sub), Ni; 1978 v K (1+1 sub), S, Ni (17)

Roberts, I. W. (Watford), 1990 v Ho; (with Huddersfield T), 1992 v A, Arg, J; (with Leicester C), 1994 v Se; 1995 v Alb (sub), Mol (7)

Roberts, Jas (Wrexham), 1913 v S, Ni (2)

Roberts, J. (Corwen), 1879 v S; 1880 v E, S; 1882 v E, S, Ni; (with Berwyn R), 1883 v E (7)

Roberts, J. (Ruthin), 1881 v S; 1882 v S (2)

Roberts, J. (Bradford C), 1906 v Ni; 1907 v Ni (2)

Roberts, J. G. (Arsenal), 1971 v S, E, Ni, Fi; 1972 v Fi, E, Ni; (with Birmingham C), 1973 v E (2), Pol, S, Ni; 1974 v Pol, E, S, Ni; 1975 v A, H, S, E; 1976 v E, S (22)

Roberts, J. H. (Bolton), 1949 v Bel (1)

Roberts, P. S. (Portsmouth), 1974 v E; 1975 v A, H, L (4)

Roberts, R. (Druids), 1884 v S; (with Bolton W), 1887 v S; 1888 v S, E; 1889 v S, E; 1890 v S; 1892 v Ni; (with Preston NE), S (9)

Roberts, R. (Wrexham), 1886 v Ni; 1887 v Ni; 1891 v Ni (3)

Roberts, R. (Rhos), 1891 v Ni; (with Crewe Alex), 1893 v E (2)

Roberts, W. (Llangollen), 1879 v E, S; 1880 v E, S; (with Berwyn R), 1881 v S; 1883 v S (6)

Roberts, W. (Wrexham), 1886 v E, S, Ni; 1887 v Ni (4)

Roberts, W. H. (Ruthin), 1882 v S; 1883 v E, S, Ni; (with Rhyl), 1884 v S (6)

Robinson, J. R. C. (Charlton Ath), 1996 v Alb (sub), Sw, Sm; 1997 v Sm, Ho (1 + sub), Ei, S; 1998 v Bel, Br; 1999 v I, D (sub), Bl, Sw, I, D (16)

Rodrigues, P. J. (Cardiff C), 1965 v Ni, Gr (2); 1966 v USSR, E, S, D; (with Leicester C), Ni, Br (2), Ch; 1967 v S; 1968 v E, S, Ni; 1969 v E, Ni, EG, R of UK; 1970 v E, S, Ni, EG; (with Sheffield W), 1971 v R, E, S, Cz, Ni; 1972 v Fi, Cz, R, E, Ni (sub); 1973 v E (3), Pol, S, Ni; 1974 v Pol (40)

Rogers, J. P. (Wrexham), 1896 v E, S, Ni (3)

Rogers, W. (Wrexham), 1931 v E, S (2)

Roose, L. R. (Aberystwyth), 1900 v Ni; (with London Welsh), 1901 v E, S, Ni; (with Stoke C), 1902 v E, S; 1904 v E; (with Everton), 1905 v S, E; (with Stoke C), 1906 v E, S, Ni; 1907 v E, S, Ni; (with Sunderland), 1908 v E, S; 1909 v E, S, Ni; 1910 v E, S, Ni; 1911 v S (24)

Rouse, R. V. (C Palace), 1959 v Ni (1)

Rowlands, A. C. (Tranmere R), 1914 v E (1)

Rowley, T. (Tranmere R), 1959 v Ni (1)

Rush, I. (Liverpool), 1980 v S (sub), Ni; 1981 v E (sub); 1982 v Ic (sub), USSR, E, S, Ni, F; 1983 v N, Y, E, Bul; 1984 v N, R, Bul, Y, S, E, Ni; 1985 v Ic, N, S, Sp; 1986 v S, S.Ar, Ei, U; 1987 v Fi (2), USSR, Cz; (with Juventus), 1988 v D, Cz, Y, Se, Ma, I; (with Liverpool), 1989 v Ho, Fi, Se, WG; 1990 v Fi, Ei; 1991 v D, Bel (2), L, Ei, Pol, WG; 1992 v G, R, N, Se; 1993 v Fa, Cy, Bel (2), RCS, Fa; 1994 v RCS, Cy, R, N, Se, Es; 1995 v Alb, Ge, Bul, G, Ge; 1996 v Mol, I (73)

Russell, M. R. (Merthyr T), 1912 v S, Ni; 1914 v E; (with Plymouth Arg), 1920 v E, S, Ni; 1921 v E, S, Ni; 1922 v E, Ni; 1923 v E, S, Ni; 1924 v E, S, Ni; 1925 v E, S; 1926 v E, S; 1928 v S; 1929 v E (23)

Sabine, H. W. (Oswestry), 1887 v Ni (1)

Saunders, D. (Brighton & HA), 1986 v Ei (sub), Ca (2); 1987 v Fi, USSR (sub); (with Oxford U), 1988 v Y, Se, Ma, I (sub); 1989 v Ho (sub), Fi; (with Derby Co), Is, Se, WG; 1990 v Fi, Ho, WG, Se, Cr; 1991 v D, Bel (2), L, Ei, Ic, Pol, WG; (with Liverpool), 1992 v Br, G, Ei, R, Ho, Arg, J; 1993 v Fa; (with Aston Villa), Cy, Bel (2), RCS, Fa; 1994 v RCS, Cy, R, N (sub); 1995 v Ge, Bul (2), G, Ge; (with Galatasaray), 1996 v G, Alb, Sm; (with Nottingham F), 1997 v Sm, Ho (2), T, Bel, S; 1998 v T, Bel, Br; (with Sheffield U), Ma, Tun; 1999 v I (sub), D, Bl; (with Benfica) Sw, I, D (69)
Savage, R. W. (Crewe Alex), 1996 v Alb (sub), Sw (sub), Sm (sub); 1997 v Ei (sub), S; (with Leicester C), 1998 v T, Bel, Jam, Tun; 1999 v I (sub), D, Bl, Sw (13)
Savin, G. (Oswestry), 1878 v S (1)
Sayer, P. (Cardiff C), 1977 v Cz, S, E, Ni; 1978 v K (2), S (7)
Scrine, F. H. (Swansea T), 1950 v E, Ni (2)
Sear, C. R. (Manchester C), 1963 v E (1)
Shaw, E. G. (Oswestry), 1882 v Ni; 1884 v S, Ni (3)
Sherwood, A. T. (Cardiff C), 1947 v E, Ni; 1948 v S, Ni; 1949 v E, S, Ni, P, Sw; 1950 v E, S, Ni, Bel; 1951 v E, S, Ni, P, Sw; 1952 v E, S, Ni, R of UK; 1953 v S, E, Ni, F, Y; 1954 v E, S, Ni, A; 1955 v S, E, Y, Ni; 1956 v E, S, Ni, A; (with Newport Co), 1957 v E, S (41)
Shone, W. A. (Oswestry), 1879 v E (1)
Shortt, W. W. (Plymouth Arg), 1947 v Ni; 1950 v Ni, Bel; 1952 v E, S, Ni, R of UK; 1953 v S, E, Ni, F, Y (12)
Showers, D. (Cardiff C), 1975 v E (sub), Ni (2)
Sidlow, C. (Liverpool), 1947 v E, S; 1948 v E, S, Ni; 1949 v S; 1950 v E (7)
Sisson, H. (Wrexham Olympic), 1885 v Ni; 1886 v S, Ni (3)
Slatter, N. (Bristol R), 1983 v S; 1984 v N (sub), Is; 1985 v Ic, Sp, Ic, N, S, Sp, N; (with Oxford U), 1986 v H (sub), S.Ar, Ca (2); 1987 v Fi (sub), Cz; 1988 v D (2), Cz, Ma, I; 1989 v Is (sub) (22)
Smallman, D. P. (Wrexham), 1974 v E (sub), S (sub), Ni; (with Everton), 1975 v H (sub), E, Ni (sub); 1976 v A (7)
Southall, N. (Everton), 1982 v Ni; 1983 v N, E, Bul, S, Ni, Br; 1984 v N, R, Bul, Y, S, E, Ni, N, Is; 1985 v Ic, Sp, Ic, N, S, Sp, N; 1986 v S, H, S.Ar, Ei; 1987 v USSR, Fi, Cz; 1988 v D, Cz, Y, Se; 1989 v Ho, Fi, Se, WG; 1990 v Fi, Ho, WG, Ei, Se, Cr; 1991 v D, Bel (2), L, Ei, Ic, Pol, WG; 1992 v Br, G, L, Ei, A, R, Ho, Arg, J; 1993 v Fa, Cy, Bel, Ei, Bel, RCS, Fa; 1994 v RCS, Cy, R, N, Se, Es; 1995 v Alb, Mol, Ge, Bul (2), G, Ge; 1996 v Mol, G, Alb, I, Sm; 1997 v Sm, Ho (2), T, Bel; 1998 v Y (92)
Speed, G. A. (Leeds U), 1990 v Cr (sub); 1991 v D, L (sub), Ei (sub), Ic, WG (sub); 1992 v Br, G (sub), L, Ei, R, Ho, Arg, J; 1993 v Fa, Cy, Bel, Ei, Bel, Fa (sub); 1994 v RCS (sub), Cy, R, N, Se; 1995 v Alb, Mol, Ge, Bul (2), G, I, Sw (sub); (with Everton), 1997 v Sm (sub), Ho (2), T, Ei, Bel, S; 1998 v T, Br; (with Newcastle U), Jam, Ma, Tun; 1999 v I, D, Sw, I, D (52)
Sprake, G. (Leeds U), 1964 v S, Ni; 1965 v S, D, Gr; 1966 v E, Ni, USSR; 1967 v S; 1968 v S, E; 1969 v S, E, Ni, WG, R of UK; 1970 v EG, I; 1971 v R, S, E, Ni; 1972 v Fi, E, S, Ni; 1973 v E (2), Pol, S, Ni; 1974 v Pol; (with Birmingham C), S, Ni; 1975 v A, H, L (37)
Stansfield, F. (Cardiff C), 1949 v S (1)
Stevenson, B. (Leeds U), 1978 v Ni; 1979 v Ma, T, S, E, Ni, Ma; 1980 v WG, T, Ic (sub); 1982 v Cz; (with Birmingham C), Sp, S, Ni, F (15)
Stevenson, N. (Swansea C), 1982 v E, S, Ni; 1983 v N (4)
Stitfall, R. F. (Cardiff C), 1953 v E; 1957 v Cz (2)
Sullivan, D. (Cardiff C), 1953 v Ni, F, Y; 1954 v Ni; 1955 v E, Ni; 1957 v E, S; 1958 v Ni, H (2), Se, Br; 1959 v S, Ni; 1960 v E, S (17)
Symons, C. J. (Portsmouth), 1992 v Ei, Ho, Arg, J; 1993 v Fa, Cy, Bel, Ei, RCS, Fa; 1994 v RCS, Cy, R; 1995 v Mol, Ge (sub), Bul, G, Ge; (with Manchester C), 1996 v Mol, G, I, Sw; 1997 v Ho (2), Ei, Bel, S; (with Fulham), 1999 v I, D, Bl, Sw (31)

Tapscott, D. R. (Arsenal), 1954 v A; 1955 v S, E, Ni, Y; 1956 v E, Ni, S, A; 1957 v Ni, Cz, EG; (with Cardiff C), 1959 v E, Ni (14)
Taylor, G. K. (C Palace), 1996 v Alb, I (sub); (with Sheffield U), Sw; 1997 v Sm (sub), Ho (sub), Ei (sub); 1998 v Bel (sub), Jam (8)
Taylor, J. (Wrexham), 1898 v E (1)
Taylor, O. D. S. (Newtown), 1893 v S, Ni; 1894 v S, Ni (4)
Thomas, A. (Druids), 1899 v Ni; 1900 v S (2)
Thomas, D. A. (Swansea T), 1957 v Cz; 1958 v EG (2)
Thomas, D. S. (Fulham), 1948 v E, S, Ni; 1949 v S (4)
Thomas, E. (Cardiff Corinthians), 1925 v E (1)
Thomas, G. (Wrexham), 1885 v E, S (2)
Thomas, H. (Manchester U), 1927 v E (1)

Thomas, M. (Wrexham), 1977 v WG, S (1+1 sub), Ni (sub); 1978 v K (sub), S, Cz, Ir, E, Ni (sub); 1979 v Ma; (with Manchester U), T, WG, Ma (sub); 1980 v Ei, WG (sub), T, E, S, Ni; 1981 v Cz, S, E, USSR; (with Everton), 1982 v Cz; (with Brighton & HA), USSR (sub), Sp, E, S (sub), Ni (sub); (with Stoke C), 1983 v N, Y, E, Bul, S, Ni, Br; 1984 v R, Bul, Y; (with Chelsea), S, E; 1985 v Ic, Sp, Ic, S, Sp, N; 1986 v S; (with WBA), H, S.Ar (sub) (51)
Thomas, M. R. (Newcastle U), 1987 v Fi (1)
Thomas, R. J. (Swindon T), 1967 v Ni; 1968 v WG; 1969 v E, Ni, I, WG, R of UK; 1970 v E, S, Ni, EG, I; 1971 v S, E, Ni, R, Cz; 1972 v Fi, Cz, R, E, S, Ni; 1973 v E (2), Pol, S, Ni; 1974 v Pol; (with Derby Co), E, S, Ni; 1975 v H (2), L (2), S, E, Ni; 1976 v A, Y, E; 1977 v Cz, S, E, Ni; 1978 v K, S; (with Cardiff C), Cz (50)
Thomas, T. (Bangor), 1898 v S, Ni (2)
Thomas, W. R. (Newport Co), 1931 v E, S (2)
Thomson, D. (Druids), 1876 v S (1)
Thomson, G. F. (Druids), 1876 v S; 1877 v S (2)
Toshack, J. B. (Cardiff C), 1969 v S, E, Ni, WG, EG, R of UK; 1970 v EG, I; (with Liverpool), 1971 v S, E, Ni, Fi; 1972 v Fi, E; 1973 v E (3), Pol, S; 1975 v A, H (2), L (2), S, E; 1976 v Y (2), E; 1977 v S; 1978 v K (2), S, Cz; (with Swansea C), 1979 v WG (sub), S, E, Ni, Ma; 1980 v WG (40)
Townsend, W. (Newtown), 1887 v Ni; 1893 v Ni (2)
Trainer, H. (Wrexham), 1895 v E, S, Ni (3)
Trainer, J. (Bolton W), 1887 v S; (with Preston NE), 1888 v S; 1889 v E; 1890 v S; 1891 v S; 1892 v Ni, S; 1893 v E; 1894 v Ni, E; 1895 v Ni, E; 1896 v S; 1897 v Ni, S, E; 1898 v S, E; 1899 v Ni, S (20)
Trollope, P. J. (Derby Co), 1997 v S; 1998 v Br (sub); (with Fulham), Jam (sub), Ma, Tun (5)
Turner, H. G. (Charlton Ath), 1937 v E, S, Ni; 1938 v E, S, Ni; 1939 v Ni, F (8)
Turner, J. (Wrexham), 1892 v E (1)
Turner, R. E. (Wrexham), 1891 v E, Ni (2)
Turner, W. H. (Wrexham), 1887 v E, Ni; 1890 v S; 1891 v E, S (5)

Van Den Hauwe, P. W. R. (Everton), 1985 v Sp; 1986 v S, H; 1987 v USSR, Fi, Cz; 1988 v D (2), Cz, Y, I; 1989 v Fi, Se (13)
Vaughan, Jas (Druids), 1893 v E, S, Ni; 1899 v E (4)
Vaughan, John (Oswestry), 1879 v S; 1880 v S; 1881 v E, S; 1882 v E, S, Ni; 1883 v E, S, Ni; (with Bolton W), 1884 v E (11)
Vaughan, J. O. (Rhyl), 1885 v Ni; 1886 v Ni, E, S (4)
Vaughan, N. (Newport Co), 1983 v Y (sub), Br; 1984 v N; (with Cardiff C), R, Bul, Y, Ni (sub), N, Is; 1985 v Sp (sub) (10)
Vaughan, T. (Rhyl), 1885 v E (1)
Vearncombe, G. (Cardiff C), 1958 v EG; 1961 v Ei (2)
Vernon, T. R. (Blackburn R), 1957 v Ni, Cz (2), EG; 1958 v E, S, EG, Se; 1959 v S; (with Everton), 1960 v Ni; 1961 v S, E, Ei; 1962 v Ni, Br (2), M; 1963 v S, E, H; 1964 v E, S; (with Stoke C), 1965 v Ni, Gr, I; 1966 v E, S, Ni, USSR, D; 1967 v Ni; 1968 v E (32)
Villars, A. K. (Cardiff C), 1974 v E, S, Ni (sub) (3)
Vizard, E. T. (Bolton W), 1911 v E, S, Ni; 1912 v E, S; 1913 v S; 1914 v E, Ni; 1920 v E; 1921 v E, S, Ni; 1922 v E, S; 1923 v E, Ni; 1924 v E, S, Ni; 1926 v E, S; 1927 v S (22)

Walley, J. T. (Watford), 1971 v Cz (1)
Walsh, I. (C Palace), 1980 v Ei, T, E, S, Ic; 1981 v T, Cz, Ei, T, S, E, USSR; 1982 v Cz (sub), Ic; (with Swansea C), Sp, S (sub), Ni (sub), F (18)
Ward, D. (Bristol R), 1959 v E; (with Cardiff C), 1962 v E (2)
Warner, J. (Swansea T), 1937 v E; (with Manchester U), 1939 v F (2)
Warren, F. W. (Cardiff C), 1929 v Ni; (with Middlesbrough), 1931 v Ni; 1933 v F, E; (with Hearts), 1937 v Ni; 1938 v Ni (6)
Watkins, A. E. (Leicester Fosse), 1898 v E, S; (with Aston Villa), 1900 v E, S; (with Millwall), 1904 v Ni (5)
Watkins, W. M. (Stoke C), 1902 v E; 1903 v E, S; (with Aston Villa), 1904 v E, S, Ni; (with Sunderland), 1905 v E, S, Ni; (with Stoke C), 1908 v Ni (10)
Webster, C (Manchester U), 1957 v Cz; 1958 v H, M, Br (4)
Whatley, W. J. (Tottenham H), 1939 v E, S (2)
White, P. F. (London Welsh), 1896 v Ni (1)
Wilcock, A. R. (Oswestry), 1890 v Ni (1)
Wilding, J. (Wrexham Olympians), 1885 v E, S, Ni; 1886 v E, Ni; (with Bootle), 1887 v E; 1888 v S, Ni; (with Wrexham), 1892 v S (9)
Williams, A. (Reading), 1994 v Es; 1995 v Alb, Mol, G (sub), Ge; 1996 v Mol, I; (with Wolverhampton W), 1998 v Br (sub), Jam; 1999 v I, D, I (12)

Williams, A. L. (Wrexham), 1931 v E (1)
Williams, A. P. (Southampton), 1998 v Br (sub), Ma (2)
Williams, B. (Bristol C), 1930 v Ni (1)
Williams, B. D. (Swansea T), 1928 v Ni, E; 1930 v E, S; (with Everton), 1931 v Ni; 1932 v E; 1933 v E, S, Ni; 1935 v Ni (10)
Williams, D. G. (Derby Co), 1988 v Cz, Y, Se, Ma, I; 1989 v Ho, Is, Se, WG; 1990 v Fi, Ho; (with Ipswich T), 1993 v Ei; 1996 v G (sub) (13)
Williams, D. M. (Norwich C), 1986 v S.Ar (sub), U, Ca (2); 1987 v Fi (5)
Williams, D. R. (Merthyr T), 1921 v E, S; (with Sheffield W), 1923 v S; 1926 v S; 1927 v E, Ni; (with Manchester U), 1929 v E, S (8)
Williams, E. (Crewe Alex), 1893 v E, S (2)
Williams, E. (Druids), 1901 v E, Ni, S; 1902 v E, Ni (5)
Williams, G. (Chirk), 1893 v S; 1894 v S; 1895 v E, S, Ni; 1898 v Ni (6)
Williams, G. E. (WBA), 1960 v Ni; 1961 v S, E, Ei; 1963 v Ni, H; 1964 v E, S, Ni; 1965 v S, E, Ni, D, Gr (2), USSR, I; 1966 v Ni, Br (2), Ch; 1967 v S, E, Ni; 1968 v Ni; 1969 v I (26)
Williams, G. G. (Swansea T), 1961 v Ni, H, Sp (2); 1962 v E (5)
Williams, G. J. J. (Cardiff C), 1951 v Sw (1)
Williams, G. O. (Wrexham), 1907 v Ni (1)
Williams, H. J. (Swansea T), 1965 v Gr (2); 1972 v R (3)
Williams, H. T. (Newport Co), 1949 v Ni, Sw; (with Leeds U), 1950 v Ni; 1951 v S (4)
Williams, J. H. (Oswestry), 1884 v E (1)
Williams, J. J. (Wrexham), 1939 v F (1)
Williams, J. T. (Middlesbrough), 1925 v Ni (1)
Williams, J. W. (C Palace), 1912 v S, Ni (2)
Williams, R. (Newcastle U), 1935 v S, E (2)

Williams, R. P. (Caernarvon), 1886 v S (1)
Williams, S. G. (WBA), 1954 v A; 1955 v E, Ni; 1956 v E, S, A; 1958 v E, S, Ni, Is (2), H (2), M, Se, Br; 1959 v E, S, Ni; 1960 v E, S, Ni; 1961 v Ni, Ei, H, Sp (2); 1962 v E, S, Ni, Br (2), M; (with Southampton), 1963 v S, E, H (2); 1964 v E, S; 1965 v S, E, D; 1966 v D (43)
Williams, W. (Druids), 1876 v S; 1878 v S; (with Oswestry), 1879 v E, S; (with Druids), 1880 v E; 1881 v E, S; 1882 v E, S, Ni; 1883 v Ni (11)
Williams, W. (Northampton T), 1925 v S (1)
Witcomb, D. F. (WBA), 1947 v E, S; (with Sheffield W), 1947 v Ni (3)
Woosnam, A. P. (Leyton Orient), 1959 v S; (with West Ham U), E; 1960 v E, S, Ni; 1961 v S, E, Ni, Ei, Sp, H; 1962 v E, S, Ni, Br; (with Aston Villa), 1963 v Ni, H (17)
Woosnam, G. (Newton White Star), 1879 v S (1)
Worthington, T. (Newtown), 1894 v S (1)
Wynn, G. A. (Wrexham), 1909 v E, S, Ni; (with Manchester C), 1910 v E; 1911 v Ni; 1912 v E, S; 1913 v E, S; 1914 v E, S (11)
Wynn, W. (Chirk), 1903 v Ni (1)

Yorath, T. C. (Leeds U), 1970 v I; 1971 v S, E, Ni; 1972 v Cz, E, S, Ni; 1973 v E, Pol, S; 1974 v Pol, E, S, Ni; 1975 v A, H (2), L (2), S; 1976 v A, E, S, Y (2), E, Ni; (with Coventry C), 1977 v WG, S (2), Cz, E, Ni; 1978 v K (2), S, Cz, WG, Ir, E, S, Ni; 1979 v T, WG, S, E, Ni; (with Tottenham H), 1980 v Ei, T, E, S, Ni, Ic; 1981 v T, Cz; (with Vancouver W), Ei, T, USSR (59)
Young, E. (Wimbledon), 1990 v Cr; (with C Palace), 1991 v D, Bel (2), L, Ei; 1992 v G, L, Ei, A); 1993 v Fa, Cy, Bel, Ei, Bel, Fa; 1994 v RCS, Cy, R, N; (with Wolverhampton W) 1996 v Alb (21)

REPUBLIC OF IRELAND

Aherne, T. (Belfast C), 1946 v P, Sp; (with Luton T), 1950 v Fi, E, Fi, Se, Bel; 1951 v N, Arg, N; 1952 v WG (2), A, Sp; 1953 v F; 1954 v F (16)
Aldridge, J. W. (Oxford U), 1986 v W, U, Ic, Cz; 1987 v Bel, S, Pol; (with Liverpool), S, Bul, Bel, Br, L; 1988 v Bul, Pol, N, E, USSR, Ho; 1989 v Ni, Tun, Sp, F (sub), H, Ma (sub), H; 1990 v WG; (with Real Sociedad), Ni, Ma, Fi (sub), T, E, Eg, Ho, R, I; 1991 v T, E (2), Pol; (with Tranmere R), 1992 v H (sub), T, W (sub), Sw (sub), US (sub), Alb, I, P (sub); 1993 v La, D, Sp, D, Alb, La, Li; 1994 v Li, Ni, CzR, I (sub), M (sub); N; 1995 v La, Ni, P, Lie; 1996 v La, P, Ho, Ru; 1997 v Mac (sub) (69)
Ambrose, P. (Shamrock R), 1955 v N, Ho; 1964 v Pol, N, E (5)
Anderson, J. (Preston NE), 1980 v Cz (sub), US (sub); 1982 v Ch, Br, Tr; (with Newcastle U), 1984 v Chn; 1986 v W, Ic, Cz; 1987 v Bul, Bel, Br, L; 1988 v R (sub), Y (sub); 1989 v Tun (16)
Andrews, P. (Bohemians), 1936 v Ho (1)
Arrigan, T. (Waterford), 1938 v N (1)

Babb, P. A. (Coventry C), 1994 v Ru, Ho, Bol, G, CzR (sub), I, M, N, Ho; (with Liverpool), 1995 v La, Lie, Ni (2), P, Lie, A; 1996 v La, P, Ho, CzR; 1997 v Ic; 1998 v Li (sub), R, Arg (sub), M; 1999 v Cro, Para (sub), Se (sub), Ni (29)
Bailham, E. (Shamrock R), 1964 v E (1)
Barber, E. (Shelbourne), 1966 v Sp; (with Birmingham C), 1966 v Bel (2)
Barry, P. (Fordsons), 1928 v Bel; 1929 v Bel (2)
Beglin, J. (Liverpool), 1984 v Chn; 1985 v M, D, I, Is, E, N, Sw; 1986 v Sw, USSR, D, W; 1987 v Bel (sub), S, Pol (15)
Bermingham, J. (Bohemians), 1929 v Bel (1)
Bermingham, P. (St James' Gate), 1935 v H (1)
Braddish, S. (Dundalk), 1978 v T (sub), Pol (2)
Bonner, P. (Celtic), 1981 v Pol; 1982 v Alg; 1984 v Ma, Is, Chn; 1985 v I, Is, E, N; 1986 v U, Ic; 1987 v Bel (2), S (2), Pol, Bul, Br, L; 1988 v Bul, R, Y, N, E, USSR, Ho; 1989 v Sp, F, H, Sp, Ma, H; 1990 v WG, Ni, Ma, W, Fi, T, E, Eg, Ho, R, I; 1991 v Mor, T, E (2), W, Pol, US; 1992 v H, Pol, T, W, Sw, Alb, I; 1993 v La, D, Sp, W, Ni, D, Alb, La, Li; 1994 v Li, Sp, Ni, Ru, Ho, Bol, CzR, I, M, N, Ho; 1995 v Lie; 1996 v M, Bol (sub) (80)
Bradshaw, P. (St James' Gate), 1939 v Sw, Pol, H (2), G (5)
Brady, F. (Fordsons), 1926 v I; 1927 v I (2)

Brady, T. R. (QPR), 1964 v A (2), Sp (2), Pol, N (6)
Brady, W. L. (Arsenal), 1975 v USSR, T, Sw, USSR, Sw, WG; 1976 v T, N, Pol; 1977 v E, T, F (2), Sp, Bul; 1978 v Bul, N; 1979 v Ni, E, D, Bul, WG; 1980 v W, Bul, E, Cy; (with Juventus), 1981 v Ho, Bel, F, Cy, Bel; 1982 v Ho, F, Ch, Br, Tr; (with Sampdoria), 1983 v Ho, Sp, Ic, Ma; 1984 v Ic, Ho, Ma, Pol, Is; (with Internazionale), 1985 v USSR, N, D, I, E, N, Sp, Sw; 1986 v Sw, USSR, D, W; (with Ascoli), 1987 v Bel, S (2), Pol; (with West Ham U), Bul, Bel, Br, L; 1988 v L, Bul; 1989 v F, H (sub), H (sub); 1990 v WG, Fi (72)
Branagan, K. G. (Bolton W), 1997 v W (1)
Breen, G. (Birmingham C), 1996 v P (sub), Cro, Ho, US, M, Bol (sub); 1997 v Lie, Mac, Ic; (with Coventry C), v Mac; 1998 v Li (sub), R, CzR, Arg, M; 1999 v Ma, Y, Para, Se, Mac (20)
Breen, T. (Manchester U), 1937 v Sw, F; (with Shamrock R), 1947 v E, Sp, P (5)
Brennan, F. (Drumcondra), 1965 v Bel (1)
Brennan, S. A. (Manchester U), 1965 v Sp; 1966 v Sp, A, Bel; 1967 v Sp, T, Sp; 1969 v Cz, D, H, Pol (sub), WG; (with Waterford), 1971 v Pol, Se, I (19)
Brown, J. (Coventry C), 1937 v Sw, F (2)
Browne, W. (Bohemians), 1964 v A, Sp, E (3)
Buckley, L. (Shamrock R), 1984 v Pol (sub); (with Waregem), 1985 v M (2)
Burke, F. (Cork Ath), 1952 v WG (1)
Burke, J. (Cork), 1934 v Bel (1)
Burke, J. (Shamrock R), 1929 v Bel (1)
Byrne, A. B. (Southampton), 1970 v D, Pol, WG; 1971 v Pol, Se (2), I (2), A; 1973 v F, USSR (sub), F, N; 1974 v Pol (14)
Byrne, D. (Shelbourne), 1929 v Bel; (with Shamrock R), 1932 v Sp; (with Coleraine), 1934 v Bel (3)
Byrne, J. (Bray Unknowns), 1928 v Bel (1)
Byrne, J. (QPR), 1985 v I, Is (sub); E (sub), Sp (sub); 1987 v S (sub), Bel (sub), Br, L (sub); 1988 v L, Bul (sub), Is, R, Y (sub), Pol (sub); (with Le Havre), 1990 v WG (sub), W, Fi, T (sub), Ma; (with Brighton & HA), 1991 v W; (with Sunderland), 1992 v T, W; (with Millwall), 1993 v W (23)
Byrne, P. (Shamrock R), 1984 v Pol, Chn; 1985 v M; 1986 v D, W (sub), U (sub), Ic (sub), Cz (8)
Byrne, P. (Dolphin), 1931 v Sp; 1932 v Ho; (with Drumcondra), 1934 v Ho (3)
Byrne, S. (Bohemians), 1931 v Sp (1)

Campbell, A. (Santander), 1985 v I (sub), Is, Sp (3)

Campbell, N. (St Patrick's Ath), 1971 v A (sub); (with Fortuna Cologne), 1972 v Ir, Ec, Ch, P; 1973 v USSR, F (sub); 1975 v WG; 1976 v N; 1977 v Sp, Bul (sub) (11)

Cannon, H. (Bohemians), 1926 v I; 1928 v Bel (2)

Cantwell, N. (West Ham U), 1954 v L; 1956 v Sp, Ho; 1957 v D, WG, E (2); 1958 v D, Pol, A; 1959 v Pol, Cz (2); 1960 v Se, Ch, Se; 1961 v N; (with Manchester U), S (2); 1962 v Cz (2), A; 1963 v Ic (2), S; 1964 v A, Sp, E; 1965 v Pol, Sp; 1966 v Sp (2), A, Bel; 1967 v Sp, T (36)

Carey, B. P. (Manchester U), 1992 v US (sub); 1993 v W; (with Leicester C), 1994 v Ru (3)

Carey, J. J. (Manchester U), 1938 v N, Cz, Pol; 1939 v Sw, Pol, H (2), G; 1946 v P, Sp; 1947 v E, Sp, P; 1948 v P, Sp; 1949 v Sw, Bel, P, Se, Sp; 1950 v Fi, E, Fi, Se; 1951 v N, Arg, N; 1953 v F, A (29)

Carolan, J. (Manchester U), 1960 v Se, Ch (2)

Carr, S. (Tottenham H), 1999 v Se, Ni, Mac (3)

Carroll, B. (Shelbourne), 1949 v Bel; 1950 v Fi (2)

Carroll, T. R. (Ipswich T), 1968 v Pol; 1969 v Pol, A, D; 1970 v Cz, Pol, WG; 1971 v Se; (with Birmingham C), 1972 v Ir, Ec, Ch, P; 1973 v USSR (2), Pol, F, N (17)

Carsley, L. K. (Derby Co), 1998 v R, Bel (1 + sub), CzR, Arg, M; 1999 v Cro (sub), Ma (sub), Para (sub); (with Blackburn R) Ni, Mac (11)

Cascarino, A. G. (Gillingham), 1986 v Sw, USSR, D; (with Millwall), 1988 v Pol, N (sub), USSR (sub), Ho (sub); 1989 v Ni, Tun, Sp, F, H, Sp, Ma, H; 1990 v WG (sub), Ni, Ma; (with Aston Villa), W, Fi, T, E, Eg, Ho (sub), R (sub), I (sub); 1991 v Mor (sub), T (sub), E (2 sub), Pol (sub), Ch (sub), US; (with Celtic), 1992 v Pol, T; (with Chelsea), W, Sw, US (sub); 1993 v W, Ni (sub), D (sub), Alb (sub), La (sub); 1994 v Li (sub), Sp (sub), Ni (sub), Ru, Bol (sub), G, CzR, Ho (sub); (with Marseille), 1995 v La (sub), Ni (sub), P (sub), Lie (sub), A (sub); 1996 v A (sub), P (sub), Ho, Ru (sub), P, Cro (sub), Ho; 1997 v Lie (sub), Mac, Ic; (with Nancy), v W, Mac, R (sub), Lie (sub); 1998 v Li (sub), Ic (sub), Li, R, Bel (2); 1999 v Cro (sub), Ma (sub), Y (sub), Para (sub), Se (sub), Ni (sub), Mac (sub) (83)

Chandler, J. (Leeds U), 1980 v Cz (sub), US (2)

Chatton, H. A. (Shelbourne), 1931 v Sp; (with Dumbarton), 1932 v Sp; (with Cork), 1934 v Ho (3)

Clarke, J. (Drogheda U), 1978 v Pol (sub) (1)

Clarke, K. (Drumcondra), 1948 v P, Sp (2)

Clarke, M. (Shamrock R), 1950 v Bel (1)

Clinton, T. J. (Everton), 1951 v N; 1954 v F, L (3)

Coad, P. (Shamrock R), 1947 v E, Sp, P; 1948 v P, Sp; 1949 v Sw, Bel, P, Se; 1951 v N (sub); 1952 v Sp (11)

Coffey, T. (Drumcondra), 1950 v Fi (1)

Colfer, M. D. (Shelbourne), 1950 v Bel; 1951 v N (2)

Collins, F. (Jacobs), 1927 v I (1)

Conmy, O. M. (Peterborough U), 1965 v Bel; 1967 v Cz; 1968 v Cz; 1970 v Cz (5)

Connolly, D. J. (Watford), 1996 v P, Ho, US, M; 1997 v R, Lie; (with Feyenoord), 1998 v Li, Ic, Li, Bel (1 + sub), CzR, M; (with Wolverhampton W), 1999 v Y (sub), Para (sub), Se, Ni (sub), Mac (sub) (18)

Connolly, H. (Cork), 1937 v G (1)

Connolly, J. (Fordsons), 1926 v I (1)

Conroy, G. A. (Stoke C), 1970 v Cz, D, H, Pol, WG; 1971 v Pol, Se (2), I; 1973 v USSR, F, USSR, N; 1974 v Pol, Br, U, Ch; 1975 v T, Sw, USSR, Sw, WG (sub); 1976 v T (sub), Pol; 1977 v E, T, Pol (27)

Conway, J. P. (Fulham), 1967 v Sp, T, Sp; 1968 v Cz; 1969 v A (sub), H; 1970 v S, Cz, D, H, Pol, WG; 1971 v I, A; 1974 v U, Ch; 1975 v WG (sub); 1976 v N, Pol; (with Manchester C), 1977 v Pol (20)

Corr, P. J. (Everton), 1949 v P, Sp; 1950 v E, Se (4)

Courtney, S. (Cork U), 1946 v P (1)

Coyle, O. C. (Bolton W), 1994 v Ho (sub) (1)

Coyne, T. (Celtic), 1992 v Sw, US, Alb (sub), US (sub), I (sub), P (sub); 1993 v W (sub), La (sub); (with Tranmere R), Ni; (with Motherwell), 1994 v Ru (sub), Ho, Bol, G (sub), CzR (sub), I, M, Ho; 1995 v Lie, Ni (sub), A; 1996 v Ru (sub); 1998 v Bel (sub) (22)

Cummins, M. P. (Luton T), 1954 v L (2); 1955 v N (2), WG; 1956 v Y, Sp; 1958 v D, Pol, A; 1959 v Pol, Cz (2); 1960 v Se, Ch, WG, Se; 1961 v S (2) (19)

Cuneen, T. (Limerick), 1951 v N (1)

Cunningham, K. (Wimbledon), 1996 v CzR, P, Cro, Ho (sub), US, Bol; 1997 v Ic (sub), W, R, Lie; 1998 v Li, Ic, Li, Bel (2), CzR; 1999 v Cro, Ma, Y, Para, Se, Ni, Mac (23)

Curtis, D. P. (Shelbourne), 1957 v D, WG; (with Bristol C), 1957 v E (2); 1958 v D, Pol, A; (with Ipswich T), 1959 v Pol; 1960 v Se, Ch, WG, Se; 1961 v N, S; 1962 v A; 1963 v Ic; (with Exeter C), 1964 v A (17)

Cusack, S. (Limerick), 1953 v F (1)

Daish, L. S. (Cambridge U), 1992 v W, Sw (sub); (with Coventry C), 1996 v CzR (sub), Cro, M (5)

Daly, G. A. (Manchester U), 1973 v Pol (sub), N; 1974 v Br (sub), U (sub); 1975 v Sw (sub), WG; 1977 v E, T, F; (with Derby Co), F, Bul; 1978 v Bul, T, D; 1979 v Ni, E, D, Bul; 1980 v Ni, E, Cy, Sw, Arg; (with Coventry C), 1981 v WG'B', Ho, Bel, Cy, W, Bel, Cz, Pol (sub); 1982 v Alg, Ch, Br, Tr; 1983 v Ho, Sp (sub); 1984 v Is (sub), Ma; (with Birmingham C), 1985 v M (sub), N, Sp, Sw; 1986 v Sw; (with Shrewsbury T), U, Ic (sub), Cz (sub); 1987 v S (sub) (48)

Daly, J. (Shamrock R), 1932 v Ho; 1935 v Sw (2)

Daly, M. (Wolverhampton W), 1978 v T, Pol (2)

Daly, P. (Shamrock R), 1950 v Fi (sub) (1)

Davis, T. L. (Oldham Ath), 1937 v G, H; (with Tranmere R), 1938 v Cz, Pol (4)

Deacy, E. (Aston Villa), 1982 v Alg (sub), Ch, Br, Tr (4)

Delap, R. J. (Derby Co), 1998 v CzR (sub), Arg (sub), M (sub) (3)

De Mange, K. J. P. P. (Liverpool), 1987 v Br (sub); (with Hull C), 1989 v Tun (sub) (2)

Dempsey, J. T. (Fulham), 1967 v Sp, Cz; 1968 v Cz, Pol; 1969 v Pol, A, D; (with Chelsea), 1969 v Cz, D; 1970 v H, WG; 1971 v Pol, Se (2), I; 1972 v Ir, Ec, Ch, P (19)

Dennehy, J. (Cork Hibernians), 1972 v Ec (sub), Ch; (with Nottingham F), 1973 v USSR (sub), Pol, F, N; 1974 v Pol (sub); 1975 v T (sub), WG (sub); (with Walsall), 1976 v Pol (sub); 1977 v Pol (sub) (11)

Desmond, P. (Middlesbrough), 1950 v Fi, E, Fi, Se (4)

Devine, J. (Arsenal), 1980 v Cz, Ni; 1981 v WG'B', Cz; 1982 v Ho, Alg; 1983 v Sp, Ma; (with Norwich C), 1984 v Ic, Ho, Is; 1985 v USSR, N (13)

Donnelly, J. (Dundalk), 1935 v H, Sw, G; 1936 v Ho, Sw, H, L; 1937 v G, H; 1938 v N (10)

Donnelly, T. (Drumcondra), 1938 v N; (Shamrock R), 1939 v Sw (2)

Donovan, D. C. (Everton), 1955 v N, Ho, N, WG; 1957 v E (5)

Donovan, T. (Aston Villa), 1980 v Cz; 1981 v WG'B'(sub) (2)

Dowdall, C. (Fordsons), 1928 v Bel; (with Barnsley), 1929 v Bel; (with Cork), 1931 v Sp (3)

Doyle, C. (Shelbourne), 1959 v Cz (1)

Doyle, D. (Shamrock R), 1926 v I (1)

Doyle, L. (Dolphin), 1932 v Sp (1)

Duff, D. A. (Blackburn R), 1998 v CzR, M; 1999 v Cro, Ma, Y, Para, Se (sub), Ni, Mac (9)

Duffy, B. (Shamrock R), 1950 v Bel (1)

Duggan, H. A. (Leeds U), 1927 v I; 1930 v Bel; 1936 v H, L; (with Newport Co), 1938 v N (5)

Dunne, A. P. (Manchester U), 1962 v A; 1963 v Ic, S; 1964 v A, Sp, Pol, N, E; 1965 v Pol, Sp; 1966 v Sp (2), A, Bel; 1967 v Sp, T, Sp; 1969 v Pol, D, H; 1970 v H; 1971 v Se, I, A; (with Bolton W), 1974 v Br (sub), U, Ch; 1975 v T, Sw, USSR, Sw, WG; 1976 v T (33)

Dunne, J. (Sheffield U), 1930 v Bel; (with Arsenal), 1936 v Sw, H, L; (with Southampton), 1937 v Sw, F; (with Shamrock R), 1938 v N (2), Cz, Pol; 1939 v Sw, Pol, H (2), G (15)

Dunne, J. C. (Fulham), 1971 v A (1)

Dunne, L. (Manchester C), 1935 v Sw, G (2)

Dunne, P. A. J. (Manchester U), 1965 v Sp; 1966 v Sp (2), WG; 1967 v T (5)

Dunne, S. (Luton T), 1953 v F, A; 1954 v F, L; 1956 v Sp, Ho; 1957 v D, WG, E; 1958 v D, Pol, A; 1959 v Pol; 1960 v WG, Se (15)

Dunne, T. (St Patrick's Ath), 1956 v Ho; 1957 v D, WG (3)

Dunning, P. (Shelbourne), 1971 v Se, I (2)

Dunphy, E. M. (York C), 1966 v Sp; (with Millwall), 1966 v WG; 1967 v T, Sp, T, Cz; 1968 v Cz, Pol; 1969 v Pol, A, D (2), H; 1970 v D, H, Pol, WG (sub); 1971 v Pol, Se (2), I (2), A (23)

Dwyer, N. M. (West Ham U), 1960 v Se, Ch, WG, Se; (with Swansea T), 1961 v W, N, S (2); 1962 v Cz (2); 1964 v Pol (sub), N, E; 1965 v Pol (14)

Eccles, P. (Shamrock R), 1986 v U (sub) (1)

Egan, R. (Dundalk), 1929 v Bel (1)

Eglington, T. J. (Shamrock R), 1946 v P, Sp; (with Everton), 1947 v E, Sp, P; 1948 v P; 1949 v Sw, P, Se; 1951 v N, Arg; 1952 v WG (2), A, Sp; 1953 v F, A; 1954 v F, L, F; 1955 v N, Ho, WG; 1956 v Sp (24)

Ellis, P. (Bohemians), 1935 v Sw, G; 1936 v Ho, Sw, L; 1937 v G, H (7)

Evans, M. J. (Southampton), 1998 v R (sub) (1)

Fagan, E. (Shamrock R), 1973 v N (sub) (1)

Fagan, F. (Manchester C), 1955 v N; 1960 v Se; (with Derby Co), v Ch, WG, Se; 1961 v W, N, S (8)

Fagan, J. (Shamrock R), 1926 v I (1)

Fairclough, M. (Dundalk), 1982 v Ch (sub), Tr (sub) (2)

Fallon, S. (Celtic), 1951 v N; 1952 v WG (2), A, Sp; 1953 v F; 1955 v N, WG (8)

Fallon, W. J. (Notts Co), 1935 v H; 1936 v H; 1937 v H, Sw, F; 1939 v Sw, Pol; (with Sheffield W), 1939 v H, G (9)

Farquharson, T. G. (Cardiff C), 1929 v Bel; 1930 v Bel; 1931 v Sp; 1932 v Sp (4)

Farrell, P. (Hibernian), 1937 v Sw, F (2)

Farrell, P. D. (Shamrock R), 1946 v P, Sp; (with Everton), 1947 v Sp, P; 1948 v P, Sp; 1949 v Sw, P (sub), Sp; 1950 v E, Fi, Se; 1951 v Arg, N; 1952 v WG (2), A, Sp; 1953 v F, A; 1954 v F (2); 1955 v N, Ho, WG; 1956 v Y, Sp; 1957 v E (28)

Farrelly, G. (Aston Villa), 1996 v P, US, Bol; (with Everton), 1998 v CzR, M (5)

Feenan, J. J. (Sunderland), 1937 v Sw, F (2)

Finucane, A. (Limerick), 1967 v T, Cz; 1969 v Cz, D, H; 1970 v S, Cz; 1971 v Se, I (1+1 sub); 1972 v A (11)

Fitzgerald, F. J. (Waterford), 1955 v Ho; 1956 v Ho (2)

Fitzgerald, P. J. (Leeds U), 1961 v W, N, S; (with Chester), 1962 v Cz (2) (5)

Fitzpatrick, K. (Limerick), 1970 v Cz (1)

Fitzsimons, A. G. (Middlesbrough), 1950 v Fi, Bel; 1952 v WG (2), A, Sp; 1953 v F, A; 1954 v F, L, F; 1955 v Ho, N, WG; 1956 v Y, Sp, Ho; 1957 v D, WG, E (2); 1958 v D, Pol, A; 1959 v Pol; (with Lincoln C), Cz (26)

Fleming, C. (Middlesbrough), 1996 v CzR (sub), P, Cro (sub), Ho (sub), US (sub), M, Bol; 1997 v Lie (sub); 1998 v R (sub), M (10)

Flood, J. J. (Shamrock R), 1926 v I; 1929 v Bel; 1930 v Bel; 1931 v Sp; 1932 v Sp (5)

Fogarty, A. (Sunderland), 1960 v WG, Se; 1961 v S; 1962 v Cz (2); 1963 v Ic (2), S (sub); 1964 v A (2); (with Hartlepools U), Sp (11)

Foley, J. (Cork), 1934 v Bel, Ho; (with Celtic), 1935 v H, Sw, G; 1937 v G, H (7)

Foley, M. (Shelbourne), 1926 v I (1)

Foley, T. C. (Northampton T), 1964 v Sp, Pol, N; 1965 v Pol, Bel; 1966 v Sp (2), WG; 1967 v Cz (9)

Foy, T. (Shamrock R), 1938 v N; 1939 v H (2)

Fullam, J. (Preston NE), 1961 v N; (with Shamrock R), 1964 v Sp, Pol, N; 1966 v A, Bel; 1968 v Pol; 1969 v Pol, A, D; 1970 v Cz (sub) (11)

Fullam, R. (Shamrock R), 1926 v I; 1927 v I (2)

Gallagher, C. (Celtic), 1967 v T, Cz (2)

Gallagher, M. (Hibernian), 1954 v L (1)

Gallagher, P. (Falkirk), 1932 v Sp (1)

Galvin, A. (Tottenham H), 1983 v Ho, Ma; 1984 v Ho (sub), Is (sub); 1985 v M, USSR, N, D, I, N, Sp; 1986 v U, Ic, Sp; 1987 v Bel (2), S, Bul, L; (with Sheffield W), 1988 v L, Bul, R, Pol, N, E, USSR, Ho; 1989 v Sp; (with Swindon T), 1990 v WG (29)

Gannon, E. (Notts Co), 1949 v Sw; (with Sheffield W), 1949 v Bel, P, Se, Sp; 1950 v F; 1951 v N; 1952 v WG, A; 1954 v L, F; 1955 v N; (with Shelbourne), N, WG (14)

Gannon, M. (Shelbourne), 1972 v A (1)

Gaskins, P. (Shamrock R), 1934 v Bel, Ho; 1935 v H, Sw, G; (with St James' Gate), 1938 v Cz, Pol (7)

Gavin, J. T. (Norwich C), 1950 v Fi (2); 1953 v F; 1954 v L; (with Tottenham H), 1955 v Ho, WG; (with Norwich C), 1957 v D (7)

Geoghegan, M. (St James' Gate), 1937 v G; 1938 v N (2)

Gibbons, A. (St Patrick's Ath), 1952 v WG; 1954 v L; 1956 v Y, Sp (4)

Gilbert, R. (Shamrock R), 1966 v WG (1)

Giles, C. (Doncaster R), 1951 v N (1)

Giles, M. J. (Manchester U), 1960 v Se, Ch; 1961 v W, N, S (2); 1962 v Cz (2), A; 1963 v Ic, S; (with Leeds U), 1964 v A (2), Sp (2), Pol, N, E; 1965 v Sp; 1966 v Sp (2), A, Bel; 1967 v Sp, T (2); 1969 v A, D, Cz; 1970 v S, Pol, WG; 1971 v I; 1973 v F, USSR; 1974 v Br, U, Ch; 1975 v USSR, T, Sw, USSR, Sw; (with WBA), 1976 v T; 1977 v E, T, F (2), Pol, Bul; (with Shamrock R), 1978 v Bul, T, Pol, N, D; 1979 v Ni, D, Bul, WG (59)

Given, S. J. J. (Blackburn R), 1996 v Ru, CzR, P, Cro, Ho, US, Bol; 1997 v Lie (2); (with Newcastle U), 1998 v Li, Ic, Li, Bel (2), CzR, Arg, M; 1999 v Cro, Ma, Y, Para, Se, Ni (23)

Givens, D. J. (Manchester U), 1969 v D, H; 1970 v S, Cz, D, H; (with Luton T) v Pol, WG; 1971 v Se, I (2), A; 1972 v Ir, Ec, P; (with QPR), 1973 v F, USSR, Pol, F, N; 1974 v Pol, Br, U, Ch; 1975 v USSR, T, Sw, USSR, Sw, WG; 1976 v T, N, Pol; 1977 v E, T, F (2), Sp, Bul; 1978 v Bul, N, D; (with Birmingham C), 1979 v Ni (sub), E, D, Bul, WG; 1980 v US (sub), Ni (sub), Sw, Arg; 1981 v Ho, Bel, Cy (sub), W; (with Neuchatel X), 1982 v F (sub) (56)

Glen, W. (Shamrock R), 1927 v I; 1929 v Bel; 1930 v Bel; 1932 v Sp; 1936 v Ho, Sw, H, L (8)

Glynn, D. (Drumcondra), 1952 v WG; 1955 v N (2)

Godwin, T. F. (Shamrock R), 1949 v P, Se, Sp; 1950 v Fi, E; (with Leicester C), Fi, Se, Bel; 1951 v N; (with Bournemouth), 1956 v Ho; 1957 v E; 1958 v D, Pol (13)

Golding, J. (Shamrock R), 1928 v Bel; 1930 v Bel (2)

Goodman, J. (Wimbledon), 1997 v W, Mac, R (sub), Lie (sub) (4)

Gorman, W. C. (Bury), 1936 v Sw, H, L; 1937 v G, H; 1938 v N, Cz, Pol; 1939 v Sw, Pol (with Brentford) H; 1947 v E, P (13)

Grace, J. (Drumcondra), 1926 v I (1)

Grealish, A. (Orient), 1976 v N, Pol; 1978 v N, D; 1979 v Ni, E, WG; (with Luton T), 1980 v W, Cz, Bul, US, Ni, E, Cy, Sw, Arg; 1981 v WG'B', Ho, Bel, F, Cy, W, Bel, Pol; (with Brighton & HA), 1982 v Ho, Alg, Ch, Br, Tr; 1983 v Ho, Sp, Ic, Sp; 1984 v Ic, Ho; (with WBA), Pol, Chn; 1985 v M, USSR, N, D, Sp (sub), Sw; 1986 v USSR, D (45)

Gregg, E. (Bohemians), 1978 v Pol, D (sub); 1979 v E (sub), D, Bul, WG; 1980 v W, Cz (8)

Griffith, R. (Walsall), 1935 v H (1)

Grimes, A. A. (Manchester U), 1978 v T, Pol, N (sub); 1980 v Bul, US, Ni, E, Cy; 1981 v WG'B' (sub), Cz, Pol; 1982 v Alg; 1983 v Sp (2); (with Coventry C), 1984 v Pol, Is; (with Luton T), 1988 v L, R (18)

Hale, A. (Aston Villa), 1962 v A; (with Doncaster R), 1963 v Ic; 1964 v Sp (2); (with Waterford), 1967 v Sp; 1968 v Pol (sub); 1969 v Pol, A, D; 1970 v S, Cz; 1971 v Pol (sub); 1972 v A (sub); 1974 v Pol (sub) (14)

Hamilton, T. (Shamrock R), 1959 v Cz (2) (2)

Hand, E. K. (Portsmouth), 1969 v Cz (sub); 1970 v Pol, WG; 1971 v Pol, A; 1973 v USSR, F, USSR, Pol, F; 1974 v Pol, Br, U, Ch; 1975 v T, Sw, USSR, Sw, WG; 1976 v T (20)

Harrington, W. (Cork), 1936 v Ho, Sw, H, L; 1938 v Pol (sub) (5)

Harte, I.P. (Leeds U), 1996 v Cro (sub), Ho, M, Bol; 1997 v Lie, Mac, Ic (sub), W, Mac (sub), R, Lie; 1998 v Li, Ic, Li, Bel (2), Arg, M; 1999 v Para (19)

Hartnett, J. B. (Middlesbrough), 1949 v Sp; 1954 v L (2)

Haverty, J. (Arsenal), 1956 v Ho; 1957 v D, WG, E (2); 1958 v D, Pol, A; 1959 v Pol; 1960 v Se, Ch; 1961 v W, N, S (2); (with Blackburn R), 1962 v Cz (2); (with Millwall), 1963 v S; 1964 v A, Sp, Pol, N, E; (with Celtic), 1965 v Pol; (with Bristol R), Sp; (with Shelbourne), 1966 v Sp (2), WG, A, Bel; 1967 v T, Sp (32)

Hayes, A. W. P. (Southampton), 1979 v D (1)

Hayes, W. E. (Huddersfield T), 1947 v E, P (2)

Hayes, W. J. (Limerick), 1949 v Bel (1)

Healey, R. (Cardiff C), 1977 v Pol; 1980 v E (sub) (2)

Heighway, S. D. (Liverpool), 1971 v Pol, Se (2), I, A; 1973 v USSR; 1975 v USSR, T, USSR, WG; 1976 v T, N; 1977 v E, F (2), Sp, Bul; 1978 v Bul, N, D; 1979 v Ni, Bul; 1980 v Bul, US, Ni, E, Cy, Arg; 1981 v Bel, F, Cy, W, Bel; (with Minnesota K), 1982 v Ho (34)

Henderson, B. (Drumcondra), 1948 v P, Sp (2)

Hennessy, J. (Shelbourne), 1965 v Pol, Bel, Sp; 1966 v WG; (with St Patrick's Ath), 1969 v A (5)

Herrick, J. (Cork Hibernians), 1972 v A, Ch (sub); (with Shamrock R), 1973 v F (sub) (3)

Higgins, J. (Birmingham C), 1951 v Arg (1)

Holmes, J. (Coventry C), 1971 v A (sub); 1973 v F, USSR, Pol, F, N; 1974 v Pol, Br; 1975 v USSR, Sw; 1976 v T, N, Pol; 1977 v E, T, F, Sp; (with Tottenham H), F, Pol, Bul; 1978 v Bul, T, Pol, N, D; 1979 v Ni, E, D, Bul; (with Vancouver W), 1984 v W (30)

Horlacher, A. F. (Bohemians), 1930 v Bel; 1932 v Sp, Ho; 1934 v Ho (sub); 1935 v H;1936 v Ho, Sw (7)

Houghton, R. J. (Oxford U), 1986 v W, U, Ic, Cz; 1987 v Bel (2), S (2), Pol, L; 1988 v L, Bul; (with Liverpool), Is, Y, N, E, USSR, Ho; 1989 v Ni, Tun, Sp, F, H, Sp, Ma, H; 1990 v Ni, Ma, Fi, E, Eg, Ho, R, I; 1991 v Mor, T, E (2), Pol, Ch, US; 1992 v H, Alb, US, I, P; (with Aston Villa), 1993 v D, Sp, Ni, D, Alb, La, Li; 1994 v Li, Sp, Ni, Bol, G (sub), I, M, N, Ho; (with C Palace), 1995 v P, A; 1996 v A, CzR; 1997 v Lie, R, Lie; (with Reading), 1998 v Li, R, Bel (1 + sub) (73)

Howlett, G. (Brighton & HA), 1984 v Chn (sub) (1)

Hoy, M. (Dundalk), 1938 v N; 1939 v Sw, Pol, H (2), G (6)

Hughton, C. (Tottenham H), 1980 v US, E, Sw, Arg; 1981 v Ho, Bel, F, Cy, W, Bel, Pol; 1982 v F; 1983 v Ho, Sp, Ma, Sp; 1984 v Ic, Ho, Ma; 1985 v M (sub), USSR, N, I, Is, E, Sp; 1986 v Sw, USSR, U, Ic; 1987 v Bel, Bul; 1988 v Is, Y, Pol, N, E, USSR, Ho; 1989 v Ni, F, H, Sp, Ma, H; 1990 v W (sub), USSR (sub), Fi, T (sub), Ma; 1991 v T; (with West Ham U), Ch; 1992 v T (53)

Hurley, C. J. (Millwall), 1957 v E; (with Sunderland), 1958 v D, Pol, A; 1959 v Cz (2); 1960 v Se, Ch, WG, Se; 1961 v W, N, S (2); 1962 v Cz (2), A; 1963 v Ic (2), S; 1964 v A (2), Sp (2), Pol, N; 1965 v Sp; 1966 v WG, A, Bel; 1967 v T, Sp, T, Cz; 1968 v Cz, Pol; 1969 v Pol, D, Cz, (with Bolton W), H (40)

Hutchinson, F. (Drumcondra), 1935 v Sw, G (2)

Irwin, D. J. (Manchester U), 1991 v Mor, T, W, E, Pol, US; 1992 v H, Pol, W, US, Alb, US (sub), I; 1993 v La, D, Sp, Ni, D, Alb, La, Li; 1994 v Li, Sp, Ni, Bol, G, I, M; 1995 v La, Lie, Ni, E, Ni, P, Lie, A; 1996 v A, P, Ho, CzR; 1997 v Lie, Mac, Ic, Mac, R; 1998 v Li, Bel, Arg (sub); 1999 v Cro, Y, Para, Mac (52)

Jordan, D. (Wolverhampton W), 1937 v Sw, F (2)

Jordan, W. (Bohemians), 1934 v Ho; 1938 v N (2)

Kavanagh, G. A. (Stoke C), 1998 v CzR (sub); 1999 v Se (sub), Ni (sub) (3)

Kavanagh, P. J. (Celtic), 1931 v Sp; 1932 v Sp (2)

Keane, R. D. (Wolverhampton W), 1998 v CzR (sub), Arg, M; 1999 v Cro, Ma, Para, Se (sub), Ni, Mac (9)

Keane, R. M. (Nottingham F), 1991 v Ch; 1992 v H, Pol, W, Sw, Alb, US; 1993 v La, D, Sp, W, Ni, D, Alb, La, Li; (with Manchester U), 1994 v Li, Sp, Ni, Bol, G, CzR (sub), I, M, N, Ho; 1995 v Ni (2); 1996 v A, Ru; 1997 v Ic, W, Mac, R, Lie; 1998 v Li, Ic, Li; 1999 v Cro, Ma, Y, Para (42)

Keane, T. R. (Swansea T), 1949 v Sw, P, Se, Sp (4)

Kearin, M. (Shamrock R), 1972 v A (1)

Kearns, F. T. (West Ham U), 1954 v L (1)

Kearns, M. (Oxford U), 1971 v Pol (sub); (with Walsall), 1974 v Pol (sub), U, Ch; 1976 v N, Pol; 1977 v E, T, F (2), Sp, Bul; 1978 v N, D; 1979 v Ni, E; (with Wolverhampton W), 1980 v US, Ni (18)

Kelly, A. T. (Sheffield U), 1993 v W (sub); 1994 v Ru (sub), G; 1995 v La, Ni, E, Ni, P, Lie, A; 1996 v A, La, P, Ho; 1997 v Mac, Ic, Mac, R; 1998 v R, Arg (sub); 1999 v Para (sub), Mac (22)

Kelly, D. T. (Walsall), 1988 v Is, R, Y; (with West Ham U), 1989 v Tun (sub); (with Leicester C), 1990 v USSR, Ma; 1991 v Mor, W (sub), Ch, US; 1992 v H; (with Newcastle U), I (sub), P; 1993 v Sp (sub), Ni; (with Wolverhampton W), 1994 v Ru, N (sub); 1995 v E, Ni; (with Sunderland), 1996 v La (sub); 1997 v N, W (sub), Mac (sub); (with Tranmere R), 1998 v Li (sub), R (sub), Bel (sub) (26)

Kelly, G. (Leeds U), 1994 v Ru, Ho, Bol (sub), G (sub), CzR, N, Ho; 1995 v La, Lie, Ni (2), P, Lie, A; 1996 v A, La, P, Ho; 1997 v W (sub), R, Lie; 1998 v Ic, Li, Bel (2), CzR, Arg, M (28)

Kelly, J. (Derry C), 1932 v Ho; 1934 v Bel; 1936 v Sw, L (4)

Kelly, J. A. (Drumcondra), 1957 v WG, E; (with Preston NE), 1962 v A; 1963 v Ic (2), S; 1964 v A (2), Sp (2), Pol; 1965 v Bel; 1966 v A, Bel; 1967 v Sp (2), T, Cz; 1968 v Pol, Cz; 1969 v Pol, A, D, Cz, D, H; 1970 v S, D, H, Pol, WG; 1971 v Pol, Se (2), I (2), A; 1972 v Ir, Ec, Ch, P; 1973 v USSR, F, USSR, Pol, F, N (47)

Kelly, J. P. V. (Wolverhampton W), 1961 v W, N, S; 1962 v Cz (2) (5)

Kelly, M. J. (Portsmouth), 1988 v Y, Pol (sub); 1989 v Tun; 1991 v Mor (4)

Kelly, N. (Nottingham F), 1954 v L (1)

Kendrick, J. (Everton), 1927 v I; (with Dolphin) 1934 v Bel, Ho; 1936 v Ho (4)

Kenna, J. J. (Blackburn R), 1995 v P (sub), Lie (sub), A (sub); 1996 v La, P, Ho, Ru (sub), CzR, P, Cro, Ho, US; 1997 v Lie, Mac, Ic, R (sub), Lie; 1998 v Li, Ic, R, Bel (1 + sub), CzR, Arg; 1999 v Cro (sub), Ma (26)

Kennedy, M. (Liverpool), 1996 v A, La (sub), P, Ru, CzR, Cro, Ho (sub), US (sub), M, Bol (sub); 1997 v R, Lie; 1998 v Li, Ic (sub), R, Bel (2), (with Wimbledon), M (sub); 1999 v Ma (sub), Se, Ni, Mac (22)

Kennedy, M. F. (Portsmouth), 1986 v Ic, Cz (sub) (2)

Kennedy, W. (St James' Gate), 1932 v Ho; 1934 v Bel, Ho (3)

Keogh, J. (Shamrock R), 1966 v WG (sub) (1)

Keogh, S. (Shamrock R), 1959 v Pol (1)

Kernaghan, A. N. (Middlesbrough), 1993 v La, D (2), Alb, La, Li; 1994 v Li; (with Manchester C), Sp, Ni, Bol (sub), CzR; 1995 v Lie, E; 1996 v A, P (sub), Ho (sub), Ru, P, Cro (sub), Ho, US, Bol (22)

Kiernan, F. W. (Shamrock R), 1951 v Arg, N; (with Southampton), 1952 v WG (2), A (5)

Kilbane, K. D. (WBA), 1998 v Ic, CzR (sub), Arg; 1999 v Se (sub), Mac (sub) (5)

Kinnear, J. P. (Tottenham H), 1967 v T; 1968 v Cz, Pol; 1969 v A; 1970 v Cz, D, H, Pol; 1971 v Se (sub), I; 1972 v Ir, Ec, Ch, P; 1973 v USSR, F; 1974 v Pol, Br, U, Ch; 1975 v USSR, T, Sw, USSR, WG; (with Brighton & HA), 1976 v T (sub) (26)

Kinsella, J. (Shelbourne), 1928 v Bel (1)

Kinsella, M. A. (Charlton Ath), 1998 v CzR, Arg; 1999 v Cro, Ma, Y, Para, Se, Ni, Mac (9)

Kinsella, O. (Shamrock R), 1932 v Ho; 1938 v N (2)

Kirkland, A. (Shamrock R), 1927 v I (1)

Lacey, W. (Shelbourne), 1927 v I; 1928 v Bel; 1930 v Bel (3)

Langan, D. (Derby Co), 1978 v T, N; 1980 v Sw, Arg; (with Birmingham C), 1981 v WG'B', Ho, Bel, F, Cy, W, Bel, Cz, Pol; 1982 v Ho, F; (with Oxford U), 1985 v N, Sp, Sw; 1986 v W, U; 1987 v Bel, S, Pol, Br (sub), L (sub); 1988 v L (26)

Lawler, J. F. (Fulham), 1953 v A; 1954 v L, F; 1955 v N, H, N, WG; 1956 v Y (8)

Lawlor, J. C. (Drumcondra), 1949 v Bel; (with Doncaster R), 1951 v N, Arg (3)

Lawlor, M. (Shamrock R), 1971 v Pol, Se (2), I (sub); 1973 v Pol (5)

Lawrenson, M. (Preston NE), 1977 v Pol; (with Brighton & HA), 1978 v Bul, Pol, N (sub); 1979 v Ni, E; 1980 v E, Cy, Sw; 1981 v Ho, Bel, F, Cy, Pol; (with Liverpool), 1982 v Ho, F; 1983 v Ho, Sp, Ic, Ma, Sp; 1984 v Ic, Ho, Ma, Is; 1985 v USSR, N, D, I, E, N; 1986 v Sw, USSR, D; 1987 v Bel, S; 1988 v Bul, Is (38)

Leech, M. (Shamrock R), 1969 v Cz, D, H; 1972 v A, Ir, Ec, P; 1973 v USSR (sub) (8)

Lennon, C. (St James' Gate), 1935 v H, Sw, G (3)

Lennox, G. (Dolphin), 1931 v Sp; 1932 v Sp (2)

Lowry, D. (St Patrick's Ath), 1962 v A (sub) (1)

Lunn, R. (Dundalk), 1939 v Sw, Pol (2)

Lynch, J. (Cork Bohemians), 1934 v Bel (1)

McAlinden, J. (Portsmouth), 1946 v P, Sp (2)

McAteer, J. W. (Bolton W), 1994 v Ru, Ho (sub), Bol (sub), G, CzR (sub), I (sub), M (sub), N, Ho (sub); 1995 v La, Lie, Ni (2 sub), Lie; (with Liverpool), 1996 v La, P, Ho (sub), Ru; 1997 v Mac, Ic, W, Mac; 1998 v Ic (sub), Li, R; 1999 v Cro, Ma, Y; (with Blackburn R), Para, Se (30)

McCann, J. (Shamrock R), 1957 v WG (1)

McCarthy, J. (Bohemians), 1926 v I; 1928 v Bel; 1930 v Bel (3)

McCarthy, M. (Manchester C), 1984 v Pol, Chn; 1985 v M, D, I, Is, E, Sp, Sw; 1986 v Sw, USSR, W (sub), U, Ic, Cz; 1987 v S (2), Pol, Bul, Bel; (with Celtic), Br, L; 1988 v Bul, Is, R, Y, N, E, USSR, Ho; 1989 v Ni, Tun, Sp, F, H, Sp; (with Lyon), 1990 v WG, Ni; (with Millwall), W, USSR, Fi, T, E, Eg, Ho, R, I; 1991 v Mor, T, E, US; 1992 v H, T, Alb (sub), US, I, P (57)

McCarthy, M. (Shamrock R), 1932 v Ho (1)

McConville, T. (Dundalk), 1972 v A; (with Waterford), 1973 v USSR, F, USSR, Pol, F (6)

McDonagh, Jacko (Shamrock R), 1984 v Pol (sub), Ma (sub); 1985 v M (sub) (3)

McDonagh, J. (Everton), 1981 v WG'B', W, Bel, Cz; (with Bolton W), 1982 v Ho, F, Ch, Br; 1983 v Ho, Sp, Ic, Ma, Sp; (with Notts Co), 1984 v Ic, Ho, Pol; 1985 v M, USSR, N, D, Sp; 1986 v Sw, USSR (with Wichita Wings) D (25)

McEvoy, M. A. (Blackburn R), 1961 v S (2); 1963 v S; 1964 v A, Sp (2), Pol, N, E; 1965 v Pol, Bel, Sp; 1966 v Sp (2); 1967 v Sp, T, Cz (17)

McGee, P. (QPR), 1978 v T, N (sub); 1979 v Ni, E, D (sub), Bul (sub); 1980 v Cz, Bul; (with Preston NE), US, Ni, Cy, Sw, Arg; 1981 v Bel (sub) (15)

McGoldrick, E. J. (C Palace), 1992 v Sw, US, I, P (sub); 1993 v D, W, Ni (sub), D; (with Arsenal), 1994 v Ni, Ru, Ho, CzR; 1995 v La (sub), Lie, E (15)

McGowan, D. (West Ham U), 1949 v P, Se, Sp (3)

McGowan, J. (Cork U), 1947 v Sp (1)

McGrath, M. (Blackburn R), 1958 v A; 1959 v Pol, Cz (2); 1960 v Se, WG, Se; 1961 v W; 1962 v Cz (2); 1963 v S; 1964 v A (2), E; 1965 v Pol, Bel, Sp; 1966 v Sp; (with Bradford PA), WG, A, Bel; 1967 v T (22)

McGrath, P. (Manchester U), 1985 v I (sub), Is, E, N (sub), Sw (sub); 1986 v Sw (sub), D, W, Ic, Cz; 1987 v Bel (2), S (2), Pol, Bul, Br, L; 1988 v L, Bul, Y, Pol, N, E, Ho; 1989 v Ni, F, H, Sp, Ma, H; (with Aston Villa), 1990 v WG, Ma, USSR, Fi, T, E, Eg, Ho, R, I; 1991 v E (2), W, Pol, Ch (sub), US; 1992 v Pol, T, Sw, US, Alb, US, I, P; 1993 v La, Sp, Ni, D, La, Li; 1994 v Sp, Ni, G, CzR, I, M, N, Ho; 1995 v La, Ni, E, Ni, P, Lie, A; 1996 v A, La, P, Ho, Ru, CzR; (with Derby Co), 1997 v W (83)

McGuire, W. (Bohemians), 1936 v Ho (1)

McKenzie, G. (Southend U), 1938 v N (2), Cz, Pol; 1939 v Sw, Pol, H (2), G (9)

Mackey, G. (Shamrock R), 1957 v D, WG, E (3)

McLoughlin, A. F. (Swindon T), 1990 v Ma, E (sub), Eg (sub); 1991 v Mor (sub), E (sub); (with Southampton), W, Ch (sub); 1992 v H (sub), W (sub); (with Portsmouth), US (1+sub), I (sub), P; 1993 v W; 1994 v Ni (sub), Ru, Ho (sub); 1995 v Lie (sub); 1996 v P, Cro, Ho, US, M, Bol (sub); 1997 v Lie, Mac, Ic, W, Mac; 1998 v Li (sub), Ic, Li, R, Bel, CzR (sub); 1999 v Y, Para (sub), Se, Ni (sub) (39)

McLoughlin, F. (Fordsons), 1930 v Bel; (with Cork), 1932 v Sp (2)

McMillan, W. (Belfast Celtic), 1946 v P, Sp (2)

McNally, J. B. (Luton T), 1959 v Cz; 1961 v S; 1963 v Ic (3)

Macken, A. (Derby Co), 1977 v Sp (1)

Madden, O. (Cork), 1936 v H (1)

Maguire, J. (Shamrock R), 1929 v Bel (1)

Malone, G. (Shelbourne), 1949 v Bel (1)

Mancini, T. J. (QPR), 1974 v Pol, Br, U, Ch; (with Arsenal), 1975 v USSR (5)

Martin, C. (Bo'ness), 1927 v I (1)

Martin, C. J. (Glentoran), 1946 v P (sub), Sp; 1947 v E; (with Leeds U), Sp; 1948 v P, Sp; (with Aston Villa), 1949 v Sw, Bel, P, Se, Sp; 1950 v Fi, E, Fi, Se, Bel; 1951 v Arg; 1952 v WG, A, Sp; 1954 v F (2), L; 1955 v N, Ho, N, WG; 1956 v Y, Sp, Ho (30)

Martin, M. P. (Bohemians), 1972 v A, Ir, Ec, Ch, P; 1973 v USSR; (with Manchester U), USSR, Pol, F, N; 1974 v Pol, Br, U, Ch; 1975 v USSR, T, Sw, USSR, Sw, WG; (with WBA), 1976 v T, N, Pol; 1977 v E, T, F (2), Sp, Pol, Bul; (with Newcastle U), 1979 v D, Bul, WG; 1980 v W, Cz, Bul, US, Ni; 1981 v WG'B', F, Bel, Cz; 1982 v Ho, F, Alg, Ch, Br, Tr; 1983 v Ho, Sp, Ma, Sp (52)

Maybury, A. (Leeds U), 1998 v CzR; 1999 v Ni (2)

Meagan, M. K. (Everton), 1961 v S; 1962 v A; 1963 v Ic; 1964 v Sp; (with Huddersfield T), 1965 v Bel; 1966 v Sp (2), A, Bel; 1967 v Sp, T, Sp, T, Cz; 1968 v Cz, Pol; (with Drogheda), 1970 v S (17)

Meehan, P. (Drumcondra), 1934 v Ho (1)

Milligan, M. J. (Oldham Ath), 1992 v US (sub) (1)

Monahan, P. (Sligo R), 1935 v Sw, G (2)

Mooney, J. (Shamrock R), 1965 v Pol, Bel (2)

Moore, A. (Middlesbrough), 1996 v CzR, Cro (sub), Ho, M, Bol; 1997 v Lie (sub), Mac (sub), Ic (sub) (8)

Moore, P. (Shamrock R), 1931 v Sp; 1932 v Ho; (with Aberdeen), 1934 v Bel, Ho; 1935 v H, G; (with Shamrock R), 1936 v Ho; 1937 v G, H (9)

Moran, K. (Manchester U), 1980 v Sw, Arg; 1981 v WG'B', Bel, F, Cy, W (sub), Bel, Cz, Pol; 1982 v F, Alg; 1983 v Ic; 1984 v Ic, Ho, Ma, Is; 1985 v M; 1986 v D, Ic, Cz; 1987 v Bel (2), S (2), Pol, Bul, Br, L; 1988 v L, Bul, Is, R, Y, Pol, N, E, USSR, Ho; (with Sporting Gijon), 1989 v Ni, Sp, H, Sp, Ma, H; 1990 v Ni, Ma; (with Blackburn R), W, USSR (sub), Ma, E, Eg, Ho, R, I; 1991 v T (sub), W, E, Pol, Ch, US; 1992 v Pol, US; 1993 v D, Sp, Ni, Alb; 1994 v Li, Sp, Ho, Bol (71)

Moroney, T. (West Ham U), 1948 v Sp; 1949 v P, Se, Sp; 1950 v Fi, E, Fi, Bel; 1951 v N (2); 1952 v WG; (with Evergreen U), 1954 v F (12)

Morris, C. B. (Celtic), 1988 v Is, R, Y, Pol, N, E, USSR, Ho; 1989 v Ni, Tun, Sp, F, H (1+1 sub); 1990 v WG, Ni, Ma (sub), W, USSR, Fi (sub), T, E, Eg, Ho, R, I; 1991 v E (2); v H (sub), Pol, W, Sw, US (2), P; (with Middlesbrough), 1993 v W (35)

Moulson, C. (Lincoln C), 1936 v H, L; (with Notts Co), 1937 v H, Sw, F (5)

Moulson, G. B. (Lincoln C), 1948 v P, Sp; 1949 v Sw (3)

Mucklan, C. (Drogheda U), 1978 v Pol (1)

Muldoon, T. (Aston Villa), 1927 v I (1)

Mulligan, P. M. (Shamrock R), 1969 v Cz, D, H; 1970 v S, Cz, D; (with Chelsea), H, Pol, WG; 1971 v Pol, Se, I; 1972 v A, Ir, Ec, Ch, P; (with C Palace), 1973 v F, USSR, Pol, F, N; 1974 v Pol, Br, U, Ch; 1975 v USSR, T, Sw, USSR, Sw; (with WBA), 1976 v T, Pol; 1977 v E, T, F (2), Pol, Bul; 1978 v Bul, N, D; 1979 v E, D, Bul (sub), WG; (with Shamrock R), 1980 v W, Cz, Bul, US (sub) (50)

Munroe, L. (Shamrock R), 1954 v L (1)

Murphy, A. (Clyde), 1956 v Y (1)

Murphy, B. (Bohemians), 1986 v U (1)

Murphy, J. (C Palace), 1980 v W, US, Cy (3)

Murray, T. (Dundalk), 1950 v Bel (1)

Newman, W. (Shelbourne), 1969 v D (1)

Nolan, R. (Shamrock R), 1957 v D, WG, E; 1958 v Pol; 1960 v Ch, WG, Se; 1962 v Cz (2); 1963 v Ic (10)

O'Brien, F. (Philadelphia F), 1980 v Cz, E, Cy (sub) (3)

O'Brien, L. (Shamrock R), 1986 v U; (with Manchester U), 1987 v Br; 1988 v Is (sub), R (sub), Y (sub), Pol (sub); 1989 v Tun; (with Newcastle U), Sp (sub); 1992 v Sw (sub); 1993 v W; (with Tranmere R), 1994 v Ru; 1996 v Cro, Ho, US, Bol; 1997 v Mac (sub) (16)

O'Brien, M. T. (Derby Co), 1927 v I; (with Walsall), 1929 v Bel; (with Norwich C), 1930 v Bel; (with Watford), 1932 v Ho (4)

O'Brien, R. (Notts Co), 1976 v N, Pol; 1977 v Sp, Pol; 1980 v Arg (sub) (5)

O'Byrne, L. B. (Shamrock R), 1949 v Bel (1)

O'Callaghan, B. R. (Stoke C), 1979 v WG (sub); 1980 v W, US; 1981 v W; 1982 v Br, Tr (6)

O'Callaghan, K. (Ipswich T), 1981 v WG'B', Cz, Pol; 1982 v Alg, Ch, Br, Tr (sub); 1983 v Sp, Ic (sub), Ma (sub), Sp (sub); 1984 v Ic, Ho, Ma; 1985 v M (sub), N (sub), D (sub), (with Portsmouth) E (sub); 1986 v Sw (sub), USSR (sub); 1987 v Br (21)

O'Connell, A. (Dundalk), 1967 v Sp; (with Bohemians), 1971 v Pol (sub) (2)

O'Connor, T. (Shamrock R), 1950 v Fi, E, Fi, Se (4)

O'Connor, T. (Fulham), 1968 v Cz; (with Dundalk), 1972 v A, Ir (sub), Ec (sub), Ch; (with Bohemians), 1973 v F (sub), Pol (sub) (7)

O'Driscoll, J. F. (Swansea T), 1949 v Sw, Bel, Se (3)

O'Driscoll, S. (Fulham), 1982 v Ch, Br, Tr (sub) (3)

O'Farrell, F. (West Ham U), 1952 v A; 1953 v A; 1954 v F; 1955 v Ho, N; 1956 v Y, Ho; (with Preston NE), 1958 v D; 1959 v Cz (9)

O'Flanagan, K. P. (Bohemians), 1938 v N, Cz, Pol; 1939 v Pol, H (2), G; (with Arsenal), 1947 v E, Sp, P (10)

O'Flanagan, M. (Bohemians), 1947 v E (1)

O'Hanlon, K. G. (Rotherham U), 1988 v Is (1)

O'Kane, P. (Bohemians), 1935 v H, Sw, G (3)

O'Keefe, E. (Everton), 1981 v W; (with Port Vale), 1984 v Chn; 1985 v M, USSR (sub), E (5)

O'Keefe, T. (Cork), 1934 v Bel; (with Waterford), 1938 v Cz, Pol (3)

O'Leary, D. (Arsenal), 1977 v E, F (2), Sp, Bul; 1978 v Bul, N, D; 1979 v E, Bul, WG; 1980 v W, Bul, Ni, E, Cy; 1981 v WG'B', Ho, Cz, Pol; 1982 v Ho, F; 1983 v Ho, Ic, Sp; 1984 v Pol, Is, Chn; 1985 v USSR, N, D, Is, E (sub), N, Sp, Sw; 1986 v Sw, USSR, D, W; 1989 v Sp, Ma, H; 1990 v WG, Ni (sub), Ma, W (sub), USSR, Fi, T, Ma, R (sub); 1991 v Mor, T, E (2), Pol, Ch; 1992 v H, Pol, T, W, Sw, US, Alb, I, P; 1993 v W (68)

O'Leary, P. (Shamrock R), 1980 v Bul, US, Ni, E (sub), Cz, Arg; 1981 v Ho (7)

O'Mahoney, M. T. (Bristol R), 1938 v Cz, Pol; 1939 v Sw, Pol, H, G (6)

O'Neill, F. S. (Shamrock R), 1962 v Cz (2); 1965 v Pol, Bel, Sp; 1966 v Sp (2), WG, A; 1967 v Sp, T, Sp, T; 1969 v Pol, A, D, Cz, D (sub), H (sub); 1972 v A (20)

O'Neill, J. (Everton), 1952 v Sp; 1953 v F, A; 1954 v F, L, F; 1955 v N, Ho, N, WG; 1956 v Y, Sp; 1957 v D; 1958 v A; 1959 v Pol, Cz (2) (17)

O'Neill, J. (Preston NE), 1961 v W (1)

O'Neill, K. P. (Norwich C), 1996 v P (sub), Cro, Ho (sub), US (sub), M, Bol; 1997 v Lie, Mac (1 + sub); 1999 v Cro, Y (sub); (with Middlesbrough) Ni (sub) (12)

O'Neill, W. (Dundalk), 1936 v Ho, Sw, H, L; 1937 v G, H, Sw, F; 1938 v N; 1939 v H, G (11)

O'Regan, K. (Brighton & HA), 1984 v Ma, Pol; 1985 v M, Sp (sub) (4)

O'Reilly, J. (Brideville), 1932 v Ho; (with Aberdeen), 1934 v Bel, Ho; (with Brideville), 1936 v Ho; Sw, H, L; (with St James' Gate), 1937 v G, H, Sw, F; 1938 v N (2), G (20)

O'Reilly, J. (Cork U), 1946 v P, Sp (2)

Peyton, G. (Fulham), 1977 v Sp (sub); 1978 v Bul, T, Pol; 1979 v D, Bul, WG; 1980 v W, Cz, Bul, E, Cy, Sw, Arg; 1981 v Ho, Bel, F, Cy; 1982 v Tr; 1985 v M (sub); 1986 v W, Cz; (with Bournemouth), 1988 v L, Pol; 1989 v Ni, Tun; 1990 v USSR, Ma; 1991 v Ch; (with Everton) 1992 v US (2), I (sub), P (33)

Peyton, N. (Shamrock R), 1957 v WG; (with Leeds U), 1960 v WG, Se (sub); 1961 v W; 1963 v Ic, S (6)

Phelan, T. (Wimbledon), 1992 v H, Pol (sub), T, W, Sw, US, I (sub), P; (with Manchester C), 1993 v La (sub), D, Sp, Ni, Alb, La, Li; 1994 v Li, Sp, Ni, Ho, Bol, G, CzR, I, M, Ho; 1995 v E; 1996 v La; (with Chelsea), Ho, Ru, P, Cro, Ho, US, M (sub), Bol; (with Everton), 1997 v W, Mac; 1998 v R (38)

Quinn, N. J. (Arsenal), 1986 v Ic (sub), Cz; 1987 v Bul (sub), Br (sub); 1988 v L (sub), Bul (sub), Is, R (sub), Pol (sub), E (sub); 1989 v Tun (sub), Sp (sub), H (sub); (with Manchester C), 1990 v USSR, Ma, Eg (sub), Ho, R, I; 1991 v Mor, T, E (2) W, Pol; 1992 v H, W (sub), US, Alb, US, I (sub), P; 1993 v La, D, Sp, Ni, D, Alb, La, Li; 1994 v Li, Sp, Ni; 1995 v La, Lie, Ni, E, Ni, P, Lie, A; 1996 v A, La, P, Ru, CzR, P (sub), Cro, Ho (sub), US; (with Sunderland), 1997 v Lie; 1998 v Li, Arg; 1999 v Ma, Y, Para, Se, Ni, Mac (69)

Reid, C. (Brideville), 1931 v Sp (1)

Richardson, D. J. (Shamrock R), 1972 v A (sub); (with Gillingham), 1973 v N (sub); 1980 v Cz (3)

Rigby, A. (St James' Gate), 1935 v H, Sw, G (3)

Ringstead, A. (Sheffield U), 1951 v Arg, N; 1952 v WG (2), A, Sp; 1953 v A; 1954 v F; 1955 v N; 1956 v Y, Sp, Ho; 1957 v E (2); 1958 v D, Pol, A; 1959 v Pol, Cz (2) (20)

Robinson, J. (Bohemians), 1928 v Bel; (with Dolphin), 1931 v Sp (2)

Robinson, M. (Brighton & HA), 1981 v WG'B', F, Cy, Bel, Pol; 1982 v Ho, F, Alg, Ch; 1983 v Ho, Sp, Ic, Ma; (with Liverpool), 1984 v Ic, Ho, Is; 1985 v USSR, N; (with QPR), N, Sp, Sw; 1986 v D (sub), W, Cz (24)

Roche, P. J. (Shelbourne), 1972 v A; (with Manchester U), 1975 v USSR, T, Sw, USSR, Sw, WG; 1976 v T (8)

Rogers, E. (Blackburn R), 1968 v Cz, Pol; 1969 v Pol, A, D, Cz, D, H; 1970 v S, D, H; 1971 v I (2), A; (with Charlton Ath), 1972 v Ir, Ec, Ch, P; 1973 v USSR (19)

Ryan, G. (Derby Co), 1978 v T; (with Brighton & HA), 1979 v E, WG; 1980 v W, Cy (sub), Sw, Arg (sub); 1981 v WG'B' (sub), F (sub), Pol (sub); 1982 v Br (sub), Ho (sub), Alg (sub), Ch (sub), Tr; 1984 v Pol, Chn; 1985 v M (18)

Ryan, R. A. (WBA), 1950 v Se, Bel; 1951 v N, Arg, N; 1952 v WG (2), A, Sp; 1953 v F, A; 1954 v F, L, F; 1955 v N; (with Derby Co), 1956 v Sp (16)

Savage, D. P. T. (Millwall), 1996 v P (sub), Cro (sub), US (sub), M, Bol (5)

Saward, P. (Millwall), 1954 v L; (with Aston Villa), 1957 v E (2); 1958 v D, Pol, A; 1959 v Pol, Cz; 1960 v Se, Ch, WG, Se; 1961 v W, N; (with Huddersfield T), 1961 v S; 1962 v A; 1963 v Ic (2) (18)

Scannell, T. (Southend U), 1954 v L (1)

Scully, P. J. (Arsenal), 1989 v Tun (sub) (1)

Sheedy, K. (Everton), 1984 v Ho (sub), Ma; 1985 v D, I, Is, Sw; 1986 v Sw, D; 1987 v S, Pol; 1988 v Is, R, Pol, E (sub), USSR; 1989 v Ni, Tun, H, Sp, Ma, H; 1990 v Ni, Ma, W (sub), USSR, Fi (sub), T, E, Eg, Ho, R, I; 1991 v W, E, Pol, Ch, US; 1992 v H, Pol, T, W; (with Newcastle U), Sw (sub), Alb; 1993 v La, W (sub) (45)

Sheridan, J. J. (Leeds U), 1988 v R, Y, Pol, N (sub); 1989 v Sp; (with Sheffield W), 1990 v W, T (sub), Ma, I (sub); 1991 v Mor (sub), T, Ch, US (sub); 1992 v H; 1993 v La; 1994 v Sp (sub), Ho, Bol, G, CzR, I, M, N, Ho; 1995 v La, Lie, Ni, E, Ni, P, Lie, A; 1996 v A, Ho (34)

Slaven, B. (Middlesbrough), 1990 v W, Fi, T (sub), Ma; 1991 v W, Pol (sub); 1993 v W (7)

Sloan, J. W. (Arsenal), 1946 v P, Sp (2)

Smyth, M. (Shamrock R), 1969 v Pol (sub) (1)

Squires, J. (Shelbourne), 1934 v Ho (1)

Stapleton, F. (Arsenal), 1977 v T, F, Sp, Bul; 1978 v Bul, N, D; 1979 v Ni, E (sub), D, WG; 1980 v W, Bul, Ni, E, Cy; 1981 v WG'B', Ho, Bel, F, Cy, Bel, Cz, Pol; (with Manchester U), 1982 v Ho, F, Alg; 1983 v Ho, Sp, Ic, Ma, Sp; 1984 v Ic, Ho, Ma, Pol, Is, Chn; 1985 v N, D, I, Is, E, N, Sw; 1986 v Sw, USSR, D, U, Ic, Cz (sub); 1987 v Bel (2), S (2), Pol, Bul, L; (with Ajax), 1988 v L, Bul, R, Y, N, E, USSR, Ho; (with Le Havre), 1989 v F, Sp, Ma; (with Blackburn R), 1990 v WG, Ma (sub) (71)

Staunton, S. (Liverpool), 1989 v Tun, Sp (2), Ma, H; 1990 v WG, Ni, Ma, W, USSR, Fi, T, Ma, E, Eg, Ho, R, I; 1991 v Mor, T, E (2), W, Pol, Ch, US; (with Aston Villa), 1992 v Pol, T, Sw, US, Alb, US, I, P; 1993 v La, Sp, Ni, D, Alb, La, Li; 1994 v Li, Sp, Ho, Bol, G, CzR, I, M, N, Ho; 1995 v La, Lie, Ni, E, Ni, P, Lie, A; 1996 v La, P, Ru; 1997 v Lie, Mac (2), W, R, Lie; 1998 v Li, Ic, Li, Bel (2), Arg; (with Liverpool), 1999 v Cro, Ma, Y, Se (78)

Stevenson, A. E. (Dolphin), 1932 v Ho; (with Everton), 1947 v E, Sp, P; 1948 v P, Sp; 1949 v Sw (7)

Strahan, F. (Shelbourne), 1964 v Pol, N, E; 1965 v Pol; 1966 v WG (5)

Sullivan, J. (Fordsons), 1928 v Bel (1)

Swan, M. M. G. (Drumcondra), 1960 v Se (sub) (1)

Synnott, N. (Shamrock R), 1978 v T, Pol; 1979 v Ni (3)

Taylor, T. (Waterford), 1959 v Pol (sub) (1)

Thomas, P. (Waterford), 1974 v Pol, Br (2)

Townsend, A. D. (Norwich C), 1989 v F, Sp (sub), Ma (sub), H; 1990 v WG (sub), Ni, Ma, W, USSR, Fi (sub), T, Ma (sub), E, Eg, Ho, R, I; (with Chelsea), 1991 v Mor, T, E (2), W, Pol, Ch, US; 1992 v Pol, W, US, Alb, US, I; 1993 v La, D, Sp, Ni, D, Alb, La, Li; (with Aston Villa), 1994 v Li, Ni, Ho, Bol, G, CzR, I, M, N, Ho; 1995 v La, Ni, E, Ni, P; 1996 v A, La, Ho, Ru, CzR, P; 1997 v Lie, Mac (2), Ic, R, Lie; 1998 v Li; (with Middlesbrough), Ic, Bel (2) (70)

Traynor, J. T. (Southampton), 1954 v L; 1962 v A; 1963 v Ic (2), S; 1964 v A (2), Sp (8)

Treacy, R. C. P. (WBA), 1966 v WG; 1967 v Sp, Cz; 1968 v Cz; (with Charlton Ath), Pol; 1969 v Pol, Cz, D; 1970 v S, D, H (sub), Pol (sub), WG (sub); 1971 v Pol, Se (sub+1), I, A; (with Swindon T), 1972 v Ir, Ec, Ch, P; 1973 v USSR, F, USSR, Pol, F, N; 1974 v Pol; (with Preston NE), Br; 1975 v USSR, Sw (2), WG; 1976 v T, N (sub), Pol (sub); (with WBA), 1977 v F, Pol; (with Shamrock R), 1978 v T, Pol; 1980 v Cz (sub) (42)

Tuohy, L. (Shamrock R), 1956 v Y; 1959 v Cz (2); (with Newcastle U), 1962 v A; 1963 v Ic (2); (with Shamrock R), 1964 v A; 1965 v Bel (8)

Turner, C. J. (Southend U), 1936 v Sw; 1937 v G, H, Sw, F; 1938 v N (2), (with West Ham U) Cz, Pol; 1939 v H (10)

Turner, P. (Celtic), 1963 v S; 1964 v Sp (2)

Vernon, J. (Belfast C), 1946 v P, Sp (2)

Waddock, A. (QPR), 1980 v Sw, Arg; 1981 v W, Pol (sub); 1982 v Alg; 1983 v Ic, Ma, Sp, Ho (sub); 1984 v Ma (sub), Ic, Ho, Is; 1985 v I, Is, E, N, Sp; 1986 v USSR; (with Millwall), 1990 v USSR, T (21)

Walsh, D. J. (Linfield), 1946 v P, Sp; (with WBA), 1947 v Sp, P; 1948 v P, Sp; 1949 v Sw, P, Se, Sp; 1950 v E, Fi, Se; 1951 v N; (with Aston Villa), Arg, N; 1952 v Sp; 1953 v A; 1954 v F (2) (20)

Walsh, J. (Limerick), 1982 v Tr (1)

Walsh, M. (Blackpool), 1976 v N, Pol; 1977 v F (sub), Pol; (with Everton), 1979 v Ni (sub); (with QPR), D (sub), Bul, WG (with Porto), 1981 v Bel (sub), Cz; 1982 v Alg (sub); 1983 v Ho, Sp (sub); (with Porto), 1984 v Ic (sub), Ma, Pol, Chn; 1985 v USSR, N (sub), D (21)

Walsh, M. (Everton), 1982 v Ch, Br, Tr; 1983 v Ic (4)

Walsh, W. (Manchester C), 1947 v E, Sp, P; 1948 v P, Sp; 1949 v Bel; 1950 v E, Se, Bel (9)

Waters, J. (Grimsby T), 1977 v T; 1980 v Ni (sub) (2)

Watters, F. (Shelbourne), 1926 v I (1)

Weir, E. (Clyde), 1939 v H (2), G (3)

Whelan, R. (St Patrick's Ath), 1964 v A, E (sub) (2)

Whelan, R. (Liverpool), 1981 v Cz (sub); 1982 v Ho (sub), F; 1983 v Ic, Ma, Sp; 1984 v Is; 1985 v USSR, N, I (sub), Is, E, N (sub), Sw; 1986 v USSR (sub), W; 1987 v Bel (sub), S, Bul, Bel, Br, L; 1988 v L, Bul, Pol, N, E, USSR, Ho; 1989 v Ni, F, H, Sp, Ma; 1990 v WG, Ni, Ma, W, Ho (sub); 1991 v Mor, E; 1992 v Sw; 1993 v La, W (sub), Li; (with Southend U), 1995 v Lie, A (53)

Whelan, M. (Manchester U), 1956 v Ho; 1957 v D, E (2) (4)

White, J. J. (Bohemians), 1928 v Bel (1)

Whittaker, R. (Chelsea), 1959 v Cz (1)

Williams, J. (Shamrock R), 1938 v N (1)

BRITISH AND IRISH INTERNATIONAL GOALSCORERS SINCE 1872

Where two players with the same surname and initials have appeared for the same country, and one or both have scored, they have been distinguished by reference to the club which appears *first* against their name in the international appearances section.

ENGLAND

Name	Goals
A'Court, A.	1
Adams, T. A.	4
Adcock, H.	1
Alcock, C. W.	1
Allen, A.	3
Allen, R.	2
Amos, A.	1
Anderson, V.	2
Anderton, D. R.	7
Astall, G.	1
Athersmith, W. C.	3
Atyeo, P. J. W.	5
Bache, J. W.	4
Bailey, N. C.	2
Baily, E. F.	5
Baker, J. H.	3
Ball, A. J.	8
Bambridge, A. L.	1
Bambridge, E. C.	11
Barclay, R.	2
Barmby, N. J.	3
Barnes, J.	11
Barnes, P. S.	4
Barton, J.	1
Bassett, W. I.	8
Bastin, C. S.	12
Beardsley, P. A.	9
Beasley, A.	1
Beattie, T. K.	1
Beckham, D. R. J.	1
Becton, F.	2
Bedford, H.	1
Bell, C.	9
Bentley, R. T. F.	9
Bishop, S. M.	1
Blackburn, F.	1
Blissett, L.	3
Bloomer, S.	28
Bond, R.	2
Bonsor, A. G.	1
Bowden, E. R.	1
Bowers, J. W.	2
Bowles, S.	
Bradford, G. R. W.	1
Bradford, J.	7
Bradley, W.	2
Bradshaw, F.	3
Brann, G.	1
Bridges, B. J.	1
Bridgett, A.	3
Brindle, T.	1
Britton, C. S.	1
Broadbent, P. F.	2
Broadis, I. A.	8
Brodie, J. B.	1
Bromley-Davenport, W.	2
Brook, E. F.	10
Brooking, T. D.	5
Brooks, J.	2
Broome, F. H.	3
Brown, A.	4
Brown, A. S.	1
Brown, G.	5
Brown, J.	3
Brown, W.	1
Buchan, C. M.	4
Bull, S. G.	4
Bullock, N.	2
Burgess, H.	4
Butcher, T.	3
Byrne, J. J.	8
Camsell, G. H.	18
Carter, H. S.	7
Carter, J. H.	4
Chadwick, E.	3
Chamberlain, M.	1
Chambers, H.	5
Channon, M. R.	21
Charlton, J.	6
Charlton, R.	49
Cheney, C. J.	1
Chivers, M.	13
Clarke, A. J.	10
Cobbold, W. N.	6
Cock, J. G.	2
Common, A.	2
Connelly, J. M.	7
Coppell, S. J.	7
Cotterill, G. H.	2
Cowans, G.	2
Crawford, R.	1
Crawshaw, T. H.	1
Crayston, W. J.	1
Creek, F. N. S.	1
Crooks, S. D.	7
Currey, E. S.	2
Currie, A. W.	3
Cursham, A. W.	2
Cursham, H. A.	5
Daft, H. B.	3
Davenport, J. K.	2
Davis, G.	1
Davis, H.	1
Day, S. H.	2
Dean, W. R.	18
Devey, J. H. G.	1
Dewhurst, F.	11
Dix, W. R.	1
Dixon, K. M.	4
Dixon, L. M.	1
Dorrell, A. R.	1
Douglas, B.	11
Drake, E. J.	6
Ducat, A.	1
Dunn, A. T. B.	2
Eastham, G.	2
Edwards, D.	5
Elliott, W. H.	3
Evans, R. E.	1
Ferdinand, L.	5
Finney, T.	30
Fleming, H. J.	9
Flowers, R.	10
Forman, Frank	1
Forman, Fred	3
Foster, R. E.	3
Fowler, R. B.	2
Francis, G. C. J.	3
Francis, T.	12
Freeman, B. C.	3
Froggatt, J.	2
Froggatt, R.	2
Galley, T.	1
Gascoigne, P. J.	10
Geary, F.	3
Gibbins, W. V. T.	3
Gilliatt, W. E.	3
Goddard, P.	1
Goodall, J.	12
Goodyer, A. C.	1
Gosling, R. C.	2
Goulden, L. A.	4
Grainger, C.	3
Greaves, J.	44
Grosvenor, A. T.	2
Gunn, W.	1
Haines, J. T. W.	2
Hall, G. W.	9
Halse, H. J.	2
Hampson, J.	5
Hampton, H.	2
Hancocks, J.	2
Hardman, H. P.	1
Harris, S. S.	2
Hassall, H. W.	4
Hateley, M.	9
Haynes, J. N.	18
Hegan, K. E.	4
Henfrey, A. G.	2
Hilsdon, G. R.	14
Hine, E. W.	4
Hinton, A. T.	1
Hirst, D. E.	1
Hitchens, G. A.	5
Hobbis, H. H. F.	1
Hoddle, G.	8
Hodgetts, D.	1
Hodgson, G.	1
Holley, G. H.	8
Houghton, W. E.	5
Howell, R.	1
Hughes, E. W.	1
Hulme, J. H. A.	4
Hunt, G. S.	1
Hunt, R.	18
Hunter, N.	2
Hurst, G. C.	24
Ince, P. E. C.	2
Jack, D. N. B.	3
Johnson, D. E.	6
Johnson, E.	2
Johnson, J. A.	2
Johnson, T. C. F.	5
Johnson, W. H.	1
Kail, E. I. L.	2
Kay, A. H.	1
Keegan, J. K.	21
Kelly, R.	8
Kennedy, R.	3
Kenyon-Slaney, W. S.	2
Keown, M. R.	1
Kevan, D. T.	8
Kidd, B.	1
Kingsford, R. K.	1
Kirchen, A. J.	2
Kirton, W. J.	1
Langton, R.	1
Latchford, R. D.	5
Latherton, E. G.	1
Lawler, C.	1
Lawton, T.	22
Lee, F.	10
Lee, J.	1
Lee, R. M.	2
Lee, S.	2
Le Saux, G. P.	1
Lindley, T.	14
Lineker, G.	48
Lofthouse, J. M.	3
Lofthouse, N.	30
Hon. A. Lyttelton	1
Mabbutt, G.	1
Macdonald, M.	6
Mannion, W. J.	11
Mariner, P.	13
Marsh, R. W.	1
Matthews, S.	11
Matthews, V.	1
McCall, J.	1
McDermott, T.	3
Medley, L. D.	1
Melia, J.	1
Mercer, D. W.	1
Merson, P. C.	3
Milburn, J. E. T.	10
Miller, H. S.	1
Mills, G. R.	3
Milward, A.	3
Mitchell, C.	5
Moore, J.	1
Moore, R. F.	2
Moore, W. G. B.	2
Morren, T.	1
Morris, F.	1
Morris, J.	3
Mortensen, S. H.	23
Morton, J. R.	1
Mosforth, W.	3
Mullen, J.	6
Mullery, A. P.	1
Neal, P. G.	5
Needham, E.	3
Nicholls, J.	1
Nicholson, W. E.	1
O'Grady, M.	3
Osborne, F. R.	3
Owen, M. J.	4
Own goals	23
Page, L. A.	1
Paine, T. L.	7
Palmer, C. L.	1
Parry, E. H.	1
Parry, R. A.	1
Pawson, F. W.	1
Payne, J.	2
Peacock, A.	3
Pearce, S.	5
Pearson, J. S.	5
Pearson, S. C.	5
Perry, W.	2
Peters, M.	20
Pickering, F.	5
Platt, D.	27
Pointer, R.	2

Quantrill, A.	1
Ramsay, A. E.	3
Revie, D. G.	4
Reynolds, J.	3
Richardson, J. R.	2
Rigby, A.	3
Rimmer, E. J.	2
Roberts, F.	2
Roberts, H.	1
Roberts, W. T.	2
Robinson, J.	3
Robson, B.	26
Robson, R.	4
Rowley, J. F.	6
Royle, J.	2
Rutherford, J.	3
Sagar, C.	1
Sandilands, R. R.	3
Sansom, K.	1
Schofield, J.	1
Scholes, P.	7
Seed, J. M.	1
Settle, J.	6
Sewell, J.	3
Shackleton, L. F.	1
Sharp, J.	1
Shearer, A.	24
Shelton, A.	1
Shepherd, A.	2
Sheringham, E. P.	9
Simpson, J.	1
Smith, A. M.	2
Smith, G. O.	11
Smith, Joe	1
Smith, J. R.	2
Smith, J. W.	4
Smith, R.	13
Smith, S.	1
Sorby, T. H.	1
Southgate, G.	1
Southworth, J.	3
Sparks, F. J.	3
Spence, J. W.	1
Spiksley, F.	5
Spilsbury, B. W.	5
Steele, F. C.	8
Stephenson, G. T.	2
Steven, T. M.	4
Stewart, J.	2
Stiles, N. P.	1
Storer, H.	1
Stone, S. B.	2
Summerbee, M. G.	1
Tambling, R. V.	1
Taylor, P. J.	2
Taylor, T.	16
Thompson, P. B.	1
Thornewell, G.	1
Tilson, S. F.	6
Townley, W. J.	2
Tueart, D.	2
Vaughton, O. H.	6
Veitch, J. G.	3
Violett, D. S.	1
Waddle, C. R.	6
Walker, W. H.	9
Wall, G.	2
Wallace, D.	1
Walsh, P.	1
Waring, T.	4
Warren, B.	2
Watson, D. V.	4
Watson, V. M.	4
Webb, G. W.	1
Webb, N.	4
Wedlock, W. J.	2
Weller, K.	1

Welsh, D.	1
Whateley, O.	2
Wheldon, G. F.	6
Whitfield, H.	1
Wignall, F.	2
Wilkes, A.	1
Wilkins, R. G.	3
Willingham, C. K.	1
Wilshaw, D. J.	10
Wilson, G. P.	1
Winckworth, W. N.	1
Windridge, J. E.	7
Wise, D. F.	1
Withe, P.	1
Wollaston, C. H. R.	1
Wood, H.	1
Woodcock, T.	16
Woodhall, G.	1
Woodward, V. J.	29
Worrall, F.	2
Worthington, F. S.	2
Wright, I. E.	9
Wright, M.	1
Wright, W. A.	3
Wylie, J. G.	1
Yates, J.	3

NORTHERN IRELAND

Anderson, T.	4
Armstrong, G.	12
Bambrick, J.	12
Barr, H. H.	1
Barron, H.	3
Best, G.	9
Bingham, W. L.	10
Black, K.	1
Blanchflower, D.	2
Blanchflower, J.	1
Brennan, B.	1
Brennan, R. A.	1
Brotherston, N.	3
Brown, J.	1
Browne, F.	2
Campbell, J.	1
Campbell, W. G.	1
Casey, T.	2
Caskey, W.	1
Cassidy, T.	1
Chambers, J.	3
Clarke, C. J.	13
Clements, D.	2
Cochrane, T.	1
Condy, J.	1
Connor, M. J.	1
Coulter, J.	1
Croft, T.	1
Crone, W.	1
Crossan, E.	1
Crossan, J. A.	10
Curran, G.	2
Cush, W. W.	5
Dalton, W.	4
D'Arcy, S. D.	1
Darling, J.	1
Davey, H. H.	1
Davis, T. L.	1
Dill, A. H.	1
Doherty, L.	1
Doherty, P. D.	3
Dougan, A. D.	8
Dowie, I.	12
Dunne, J.	4
Elder, A. R.	1
Emerson, W.	1
English, S.	1
Feeney, W	1

Ferguson, W.	1
Ferris, J.	1
Ferris, R. O.	1
Finney, T.	2
Gaffkin, J.	4
Gara, A.	3
Gaukrodger, G.	1
Gibb, J. T.	2
Gibb, T. J.	1
Gillespie, K. R.	1
Gillespie, W.	12
Goodall, A. L.	2
Griffin, D. J.	1
Gray, P.	5
Halligan, W.	1
Hamill, M.	1
Hamilton, B.	4
Hamilton, W. R.	5
Hannon, D. J.	1
Harkin, J. T.	2
Harvey, M.	3
Hill, C. F.	1
Hughes, M.	3
Humphries, W.	1
Hunter, A. *(Distillery)*	1
Hunter, A. *(Blackburn R)*	1
Hunter, B. V.	1
Irvine, R. W.	3
Irvine, W. J.	8
Johnston, H.	2
Johnston, S.	2
Johnston, W. C.	1
Jones, S.	1
Jones, J.	1
Kelly, J.	4
Kernaghan, N.	1
Kirwan, J.	2
Lacey, W.	3
Lemon, J.	2
Lennon, N. F.	2
Lockhart, N.	3
Lomas, S. M.	2
Magilton, J.	5
Mahood, J.	2
Martin, D. K.	3
Maxwell, J.	2
McAdams, W. J.	7
McAllen, J.	1
Mcauley, J. L.	1
McCandless, J.	3
McCaw, J. H.	1
McClelland, J.	1
McCluggage, A.	2
McCracken, W.	1
McCrory, S.	1
McCurdy, C.	1
McDonald, A.	3
McGarry, J. K.	1
McGrath, R. C.	4
McIlroy, J.	10
McIlroy, S. B.	5
McKnight, J.	2
McLaughlin, J. C.	6
McMahon, G. J.	2
McMordie, A. S.	3
McMorran, E. J.	4
McParland, P. J.	10
McWha, W. B. R.	1
Meldon, J.	1
Mercer, J. T.	1
Millar, W.	1
Milligan, D.	1
Milne, R. G.	2
Molyneux, T. B.	1

Moreland, V.	1
Morgan, S.	3
Morrow, S. J.	1
Morrow, W. J.	1
Mulryne, P. P.	1
Murphy, N.	1
Neill, W. J. T.	2
Nelson, S.	1
Nicholl, C. J.	3
Nicholl, J. M.	1
Nicholson, J. J.	6
O'Boyle, G.	1
O'Hagan, C.	2
O'Kane, W. J.	1
O'Neill, J.	2
O'Neill, M. A.	4
O'Neill, M. H.	8
Own goals	6
Patterson, D. J.	1
Peacock, R.	2
Peden, J.	7
Penney, S.	2
Pyper, James	2
Pyper, John	1
Quinn, J. M.	12
Quinn, S. J.	1
Reynolds, J.	1
Rowland, K.	1
Rowley, R. W. M.	2
Sheridan, J.	2
Sherrard, J.	1
Sherrard, W. C.	2
Simpson, W. J.	5
Sloan, H. A. de B.	4
Smyth, S.	5
Spence, D. W.	3
Stanfield, O. M.	11
Stevenson, A. E.	5
Stewart, I.	2
Taggart, G. P.	7
Thompson, F. W.	1
Torrans, S.	1
Tully, C. P.	3
Turner, E.	1
Walker, J.	1
Walsh, D. J.	5
Welsh, E.	1
Whiteside, N.	9
Whiteside, S.	1
Williams, J. R.	1
Williamson, J.	1
Wilson, D. J.	1
Wilson, K. J.	6
Wilson, S. J.	7
Wilton, J. M.	1
Young, S.	2

SCOTLAND

Aitken, R. *(Celtic)*	1
Aitken, R. *(Dumbarton)*	1
Aitkenhead, W. A. C.	2
Alexander, D.	1
Allan, D. S.	4
Allan, J.	2
Anderson, F.	1
Anderson, W.	4
Andrews, P.	1
Archibald, A.	1
Archibald, S.	4
Baird, D.	2
Baird, J. C.	2

Stewart, R.	1	Deacy, N.	4	Morgan-Owen, M. M.	2	**REPUBLIC OF**	
Stewart, W. E.	1	Doughty, J.	6	Morris, A. G.	9	**IRELAND**	
Strachan, G.	5	Doughty, R.	2	Morris, H.	2	Aldridge, J.	19
Sturrock, P.	3	Durban, A.	2	Morris, R.	1	Ambrose, P.	1
		Dwyer, P.	2	Morris, S.	2	Anderson, J.	1
Taylor, J. D.	1					Bermingham, P.	1
Templeton, R.	1	Edwards, G.	2	Nicholas, P.	2	Bradshaw, P.	4
Thomson, A.	1	Edwards, R. I.	4			Brady, L.	9
Thomson, C.	4	England, H. M.	4			Breen, G.	3
Thomson, R.	1	Evans, I.	1	O'Callaghan, E.	3	Brown, D.	1
Thomson, W.	1	Evans, J.	1	O'Sullivan, P. A.	1	Byrne, J. (*Bray*)	1
Thornton, W.	1	Evans, R. E.	2	Owen, G.	2	Byrne, J. (*QPR*)	4
		Evans, W.	1	Owen, W.	4		
Waddell, T. S.	1	Eyton-Jones, J. A.	1	Owen, W. P.	6	Cantwell, J.	14
Waddell, W.	6			Own goals	13	Carey, J.	3
Walker, J.	2	Flynn, B.	7			Carroll, T.	1
Walker, R.	7	Ford, T.	23	Palmer, D.	3	Cascarino, A.	19
Walker, T.	9	Foulkes, W. I.	1	Parry, T. D.	3	Coad, P.	3
Wallace, I. A.	1	Fowler, J.	3	Paul, R.	1	Connolly, D. J.	7
Wark, J.	7			Peake, E.	1	Conroy, T.	2
Watson, J. A. K.	1	Giles, D.	2	Pembridge, M.	5	Conway, J.	3
Watt, F.	2	Giggs, R. J.	5	Perry, E.	1	Coyne, T.	6
Watt, W. W.	1	Glover, E. M.	7	Phillips, C.	5	Cummins, G.	5
Weir, A.	1	Godfrey, B. C.	2	Phillips, D.	2	Curtis, D.	8
Weir, J. B.	1	Green, A. W.	3	Powell, A.	1		
White, J. A.	3	Griffiths, A. T.	6	Powell, D.	1	Daly, G.	13
Wilson, A.	2	Griffiths, M. W.	2	Price, J.	4	Davis, T.	4
Wilson, A. N.	13	Griffiths, T. P.	3	Price, P.	1	Dempsey, J.	1
Wilson, D. (*Queen's*				Pryce-Jones, W. E.	3	Dennehy, M.	2
Park)	2	Harris, C. S.	1	Pugh, D. H.	2	Donnelly, J.	4
Wilson, D. (*Rangers*)	9	Hartson, J.	2			Donnelly, T.	1
Wilson, H.	1	Hersee, R.	1	Reece, G. I.	2	Duffy, B.	1
Wylie, T. G.	1	Hewitt, R.	1	Rees, R. R.	3	Duggan, H.	1
		Hockey, T.	1	Richards, R. W.	1	Dunne, J.	13
Young, A.	5	Hodges, G.	2	Roach, J.	2	Dunne, L.	1
		Hole, W. J.	1	Robbins, W. W.	4		
		Hopkins, I. J.	2	Roberts, J. (*Corwen*)	1	Eglington, T.	2
WALES		Horne, B.	2	Roberts, Jas.	1	Ellis, P.	2
Allchurch, I. J.	23	Howell, E. G.	3	Roberts, P. S.	1		
Allen, M.	3	Hughes, L. M.	16	Roberts, R. (*Druids*)	1	Fagan, F.	5
Astley, D. J.	12			Roberts, W. (*Llangollen*)	2	Fallon, S.	2
Atherton, R. W.	2	James, E.	2	Roberts, W. (*Wrexham*)	1	Fallon, W.	2
		James, L.	10	Roberts, W. H.	1	Farrell, P.	3
Bamford, T.	1	James, R.	7	Robinson, J. R. C.	2	Fitzgerald, P.	2
Barnes, W.	1	Jarrett, R. H.	3	Rush, I.	28	Fitzgerald, J.	1
Bellamy, C. D.	2	Jenkyns, C. A.	1	Russell, M. R.	1	Fitzsimmons, A.	7
Blackmore, C. G.	1	Jones, A.	1			Flood, J. J.	4
Blake, N. A.	2	Jones, Bryn	6	Sabine, H. W.	1	Fogarty, A.	3
Bodin, P. J.	3	Jones, B. S.	2	Saunders, D.	21	Fullam, J.	1
Boulter, L. M.	1	Jones, Cliff	16	Savage, R. W.	1	Fullam, R.	1
Bowdler, J. C. H.	3	Jones, C. W.	1	Shaw, E. G.	2		
Bowen, D. L.	1	Jones, D. E.	1	Sisson, H.	4	Galvin, A.	1
Bowen, M.	3	Jones, Evan	1	Slatter, N.	2	Gavin, J.	2
Boyle, T.	1	Jones, H.	1	Smallman, D. P.	1	Geoghegan, M.	2
Bryan, T.	1	Jones, I.	1	Speed, G. A.	3	Giles, J.	5
Burgess, W. A. R.	1	Jones, J. L.	1	Symons, C. J.	2	Givens, D.	19
Burke, T.	1	Jones, J. O.	1			Glynn, D.	1
Butler, W. T.	1	Jones, J. P.	1	Tapscott, D. R.	4	Grealish, T.	8
		Jones, Leslie J.	1	Thomas, M.	4	Grimes, A. A.	1
Chapman, T.	2	Jones, R. A.	2	Thomas, T.	1		
Charles, J.	1	Jones, W. L.	6	Toshack, J. B.	12	Hale, A.	2
Charles, M.	6			Trainer, H.	2	Hand, E.	2
Charles, W. J.	15	Keenor, F. C.	2			Harte, I. P.	2
Clarke, R. J.	5	Krzywicki, R. L.	1	Vaughan, John	2	Haverty, J.	3
Coleman, C.	4			Vernon, T. R.	8	Holmes, J.	1
Collier, D. J.	1	Leek, K.	5	Vizard, E. T.	1	Horlacher, A.	2
Crosse, K.	1	Lewis, B.	4			Houghton, R.	6
Cumner, R. H.	1	Lewis, D. M.	2	Walsh, I.	7	Hughton, C.	1
Curtis, A.	6	Lewis, W.	8	Warren, F. W.	3	Hurley, C.	2
Curtis, E. R.	3	Lewis, W. L.	3	Watkins, W. M.	4		
		Lovell, S.	1	Wilding, J.	4	Irwin, D.	4
Davies, D. W.	1	Lowrie, G.	2	Williams, A.	1		
Davies, E. Lloyd	1			Williams, D. R.	2	Jordan, D.	1
Davies, G.	2	Mahoney, J. F.	1	Williams, G. E.	1		
Davies, L. S.	6	Mays, A. W.	1	Williams, G. G.	1	Kavanagh, G. A.	1
Davies, R. T.	9	Medwin, T. C.	6	Williams, W.	1	Keane, R. D.	2
Davies, R. W.	6	Melville, A. K	3	Woosnam, A. P.	3	Keane, R. M.	5
Davies, S.	5	Meredith, W. H.	11	Wynn, G. A.	1	Kelly, D.	9
Davies, W.	6	Mills, T. J.	1			Kelly, G.	1
Davies, W. H.	1	Moore, G.	1	Yorath, T. C.	2	Kelly, J.	2
Davies, William	5	Morgan, J. R.	2	Young, E.	1	Kennedy, M.	1
Davis, W. O.	1	Morgan-Owen, H.	1			Kernaghan, A. N.	1

Lacey, W.	1	Moore, P.	7	Own goals	7	Stapleton, F.	20
Lawrenson, M.	5	Moran, K.	6			Staunton, S.	5
Leech, M.	2	Moroney, T.	1	Quinn, N.	18	Strahan, J.	1
		Mulligan, P.	1			Sullivan, J.	1
McAteer, J. W.	1			Ringstead, A.	7		
McCann, J.	1	O'Callaghan, K.	1	Robinson, M.	4	Townsend, A. D.	7
McCarthy, M.	2	O'Connor, T.	2	Rogers, E.	5	Treacy, R.	5
McEvoy, A.	6	O'Farrell, F.	2	Ryan, G.	1	Touhy, L.	4
McGee, P.	4	O'Flanagan, K.	3	Ryan, R.	3		
McGrath, P.	8	O'Keefe, E.	1			Waddock, G.	3
McLoughlin, A. F.	2	O'Leary, D. A.	1	Sheedy, K.	9	Walsh, D.	5
Mancini, T.	1	O'Neill, F.	1	Sheridan, J.	5	Walsh, M.	3
Martin, C.	6	O'Neill, K. P.	4	Slaven, B.	1	Waters, J.	1
Martin, M.	4	O'Reilly, J. (*Brideville*)	2	Sloan, W.	1	White, J. J.	2
Mooney, J.	1	O'Reilly, J. (*Cork*)	1	Squires, J.	1	Whelan, R.	3

Alan Shearer is challenged by the Swedish defender Joachim Bjorklund in the European Championship qualifier at Wembley. Shearer remains England's leading goalscorer among contemporary internationals. He won his first full cap for England against France on 19 February 1992 and scored one of the goals in a 2-0 win. He continues to be the most expensive English player, having been signed by Newcastle United from Blackburn Rovers in July 1996 for £15 million. (ASP)

SOUTH AMERICA

COPA LIBERTADORES 1997

Results missing from last edition

SEMI-FINALS, FIRST LEG
Racing 3, Sporting Cristal 2
Cruzeiro 1, Colo Colo 0

SEMI-FINALS, SECOND LEG
Sporting Cristal 4, Racing 1
Colo Colo 3, Cruzeiro 2
(Cruzeiro won 4-1 on penalties)

FINAL, FIRST LEG
Sporting Cristal 0, Cruzeiro 0

FINAL, SECOND LEG
Cruzeiro 1, Sporting Cristal 0

COPA LIBERTADORES 1998

Results missing from last edition

SECOND ROUND, SECOND LEG
Cruzeiro 0, Vasco da Gama 0

QUARTER-FINALS, FIRST LEG
Gremio 1, Vasco da Gama 1

QUARTER-FINALS, SECOND LEG
Vasco da Gama 1, Gremio 0

SEMI-FINALS, FIRST LEG
Barcelona 1, Cerro Porteno 0
Vasco da Gama 1, River Plate 0

SEMI-FINALS, SECOND LEG
Cerro Porteno 2, Barcelona 1
(Barcelona won 4-3 on penalties)
River Plate 1, Vasco da Gama 1

FINAL, FIRST LEG
Vasco da Gama 2, Barcelona 0

FINAL, SECOND LEG
Barcelona 1, Vasco da Gama 2

COPA LIBERTADORES 1999

Preliminary

Group	P	W	D	L	F	A	Pts
Monterrey	6	3	1	2	13	9	10
Estudiantes (Ven)	6	3	1	2	9	9	10
Necaxa	6	2	3	1	5	3	9
Univ. Los Andes	6	1	1	4	5	11	4

Group 1	P	W	D	L	F	A	Pts
Nacional (U)	6	4	0	2	9	8	12
Estudiantes (Ven)	6	3	0	3	9	14	9
Bella Vista	6	2	1	3	9	6	7
Monterrey	6	2	1	3	10	9	7

Group 2	P	W	D	L	F	A	Pts
Velez Sarsfield	6	2	3	1	6	3	9
Dep Cali	6	3	0	3	4	8	9
River Plate	6	2	2	2	8	8	8
Once Caldas	6	2	1	3	7	6	7

Group 3	P	W	D	L	F	A	Pts
Corinthians	6	4	0	2	16	8	12
Palmeiras	6	3	1	2	12	10	10
Cerro Porteno	6	2	1	3	14	20	7
Olimpia	6	1	2	3	11	15	5

Group 4	P	W	D	L	F	A	Pts
Univ. Catolica	6	3	2	1	9	5	11
Colo Colo	6	2	2	2	5	7	8
Universitario	6	2	1	3	7	8	7
Sporting Cristal	6	0	5	1	7	8	5

Group 5	P	W	D	L	F	A	Pts
LDU	6	3	1	2	10	8	10
Emelec	6	3	0	3	9	12	9
Wilstermann	6	2	2	2	9	9	8
Blooming	6	2	1	3	5	4	7

SECOND ROUND, FIRST LEG
Bella Vista 2, Univ. Catolica 2
Wilstermann 1, Corinthians 1
Cerro Porteno 5, Nacional 0
Palmeiras 1, Vasco da Gama 1
Universitario 0, Velez Sarsfield 0
River Plate 1, LDU 0
Emelec 1, Estudiantes 3
Dep Cali 2, Colo Colo 0

SECOND ROUND, SECOND LEG
Univ. Catolica 1, Bella Vista 3
Nacional 2, Cerro Porteno 1
Estudiantes 0, Emelec 1
Vasco da Gama 2, Palmeiras 4
Velez Sarsfield 4, Universitario 0
Corinthians 5, Wilstermann 2

LDU 1, River Plate 0
(River Plate won 5-4 on penalties)
Colo Colo 1, Dep Cali 0

QUARTER-FINALS, FIRST LEG
River Plate 2, Velez Sarsfield 0
Palmeiras 2, Corinthians 0
Estudiantes 3, Cerro Porteno 0
Dep Cali 2, Bella Vista 1

QUARTER-FINALS, SECOND LEG
Velez Sarsfield 1, River Plate 0
Cerro Porteno 4, Estudiantes 0
Bella Vista 1, Dep Cali 1
Corinthians 2, Palmeiras 0
(Palmeiras won 4-2 on penalties)

SEMI-FINALS, FIRST LEG
River Plate 1, Palmeiras 0
Dep Cali 4, Cerro Porteno 0

SEMI-FINALS, SECOND LEG
Palmeiras 3, River Plate 0
Cerro Porteno 3, Dep Cali 2

FINAL, FIRST LEG
Dep Cali 1, Palmeiras 0

FINAL, SECOND LEG
Palmeiras 2, Dep Cali 1
(Palmeiras won 4-3 on penalties.)

MERCONORTE CUP

Group A	P	W	D	L	F	A	Pts
Millonarios	6	3	1	2	7	8	10
Emelec	6	2	3	1	9	6	9
America	6	1	4	1	9	9	7
Sporting Cristal	6	0	4	2	5	7	4

SEMI-FINALS, FIRST LEG
El Nacional 1, Dep Cali 2
Millonarios 0, Atletico Nacional 2

Group B	P	W	D	L	F	A	Pts
Atletico Nacional	6	3	2	1	14	7	11
Alianza	6	2	2	2	8	6	8
The Strongest	6	2	2	2	5	9	8
Barcelona	6	1	2	3	5	10	5

SEMI-FINALS, SECOND LEG
Atletico Nacional 1, Millonarios 2
Dep Cali 1, El Nacional 2
(Dep Cali won 5-4 on penalties)

Group C	P	W	D	L	F	A	Pts
Dep Cali	6	3	2	1	7	3	11
El Nacional	6	3	1	2	6	6	10
Caracas	6	2	1	3	6	8	7
Universitario	6	1	2	3	6	8	5

FINAL, FIRST LEG
Atletico Nacional 3, Dep Cali 1

FINAL, SECOND LEG
Dep Cali 0, Atletico Nacional 1

MERCOSUR CUP

Group A	P	W	D	L	F	A	Pts
Cruzeiro	6	3	1	2	15	7	10
San Lorenzo	6	3	1	2	11	8	10
Sao Paulo	6	2	1	3	8	12	7
Colo Colo	6	2	1	3	5	12	7

Group B	P	W	D	L	F	A	Pts
Palmeiras	6	6	0	0	16	3	18
Nacional (U)	6	3	0	3	10	14	9
Independiente	6	2	0	4	12	15	6
Univ. de Chile	6	1	0	5	7	12	3

Group C	P	W	D	L	F	A	Pts
Racing	6	4	2	0	9	4	14
Olimpia	6	3	1	2	13	12	10
Corinthians	6	1	2	3	7	8	5
Penarol	6	0	3	3	6	11	3

Group D	P	W	D	L	F	A	Pts
Velez Sarsfield	6	3	2	1	7	6	11
Boca Juniors	6	3	0	3	11	7	9
Flamengo	6	3	0	3	7	8	9
Cerro Porteno	6	1	2	3	9	13	5

Group E	P	W	D	L	F	A	Pts
River Plate (A)	6	2	3	1	8	7	9
Vasco da Gama	6	2	3	1	4	3	9
Gremio	6	2	1	3	10	9	7
Univ. Catolica	6	1	3	2	8	9	6

QUARTER FINALS, FIRST LEG
Velez Sarsfield 3, Olimpia 4
River Plate 1, Cruzeiro 2
San Lorenzo 0, Racing 0
Palmeiras 3, Boca Juniors 1

QUARTER-FINALS, SECOND LEG
Olimpia 2, Velez Sarsfield 1
Cruzeiro 2, River Plate 0

Racing 1, San Lorenzo 1
(San Lorenzo won 2-0 on penalties)
Boca Juniors 1, Palmeiras 1

SEMI-FINALS, FIRST LEG
Palmeiras 2, Olimpia 0
Cruzeiro 1, San Lorenzo 0

SEMI-FINALS, SECOND LEG
Olimpia 0, Palmeiras 1
(Match abandoned 69 minutes)
San Lorenzo 1, Cruzeiro 1

FINAL, FIRST LEG
Cruzeiro 2, Palmeiras 1

FINAL, SECOND LEG
Palmeiras 3, Cruzeiro 1

PLAY-OFF
Palmeiras 1, Cruzeiro 0
(Third game played as each team had won one match)

CONMEBOL CUP

FIRST ROUND, FIRST LEG
Wilstermann 0, Gimnasia 0
Melgar 1, LDU 3
Dep. Chacao 2, Atletico Quindio 2
Santos 2, Once Caldas 1
River Plate (U) 0, Huracan Buceo 0
Rosario Central 2, Audax Italiano 0
Atletico Mineiro 0, Cerro Cora 0
Sampaio 0, America 0

FIRST ROUND, SECOND LEG
Gimnasia 1, Wilstermann 1
(Wilstermann won 4-2 on penalties)
Once Caldas 2, Santos 1
(Santos won 3-2 on penalties)
Atletico Quindio 2, Dep. Chacao 1
LDU 3, Melgar 1
Audax Italiano 1, Rosario Central 0
Huracan Buceo 4, River Plate (U) 1
Cerro Cora 0, Atletico Mineiro 0
(Atletico Mineiro won 4-2 on penalties)
America 1, Sampaio 3

SECOND ROUND, FIRST LEG
Sampaio 1, Atletico Quindio 0

LDU 2, Santos 2
Atletico Mineiro 3, Wilstermann 1
Huracan Buceo 2, Rosario Central 3

SECOND ROUND, SECOND LEG
Atletico Quindio 0, Sampaio 1
Santos 3, LDU 0
Wilstermann 0, Atletico Mineiro 1
Rosario Central 2, Huracan Buceo 0

SEMI-FINALS, FIRST LEG
Rosario Central 1, Atletico Mineiro 1
Santos 0, Sampaio 0

SEMI-FINALS, SECOND LEG
Atletico Mineiro 0, Rosario Central 1
Sampaio 1, Santos 5

FINAL, FIRST LEG
Santos 1, Rosario Central 0

FINAL, SECOND LEG
Rosario Central 0, Santos 0

COPA AMERICA 1999 (in Paraguay)

GROUP A
Peru 3, Japan 2
Paraguay 0, Bolivia 0
Paraguay 4, Japan 0
Peru 1, Bolivia 0
Paraguay 1, Peru 0
Japan 1, Bolivia 1

GROUP B
Chile 0, Mexico 1
Brazil 7, Venezuela 0
Brazil 2, Mexico 1
Chile 3, Venezuela 0
Mexico 3, Venezuela 1
Brazil 1, Chile 0

GROUP C
Uruguay 0, Colombia 1
Argentina 3, Ecuador 1
Uruguay 2, Ecuador 1
Argentina 0, Colombia 3

Colombia 2, Ecuador 1
Argentina 2, Uruguay 0

QUARTER-FINALS
Peru 3, Mexico 3
(Mexico won 4-2 on penalties).
Paraguay 1, Uruguay 1
(Uruguay won 5-3 on penalties).
Colombia 2, Chile 3
Brazil 2, Argentina 1

SEMI-FINALS
Uruguay 1, Chile 1
(Uruguay won 5-3 on penalties).
Brazil 2, Mexico 0

MATCH FOR THIRD PLACE
Chile 1, Mexico 2

FINAL
Brazil 3, Uruguay 0

AFRICAN NATIONS' CUP 1999

Group 1

	P	W	D	L	F	A	Pts
Cameroon	4	3	1	0	8	1	10
Eritrea	4	1	1	2	4	4	4
Mozambique	4	1	0	3	4	9	3

Group 2

	P	W	D	L	F	A	Pts
Morocco	4	2	2	0	6	4	8
Togo	4	1	1	2	5	6	4
Guinea	4	1	1	2	3	4	4

Group 3

	P	W	D	L	F	A	Pts
Ivory Coast	6	3	2	1	7	2	11
Congo	6	3	1	2	6	5	10
Mali	6	2	3	1	5	3	9
Namibia	6	0	2	4	2	10	2

Group 4

	P	W	D	L	F	A	Pts
South Africa	6	3	2	1	10	5	11
Gabon	6	3	1	2	10	10	10
Mauritius	6	1	3	2	6	8	6
Angola	6	1	2	3	7	10	5

Group 5

	P	W	D	L	F	A	Pts
Burkina Fasco	4	2	2	0	8	5	8
Senegal	4	1	2	1	4	4	5
Burundi	4	1	0	3	3	6	3

Group 6

	P	W	D	L	F	A	Pts
Zambia	6	5	1	0	9	2	16
DR Congo	6	3	1	2	7	6	10
Madagascar	6	1	2	3	6	10	5
Kenya	6	0	2	4	3	7	2

Group 7

	P	W	D	L	F	A	Pts
Tunisia	6	5	0	1	13	3	15
Algeria	6	2	1	3	8	7	7
Liberia	6	2	1	3	7	8	7
Uganda	6	2	0	4	3	13	6

Eritrea and Senegal qualify for play-off group with Zimbabwe. Egypt qualify as holders; Ghana and Nigeria qualify as co-hosts.

UEFA UNDER-21 CHAMPIONSHIP
1998–2000

GROUP 1
Belarus 0, Denmark 2
Wales 1, Italy 2
Denmark 2, Wales 2
Italy 1, Switzerland 0
Switzerland 2, Denmark 0
Wales 0, Belarus 0
Denmark 1, Italy 2
Switzerland 1, Wales 0
Italy 4, Belarus 1
Denmark 2, Belarus 0
Italy 6, Wales 2
Wales 1, Denmark 2
Switzerland 0, Italy 0

GROUP 2
Latvia 1, Georgia 2
Georgia 0, Albania 1
Slovenia 1, Norway 3
Norway 4, Albania 1
Greece 3, Georgia 2
Slovenia 0, Latvia 1
Norway 2, Latvia 0
Greece 2, Slovenia 2
Albania 0, Greece 5
Greece 2, Norway 1
Georgia 0, Slovenia 0
Latvia 0, Greece 2
Georgia 0, Norway 3
Latvia 0, Albania 0
Norway 0, Georgia 0
Albania 1, Norway 2
Georgia 1, Greece 1
Latvia 1, Slovenia 1
Albania 1, Slovenia 4
Greece 6, Latvia 0

GROUP 3
Turkey 2, N Ireland 0
N Ireland 1, Finland 1
Turkey 2, Germany 0
Moldova 0, Germany 2
Turkey 1, Finland 1
Finland 1, Moldova 0
N Ireland 1, Moldova 1
N Ireland 1, Germany 0
Turkey 2, Moldova 0
Moldova 0, N Ireland 0
Germany 2, Finland 0
Germany 2, Moldova 0

Finland 0, Turkey 0
Moldova 1, Finland 1

GROUP 4
Ukraine 1, Russia 0
Armenia 3, Iceland 1
Russia 2, France 1
Ukraine 8, Armenia 0
Iceland 1, Russia 2
Iceland 0, France 2
France 4, Ukraine 0
Armenia 0, Russia 2
Ukraine 5, Iceland 1
France 3, Armenia 1
Iceland 2, Armenia 0
France 2, Russia 0
Armenia 1, Ukraine 1
Russia 3, Iceland 0

GROUP 5
Sweden 0, England 2
England 1, Bulgaria 0
Poland 5, Luxembourg 0
Bulgaria 2, Sweden 1
Luxembourg 0, England 5
Bulgaria 2, Poland 2
Sweden 3, Luxembourg 0
England 5, Poland 0
Poland 2, Sweden 0
Luxembourg 0, Bulgaria 3
England 3, Sweden 0
Poland 3, Bulgaria 3
Bulgaria 0, England 1
Luxembourg 0, Poland 4

GROUP 6
Austria 0, Israel 1
Cyprus 1, Spain 3
Cyprus 2, Austria 1
Holland 3, Israel 0
Israel 0, Spain 4
Holland 3, Austria 2
Cyprus 0, Holland 3
Spain 4, Austria 0
Israel 1, Cyprus 1
Holland 0, Spain 1
Austria 0, Holland 1
Spain 4, Holland 1
Israel 2, Austria 1
Holland 5, Cyprus 1

GROUP 7
Portugal 1, Romania 1
Azerbaijan 2, Hungary 1
Slovakia 1, Portugal 0
Hungary 1, Romania 2
Hungary 0, Portugal 3
Slovakia 2, Azerbaijan 1
Portugal 5, Azerbaijan 0
Romania 0, Slovakia 1
Azerbaijan 0, Romania 2
Slovakia 4, Hungary 1
Romania 2, Hungary 1
Portugal 1, Slovakia 1
Romania 1, Azerbaijan 1
Hungary 3, Slovakia 0

GROUP 8
Republic of Ireland 2, Croatia 2
Malta 0, Croatia 3
Republic of Ireland 2, Malta 1
Croatia 4, Macedonia 0
Macedonia 1, Malta 0
Yugoslavia 1, Republic of Ireland 1
Malta 5, Macedonia 1
Malta 1, Yugoslavia 5
Macedonia 0, Croatia 2
Republic of Ireland 0, Macedonia 0
Yugoslavia 7, Malta 0

GROUP 9
Lithuania 0, Scotland 0
Scotland 2, Estonia 0
Bosnia 0, Czech Republic 0
Lithuania 0, Belgium 1
Lithuania 4, Bosnia 0
Czech Republic 3, Estonia 0
Belgium 2, Scotland 0
Belgium 0, Czech Republic 2
Bosnia 3, Estonia 2
Scotland 2, Belgium 2
Czech Republic 1, Lithuania 0
Lithuania 4, Estonia 1
Scotland 0, Czech Republic 1
Belgium 4, Bosnia 0
Bosnia 1, Lithuania 2
Estonia 0, Czech Republic 3
Czech Republic 3, Scotland 2
Estonia 0, Lithuania 2

WORLD YOUTH CHAMPIONSHIP UNDER-20

5 Apr
USA 1
England 0
England: Taylor (Arsenal); Cooper (Nottingham Forest), Haslam (Sheffield Wednesday), Wright S (Liverpool), Cole A (Arsenal), Piercy (Tottenham H) [Lincoln (Arsenal)], Vernazza (Arsenal), Nicholls (Charlton Athletic) [Murphy N (Liverpool)], Etherington (Peterborough United), Oliver (West Bromwich Albion) [Johnson A (Birmingham City)], Dudley (Notts County).

8 Apr
Cameroon 1
England 0
England: Taylor (Arsenal); Cooper (Nottingham Forest), Haslam (Sheffield Wednesday), Wright S (Liverpool), Cole A (Arsenal), Lincoln (Arsenal), Vernazza

(Arsenal), Nicholls (Charlton Athletic) [Chambers J (West Bromwich Albion)], Etherington (Peterborough United), Johnson A (Birmingham City), Dudley (Notts County) [Piercy (Tottenham Hotspur)] [Chambers A (West Bromwich Albion)].

11 Apr
Japan 2
England 0
England: Rachubka (Manchester United); Cooper (Nottingham Forest) [Chambers J (West Bromwich Albion)], Haslam (Sheffield Wednesday), Wright S (Liverpool), Murphy N (Liverpool), Lincoln (Arsenal) [Crouch (Tottenham Hotspur)], Vernazza (Arsenal), Nicholls (Charlton Athletic), Etherington (Peterborough United), Johnson A (Birmingham City), Dudley (Notts County) [Chambers A (West Bromwich Albion)].

17th UEFA UNDER-16 CHAMPIONSHIP

(Finals in Czech Republic)

GROUP A
Israel 3, Finland 2
Portugal 2, Switzerland 2
Finland 1, Switzerland 4
Israel 1, Portugal 2
Finland 2, Portugal 3
Switzerland 1, Israel 3

GROUP B
Hungary 1, England 1
Slovakia 2, Sweden 0
Hungary 1, Slovakia 2
England 2, Sweden 1
England 3, Slovakia 1
Sweden 2, Hungary 1

GROUP C
Russia 1, Poland 2
Spain 2, Croatia 0
Croatia 1, Poland 1
Spain 1, Russia 0
Croatia 0, Russia 1
Poland 0, Spain 3

GROUP D
Denmark 0, Greece 1
Czech Republic 0, Germany 1
Germany 2, Greece 0
Czech Republic 1, Denmark 0
Germany 0, Denmark 2
Greece 0, Czech Republic 2

QUARTER-FINALS
Spain 5, Israel 1
Portugal 1, Poland 2
Germany 6, Slovakia 0
England 0, Czech Republic 1

SEMI-FINALS
Spain 4, Germany 0
Poland 3, Czech Republic 2

3RD/4TH PLACE
Germany 2, Czech Republic 1

FINAL
Spain 4, Poland 1

14th UEFA UNDER-18 CHAMPIONSHIP

(Finals in Cyprus)

GROUP A
Lithuania 1, Germany 7
Portugal 1, Spain 2
Portugal 2, Lithuania 0
Spain 1, Germany 4
Germany 0, Portugal 2
Spain 2, Lithuania 1

GROUP B
Croatia 2, Republic of Ireland 5
Cyprus 1, England 2
Croatia 3, Cyprus 0

Republic of Ireland 0, England 1
England 0, Croatia 3
Republic of Ireland 3, Cyprus 0

3RD/4TH PLACE
Croatia 0, Portugal 0
Croatia won 5-4 on penalties.

FINAL
Republic of Ireland 1, Germany 1
Republic of Ireland won 4-3 on penalties.

15th UEFA UNDER-18 CHAMPIONSHIP

Qualifying Tournament

GROUP 1
England 1, Spain 1
Israel 2, Andorra 0
England 8, Andorra 0
Spain 2, Israel 0
England 2, Israel 1
Spain 9, Andorra 0

	P	W	D	L	F	A	Pts
Spain	3	2	1	0	12	1	7
England	3	2	1	0	11	2	7
Israel	3	1	0	2	3	4	3
Andorra	3	0	0	3	0	19	0

(Finals held in Sweden July 1999).

WORLD YOUTH CHAMPIONSHIP

In Nigeria

GROUP A
Nigeria 1, Costa Rica 1
Germany 4, Costa Rica 0
Nigeria 2, Germany 0
Costa Rica 1, Paraguay 3
Nigeria 1, Paraguay 2
Costa Rica 2, Germany 1

GROUP B
Ghana 1, Croatia 1
Argentina 1, Kazakhstan 0
Ghana 1, Argentina 0
Croatia 5, Kazakhstan 1
Ghana 3, Kazakhstan 0
Croatia 0, Argentina 0

GROUP C
Australia 3, Saudi Arabia 1
Mexico 1, Republic of Ireland 0
Australia 1, Mexico 3
Saudi Arabia 0, Republic of Ireland 2
Australia 0, Republic of Ireland 4
Saudi Arabia 1, Mexico 1

GROUP D
Uruguay 1, Mali 2

South Korea 1, Portugal 3
Uruguay 1, South Korea 0
Mali 2, Portugal 1
Uruguay 0, Portugal 0
Mali 2, South Korea 4

GROUP E
Cameroon 2, Japan 1
England 0, USA 1
Cameroon 1, England 0
Japan 3, USA 1
Cameroon 1, USA 3
Japan 2, England 0

GROUP F
Zambia 4, Honduras 3
Spain 2, Brazil 0
Zambia 0, Spain 0
Honduras 0, Brazil 3
Zambia 1, Brazil 5
Honduras 1, Spain 3

SECOND ROUND
Ghana 2, Costa Rica 0
Nigeria 1, Republic of Ireland 1
Nigeria won 5-3 on penalties

Brazil 4, Croatia 0
Paraguay 2, Uruguay 2
Uruguay won 10-9 on penalties
Spain 3, USA 2
Japan 1, Portugal 1
Japan won 5-4 on penalties
Mexico 4, Argentina 1
Mali 5, Cameroon 4

QUARTER-FINALS
Uruguay 2, Brazil 1
Mali 3, Nigeria 1
Japan 2, Mexico 0
Spain 1, Ghana 1
Spain won 8-7 on penalties

SEMI-FINALS
Spain 3, Mali 1
Japan 2, Uruguay 1

MATCH FOR THIRD PLACE
Mali 1, Uruguay 0

FINAL
Spain 4, Japan 0

OLYMPIC FOOTBALL

Previous medallists

1896 Athens*	1 Denmark	1932 Los Angeles		1968 Mexico City	1 Hungary	
	2 Greece		no tournament		2 Bulgaria	
1900 Paris*	1 Great Britain	1936 Berlin	1 Italy		3 Japan	
	2 France		2 Austria	1972 Munich	1 Poland	
1904 St Louis**	1 Canada		3 Norway		2 Hungary	
	2 USA	1948 London	1 Sweden		3 E Germany/USSR	
1908 London	1 Great Britain		2 Yugoslavia	1976 Montreal	1 East Germany	
	2 Denmark		3 Denmark		2 Poland	
	3 Holland	1952 Helsinki	1 Hungary		3 USSR	
1912 Stockholm	1 England		2 Yugoslavia	1980 Moscow	1 Czechoslovakia	
	2 Denmark		3 Sweden		2 East Germany	
	3 Holland	1956 Melbourne	1 USSR		3 USSR	
1920 Antwerp	1 Belgium		2 Yugoslavia	1984 Los Angeles	1 France	
	2 Spain		3 Bulgaria		2 Brazil	
	3 Holland	1960 Rome	1 Yugoslavia		3 Yugoslavia	
1924 Paris	1 Uruguay		2 Denmark	1988 Seoul	1 USSR	
	2 Switzerland		3 Hungary		2 Brazil	
	3 Sweden	1964 Tokyo	1 Hungary		3 West Germany	
1928 Amsterdam	1 Uruguay		2 Czechoslovakia	1992 Barcelona	1 Spain	
	2 Argentina		3 East Germany		2 Poland	
	3 Italy				3 Ghana	
				1996 Atlanta	1 Nigeria	
					2 Argentina	
					3 Brazil	

* No official tournament
** No official tournament but gold medal later awarded by IOC

Sydney 2000

QUALIFYING TOURNAMENT

European Zone

(See results in European Under-21 Tournament)

Asian Zone

GROUP 1
Yemen 0, Qatar 3
UAE 6, Yemen 1
UAE 0, Qatar 1
Qatar 3, Yemen 1
Yemen 0, UAE 5

GROUP 2
Oman 2, Kuwait 2
Syria 1, Kuwait 2
Oman 1, Syria 5
Kuwait 3, Syria 2
Syria 0, Oman 1
Kuwait 3, Oman 1

GROUP 3
Jordan, Saudi Arabia, Iraq

GROUP 4
Iran 2, Bahrain 1
Bahrain 2, Lebanon 1
Lebanon 2, Iran 0

GROUP 5
Uzbekistan 3, Kyrgyzstan 0
Tajikistan 1, Turkmenistan 2
Uzbekistan 3, Tajikistan 0
Tajikistan 0, Kazakhstan 0

Turkmenistan 1, Uzbekistan 1
Kyrgyzstan 1, Tajikistan 0
Kazakhstan 4, Turkmenistan 1
Uzbekistan 0, Kazakhstan 2
Turkmenistan 3, Kyrgyzstan 0
Kyrgyzstan 2, Turkmenistan 1
Kazakhstan 3, Uzbekistan 1
Tajikistan 1, Kyrgyzstan 2
Turkmenistan 3, Kazakhstan 2

GROUP 6
Hong Kong, Nepal, Philippines, Japan, Malaysia

GROUP 7
Myanmar 0, North Korea 1
Vietnam 0, China 4
Myanmar 0, China 4
Vietnam 1, North Korea 2
North Korea 0, China 1
Vietnam 1, Myanmar 2

GROUP 8
Taiwan 1, Indonesia 2
South Korea 5, Sri Lanka 0
Indonesia 2, Sri Lanka 1
South Korea 7, Taiwan 0
Taiwan 4, Sri Lanka 1
South Korea 7, Indonesia 0

GROUP 9
Thailand and India

Concacaf Zone

CARIBBEAN GROUP 1
Guyana, Surinam, Aruba, Antigua

CARIBBEAN GROUP 2
Dominican Republic, St Kitts & Nevis

CARIBBEAN GROUP 3
Bahamas, Cuba, Haiti, Dominica

CARIBBEAN GROUP 4
St Vincent 1, Trinidad & Tobago 5
Trinidad & Tobago 4, St Vincent 0
St Lucia 2, Barbados 1
Barbados 4, St Lucia 1

African Zone

PRELIMINARY COMPETITION
Kenya 1, Tanzania 0
Uganda 2, Sudan 1
Namibia 0, Mozambique 0
Botswana 3, Swaziland 0
Congo Brazzaville 1, Guinea 0
Seychelles 0, Mauritius 2
Guinea 1, Congo Brazzaville 1
Mauritius 4, Seychelles 0
Mozambique 3, Namibia 3
Sudan 0, Uganda 0
Swaziland 2, Botswana 2
Tanzania 2, Kenya 0

ENGLAND UNDER-21 RESULTS 1976–99

EC UEFA Competition for Under-21 Teams

Year	Date		Venue	Eng	Alb
			v ALBANIA	**Eng**	**Alb**
EC1989	Mar	7	Shkroda	2	1
EC1989	April	25	Ipswich	2	0
			v ANGOLA	**Eng**	**Ang**
1995	June	10	Toulon	1	0
1996	May	28	Toulon	0	2
			v ARGENTINA	**Eng**	**Arg**
1998	May	18	Toulon	0	2
			v AUSTRIA	**Eng**	**Aus**
1994	Oct	11	Kapfenberg	3	1
1995	Nov	14	Middlesbrough	2	1
			v BELGIUM	**Eng**	**Bel**
1994	June	5	Marseille	2	1
1996	May	24	Toulon	1	0
			v BRAZIL	**Eng**	**B**
1993	June	11	Toulon	0	0
1995	June	6	Toulon	0	2
1996	June	1	Toulon	1	2
			v BULGARIA	**Eng**	**Bul**
EC1979	June	5	Pernik	3	1
EC1979	Nov	20	Leicester	5	0
1989	June	5	Toulon	2	3
EC1998	Oct	9	West Ham	1	0
EC1999	June	8	Vratsa	1	0
			v CROATIA	**Eng**	**Cro**
1996	Apr	23	Sunderland	0	1
			v CZECHOSLOVAKIA	**Eng**	**Cz**
1990	May	28	Toulon	2	1
1992	May	26	Toulon	1	2
1993	June	9	Toulon	1	1
			v CZECH REPUBLIC	**Eng**	**CzR**
1998	Nov	17	Ipswich	0	1
			v DENMARK	**Eng**	**Den**
EC1978	Sept	19	Hvidovre	2	1
EC1979	Sept	11	Watford	1	0
EC1982	Sept	21	Hvidovre	4	1
EC1983	Sept	20	Norwich	4	1
EC1986	Mar	12	Copenhagen	1	0
EC1986	Mar	26	Manchester	1	1
1988	Sept	13	Watford	0	0
1994	Mar	8	Brentford	1	0
			v EAST GERMANY	**Eng**	**EG**
EC1980	April	16	Sheffield	1	2
EC1980	April	23	Jena	0	1
			v FINLAND	**Eng**	**Fin**
EC1977	May	26	Helsinki	1	0
EC1977	Oct	12	Hull	8	1
EC1984	Oct	16	Southampton	2	0
EC1985	May	21	Mikkeli	1	3
			v FRANCE	**Eng**	**Fra**
EC1984	Feb	28	Sheffield	6	1
EC1984	Mar	28	Rouen	1	0
1987	June	11	Toulon	0	2
EC1988	April	13	Besancon	2	4
EC1988	April	27	Highbury	2	2
1988	June	12	Toulon	2	4
1990	May	23	Toulon	7	3
1991	June	3	Toulon	1	0
1992	May	28	Toulon	0	0
1993	June	15	Toulon	1	0
1994	May	31	Aubagne	0	3
1994	Sept	6	Leicester	0	0
1995	June	10	Toulon	0	2
1998	May	14	Toulon	1	1
1999	Feb	9	Derby	2	1
			v GEORGIA	**Eng**	**Geo**
EC1996	Nov	8	Batumi	1	0
EC1997	April	29	Charlton	0	0
			v GERMANY	**Eng**	**Ger**
1991	Sept	10	Scunthorpe	2	1

Year	Date		Venue	Eng	Gre
			v GREECE	**Eng**	**Gre**
EC1982	Nov	16	Piraeus	0	1
EC1983	Mar	29	Portsmouth	2	1
1989	Feb	7	Patras	0	1
EC1997	Nov	13	Heraklion	0	2
EC1997	Dec	17	Norwich	4	2
			v HOLLAND	**Eng**	**H**
EC1993	April	27	Portsmouth	3	0
EC1993	Oct	12	Utrecht	1	1
			v HUNGARY	**Eng**	**Hun**
EC1981	June	5	Keszthely	2	1
EC1981	Nov	17	Nottingham	2	0
EC1983	April	26	Newcastle	1	0
EC1983	Oct	11	Nyiregyhaza	2	0
1990	Sept	11	Southampton	3	1
1992	May	12	Budapest	2	2
1999	April	27	Budapest	2	2
			v ITALY	**Eng**	**Italy**
EC1978	Mar	8	Manchester	2	1
EC1978	April	5	Rome	0	0
EC1984	April	18	Manchester	3	1
EC1984	May	2	Florence	0	1
EC1986	April	9	Pisa	0	2
EC1986	April	23	Swindon	1	1
EC1997	Feb	12	Bristol	1	0
EC1997	Oct	10	Rieti	0	0
			v ISRAEL	**Eng**	**Isr**
1985	Feb	27	Tel Aviv	2	1
			v LATVIA	**Eng**	**Lat**
1995	April	25	Riga	1	0
1995	June	7	Burnley	4	0
			v LUXEMBOURG	**Eng**	**Lux**
EC1998	Oct	13	Greven Macher	5	0
			v MALAYSIA	**Eng**	**Mal**
1995	June	8	Toulon	2	0
			v MEXICO	**Eng**	**Mex**
1988	June	5	Toulon	2	1
1991	May	29	Toulon	6	0
1992	May	25	Toulon	1	1
			v MOLDOVA	**Eng**	**Mol**
EC1996	Aug	31	Chisinau	2	0
EC1997	Sept	9	Wycombe	1	0
			v MOROCCO	**Eng**	**Mor**
1987	June	7	Toulon	2	0
1988	June	9	Toulon	1	0
			v NORWAY	**Eng**	**Nor**
EC1977	June	1	Bergen	2	1
EC1977	Sept	6	Brighton	6	0
1980	Sept	9	Southampton	3	0
1981	Sept	8	Drammen	0	0
EC1992	Oct	13	Peterborough	0	2
EC1993	June	1	Stavanger	1	1
1995	Oct	10	Stavanger	2	2
			v POLAND	**Eng**	**Pol**
EC1982	Mar	17	Warsaw	2	1
EC1982	April	7	West Ham	2	2
EC1989	June	2	Plymouth	2	1
EC1989	Oct	10	Jastrzebie	3	1
EC1990	Oct	16	Tottenham	0	1
EC1993	May	28	Zdroj	4	1
EC1993	Sept	7	Millwall	1	2
EC1996	Oct	8	Wolverhampton	0	0
EC1997	May	30	Katowice	1	1
EC1999	Mar	26	Southampton	5	0
			v PORTUGAL	**Eng**	**Por**
1987	June	13	Toulon	0	0
1990	May	21	Toulon	0	1
1993	June	7	Toulon	0	0
1994	June	7	Toulon	2	0
1995	Sept	2	Lisbon	0	2
1996	May	30	Toulon	1	3

England Under-21 Results 1976–99

v REPUBLIC OF IRELAND				Eng	RoI
1981	Feb	25	Liverpool	1	0
1985	Mar	25	Portsmouth	3	2
1989	June	9	Toulon	0	0
EC1990	Nov	13	Cork	3	0
EC1991	Mar	26	Brentford	3	0
1994	Nov	15	Newcastle	1	0
1995	Mar	27	Dublin	2	0

v ROMANIA				Eng	Rom
EC1980	Oct	14	Ploesti	0	4
EC1981	April	28	Swindon	3	0
EC1985	April	30	Brasov	0	0
EC1985	Sept	10	Ipswich	3	0

v RUSSIA				Eng	Rus
1994	May	30	Bandol	2	0

v SAN MARINO				Eng	SM
EC1993	Feb	16	Luton	6	0
EC1993	Nov	17	San Marino	4	0

v SENEGAL				Eng	Sen
1989	June	7	Toulon	6	1
1991	May	27	Toulon	2	1

v SCOTLAND				Eng	Sco
1977	April	27	Sheffield	1	0
EC1980	Feb	12	Coventry	2	1
EC1980	Mar	4	Aberdeen	0	0
EC1982	April	19	Glasgow	1	0
EC1982	April	28	Manchester	1	1
EC1988	Feb	16	Aberdeen	1	0
EC1988	Mar	22	Nottingham	1	0
1993	June	13	Toulon	1	0

v SOUTH AFRICA				Eng	SA
1998	May	16	Toulon	3	1

v SPAIN				Eng	Spa
EC1984	May	17	Seville	1	0
EC1984	May	24	Sheffield	2	0
1987	Feb	18	Burgos	2	1
1992	Sept	8	Burgos	1	0

v SWEDEN				Eng	Swe
1979	June	9	Vasteras	2	1
1986	Sept	9	Ostersund	1	1
EC1988	Oct	18	Coventry	1	1
EC1989	Sept	5	Uppsala	0	1
EC1998	Sept	4	Sundvall	2	0
EC1999	June	4	Huddersfield	3	0

v SWITZERLAND				Eng	Swit
EC1980	Nov	18	Ipswich	5	0
EC1981	May	31	Neuenburg	0	0
1988	May	28	Lausanne	1	1
1996	April	1	Swindon	0	0
1998	Mar	24	Brugglifeld	0	2

v USA				Eng	USA
1989	June	11	Toulon	0	2
1994	June	2	Toulon	3	0

v TURKEY				Eng	Tur
EC1984	Nov	13	Bursa	0	0
EC1985	Oct	15	Bristol	3	0
EC1987	April	28	Izmir	0	0
EC1987	Oct	13	Sheffield	1	1
EC1991	April	30	Izmir	2	2
1991	Oct	15	Reading	2	0
EC1992	Nov	17	Orient	0	1
EC1993	Mar	30	Izmir	0	0

v USSR				Eng	USSR
1987	June	9	Toulon	0	0
1988	June	7	Toulon	1	0
1990	May	25	Toulon	2	1
1991	May	31	Toulon	2	1

v WALES				Eng	Wales
1976	Dec	15	Wolverhampton	0	0
1979	Feb	6	Swansea	1	0
1990	Dec	5	Tranmere	0	0

v WEST GERMANY				Eng	WG
EC1982	Sept	21	Sheffield	3	1
EC1982	Oct	12	Bremen	2	3
1987	Sept	8	Ludenscheid	0	2

v YUGOSLAVIA				Eng	Yugo
EC1978	April	19	Novi Sad	1	2
EC1978	May	2	Manchester	1	1
EC1986	Nov	11	Peterborough	1	1
EC1987	Nov	10	Zemun	5	1

ENGLAND B RESULTS 1949–99

Year	Date		Venue		
			v ALGERIA	Eng	Alg
1990	Dec	11	Algiers	0	0
			v AUSTRALIA	Eng	Aust
1980	Nov	17	Birmingham	1	0
			v AUSTRIA	Eng	Aus
1979†	June	12	Klagenfurt	1	0

†Abandoned 60 mins; waterlogged pitch.

			v CHILE	Eng	Ch
1998	Feb	10	West Bromwich	1	2
			v CIS	Eng	CIS
1992	April	28	Moscow	1	1
			v CZECHOSLOVAKIA	Eng	Cz
1978	Nov	28	Prague	1	0
1990	April	24	Sunderland	2	0
1992	Mar	24	Budejovice	1	0
			v FINLAND	Eng	Fin
1949	May	15	Helsinki	4	0
			v FRANCE	Eng	Fra
1952	May	22	Le Havre	1	7
1992	Feb	18	Loftus Road	3	0
			v WEST GERMANY	Eng	WG
1954	Mar	24	Gelsenkirchen	4	0
1955	Mar	23	Sheffield	1	1
1978	Feb	21	Augsburg	2	1

			v HOLLAND	Eng	Hol
1949	May	18	Amsterdam	4	0
1950	Feb	22	Newcastle	1	0
1952	Mar	26	Amsterdam	1	0
			v ICELAND	Eng	Ice
1989	May	19	Reykjavik	2	0
1991	April	27	Watford	1	0
			v ITALY	Eng	Italy
1950	May	11	Milan	0	5
1989	Nov	14	Brighton	1	1
			v LUXEMBOURG	Eng	Lux
1950	May	21	Luxembourg	2	1
			v MALAYSIA	Eng	Mal
1978	May	30	Kuala Lumpur	1	1
			v MALTA	Eng	Mal
1987	Oct	14	Ta'Qali	2	0
			v NEW ZEALAND	Eng	NZ
1978	June	7	Christchurch	4	0
1978	June	11	Wellington	3	1
1978	June	14	Auckland	4	0
1979	Oct	15	Leyton	4	1
1984	Nov	13	Nottingham	2	0
			v NORTHERN IRELAND	Eng	NI
1994	May	10	Sheffield	4	2

1989	May	22	**v NORWAY** Stavanger	Eng 1	Nor 0

1990	Mar	27	**v REPUBLIC OF IRELAND** Cork	Eng 1	RoI 4
1994	Dec	13	Liverpool	2	0

1998	Apr	21	**v RUSSIA** Loftus Road	Eng 4	Rus 1

1953	Mar	11	**v SCOTLAND** Edinburgh	Eng 2	Sco 2
1954	Mar	3	Sunderland	1	1
1956	Feb	29	Dundee	2	2
1957	Feb	6	Birmingham	4	1

1978	June	18	**v SINGAPORE** Singapore	Eng 8	Sin 0

1980	Mar	26	**v SPAIN** Sunderland	Eng 1	Sp 0
1981	Mar	25	Granada	2	3

1991*	Dec	18	Castellon	Eng 1	Sp 0

*Spanish Olympic XI

1950	Jan	18	**v SWITZERLAND** Sheffield	Eng 5	Swit 0
1954	May	22	Basle	0	2
1956	Mar	21	Southampton	4	1
1989	May	16	Winterthur	2	0
1991	May	20	Walsall	2	1

1980	Oct	14	**v USA** Manchester	Eng 1	USA 0

1991	Feb	5	**v WALES** Swansea	Eng 1	Wales 0

1954	May	16	**v YUGOSLAVIA** Ljubljana	Eng 1	Yugo 2
1955	Oct	19	Manchester	5	1
1989	Dec	12	Millwall	2	1

Frank Lampard, the West Ham United midfield player, captained the successful England Under-21 team during the 1998–99 season. The son of West Ham United assistant manager Frank Lampard, who made 663 senior appearances for the club, Lampard junior came to prominence in the club's record-breaking South East Counties League Championship winning side in 1995–96. He also collected a runners-up medal in the FA Youth Cup Final the same season. (ASP)

BRITISH AND IRISH UNDER-21 TEAMS
1998–99

ENGLAND UNDER-21 INTERNATIONALS

4 Sept
Sweden (0) 0
England (1) 2 *(Carragher 8, Lampard 86 (pen))*   5266
England: Wright; Dyer K (Curtis 78), Ball, Mills, Brown, Upson, Lampard, Carragher, Heskey, Jansen (Euell 81), Hendrie (Clemence 88).

9 Oct
England (0) 1 *(Lampard 61 (pen))*
Bulgaria (0) 0   11,577
England: Wright; Dyer K (Mills 63), Ball, Curtis, Brown, Upson, Lampard, Carragher, Heskey (Euell 90), Jansen (Morris 74), Hendrie.

13 Oct
Luxembourg (0) 0
England (2) 5 *(Hendrie 27, Upson 34, Lampard 52, Cort 68, 85)*   3500
England: Wright; Curtis, Ball, Mills, Brown, Upson, Lampard (Johnson 75), Carragher, Heskey, Jansen (Cort 59), Hendrie (Morris 49).

17 Nov
England (0) 0
Czech Republic (0) 1 *(Dosek 41)*   13,768
England: Simonsen; Dyer K, Ball (Beattie 79), Curtis, Brown (Johnson 79), Barry, Lampard, Carragher, Davies, Cort (Cadamarteri 70), Morris (Dunn 46).

9 Feb
England (0) 2 *(Bowyer 54, Upson 62)*
France (1) 1 *(Christanual 21)*   32,865
England: Simonsen; Curtis, Upson (Marshall L 88), O'Brien, Barry, Williams, Lampard (Jansen 46), Carragher, Bridges (Beattie 46), Bowyer (Cresswell 68), Hendrie.

26 Mar
England (1) 5 *(Bowyer 41, 80, Lampard 54 (pen), 59, Hendrie 71)*
Poland (0) 0   15,202
England: Wright; Mills, Ball, Johnson, Brown, Carragher, Lampard (Mullins 79), Beattie, Jansen (Euell 61), Bowyer, Hendrie (Curtis 73).

27 Apr
Hungary (2) 2 *(Rosa 3, 25)*
England (0) 2 *(Mills 53, Beattie 56 (pen))*   5000
England: Wright; Curtis, Griffin (Bridge 28), Mills, Young, Barry (Vassell 60), Greening, Mullins, Beattie (Cort 67), Euell (Cresswell 46), Woodhouse.

4 June
England (2) 3 *(Cort 30, 80, Cresswell 45)*
Sweden (0) 0   13,045
England: Wright; Dyer K, Johnson, Mills, Brown, Robinson, Lampard, Carragher, Cresswell (Greening 71), Cort, Woodhouse (Curtis 57).

8 June
Bulgaria (0) 0
England (0) 1 *(Cort 87)*   2000
England: Simonsen; Curtis, Johnson, Mullins, Brown, Robinson, Greening, Carragher, Cresswell, Cort, Woodhouse.

SCOTLAND UNDER-21 INTERNATIONALS

4 Sept
Lithuania (0) 0
Scotland (0) 0   500
Scotland: Alexander; McEwan, McCluskey, Archibald, Buchan, Easton, Brebner, Strachan (Mason), Campbell, Burchill (Notman), Graham (Elliot).

9 Oct
Scotland (1) 2 *(Dargo 6, Dalglish 74)*
Estonia (0) 0   2676
Scotland: Alexander; Anderson R (McEwan), Buchan, Wilson, Naysmith, Campbell (Burchill), Easton, Strachan, Brebner, Dalglish, Dargo (Notman).

14 Oct
Belgium (2) 2 *(Moraye 38, 44)*
Scotland (0) 0   2000
Scotland: Alexander; McEwan, Buchan, Wilson, Naysmith, Campbell (Dargo), Easton (Paterson), Strachan, Brebner, Dalglish (Notman), Burchill.

18 Nov
Scotland (1) 2 *(Dargo 40, 69)*
Belgium (2) 2 *(Somers 8, Vanderpaar 14 (pen))*   5087
Scotland: Alexander; McEwan, Anderson R, Wilson, Naysmith, Strachan (Paterson), Ferguson (Easton), Campbell (Notman), Brebner, Dargo, Burchill.

30 Mar
Scotland (0) 0
Czech Republic (0) 1 *(Sionko 46)*   3681
Scotland: Alexander; McEwan (Teale), Naysmith, Hughes, Lauchlan, Buchan, Campbell (Young), Dalglish, McCulloch (Dargo), Brebner, Burchill.

27 Apr
Germany (1) 2 *(Nehrbauer 21, Reich 80 (pen))*
Scotland (0) 1 *(Thompson 84)*   1500
Scotland: Alexander (Mathieson); Nicholson (Young), Naysmith, Anderson R, Wilson, Lauchlan (McAnespie), Campbell (Teale), Buchan (McEwan), Dargo (Anderson I), Brebner, McCulloch (Thompson).

31 May
Republic of Ireland (0) 0
Scotland (1) 1 *(Thompson 45)*   3816
Scotland: Gallacher; Anderson R, Naysmith, Hughes, Wilson, Buchan, Campbell (Teale), Burchill (O'Brien), Thompson, Brebner, Anderson I (Rae).

4 June
Scotland (1) 1 *(Burchill 38)*
Northern Ireland (1) 1 *(Healy 13 (pen))*   2569
Scotland: Gallacher; Nicholson, Hughes, Rae, Anderson R, Lauchlan, Campbell (Tarrant), Burchill (Dargo), Thompson (O'Brien), Brebner, Anderson I.

8 June
Czech Republic (1) 3 *(Dosek 10, Hienz 74, Sionko 86)*
Scotland (0) 2 *(Thompson 51, Hughes 69)*   3141
Scotland: Gallacher; Anderson R (Nicholson), Naysmith (O'Brien), Rae, Wilson, Lauchlan, Hughes, Burchill, Thompson, Brebner, Anderson I (Campbell).

WALES UNDER-21 INTERNATIONALS

4 Sept
Wales (1) 1 *(Bellamy 45)*
Italy (2) 2 *(Mezzano 13, Comandin 25)*   650
Wales: Tony Williams; Green (Price 23), Roberts G, Jones, Jarman, Hughes, Llewellyn, Bellamy (Roberts N 87), Haworth, Oster, Andrew Williams.

9 Oct
Denmark (1) 2 *(Rommedahl 16, Madsen 62)*
Wales (2) 2 *(Haworth 8, Thomas J 45)*   709
Wales: Tony Williams; Price, Roberts G, Green (Andrew Williams 65), Williams D, Gabbidon, Davies, Jones (Wright 69), Haworth, Llewellyn, Thomas (Gibson 79).

13 Oct
Wales (0) 0
Belarus (0) 0 402
Wales: Tony Williams; Price, Roberts G, Green, Williams D, Andrew Williams, Davies, Jones, Haworth, Llewellyn, Thomas J (Gibson 68).

18 Nov
Portugal (2) 3 *(Soares 19, Pacheco 38, Moreira 88)*
Wales (0) 0 7000
Wales: Tony Williams; Price, Roberts G (Hopkins), Gibson, Gabbidon, Jarman, Low, Holloway, Roberts N, Tipton (Jeanne), Thomas J (Earnshaw).

30 Mar
Switzerland (0) 1 *(Yakin 2)*
Wales (0) 0 1050
Wales: Tony Williams; Green, Andrew Williams, Gabbidon, Hughes, Jones, Roberts S (Maxwell 68), Davies, Haworth, Jeanne (Tipton 68), Oster.

4 June
Italy (1) 6 *(Ventola 8, 71, 90, Pirlo 59, Comandini 75, Bannuchi 79)*
Wales (1) 2 *(Jeanne 30, Jones 66)* 7000
Wales: Tony Williams; Green, Andrew Williams, Jones, Hughes, Williams D (Gabbidon 79), Jeanne, Earnshaw (Evans 55 (Roberts S 79)), Llewellyn, Davies, Maxwell.

8 June
Wales (1) 1 *(Evans 6)*
Denmark (1) 2 *(Smith 2, Alkhag 70)* 881
Wales: Tony Williams; Gabbidon, Roberts G, Holloway, Williams D, Evans, Roberts S (Roberts C 19), Davies, Martin (Davies D 62), Green, Earnshaw (Jelleyman 82).

NORTHERN IRELAND
UNDER-21 INTERNATIONALS

4 Sept
Turkey (0) 2 *(Korprulu 57, Albayrak 69)*
Northern Ireland (0) 0 3739
Northern Ireland: Carroll; Griffin, McGlinchey, Feeney, Burns, Waterman, Johnson (Lyttle 89), McVeigh (Fitzgerald 75), Coote (McKnight 75), Jeff Whitley, Friars.

9 Oct
Northern Ireland (1) 1 *(Coote 17)*
Finland (1) 1 *(Niemi 29)* 2000
Northern Ireland: Carroll; Griffin, McGlinchey, Jeff Whitley, Burns, Waterman, Johnson, Feeney, Coote, Fitzgerald (Graham 65), Friars (Elliott 87).

17 Nov
Northern Ireland (0) 1 *(Healy 73)*
Moldova (1) 1 *(Lunga 43)* 1920
Northern Ireland: Carroll; Lyttle, McGlinchey, Jeff Whitley, Burns, Waterman, Graham (Healy 65), Feeney, Coote, McVeigh (McKnight 65), Friars.

26 Mar
Northern Ireland (0) 1 *(Hertzsch 52 (og))*
Germany (0) 0 2534
Northern Ireland: Carroll; Griffin, McGlinchey, Jeff Whitley, Burns, Waterman, Johnson (Feeney 80), McVeigh, Coote (Healy 85), Mulryne, Friars.

30 Mar
Moldova (0) 0
Northern Ireland (0) 0 2000
Northern Ireland: Carroll; Griffin, McGlinchey, Lyttle, Burns, Waterman, Johnson, McVeigh, Coote, Mulryne, Friars.

2 June
Republic of Ireland (1) 1 *(Ferguson 6)*
Northern Ireland (0) 0 605
Northern Ireland: Carroll; Griffin, McGlinchey, Burns, Waterman, Jeff Whitley, Johnson, Feeney (Healy 68), Coote, McVeigh (Graham 68), Elliott (Clarke 77).

4 June
Scotland (1) 1 *(Burchill 38)*
Northern Ireland (1) 1 *(Healy 13 (pen))* 2569
Northern Ireland: Wells; Lyttle, McGlinchey, Griffin, Morgan, Jeff Whitley, Feeney, Graham, Kirk (Waterman 66), Healy, Clarke (Elliott 66).

REPUBLIC OF IRELAND
UNDER-21 INTERNATIONALS

4 Sept
Republic of Ireland (1) 2 *(Conlon 2, Baker 59)*
Croatia (0) 2 *(Tomic 58, Sokota 78)* 4500
Republic of Ireland: O'Reilly; Worrell, Coughlan (Darcy 50), Ryan, Boxall (Folan 86), Inman, Morgan, Mahon (Baker 50), Kilbane, Clare, Conlon.

13 Oct
Republic of Ireland (1) 2 *(Clare 29, Worrell 90)*
Malta (1) 1 *(Licari 27)* 4500
Republic of Ireland: O'Reilly; Boxall, Worrell, Hawkins, Ryan, Inman (Folan 77), Morgan, Mahon (McPhail 56), Kilbane, Clare, Lee.

18 Nov
Yugoslavia (1) 1 *(Ivic 6)*
Republic of Ireland (0) 1 *(Kilbane 90 (pen))* 2000
Republic of Ireland: O'Reilly; Boxall (Barry-Murphy 43), Ryan, Worrell, Coughlan (Darcy 39), Dunne, Mahon (Inman 59), Morgan, Lee, Baker, Kilbane.

27 Apr
Republic of Ireland (0) 0
Sweden (1) 3 *(Andersson 24, Wahlstedt 55, 90)* 1800
Republic of Ireland: O'Connor; Worrell (Baker 63), Hawkins (Lynch 59), O'Brien, Barry-Murphy, Maybury, Morgan (Cummins 46), Mahon, McKeever (Armstrong 59), Clare (Grant 63), Fenn (Molloy 60).

31 May
Republic of Ireland (0) 0
Scotland (1) 1 *(Thompson 45)* 3816
Republic of Ireland: O'Reilly; Boxall, Maybury, Quinn, Hawkins, Worrell, McPhail, Fenn, Lee (Conlon 66), Rowlands, Mahon (McKeever 50).

2 June
Republic of Ireland (1) 1 *(Ferguson 6)*
Northern Ireland (0) 0 605
Republic of Ireland: O'Connor; Worrell (Maybury 46), Ryan, McClare, Hawkins (Mahon 62), Ferguson, Folan, Barry-Murphy, Molloy, Conlon, McKeever (McPhail 75).

8 June
Republic of Ireland (0) 0
Macedonia (0) 0 2000
Republic of Ireland: O'Reilly; Boxall, Hawkins, Ferguson, Worrell, Rowlands, Quinn (McClare 78), McPhail, Mahon, Grant, Fenn (Molloy 66).

UEFA awarded the Republic of Ireland a 3-0 win; Macedonia fielded a suspended player).

B INTERNATIONALS

9 Feb
Wales (0) 1 *(Williams 72)*
Northern Ireland (0) 0 1270
Wales: Ward (Coyne 48); Trollope, Lloyd, Page, Edwards, Mardon (Hughes 48), Oster (Davies 58), Robinson, Nogan (Williams 71), Lloyd-Williams (Roberts N 86), Coates.
Northern Ireland: Taylor; Griffin (Jeff Whitley 46), McGlinchey, Sonner, McGibbon (Hunter 46), Williams M, Hamill, Jim Whitley, Ferguson (Coote 78), Black (Healy 66), O'Neill.

9 Feb
Republic of Ireland (3) 4 *(Fenn 1, 3, Clare 13, 51)*
National League Selection (1) 3 *(Coughlan 40, Gormley 56 (pen) Cousins 62)* 1125
Republic of Ireland: Kiely (Colgan 46); Worrell, Quinn, Butler, Hardy, Finnan, Holland (Savage 46), Whalley (Kavanagh 46), Moore, Clare, Fenn (Scully 72).

BRITISH UNDER-21 APPEARANCES 1976–1999

ENGLAND

Ablett, G. (Liverpool), 1988 v F (1)
Adams, A. (Arsenal), 1985 v Ei, Fi; 1986 v D; 1987 v Se, Y (5)
Adams, N. (Everton), 1987 v Se (1)
Allen, B. (QPR), 1992 v H, M, Cz, F; 1993 v N (sub), T, P, Cz (sub) (8)
Allen, C. A. (Oxford U), 1995 v Br (sub), F (sub) (2)
Allen, C. (QPR), 1980 v EG (sub); (with C Palace), 1981 v N, R (3)
Allen, M. (QPR), 1987 v Se (sub); 1988 v Y (sub) (2)
Allen, P. (West Ham U), 1985 v Ei, R; (with Tottenham H, 1986 v R (3)
Allen, R. W. (Tottenham H), 1998 v F (sub), S.Af, Arg (sub) (3)
Anderson, V. A. (Nottingham F), 1978 v I (1)
Anderton, D. R. (Tottenham H), 1993 v Sp, Sm, Ho, Pol, N, P, Cz, Br, S, F; 1994 v Pol, Sm (12)
Andrews, I. (Leicester C), 1987 v Se (1)
Ardley, N. C. (Wimbledon), 1993 v Pol, N, P, Cz, Br, S, F, 1994 v Pol (sub), Ho, Sm (10)
Ashcroft, L. (Preston NE), 1992 v H (sub) (1)
Atherton, P. (Coventry C), 1992 v T (1)
Atkinson, B. (Sunderland), 1991 v W (sub), Sen, M, USSR (sub); F; 1992 v Pol (sub) (6)
Awford, A. T. (Portsmouth), 1993 v Sp, N, T, P, Cz, Br, S, F; 1994 v Ho (9)

Bailey, G. R. (Manchester U), 1979 v W, Bul; 1980 v D, S (2), EG; 1982 v N; 1983 v D, Gr; 1984 v H, F (2), I, Sp (14)
Baker, G. E. (Southampton), 1981 v N, R (2)
Ball, M. J. (Everton), 1999 v Se, Bul, L, CzR, Pol (5)
Barker, S. (Blackburn R), 1985 v Is (sub), Ei, R; 1986 v I (4)
Barmby, N. J. (Tottenham H), 1994 v D; 1995 v P, A (sub); (with Everton), 1998 v Sw (4)
Bannister, G. (Sheffield W), 1982 v Pol (1)
Barnes, J. (Watford), 1983 v D, Gr (2)
Barnes, P. S. (Manchester C), 1977 v W (sub), S, Fi, N; 1978 v N, Fi, I (2), Y (9)
Barrett, E. D. (Oldham Ath), 1990 v P, F, USSR, Cz (4)
Barry, G. (Aston Villa), 1999 v CzR, F, H (3)
Bart-Williams, C. G. (Sheffield W), 1993 v Sp, N, T; 1994 v D, Ru, F, Bel, P; 1995 v P, A, Ei (2), La (2); (with Nottingham F) 1996 v P (sub), A (16)
Batty, D. (Leeds U), 1988 v Sw (sub); 1989 v Gr (sub), Bul, Sen, Ei, US; 1990 v Pol (7)
Bazeley, D. S. (Watford), 1992 v H (sub) (1)
Beagrie, P. (Sheffield U), 1988 v WG, T (2)
Beardsmore, R. (Manchester U), 1989 v Gr, Alb (sub), Pol, Bul, USA (5)
Beattie, J. S. (Southampton), 1999 v CzR (sub), F (sub), Pol, H (4)
Beckham, D. R. J. (Manchester U), 1995 v Br, Mal, An, F; 1996 v P, A (sub), Bel, An, P (9)
Bent, M. N. (Crystal Palace), 1998 v S.Af (sub), Arg (2)
Beeston, C. (Stoke C), 1988 v USSR (1)
Bertschin, K. E. (Birmingham C), 1977 v S; 1978 v Y (2) (3)
Birtles, G. (Nottingham F), 1980 v Bul, EG (sub) (2)
Blackwell, D. R. (Wimbledon), 1991 v W, T, Sen (sub), M, USSR, F (6)
Blake, M. A. (Aston Villa), 1990 v F (sub), Cz (sub); 1991 v H, Pol, Ei (2), W; 1992 v Pol (8)
Blissett, L. L. (Watford), 1979 v W, Bul (sub), Se; 1980 v D (4)
Booth, A. D. (Huddersfield T), 1995 v La (2 subs); 1996 v N (3)
Bowyer, L. D. (Charlton Ath), 1996 v N (sub), Bel, P, Br; (with Leeds U), 1997 v Mol, I, Sw, Ge; 1998 v Mol; 1999 v F, Pol (11)
Bracewell, P. (Stoke C), 1983 v D, Gr (1 + 1 sub), H; 1984 v D, H, F (2), I (2), Sp (2); 1985 v T (13)
Bradbury, L. M. (Portsmouth), 1997 v Pol; (with Manchester C), 1998 v Mol (sub), I (sub) (3)
Branch, P. M. (Everton), 1997 v Pol (sub) (1)
Bradshaw, P. W. (Wolverhampton W), 1977 v W, S; 1978 v Fi, Y (4)
Breacker, T. (Luton T), 1986 v I (2) (2)
Brennan, M. (Ipswich T), 1987 v Y, Sp, T, Mor, F (5)
Bridge, W. M. (Southampton), 1999 v H (sub) (1)
Bridges, M. (Sunderland), 1997 v Sw (sub); 1999 v F (2)
Brightwell, I. (Manchester C), 1989 v D, Alb; 1990 v Se (sub), Pol (4)

Briscoe, L. S. (Sheffield W), 1996 v Cro, Bel (sub), An, Br; 1997 v Sw (sub) (5)
Brock, K. (Oxford U), 1984 v I, Sp (2); 1986 v I (4)
Broomes, M. C. (Blackburn R), 1997 v Sw, Ge (2)
Brown, M. R. (Manchester C), 1996 v Cro, Bel, An, P (4)
Brown, W. M. (Manchester U), 1999 v Se, Bul, L, CzR, Pol, Se, Bul (7)
Bull, S. G. (Wolverhampton W), 1989 v Alb (2) Pol; 1990 v Se, Pol (5)
Bullock, M. J. (Barnsley), 1998 v Gr (sub) (1)
Burrows, D. (WBA), 1989 v Se (sub); (with Liverpool), Gr, Alb (2), Pol; 1990 v Se, Pol (7)
Butcher, T. I. (Ipswich T), 1979 v Se; 1980 v D, Bul, S (2), EG (2) (7)
Butt, N. (Manchester U), 1995 v Ei (2), La; 1996 v P, A; 1997 v Ge, Pol (7)
Butters, G. (Tottenham H), 1989 v Bul, Sen (sub), Ei (sub) (3)
Butterworth, I. (Coventry C), 1985 v T, R; (with Nottingham F), 1986 v R, T, D (2), I (2) (8)

Cadamarteri, D. L. (Everton), 1999 v CzR (sub) (1)
Caesar, G. (Arsenal), 1987 v Mor, USSR (sub), F (3)
Callaghan, N. (Watford), 1983 v D, Gr (sub), H (sub); 1984 v D, H, F (2), I, Sp (9)
Campbell, K. J. (Arsenal), 1991 v H, T (sub); 1992 v G, T (4)
Campbell, S. (Tottenham), 1994 v D, Ru, F, US, Bel, P; 1995 v P, A, Ei; 1996 v N, A (11)
Carbon, M. P. (Derby Co), 1996 v Cro (sub); 1997 v Ge, I, Sw (4)
Carr, C. (Fulham), 1985 v Ei (sub) (1)
Carr, F. (Nottingham F), 1987 v Se, Y, Sp (sub), Mor, USSR; 1988 v WG (sub), T, Y, F (9)
Carragher, J. L. (Liverpool), 1997 v I (sub), Sw, Ge, Pol; 1998 v Mol (sub), I, Gr, Sw (sub), F, S.Af, Arg; 1999 v Se, Bul, L, CzR, F, Pol, Se, Bul (19)
Casper, C. M. (Manchester U), 1995 v Mal (1)
Caton, T. (Manchester C), 1982 v N, H (sub), Pol (2), S; 1983 v WG (2), Gr; 1984 v D, H, F (2), I (2) (14)
Challis, T. M. (QPR), 1996 v An, P (2)
Chamberlain, M. (Stoke C), 1983 v Gr; 1984 v F (sub), I, Sp (4)
Chapman, L. (Stoke C), 1981 v Ei (1)
Charles, G. A. (Nottingham F), 1991 v H, W (sub), Ei; 1992 v T (4)
Chettle, S. (Nottingham F), 1988 v M, USSR, Mor, F; 1989 v D, Se, Gr, Alb (2), Bul; 1990 v Se, Pol (12)
Clark, L. R. (Newcastle U), 1992 v Cz, F; 1993 v Sp, N, T, Ho (sub), Pol (sub), Cz, Br, S; 1994 v Ho (11)
Clegg, M. J. (Manchester U), 1998 v Fr (sub), S.Af (sub) (2)
Clemence, S. N. (Tottenham H), 1999 v Se (sub) (1)
Clough, N. (Nottingham F), 1986 v D (sub); 1987 v Se, Y, T, USSR (sub), P; 1988 v WG, T, Y, S (2), M, Mor, F (15)
Cole, A. A. (Arsenal), 1992 v H, Cz (subs); (with Bristol C), 1993 v Sm; (with Newcastle U), Pol, N; 1994 v Pol, Ho (8)
Coney, D. (Fulham), 1985 v T (sub); 1986 v R; 1988 v T, WG (4)
Connor, T. (Brighton & HA), 1987 v Y (1)
Cooke, R. (Tottenham H), 1986 v D (sub) (1)
Cooke, T. J. (Manchester U), 1996 v Cro, Bel, An (sub), P (4)
Cooper, C. (Middlesbrough), 1988 v F (2), M, USSR, Mor; 1989 v D, Se, Gr (8)
Corrigan, J. T. (Manchester C), 1978 v I (2), Y (3)
Cort, C. E. R. (Wimbledon), 1999 v L (sub), CzR, H (sub), Se, Bul (5)
Cottee, A. (West Ham U), 1985 v Fi (sub), Is (sub), Ei, R, Fi; 1987 v Sp, P; 1988 v WG (8)
Couzens, A. J. (Leeds U), 1995 v Mal (sub), An, F (sub) (3)
Cowans, G. S. (Aston Villa), 1979 v W, Se; 1980 v Bul, EG; 1981 v R (5)
Cox, N. J. (Aston Villa), 1993 v T, Ho, Pol, N; 1994 v Pol, Sm (6)
Cranson, I. (Ipswich T), 1985 v Fi, Is, R; 1986 v R, I (5)
Cresswell, R. P. W. (York C), 1999 v F (sub); (with Sheffield W) H (sub), Se, Bul (4)
Croft, G. (Grimsby T), 1995 v Br, Mal, An, F (4)
Crooks, G. (Stoke C), 1980 v Bul, S (2), EG (sub) (4)
Crossley, M. G. (Nottingham F), 1990 v P, USSR, Cz (3)
Cundy, J. V. (Chelsea), 1991 v Ei (2); 1992 v Pol (3)

Cunningham, L. (WBA), 1977 v S, Fi, N (sub); 1978 v N, Fi, I (6)

Curbishley, L. C. (Birmingham C), 1981 v Sw (1)

Curtis, J. C. K. (Manchester U), 1998 v I (sub), Gr, Sw, F, S.Af, Arg; 1999 v Se (sub), Bul, L, CzR, F, Pol (sub), H, Se (sub), Bul (15)

Daniel, P. W. (Hull C), 1977 v S, Fi, N; 1978 v Fi, I, Y (2) (7)

Davies, K. C. (Southampton), 1998 v Gr (sub); (with Blackburn R), 1999 v CzR (2)

Davis, K. G. (Luton T), 1995 v An; 1996 v Cro (sub), P (3)

Davis, P. (Arsenal), 1982 v Pol, S; 1983 v D, Gr (1 + 1 sub), H (sub); 1987 v T; 1988 v WG, T, Y, Fr (11)

Day, C. N. (Tottenham H), 1996 v Cro, Bel, Br; (with Crystal Palace), 1997 v Mol, Ge, Sw (6)

D'Avray, M. (Ipswich T), 1984 v I, Sp (sub) (2)

Deehan, J. M. (Aston Villa), 1977 v N; 1978 v N, Fi, I; 1979 v Bul, Se (sub); 1980 v D (7)

Dennis, M. E. (Birmingham C), 1980 v Bul; 1981 v N, R (3)

Dichio, D. S. E. (QPR), 1996 v N (sub) (1)

Dickens, A. (West Ham U), 1985 v Fi (sub) (1)

Dicks, J. (West Ham U), 1988 v Sw (sub), M, Mor, F (4)

Digby, F. (Swindon T), 1987 v Sp (sub), USSR, P; 1988 v T; 1990 v Pol (5)

Dillon, K. P. (Birmingham C), 1981 v R (1)

Dixon, K. (Chelsea), 1985 v Fi (1)

Dobson, A. (Coventry C), 1989 v Bul, Sen, Ei, US (4)

Dodd, J. R. (Southampton), 1991 v Pol, Ei, T, Sen, M, F; 1992 v G, Pol (8)

Donowa, L. (Norwich C), 1985 v Is, R (sub), Fi (sub) (3)

Dorigo, A. (Aston Villa), 1987 v Se, Sp, T, Mor, USSR, F, P; 1988 v WG, Y, S (2) (11)

Dozzell, J. (Ipswich T), 1987 v Se, Y (sub), Sp, USSR, F, P; 1989 v Se, Gr (sub); 1990 v Se (sub) (9)

Draper, M. A. (Notts Co), 1991 v Ei (sub); 1992 v G, Pol (3)

Duberry, M. W. (Chelsea), 1997 v Mol, Pol, Ge; 1998 v Mol, Gr (5)

Dunn, D. J. I. (Blackburn R), 1999 v CzR (sub) (1)

Duxbury, M. (Manchester U), 1981 v Sw (sub), Ei (sub), R (sub), Sw; 1982 v N; 1983 v WG (2) (7)

Dyer, B. A. (Crystal Palace), 1994 v Ru, F, US, Bel, P; 1995 v P (sub); 1996 v Cro; 1997 v Mol, Ge; 1998 v Mol, Gr (10)

Dyer, K. C. (Ipswich T), 1998 v Mol, I, Gr, Sw, S.Af, Arg; 1999 v Se, Bul, CzR, Se (10)

Dyson, P. I. (Coventry C), 1981 v N, R, Sw, Ei (4)

Eadie, D. M. (Norwich C), 1994 v F (sub), US; 1997 v Mol, Ge (2), I; 1998 v I (7)

Ebbrell, J. (Everton), 1989 v Sen, Ei, US (sub); 1990 v P, F, USSR, Cz; 1991 v H, Pol, Ei, W, T; 1992 v G, T (14)

Edghill, R. A. (Manchester C), 1994 v D, Ru; 1995 v A (3)

Ehiogu, U. (Aston Villa), 1992 v H, M, Cz, F; 1993 v Sp, N, T, Sm, T, Ho, Pol, N; 1994 v Ho, Sm (15)

Elliott, P. (Luton T), 1985 v Fi; 1986 v T, D (3)

Elliott, R. J. (Newcastle U), 1996 v P, A (2)

Elliott, S. W. (Derby Co), 1998 v F, Arg (sub) (2)

Euell, J. J. (Wimbledon), 1998 v F, Arg (sub); 1999 v Se (sub), Bul (se), Pol (sub), H (6)

Fairclough, C. (Nottingham F), 1985 v T, Is, Ei; 1987 v Sp, T; (with Tottenham H), 1988 v Y, F (7)

Fairclough, D. (Liverpool), 1977 v W (1)

Fashanu, J. (Norwich C), 1980 v EG; 1981 v N (sub), R, Sw, Ei (sub), H; (with Nottingham F), 1982 v N, H, Pol, S; 1983 v WG (sub) (11)

Fear, P. (Wimbledon), 1994 v Ru, F, US (sub) (3)

Fenton, G. A. (Aston Villa), 1995 v Ei (1)

Fenwick, T. W. (C Palace), 1981 v N, R, Sw, Ei; (with QPR), R; 1982 v N, H, S (2); 1983 v WG (2) (11)

Ferdinand, R. G. (West Ham U), 1997 v Sw, Ge; 1998 v I, Gr (4)

Fereday, W. (QPR), 1985 v T, Ei (sub). Fi; 1986 v T (sub), I (5)

Flitcroft, G. W. (Manchester C), 1993 v Sm, Hol, N, P, Cz, Br, S, F; 1994 v Pol, Ho (10)

Flowers, T. (Southampton), 1987 v Mor, F; 1988 v WG (sub) (3)

Ford, M. (Leeds U), 1996 v Cro; 1997 v Mol (2)

Forster, N. M. (Brentford), 1995 v Br, Mal, An, F (4)

Forsyth, M. (Derby Co), 1988 v Sw (1)

Foster, S. (Brighton & HA), 1980 v EG (sub) (1)

Fowler, R. B. (Liverpool), 1994 v Sm, Ru (sub), F, US; 1995 v P, A; 1996 v P, A (8)

Froggatt, S. J. (Aston Villa), 1993 v Sp, Sm (sub) (2)

Futcher, P. (Luton T), 1977 v W, S, Fi, N; (with Manchester C), 1978 v N, Fi, I (2), Y (2); 1979 v D (11)

Gabbiadini, M. (Sunderland), 1989 v Bul, USA (2)

Gale, A. (Fulham), 1982 v Pol (1)

Gallen, K. A. (QPR), 1995 v Ei, La (2); 1996 v Cro (4)

Gascoigne, P. (Newcastle U), 1987 v Mo, USSR, P; 1988 v WG, Y, S (2), F (2), Sw, M, USSR (sub), Mor (13)

Gayle, H. (Birmingham C), 1984 v I, Sp (2) (3)

Gernon, T. (Ipswich T), 1983 v Gr (1)

Gerrard, P. W. (Oldham Ath), 1993 v T, Ho, Pol, N, P, Cz, Br, S, F; 1994 v D, Ru; 1995 v P, A, Ei (2), La (2); 1996 v P (18)

Gibbs, N. (Watford), 1987 v Mor, USSR, F, P; 1988 v T (5)

Gibson, C. (Aston Villa), 1982 v N (1)

Gilbert, W. A. (C Palace), 1979 v W, Bul; 1980 v Bul; 1981 v N, R, Sw, R, Sw, H; 1982 v N (sub), H (11)

Goddard, P. (West Ham U), 1981 v N, Sw, Ei (sub); 1982 v N (sub), Pol, S; 1983 v WG (2) (8)

Gordon, D. (Norwich C), 1987 v T (sub), Mor (sub), F, P (4)

Gordon, D. D. (Crystal Palace), 1994 v Ru, F, US, Bel, P; 1995 v P, A, Ei (2), La (2); 1996 v P, N (13)

Grant, A. J. (Everton), 1996 v An (sub) (1)

Granville, D. P. (Chelsea), 1997 v Ge (sub), Pol; 1998 v Mol (3)

Gray, A. (Aston Villa), 1988 v S, F (2)

Greening, J. (Manchester U), 1999 v H, Se (sub), Bul (3)

Griffin, A. (Newcastle U), 1999 v H (1)

Guppy, S. A. (Leicester C), 1998 v Sw (1)

Haigh, P. (Hull C), 1977 v N (sub) (1)

Hall, M. T. J. (Coventry C), 1997 v Pol (2), I, Sw, Ge; 1998 v Mol, Gr (2) (8)

Hall, R. A. (Southampton), 1992 v H (sub), F; 1993 v Sm, T, Ho, Pol, P, Cz, Br, S, F (11)

Hamilton, D. V. (Newcastle U), 1997 v Pol (1)

Hardyman, P. (Portsmouth), 1985 v Ei; 1986 v D (2)

Hateley, M. (Coventry C), 1982 v Pol, S; 1983 v Gr (2), H; (with Portsmouth), 1984 v F (2), I, Sp (2) (10)

Hayes, M. (Arsenal), 1987 v Sp, T; 1988 v F (sub) (3)

Hazell, R. J. (Wolverhampton W), 1979 v D (1)

Heaney, N. A. (Arsenal), 1992 v H, M, Cz, F; 1993 v N, T (6)

Heath, A. (Stoke C), 1981 v R, Sw, H; 1982 v N, H; (with Everton), Pol, S; 1983 v WG (8)

Hendon, I. M. (Tottenham H), 1992 v H, M, Cz, F; 1993 v Sp, N, T (7)

Hendrie, L. A. (Aston Villa), 1996 v Cro; 1998 v Sw (sub); 1999 v Se, Bul, L, F, Pol (7)

Hesford, I. (Blackpool), 1981 v Ei (sub), Pol (2), S (2); 1983 v WG (2) (7)

Heskey, E. W. I. (Leicester C), 1997 v I, Ge, Pol (2); 1998 v I, Gr (2), Sw, F, S.Af, Arg; 1999 v Se, Bul, L (14)

Hilaire, V. (C Palace), 1980 v Bul, S (1+1 sub), EG (2); 1981 v N, R, Sw (sub); 1982 v Pol (sub) (9)

Hill, D. R. L. (Tottenham H), 1995 v Br, Mal, An, F (4)

Hillier, D. (Arsenal), 1991 v T (1)

Hinchcliffe, A. (Manchester C), 1989 v D (1)

Hinshelwood, P. A. (C Palace), 1978 v N; 1980 v EG (2)

Hirst, D. (Sheffield W), 1988 v USSR, F; 1989 v D, Bul (sub), Sen, Ei, US (7)

Hislop, N. S. (Newcastle U), 1992 v Sw (1)

Hoddle, G. (Tottenham H), 1977 v W (sub); 1978 v Fi (sub), I (2), Y; 1979 v D, W, Bul; 1980 v S (2), EG (2) (12)

Hodge, S. (Nottingham F), 1983 v Gr (sub); 1984 v D, F, I, Sp (2); (with Aston Villa), 1986 v N, T (8)

Hodgson, D. J. (Middlesbrough), 1981 v N, R (sub), Sw, Ei; 1982 v Pol; 1983 v WG (6)

Holdsworth, D. (Watford), 1989 v Gr (sub) (1)

Holland, C. J. (Newcastle U), 1995 v La; 1996 v N (sub), A (sub), Cro, Bel, An, Br; 1997 v Mol, Pol, Sw (10)

Holland, P. (Mansfield T), 1995 v Br, Mal, An, F (4)

Holloway, D. (Sunderland), 1998 v Sw (sub) (1)

Horne, B. (Millwall), 1989 v Gr (sub), Pol, Bul, Ei, US (5)

Howe, E. J. F. (Bournemouth), 1998 v S.Af (sub), Arg (2)

Hucker, P. (QPR), 1984 v I, Sp (2)

Huckerby, D. (Coventry C), 1997 v I (sub), Sw, Ge (sub), Pol (sub) (4)

Hughes, S. J. (Arsenal), 1997 v I, Sw, Ge, Pol; 1998 v Mol, I, Gr, Sw (sub) (8)

Humphreys, R. J. (Sheffield W), 1997 v Pol, Ge (sub), Sw (3)

Impey, A. R. (QPR), 1993 v T (1)
Ince, P. (West Ham U), 1989 v Alb; 1990 v Se (2)

Jackson, M. A. (Everton), 1992 v H, M, Cz, F; 1993 v Sm (sub), T, Ho, Pol, N; 1994 v Pol (10)
James, D. (Watford), 1991 v Ei (2), T, Sen, M, USSR, F; 1992 v G, T, Pol (10)
James, J. C. (Luton T), 1990 v F, USSR (2)
Jansen, M. B (Crystal Palace), 1999 v Se, Bul, L; (with Blackburn R) F (sub), Pol (5)
Jemson, N. B. (Nottingham F), 1991 v W (1)
Joachim, J. K. (Leicester C), 1994 v D (sub); 1995 v P, A, Ei, Br, Mal, An, F; 1996 v N (9)
Johnson, S. A. M. (Crewe Alex), 1999 v L (sub), CzR (sub), F (sub), Pol; (with Derby Co) Se, Bul (6)
Johnson, T. (Notts Co), 1991 v H (sub), Ei (sub); 1992 v G, T, Pol; (with Derby Co), M, Cz (sub) (7)
Johnston, C. P. (Middlesbrough), 1981 v N, Ei (2)
Jones, D. R. (Everton), 1977 v W (1)
Jones, C. H. (Tottenham H), 1978 v Y (sub) (1)
Jones, R. (Liverpool), 1993 v Sm, Ho (2)

Keegan, G. A. (Manchester C), 1977 v W (1)
Kenny, W. (Everton), 1993 v T (1)
Keown, M. (Aston Villa), 1987 v Sp, Mor, USSR, P; 1988 v T, S, F (2) (8)
Kerslake, D. (QPR), 1986 v T (1)
Kilcline, B. (Notts C), 1983 v D, Gr (2)
King, A. E. (Everton), 1977 v W; 1978 v Y (2)
Kitson, P. (Leicester C), 1991 v Sen (sub), M, F; 1992 v Pol; (with Derby Co), M, Cz, F (7)
Knight, A. (Portsmouth), 1983 v Gr, H (2)
Knight, I. (Sheffield W), 1987 v Se (sub), Y (2)
Kozluk, R. (Derby Co), 1998 v F, Arg (sub) (2)

Lake, P. (Manchester C), 1989 v D, Alb (2), Pol; 1990 v Pol (5)
Lampard, F. J. (West Ham U), 1998 v Gr (2), Sw, F, S.Af, Arg; 1999 v Se, Bul, L, CzR, F, Pol, Se (13)
Langley, T. W. (Chelsea), 1978 v I (sub) (1)
Lee, D. J. (Chelsea), 1990 v F; 1991 v H, Pol, Ei (2), T, Sen, USSR, F; 1992 v Pol (10)
Lee, R. (Charlton Ath), 1986 v I (sub); 1987 v Se (sub) (2)
Lee, S. (Liverpool), 1981 v R, Sw, H; 1982 v S; 1983 v WG (2) (6)
Le Saux, G. (Chelsea), 1990 v P, F, USSR, Cz (4)
Lowe, D. (Ipswich T), 1988 v F, Sw (sub) (2)
Lukic, J. (Leeds U), 1981 v N, R, Ei, R, Sw, H; 1982 v H (7)
Lund, G. (Grimsby T), 1985 v T; 1986 v R, T (3)

McCall, S. H. (Ipswich T), 1981 v Sw, H; 1982 v H, S; 1983 v WG (2) (6)
McDonald, N. (Newcastle U), 1987 v Se (sub), Sp, T; 1988 v WG, Y (sub) (5)
McGrath, L. (Coventry C), 1986 v D (1)
MacKenzie, S. (WBA), 1982 v N, S (2) (3)
McLeary, A. (Millwall), 1988 v Sw (1)
McMahon, S. (Everton), 1981 v Ei; 1982 v Pol; 1983 v D, Gr (2); (with Aston Villa) 1984 v H (6)
McManaman, S. (Liverpool), 1991 v W, M (sub); 1993 v N, T, Sm, T; 1994 v Pol (7)
Mabbutt, G. (Bristol R), 1982 v Pol (2), S; (with Tottenham H), 1983 v D; 1984 v F; 1986 v D, I (7)
Makin, C. (Oldham Ath), 1994 v Ru (sub), F, US, Bel, P (5)
Marriott, A. (Nottingham F), 1992 v M (1)
Marsh, S. T. (Oxford U), 1998 v F (1)
Marshall, A. J. (Norwich C), 1995 v Mal, An; 1997 v Pol, I (4)
Marshall, L. K. (Norwich C), 1999 v F (sub) (1)
Martin, L. (Manchester U), 1989 v Gr (sub), Alb (sub) (2)
Martyn, N. (Bristol R), 1988 v S (sub), M, USSR, Mor, F; 1989 v D, Se, Gr, Alb (2); 1990 v Se (11)
Matteo, D. (Liverpool), 1994 v F (sub), Bel, P; 1998 v Sw (4)
Matthew, D. (Chelsea), 1990 v P, USSR (sub), Cz; 1991 v Ei, M, USSR, F; 1992 v G (sub), T (9)
May, A. (Manchester C), 1986 v I (sub) (1)
Merson, P. (Arsenal), 1989 v D, Gr, Pol (sub); 1990 v Pol (4)
Middleton, J. (Nottingham F), 1977 v Fi, N; (with Derby Co), 1978 v N (3)
Miller, A. (Arsenal), 1988 v Mor (sub); 1989 v Sen; 1991 v H, Pol (4)

Mills, D. J. (Charlton Ath), 1999 v Se, Bul (sub), L, Pol, H, Se (6)
Mills, G. R. (Nottingham F), 1981 v R; 1982 v N (2)
Mimms, R. (Rotherham U), 1985 v Is (sub), Ei (sub); (with Everton), 1986 v I (3)
Minto, S. C. (Charlton Ath), 1991 v W; 1992 v H, M, Cz; 1993 v T; 1994 v Ho (6)
Moore, I. (Tranmere R), 1996 v Cro (sub), Bel (sub), An, P, Br; 1997 v Mol (sub); (with Nottingham F), Sw (sub) (7)
Moran, S. (Southampton), 1982 v N (sub); 1984 v F (2)
Morgan, S. (Leicester C), 1987 v Se, Y (2)
Morris, J. (Chelsea), 1997 v Pol (sub), Sw (sub), Ge (sub); 1999 v Bul (sub), L (sub), CzR (6)
Mortimer, P. (Charlton Ath), 1989 v Sen, Ei (2)
Moses, A. P. (Barnsley), 1997 v Pol; 1998 v Gr (sub) (2)
Moses, R. M. (WBA), 1981 v N (sub), Sw, Ei, R, Sw, H; 1982 v N (sub); (with Manchester U), H (8)
Mountfield, D. (Everton), 1984 v Sp (1)
Muggleton, C. D. (Leicester C), 1990 v F (1)
Mullins, H. I. (Crystal Palace), 1999 v Pol (sub), H, Bul (3)
Murphy, D. B. (Liverpool), 1998 v Mol, Gr (sub) (2)
Murray, P. (QPR), 1997 v I, Pol; 1998 v I, Gr (4)
Mutch, A. (Wolverhampton W), 1989 v Pol (1)
Myers. A. (Chelsea), 1995 v Br, Mal, An (sub), F (4)

Nethercott, S. (Tottenham), 1994 v D, Ru, F, US, Bel, P; 1995 v La (2) (8)
Neville, P. J. (Manchester U), 1995 v Br, Mal, An, F; 1996 v P, N (sub); 1997 v Ge (7)
Newell, M. (Luton T), 1986 v D (1 + 1 sub), I (1 + 1 sub) (4)
Newton, E. J. I. (Chelsea), 1993 v T (sub); 1994 v Sm (2)
Newton, S. O. (Charlton Ath), 1997 v Mol, Pol, Ge (3)
Nicholls, A. (Plymouth Arg), 1994 v F (1)

Oakes, M. C. (Aston Villa), 1994 v D (sub), F (sub), US, Bel, P; 1996 v A (6)
Oakes, S. J. (Luton T), 1993 v Br (sub) (1)
Oakley, M. (Southampton), 1997 v Ge; 1998 v F, S.Af, Arg (4)
O'Brien, A. J. (Bradford C), 1999 v F (1)
O'Connor, J. (Everton), 1996 v Cro, An, Br (3)
Oldfield, D. (Luton T), 1989 v Se (1)
Olney, I. A. (Aston Villa), 1990 v P, F, USSR, Cz; 1991 v H, Pol, Ei (2), T; 1992 v Pol (sub) (10)
Ord, R. J. (Sunderland), 1991 v W, M, USSR (3)
Osman, R. C. (Ipswich T), 1979 v W (sub), Se; 1980 v D, S (2), EG (2) (7)
Owen, G. A. (Manchester C), 1977 v S, Fi, N; 1978 v N, Fi, I (2), Y; 1979 v D, W; (with WBA), Bul, Se (sub); 1980 v D, S (2), EG; 1981 v Sw, R; 1982 v N (sub), H; 1983 v WG (2) (22)
Owen, M. J. (Liverpool), 1998 v Gr (1)

Painter, I. (Stoke C), 1986 v I (1)
Palmer, C. (Sheffield W), 1989 v Bul, Sen, Ei, US (4)
Parker, G. (Hull C), 1986 v I (2); (with Nottingham F), F; 1987 v Se, Y (sub), Sp (6)
Parker, P. (Fulham), 1985 v Fi, T, Is (sub), Ei, R, Fi; 1986 v T, D (8)
Parkes, P. B. F. (QPR), 1979 v D (1)
Parkin, S. (Stoke C), 1987 v Sp (sub); 1988 v WG (sub), T, S (sub), F (5)
Parlour, R. (Arsenal), 1992 v H, M, Cz, F; 1993 v Sp, N, T; 1994 v D, Ru, Bel, P; 1995 v A (12)
Peach, D. S. (Southampton), 1977 v S, Fi, N; 1978 v N, I (2) (6)
Peake, A. (Leicester C), 1982 v Pol (1)
Pearce, I. A. (Blackburn R), 1995 v Ei, La; 1996 v N (3)
Pearce, S. (Nottingham F), 1987 v Y (1)
Pickering, N. (Sunderland), 1983 v D (sub), Gr, H; 1984 v F (sub + 1), I (2), Sp; 1985 v Is, R, Fi; 1986 v R, T; (with Coventry C), D, I (15)
Platt, D. (Aston Villa), 1988 v M, Mor, F (3)
Plummer, C. S. (QPR), 1996 v Cro (sub), Bel, An, P (sub), Br (5)
Pollock, J. (Middlesbrough), 1995 v Ei (sub); 1996 v N, A (3)
Porter, G. (Watford), 1987 v Sp (sub), T, Mor, USSR, F, P (sub); 1988 v T (sub), Y, S (2), F, Sw (12)
Potter, G. S. (Southampton), 1997 v Mol (1)
Pressman, K. (Sheffield W), 1989 v D (sub) (1)

Walker, D. (Nottingham F), 1985 v Fi; 1987 v Se, T; 1988 v WG, T, S (2) (7)

Walker, I. M. (Tottenham H), 1991 v W; 1992 v H, Cz, F; 1993 v Sp, N, T, Sm; 1994 v Pol (9)

Walsh, G. (Manchester U), 1988 v WG, Y (2)

Walsh, P. M. (Luton T), 1983 v D (sub), Gr (2), H (4)

Walters, K. (Aston Villa), 1984 v D (sub), H (sub); 1985 v Is, Ei, R; 1986 v R, T, D, I (sub) (9)

Ward, P. D. (Brighton & HA), 1978 v N; 1980 v EG (2)

Warhurst, P. (Oldham Ath), 1991 v H, Pol, W, Sen, M (sub), USSR, F (sub); (with Sheffield W), 1992 v G (8)

Watson, D. (Norwich C), 1984 v D, F (2), I (2), Sp (2) (7)

Watson, D. N. (Barnsley), 1994 v Ho, Sm; 1995 v Br, F; 1996 v N (5)

Watson, G. (Sheffield W), 1991 v Sen, USSR (2)

Watson, S. C. (Newcastle U), 1993 v Sp (sub), N; 1994 v Sm (sub), D; 1995 v P, A, Ei (2), La (2); 1996 v N, A (12)

Webb, N. (Portsmouth), 1985 v Ei; (with Nottingham F), 1986 v D (2) (3)

Whelan, P. J. (Ipswich T), 1993 v Sp, T (sub), P (3)

Whelan, N. (Leeds U), 1995 v A (sub), Ei (2)

White, D. (Manchester C), 1988 v S (2), F, USSR; 1989 v Se; 1990 v Pol (6)

Whyte, C. (Arsenal), 1982 v S (1+1 sub); 1983 v D, Gr (4)

Wicks, S. (QPR), 1982 v S (1)

Wilkins, R. C. (Chelsea), 1977 v W (1)

Wilkinson, P. (Grimsby T), 1985 v Ei, R (sub); (with Everton), 1986 v R (sub), I (4)

Williams, D. (Sunderland), 1998 v Sw (sub); 1999 v F (2)

Williams, P. (Charlton Ath), 1989 v Bul, Sen, Ei, US (sub) (4)

Williams, P. D. (Derby Co), 1991 v Sen, M, USSR; 1992 v G, T, Pol (6)

Williams, S. C. (Southampton), 1977 v S, Fi, N; 1978 v N, I (1 + 1 sub), Y (2); 1979 v D, Bul, Se (sub); 1980 v D, EG (2) (14)

Winterburn, N. (Wimbledon), 1986 v I (1)

Wise, D. (Wimbledon), 1988 v Sw (1)

Woodcook, A. S. (Nottingham F), 1978 v Fi, I (2)

Woodhouse, C. (Sheffield U), 1999 v H, Se, Bul (3)

Woods, C. C. E. (Nottingham F), 1979 v W (sub), Se; (with QPR), 1980 v Bul, EG; 1981 v Sw; (with Norwich C), 1984 v D (6)

Wright, A. G. (Blackburn), 1993 v Sp, N (2)

Wright, M. (Southampton), 1983 v Gr, H; 1984 v D, H (4)

Wright, R. I. (Ipswich T), 1997 v Ge, Pol; 1998 v Mol, I, Gr (2), S.Af; 1999 v Se, Bul, L, Pol, H, Se (14)

Wright, W. (Everton), 1979 v D, W, Bul; 1980 v D, S (2) (6)

Yates, D. (Notts Co), 1989 v D (sub), Bul, Sen, Ei, US (5)

Young, L. P. (Tottenham H), 1999 v H (1)

SCOTLAND

Aitken, R. (Celtic), 1977 v Cz, W, Sw; 1978 v Cz, W; 1979 v P, A; 1980 v Bel, E; 1984 v EG, Y (2); 1985 v WG, Ic, Sp (16)

Albiston, A. (Manchester U), 1977 v Cz, W, Sw; 1978 v Sw, Cz (5)

Alexander, N. (Stenhousemuir), 1997 v P; 1998 v Bl, Ei, I; (with Livingston), 1999 v Li, Es, Bel (2), CzR, G (10)

Anderson, I. (Dundee), 1997 v Co (sub), US, CzR, P; 1998 v Bl, La, Fi, D (sub), Ei (sub), Ni; 1999 v G (sub), Ei, Ni, CzR (14)

Anderson, R. (Aberdeen), 1997 v Es, A, Se; 1998 v La (sub), Fi, Ei, I; 1999 v Es, Bel, G, Ei, Ni, CzR (13)

Anthony, M. (Celtic), 1997 v La (sub), Es (sub), Col (3)

Archdeacon, O. (Celtic), 1987 v WG (sub) (1)

Archibald, A. (Partick T), 1998 v Fi, Ei, Ni, I; 1999 v Li (5)

Archibald, S. (Aberdeen), 1980 v B, E (2), WG; (with Tottenham H), 1981 v D (5)

Bagen, D. (Kilmarnock), 1997 v Es, A (sub), Se (sub), Bl (4)

Bain, K. (Dundee), 1993 v P, I, Ma, P (4)

Baker, M. (St. Mirren), 1993 v F, M, E; 1994 v Ma, A; 1995 v Gr, M, F (sub), Sk (sub); 1996 v H (sub) (10)

Bannon, E. J. P. (Hearts), 1979 v US; (with Chelsea), P, N (2); (with Dundee U), 1980 v Bel, WG, E (7)

Beattie, J. (St Mirren), 1992 v D, US, P, Y (4)

Beaumont, D. (Dundee U), 1985 v Ic (1)

Bell, D. (Aberdeen), 1981 v D; 1984 v Y (2)

Bernard, P. R. J. (Oldham Ath), 1992 v R (sub), D, Se (sub), US; 1993 v Sw, P, I, Ma, P, F, Bul, M, E; 1994 v I, Ma (15)

Bett, J. (Rangers), 1981 v Se, D; 1982 v Se, D, I, E (2) (7)

Black, E. (Aberdeen), 1983 v EG, Sw (2), Bel; 1985 v Ic, Sp (2), Ic (8)

Blair, A. (Coventry C), 1980 v E; 1981 v Se; (with Aston Villa), 1982 v Se, D, I (5)

Bollan, G. (Dundee U), 1992 v D, G (sub), US, P, Y; 1993 v Sw, P, I, P, F, Bul, M, E; 1994 v Sw; 1995 v Gr; (with Rangers) v Ru, Sm (17)

Bonar, P. (Raith R), 1997 v A, La, Es (sub), Se (4)

Booth, S. (Aberdeen), 1991 v R (sub), Bul (sub + 1), Pol, F (sub); 1992 v Sw, R, D, Se, US, P, Y; 1993 v Ma, P (14)

Bowes, M. J. (Dunfermline Ath), 1992 v D (sub) (1)

Bowman, D. (Hearts), 1985 v WG (sub) (1)

Boyack, S. (Rangers), 1997 v Se (1)

Boyd, T. (Motherwell), 1987 v WG, Ei (2), Bel; 1988 v Bel (5)

Brazil, A. (Hibernian), 1978 v W (1)

Brazil, A. (Ipswich T), 1979 v N; 1980 v Bel (2), E (2), WG; 1981 v Se; 1982 v Se (8)

Brebner, G. I. (Manchester U), 1997 v Col, CzR (sub), US (sub), P; 1998 v Bl, La, Fi, D; (with Reading), 1999 v Li, Es, Bel (2), CzR, G, Ei, Ni, CzR (17)

Brough, J. (Hearts), 1981 v D (1)

Browne, P. (Raith R), 1997 v A (1)

Buchan, J. (Aberdeen), 1997 v Se, Col, CzR, P; 1998 v Bl, La, Fi; 1999 v Li, Es, Bel, CzR, G, Ei (13)

Burchill, M. (Celtic), 1998 v Fi, D (sub); 1999 v Li, Es (sub), Bel (2), CzR, Ei, Ni, CzR (10)

Burke, A. (Kilmarnock), 1997 v Es, A, Bl (sub); 1998 v Ei (sub) (4)

Burley, G. E. (Ipswich T), 1977 v Cz, W, Sw; 1978 v Sw, Cz (5)

Burley, C. (Chelsea), 1992 v D; 1993 v Sw, P, I, P; 1994 v Sw, I (sub) (7)

Burns, H. (Rangers), 1985 v Sp, Ic (sub) (2)

Burns, T. (Celtic), 1977 v Cz, W, E; 1978 v Sw; 1982 v E (5)

Campbell, S. (Dundee), 1989 v N (sub), Y, F (3)

Campbell, S. P. (Leicester C), 1998 v Fi (sub), D, Ei, Ni (sub), I; 1999 v Li, Es, Bel (2), CzR, G, Ei, Ni, CzR (sub) (14)

Carey, L. A. (Bristol C), 1998 v D (1)

Casey, J. (Celtic), 1978 v W (1)

Christie, M. (Dundee), 1992 v D, P (sub), Y (3)

Clark, R. (Aberdeen), 1977 v Cz, W, Sw (3)

Clarke, S. (St Mirren), 1984 v Bel, EG, Y; 1985 v WG, Ic, Sp (2), Ic (8)

Cleland, A. (Dundee U), 1990 v F, N (2); 1991 v R, Sw, Bul; 1992 v Sw, R, G, Se (2) (11)

Collins, J. (Hibernian), 1988 v Bel, E; 1989 v N, Y, F; 1990 v Y, F, N (8)

Connolly, P. (Dundee U), 1991 v R (sub), Sw, Bul (3)

Connor, R. (Ayr U), 1981 v Se; 1982 v Se (2)

Cooper, D. (Clydebank), 1977 v Cz, W, Sw, E; (with Rangers), 1978 v Sw, Cz (6)

Cooper, N. (Aberdeen), 1982 v D, E (2); 1983 v Bel, EG, Sw (2); 1984 v Bel, EG, Y; 1985 v Ic, Sp, Ic (13)

Crabbe, S. (Hearts), 1990 v Y (sub), F (2)

Craig, M. (Aberdeen), 1998 v Bl, La (2)

Craig, T. (Newcastle U), 1977 v E (1)

Crainie, D. (Celtic), 1983 v Sw (sub) (1)

Crawford, S. (Raith R), 1994 v A, Eg, P, Bel; 1995 v Fi, Ru,Gr, Ru, Sm, M, F (sub), Sk (sub), Br (sub); 1996 v Gr, Fi (sub), H (1 + sub), Sp (sub), F (sub) (19)

Creaney, G. (Celtic), 1991 v Sw, Bul (2), Pol, F; 1992 v Sw, R, G (2), Se (2) (11)

Dailly, C. (Dundee U), 1991 v R; 1992 v US, R; 1993 v Sw, P, I, Ic, P, F, Bul, M, E; 1994 v Sw, I, Ma, A, Eg, P, Bel; 1995 v Fi, Ru, Gr, Ru, Sm, M, F, Sk, Br; 1996 v Fi, Sm, H (2), Sp, F (34)

Dalglish, P. (Newcastle U), 1999 v Es, Bel, CzR (3)

Dargo, C. (Raith R), 1998 v Fi, Ei, Ni (sub), I; 1999 v Es, Bel (1+sub), CzR (sub), G, Ni (sub) (10)

Davidson, C. (St Johnstone), 1997 v Se, Bl (2)

Dawson, A. (Rangers), 1979 v P, N (2); 1980 v B (2), E (2), WG (8)

Deas, P. A. (St Johnstone), 1992 v D (sub); 1993 v Ma (2)

Dennis, S. (Raith R), 1992 v Sw (1)

Dickov, P. (Arsenal), 1992 v Y; 1993 v F, M, E (4)

Dodds, D. (Dundee U), 1978 v W (1)

Dods, D. (Hibernian), 1997 v La, Es, Se (2), Bl (5)

Donald, G. S. (Hibernian), 1992 v US (sub), P, Y (sub) (3)

Donnelly, S. (Celtic), 1994 v Eg, P, Bel; 1995 v Fi, Gr (sub); 1996 v Gr (sub), Sm, H (2), Sp, F (11)
Dow, A. (Dundee), 1993 v Ma (sub), Ic; (with Chelsea) 1994 v I (3)
Duffy, J. (Dundee), 1987 v Ei (1)
Durie, G. S. (Chelsea), 1987 v WG, Ei, Bel; 1988 v Bel (4)
Durrant, I. (Rangers), 1987 v WG, Ei, Bel; 1988 v E (4)
Doyle, J. (Partick Th), 1981 v D, I (sub) (2)

Easton, C. (Dundee U), 1997 v Col, US, CzR, P; 1998 v Bl, Fi, D, Ei, Ni, I; 1999 v Li, Es, Bel (1+sub) (14)
Elliot, B. (Celtic), 1998 v Ni; 1999 v Li (sub) (2)

Ferguson, B. (Rangers), 1997 v Col (sub), US, CzR, P; 1998 v Bl, La, Fi, D (sub), Ei, Ni, I; 1999 v Bel (12)
Ferguson, D. (Rangers), 1987 v WG, Ei, Bel; 1988 v E; 1990 v Y (5)
Ferguson, D. (Dundee U), 1992 v D, G, Se (2); 1993 v Sw, I, Ma (7)
Ferguson, D. (Manchester U), 1992 v US, P (sub), Y; 1993 v Sw, Ma (5)
Ferguson, I. (Dundee), 1983 v EG (sub), Sw (sub); 1984 v Bel (sub), EG (4)
Ferguson, I. (Clyde), 1987 v WG (sub), Ei; (with St Mirren), Ei, Bel; 1988 v Bel; (with Rangers), E (sub) (6)
Ferguson, R. (Hamilton A), 1977 v E (1)
Findlay, W. (Hibernian), 1991 v R, Pol, Bul (2), Pol (5)
Fitzpatrick, A. (St Mirren), 1977 v W (sub), Sw (sub), E; 1978 v Sw, Cz (5)
Flannigan, C. (Clydebank), 1993 v Ic (sub) (1)
Fleck, R. (Rangers), 1987 v WG (sub), Ei, Bel; (with Norwich C), 1988 v E (2); 1989 v Y (6)
Freedman, D. A. (Barnet), 1995 v Ru (sub + 1), Sm, M, F, Sk, Br; (with C Palace) 1996 v Sm (sub) (8)
Fridge, L. (St Mirren), 1989 v F; 1990 v Y (2)
Fullarton, J. (St. Mirren), 1993 v F, Bul; 1994 v Ma, A, Eg, P, Bel; 1995 v M, F, Sk, Br; 1996 v Gr, Fi, H (sub + 1), Sp (sub), F (17)
Fulton, M. (St Mirren), 1980 v Bel, WG, E; 1981 v Se, D (sub) (5)
Fulton, S. (Celtic), 1991 v R, Sw, Bul, Pol, F; 1992 v G (2) (7)

Gallacher, K. (Dundee U), 1987 v WG, Ei (2), Bel (sub); 1988 v E (2); 1990 v Y (7)
Gallacher, P. (Dundee U), 1999 v Ei, Ni, CzR (3)
Galloway, M. (Hearts), 1989 v F; (with Celtic), 1990 v N (2)
Gardiner, J. (Hibernian), 1993 v F (1)
Geddes, R. (Dundee), 1982 v Se, D, E (2); 1988 v E (5)
Gemmill, S. (Nottingham F), 1992 v Sw, R (sub), G (sub), Se (sub) (4)
Germaine, J. (WBA), 1997 v Se (1)
Gilles, R. (St Mirren), 1997 v A (1 + sub), La, Es (2), Se, Bl (7)
Gillespie, G. (Coventry C), 1979 v US; 1980 v E; 1981 v D; 1982 v Se, D, I (2), E (8)
Glass, S. (Aberdeen), 1995 v M, F, Sk, Br; 1996 v Gr, Fi, H, Sp; 1997 v A (2), Es (11)
Glover, L. (Nottingham F), 1988 v Bel (sub); 1989 v N; 1990 v Y (3)
Goram, A. (Oldham Ath), 1987 v Ei (1)
Gough, C. R. (Dundee U), 1983 v EG, Sw, Bel; 1984 v Y (2) (5)
Graham, D. (Rangers), 1998 v Bl (sub), La (sub), Fi (sub), D, Ei (sub), Ni, I; 1999 v Li (8)
Grant, P. (Celtic), 1985 v WG, Ic, Sp; 1987 v WG, Ei (2), Bel; 1988 v Bel, E (2) (10)
Gray S. (Celtic), 1995 v F, Sk, Br; 1996 v Gr, H, Sp, F (7)
Gray, S. (Aberdeen), 1987 v WG (1)
Gunn, B. (Aberdeen), 1984 v EG, Y (2); 1985 v WG, Ic, Sp (2), Ic; 1990 v F (9)

Hagen, D. (Rangers), 1992 v D (sub), US (sub), P, Y; 1993 v Sw (sub), P, Ic, P (8)
Hamilton, B. (St Mirren), 1989 v Y, F (sub); 1990 v F, N (4)
Hamilton, J. (Dundee) 1995 v Sm (sub), Br; 1996 v Fi (sub), Sm, H (sub), Sp (sub), F; 1997 v A, La, Es, Se; (with Hearts), Es, A, Se (14)
Handyside, P. (Grimsby T), 1993 v Ic (sub), Bul, M, E; 1995 v Ru; 1996 v Fi, Sm (7)
Hannah, D. (Dundee U), 1993 v F (sub), Bul, M; 1994 v A, Eg, P, Bel; 1995 v Fi, Ru (sub), Gr, Ru, M, F, Sk, Br; 1996 v Gr (16)

Harper, K. (Hibernian), 1995 v Ru (sub); 1996 v Fi; 1997 v A (2), La, Es, Se (7)
Hartford, R. A. (Manchester C), 1977 v Sw (1)
Hartley, P. (Millwall), 1997 v A (sub) (1)
Hegarty, P. (Dundee U), 1987 v WG, Bel; 1988 v E (2); 1990 v F, N (6)
Hendry, J. (Tottenham H), 1992 v D (sub) (1)
Hetherston, B. (St Mirren), 1997 v Es (sub) (1)
Hewitt, J. (Aberdeen), 1982 v I; 1983 v EG, Sw (2); 1984 v Bel, Y (sub) (6)
Hogg, G. (Manchester U), 1984 v Y; 1985 v WG, Ic, Sp (4)
Hood, G. (Ayr U), 1993 v F, E (sub); 1994 v A (3)
Horn, R. (Hearts), 1997 v US, CzR, P; 1998 v Bl, La, D (sub) (6)
Howie, S. (Cowdenbeath), 1993 v Ma, Ic, P; 1994 v Sw, I (5)
Hughes, R. D. (Bournemouth), 1999 v CzR, Ei, Ni, CzR (4)
Hunter, G. (Hibernian), 1987 v Ei (sub); 1988 v Bel, E (3)
Hunter, P. (East Fife), 1989 v N (sub), F (sub); 1990 v F (sub) (3)

James, K. F. (Falkirk), 1997 v Bl (1)
Jardine, I. (Kilmarnock), 1979 v US (1)
Jess, E. (Aberdeen), 1990 v F (sub), N (sub); 1991 v R, Sw, Bul (2), Pol, F; 1992 v Sw, R, G (2), Se (1 + 1 sub) (14)
Johnson, G. I. (Dundee U), 1992 v US, P, Y; 1993 v Sw, P, Ma (6)
Johnston, A. (Hearts), 1994 v Bel; 1995 v Ru, 1996 v Sp (3)
Johnston, F. (Falkirk), 1993 v Ic (1)
Johnston, M. (Partick Th), 1984 v EG (sub); (with Watford), Y (2) (3)
Jupp, D. A. (Fulham), 1995 v Fi, Ru (2), Sm, M, F, Sk, Br; 1997 v Se (9)

Kirkwood, D. (Hearts), 1990 v Y (1)
Kerr, S. (Celtic), 1993 v Bul, M, E; 1994 v Ma, A, Eg, P, Bel; 1995 v Fi, Gr (10)

Lambert, P. (St Mirren), 1991 v R, Sw, Bul (2), Pol, F; 1992 v Sw, R, G (2), Se (11)
Lauchlan, J. (Kilmarnock), 1998 v Ei, Ni, I; 1999 v CzR, G, Ni, CzR (7)
Lavety, B. (St. Mirren), 1993 v Ic, Bul (sub), M (sub), E; 1994 v Ma, A (sub), Eg (sub), Bel (sub); 1995 v Fi (sub) (9)
Lavin, G. (Watford), 1993 v F, Bul, M; 1994 v Ma, Eg, P, Bel (7)
Leighton, J. (Aberdeen), 1982 v I (1)
Levein, C. (Hearts), 1985 v Sp, Ic (2)
Liddell, A. M. (Barnsley), 1994 v Ma (sub); 1995 v Sm (sub), M (sub), F, Sk; 1996 v Gr, Fi, Sm, H (2), Sp, F (sub) (12)
Lindsey, J. (Motherwell), 1979 v US (1)
Locke, G. (Hearts), 1994 v Ma, A, Eg, P; 1995 v Fi; 1996 v Fi, H; 1997 v Es, A, Bl (10)
Love, G. (Hibernian), 1995 v Ru (1)

McAllister, G. (Leicester C), 1990 v N (1)
McAlpine, H. (Dundee U), 1983 v EG, Sw (2), Bel; 1984 v Bel (5)
McAnespie, K. (St Johnstone), 1998 v Fi (sub); 1999 v G (sub) (2)
McAuley, S. (St. Johnstone), 1993 v P (sub) (1)
McAvennie, F. (St Mirren), 1982 v I, E; 1985 v Is, Ei, R (5)
McBride, J. (Everton), 1981 v D (1)
McBride, J. P. (Celtic), 1998 v Ni (sub), I (sub) (2)
McCall, S. (Bradford C), 1988 v E; (with Everton), 1990 v F (2)
McCann, N. (Dundee), 1994 v A, Eg, P, Bel; 1995 v Fi, Gr (sub), Sm; 1996 v Fi, Sm (9)
McClair, B. (Celtic), 1984 v Bel (sub), EG, Y (1 + 1 sub); 1985 v WG, Ic, Sp, Ic (8)
McCluskey, G. (Celtic), 1979 v US, P; 1980 v Bel (2); 1982 v D, I (6)
McCluskey, S. (St Johnstone), 1997 v Es (2), A, Se, Col, US, CzR; 1998 v Bl, La, D, Ei (sub), Ni, I; 1999 v Li (14)
McCoist, A. (Rangers), 1984 v Bel (1)
McConnell, I. (Clyde), 1997 v A (sub) (1)
McCulloch, A. (Kilmarnock), 1981 v Se (1)
McCulloch, I. (Notts Co), 1982 v E (2)

McCulloch, L. (Motherwell), 1997 v La (sub), Es (1 + sub), Se (sub + 1), A (sub), Col (sub); 1998 v Bl (sub), Fi (sub), D, Ei, Ni; 1999 v CzR, G (14)

MacDonald, J. (Rangers), 1980 v WG (sub); 1981 v Se; 1982 v Se (sub), L, I (2), E (2 sub) (8)

McDonald, C. (Falkirk), 1995 v Fi (sub), Ru, M (sub), F (sub), Br (sub) (5)

McEwan, C. (Clyde), 1997 v Col, US (sub), CzR (sub), P; (with Raith R), 1998 v Bl, La, Fi, D, Ei, Ni, I; 1999 v Li, Es (sub), Bel (2), CzR, G (sub) (17)

McFarlane, D. (Hamilton A), 1997 v Col, US (sub), P (sub) (3)

McGarry, S. (St Mirren), 1997 v US, CzR, P (sub) (3)

McGarvey, F. (St Mirren), 1977 v E; 1978 v Cz; (with Celtic), 1982 v D (3)

McGarvey, S. (Manchester U), 1982 v E (sub); 1983 v Bel, Sw; 1984 v Bel (4)

McGhee, M. (Aberdeen), 1981 v D (1)

McGinnis, G. (Dundee U), 1985 v Sp (1)

McGrillen, P. (Motherwell), 1994 v Sw (sub), I (2)

McInally, J. (Dundee U), 1989 v F (1)

McKenzie, R. (Hearts), 1997 v Es, Bl (2)

McKimmie, S. (Aberdeen), 1985 v WG, Ic (2) (3)

McKinlay, T. (Dundee), 1984 v EG (sub); 1985 v WG, Ic, Sp (2), Ic (6)

McKinlay, W. (Dundee U), 1989 v N, Y (sub); F; 1990 v Y, F, N (6)

Mcᶜᵛⁱⁿⁿon, R. (Dundee U), 1991 v R, Pol (sub); 1992 v G (2), Se (2) (6)

McLaren, A, (Hearts), 1989 v F; 1990 v Y, N; 1991 v Sw, Bul, Po1, F; 1992 v R, G, Se (2) (11)

McLaren, A. (Dundee U), 1993 v I, Ma (sub); 1994 v Sw, I (sub) (4)

McLaughlin, B. (Celtic), 1995 v Ru, Sm, M, Sk (sub), Br (sub); 1996 v Gr (sub), Sm (sub), H (8)

McLaughlin, J. (Morton), 1981 v D; 1982 v Se, D, I, E (2); 1983 v EG, Sw (2), Bel (10)

McLeish, A. (Aberdeen), 1978 v W; 1979 v US; 1980 v Bel, E (2); 1987 v Ei (6)

McLeod, A. (Hibernian), 1979 v P, N (2) (3)

McLeod, J. (Dundee U), 1989 v N; 1990 v F (2)

MacLeod, M. (Dumbarton), 1979 v US; (with Celtic), P (sub), N (2); 1980 v Bel (5)

McMillan, S. (Motherwell), 1997 v A (sub + sub), Se, Bl (4)

McNab, N. (Tottenham H), 1978 v W (1)

McNally, M. (Celtic), 1991 v Bul; 1993 v Ic (2)

McNamara, J. (Dunfermline Ath), 1994 v A, Bel; 1995 v Gr, Ru, Sm; 1996 v Gr, Fi; (with Celtic), Sm, H (2), Sp, F (12)

McNichol, J. (Brentford), 1979 v P, N (2); 1980 v Bel (2), WG, E (7)

McNiven, D. (Leeds U), 1977 v Cz, W (sub), Sw (sub) (3)

McNiven, S. A. (Oldham Ath), 1996 v Sm (sub) (1)

McPherson, D. (Rangers), 1984 v Bel; 1985 v Sp; (with Hearts), 1989 v N, Y (4)

McQuilken, J. (Celtic), 1993 v Bul, E (2)

McStay, P. (Celtic), 1983 v EG, Sw (2); 1984 v Y (2) (5)

McWhirter, N. (St Mirren), 1991 v Bul (sub) (1)

Main, A. (Dundee U), 1988 v E; 1989 v Y; 1990 v N (3)

Malpas, M. (Dundee U), 1983 v Bel, Sw (1+1 sub); 1984 v Bel, EG, Y (2); 1985 v Sp (8)

Marshall, S. R. (Arsenal), 1995 v Ru, Gr; 1996 v H, Sp, F (5)

Mason, G. R. (Manchester C), 1999 v Li (sub) (1)

Mathieson, D. (Queen of the South), 1997 v Col; 1998 v La; 1999 v G (sub) (3)

May, E. (Hibernian), 1989 v Y (sub), F (2)

Meldrum, C. (Kilmarnock), 1996 v F (sub); 1997 v A (2), La, Es, Se (6)

Melrose, J. (Partick Th), 1977 v Sw; 1979 v US, P, N (2); 1980 v Bel (sub), WG, E (8)

Miller, C. (Rangers), 1995 v Gr, Ru; 1996 v Gr, Sp, F; 1997 v A, La, Es (8)

Miller, J. (Aberdeen), 1987 v Ei (sub); 1988 v Bel; (with Celtic), E; 1989 v N, Y; 1990 v F, N (7)

Miller, W. (Aberdeen), 1978 v Sw, Cz (2)

Miller, W. (Hibernian), 1991 v R, Sw, Bul, Pol, F; 1992 v R, G (sub) (7)

Milne, R. (Dundee U), 1982 v Se (sub); 1984 v Bel, EG (3)

Money, I. C. (St Mirren), 1987 v Ei; 1988 v Bel; 1989 v N (3)

Muir, L. (Hibernian), 1977 v Cz (sub) (1)

Murray, N. (Rangers), 1993 v P (sub), Ma, Ic, P; 1994 v Sw, I; 1995 v Fi, Ru, Gr, Sm; 1996 v Gr (sub), Fi, Sm, H (2), F (16)

Murray, R. (Bournemouth), 1993 v Ic (sub) (1)

Narey, D. (Dundee U), 1977 v Cz, Sw; 1978 v Sw, Cz (4)

Naysmith, G. (Hearts), 1997 v La, Es (1 + sub), Se, A, Col, US, CzR, P; 1998 v La, D; 1999 v Es, Bel (2), CzR, G, Ei, CzR (18)

Nevin, P. (Chelsea), 1985 v WG, Ic, Sp (2), Ic (5)

Nicholas, C. (Celtic), 1981 v Se; 1982 v Se; 1983 v EG, Sw, Bel; (with Arsenal), 1984 v Y (6)

Nicholson, B. (Rangers), 1999 v G, Ni, CzR (sub) (3)

Nicol, S. (Ayr U), 1981 v Se; 1982 v Se, D; (with Liverpool), I (2), E (2); 1983 v EG, Sw (2), Bel; 1984 v Bel, EG, Y (14)

Nisbet, S. (Rangers), 1989 v N, Y, F; 1990 v Y, F (5)

Notman, A. M. (Manchester U), 1999 v Li (sub), Es, Bel (sub+sub) (4)

O'Brien, B. (Blackburn R), 1999 v Ei (sub), Ni (sub), CzR (sub) (3)

O'Donnell, P. (Motherwell), 1992 v Sw (sub), R, D, G (2), Se (1 + 1 sub); 1993 v P (8)

O'Neil, B. (Celtic), 1992 v D, G, Se (2); 1993 v Sw, P, I (7)

O'Neil, J. (Dundee U), 1991 v Bul (sub) (1)

O'Neill, M. (Clyde), 1995 v Ru (sub), F, Sk, Br; 1997 v Se (sub), Bl (sub) (6)

Orr, N. (Morton), 1978 v W (sub); 1979 v US, P, N (2); 1980 v Bel, E (7)

Parlane, D. (Rangers), 1977 v W (1)

Paterson, C. (Hibernian), 1981 v Se; 1982 v I (2)

Paterson, J. (Dundee U), 1997 v Col, US, CzR; 1999 v Bel (sub+sub) (5)

Payne, G. (Dundee U), 1978 v Sw, Cz, W (3)

Peacock, L. A. (Carlisle U), 1997 v Bl (1)

Pressley, S. (Rangers), 1993 v Ic, F, Bul, M, E; 1994 v Sw, I, M, A, Eg, P, Bel; 1995 v Fi; (with Coventry C), Ru (2), Sm, M, F, Sk, Br; (with Dundee U), 1996 v Gr, Sm, H (2), Sp, F (26)

Provan, D. (Kilmarnock), 1977 v Cz (sub) (1)

Rae, A. (Millwall), 1991 v Bul (sub + 1), F (sub); 1992 v Sw, R, G (sub), Se (2) (8)

Rae, G. (Dundee), 1999 v Ei (sub), Ni, CzR (3)

Redford, I. (Rangers), 1981 v Se (sub); 1982 v Se, D, I (2), E (6)

Reid, B. (Rangers), 1991 v F; 1992 v D, US, P (4)

Reid, C. (Hibernian), 1993 v Sw, P, I (3)

Reid, M. (Celtic), 1982 v E; 1984 v Y (2)

Reid, R. (St Mirren), 1977 v W, Sw, E (3)

Renicks, S. (Hamilton A), 1997 v Bl (1)

Rice, B. (Hibernian), 1985 v WG (1)

Richardson, L. (St Mirren), 1980 v WG, E (sub) (2)

Ritchie, A. (Morton), 1980 v Bel (1)

Ritchie, P. R. (Hearts), 1996 v H; 1997 v A (2), La, Es (2), Se (7)

Robertson, A. (Rangers) 1991 v F (1)

Robertson, C. (Rangers), 1977 v E (sub) (1)

Robertson, D. (Aberdeen), 1987 v Ei (sub); 1988 v E (2); 1989 v N, Y; 1990 v Y, N (7)

Robertson, H. (Aberdeen), 1994 v Eg; 1995 v Fi (2)

Robertson, J. (Hearts), 1985 v WG, Ic (sub) (2)

Robertson, L. (Rangers), 1993 v F, M (sub), E (sub) (3)

Robertson, S. (St Johnstone), 1998 v Fi, Ni (2)

Roddie, A. (Aberdeen), 1992 v US, P; 1993 v Sw (sub), P, Ic (5)

Ross, T. W. (Arsenal), 1977 v W (1)

Rowson, D. (Aberdeen), 1997 v La, Es, Se (2), Bl (5)

Russell, R. (Rangers), 1978 v W; 1980 v Bel; 1984 v Y (3)

Salton, D. B. (Luton T), 1992 v D, US, P, Y; 1993 v Sw, I (6)

Scott, P. (St Johnstone), 1994 v A (sub), Eg (sub), P, Bel (4)

Scrimgour, D. (St Mirren), 1997 v US, CzR; 1998 v D (3)

Seaton, A. (Falkirk), 1998 v Bl (sub) (1)

Shannon, R. (Dundee), 1987 v WG, Ei (2), Bel; 1988 v Bel, E (2) (7)

Sharp, G. (Everton), 1982 v E (1)

Sharp, R. (Dunfermline Ath), 1990 v N (sub); 1991 v R, Sw, Bul (4)

Sheerin, P. (Southampton), 1996 v Sm (1)

Shields, G. (Rangers), 1997 v A, La (2)

Simpson, N. (Aberdeen), 1982 v I (2), E; 1983 v EG, Sw (2), Bel; 1984 v Bel, EG, Y; 1985 v Sp (11)

Sinclair, D. (Dumbarton), 1977 v E (1)

Skilling, M. (Kilmarnock), 1993 v Ic (sub); 1994 v I (2)

Smith, B. M. (Celtic), 1992 v G (2), US, P, Y (5)

Smith, G. (Rangers), 1978 v W (1)
Smith, H. G. (Hearts), 1987 v WG, Bel (2)
Sneddon, A. (Celtic), 1979 v US (1)
Speedie, D. (Chelsea), 1985 v Sp (1)
Spencer, J. (Rangers), 1991 v Sw (sub), F; 1992 v Sw (3)
Stanton, P. (Hibernian), 1977 v Cz (1)
Stark, W. (Aberdeen), 1985 v Ic (1)
Stephen, R. (Dundee), 1983 v Bel (sub) (1)
Stevens, G. (Motherwell), 1977 v E (1)
Stewart, J. (Kilmarnock), 1978 v Sw, Cz; (with Middlesbrough), 1979 v P (3)
Stewart, R. (Dundee U), 1979 v P, N (2); (with West Ham U), 1980 v Bel (2), E (2), WG; 1981 v D; 1982 v I (2), E (12)
Stillie, D. (Aberdeen), 1995 v Ru (2), Sm, M, F, Sk, Br; 1996 v Gr, Fi, Sm, H (2), Sp, F (14)
Strachan, G. D. (Aberdeen), 1980 v Bel (1)
Strachan, G. D. (Coventry C), 1998 v D, Ei; 1999 v Li, Es, Bel (2) (6)
Sturrock, P. (Dundee U), 1977 v Cz, W, Sw, E; 1978 v Sw, Cz; 1982 v Se, I, E (9)
Sweeney, S. (Clydebank), 1991 v R, Sw (sub), Bul (2), Pol; 1992 v Sw, R (7)

Tarrant, N. K. (Aston Villa), 1999 v Ni (sub) (1)
Teale, G. (Clydebank), 1997 v La (sub), Es, Bl; (with Ayr U), 1999 v CzR (sub), G (sub), Ei (sub) (6)
Telfer, P. (Luton T), 1993 v Ma, P; 1994 v Sw (3)
Thomas, K. (Hearts), 1993 v F (sub), Bul, M, E; 1994 v Sw, Ma; 1995 v Gr; 1997 v A (8)
Thompson, S. (Dundee U), 1997 v US, CzR, P; 1998 v Bl, La; 1999 v G (sub), Ei, Ni, CzR (9)
Thomson, W. (Partick Th), 1977 v E (sub); 1978 v W; (with St Mirren), 1979 v US, N (2); 1980 v Bel (2), E (2), WG (10)
Tolmie, J. (Morton), 1980 v Bel (sub) (1)
Tortolano, J. (Hibernian), 1987 v WG, Ei (2)
Tweed, S. (Hibernian), 1993 v Ic; 1994 v Sw, I (3)

Walker, A. (Celtic), 1988 v Bel (1)
Wallace, I. (Coventry C), 1978 v Sw (1)
Walsh, C. (Nottingham F), 1984 v EG, Sw (2), Bel; 1984 v EG (5)
Wark, J. (Ipswich T), 1977 v Cz, W, Sw; 1978 v W; 1979 v P; 1980 v E (2), WG (8)
Watson, A. (Aberdeen), 1981 v Se, D; 1982 v D, I (sub) (4)
Watson, K. (Rangers), 1977 v E; 1978 v Sw (sub) (2)
Watt, M. (Aberdeen), 1991 v R, Sw, Bul (2), Pol, F; 1992 v Sw, R, G (2), Se (2) (12)
Whiteford, A. (St Johnstone), 1997 v US (1)
Whyte, D. (Celtic), 1987 v Ei (2), Bel; 1988 v E (2); 1989 v N, Y; 1990 v Y, N (9)
Will, J. A. (Arsenal), 1992 v D (sub), Y; 1993 v Ic (sub) (3)
Wilson, S. (Rangers), 1999 v Es, Bel (2), G, Ei, CzR (6)
Wilson, T. (St Mirren), 1983 v Sw (sub) (1)
Wilson, T. (Nottingham F), 1988 v E; 1989 v N, Y; 1990 v F (4)
Winnie, D. (St Mirren), 1988 v Bel (1)
Wright, P. (Aberdeen), 1989 v Y, F; (with QPR), 1990 v Y (sub) (3)
Wright, S. (Aberdeen), 1991 v Bul, Pol, F; 1992 v Sw, G (2), Se (2); 1993 v Sw, P, I, Ma; 1994 v I, Ma (14)
Wright, T. (Oldham Ath), 1987 v Bel (sub) (1)

Young, D. (Aberdeen), 1997 v Es (sub), Se, Col, CzR (sub), P; 1998 v La (sub); 1999 v CzR (sub), G (sub) (8)

WALES
Aizlewood, M. (Luton T), 1979 v E; 1981 v Ho (2)

Baddeley, L. M. (Cardiff C), 1996 v Mol (sub), G (sub) (2)
Balcombe, S. (Leeds U), 1982 v F (sub) (1)
Barnhouse, D. J. (Swansea), 1995 v Mol; 1996 v Mol, Sm (3)
Bater, P. T. (Bristol R), 1977 v E, S (2)
Bellamy, C. D. (Norwich C), 1996 v Sm (sub); 1997 v Sm, T, Bel; 1998 v T, Bel, I; 1999 v I (8)
Bird, A. (Cardiff C), 1993 v Cy (sub); 1994 v Cy (sub); 1995 v Mol, Ge (sub), Bul; 1996 v G (sub) (6)
Blackmore, C. (Manchester U), 1984 v N, Bul, Y (3)
Blake, N. (Cardiff C), 1991 v Pol (sub); 1993 v Cy, Bel, RCS; 1994 v RCS (5)
Blaney, S. D. (West Ham U), 1997 v Sm, Ho, T (3)

Bodin, P. (Cardiff C), 1983 v Y (1)
Bowen, J. P. (Swansea C), 1993 v Cy, Bel (2); 1994 v RCS, R (sub) (5)
Bowen, M. (Tottenham H), 1983 v N; 1984 v Bul, Y (3)
Boyle, T. (C Palace), 1982 v F (1)
Brace, D. P. (Wrexham), 1995 v Ge, Bul (2); 1997 v Sm Ho; 1998 v T (6)

Cegielski, W. (Wrexham), 1977 v E (sub), S (2)
Chapple, S. R. (Swansea C), 1992 v R; 1993 v Cy, Bel (2), RCS; 1994 v RCS; Bul (2) (8)
Charles, J. M. (Swansea C), 1979 v E; 1981 v Ho (2)
Clark, J. (Manchester U), 1978 v S; (with Derby Co), 1979 v E (2)
Coates, J. S. (Swansea C), 1996 v Mol, G; 1997 v Ho, T (sub); 1998 v T (sub) (5)
Coleman, C. (Swansea C), 1990 v Pol; 1991 v E, Pol (3)
Coyne, D. (Tranmere R), 1992 v R; 1994 v Cy (sub), R; 1995 v Mol, Ge, Bul (2) (7)
Curtis, A. T. (Swansea C), 1977 v E (1)

Davies, A. (Manchester U), 1982 v F (1), Ho; 1983 v N, Y, Bul (6)
Davies, D. (Barry T), 1999 v D (sub) (1)
Davies, G. M. (Hereford U), 1993 v Bel, RCS; 1995 v Mol (sub), Ge, Bul (2); (with C Palace) 1996 v Mol (7)
Davies, I. C. (Norwich C), 1978 v S (sub) (1)
Davies, S. (Peterborough U), 1999 v D, Bl, Sw, I, D (5)
Deacy, N. (PSV Eindhoven), 1977 v S (1)
Dibble, A. (Cardiff C), 1983 v Bul; 1984 v N, Bul (3)
Doyle, S. C. (Preston NE), 1979 v E (sub); (with Huddersfield T), 1984 v N (2)
Dwyer, P. J. (Cardiff C), 1979 v E (1)

Earnshaw, R. (Cardiff C), 1999 v P (sub), I, D (3)
Ebdon, M. (Everton), 1990 v Pol; 1991 v E (2)
Edwards, C. N. H. (Swansea C), 1996 v G; 1997 v Sm, Ho (2), T, Bel; 1998 v T (7)
Edwards, R. I. (Chester), 1977 v S; 1978 v W (2)
Edwards, R. W. (Bristol C), 1991 v Pol; 1992 v R; 1993 v Cy, Bel (2), RCS; 1994 v RCS, Cy, R; 1995 v Ge, Bul; 1996 v Mol, G (13)
Evans, A. (Bristol R), 1977 v E (1)
Evans, K. (Leeds U), 1999 v I (sub), D (2)
Evans, P. S. (Shrewsbury T), 1996 v G (1)
Evans, T. (Cardiff C), 1995 v Bul (sub); 1996 v Mol, G (3)

Foster, M. G. (Tranmere R), 1993 v RCS (1)
Freestone, R. (Chelsea), 1990 v Pol (1)

Gabbidon, D. L. (WBA), 1999 v D, P, Sw, I (sub), D (5)
Gale, D. (Swansea C), 1983 v Bul; 1984 v N (sub) (2)
Gibson, N. D. (Tranmere R), 1999 v D (sub), Bl (sub), P (3)
Giggs, R. (Manchester U), 1991 v Pol (1)
Giles, D. C. (Cardiff C), 1977 v S; 1978 v S; (with Swansea C), 1981 v Ho; (with C Palace), 1983 v Y (4)
Giles, P. (Cardiff C), 1982 v F (2), Ho (3)
Graham, D. (Manchester U), 1991 v E (1)
Green, R. M. (Wolverhampton W), 1998 v I; 1999 v I, D, Bl, Sw, I, D (7)
Griffith, C. (Cardiff C), 1990 v Pol (1)
Griffiths, C. (Shrewsbury T), 1991 v Pol (sub) (1)

Hall, G. D. (Chelsea), 1990 v Pol (1)
Hartson, J. (Luton T), 1994 v Cy, R; 1995 v Mol, Ge, Bul; (with Arsenal), 1996 v G, Sm; 1997 v Sm, Ho (9)
Haworth, S. O. (Cardiff C), 1997 v Ho, T, Bel; (with Coventry C), 1998 v T, Bel; I; 1999 v I, D; (with Wigan Ath) Bl, Sw (10)
Hodges, G. (Wimbledon), 1983 v Y (sub), Bul (sub); 1984 v N, Bul, Y (5)
Holden, A. (Chester C), 1984 v Y (sub) (1)
Holloway, C. D. (Exeter C), 1999 v P, D (2)
Hopkins, J. (Fulham), 1982 v F (sub), Ho; 1983 v N, Y, Bul (5)
Hopkins, S. A. (Wrexham), 1999 v P (sub) (1)
Huggins, D. N. (Bristol C), 1996 v Sm (1)
Hughes, D. R. (Southampton), 1994 v R (1)
Hughes, R. D. (Aston Villa), 1996 v Sm; 1997 v Sm (sub), Ho (2), T, Bel; 1998 v T, Bel, I; 1999 v I, Sw, I (12)
Hughes, I. (Bury), 1992 v R; 1993 v Cy, Bel (sub), RCS; 1994 v Cy, R; 1995 v Mol, Ge, Bul; 1996 v Mol (sub), G (11)
Hughes, L. M. (Manchester U), 1983 v N, Y; 1984 v N, Bul, Y (5)
Hughes, W. (WBA), 1977 v E, S; 1978 v S (3)

Jackett, K. (Watford), 1981 v Ho; 1982 v F (2)
James, R. M. (Swansea C), 1977 v E, S; 1978 v S (3)
Jarman, L. (Cardiff C), 1996 v Sm; 1997 v Sm, Ho (2), Bel; 1998 v T, Bel; 1999 v I, P (9)
Jeanne, L. C. (QPR), 1999 v P (sub), Sw, I (3)
Jelleyman, G. A. (Peterborough U), 1999 v D (sub) (1)
Jenkins, L. D. (Swansea C), 1998 v T (sub) (1)
Jenkins, S. R. (Swansea C), 1993 v Cy (sub), Bel (2)
Jones, F. (Wrexham), 1981 v Ho (1)
Jones, L. (Cardiff C), 1982 v F (2), Ho (3)
Jones, M. G. (Leeds U), 1998 v Bel; 1999 v I, D, Bl, Sw, I (6)
Jones, P. L. (Liverpool), 1992 v R; 1993 v Cy, Bel (2), RCS; 1994 v RCS (sub), Cy, R; 1995 v Mol, Ge; 1996 v Mol, G (12)
Jones, R. (Sheffield W), 1994 v R; 1995 v Bul (2) (3)
Jones, V. (Bristol R), 1979 v E; 1981 v Ho (2)

Kendall, M. (Tottenham H), 1978 v S (1)
Kenworthy, J. R. (Tranmere R), 1994 v Cy; 1995 v Mol, Bul (3)
Knott, G. R. (Tottenham H), 1996 v Sm (1)

Law, B. J. (QPR), 1990 v Pol; 1991 v E (2)
Letheran, G. (Leeds U), 1977 v E, S (2)
Lewis, D. (Swansea C), 1982 v F (2), Ho; 1983 v N, Y, Bul; 1984 v N, Bu1, Y (9)
Lewis, J. (Cardiff C), 1983 v N (1)
Llewellyn, C. M. (Norwich C), 1998 v T (sub), Bel (sub), I; 1999 v I, D, Bl, I (7)
Loveridge, J. (Swansea C), 1982 v Ho; 1983 v N, Bul (3)
Low, J. D. (Bristol R), 1999 v P (1)
Lowndes, S. R. (Newport Co), 1979 v E; 1981 v Ho; (with Millwall), 1984 v Bul, Y (4)

McCarthy, A. J. (QPR), 1994 v RCS, Cy, R (3)
Maddy, P. (Cardiff C), 1982 v Ho; 1983 v N (sub) (2)
Margetson, M. W. (Manchester C), 1992 v R; 1993 v Cy, Bel (2), RCS; 1994 v RCS, Cy (7)
Martin, A. P. (Crystal Palace), 1999 v D (1)
Marustik, C. (Swansea C), 1982 v F (2); 1983 v Y, Bul; 1984 v N, Bul, Y (7)
Maxwell, L. J. (Liverpool), 1999 v Sw (sub), I (2)
Meaker, M. J. (QPR), 1994 v RCS (sub), R (sub) (2)
Melville, A. K. (Swansea C), 1990 v Pol; (with Oxford U), 1991 v E (2)
Micallef, C. (Cardiff C), 1982 v F, Ho; 1983 v N (3)
Morgan, A. M. (Tranmere R), 1995 v Mol, Bul; 1996 v Mol, G (4)
Mountain, P. D. (Cardiff C), 1997 v Ho, T (2)

Nardiello, D. (Coventry C), 1978 v S (1)
Neilson, A. B. (Newcastle U), 1993 v Cy, Bel (2), RCS; 1994 v RCS, Cy, R (7)
Nicholas, P. (C Palace), 1978 v S; 1979 v E; (with Arsenal), 1982 v F (3)
Nogan, K. (Luton T), 1990 v Pol; 1991 v E (2)
Nogan, L. (Oxford U) 1991 v E (1)

Oster, J. M. (Grimsby T), 1997 v Sm (sub), Ho (sub), T, Bel; (with Everton), 1998 v T, Bel, I; 1999 v I, Sw (9)
Owen, G. (Wrexham), 1991 v E (sub), Pol; 1992 v R; 1993 v Cy, Bel (2); 1994 v Cy, R (8)

Page, R. J. (Watford), 1995 v Mol, Ge, Bul; 1996 v Mol (4)
Partridge, D. W. (West Ham U), 1997 v T (1)
Pascoe, C. (Swansea C), 1983 v Bul (sub); 1984 v N (sub), Bul, Y (4)
Pembridge, M. (Luton T), 1991 v Pol (1)
Perry, J. (Cardiff C), 1990 v Pol; 1991 v E, Pol (3)
Peters, M. (Manchester C), 1992 v R; (with Norwich C), 1993 v Cy, RCS (3)
Phillips, D. (Plymouth Arg), 1984 v N, Bul, Y (3)
Phillips, L. (Swansea C), 1979 v E; (with Charlton Ath), 1983 v N (2)
Pontin, K. (Cardiff C), 1978 v S (1)
Powell, L. (Southampton), 1991 v Pol (sub); 1992 v R (sub); 1993 v Bel (sub); 1994 v RCS (4)
Price, J. J. (Swansea C), 1998 v I (sub); 1999 v I (sub), D, Bl, P (5)
Price, P. (Luton T), 1981 v Ho (1)
Pugh, D. (Doncaster R), 1982 v F (2) (2)
Pugh, S. (Wrexham), 1993 v Bel (2 subs) (2)

Ramasut, M. W. T. (Bristol R), 1997 v Ho, Bel; 1998 v T, I (4)
Ratcliffe, K. (Everton), 1981 v Ho; 1982 v F (2)

Ready, K. (QPR), 1992 v R; 1993 v Bel (2); 1994 v RCS, Cy (5)
Rees, A. (Birmingham C), 1984 v N (1)
Rees, J. (Luton T), 1990 v Pol; 1991 v E, Pol (3)
Roberts, A. (QPR), 1991 v E, Pol (2)
Roberts, C. J. (Cardiff C), 1999 v D (sub) (1)
Roberts, G. (Hull C), 1983 v Bul (1)
Roberts, G. W. (Liverpool), 1997 v Ho, T, Bel; 1998 v T, I; 1999 v I, D, Bl, P; (with Panionios) D (10)
Roberts, J. G. (Wrexham), 1977 v E (1)
Roberts, N. W. (Wrexham), 1999 v I (sub), P (2)
Roberts, P. (Porthmadog), 1997 v Ho (sub) (1)
Roberts, S. I. (Swansea C), 1999 v Sw, I (sub), D (3)
Robinson, C. P. (Wolverhampton W), 1996 v Sm; 1997 v Sm, Ho (2), T, Bel (6)
Robinson, J. (Brighton & HA), 1992 v R; (with Charlton Ath), 1993 v Bel; 1994 v RCS, Cy, R (5)
Rowlands, A. J. R. (Manchester C), 1996 v Sm; 1997 v Sm, Ho (1 + sub), T (sub) (5)
Rush, I. (Liverpool), 1981 v Ho; 1982 v F (2)

Savage, R. W. (Crewe Alex), 1995 v Bul; 1996 v Mol, G (3)
Sayer, P. A. (Cardiff C), 1977 v E, S (2)
Searle, D. (Cardiff C), 1991 v Pol (sub); 1992 v R; 1993 v Cy, Bel (2), RCS; 1994 v RCS (6)
Slatter, N. (Bristol R), 1983 v N, Y, Bul; 1984 v N, Bul, Y (6)
Speed, G. A. (Leeds U), 1990 v Pol; 1991 v E, Pol (3)
Stevenson, N. (Swansea C), 1982 v F, Ho (2)
Stevenson, W. B. (Leeds U), 1977 v E, S; 1978 v S (3)
Symons, K. (Portsmouth), 1991 v E, Pol (2)

Taylor, G. K. (Bristol R), 1995 v Ge, Bul (2); 1996 v Mol (4)
Thomas, D. J. (Watford), 1998 v T, Bel (2)
Thomas, J. A. (Blackburn R), 1996 v Sm; 1997 v Sm, Ho (2), T, Bel; 1998 v Bel; 1999 v D, Bl, P (10)
Thomas, Martin R. (Bristol R), 1979 v E; 1981 v Ho (2)
Thomas, Mickey R. (Wrexham), 1977 v E; 1978 v S (2)
Thomas, D. G. (Leeds U), 1977 v E; 1979 v E; 1984 v N (3)
Tibbott, L. (Ipswich T), 1977 v E, S (2)
Tipton, M. J. (Oldham Ath), 1998 v I (sub); 1999 v P, Sw (sub) (3)
Twiddy, C. (Plymouth Arg), 1995 v Mol, Ge; 1996 v G (sub) (3)

Vaughan, N. (Newport Co), 1982 v F, Ho (2)

Walsh, I. P. (C Palace), 1979 v E; (with Swansea C), 1983 v Bul (2)
Walton, M. (Norwich C.), 1991 v Pol (sub) (1)
Ward, D. (Notts Co), 1996 v Mol, G (2)
Williams, A. P. (Southampton), 1998 v Bel, I; 1999 v I, D (sub), Bl, Sw, I (7)
Williams, A. S. (Blackburn R), 1996 v Sm; 1997 v Sm, Ho, Bel; 1998 v T, Bel, I; 1999 v I, D, Bl, P, Sw, I, D (14)
Williams, D. (Bristol R), 1983 v Y (1)
Williams, D. I. L. (Liverpool), 1998 v I; 1999 v D, Bl; (with Wrexham) I, D (5)
Williams, E. (Caernarfon T), 1997 v Ho (sub), T (sub) (2)
Williams, G. (Bristol R), 1983 v Y, Bul (2)
Williams, S. J. (Wrexham), 1995 v Mol, Ge, Bul (2) (4)
Wilmot, R. (Arsenal), 1982 v F (2), Ho; 1983 v N, Y; 1984 v Y (6)
Wright, A. A. (Oxford U), 1998 v Bel, I (sub); 1999 v D (sub) (3)

Young, S. (Cardiff C), 1996 v Sm; 1997 v Sm, Ho (2), Bel (sub) (5)

NORTHERN IRELAND
Bailie, N. (Linfield), 1990 v Is; 1994 v R (sub) (2)
Beatty, S. (Chelsea), 1990 v Is; (with Linfield), 1994 v R (2)
Black, K. T. (Luton T), 1990 v Is (1)
Blackledge, G. (Portadown), 1978 v Ei (1)
Boyle, W. S. (Leeds U), 1998 v Sw (sub), S (sub) (2)
Brotherston, N. (Blackburn R), 1978 v Ei (sub) (1)
Burns, L. (Port Vale), 1998 v Sw, S, Ei; 1999 v T, Fi, Mol, G, Mol, Ei (9)

Carroll, R. E. (Wigan Ath), 1998 v S, Ei; 1999 v T, Fi, Mol, G, Mol, Ei (8)
Clarke, R. (Portadown), 1999 v Ei (sub), S (2)
Connell, T. E. (Coleraine), 1978 v Ei (sub) (1)

Coote, A. (Norwich C), 1998 v Sw (sub), S, Ei; 1999 v T, Fi, Mol, G, Mol, Ei (9)

Devine, D. (Omagh T), 1994 v R (1)
Devine, J. (Glentoran), 1990 v Is (1)
Donaghy, M. M. (Larne), 1978 v Ei (1)
Dowie, I. (Luton T), 1990 v Is (1)

Elliott, S. (Glentoran), 1999 v Fi (sub), Ei, S (sub) (3)

Feeney, L. (Linfield), 1998 v Ei (sub); 1999 v T, Fi, Mol; (with Rangers) G (sub), Ei, S (7)
Fitzgerald, D. (Rangers), 1998 v Sw, S; 1999 v T (sub), Fi (4)
Friars, S. M. (Liverpool), 1998 v Sw, S, Ei; (with Ipswich T), 1999 v T, Fi, Mol, G, Mol (8)

Gillespie, K. R. (Manchester U), 1994 v R (1)
Glendinning, M. (Bangor), 1994 v R (1)
Graham, G. L. (Crystal Palace), 1999 v S (1)
Graham, R. S. (QPR), 1999 v Fi (sub), Mol, Ei (sub) (3)
Gray, P. (Luton T), 1990 v Is (sub) (1)
Griffin, D. J. (St Johnstone), 1998 v S (sub), Ei; 1999 v T, Fi, G, Mol, Ei, S (8)

Hamilton, W. R. (Linfield), 1978 v Ei (1)
Harvey, J. (Arsenal), 1978 v Ei (1)
Hayes, T. (Luton T), 1978 v Ei (1)
Healy, D. J. (Manchester U), 1999 v Mol (sub), G (sub), Ei (sub), S (4)
Hughes, M. E. (Manchester C), 1990 v Is (sub)

Johnson, D. (Blackburn R), 1998 v Sw, S, Ei; 1999 v T, Fi, G, Mol, Ei (8)
Johnston, B. (Cliftonville), 1978 v Ei (1)

Kee, P. V. (Oxford U), 1990 v Is (1)
Kelly, N. (Oldham Ath), 1990 v Is (sub) (1)
Kirk, A. (Hearts), 1999 v S (1)

Lennon, N. F. (Manchester C), 1990 v Is; (with Crewe Alex), 1994 v R (2)
Lyttle, G. (Celtic), 1998 v Sw, S; (with Peterborough U), 1999 v T (sub), Mol (2), S (6)

Magee, J. (Bangor), 1994 v R (sub) (1)
Magilton, J. (Liverpool), 1990 v Is (1)
Matthews, N. P. (Blackpool), 1990 v Is (1)
McBride, J. (Glentoran), 1994 v R (sub) (1)
McCallion, E. (Coleraine), 1998 v Sw (sub) (1)
McCoy, R. K. (Coleraine), 1990 v Is (1)
McCreery, D. (Manchester U), 1978 v Ei (1)
McGibbon, P. C. G. (Manchester U), 1994 v R (1)
McGlinchey, B. (Manchester C), 1998 v Sw, S, Ei; 1999 v T, Fi, Mol, G, Mol, Ei, S (10)
McIlroy, T. (Linfield), 1994 v R (sub) (1)
McKnight, P. (Rangers), 1998 v Sw; 1999 v T (sub), Mol (sub) (3)
McMahon, G. J. (Tottenham H),1994 v R (sub) (1)
McVeigh, P. (Tottenham H), 1998 v S (sub), Ei; 1999 v T, Mol, G, Mol, Ei (7)
Millar, W. P. (Port Vale), 1990 v Is (1)
Moreland, V. (Glentoran), 1978 v Ei (sub) (1)
Morgan, M, P. T. (Preston NE), 1999 v S (1)
Mulryne, P. P. (Manchester U), Sw, S, Ei; (with Norwich C), 1999 v G, Mol (5)
Murray, W. (Linfield), 1978 v Ei (sub) (1)

Nicholl, J. M. (Manchester U), 1978 v Ei (1)

O'Hara, G. (Leeds U), 1994 v R (1)
O'Neill, M. A. M. (Hibernian), 1994 v R (1)
O'Neill, J. P. (Leicester C), 1978 v Ei (1)

Patterson, D. J. (Crystal Palace), 1994 v R (1)

Quinn, S. J. (Blackpool), 1994 v R (1)

Robinson, S. (Tottenham H), 1994 v R (1)

Sloan, T. (Ballymena U), 1978 v Ei (1)

Taylor, M. S. (Fulham), 1998 v Sw (1)

Waterman, D. G. (Portsmouth), 1998 v Sw, S, Ei; 1999 v T, Fi, Mol, G, Mol, Ei, S (sub) (10)
Wells, D. P. (Barry T), 1999 v S (1)
Whitley, Jeff (Manchester C), 1998 v Sw, S, Ei; 1999 v T, Fi, Mol, G, Ei, S (9)

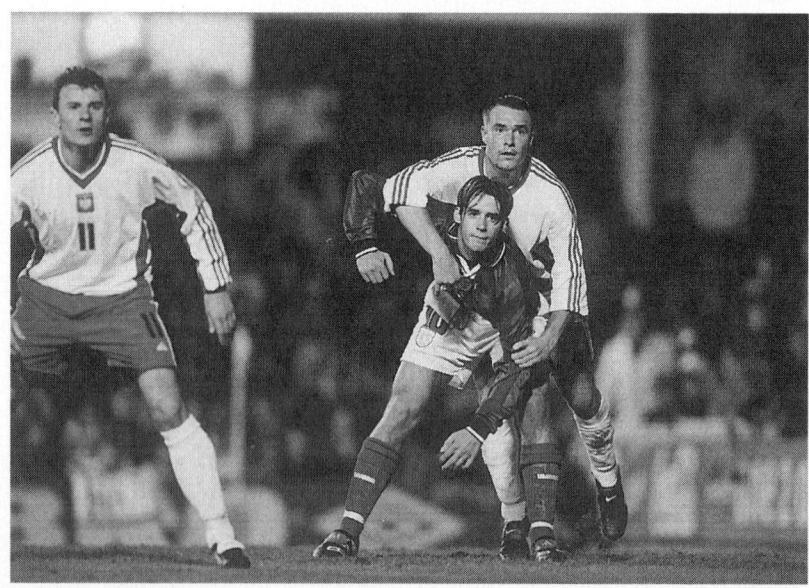

Matt Jansen, the England Under-21 international, is well-covered by a Polish defender during the UEFA Championship match. (Actionimages)

INTERNATIONAL RECORDS

MOST GOALS IN AN INTERNATIONAL

Record			
	Sophus Nielsen (Denmark) 10 goals v France, at White City (Olympics)		22.10.1908
	Gottfried Fuchs (Germany) 10 goals v Russia, in Stockholm (Olympics)		1.7.1912
World Cup	Gary Cole (Australia) 7 goals v Fiji, in Melbourne		14.8.1981
	Karim Bagheri (Iran) 7 goals v Maldives, in Damascus		2.6.1997
England	Malcolm Macdonald (Newcastle U) 5 goals v Cyprus, at Wembley		16.4.1975
	Willie Hall (Tottenham H) 5 goals v Ireland, at Old Trafford		16.11.1938
	Steve Bloomer (Derby Co) 5 goals v Wales, at Cardiff		16.3.1896
	Howard Vaughton (Aston Villa) 5 goals v Ireland, at Belfast		18.2.1882
Ireland	Joe Bambrick (Linfield) 6 goals v Wales, at Belfast		1.2.1930
Wales	John Price (Wrexham) 4 goals v Ireland, at Wrexham		25.2.1882
	Mel Charles (Cardiff C) 4 goals v Ireland, at Cardiff		11.4.1962
	Ian Edwards (Chester) 4 goals v Malta, at Wrexham		25.10.1978

MOST GOALS IN AN INTERNATIONAL CAREER

		Goals	Games
England	Bobby Charlton (Manchester U)	49	106
Scotland	Denis Law (Huddersfield T, Manchester C, Torino, Manchester U)	30	55
	Kenny Dalglish (Celtic, Liverpool)	30	102
Ireland	Colin Clarke (Bournemouth, Southampton, QPR, Portsmouth)	13	38
Wales	Ian Rush (Liverpool, Juventus)	28	73
Republic of Ireland	Frank Stapleton (Arsenal, Manchester U, Ajax, Derby Co, Le Havre, Blackburn R)	20	70

HIGHEST SCORES

World Cup Match	Iran	17	Maldives	0	1997
European Championship	Spain	12	Malta	1	1983
Olympic Games	Denmark	17	France	1	1908
	Germany	16	USSR	0	1912
Other International Match	Germany	13	Finland	0	1940
	Spain	13	Bulgaria	0	1933
European Cup	Feyenoord	12	K R Reykjavik	2	1969
European Cup-Winners' Cup	Sporting Lisbon	16	Apoel Nicosia	1	1963
Fairs & UEFA Cups	Ajax	14	Red Boys	0	1984

GOALSCORING RECORDS

World Cup Final	Geoff Hurst (England) 3 goals v West Germany	1966
World Cup Final tournament	Just Fontaine (France) 13 goals	1958
Career	Artur Friedenreich (Brazil) 1329 goals	1910–30
	Pelè (Brazil) 1281 goals	*1956–78
	Franz 'Bimbo' Binder (Austria, Germany) 1006 goals	1930–50

*Pelé subsequently scored two goals in Testimonial matches making his total 1283.

MOST CAPPED INTERNATIONALS IN BRITISH ISLES

England	Peter Shilton	125 appearances	1970–90
Northern Ireland	Pat Jennings	119 appearances	1964–86
Scotland	Kenny Dalglish	102 appearances	1971–86
Wales	Neville Southall	92 appearances	1982–97
Republic of Ireland	Paul McGrath	83 appearances	1984–97

BRITISH & IRISH INTERNATIONAL MANAGERS

England
Walter Winterbottom 1946–1962 (after period as coach); Alf Ramsey 1963–1974; Joe Mercer (caretaker) 1974; Don Revie 1974–1977; Ron Greenwood 1977–1982; Bobby Robson 1982–1990; Graham Taylor 1990–1993; Terry Venables (coach) 1994–1996; Glenn Hoddle 1996–1999; Kevin Keegan from May 1999.

Northern Ireland
Billy Bingham 1967–1971; Terry Neill 1971–1975; Dave Clements (player-manager) 1975–1976; Danny Blanchflower 1976–1979; Billy Bingham 1980–1993; Bryan Hamilton 1994–1998; Lawrie McMenemy from February 1998

Scotland
Bobby Brown 1967–1971; Tommy Docherty 1971–1972; Willie Ormond 1973–1977; Ally MacLeod 1977–1978;

Jock Stein 1978–1985; Alex Ferguson (caretaker) 1985–1986 Andy Roxburgh (coach) 1986–1993; Craig Brown from September 1993.

Wales
Mike Smith 1974–1979; Mike England 1980–1988; David Williams (caretaker) 1988; Terry Yorath 1988–1993; John Toshack 1994 for one match; Mike Smith 1994–1995; Bobby Gould 1995–1999.

Republic of Ireland
Liam Tuohy 1971–1972; Johnny Giles 1973–1980 (after period as player-manager); Eoin Hand 1980–1985; Jack Charlton 1986–1996; Mick McCarthy from February 1996.

FA SCHOOLS & YOUTH GAMES 1998–99

ENGLAND UNDER-18

19 July*

Cyprus 1   England 2

England: Simonsen (Tranmere Rovers); Ball (Everton), Cooper (Nottingham Forest), Woodgate (Leeds United) [Young (Tottenham Hotspur) 75], Upson (Arsenal), Griffin (Newcastle United), Vernazz (Arsenal), Matthews (Leeds United), Cadamarteri (Everton) [Smith (Leeds United) 65], Johnson (Crewe Alexandra), Fenton N (Manchester City).

21 July*

Republic of Ireland 0   England 1 *(Smith 85)*

England: Simonsen (Tranmere Rovers); Ball (Everton), Cooper (Nottingham Forest) [Vernazza (Arsenal) 46], Woodgate (Leeds United), Upson (Arsenal), Matthews (Leeds United), Johnson (Crewe Alexandra), Ormerod (Middlesbrough) [Griffin (Newcastle United) 60], Young (Tottenham Hotspur), Dunn (Blackburn Rovers), Smith (Leeds United).

23 July*

England 0   Croatia 3

England: Simonsen (Tranmere Rovers); Ball (Everton), Upson (Arsenal), Vernazza (Arsenal), Matthews (Leeds United), Johnson (Crewe Alexanra) [Griffin (Newcastle United) 60], Ormerod (Middlesbrough) [Piercy (Tottenham Hotspur 60)], Young (Tottenham Hotspur) [Woodgate (Leeds United) 75], Fenton N (Manchester City), Dunn (Blackburn Rovers), Smith (Leeds United).

2 Sept+

Republic of Ireland 0   England 5 *(Vassell 36, 72, Gerrard 24, Milligan 17, Jeffers 77)*

England: Taylor (Arsenal) [Ghent (Aston Villa)]; Wright D (Crewe Alexandra), Naylor (Wolverhampton Wanderers) [Woodhouse (Sheffield United)], Wellens (Manchester United) [Riggott (Derby County)], Woodgate (Leeds United) [Jeffers (Everton)], Wright S (Liverpool), Chadwick (Manchester United), Vassell (Aston Villa), Bridge (Southampton) [Etherington (Peterborough United)], Gerrard (Liverpool) [Roche (Manchester United)], Milligan (Everton) [Russell (Norwich City)].

13 Oct+

Italy 2   England 4 *(Milligan 17, 40, Vassell 32, Gerrard 89)*

England: Taylor (Arsenal); Wright D (Crewe Alexandra) [Roche (Manchester United) 46], Woodhouse (Sheffield United), Gerrard (Liverpool), Wright S (Liverpool), Barry (Aston Villa), Chadwick (Manchester United) [Riggott (Derby County) 87], Parker (Charlton Athletic), Vassell (Aston Villa) [Smith (Leeds United) 68], Milligan (Everton) [Wellens (Manchester United) 57], Bridge (Southampton) [Wheatcroft (Manchester United) 46] [Russell (Norwich City) 83].

8 Mar+

Spain 1   England 1 *(Wright S 20)*

England: Taylor (Arsenal); Wright D (Crewe Alexandra), Naylor (Wolverhampton Wanderers), Wellens (Manchester United), Wright S (Liverpool), King (Tottenham Hotspur), Chadwick (Manchester United), Parker (Charlton Athletic) [Cole (West Ham United) 63], Vassell (Aston Villa), Milligan (Everton), Bridge (Southampton) [Morris (Sheffield United) 46].

10 Mar**

England 8 *(Parker 15, Milligan 17 (pen) 87 (pen), Chadwick 19, Vassell 28, King 62, Cole 64, Etherington 73)*   **Andorra 0**

England: Taylor (Arsenal); Wright D (Crewe Alexandra) [Roche (Manchester United 46], Naylor (Wolverhampton Wanderers) [Regan (Everton) 67], Cole (West Ham United), Wright S (Liverpool), King (Tottenham Hotspur), Chadwick (Manchester United), Parker (Charlton Athletic), Vassell (Aston Villa), Milligan (Everton), Bridge (Southampton) [Etherington (Peterborough United) 46].

12 Mar**

England 2 *(Vassell 7, Wright S 37)*   **Israel 1**

England: Taylor (Arsenal); Wellens (Manchester United), Wright S (Liverpool), King (Tottenham Hotspur), Parker (Charlton Athletic), Vassell (Aston Villa) [Johnson A (Birmingham City) 89], Milligan (Everton) [Dixon (Leeds United) 72], Regan (Everton), Cole (West Ham United), Roche (Manchester United), Etherington (Peterborough United) [Chadwick (Manchester United) 77].

ENGLAND UNDER-16 *Missing from last year's edition*

14 Nov 1997+

Poland 2   England 1

England: Murray (Wolverhampton Wanderers) [Rachubka (Manchester United) 40]; Maley (Sunderland), Hall D (Coventry City), Stanton (Scunthorpe United) [Senda (Southampton) 60], Barry (Aston Villa), Osman (Everton) [Lyons (Derby County) 40], Turner (Nottingham Forest), Blois (Norwich City) [Reid (Millwall) 60], Proudlock (Wolverhampton Wanderers) [Coppinger (Darlington) 40], Jeffers (Everton), Etherington (Peterborough United).

9 Dec 1997+

England 1 *(Taylor 39)*   **Northern Ireland 0**

England: Hodgson (Manchester City) [Bywater (Rochdale) 40]; Wright R (Preston North End) [Walker (Manchester United) 40], Hall D (Coventry City), Pilkington (Everton), Taylor (Middlesbrough), Pead (Coventry City), Webber (Manchester United), Turner (Nottingham Forest) [Noble (Arsenal) 65], Mike (Manchester City) [McStea (Middlesbrough) 40], Armstrong (Liverpool), Torpey (Liverpool) [Clarke (Everton) 65].

10 Dec 1997+

England 5 *(Cole 2, Senda, Coppinger, Etherington)*

Northern Ireland 0

England: Rachubka (Manchester United) [Murray (Wolverhampton Wanderers) 40]; Maley (Sunderland), Evans G (Leeds United) [Osman (Everton) 40], Stanton (Scunthorpe United), Barry (Aston Villa), Cole (West Ham United), Senda (Southampton), Blois (Norwich City), Reid (Millwall) [Standing (Aston Villa) 40], Coppinger (Darlington), Etherington (Peterborough United) [Lyons (Derby County) 40].

3 Mar 1998#

England 3 *(Cole, Armstrong, Mike)*   **Bosnia 1**

England: Rachubka (Manchester United); Canoville (Millwall), Hanson (Middlesbrough), Hall D (Coventry City) [Blois (Norwich City) 63], Barry (Aston Villa), Osman (Everton), Senda (Southampton) [Mike (Manchester City) 47], Cole (West Ham United), Webber (Manchester United), Armstrong (Liverpool) [Lyons (Derby County) 74], Etherington (Peterborough United).

5 Mar 1998#

England 1 *(Canoville)*   **Croatia 1**

England: Rachubka (Manchester United); Canoville (Millwall), Hanson (Middlesbrough), Hall D (Coventry City), Barry (Aston Villa), Osman (Everton), Webber (Manchester United), Blois (Norwich City), Armstrong (Liverpool) [Senda (Southampton) 68], Cole (West Ham United), Etherington (Peterborough United) [Mike (Manchester City) 64].

7 Mar 1998#

Slovakia 0   England 0

England: Rachubka (Manchester United); Canoville (Millwall), Hanson (Middlesbrough), Stanton (Scunthorpe United), Barry (Aston Villa), Osman (Everton), Mike (Manchester City), Lyons (Derby County), Armstrong (Liverpool), Cole (West Ham United), Etherington (Peterborough United).

6 Apr 1998+

England 2 *(Lyons, Coppinger)*   **Norway 1**

England: Kirkland (Coventry City); Stanton (Scunthorpe United), Hanson (Middlesbrough), Hall D (Coventry City), Barry (Aston Villa), Lyons (Derby County), Turner (Nottingham Forest), Standing (Aston Villa), Reid (Millwall), Coppinger (Newcastle United), Warnock (Liverpool).

23 June 1998~

USA 4   England 1 *(Cole 85)*

England: Hodgson (Manchester City) [Evans (Chelsea) 40]; Wright R (Preston North End), McCready (Crewe Alexandra) [Pead (Coventry City) 40], Parnaby (Middlesbrough), Taylor (Middlesbrough), Clarke (Everton), Webber (Manchester United) [Pilkington (Everton) 40], Cole (West Ham United), Mike (Manchester City), Armstrong (Liverpool), Torpey (Liverpool) [Walker (Manchester United) 40].

26 June 1998~

USA 2   England 3 *(Cole 12, 43, 77)*

England: Evans (Chelsea) [Hodgson (Manchester City) 40]; Pead (Coventry City), McCready (Crewe Alexandra) [Wright R (Preston North End) 40], Taylor (Middlesbrough), Pilkington (Everton), Parnaby (Middlesbrough), Walker (Manchester United), Cole (West Ham United), Mike (Manchester City) [Torpey (Liverpool) 40], Armstrong (Liverpool) [Webber (Manchester United) 40], Clarke (Everton).

17 Nov 1998+

England 2 *(Nardiello, Knight)*   **Scotland 0**

England: Crookes (Liverpool); Parnaby (Middlesbrough), O'Brien (Liverpool), Clarke (Everton), Szmid (Manchester United), Britton (Arsenal), Rose (Manchester United), Keenan (Chelsea), Hamshaw (Sheffield Wednesday), Defoe (Charlton Athletic), Nardiello (Manchester United). *Subs all used:* Evans (Chelsea), McGhie (Sunderland), Knight (Chelsea), Jenkins (Wimbledon), McMaster (Leeds United), Richardson (Leeds United), Bothroyd (Arsenal), Davis (Manchester United).

12 Jan 1999+

Turkey 0   England 2 *(Fallon 55, 70)*

England: Evans (Chelsea) [Howarth (York City) 70]; Richardson (Leeds United) [Nardiello (Manchester United) 70], Jenkins (Wimbledon) [Keenan (Chelsea) 68], Davies (Southampton), Clarke (Everton), Parnaby (Middlesbrough), Szmid (Manchester United) [Bewers (Aston Villa) 70], Noble (Arsenal) [O'Brien (Liverpool) 40], Bothroyd (Arsenal) [Fallon (Barnsley) 40], Defoe (Charlton Athletic) [Knight (Chelsea) 40], Britton (Arsenal).

22 Feb 1999#

Armenia 1   England 2 *(Hamshaw 76, McMaster 79)*

England: Evans (Chelsea); Richardson (Leeds United), Jenkins (Wimbledon), Davies (Southampton) [Hamshaw (Sheffield Wednesday) 72], Clarke (Everton), Parnaby (Middlesbrough), O'Brien (Liverpool), McMaster (Leeds United), Fallon (Barnsley) [Bothroyd (Arsenal) 63], Knight (Chelsea), Rose (Manchester United) [Davis (Manchester United) 55].

26 Feb 1999#

England 2 *(Jenkins 3, Knight 50)*   **Cyprus 0**

England: Evans (Chelsea); Richardson (Leeds United), Jenkins (Wimbledon), Davies (Southampton), Clarke (Everton), Parnaby (Middlesbrough), O'Brien (Liverpool), McMaster (Leeds United) [Szmid (Manchester United) 76], Fallon (Barnsley) [Bothroyd (Arsenal) 72], Knight (Chelsea), Davis (Manchester United) [Defoe (Charlton Athletic) 80].

30 Mar 1999+

England 1 *(Parnaby 83)*   **Turkey 0**

England: Howarth (York City); Richardson (Leeds United), Jenkins (Wimbledon) [Davies (Southampton) 40], O'Brien (Liverpool) [Dunfield (Manchester City) 79], Clarke (Everton), Parnaby (Middlesbrough), Hylton (Aston Villa), McMaster (Leeds United) [Davis (Manchester United) 68], Szmid (Manchester United) [Defoe (Charlton Athletic) 45], Fallon (Barnsley) [Bewers (Aston Villa) 45], Farrell (Leeds United) [Knight (Chelsea) 68].

25 Apr 1999#

Hungary 1   England 1 *(Fallon 70)*

England: Evans (Chelsea); Richardson (Leeds United), Jenkins (Wimbledon) [Davis (Manchester United) 67], Davies (Southampton) [Hamshaw (Sheffield Wednesday) 67], Clarke (Everton), Parnaby (Middlesbrough), O'Brien (Liverpool), McMaster (Leeds United), Fallon (Barnsley) [Farrell (Leeds United) 78], Knight (Chelsea), Szmid (Manchester United).

27 Apr 1999#

Sweden 1   England 2 *(Fallon 50, 81)*

England: Evans (Chelsea); Richardson (Leeds United), Jenkins (Wimbledon), Bewers (Aston Villa), Parnaby (Middlesbrough), Szmid (Manchester United) [Davis (Manchester United) 65], O'Brien (Liverpool), McMaster (Leeds United), Fallon (Barnsley), Knight (Chelsea) [Bothroyd (Arsenal) 70], Hamshaw (Sheffield Wednesday).

29 Apr 1999#

Slovakia 1   England 3 *(Farrell 28, Bothroyd 42, Knight 79)*

England: Evans (Chelsea); Jenkins (Wimbledon), Clarke (Everton), Bewers (Aston Villa), Parnaby (Middlesbrough), O'Brien (Liverpool) [Britton (Arsenal) 86], McMaster (Leeds United), Davis (Manchester United), Hamshaw (Sheffield Wednesday), Farrell (Leeds United), Bothroyd (Arsenal) [Fallon (Barnsley) 79].

2 May 1999#

England 0   Czech Republic 1

England: Evans (Chelsea); Richardson (Leeds United), Jenkins (Wimbledon), Clarke (Everton), Parnaby (Middlesbrough) [Hamshaw (Sheffield Wednesday) 35], Bewers (Aston Villa), O'Brien (Liverpool), McMaster (Leeds United) [Davis (Manchester United) 85], Szmid (Manchester United) [Bothroyd (Arsenal) 60], Fallon (Barnsley), Knight (Chelsea).

* Under-18 Championship 1997-98; + Friendly; ** UEFA Under-18; # UEFA Under-16; ~ USA Tour; ##Adidas Victory Shield; = Montaigu Tournament.

WOMEN'S FOOTBALL 1998–99

Arsenal Ladies still remain the team to beat, having recorded another and coincidentally the same 'Double' last season as they achieved the season before, that of the AXA sponsored FA Women's Cup and the FA Women's Premier League Cup. They also finished as runners up to an excellent Croydon Ladies team who annexed the FA Women's Premier National League title. Briefly Croydon's Championship margin was three points with forty-six from their eighteen matches. Arsenal's Cup victories were respectively by 2-0 over Southampton Saints at Charlton Athletic's ground in front of 6450 spectators and by 3-1 at Everton.

The Champions of the FAWPL Northern Division were Aston Villa with forty-five points from eighteen games with Blyth Spartans Kestrels in second place eight points behind. In the Southern section were Reading Royals who had been newly promoted with forty-one points from eighteen games with the Whitehawk second two points adrift.

The number of teams entering all competitions has made the sport for women the fastest growing in the country and the FA have indicated that they propose 'to make women's football the top female sport in the next millennium'. To bolster this concept the FA launched its 'Talent Development Plan' aimed at identifying and developing young players from the age of ten through to the England Senior team, following the men's structure by establishing a network of Centres of Excellence. It is also intended to develop the Under 16 and Under 18 International Squads. In all the budget for 1999/2000 exceeds one million pounds.

The current structure of women's football consists of Mr Ray Kiddell, the Chairman of the FA Women's Football Committee; Kelly Simmons, the Women's Football Co-ordinator plus five Regional Directors. These are Julie Lewis (the North-East); Ros Potts (South-East); Lucy Wellings (South-West); Donna McIvor (East Midlands) and Rachel Pavlou (West Midlands and North-West), whilst Tessa Hayward is an administrator who makes up the team.

Hope Powell is and was the first full time National Coach and the Secretary of the FA Women's Premier League is Ms Sue Barwick. Although there is a Women's Football department at the FA's Headquarters at Lancaster Gate, most of the administrative functions are carried out from the FA's other address at 9 Wylotts Place, Potters Bar, Hertfordshire EN6 2JD – Phone Number 01707-671805. Fax 01707-644190.

KEN GOLDMAN

FA WOMEN'S PREMIER LEAGUE

RESULTS 1998–99 Season:

National Division

Champions: Croydon

	Arsenal	Bradford City	Croydon	Doncaster Belles	Everton	Ilkeston Town	Liverpool	Millwall Lionesses	Southampton Saints	Tranmere Rovers
Arsenal	—	6-0	3-3	2-2	4-1	6-0	2-0	1-0	2-1	3-1
Bradford City	0-3	—	2-6	1-5	2-3	3-2	1-3	1-1	1-0	0-0
Croydon	2-2	4-0	—	0-0	1-0	5-0	2-1	2-1	4-0	4-0
Doncaster Belles	1-3	3-0	0-1	—	1-2	1-0	1-0	2-1	2-2	3-0
Everton	2-2	5-0	0-0	1-2	—	2-1	1-0	2-0	0-1	0-4
Ilkeston Town	0-9	1-1	1-4	1-1	1-0	—	0-3	0-2	0-2	3-4
Liverpool	0-5	5-1	0-3	1-2	1-2	2-1	—	1-1	3-0	5-0
Millwall Lionesses	0-1	1-1	0-4	1-1	0-3	3-1	1-0	—	1-1	0-2
Southampton Saints	1-5	5-1	1-3	2-2	0-4	0-1	2-1	2-0	—	0-2
Tranmere Rovers	1-0	5-0	0-5	1-3	0-2	3-1	2-2	1-1	3-0	—

National Division	P	W	D	L	F	A	GD	Pts
Croydon	18	14	4	0	53	11	+42	46
Arsenal	18	13	4	1	59	15	+44	43
Doncaster Belles	18	9	6	3	32	19	+13	33
Everton	18	10	2	6	30	20	+10	32
Tranmere Rovers	18	8	3	7	29	32	−3	27
Liverpool	18	6	2	10	28	27	+1	20
Southampton Saints	18	5	3	10	20	35	−15	18
Millwall Lionesses	18	3	6	9	14	26	−12	15
Bradford City	18	2	4	12	15	68	−53	10
Ilkeston Town	18	2	2	14	14	51	−37	8

RESULTS 1998–99 Season:

Northern Division

Champions: Aston Villa

	Arnold Town	Aston Villa	Berkhamsted Town	Blyth Spartans K	Coventry City	Garswood Saints	Huddersfield Town	Leeds United	Sheffield Wednesday	Wolverhampton W
Arnold Town	—	0-3	0-3	0-1	2-0	1-3	1-1	0-2	1-4	2-5
Aston Villa	7-0	—	12-1	1-1	4-0	1-0	4-2	2-1	1-0	3-1
Berkhamsted Town	1-0	0-2	—	3-2	3-0	5-6	3-0	2-3	0-2	3-3
Blyth Spartans K	1-1	3-0	2-0	—	7-0	3-0	5-1	3-0	1-3	0-1
Coventry City	1-0	0-6	3-0	0-2	—	0-2	2-3	2-2	1-6	0-4
Garswood Saints	5-0	2-2	2-1	1-1	1-2	—	5-0	1-1	1-4	2-2
Huddersfield Town	2-2	1-4	1-4	2-4	3-2	1-4	—	1-7	1-5	1-1
Leeds United	10-0	1-1	10-1	2-3	11-0	4-1	3-1	—	5-5	1-1
Sheffield Wednesday	1-0	1-2	2-5	1-1	4-1	0-0	7-2	2-3	—	1-1
Wolverhampton W	3-0	0-2	4-0	1-4	3-0	1-3	4-1	3-1	2-1	—

Northern Division	P	W	D	L	F	A	GD	Pts
Aston Villa	18	14	3	1	57	14	+43	45
Blyth Spartans K	18	11	4	3	44	17	+27	37
Leeds United	19	9	5	4	67	29	+38	32
Wolverhampton W	18	9	5	4	40	25	+15	32
Sheffield Wednesday	18	9	4	5	49	28	+21	31
Garswood Saints	18	8	5	5	39	29	+10	29
Berkhamsted Town	18	7	1	10	35	54	−19	22
Coventry City	18	3	1	14	14	63	−49	10
Huddersfield Town	18	2	3	13	24	67	−43	9
Arnold Town	18	1	3	14	10	53	−43	6

RESULTS 1998–99 Season:

Southern Division

Champions: Reading

	Barnet	Barry Town	Brighton & Hove A	Ipswich Town	Langford	Leyton Orient	Reading Royals	Three Bridges	Whitehawk	Wimbledon
Barnet	—	3-3	0-3	2-3	3-2	2-0	2-3	2-2	1-1	0-4
Barry Town	2-1	—	1-1	3-0	1-0	1-0	1-3	0-2	0-2	1-2
Brighton & Hove A	3-2	1-1	—	3-2	1-1	4-2	1-1	4-0	1-4	3-0
Ipswich Town	1-3	1-2	1-3	—	1-4	3-2	0-6	1-2	1-4	0-3
Langford	6-0	0-1	0-0	3-1	—	5-2	0-4	0-1	0-1	4-0
Leyton Orient	3-2	0-0	0-2	3-2	1-5	—	1-7	1-1	1-5	4-8
Reading Royals	6-0	1-1	3-1	4-0	0-2	2-1	—	4-0	2-1	8-2
Three Bridges	3-1	2-3	1-0	5-3	1-0	1-2	4-1	—	2-3	3-1
Whitehawk	6-0	6-0	1-1	6-2	7-0	4-0	0-2	0-1	—	4-0
Wimbledon	1-4	2-0	1-3	4-0	3-2	4-1	4-3	1-4	1-1	—

Southern Division	P	W	D	L	F	A	GD	Pts
Reading Royals	18	13	2	3	60	21	+39	41
Whitehawk	18	12	3	3	56	15	+41	39
Three Bridges	18	11	2	5	35	27	+8	35
Brighton & Hove A	18	9	6	3	35	21	+14	33
Wimbledon	18	9	1	8	41	45	−4	28
Barry Town	18	7	5	6	21	27	−6	26
Langford	18	7	2	9	34	28	+6	23
Barnet	18	4	3	11	28	52	−24	15
Leyton Orient	18	3	2	13	24	58	−34	11
Ipswich Town	18	2	0	16	22	62	−40	6

AXA FA WOMEN'S CUP 1998–99

PRELIMINARY ROUND

Newton Aycliffe v Preston AFC	0-11
Brighouse v Thorpe United	2-1
Brazil Girls v Bolton Wanderers (Supp)	3-1
Worksop Town v Lincoln City	8-2
Lichfield Diamonds v Telford United	0-2
Kidderminster Harriers v Tamworth	2-0
UG Sports v Billericay Town	5-2
Witney Town v Watford	0-8
St Margaretsbury v HP Needham Market	0-3
QPRLSA v Newport Pagnell United	4-5
Woking v Tring Town	5-1
Corfe Hills United v Newport Strikers	1-5

Hemsworth withdrew v Ilkeston w.o.	
Leicester City v Kidderminster Harriers	3-3, 1-2
Highfield Rangers v Bloxwich Town	3-0
Worcester City v Mansfield Town	0-3
Shrewsbury Town v Worksop Town	2-1
Chesterfield v Melton Mowbray	9-0
Rea Valley Rovers v Atherstone United	4-2
Loughborough Students v Kettering Amazons	9-1
Birmingham City v Belper Town	5-0
Newcastle Town v Derby County	4-3
Steel City Wanderers v Nettleham	0-3
Chelmsford w.o. v Redhill withdrew	
Chesham United v Woking	3-1
Redbridge Wanderers v Chelsea	0-2
Newport Pagnell United v Gillingham Girls	3-4
Barking v West Ham United	3-3, 3-3
West Ham United won 5-3 on penalties	
Basingstoke Town v London Womens	2-1
Hassocks v Hastings Town	6-0
Bishop's Stortford v Canary Racers	0-15
UG Sports v Clapton	4-4, 0-2
Charlton v Hendon	11-0
Fulham v Wembley Mill Hill	2-3
HP Needham Market v Welwyn Garden City	7-2
Bedford Bells v Kings Lynn	7-0
Abbey Rangers v Hampton	3-5
Walkern v Slough Town	2-3
Camberley Town v Maidstone United	6-0
Luton v Risborough Rangers	2-4
Cambridge United v Surbiton	3-1
Enfield v Queens Park Rangers	3-1
Teynham Gunners v Newham	4-3
Malling v Hackney	3-2
Tottenham Hotspur v Northampton Town & County	6-1
Watford v Dulwich Hamlet	5-0
Stanway v Denham United	0-9

FIRST ROUND

Rochdale v Leeds City Vixens	1-7
Norton v Stockport County	0-6
Darlington v Stockport	2-10
Doncaster Rovers v Kirklees	7-0
Mond Rangers v Bangor City	0-7
Warrington Grange v Stockport Celtic	0-3
Manchester United v Chorley	5-1
Blackburn Rangers v Blackburn Rovers	1-10
Scunthorpe United v Blackpool (Wren) Rovers	2-2, 1-2
Newsham PH v Carlisle Wanderers	3-1
Bury v Deans	6-2
Liverpool Hope Feds v Hull City	3-1
Preston North End v Middlesbrough	3-5
Manchester City v Brazil Girls	6-2
Trafford v Brighouse	3-1
Leeds Athletics v Preston AFC	0-5
Selby Town v Barnsley	0-1
Newcastle v Oldham Athletic	0-5
Wigan v Sheffield Hallam United	4-2
Telford United v Stafford Rangers	9-1

London Ladies v Haverhill Rovers	0-6
Cam Bulldog v North Moulton	10-3
Keynsham Town v Okeford United	1-6
Oxford United v Barnstaple Town	5-0
Newton Abbot withdrew v Cardiff County w.o.	
Truro City v Saltash Pilgrims	1-8
Swindon Town v Newport Strikers	2-1
Elmore Eagles v Clevedon	4-0
Swindon Spitfires v Bath City	1-4
Portsmouth v City of Gloucester	19-0
Bristol Rovers v Bristol City	2-0
South Coast Rangers v Exeter Rangers	4-1
Plymouth Activate withdrew v Sherborne w.o.	

SECOND ROUND

Stockport Celtic v Manchester City	2-6
Liverpool Hope Feds v Garswood Saints	1-4
Barnsley v Wigan	2-3
Huddersfield Town v Preston AFC	6-0
Stockport County v Bangor City	1-4
Stockport v Oldham Athletic	3-3, 3-4
Blyth Spartans Kestrels v Manchester United	9-1
Newsham PH v Leeds City Vixens	0-7
Leeds United v Sheffield Wednesday	2-3
Trafford v Bury	6-2
Blackburn Rovers v Middlesbrough	5-4
Doncaster Rovers v Blackpool (Wren) Rovers	5-1
Mansfield Town v Shrewsbury Town	1-1, 2-1
Rea Valley Rovers v Aston Villa	1-6
Nettleham v Highfield Rangers	0-3
Coventry City v Chesterfield	2-1
Birmingham City v Wolverhampton Wanderers	2-3
Arnold Town v Loughborough Students	2-0
Telford United v Newcastle Town	0-2
Ilkeston v Kidderminster Harriers	6-3
Risborough Rangers v Whitehawk	0-4
Teynham Gunners v Charlton	0-13
Hampton v Chelsea	2-5
Slough Town v Chesham United	3-4
Chelmsford v Watford	1-1, 1-5
Denham United v Basingstoke Town	6-0
Enfield v Langford	0-5
Camberley Town v Gillingham Girls	2-0
West Ham United v HP Needham Market	3-1
Wimbledon v Berkhamsted Town	0-1
Leyton Orient w.o. v Malling unable to field a team	
Three Bridges v Ipswich Town	4-1
Wembley Mill Hill v Barnet	4-3
Tottenham Hotspur v Cambridge United	7-0
Clapton withdrew v Brighton & Hove Albion w.o.	
Canary Racers v Haverhill Rovers	10-1
Bedford Bells v Hassocks	3-0
Bath City v Barry Town	0-5
Saltash Pilgrims v Portsmouth	6-2
Sherborne v Oxford United	1-4
Cardiff County w.o. v Cam Bulldog	withdrew
Swindon Town v South Coast Rangers	4-1
Bristol Rovers v Okeford United	6-0
Reading Royals v Elmore Eagles	7-1

THIRD ROUND

Huddersfield Town v Wolverhampton Wanderers	1-2
Blackburn Rovers v Wigan	4-2
Leeds City Vixens v Trafford	3-0
Bangor City v Garswood Saints	2-0
Sheffield Wednesday v Doncaster Rovers	8-1
Highfield Rangers v Coventry City	1-3
Ilkeston v Manchester City	2-1
Oldham Athletic v Aston Villa	2-5
Blyth Spartans Kestrels w.o. v Newcastle Town withdrew	

Arnold Town v Mansfield Town	2-0
Langford v Charlton	4-1
Watford v Chesham United	9-0
Cardiff County v Wembley Mill Hill	0-2
Camberley Town v Canary Racers	0-3
Reading Royals v Saltash Pilgrims	9-2
Chelsea v Denham United	1-0
Brighton & Hove Albion v Barry Town	4-2
Tottenham Hotspur v Oxford United	2-0
West Ham United v Bedford Bells	1-1, 0-2
Berkhamsted Town v Whitehawk	3-1
Bristol Rovers v Swindon Town	4-2
Three Bridges v Leyton Orient	5-2

FOURTH ROUND

Aston Villa v Millwall Lionesses	0-1
Everton v Wembley Mill Hill	4-2
Wolverhampton Wanderers v Bradford City	1-0
Leeds City Vixens v Southampton Saints	1-2
Tottenham Hotspur v Three Bridges	0-1
Canary Racers v Doncaster Belles	0-6
Langford v Arnold Town	5-0
Bristol Rovers v Berkhamsted Town	2-5
Reading Royals v Blackburn Rovers	7-2
Chelsea v Arsenal	0-11
Tranmere Rovers v Liverpool	2-1
Blyth Spartans Kestrels v Croydon	1-3
Ilkeston v Sheffield Wednesday	0-4
Bangor City v Bedford Bells	2-2, 1-2
Watford v Ilkeston Town	3-1
Brighton & Hove Albion v Coventry City	2-1

FIFTH ROUND

Three Bridges v Tranmere Rovers	0-1
Reading Royals v Brighton & Hove Albion	1-0
Langford v Sheffield Wednesday	0-1
Watford v Bedford Bells	1-0
Wolverhampton Wanderers v Doncaster Belles	0-2
Berkhamsted Town v Southampton Saints	1-5
Arsenal v Everton	1-0
Croydon v Millwall Lionesses	1-0

SIXTH ROUND

Doncaster Belles v Croydon	2-0
Watford v Arsenal	1-5
Sheffield Wednesday v Southampton Saints	0-5
Reading Royals v Tranmere Rovers	3-5

SEMI-FINALS

Arsenal v Doncaster Belles	2-0
Southampton Saints v Tranmere Rovers	2-1

FINAL (at The Valley)

3 MAY

Arsenal (2) 2 *(Hayes 12 (og), Wheatley 40)*

Southampton Saints (0) 0   6450

Arsenal: Reed; White, Slee, Harwood (Mapes), Pealling, Williams, Grant, Lorton (Rockall), Wheatley, Spacey, Yankey (Downham).

Southampton Saints: Beer; Short, Hayes, Armstrong, Beesley (O'Brien); McArthur, Fisher, Gould (Langrish), Ritchie, Stainer (Poore), Dimsdale.

Referee: Mrs. W. Toms (Poole).

AXA FA WOMEN'S PREMIER LEAGUE CUP 1998–99

FIRST ROUND
Liverpool v Ipswich Town	5-1
Langford v Bradford City	2-1
Wolverhampton Wanderers v Reading Royals	3-2
Leeds United v Ilkeston Town	3-0
Everton v Millwall Lionesses	0-0
Everton won 3-0 on penalties	
Wimbledon v Sheffield Wednesday	5-3
Leyton Orient v Barry Town	2-4
Huddersfield Town v Garswood Saints	1-2
Three Bridges v Doncaster Belles	0-6
Aston Villa v Tranmere Rovers	1-5
Whitehawk v Arnold Town	3-2
Southampton Saints v Blyth Spartans Kestrels	3-3
Blyth Spartans Kestrels won 4-3 on penalties	
Barnet v Brighton & Hove Albion	0-2
Coventry City v Berkhamsted Town	0-1

SECOND ROUND
Doncaster Belles v Croydon	1-1, 1-3
Arsenal v Wolverhampton Wanderers	9-0

Everton v Wimbledon	4-0
Tranmere Rovers v Berkhamsted Town	9-1
Blyth Spartans Kestrels v Brighton & Hove Albion	4-3
Liverpool v Whitehawk	3-4
Langford v Barry Town	5-0
Leeds United v Garswood Saints	2-3

THIRD ROUND
Whitehawk v Langford	2-0
Tranmere Rovers w.o. v Garswood Saints excluded	
Arsenal v Croydon	1-0
Everton v Blyth Spartans Kestrels	5-0

SEMI-FINALS
Everton v Tranmere Rovers	2-1
Arsenal v Whitehawk	4-1

FINAL
Arsenal v Everton	3-1

ENGLAND INTERNATIONALS

WORLD CUP

QUALIFYING GROUP 3
	P	W	D	L	F	A	Pts
Norway	6	4	1	1	13	5	13
Germany	6	4	0	2	9	5	12
Holland	6	2	1	3	5	10	7
England	6	1	0	5	3	10	3

Play-off: Romania 1, England 4; England 2, Romania 1.

UEFA UNDER-18

England 1, Holland 1
Faroes 0, Republic of Ireland 2
Holland 2, Faroes 0
England 5, Republic of Ireland 0
Republic of Ireland 1, Holland 3
England 7, Faroes 0

	P	W	D	L	F	A	Pts
England	3	2	1	0	13	1	7
Holland	3	2	1	0	5	2	7
Republic of Ireland	3	1	0	2	3	8	3
Faroes	3	0	0	3	0	11	0

QUARTER-FINALS
England 1, Norway 3
Norway 1, England 0
Friendly: England 3, Finland 0

UNDER-16

England 2, Scotland 0
England 1, USA 5
England 2, Republic of Ireland 1
England 2, Wales 0

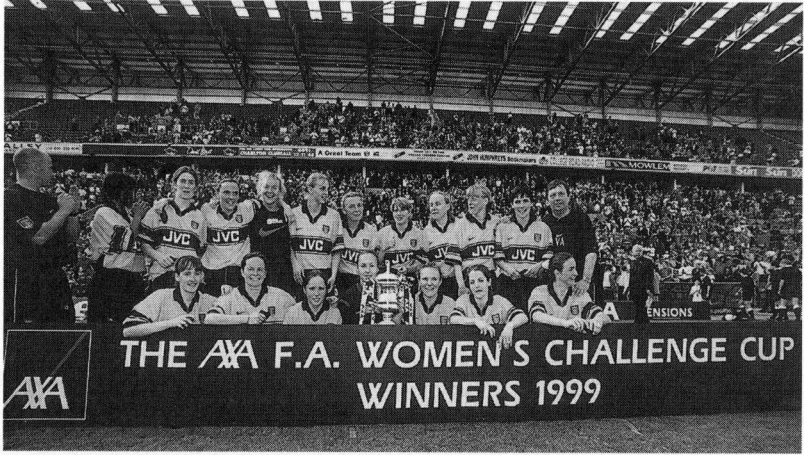

Arsenal ladies team celebrate victory in the AXA FA Women's Challenge Cup Final. They beat Southampton Saints 2-0 at Charlton. (Actionimages)

NATIONWIDE CONFERENCE 1998–99

NATIONWIDE CONFERENCE TABLE 1998–99

		Home			Goals		Away			Goals		
	P	W	D	L	F	A	W	D	L	F	A	Pts
Cheltenham Town	42	11	9	1	35	14	11	5	5	36	22	80
Kettering Town	42	11	5	5	31	16	11	5	5	27	21	76
Hayes	42	12	3	6	34	25	10	5	6	29	25	74
Rushden & Diamonds	42	11	4	6	41	22	9	8	4	30	20	72
Yeovil Town	42	8	4	9	35	32	12	7	2	33	22	71
Stevenage Borough	42	9	9	3	37	23	8	8	5	25	22	68
Northwich Victoria	42	11	3	7	29	21	8	6	7	31	30	66
Kingstonian	42	9	7	5	25	19	8	6	7	25	30	64
Woking	42	9	5	7	27	20	9	4	8	24	25	63
Hednesford Town	42	9	8	4	30	24	6	8	7	19	20	61
Dover Athletic	42	7	9	5	27	21	8	4	9	27	27	58
Forest Green Rovers	42	9	5	7	28	22	6	8	7	27	28	58
Hereford United	42	9	5	7	25	17	6	5	10	24	29	55
Morecambe	42	9	5	7	31	29	6	3	12	29	47	53
Kidderminster Harriers	42	9	4	8	32	22	5	5	11	24	30	51
Doncaster Rovers	42	7	5	9	26	26	5	7	9	25	29	48
Telford United	42	7	8	6	24	24	3	8	10	20	36	46
Southport	42	6	9	6	29	28	4	6	11	18	31	45
Barrow	42	7	5	9	17	23	4	5	12	23	40	43
Welling United	42	4	7	10	18	30	5	7	9	26	35	41
Leek Town	42	5	5	11	34	42	3	3	15	14	34	32
Farnborough Town	42	6	5	10	29	48	1	6	14	12	41	32

ATTENDANCES BY CLUB 1998–99

	Aggregate 1998–99	Average 1998–99	Average 1997–98	% Change
Barrow	34,108	1,624	1,325	+22.6
Cheltenham Town	65,354	3,112	1,837	+69.4
Doncaster Rovers	70,979	3,380	1,715	+97.1
Dover Athletic	22,750	1,083	1,069	+1.3
Farnborough Town	16,513	786	816	–3.7
Forest Green Rovers	17,925	854	697	+22.5
Hayes	15,967	760	661	+15.0
Hednesford Town	22,852	1,088	1,418	–23.3
Hereford United	41,494	1,976	2,477	–20.2
Kettering Town	42,700	2,033	1,491	+36.4
Kidderminster Harriers	40,823	1,944	2,023	–3.9
Kingstonian	27,307	1,300	700	+85.7
Leek Town	12,747	607	782	–22.4
Morecambe	24,425	1,163	1,532	–24.1
Northwich Victoria	23,949	1,140	1,101	+3.5
Rushden & Diamonds	63,924	3,044	2,552	+19.3
Southport	24,320	1,158	1,055	+9.8
Stevenage Borough	53,581	2,551	2,252	+13.3
Telford United	18,023	858	799	+7.4
Welling United	14,316	682	709	–3.8
Woking	46,942	2,235	2,801	–20.2
Yeovil Town	50,519	2,406	2,457	–2.0
Conference Total:	751,518	1,627	1,476	+ 10.23

HIGHEST ATTENDANCES 1998–99

6,312	Rushden & Diamonds	1-2	Cheltenham Town	3.4.99
6,150	Cheltenham Town	3-2	Yeovil Town	22.4.99
5,400	Cheltenham Town	0-0	Welling United	1.5.99
5,202	Cheltenham Town	3-0	Kettering Town	20.3.99
5,039	Kettering Town	0-0	Rushden & Diamonds	27.3.99
4,700	Rushden & Diamonds	1-2	Kettering Town	1.5.99
4,629	Doncaster Rovers	0-0	Stevenage Borough	26.3.99
4,577	Rushden & Diamonds	1-3	Doncaster Rovers	23.1.99
4,569	Doncaster Rovers	1-1	Kettering Town	31.8.98
4,518	Cheltenham Town	1-0	Kidderminster Harriers	5.4.99
4,413	Doncaster Rovers	0-2	Yeovil Town	13.2.99
4,319	Stevenage Borough	0-0	Rushden & Diamonds	26.12.98
4,307	Rushden & Diamonds	2-0	Woking	28.12.98
4,253	Doncaster Rovers	2-1	Morecambe	16.1.99
4,051	Cheltenham Town	1-0	Rushden & Diamonds	28.11.98
3,937	Stevenage Borough	2-2	Kettering Town	28.12.98
3,772	Woking	0-1	Kingstonian	1.1.99

NATIONWIDE CONFERENCE LEADING GOALSCORERS 1998–99

Conf.		FAC	ECT	UT
26	Carl Alford (Stevenage Borough)	+	4	—	3
20	Warren Patmore (Yeovil Town)	+	4	—	2
19	John Norman (Morecambe)	+	2	2	—
18	Lee Charles (Hayes)	+	—	1	2
	Neil Grayson (Cheltenham Town)	+	—	—	5
	Hugh McAuley (Leek Town)	+	—	1	—
17	Darren Collins (Rushden & Diamonds)	+	2	—	—
15	Dennis Bailey (Cheltenham Town)	+	1	6	1
	Adrian Foster (Rushden & Diamonds)	+	—	1	—
	Paul Tait (Northwich Victoria)	+	—	1	—
13	Darran Hay (Woking)	+	5	—	5
	Mark Hynes (Dover Athletic)	+	4	—	1
	Adie Mike (Hednesford Town)	+	3	—	—
12	Ian Duerden (Doncaster Rovers)	+	2	4	—
	Marc McGregor (Forest Green Rovers)	+	—	—	3
	Brett McNamara (Kettering Town)	+	—	—	2
	Steve West (Woking)	+	—	—	1
11	Scott Huckerby (Telford United)	+	3	—	2
	Leroy May (Kidderminster Harriers)	+	—	1	—
10	Lee Hudson (Kettering Town)	+	—	—	1
	Neil Illman (Northwich Victoria)	+	—	1	1
	Richard Leadbeater (Stevenage Borough)	+	—	—	—
	David Leworthy (Kingstonian)	+	2	—	5
	Owen Pickard (Yeovil Town)	+	—	—	2
	Martin Randall (Hayes)	+	2	—	—

FAC: FA Cup; ECT: Endsleigh Challenge Trophy; UT Umbro Trophy.

CLUB REVIEW

	FC	FAT	SCC	FAC
Barrow	19	2	1	3q
1997-98	1UL	4	-	1q
Cheltenham Town	1	SF	SF	1
	2	F	1	3
Doncaster Rovers	16	2	W	2
	24D3	–	–	1
Dover Athletic	11	3	1	4q
	13	SF	1	2q
Farnborough Town	22	3	F	4q
	18	1	3	1
Forest Green Rovers	12	F	1	3q
	1DM	2q	–	2q
Hayes	3	2	QF	1
	12	QF	SF	1
Hednesford Town	10	3	2	2
	7	3	QF	2
Hereford United	13	2	QF	3q
	6	2	2	3
Kettering Town	2	3	1	3q
	14	2	2	3q
Kidderminster H.	15	2	2	1
	17	2	2	4q
Kingstonian	8	F	1	2
	1RL	1q	–	4q
Leek Town	21	2	1	4q
	19	2	2	1q
Morecambe	14	2	SF	4q
	5	2	W	1
Northwich Victoria	7	QF	QF	3q
	9	3	SF	1
Rushden & D'mnds	4	4	2	3
	4	2	1	4q
Southport	18	QF	2	3
	16	F	1	1
Stevenage Borough	6	4	2	2
	15	QF	2	4
Telford United	17	4	1	1
	20	2	2	1q
Welling United	20	2	1	1
	10	1	1	2q
Woking	9	5	QF	1
	3	1	F	1
Yeovil Town	5	5	2	3
	11	1	3	4q

HIGHEST AGGREGATE SCORE

5-4 Doncaster Rovers v Dover Athletic 19.12.98
6-3 Yeovil Town v Farnborough Town 28.12.98

LARGEST HOME MARGIN

7-0 Leek Town v Morecambe 25.8.98
6-0 Kettering Town v Morecambe 9.1.99
5-0 Rushden & Diamonds v Hayes 31.8.98
5-0 Forest Green Rovers v Kidderminster 13.3.99 Harriers
5-0 Stevenage Borough v Woking 12.4.99

LARGEST AWAY MARGIN

1-6 Farnborough Town v Morecambe 12.12.98
1-6 Farnborough Town v Northwich Victoria 20.3.98
1-5 Farnborough Town v Hayes 6.2.99
1-5 Kingstonian v Rushden & Diamonds 25.8.98

CONSECUTIVE VICTORIES

7 Cheltenham Town, Rushden & Diamonds
6 Hayes, Woking

CONSECUTIVE DEFEATS

10 Leek Town
5 Woking

MATCHES WITHOUT DEFEAT

17 Cheltenham Town
13 Hereford United
12 Halifax Town
14 Cheltenham Town, Yeovil Town
9 Dover Athletic, Hednesford Town, Kingstonian
8 Forest Green Rovers, Kettering Town, Rushden & Diamonds

MATCHES WITHOUT SUCCESS

18 Leek Town
15 Southport
14 Farnborough Town

NATIONWIDE CONFERENCE 1998–99

APPEARANCES AND GOALSCORERS

Barrow
Appearances: Bauress, G. 25; Challender, G. 12; Coates, M. 15(6); Coathup, L. 4(2); Davis, C. 12; Dawson, B. 12(2); Dobie, M. 5; Doherty, N. 3(2); Fensome, A. 26(2); Foster, I. 14(14); Haddon, P. 10(3); Heyward, A. 13(1); Higgins, D. 36(1); Hill, A. 8(2); Johnston, E. 30(2); Jones, P. 30; Keilty, G. 8(8); Kennedy, E. 13(2); Lewis, G. 4(2); Macauley, C. 23; Maddox, M. 3(1); Marginson, K. 2(11); Marsh, M. 16(1); McAlinden, N. 0; McDonald, R. 1; McIntyre, K. 5; Morton, N. 17(2); Mutch, A. 19(3); Naylor, R. 4; O'Keefe, L. 20(3); O'Toole, J. 5; Orr, C. 0; Parks, T. 18; Robertson, P. 5; Sandwith, K. 10(2); Seagraves, M. 13; Smith, M. 4(1); Southworth, B. 1; Woods, A. 1; Wright, A. 0(3).
Goals (40): Coates, M. 5, Dawson, B. 3, Foster, I. 7, Heyward, A. 3, Johnston, E. 2, Jones, P. 1, Macauley, C. 1, Marginson, K. 2, Morton, N. 4, Mutch, A. 8, O'Keefe, L. 1, Seagraves, M. 1, OG, 2.

Cheltenham Town
Appearances: Bailey, D. 7(1); Banks, C. 34(1); Bloomer, R. 15(14); Book, S. 42; Bragg, D. 0; Brough, J. 36(4); Casey, R. 0; Duff, M. 41; Eaton, J. 28(7); Freeman, M. 36(1); Gannaway, R. 0; Grayson, N. 38(2); Hopkins, G. 0; Howarth, N. 4(4); Howells, L. 37(1); Jackson, M. (1); Knight, K. 9(13); Milton, R. 6(11); Murphy, S. 0; Norton, D. 35(1); Smith, J. 3(5); Victory, J. 42; Walker, C. 16(7); Walker, R. 14(2); Watkins, D. 9(10); Yates, M. 12.
Goals (71): Bailey, D. 2, Banks, C. 1, Brough, J. 4, Duff, M. 2, Eaton, J. 9, Freeman, M. 5, Grayson, N. 18, Howells, L. 6, Knight, K. 3, Norton, D. 3, Smith, J. 1, Victory, J. 5, Walker, C. 4, Watkins, D. 6, OG, 2.

Doncaster Rovers
Appearances: Barnwell-Edinboro, J. 6(4); Beckett, D. 3(7); Bradley, M. 1; Brookes, D. 0(3); Calidwell, M. 6(6); Cunningham, H. 0(1); Duerdon, I. 24(2); Esdaille, D. 0; Foster, M. 4(1); George, D. 2(10); Goodwin, S. 21(4); Haywood, A. 2; Hume, M. 15(9); Jones, D. 0(1); Kirkwood, G. 23(10); Linares-Ybarra, I. 4(2); Maamria, N. 18(9); Maxfield, S. 27(6); McIntryre, K. 29; Minett, J. 20(5); Nichol, S. 25; Penney, D. 30(1); Powell, R. 0; Ridley, M. 0; Rimmer, S. 2; Shaw, S. 35; Sheridan, J. 7; Snodin, G. 1(1); Snodin, I. 10(1); Southall, N. 9; Sutherland, C. 34; Warren, L. 38(2); Watson, A. 3(1); Wild, R. 0; Woods, A. 33; Wright, T. 24.
Goals (51): Barnwell-Edinboro, J. 1, Beckett, D. 1, Duerdon, I. 12, Goodwin, S. 5, Hume, M. 7, Kirkwood, G. 8, Maamria, N. 3, Maxfield, S. 1, Minett, J. 1, Penney, D. 6, Sutherland, C. 2, Watson, A. 1, Wright, T. 1, OG, 2.

Dover Athletic
Appearances: Adams, D. 9(2); Adams, K. 9(2); Beard, S. 10(1); Brady, M. 4(1); Brown, S. 7; Budden, J. 36(1); Carruthers, M. 10(2); Clarke, D. 32(1); Daniels, S. 4; Elliott, S. 1(2); Gooden, R. 2(9); Harrison, A. 1(1); Henry, L. 7(3); Hogg, A. 0; Hynes, M. 16(8); Iorfa, D. 1(2); Le Bihan, N. 34; Leberl, J. 30; Mitten, C. 41; Moore, A. 9(7); Munday, S. 20; Norman, S. 1(5); Palmer, L. 33(4); Reina, R. 23(3); Shearer, L. 26; Strouts, J. 17(1); Vasittart, J. 18(6); Virgo, J. 32(4); Wormull, S. 29(1).
Goals (54): Adams, K. 1, Adams, D. 2, Brady, M. 1, Brown, S. 1, Budden, J. 4, Carruthers, M. 7, Clarke, D. 1, Daniels, S. 1, Henry, L. 2, Hynes, M. 10, Iorfa, D. 1, Le Bihan, N. 3, Leberl, J. 1, Reina, R. 4, Shearer, L. 2, Vasittart, J. 5, Virgo, J. 4, Wormull, S. 2.

Farnborough Town
Appearances: Bailey, D. 30; Baker, N. 23(9); Baker, S. 23(3); Bass, D. 2; Bennetts, N. 0(3); Boothe, C. 9(1); Cheeseman, K. 0(1); Coles, D. 1; Davis, N. 4(1); Day, J. 1(5); Harding, D. 0; Harford, P. 8; Harlow, D. 4(1); Harte, S. 25(1); Hayward, D. 5(4); Henrikson, T. 3; Hooper, N. 9(5); Horner, R. 10(1); Hutt, M. 1; Jansen, N. 1; Kemp, S. 0; Lake, S. 2(2); Low, J. 3(1); Mackenzie, S. 36; McKimm, S. 15; Miller, B. 27(5); Radford, J. 1; Robson, D. 37(2); Rowlands, K. 14(9); Rust, N. 0; Simpson, C. 1(4); Simpson, P. 3; Stemp, W. 26(1); Taylor, A. 17(6); Underwood, J. 22(5); West, M. 33(7); White, C. 13(1); Wingfield, P. 28(1); Wye, L. 23(1).
Goals (41): Bailey, D. 13, Baker, N. 2, Boothe, C. 1, Harford, P. 1, Harte, S. 1, Horner, R. 1, Low, J. 2, Miller, B. 2, Robson, D. 2, Rowlands, K. 2, Simpson, C. 1, Underwood, J. 1, West, M. 8, Wingfield, P. 2, Wye, L. 1, OG, 1.

Forest Green Rovers
Appearances: Bailey, D. 25(2); Birkby, D. 8(4); Callinan, T. 1; Catley, A. 1(1); Catley, A. 1(1); Chapple, S. 5(7); Cook, R. 28(9); Coupe, M. 17(8); Drysdale, J. 26(1); Evans, R. 0(1); Forbes, D. 39; Hallam, M. 13(3); Hedges, I. 32(1); Hodson, B. 3(1); Honor, C. 30; Hunt, P. 22; Jackson, T. 0(3); Kilgour, M. 25(2); McGregor, M. 19(9); Mehew, D. 13(1); Mogg, D. 0; Perrin, S. 8; Rollo, J. 7(9); Shuttlewood, J. 34; Smart, G. 16(13); Smith, C. 2(7); Sykes, A. 35(3); Westlake, T. 1; Wigg, N. 25(5); Winter, S. 9(1); Winter, A. 35(3).
Goals (55): Cook, R. 5, Coupe, M. 2, Drysdale, J. 3, Hallam, M. 3, Hedges, I. 3, Hunt, P. 8, Kilgour, M. 1, McGregor, M. 12, Mehew, D. 5, Smart, G. 1, Sykes, A. 8, Winter, S. 2, Winter, S. 1, OG, 1.

Hayes
Appearances: Asselman, E. 5(1); Ballarp, K. 0; Boothe, C. 4(6); Buglione, M. 5(8); Bunce, N. 31(1); Catlin, N. 5(4); Charles, L. 38(3); Coates, M. 1(1); Coppard, D. 0; Davies, K. 0; Delisser, A. 9(7); Domingos, A. 1(5); Flynn, L. 42; Goodliff, J. 34(1); Hall, M. 16(6); Hodson, B. 20(7); Hodson, M. 6; Lyons, J. 0; Meara, R. 36; Metcalfe, C. 15(6); Moore, B. 17(8); Norman, P. 7(5); Paul, K. 0(1); Randall, M. 33(6); Roddis, N. 20(6); Sparks, C. 35; Spencer, R. 6(2); Taylor, L. 2(2); Townsend, R. 0; Watts, A. 38(5); Wilkinson, D. 39.
Goals (63): Buglione, M. 1, Bunce, N. 3, Catlin, N. 1, Charles, L. 18, Domingos, A. 1, Flynn, L. 4, Hall, M. 3, Hodson, B. 7, Metcalfe, C. 1, Moore, B. 3, Norman, P. 1, Randall, M. 10, Sparks, C. 3, Watts, A. 3, Wilkinson, D. 2, OG, 2.

Hednesford Town
Appearances: Amos, N. 2(5); Anderson, D. 0; Beeston, C. 21; Bignall, M. 1(2); Blades, P. 11; Bradley, R. 30; Brindley, C. 39; Broadhurst, N. 0(1); Carty, P. 20(3); Colkin, L. 31; Comyn, A. 31; Cooksley, S. 13; Davis, N. 21(1); Davis, P. 1; Dennison, R. 3(2); Devine, S. 1(1); Fitzpatrick, G. 17(3); Francis, D. 0(4); Griffiths, T. 0; Hall, M. 0; Hayward, A. 15(2); Jackson, L. 1(2); Kelly, J. 11(6); Kimming, G. 27(3); King, S. 0; Lake, S. 18(3); Mike, A. 13; Morgan, P. 29; O'Connor, S. 5(5); O'Connor, J. 3(2); Preece, D. 11(1); Sedgemore, J. 24(2); Stanbrook, C. 0; Szewczyk, P. 4(5); Twynham, G. 4(1); Ware, P. 36(5).
Goals (49): Beeston, C. 1, Bignall, M. 1, Bradley, R. 1, Brindley, C. 3, Carty, P. 1, Comyn, A. 2, Davis, N. 8, Fitzpatrick, G. 2, Hayward, A. 3, Kelly, J. 1, Kimming, G. 8, Lake, S. 2, Mike, A. 3, O'Connor, J. 2, O'Connor, S. 2, Sedgemore, J. 2, Szewczyk, P. 2, Ware, P. 5.

Hereford United
Appearances: Boden, C. 4; Clarke, M. 7; Collins, K. 6; Cook, G. 14(13); Cowe, S. 12(3); Cross, M. 3(5); Dennison, R. 17(2); Downing, K. 10(2); Duce, M. 13(5); Dyer, W. 2(4); Evans, S. 20; Fenings, P. 5(5); Hill, J. 0; James, A. 28; Jones, M. 4; Lane, C. 36; Leadbetter, A. 16; Mahon, G. 16; Martin, D. 1; Parry, P. 19(4); Quy, A. 38; Roberts, C. 7(2); Rogerson, I. 32(2); Shirley, J. 0(2); Snape, J. 22(1); Taylor, R. 40; Walker, R. 12; Williams, G. 31(7); Wright, I. 35.
Goals (49): Cook, G. 3, Cowe, S. 2, Dennison, R. 1, Downing, K. 2, Duce, M. 3, Dyer, W. 1, Evans, S. 1, Fenings, P. 2, James, A. 1, Leadbetter, R. 6, Mahon, G. 3, Parry, P. 3, Roberts, C. 2, Rogerson, I. 1, Snape, J. 1, Taylor, R. 1, Walker, R. 3, Williams, G. 6, Wright, I. 7.

Kettering
Appearances: Adams, C. 36(3); Barclay, D. 2; Brown, P. 37(1); Cox, P. 38(1); Eastwood, P. 2(1); Fisher, M. 34(1); Glynn, M. 1; Haydon, N. 7; Hayes, A. 5(5); Hone, M. 25(7); Hopkins, C. 0(2); Hudson, N. 24(10); Mason, A. 4(3); Matthews, M. 38(1); McNamara, B. 37(4); Mutchell, R. 3(1); Norman, C. 41; Raynor, P. 27; Ridgway, I. 0(6); Sollitt, A. 32; Thompson, P. 0(3); Tucker, M. 0; Vowden, C. 42; Warne, P. 3; Wilde, A. 2(3); Wilkes, T. 2(6); Williams, S. 8(4); Williamson, D. 0(3); Wilson, S. 10; Wright, B. 5(6).
Goals (58): Adams, C. 2, Brown, P. 8, Fisher, M. 2, Hudson, N. 10, Mason, A. 1, Matthews, M. 1, McNamara, B. 12, Norman, C. 9, Raynor, P. 2, Vowden, C. 4, Warne, P. 2, Wilkes, T. 1, Williams, S. 3, OG, 1.

Kidderminster Harriers
Appearances: Acton, D. 1; Arnold, I. 20(2); Beard, M. 0(2); Bennett, G. 0; Bignall, M. 5(3); Brock, S. 42; Cunnington, S. 24(3); Davies, P. 1; Deakin, J. 26(6); Druce, M. 15; Ford, J. 16; Glover, D. 17; Hadley, S. 20(3); Hines, L. 16(1); Hinton, C. 30(2);

May, L. 25(8); Payne, S. 12(3); Purdie, J. 4(2); Robinson, A. 2(3); Skelding, J. 9; Smith, A. 22(2); Taylor, S. 27(1); Thomas, C. 5(5); Webb, P. 31(3); Weir, M. 33; Willetts, K. 19(1); Wolsey, M. 8(11); Yates, M. 22.

Goals (56): Arnold, I. 5, Cunnington, S. 2, Deakin, J. 2, Druce, M. 1, Ford, J. 4, Hadley, S. 7, Hines, L. 1, May, L. 11, Payne, S. 4, Robinson, A. 1, Taylor, S. 4, Thomas, C. 2, Webb, P. 1, Weir, M. 1, Willetts, K. 7, Yates, M. 2, OG, 1.

Kingstonian

Appearances: Akuamoah, E. 29(4); Barrett, S. 6; Boylan, L. 5; Brown, W. 8(2); Brown, S. 3; Coates, M. 1; Corbett, S. 10(15); Crossely, M. 35; Culverhouse, I. 1; Dixon, F. 0(1); Drewitt, G. 0(2); Farrelly, S. 22; Francis, D. 7(9); Francis, J. 6(3); Harris, M. 40; Holligan, G. 5(12); John, J. 11; Langley, S. 2; Lester, M. 1(2); Leworthy, D. 33(1); Luckett, C. 41(1); Mustafa, T. 36; Nyamah, K. 4; Patterson, G. 35; Pitcher, G. 37; Rattray, K. 25(8); Smith, D. 8(1); Stewart, S. 35; Thomas, D. 1(1); Tranter, C. 3(5); Watkinson, R. 0(1); White, T. 4(1); Willgrass, A. 6(1).

Goals (50): Akuamoah, E. 7, Boylan, L. 1, Brown, W. 1, Corbett, S. 3, Crossely, M. 2, Francis, J. 1, Harris, M. 1, Holligan, G. 5, Leworthy, D. 10, Luckett, C. 5, Mustafa, T. 3, Patterson, G. 2, Pitcher, G. 5, Rattray, K. 2, Stewart, S. 1, Tranter, C. 1.

Leek Town

Appearances: Agana, T. 15(5); Baker, D. 0(1); Beeby, M. 30(1); Burnskill, I. 31(6); Callan, A. 13(5); Circuit, S. 31(1); Cunningham, D. 5(1); Diskin, J. 22(3); Ellis, N. 19(6); Hawtin, D. 17(4); Heverin, M. 0(4); Ingham, G. 42; James, C. 37; March, S. 22(3); McAuley, H. 33(1); McCord, B. 15(2); Mike, A. 25(1); Morgan, L. 3(1); Newland, R. 0; O'Toole, G. 14(2); Parker, J. 19(1); Pascoe, J. 29(3); Price, S. 11(3); Riley, K. 7(4); Tobin, S. 0(4); Trott, D. 3; Williams, S. 3(1).

Goals (48): Agana, T. 3, Beeby, M. 1, Callan, A. 1, Circuit, S. 1, Cunningham, D. 3, Ellis, N. 3, Hawtin, D. 4, Heverin, M. 1, McAuley, H. 18, Mike, A. 10, Morgan, L. 1, Parker, J. 1, OG, 1.

Morecambe

Appearances: Banks (C), A. 7(1); Banks, (M) A. 14; Brown, G. 6(1); Burns, P. 27(4); Ceroalo, M. 9(14); Curtis, W. 7(11); Drummond, S. 31(6); Fensome, A. 11; Gardner, D. 18(1); Haddow, P. 3(2); Hall, D. 24; Hardixer, J. 1; Heald, A. 2; Healy, B. 16; Hughes, A. 4; Jackson, J. 28(1); Keeling, B. 13(10); Kennedy, J. 20; Knowles, M. 7(1); Lyons, D. 19(12); Mayers, K. 26(4); McGuire, P. 0(1); McIlharghey, S. 24; McKearney, D. 32(2); Milner, A. 3; Morton, N. 4(2); Norman, J. 38(3); Rushton, P. 12(8); Shannick, D. 9(11); Shirley, M. 26(6); Waller, M. 8.

Goals (60): Banks (C), A. 1, Ceroalo, M. 5, Curtis, W. 3, Drummond, S. 5, Gardner, D. 2, Heald, A. 1, Healy, B. 2, Jackson, J. 6, Keeling, B. 1, Lyons, D. 6, Mayers, K. 2, McKearney, D. 1, Milner, A. 1, Norman, J. 19, Shirley, M. 2, Takano K. 2, OG, 1.

Northwich Victoria

Appearances: Bates, J. 26(3); Birch, M. 42; Cooke, I. 8(14); Crookes, D. 24(1); Devlin, M. 15(3); Duffy, C. 30(8); Filson, M. 3(1); Fletcher, G. 0; Gardiner, M. 0(2); Greygoose, D. 22; Illman, N. 25(9); Key, L. 18; Mayes, D. 0; O'Toole, J. 2; Owen, V. 23(1); Peel, N. 10(1); Robertson, J. 34(1); Simpson, W. 32(2); Tait, P. 35(5); Terry, S. 33(4); Vicary, D. 30(6); Walters, W. 30; Ward, D. 6(8); Webster, J. 4(5); Williams, C. 8(11).

Goals (60): Birch, M. 1, Cooke, I. 4, Crookes, D. 1, Devlin, M. 2, Filson, M. 1, Illman, N. 10, Owen, V. 3, Peel, N. 1, Simpson, W. 2, Tait, P. 15, Terry, S. 4, Vicary, D. 5, Walters, S. 9, Williams, C. 2.

Rushden & Diamonds

Appearances: Archer, L. 1(2); Berry, S. 1(1); Bradshaw, D. 34; Brady, J. 31(4); Branston, G. 9; Burgess, A. 0; Butterworth, G. 18(2); Challinor, J. 0; Collett, A. 4; Collins, D. 31; Cooper, M. 17(1); Corry, S. 1; Cramman, K. 2; De Souza, M. 19(5); Feuer, A. 3; Foster, A. 19(5); Gayle, M. 14; Hamsher, J. 11(4); Hanlon, R. 1(4); Heggs, C. 21(4); Kyriacou, P. 0; McElhatton, M. 30(3); Mehew, D. 1(1); Mills, G. 0; Milson, M. 12(2); Ndekwe, M. 0(2); Rawle, M. 0(1); Rodwell, J. 29; Smith, M. 20; Underwood, P. 39; Van Der Velden, C. 12; Warburton, R. 10; West, C. 12(2); Whyte, C. 17(2); Wilson, P. 14; Wooding, T. 25(5).

Goals (71): Brady, J. 2, Collins, D. 17, Cooper, M. 6. De Souza, M. 7, Foster, A. 15, Hamsher, J. 1, Hanlon, R. 1, Heggs, C. 4, McElhatton, M. 4, Milson, M. 1, Rodwell, J. 2, Underwood, P. 2, West, C. 3, Whyte, C. 1, Wooding, T. 4, OG, 1.

Southport

Appearances: Arnold, I. 5; Bagnall, J. 2; Bolland, P. 26(2); Butler, R. 22(2); Courtney, G. 0(1); Dobbin, J. 3; Elam, L. 26(1); Farley, A. 34(2); Farrell, M. 0; Formby, K. 20(9); Furlong, L. 17(5); Futcher, P. 12(2); Gamble, D. 31(2); Gouck, A. 34; Graves, S. 1(2); Guyett, S. 34; Horner, P. 28(3); Lalley, A. 0; Lowe, R. 0; Marsh, M. 1; Morgan, J. 1; Mutch, A. 0(1); Newman, J. 3(2);

O'Reilly, J. 13(1); Quinn, S. 4(7); Ross, B. 12(10); Ryan, T. 38; Stewart, W. 30; Stuart, M. 9; Taylor, P. 1(1); Thompson, D. 24(13); Trundle, L. 21(1); Whittaker, A. 1(4).

Goals (47): Arnold, I. 2, Bolland, P. 5, Elam, L. 7, Furlong, L. 4, Gamble, D. 2, Gouck, A. 1, Guyett, S. 6, Horner, P. 2, O'Reilly, J. 5, Quinn, S. 1, Ross, B. 3, Ryan, T. 1, Stuart, M. 1, Thompson, D. 1, Trundle, L. 4, Whittaker, A. 1, OG, 1.

Stevenage Borough

Appearances: Alford, C. 40(1); Barnwell-Edinboro, J. 13; Barr, G. 1(0); Beevor, S. 32(4); Berry, S. 27; Blackwell, N. 0; Brooker, P. 10; Butler, S. 6(3); Coll, O. 0; Dillnutt, J. 5; Flain, S. 0; Gallacher, D. 0; Gridelet, P. 1; Harrison, R. 14; Harvey, L. 33; Highton, B. 0(1); Howarth, L. 30(3); Jackson, E. 7; Kean, R. 1(2); Kirby, R. 18(1); Leadbetter, R. 10(1); Love, M. 30(4); Mahorn, P. 2(4); McAree, R. 3; Mean, J. 0; Mitchell, J. 0; Naylor, D. 17(6); Pearson, C. 10(7); Peel, N. 2(2); Perkins, S. 3(2); Plummer, D. 18(5); Reinelt, R. 7(2); Rogers, D. 8(3); Samuels, D. 6(2); Smith, M. 42; Statham, B. 3; Strouts, J. 17(1); Taylor, C. 28; Taylor, R. 0; Telemaque, R. 1(5); Thompson, P. 3(10); Trott, R. 15(2); Twidell, D. 0.

Goals (62): Alford, C. 26, Barnwell-Edinboro, J. 4, Beevor, S. 4, Brooker, P. 1, Butler, S. 3. Harrison, R. 1, Howarth, L. 1, Kean, R. 1, Leadbetter, R. 4, Love, M. 3, Pearson, C. 3, Plummer, D. 2, Strouts, J. 5, Telemaque, R. 1, Thompson, P. 1, Trott, R. 2.

Telford United

Appearances: Bailey, D. 7; Beazeley, A. 2; Bentley, J. 35(1); Bytheway, M. 4(5); Bywater, P. 2; Cadette, N. 3; Campbell, N. 4; Cartwright, N. 2; Challinor, P. 18(7); Corns, S. 6(3); Davis, C. 4; Doyle, M. 30(1); Dudley, C. 1; Fee, G. 18(1); Fitzpatrick, G. 17; Fowler, L. 29(2); Gray, B. 2(9); Hodson, S. 5(1); Huckerby, S. 33(8); Jones, M. 3; Jones, M. 22(5); Lyne, N. 6(1); Macauley, C. 15; McCord, B. 4(1); Murphy, G. 27(11); Mutch, A. 3(1); Naylor, M. 20(2); Norman, D. 4(1); Palmer, S. 19(7); Read, D. 10; Sandwith, K. 12; Shakespeare, C. 26(2); Turner, J. 1(1); Turner, G. 9(5); Wilkes, T. 3(2); Williams, D. 37.

Goals (44): Bentley, J. 4, Campbell, N. 1, Doyle, M. 1, Fitzpatrick, G. 4. Gray, B. 1, Huckerby, S. 11, Jones, M. 1, Murphy, G. 8, Naylor, M. 1, Norbury, M. 2, Palmer, S. 7, Turner, G. 3.

Welling United

Appearances: Adams, D. 16(2); Allardyce, C. 3; Anderson, L. 6; Appiah, S. 8(13); Brown, D. 34(4); Browne, S. 21(4); Cooper, M. 19(5); Dennis, K. 4; Dolby, T. 21(8); Farley, J. 23(1); Hanlon, R. 7; Harford, P. 1; Harle, M. 7; Harris, A. 1; Hunter, A. 9(1); Hynes, M. 14(1); King, T. 1; Knight, G. 41; Lewis, B. 0(1); Linger, P. 12(10); McDonald, D. 19; Piper, L. 1(1); Powell, R. 3(7); Rivere, A. 13(3); Rowe, E. 9; Rutherford, M. 37; Side, C. 0(1); Skiverton, S. 35; Trebble, N. 16; Ugbah, J. 29(2); Vercesi, R. 10(2); Watts, L. 40; Witter, T. 8.

Goals (44): Adams, D. 6, Appiah, S. 1, Brown, D. 1, Browne, S. 7, Cooper, M. 3, Dolby, T. 6, Farley, J. 1, Hanlon, R. 4, Hynes, M. 3, Linger, P. 3, Rowe, E. 2, Rutherford, M. 1, Trebble, N. 3, Ugbah, J. 1, Vercesi, R. 1, OG, 1.

Woking

Appearances: Alighieri, D. 0; Batty, L. 29; Betsey, K. 7; Bolt, P. 31(6); Coward, R. 1; Danzey, M. 34; Ellis, A. 28(5); Flahavan, D. 12; French, S. 3(4); Girdler, S. 23(3); Goddard, R. 11; Gridelet, P. 17; Hay, D. 25(10); Hollingdale, R. 28; Kamara, B. 3(2); Mcaree, R. 0(1); Panter, D. 0; Payne, G. 30(4); Perkins, S. 20(3); Saunders, E. 32(1); Smith, S. 39; Statham, B. 6; Steele, S. 23(6); Sutton, W. 6; Taylor, R. 17(1); Timothy, D. 3(1); West, S. 25(7).

Goals (51): Betsey, K. 2, Bolt, P. 4, Danzey, M. 2, Girdler, S. 1, Goddard, R. 2, Gridelet, P. 1. Hay, D. 13, Hollingdale, R. 1, Payne, G. 7, Perkins, S. 3, Saunders, E. 1, Steele, S. 1, West, S. 12.

Yeovil Town

Appearances: Appleton, A. 0(3); Birkby, D. 0(1); Brown, K. 38; Chandler, D. 15(4); Collier, L. 0; Cousin, R. 39(1); Dale, C. 4(5); Davey, J. 0; Fishlock, M. 37; Franklyn, D. 2(3); Groves, L. 0(1); Hannigan, A. 38; Hayfield, M. 15(1); Keeling, D. 10(9); McGrath, S. 2; Miller, J. 0; Mountain, P. 0; Parmenter, S. 0(1); Patmore, W. 38; Pennock, A. 37; Pickard, G. 26(3); Piper, D. 32(4); Pitman, J. 5(2); Pounder, A. 14(13); Rigby, M. 5; Simpson, P. 10(4); Smith, R. 6(3); Smith, B. 22(10); Smith, N. 0; Steele, P. 3; Stott, S. 35(1); Thompson, S. 35; Tonkin, A. 0(1); Winstone, S. 0(2).

Goals (68): Appleton, A. 1, Chandler, D. 1, Cousin, R. 1, Dale, C. 4, Fishlock, M. 2, Franklyn, D. 2, Groves, L. 1, Hannigan, A. 4, Hayfield, M. 1, Keeling, D. 5, Patmore, W. 20, Pickard, G. 10, Piper, D. 1, Pounder, A. 2, Smith, B. 2, Stott, S. 6, Thompson, S. 4, OG, 1.

NATIONWIDE CONFERENCE: MEMBERS CLUBS SEASON 1999-2000

Club: ALTRINCHAM
Colours: Red and White Stripe shirts,black shorts
Ground: Moss Lane
Tel: 0161 928 1045
Year Formed: 1903
Record Gate: 10,275 (1925 Altrincham Boys v
  Sunderland Boys)
Nickname: The Robins
Manager: Bernard Taylor
Secretary: Graham Heathcote

Club: BARROW
Colours: White shirts blue trim, white shorts blue trim
Ground: Holker Street Stadium, Wilkie Road, Barrow in
  Furness, Cumbria LA14 5UW
Tel: 01229 820346
Year Formed: 1901
Record Gate: 6,002 (v Enfield 1988)
Nickname: Bluebirds
Manager: Owen Brown
Secretary: Patricia Brewer

Club: CHELTENHAM TOWN
Colours: Red and white striped shirts, white shorts
Ground: Whaddon Road, Cheltenham, Glos, GL52 5NA
Tel: 01242 573558
Year Formed: 1892
Record Gate: 8236 (1956 v Reading)
Nickname: The Robins
Manager: Steve Cotterill
Secretary: Reg Woodward

Club: DONCASTER ROVERS
Colours: White shirts red trim, white shorts red trim
Ground: Belle Vue, Doncaster, DN4 5HT
Tel: 01302 539441
Year Formed: 1879
Record Gate: 37,149 (v Hull City 1948)
Nickname: Rovers
Manager: Ian Snodin
Secretary: Joan Oldale

Club: DOVER ATHLETIC
Colours: White shirts, black shorts
Ground: Crabble Athletic Ground, Lewisham Road,
  River, Dover, Kent CT17 0PB
Tel: 01304 822373
Year Formed: 1983
Record Gate: 4035 (1992 v Bromsgrove Rovers)
Nickname: The Lillywhites
Manager: Bill Williams
Secretary: John Durrant

Club: FARNBOROUGH TOWN
Colours: Yellow and blue shirts, blue shorts
Ground: Cherrywood Road, Farnborough, Hampshire
  GU14 8UD
Tel: 01252 541469
Year Formed: 1967
Record Gate: 3069 (1991 v Colchester U)
Nickname: Boro
Manager: Alan Taylor
Secretary: Terry Parr

Club: FOREST GREEN ROVERS
Colours: Black and white striped shirts, black shorts
Ground: The Lawn, Nympsfield Road, Forest Green,
  Nailsworth, Glos GL6 0ET
Tel: 01453 834860
Year Formed: 1890
Record Gate: 3,002 (1999 v St. Albans City)
Nickname: Rovers
Manager: Frank Gregan
Managing Director: Colin Peake

Club: HAYES
Colours: Red and white striped shirts, black shorts
Ground: Townfield House, Church Road, Hayes,
  Middlesex UB3 3LE
Tel: 0181 573 2075
Year formed: 1909
Record Gate: 15,370 (1951 v Bromley)
Nickname: Missioners
Manager: Terry Brown
Secretary: John Bond (Jnr)

Club: HEDNESFORD TOWN
Colours: White shirts with black trim, black shorts, red
  and white trim
Ground: Keys Park, Hill Street, Hednesford,
  Staffordshire WS12 5DW
Tel: 01543 422870
Year Formed: 1880
Record Gate: 10,000 (1927 v Walsall)
Nickname: The Pitmen
Manager: John Baldwin
Secretary: Richard Murning

Club: HEREFORD UNITED
Colours: White, shirts, black shorts
Ground: Edgar Street, Hereford, HR4 9JU
Tel: 01432 276666
Year Formed: 1924
Record Gate: 18,114 (1958 v Sheffield Wednesday)
Nickname: United
Manager: Graham Turner
Secretary: Joan Fennessy

Club: KETTERING TOWN
Colours: Red and black shirts, red shorts
Ground: Rockingham Road, Kettering, Northants
  NN16 9AW
Tel: 01536 483028/410815
Year Formed: 1875
Record Gate: 11,536 (1947 v Peterborough)
Nickname: The Poppies
Manager: Peter Morris
Secretary: Gerry Knowles

Club: KIDDERMINSTER HARRIERS
Colours: Red and white halved shirts, red shorts
Ground: Aggborough, Hoo Road, Kidderminster
  DY10 1NB
Tel: 01562 823931
Year Formed: 1886
Record Gate: 9155 (1948 v Hereford)
Nickname: The Harriers
Manager: Jan Molby
Secretary: Roger Barlow

Club: KINGSTONIAN
Colours: Red and white hooped shirts, white shorts
Ground: Kingsmeadow Stadium
Tel: 0181 547 3335
Year Formed: 1885
Record Gate: 4,582 (v Chelsea 1995)
Nickname: The K's
Manager: Geoff Chapple
Secretary: Derek Powell

Club: LEEK TOWN
Colours: Blue shirts yellow collar and cuffs, blue and
  yellow striped shorts
Ground: Harrison Park, Macclesfield Road, Leek, Staffs
  ST13 8LD
Tel: 01538 399278
Year Formed: 1947
Record Gate: 5312 (1973 v Macclesfield Town)
Nickname: The Blues
Manager: Ernie Moss
Secretary: Michael Rowley

Club: MORECAMBE
Colours: Red shirts, black shorts
Ground: Christie Park, Lancaster Road, Morecambe,
 Lancashire LA4 5TJ
Tel: 01524 411797
Year Formed: 1920
Record Gate: 9326 (1962 FA Cup Third Round Proper v
 Weymouth)
Nickname: The Shrimps
Manager: Jim Harvey
Secretary: Neil Marsdin

Club: NORTHWICH VICTORIA
Colours: Green shirts, white shorts
Ground: The Drill Field, Northwich, Cheshire CW9 5HN
Tel: 01606 41450
Year Formed: 1874
Record Gate: 11,290 (1949 v Witton A) 12,000 (1977 v
 Watford FAC4)
Nickname: The Vics
Manager: Mark Gardner
Secretary: Derek Nuttall

Club: NUNEATON BOROUGH
Colours: Blue and White Stripe shirts, Navy shorts with
 royal/white piping
Ground: Manor Park
Tel: 024 76385738
Year Formed: 1937
Record Gate: 22,114 (1967 v Rotherham, FA Cup 3rd
 Round)
Nickname: The Boro
Manager: Brendan Phillips
Secretary: Peter Humphreys

Club: RUSHDEN & DIAMONDS
Colours: White and blue shirts, blue shorts
Ground: Nene Park, Station Road, Irthlingborough,
 Northants NN9 5QF
Tel: 01933 652000
Year Formed: 1992
Record Gate: 6,431 (1999 v Leeds United)
Nickname: Diamonds
Head Coach: Brian Talbot
Secretary: David Joyce

Club: SCARBOROUGH
Colours: Red with thin white stripes, red shorts
Ground: The McCain Stadium
Tel: 01723 375094
Year Formed: 1879
Record Gate: 11,130 (1987 v Luton FA Cup 3rd Round)
Nickname: The Boro
Manager: Colin Addison
Secretary: Gillian Russell

Club: SOUTHPORT
Colours: Old gold and black shirts, black shorts
Ground: Haig Avenue, Southport PR8 6JZ
Tel: 01704 533422
Year Formed: 1881
Record Gate: 20,010 (1932 v Newcastle United)
Nickname: The Sandgrounders
Manager: Paul Futcher
Secretary: Ken Hilton

Club: STEVENAGE BOROUGH
Colours: Red shirts, black shorts
Ground: Broadhall Way, Stevenage, Herts SG2 8RH
Tel: 01438 223 223
Year Formed: 1976
Record Gate: 15,365 (1997 v Birmingham City at St
 Andrews)
Nickname: The Boro
Manager: Richard Hill
Secretary: Roger Austin

Club: SUTTON UNITED
Colours: Chocolate and Amber Quarters, Chocolate
Ground: Borough Sports Ground
Tel: 0181 644 4440
Year Formed: 1898
Record Gate: 14,000 (1970 v Leeds United FA Cup 4th
 Round)
Nickname: The U's
Manager: John Rains
Secretary: Brian Williams

Club: TELFORD UNITED
Colours: White shirts black/orange trim, black shorts
 black trim
Ground: Bucks Head, Watling Street, Telford TF1 2NJ
Tel: 01952 640064
Year Formed: 1877
Record Gate: 13,000 (1935 v Shrewsbury)
Nickname: The Lilywhites
Manager: Alan Lewer
Secretary: Mike Ferriday

Club: WELLING UNITED
Colours: Red shirts, red shorts
Ground: Park View Road Ground, Welling, Kent
 DA16 1SY
Tel: 0181-301 1196
Year Formed: 1963
Record Gate: 4020 (1989 v Gillingham)
Nickname: The Wings
Manager: Brian McDermott
Secretary: Barrie Hobbins

Club: WOKING
Colours: Red and white halved shirts, black shorts
Ground: Kingfield Sports Ground, Kingfield, Woking,
 Surrey GU22 9AA
Tel: 01483 772470
Year Formed: 1889
Record Gate: 6084 (1997 v Coventry City)
Nickname: The Cardinals
Manager: John McGovern
Secretary: Phil Ledger, JP

Club: YEOVIL TOWN
Colours: Green and white shirts, white shorts
Ground: Huish Park, Lufton Way, Yeovil, Somerset
 BA22 8YF
Tel: 01935 423662
Year Formed: 1896
Record Gate: 8612 (1993 v Arsenal)
Nickname: The Glovers
Coach: Colin Lippiatt
Secretary: Jean Cotton

NATIONWIDE CONFERENCE RESULTS 1998-99

	Barrow	Cheltenham Town	Doncaster Rovers	Dover Athletic	Farnborough Town	Forest Green Rovers	Hayes	Hednesford Town	Hereford United	Kettering Town	Kidderminster Harriers	Kingstonian	Leek Town	Morecambe	Northwich Victoria	Rushden & Diamonds	Southport	Stevenage Borough	Telford United	Welling United	Woking	Yeovil Town
Barrow	—	1-1	2-2	1-0	1-0	2-1	0-1	0-2	0-1	0-0	0-4	0-1	2-1	2-1	0-1	0-2	0-0	0-1	1-1	2-1	1-2	2-0
Cheltenham Town	4-1	—	2-1	1-1	0-0	1-1	3-3	0-0	2-2	3-0	1-0	1-0	0-0	4-1	0-1	1-0	3-0	3-0	2-0	0-0	1-1	3-2
Doncaster Rovers	2-1	2-2	—	5-4	1-2	0-1	0-1	0-1	3-1	1-1	1-0	1-0	0-1	2-1	2-2	1-1	0-1	0-0	2-1	4-1	0-1	0-2
Dover Athletic	1-1	0-0	5-4	—	2-1	1-1	0-0	0-0	3-1	0-1	0-1	0-1	0-1	2-3	0-0	1-2	2-1	1-1	1-1	1-2	3-2	1-2
Farnborough Town	2-2	2-4	1-0	2-1	—	2-2	1-5	0-1	0-4	1-3	2-4	5-1	2-1	1-6	1-6	0-2	1-1	1-0	3-1	1-1	2-1	0-0
Forest Green Rovers	1-1	1-2	0-1	1-1	2-2	—	1-2	1-0	2-1	1-0	5-0	4-2	3-1	2-2	3-1	0-2	1-0	1-2	1-1	3-2	0-2	1-2
Hayes	1-0	3-2	0-1	0-0	0-0	1-2	—	0-0	1-2	1-1	2-1	1-0	2-0	1-2	1-0	2-1	3-0	2-2	4-3	1-2	2-2	1-1
Hednesford Town	1-0	3-2	2-0	1-0	1-0	0-3	0-0	—	3-1	0-2	2-1	3-0	1-0	1-0	1-0	1-1	3-1	2-2	1-1	3-2	2-1	2-3
Hereford United	3-0	0-2	1-1	2-0	0-0	1-1	0-1	3-1	—	1-1	1-3	1-2	1-0	2-0	2-2	2-1	1-0	0-1	0-0	1-1	0-1	0-1
Kettering Town	2-0	0-2	1-0	0-2	2-0	4-0	1-0	1-0	1-1	—	1-1	2-0	1-0	6-0	0-0	3-2	2-1	1-2	2-1	0-1	3-0	1-2
Kidderminster Harriers	1-2	0-1	0-1	1-0	4-1	2-1	0-1	1-2	1-0	1-1	—	2-0	2-1	5-2	4-0	0-0	0-2	2-0	3-0	2-1	3-2	0-1
Kingstonian	5-1	1-2	3-3	1-0	2-0	2-2	1-1	1-1	2-0	1-2	0-1	—	3-0	0-0	1-1	0-0	0-0	1-0	1-0	2-4	0-0	0-0
Leek Town	3-1	0-2	2-1	2-0	1-1	0-1	1-4	1-3	3-2	1-2	1-0	0-1	—	7-0	0-3	1-5	1-1	1-1	1-1	2-1	0-3	0-0
Morecambe	3-2	0-2	1-1	0-4	4-0	0-2	2-3	3-1	1-0	3-1	1-4	3-0	7-0	—	3-1	2-3	1-2	0-1	0-1	3-0	0-1	2-4
Northwich Victoria	1-0	1-0	1-2	1-0	1-0	3-1	2-1	1-1	1-0	4-0	2-1	2-2	2-2	1-1	—	2-3	3-1	2-1	1-1	3-1	0-3	1-1
Rushden & Diamonds	4-0	1-2	1-3	2-2	3-0	1-0	5-0	1-0	1-0	1-2	1-0	0-0	0-2	0-3	1-2	—	3-1	1-1	2-3	5-2	2-0	1-2
Southport	0-4	0-2	3-2	3-0	1-0	4-0	1-2	3-1	1-1	0-1	1-1	2-3	3-1	3-1	2-2	2-1	—	1-1	2-1	1-1	0-0	1-2
Stevenage Borough	1-2	2-2	1-0	1-0	2-2	1-1	2-1	3-1	0-0	2-2	3-0	0-0	2-0	1-0	1-3	0-1	0-0	—	2-2	0-0	5-0	2-3
Telford United	1-1	0-3	0-2	1-1	3-1	2-1	2-1	1-1	0-3	3-0	0-0	1-1	0-0	3-1	3-0	0-0	0-0	2-2	—	0-1	1-0	1-1
Welling United	1-1	2-1	1-1	0-3	3-1	0-2	0-2	3-2	0-1	0-0	2-1	3-3	1-3	2-3	2-3	2-2	1-0	0-3	2-2	—	0-1	2-2
Woking	2-3	1-0	2-0	1-2	4-0	1-1	2-0	1-1	2-2	0-2	0-0	1-1	1-0	3-2	2-1	1-1	2-3	1-1	0-1	0-0	—	1-2
Yeovil Town	1-0	2-2	2-2	1-1	6-3	0-4	1-1	2-1	0-1	2-1	3-1	1-3	2-0	0-3	1-2	0-1	3-1	1-3	4-0	1-3	0-1	—

THE BOB LORD CHALLENGE TROPHY 1998–99

First Round

Barrow 2 *(O'Keefe, Mutch)* Leek Town 1 *(McAuley)*	891
Dover Athletic 2 *(Elliott 2)* Stevenage Borough 3 *(Perkins 2, Thompson)*	605
Farnborough Town 4 *(Bailey 2, Baker, Rowlands)* Kingstonian 2 *(Luckett, Holligan)*	540
Forest Green Rovers 2 *(Birkby, Drysdale)* Kidderminster Harriers 4 *(Hadley 2, May, Willetts)*	446
Kettering Town 0 Hayes 3 *(Hodson 2, OG)*	651
Southport 2 *(O'Reilly, Gamble)* ' Telford United 1 *(Murphy)*	634

Second Round

Doncaster Rovers 2 *(Hume 2)* Southport 0	947
Farnborough Town 3 *(Bailey 3)* Rushden & Diamonds 1 *(Foster)*	313
Hayes 3 *(Charles, Moore 2)* Welling United 2 *(Appiah, Ugbah)*	227
Hednesford Town 1 *(Dennison)* Northwich Victoria 3 *(Vicary, Illman, Cooke)*	318
Kidderminster Harriers 1 *(Arnold)* Hereford United 2 *(Parry, Druce)*	645
Morecambe 2 *(Norman, Hughes)* Barrow 0	567

Stevenage Borough 0 Cheltenham Town 1 *(Eaton)*	604
Woking 3 *(Bolt 2, Payne)* Yeovil Town 0	580

Third Round

Cheltenham Town 2 *(Hopkins 2)* Hayes 1 *(Norman)*	469
Doncaster Rovers 3 *(Barnwell Edinboro 2, George)* Northwich Victoria 2 *(Tait, Vicary)*	1877
Farnborough Town 4 *(West 2, Underwood, Bailey)* Woking 3 *(Coward, Bolt 2)*	592
Hereford United 2 *(Cowe, Cook)* Morecambe 3 *(Lyons, 2 Norman)*	567

Semi-Final (two legs)

Farnborough Town 2 *(Robson, Wingfield)* Cheltenham Town 0 *(Played over one leg)*	260
Morecambe 1 *(Keeling)* Doncaster Rovers 2 *(Duerden 2)*	1302
Doncaster Rovers 1 *(Watson)* Morecambe 0	3297

Final (two legs)

Farnborough Town 0 Doncaster Rovers 1 *(Penney)*	643
Doncaster Rovers 3 *(Duerden 2, Sutherland)* Farnborough Town 0	7160

THE MAIL ON SUNDAY
Monthly Awards

	Goalscorer Of The Month	Team Performance Of The Month	Manager Of The Month
AUGUST	Adrian Foster *Rushden & Diamonds*	*Leek Town* (7-0 v Morecambe (H) 25/8)	Brian Talbot *Rushden & Diamonds*
SEPTEMBER	Steve West *Woking*	*Telford United* (3-2 v Rushden & Diamonds (A) 12/9)	Terry Brown *Hayes*
OCTOBER	Gavin Holligan *Kingstonian* Neil Davis *Hednesford Town* Adie Mike *Leek Town* Brian Ross *Southport*	*Hereford United* (3-0 v Stevenage Borough (A) 10/10)	Paul Fairclough *Stevenage Borough*
NOVEMBER	Carl Alford *Stevenage Borough*	*Woking* (1-0 v Cheltenham Town (H) 7/11)	Colin Lippiatt *Yeovil Town*
DECEMBER	John Norman *Morecambe*	*Doncaster Rovers* (5-4 v Dover Athletic (H) 19/12)	Peter Morris *Kettering Town*
JANUARY	Ian Duerden *Doncaster Rovers*	*Doncaster Rovers* (3-1 v Rushden & Diamonds (A) 23/1)	Frank Gregan *Forest Green Rovers*
FEBRUARY	David Leworthy *Kingstonian*	*Barrow* (2-0 v Yeovil Town (H) 20/2)	Steve Cotterill *Cheltenham Town*
MARCH	Mark McGregor *Forest Green Rovers*	*Northwich Victoria* (6-1 v Farnborough Town (A) 20/3)	Colin Lippiatt *Yeovil Town*
APRIL/MAY	Carl Alford *Stevenage Borough*	*Barrow* (2-1 v Stevenage Borough (A) 17/4)	Peter Morris *Kettering Town*

UNIBOND LEAGUE 1998–99

Premier Division

	P	W	D	L	F	A	W	D	L	F	A	Pts
			Home		*Goals*			*Away*		*Goals*		
Altrincham	42	12	8	1	32	13	11	3	7	35	20	80
Worksop Town	42	16	3	2	37	15	6	7	8	29	33	76
Guiseley	42	15	3	3	41	17	6	6	9	23	30	72
Bamber Bridge	42	9	8	4	39	30	9	7	5	24	18	69
Gateshead	42	10	4	7	37	28	8	7	6	32	30	65
Gainsborough Trinity	42	10	4	7	35	28	9	4	8	30	31	65
Whitby Town	42	10	4	7	38	29	7	9	5	39	33	64
Leigh RMI	42	6	10	5	30	26	10	5	6	33	28	63
Hyde United	42	9	6	6	37	22	7	5	9	24	26	59
Stalybridge Celtic	42	13	5	3	43	23	3	6	12	28	40	59
Winsford United	42	6	8	7	26	27	8	7	6	30	25	57
Runcorn	42	6	8	7	21	25	6	11	4	25	24	55
Emley	42	6	9	6	23	24	6	8	7	24	25	53
Blyth Spartans	42	7	5	9	29	32	7	4	10	27	32	51
Colwyn Bay	42	6	6	9	27	32	6	7	8	33	39	49
Frickley Athletic	42	6	6	9	28	32	5	9	7	27	39	48
Marine	42	6	7	8	37	41	4	10	7	24	28	47
Spennymoor United	42	7	7	7	27	26	5	4	12	25	45	47
Lancaster City	42	7	7	7	28	25	4	6	11	22	37	46
Bishop Auckland	42	5	10	6	25	31	5	5	11	24	36	45
Chorley	42	3	8	10	26	37	5	7	9	19	31	39
Accrington Stanley	42	5	5	11	24	37	4	4	13	23	40	36

Division One

	P	W	D	L	F	A	W	D	L	F	A	Pts
			Home		*Goals*			*Away*		*Goals*		
Droylsden	42	16	3	2	54	24	10	5	6	43	31	86
Hucknall Town (3)	42	14	5	2	45	19	12	6	3	35	19	86
Ashton United	42	13	6	2	40	20	9	6	6	39	26	78
Lincoln United	42	13	3	5	57	32	7	9	5	37	33	72
Eastwood Town	42	11	7	3	39	24	9	1	11	26	45	68
Radcliffe Borough	42	11	4	6	45	33	8	4	9	33	29	65
Burscough	42	12	2	7	33	24	7	6	8	34	37	65
Witton Albion	42	11	4	6	45	25	7	5	9	25	38	63
Bradford Park Avenue	42	9	6	6	35	26	8	5	8	29	29	62
Stocksbridge Park Steels	42	7	7	7	31	34	9	6	6	33	26	61
Harrogate Town	42	9	3	9	42	40	8	4	9	33	37	58
Gretna	42	8	7	6	40	38	8	3	10	33	42	58
Belper Town	42	10	6	5	34	25	5	5	11	24	32	56
Trafford	42	8	6	7	22	20	6	5	10	28	38	53
Netherfield Kendal	42	7	3	11	30	36	6	7	8	21	28	49
Flixton	42	8	6	7	31	28	4	6	11	19	36	48
Matlock Town	42	8	2	11	31	33	6	4	11	22	39	48
Farsley Celtic	42	8	6	7	31	27	3	7	11	25	46	46
Whitley Bay	42	6	5	10	26	31	4	4	13	27	46	39
Congleton Town	42	6	8	7	32	38	2	7	12	33	53	39
Great Harwood Town	42	5	5	11	28	32	5	3	13	23	41	38
Alfreton Town	42	4	6	11	24	42	5	2	14	29	44	35

(3) – 3 points deducted for breach of rule

LEADING GOALSCORERS

(In order of League Goals)

Premier Division

Lge	Cup	Tot	
26	10	36	Tony Carroll (Chorley – 24+10 for Radcliffe Borough)
24	5	34	Mark Carter (Runcorn – 19+5 for Ashton United)
22	10	32	Billy O'Callaghan (Accrington Stanley)
20	9	29	Deiniol Graham (Colwyn Bay)
19	7	26	John Morgan (Marine)
18	6	24	Simon Yeo (Hyde United)
18	4	22	Leroy Chambers (Altrincham)
17	7	24	Peter Thomson (Lancaster City)
17	5	22	Carl Chillingsworth (Whitby Town)
17	5	22	Paul Heavey (Accrington Stanley – 11+2 for Congleton Town)
16	3	19	Phil Stafford (Worksop Town)
16	1	17	Keith Fletcher (Blyth Spartans)

First Division

Lge	Cup	Tot	
24	9	33	Robbie Whellans (Farsley Celtic)
23	8	31	Peter Morgan (Eastwood Town)
22	2	24	Glen Robson (Harrogate Town – 1 for Spennymoor United)
21	5	26	Mark Wilde (Burscough)
18	7	25	Jody Banin (Flixton)
17	4	21	Rick Ranshaw (Lincoln United)
16	6	22	Jimmy Bell (Ashton United)
16	5	21	Carl Holmes (Droylsden)
16	5	21	Gary Hurlstone (Stocksbridge Park Steels)
16	4	20	Martin Pemberton (Harrogate Town)

UNIBOND CLUB OF THE MONTH AWARD

Aug/Sept	Worksop Town
October	Frickley Athletic
November	Emley
December	Altrincham
January	Altrincham
February	Whitby Town
March	Leigh RMI
April	Altrincham

UNIBOND CLUB OF THE MONTH AWARD

Aug/Sept	Belper Town
October	Lincoln United
November	Droylsden
December	Droylsden
January	Ashton United
February	Harrogate Town
March	Radcliffe Borough
April	Hucknall Town

ATTENDANCES

Premier Division
Aggregate: 172,186

First Division
Aggregate: 78,632

UNIBOND LEAGUE — PREMIER DIVISION RESULTS 1998–99

	Accrington Stanley	Altrincham	Bamber Bridge	Bishop Auckland	Blyth Spartans	Chorley	Colwyn Bay	Emley	Frickley Athletic	Gainsborough Trinity	Gateshead	Guiseley	Hyde United	Lancaster City	Leigh RMI	Marine	Runcorn	Spennymoor United	Stalybridge Celtic	Whitby Town	Winsford United	Worksop Town
Accrington Stanley	—	1-4	0-5	0-1	1-3	0-0	1-2	2-0	1-1	2-1	1-3	2-0	1-1	1-1	1-2	3-2	1-2	2-3	2-0	1-1	0-2	1-3
Altrincham	2-1	—	0-1	0-0	0-0	4-0	1-1	1-0	1-1	1-1	1-0	1-0	2-1	1-2	1-0	4-1	3-0	2-1	2-1	1-1	1-1	2-0
Bamber Bridge	1-1	0-1	—	2-2	1-0	1-0	1-1	1-2	3-2	1-4	3-1	4-1	1-1	4-3	1-1	2-2	1-2	5-1	2-1	1-1	1-1	3-2
Bishop Auckland	2-1	2-1	2-2	—	2-2	1-0	0-1	1-1	2-2	2-1	2-2	1-0	0-1	1-1	0-0	0-2	1-2	1-1	3-3	1-1	0-2	2-1
Blyth Spartans	0-1	2-1	2-2	2-1	—	4-4	0-2	1-1	2-2	0-2	2-2	4-1	1-2	1-0	4-1	2-1	1-1	4-0	3-2	0-5	0-3	0-1
Chorley	4-0	0-2	2-2	2-0	0-0	—	1-2	3-3	1-1	0-2	1-2	0-2	1-3	2-0	3-3	1-0	1-3	2-2	1-2	2-2	2-2	1-3
Colwyn Bay	3-1	1-1	0-1	0-3	2-0	2-1	—	3-3	0-2	3-4	2-2	0-0	2-1	0-0	0-1	1-0	1-1	1-0	1-2	3-1	2-2	3-1
Emley	3-1	1-1	2-1	2-0	3-3	1-1	0-0	—	1-1	0-0	2-1	0-0	1-3	0-0	0-1	1-0	1-1	1-0	1-2	3-1	1-2	2-2
Frickley Athletic	0-0	0-3	0-1	2-1	2-0	2-2	2-1	1-1	—	1-2	0-2	1-2	3-0	3-2	0-1	1-1	1-1	1-2	3-2	3-3	3-1	2-3
Gainsborough Trinity	0-4	0-3	0-1	4-1	3-4	3-0	3-1	1-2	4-1	—	1-1	1-0	3-0	1-0	2-0	3-0	1-1	3-1	1-4	2-0	0-0	3-1
Gateshead	3-0	0-1	2-0	1-0	0-1	0-0	1-0	1-0	1-1	0-2	—	1-0	0-3	7-1	2-0	3-0	2-2	0-1	2-1	1-1	2-1	2-1
Guiseley	4-0	2-0	1-0	1-0	1-2	4-0	2-2	1-1	3-1	1-0	1-0	—	1-0	1-0	2-0	1-1	2-0	3-0	1-1	0-3	2-3	0-0
Hyde United	3-2	0-1	1-1	5-0	0-1	3-4	2-2	0-1	2-0	3-1	1-0	3-1	—	1-1	1-2	1-1	2-0	3-0	1-1	3-2	1-0	0-0
Lancaster City	1-0	0-0	3-2	2-4	2-2	0-1	4-1	1-1	5-0	0-1	1-0	1-3	1-0	—	1-2	0-0	1-1	0-3	3-0	0-1	1-0	2-0
Leigh RMI	1-2	3-2	0-1	1-1	3-2	3-2	3-2	0-0	2-0	3-0	2-0	2-0	1-2	1-2	—	0-0	0-0	1-1	3-0	0-1	1-0	1-1
Marine	3-2	2-1	1-2	2-2	1-3	4-1	1-4	2-2	1-4	1-2	1-1	1-1	1-0	2-1	1-1	—	1-4	5-2	2-2	2-2	2-2	0-0
Runcorn	2-0	3-1	2-1	0-1	2-1	4-0	2-1	1-1	0-1	1-1	3-1	0-0	2-0	1-2	2-4	0-2	—	2-0	1-0	2-0	1-0	1-2
Spennymoor United	2-0	3-1	2-2	3-0	2-1	2-2	4-1	2-1	0-1	0-0	0-3	2-2	2-1	3-1	4-4	0-2	0-0	—	1-0	2-0	1-0	3-0
Stalybridge Celtic	1-3	3-1	3-1	1-2	1-0	2-1	0-0	0-1	2-2	0-2	3-1	2-2	2-3	3-1	4-4	0-2	1-2	3-0	—	2-0	1-0	2-1
Whitby Town	3-2	1-4	1-1	3-1	2-1	1-1	4-3	1-0	4-0	5-1	1-2	0-0	2-3	1-2	4-4	0-2	0-0	4-1	4-1	—	1-2	1-1
Winsford United	2-2	2-1	1-0	1-2	2-2	1-2	1-1	3-2	2-2	2-0	2-1	0-1	0-2	1-0	2-0	2-2	0-0	1-1	1-2	0-2	—	1-0
Worksop Town	1-0	3-1	1-1	3-1	1-0	2-0	1-2	0-2	2-0	1-1	2-0	3-1	2-0	3-0	2-1	1-1	2-1	2-1	2-1	2-1	1-0	—

UNIBOND LEAGUE — FIRST DIVISION RESULTS 1998-99

Column key (home team down the left, away team across the top):
1 Alfreton Town · 2 Ashton United · 3 Belper Town · 4 Bradford Park Avenue · 5 Burscough · 6 Congleton Town · 7 Droylsden · 8 Eastwood Town · 9 Farsley Celtic · 10 Flixton · 11 Great Harwood Town · 12 Gretna · 13 Harrogate Town · 14 Hucknall Town · 15 Lincoln United · 16 Matlock Town · 17 Netherfield Kendal · 18 Radcliffe Borough · 19 Stocksbridge Park Steels · 20 Trafford · 21 Whitley Bay · 22 Witton Albion

Home \ Away	1	2	3	4	5	6	7	8	9	10	11	12	13	14	15	16	17	18	19	20	21	22
Alfreton Town	—	1-7	0-3	2-2	0-1	2-1	0-2	3-0	2-2	0-0	1-3	0-1	1-1	1-2	2-2	3-2	1-2	1-1	1-3	0-3	2-1	1-3
Ashton United	4-2	—	1-0	1-0	3-1	1-1	1-1	2-0	3-0	2-0	3-0	4-2	3-2	0-0	1-1	1-0	1-1	2-1	0-2	1-1	6-3	0-2
Belper Town	1-2	0-2	—	3-1	2-0	2-2	3-0	0-3	2-1	0-0	0-1	1-1	2-2	0-0	4-1	1-3	1-2	3-3	0-0	1-2	5-3	2-2
Bradford Park Avenue	2-1	2-3	3-1	—	1-1	4-0	0-5	3-1	1-2	2-1	0-1	4-2	0-1	2-2	3-1	3-1	1-1	1-2	1-1	0-0	0-0	5-0
Burscough	2-1	2-2	2-1	1-1	—	3-2	1-3	2-0	1-0	3-0	0-2	2-0	2-0	0-3	2-1	0-1	0-1	1-0	1-2	2-2	2-1	4-0
Congleton Town	2-1	1-1	1-0	0-0	3-2	—	0-1	1-2	3-1	1-2	1-1	2-2	1-0	2-4	1-7	3-4	0-0	2-6	0-4	3-1	2-2	1-1
Droylsden	1-0	2-1	4-1	0-0	4-2	2-4	—	1-3	3-3	1-2	1-1	2-0	1-0	4-2	5-1	2-0	1-1	3-2	3-1	2-0	2-1	5-0
Eastwood Town	2-2	2-1	1-0	4-5	2-2	2-0	2-0	—	1-1	1-3	3-0	2-0	2-1	4-2	5-1	3-0	3-0	3-2	2-2	2-0	2-1	2-0
Farsley Celtic	3-1	1-1	2-1	0-2	1-4	2-0	2-0	2-0	—	4-0	3-1	1-0	1-1	0-3	0-2	3-0	1-1	0-0	4-3	0-2	1-2	0-1
Flixton	2-0	2-0	0-0	0-2	2-2	2-0	1-1	2-0	0-2	—	1-0	2-3	1-1	0-3	0-0	2-2	1-0	1-0	2-0	1-2	2-0	2-3
Great Harwood Town	5-1	1-4	0-1	3-4	2-5	5-2	2-2	0-0	2-0	0-1	—	2-3	0-1	1-0	1-4	0-1	4-0	1-2	0-0	1-2	5-1	2-3
Gretna	2-1	0-2	1-1	3-2	1-1	2-2	2-5	2-4	0-1	1-1	3-0	—	2-2	1-1	2-5	3-2	1-3	2-2	1-1	4-2	2-2	2-1
Harrogate Town	0-4	0-2	5-3	0-1	0-4	2-2	3-0	2-1	1-1	1-1	0-1	2-2	—	2-2	4-0	4-0	0-2	1-2	1-0	1-1	1-0	2-1
Hucknall Town	2-1	4-0	1-0	2-2	1-0	1-1	1-0	2-4	0-3	0-3	1-0	1-1	2-3	—	1-0	1-0	1-0	1-2	2-2	2-1	2-3	2-3
Lincoln United	4-0	1-1	1-2	1-3	0-1	7-0	2-2	3-3	1-1	1-1	7-0	1-2	3-0	4-0	—	1-2	6-3	5-1	1-0	5-3	1-0	0-1
Matlock Town	0-3	1-0	1-3	3-1	0-1	1-1	2-0	3-0	3-0	2-2	0-1	3-2	4-0	1-0	0-2	—	6-0	3-1	2-0	2-1	2-3	3-1
Netherfield Kendal	1-0	1-1	1-2	1-1	0-1	1-1	2-0	3-0	1-1	1-0	4-0	1-3	0-2	1-0	4-0	1-2	—	3-1	0-4	4-2	1-3	1-3
Radcliffe Borough	2-3	2-1	3-3	1-2	1-0	1-1	0-3	3-2	0-0	1-0	1-2	2-2	1-2	1-2	2-4	3-1	0-3	—	0-1	4-1	2-1	1-0
Stocksbridge Park Steels	2-2	0-3	0-0	1-1	1-2	1-1	2-0	2-2	4-3	2-0	0-0	1-1	1-0	2-2	4-3	2-0	0-3	2-4	—	1-0	4-1	3-1
Trafford	3-2	2-1	1-1	0-0	2-2	3-2	2-0	1-0	1-0	1-2	1-2	4-1	1-1	2-1	1-0	2-1	1-0	4-1	1-3	—	1-1	1-0
Whitley Bay	0-2	1-3	1-0	1-0	2-1	4-0	2-3	2-1	0-1	2-0	2-0	2-2	1-0	2-3	1-0	1-2	2-2	2-1	1-2	1-1	—	0-0
Witton Albion	4-0	1-2	4-2	2-1	4-0	5-0	2-1	5-1	2-0	2-3	2-3	2-1	2-1	2-3	4-1	1-3	1-3	1-0	4-1	0-1	2-0	—

UNIBOND CHALLENGE CUP

FIRST ROUND
Accrington Stanley 1, Gretna 0
Bradford Park Avenue 3, Whitley Bay 1
Burscough 2, Bamber Bridge 1 *(aet; after 0-0 draw)*
Congleton Town 2, Belper Town 3
Droylsden 2, Flixton 0
Eastwood Town 0, Alfreton Town 1 *(after 1-1 draw)*
Great Harwood Town 1, Netherfield Kendal 0
Harrogate Town 0, Farsley Celtic 4
Hucknall Town 4, Stocksbridge Park Steels 1
Matlock Town 2, Lincoln United 5
Radcliffe Borough 3, Witton Albion 4 *(aet; after 1-1 draw)*
Trafford 3, Ashton United 1 *(after 0-0 draw)*

SECOND ROUND
Accrington Stanley 2, Great Harwood Town 0
Alfreton Town 3, Belper Town 2
Bishop Auckland 2, Farsley Celtic 4 *(after 3-3 draw)*
Blyth Spartans 3, Bradford Park Avenue 1
Droylsden 4, Hyde United 1
Gainsborough Trinity 3, Lincoln United 1
Guiseley 1, Spennymoor United 0 *(after 1-1 draw)*
Hucknall Town 3, Emley 2 *(after 2-2 draw)*
Lancaster City 1, Trafford 2
Leigh 0, Burscough 1
Marine 1, Chorley 2 *(after 1-1 draw)*
Runcorn 0, Colwyn Bay 3

Stalybridge Celtic 1, Altrincham 0
Whitby Town 1, Gateshead 2
Winsford United 2, Witton Albion 2 *(aet; after 1-1 draw Witton Albion won 4-3 on penalties)*
Worksop Town 1, Frickley Athletic 3

THIRD ROUND
Accrington Stanley 2, Chorley 0 *(after 0-0 draw)*
Colwyn Bay 2, Droylsden 3 *(after 2-2 draw)*
Gainsborough Trinity 0, Farsley Celtic 1 *(after 0-0 draw)*
Gateshead 0, Farsley Celtic 1 *(after 0-0 draw)*
Guiseley 3, Frickley Athletic 1
Hucknall Town 1, Alfreton Town 0
Stalybridge Celtic 4, Witton Albion 1 *(after 1-1 draw)*
Trafford 0, Burscough 1 *(after 0-0 draw)*

FOURTH ROUND
Blyth Spartans 4, Droylsden 3
Guiseley 2, Accrington Stanley 1 *(after 1-1 draw)*
Farsley Celtic 0, Hucknall Town 1 *(after 0-0 draw)*
Stalybridge Celtic 5, Burscough 2

SEMI-FINALS
Blyth Spartans 0, Guiseley 2
Hucknall Town 1, Stalybridge Celtic 2 *(after 1-1 draw)*

FINAL
Stalybridge Celtic 2, Guiseley 1

UNIBOND LEAGUE PRESIDENT'S CUP

FIRST ROUND
Droylsden 0, Hyde United 0 *(aet; after 2-2 draw Droylsden won 5-4 on penalties)*
Eastwood Town 1, Guiseley 3
Farsley Celtic 3, Worksop Town 4 *(aet; after 2-2 draw)*
Gainsborough Trinity 6, Lincoln United 2
Leigh 2, Aston United 1
Stalybridge Celtic 5, Marine 0
Winsford United 0, Altrincham 1 *(after 2-2 draw)*
Witton Albion 1, Runcorn 3 *(after 1-1 draw)*

SECOND ROUND
Guiseley 1, Droylsden 2
Leigh 2, Altrincham 1 *(after 1-1 draw)*

Stalybridge Celtic 2, Gainsborough Trinity 1 *(after 2-2 draw)*
Worksop Town 1, Runcorn 3

SEMI-FINALS (TWO LEGS)
Leigh 1, Runcorn 0
Runcorn 1, Leigh 1
Droylsden 1, Stalybridge Celtic 1
Stalybridge Celtic 2, Droylsden 3

FINAL
Leigh 1, Droylsden 2

UNIFILLA FIRST DIVISION CUP

FIRST ROUND
Belper Town 2, Matlock Town 3
Burscough 2, Great Harwood Town 0
Flixton 1, Netherfield Kendal 0 *aet*
Gretna 1, Whitley Bay 0
Hucknall Town 5, Harrogate Town 3
Stocksbridge Park Steels 1, Congleton Town 2

SECOND ROUND
Ashton United 2, Flixton 0
Eastwood Town 0, Bradford Park Avenue 1
Farsley Celtic 1, Alfreton Town 3
Lincoln United 0, Hucknall Town 4
Matlock Town 3, Congleton Town 1
Radcliffe Borough 2, Burscough 0

Trafford 0, Droylsden 2
Witton Albion 2, Gretna 2
(aet; Witton Albion won 5-3 on penalties)

THIRD ROUND
Alfreton Town 0, Ashton United 3
Droylsden 1, Bradford Park Avenue 0
Hucknall Town 1, Radcliffe Borough 2 *aet*
Matlock Town 1, Witton Albion 2

SEMI-FINALS
Ashton United 3, Radcliffe Borough 2
Witton Albion 1, Droylsden 2

FINAL
Droylsden 0, Ashton United 1

DR MARTENS LEAGUE 1998–99

Premier Division

	P	W	D	L	F	A	Pts	GD
Nuneaton Borough	42	27	9	6	91	33	90	58
Boston United	42	17	16	9	69	51	67	18
Ilkeston Town	42	18	13	11	72	59	67	13
Bath City	42	18	11	13	70	44	65	26
Hastings Town	42	18	11	13	57	49	65	8
Gloucester City	42	18	11	13	57	52	65	5
Worcester City	42	18	9	15	58	54	63	4
Halesowen Town	42	17	11	14	72	60	62	12
Tamworth	42	19	5	18	60	67	62	–7
King's Lynn	42	17	10	15	53	46	61	7
Crawley Town	42	17	10	15	57	58	61	–1
Salisbury City	42	16	12	14	56	61	60	–5
Burton Albion	42	17	7	18	58	52	58	6
Weymouth	42	14	14	14	56	53	56	3
Merthyr Tydfil	42	15	8	19	52	62	53	–10
Atherstone United	42	12	14	16	47	52	50	–5
Grantham Town	42	14	8	20	51	58	50	–7
Dorchester Town	42	11	15	16	49	63	48	–14
Rothwell Town	42	13	9	20	47	67	48	–20
Cambridge City	42	11	12	19	47	68	45	–21
Gresley Rovers	42	12	8	22	49	73	44	–24
Bromsgrove Rov*	42	8	7	27	38	84	30	–46

* 1 point deducted

Midland Division

	P	W	D	L	F	A	Pts	GD
Clevedon Town	42	28	8	6	83	35	92	48
Newport AFC	42	26	7	9	92	51	85	41
Redditch United*	42	22	12	8	81	45	75	36
Hinckley United	42	20	12	10	58	40	72	18
Stafford Rangers	42	21	8	13	92	61	71	31
Bilston Town	42	20	11	11	79	69	71	10
Solihull Borough	42	19	12	11	76	53	69	23
Moor Green	42	20	7	15	70	61	67	9
Blakenall Town	42	17	14	11	65	54	65	11
Shepshed Dynamo	42	17	12	13	62	54	63	8
Sutton Coldfield Town	42	17	8	17	46	57	59	–11
Stourbridge	42	16	10	16	60	54	58	6
Evesham United	42	16	9	17	64	63	57	1
Wisbech Town	42	16	9	17	59	66	57	–7
Weston-Super-Mare	42	15	10	17	59	56	55	3
Bedworth United	42	15	9	18	63	52	54	11
Cinderford Town	42	13	8	21	61	74	47	–13
Stamford AFC	42	13	7	22	60	75	46	–15
Paget Rangers	42	11	12	19	49	58	45	–9
VS Rugby	42	12	9	21	53	74	45	–21
Racing Club Warwick	42	5	8	29	38	93	23	–55
Bloxwich Town	42	1	2	39	26	151	5	–125

* 3 points deducted

Southern Division

	P	W	D	L	F	A	Pts	GD
Havant & Waterlooville	42	29	7	6	85	32	94	53
Margate	42	27	8	7	84	33	89	51
Folkestone Invicta	42	26	8	8	92	47	86	45
Newport IOW	42	23	7	12	68	40	76	28
Chelmsford City	42	20	12	10	91	51	72	40
Raunds Town	42	19	13	10	87	50	70	37
Ashford Town	42	17	12	13	59	54	63	5
Baldock Town	42	17	9	16	60	59	60	1
Fisher Athletic	42	16	11	15	58	52	59	6
Bashley	42	17	7	18	74	77	58	–3
Witney Town	42	15	12	15	56	48	57	8
Cirencester Town	42	16	8	18	61	66	56	–5
Sittingbourne	42	12	18	12	54	56	54	–2
Dartford	42	14	10	18	48	54	52	–6
Erith & Belvedere	42	15	7	20	48	64	52	–16
Tonbridge Angels	42	12	15	15	48	59	51	–11
St Leonards	42	14	8	20	57	72	50	–15
Fleet Town	42	12	11	19	54	72	47	–18
Corby Town	42	10	10	22	48	73	40	–25
Yate Town	42	10	7	25	37	79	37	–42
Andover	42	6	10	26	48	115	28	–67
Brackley Town	42	6	8	28	41	105	26	–64

LEADING GOALSCORERS
(League and Cup)

Premier Division

S. Piearce (Halesowen Town)	27
D. Laws (Weymouth)	25
M. Paul (Bath City)	24
A. Kiwomya (Nuneaton Borough)	19
B. Abbey (Crawley Town)	18
S. Keeble (King's Lynn)	18
M. Owen (Worcester City)	17
D. O'Hagan (Dorchester Town)	16
C. Griffith (Merthyr Tydfil)	15

Midland Division

K. Bayliss (Newport AFC)	29
A. Cook (Clevedon Town)	29
S. Voice (Bilston Town)	25
A. Eccleston (Stafford Rangers)	23
R. Mitchell (Stafford Rangers)	23
J. Bevan (Cinderford Town)	17
N. Kirk (Sutton Coldfield Town)	16
L. Palmer (Blakenall)	16

Southern Division

J. Taylor (Bashley)	32
I. Cambridge (Chelmsford City)	31
K. Slinn (Raunds Town)	28
S. Lawrence (Folkestone Invicta)	23
S. Tate (Havant & Waterlooville)	22
P. Sykes (Margate)	21
I. Bramble (Chelmsford City)	20
P. Andrews (Bashley)	19
D. Arter (Tonbridge Angels)	18
M. Frampton (Fleet Town)	18
K. Miles (St. Leonards)	18

DR MARTENS LEAGUE CUP

PRELIMINARY ROUND, FIRST LEG
Ilkeston Town 4, Wisbech Town 1
Sittingbourne 0, Ashford Town 5

PRELIMINARY ROUND, SECOND LEG
Wisbech Town 3, Ilkeston Town 3
Ashford Town 1, Sittingbourne 0

FIRST ROUND, FIRST LEG
Andover 1, Newport (IW) 2
Ashford Town 2, Hastings Town 3
Bashley 1, Salisbury City 1
Blakenall 2, Solihull Borough 2
Bloxwich Town 2, Stourbridge 4
Cambridge City 4, Brackley Town 3
Clevedon Town 1, Witney Town 0
Dorchester Town 3, Fleet Town 1
Evesham United 1, Redditch United 4
Gloucester City 1, Cirencester Town 0
Grantham Town 4, Ilkeston Town 0
Halesowen Town 1, Bromsgrove Rovers 0
Margate 3, Folkestone Invicta 3
Merthyr Tydfil 2, Bath City 3
Moor Green 2, Burton Albion 2
Raunds Town 3, Baldock Town 1
Rothwell Town 1, Chelmsford City 0
Boston United 5, Kings Lynn 0
Dartford 1, Tonbridge Angels 1
Erith & Belvedere 0, Crawley Town 1
Newport AFC 4, Cinderford Town 2
Racing Club Warwick 3, Stafford Rangers 1
St Leonards Stamcroft 2, Fisher Athletic 2
VS Rugby 1, Bedworth United 1
Havant & Waterlooville 2, Weymouth 3
Shepshed Dynamo 5, Paget Rangers 1
Tamworth 4, Gresley Rovers 1
Worcester City 1, Bilston Town 1
Weston-Super-Mare 3, Yate Town 2
Sutton Coldfield Town 2, Hinckley United 0
Atherstone United 2, Nuneaton Borough 1
Corby Town 1, Stamford AFC 0

FIRST ROUND, SECOND LEG
Burton Albion 4, Moor Green 1
Bath City 4, Merthyr Tydfil 3
Bedworth United 1, VS Rugby 0
Cinderford Town 1, Newport AFC 1
Cirencester Town 1, Gloucester City 3
Fleet Town 0, Dorchester Town 0
Hastings Town 1, Ashford Town 2
Newport (IW) 5, Andover 1
Weymouth 1, Havant & Waterlooville 1
Witney Town 4, Clevedon Town 2
Fisher Athletic 0, St Leonards Stamcroft 2
Folkestone Invicta 2, Margate 0
Ilkeston Town 1, Grantham Town 0
Stamford AFC 3, Corby Town 0
Hinckley United 0, Sutton Coldfield Town 2
Tonbridge Angels 5, Dartford 1
Yate Town 2, Weston-Super-Mare 2
Bilston Town 3, Worcester City 1
Paget Rangers 1, Shepshed Dynamo 0
Crawley Town 5, Erith & Belvedere 0
Redditch United 2, Evesham 1
Stafford Rangers 3, Racing Club Warwick 2
Stourbridge 3, Bloxwich 1

Bromsgrove Rovers 1, Halesowen Town 2
Solihull Borough 4, Blakenall 0
Nuneaton Borough 1, Atherstone United 3
Baldock Town 4, Raunds Town 1
Kings Lynn 2, Boston United 1
Gresley Rovers 0, Tamworth 4
Salisbury City 2, Bashley 2
Brackley Town 1, Cambridge City 4
Chelmsford City 0, Rothwell Town 3

SECOND ROUND
Bashley 1, Weymouth 1
Replay Weymouth 1, Bashley 3
Bedworth United 1, Tamworth 1
Replay Tamworth 1, Bedworth United 5
Bath City 0, Witney Town 0
Replay Witney Town 3, Bath City 1
Dorchester Town 4, Newport (IW) 2
Tonbridge Angels 0, Cambridge City 2
Newport AFC 2, Weston-Super-Mare 0
Solihull Borough 2, Redditch United 1
St Leonards Stamcroft 3, Crawley Town 2
Stourbridge 2, Gloucester City 0
Folkestone Invicta 2, Hastings Town 1
Grantham Town 0, Rothwell Town 0
Replay Rothwell Town 1, Grantham Town 0
Halesowen Town 4, Bilston Town 2
Boston United 1, Stamford AFC 0
Atherstone United 1, Burton Albion 1
Replay Burton Albion 2, Atherstone United 1
Racing Club Warwick 0, Sutton Coldfield Town 3
Shepshed Dynamo 4, Baldock Town 2

THIRD ROUND
Folkestone Invicta 2, St Leonards Stamcroft 3
Witney Town 1, Dorchester Town 2
Rothwell Town 1, Boston United 3
Bilston Town 1, Burton Albion 1
Replay Burton Albion 0, Bilston Town 0
Cambridge City 4, Shepshed Dynamo 2
Newport AFC 0, Bashley 2
Sutton Coldfield Town 2, Bedworth United 1
Stourbridge 2, Solihull Borough 1

FOURTH ROUND
Bashley 0, Dorchester Town 3
Stourbridge 0, Boston United 2
Cambridge City 0, St Leonards Stamcroft 0
Replay St Leonards Stamcroft 1, Cambridge City 1
Sutton Coldfield Town 1, Burton Albion 0

SEMI-FINALS, FIRST LEG
Dorchester Town 0, Cambridge City 3
Boston United 2, Sutton Coldfield Town 2

SEMI-FINALS, SECOND LEG
Cambridge City 1, Dorchester Town 3
Sutton Coldfield Town 1, Boston United 0

FINAL, FIRST LEG
Sutton Coldfield Town 2, Cambridge City 1

FINAL, SECOND LEG
Cambridge City 0, Sutton Coldfield Town 0

DR MARTENS LEAGUE — PREMIER DIVISION RESULTS 1998–99

	Atherstone United	Bath City	Boston United	Bromsgrove Rovers	Burton Albion	Cambridge City	Crawley Town	Dorchester Town	Gloucester City	Grantham Town	Gresley Rovers	Halesowen Town	Hastings Town	Ilkeston Town	King's Lynn	Merthyr Tydfil	Nuneaton Borough	Rothwell Town	Salisbury City	Tamworth	Weymouth	Worcester City
Atherstone United	—	2-1	0-0	5-1	2-2	0-1	2-1	3-1	1-2	1-1	2-1	0-2	1-1	3-3	1-2	2-1	0-2	2-2	2-0	0-1	0-0	1-1
Bath City	3-1	—	1-1	3-0	0-2	1-1	2-2	0-1	1-2	1-1	3-0	0-0	1-1	1-2	2-0	3-0	1-3	2-0	3-5	3-0	2-1	0-0
Boston United	0-0	8-0	—	2-2	0-0	4-1	3-0	5-1	1-0	3-0	4-1	2-0	1-1	0-1	0-1	0-3	2-3	0-0	3-1	2-0	2-1	3-1
Bromsgrove Rovers	0-0	3-0	2-2	—	0-0	4-1	3-1	1-2	4-2	4-2	0-0	2-5	2-1	0-2	1-0	0-1	0-4	3-0	0-2	2-1	2-2	0-2
Burton Albion	0-3	0-2	0-0	0-0	—	4-1	1-2	7-0	5-3	0-1	1-0	0-1	3-1	1-2	0-1	0-1	1-1	0-0	1-2	2-1	1-2	0-1
Cambridge City	3-1	1-4	4-1	4-1	4-1	—	0-0	0-0	1-1	1-0	1-2	1-1	3-1	0-1	2-1	1-2	1-1	2-2	1-3	1-0	1-0	3-0
Crawley Town	3-0	2-2	2-0	3-1	1-2	0-0	—	1-1	0-0	3-2	2-0	2-0	1-2	0-1	3-1	0-2	0-3	1-0	1-1	0-1	2-1	2-1
Dorchester Town	2-1	0-0	0-1	0-1	7-0	1-1	1-1	—	4-1	2-0	1-0	1-1	2-3	1-1	2-1	1-1	0-1	3-1	4-0	0-1	1-1	1-2
Gloucester City	0-0	2-2	0-1	3-1	5-3	1-1	1-2	0-0	—	0-0	0-0	2-0	1-2	3-1	2-1	2-1	1-0	2-1	1-2	1-2	0-0	0-2
Grantham Town	1-1	1-3	4-3	4-1	4-2	1-0	2-0	4-1	0-1	—	3-1	2-0	0-0	3-1	0-1	5-3	2-0	3-0	2-1	2-3	2-0	0-3
Gresley Rovers	2-1	1-0	4-1	1-3	1-0	1-2	1-2	2-0	2-3	0-1	—	2-0	3-3	4-1	2-1	0-0	0-3	1-3	4-1	3-0	1-2	1-1
Halesowen Town	3-1	2-2	1-3	1-4	0-1	2-0	2-0	3-1	0-1	2-0	3-4	—	3-3	3-0	0-1	2-0	2-0	4-0	3-3	1-2	2-2	0-0
Hastings Town	0-0	0-2	1-0	1-2	2-1	0-1	3-0	1-0	0-0	1-1	1-2	2-0	—	3-3	3-0	0-2	0-4	1-1	3-2	3-5	0-1	1-0
Ilkeston Town	1-2	1-3	2-0	2-1	0-2	0-1	3-1	5-2	4-3	1-1	4-1	2-2	3-3	—	1-1	2-0	0-1	3-0	3-0	4-2	1-1	3-0
King's Lynn	0-0	1-2	2-1	0-3	0-1	2-1	3-1	1-1	2-0	1-0	4-0	1-1	1-1	0-0	—	3-0	2-4	2-0	3-3	6-0	1-2	2-0
Merthyr Tydfil	2-0	0-2	1-3	3-3	0-1	0-1	2-1	1-1	0-1	1-0	1-2	1-0	1-2	3-0	0-1	—	2-1	4-1	0-1	2-0	1-1	0-1
Nuneaton Borough	1-0	1-1	6-0	4-0	1-1	2-4	2-1	0-0	0-1	2-0	3-1	4-3	0-0	1-2	4-0	6-1	—	2-0	1-0	2-1	4-2	2-0
Rothwell Town	2-0	1-1	2-0	2-0	0-0	3-3	1-1	1-1	0-1	0-1	2-0	2-1	1-0	3-1	0-2	4-0	2-0	—	1-0	1-0	1-0	1-2
Salisbury City	0-2	3-2	1-0	4-1	1-2	1-3	0-2	3-3	1-1	1-0	2-2	1-2	1-0	0-0	2-2	1-0	1-1	1-0	—	2-1	1-0	2-0
Tamworth	2-1	1-1	1-0	6-1	2-1	2-1	3-1	1-0	1-2	1-1	0-1	3-1	1-5	2-2	0-2	4-2	1-1	3-2	2-1	—	1-3	0-1
Weymouth	0-1	2-1	1-3	1-2	1-2	1-0	1-3	2-1	5-3	1-0	3-1	1-2	1-2	1-1	1-0	0-0	1-1	5-0	1-1	0-3	—	2-1
Worcester City	1-2	0-3	3-1	4-2	0-1	3-0	1-2	2-2	1-2	1-2	3-3	3-4	1-1	3-0	3-2	6-1	0-4	1-0	0-0	1-0	3-0	—

DR MARTENS LEAGUE — MIDLAND DIVISION RESULTS 1998-99

Home \ Away	Bedworth United	Bilston Town	Blakenall	Bloxwich Town	Cinderford Town	Clevedon Town	Evesham United	Hinckley United	Moor Green	Newport AFC	Paget Rangers	Racing Club Warwick	Redditch United	Shepshed Dynamo	Solihull Borough	Stafford Rangers	Stamford AFC	Stourbridge	Sutton Coldfield Town	VS Rugby	Weston-Super-Mare	Wisbech Town
Bedworth United	—	1-1	0-1	5-1	1-0	0-1	2-1	0-0	2-0	0-1	1-1	0-0	1-1	0-1	1-2	0-2	3-1	0-1	1-2	2-0	1-1	0-2
Bilston Town	1-1	—	2-2	5-2	4-2	0-1	2-2	2-1	3-2	5-2	1-1	1-0	0-0	3-2	3-1	1-2	1-1	1-0	2-1	2-4	0-3	3-1
Blakenall	2-0	1-1	—	2-0	1-0	2-5	0-1	3-0	0-2	3-3	1-0	1-0	3-3	1-1	2-1	2-1	1-4	1-1	1-1	3-0	1-1	1-1
Bloxwich Town	0-5	1-6	0-2	—	1-4	1-4	0-4	0-3	1-5	0-6	1-2	1-4	0-5	1-2	2-6	1-6	2-5	0-2	0-2	1-1	0-1	1-3
Cinderford Town	1-4	1-2	2-2	1-4	—	1-4	3-2	0-1	2-3	2-5	1-1	1-2	1-2	1-2	0-1	2-3	1-1	2-1	0-1	1-2	2-1	2-3
Clevedon Town	3-4	3-0	1-2	1-4	1-4	—	1-1	2-2	1-1	2-1	1-1	1-2	3-0	2-1	2-1	2-3	2-2	0-0	2-0	5-1	2-0	0-2
Evesham United	2-1	1-2	0-2	0-2	1-1	0-1	—	2-2	1-0	0-2	0-1	0-0	1-1	0-0	1-1	3-2	1-0	0-5	2-0	3-1	2-0	5-1
Hinckley United	0-0	1-2	0-2	2-0	2-0	0-2	2-2	—	5-1	0-0	2-1	3-0	1-1	3-0	4-1	1-0	1-2	0-5	1-0	1-1	1-1	0-0
Moor Green	1-2	1-3	2-1	0-1	1-2	2-3	3-0	1-1	—	4-1	2-1	3-1	0-3	2-0	0-0	4-2	3-2	3-1	2-1	0-1	1-2	1-1
Newport AFC	1-0	5-0	3-0	4-0	4-1	1-1	3-0	1-1	3-2	—	2-1	3-1	1-1	1-1	4-1	3-1	2-1	4-2	4-0	3-2	2-1	4-1
Paget Rangers	2-2	0-2	3-3	6-0	0-0	0-3	3-0	0-1	3-2	4-1	—	1-1	1-3	2-3	0-5	1-4	1-2	1-0	2-3	5-2	2-2	0-3
Racing Club Warwick	1-3	1-2	2-2	3-2	1-2	0-1	0-4	0-1	1-3	0-1	1-1	—	1-3	2-3	1-0	1-4	1-1	1-0	1-1	2-2	0-4	0-3
Redditch United	2-0	1-0	0-0	4-1	2-3	0-1	3-0	6-0	3-0	1-1	2-1	1-1	—	1-4	4-1	0-0	2-0	0-3	3-0	1-0	0-2	1-1
Shepshed Dynamo	2-0	2-1	0-0	1-1	1-1	0-1	2-2	2-3	2-2	3-1	2-1	1-1	3-5	—	4-1	0-0	5-1	3-1	3-0	1-0	0-0	3-0
Solihull Borough	1-0	1-1	5-3	7-0	3-0	0-0	3-0	3-1	3-0	1-0	1-1	2-1	1-1	1-1	—	0-0	2-1	1-1	2-0	0-0	3-0	1-0
Stafford Rangers	1-2	6-3	4-0	7-0	2-2	0-0	7-3	1-1	1-2	4-1	1-1	6-1	1-0	3-1	3-1	—	3-0	5-1	5-1	3-0	3-1	5-1
Stamford AFC	1-2	2-2	1-0	1-0	1-1	0-1	3-1	1-1	1-0	3-1	1-1	4-1	2-1	0-1	2-2	4-1	—	3-0	3-1	0-0	1-2	4-2
Stourbridge	2-6	1-0	2-2	3-1	2-2	1-2	1-0	0-1	0-2	3-4	2-0	4-1	0-3	0-2	2-2	0-1	1-0	—	1-0	0-2	2-0	3-2
Sutton Coldfield Town	1-0	3-3	2-0	2-3	2-2	3-1	1-1	0-1	2-2	1-0	1-2	3-1	2-3	1-0	1-1	1-1	3-1	0-3	—	0-2	0-1	1-0
VS Rugby	4-4	3-3	0-1	3-3	1-2	1-3	2-1	1-1	0-2	1-2	2-1	2-1	2-1	1-0	3-3	2-1	3-1	0-2	0-2	—	1-0	0-1
Weston-Super-Mare	0-3	4-2	0-3	3-0	2-0	4-2	2-3	1-1	3-0	2-0	2-0	2-0	0-1	2-2	3-0	2-0	3-1	0-0	4-2	2-0	—	1-2
Wisbech Town	2-1	2-3	1-0	3-0	2-0	0-2	2-3	0-1	1-1	0-3	1-1	4-0	0-3	3-2	0-1	0-1	0-0	3-3	1-1	3-1	2-1	—

DR MARTENS LEAGUE — SOUTHERN DIVISION RESULTS 1998-99

	Andover	Ashford Town	Baldock Town	Bashley	Brackley Town	Chelmsford City	Cirencester Town	Corby Town	Dartford	Erith & Belvedere	Fisher Athletic London	Fleet Town	Folkestone Invicta	Havant & Waterlooville	Margate	Newport IOW	Raunds Town	Sittingbourne	St Leonards Stamcroft	Trowbridge Angels	Witney Town	Yate Town
Andover	—	1-5	2-2	1-1	3-2	1-3	0-2	1-2	1-1	3-1	2-5	0-0	0-4	0-4	1-3	0-2	1-2	2-2	1-3	2-2	3-1	1-1
Ashford Town	1-1	—	2-1	1-3	4-1	2-1	2-1	4-1	0-3	2-0	1-1	3-1	0-2	0-3	1-2	1-0	0-1	0-0	3-0	0-2	3-1	0-0
Baldock Town	2-2	2-1	—	3-1	1-2	1-1	1-1	2-0	3-2	2-1	0-1	3-1	0-3	0-5	0-1	1-0	3-3	4-1	0-2	0-2	1-0	5-0
Bashley	3-1	1-3	1-5	—	3-1	1-4	4-2	1-0	1-0	1-3	3-1	2-1	4-1	2-2	2-1	1-3	3-0	3-0	2-1	1-2	1-0	2-1
Brackley Town	1-0	4-1	0-1	2-1	—	1-5	1-3	2-0	0-0	1-1	1-3	1-1	2-2	4-6	1-2	1-3	4-2	1-2	2-1	1-0	0-2	3-0
Chelmsford City	4-0	3-0	3-0	0-1	6-1	—	2-2	3-0	3-0	1-1	0-1	1-1	2-1	0-2	2-3	4-3	3-2	1-4	1-1	3-0	0-4	5-3
Cirencester Town	1-4	1-1	1-1	1-1	2-1	2-2	—	2-0	2-0	2-0	3-3	0-0	0-2	1-3	0-2	3-0	2-1	2-0	3-0	1-1	2-2	1-1
Corby Town	4-0	1-3	1-3	0-3	3-0	3-1	1-1	—	1-2	1-3	2-1	3-5	1-3	0-2	3-1	5-1	0-0	0-0	1-4	0-1	1-1	5-1
Dartford	3-1	0-0	1-2	2-1	6-1	2-1	4-1	2-0	—	2-0	2-0	1-1	3-4	0-2	0-0	0-2	0-1	1-1	0-0	1-1	0-0	1-0
Erith & Belvedere	0-1	2-1	0-0	0-3	3-2	1-0	0-1	0-2	1-2	—	1-2	3-3	1-1	2-0	0-2	0-3	3-1	2-2	3-1	1-1	0-1	0-2
Fisher Athletic London	2-0	0-1	1-2	2-1	2-0	0-2	4-1	2-1	2-1	2-0	—	1-1	0-1	2-3	0-1	0-0	1-2	0-0	1-0	1-0	1-3	2-1
Fleet Town	3-3	3-3	0-0	0-0	3-0	1-0	0-4	1-1	2-1	4-1	3-3	—	4-0	4-6	0-1	0-1	4-0	3-3	2-0	2-0	2-0	1-0
Folkestone Invicta	6-2	2-1	4-0	3-0	4-0	3-2	3-2	1-3	1-2	2-1	0-0	4-0	—	0-1	2-0	3-0	3-2	0-3	0-2	1-1	2-1	3-2
Havant & Waterlooville	5-1	2-0	2-0	3-1	3-1	0-3	3-0	2-0	1-1	2-1	2-0	2-0	0-1	—	1-0	3-0	3-1	1-0	2-1	3-1	2-0	2-0
Margate	4-1	1-1	3-0	2-0	2-0	2-2	3-0	6-0	2-2	0-2	1-2	1-2	1-0	2-0	—	1-2	2-0	3-0	2-1	3-0	2-0	3-0
Newport IOW	2-0	1-1	0-1	4-0	2-0	1-1	2-1	3-0	1-0	1-1	2-0	4-0	2-1	1-0	1-2	—	2-0	1-1	2-2	0-0	0-0	4-0
Raunds Town	10-0	1-1	1-1	1-1	4-2	3-3	1-0	3-1	7-0	1-3	2-2	4-0	2-2	0-1	0-1	2-0	—	3-2	2-1	5-1	2-0	3-0
Sittingbourne	4-1	0-0	3-3	1-0	0-0	1-1	3-0	1-0	2-1	7-1	1-1	0-2	0-3	0-1	1-1	1-0	0-1	—	0-0	1-2	0-0	2-2
St Leonards Stamcroft	3-1	1-2	1-0	1-2	1-0	0-4	1-2	1-1	1-0	0-1	2-2	2-0	0-2	0-4	1-6	2-2	0-2	1-2	—	1-0	5-1	2-1
Trowbridge Angels	4-1	2-2	1-0	3-3	1-1	1-1	1-3	4-0	1-3	1-3	1-1	0-0	1-1	0-4	2-3	0-0	1-4	2-2	1-4	—	1-0	1-0
Witney Town	4-2	0-2	1-0	1-0	8-1	1-0	2-1	0-2	0-1	0-2	1-2	3-1	0-4	1-1	1-1	0-1	0-1	3-0	1-2	0-2	—	0-0
Yate Town	1-2	1-0	3-1	2-1	2-1	1-2	0-1	1-1	1-0	0-1	2-1	1-3	2-1	2-0	0-1	0-4	0-3	2-2	3-1	2-1	0-0	—

RYMAN FOOTBALL LEAGUE 1998–99

Premier Division

	P	Home W	D	L	Away W	D	L	Total W	D	L	Goals F	A	GD	Pts
Sutton United	42	14	3	4	13	4	4	27	7	8	89	39	+50	88
Aylesbury United	42	12	3	6	11	5	5	23	8	11	67	38	+29	77
Dagenham & Redbridge	42	10	8	3	10	5	6	20	13	9	71	44	+27	73
Purfleet	42	15	2	4	7	5	9	22	7	13	71	52	+19	73
Enfield	42	13	4	4	8	5	8	21	9	12	73	49	+24	72
St Albans City	42	10	8	3	7	9	5	17	17	8	71	52	+19	68
Aldershot Town	42	11	4	6	5	10	6	16	14	12	83	48	+35	62
Basingstoke Town	42	10	7	4	7	3	11	17	10	15	63	53	+10	61
Harrow Borough	42	10	5	6	7	4	10	17	9	16	72	66	+6	60
Gravesend & Northfleet	42	11	2	8	7	4	10	18	6	18	54	53	+1	60
Slough Town	42	8	6	7	8	5	8	16	11	15	60	53	+7	59
Billericay Town	42	9	5	7	6	8	7	15	13	14	54	56	−2	58
Hendon	42	9	6	6	7	3	11	16	9	17	70	71	−1	57
Boreham Wood	42	9	8	4	5	7	9	14	15	13	59	63	−4	57
Chesham United	42	8	5	8	7	4	10	15	9	18	58	79	−21	54
Dulwich Hamlet	42	11	4	6	3	4	14	14	8	20	53	63	−10	50
Heybridge Swifts	42	8	4	9	5	5	11	13	9	20	51	85	−34	48
Walton & Hersham	42	8	3	10	4	4	13	12	7	23	50	77	−27	43
Hampton	42	6	9	6	4	3	14	10	12	20	41	71	−30	42
Carshalton Athletic	42	7	5	9	3	5	13	10	10	22	47	82	−35	40
Bishops Stortford	42	5	4	12	4	6	11	9	10	23	49	90	−41	37
Bromley	42	5	7	9	3	4	14	8	11	23	50	72	−22	35

Division One

	P	Home W	D	L	Away W	D	L	Total W	D	L	Goals F	A	GD	Pts
Canvey Island	42	17	1	3	11	5	5	28	6	8	76	41	+35	90
Hitchin Town	42	16	4	1	9	6	6	25	10	7	75	38	+37	85
Wealdstone	42	14	4	3	12	2	7	26	6	10	75	48	+27	84
Braintree Town	42	9	5	7	11	5	5	20	10	12	75	48	+27	70
Bognor Regis Town	42	11	3	7	9	5	7	20	8	14	63	44	+19	68
Grays Athletic	42	12	3	6	7	8	6	19	11	12	56	42	+14	68
Oxford City	42	9	7	5	7	7	7	16	14	12	58	51	+7	62
Croydon	42	10	5	6	6	8	7	16	13	13	53	53	0	61
Chertsey Town	42	7	8	6	7	8	6	14	16	12	57	57	0	58
Romford	42	7	6	8	7	9	5	14	15	13	58	63	−5	57
Maidenhead United	42	3	7	11	10	8	3	13	15	14	50	46	+4	54
Worthing	42	5	8	8	8	5	8	13	13	16	47	61	−14	52
Leyton Pennant	42	6	7	8	7	5	9	13	12	17	62	70	−8	51
Uxbridge	42	5	7	9	8	4	9	13	11	18	54	51	+3	50
Barton Rovers	42	6	8	7	5	7	9	11	15	16	43	49	−6	48
Yeading	42	6	6	9	6	4	11	12	10	20	51	55	−4	46
Leatherhead	42	10	4	7	2	5	14	12	9	21	48	59	−11	45
Whyteleafe	42	9	3	9	4	3	14	13	6	23	51	72	−21	45
Staines Town	42	6	10	5	4	5	12	10	15	17	33	57	−24	45
Molesey	42	3	11	7	5	9	7	8	20	14	35	52	−17	44
Wembley	42	6	4	11	4	6	11	10	10	22	36	71	−35	40
Berkhamsted Town	42	6	5	10	4	2	15	10	7	25	53	81	−28	37

Division Two

	P	Home W	D	L	Away W	D	L	Total W	D	L	Goals F	A	GD	Pts
Bedford Town	42	16	4	1	13	5	3	29	7	6	89	31	+58	94
Harlow Town	42	16	3	2	11	5	5	27	8	7	100	47	+53	89
Thame United	42	14	4	3	12	4	5	26	8	8	89	50	+39	86
Hemel Hempstead Town	42	12	4	5	9	8	4	21	12	9	90	50	+40	75
Windsor & Eton	42	14	1	6	8	5	8	22	6	14	84	55	+29	72
Banstead Athletic	42	11	5	5	10	3	8	21	8	13	83	62	+21	71
Northwood	42	10	4	7	10	3	8	20	7	15	67	68	−1	67
Tooting & Mitcham Utd	42	9	5	7	10	4	7	19	9	14	63	62	+1	66
Chalfont St Peter	42	9	5	7	7	7	7	16	12	14	70	71	−1	60
Metropolitan Police	42	10	4	7	7	4	10	17	8	17	61	58	+3	59
Leighton Town	42	9	5	7	7	5	9	16	10	16	60	64	−4	58
Horsham	42	12	0	9	5	6	10	17	6	19	74	67	+7	57
Marlow	42	9	6	6	7	3	11	16	9	17	72	68	+4	57
Edgware Town	42	5	7	9	3	9	9	14	10	18	65	68	−3	52
Witham Town	42	6	9	6	6	6	9	12	15	15	64	64	0	51
Hungerford Town	42	9	5	7	4	7	10	13	12	17	59	61	−2	51
Wivenhoe Town	42	4	7	10	10	1	10	14	8	20	71	83	−12	50
Wokingham Town	42	7	2	12	7	2	12	14	4	24	44	79	−35	46
Barking	42	8	5	8	2	6	13	10	11	21	50	75	−25	41
Hertford Town	42	8	1	12	3	1	17	11	2	29	44	96	−52	35
Bracknell Town	42	4	4	13	6	6	12	7	10	25	48	92	−44	31
Abingdon Town	42	3	4	14	3	2	16	6	6	30	48	124	−76	24

Division Three

	P	Home			Away			Total			Goals			Pts
		W	D	L	W	D	L	W	D	L	F	A	GD	
Ford United	38	15	2	2	12	3	4	27	5	6	110	42	+68	86
Wingate & Finchley	38	11	3	5	14	2	3	25	5	8	79	38	+41	80
Cheshunt	38	14	5	0	9	5	5	23	10	5	70	41	+29	79
Lewes	38	15	2	2	10	1	8	25	3	10	86	45	+41	78
Epsom & Ewell	38	10	2	7	9	3	7	19	5	14	61	51	+10	62
Ware	38	12	1	6	7	3	9	19	4	15	79	60	+19	61
Tilbury	38	8	4	7	9	4	6	17	8	13	74	52	+22	59
Croydon Athletic	38	9	4	6	7	6	6	16	10	12	82	59	+23	58
East Thurrock United	38	8	7	4	7	6	6	15	13	10	74	56	+18	58
Egham Town	38	6	6	7	10	2	7	16	8	14	65	58	+7	56
Corinthian-Casuals	38	8	4	7	8	3	8	16	7	15	70	71	−1	55
Southall	38	7	4	8	7	5	7	14	9	15	68	66	+2	51
Camberley Town	38	10	3	6	4	5	10	14	8	16	66	77	−11	50
Aveley	38	6	4	9	6	3	10	12	7	19	50	67	−17	43
Flackwell Heath	38	8	4	7	3	5	11	11	9	18	59	70	−11	42
Hornchurch	38	6	4	9	4	5	10	10	9	19	48	73	−25	39
Clapton	38	7	1	11	4	5	10	11	6	21	48	89	−41	39
Dorking	38	3	4	12	5	3	11	8	7	23	52	98	−46	31
Kingsbury Town	38	4	2	13	2	1	16	6	3	29	40	98	−58	21
Tring Town	38	4	5	10	1	1	17	5	6	27	38	108	−70	21

LEADING GOALSCORERS

	Premier Division	*Lge*	*RLC*	*PC*
40	Gary Abbott (Aldershot Town)	33	7	
28	Steve Clark (St Albans City)	28		
28	George Georgiou (Purfleet)	22	4	2
27	Mark Watson (Sutton United)	24	3	
26	Ian Mancey (Basingstoke Town)	23		3

	Division One			
27	Neil Selby (Chertsey Town)	26	1	
24	Billy Read (Leyton Pennant)	20	4	
23	Steve Tilson (Canvey Island)	20	2	1
20	Neil Scammell (Bognor Regis Town)	19	1	
20	Brian Jones (Wealdstone)	18		2

	Division Two			*VT*
30	Julian Hazel (Wivenhoe Town)	25		5
28	Dennis Greene (Windsor & Eton)	25		3
27	Robert Gibson (Marlow)	21	1	5
25	Warren Burton (Banstead Athletic)	20	3	2
24	Wayne Cort (Harlow Town)	24		

	Division Three			
38	Jeff Wood (Ford United)	35	3	
30	Deal Callcut (Ware)	28	2	
29	Clayton Whittle (Egham Town)	26	1	2
28	Ben Strevens (Wingate & Finchley)	28		
26	Del Francois (Tilbury)	23	2	1

Lge: Ryman League; RLC: Ryman League Cup; PC: Puma Cup; VT: Vandanel Trophy

ATTENDANCES

Premier Divison
Aggregate: 264,042
Highest Individual crowd: 2810 Basingstoke Town v Aldershot Town

Division One
Aggregate: 92,973
Highest Individual crowd: 1058 Worthing v Bognor Regis Town

Division Two
Aggregate: 60,954
Highest Individual crowd: 806 Bedford Town v Leighton Town

Division Three
Aggregate: 28,668
Highest Individual crowd: 380 Wingate & Finchley v Cheshunt

PREVIOUS SEASONS

SEASON	CLUBS	GAMES	AGG	AVE
1988–1989	86	1764	323,197	183
1989–1990	87	1806	387,441	215
1990–1991	88	1848	404,703	219
1991–1992	86	1764	397,553	225
1992–1993	85	1724	430,518	247
1993–1994	87	1806	423,306	234
1994–1995	87	1806	433,703	240
1995–1996	86	1764	440,285	250
1996–1997	83	1658	461,944	278
1997–1998	86	1766	456,454	258
1998–1999	86	1766	446,637	253

RYMAN FOOTBALL LEAGUE—PREMIER DIVISION RESULTS 1998-99

	Aldershot Town	Aylesbury United	Basingstoke Town	Billericay Town	Bishop's Stortford	Boreham Wood	Bromley	Carshalton Athletic	Chesham United	Dagenham & Redbridge	Dulwich Hamlet	Enfield	Gravesend & Northfleet	Hampton	Harrow Borough	Hendon	Heybridge Swifts	Purfleet	St Albans City	Slough Town	Sutton United	Walton & Hersham
Aldershot Town	—	0-1	2-1	1-1	0-8	1-1	3-0	4-0	0-0	4-3	3-1	3-1	3-0	5-0	5-2	0-2	1-1	1-1	1-2	1-1	1-2	7-2
Aylesbury United	0-1	—	2-1	3-0	0-3	1-6	2-1	2-0	0-3	0-1	3-0	1-2	2-0	3-0	2-0	1-0	0-1	2-1	0-0	0-0	1-4	1-0
Basingstoke Town	2-1	3-2	—	0-1	3-1	1-1	1-1	2-1	4-0	1-1	2-1	1-0	2-2	1-0	2-1	1-1	2-2	3-2	1-2	0-2	1-2	0-0
Billericay Town	1-1	3-0	0-1	—	3-2	1-0	2-2	2-0	3-0	1-2	1-0	0-1	0-2	2-0	2-2	2-1	2-1	0-1	3-3	1-2	1-2	1-0
Bishop's Stortford	0-8	0-3	3-1	3-2	—	2-0	1-3	1-2	5-2	0-3	2-1	1-2	3-1	4-2	0-3	0-3	1-3	0-0	1-1	0-1	0-1	1-0
Boreham Wood	1-1	1-6	1-1	1-0	2-0	—	0-3	4-4	0-0	0-2	4-0	4-3	3-1	0-0	1-0	2-0	1-1	2-1	1-1	1-0	2-0	0-0
Bromley	1-1	0-1	1-1	2-2	1-3	0-3	—	2-3	0-1	0-0	0-3	2-1	0-1	2-4	3-0	1-4	6-1	2-1	0-1	2-1	1-1	1-1
Carshalton Athletic	0-2	3-3	1-0	1-3	1-2	4-4	1-1	—	0-1	0-0	2-0	2-1	1-2	2-2	1-2	1-3	1-2	3-3	1-1	0-3	1-0	1-3
Chesham United	0-0	1-0	0-2	3-3	5-2	0-0	3-1	3-0	—	2-5	0-0	2-0	3-2	4-0	1-4	0-2	1-0	0-1	2-1	1-0	0-3	1-2
Dagenham & Redbridge	0-1	1-0	2-0	1-2	0-3	0-2	3-3	5-0	0-0	—	1-0	3-3	0-0	2-1	1-0	6-0	3-0	1-2	2-2	3-0	0-0	3-1
Dulwich Hamlet	4-3	0-1	2-0	2-4	2-1	4-0	2-0	0-0	3-2	1-2	—	0-1	1-0	0-0	0-2	3-1	4-3	1-2	2-2	2-2	2-1	3-2
Enfield	4-0	2-3	3-2	1-0	1-2	4-3	3-0	1-0	2-2	4-0	2-1	—	0-2	3-0	5-0	2-1	4-1	1-1	0-0	2-1	1-1	3-2
Gravesend & Northfleet	2-1	1-2	1-0	0-0	3-1	3-1	1-2	3-1	0-2	2-0	0-1	0-3	—	3-0	2-0	0-1	3-2	2-3	0-1	1-2	2-1	2-0
Hampton	0-0	0-0	2-1	3-3	4-2	0-0	2-1	1-1	0-1	1-2	0-0	0-2	1-0	—	4-0	3-1	4-0	5-0	1-2	2-2	0-3	2-0
Harrow Borough	1-0	1-4	0-0	0-0	0-3	1-0	2-0	8-2	5-4	2-1	3-2	0-0	0-1	4-0	—	0-0	2-0	1-2	0-0	0-2	0-3	0-1
Hendon	1-1	3-3	2-1	3-3	0-3	2-0	2-1	1-1	2-1	2-2	1-1	2-0	0-0	1-2	1-2	—	6-1	0-0	4-3	5-2	0-3	0-3
Heybridge Swifts	1-1	1-1	3-9	2-0	1-3	1-1	1-0	0-2	0-4	1-2	0-2	2-2	3-2	3-0	2-4	1-0	—	2-0	0-3	2-1	5-2	0-3
Purfleet	1-1	0-0	2-1	0-2	0-0	2-1	2-1	4-2	3-0	3-0	1-1	0-1	2-1	4-0	4-0	4-0	2-0	—	1-0	0-4	2-4	1-0
St Albans City	1-1	2-1	4-2	3-1	1-1	1-1	1-0	3-0	2-3	2-2	1-0	2-1	0-2	3-1	1-1	4-2	1-1	2-0	—	3-3	1-3	6-1
Slough Town	2-2	1-0	1-0	1-1	0-1	1-0	4-1	1-1	3-1	0-1	2-0	2-2	4-0	3-0	0-3	1-1	0-1	2-3	1-0	—	2-2	1-1
Sutton United	5-0	1-2	1-2	4-1	0-1	2-0	2-1	3-0	2-0	3-1	3-1	1-1	1-1	3-2	2-1	4-1	1-1	2-1	2-3	0-1	—	5-0
Walton & Hersham	0-4	0-2	2-1	3-4	1-0	0-0	1-0	3-2	9-1	0-1	3-1	0-4	1-3	0-1	2-2	0-3	0-1	1-0	1-0	2-0	0-2	—

RYMAN FOOTBALL LEAGUE—DIVISION ONE RESULTS 1998-99

	Barton Rovers	Berkhamsted Town	Bognor Regis Town	Braintree Town	Canvey Island	Chertsey Town	Croydon	Grays Athletic	Hitchin Town	Leatherhead	Leyton Pennant	Maidenhead United	Molesey	Oxford City	Romford	Staines Town	Uxbridge	Wealdstone	Wembley	Whyteleafe	Worthing	Yeading
Barton Rovers	—	2-0	1-0	1-3	0-1	1-1	2-0	0-1	0-0	0-0	0-2	1-1	2-1	0-0	1-1	0-0	1-0	0-3	0-1	2-0	0-0	2-1
Berkhamsted Town	2-1	—	1-3	6-0	2-0	3-3	2-2	1-4	1-2	3-2	2-0	0-3	0-1	0-2	3-3	5-0	0-0	4-1	1-1	2-1	0-1	0-3
Bognor Regis Town	1-0	1-3	—	4-0	0-0	3-1	1-2	0-1	6-1	3-0	0-1	3-1	0-0	0-1	1-1	1-0	2-0	2-0	4-1	3-1	1-2	1-3
Braintree Town	1-1	0-2	4-0	—	0-2	1-2	3-2	1-1	3-0	3-0	8-2	2-2	0-0	1-2	1-3	4-0	2-4	1-0	0-1	2-0	4-0	1-0
Canvey Island	0-2	1-3	0-0	2-1	—	1-2	2-1	2-1	1-3	1-0	6-1	0-4	0-2	0-1	0-2	2-0	1-0	4-2	3-0	1-1	2-0	3-1
Chertsey Town	2-1	3-3	3-1	0-3	1-2	—	1-4	1-0	1-4	2-0	1-1	2-2	0-1	2-0	2-2	1-1	2-1	0-1	1-1	2-0	2-2	2-0
Croydon	1-0	2-2	2-0	0-0	3-0	2-0	—	4-0	1-0	4-0	2-1	0-0	2-4	1-0	1-1	2-0	2-2	2-3	0-0	0-2	1-2	2-1
Grays Athletic	2-2	1-4	1-3	1-1	0-1	2-2	2-0	—	1-0	2-1	2-3	0-2	1-0	1-0	0-1	1-2	1-0	1-1	4-1	2-0	1-0	3-0
Hitchin Town	1-1	1-2	4-0	3-0	1-3	1-4	1-0	4-0	—	2-1	1-0	2-2	1-0	3-3	0-0	1-0	2-1	3-1	3-0	3-2	5-0	2-1
Leatherhead	4-2	3-2	3-0	3-0	1-0	2-0	4-0	2-1	0-4	—	1-0	0-1	0-3	2-2	4-1	0-1	2-0	0-1	1-1	4-1	1-0	2-0
Leyton Pennant	3-0	2-0	0-1	8-2	6-1	1-1	2-1	2-3	1-0	1-3	—	3-1	2-2	2-1	2-2	4-1	2-3	1-2	0-0	0-1	1-2	2-1
Maidenhead United	0-2	0-3	3-1	2-2	0-4	2-2	0-0	0-2	0-0	1-0	1-2	—	1-1	2-2	0-2	2-1	0-2	0-2	0-1	1-1	0-0	0-1
Molesey	0-6	0-1	0-0	0-0	0-2	0-1	2-4	1-0	0-3	1-0	1-4	0-4	—	0-0	0-1	1-1	0-4	2-0	0-0	0-0	3-4	1-1
Oxford City	2-0	0-2	0-1	1-2	0-1	2-0	1-0	1-0	1-1	3-2	3-2	0-1	2-1	—	2-2	2-2	1-3	3-1	3-0	0-1	2-2	2-2
Romford	2-2	3-3	1-1	1-3	0-2	2-2	1-1	0-1	1-2	4-1	3-2	0-3	0-0	1-0	—	1-0	0-0	0-4	3-4	3-1	2-1	3-4
Staines Town	0-0	5-0	1-0	4-0	2-0	1-1	2-0	1-2	2-1	0-0	1-1	1-1	1-0	0-0	1-2	—	0-1	2-2	2-1	1-0	0-1	0-0
Uxbridge	1-0	0-0	2-0	2-4	1-0	2-1	2-2	1-0	0-1	1-1	2-2	1-1	0-0	0-3	2-3	2-2	—	0-1	4-0	5-0	1-2	2-0
Wealdstone	5-2	4-1	2-0	1-0	4-2	0-1	2-3	1-1	0-1	1-0	1-0	0-3	2-2	2-0	1-0	3-1	2-1	—	1-0	2-1	4-1	2-0
Wembley	1-1	1-1	4-1	0-1	3-0	1-1	0-0	4-1	0-3	1-0	1-4	0-0	1-1	4-1	2-0	2-0	1-2	0-2	—	2-1	1-2	1-1
Whyteleafe	3-4	2-1	3-1	2-0	1-1	2-0	0-2	2-0	1-1	1-0	0-2	3-2	1-3	0-1	2-1	3-0	3-0	0-2	1-0	—	1-1	1-3
Worthing	0-0	0-1	1-2	4-0	2-0	2-2	1-2	1-0	1-1	0-1	1-1	0-1	1-1	2-4	3-0	0-1	0-0	1-2	5-3	1-2	—	0-1
Yeading	0-1	0-3	1-3	1-0	3-1	2-0	2-1	3-0	1-1	4-1	1-1	0-2	3-0	0-0	2-2	1-2	0-1	0-1	3-0	2-1	3-0	—

RYMAN FOOTBALL LEAGUE—DIVISION TWO RESULTS 1998-99

	Abingdon Town	Banstead Athletic	Barking	Bedford Town	Bracknell Town	Chalfont St Peter	Edgware Town	Harlow Town	Hemel Hempstead Town	Hertford Town	Horsham	Hungerford Town	Leighton Town	Marlow	Metropolitan Police	Northwood	Thame United	Tooting & Mitcham United	Windsor & Eton	Witham Town	Wivenhoe Town	Wokingham Town
Abingdon Town	—	1-2	0-0	0-3	0-1	2-2	0-2	3-2	2-5	4-1	3-2	0-4	2-2	0-4	2-4	1-4	2-6	0-2	1-6	2-3	2-4	1-1
Banstead Athletic	4-1	—	1-0	3-1	3-1	5-1	1-1	2-2	0-4	5-1	4-4	1-1	0-1	4-1	2-0	2-0	1-3	1-1	1-0	0-1	4-1	1-3
Barking	4-2	2-2	—	1-1	0-2	2-0	1-0	5-0	0-3	4-0	3-2	2-0	2-3	0-3	0-1	0-1	1-1	4-3	1-0	1-0	1-2	1-2
Bedford Town	1-0	1-1	1-1	—	0-2	3-0	0-1	3-0	1-1	5-0	3-0	2-0	0-1	2-1	1-0	6-0	4-0	2-0	3-0	1-0	0-0	4-1
Bracknell Town	0-5	3-0	4-0	0-2	—	4-4	7-1	2-2	1-0	3-1	0-1	0-1	2-3	0-1	1-1	0-2	1-2	0-0	0-1	1-5	1-4	1-2
Chalfont St Peter	6-2	0-2	3-1	1-2	4-0	—	1-1	1-4	0-0	3-1	0-1	3-2	3-1	0-0	2-0	2-3	0-2	0-0	3-2	1-0	5-2	1-2
Edgware Town	2-1	2-5	4-1	0-1	7-1	1-1	—	6-0	1-1	4-1	0-2	0-0	1-1	0-2	1-1	0-4	0-1	1-2	2-2	2-2	1-2	3-0
Harlow Town	3-1	2-1	1-0	3-0	2-2	2-0	6-0	—	1-3	4-0	3-1	2-2	1-4	6-1	3-0	3-0	5-1	7-0	1-1	4-0	3-0	1-1
Hemel Hempstead Town	3-0	0-1	3-0	2-1	1-0	4-1	1-4	1-3	—	2-1	3-0	0-0	2-1	3-1	4-1	1-1	0-0	4-5	1-3	2-2	1-2	1-2
Hertford Town	3-2	6-2	3-2	0-2	1-0	0-2	0-2	3-1	3-1	—	0-1	2-1	2-1	1-0	0-1	1-3	0-0	0-1	2-1	0-3	3-1	0-1
Horsham	3-1	2-3	2-0	0-2	0-0	0-1	2-1	6-0	1-4	3-1	—	0-3	2-0	6-2	3-0	1-3	4-2	3-0	3-0	3-1	1-3	7-0
Hungerford Town	2-0	3-2	1-1	1-4	2-0	1-2	4-1	2-2	2-0	2-0	0-1	—	1-1	0-0	0-2	1-1	1-0	2-1	0-1	0-1	1-2	1-0
Leighton Town	3-0	2-0	5-3	1-4	2-2	2-2	4-2	1-1	2-3	7-2	3-1	2-3	—	4-2	0-2	0-1	0-5	1-2	1-1	3-2	1-4	2-1
Marlow	9-1	1-0	2-2	0-2	2-2	0-2	4-2	1-1	2-0	0-0	2-2	1-0	0-0	—	4-3	2-0	4-2	1-2	2-2	1-3	1-2	2-1
Metropolitan Police	0-1	0-5	4-0	2-4	7-1	1-1	1-2	1-1	1-1	2-0	2-0	0-2	1-0	1-0	—	2-1	0-2	0-1	0-1	3-3	5-2	3-0
Northwood	5-0	0-2	2-1	1-1	3-0	4-0	2-1	3-0	1-0	2-3	0-3	1-1	1-0	1-0	1-0	—	0-2	4-2	0-7	2-0	4-1	4-1
Thame United	4-0	3-3	1-0	1-2	4-0	4-0	3-0	1-0	1-0	2-0	2-2	3-3	1-1	3-1	0-3	2-0	—	0-2	4-1	5-3	4-1	2-1
Tooting & Mitcham United	4-0	0-1	3-1	1-5	1-1	1-1	1-2	7-0	1-1	3-1	1-1	4-0	2-1	0-2	2-1	0-1	1-2	—	1-6	1-1	2-1	4-0
Windsor & Eton	6-0	4-0	1-2	3-0	5-2	4-0	1-1	1-1	0-2	4-1	0-2	1-0	1-0	0-2	1-0	4-1	1-1	2-1	—	2-1	1-4	1-4
Witham Town	2-2	1-0	1-1	0-0	0-2	1-5	3-0	4-0	1-5	1-3	2-0	1-1	4-1	2-1	2-0	0-0	1-3	1-1	1-1	—	1-2	4-2
Wivenhoe Town	0-0	1-3	1-1	0-2	2-2	1-5	1-2	3-0	2-0	3-1	4-1	2-2	1-2	3-1	1-1	1-2	1-3	0-1	2-3	1-1	—	7-1
Wokingham Town	0-1	0-3	2-3	2-0	0-0	0-3	0-0	1-1	1-2	0-1	2-1	1-2	0-1	0-3	0-1	3-0	0-3	0-2	1-0	1-0	2-0	—

RYMAN FOOTBALL LEAGUE—DIVISION THREE RESULTS 1998-99

	Aveley	Camberley Town	Cheshunt	Clapton	Corinthian-Casuals	Croydon Athletic	Dorking	East Thurrock United	Egham Town	Epsom & Ewell	Flackwell Heath	Ford United	Hornchurch	Kingsbury Town	Lewes	Southall	Tilbury	Tring Town	Ware	Wingate & Finchley
Aveley	—	0-1	2-1	2-4	2-3	0-1	2-1	2-0	1-0	1-1	0-0	1-1	2-0	1-0	0-2	1-2	0-1	3-3	1-3	2-3
Camberley Town	4-2	—	1-3	2-2	2-3	3-0	4-2	2-3	9-0	2-1	2-1	1-0	1-0	1-1	1-2	3-3	1-6	3-0	2-1	1-2
Cheshunt	3-1	6-2	—	2-0	2-2	4-2	3-0	3-3	2-1	1-1	2-0	0-0	1-0	2-1	2-0	2-0	3-1	3-0	2-1	2-2
Clapton	2-0	0-1	0-0	—	0-1	2-1	1-2	1-0	0-3	0-4	2-1	1-9	2-3	4-1	0-2	0-4	3-1	5-2	0-4	0-4
Corinthian-Casuals	5-1	1-4	3-0	4-2	—	4-4	0-1	1-1	1-4	3-0	2-1	2-3	5-1	2-1	3-3	2-2	3-4	2-0	0-5	0-1
Croydon Athletic	0-0	2-1	2-2	4-2	3-1	—	2-3	0-2	0-1	2-3	2-2	6-2	2-1	5-1	1-0	5-1	1-3	9-1	2-2	0-1
Dorking	1-1	3-0	0-1	0-3	0-2	1-5	—	1-1	0-4	2-2	2-4	2-7	1-3	0-1	1-5	0-5	1-1	3-0	2-5	2-1
East Thurrock United	3-0	1-1	0-1	1-1	1-0	0-0	2-2	—	2-2	2-4	4-1	1-1	2-3	4-0	0-1	1-2	1-2	4-0	4-1	2-0
Egham Town	0-1	2-0	1-2	2-2	1-0	1-1	1-1	1-1	—	0-2	3-0	2-3	2-2	2-0	1-2	1-2	1-1	2-1	3-1	1-2
Epsom & Ewell	1-0	1-1	0-0	3-0	1-2	2-0	2-1	1-1	0-2	—	4-2	0-5	2-0	4-0	2-3	0-1	0-1	2-1	1-2	0-2
Flackwell Heath	3-4	6-0	2-0	3-0	4-1	1-1	4-2	3-2	1-0	4-2	—	1-2	0-0	4-2	1-0	1-4	0-5	4-0	2-1	0-4
Ford United	4-2	5-0	7-0	1-0	1-1	4-1	2-1	4-2	3-0	1-6	2-0	—	1-1	3-0	2-0	0-3	0-1	5-1	2-0	2-3
Hornchurch	1-4	1-0	1-4	1-3	1-2	1-4	3-0	0-2	1-5	2-0	1-1	1-4	—	2-1	2-1	0-0	4-3	0-0	1-1	0-2
Kingsbury Town	5-2	2-2	1-2	1-2	2-0	1-0	4-2	0-4	1-4	3-0	1-1	1-4	2-0	—	1-2	2-0	2-0	1-2	0-3	1-6
Lewes	4-1	6-2	3-2	9-0	6-2	1-1	6-1	3-3	4-1	2-3	1-0	3-0	2-1	2-0	—	5-0	3-1	3-1	1-0	1-2
Southall	0-1	2-0	0-2	1-1	3-3	2-3	4-4	1-2	1-2	0-1	1-4	0-3	0-0	2-0	5-0	—	3-1	3-1	2-1	1-1
Tilbury	0-1	1-1	0-1	3-1	2-0	2-2	0-1	1-2	1-1	0-1	1-1	0-1	4-3	2-0	3-1	4-1	—	2-1	3-1	3-1
Tring Town	0-3	1-1	1-1	1-0	0-2	1-5	1-3	4-0	2-1	2-1	1-3	1-3	0-0	1-2	3-1	0-2	2-1	—	1-0	2-1
Ware	4-3	2-4	0-3	3-1	3-1	0-2	4-2	4-2	2-3	2-0	2-0	0-2	4-1	5-1	2-1	3-0	3-3	1-0	—	3-2
Wingate & Finchley	0-0	3-0	0-0	5-0	2-1	0-1	2-1	2-2	0-1	1-0	6-2	3-2	0-2	4-0	1-2	4-0	3-1	2-1	0-3	—

RYMAN LEAGUE CUP 1998–99

PRELIMINARY ROUND
Abingdon Town 2, Epsom & Ewell 1
Aveley 2, Ford United 2
Replay Ford United 2, Aveley 0
Banstead Athletic 1, Witham Town 0
Barking 0, Harlow Town 4
Bedford Town 2, Braintree Town 1
Bracknell Town 0, Tooting & Mitcham United 4
Camberley Town 2, Tring Town 0
East Thurrock United 2, Wokingham Town 0
Hemel Hempstead Town 1, Edgware Town 0
Hertford Town 1, Lewes 2
Kingsbury Town 0, Leighton Town 3
Marlow 5, Flackwell Heath 2
Southall 0, Hungerford Town 1
Wingate & Finchley 1, Chalfont St Peter 2
Wivenhoe Town 1, Windsor & Eton 2
Ware 0, Thame United 0
Replay Thame United 0, Ware 2
Dorking 2, Croydon Athletic 3
Metropolitan Police 3, Tilbury 3
Replay Tilbury 0, Metropolitan Police 2
Egham Town 1, Clapton 1
Egham Town removed from competition
Corinthian-Casuals 4, Horsham 0
Wealdstone 4, Northwood 1
Hornchurch 1, Cheshunt 1
Replay Cheshunt 3, Hornchurch 1
Cheshunt removed from competition

FIRST ROUND
Abingdon Town 0, Slough Town 1
Aylesbury United 1, Leyton Pennant 4
Barton Rovers 2, Camberley Town 1
Bognor Regis Town 2, Chesham United 2
Replay Chesham United 2, Bognor Regis Town 1
Boreham Wood 2, Enfield 0
Bromley 3, Tooting & Mitcham United 0
Carshalton Athletic 4, Banstead Athletic 3
Chertsey Town 3, Chalfont St Peter 2
Dulwich Hamlet 2, Sutton United 3
Harrow Borough 3, East Thurrock United 2
Hemel Hempstead Town 0, Romford 1
Heybridge Swifts 3, Walton & Hersham 2
Hitchin Town 0, Aldershot Town 1
Leatherhead 2, Corinthian-Casuals 1
Leighton Town 0, Uxbridge 2
Maidenhead United 3, Lewes 1
Purfleet 4, Oxford City 2
St Albans City 1, Hendon 4
Staines Town 1, Yeading 0
Wembley 1, Hampton 1
Replay Hampton 5, Wembley 0
Whyteleafe 0, Gravesend & Northfleet 5
Windsor & Eton 0, Hungerford Town 1
Worthing 0, Billericay Town 1
Grays Athletic 1, Metropolitan Police 3
Hornchurch 0, Canvey Island 3
Clapton 1, Marlow 5

Wealdstone 4, Berkhamsted Town 1
Wealdstone removed from competition
Ware 1, Dagenham & Redbridge 2
Croydon Athletic 2, Harlow Town 2
Replay Harlow Town 1, Croydon Athletic 1
Croydon Athletic won 5-4 on penalties
Molesey 1, Bishop's Stortford 2
Croydon 2, Basingstoke Town 4
Bedford Town 6, Ford United 2

SECOND ROUND
Boreham Wood 3, Hungerford Town 1
Heybridge Swifts 1, Bromley 2
Metropolitan Police 3, Marlow 4
Sutton United 4, Billericay Town 0
Carshalton Athletic 1, Uxbridge 2
Croydon Athletic 0, Maidenhead United 2
Berkhamsted Town 3, Canvey Island 1
Harrow Borough 1, Bedford Town 0
Chertsey Town 4, Aldershot Town 4
Replay Aldershot Town 5, Chertsey Town 0
Leatherhead 6, Leyton Pennant 4
Staines Town 1, Slough Town 3
Hendon 2, Gravesend & Northfleet 1
Chesham United 2, Dagenham & Redbridge 1
Bishop's Stortford 5, Basingstoke Town 4
Bishop's Stortford removed from competition
Romford 1, Barton Rovers 2
Purfleet 5, Hampton 0
Purfleet removed from competition

THIRD ROUND
Hampton 2, Leatherhead 5
Berkhamsted Town 3, Aldershot Town 3
Replay Aldershot Town 1, Berkhamsted Town 0
Marlow 2, Hendon 1
Barton Rovers 0, Boreham Wood 3
Maidenhead United 4, Slough Town 2
Chesham United 0, Bromley 3
Sutton United 2, Basingstoke Town 0
Uxbridge 1, Harrow Borough 0

FOURTH ROUND
Leatherhead 0, Aldershot Town 1
Boreham Wood 5, Marlow 1
Maidenhead United 5, Sutton United 4
Uxbridge 0, Bromley 2

SEMI-FINALS, FIRST LEG
Maidenhead United 2, Boreham Wood 3
Bromley 1, Aldershot Town 3

SEMI-FINALS, SECOND LEG
Aldershot Town 1, Bromley 2
Boreham Wood 1, Maidenhead United 0

FINAL
Aldershot Town 2, Boreham Wood 1
(at Slough Town)

PUMA CUP

FIRST ROUND
Basingstoke Town 4, Croydon 1
Leatherhead 0, Whyteleafe 1
Worthing 3, Maidenhead United 1
Slough Town 1, Bromley 0
Chesham United 4, Barton Rovers 1
Harrow Borough 1, Leyton Pennant 0
Wembley 0, Bishop's Stortford 2
Romford 1, Staines Town 0
Sutton United 1, Walton & Hersham 3
Boreham Wood 2, Braintree Town 0
Enfield 2, St Albans City 0
Grays Athletic 0, Wealdstone 1

SECOND ROUND
Basingstoke Town 3, Bognor Regis Town 0
Berkhamsted Town 1, Aylesbury United 1

Berkhamsted Town won 4-2 on penalties
Boreham Wood 1, Canvey Island 1
Canvey Island won 3-0 on penalties
Carshalton Athletic 2, Chertsey Town 0
Chesham United 2, Dagenham & Redbridge 1
Dulwich Hamlet 1, Hampton 0
Enfield 1, Bishop's Stortford 0
Harrow Borough 1, Romford 3
Hendon 2, Heybridge Swifts 1
Oxford City 2, Molesey 1
Purfleet 2, Billericay Town 1
Walton & Hersham 2, Slough Town 0
Uxbridge 0, Hitchin Town 2
Whyteleafe 0, Gravesend & Northfleet 1
Worthing 6, Aldershot Town 0
Yeading 2, Wealdstone 5

THIRD ROUND
Enfield 0, Purfleet 2
Oxford City 2, Wealdstone 4
Hitchin Town 3, Romford 1
Dulwich Hamlet 3, Basingstoke Town 1
Carshalton Athletic 2, Walton & Hersham 0
Whyteleafe 0, Worthing 2
Canvey Island 0, Hendon 2
Berkhamsted Town 0, Chesham United 5

FOURTH ROUND
Dulwich Hamlet 1, Wealdstone 0
Hitchin Town 0, Purfleet 2

Worthing 3, Carshalton Athletic 0
Chesham United 0, Hendon 1

SEMI-FINALS
Dulwich Hamlet 0, Hendon 2
Purfleet 0, Worthing 1

FINAL
Hendon 1, Worthing 0
(at Sutton United)

VANDANEL TROPHY

FIRST ROUND
Wokingham Town 0, Marlow 5
Barking 3, Ware 1
Bracknell Town 1, Thame United 3
Dorking 1, Lewes 2
Tilbury 1, Northwood 2
Windsor & Eton 1, Flackwell Heath 0
Wingate & Finchley 0, Leighton Town 4
Harlow Town 1, Ford United 0
Chalfont St Peter 4, Kingsbury Town 1
Egham Town 1, Hungerford Town 0

SECOND ROUND
Marlow 3, Lewes 2
Abingdon Town 2, Egham Town 3
Banstead Athletic 4, Camberley Town 2
Bedford Town 1, Cheshunt 0
Clapton 0, Edgware Town 2
Corinthian Casuals 0, Metropolitan Police 1
East Thurrock United 2, Hertford Town 3
Harlow Town 6, Aveley 0
Hemel Hempstead Town 0, Windsor & Eton 2
Hornchurch 1, Barking 3
Leighton Town 2, Northwood 1
Southall 2, Croydon Athletic 0
Thame United 3, Chalfont St Peter 2
Tooting & Mitcham United 4, Horsham 1

Tring Town 0, Epsom & Ewell 2
Wivenhoe Town 3, Witham Town 1

THIRD ROUND
Tooting & Mitcham United 3, Metropolitan Police 1
Wivenhoe Town 4, Barking 1
Banstead Athletic 1, Epsom & Ewell 4
Bedford Town 1, Leighton Town 3
Harlow Town 0, Edgware Town 1
Hertford Town 0, Windsor & Eton 2
Marlow 4, Egham Town 0
Thame United 1, Southall 3

FOURTH ROUND
Tooting & Mitcham United 2, Epsom & Ewell 1
Leighton Town 2, Wivenhoe Town 1
Southall 0, Marlow 1
Windsor & Eton 4, Edgware Town 1

SEMI-FINALS
Windsor & Eton 3, Marlow 0
Leighton Town 3, Tooting & Mitcham United 2

FINAL
Leighton Town 1, Windsor & Eton 0
(at Chesham United)

CUP ATTENDANCES

Ryman League Cup	17,833
Puma Cup	5,884
Vandanel Trophy	3,031

AWARDS

William Hill Managers of the Season Awards

Premier Division	John Rains	Sutton United
Division One	Jeff King	Canvey Island
Division Two	Jason Reed	Bedford Town
Division Three	Dennis Elliott	Ford United

FA UMBRO TROPHY 1998–99

FIRST ROUND

Belper Town v Radcliffe Borough	1-3
Farsley Celtic v Accrington Stanley	1-1, 1-4
Ashton United v Bloxwich Town	6-0
Stafford Rangers v Lancaster City	4-2
Redditch United v VS Rugby	3-0
Bilston Town v Hyde United	3-4
Hinckley United v Congleton Town	2-1
Stalybridge Celtic v Flixton	2-1
Sutton Coldfield Town v Bamber Bridge	2-2, 1-2
Bradford Park Avenue v Stourbridge	3-0
Eastwood Town v Runcorn	2-2, 1-2
Spennymoor United v Trafford	0-1
Gateshead v Paget Rangers	2-2, 0-1
Stocksbridge Park Steels v Boston United	1-1, 0-1
Marine v Frickley Athletic	2-3
Gresley Rovers v Stamford	1-0
Blyth Spartans v Whitby Town	2-2, 1-3
Burton Albion v Grantham Town	0-0, 3-0
Halesowen Town v Guiseley	0-2
Blakenall v Ilkeston Town	2-0
Gretna v Solihull Borough	2-1
Winsford United v Gainsborough Trinity	0-1
Bishop Auckland v Matlock Town	4-2
Dagenham & Redbridge v Wealdstone	1-0
(abandoned 18 minutes; waterlogged pitch)	1-1, 5-0
Maidenhead United v Yate Town	1-1, 2-1
Whyteleafe v Bishop's Stortford	3-1
Dorchester Town v Bath City	0-2
Bashley v Staines Town	4-0
Molesey v Boreham Wood	1-2
Cirencester Town v Cinderford Town	1-0
Braintree Town v Fleet Town	4-1
Walton & Hersham v Weston-Super-Mare	2-2, 0-2
Salisbury City v Carshalton Athletic	2-1
Chertsey Town v Gloucester City	0-5
Folkestone Invicta v Hampton	2-1
Weymouth v Kings Lynn	1-0
Harrow Borough v Cambridge City	4-2
Leyton Pennant v Purfleet	4-3
Canvey Island v Wisbech Town	1-0
Erith & Belvedere v Newport (IW)	1-1, 3-4
Croydon v Baldock Town	0-2
Wembley v Witney Town	1-2
Hastings Town v Chelmsford City	2-2, 1-0
St Leonards v Enfield	2-4
Worcester City v Billericay Town	2-1
Brackley Town v Grays Athletic	1-4
Leatherhead v Crawley Town	1-2
Newport AFC v Heybridge Swifts	2-4

SECOND ROUND

Gainsborough Trinity v Harrogate Town	4-1
Altrincham v Burscough	2-2, 3-1
Burton Albion v Bamber Bridge	5-0
Kidderminster Harriers v Lincoln United	2-2, 1-2
Hinckley United v Gresley Rovers	2-0
Trafford v Chorley	1-3
Witton Albion v Bradford Park Avenue	0-2
Tamworth v Stalybridge Celtic	1-3
Doncaster Rovers v Frickley Athletic	0-2
Redditch United v Corby Town	3-2
Radcliffe Borough v Great Harwood Town	5-1
Boston United v Worksop Town	1-1, 4-0
Bromsgrove Rovers v Hednesford Town	1-2
Colwyn Bay v Stafford Rangers	3-2
Bishop Auckland v Guiseley	1-1, 1-3
Nuneaton Borough v Hyde United	1-1, 0-1
Runcorn v Moor Green	3-0
Atherstone United v Southport	0-0, 1-2
Hucknall Town v Barrow	2-1
Alfreton Town v Droylsden	1-2
Northwich Victoria v Netherfield Kendal	3-0
Emley v Whitley Bay	1-0
Blakenall v Telford United	1-1, 1-2
Paget Rangers v Accrington Stanley	0-2
Ashton United v Leek Town	1-0
Gretna v Shepshed Dynamo	1-1, 0-2
Whitby Town v Bedworth United	4-0
Leigh RMI v Morecambe	4-1
Cirencester Town v Dulwich Hamlet	0-3

Stevenage Borough v Uxbridge	4-0
Rushden & Diamonds v Bath City	2-0
Hayes v Folkestone Invicta	1-1, 2-3
Merthyr Tydfil v Basingstoke Town	0-2
Gloucester City v Kingstonian	1-2
Ashford Town v Hastings Town	0-2
Aldershot Town v Bromley	3-1
Romford v Worthing	3-3, 3-4
Maidenhead United v Clevedon Town	1-0
Fisher Athletic v Worcester City	1-1, 1-5
Dover Athletic v Welling United	4-1
Kettering Town v Andover	4-0
Forest Green Rovers v Boreham Wood	4-1
Yeovil Town v Tonbridge Angels	1-0
Leyton Pennant v St Albans City	0-3
Margate v Havant & Waterlooville	1-3
Slough Town v Baldock Town	3-1
Woking v Salisbury City	2-1
Farnborough Town v Dartford	1-1, 2-1
Cheltenham Town v Bashley	2-1
Newport (IW) v Gravesend & Northfleet	1-0
Hereford United v Hitchin Town	1-1, 1-2
Heybridge Swifts v Sutton United	1-2
Crawley Town v Sittingbourne	2-2, 5-1
Dagenham & Redbridge v Barton Rovers	3-2
Weymouth v Braintree Town	2-1
Aylesbury United v Harrow Borough	1-1, 3-2
Racing Club Warwick v Raunds Town	1-1, 0-2
Grays Athletic v Whyteleafe	2-3
Evesham United v Canvey Island	1-1, 0-5
Oxford City v Enfield	0-1
Bognor Regis Town v Witney Town	1-3
Weston-Super-Mare v Berkhamsted Town	1-1, 2-0
Yeading v Chesham United	3-3, 0-4
Hendon v Rothwell Town	1-1, 2-1

THIRD ROUND

Radcliffe Borough v Northwich Victoria	1-2
Colwyn Bay v Hednesford Town	1-1, 2-2
Colwyn Bay won 5-4 on penalties	
Shepshed Dynamo v Emley	1-1, 1-3
Altrincham v Burton Albion	1-0
Accrington Stanley v Ashton United	1-3
Stalybridge Celtic v Hinckley United	0-3
Lincoln United v Bradford Park Avenue	2-5
Whitby Town v Frickley Athletic	2-1
Droylsden v Telford United	2-3
Chorley v Guiseley	1-1, 1-2
Leigh RMI v Southport	0-1
Runcorn v Hyde United	2-1
Gainsborough Trinity v Boston United	1-4
Hucknall Town v Redditch United	1-3
Basingstoke Town v Yeovil Town	0-2
Hitchin Town v Enfield	3-3, 1-0
Worthing v Hendon	0-2
Hastings Town v St Albans City	0-3
Weston-Super-Mare v Raunds Town	2-2, 1-0
Stevenage Borough v Dover Athletic	3-2
Forest Green Rovers v Witney Town	4-0
Weymouth v Sutton United	1-0
Kingstonian v Kettering Town	5-2
Crawley Town v Chesham United	2-3
Dulwich Hamlet v Whyteleafe	1-2
Cheltenham Town v Canvey Island	2-1
Aldershot Town v Maidenhead United	1-0
Slough Town v Rushden & Diamonds	1-2
Aylesbury United v Newport (IW)	2-0
Dagenham & Redbridge v Farnborough Town	1-1, 1-1
Dagenham & Redbridge won 4-2 on penalties	
Havant & Waterlooville v Worcester City	0-1
Woking v Folkestone Invicta	8-4

FOURTH ROUND

Runcorn v Southport	2-3
Dagenham & Redbridge v Telford United	4-0
Chesham United v Hendon	0-2
Yeovil Town v Hinckley United	3-2
Woking v Rushden & Diamonds	0-0, 2-1
Ashton United v St Albans City	2-2, 1-2
Colwyn Bay v Bradford Park Avenue	3-1

Hitchin Town v Weston-Super-Mare	2-1
Aylesbury United v Whitby Town	0-1
Boston United v Redditch United	2-0
Whyteleafe v Kingstonian	0-3
Guiseley v Emley	0-2
Aldershot Town v Altrincham	1-2
Weymouth v Forest Green Rovers	1-2
Cheltenham Town v Stevenage Borough	0-0, 1-0
(abandoned 45 minutes; snow)	0-0
Cheltenham Town won 5-4 on penalties	
Northwich Victoria v Worcester City	1-0

FIFTH ROUND

Hitchin Town v Forest Green Rovers	1-2
Northwich Victoria v Colwyn Bay	3-1
Boston United v Altrincham	2-0
Kingstonian v Yeovil Town	1-0
Emley v Whitby Town	2-0
Cheltenham Town v Hendon	3-0
Woking v Southport	0-0, 0-1
Dagenham & Redbridge v St Albans City	1-2

SIXTH ROUND

Northwich Victoria v Kingstonian	0-2
Emley v Cheltenham Town	0-1

Forest Green Rovers v Southport	4-1
St Albans City v Boston United	2-1

SEMI-FINAL (First Leg)

Kingstonian v Cheltenham Town	2-2
St Albans City v Forest Green Rovers	1-1

SEMI-FINAL (Second Leg)

Cheltenham Town v Kingstonian	1-3
Forest Green Rovers v St Albans City	3-2

FINAL (at Wembley)

15 MAY

Forest Green Rovers (0) 0

Kingstonian (0) 1 *(Mustafa 49)*   20,037

Forest Green Rovers: Shuttlewood; Hedges, Kilgour, Forbes, Bailey (Smart), Honor (Winter), Wigg (Cook), Drysdale, Sykes, McGregor, Mehew.
Kingstonian: Farrelly; Stewart, Crossley, Harris, Mustafa, Patterson, Luckett, Rattray, Pitcher, Akuamoah, Leworthy (Francis).
Referee: A. Wilkie (Chester-le-Street).

Kingstonian players at Wembley following their FA Umbro Trophy win over Forest Green Rovers. (Actionimages)

FA CARLSBERG VASE 1998–99

FIRST QUALIFYING ROUND

Goole AFC v Fleetwood Freeport	1-0
Marske United v Shildon	1-5
Woodley Sports w.o. v Blackpool (Wren) Rovers withdrew	
Sheffield v Consett	1-5
Liversedge v Chadderton	3-2
Glasshoughton Welfare v Maltby Main	2-4
Newcastle Blue Star v Ossett Town	1-3
Parkgate v Shotton Comrades	0-2
Kirby Muxloe v Stafford Town	1-0
Ludlow Town v Nettleham	1-3
Boston Town v Handrahan Timbers	1-2
Studley BKL v Kington Town	0-8
Malvern Town v Bilston Community College	2-0
Highfield Rangers v Barrow Town	3-1
Downes Sports v Stourport Swifts	1-3
Mickleover Sports v Kings Norton Town	3-2
Mildenhall Town v Toddington Rovers	4-1
Buckingham Athletic v Viking Sports	4-1
Kempston Rovers v Hullbridge Sports	0-1
Bedford United v Ruislip Manor	1-2
Sawbridgeworth Town v Wivenhoe Town	1-2
Islington St Marys v Burnham	2-1
Kingsbury Town v Milton Keynes City	0-2
Downham Town v East Thurrock United	0-1
Cockfosters v Stowmarket Town	1-2
Brimsdown Rovers v Southend Manor	1-3
Slade Green v Merstham	0-1
Sheppey United v Erith Town	3-2
Lordswood v Newbury AFC	1-3
Greenwich Borough v Beckenham Town	1-2
East Cowes Victoria v Hungerford Town	1-2
Redhill v Whitehawk	2-1
Blackfield & Langley v Eastleigh	1-4
Cray Wanderers v Abingdon United	0-1
Fareham Town v Lancing	3-0
Truro City v Willand Rovers	2-0
Street v Frome Town	2-1
Harrow Hill v Pershore Town	1-3
Highworth Town v Brislington	0-2

SECOND QUALIFYING ROUND

Shildon v Maine Road	2-3
Crook Town v Bootle	2-3
Pickering Town v Washington	1-2
South Shields v Ashington	1-0
Armthorpe Welfare v Goole	0-2
Prescot Cables v Holker Old Boys	5-1
Tadcaster Albion v Selby Town	1-3
Skelmersdale United v Liversedge	1-2
Thackley v Brodsworth	0-1
Stockton v Chester-Le-Street Town	2-4
Cheadle Town v Ramsbottom United	2-3
Rossendale United v East Manchester	2-1
Hall Road Rangers v St Helens Town	1-2
Yorkshire Amateur v Vauxhall GM	0-8
Grimethorpe Miners Welfare v Hallam	0-3
Peterlee Newtown v Rossington Main	2-3
Salford City v Northallerton Town	2-0
Hebburn v Ossett Albion	0-1
Garforth Town v Willington	5-1
Ryhope CA v Morpeth Town	0-2
Louth United v Jarrow Roofing Boldon CA	2-1
Maltby Main v Brandon United	0-3
Atherton Collieries v Harrogate Railway	4-4, 1-2
Oldham Town v Easington Colliery	2-5
Eccleshill United v Penrith	5-0
Ossett Town v Whickham	2-0
Woodley Sports v Prudhoe Town	2-0
Shotton Comrades v West Allotment Celtic	1-3
Evenwood Town v Consett	1-3
Bacup Borough v Darwen	1-0
(abandoned 60 minutes: floodlight failure)	
Worsbro Bridge MW v Horden CW	1-3
	3-1
Nantwich Town v Glapwell	4-1
Rushall Olympic v Nettleham	3-1
Pelsall Villa v Sandiacre Town	2-2, 2-1
Gornal Athletic v Walsall Wood	4-0
Ibstock Welfare v Stourport Swifts	3-1
Lye Town v Gedling Town	4-4, 0-3

West Midlands Police v Stewarts & Lloyds	2-2, 1-0
Bridgnorth Town v Highfield Rangers	1-5
Kings Heath v Bolehall Swifts	1-2
Wednesfield v Kirby Muxloe	4-5
Glossop North End v Sandwell Borough	2-1
Long Eaton United v Oldbury United	1-4
Mickleover Sports v Shirebrook Town	3-3, 3-1
Rainworth MW v Holbeach United	3-0
Blackstone v Leek CSOB	4-2
Friar Lane OB v Stratford Town	3-4
Holwell Sports v Highgate United	10-1
Willenhall Town v Barwell	2-0
Meir KA v Malvern Town	8-0
Long Buckby v Handrahan Timbers	2-5
Borrowash Victoria v Heanor Town	0-1
Chasetown v Tividale	7-0
Knypersley Victoria v Arnold Town	1-1, 0-2
Newcastle Town v Desborough Town	1-1, 2-1
Staveley MW v Dunkirk	2-1
St Andrews v Halesowen Harriers	3-2
Stapenhill v Anstey Nomads	1-0
Westfields v Shifnal Town	2-1
Boldmere St Michaels v Bourne Town	3-0
Kington Town v Kimberley Town	6-4
Mildenhall Town v Brightlingsea United	2-0
Swaffham Town v Ruislip Manor	2-1
Flackwell Heath v Stansted	1-1, 1-4
Bury Town v Beaconsfield SYCOB	1-3
March Town United v Clapton	1-2
Stowmarket Town v Brook House	3-0
Wingate & Finchley v Ilford	0-4
Yaxley v Soham Town Rangers	7-2
Clacton Town v Hadleigh United	3-1
Islington St Marys v Southend Manor	2-1
Barkingside v Southall	2-1
Biggleswade Town v Bedford Town	1-4
Needham Market v Saffron Walden Town	1-2
Amersham Town v Tiptree United	1-2
Potton United v Wellingborough Town	0-5
Somersham Town v Hornchurch	0-6
East Thurrock United v Felixstowe Port & Town	1-0
Wivenhoe Town v Harlow Town	2-4
Tilbury v Burnham Ramblers	4-0
Thetford Town v Hoddesdon Town	2-0
Fakenham Town v Norwich United	2-0
Edgware Town v Harwich & Parkeston	4-2
Concord Rangers v Ware	1-3
Milton Keynes City v Letchworth	0-2
Watton United v Wootton Blue Cross	1-0
Newmarket Town v Cornard United	3-0
Buckingham Athletic v Witham Town	3-1
Bowers United v Maldon Town	4-1
St Neots Town v Hullbridge Sports	4-4, 1-1
St Neots Town won 5-4 on penalties	
Royston Town v Banbury United	2-1
Warboys Town v Chalfont St Peter	0-3
Tring Town v Ford United	0-1
Great Yarmouth Town v Halstead Town	1-0
Bicester Town v Hertford Town	2-2, 1-0
Welwyn Garden City v London Colney	3-2
Waltham Abbey v Ipswich Wanderers	3-0
Eynesbury Rovers v Haverhill Rovers	4-1
Basildon United v Langford	2-1
Ford Sports Daventry v Hillingdon Borough	4-2
Whitton United v Leighton Town	0-3
Harpenden Town v Stanway Rovers	3-0
Aveley v Gorleston	3-0
Hanwell Town v Lowestoft Town	1-2
Hemel Hempstead Town v Cheshunt	2-4
Merstham v Eastbourne Town	2-1
Ringmer v Whitchurch United	2-0
Kintbury Ranges v Hassocks	2-3
Totton AFC v Cobham	0-1
Epsom & Ewell v Bracknell Town	2-1
Wick v Hailsham Town	5-0
Raynes Park Vale v Croydon Athletic	0-0, 0-1
Carterton Town v Sidley United	0-0, 0-1
Didcot Town v Farnham Town	5-3
Ash United v Three Bridges	2-1
Dorking v Chichester City	1-2
Redhill v Hythe United	3-2
Abingdon United v East Grinstead Town	2-0

Romsey Town v Hungerford Town	1-9
East Preston v Pagham	1-2
Portsmouth Royal Navy v Chipstead	0-2
Metropolitan Police v Fareham Town	0-1
Oakwood v Southwick	2-4
Chatham Town v Cove	2-4
Ramsgate v Newbury AFC	3-0
Corinthian-Casuals v Crowborough Athletic	5-1
Saltdean United v Windsor & Eton	2-4
Sheppey United v BAT Sports	2-0
Beckenham Town v Horsham YMCA	0-2
Sandhurst Town v Bournemouth	4-2
Camberley Town v Portfield	1-0
Reading Town v Ashford Town (Middlesex)	2-1
Bedfont v Selsey	3-1
Lewes v Egham Town	1-4
Gosport Borough v Langney Sports	1-0
Horsham v Canterbury City	0-2
Thamesmead Town v Christchurch	1-0
North Leigh v Arundel	4-1
Godalming & Guildford v Deal Town	0-4
Tunbridge Wells v Wantage Town	3-0
Shoreham v Eastleigh	0-3
Brockenhurst v Chard Town	5-1
Westbury United v Melksham Town	1-4
Bemerton Heath Harlequins v Warminster Town	3-0
Street v Devizes Town	0-2
Brislington v Glastonbury	4-0
Downton v Pershore Town	1-2
Newquay v Hallen	3-2
Backwell United v Paulton Rovers	0-2
Bideford v Welton Rovers	2-1
Barnstaple Town v Odd Down	1-1, 4-1
St Blazey v Almondsbury Town	5-1
Bridport v Calne Town	7-2
Elmore v Ilfracombe Town	1-4
Wellington Town v Shortwood United	1-0
Bridgwater Town v Falmouth Town	0-1
Keynsham Town v Minehead Town	1-3
Tuffley Rovers v Truro City	0-1
Bishop Sutton v Dawlish Town	0-1
Fairford Town v Torrington	2-0

FIRST ROUND

West Auckland Town v Bootle	1-0
Maine Road v Brodsworth	2-2, 3-1
St Helens Town v Brigg Town	2-1
Curzon Ashton v Hallam	1-3
Paulton Victoria v Louth United	0-2
Liversedge v Rossendale United	4-2
Guisborough Town v Ossett Town	1-2
Chester-Le-Street Town v Durham City	2-1
Washington v Prescot Cables	1-6
Warrington Town v Ossett Albion	3-1
Selby Town v Consett	2-3
Morpeth Town v Denaby United	2-1
Rossington Main v Goole	2-5
Seaham Red Star v West Allotment Celtic	3-1
Easington Colliery v Salford City	2-0
Atherton LR v Billingham Synthonia	1-5
Darwen v Eccleshill United	1-3
Worsbro Bridge MW v Garforth Town	1-4
Ramsbottom United v Woodley Sports	4-1
Brandon United v Harrogate Railway	5-1
Vauxhall GM v South Shields	1-0
Arnold Town v Kirby Muxloe	3-1
West Midlands Police v Holwell Sports	1-3
Stratford Town v Chasetown	1-2
Boldmere St Michaels v Mickleover Sports	2-3
Rainworth MW v Rushall Olympic	0-7
Gornal Athletic v Staveley MW	0-2
Ibstock Welfare v Westfields	2-1
Stapenhill v St Andrews	1-2
Gedling Town v Kington Town	0-3
Rocester v Handrahan Timbers	5-0
Northampton Spencer v Nantwich Town	2-4
Pelsall Villa v Oldbury United	1-3
Heanor Town v Blackstone	7-2
Birstall United v Glossop North End	3-0
Bolehall Swifts v Ely City	2-0
Meir KA v Willenhall Town	2-0
Newcastle Town v Highfield Rangers	0-1
Redhill v Sheppey United	2-1
Welwyn Garden City v Windsor & Eton	1-3
Bowers United v Waltham Abbey	3-0

Newmarket Town v Barking	2-2, 2-2
Newmarket Town won 4-2 on penalties	
Ilford v Yaxley	0-3
Swaffham Town v Royston Town	1-2
Hungerford Town v Gosport Borough	1-0
Tunbridge Wells v Leighton Town	2-1
Barkingside v Croydon Athletic	1-0
Fareham Town v Letchworth	0-1
Buckingham Town v Marlow	4-2
St Neots Town v Pagham	4-1
Lowestoft Town v Wellingborough Town	3-1
Canterbury City v Northwood	0-1
Tiptree United v Cowes Sports	4-1
Sidley United v Clapton	4-2
Basildon United v Beaconsfield SYCOB	3-0
Ware v Hassocks	0-3
Stowmarket Town v Littlehampton Town	6-1
Aveley v Whitstable Town	2-1
Fakenham Town v Egham Town	3-2
Merstham v Deal Town	1-5
Saffron Walden Town v Chalfont St Peter	1-0
Buckingham Athletic v Islington St Marys	3-2
Hornchurch v Cheshunt	0-1
Thetford Town v Corinthian-Casuals	3-2
Diss Town v Edgware Town	1-0
Abingdon United v North Leigh	0-2
Horsham YMCA v Ringmer	1-0
Ford United v Bedfont	4-4, 1-0
Cobham v Peacehaven & Telscombe	6-2
Reading Town v Bicester Town	1-2
Thamesmead Town v Watton United	5-0
Cove v Camberley Town	0-6
Didcot Town v Harlow Town	0-3
Tilbury v Wick	1-3
Great Yarmouth Town v East Thurrock United	0-2
Mildenhall Town v Sandhurst Town	3-1
Chipstead v Arlesey Town	3-2
Thatcham Town v Chichester City	4-0
Eastleigh v Clacton Town	0-1
Stotfold v Ford Sports Daventry	1-0
Harpenden Town v Ramsgate	0-1
Epsom & Ewell v Stansted	1-1, 5-0
Southwick v Ash United	2-4
Bedford Town v Eynesbury Rovers	3-1
Devizes Town v Brislington	0-1
Minehead Town v Falmouth Town	2-1
EFC Cheltenham v Barnstaple Town	1-2
Newquay v Brockenhurst	2-0
Fairford Town v Truro City	2-1
St Blazey v Mangotsfield United	1-0
Bideford v Wellington Town	2-3
Pershore Town v Ilfracombe Town	0-2
Dawlish Town v Bodmin Town	3-1
Bridport v Paulton Rovers	2-1
Melksham Town v Wimborne Town	3-1
Bemerton Heath Harlequins v Chippenham Town	2-1

SECOND ROUND

Ossett Town v Seaham Red Star	2-3
Garforth Town v Prescot Cables	4-2
Bedlington Terriers v Ramsbottom United	3-0
North Ferriby United v Workington	0-1
Billingham Synthonia v Tow Law Town	2-5
Clitheroe v West Auckland Town	1-0
Eccleshill United v Hallam	3-2
Dunston FB v Maine Road	2-1
Vauxhall GM v Easington Colliery	4-2
Mossley v Consett	3-1
St Helens Town v Morpeth Town	2-2, 4-0
Brandon United v Liversedge	3-1
Billingham Town v Chester-Le-Street Town	2-1
Warrington Town v Louth United	2-0
Heanor Town v Rushall Olympic	4-2
Mickleover Sports v Stotfold	2-1
Spalding United v Rocester	5-2
Birstall United v Oadby Town	0-1
Highfield Rangers v Holwell Sports	3-1
Staveley MW v Nantwich Town	1-0
Arnold Town v Wroxham	3-4
Chasetown v Histon	1-0
St Andrews v Buxton	3-2
Goole v Meir KA	3-1
Ibstock Welfare v Bedford Town	0-5
Kidsgrove Athletic v Bolehall Swifts	5-3
Kington Town v Oldbury United	4-5

Fakenham Town v Epsom & Ewell	2-1
Lowestoft Town v Tooting & Mitcham United	1-3
Saffron Walden Town v Sudbury Town	1-2
Tunbridge Wells v Ash United	2-6
Abingdon Town v Letchworth	0-1
Banstead Athletic v Hassocks	2-1
Thatcham Town v Ramsgate	1-3
Barkingside v Tiptree United	2-1
Harlow Town v Great Wakering Rovers	4-3
Woodbridge Town v Redhill	3-2
Mildenhall Town v Herne Bay	0-1
Thamesmead Town v Brache Sparta	1-2
Newmarket Town v Aveley	5-0
Northwood v Buckingham Athletic	3-1
Clacton Town v Buckingham Town	3-1
Burgess Hill Town v Camberley Town	2-2, 0-4
Chipstead v Windsor & Eton	7-2
Thetford Town v Sudbury Wanderers	0-4
Horsham YMCA v Deal Town	0-5
Royston Town v North Leigh	1-0
Potters Bar Town v Ford United	0-1
Cobham v Stowmarket Town	5-2
Bowers United v Basildon United	1-0
Diss Town v Yaxley	4-4, 3-1
Wokingham Town v Sidley United	0-1
Cheshunt v Wick	0-1
East Thurrock United v St Neots Town	2-1
Bicester Town v Thame United	1-3
Bemerton Heath Harlequins v Swindon Supermarine	3-0
Newquay v Hungerford Town	1-3
Taunton Town v Bridport	4-0
Ilfracombe Town v Tiverton Town	0-5
Minehead Town v Melksham Town	0-2
Dawlish Town v Fairford Town	3-2
Lymington & New Milton v Wellington Town	1-0
Brislington v Porthleven	3-3, 0-1
Barnstaple Town v St Blazey	1-5

THIRD ROUND

Highfield Rangers v Garforth Town	1-2
Staveley MW v Dunston FB	0-2
Bedlington Terriers v Mickleover Sports	4-1
Abandoned 54 minutes; floodlight failure,	0-3
Abandoned; floodlight failure,	2-0
St Helens Town v Eccleshill United	3-1
Brandon United v Goole	2-3
Warrington Town v Heanor Town	2-1
Mossley v St Andrews	3-0
Billingham Town v Clitheroe	0-2
Seaham Red Star v Vauxhall GM	0-2
Workington v Tow Law Town	1-1, 4-3
Kidsgrove Athletic v Oadby Town	3-1
East Thurrock United v Harlow Town	3-4
Royston Town v Sudbury Town	0-3
Thame United v Letchworth	2-1
Sudbury Wanderers v Brache Sparta	3-1
Bowers United v Diss Town	4-0
Barkingside v Oldbury United	1-7
Spalding United v Northwood	2-2, 1-2
Fakenham Town v Bedford Town	1-4
Chasetown v Wroxham	0-1
Ford United v Newmarket Town	4-3
Woodbridge Town v Clacton Town	1-0
Melksham Town v Ash United	1-2
Herne Bay v Banstead Athletic	0-2

Taunton Town v Dawlish Town	1-0
Deal Town v Tiverton Town	1-2
St Blazey v Porthleven	2-1
Ramsgate v Bemerton Heath Harlequins	0-3
Lymington & New Milton v Hungerford Town	4-0
Chipstead v Tooting & Mitcham United	2-2, 2-3
Wick v Sidley United	3-2
Cobham v Camberley Town	1-2

FOURTH ROUND

Sudbury Wanderers v Garforth Town	2-0
Clitheroe v St Helens Town	1-0
Bedlington Terriers v Banstead Athletic	7-3
Sudbury Town v Northwood	0-1
Wick v Vauxhall GM	0-5
Warrington Town v Thame United	0-2
Camberley Town v Tooting & Mitcham United	1-0
Goole v Bemerton Heath Harlequins	0-1
Harlow Town v Taunton Town	1-2
Ash United v Tiverton Town	1-5
Bedford Town v Wroxham	3-1
Ford United v Kidsgrove Athletic	4-2
Lymington & New Milton v Mossley	1-0
St Blazey v Dunston FB	1-5
Bowers United v Woodbridge Town	1-2
Oldbury United v Workington	0-4

FIFTH ROUND

Woodbridge Town v Camberley Town	2-1
Bedford Town v Tiverton Town	1-2
Dunston FB v Lymington & New Milton	1-4
Ford United v Bedlington Terriers	1-2
Workington v Sudbury Wanderers	3-0
Thame United v Vauxhall GM	2-1
Taunton Town v Northwood	5-2
Clitheroe v Bemerton Heath Harlequins	1-0

SIXTH ROUND

Taunton Town v Lymington & New Milton	3-1
Tiverton Town v Clitheroe	4-0
Woodbridge Town v Thame United	0-2
Bedlington Terriers v Workington	1-0

SEMI-FINALS (Two Legs)

Taunton Town v Tiverton Town	0-3, 1-2
Bedlington Terriers v Thame United	5-0, 0-0

FINAL (at Wembley)

16 MAY

Bedlington Terriers (0) 0

Tiverton Town (0) 1 *(Rogers 88)*   13,878

Bedlington Terriers: O'Connor; Bowes, Melrose, Teasdale, Pike, Bond, Cross, Middleton (Renforth), Boon (Ludlow), Milner, Gibb.
Tiverton Town: Edwards; Tallon, Tatterton, Saunders, Fallon, Nancekivell (Rogers), Daly, Conning (Pears), Leonard, Varley, Everett.
Referee: W. Burns (Scarborough).

THE TIMES FA YOUTH CUP 1998–99

FIRST QUALIFYING ROUND

Prescot Cables v Yorkshire Amateur	2-0
Lancaster City v Stocksbridge Park Steels	1-1, 1-0
Warrington Town withdrew v Runcorn w.o.	
Harrogate Town v Brigg Town	1-1, 3-1
Northwich Victoria v Rossendale United	3-0
Altrincham v Marine	1-0
Flixton v Chadderton	1-0
Farsley Celtic v Stalybridge Celtic	5-0
Southport withdrew v Worksop Town w.o.	
Garforth Town v Ashton United	5-1
Walsall Wood v Tamworth	2-0
Racing Club Warwick v Stourbridge	2-2, 3-1
Halesowen Town v Nantwich Town	1-2
Hinckley United v Congleton Town	5-3
Bedworth United v Bolehall Swifts	1-2
Nuneaton Borough v Boldmere St Michaels	3-0
VS Rugby v Wednesfield	1-5
Lincoln United v Barwell Athletic	2-2, 6-1
Burton Albion v Atherstone United	8-2
Belper Town v Kidderminster Harriers	2-7
Matlock Town v Holwell Sports	0-1
Gornal Athletic v Chasetown	2-1
Gresley Rovers v Bromsgrove Rovers	3-1
Birstall United v Redditch United	3-0
Concord Rangers v Stevenage Borough	2-7
Rushden & Diamonds v Cheshunt	3-0
Staines Town v Hayes	1-3
Witham Town v Harpenden Town	0-3
Newmarket Town v Leyton	3-1
Ilford v Hemel Hempstead Town	2-2, 2-6
Bedford Town v Harlow Town	3-1
Southend Manor v Barking	5-0
Beaconsfield SYCOB v Braintree Town	2-0
Chelmsford City v Kingsbury Town	5-1
Cambridge City v Northwood	4-0
Wisbech Town v Fakenham Town	3-1
Hampton w.o. v Royston Town withdrew	
Somersham Town v Bishop's Stortford	1-4
Great Wakering Rovers v Northampton Spencer	5-2
Romford v Hendon	2-1
Hanwell Town withdrew v Burnham Ramblers w.o.	
Wivenhoe Town withdrew v Wembley w.o.	
Hillingdon Borough v Wellingborough Town	4-4, 1-2
Uxbridge v Marlow	3-4
Hitchin Town v Welwyn Garden City	3-1
Hullbridge Sports v Buckingham Town	5-0
Ruislip Manor v Sudbury Wanderers	6-1
Bracknell Town v Merstham	6-0
Basingstoke Town v Molesey	0-0, 0-3
Bromley v Eastleigh	4-3
Burgess Hill Town v Sutton United	2-2, 0-1
Reading Town v Fisher Athletic	0-0, 7-0
Wokingham Town v Blackfield & Langley	2-6
Ashford Town (Middlesex) v Croydon	2-0
Eastbourne Town v Whitstable Town	5-1
Walton & Hersham v Thamesmead Town	4-2
Tonbridge Angels v Romsey Town	4-2
Dartford v Pagham	3-1
Crawley Town v Croydon Athletic	2-4
Erith & Belvedere v Chatham Town	2-4
Saltdean United v North Leigh	3-4
Newbury AFC v Leatherhead	0-0, 5-3
Langney Sports v Banstead Athletic	2-6
Dorking v Folkestone Invicta	1-1, 0-1
Aldershot Town v Bashley	4-1
Chichester City v Kingstonian	
Woking w.o. v Hythe United withdrew	
Oxford City w.o. v Slough Town withdrew	
Camberley Town v Chipstead	1-4
Didcot Town v Maidenhead United	3-0
Herne Bay v Thatcham Town	1-2
Welling United v Tooting & Mitcham United	3-2
Odd Down v Evesham United	1-4
Salisbury City v Cinderford Town	2-1
Forest Green Rovers v Gloucester City	1-1, 2-1
Yate Town v Chippenham Town	1-2
Malvern Town v Weston-Super-Mare	2-6
Pershore Town v Weymouth	2-0

Newport AFC v Yeovil Town	4-0
Cirencester Town v Paulton Rovers	4-0

SECOND QUALIFYING ROUND

Runcorn v Northwich Victoria	2-2, 2-0
Prescot Cables v Lancaster City	1-1, 0-0
Lancaster City won 5-4 on penalties.	
Harrogate Town v Emley	1-1, 1-2
Altrincham v Frickley Athletic	3-0
Flixton v Farsley Celtic	1-2
Worksop Town v Garforth Town	0-1
Billingham Town v Burscough	1-2
Wednesfield withdrew v Racing Club Warwick w.o.	
Gornal Athletic v Walsall Wood	0-2
Bolehall Swifts v Leek Town	4-1
Birstall United v Hinckley United	3-5
Willenhall Town v Kidderminster Harriers	1-7
Bilston Town v Holwell Sports	4-3
Nuneaton Borough v Nantwich Town	1-1, 2-0
Gresley Rovers v Burton Albion	0-2
Lincoln United v Ilkeston Town	3-2
Viking Sports v Beaconsfield SYCOB	4-1
Cambridge City w.o. v Hoddesdon Town withdrew	
Wembley v Waltham Abbey	10-1
Chesham United v Sudbury Wanderers	6-0
Hampton v Chelmsford City	7-1
St Albans City v Hullbridge Sports	2-2, 1-3
Hemel Hempstead Town v Rushden & Diamonds	1-2
Newmarket Town v Ipswich Wanderers	1-2
Maldon Town v Potters Bar Town	2-3
Bishop's Stortford v Basildon United	1-0
Hornchurch v Banbury United	7-0
Hayes v Soham Town Rangers	5-0
Leighton Town v Southend Manor	6-1
Bowers United v Harpenden Town	1-1, 1-4
Wellingborough Town v Amersham Town	6-1
Stanway Rovers v Bedford Town	0-3
Histon v Stevenage Borough	1-5
Hitchin Town v Marlow	4-1
Great Wakering Rovers v Rothwell Town	2-2, 0-2
Romford v Wisbech Town	2-2, 3-0
Islington St Marys v Burnham Ramblers	2-4
Bedfont v Walton & Hersham	1-3
Dartford v Corinthian Casuals	6-0
Bashley v Thatcham Town	1-0
Sittingbourne v Didcot Town	4-3
Chatham Town v Tonbridge Angels	3-1
Carshalton Athletic v Chipstead	3-3, 4-6
Wokingham Town v Basingstoke Town	0-3
Fisher Athletic v Horsham YMCA	2-0
Thame United v Cobham	4-1
North Leigh v Dulwich Hamlet	1-1, 0-1
Margate v Abingdon United	0-3
Eastleigh w.o. v Hastings Town withdrew	
Farnborough Town v Eastbourne Town	7-1
Three Bridges v Burgess Hill Town	0-5
Chichester City v Dover Athletic	1-1, 2-4
Welling United v Croydon	4-1
Southwick v Bracknell Town	0-3
Oxford City v Woking	2-0
Leatherhead v Egham Town	12-0
Langney Sports v Crawley Town	1-0
Whyteleafe v Folkestone Invicta	5-6
Chippenham Town v Cirencester Town	0-4
Weston-Super-Mare v Mangotsfield United	4-2
Evesham United v Forest Green Rovers	2-4
Hereford United v Warminster Town	5-0
Cheltenham Town v Salisbury City	4-2
Pershore Town v Newport AFC	0-4

THIRD QUALIFYING ROUND

Burscough v Farsley Celtic	1-0
Lincoln United v Lancaster City	5-1
Altrincham v Emley	5-0
Garforth Town v Runcorn	1-6
Burton Albion v Racing Club Warwick	0-2
Cheltenham Town v Nuneaton Borough	1-1, 0-6
Bolehall Swifts v Walsall Wood	2-3
Bilston Town v Kidderminster Harriers	2-3
Cirencester Town v Newport AFC	2-0

Forest Green Rovers v Weston-Super-Mare	1-5
Hinckley United v Hereford United	3-1
Wellingborough Town v Harpenden Town	7-1
Leighton Town v Hitchin Town	2-2, 1-5
Rothwell Town v Viking Sports	0-2
Thame United v Chesham United	0-2
Wembley v Romford	1-2
Potters Bar Town v Rushden & Diamonds	0-4
Ipswich Wanderers v Bedford Town	0-1
Bishop's Stortford v Hampton	4-3
Stevenage Borough v Hayes	1-1, 4-0
Hullbridge Sports v Hornchurch	3-2
Burnham Ramblers v Cambridge City	4-5
Fisher Athletic v Walton & Hersham	0-5
Farnborough Town v Bashley	6-1
Oxford City v Basingstoke Town	1-1, 2-3
Bracknell Town v Burgess Hill Town	0-4
Dulwich Hamlet v Eastleigh	1-2
Chatham Town v Chipstead	3-0
Abingdon United v Sittingbourne	0-3
Langney Sports v Dartford	1-0
Folkestone Invicta v Leatherhead	2-3
Welling United v Dover Athletic	2-1

FIRST ROUND

Rochdale v Scarborough	2-0
Runcorn v Hull City	1-6
Chesterfield v Rotherham United	1-3
Lincoln United v Wigan Athletic	2-5
Burscough v York City	2-3
Scunthorpe United v Blackpool	3-1
Oldham Athletic v Burnley	2-0
Altrincham v Hartlepool United	0-1
Chester City v Manchester City	2-2, 0-2
Wrexham v Mansfield Town	1-1, 0-2
Preston North End v Halifax Town	1-0
Carlisle United v Darlington	1-1, 1-0
Plymouth Argyle v Shrewsbury Town	3-0
Kidderminster Harriers v Cardiff City	1-5
Rushden & Diamonds v Reading	0-3
Nuneaton Borough v Swansea City	2-2, 1-3
Racing Club Warwick v Walsall	1-4
Stoke City v Cirencester Town	3-0
Notts County v Weston-Super-Mare	4-0
Bolehall Swifts v Cambridge United	1-7
Wellingborough Town v Exeter City	2-5
Torquay United v Lincoln City	0-2
Peterborough United v Bristol Rovers	3-1
Hinckley United v Basingstoke Town	1-0
Fulham v Farnborough Town	1-1, 3-1
Barnet v Walton & Hersham	2-1
AFC Bournemouth v Leyton Orient	2-4
Brentford v Wycombe Wanderers	4-1
Southend United v Sittingbourne	7-0
Brighton & Hove Albion v Hitchin Town	6-1
Gillingham v Chatham Town	3-1
Romford v Eastleigh	3-1
Burgess Hill Town v Chesham United	1-1, 3-2
Langney Sports v Welling United	2-2, 1-2
Bishop's Stortford v Hullbridge Sports	1-1, 1-0
Luton Town v Colchester United	0-1
Leatherhead v Stevenage Borough	0-6
Enfield v Bedford Town	2-1
Northampton Town v Cambridge City	3-1
Millwall v Viking Sports	4-0

SECOND ROUND

Mansfield Town v Preston North End	1-2
Hartlepool United v Rotherham United	5-1
Manchester City v Carlisle United	6-0
Stoke City v Oldham Athletic	0-0, 1-0
Lincoln City v Scunthorpe United 0-0, *(abandoned 8 minutes; fog)*	0-4
Wigan Athletic v York City	0-3
Hull City v Rochdale	5-4
Peterborough United v Cardiff City	2-1
Cambridge United v Swansea City	0-0, 1-0
Walsall v Plymouth Argyle	1-0
Northampton Town v Stevenage Borough	1-1, 2-0
Exeter City v Notts County	0-2
Hinckley United v Reading	2-2, 1-2
Southend United v Brentford	0-2

Burgess Hill Town v Millwall	0-7
Bishop's Stortford v Romford	1-1, 2-3
Welling United v Barnet	1-2
Brighton & Hove Albion v Fulham	2-0
Gillingham v Enfield	0-0, 3-0
Leyton Orient v Colchester United	3-1

THIRD ROUND

Bury v Newcastle United	0-0, 1-3
Barnet v Hartlepool United	0-0, 0-3
Manchester United v Everton	2-2, 0-4
Manchester City v Sheffield Wednesday	2-3
Derby County v Charlton Athletic	1-4
Huddersfield Town v Bradford City	4-0
Watford v Romford	4-0
Scunthorpe United v Portsmouth	2-1
Queens Park Rangers v Birmingham City	4-0
Southampton v Liverpool	1-2
Grimsby United v Arsenal	1-5
Northampton Town v Chelsea	0-1
Tottenham Hotspur v Walsall	0-0, 0-0
Walsall won 4-2 on penalties.	
Crewe Alexandra v Brentford	2-0
Crystal Palace v Tranmere Rovers	1-0
Port Vale v Notts County	1-1, 2-3
Stockport County v West Ham United	2-3
Gillingham v Leicester City	1-3
Bolton Wanderers v Barnsley	0-0, 3-2
Stoke City v York City	0-3
Middlesbrough v Wolverhampton Wanderers	2-1
Norwich City v Blackburn Rovers	0-3
Sheffield United v Leyton Orient	2-1
Oxford United v Wimbledon	1-1, 0-2
Brighton & Hove Albion v Coventry City	1-1, 0-2
Preston North End v Peterborough United	4-2
Cambridge United v Ipswich Town	0-1
West Bromwich Albion v Nottingham Forest	1-1, 1-2
Aston Villa v Hull City	5-1
Millwall v Reading	2-0
Sunderland v Bristol City	2-1
Swindon Town v Leeds United	2-2, 1-0

FOURTH ROUND

Liverpool v Wimbledon	1-2
Aston Villa v Huddersfield Town	4-1
Crewe Alexandra v Queens Park Rangers	0-1
Everton v Swindon Town	1-1, 5-1
Scunthorpe United v Middlesbrough	0-0, 1-2
Hartlepool United v Watford	2-5
Sheffield Wednesday v Leicester City	1-0
Walsall v West Ham United	1-4
Charlton Athletic v Crystal Palace	0-2
Preston North End v Arsenal	1-4
Newcastle United v Chelsea	0-0, 2-1
Blackburn Rovers v Sheffield United	1-2
Ipswich Town v York City	1-1, 0-2
Coventry City v Notts County	3-0
Millwall v Bolton Wanderers	4-0
Nottingham Forest v Sunderland	1-1, 4-0

FIFTH ROUND

Newcastle United v Middlesbrough	0-0, 5-0
York City v West Ham United	1-1, 0-5
Queens Park Rangers v Nottingham Forest	2-2, 2-4
Sheffield United v Coventry City	1-1, 0-4
Arsenal v Crystal Palace	0-0, 1-0
Aston Villa v Watford	2-0
Sheffield Wednesday v Everton	1-1, 1-3
Millwall v Wimbledon	1-2

SIXTH ROUND

Arsenal v West Ham United	0-0, 0-4
Wimbledon v Coventry City	0-3
Nottingham Forest v Newcastle United	2-3
Everton v Aston Villa	1-0

SEMI-FINALS (TWO LEGS)

West Ham United v Everton	3-0, 0-1
Newcastle United v Coventry City	0-4, 2-1

FINAL FIRST LEG

7 MAY

Coventry City (0) 0
West Ham United (0) 3 *(Newton 70, Angus 75,*
Brayley 78)   11,500
Coventry City: Kirkland; Mooney, Lewis, Betts, Burrows
M, Cudworth, Graham (Grant), Pead (Doyle), Eribenne,
McSheffrey, McPhee.
West Ham United: Bywater; Newton, Taylor, Forbes,
Iriekpen, Angus, Carrick (Omonua), Cole, Garcia,
Brayley (Riddle), Ferrante.
Referee: R. Harris (Oxford).

FINAL SECOND LEG

14 MAY

West Ham United (3) 6 *(Brayley 3, 59, Newton 28, Garcia*
34 (pen), 70, Carrick 64)
Coventry City (0) 0   18,438
West Ham United: Bywater; Newton (Cooper), Taylor,
Forbes, Iriekpen, Angus, Carrick, Cole, Garcia, Brayley,
Ferrante.
Coventry City: Kirkland; Mooney, Lewis (Strachan C),
Burrows M, Cudworth, Betts (Doyle), Graham (Grant),
Pead, Davenport, McSheffrey, McPhee.
Referee: R. Harris (Oxford).

SEMI-PROFESSIONAL INTERNATIONALS

2 Mar

England 4 *(Grayson 2, Charles, own goal)*
Italy 1   1012
England: Book (Cheltenham Town) [Gothard
(Dagenham & Redbridge)]; Shaw (Doncaster Rovers)
[Wormull (Dover Athletic)], Underwood (Rushden &
Diamonds), Danzey (Woking) [Comyn (Hednesford
Town)], Smith (Stevenage Borough), Ryan (Southport),
Yates (Cheltenham Town), Butterworth (Rushden &
Diamonds), Patmore (Yeovil Town) [Watkins
(Cheltenham Town)], Grayson (Cheltenham Town),
Patterson (Kingstonian) [Charles (Hayes)].

30 Mar

Holland 1 *(Knijn)*
England 1 *(Patmore)*   1300
England: Book (Cheltenham Town); Shaw (Doncaster
Rovers), Underwood (Rushden & Diamonds) [Fishlock

(Yeovil Town)], Danzey (Woking), Smith (Stevenage
Borough), Ryan (Southport), Stott (Yeovil Town)
[Williams (Nuneaton Borough)], Butterworth (Rushden
& Diamonds), Patmore (Yeovil Town) [Comyn
(Hednesford Town)], Grayson (Cheltenham Town)
(Charles [Hayes]), Patterson (Kingstonian).

23 May

England 2 *(Patmore, Pitcher)*
Wales 1   507
England: Book (Cheltenham Town) [Gothard
(Dagenham & Redbridge)]; Williams (Nuneaton
Borough) [Comyn (Hednesford Town)], Wormull
(Dover Athletic) [Howells (Cheltenham Town)], Banks
(Cheltenham Town), Smith (Stevenage Borough), Ryan
(Southport), Yates (Cheltenham Town) [Stott (Yeovil
Town)], Butterworth (Rushden & Diamonds), Patmore
(Yeovil Town), Grayson (Cheltenham Town), Pitcher
(Kingstonian) [Charles (Hayes)].

FA XI REPRESENTATIVE MATCHES

8 Dec

FA XI 0
Southern League 0   224
FA XI: Book (Cheltenham Town) [Brock
(Kidderminster Harriers)]; Duff (Cheltenham Town),
Victory (Cheltenham Town), Banks (Cheltenham Town),
Cousins (Yeovil Town) [Wright (Hereford United)],
Walker (Cheltenham Town), Howells (Cheltenham
Town), Milton (Cheltenham Town), Eaton (Cheltenham
Town), Watkins (Cheltenham Town) [Hunt (Forest
Green Rovers), Drysdale (Forest Green Rovers) [Honor
(Forest Green Rovers)].

9 Dec

FA XI 1 *(Akuamoah)*
Isthmian League 1   158
FA XI: Taylor (Stevenage Borough) [Farrelly
(Kingstonian)]; Harvey (Stevenage Borough), Fishlock
(Yeovil Town), Crossley (Kingstonian) [Beevor
(Stevenage Borough)], Smith (Stevenage Borough),
Danzey (Woking), Perkins (Woking) [Miller
(Farnborough Town)], Berry (Stevenage Borough),
Patmore (Yeovil Town) [West (Woking)], Akuamoah
(Kingstonian), Patterson (Kingstonian).

5 Jan

FA XI 3 *(Grayson 2, Cox)*
Combined Services 0   120
FA XI: Sollitt (Kettering Town) [Morgan (Hednesford
Town)]; Carty (Hednesford Town), Comyn (Hednesford

Town), Vowden (Kettering Town), Norman (Kettering
Town) [Cox (Kettering Town)], Williams (Nuneaton
Borough) [Wolseley (Kidderminster Harriers)], Grayson
(Cheltenham Town), Hudson (Kettering Town), Foster
(Rushden & Diamonds), Taylor (Kidderminster
Harriers) [Beard (Kidderminster Harriers)].

1 Feb

FA XI 4 *(Charles 2, Docking, Pope)*
British Universities 0   156
FA XI: Bastock (Boston United) [Heeps (Bedford
Town)]; Vickers (St Albans City), Sparkes (Hayes), Pope
(Histon) [Nedemovic (Soham Town Rangers)], Gowshall
(Boston United) [Leonard (Soham Town Rangers)],
Haylock (Newmarket Town), St Hilaire (Billericay
Town), Docking (Soham Town Rangers) [Stanhope
(Boston United)], Charles (Hayes), Lewis (Hendon),
Braybrooke (Soham Town Rangers).

21 May

FA XI 1 *(Ryan)*
Highland League 1   400
FA XI: Gothard (Dagenham & Redbridge); Yates
(Cheltenham Town), Wormull (Dover Athletic), Comyn
(Hednesford Town), Smith (Stevenage Borough), Ryan
(Southport), Howells (Cheltenham Town) [Pitcher
(Kingstonian)], Butterworth (Rushden & Diamonds),
Patmore (Yeovil Town), Charles (Hayes) [Grayson
(Cheltenham Town)], Patterson (Kingstonian) [Williams
(Nuneaton Borough)].

FA UMBRO SUNDAY CUP 1998–99

FIRST ROUND

Albion Sports v A3	1-2
East Bowling Unity v Bulford	3-0
Dudley & Weetslade v Hartlepool Staincliffe Hotel	1-0
Littlewoods Athletic v Queens Park AFC	1-1, 3-2
Mainstay v Allerton	1-3
Albion Broseley v Caldway	2-1
Crown withdrew v Idsall Rangers w.o.	
Shankhouse v Tithebarn	0-3
Sandon v Mode Force Rouke's	4-1
Blue Union v Lobster	4-2
Humbledon Plains Farm v Clubmoor Nalgo	2-1
Pineapple v Newfield	2-1
Packaging DKS v Britannia	0-3
Hartlepool Lion Hotel v Nicosia	3-1
Orchard Park v Seymour	3-1
Stanley Road v Keith J Alarms	3-5
Birmingham Celtic v Manfast	4-1
Brookvale Athletic v Park Inn	6-2
Mackadown Lane S&S v Greyhound Dog	3-5
Cheadle United v Leominster British Legion	8-0
Sandwell withdrew v Heathfield w.o.	
Melton Youth Old Boys v Leicester City Bus	5-1
Oxford Road Social v Bournemouth	7-0
Courage v Bournemouth Electric	1-2
Peppard v BRSC Aidan	0-2
Reading Borough v Hanham Sunday	3-0
Gossoms End v Duke of York	1-2
Holderness United v Ouzavich	0-3
Shenley Hotel v Old Oak	3-1
Belstone w.o. v Snodland WMC withdrew	
Hammer v Royal Ascot	3-1
Luton Old Boys (Sunday) v Sawston Keys	1-0
Winchesterow withdrew v Active Signs w.o.	
Winter Royals v Oakwood Sports	5-2

SECOND ROUND

Blue Union v Allerton	1-2
Britannia v Humbledon Plains Farm	1-6
Pineapple v Slade Celtic	1-0
Idsall Rangers v Keith J Alarms	1-5
A3 v Hartlepool Lion Hotel	1-1, 2-2
Hartlepool Lion Hotel won 7-6 on penalties	
Lodge Cottrell v Clifton Albion	7-0
Northwood v Salerno	1-2
Birmingham Celtic v Tithebarn	1-0
Grosvenor Park v Cheadle United	1-5
Bolton Woods v Dudley & Weetslade	2-1
Sandon v East Bowling Unity	2-2, 2-0
Marston Sports v Littlewoods Athletic	1-2
Olympic Star v Orchard Park	2-1
Brookvale Athletic v Eden Vale	1-1, 1-2
Greyhound Dog v Albion Broseley	2-1
Celtic SC (Luton) v Melton Youth Old Boys	3-1
Active Signs v St Josephs (South Oxhey)	1-2
Pitsea v Oakview	1-0
Winter Royals v New Inn Keynsham	3-2
Watford Labour v The Cutters Friday	6-1

Hammer v Lebeq Tavern Courage	0-1
Warriors v Duke of York	2-2, 3-1
Azaad Sports v Shenley Hotel	2-1
Luton Old Boys (Sunday) v BRSC Aidan	0-1
Ouzavich v Fryerns	0-2
Belstone v Bournemouth Electric	1-1, 1-5
Reading Borough v Little Paxton	0-2
Coach & Horses v Oxford Road Social	4-0
St Josephs (Luton) v Heathfield	2-0
Sandford v Continental	4-5
Beaufort v Theale (Sunday)	1-3
bye: Caversham Park Village	

THIRD ROUND

Littlewoods Athletic v Olympic Star	3-0
Hartlepool Lion Hotel v Cheadle United	1-2
Salerno v Birmingham Celtic	1-1, 2-3
Pineapple v Lodge Cottrell	2-3
Allerton v Keith J Alarms	3-1
Eden Vale v Sandon	0-1
Humbledon Plains Farm v Bolton Woods	1-2
Pitsea v BRSC Aidan	4-0
Caversham Park Village v Warriors	2-0
Fryerns v Theale (Sunday)	1-3
St Josephs (Luton) v Lebeq Tavern Courage	3-1
Winter Royals v Bournemouth Electric	1-2
Little Paxton v Azaad Sports	1-0
Continental v Coach & Horses	3-0
Greyhound Dog v Celtic SC (Luton)	2-3
Watford Labour v St Josephs (South Oxhey)	2-4

FOURTH ROUND

Sandon v Continental	3-0
Bournemouth Electric v Theale (Sunday)	1-3
Cheadle United v Celtic SC (Luton)	1-0
Lodge Cottrell v St Josephs (South Oxhey)	6-0
Little Paxton v Birmingham Celtic	2-1
St Josephs (Luton) v Allerton	2-0
Caversham Park Village v Littlewoods Athletic	0-6
Pitsea v Bolton Woods	2-1

FIFTH ROUND

Sandon v Littlewoods Athletic	0-1
Cheadle United v Lodge Cottrell	0-1
Pitsea v St Josephs (Luton)	1-5
Theale (Sunday) v Little Paxton	0-1

SEMI-FINALS

Little Paxton v Littlewoods Athletic	2-0
St Josephs (Luton) v Lodge Cottrell	3-1

FINAL

Little Paxton v St Josephs (Luton)	2-2
Little Paxton won 4-3 on penalties	

FA COUNTY YOUTH CHALLENGE CUP 1998–99

FIRST ROUND

Shropshire v Nottinghamshire	3-1
Cumberland v Sheffield & Hallamshire	1-0
Lancashire v Manchester	1-3
Liverpool v Cheshire	1-2
Cambridgeshire v Kent	2-1
Surrey v Leicestershire & Rutland	3-2
Suffolk v Middlesex	0-4
Essex v Birmingham	1-0
Wiltshire v Oxfordshire	1-3
Gloucestershire v Berks & Bucks	0-4
Herefordshire v Somerset	2-1

Oxfordshire v Devon	4-1
Berks & Bucks v Cornwall	1-1, 0-1

THIRD ROUND

North Riding v West Riding	2-4
Durham v East Riding	2-0
Lincolnshire v Cumberland	1-0
Cornwall v Oxfordshire	3-2
Worcestershire v Dorset	6-1
Army v Northamptonshire	2-3
Sussex v Cambridgeshire	3-0
Norfolk v London	4-5

SECOND ROUND

Manchester v Cumberland	0-1
Northumberland v West Riding	2-3
North Riding v Cheshire	3-1
Durham v Shropshire	3-2
Westmorland v East Riding	1-3
Lincolnshire v Staffordshire	5-3
Surrey v Northamptonshire	0-1
Cambridgeshire v Hertfordshire	3-2
London v Essex	4-3
Middlesex v Worcestershire	0-3
Huntingdonshire v Sussex	1-3
Bedfordshire v Norfolk	2-5
Dorset v Herefordshire	3-1
Army v Hampshire	4-1

FOURTH ROUND

Northamptonshire v Sussex	2-3
Durham v West Riding	3-2
Cornwall v London	6-0
Worcestershire v Lincolnshire	2-3

SEMI-FINALS

Sussex v Lincolnshire	3-1
Durham v Cornwall	3-1

FINAL

Durham v Sussex	1-0

FA SCHOOLS & YOUTH GAMES 1998–99

ENGLAND UNDER-15

2 Oct##

Wales 2　England 4 *(Wood 28, 58, Brown 50, 62)*

England: Allaway (Reading); Duncan (Queens Park Rangers), [Pennant (Notts County) 50], Willetts (Everton), Clark (Manchester United), Otsemobor (Liverpool), Bowditch (Tottenham Hotspur), Sherman (Leeds United), Spicer (Arsenal), Wood (Manchester United), Brown (Bristol City) [Johnson (Leeds United) 62], Prince (Liverpool) [Howard (Southampton) 40].

6 Nov##

Northern Ireland 1　England 3 *(Moore 5, Clark 22, 30)*

England: Bell (Newcastle United) [Jowsey (Scarborough) 66]; Thornton (Chelsea), Emanuel (Bristol City), Clark (Manchester United), O'Hanlon (Everton), Bowditch (Tottenham Hotspur), Dove (Middlesbrough) [Linwood (Tranmere Rovers) 71], Cooke (Manchester United), Howard (Southampton), Moore (Aston Villa), Johnson (Leeds United) [Austin (Barnsley) 40].

20 Nov##

England 0　Scotland 1

England: Lonergan (Preston North End) [Allaway (Reading) 20]; Sherman (Leeds United), Austin (Barnsley), Clark (Manchester United), O'Hanlon (Everton), Otsemobor (Liverpool), Pennant (Notts County) [Willetts (Everton) 80], Spicer (Arsenal), Wood (Manchester United), Brown (Bristol City), Prince (Liverpool) [Dove (Middlesbrough) 58].

12 Mar+

England 0　Republic of Ireland 0

England: Lonergan (Preston North End); Sherman (Leeds United) [Muirhead (Manchester United) 60], Austin (Barnsley) [Willetts (Everton) 45], Clark (Manchester United), O'Hanlon (Everton) [Parker (Birmingham City)], Fox (Exeter City), Pennant (Arsenal), Spicer (Arsenal) [Cooke (Manchester United)], Wood (Manchester United) [Albiston (Manchester United)], Chopra (Newcastle United) [Jenas (Nottingham Forest)], Dove (Middlesbrough) [Howard (Southampton) 45].

2 Apr=

England 2 *(Chopra 20, 50)*　**China 1**

England: Allaway (Reading); Duncan (Queens Park Rangers), Willetts (Everton), Clark (Manchester United), O'Hanlon (Everton), Johnson (Leeds United) [Howard (Southampton) 30], Pennant (Arsenal) [Muirhead (Manchester United) 55], Spicer (Arsenal), Brown (Bristol City) [Wood (Manchester United) 50], Chopra (Newcastle United), Austin (Barnsley).

3 Apr=

England 2 *(Brown 40, 50)*　**Cameroon 0**

England: Allaway (Reading); Austin (Barnsley) [Duncan (Queens Park Rangers)], Willetts (Everton), Clark (Manchester United), O'Hanlon (Everton), Fox (Exeter City) [Otsemobor (Liverpool)], Pennant (Arsenal), Spicer (Arsenal), Wood (Manchester United) [Chopra (Newcastle United)], Howard (Southampton), Brown (Bristol City) [Johnson (Leeds United)].

4 Apr=

England 0　Italy 1

England: Allaway (Reading); Duncan (Queens Park Rangers), Willetts (Everton), Clark (Manchester United), O'Hanlon (Everton), Otsemobor (Liverpool) [Muirhead (Manchester United) 45], Johnson (Leeds United) [Pennant (Arsenal) 30], Spicer (Arsenal), Wood (Manchester United) [Brown (Bristol City) 35], Howard (Southampton), Prince (Liverpool).

5 Apr=

England 1 *(Pennant 50)*　**Gabon 2**

England: Lonergan (Preston North End); Duncan (Queens Park Rangers), Willetts (Everton), Clark (Manchester United), O'Hanlon (Everton), Otsemobor (Liverpool) [Muirhead (Manchester United)], Pennant (Arsenal), Fox (Exeter City) [Wood (Manchester United)], Brown (Bristol City), Howard (Southampton), Prince (Liverpool) [Chopra (Newcastle United)].

+ Friendly; ##Adidas Victory Shield; = Montaigu Tournament.

UNIVERSITY FOOTBALL 1998–99

115th UNIVERSITY MATCH

(at Craven Cottage, Fulham, att: 2000)

Oxford 1, Cambridge 0 (h-t 0-0)

Oxford: Rutter; Spencer, O'Brien, Wardle, Humphries, Fowler, Goff, Falconer, Cairnes, Rishworth, Davies.
Subs: Lowe, Williams, Fletcher, Griffin.
Scorer: Cairnes 88.
Cambridge: Haines; Hayden, Jennings, Mowat, Kerr, Pett, Ball, Fearnley A, Walsh, Williamson, Fearnley T.
Subs: Madden, Walford, Glamocak, Brooksbank.
Referee: U. Rennie (Sheffield).
Cambridge have not won the fixture for eleven years, but still lead Oxford by 45 wins to 44 with 26 drawn.

LONDON UNIVERSITY XI REPRESENTATIVE MATCH RESULTS

Old Boys' League	Lost	0-2
Southern Amateur League	Lost	0-2
SE Region BUSA	Lost	1-5
Lloyd's of London	Lost	1-2
Royal Navy U-21	Lost	0-3
Metropolitan Police	Won	2-0
Cambridge University	Lost	0-3
Army Crusaders	Won	5-0
Oxford University	Lost	1-4
Amateur Football Alliance	Lost	2-3

UNIVERSITY OF LONDON INTER-COLLEGIATE MEN'S LEAGUE

PREMIER DIVISION	P	W	D	L	F	A	Pts
Imperial College	14	10	3	1	43	16	33
London School of Economics	14	8	2	4	18	14	26
University College	14	8	1	5	32	17	25
Goldsmiths' College	14	6	1	7	18	22	19
King's College	14	5	3	6	20	16	18
Royal Holloway College	14	5	1	8	15	26	16
Q Mary Westfield College	14	4	3	7	26	28	15
Royal School of Mines (IC)	14	2	2	10	12	45	8

DIVISION ONE	P	W	D	L	F	A	Pts
GKT (ex UMDS)	16	12	1	3	57	38	43
University College Res	18	13	2	3	49	27	41
Imperial College Sch Med	16	12	0	4	58	26	36
London School Economics Res	18	8	2	8	28	25	26
R Lon'n & St Bart's Med Sch	18	7	1	10	28	41	22
UCL & Middx Hosp Med Sch	18	6	3	9	48	48	21
Goldsmiths' College Res.	18	7	0	11	34	43	21
Q Mary Westfield College Res	18	6	2	10	29	40	20
Royal Holloway College Res	18	5	2	11	37	52	17
Royal Veterinary College	18	5	1	12	33	61	16

DIVISION TWO	P	W	D	L	F	A	Pts
Imperial College Res.	17	12	1	4	54	22	37
Royal Holloway College 3rd	18	11	3	4	51	19	36
Imperial College Sch M Res	18	11	3	4	30	20	36
Sch Slav & E.Europ'n Stud	17	12	0	5	30	18	36
University College 3rd	18	8	2	8	35	27	26
London Sch Economics 3rd	18	7	3	8	22	34	24
King's College 3rd	18	7	1	10	40	55	22
Royal Free Hosp Sch Med	17	7	1	9	24	23	12
Imperial College 3rd	17	5	3	9	19	41	8
GKT Res	18	1	1	16	10	56	4

Division Three–10 Teams–Won by King's College 3rd
Division Four–10 Teams–Won by King's College 4th
Division Five–9 Teams–Won by R London & St Barts Res
Division Six–9 Teams–Won by Sch Slavonic & E Euro St
Challenge Cup–Imperial 5, Queen Mary Westfield 1
Upper Reserves Cup–UC Res 4, R Holloway College 3rd 0
Lower Reserves Cup–King's 4th 5, King's 5th 2
United Hospitals Senior Cup–No results advised
Junior Cup–No results advised

BRITISH UNIVERSITIES SPORTS ASSOCIATION CHAMPIONSHIP

Finals (Men)
First XI
Manchester 2, Luton 0
Second XI
Loughborough 5, UWIC 0
Third XI
Crewe & Alsager 3, Oxford Brookes 0
Fourth XI
Loughborough 3, Brunel (West London) 2
Shield
Crewe & Alsager 3, Reading 2

Women's
Edinburgh 4, St Mark & St John 1

BUSA Games (Men's)
Northern Ireland 0, Scotland 1; England 0, Wales 2; Wales 0, Scotland 1; Northern Ireland 1, England 2; England 3, Scotland 0; Wales 3, Northern Ireland 1.

Final placings:
1 Wales, 2 England, 3 Scotland, 4 Northern Ireland.

BUSA Games (Women's)
England 3, Northern Ireland 0; England 8, Wales 0; Scotland 5, England 1; Wales 3, Northern Ireland 0; Northern Ireland 0, Scotland 7; Northern Ireland 1, Wales 1; Scotland 10, Wales 0.

Final placings:
1 Scotland, 2 England, 3 Northern Ireland, 4 Wales.

Men's International
English Universities v RAF 4-1; v Prison Service 3-1; v Reme 2-1.

Women's International
English Universities v Aston Villa 1-0; v Civil Service 2-3; v Combined Irish Colleges 2-2.

UNIVERSITY OF LONDON INTER-COLLEGIATE WOMEN'S LEAGUE

PREMIER DIVISION	P	W	D	L	F	A	Pts
R Lon Hosp & Q Mary Westfield	14	13	1	0	94	7	40
Royal Holloway College	14	11	1	2	100	9	34
University College	14	10	1	3	51	23	31
London School of Economics	14	7	0	7	51	29	21
King's College	14	5	1	7	33	43	16
Imperial College	14	5	0	9	28	57	15
Wye College	14	1	1	11	16	84	4
St George's Hospital	14	0	1	13	10	131	1

DIVISION ONE	P	W	D	L	F	A	Pts
SOAS	18	14	2	1	85	8	44
Goldsmiths' College	18	14	2	2	60	14	44
GKT	18	11	0	6	66	30	33
Royal Veterinary	18	10	0	8	30	12	30
Royal Free Hospital	18	10	0	8	47	30	30
University Col & Mx Hosp	18	8	0	10	34	57	24
Royal Holloway College Res	18	6	1	8	22	43	19
University College Res	18	6	1	11	22	59	19
GKT Res	18	3	0	15	5	106	9
Royal Free Hospital Res	18	2	0	16	6	18	6

Womens' Challenge Cup–Q Mary Westfield 4, Royal Holloway 2

SCHOOLS FOOTBALL 1998–99

GOODYEAR CENTENARY SHIELD 1998–99

UNDER-18	P	W	D	L	F	A	Pts
Northern Ireland	3	2	1	0	5	3	5
England	3	1	2	0	3	2	4
Wales	3	1	0	2	5	6	2
Scotland	3	0	1	2	1	3	1

ESFA UNDER-18 1998–99

England 0, Republic of Ireland 2 - Ipswich, 6 February
England 1, Northern Ireland 1 - Darlington, 12 February
England 2, Wales 1 - Wolverhampton, 4 March
England 0, Scotland 0 - Edinburgh, 26 March
England 0, Hungary 3 - Budapest, 13 April
England 1, Holland 2 - Wembley, 8 May
Overall Record Played 6, Won 1, Drew 2, Lost 3, Goals For 4, Goals Against 9
Scorers: Rummery (2), Cripps, Foster.

ESFA WAGONWHEELS 5-A-SIDE COMPETITION U.12 FINALS

BOYS FINAL:
Meadows School (Chesterfield) 3, Welling School (North Kent) 0
Staged at Aston Villa Sports Centre 6 March

GIRLS FINAL:
Abraham Darby School (Telford) 4, Eastlea School (Newham) 1

ESFA U.11 ADIDAS PREDATOR PREMIER FINAL 7-A-SIDE TROPHY

FINAL:
Vale of White Horse Schools FA 0, Carlisle Schools FA 0
Trophy Shared.
Played at Wembley, 8 May.

ESFA U.11 ADIDAS PREDATOR FINAL 6-A-SIDE TROPHY

FINAL:
St Mary's Primary School (Hendon) 2, Avondale Primary School (Darwen) 1
Played at Wembley, 8 May.

ESFA U.11 SMALL PRIMARY SCHOOLS FINAL 6-A-SIDE COMPETITION

FINAL:
Holy Cross Primary School (Nottingham) 2, Great Dalby Primary School (Leicester) 1 aet.
Played at Leicester City, 29 March.

ESFA SNICKERS U.19 SCHOOLS AND COLLEGES COMPETITION

FINAL:
Cirencester College (Gloucestershire) 2, Sheffield College (South Yorkshire) 0
Played at West Bromwich, 10 May.

ESFA MARS U.19 INDIVIDUAL SCHOOLS COMPETITION

FINAL:
Ardingly College (Sussex) 2, Archbishop Beck School (Merseyside) 1
Played at West Bromwich, 10 May.

ESFA U.19 INTER-COUNTY PREMIER LEAGUE COMPETITION

FINAL:
Northumberland 0, Dorset 0 *aet*
Trophy Shared.
Played at Berwick Rangers, 13 May.

ESFA GOODYEAR U.16 INDIVIDUAL SCHOOLS COMPETITION

FINAL:
Cramlington High School (Northumberland) 4, Crown Woods School (Inner London) 1
Played at Wolverhampton, 2 May.

ESFA U.16 INTER-COUNTY PREMIER LEAGUE COMPETITION

FINAL:
Northumberland 3, Essex 2
Played at Middlesbrough, 4 May.

ESFA U.16 INTER-COUNTY GIRLS UNITED NORWEST CO-OP TROPHY

FINAL:
Hampshire 3, Durham 1
Played at Tranmere, 14 May.

ESFA U.16 INDIVIDUAL GIRLS SCHOOLS UNITED NORWEST CO-OP CUP

FINAL:
Meole Brace School (Shropshire) 4, Holmfirth School (West Yorkshire) 1
Played at Tranmere, 14 May.

EFSA U.15 HEINZ TROPHY

FINAL (two legs):
South Notts 3, Bishop Auckland 0
Played at Mansfield, 11 May.
Bishop Auckland 0, South Notts 0
Played at Bishop Auckland, 19 May.

ESFA U.14 HEINZ KETCHUP CUP

FINAL:
Cardinal Newman High School (Luton) 2, Kingsdown School (Swindon) 1
Played at Arsenal, 17 May.

BOODLE & DUNTHORNE INDEPENDENT SCHOOLS FA CUP 1997–98

PRELIMINARY ROUND
Forest 4, Oswestry 1
QEGS, Blackburn 3, Winchester 1
Wellingborough 4, St Edmund's 0
Aldenham 2, Alleyn's 3
Ardingly 6, Batley GS 0

FIRST ROUND
City of London 1, Victoria College, Jersey 2
Chigwell 0, Lancing 3

Wolverhampton GS 3, Malvern 2
Highgate 2, Manchester GS 3
Repton 2, Brentwood 2
(aet; Repton won 6-5 on penalties)
Ardingly 7, Kimbolton 0
Bolton 4, KES, Witley 0
Haileybury 1, St Bede's 5
King's, Chester 5, John Lyon 0
Wellingborough 1, Westminster 2
Hampton 2, QEGS, Blackburn 1
Grange 1, Shrewsbury 3
Bradfield 4, Alleyn's 2 *aet*
Eton 5, Forest 1
Charterhouse 2, Latymer Upper 3
Hulme GS 1, Bury GS 0

SECOND ROUND
Westminster 1, Bolton 1
(aet; Bolton won 5-4 on penalties)
Lancing 0, Wolverhampton GS 4
Shrewsbury 9, Victoria College, Jersey 2
Eton 1, Ardingly 1
(aet; Ardingly won 4-2 on penalties)
Repton 5, St Bede's 1 *(aet)*
Latymer Upper 2, Bradfield 2
(aet; Bradfield won 5-4 on penalties)

Hulme GS 2, Manchester GS 1 *(aet)*
Hampton 2, King's, Chester 1

THIRD ROUND
Repton 1, Bolton 0
Shrewsbury 1, Wolverhampton GS 2
Hampton 1, Bradfield 0
Ardingly 1, Hulme GS 0

SEMI-FINALS
Hampton 2, Ardingly 0
Repton 3, Wolverhampton GS 3
(aet; Wolverhampton GS won 5-4 on penalties)

FINAL (at Leicester City)
Hampton 2 *(Nasrallah, Stone)*
Wolverhampton GS 1 *(Turner)*   1012
Hampton: J Comber; R Dixon, M Waldron, Chun Yip Chow, D Sims, B Naidu, A Stone, K Warren, A Nasrallah (T Jackson), A Fleming, M Sexton.
Wolverhampton GS: C Lancaster; A Bate, J Collins, T Smyth, A Skedgel (R Bolton), J Carter, J Skedgel, T Baker, B Bond (S Drury), A Turner, A Benbow.
Referee: D. Elleray (Harrow).

Back Row (Left to Right): Mark Wallington (goalkeeper coach), Michael Feeley, Ryan Rummery, Russell Burden, Neil Morris, Kristian Rogers (GK), Neil Dix, Matthew Smith (GK), David Duffy, Elliot Onochie, Graham Taylor, Arthur Tabor (Doctor), Alan Gallafant (Physio).
Front Row (Left to Right): Dave Cook (Manager), Craig Cripps, Billy Sobey, Alan Marsh, Geoff Lee (Vice Chairman), John Robson (Chairman), Daniel Dawson, James Hughes, Sam Allison, Malcolm Hurd (Assistant Manager).

AVON INSURANCE COMBINATION 1998–99

Charlton Athletic retained their Avon Insurance Combination title by beating off the challenge of both Tottenham Hotspur and Chelsea and the final margin of three points gave Charlton their third ever Football Combination title. Ipswich, Watford, Southampton and Peterborough at one time or another throughout the season, also harboured hopes of winning what was one of the most open and competitive championship challenges of recent seasons.

Ably coached by Gary Stevens, Charlton fielded a potent mixture of experience and youth with Shaun Newton, Scott Parker, Paul Konchesky and Mark McCammon all impressing.

Tottenham's late unbeaten run of twelve games just failed to bring them title success but Rory Allen and Paul McVeigh scored consistently and restated their undoubted talent.

Chelsea fielded a predominantly young side and Sam Dalla Bona top scorer in both the reserves and youth team, Sam Parkin and John Terry all showed up well.

Ipswich provided the League's leading scorer in Neil Midgley whose twenty goals narrowly beat the challengers of Fulham's Kevin Betsy and Norwich's Adrian Coote.

Peterborough enjoyed a fine season in the Avon Insurance Combination and showcased a number of talented youngsters such as Tony Shields and Matthew Hann.

The main purpose of the Combination is to encourage the development of young talent and names to watch out for in the near future include Arsenal's Stuart Taylor, Barnet striker Marlon King, Crystal Palace's Stephen Evans, Titus Bramble of Ipswich and Colchester's Lomana Tresor Lua-Lua.

Stars who graced the Avon Insurance Combination during the season included Tony Adams, Matt Le Tissier, Ian Wright, Dan Petrescu, John Scales and Steve Bould.

Northampton Town won the Avon Insurance Enterprise Award and attracted over 4,700 spectators to their match with Arsenal.

Avon Insurance are about to enter the sixth season of their sponsorship which has been extended to the end of the 2002–03 season by which time it will be one of the longest lasting sponsorships in English football.

	P	W	D	L	F	A	GD	Pts
Charlton Ath	28	19	3	6	60	24	+36	60
Tottenham H	28	18	3	7	56	24	+32	57
Chelsea	28	18	3	7	39	22	+17	57
Ipswich T	28	17	4	7	62	32	+30	55
Watford	28	14	9	5	56	28	+27	51
Southampton	28	15	4	9	53	37	+16	49
Peterborough U	28	14	6	8	50	35	+15	48
Fulham	28	14	5	9	63	44	+19	47
Arsenal	28	13	6	9	47	32	+15	45
Colchester U	28	13	4	11	46	43	+3	43
West Ham U	28	11	8	9	56	40	+16	41
Norwich C	28	12	5	11	38	34	+4	41
Northampton T	28	12	5	11	35	41	–6	41
Luton T	28	11	7	10	45	43	+2	40
QPR	28	11	5	12	44	34	+10	38
Portsmouth	28	11	5	12	40	37	+3	38
Wimbledon	28	9	11	8	38	38	0	38
Brighton & HA	28	9	10	9	27	31	–4	37
Bournemouth	28	10	6	12	43	39	+4	36
Crystal Palace	28	9	6	13	43	50	–7	33
Oxford U	28	10	3	15	33	52	–19	33
Reading	28	9	4	15	31	41	–10	31
Swindon T	28	8	6	14	26	47	–21	30
Cambridge U	28	8	6	14	41	65	–24	30
Barnet	28	8	5	15	33	65	–32	29
Millwall	28	7	6	15	33	58	–25	27
Brentford	28	5	7	16	25	56	–31	22
Wycombe W	28	5	7	16	24	58	–34	22
Gillingham	28	4	5	19	21	57	–36	17

1998–99 SEASON SUMMARY
Champions – Charlton Athletic
Top Scorer – Neil Midgley (Ipswich Town)
Fair Play Award – Peterborough United
Avon Insurance Enterprise Award – Northampton Town
Avon Insurance Programme Award – Fulham

Charlton Athletic Avon Insurance Combination Champions
League Appearances: Allen 6; Allman 11+8; Balmer 3; Barnes 3; Barness 14; Beale 1+3; Bowen 5; Bright 10; Brown 8; Doherty 5+3; Emblen 2; Ford 1+2; Fortune 15+2; Grahn 1; Hales 2+3; Hegley 1; Hockley 1; Holmes 17+1; Ifejiagwa 6; Ilic 4; Izzet 3+4; James 9+2; Jones K 7; Jones S 8; Konchesky 23; Lee 16+3; Lisbie 15; Longo 1; MacDonald 7+10; McCammon 9+1; McCarthy 0+2; Mendonca 6; Mortimer 10; Newton 10; Nicholls 11; Parker 16+2; Petterson 5; Piper 0+1; Poole 1; Redfearn 1; Robinson 1; Royce 8; Rufus 1; Sakiri 1; Salmon 9; Smith 1; Stevens 0+1; Tiler 1; Toms 7+1; Turner 1; Webster 0+2; Youds 3.
Goals: McCammon 7, Parker 7, Allen 5, Barness 5, Konchesky 5; Lisbie 5; Bright 4, Jones S 4, Hales 3, MacDonald 3, Newton 3, Holmes 2, Mendonca 2, Fortune 1, Jones K 1, Nicholls 1, own goals 2.

PONTIN'S LEAGUE 1998-99

On 4 May 1999 Sunderland confirmed the Pontin's League title for the first time in their history by beating Derby County 4-1 at the Stadium of Light, watched by a crowd of 23,378. The title had been handed to them the previous day when Manchester United lost 1-0 to Preston.

Sunderland and United had been strong contenders for the championship throughout. United with their final four matches all at home (on Bury's Gigg Lane ground) might have been slight favourites in the end, but lost three of them.

Interest in Sunderland's season on the back of their first team's performances was such that on 17 December 1998 Sunderland reserves lying second in the Premier Division, were at home to leaders Manchester United. The kick-off had to be delayed half an hour because of the crowd, but there were still some 3000 spectators trying to gain admission when play started. The official attendance was 20,583. Sunderland won 2-0 with goals from Danny Dichio and Michael Proctor.

This still left United with a two point advantage and a game in hand of their nearest rivals. The previous evening Everton had kept up their challenge with a 3-0 win at Derby County, a point behind Sunderland. Everton faded a little after this and Liverpool were the only other serious rivals.

However, when Liverpool were the visitors to Sunderland on 27 January 1999 the home club decided to allow spectators in free of charge. There were doubts raised that this would infringe the competition's rules and the match officially discounted. But after a crowd of 33,517 was recorded, the League accepted the fixture as a genuine one. It was believed to be the highest gate ever recorded in the Central League. A collection made on the evening for local charities raised £7,000.

More milestones were recorded the same week when MUTV, Manchester United's own television channel broke new ground by covering their first ever 'live' Pontin's League game, having previously transmitted recorded matches only. The game at Bury's Gigg Lane ground against Derby County ended in a 4-0 win for United.

Sunderland's average gate was over 8000 compared with 1600 the previous season. Reserve coach Adrian Heath became manager of Sheffield United in the summer.

PONTIN'S LEAGUE CUP
GROUP 1
Middlesbrough 1, Darlington 1; Hartlepool United 1, Darlington 0; Middlesbrough 2, Scarborough 2; Newcastle United 3, Hartlepool United 2; Darlington 3, Scarborough 0; Scarborough 3, Hartlepool United 4; Darlington 4, Newcastle United 1; Hartlepool United 0, Middlesbrough 4; Newcastle United 1, Middlesbrough 2; Scarborough 2, Newcastle United 1

Group 2
Halifax Town 5, Hull City 3; Barnsley 2, Rotherham United 0; Rotherham United 1, Halifax Town 0; Halifax Town 1, Barnsley 2; Rotherham United 0, York City 0; Barnsley 1, York City 2; York City 0, Hull City 2; York City 2, Halifax Town 1; Hull City 1, Rotherham United 4; Hull City 2, Barnsley 0

Group 3
Tranmere Rovers 2, West Bromwich Albion 1; Manchester City 2, Tranmere Rovers 3; Manchester City 0, West Bromwich Albion 0; West Bromwich Albion 2, Manchester City 2; Tranmere Rovers 4, Manchester City 3; West Bromwich Albion 1, Tranmere Rovers 1

Group 4
Huddersfield Town 2, Sheffield United 2; Chesterfield 1, Sheffield United 0; Chesterfield 0, Huddersfield Town 3; Sheffield United 1, Huddersfield Town 1; Sheffield United 1, Chesterfield 1; Huddersfield Town 1, Chesterfield 1

Group 5
Bury 1, Stoke City 0; Oldham Athletic 1, Stockport County 3; Bury 1, Oldham Athletic 2; Stockport County 1, Bury 2; Stoke City 1, Stockport County 5; Oldham Athletic 0, Stoke City 2; ; **Group 6;** Bradford City 2, Leicester City 2; Notts County 1, Scunthorpe United 1; Scunthorpe United 1, Leicester City 4; Bradford City 3, Scunthorpe United 0; Leicester City 2, Notts County 1; Notts County 0, Bradford City 2

QUARTER-FINALS
Tranmere Rovers 4, Huddersfield Town 1; Rotherham United 0, Middlesbrough 0 (*aet; Rotherham United won 5-3 on penalties*); Stockport County 3, York City 2; Darlington 0, Bradford City 2

SEMI-FINALS
Tranmere Rovers 4, Rotherham United 1; Stockport County 3, Bradford City 1

FINAL
Tranmere Rovers 2, Stockport County 1;

Sunderland Pontin's League Appearances: Aiston 1+1; Ball 1; Beavers 8+2; Bridges 9; Butler P 1; Butler T 3+2; Byrne 1; Clark 1; Convery 0+1; Craddock 19; Dichio 14; Dickman 6; Duke 15+1; Gray 2; Harrison 10; Harte 0+1; Heckingbottom 9+1; Holloway 12; Ingram 1+1; Johnston 1; Lamb 0+3; Lumsdon 14+1; McCann 11; McCartney 8+3; McGill 1+4; McNeil 0+1; Maley 14+3; Makin 1; Marriott 23; Mullin 9+1; Pitts 3+1; Proctor 6+6; Quinn 1; Rae 3; Scott 4; Smith 17; Summerbee 2; Thirlwell 16+2; Wainwright 9+1; Weaver 1; Williams 7.

Goals: Proctor 7, Bridges 6, Smith 6, Dichio 5, Craddock 4, Mullin 3, Wainwright 3, Beavers 2, McCann 2, Thirlwell 2, Harrison 1, Heckingbottom 1, Johnston 1, Lumsdon 1, Quinn 1, Scott 1.

Premier Division	P	W	D	L	F	A	Pts
Sunderland	24	14	7	3	46	18	49
Liverpool	24	13	7	4	28	16	46
Manchester U	24	13	4	7	48	28	43
Nottingham F	24	11	6	7	35	26	39
Everton	24	11	5	8	34	28	38
Blackburn R	24	8	7	9	31	26	31
Leeds U	24	9	3	12	40	43	30
Leicester C	24	8	6	10	30	41	30
Aston Villa	24	8	5	11	36	37	29
Stoke C	24	7	7	10	24	32	28
Preston NE	24	7	5	12	20	42	26
Birmingham C	24	5	9	10	24	33	24
Derby Co	24	3	7	14	26	52	16

Division One	P	W	D	L	F	A	Pts
Coventry C	24	12	6	6	36	21	42
Oldham Ath	24	13	3	8	36	31	42
Middlesbrough	24	12	5	7	48	38	41
Port Vale	24	11	4	9	31	30	37
Manchester C	24	10	6	8	53	38	36
Sheffield W	24	9	8	7	26	23	35
WBA	24	8	9	7	35	32	33
Wolverhampton W	24	10	3	11	43	45	33
Tranmere R	24	12	12	4	41	32	32
Bolton W	24	8	4	12	25	35	28
Barnsley	24	6	9	9	27	35	27
Burnley	24	6	8	10	20	35	26
Grimsby T	24	5	5	14	20	46	20

Division Two	P	W	D	L	F	A	Pts
Newcastle U	24	14	6	4	46	17	48
Huddersfield T	24	13	5	6	41	25	44
Shrewsbury T	24	9	9	6	29	24	36
Wrexham	24	11	3	10	41	37	36
Bradford C	24	10	4	10	41	41	34
Sheffield U	24	9	7	8	27	29	34
Stockport Co	24	9	6	9	41	32	33
York C	24	8	9	7	35	28	33
Rotherham U	24	9	6	9	36	33	33
Scarborough	24	9	4	11	30	39	31
Notts Co	24	7	6	11	31	48	27
Lincoln C	24	7	3	14	31	47	24
Blackpool	24	3	8	13	25	48	17

Division Three	P	W	D	L	F	A	Pts
Scunthorpe U	22	13	5	4	48	27	44
Walsall	22	12	6	4	49	26	42
Hartlepool U	22	11	6	5	44	32	39
Rochdale	22	10	6	6	33	27	36
Bury	22	10	5	7	42	33	35
Chesterfield	22	10	4	8	28	30	34
Wigan Ath	22	9	4	9	32	30	31
Darlington	22	9	3	10	36	37	30
Halifax T	22	5	5	12	29	43	20
Chester C	22	5	5	12	23	47	20
Hull C	22	4	7	11	21	38	19
Carlisle U	22	5	2	15	31	46	17

NON-LEAGUE TABLES 1998–99

ENDSLEIGH INSURANCE MIDLAND FOOTBALL COMBINATION

Premier Division	P	W	D	L	F	A	Pts
Alveston	34	21	8	5	74	32	71
Cheslyn Hay	34	18	10	6	61	42	64
Southam United	34	16	10	8	70	49	58
Kings Heath	34	17	6	11	66	51	57
Massey Ferguson	34	15	10	9	57	51	55
Meir KA	34	15	9	10	69	47	54
Studley BKL	34	14	11	9	67	43	53
GPT (Coventry)	34	15	8	11	67	65	53
Handrahan Timbers	34	14	10	10	56	47	52
Bolehall Swifts	34	13	8	13	58	48	47
Highgate United	34	13	7	14	69	59	46
Feckenham	34	10	14	10	45	42	44
Coventry Sphinx	34	12	7	15	53	64	43
Alvechurch	34	12	4	18	61	77	40
Continental Star*	34	11	7	16	57	69	37
Kenilworth Town	34	8	8	18	37	67	32
Coleshill Town	34	6	6	22	46	78	24
Dudley Sports	34	2	5	27	27	109	11

*3 points deducted
Bilston Community College resigned – records expunged

Division One	P	W	D	L	F	A	Pts
Northfield Town	30	22	2	6	95	32	68
Knowle	30	20	4	6	78	33	64
Blackheath E'drives	30	19	7	4	83	45	64
Alvis	30	16	3	11	69	66	51
Thimblemill REC	30	14	5	11	67	43	47
Chelmsley Town	30	15	2	13	61	58	47
Holly Lane	30	13	6	11	59	51	45
Wellesbourne	30	14	2	14	57	55	44
Shirley Town	30	12	4	14	50	74	40
Burntwood	30	10	6	14	70	71	36
Hams Hall	30	9	9	12	52	54	36
Studley BKL Res	30	10	5	15	49	58	35
Kings Norton Town Res	30	9	3	18	52	82	30
Loughborough Athletic	30	10	0	20	38	84	30
West Mids Fire Service	30	8	5	17	40	68	29
Colletts Green	30	5	5	20	40	86	20

Swan Sports resigned – records expunged

COURAGE COMBINED COUNTIES LEAGUE

Premier Division	P	W	D	L	F	A	Pts
Ash United	40	31	3	6	115	46	96
Cobham	40	24	11	5	108	50	83
Chipstead	40	25	8	7	82	39	83
Ashford Town	40	24	7	9	102	50	79
Bedfont	40	23	5	12	97	66	74
Godalming & Guildford	40	23	3	14	79	58	72
Reading Town	40	21	7	12	73	55	70
Wallingford	40	20	9	11	104	62	69
Westfield	40	19	8	13	52	45	65
Chessington & Hook	40	18	4	18	77	67	58
Merstham	40	16	8	16	75	67	56
Raynes Park Vale	40	16	8	16	73	70	56
Farnham Town	40	16	7	17	89	73	55
Feltham	40	16	7	17	53	57	55
Sandhurst Town	40	13	8	19	63	92	47
Viking Sports	40	12	5	23	56	97	41
Walton Casuals	40	9	6	25	60	88	33
Cranleigh	40	9	4	27	60	122	31
Netherne Village	40	9	4	27	51	120	31
Hartley Wintney	40	7	9	24	50	87	30
Cove	40	3	1	36	27	135	10

UNIJET SUSSEX COUNTY LEAGUE

Division One	P	W	D	L	F	A	Pts
Burgess Hill Town	38	28	5	5	106	24	89
Saltdean United	38	26	8	4	100	35	86
Horsham YMCA	38	24	7	7	97	50	79
Langney Sports	38	20	6	12	69	43	66
Shoreham	38	19	8	11	80	57	65
Wick	38	18	7	13	65	49	61
East Preston	38	18	6	14	69	57	60
Eastbourne United	38	17	8	13	59	51	59
Pagham	38	16	11	11	42	39	59
Eastbourne Town	38	14	12	12	61	62	54
Redhill	38	14	11	13	79	60	53
Portfield	38	12	13	13	62	66	49
Hassocks	38	13	7	18	51	51	46
Whitehawk	38	11	10	17	50	61	43
Chichester City	38	10	11	17	44	66	41
Littlehampton	38	10	7	21	38	87	37
Ringmer	38	8	11	19	35	64	35
Selsey	38	7	8	23	42	93	29
Hailsham Town	38	7	4	27	40	101	25
Broadbridge Heath	38	4	8	26	32	105	20

Division Two	P	W	D	L	F	A	Pts
Sidley United	34	26	4	4	72	23	82
Three Bridges V	34	23	4	7	74	35	73
Crawley Down	34	22	7	5	66	35	73
Southwick	34	18	9	7	84	34	63
Mile Oak	34	18	8	8	63	49	62
Storrington	34	18	6	10	54	30	60
Sidlesham	34	17	6	11	70	38	57
Arundel	34	16	9	9	57	43	57
Lancing	34	10	11	13	50	55	41
Lingfield	34	10	9	15	54	56	39
Shinewater Association	34	10	9	15	47	58	39
Peacehaven & Telscombe	34	8	12	14	50	67	36
East Grinstead Town	34	10	5	19	50	78	35
Worthing United	34	8	9	17	48	73	33
Oakwood	34	10	3	21	37	72	33
Withdean	34	5	12	17	43	67	27
Crowborough Athletic	34	7	6	21	45	80	27
Newhaven	34	2	7	25	26	97	13

LANCASHIRE FOOTBALL LEAGUE

Division One	P	W	D	L	F	A	Pts
Tranmere Rovers A	20	15	3	2	53	11	48
Burnley A	20	15	3	2	46	12	48
Wrexham A	20	10	5	5	63	38	35
Oldham Athletic A	20	10	3	7	40	30	33
Bury A	20	9	6	5	27	20	33
Macclesfield Town Res	20	9	5	6	41	22	32
Southport Res	20	7	3	10	35	42	24
Morecambe A	20	6	2	12	26	66	20
Leek Town Res	20	4	4	12	20	48	16
Marine Res	20	3	5	12	26	36	14
Accrington Stanley Res	20	1	3	16	13	66	6

MANCHESTER LEAGUE

Premier Division	P	W	D	L	F	A	Pts
Stand Athletic	28	19	5	4	76	35	62
East Manchester	28	15	5	8	56	45	50
Monton Amateurs	28	13	7	8	47	38	46
Wythenshawe Am	28	12	9	7	44	36	45
Mitchell Shackleton	28	13	4	11	58	47	43
Prestwich Heys	28	11	6	11	52	48	39
Springhead	28	10	6	12	43	46	36
Elton Fold	28	11	3	14	40	50	36
Dukinfield Town	28	10	6	12	38	49	36
Atherton Town	28	9	8	11	44	43	35
BICC	28	8	11	9	62	62	35
Urmston	28	9	5	14	44	60	32
Failsworth Town	28	9	5	14	42	61	32
Little Hulton United	28	8	6	14	43	55	30
Stockport Georgians	28	7	6	15	33	52	27

NORTH-WESTERN TRAINS LEAGUE

Divison One

	P	W	D	L	F	A	Pts
Workington	40	27	9	4	86	28	90
Mossley	40	27	7	6	91	38	88
Vauxhall GM	40	26	7	7	92	40	85
Newcastle Town	40	25	9	6	86	33	84
Kidsgrove Athletic	40	24	7	9	90	47	79
Prescot Cables	40	21	9	10	78	44	72
Skelmersdale United	40	21	8	11	82	48	71
St Helens Town	40	22	5	13	77	58	71
Leek CSOB	40	14	11	15	52	58	53
Salford City	40	15	7	18	63	73	52
Ramsbottom United	40	14	8	18	54	64	50
Clitheroe	40	14	6	20	68	58	48
Maine Road	40	14	6	20	50	71	48
Rossendale United	40	14	5	21	59	81	47
Nantwich Town	40	12	6	22	54	68	42
Glossop North End	40	12	6	22	53	81	42
Cheadle Town	40	12	6	22	56	97	42
Atherton LR	40	10	9	21	45	73	39
Atherton Collieries	40	9	7	24	50	88	34
Bootle	40	9	7	24	41	84	34
Holker Old Boys	40	4	3	33	21	116	15

Division Two

	P	W	D	L	F	A	Pts
Fleetwood	36	21	8	7	102	34	71
Abbey Hey	36	20	6	10	70	35	66
Squires Gate	36	17	14	5	53	31	65
Warrington Town	36	18	9	9	82	46	63
Woodley Sports	36	17	10	9	60	38	61
Castleton Gabriels	36	17	10	9	71	56	61
Formby	36	17	7	12	81	59	58
Darwen	36	13	12	11	64	53	51
Chadderton	36	11	17	8	42	38	50
Tetley Walker	36	14	8	14	62	64	50
Bacup Borough	36	11	14	11	47	61	47
Daisy Hill	36	12	9	15	51	63	45
Nelson	36	11	11	14	51	49	44
Curzon Ashton	36	12	7	17	56	58	43
Maghull	36	11	10	15	50	70	43
Colne	36	11	7	18	53	70	40
Ashton Town	36	11	6	19	35	59	39
Oldham Town	36	5	7	24	35	99	22
Blackpool Mechanics	36	4	6	26	40	122	18

JPL WADE NORTHERN FOOTBALL ALLIANCE

Premier Division

	P	W	D	L	F	A	Pts
West Allotment Celtic	28	21	4	3	75	31	67
Ponteland United	28	20	4	4	71	25	64
Ryton	28	17	5	6	63	35	56
Northbank Carlisle	28	15	3	10	52	38	48
Hebburn Reyrolle	28	12	3	13	52	52	39
N/C Benfield Park	28	11	4	13	38	51	37
Shankhouse*	28	11	6	11	41	36	36
Lemington Social Club	28	11	3	14	36	51	36
Seaton Delaval Am	28	9	7	12	49	53	34
Carlisle City	28	10	4	14	44	51	34
Spittal Rovers	28	9	6	13	41	59	33
N/S St Columbas	28	8	7	13	46	56	31
Winlaton Hallgarth	28	8	4	16	50	68	28
Walker Central	28	8	4	16	33	56	28
Walker Ledwood Fos*	28	6	4	18	27	56	19

Division One

	P	W	D	L	F	A	Pts
Percy Main Amateurs	26	20	4	2	83	20	64
Coxlodge Social Club	26	17	3	6	100	42	54
Newcastle University	26	15	7	4	90	35	52
Heaton Stannington	26	11	9	6	68	49	42
Newbiggin CW	26	12	5	9	56	57	41
Amble Town*	26	13	3	10	58	55	39
Proctor & Gamble	26	11	6	9	44	49	39
Heddon Institute	26	10	7	9	64	60	37
Morpeth Town A	26	9	5	12	45	50	32
Highfields United	26	9	3	14	56	72	30
Gosforth Bohemians	26	7	5	14	33	65	26
Ashington Hirst	26	6	4	16	41	68	22
Hexham Swinton	26	6	2	18	41	101	20
Heaton Newton Park*	26	3	3	20	44	100	9

Division Two

	P	W	D	L	F	A	Pts
Amble Vikings	22	16	6	0	62	23	54
Cullercoats	22	15	3	4	81	32	48
Chopwell Top Club	22	14	6	2	66	25	48
Rutherford	22	12	6	4	52	26	42
Wark	22	9	7	6	42	34	34
Northern Social Club	22	9	2	11	55	66	29
Wallington*	22	8	6	8	39	47	27
Otterburn*	22	6	5	11	44	44	20
Hexham Border Co	22	4	5	13	41	78	17
N/C British Tele*	22	5	3	14	32	49	15
Stobhill Rangers	22	3	6	13	32	72	15
Shiremoor G Horse*	22	2	3	17	32	82	6

*3 points deducted

CARLSBERG WEST CHESHIRE LEAGUE

Division One

	P	W	D	L	F	A	Pts
Cammell Laird	30	23	5	2	82	25	74
Heswall	30	22	5	3	74	34	71
Poulton Victoria	30	19	5	6	93	51	62
Vauxhall Motors	30	15	7	8	78	62	52
Stork	30	16	3	11	64	37	51
Ashville	30	14	6	10	51	45	48
Mersey Royal	30	13	4	13	59	47	43
General Chemicals	30	13	3	14	57	52	42
Shell	30	8	10	12	48	55	34
Capenhurst	30	9	5	16	54	77	32
Christleton	30	9	4	17	44	68	31
Blacon Youth Club	30	9	3	18	41	78	30
Mond Rangers	30	8	5	17	48	76	29
Merseyside Police	30	7	7	16	60	83	28
Newton	30	7	7	16	45	70	28
Bromborough Pool	30	7	3	20	38	76	24

INTERLINK EXPRESS MIDLAND FOOTBALL ALLIANCE

	P	W	D	L	F	A	Pts
Rocester	38	25	7	6	80	36	82
Kings Norton Town	38	25	5	8	65	29	80
Oldbury United	38	19	9	10	67	42	66
Boldmere St Michaels	38	19	8	11	56	49	65
Barwell	38	17	10	11	69	54	61
Halesowen Harriers	38	17	8	13	65	63	59
Rushall Olympic	38	16	10	12	57	44	58
Shifnal Town	38	16	8	14	59	60	56
West Midlands Police	38	15	10	13	50	52	55
Chasetown	38	12	17	9	48	38	53
Bridgnorth Town	38	14	11	13	44	40	53
Stourport Swifts	38	13	11	14	56	50	50
Knypersley Victoria	38	13	8	17	59	61	47
Willenhall Town	38	13	8	17	51	53	47
Wednesfield	38	12	6	20	63	72	42
Pelsall Villa	38	11	7	20	41	67	40
Stapenhill	38	11	5	22	51	82	38
Sandwell Borough	38	10	7	21	37	65	37
Pershore Town	38	8	11	19	47	64	35
Stratford Town	38	7	8	23	39	83	29

JEWSON SOUTH WESTERN LEAGUE

	P	W	D	L	F	A	Pts
St Blazey	32	23	5	4	69	25	74
Porthleven	32	22	7	3	102	36	73
Truro City	32	18	8	6	65	37	62
Falmouth Town	32	17	8	7	57	35	59
Wadebridge Town	32	17	6	9	63	34	57
Millbrook	32	17	5	10	55	52	56
Saltash United	32	15	7	10	56	45	52
Bodmin Town	32	15	5	12	65	57	50
Penzance	32	12	7	13	58	62	43
Holsworthy	32	11	8	13	50	55	41
Ply Parkway	32	10	6	16	50	74	36
Liskeard Athletic	32	8	9	15	47	62	33
Tavistock	32	8	8	16	32	47	32
Newquay	32	10	2	20	40	64	32
St Austell	32	7	5	20	29	67	26
Torpoint Athletic	32	5	5	22	39	73	20
Launceston	32	4	5	23	33	105	17

WINSTONLEAD KENT LEAGUE

Premier Division

	P	W	D	L	F	A	Pts
Ramsgate	36	26	5	5	93	24	83
Deal Town	36	24	9	3	78	24	81
Greenwich Borough	36	24	4	8	64	28	76
Thamesmead Town	36	20	14	2	57	19	74
Crockenhill**	36	19	10	7	62	38	66
Chatham Town	36	18	11	7	61	40	65
VCD Athletic	36	16	9	11	61	51	57
Whitstable Town	36	15	9	12	60	52	54
Beckenham Town	36	13	11	12	51	47	50
Slade Green	36	11	11	14	58	49	44
Sheppey United*	36	11	8	17	50	59	44
Herne Bay	36	9	9	18	34	51	36
Lordswood	36	8	12	16	47	71	36
Cray Wanderers*	36	8	9	19	53	68	35
Canterbury City	36	9	8	19	34	73	35
Faversham Town**	36	9	5	22	41	80	29
Erith Town	36	8	5	23	33	79	29
Hythe United	36	7	7	22	38	65	28
Tunbridge Wells	36	5	8	23	46	105	23

Division One

	P	W	D	L	F	A	Pts
Deal Town	36	28	6	2	114	25	90
Dover Athletic	36	28	2	6	109	33	86
Margate*	36	23	11	2	85	25	82
Swanley Furness*	36	20	4	12	69	46	67
Thamesmead Town*	36	18	9	9	91	65	65
Folkestone Invicta	36	19	7	10	98	70	64
Ramsgate	36	17	10	9	74	62	61
Hastings Town	36	15	9	12	54	67	54
Lordswood	36	15	6	15	65	69	51
Dartford	36	14	7	15	60	64	49
Sittingbourne**	36	13	10	13	57	57	46
Chatham Town	36	13	4	19	57	79	43
Beckenham Town**	36	11	8	17	46	43	39
Herne Bay	36	10	7	19	54	75	37
Canterbury City	36	11	4	21	42	91	37
Cray Wanderers	36	8	6	22	46	83	30
Hythe United	36	7	3	26	39	94	24
Crockenhill	36	4	10	22	45	94	22
Whitstable Town	36	5	3	28	32	86	18

*= points awarded   **= points deducted

SCHWEPPES ESSEX SENIOR LEAGUE

	P	W	D	L	F	A	Pts
Bowers United	26	21	3	2	78	16	66
Gt Wakering Rovers	26	20	2	4	73	26	62
Saffron Walden Town	26	16	8	2	49	20	56
Burnham Ramblers	26	14	6	6	61	25	48
Southend Manor	26	11	9	6	49	40	42
Ilford	26	13	3	10	49	44	42
Basildon United (–3)	26	13	5	8	46	35	41
Hullbridge Sports	26	8	3	15	42	38	27
Concord Rangers (–4)	26	8	7	11	33	48	27
Brentwood	26	5	6	15	30	60	21
Stansted	26	6	3	17	40	88	21
East Ham United	26	5	5	16	33	88	20
Sawbridgeworth Town	26	4	6	16	19	47	18
Eton Manor	26	3	4	19	36	63	13

SCREWFIX DIRECT LEAGUE

Premier Division

	P	W	D	L	F	A	Pts
Taunton Town	38	33	3	2	134	33	102
Tiverton Town	38	29	4	5	118	27	91
Chippenham Town	38	25	7	6	93	41	82
Melksham Town	38	20	10	8	73	44	70
Paulton Rovers	38	18	12	8	70	42	66
Brislington	38	18	10	10	74	44	64
Yeovil Town Res	38	18	4	16	70	66	58
Bridport	38	16	7	15	61	68	55
Bridgwater Town	38	15	9	14	68	51	54
Backwell United	38	15	7	16	56	48	52
Mangotsfield United	38	14	9	15	60	58	51
Barnstaple Town	38	14	8	16	72	55	50
Bristol Manor Farm	38	15	4	19	61	57	49
Elmore	38	14	6	18	68	82	48
Bishop Sutton	38	12	7	19	67	81	43
Westbury United	38	9	8	21	42	103	35
Bideford	38	10	1	27	40	108	31
Odd Down	38	5	15	18	44	86	30
Keynsham Town	38	6	7	25	33	99	25
Calne Town	38	3	4	31	34	143	13

Division One

	P	W	D	L	F	A	Pts
Minehead	36	31	4	1	124	25	97
Dawlish Town	36	27	6	3	83	28	87
Street	36	27	4	5	85	36	85
Devizes Town	36	20	7	9	79	43	67
Clyst Rovers	36	21	4	11	76	51	67
Wellington	36	20	6	10	71	42	66
Exmouth Town	36	20	4	12	80	49	64
Pewsey Vale	36	18	4	14	72	46	58
Corsham Town	36	15	10	11	47	58	55
Welton Rovers	36	13	7	16	61	58	46
Bitton	36	12	9	15	67	59	45
Larkhall Athletic	36	13	5	18	51	65	44
Ilfracombe Town	36	12	7	17	61	71	43
Torrington	36	13	0	23	56	79	39
Warminster Town	36	9	3	24	40	79	30
Chard Town	36	9	2	25	49	102	29
Frome Town	36	7	5	24	44	102	26
Glastonbury	36	3	6	27	47	111	15
Heavitree United	36	4	3	29	31	120	15

JEWSON (EAST COUNTIES) LEAGUE

Premier Division

	P	W	D	L	F	A	Pts
Wroxham	42	27	10	5	88	36	91
Fakenham Town	42	25	10	7	96	50	85
Great Yarmouth Town	42	23	9	10	69	36	78
Histon	42	19	17	6	80	53	74
Lowestoft Town	42	19	12	11	78	53	69
Felixstowe Port & Town	42	20	9	13	78	56	69
Soham Town Rangers	42	19	12	11	77	73	69
Newmarket Town	42	19	11	12	68	55	68
Sudbury Town	42	20	8	14	75	67	68
Sudbury Wanderers	42	17	8	17	72	62	59
Bury Town	42	15	14	13	47	46	59
Diss Town	42	14	15	13	54	59	57
Maldon Town	42	16	8	18	69	69	56
Halstead Town	42	14	11	17	59	71	53
Warboys Town	42	14	10	18	70	86	52
Stowmarket Town	42	12	11	19	59	72	47
Gorleston	42	12	10	20	52	78	46
Harwich & Parkeston	42	9	14	19	42	63	41
Woodbridge Town	42	9	11	22	49	73	38
Watton United	42	9	10	23	53	83	37
Ipswich Wanderers	42	5	13	24	49	82	28
Ely City	42	3	11	28	39	100	20

Division One

	P	W	D	L	F	A	Pts
Clacton Town	34	22	9	3	93	26	75
Mildenhall Town	34	21	8	5	79	26	71
Downham Town	34	21	4	9	65	47	67
Tiptree United	34	20	5	9	76	47	65
Needham Market	34	18	7	9	76	43	61
Swaffham Town	34	18	7	9	56	35	61
Dereham Town	34	17	7	10	62	41	58
Chatteris Town	34	16	6	12	51	51	54
Cornard United	34	14	11	9	49	42	53
Whitton United	34	13	9	12	52	57	48
Stanway Rovers	34	11	10	13	43	48	43
Haverhill Rovers	34	9	11	14	38	54	38
Norwich United	34	10	6	18	38	59	36
Brightlingsea United	34	7	11	16	53	68	32
March Town United	34	8	6	20	43	71	30
Hadleigh United	34	7	3	24	34	78	24
Somersham Town	34	5	8	21	33	86	23
Thetford Town	34	3	4	27	32	94	13

SOUTH EAST COUNTIES LEAGUE

	P	W	D	L	F	A	Pts
Luton Town	30	20	6	4	59	25	66
Leyton Orient	30	19	7	4	67	32	64
Brentford	30	19	4	7	74	34	61
Cambridge United	30	12	9	9	57	53	45
Bristol Rovers	30	12	7	11	52	51	43
Barnet	30	12	7	11	40	44	43
Reading	30	9	12	9	36	38	39
Wycombe Wanderers	30	9	11	10	35	37	38
Brighton & Hove Albion	30	10	7	13	48	47	37
Swindon Town	30	10	7	13	41	43	37
Colchester United	30	11	3	16	47	49	36
Portsmouth	30	8	10	12	41	56	34
Oxford United	30	9	7	14	36	53	34
AFC Bournemouth	30	10	3	17	43	66	33
Southend United	30	8	5	17	37	55	29
Gillingham	30	7	5	18	35	66	26

REDFERNS INTERNATIONAL REMOVERS CENTRAL MIDLANDS LEAGUE

Supreme Division	P	W	D	L	F	A	Pts
Mickleover Sports	36	28	3	5	134	44	87
Dunkirk	36	26	4	6	109	38	82
Goole	36	24	9	3	93	23	81
Nettleham	36	21	7	8	69	38	70
Heanor Town	36	21	6	9	98	41	69
Gedling Town	36	18	6	12	76	52	60
Shirebrook Town	36	16	10	10	72	51	58
S. Normanton Athletic	36	17	7	12	74	57	58
Hucknall Rolls Royce	36	17	5	14	64	47	56
Sandiacre Town	36	16	7	13	65	70	55
Clipstone Welfare	36	15	5	16	75	86	50
Blidworth Welfare	36	14	5	17	51	70	47
Sneinton	36	13	6	17	61	71	45
Long Eaton United	36	12	6	18	53	74	42
Graham Street Prims	36	9	6	21	46	92	33
Collingham	36	7	6	23	38	101	27
Kimberley Town	36	5	5	26	51	116	20
Grimethorpe MW	36	3	7	26	27	92	16
Harworth Colliery Inst	36	4	2	30	36	129	14

Premier Division	P	W	D	L	F	A	Pts
Lincoln Moorlands	28	26	2	0	96	17	80
Welbeck Colliery	28	18	5	5	67	40	59
Shardlow St James	28	17	4	7	78	48	55
Selston	28	16	5	7	79	45	53
Blackwell MW	28	14	5	9	51	46	47
Holbrook	28	12	6	10	58	49	42
Thorne Colliery	28	10	9	9	59	44	39
Yorkshire Main	28	10	9	9	41	59	39
Askern Welfare	28	11	3	14	59	55	36
Stanton Ilkeston	28	11	3	14	55	64	36
Radford	28	9	6	13	48	63	33
Gr'nwood Meadows (–1)	28	8	4	16	47	75	27
Teversal Grange	28	5	4	19	38	70	19
Mexborough Athletic	28	3	5	20	29	77	14
Mickleover RBL	28	4	2	22	34	87	14

NORTHERN COUNTIES (EAST) LEAGUE

Premier Division	P	W	D	L	F	A	Pts
Ossett Albion	38	23	5	10	86	50	74
Ossett Town	38	22	7	9	76	44	73
Brigg Town	38	20	12	6	78	43	72
Hallam	38	22	5	11	95	63	71
North Ferriby United	38	19	12	7	92	50	69
Liversedge	38	21	4	13	87	63	67
Arnold Town	38	19	7	12	78	56	64
Denaby United	38	15	12	11	66	60	57
Garforth Town	38	15	9	14	74	70	54
Buxton	38	14	10	14	54	53	52
Selby Town	38	15	7	16	59	61	52
Sheffield	38	15	6	17	55	58	51
Armthorpe Welfare	38	13	11	14	46	50	50
Glasshoughton Welfare	38	13	9	16	58	71	48
Thackley	38	14	5	19	65	77	47
Eccleshill United	38	12	6	20	56	74	42
Staveley MW*	38	9	11	18	50	84	36
Maltby Main†	38	8	6	24	51	87	26
Pontefract Collieries	38	7	7	24	37	86	26
Pickering Town	38	5	7	26	44	107	22

Division One	P	W	D	L	F	A	Pts
Harrogate Railway Ath	24	15	6	3	58	29	51
Brodsworth MW	24	13	3	8	52	42	42
Glapwell	24	12	6	6	47	39	42
Parkgate	24	12	5	7	61	32	41
Borrowash Victoria	24	12	5	7	48	38	41
Worsbrough Bridge MW	24	9	6	9	49	42	33
Hall Road Rangers	24	9	6	9	44	49	33
Hatfield Main*	24	10	3	11	27	47	32
Louth United	24	9	3	12	37	33	30
Yorkshire Amateurs	24	6	7	11	41	49	25
Tadcaster Albion	24	6	6	12	33	51	24
Rossington Main	24	6	4	14	37	51	22
Winterton Rangers	24	3	8	13	22	54	17

† 4 points deducted   * 2 points deducted

BANKS'S BREWERY WEST MIDLANDS LEAGUE

Premier Division	P	W	D	L	F	A	Pts
Kington Town	40	32	3	5	120	39	99
Cradley Town	40	28	3	9	98	40	87
Stafford Town	40	27	5	8	89	38	86
W'ton Casuals	40	24	5	11	97	72	77
Smethwick Rangers	40	21	8	11	88	52	71
Darlaston Town	40	21	7	12	81	63	70
Bandon	40	19	7	14	72	53	64
Malvern Town	40	16	12	12	76	62	60
Tipton Town	40	17	6	17	62	75	57
Bustleholme	40	16	7	17	63	71	55
Gornal Athletic	40	14	11	15	68	65	53
Lye Town	40	12	15	13	56	54	51
Star	40	14	8	18	55	63	50
Dudley Town	40	11	13	16	52	67	46
Tividale	40	12	9	19	55	69	45
Brierley Hill Town	40	11	12	17	57	74	45
Westfields	40	9	15	16	57	67	42
Ludlow Town	40	12	5	23	46	82	41
Ettingshall HT	40	10	9	21	62	87	39
Walsall Wood	40	5	7	28	43	99	22
W'ton United	40	1	9	30	33	138	12

Division One (North)	P	W	D	L	F	A	Pts
Heath Hayes	28	19	5	4	75	28	62
Little Drayton Rgrs (–3)	28	19	6	3	74	24	60
Lucas Flight Controls	28	18	4	6	91	37	58
Great Wyrley	28	17	5	6	75	35	56
Brereton Social	28	16	8	4	83	48	56
Newport	28	17	5	6	62	40	56
Cannock Chase	28	14	7	7	63	43	49
Sedgley White Lions	28	11	7	10	44	38	40
Morda United	28	9	3	16	55	72	30
Shifnal Town Res	28	9	2	17	42	66	29
W'ton Casuals Res	28	8	4	16	53	79	28
Wyrley Rangers	28	6	5	17	39	92	23
W'ton Town	28	3	7	18	35	71	16
Corestone Services	28	2	8	18	37	105	14
Walsall Wood Res (–1)	28	2	4	22	25	75	9

Division One (South)	P	W	D	L	F	A	Pts
Wellington	26	22	1	3	115	17	67
Causeway United	26	21	1	4	75	24	64
Leominster Town	26	13	5	8	57	48	44
Bromyard Town	26	13	3	10	43	34	42
Tividale Res	26	12	4	10	48	49	40
Sikh Hunters	26	12	3	11	68	70	39
H'owen Harriers Res	26	11	4	11	59	51	37
Malvern Town Res	26	9	7	10	45	54	34
Cradley Town Res	26	10	2	14	43	50	32
Hinton	26	10	2	14	53	68	32
Pershore Town Res	26	9	4	13	28	50	31
Mahal	26	7	5	14	42	67	26
Lye Town Res	26	8	1	17	44	91	25
Borgfeld Celtic	26	3	2	21	36	83	11

COMPLETE MUSIC HELLENIC LEAGUE

Premier Division	P	W	D	L	F	A	Pts
Burnham	36	26	6	4	88	31	84
Carterton Town	36	25	6	5	82	34	81
Highworth Town	36	21	6	9	92	47	69
Banbury United	36	20	9	7	73	33	69
North Leigh	36	18	11	7	77	44	65
EFC Cheltenham	36	17	5	14	60	36	56
Abingdon United	36	17	5	14	61	55	56
Tuffley Rovers	36	16	6	14	63	55	54
Didcot Town	36	16	5	15	58	52	53
Bicester Town	36	15	8	13	58	60	53
Cirencester Academy	36	12	11	13	42	56	47
Hallen	36	10	14	12	45	48	44
Fairford Town	36	10	10	16	42	50	40
Swindon Supermarine	36	10	9	17	41	59	39
Shortwood United	36	9	11	16	37	61	38
Almondsbury Town	36	8	7	21	47	82	31
Wantage Town	36	8	5	23	36	90	29
Kintbury Rangers (–6)	36	8	8	20	48	89	26
Harrow Hill	36	4	2	30	31	99	14

Division One	P	W	D	L	F	A	Pts
Pegasus Juniors	32	22	7	3	96	47	73
Ardley United	32	19	5	8	66	46	62
Forest Green Rovers Res	32	18	6	8	71	40	60
Milton United	32	18	6	8	62	45	60
Wootton Bassett Town	32	17	7	8	64	43	58
Ross Town	32	15	7	10	57	41	52
Letcombe	32	13	9	10	56	45	48
Cheltenham Saracens	32	13	5	14	56	61	44
Worcester College OB	32	11	5	16	42	59	38
Kidlington	32	10	8	13	51	71	38
Purton	32	9	9	14	41	62	36
Bishops Cleeve	32	9	7	16	55	66	34
Easington Sports	32	8	8	16	47	56	32
Cirencester United	32	8	7	17	49	55	31
Clanfield	32	9	4	19	40	71	31
Watlington Town	32	7	9	16	49	69	30
Headington Amateurs	32	6	11	15	44	64	29

EVERARDS BREWERY LEICESTERSHIRE SENIOR LEAGUE

Premier Division	P	W	D	L	F	A	Pts
Oadby Town	34	25	4	5	90	28	79
Birstall United	34	24	7	3	77	27	79
Holwell Sports	34	23	5	6	100	45	74
Highfield Rangers	34	21	3	10	60	39	66
St Andrews	34	18	6	10	87	51	60
Quorn	34	14	9	11	79	70	51
Kirby Muxloe	34	14	8	12	61	54	50
Anstey Nomads	34	14	6	14	57	54	48
Thringstone United	34	11	10	13	56	63	43
Barrow Town	34	12	6	16	48	60	42
Cottesmore Amateurs	34	13	3	18	50	72	42
Downes Sports	34	11	8	15	49	54	41
Coalville Town	34	10	9	15	53	63	39
Ibstock Welfare	34	8	11	15	54	60	35
Lutterworth Town	34	8	11	15	44	59	35
Aylestone Park OB	34	8	6	20	45	90	30
Ellistown	34	3	11	20	24	93	20
Friar Lane OB	34	4	7	23	33	85	19

Division One	P	W	D	L	F	A	Pts
Thurmaston Town	34	30	4	0	113	21	94
Thurnby Rangers	34	25	3	6	114	39	78
Blaby & Whetstone	34	21	8	5	72	33	71
Leics YMCA	34	20	5	9	98	48	65
Huncote S & S	34	17	7	10	76	53	58
Stoney Stanton	34	17	6	11	66	50	57
Fosse Imps	34	16	6	12	83	66	54
Anstey Town	34	14	5	15	59	58	47
Leics Constabulary	34	14	5	15	60	61	47
Narborough	34	13	7	14	65	74	46
Sileby Town	34	13	6	15	58	58	45
Bardon Hill	34	13	5	16	69	61	44
Loughborough Dynamo	34	12	6	16	68	75	42
Earl Shilton Alb	34	11	5	18	53	76	38
Asfordby Ams	34	8	12	14	63	76	36
Saffron Dynamo	34	8	5	21	53	76	29
North Kilworth	34	3	3	28	32	130	12
Harborough Town	34	1	2	31	21	168	5

JEWSON WESSEX LEAGUE

Division One	P	W	D	L	F	A	Pts
Lymington & New M	38	27	6	5	92	31	87
Thatcham Town	38	23	9	6	92	46	78
AFC Newbury	38	22	11	5	81	39	77
Eastleigh	38	22	8	8	69	43	74
Christchurch	38	22	7	9	72	53	73
Wimborne Town	38	18	14	6	81	34	68
Cowes Sports	38	19	8	11	77	54	65
Moneyfields	38	17	8	13	69	62	59
AFC Totton	38	15	10	13	60	50	55
Bemerton Heath H	38	17	4	17	59	54	55
Brockenhurst	38	14	7	17	52	61	49
Bournemouth	38	12	10	16	46	63	46
Fareham Town	38	11	12	15	58	67	45
Gosport Borough	38	11	11	16	66	71	44
BAT	38	10	13	15	55	65	43
East Cowes Vics	38	10	4	24	48	103	34
Hamble ASSC	38	6	9	23	37	68	27
Portsmouth RN	38	6	9	23	42	81	27
Whitchurch United	38	5	11	22	36	76	26
Downton	38	4	7	27	40	111	19

SPARTAN SOUTH MIDLANDS LEAGUE

Premier Division	P	W	D	L	F	A	Pts
Barkingside	44	30	6	8	97	44	96
Potters Bar Town	44	29	7	8	109	30	94
London Colney	44	29	5	10	98	28	92
Beaconsfield SYCOB	44	25	9	10	85	40	84
Brook House	44	24	11	9	74	42	83
Hoddesdon Town	44	24	7	13	80	60	79
Toddington Rovers	44	22	12	10	72	48	78
Ruislip Manor	44	22	10	12	89	60	76
Royston Town	44	19	11	14	73	62	68
Hillingdon Borough (−4)	44	20	9	15	72	61	65
Waltham Abbey	44	16	13	15	79	64	61
Brache Sparta	44	17	6	21	80	74	57
Arlesey Town	44	16	8	20	61	70	56
New Bradwell St Peter	44	15	11	18	56	70	56
Buckingham Athletic	44	15	9	20	65	101	54
Milton Keynes City	44	13	10	21	68	88	49
Islington St Mary's	44	11	14	19	55	85	47
Somersett Ambury V&E	44	13	6	25	50	103	45
St Margaretsbury (−3)	44	12	10	22	75	98	43
Haringey Borough	44	9	11	24	49	87	38
Welwyn Garden City	44	10	6	28	63	95	36
Harpenden Town	44	9	9	26	47	86	36
Brimsdown Rovers	44	3	6	35	35	136	15

Senior Division	P	W	D	L	F	A	Pts
Holmer Green	42	30	6	6	121	42	96
Hanwell Town	42	30	6	6	105	44	96
Tring Athletic	42	28	8	6	109	35	92
Milton Keynes	42	28	6	8	104	47	90
Biggleswade Town	42	25	6	11	99	62	81
Bedford United	42	23	8	11	65	52	77
Letchworth	42	18	13	11	83	54	67
Biggleswade United	42	19	7	16	86	66	64
Leverstock Green	42	17	13	12	73	63	64
Cockfosters	42	17	11	14	76	62	62
Greenacres (Hemel)	42	19	4	19	71	61	61
Langford	42	18	7	17	71	80	61
Shillington	42	16	9	17	72	73	57
Amersham Town	42	14	10	18	71	82	52
Caddington	42	14	10	18	75	93	52
Totternhoe	42	12	10	20	56	71	46
Luton Old Boys	42	10	9	23	39	78	39
Stony Stratford Town	42	8	11	23	58	98	35
Risborough Rangers	42	8	6	28	41	97	30
Harefield United	42	8	5	29	48	112	29
Winslow United	42	7	5	30	42	104	26
Houghton Town	42	6	4	32	43	132	22

Division One	P	W	D	L	F	A	Pts
Bridger Packing	32	27	3	2	92	21	84
Ampthill Town	32	26	3	3	106	33	81
De Havilland	32	26	2	4	102	23	80
Mursley United	32	21	5	6	72	26	68
Dunstable Town '98'	32	19	6	7	72	42	63
Scot	32	16	3	13	60	58	51
Pitstone & Ivinghoe	32	14	4	14	80	65	46
Walden Rangers	32	14	4	14	61	47	46
Old Dunstablians	32	14	4	14	65	59	46
Kent Athletic	32	12	8	12	58	44	44
The 61 FC (Luton)	32	10	7	15	57	87	37
Flamstead (−1)	32	10	4	18	63	84	33
Leighton Athletic	32	7	6	19	39	76	27
Old Bradwell United (−3)	32	9	3	20	49	96	27
Abbey National (MK)	32	4	8	20	41	75	20
Newport Athletic	32	4	2	26	37	123	14
Markyate	32	2	2	28	25	120	8

*= 1 point deducted   *= 3 points deducted

OPTIMUM INTERIORS CENTRAL CONFERENCE

Division One	P	W	D	L	F	A	Pts
Stoke City	18	11	3	4	42	20	36
Gloucester City	18	9	2	7	31	34	29
Rushden & Diamonds	18	7	7	4	44	30	28
Kidderminster Harriers	18	8	3	7	48	38	27
Hednesford Town	18	7	6	5	34	32	27
Worcester City	18	9	0	9	38	42	27
Cheltenham Town	18	7	3	8	40	37	24
Hereford United	18	6	3	9	30	36	21
Telford United	18	4	5	9	31	48	17
Bromsgrove Rovers	18	3	6	9	24	45	15

UNITED COUNTIES LEAGUE

Premier Division	P	W	D	L	F	A	Pts
Spalding United	38	30	3	5	106	29	93
Desborough Town	38	24	6	8	82	41	78
Cogenhoe United	38	23	5	10	89	47	74
N'pton Spencer	38	20	6	12	78	46	66
S & L Corby	38	19	9	10	70	45	66
Bourne Town	38	18	9	11	75	69	63
Stotfold	38	17	11	10	57	43	62
Boston Town	38	17	10	11	68	44	61
Buckingham Town	38	17	9	12	71	52	60
Yaxley	38	18	5	15	87	75	59
Wellingborough Town	38	16	6	16	57	57	54
Blackstone	38	16	5	17	59	56	53
St Neots Town	38	15	6	17	70	73	51
Wootton Blue Cross	38	13	8	17	54	77	47
Holbeach United	38	12	10	16	62	65	46
Ford Sports	38	12	9	17	50	57	45
Kempston Rovers	38	10	6	22	46	75	36
Eynesbury Rovers	38	6	7	25	42	100	25
Long Buckby	38	3	6	29	26	99	15
Potton United	38	2	8	28	21	120	14

Division One	P	W	D	L	F	A	Pts
Bugbrooke St Michael	34	24	6	4	104	29	78
Higham Town	34	23	6	5	101	28	75
Rothwell Corinthians	34	18	10	6	78	52	64
W Whitworths	34	19	6	9	73	43	63
Cottingham	34	18	9	7	80	51	63
N'pton Vanaid	34	17	10	7	51	26	61
Blisworth	34	15	10	9	69	53	55
Thrapston Town	34	14	8	12	66	63	50
Newport Pagnell Town	34	14	7	13	78	79	49
Daventry Town	34	14	4	16	56	55	46
ON Chenecks	34	13	6	15	52	61	45
Olney Town	34	11	8	15	56	49	41
Woodford United	34	10	9	15	56	74	39
St Ives Town	34	7	12	15	31	62	33
Irchester United	34	9	4	21	44	96	31
Sharnbrook	34	5	8	21	35	94	23
Harrowby United	34	5	4	25	49	105	19
Burton Park Wanderers	34	3	7	24	28	87	16

HIGHLAND LEAGUE

	P	W	D	L	F	A	Pts
Peterhead	30	24	4	2	89	19	76
Huntly	30	23	3	4	86	38	72
Keith	30	22	4	4	92	41	70
Elgin City	30	21	1	8	71	39	64
Fraserburgh	30	18	6	6	86	39	60
Clachnacuddin	30	16	8	6	80	45	56
Cove Rangers	30	16	5	9	88	48	53
Forres Mechanics	30	11	6	13	60	60	39
Brora Rangers	30	11	5	14	61	63	38
Deveronvale	30	11	4	15	57	72	37
Rothes	30	8	5	17	46	64	29
Buckie Thistle	30	8	4	18	36	60	28
Lossiemouth	30	8	4	18	40	67	28
Wick Academy	30	7	2	21	33	85	23
Nairn County	30	3	2	25	32	114	11
Fort William	30	1	1	28	24	127	4

ARNOTT INSURANCE NORTHERN LEAGUE

Division One	P	W	D	L	F	A	Pts
Bedlington Terriers	38	33	2	3	128	37	101
Tow Law Town	38	23	6	9	80	49	75
Chester-le-Street Town	38	17	14	7	71	46	65
Dunston Fed	38	18	10	10	75	53	64
West Auckland Town	38	19	7	12	67	62	64
Guisborough Town	38	18	5	15	68	65	59
Seaham Red Star	38	16	7	15	62	59	55
Consett	38	15	7	16	72	64	52
Morpeth Town	38	15	6	17	54	60	51
Stockton	38	15	6	17	68	77	51
Billingham Syn (–3)	38	15	7	16	60	56	49
Marske United	38	13	9	16	58	63	48
Crook Town	38	13	7	18	51	60	46
South Shields	38	10	15	13	58	66	45
Billingham Town (–3)	38	13	9	16	66	81	45
Jarrow Roofing	38	11	10	17	62	85	43
Easington Colliery	38	11	6	21	67	78	39
Newcastle Blue Star (–3)	38	12	5	21	59	83	38
Penrith (–3)	38	10	8	20	59	82	35
Shildon	38	6	8	24	48	107	26

HAMPSHIRE LEAGUE

Division One	P	W	D	L	F	A	Pts
Alton Town	36	28	6	2	117	28	90
Poole Town	36	27	6	3	124	42	87
Colden Common	36	21	6	9	54	38	69
Blackfield-Langley	36	18	3	15	89	81	57
New Street	36	17	5	14	83	67	56
Brading Town	36	15	9	12	66	51	54
Fleet Spurs	36	15	8	13	73	53	53
Stockbridge	36	14	9	13	67	66	51
Fleetlands	36	15	6	15	71	78	51
Liss Athletic	36	15	5	16	63	57	50
Locksheath	36	15	5	16	66	64	50
Mayflower	36	14	7	15	54	61	49
Horndean	36	12	9	15	67	71	45
Pirelli General	36	12	7	17	60	66	43
Hayling United	36	11	6	19	40	60	39
Vosper Thornycroft	36	11	6	19	56	77	39
Winchester City	36	10	6	19	47	86	36
Bishopstoke	36	8	5	23	37	106	29
Romsey Town	36	5	4	27	40	122	19

FA ACADEMY LEAGUE UNDER-19 1998–99

GROUP A	P	W	D	L	F	A	GD	Pts
Everton	22	12	4	6	39	25	+14	40
Manchester U	22	12	4	6	38	25	+13	40
Crewe Alex	22	11	6	5	30	19	+11	39
Blackburn R	22	11	3	8	46	29	+17	36
Liverpool	22	9	9	4	33	17	+16	36
Aston Villa	22	7	4	11	34	44	–10	25
Manchester C	22	4	3	15	20	50	–30	15
Bolton W	22	3	3	16	28	63	–35	12

GROUP B	P	W	D	L	F	A	GD	Pts
Fulham	22	12	3	7	34	27	+7	39
Crystal Palace	22	12	2	8	46	35	+11	38
Chelsea	22	11	4	7	43	36	+7	37
Charlton Ath	22	10	7	5	37	30	+7	37
Wimbledon	22	7	9	6	32	33	–1	30
Bristol C	22	7	5	10	34	39	–5	26
QPR	22	6	6	10	32	39	–7	24
Southampton	22	5	4	13	29	50	–21	19

GROUP C	P	W	D	L	F	A	GD	Pts
Nottingham F	22	13	6	3	53	23	+30	45
Sheffield W	22	10	5	7	37	36	+1	35
Sunderland	22	8	9	5	34	26	+8	33
Leeds U	22	10	3	9	34	37	–3	33
Barnsley	22	8	6	8	36	28	+8	30
Derby Co	22	8	5	9	34	35	–1	29
Middlesbrough	22	8	5	9	27	42	–15	29
Newcastle U	22	7	4	11	32	43	–11	25
Leicester C	22	5	5	12	27	37	–10	20

GROUP D	P	W	D	L	F	A	GD	Pts
West Ham U	22	17	3	2	53	20	+33	54
Arsenal	22	12	2	8	36	27	+9	38
Watford	22	9	6	7	37	40	–3	33
Tottenham H	22	8	6	8	35	31	+4	30
Coventry C	22	9	2	11	43	38	+5	29
Peterborough U	22	7	7	8	33	34	–1	28
Millwall	22	7	3	12	29	38	–9	24
Ipswich T	22	4	5	13	31	44	–13	17
Norwich C	22	5	2	15	23	49	–26	17

UNDER-19 PLAY-OFFS

Preliminary Round
Ipswich T 2 Leicester C 4
Newcastle U 0 Norwich C 6

First Round
Everton 7 Leicester C 1
Charlton Ath 3 Barnsley 1
Sunderland 3 Bristol C 0
Arsenal 4 Manchester C 0
Manchester U 4 Millwall 1
Chelsea 3 Derby Co 2
Leeds U 0 Wimbledon 3
West Ham U 2 Bolton W 1
Nottingham F 3 Southampton 0
Blackburn R 5 Coventry C 2

Watford 3 Aston V 1
Crystal Palace 1 Middlesbrough 2
Sheffield W 2 QPR 0
Crewe Alex 3 Peterborough U 0
Tottenham H 2 Liverpool 1
Fulham 5 Norwich C 0

Seond Round
Everton 4 Charlton Ath 0
Arsenal 3 Sunderland 1
Manchester U 1 Chelsea 2 *(aet)*
West Ham U 2 Wimbledon 1
Nottingham F 1 Blackburn R 0
Middlesbrough 2 Watford 1

Sheffield W 1 Crewe Alex 1 *(aet)*
(Sheffield W won 3-0 on penalties)
Fulham 1 Tottenham H 2

Third Round
Everton 2 Arsenal 1
Nottingham F 3 Middlesbrough 2
West Ham U 2 Chelsea 1 *(aet)*
(West Ham U won 5-3 on penalties)
Tottenham H 0 Sheffield W 2

Semi-Finals
West Ham U 1 Everton 0
Nottingham F 2 Sheffield W 3 *(aet)*

Final
West Ham U 1 Sheffield W 0 *(aet)*

FA ACADEMY LEAGUE UNDER-17 1998–99

GROUP A	P	W	D	L	F	A	GD	Pts
Manchester U	22	14	7	1	66	20	+46	49
Blackburn R	22	14	5	3	56	23	+33	47
Liverpool	22	9	10	3	47	36	+11	37
Everton	22	10	5	7	44	33	+11	35
Manchester C	22	9	6	7	49	42	+7	33
Crewe Alex	22	6	8	8	30	32	–2	26
Aston Villa	22	7	3	12	27	54	–27	24

GROUP B	P	W	D	L	F	A	GD	Pts
Wimbledon	22	8	6	8	29	33	–4	30
Bristol C	22	8	4	10	40	42	–2	28
QPR	22	7	7	8	48	51	–3	28
Crystal Palace	22	7	6	9	25	37	–12	27
Southampton	22	7	4	11	37	50	–13	25
Fulham	22	5	4	13	37	69	–32	19
Charlton Ath	22	3	6	13	29	51	–22	15

GROUP C	P	W	D	L	F	A	GD	Pts
Newcastle U	22	16	3	3	45	19	+26	51
Leeds U	22	11	4	7	55	33	+22	37
Sunderland	22	11	4	7	39	24	+15	37
Sheffield W	22	11	2	9	45	41	+4	35
Leicester C	22	9	4	9	33	35	–2	31
Nottingham F	22	8	5	9	30	34	–4	29
Barnsley	22	8	3	11	29	44	–15	27
Middlesbrough	22	7	4	11	31	37	–6	25
Derby Co	22	5	3	14	25	54	–29	18

GROUP D	P	W	D	L	F	A	GD	Pts
Arsenal	22	15	4	3	54	23	+31	49
West Ham U	22	12	5	5	42	23	+19	41
Coventry C	22	11	1	10	52	42	+10	34
Tottenham H	22	6	9	7	26	32	–6	27
Watford	22	7	3	12	45	53	–8	24
Millwall	22	6	2	14	15	31	–16	20
Peterborough U	22	3	3	16	29	61	–32	12

UNDER-17 PLAY-OFFS

First Round
Crystal Palace 3 Leicester C 4 *(aet)*
Sunderland 2 Fulham 1
West Ham U 2 Aston Villa 3
Blackburn R 4 Peterborough U 0
QPR 1 Nottingham F 2
Sheffield W 3 Southampton 1
Arsenal 2 Derby Co 0
Everton 1 Watford 0
Coventry C 1 Crewe Alex 3
Leeds U 4 Charlton Ath 1
Liverpool 2 Millwall 0

Tottenham H 0 Manchester C 2
Wimbledon 4 Middlesbrough 2

Second Round
Manchester U 5 Leicester C 4 *(aet)*
Aston Villa 1 Sunderland 7
Blackburn R 4 Nottingham F 0
Arsenal 5 Sheffield W 0
Newcastle U 4 Watford 1
Barnsley 0 Crewe Alex 4
Leeds 1 Liverpool 1 *(aet)*
(Liverpool won 5-4 on penalties)
Wimbledon 1 Manchester C 3

Third Round
Manchester U 3 Sunderland 0
Arsenal 2 Blackburn R 2 *(aet)*
(Blackburn R won 6-5 on penalties)
Newcastle U 2 Crewe Alex 0
Manchester C 4 Liverpool 1

Semi-Finals
Manchester U 1 Blackburn R 5 *(aet)*
Newcastle U 1 Manchester C 2

Final
Blackburn R 4 Manchester C 3 *(aet)*

AMATEUR FOOTBALL ALLIANCE 1998–99

AFA SENIOR CUP

1st Round Proper
Old Foresters 0, 2 Old Ignatians
Pegasus 1, 3 Old Aloysians
Parkfield 0, 5 E Barnet O Grammarians
Old Stationers 2*, 3* Old Chigwellians
Old Buckwellians 3, 4 St Mary's College
Lancing Old Boys 0, 3 Old Finchleians
Old Wokingians 0, 2 Latymer Old Boys
Lensbury 2*, 5* Old Salesians
Bank of England wo, wd Old Tollingtonians
Civil Service 2, 1 Alexandra Park
Alleyn Old Boys 6, 3 Old Woodhouseians
Norsemen 3, 1 South Bank
Old Tiffinian 4, 0 Centymca
West Wickham 3*, 1* Old Grammarians
Old Sinjuns 2, 3 Ealing Association
Old Hamptonians 1, 2 Old Salopians
Wake Green 0, 2 Old Suttonians
Crouch End Vampires 1, 0 Nat'l Westminster Bank
Westerns 4, 2 Old Malvernian
Polytechnic 1, 2 Old Reptonian
Old Salvatorians 0, 1 Hale End Athletic
Hon Artillery Company 5, 1 Old Parmiterians
UCL Academicals 1, 4 Old Actonians Assn
Kingsburians 1, 2 Old Manorians
Old Bromleians 0, 4 Nottsborough
Old Latymerians 3, 1 Albanian
Midland Bank 1, 2 City of London
Carshalton 4, 1 William Fitt
Cuaco 2, 0 Winchmore Hill
Old Minchendenians 1*:0, 1*:7 Old Tenisonians
Mill Hill Village 4, 3 Old Owens
Hadley 0, 4 Old Esthameians
(* *after extra time*)

2nd Round Proper
Old Ignatians 1, 3 Old Aloysians
E Barnet O Grammarians 2, 0 Old Chigwellians

St Mary's College 1, 2 Old Finchleians
Latymer Old Boys 1, 2 Old Salesians
Bank of England 2*, 3* Civil Service
Alleyn Old Boys 0, 1 Norsemen
Old Tiffinian 4, 1 West Wickham
Ealing Association 0, 2 Old Salopians
Old Suttonians 1, 2 Crouch End Vampires
Westerns 2, 5 Old Reptonian
Hale End Athletic 1, 2 Hon Artillery Company
Old Actonians Assn 3, 2 Old Manorians
Nottsborough 3, 2 City of London
Old Latymerians 3, 4 Carshalton
Cuaco 0, 6 Old Tenisonians
Mill Hill Village 3, 0 Old Esthameians

3rd Round Proper
Old Aloysians 5, 3 E Barnet O Grammarians
Old Finchleians 5, 2 Old Salesians
Civil Service 4, 1 Norsemen
Old Tiffinian 1, 3 Old Salopians
Crouch End Vampires 3, 1 Old Reptonian
Hon Artillery Company 4, 3 Old Actonians Assn
Nottsborough 1, 0 Carshalton
Old Tenisonians 2, 1 Mill Hill Village

4th Round Proper
Old Aloysians 1, 2 Old Finchleians
Civil Service 0*:2, 0*:0 Old Salopians
Crouch End Vampires 2*, 3* Hon Artillery Company
Nottsborough 3*:1, 3*:0 Old Tenisonians

Semi-finals
Old Finchleians 4*, 2* Civil Service
Hon Artillery Company 3, 2 Nottsborough

Final
Old Finchleians 4, 1 Hon Artillery Company

OTHER AFA CUP RESULTS

Intermediate
Barclays Bank Res 3, 0 Carshalton Res
Junior
Albanian 3rd 1, 0 Barclays Bank 3rd
Minor
Barclays Bank 4th 3, 1 Polytechnic 4th
Senior Novets
Polytechnic 5th 2, 1 Old Finchleians 5th
Intermediate Novets
Old Actonians Assn 6th 1*, 2* Natwest Bank 6th
Junior Novets
Old Actonians Assn 9th 4, 0 Midland Bank 7th
Veterans
Winchmore Hill 3, 1 Alexandra Park
Open Veterans
P L A 2, 1 Winchmore Hill
Youth – U16
Norsemen 4, 0 Old Parmiterians
Essex Senior
Old Parkonians 2, 0 Old Parmiterians
Middlesex Senior
Old Actonians Assn 2, 0 Lensbury
Surrey Senior
Carshalton 2*, 0* Old Salesians
Essex Intermediate
Old Parkonians Res 2, 1 Old Buckwellians Res
Kent Intermediate
Morgan Guaranty 1st 1, 2 Old Sedcopians Res
Middlesex Intermediate
Old Aloysians Res 4*, 3* Barclays Bank Res
Surrey Intermediate
Carshalton Res 3, 2 Nottsborough Res
Greenland Memorial
Old Aloysians 5, 1 Norsemen
(* *after extra time*)

AFA REPRESENTATIVE XI

v Oxford University   Lost 1-4
v Army FA   Lost 2-3
v Royal Navy FA   Lost 2-4

v London University   Won 3-1
v London FA   Won 1-0

ARTHUR DUNN CUP FINAL

Old Salopians 3, 1 Lancing Old Boys

ARTHURIAN LEAGUE

PREMIER DIVISION	P	W	D	L	F	A	Pts
Old Chigwellians	16	12	1	3	32	19	25
Old Foresters	16	11	2	3	28	18	24
Old Salopians	16	8	2	6	43	29	18
Old Carthusians	16	9	0	7	28	18	18
Old Brentwoods	16	7	2	7	26	29	16
Lancing Old Boys	16	6	0	10	26	31	12
Old Reptonians	16	5	2	9	19	33	12
Old Bradfieldians	16	4	3	9	18	28	11
Old Etonians	16	4	0	12	21	36	8

DIVISION 1	P	W	D	L	F	A	Pts
Old Cholmeleians	14	11	3	0	57	15	24#
Old Malvernians	14	7	2	5	33	28	16
Old Witleians	14	7	2	5	35	32	16
Old Aldenhamians	14	6	2	6	33	35	14
Old Harrovians	14	6	1	7	46	39	13
Old Haberdashers	14	5	2	7	17	37	12
Old Wykehamists	14	4	3	7	37	45	11
Old Wellingburians	14	2	1	11	19	46	5

DIVISION 2	P	W	D	L	F	A	Pts
Old Brentwoods Res	16	11	4	1	44	21	26
Old Etonians Res	16	9	3	4	41	23	21
Old Cholmeleians Res	16	8	6	2	26	13	21#
Old Chigwellians Res	16	6	2	8	34	33	14
Old Etonians 3rd	16	5	4	7	23	22	14
Lancing Old Boys Res	16	5	3	8	29	45	13
Old Foresters Res	16	5	2	9	19	34	12
Old Cholmeleians 3rd	16	4	4	8	25	40	11#
Old Millhillians	16	4	2	10	29	39	10

DIVISION 3

	P	W	D	L	F	A	Pts
Old Salopians Res	14	8	2	4	52	22	18
Old Carthusians Res	14	8	2	4	45	20	18
Old Westminsters	14	7	3	4	40	23	17
Old Foresters 3rd	14	8	1	5	30	33	17
Old Reptonians Res	14	7	1	6	32	48	15
Old Harrovians Res	14	7	0	7	37	34	14
Old Cholmeleians 4th	14	4	1	9	26	49	8#
Old Brentwoods 3rd	14	1	2	11	21	54	4

(# 1 point deducted - breach of rule)

Division 4–8 Teams – Won by Old Aldenhamians Res
Division 5–6 Teams – Won by Old Carthusians 3rd
Junior League Cup
Old Chigwellians Res 4, 2 Old Haberdashers Res
Derrik Moore Veterans Cup
Old Etonians 3, 1 Old Ardinians
Jim Dixson VI-a-Side–Won by Old Millhillians

LONDON FINANCIAL FA

DIVISION ONE

	P	W	D	L	F	A	Pts
Morgan Guaranty	14	9	2	3	49	26	29
Royal Sun Alliance	14	9	2	3	43	27	29
Dresdner Kleinwort Benson	14	6	4	4	34	26	22
Coutts & Co	14	7	0	7	32	29	21
Granby	14	5	6	3	23	28	21
GE Capital Ins Services	14	3	6	5	28	28	15
Bank America	14	3	3	8	24	38	12
Royal Bank of Scotland	14	1	3	10	26	57	6

Allied Irish Bank withdrawn – record expunged

DIVISION TWO

	P	W	D	L	F	A	Pts
Citibank	16	12	1	3	56	16	37
Eagle Star	16	12	0	4	53	26	36
Standard Chartered Bank	16	9	4	3	53	25	31
Chase Manhattan Bank	16	10	1	5	47	25	31
J&H Marsh & McLennan	16	7	5	4	39	37	26
Foreign & Commonwealth Office	16	7	2	7	31	37	23
Temple Bar	16	3	3	10	32	42	12
Century Life	16	2	2	12	24	59	8
Salomon Smith Barney	16	0	2	14	23	91	2

DIVISION THREE

	P	W	D	L	F	A	Pts
Mount Pleasant P O	14	12	1	1	74	18	37
Abbey National	14	10	1	3	54	24	31
C Hoare & Co	14	6	1	7	37	35	19
Bank America Res	14	6	1	7	29	42	19
Lincoln	14	5	3	6	38	35	18
ANZ Banking Group	14	5	1	8	19	32	16
Royal Bank of Scotland Res	14	5	1	8	24	42	16
Noble Lowndes	14	2	1	11	14	61	7

Credit Suisse Finan'l Products withdrawn – record expunged

DIVISION FOUR

	P	W	D	L	F	A	Pts
Customs & Excise	18	14	2	2	73	33	44
Eagle Star Res	18	13	0	5	59	29	39
Royal Sun Alliance Res	18	9	7	2	42	28	34
British Gas (Bromley)	18	7	4	7	41	34	25
Granby Res	18	6	6	6	35	33	24
Citibank Res	18	6	4	8	50	57	22
J&H Marsh & McLennan Res	18	5	4	9	43	50	19
Coutts & Co. Res	18	6	2	10	25	48	17*
Royal Sun Alliance 3rd	18	4	4	10	24	48	16
Temple Bar Res	18	1	5	12	24	58	8

* 3 pts deducted – playing ineligible player

DIVISION FIVE

	P	W	D	L	F	A	Pts
Cabinet Office & Treasury	16	13	3	0	82	20	42
Chelsea Exiles	16	13	1	2	97	26	40
Bank of Ireland	16	11	3	2	67	22	36
Gaflac	16	8	0	8	56	53	24
Temple Bar 3rd	16	6	2	8	43	47	20
R Bank of Scotland 3rd	16	5	0	11	29	51	15
Noble Lowndes Res	16	4	2	10	26	63	14
Standard Chartered Res	16	4	1	11	35	68	13
Eagle Star 3rd	16	2	0	14	30	115	6

Challenge Cup–Bank of England 2, Midland Bank 1
Senior Cup–Morgan Guaranty 2, GE Capital 1
Senior Plate–Chase Manhattan 4, Standard Chartered Bank 1

Junior Cup–R Sun Alliance Res 2, Eagle Star Res 1
Junior Plate–C Hoare & Co 4, Granby Res 1
Minor Cup–Bank of Ireland 3, Cabinet Office & Treasury 4
Minor Plate–Chelsea Exiles 2, R. Bank of Scotland 3rd 1
Veterans' Cup–Lensbury 4*, Lloyds Bank 2*
W A Jewell Memorial V-a-S–Won by Morgan Guaranty
Saunders Shield V-a-S–Won by Chase Manhattan Bank 'B'
Sportsmanship Shield–Won by Gaflac

Representative Matches
v Southern Olympian League–Drawn 1-1
v Royal Marines–Lost 0-3
v Southern Amateur League 'B'–Lost 2-6
v Old Boys' League–Drawn 4-6
v Bristol Insurance Institute–Lost 1-6

LONDON LEGAL LEAGUE

DIVISION ONE

	P	W	D	L	F	A	Pts
Wilde Sapte	18	13	4	1	61	19	30
Clifford Chance	18	10	5	3	37	20	25
Gray's Inn	18	10	3	5	36	20	23
Slaughter & May	18	10	2	6	53	28	22
Linklaters & Paines	18	9	4	5	25	30	22
Rosling King	18	9	3	6	41	34	21
Lovell White Durrant	18	7	4	7	29	31	18
Cameron McKenna	18	4	2	12	28	69	10
Pegasus	18	2	1	15	21	51	5
Herbert Smith	18	1	2	15	25	54	4

DIVISION TWO

	P	W	D	L	F	A	Pts
KPMG	18	15	0	3	69	19	30
Taylor Joynson Garrett	18	11	3	4	36	24	25
Norton Rose	18	11	2	5	41	27	24
Nabarro Nathanson	18	10	2	6	36	29	22
Stephenson Harwood	18	8	2	8	46	26	18
Kennedy's	18	7	2	9	30	32	16
Freshfields	18	6	4	8	23	36	16
Denton Hall	18	6	1	11	34	54	13
DJ Freeman	18	6	0	12	31	45	12
Allen & Overy	18	2	0	16	17	71	4

DIVISION THREE

	P	W	D	L	F	A	Pts
Watson Farley & Williams	22	18	3	1	54	14	39
Simmons & Simmons	22	15	4	3	52	23	34
Nicholson Graham & Jones	22	14	4	4	65	23	32
Barlow Lyde & Gilbert	22	12	4	6	34	24	28
Eversheds	22	12	1	9	49	32	25
Richards Butler	22	9	3	10	43	46	21
Baker & McKenzie	22	10	1	11	35	55	21
Edward Lewis	22	7	4	11	25	45	18
Titmuss Sainer Dechert	22	6	5	11	20	34	17
SJ Berwin	22	7	1	14	24	44	15
Macfarlanes	22	6	2	14	18	58	14
Hammond Suddards	22	1	0	21	6	27	2

League Challenge Cup–Gray's Inn 2, Slaughter & May 1
Weavers Arms Cup–Linklaters 2, Watson Farley & Williams 0

LONDON OLD BOYS' CUPS

Senior–Phoenix Old Boys 1, Old Ignatians 0
Intermediate–Old Manorians Res 2, Latymer Old Boys Res 1
Junior–Phoenix Old Boys 3rd 2, Old Reigatians 3rd 0
Minor–Old Meadonians 4th 2, Old Actonians 4th 0
Novets–Old Actonians Ass'n 5th 0, Old Suttonians 5th 7
Drummond–Leyton County Old Boys 6th 2, Glyn Old Boys 6th 1
Nemean–Old Actonins 9th 7, Old Suttonians 8th 1
Veterans–Old Finchleians Vets 0, Old Tenisonians Vets 3

OLD BOYS' INVITATION CUPS

Senior–Old Finchleians 4*, Old Tenisonians 3*
Junior–E Barnet O Grammarians Res 2, Old Stationers Res 0
Minor–E Barnet O Grammarians 3rd 2, Old Finchleians 3rd 3
4th XI–Old Esthameians 4th 1*†, Old Tenisonians 4th 1*
5th XI–Old Minchendenians 1*, Old Tenisonians 5th 2*
6th XI–E Barnet O Grammarians 6th 1, Glyn Old Boys 6th 3
7th XI–Old Bromleians 7th 4, Old Finchleians 7th 1
Veterans' XI–Old Tenisonians Vets 6, Old Finchleians Vets 2
(* after extra time; †won on penalties)

OLD BOYS' LEAGUE

Premier Division	P	W	D	L	F	A	Pts
Old Ignatians	20	15	2	3	55	23	32
Old Tenisonians	20	12	6	2	39	19	30
Old Aloysians	20	13	3	4	57	28	29
Old Salvatorians	20	9	4	7	41	35	22
Old Meadonians	20	10	2	8	38	33	22
Old Hamptonians	20	9	3	8	33	34	21
Old Vaughanians	20	6	4	10	23	24	16
Cardinal Manning OB	20	5	6	9	32	42	16
Old Buckwellians	20	6	3	11	48	60	15
Glyn Old Boys	20	4	2	14	17	51	10
Enfield Old Grammarians	20	1	5	14	23	57	7

Senior Division One	P	W	D	L	F	A	Pts
Old Wilsonians	20	16	2	2	67	24	34
Phoenix Old Boys	20	12	5	3	46	28	29
Old Suttonians	20	9	3	8	36	35	21
Shene Old Grammarians	20	8	5	7	38	44	21
Old Manorians	20	7	5	8	35	35	19
Old Dorkinians	20	6	6	8	37	40	18
Old Kingsburians	20	6	6	8	36	40	18
Old Isleworthians	20	7	4	9	37	48	18
Latymer Old Boys	20	7	3	10	33	37	17
Old Tiffinians	20	3	7	8	21	35	13
Old Reigatians	20	5	2	13	23	43	12

Senior Division Two	P	W	D	L	F	A	Pts
Old Minchendenians	18	11	5	2	60	35	27
Old Vaughanians Res	18	11	3	4	40	24	25
John Fisher Old Boys	18	9	6	3	44	24	24
Old Danes	18	8	4	6	55	36	20
Chertsey Old Salesians	18	7	4	7	32	51	18
Clapham Old Xaverians	18	5	5	8	41	49	15
Old Meadonians Res	18	6	2	10	45	60	14
Old Sinjuns	18	5	3	10	52	51	13
Old Tenisonians Res	17	6	3	8	30	40	13#
Old Camdenians	17	3	1	13	28	57	5#

Senior Division 3	P	W	D	L	F	A	Pts
Latymer Old Boys Res	21	16	2	3	57	28	34
Phoenix Old Boys Res	22	11	5	6	50	39	27
Q. Mary College OB	22	10	5	7	55	49	25
Old Uffingtonians	22	11	2	9	59	49	24
Old Aloysians Res	22	10	3	9	57	51	23
Old Addeyans	22	8	6	8	50	39	22
Old Hamptonians Res	22	9	4	9	34	54	22
Old Salvatorians Res	21	6	8	7	31	43	20
Old Sedcopians	22	6	7	9	57	48	19
Old Wokingians	22	6	7	9	43	34	19
Old Dorkinians Res	22	6	2	14	42	68	12#
Mill Hill County OB	22	5	3	14	42	75	11#

(# 2 points deducted for breach of rule)

Intermediate Divisions:
North–11 Teams Won by Old Manorians Res
South–12 Teams Won by Old Wilsonians Res
Division One North–11 Teams Won by Old Tollingtonians
Division One South–10 Teams Won by Old Paulines
Division One West–11 Teams Won by Old Danes Res
Division Two North–11 Teams Won by Old Tollingtonians Res
Division Two South–11 Teams Won by Chertsey Old Salesians 3rd
Division Two West–11 Teams Won by Cardinal Manning Old Boys 3rd
Division Three North–11 Teams Won by Old Tollingtonians 3rd
Division Three South–11 Teams Won by Glyn Old Boys 4th
Division Three West–11 Teams Won by Old Kingsburians 4th
Division Four North–11 Teams Won by Leyton County Old Boys 4th
Division Four South–10 Teams Won by Old Sedcopians 3rd
Division Four West–11 Teams Won by Holland Park Old Boys Res
Division Five North–9 Teams Won by Leyton County Old Boys 5th
Division Five South–11 Teams Won by Old Sedcopians 4th
Division Five West–12 Teams Won by Old Manorians 6th
Division Six North–8 Teams Won by Old Buckwellians 5th
Division Six South–11 Teams Won by John Fisher Old Boys 4th
Division Six West–10 Teams Won by Old Salvatorians 9th
Division Seven South–10 Teams Won by Old Paulines Res
Division Eight South–8 Teams Won by Old Paulines 3rd
Division Nine South–10 Teams Won by Glyn Old Boys 8th

MIDLAND AMATEUR ALLIANCE

PREMIER DIVISION	P	W	D	L	F	A	Pts
Old Elizabethans	20	16	3	1	63	21	51
Beeston Old Boys Assn	20	16	1	3	75	29	49
Lady Bay	20	13	3	4	60	34	42
ASC Dayncourt	20	10	3	7	60	41	33
Kirton Brick Works	20	10	3	7	53	36	33
Bassingfield	20	8	4	8	58	52	28
Pannell Kerr Foster Steelers	20	7	2	11	40	47	23
Prince of Wales	20	6	2	12	36	52	20
Parkhead Academicals	20	5	3	12	26	53	18
Tibshelf Old Boys	20	3	2	15	34	86	11
Dynamo Baptist	20	2	2	16	23	77	8

DIVISION ONE	P	W	D	L	F	A	Pts
Nottingham Irish Centre	26	23	1	2	120	35	70
Beeston Town 'A'	26	19	1	6	112	38	58
Caribbean Cavaliers	26	17	5	4	69	26	56
Old Elizabethans Res	26	18	2	6	88	51	56
Ollerton Town 'A'	26	11	6	9	59	65	39
Dukeries Hotel	26	11	4	11	53	54	37
Radcliffe Olympic 'A'	26	10	6	10	52	61	36
Nottinghamshire	26	8	7	11	49	49	31
Magdala Amateurs 'A'	26	9	4	13	54	55	31
Derbyshire Amateurs 'A'	26	9	4	13	48	68	31
Woodborough United	26	7	4	15	45	76	25
Bassingfield Res	26	7	3	16	48	85	24
Ilkeston Rangers	26	6	4	16	49	88	22
County Nalgo	26	0	3	23	26	121	3

DIVISION TWO	P	W	D	L	F	A	Pts
Arnold & Carlton College	26	21	2	3	87	32	65
Hucknall Sports YC	26	18	5	3	96	38	59
ASC Dayncourt Res	26	17	5	4	109	45	56
Gresham United	26	13	5	8	77	48	44
Cadland Chilwell	26	13	5	8	66	51	44
Nottinghamshire Res	26	12	4	10	62	60	40
Southwell Amateurs	26	10	5	11	61	60	35
Old Elizabethans 3rd	26	8	9	9	56	63	33
Lady Bay Res	26	9	5	12	82	90	32
Brunts Old Boys	26	9	3	14	47	65	30
Prince of Wales Res	26	7	3	16	39	62	24
Magdala Amateurs Res	26	5	3	17	59	104	21
Ilkeston Rangers Res	26	3	7	16	41	100	16
Beeston Old Boys Res	26	4	3	19	42	106	15

DIVISION THREE	P	W	D	L	F	A	Pts
Gedling Town YC	20	17	1	2	76	16	52
Fleet Cars	20	16	0	4	78	40	48
Old Bemrosians	20	14	0	6	61	48	42
Acrumac	20	13	1	6	64	36	40
ASC Dayncourt 3rd	20	10	3	7	56	39	33
Prince of Wales 3rd	20	10	0	10	58	46	30
E Mid Training & Ed. Centre	20	8	2	10	55	63	26
Derbyshire Amateurs 3rd	24	7	3	10	52	58	24
Nottinghamshire 3rd	20	4	1	15	33	85	13
Tibshelf Old Boys 3rd	20	3	1	16	13	73	10
Dynamo Baptist Res	20	2	0	18	27	69	6

League Cups:
Senior–FC Beeston 2, Kirton Brick Works 1
Intermediate–Arnold & Carlton 4, Gresham United 2
Minor–Gedling Town YC 5, EMTEC 2

SOUTHERN AMATEUR LEAGUE

SENIOR SECTION:

FIRST DIVISION	P	W	D	L	F	A	Pts
Old Actonians Association	22	15	5	2	52	19	50
Barclays Bank	22	14	4	4	57	35	46
Carshalton	22	10	6	6	59	36	36
Crouch End Vampires	22	10	6	6	45	29	36
National Westminster Bank	22	9	4	9	36	38	31
Polytechnic	22	9	5	8	45	37	29***
East Barnet Old Grammarians	22	7	6	9	28	48	27
Lloyds Bank	22	6	7	9	38	37	25
Old Parmiterians	22	8	1	13	34	44	25
Norsemen	22	5	7	10	35	50	22
Lensbury	22	5	7	10	38	56	21*
West Wickham	22	2	6	14	27	55	12

(Point deducted for breach of League Rule)*

SECOND DIVISION

	P	W	D	L	F	A	Pts
Old Bromleians	22	12	8	2	53	26	44
Old Owens	22	12	7	3	45	28	43
Old Salesians	22	13	3	6	56	35	42
Midland Bank	22	11	4	7	42	30	37
Old Parkonians	22	11	3	8	38	31	36
Old Esthameians	22	9	8	5	39	29	35
Civil Service	22	10	3	9	41	40	33
Alexandra Park	22	8	7	7	44	44	31
South Bank	22	5	7	10	32	47	22
Old Stationers	22	4	5	13	32	55	17
Winchmore Hill	22	2	6	14	31	58	12
Old Lyonians	22	3	3	16	27	57	12

THIRD DIVISION

	P	W	D	L	F	A	Pts
Alleyn Old Boys	22	16	4	2	73	21	52
Old Finchleians	22	15	3	4	84	38	48
Broomfield	22	15	3	6	52	36	48
Bank of England	22	13	3	6	49	28	42
Cuaco	22	10	4	8	49	45	34
Merton	22	8	5	9	41	43	29
Old Latymerians	22	6	8	8	40	37	26
Old Westminster Citizens	22	7	5	10	42	46	26
Southgate Olympic	22	7	3	12	36	54	24
Kew Association	22	6	5	11	42	50	23
Ibis	22	2	7	13	30	69	13
Brentham	22	1	2	19	32	103	5

RESERVE TEAMS SECTION – Divisional Champions:
First Division–12 Teams – East Barnet Old Grammarians Res
Second Division–12 Teams – Midland Bank Res
Third Division–12 Teams – Merton Res

3RD TEAMS SECTION:
First Division–12 Teams – East Barnet Old Grammarians 3rd
Second Division–12 Teams – Old Owens 3rd
Third Division–12 Teams – Old Finchleians 3rd

4TH TEAMS SECTION:
First Division–12 Teams – Old Actonians Association 4th
Second Division–12 Teams – Old Parmiterians 4th
Third Division–12 Teams – Old Finchleians 4th

5TH TEAMS SECTION:
First Division–11 Teams – Old Actonians Association 5th
Second Division–11 Teams – Civil Service 5th
Third Division–10 Teams – Old Finchleians 5th

6TH TEAMS SECTION:
First Division–9 Teams – Old Actonians Association 6th
Second Division–7 Teams – Carshalton 6th
Third Division–7 Teams – Old Finchleians 6th

MINOR SECTION:
First Division–10 Teams – Old Stationers 7th
Second Division–10 Teams – National Westminster Bank 7th
Third Division–10 Teams – Old Parmiterians 8th
Fourth Division–10 Teams – Old Finchleians 8th

CHALLENGE CUPS (Entries):
Junior (22)–Norsemen 3rd 2
   Barclays Bank 3rd 1

Minor (22)–Barclays Bank 4th 2
   Crouch End Vampires 1

Senior Novets (19)–Polytechnic 5th 1:5p
   Midland Bank 5th 1:4p
Intermediate Novets (16)–National Westminster Bank 6th 2
   Old Parmiterians 6th 1

Junior Novets (28–Winchmore Hill 7th 3
   National Westminster Bank 7th 0

Hamilton Trophy for Hospitality & Sportsmanship–Cuaco
Wilkinson Sword for Disciplinary Conduct–Cuaco

SOUTHERN OLYMPIAN LEAGUE

SENIOR SECTION:

DIVISION ONE

	P	W	D	L	F	A	Pts
Nottsborough	17	11	4	2	56	19	26
Old Woodhouseians	18	11	4	3	34	19	26
Hale End Athletic	18	11	2	5	37	36	24
Old Grammarians	18	8	5	5	36	25	20*
City of London	17	7	2	8	28	33	16
Hon Artillery Company	17	6	3	8	32	30	15
Parkfield	17	6	2	9	39	41	14
Ulysses	18	5	4	9	27	36	14
Southgate County	18	5	3	10	31	55	12*
St Mary's College	18	2	3	13	34	50	5**

DIVISION TWO

	P	W	D	L	F	A	Pts
UCL Academicals	18	12	4	2	45	23	28
Mill Hill Village	18	10	5	3	48	28	25
Pegasus	17	8	4	5	50	38	20
Fulham Compton Old Boys	18	9	3	6	46	44	20*
Hadley	18	9	1	8	42	39	19
Old Bealonians	18	8	3	7	43	41	19
Albanian	17	7	2	8	40	26	16
Wandsworth Borough	18	6	3	9	36	50	15
Ealing Association	18	4	3	11	24	44	11
BBC	18	1	2	15	24	65	4

DIVISION THREE

	P	W	D	L	F	A	Pts
Old Colfeians	18	14	2	2	55	20	30
University of Hertford	18	13	3	2	63	31	29
Brent	17	9	3	5	34	25	21
Tesco Country Club	17	9	3	5	43	33	18***
London Welsh	18	8	1	9	42	42	17
Inland Revenue	18	6	2	10	41	45	14
Duncombe Sports	18	6	4	8	36	39	13***
The Comets	18	5	3	10	36	55	13
Hampstead Heathens	18	5	0	13	40	63	10
Westerns	18	2	3	13	26	57	7

DIVISION FOUR

	P	W	D	L	F	A	Pts
Mayfield Athletic	14	11	1	2	23	30	23
Kings Old Boys	14	8	3	3	23	26	19
The Cheshunt Club	14	8	3	3	21	19	18*
Centymca	14	4	6	4	26	32	14
London Airways	14	5	3	6	24	27	13
Witan	14	6	1	7	19	27	13
Birkbeck College	14	2	2	10	14	40	6
Economicals	14	1	3	10	17	45	5

(* *point deducted for disciplinary breach*)

Intermediate Section:
Divisional Champions
Division One–10 Teams Won by Nottsborough Res
Division Two–10 Teams Won by Mill Hill Village Res
Division Three–10 Teams Won by Albanian 4th
Division Four–Disbanded

Junior Section:
Division One N–10 Teams Won by Old Woodhouseians 3rd
Division Two N–10 Teams Won by Parkfield 5th
Division Three N–9 Teams Won by Old Woodhouseians 4th
Division Four N–9 Teams Won by Parkfield 7th
Division One S&W–10 Teams Won by Centymca Res
Division Two S&W–10 Teams Won by Old Grammarians 3rd
Division Three S&W–10 Teams Won by Ealing Association 4th
Senior Challenge Bowl–Won by Albanian
Senior Challenge Shield–Won by Old Colfeians
Intermediate Challenge Cup–Won by Southgate County Res
Intermediate Challenge Shield–Won by Hon Artillery Company Res
Junior Challenge Cup–Won by Mill Hill Village 3rd
Junior Challenge Shield–Won by BBC 3rd
Mander Cup–Won by Albanian 4th
Mander Shield–Won by BBC 4th
Burntwood Trophy–Won by Albanian 5th
Burntwood Shield–Won by Ealing Association 5th
Thomas Parmiter Cup–Won by Parkfield 6th
Thomas Parmiter Shield–Won by Old Finchleians 6th
Veterans' Challenge Cup–Won by Old Finchleians Vets
Veterans' Challenge Shield–Won by Centymca Vets

RECORDS

Major British Records

HIGHEST WINS

First-Class Match	Arbroath *(Scottish Cup 1st Round)*	36	Bon Accord	0	12 Sept 1885
International Match	England	13	Ireland	0	18 Feb 1882
FA Cup	Preston NE *(1st Round)*	26	Hyde U	0	15 Oct 1887
League Cup	West Ham U *(2nd Round, 2nd Leg)*	10	Bury	0	25 Oct 1983
	Liverpool *(2nd Round, 1st Leg)*	10	Fulham	0	23 Sept 1986

FA PREMIER LEAGUE

	(Home)	Manchester U	9	Ipswich T	0	4 March 1995
	(Away)	Nottingham F	1	Manchester U	8	6 Feb 1999

FOOTBALL LEAGUE

Division 1	*(Home)*	WBA	12	Darwen	0	4 April 1892
		Nottingham F	12	Leicester Fosse	0	21 April 1909
	(Away)	Newcastle U	1	Sunderland	9	5 Dec 1908
		Cardiff C	1	Wolverhampton W	9	3 Sept 1955
Division 2	*(Home)*	Newcastle U	13	Newport Co	0	5 Oct 1946
	(Away)	Burslem PV	0	Sheffield U	10	10 Dec 1892
Division 3	*(Home)*	Gillingham	10	Chesterfield	0	5 Sept 1987
	(Away)	Halifax T	0	Fulham	8	16 Sept 1969
Division 3(S)	*(Home)*	Luton T	12	Bristol R	0	13 April 1936
	(Away)	Northampton T	0	Walsall	8	2 Feb 1947
Division 3(N)	*(Home)*	Stockport Co	13	Halifax T	0	6 Jan 1934
	(Away)	Accrington S	0	Barnsley	9	3 Feb 1934
Division 4	*(Home)*	Oldham Ath	11	Southport	0	26 Dec 1962
	(Away)	Crewe Alex	1	Rotherham U	8	8 Sept 1973
Aggregate Division 3(N)		Tranmere R	13	Oldham Ath	4	26 Dec 1935

SCOTTISH LEAGUE

Premier	*(Home)*	Aberdeen	8	Motherwell	0	26 March 1979
Division	*(Away)*	Hamilton A	0	Celtic	8	5 Nov 1988
Division 1	*(Home)*	Celtic	11	Dundee	0	26 Oct 1895
	(Away)	Airdrieonians	1	Hibernian	11	24 Oct 1950
Division 2	*(Home)*	Airdrieonians	15	Dundee Wanderers	1	1 Dec 1894
	(Away)	Alloa Ath	0	Dundee	10	8 March 1947

LEAGUE CHAMPIONSHIP HAT-TRICKS

Huddersfield T	1923–24 to 1925–26
Arsenal	1932–33 to 1934–35
Liverpool	1981–82 to 1983–84

MOST GOALS FOR IN A SEASON

		Goals	*Games*	*Season*
FA PREMIER LEAGUE				
	Newcastle U	82	42	1993–94
FOOTBALL LEAGUE				
Division 1	Aston V	128	42	1930–31
Division 2	Middlesbrough	122	42	1926–27
Division 3(S)	Millwall	127	42	1927–28
Division 3(N)	Bradford C	128	42	1928–29
Division 3	QPR	111	46	1961–62
Division 4	Peterborough U	134	46	1960–61
SCOTTISH LEAGUE				
Premier Division	Rangers	101	44	1991–92
	Dundee U	90	36	1982–83
	Celtic	90	36	1982–83
	Celtic	90	44	1986–87
Division 1	Hearts	132	34	1957–58
Division 2	Raith R	142	34	1937–38
New Division 1	Dunfermline Ath	93	44	1993–94
	Motherwell	92	39	1981–82
New Division 2	Ayr U	95	39	1987–88
New Division 3	Alloa	78	36	1997–98

FEWEST GOALS FOR IN A SEASON

		Goals	Games	Season
FA PREMIER LEAGUE				
	Leeds U	28	38	1996–97
FOOTBALL LEAGUE	(minimum 42 games)			
Division 1	Stoke C	24	42	1984–85
Division 2	Watford	24	42	1971–72
	Leyton Orient	30	46	1994–95
Division 3(S)	Crystal Palace	33	46	1950–51
Division 3(N)	Crewe Alex	32	42	1923–24
Division 3	Stockport Co	27	46	1969–70
Division 4	Crewe Alex	29	46	1981–82
SCOTTISH LEAGUE	(minimum 30 games)			
Premier Division	Hamilton A	19	36	1988–89
	Dunfermline Ath	22	44	1991–92
Division 1	Brechin C	30	44	1993–94
	Ayr U	20	34	1966–67
Division 2	Lochgelly U	20	38	1923–24
New Division 1	Stirling Alb	18	39	1980–81
	Dumbarton	23	36	1995–96
New Division 2	Brechin C	22	36	1994–95
New Division 3	Alloa	26	36	1995–96

MOST GOALS AGAINST IN A SEASON

		Goals	Games	Season
FA PREMIER LEAGUE				
	Swindon T	100	42	1993–94
FOOTBALL LEAGUE				
Division 1	Blackpool	125	42	1930–31
Division 2	Darwen	141	34	1898–99
Division 3(S)	Merthyr T	135	42	1929–30
Division 3(N)	Nelson	136	42	1927–28
Division 3	Accrington S	123	46	1959–60
Division 4	Hartlepools U	109	46	1959–60
SCOTTISH LEAGUE				
Premier Division	Morton	100	36	1984–85
	Morton	100	44	1987–88
Division 1	Leith Ath	137	38	1931–32
Division 2	Edinburgh C	146	38	1931–32
New Division 1	Queen of the S	99	39	1988–89
	Cowdenbeath	109	44	1992–93
New Division 2	Meadowbank T	89	39	1977–78
New Division 3	Albion R	82	36	1994–95

FEWEST GOALS AGAINST IN A SEASON

		Goals	Games	Season
FA PREMIER LEAGUE				
	Arsenal	17	38	1998–99
FOOTBALL LEAGUE	(minimum 42 games)			
Division 1	Liverpool	16	42	1978–79
Division 2	Manchester U	23	42	1924–25
	West Ham U	34	46	1990–91
Division 3(S)	Southampton	21	42	1921–22
Division 3(N)	Port Vale	21	46	1953–54
Division 3	Gillingham	20	46	1995–96
Division 4	Lincoln C	25	46	1980–81
SCOTTISH LEAGUE	(minimum 30 games)			
Premier Division	Rangers	19	36	1989–90
	Rangers	23	44	1986–87
	Celtic	23	44	1987–88
Division 1	Celtic	14	38	1913–14
Division 2	Morton	20	38	1966–67
New Division 1	St Johnstone	23	36	1996–97
	Hibernian	24	39	1980–81
	Falkirk	32	44	1993–94
New Division 2	St Johnstone	24	39	1987–88
	Stirling Alb	24	39	1990–91
New Division 3	Brechin C	21	36	1995–96

MOST POINTS IN A SEASON

FOOTBALL LEAGUE	(under old system of two points for a win)	Points	Games	Season
Division 1	Liverpool	68	42	1978–79
Division 2	Tottenham H	70	42	1919–20
Division 3	Aston V	70	46	1971–72
Division 3(S)	Nottingham F	70	46	1950–51
	Bristol C	70	46	1954–55
Division 3(N)	Doncaster R	72	42	1946–47
Division 4	Lincoln C	74	46	1975–76
SCOTTISH LEAGUE				
Premier Division	Aberdeen	59	36	1984–85
	Rangers	73	44	1992–93
Division 1	Rangers	76	42	1920–21
Division 2	Morton	69	38	1966–67
New Division 1	St Mirren	62	39	1976–77
	Falkirk	66	44	1993–94
New Division 2	Forfar Ath	63	39	1983–84
FA PREMIER LEAGUE	(three points for a win)			
	Manchester U	92	42	1993–94
FOOTBALL LEAGUE				
Division 1	Sunderland	105	46	1998–99
	Everton	90	42	1984–85
	Liverpool	90	40	1987–88
Division 2	Fulham	101	46	1998–99
Division 3	Notts Co	99	46	1997–98
Division 4	Swindon T	102	46	1985–86
SCOTTISH LEAGUE				
Premier Division	Rangers	87	36	1995–96
New Division 1	Hibernian	89	36	1998–99
New Division 2	Stirling Alb	81	36	1995–96
New Division 3	Forfar Ath	80	36	1994–95

FEWEST POINTS IN A SEASON

FA PREMIER LEAGUE		Points	Games	Season
	Ipswich T	27	42	1994–95
FOOTBALL LEAGUE	(minimum 34 games)			
Division 1	Stoke C	17	42	1984–85
Division 2	Doncaster R	8	34	1904–05
	Loughborough T	8	34	1899–1900
	Walsall	31	46	1988–89
Division 3	Doncaster R	20	46	1997–98
Division 3(S)	Merthyr T	21	42	1924–25 & 1929–30
	QPR	21	42	1925–26
Division 3(N)	Rochdale	11	40	1931–32
Division 4	Workington	19	46	1976–77
SCOTTISH LEAGUE	(minimum 30 games)			
Premier Division	St Johnstone	11	36	1975–76
	Morton	16	44	1987–88
Division 1	Stirling Alb	6	30	1954–55
Division 2	Edinburgh C	7	34	1936–37
New Division 1	Queen of the S	10	39	1988–89
	Cowdenbeath	13	44	1992–93
New Division 2	Berwick R	16	39	1987–88
	Stranraer	16	39	1987–88
New Division 3	Albion R	18	36	1994–95

MOST WINS IN A SEASON

FA PREMIER LEAGUE		Wins	Games	Season
	Manchester U	27	42	1993–94
	Blackburn R	27	42	1994–95
FOOTBALL LEAGUE				
Division 1	Tottenham H	31	42	1960–61
Division 2	Tottenham H	32	42	1919–20
Division 3(S)	Millwall	30	42	1927–28
	Plymouth Arg	30	42	1929–30
	Cardiff C	30	42	1946–47
	Nottingham F	30	46	1950–51
	Bristol C	30	46	1954–55

Division 3(N)	Doncaster R	33	42	1946–47
Division 3	Aston V	32	46	1971–72
Division 4	Lincoln C	32	46	1975–76
	Swindon T	32	46	1985–86

SCOTTISH LEAGUE

Premier Division	Rangers	27	36	1995–96
	Aberdeen	27	36	1984–85
	Rangers	33	44	1991–92
	Rangers	33	44	1992–93
Division 1	Rangers	35	42	1920–21
Division 2	Morton	33	38	1966–67
New Division 1	Hibernian	28	36	1998–99
New Division 2	Forfar Ath	27	39	1983–84
	Ayr U	27	39	1987–88
New Division 3	Forfar Ath	25	36	1994–95

RECORD HOME WINS IN A SEASON

Brentford won all 21 games in Division 3(S), 1929–30

UNDEFEATED AT HOME

Liverpool 85 games (63 League, 9 League Cup, 7 European, 6 FA Cup), Jan 1978–Jan 1981

RECORD AWAY WINS IN A SEASON

Doncaster R won 18 of 21 games in Division 3(N), 1946–47

FEWEST WINS IN A SEASON

FA PREMIER LEAGUE		*Wins*	*Games*	*Season*
	Swindon T	5	42	1993–94
FOOTBALL LEAGUE				
Division 1	Stoke C	3	22	1889–90
	Woolwich Arsenal	3	38	1912–13
	Stoke C	3	42	1984–85
Division 2	Loughborough T	1	34	1899–1900
	Walsall	5	46	1988–89
Division 3(S)	Merthyr T	6	42	1929–30
	QPR	6	42	1925–26
Division 3(N)	Rochdale	4	40	1931–32
Division 3	Rochdale	2	46	1973–74
Division 4	Southport	3	46	1976–77
SCOTTISH LEAGUE				
Premier Division	St Johnstone	3	36	1975–76
	Kilmarnock	3	36	1982–83
	Morton	3	44	1987–88
Division 1	Vale of Leven	0	22	1891–92
Division 2	East Stirlingshire	1	22	1905–06
	Forfar Ath	1	38	1974–75
New Division 1	Queen of the S	2	39	1988–89
	Cowdenbeath	3	44	1992–93
New Division 2	Forfar Ath	4	26	1975–76
	Stranraer	4	39	1987–88
New Division 3	Albion R	5	36	1994–95

MOST DEFEATS IN A SEASON

FA PREMIER LEAGUE		*Defeats*	*Games*	*Season*
	Ipswich T	29	42	1994–95
FOOTBALL LEAGUE				
Division 1	Stoke C	31	42	1984–85
Division 2	Tranmere R	31	42	1938–39
	Chester C	33	46	1992–93
Division 3	Doncaster R	34	46	1997–98
Division 3(S)	Merthyr T	29	42	1924–25
	Walsall	29	46	1952–53
	Walsall	29	46	1953–54
Division 3(N)	Rochdale	33	40	1931–32
Division 4	Newport Co	33	46	1987–88

SCOTTISH LEAGUE

Premier Division	Morton	29	36	1984–85
Division 1	St Mirren	31	42	1920–21
Division 2	Brechin C	30	36	1962–63
	Lochgelly	30	38	1923–24
New Division 1	Queen of the S	29	39	1988–89
	Dumbarton	31	36	1995–96
	Cowdenbeath	34	44	1992–93
New Division 2	Berwick R	29	39	1987–88
New Division 3	Albion R	28	36	1994–95

HAT-TRICKS

Career 34 Dixie Dean (Tranmere R, Everton, Notts Co, England)
Division 1 (one season post-war) 6 Jimmy Greaves (Chelsea), 1960–61
Three for one team one match
West, Spouncer, Hooper, Nottingham F v Leicester Fosse, Division 1, 21 April 1909
Barnes, Ambler, Davies, Wrexham v Hartlepools U, Division 4, 3 March 1962
Adcock, Stewart, White, Manchester C v Huddersfield T, Division 2, 7 Nov 1987
Loasby, Smith, Wells, Northampton T v Walsall, Division 3S, 5 Nov 1927
Bowater, Hoyland, Readman, Mansfield T v Rotherham U, Division 3N, 27 Dec 1932

FEWEST DEFEATS IN A SEASON
(Minimum 20 games)

		Defeats	Games	Season
FA PREMIER LEAGUE				
	Manchester U	3	38	1998–99
	Chelsea	3	38	1998–99
FOOTBALL LEAGUE				
Division 1	Preston NE	0	22	1888–89
	Arsenal	1	38	1990–91
	Liverpool	2	40	1987–88
	Leeds U	2	42	1968–69
Division 2	Liverpool	0	28	1893–94
	Burnley	2	30	1897–98
	Bristol C	2	38	1905–06
	Leeds U	3	42	1963–64
	Chelsea	5	46	1988–89
Division 3	QPR	5	46	1966–67
	Bristol R	5	46	1989–90
	Notts Co	5	46	1997–98
Division 3(S)	Southampton	4	42	1921–22
	Plymouth Arg	4	42	1929–30
Division 3(N)	Port Vale	3	46	1953–54
	Doncaster R	3	42	1946–47
	Wolverhampton W	3	42	1923–24
Division 4	Lincoln C	4	46	1975–76
	Sheffield U	4	46	1981–82
	Bournemouth	4	46	1981–82
SCOTTISH LEAGUE				
Premier Division	Rangers	3	36	1995–96
	Celtic	3	44	1987–88
Division 1	Rangers	0	18	1898–99
	Rangers	1	42	1920–21
Division 2	Clyde	1	36	1956–57
	Morton	1	36	1962–63
	St Mirren	1	36	1967–68
New Division 1	Partick T	2	26	1975–76
	St Mirren	2	39	1976–77
	Raith R	4	44	1992–93
	Falkirk	4	44	1993–94
New Division 2	Raith R	1	26	1975–76
	Clydebank	3	26	1975–76
	Forfar Ath	3	39	1983–84
	Raith R	3	39	1986–87
	Livingston	3	36	1998–99
New Division 3	Forfar Ath	6	36	1994–95
	Inverness T	6	36	1996–97

MOST DRAWN GAMES IN A SEASON

		Draws	Games	Season
FA PREMIER LEAGUE				
	Manchester C	18	42	1993–94
	Sheffield U	18	42	1993–94
	Southampton	18	42	1994–95
FOOTBALL LEAGUE				
Division 1	Norwich C	23	42	1978–79
Division 3	Cardiff C	23	46	1997–98
	Hartlepool U	23	46	1997–98
Division 4	Exeter C	23	46	1986–87
SCOTTISH LEAGUE				
Premier Division	Aberdeen	21	44	1993–94
New Division 1	East Fife	21	44	1986–87

MOST GOALS IN A GAME

FA PREMIER LEAGUE	Andy Cole (Manchester U) 5 goals v Ipswich T	4 Mar 1995
FOOTBALL LEAGUE		
Division 1	Ted Drake (Arsenal) 7 goals v Aston V	14 Dec 1935
	James Ross (Preston NE) 7 goals v Stoke	6 Oct 1888
Division 2	Tommy Briggs (Blackburn R) 7 goals v Bristol R	5 Feb 1955
	Neville Coleman (Stoke C) 7 goals v Lincoln C	23 Feb 1957
Division 3(S)	Joe Payne (Luton T) 10 goals v Bristol R	13 April 1936
Division 3(N)	Bunny Bell (Tranmere R) 9 goals v Oldham Ath	26 Dec 1935
Division 3	Steve Earle (Fulham) 5 goals v Halifax T	16 Sept 1969
	Barrie Thomas (Scunthorpe U) 5 goals v Luton T	24 April 1965
	Keith East (Swindon T) 5 goals v Mansfield T	20 Nov 1965
	Alf Wood (Shrewsbury T) 5 goals v Blackburn R	2 Oct 1971
	Tony Caldwell (Bolton W) 5 goals v Walsall	10 Sept 1983
	Andy Jones (Port Vale) 5 goals v Newport Co	4 May 1987
	Steve Wilkinson (Mansfield T) 5 goals v Birmingham C	3 April 1990
Division 4	Bert Lister (Oldham Ath) 6 goals v Southport	26 Dec 1962
FA CUP	Ted MacDougall (Bournemouth) 9 goals v Margate (*1st Round*)	20 Nov 1971
LEAGUE CUP	Frankie Bunn (Oldham Ath) 6 goals v Scarborough	25 Oct 1989
SCOTTISH LEAGUE		
Premier Division	Paul Sturrock (Dundee U) 5 goals v Morton	17 Nov 1984
Division 1	Jimmy McGrory (Celtic) 8 goals v Dunfermline Ath	14 Sept 1928
Division 2	Owen McNally (Arthurlie) 8 goals v Armadale	1 Oct 1927
	Jim Dyet (King's Park) 8 goals v Forfar Ath	2 Jan 1930
	John Calder (Morton) 8 goals v Raith R	18 April 1936
	Norman Hayward (Raith R) 8 goals v Brechin C	20 Aug 1937
SCOTTISH CUP	John Petrie (Arbroath) 13 goals v Bon Accord (*1st Round*)	12 Sept 1885

MOST LEAGUE GOALS IN A SEASON

		Goals	Games	Season
FA PREMIER LEAGUE	Andy Cole (Newcastle U)	34	40	1993–94
	Alan Shearer (Blackburn R)	34	42	1994–95
Division 1	Dixie Dean (Everton)	60	39	1927–28
Division 2	George Camsell (Middlesbrough)	59	37	1926–27
Division 3(S)	Joe Payne (Luton T)	55	39	1936–37
Division 3(N)	Ted Harston (Mansfield T)	55	41	1936–37
Division 3	Derek Reeves (Southampton)	39	46	1959–60
Division 4	Terry Bly (Peterborough U)	52	46	1960–61
FA CUP	Sandy Brown (Tottenham H)	15	8	1900–01
LEAGUE CUP	Clive Allen (Tottenham H)	12	9	1986–87
SCOTTISH LEAGUE				
Division 1	William McFadyen (Motherwell)	52	34	1931–32
Division 2	Jim Smith (Ayr U)	66	38	1927–28

MOST LEAGUE GOALS IN A CAREER

		Goals	Games	Season
FOOTBALL LEAGUE				
Arthur Rowley	WBA	4	24	1946–48
	Fulham	27	56	1948–50
	Leicester C	251	303	1950–58
	Shrewsbury T	152	236	1958–65
		434	619	
SCOTTISH LEAGUE				
Jimmy McGrory	Celtic	1	3	1922–23
	Clydebank	13	30	1923–24
	Celtic	396	375	1924–38
		410	408	

MOST CUP GOALS IN A CAREER

FA CUP (post-war)

Ian Rush 43 (Chester, Liverpool)
Pre-war: Henry Cursham 48 (Notts Co)

LEAGUE CUP

Geoff Hurst 49 (West Ham U, Stoke C)
Ian Rush 49 (Chester, Liverpool, Newcastle U)

A CENTURY OF LEAGUE AND CUP GOALS IN CONSECUTIVE SEASONS

George Camsell	Middlesbrough	59 Lge	5 Cup		1926–27
(101 goals)		33	4		1927–28
Steve Bull	Wolverhampton W	34 Lge	18 Cup		1987–88
(102 goals)		37	13		1988–89

(Camsell's cup goals were all scored in the FA Cup; Bull had 12 in the Sherpa Van Trophy, 3 Littlewoods Cup, 3 FA Cup in 1987–88; 11 Sherpa Van Trophy, 2 Littlewoods Cup in 1988–89.)

LONGEST SEQUENCE OF CONSECUTIVE SCORING (Individual)

FA PREMIER LEAGUE
Mark Stein (Chelsea)   9 in 7 games   1993–94
FOOTBALL LEAGUE RECORD
Dixie Dean (Everton)   23 in 12 games   1930–31

LONGEST WINNING SEQUENCE

FOOTBALL LEAGUE		*Games*	*Season*
Division 1	Tottenham H	13	1959–60 (2)
			and 1960–61 (11)
	Preston NE	13	1891–92
	Sunderland	13	1891–92
Division 2	Manchester U	14	1904–05
	Bristol C	14	1905–06
	Preston NE	14	1950–51
Division 3	Reading	13	1985–86
From Season's start			
Division 1	Tottenham H	11	1960–61
Division 3	Reading	13	1985–86

LONGEST WINNING SEQUENCE IN A SEASON

FOOTBALL LEAGUE		*Games*	*Season*
Division 1	Tottenham H	11	1960–61
Division 2	Manchester U	14	1904–05
Division 2	Bristol C	14	1905–06
Division 2	Preston NE	14	1950–51
SCOTTISH LEAGUE			
Division 2	Morton	23	1963–64

LONGEST UNBEATEN SEQUENCE

FOOTBALL LEAGUE		*Games*	*Seasons*
Division 1	Nottingham F	42	Nov 1977–Dec 1978

LONGEST UNBEATEN CUP SEQUENCE

Liverpool   25 rounds   League/Milk Cup   1980–84

LONGEST UNBEATEN SEQUENCE IN A SEASON

FOOTBALL LEAGUE		*Games*	*Season*
Division 1	Burnley	30	1920–21

LONGEST UNBEATEN START TO A SEASON

FOOTBALL LEAGUE		*Games*	*Season*
Division 1	Leeds U	29	1973–74
Division 1	Liverpool	29	1987–88

LONGEST SEQUENCE WITHOUT A WIN IN A SEASON

FOOTBALL LEAGUE		*Games*	*Season*
Division 2	Cambridge U	31	1983–84

LONGEST SEQUENCE WITHOUT A WIN FROM SEASON'S START

Division 1	Sheffield U	16	1990–91

LONGEST SEQUENCE OF CONSECUTIVE DEFEATS

FOOTBALL LEAGUE		*Games*	*Season*
Division 2	Darwen	18	1898–99

GOALKEEPING RECORDS (WITHOUT CONCEDING A GOAL)

British record (all competitive games)
Chris Woods, Rangers, in 1196 minutes from 26 November 1986 to 31 January 1987.
Football League
Steve Death, Reading, 1103 minutes from 24 March to 18 August 1979.

PENALTIES

		Goals	*Season*
Most in a Season (individual)			
Division 1	Francis Lee (Manchester C)	13	1971–72
Most awarded in one game			
Five	Crystal Palace (4 – 1 scored, 3 missed) v Brighton & HA (1 scored), Div 2		1988–89
Most saved in a Season			
Division 1	Paul Cooper (Ipswich T)	8 (of 10)	1979–80

MOST LEAGUE APPEARANCES (750+ matches)

1005 Peter Shilton (286 Leicester City, 110 Stoke City, 202 Nottingham Forest, 188 Southampton, 175 Derby County, 34 Plymouth Argyle, 1 Bolton Wanderers, 9 Leyton Orient)1966–97
879 Graeme Armstrong (204 Stirling A, 83 Berwick R, 353 Meadowbank T, 239 Stenhousemuir) 1975–99
863 Tommy Hutchison (165 Blackpool, 314 Coventry City, 46 Manchester City, 92 Burnley 178 Swansea City, 68 Alloa) 1965–91
824 Terry Paine (713 Southampton, 111 Hereford United) 1957–77
842 Tony Ford (355 Grimsby T, 9 Sunderland (loan), 112 Stoke C, 114 WBA, 68 Grimsby T, 5 Bradford C (loan), 76 Scunthorpe U, 103 Mansfield T) 1975–98
782 Robbie James (484 Swansea C, 48 Stoke C, 87 QPR, 23 Leicester C, 89 Bradford C, 51 Cardiff C) 1973–94
777 Alan Oakes (565 Manchester C, 211 Chester C, 1 Port Vale) 1959–84
771 John Burridge (27 Workington, 134 Blackpool, 65 Aston Villa, 6 Southend U (loan), 88 Crystal Palace, 39 QPR, 74 Wolverhampton W, 6 Derby Co (loan), 109 Sheffield U, 62 Southampton, 67 Newcastle U, 65 Hibernian, 3 Scarborough, 4 Lincoln C, 3 Aberdeen, 3 Dumbarton, 3 Falkirk, 4 Manchester C, 3 Darlington, 6 Queen of the South) 1968–96
770 John Trollope (all for Swindon Town) 1960–80†
764 Jimmy Dickinson (all for Portsmouth) 1946–65
761 Roy Sproson (all for Port Vale) 1950–72
758 Ray Clemence (48 Scunthorpe United, 470 Liverpool, 240 Tottenham Hotspur) 1966–87
758 Billy Bonds (95 Charlton Ath, 663 West Ham U) 1964–88
757 Pat Jennings (48 Watford, 472 Tottenham Hotspur, 237 Arsenal) 1963–86
757 Frank Worthington (171 Huddersfield T, 210 Leicester C, 84 Bolton W, 75 Birmingham C, 32 Leeds U, 195 Sunderland, 34 Southampton, 31 Brighton & HA, 59 Tranmere R, 23 Preston NE, 19 Stockport Co) 1966–88
† record for one club

Consecutive
401 Harold Bell (401 Tranmere R; 459 in all games) 1946–55

FA CUP
88 Ian Callaghan (79 Liverpool, 7 Swansea C, 2 Crewe Alex)

Most Senior Matches
1390 Peter Shilton (1005 League, 86 FA Cup, 102 League Cup, 125 Internationals, 13 Under-23, 4 Football League XI, 20 European Cup, 7 Texaco Cup, 5 Simod Cup, 4 European Super Cup, 4 UEFA Cup, 3 Screen Sport Super Cup, 3 Zenith Data Systems Cup, 2 Autoglass Trophy, 2 Charity Shield, 2 Full Members Cup, 1 Anglo-Italian Cup, 1 Football League play-offs, 1 World Club Championship)

MOST FA CUP FINAL GOALS

Ian Rush (Liverpool) 5: 1986(2), 1989(2), 1992(1)

MOST LEAGUE MEDALS

Phil Neal (Liverpool) 8: 1976, 1977, 1979, 1980, 1982, 1983, 1984, 1986
Alan Hansen (Liverpool) 8: 1979, 1980, 1982, 1983, 1984, 1986, 1988, 1990

OTHER RECORDS

YOUNGEST PLAYERS
FA Premier League Andy Campbell, 16 years, 352 days, Middlesbrough v Sheffield W, 5.4.96.
FA Premier League scorer Andy Turner, 17 years 166 days, Tottenham H v Everton, 5.9.92.
Football League Albert Geldard, 15 years 158 days, Bradford Park Avenue v Millwall, Division 2, 16.9.29; and Ken Roberts, 15 years 158 days, Wrexham v Bradford Park Avenue, Division 3N, 1.9.51
Football League scorer
Ronnie Dix, 15 years 180 days, Bristol Rovers v Norwich City, Division 3S, 3.3.28.
Division 1
Derek Forster, 15 years 185 days, Sunderland v Leicester City, 22.8.84.
Division 1 scorer
Jason Dozzell, 16 years 57 days as substitute Ipswich Town v Coventry City, 4.2.84
Division 1 hat-tricks
Alan Shearer, 17 years 240 days, Southampton v Arsenal, 9.4.88
Jimmy Greaves, 17 years 10 months, Chelsea v Portsmouth, 25.12.57
FA Cup (any round)
Andy Awford, 15 years 88 days as substitute Worcester City v Boreham Wood, 3rd Qual. rd, 10.10.87
FA Cup proper
Scott Endersby, 15 years 288 days, Kettering v Tilbury, 1st rd, 26.11.77

FA Cup Final
James Prinsep, 17 years 245 days, Clapham Rovers v Old Etonians, 1879
FA Cup Final scorer
Norman Whiteside, 18 years 18 days, Manchester United v Brighton & Hove Albion, 1983
FA Cup Final captain
David Nish, 21 years 212 days, Leicester City v Manchester City, 1969
League Cup Final scorer
Norman Whiteside, 17 years 324 days, Manchester United v Liverpool, 1983
League Cup Final captain
Barry Venison, 20 years 7 months 8 days, Sunderland v Norwich City, 1985

OLDEST PLAYERS
Football League
Neil McBain, 52 years 4 months, New Brighton v Hartlepools United, Div 3N, 15.3.47 (McBain was New Brighton's manager and had to play in an emergency)
Division 1
Stanley Matthews, 50 years 5 days, Stoke City v Fulham, 6.2.65

SENDINGS-OFF

Season	314 (League alone)	1994–95
Day	15 (3 League, 12 FA Cup*)	20 Nov 1982
	worst overall FA Cup total	
League	13	14 Dec 1985; 19 Aug 1995; 9 Sept 1995
Weekend	15	22/23 Dec 1990
FA Cup Final	Kevin Moran, Manchester U v Everton	1985
Quickest	Mark Smith, Crewe Alex v Darlington (away) Div 3: 19 secs	12 March 1994
Most one game	Four: Northampton T (0) v Hereford U (4) Div 3	11 Nov 1992
	Four: Crewe Alex (2) v Bradford PA (2) Div 3N	8 Jan 1955
	Four: Sheffield U (1) v Portsmouth (3) Div 2	13 Dec 1986
	Four: Port Vale (2) v Northampton T (2) Littlewoods Cup	18 Aug 1987
	Four: Brentford (2) v Mansfield T (2) Div 3	12 Dec 1987
	Four: Shrewsbury T (1) v Rotherham U (3) Div 3	4 Oct 1997

RECORD ATTENDANCES

FA Premier League	55,316	Manchester U v Southampton	27.2.99
Football League	83,260	Manchester U v Arsenal, Maine Road	17.1.1948
Scottish League	118,567	Rangers v Celtic, Ibrox Stadium	2.1.1939
FA Cup Final	126,047*	Bolton W v West Ham U, Wembley	28.4.1923
European Cup	135,826	Celtic v Leeds U, semi-final at Hampden Park	15.4.1970
Scottish Cup	146,433	Celtic v Aberdeen, Hampden Park	24.4.37
World Cup	199,854†	Brazil v Uruguay, Maracana, Rio	16.7.50

* It has been estimated that as many as 70,000 more broke in without paying.
† 173,830 paid.

TOP TEN TRANSFERS

Player	*From*	*To*	*Month*	*Fee*
Christian Vieri	Lazio	Internazionale	June 1999	£31m
Denilson	Sao Paulo	Real Betis	August 1998	£21.4m
Marcio Amoroso	Udinese	Parma	June 1999	£18m
Ronaldo	Barcelona	Internazionale	July 1997	£18m
Juan Sebastian Veron	Parma	Lazio	June 1999	£17.5m
Christian Vieri	Atletico Madrid	Lazio	June 1997	£17m
Rivaldo	La Coruna	Barcelona	August 1997	£16m
Andriy Shevchenko	Kiev Dynamo	AC Milan	June 1999	£15.7m
Vincenzo Montella	Sampdoria	Roma	June 1999	£15.3m
Alan Shearer	Blackburn R	Newcastle U	July 1996	£15m

CENTENARY YEAR UNDER-21 MATCH

25 November 1998

Italian League (0) 1, *(Esposito 80 (pen))*

Football League (0) 1 *(Evers 63)*

Football League Under-21: Wright (Ipswich T); O'Brien (Bradford C), Marsh (Oxford U), Robinson (Watford), Marshall (Norwich C), Evers (Luton T) [Rowlands (Brentford) 77], Mullins (Crystal Palace), Johnson (Crewe Alex), Powell (Oxford U) [Howe (Bournemouth) 46], Bridges (Sunderland), Branch (Everton) [Ranking (Bradford C) 71].

IMPORTANT ADDRESSES

The Football Association: The Secretary, 16 Lancaster Gate, London W2 3LW. *0171 262 4542*

Scotland: David Taylor, 6 Park Gardens, Glasgow G3 7YE. *0141 332 6372*
Northern Ireland (Irish FA): D. I. Bowen, 20 Windsor Avenue, Belfast BT9 6EG. *01232 669458*
Wales: A. Evans, 3 Westgate Street, Cardiff, South Glamorgan CF1 1JF. *01222 372325*
Republic of Ireland (FA of Ireland): B. O'Byrne, 80 Merrion Square South, Dublin 2. *00353 16766864*

International Federation (FIFA): M. Zen-Ruffinen, P. O. Box 85 8030 Zurich, Switzerland. *00 411 384 9595. Fax: 00 411 384 9696*
Union of European Football Associations: G. Aigner, Chemin de la Redoute 54, Case Postale 303 CH-1260 Nyon, Switzerland. *0041 22 994 44 44. Fax: 0041 22 994 44 88*

THE LEAGUES

The Premier League: The Secretary, 11 Connaught Place, London W2 2ET *0171-298-1600*
The Football League: J. D. Dent, F.C.I.S., The Football League, Unit 5, Edward VII Quay, Navigation Way, Preston, Lancashire PR2 2YF. *01772 325800. Fax 01772 325801*
Scottish Premier League: R. Mitchell, Hampden Park, Somerville Drive, Glasgow G42 9BA. *0141 646 6962*
The Scottish League: P. Donald, 188 West Regent Street, Glasgow G2 4RY. *0141 248 3844*
The Irish League: H. Wallace, 87 University Street, Belfast BT7 1HP. *01232 242888*
Football League of Ireland: E. Morris, 80 Merrion Square South, Dublin 2. *003531 765120*
The Nationwide Football Conference: J. A. Moules, Collingwood House, Crossways, Dartford DA2 6QQ. *01322 303120*
Central League: A. Williamson, The Football League, Unit 5, Edward VII Quay, Navigation Way, Preston, Lancashire PR2 2YF. *01772 325800. Fax 01772 325801*
North West Counties League: M. Darby, 87 Hillary Road, Hyde, Cheshire SK14 4EB.
Eastern Counties League: B. A. Badcock, 41 The Copse, Southwood, Farnborough, Hampshire GU14 0QD. *01252 387588*
Football Combination: N. Chamberlain, 2 Vicarage Close, Old Costessey, Norwich NR8 5DL. *01603 743998*
Hellenic League: B. King, 83 Queens Road, Carterton, Oxon OX18 3YF. *01793 493502*
Kent League: R. Vinter, Bakery House, The Street, Chilham, Canterbury, Kent CT4 8BX. *01227 730457*
Leicestershire Senior League: R. J. Holmes, 8 Huntsman Close, Markfield, Leics LE67 9XE. *01530 243093*
Manchester League: J. Hall, 31 Sunhill Close, Rochdale, OL16 4RU. *01706 719829*
Midland Combination: N. Harvey, 115 Millfield Road, Handsworth Wood, Birmingham B20 1ED. *0121 357 4172*
Northern Premier: R. D. Bayley, 22 Woburn Drive, Hale, Altrincham, Cheshire WA15 8LZ. *0161-980 7007*
Northern League: T. Golightly, 85 Park Road North, Chester-le-Street, Co Durham DH3 3SA. *0191 3882056*

Isthmian League: N. Robinson, 226 Rye Lane, Peckham SE15 4NL. *020 8409 1978. Fax: 020 7639 5726*
South-East Counties League: A. Leather, 66 Green Acres, Chichester Road, Croydon, Surrey CR0 5UX. *0181-681 7100*
Southern League: D. J. Strudwick, P. O. Box 90, Worcester, WR3 8RX. *01905 757509*
Spartan South Midlands League: M. Mitchell, 26 Leighton Court, Dunstable, Beds LU6 1EW. *01582 667291*
South Western League: M. Goodenough, Rose Cottage, Horrelsford, Milton Damerel, Holsworthy, Devon EX22 7NJ. *01409 261402*
United Counties League: R. Gamble, 8 Bostock Avenue, Northampton NN4 1LW. *01604 637766*
Western League: K. A. Clarke, 32 Westmead Lane, Chippenham, Wilts SN15 3HZ. *01249 464467*
West Midlands Regional League: N. R. Juggins, 14 Badger Way, Blackwell, Bromsgrove, Worcs B60 1EX. *0121 447 8167*
Northern Counties (East): B. Wood, 6 Restmore Avenue, Guiseley, Leeds LS20 9DG. *01943 874558*
Central Midlands Football League: Frank Harwood, 103 Vestry Road, Oakwood, Derby, Derbyshire DE21 2BN. *01332 832372*
Combined Counties League: Clive R. Tidey, 22 Silo Road, Farncombe, Godalming, Surrey GU7 3PA. *01483 428453*
Essex Senior League: David Walls, 77 Thorpedene Gardens, Shoeburyness, Essex SS3 9JE. *01702 294047*
Lancashire Football League: Barbara Howarth, 465 Whalley Road, Clayton-le-Moors, Accrington, Lancs BB5 5RP. *01254 388080*
Midland Football Alliance: Bob Thomas, 416 Bloxwich Road, Leamore, Walsall WS3 2UY. *01922 710565*
North West Counties Football League: Mike Darby, 87 Hillary Road, Hyde, Cheshire SK14 4EB. *0161 368 6243*
Wessex League: Tom Lindon, 63 Downs Road, South Wonston, Winchester, Hants SO21 3EW. *01962 884760*
South Western League: Wendy Donohue, 115 Longfield, Falmouth, Cornwall TR11 4SL. *01326 316642*

COUNTY FOOTBALL ASSOCIATIONS

Bedfordshire: P. D. Brown, Century House, Skimpot Road, Dunstable, Beds LU5 4JU. *01582 565111*
Berks and Bucks: B. G. Moore, 15a London Street, Faringdon, Oxon SN7 7HD. *01367 242099*
Birmingham County: M. Pennick, County FA Offices, Rayhall Lane, Great Barr, Birmingham B43 6JF. *0121 357 4278*
Cambridgeshire: R. K. Pawley, 3 Signet Court, Swanns Road, Cambridge CB5 8LA. *01223 576770*
Cheshire: Mrs M. Dunford, The Cottage, Hartford Moss Rec Centre, Winnington, Northwich CW8 4BG. *01606 871166*
Cornwall: B. Cudmore, 1 High Cross Street, St. Austell, Cornwall PL25 4AB. *01726 74080*
Cumberland: J. A. Murphy, 17 Oxford Street, Workington, Cumbria CA14 2AL. *01900 872310*
Derbyshire: K. Compton, The Grandstand, Moorways Stadium, Moor Lane, Derby DE24 8FB. *01332 361422*
Devon County: C. Davidson, County HQ, Coach Road, Newton Abbot, Devon TQ12 1EJ. *01626 332077*
Dorset County: P. Hough, County Ground, Blandford

Close, Hamsworthy, Poole, Dorset BH15 4BF. *01202 682375*
Durham: J. Topping, 'Codeslaw', Ferens Park, Durham DH1 1JZ. *0191 3848653*
East Riding County: D. R. Johnson, 50 Boulevard, Hull HU3 2TB. *01482 221158*
Essex County: P. Sammons, 31 Mildmay Road, Chelmsford, Essex CM2 0DN. *01245 357727*
Gloucestershire: P. Britton, Oaklands Park, Almondsbury, Bristol BS32 4AG. *01454 615888*
Guernsey: D. Dorey, Haut Regard, St. Clair Hill, St. Sampson's, Guernsey, GY2 4DT, CI. *01481 246231*
Hampshire: R. G. Barnes, William Pickford House, 8 Ashwood Gardens, off Winchester Road, Southampton SO16 7PW. *01703 791110*
Herefordshire: J. S. Lambert, 1 Murfield Close, Holmer, Hereford HR1 1QB. *01432 270308*
Hertfordshire: R. G. Kibble, County Ground, Baldock Road, Letchworth, Herts SG6 2EN. *01462 677622*
Huntingdonshire: M. M. Armstrong, Cromwell Chambers, 8 St Johns Street, Huntingdon, Cambs PE18 6DD. *01480 414412*

Isle of Man: Mrs A. Garrett, P.O. Box 53, The Bowl, Douglas IOM IM99 1GY. *01624 615576*

Jersey: S. Monks, Rocqueberg View Guest House, Rue De Samares, St. Clement, Jersey JE2 6LS. *01534 852642*

Kent County: K. T. Masters, 69 Maidstone Road, Chatham, Kent ME4 6DT. *01634 843824*

Lancashire: J. Kenyon, County Ground, Thurston Road, Leyland, Preston, Lancs PR5 1LF. *01772 624000*

Leicestershire and Rutland: R. E. Barston, Holmes Park, Dog and Gun Lane, Whetstone, Leicester LE8 3LJ. *0116 2867828*

Lincolnshire: J. Griffin, PO Box 26, 12 Dean Road, Lincoln LN2 4DP. *01522 524917*

Liverpool County: F. L. J. Hunter, Liverpool Soccer Centre, Walton Hall Park, Walton Hall Avenue, Liverpool L4 9XP. *0151 523 4488*

London: D. Fowkes, 6 Aldworth Grove, London SE13 6HY. *0181 690 9626*

Manchester County: P. Smith, Brantingham Road, Chorlton, Manchester M21 0TT. *0161-881 0299*

Middlesex County: P. J. Clayton, 39 Roxborough Road, Harrow, Middx HA1 1NS. *0181 424 8524*

Norfolk County: R. J. Howlett, Plantation Park, Blofield, Norwich, Norfolk, NR13 4PL. *01603 717177*

Northamptonshire: B. Walden, 2 Duncan Close, Moulton Park, Northampton NN3 6WL. *01604 670741*

North Riding County: M. Jarvis, Southlands Centre, Ormesby Road, Middlesbrough TS3 0HB. *01642 318603*

Northumberland: R. E. Maughan, Seymour House, 10 Brenkley Way, Blezard Bus Park, Seaton Burn, Newcastle upon Tyne NE13 6DT. *0191 236 8020*

Nottinghamshire: M. Kilbee, 7 Clarendon Street, Nottingham NG1 5HS. *0115 9418954*

Oxfordshire: R. Leaver, Rondamician, West End Lane, Merton, Bicester, Oxon OX6 0NG. *01865 331360*

Sheffield and Hallamshire: G. Thompson, Clegg House, 5 Onslow Road, Sheffield S11 7AF. *01142 670068*

Shropshire: D. Rowe, Gay Meadow, Abbey Foregate, Shrewsbury SY2 6AB. *01743 362769*

Somerset & Avon (South): Mrs H. Marchment, 30 North Road, Midsomer Norton, Bath BA3 2QD. *01761 410280*

Staffordshire: B. J. Adshead, County Showground, Weston Road, Stafford ST18 0DB. *01785 256994*

Suffolk County: W. M. Steward, 2 Millfields, Haughley, Stowmarket, Suffolk IP14 3PU. *01449 673481*

Surrey County: R. Ward, 321 Kingston Road, Leatherhead, Surrey KT22 7TU. *01372 373543*

Sussex County: D. M. Worsfold, County Office, Culver Road, Lancing, Sussex BN15 9AX. *01903 753547*

Westmorland: P. G. Ducksbury, Unit 1, Angel Court, 21 Highgate, Kendal, Cumbria LA9 4DA. *01539 730946*

West Riding County: R. Carter, Fleet Lane, Woodlesford, Leeds LS26 8NX. *0113 2821222*

Wiltshire: G. Benson, 16 Robins Green, Covingham, Swindon SN3 5AY. *01793 525245*

Worcestershire: M. R. Leggett Fermain, 12 Worcester Road, Evesham, Worcs WR11 4JU. *01386 443215*

OTHER USEFUL ADDRESSES

Amateur Football Alliance: M. L. Brown, 55 Islington Park Street, London N1 1QB. *0171 359 3493*

English Schools FA: M. R. Berry, 1/2 Eastgate Street, Stafford ST16 2NN. *01785 51142*

Oxford University: M. H. Matthews, University College, Oxford OX1 4BH. *01865 276648*

Cambridge University: Dr J. A. Little, St Catherine's College, Cambridge CB2 1RL. *01223 338366*

Army: Major T. C. Knight ASCB (MOD), Clayton Barracks, Thornhill Road, Aldershot, Hants GU11 2BG. *01252 348571/4*

Royal Air Force: WG CDR R. N. Williams, RAF, FA OC OPS WG RAF Linton on Ouse, York YO30 2AA. *01347 848261 ext. 7847*

Royal Navy: Lt-Cdr J. Danks, R.N. Sports Office, H.M.S. Temeraire, Portsmouth, Hants PO1 2HB. *01705 722671*

British Universities Sports Association: G. Gregory-Jones, Chief Executive: BUSA, 8 Union Street, London SE1 1SZ. *0171 357 8555*

British Olympic Association: 6 John Prince's Place, London W1M 0DH. *0171 408 2029*

National Federation of Football Supporters' Clubs: Chairman: Ian D. Todd MBE, 8 Wyke Close, Wyke Gardens, Isleworth, Middlesex TW7 5PE. *0181 847 2905 (and fax)*. Mobile: *0961 558908*. National Secretary: Mark Agate, "The Stadium", 14 Coombe Close, Lordswood, Chatham, Kent ME5 8NU. *01634 319461 (and fax)*

National Playing Fields Association: Col R. Satterthwaite, O.B.E., 578b Catherine Place, London, SW1.

The Scottish Football Commercial Managers Association: J. E. Hillier (Chairman), c/o Keith FC Promotions Office, 60 Union Street, Keith, Banffshire, Scotland.

Professional Footballers' Association: G. Taylor, 2 Oxford Court, Bishopsgate, Off Lower Mosley Street, Manchester M2 3WQ. *0161 236 0575*

Referees' Association: A. Smith, 1 Westhill Road, Coundon, Coventry CV6 2AD *01203 601701*

Women's Football Alliance: Miss K. Simmons, 9 Wyllyotts Place, Potters Bar, Herts EN6 2JD. *01707 651840*

Institute of Football Management and Administration: 44 Holy Walk, Leamington Spa, Warwickshire, CV32 4YS. *01926 882313. Fax: 01926 886829*

Football Administrators Association: as above.

Commercial and Marketing Managers Association: as above.

Management Statts Association: as above.

League Managers Association: as above.

The Association of Football Statisticians: R. J. Spiller, PO Box 5828, Basildon, Essex SS15 5GQ. *01268 416020 (and fax 01268-543559)*

The Football Programme Directory: David Stacey, 'The Beeches', 66 Southend Road, Wickford, Essex SS11 8EN. *01268 732041 (and fax)*

England Football Supporters Association: Publicity Officer, David Stacey, 'The Beeches', 66 Southend Road, Wickford, Essex SS11 8EN. *01268 732041 (and fax)*

World Cup (1966) Association: as above.

The Ninety-Two Club: 104 Gilda Crescent, Whitchurch, Bristol BS14 9LD.

Scottish 38 Club: Mark Byatt, 6 Greenfields Close, Loughton, Essex IG10 3HG. *0181 508 6088*

The Football Trust: Second Floor, Walkden House, 10 Melton Street, London NW1 2EJ. *0171 388 4504*

Association of Provincial Football Supporters Clubs in London: Stephen Moon, 32 Westminster Gardens, Barking, Essex IG11 0BJ. *0181 594 2367.*

World Association of Friends of English Football: Carlisle Hill, Gluck, Habichthof 2, D24939 Flensburg, Germany. *0049 461 4700222.*

Football Postcard Collectors Club: PRO: Bryan Horsnell, 275 Overdown Road, Tilehurst, Reading RG31 6NX. *Telephone and Fax: 0118 9424448.*

UK Programme Collectors Club: Secretary, John Litster, 46 Milton Road, Kirkcaldy, Fife KY1 1TL. *01592 268718. Fax: 01592 595069*

Programme Monthly: as above.

Scottish Football Historians Association: as above.

Phil Gould (Licensed Football Agent), c/o Whoppit Management Ltd, P. O. Box 27204, London N11 2WS. *07071 732 468. Fax: 07070 732 469*

The Scandinavian Union of Supporters of British Football: Postboks, 15 Stovner, N-0913 Oslo, Norway.

FOOTBALL AWARDS 1999

FOOTBALLER OF THE YEAR

The Football Writers' Association Award for the Footballer of the Year went to David Ginola of Tottenham Hotspur and France.

THE PFA AWARDS 1999

Player of the Year: David Ginola, Tottenham Hotspur.
Young Player of the Year: Nicolas Anelka, Arsenal.
Merit Award: Tony Ford, Mansfield Town.

THE SCOTTISH PFA AWARDS 1999

Player of the Year: Henrik Larsson, Celtic.

SCOTTISH FOOTBALL WRITERS ASSOCIATION

Player of the Year: Henrik Larsson, Celtic.

EUROPEAN FOOTBALLER OF THE YEAR 1998

Zinedine Zidane (Juventus).

WORLD PLAYER OF THE YEAR 1998

Zinedine Zidane (Juventus).

CARLING AWARD WINNERS 1998–99

Month	Manager	Player
August	Alan Curbishley	Michael Owen
September	John Gregory	Alan Shearer
October	Martin O'Neill	Roy Keane
November	Harry Redknapp	Dion Dublin
December	Brian Kidd	David Ginola
January	Alex Ferguson	Dwight Yorke
February	Alan Curbishley	Nicolas Anelka
March	David O'Leary	Ray Parlour
April	Alex Ferguson	Sol Campbell

David Ginola won both the Football Writers' Association Player of the Year Award, as well as the one voted on by his professional colleagues. (Colorsport)

LEAGUE MANAGERS ASSOCIATION

The League Managers Association is the official representative body for professional football managers with its headquarters in Leamington Spa and which was inaugurated under its present title the same year as the FA Premier League was formed.

It was Watford and former England manager Graham Taylor whose vision prompted the formation of the Association as the profile and demands on Premiership and Football League managers increased.

The intervening years have, without doubt, been the most eventful in the long history of the game. The formation of the Premier League itself with the escalating television revenues it promoted was followed by the Bosman judgement and the huge effect that has had on football's transfer market, all of which had a direct effect on the role of the football manager.

Taylor's own motivation was the belief that managers possessed a vast store of knowledge and experience which was not being transmitted back for the benefit of the game as a whole. The managers lacked a channel through which to express their views to legislators and decision-makers.

Both the Premier League and the Football Association were quick to recognise that the newly formed LMA could make a useful contribution to the debates, which would ultimately reshape the game in this country. Today it is involved in close dialogue with all the game's official administrative bodies with its views valued and sought.

One of the most significant early breakthroughs was the introduction into Premier League regulations of a Code of Conduct governing the appointment of managers and the termination of their contracts. A similar agreement with the Football League has meant that LMA members now have greater protection in the event of losing their jobs than they have ever had with similar safeguards for clubs in relation to their own managers being 'poached' by another club.

There have been numerous other initiatives in regard, for instance, to reserve team football and the review of disciplinary procedures, both of which, at the time, had remained unchanged for many years and were no longer serving the game's best interests.

Various discussion papers have been produced by the Association including one about management structures abroad and the use of a head coach for the senior squad only. This system has since been widely introduced among Premiership clubs.

Other projects have included a study of the youth development of Italian club Parma FC and Ajax of Holland and The Italian Approach, an appraisal of the methods used by Italian clubs in the development of players as professional footballers.

In regard to the welfare of its own members the LMA has streamlined a beneficial pension package and a mechanism whereby all their members' contracts can be professionally scrutinised before being signed.

The LMA has also, during the 1998–99 season, introduced a Performance of the Week award, sponsored by Scottish Mutual, which has proved extremely popular and which is judged weekly by a panel of committee members from both the Premiership and the three divisions of the Football League.

Several of the managers who helped launch the Association are still actively participating in its activities. Howard Wilkinson, the FA's Director of Coaching, is the Chairman, while Sir Alex Ferguson remains a stalwart committee member.

Initially the Chief Executive post was filled by the late John Camkin, former journalist, broadcaster, and director of Coventry City whose energy and ideas were vital to the LMA in its early days.

Frank Clark was to follow him until he became manager of Nottingham Forest and Steve Coppell, Jim Smith and Gordon Milne all had stints in the post until 1996.

It was then that the LMA appointed the former Peterborough, Wolves, Notts County, Walsall and Northampton Town manager John Barnwell as its Chief Executive, with the long-serving Olaf Dixon as his Deputy. John has been a major driving force over the past three years in ensuring that the LMA has an increasingly active role in the running of football and the welfare of its professional managers.

REFEREEING AND THE REFEREES

REFEREES AND THE LAWS OF THE GAME

There is considerable hope that the 1999–2000 season will see much more respect being paid to referees and their Assistants by all sections of the game. A number were physically attacked by players or spectators last season leading to the FA Premier League introducing a system whereby now their referees are escorted to and from matches. Likewise FIFA have been at pains to point out that racist remarks on the field constitute a dismissal offence and they have recently instructed referees to be more draconian in their approach to swearing which is also an offence warranting dismissal. Limited experiments will continue with moving the ball forward 9.15 metres (10 yards), where players show dissent from decisions, delay restarts or fail to retreat the required distance at free kicks. There is considerable expectation that this will be eventually implemented into the Laws.

Changes in the Laws and their sub-rules for 1999–2000 are few. Perhaps the most important is that 'any simulating action anywhere on the field which is intended to deceive the referee must be sanctioned as unsporting behaviour'. This will of course mean that 'diving', 'feigning injury' or pretence that an offence has been committed when it has not will result in the culprit receiving a yellow card and a caution. There are minor changes to allow what are known as 'flying substitutes' in matches involving the Under 16's, Women's football and Veterans' football (over 35) but only as sanctioned by individual national associations. As more and more games are using multiple footballs to speed up matches, the referee must ensure that they all meet the strict requirements. Fourth officials are now able to report to the referee irresponsible behaviour by occupants of the technical area or the unsatisfactory equipment of substitutes before they enter the field of play.

Lastly another experiment which may become of the greatest value to professional rather than amateur football (where there would be insufficient officials) is the authorisation of the concept of a two-referee system. The International FA Board who deal with the Laws are instructing a sub-committee to work out the details which are not available at the time of going to print.

The list of the officials both in the 'middle' and 'on the line' in the Premier and Nationwide Leagues who, together, make up the National List, are set out below and those on the Premiership are marked with a # and those new to that List are given an asterisk *.

This season there are twenty-two Premier League referees so five new names have been added to the list. They are Steven Bennett (Kent), Andy D'Urso (Essex), Mark Halsey (Herts), Barry Knight (Kent) and Alan Wiley (Staffs). Newly appointed Assistant Referees to the Premier League are Messrs P. Barston, R. Booth, A. Garratt, G. Hegley and T. Kettle. Upgraded from Assistant to Referee are Richard Beeby, Phil Joslin, Alan Kaye, Trevor Parkes, Michael Ryan and Steve Tomlin.

David Elleray remains the Senior Referee and last season's major honours went to Peter Jones (FA Cup Final) and Terry Heilbron (Worthington Cup Final). The first honour of the new season goes to Graham Barber who referees the FA Charity Shield match between Manchester United and Arsenal.

KEN GOLDMAN

NATIONAL LIST OF REFEREES FOR SEASON 1999–2000

#Alcock, P.E. (Halstead, Kent)
Baines, S.J. (Chesterfield)
#Barber, G.P. (Tring, Herts)
#Barry, N.S. (Scunthorpe)
Bates, A. (Stoke-on-Trent)
*Beeby, R.J. (Northampton)
#Bennett, S.G. (Orpington, Kent)
Brandwood, M.J. (Lichfield, Staffs)
Burns, W.C. (Scarborough)
Butler, A.N. (Sutton-in-Ashfield)
Cable, L.E. (Woking)
Cain, G. (Seaforth, Merseyside)
Cowburn, M.G. (Blackpool)
Crick, D.R. (Worcester Park, Surrey)
Danson, P.S. (Leicester)
Dean, M.L. (Heswall, Wirral)
Down, P. (Stoke-on-Trent)
#Dunn, S.W. (Bristol)
#Durkin, P.A. (Portland, Dorset)
#D'Urso, A.P. (Billericay, Essex)
#Elleray, D.R. (Harrow-on-the-Hill)
Fletcher, M. (Warley, West Midlands)
Foy, C.J. (St Helens, Merseyside)
Frankland, G.B. (Middlesbrough)
Furnandiz, R.D. (Doncaster)
#Gallagher, D.J. (Banbury, Oxon)

Hall, A.R. (Birmingham)
#Halsey, M.R. (Welwyn Garden City, Herts)
#Harris, R.J. (Oxford)
Heilbron, T. (Newton Aycliffe)
Hill, K.D. (Royston, Herts)
Jones, M.J. (Chester)
#Jones, P. (Loughborough)
Jones, T. (Barrow-in-Furness)
Jordan, W.M. (Tring, Herts)
*Joslin, P.J. (Newark, Nottinghamshire)
*Kaye, A. (Wakefield)
Kirkby, J.A. (Sheffield)
#Knight, B. (Orpington, Kent)
Laws, D. (Whitley Bay)
Laws, G. (Whitley Bay)
Leach, K.A. (Codsall, Staffs)
Leake, A.R. (Darwen, Lancashire)
#Lodge, S.J. (Barnsley)
Lomas, E. (Manchester)
Lynch, K.M. (Kirk Hammerton, Nr York)
Mathieson, S.W. (Stockport)
Messias, M.D. (York)
Olivier, R.J. (Sutton Coldfield)
*Parkes, T.A. (Birmingham)
Pearson, R. (Peterlee, Durham)

Pike, M.S (Barrow-in-Furness)
#Poll, G. (Tring, Hertfordshire)
Pugh, D. (Bebington, Wirral)
#Reed, M.D. (Birmingham)
Rejer, P. (Tipton, West Midlands)
#Rennie, U.D. (Sheffield)
Richards, P.R. (Preston)
#Riley, M.A. (Leeds)
Robinson, J.P. (Hull)
*Ryan, M. (Preston)
Stretton, F.G. (Nottingham)
Styles, R. (Waterlooville, Hants)
Taylor, P. (Cheshunt, Hertfordshire)
*Tomlin, S.G. (Lewes, East Sussex)
Walton, P. (Long Buckby, Northants)
Warren, M.R. (Walsall)
#Wiley, A.G. (Burntwood, Staffs)
Wilkes, C.R. (Gloucester)
#Wilkie, A.B. (Chester-le-Street)
#Willard, G.S. (Worthing, West Sussex)
#Winter, J.T. (Stockton-on-Tees)
Wolstenholme, E.K. (Blackburn)
*New for season 1999–2000.
#Premier League referee.

ASSISTANT REFEREES

Armstrong, P. (Thatcham, Berks)
Artis, S.G. (Norwich)
Aston, G.A. (Kingswinford)
Atkins, G. (Bradford)
Atkinson, M. (Leeds)
Babski, D.S. (Scunthorpe)
*Baker, B.D. (Andover, Hampshire)

Baker, B.L. (Warminster, Wiltshire)
Baker, L. (Watchet, Somerset)
Bannister, N. (Goole, E Yorkshire)
Barker, C. (York)
Barnes, K.G. (Swindon)
Barnes, P.W. (Crowland, Lincolnshire)

*Barrett, G.P. (Grays, Essex)
Barston, P.S. (Loughborough)
Bassindale, C. (Doncaster)
Beale, G.A. (Taunton)
Bello, B. (Manchester)
Bentley, I.F. (Mitcham, Surrey)
Bishop, M.E. (Southfleet, Kent)

Blanchard, I. (Hull)
Bone, R. (Orpington, Kent)
Booth, D.A. (Barnsley)
Booth, R.J. (Sutton-in-Ashfield, Notts)
Boyeson, C. (Hull)
Brammer, D.S. (Weston-super-Mare)
Brand, S.R. (Wirral)
*Bratt, S.J. (Blakenhall, West Midlands)
Brayne, R.E. (Harlow, Essex)
Brittain, G.M. (Doncaster)
*Broadhurst, P. (West Kirby, Wirral)
Brown, A.R. (Preston)
Bryan, D.S. (Stamford)
Buller, K.R. (Bridgwater)
Burton, R. (Burton-on-Trent)
Butler, A.N. (Wigan)
Cairns, M.J. (Basingstoke)
Canadine, P. (Rotherham)
Carter, J.E. (Sunderland)
Castle, S. (Wolverhampton)
*Chapman, G.J. (Stroud, Gloucestershire)
Chittenden, S. (St Albans)
*Clattenburg, M. (Cramlington, Northumberland)
Clingo, S.G. (Kings Lynn, Norfolk)
Clyde, A.L. (Doncaster)
Cockwill, N.R. (Barnstaple, North Devon)
Coffey, S. (Liverpool)
Conn, A. (Royston, Hertfordshire)
Cooper, M.A. (Walsall)
Cooper, R.J. (Tynemouth)
Curson, B. (Hinckley, Leicestershire)
*Deadman, D. (Hertford)
Dearing, M.D. (Northolt, Middlesex)
*Denniff, A.P. (Sheffield)
Desmond, R.P. (Swindon)
Devine, J.P. (Middlesbrough)
Dexter, M.C. (Leicester)
Downs, D.G. (Shefford, Bedfordshire)
Drysdale, D. (Lincoln)
Eastwood, P. (Manchester)
Ebbage, M. (Burnham, Buckinghamshire)
Edwards, C.D. (Oldham)
Evans, E.M. (Manchester)
Evans, R.J. (Beckenham, Kent)
*Evetts, G.S. (Hoddesdon, Hertfordshire)
Foulkes, G.W. (Liverpool)
Francis, C.J. (Ely, Cambridgeshire)
Gagen, S.L. (New Malden, Surrey)
Garratt, A.M. (Walsall)
Garrett, L.P. (Southend)
Gosling, I.J. (Ashford, Kent)
Gould, R. (Swadlincote, Derbyshire)
*Greaves, A.J. (Doncaster)
Green, A.J. (Hinckley, Leicestershire)
Griffin, P.J. (Hornchurch, Essex)
Griffiths, S.J. (Macclesfield)
*Griggs, R.P. (Cambridge)
Habgood, S.D. (Chippenham, Wiltshire)
Hall, G.A. (Hixon, Nr Stafford)
Hancox, N. (Walsall Wood, W Midlands)
Harris, I.R. (Torpoint, Cornwall)
Harvey, A.C. (Croxley Green, Hertfordshire)
Hawken, M.A. (St Austell, Cornwall)
Hawkes, K.J. (Quedgeley, Gloucestershire)
Haxby, M.D. (New Brighton, Wirral)

Head, S.C. (Stokenchurch, Buckinghamshire)
Hegley, G.K. (Bishops Stortford)
*Higgins, L.G. (Manchester)
Hills, C.J. (Ely, Cambridgeshire)
Hine, D.J. (Worcester)
Hogg, A.S. (Sheffield)
Holbrook, J.H. (Telford)
Horlick, D.M. (Liverpool)
Horton, A.J. (Wolverhampton)
Howells, A.C. (Port Talbot)
Howes, T.P. (Norwich)
Hubbard, J.R. (Leicester)
*Ilderton, E.L. (Whitley Bay)
Ingram, K.R. (Kingswinford)
Ives, G.L. (Hornchurch)
Ives, M. (Biggleswade, Bedfordshire)
James, R.G. (Milton Keynes)
Jones, L.C. (Bournemouth)
Jones, N.L. (Plymouth)
Kasey, J.R. (Epsom, Surrey)
Kellett, D.G. (Bradford)
Kettle, T.M. (Shawbury, Shropshire)
King, E.A. (Northumberland)
Lee, R. (Brentwood, Essex)
Lewis, R.L. (Shrewsbury)
Lilley, S.J. (Bury St Edmunds)
Lockhart, R. (Newcastle-upon-Tyne)
McGee, A. (Knowsley Village, Merseyside)
McGirl, P.J. (Bedford)
*McGuffog, P. (Manchester)
Martin, A.J. (Penkridge, Staffordshire)
Martin, E.A.C. (Williton, Somerset)
Martin, R.W. (Sheffield)
Mason, L.S. (Bolton)
Massey, T. (Stockport)
Maynard, M.A. (Hertford)
Maynard, R.R. (Bristol)
Mazonowicz, M.J. (Swindon)
Meads, C.J. (Wetherby)
Melin, P.W. (Frimley, Surrey)
Melinn, R.J. (Bridgwater)
Mellor, G.S. (Rotherham)
Merchant, K. (West Ewell, Surrey)
*Miller, D. (Bristol)
*Miller, K.J. (Cowpen, Northumberland)
*Miller, N.S. (Witton Gilbert, Durham)
Morrison, D.P. (Littleover, Derbyshire)
Mullarkey, M. (Exeter)
Nicholson, A.R. (Halifax)
Nicholson, P.W. (Burnhope, Durham)
Nind, K.J. (Bromsgrove)
Norman, P.V. (Sherborne, Dorset)
North, M.J. (Bournemouth)
Oliver, C.W. (Ashington, Northumberland)
Parish, G.B. (Harlow)
Parker, K.E. (Hartlepool)
Pashley, R.A. (Chesterfield)
Pawson, P.M. (Sheffield)
Payne, R.G. (Flitwick, Bedfordshire)
Peacock, D. (Redcar, Cleveland)
Pearce, J.E. (Dagenham)
Pearson, G.D. (Kidderminster)
Penn, A.M. (Kingswinford)
Penton, C. (Woodlingdean, E Sussex)
Perkin, N.F. (Gravesend)
Perlejewski, A.K. (Ryme Intrinseca, Dorset)
Pettitt, J.W. (Welling, Kent)
Pike K. (Gillingham, Dorset)
Pollard, T.J. (Bury St Edmunds)
Pollock, R.M. (Maghull, Merseyside)
Postles, M.D. (Coneyhurst

Common, W Sussex)
Powell, K. (Hartlepool)
Probert, L.W. (Bridgwater)
*Proctor-Green, S.R.M. (Rotherham)
Prosser, P.J. (Innsworth, Gloucestershire)
*Ramsay, W. (Coventry)
Rawcliffe, A. (Manchester)
Reynolds, K.S. (East Barnet)
Richards, D.C. (Llanelli, Carmarthenshire)
Robinson, M.G. (Darlington)
Ross, J.J. (London)
Rushton, G.N. (Nelson, Lancashire)
*Sainsbury, A. (Devizes, Wiltshire)
Salisbury, G. (Preston)
Sharp, P.R. (St Albans)
Shaw, G. (Bramhall, Cheshire)
Shaw, I.D. (Crewe)
Shaw, M.A. (Macclesfield)
Shaw, W. (Blackburn)
Sheffield, J.A. (Burntwood, Staffordshire)
*Short, M. (Barnsley)
Short, M.L. (Grantham, Lincolnshire)
*Singh, J. (Hounslow, Middlesex)
Smith, A.N. (Castleford, W Yorkshire)
Smith, J.P. (Bramhall, Cheshire)
Smith, R.A. (Loughborough)
Smith, R.G. (Chelmsford)
Spicer, D.R. (Totten, Hampshire)
Stott, G.T. (Manchester)
Sygmuta, B.C. (Northallerton)
Tanner, S.J. (Bristol)
Tarry, E.J. (Manchester)
Taylor, J.T. (Blackburn)
Thiarra, S.S. (Bedford)
Thorpe, M. (Ipswich)
Tiffin, R. (Houghton-le-Spring)
Tincknell, S.W. (Watford)
Tingey, M. (High Wycombe, Buckinghamshire)
Toms, Mrs W. (Poole)
Torrance, K.R. (Camberley, Surrey)
Townsend, K.N. (Brierley Hill, W Midlands)
Turner, G.B. (Chesterfield)
Unsworth, D. (Bolton)
Vosper, P.A. (London)
Wade, B. (Isle of Wight)
Wallace, G. (New Herrington, Tyne & Wear)
Walsh, E.J. (Bromsgrove)
Ward, M.B. (Milton Keynes)
Webb, A.J. (Winnersh, Berkshire)
Webb, H.M. (Rotherham)
Webster, C.H. (Shotley Bridge, Durham)
*West, M. (Foxhole, Nr St Austell, Cornwall)
Whitby, D. (Liverpool)
Whitehouse, I. (Calne, Wiltshire)
Wilkins, A.M. (Gravesend, Kent)
Williams, M.A. (Hereford)
*Williamson, I.G. (Theale, Berkshire)
Wing, P.B. (Burbage, Leicestershire)
Wood, A.R. (Birkenhead)
Wood, D. (Ilkley, W Yorkshire)
Wood, P.M. (Fleetwood, Lancashire)
Woodroffe, J.D. (Wicken, Cambridgeshire)
Woolmer, K.A. (Northampton)
Yates, N.A. (Blackburn)
Yerby, M.S. (Ashford, Kent)
*Young, G.R. (Dunstable, Bedfordshire)
Zipfel, R.J. (Thetford, Norfolk)
*New for season 1999/2000.

FOOTBALL AND THE LAW

Football and the Law have come a long way since the Victorian style named solicitor Ebenezer Cobb Morley in London's King's Bench Walk Temple, as uncovered by the indefatigable historian Bryon Butler, co-ordinated the then differential club, school and university rules of play which became the Laws of the Game and The Football Association on 26th October 1863. Eight years later in 1871 a Justice of the Peace, Charles Alcock, conceived the world's oldest and greatest national knock-out *Challenge* Cup Competition for the Association, based upon Harrow School's cock-house knock out system. Six years further forward the barrister old Etonian Alfred Lyttelton, great uncle of jazzman Humphrey, gained his England soccer cap in 1877, before more at cricket for England, to become the first Double International at both seasonal games and three decades later in the early 1900's the professional practising solicitor, Harold Hardman, added an Olympic Soccer gold winning to his winners' and losers' full F.A. Cup medals, as an *amateur* outside left, good enough to keep out of the full England XI the leading professionals of their day. Half a century later, in the early 1950's with the guidance of the schoolmasterly Sir Stanley Rous, he was able to lead Sir Matt Busby and Manchester United as Chairman of the Club into Europe by outsmarting the bureaucratic and parochial minded Football League who had denied the similar claims of Chelsea a year earlier.

What they all would have made of last seasons turmoil with the departures from office of the solicitor chairman of the F.A., Keith Wiseman, and m'learned friend, Peter Leaver, Q.C., from Chief Executiveship of the Premier League, in well publicised controversial circumstances, even before Manchester United's withdrawal from the F.A. Challenge Cup Competition to play in Brazil for enigmatic reasons under debatable Government pressure, is impossible to tell. What is more certain is that their respective intelligencies, integrity and genuine love for the game they served so honourably and loyally throughout their lives would have come up at least with some constructive thoughts about comprehensive insurance for injured players at all levels contemplated by Ted Drake's lesser known but more lastingly significant namesake, Sir Maurice Drake, as Mr. Justice Drake in his landmark judgement it had rejected Paul Elliott's compensation claim against Dean Saunders and Liverpool for his crucial cruciate ligament injury which ended his playing career, in London's High Court, during 1993.

Six years on in 1999 the obscene monies floating around the game, and the self-serving selfish administrators at all levels have remained stunningly silent about any attempts to activate this ideal commercial benefit for players at all levels which include the members of the 43,000 registered F.A. Clubs outside the Premier and Nationwide Leagues, irrespective of those unregistered on Hackney Marshes and comparable open spaces.

Gordon Taylor at the P.F.A. regularly reports 40–50 professionals retiring each year through injury. Gordon Watson of Bradford City did not retire but refused to re-sign under the Bosman European Court of Justice Judgement, after he had obtained a £900,000 damages award in the High Court from a tackle by Kevin Gray playing for Huddersfield during early 1998. At the time when a Court of Appeal in London was dismissing Huddersfield Town's challenge to the legal basis for the judgement, a Bradford County Court judge was applying well-known legal criteria of recklessness to award a 16 year old schoolboy, Maxwell Casson, at the time of his injuries, a £3,000 interim award for a broken ankle caused by the Army in a Work Experience makeshift football match at Strensel Barracks in Yorkshire.

Each of these cases is the tip of an iceberg which can never melt while compensation for injuries can be claimed as in any other circumstance such as road traffic accidents, through the courts, and comprehensive insurance remains untackled. Different considerations apply for criminal injuries and criminality on and off the field. Parliament kicked into touch BSkyB's bid for Manchester United. A new law to control soccer hooligans is in the pipeline, and the High Court has yet to adjudicate on a commercial row between the Premier League and the Office of Fair Trading.

How far fair play still exists in the game each reader must judge for him or herself. What is certain is that lawyers of a different breed are required to serve sport and football today from those early pioneers who created a different game from the one so much in need of the law today, off as well as on the field of play.

EDWARD GRAYSON

The FOOTBALL TRUST
Helping the game

The Football Trust has been providing vital support for the game at every level throughout the UK for nearly 25 years.

The Chancellor of the Exchequer has delivered a budget for football. The Rt. Hon Gordon Brown MP announced a reduction in pool betting duty from 26.5% to 17.5%. This reduction will ensure that the pools companies are able to continue their annual contribution to the Football Trust until at least March 2002.

All this spells good news for the Trust and even better news for our national game. With their support and the continued commitment of our funding partners the Trust can tackle new investment priorities and broaden the Trust's remit.

The Trust has never been more needed. The more equitable distribution of football's new found wealth is a key issue in the game. There is money aplenty at the very top of the game but many Football League clubs still struggle to survive. There is compelling evidence that grass roots facilities, at schools and in the parks, are in desperate need of repair and crying out for investment.

The Trust is unique. It brings all of football's major players together round one table. It is the established vehicle for grant aiding football with funding from the FA Premier League, the Football Association, the English Sports Council, the Football League and the Professional Footballers Association flowing through the Trust for the benefit of our national game.

It has formed a partnership in Scotland with the SFA and the Scottish Sports Council for the benefit of Scottish football and we hope, with Government support, to make similar arrangements in Wales and Northern Ireland.

The Taylor Report has transformed football and the Trust has played a huge part in that transformation. The Trust has grant aided 150 new and refurbished stands, 55 new community and family and disabled facilities along with stadium control rooms, first aid rooms and classrooms.

England has successfully hosted a major international football championship for the first time in 30 years. The venues chosen for EURO 96 were excellent examples of the tremendous progress we have made.

We have new grounds at Chester City, Millwall, Northampton Town, Middlesbrough, Huddersfield Town, Sunderland, Bolton Wanderers, Derby County, Stoke City and Reading and ten more clubs have ambitions to relocate.

Thanks to the Trust's investment this country can now boast the finest football grounds in the world. Grounds to grace the 2006 World Cup.

In addition the Trust has provided support for essential safety and improvement work at grounds at every level, from the top of the game to the grass roots throughout the United Kingdom. It has schemes for providing strip and equipment for schoolboy and schoolgirl teams, women's football, pitches and dressing rooms for local clubs along with contributions to many football related charitable organisations.

The Football in the Community Programme owes its existence to the Trust and our investment of some £5.5m. Substantial investment has been made in training facilities and youth development.

This year alone the Trust made over 120 grant offers. This funding went to a wide range of initiatives and facilities such as the Kick Racism out of Football campaign, the Learning through Football initiative, Women's football and a new stand at Port Vale.

THE NEW REMIT

With Government support and the continued commitment of our funding partners – *The FA Premier League, The Football Association, Sport England, The Football League and The PFA* – the Trust can tackle new funding initiatives and broaden the Trust's remit, creating a long-term partnership and strategy for our national game.

The Trust can tackle new areas such as player development and education and to ensure greater investment in the grass roots, including community based facilities, schools, building links between clubs and communities, supporting inner city schemes, encouraging the development of education centres at football and support for park teams. The Trust can play a significant role in countering social exclusion.

The commitment of the Government and the new funding partners to draw on the Trust's huge grant aid experience and expertise will have the support of everyone who cares about the future of our national game.

BOB HENNESSY

The Football Trust
Taylor Work @ 31 May 1999

PREMIER LEAGUE	Project cost £000	Grant aid £000	
Arsenal	20,000	1,894	9%
Aston Villa	11,026	1,884	17%
Blackburn Rovers	17,600	1,775	10%
Charlton Athletic	6,571	2,058	31%
Chelsea	7,700	2,000	26%
Coventry City	4,500	2,000	44%
Derby County	20,020	2,904	15%
Everton	2,650	1,300	49%
Leeds United	7,200	1,938	27%
Leicester City	5,250	1,940	37%
Liverpool	9,000	1,994	22%
Manchester United	10,000	1,400	14%
Middlesbrough	10,009	2,507	25%
Newcastle United	5,500	2,000	36%
Nottingham Forest	8,700	1,903	22%
Sheffield Wednesday	4,179	1,984	47%
Southampton	23,000	3,500	15%
Tottenham Hotspur	10,000	1,998	20%
West Ham United	4,900	2,000	41%
Wimbledon	0	0	n/a
	187,805	38,979	21%

FOOTBALL LEAGUE DIVISION ONE

Barnsley	5,000	2,000	40%
Birmingham City	4,000	2,000	50%
Bolton Wanderers	20,000	2,500	13%
Bradford City	4,500	2,004	45%
Bristol City	2,167	1,185	55%
Bury	3,315	2,060	62%
Crewe Alexandra	3,456	2,082	60%
Crystal Palace	3,964	2,000	50%
Grimsby Town	750	460	61%
Huddersfield Town	14,450	2,500	17%
Ipswich Town	309	207	67%
Norwich City	3,000	2,000	67%
Oxford United	16,000	2,000	13%
Port Vale	6,138	2,151	35%
Portsmouth	2,450	1,400	57%
Queens Park Rangers	2,969	1,466	49%
Sheffield United	5,600	2,000	36%
Stockport County	1,539	973	63%
Sunderland	12,000	2,500	21%
Swindon Town	3,180	963	30%
Tranmere Rovers	2,670	2,000	75%
Watford	4,100	1,800	44%
West Bromich Albion	3,900	2,000	51%
Wolverhampton Wanderers	6,600	1,750	27%
	132,057	42,001	32%

FOOTBALL LEAGUE DIVISION TWO

AFC Bournemouth	0	0	n/a
Blackpool	31	25	81%
Bristol Rovers	51	34	66%
Burnley	4,800	2,000	42%
Chesterfield	0	0	n/a
Colchester United	155	118	76%
Fulham	0	0	n/a
Gillingham	4,900	2,250	46%
Lincoln City	1,004	789	79%
Luton Town	615	451	73%
Macclesfield Town	0	0	n/a
Manchester City	5,000	2,000	40%
Millwall	15,800	3,500	22%
Northampton Town	4,500	1,000	22%
Notts County	3,200	2,000	63%
Oldham Athletic	3,174	1,604	51%
Preston North End	5,400	1,006	19%
Reading	17,847	2,500	14%
Stoke City	13,600	2,500	18%
Walsall	29	25	86%
Wigan Athletic	29,000	1,000	3%
Wrexham	2,700	1,000	37%
Wycombe Wanderers	1,798	1,000	56%
York City	330	228	69%
	113,934	25,030	22%

FOOTBALL LEAGUE DIVISION THREE

Barnet	0	0	n/a
Brentford	308	231	75%
Brighton & Hove Albion	0	0	n/a
Cambridge United	102	72	71%
Cardiff City	1,306	524	40%
Carlisle	2,141	1,002	47%
Chester City	3,500	500	14%
Darlington	4,000	750	19%
Exeter City	0	0	n/a
Halifax Town	0	0	n/a
Hartlepool United	1,737	1,177	68%
Hull City	68	55	81%
Leyton Orient	1,100	750	68%
Mansfield Town	4,575	1,250	27%
Peterborough United	1,656	1,150	69%
Plymouth Argyle	26	18	69%
Rochdale	1,848	750	41%
Rotherham United	336	285	85%
Scarborough	1,081	750	69%
Scunthorpe United	0	0	n/a
Shrewsbury Town	247	186	75%
Southend United	1,393	893	64%
Swansea City	0	0	n/a
Torquay United	960	506	53%
	26,384	10,849	41%

FOOTBALL CLUB CHAPLAINCY

This year's Chaplain's article has been especially provided by one of the chaplains involved in the new Academies now being established at senior clubs.

SENTIMENT
"There's no sentiment in football" they used to comment 15 years ago as the one year apprentice was shown the exit door aged 17, or the young pro aged 21, or the seasoned player aged 35. The manager would describe the task of telling a player he was no longer good enough, fast enough, strong enough or young enough as "the hardest part of the job". But it had to be done, and the drop-out from professional football was known within the game to be both a very high percentage and a blow from which some struggled to recover. What else apart from football had they been prepared for, trained for? What other skills apart from footballing ones had they been given? From an increasingly early age, expectations of a glittering football career had filled the dreams of the young lad, his family, his friends, and maybe some eager hangers-on. The glitter had faded and then been completely snuffed out with the words in the manager's office, "I'm afraid the Club is not offering you a contract".

CONCERN
The Chaplain's concern has always been for the whole person (spirit, mind and body) and not just for the footballer, but for life after the playing days as well as for the action on the pitch. The chaplain also seeks to serve the whole club and not just the playing staff: each person's worth is measured not in transfer fee income but is seen in terms of their being made in God's image and being valued as worth Christ's death for them. The sight of demoralised youngsters leaving the Club without a qualification or appetite for anything else was a sorry for concerned cleaners and secretaries as well as for managers, fellow players and youth team coaches. Many would try and encourage, counsel a bigger perspective and hope they would prosper in the years ahead.

DIFFERENT
The situation now is very different. Fifteen years ago a 16-year-old apprentice would have one year to win himself a contract and much of that year would be spent in cleaning boots and in menial jobs while he adapted to the pressure of a hard baptism into an adult world. Now most League clubs are adopting the three year football scholarship for their 16-year-olds. There will be a paid employee at most clubs specifically concerned for the education and welfare of the young person. Alongside the education provided for the apprentice (now called "scholar") there is a series of lifelong learning "core skills" that are covered over the three years: the skills will include social skills, drugs awareness, media skills and two skills that many of the club chaplains will be helping with, "relationships" and "pastoral care" (for example in cases of family breakdown, bereavement, illness). Chaplains have always known the very human needs of footballers and of all employees at a football club. It is very encouraging to see the football world express its concern for the players in the new Academies and for their life beyond football. The Footballers Further Education and Vocational Training Society tries to look after players not only during their professional career but also after it has finished". That is a great sentiment and one which from their experience every chaplain will applaud with feeling. Life off the pitch as well as on it should be lived to the fullness of each person's talent and potential.

THE REV

OFFICIAL CHAPLAINS TO FA PREMIERSHIP AND FOOTBALL LEAGUE CLUBS

Rev John Bingham—Chesterfield
Rev Richard Chewter—Exeter C
Rev Michael Lowe—AFC Bournemouth
Rev Andrew Taggart—Torquay U
Rev David Jeans—Sheffield W
Rev Nigel Sands—Crystal Palace
Rev Graham Spencer—Leicester C
Rev Philip Miller—Ipswich T
Rev Allen Bagshawe—Hull C
Rev David Tully—Newcastle U
Rev Derek Cleave—Bristol City
Rev Brian Rice—Hartlepool U
Revs Andy Cowley and John Graham—Watford
Rev Michael Chantry—Oxford U
Rev Michael Futens—Derby C
Rev Ken Hawkins—Birmingham C
Rev Simon Stevenette—Bristol R
Rev Cannon Michael Hunter—Grimsby T
Rev Chris Cullwick—York C
Rev Stephen Cooper—Middlesbrough
Rev Tony Porter—Manchester C
Fr Joe Jordan—Cardiff City
Fr Andrew McMahon—Southampton
Rev Henry Corbett and Rev Harry Ross—Everton
Rev Jeff Howden—Plymouth Argyle

Rev Mervyn Terrett—Luton T
Rev Peter Bye—Carlisle U
Rev David Langdon—QPR
Rev Gary Piper—Fulham
Rev Peter Amos—Barnsley
Rev Barry Kirk—Reading
Rev Martin Short—Bradford C
Rev John Boyers—Manchester U
Rev Martin Butt—Walsall
Rev Steve Riley and Capt Andrew Vertigan—Leeds U
Rev Fr Alan Poulter and Fr Gerald Courell—Tranmere R
Rev Mark Kichenside and Rev Jeffrey Heskins—Charlton Ath
Rev Owen Beament—Millwall
Rev Elwin Cockett—West Ham U
Rev Mick Woodhead—Sheffield U
Rev Alan Comfort—Leyton Orient
Rev John Hall-Matthews—Wolverhampton W
Rev Mark Cockayne—Doncaster R
Rev Ken Baker—Northampton T
Rev Steve Halliwell—Barnet
Rev Richard Havton—Gillingham
Rev Clive Andrews—Notts Co
Rev Chris Nelson—Preston North End
Rev Paul Brown—Wrexham
Major Graham Carey—Portsmouth

The chaplains hope that those who read this page will see the value and benefit of chaplaincy work in football and will take appropriate steps to spread the word where this is possible. They would also like to thank the editors of the Rothmans Yearbook for their continued support for this specialist and growing area of work.
    The following addresses may be helpful: SCORE (Sports Chaplaincy Offering Resources and Encouragement), PO Box 123, Sale, Manchester M33 4ZA and Christians in Sport, PO Box 93, Oxford OX2 7YP.

OBITUARIES

Charlie Adam (b Glasgow 22.3.19; d 30.9.97). A winger who served Leicester City and Mansfield Town in the years immediately after the Second World War. Although he joined Leicester as a 19-year-old in 1938, Charlie didn't make the first of 158 League appearances (22 goals) for the Foxes until 1946. In July, 1952, he moved to Mansfield Town where he had a further 94 appearances in the League scoring seven times.

Gilbert Alldis (b Birkenhead 26.1.20; d 8.1.98). Gilbert started out with Tranmere Rovers prior to the outset of the Second World War and made his debut in 1938. He continued with Rovers after hostilities, playing mainly as a forward. He had 73 League outings (4 goals) before moving to New Brighton in July, 1950, where he had 12 League outings.

Percy Ames (b Bedford 13.12.31; d 4.12.98). Percy spent four years with Tottenham in the early fifties without playing a League game, then moved to Colchester United in May, 1955 and became the regular custodian. In ten years at Layer Road he amassed 397 League appearances, which included an incredible run of 230 consecutive outings between February, 1956 and January, 1961!

Alex Anderson (b Monifieth 15.11.21; d 18.1.99). A full-back, Alex signed for Southampton in November, 1949, following spells with St Johnstone, East Fife and Forfar Athletic. After 20 League appearances for the Saints, he moved to Exeter City in June, 1952, but following just six League outings he moved to Dundee United where he completed his first class playing career.

Doug 'Sam' Baldie (b Scoon 16.4.21; d Bristol 10.11.98). A forward, Sam played for Bristol Rovers in 1945, before signing amateur forms with Luton Town in November of that year. Having made no first team appearances for the Hatters, he returned to Bristol Rovers the following year and scored four times in eight League outings. In 1948, after two seasons at Eastville, he joined Chippenham United and three years later moved on to Minehead.

Jackie Blanchflower (b Belfast 7.3.33; d 2.9.98). Signed for Manchester United in March, 1950, having come through the junior ranks at Old Trafford, and made his League debut in 1951. Jackie was originally an inside-forward but was converted to a half-back. He played alongside his brother in the Northern Ireland team and he won a total of 12 caps, helping his country reach the 1958 World Cup finals. Jackie won Championship medals with United in 1956 and 1957 and in the latter year he played in the FA Cup final. But he spent most of the 2-1 defeat against Aston Villa in goal, following an early injury to Ray Wood. He made 104 League appearances for United scoring 26 times, and played in a further five European Champions' Cup games, made one appearance in the Charity Shield, and had six FA Cup outings.

Ray Bowden (b Looe 13.9.09; d 9.98). Ray started out with his local club Looe in the Plymouth and District league and scored over 100 goals in one season as a teenager before being spotted by Argyle. The slightly built youngster made his Plymouth debut in the 1926-27 season and went on to score a phenomenal 83 goals in 145 League games for the Pilgrims. He won a Third Division South Championship medal in 1930 and toured Canada with the FA a year later. In March, 1933, the prolific Argyle forward line, which included greats Jack Leslie and Sammy Black, was one major player light when Ray moved to Arsenal for £5,000. It was, at the time, a record fee for both Argyle and Arsenal. At Highbury, Ray went on to win the first of six England caps and won Championship medals in 1934 and 1935 (he didn't qualify for a medal in 1933, due to insufficient matches following his transfer). He won a Charity Shield medal in 1934 scoring against Everton and went on to gain an FA Cup winners' medal in 1936, following the Gunners' victory over Sheffield United. In 1937, he moved to Newcastle United for £5,000, where he played until the outbreak of the war, scoring a hat-trick in the third match of the 1939-40 season, just days before hostilities were declared.

Alf Boyd (b Dundee 22.10.20; d 3.7.98). A half-back, Alf started out with St. Johnstone just prior to the outbreak of the Second World War and rejoined the club after hostilities had ended. But his stay was brief because he became a Dundee player and was a member of the Dens Park side that won the Second Division title in 1947. He was skipper when the club won the Scottish League Cup in the 1951-52 campaign and he scored the winner against Rangers. 1952 also saw a Scottish Cup final appearance, but Dundee were beaten 4-0 by Motherwell. But that loss was compensated by another victory in the League Cup in 1952-53. Alf toured South Africa with Dundee in 1953, and decided to remain in the country, becoming manager of Durban City before moving to Johannesburg.

Harold Brook (b Sheffield 15.10.21; d 11.98). Harold played 229 League games for Sheffield United between 1946 and 1954, scoring 89 goals. In his penultimate season with the Blades (1952-53) he helped the club win the Second Division title. In July, 1954, he signed for Leeds and hit a further 46 League goals in 102 games, including 16 in 1954-55, when he finished Leeds' top scorer. In March, 1958, he left Elland Road and had a short spell with Lincoln City, for whom he made four League appearances (1 goal) before retiring.

Laurie Brown (b Shildon 22.8.37; d 30.9.98). A former England amateur international, Laurie won 14 caps for his country and represented Great Britain at the Olympic Games in 1960. The big centre-half started out with Bishop Auckland, joined Darlington as an amateur in 1958, but after only three League games he was signed by Northampton Town as a fully-fledged professional. At the County Ground he was used as a forward and scored 21 times in 33 League outings. This prompted Arsenal to snap him up for £35,000 and he made 101 appearances, mainly as a defender, between 1961 and 1964. He then moved to Spurs for £40,000, where he remained until the summer of 1966, having made a further 62 League appearances. When Norwich City stepped in and he had just over two years at Carrow Road, during which time he played 80 League games. In December, 1968, he became player-manager of Bradford Park Avenue, but the famous old Yorkshire club lost their League status and, after 36 appearances, he left to take up similar posts with first Altrincham and then King's Lynn, before accepting a purely managerial position with Stockton.

Tom Bushby (b Shildon 21.8.14; d 25.12.98). Tom started out with Wolves as an amateur, before signing for Southend in 1934. It was the first of four coastal clubs for the wing half, who made 40 League appearances and scored 12 goals for United. In 1939, he joined Portsmouth, a month after they had lifted the FA Cup. War then intervened, although Tom did make 77 appearances overall for Pompey during hostilities and scored 12 times. In September, 1946, he moved along the Hampshire coast to Southampton, but after just three League games, he joined Cowes on the Isle of Wight.

Ronald 'Sammy' Collins (b Bristol 13.1.23; d 1.6.98). A goalscoring inside-forward or winger, Sammy started out with Bristol City in the 1945-46 season and made 14 League appearances after the war before joining Torquay United in June, 1948. He became a regular at Plainmoor in the 1951-52 season and finished top goalscorer for the Gulls in 1955-56 with 40 goals and that particular season he was the leading scorer in the entire Football League. He completed a fine career with Torquay in 1957, having amassed 204 goals in 358 League games.

Harry Colville (b 12.12.24; d 16.3.99). A centre-half, Harry began with Falkirk, but by 1946 he had moved to Raith Rovers. Success was just around the corner and in the 1948-49 season, he helped the club win the Scottish Second Division title and reach the League Cup final. Following 185 League outings, he joined Dunfermline before returning to

Falkirk in 1955 where, in his first season back at Brockville Park, he made 21 League appearances in the number five shirt. He completed his first class playing career with Falkirk, before becoming manager of Cowdenbeath.

Jimmy Constantine (b Ashton-under-Lyne 16.2.20; d 4.9.98). A centre-forward, Jimmy signed for Manchester City six months before the end of the Second World War and won a Second Division Championship medal in the first official season following hostilities (1946-47), scoring 12 times in 18 appearances, which included a hat-trick against Millwall on his League debut. However, an injury saw him lose his first team place and, in August, 1947, he was snapped up by Bury and, in that initial season, he scored 14 goals in 32 League games. Millwall were again on the receiving end as he poached yet another hat-trick against them at The Den. At the end of that campaign, the Lions signed him and he became a big hit, amassing a fantastic 75 goals in 141 League games, as well as being the club's leading scorer in three out of four seasons. In 1952, he was allowed to join non-League Tonbridge and hit a further 76 goals in two seasons before injury forced him to retire and become the club's trainer. But injuries to his first teamers forced his return at the end of the 1956-57 season and he scored twice in his comeback game. Jimmy continued playing into the 1957-58 campaign, but broke a leg during the course of the season. He was nevertheless undeterred and made another return in 1960-61 before finally calling it a day in 1962, although he still gained great enjoyment playing at local level into his fifties.

Norman Coupe (b Cumwhinton 15.7.24; d 22.4.98). A former Royal Marine, Norman took part in the D-Day landings. A couple of years after the war he joined his local club, Carlisle United (September, 1947). A full-back, he made 31 League appearances for the Cumbrians before being transferred to Rochdale in October, 1951. After 8 League outings, he joined Workington in 1952, where he made six League appearances.

Frank Curran (b Ryton 31.5.17; d 24.9.98). Frank started out with Southport in the mid-thirties and had 16 League outings, scoring three times, before a move took him to Accrington Stanley in February, 1937. After 34 League games and 14 goals, the inside-forward joined Bristol Rovers in June, 1938. Frank spent a season at Eastville, but he enjoyed a productive period, netting 21 goals in 27 League matches, to become the club's top scorer in the 1938-39 season. In the summer of '39, he moved across Bristol to join City, but the outbreak of the war interrupted his career after three League games of the new season. During hostilities he played for City, Everton, Southport, Accrington, Bristol Rovers and Swindon, but rejoined Rovers in 1946 and in the first season following the war he made 11 League appearances and scored three times. Later that season, he had a short spell with then non-League Shrewsbury before transferring to Tranmere Rovers in June, 1947, where he scored seven goals in 17 League outings. He retired in 1953, following a further spell with Shrewsbury.

John Dickson (b 1949; d 12.1.98). A prolific scorer for Cowdenbeath, he finished as the club's (and Scotland's) top marksman in the 1969-70 season with 31 League goals, following Beath's promotion to the First Division. He again topped the club's goalscoring charts in 1970-71, before being transferred to St Mirren in 1972. In the mid-seventies he had a successful spell with Ayr United, helping them to Premier League status. In 1977, John became player-coach of Elgin City, before seeing out his first class career with East Fife.

Gottfried Dienst (b Switzerland 9.9.19; d 6.98). Well-known referee who officiated the 1966 World Cup final and awarded Geoff Hurst's controversial third goal in England's favour against West Germany.

Ronnie Dix (b Bristol 5.9.12; d 2.4.98). An inside-forward, Ronnie started out with Bristol Rovers and made his debut in February, 1928. The following month, he became the youngest player to score a goal in the Football League when he opened his account against Norwich City aged just 15 years and 180 days! He made 101 League appearances for Rovers and scored 33 times. In May, 1932 he moved to Blackburn Rovers (14 League goals in 38 games), but the following year he was off to Aston Villa, where he remained until 1937, scoring 30 goals in 97 League outings. Derby County was his next stop, and he managed to find the net another 30 times in 94 League games. It was this sort of form that led to his international call-up and on the 9th November, 2.1938 he was on the scoresheet for England in a 4-0 victory over Norway at St James' Park. Just prior to the outbreak of the Second World War, Ronnie was transferred to Tottenham, but did not make his debut until after hostilities, in September, 1946, to become the fourth oldest Spurs debutant at the age of 34. He spent three years at White Hart Lane before ending his League career with Reading for whom he made 44 League appearances, scoring 13 times.

Jim Ellis (b Baldridgeburn 1924; d 1.99). Jim saw service with Airdrieonians, Cowdenbeath, East Fife, Raith Rovers and Dunfermline Athletic during the 1940s and early fifties.

Harry Everett (b Worksop 11.11.20; d 29.8.98). A defender with Mansfield Town for whom he made 16 League appearances immediately after the Second World War.

Peter Farrell (b Dublin 16.8.22; d 3.99). Peter doubled up as a wing-half or an inside-forward and joined Everton from Shamrock Rovers in August, 1946. He gave the club wonderful service, making 422 League appearances (13 goals) and was an inspirational skipper. He also won 28 caps for the Republic of Ireland, but it was as an inside-right against England in 1949, that he helped the Irish to victory by scoring one of the goals in their 2-0 success at Goodison Park. He also made seven appearances as a wing-half for Northern Ireland in the late forties, when it was accepted for the North to select players born in the Republic for Home International fixtures. In October, 1957, Peter left Goodison to become player-manager of Tranmere Rovers, where he remained until December, 1960. Following 114 League appearances for the Prenton Park club, he was appointed player-manager of Holyhead Town, whom he led to the Championship of the Welsh League (North).

Archie Ferguson (b Lochore 9.12.18; d 19.3.98). Archie played pre-war football for Raith Rovers, but his career was interrupted when he joined the Army. He served in the Middle East and Europe and was evacuated from Dunkirk in 1941. At the end of the war he was stationed near Doncaster and became goalkeeper for Rovers between 1946 and July, 1948, making 61 appearances, before joining Wrexham. He went on to make 126 League appearances for the Robins and played in the 1950 Welsh Cup final against Swansea Town. He completed his first class career with Dunfermline, whom he joined in 1953.

Albert Gage (b Walthamstow 20.9.22; d 5.96). A goalkeeper who signed amateur forms with Fulham in 1939, before moving across London to Clapton Orient in 1943. He returned to Craven Cottage the following year and also guested for Stockport County, before signing for Aldershot in 1946. He made 39 League appearances for the Hampshire club and then left England for Canada. Upon his return to Britain in 1948, he rejoined Fulham but, before he had made a League appearance, he was signed by Gillingham in 1950 and had 40 League outings for the Kent club.

Matt Gillies (b Loganlea 12.8.21; d 12.98). Originally an amateur with Motherwell, Matt joined Bolton during the Second World War, while serving with the RAF. He made his official League debut after hostilities and became centre-half and captain of the Wanderers. Following 145 League appearances, he moved to Leicester City for £9,500 in January, 1952. Two years later, he was celebrating the Second Division Championship, but City's stay in the top flight was brief. A season later (1954-55), they were relegated to Division Two and Matt called it a day on the playing side. In 1957, City returned to the First Division and he eventually became caretaker-manager in November, 1958, assuming overall control of the Filberts two months later. He was manager when the club reached the FA Cup final in 1961 and 1963 and in 1964 he led the Foxes to victory in the then two-legged League Cup final. Leicester also reached the final in 1965, but lost to Chelsea. In December, 1968, Matt resigned and took over at Nottingham Forest during the opening weeks of 1969. But his tenure at the City Ground ended with his dismissal in 1972.

Archie Glen (b Coalburn 16.4.29; d 30.8.98). An inside-forward in the early part of his career, Archie signed for Aberdeen in April, 1947, and made his debut against Rangers two years later. He became a regular in 1953-54, but as a half-back, and he achieved lasting fame in Aberdeen folklore when his penalty against Clyde at the end of the 1954-55 season saw the Dons win the Championship. He won two caps for Scotland, a League Cup medal (1955-56) and Scottish Cup runners-up medals in 1954 and 1959, before retiring in 1960.

Ken Goldstraw (b Leek 18.9.17; d 10.1.99). Ken played for Walsall and Swindon Town prior to the Second World War, but then national service terminated his playing career.

Reg Goodacre (b Billingborough 1908; d 28.9.98). Reg was a full-back who spent three years with West Ham United in the early thirties. In 1933, he joined Mansfield Town and had 18 League outings, scoring once. In 1934, he signed for Peterborough United, but a year later he was on his way to Gainsborough Trinity, for whom he played until he retired.

Dennis Gordon (b Wolverhampton 7.6.24; d 5.98). Dennis began with Oxford City before being snapped up by West Bromwich Albion in September, 1947. After 27 appearances and two goals in almost three years with the Baggies, he joined Brighton and Hove Albion and became a great favourite at the Goldstone, making 276 League appearances between 1952 and 1960 and scoring 63 goals from his position on the wing. He won a Third Division South Championship medal with the Albion in 1958.

Thomas John 'Jock' Govan (b Larkhall 16.1.23; d 19.2.99). A full-back who made his debut for Hibernian during the Second World War and went on to become an important member of the side when Hibs reached the Scottish Cup final in 1947 and the League Cup final in the 1950-51 season. Jock also contributed to the Easter Road club claiming three Scottish League titles in 1948, 1951 and 1952. He made his Scotland debut in November, 1947 against Wales at Hampden Park and made five further appearances in the international shirt, culminating in a 3-2 victory over Northern Ireland in November, 1948. Six years later, he joined Ayr United, where he saw out his first class playing career.

James Steve Griffiths (b Barnsley 23.1.14; d 10.6.98). Steve began with Chesterfield in October, 1934, but having made no first team appearances in almost three years he joined Halifax Town, where he scored 14 times in 76 League games. In June, 1939, the inside-forward moved to Portsmouth, where he hit 21 goals in 42 wartime games. After hostilities, he joined Aldershot and scored a further nine times in 42 League outings. In June, 1947, he signed for his hometown team, Barnsley, and had an impressive goals tally of 29 in 65 League games before departing for York City in June, 1951. He was still playing at the age of 39, but retired in 1953 having hit 12 goals in 74 League matches for the Minstermen.

Gladstone Guest (b Rotherham 26.6.17; d 7.98). A free-scoring inside-forward, Gladstone was one of the many whose League career was hampered by the outbreak of the Second World War. He joined Rotherham in 1939, but was unable to make his League debut until 1946. In 1951, he skippered the side to the Championship of the Third Division North and had the heartbreak of missing out on promotion to the First Division in 1955 on goal average. Gladstone amassed 356 League appearances for his one and only League club and scored 130 goals. After completing his playing career for Rotherham, he became the club's groundsman until the early eighties.

Harry Haddock (b Glasgow 26.7.25; d 18.12.98). A cultured full-back for Clyde, whom he joined in 1949, Harry enjoyed great success at club and international level, particularly in the mid-fifties, when Clyde won the Scottish Cup in 1955 and again in 1958. He also helped the club win the Second Division title in 1957. Harry made his international debut for Scotland in December, 1954 against Hungary at Hampden. He then played a further four times that season in the left-back position, before waiting three years (1958) to make his sixth and final international appearance. Despite being of slight build, he was reputed to have the longest throw in Scottish football during the fifties.

Walter Hanlon (b Glasgow 23.9.19; d 23.4.99). A clever, diminutive outside-left who joined Brighton and Hove Albion from Clyde in August, 1946, and went on to make 72 League appearances, scoring four times for the club before moving along the south coast to Bournemouth in May, 1948. With the Dean Court side, Wally scored three times in 19 League outings, before joining Crystal Palace in July, 1949, where he made 125 League appearances and hit eight goals, including one on his debut against Exeter City. He was immensely popular at Palace and on the eve of the 1954 FA Cup final, he had a benefit match against a London XI, which Palace won 6-5 and Wally scored the winner in the final seconds! In 1955, he moved on to Sudbury Town.

John Hardman (b Bury 17.12.40; d 3.98). A half-back, John signed for Rochdale in August, 1960, and went on to play until 1967, making 40 League appearances and scoring two goals.

Joe Hayes (b Kearsley 20.1.36; d 1999). Joe was a free-scoring inside-forward who made his name with Manchester City in the fifties and early sixties. He signed for City in August, 1953, and went on to make 331 League appearances, amassing an impressive total of 142 goals. In 1956, he won a runners-up medal at Wembley after City were beaten by Newcastle in the FA Cup final. A year later, City reached Wembley again. This time he celebrated two-fold, scoring City's first goal, as they beat Birmingham 3-1. In 1958, Joe made two Under-23 appearances for England against Scotland and Wales. After almost 12 years with City, Joe moved to Barnsley and, in the 1965-66 season, he made 25 League appearances and scored three times.

Gordon Hodgson (b Newcastle 13.10.52; d 4.99). Gordon signed for his local club, Newcastle United, in July, 1971, and that same year he represented England at Youth international level. After almost three years and nine League appearances, the midfielder joined Mansfield Town where he had a productive period, with 184 League outings and 23 goals. In 1975, he helped the club win the Fourth Division title and, two years later, they were Champions of Division Three. In September, 1978, Gordon was snapped up by Oxford United, where he made 67 League appearances (3 goals), before moving on to Peterborough United in August, 1980. With the Posh, he had a further 83 League outings and scored five times.

Roy Hollis (b Great Yarmouth 11.12.25; d 12.11.98). Roy was a dominating centre-forward who started out with Yarmouth Town in 1946, but went on to find fame with Norwich City, for whom he hit a hat-trick on his debut in 1948. Two years later, he scored five times against Walsall in an 8-0 win. In December, 1952, Spurs signed him and he scored twice on his debut, an FA Cup tie against Tranmere Rovers. But after just three League games and one goal, Southend United snapped him up in February, 1954. He scored at the rate of one every two games, amassing a fantastic 122 League goals in 240 games plus 15 FA Cup goals in a mere 20 ties. Following his League career with Southend, whom he left in 1960, Roy continued at non-League level with Chelmsford City. Yarmouth Town and Lowestoft Town.

Henry Horton (b Malvern 18.4.23; d 2.11.98). A wing-half, Henry started out with Worcester City before joining Blackburn Rovers in January, 1947. He made 92 League appearances for Rovers, scoring five times, then joined Southampton in June, 1951 for £10,000. At The Dell he scored 11 goals in 75 League games before moving to Bradford Park Avenue in May, 1954. After 27 League appearances, Henry retired from the game and pursued his cricket career with first Worcestershire and then Hampshire, with whom he won the County Championship in 1961. Following the conclusion of his playing career, Henry became an umpire and later coached Worcestershire.

William Houliston (b Dumfries 4.4.21; d 10.2.99). A centre-forward, who made his debut for his local club, Queen of the South, in October, 1945. Billy became a regular goalscorer for Queens and, in January, 1948, he was selected to play for the Scottish League against the Irish League and he hit a brace in the 3-0 win. He had two further outings for the Scottish League, a one-all draw with the Football League in March, 1948, then scored against the League of Ireland in September of that year. On the 17th November, 1948, Billy made his Scotland debut against Northern Ireland and celebrated with two goals in a 3-2 victory. In early April, the following year, he was part of the Scotland team that won 3-1 in impressive style against England at Wembley. Three weeks later, he was again victorious in the dark blue shirt, this time in a 2-0 win over France at Hampden Park. He made one further appearance for the Scottish League before leaving Queen of the South in 1952, bound for Berwick Rangers, then Third Lanark. He was Chairman of Queens from 1962 until 1994.

Leslie Howe (b 5.3.12; d 23.2.99). Leslie started out as an amateur with Tottenham in October, 1928, signing as a professional in 1930. A wing-half or central defender, he made 165 League appearances, scoring 26 goals before the outbreak of World War Two.

Kevin Howley (b 1924; d 7.97). A FIFA referee, who officiated in two World Cup tournaments, a UEFA Cup final and the 1960 FA Cup final between Blackburn Rovers and Wolves.

Thomas Gwyn Hughes (b Blaenaeu Ffestiniog 7.5.22; d 14.3.99). Gwyn was a great servant to Northampton after the end of the war and played for the Cobblers until 1956. During that period he made 224 League appearances and scored 15 goals. Normally an inside-forward, he played for Northampton in every half-back and forward position.

Arthur Jefferson (b Goldthorpe 14.12.16; d 7.98). Arthur started out with Peterborough United, but moved to Queens Park Rangers as a 19-year-old in February, 1936. The war limited his appearances, but he resumed his Loftus Road career following hostilities and skippered the club to the Third Division South title in 1948. A great exponent of the sliding tackle, Arthur, known affectionately as 'Rubber Legs', gave QPR great service until 1950, making 213 League appearances, including 89 pre-war. He then moved to Aldershot for £5,000, a substantial sum in those days, and played for the Shots until the age of 38, appearing in 170 League matches.

George Jewett (b Bitterne 2.4.06; d 1998). George signed for his local club, Southampton, in the late twenties, but after making second-eleven appearances he joined Watford. He turned out 29 times for the Hornets in League games, before moving to Crystal Palace, where he had a single outing.

Thomas 'Tucker' Johnson (b Gateshead 21.9.21; d 3.99). An inside-forward, who made 52 League appearances (19 goals) for his local club, Gateshead, immediately after the war. In August, 1948, he joined Nottingham Forest and had an impressive scoring rate, scoring 27 times in 68 League games.

John 'Jack' Jones (b 1916; d 11.3.99). With his strong and muscular approach, Jack was a big hit with Third Lanark in the years leading up to the Second World War. The 1938-39 season was one to be remembered for the popular forward, who scored a total of 28 goals. He played for the club during hostilities, before moving on to Stranraer in 1947.

Norman Kitchen (b Sunderland 26.7.11; d 8.11.98). A winger for Hull City in the mid-thirties, Norman scored on his League debut for the Tigers in February, 1936. But his career at Anlaby Road was brief; he signed for Southport five months later and scored 13 goals in 58 League matches for the seaside club.

Walter Lappage (b Sutton-in-Ashfield 1927; d 30.8.98). A half-back, Walter had one outing for Mansfield Town in 1945-46 and was released at the end of that season.

Joseph 'Robin' Lawler (b Drumcondra 28.2.25; d 17.4.98). An Irish Cup winner with Belfast Celtic in 1947, Robin became a Fulham player in March, 1949. He made the first team at Craven Cottage in 1952 and totalled 281 League appearances with his one and only Football League club before leaving for Yiewsley in 1962. A wing-half, he helped Fulham reach the semi-final of the FA Cup in 1958 and the First Division a year later, when the Cottagers were promoted to the top flight. He also won eight caps for the Republic of Ireland.

Brian Lewis (b Woking 26.1.43; d 14.12.98). A clever inside-forward who signed for Crystal Palace in April, 1960. After 32 League games and four goals, he moved to Portsmouth in July, 1963 and had three-and-a-half years (134 League outings; 23 goals) at Fratton Park before being signed for £25,000 by Coventry City in January, 1967. The Sky Blues finished the campaign as Second Division winners and Brian won a Championship medal. In July, 1968, he was off to Luton Town, newly promoted to the Third Division. In his first season, he finished as the Hatters' top scorer (22 goals). Eighteen months later and he was on his travels once more, this time to Oxford United for £10,000, where he scored four times in 14 outings. In December, 1970, Brian moved to Fourth Division Colchester United for £5,000 and was a member of the side that knocked mighty Leeds out of the FA Cup at the Fifth Round stage, in February, 1971. In April of the following year, after 17 goals in 46 League appearances, Brian rejoined Pompey for £8,500 where he had a further 60 League outings and scored 8 times before leaving Fratton for non-League Hastings in 1975.

John Liddell (b Stirling 13.12.33; 16.3.99). John joined Oldham Athletic a month into the 1960-61 season, having scored 36 goals for St Johnstone the previous campaign, a feat that contributed largely to the club winning the Scottish Second Division Championship. With the Latics he scored nine times in 18 League games, but following only five appearances and one goal in the 1961-62 season, John left for Worcester City. He later retired after a spell at Mossley.

Ian Main (b Weston-Super-Mare 31.10.59; d 16.9.98). A former England Under-18 goalkeeper, Ian was an apprentice with Stoke City, but was released as a teenager and moved to Gloucester City. In the 1978-79 season he joined Exeter City, originally on a non-contract basis, and made his League debut in the 2-0 victory at home to Rotherham United on the 31st March, 1979, keeping his place until the end of the campaign. Ian played 78 League games for the Grecians, renewing his acquaintance with the city from whose university he had earlier graduated. His final League appearance was in a 3-3 draw at home to Portsmouth in May, 1982. He later joined the Devon and Cornwall police force and was a keen rugby and squash player.

George Male (b West Ham 8.5.10; d 19.2.98). Partnered Eddie Hapgood at full-back in the great Arsenal side of the thirties, making his League debut as a half-back in the 1930-31 season. George's FA Cup debut came in the 1932 FA Cup final defeat by Newcastle. He was subsequently converted to a right-back and won four Championship medals and one FA Cup winners' medal leading up to the outbreak of the Second World War. He also contributed to the Gunners'

1948 title success, but in making only eight League appearances, he didn't obtain a medal. George also won 19 England international caps and skippered his country on six occasions. Following his playing career, he took a coaching position at Highbury, then became a scout. He served Arsenal for 45 years before retiring in 1975.

Arthur Mann (b Burntisland 23.1.48; d 3.2.99). Arthur was originally with Hearts and played in the 1968 Scottish Cup final defeat against Dunfermline. In November of that year, he moved to Manchester City, and won a League Cup final medal, following victory over West Bromwich Albion in 1970. At home in either a full-back role or in midfield, Arthur made 35 League appearances for City, had a short loan spell to Blackpool, then moved permanently to Notts County in July, 1972. At Meadow Lane, he amassed 253 League appearances, scoring 21 goals, helping the club to win promotion from the Third Division in 1973. In June, 1979, he left County for Shrewsbury, but after eight League outings and one goal, he joined Mansfield Town four months later. He played 116 League games for the Stags (three goals), before turning to non-League football in the early eighties. Arthur had spells with Boston, Telford and Kettering, then became assistant manager at Grimsby Town in 1989 and occupied a similar post at West Bromwich Albion in the mid-nineties.

Johnny Maule (b 1922; d 22.1.98). Johnny won a Scottish League Cup final runners-up medal with Raith in the 1948-49 season, but celebrated later that campaign when Rovers won the Championship of the Scottish Second Division. He temporarily retired through injury in 1953, but returned to play for Third Lanark.

Bobby McEwan (b Worcester 28.3.42; d 15.12.98). A pillar of the Worcester City defence from 1958 to 1975, Bobby holds the club's appearance record, having totalled a phenomenal 596 first team outings. After leaving Worcester, he had a spell with Bromsgrove Rovers.

William McFarlane (b Fallin 1.10.23; d 13.10.98). A clever winger who played for Hearts just after the war, having originally signed for them in 1942. In May, 1947, he was a member of the Scotland side that won 6-0 in Luxembourg, his sole international appearance. He also represented the Scottish League when they beat the Irish League 7-4 the previous month. In 1951, he left Tynecastle to join Stirling Albion, for whom he scored six goals in 54 League outings.

Tom McGarrity (b Scotstoun 24.11.22; d 17.3.99). Following service with the RAF during the war, Tom played as an inside-forward for Morton, while training as a physiotherapist. In November, 1952, he signed for Southampton and scored on his Saints debut. He retired from professional football at the end of the 1952-53 season, having made five League appearances, to take up a career at the John Radcliffe Hospital in Oxford. Tom continued playing at amateur level and also became a coach with Oxford United.

Frank McGorrighan (b Easington 28.3.42; d 1998). Frank played for Middlesbrough and Carlisle United as an inside-forward during the Second World War. He joined Hull City in August, 1946, and made 20 League appearances, scoring twice before departing for Blackburn Rovers in February, 1947. Following five League games, he returned to Hull but, in August, 1948, six League outings later, he was signed by Southport. But his stay was brief and after four games, he retired.

John McGrath (b Manchester 23.8.38; d 25.12.98). John was an imposing figure on a football field who gave everything to the cause; a centre-half noted for his no-nonsense challenges, but a man who also possessed the ability to play himself out of trouble. He signed for Bury in October, 1955, after a short spell as an amateur with Bolton Wanderers, and won a Third Division Championship medal with the Shakers in 1961, even though he was prized away by Newcastle in February of that year, following 148 League games and two goals. In March, 1961, he made his England Under-23 debut against West Germany and celebrated as the intermediates won 4-1. John enjoyed further success at St James' Park, winning a Second Division Championship medal in 1965. After amassing 170 League appearances for the Magpies he was sought by Southampton and arrived at The Dell in February, 1968. He was a colossus at the heart of the Saints defence, which included other never-say-die performers like Dennis Hollywood, Jimmy Gabriel and David Walker. A young Paul Bennett eventually took his first team place and, in December, 1972, after 168 League games and one goal he went to Brighton and Hove Albion, but only for a short three match loan spell. John returned to Southampton to take up a coaching position in 1975. Four years later, he was appointed boss of Port Vale and achieved promotion from the Fourth Division in 1983. In January, 1984, he took the vacant manager's job at Chester, but moved on to Preston North End two years later, and won promotion to the Third Division in 1987. He departed North End in 1990 and took over at Halifax the following year where he remained until resigning in December, 1992.

Joe McLelland (b Edinburgh 1936; d 4.99). Joe was a committed full-back for Hibernian, whom he joined in 1956. He played in the 1958 Scottish Cup final against Clyde and received a runners-up medal after the narrow 1-0 defeat. He also played for the club when they embarked on a European Fairs Cup (UEFA Cup) campaign in 1960-61, reaching the semi-finals in the process.

Maurice Milne (b Dundee 21.10.32; d 8.8.98). Maurice joined Dundee United in 1954, where his skills on the left-wing made him a favourite at Tannadice. In May, 1957, he moved to Norwich City, but left to join Gloucester City the following year after just five games in the 1957-58 season. In 1959, he returned to Scotland to join Dunfermline, but was forced to retire through injury shortly after his move.

Roy Milne (b Falkirk 27.4.21; d 29.6.98). Roy signed for Celtic during the war and played in the left-back berth after hostilities. Celtic released him in 1952 and he settled in the United States and played club football on the East and West coasts. He also made international appearances before turning to management. Roy returned to Scotland in 1973 and became a hotelier near Stirling.

Fred Morris (b Oswestry 15.6.29; d 20.11.98). A fleet-of-foot outside-right who served six League clubs between 1950 and 1962. Fred signed for Walsall from Oswestry Town in May, 1950 and made 210 League appearances scoring 43 times. In March, 1957, he moved on to Mansfield and hit a further 17 goals in 56 League outings before Liverpool paid £7,000 for his services in February, 1958. After 14 goals in 47 League matches, he left Anfield for Crewe in June, 1960. His stay at Gresty Road was brief, however, and after only eight games and one goal he signed for Gillingham in January, 1961. Ten League games and one goal later and he was on the move once more, this time to Chester, in the summer of 1961. Fred spent a season at Sealand Road and made 29 League appearances for City, scoring three times. The following close season (1962), he left the Football League to join Altrincham.

Bobby Nash (b Hammersmith 8.2.46; d 2.98). A full-back who signed for Queens Park Rangers in February, 1964, after progressing through the club's junior ranks. He made 17 League appearances for the West Londoners before being transferred to Exeter City in June, 1966. He made one appearance for the Grecians and then spent the remainder of his career outside the League with Hastings United, Rye Town and Three Bridges.

Bernard John 'Len' Newcombe (b 28.2.31; d 8.98). An outside-left who signed for Fulham in May, 1948, and made 23 League appearances (three goals) before moving across London to Brentford in April, 1956. For the Bees he had 84 League outings and scored 10 times.

Jackie Blanchflower (Colorsport)

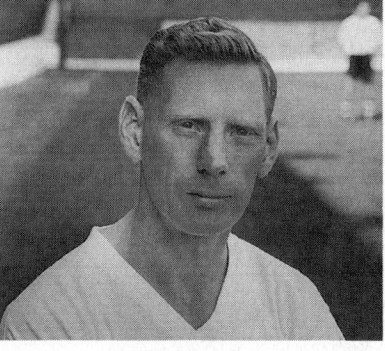

Syd Owen (Colorsport)

John Osborne (b Barlborough 1.12.40; d 11.98). John started out with Chesterfield, signing for the Spireites in September, 1960. He made 110 League appearances for the club, 109 in goal, and one at centre-forward! In January, 1967, he was snapped up by West Bromwich Albion and went on to give sterling service to the Baggies in an eleven year period, amassing 250 League appearances in the process. In 1968, he won an FA Cup winners' medal, following a 1-0 victory over Everton and in 1970 he won a runners-up medal after Albion had reached the League Cup final. Following his playing career, he became commercial manager at Worcestershire County Cricket Club.

Syd Owen (b Small Heath 29.2.22; d 1.99). As club captain and centre-half, Syd was the mainstay of Luton's defence during their productive run of the 1950s. Before his move to the Hatters, he had previously been with Birmingham City. Following five League appearances, he joined Luton in June, 1947 for £1,500. What followed was a long and loyal association. Syd became skipper in the 1950-51 season and his solid performances earned him the first of three England caps in May, 1954. The following year he was at his pivotal best as Luton were promoted to the First Division. In 1959, he helped steer the club to the FA Cup final, a feat which earned him the Footballer of the Year accolade. He then had a brief period as manager at Kenilworth Road then, in May, 1960, he was appointed chief coach at Leeds United, and remained at Elland Road until the mid-seventies. In October, 1975, he took the assistant manager's post at Birmingham City. Two years later, he became coach at Hull City, but only for a three month period. In May, 1978, he was appointed youth team coach with Manchester United, before eventually becoming a scout at Old Trafford, a position he held until 1982 before retiring.

Tommy Pearson (b Edinburgh 16.3.13; d 1.3.99). An outside-left who signed for Newcastle United as a 20-year-old, Tommy played for the club before, during and after the Second World War, amassing 212 League games and scoring 46 goals. He was capped twice by Scotland in 1947 against England and Belgium but, he also played *for* England in a wartime international *against* Scotland. He was attending an international between the two countries at Newcastle in December, 1939, when news of a car crash, involving England winger Eric Brook, was announced. Tommy took his place and was on the victorious side against his countrymen, England winning 2-1. In February, 1948, Tommy joined Aberdeen and represented the Scottish League against the League of Ireland two months later. He enjoyed a successful period at Pittodrie, playing into his forties, before retiring in 1953, having scored 16 goals in a total of 115 League and Cup games.

Edwin Perry (b Rhymney 19.1.09; d 11.98). Eddie was a centre-forward who began with Merthyr Town in the late twenties, but was snapped up by Bournemouth when he impressed in an FA Cup tie against them. After two years on the south coast, he was transferred to Thames FC, but Fulham prized him away in May, 1931, following his goalscoring exploits. After 36 goals in 62 League outings for the Cottagers, he moved to Doncaster Rovers, where he netted 32 goals in 98 League games and was capped three times by Wales. He returned to Fulham just prior to the outbreak of the war and guested for Brentford during hostilities. He had a ten-year spell between 1946 and 1956 as a coach with Fulham, then went on to manage Southend United until 1960.

Jimmy Philp (b 1914; d 25.3.98). Jimmy was a great favourite at East Fife, whom he joined from Hearts in 1946. A talented defender, he was in the East Fife side that won the Scottish League Cup in the 1947-48 season. He later played for Brechin City, before rejoining the Fifeshire club where he served as a trainer, groundsman and kitman.

Tommy Powell (b Derby 12.4.25; d 9.9.98). A one-club man, Tommy joined Derby County in 1942 and played for the Rams during the war years, as well as serving in the Army. He made his debut in 1948 and made 381 League appearances, scoring 58 goals, and set up many others with his deft passing ability from his position of inside-forward or on the right wing. In 1957, Tommy won a Third Division North Championship medal before retiring at the top level through injury in 1961.

Gareth Price (b Swindon 21.2.70; d 31.8.98). Gareth started out with Nottingham Forest as an amateur before moving to Mansfield Town in the late eighties. He left the Stags without making any League appearances and joined Bury. He made his League debut for the Shakers as a substitute against Huddersfield on the 16th April, 1990, and celebrated a six-nil victory. Gareth made a further three appearances for Bury in 1990-91, before playing non-League with Kettering, Gainsborough and Ashfield United. A serious illness then prohibited him from playing.

Sir Alf Ramsey (b Dagenham 22.1.20; d 28.4.99). Alf began as an amateur with Portsmouth, but in 1940 he joined Southampton, turning professional in 1944. He made his debut for the Saints in 1946 and won the first of 32 caps for England when he made his international debut against Switzerland on the 2nd December, 1948. After 90 League appearances and eight goals, he joined Tottenham in May, 1949, for £21,000 which was, at the time, a record for a full-back. As part of the transfer, a Spurs player went to The Dell. In his first season at White Hart Lane, Spurs won the Second Division title, then followed that up with the League Championship in 1951. His final appearance for England was against Hungary in November, 1953, and he scored from the penalty spot in the 6-3 defeat at Wembley. He also made one appearance for the England 'B' side against Switzerland and represented the Football League on four occa-

Sir Alf Ramsey (Colorsport)   Dennis Viollet (Colorsport)

sions. In August, 1955, he was appointed manager of Ipswich Town and, two years later, guided Town to the Championship of the Third Division (South). In 1961, he piloted another promotion, this time to the First Division and, in the very next campaign of 1961-62, Ipswich achieved a stunning Championship success. In October, 1962, he was appointed England manager. His first game in charge, on the 27th February, 1963, saw England's elimination from the European Nations' Cup (now European Championship) after a 5-2 defeat in France. Despite this initial set-back, he proclaimed England would win the next World Cup in 1966. His prophetic words proved well-founded following England's 4-2 win over West Germany in the final at Wembley. In 1967, he was knighted for his services to football and the following year he guided England to third place in the European Nations' Cup, still their best ever position in the tournament. In 1970, he saw England eliminated in the quarter-finals of the World Cup, when they lost 3-2 to West Germany. There was more World Cup heartache when England failed to beat Poland in a qualifying match at Wembley in October, 1973, and lost their opportunity to go to the 1974 finals in the process. Sir Alf was relieved of the England manager's job in May, 1974. He became a director of Birmingham City in January, 1976, and had a short spell as care-taker boss at St. Andrews between September, 1977 and March, 1978. His final appointment in 1980 saw him take the post of technical director with Panathinaikos, but his stay with the Athenian club only lasted a few months.

Ron Reynolds (b Haslemere 2.6.28; d 6.99). Ron came through the juniors at Aldershot before making his League debut in goal in the 1946-47 season, when the Shots were in the Third Division South. He played 115 League games for the Hampshire club, before moving to Tottenham Hotspur in July, 1950, where he spent almost ten years. Spurs had just won the Second Division title and in their first season back in the top flight they relieved Portsmouth of the League Championship trophy (1950-51). While Ron was at White Hart Lane, Tottenham twice finished First Division runners-up in 1951-52 and again in 1956-57. After 86 appearances in the Spurs green jersey, he moved to Southampton in March, 1960, and went on to make another 91 League appearances. At the end of his first campaign at The Dell (1959-60), the Saints won the Third Division Championship.

Tommy Robertson (b Perth 1929; d 6.3.99). A wing-half, Tommy started out with Southend in the late forties, but did not make a first team appearance. He joined his local club St Johnstone, for whom he played until the mid-fifties, before emigrating to Canada.

Augustus Scott (b Sunderland 19.2.21; d 28.11.98). Signed by Luton Town prior to the Second World War, Augie never played a first team game for the Hatters and joined Southampton in July, 1947. The little inside-forward spent more than four year with the Saints, scoring ten goals in 49 games. In August, 1951, he moved to Colchester United, where he had a further 120 League outings and scored 11 times.

Dick Sheppard (b Bristol 14.2.45; d 18.10.98). Dick signed for West Bromwich Albion in February, 1963 and made his debut in goal two years later. He appeared for the Baggies in the 1967 League Cup final and received a runners-up medal following the 3-2 reversal against Queens Park Rangers. In June, 1969, after 39 League appearances, he returned to his place of birth to join Bristol Rovers. Dick was Rovers' hero when they won the Watney Cup final in 1972, saving a spot-kick from Sheffield United's Ted Hemsley in the penalty shoot-out. He also saved a George Best penalty in a Third Round League Cup replay at Manchester United in October, 1972, as Rovers went through 2-1 at Old Trafford, following a one-all draw in front of more than 33,000 at Eastville! In January, 1973, he suffered a serious head injury at home to Tranmere, and only made one further appearance for Rovers, at the end of 1974. In between he had two games on loan to then Fourth Division Torquay United, making him an elite member of a group of players who have appeared in all four Divisions of the Football League.

John Trevor Smith (b West Stanley 8.9.10; d 23.10.98). An inside-forward, who signed for Charlton Athletic in May, 1933, following an unsuccessful trial with Portsmouth three years earlier. He made 23 League appearances for the Haddicks, scoring six goals, before moving on to Fulham in March, 1935. After finding the net 19 times in 93 League games, he joined Crystal Palace three years later and had 147 outings, scoring 54 goals, which included wartime appear-ances. In June, 1947, he signed for Watford and had a further 10 first team League outings.

Tom Smith (b Fenwick 4.10.09; d 21.6.98). Tom was a dominating centre-half with Kilmarnock, whom he joined at the end of the twenties and played for with distinction until December, 1936. During that period he won a Scottish Cup run-ners-up medal (1932) after Killie were beaten by Rangers in the replayed final, made his Scotland debut against England (1934), and in October, 1936 represented the Scottish League against the Football League. Two months later, he was on his way to Preston North End and was the proud captain when North End lifted the FA Cup following vic-tory over Huddersfield Town in the 1938 final. That same year he won his second cap and celebrated as Scotland beat England at Wembley. He continued to play for Preston during the war years and also guested for Burnley, Rochdale and Manchester United. Following hostilities, Tom rejoined Kilmarnock to become secretary/manager, before return-ing to Lancashire to live.

Ian Stewart (b 1940; d 18.5.98). An inside-forward, Ian spent six seasons with East Fife (1959-65) and scored 80 goals in 198 League games, before seeing out his career with Clyde and Arbroath.

Alex Stott (d. 19.12.98). Alex joined Dundee from Portsmouth in 1947 and hit 39 goals for the club in the 1948-49 season, as Dundee finished runners-up to Rangers in the Scottish First Division. In the autumn of 1949, Partick Thistle secured the centre-forward's services for £6,000 and he hit 76 goals, before moving on to Hamilton Academicals in January, 1954, scoring a brace on his debut.

Fred Thompson (b Swindon 24.11.37; d 22.5.98). Fred was a half-back who played for his local club Swindon Town. He signed for the club in September, 1955, having made his debut the previous season, and had 21 League outings, scoring once, before joining Trowbridge in 1962. Two years later he became player/manager of Chippenham, where he remained until the early seventies.

Andy Thomson (b Belshill 4.12.79; d 4.12.98). Andy became a professional with Motherwell as a 17-year-old. He was destined to make a career from football, but died tragically of heart seizure.

Robert Stanley Thursby (b Lincoln 5.3.09; d 1998). A winger who played for Lincoln City whom he joined as an amateur in 1929. He made 21 League appearances and scored six times.

Willie Toner (b Glasgow 18.12.29; d 3.99). Willie was a robust, but skilful centre-half who had spells with Queen's Park and Celtic before joining Sheffield United in May, 1951. Two years later, he was the proud recipient of a Second Division Championship medal. He made 55 League appearances for the Blades and scored twice before a move took him back to Scotland, when Kilmarnock snapped him up for £2,000. Willie enjoyed a successful career with Killie and helped them reach the final of the Scottish Cup in 1957, which they lost to Falkirk, following a replay. In October, 1959, he won his first cap against Wales in Cardiff and followed that with an appearance versus Northern Ireland at Hampden Park. Willie also had five outings for the Scottish League team. In 1960, he returned to Hampden to play in the Scottish Cup final against Rangers, but once more had to be content with a runners-up medal. The following season (1960-61), Killie were League Cup finalists, but lost to Rangers again. In April, 1963, he moved on to Hibernian, but six months later he was at Ayr United. In October, 1964, Willie took up his first managerial post at Dumbarton, where he remained for three years.

George Ure (b Dundee 1919; d 26.3.99). George played in the left-back position for Dundee United before and after the Second World War, as well as being with Brechin City, Falkirk and Hearts.

Dennis Viollet (b Manchester 20.9.33; d 6.3.99). An inside-forward who had a wonderful goalscoring record for both Manchester United and Stoke City. Dennis signed professional forms for United in September, 1950, and went on to make 259 League appearances for the Red Devils, scoring 160 goals. His 20 League goals in the 1955-56 campaign helped secure the First Division Championship and a further 16 strikes the following season ensured the title stayed at Old Trafford. In 1958, he survived the Munich air crash and went on to win a runners-up medal when United were beaten by Bolton in the Cup final. In the 1959-60 season, he hit 32 goals to become United's highest League scorer in a season and on the 22nd May, 1960 he made his England debut in Budapest against Hungary. A further cap followed in September, 1961, when he scored in the 4-1 victory over Luxembourg at Highbury. He joined Stoke City in January, 1962 for £25,000 and the following year celebrated as Stoke won the Second Division title. In 1964, Dennis won a League Cup runners-up medal, following a 4-3 aggregate defeat against Leicester City. He amassed 182 League games for the Potters and scored 59 goals before joining the North American Soccer League. In the late sixties, he returned to England to play for Witton Albion, then became player-coach with Linfield, winning the Irish Cup in 1970. He emigrated to the United States in 1974.

Bobby Walker (b Stirling 16.3.12; d 14.10.98). Former Motherwell, Falkirk and Exeter City goalkeeper who became a player-coach in Malta and in 1939 emigrated to Australia, where he held nearly every top official post in Australian Soccer. He also became manager of a provincial newspaper and jointly formed the national magazine, Soccer World.

George Watson (b Errol 1912; d 1998). George played for Dundee United before the outbreak of the Second World War and emigrated to Canada in 1947.

Charlie Watkins (b Glasgow 14.1.21; d 2.98). Originally a half-back with Glasgow Rangers, Charlie joined Luton Town in September, 1948, and played 217 League games for the Hatters, scoring 16 times. His final season at Kenilworth Road coincided with the club winning promotion to the First Division as runners-up to Birmingham City.

Richard Whittaker (b Dublin 10.10.34; d 18.9.98). Richard signed for Chelsea in May, 1952 and spent more than eight years at Stamford Bridge. But first team opportunities were limited and he made 48 League appearances before he joined Peterborough United in September, 1960. The previous year he had won a cap for the Republic of Ireland against Czechoslovakia. There was more success for the Irish defender at Peterborough, when he helped the Posh win the Fourth Division title in 1961. Two years and 82 League games later, he was on his way to Queens Park Rangers, where he had 17 League outings, before completing his career with Corby and Stamford Town.

Ernie Whittle (b Lanchester 25.11.25; d 8.5.98). A forward, who began with Newcastle United during the war, then moved to Lincoln City in 1950 without ever making a League appearance for the Magpies. He enjoyed great success at Sincil Bank, winning a Third Division North Championship medal in 1952, as part of the Lincoln team that netted 121 goals in the campaign! Ernie bagged 19 of them. In all he scored 62 times in 145 League games before moving to Workington in March, 1954 and found the net a further 45 times in 112 League games. He joined Chesterfield in November, 1956 and made 15 League appearances, scoring four times, before completing his first class career with Bradford Park Avenue, with whom he bagged a further 6 goals in 18 games during the 1957-58 season.

John 'Jock' Whyte (b West Calder 7.5.21; d 17.10.98). Jock started out with Falkirk and won a runners-up medal against East Fife in the 1947-48 Scottish League Cup final. The full-back joined Bradford City in August, 1950 and went on to make 236 League appearances, scoring twice, before moving to then non-League Wigan in July, 1957.

THE FA CARLING PREMIERSHIP
and NATIONWIDE FOOTBALL LEAGUE
FIXTURES 1999–2000

Saturday 7 August 1999
FA Carling Premiership
Arsenal v Leicester C
Chelsea v Sunderland
Coventry C v Southampton
Leeds U v Derby Co
Middlesbrough v Bradford C
Newcastle U v Aston Villa
Sheffield W v Liverpool
Watford v Wimbledon
West Ham U v Tottenham H

Nationwide Football League Division 1
Birmingham C v Fulham
Blackburn R v Port Vale
Charlton Ath v Barnsley
Crystal Palace v Crewe Alex
Grimsby T v Stockport Co
Ipswich T v Nottingham F
Portsmouth v Sheffield U
QPR v Huddersfield T
Tranmere R v Bolton W
Walsall v Swindon T
WBA v Norwich C

Nationwide Football League Division 2
AFC Bournemouth v Cambridge U
Blackpool v Wrexham
Bristol R v Brentford
Bury v Gillingham
Cardiff C v Millwall
Chesterfield v Colchester U
Notts Co v Luton T
Oldham Ath v Preston NE
Reading v Bristol C
Stoke C v Oxford U
Wigan Ath v Scunthorpe U
Wycombe W v Burnley

Nationwide Football League Division 3
Brighton & HA v Mansfield T
Carlisle U v Leyton Orient
Cheltenham T v Rochdale
Chester C v Barnet
Exeter C v Hull C
Halifax T v Darlington
Lincoln C v Rotherham U
Macclesfield T v Northampton T
Peterborough U v Hartlepool U
Shrewsbury T v Torquay U
Southend U v Plymouth Arg
York C v Swansea C

Sunday 8 August 1999
FA Carling Premiership
Everton v Manchester U (4.00)

Nationwide Football League Division 1
Manchester C v Wolverhampton W
(1.00)

Monday 9 August 1999
FA Carling Premiership
Tottenham H v Newcastle U (8.00)

Tuesday 10 August 1999
FA Carling Premiership
Derby Co v Arsenal (8.00)
Sunderland v Watford
Wimbledon v Middlesbrough

Wednesday 11 August 1999
FA Carling Premiership
Aston Villa v Everton
Leicester C v Coventry C
Liverpool v West Ham U
Manchester U v Sheffield W (8.00)
Southampton v Leeds U

Friday 13 August 1999
Nationwide Football League Division 1
Huddersfield T v Blackburn R

Saturday 14 August 1999
FA Carling Premiership
Bradford C v Sheffield W
Derby Co v Middlesbrough
Leicester C v Chelsea
Liverpool v Watford
Manchester U v Leeds U
Sunderland v Arsenal
Tottenham H v Everton
Wimbledon v Coventry C

Nationwide Football League Division 1
Barnsley v Crystal Palace
Bolton W v QPR
Fulham v Manchester C
Norwich C v Birmingham C
Nottingham F v Grimsby T
Port Vale v WBA
Sheffield U v Walsall
Stockport Co v Tranmere R
Wolverhampton W v Portsmouth

Nationwide Football League Division 2
Brentford v Oldham Ath
Bristol C v AFC Bournemouth
Burnley v Chesterfield
Cambridge U v Reading
Colchester U v Notts Co
Gillingham v Bristol R
Luton T v Blackpool
Millwall v Wigan Ath
Oxford U v Cardiff C
Preston NE v Stoke C
Scunthorpe U v Wycombe W
Wrexham v Bury

Nationwide Football League Division 3
Barnet v Exeter C
Darlington v Macclesfield T
Hartlepool U v Halifax T
Hull C v Lincoln C
Leyton Orient v Brighton & HA
Mansfield T v Cheltenham T
Northampton T v Peterborough U
Plymouth Arg v Shrewsbury T
Rochdale v Southend U
Rotherham U v Chester C
Swansea C v Carlisle U
Torquay U v York C

Sunday 15 August 1999
FA Carling Premiership
Southampton v Newcastle U (4.00)

Nationwide Football League Division 1
Swindon T v Ipswich T (1.00)

Monday 16 August 1999
FA Carling Premiership
Aston Villa v West Ham U (8.00)

Friday 20 August 1999
Nationwide Football League Division 1
WBA v Nottingham F

Nationwide Football League Division 2
Cardiff C v Wrexham (7.30)

Saturday 21 August 1999
FA Carling Premiership
Chelsea v Aston Villa
Coventry C v Derby Co
Everton v Southampton
Leeds U v Sunderland
Middlesbrough v Liverpool
Newcastle U v Wimbledon
Sheffield W v Tottenham H
Watford v Bradford C
West Ham U v Leicester C

Nationwide Football League Division 1
Birmingham C v Port Vale
Blackburn R v Barnsley
Charlton Ath v Norwich C
Crystal Palace v Swindon T
Grimsby T v Fulham
Ipswich T v Bolton W
Manchester C v Sheffield U
Portsmouth v Stockport Co
QPR v Wolverhampton W
Tranmere R v Huddersfield T
Walsall v Crewe Alex

Nationwide Football League Division 2
AFC Bournemouth v Colchester U
Blackpool v Gillingham
Bristol R v Oxford U
Bury v Brentford
Chesterfield v Cambridge U
Notts Co v Scunthorpe U
Oldham Ath v Burnley
Reading v Luton T
Wigan Ath v Bristol C
Wycombe W v Preston NE

Nationwide Football League Division 3
Brighton & HA v Torquay U
Carlisle U v Hartlepool U
Cheltenham T v Hull C
Chester C v Northampton T
Exeter C v Rotherham U
Halifax T v Plymouth Arg
Lincoln C v Barnet
Macclesfield T v Swansea C
Peterborough U v Leyton Orient
Shrewsbury T v Darlington
Southend U v Mansfield T
York C v Rochdale

Sunday 22 August 1999
FA Carling Premiership
Arsenal v Manchester U (4.00)

Nationwide Football League Division 2
Stoke C v Millwall (1.00)

Monday 23 August 1999
FA Carling Premiership
Leeds U v Liverpool (8.00)

Tuesday 24 August 1999
FA Carling Premiership
Middlesbrough v Leicester C
Watford v Aston Villa

Wednesday 25 August 1999
FA Carling Premiership
Arsenal v Bradford C
Coventry C v Manchester U
Everton v Wimbledon (8.00)
Newcastle U v Sunderland
Sheffield W v Derby Co
West Ham U v Southampton

Friday 27 August 1999
Nationwide Football League Division 1
Crewe Alex v Grimsby T
Stockport Co v Birmingham C

Nationwide Football League Division 3
Northampton T v Lincoln C

Saturday 28 August 1999
FA Carling Premiership
Aston Villa v Middlesbrough
Bradford C v West Ham U
Derby Co v Everton
Liverpool v Arsenal
Southampton v Sheffield W
Tottenham H v Leeds U
Wimbledon v Chelsea

Nationwide Football League Division 1
Barnsley v Portsmouth
Bolton W v Manchester C
Fulham v Charlton Ath
Huddersfield T v Crystal Palace
Norwich C v Blackburn R
Nottingham F v QPR
Port Vale v Tranmere R
Sheffield U v Ipswich T
Swindon T v WBA
Wolverhampton W v Walsall

Nationwide Football League Division 2
Brentford v Blackpool
Bristol C v Bury
Burnley v Stoke C
Cambridge U v Notts Co
Colchester U v Reading
Gillingham v Wycombe W
Luton T v Cardiff C
Millwall v Chesterfield
Oxford U v Oldham Ath
Preston NE v Wigan Ath
Scunthorpe U v AFC Bournemouth
Wrexham v Bristol R

Nationwide Football League Division 3
Barnet v York C
Darlington v Brighton & HA
Hartlepool U v Cheltenham T
Hull C v Macclesfield T
Leyton Orient v Halifax T
Mansfield T v Carlisle U
Plymouth Arg v Peterborough U
Rochdale v Exeter C
Rotherham U v Shrewsbury T
Swansea C v Southend U
Torquay U v Chester C

Sunday 29 August 1999
FA Carling Premiership
Sunderland v Coventry C (4.00)

Monday 30 August 1999
FA Carling Premiership
Leicester C v Watford (8.00)
Manchester U v Newcastle U (1.00)

Nationwide Football League Division 1
Birmingham C v Crewe Alex (3.00)
Blackburn R v Bolton W (3.00)
Grimsby T v Swindon T (3.00)
Ipswich T v Barnsley (3.00)
Manchester C v Nottingham F (3.00)
Portsmouth v Huddersfield T (3.00)
Tranmere R v Sheffield U (3.00)
Walsall v Norwich C (3.00)
WBA v Fulham (3.00)

Nationwide Football League Division 2
Blackpool v Oxford U (3.00)
Bristol R v Burnley (3.00)
Bury v Colchester U (3.00)
Cardiff C v Scunthorpe U (3.00)
Chesterfield v Bristol C (3.00)
Notts Co v Brentford (3.00)
Oldham Ath v Millwall (3.00)
Stoke C v Gillingham (3.00)
Wigan Ath v Cambridge U (3.00)

Nationwide Football League Division 3
Carlisle U v Plymouth Arg (3.00)
Cheltenham T v Barnet (3.00)
Chester C v Rochdale (3.00)
Exeter C v Mansfield T (3.00)
Lincoln C v Swansea C (3.00)
Macclesfield T v Rotherham U (3.00)
Peterborough U v Darlington (3.00)
Southend U v Leyton Orient (3.00)
York C v Northampton T (3.00)

Tuesday 31 August 1999
Nationwide Football League Division 1
Charlton Ath v Stockport Co (8.00)
Crystal Palace v Wolverhampton W (8.00)
QPR v Port Vale (8.00)

Nationwide Football League Division 2
AFC Bournemouth v Luton T
Wycombe W v Wrexham

Nationwide Football League Division 3
Halifax T v Torquay U
Shrewsbury T v Hartlepool U (7.30)

Wednesday 1 September 1999
Nationwide Football League Division 2
Reading v Preston NE

Nationwide Football League Division 3
Brighton & HA v Hull C (8.00)

Friday 3 September 1999
Nationwide Football League Division 1
Barnsley v Tranmere R
Port Vale v Grimsby T

Nationwide Football League Division 3
Mansfield T v Peterborough U
Rochdale v Halifax T

Saturday 4 September 1999
Nationwide Football League Division 1
Crewe Alex v WBA
Fulham v Portsmouth
Huddersfield T v Ipswich T
Norwich C v Manchester C
Nottingham F v Walsall
Sheffield U v Crystal Palace
Stockport Co v QPR
Swindon T v Blackburn R
Wolverhampton W v Charlton Ath

Nationwide Football League Division 2
Brentford v Cardiff C
Bristol C v Blackpool (12.00)
Burnley v AFC Bournemouth
Cambridge U v Stoke C
Colchester U v Wigan Ath (1.00)
Gillingham v Oldham Ath
Luton T v Bury

Millwall v Reading
Oxford U v Wycombe W
Preston NE v Chesterfield
Scunthorpe U v Bristol R
Wrexham v Notts Co

Nationwide Football League Division 3
Darlington v Exeter C
Hartlepool U v Southend U (12.00)
Hull C v Chester C
Leyton Orient v Shrewsbury T
Northampton T v Carlisle U
Plymouth Arg v Brighton & HA
Rotherham U v York C
Swansea C v Cheltenham T
Torquay U v Lincoln C

Sunday 5 September 1999
Nationwide Football League Division 1
Bolton W v Birmingham C (1.00)

Nationwide Football League Division 3
Barnet v Macclesfield T

Friday 10 September 1999
Nationwide Football League Division 1
Barnsley v Stockport Co

Saturday 11 September 1999
FA Carling Premiership
Arsenal v Aston Villa
Chelsea v Newcastle U
Coventry C v Leeds U
Liverpool v Manchester U (11.30)
Middlesbrough v Southampton
Sheffield W v Everton
Sunderland v Leicester C
West Ham U v Watford
Wimbledon v Derby Co

Nationwide Football League Division 1
Birmingham C v WBA
Blackburn R v Tranmere R
Charlton Ath v Bolton W
Grimsby T v Walsall
Manchester C v Crystal Palace
Norwich C v Crewe Alex
Port Vale v Fulham
Portsmouth v Ipswich T
QPR v Sheffield U
Swindon T v Nottingham F
Wolverhampton W v Huddersfield T

Nationwide Football League Division 2
AFC Bournemouth v Reading
Bristol C v Millwall
Cambridge U v Brentford
Chesterfield v Stoke C
Colchester U v Scunthorpe U
Luton T v Wrexham
Notts Co v Blackpool
Oldham Ath v Bury
Oxford U v Gillingham
Preston NE v Burnley
Wigan Ath v Bristol R
Wycombe W v Cardiff C

Nationwide Football League Division 3
Carlisle U v Lincoln C
Chester C v Exeter C
Halifax T v Brighton & HA
Macclesfield T v Southend U
Mansfield T v Leyton Orient
Northampton T v Hartlepool U
Plymouth Arg v Rotherham U
Rochdale v Darlington
Swansea C v Barnet
Torquay U v Hull C
York C v Peterborough U

Sunday 12 September 1999
FA Carling Premiership
Bradford C v Tottenham H (4.00)

Nationwide Football League Division 3
Cheltenham T v Shrewsbury T (1.00)

Saturday 18 September 1999
FA Carling Premiership
Aston Villa v Bradford C
Derby Co v Sunderland
Everton v West Ham U
Leicester C v Liverpool
Manchester U v Wimbledon
Southampton v Arsenal
Watford v Chelsea

Nationwide Football League Division 1
Bolton W v Barnsley
Crewe Alex v Swindon T
Crystal Palace v Grimsby T
Fulham v QPR
Huddersfield T v Norwich C
Ipswich T v Birmingham C
Sheffield U v Charlton Ath
Stockport Co v Port Vale
Tranmere R v Portsmouth
Walsall v Manchester C
WBA v Blackburn R

Nationwide Football League Division 2
Blackpool v AFC Bournemouth
Brentford v Luton T
Bristol R v Oldham Ath
Burnley v Colchester U
Bury v Wycombe W
Cardiff C v Notts Co
Gillingham v Preston NE
Millwall v Cambridge U
Reading v Chesterfield
Scunthorpe U v Bristol C
Stoke C v Wigan Ath
Wrexham v Oxford U

Nationwide Football League Division 3
Barnet v Northampton T
Brighton & HA v Chester C
Darlington v Mansfield T
Exeter C v York C
Hartlepool U v Plymouth Arg
Hull C v Swansea C
Leyton Orient v Torquay U
Lincoln C v Macclesfield T
Peterborough U v Cheltenham T
Rotherham U v Rochdale
Shrewsbury T v Carlisle U
Southend U v Halifax T

Sunday 19 September 1999
FA Carling Premiership
Leeds U v Middlesbrough (4.00)
Newcastle U v Sheffield W
Tottenham H v Coventry C

Nationwide Football League Division 1
Nottingham F v Wolverhampton W (1.00)

Friday 24 September 1999
Nationwide Football League Division 3
Mansfield T v Shrewsbury T

Saturday 25 September 1999
FA Carling Premiership
Arsenal v Watford
Coventry C v West Ham U
Derby Co v Bradford C
Leeds U v Newcastle U
Leicester C v Aston Villa
Manchester U v Southampton
Middlesbrough v Chelsea
Sunderland v Sheffield W

Nationwide Football League Division 1
Barnsley v Huddersfield T
Birmingham C v QPR
Blackburn R v Walsall
Bolton W v Nottingham F

Fulham v Crewe Alex
Port Vale v Swindon T
Portsmouth v Grimsby T
Sheffield U v Wolverhampton W
Stockport Co v Norwich C
Tranmere R v Charlton Ath
WBA v Crystal Palace

Nationwide Football League Division 2
AFC Bournemouth v Bury
Blackpool v Wycombe W
Brentford v Preston NE
Bristol C v Burnley
Cambridge U v Gillingham
Cardiff C v Wigan Ath
Luton T v Oxford U
Millwall v Colchester U
Notts Co v Bristol R
Reading v Oldham Ath
Scunthorpe U v Chesterfield
Wrexham v Stoke C

Nationwide Football League Division 3
Brighton & HA v Cheltenham T
Chester C v Lincoln C
Darlington v Plymouth Arg
Exeter C v Macclesfield T
Halifax T v Carlisle U
Hull C v York C
Leyton Orient v Hartlepool U
Rochdale v Swansea C
Rotherham U v Northampton T
Southend U v Peterborough U
Torquay U v Barnet

Sunday 26 September 1999
FA Carling Premiership
Wimbledon v Tottenham H (4.00)

Nationwide Football League Division 1
Ipswich T v Manchester C (1.00)

Monday 27 September 1999
FA Carling Premiership
Liverpool v Everton (8.00)

Friday 1 October 1999
Nationwide Football League Division 1
Nottingham F v Barnsley

Nationwide Football League Division 2
Colchester U v Wrexham

Saturday 2 October 1999
FA Carling Premiership
Aston Villa v Liverpool
Bradford C v Sunderland
Everton v Coventry C
Sheffield W v Wimbledon
West Ham U v Arsenal

Nationwide Football League Division 1
Charlton Ath v Birmingham C
Crystal Palace v Portsmouth
Grimsby T v Ipswich T
Huddersfield T v Sheffield U
Manchester C v Port Vale
Norwich C v Fulham
QPR v Blackburn R
Swindon T v Bolton W
Walsall v Stockport Co

Nationwide Football League Division 2
Bristol R v Blackpool
Burnley v Brentford
Bury v Cardiff C
Chesterfield v AFC Bournemouth
Gillingham v Millwall
Oldham Ath v Notts Co
Oxford U v Bristol C
Preston NE v Cambridge U
Stoke C v Scunthorpe U
Wigan Ath v Luton T
Wycombe W v Reading

Nationwide Football League Division 3
Barnet v Hull C
Carlisle U v Southend U
Cheltenham T v Rotherham U
Hartlepool U v Darlington
Lincoln C v Exeter C
Macclesfield T v Torquay U
Northampton T v Rochdale
Peterborough U v Brighton & HA
Plymouth Arg v Leyton Orient
Shrewsbury T v Halifax T
Swansea C v Mansfield T
York C v Chester C

Sunday 3 October 1999
FA Carling Premiership
Chelsea v Manchester U (4.00)
Newcastle U v Middlesbrough
Tottenham H v Leicester C (4.00)
Watford v Leeds U

Nationwide Football League Division 1
Crewe Alex v Tranmere R (1.00)
Wolverhampton W v WBA (1.00)

Monday 4 October 1999
FA Carling Premiership
Southampton v Derby Co (8.00)

Friday 8 October 1999
Nationwide Football League Division 1
Walsall v Birmingham C

Nationwide Football League Division 3
Swansea C v Rotherham U

Saturday 9 October 1999
Nationwide Football League Division 1
Charlton Ath v Blackburn R
Crewe Alex v Sheffield U
Crystal Palace v Ipswich T
Grimsby T v WBA
Huddersfield T v Port Vale
Manchester C v Portsmouth
Norwich C v Barnsley
QPR v Tranmere R
Swindon T v Stockport Co
Wolverhampton W v Bolton W

Nationwide Football League Division 2
Bristol R v Cardiff C
Bury v Notts Co
Chesterfield v Blackpool
Colchester U v Brentford
Gillingham v Wrexham
Oldham Ath v Luton T
Oxford U v Millwall
Preston NE v Bristol C
Stoke C v Reading
Wigan Ath v AFC Bournemouth
Wycombe W v Cambridge U

Nationwide Football League Division 3
Barnet v Rochdale
Carlisle U v Brighton & HA
Cheltenham T v Southend U
Hartlepool U v Hull C
Lincoln C v Darlington
Macclesfield T v Halifax T
Northampton T v Torquay U
Peterborough U v Chester C
Plymouth Arg v Mansfield T
Shrewsbury T v Exeter C
York C v Leyton Orient

Sunday 10 October 1999
Nationwide Football League Division 1
Nottingham F v Fulham

Nationwide Football League Division 2
Burnley v Scunthorpe U (1.00)

Friday 15 October 1999
Nationwide Football League Division 2
Cambridge U v Colchester U

Saturday 16 October 1999
FA Carling Premiership
Arsenal v Everton
Coventry C v Newcastle U
Derby Co v Tottenham H
Leeds U v Sheffield W
Leicester C v Southampton
Liverpool v Chelsea
Manchester U v Watford
Wimbledon v Bradford C

Nationwide Football League Division 1
Barnsley v Wolverhampton W
Birmingham C v Crystal Palace
Blackburn R v Grimsby T
Bolton W v Huddersfield T
Fulham v Swindon T
Ipswich T v QPR
Port Vale v Norwich C
Portsmouth v Charlton Ath
Sheffield U v Nottingham F
Stockport Co v Crewe Alex
Tranmere R v Manchester C
WBA v Walsall

Nationwide Football League Division 2
AFC Bournemouth v Stoke C
Blackpool v Bury
Brentford v Oxford U
Cardiff C v Oldham Ath
Luton T v Gillingham
Millwall v Burnley
Notts Co v Wycombe W
Reading v Wigan Ath
Scunthorpe U v Preston NE
Wrexham v Chesterfield

Nationwide Football League Division 3
Brighton & HA v York C
Chester C v Macclesfield T
Darlington v Cheltenham T
Exeter C v Carlisle U
Halifax T v Peterborough U
Hull C v Northampton T
Leyton Orient v Lincoln C
Mansfield T v Hartlepool U
Rochdale v Plymouth Arg
Rotherham U v Barnet
Southend U v Shrewsbury T
Torquay U v Swansea C

Sunday 17 October 1999
FA Carling Premiership
Middlesbrough v West Ham U (4.00)

Nationwide Football League Division 2
Bristol C v Bristol R (1.00)

Monday 18 October 1999
FA Carling Premiership
Sunderland v Aston Villa (8.00)

Tuesday 19 October 1999
Nationwide Football League Division 1
Barnsley v Swindon T
Birmingham C v Manchester C (8.00)
Bolton W v Crewe Alex (8.00)
Fulham v Wolverhampton W
Ipswich T v Charlton Ath
Port Vale v Nottingham F
Portsmouth v Walsall
Sheffield U v Norwich C
Stockport Co v Huddersfield T
Tranmere R v Grimsby T
WBA v QPR

Nationwide Football League Division 2
AFC Bournemouth v Bristol R
Blackpool v Oldham Ath
Brentford v Gillingham

Bristol C v Colchester U
Cambridge U v Burnley
Cardiff C v Stoke C
Luton T v Wycombe W
Millwall v Preston NE
Notts Co v Chesterfield
Scunthorpe U v Oxford U (7.30)
Wrexham v Wigan Ath (7.30)

Nationwide Football League Division 3
Brighton & HA v Shrewsbury T (8.00)
Chester C v Cheltenham T
Darlington v Carlisle U (7.30)
Exeter C v Swansea C
Halifax T v York C
Hull C v Plymouth Arg
Leyton Orient v Barnet
Mansfield T v Northampton T
Rochdale v Macclesfield T
Rotherham U v Hartlepool U
Southend U v Lincoln C
Torquay U v Peterborough U

Wednesday 20 October 1999
Nationwide Football League Division 1
Blackburn R v Crystal Palace

Nationwide Football League Division 2
Reading v Bury

Friday 22 October 1999
Nationwide Football League Division 3
Swansea C v Rochdale

Saturday 23 October 1999
FA Carling Premiership
Aston Villa v Wimbledon
Bradford C v Leicester C
Chelsea v Arsenal
Everton v Leeds U
Sheffield W v Coventry C
Southampton v Liverpool
Tottenham H v Manchester U
West Ham U v Sunderland

Nationwide Football League Division 1
Charlton Ath v WBA
Crewe Alex v Barnsley
Crystal Palace v Tranmere R
Grimsby T v Birmingham C
Huddersfield T v Fulham
Manchester C v Blackburn R
Nottingham F v Stockport Co
QPR v Portsmouth
Swindon T v Sheffield U
Walsall v Ipswich T
Wolverhampton W v Port Vale

Nationwide Football League Division 2
Bristol R v Notts Co
Burnley v Bristol C
Bury v AFC Bournemouth
Chesterfield v Scunthorpe U
Colchester U v Millwall
Gillingham v Cambridge U
Oldham Ath v Reading
Oxford U v Luton T
Preston NE v Brentford
Stoke C v Wrexham
Wigan Ath v Cardiff C
Wycombe W v Blackpool

Nationwide Football League Division 3
Barnet v Torquay U
Carlisle U v Halifax T
Cheltenham T v Brighton & HA
Hartlepool U v Leyton Orient
Lincoln C v Chester C
Macclesfield T v Exeter C
Northampton T v Rotherham U
Peterborough U v Southend U
Plymouth Arg v Darlington
Shrewsbury T v Mansfield T
York C v Hull C

Sunday 24 October 1999
FA Carling Premiership
Watford v Middlesbrough (4.00)

Nationwide Football League Division 1
Norwich C v Bolton W (1.00)

Monday 25 October 1999
FA Carling Premiership
Newcastle U v Derby Co (8.00)

Tuesday 26 October 1999
Nationwide Football League Division 1
Charlton Ath v Tranmere R (8.00)
Crewe Alex v Fulham
Crystal Palace v WBA
Grimsby T v Portsmouth
Huddersfield T v Barnsley
Norwich C v Stockport Co
Swindon T v Port Vale
Walsall v Blackburn R
Wolverhampton W v Sheffield U

Wednesday 27 October 1999
Nationwide Football League Division 1
Manchester C v Ipswich T
Nottingham F v Bolton W
QPR v Birmingham C (8.00)

Saturday 30 October 1999
FA Carling Premiership
Arsenal v Newcastle U
Derby Co v Chelsea
Leeds U v West Ham U
Leicester C v Sheffield W
Manchester U v Aston Villa
Middlesbrough v Everton
Sunderland v Tottenham H
Wimbledon v Southampton

Nationwide Football League Division 1
Barnsley v Nottingham F
Birmingham C v Charlton Ath
Blackburn R v QPR
Bolton W v Swindon T
Fulham v Norwich C
Ipswich T v Grimsby T
Port Vale v Manchester C
Portsmouth v Crystal Palace
Sheffield U v Huddersfield T
Stockport Co v Walsall
Tranmere R v Crewe Alex

Sunday 31 October 1999
FA Carling Premiership
Coventry C v Watford (4.00)

Nationwide Football League Division 1
WBA v Wolverhampton W (1.00)

Monday 1 November 1999
FA Carling Premiership
Liverpool v Bradford C (8.00)

Tuesday 2 November 1999
Nationwide Football League Division 1
Crewe Alex v Charlton Ath

Nationwide Football League Division 2
Brentford v Reading
Bristol R v Bury
Burnley v Wrexham
Cambridge U v Scunthorpe U
Cardiff C v Blackpool
Gillingham v Bristol C
Millwall v Luton T
Oldham Ath v Wycombe W
Oxford U v Colchester U
Preston NE v AFC Bournemouth
Wigan Ath v Chesterfield

Nationwide Football League Division 3
Carlisle U v York C

Darlington v Leyton Orient (7.30)
Halifax T v Cheltenham T
Hartlepool U v Barnet (7.30)
Lincoln C v Peterborough U
Macclesfield T v Mansfield T
Northampton T v Swansea C
Plymouth Arg v Exeter C
Rochdale v Hull C
Rotherham U v Torquay U
Shrewsbury T v Chester C (7.30)
Southend U v Brighton & HA

Wednesday 3 November 1999
Nationwide Football League Division 2
Stoke C v Notts Co

Friday 5 November 1999
Nationwide Football League Division 1
Port Vale v Crewe Alex

Nationwide Football League Division 3
Swansea C v Halifax T

Saturday 6 November 1999
FA Carling Premiership
Aston Villa v Southampton
Bradford C v Coventry C
Chelsea v West Ham U
Liverpool v Derby Co
Manchester U v Leicester C
Middlesbrough v Sunderland
Sheffield W v Watford
Tottenham H v Arsenal

Nationwide Football League Division 1
Barnsley v Sheffield U
Blackburn R v Ipswich T
Bolton W v Crystal Palace
Charlton Ath v Walsall
Huddersfield T v Swindon T
Norwich C v Nottingham F
Portsmouth v Birmingham C
QPR v Manchester C
Stockport Co v Fulham
Tranmere R v WBA
Wolverhampton W v Grimsby T

Nationwide Football League Division 2
AFC Bournemouth v Cardiff C
Blackpool v Wigan Ath
Bristol C v Cambridge U
Bury v Stoke C
Chesterfield v Oldham Ath
Colchester U v Preston NE
Luton T v Burnley
Notts Co v Gillingham
Scunthorpe U v Millwall
Wrexham v Brentford
Wycombe W v Bristol R

Nationwide Football League Division 3
Barnet v Darlington
Brighton & HA v Hartlepool U
Cheltenham T v Carlisle U
Chester C v Plymouth Arg
Exeter C v Southend U
Hull C v Rotherham U
Leyton Orient v Northampton T
Mansfield T v Lincoln C
Peterborough U v Shrewsbury T
Torquay U v Rochdale
York C v Macclesfield T

Sunday 7 November 1999
FA Carling Premiership
Wimbledon v Leeds U (4.00)

Nationwide Football League Division 2
Reading v Oxford U (1.00)

Monday 8 November 1999
FA Carling Premiership
Newcastle U v Everton (8.00)

Friday 12 November 1999
Nationwide Football League Division 2
Gillingham v AFC Bournemouth

Saturday 13 November 1999
Nationwide Football League Division 1
Birmingham C v Blackburn R
Crewe Alex v Wolverhampton W
Crystal Palace v QPR
Fulham v Barnsley
Grimsby T v Charlton Ath
Ipswich T v Tranmere R
Manchester C v Stockport Co
Sheffield U v Bolton W
Swindon T v Norwich C
Walsall v Port Vale
WBA v Portsmouth

Nationwide Football League Division 2
Brentford v Scunthorpe U
Bristol R v Reading
Burnley v Blackpool
Cambridge U v Luton T
Cardiff C v Chesterfield
Millwall v Wrexham
Oldham Ath v Colchester U
Oxford U v Bury
Preston NE v Notts Co
Stoke C v Bristol C
Wigan Ath v Wycombe W

Nationwide Football League Division 3
Carlisle U v Peterborough U
Darlington v Torquay U
Halifax T v Exeter C
Hartlepool U v Chester C
Lincoln C v York C
Macclesfield T v Brighton & HA
Northampton T v Cheltenham T
Plymouth Arg v Barnet
Rochdale v Mansfield T
Rotherham U v Leyton Orient
Shrewsbury T v Swansea C
Southend U v Hull C

Sunday 14 November 1999
Nationwide Football League Division 1
Nottingham F v Huddersfield T (1.00)

Saturday 20 November 1999
FA Carling Premiership
Arsenal v Middlesbrough
Derby Co v Manchester U
Everton v Chelsea
Leeds U v Bradford C
Leicester C v Wimbledon
Southampton v Tottenham H
Sunderland v Liverpool
Watford v Newcastle U

Nationwide Football League Division 1
Barnsley v Birmingham C
Blackburn R v Fulham
Bolton W v Grimsby T
Charlton Ath v Manchester C
Huddersfield T v WBA
Port Vale v Crystal Palace
Portsmouth v Crewe Alex
QPR v Walsall
Stockport Co v Sheffield U
Tranmere R v Nottingham F
Wolverhampton W v Swindon T

Sunday 21 November 1999
FA Carling Premiership
West Ham U v Sheffield W (4.00)

Nationwide Football League Division 1
Norwich C v Ipswich T (1.00)

Monday 22 November 1999
FA Carling Premiership
Coventry C v Aston Villa (8.00)

Tuesday 23 November 1999
Nationwide Football League Division 1
Birmingham C v Tranmere R
Crewe Alex v Blackburn R
Crystal Palace v Norwich C
Fulham v Bolton W
Grimsby T v QPR
Sheffield U v Port Vale
Swindon T v Charlton Ath
Walsall v Huddersfield T
WBA v Stockport Co

Nationwide Football League Division 2
AFC Bournemouth v Brentford
Blackpool v Millwall
Bristol C v Oldham Ath
Bury v Wigan Ath
Chesterfield v Bristol R
Luton T v Preston NE
Notts Co v Oxford U
Scunthorpe U v Gillingham (7.30)
Wrexham v Cambridge U (7.30)
Wycombe W v Stoke C

Nationwide Football League Division 3
Barnet v Carlisle U
Brighton & HA v Lincoln C (8.00)
Cheltenham T v Plymouth Arg
Chester C v Southend U
Exeter C v Northampton T
Hull C v Halifax T
Leyton Orient v Rochdale
Mansfield T v Rotherham U
Peterborough U v Macclesfield T
Swansea C v Darlington
Torquay U v Hartlepool U
York C v Shrewsbury T

Wednesday 24 November 1999
Nationwide Football League Division 1
Ipswich T v Wolverhampton W
Manchester C v Barnsley
Nottingham F v Portsmouth

Nationwide Football League Division 2
Colchester U v Cardiff C
Reading v Burnley

Friday 26 November 1999
Nationwide Football League Division 1
Walsall v Fulham

Saturday 27 November 1999
FA Carling Premiership
Arsenal v Derby Co
Coventry C v Leicester C
Everton v Aston Villa
Leeds U v Southampton
Middlesbrough v Wimbledon
Newcastle U v Tottenham H
Sheffield W v Manchester U
Watford v Sunderland
West Ham U v Liverpool

Nationwide Football League Division 1
Birmingham C v Swindon T
Blackburn R v Stockport Co
Charlton Ath v Port Vale
Crystal Palace v Nottingham F
Ipswich T v Crewe Alex
Manchester C v Huddersfield T
Portsmouth v Bolton W
QPR v Barnsley
Tranmere R v Wolverhampton W
WBA v Sheffield U

Nationwide Football League Division 2
AFC Bournemouth v Millwall
Blackpool v Cambridge U
Bristol R v Luton T
Bury v Preston NE
Cardiff C v Gillingham
Chesterfield v Oxford U
Notts Co v Bristol C

Oldham Ath v Wrexham
Reading v Scunthorpe U
Stoke C v Colchester U
Wigan Ath v Burnley
Wycombe W v Brentford

Nationwide Football League Division 3
Brighton & HA v Northampton T
Carlisle U v Rotherham U
Cheltenham T v Leyton Orient
Chester C v Swansea C
Exeter C v Torquay U
Halifax T v Mansfield T
Lincoln C v Rochdale
Macclesfield T v Hartlepool U
Peterborough U v Barnet
Shrewsbury T v Hull C
Southend U v Darlington
York C v Plymouth Arg

Sunday 28 November 1999
FA Carling Premiership
Chelsea v Bradford C (4.00)

Nationwide Football League Division 1
Grimsby T v Norwich C (1.00)

Friday 3 December 1999
Nationwide Football League Division 1
Wolverhampton W v Manchester C

Nationwide Football League Division 2
Colchester U v Chesterfield

Saturday 4 December 1999
FA Carling Premiership
Aston Villa v Newcastle U
Bradford C v Middlesbrough
Derby Co v Leeds U
Leicester C v Arsenal (11.30)
Manchester U v Everton
Southampton v Coventry C
Sunderland v Chelsea
Wimbledon v Watford

Nationwide Football League Division 1
Barnsley v Charlton Ath
Bolton W v Tranmere R
Crewe Alex v Crystal Palace
Fulham v Birmingham C
Huddersfield T v QPR
Norwich C v WBA
Port Vale v Blackburn R
Sheffield U v Portsmouth
Stockport Co v Grimsby T
Swindon T v Walsall

Nationwide Football League Division 2
Brentford v Bristol R
Bristol C v Reading
Burnley v Wycombe W
Cambridge U v AFC Bournemouth
Gillingham v Bury
Luton T v Notts Co
Millwall v Cardiff C
Oxford U v Stoke C
Preston NE v Oldham Ath
Scunthorpe U v Wigan Ath
Wrexham v Blackpool

Nationwide Football League Division 3
Barnet v Chester C
Darlington v Halifax T
Hartlepool U v Peterborough U
Hull C v Exeter C
Leyton Orient v Carlisle U
Mansfield T v Brighton & HA
Northampton T v Macclesfield T
Plymouth Arg v Southend U
Rochdale v Cheltenham T
Rotherham U v Lincoln C
Swansea C v York C
Torquay U v Shrewsbury T

Sunday 5 December 1999
FA Carling Premiership
Liverpool v Sheffield W (4.00)

Nationwide Football League Division 1
Nottingham F v Ipswich T (1.00)

Monday 6 December 1999
FA Carling Premiership
Tottenham H v West Ham U (8.00)

Friday 10 December 1999
Nationwide Football League Division 3
Brighton & HA v Rochdale (8.00)
Southend U v Barnet

Saturday 11 December 1999
Nationwide Football League Division 2
Blackpool v Reading
Brentford v Chesterfield
Bristol R v Colchester U
Bury v Cambridge U
Cardiff C v Bristol C
Gillingham v Burnley
Luton T v Stoke C
Notts Co v AFC Bournemouth
Oldham Ath v Wigan Ath
Oxford U v Preston NE
Wrexham v Scunthorpe U
Wycombe W v Millwall

Nationwide Football League Division 3
Carlisle U v Torquay U
Cheltenham T v Macclesfield T
Darlington v Chester C
Halifax T v Rotherham U
Hartlepool U v Swansea C
Leyton Orient v Exeter C
Mansfield T v York C
Peterborough U v Hull C
Plymouth Arg v Lincoln C
Shrewsbury T v Northampton T

Tuesday 14 December 1999
Nationwide Football League Division 3
Lincoln C v Hartlepool U

Friday 17 December 1999
Nationwide Football League Division 1
Ipswich T v WBA
Tranmere R v Norwich C
Wolverhampton W v Birmingham C

Nationwide Football League Division 2
Bristol C v Wycombe W
Colchester U v Luton T

Nationwide Football League Division 3
Northampton T v Plymouth Arg
York C v Southend U

Saturday 18 December 1999
FA Carling Premiership
Arsenal v Wimbledon
Aston Villa v Sheffield W
Bradford C v Newcastle U
Leicester C v Derby Co
Liverpool v Coventry C
Middlesbrough v Tottenham H
Sunderland v Southampton
Watford v Everton
West Ham U v Manchester U

Nationwide Football League Division 1
Barnsley v Walsall
Bolton W v Stockport Co
Crystal Palace v Fulham
Huddersfield T v Grimsby T
Manchester C v Swindon T
Nottingham F v Crewe Alex
Portsmouth v Port Vale
QPR v Charlton Ath

Nationwide Football League Division 2
AFC Bournemouth v Oxford U
Burnley v Cardiff C
Cambridge U v Oldham Ath
Chesterfield v Gillingham
Millwall v Notts Co
Preston NE v Blackpool
Reading v Wrexham
Scunthorpe U v Bury
Stoke C v Bristol R
Wigan Ath v Brentford

Nationwide Football League Division 3
Barnet v Mansfield T
Chester C v Halifax T
Exeter C v Hartlepool U
Hull C v Carlisle U
Lincoln C v Shrewsbury T
Macclesfield T v Leyton Orient
Rochdale v Peterborough U
Rotherham U v Darlington
Swansea C v Brighton & HA
Torquay U v Cheltenham T

Sunday 19 December 1999
FA Carling Premiership
Chelsea v Leeds U (4.00)

Nationwide Football League Division 1
Sheffield U v Blackburn R (1.00)

Sunday 26 December 1999
FA Carling Premiership
Coventry C v Arsenal (5.00)
Derby Co v Aston Villa
Everton v Sunderland
Leeds U v Leicester C
Manchester U v Bradford C
Newcastle U v Liverpool
Sheffield W v Middlesbrough
Southampton v Chelsea
Tottenham H v Watford (12.00)
Wimbledon v West Ham U (12.00)

Nationwide Football League Division 1
Birmingham C v Sheffield U
Blackburn R v Nottingham F
Charlton Ath v Crystal Palace (12.00)
Crewe Alex v Huddersfield T
Fulham v Ipswich T (12.00)
Grimsby T v Barnsley
Norwich C v QPR
Port Vale v Bolton W
Stockport Co v Wolverhampton W
Swindon T v Portsmouth
Walsall v Tranmere R
WBA v Manchester C (12.00)

Nationwide Football League Division 2
Blackpool v Stoke C
Brentford v Bristol C (12.00)
Bristol R v Millwall
Bury v Burnley
Cardiff C v Reading
Gillingham v Colchester U
Luton T v Chesterfield
Notts Co v Wigan Ath
Oldham Ath v Scunthorpe U
Oxford U v Cambridge U
Wrexham v Preston NE
Wycombe W v AFC Bournemouth

Nationwide Football League Division 3
Brighton & HA v Barnet
Carlisle U v Rochdale
Cheltenham T v Exeter C
Darlington v Hull C
Halifax T v Lincoln C (1.00)
Hartlepool U v York C (1.00)
Leyton Orient v Swansea C (12.00)
Mansfield T v Chester C
Peterborough U v Rotherham U
Plymouth Arg v Torquay U
Shrewsbury T v Macclesfield T (12.00)
Southend U v Northampton T

Tuesday 28 December 1999
FA Carling Premiership
Arsenal v Leeds U (3.00)
Bradford C v Everton (3.00)
Leicester C v Newcastle U (3.00)
Liverpool v Wimbledon (3.00)
Sunderland v Manchester U (8.00)
Watford v Southampton (3.00)
West Ham U v Derby Co (3.00)

Nationwide Football League Division 1
Barnsley v Port Vale (3.00)
Bolton W v WBA (3.00)
Crystal Palace v Walsall (3.00)
Huddersfield T v Charlton Ath (12.00)
Ipswich T v Stockport Co (3.00)
Manchester C v Grimsby T (3.00)
Nottingham F v Birmingham C (3.00)
Portsmouth v Blackburn R (3.00)
QPR v Crewe Alex (3.00)
Sheffield U v Fulham (3.00)
Tranmere R v Swindon T (3.00)
Wolverhampton W v Norwich C (3.00)

Nationwide Football League Division 2
AFC Bournemouth v Wrexham (3.00)
Bristol C v Luton T (3.00)
Burnley v Oxford U (3.00)
Cambridge U v Cardiff C (3.00)
Chesterfield v Bury (3.00)
Millwall v Brentford (3.00)
Preston NE v Bristol R (3.00)
Reading v Notts Co (3.00)
Scunthorpe U v Blackpool (3.00)
Stoke C v Oldham Ath (3.00)
Wigan Ath v Gillingham (3.00)

Nationwide Football League Division 3
Barnet v Halifax T (3.00)
Chester C v Leyton Orient (3.00)
Exeter C v Peterborough U (3.00)
Hull C v Mansfield T (3.00)
Macclesfield T v Carlisle U (3.00)
Northampton T v Darlington (3.00)
Rochdale v Shrewsbury T (3.00)
Rotherham U v Brighton & HA (3.00)
Swansea C v Plymouth Arg (3.00)
Torquay U v Southend U (3.00)
York C v Cheltenham T (3.00)

Wednesday 29 December 1999
FA Carling Premiership
Aston Villa v Tottenham H
Chelsea v Sheffield W (8.00)
Middlesbrough v Coventry C

Nationwide Football League Division 2
Colchester U v Wycombe W

Monday 3 January 2000
FA Carling Premiership
Coventry C v Chelsea (3.00)
Derby Co v Watford (3.00)
Everton v Leicester C (3.00)
Leeds U v Aston Villa (3.00)
Manchester U v Middlesbrough (3.00)
Newcastle U v West Ham U (3.00)
Sheffield W v Arsenal (3.00)
Southampton v Bradford C (3.00)
Tottenham H v Liverpool (3.00)
Wimbledon v Sunderland (3.00)

Nationwide Football League Division 1
Birmingham C v Huddersfield T (3.00)
Blackburn R v Wolverhampton W (3.00)
Charlton Ath v Nottingham F (3.00)
Crewe Alex v Manchester C (3.00)
Fulham v Tranmere R (3.00)
Grimsby T v Sheffield U (3.00)
Norwich C v Portsmouth (3.00)

Port Vale v Ipswich T (3.00)
Stockport Co v Crystal Palace (3.00)
Swindon T v QPR (3.00)
Walsall v Bolton W (3.00)
WBA v Barnsley (3.00)

Nationwide Football League Division 2
Blackpool v Colchester U (3.00)
Brentford v Stoke C (3.00)
Bristol R v Cambridge U (3.00)
Cardiff C v Preston NE (3.00)
Gillingham v Reading (3.00)
Luton T v Scunthorpe U (3.00)
Notts Co v Burnley (3.00)
Oldham Ath v AFC Bournemouth (3.00)
Oxford U v Wigan Ath (3.00)
Wrexham v Bristol C (3.00)
Wycombe W v Chesterfield (3.00)

Nationwide Football League Division 3
Brighton & HA v Exeter C (3.00)
Carlisle U v Chester C (3.00)
Cheltenham T v Lincoln C (3.00)
Darlington v York C (3.00)
Halifax T v Northampton T (3.00)
Hartlepool U v Rochdale (3.00)
Leyton Orient v Hull C (3.00)
Mansfield T v Torquay U (3.00)
Peterborough U v Swansea C (3.00)
Plymouth Arg v Macclesfield T (3.00)
Shrewsbury T v Barnet (3.00)
Southend U v Rotherham U (3.00)

Tuesday 4 January 2000
Nationwide Football League Division 2
Bury v Millwall

Saturday 8 January 2000
FA Carling Premiership
Bradford C v Chelsea

Nationwide Football League Division 2
AFC Bournemouth v Notts Co
Bristol C v Cardiff C
Burnley v Gillingham
Cambridge U v Bury
Chesterfield v Brentford
Colchester U v Bristol R
Millwall v Wycombe W
Preston NE v Oxford U
Reading v Blackpool
Scunthorpe U v Wrexham
Stoke C v Luton T
Wigan Ath v Oldham Ath

Nationwide Football League Division 3
Barnet v Southend U
Chester C v Darlington
Exeter C v Leyton Orient
Hull C v Peterborough U
Lincoln C v Plymouth Arg
Macclesfield T v Cheltenham T
Northampton T v Shrewsbury T
Rochdale v Brighton & HA
Rotherham U v Halifax T
Swansea C v Hartlepool U
Torquay U v Carlisle U
York C v Mansfield T

Wednesday 12 January 2000
FA Carling Premiership
Chelsea v Tottenham H

Saturday 15 January 2000
FA Carling Premiership
Arsenal v Sunderland
Chelsea v Leicester C
Coventry C v Wimbledon
Everton v Tottenham H
Leeds U v Newcastle U
Middlesbrough v Derby Co
Newcastle U v Southampton
Sheffield W v Bradford C

Watford v Liverpool
West Ham U v Aston Villa

Nationwide Football League Division 1
Birmingham C v Norwich C
Blackburn R v Huddersfield T
Charlton Ath v Crewe Alex
Crystal Palace v Barnsley
Grimsby T v Nottingham F
Ipswich T v Swindon T
Manchester C v Fulham
Portsmouth v Wolverhampton W
QPR v Bolton W
Tranmere R v Stockport Co
Walsall v Sheffield U
WBA v Port Vale

Nationwide Football League Division 2
AFC Bournemouth v Bristol C
Blackpool v Luton T
Bristol R v Gillingham
Bury v Wrexham
Cardiff C v Oxford U
Chesterfield v Burnley
Notts Co v Colchester U
Oldham Ath v Brentford
Reading v Cambridge U
Stoke C v Preston NE
Wigan Ath v Millwall
Wycombe W v Scunthorpe U

Nationwide Football League Division 3
Brighton & HA v Leyton Orient
Carlisle U v Swansea C
Cheltenham T v Mansfield T
Chester C v Rotherham U
Exeter C v Barnet
Halifax T v Hartlepool U
Lincoln C v Hull C
Macclesfield T v Darlington
Peterborough U v Northampton T
Shrewsbury T v Plymouth Arg
Southend U v Rochdale
York C v Torquay U

Saturday 22 January 2000
FA Carling Premiership
Aston Villa v Chelsea
Bradford C v Watford
Derby Co v Coventry C
Leicester C v West Ham U
Liverpool v Middlesbrough
Manchester U v Arsenal
Southampton v Everton
Sunderland v Leeds U
Tottenham H v Sheffield W
Wimbledon v Newcastle U

Nationwide Football League Division 1
Barnsley v Blackburn R
Bolton W v Ipswich T
Crewe Alex v Walsall
Fulham v Grimsby T
Huddersfield T v Tranmere R
Norwich C v Charlton Ath
Nottingham F v WBA
Port Vale v Birmingham C
Sheffield U v Manchester C
Stockport Co v Portsmouth
Swindon T v Crystal Palace
Wolverhampton W v QPR

Nationwide Football League Division 2
Brentford v Bury
Bristol C v Wigan Ath
Burnley v Oldham Ath
Cambridge U v Chesterfield
Colchester U v AFC Bournemouth
Gillingham v Blackpool
Luton T v Reading
Millwall v Stoke C
Oxford U v Bristol R
Preston NE v Wycombe W
Scunthorpe U v Notts Co
Wrexham v Cardiff C

Nationwide Football League Division 3
Barnet v Lincoln C
Darlington v Shrewsbury T
Hartlepool U v Carlisle U
Hull C v Cheltenham T
Leyton Orient v Peterborough U
Mansfield T v Southend U
Northampton T v Chester C
Plymouth Arg v Halifax T
Rochdale v York C
Rotherham U v Exeter C
Swansea C v Macclesfield T
Torquay U v Brighton & HA

Saturday 29 January 2000
Nationwide Football League Division 1
Birmingham C v Stockport Co
Blackburn R v Norwich C
Charlton Ath v Fulham
Crystal Palace v Huddersfield T
Grimsby T v Crewe Alex
Ipswich T v Sheffield U
Manchester C v Bolton W
Portsmouth v Barnsley
QPR v Nottingham F
Tranmere R v Port Vale
Walsall v Wolverhampton W
WBA v Swindon T

Nationwide Football League Division 2
AFC Bournemouth v Scunthorpe U
Blackpool v Brentford
Bristol R v Wrexham
Bury v Bristol C
Cardiff C v Luton T
Chesterfield v Millwall
Notts Co v Cambridge U
Oldham Ath v Oxford U
Reading v Colchester U
Stoke C v Burnley
Wigan Ath v Preston NE
Wycombe W v Gillingham

Nationwide Football League Division 3
Brighton & HA v Darlington
Carlisle U v Mansfield T
Cheltenham T v Hartlepool U
Chester C v Torquay U
Exeter C v Rochdale
Halifax T v Leyton Orient
Lincoln C v Northampton T
Macclesfield T v Hull C
Peterborough U v Plymouth Arg
Shrewsbury T v Rotherham U
Southend U v Swansea C
York C v Barnet

Friday 4 February 2000
Nationwide Football League Division 3
Mansfield T v Exeter C
Swansea C v Lincoln C

Saturday 5 February 2000
FA Carling Premiership
Aston Villa v Watford
Bradford C v Arsenal
Derby Co v Sheffield W
Leicester C v Middlesbrough
Liverpool v Leeds U
Manchester U v Coventry C
Southampton v West Ham U
Sunderland v Newcastle U
Tottenham H v Chelsea
Wimbledon v Everton

Nationwide Football League Division 1
Barnsley v Ipswich T
Bolton W v Blackburn R
Crewe Alex v Birmingham C
Fulham v WBA
Huddersfield T v Portsmouth
Norwich C v Walsall
Nottingham F v Manchester C
Port Vale v QPR
Sheffield U v Tranmere R

Stockport Co v Charlton Ath
Swindon T v Grimsby T
Wolverhampton W v Crystal Palace

Nationwide Football League Division 2
Brentford v Notts Co
Bristol C v Chesterfield
Burnley v Bristol R
Cambridge U v Wigan Ath
Colchester U v Bury
Gillingham v Stoke C
Luton T v AFC Bournemouth
Millwall v Oldham Ath
Oxford U v Blackpool
Preston NE v Reading
Scunthorpe U v Cardiff C
Wrexham v Wycombe W

Nationwide Football League Division 3
Barnet v Cheltenham T
Darlington v Peterborough U
Hartlepool U v Shrewsbury T
Hull C v Brighton & HA
Leyton Orient v Southend U
Northampton T v York C
Plymouth Arg v Carlisle U
Rochdale v Chester C
Rotherham U v Macclesfield T
Torquay U v Halifax T

Saturday 12 February 2000
FA Carling Premiership
Arsenal v Liverpool
Chelsea v Wimbledon
Coventry C v Sunderland
Everton v Derby Co
Leeds U v Tottenham H
Middlesbrough v Aston Villa
Newcastle U v Manchester U
Sheffield W v Southampton
Watford v Leicester C
West Ham U v Bradford C

Nationwide Football League Division 1
Birmingham C v Bolton W
Blackburn R v Swindon T
Charlton Ath v Wolverhampton W
Crystal Palace v Sheffield U
Grimsby T v Port Vale
Ipswich T v Huddersfield T
Manchester C v Norwich C
Portsmouth v Fulham
QPR v Stockport Co
Tranmere R v Barnsley
Walsall v Nottingham F
WBA v Crewe Alex

Nationwide Football League Division 2
AFC Bournemouth v Burnley
Blackpool v Bristol C
Bristol R v Scunthorpe U
Bury v Luton T
Cardiff C v Brentford
Chesterfield v Preston NE
Notts Co v Wrexham
Oldham Ath v Gillingham
Reading v Millwall
Stoke C v Cambridge U
Wigan Ath v Colchester U
Wycombe W v Oxford U

Nationwide Football League Division 3
Brighton & HA v Plymouth Arg
Carlisle U v Northampton T
Chester C v Hull C
Exeter C v Darlington
Halifax T v Rochdale
Lincoln C v Torquay U
Macclesfield T v Barnet
Peterborough U v Mansfield T
Shrewsbury T v Leyton Orient
Southend U v Hartlepool U
York C v Rotherham U

Sunday 13 February 2000
Nationwide Football League Division 3
Cheltenham T v Swansea C (12.00)

Saturday 19 February 2000
Nationwide Football League Division 1
Barnsley v QPR
Bolton W v Portsmouth
Crewe Alex v Ipswich T
Fulham v Walsall
Huddersfield T v Manchester C
Norwich C v Grimsby T
Nottingham F v Crystal Palace
Port Vale v Charlton Ath
Sheffield U v WBA
Stockport Co v Blackburn R
Swindon T v Birmingham C
Wolverhampton W v Tranmere R

Nationwide Football League Division 2
Brentford v Wycombe W
Bristol C v Notts Co
Burnley v Wigan Ath
Cambridge U v Blackpool
Colchester U v Stoke C
Gillingham v Cardiff C
Luton T v Bristol R
Millwall v AFC Bournemouth
Oxford U v Chesterfield
Preston NE v Bury
Scunthorpe U v Reading
Wrexham v Oldham Ath

Nationwide Football League Division 3
Barnet v Peterborough U
Darlington v Southend U
Hartlepool U v Macclesfield T
Hull C v Shrewsbury T
Leyton Orient v Cheltenham T
Mansfield T v Halifax T
Northampton T v Brighton & HA
Plymouth Arg v York C
Rochdale v Lincoln C
Rotherham U v Carlisle U
Swansea C v Chester C
Torquay U v Exeter C (12.00)

Saturday 26 February 2000
FA Carling Premiership
Arsenal v Southampton
Bradford C v Aston Villa
Chelsea v Watford
Coventry C v Tottenham H
Liverpool v Leicester C
Middlesbrough v Leeds U
Sheffield W v Newcastle U
Sunderland v Derby Co
West Ham U v Everton
Wimbledon v Manchester U

Nationwide Football League Division 1
Barnsley v Bolton W
Birmingham C v Ipswich T
Blackburn R v WBA
Charlton Ath v Sheffield U
Grimsby T v Crystal Palace
Manchester C v Walsall
Norwich C v Huddersfield T
Port Vale v Stockport Co
Portsmouth v Tranmere R
QPR v Fulham
Swindon T v Crewe Alex
Wolverhampton W v Nottingham F

Nationwide Football League Division 2
AFC Bournemouth v Blackpool
Bristol C v Scunthorpe U
Cambridge U v Millwall
Chesterfield v Reading
Colchester U v Burnley
Luton T v Brentford
Notts Co v Cardiff C
Oldham Ath v Bristol R
Oxford U v Wrexham
Preston NE v Gillingham

Wigan Ath v Stoke C
Wycombe W v Bury

Nationwide Football League Division 3
Carlisle U v Shrewsbury T
Cheltenham T v Peterborough U
Chester C v Brighton & HA
Halifax T v Southend U
Macclesfield T v Lincoln C
Mansfield T v Darlington
Northampton T v Barnet
Plymouth Arg v Hartlepool U
Rochdale v Rotherham U
Swansea C v Hull C
Torquay U v Leyton Orient
York C v Exeter C

Friday 3 March 2000
Nationwide Football League Division 2
Cardiff C v Wycombe W (7.30)

Nationwide Football League Division 3
Southend U v Macclesfield T

Saturday 4 March 2000
FA Carling Premiership
Aston Villa v Arsenal
Derby Co v Wimbledon
Everton v Sheffield W
Leeds U v Coventry C
Leicester C v Sunderland
Manchester U v Liverpool
Newcastle U v Chelsea
Southampton v Middlesbrough
Tottenham H v Bradford C
Watford v West Ham U

Nationwide Football League Division 1
Bolton W v Charlton Ath
Crewe Alex v Norwich C
Crystal Palace v Manchester C
Fulham v Port Vale
Huddersfield T v Wolverhampton W
Ipswich T v Portsmouth
Nottingham F v Swindon T
Sheffield U v QPR
Stockport Co v Barnsley
Tranmere R v Blackburn R
Walsall v Grimsby T
WBA v Birmingham C

Nationwide Football League Division 2
Blackpool v Notts Co
Brentford v Cambridge U
Bristol R v Wigan Ath
Burnley v Preston NE
Bury v Oldham Ath
Gillingham v Oxford U
Millwall v Bristol C
Reading v AFC Bournemouth
Scunthorpe U v Colchester U
Stoke C v Chesterfield
Wrexham v Luton T

Nationwide Football League Division 3
Barnet v Swansea C
Brighton & HA v Halifax T
Darlington v Rochdale
Exeter C v Chester C
Hartlepool U v Northampton T
Hull C v Torquay U
Leyton Orient v Mansfield T
Lincoln C v Carlisle U
Peterborough U v York C
Rotherham U v Plymouth Arg
Shrewsbury T v Cheltenham T

Tuesday 7 March 2000
Nationwide Football League Division 1
Birmingham C v Portsmouth
Crewe Alex v Port Vale
Crystal Palace v Bolton W
Fulham v Stockport Co
Grimsby T v Wolverhampton W
Ipswich T v Blackburn R

Sheffield U v Barnsley
Swindon T v Huddersfield T
Walsall v Charlton Ath
WBA v Tranmere R

Nationwide Football League Division 2
Brentford v Wrexham
Bristol R v Wycombe W
Burnley v Luton T
Cambridge U v Bristol C
Cardiff C v AFC Bournemouth
Gillingham v Notts Co
Millwall v Scunthorpe U
Oldham Ath v Chesterfield
Oxford U v Reading
Preston NE v Colchester U
Wigan Ath v Blackpool

Nationwide Football League Division 3
Carlisle U v Cheltenham T
Darlington v Barnet (7.30)
Halifax T v Swansea C
Hartlepool U v Brighton & HA (7.30)
Lincoln C v Mansfield T
Macclesfield T v York C
Northampton T v Leyton Orient
Plymouth Arg v Chester C
Rochdale v Torquay U
Rotherham U v Hull C
Shrewsbury T v Peterborough U
(7.30)
Southend U v Exeter C

Wednesday 8 March 2000
Nationwide Football League Division 1
Manchester C v QPR
Nottingham F v Norwich C

Nationwide Football League Division 2
Stoke C v Bury

Saturday 11 March 2000
FA Carling Premiership
Aston Villa v Coventry C
Bradford C v Leeds U
Chelsea v Everton
Liverpool v Sunderland
Manchester U v Derby Co
Middlesbrough v Arsenal
Newcastle U v Watford
Sheffield W v West Ham U
Tottenham H v Southampton
Wimbledon v Leicester C

Nationwide Football League Division 1
Barnsley v Manchester C
Blackburn R v Crewe Alex
Bolton W v Fulham
Charlton Ath v Swindon T
Huddersfield T v Walsall
Norwich C v Crystal Palace
Port Vale v Sheffield U
Portsmouth v Nottingham F
QPR v Grimsby T
Stockport Co v WBA
Tranmere R v Birmingham C
Wolverhampton W v Ipswich T

Nationwide Football League Division 2
AFC Bournemouth v Preston NE
Blackpool v Cardiff C
Bristol C v Gillingham
Bury v Bristol R
Chesterfield v Wigan Ath
Colchester U v Oxford U
Luton T v Millwall
Notts Co v Stoke C
Reading v Brentford
Scunthorpe U v Cambridge U
Wrexham v Burnley
Wycombe W v Oldham Ath

Nationwide Football League Division 3
Barnet v Hartlepool U
Brighton & HA v Southend U

Cheltenham T v Halifax T
Chester C v Shrewsbury T
Exeter C v Plymouth Arg (12.00)
Hull C v Rochdale
Leyton Orient v Darlington
Mansfield T v Macclesfield T
Peterborough U v Lincoln C
Swansea C v Northampton T
Torquay U v Rotherham U
York C v Carlisle U

Friday 17 March 2000
Nationwide Football League Division 2
Cardiff C v Colchester U (7.30)

Saturday 18 March 2000
FA Carling Premiership
Arsenal v Tottenham H
Coventry C v Bradford C
Derby Co v Liverpool
Everton v Newcastle U
Leeds U v Wimbledon
Leicester C v Manchester U
Southampton v Aston Villa
Sunderland v Middlesbrough
Watford v Sheffield W
West Ham U v Chelsea

Nationwide Football League Division 1
Birmingham C v Barnsley
Crewe Alex v Portsmouth
Crystal Palace v Port Vale
Fulham v Blackburn R
Grimsby T v Bolton W
Ipswich T v Norwich C
Manchester C v Charlton Ath
Nottingham F v Tranmere R
Sheffield U v Stockport Co
Swindon T v Wolverhampton W
Walsall v QPR
WBA v Huddersfield T

Nationwide Football League Division 2
Brentford v AFC Bournemouth
Bristol R v Chesterfield
Burnley v Reading
Cambridge U v Wrexham
Gillingham v Scunthorpe U
Millwall v Blackpool
Oldham Ath v Bristol C
Oxford U v Notts Co
Preston NE v Luton T
Stoke C v Wycombe W
Wigan Ath v Bury

Nationwide Football League Division 3
Carlisle U v Barnet
Darlington v Swansea C
Halifax T v Hull C
Hartlepool U v Torquay U
Lincoln C v Brighton & HA
Macclesfield T v Peterborough U
Northampton T v Exeter C
Plymouth Arg v Cheltenham T
Rochdale v Leyton Orient
Rotherham U v Mansfield T
Shrewsbury T v York C
Southend U v Chester C

Tuesday 21 March 2000
Nationwide Football League Division 1
Barnsley v Fulham
Bolton W v Sheffield U (8.00)
Charlton Ath v Grimsby T (8.00)
Huddersfield T v Nottingham F
Norwich C v Swindon T
Port Vale v Walsall
Portsmouth v WBA
Stockport Co v Manchester C
Tranmere R v Ipswich T
Wolverhampton W v Crewe Alex

Nationwide Football League Division 2
AFC Bournemouth v Gillingham
Blackpool v Burnley

Bristol C v Stoke C
Bury v Oxford U
Chesterfield v Cardiff C
Colchester U v Oldham Ath
Luton T v Cambridge U
Notts Co v Preston NE
Scunthorpe U v Brentford (7.30)
Wrexham v Millwall (7.30)
Wycombe W v Wigan Ath

Nationwide Football League Division 3
Barnet v Plymouth Arg
Brighton & HA v Macclesfield T
(8.00)
Cheltenham T v Northampton T
Chester C v Hartlepool U
Exeter C v Halifax T
Hull C v Southend U
Leyton Orient v Rotherham U
Mansfield T v Rochdale
Peterborough U v Carlisle U
Swansea C v Shrewsbury T
Torquay U v Darlington
York C v Lincoln C

Wednesday 22 March 2000
Nationwide Football League Division 1
Blackburn R v Birmingham C
QPR v Crystal Palace (8.00)

Nationwide Football League Division 2
Reading v Bristol R

Saturday 25 March 2000
FA Carling Premiership
Arsenal v Coventry C
Aston Villa v Derby Co
Bradford C v Manchester U
Chelsea v Southampton
Leicester C v Leeds U
Liverpool v Newcastle U
Middlesbrough v Sheffield W
Sunderland v Everton
Watford v Tottenham H
West Ham U v Wimbledon

Nationwide Football League Division 1
Barnsley v Grimsby T
Bolton W v Port Vale
Crystal Palace v Charlton Ath
Huddersfield T v Crewe Alex
Ipswich T v Fulham
Manchester C v WBA
Nottingham F v Blackburn R
Portsmouth v Swindon T
QPR v Norwich C
Sheffield U v Birmingham C
Tranmere R v Walsall
Wolverhampton W v Stockport Co

Nationwide Football League Division 2
AFC Bournemouth v Wycombe W
Bristol C v Brentford
Burnley v Bury
Cambridge U v Oxford U
Chesterfield v Luton T
Colchester U v Gillingham
Millwall v Bristol R
Preston NE v Wrexham
Reading v Cardiff C
Scunthorpe U v Oldham Ath
Stoke C v Blackpool
Wigan Ath v Notts Co

Nationwide Football League Division 3
Barnet v Brighton & HA
Chester C v Mansfield T
Exeter C v Cheltenham T
Hull C v Darlington
Lincoln C v Halifax T
Macclesfield T v Shrewsbury T
Northampton T v Southend U
Rochdale v Carlisle U

Rotherham U v Peterborough U
Swansea C v Leyton Orient
Torquay U v Plymouth Arg (12.00)
York C v Hartlepool U

Saturday 1 April 2000
FA Carling Premiership
Coventry C v Liverpool
Derby Co v Leicester C
Everton v Watford
Leeds U v Chelsea
Manchester U v West Ham U
Newcastle U v Bradford C
Sheffield W v Aston Villa
Southampton v Sunderland
Tottenham H v Middlesbrough
Wimbledon v Arsenal

Nationwide Football League Division 1
Birmingham C v Wolverhampton W
Blackburn R v Sheffield U
Charlton Ath v QPR
Crewe Alex v Nottingham F
Fulham v Crystal Palace
Grimsby T v Huddersfield T
Norwich C v Tranmere R
Port Vale v Portsmouth
Stockport Co v Bolton W
Swindon T v Manchester C
Walsall v Barnsley
WBA v Ipswich T

Nationwide Football League Division 2
Blackpool v Preston NE
Brentford v Wigan Ath
Bristol R v Stoke C
Bury v Scunthorpe U
Cardiff C v Burnley
Gillingham v Chesterfield
Luton T v Colchester U
Notts Co v Millwall
Oldham Ath v Cambridge U
Oxford U v AFC Bournemouth
Wrexham v Reading
Wycombe W v Bristol C

Nationwide Football League Division 3
Brighton & HA v Swansea C
Carlisle U v Hull C
Cheltenham T v Torquay U
Darlington v Rotherham U
Halifax T v Chester C
Hartlepool U v Exeter C
Leyton Orient v Macclesfield T
Mansfield T v Barnet
Peterborough U v Rochdale
Plymouth Arg v Northampton T
Shrewsbury T v Lincoln C
Southend U v York C

Saturday 8 April 2000
FA Carling Premiership
Arsenal v Sheffield W
Aston Villa v Leeds U
Bradford C v Southampton
Chelsea v Coventry C
Leicester C v Everton
Middlesbrough v Manchester U
Sunderland v Wimbledon
Watford v Derby Co
West Ham U v Newcastle U

Nationwide Football League Division 1
Barnsley v WBA
Bolton W v Walsall
Crystal Palace v Stockport Co
Huddersfield T v Birmingham C
Ipswich T v Port Vale
Manchester C v Crewe Alex
Nottingham F v Charlton Ath
Portsmouth v Norwich C
QPR v Swindon T
Sheffield U v Grimsby T
Wolverhampton W v Blackburn R

Nationwide Football League Division 2
AFC Bournemouth v Oldham Ath
Bristol C v Wrexham
Burnley v Notts Co
Cambridge U v Bristol R
Chesterfield v Wycombe W
Colchester U v Blackpool
Millwall v Bury
Preston NE v Cardiff C
Reading v Gillingham
Scunthorpe U v Luton T
Stoke C v Brentford
Wigan Ath v Oxford U

Nationwide Football League Division 3
Barnet v Shrewsbury T
Chester C v Carlisle U
Exeter C v Brighton & HA
Hull C v Leyton Orient
Lincoln C v Cheltenham T
Macclesfield T v Plymouth Arg
Northampton T v Halifax T
Rochdale v Hartlepool U
Rotherham U v Southend U
Swansea C v Peterborough U
Torquay U v Mansfield T
York C v Darlington

Sunday 9 April 2000
FA Carling Premiership
Liverpool v Tottenham H

Nationwide Football League Division 1
Tranmere R v Fulham (2.00)

Saturday 15 April 2000
FA Carling Premiership
Coventry C v Middlesbrough
Derby Co v West Ham U
Everton v Bradford C
Leeds U v Arsenal
Manchester U v Sunderland
Newcastle U v Leicester C
Sheffield W v Chelsea
Southampton v Watford
Tottenham H v Aston Villa
Wimbledon v Liverpool

Nationwide Football League Division 1
Birmingham C v Nottingham F
Blackburn R v Portsmouth
Charlton Ath v Huddersfield T
Crewe Alex v QPR
Fulham v Sheffield U
Grimsby T v Manchester C
Norwich C v Wolverhampton W
Port Vale v Barnsley
Stockport Co v Ipswich T
Swindon T v Tranmere R
Walsall v Crystal Palace
WBA v Bolton W

Nationwide Football League Division 2
Blackpool v Scunthorpe U
Brentford v Millwall
Bristol R v Preston NE
Bury v Chesterfield
Cardiff C v Cambridge U
Gillingham v Wigan Ath
Luton T v Bristol C
Notts Co v Reading
Oldham Ath v Stoke C
Oxford U v Burnley
Wrexham v AFC Bournemouth
Wycombe W v Colchester U

Nationwide Football League Division 3
Brighton & HA v Rotherham U
Carlisle U v Macclesfield T
Cheltenham T v York C
Darlington v Northampton T
Halifax T v Barnet
Hartlepool U v Lincoln C
Leyton Orient v Chester C
Mansfield T v Hull C

Peterborough U v Exeter C
Plymouth Arg v Swansea C
Shrewsbury T v Rochdale
Southend U v Torquay U

Friday 21 April 2000
Nationwide Football League Division 2
Wycombe W v Notts Co

Nationwide Football League Division 3
Northampton T v Hull C

Saturday 22 April 2000
FA Carling Premiership
Aston Villa v Leicester C
Bradford C v Derby Co
Chelsea v Middlesbrough
Everton v Liverpool
Newcastle U v Leeds U
Sheffield W v Sunderland
Southampton v Manchester U
Tottenham H v Wimbledon
Watford v Arsenal
West Ham U v Coventry C

Nationwide Football League Division 1
Charlton Ath v Portsmouth
Crewe Alex v Stockport Co
Crystal Palace v Birmingham C
Grimsby T v Blackburn R
Huddersfield T v Bolton W
Manchester C v Tranmere R
Norwich C v Port Vale
Nottingham F v Sheffield U
QPR v Ipswich T
Swindon T v Fulham
Walsall v WBA
Wolverhampton W v Barnsley

Nationwide Football League Division 2
Bristol R v Bristol C
Burnley v Millwall
Bury v Blackpool
Chesterfield v Wrexham
Colchester U v Cambridge U
Gillingham v Luton T
Oldham Ath v Cardiff C
Oxford U v Brentford
Preston NE v Scunthorpe U
Stoke C v AFC Bournemouth
Wigan Ath v Reading

Nationwide Football League Division 3
Barnet v Rotherham U
Carlisle U v Exeter C
Cheltenham T v Darlington
Hartlepool U v Mansfield T
Lincoln C v Leyton Orient
Macclesfield T v Chester C
Peterborough U v Halifax T
Plymouth Arg v Rochdale
Shrewsbury T v Southend U
Swansea C v Torquay U
York C v Brighton & HA

Monday 24 April 2000
FA Carling Premiership
Coventry C v Everton (3.00)
Derby Co v Southampton (3.00)
Liverpool v Aston Villa (3.00)
Manchester U v Chelsea (3.00)
Middlesbrough v Newcastle U (3.00)
Sunderland v Bradford C (3.00)
Wimbledon v Sheffield W (3.00)

Nationwide Football League Division 1
Barnsley v Norwich C (3.00)
Birmingham C v Walsall (3.00)
Blackburn R v Charlton Ath (3.00)
Bolton W v Wolverhampton W (3.00)
Fulham v Nottingham F (3.00)
Ipswich T v Crystal Palace (3.00)
Port Vale v Huddersfield T (3.00)
Portsmouth v Manchester C (3.00)
Sheffield U v Crewe Alex (3.00)

Stockport Co v Swindon T (3.00)
Tranmere R v QPR (3.00)
WBA v Grimsby T (3.00)

Nationwide Football League Division 2
Blackpool v Bristol R (3.00)
Brentford v Burnley (3.00)
Bristol C v Oxford U (3.00)
Cambridge U v Preston NE (3.00)
Cardiff C v Bury (3.00)
Luton T v Wigan Ath (3.00)
Millwall v Gillingham (3.00)
Notts Co v Oldham Ath (3.00)
Reading v Wycombe W (3.00)
Scunthorpe U v Stoke C (3.00)
Wrexham v Colchester U (3.00)

Nationwide Football League Division 3
Chester C v York C (3.00)
Darlington v Hartlepool U (3.00)
Exeter C v Lincoln C (3.00)
Halifax T v Shrewsbury T (2.00)
Hull C v Barnet (3.00)
Leyton Orient v Plymouth Arg (3.00)
Mansfield T v Swansea C (3.00)
Rochdale v Northampton T (3.00)
Rotherham U v Cheltenham T (3.00)
Southend U v Carlisle U (3.00)
Torquay U v Macclesfield T (3.00)

Tuesday 25 April 2000
FA Carling Premiership
Arsenal v West Ham U
Leeds U v Watford
Leicester C v Tottenham H

Nationwide Football League Division 3
AFC Bournemouth v Chesterfield

Wednesday 26 April 2000
Nationwide Football League Division 3
Brighton & HA v Peterborough U

Saturday 29 April 2000
FA Carling Premiership
Aston Villa v Sunderland
Bradford C v Wimbledon
Chelsea v Liverpool
Everton v Arsenal
Newcastle U v Coventry C
Sheffield W v Leeds U
Southampton v Leicester C
Tottenham H v Derby Co
Watford v Manchester U
West Ham U v Middlesbrough

Nationwide Football League Division 1
Charlton Ath v Ipswich T
Crewe Alex v Bolton W
Crystal Palace v Blackburn R
Grimsby T v Tranmere R
Huddersfield T v Stockport Co
Manchester C v Birmingham C
Norwich C v Sheffield U
Nottingham F v Port Vale
QPR v WBA
Swindon T v Barnsley
Walsall v Portsmouth
Wolverhampton W v Fulham

Nationwide Football League Division 2
Bristol R v AFC Bournemouth
Burnley v Cambridge U
Bury v Reading
Chesterfield v Notts Co
Colchester U v Bristol C
Gillingham v Brentford
Oldham Ath v Blackpool
Oxford U v Scunthorpe U
Preston NE v Millwall
Stoke C v Cardiff C
Wigan Ath v Wrexham
Wycombe W v Luton T

Nationwide Football League Division 3
Barnet v Leyton Orient
Carlisle U v Darlington
Cheltenham T v Chester C
Hartlepool U v Rotherham U
Lincoln C v Southend U
Macclesfield T v Rochdale
Northampton T v Mansfield T
Peterborough U v Torquay U
Plymouth Arg v Hull C
Shrewsbury T v Brighton & HA
Swansea C v Exeter C
York C v Halifax T

Saturday 6 May 2000
FA Carling Premiership
Arsenal v Chelsea
Coventry C v Sheffield W
Derby Co v Newcastle U
Leeds U v Everton
Leicester C v Bradford C
Liverpool v Southampton
Manchester U v Tottenham H
Middlesbrough v Watford
Sunderland v West Ham U
Wimbledon v Aston Villa

Nationwide Football League Division 2
AFC Bournemouth v Wigan Ath
Blackpool v Chesterfield
Brentford v Colchester U
Bristol C v Preston NE
Cambridge U v Wycombe W
Cardiff C v Bristol R
Luton T v Oldham Ath
Millwall v Oxford U
Notts Co v Bury
Reading v Stoke C
Scunthorpe U v Burnley
Wrexham v Gillingham

Nationwide Football League Division 3
Brighton & HA v Carlisle U
Chester C v Peterborough U
Darlington v Lincoln C
Exeter C v Shrewsbury T
Halifax T v Macclesfield T
Hull C v Hartlepool U
Leyton Orient v York C
Mansfield T v Plymouth Arg
Rochdale v Barnet
Rotherham U v Swansea C
Southend U v Cheltenham T
Torquay U v Northampton T

Sunday 7 May 2000
Nationwide Football League Division 1
Barnsley v Crewe Alex (1.30)
Birmingham C v Grimsby T (1.30)
Blackburn R v Manchester C (1.30)
Bolton W v Norwich C (1.30)
Fulham v Huddersfield T (1.30)
Ipswich T v Walsall (1.30)
Port Vale v Wolverhampton W (1.30)
Portsmouth v QPR (1.30)
Sheffield U v Swindon T (1.30)
Stockport Co v Nottingham F (1.30)
Tranmere R v Crystal Palace (1.30)
WBA v Charlton Ath (1.30)

Sunday 14 May 2000
FA Carling Premiership
Aston Villa v Manchester U (4.00)
Bradford C v Liverpool (4.00)
Chelsea v Derby Co (4.00)
Everton v Middlesbrough (4.00)
Newcastle U v Arsenal (4.00)
Sheffield W v Leicester C (4.00)
Southampton v Wimbledon (4.00)
Tottenham H v Sunderland (4.00)
Watford v Coventry C (4.00)
West Ham U v Leeds U (4.00)

FA CARLING PREMIERSHIP FIXTURES 1999-2000

Copyright © The FA Premier League Ltd 1999. Copyright Licence No. AP.99.005. Compiled in association with SEMA Group.

	Arsenal	Aston Villa	Bradford C	Chelsea	Coventry C	Derby Co	Everton	Leeds U	Leicester C	Liverpool	Manchester U	Middlesbrough	Newcastle U	Sheffield W	Southampton	Sunderland	Tottenham H	Watford	West Ham U	Wimbledon
Arsenal	–	11.9	25.8	6.5	25.3	27.11	16.10	28.12	7.8	12.2	22.8	20.11	30.10	8.4	26.2	15.1	18.3	25.9	25.4	18.12
Aston Villa	4.3	–	18.9	22.1	11.3	25.3	11.8	8.4	22.4	2.10	14.5	28.8	4.12	18.12	6.11	29.4	29.12	5.2	16.8	23.10
Bradford C	5.2	26.2	–	8.1	6.11	22.4	28.12	11.3	23.10	14.5	25.3	4.12	18.12	14.8	8.4	2.10	12.9	22.1	28.8	29.4
Chelsea	23.10	21.8	28.11	–	8.4	14.5	11.3	19.12	15.1	29.4	3.10	22.4	11.9	29.12	25.3	7.8	12.1	26.2	6.11	12.2
Coventry C	26.12	22.11	18.3	3.1	–	21.8	24.4	11.9	27.11	1.4	25.8	15.4	16.10	6.5	7.8	12.2	26.2	31.10	25.9	15.1
Derby Co	10.8	26.12	25.9	30.10	22.1	–	28.8	4.12	1.4	18.3	20.11	14.8	6.5	5.2	24.4	18.9	16.10	3.1	15.4	4.3
Everton	29.4	27.11	15.4	20.11	2.10	28.8	–	23.10	3.1	22.4	8.8	14.5	18.3	4.3	21.8	26.12	15.1	1.4	18.9	25.8
Leeds U	15.4	3.1	20.11	1.4	4.3	7.8	6.5	–	26.12	23.8	15.1	19.9	25.9	16.10	27.11	21.8	12.2	25.4	30.10	18.3
Leicester C	4.12	25.9	6.5	14.8	11.8	18.12	8.4	25.3	–	18.9	18.3	5.2	28.12	30.10	16.10	4.3	25.4	30.8	17.10	20.11
Liverpool	28.8	24.4	1.11	16.10	18.12	6.11	27.9	5.2	26.2	–	11.9	22.1	25.3	5.12	6.5	11.3	9.4	14.8	1.4	28.12
Manchester U	22.1	30.10	26.12	24.4	5.2	11.3	4.12	14.8	6.11	11.9	–	3.1	30.8	11.8	25.9	15.4	18.12	6.5	1.4	20.11
Middlesbrough	11.3	12.2	7.8	4.3	29.4	15.1	30.10	26.2	24.8	4.3	3.1	–	24.4	25.3	11.9	6.11	6.5	16.10	3.1	10.8
Newcastle U	14.5	7.8	1.4	15.4	16.10	25.10	8.11	22.4	15.4	26.12	12.2	3.10	–	19.9	15.1	25.8	27.11	6.11	8.4	2.10
Sheffield W	3.1	1.4	15.1	26.12	23.10	25.8	11.9	29.4	14.5	7.8	8.4	26.12	19.9	–	12.2	22.4	21.8	18.3	11.3	24.4
Southampton	18.9	18.3	3.1	4.12	7.8	4.10	22.1	11.8	29.4	23.10	22.4	4.3	15.8	28.8	–	1.4	20.11	15.4	25.8	30.10
Sunderland	14.8	18.10	24.4	5.2	29.8	26.2	25.3	22.1	11.9	20.11	28.12	18.3	5.2	25.9	18.12	–	30.10	10.8	6.5	8.4
Tottenham H	6.11	15.4	4.3	22.1	19.9	29.4	14.8	28.8	3.10	3.1	23.10	1.4	9.8	22.1	11.3	14.5	–	25.3	7.8	26.9
Watford	22.4	24.8	21.8	18.9	14.5	8.4	18.12	3.10	12.2	15.1	29.4	24.10	20.11	18.3	28.12	27.11	25.3	–	11.9	4.12
West Ham U	2.10	15.1	12.2	18.3	22.4	28.12	26.2	14.5	21.8	27.11	18.12	29.4	8.4	21.11	25.8	23.10	7.8	4.3	–	25.3
Wimbledon	1.4	6.5	16.10	28.8	14.8	11.9	5.2	7.11	11.3	15.4	26.2	10.8	22.1	24.4	30.10	3.1	26.9	26.12	26.12	–

NATIONWIDE FOOTBALL LEAGUE FIXTURES 1999–2000

Copyright © The FA Premier League Ltd 1999. Copyright Licence No. AP.99.005. Compiled in association with SEMA Group.

DIVISION ONE

	Barnsley	Birmingham C	Blackburn R	Bolton W	Charlton Ath	Crewe Alex	Crystal Palace	Fulham	Grimsby T	Huddersfield T	Ipswich T	Manchester C	Norwich C	Nottingham F	Port Vale	Portsmouth	QPR	Sheffield U	Stockport Co	Swindon T	Tranmere R	Walsall	WBA	Wolverhampton W
Barnsley	–	20.11	22.1	26.2	4.12	7.5	14.8	21.3	25.3	25.9	5.2	11.3	24.4	30.10	28.12	28.8	19.2	6.11	10.9	19.10	3.9	18.12	8.4	16.10
Birmingham C	18.3	–	13.11	12.2	30.10	30.8	16.10	7.8	7.5	3.1	26.2	19.10	15.1	15.4	21.8	7.3	25.9	29.1	29.1	27.11	23.11	24.4	11.9	1.4
Blackburn R	21.8	22.3	–	30.8	24.4	11.3	20.10	20.11	16.10	15.1	6.11	7.5	29.1	26.12	7.8	15.4	30.10	1.4	27.11	12.2	11.9	25.9	26.2	3.1
Bolton W	18.9	5.9	5.2	–	4.3	19.10	6.11	11.3	16.10	16.10	22.1	28.8	7.5	3.1	25.3	19.2	14.8	21.3	18.12	30.10	4.12	8.4	28.12	24.4
Charlton Ath	7.8	2.10	9.10	11.9	–	15.1	26.12	29.1	20.11	16.10	29.4	20.11	21.8	3.1	27.11	22.4	1.4	26.2	18.12	11.3	26.10	22.1	23.10	12.2
Crewe Alex	23.10	5.2	23.11	29.4	2.11	–	4.12	26.10	27.8	26.12	19.2	4.9	4.3	1.4	7.3	18.3	15.4	9.10	22.4	18.9	3.10	22.1	4.9	13.11
Crystal Palace	15.1	22.4	29.4	7.3	4.12	7.8	–	18.12	18.9	26.12	9.10	3.1	23.11	1.4	18.3	4.9	13.11	15.4	8.4	21.8	28.8	28.12	26.10	31.8
Fulham	13.11	4.12	18.3	23.11	13.11	25.3	1.4	–	22.1	7.5	9.10	14.8	30.10	27.11	18.3	4.9	23.11	15.4	8.4	21.8	3.1	28.12	22.1	3.10
Grimsby T	26.12	23.10	22.4	18.3	26.12	27.8	1.4	18.12	–	1.4	2.10	15.4	30.10	4.9	12.2	26.10	4.12	3.1	7.8	6.11	3.1	19.2	5.2	7.3
Huddersfield T	26.10	8.4	13.8	22.4	16.10	25.3	28.8	21.8	1.4	–	4.9	19.2	18.9	8.4	5.2	26.10	4.12	7.8	29.4	6.11	22.1	11.3	20.11	4.3
Ipswich T	30.8	18.9	7.3	21.8	24.11	27.11	23.10	15.1	18.12	12.2	–	26.9	18.3	21.3	9.10	5.2	16.10	29.1	28.12	6.11	13.11	7.5	17.12	24.11
Manchester C	24.11	29.4	23.10	18.3	29.4	4.9	26.9	15.1	30.10	27.11	26.9	–	12.2	30.8	8.4	3.1	8.3	21.8	13.11	18.12	22.4	26.2	25.3	8.8
Norwich C	9.10	14.8	28.8	7.8	14.8	4.3	4.9	20.11	2.10	22.1	4.9	12.2	–	16.10	22.4	3.1	26.12	29.4	26.10	21.3	1.4	5.2	4.12	15.4
Nottingham F	1.10	28.12	25.3	27.10	8.4	18.12	19.2	10.10	14.8	14.11	5.12	4.9	8.3	–	29.4	24.11	28.8	22.4	23.10	4.3	18.3	4.9	22.1	19.9
Port Vale	15.4	22.1	4.12	25.3	19.2	7.3	18.3	8.4	11.3	30.10	13.11	18.12	8.3	30.10	–	1.4	5.2	11.3	26.2	25.9	28.8	19.10	14.8	7.5
Portsmouth	29.1	6.11	28.12	27.11	16.10	5.11	30.10	11.9	3.9	18.12	24.4	8.4	11.3	18.12	–	7.8	7.8	21.8	25.3	26.2	19.10	21.3	15.1	21.8
QPR	27.11	27.10	2.10	15.1	18.12	28.12	22.3	6.11	11.3	7.8	22.4	6.11	25.3	29.1	31.8	23.10	–	11.9	11.9	8.4	9.10	20.11	29.4	21.8
Sheffield U	7.3	25.3	19.12	19.2	18.9	24.4	4.9	28.12	8.4	30.10	22.1	21.3	19.10	16.10	23.11	4.12	4.3	–	18.3	7.5	5.2	14.8	19.2	25.9
Stockport Co	4.3	27.8	19.2	4.9	5.2	16.10	3.1	6.11	4.12	19.10	29.4	21.3	25.9	8.4	18.9	22.1	4.9	20.11	–	24.4	14.8	30.10	11.3	26.12
Swindon T	29.4	19.2	4.9	3.1	23.11	26.2	22.1	9.4	5.2	7.3	15.8	1.4	13.11	30.8	26.10	26.12	3.1	23.10	9.10	–	15.4	4.12	28.8	18.3
Tranmere R	12.2	11.3	4.3	7.8	7.3	30.10	7.5	9.4	19.10	21.8	21.3	16.10	18.12	20.11	29.1	29.4	18.3	30.8	15.1	28.12	–	25.3	26.12	27.11
Walsall	1.4	8.10	26.10	3.1	7.3	7.5	15.4	25.9	30.8	24.4	18.3	1.4	30.8	18.9	13.11	29.4	18.3	15.1	2.10	7.8	26.12	–	22.4	29.1
WBA	3.1	4.3	18.9	15.4	7.3	12.2	25.9	30.8	24.4	18.3	20.8	26.12	7.8	12.2	20.8	13.11	19.10	27.11	23.11	29.1	7.3	16.10	–	31.10
Wolverhampton W	22.4	17.12	8.4	9.10	4.9	21.3	5.2	29.4	6.11	11.9	11.3	26.2	28.12	26.2	23.10	14.8	22.1	25.3	25.3	20.11	19.2	28.8	3.10	–

NATIONWIDE FOOTBALL LEAGUE FIXTURES 1999–2000

Copyright © The FA Premier League Ltd 1999. Copyright Licence No. AP.99.005. Compiled in association with SEMA Group.

DIVISION TWO

	Blackpool	AFC Bournemouth	Brentford	Bristol C	Bristol R	Burnley	Bury	Cambridge U	Cardiff C	Chesterfield	Colchester U	Gillingham	Luton T	Millwall	Notts Co	Oldham Ath	Oxford U	Preston NE	Reading	Scunthorpe U	Stoke C	Wigan Ath	Wrexham	Wycombe W
Blackpool	–	18.9	29.1	12.2	24.4	21.3	16.10	27.11	11.3	6.5	3.1	21.8	15.1	23.11	4.3	19.10	30.8	1.4	11.12	15.4	26.12	6.11	7.8	25.9
AFC Bournemouth	26.2	–	23.11	15.1	19.10	12.2	25.9	7.8	6.11	25.4	21.8	21.3	31.8	27.11	8.1	8.4	18.12	11.3	11.9	29.1	16.10	6.5	28.12	25.3
Brentford	28.8	18.3	–	26.12	4.12	24.4	22.1	4.3	4.9	11.12	6.5	19.10	18.9	15.4	5.2	14.8	16.10	25.9	2.11	13.11	3.1	1.4	7.3	19.2
Bristol C	4.9	14.8	25.3	–	17.10	25.9	22.1	4.3	8.1	5.2	19.10	11.3	28.12	15.4	5.2	23.11	24.4	6.5	4.12	26.2	21.3	22.1	8.4	17.12
Bristol R	2.10	29.4	7.8	2.10	–	30.8	2.11	3.1	9.10	18.3	11.12	15.1	27.11	26.12	23.10	18.9	15.4	6.5	13.11	12.2	1.4	4.3	29.1	7.3
Burnley	13.11	4.9	2.10	23.10	5.2	–	25.3	11.12	18.12	14.8	11.12	8.1	7.3	22.4	8.4	22.1	28.12	4.3	18.3	10.10	28.8	19.2	2.11	7.3
Bury	22.4	23.10	21.8	29.1	11.3	26.12	–	11.12	8.1	24.4	4.9	8.4	22.4	4.1	9.10	22.1	28.12	4.3	18.3	20.10	8.3	4.9	18.3	26.2
Cambridge U	19.2	4.12	11.9	7.3	21.8	19.10	8.1	–	7.8	13.11	25.9	25.9	13.11	18.9	11.12	4.3	4.9	24.4	14.8	2.11	4.9	5.2	18.3	4.12
Cardiff C	2.11	7.3	12.2	11.12	7.3	1.4	24.4	15.4	–	22.1	27.11	13.11	29.1	26.2	18.9	16.10	25.3	3.1	14.8	30.8	4.9	5.2	20.8	6.5
Chesterfield	9.10	2.10	8.1	30.8	23.11	13.11	22.1	15.4	21.3	–	7.8	18.12	25.3	7.8	29.4	16.10	27.11	3.1	26.12	23.10	19.10	25.9	20.8	3.3
Colchester U	8.4	22.1	9.10	29.4	8.1	26.2	5.2	22.4	24.11	3.12	–	25.3	17.12	23.10	14.8	21.3	11.3	6.11	28.8	11.9	19.2	4.9	1.10	29.12
Gillingham	22.1	12.11	29.4	2.11	14.8	11.12	4.12	12.12	19.2	1.4	25.3	–	22.4	2.10	29.4	4.9	4.3	6.11	3.1	11.9	5.2	15.4	9.10	29.12
Luton T	14.8	5.2	26.2	2.11	14.8	6.11	16.10	4.9	21.3	4.3	2.10	11.3	–	10.10	18.12	6.5	25.9	23.11	22.1	3.1	5.2	15.4	11.9	19.10
Millwall	18.3	19.2	28.12	4.3	25.3	16.10	8.4	18.9	4.12	22.1	2.11	21.3	11.3	–	18.12	5.2	6.5	19.10	4.9	7.3	22.1	14.8	13.11	8.1
Notts Co	11.9	11.12	30.8	27.11	25.9	3.1	6.5	29.1	26.2	19.10	7.3	4.12	11.3	18.12	–	24.4	23.11	21.3	4.9	21.8	11.3	14.8	12.2	16.10
Oldham Ath	29.4	3.1	15.1	18.3	26.2	21.8	15.4	1.4	22.4	8.1	12.2	11.9	23.10	30.8	2.10	–	28.8	7.8	23.10	29.4	15.4	11.12	27.11	2.11
Oxford U	5.2	1.4	22.4	2.11	22.1	14.8	13.11	26.12	14.8	8.4	27.11	23.10	9.10	28.8	2.10	28.8	–	29.1	5.2	27.11	4.12	3.1	26.2	4.9
Preston NE	18.12	2.11	23.10	28.12	2.10	11.9	19.2	2.10	14.8	18.9	6.11	8.4	23.10	9.10	18.3	28.8	8.1	–	11.12	1.9	7.3	26.12	27.11	2.11
Reading	8.1	4.3	11.3	22.3	4.9	6.5	20.10	2.10	25.3	18.9	29.1	12.2	21.8	29.4	13.11	4.12	25.9	1.9	–	27.11	6.5	16.10	18.12	24.4
Scunthorpe U	28.12	28.8	21.3	11.3	4.9	6.5	8.3	11.3	5.2	25.3	18.9	28.12	12.2	21.8	28.12	25.9	19.10	16.10	19.2	–	24.4	4.12	8.1	14.8
Stoke C	25.3	22.4	8.4	18.9	13.11	21.8	3.1	12.2	29.4	23.10	2.11	22.8	8.1	22.8	3.11	25.3	19.10	7.8	9.10	16.10	–	18.9	26.2	14.8
Wigan Ath	7.3	9.10	18.12	13.11	21.8	3.1	9.10	30.8	6.11	8.1	30.8	28.12	2.10	8.1	8.4	8.1	7.8	15.1	19.2	7.8	26.2	–	18.9	13.11
Wrexham	4.12	15.4	6.11	21.8	28.8	11.3	18.3	23.11	6.11	19.2	21.3	4.3	21.3	15.1	4.9	19.2	18.9	26.12	1.4	11.12	25.9	19.10	–	5.2
Wycombe W	23.10	26.12	27.11	1.4	6.11	7.8	26.2	27.11	6.5	3.3	29.12	21.8	29.4	8.1	16.10	11.3	12.2	21.8	2.10	15.1	23.11	21.3	31.8	–

NATIONWIDE FOOTBALL LEAGUE FIXTURES 1999–2000

Copyright © The FA Premier League Ltd 1999. Copyright Licence No. AP.99.005. Compiled in association with SEMA Group.

DIVISION THREE

	Barnet	Brighton & HA	Carlisle U	Cheltenham T	Chester C	Darlington	Exeter C	Halifax T	Hartlepool U	Hull C	Leyton O	Lincoln C	Macclesfield T	Mansfield T	Northampton T	Peterborough U	Plymouth Arg	Rochdale	Rotherham U	Shrewsbury T	Southend U	Swansea C	Torquay U	York C
Barnet	—	25.3	23.11	18.3	30.8	6.11	14.8	28.12	11.3	2.10	29.4	22.1	5.9	18.12	18.9	19.2	21.3	13.11	6.5	8.4	8.1	4.3	23.10	28.8
Brighton & HA	26.12	—	6.5	7.3	26.2	29.1	3.1	4.3	6.11	1.9	15.1	23.11	13.11	4.12	19.2	2.10	4.9	8.1	28.12	19.10	11.3	1.4	21.8	16.10
Carlisle U	18.3	9.10	—	7.3	8.4	29.4	22.4	23.10	21.8	1.4	7.8	11.9	28.12	14.8	4.9	21.3	5.2	25.3	19.2	26.2	2.10	15.1	11.12	2.11
Cheltenham T	30.8	23.10	6.11	—	19.10	22.4	26.12	11.3	29.1	21.8	27.11	3.1	8.1	14.8	13.11	18.9	18.3	4.12	24.4	12.9	9.10	13.2	1.4	15.4
Chester C	7.8	26.2	8.4	19.10	—	8.1	11.9	18.12	21.3	12.2	28.12	25.9	16.10	25.3	21.4	2.10	7.3	30.8	11.3	11.3	23.11	27.11	29.1	24.4
Darlington	7.3	28.8	19.10	16.10	15.4	—	4.9	4.12	24.4	26.12	2.11	6.5	14.8	26.2	26.2	22.1	30.8	23.10	18.12	22.1	19.2	18.3	13.11	3.1
Exeter C	15.1	8.4	16.10	25.3	14.8	12.2	—	21.3	18.12	7.8	8.1	24.4	11.3	19.2	8.4	2.11	28.8	22.1	9.10	6.5	6.5	19.10	27.11	18.9
Halifax T	15.4	11.9	25.9	2.11	18.12	7.8	21.3	—	15.1	18.3	24.4	26.12	11.3	8.4	21.4	2.10	22.4	2.11	8.1	24.4	26.2	7.3	31.8	19.10
Hartlepool U	2.11	7.3	22.1	28.8	21.3	2.10	18.12	15.1	—	9.10	7.3	6.5	27.11	16.10	11.9	7.8	26.2	1.4	19.10	5.2	4.9	11.12	18.3	26.12
Hull C	24.4	5.2	18.12	22.1	12.2	25.3	7.8	18.3	15.1	—	23.10	16.10	29.1	15.4	21.4	11.12	29.4	2.11	7.3	19.2	21.3	18.9	4.3	25.9
Leyton O	19.10	14.8	4.12	19.2	28.12	11.3	8.1	28.8	25.9	3.1	—	22.4	18.12	11.9	7.3	21.8	23.10	13.11	13.11	4.9	5.2	26.12	18.9	6.5
Lincoln C	21.8	18.3	4.3	8.4	25.9	9.10	24.4	25.3	14.12	15.1	22.4	—	26.2	28.8	11.3	11.3	11.12	27.11	23.11	18.12	29.4	30.8	12.2	13.11
Macclesfield T	12.2	13.11	28.12	8.1	16.10	15.1	11.3	9.10	27.11	29.1	18.12	26.2	—	2.11	29.1	23.11	3.1	29.4	19.10	25.3	11.9	21.8	2.10	7.3
Mansfield T	1.4	4.12	14.8	14.8	25.3	26.2	19.2	8.4	16.10	15.4	11.9	28.8	2.11	—	29.4	3.9	8.4	13.11	18.3	24.9	22.1	24.4	3.1	11.12
Northampton T	26.2	19.2	4.9	13.11	21.4	26.2	8.4	21.4	11.9	21.4	7.3	11.3	29.1	19.10	—	14.8	29.1	3.1	23.10	28.8	23.10	2.11	15.1	5.2
Peterborough U	27.11	2.10	21.3	18.9	2.10	22.1	2.11	2.10	7.8	11.12	21.8	11.3	23.11	15.1	14.8	—	17.12	14.8	26.12	6.11	4.12	3.1	29.4	4.3
Plymouth Arg	13.11	4.9	5.2	18.3	7.3	30.8	28.8	22.4	26.2	29.4	23.10	11.12	3.1	9.10	29.1	17.12	—	22.4	11.9	14.8	14.8	15.4	26.12	19.2
Rochdale	6.5	8.1	25.3	4.12	30.8	23.10	22.1	2.11	1.4	2.11	13.11	27.11	29.4	13.11	3.1	14.8	22.4	—	1.4	28.12	28.12	25.9	7.3	22.1
Rotherham U	16.10	28.12	19.2	24.4	21.8	18.12	9.10	8.1	19.10	7.3	13.11	23.11	19.10	18.3	23.10	26.12	11.9	1.4	—	28.8	8.4	6.5	2.11	4.9
Shrewsbury T	3.1	29.4	18.9	4.3	11.3	21.8	2.10	2.10	31.8	27.11	30.8	18.12	25.3	24.9	28.8	6.11	14.8	28.12	28.8	—	22.4	13.11	7.8	18.3
Southend U	11.12	2.11	24.4	6.5	23.11	27.11	7.3	18.9	12.2	13.11	12.2	29.4	11.9	22.1	23.10	4.12	14.8	28.12	8.4	22.4	—	29.1	15.4	1.4
Swansea C	11.9	18.12	14.8	4.9	27.11	21.3	29.4	5.11	23.11	26.2	25.3	30.8	21.8	24.4	2.11	3.1	15.4	25.9	6.5	13.11	28.8	—	22.4	16.10
Torquay U	25.9	22.1	8.1	18.12	29.1	8.4	26.2	5.2	11.9	23.10	26.2	12.2	2.10	3.1	15.1	2.11	29.1	25.3	29.4	7.8	28.12	22.4	—	14.8
York C	29.1	22.4	11.3	28.12	2.10	3.1	8.4	29.4	25.3	23.10	9.10	13.11	7.3	11.12	5.2	4.3	19.2	22.1	4.9	18.3	6.11	16.10	15.1	—

OTHER FIXTURES 1999–2000

July 1999

1 Thu	England v France – Under 16 Mini-Tournament at Northwich Victoria FC (7.05pm)
3 Sat	France v Argentina – Under 16 Mini-Tournament at Kingstonian FC (3.30pm)
	UEFA Intertoto Cup 2nd Round (1)
4 Sun	England v Argentina – Under 16 Mini-Tournament at Wembley Stadium (3.00pm)
	England v Scotland – Under 16 Women's International at Wembley Stadium (1.00pm)
10 Sat	UEFA Intertoto Cup 2nd Round (2)
13/14 Tue/Wed	UEFA Champions League 1st Qualifying Stage (1)
17 Sat	UEFA Intertoto Cup 3rd Round (1)
20/21 Tue/Wed	UEFA Champions League 1st Qualifying Stage (2)
24 Sat	UEFA Intertoto Cup 3rd Round (2)
27/28 Tue/Wed	UEFA Champions League 2nd Qualifying Stage (1)
28 Wed	UEFA Intertoto Cup Semi-Final (1)
31 Sat	Official Start of Season

August

1 Sun	One-2-One F.A. Charity Shield
	Nordic Under 16 Tournament in England (ends 8 Aug)
3/4 Tue/Wed	UEFA Champions League 2nd Qualifying Stage (2)
4 Wed	UEFA Intertoto Cup Semi-Final (2)
7 Sat	F.A. Carling Premier League and Nationwide Leagues starting date
10 Tue	UEFA Intertoto Cup Final (1)
10/11 Tue/Wed	UEFA Champions League 3rd Qualifying Stage (1)
11 Wed	Worthington Cup 1 (1)
12 Thu	UEFA Cup Qualifying Round (1)
14 Sat	Nationwide Conference starting date
18 Wed	International (Friendly)
21 Sat	F.A. Cup Sponsored by AXA Preliminary Round
22 Sun	Denmark v England (Women's Friendly International)
24 Tue	UEFA Intertoto Cup Final (2)
24/25 Tue/Wed	UEFA Champions League 3rd Qualifying Stage (2)
25 Wed	Worthington Cup 1 (2)
26 Thu	UEFA Cup Qualifying Round (2)
30 Mon	Bank Holiday

September

4 Sat	England v Luxembourg UEFA European Championship
	F.A. Cup Sponsored by AXA 1Q
	The Times F.A. Youth Cup 1Q*
8 Wed	Poland v England UEFA European Championship
11 Sat	F.A. Carlsberg Vase 1Q
12 Sun	AXA F.A. Women's Cup EP
14/15 Tue/Wed	UEFA Champions League 1st Group – Match 1
15 Wed	Worthington Cup 2 (1)
16 Thu	UEFA Cup 1 (1)
	England v France (Women's Friendly International)

18 Sat	F.A. Cup Sponsored by AXA 2Q
21/22 Tue/Wed	UEFA Champions League 1st Group – Match 2
22 Wed	Worthington Cup 2 (2)
25 Sat	F.A. Carlsberg Vase 2Q
	The Times F.A. Youth Cup 2Q*
26 Sun	AXA F.A. Women's Cup P
28/29 Tue/Wed	UEFA Champions League 1st Group – Match 3
30 Thu	UEFA Cup 1 (2)

October

2 Sat	F.A. Cup Sponsored by AXA 3Q
9 Sat	F.A. Umbro Trophy 1
	The Times F.A. Youth Cup 3Q*
	F.A. County Youth Cup 1*
10 Sun	AXA F.A. Women's Cup 1
	England v Belgium – Friendly International at Sunderland FC (3.00pm)
13 Wed	Worthington Cup 3
15 Fri	England v Northern Ireland (Victory Shield – Under 15 Schoolboy team)
16 Sat	F.A. Cup Sponsored by AXA 4Q
	Switzerland v England (Women's UEFA International)
17 Sun	F.A. Umbro Sunday Cup 1
19/20 Tue/Wed	UEFA Champions League 1st Group – Match 4
21 Thu	UEFA Cup 2 (1)
23 Sat	F.A. Carlsberg Vase 1P
26/27 Tue/Wed	UEFA Champions League 1st Group – Match 5
28 Thu	England v Wales (Victory Shield – Under 15 Schoolboy team)
30 Sat	F.A. Cup Sponsored by AXA 1P
	The Times F.A. Youth Cup 1P*

November

2/3 Tue/Wed	UEFA Champions League 1st Group – Match 6
4 Thu	UEFA Cup 2 (2)
7 Sun	AXA F.A. Women's Cup 2
10 Wed	F.A. Cup Sponsored by AXA 1P Replay
11 Thu	Scotland v England (Victory Shield – Under 15 Schoolboy team)
13 Sat	Possible Play-Off for UEFA European Championship
	F.A. Carlsberg Vase 2P
	The Times F.A. Youth Cup 2P*
	F.A. County Youth Cup 2*
	Under 18 UEFA Three Team Mini-Tournament in England (ends 20 Nov)
14 Sun	F.A. Umbro Sunday Cup 2
17 Wed	Possible Play-Off for UEFA European Championship
20 Sat	F.A. Cup Sponsored by AXA 2P
23/24 Tue/Wed	UEFA Champions League 2nd Group – Match 1
25 Thu	UEFA Cup 3 (1)
27 Sat	F.A. Umbro Trophy 2

December

1 Wed	Worthington Cup 4
	F.A. Cup Sponsored by AXA 2P Replay
4 Sat	F.A. Carlsberg Vase 3P
5 Sun	F.A. Umbro Sunday Cup 3
6 Mon	F.A. XI v Northern Premier League

7 Tue	FIFA World Cup – Draw for Preliminary Competition
	F.A. XI v Southern League
7/8 Tue/Wed	UEFA Champions League 2nd Group – Match 2
8 Wed	F.A. XI v Isthmian League
9 Thu	UEFA Cup 3 (2)
11 Sat	F.A. Cup Sponsored by AXA 3P
	The Times F.A. Youth Cup 3P*
12 Sun	AXA F.A. Women's Cup 3
15 Wed	Worthington Cup 5
18 Sat	F.A. County Youth Cup 3*
22 Wed	F.A. Cup Sponsored by AXA 3P Replay
26 Sun	Boxing Day
27 Mon	Bank Holiday
28 Tue	Bank Holiday

January 2000

1 Sat	New Year's Day
3 Mon	Bank Holiday
8 Sat	F.A. Cup Sponsored by AXA 4P
9 Sun	AXA F.A. Women's Cup 4
10 Mon	F.A. XI v Combined Services
12 Wed	Worthington Cup Semi-Final (1)
15 Sat	F.A. Umbro Trophy 3
19 Wed	F.A. Cup Sponsored by AXA 4P Replay
22 Sat	F.A. Carlsberg Vase 4P
	The Times F.A. Youth Cup 4P*
23 Sun	F.A. Umbro Sunday Cup 4
26 Wed	Worthington Cup Semi-Final (2)
29 Sat	F.A. Cup Sponsored by AXA 5P
	F.A. County Youth Cup 4*

February

5 Sat	F.A. Umbro Trophy 4
6 Sun	AXA F.A. Women's Cup 5
9 Wed	F.A. Cup Sponsored by AXA 5P Replay
12 Sat	F.A. Carlsberg Vase 5P
	The Times F.A. Youth Cup 5P*
19 Sat	F.A. Cup Sponsored by AXA 6P
20 Sun	England v Poland (Women's UEFA International)
	F.A. Umbro Sunday Cup 5
23 Wed	International (Friendly)
26 Sat	F.A. Umbro Trophy 5
27 Sun	AXA F.A. Women's Cup 6
	Worthington Cup Final
29 Tue	England Semi-Professional International
29/1 Tue/Wed	UEFA Champions League 2nd Group – Match 3

March

1 Wed	F.A. Cup Sponsored by AXA 6P Replay
2 Thu	UEFA Cup 4 (1)
4 Sat	F.A. Carlsberg Vase 6P
	The Times F.A. Youth Cup 6P*
7 Tue	Under 16 UEFA Three Team Mini-Tournament in Luxembourg (ends 12 March)
7/8 Tue/Wed	UEFA Champions League 2nd Group – Match 4
9 Thu	UEFA Cup 4 (2)
	England v Norway (Women's UEFA International)
11 Sat	F.A. Umbro Trophy 6
	F.A. County Youth Cup Semi-Final*
14/15 Tue/Wed	UEFA Champions League 2nd Group – Match 5
16 Thu	UEFA Cup Quarter-Final (1)
18 Sat	F.A. Carlsberg Vase SF1
19 Sun	F.A. Umbro Sunday Cup SF

21 Tue	England Semi-Professional International
21/22 Tue/Wed	UEFA Champions League 2nd Group – Match 6
23 Thu	UEFA Cup Quarter-Final (2)
24 Fri	England v Holland (Under 15 Schoolboy Friendly International)
25 Sat	F.A. Carlsberg Vase SF2
	The Times F.A. Youth Cup SF1*
26 Sun	AXA F.A. Women's Cup SF
29 Wed	International (Friendly)

April

1 Sat	F.A. Umbro Trophy SF1
4/5 Tue/Wed	UEFA Champions League Quarter-Final (1)
6 Thu	UEFA Cup Semi-Final (1)
7 Fri	England v Italy (Under 15 Schoolboy Friendly International)
9 Sun	F.A. Cup Sponsored by AXA Semi-Final
15 Sat	F.A. Umbro Trophy SF2
	The Times F.A. Youth Cup SF2*
18/19 Tue/Wed	UEFA Champions League Quarter-Final (2)
20 Thu	UEFA Cup Semi-Final (2)
21 Fri	Good Friday
22 Sat	Portugal v England (Women's UEFA International)
24 Mon	Easter Monday
26 Wed	International (Friendly)
29 Sat	F.A. County Youth Cup Final (fixed date)

May

1 Mon	AXA F.A. Women's Cup Final
3 Wed	UEFA Champions League Semi-Final (1)
5 Fri	The Times F.A. Youth Cup Final 1st Leg (fixed date)
6 Sat	F.A. Carlsberg Vase Final
	Final Nationwide League fixtures Divs 2&3
	Final Nationwide Conference fixtures
7 Sun	Final Nationwide League fixtures Div 1
10 Wed	UEFA Champions League Semi-Final (2)
12 Fri	The Times F.A. Youth Cup Final 2nd Leg (fixed date)
13 Sat	F.A. Umbro Trophy Final
14 Sun	Nationwide League Play-Off Semi-Final (1)
	Final F.A. Carling Premier League fixtures
	England v Switzerland (Women's UEFA International)
17 Wed	UEFA Cup Final
	Nationwide League Play-Off Semi-Final (2)
20 Sat	F.A. Cup Sponsored by AXA Final
24 Wed	UEFA Champions League Final
27 Sat	Nationwide League 3rd Division Play-Off
28 Sun	Nationwide Leage 2nd Division Play-Off
29 Mon	Nationwide League 1st Division Play-Off

June

3 Sat	Possible International Friendly
4 Sun	Possible International Friendly
	Norway v England (Women's UEFA International)
10 Sat	European Championship Commences (ends 2 July)

* = closing date
to be dated – F.A. Umbro Sunday Cup Final

STOP PRESS

Geoff Thompson new FA Chairman ... Man U to opt out of FA Cup to play in Brazilian tournament ... FL to re-introduce goal difference, adopt names and squad nos. and three from five subs ... WC 2002 could start in May and FIFA postpone vote for 2006 to July ... England win an Under-16 tournament ... Granada in £22m league with Liverpool ... Tony Banks denies bullying Man U ... Arsenal, Charlton and Swansea may move grounds ... Dave Ewing, Man City FA Cup hero dies at 70 and Laurie Scott (Arsenal and England) at 84 ... After 544 random examinations, two players test positive for drugs ... Rules tightened on imports ... FIFA announce anti-cheating purge ... 10 yard free kick experiment to continue ... West Ham beat Jokerit in the Inter-Toto Cup and Chelsea will play either Rapid Bucharest or Skonto Riga in the Champions League ... Denis Smith axed at WBA ... Schwarz record move stalls, Anelka's collapses ... 12 club Scots PL in a year.

Top Transfers: Chris Sutton, Blackburn R to **Chelsea** £10m; Dietmar Hamann, Newcastle U to **Liverpool** £8m; Kieron Dyer, Ipswich T to **Newcastle U** £6m; Eyal Berkovic, West Ham U to **Celtic** £5,750,000; Elena Marcelino, Mallorca to **Newcastle U** £5m; Michael Duberry, Chelsea to **Leeds U** £5m; Michael Bridges, Sunderland to **Leeds U** £5m.

Other moves completed and pending: **Arsenal:** Oleg Luzhny (Dynamo Kiev); Stefan Malz (Munich 1860); Silvinho (Corinthians); Moritz Volz (Schalke); **Aston Villa:** George Boateng (Coventry C); Nagun Grayeb (Graiev) (Hapoel Haifa); David James (Liverpool); **Bradford C:** Matt Clarke (Sheffield W); Gunnar Halle (Leeds U); Andy Myers (Chelsea); Lee Sharpe (Leeds U); David Wetherall (Leeds U); **Chelsea:** Didier Deschamps (Juventus); Jes Hogh (Fenerbahce); Mario Melchiot (Ajax); **Coventry C:** Youssef Chippo (Porto); Mustapha Hadji (La Coruna); Morten Hyldgaard (Ikast); **Derby Co:** Esteban Fuertes (Colon); Seth Johnson (Crewe Alex); Andy Oakes (Hull C); **Everton:** Kevin Campbell (Trabzonspor); Richard Gough (San Jose); **Leeds U:** Eirik Bakke (Sogndal); Danny Mills (Charlton Ath); **Liverpool:** Titi Camara (Marseille); Stephane Henchoz (Blackburn R); Sami Hyypia (Willem II); Erik Meijer (Leverkusen); Vladimir Smicer (Lens); Sander Westerveld (Vitesse); **Manchester U:** Mark Bosnich (Aston Villa); **Newcastle U:** Franck Dumas (Monaco); Alain Goma (Paris St Germain); **Sheffield W:** Gilles De Bilde (PSV Eindhoven); Gerald Sibon (Ajax); **Southampton:** Dean Richards (Wolverhampton W); **Sunderland:** Steve Bould (Arsenal); Carsten Fredgaard (Lyngby); Thomas Helmer (Bayern Munich); Michael Ingham (Cliftonville); **Tottenham H:** Willem Korsten (Vitesse); Chris Perry (Wimbledon); **Watford:** Dominic Foley (Wolverhampton W); Des Lyttle (Nottingham F); Mark Williams (Chesterfield); **West Ham U:** Paulo Wanchope (Derby Co); **Wimbledon:** Walid Badir (Hapoel Petah Tikva); Kelvin Davis (Luton T); Tore Pedersen (Blackburn R); Chris Willmott (Luton T).

Jason Crowe, Arsenal to Portsmouth; Stan Collymore, Aston Villa to Fulham (loan); Ricardo Scimeca, Aston Villa to Nottingham F; Dmitri Kharine, Chelsea to Celtic; Eddie Newton, Chelsea to Birmingham C; Willie Boland, Coventry C to Cardiff C; Adam Eaton, Everton to Preston NE; Paul Dalglish, Newcastle U to Norwich C; Peter Keen, Newcastle U to Carlisle U; Paddy Kelly, Newcastle U to Livingston; Steve Basham, Southampton to Preston NE; Steve Jenkins, Southampton to Brentford; Lee Clark, Sunderland to Fulham; Andy Melville, Sunderland to Fulham; Rory Allen, Tottenham H to Portsmouth; Andy Sinton, Tottenham H to Wolverhampton W; Simon Brown, Tottenham H to Colchester U; Tony Daley, Watford to Walsall; Darren Bazeley, Watford to Wolverhampton W; Lee Hodges, West Ham U to Scunthorpe U; Joe Keith, West Ham U to Colchester U; Mark Kennedy, Wimbledon to Manchester C; Nicky Forster, Birmingham C to Reading; Martin Gray, Oxford U to Darlington; Kenny Irons, Tranmere R to Huddersfield T; Chris Lucketti, Bury to Huddersfield T; Kevin Nicholls, Charlton Ath to Wigan Ath; John Varty, Carlisle U to Rotherham U; Daniel Brown, Leyton Orient to Barnet; Sagi Burton, Crystal Palace to Colchester U; Matt Hocking, Hull C to York C; Dean Kiely, Bury to Charlton Ath; Simon Donnelly, Celtic to Sheffield W; Phil O'Donnell, Celtic to Sheffield W; Neil Heaney, Manchester C to Darlington; Scott Sellars, Bolton W to Huddersfield T; Neil Shipperley, Nottingham F to Barnsley; Joshua Low, Bristol R to Leyton Orient; Darren Freeman, Brentford to Brighton & HA; Sean Dyche, Bristol C to Millwall; Andy Petterson, Charlton Ath to Portsmouth; Alan Lee, Aston Villa to Burnley; Michael Black, Arsenal to Tranmere R; Peter Fear, Wimbledon to Oxford U; Patricio Graff, Feyenoord to Ipswich T; Mark Paul, Southampton to Hull C; Olivier Tebily, Sheffield U to Celtic; Bruno Leal, Sporting Lisbon to Southampton; Matthew Brazier, Fulham to Cardiff C; Danny Coyne, Tranmere R to Grimsby T; Bradley Allen, Charlton Ath to Grimsby T; Michael Gilkes, Wolverhampton W to Millwall; Guy Whittingham, Sheffield W to Portsmouth; Russell Perrett, Portsmouth to Cardiff C; Paul Tait, Northwich Vic to Crewe Alex; Shaun Murray, WBA to Sheffield U; John Mullin, Sunderland to Burnley; Geoff Thomas, Nottingham F to Barnsley; Nick Henry, Sheffield U to Tranmere R; Frazer Toms, Charlton Ath to Barnet; Marcus Hahnemann, Colorado to Fulham; Jermaine Wright, Crewe Alex to Ipswich T; Rob Steiner, Bradford C to QPR; Jacques Williams, Bordeaux to Birmingham C; Tresor Luntala, Rennes to Birmingham C; Jean Yves de Blasiis, RS Paris to Norwich C; Steve Anthrobus, Crewe Alex to Oxford U; Tommy Widdrington, Grimsby T to Port Vale; Stephen Hughes, Arsenal to Fulham (loan); Clyde Wijnhard, Leeds U to Huddersfield T; Dirk Heinen, Leverkusen to Liverpool.

Leaving the country: Kaba Diawara, Arsenal to Marseille; Fabian Caballero, Arsenal to Tembetary; Olivier Dacourt, Everton to Lens; Ibrahim Bakayoko, Everton to Marseille; Pontus Kamark, Leicester C to AIK Stockholm; Steve McManaman, Liverpool to Real Madrid; Jean-Michel Ferri, Liverpool to Sochaux; Peter Schmeichel, Manchester U to Sporting Lisbon; Philippe Albert, Newcastle U to Charleroi; Ralf Keidel, Newcastle U to Duisburg; Dejan Stefanovic, Sheffield W to Perugia; Roger Nilsen, Tottenham H to Graz; Marco Materazzi, Everton to Perugia; Pierre Van Hooijdonk, Nottingham F to Vitesse; Philippe Clement, Coventry C to FC Brugge; Sean Dundee, Liverpool to Stuttgartt.

Coaching and admin moves: Peter Storrie, Chief Executive at Southend; Chris Waddle, Sheffield W Reserve Team Coach; Neale Cooper as Carlisle No. 2; Bobby Robson, FA Coaching Consultant.

One for next year's edition: Wigan's third scorer v Northampton T 29.4.99 was McGibbon not Balmer.

*If you enjoyed this book here is a selection of
other bestselling sports titles from Headline*

ROTHMANS BOOK OF FOOTBALL RECORDS	Jack Rollin	£25.00 ☐
PLAYFAIR FOOTBALL WHO'S WHO 2000	Jack Rollin	£6.99 ☐
PLAYFAIR FOOTBALL ANNUAL 1999–2000	Glenda Rollin	£4.99 ☐
KICKING WITH BOTH FEET	Frank Clark	£16.99 ☐
RED VOICES	Stephen F. Kelly	£17.99 ☐
CHERRIES IN THE RED	Trevor Watkins	£16.99 ☐
LEFT FOOT FORWARD	Garry Nelson	£5.99 ☐
FERGIE	Stephen F. Kelly	£6.99 ☐
DERBY DAYS	Dougie and Eddy Brimson	£6.99 ☐
MANCHESTER UNITED RUINED MY LIFE	Colin Shindler	£5.99 ☐

Headline books are available at your local bookshop or newsagent. Alternatively, books can be ordered direct from the publisher. Just tick the titles you want and fill in the form below. Prices and availability subject to change without notice.

Buy four books from the selection above and get free postage and packaging and delivery within 48 hours. Just send a cheque or postal order made payable to *Bookpoint Ltd* to the value of the total cover price of the four books. Alternatively, if you wish to buy fewer than four books the following postage and packaging applies:

UK and BFPO: £4.30 for one book; £6.30 for two books; £8.30 for three books.

Overseas and Eire: £4.80 for one book; £7.10 for two or three books (surface mail).

Please enclose a cheque or postal order made payable to *Bookpoint Limited*, and send to: Headline Book Publishing Ltd, 39 Milton Park, Abingdon, OXON OX14 4TD, UK.

E-mail address: orders@bookpoint.co.uk

If you would prefer to pay by credit card, our call team would be delighted to take your order by telephone. Our direct line is 01235 400 414 (lines open 9.00 am–6.00 pm Monday to Saturday, 24 hour message answering service). Alternatively you can send a fax on 01235 400 454.

Name ....

Address ....

....

....

If you would prefer to pay by credit card, please complete:

Please debit my Visa/Access/Diner's Card/American Express (delete as applicable) card number:

Signature .... Expiry Date ....